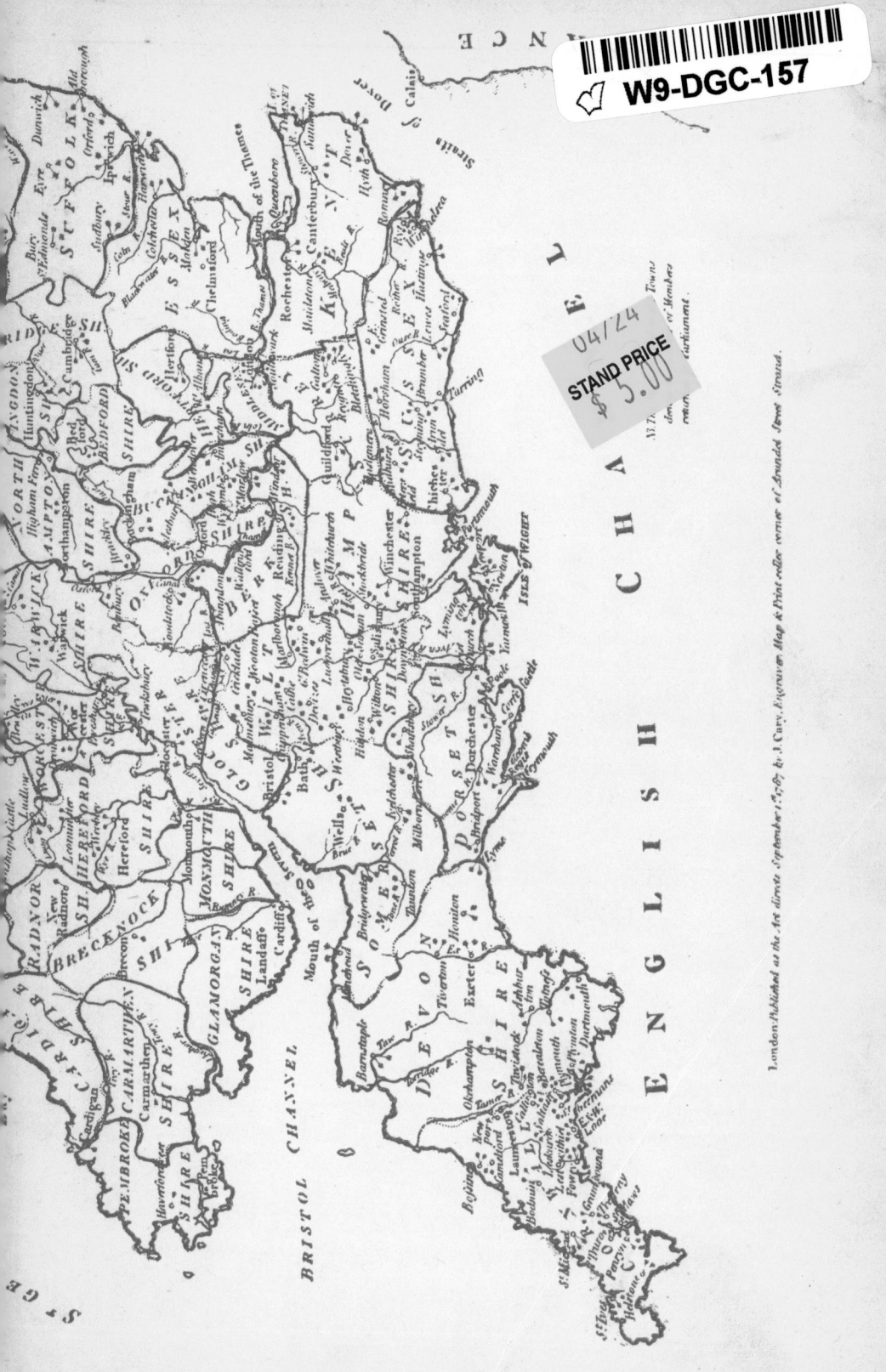

ENGLISH POETRY AND PROSE OF THE ROMANTIC MOVEMENT

ENGLISH POETRY

AND PROSE OF THE

ROMANTIC MOVEMENT

Revised Edition

Edited by GEORGE BENJAMIN WOODS
American University

SCOTT, FORESMAN AND COMPANY
Chicago, Atlanta, Dallas, New York

"Tintern Abbey," from Samuel Ireland's
"Picturesque Views of the
River Wye" 1797.

TO MY WIFE, WHO HAS SHARED
THE PLEASURE AND THE LABOR OF
PREPARING THIS BOOK

Illustration for Gray's "Ode on the Spring." From "Designs by Mr. R. Bentley for Six Poems by Mr. T. Gray," London ... R. Dodsley ... MDCCLIII

Preface

THE text of this revised edition remains almost the same as that of the previous book, which has served college and university classes since 1916. But there are now added reproductions of original illustrations from the Romantic period and a large number of new selections from William Blake. In addition, the critical notes and bibliographies have been divided into separate sections for easier use and have been brought up to date. The large number of bibliographical entries published since 1916 give striking evidence of the vitality of the Romantic period of English literature and of the continuing interest in the writers of that period.

The selections included in this volume have been chosen with a twofold intention: first, to provide in one book all the material, with the single exception of the novel, necessary to acquaint the student with the best and most characteristic work of the men who made the years 1798 to 1832 one of the notable epochs of English literature; secondly, to add to this body of prose and verse on which critical appreciation has set the seal of final approval enough of what preceded and accompanied the triumph of the Romantic temper to show the inception of the movement, its growth, its contrasts, its failings. Selections from Percy's *Reliques of Ancient English Poetry* and from Scott's *The Minstrelsy of the Scottish Border* are included because of the recognized influence of both of these collections upon the Romantic Movement; Percy and Scott were the most conspicuous of the group of antiquarians who were consciously concerned with the revival of interest in medieval ballads and romances. It seemed advisable also that the Gothic revival, another important phase of Romanticism, should be given representation, and therefore selections have been included from Walpole's *The Castle of Otranto* and from Beckford's *The History of the Caliph Vathek*. With these exceptions the novelists have been excluded, inasmuch as a novel does not readily lend itself to selection and had best be studied in its entirety.

It has been the aim to include, whenever possible, literary wholes; but in some cases the desire adequately to illustrate all the Romantic interests of a given writer has made it necessary to include only extracts from the longer works. As a rule these extracts are distinctly characteristic in themselves as well as self-explanatory; where needed, summaries of omitted portions have been supplied in the notes. In the case of such works as *Don Juan* and *The Prelude*, enough is given to make the use of other books virtually unnecessary. As it was impossible to give space to all of any one of

Scott's longer poems, two cantos of *The Lady of the Lake* have been included as representative of this side of Scott's work.

The selections under each author are arranged in the order of writing, so far as this could be determined, except that in the case of writers from whom both poetry and prose are included, the selections of poetry are placed first. (This division is not made, however, in the writings of Blake, who often used both poetry and prose under a single major title.) Dates of writing and publication, when known, are given at the beginning of each selection; dates of writing are printed in italics. Asterisks are used as the authors used them and usually denote that the selection in which they occur was left incomplete. Unless the original spelling is distinctly important, as it is in the case of Chatterton's poems and Blake's writings, modern spelling is employed. In the references to pages in this volume, the letter *a* is used to indicate the first column on the page; the letter *b* to indicate the second column. Brief glossarial notes are given at the foot of the page; additional notes, both explanatory and critical in character, are given in the appendix. In this revised edition the critical notes are presented in the order in which authors and titles appear in the text. The bibliographies are presented in the alphabetical order of the authors represented in the text. Included in the appendix also are selections from the writings of Pope, Johnson, and Burke, a table showing historical backgrounds for the principal writers of the Romantic era, a glossary of proper names occurring in the text, and an index of authors, titles, first lines of poems, and first lines of lyrics found in the dramas and other long works printed in this volume.

I express my thanks to the Houghton Mifflin Company, to Ginn and Company, to the Macmillan Company, to the John Lane Company, and to E. P. Dutton and Company for permission to quote extracts from their publications; to the Librarian of the Harvard University Library for the use of a number of books which otherwise would have been inaccessible to me; to Professor Arthur W. Craver, of Miami University, Professor George Benedict, of Brown University, and to Professor Fred A. Dudley, of The State College of Washington, for suggestions regarding individual writers and selections; to Miss Iva Firkins, of the Library of the University of Minnesota, and to Mr. R. L. Walkley, of the Minneapolis Public Library, for help in preparing the bibliographies; to Professor Karl J. Holzknecht, of New York University, for selecting and preparing the illustrations used in the text; to the New York Public Library, Newberry Library of Chicago, and the University of Chicago library for providing access to the authentic illustrations and maps used in this edition; and to several of my colleagues and students who have been generous of their time in supplying necessary information or other help. I wish to give special recognition to the late Professor Lindsay Todd Damon, of Brown University, whose careful supervision and keen critical judgment made for countless improvements throughout the original book, and whose editorial principles I have tried to follow again in this edition.

George B. Woods

June 1950   American University

Romanticism in Illustration

It may be impossible to define romanticism satisfactorily; it is a little less difficult to illustrate it. Scholars and critics equate the romantic temper to liberalism in the arts, to aspiration, to escapism, to mysticism, to the addition of strangeness to beauty. They find it in the predominance of the imagination over reason and a sense of fact, in an emphasis upon imaginative associations rather than the more obvious connotations of ideas, or in a revival of wonder and mystery and warmth and feeling in art. In the last analysis the romantic spirit is a state of mind, a way of looking at life for purposes of art; it has always been and it may occur at any time; it was especially dominant in the late eighteenth and the early nineteenth centuries.

Definitions are at best abstract and coldly inadequate and unspecific. Somehow, it is the very essence of romanticism that it should seem disorderly and confused rather than clearly conceived and systematic. But its earmarks are easily recognizable, and within a limited space the illustrations of this volume have been chosen to present in a more specific way some of the characteristic aspects of romanticism, and to supplement the literary selections in the book.

Sentimental contemplation. Thomas Bewick's representation of Goldsmith's sentimental *Traveller*, seated on a crag in the Alps (pictured on this page), is that of a melancholy young man living again his experiences in the countries he has visited, and luxuriating in the emotions aroused by reflection and contemplation. Taking sentimental journeys was an innocent diversion approved in the eighteenth century (Goldsmith, Sterne), and also in the early nine-

The Traveller. A wood engraving by Thomas Bewick for "Poems of Goldsmith and Parnell," London, 1795.

teenth (Byron, *Childe Harold*). Bewick was illustrating these lines from Goldsmith:

E'en now, where Alpine solitudes ascend,
I sit me down a pensive hour to spend;
And placed on high, above the storm's career,
Look downwards, where an hundred realms appear;
Lakes, forests, cities, plains, extending wide,
The pomp of kings, the shepherd's pride.

The figure in the background of the frontispiece for Gray's poems (p. xxx) is representative of this same theme.

The return to nature. Similarly, the design on the title-page, which represents Tintern Abbey, is suggestive of both the sentimental traveler and the return to nature. The engraving is taken from Samuel Ireland's *Picturesque Views on the River Wye*, published in 1797, just the year before William Wordsworth revisited this romantic district and wrote his famous poem (see pp. 259-63) on the significance which such woodland, hill, and river scenery had come to have for him. "O sylvan Wye," he wrote:

> thou wanderer thro' the woods,
> How often has my spirit turned to thee!

Thus, for the Romantic, nature became a great restorative and a spiritual guide in life. Wordsworth, Coleridge, Southey, De Quincey— many of the poets of this period —were "Lakers," who found their inspiration in the famous Lake District (see "The Grange in Borrowdale," p. xvi) and made it their home or wrote about the scenery (see Gray's *Journals*, pp. 73-5). It was recollections of such beauty as the Wye Valley and the Lake District which the impressionable contemplative traveler stored up for future solace:

> well pleased to recognize
> In nature and the language of the sense
> The anchor of my purest thoughts, the nurse,
> The guide, the guardian of my heart, and soul
> Of all my moral being.

The love of "natural" nature. But nature alone was not enough; it was nature unspoiled, unpruned, unrestrained, and free that had for the Romantic a special appeal. Pictured on this and the opposite page are two engravings from Richard Payne Knight's *The Landscape: a Didactic Poem* (1794). Knight's poetry is not superlative, and it is interestingly incongruous that he should phrase his romantic thoughts in classical heroic couplets, but his work is significant of a trend. *Nature Unimproved* is romantic; *Nature Improved* is classical. Knight's preference is for the former:

"Nature 'Unimproved.'" A drawing by T. Hearne in "The Landscape, a Didactic Poem" by Richard Payne Knight, 1794.

x

So let th' approach and entrance to your place
Display no glitter, and affect no grace;
But still in careless easy curves proceed,
Through the rough thicket or the flow'ry mead;
Till bursting from some deep-imbower'd shade
Some narrow valley, or some op'ning glade,
Well mix'd and blended in the scene you shew
The stately mansion rising to the view.
But mix'd and blended, ever let it be
A mere component part of what you see.

He disapproves of tampering with nature or with any attempt to restrain it or improve upon it:

Shav'd to the brink, our brooks are taught to flow
Where no obtruding leaves or branches grow;

While clumps of shrubs bespot each winding vale,
Open alike to ev'ry gleam and gale;
Each secret haunt, and deep recess display'd
And intricacy banish'd with its shade . . .
Which hung, reflected o'er the glassy flood;
Where screen'd and shelter'd from the heats of day,
Oft on the moss-grown stone repos'd I lay
And tranquil view'd the limpid stream below,
Brown with o'erhanging shade, in circling eddies flow . . .
Walls, mellow'd into harmony by time
O'er which fantastic creepers us'd to climb.

The influence of Milton and earlier poets. Notable in the literary selections of this book is the influence of early poets, especially Spenser and Milton, upon the budding romantics. Hence Blake's illustration to Milton's *L'Allegro*, "Mirth and her Companions," is reproduced on page 232.

"Nature 'Improved.'" A drawing by T. Hearne in "The Landscape, a Didactic Poem" by Richard Payne Knight, 1794.

The Sad Historian. A wood engraving by John Bewick for "Poems by Goldsmith and Parnell," London, 1795.

Emotional sympathy with humble life and idealization of it. Thomas Bewick's wood engraving reproduced above represents these lines[1] from Oliver Goldsmith's *The Deserted Village*:

. . . yon widow'd solitary thing,
That feebly bends beside the plashy spring;
She, wretched matron, forced, in age, for
    bread,
To strip the brook with mantling cresses
    spread,
To pick her wintry fagot from the thorn,
To seek her nightly shed, and weep till
    morn;
She only left, of all the harmless train,
The sad historian of the pensive plain.

The woodcut reinforces Goldsmith's effort to arouse a sympathetic tear for misfortune in humble life.

[1] This and the next quotation from Goldsmith, although omitted from this book as not properly or wholly romantic, were more and more open in the late eighteenth century to romantic interpretation.

"The Departure," another of Bewick's engravings for Goldsmith's *The Deserted Village,* has the same warmth and significance. It was meant to accompany these lines:

When the poor exiles, every pleasure past,
Hung round their bowers, and fondly looked
    their last,
And took a long farewell, and wished in
    vain,
For seats like these beyond the western
    main . . .
The good old sire the first prepared to go
To new-found worlds, and wept for others'
    woe;
But for himself, in conscious virtue brave,
He only wished for worlds beyond the
    grave.
His lovely daughter, lovelier in her tears,
The fond companion of his helpless years,
Silent went next, neglectful of her charms,
And left a lover's for a father's arms.

Such poems and their illustrations were forerunners of Wordsworth, just as Thomas Gainsborough (1727-1788), in his land-

The Departure. A wood engraving by Thomas Bewick for "Poems of Goldsmith and Parnell," London, 1795.

View of Ruins after the old Roman Manner, for the Termination of Walks, Avenues, etc. Designed by Batty Langley in his "New Principles of Gardening," 1728.

scapes and genre painting, was the anticipator by more than a decade of the idealization of life with nature that is one of the characteristics of Wordsworth's poetry. Blake's *Songs* (see pp. 168 ff., 181 ff.) also represent this interest in simple life, in childhood, and in the emotions of humble life. On the other hand it is interesting to note that George Crabbe's *The Village* (p. 154) was written as a realistic antithesis to Goldsmith's idyllic sentimentalism.

Gothicism and a sentimental interest in the relics of an idealized past. Horace Walpole's cardboard castle at Strawberry Hill (p. 1199) and his *Castle of Otranto* were alike products of his medieval enthusiasms (see his preface, p. 1248b). The novel is as artificial as the villa, the villa as the book; both express a taste not for real medieval-

ism, but for Coney Island Gothic. Sir Walter Scott built himself a similar house at Abbotsford; so did William Beckford at Fonthill Abbey. The absurdities of the style are satirized in Cockolorum Hall in Chapter XXII of R. S. Surtees' *Handley Cross*.

Of similar nature were the artificial ruins "in the Roman manner" which were occasionally erected at the ends of avenues and walks to give a proper romantic aspect to the view. Reproduced above is an engraving taken from Batty Langley's *New Principles of Gardening* (1728).

Sympathy for rural life and activities. The reposing cattle in Bentley's design for Gray's *Ode on the Spring* (see p. 57 for this poem) illustrate the swing away from the town, which is man-made, to the country, made by God. This illustration appears on the back of the dedication page.

From "The Grave, A Poem," by Robert Blair.
Original Designs [by William Blake].

Illustrated by Twelve Etchings executed from

The pleasures of melancholy and sentiments on the graveyard and the tomb. Such
thoughts shade all the way from the sober
grey of Gray's *Elegy* to the deep funereal
sable of Blair's *The Grave* (p. 37). Blake's
illustrations to *The Grave* are famous and
were dedicated to Queen Charlotte. (See
*Dedication of the Illustrations to Blair's
"The Grave," To the Queen*, p. 195.) The
two etchings selected here are representative, as are Blake's descriptions:

Death's Door

'Tis but a Night, a long and moonless Night
We make the Grave our Bed, and then are
gone.

(The Door opening, there seems to make
utter darkness visible: age, on crutches, hurried by a tempest into it. Above is the renovated man seated in light and glory.)

*The Soul Exploring the Recesses of the
Grave:* (The Soul, prior to the dissolution
of the Body, exploring through and beyond
the tomb, and there discovering the emblems
of mortality and immortality.)

Similarly, Bentley's frontispiece to Gray's
Elegy (shown on the next page) is also romantically funereal, and at the same time
Gothic. On one side is a Gothic gateway in
ruins; on the other the implements and employments of the poor and humble. Through
the arch appear a village church built out

xiv

of the remains of an abbey, and a church-yard where the rude forefathers of the village sleep. A countryman is showing an epitaph to a passer-by.

Symbolism and mysticism. The romantic mind adored symbols, and some of its most representative figures, like William Blake, are among the world's greatest mystics. See Bentley's "Frontispiece for a Collection of Gray's Poems," which serves in this book to introduce the section "Eighteenth Century Forerunners" (see page xxx). Here the ornaments allude to the chief subjects of the poems. The altar, the chaplet of flowers, and the rustic pipe allude to the *Ode on the Spring;* the boy with hobby-horse and book, to the *Ode on the Distant Prospect of Eton College;* the cat-Arion, or cat with a lyre riding on a dolphin's back, refers to that line from the *Ode on the*

Death of a Favorite Cat Drowned in a Tub of Gold Fishes:

No Dolphin came, no Nereid stirr'd.

The monkey with violin and lawyer's wig alludes to Lord Keeper Hatton's dancing in *The Long Story;* the Roman sepulchral altar inscribed DIIS MANIBUS SACRUM, with the spade and skull, to the *Elegy.* The monkey painting, the lyre, the pen and crayon, are allusive to the poems and drawings. Everything has significance.

Symbolic also are the illustrations of and by William Blake, the most romantic of the Romantic artists. Blake's poetry can best be understood by reference to his illustrations of it. He invented a method of "illuminated printing" in which both words and decoration were drawn on a copper plate with an impervious medium, like

Illustration for Gray's "Elegy." From "Designs by Mr. R. Bentley for Six Poems by Mr. T. Gray," London, . . . R. Dodsley, . . . MDCCLIII.

"dragon's blood," and the copper then etched away by acid. Text and design then remained in relief and could be printed in any tint that pleased the artist, the print being either left plain or colored by hand with water colors. In the original edition, Blake's illustrations which accompany and are part of the design of the lyrics that make up *Songs of Innocence* and *Songs of Experience* are delicately washed with water color. These designs illustrate as nothing else can the quality of Blake's imagination. Similarly, the illustration from *America: A Prophecy* (p. 180) is a revelation in another medium of the poet's mind and of the mystic images he wished to conjure up as accompaniment to the thoughts he expressed in words.

Orientalism. Comparable to the Gothicism and late eighteenth century interest in the romantic past is the equally zealous

Oriental exoticism of the early nineteenth century (see Beckford's *Vathek*, Moore's *Lalla Rookh*, and Byron's Oriental tales). On page 1202 is a representation of the Saracenic-Indo-Chinese confection which John Nash produced for George IV at Brighton, transforming a restrained classical mansion into a kind of Aladdin's Palace.

Other aspects of Romanticism which cannot be represented pictorially—like humanitarianism and the interest in man's inalienable rights (Cowper, Burns, Byron, Shelley, Hood, Hawker, Hemans, Elliot); the collection and imitation of popular ballads (Percy, Coleridge, Scott, Campbell); Celtic and Scandinavian mythology and literature (Ossian, Gray)—are amply represented in the literary selections in this book.

Karl J. Holzknecht
June 1950   New York University

"*The Grange in Borrowdale,*" *an engraving by Joseph Farington. From* "*The Lakes of Lancashire, Westmorland, and Cumberland*" (1816).

Contents

WILLIAM BLAKE 1757-1827

ROBERT BURNS 1759-1796

xxv

℞ *Illustrations*

Frontispiece for a Collection of Gray's Poems. From "Designs by Mr. R. Bentley for Six Poems by Mr. T. Gray," London, ... R. Dodsley, ... MDCCLIII

Eighteenth Century Forerunners

Anne, Countess of Winchilsea 1661-1720

THE TREE
1880

Fair tree, for thy delightful shade
'T is just that some return be made;
Sure some return is due from me
To thy cool shadows and to thee.
5 When thou to birds dost shelter give
Thou music dost from them receive;
If travellers beneath thee stay
Till storms have worn themselves away,
That time in praising thee they spend,
10 And thy protecting pow'r commend;
The shepherd here, from scorching freed,
Tunes to thy dancing leaves his reed,
Whilst his lov'd nymph in thanks bestows
Her flow'ry chaplets on thy boughs.
15 Shall I then only silent be,
And no return be made by me?
No! let this wish upon thee wait,
And still to flourish be thy fate;
To future ages mayst thou stand
20 Untouch'd by the rash workman's hand,
Till that large stock of sap is spent
Which gives thy summer's ornament;
Till the fierce winds, that vainly strive
To shock thy greatness whilst alive,
25 Shall on thy lifeless hour attend,
Prevent[1] the axe, and grace thy end,
Their scatter'd strength together call
And to the clouds proclaim thy fall;
Who then their ev'ning dews may spare,
30 When thou no longer art their care,
But shalt, like ancient heroes, burn,
And some bright hearth be made thy urn.

From THE PETITION FOR AN ABSOLUTE RETREAT
1713

Give me, O indulgent Fate!
Give me yet, before I die,
A sweet, but absolute retreat,
'Mongst paths so lost, and trees so high,

[1] come before; anticipate

5 That the world may ne'er invade,
Through such windings and such shade.
My unshaken liberty.

No intruders thither come,
Who visit, but to be from home;
10 None who their vain moments pass,
Only studious of their glass.
News, that charm to list'ning ears,
That false alarm to hopes and fears,
That common theme for every fop,
15 From the statesman to the shop,
In those coverts ne'er be spread.
Of who's deceas'd, or who's to wed,
Be no tidings thither brought,
But silent, as a midnight thought,
20 Where the world may ne'er invade,
Be those windings, and that shade!

Courteous Fate! afford me there
A table spread without my care
With what the neighb'ring fields impart,
25 Whose cleanliness be all its art.
When of old the calf was drest —
Tho' to make an angel's feast —
In the plain, unstudied sauce
Nor truffle,[1] nor morillia[1] was;
30 Nor could the mighty patriarch's board
One far-fetch'd ortolane[2] afford.
Courteous Fate, then give me there
Only plain and wholesome fare.
Fruits indeed, would Heaven bestow,
35 All, that did in Eden grow,—
All, but the forbidden tree,
Would be coveted by me:
Grapes, with juice so crowded up
As breaking[3] thro' the native cup;
40 Figs, yet growing, candied o'er
By the sun's attracting power;
Cherries, with the downy peach,
All within my easy reach;
Whilst, creeping near the humble ground,
45 Should the strawberry be found,
Springing wheresoe'er I strayed,
Thro' those windings and that shade.

[1] A kind of edible fungus.   ing, often served as a delicacy.
[2] A small bird, the common European bunt-   [3] as if about to break

1

For my garments, let them be
What may with the time agree;
50 Warm, when Phœbus does retire,
And is ill-supplied by fire;
But when he renews the year
And verdant all the fields appear,
Beauty every thing resumes,
55 Birds have dropt their winter-plumes;
When the lily full display'd
Stands in purer white array'd
Than that vest which heretofore
The luxurious monarch[1] wore
60 When from Salem's gates he drove
To the soft retreat of love,
Lebanon's all burnish'd house,
And the dear Egyptian spouse,—
Clothe me, Fate, tho' not so gay,
65 Clothe me light, and fresh as May.
In the fountains let me view
All my habit cheap and new,
Such as, when sweet zephyrs fly,
With their motions may comply,
70 Gently waving, to express
Unaffected carelessness.
No perfumes have there a part,
Borrow'd from the chemist's art;
But such as rise from flow'ry beds,
75 Or the falling jasmine sheds!
'Twas the odor of the field
Esau's rural coat did yield
That inspir'd his father's prayer
For blessings of the earth and air.
80 Of gums or powders had it smelt,
The supplanter, then unfelt,
Easily had been descry'd
For one that did in tents abide,
For some beauteous handmaid's joy
85 And his mother's darling boy.[2]
Let me then no fragrance wear
But what the winds from gardens bear
In such kind, surprising gales
As gather'd from Fidentia's vales
90 All the flowers that in them grew;
Which intermixing, as they flew,
In wreathen garlands dropt again
On Lucullus, and his men,
Who, cheer'd by the victorious sight
95 Trebl'd numbers put to flight.
Let me, when I must be fine,
In such natural colors shine;
Wove, and painted by the sun,
Whose resplendent rays to shun,
100 When they do too fiercely beat,
Let me find some close retreat
Where they have no passage made
Thro' those windings, and that shade.

.   .   .   .   .

[1] Solomon. *I Kings,* 7 :1-12.
[2] *Genesis,* 25-27.

TO THE NIGHTINGALE
1713

Exert thy voice, sweet harbinger of
    Spring!
    This moment is thy time to sing,
    This moment I attend to praise,
And set my numbers to thy lays.
5   Free as thine shall be my song;
    As thy music, short, or long.
Poets, wild as thee, were born,
    Pleasing best when unconfin'd,
    When to please is least design'd,
10 Soothing but their cares to rest;
    Cares do still their thoughts molest,
    And still th' unhappy poet's breast,
Like thine, when best he sings, is plac'd
    against a thorn.[1]
She begins; let all be still!
15   Muse, thy promise now fulfil!
Sweet, oh! sweet, still sweeter yet!
Can thy words such accents fit?
Canst thou syllables refine,
Melt a sense that shall retain
20 Still some spirit of the brain,
Till with sounds like these it join?
    'Twill not be! then change thy note;
Let division[2] shake thy throat.
Hark! division now she tries;
25 Yet as far the muse outflies.
Cease then, prithee, cease thy tune;
Trifler, wilt thou sing till June?
Till thy bus'ness all lies waste,
And the time of building's past!
30   Thus we poets that have speech,
Unlike what thy forests teach,
    If a fluent vein be shown
    That's transcendent to our own,
Criticise, reform, or preach,
35 Or censure what we cannot reach.

A NOCTURNAL REVERIE
1713

In such a night, when every louder wind
Is to its distant cavern safe confin'd,
And only gentle zephyr fans his wings,
And lonely Philomel, still waking, sings;
5 Or from some tree, fam'd for the owl's
    delight,
She, hollowing clear, directs the wand'rer
    right;
In such a night, when passing clouds
    give place,
Or thinly veil the Heav'ns mysterious
    face;
When in some river, overhung with green,

[1] A popular superstition. See Young's *Night
    Thoughts,* 1, 439 ff.
[2] A series of notes to be sung in one breath to
    each syllable.

10 The waving moon and trembling leaves
   are seen;
When freshen'd grass now bears itself
   upright,
And makes cool banks to pleasing rest
   invite,
When spring the woodbine and the
   bramble-rose,
And where the sleepy cowslip shelter'd
   grows;
15 Whilst now a paler hue the foxglove
   takes,
Yet chequers still with red the dusky
   brakes;
When scatter'd glow-worms, but in twilight fine,
Show trivial beauties watch their hour
   to shine,
Whilst Salisb'ry stands the test of every
   light
20 In perfect charms and perfect virtue
   bright;
When odors which declin'd repelling
   day
Thro' temp'rate air uninterrupted stray;
When darken'd groves their softest
   shadows wear,
And falling waters we distinctly hear;
25 When thro' the gloom more venerable
   shows
Some ancient fabric, awful in repose,
While sunburnt hills their swarthy looks
   conceal
And swelling haycocks thicken up the
   vale;
When the loos'd horse now, as his pasture leads,
30 Comes slowly grazing thro' th' adjoining
   meads,
Whose stealing pace, and lengthen'd
   shade we fear,
Till torn up forage in his teeth we hear;
When nibbling sheep at large pursue
   their food,
And unmolested kine re-chew the cud;
35 When curlews cry beneath the village-
   walls,
And to her straggling brood the partridge calls;
Their shortliv'd jubilee the creatures
   keep,
Which but endures whilst tyrant-man
   does sleep;
When a sedate content the spirit feels,
40 And no fierce light disturb, whilst it
   reveals;
But silent musings urge the mind to seek
Something too high for syllables to
   speak;

Till the free soul to a compos'dness
   charm'd,
Finding the elements of rage disarm'd,
45 O'er all below a solemn quiet grown,
Joys in th' inferior world and thinks it
   like her own:
In such a night let me abroad remain
Till morning breaks and all's confus'd
   again;
Our cares, our toils, our clamors are
   renew'd,
50 Or pleasures, seldom reach'd, again pursu'd.

Thomas Parnell 1679-1718

A FAIRY TALE

IN THE ANCIENT ENGLISH STYLE
1721

In Britain's isle and Arthur's days,
When midnight faeries daunc'd the
   maze,
Liv'd Edwin of the green;
Edwin, I wis,[1] a gentle youth,
5 Endow'd with courage, sense, and truth
   Though badly shap'd he been.

His mountain back mote well be said
To measure heighth against his head,
   And lift itself above:
10 Yet spite of all that nature did
To make his uncouth form forbid,
   This creature dar'd to love.

He felt the charms of Edith's eyes,
Nor wanted hope to gain the prize,
15   Could ladies look within;
But one Sir Topaz dress'd with art,
And, if a shape could win a heart,
   He had a shape to win.

Edwin, if right I read my song,
20 With slighted passion pac'd along
   All in the moony light:
'Twas near an old enchaunted court,
Where sportive faeries made resort
   To revel out the night.

25 His heart was drear, his hope was
   cross'd,
'Twas late, 'twas farr, the path was lost
   That reach'd the neighbor-town;
With weary steps he quits the shades,
Resolv'd, the darkling dome he treads,
30   And drops his limbs adown.

But scant he lays him on the floor,
When hollow winds remove the door,
[1] know

A trembling rocks the ground:
And, well I ween[1] to count aright,
35 At once an hundred tapers light
    On all the walls around.

Now sounding tongues assail his ear,
Now sounding feet approachen near,
    And now the sounds encrease;
40 And from the corner where he lay
He sees a train profusely gay
    Come pranckling o'er the place.

But, trust me, gentles, never yet
Was dight[2] a masking half so neat,
45   Or half so rich before;
The country lent the sweet perfumes,
The sea the pearl, the sky the plumes,
    The town its silken store.

Now whilst he gaz'd, a gallant drest
50 In flaunting robes above the rest,
    With awfull accent cried,
What mortal of a wretched mind,
Whose sighs infect the balmy wind,
    Has here presumed to hide?

55 At this the swain, whose venturous soul
No fears of magic art controul,
    Advanc'd in open sight;
"Nor have I cause of dreed," he said,
"Who view, by no presumption led,
60   Your revels of the night.

" 'Twas grief for scorn of faithful love,
Which made my steps unweeting[3] rove
    Amid the nightly dew."
'Tis well, the gallant cries again,
65 We faeries never injure men
    Who dare to tell us true.

Exalt thy love-dejected heart,
Be mine the task, or ere we part,
    To make thee grief resign;
70 Now take the pleasure of thy chaunce;
Whilst I with Mab my partner daunce,
    Be little Mable thine.

He spoke, and all a sudden there
Light musick floats in wanton air;
75   The monarch leads the queen;
The rest their faerie partners found,
And Mable trimly tript the ground
    With Edwin of the green.

The dauncing past, the board was laid,
80 And siker[4] such a feast was made
    As heart and lip desire;

Withouten hands the dishes fly,
The glasses with a wish come nigh,
    And with a wish retire.

85 But now to please the faerie king,
Full every deal[1] they laugh and sing,
    And antick feats devise;
Some wind and tumble like an ape,
And other-some transmute their shape
90   In Edwin's wondering eyes.

Till one at last that Robin hight,[2]
Renown'd for pinching maids by night,
    Has hent[3] him up aloof;
And full against the beam he flung,
95 Where by the back the youth he hung
    To spraul unneath the roof.

From thence, "Reverse my charm," he
    cries,
"And let it fairly now suffice
    The gambol has been shown."
100 But Oberon answers with a smile,
Content thee, Edwin, for a while,
    The vantage is thine own.

Here ended all the phantome play;
They smelt the fresh approach of day,
105   And heard a cock to crow;
The whirling wind that bore the crowd
Has clapp'd the door, and whistled loud,
    To warn them all to go.

Then screaming all at once they fly
110 And all at once the tapers die;
    Poor Edwin falls to floor;
Forlorn his state, and dark the place,
Was never wight in sike[4] a case
    Through all the land before.

115 But soon as Dan[5] Apollo rose,
Full jolly creature home he goes,
    He feels his back the less;
His honest tongue and steady mind
Han rid him of the lump behind
120   Which made him want success.

With lusty livelyhed[6] he talks
He seems a daunceing as he walks;
    His story soon took wind;
And beauteous Edith sees the youth,
125 Endow'd with courage, sense, and truth,
    Without a bunch behind.

The story told, Sir Topaz mov'd,
The youth of Edith erst approv'd,[7]

---

[1] think
[2] dressed
[3] unknowing
[4] certainly

[1] all the time (or, possibly, all the company)
[2] was called
[3] seized
[4] such
[5] Lord; master (from Latin *dominus*, master)
[6] liveliness
[7] the youth formerly approved by Edith

To see the revel scene:
130 At close of eve he leaves his home,
And wends to find the ruin'd dome
All on the gloomy plain.

As there he bides, it so befell,
The wind came rustling down a dell,
135　A shaking seiz'd the wall:
Up spring the tapers as before,
The faeries bragly[1] foot the floor,
And musick fills the hall.

But certes[2] sorely sunk with woe
140 Sir Topaz sees the elfin show,
His spirits in him die:
When Oberon cries, "A man is near,
A mortall passion, cleeped[3] fear,
Hangs flagging in the sky."

145 With that Sir Topaz, hapless youth!
In accents faultering ay for ruth
Intreats them pity graunt;
For als he been a mister wight[4]
Betray'd by wandering in the night
150　To tread the circled haunt.

"Ah losell[5] vile!" at once they roar,
"And little skill'd of faerie lore,
Thy cause to come we know;
Now has thy kestrell[6] courage fell;
155 And faeries, since a lie you tell,
Are free to work thee woe."

Then Will,[7] who bears the wispy fire
To trail the swains among the mire,
The caitive upward flung;
160 There like a tortoise in a shop
He dangled from the chamber-top,
Where whilome Edwin hung.

The revel now proceeds apace,
Deffly[8] they frisk it o'er the place,
165　They sit, they drink, and eat;
The time with frolick mirth beguile,
And poor Sir Topaz hangs the while
Till all the rout retreat.

By this the starrs began to wink,
170 They shriek, they fly, the tapers sink,
And down ydrops the knight:
For never spell by faerie laid
With strong enchantment bound a glade
Beyond the length of night.

175 Chill, dark, alone, adreed,[1] he lay,
Till up the welkin[2] rose the day,
Then deem'd the dole was o'er:
But wot ye well his harder lot?
His seely[3] back the bunch has got
180　Which Edwin lost afore.

This tale a **Sibyl**-nurse[4] ared;[5]
She softly strok'd my youngling head,
And when the tale was done,
"Thus some are born, my son," she cries,
185 "With base impediments to rise,
And some are born with none.

But virtue can itself advance
To what the favorite fools of chance
By fortune seem'd design'd;
190 Virtue can gain the odds of fate,
And from itself shake off the weight
Upon th' unworthy mind."

A NIGHT-PIECE ON DEATH
1721

By the blue taper's trembling light,
No more I waste the wakeful night,
Intent with endless view to pore
The schoolmen and the sages o'er:
5 Their books from wisdom widely stray,
Or point at best the longest way.
I'll seek a readier path, and go
Where wisdom's surely taught below.

How deep yon azure dyes the sky,
10 Where orbs of gold unnumber'd lie,
While through their ranks in silver pride
The nether crescent seems to glide!
The slumbering breeze forgets to breathe,
The lake is smooth and clear beneath,
15 Where once again the spangled show
Descends to meet our eyes below.
The grounds which on the right aspire,
In dimness from the view retire:
The left presents a place of graves,
20 Whose wall the silent water laves.
That steeple guides thy doubtful sight
Among the livid gleams of night.
There pass, with melancholy state,
By all the solemn heaps of fate,
25 And think, as softly-sad you tread
Above the venerable dead,
"Time was, like thee they life possest,
And time shall be that thou shalt rest."

---

[1] proudly; finely
[2] certainly
[3] called
[4] because he is a poor fellow
[5] worthless person
[6] A term often used in

contempt, as of a mean kind of hawk. A kestrel is a common European falcon.
[7] Will-o'-the-wisp.
[8] deftly

[1] afraid
[2] sky
[3] poor
[4] An old woman professing to have the

gift of prophecy, like that ascribed to the ancient Sibyls.
[5] told

Those graves, with bending osier[1] bound,
30 That nameless heave the crumbled
    ground,
Quick to the glancing thought disclose,
Where toil and poverty repose.

The flat smooth stones that bear a name,
The chisel's slender help to fame,
35 (Which ere our set of friends decay
Their frequent steps may wear away,)
A middle race of mortals own,
Men, half ambitious, all unknown.

The marble tombs that rise on high,
40 Whose dead in vaulted arches lie,
Whose pillars swell with sculptur'd
    stones,
Arms, angels, epitaphs, and bones,
These, all the poor remains of state,
Adorn the rich, or praise the great;
45 Who while on earth in fame they live,
Are senseless of the fame they give.

Hah! while I gaze, pale Cynthia fades,
The bursting earth unveils the shades!
All slow, and wan, and wrapp'd with
    shrouds,
50 They rise in visionary crowds,
And all with sober accent cry,
"Think, mortal, what it is to die."

Now from yon black and funeral yew,[2]
That bathes the charnel-house with dew,
55 Methinks I hear a voice begin;
(Ye ravens, cease your croaking din,
Ye tolling clocks, no time resound
O'er the long lake and midnight ground!)
It sends a peal of hollow groans,
60 Thus speaking from among the bones:

"When men my scythe and darts supply,
How great a king of fears am I!
They view me like the last of things:
They make, and then they dread, my
    stings.
65 Fools! if you less provok'd your fears,
No more my spectre-form appears.
Death's but a path that must be trod,
If man would ever pass to God;
A port of calms, a state of ease
70 From the rough rage of swelling seas.

"Why then thy flowing sable stoles,
Deep pendant cypress,[3] mourning poles,[4]
Loose scarfs to fall athwart thy weeds,

Long palls, drawn hearses, cover'd
    steeds,
75 And plumes of black, that, as they tread,
Nod o'er the scutcheons of the dead?

"Nor can the parted body know,
Nor wants the soul, these forms of woe,
As men who long in prison dwell,
80 With lamps that glimmer round the cell,
Whene'er their suffering years are run,
Spring forth to greet the glittering sun:
Such joy, though far transcending sense,
Have pious souls at parting hence.
85 On earth, and in the body plac'd,
A few, and evil years they waste;
But when their chains are cast aside,
See the glad scene unfolding wide,
Clap the glad wing, and tower away,
90 And mingle with the blaze of day."

A HYMN TO CONTENTMENT
1721

Lovely, lasting peace of mind!
Sweet delight of human-kind!
Heavenly-born, and bred on high,
To crown the favorites of the sky
5 With more of happiness below,
Than victors in a triumph know!
Whither, O whither art thou fled,
To lay thy meek, contented head?
What happy region dost thou please
10 To make the seat of calms and ease?

Ambition searches all its sphere
Of pomp and state, to meet thee there.
Encreasing avarice would find
Thy presence in its gold enshrin'd.
15 The bold adventurer ploughs his way
Through rocks amidst the foaming sea,
To gain thy love; and then perceives
Thou wert not in the rocks and waves.
The silent heart, which grief assails,
20 Treads soft and lonesome o'er the vales.
Sees daisies open, rivers run,
And seeks, as I have vainly done,
Amusing thought, but learns to know
That solitude's the nurse of woe.
25 No real happiness is found
In trailing purple o'er the ground;[1]
Or in a soul exalted high,
To range the circuit of the sky,
Converse with stars above, and know
30 All Nature in its forms below;
The rest it seeks, in seeking dies,
And doubts at last, for knowledge, rise.

Lovely, lasting peace, appear!
This world itself, if thou art here,

---

[1] willow
[2] The yew is a common tree in graveyards.
[3] A kind of thin cloth, often used for mourning.
[4] A pole (pile) is a fabric with a heavy nap.

[1] in wearing the purple robes of royalty

35 Is once again with Eden blest,
And man contains it in his breast.

'Twas thus, as under shade I stood,
I sung my wishes to the wood,
And, lost in thought, no more perceiv'd
40 The branches whisper as they wav'd;
It seem'd as all the quiet place
Confess'd the presence of the Grace.
When thus she spoke: "Go rule thy will;
Bid thy wild passions all be still,
45 Know God, and bring thy heart to know
The joys which from religion flow:
Then every Grace shall prove its guest,
And I'll be there to crown the rest."

Oh! by yonder mossy seat,
50 In my hours of sweet retreat,
Might I thus my soul employ
With sense of gratitude and joy!
Rais'd as ancient prophets were,
In heavenly vision, praise, and prayer;
55 Pleasing all men, hurting none,
Pleas'd and bless'd with God alone:
Then while the gardens take[1] my sight,
With all the colors of delight,
While silver waters glide along,
60 To please my ear, and court my song,
I'll lift my voice, and tune my string,
And Thee, great Source of Nature, sing.

The sun, that walks his airy way,
To light the world, and give the day;
65 The moon, that shines with borrow'd
light;
The stars, that gild the gloomy night;
The seas, that roll unnumber'd waves;
The wood, that spreads its shady leaves;
The field, whose ears conceal the grain,
70 The yellow treasure of the plain;
All of these, and all I see,
Should be sung, and sung by me:
They speak their Maker as they can,
But want and ask the tongue of man.

75 Go search among your idle dreams,
Your busy or your vain extremes,
And find a life of equal bliss,
Or own the next begun in this.

Allan Ramsay 1685?-1758

THE HIGHLAND LADDIE
1721

The Lawland lads think they are fine,
But O they're vain and idly gaudy;
How much unlike that gracefu' mien
And manly looks of my Highland
laddie!

[1] charm: bewitch

Chorus

5 O my bonny, bonny Highland laddie!
My handsome, charming Highland lad-
die!
May Heaven still guard and love reward
Our Lawland lass and her Highland
laddie!

If I were free at will to chuse
10 To be the wealthiest Lawland lady,
I'd take young Donald without trews,[1]
With bonnet blew and belted plaidy.

The brawest[2] beau in borrows town,[3]
In a' his airs, with art made ready,
15 Compared to him, he's but a clown;
He's finer far in 's tartan[4] plaidy.

O'er benty[5] hill with him I'll run,
And leave my Lawland kin and dady;
Frae winter's cauld and summer's sun
20 He'll screen me with his Highland
plaidy.

A painted room and silken bed
May please a Lawland laird and lady,
But I can kiss and be as glad
Behind a bush in 's Highland plaidy.

25 Few compliments between us pass:
I ca' him my dear Highland laddie;
And he ca's me his Lawland lass,
Syne rows[6] me in his Highland plaidy.

Nae greater joy I'll e'er pretend
30 Than that his love prove true and
steady,
Like mine to him, which ne'er shall end
While Heaven preserve my Highland
laddie.

MY PEGGY
1721

My Peggy is a young thing
Just enter'd in her teens,
Fair as the day, and sweet as May,
Fair as the day, and always gay.
5 My Peggy is a young thing,
And I'm na very auld,
Yet weel I like to meet her at
The wauking o' the fauld.[7]

My Peggy speaks sae sweetly,
10 Whene'er we meet alane,

[1] trousers
[2] finest
[3] royal borough
[4] woolen cloth check-
ered with narrow
bands of various
colors
[5] covered with coarse
grass
[6] then rolls
[7] watching of the
sheep-fold

I wish nae mair to lay my care,
I wish nae mair o' a' that's rare,
  My Peggy speaks sae sweetly,
    To a' the lave[1] I'm cauld,
15 But she gars[2] a' my spirits glow
    At wauking o' the fauld.

  My Peggy smiles sae kindly
    Whene'er I whisper love,
That I look doun on a' the toun,
20 That I look doun upon a croun.
  My Peggy smiles sae kindly,
    It maks me blythe an' bauld,
An' naething gies me sic[3] delight
    As wauking o' the fauld.

25   My Peggy sings sae saftly
    When on my pipe I play,
By a' the rest it is confest,
By a' the rest that she sings best.
  My Peggy sings sae saftly,
30   And in her sangs are tauld
Wi' innocence, the wale o' sense,[4]
    At wauking o' the fauld.

SWEET WILLIAM'S GHOST
1724

There came a ghost to Margret's door,
  With many a grievous grone,
And ay he tirled at the pin,[5]
  But answer made she none.

5 Is this my father Philip?
  Or is't my brother John?
Or is't my true love Willie,
  From Scotland new come home?

'Tis not thy father Philip,
10   Nor yet thy brother John:
But 'tis thy true love Willie
  From Scotland new come home.

O sweet Margret! O dear Margret!
  I pray thee speak to mee:
15 Give me my faith and troth, Margret,
  As I gave it to thee.

Thy faith and troth thou'se nevir get,
  Of me shalt nevir win,
Till that thou come within my bower,
20   And kiss my cheek and chin.

If I should come within thy bower,
  I am no earthly man:
And should I kiss thy rosy lipp,
  Thy days will not be lang.

25 O sweet Margret! O dear Margret!
  I pray thee speak to mee:
Give me my faith and troth, Margret,
  As I gave it to thee.

Thy faith and troth thou'se nevir get,
30   Of me shalt nevir win,
Till thou take me to yon kirk yard,
  And wed me with a ring.

My bones are buried in a kirk yard
  Afar beyond the sea,
35 And it is but my sprite, Margret,
  That's speaking now to thee.

She stretched out her lily-white hand,
  As for to do her best:
Hae there your faith and troth, Willie,
40   God send your soul good rest.

Now she has kilted[1] her robes of green,
  A piece below her knee:
And a' the live-lang winter night
  The dead corps followed shee.

45 Is there any room at your head, Willie?
  Or any room at your feet?
Or any room at your side, Willie?
  Wherein that I may creep?

There's nae room at my head, Margret,
50   There's nae room at my feet,
There's nae room at my side, Margret,
  My coffin is made so meet.[2]

Then up and crew the red red cock,
  And up then crew the gray:
55 'Tis time, 'tis time, my dear Margret,
  That I were gane away.

No more the ghost to Margret said,
  But, with a grievous grone,
Evanish'd in a cloud of mist,
60   And left her all alone.

O stay, my only true love, stay,
  The constant Margret cried:
Wan grew her cheeks, she clos'd her een,
  Stretch'd her saft limbs, and died.

[1] rest
[2] makes
[3] such
[4] soul of sense
[5] A tirling was formerly used instead of a knocker; it consisted of a notched metal bar (the pin) with a loose metal ring, which was drawn over it to make a sound.

[1] tucked up   [2] close-fitting

THROUGH THE WOOD, LADDIE
1724

O Sandy, why leaves thou thy Nelly to
    mourn?
    Thy presence would ease me
    When naething could please me,
Now dowie[1] I sigh on the bank of the
    burn,[2]
5 Ere through the wood, laddie,—until thou
    return.

Though woods now are bonny, and morn-
    ings are clear,
    While lavrocks[3] are singing
    And primroses springing,
Yet nane of them pleases my eye or my
    ear,
10 When through the wood, laddie, ye dinna
    appear.

That I am forsaken some spare no to tell;
    I'm fashed[4] wi' their scorning
    Baith evening and morning;
Their jeering aft gaes to my heart wi'
    a knell,
15 When through the wood, laddie, I wan-
    der mysel'.

Then stay, my dear Sandie, nae langer
    away,
    But quick as an arrow,
    Haste here to thy marrow,[5]
Wha's living in languor till that happy
    day,
20 When through the wood, laddie, we'll
    dance, sing, and play.

AN[6] THOU WERE MY AIN THING
1724
Chorus

An thou were my ain thing,
I would love thee, I would love thee;
An thou were my ain thing
How dearly I would love thee.

5 Like bees that suck the morning dew,
Frae flowers of sweetest scent and hue,
Sae wad I dwell upon thy mow[7]
    And gar[8] the gods envy me.

Sae lang's I had the use of light
10 I'd on thy beauties feast my sight,
Syne in saft whispers through the night
    I'd tell how much I loved thee.

How fair and ruddy is my Jean!
She moves a goddess o'er the green.
15 Were I a king thou should be queen—
    Nane but myself aboon thee.

I'ld grasp thee to this breast of mine,
Whilst thou like ivy on the vine
Around my stronger limbs should twine,
20   Formed handy to defend thee.

Time's on the wing and will not stay,
In shining youth let's make our hay;
Since love admits of no delay,
    O let na scorn undo thee.

25 While love does at his altar stand,
Hae,[1] here's my heart, gie me thy hand,
And with ilk[2] smile thou shalt command
The will of him who loves thee.

Chorus

An thou were my ain thing
30 I would love thee, I would love thee;
An thou were my ain thing,
    How dearly I would love thee.

From THE GENTLE SHEPHERD
1725
SCENE IV.

Behind a tree upon the plain,
    Pate and his Peggy meet:
In love, without a vicious stain,
The bonny lass and cheerfu' swain
    Change vows an' kisses sweet.

PATIE AND PEGGY

Peggy. O Patie, let me gang, I
    maunna stay;
We're baith cry'd hame, an' Jenny
    she's away.
    Patie. I'm laith to part sae soon, now
    we're alane,
An' Roger he's awa' wi' Jenny gane;
5 They're as content, for aught I hear or
    see,
To be alane themsells, I judge, as we.
Here, where primroses thickest paint the
    green,
Hard by this little burnie[3] let us lean.
Hark, how the lav'rocks[4] chant aboon our
    heads,
10 How saft the westlin winds sough thro'
    the reeds!
    Peggy. The scented meadows,—birds,
    —an' healthy breeze,
For aught I ken, may mair than Peggy
    please.
    Patie. Ye wrang me sair, to doubt my
    being kind;

---

[1] gloomy   [5] mate
[2] brook   [6] if
[3] larks   [7] mouth
[4] bothered   [8] make

[1] have   [3] brook
[2] each   [4] larks

In speaking sae, ye ca' me dull an' blind;
15 Gif I cou'd fancy aught's sae sweet or
    fair
As my dear Meg, or worthy o' my care.
Thy breath is sweeter than the sweetest
    brier,
Thy cheek an' breast the finest flow'rs
    appear.
Thy words excel the maist delightfu'
    notes,
20 That warble thro' the merl or mavis'[1]
    throats.
Wi' thee I tent[2] nae flow'rs that busk[3]
    the field,
Or riper berries that our mountains
    yield.
The sweetest fruits that hing upon the
    tree
Are far inferior to a kiss o' thee.
25   *Peggy.* But, Patrick, for some wicked
    end, may fleetch,[4]
An' lambs shou'd tremble when the foxes
    preach.
I daurna stay; ye joker, let me gang:
Anither lass may gar[5] you change your
    sang;
Your thoughts may flit, and I may thole[6]
    the wrang.
30   *Patie.* Sooner a mother shall her
    fondness drap,
An' wrang the bairn sits smiling on her
    lap:
The sun shall change, the moon to change
    shall cease,
The gaits to clim,[7]—the sheep to yield
    their fleece,
Ere aught by me be either said or done,
35 Shall skaith[8] our love, I swear by a' aboon.
   Peggy. Then keep your aith.—But
    mony lads will swear,
An' be mansworn to twa in hauf-a-year.
Now I believe ye like me wonder weel;
But if a fairer face your heart shou'd
    steal,
40 Your Meg, forsaken, bootless might
    relate,
How she was dawted[9] anes by faithless
    Pate.
   Patie. I'm sure I canna change; ye
    needna fear;
Tho' we're but young, I've looed you
    mony a year.
I mind it weel, when thou cou'dst hardly
    gang,[10]

45 Or lisp out words, I choos'd ye frae the
    thrang
O' a the bairns, an' led thee by the
    hand,
Aft to the tansy knowe,[1] or rashy[2] strand,
Thou smiling by my side:—I took delyte
To pou the rashes green, wi' roots sae
    white;
50 O' which, as weel as my young fancy
    cou'd,
For thee I plet[3] the flow'ry belt an'
    snood.[4]
   Peggy. When first thou gade wi'
    shepherds to the hill,
An' I to milk the ewes first try'd my
    skill,
To bear a leglen[5] was nae toil to me,
55 When at the bught[6] at e'en I met wi'
    thee.
Patie. When corn grew yellow, an' the
    heather-bells
Bloom'd bonny on the muir[7] an' rising
    fells,
Nae birns,[8] or briers, or whins,[9] e'er
    troubl'd me
Gif I cou'd find blae-berries ripe for thee.
60   *Peggy.* When thou didst wrestle, run,
    or putt the stane,
An' wan the day, my heart was flight-
    'rin fain;[10]
At a' these sports thou still gie joy to
    me;
For nane can wrestle, run, or putt wi'
    thee.
   Patie. Jenny sings saft the *Broom o'
    Cowdenknowes,*
65 An' Rosie lilts[11] the *Milking o' the
    Ewes;*
There's nane like Nancy *Jenny Nettles*
    sings;
At turns[12] in *Maggy Lauder,* Marion
    dings:[13]
But when my Peggy sings, wi' sweeter
    skill,
The *Boatman,* or the *Lass o' Patie's Mill,*
70 It is a thousand times mair sweet to
    me;
Tho' they sing weel, they canna sing like
    thee.
   Peggy. How eith[14] can lasses trow
    what they desire!

---

[1] blackbird or thrush's
[2] tend; watch
[3] adorn
[4] flatter
[5] make
[6] endure
[7] goats to climb
[8] harm
[9] made much of; caressed
[10] walk

[1] knoll overgrown with tansies
[2] overgrown with rashes,—*i. e.,* rushes
[3] plaited; wove
[4] headband
[5] milk-pail
[6] the pen in which the ewes were milked
[7] heath
[8] charred stems of heather
[9] spiny evergreen shrubs
[10] fluttering with gladness
[11] sings with spirit
[12] A turn is an ornament in music.
[13] excels
[14] easily

An', roos'd by them we love, blaws up
    that fire;[1]
But wha looes best, let time an' carriage[2]
    try;
75 Be constant, an' my love shall time defy.
Be still as now; an' a' my care shall
    be
How to contrive what pleasant is for
    thee.
    Patie. Were thou a giglet gawky[3] like
      the lave,[4]
That little better than our nowt[5] be-
    have;
80 At naught they'll ferly;[6] senseless tales
    believe;
Be blythe for silly heghts,[7] for trifles
    grieve:—
Sic ne'er cou'd win my heart, that kenna
    how
Either to keep a prize, or yet prove
    true;
But thou, in better sense without a flaw,
85 As in thy beauty, far excels them a':
Continue kind, an' a' my care shall be,
How to contrive what pleasing is for
    thee.
    Peggy. Agreed.—But hearken! yon's
      auld aunty's cry,
I ken they'll wonder what can mak us
    stay.
90   *Patie.* An' let them ferly.—Now a
    kindly kiss,
Or five-score guid anes wadna be amiss;
An' syne we'll sing the sang, wi' tunefu'
    glee,
That I made up last owk[8] on you and
    me.
    Peggy. Sing first, syne claim your
    hire.
95   *Patie.* Weel, I agree.

Patie sings.

By the delicious warmness of thy mouth,
An' rowing een[9] that smiling tell the
    truth,
I guess, my lassie, that, as weel as I,
You're made for love, an' why should ye
    deny.

Peggy sings.

100 But ken ye, lad, gin we confess o'er soon,
Ye think us cheap, an' syne the wooing's
    done:

The maiden that o'er quickly tines[1] her
    power,
Like unripe fruit, will taste but hard an'
    sour.

Patie sings.

But gin they hing o'er lang upon the
    tree,
105 Their sweetness they may tine; an' sae
    may ye.
Red-cheeked ye completely ripe appear,
An' I hae thol'd[2] and woo'd a lang half-
    year.

Peggy, singing, fa's into Patie's arms.

Then dinna pu' me, gently thus I fa'
Into my Patie's arms, for good an' a',
110 But stint your wishes to this kind em-
    brace,
An' mint[3] nae farer till we've got the
    grace.

Patie, wi' his left hand about her waist.

O charming armfu'! hence, ye cares,
    away,
I'll kiss my treasure a' the live-lang day:
A' night I'll dream my kisses o'er again,
115 Till that day come that ye'll be a' my
    ain.

Sung by both.

Sun, gallop down the westlin skies,
    Gang soon to bed, an' quickly rise;
O lash your steeds, post time away,
    And haste about our bridal day!
120 An' if ye're wearied, honest light,
    Sleep, gin ye like, a week that night.

PREFACE TO THE EVERGREEN
1724

    I have observed that readers of the best
and most exquisite discernment frequently
complain of our modern writings as filled
with affected delicacies and studied re-
5 finements, which they would gladly exchange for that natural strength of
thought and simplicity of style our forefathers practiced. To such, I hope, the
following collection of poems will not be
10 displeasing.
    When these good old bards wrote, we
had not yet made use of imported trim-
ming upon our clothes, nor of foreign
embroidery in our writings. Their poetry
15 is the product of their own country, not

---

[1] the fire of love, kindled by those we
  love, burns up
[2] actions
[3] frivolous simpleton
[4] rest
[5] cattle
[6] wonder
[7] promises
[8] week
[9] rolling eyes

[1] loses
[2] have suffered
[3] attempt

pilfered and spoiled in the transportation from abroad. Their images are native, and their landscapes domestic; copied from those fields and meadows we every day behold.

The morning rises (in the poet's description) as she does in the Scottish horizon. We are not carried to Greece or Italy for a shade, a stream, or a breeze. The groves rise in our own valleys; the rivers flow from our own fountains; and the winds blow upon our own hills. I find not fault with those things as they are in Greece or Italy; but with a Northern poet for fetching his materials from these places in a poem of which his own country is the scene, as our hymners to the spring and makers of pastorals frequently do.

This miscellany will likewise recommend itself by the diversity of subjects and humor it contains. The grave description and the wanton story, the moral saying and the mirthful jest, will illustrate and alternately relieve each other.

The reader whose temper is spleened with the vices and follies now in fashion, may gratify his humor with the satires he will here find upon the follies and vices that were uppermost two or three hundred years ago. The man whose inclinations are turned to mirth will be pleased to know how the good fellow of a former age told his jovial tale; and the lover may divert himself with the old fashioned sonnet of an amorous poet in Queen Margaret and Queen Mary's days.[1] In a word, the following collection will be such another prospect to the eye of the mind as to the outward eye is the various meadow, where flowers of different hue and smell are mingled together in a beautiful irregularity.

I hope also the reader, when he dips into these poems, will not be displeased with this reflection, that he is stepping back into the times that are past and that exist no more. Thus, the manners and customs

[1] The sixteenth century.

then in vogue, as he will find them here described, will have all the air and charm of novelty; and that seldom fails of exciting attention and pleasing the mind. Besides, the numbers in which these images are conveyed, as they are not now commonly practiced, will appear new and amusing.

The different stanza and varied cadence will likewise much soothe and engage the ear, which in poetry especially must be always flattered. However, I do not expect that these poems should please everybody; nay, the critical reader must needs find several faults, for I own that there will be found in these volumes two or three pieces whose antiquity is their greatest value. Yet still I am persuaded there are many more that shall merit approbation and applause than censure and blame. The best works are but a kind of miscellany, and the cleanest corn is not without some chaff; no, not after often winnowing. Besides, dispraise is the easiest part of learning, and but at best the offspring of uncharitable wit. Every clown can see that the furrow is crooked; but where is the man that will plow me one straight?

There is nothing can be heard more silly than one's expressing his ignorance of his native language; yet, such there are who can vaunt of acquiring a tolerable perfection in the French or Italian tongues if they have been a fortnight in Paris, or a month in Rome. But show them the most elegant thoughts in a Scots dress, they as disdainfully as stupidly condemn it as barbarous. But the true reason is obvious: every one that is born never so little superior to the vulgar would fain distinguish themselves from them by some manner or other, and such, it would appear, cannot arrive at a better method. But this affected class of fops give no uneasiness, not being numerous; for the most part of our gentlemen, who are generally masters of the most useful and politest languages, can take pleasure (for a change) to speak and read their own.

William Hamilton 1704-1754

THE BRAES[1] OF YARROW

IN IMITATION OF THE ANCIENT SCOTS
MANNER
1724

A. Busk[2] ye, busk ye, my bonny bonny
  bride,
  Busk ye, busk ye, my winsome marrow,[3]
  Busk ye, busk ye, my bonny bonny
  bride,
  And think nae mair on the Braes
  of Yarrow.

5 *B.* Where gat ye that bonny bonny bride?
  Where gat ye that winsome mar-
  row?
A. I gat her where I dare na weil be seen,
  Puing the birks[4] on the Braes of
  Yarrow.

  Weep not, weep not, my bonny bonny
  bride,
10 Weep not, weep not, my winsome
  marrow;
  Nor let thy heart lament to leive
  Puing the birks on the Braes of
  Yarrow.

B. Why does she weep, thy bonny bonny
  bride?
  Why does she weep, thy winsome
  marrow?
15 And why dare ye nae mair weil be
  seen
  Puing the birks on the Braes of
  Yarrow?

A. Lang maun she weep, lang maun she,
  maun she weep,
  Lang maun she weep with dule[5] and
  sorrow;
  And lang maun I nae mair weil be
  seen
20 Puing the birks on the Braes of
  Yarrow.

  For she has tint[6] her luver, luver
  dear,
  Her luver dear, the cause of sor-
  row;
  And I hae slain the comliest swain
  That eir pu'd birks on the Braes of
  Yarrow.

25 Why rins thy stream, O Yarrow,
  Yarrow, reid?
  Why on thy braes heard the voice
  of sorrow?
  And why yon melancholious weids
  Hung on the bonny birks of
  Yarrow?

  What's yonder floats on the rueful
  rueful flude?
30 What's yonder floats? O dule and
  sorrow!
  O 'tis he the comely swain I slew
  Upon the duleful Braes of Yarrow.

  Wash, O wash his wounds, his wounds
  in tears,
  His wounds in tears with dule and
  sorrow;
35 And wrap his limbs in mourning
  weids,
  And lay him on the Braes of
  Yarrow.

  Then build, then build, ye sisters,
  sisters sad,
  Ye sisters sad, his tomb with
  sorrow;
  And weep around in waeful wise
40 His hapless fate on the Braes of
  Yarrow.

  Curse ye, curse ye, his useless, useless
  shield,
  My arm that wrought the deed of
  sorrow,
  The fatal spear that pierc'd his
  breast,
  His comely breast on the Braes of
  Yarrow.

45 Did I not warn thee, not to, not to
  luve?
  And warn from fight? but to my
  sorrow
  Too rashly bauld a stronger arm
  Thou mett'st, and fell'st on the
  Braes of Yarrow.

C. Sweet smells the birk, green grows,
  green grows the grass,
50 Yellow on Yarrow's bank the
  gowan,[1]
  Fair hangs the apple frae the rock,
  Sweet the wave of Yarrow flowan.[2]

A. Flows Yarrow sweet? as sweet, as
  sweet flows Tweed,
  As green its grass, its gowan as
  yellow,

[1] banks
[2] array; adorn
[3] mate
[4] pulling the birches
[5] grief
[6] lost

[1] the daisy   [2] flowing

55 As sweet smells on its braes the birk,
    The apple frae its rock as mellow.

Fair was thy luve, fair, fair indeed
    thy luve,
  In flow'ry bands thou didst him
    fetter;
Tho' he was fair, and weil beluv'd
    again
60   Than me he never luv'd thee better.

Busk ye, then busk, my bonny bonny
    bride,
Busk ye, busk ye, my winsome
    marrow,
Busk ye, and luve me on the banks of
    Tweed,
  And think nae mair on the Braes
    of Yarrow.

65 *C.* How can I busk, a bonny bonny bride?
  How can I busk, a winsome marrow?
  How luve him upon the banks of
    Tweed,
    That slew my luve on the Braes of
    Yarrow?

O Yarrow fields, may never, never
    rain
70 Nor dew thy tender blossoms cover,
For there was basely slain my luve,
  My luve, as he had not been a lover.

The boy put on his robes, his robes of
    green,
  His purple vest, 'twas my awn
    sewing:
75 Ah! wretched me! I little, little
    kenn'd
  He was in these to meet his ruin.

The boy took out his milk-white, milk-
    white steed,
  Unheedful of my dule and sorrow:
But ere the to-fall[1] of the night
80   He lay a corps on the Braes of
    Yarrow.

Much I rejoyc'd that waeful, waeful
    day;
  I sang, my voice the woods return-
    ing:
But lang ere night the spear was
    flown,
  That slew my luve, and left me
    mourning.

85 What can my barbarous, barbarous
    father do,
  But with his cruel rage pursue me?

[1] close

My luver's blood is on thy spear,
  How canst thou, barbarous man,
    then wooe me?

My happy sisters may be, may be
    proud
90   With cruel and ungentle scoffin',
May bid me seek on Yarrow's Braes
  My luver nailed in his coffin.

My brother Douglas may upbraid, up-
    braid,
  And strive with threatning words
    to muve me:
95 My luver's blood is on thy spear,
  How canst thou ever bid me luve
    thee?

Yes, yes, prepare the bed, the bed of
    luve,
  With bridal sheets my body cover,
Unbar, ye bridal maids, the door,
100   Let in the expected husband lover.

But who the expected husband, hus-
    band is?
  His hands, methinks, are bath'd in
    slaughter:
Ah me! what ghastly spectre's yon
  Comes in his pale shroud, bleeding
    after?

105 Pale as he is, here lay him, lay him
    down,
  O lay his cold head on my pillow;
Take aff, take aff, these bridal weids,
  And crown my careful head with
    willow.

Pale tho' thou art, yet best, yet best
    beluv'd,
110   O could my warmth to life restore
    thee!
Yet lye all night between my breists,
  No youth lay ever there before thee.

Pale, pale indeed, O luvely, luvely
    youth!
  Forgive, forgive so foul a slaughter:
115 And lye all night between my
    breists;
  No youth shall ever lye there after.

A. Return, return, O mournful, mourn-
    ful bride,
  Return, and dry thy useless sorrow:
Thy luver heeds none of thy sighs,
    He lyes a corps on the Braes of
    Yarrow.

David Mallet 1705-1765

WILLIAM AND MARGARET
1724

'Twas at the silent solemn hour,
  When night and morning meet;
In glided Margaret's grimly ghost,
4 And stood at William's feet.

Her face was like an April morn
  Clad in a wintry cloud;
And clay-cold was her lily hand
8 That held her sable shroud.

So shall the fairest face appear,
  When youth and years are flown:
Such is the robe that kings must wear,
12 When death has reft their crown.

Her bloom was like the springing flower,
  That sips the·silver dew;
The rose was budded in her cheek,
16 Just opening to the view.

But love had, like the canker-worm,
  Consumed her early prime;
The rose grew pale, and left her cheek,
20 She died before her time.

"Awake!" she cried, "thy true love
    calls,
  Come from her midnight grave;
Now let thy pity hear the maid
24 Thy love refused to save.

"This is the dark and dreary hour
  When injured ghosts complain;
When yawning graves give up their
    dead,
28 To haunt the faithless swain.

"Bethink thee, William, of thy fault,
  Thy pledge and broken oath!
And give me back my maiden vow,
32 And give me back my troth.

"Why did you promise love to me,
  And not that promise keep?
Why did you swear my eyes were bright,
36 Yet leave those eyes to weep?

"How could you say my face was fair,
  And yet that face forsake?
How could you win my virgin heart,
40 Yet leave that heart to break?

"Why did you say my lip was sweet,
  And make the scarlet pale?
And why did I, young, witless maid!
44 Believe the flattering tale?

"That face, alas! no more is fair,
  Those lips no longer red:
Dark are my eyes, now closed in death,
48 And every charm is fled.

"The hungry worm my sister is;
  This winding-sheet I wear:
And cold and weary lasts our night,
52 Till that last morn appear.

"But hark! the cock has warned me
    hence;
  A long and last adieu!
Come see, false man, how low she lies,
56 Who died for love of you."

The lark sung loud; the morning smiled
  With beams of rosy red:
Pale William quaked in every limb,
60 And raving left his bed.

He hied him to the fatal place
  Where Margaret's body lay;
And stretched him on the green-grass
    turf
64 That wrapt her breathless clay.

And thrice he called on Margaret's name,
  And thrice he wept full sore;
Then laid his cheek to her cold grave,
68 And word spake never more!

THE BIRKS[1] OF ENDERMAY

The smiling morn, the breathing spring,
  Invite the tuneful birds to sing:
And while they warble from each spray,
  Love melts the universal lay.
5 Let us, Amanda, timely wise,
  Like them improve the hour that flies;
And, in soft raptures, waste the day,
  Among the shades of Endermay.

For soon the winter of the year,
10 And age, life's winter, will appear:
  At this, thy living bloom must fade;
  As that will strip the verdant shade.
  Our taste of pleasure then is o'er;
  The feather'd songsters love no more:
15 And when they droop, and we decay,
  Adieu the shades of Endermay!

[1] birches

John Dyer 1700?-1758?

GRONGAR HILL
1726

Silent nymph[1] with curious eye,
Who, the purple ev'ning, lie
On the mountain's lonely van,
Beyond the noise of busy man,
5 Painting fair the form of things,
While the yellow linnet sings,
Or the tuneful nightingale
Charms the forest with her tale,
Come, with all thy various hues,
10 Come, and aid thy sister Muse;
Now while Phoebus, riding high,
Gives lustre to the land and sky,
Grongar Hill invites my song;
Draw the landskip bright and strong;
15 Grongar, in whose mossy cells,
Sweetly musing Quiet dwells;
Grongar, in whose silent shade,
For the modest Muses made,
So oft I have, the ev'ning still,
20 At the fountain of a rill,
Sat upon a flow'ry bed,
With my hand beneath my head,
While stray'd my eyes o'er Towy's flood,
Over mead and over wood,
25 From house to house, from hill to hill,
Till Contemplation had her fill.
About his chequer'd sides I wind,
And leave his brooks and meads behind,
And groves and grottoes where I lay,
30 And vistoes[2] shooting beams of day.
Wide and wider spreads the vale,
As circles on a smooth canal:
The mountains round, unhappy fate!
Sooner or later, of all height,
35 Withdraw their summits from the skies,
And lessen as the others rise:
Still the prospect wider spreads,
Adds a thousand woods and meads;
Still it widens, widens still,
40 And sinks the newly-risen hill.
Now I gain the mountain's brow,
What a landskip lies below!
No clouds, no vapors intervene;
But the gay, the open scene
45 Does the face of Nature show
In all the hues of heaven's bow,
And, swelling to embrace the light,
Spreads around beneath the sight.
Old castles on the cliffs arise,
50 Proudly tow'ring in the skies;
Rushing from the woods, the spires
Seem from hence ascending fires;
Half his beams Apollo sheds

On the yellow mountain-heads,
55 Gilds the fleeces of the flocks,
And glitters on the broken rocks.
Below me trees unnumber'd rise,
Beautiful in various dyes;
The gloomy pine, the poplar blue,
60 The yellow beech, the sable yew,
The slender fir, that taper grows,
The sturdy oak with broad-spread boughs,
And beyond the purple grove,
Haunt of Phillis, queen of love!
65 Gaudy as the op'ning dawn,
Lies a long and level lawn,[1]
On which a dark hill, steep and high,
Holds and charms the wand'ring eye:
Deep are his feet in Towy's flood,
70 His sides are cloth'd with waving wood,
And ancient towers crown his brow,
That cast an awful look below;
Whose ragged walls the ivy creeps,
And with her arms from falling keeps;
75 So both a safety from the wind
On mutual dependence find.
'Tis now the raven's bleak abode;
'Tis now th' apartment of the toad;
And there the fox securely feeds,
80 And there the pois'nous adder breeds,
Conceal'd in ruins, moss, and weeds;
While, ever and anon, there falls
Huge heaps of hoary moulder'd walls.
Yet Time has seen, that lifts the low,
85 And level lays the lofty brow,
Has seen this broken pile compleat,[2]
Big with the vanity of state:
But transient is the smile of Fate!
A little rule, a little sway,
90 A sunbeam in a winter's day,
Is all the proud and mighty have
Between the cradle and the grave.
And see the rivers how they run
Thro' woods and meads, in shade and
    sun!
95 Sometimes swift and sometimes slow,
Wave succeeding wave, they go
A various journey to the deep,
Like human life to endless sleep:
Thus is Nature's vesture wrought,
100 To instruct our wand'ring thought;
Thus she dresses green and gay,
To disperse our cares away.
Ever charming, ever new,
When will the landskip tire the view!
105 The fountain's fall, the river's flow,
The woody valleys warm and low;
The windy summit, wild and high,
Roughly rushing on the sky!
The pleasant seat, the ruin'd tow'r,

---

[1] The muse of painting.   [2] vistas; prospects

[1] grassy field   [2] *Compleat* rimes with *state.*

110 The naked rock, the shady bow'r;
The town and village, dome and farm,
Each give each a double charm,
As pearls upon an Ethiop's arm.
See on the mountain's southern side,
115 Where the prospect opens wide,
Where the ev'ning gilds the tide,
How close and small the hedges lie!
What streaks of meadows cross the eye!
A step, methinks, may pass the stream,
120 So little distant dangers seem;
So we mistake the Future's face,
Ey'd thro' Hope's deluding glass;
As yon summits soft and fair,
Clad in colors of the air,
125 Which, to those who journey near,
Barren, brown, and rough appear;
Still we tread the same coarse way;
The present's still a cloudy day.
O may I with myself agree,
130 And never covet what I see;
Content me with an humble shade,
My passions tam'd, my wishes laid;
For while our wishes wildly roll,
We banish quiet from the soul;
135 'Tis thus the busy beat the air,
And misers gather wealth and care.
Now, ev'n now, my joys run high,
As on the mountain-turf I lie;
While the wanton Zephyr sings,
140 And in the vale perfumes his wings;
While the waters murmur deep;
While the shepherd charms[1] his sheep;
While the birds unbounded fly,
And with music fill the sky,
145 Now, ev'n now, my joys run high.
Be full, ye courts! be great who will;
Search for Peace with all your skill:
Open wide the lofty door,
Seek her on the marble floor:
150 In vain ye search, she is not there;
In vain ye search the domes of Care!
Grass and flowers Quiet treads,
On the meads and mountain-heads,
Along with Pleasure close ally'd,
155 Ever by each other's side,
And often, by the murm'ring rill,
Hears the thrush, while all is still,
Within the groves of Grongar Hill.

THE FLEECE
1757

From Book I

Ah, gentle shepherd, thine the lot to
tend
400 Of all, that feel distress, the most assail'd,

[1] controls or calms by playing upon his pipe

Feeble, defenceless: lenient be thy care:
But spread around thy tenderest diligence
In flow'ry spring-time, when the new-
dropt lamb,
Tottering with weakness by his mother's
side,
405 Feels the fresh world about him; and
each thorn,
Hillock, or furrow, trips his feeble feet:
Oh, guard his meek sweet innocence from
all
Th' innumerous ills, that rush around
his life;
Mark the quick kite, with beak and
talons prone,
410 Circling the skies to snatch him from
the plain;
Observe the lurking crows; beware the
brake,
There the sly fox the careless minute
waits;
Nor trust thy neighbor's dog, nor earth,
nor sky:
Thy bosom to a thousand cares divide.
415 Eurus oft sings his hail; the tardy fields
Pay not their promised food; and oft
the dam
O'er her weak twins with empty udder
mourns,
Or fails to guard, when the bold bird of
prey
Alights, and hops in many turns around,
420 And tires her also turning: to her aid
Be nimble, and the weakest in thine arms
Gently convey to the warm cote, and oft,
Between the lark's note and the nightin-
gale's,
His hungry bleating still with tepid milk:
425 In this soft office may thy children join,
And charitable habits learn in sport:
Nor yield him to himself, ere vernal airs
Sprinkle thy little croft with daisy
flowers:
Nor yet forget him: life has rising ills:
430 Various as ether[1] is the pastoral care:
Through slow experience, by a patient
breast,
The whole long lesson gradual is at-
tained,
By precept after precept, oft received
With deep attention: such as Nuceus
sings
435 To the full vale near Soare's enamor'd
brook,
While all is silence: sweet Hincklean
swain!

[1] The substance supposed to fill the upper regions
of space.

Whom rude obscurity severely clasps:
The muse, howe'er, will deck thy simple
    cell
With purple violets and primrose flowers,
440 Well-pleased thy faithful lessons to re-
    pay.

. . . . .

James Thomson 1700-1748

THE SEASONS

From WINTER
1725   1726

See, Winter comes to rule the varied
    year,
Sullen and sad, with all his rising train—
Vapors, and clouds, and storms. Be these
    my theme;
These, that exalt the soul to solemn
    thought
5 And heavenly musing. Welcome, kin-
    dred glooms!
Cogenial[1] horrors, hail! With frequent
    foot,
Pleased have I, in my cheerful morn of
    life,
When nursed by careless solitude I lived
And sung of Nature with unceasing joy,
20 Pleased have I wandered through your
    rough domain;
Trod the pure virgin-snows, myself as
    pure;
Heard the winds roar, and the big tor-
    rent burst;
Or seen the deep-fermenting tempest
    brewed
In the grim evening-sky. Thus passed
    the time,
15 Till through the lucid chambers of the
    south
Looked out the joyous Spring—looked
    out and smiled.

. . . . . .

    Then comes the father of the tempest
    forth,
Wrapt in black glooms. First, joyless
    rains obscure
Drive through the mingling skies with
    vapor foul,
75 Dash on the mountain's brow, and shake
    the woods
That grumbling wave below. The un-
    sightly plain
Lies a brown deluge; as the low-bent
    clouds
Pour flood on flood, yet unexhausted still
Combine, and, deepening into night, shut
    up

[1] congenial

80 The day's fair face. The wanderers of
    heaven,
Each to his home, retire; save those
    that love
To take their pastime in the troubled air,
Or skimming flutter round the dimply
    pool.
The cattle from the untasted fields return
85 And ask, with meaning low, their wonted
    stalls,
Or ruminate in the contiguous shade.
Thither the household feathery people
    crowd,
The crested cock, with all his female
    train,
Pensive and dripping; while the cottage-
    hind
90 Hangs o'er the enlivening blaze, and
    taleful there
Recounts his simple frolic: much he
    talks,
And much he laughs, nor recks the storm
    that blows
Without, and rattles on his humble roof.
    Wide o'er the brim, with many a tor-
    rent swelled,
95 And the mixed ruin of its banks o'er-
    spread,
At last the roused-up river pours along:
Resistless, roaring, dreadful, down it
    comes,
From the rude mountain and the mossy
    wild,
Tumbling through rocks abrupt, and
    sounding far;
100 Then o'er the sanded valley floating
    spreads,
Calm, sluggish, silent; till again, con-
    strained
Between two meeting hills, it bursts a
    way
Where rocks and woods o'erhang the
    turbid stream;
There, gathering triple force, rapid and
    deep,
105 It boils, and wheels, and foams, and
    thunders through.

. . . . . .

    Ah! little think the gay licentious
    proud,
Whom pleasure, power, and affluence
    surround—
They, who their thoughtless hours in
    giddy mirth,
325 And wanton, often cruel, riot waste—
Ah! little think they, while they dance
    along,
How many feel, this very moment, death
And all the sad variety of pain;

How many sink in the devouring flood,
330 Or more devouring flame; how many
    bleed,
By shameful variance betwixt man and
    man;
How many pine in want, and dungeon-
    glooms,
Shut from the common air and common
    use
Of their own limbs; how many drink the
    cup
335 Of baleful grief, or eat the bitter bread
Of misery; sore pierced by wintry winds,
How many shrink into the sordid hut
Of cheerless poverty; how many shake
With all the fiercer tortures of the mind,
340 Unbounded passion, madness, guilt, re-
    morse—
Whence, tumbled headlong from the
    height of life,
They furnish matter for the tragic muse;
Even in the vale, where wisdom loves to
    dwell,
With friendship, peace, and contempla-
    tion joined,
345 How many, racked with honest passions,
    droop
In deep retired distress; how many stand
Around the death-bed of their dearest
    friends,
And point the parting anguish! Thought
    fond man
Of these, and all the thousand nameless
    ills
350 That one incessant struggle render life,
One scene of toil, of suffering, and of
    fate,
Vice in his high career would stand
    appalled,
And heedless rambling Impulse learn to
    think;
The conscious heart of Charity would
    warm,
355 And her wide wish Benevolence dilate;
The social tear would rise, the social
    sigh;
And, into clear perfection, gradual
    bliss,
Refining still, the social passions work.
    And here can I forget the generous
    band
360 Who, touched with human woe, redressive
    searched
Into the horrors of the gloomy jail?[1]

Unpitied and unheard where misery
    moans,
Where sickness pines, where thirst and
    hunger burn,
And poor misfortune feels the lash of
    vice;
365 While in the land of liberty—the land
Whose every street and public meeting
    glow
With open freedom—little tyrants raged,
Snatched the lean morsel from the starv-
    ing mouth,
Tore from cold wintry limbs the tattered
    weed,
370 Even robbed them of the last of com-
    forts, sleep,
The free-born Briton to the dungeon
    chained
Or, as the lust of cruelty prevailed,
At pleasure marked him with inglorious
    stripes,
And crushed out lives, by secret bar-
    barous ways,
375 That for their country would have toiled
    or bled.
O great design! if executed well,
With patient care and wisdom-tempered
    zeal.
Ye sons of mercy! yet resume the search;
Drag forth the legal monsters into light,
380 Wrench from their hands Oppression's
    iron rod,
And bid the cruel feel the pains they
    give.
Much still untouched remains; in this
    rank age,
Much is the patriot's weeding hand re-
    quired.
The toils of law—what dark insidious
    men
385 Have cumbrous added to perplex the
    truth
And lengthen simple justice into trade—
How glorious were the day that saw
    these broke,
And every man within the reach of right!
     ·   ·   ·   ·   ·   ·

From SUMMER
1726   1727

516 Still let me pierce into the midnight
    depth
Of yonder grove, of wildest largest
    growth,
That, forming high in air a woodland
    quire,
Nods o'er the mount beneath. At every
    step,

---

[1] A committee appointed in 1729 to investigate
    the conditions of jails and prisons, who dis-
    covered that the wardenships of prisons were
    bought by men who were accustomed to exact
    heavy fees from prisoners on the penalty of
    severe punishment.

520 Solemn and slow the shadows blacker fall,
And all is awful listening gloom around.
These are the haunts of meditation, these
The scenes where ancient bards the inspiring breath
Ecstatic felt, and, from this world retired,
525 Conversed with angels and immortal forms,
On gracious errands bent—to save the fall
Of virtue struggling on the brink of vice;
In waking whispers and repeated dreams
To hint pure thought, and warn the favored soul,
530 For future trials fated, to prepare;
To prompt the poet, who devoted gives
His muse to better themes; to soothe the pangs
Of dying worth, and from the patriot's breast
(Backward to mingle in detested war,
535 But foremost when engaged) to turn the death;
And numberless such offices of love,
Daily and nightly, zealous to perform.

·   ·   ·   ·   ·   ·

585   Thus up the mount, in airy vision rapt,
I stray, regardless whither; till the sound
Of a near fall of water every sense
Wakes from the charm of thought: swift-shrinking back,
I check my steps and view the broken scene.
590   Smooth to the shelving brink a copious flood
Rolls fair and placid; where, collected all
In one impetuous torrent, down the steep
It thundering shoots, and shakes the country round.
At first, an azure sheet, it rushes broad;
595 Then, whitening by degrees as prone it falls,
And from the loud-resounding rocks below
Dashed in a cloud of foam, it sends aloft
A hoary mist and forms a ceaseless shower.
Nor can the tortured wave here find repose;
600 But, raging still amid the shaggy rocks,
Now flashes o'er the scattered fragments, now
Aslant the hollow channel rapid darts;

And, falling fast from gradual slope to slope,
With wild infracted course and lessened roar
605 It gains a safer bed, and steals at last
Along the mazes of the quiet vale.
Invited from the cliff, to whose dark brow
He clings, the steep-ascending eagle soars
With upward pinions through the flood of day,
610 And, giving full his bosom to the blaze,
Gains on the Sun; while all the tuneful race,
Smit by afflictive noon, disordered droop
Deep in the thicket, or, from bower to bower
Responsive, force an interrupted strain.
615 The stock-dove only through the forest coos,
Mournfully hoarse; oft ceasing from his plaint,
Short interval of weary woe! again
The sad idea of his murdered mate,
Struck from his side by savage fowler's guile,
620 Across his fancy comes; and then resounds
A louder song of sorrow through the grove.
Beside the dewy border let me sit,
All in the freshness of the humid air,
There on that hollowed rock, grotesque and wild,
625 An ample chair moss-lined and over head
By flowering umbrage shaded; where the bee
Strays diligent, and with the extracted balm
Of fragrant woodbine loads his little thigh.

·   ·   ·   ·   ·   ·

1371   The Sun has lost his rage: his downward orb
Shoots nothing now but animating warmth
And vital lustre; that with various ray,
Lights up the clouds, those beauteous robes of heaven,
1375 Incessant rolled into romantic shapes,
The dream of waking fancy! Broad below,
Covered with ripening fruits, and swelling fast
Into the perfect year, the pregnant earth
And all her tribes rejoice. Now the soft hour

1380 Of walking comes for him who lonely loves
     To seek the distant hills, and there con-
          verse
     With nature, there to harmonize his heart,
     And in pathetic song to breathe around
     The harmony to others. Social friends,
1385 Attuned to happy unison of soul—
     To whose exulting eye a fairer world,
     Of which the vulgar never had a glimpse,
     Displays its charms; whose minds are
          richly fraught
     With philosophic stores, superior light;
1390 And in whose breast enthusiastic burns
     Virtue, the sons of interest deem ro-
          mance—
     Now called abroad, enjoy the falling day:
     Now to the verdant portico of woods,
     To nature's vast lyceum, forth they walk;
1395 By that kind school where no proud mas-
          ter reigns,
     The full free converse of the friendly
          heart,
     Improving and improved. Now from the
          world,
     Sacred to sweet retirement, lovers steal,
     And pour their souls in transport, which
          the sire
1400 Of love approving hears, and calls it
          good. . . . . .

From AUTUMN
1730

950   But see the fading many-colored woods,
     Shade deepening over shade, the country
          round
     Imbrown; a crowded umbrage, dusk and
          dun,
     Of every hue from wan declining green
     To sooty dark. These now the lonesome
          muse,
955 Low-whispering, lead into their leaf-
          strown walks,
     And give the season in its latest view.
     Meantime, light shadowing all, a sober
          calm
     Fleeces[1] unbounded ether; whose least
          wave
     Stands tremulous, uncertain where to turn
960 The gentle current; while, illumined wide,
     The dewy-skirted clouds imbibe the sun,
     And through their lucid veil his softened
          force
     Shed o'er the peaceful world. Then is
          the time
     For those whom wisdom and whom na-
          ture charm
965 To steal themselves from the degenerate
          crowd,

¹ spreads over like a fleece

And soar above this little scene of
     things—
To tread low-thoughted vice beneath
     their feet,
To soothe the throbbing passions into
     peace,
And woo lone Quiet in her silent walks.
970 Thus solitary, and in pensive guise,
Oft let me wander o'er the russet mead,
And through the saddened grove, where
     scarce is heard
One dying strain to cheer the woodman's
     toil.
Haply some widowed songster pours his
     plaint
975 Far in faint warblings through the
     tawny[1] copse;
While congregated thrushes, linnets,
     larks,
And each wild throat whose artless
     strains so late
Swelled all the music of the swarming
     shades,
Robbed of their tuneful souls, now shiv-
     ering sit
980 On the dead tree, a dull despondent
     flock,
With not a brightness waving o'er their
     plumes,
And naught save chattering discord in
     their note.
Oh, let not, aimed from some inhuman
     eye,
The gun the music of the coming year
985 Destroy, and harmless, unsuspecting
     harm,
Lay the weak tribes, a miserable prey,
In mingled murder fluttering on the
     ground!
  The pale descending year, yet pleasing
     still,
A gentler mood inspires; for now the
     leaf
990 Incessant rustles from the mournful
     grove,
Oft startling such as studious walk be-
     low,
And slowly circles through the waving
     air.
But, should a quicker breeze amid the
     boughs
Sob, o'er the sky the leafy deluge
     streams;
995 Till, choked and matted with the dreary
     shower,
The forest-walks, at every rising gale,
Roll wide the wither'd waste, and whistle
     bleak.

¹ yellowish brown

Fled is the blasted verdure of the fields;
And, shrunk into their beds, the flowery
    race
1000 Their sunny robes resign. Even what
    remained
Of bolder fruits falls from the naked
    tree;
And—woods, fields, gardens, orchards,
    all around—
The desolated prospect thrills the soul.
    He comes! he comes! in every breeze
    the Power
1005 Of Philosophic Melancholy comes!
His near approach the sudden-starting
    tear,
The glowing cheek, the mild dejected air,
The softened feature, and the beating
    heart,
Pierced deep with many a virtuous pang,
    declare.
1010 O'er all the soul his sacred influence
    breathes;
Inflames imagination; through the breast
Infuses every tenderness; and far
Beyond dim earth exalts the swelling
    thought.
Ten thousand thousand fleet ideas, such
1015 As never mingled with the vulgar dream,
Crowd fast into the mind's creative eye.
As fast the correspondent passions rise,
As varied, and as high—devotion raised
To rapture, and divine astonishment;
1020 The love of nature unconfined, and, chief,
Of human race; the large ambitious wish
To make them blest; the sigh for suffer-
    ing worth
Lost in obscurity; the noble scorn
Of tyrant pride; the fearless great re-
    solve;
1025 The wonder which the dying patriot
    draws,
Inspiring glory through remotest time;
The awakened throb for virtue and for
    fame;
The sympathies of love and friendship
    dear,
With all the social offspring of the heart.
1030   Oh! bear me then to vast embowering
    shades,
To twilight groves, and visionary vales,
To weeping grottoes, and prophetic
    glooms;
Where angel forms athwart the solemn
    dusk,
Tremendous, sweep, or seem to sweep
    along;
1035 And voices more than human, through
    the void
Deep-sounding, seize the enthusiastic ear.

              Meanwhile the moon,
Full-orbed and breaking through the
    scattered clouds,
1090 Shows her broad visage in the crimsoned
    east.
Turned to the sun direct, her spotted
    disk
(Where mountains rise, umbrageous
    dales descend,
And caverns deep, as optic tube descries)
A smaller earth, gives all his blaze
    again,
1095 Void of its flame, and sheds a softer
    day.
Now through the passing cloud she seems
    to stoop,
Now up the pure cerulean rides sublime.
Wide the pale deluge floats, and stream-
    ing mild
O'er the skied mountain to the shad-
    owy vale,
1100 While rocks and floods reflect the quiv-
    ering gleam,
The whole air whitens with a boundless
    tide
Of silver radiance trembling round the
    world.

     O Nature! all-sufficient! over all
Enrich me with the knowledge of thy
    works;
Snatch me to heaven; thy rolling won-
    ders there,
1355 World beyond world, in infinite extent
Profusely scattered o'er the blue im-
    mense,
Show me; their motions, periods, and
    their laws
Give me to scan; through the disclosing
    deep
Light my blind way: the mineral strata
    there;
1360 Thrust blooming thence the vegetable
    world;
O'er that the rising system, more com-
    plex,
Of animals; and, higher still, the mind,
The varied scene of quick-compounded
    thought,
And where the mixing passions endless
    shift;
1365 These ever open to my ravished eye—
A search, the flight of time can ne'er
    exhaust!
But, if to that unequal—if the blood
In sluggish streams about my heart forbid
That best ambition—under closing shades
1370 Inglorious lay me by the lowly brook,

And whisper to my dreams. From thee
begin,
Dwell all on thee, with thee conclude
my song;
And let me never, never stray from thee!

A HYMN ON THE SEASONS
1730

These, as they change, Almighty Father!
these
Are but the varied God. The rolling year
Is full of thee. Forth in the pleasing
spring
Thy beauty walks, thy tenderness and
love.
5 Wide flush the fields; the softening air
is balm;
Echo the mountains round; the forest
smiles;
And every sense, and every heart, is joy.
Then comes thy glory in the summer-
months,
With light and heat refulgent.[1] Then thy
sun
10 Shoots full perfection through the swelling year:
And oft thy voice in dreadful thunder
speaks,
And oft, at dawn, deep noon, or falling
eve,
By brooks and groves, in hollow-whis-
pering gales,
Thy bounty shines in autumn unconfined,
15 And spreads a common feast for all
that lives.
In winter awful thou! with clouds and
storms
Around thee thrown, tempest o'er tempest rolled,
Majestic darkness! on the whirlwind's
wing
Riding sublime, thou bidst the world
adore,
20 And humblest nature with thy northern
blast.

Mysterious round! what skill, what
force divine,
Deep-felt in these appear! a simple train,
Yet so delightful mixed, with such kind
art,
Such beauty and beneficence combined,
25 Shade unperceived so softening into
shade,
And all so forming an harmonious
whole

[1] brilliant: radiant

That, as they still succeed, they ravish
still.
But, wandering oft with brute unconscious gaze,
Man marks not thee, marks not the
mighty hand
30 That, ever busy, wheels the silent spheres,
Works in the secret deep, shoots steaming thence
The fair profusion that o'erspreads the
spring,
Flings from the sun direct the flaming
day,
Feeds every creature, hurls the tempest
forth,
35 And, as on earth this grateful change
revolves,
With transport touches all the springs
of life.

Nature, attend! join, every living soul
Beneath the spacious temple of the
sky,
In adoration join; and ardent raise
40 One general song! To him, ye vocal
gales,
Breathe soft, whose spirit in your freshness breathes:
Oh! talk of him in solitary glooms,
Where, o'er the rock, the scarcely-wav-
ing pine
Fills the brown shade with a religious
awe.
45 And ye, whose bolder note is heard afar,
Who shake the astonished world, lift
high to heaven
The impetuous song, and say from whom
you rage.
His praise, ye brooks, attune, ye trembling rills;
And let me catch it as I muse along.
50 Ye headlong torrents, rapid and profound;
Ye softer floods, that lead the humid
maze
Along the vale; and thou, majestic main,
A secret world of wonders in thyself,
Sound his stupendous praise, whose
greater voice
55 Or bids you roar or bids your roarings
fall.
Soft roll your incense, herbs, and fruits,
and flowers,
In mingled clouds to him, whose sun
exalts,
Whose breath perfumes you, and whose
pencil paints.
Ye forests, bend; ye harvests, wave to
him—

60 Breathe your still song into the reaper's
    heart
    As home he goes beneath the joyous
      moon.
    Ye that keep watch in heaven, as earth
      asleep
    Unconscious lies, effuse[1] your mildest
      beams,
    Ye constellations! while your angels
      strike
65 Amid the spangled sky the silver lyre.
    Great source of day! best image here
      below
    Of thy Creator, ever pouring wide
    From world to world the vital ocean
      round!
    On nature write with every beam his
      praise.
70 The thunder rolls: be hushed the pros-
      trate world
    While cloud to cloud returns the solemn
      hymn.
    Bleat out afresh, ye hills; ye mossy
      rocks,
    Retain the sound; the broad responsive
      low,
    Ye valleys, raise; for the Great Shep-
      herd reigns,
75 And his unsuffering kingdom yet will
      come.
    Ye woodlands all, awake: a boundless
      song
    Burst from the groves; and, when the
      restless day,
    Expiring, lays the warbling world asleep,
    Sweetest of birds, sweet Philomela!
      charm
80 The listening shades, and teach the night
      his praise!
    Ye, chief, for whom the whole creation
      smiles,
    At once the head, the heart, the tongue
      of all,
    Crown the great hymn! In swarming
      cities vast,
    Assembled men, to the deep organ
      join
85 The long-resounding voice, oft breaking
      clear
    At solemn pauses through the swelling
      bass;
    And, as each mingling flame increases
      each,
    In one united ardor rise to heaven.
    Or, if you rather choose the rural shade,
90 And find a fane in every sacred grove,
    There let the shepherd's flute, the vir-
      gin's lay,

[1] send forth

    The prompting seraph, and the poet's
      lyre
    Still sing the God of Seasons as they roll.
    For me, when I forget the darling theme,
95 Whether the blossom blows, the summer-
      ray
    Russets the plain, inspiring autumn
      gleams,
    Or winter rises in the blackening east,
    Be my tongue mute, my fancy paint no
      more.
    And, dead to joy, forget my heart to beat!
100   Should fate command me to the far-
      thest verge
    Of the green earth, to distant barbarous
      climes,
    Rivers unknown to song, where first the
      sun
    Gilds Indian mountains, or his setting
      beam
    Flames on the Atlantic isles, 'tis nought
      to me;
105 Since God is ever present, ever felt,
    In the void waste as in the city full,
    And where he vital spreads there must
      be joy.
    When even at last the solemn hour shall
      come,
    And wing my mystic flight to future
      worlds,
110 I cheerful will obey; there, with new
      powers,
    Will rising wonders sing: I cannot go
    Where universal love not smiles around,
    Sustaining all yon orbs and all their
      sons;
    From seeming evil still educing good,
115 And better thence again, and better still,
    In infinite progression. But I lose
    Myself in him, in light ineffable!
    Come then, expressive Silence, muse his
      praise.

THE CASTLE OF INDOLENCE
1736-48   1748
From CANTO I

    The Castle hight[1] of Indolence,
      And its false luxury;
    Where for a little time alas!
      We lived right jollily.

O mortal man, who livest here by toil,
Do not complain of this thy hard
    estate;
That like an emmet[2] thou must ever
    moil
Is a sad sentence of an ancient date:[3]

[1] called: named
[2] ant
[3] "In the sweat of thy face shalt thou eat
bread."—*Genesis*, 3:19.

And, certes, there is for it reason
    great;
For, though sometimes it makes thee
    weep and wail,
And curse thy stars, and early drudge
    and late,
Withouten that would come an heavier
    bale,
Loose life, unruly passions, and diseases
    pale.

10 In lowly dale, fast by a river's side,
    With woody hill o'er hill encompassed
    round,
A most enchanting wizard did abide,
Than whom a fiend more fell is no-
    where found.
It was, I ween,[1] a lovely spot of
    ground;
15 And there a season atween June and
    May,
Half prankt with spring, with summer
    half imbrowned,
A listless climate made, where, sooth
    to say,
No living wight could work, ne carèd
    even for play.

Was nought around but images of rest:
20 Sleep-soothing groves, and quiet lawns
    between;
And flowery beds that slumbrous in-
    fluence kest,[2]
From poppies breathed; and beds of
    pleasant green,
Where never yet was creeping creature
    seen.
Meantime unnumbered glittering stream-
    lets played,
25 And hurlèd everywhere their waters
    sheen;
That, as they bickered through the
    sunny glade,
Though restless still themselves, a lulling
    murmur made.

Joined to the prattle of the purling
    rills,
Were heard the lowing herds along
    the vale,
And flocks loud-bleating from the dis-
    tant hills,
And vacant[3] shepherds piping in the
    dale:
And now and then sweet Philomel
    would wail,
Or stock-doves plain amid the forest
    deep,

That drowsy rustled to the sighing
    gale;
35 And still a coil the grasshopper did
    keep;
Yet all these sounds yblent[1] inclinèd all
    to sleep.

Full in the passage of the vale, above,
A sable, silent, solemn forest stood;
Where nought but shadowy forms were
    seen to move,
40 As Idless fancied in her dreaming
    mood.
And up the hills, on either side, a wood
Of blackening pines, ay waving to and
    fro,
Sent forth a sleepy horror through the
    blood;
And where this valley winded out,
    below,
45 The murmuring main was heard, and
    scarcely heard, to flow.

A pleasing land of drowsyhed it was:
Of dreams that wave before the half-
    shut eye;
And of gay castles in the clouds that
    pass,
For ever flushing round a summer sky:
50 There eke the soft delights, that witch-
    ingly
Instil a wanton sweetness through the
    breast,
And the calm pleasures always hov-
    ered nigh;
But whate'er smacked of noyance, or
    unrest,
Was far far off expelled from this deli-
    cious nest.

55 The landskip such, inspiring perfect
    ease;
Where Indolence (for so the wizard
    hight)[2]
Close-hid his castle mid embowering
    trees,
That half shut out the beams of Phoe-
    bus bright,
And made a kind of checkered day
    and night.
60 Meanwhile, unceasing at the massy
    gate,
Beneath a spacious palm, the wicked
    wight
Was placed; and, to his lute, of cruel
    fate
And labor harsh complained, lamenting
    man's estate.

---

[1] think   [2] cast   [3] care-free   [1] blended   [2] was called

Thither continual pilgrims crowded
   still
65 From all the roads of earth that pass
   there by:
For, as they chaunced to breathe on
   neighboring hill,
The freshness of this valley smote
   their eye,
And drew them ever and anon more
   nigh,
Till clustering round the enchanter
   false they hung,
70 Ymolten[1] with his syren melody;
While o'er th' enfeebling lute his
   hand he flung,
And to the trembling chord these tempting verses sung:

"Behold! ye pilgrims of this earth,
   behold!
See all but man with unearned pleasure gay.
75 See her bright robes the butterfly unfold,
Broke from her wintry tomb in prime
   of May.
What youthful bride can equal her
   array?
Who can with her for easy pleasure
   vie?
From mead to mead with gentle wing
   to stray,
80 From flower to flower on balmy gales
   to fly,
Is all she has to do beneath the radiant
   sky.

"Behold the merry minstrels of the
   morn,
The swarming songsters of the careless grove,
Ten thousand throats that, from the
   flowering thorn,
85 Hymn their good God, and carol sweet
   of love,
Such grateful kindly raptures them
   emove![2]
They neither plough nor sow; ne,[3] fit
   for flail,
E'er to the barn the nodding sheaves
   they drove;
Yet theirs each harvest dancing in
   the gale,
90 Whatever crowns the hill, or smiles
   along the vale.

"Outcast of Nature, man! the wretched
   thrall
Of bitter-dropping sweat, of sweltry
   pain,
Of cares that eat away thy heart with
   gall,
95 And of the vices, an inhuman train,
That all proceed from savage thirst
   of gain:
For when hard-hearted Interest first
   began
To poison earth, Astraea left the plain;
Guile, Violence, and Murder seized on
   man,
And, for soft milky streams, with blood
   the rivers ran.

100 "Come, ye, who still the cumbrous
   load of life
Push hard up hill; but, as the farthest
   steep
You trust to gain, and put an end to
   strife,
Down thunders back the stone with
   mighty sweep,
And hurls your labors to the valley
   deep,
105 Forever vain: come, and withouten fee
I in oblivion will your sorrows steep,
Your cares, your toils; will steep you
   in a sea
Of full delight: O come, ye weary
   wights, to me!

"With me, you need not rise at early
   dawn,
110 To pass the joyless day in various
   stounds;[1]
Or, louting low, on upstart fortune
   fawn,
And sell fair honor for some paltry
   pounds;
Or through the city take your dirty
   rounds
To cheat, and dun, and lie, and visit
   pay,
115 Now flattering base, now giving secret
   wounds;
Or prowl in courts of law for human
   prey,
In venal senate thieve, or rob on broad
   highway.

"No cocks, with me, to rustic labor
   call,
From village on to village sounding
   clear;

---

[1] melted   [3] nor
[2] move (cf. emotion)

[1] aches; sorrows

120 To tardy swain no shrill-voiced matrons squall;
No dogs, no babes, no wives to stun
  your ear;
No hammers thump; no horrid blacksmith sear,
Ne noisy tradesman your sweet slumbers start
With sounds that are a misery to hear:
125 But all is calm as would delight the
  heart
Of Sybarite[1] of old, all nature, and all
  art.

"Here nought but candor reigns, indulgent ease,
Good-natured lounging, sauntering up
  and down:
They who are pleased themselves must
  always please;
130 On others' ways they never squint a
  frown,
Nor heed what haps in hamlet or in
  town.
Thus, from the source of tender Indolence,
With milky blood the heart is over-
  flown,
Is soothed and sweetened by the social
  sense;
135 For interest, envy, pride, and strife are
  banished hence.

"What, what is virtue but repose of
  mind?
A pure ethereal calm that knows no
  storm,
Above the reach of wild ambition's
  wind,
Above those passions that this world
  deform,
140 And torture man, a proud malignant
  worm!
But here, instead, soft gales of passion
  play,
And gently stir the heart, thereby to
  form
A quicker sense of joy; as breezes
  stray
Across the enlivened skies, and make
  them still more gay.

145 "The best of men have ever loved repose:
They hate to mingle in the filthy fray;
Where the soul sours, and gradual
  rancor grows,

[1] An inhabitant of Sybaris, Italy, a city noted
for luxurious living.

Imbittered more from peevish day to
  day.
Even those whom fame has lent her
  fairest ray,
150 The most renowned of worthy wights
  of yore,
From a base world at last have stolen
  away:
So Scipio, to the soft Cumaean shore
Retiring, tasted joy he never knew before.

"But if a little exercise you chuse,
155 Some zest for ease, 'tis not forbidden
  here.
Amid the groves you may indulge the
  muse,
Or tend the blooms, and deck the vernal year;
Or softly stealing, with your watery
  gear,
Along the brooks, the crimson-spotted
  fry
160 You may delude: the whilst, amused,
  you hear
Now the hoarse stream, and now the
  zephyr's sigh,
Attunèd to the birds, and woodland
  melody.

"O grievous folly! to heap up estate,
Losing the days you see beneath the
  sun;
165 When, sudden, comes blind unrelenting fate,
And gives the untasted portion you
  have won
With ruthless toil, and many a wretch
  undone,
To those who mock you gone to Pluto's
  reign,
There with sad ghosts to pine, and
  shadows dun:
170 But sure it is of vanities most vain,
To toil for what you here untoiling may
  obtain."

He ceased. But still their trembling
  ears retained
The deep vibrations of his witching
  song;
That, by a kind of magic power, constrained
175 To enter in, pell-mell, the listening
  throng.
Heaps poured on heaps, and yet they
  slipt along
In silent ease: as when, beneath the
  beam

Of summer moons, the distant woods
    among,
Or by some flood all silvered with the 215
    gleam,
180 The soft-embodied fays through airy
    portal stream.

By the smooth demon so it ordered was,
And here his baneful bounty first
    began:
Though some there were who would
    not further pass,
And his alluring baits suspected han.[1] 220
185 The wise distrust the too fair-spoken
    man.
Yet through the gate they cast a wish-
    ful eye:
Not to move on, perdie,[2] is all they
    can;
For, do their very best, they cannot
    fly,
But often each way look, and often 225
    sorely sigh.

190 When this the watchful wicked wizard
    saw,
With sudden spring he leaped upon
    them strait;
And, soon as touched by his unhal-
    lowed paw,
They found themselves within the
    cursèd gate,
Full hard to be repassed, like that of 230
    Fate.
195 Not stronger were of old the giant-
    crew,
Who sought to pull high Jove from
    regal state,[3]
Though feeble wretch he seemed, of
    sallow hue:
Certes, who bides his grasp, will that
    encounter rue.

.   .   .   .   .   .

Waked by the crowd, slow from his
    bench arose
A comely full-spread porter, swoln
    with sleep:
210 His calm, broad, thoughtless aspect
    breathed repose;
And in sweet torpor he was plungèd
    deep,
Ne could himself from ceaseless yawn- 240
    ing keep;
While o'er his eyes the drowsy liquor
    ran,

Through which his half-waked soul
    would faintly peep.
Then, taking his black staff, he called
    his man,
And roused himself as much as rouse
    himself he can.

The lad leaped lightly at his master's
    call.
He was, to weet,[1] a little roguish page,
Save sleep and play who minded
    nought at all,
Like most the untaught striplings of
    his age.
This boy he kept each band to disen-
    gage,
Garters and buckles, task for him
    unfit,
But ill-becoming his grave personage,
And which his portly paunch would
    not permit.
So this same limber page to all per-
    formèd it.

Meantime the master-porter wide dis-
    played
Great store of caps, of slippers, and of
    gowns,
Wherewith he those who entered in
    arrayed,
Loose as the breeze that plays along
    the downs,
And waves the summer woods when
    evening frowns.
O fair undress, best dress! it checks
    no vein,
But every flowing limb in pleasure
    drowns,
And heightens ease with grace. This
    done, right fain
Sir Porter sat him down, and turned to
    sleep again.

235 Thus easy robed, they to the fountain
    sped,
That in the middle of the court up-
    threw
A stream, high-spouting from its liquid
    bed,
And falling back again in drizzly dew:
There each deep draughts, as deep he
    thirsted, drew;
It was a fountain of Nepenthe[2] rare:
Whence, as Dan[3] Homer sings,[4] huge
    pleasaunce grew,

---

[1] have
[2] An oath from the French, *par Dieu*, by God.
[3] The Titans, who rebelled against Jupiter.

[1] as far as one could tell
[2] A drug which causes forgetfulness of pain and sorrow.
[3] Lord; master
[4] *Odyssey*, 4, 220 ff.

And sweet oblivion of vile earthly
 care,
Fair gladsome waking thoughts, and
 joyous dreams more fair.

This rite performed, all inly pleased
 and still,
245 Withouten trump[1] was proclamation
 made:—
"Ye sons of Indolence, do what you
 will;
And wander where you list, through
 hall or glade:
Be no man's pleasure for another's
 staid:
Let each as likes him best his hours
 employ,
250 And curst be he who minds his neighbor's trade!
Here dwells kind ease, and unreprov-
 ing joy:
He little merits bliss who others can
 annoy."

Strait of these endless numbers,
 swarming round
As thick as idle motes in sunny
 ray,
255 Not one eftsoons[2] in view was to be
 found,
But every man strolled off his own
 glad way.
Wide o'er this ample court's blank
 area,
With all the lodges that thereto per-
 tained,
No living creature could be seen to
 stray;
260 While solitude and perfect silence
 reigned:
So that to think you dreamt you almost
 was constrained.

As when a shepherd of the Hebrid
 Isles,
Placed far amid the melancholy main,
(Whether it be lone fancy him be-
 guiles,
265 Or that aerial beings sometimes deign
To stand embodied to our senses plain)
Sees on the naked hill, or valley low,
The whilst in ocean Phoebus dips his
 wain,[3]
A vast assembly moving to and fro;
270 Then all at once in air dissolves the
 wondrous show.

[1] trumpet
[2] immediately
[3] while the sun-god dips his wagon,—*i. e.*, while
the sun is setting

Ye gods of quiet, and of sleep profound,
Whose soft dominion o'er this castle
 sways,
And all the widely-silent places round,
Forgive me, if my trembling pen displays
275 What never yet was sung in mortal
 lays.
But how shall I attempt such arduous
 string?
I who have spent my nights and
 nightly days
In this soul-deadening place, loose-
 loitering—
Ah! how shall I for this uprear my
 moulted wing?

280 Come on, my muse, nor stoop to low
 despair,
Thou imp of Jove, touched by celestial
 fire!
Thou yet shalt sing of war, and actions
 fair,
Which the bold sons of Britain will
 inspire;
Of ancient bards thou yet shalt sweep
 the lyre;
285 Thou yet shalt tread in tragic pall the
 stage,
Paint love's enchanting woes, the
 hero's ire,
The sage's calm, the patriot's noble
 rage,
Dashing corruption down through every
 worthless age.

The doors, that knew no shrill alarming bell,
290 Ne cursèd knocker plied by villain's
 hand,
Self-opened into halls, where, who can
 tell
What elegance and grandeur wide expand
The pride of Turkey and of Persia
 land?
Soft quilts on quilts, on carpets carpets spread,
295 And couches stretched around in seemly
 band;
And endless pillows rise to prop the
 head;
So that each spacious room was one full-
 swelling bed.

And everywhere huge covered tables
 stood.
With wines high-flavored and rich
 viands crowned;

300 Whatever sprightly juice or tasteful
        food
     On the green bosom of this Earth are
        found,
     And all old Ocean genders in his
        round—
     Some hand unseen these silently dis-
        played,
     Even undemanded by a sign or sound;
305 You need but wish, and, instantly
        obeyed,
     Fair-ranged the dishes rose, and thick
        the glasses played.

     Here freedom reigned without the
        least alloy;
     Nor gossip's tale, nor ancient maid-
        en's gall,
     Nor saintly spleen durst murmur at
        our joy,
310 And with envenomed tongue our
        pleasures pall.
     For why? there was but one great
        rule for all;
     To wit, that each should work his own
        desire,
     And eat, drink, study, sleep, as it may
        fall,
     Or melt the time in love, or wake the
        lyre,
315 And carol what, unbid, the Muses might
        inspire.

     The rooms with costly tapestry were
        hung,
     Where was inwoven many a gentle
        tale,
     Such as of old the rural poets sung
     Or of Arcadian or Sicilian vale:
320 Reclining lovers, in the lonely dale,
     Poured forth at large the sweetly tor-
        tured heart;
     Or, looking tender passion, swelled the
        gale,
     And taught charmed echo to resound
        their smart;
     While flocks, woods, streams around, re-
        pose and peace impart.

325 Those pleased the most, where, by a
        cunning hand,
     Depeinten[1] was the patriarchal age;
     What time Dan Abraham left the Chal-
        dee land,
     And pastured on from verdant stage
        to stage,
     Where fields and fountains fresh
        could best engage.[2]

     [1] depicted; painted   [2] *Genesis*, 11:31.

330 Toil was not then. Of nothing took
        they heed,
     But with wild beasts the silvan war to
        wage,
     And o'er vast plains their herds and
        flocks to feed:
     Blest sons of nature they! true golden
        age indeed!

     Sometimes the pencil, in cool airy halls,
335 Bade the gay bloom of vernal land-
        skips rise,
     Or Autumn's varied shades imbrown
        the walls:
     Now the black tempest strikes the
        astonished eyes;
     Now down the steep the flashing tor-
        rent flies;
     The trembling sun now plays o'er
        ocean blue,
340 And now rude mountains frown amid
        the skies;
     Whate'er Lorrain light-touched with
        softening hue,
     Or savage Rosa dashed, or learnèd
        Poussin drew.

     Each sound too here to languishment
        inclined,
     Lulled the weak bosom, and inducèd
        ease.
345 Aerial music in the warbling wind,
     At distance rising oft, by small de-
        grees,
     Nearer and nearer came, till o'er the
        trees
     It hung, and breathed such soul-dis-
        solving airs
     As did, alas! with soft perdition
        please:
350 Entangled deep in its enchanting
        snares,
     The listening heart forgot all duties and
        all cares.

     A certain music, never known before,
     Here soothed the pensive melancholy
        mind;
     Full easily obtained. Behoves no more,
355 But sidelong to the gently-waving wind
     To lay the well-tuned instrument re-
        clined;
     From which, with airy flying fingers
        light,
     Beyond each mortal touch the most
        refined,
     The god of winds drew sounds of deep
        delight:
360 Whence, with just cause, the Harp of
        Æolus it hight.

Ah me! what hand can touch the
    strings so fine?
Who up the lofty diapasan[1] roll
Such sweet, such sad, such solemn airs
    divine,
Then let them down again into the
    soul?
365 Now rising love they fanned; now
    pleasing dole
They breathed, in tender musings,
    through the heart;
And now a graver sacred strain they
    stole,
As when seraphic hands an hymn im-
    part:
Wild warbling Nature all, above the
    reach of Art!

370 Such the gay splendor, the luxurious
    state,
Of Caliphs[2] old, who on the Tygris'
    shore,
In mighty Bagdat, populous and
    great,
Held their bright court, where was of
    ladies store;
And verse, love, music still the gar-
    land wore;
375 When sleep was coy, the bard in wait-
    ing there
Cheered the lone midnight with the
    muse's lore;
Composing music bade his dreams be
    fair,
And music lent new gladness to the
    morning air.

Near the pavilions where we slept,
    still ran
380 Soft-tinkling streams, and dashing
    waters fell,
And sobbing breezes sighed, and oft
    began
(So worked the wizard) wintry storms
    to swell,
As heaven and earth they would to-
    gether mell:[3]
At doors and windows, threatening,
    seemed to call
385 The demons of the tempest, growling
    fell;
Yet the least entrance found they none
    at all;
Whence sweeter grew our sleep, secure
    in massy hall.

[1] entire compass of tones
[2] Caliph is the title of the successors of Moham-
    med, now claimed by the Sultan of Turkey.
[3] mingle

And hither Morpheus sent his kindest
    dreams,
Raising a world of gayer tinct and
    grace;
390 O'er which were shadowy cast Elysian
    gleams,
That played in waving lights from
    place to place,
And shed a roseate smile on nature's
    face.
Not Titian's pencil e'er could so
    array,
So fleece with clouds the pure ethereal
    space;
395 Ne could it e'er such melting forms
    display,
As loose on flowery beds all languishingly
    lay.

.   .   .   .   .

One great amusement of our house-
    hold was—
In a huge crystal magic globe to spy,
435 Still as you turned it, all things that
    do pass
Upon this ant-hill earth; where con-
    stantly
Of idly-busy men the restless fry
Run bustling to and fro with foolish
    haste
In search of pleasures vain, that from
    them fly,
440 Or which, obtained, the caitiffs dare
    not taste:
When nothing is enjoyed, can there be
    greater waste?

Of Vanity the Mirror this was called.
Here you a muckworm of the town
    might see
At his dull desk, amid his ledgers
    stalled,
445 Eat up with carking care and penurie,
Most like to carcase parched on gal-
    low-tree.
"A penny savèd is a penny got"—
Firm to this scoundrel maxim keepeth
    he,
Ne of its rigor will he bate a jot,
450 Till it has quenched his fire, and ban-
    ishèd his pot.

Strait from the filth of this low grub,
    behold!
Comes fluttering forth a gaudy spend-
    thrift heir,
All glossy gay, enamelled all with gold,
The silly tenant of the summer-air.
455 In folly lost, of nothing takes he care;

Pimps, lawyers, stewards, harlots, flatterers vile,
And thieving tradesmen him among
   them share:
His father's ghost from Limbo-lake 620
   the while
Sees this, which more damnation doth
   upon him pile.

460   This globe portrayed the race of
     learned men,
   Still at their books, and turning o'er
     the page,
   Backwards and forwards: oft they
     snatch the pen
   As if inspired, and in a Thespian[1]
     rage;
   Then write, and blot, as would your
     ruth engage.
465   Why, authors, all this scrawl and
     scribbling sore?
   To lose the present, gain the future
     age,
   Praisèd to be when you can hear no
     more,
And much enriched with fame when use-
   less worldly store!

.   .   .   .   .   .

   A bard here dwelt, more fat than bard
     beseems
605   Who, void of envy, guile, and lust of
     gain,
   On virtue still, and nature's pleasing
     themes,
   Poured forth his unpremeditated strain,
   The world forsaking with a calm dis-
     dain:
   Here laughed he careless in his easy
     seat;
610   Here quaffed, encircled with the joy-
     ous train;
   Oft moralizing sage; his ditty sweet
He loathèd much to write, ne carèd to
   repeat.[2]

   Full oft by holy feet our ground was
     trod;
   Of clerks[3] good plenty here you mote
     espy.
615   A little, round, fat, oily man of God
   Was one I chiefly marked among the
     fry:
   He had a roguish twinkle in his eye,

[1] tragic (Thespis was the reputed founder of
 tragedy.)
[3] Lines 604-12 contain a portrait of Thomson
 himself; with the exception of l. 604, the
 stanza is ascribed to Lord Lyttleton, an English author and politician.
[3] clergyman; priests

And shone all glittering with ungodly
   dew,
If a tight[1] damsel chanced to trippen
   by;
Which when observed, he shrunk into
   his mew,[2]
And straight would recollect his piety
   anew.[3]

.   .   .   .   .   .

TELL ME, THOU SOUL OF HER I LOVE

Tell me, thou soul of her I love,
   Ah! tell me, whither art thou fled?
To what delightful world above,
   Appointed for the happy dead?

5 Or dost thou free at pleasure roam,
   And sometimes share thy lover's woe
Where, void of thee, his cheerless home
   Can now, alas! no comfort know?

Oh! if thou hoverest round my walk,
10   While, under every well-known tree,
I to thy fancied shadow talk,
   And every tear is full of thee—

Should then the weary eye of grief
   Beside some sympathetic stream
15 In slumber find a short relief,
   Oh, visit thou my soothing dream!

TO AMANDA

Come, dear Amanda, quit the town,
   And to the rural hamlets fly;
Behold! the wintry storms are gone,
   A gentle radiance glads the sky.

5 The birds awake, the flowers appear,
   Earth spreads a verdant couch for thee;
'Tis joy and music all we hear,
   'Tis love and beauty all we see.

Come, let us mark the gradual spring,
10   How peeps the bud, the blossom blows;
Till Philomel begins to sing,
   And perfect May to swell the rose.

Even so thy rising charms improve,
   As life's warm season grows more
     bright;
15 And, opening to the sighs of love,
   Thy beauties glow with full delight.

[1] comely; neat
[2] study
[3] Lines 613-21 contain a portrait of the Rev.
 Patrick Murdock, Thomson's friend and biographer.

Edward Young 1683-1765

NIGHT THOUGHTS
1742

From NIGHT I. ON LIFE, DEATH, AND
IMMORTALITY

Tired nature's sweet restorer, balmy
  Sleep!
He, like the world, his ready visit pays
Where Fortune smiles; the wretched he
  forsakes,
Swift on his downy pinion flies from woe,
5 And lights on lids unsullied with a
  tear.
  From short (as usual) and disturbed
    repose,
I wake: how happy they who wake no
  more!
Yet that were vain, if dreams infest the
  grave.
I wake, emerging from a sea of dreams
10 Tumultuous, where my wrecked, despond-
  ing thought
From wave to wave of fancied misery
At random drove, her helm of reason
  lost;
Though now restored, 'tis only change
  of pain,
A bitter change! severer for severe.
15 The day too short for my distress; and
  Night,
Even in the zenith of her dark domain,
Is sunshine to the color of my fate.
  Night, sable goddess! from her ebon
    throne,
In rayless majesty, now stretches forth
20 Her leaden scepter o'er a slumbering
  world.
Silence how dead! and darkness how
  profound!
Nor eye nor list'ning ear an object finds:
Creation sleeps. 'Tis as the general pulse
Of life stood still, and Nature made a
  pause,
25 An awful pause, prophetic of her end.
And let her prophecy be soon fulfilled!
Fate, drop the curtain! I can lose no
  more.
  Silence and Darkness, solemn sisters,
    twins
From ancient Night, who nurse the ten-
  der thought
30 To reason, and on reason build resolve
(That column of true majesty in man),
Assist me! I will thank you in the grave,
The grave your kingdom; there this frame
  shall fall
A victim sacred to your dreary shrine.
   .   .   .   .   .

The bell strikes one: we take no note
  of time,
55 But from its loss. To give it, then, a
  tongue,
Is wise in man. As if an angel spoke,
I feel the solemn sound. If heard aright,
It is the knell of my departed hours:
Where are they? With the years beyond
  the flood.
60 It is the signal that demands despatch;
How much is to be done! my hopes and
  fears
Start up alarmed, and o'er life's narrow
  verge
Look down—on what? a fathomless
  abyss;
A dread eternity; how surely mine!
65 And can eternity belong to me,
Poor pensioner on the bounties of an
  hour?
How poor, how rich, how abject, how
  august,
How complicate, how wonderful, is
  man!
How passing wonder He who made him
  such!
70 Who centred in our make such strange
  extremes,
From different natures marvellously
  mixed,
Connection exquisite of distant worlds!
Distinguished link in being's endless
  chain!
Midway from nothing to the Deity!
75 A beam ethereal, sullied, and absorpt!
Though sullied and dishonored, still
  divine!
Dim miniature of greatness absolute!
An heir of glory! a frail child of dust!
Helpless immortal! insect infinite!
80 A worm! a god!—I tremble at myself,
And in myself am lost! At home a
  stranger,
Thought wanders up and down, sur-
  prised, aghast,
And wondering at her own. How reason
  reels!
O, what a miracle to man is man!
85 Triumphantly distressed! What joy!
  what dread!
Alternately transported and alarmed!
What can preserve my life? or what
  destroy?
An angel's arm can't snatch me from the
  grave;
Legions of angels can't confine me there.
   .   .   .   .   .
The spritely lark's shrill matin wakes the
  morn.

Grief's sharpest thorn hard pressing on
  my breast,
440 I strive, with wakeful melody, to cheer
The sullen gloom, sweet Philomel! like
  thee,
And call the stars to listen: every star
Is deaf to mine, enamor'd of thy lay.
Yet be not vain; there are, who thine
  excel,
445 And charm thro' distant ages: wrapt in
  shade,
Pris'ner of darkness! to the silent hours,
How often I repeat their rage divine.
To lull my griefs, and steal my heart
  from woe!
I roll their raptures, but not catch their
  fire.
450 Dark, tho' not blind, like thee, Mæonides!
Or, Milton! thee; ah could I reach your
  strain
Or his, who made Mæonides our own.[1]
Man too he sung: immortal man I sing;
Oft bursts my song beyond the bounds
  of life
455 What, now, but immortality can please?
O had he press'd his theme, pursu'd the
  track,
Which opens out of darkness into day!
O had he, mounted on his wing of fire,
Soar'd where I sink, and sung immortal
  man!
460 How had it blest mankind, and rescu'd
  me!

From NIGHT III. NARCISSA

Then welcome, death! thy dread har-
  bingers,
Age and disease; disease, tho' long my
  guest;
That plucks my nerves, those tender
  strings of life;
490 Which, pluckt a little more, will toll the
  bell,
That calls my few friends to my funeral;
Where feeble nature drops, perhaps, a
  tear,
While reason and religion, better taught,
Congratulate the dead, and crown his tomb
495 With wreath triumphant. Death is victory;
It binds in chains the raging ills of life:
Lust and ambition, wrath and avarice,
Dragg'd at his chariot-wheel, applaud his
  power.
That ills corrosive, cares importunate,
500 Are not immortal too, O death! is thine.

----
[1] Pope, who translated the *Odyssey* and the *Iliad*
  of Homer.

Our day of dissolution!—name it right;
'Tis our great pay-day; 'tis our harvest,
  rich
And ripe: What tho' the sickle, sometimes keen,
Just scars us as we reap the golden
  grain?
505 More than thy balm, O Gilead![1] heals
  the wound.
Birth's feeble cry, and death's deep dismal groan,
Are slender tributes low-taxt nature pays
For mighty gain: the gain of each, a
  life!
But O! the last the former so transcends,
510 Life dies, compar'd: life lives beyond
  the grave.
  And feel I, death! no joy from thought
  of thee,
Death, the great counsellor, who man
  inspires
With ev'ry nobler thought and fairer
  deed!
Death, the deliverer, who rescues man!
515 Death, the rewarder, who the rescu'd
  crowns!
Death, that absolves my birth; a curse
  without it!
Rich death, that realizes all my cares,
Toils, virtues, hopes; without it a chimera!
Death, of all pain the period, not of joy;
520 Joy's source, and subject, still subsist
  unhurt;
One, in my soul; and one, in her great
  sire;
Tho' the four winds were warring for
  my dust.
Yes, and from winds, and waves, and
  central night,
Tho' prison'd there, my dust too I reclaim,
525 (To dust when drop proud nature's
  proudest spheres,)
And live entire. Death is the crown of
  life:
Were death denied, poor man would live
  in vain;
Were death denied, to live would not be
  life;
Were death denied, ev'n fools would wish
  to die.
530 Death wounds to cure: we fall; we rise;
  we reign!
Spring from our fetters; fasten in the
  skies;
Where blooming Eden withers in our
  sight:

----
[1] *Genesis*, 37 :25 ; *Numbers*, 32 :1-30.

Death gives us more than was in Eden lost.
This king of terrors is the prince of
  peace.
535 When shall I die to vanity, pain, death?
When shall I die?—When shall I live for
  ever?

From Night V. The Relapse

125   Let Indians, and the gay, like Indians,
  fond
Of feather'd fopperies, the sun adore:
Darkness has more divinity for me;
It strikes thought inward; it drives back
  the soul
To settle on herself, our point supreme!
130 There lies our theatre! there sits our
  judge.
Darkness the curtain drops o'er life's
  dull scene;
'Tis the kind hand of Providence stretcht
  out
'Twixt man and vanity; 'tis reason's
  reign,
And virtue's too; these tutelary shades
135 Are man's asylum from the tainted
  throng.
Night is the good man's friend, and
  guardian too
It no less rescues virtue, than inspires.

.   .   .   .   .   .

From Night VI. The Infidel Reclaimed

Our senses, as our reason, are divine.
But for the magic organ's powerful
  charm,
430 Earth were a rude, uncolor'd chaos still.
Objects are but th' occasion; ours th'
  exploit;
Ours is the cloth, the pencil, and the
  paint,
Which nature's admirable picture draws;
And beautifies creation's ample dome.
435 Like Milton's Eve, when gazing on the
  lake,[1]
Man makes the matchless image, man
  admires:
Say then, shall man, his thoughts all sent
  abroad,
Superior wonders in himself forgot,
His admiration waste on objects round,
440 When heaven makes him the soul of all
  he sees
Absurd: not rare! so great, so mean, is
  man.

.   .   .   .   .   .

Nature, thy daughter, ever changing birth
Of thee the Great Immutable, to man

[1] *Paradise Lost*, 4, 456 ff.

Speaks wisdom; is his oracle supreme;
695 And he who most consults her, is most
  wise.
Lorenzo, to this heavenly Delphos haste;
And come back all-immortal; all divine:
Look nature through, 'tis revolution all;
All change; no death. Day follows
  night; and night
700 The dying day; stars rise, and set, and
  rise;
Earth takes th' example. See, the summer gay,
With her green chaplet, and ambrosial
  flowers,
Droops into pallid autumn: winter gray,
Horrid with frost, and turbulent with
  storm,
705 Blows autumn, and his golden fruits
  away;
Then melts into the spring: soft spring,
  with breath
Favonian,[1] from warm chambers of the
  south,
Recalls the first. All, to re-flourish, fades;
As in a wheel, all sinks, to re-ascend.
710 Emblems of man, who passes, not expires.

From Night IX. The Consolation

As when a traveller, a long day past,
In painful search of what he cannot find,
At night's approach, content with the
  next cot,
There ruminates awhile, his labor lost;
5 Then cheers his heart with what his fate
  affords,
And chants his sonnet to deceive the
  time,
Till the due season calls him to repose:
Thus I, long-travell'd in the ways of
  men,
And dancing, with the rest, the giddy
  maze,
10 Where disappointment smiles at hope's
  career;
Warn'd by the languor of life's evening
  ray,
At length have hous'd me in an humble
  shed;
Where, future wand'ring banish'd from
  my thought,
And waiting, patient, the sweet hour of
  rest,
15 I chase the moments with a serious song.
Song soothes our pains; and age has
  pains to soothe.

.   .   .   .   .   .

[1] gentle, like Favonius, the west wind

From CONJECTURES ON ORIGINAL
COMPOSITION
1759   *1759*

. . . . . .

But there are who write with vigor and
success, to the world's delight and their
own renown. These are the glorious fruits
where genius prevails. The mind of a man
of genius is a fertile and pleasant field,
pleasant as Elysium, and fertile as Tempe; 10
it enjoys a perpetual spring. Of that
spring, originals are the fairest flowers;
imitations are of quicker growth but
fainter bloom. Imitations are of two
kinds: one of nature, one of authors. The 15
first we call originals, and confine the term
imitation to the second. I shall not enter
into the curious enquiry of what is or is
not, strictly speaking, original, content
with what all must allow, that some com- 20
positions are more so than others; and
the more they are so, I say, the better.
Originals are and ought to be great favorites, for they are great benefactors; they
extend the republic of letters, and add a 25
new province to its dominion. Imitators
only give us a sort of duplicates of what
we had, possibly much better, before, increasing the mere drug of books, while all
that makes them valuable, knowledge and 30
genius, are at a stand. The pen of an
original writer, like Armida's wand, out
of a barren waste calls a blooming spring.
Out of that blooming spring, an imitator
is a transplanter of laurels, which some- 35
times die on removal, always languish in
a foreign soil. . . .

We read imitation with somewhat of his
languor who listens to a twice-told tale.
Our spirits rouse at an original that is a 40
perfect stranger, and all throng to learn
what news from a foreign land. And
though it comes like an Indian prince,
adorned with feathers only, having little
of weight, yet of our attention it will rob 45
the more solid, if not equally new. Thus
every telescope is lifted at a new-discov-
ered star; it makes a hundred astronomers
in a moment, and denies equal notice to
the sun. But if an original, by being as 50
excellent as new, adds admiration to surprise, then are we at the writer's mercy;
on the strong wind of his imagination, we
are snatched from Britain to Italy, from
climate to climate, from pleasure to pleas- 55
ure; we have no home, no thought, of our
own till the magician drops his pen. And
then falling down into ourselves, we awake
to flat realities, lamenting the change,
like the beggar who dreampt himself a
prince. . . .

But why are originals so few? Not
because the writer's harvest is over, the 5
great reapers of antiquity having left
nothing to be gleaned after them; nor
because the human mind's teeming time
is past, or because it is incapable of putting forth unprecedented births; but be- 10
cause illustrious examples engross, prejudice, and intimidate. They engross our
attention, and so prevent a due inspection
of ourselves; they prejudice our judgment in favor of their abilities, and so 15
lessen the sense of our own; and they
intimidate us with the splendor of their
renown, and thus under diffidence bury
our strength. Nature's impossibilities and
those of diffidence lie wide asunder. . . . 20

Had Milton never wrote, Pope had been
less to blame. But when in Milton's
genius, Homer, as it were, personally rose
to forbid Britons doing him that ignoble
wrong,[1] it is less pardonable, by that 25
effeminate decoration, to put Achilles in
petticoats a second time. How much nobler
had it been, if his numbers had rolled on
in full flow, through the various modulations of masculine melody, into those gran- 30
deurs of solemn sound which are indispensably demanded by the native dignity
of heroic song! How much nobler, if he
had resisted the temptation of that Gothic
demon,[2] which modern poesy tasting, be- 35
came mortal! O how unlike the deathless,
divine harmony of three great names (how
justly joined!) of Milton, Greece, and
Rome! His verse, but for this little speck
of mortality in its extreme parts, as his 40
hero had in his heel, like him, had been
invulnerable and immortal.[3] But unfortunately, that was undipt in Helicon, as
this in Styx. Harmony as well as eloquence
is essential to poesy; and a murder of his 45
music is putting half Homer to death.
Blank is a term of diminution; what we
mean by blank verse is verse unfallen,
uncurst; verse reclaimed, reënthroned in
the true language of the gods, who never 50
thundered, nor suffered their Homer to
thunder, in rhyme. . . .

When such an ample area for renowned
adventure in original attempts lies before

[1] Pope's offense in translating Homer was doubled
by the use of rhyming couplets.
[2] rhyme
[3] According to popular legend, Achilles, the hero of
the *Iliad*, was plunged by his mother into the
waters of Styx, and his whole body made invulnerable, except the heel by which he was held.

us, shall we be as mere leaden pipes, conveying to the present age small streams of excellence from its grand reservoir of antiquity, and those too, perhaps, mudded
5 in the pass? Originals shine like comets; have no peer in their path; are rivaled by none, and the gaze of all. All other compositions (if they shine at all) shine in clusters, like the stars in the galaxy,
10 where, like bad neighbors, all suffer from all, each particular being diminished and almost lost in the throng.

If thoughts of this nature prevailed, if ancients and moderns were no longer con-
15 sidered as masters and pupils, but as hard-matched rivals for renown, then moderns, by the longevity of their labors, might one day become ancients themselves. And old time, that best weigher of merits, to keep
20 his balance even, might have the golden weight of an Augustan age[1] in both his scales; or rather our scale might descend, and that of antiquity (as a modern match for it strongly speaks) might kick the beam.

Robert Blair 1699-1746

From THE GRAVE
1743

While some affect[2] the sun, and some the shade,
Some flee the city, some the hermitage,
Their aims as various as the roads they take
In journeying through life; the task be mine
5 To paint the gloomy horrors of the tomb;
Th' appointed place of rendezvous, where all
These travellers meet. Thy succors I implore,
Eternal King! whose potent arm sustains
The keys of hell and death.—The Grave, dread thing!
10 Men shiver when thou'rt nam'd: nature, appall'd,
Shakes off her wonted firmness.—Ah, how dark
Thy long-extended realms, and rueful wastes!

[1] A period when literature is at the height of purity and refinement, so called because the reign of Augustus Cæsar (31 B. C.-14 A. D.) was the golden age of Latin literature. The term is commonly applied in English literature to the time of Queen Anne (1702-14) because the writers of that period modeled their work upon that of the ancients.
[2] choose; prefer

Where nought but silence reigns, and night, dark night,
Dark as was chaos, ere the infant sun
15 Was roll'd together, or had tried his beams
Athwart the gloom profound.—The sickly taper
By glimmering through thy low-brow'd misty vaults,
(Furr'd round with mouldy damps and ropy slime)
Lets fall a supernumerary horror,
20 And only serves to make thy night more irksome.
Well do I know thee by thy trusty yew,[1]
Cheerless, unsocial plant! that loves to dwell
Midst skulls and coffins, epitaphs and worms:
Where light-heel'd ghosts and visionary shades,
25 Beneath the wan cold moon (as fame reports)
Embodied, thick, perform their mystic rounds.
No other merriment, dull tree! is thine.
See yonder hallow'd fane;—the pious work
Of names once fam'd, now dubious or forgot,
30 And buried midst the wreck of things which were;
There lie interr'd the more illustrious dead.
The wind is up: hark! how it howls! Methinks
Till now I never heard a sound so dreary:
Doors creak, and windows clap, and night's foul bird,
35 Rook'd in the spire, screams loud: the gloomy aisles,
Black-plaster'd, and hung round with shreds of 'scutcheons
And tatter'd coats of arms, send back the sound
Laden with heavier airs, from the low vaults,
The mansions of the dead.—Rous'd from their slumbers,
40 In grim array the grisly spectres rise,
Grin horrible, and, obstinately sullen,
Pass and repass, hush'd as the foot of night.
Again the screech-owl shrieks: ungracious sound!

[1] The yew is a common tree in graveyards.

I'll hear no more; it makes one's blood
run chill.
45   Quite round the pile, a row of reverend elms,
(Coeval near with that) all ragged
show,
Long lash'd by the rude winds. Some
rift half down
Their branchless trunks; others so thin
a-top,
That scarce two crows could lodge in the
same tree.
50 Strange things, the neighbors say, have
happen'd here:
Wild shrieks have issued from the hollow
tombs:
Dead men have come again, and walk'd
about;
And the great bell has toll'd, unrung,
untouch'd.
(Such tales their cheer, at wake or
gossiping,[1]
55 When it draws near the witching time
of night.)
Oft in the lone church yard at night
I've seen,
By glimpse of moonshine chequering
through the trees,
The school-boy, with his satchel in his
hand,
Whistling aloud to bear his courage
up,
60 And lightly tripping o'er the long flat
stones,
(With nettles skirted, and with moss
o'ergrown,)
That tell in homely phrase who lie below.
Sudden he starts, and hears, or thinks
he hears,
The sound of something purring at his
heels;
65 Full fast he flies, and dares not look
behind him,
Till out of breath he overtakes his
fellows;
Who gather round, and wonder at the
tale
Of horrid apparition, tall and ghastly,
That walks at dead of night, or takes his
stand
70 O'er some new-open'd grave; and
(strange to tell!)
Evanishes at crowing of the cock.
The new-made widow, too, I've sometimes 'spied,
Sad sight! slow moving o'er the prostrate dead:

[1] christening

Listless, she crawls along in doleful
black,
75 Whilst bursts of sorrow gush from either
eye,
Fast falling down her now untasted
cheek:
Prone on the lowly grave of the dear
man
She drops; whilst busy, meddling memory,
In barbarous succession musters up
80 The past endearments of their softer
hours,
Tenacious of its theme. Still, still she
thinks
She sees him, and, indulging the fond
thought,
Clings yet more closely to the senseless
turf,
Nor heeds the passenger who looks that
way.
85   Invidious grave!—how dost thou rend
in sunder
Whom love has knit, and sympathy
made one!
A tie more stubborn far than nature's
band.
Friendship! mysterious cement of the
soul;
Sweetener of life, and solder of society!
90 I owe thee much: thou hast deserved
from me,
Far, far beyond what I can ever pay.
Oft have I proved the labors of thy love,
And the warm efforts of the gentle
heart,
Anxious to please.—Oh! when my friend
and I
95 In some thick wood have wander'd heedless on,
Hid from the vulgar eye, and sat us
down
Upon the sloping cowslip-cover'd bank,
Where the pure limpid stream has slid
along
In grateful errors[1] through the underwood,
100 Sweet murmuring,—methought the shrill-
tongued thrush
Mended his song of love; the sooty
blackbird
Mellow'd his pipe, and soften'd every
note;
The eglantine smelt sweeter, and the
rose
Assumed a dye more deep; whilst every
flower
105 Vied with its fellow-plant in luxury

[1] wanderings

Of dress.—Oh! then the longest summer's day
Seem'd too, too much in haste: still the
full heart
Had not imparted half! 'twas happiness
Too exquisite to last. Of joys departed,
110 Not to return, how painful the remembrance!

. . . . . .

Poor man!—how happy once in thy
first state!
When yet but warm from thy great
Maker's hand,
He stamp'd thee with his image, and,
well pleased,
Smiled on his last fair work.—Then all
was well.
545 Sound was the body, and the soul serene;
Like two sweet instruments, ne'er out of
tune,
That play their several parts.—Nor head,
nor heart,
Offer'd to ache: nor was there cause
they should;
For all was pure within: no fell remorse,
550 Nor anxious casting-up of what might be,
Alarm'd his peaceful bosom.—Summer
seas
Show not more smooth, when kissed by
southern winds
Just ready to expire.—Scarce importuned,
The generous soil, with a luxuriant hand,
555 Offer'd the various produce of the year,
And everything most perfect in its kind.
Blessed! thrice-blessed days!—But ah,
how short!
Blest as the pleasing dreams of holy
men;
But fugitive like those, and quickly gone.
560 O slippery state of things!—What sudden turns!
What strange vicissitudes in the first
leaf
Of man's sad history!—Today most
happy,
And ere tomorrow's sun has set, most
abject!
How scant the space between these vast
extremes!

. . . . . .

Sure the last end
Of the good man is peace. How calm
his exit!
Night-dews fall not more gently to the
ground,
715 Nor weary worn-out winds expire so soft.
Behold him! in the evening tide of life,

A life well spent, whose early care it was
His riper years should not upbraid his
green
By unperceiv'd degrees he wears away;
720 Yet like the sun seems larger at his
setting!
High in his faith and hopes, look! how
he reaches
After the prize in view! and, like a bird
That's hamper'd, struggles hard to get
away!
Whilst the glad gates of sight are wide
expanded
725 To let new glories in, the first fair fruits
Of the fast-coming harvest! Then! O
then!
Each earth-born joy grows vile, or dis-
appears,
Shrunk to a thing of nought. O how he
longs
To have his passport sign'd, and be dismiss'd!
730 'Tis done, and now he's happy! The
glad soul
Has not a wish uncrown'd. Even the lag
flesh
Rests too in hope of meeting once again
Its better half, never to sunder more.
Nor shall it hope in vain: the time
draws on
735 When not a single spot of burial-earth,
Whether on land, or in the spacious sea,
But must give back its long-committed
dust
Inviolate: and faithfully shall these
Make up the full account; not the least
atom
740 Embezzled, or mislaid, of the whole tale.[1]
Each soul shall have a body ready-
furnished;
And each shall have his own. Hence, ye
profane:
Ask not how this can be. Sure the same
power
That reared the piece at first, and took it
down,
745 Can reassemble the loose scatter'd parts,
And put them as they were: Almighty
God
Has done much more: Nor is his arm
impair'd
Through length of days; and what he
can he will:
His faithfulness stands bound to see it
done.
750 When the dread trumpet sounds, the
slumbering dust,
Not unattentive to the call, shall wake;

[1] number; count

And every joint possess its proper place,
With a new elegance of form, unknown
To its first state. Nor shall the con-
    scious soul
755 Mistake its partner; but amidst the
    crowd,
Singling its other half, into its arms
Shall rush, with all the impatience of a
    man
That's new come home, who having long
    been absent,
With haste runs over every different
    room,
760 In pain to see the whole. Thrice happy
    meeting!
Nor time, nor death, shall ever part them
    more.
    'Tis but a night, a long and moonless
    night;
We make the grave our bed, and then
    are gone.
Thus, at the shut of even, the weary
    bird
765 Leaves the wide air, and in some lonely
    brake
Cowers down, and dozes till the dawn of
    day;
Then claps his well fledg'd wings and
    bears away.

William Shenstone 1714-1763

From THE SCHOOLMISTRESS

IN IMITATION OF SPENSER
1736   1737

Ah me! full sorely is my heart for-
    lorn,
To think how modest worth neglected
    lies;
While partial fame doth with her
    blasts adorn
Such deeds alone, as pride and pomp
    disguise;
5 Deeds of ill sort, and mischievous em-
    prize:
Lend me thy clarion, goddess! let me
    try
To sound the praise of merit, ere it
    dies;
Such as I oft have chaunced to espy,
Lost in the dreary shades of dull ob-
    scurity.

10 In ev'ry village mark'd with little
    spire,
Embow'r'd in trees, and hardly known
    to fame,
There dwells, in lowly shed, and mean
    attire.

A matron old, whom we school-
    mistress name;
Who boasts unruly brats with birch
    to tame;
15 They grieven sore, in piteous durance
    pent,
Aw'd by the pow'r of this relentless
    dame;
And oft-times, on vagaries idly bent,
For unkempt hair, or talk unconn'd, are
    sorely shent.[1]

And all in sight doth rise a birchen tree,
20 Which learning near her little dome
    did stowe;
Whilom a twig of small regard to see,
Tho' now so wide its waving branches
    flow;
And work the simple vassals mickle[2]
    woe;
For not a wind might curl the leaves
    that blew,
25 But their limbs shudder'd, and their
    pulse beat low;
And as they look'd they found their
    horrow grew,
And shap'd it into rods, and tingled at
    the view.

So have I seen (who has not, may
    conceive)
A lifeless phantom near a garden
    placed,
30 So doth it wanton birds of peace be-
    reave
Of sport, of song, of pleasure, of re-
    past;
They start, they stare, they wheel,
    they look aghast;
Sad servitude! such comfortless annoy
May no bold Briton's riper age e'er
    taste!
35 Ne superstition clog his dance of joy,
Ne vision empty, vain, his native bliss
    destroy.

Near to this dome is found a patch so
    green,
On which the tribe their gambols do
    display.
And at the door imprisoning board is
    seen,
40 Lest weakly wights of smaller size
    should stray;
Eager, perdie,[3] to bask in sunny day!
The noises intermixed, which thence
    resound,

----

¹ punished   ³ certainly (originally,
² much   an oath)

Do learning's little tenement betray;
Where sits the dame, disguised in look
    profound,
45 And eyes her fairy throng, and turns
    her wheel around.

Her cap, far whiter than the driven
    snow,
Emblem right meet of decency does
    yield:
Her apron, dyed in grain, as blue, I
    trow,
As is the harebell that adorns the
    field;
50 And in her hand, for scepter, she does
    wield
Tway birchen sprays; with anxious
    fear entwined,
With dark distrust, and sad repent-
    ance filled;
And steadfast hate, and sharp afflic-
    tion joined,
And fury uncontrolled, and chastisement
    unkind.

55 Few but have kenn'd, in semblance
    meet portray'd,
The childish faces, of old Aeol's train,
Libs, Notus, Auster: these in frowns
    array'd,
How then would fare on earth, or sky,
    or main,
Were the stern god to give his slaves
    the rein?
60 And were not she rebellious breasts to
    quell,
And were not she her statutes to main-
    tain,
The cot no more, I ween, were deem'd
    the cell
Where comely peace of mind, and decent
    order dwell.

A russet stole was o'er her shoulders
    thrown;
65 A russet kirtle fenced the nipping air;
'Twas simple russet, but it was her
    own;
'Twas her own country bred the flock
    so fair!
'Twas her own labor did the fleece pre-
    pare;
And, sooth to say, her pupils ranged
    around,
70 Through pious awe, did term it pass-
    ing rare;
For they in gaping wonderment abound,
And think, no doubt, she been the great-
    est wight on ground.

Albeit ne[1] flatt'ry did corrupt her
    truth,
Ne[1] pompous title did debauch her
    ear;
75 Goody, good-woman, gossip,[2] n'aunt,
    forsooth,
Or dame, the sole additions[3] she did
    hear;
Yet these she challeng'd, these she
    held right dear:
Ne would esteem him act as mought
    behove,
Who should not honor'd eld with these
    revere:
80 For never title yet so mean could
    prove,
But there was eke a mind which did that
    title love.

One ancient hen she took delight to
    feed,
The plodding pattern of the busy
    dame;
Which, ever and anon, impelled by
    need,
85 Into her school, begirt with chickens,
    came;
Such favor did her past deportment
    claim;
And, if neglect had lavished on the
    ground
Fragment of bread, she would collect
    the same;
For well she knew, and quaintly could
    expound,
90 What sin it were to waste the smallest
    crumb she found.

Herbs, too, she knew, and well of each
    could speak,
That in her garden sipped the silvery
    dew;
Where no vain flower disclosed a
    gaudy streak,
But herbs for use and physic, not a
    few,
95 Of gray renown, within those borders
    grew:
The tufted basil, pun-provoking thyme,
Fresh balm, and marigold of cheerful
    hue:
The lowly gill, that never dares to
    climb;
And more I fain would sing, disdaining
    here to rhyme.

.   .   .   .   .

[1] neither—nor   [3] titles; descriptive
[2] sponsor at a baptism   terms added

Here oft the dame, on Sabbath's decent eve,
Hymnèd such psalms as Sternhold forth did mete;
120 If winter 'twere, she to her hearth did cleave,
But in her garden found a summer-seat:
Sweet melody! to hear her then repeat
How Israel's sons, beneath a foreign king,
While taunting foemen did a song entreat,[1]
125 All, for the nonce,[2] untuning every string,
Uphung their useless lyres—small heart had they to sing.

For she was just, and friend to virtuous lore,
And passed much time in truly virtuous deed;
And in those elfins' ears would oft deplore
130 The times, when truth by popish rage did bleed,
And tortuous death was true devotion's meed;
And simple faith in iron chains did mourn,
That nould[3] on wooden image place her creed;
And lawny saints[4] in smouldering flames did burn:
135 Ah! dearest Lord! forfend[5] thilk[6] days should e'er return.

In elbow chair, like that of Scottish stem[7]
By the sharp tooth of cank'ring eld defac'd,
In which, when he receives his diadem,
Our sov'reign prince and liefest[8] liege is plac'd,
140 The matron sate; and some with rank she grac'd,
(The source of children's and of courtier's pride!)
Redress'd affronts, for vile affronts there pass'd;

And warn'd them not the fretful to deride,
But love each other dear, whatever them betide.

145 Right well she knew each temper to descry:
To thwart the proud, and the submiss to raise;
Some with vile copper prize exalt on high,
And some entice with pittance small of praise;
And other some with baleful sprig she 'frays.[1]
150 Ev'n absent, she the reins of pow'r doth hold,
While with quaint[2] arts the giddy crowd she sways,
Forewarned, if little bird their pranks behold,
'Twill whisper in her ear and all the scene unfold.

Lo, now with state she utters the command!
155 Eftsoons[3] the urchins to their tasks repair:
Their books of stature small they take in hand,[4]
Which with pellucid horn securèd are,
To save from finger wet the letters fair;
The work so gay, that on their back is seen,
160 St. George's high atchievements does declare,
On which thilk[5] wight that has y-gazing been
Kens the forth-coming rod—unpleasing sight, I ween!

Ah, luckless he, and born beneath the beam
Of evil star! it irks me whilst I write;
165 As erst the bard[6] by Mulla's silver stream,
Oft, as he told of deadly dolorous plight,
Sighed as he sung, and did in tears indite:

---

[1] *Psalms*, 137.
[2] for the occasion
[3] would not
[4] saints clad in lawn
[5] forbid
[6] those same
[7] The Scottish coronation chair at Scone rested upon a large stone of supposed miraculous power. **It was taken to England in 1297 by Edward I. and** since that time it has been a part of the chair in which English sovereigns are crowned.
[8] most loved

[1] frightens
[2] clever
[3] at once
[4] The book was a piece of board on which were printed the alphabet, the nine digits, and sometimes the Lord's Prayer. The front side was protected with a thin transparent piece of horn; the back was decorated with a sketch of St. George and the dragon.
[5] that same
[6] Spenser, whose home at Kilcolman Castle, in Ireland, was near the river Mulla.

For, brandishing the rod, she doth
   begin
To loose the brogues;[1] the stripling's late delight,
170 And down they drop; appears his
   dainty skin,
  Fair as the furry coat of whitest
   ermelin.[2]

O ruthful scene! when from a nook
   obscure
His little sister doth his peril see,
All playful as she sate she grows demure;
175 She finds full soon her wonted spirits
   flee;
She meditates a pray'r to set him
   free:
Nor gentle pardon could this dame
   deny
(If gentle pardon could with dames
   agree)
To her sad grief that swells in either
   eye,
180 And wrings her so that all for pity she
   could die.

No longer can she now her shrieks
   command;
And hardly she forbears, through
   aweful fear,
To rushen forth and with presumptuous hand
To stay harsh justice in its mid career.
185 On thee she calls, on thee, her parent
   dear!
(Ah, too remote to ward the shameful
   blow!)
She sees no kind domestic visage
   near,
And soon a flood of tears begins to
   flow,
And gives a loose at last to unavailing
   woe.

190 But ah, what pen his piteous plight
   may trace,
Or what device his loud laments explain—
The form uncouth[3] of his disguisèd
   face,
The pallid hue that dyes his looks
   amain,[4]
The plenteous show'r that does his
   cheek distain,—
195 When he, in abject wise, implores the
   dame,

Ne hopeth aught of sweet reprieve to
   gain,
Or when from high she levels well her
   aim,
And through the thatch his cries each
   falling stroke proclaim?

The other tribe, aghast, with sore dismay
200 Attend, and conn their tasks with
   mickle[1] care;
By turns, astonied, ev'ry twig survey,
And from their fellow's hateful
   wounds beware,
Knowing, I wist,[2] how each the same
   may share;
Till fear has taught them a performance meet,
205 And to the well-known chest the dame
   repair,
Whence oft with sugared cates[3] she
   doth 'em greet,
And ginger-bread y-rare—now, certes,
   doubly sweet!

   . . . .

But now Dan[4] Phœbus gains the
   middle sky,
And liberty unbars her prison door;
And like a rushing torrent out they
   fly;
265 And now the grassy cirque[5] han[6]
   covered o'er
With boisterous revel rout and wild
   uproar;
A thousand ways in wanton rings they
   run.
Heaven shield their short-lived pastimes I implore;
For well may freedom erst so dearly
   won
270 Appear to British elf more gladsome
   than the sun.

Enjoy, poor imps! enjoy your sportive
   trade,
And chase gay flies, and cull the fairest flowers;
For when my bones in grass-green sods
   are laid,
O never may ye taste more careless
   hours
275 In knightly castles or in ladies'
   bowers.
O vain to seek delight in earthly
   thing!

---

[1] trousers   [3] unusual
[2] ermine   [4] completely

[1] much   [4] Lord; master
[2] know   [5] circle
[3] dainties   [6] have

But most in courts, where proud ambition towers;
Deluded wight! who weens fair peace
can spring
Beneath the pompous dome of kesar[1] or
of king.

. . . . . .

Mark Akenside 1721-1770

THE PLEASURES OF THE IMAGINATION
1738-43   1744-70

From PART I
1757

From Heaven my strains begin; from
Heaven descends
100 The flame of genius to the chosen breast,
And beauty with poetic wonder join'd,
And inspiration. Ere the rising sun
Shone o'er the deep, or 'mid the vault of
night
The moon her silver lamp suspended;
ere
105 The vales with springs were water'd,
or with groves
Of oak or pine the ancient hills were
crown'd;
Then the Great Spirit, whom his works
adore,
Within his own deep essence view'd the
forms,
The forms eternal of created things:
The radiant sun; the moon's nocturnal
lamp;
110 The mountains and the streams; the
ample stores
Of earth, of heaven, of nature. From
the first,
On that full scene his love divine he
fix'd,
His admiration; till, in time complete,
What he admir'd and lov'd, his vital
power
115 Unfolded into being. Hence the breath
Of life informing each organic frame;
Hence the green earth, and wild-resound-
ing waves;
Hence light and shade, alternate;
warmth and cold;
And bright autumnal skies, and vernal
showers,
120 And all the fair variety of things.
But not alike to every mortal eye
Is this great scene unveil'd. For while
the claims
Of social life to different labors urge

[1] kaiser; emperor

The active powers of man, with wisest
care
125 Hath Nature on the multitude of minds
Impress'd a various bias; and to each
Decreed its province in the common toil.
To some she taught the fabric of the
sphere,
The changeful moon, the circuit of the
stars,
130 The golden zones of heaven: to some she
gave
To search the story of eternal thought;
Of space and time; of fate's unbroken
chain,
And will's quick movement: others by
the hand
She led o'er vales and mountains, to
explore
135 What healing virtue dwells in every vein
Of herbs or trees. But some to nobler
hopes
Were destin'd: some within a finer
mould
She wrought, and temper'd with a purer
flame.
To these the Sire Omnipotent unfolds,
140 In fuller aspects and with fairer lights,
This picture of the world. Through
every part
They trace the lofty sketches of his
hand:
In earth or air, the meadow's flowery
store,
The moon's mild radiance, or the virgin's mien
145 Dress'd in attractive smiles, they see portray'd
(As far as mortal eyes the portrait scan)
Those lineaments of beauty which delight
The Mind Supreme. They also feel their
force,
Enamor'd: they partake the eternal joy.
150 For as old Memnon's image long renown'd
Through fabling Egypt, at the genial
touch
Of morning, from its inmost frame sent
forth
Spontaneous music; so doth Nature's
hand,
To certain attributes which matter
claims,
155 Adapt the finer organs of the mind:
So the glad impulse of those kindred
powers
(Of form, of color's cheerful pomp, of
sound
Melodious, or of motion aptly sped)

Detains the enliven'd sense; till soon
the soul
Feels the deep concord, and assents
through all
160 Her functions. Then the charm by fate
prepar'd
Diffuseth its enchantment. Fancy dreams,
Rapt into high discourse with prophets
old,
And wandering through Elysium, Fancy
dreams
Of sacred fountains, of o'ershadowing
groves,
165 Whose walks with godlike harmony resound:
Fountains, which Homer visits; happy
groves,
Where Milton dwells: the intellectual
power,
On the mind's throne, suspends his
graver cares,
And smiles: the passions, to divine repose,
170 Persuaded yield: and love and joy alone
Are waking; love and joy, such as await
An angel's meditation. O! attend,
Whoe'er thou art whom these delights
can touch;
Whom Nature's aspect, Nature's simple
garb,
175 Can thus command; O! listen to my
song;
And I will guide thee to her blissful
walks,
And teach thy solitude her voice to hear,
178 And point her gracious features to thy
view.

. . . . . .

For, amid
The various forms, which this full world
presents
Like rivals to his[1] choice, what human
breast
230 E'er doubts, before the transient and
minute,
To prize the vast, the stable, the sublime?
Who, that from heights aërial sends his
eye
Around a wild horizon, and surveys
Indus or Ganges rolling his broad wave
235 Through mountains, plains, thro' spacious cities old,
And regions dark with woods, will turn
away
To mark the path of some penurious[2]
rill

[1] man's   [2] scanty

Which murmureth at his feet? Where
does the soul
Consent her soaring fancy to restrain,
240 Which bears her up, as on an eagle's
wings,
Destin'd for highest heaven; or which
of fate's
Tremendous barriers shall confine her
flight
To any humbler quarry?[1] The rich
earth
Cannot detain her; nor the ambient[2]
air
245 With all its changes. For a while with
joy
She hovers o'er the sun, and views the
small
Attendant orbs, beneath his sacred beam,
Emerging from the deep, like cluster'd
isles
Whose rocky shores to the glad sailor's
eye
250 Reflect the gleams of morning: for a
while
With pride she sees his firm, paternal
sway
Bend the reluctant planets to move each
Round its perpetual year. But soon she
quits
That prospect: meditating loftier views,
255 She darts adventurous up the long career
Of comets; through the constellations
holds
Her course, and now looks back on all
the stars
Whose blended flames as with a milky
stream
Part the blue region. Empyréan tracts,[3]
260 Where happy souls beyond this concave
heaven
Abide, she then explores, whence purer
light
For countless ages travels through the
abyss,
Nor hath in sight of mortals yet arriv'd.
Upon the wide creation's utmost shore
265 At length she stands, and the dread
space beyond
Contemplates, half-recoiling: nathless[4]
down
The gloomy void, astonish'd, yet un-
quell'd,
She plungeth; down the unfathomable
gulf,
Where God alone hath being. There her
hopes

[1] object p u r s u e d or
hunted
[2] surrounding on a l l
sides
[3] T h e highest heaven,
far above the sky.
[4] nevertheless

270 Rest at the fated goal. For, from the
      birth
Of human kind, the Sovereign Maker
      said
That not in humble, nor in brief delight,
Not in the fleeting echoes of renown,
Power's purple robes, nor Pleasure's
      flowery lap,
275 The soul should find contentment; but,
      from these
Turning disdainful to an equal good,
Through Nature's opening walks enlarge
      her aim,
Till every bound at length should dis-
      appear,
And infinite perfection fill the scene.

     .   .   .   .   .

           Then tell me (for ye know)
Doth Beauty ever deign to dwell where
      use
And aptitude are strangers? is her
      praise
405 Confess'd in aught whose most peculiar
      ends
Are lame and fruitless? or did Nature
      mean
This pleasing call the herald of a lie,
To hide the shame of discord and dis-
      ease,
And win each fond admirer into snares,
410 Foil'd, baffled? No; with better provi-
      dence
The general mother, conscious how infirm
Her offspring tread the paths of good
      and ill,
Thus, to the choice of credulous desire,
Doth objects the completest of their tribe
415 Distinguish and commend. Yon flowery
      bank,
Cloth'd in the soft magnificence of
      Spring,
Will not the flocks approve it? will they
      ask
The reedy fen for pasture? That clear
      rill
Which trickleth murmuring from the
      mossy rock,
420 Yields it less wholesome beverage to the
      worn
And thirsty traveller, than the standing
      pool
With muddy weeds o'ergrown? Yon
      ragged vine,
Whose lean and sullen clusters mourn
      the rage
Of Eurus, will the wine-press or the
      bowl
425 Report of her, as of the swelling grape

Which glitters through the tendrils, like
      a gem
When first it meets the sun? Or what
      are all
The various charms to life and sense
      adjoin'd?
Are they not pledges of a state entire,
430 Where native order reigns, with every
      part
In health, and every function well per-
      form'd?
    Thus then at first was Beauty sent
      from Heaven,
The lovely ministress of Truth and Good
In this dark world; for Truth and Good
      are one;
435 And Beauty dwells in them, and they in
      her,
With like participation.

     .   .   .   .   .

           All her works
Well-pleas'd thou didst behold: the
      gloomy fires
Of storm or earthquake, and the purest
      light
Of summer; soft Campania's new-born
      rose,
580 And the slow weed which pines on Rus-
      sian hills,
Comely alike to thy full vision stand:
To thy surrounding vision, which unites
All essences and powers of the great
      world
In one sole order, fair alike they stand,
585 As features well consenting, and alike
Requir'd by Nature ere she could attain
Her just resemblance to the perfect
      shape
Of universal Beauty, which with thee
Dwelt from the first.

     .   .   .   .   .

FOR A GROTTO
1758

To me, whom in their lays the shepherds
      call
Actaea, daughter of the neighboring
      stream,
This cave belongs. The fig-tree and the
      vine,
Which o'er the rocky entrance down-
      ward shoot,
5 Were placed by Glycon. He, with cow-
      slips pale,
Primrose, and purple lychnis, decked the
      green
Before my threshold, and my shelving
      walls

With honeysuckle covered. Here, at
   noon,
Lulled by the murmur of my rising
   fount,
10 I slumber; here my clustering fruits I
   tend;
Or from the humid flowers, at break of
   day,
Fresh garlands weave, and chase from
   all my bounds
Each thing impure or noxious. Enter in,
O stranger, undismayed. Nor bat nor
   toad
15 Here lurks: and if thy breast of blameless thoughts
Approve[1] thee, not unwelcome shalt thou
   tread
My quiet mansion; chiefly, if thy name
Wise Pallas and the immortal Muses
   own.

ODE

TO THE EVENING STAR

Tonight retired, the queen of heaven[2]
   With young Endymion stays;
And now to Hesper it is given
Awhile to rule the vacant sky,
5 Till she shall to her lamp supply
   A stream of brighter rays.

O Hesper, while the starry throng
   With awe thy path surrounds,
Oh, listen to my suppliant song,
10 If haply now the vocal sphere
Can suffer thy delighted ear
   To stoop to mortal sounds.

So may the bridegroom's genial strain
   Thee still invoke to shine;
15 So may the bride's unmarried train
To Hymen chaunt their flattering vow,
Still that his lucky torch may glow
   With lustre pure as thine.

Far other vows must I prefer
20   To thy indulgent power.
Alas! but now I paid my tear
On fair Olympia's[3] virgin tomb;
And lo, from thence, in quest I roam
   Of Philomela's bower.

25 Propitious send thy golden ray,
   Thou purest light above!
Let no false flame seduce to stray
Where gulf or steep lie hid for harm;
But lead where music's healing charm
30   May soothe afflicted love.

To them, by many a grateful song
   In happier seasons vow'd,
These lawns,[1] Olympia's haunts, belong:
Oft by yon silver stream we walk'd,
35 Or fix'd,[2] while Philomela talk'd,
   Beneath yon copses stood.

Nor seldom, where the beechen boughs
   That roofless tower invade,
We came, while her enchanting Muse
40 The radiant moon above us held:
Till, by a clamorous owl compell'd
   She fled the solemn shade.

But hark! I hear her liquid tone!
   Now Hesper guide my feet!
45 Down the red marl[3] with moss o'ergrown,
Through yon wild thicket next the plain,
Whose hawthorns choke the winding lane
   Which leads to her retreat.

See the green space: on either hand
50   Enlarged it spreads around:
See, in the midst she takes her stand,
Where one old oak his awful shade
Extends o'er half the level mead,
   Enclosed in woods profound.

55 Hark! how through many a melting note
   She now prolongs her lays:
How sweetly down the void they float!
The breeze their magic path attends;
The stars shine out; the forest bends;
60   The wakeful heifers graze.

Whoe'er thou art whom chance may bring
   To this sequester'd spot,
If then the plaintive Siren sing,
Oh softly tread beneath her bower
65 And think of Heaven's disposing power,
   Of man's uncertain lot.

Oh think; o'er all this mortal stage
   What mournful scenes arise:
What ruin waits on kingly rage;
70 How often virtue dwells with woe;
How many griefs from knowledge flow;
   How swiftly pleasure flies!

Oh sacred bird! let me at eve,
   Thus wandering all alone,
75 Thy tender counsel oft receive,
Bear witness to thy pensive airs,
And pity Nature's common cares,
   Till I forget my own.

---

[1] prove; confirm
[2] Diana, the moon.
[3] Olympia is the poet's beloved.

[1] green fields
[2] attentive; motion-less
[3] A kind of soft earthy deposit.

William Collins 1721-1759

A SONG FROM SHAKESPEAR'S CYMBELYNE

SUNG BY GUIDERUS AND ARVIRAGUS OVER
FIDELE, SUPPOS'D TO BE DEAD[1]

1744

To fair Fidele's grassy tomb
  Soft maids and village hinds[2] shall
    bring
Each op'ning sweet, of earliest bloom,
  And rifle all the breathing spring.

5 No wailing ghost shall dare appear,
  To vex with shrieks this quiet grove:
But shepherd lads assemble here,
  And melting virgins own their love.

No wither'd witch shall here be seen,
10 No goblins lead their nightly crew:
The female fays shall haunt the green,
  And dress thy grave with pearly dew.

The redbreast oft at ev'ning hours
  Shall kindly lend his little aid,
15 With hoary moss, and gather'd flow'rs,
  To deck the ground where thou art
    laid.

When howling winds, and beating rain,
  In tempests shake the sylvan cell,
Or midst the chace on ev'ry plain,
20 The tender thought on thee shall
    dwell.

Each lonely scene shall thee restore,
  For thee the tear be duly shed:
Belov'd, till life could charm no more;
  And mourn'd, till Pity's self be dead.

ODE TO SIMPLICITY
1746

O thou by Nature taught
To breathe her genuine thought,
In numbers warmly pure, and sweetly
  strong:
  Who first, on mountains wild,
5 In Fancy, loveliest child,
Thy babe or Pleasure's, nurs'd the
  pow'rs of song!

Thou who with hermit heart
Disdain'st the wealth of art,

---

[1] *Cymbeline*, IV, 2, 215-229, furnished the inspiration for this song. The brothers there mourn for their sister Imogen, who is disguised as Fidele, and who they think is dead.
[2] rustics; peasants

And gauds,[1] and pageant weeds, and
  trailing pall,
10 But com'st a decent[2] maid
  In Attic robe array'd,
O chaste, unboastful nymph, to thee I
  call!

By all the honey'd store
On Hybla's thymy[3] shore,
15 By all her blooms, and mingled murmurs
  dear,
  By her[4] whose lovelorn woe
  In ev'ning musings slow
Sooth'd sweetly sad Electra's poet's[5]
  ear:

By old Cephisus deep,
20 Who spread his wavy sweep
In warbled wand'rings round thy green
  retreat,[6]
  On whose enamell'd side
  When holy Freedom died,[7]
No equal haunt allur'd thy future feet:

25 O sister meek of Truth,
  To my admiring youth
Thy sober aid and native charms infuse!
  The flow'rs that sweetest breathe,
  Tho' Beauty cull'd the wreath,
30 Still ask thy hand to range their order'd
  hues.

While Rome could none esteem
But virtue's[8] patriot theme,
You lov'd her hills, and led her laureate
  band:
  But staid to sing alone
35 To one distinguish'd throne,[9]
And turned thy face, and fled her alter'd
  land.

No more, in hall or bow'r,
The passions own thy pow'r;
Love, only love, her forceless numbers
  mean:[10]
40 For thou hast left her shrine;
  Nor olive more, nor vine,
Shall gain thy feet to bless the servile
  scene.

---

[1] ornaments of dress
[2] decorous; proper
[3] overgrown with thyme
[4] "The nightingale, for whom Sophocles seems to have entertained a peculiar fondness."—Collins.
[5] Sophocles, the author of the Greek tragedy *Electra*.
[6] Athens.
[7] When Greece was conquered by Alexander, in 335 B. C.
[8] heroic manhood's
[9] The throne of Augustus Cæsar, the patron of Virgil and Horace.
[10] An allusion to the artificial love poetry of medieval Italy.

Tho' taste, tho' genius bless
To some divine excess,
45 Faints the cold work till thou inspire the
    whole;
What each, what all supply,
May court, may charm our eye,
Thou, only thou, canst raise the meeting
    soul!

Of these let others ask,
50 To aid some mighty task;
I only seek to find my temp'rate vale:
Where oft my reed[1] might sound
To maids and shepherds round,
And all thy sons, O Nature, learn my
    tale.

ODE ON THE POETICAL CHARACTER
1746
STROPHE

As once, if not with light regard[2]
I read aright that gifted bard[3]
(Him whose school above the rest
His loveliest Elfin Queen has blest),
5 One, only one, unrivall'd fair[4]
Might hope the magic girdle wear,
At solemn turney hung on high,
The wish of each love-darting eye;
Lo! to each other nymph in turn applied,
10 As if, in air unseen, some hov'ring
    hand,
Some chaste and angel friend to virgin
    fame,
With whisper'd spell had burst the
    starting band,
It left unblest her loath'd, dishonor'd
    side;
Happier hopeless fair, if never
15 Her baffled hand with vain endeavor
Had touch'd that fatal zone to her de-
    nied!
Young Fancy[5] thus, to me divinest
    name,
To whom, prepar'd and bath'd in
    heav'n,
The cest[6] of amplest pow'r is giv'n,
20 To few the godlike gift assigns,
To gird their blest, prophetic loins,
And gaze her visions wild, and feel un-
    mix'd her flame!

EPODE

The band, as fairy legends say,
Was wove on that creating day

25 When He who call'd with thought to
    birth
Yon tented sky, this laughing earth,
And drest with springs and forests tall,
And pour'd the main engirting all,
Long by the lov'd enthusiast woo'd,
30 Himself in some diviner mood,
Retiring, sate with her alone,
And plac'd her on his sapphire throne,[1]
The whiles, the vaulted shrine around,
Seraphic wires were heard to sound,
35 Now sublimest triumph swelling,
Now on love and mercy dwelling;
And she, from out the veiling cloud,
Breath'd her magic notes aloud:
And thou, thou rich-hair'd Youth of
    Morn,[2]
40 And all thy subject life, was born!
The dang'rous Passions kept aloof,
Far from the sainted growing woof:
But near it sate ecstatic Wonder,
List'ning the deep applauding thunder;
45 And Truth, in sunny vest array'd,
By whose[3] the tarsel's[4] eyes were made;
All the shad'wy tribes of mind
In braided[5] dance their murmurs join'd,
And all the bright uncounted Pow'rs
50 Who feed on heav'n's ambrosial flow'rs.
Where is the bard whose soul can now
Its high presuming hopes avow?
Where he who thinks, with rapture blind,
This hallow'd work for him design'd?

ANTISTROPHE

55 High on some cliff, to heav'n up-pil'd,
Of rude access, of prospect wild,
Where, tangled round the jealous[6] steep,
Strange shades o'er-brow the valleys
    deep,
And holy genii guard the rock,
60 Its glooms embrown, its springs unlock,
While on its rich ambitious head
An Eden, like his own, lies spread,
I view that oak, the fancied glades
    among,
By which as Milton lay, his ev'ning ear,
65 From many a cloud that dropp'd ethereal
    dew,
Nigh spher'd[7] in heav'n its native strains
    could hear,
On which that ancient trump he reach'd
    was hung:
Thither oft, his glory greeting,

[1] The symbol of pas-
  toral poetry.
[2] attention
[3] Spenser.
[4] Amoret, not Flori-
  mel, as Collins sug-
gested. See *The
Faerie Queene*, IV,
5, st. 16-19.
[5] Imagination
[6] cestus; girdle

[1] The blue or upper
  heavens, above the
  sky.
[2] The sun.
[3] That is, by whose
  eyes.
[4] male falcon's
[5] intricate
[6] difficult of approach
[7] in one of the spheres
  in which the heav-
  enly bodies were
  supposed to be fixed

From Waller's myrtle shades retreat-
    ing,[1]
70 With many a vow from Hope's aspiring
    tongue,
    My trembling feet his guiding steps
       pursue;
    In vain—such bliss to one alone
    Of all the sons of soul was known,[2]
    And Heav'n and Fancy, kindred
       pow'rs,
75 Have now o'erturn'd th' inspiring
       bow'rs,
    Or curtain'd close such scene from ev'ry
       future view.

ODE WRITTEN IN THE BEGINNING
OF THE YEAR 1746
1746   1746

How sleep the brave who sink to rest
By all their country's wishes blest!
When Spring, with dewy fingers cold,
Returns to deck their hallow'd mold,
5 She there shall dress a sweeter sod
Than Fancy's feet have ever trod.

By fairy hands their knell is rung,
By forms unseen their dirge is sung;
There Honor comes, a pilgrim gray,
10 To bless the turf that wraps their clay;
And Freedom shall awhile repair,
To dwell a weeping hermit there!

ODE TO EVENING
1746

If ought of oaten stop,[3] or pastoral song,
May hope, chaste Eve, to sooth thy
    modest ear,
    Like thy own solemn springs,
    Thy springs and dying gales,

5 O nymph reserv'd, while now the bright-
    hair'd sun
Sits in yon western tent, whose cloudy
    skirts,
    With brede[4] ethereal wove,
    O'erhang his wavy bed:

Now air is hush'd, save where the weak-
    ey'd bat,
10 With short shrill shriek, flits by on
    leathern wing,
    Or where the beetle winds
    His small but sullen horn,

As oft he rises 'midst the twilight path,
Against the pilgrim borne in heedless
15   hum:
    Now teach me, maid compos'd,
    To breathe some soften'd strain,

Whose numbers, stealing thro' thy
    dark'ning vale,
May not unseemly with its stillness suit,
    As, musing slow, I hail
20   Thy genial lov'd return!

For when thy folding-star arising shews
His paly[1] circlet, at his warning lamp
    The fragrant Hours, and elves
    Who slept in flow'rs the day,

25 And many a nymph who wreaths her
    brows with sedge,
And sheds the fresh'ning dew, and,
    lovelier still,
    The pensive Pleasures sweet,
    Prepare thy shadowy car.

Then lead, calm vot'ress, where some
    sheety lake
30 Cheers the lone heath, or some time-
    hallow'd pile
    Or upland fallows gray
    Reflect its last cool gleam.

But when chill blust'ring winds, or driv-
    ing rain,
Forbid my willing feet, be mine the hut
35   That from the mountain's side
    Views wilds, and swelling floods,

And hamlets brown, and dim-discover'd
    spires,
And hears their simple bell, and marks
    o'er all
    Thy dewy fingers draw
40   The gradual dusky veil.

While Spring shall pour his show'rs, as
    oft he wont,[2]
And bathe thy breathing tresses, meek-
    est Eve;
    While Summer loves to sport
    Beneath thy ling'ring light;

45 While sallow Autumn fills thy lap with
    leaves;
Or Winter, yelling thro' the troublous
    air,
    Affrights thy shrinking train,
    And rudely rends thy robes;

---

[1] An allusion to t h e
love poems of Ed-
mund Waller. The
myrtle was sacred
to Venus.

[2] Milton.

[3] anything played upon
the shepherd's oaten
pipe

[4] braid; embroidery

[1] pale

[2] is accustomed to do

So long, sure-found beneath the sylvan
 shed,
50 Shall Fancy, Friendship, Science, rose-
 lipp'd Health,
 Thy gentlest influence own,
 And hymn thy fav'rite name!

THE PASSIONS

AN ODE FOR MUSIC
1746

When Music, heav'nly maid, was young,
While yet in early Greece she sung,
The Passions oft, to hear her shell,[1]
Throng'd around her magic cell,
5 Exulting, trembling, raging, fainting,
Possest beyond the Muse's painting;
By turns they felt the glowing mind
Disturb'd, delighted, rais'd, refin'd:
Till once, 't is said, when all were fir'd,
10 Fill'd with fury, rapt, inspir'd,
From the supporting myrtles round
They snatch'd her instruments of sound;
And as they oft had heard apart
Sweet lessons of her forceful art,
15 Each, for madness rul'd the hour,
Would prove his own expressive pow'r.

First Fear his hand, its skill to try,
 Amid the chords bewilder'd laid,
And back recoil'd, he knew not why,
20 Ev'n at the sound himself had made.

Next Anger rush'd; his eyes, on fire,
 In lightnings own'd his secret stings;
In one rude clash he struck the lyre,
 And swept with hurried hand the
  strings.

25 With woful measures wan Despair
 Low sullen sounds his grief beguil'd;
A solemn, strange, and mingled air;
 'Twas sad by fits, by starts 'twas wild.

But thou, O Hope, with eyes so fair,
30 What was thy delightful measure?
Still it whisper'd promis'd pleasure,
 And bad the lovely scenes at distance
  hail!
Still would her touch the strain prolong,
 And from the rocks, the woods, the
  vale,
35 She call'd on Echo still thro' all the
  song;
 And where her sweetest theme she
  chose,

A soft responsive voice was heard at
 ev'ry close,
And Hope enchanted smil'd, and wav'd
 her golden hair.

And longer had she sung,—but with a
 frown
40 Revenge impatient rose;
He threw his blood-stain'd sword in
  thunder down
 And with a with'ring look
The war-denouncing[1] trumpet took,
And blew a blast so loud and dread,
45 Were ne'er prophetic sounds so full of
 woe.
 And ever and anon he beat
 The doubling drum with furious
  heat;
 And tho' sometimes, each dreary pause
  between,
 Dejected Pity, at his side,
50 Her soul-subduing voice apply'd,
 Yet still he kept his wild unalter'd
  mien,
While each strain'd ball of sight seem'd
 bursting from his head.

Thy numbers, Jealousy, to nought were
 fix'd,
 Sad proof of thy distressful state;
55 Of diff'ring themes the veering song was
 mix'd,
 And now it courted Love, now raving
  call'd on Hate.

With eyes uprais'd, as one inspir'd,
Pale Melancholy sate retir'd,
And from her wild sequester'd seat,
60 In notes by distance made more sweet,
Pour'd thro' the mellow horn her pen-
 sive soul:
And, dashing soft from rocks around,
Bubbling runnels join'd the sound;
Thro' glades and glooms the mingled
 measure stole;
65 Or o'er some haunted stream with
  fond delay
 Round an holy calm diffusing,
 Love of peace and lonely musing,
In hollow murmurs died away.

But O how alter'd was its sprightlier
 tone,
70 When Cheerfulness, a nymph of health-
 iest hue,
 Her bow across her shoulder flung,
 Her buskins gemm'd with morning dew,

---

[1] lyre (The first lyre is said to have been made
from a tortoise shell.)

[1] announcing

Blew an inspiring air, that dale and
    thicket rung,
The hunter's call to faun and dryad
    known!
75 The oak-crown'd sisters,[1] and their
    chaste-ey'd queen,[2]
Satyrs, and sylvan boys, were seen,
Peeping from forth their alleys green;
Brown Exercise rejoic'd to hear,
    And Sport leapt up, and se;z'd his
    beechen spear.

80 Last came Joy's ecstatic trial.
He, with viny crown advancing,
    First to the lively pipe his hand ad-
    drest;
But soon he saw the brisk awak'ning
    viol,
Whose sweet entrancing voice he lov'd
    the best.
85 They would have thought, who heard
    the strain,
    They saw in Tempe's vale her native
    maids,
    Amidst the festal sounding shades,
To some unwearied minstrel dancing,
While, as his flying fingers kiss'd the
    strings,
90 Love fram'd with Mirth a gay fan-
    tastic round;
    Loose were her tresses seen, her zone[3]
    unbound,
    And he, amidst his frolic play,
As if he would the charming air repay,
Shook thousand odors from his dewy
    wings.

95 O Music, sphere-descended maid,
Friend of Pleasure, Wisdom's aid,
Why, goddess, why, to us deny'd,
Lay'st thou thy ancient lyre aside?
As in that lov'd Athenian bow'r
100 You learn'd an all-commanding pow'r,
Thy mimic soul, O nymph endear'd,
Can well recall what then it heard.
Where is thy native simple heart,
Devote to Virtue, Fancy, Art?
105 Arise as in that elder time,
Warm, energic, chaste, sublime!
Thy wonders, in that godlike age,
Fill thy recording sister's page—
'Tis said, and I believe the tale,
110 Thy humblest reed could more prevail,
Had more of strength, diviner rage,
Than all which charms this laggard age,
Ev'n all at once together found,
Cæcilia's mingled world of sound.

[1] wood nymphs   [2] Diana   [3] girdle

115 O bid our vain endeavors cease,
Revive the just designs of Greece,
Return in all thy simple state,
Confirm the tales her sons relate!

ODE ON THE DEATH OF MR. THOMSON
    1748   1749

In yonder grave a druid lies,
    Where slowly winds the stealing wave.
The year's best sweets shall duteous rise
    To deck its poet's sylvan grave.

5 In yon deep bed of whisp'ring reeds
    His airy harp[1] shall now be laid,
That he whose heart in sorrow bleeds
    May love thro' life the soothing shade.

Then maids and youths shall linger here;
10   And while its sounds at distance swell,
Shall sadly seem in Pity's ear
    To hear the Woodland Pilgrim's knell.

Remembrance oft shall haunt the shore
    When Thames in summer wreaths is
    drest,
15 And oft suspend the dashing oar
    To bid his gentle spirit rest.

And oft as Ease and Health retire
    To breezy lawn, or forest deep,
The friend shall view yon whit'ning
    spire,
20   And mid the varied landscape weep.

But thou who own'st that earthy bed,
    Ah, what will ev'ry dirge avail,
Or tears which Love and Pity shed,
    That mourn beneath the gliding sail?

25 Yet lives there one whose heedless eye
    Shall scorn thy pale shrine glimm'ring
    near?
With him, sweet bard, may Fancy die,
    And Joy desert the blooming year!

But thou, lorn stream, whose sullen tide
30   No sedge-crown'd sisters now attend,
Now waft me from the green hill's side
    Whose cold turf hides the buried
    friend.

And see, the fairy valleys fade;
    Dun night has veil'd the solemn view.

[1] The Harp of Æolus. See Thomson's *The Castle
of Indolence*, 1, 360; also his *Ode to Æolus's
Harp.*

35 Yet once again, dear parted shade,
   Meek Nature's child, again adieu!

The genial meads, assign'd to bless
   Thy life, shall mourn thy early doom;
Their hinds and shepherd girls shall dress
40   With simple hands thy rural tomb.

Long, long, thy stone and pointed clay
   Shall melt the musing Briton's eyes;
O vales and wild woods, shall he say,
   In yonder grave your druid lies!

AN ODE ON THE POPULAR SUPER-STITIONS OF THE HIGHLANDS OF SCOTLAND

CONSIDERED AS THE SUBJECT OF POETRY
1749   1788

H——,[1] thou return'st from Thames,
   whose naiads long
Have seen thee ling'ring, with a fond
   delay,
'Mid those soft friends, whose hearts,
   some future day,
Shall melt, perhaps, to hear thy tragic
   song.
5 Go, not unmindful of that cordial
   youth[2]
Whom, long-endear'd, thou leav'st by
   Lavant's side;
Together let us wish him lasting truth,
   And joy untainted, with his destined
   bride.
Go! nor regardless, while these numbers
   boast
10   My short-liv'd bliss, forget my social
   name;
But think far off how, on the Southern
   coast,
   I met thy friendship with an equal
   flame!
Fresh to that soil thou turn'st, whose
   ev'ry vale
Shall prompt the poet, and his song
   demand:
15 To thee thy copious subjects ne'er shall
   fail;
   Thou need'st but take the pencil to
   thy hand,
And paint what all believe who own thy
   genial land.[3]

There must thou wake perforce thy Doric[1]
   quill;
'Tis Fancy's land to which thou sett'st
   thy feet,
20 Where still, 'tis said, the fairy people
   meet
Beneath each birken shade on mead or
   hill.
There each trim lass that skims the
   milky store
To the swart tribes[2] their creamy bowl
   allots;
By night they sip it round the cottage
   door,
25 While airy minstrels warble jocund
   notes.
There ev'ry herd, by sad experience,
   knows
How, wing'd with fate, their elf-shot
   arrows fly;
When the sick ewe her summer food
   foregoes,
Or, stretch'd on earth, the heart-smit
   heifers lie.
30 Such airy beings awe th' untutor'd
   swain:
Nor thou, though learn'd, his homelier
   thoughts neglect;
Let thy sweet Muse the rural faith sustain:
   These are the themes of simple, sure
   effect,
That add new conquests to her boundless
   reign,
35 And fill, with double force, her heart-
   commanding strain.

Ev'n yet preserv'd, how often may'st
   thou hear,
   Where to the pole the boreal[3] mountains run,
Taught by the father to his list'ning
   son,
Strange lays, whose pow'r had charm'd
   a Spenser's ear.
40 At ev'ry pause, before thy mind possest,
   Old Runic bards[4] shall seem to rise
   around,
With uncouth[5] lyres, in many-color'd
   vest,[6]
   Their matted hair with boughs fantastic crown'd:

---

[1] John Home (1722-1808), a Scottish clergyman and dramatist, whose tragedy of *Agis* was refused by Garrick, the noted English actor, when it was brought to him in London in 1749.
[2] John Barrow, who had introduced Collins and Home.
[3] acknowledge it as their country

[1] simple; natural (Doric was the oldest and simplest style of architecture used by the Greeks.)
[2] Brownies.
[3] northern
[4] poets of the northern countries who wrote poems in runes, their early alphabet
[5] strange; of unusual shape
[6] garment

Whether thou bid'st the well-taught
    hind repeat
45 The choral dirge that mourns some
    chieftain brave,
When ev'ry shrieking maid her bosom
    beat,
And strew'd with choicest herbs his
    scented grave;
Or, whether, sitting in the shepherd's
    shiel,[1]
Thou hear'st some sounding tale of
    war's alarms,
50 When, at the bugle's call, with fire and
    steel,
The sturdy clans pour'd forth their
    bony swarms,
And hostile brothers met to prove each
    other's arms.

'Tis thine to sing, how, framing hideous
    spells,
    In Sky's lone isle the gifted wizard
    seer,
55 Lodg'd in the wintry cave with [Fate's
    fell spear]
Or in the depth of Uist's dark forests
    dwells:
How they whose sight such dreary
    dreams engross,
    With their own visions oft astonish'd
    droop,
When o'er the wat'ry strath[2] or quaggy
    moss
60 They see the gliding ghosts unbodied
    troop;
Or if in sports, or on the festive green,
    Their [destined] glance some fated
    youth descry,
Who, now perhaps in lusty vigor seen
    And rosy health, shall soon lamented
    die.
65 For them the viewless forms of air obey,
    Their bidding heed, and at their beck
    repair.
They know what spirit brews the storm-
    ful day,
    And, heartless,[3] oft like moody mad-
    ness stare
To see the phantom train their secret
    work prepare.

70 [To monarchs dear, some hundred miles
    astray,
    Oft have they seen Fate give the fatal
    blow!
The seer, in Sky, shriek'd as the blood
    did flow,

When headless Charles[1] warm on the
    scaffold lay!
As Boreas threw his young Aurora
    forth,
75 In the first year of the first George's
    reign,
And battles rag'd in welkin[2] of the
    North,
    They mourn'd in air, fell, fell Rebel-
    lion slain!
And as, of late, they joy'd in Preston's
    fight,
    Saw at sad Falkirk all their hopes
    near crown'd,
80 They rav'd, divining, thro' their second
    sight,
    Pale, red Culloden, where these hopes
    were drown'd!
Illustrious William![3] Britain's guardian
    name!
    One William sav'd us from a tyrant's
    stroke;
He, for a sceptre, gain'd heroic fame;
85 But thou, more glorious, Slavery's
    chain hast broke,
To reign a private man, and bow to
    Freedom's yoke!

These, too, thou'lt sing! for well thy
    magic Muse
    Can to the topmost heav'n of grandeur
    soar!
Or stoop to wail the swain that is no
    more!
90 Ah, homely swains! your homeward
    steps ne'er lose;
Let not dank Will[4] mislead you to the
    heath:
    Dancing in mirky night, o'er fen and
    lake,
He glows, to draw you downward to
    your death,
    In his bewitch'd, low, marshy willow
    brake!]
95 What tho' far off, from some dark dell
    espied,
    His glimm'ring mazes cheer th' ex-
    cursive sight,
Yet turn, ye wand'rers, turn your steps
    aside,
    Nor trust the guidance of that faith-
    less light;
For, watchful, lurking 'mid th' unrus-
    tling reed.
100 At those mirk[5] hours the wily monster
    lies,

---

[1] summer hut   [3] dismayed
[2] valley cut by a river

[1] Charles I.   trasted with Wil-
[2] the sky   liam of Orange (1. 84).
[3] William, Duke of   [4] Will-o'-the-wisp
    Cumberland, is con-   [5] murky; dark

And listens oft to hear the passing steed,
  And frequent round him rolls his
    sullen eyes,
If chance his savage wrath may some
    weak wretch surprise.

Ah, luckless swain, o'er all unblest in-
    deed!
105 Whom, late bewilder'd in the dank,
    dark fen,
  Far from his flocks and smoking ham-
    let then,
To that sad spot [where hums the sedgy
    weed]
On him, enrag'd, the fiend, in angry
    mood,
  Shall never look with Pity's kind con-
    cern,
110 But instant, furious, raise the whelming
    flood
  O'er its drown'd bank, forbidding all
    return.
Or, if he meditate his wish'd escape
  To some dim hill that seems uprising
    near,
  To his faint eye the grim and grisly
    shape,
115 In all its terrors clad, shall wild
    appear.
Meantime, the wat'ry surge shall round
    him rise,
  Pour'd sudden forth from ev'ry swell-
    ing source.
What now remains but tears and hope-
    less sighs?
  His fear-shook limbs have lost their
    youthly force,
120 And down the waves he floats, a pale
    and breathless corse.

For him, in vain, his anxious wife shall
    wait,
  Or wander forth to meet him on his
    way;
For him, in vain, at to-fall[1] of the
    day,
  His babes shall linger at th' unclosing
    gate.
125 Ah, ne'er shall he return! Alone, if
    night
  Her travell'd limbs in broken slumbers
    steep,
With dropping willows drest, his mourn-
    ful sprite
  Shall visit sad, perchance, her silent
    sleep:
Then he, perhaps, with moist and wat'ry
    hand,

130 Shall fondly seem to press her shud-
    d'ring cheek,
  And with his blue-swoln face before her
    stand,
  And, shiv'ring cold, these piteous ac-
    cents speak:
"Pursue, dear wife, thy daily toils
    pursue
  At dawn or dusk, industrious as be-
    fore;
135 Nor e'er of me one hapless thought
    renew,
  While I lie welt'ring on the ozier'd[1]
    shore,
Drown'd by the kælpie's[2] wrath, nor e'er
    shall aid thee more!"

Unbounded is thy range; with varied
    style
  Thy Muse may, like those feath'ry
    tribes which spring
140 From their rude rocks, extend her
    skirting wing
Round the moist marge of each cold
    Hebrid isle,
  To that hoar pile which still its ruin
    shows:[3]
  In whose small vaults a pigmy-folk is
    found,
Whose bones the delver with his spade
    upthrows,
145 And culls them, wond'ring, from the
    hallow'd ground!
Or thither, where, beneath the show'ry
    West,
  The mighty kings of three fair realms
    are laid:[4]
  Once foes, perhaps, together now they
    rest;
No slaves revere them, and no wars
    invade:
150 Yet frequent now, at midnight's solemn
    hour,
  The rifted mounds their yawning cells
    unfold,
  And forth the monarchs stalk with
    sov'reign pow'r,
In pageant robes, and wreath'd with
    sheeny gold,
  And on their twilight tombs aërial coun-
    cil hold.

[1] covered with willows
[2] water spirit's
[3] A stone vault in the Island of Benbecula, said to contain many small bones thought by the inhabitants to be the bones of pygmies. See M. Martin's *Description of the Western Islands of Scotland.*
[4] The Island of Iona was said to contain the tombs of the kings of Scotland, Ireland, and Norway. See Martin's *Description.*

[1] close

155 But O, o'er all, forget not Kilda's race,
    On whose bleak rocks, which brave the
        wasting tides,
    Fair Nature's daughter, Virtue, yet
        abides.
    Go, just as they, their blameless manners
        trace!
    Then to my ear transmit some gentle
        song
160   Of those whose lives are yet sincere
        and plain,
    Their bounded walks the rugged cliffs
        along,
    And all their prospect but the wintry
        main.
    With sparing temp'rance, at the needful
        time,
    They drain the sainted spring, or,
        hunger-prest,
165 Along th' Atlantic rock undreading
        climb,
    And of its eggs despoil the solan's[1]
        nest.
    Thus blest in primal innocence they
        live,
    Suffic'd and happy with that frugal
        fare
    Which tasteful toil[2] and hourly danger
        give.
170   Hard is their shallow soil, and bleak
        and bare;
    Nor ever vernal bee was heard to mur-
        mur there!

    Nor need'st thou blush, that such false
        themes engage
    Thy gentle[3] mind, of fairer stores
        possest;
    For not alone they touch the village
        breast,
175 But fill'd in elder time th' historic page.
    There Shakespeare's self, with ev'ry gar-
        land crown'd,—
    [Flew to those fairy climes his fancy
        sheen!]—
    In musing hour, his wayward Sisters[4]
        found,
    And with their terrors drest the magic
        scene.
180 From them he sung, when, 'mid his bold
        design,
    Before the Scot afflicted and aghast,
    The shadowy kings of Banquo's fated line
    Thro' the dark cave in gleamy pageant
        past.

Proceed, nor quit the tales which, simply
    told,
185   Could once so well my answ'ring bosom
        pierce;
Proceed! in forceful sounds and colors
    bold,
    The native legends of thy land re-
        hearse;
    To such adapt thy lyre and suit thy
        pow'rful verse.

In scenes like these, which, daring to
    depart
190   From sober truth, are still to nature
        true,
    And call forth fresh delight to Fancy's
        view,
    Th' heroic muse employ'd her Tasso's
        art!
    How have I trembled, when, at Tancred's
        stroke,
    Its gushing blood the gaping cypress
        pour'd;[1]
195 When each live plant with mortal ac-
        cents spoke,
    And the wild blast upheav'd the
        vanish'd sword!
    How have I sat, when pip'd the pensive
        wind,
    To hear his harp, by British Fairfax
        strung,—
Prevailing poet, whose undoubting mind
200   Believ'd the magic wonders which he
        sung!
Hence at each sound imagination glows;
    [*The MS. lacks a line here.*]
Hence his warm lay with softest sweet-
    ness flows;
    Melting it flows, pure, num'rous,
        strong, and clear,
205 And fills th' impassion'd heart, and wins
    th' harmonious ear.

All hail, ye scenes that o'er my soul
    prevail,
Ye [splendid] friths[2] and lakes which,
    far away,
    Are by smooth Annan fill'd, or past'ral
        Tay,
    Or Don's romantic springs; at distance,
        hail!
210 The time shall come when I, perhaps, may
    tread
    Your lowly glens, o'erhung with spread-
        ing broom,
    Or o'er your stretching heaths by fancy
        led:

---

[1] gannet's (a kind of wild goose)
[2] toil which makes food appetizing
[3] well-born; cultivated
[4] *Macbeth*, IV. 1. The wayward Sisters are the weird Sisters,— *i. e.*, the Sisters of Destiny.

[1] Tasso, *Jerusalem Delivered*, 13, 41-43.
[2] bays

[The MS. lacks a line here.]
Then will I dress once more the faded
    bow'r,
215 Where Jonson sat in Drummond's[1]
    [classic] shade,
Or crop from Tiviot's dale each [lyric
    flower]
And mourn on Yarrow's banks [where
    Willy's[2] laid!]
Meantime, ye Pow'rs that on the plains
    which bore
The cordial youth,[3] on Lothian's plains,
    attend,
220 Where'er he dwell, on hill or lowly muir,
To him I lose your kind protection
    lend,
And, touch'd with love like mine, pre-
    serve my absent friend!

Thomas Gray 1716-1771

ODE ON THE SPRING
1742   1748

Lo! where the rosy-bosom'd Hours,
    Fair Venus' train, appear,
Disclose[4] the long-expecting[5] flowers,
    And wake the purple[6] year!
5 The Attic warbler[7] pours her throat,
    Responsive to the cuckoo's note,
      The untaught harmony of spring:
While, whisp'ring pleasure as they fly,
Cool Zephyrs thro' the clear blue sky
10   Their gather'd fragrance fling.

Where'er the oak's thick branches
      stretch
    A broader browner shade,
Where'er the rude and moss-grown beech
    O'er-canopies the glade,
15 Beside some water's rushy brink
With me the Muse shall sit, and think
    (At ease reclin'd in rustic state)
How vain the ardor of the crowd,
How low, how little are the proud,
20   How indigent the great!

Still is the toiling hand of Care;
    The panting herds repose;
Yet hark, how thro' the peopled air
    The busy murmur glows!
25 The insect-youth are on the wing,
    Eager to taste the honied spring,

And float amid the liquid noon;
Some lightly o'er the current skim,
Some show their gayly-gilded trim
30   Quick-glancing to the sun.

To Contemplation's sober eye
    Such is the race of man:
And they that creep, and they that fly,
    Shall end where they began.
35 Alike the busy and the gay
But flutter thro' life's little day,
    In Fortune's varying colors drest:
Brush'd by the hand of rough Mischance,
Or chill'd by Age, their airy dance
40   They leave, in dust to rest.

Methinks I hear, in accents low,
    The sportive kind reply:
Poor moralist! and what art thou?
    A solitary fly!
45 Thy joys no glittering female meets,
No hive hast thou of hoarded sweets,
    No painted plumage to display:
On hasty wings thy youth is flown;
Thy sun is set, thy spring is gone—
50   We frolic while 'tis May.

ODE ON A DISTANT PROSPECT OF ETON COLLEGE
1742   1747

Ye distant spires, ye antique towers,
    That crown the wat'ry glade,
Where grateful Science still adores
    Her Henry's holy shade;[1]
5 And ye, that from the stately brow
Of Windsor's heights th' expanse below
    Of grove, of lawn, of mead survey,
Whose turf, whose shade, whose flowers
      among
Wanders the hoary Thames along
10   His silver-winding way:

Ah, happy hills! ah, pleasing shade!
    Ah, fields belov'd in vain!
Where once my careless childhood
      stray'd,
    A stranger yet to pain!
15 I feel the gales that from ye blow
A momentary bliss bestow,
    As waving fresh their gladsome wing,
My weary soul they seem to soothe,
And, redolent of joy and youth,
20   To breathe a second spring.

Say, father Thames, for thou hast seen
    Full many a sprightly race,

---

[1] Ben Jonson visited the poet William Drummond, at Hawthornden, near Edinburgh, in 1619.
[2] In the old ballad "Willie Drowned in Yarrow."
[3] Drummond   [4] open; expand   [5] awaiting
[6] *Purple* is here used in its classical sense of *bright.*
[7] The nightingale, common in Attica, and often referred to in Greek literature

[1] Eton College was founded by Henry VI in 1440.

Disporting on thy margent green,
The paths of pleasure trace;
25 Who foremost now delight to cleave,
With pliant arm, thy glassy wave?
The captive linnet which enthral?
What idle progeny succeed
To chase the rolling circle's speed,
30 Or urge the flying ball?

While some, on earnest business bent,
Their murm'ring labors ply
'Gainst graver hours that bring con-
straint
To sweeten liberty,
35 Some bold adventurers disdain
The limits of their little reign,
And unknown regions dare descry;
Still as they run they look behind,
They hear a voice in every wind,
40 And snatch a fearful joy.

Gay hope is theirs by fancy fed,
Less pleasing when possest;
The tear forgot as soon as shed;
The sunshine of the breast;
45 Theirs buxom health, of rosy hue,
Wild wit, invention ever-new,
And lively cheer, of vigor born;
The thoughtless day, the easy night,
The spirits pure, the slumbers light,
50 That fly th' approach of morn.

Alas! regardless of their doom
The little victims play;
No sense have they of ills to come,
Nor care beyond today:
55 Yet see, how all around 'em wait
The ministers of human Fate,
And black Misfortune's baleful train!
Ah, show them where in ambush stand,
To seize their prey, the murth'rous band!
60 Ah, tell them they are men!

These shall the fury Passions tear,
The vultures of the mind:
Disdainful Anger, pallid Fear,
And Shame that sculks behind;
65 Or pining Love shall waste their youth,
Or Jealousy, with rankling tooth,
That inly gnaws the secret heart;
And Envy wan, and faded Care,
Grim-visag'd comfortless Despair,
70 And Sorrow's piercing dart.

Ambition this shall tempt to rise,
Then whirl the wretch from high,
To bitter Scorn a sacrifice,
And grinning Infamy.
75 The stings of Falsehood those shall try,

And hard Unkindness' alter'd eye,
That mocks the tear it forc'd to flow;
And keen Remorse with blood defil'd,
And moody Madness laughing wild
80 Amid severest woe.

Lo! in the vale of years beneath
A griesly troop are seen,
The painful family of Death,
More hideous than their queen:
85 This racks the joints; this fires the
veins;
That every laboring sinew strains;
Those in the deeper vitals rage;
Lo! Poverty to fill the band,
That numbs the soul with icy hand,
90 And slow-consuming Age.

To each his suff'rings: all are men,
Condemn'd alike to groan;
The tender for another's pain,
Th' unfeeling for his own.
95 Yet, ah! why should they know their
fate?
Since sorrow never comes too late,
And happiness too swiftly flies,
Thought would destroy their paradise.
No more;—where ignorance is bliss,
100 'Tis folly to be wise.

HYMN TO ADVERSITY
1742   1748

Daughter of Jove, relentless power,
Thou tamer of the human breast,
Whose iron scourge and tort'ring hour
The bad affright, afflict the best!
5 Bound in thy adamantine chain,
The proud are taught to taste of pain,
And purple tyrants vainly groan
With pangs unfelt before, unpitied and
alone.

When first thy sire to send on earth
10 Virtue, his darling child, design'd,
To thee he gave the heav'nly birth,
And bade to form her infant mind.
Stern, rugged nurse! thy rigid lore
With patience many a year she bore;
15 What sorrow was, thou bad'st her
know,
And from her own she learn'd to melt
at others' woe.

Scar'd at thy frown terrific, fly
Self-pleasing Folly's idle brood,
Wild Laughter, Noise, and thoughtless
Joy,
20 And leave us leisure to be good.

Light they disperse, and with them go
  The summer friend, the flattering foe;
By vain Prosperity receiv'd,
To her they vow their truth, and are
  again believ'd.

25   Wisdom in sable garb array'd,
  Immers'd in rapt'rous thought profound,
And Melancholy, silent maid,
  With leaden eye that loves the
  ground,
  Still on thy solemn steps attend;
30 Warm Charity, the gen'ral friend,
  With Justice, to herself severe,
And Pity, dropping soft the sadly-
  pleasing tear.

Oh! gently on thy suppliant's head,
  Dread goddess, lay thy chast'ning
  hand!
35 Not in thy Gorgon[1] terrors clad,
  Not circled with the vengeful band[2]
  (As by the impious thou art seen),
With thund'ring voice, and threat'ning
  mien,
  With screaming Horror's fun'ral cry,
40 Despair, and fell Disease, and ghastly
  Poverty:

Thy form benign, O goddess, wear;
  Thy milder influence impart;
Thy philosophic train be there
  To soften, not to wound, my heart.
45 The gen'rous spark extinct revive;
  Teach me to love, and to forgive,
Exact my own defects to scan,
What others are to feel, and know my-
  self a man.

ELEGY WRITTEN IN A COUNTRY
CHURCH YARD
1742-50   1751

The curfew tolls the knell of parting day;
  The lowing herd winds slowly o'er the
  lea;
The ploughman homeward plods his
  weary way,
  And leaves the world to darkness and
  to me.

5 Now fades the glimmering landscape on
  the sight,
  And all the air a solemn stillness
  holds,

[1] death-dealing (See Glossary.)
[2] The Furies.

Save where the beetle wheels his droning
  flight,
  And drowsy tinklings lull the distant
  folds;

Save that from yonder ivy-mantled tow'r,
10 The moping owl does to the moon
  complain
Of such as, wand'ring near her secret
  bow'r,
  Molest her ancient solitary reign.

Beneath those rugged elms, that yew-
  tree's shade,
  Where heaves the turf in many a
  mould'ring heap,
15 Each in his narrow cell forever laid,
  The rude[1] forefathers of the hamlet
  sleep.

The breezy call of incense-breathing
  Morn,
  The swallow twitt'ring from the straw-
  built shed,
The cock's shrill clarion, or the echoing
  horn,
20 No more shall rouse them from their
  lowly bed.

For them no more the blazing hearth
  shall burn,
  Or busy housewife ply her evening
  care;
No children run to lisp their sire's return,
  Or climb his knees the envied kiss to
  share.

25 Oft did the harvest to their sickle yield,
  Their furrow oft the stubborn glebe[2]
  has broke:
How jocund did they drive their team
  afield!
  How bow'd the woods beneath their
  sturdy stroke!

Let not Ambition mock their useful toil,
30 Their homely joys, and destiny obscure;
Nor Grandeur hear with a disdainful
  smile
  The short and simple annals of the
  poor.

The boast of heraldry,[3] the pomp of
  pow'r,
  And all that beauty, all that wealth
  e'er gave,

[1] simple-living   [2] sod   [3] high descent

35 Awaits alike th' inevitable hour:
     The paths of glory lead but to the
       grave.

Nor you, ye proud, impute to these the
     fault,
   If Memory o'er their tomb no trophies
     raise,
Where through the long-drawn aisle and
     fretted vault
40   The pealing anthem swells the note of
     praise.

Can storied[1] urn, or animated[2] bust,
   Back to its mansion call the fleeting
     breath?
Can Honor's voice provoke[3] the silent
     dust,
   Or Flatt'ry soothe the dull cold ear of
     Death?

45 Perhaps in this neglected spot is laid
     Some heart once pregnant with celes-
       tial fire;
Hands that the rod of empire might
     have sway'd,
   Or wak'd to extasy the living lyre.

But Knowledge to their eyes her ample
     page,
50   Rich with the spoils of time, did ne'er
     unroll;
Chill Penury repress'd their noble
     rage,[4]
   And froze the genial[5] current of the
     soul.

Full many a gem of purest ray serene
   The dark unfathom'd caves of ocean
     bear;
55 Full many a flower is born to blush
     unseen,
   And waste its sweetness on the desert
     air.

Some village Hampden that with daunt-
     less breast,
   The little tyrant of his fields with-
     stood,
Some mute inglorious Milton, here may
     rest,
60   Some Cromwell guiltless of his coun-
     try's blood.[6]

Th' applause of list'ning senates to
     command,
   The threats of pain and ruin to de-
     spise,
To scatter plenty o'er a smiling land,
   And read their history in a nation's
     eyes,

65 Their lot forbad: nor circumscrib'd alone
     Their growing virtues, but their crimes
       confined
Forbad to wade thro' slaughter to a throne,
   And shut the gates of mercy on man-
     kind,

The struggling pangs of conscious truth
     to hide,
70   To quench the blushes of ingenuous
     shame,
Or heap the shrine of Luxury and Pride
   With incense kindled at the Muse's
     flame.

Far from the madding crowd's ignoble
     strife,
   Their sober wishes never learn'd to
     stray;
75 Along the cool sequester'd vale of life
   They kept the noiseless tenor of their
     way.

Yet ev'n these bones from insult to pro-
     tect,
   Some frail memorial still[1] erected
     nigh,
With uncouth[2] rhymes and shapeless
     sculpture deck'd,
80   Implores the passing tribute of a sigh.

Their name, their years, spelt by th' un-
     letter'd Muse,
   The place of fame and elegy supply;
And many a holy text around she strews,
   That teach the rustic moralist to die.

85 For who, to dumb Forgetfulness a prey,
     This pleasing anxious being e'er re-
       sign'd,
Left the warm precincts of the cheerful
     day,
   Nor cast one longing, ling'ring look
     behind?

On some fond breast the parting soul
     relies,
90   Some pious drops the closing eye re-
     quires;

---

[1] inscribed with a story
[2] lifelike
[3] arouse; call forth
[4] enthusiasm
[5] warming; giving life
[6] In the eighteenth

century, Cromwell
was regarded as one
who had sacrificed
his country to his
ambition. See l. 67.

---

[1] always; habitually   [2] strange; odd

E'en from the tomb the voice of Nature
cries,
E'en in our ashes live their wonted 120
fires.

For thee, who, mindful of th' unhonor'd
dead,
Dost in these lines their artless tale
relate,
95 If chance,[1] by lonely Contemplation led,
Some kindred spirit shall enquire thy
fate,—

Haply some hoary-headed swain may say,
"Oft have we seen him at the peep of
dawn
Brushing with hasty steps the dews
away,
100 To meet the sun upon the upland lawn.

"There, at the foot of yonder nodding
beech,
That wreathes its old fantastic roots
so high,
His listless length at noontide would he
stretch,
And pore upon the brook that babbles
by.

105 "Hard by yon wood, now smiling as in
scorn,
Mutt'ring his wayward fancies, he
would rove;
Now drooping, woful-wan, like one forlorn,
Or craz'd with care, or cross'd in
hopeless love.

"One morn I miss'd him on the custom'd hill,
110 Along the heath, and near his fav'rite
tree;
Another came; nor yet beside the rill,
Nor up the lawn, nor at the wood was
he;

"The next, with dirges due, in sad array
Slow through the church-way path we
saw him borne:—
115 Approach and read (for thou can'st
read) the lay
Grav'd on the stone beneath yon aged
thorn."[2]

THE EPITAPH

Here rests his head upon the lap of
Earth
A youth, to Fortune and to Fame un-
known:

[1] perchance   [2] hawthorn tree

Fair Science frown'd not on his humble
birth,
And Melancholy mark'd him for her
own.

Large was his bounty, and his soul sincere;
Heaven did a recompense as largely
send:
He gave to Mis'ry all he had, a tear,
He gain'd from Heav'n ('twas all he
wish'd) a friend.

125 No farther seek his merits to disclose,
Or draw his frailties from their dread
abode
(There they alike in trembling hope
repose),
The bosom of his Father and his God.

THE PROGRESS OF POESY
1754   1757
I. 1

Awake, Æolian lyre,[1] awake,
And give to rapture all thy trembling
strings!
From Helicon's harmonious springs
A thousand rills their mazy progress
take;
5 The laughing flowers that round them
blow,
Drink life and fragrance as they flow.
Now the rich stream of music winds
along,
Deep, majestic, smooth, and strong,
Thro' verdant vales, and Ceres' golden
reign:
10 Now rolling down the steep amain,
Headlong, impetuous, see it pour;
The rocks and nodding groves rebellow
to the roar.

I. 2

Oh! sov'reign of the willing soul,
Parent of sweet and solemn-breathing
airs,
15 Enchanting shell![2] the sullen Cares
And frantic Passions hear thy soft
control.
On Thracia's hills the Lord of War[3]
Has curb'd the fury of his car.
And dropt his thirsty lance at thy com-
mand.

[1] Invoked here as the equivalent of poetry in the
lighter and softer moods, like that of Pindar,
the famous Greek lyric poet, of Æolia, Asia
Minor.
[2] The first lyre is said to have been made from
a tortoise shell.
[3] Mars, whose favorite haunt was said to be
Thrace.

20 Perching on the scept'red hand
Of Jove, thy magic lulls the feather'd
    king[1]
With ruffled plumes and flagging wing;
Quench'd in dark clouds of slumber lie
The terror of his beak, and lightnings of
    his eye.

I. 3

25 Thee, the voice, the dance, obey,
Temper'd to thy warbled lay.
    O'er Idalia's velvet-green
    The rosy-crownèd Loves are seen
On Cytherea's day;
30 With antic Sports, and blue-eyed Pleas-
    ures,
Frisking light in frolic measures;
    Now pursuing, now retreating,
    Now in circling troops they meet;
To brisk notes in cadence beating,
35   Glance their many-twinkling feet.
Slow melting strains their Queen's ap-
    proach declare:
Where'er she turns, the Graces hom-
    age pay.
With arms sublime,[2] that float upon the
    air,
    In gliding state she wins her easy
    way;
40 O'er her warm cheek and rising bosom,
    move
The bloom of young Desire and purple
    light of Love.

II. 1

Man's feeble race what ills await!
Labor, and Penury, the racks of Pain,
Disease, and Sorrow's weeping train,
45   And Death, sad refuge from the storms
    of Fate!
The fond[3] complaint, my song, disprove,
And justify the laws of Jove.
Say, has he giv'n in vain the heav'nly
    Muse?
Night and all her sickly dews,
50 Her spectres wan, and birds of boding
    cry,
He gives to[4] range the dreary sky;
Till down the eastern cliffs afar
Hyperion's march they spy, and glitt'ring
    shafts of war.

II. 2

In climes beyond the solar road,
55 Where shaggy forms o'er ice-built moun-
    tains roam,
The Muse has broke the twilight-gloom

To cheer the shiv'ring native's dull
    abode.
And oft, beneath the od'rous shade
Of Chili's boundless forests laid,
60 She deigns to hear the savage youth repeat,
In loose numbers wildly sweet,
Their feather-cinctur'd chiefs, and dusky
    loves.
Her track, where'er the goddess roves,
Glory pursue, and gen'rous Shame,
65 Th' unconquerable Mind, and Freedom's
    holy flame.

II. 3

Woods, that wave o'er Delphi's steep,
Isles, that crown th' Ægean deep,
    Fields, that cool Ilissus laves,
    Or where Mæander's amber waves
70 In lingering lab'rinths creep,
    How do your tuneful echoes languish,
    Mute, but to the voice of Anguish?
Where each old poetic mountain
    Inspiration breath'd around;
75 Ev'ry shade and hallow'd fountain
    Murmur'd deep a solemn sound;
Till the sad Nine, in Greece's evil hour,[1]
    Left their Parnassus for the Latian
    plains.
Alike they scorn the pomp of tyrant
    Power,
80   And coward Vice, that revels in her
    chains.
When Latium had her lofty spirit lost,
They sought, O Albion, next, thy sea-
    encircled coast.

III. 1

Far from the sun and summer-gale,
In thy green lap was Nature's darling[2]
    laid,
85 What time, where lucid Avon stray'd,
    To him the mighty mother did unveil
Her awful face: the dauntless child
Stretch'd forth his little arms and smil'd,
"This pencil take," she said, "whose
    colors clear
90 Richly paint the vernal year.
Thine too these golden keys, immortal boy!
This can unlock the gates of Joy;
Of Horror that, and thrilling Fears,
Or ope the sacred source of sympathetic
    tears."

III. 2

95   Nor second he,[3] that rode sublime
Upon the seraph-wings of Ecstasy,

---

[1] Jove's eagle.
[2] uplifted
[3] foolish
[4] allows to

[1] When Grecian civil-
ization declined be-
fore the rising pow-
er of Rome, during
the second century
B. C.
[2] Shakespeare.
[3] Milton.

The secrets of th' Abyss to spy.
  He pass'd the flaming bounds of
    Place and Time:
The living throne, the sapphire blaze,
100 Where angels tremble while they gaze,
He saw; but, blasted with excess of light,
  Clos'd his eyes in endless night.
Behold, where Dryden's less presump-
    tuous car,
  Wide o'er the fields of Glory bear
105 Two coursers of ethereal race,[1]
With necks in thunder cloth'd, and long-
    resounding pace!

III. 3

Hark! his hands the lyre explore:
Bright-eyed Fancy, hov'ring o'er,
Scatters from her pictur'd urn
110 Thoughts that breathe, and words that
    burn.
  But ah! 'tis heard no more!
  Oh! lyre divine, what daring spirit[2]
  Wakes thee now? Tho' he inherit
Nor the pride, nor ample pinion,
115   That the Theban Eagle[3] bear,
Sailing with supreme dominion
Thro' the azure deep of air:
Yet oft before his infant eyes would run
  Such forms as glitter in the Muse's
    ray,
120 With Orient[4] hues, unborrow'd of the
    sun:
  Yet shall he mount, and keep his dis-
    tant way
Beyond the limits of a vulgar fate,
Beneath the good how far—but far above
    the great.

THE BARD
1754-57   1757
I. 1

"Ruin seize thee, ruthless King![5]
  Confusion[6] on thy banners wait;
Tho' fann'd by Conquest's crimson
    wing,
  They mock the air with idle state.
5 Helm, nor hauberk's twisted mail,
Nor e'en thy virtues, tyrant, shall avail
To save thy secret soul from nightly
    fears,
From Cambria's curse, from Cambria's
    tears!''
Such were the sounds that o'er the
    crested pride

---

[1] "Meant to express the stately march and sounding energy of Dryden's rhymes."—Gray.
[2] Gray himself.
[3] P i n d a r, who compares himself to an eagle in *Olympian Odes*, 2, 159.
[4] bright, like the East
[5] Edward I.
[6] destruction

---

10   Of the first Edward scatter'd wild
    dismay,
As down the steep of Snowdon's shaggy
    side
  He wound with toilsome march his
    long array.
Stout Glo'ster stood aghast in speech-
    less trance;
"To arms!'' cried Mortimer, and couch'd
    his quiv'ring lance.

I. 2
15 On a rock, whose haughty brow
Frowns o'er cold Conway's foaming
    flood,
  Robed in the sable garb of woe,
With haggard eyes the poet stood
(Loose his beard, and hoary hair
20 Stream'd, like a meteor, to the troubled
    air)
And with a master's hand, and proph-
    et's fire,
Struck the deep sorrows of his lyre:
  "Hark, how each giant-oak and desert
    cave
Sighs to the torrent's awful voice be-
    neath!
25 O'er thee, oh King! their hundred arms
    they wave,
  Revenge on thee in hoarser murmurs
    breathe,
Vocal no more, since Cambria's fatal
    day,
To high-born Hoel's harp, or soft Llew-
    ellyn's lay.

I. 3
  "Cold is Cadwallo's tongue,
30   That hush'd the stormy main;
Brave Urien sleeps upon his craggy bed;
Mountains, ye mourn in vain
Modred, whose magic song
Made huge Plinlimmon bow his cloud-topt
    head.
35   On dreary Arvon's shore they lie,
Smear'd with gore, and ghastly pale;
Far, far aloof th' affrighted ravens sail;
  The famish'd eagle screams, and passes
    by.
Dear lost companions of my tuneful art,
40   Dear as the light that visits these sad
    eyes,
Dear as the ruddy drops that warm my
    heart,
  Ye died amidst your dying country's
    cries—
No more I weep. They do not sleep!
  On yonder cliffs, a griesly band,
45 I see them sit; they linger yet,

Avengers of their native land:
With me in dreadful harmony they join,
And weave with bloody hands the tissue
   of thy line.

II. 1

"Weave the warp,[1] and weave the
   woof,
50 The winding-sheet of Edward's race;
   Give ample room, and verge[2] enough
The characters of hell to trace.
Mark the year, and mark the night,
When Severn shall re-echo with affright
55 The shrieks of death, thro' Berkley's
   roofs that ring,
Shrieks of an agonizing king![3]
   She-wolf of France,[4] with unrelenting
     fangs,
That tear'st the bowels of thy mangled
   mate,
From thee be born, who o'er thy country hangs
60 The scourge of Heav'n.[5] What Terrors
   round him wait!
Amazement[6] in his van, with Flight
   combin'd,
And Sorrow's faded form, and Solitude
   behind.

II. 2

"Mighty victor, mighty lord!
Low on his funeral couch he lies!
65   No pitying heart, no eye, afford
A tear to grace his obsequies.
Is the Sable Warrior[7] fled?
Thy son is gone; he rests among the
   dead.
The swarm, that in thy noontide beam
   were born?
70 Gone to salute the rising morn.[8]
Fair laughs the morn, and soft the zephyr
   blows,
   While proudly riding o'er the azure
     realm,
In gallant trim the gilded vessel goes;
   Youth on the prow, and Pleasure at
     the helm;
75 Regardless of the sweeping Whirlwind's
   sway,
That, hush'd in grim repose, expects his
   ev'ning prey.

II. 3

"Fill high the sparkling bowl;
The rich repast prepare;
   Reft of a crown, he yet may share
     the feast:
80 Close by the regal chair
   Fell Thirst and Famine scowl
A baleful smile upon their baffled
   guest.
Heard ye the din of battle bray,[1]
   Lance to lance, and horse to horse?
85 Long years of havoc urge their des-
   tined course,
And thro' the kindred squadrons mow
   their way.
Ye towers of Julius,[2] London's lasting
   shame,
With many a foul and midnight murther
   fed,
Revere his consort's[3] faith, his father's[4]
   fame,
90 And spare the meek usurper's[5] holy head!

Above, below,[6] the rose of snow,
   Twin'd with her blushing foe, we
     spread:[7]
The bristled Boar[8] in infant-gore
   Wallows beneath the thorny shade.
95 Now, brothers, bending o'er th' accursed
   loom,
Stamp we our vengeance deep, and ratify
   his doom!

III. 1

"Edward, lo! to sudden fate
(Weave we the woof: the thread is
   spun.)
   Half of thy heart we consecrate.[9]
100 (The web is wove. The work is done.)
Stay, oh stay! nor thus forlorn
Leave me unbless'd, unpitied, here to
   mourn!
In yon bright track, that fires the western skies,
They melt, they vanish from my eyes.
105 But oh! what solemn scenes on Snowdon's height,

---

[1] The warp is the threads extended lengthwise in the loom in weaving; the woof is the threads that cross the warp.
[2] space
[3] Edward II, who was murdered in Berkley Castle.
[4] Isabel of France, the adulterous queen of Edward II.
[5] Edward III, who scourged France.
[6] confusion
[7] The Black Prince, who did not live to succeed his father.
[8] Richard II.
[1] The Wars of the Roses.
[2] The Tower of London, part of which was said to have been built by Julius Caesar.
[3] Margaret of Anjou.
[4] Henry V.
[5] Henry VI, who was deposed in 1461.
[6] That is, in the loom.
[7] The white and the red roses, emblems of the Houses of York and Lancaster, were united by the marriage of Henry VII and Elizabeth of York.
[8] Richard III, whose badge was a silver boar, and who murdered the two young sons of Edward IV, who stood between him and the throne.
[9] Eleanor, queen of Edward I, lost her life in saving her husband's by sucking the poison from a dagger-wound.

Descending slow, their glittering skirts
   unroll?
Visions of glory, spare my aching sight!
Ye unborn ages, crowd not on my soul! 140
No more our long-lost Arthur we bewail.[1]
110 All hail, ye genuine kings,[2] Britannia's
   issue, hail!

III. 2

"Girt with many a baron bold
Sublime[3] their starry fronts they rear;
  And gorgeous dames, and statesmen
   old
In bearded majesty, appear.
115 In the midst a form divine![4]
Her eye proclaims her of the Briton line;
Her lion-port, her awe-commanding face,
Attemper'd sweet to virgin-grace.
What strings symphonious tremble in the
   air,
120   What strains of vocal transport round
   her play!
Hear from the grave, great Taliessin,
   hear;
  They breathe a soul to animate thy
   clay.
Bright Rapture calls, and soaring as she
   sings,
Waves in the eye of Heav'n her many-
   color'd wings.

III. 3

125   "The verse adorn again
  Fierce War, and faithful Love,
And Truth severe, by fairy Fiction
   drest.[5]
  In buskin'd[6] measures move
Pale Grief, and pleasing Pain,
130 With Horror, tyrant of the throbbing
   breast.[7]
  A voice, as of the cherub-choir,
Gales from blooming Eden bear;[8]
And distant warblings lessen on my ear,
  That, lost in long futurity, expire.
135 Fond[9] impious man, think'st thou yon
   sanguine cloud,
  Rais'd by thy breath, has quench'd
   the orb of day?
Tomorrow he repairs the golden flood,

And warms the nations with redoubled
   ray.
Enough for me; with joy I see
  The diff'rent doom our Fates assign.
Be thine Despair, and scept'red Care,
To triumph, and to die, are mine."
He spoke, and headlong from the moun-
   tain's height
Deep in the roaring tide he plunged to
   endless night.

ODE ON THE PLEASURE ARISING FROM VICISSITUDE[1]
1754   1775

Now the golden Morn aloft
  Waves her dew-bespangled wing;
With vermeil cheek and whisper soft
  She wooes the tardy Spring;
5 Till April starts, and calls around
The sleeping fragrance from the ground,
And lightly o'er the living scene
Scatters his freshest, tenderest green.

New-born flocks, in rustic dance,
10   Frisking ply their feeble feet;
Forgetful of their wintry trance
  The birds his presence greet:
But chief, the sky-lark warbles high
His trembling thrilling ecstasy,
15 And, lessening from the dazzled sight,
Melts into air and liquid light.

Rise, my soul! on wings of fire,
  Rise the rapt'rous choir among!
Hark! 'tis Nature strikes the lyre,
20   And leads the gen'ral song.

   *   *   *   *   *   *

Yesterday the sullen year
  Saw the snowy whirlwind fly;
Mute was the music of the air,
  The herd stood drooping by:
25 Their raptures now that wildly flow,
No yesterday nor morrow know;
'Tis man alone that joy descries
With forward and reverted eyes.

Smiles on past Misfortune's brow
30   Soft Reflection's hand can trace,
And o'er the cheek of Sorrow throw
  A melancholy grace;
While Hope prolongs our happier hour,
Or deepest shades, that dimly lower[2]
35 And blacken round our weary way,
Gilds with a gleam of distant day.

---

1 It was predicted and commonly believed that King Arthur would return from fairy-land to reign over Britain.
2 The House of Tudor, which was of Welsh blood.
3 lifted up
4 Queen Elizabeth.
5 An allusion to *The Faerie Queene* of Spenser.
6 tragic (The buskin was a high-heeled shoe worn by actors in Greek tragedy.)
7 An allusion to Shakespeare.
8 An allusion to Milton.
9 foolish

1 regular change from one condition to another
2 lour; appear gloomy

Still, where rosy Pleasure leads,
  See a kindred Grief pursue;
Behind the steps that Misery treads,
40   Approaching Comfort view:
The hues of Bliss more brightly glow,
Chastis'd[1] by sabler tints of woe,
And blended form, with artful strife,
The strength and harmony of life.

45 See the wretch, that long has tost
  On the thorny bed of pain,
At length repair his vigor lost,
  And breathe and walk again:
The meanest floweret of the vale,
50 The simplest note that swells the gale,
The common sun, the air, the skies,
To him are opening Paradise.

Humble Quiet builds her cell,
  Near the source whence pleasure flows;
55 She eyes the clear crystalline well,
  And tastes it as it goes.

*   *   *   *   *   *

SONG
1761

Thyrsis, when we parted, swore
  Ere the spring he would return—
Ah! what means yon violet flower?
  And the buds that deck the thorn?
5 'Twas the lark that upward sprung!
  'Twas the nightingale that sung!

Idle notes! untimely green!
  Why this unavailing haste?
Western gales and skies serene
10 Speak not always winter past.
Cease, my doubts, my fears to move,
Spare the honor of my love.

THE FATAL SISTERS
1761   1768

Now the storm begins to lower
  (Haste, the loom of hell prepare!)
Iron-sleet of arrowy shower
  Hurtles in the darken'd air.

5 Glitt'ring lances are the loom,
  Where the dusky warp we strain,
Weaving many a soldier's doom,
  Orkney's woe, and Randver's bane.

See the griesly texture grow!
10 'Tis of human entrails made;
And the weights, that play below,
  Each a gasping warrior's head.

Shafts for shuttles, dipt in gore
  Shoot the trembling cords along.
15 Sword, that once a monarch bore,
  Keep the tissue close and strong.

Mista, black, terrific maid,
  Sangrida, and Hilda, see,
Join the wayward work to aid:
20 'Tis the woof of victory.

Ere the ruddy sun be set,
  Pikes must shiver, javelins sing,
Blade with clattering buckler meet,
  Hauberk crash, and helmet ring.

25 (Weave the crimson web of war!)
  Let us go, and let us fly
Where our friends the conflict share,
  Where they triumph, where they die.

As the paths of fate we tread,
30 Wading through th' ensanguin'd field,
Gondula, and Geira, spread
  O'er the youthful king[1] your shield.

We the reins to slaughter give;
  Ours to kill, and ours to spare:
35 Spite of danger he shall live.
  (Weave the crimson web of war!)

They, whom once the desert-beach
  Pent within its bleak domain,
Soon their ample sway shall stretch
40 O'er the plenty of the plain.

Low the dauntless earl is laid,
  Gor'd with many a gaping wound:
Fate demands a nobler head;
  Soon a king[2] shall bite the ground.

45 Long his loss shall Eirin weep,
  Ne'er again his likeness see;
Long her strains in sorrow steep,
  Strains of immortality!

Horror covers all the heath,
50 Clouds of carnage blot the sun.
Sisters, weave the web of death!
  Sisters, cease; the work is done.

Hail the task, and hail the hands!
  Songs of joy and triumph sing!
55 Joy to the victorious bands;
  Triumph to the younger king.

Mortal, thou that hear'st the tale,
  Learn the tenor of our song.

---

[1] chastened

[1] Sigtrygg (Sictryg).   [2] Brian.

Scotland, thro' each winding vale
60 Far and wide the notes prolong.

Sisters, hence with spurs of speed!
  Each her thundering falchion wield;
Each bestride her sable steed.
  Hurry, hurry to the field!

THE DESCENT OF ODIN
1761   1768

Uprose the King of Men with speed,
And saddled straight his coal-black steed;
Down the yawning steep he rode,
That leads to Hela's drear abode.
5 Him the Dog of Darkness spied;
His shaggy throat he open'd wide,
While from his jaws, with carnage fill'd,
Foam and human gore distill'd,
Hoarse he bays with hideous din,
10 Eyes that glow, and fangs that grin;
And long pursues with fruitless yell,
The Father of the powerful spell.
Onward still his way he takes
(The groaning earth beneath him shakes),
15 Till full before his fearless eyes
The portals nine of hell arise.
Right against the eastern gate,[1]
By the moss-grown pile he sate,
Where long of yore to sleep was laid
20 The dust of the prophetic maid.[2]
Facing to the northern clime,
Thrice he trac'd the Runic[3] rhyme;
Thrice pronounc'd, in accents dread,
The thrilling verse that wakes the dead;
25 Till from out the hollow ground
Slowly breath'd a sullen sound.

Prophetess. What call unknown, what
    charms, presume
To break the quiet of the tomb?
Who thus afflicts my troubled sprite,
30 And drags me from the realms of night?
Long on these mould'ring bones have
    beat
The winter's snow, the summer's heat,
The drenching dews, and driving rain!
Let me, let me sleep again!
35 Who is he, with voice unblest,
That calls me from the bed of rest?

Odin. A traveller, to thee unknown,
Is he that calls, a warrior's son.
Thou the deeds of light shalt know;

40 Tell me what is done below;
For whom yon glitt'ring board is spread,
Dress'd for whom yon golden bed?

Prophetess. Mantling[1] in the goblet see
The pure bev'rage of the bee;[2]
45 O'er it hangs the shield of gold;
'Tis the drink of Balder bold:
Balder's head to death is giv'n;
Pain can reach the sons of Heav'n!
Unwilling I my lips unclose:
50 Leave me, leave me to repose!

Odin. Once again my call obey:
Prophetess, arise, and say
What dangers Odin's child await;
Who the author of his fate?

55 *Prophetess.* In Hoder's hand the hero's
    doom;
His brother sends him to the tomb.
Now my weary lips I close:
Leave me, leave me to repose!

Odin. Prophetess, my spell obey:
60 Once again arise, and say
Who th' avenger of his guilt;
By whom shall Hoder's blood be spilt?

Prophetess. In the caverns of the west,
By Odin's fierce embrace comprest,
65 A wond'rous boy shall Rinda bear,
Who ne'er shall comb his raven-hair,
Nor wash his visage in the stream,
Nor see the sun's departing beam,
Till he on Hoder's corse shall smile
70 Flaming on the fun'ral pile.
Now my weary lips I close:
Leave me, leave me to repose!

Odin. Yet a while my call obey:
Prophetess, awake, and say
75 What virgins these, in speechless woe,
That bend to earth their solemn brow,
That their flaxen tresses tear,
And snowy veils that float in air.
Tell me whence their sorrows rose;
80 Then I leave thee to repose.

Prophetess. Ha! no traveller art thou!
King of Men, I know thee now;
Mightiest of a mighty line—

Odin. No boding maid of skill divine
85 Art thou, nor prophetess of good;
But mother of the giant-brood!

---

[1] *L'Allegro,* 59.
[2] Hela (or perhaps Angerbode, the "mother of
the giant-brood," Fenris, Hela, and the Midgard Serpent).
[3] magic (Runes were the characters used in
writing by the early Germanic peoples; they
were supposed to possess magic power.)

[1] taking on a froth
[2] mead, a fermented drink made of honey

Prophetess. Hie thee hence, and boast
    at home,
That never shall enquirer come
To break my iron-sleep again,
90 Till Lok has burst his tenfold chain;
Never, till substantial Night
Has reassum'd her ancient right;
Till wrapt in flames, in ruin hurl'd,
Sinks the fabric of the world.

THE TRIUMPHS OF OWEN

A FRAGMENT
1764   1768

Owen's praise demands my song,
Owen swift, and Owen strong;
Fairest flower of Roderic's stem,
Gwyneth's shield, and Britain's gem.
5 He nor heaps his brooded stores,
Nor on all profusely pours;
Lord of every regal art,
Liberal hand, and open heart.
Big with hosts of mighty name,
10 Squadrons three against him came;
This the force of Eirin hiding,
Side by side as proudly riding,
On her shadow long and gay
Lochlin plows the wat'ry way;
15 There the Norman sails afar
Catch the winds and join the war:
Black and huge along they sweep,
Burthens of the angry deep.

Dauntless on his native sands
20 The dragon-son[1] of Mona stands;
In glitt'ring arms and glory drest,
High he rears his ruby crest.
There the thund'ring strokes begin,
There the press, and there the din;
25 Talymalfra's rocky shore
Echoing to the battle's roar.
Check'd by the torrent-tide of blood,
Backward Meinai rolls his flood;
While, heap'd his master's feet around,
30 Prostrate warriors gnaw the ground.
Where his glowing eye-balls turn,
Thousand banners round him burn:
Where he points his purple spear,
Hasty, hasty rout is there,
35 Marking with indignant eye
Fear to stop, and shame to fly.
There confusion, terror's child,

[1] As a descendant of Cadwallader, a famous British king, Owen wore the device of a red dragon.

Conflict fierce, and ruin wild,
Agony, that pants for breath,
40 Despair and honorable death.

*   *   *   *   *

THE DEATH OF HOEL

AN ODE, SELECTED FROM THE GODODIN
1764   1775

Had I but the torrent's might,
With headlong rage and wild affright
Upon Deïra's squadron's hurl'd
To rush, and sweep them from the world!
5 Too, too secure in youthful pride,
By them, my friend, my Hoel, died,
Great Cian's son: of Madoc old
He ask'd no heaps of hoarded gold;
Alone in nature's wealth array'd.
10 He ask'd and had the lovely maid.

To Cattraeth's vale in glitt'ring row
Thrice two hundred warriors go:
Every warrior's manly neck
Chains of regal honor deck,
15 Wreath'd in many a golden link:
From the golden cup they drink
Nectar that the bees produce,[1]
Or the grape's ecstatic juice.
Flush'd with mirth and hope they burn:
20 But none from Cattraeth's vale return,
Save Aëron brave, and Conan strong,
(Bursting through the bloody throng)
And I, the meanest of them all,
That live to weep and sing their fall.

CARÀDOC
1764   1775

Have ye seen the tusky boar,
Or the bull, with sullen roar,
On surrounding foes advance?
So Caràdoc bore his lance.

CONAN
1764   1775

Conan's name, my lay, rehearse,
Build to him the lofty verse,
Sacred tribute of the bard,
Verse, the hero's sole reward.
5 As the flame's devouring force;
As the whirlwind in its course;
As the thunder's fiery stroke,
Glancing on the shiver'd oak;
Did the sword of Conan mow
10 The crimson harvest of the foe.

[1] mead, a fermented drink made of honey

From JOURNAL IN FRANCE
1739   1884
SEPT. 17

Journey to Geneva. The road runs over a mountain, which gives you the first taste of the Alps, in its magnificent rudeness, and steep precipices. Set out from Echelles on horseback to see the Grande Chartreuse; the way to it up a vast mountain, in many places the road not two yards broad; on one side the rock hanging over you, and on the other side a monstrous precipice. In the bottom runs a torrent, called *Les Guiers morts,* that works its way among the rocks with a mighty noise, and frequent falls. You here meet with all the beauties so savage and horrid a place can present you with; rocks of various and uncouth figures, cascades pouring down from an immense height out of hanging groves of pine trees, and the solemn sound of the stream that roars below, all concur to form one of the most poetical scenes imaginable.

From GRAY'S LETTERS
1735-71   1814-84
To MRS. DOROTHY GRAY
LYONS, *Oct.* 13, N. S. *1739.*

It is now almost five weeks since I left Dijon, one of the gayest and most agreeable little cities of France, for Lyons, its reverse in all these particulars. It is the second in the kingdom in bigness and rank, the streets excessively narrow and nasty; the houses immensely high and large (that, for instance where we are lodged, has twenty-five rooms on a floor, and that for five stories); it swarms with inhabitants like Paris itself, but chiefly a mercantile people, too much given up to commerce, to think of their own, much less of a stranger's diversions. We have no acquaintance in the town, but such English as happen to be passing through here, in their way to Italy and the south, which at present happen to be near thirty in number. It is a fortnight since we set out from hence upon a little excursion to Geneva. We took the longest road, which lies through Savoy, on purpose to see a famous monastery, called the grand Chartreuse, and had no reason to think our time lost. After having travelled seven days very slow (for we did not change horses, it being impossible for a chaise to go post[1] in these roads) we arrived at a

[1] rapidly, like one relaying letters, messages, etc.

little village, among the mountains of Savoy, called Echelles; from thence we proceeded on horses, who are used to the way, to the mountain of the Chartreuse. It is six miles to the top; the road runs winding up it, commonly not six feet broad; on one hand is the rock, with woods of pine-trees hanging over head; on the other, a monstrous precipice, almost perpendicular, at the bottom of which rolls a torrent, that sometimes tumbling among the fragments of stone that have fallen from on high, and sometimes precipitating itself down vast descents with a noise like thunder, which is still made greater by the echo from the mountains on each side, concurs to form one of the most solemn, the most romantic, and the most astonishing scenes I ever beheld. Add to this the strange views made by the crags and cliffs on the other hand; the cascades that in many places throw themselves from the very summit down into the vale, and the river below; and many other particulars impossible to describe; you will conclude we had no occasion to repent our pains. This place St. Bruno chose to retire to, and upon its very top founded the aforesaid convent, which is the superior of the whole order. When we came there, the two fathers, who are commissioned to entertain strangers (for the rest must neither speak one to another, nor to any one else), received us very kindly; and set before us a repast of dried fish, eggs, butter, and fruits, all excellent in their kind, and extremely neat. They pressed us to spend the night there, and to stay some days with them; but this we could not do, so they led us about their house, which is, you must think, like a little city; for there are 100 fathers, besides 300 servants, that make their clothes, grind their corn, press their wine, and do everything among themselves. The whole is quiet, orderly, and simple; nothing of finery, but the wonderful decency, and the strange situation, more than supply the place of it. In the evening we descended by the same way, passing through many clouds that were then forming themselves on the mountain's side. Next day we continued our journey by Chamberry, which, though the chief city of the Dutchy, and residence of the King of Sardinia, when he comes into this part of his dominions, makes but a very mean and insignificant appearance; we lay at Aix, once famous for its hot baths, and the next night at Annecy; the

day after, by noon, we got to Geneva.
I have not time to say anything about it,
nor of our solitary journey back again.

• • •

To Richard West

TURIN, *Nov.* 16, N. S. *1739.*

After eight days' journey through
Greenland, we arrived at Turin. You approach it by a handsome avenue of nine
miles long, and quite strait. The entrance
is guarded by certain vigilant dragons,
called Douâniers,[1] who mumbled us for
some time. The city is not large, as
being a place of strength, and consequently confined within its fortifications;
it has many beauties and some faults;
among the first are streets all laid out by
the line, regular uniform buildings, fine
walks that surround the whole, and in
general a good lively clean appearance.
But the houses are of brick plastered,
which is apt to want repairing; the windows of oiled paper, which is apt to be
torn; and everything very slight, which
is apt to tumble down. There is an excellent opera, but it is only in the carnival;
balls every night, but only in the carnival; masquerades too, but only in the
carnival. This carnival lasts only from
Christmas to Lent; one half of the remaining part of the year is passed in remembering the last, the other in expecting the
future carnival. We cannot well subsist
upon such slender diet, no more than upon
an execrable Italian comedy, and a puppet-show, called *Rappresentazione d'un
anima dannata,*[2] which, I think, are all
the present diversions of the place; except
the Marquise de Cavaillac's Conversa-
zione, where one goes to see people play at
ombre and taroc, a game with seventy-
two cards all painted with suns and moons
and devils and monks. Mr. Walpole has
been at court; the family are at present
at a country palace, called La Venerie.
The palace here in town is the very
quintessence of gilding and looking-glass;
inlaid floors, carved panels, and painting,
wherever they could stick a brush. I own
I have not, as yet, anywhere met with
those grand and simple works of art that
are to amaze one, and whose sight one is
to be the better for; but those of Nature
have astonished me beyond expression.
In our little journey up to the Grande
Chartreuse, I do not remember to have

gone ten paces without an exclamation,
that there was no restraining: not a precipice, not a torrent, not a cliff, but is
pregnant with religion and poetry. There
are certain scenes that would awe an
atheist into belief, without the help of
other argument. One need not have a
very fantastic imagination to see spirits
there at noon-day. You have Death perpetually before your eyes, only so far
removed as to compose the mind without
frighting it. I am well persuaded St.
Bruno was a man of no common genius
to choose such a situation for his retirement, and perhaps should have been a
disciple of his, had I been born in his
time. You may believe Abelard and
Heloïse were not forgot upon this occasion. If I do not mistake, I saw you too
every now and then at a distance along
the trees; *il me semble, que j'ai vu ce
chien de visage là quelque part.*[1] You
seemed to call to me from the other side
of the precipice, but the noise of the
river below was so great, that I really
could not distinguish what you said; it
seemed to have a cadence like verse. In
your next you will be so good to let me
know what it was. The week we have
since passed among the Alps has not
equalled the single day upon that mountain, because the winter was rather too
far advanced, and the weather a little
foggy. However, it did not want its beauties; the savage rudeness of the view is
inconceivable without seeing it. I reckoned in one day thirteen cascades, the
least of which was, I dare say, one hundred feet in height. I had Livy in the
chaise with me, and beheld his *"Nives
cælo propè immistæ, tecta informia im-
posita rupibus, pecora jumentaque torrida
frigore, homines intonsi and inculti, ani-
malia inanimaque omnia rigentia gelu;
omnia confragosa, præruptaque."*[2] The
creatures that inhabit them are, in all
respects, below humanity; and most of
them, especially women, have the *tu-
midum guttur,*[3] which they call *goscia.*
Mont Cenis, I confess, carries the permission mountains have of being frightful
rather too far; and its horrors were ac-

---

[1] custom-house officers

[2] Representation of a lost soul.

[1] it seems to me that I have seen that dog-face somewhere

[2] Snows almost mingling with the sky, the shape-less huts situated on the cliffs, the cattle and beasts of burden withered by the cold, the men unshorn and wildly dressed, all things—animate and inanimate—stiffened with frost, everything broken and jagged.—Livy, *History of Rome,* 21 :32.

[3] swollen throat

companied with too much danger to give one time to reflect upon their beauties. There is a family of the Alpine monsters I have mentioned, upon its very top, that in the middle of winter calmly lay in their stock of provisions and firing, and so are buried in their hut for a month or two under the snow. When we were down it, and got a little way into Piedmont, we began to find *"Apricos quosdam colles, rivosque prope sylvas, and jam humano cultu digniora loca."*[1] I read Silius Italicus too, for the first time; and wished for you, according to custom. We set out for Genoa in two days' time.

To Horace Walpole
[1760.]

I am so charmed with the two specimens of Erse poetry,[2] that I cannot help giving you the trouble to enquire a little farther about them, and should wish to see a few lines of the original, that I may form some slight idea of the language, the measures, and the rhythm.

Is there anything known of the author or authors, and of what antiquity are they supposed to be? Is there any more to be had of equal beauty, or at all approaching to it? I have been often told that the poem called *Hardicanute* (which I always admired and still admire) was the work of somebody that lived a few years ago. This I do not at all believe, though it has evidently been retouched in places by some modern hand: but however, I am authorized by this report to ask whether the two poems in question are certainly antique and genuine. I make this enquiry in quality of an antiquary, and am not otherwise concerned about it: for, if I were sure that any one now living in Scotland had written them to divert himself, and laugh at the credulity of the world, I would undertake a journey into the Highlands only for the pleasure of seeing him.

To Richard Stonehewer
London, *June 29, 1760.*

I have received another Scotch packet with a third specimen, inferior in kind

---

[1] Some sunny hills and rivulets flowing beside woods, and scenes more worthy the abode of man.—Livy, *History of Rome*, 21:37.
[2] Specimens of the Ossianic poems, which Macpherson declared he had collected in the Scottish Highlands, and had translated from the Gaelic or Erse language.

(because it is merely description), but yet full of nature and noble wild imagination. Five bards pass the night at the castle of a chief (himself a principal bard); each goes out in his turn to observe the face of things, and returns with an extempore picture of the changes he has seen; it is an October night (the harvest-month of the Highlands). This is the whole plan; yet there is a contrivance, and a preparation of ideas, that you would not expect. The oddest thing is, that every one of them sees ghosts (more or less). The idea that struck and surprised me most, is the following. One of them (describing a storm of wind and rain) says—

Ghosts ride on the tempest tonight:
Sweet is their voice between the gusts of wind;
Their songs are of other worlds!

Did you never observe (while rocking winds are piping loud[1]) that pause, as the gust is recollecting itself, and rising upon the ear in a shrill and plaintive note, like the swell of an Æolian harp? I do assure you there is nothing in the world so like the voice of a spirit. Thomson had an ear sometimes: he was not deaf to this; and has described it gloriously, but given it another different turn, and of more horror. I cannot repeat the lines: it is in his "Winter."[2] There is another very fine picture in one of them. It describes the breaking of the clouds after the storm before it is settled into a calm, and when the moon is seen by short intervals.

The waves are tumbling on the lake,
And lash the rocky sides.
The boat is brim-full in the cove,
The oars on the rocking tide.
Sad sits a maid beneath a cliff,
And eyes the rolling stream;
Her Lover promised to come,
She saw his boat (when it was evening) on the lake;
Are these his groans in the gale?
Is this his broken boat on the shore?[3]

To Thomas Wharton
[July, 1760.]

If you have seen Stonehewer, he has probably told you of my old Scotch (or rather Irish) poetry. I am gone mad about them. They are said to be translations (literal and in prose) from the Erse tongue, done by one Macpherson, a young

---

[1] *Il Penseroso*, 126.
[2] See ll. 67-71; 149-52; 175-201.
[3] These lines were published in a note to Macpherson's *Croma*.

clergyman in the Highlands. He means to publish a collection he has of these specimens of antiquity; but what plagues me is, I cannot come at any certainty on that head. I was so struck, so *extasié*[1] with their infinite beauty, that I writ into Scotland to make a thousand enquiries. The letters I have in return are ill wrote, ill reasoned, unsatisfactory, calculated (one would imagine) to deceive one, and yet not cunning enough to do it cleverly. In short, the whole external evidence would make one believe these fragments (for so he calls them, though nothing can be more entire) counterfeit; but the internal is so strong on the other side, that I am resolved to believe them genuine, spite of the devil and the kirk. It is impossible to convince me that they were invented by the same man that writes me these letters. On the other hand, it is almost as hard to suppose, if they are original, that he should be able to translate them so admirably. What can one do? Since Stonehewer went, I have received another of a very different and inferior kind (being merely descriptive), much more modern than the former (he says), yet very old too. This too in its way is extremely fine. In short, this man is the very dæmon of poetry, or he has lighted on a treasure hid for ages. The Welch poets are also coming to light. I have seen a discourse in MS. about them (by one Mr. Evans, a clergyman) with specimens of their writings. This is in Latin, and though it don't approach the other, there are fine scraps among it. . . . . . .

To The Reverend William Mason
PEMBROKE HALL, *August 7, 1760.*

The Erse fragments have been published five weeks ago in Scotland, though I had them not (by a mistake) till the other day. As you tell me new things do not reach you soon at Aston, I inclose what I can; the rest shall follow, when you tell me whether you have not got the pamphlet already. I send the two which I had before, for Mr. Wood, because he has not the affectation of not admiring. I continue to think them genuine, though my reasons for believing the contrary are rather stronger than ever: but I will have them antique, for I never knew a Scotchman of my own time that could read, much less write, poetry; and such poetry too! I have one

[1] enraptured

(from Mr. Macpherson) which he has not printed: it is mere description, but excellent, too, in its kind. If you are good, and will learn to admire, I will transcribe it.

As to their authenticity, I have made many enquiries, and have lately procured a letter from Mr. David Hume (the historian), which is more satisfactory than anything I have yet met with on that subject. He says—

"Certain it is that these poems are in everybody's mouth in the Highlands, have been handed down from father to son, and are of an age beyond all memory and tradition. Adam Smith, the celebrated professor in Glasgow, told me that the piper of the Argyleshire Militia repeated to him all of those which Mr. Macpherson had translated, and many more of equal beauty. Major Mackay (Lord Rae's brother) told me that he remembers them perfectly well; as likewise did the Laird of Macfarlane (the greatest antiquarian we have in this country), and who insists strongly on the historical truth as well as the poetical beauty of these productions. I could add the Laird and Lady Macleod, with many more, that live in different parts of the Highlands, very remote from each other, and could only be acquainted with what had become (in a manner) national works. There is a country surgeon in Lochaber who has by heart the entire epic poem[1] mentioned by Mr. Macpherson in his preface; and, as he is old, is perhaps the only person living that knows it all, and has never committed it to writing, we are in the more haste to recover a monument which will certainly be regarded as a curiosity in the republic of letters: we have, therefore, set about a subscription of a guinea or two guineas apiece, in order to enable Mr. Macpherson to undertake a mission into the Highlands to recover this poem, and other fragments of antiquity."

He adds, too, that the names of Fingal, Ossian, Oscar, etc., are still given in the Highlands to large mastiffs, as we give to ours the names of Cæsar, Pompey, Hector, etc.

To The Reverend William Mason
1765.

Res est sacra miser[2] (says the poet), but I say it is the happy man that is the sacred thing, and therefore let the profane

[1] *Fingal.*   [2] A wretched person is a sacred object.

keep their distance. He is one of Lucretius' gods, supremely blessed in the contemplation of his own felicity, and what has he to do with worshippers? This, mind, is the first reason why I did not come to York: the second is, that I do not love confinement, and probably by next summer may be permitted to touch whom, and where, and with what I think fit, without giving you any offence: the third and last, and not the least perhaps, is, that the finances were at so low an ebb that I could not exactly do what I wished, but was obliged to come the shortest road to town and recruit them. I do not justly know what your taste in reasons may be, since you altered your condition, but there is the ingenious, the petulant, and the dull; for you any one would have done, for in my conscience I do not believe you care a halfpenny for any reasons at present; so God bless ye both, and give ye all ye wish, when ye are restored to the use of your wishes.

I am returned from Scotland charmed with my expedition; it is of the Highlands I speak; the Lowlands are worth seeing once, but the mountains are ecstatic, and ought to be visited in pilgrimage once a year. None but those monstrous creatures of God know how to join so much beauty with so much horror. A fig for your poets, painters, gardeners, and clergymen, that have not been among them; their imagination can be made of nothing but bowling-greens, flowering shrubs, horse-ponds, Fleet ditches, shell grottoes, and Chinese rails.[1] Then I had so so beautiful an autumn, Italy could hardly produce a nobler scene, and this so sweetly contrasted with that perfection of nastiness, and total want of accommodation, that Scotland only can supply. Oh, you would have blessed yourself. I shall certainly go again; what a pity it is I cannot draw, nor describe, nor ride on horseback.

Stonehewer is the busiest creature upon earth except Mr. Fraser; they stand pretty tight, for all his Royal Highness. Have you read (oh no, I had forgot) Dr. Lowth's pamphlet against your uncle the Bishop? Oh, how he works him. I hear he will soon be on the same bench. Today Mr. Hurd came to see me, but we had not a word of that matter; he is grown pure

[1] Terms similar to those used by Mason in his poetry, and indicating popular architectural ornaments of the 18th century.

and plump, just of the proper breadth for a celebrated town-preacher. There was Dr. Balguy too; he says Mrs. Mason is very handsome, so you are his friend forever. Lord Newnham, I hear, has ill health of late; it is a nervous case, so have a care. How do your eyes do?

Adieu: my respects to the bride. I would kiss her, but you stand by and pretend it is not the fashion, though I know they do so at Hull.—I am ever yours,

T. G.

From JOURNAL IN THE LAKES
1769   1775

Sept. 30, 1769. . . . On the ascent of the hill above Appleby the thick hanging wood and the long reaches of the Eden (rapid, clear, and full as ever) winding below with views of the castle and town, gave much employment to the mirror; but the sun was wanting and the sky overcast. . . . In the afternoon walked up the Beacon-hill a mile to the top, saw Whinfield and Lowther Parks, and through an opening in the bosom of that cluster of mountains, which the Doctor well remembers, the lake of Ulz-water, with the craggy tops of a hundred nameless hills.

October 3. Wind at S. E.; a heavenly day. Rose at 7, and walked out under the conduct of my landlord to Borrodale. The grass was covered with a hoar frost, which soon melted, and exhaled in a thin blueish smoke. Crossed the meadows obliquely, catching a diversity of views among the hills over the lake and islands, and changing prospect at every ten paces; left Cockshut and Castlehill (which we formerly mounted) behind me, and drew near the foot of Walla-crag, whose bare and rocky brow, cut perpendicularly down above 400 feet, as I guess, awfully overlooks the way; our path here tends to the left, and the ground gently rising, and covered with a glade of scattering trees and bushes on the very margin of the water, opens both ways the most delicious view, that my eyes ever beheld. Behind you are the magnificent heights of Walla-crag; opposite lie the thick hanging woods of Lord Egremont, and Newland valley, with green and smiling fields embosomed in the dark cliffs; to the left the jaws of Borrodale, with that turbulent chaos of mountain behind mountain, rolled in confusion; beneath you, and stretching far away to the right, the shining purity of the Lake, just ruffled by the breeze, enough to shew it is alive, reflecting rocks, woods, fields, and inverted tops of mountains, with the white buildings of Keswick, Crosthwait church, and Skiddaw for a background at a distance. Oh! Doctor! I never wished more for you; and pray think, how the glass played its part in such a spot, which is called Carf-close-reeds; I choose to set down these barbarous names, that any body may enquire on the place, and easily find the particular station, that I mean. This scene continues to Borrow-gate, and a little farther, passing a brook called Barrow-beck, we entered Borrodale. The crags, named Lodoor-banks, now begin to impend terribly over your way; and more terribly, when you hear, that three years since an immense mass of rock tumbled at once from the brow, and barred all access to the dale (for this is the only road) till they could work their way through it. Luckily no one was passing at the time of this fall; but down the side of the mountain, and far into the lake lie dispersed the huge fragments of this ruin in all shapes and in all directions. Something farther we turned aside into a coppice, ascending a little in front of Lodoor waterfall, the height appears to be about 200 feet, the quantity of water not great, though (these days excepted) it had rained daily in the hills for nearly two months before: but then the stream was nobly broken, leaping from rock to rock, and foaming with fury. On one side a towering crag, that spired up to equal, if not overtop, the neighboring cliffs (this lay all in shade and darkness) on the other hand a rounder broader projecting hill shagged with wood and illumined by the sun, which glanced sideways on the upper part of the cataract. The force of the water wearing a deep channel in the ground hurries away to join the lake. We descended again, and passed the stream over a rude bridge. Soon after we came under Gowder crag, a hill more formidable to the eye and to the apprehension than that of Lodoor; the rocks a-top, deep-cloven perpendicularly by the rains, hanging loose and nodding forwards, seem just starting from their base in shivers; the whole way down, and the road on both sides is strewed with piles of the fragments strangely thrown across each other, and of a dreadful bulk. The place reminds one of those passes in the Alps, where the guides tell you to move on with speed, and say nothing, lest the agitation of the air should loosen the snows above, and bring down a mass, that would overwhelm a caravan. I took their counsel here and hastened on in silence. . . . Walked leisurely home the way we came, but saw a new landscape: the features indeed were the same in part, but many new ones were disclosed by the midday sun, and the tints were entirely changed. Take notice this was the best or perhaps the only day for going up Skiddaw, but I thought it better employed: it was perfectly serene, and hot as midsummer.

In the evening walked alone down to the Lake by the side of Crow-Park after sun-set and saw the solemn coloring of night draw on, the last gleam of sunshine fading away on the hill-tops, the deep serene of the waters, and the long shadows of the mountains thrown across them, till they nearly touched the hithermost shore. At distance heard the murmur of many waterfalls not audible in the day-time. Wished for the moon, but she was *dark to me and silent, hid in her vacant interlunar cave.*

October 8. Past by the little chapel of Wiborn, out of which the Sunday congregation were then issuing. Past a beck near Dunmailraise and entered Westmoreland a second time, now begin to see Helm-crag distinguished from its rugged neighbors not so much by its height, as by the strange broken outline of its top, like some gigantic building demolished, and the stones that composed it flung across each other in wild confusion. Just beyond it opens one of the sweetest landscapes that art ever attempted to imitate. The bosom of the mountains spreading here into a broad basin discovers in the midst Grasmere-water; its margin is hollowed into small bays with bold eminences: some of them rocks, some of soft turf that half conceal and vary the figure of the little lake they command. From the shore a low promontory pushes itself far into the water, and on it stands a white village with the parish-church rising in the midst of it, hanging enclosures, corn-fields, and meadows green as an emerald, with their trees and hedges, and cattle fill up the whole space from the edge of the water. Just opposite to you is a large farm-house at the bottom of a steep smooth lawn embosomed in old woods, which climb half way up the mountain's side, and discover above them a broken line of crags, that crown the scene. Not a single red tile, no flaming gentleman's house, or garden walls break in upon the repose of this little unsuspected paradise, but all is peace, rusticity, and happy poverty in its neatest, most becoming attire.

Thomas Warton 1728-1790

From THE PLEASURES OF MELANCHOLY
1745   1747

Mother of musings, Contemplation sage,
Whose grotto stands upon the topmost rock
Of Teneriff; 'mid the tempestuous night,
On which, in calmest meditation held,
5 Thou hear'st with howling winds the beating rain
And drifting hail descend; or if the skies
Unclouded shine, and thro' the blue serene
Pale Cynthia rolls her silver-axled car,
Whence gazing stedfast on the spangled vault
10 Raptur'd thou sitt'st, while murmurs indistinct
Of distant billows sooth thy pensive ear
With hoarse and hollow sounds; secure, self-blest,
There oft thou listen'st to the wild uproar
Of fleets encount'ring, that in whispers low
15 Ascends the rocky summit, where thou dwell'st
Remote from man, conversing with the spheres!
O lead me, queen sublime, to solemn glooms
Congenial with my soul; to cheerless shades,
To ruin'd seats, to twilight cells and bow'rs,
20 Where thoughtful Melancholy loves to muse,
Her fav'rite midnight haunts. The laughing scenes
Of purple Spring, where all the wanton train
Of Smiles and Graces seem to lead the dance

In sportive round, while from their hand they show'r
25 Ambrosial blooms and flow'rs, no longer charm;
Tempe, no more I court thy balmy breeze,
Adieu green vales! ye broider'd meads, adieu!
    Beneath yon ruined abbey's moss-grown piles
Oft let me sit, at twilight hour of eve,
30 Where through some western window the pale moon
Pours her long-levelled rule of streaming light,
While sullen, sacred silence reigns around,
Save the lone screech-owl's note, who builds his bow'r
Amid the mould'ring caverns dark and damp,
35 Or the calm breeze that rustles in the leaves
Of flaunting ivy, that with mantle green
Invests some wasted tow'r. Or let me tread
Its neighb'ring walk of pines, where mused of old
The cloistered brothers: through the gloomy void
40 That far extends beneath their ample arch
As on I pace, religious horror wraps
My soul in dread repose. But when the world
Is clad in midnight's raven-colored robe,
'Mid hollow charnel let me watch the flame
45 Of taper dim, shedding a livid glare
O'er the wan heaps, while airy voices talk
Along the glimm'ring walls, or ghostly shape,
At distance seen, invites with beck'ning hand
My lonesome steps through the far-winding vaults.
50 Nor undelightful is the solemn noon
Of night, when, haply wakeful, from my couch
I start: lo, all is motionless around!
Roars not the rushing wind; the sons of men
And every beast in mute oblivion lie;
55 All Nature's hushed in silence and in sleep:
O then how fearful is it to reflect
That through the still globe's awful solitude

No being wakes but me! till stealing
    sleep
My drooping temples bathes in opiate
    dews.
60 Nor then let dreams, of wanton folly
    born,
My senses lead through flow'ry paths of
    joy:
But let the sacred genius of the night
Such mystic visions send as Spenser saw[1]
When through bewild'ring Fancy's magic
    maze,
65 To the fell house of Busyrane, he led
Th' unshaken Britomart; or Milton
    knew,
When in abstracted thought he first con-
    ceived
All heav'n in tumult, and the seraphim
Come tow'ring, arm'd in adamant and
    gold.[2]

. . . . . .

Thro' Pope's soft song tho' all the
    Graces breathe,
And happiest art adorn his Attic[3] page;
155 Yet does my mind with sweeter trans-
    port glow,
As at the root of mossy trunk reclin'd,
In magic Spenser's wildly-warbled song[4]
I see deserted Una wander wide
Thro' wasteful solitudes, and lurid
    heaths,
160 Weary, forlorn; than when the fated
    fair
Upon the bosom bright of silver Thames
Launches in all the lustre of brocade,
Amid the splendors of the laughing Sun.[5]
The gay description palls upon the sense,
165 And coldly strikes the mind with feeble
    bliss.

. . . . . .

From ODE ON THE APPROACH OF
SUMMER
1753

Hence, iron-scepter'd Winter, haste
    To bleak Siberian waste!
Haste to thy polar solitude;
    Mid cataracts of ice,
5 Whose torrents dumb are stretch'd in
    fragments rude
    From many an airy precipice,
Where, ever beat by sleety show'rs,
    Thy gloomy Gothic castle tow'rs,
Amid whose howling iles[6] and halls,
10 Where no gay sunbeam paints the walls,

[1] *T h e Faerie Queene*,
  III. 11-12.
[2] *Paradise Lost*, 6, 110.
[3] m a r k e d by classic
  qualities
[4] *The Faerie Queene*, I,
  3 and 6.
[5] Pope, *The Rape of
  the Lock*, 2, 1 ff.
[6] aisles

On ebon throne thou lov'st to shroud
Thy brows in many a murky cloud.

. . . . . .

Haste thee, nymph! and hand in hand,
With thee lead a buxom band;
Bring fantastic-footed Joy,
60 With Sport, that yellow-tressed boy:
Leisure, that through the balmy sky
Chases a crimson butterfly.
Bring Health, that loves in early dawn
To meet the milk-maid on the lawn;
65 Bring Pleasure, rural nymph, and Peace,
Meek, cottage-loving shepherdess!
And that sweet stripling, Zephyr, bring,
Light, and forever on the wing,
Bring the dear Muse, that loves to lean
70 On river-margins, mossy green.
But who is she, that bears thy train,
Pacing light the velvet plain?
The pale pink binds her auburn hair,
Her tresses flow with pastoral air;
75 'Tis May, the Grace—confest she stands
By branch of hawthorn in her hands:
Lo! near her trip the lightsome Dews,
Their wings all ting'd in iris-hues;[1]
With whom the pow'rs of Flora play,
80 And paint with pansies all the way.
Oft when thy season, sweetest queen,
Has dress'd the groves in liv'ry green;
When in each fair and fertile field
Beauty begins her bow'r to build!
85 While Evening, veil'd in shadows brown,
Puts her matron-mantle on,
And mists in spreading streams convey
More fresh the fumes of new-shorn hay:
Then, goddess, guide my pilgrim feet
Contemplation hoar to meet,
90 As slow he winds in museful mood,
Near the rush'd marge of Cherwell's
    flood;
Or o'er old Avon's magic edge,
Whence Shakespeare cull'd the spiky
    sedge,
All playful yet, in years unripe,
95 To frame a shrill and simple pipe.
There thro' the dusk but dimly seen,
Sweet ev'ning-objects intervene:
His wattled cotes the shepherd plants,
Beneath her elm the milk-maid chants,
100 The woodman, speeding home, awhile
Rests him at a shady stile.
Nor wants there fragrance to dispense
Refreshment o'er my soothed sense;
Nor tangled woodbine's balmy bloom,
105 Nor grass besprent[2] to breathe perfume:
Nor lurking wild-thyme's spicy sweet
To bathe in dew my roving feet:

[1] colors of the rainbow [2] sprinkled over

Nor wants there note of Philomel,
Nor sound of distant-tinkling bell:
110 Nor lowings faint of herds remote,
Nor mastiff's bark from bosom'd cot:
Rustle the breezes lightly borne
O'er deep embattled ears of corn:
Round ancient elm, with humming noise,
115 Full loud the chaffer-swarms[1] rejoice.

． ． ． ． ．

THE CRUSADE
1777

Bound for holy Palestine,
Nimbly we brush'd the level brine,
All in azure steel array'd;
O'er the wave our weapons play'd,
5 And made the dancing billows glow;
High upon the trophied prow,
Many a warrior-minstrel swung
His sounding harp, and boldly sung:
"Syrian virgins, wail and weep,
10 English Richard plows the deep!
Tremble, watchmen, as ye spy
From distant towers, with anxious eye,
The radiant range of shield and lance
Down Damascus' hills advance:
15 From Sion's turrets as afar
Ye ken the march of Europe's war!
Saladin, thou paynim king,
From Albion's isle revenge we bring!
On Acon's spiry citadel,
20 Though to the gale thy banners swell,
Pictur'd with the silver moon;
England shall end thy glory soon!
In vain, to break our firm array,
Thy brazen drums hoarse discord bray:
25 Those sounds our rising fury fan:
English Richard in the van,
On to victory we go,
A vaunting infidel the foe."
Blondel led the tuneful band,
30 And swept the wire with glowing hand.
Cyprus, from her rocky mound,
And Crete, with piny verdure crown'd,
Far along the smiling main
Echoed the prophetic strain.
35 Soon we kiss'd the sacred earth
That gave a murder'd Saviour birth;
Then, with ardor fresh endu'd,
Thus the solemn song renew'd:—
"Lo, the toilsome voyage past,
40 Heaven's favor'd hills appear at last!
Object of our holy vow,
We tread the Tyrian valleys now.
From Carmel's almond-shaded steep
We feel the cheering fragrance creep:
45 O'er Engaddi's shrubs of balm

[1] swarms of beetles

Waves the date-empurpled palm;
See Lebanon's aspiring head
Wide his immortal umbrage spread!
Hail Calvary, thou mountain hoar,
50 Wet with our Redeemer's gore!
Ye trampled tombs, ye fanes forlorn,
Ye stones, by tears of pilgrims worn;
Your ravish'd honors to restore,
Fearless we climb this hostile shore!
55 And thou, the sepulchre of God!
By mocking pagans rudely trod,
Bereft of every awful rite,
And quench'd thy lamps that beam'd
so bright;
For thee, from Britain's distant coast,
60 Lo, Richard leads his faithful host!
Aloft in his heroic hand,
Blazing, like the beacon's brand,
O'er the far-affrighted fields,
Resistless Kaliburn he wields.
65 Proud Saracen, pollute no more
The shrines by martyrs built of yore!
From each wild mountain's trackless
crown
In vain thy gloomy castles frown:
Thy battering engines, huge and high,
70 In vain our steel-clad steeds defy;
And, rolling in terrific state,
On giant-wheels harsh thunders grate.
When eve has hush'd the buzzing
camp,
Amid the moonlight vapors damp,
75 Thy necromantic forms, in vain,
Haunt us on the tented plain:
We bid those spectre-shapes avaunt,
Ashtaroth, and Termagaunt!
With many a demon, pale of hue,
80 Doom'd to drink the bitter dew
That drops from Macon's sooty tree,
'Mid the dread grove of ebony.
Nor magic charms, nor fiends of hell,
The Christian's holy courage quell.
85 Salem, in ancient majesty
Arise, and lift thee to the sky!
Soon on thy battlements divine
Shall wave the badge of Constantine.
Ye Barons, to the sun unfold
90 Our Cross with crimson wove and gold!"

SONNETS
1777

WRITTEN IN A BLANK LEAF OF DUGDALE'S
MONASTICON

Deem not devoid of elegance the sage,
By Fancy's genuine feelings unbeguiled,
Of painful pedantry the poring child,
Who turns, of these proud domes, th'
historic page,

5 Now sunk by Time, and Henry's fiercer
  rage.[1]
Think'st thou the warbling Muses never
  smiled
On his lone hours? Ingenuous views
  engage
His thoughts, on themes, unclassic falsely
  styled,
10 Intent. While cloistered Piety displays
Her mouldering roll, the piercing eye
  explores
New manners, and the pomp of elder
  days,
Whence culls the pensive bard his pictured stores.
Nor rough nor barren are the winding
  ways
Of hoar Antiquity, but strown with
  flowers.

WRITTEN AT STONEHENGE

Thou noblest monument of Albion's isle!
Whether by Merlin's aid from Scythia's
  shore,
To Amber's fatal plain Pendragon bore,
Huge frame of giant-hands, the mighty
  pile,
5 T' entomb his Britons slain by Hen-
  gist's guile:
Or Druid priests, sprinkled with human
  gore,
Taught 'mid thy massy maze their mystic lore:
Or Danish chiefs, enrich'd with savage
  spoil,
To Victory's idol vast, an unhewn
  shrine,
10 Rear'd the rude heap: or, in thy hallow'd
  round,
Repose the kings of Brutus' genuine
  line;
Or here those kings in solemn state
  were crown'd:
Studious to trace thy wondrous origine,
We muse on many an ancient tale
  renown'd.

WHILE SUMMER SUNS O'ER THE GAY PROSPECT PLAY'D

While summer suns o'er the gay pros-
  pect play'd,
Through Surry's verdant scenes, where
  Epsom spreads

[1] Henry VIII's disruption of the monasteries.

'Mid intermingling elms her flowery
  meads,
And Hascombe's hill, in towering groves
  array'd,
5 Rear'd its romantic steep, with mind
  serene,
I journey'd blithe. Full pensive I return'd;
For now my breast with hopeless passion
  burn'd,
Wet with hoar mists appear'd the gaudy
  scene,
Which late in careless indolence I
  pass'd;
10 And Autumn all around those hues had
  cast
Where past delight my recent grief
  might trace.
Sad change, that Nature a congenial
  gloom
Should wear, when most, my cheerless
  mood to chase,
I wish'd her green attire, and wonted
  bloom!

ON KING ARTHUR'S ROUND TABLE AT WINCHESTER

Where Venta's Norman castle still up-
  rears
Its rafter'd hall, that o'er the grassy
  foss,
And scatter'd flinty fragments clad in
  moss,
On yonder steep in naked state appears;
5 High-hung remains, the pride of warlike years,
Old Arthur's board: on the capacious
  round
Some British pen has sketch'd the names
  renown'd,
In marks obscure, of his immortal
  peers.
Though join'd by magic skill, with
  many a rhyme,
10 The Druid frame, unhonor'd, falls a
  prey
To the slow vengeance of the wizard
  Time,
And fade the British characters away;
Yet Spenser's page, that chants in verse
  sublime
Those chiefs, shall live, unconscious of
  decay.

From OBSERVATIONS ON THE FAIRY
QUEEN OF SPENSER
1754

. . . .

It is absurd to think of judging either Ariosto or Spenser by precepts which they did not attend to. We who live in the days of writing by rule are apt to try every composition by those laws which we have been taught to think the sole criterion of excellence. Critical taste is universally diffused, and we require the same order and design which every modern performance is expected to have, in poems where they never were regarded or intended. Spenser, and the same may be said of Ariosto, did not live in an age of planning. His poetry is the careless exuberance of a warm imagination and a strong sensibility. It was his business to engage the fancy, and to interest the attention by bold and striking images, in the formation and the disposition of which, little labor or art was applied. The various and the marvellous were the chief sources of delight. Hence we find our author ransacking alike the regions of reality and romance, of truth and fiction, to find the proper decoration and furniture for his fairy structure. Born in such an age, Spenser wrote rapidly from his own feelings, which at the same time were naturally noble. Exactness[1] in his poem would have been like the cornice which a painter introduced in the grotto of Calypso. Spenser's beauties are like the flowers in Paradise,

Which not nice Art
In beds and curious knots, but Nature boon
Pour'd forth profuse, on hill, and dale, and plain ;
Both where the morning sun first warmly smote
The open field, or where the unpierc'd shade
Imbrown'd the noon-tide bowers.
—*Paradise Lost*, 4, 241.

If *The Fairy Queen* be destitute of that arrangement and economy which epic severity requires, yet we scarcely regret the loss of these while their place is so amply supplied by something which more powerfully attracts us; something which engages the affections, the feelings of the heart, rather than the cold approbation of the head. If there be any poem whose graces please because they are situated beyond the reach of art, and where the force and faculties of creative imagination delight because they are unassisted

and unrestrained by those of deliberate judgment, it is this. In reading Spenser, if the critic is not satisfied, yet the reader is transported. (I, 15-16.)

. . . .

I cannot dismiss this section without a wish that this neglected author [Chaucer], whom Spenser proposed as the pattern of his style, and to whom he is indebted for many noble inventions, should be more universally studied. This is at least what one might expect in an age of research and curiosity. Chaucer is regarded rather as an old, than as a good, poet. We look upon his poems as venerable relics, not as beautiful compositions; as pieces better calculated to gratify the antiquarian than the critic. He abounds not only in strokes of humor, which is commonly supposed to be his sole talent, but of pathos and sublimity not unworthy a more refined age. His old manners, his romantic arguments, his wildness of painting,[1] his simplicity and antiquity of expression, transport us into some fairy region, and are all highly pleasing to the imagination. It is true that his uncouth[2] and unfamiliar language disgusts and deters many readers; but the principal reason of his being so little known and so seldom taken into hand, is the convenient opportunity of reading him with pleasure and facility in modern imitations. For when translation, and such, imitations from Chaucer may be justly called, at length becomes substituted as the means of attaining a knowledge of any difficult and ancient author, the original not only begins to be neglected and excluded as less easy, but also despised as less ornamental and elegant. Thus the public taste becomes imperceptibly vitiated, while the genuine model is superseded, and gradually gives way to the establishment of a more specious but false resemblance. Thus, too many readers, happy to find the readiest accommodation for their indolence and their illiteracy, think themselves sufficient masters of Homer from Pope's translation; and thus, by an indiscreet comparison, Pope's translation is commonly preferred to the Grecian text, in proportion as the former is

[1] conformity to set rules (The eighteenth century was devoted to "exactness" in form and style of writing.)

[1] Chaucer's descriptions are noted for their naturalness and truth rather than for their wildness ; and although he was fond of the medieval romances, his material is largely realistic.
[2] This judgment is due to ignorance of Middle English. Chaucer's language is in no sense uncouth.

furnished with more frequent and shining metaphors, more lively descriptions, and in general appears to be more full and florid, more elaborate and various.
5 (I, 196-198.)

. . . . . .

Mechanical critics will perhaps be disgusted at the liberties I have taken in introducing so many anecdotes of ancient
10 chivalry. But my subject required frequent proofs of this sort. Nor could I be persuaded that such enquiries were, in other respects, either useless or ridiculous; as they tended, at least, to illus-
15 trate an institution of no frivolous or indifferent nature. Chivalry is commonly looked upon as a barbarous sport or extravagant amusement of the dark ages. It had, however, no small influence on the
20 manners, policies, and constitutions of ancient times, and served many public and important purposes. It was the school of fortitude, honor, and affability. Its exercises, like the Grecian games,
25 habituated the youth to fatigue and enterprise, and inspired the noblest sentiments of heroism. It taught gallantry and civility to a savage and ignorant people, and humanized the native ferocity of the
30 Northern nations. It conduced to refine the manners of the combatants by exciting an emulation in the devices and accoutrements, the splendor and parade, of their tilts and tournaments; while its mag-
35 nificent festivals, thronged with noble dames and courteous knights, produced the first efforts of wit and fancy.
I am still further to hope that, together with other specimens of obsolete litera-
40 ture in general hinted at before, the many references I have made in particular to romances, the necessary appendage of ancient chivalry, will also plead their pardon. For however monstrous and unnat-
45 ural these compositions may appear to this age of reason and refinement, they merit more attention than the world is willing to bestow. They preserve many curious historical facts, and throw consid-
50 erable light on the nature of the feudal system. They are the pictures of ancient usages and customs; and represent the manners, genius, and character of our ancestors. Above all, such are their terrible
55 Graces of magic and enchantment, so magnificently marvellous are their fictions and fablings, that they contribute, in a wonderful degree, to rouse and invigorate all the powers of imagination; to

store the fancy with those sublime and alarming images which poetry best delights to display. (II, 266-268.)

Joseph Warton 1722-1800

THE ENTHUSIAST: OR THE LOVER OF NATURE
1740   1744

Ye green-rob'd Dryads, oft at dusky eve
By wondering shepherds seen, to forests brown,
To unfrequented meads, and pathless wilds,
Lead me from gardens deck'd with art's vain pomps.
5 Can gilt alcoves, can marble-mimic gods,
Parterres embroider'd, obelisks, and urns,
Of high relief; can the long, spreading lake,
Or vista lessening to the sight; can Stow,
With all her Attic fanes, such raptures raise,
10 As the thrush-haunted copse, where lightly leaps
The fearful fawn the rustling leaves along,
And the brisk squirrel sports from bough to bough,
While from an hollow oak, whose naked roots
O'erhang a pensive rill, the busy bees
15 Hum drowsy lullabies? The bards of old,
Fair Nature's friends, sought such retreats, to charm
Sweet Echo with their songs; oft too they met,
In summer evenings, near sequester'd bowers,
Or mountain-nymph, or Muse, and eager learnt
20 The moral strains she taught to mend mankind.
As in a secret grot, Ægeria stole
With patient Numa, and in silent night
Whisper'd him sacred laws, he list'ning sat,
Rapt with her virtuous voice, old Tiber lean'd
25 Attentive on his urn, and hush'd his waves.
Rich in her weeping country's spoils, Versailles

May boast a thousand fountains, that
    can cast
The tortur'd waters to the distant
    Heav'ns;
Yet let me choose some pine-topt preci-
    pice
30 Abrupt and shaggy, whence a foamy
    stream,
Like Anio, tumbling roars; or some bleak
    heath,
Where straggling stands the mournful
    juniper,
Or yew-tree scath'd; while in clear pros-
    pect round,
From the grove's bosom spires emerge,
    and smoke
35 In bluish wreaths ascends, ripe harvests
    wave,
Low lonely cottages, and ruin'd tops
Of Gothic battlements appear, and
    streams
Beneath the sun-beams twinkle.—The
    shrill lark,
That wakes the woodman to his early
    task,
40 Or love-sick Philomel, whose luscious
    lays
Soothe lone night-wanderers, the moan-
    ing dove
Pitied by list'ning milk-maid, far excel
The deep-mouth'd viol, the soul-lulling
    lute,
And battle-breathing trumpet. Artful
    sounds!
45 That please not like the choristers of
    air,
When first they hail th' approach of
    laughing May.
    Can Kent design like Nature? Mark
    where Thames
Plenty and pleasure pours through Lin-
    coln's meads;
Can the great artist, though with taste
    supreme
50 Endu'd, one beauty to this Eden add?
Though he, by rules unfetter'd, boldly
    scorns
Formality and method, round and
    square
Disdaining, plans irregularly great.
    Creative Titian, can thy vivid strokes,
55 Or thine, O graceful Raphael, dare to
    vie
With the rich tints that paint the breath-
    ing mead?
The thousand-color'd tulip, violet's
    bell
Snow-clad and meek, the vermil-tinctur'd
    rose,

And golden crocus?—Yet with these the
    maid,
60 Phillis or Phoebe, at a feast or wake
Her jetty locks enamels; fairer she,
In innocence and homespun vestments
    dress'd,
Than if cerulean sapphires at her ears
Shone pendant, or a precious diamond-
    cross
65 Heav'd gently on her panting bosom
    white.
    Yon shepherd idly stretch'd on the
    rude rock,
List'ning to dashing waves, and sea-
    mew's clang
High-hovering o'er his head, who views
    beneath
The dolphin dancing o'er the level brine,
70 Feels more true bliss than the proud
    admiral,
Amid his vessels bright with burnish'd
    gold
And silken streamers, though his lordly
    nod
Ten thousand war-worn mariners re-
    vere.
And great Aeneas gaz'd with more de-
    light
75 On the rough mountain shagg'd with
    horrid shades,
(Where cloud-compelling Jove, as fancy
    dream'd,
Descending, shook his direful aegis black)
Than if he enter'd the high Capitol
On golden columns rear'd, a conquer'd
    world
80 Exhausted, to enrich its stately head.
More pleas'd he slept in poor Evander's
    cot
On shaggy skins, lull'd by sweet night-
    ingales,
Than if a Nero, in an age refin'd,
Beneath a gorgeous canopy had plac'd
85 His royal guest, and bade his minstrels
    sound
Soft slumb'rous airs, to sooth his rest.
    Happy the first of men, ere yet con-
    fin'd
To smoky cities; who in sheltering
    groves,
Warm caves, and deep-sunk vallies liv'd
    and lov'd,
90 By cares unwounded; what the sun and
    showers,
And genial earth untillag'd, could pro-
    duce,
They gather'd grateful, or the acorn
    brown
Or blushing berry; by the liquid lapse

Of murm'ring waters call'd to slake
    their thirst,
95 Or with fair nymphs their sun-brown
    limbs to bathe;
With nymphs who fondly clasp'd their
    fav'rite youths,
Unaw'd by shame, beneath the beechen
    shade,
Nor wiles, nor artificial coyness knew.
Then doors and walls were not; the melt-
    ing maid
100 Nor frown of parents fear'd, nor hus-
    band's threats;
Nor had curs'd gold their tender hearts
    allur'd:
Then beauty was not venal. Injur'd
    Love,
O! whither, god of raptures, art thou
    fled?
While Avarice waves his golden wand
    around,
105 Abhorr'd magician, and his costly cup
Prepares with baneful drugs, t' enchant
    the souls
Of each low-thoughted fair to wed for
    gain.
    In Earth's first infancy (as sung the
    bard
Who strongly painted what he boldly
    thought),
110 Though the fierce north oft smote with
    iron whip
Their shiv'ring limbs, though oft the
    bristly boar
Or hungry lion, 'woke them with their
    howls,
And scar'd them from their moss-grown
    caves, to rove
115 Houseless and cold in dark tempestuous
    nights;
Yet were not myriads in embattl'd fields
Swept off at once, nor had the raging
    seas
O'erwhelm'd the found'ring bark and
    shrieking crew;
In vain the glassy ocean smil'd to tempt
120 The jolly sailor, unsuspecting harm,
For Commerce ne'er had spread her
    swelling sails,
Nor had the wond'ring Nereids ever
    heard
The dashing oar: then famine, want, and
    pain,
Sunk to the grave their fainting limbs;
    but us,
125 Diseaseful dainties, riot, and excess,
And feverish luxury destroy. In brakes
Or marshes wild unknowingly they
    cropp'd

Herbs of malignant juice; to realms
    remote
While we for powerful poisons madly
    roam,
130 From every noxious herb collecting
    death.
What though unknown to those primeval
    sires
The well-arch'd dome, peopled with
    breathing forms
By fair Italia's skilful hand, unknown
The shapely column, and the crumbling
    busts
135 Of awful ancestors in long descent?
Yet why should man, mistaken, deem it
    nobler
To dwell in palaces, and high-roof'd
    halls,
Than in God's forests, architect su-
    preme!
Say, is the Persian carpet, than the
    field's
140 Or meadow's mantle gay, more richly
    wov'n;
Or softer to the votaries of ease
Than bladed grass, perfum'd with dew-
    dropt flow'rs?
O taste corrupt! that luxury and pomp,
In specious names of polish'd manners
    veil'd,
145 Should proudly banish Nature's simple
    charms!
All beauteous Nature! by thy boundless
    charms
Oppress'd, O where shall I begin thy
    praise,
Where turn th' ecstatic eye, how ease
    my breast
That pants with wild astonishment and
    love!
150 Dark forests, and the op'ning lawn, re-
    fresh'd
With ever-gushing brooks, hill, meadow,
    dale,
The balmy bean-field, the gay-clover'd
    close,
So sweetly interchang'd, the lowing ox,
The playful lamb, the distant waterfall
155 Now faintly heard, now swelling with
    the breeze,
The sound of pastoral reed from hazel-
    bower,
The choral birds, the neighing steed,
    that snuffs
His dappled mate, stung with intense
    desire,
The ripen'd orchard when the ruddy orbs
160 Betwixt the green leaves blush, the
    azure skies,

The cheerful Sun that through Earth's
    vitals pours
Delight and health, and heat; all, all
    conspire
To raise, to sooth, to harmonize the
    mind,
To lift on wings of praise, to the great
    Sire
165 Of being and of beauty, at whose nod
Creation started from the gloomy vault
Of dreary Chaos, while the griesly
    king
Murmur'd to feel his boisterous power
    confin'd.
    What are the lays of artful Addison,
170 Coldly correct, to Shakespear's war-
    blings wild?
Whom on the winding Avon's willow'd
    banks
Fair Fancy found, and bore the smiling
    babe
To a close cavern: (still the shepherds
    show
The sacred place, whence with religious
    awe
175 They hear, returning from the field at
    eve,
Strange whisp'rings of sweet music
    through the air)
Here, as with honey gather'd from the
    rock,
She fed the little prattler, and with
    songs
Oft sooth'd his wand'ring ears, with deep
    delight
180 On her soft lap he sat, and caught the
    sounds.
    Oft near some crowded city would I
    walk,
Listening the far-off noises, rattling
    cars,
Loud shouts of joy, sad shrieks of sor-
    row, knells
Full slowly tolling, instruments of trade,
185 Striking mine ears with one deep-swell-
    ing hum.
Or wand'ring near the sea, attend the
    sounds
Of hollow winds, and ever-beating waves.
Ev'n when wild tempests swallow up the
    plains,
And Boreas' blasts, big hail, and rains
    combine
190 To shake the groves and mountains,
    would I sit,
Pensively musing on the outrageous
    crimes
That wake Heaven's vengeance: at such
    solemn hours,

Demons and goblins through the dark
    air shriek,
While Hecat, with her black-brow'd sis-
    ters nine,
195 Rides o'er the Earth, and scatters woes
    and death.
Then too, they say, in drear Egyptian wilds
The lion and the tiger prowl for prey
With roarings loud! the list'ning trav-
    eller
Starts fear struck, while the hollow echo-
    ing vaults
200 Of pyramids increase the deathful
    sounds.
    But let me never fail in cloudless
    nights,
When silent Cynthia in her silver car
Through the blue conclave slides, when
    shine the hills,
Twinkle the streams, and woods look
    tipp'd with gold,
205 To seek some level mead, and there
    invoke
Old Midnight's sister, Contemplation
    sage,
(Queen of the rugged brow and stern-
    fixt eye)
To lift my soul above this little Earth,
This folly-fetter'd world: to purge my
    ears,
210 That I may hear the rolling planets'
    song,
And tuneful turning spheres: if this be
    barr'd,
The little Fays that dance in neighboring
    dales,
Sipping the night-dew, while they laugh
    and love,
Shall charm me with aërial notes.—As
    thus
215 I wander musing, lo, what awful forms
Yonder appear! sharp-ey'd Philosophy
Clad in dun robes, an eagle on his
    wrist,
First meets my eye; next, virgin Solitude
Serene, who blushes at each gazer's
    sight;
220 Then Wisdom's hoary head, with crutch
    in hand,
Trembling, and bent with age; last Vir-
    tue's self
Smiling, in white array'd, who with her
    leads
Sweet Innocence, that prattles by her
    side,
A naked boy!—Harass'd with fear I
    stop,
225 I gaze, when Virtue thus—"Who'er
    thou art,

Mortal, by whom I deign to be beheld
In these my midnight-walks; depart,
    and say,
That henceforth I and my immortal
    train
Forsake Britannia's isle; who fondly
    stoops
230 To Vice, her favorite paramour.''—She
    spoke,
And as she turn'd, her round and rosy
    neck
Her flowing train, and long ambrosial
    hair,
Breathing rich odors, I enamor'd view.
  O who will bear me then to western
    climes,
235 (Since Virtue leaves our wretched land)
    to fields
Yet unpolluted with Iberian swords:
The isles of Innocence, from mortal
    view
Deeply retir'd, beneath a plantane's
    shade,
Where Happiness and Quest sit en-
    thron'd,
240 With simple Indian swains, that I may
    hunt
The boar and tiger through savannahs[1]
    wild,
Through fragrant deserts, and through
    citron groves?
There, fed on dates and herbs, would I
    despise
The far-fetch'd cates of luxury, and
    hoards
245 Of narrow-hearted avarice; nor heed
The distant din of the tumultuous world.
So when rude whirlwinds rouse the roar-
    ing main,
Beneath fair Thetis sits, in coral caves,
Serenely gay, nor sinking sailor's cries
250 Disturb her sportive nymphs, who round
    her form
The light fantastic dance, or for her
    hair
Weave rosy crowns, or with according
    lutes
Grace the soft warbles of her honied
    voice.

ODE TO FANCY
1746

O parent of each lovely Muse,   .
Thy spirit o'er my soul diffuse,
O'er all my artless songs preside,
My footsteps to thy temple guide,
5 To offer at thy turf-built shrine,

[1] tropical grasslands containing scattered trees

In golden cups no costly wine.
No murder'd fatling of the flock,
But flowers and honey from the rock.
O nymph with loosely-flowing hair,
10 With buskin'd[1] leg, and bosom bare,
Thy waist with myrtle-girdle bound,
Thy brows with Indian feathers crown'd,
Waving in thy snowy hand
An all-commanding magic wand,
15 Of pow'r to bid fresh gardens blow,
'Mid cheerless Lapland's barren snow,
Whose rapid wings thy flight convey
Thro' air, and over earth and sea,
While the vast various landscape lies
20 Conspicuous to thy piercing eyes.
O lover of the desert, hail!
Say, in what deep and pathless vale,
Or on what hoary mountain's side,
'Mid fall of waters, you reside,
25 'Mid broken rocks, a rugged scene,
With green and grassy dales between.
Mid forests dark of aged oak,
Ne'er echoing with the woodman's stroke,
Where never human art appear'd,
30 Nor ev'n one straw-roof'd cot was reared,
Where Nature seems to sit alone,
Majestic on a craggy throne;
Tell me the path, sweet wand'rer, tell,
To thy unknown sequest'red cell,
35 Where woodbines cluster round the
    door,
Where shells and moss o'erlay the floor,
And on whose top an hawthorn blows,
Amid whose thickly-woven boughs
Some nightingale still builds her nest,
40 Each evening warbling thee to rest:
Then lay me by the haunted stream,
Rapt in some wild, poetic dream,
In converse while methinks I rove
With Spenser through a fairy grove;
45 Till, suddenly awak'd, I hear
Strange whisper'd music in my ear,
And my glad soul in bliss is drown'd
By the sweetly-soothing sound!
Me, goddess, by thy right hand lead
50 Sometimes through the yellow mead,
Where Joy and white-rob'd Peace resort,
And Venus keeps her festive court,
Where Mirth and Youth each evening
    meet,
And lightly trip with nimble feet,
55 Nodding their lily-crowned heads,
Where Laughter, rose-lipp'd Hebe, leads;
Where Echo walks steep hills among,
List'ning to the shepherd's song:
Yet not these flowery fields of joy
60 Can long my pensive mind employ.
Haste, Fancy, from the scenes of folly,

[1] clad in a buskin, or half-boot

To meet the matron Melancholy,
Goddess of the tearful eye,
That loves to fold her arms, and sigh;
65 Let us with silent footsteps go
To charnels and the house of woe,
To Gothic churches, vaults, and tombs,
Where each sad night some virgin comes,
With throbbing breast, and faded cheek,
70 Her promis'd bridegroom's urn to seek;
Or to some abbey's mould'ring tow'rs,
Where, to avoid cold wintry show'rs,
The naked beggar shivering lies,
While whistling tempests round her
    rise,
75 And trembles lest the tottering wall
Should on her sleeping infants fall.
Now let us louder strike the lyre,
For my heart glows with martial fire,
I feel, I feel, with sudden heat,
My big tumultuous bosom beat;
80 The trumpet's clangors pierce my
    ear,
A thousand widows' shrieks I hear,
Give me another horse, I cry,
Lo! the base Gallic squadrons fly;
85 Whence is this rage?—what spirit,
    say
To battle hurries me away?
'Tis Fancy, in her fiery car,
Transports me to the thickest war,
There whirls me o'er the hills of slain,
90 Where Tumult and Destruction reign;
Where mad with pain, the wounded
    steed
Tramples the dying and the dead;
Where giant Terror stalks around,
With sullen joy surveys the ground,
95 And, pointing to th' ensanguin'd field,
Shakes his dreadful gorgon shield!
O guide me from this horrid scene,
To high-arch'd walks and alleys green,
Which lovely Laura seeks to shun
100 The fervors of the mid-day sun;
The pangs of absence, O remove!
For thou canst place me near my love,
Canst fold in visionary bliss,
And let me think I steal a kiss,
105 While her ruby lips dispense
Luscious nectar's quintessence!
When young-eyed Spring profusely
    throws
From her green lap the pink and rose,
When the soft turtle of the dale
110 To Summer tells her tender tale,
When Autumn cooling caverns seeks,
And stains with wine his jolly cheeks;
When Winter, like poor pilgrim old,
Shakes his silver beard with cold;
115 At every season let my ear

Thy solemn whispers, Fancy, hear.
O warm, enthusiastic maid,
Without thy powerful, vital aid,
That breathes an energy divine,
120 That gives a soul to every line,
Ne'er may I strive with lips profane
To utter an unhallow'd strain,
Nor dare to touch the sacred string,
Save when with smiles thou bid'st me
    sing.
125 O hear our prayer, O hither come
From thy lamented Shakespear's tomb,
On which thou lov'st to sit at eve,
Musing o'er thy darling's grave;
O queen of numbers, once again
130 Animate some chosen swain,
Who, fill'd with unexhausted fire,
May boldly smite the sounding lyre,
Who with some new unequall'd song,
May rise above the rhyming throng,
135 O'er all our list'ning passions reign,
O'erwhelm our souls with joy and pain,
With terror shake, and pity move,
Rouse with revenge, or melt with love,
O deign t' attend his evening walk,
140 With him in groves and grottos talk;
Teach him to scorn with frigid art
Feebly to touch th' unraptur'd heart;
Like lightning, let his mighty verse
The bosom's inmost foldings pierce;
145 With native beauties win applause
Beyond cold critics' studied laws;
O let each Muse's fame increase,
O bid Britannia rival Greece.

From ESSAY ON THE GENIUS AND WRITINGS OF POPE
1756-82

. . . .

Thus have I endeavored to give a critical account, with freedom, but it is hoped with impartiality, of each of Pope's works; by which review it will appear, 5 that the largest portion of them is of the didactic, moral, and satyric kind; and consequently, not of the most poetic species of poetry; whence it is manifest, that good sense and judgment were his characteristical excellencies, rather than fancy 10 and invention: not that the author of *The Rape of the Lock,* and *Eloisa,* can be thought to want imagination; but because his imagination was not his predominant talent, because he indulged it not, and be- 15 cause he gave not so many proofs of this talent as of the other. This turn of mind led him to admire French models; he studied Boileau attentively; formed himself upon him, as Milton formed himself upon the Grecian and Italian sons of Fancy. He stuck to describing modern manners; but those manners, because they are familiar, uniform, and polished, are, in their very nature, unfit for any lofty effort of the Muse. He gradually became one of the most correct, even, and exact poets that ever wrote; polishing his pieces with a care and assiduity, that no business or avocation ever interrupted; so that if he does not frequently ravish and transport his reader, yet he does not disgust him with unexpected inequalities, and absurd improprieties. Whatever poetical enthusiasm he actually possessed, he withheld and stifled. The perusal of him affects not our minds with such strong emotions as we feel from Homer and Milton; so that no man of a true poetical spirit, is master of himself while he reads them. Hence, he is a writer fit for universal perusal; adapted to all ages and stations; for the old and for the young; the man of business and the scholar. He who would think *The Faery Queen, Palamon and Arcite, The Tempest* or *Comus,* childish and romantic, might relish Pope. Surely, it is no narrow and niggardly encomium, to say he is the great Poet of Reason, the first of ethical authors in verse. And this species of writing is, after all, the surest road to an extensive reputation. It lies more level to the general capacities of men, than the higher flights of more genuine poetry. We all remember when even a Churchill was more in vogue than a Gray. He that treats of fashionable follies and the topics of the day, that describes present persons and recent events, finds many readers, whose understandings and whose passions he gratifies. The name of Chesterfield on one hand, and of Walpole on the other, failed not to make a poem bought up and talked of. And it cannot be doubted that the Odes of Horace which celebrated, and the Satires which ridiculed, well-known and real characters at Rome, were more frequently cited, than the Æneid and the Georgic of Virgil.

Where then, according to the question proposed at the beginning of this Essay, shall we with justice be authorized to place our admired Pope? Not, assuredly, in the same rank with Spenser, Shakespeare, and Milton; however justly we may applaud the *Eloisa* and *Rape of the Lock;* but, considering the correctness, elegance, and utility of his works, the weight of sentiment, and the knowledge of man they contain, we may venture to assign him a place, next to Milton, and just above Dryden. Yet, to bring our minds steadily to make this decision, we must forget, for a moment, the divine *Music Ode* of Dryden; and may, perhaps, then be compelled to confess, that though Dryden be the greater genius, yet Pope is the better artist.

The preference here given to Pope above other modern English poets, it must be remembered, is founded on the excellencies of his works in general, and taken all together; for there are parts and passages in other modern authors, in Young and in Thomson, for instance, equal to any of Pope; and he has written nothing in a strain so truly sublime, as *The Bard* of Gray.

James Macpherson 1738-1796

CARTHON: A POEM
1760

A tale of the times of old! The deeds of days of other years!

The murmur of thy streams, O Lora! brings back the memory of the past. The sound of thy woods, Garmallar, is lovely in mine ear. Dost thou not behold, Malvina, a rock with its head of heath? Three aged pines bend from its face; green is the narrow plain at its feet; there the flower of the mountain grows, and shakes its white head in the breeze. The thistle is there alone, shedding its aged beard. Two stones, half sunk in the ground, shew their heads of moss. The deer of the mountain avoids the place, for he beholds a dim ghost standing there. The mighty lie, O Malvina! in the narrow plain of the rock.

A tale of the times of old! the deeds of days of other years!

Who comes from the land of strangers, with his thousands around him? the sunbeam pours its bright stream before him; his hair meets the wind of his hills. His face is settled from war. He is calm as the evening beam that looks from the cloud of the west, on Cona's silent vale. Who is it but Comhal's son, the king of mighty deeds! He beholds his hills with joy, he bids a thousand voices rise. "Ye have fled over your fields, ye sons of the distant land! The king of the world sits in his hall, and hears of his people's flight. He lifts his red eye of pride; he takes his father's sword. Ye have fled over your fields, sons of the distant land!''

Such were the words of the bards, when they came to Selma's halls. A thousand lights from the stranger's land rose in the midst of the people. The feast is spread around; the night passed away in joy. "Where is the noble Clessámmor?" said the fair-haired Fingal. "Where is the brother of Morna, in the hour of my joy? Sullen and dark he passes his days in the vale of echoing Lora: but, behold, he comes from the hill, like a steed in his strength, who finds his companions in the breeze, and tosses his bright mane in the wind. Blest be the soul of Clessámmor, why so long from Selma?''

"Returns the chief," said Clessámmor, "in the midst of his fame? Such was the renown of Comhal in the battles of his youth. Often did we pass over Carun to the land of the strangers: our swords returned, not unstained with blood: nor did the kings of the world rejoice. Why do I remember the times of our war? My hair is mixed with gray. My hand forgets to bend the bow: I lift a lighter spear. O that my joy would return, as when I first beheld the maid; the white-bosomed daughter of the strangers, Moina, with the dark-blue eyes!''

"Tell," said the mighty Fingal, "the tale of thy youthful days. Sorrow, like a cloud on the sun, shades the soul of Clessámmor. Mournful are thy thoughts, alone, on the banks of the roaring Lora. Let us hear the sorrow of thy youth, and the darkness of thy days!''

"It was in the days of peace," replied the great Clessámmor, "I came in my bounding ship, to Balclutha's walls of towers. The winds had roared behind my sails, and Clutha's streams received my dark-bosomed ship. Three days I remained in Reuthámir's halls, and saw his daughter, that beam of light. The joy of the shell[1] went round, and the aged hero gave the fair. Her breasts were like foam on the wave, and her eyes like stars of light: her hair was dark as the raven's wing: her soul was generous and mild. My love for Moina was great: my heart poured forth in joy.

"The son of a stranger came; a chief who loved the white-bosomed Moina. His words were mighty in the hall; he often half-unsheathed his sword. 'Where,' said

he, 'is the mighty Comhal, the restless wanderer of the heath? Comes he, with his host, to Balclutha, since Clessámmor is so bold?' 'My soul,' I replied, 'O warrior! burns in a light of its own. I stand without fear in the midst of thousands, though the valiant are distant far. Stranger! thy words are mighty, for Clessámmor is alone. But my sword trembles by my side, and longs to glitter in my hand. Speak no more of Comhal, son of the winding Clutha!'

"The strength of his pride arose. We fought; he fell beneath my sword. The banks of Clutha heard his fall; a thousand spears glittered around. I fought: the strangers prevailed: I plunged into the stream of Clutha. My white sails rose over the waves, and I bounded on the dark-blue sea. Moina came to the shore, and rolled the red eye of her tears: her loose hair flew on the wind; and I heard her mournful, distant cries. Often did I turn my ship; but the winds of the East prevailed. Nor Clutha ever since have I seen, nor Moina of the dark-brown hair. She fell in Balclutha, for I have seen her ghost. I knew her as she came through the dusky night, along the murmur of Lora: she was like the new moon, seen through the gathered mist: when the sky pours down its flaky snow, and the world is silent and dark.''

"Raise, ye bards," said the mighty Fingal, "the praise of unhappy Moina. Call her ghost, with your songs, to our hills, that she may rest with the fair of Morven, the sunbeams of other days, the delight of heroes of old. I have seen the walls of Balclutha, but they were desolate. The fire had resounded in the halls: and the voice of the people is heard no more. The stream of Clutha was removed from its place, by the fall of the walls. The thistle shook there its lonely head: the moss whistled to the wind. The fox looked out from the windows, the rank grass of the wall waved round its head. Desolate is the dwelling of Moina, silence is in the house of her fathers. Raise the song of mourning, O bards! over the land of strangers. They have but fallen before us: for one day we must fall. Why dost thou build the hall, son of the winged days? Thou lookest from thy towers to-day; yet a few years, and the blast of the desert comes; it howls in thy empty court, and whistles round thy half-worn shield. And let the blast of the desert come! we

---

[1] "To 'rejoice in the shell' is a phrase for feasting sumptuously and drinking freely."—Macpherson.

shall be renowned in our day! The mark of my arm shall be in battle; my name in the song of bards. Raise the song; send round the shell: let joy be heard in my hall. When thou, sun of heaven, shalt fail! if thou shalt fail, thou mighty light! if thy brightness is for a season, like Fingal, our fame shall survive thy beams!''

Such was the song of Fingal, in the day of his joy. His thousand bards leaned forward from their seats, to hear the voice of the king. It was like the music of harps on the gale of the spring. Lovely were thy thoughts, O Fingal! why had not Ossian the strength of thy soul? But thou standest alone, my father! who can equal the king of Selma?

The night passed away in song; morning returned in joy. The mountains shewed their gray heads; the blue face of ocean smiled. The white wave is seen tumbling round the distant rock; a mist rose, slowly, from the lake. It came in the figure of an aged man along the silent plain. Its large limbs did not move in steps; for a ghost supported it in mid-air. It came towards Selma's hall, and dissolved in a shower of blood.

The king alone beheld the sight; he foresaw the death of the people. He came in silence to his hall; and took his father's spear. The mail rattled on his breast. The heroes rose around. They looked in silence on each other, marking the eyes of Fingal. They saw battle in his face: the death of armies on his spear. A thousand shields at once are placed on their arms; they drew a thousand swords. The hall of Selma brightened around. The clang of arms ascends. The gray dogs howl in their place. No word is among the mighty chiefs. Each marked the eyes of the king; and half-assumed his spear.

''Sons of Morven,'' begun the king, ''this is no time to fill the shell. The battle darkens near us; death hovers over the land. Some ghost, the friend of Fingal, has forewarned us of the foe. The sons of the stranger come from the darkly-rolling sea. For, from the water, came the sign of Morven's gloomy danger. Let each assume his heavy spear, each gird on his father's sword. Let the dark helmet rise on every head; the mail pour its lightning from every side. The battle gathers like a storm; soon shall ye hear the roar of death.''

The hero moved on before his host, like a cloud before a ridge of green fire, when it pours on the sky of night, and mariners foresee a storm. On Cona's rising heath they stood: the white-bosomed maids beheld them above like a grove; they foresaw the death of the youth, and looked towards the sea with fear. The white wave deceived them for distant sails; the tear is on their cheek! The sun rose on the sea, and we beheld a distant fleet. Like the mist of ocean they came, and poured their youth upon the coast. The chief was among them, like the stag in the midst of the herd. His shield is studded with gold; stately strode the king of spears. He moved toward Selma; his thousands moved behind.

''Go, with a song of peace,'' said Fingal; ''go, Ullin, to the king of swords. Tell him that we are mighty in war; that the ghosts of our foes are many. But renowned are they who have feasted in my halls; they show the arms of my fathers in a foreign land: the sons of the strangers wonder, and bless the friends of Morven's race; for our names have been heard afar: the kings of the world shook in the midst of their host.''

Ullin went with his song. Fingal rested on his spear: he saw the mighty foe in his armor: he blest the stranger's son. ''How stately art thou, son of the sea!'' said the king of woody Morven. ''Thy sword is a beam of fire by thy side: thy spear is a pine that defies the storm. The varied face of the moon is not broader than thy shield. Ruddy is thy face of youth! soft the ringlets of thy hair! But this tree may fall; and his memory be forgot! The daughter of the stranger will be sad, looking to the rolling sea: the children will say, 'We see a ship; perhaps it is the king of Balclutha.' The tear starts from their mother's eye. Her thoughts are of him who sleeps in Morven!''

Such were the words of the king, when Ullin came to the mighty Carthon; he threw down the spear before him; he raised the song of peace. ''Come to the feast of Fingal, Carthon, from the rolling sea! partake of the feast of the king, or lift the spear of war! The ghosts of our foes are many: but renowned are the friends of Morven! Behold that field, O Carthon! many a green hill rises there, with mossy stones and rustling grass: these are the tombs of Fingal's foes, the sons of the rolling sea!''

"Dost thou speak to the weak in arms!" said Carthon, "bard of the woody Morven? Is my face pale for fear, son of the peaceful song? Why, then, dost thou think to darken my soul with the tales of those who fell? My arm has fought in battle; my renown is known afar. Go to the feeble in arms, bid them yield to Fingal. Have not I seen the fallen Balclutha? And shall I feast with Comhal's son? Comhal, who threw his fire in the midst of my father's hall? I was young, and knew not the cause, why the virgins wept. The columns of smoke pleased mine eye, when they rose above my walls! I often looked back with gladness when my friends fled along the hill. But when the years of my youth came on, I beheld the moss of my fallen walls. My sigh arose with the morning, and my tears descended with night. 'Shall I not fight,' I said to my soul, 'against the children of my foes?' And I will fight, O bard! I feel the strength of my soul."

His people gathered round the hero, and drew at once their shining swords. He stands in the midst, like a pillar of fire, the tear half-starting from his eye; for he thought of the fallen Balclutha. The crowded pride of his soul arose. Sidelong he looked up to the hill, where our heroes shone in arms; the spear trembled in his hand. Bending forward, he seemed to threaten the king.

"Shall I," said Fingal to his soul, "meet, at once, the youth? Shall I stop him, in the midst of his course, before his fame shall arise? But the bard, hereafter, may say, when he sees the tomb of Carthon, Fingal took his thousands to battle, before the noble Carthon fell. No: bard of the times to come! thou shalt not lessen Fingal's fame. My heroes will fight the youth, and Fingal behold the war. If he overcomes, I rush, in my strength, like the roaring stream of Cona. Who, of my chiefs will meet the son of the rolling sea? Many are his warriors on the coast, and strong is his ashen spear!"

Cathul rose, in his strength, the son of the mighty Lormar: three hundred youths attend the chief, the race of his native streams. Feeble was his arm against Carthon: he fell, and his heroes fled. Connal resumed the battle, but he broke his heavy spear: he lay bound on the field: Carthon pursued his people.

"Clessámmor!" said the king of Morven, "where is the spear of thy strength? Wilt thou behold Connal bound; thy friend, at the stream of Lora? Rise, in the light of thy steel, companion of valiant Comhal! Let the youth of Balclutha feel the strength of Morven's race." He rose in the strength of his steel, shaking his grizzly locks. He fitted the steel to his side; he rushed, in the pride of valor.

Carthon stood on a rock; he saw the hero rushing on. He loved the dreadful joy of his face: his strength, in the locks of age! "Shall I lift that spear," he said, "that never strikes, but once, a foe? Or shall I, with the words of peace, preserve the warrior's life? Stately are his steps of age! lovely the remnant of his years! Perhaps it is the husband of Moina; the father of car-borne Carthon. Often have I heard that he dwelt at the echoing stream of Lora."

Such were his words, when Clessámmor came, and lifted high his spear. The youth received it on his shield, and spoke the words of peace. "Warrior of the aged locks! Is there no youth to lift the spear? Hast thou no son to raise the shield before his father to meet the arm of youth? Is the spouse of thy love no more? or weeps she over the tombs of thy sons? Art thou of the kings of men? What will be the fame of my sword should'st thou fall?"

"It will be great, thou son of pride!" begun the tall Clessámmor. "I have been renowned in battle; but I never told my name to a foe.[1] Yield to me, son of the wave, then shalt thou know, that the mark of my sword is in many a field." "I never yielded, king of spears!" replied the noble pride of Carthon: "I have also fought in war; I behold my future fame. Despise me not, thou chief of men! my arm, my spear is strong. Retire among thy friends; let younger heroes fight." "Why dost thou wound my soul?" replied Clessámmor, with a tear. "Age does not tremble on my hand; I still can lift the sword. Shall I fly in Fingal's sight: in the sight of him I love? Son of the sea! I never fled: exalt thy pointed spear."

They fought like two contending winds,

[1] "To tell one's name to an enemy was reckoned, in those days of heroism, a manifest evasion of fighting him; for if it was once known that friendship subsisted of old between the ancestors of the combatants, the battle immediately ceased, and the ancient amity of their forefathers was renewed. 'A man who tells his name to his enemy,' was of old an ignominious term for a coward."—Macpherson.

that strive to roll the wave. Carthon bade his spear to err; he still thought that the foe was the spouse of Moina. He broke Clessámmor's beamy spear in twain: he seized his shining sword. But as Carthon was binding the chief, the chief drew the dagger of his fathers. He saw the foe's uncovered side, and opened there a wound.

Fingal saw Clessámmor low: he moved in the sound of his steel. The host stood silent in his presence; they turned their eyes to the king. He came like the sullen noise of a storm before the winds arise: the hunter hears it in the vale, and retires to the cave of the rock. Carthon stood in his place: the blood is rushing down his side: he saw the coming down of the king; his hopes of fame arose; but pale was his cheek: his hair flew loose, his helmet shook on high: the force of Carthon failed; but his soul was strong.

Fingal beheld the hero's blood; he stopt the uplifted spear. "Yield, king of swords!" said Comhal's son; "I behold thy blood. Thou hast been mighty in battle, and thy fame shall never fade." "Art thou the king so far renowned?" replied the car-borne Carthon. "Art thou that light of death, that frightens the kings of the world? But why should Carthon ask? for he is like the stream of his hills, strong as a river in his course, swift as the eagle of heaven. O that I had fought with the king, that my fame might be great in song! that the hunter, beholding my tomb, might say he fought with the mighty Fingal. But Carthon dies unknown; he has poured out his force on the weak."

"But thou shalt not die unknown," replied the king of woody Morven: "my bards are many, O Carthon! Their songs descend to future times. The children of years to come shall hear the fame of Carthon, when they sit round the burning oak, and the night is spent in songs of old. The hunter, sitting in the heath, shall hear the rustling blast, and, raising his eyes, behold the rock where Carthon fell. He shall turn to his son, and shew the place where the mighty fought: 'There the king of Balclutha fought, like the strength of a thousand streams.'"

Joy rose in Carthon's face: he lifted his heavy eyes. He gave his sword to Fingal, to lie within his hall, that the memory of Balclutha's king might remain in Morven. The battle ceased along the field, the bard had sung the song of peace. The chiefs gathered round the falling Carthon; they heard his words with sighs. Silent they leaned on their spears, while Balclutha's hero spoke. His hair sighed in the wind, and his voice was sad and low.

"King of Morven," Carthon said, "I fall in the midst of my course. A foreign tomb receives, in youth, the last of Reuthámir's race. Darkness dwells in Balclutha: the shadows of grief in Crathmo. But raise my remembrance on the banks of Lora, where my fathers dwelt. Perhaps the husband of Moina will mourn over his fallen Carthon." His words reached the heart of Clessámmor: he fell in silence on his son. The host stood darkened around: no voice is on the plain. Night came: the moon, from the east, looked on the mournful field; but still they stood, like a silent grove that lifts its head on Gormal, when the loud winds are laid, and dark autumn is on the plain.

Three days they mourned above Carthon; on the fourth his father died. In the narrow plain of the rock they lie; a dim ghost defends their tomb. There lovely Moina is often seen, when the sunbeam darts on the rock, and all around is dark. There she is seen, Malvina! but not like the daughters of the hill. Her robes are from the stranger's land; and she is still alone!

Fingal was sad for Carthon; he commanded his bards to mark the day when shadowy autumn returned. And often did they mark the day, and sing the hero's praise. "Who comes so dark from ocean's roar, like autumn's shadowy cloud? Death is trembling in his hand! his eyes are flames of fire! Who roars along dark Lora's heath? Who but Carthon, king of swords! The people fall! see how he strides, like the sullen ghost of Morven! But there he lies, a goodly oak which sudden blasts overturned! When shalt thou rise, Balclutha's joy? When, Carthon, shalt thou arise? Who comes so dark from ocean's roar, like autumn's shadowy cloud?" Such were the words of the bards, in the day of their mourning: Ossian often joined their voice, and added to their song. My soul has been mournful for Carthon; he fell in the days of his youth: and thou, O Clessámmor! where is thy dwelling in the wind? Has the youth forgot his wound? Flies he,

on clouds, with thee? I feel the sun, O
Malvina! leave me to my rest. Perhaps
they may come to my dreams; I think I
hear a feeble voice! The beam of heaven
delights to shine on the grave of Carthon: 5
I feel it warm around!

O thou that rollest above, round as the
shield of my fathers! Whence are thy
beams, O sun! thy everlasting light? Thou
comest forth, in thy awful beauty; the 10
stars hide themselves in the sky; the
moon, cold and pale, sinks in the western
wave; but thou thyself movest alone.
Who can be a companion of thy course?
The oaks of the mountains fall: the moun- 15
tains themselves decay with years; the
ocean shrinks and grows again: the moon
herself is lost in heaven; but thou art for
ever the same, rejoicing in the brightness
of thy course. When the world is dark 20
with tempests, when thunder rolls and
lightning flies, thou lookest in thy beauty
from the clouds, and laughest at the storm.
But to Ossian, thou lookest in vain; for
he beholds thy beams no more; whether 25
thy yellow hair flows on the eastern
clouds, or thou tremblest at the gates of
the west. But thou art, perhaps, like me,
for a season; thy years will have an end.
Thou shalt sleep in thy clouds, careless 30
of the voice of the morning. Exult then,
O sun, in the strength of thy youth! Age is
dark and unlovely; it is like the glimmering
light of the moon, when it shines through
broken clouds, and the mist is on the hills; 35
the blast of the north is on the plain; the
traveller shrinks in the midst of his journey.

OINA-MORUL: A POEM
1760
40

As flies the unconstant sun, over Lar-
mon's grassy hill, so pass the tales of
old along my soul by night! When bards
are removed to their place, when harps
are hung in Selma's hall, then comes a 45
voice to Ossian, and awakes his soul! It
is the voice of years that are gone! they
roll before me with all their deeds! I
seize the tales as they pass, and pour them
forth in song. Nor a troubled stream is 50
the song of the king, it is like the rising
of music from Lutha of the strings.
Lutha of many strings, not silent are thy
streamy rocks, when the white hands of
Malvina move upon the harp! Light of the 55
shadowy thoughts, that fly across my soul,
daughter of Toscar of helmets, wilt thou not
hear the song? We call back, maid of
Lutha, the years that have rolled away!

It was in the days of the king, while
yet my locks were young, that I marked
Con-cathlin on high, from ocean's nightly
wave. My course was towards the isle of
Fuärfed, woody dweller of seas! Fingal had
sent me to the aid of Mal-orchol, king of
Fuärfed wild: for war was around him, and
our fathers had met at the feast.

In Col-coiled, I bound my sails; I sent
my sword to Mal-orchol of shells.[1] He
knew the signal of Albion, and his joy
arose. He came from his own high hall,
and seized my hand in grief. "Why
comes the race of heroes to a falling
king? Ton-thormod of many spears is
the chief of wavy Sar-dronlo. He saw,
and loved my daughter, white-bosomed
Oina-morul. He sought; I denied the
maid, for our fathers had been foes. He
came with battle to Fuärfed; my people
are rolled away. Why comes the race of
heroes to a falling king?"

"I come not," I said, "to look, like a
boy, on the strife. Fingal remembers Mal-
orchol, and his hall for strangers. From
his waves, the warrior descended on thy
woody isle. Thou wert no cloud before
him. Thy feast was spread with songs.
For this my sword shall rise, and thy
foes perhaps may fail. Our friends are
not forgot in their danger, though distant
is our land."

"Descendant of the daring Trenmor,
thy words are like the voice of Cruth-
loda, when he speaks from his parting
cloud, strong dweller of the sky! Many
have rejoiced at my feast; but they all
have forgot Mal-orchol. I have looked
towards all the winds; but no white sails
were seen. But steel resounds in my hall;
and not the joyful shells. Come to my
dwelling, race of heroes! dark-skirted
night is near. Hear the voice of songs,
from the maid of Fuärfed wild."

We went. On the harp arose the white
hands of Oina-morul. She waked her own
sad tale, from every trembling string. I
stood in silence; for bright in her locks
was the daughter of many isles! Her
eyes were two stars, looking forward
through a rushing shower. The mariner
marks them on high, and blesses the lovely
beams. With morning we rushed to battle,
to Tormul's resounding stream: the foe
moved to the sound of Ton-thormod's
bossy shield. From wing to wing the strife

---

[1] "The ancient Scots, as well as the present Highlanders, drunk in shells; hence it is that we so
often meet in the old poetry with 'chief of
shells' and 'the hall of shells.'"—Macpherson.

was mixed. I met Ton-thormod in fight. Wide flew his broken steel. I seized the king in war. I gave his hand, bound fast with thongs, to Mal-orchol, the giver of shells. Joy rose at the feast of Fuär- 5 fed, for the foe had failed. Ton-thormod turned his face away, from Oina-morul of isles!

"Son of Fingal," begun Mal-orchol, "not forgot shalt thou pass from me. A 10 light shall dwell in thy ship, Oina-morul of slow-rolling eyes. She shall kindle glad-ness along thy mighty soul. Nor unheeded shall the maid move in Selma, through the dwellings of kings!" 15

In the hall I lay in night. Mine eyes were half-closed in sleep. Soft music came to mine ear: it was like the rising breeze, that whirls, at first, the thistle's beard, then flies, dark-shadowy, over the 20 grass. It was the maid of Fuärfed wild! she raised the nightly song; she knew that my soul was a stream, that flowed at pleas-ant sounds. "Who looks," she said, "from his rock on ocean's closing mist? 25 His long locks, like the raven's wing, are wandering on the blast. Stately are his steps in grief! The tears are in his eyes! His manly breast is heaving over his bursting soul! Retire, I am distant far, 30 a wanderer in lands unknown. Though the race of kings are around me, yet my soul is dark. Why have our fathers been foes, Ton-thormod, love of maids!"

"Soft voice of the streamy isle," I said, 35 "why dost thou mourn by night? The race of daring Trenmor are not the dark in soul. Thou shalt not wander by streams unknown, blue-eyed Oina-morul! Within this bosom is a voice; it comes not 40 to other ears: it bids Ossian hear the hapless, in their hour of woe. Retire, soft singer by night! Ton-thormod shall not mourn on his rock!"

With morning I loosed the king. I 45 gave the long-haired maid. Mal-orchol heard my words in the midst of his echo-ing halls. "King of Fuärfed wild, why should Ton-thormod mourn? He is of the race of heroes, and a flame in war. 50 Your fathers have been foes, but now their dim ghosts rejoice in death. They stretch their hands of mist to the same shell in Loda. Forget their rage, ye warriors! It was the cloud of other 55 years."

Such were the deeds of Ossian, while yet his locks were young; though loveli-ness, with a robe of beams, clothed the

daughter of many isles. We call back, maid of Lutha, the years that have rolled away!

From FINGAL: AN ANCIENT EPIC POEM
1762
Book I

Cuthullin sat by Tura's wall; by the tree of the rustling sound. His spear leaned against the rock. His shield lay on the grass by his side. Amid his thoughts of mighty Cairbar, a hero slain by the chief in war, the scout of ocean comes, Moran the son of Fithil!

"Arise," says the youth, "Cuthullin, arise. I see the ships of the north! Many, chief of men, are the foe. Many the heroes of the sea-borne Swaran!" "Moran!" replied the blue-eyed chief, "thou ever tremblest, son of Fithil! Thy fears have increased the foe. It is Fingal, king of deserts, with aid to green Erin of streams." "I beheld their chief," says Moran, "tall as a glittering rock. His spear is a blasted pine. His shield the rising moon! He sat on the shore, like a cloud of mist on the silent hill! Many, chief of heroes! I said, many are our hands of war. Well art thou named, the mighty man; but many mighty men are seen from Tura's windy walls."

"He spoke, like a wave on a rock: 'Who in this land appears like me? Heroes stand not in my presence: they fall to earth from my hand. Who can meet Swaran in fight? Who but Fingal, king of Selma of storms? Once we wrestled on Malmor; our heels overturned the woods. Rocks fell from their place; rivulets, changing their course, fled murmuring from our side. Three days we renewed the strife; heroes stood at a distance and trembled. On the fourth, Fingal says that the king of the ocean fell! but Swaran says he stood! Let dark Cuthullin yield to him, that is strong as the storms of his land!' "

"No!" replied the blue-eyed chief, "I never yield to mortal man! Dark Cuth-ullin shall be great or dead! Go, son of Fithil, take my spear. Strike the sounding shield of Semo. It hangs at Tura's rus-tling gate. The sound of peace is not its voice! My heroes shall hear and obey." He went. He struck the bossy shield. The hills, the rocks reply. The sound spreads along the wood: deer start by the lake of roes. Curach leaps from the sounding rock; and Connal of the bloody spear! Crugal's breast of snow beats high. The son of Favi leaves the dark-brown hind. It is the shield of war, said Ronnar! the spear of Cuthullin, said Lugar! Son of the sea, put on thy arms! Calmar, lift thy sounding steel! Puno! dreadful hero, arise! Cairbar, from thy red tree of Cromla! Bend thy knee, O Eth! descend from the streams of Lena. Ca-olt, stretch thy side as thou movest along the whistling heath of Mora: thy side that is white as the foam of the troubled sea, when the dark winds pour it on rocky Cuthon.

Now I behold the chiefs, in the pride of their former deeds! Their souls are kindled at the battles of old; at the actions of other times. Their eyes are flames of fire. They roll in search of the foes of the land. Their mighty hands are on their swords. Lightning pours from their sides of steel. They come like streams from the mountains; each rushes roaring from the hill. Bright are the chiefs of battle, in the armor of their fathers. Gloomy and dark their heroes follow, like the gathering of the rainy clouds behind the red meteors of heaven. The sounds of crashing arms ascend. The gray dogs howl between. Unequal bursts the song of battle. Rocking Cromla echoes round. On Lena's dusky heath they stand, like mist that shades the hills of autumn: when broken and dark it settles high, and lifts its head to heaven!

"Hail," said Cuthullin, "sons of the narrow vales! hail, hunters of the deer! Another sport is drawing near. It is like the dark rolling of that wave on the coast! Or shall we fight, ye sons of war! or yield green Erin to Lochlin? O Connal! speak, thou first of men! thou breaker of the shields! thou hast often fought with Locklin: wilt thou lift thy father's spear?"

"Cuthullin!" calm the chief replied, "the spear of Connal is keen. It delights to shine in battle; to mix with the blood of thousands. But though my hand is bent on war, my heart is for the peace of Erin. Behold, thou first in Cormac's war, the sable fleet of Swaran. His masts are many on our coast, like reeds in the lake of Lego. His ships are forests clothed with mists, when the trees yield by turns to the squally wind. Many are his chiefs in battle. Connal is for peace! Fingal would shun his arm, the first of mortal men! Fingal, who scatters the mighty, as stormy winds the heath; when streams roar through echoing Cona: and night settles with all her clouds on the hill!"

"Fly, thou man of peace," said Calmar; "fly," said the son of Matha; "go, Connal, to thy silent hills, where the spear never brightens in war! Pursue the dark-brown deer of Cromla: stop with thine arrows the bounding roes of Lena. But, blue-eyed son of Semo, Cuthullin, ruler of the field, scatter thou the sons of Lochlin! roar through the ranks of their pride. Let no vessel of the kingdom of snow bound on the dark-rolling waves of Inistore. Rise, ye dark winds of Erin, rise! roar, whirlwinds of Lara of hinds! Amid the tempest let me die, torn, in a cloud, by angry ghosts of men; amid the tempest let Calmar die, if ever chase was sport to him, so much as the battle of shields!"

"Calmar!" Connal slow replied, "I never fled, young son of Matha! I was swift with my friends in fight; but small is the fame of Connal! The battle was won in my presence; the valiant overcame! But, son of Semo, hear my voice, regard the ancient throne of Cormac. Give wealth and half the land for peace, till Fingal shall arrive on our coast. Or, if war be thy choice, I lift the sword and spear. My joy shall be in the midst of thousands; my soul shall lighten through the gloom of the fight!"

"To me," Cuthullin replies, "pleasant is the noise of arms! pleasant as the thunder of heaven, before the shower of spring! But gather all the shining tribes, that I may view the sons of war! Let them pass along the heath, bright as the sunshine before a storm; when the west wind collects the clouds, and Morven echoes over all her oaks! But where are my friends in battle? the supporters of my arm in danger? Where art thou, white-bosomed Câthba? Where is that cloud in war, Duchômar? Hast thou left me, O Fergus! in the day of the storm? Fergus, first in our joy at the feast! son of Rossa! arm of death! comest thou like a roe from Malmor? like a hart from thy echoing hills? Hail, thou son of Rossa! what shades the soul of war?"

"Four stones," replied the chief, "rise on the grave of Câthba. These hands have laid in earth Duchômar, that cloud in war! Câthba, son of Torman! thou wert a sunbeam in Erin. And thou, O valiant Duchômar! a mist of the marshy Lano, when it moves on the plains of autumn, bearing the death of thousands along. Morna! fairest of maids! calm is thy sleep in the cave of the rock! Thou hast fallen in darkness, like a star that shoots across the desert, when the traveller is alone, and mourns the transient beam!''

"Say," said Semo's blue-eyed son, "say how fell the chiefs of Erin. Fell they by the sons of Lochlin, striving in the battle of heroes? Or what confines the strong in arms to the dark and narrow house?''

"Câthba," replied the hero, "fell by the sword of Duchômar at the oak of the noisy streams. Duchômar came to Tura's cave; he spoke to the lovely Morna. 'Morna, fairest among women, lovely daughter of strong-armed Cormac! Why in the circle of stones? in the cave of the rock alone? The stream murmurs along. The old tree groans in the wind. The lake is troubled before thee; dark are the clouds of the sky! But thou art snow on the heath; thy hair is the mist of Cromla; when it curls on the hill; when it shines to the beam of the west! Thy breasts are two smooth rocks seen from Branno of streams. Thy arms, like two white pillars in the halls of the great Fingal.'

"'From whence,' the fair-haired maid replied, 'from whence, Duchômar, most gloomy of men? Dark are thy brows and terrible! Red are thy rolling eyes! Does Swaran appear on the sea? What of the foe, Duchômar?'—'From the hill I return, O Morna, from the hill of the dark-brown hinds. Three have I slain with my bended yew. Three with my long-bounding dogs of the chase. Lovely daughter of Cormac, I love thee as my soul! I have slain one stately deer for thee. High was his branchy head; and fleet his feet of wind.'—'Duchômar!' calm the maid replied, 'I love thee not, thou gloomy man! hard is thy heart of rock; dark is thy terrible brow. But Câthba, young son of Torman, thou art the love of Morna. Thou art a sunbeam, in the day of the gloomy storm. Sawest thou the son of Torman, lovely on the hill of his hinds? Here the daughter of Cormac waits the coming of Câthba!'

"'Long shall Morna wait,' Duchômar said, 'long shall Morna wait for Câthba! Behold this sword unsheathed! Here

wanders the blood of Câthba. Long shall Morna wait. He fell by the stream of Branno! On Croma I will raise his tomb, daughter of blue-shielded Cormac! Turn on Duchômar thine eyes; his arm is strong as a storm.' — 'Is the son of Torman fallen?' said the wildly-bursting voice of the maid. 'Is he fallen on his echoing hills, the youth with the breast of snow? the first in the chase of hinds? the foe of the strangers of ocean? Thou art dark[1] to me, Duchômar, cruel is thine arm to Morna! Give me that sword, my foe! I love the wandering blood of Câthba!'

"He gave the sword to her tears. She pierced his manly breast! He fell, like the bank of a mountain-stream, and stretching forth his hand, he spoke: 'Daughter of blue-shielded Cormac! Thou hast slain me in youth! The sword is cold in my breast! Morna, I feel it cold. Give me to Moina the maid. Duchômar was the dream of her night! She will raise my tomb; the hunter shall raise my fame. But draw the sword from my breast. Morna, the steel is cold!' She came, in all her tears, she came; she drew the sword from his breast. He pierced her white side! He spread her fair locks on the ground! Her bursting blood sounds from her side: her white arm is stained with red. Rolling in death she lay. The cave re-echoed to her sighs.''

"Peace," said Cuthullin, "to the souls of the heroes! their deeds were great in fight. Let them ride around me on clouds. Let them shew their features of war. My soul shall then be firm in danger; mine arm like the thunder of heaven! But be thou on a moonbeam, O Morna! near the window of my rest; when my thoughts are of peace; when the din of arms is past. Gather the strength of the tribes! Move to the wars of Erin! Attend the car of my battles! Rejoice in the noise of my course! Place three spears by my side: follow the bounding of my steeds! that my soul may be strong in my friends, when battle darkens round the beams of my steel!''

As rushes a stream of foam from the dark shady deep of Cromla, when the thunder is travelling above, and dark-brown night sits on half the hill, through the breaches of the tempest look forth the dim faces of ghosts. So fierce, so vast, so ter-

[1] "She alludes to his name the 'dark man.' "—Macpherson.

rible, rushed on the sons of Erin. The chief, like a whale of ocean, whom all his billows pursue, poured valor forth as a stream, rolling his might along the shore. The sons of Lochlin heard the noise, as the sound of a winter-storm. Swaran struck his bossy shield: he called the son of Arno, "What murmur rolls along the hill, like the gathering flies of the eve? The sons of Erin descend, or rustling winds 10 roar in the distant wood! Such is the noise of Gormal, before the white tops of my waves arise. O son of Arno! ascend the hill; view the dark face of the heath!"

He went. He, trembling, swift returned. 15 His eyes rolled wildly round. His heart beat high against his side. His words were faltering, broken, slow. "Arise, son of ocean, arise, chief of the dark-brown shields! I see the dark, the mountain- 20 stream of battle! the deep-moving strength of the sons of Erin! The car of war comes on, like the flame of death! the rapid car of Cuthullin, the noble son of Semo! It bends behind like a wave near a rock; like the sun- 25 streaked mist of the heath. Its sides are embossed with stones, and sparkle like the sea round the boat of night. Of polished yew is its beam; its seat of the smoothest bone. The sides are replenished with spears; the 30 bottom is the footstool of heroes! Before the right side of the car is seen the snorting horse! the high-maned, broad breasted, proud, wide-leaping, strong steed of the hill. Loud and resounding is his 35 hoof; the spreading of his mane above is like a stream of smoke on a ridge of rocks. Bright are the sides of the steed! his name is Sulin-Sifadda.

"Before the left side of the car is seen 40 the snorting horse! The thin-maned, high-headed, strong-hoofed, fleet, bounding son of the hill: his name is Dusronnal, among the stormy sons of the sword! A thousand thongs bind the car on high. Hard pol- 45 ished bits shine in a wreath of foam. Thin thongs, bright studded with gems, bend on the stately necks of the steeds. The steeds that, like wreaths of mist, fly over the streamy vales! The wildness of 50 deer is in their course, the strength of eagles descending on the prey. Their noise is like the blast of winter, on the sides of the snow-headed Gormal.

"Within the car is seen the chief; the 55 strong-armed son of the sword. The hero's name is Cuthullin, son of Semo, king of shells.[1] His red cheek is like my

[1] See p. 91, n. 1.

polished yew. The look of his blue-rolling eye is wide, beneath the dark arch of his brow. His hair flies from his head like a flame, as bending forward he wields the spear. Fly, king of ocean, fly! He 5 comes like a storm along the streamy vale!"

"When did I fly?" replied the king. "When fled Swaran from the battle of spears? When did I shrink from danger, chief of the little soul? I met the storm 10 of Gormal, when the foam of my waves beat high. I met the storm of the clouds; shall Swaran fly from a hero? Were Fingal himself before me, my soul should not darken with fear. Arise to battle, my 15 thousands! pour round me like the echoing main. Gather round the bright steel of your king; strong as the rocks of my land, that meet the storm with joy, and stretch their dark pines to the wind!" 20

Like autumn's dark storms pouring from two echoing hills, towards each other approached the heroes. Like two deep streams from high rocks meeting, mixing, roaring on the plain; loud, rough, and dark in battle meet Lochlin and Inis-fail. Chief mixes his strokes with chief, and man with man; steel, clanging, sounds on steel. Helmets are cleft on high. Blood bursts and smokes around. Strings mur- 30 mur on the polished yews. Darts rush along the sky. Spears fall like the circles of light, which gild the face of night. As the noise of the troubled ocean, when roll the waves on high; as the last peal of 35 thunder in heaven, such is the din of war! Though Cormac's hundred bards were there to give the fight to song; feeble was the voice of a hundred bards to send the deaths to future times! For many were the deaths of heroes; wide poured the blood of the brave!

Mourn, ye sons of song, mourn the death of the noble Sithállin. Let the sighs of Fióna rise, on the lone plains of her 45 lovely Ardan. They fell, like two hinds of the desert, by the hands of the mighty Swaran; when, in the midst of thousands, he roared, like the shrill spirit of a storm. He sits dim on the clouds of the north, 50 and enjoys the death of the mariner. Nor slept thy hand by thy side, chief of the isle of mist![1] many were the deaths of thine arm, Cuthullin, thou son of Semo! His sword was like the beam of heaven 55 when it pierces the sons of the vale; when the people are blasted and fall, and all

[2] The Isle of Sky, off the coast of Scotland.

the hills are burning around. Dusronnal snorted over the bodies of heroes. Sifadda bathed his hoof in blood. The battle lay behind them, as groves overturned on the desert of Cromla; when the blast has passed the heath, laden with the spirits of night!

Weep on the rocks of roaring winds, O maid of Inistore! Bend thy fair head over the waves, thou lovelier than the ghost of the hills, when it moves in a sunbeam, at noon, over the silence of Morven! He is fallen! thy youth is low! pale beneath the sword of Cuthullin! No more shall valor raise thy love to match the blood of kings. Trenar, graceful Trenar died, O maid of Inistore! His gray dogs are howling at home! they see his passing ghost. His bow is in the hall unstrung. No sound is in the hall of his hinds!

As roll a thousand waves to the rocks, so Swaran's host came on. As meets a rock a thousand waves, so Erin met Swaran of spears. Death raises all his voices around, and mixes with the sounds of shields. Each hero is a pillar of darkness; the sword a beam of fire in his hand. The field echoes from wing to wing, as a hundred hammers that rise, by turns, on the red son of the furnace. Who are these on Lena's heath, these so gloomy and dark? Who are these like two clouds, and their swords like lightning above them? The little hills are troubled around; the rocks tremble with all their moss. Who is it but Ocean's son and the car-borne chief of Erin? Many are the anxious eyes of their friends, as they see them dim on the heath. But night conceals the chiefs in clouds, and ends the dreadful fight!

It was on Cromla's shaggy side that Dorglas had placed the deer; the early fortune of the chase, before the heroes left the hill. A hundred youths collect the heath; ten warriors wake the fire; three hundred choose the polished stones. The feast is smoking wide! Cuthullin, chief of Erin's war, resumed his mighty soul. He stood upon his beamy spear, and spoke to the son of songs; to Carril of other times, the gray-haired son of Kinfena. "Is this feast spread for me alone and the king of Lochlin on Erin's shore; far from the deer of his hills, and sounding halls of his feasts? Rise, Carril of other times; carry my words to Swaran. Tell him from the roaring of waters, that Cuthullin gives his feast. Here let him

listen to the sound of my groves, amidst the clouds of night, for cold and bleak the blustering winds rush over the foam of his seas. Here let him praise the trembling harp, and hear the songs of heroes!''

Old Carril went, with softest voice. He called the king of dark-brown shields! "Rise from the skins of thy chase; rise, Swaran, king of groves! Cuthullin gives the joy of shells. Partake the feast of Erin's blue-eyed chief!'' He answered like the sullen sound of Cromla before a storm. "Though all thy daughters, Inisfail! should stretch their arms of snow; should raise the heavings of their breasts, and softly roll their eyes of love; yet, fixed as Lochlin's thousand rocks, here Swaran should remain, till morn, with the young beams of the east, shall light me to the death of Cuthullin. Pleasant to my ear is Lochlin's wind! It rushes over my seas! It speaks aloft in all my shrouds, and brings my green forests to my mind: the green forests of Gormal, which often echoed to my winds, when my spear was red in the chase of the boar. Let dark Cuthullin yield to me the ancient throne of Cormac, or Erin's torrents shall show from their hills the red foam of the blood of his pride!''

"Sad is the sound of Swaran's voice," said Carril of other times! "Sad to himself alone,'' said the blue-eyed son of Semo. "But, Carril, raise the voice on high; tell the deeds of other times. Send thou the night away in song; and give the joy of grief. For many heroes and maids of love, have moved on Inis-fail, and lovely are the songs of woe that are heard in Albion's rocks, when the noise of the chase is past, and the streams of Coma answer to the voice of Ossian.''

"In other days,'' Carril replies, "came the sons of Ocean to Erin; a thousand vessels bounded on waves to Ullin's lovely plains. The sons of Inis-fail arose to meet the race of dark-brown shields. Cairbar, first of men, was there, and Grudar, stately youth! Long had they strove for the spotted bull, that lowed on Golbun's echoing heath. Each claimed him as his own. Death was often at the point of their steel! Side by side the heroes fought; the strangers of Ocean fled. Whose name was fairer on the hill, than the name of Cairbar and Grudar! But ah! why ever lowed the bull, on Golbun's echoing heath. They saw him leaping like snow. The wrath of the chiefs returned!

"On Lubar's grassy banks they fought; Grudar fell in his blood. Fierce Cairbar came to the vale, where Brassolis, fairest of his sisters, all alone, raised the song of grief. She sung of the actions of Grudar, the youth of her secret soul! She mourned him in the field of blood, but still she hoped for his return. Her white bosom is seen from her robe, as the moon from the clouds of night, when its edge heaves white on the view, from the darkness which covers its orb. Her voice was softer than the harp to raise the song of grief. Her soul was fixed on Grudar. The secret look of her eye was his. 'When shalt thou come in thine arms, thou mighty in the war?'

"'Take, Brassolis,' Cairbar came and said, 'take, Brassolis, this shield of blood. Fix it on high within my hall, the armor of my foe!' Her soft heart beat against her side. Distracted, pale, she flew. She found her youth in all his blood; she died on Cromla's heath. Here rests their dust, Cuthullin! these lonely yews sprung from their tombs, and shade them from the storm. Fair was Brassolis on the plain! Stately was Grudar on the hill! The bard shall preserve their names, and send them down to future times!"

"Pleasant is thy voice, O Carril," said the blue-eyed chief of Erin. "Pleasant are the words of other times! They are like the calm shower of spring, when the sun looks on the field, and the light cloud flies over the hills. O strike the harp in praise of my love, the lonely sunbeam of Dunscaith! Strike the harp in the praise of Bragéla, she that I left in the isle of mist, the spouse of Semo's son! Dost thou raise thy fair face from the rock to find the sails of Cuthullin? The sea is rolling distant far; its white foam deceives thee for my sails. Retire, for it is night, my love; the dark winds sing in thy hair. Retire to the halls of my feasts; think of the times that are past. I will not return till the storm of war is ceased. O Connal! speak of war and arms, and send her from my mind. Lovely with her flowing hair is the white-bosomed daughter of Sorglan."

Connal, slow to speak, replied, "Guard against the race of Ocean. Send thy troop of night abroad, and watch the strength of Swaran. Cuthullin! I am for peace till the race of Selma come,

till Fingal come, the first of men, and beam, like the sun, on our fields!" The hero struck the shield of alarms, the warriors of the night moved on! The rest lay in the heath of the deer, and slept beneath the dusky wind. The ghosts of the lately dead were near,[1] and swam on the gloomy clouds. And far distant, in the dark silence of Lena, the feeble voices of death were faintly heard.

Richard Hurd 1720-1808

From LETTERS ON CHIVALRY AND ROMANCE

1762   *1762*

LETTER I

The ages we call barbarous present us with many a subject of curious speculation. What, for instance, is more remarkable than the Gothic chivalry? or than the spirit of romance, which took its rise from that singular institution?

Nothing in human nature, my dear friend, is without its reasons. The modes and fashions of different times may appear, at first sight, fantastic and unaccountable. But they who look nearly into them discover some latent cause of their production.

Nature once known, no prodigies remain,[3]

as sings our philosophical bard; but to come at this knowledge is the difficulty. Sometimes a close attention to the workings of the human mind is sufficient to lead us to it. Sometimes more than that, the diligent observation of what passes without us, is necessary.

This last I take to be the case here. The prodigies[2] we are now contemplating had their origin in the barbarous ages. Why, then, says the fastidious modern, look any farther for the reason? Why not resolve them at once into the usual caprice and absurdity of barbarians?

This, you see, is a short and commodious philosophy. Yet barbarians have their own, such as it is, if they are not enlightened by our reason. Shall we then condemn them unheard, or will it not be fair to let them have the telling of their own story?

Would we know from what causes the

---

[1] "It was long the opinion of the ancient Scots that a ghost was heard shrieking near the place where a death was to happen soon after."—Macpherson.
[2] Pope, *Moral Essays*, Epistle 1, 208.
[3] Modes and fashions of medieval chivalry.

institution of chivalry was derived? The time of its birth, the situation of the barbarians, amongst whom it arose, must be considered. Their wants, designs, and policies must be explored. We must in-quire when and where and how it came to pass that the western world became familiarized to this prodigy, which we now start at.

Another thing is full as remarkable, and concerns us more nearly. The spirit of chivalry was a fire which soon spent itself; but that of romance, which was kindled at it, burnt long, and continued its light and heat even to the politer ages. The greatest geniuses of our own and foreign countries, such as Ariosto and Tasso in Italy, and Spenser and Milton in England, were seduced by these bar-barities of their forefathers, were even charmed by the Gothic romances.[1] Was this caprice and absurdity in them? Or, may there not be something in the Gothic romance peculiarly suited to the views of a genius, and to the ends of poetry? And may not the philosophic moderns have gone too far, in their perpetual ridi-cule and contempt of it?

To form a judgment in the case, the rise, progress, and genius of Gothic chiv-alry must be explained.

The circumstances in the Gothic fictions and manners, which are proper to the ends of poetry (if any such there be) must be pointed out.

Reasons for the decline and rejection of the Gothic taste in later times must be given.

You have in these particulars both the subject and the plan of the following Letters.

LETTER VI

Let it be no surprise to you that, in the close of my last Letter, I presumed to bring the *Gierusalemme Liberata* into com-petition with the *Iliad*.

So far as the heroic and Gothic man-ners are the same, the pictures of each, if well taken, must be equally entertain-ing. But I go further, and maintain that the circumstances in which they differ are clearly to the advantage of the Gothic designers.

You see, my purpose is to lead you from this forgotten chivalry to a more amusing subject; I mean the poetry we still read, and which was founded upon it.

[1] Medieval romances of chivalry.

Much has been said, and with great truth, of the felicity of Homer's age, for poetical manners. But as Homer was a citizen of the world, when he had seen in Greece, on the one hand, the manners he has described, could he, on the other hand, have seen in the west the manners of the feudal ages, I make no doubt but he would certainly have preferred the lat-ter. And the grounds of this preference would, I suppose, have been the improved gallantry of the feudal times and the superior solemnity of their superstitions.

If any great poet, like Homer, had lived amongst, and sung of, the Gothic knights (for after all, Spenser and Tasso came too late, and it was impossible for them to paint truly and perfectly what was no longer seen or believed) this preference, I persuade myself, had been very sensible. But their fortune was not so happy.

—omnes illacrymabiles
Urgentur, ignotique longâ
Nocte, carent quia vate sacro.[1]

As it is, we may take a guess of what the subject was capable of affording to real genius from the rude sketches we have of it in the old romancers. And it is but looking into any of them to be con-vinced that the gallantry which inspirited the feudal times was of a nature to fur-nish the poet with finer scenes and sub-jects of description in every view, than the simple and uncontrolled barbarity of the Grecian.

The principal entertainment arising from the delineation of these consists in the exercise of the boisterous passions, which are provoked and kept alive from one end of the *Iliad* to the other, by every imaginable scene of rage, revenge, and slaughter. In the other, together with these, the gentler and more humane affec-tions are awakened in us by the most interesting displays of love and friend-ship; of love, elevated to its noblest heights; and of friendship, operating on the purest motives. The mere variety of these paintings is a relief to the reader, as well as writer. But their beauty, nov-elty, and pathos give them a vast advan-tage on the comparison.

Consider, withal, the surprises, acci-dents, adventures which probably and naturally attend on the life of wandering knights; the occasion there must be for

[1] All are overwhelmed with the long night of death, unwept and unknown because they lack a sacred bard.—Horace, *Odes*, IV, 9, 26 ff.

describing the wonders of different countries, and of presenting to view the manners and policies of distant states: all which make so conspicuous a part of the materials of the greater poetry.

So that, on the whole, though the spirit, passions, rapine, and violence of the two sets of manners were equal, yet there was a dignity, a magnificence, a variety in the feudal, which the other wanted.

As to religious machinery, perhaps the popular system of each was equally remote from reason, yet the latter had something in it more amusing, as well as more awakening to the imagination.

The current popular tales of elves and fairies were even fitter to take the credulous mind, and charm it into a willing admiration of the specious miracles, which wayward fancy delights in, than those of the old traditionary rabble of pagan divinities. And then, for the more solemn fancies of witchcraft and incantation, the horrors of the Gothic were above measure striking and terrible. The mummeries of the pagan priests were childish, but the Gothic enchanters shook and alarmed all nature.

We feel this difference very sensibly in reading the ancient and modern poets. You would not compare the Canidia of Horace with the Witches in *Macbeth*. And what are Virgil's myrtles dropping blood,[1] to Tasso's enchanted forest?[2]

Ovid indeed, who had a fancy turned to romance, makes Medea, in a rant, talk wildly. But was this the common language of their other writers? The enchantress in Virgil says coolly of the very chiefest prodigies of her charms and poisons,

His ego sæpè lupum fieri, & se condere sylvis
Mœrin; sæpè animas imis excire sepulchris,
Atque satas alio vidi traducere messes.[3]

The admirable poet has given an air of the marvellous to his subject, by the magic of his expression. Else, what do we find here, but the ordinary effects of melancholy, the vulgar superstition of evoking spirits, and the supposed influence of fascination on the hopes of rural industry.

Non isthic obliquo oculo mihi commoda quisquam
Limat[1] . . .

says the poet of his country-seat, as if this security from a fascinating eye were a singular privilege, and the mark of a more than common good fortune.

Shakespear, on the other hand, with a terrible sublime (which not so much the energy of his genius, as the nature of his subject drew from him) gives us another idea of the rough magic, as he calls it, of fairy enchantment.

I have bedimm'd
The noon-tide sun, call'd forth the mutinous winds,
And 'twixt the green sea and the azure vault
Set roaring war; to the dread rattling thunder
Have I giv'n fire, and rifted Jove's stout oak
With his own bolt. The strong-bas'd promontory
Have I made shake, and by the spurs pluck'd up
The pine and cedar. Graves, at my command,
Have open'd, and let forth their sleepers.[2]

The last circumstance, you will say, is but the *animas imis excire sepulchris*[3] of the Latin poet. But a very significant word marks the difference. The pagan necromancers had a hundred little tricks by which they pretended to call up the ghosts, or shadows of the dead; but these, in the ideas of paganism, were quite another thing from Shakespear's sleepers.

This may serve for a cast of Shakespear's magic. And I can't but think that, when Milton wanted to paint the horrors of that night (one of the noblest parts in his *Paradise Regained*) which the Devil himself is feigned to conjure up in the wilderness, the Gothic language and ideas helped him to work up his tempest with such terror. You will judge from these lines:

Nor staid the terror there:
Infernal ghosts and hellish furies round
Environ'd thee; some howl'd, some yell'd, some shriek'd,
Some bent at thee their fiery darts.[4]

But above all from the following,

Thus pass'd the night so foul, till morning fair
Came forth with pilgrim steps in amice[5] gray,
Who with her *radiant finger* still'd the roar
Of thunder, chas'd the clouds, and laid the winds
And *griesly specters*.[6]

Where the *radiant finger* points at the potent wand of the Gothic magicians, which could reduce the calm of nature, upon occasion, as well as disturb it; and the *griesly specters laid* by the approach

---

[1] *Æneid*, 3, 23 ff.
[2] *Jerusalem Delivered*, 13, st. 43 ff.
[3] Often I have seen Moeris become a wolf, and hide himself in the forest, and often I have seen him call forth souls from the depths of the tomb, and I have seen him remove crops from one place to another.—*Eclogues*, 8, 97 ff.

[1] No one here lessens, with an envious look, my advantages. — H o r a c e, *Epistles*, I, 14, 27.
[2] *The Tempest*, V, 1, 41 ff.
[3] Virgil, quoted above.
[4] *Paradise Regained*, 4, 421 ff.
[5] A kind of hooded cloak lined with fur.
[6] *Paradise Regained*, 4, 426 ff.

of morn, were apparently of their raising, as a sagacious critic perceived when he took notice "how very injudicious it was to retail the popular superstition in this place."

After all, the conclusion is not to be drawn so much from particular passages, as from the general impression left on our minds in reading the ancient and modern poets. And this is so much in favor of the latter that Mr. Addison scruples not to say, "The ancients have not much of this poetry among them; for, indeed, almost the whole substance of it owes its original to the darkness and superstition of later ages—Our forefathers looked upon nature with more reverence and horror, before the world was enlightened by learning and philosophy, and loved to astonish themselves with the apprehensions of Witchcraft, Prodigies, Charms, and Inchantments. There was not a village in England, that had not a Ghost in it; the churchyards were all haunted; every large common had a circle of fairies belonging to it; and there was scarce a Shepherd to be met with who had not seen a spirit."

We are upon enchanted ground, my friend; and you are to think yourself well used that I detain you no longer in this fearful circle. The glimpse you have had of it will help your imagination to conceive the rest. And without more words you will readily apprehend that the fancies of our modern bards are not only more gallant, but, on a change of the scene, more sublime, more terrible, more alarming, than those of the classic fablers. In a word, you will find that the manners they paint, and the superstitions they adopt, are the more poetical for being Gothic.

Horace Walpole 1717-1797

From THE CASTLE OF OTRANTO
1764
CHAPTER I

Manfred, Prince of Otranto, had one son and one daughter. The latter, a most beautiful virgin aged eighteen, was called Matilda. Conrad, the son, was three years younger, a homely youth, sickly, and of no promising disposition; yet he was the darling of his father, who never showed any symptoms of affection to Matilda. Manfred had contracted a marriage for his son with the Marquis of Vicenza's daughter, Isabella; and she had already

been delivered by her guardians into the hands of Manfred that he might celebrate the wedding as soon as Conrad's infirm state of health would permit. Manfred's impatience for this ceremonial was remarked by his family and neighbors. The former indeed, apprehending the severity of their Prince's disposition, did not dare to utter their surmises on this precipitation. Hippolita, his wife, an amiable lady, did sometimes venture to represent the danger of marrying their only son so early, considering his great youth and greater infirmities; but she never received any other answer than reflections on her own sterility, who had given him but one heir. His tenants and subjects were less cautious in their discourses. They attributed this hasty wedding to the Prince's dread of seeing accomplished an ancient prophecy, which was said to have pronounced that the castle and lordship of Otranto should pass from the present family whenever the real owner should be grown too large to inhabit it. It was difficult to make any sense of this prophecy; and still less easy to conceive what it had to do with the marriage in question. Yet these mysteries or contradictions did not make the populace adhere the less to their opinion.

Young Conrad's birthday was fixed for his espousals. The company was assembled in the chapel of the castle, and everything ready for beginning the divine office, when Conrad himself was missing. Manfred, impatient of the least delay, and who had not observed his son retire, dispatched one of his attendants to summon the young prince. The servant, who had not staid long enough to have crossed the court to Conrad's apartment, came running back breathless, in a frantic manner, his eyes staring, and foaming at the mouth. He said nothing, but pointed to the court. The company were struck with terror and amazement. The Princess Hippolita, without knowing what was the matter, but anxious for her son, swooned away. Manfred, less apprehensive than enraged at the procrastination of the nuptials, and at the folly of his domestic, asked imperiously what was the matter. The fellow made no answer, but continued pointing towards the court-yard; and at last, after repeated questions put to him, cried out, "Oh! the helmet! the helmet!" In the meantime, some of the company had run into the court, from whence was heard a confused noise of shrieks, horror, and surprise. Manfred, who began to be alarmed at not seeing his son, went himself to get information of what occasioned this strange confusion. Matilda remained endeavoring to assist her mother, and Isabella staid for the same purpose and to avoid showing any impatience for the bridegroom, for whom, in truth, she had conceived little affection.

The first thing that struck Manfred's eyes was a group of his servants endeavoring to raise something that appeared to him a mountain of sable plumes. He gazed without believing his sight. "What are ye doing?" cried Manfred, wrathfully. "Where is my son?" A volley of voices replied, "Oh! my lord! the prince! the prince! the helmet! the helmet!" Shocked with these lamentable sounds, and dreading he knew not what, he advanced hastily, but with a sight for a father's eyes! He beheld his child dashed to pieces and almost buried under an enormous helmet, an hundred times more large than any casque ever made for human being, and shaded with a proportionable quantity of black feathers.

The horror of the spectacle, the ignorance of all around how this misfortune had happened, and above all, the tremendous phenomenon before him, took away the Prince's speech. Yet his silence lasted longer than even grief could occasion. He fixed his eyes on what he wished in vain to believe a vision; and seemed less attentive to his loss than buried in meditation on the stupendous object that had occasioned it. He touched, he examined the fatal casque; nor could even the bleeding mangled remains of the young Prince divert the eyes of Manfred from the portent before him. All who had known his partial fondness for young Conrad were as much surprised at their Prince's insensibility, as thunder-struck themselves at the miracle of the helmet. They conveyed the disfigured corpse into the hall, without receiving the least direction from Manfred. As little was he attentive to the ladies who remained in the chapel. On the contrary, without mentioning the unhappy princesses, his wife and daughter, the first sounds that dropped from Manfred's lips were, "Take care of the Lady Isabella."

The domestics, without observing the singularity of this direction, were guided by their affection to their mistress to consider it as peculiarly addressed to her

situation, and flew to her assistance. They conveyed her to her chamber more dead than alive, and indifferent to all the strange circumstances she heard except the death of her son. Matilda, who doted on her mother, smothered her own grief and amazement, and thought of nothing but assisting and comforting her afflicted parents. Isabella, who had been treated by Hippolita like a daughter, and who returned that tenderness with equal duty and affection, was scarce less assiduous about the Princess, at the same time endeavoring to partake and lessen the weight of sorrow which she saw Matilda strove to suppress, for whom she had conceived the warmest sympathy of friendship. Yet her own situation could not help finding its place in her thoughts. She felt no concern for the death of young Conrad, except commiseration; and she was not sorry to be delivered from a marriage which had promised her little felicity, either from her destined bridegroom or from the severe temper of Manfred, who, though he had distinguished her by great indulgence, had imprinted her mind with terror, from his causeless rigor to such amiable princesses as Hippolita and Matilda.

While the ladies were conveying the wretched mother to her bed, Manfred remained in the court, gazing on the ominous casque, and regardless of the crowd which the strangeness of the event had now assembled around him. The few words he articulated tended solely to inquiries whether any man knew from whence it could have come. Nobody could give him the least information. However, as it seemed to be the sole object of his curiosity, it soon became so to the rest of the spectators, whose conjectures were as absurd and improbable as the catastrophe itself was unprecedented. In the midst of their senseless guesses, a young peasant, whom rumor had drawn thither from a neighboring village, observed that the miraculous helmet was exactly like that on the figure in black marble of Alfonso the Good, one of their former princes in the church of St. Nicholas. "Villain! What sayest thou?" cried Manfred, starting from his trance in a tempest of rage, and seizing the young man by the collar. "How darest thou utter such treason? Thy life shall pay for it." The spectators, who as little comprehended the cause of the Prince's fury as all the rest they had seen, were at a loss to unravel this new circumstance. The young peasant himself was still more astonished, not conceiving how he had offended the Prince; yet recollecting himself, with a mixture of grace and humility, he disengaged himself from Manfred's gripe, and then with an obeisance which discovered more jealousy of innocence than dismay, he asked, with respect, of what he was guilty. Manfred, more enraged at the vigor, however decently exerted, with which the young man had shaken off his hold, than appeared by his submission, ordered his attendants to seize him, and if he had not been withheld by his friends, whom he had invited to the nuptials, would have poignarded the peasant in their arms.

During this altercation, some of the vulgar spectators had run to the great church, which stood near the castle, and came back open-mouthed, declaring that the helmet was missing from Alfonso's statue. Manfred, at this news, grew perfectly frantic; and, as if he sought a subject on which to vent the tempest within him, he rushed again on the young peasant crying, "Villain! Monster! Sorcerer! 'Tis thou hast done this! 'Tis thou hast slain my son!" The mob, who wanted some object within the scope of their capacities on whom they might discharge their bewildered reasonings, caught the words from the mouth of their lord and reëchoed, "Ay, ay; 'tis he; 'tis he; he has stolen the helmet from good Alfonso's tomb and dashed out the brains of our young Prince with it," never reflecting how enormous the disproportion was between the marble helmet that had been in the church and that of steel before their eyes, nor how impossible it was for a youth, seemingly not twenty, to wield a piece of armor of so prodigious a weight.

The folly of these ejaculations brought Manfred to himself. Yet whether provoked at the peasant having observed the resemblance between the two helmets, and thereby led to the farther discovery of the absence of that in the church, or wishing to bury any fresh rumors under so impertinent a supposition, he gravely pronounced that the young man was certainly a necromancer, and that till the church could take cognizance of the affair, he would have the magician, whom they had thus detected, kept prisoner under the helmet itself, which he ordered his attendants to raise and place the young man under it, declaring he should be kept there without food, with which his own infernal art might furnish him.

It was in vain for the youth to represent against this preposterous sentence. In vain did Manfred's friends endeavor to divert him from this savage and illgrounded resolution. The generality were charmed with their lord's decision, which, to their apprehensions, carried great appearance of justice, as the magician was to be punished by the very instrument with which he had offended. Nor were they struck with the least compunction at the probability of the youth being starved, for they firmly believed that by his diabolic skill he could easily supply himself with nutriment.

Manfred thus saw his commands even cheerfully obeyed; and appointing a guard with strict orders to prevent any food being conveyed to the prisoner, he dismissed his friends and attendants, and retired to his own chamber after locking the gates of the castle, in which he suffered none but his domestics to remain.

In the meantime, the care and zeal of the young ladies had brought the Princess Hippolita to herself, who amidst the transports of her own sorrow frequently demanded news of her lord, would have dismissed her attendants to watch over him, and at last enjoined Matilda to leave her and visit and comfort her father. Matilda, who wanted no affectionate duty to Manfred though she trembled at his austerity, obeyed the orders of Hippolata, whom she tenderly recommended to Isabella; and enquiring of the domestics for her father, was informed that he was retired to his chamber and had commanded that nobody should have admittance to him. Concluding that he was immersed in sorrow for the death of her brother, and fearing to renew his tears by the sight of his sole remaining child, she hesitated whether she should break in upon his affliction. Yet, solicitude for him, backed by the commands of her mother, encouraged her to venture disobeying the orders he had given, a fault she had never been guilty of before. The gentle timidity of her nature made her pause for some minutes at the door. She heard him traverse his chamber backwards and forwards with disordered steps, a mood which increased her apprehensions. She was, however, just going to beg admittance when Manfred suddenly opened his door; and as it was now twilight, concurring with the disorder of his mind, he did not distinguish the person, but asked angrily who it was. Matilda replied trembling, "My dearest father, it is I, your daughter." Manfred stepping back hastily, cried, "Begone! I do not want a daughter," and flinging back abruptly, clapped the door against the terrified Matilda.

She was too well acquainted with her father's impetuosity to venture a second intrusion. When she had a little recovered the shock of so bitter a reception, she wiped away her tears to prevent the additional stab that the knowledge of it would give to Hippolita, who questioned her in the most anxious terms on the health of Manfred and how he bore his loss. Matilda assured her he was well and supported his misfortune with manly fortitude. "But will he not let me see him?" said Hippolita mournfully; "will he not permit me to blend my tears with his and shed a mother's sorrows in the bosom of her lord? Or do you deceive me, Matilda? I know how Manfred doted on his son. Is not the stroke too heavy for him? Has he not sunk under it? You do not answer me. Alas! I dread the worst! Raise me, my maidens; I will, I will see my lord. Bear me to him instantly. He is dearer to me even than my children." Matilda made signs to Isabella to prevent Hippolita's rising; and both those lovely young women were using their gentle violence to stop and calm the Princess, when a servant, on the part of Manfred, arrived and told Isabella that his lord demanded to speak with her.

"With me!" cried Isabella. "Go!" said Hippolita, relieved by a message from her lord; "Manfred cannot support the sight of his own family. He thinks you less disordered than we are, and dreads the shock of my grief. Console him, dear Isabella, and tell him I will smother my own anguish rather than add to his."

As it was now evening, the servant who conducted Isabella bore a torch before her. When they came to Manfred, who was walking impatiently about the gallery, he started and said hastily: "Take away that light, and begone!" Then shutting the door impetuously, he flung himself upon a bench against the wall, and bade Isabella sit by him. She obeyed trembling. "I sent for you lady," said he, and then stopped under great appearance of confusion. "My lord!" "Yes, I sent for

you on a matter of great moment," resumed he. "Dry your tears, young lady. You have lost your bridegroom. Yes, cruel fate! and I have lost the hopes of my race! But Conrad was not worthy of your beauty." "How! my lord," said Isabella. "Sure you do not suspect me of not feeling the concern I ought! My duty and affection would have always"— "Think no more of him," interrupted Manfred; "he was a sickly puny child; and heaven has perhaps taken him away that I might not trust the honors of my house on so frail a foundation. The line of Manfred calls for numerous supports. My foolish fondness for that boy blinded the eyes of my prudence; but it is better as it is. I hope in a few years to have reason to rejoice at the death of Conrad."

Words cannot paint the astonishment of Isabella. At first, she apprehended that grief had disordered Manfred's understanding. Her next thought suggested that this strange discourse was designed to ensnare her. She feared that Manfred had perceived her indifference for his son; and in consequence of that idea she replied: "Good my lord, do not doubt my tenderness. My heart would have accompanied my hand. Conrad would have engrossed all my care; and wherever fate shall dispose of me, I shall always cherish his memory, and regard your highness and the virtuous Hippolita as my parents." "Curse on Hippolita!" cried Manfred. "Forget her from this moment, as I do. In short, lady, you have missed a husband undeserving of your charms. They shall now be better disposed of. Instead of a sickly boy, you shall have a husband in the prime of his age, who will know how to value your beauties, and who may expect a numerous offspring." "Alas! my lord," said Isabella; "my mind is too sadly engrossed by the recent catastrophe in your family to think of another marriage. If ever my father returns, and it shall be his pleasure, I shall obey, as I did when I consented to give my hand to your son. But until his return, permit me to remain under your hospitable roof, and employ the melancholy hours in assuaging yours, Hippolita's and the fair Matilda's affliction."

"I desired you once before," said Manfred, angrily, "not to name that woman. From this hour she must be a stranger to you as she must be to me. In short, Isabella, since I cannot give you my son,

I offer you myself.'' ''Heavens!'' cried Isabella, waking from her delusion; ''what do I hear? You! my lord! you! my father-in-law! the father of Conrad! the husband of the virtuous Hippolita!'' ''I tell you,'' said Manfred, imperiously, ''Hippolita is no longer my wife; I divorce her from this hour. Too long has she cursed me by her unfruitfulness. My fate depends on having sons; and this night I trust will give a new date to my hopes.'' At those words he seized the cold hand of Isabella, who was half dead with fright and horror. She shrieked and started from him. Manfred rose to pursue her, when the moon, which was now up and gleamed in at the opposite casement, presented to his sight the plumes of the fatal helmet, which rose to the height of the windows, waving backwards and forwards, in a tempestuous manner, and accompanied with a hollow and rustling sound. Isabella, who gathered courage from her situation, and who dreaded nothing so much as Manfred's pursuit of his declaration, cried: ''Look! my lord. See! heaven itself declares against your impious intentions.'' ''Heaven nor hell shall impede my designs,'' said Manfred, advancing again to seize the Princess. At that instant the portrait of his grandfather, which hung over the bench where they had been sitting, uttered a deep sigh and heaved its breast. Isabella, whose back was turned to the picture, saw not the motion, nor knew whence the sound came, but started, and said: ''Hark! my lord! What sound was that?'' and at the same time made towards the door. Manfred, distracted between the flight of Isabella, who had now reached the stairs, and yet unable to keep his eyes from the picture, which began to move, had, however, advanced some steps after her, still looking backwards on the portrait, when he saw it quit its panel and descend on the floor with a grave and melancholy air. ''Do I dream?'' cried Manfred, returning; ''or are the devils themselves in league against me? Speak, infernal spectre! Or, if thou art my grandsire, why dost thou too conspire against thy wretched descendant, who too dearly pays for—'' Ere he could finish the sentence, the vision sighed again, and made a sign to Manfred to follow him. ''Lead on!'' cried Manfred; ''I will follow thee to the gulf of perdition.'' The spectre marched sedately, but dejected, to the end of the gallery and turned into a chamber on the right-hand. Manfred accompanied him at a little distance, full of anxiety and horror, but resolved. As he would have entered the chamber, the door was clapped to with violence by an invisible hand. The Prince, collecting courage from this delay, would have forcibly burst open the door with his foot, but found that it resisted his utmost efforts. ''Since hell will not satisfy my curiosity,'' said Manfred, ''I will use the human means in my power for preserving my race; Isabella shall not escape me.''

That lady, whose resolution had given way to terror the moment she had quitted Manfred, continued her flight to the bottom of the principal staircase. There she stopped, not knowing whither to direct her steps, nor how to escape from the impetuosity of the Prince. The gates of the castle she knew were locked, and guards placed in the court. Should she, as her heart prompted her, go and prepare Hippolita for the cruel destiny that awaited her, she did not doubt but Manfred would seek her there, and that his violence would incite him to double the injury he meditated, without leaving room for them to avoid the impetuosity of his passions. Delay might give him time to reflect on the horrid measures he had conceived, or produce some circumstance in her favor if she could, for that night at least, avoid his odious purpose. Yet, where conceal herself? How avoid the pursuit he would infallibly make throughout the castle? As these thoughts passed rapidly through her mind, she recollected a subterraneous passage which led from the vaults of the castle to the church of St. Nicholas. Could she reach the altar before she was overtaken, she knew even Manfred's violence would not dare to profane the sacredness of the place; and she determined, if no other means of deliverance offered, to shut herself up forever among the holy virgins, whose convent was contiguous to the cathedral. In this resolution, she seized a lamp that burned at the foot of the staircase, and hurried towards the secret passage.

The lower part of the castle was hollowed into several intricate cloisters; and it was not easy for one under so much anxiety to find the door that opened into the cavern. An awful silence reigned throughout those subterraneous regions, except now and then some blasts of wind that shook the doors she had passed, and which, grating on the rusty hinges, were reëchoed through that long labyrinth of darkness. Every murmur struck her with new terror; yet, more she dreaded to hear the wrathful voice of Manfred urging his domestics to pursue her. She trod as softly as impatience would give her leave; yet frequently stopped and listened to hear if she was followed. In one of those moments she thought she heard a sigh. She shuddered, and recoiled a few paces. In a moment she thought she heard the step of some person. Her blood curdled: she concluded it was Manfred. Every suggestion that horror could inspire rushed into her mind. She condemned her rash flight, which had thus exposed her to his rage in a place where her cries were not likely to draw anybody to her assistance. Yet, the sound seemed not to come from behind,—if Manfred knew where she was, he must have followed her. She was still in one of the cloisters, and the steps she heard were too distinct to proceed from the way she had come. Cheered with this reflection, and hoping to find a friend in whoever was not the Prince, she was going to advance, when a door that stood ajar at some distance to the left was opened gently. But ere her lamp, which she held up, could discover who opened it, the person retreated precipitately on seeing the light.

Isabella, whom every incident was sufficient to dismay, hesitated whether she should proceed. Her dread of Manfred soon outweighed every other terror. The very circumstance of the person avoiding her gave her a sort of courage. It could only be, she thought, some domestic belonging to the castle. Her gentleness had never raised her an enemy, and conscious innocence bade her hope that, unless sent by the Prince's order to seek her, his servants would rather assist than prevent her flight. Fortifying herself with these reflections, and believing by what she could observe that she was near the mouth of the subterraneous cavern, she approached the door that had been opened; but a sudden gust of wind that met her at the door extinguished her lamp and left her in total darkness.

Words cannot paint the horror of the Princess's situation. Alone in so dismal a place, her mind imprinted with all the terrible events of the day, hopeless of escaping, expecting every moment the arrival of Manfred, and far from tranquil on knowing she was within reach of somebody, she knew not whom, who for some cause seemed concealed thereabouts,—all these thoughts crowded on her distracted mind, and she was ready to sink under her apprehensions. She addressed herself to every saint in heaven, and inwardly implored their assistance. For a considerable time she remained in an agony of despair. At last, as softly as was possible, she felt for the door, and having found it, entered trembling into the vault from whence she had heard the sigh and steps. It gave her a kind of momentary joy to perceive an imperfect ray of clouded moonshine gleam from the roof of the vault, which seemed to be fallen in, and from whence hung a fragment of earth or building, she could not distinguish which, that appeared to have been crushed inwards. She advanced eagerly towards this chasm, when she discerned a human form standing close against the wall.

She shrieked, believing it the ghost of her betrothed Conrad. The figure advancing said in a submissive voice: "Be not alarmed, lady; I will not injure you." Isabella, a little encouraged by the words and tone of voice of the stranger, and recollecting that this must be the person who had opened the door, recovered her spirits enough to reply: "Sir, whoever you are, take pity on a wretched princess standing on the brink of destruction. Assist me to escape from this fatal castle, or in a few moments I may be made miserable forever." "Alas!" said the stranger, "what can I do to assist you? I will die in your defence; but I am unacquainted with the castle, and want—" "Oh!" said Isabella, hastily interrupting him, "help me but to find a trap-door that must be hereabout, and it is the greatest service you can do me, for I have not a minute to lose." Saying these words, she felt about on the pavement, and directed the stranger to search likewise for a smooth piece of brass inclosed in one of the stones. "That," said she, "is the lock, which opens with a spring, of which I know the secret. If we can find that, I may escape; if not, alas! courteous stranger, I fear I shall have involved you in my misfortunes. Manfred will suspect you for the accomplice of my flight, and you will fall a victim to his resentment." "I value not my life," said the stranger; "and it will be some comfort to lose it in trying to deliver you from his tyranny."

"Generous youth," said Isabella, "how shall I ever requite—" As she uttered those words, a ray of moonshine streaming through a cranny of the ruin above shone directly on the lock they sought. "Oh! transport!" said Isabella, "here is the trap-door!" And taking out a key, she touched the spring, which starting aside discovered an iron ring. "Lift up the door," said the Princess. The stranger obeyed; and beneath appeared some stone steps descending into a vault totally dark. "We must go down here," said Isabella. "Follow me. Dark and dismal as it is, we cannot miss our way; it leads directly to the church of St. Nicholas. But perhaps," added the Princess, modestly, "you have no reason to leave the castle; nor have I farther occasion for your service. In few minutes I shall be safe from Manfred's rage. Only let me know to whom I am so much obliged." "I will never quit you," said the stranger eagerly, "until I have placed you in safety. Nor think me, Princess, more generous than I am. Though you are my principal care—" The stranger was interrupted by a sudden noise of voices that seemed approaching, and they soon distinguished these words: "Talk not to me of necromancers. I tell you she must be in the castle. I will find her in spite of enchantment." "Oh, heavens!" cried Isabella, "it is the voice of Manfred! Make haste or we are ruined! And shut the trap-door after you." Saying this, she descended the steps precipitately, and as the stranger hastened to follow her he let the door slip out of his hands. It fell, and the spring closed over it. He tried in vain to open it, not having observed Isabella's method of touching the spring; nor had he many moments to make an essay. The noise of the falling door had been heard by Manfred, who directed by the sound, hastened thither, attended by his servants with torches. "It must be Isabella," cried Manfred before he entered the vault; "she is escaping by the subterraneous passage, but she cannot have got far." What was the astonishment of the Prince when, instead of Isabella, the light of the torches discovered to him the young peasant whom he thought confined under the fatal helmet. "Traitor!" said Manfred; "how camest thou here? I thought thee in durance above in the court." "I am no traitor," replied the young man boldly;

"nor am I answerable for your thoughts." "Presumptuous villain!" cried Manfred; "dost thou provoke my wrath? Tell me: How hast thou escaped from above? Thou hast corrupted thy guards, and their lives shall answer it." "My poverty," said the peasant calmly, "will disculpate them. Though the ministers of a tyrant's wrath, to thee they are faithful and but too willing to execute the orders which you unjustly imposed upon them." "Art thou so hardy as to dare my vengeance?" said the Prince. "But tortures shall force the truth from thee. Tell me; I will know thy accomplices." "There was my accomplice," said the youth, smiling, and pointing to the roof. Manfred ordered the torches to be held up, and perceived that one of the cheeks of the enchanted casque had forced its way through the pavement of the court as his servants had let it fall over the peasant, and had broken through into the vault, leaving a gap through which the peasant had pressed himself some minutes before he was found by Isabella. "Was that the way by which thou didst descend?" said Manfred. "It was," said the youth. "But what noise was that," said Manfred, "which I heard as I entered the cloister?" "A door clapped," said the peasant; "I heard it as well as you." "What door?" said Manfred hastily. "I am not acquainted with your castle," said the peasant; "this is the first time I ever entered it, and this vault the only part of it within which I ever was." "But I tell thee," said Manfred, wishing to find out if the youth had discovered the trap-door, "it was this way I heard the noise; my servants heard it too—" "My lord," interrupted one of them officiously, "to be sure it was the trap-door, and he was going to make his escape." "Peace! blockhead," said the Prince angrily; "if he was going to escape, how should he come on this side? I will know from his own mouth what noise it was I heard. Tell me truly; thy life depends on thy veracity." "My veracity is dearer to me than my life," said the peasant; "nor would I purchase the one by forfeiting the other." "Indeed! young philosopher!" said Manfred contemptuously. "Tell me then: What was the noise I heard?" "Ask me what I can answer," said he; "and put me to death instantly if I tell you a lie." Manfred, growing impatient at the steady valor and indifference of the youth, cried:

"Well then, thou man of truth! answer. Was it the fall of the trap-door that I heard?" "It was," said the youth. "It was!" said the Prince; "and how didst thou come to know there was a trap-door here?" "I saw the plate of brass by a gleam of moonshine," replied he. "But what told thee it was a lock?" said Manfred. "How didst thou discover the secret of opening it?" "Providence, that delivered me from the helmet, was able to direct me to the spring of a lock," said he. "Providence should have gone a little farther and have placed thee out of the reach of my resentment," said Manfred. "When Providence had taught thee to open the lock, it abandoned thee for a fool who did not know how to make use of its favors. Why didst thou not pursue the path pointed out for thy escape? Why didst thou shut the trap-door before thou hadst descended the steps?" "I might ask you, my lord," said the peasant, "how I, totally unacquainted with your castle, was to know that those steps led to any outlet. But I scorn to evade your questions. Wherever those steps lead to, perhaps I should have explored the way, I could not be in a worse situation than I was. But the truth is, I let the trap-door fall. Your immediate arrival followed. I had given the alarm; what imported it to me whether I was seized a minute sooner or a minute late?" "Thou art a resolute villain for thy years," said Manfred; "yet on reflection I suspect thou dost but trifle with me. Thou hast not yet told me how thou didst open the lock." "That I will show you, my lord," said the peasant, and taking up a fragment of stone that had fallen from above, he laid himself on the trap-door and began to beat on the piece of brass that covered it, meaning to gain time for the escape of the Princess. This presence of mind, joined to the frankness of the youth, staggered Manfred. He even felt a disposition towards pardoning one who had been guilty of no crime. Manfred was not one of those savage tyrants who wanton in cruelty unprovoked. The circumstances of his fortune had given an asperity to his temper, which was naturally humane; and his virtues were always ready to operate when his passions did not obscure his reason.

While the Prince was in this suspense, a confused noise of voices echoed through the distant vaults. As the sound approached, he distinguished the clamors of some of his domestics, whom he had dispersed through the castle in search of Isabella, calling out: "Where is my lord? Where is the Prince?" "Here I am," said Manfred, as they came nearer. "Have you found the Princess?" The first that arrived replied: "Oh! my lord! I am glad we have found you." "Found me!" said Manfred. "Have you found the Princess?" "We thought we had, my lord," said the fellow, looking terrified; "but—" "But what?" cried the Prince. "Has she escaped?" "Jaquez and I, my lord—" "Yes, I and Diego," interrupted the second, who came up in still greater consternation. "Speak one of you at a time," said Manfred. "I ask you, Where is the Princess?" "We do not know," said they both together; "but we are frightened out of our wits." "So I think, blockheads," said Manfred. "What is it has scared you thus?" "Oh! my lord!" said Jaquez, "Diego has seen such a sight! Your highness would not believe our eyes." "What new absurdity is this?" cried Manfred. "Give me a direct answer, or by heaven—" "Why, my lord, if it please your highness to hear me," said the poor fellow, "Diego and I—" "Yes, I and Jaquez," cried his comrade— "Did not I forbid you to speak both at a time?" said the Prince. "You, Jaquez, answer; for the other fool seems more distracted than thou art." "What is the matter, my gracious lord?" said Jaquez. "If it please your highness to hear me, Diego and I according to your highness's orders went to search for the young lady; but being comprehensive that we might meet the ghost of my young lord, (God rest his soul!) as he has not received Christian burial—" "Sot!" cried Manfred, in a rage; "is it only a ghost then that thou hast seen?" "Oh! worse! worse! my lord," cried Diego. "I had rather have seen ten whole ghosts—" "Grant me patience!" said Manfred; "these blockheads distract me. Out of my sight, Diego! And thou, Jaquez, tell me in one word: Art thou sober? Art thou raving? Thou wast wont to have some sense. Hast the other sot frightened himself and thee too? Speak! What is it he fancies he has seen?" "Why, my lord," replied Jaquez, trembling, "I was going to tell your highness that since the calamitous misfortune of my young lord (God rest his precious soul!), not one of us, your highness's faithful servants—indeed we are, my lord, though poor men—I say, not one of us has dared to set a foot about the castle but two together. So Diego and I, thinking that my young lady might be in the great gallery, went up there to look for her, and tell her your highness wanted something to impart to her—'' ''O blundering fools!'' cried Manfred. ''And in the meantime she has made her escape because you were afraid of goblins! Why, thou knave! she left me in the gallery; I came from thence myself.'' ''For all that, she may be there still for ought I know,'' said Jaquez; ''but the devil shall have me before I seek her there again! Poor Diego! I do not believe he will ever recover it.'' ''Recover what?'' said Manfred. ''Am I never to learn what it is has terrified these rascals? But I lose my time. Follow me, slave; I will see if she is in the gallery.'' ''For heaven's sake, my dear good lord,'' cried Jaquez, ''do not go to the gallery! Satan himself I believe is in the great chamber next to the gallery.'' Manfred, who hitherto had treated the terror of his servants as an idle panic, was struck at this new circumstance. He recollected the apparition of the portrait and the sudden closing of the door at the end of the gallery. His voice faltered, and he asked with disorder: ''What is in the great chamber?'' ''My lord,'' said Jaquez, ''when Diego and I came into the gallery, he went first, for he said he had more courage than I. So when we came into the gallery, we found nobody. We looked under every bench and stool; and still we found nobody.'' ''Were all the pictures in their places?'' said Manfred. ''Yes, my lord,'' answered Jaquez; ''but we did not think of looking behind them.'' ''Well, well!'' said Manfred; ''proceed.'' ''When we came to the door of the great chamber,'' continued Jaquez, ''we found it shut—'' ''And could not you open it?'' said Manfred. ''Oh! yes, my lord; would to heaven we had not!'' replied he. ''Nay, it was not I neither; it was Diego. He was grown fool-hardy, and would go on though I advised him not. If ever I open a door that is shut, again—'' ''Trifle not,'' said Manfred, shuddering; ''but tell me what you saw in the great chamber on opening the door.'' ''I! my lord!'' said Jaquez; ''I saw nothing; I was behind Diego. But I heard the noise.'' ''Jaquez,'' said Man-

fred, in a solemn tone of voice, ''tell me, I adjure thee by the souls of my ancestors: What was it thou sawest? What was it thou heardst?'' ''It was Diego saw it, my lord; it was not I,'' replied Jaquez; ''I only heard the noise. Diego had no sooner opened the door than he cried out and ran back. I ran back too, and said: 'Is it the ghost? the ghost?' 'No, no,' said Diego, and his hair stood an end; 'it is a giant, I believe. He is all clad in armor, for I saw his foot and part of his leg, and they are as large as the helmet below in the court.' As he said these words, my lord, we heard a violent motion and the rattling of armor as if the giant was rising, for Diego has told me since that he believes the giant was lying down, for the foot and leg were stretched at length on the floor. Before we could get to the end of the gallery, we heard the door of the great chamber clap behind us; but we did not dare turn back to see if the giant was following us. Yet now I think on it, we must have heard him if he had pursued us—But for heaven's sake, good my lord, send for the chaplain and have the castle exorcised, for, for certain, it is enchanted.'' ''Ay, pray do, my lord,'' cried all the servants at once, ''or we must leave your highness's service.'' ''Peace, dotards,'' said Manfred; ''and follow me. I will know what all this means.'' ''We! my lord,'' cried they with one voice; ''we would not go up to the gallery for your highness's revenue.'' The young peasant, who had stood silent, now spoke. ''Will your highness,'' said he, ''permit me to try this adventure? My life is of consequence to nobody. I fear no bad angel, and have offended no good one.'' ''Your behavior is above your seeming,'' said Manfred, viewing him with surprise and admiration. ''Hereafter, I will reward your bravery; but now,'' continued he with a sigh, ''I am so circumstanced that I dare trust no eyes but my own; however, I give you leave to accompany me.''

Manfred, when he first followed Isabella from the gallery, had gone directly to the apartment of his wife, concluding the Princess had retired thither. Hippolita, who knew his step, rose with anxious fondness to meet her lord, whom she had not seen since the death of their son. She would have flown in a transport mixed of joy and grief to his bosom, but he pushed her rudely off, and said, ''Where is Isabella?'' ''Isabella! my lord!'' said the astonished Hippolita. ''Yes, Isabella!'' cried Manfred imperiously. ''I want Isabella.'' ''My lord,'' replied Matilda, who perceived how much his behavior had shocked her mother, ''she has not been with us since your highness summoned her to your apartment.'' ''Tell me where she is,'' said the Prince; ''I do not want to know where she has been.'' ''My good lord,'' said Hippolita, ''your daughter tells you the truth: Isabella left us by your command, and has not returned since. But, my good lord, compose yourself; retire to your rest. This dismal day has disordered you. Isabella shall wait your orders in the morning.'' ''What then! you know where she is!'' cried Manfred. ''Tell me directly, for I will not lose an instant. And you, woman,'' speaking to his wife, ''order your chaplain to attend me forthwith.'' ''Isabella,'' said Hippolita calmly, ''is retired, I suppose, to her chamber. She is not accustomed to watch at this late hour. Gracious my lord,'' continued she, ''let me know what has disturbed you. Has Isabella offended you?'' ''Trouble me not with questions,'' said Manfred; ''but tell me where she is.'' ''Matilda shall call her,'' said the Princess. ''Sit down, my lord, and resume your wonted fortitude.'' ''What, art thou jealous of Isabella,'' replied he, ''that you wish to be present at our interview?'' ''Good heavens! my lord,'' said Hippolita, ''what is it your highness means?'' ''Thou wilt know ere many minutes are passed,'' said the cruel Prince. ''Send your chaplain to me, and wait my pleasure here.'' At these words he flung out of the room in search of Isabella, leaving the amazed ladies thunder-struck with his words and frantic deportment, and lost in vain conjectures on what he was meditating.

Manfred was now returning from the vault attended by the peasant and a few of his servants whom he had obliged to accompany him. He ascended the staircase without stopping till he arrived at the gallery, at the door of which he met Hippolita and her chaplain. When Diego had been dismissed by Manfred, he had gone directly to the Princess's apartment with the alarm of what he had seen. That excellent lady, who no more than Manfred doubted of the reality of the vision, yet affected to treat it as a delirium of the servant. Willing, however, to save her lord from any additional shock, and prepared by a series of grief not to tremble at any accession to it, she determined to make herself the first sacrifice if fate had marked the present hour for their destruction. Dismissing the reluctant Matilda to her rest, who in vain sued for leave to accompany her mother, and attended only by her chaplain, Hippolita had visited the gallery and great chamber, and now with more serenity of soul than she had felt for many hours, she met her lord and assured him that the vision of the gigantic leg and foot was all a fable, and no doubt an impression made by fear and the dark and dismal hour of the night on the minds of his servants. She and the chaplain had examined the chamber, and found every thing in the usual order. Manfred, though persuaded like his wife that the vision had been no work of fancy, recovered a little from the tempest of mind into which so many strange events had thrown him. Ashamed, too, of his inhuman treatment of a princess who returned every injury with new marks of tenderness and duty, he felt returning love forcing itself into his eyes; but not less ashamed of feeling remorse towards one against whom he was inwardly meditating a yet more bitter outrage, he curbed the yearnings of his heart and did not dare to lean even towards pity. The next transition of his soul was to exquisite villainy. Presuming on the unshaken submission of Hippolita, he flattered himself that she would not only acquiesce with patience to a divorce, but would obey, if it was his pleasure, in endeavoring to persuade Isabella to give him her hand. But ere he could indulge this horrid hope, he reflected that Isabella was not to be found. Coming to himself, he gave orders that every avenue to the castle should be strictly guarded, and charged his domestics on pain of their lives to suffer nobody to pass out. The young peasant, to whom he spoke favorably, he ordered to remain in a small chamber on the stairs, in which there was a pallet-bed, and the key of which he took away himself, telling the youth he would talk with him in the morning. Then dismissing his attendants, and bestowing a sullen kind of half-nod on Hippolita, he retired to his own chamber.

Thomas Percy 1729-1811

From RELIQUES OF ANCIENT
ENGLISH POETRY
1765

ROBIN HOOD AND GUY OF GISBORNE

When shaws[1] beene sheene,[2] and shradds[3]
    full fayre,
And leaves both large and longe,
Itt is merrye walking in the fayre forrèst
    To heare the small birdes songe.

5 The woodweele[4] sang, and wold not cease,
    Sitting upon the spraye,
Soe lowde, he wakened Robin Hood,
    In the greenwood where he lay.

"Now by my faye,"[5] sayd jollye Robìn.
10   "A sweaven[6] I had this night;
I dreamt me of tow wighty yemen,[7]
    That fast with me can[8] fight.

Methought they did mee beate and binde,
    And tooke my bow mee froe;
15 Iff I be Robin alive in this lande,
    Ile be wroken[9] on them towe."

"Sweavens are swift, master," quoth John,
    "As the wind blowes ore the hill;
For if itt be never so loude this night,
20   Tomorrow it may be still."

"Buske[10] yee, bowne yee, my merry men
    all,
And John shall goe with mee,
For Ile goe seeke yond wight yeomen,
    In greenwood where the[11] bee."

25 Then they cast on their gownes of grene,
    And tooke theyr bowes each one;
And they away to the greene forrèst
    A-shooting forth are gone;

Untill they came to the merry greenwood,
30   Where they had gladdest bee,
There were the ware of a wight yeomàn,
    His body leaned to a tree.

A sword and a dagger he wore by his side,
    Of manye a man the bane;
35 And he was clad in his capull-hyde,[12]
    Topp and tayll and mayne.

"Stand you still, master," quoth Little
    John,
    "Under this tree so grene,

And I will go to yond wight yeoman
40   To know what he doth meane."

"Ah! John, by me thou settest noe store,
    And that I farley[1] finde:
How offt send I my men beffore
    And tarry my selfe behinde?

45 "It is no cunning a knave to ken,
    And a man but heare him speake;
And itt were not for bursting of my bowe,
    John, I thy head wold breake."

As often wordes they breeden bale,
50   So they parted Robin and John;
And John is gone to Barnesdale;
    The gates[2] he knoweth eche one.

But when he came to Barnesdale,
    Great heavinesse there hee hadd,
55 For he found tow of his owne fellòwes
    Were slaine both in a slade.[3]

And Scarlette he was flying a-foote
    Fast over stocke and stone,
For the proud sheriffe with seven score men
60   Fast after him is gone.

"One shoote now I will shoote," quoth
    John,
    "With Christ his might and mayne:
Ile make yond fellow that flyes soe fast,
    To stopp he shall be fayne."

65 Then John bent up his long bende-bowe,[4]
    And fetteled[5] him to shoote:
The bow was made of tender boughe,
    And fell down to his foote.

"Woe worth, woe worth thee,[6] wicked
    wood,
70   That ere thou grew on a tree;
For now this day thou art my bale,
    My boote[7] when thou shold bee."

His shoote it was but loosely shott,
    Yet flewe not the arrowe in vaine,
75 For itt mett one of the sheriffes men,
    Good William a Trent was slaine.

It had bene better of William a Trent
    To have bene abed with sorrowe,
Than to be that day in the green wood slade
80   To meet with Little Johns arrowe.

But as it is said, when men be mett
    Fyve can doe more than three,

---

[1] groves
[2] beautiful
[3] coppices
[4] woodlark
[5] faith
[6] dream
[7] two strong yemen
[8] for *gan*, did
[9] avenged
[10] make ready (*buske* and *bowne* are doublets)
[11] they
[12] horse-hide

---

[1] strange
[2] ways; paths
[3] valley; ravine
[4] bent, or curved, bow
[5] made ready
[6] woe be to thee
[7] help

The sheriffe hath taken Little John,
And bound him fast to a tree.

85 "Thou shalt be drawen by dale and downe,[1]
And hanged hye on a hill."
"But thou mayst fayle of thy purpose,"
quoth John,
"If itt be Christ his will."

Let us leave talking of Little John,
90 And thinke of Robin Hood,
How he is gone to the wight yemàn,
Where under the leaves he stood.

"Good morrowe, good fellowe," sayd
Robin so fayre,
"Good morrowe, good fellow," quoth
he:
95 "Methinkes by this bowe thou beares in
thy hande
A good archere thou sholdst bee."

"I am wilfulle[2] of my waye," quo' the
yeman,
"And of my morning tyde."
"Ile lead thee through the wood," sayd
Robin;
100 "Good fellow, Ile be thy guide."

"I seeke an outlàwe," the straunger sayd,
"Men call him Robin Hood;
Rather Ild meet with that proud outlàwe,
Than fortye pound soe good."

105 "Now come with me, thou wighty yeman,
And Robin thou soone shalt see:
But first let us some pastime find
Under the greenwood tree.

"First let us some masterye[3] make
110 Among the woods so even,
We may chance to meet with Robin Hood
Here att some unsett steven."[4]

They cutt them downe two summer
shroggs,[5]
That grew both under a breere,
115 And sett them threescore rood in
twaine[6]
To shoot the prickes y-fere:[7]

"Leade on, good fellowe," quoth Robin
Hood,
"Leade on, I doe bidd thee."
"Nay by my faith, good fellowe, hee sayd,
120 "My leader thou shalt be."

The first time Robin shot at the pricke,
He mist but an inch it froe:
The yeoman he was an archer good,
But he cold never shoote soe.

125 The second shoote had the wightye yeman,
He shote within the garlànde:[1]
But Robin he shott far better than hee,
For he clave the good pricke wande.

"A blessing upon thy heart," he sayd;
130 "Good fellowe, thy shooting is goode;
For an thy hart be as good as thy hand,
Thou wert better then Robin Hoode.

"Now tell me thy name, good fellowe,"
sayd he,
"Under the leaves of lyne."[2]
135 "Nay by my faith," quoth bolde Robìn,
"Till thou have told me thine."

"I dwell by dale and downe," quoth hee,
"And Robin to take Ime sworne;
And when I am called by my right name
140 I am Guye of good Gisbòrne."

"My dwelling is in this wood," sayes
Robin,
"By thee I set right nought:
I am Robin Hood of Barnèsdale,
Whom thou so long hast sought."

145 He that had neither beene kithe nor kin,
Might have seene a full fayre sight,
To see how together these yeomen went
With blades both browne and bright.

To see how these yeomen together they
fought
150 Two howres of a summers day:
Yett neither Robin Hood nor Sir Guy
Them fettled to flye away.

Robin was reachles[3] on a roote,
And stumbled at that tyde;[4]
155 And Guy was quick and nimble with-all,
And hitt him ore the left side.

"Ah, deere Lady," sayd Robin Hood.
"thou
That art both mother and may,[5]
I think it was never mans destinye
160 To dye before his day."

[1] valley and hill	[5] wands
[2] astray	[6] apart
[3] trial of skill	[7] the wands (targets)
[4] unexpected hour	together

[1] the ring within which the prick or target was set to be shot at	[2] linden
	[3] careless
	[4] time
	[5] maiden

Robin thought on our ladye deere,
　And soone leapt up againe,
And strait he came with a backward[1]
　　　stroke,
　And he Sir Guy hath slayne.

165 He took Sir Guys head by the hayre,
　And stuck itt upon his bowes end:
"Thou hast beene a traytor all thy life,
　Which thing must have an ende."

Robin pulled forth an Irish kniffe,
170　And nicked Sir Guy in the face,
That he was never on woman born,
　Cold tell whose head it was.

Saies, "Lye there, lye there, now Sir Guye,
　And with me be not wrothe,
175 If thou have had the worst strokes at
　　　my hand,
　Thou shalt have the better clothe."

Robin did off his gowne of greene,
　And on Sir Guy did throwe,
And hee put on that capull-hyde,
180　That cladd him topp to toe.

"The bowe, the arrowes, and litle horne,
　Now with me I will beare;
For I will away to Barnèsdale,
　To see how my men doe fare."

185 Robin Hood sett Guyes horne to his mouth,
　And a loud blast in it did blow,
That beheard the sheriffe of Nottingham,
　As he leaned under a lowe.[2]

"Hearken, hearken," sayd the sheriffe,
190　"I heare now tydings good,
For yonder I heare Sir Guyes horne blowe,
　And he hath slaine Robin Hoode.

"Yonder I heare Sir Guyes horne blowe,
　Itt blowes soe well in tyde,
195 And yonder comes that wightye yeoman,
　Cladd in his capull-hyde.

"Come hyther, come hyther, thou good
　　　Sir Guy,
　Aske what thou wilt of mee."
"O I will none of thy gold," sayd Robin,
200　"Nor I will none of thy fee:[3]

"But now I have slaine the master," he
　　　sayes,
　"Let me goe strike the knave;

For this is all the rewarde I aske;
　Nor noe other will I have."

205 "Thou art a madman," said the sheriffe,
　"Thou sholdst have had a knightes fee:
But seeing thy asking hath beene soe bad,
　Well granted it shale be."

When Little John heard his master speake,
210　Well knewe he it was his steven:[1]
"Now shall I be looset," quoth Little John,
　"With Christ his might in heaven."

Fast Robin hee hyed him to Little John,
　He thought to loose him belive;[2]
215 The sheriffe and all his companye
　Fast after him can drive.

"Stand abacke, stand abacke," sayd
　　　Robin;
　"Why draw you mee soe neere?
Itt was never the use in our countryè,
220　Ones shrift another shold heere."

But Robin pulled forth an Irysh knife,
　And losed John hand and foote,
And gave him Sir Guyes bow into his hand,
　And bade it be his boote.

225 Then John he took Guyes bow in his hand,
　His boltes and arrowes eche one:
When the sheriffe saw Little John bend
　　　his bow,
　He fettled him to be gone.

Towards his house in Nottingham towne
230　He fled full fast away;
And soe did all his companye:
　Not one behind wold stay.

But he cold neither runne soe fast,
　Nor away soe fast cold ryde,
235 But Little John with an arrowe soe broad
　He shott him into the backe-syde.

THE ANCIENT BALLAD OF CHEVY-CHASE

THE FIRST FIT[3]

The Persè owt[4] of Northombarlande,
　And a vowe to God mayd he,
That he wolde hunte in the mountayns
　Off Chyviat within dayes thre,
5 In the mauger of[5] doughtè Dogles,
　And all that ever with him be.

---

[1] back-hand
[2] hill
[3] property held on feu-
　　dal tenure
[1] voice
[2] quickly
[3] division of the song
[4] came out
[5] in spite of

The fattiste hartes in all Cheviat
  He sayd he wold kill, and cary them
    away:
"Be my feth," sayd the dougheti Doglas
  agayn,
10 "I wyll let[1] that hontyng yf that I
    may."

Then the Persè owt of Banborowe cam,
  With him a myghtye meany,[2]
With fifteen hondrith archares bold;
  The wear[3] chosen out of shyars thre.

15 This begane on a Monday at morn
  In Cheviat the hillys so he;[4]
The chyld may rue that ys un-born,
  It was the mor pittè.

The dryvars[5] thorowe the woodes went
20 For to reas the dear;
Bomen bickarte[6] uppone the bent[7]
  With ther browd aras[8] cleare.

Then the wyld[9] thorowe the woodes went
  On every syde shear;[10]
25 Grea-hondes thorowe the greves[11] glent[12]
  For to kyll thear dear.

The begane in Chyviat the hyls above
  Yerly[13] on a Monnyn day;
Be that[14] it drewe to the oware off none[15]
30 A hondrith fat hartes ded ther lay.

The blewe a mort[16] uppone the bent,
  The semblyd on sydis shear;
To the quyrry[17] then the Persè went
  To se the bryttlyng[18] off the deare.

35 He sayd, "It was the Duglas promys
  This day to meet me hear;
But I wyste he wold faylle verament:"[19]
  A gret oth the Persè swear.

At the laste a squyar of Northombelonde
40 Lokyde at his hand full ny,
He was war ath[20] the doughetie Doglas
  comynge:
  With him a mightè meany,

Both with spear, byll, and brande:[21]
  Yt was a myghti sight to se.

45 Hardyar men both off hart nar hande
  Wear not in Christiantè.

The wear twenty hondrith spear-men good
  Withouten any fayle;[1]
The wear borne a-long be the watter a
  Twyde
50 Yth[2] bowndes of Tividale.

"Leave off the brytlyng of the dear," he
  sayde,
  "And to your bowys look ye tayk good
    heed,
For never sithe ye wear on your mothars
  borne
  Had ye never so mickle[3] need."

55 The dougheti Dogglas on a stede
  He rode att his men beforne;
His armor glytteryde as dyd a glede;[4]
  A bolder barne[5] was never born.

"Tell me what men ye ar," he says,
60 "Or whos men that ye be:
Who gave youe leave to hunte in this
  Chyviat chays in the spyt of me?"

The first mane that ever him an answear
  mayd,
  Yt was the good lord Persè:
65 "We wyll not tell the what men we ar,"
  he says,
  "Nor whos men that we be;
But we wyll hount hear in this chays
  In the spyte of thyne, and of the.

"The fattiste hartes in all Chyviat
70 We have kyld, and cast[6] to carry them
    a-way."
"Be my troth, sayd the doughtè Dogglas
  agayn,
  "Ther-for the ton[7] of us shall de this
    day."

Then sayd the doughtè Doglas
  Unto the lord Persè:
75 "To kyll all thes giltless men,
  A-las! it wear great pittè.

"But, Persè, thowe art a lord of lande,
  I am a yerle callyd within my contre;
Let all our men uppone a parti[8] stande;
80 And do the battell off the and of me."

[1] prevent	[12] darted
[2] band	[13] early
[3] they were	[14] when
[4] high	[15] hour of noon
[5] stalkers	[16] death-note
[6] swiftly coursed	[17] slaughtered game
[7] field	[18] cutting up
[8] arrows	[19] truly
[9] wild deer	[20] aware of
[10] several	[21] pike and sword
[11] groves	

[1] without any doubt	[5] man
[2] in the	[6] intend
[3] much	[7] one
[4] glowing coal	[8] to one side

"Nowe Cristes corse[1] on his crowne,"
   sayd the lord Persè,
"Who-soever ther-to says nay.
Be my troth, doughtè Doglas," he says,
   "Thow shalt never se that day;

85 "Nethar in Ynglonde, Skottlonde, nar
     France,
   Nor for no man of a woman born,
But and fortune be my chance,[2]
   I dar met him on[3] man for on."

Then bespayke a squyar off Northombar-
     londe,
90   Ric.[4] Wytharynton was his nam;
"It shall never be told in Sothe-Yng-
     londe," he says,
   "To kyng Herry the fourth for sham.

"I wat[5] youe byn[6] great lordes twaw,
   I am a poor squyar of lande;
95 I wyll never se my captayne fight on a
     fylde,
   And stande my-selffe, and looke on,
But whyll I may my weppone welde,
   I wyll not fayl both harte and hande."

That day, that day, that dredfull day:
100   The first Fit here I fynde,[7]
And you wyll here any mor athe[8] hountyng
     athe Chyviat,
   Yet ys ther mor behynde.

THE SECOND FIT

The Yngglishe men hade ther bowys
     yebent,
   Ther hartes were good yenoughe;
105 The first of arros that the shote off,
   Seven skore spear-men the sloughe.[9]

Yet bydys[10] the yerle Doglas uppon the
     bent,
   A captayne good yenoughe,
And that was sene verament,
110   For he wrought hom[11] both woo and
     wouche.[12]

The Dogglas pertyd his ost in thre,
   Lyk a cheffe cheften off pryde,[13]
With suar[14] speares off myghttè tre[15]
   The cum in on every syde.

115 Thrughe our Yngglishe archery[1]
   Gave many a wounde full wyde;
Many a doughetè the garde[2] to dy,
   Which ganyde them no pryde.[3]

The Yngglyshe men let thear bowys be,
120   And pulde owt brandes that wer bright;
It was a hevy syght to se
   Bryght swordes on basnites[4] lyght.

Thorowe ryche male,[5] and myneyeple,[6]
   Many sterne the stroke downe streght:[7]
125 Many a freyke,[8] that was full free,
   Ther undar foot dyd lyght.

At last the Duglas and the Persè met,
   Lyk to captayns of myght and mayne;
The swapte[9] togethar tyll the both swat[10]
130   With swordes, that were of fyn myllàn.[11]

Thes worthè freckys for to fyght
   Ther-to the wear full fayne,
Tyll the bloode owte off thear basnetes
     sprente,[12]
   As ever dyd heal or rayne.

135 "Hold the, Persè," sayd the Doglas,
   And i' feth I shall the brynge
Wher thowe shalte have a yerls wagis[13]
   Of Jamy our Scottish kynge.

"Thoue shalte have thy ransom fre,
140   I hight the hear[14] this thinge,
For the manfullyste man yet art thowe,
   That ever I conqueryd in filde fightyng."

"Nay, then," sayd the lord Persè,
   "I tolde it the beforne,
145 That I wolde never yeldyde be
   To no man of a woman born."

With that ther cam an arrowe hastely
   Forthe off a mightie wane,[15]
Hit hathe strekene the yerle Duglas
150   In at the brest bane.

Thoroue lyvar and longs bathe[16]
   The sharp arrowe ys gane,
That never after in all his lyffe days,
   He spake mo wordes but ane,

---

[1] curse
[2] if fortune favors me
[3] one
[4] Richard
[5] know
[6] are
[7] finish
[8] of the
[9] they slew
[10] abides
[11] them
[12] harm
[13] like a proud leading chieftain
[14] sure; trusty
[15] strong wood

[1] among our English archers
[2] they made
[3] which won them no pride
[4] helmets
[5] armor
[6] gauntlet
[7] many bold ones they struck down straightway
[8] man
[9] they smote
[10] they both sweat
[11] Milan steel
[12] sprang
[13] an earl's wages
[14] promise thee here
[15] "one; m a n."—Percy.
[16] liver and lungs both

155 That was, "Fyghte ye, my merry men,
  whyllys ye may,
  For my lyff days ben gan."

The Persè leanyde on his brande,
 And sawe the Duglas de;
He tooke the dede man be the hande,
160 And sayd, "Wo ys me for the!

"To have savyde thy lyffe, I wold have
  pertyd with
 My landes for years thre,
For a better man of hart, nare of hande
Was not in all the north countrè."

165 Off all that se[1] a Skottishe knyght,
 Was callyd Sir Hewe the Mongon-byrry,
He sawe the Duglas to the deth was
  dyght;[2]
He spendyd a spear a trusti tre:[3]

He rod uppon a corsiare
170 Throughe a hondrith archery;
He never styntyde, nar never blane,[4]
 Tyll he cam to the good lord Persè.

He set uppone the lord Persè
 A dynte, that was full soare;
175 With a suar spear of a myghtè tre
 Clean thorow the body he the Persè bore,

Athe tothar syde, that a man myght se,
 A large cloth yard and mare:[5]
Towe bettar captayns wear nat in Christiantè,
180 Then that day slain wear thare.

An archer off Northomberlonde
 Say[6] slean was the lord Persè,
He bar a bende-bow[7] in his hande,
 Was made off trusti tre:

185 An arow, that a cloth yarde was lang,
 To th' hard stele halyde[8] he;
A dynt, that was both sad and soar,
 He sat[9] on Sir Hewe the Mongon-byrry.

The dynt yt was both sad and sar,
190 That he of Mongon-byrry sete;
The swane-fethars, that his arrowe bar,
 With his hart blood the wear wete.

Ther was never a freake wone foot wold fle,
 But still in stour[10] dyd stand,

195 Heawing on yche othar, whyll the myght
  dre,[1]
 With many a bal-ful brande.

This battell begane in Chyviat
 An owar befor the none,
And when even-song bell was rang
200 The battell was nat half done.

The tooke "on"[2] on ethar hand
 Be the lyght off the mone;
Many hade no strength for to stande,
 In Chyviat the hyllys abone.[3]

205 Of fifteen hondrith archars of Ynglonde
 Went away but fifti and thre;
Of twenty hondrith spear-men of Skot-
  londe,
 But even five and fifti:

But all wear slayne Cheviat within:
210 The hade no strengthe to sand on hie;
The chylde may rue that ys un-borne,
 It was the mor pittè.

Thear was slayne with the lord Persè
 Sir John of Agerstone,
215 Sir Roge[4] the hinde[5] Hartly,
 Sir Wyllyam the bolde Hearone.

Sir Jorg the worthè Lovele
 A knyght of great renowen,
Sir Raff[6] the ryche Rugbè
220 With dyntes wear beaten dowene.

For Wetharryngton my harte was wo,
 That ever he slayne shulde be;
For when both his leggis wear hewyne in to,
 He knyled and fought on hys kne.

225 Ther was slayne with the dougheti Douglas
 Sir Hewe the Mongon-byrry,
Sir Davye Lwdale,[7] that worthè was,
 His sistars son was he:

Sir Charles a Murrè, in that place,
230 That never a foot wolde fle;
Sir Hewe Maxwell, a lorde he was,
 With the Duglas dyd he dey.

So on the morrowe the mayde them
  byears[8]
 Off byrch, and hasell so gray;

---

[1] saw
[2] doomed; promised
[3] spanned,—*i.e.*, placed in rest, a spear of strong wood
[4] stopped nor ever ceased
[5] more
[6] saw
[7] bent, or curved, bow
[8] drew to the hard steel,—*i. e.*, the head
[9] set
[10] stress of battle

[1] endure
[2] Percy's addition to the MS. The phrase may mean "they continued fighting."
[3] above
[4] Roger
[5] courteous
[6] Ralph
[7] Pronounced as if spelled Lewdale.
[8] they made them biers

235 Many wedous with wepyng tears
    Cam to fach ther makys[1] a-way.

Tivydale may carpe off[2] care,
    Northombarlond may mayk grat mone,
For towe such captayns, as slayne wear
        thear,
240 On the March-perti[3] shall never be none.

Word ys commen to Edden-burrowe,
    To Jamy the Skottishe kyng,
That dougheti Duglas, lyff-tenant of the
        Merches,
    He lay slean Chyviot with-in.

245 His handdes dyd he weal[4] and wryng,
    He sayd, "Alas, and woe ys me!
Such another captayn Skotland within,"
    He sayd, "y-feth[5] shuld never be."

Worde ys commyn to lovly Londone
250 Till the fourth Harry our kyng,
That lord Persè, leyff-tennante of the
        Merchis,
    He lay slayne Chyviat within.

"God have merci on his soll," sayd
        kyng Harry,
    "Good lord, yf thy will it be!
255 I have a hondrith captayns in Yng-
        londe," he sayd,
    "As good as ever was hee:
But Persè, and I brook[6] my lyffe,
    Thy deth well quyte[7] shall be."

As our noble kyng made his a-vowe,
260 Lyke a noble prince of renowen,
For the deth of the lord Persè,
    He dyd the battel of Hombyll-down:

Wher syx and thritte Skottish knyghtes
    On a day were beaten down:
265 Glendale glytteryde on[8] ther armor
        bryght,
    Over castill, towar, and town.

This was the hontynge off the Cheviat;
    That tear begane this spurn:[9]
Old men that knowen the grownde well
        yenoughe,
270 Call it the Battell of Otterburn.

At Otterburn began this spurne
    Uppon a Monnyn day:

Ther was the dougghtè Doglas slean,
    The Persè never went away.

275 Ther was never a tym on the March-partes
    Sen the Doglas and the Persè met,
But yt was marvele, and[1] the redde blude
        ronne not,
    As the reane doys[2] in the stret.

Jhesue Christ our balys bete,[3]
280 And to the[4] blys us brynge!
Thus was the hountynge of the Chevyat:
    God send us all good ending!

Sir Patrick Spence

The king sits in Dumferling toune,
    Drinking the blude-reid wine:
"O quhar[5] will I get guid sailòr,
    To sail this schip of mine?"

5 Up and spak an eldern knicht,
    Sat at the kings richt kne:
"Sir Patrick Spence is the best sailòr,
    That sails upon the se."

The king has written a braid[6] letter,
10 And signd it wi' his hand;
And sent it to Sir Patrick Spence,
    Was walking on the sand.

The first line that Sir Patrick red,
    A loud lauch[7] lauched he:
15 The next line that Sir Patrick red,
    The teir blinded his ee.

"O quha[8] is this has don this deid,
    This ill deid don to me;
To send me out this time o' the zeir,[9]
20 To sail upon the se?

"Mak hast, mak haste, my mirry men all,
    Our guid schip sails the morne;"
"O say na sae, my master deir,
    For I feir a deadlie storme.

25 "Late, late yestreen I saw the new moone,
    Wi' the auld moone in hir arme;
And I feir, I feir, my deir mastèr,
    That we will com to harme."

O our Scots nobles wer richt laith[10]
30 To weet their cork-heild schoone;

---

[1] fetch their mates
[2] talk of
[3] border side
[4] clench
[5] in faith

[6] if I enjoy
[7] paid for
[8] with
[9] that there began this
    fight

[1] if
[2] rain does
[3] evils remedy
[4] thy
[5] where

[6] open; clear
[7] laugh
[8] who
[9] year
[10] loth

Bot lang owre[1] a' the play wer playd,
Thair hats they swam aboone.[2]

O lang, lang, may thair ladies sit
Wi' thair fans into their hand,
35 Or eir they se Sir Patrick Spence
Cum sailing to the land.

O lang, lang, may the ladies stand
Wi' thair gold kems[3] in their hair,
Waiting for thair ain deir lords,
40 For they'll se thame na mair.

Have owre,[4] have owre to Aberdour,
It's fiftie fadom deip:
And thair lies guid Sir Patrick Spence,
Wi' the Scots lords at his feit.

EDOM O' GORDON

It fell about the Martinmas,
Quhen[5] the wind blew schril and cauld,
Said Edom o' Gordon to his men,
"We maun draw to a hauld."[6]

5 "And quhat[7] a hauld sall we draw till,
My mirry men and me?"
"We wul gae to the house o' the Rodes,
To see that fair ladìe."

The lady stude on her castle wa',
10 Beheld baith dale and down:[8]
There she was ware of a host of men
Cum ryding towards the toun.[9]

"O see ze[10] nat, my mirry men a'?
O see ze nat quhat I see?
15 Methinks I see a host of men:
I marveil quha[11] they be."

She weend[12] it had been hir luvely lord,
As he came ryding hame;
It was the traitor Edom o' Gordon,
20 Quha reckt nae sin nor shame.

She had nae sooner buskit[13] hirsel,
And putten on hir goun,
But Edom o' Gordon and his men
Were round about the toun.

25 They had nae sooner supper sett,
Nae sooner said the grace,
But Edom o' Gordon and his men
Were light about the place.

The lady ran up to hir towir head,
30 Sa fast as she could hie,
To see if by hir fair speechès
She could wi' him agree.

But quhan he see[1] this lady saif,
And hir yates all locked fast,
35 He fell into a rage of wrath,
And his look was all aghast.

"Cum doun to me, ze lady gay,
Cum doun, cum doun to me:
This night sall ye lig[2] within mine armes,
40 Tomorrow my bride sall be."

"I winnae[3] cum doun, ze fals Gordòn,
I winnae cum doun to thee;
I winnae forsake my ain dear lord,
That is sae far frae me."

45 "Give owre zour[4] house, ze lady fair,
Give owre zour house to me,
Or I sall brenn[5] yoursel therein,
Bot and zour babies three."[6]

"I winnae give owre, ze false Gordòn,
50 To nae sik[7] traitor as zee;
And if ze brenn my ain dear babes,
My lord sall make ze drie."[8]

"But reach my pistoll, Glaud my man,
And charge ze weil my gun:
55 For, but an I pierce that bluidy butcher,
My babes we been undone."

She stude upon hir castle wa',
And let twa bullets flee:
She mist that bluidy butchers hart,
60 And only raz'd his knee.

"Set fire to the house," quo' fals Gordòn,
All wood wi' dule and ire:[9]
"Fals lady, ze sall rue this deid,
As ze bren in the fire."

65 "Wae worth, wae worth ze,[10] Jock my man,
I paid ze weil zour fee;[11]
Quhy pow[12] ze out the ground-wa stane,
Lets in the reek[13] to me?

And ein[14] wae worth ze, Jock my man,
70 I paid ze weil zour hire;

---

1 but long before
2 swam above,—*i. e.,*
 floated on water
3 combs
4 half way over
5 when
6 we must draw to-
 wards (go take) a
 stronghold
7 what
8 valley and hill
9 farm (with its col-
 lection of buildings)
10 ye
11 who
12 thought
13 dressed

1 saw
2 lie
3 will not
4 your
5 burn
6 both you and your
 babies three
7 no such
8 suffer; pay dearly
9 all mad with pain
 and wrath
10 woe be to thee
11 wages
12 pull
13 smoke
14 even

Quhy pow ze out the ground-wa stane,
   To me lets in the fire?''

"Ze paid me weil my hire, lady;
   Ze paid me weil my fee:
75 But now Ime Edom o' Gordon's man
   Maun either doe or die.[1]

O than bespaik hir little son,
   Sate on the nourice' knee:
Sayes, "Mither deare, gi owre this house,
80   For the reek it smithers me.''

"I wad gie a' my gowd,[2] my childe,
   Sae wad I a' my fee,[3]
For ane blast o' the westlin wind,
   To blaw the reek frae thee.''

85 O then bespaik hir dochter dear,
   She was baith jimp[4] and sma:
"O row[5] me in a pair o' sheits,
   And tow[6] me owre the wa.''

The rowd hir in a pair o' sheits,
90   And towd hir owre the wa:
But on the point of Gordons spear
   She gat a deadly fa.

O bonnie bonnie was hir mouth,
   And cherry were hir cheiks,
95 And clear clear was hir zellow hair,
   Whareon the reid bluid dreips.

Then wi' his spear he turnd hir owre,
   O gin hir face was wan![7]
He sayd, "Ze are the first that eir
100   I wisht alive again.''

He turnd hir owre and owre again,
   O gin hir skin was whyte!
"I might ha spared that bonnie face,
   To hae been sum mans delyte.

105 "Busk and boun,[8] my merry men a',
   For ill dooms I doe guess;
I cannae luik in that bonnie face,
   As it lyes on the grass.''

"Thame, luiks to freits, my master deir,
110   Then freits wil follow thame:[9]
Let it neir be said brave Edom o' Gordon
   Was daunted by a dame.''

But quhen the ladye see the fire
   Cum flaming owre hir head,
115 She wept and kist her children twain,
   Sayd, "Bairns, we been but dead.''

The Gordon then his bougill blew,
   And said, "Awa', awa';
This house o' the Rodes is a' in flame,
120   I hauld it time to ga'.''

O then bespyed hir ain dear lord,
   As hee cam owr the lee;
He sied his castle all in blaze
   Sa far as he could see.

125 Then sair, O sair his mind misgave,
   And all his hart was wae;
"Put on, put on, my wighty[1] men,
   So fast as ze can gae.

"Put on, put on, my wighty men,
130   Sa fast as ze can drie;[2]
For he that is hindmost of the thrang
   Sall neir get guid o' me.''

Than sum they rade, and sum they rin,
   Fou fast out-owr the bent;[3]
135 But eir the foremost could get up,
   Baith lady and babes were brent.

He wrang his hands, he rent his hair,
   And wept in teenefu'[4] muid:
"O traitors, for this cruel deid
140   Ze sall weep teirs o' bluid.''

And after the Gordon he is gane,
   Sa fast as he might drie;
And soon i' the Gordon's foul hartis bluid
   He's wroken[5] his dear ladie.

LORD THOMAS AND FAIR ELLINOR

Lord Thomas he was a bold forrestèr,
   And a chaser of the kings deere;
Faire Ellinor was a fine womàn,
   And Lord Thomas he loved her deare.

5 "Come riddle my riddle, dear mother,''
   he sayd,
"And riddle us both as one:[6]
Whether I shall marrye with faire Ellinòr,
   And let the browne girl alone?''

"The browne girl she has got houses and
     lands,
10   Faire Ellinor she has got none,

---

[1] must either do or die
[2] gold
[3] property held on feudal tenure
[4] slender
[5] roll
[6] let down with a rope
[7] Oh, but her f a c e was wan! (A Scottish idiom expressing great admiration.)
[8] get ready and go
[9] Them that look after omens of ill luck, ill luck will follow.

[1] strong
[2] are able
[3] field
[4] sorrowful
[5] avenged
[6] let us s o l v e it together

And therefore I charge thee on my blessing,
  To bring me the browne girl home.''

And as it befelle on a high holidaye,
  As many there are beside,
15 Lord Thomas he went to faire Ellinòr,
  That should have been his bride.

And when he came to fair Ellinors bower,
  He knocked there at the ring,[1]
And who was so readye as faire Ellinòr,
20 To let Lord Thomas withinn.

''What newes, what newes, Lord Thomas?''
    she sayd,
''What newes dost thou bring to mee?''
''I am come to bid thee to my weddìng,
  And that is bad newes for thee.''

25 ''O God forbid, Lord Thomas,'' she sayd,
  ''That such a thing should be done;
I thought to have been the bride my selfe,
  And thou to have been the bridegroome.''

''Come riddle my riddle, dear mother,''
    she sayd,
30 ''And riddle it all in one;
Whether I shall goe to Lord Thomas his
    wedding,
  Or whether shall tarry at home?''

''There are manye that are your friendes,
    daughtèr,
  And manye a one your foe,
35 Therefore I charge you on my blessing,
  To Lord Thomas his wedding don't
    goe.''

''There are manye that are my friendes,
    mothèr;
  But were every one my foe,
Betide me life, betide me death,
40 To Lord Thomas his wedding I'ld
    goe.''

She cloathed herself in gallant attire,
  And her merrye men all in greene;
And as they rid through every towne,
  They took her to be some queene.

45 But when she came to Lord Thomas his
    gate,
  She knocked there at the ring;
And who was so readye as Lord Thomàs,
  To lett fair Ellinor in.

''Is this your bride?'' fair Ellinor sayd;
50 ''Methinks she looks wonderous browne;

[1] hammer of the door-knocker

Thou mightest have had as faire a womàn,
  As ever trod on the grounde.''

''Despise her not, fair Ellin,'' he sayd,
  ''Despise her not unto mee;
55 For better I love thy little fingèr,
  Than all her whole bodèe.''

This browne bride had a little penknife,
  That was both long and sharpe,
And betwixt the short ribs and the long,
60 She prick'd faire Ellinor's harte.

''O Christ thee save,'' Lord Thomas, hee
    sayd,
  ''Methinks thou lookst wonderous wan;
Thou usedst to look with as fresh a colòur,
  As ever the sun shone on.''

65 ''Oh, art thou blind, Lord Thomas?''
    she sayd,
  ''Or canst thou not very well see?
Oh! dost thou not see my owne hearts
    bloode
Run trickling down my knee?''

Lord Thomas he had a sword by his side;
70 As he walked about the halle,
He cut off his brides head from her
    shouldèrs,
  And threw it against the walle.

He set the hilte against the grounde,
  And the point against his harte.
75 There never three lovers together did meete,
  That sooner againe did parte.

James Beattie 1735-1803

RETIREMENT
1758

When in the crimson cloud of even
  The lingering light decays,
And Hesper on the front of heaven
  His glittering gem displays;
5 Deep in the silent vale, unseen,
  Beside a lulling stream,
A pensive Youth, of placid mien,
  Indulged this tender theme:

''Ye cliffs, in hoary grandeur piled
10 High o'er the glimmering dale;
Ye woods, along whose windings wild
  Murmurs the solemn gale:
Where Melancholy strays forlorn,
  And Woe retires to weep,
15 What time the wan Moon's yellow horn
  Gleams on the western deep!

"To you, ye wastes, whose artless
          charms
    Ne'er drew Ambition's eye,
    'Scaped[1] a tumultuous world's alarms,
20   To your retreats I fly.
    Deep in your most sequester'd bower
    Let me at last recline,
    Where Solitude, mild, modest power,
    Leans on her ivied shrine.

25 "How shall I woo thee, matchless fair?
    Thy heavenly smile how win?
    Thy smile that smooths the brow of Care,
    And stills the storm within.
    O wilt thou to thy favorite grove
30   Thine ardent votary bring,
    And bless his hours, and bid them move
    Serene, on silent wing?

    "Oft let Remembrance soothe his mind
    With dreams of former days,
35 When, in the lap of Peace reclined,
    He framed his infant lays;
    When Fancy roved at large, nor Care
    Nor cold Distrust alarm'd,
    Nor Envy, with malignant glare,
40   His simple youth had harm'd.

    " 'Twas then, O Solitude, to thee
    His early vows were paid,
    From heart sincere, and warm, and free,
    Devoted to the shade.
45 Ah! why did Fate his steps decoy
    In stormy paths to roam,
    Remote from all congenial joy?—
    O take the wanderer home!

    "Thy shades, thy silence, now be mine,
50   Thy charms my only theme;
    My haunt the hollow cliff, whose pine
    Waves o'er the gloomy stream,
    Whence the scared owl on pinions gray
    Breaks from the rustling boughs,
55 And down the lone vale sails away
    To more profound repose.

    "Oh, while to thee the woodland pours
    Its wildly-warbling song,
    And balmy from the banks of flowers
60   The Zephyr breathes along,
    Let no rude sound invade from far,
    No vagrant foot be nigh,
    No ray from Grandeur's gilded car
    Flash on the startled eye.

65 "But if some pilgrim through the glade
    Thy hallow'd bowers explore,
    O guard from harm his hoary head,
    And listen to his lore;
    ¹ escaped from

For he of joys divine shall tell,
70   That wean from earthly woe,
    And triumph o'er the mighty spell
    That chains this heart below.

    "For me no more the path invites
    Ambition loves to tread;
75 No more I climb those toilsome heights,
    By guileful Hope misled;
    Leaps my fond fluttering heart no more
    To Mirth's enlivening strain;
    For present pleasure soon is o'er,
80   And all the past is vain."

THE MINSTREL; OR, THE PROGRESS
OF GENIUS
1766-71   1771
From Book I

    Ah! who can tell how hard it is to
          climb
    The steep where Fame's proud temple
          shines afar?
    Ah! who can tell how many a soul
          sublime
    Has felt the influence of malignant
          star,
5   And waged with Fortune an eternal
          war—
    Check'd by the scoff of Pride, by
          Envy's frown,
    And Poverty's unconquerable bar—
    In life's low vale remote has pined
          alone,
    Then dropp'd into the grave, unpitied
          and unknown?

10   And yet the languor of inglorious
          days,
    Not equally oppressive is to all;
    Him who ne'er listen'd to the voice of
          praise,
    The silence of neglect can ne'er appal.
    There are, who, deaf to mad Ambi-
          tion's call,
15   Would shrink to hear th' obstrep-
          erous trump of Fame;
    Supremely blest, if to their portion
          fall
    Health, competence, and peace. Nor
          higher aim
    Had he whose simple tale these artless
          lines proclaim.

    The rolls of fame I will not now
          explore;
20   Nor need I here describe, in learned
          lay,

How forth the Minstrel far'd in days
    of yore,
50 Right glad of heart, though homely in
    array;
His waving locks and beard all hoary
    gray;
While from his bending shoulder, de-
    cent hung
25 His harp, the sole companion of his
    way,
Which to the whistling wild responsive
    rung:
And ever as he went some merry lay he
    sung.

Fret not thyself, thou glittering child
    of pride,
That a poor villager inspires my
    strain;
30 With thee let Pageantry and Power
    abide:
The gentle Muses haunt the sylvan
    reign;
Where through wild groves at eve the
    lonely swain
Enraptured roams, to gaze on Nature's
    charms:
They hate the sensual and scorn the
    vain,
35 The parasite their influence never
    warms,
Nor him whose sordid soul the love of
    gold alarms.

Though richest hues the peacock's
    plumes adorn,
Yet horror screams from his discord-
    ant throat.
Rise, sons of harmony, and hail the
    morn,
40 While warbling larks on russet pinions
    float:
Or seek at noon the woodland scene
    remote,
Where the gray linnets carol from the
    hill.
Oh, let them ne'er, with artificial
    note,
To please a tyrant, strain the little
    bill,
45 But sing what Heaven inspires, and
    wander where they will!

Liberal, not lavish, is kind Nature's
    hand;
Nor was perfection made for man
    below;
Yet all her schemes with nicest art
    are plann'd;

Good counteracting ill, and gladness
    woe.
50 With gold and gems if Chilian moun-
    tains glow;
If bleak and barren Scotia's hills
    arise;
There plague and poison, lust and
    rapine grow;
Here, peaceful are the vales, and pure
    the skies,
And Freedom fires the soul, and spar-
    kles in the eyes.

55 Then grieve not, thou, to whom th'
    indulgent Muse
Vouchsafes a portion of celestial fire;
Nor blame the partial Fates, if they
    refuse
Th' imperial banquet and the rich
    attire.
Know thine own worth, and reverence
    the lyre.
60 Wilt thou debase the heart which God
    refined?
No; let thy heaven-taught soul to
    Heaven aspire,
To fancy, freedom, harmony resign'd;
Ambition's grovelling crew forever left
    behind.

Canst thou forego the pure ethereal
    soul
65 In each fine sense so exquisitely keen,
On the dull couch of Luxury to loll,
Stung with disease, and stupefied with
    spleen;
Fain to implore the aid of Flattery's
    screen,
Even from thyself thy loathsome heart
    to hide
70 (The mansion then no more of joy
    serene),
Where fear, distrust, malevolence
    abide,
And impotent desire, and disappointed
    pride?

Oh, how canst thou renounce the
    boundless store
Of charms which Nature to her votary
    yields?
75 The warbling woodland, the resound-
    ing shore,
The pomp of groves, and garniture of
    fields;
All that the genial ray of morning
    gilds,
And all that echoes to the song of
    even,

All that the mountain's sheltering
    bosom shields,
80 And all the dread magnificence of
    heaven,
Oh, how canst thou renounce, and hope
    to be forgiven?

These charms shall work thy soul's
    eternal health,
And love, and gentleness, and joy
    impart.
But these thou must renounce, if lust
    of wealth
85 E'er win its way to thy corrupted
    heart:
For, ah! it poisons like a scorpion's
    dart;
Prompting th' ungenerous wish, the
    selfish scheme,
The stern resolve, unmoved by pity's
    smart,
The troublous day, and long distress-
    ful dream.
90 Return, my roving Muse, resume thy
    purposed theme.

There lived in Gothic days,[1] as legends
    tell,
A shepherd swain, a man of low de-
    gree,
Whose sires, perchance, in Fairyland
    might dwell,
Sicilian groves, or vales of Arcady;
95 But he, I ween, was of the north coun-
    trie;[2]
A nation famed for song, and beauty's
    charms;
Zealous, yet modest; innocent, though
    free;
Patient of toil: serene amidst alarms;
Inflexible in faith: invincible in arms.

100 The shepherd swain of whom I men-
    tion made,
On Scotia's mountains fed his little
    flock;
The sickle, scythe, or plough he never
    sway'd;
An honest heart was almost all his
    stock;
His drink the living water from the
    rock;
105 The milky dams supplied his board,
    and lent
Their kindly fleece to baffle winter's
    shock;

[1] In the Middle Ages.
[2] The "North Countrie" was the traditional
   dwelling place of fairies, demons, giants, etc.

And he, though oft with dust and
    sweat besprent,
Did guide and guard their wanderings,
    wheresoe'er they went.

.   .   .   .   .   .

And oft he traced the uplands, to
    survey,
165 When o'er the sky advanced the kin-
    dling dawn,
The crimson cloud, blue main, and
    mountain gray,
And lake, dim-gleaming on the smoky
    lawn:
Far to the west the long, long vale
    withdrawn,
Where twilight loves to linger for a
    while;
170 And now he faintly kens the bounding
    fawn,
And villager abroad at early toil.
But, lo! the sun appears, and heaven,
    earth, ocean smile!

And oft the craggy cliff he loved to
    climb,
When all in mist the world below was
    lost.
175 What dreadful pleasure! there to
    stand sublime,
Like shipwreck'd mariner on desert
    coast,
And view the enormous waste of
    vapor, toss'd
In billows, lengthening to th' horizon
    round,
Now scoop'd in gulfs, with mountains
    now emboss'd!
180 And hear the voice of Mirth and Song
    rebound,
Flocks, herds, and waterfalls, along the
    hoar profound!

In truth he was a strange and way-
    ward wight,
Fond of each gentle and each dread-
    ful scene.
In darkness, and in storm, he found
    delight;
185 Nor less than when on ocean-wave
    serene
The southern sun diffused his dazzling
    shene,
Even sad vicissitude amused his soul;
And if a sigh would sometimes inter-
    vene,
And down his cheek a tear of pity roll,
190 A sigh, a tear, so sweet, he wish'd not
    to control.

.   .   .   .   .   .

280 When the long-sounding curfew from
        afar
    Loaded with loud lament the lonely
        gale,
    Young Edwin, lighted by the evening
        star,
    Lingering and listening, wander'd
        down the vale.
    There would he dream of graves, and
        corses pale,
285 And ghosts that to the charnel-
        dungeon throng,
    And drag a length of clanking chain,
        and wail,
    Till silenced by the owl's terrific
        song,
    Or blast that shrieks by fits the shudder-
        ing isles along.

    Or, when the setting moon, in crimson
        dyed,
290 Hung o'er the dark and melancholy
        deep,
    To haunted stream, remote from man,
        he hied,
    Where fays of yore their revels wont
        to keep;
    And there let Fancy rove at large, till
        sleep
    A vision brought to his entranced
        sight.
295 And first, a wildly murmuring wind
        'gan creep
    Shrill to his ringing ear; then tapers
        bright,
    With instantaneous gleam, illumed the
        vault of night.

    Anon in view a portal's blazon'd
        arch
    Arose; the trumpet bids the valves un-
        fold,
300 And forth an host of little warriors
        march,
    Grasping the diamond lance and targe
        of gold.
    Their look was gentle, their demeanor
        bold,
    And green their helms, and green their
        silk attire;
    And here and there, right venerably
        old,
305 The long-rob'd minstrels wake the
        warbling wire,
    And some with mellow breath the mar-
        tial pipe inspire.

    With merriment and song and timbrels
        clear,

    A troop of dames from myrtle bowers
        advance;
    The little warriors doff the targe and
        spear,
310 And loud enlivening strains provoke the
        dance.
    They meet, they dart away, they wheel
    To right, to left, they thrid the flying
        maze;
    Now bound aloft with vigorous spring,
        then glance
    Rapid along: with many-color'd rays
315 Of tapers, gems, and gold, the echoing
        forests blaze.

    The dream is fled. Proud harbinger
        of day,
    Who scar'd'st the vision with thy cla-
        rion shrill,
    Fell chanticleer! who oft hath reft
        away
    My fancied good, and brought substan-
        tial ill!
320 O to thy cursed scream, discordant
        still,
    Let Harmony aye shut her gentle ear:
    Thy boastful mirth let jealous rivals
        spill,
    Insult thy crest, and glossy pinions
        tear,
    And ever in thy dreams the ruthless fox
        appear!

325 Forbear, my Muse. Let Love attune
        thy line.
    Revoke the spell. Thine Edwin frets
        not so.
    For how should he at wicked chance
        repine
    Who feels from every change amuse-
        ment flow?
    Even now his eyes with smiles of rap-
        ture glow,
330 As on he wanders through the scenes
        of morn,
    Where the fresh flowers in living lustre
        blow,
    Where thousand pearls the dewy lawns
        adorn,
    A thousand notes of joy in every breeze
        are born.

    But who the melodies of morn can
        tell?
335 The wild brook babbling down the
        mountain side,
    The lowing herd; the sheep-fold's
        simple bell;

The pipe of early shepherd dim descried
In the lone valley; echoing far and 475
wide,
The clamorous horn along the cliffs
above;
340 The hollow murmur of the ocean-tide;
The hum of bees, the linnet's lay of
love,
And the full choir that wakes the universal grove.

The cottage curs at early pilgrim bark;
Crown'd with her pail the tripping 480
milkmaid sings;
345 The whistling ploughman stalks afield;
and hark!
Down the rough slope the ponderous
wagon rings;
Through rustling corn the hare astonish'd springs;
Slow tolls the village clock the drowsy
hour;
The partridge bursts away on whir- 485
ring wings;
350 Deep mourns the turtle[1] in sequester'd
bower,
And shrill lark carols clear from her
aërial tower.

O Nature, how in every charm supreme!
Whose votaries feast on raptures ever 490
new!
O for the voice and fire of seraphim,
355 To sing thy glories with devotion due!
Blest be the day I 'scaped the wrangling crew,
From Pyrrho's maze, and Epicurus'
sty;
And held high converse with the godlike few,
Who to th' enraptur'd heart, and ear, 495
and eye,
360 Teach beauty, virtue, truth, and love,
and melody.

.   .   .   .   .   .

Oft when the winter storm had ceas'd 515
to rave,
470 He roam'd the snowy waste at even,
to view
The cloud stupendous, from th' Atlantic wave
High-towering, sail along th' horizon
blue;
Where, midst the changeful scenery,
ever new,   520

[1] turtledove

Fancy a thousand wondrous forms
descries,
More wildly great than ever pencil
drew,—
Rocks, torrents, gulfs, and shapes of
giant size,
And glitt'ring cliffs on cliffs, and fiery
ramparts rise.

Thence musing onward to the sounding
shore,
The lone enthusiast oft would take his
way,
Listening, with pleasing dread, to the
deep roar
Of the wide-weltering waves. In black
array,
When sulphurous clouds roll'd on th'
autumnal day,
Even then he hasten'd from the haunt
of man,
Along the trembling wilderness to
stray,
What time the lightning's fierce career
began,
And o'er Heav'n's rending arch the rattling thunder ran.

Responsive to the lively pipe, when all
In sprightly dance the village youth
were join'd,
Edwin, of melody aye held in thrall,
From the rude gambol far remote reclin'd,
Sooth'd with the soft notes warbling
in the wind,
Ah! then all jollity seem'd noise and
folly,
To the pure soul by Fancy's fire refin'd;
Ah! what is mirth but turbulence unholy,
When with the charm compar'd of heavenly melancholy?

.   .   .   .   .   .

Meanwhile, whate'er of beautiful, or
new,
Sublime, or dreadful, in earth, sea, or
sky,
By chance, or search, was offer'd to
his view,
He scann'd with curious and romantic
eye.
Whate'er of lore tradition could supply
From Gothic tale, or song, or fable
old,
Rous'd him, still keen to listen and to
pry.

At last, though long by penury controll'd
And solitude, his soul her graces 'gan
unfold.

Thus on the chill Lapponian's dreary
land,
For many a long month lost in snow
profound,
525 When Sol from Cancer sends the season bland,
And in their northern caves the storms
are bound;
From silent mountains, straight, with
startling sound,
Torrents are hurl'd; green hills
emerge; and, lo!
The trees are foliage, cliffs with flowers
are crown'd;
530 Pure rills through vales of verdure
warbling go;
And wonder, love, and joy, the peasant's
heart o'erflow.

Here pause, my Gothic lyre, a little
while,
The leisure hour is all that thou canst
claim.
But on this verse if Montagu should
smile,
535 New strains ere long shall animate thy
frame.
And her applause to me is more than
fame;
For still with truth accords her taste
refin'd.
At lucre or renown let others aim,
I only wish to please the gentle
mind,
540 Whom Nature's charms inspire, and love
of humankind.

Thomas Chatterton 1752-1770
BRISTOWE TRAGEDIE;

OR, THE DETHE OF SYR CHARLES BAWDIN
1768   1772

The feathered songster chaunticleer
Han[1] wounde hys bugle horne,
And tolde the earlie villager
The commynge of the morne:

5 Kynge Edwarde[2] sawe the ruddie streakes
Of lyghte eclypse the greie;
And herde the raven's crokynge throte
Proclayme the fated daie.

¹ has   ² Edward IV.

"Thou'rt righte," quod[1] hee, "for, by the
Godde
10 That syttes enthron'd on hyghe!
Charles Bawdin, and hys fellowes twaine,
To-daie shall surelie die."

Thenne wythe a jugge of nappy[2] ale
Hys knyghtes dydd onne hymm waite;
15 "Goe tell the traytour thatt to-daie
Hee leaves thys mortall state."

Sir Canterlone thenne bendedd lowe,
With harte brymm-fulle of woe;
Hee journey'd to the castle-gate
20 And to Syr Charles dydd goe.

But whenne hee came, hys children
twaine,
And eke hys lovynge wyfe,
Wythe brinie tears dydd wett the floore,
For goode Syr Charleses lyfe.

25 "O goode Syr Charles!" sayd Canter-
lone,
"Badde tydyngs I doe brynge."
"Speke boldlie, manne," sayd brave Syr
Charles,
"Whatte says thie traytor kynge?"

"I greeve to telle; before yonne sonne
30 Does fromme the welkin flye,
Hee hathe uppone hys honnour sworne,
Thatt thou shalt surelie die."

"Wee all must die," quod brave Syr
Charles;
"Of thatte I'm not affearde;
35 Whatte bootes to lyve a little space?
Thanke Jesu, I'm prepar'd:

"Butt telle thye kynge, for myne hee's
not,
I'de sooner die to-daie
Thanne lyve hys slave, as manie are,
40 Though I shoulde lyve for aie."

Thenne Canterlone hee dydd goe out,
To telle the maior straite
To gett all thynges ynne reddyness
For goode Syr Charles's fate.

45 Thenne Maisterr Canynge saughte the
kynge,
And felle down onne hys knee;
"I'm come," quod hee, "unto your
grace
To move your clemencye."

¹ quoth ; said   ² sparkling

Thenne quod the kynge, ''Youre tale
    speke out,
50   You have been much oure friende;
Whatever youre request may bee,
    We wylle to ytte attende.''

''My nobile leige! alle my request,
    Ys for a nobile knyghte,
55 Who, tho' mayhap hee has donne wronge,
    Hee thoughte ytte style was ryghte:

''Hee has a spouse and children twaine,
    Alle rewyn'd[1] are for aie;
Yff that you are resolv'd to lett
60   Charles Bawdin die to-daie.''

''Speke nott of such a traytour vile,''
    The kynge ynn furie sayde;
''Before the evening starre doth sheene,
    Bawdin shall loose hys hedde:

65 ''Justice does loudlie for hym calle,
    And hee shalle have hys meede:
Speke, Maister Canynge! Whatte thynge
    else
    Att present doe you neede?''

''My nobile leige!'' good Canynge sayde,
70   ''Leave justice to our Godde,
And laye the yronne rule asyde;
    Be thyne the olyve rodde.[2]

''Was Godde to serche our hertes and
    reines,[3]
    The best were synners grete;
75 Christ's vycarr only knowes ne synne,
    Ynne all thys mortall state.

''Lette mercie rule thyne infante reigne,
    'T wylle faste thye crowne fulle sure;
From race to race thye familie
80   Alle sov'reigns shall endure:

''But yff wythe bloode and slaughter thou
    Beginne thy infante reigne,
Thy crowne upponne thy childrennes brows
    Wylle never long remayne.''

85 ''Canynge, awaie! thys traytour vile
    Has scorn'd my power and mee;
Howe canst thou thenne for such a manne
    Intreate my clemencye?''

''Mie nobile leige! the trulie brave
90   Wylle val'rous actions prize;

Respect a brave and nobile mynde
    Altho' ynne enemies.''

''Canynge, awaie! By Godde ynne Heav'n
    That dydd mee being gyve,
95 I wylle nott taste a bitt of breade
    Whilst thys Syr Charles dothe lyve.

''Bie Marie, and alle Seinctes ynne Heav'n,
    Thys sunne shall be hys laste;''
Thenne Canynge dropt a brinie teare,
100   And from the presence paste.

With herte brymm-fulle of gnawynge
    grief,
Hee to Syr Charles dydd goe,
And satt hymm downe uponne a stoole,
    And teares beganne to flowe.

105 ''Wee alle must die,'' quod brave Syr
    Charles;
''Whatte bootes ytte howe or whenne;
Dethe ys the sure, the certaine fate
    Of all wee mortall menne.

''Saye why, my friend, thie honest soul
110   Runns overr att thyne eye;
Is ytte for my most welcome doome
    Thatt thou dost child-lyke crye?''

Quod godlie Canynge, ''I doe weepe,
    Thatt thou soe soone must dye,
115 And leave thy sonnes and helpless wyfe;
    'Tys thys thatt wettes myne eye.''

''Thenne drie the tears thatt out thyne eye
    From godlie fountaines sprynge;
Dethe I despise, and alle the power
120   Of Edwarde, traytor kynge.

''Whan through the tyrant's welcom means
    I shall resigne my lyfe,
The Godde I serve wylle soone provyde
    For bothe mye sonnes and wyfe.

125 ''Before I sawe the lyghtsome sunne,
    Thys was appointed mee;
Shall mortal manne repyne or grudge
    What Godde ordeynes to bee?

''Howe oft ynne battaile have I stoode,
130   Whan thousands dy'd arounde;
Whan smokynge streemes of crimson
    bloode
Imbrew'd the fatten'd grounde:

''Howe dydd I knowe thatt ev'ry darte,
    That cutte the airie waie,
135 Myghte nott fynde passage toe my harte,
    And close myne eyes for aie?

---

[1] ruined   [3] kidneys
[2] the rod of peace

"And shall I nowe, forr feere of dethe,
　Looke wanne and bee dysmayde?
Ne! fromm my herte flie childyshe feere,
140　Bee alle the manne display'd.

"Ah!" goddelyke Henrie![1] Godde for-
　　fende,[2]
And guarde thee and thye sonne,
Yff 'tis hys wylle; but yff 'tis nott,
　Why thenne hys wylle bee donne.

145 "My honest friende, my faulte has beene
　To serve Godde and mye prynce;
And thatt I no tyme-server am,
　My dethe wylle soone convynce.

"Ynne Londonne citye was I borne,
150　Of parents of grete note;
My fadre dydd a nobile armes
　Emblazon onne hys cote:

"I make ne doubte butt hee ys gone
　Where ever I hope to goe;
155 Where wee for ever shall bee blest,
　From oute the reech of woe.

"Hee taughte mee justice and the laws
　Wyth pitie to unite;
And eke hee taughte mee howe to knowe
160　The wronge cause fromme the ryghte:

"Hee taughte mee wyth a prudent hande
　To feede the hungrie poore,
Ne lette mye servants dryve awaie
　The hungrie fromme my doore:

165 "And none can saye butt alle mye lyfe
　I have hys wordyes kept;
And summ'd the actyonns of the daie
　Eche nyghte before I slept.

"I have a spouse, goe aske of her
170　Yff I defyl'd her bedde?
I have a kynge, and none can laie
　Blacke treason onne my hedde.

"Ynne Lent, and onne the holie eve,
　Fromme fleshe I dydd refrayne;
175 Whie should I thenne appeare dismay'd
　To leave thys worlde of payne?

"Ne, hapless Henrie! I rejoyce,
　I shall ne see thye dethe;
Moste willynglie ynne thye just cause
180　Doe I resign my brethe.

"Oh, fickle people! rewyn'd londe!
　Thou wylt kenne peace ne moe;
Whyle Richard's sonnes[1] exalt themselves,
　Thye brookes wythe bloude wylle flowe.

185 "Saie, were ye tyr'd of godlie peace,
　And godlie Henrie's reigne,
Thatt you dyd choppe[2] you easie daies
　For those of bloude and peyne?

"Whatte tho' I onne a sledde bee drawne,
190　And mangled by a hynde,[3]
I doe defye the traytor's pow'r,
　Hee can ne harm my mynde;

"Whatte tho', uphoisted onne a pole,
　Mye lymbes shall rotte ynne ayre,
195 And ne ryche monument of brasse
　Charles Bawdin's name shall bear;

"Yett ynne the holie booke above,
　Whyche tyme can't eate awaie,
There wythe the servants of the Lorde
200　Mye name shall lyve for aie.

"Thenne welcome dethe; for lyfe eterne
　I leave thys mortall lyfe:
Farewell, vayne worlde, and alle that's
　　deare,
　Mye sonnes and lovynge wyfe!

205 "Nowe dethe as welcome to mee comes,
　As e'er the moneth of Maie;
Nor woulde I even wyshe to lyve,
　Wyth my dere wyfe to staie."

Quod Canynge, " 'Tys a goodlie thynge
210　To bee prepar'd to die;
And from thys world of peyne and grefe
　To Godde ynne Heav'n to flie."

And nowe the belle beganne to tolle,
　And claryonnes to sounde;
215 Syr Charles hee herde the horses' feete
　A-prauncyng onne the grounde:

And just before the officers
　His lovynge wyfe came ynne,
Weepynge unfeigned teeres of woe,
220　Wythe loude and dysmalle dynne.

"Sweet Florence! nowe I praie forbere,
　Ynne quiet lett mee die;
Praie Godde thatt ev'ry Christian soule
　Maye looke onne dethe as I.

---

[1] Henry VI, noted for his piety, who had been
　deposed and held captive by Edward IV.
[2] defend (The word is misused; it means forbid.)

[1] Richard, Duke of York, was father of Edward
　IV and Richard III.
[2] exchange
[3] peasant

225 "Sweet Florence! why these brinie teeres?
　　Theye washe my soule awaie,
And almost make mee wyshe for lyfe,
　　Wythe thee, sweete dame, to staie.

　" 'T ys butt a journie I shalle goe
230　Untoe the lande of blysse;
Nowe, as a proofe of husbande's love,
　　Receive thys holie kysse.''

Thenne Florence, fault'ring ynne her saie,
　　Tremblynge these wordyes spoke,
235 "Ah, cruele Edwarde! bloudie kynge!
　　Mye herte ys welle nyghe broke:

"Ah, sweete Syr Charles! why wylt thou
　　　goe,
　　Wythoute thye lovynge wyfe?
The cruelle axe thatt cuttes thye necke,
240　Ytte eke shall ende mye lyfe.''

And nowe the officers came ynne
　　To brynge Syr Charles awaie,
Whoe turnedd toe hys lovynge wyfe,
　　And thus to her dydd saie:

245 "I goe to lyfe, and nott to dethe;
　　Truste thou ynne Godde above,
And teache thye sonnes to feare the Lorde,
　　And ynne theyre hertes hym love:

"Teache them to runne the nobile race
250　Thatt I theyre fader runne;
Florence! shou'd dethe thee take—adieu!
　　Yee officers leade onne.''

Thenne Florence rav'd as anie madde,
　　And dydd her tresses tere;
255 "Oh! staie, mye husbande! lorde, and
　　　lyfe!''—
　　Syr Charles thenne dropt a teare.

'Tyll tyredd oute wythe ravynge loud,
　　Shee fellen onne the flore;
Syr Charles exerted alle hys myghte,
260　And march'd fromme oute the dore.

Uponne a sledde hee mounted thenne,
　　Wythe lookes full brave and swete;
Lookes thatt enshone[1] ne more concern
　　Thanne anie ynne the strete.

265 Before hym went the council-menne,
　　Ynne scarlett robes and golde,
And tassils spanglynge ynne the sunne,
　　Muche glorious to beholde:

The Freers of Seincte Augustyne next
270　Appeared to the syghte,
Alle cladd ynne homelie russett weedes,[1]
　　Of godlie monkysh plyghte.[2]

Ynne diffraunt partes a godlie psaume
　　Moste sweetlie theye dydd chaunt;
275 Behynde theyre backes syx mynstrelles
　　　came,
　　Who tun'd the strunge bataunt.[3]

Thenne fyve-and-twentye archers came;
　　Echone[4] the bowe dydd bende,
From rescue of Kynge Henrie's friends
280　Syr Charles forr to defend.

Bolde as a lyon came Syr Charles,
　　Drawne onne a cloth-layde sledde,
Bye two blacke stedes ynne trappynges
　　　white,
　　Wyth plumes uponne theyre hedde:

285 Behynde hym five-and-twentye moe
　　Of archers stronge and stoute,
Wyth bended bowe echone ynne hande,
　　Marched ynne goodlie route;

Seincte Jameses Freers marched next,
290　Echone hys parte dydd chaunt;
Behynde theyre backes syx mynstrelles
　　　came,
　　Who tun'd the strunge bataunt:

Thenne came the maior and eldermenne,
　　Ynne clothe of scarlett deck't;
295 And theyre attendyng menne echone,
　　Lyke Easterne princes trickt.[5]

And after them a multitude
　　Of citizenns dydd thronge;
The wyndowes were all fulle of heddes,
300　As hee dydd passe alonge.

And whenne hee came to the hyghe crosse,
　　Syr Charles dydd turne and saie,
"O Thou, thatt savest manne fromme
　　　synne,
　　Washe mye soule clean thys daie!''

305 Att the grete mynsterr wyndowe sat
　　The kynge ynne myckle[6] state,
To see Charles Bawdin goe alonge
　　To hys most welcom fate.

Soone as the sledde drewe nyghe enowe
310　Thatt Edwarde hee myghte heare,

---

[1] showed (an invented form)

[1] homespun clothes
[2] weave; texture
[3] No such musical in-
　　strument is known.
　　The word is really
[4] each one
[5] decked out
[6] great; much
　　an adjective, mean-
　　ing *eager.*

The brave Syr Charles hee dydd stande
    uppe,
And thus hys wordes declare:

"Thou seest mee, Edwarde! traytour vile!
    Expos'd to infamie;
315 Butt bee assur'd, disloyall manne,
    I 'm greaterr nowe thanne thee!

"Bye foule proceedyngs, murdre, bloude,
    Thou wearest nowe a crowne;
And hast appoynted mee to dye,
320   By power nott thyne owne.

"Thou thynkest I shall die to-daie;
    I have beene dede 'till nowe,
And soone shall lyve to weare a crowne
    For aie uponne my browe:

325 "Whylst thou, perhapps, for som few
    yeares,
    Shalt rule thys fickle lande,
To lett them knowe howe wyde the rule
    'Twixt kynge and tyrant hande:

"Thye pow'r unjust, thou traytour slave!
330   Shall falle onne thye owne hedde"—
Fromme out of hearyng of the kynge
    Departed thenne the sledde.

Kynge Edwarde's soule rush'd to hys face,
    Hee turn'd hys hedde awaie,
335 And to hys broder Gloucester[1]
    Hee thus dydd speke and saie:

"To hym that soe-much-dreaded dethe
    No ghastlie terrors brynge,
Beholde the manne! hee spake the truthe,
340   Hee's greater thanne a kynge!"

"Soe lett hym die!" Duke Richard sayde;
    "And maye echone oure foes
Bende downe theyre neckes to bloudie axe
    And feede the carryon crowes."

345 And nowe the horses gentlie drewe
    Syr Charles uppe the hyghe hylle;
The axe dydd glysterr ynne the sunne,
    His pretious bloude to spylle.

Syr Charles dydd uppe the scaffold goe,
350   As uppe a gilded carre
Of victorye, bye val'rous chiefs
    Gayn'd ynne the bloudie warre:

And to the people hee dydd saie,
    "Beholde you see mee dye,

1 The Duke of Gloucester, afterward Richard III.

355 For servynge loyally mye kynge,
    Mye kynge most ryghtfullie.

"As longe as Edwarde rules thys land,
    Ne quiet you wylle knowe:
Youre sonnes and husbandes shalle bee
    slayne
360   And brookes wythe bloude shalle
    flowe.

"You leave youre goode and lawfulle
    kynge,
    Whenne ynne adversitye;
Lyke mee, untoe the true cause stycke,
    And for the true cause dye."

365 Thenne hee, wyth preestes, uponne hys
    knees,
    A pray'r to Godde dydd make,
Beseechynge hym unto hymselfe
    Hys partynge soule to take.

Thenne, kneelynge downe, hee layd hys
    hedde
370   Most seemlie onne the blocke;
Whyche fromme hys bodie fayre at once
    The able heddes-manne stroke:

And oute the bloude beganne to flowe,
    And rounde the scaffolde twyne;
375 And teares, enowe to wash't awaie,
    Dydd flow fromme each mann's eyne.

The bloudie axe hys bodie fayre
    Ynnto foure parties cutte;
And ey'rye parte, and eke hys hedde,
380   Uponne a pole was putte.

One parte dydd rotte onne Kynwulph-
    hylle,
    One onne the mynster-tower,
And one from off the castle-gate
    The crowen[1] dydd devoure;

385 The other onne Seyncte Powle's goode
    gate,
    A dreery spectacle;
Hys hedde was plac'd onne the hyghe
    crosse,
    Ynne hyghe-streete most nobile.

Thus was the ende of Bawdin's fate:
390   Godde prosper longe oure kynge,
And grante hee maye, wyth Bawdin's
    soule,
    Ynne heav'n Godd's mercie synge!

1 crows

THE ACCOUNTE OF W. CANYNGES FEAST
1768   1772

Thorowe the halle the belle han sounde;[1]
Byelecoyle doe the grave beseeme;[2]
The ealdermenne doe sytte arounde,
Ande snoffelle oppe[3] the cheorte[4] steeme,
5 Lyche asses wylde ynne desarte waste
Swotelye[5] the morneynge ayre doe
      taste.

Syke keene[6] thie ate; the minstrels plaie,
The dynne of angelles doe theie keepe;[7]
Heie stylle,[8] the guestes ha ne[9] to saie,
10 Butte nodde yer[10] thankes ande falle
      aslape.
Thus echone daie bee I to deene,[11]
Gyf[12] Rowley, Iscamm, or Tyb. Gorges[13]
be ne seene.

From ÆLLA: A TRAGYCAL ENTERLUDE
1768   1777

I. Mynstrelles Songe

Fyrste Mynstrelle

The boddynge[14] flourettes bloshes atte
      the lyghte;
The mees[15] be sprenged[16] wyth the
      yellowe hue;
Ynn daiseyd mantels ys the mountayne
      dyghte;
The nesh[17] yonge coweslepe bendethe
      wyth the dewe;
5 The trees enlefèd,[18] yntoe heavenne
      straughte,[19]
Whenn gentle wyndes doe blowe, to
      whestlyng dynne ys brought.

The evenynge commes, and brynges the
      dewe alonge;
The roddie welkynne sheeneth to the
      eyne;[20]
Arounde the alestake[21] mynstrelles synge
      the songe;
10 Yonge ivie rounde the doore poste do
      entwyne;

I laie mee onn the grasse; yette, to
      mie wylle,
Albeytte alle ys fayre, there lackethe
      somethynge stylle.

Seconde Mynstrelle

So Adam thoughtenne, whann, ynn
      Paradyse,
All heavenn and erthe dyd hommage
      to hys mynde;
15 Ynn womman alleyne[1] mannès pleas-
      aunce lyes;
As instrumentes of joie were made the
      kynde.[2]
Go, take a wyfe untoe thie armes, and
      see
Wynter and brownie hylles wyll have a
      charme for thee.

Thyrde Mynstrelle

Whanne Autumpne blake[3] and sonne-
      brente doe appere,
20 With hys goulde honde guylteynge[4] the
      falleynge lefe,
Bryngeynge oppe Wynterr to folfylle
      the yere,
Beerynge uponne hys backe the ripèd
      shefe;
Whan al the hyls wythe woddie sede[5]
      ys whyte;
Whanne levynne fyres[6] and lemes[7] do mete
      from far the syghte:[8]
25 Whann the fayre apple, rudde as even
      skie,[9]
Do bende the tree unto the fructyle[10]
      grounde;
When joicie peres, and berries of
      blacke die,
Doe daunce yn ayre, and call the
      eyne[11] arounde;
Thann, bee the even foule or even fayre,
30 Meethynckes mie hartys[12] joie ys steynced[13]
      wyth somme care.

Seconde Mynstrelle

Angelles bee wroghte to bee of neidher
      kynde;[14]
Angelles alleyne fromme chafe[15] desyre
      bee free:

---

[1] has sounded
[2] f a i r welcoming do
      t h e dignified per-
      sonages appear
[3] snuff up
[4] savory; pleasant
[5] sweetly
[6] so keenly
[7] they play music like
      that of angels
[8] t h e y s t i l l,—*i. e.*,
      when the musicians
      cease playing
[9] have nothing
[10] their
[11] thus every day am
      I to dine
[12] if
[13] Imaginary boon com-
      panions of Canynge.
[14] budding
[15] meadows
[16] are sprinkled
[17] tender
[18] leafed out
[19] stretched
[20] the ruddy sky shines
      to the eye
[21] A stake serving as
      the sign of an ale-
      house.

[1] alone
[2] species,—*i. e.*, woman-
      kind
[3] b l e a k ; bare (In
      Chatterton's glos-
      sary, it is defined as
      naked.)
[4] gilding
[5] willow seed
[6] lightning
[7] gleams
[8] as far as the eye can
      see
[9] ruddy as evening sky
[10] fruitful
[11] eyes
[12] heart's
[13] stained
[14] are made to be of
      neither sex
[15] hot

Dheere[1] ys a somwhatte evere yn the
    mynde,
Yatte,[2] wythout wommanne, cannot
    styllèd bee;
35 Ne seyncte yn celles, botte,[3] havynge
    blodde and tere,[4]
Do fynde the spryte to joie on syghte of
    wommanne fayre;

Wommen bee made, notte for hem-
    selves, botte manne,
Bone of hys bone, and chyld of hys
    desire;
Fromme an ynutyle membere[5] fyrste
    beganne,
40 Ywroghte with moche of water, lyttele
    fyre;
Therefore theie seke the fyre of love,
    to hete
The milkyness of kynde,[6] and make hem-
    selves complete.

Albeytte wythout wommen menne were
    pheeres[7]
To salvage kynde,[8] and wulde botte lyve
    to slea,
45 Botte wommenne efte[9] the spryghte of
    peace so cheres,
Tochelod yn[10] Angel joie heie[11] Angeles
    bee:
Go, take thee swythyn[12] to thie bedde
    a wyfe;
Bee bante[13] or blessed hie[14] yn proovynge
    marryage lyfe.

2. Mynstrelles Songe

O! synge untoe mie roundelaie,[15]
O! droppe the brynie teare wythe mee,
Daunce ne moe atte hallie daie,[16]
Lycke a reynynge[17] ryver bee;
5   Mie love ys dedde,
    Gon to hys death-bedde,
    Al under the wyllowe tree.

Blacke hys cryne[18] as the wyntere nyghte,
Whyte hys rode[19] as the sommer snowe,
10 Rodde[20] hys face as the mornynge lyghte,
Cale[21] he lyes ynne the grave belowe;
    Mie love ys dedde,

Gon to hys deathe-bedde,
Al under the wyllowe tree.

15 Swote[1] hys tyngue as the throstles note,
Quycke ynn daunce as thoughte canne bee,
Defte hys taboure,[2] codgelle stote,[3]
O! hee lyes bie the wyllowe tree:
20   Mie love ys dedde,
    Gonne to hys deathe-bedde,
    Alle underre the wyllowe tree.

Harke! the ravenne flappes hys wynge,
In the briered delle belowe;
Harke! the dethe-owle loude dothe synge,
25 To the nyghte-mares as heie[4] goe;
    Mie love ys dedde,
    Gonne to hys deathe-bedde,
    Al under the wyllowe tree.

See! the whyte moone sheenes onne hie;
30 Whyterre ys mie true loves shroude;
Whyterre yanne[5] the mornynge skie,
Whyterre yanne the evenynge cloude;
    Mie love ys dedde,
    Gon to hys deathe-bedde,
35   Al under the wyllowe tree.

Heere, uponne mie true loves grave,
Schalle the baren fleurs be layde,
Nee one hallie Seyncte to save
Al the celness of a mayde.[6]
40   Mie love ys dedde,
    Gonne to hys deathe-bedde,
    Alle under the wyllowe tree.

Wythe mie hondes I'lle dente[7] the brieres
Rounde his hallie corse to gre,[8]
45 Ouphante[9] fairie lyghte youre fyres,
Heere mie boddie stylle schalle bee.
    Mie love ys dedde,
    Gon to hys deathe-bedde,
    Al under the wyllowe tree.

50 Comme, wythe acorne-coppe and thorne,
Drayne mie hartys blodde awaie;
Lyfe and all yttes goode I scorne,
Daunce bie nete,[10] or feaste by daie.
    Mie love ys dedde,
55   Gon to hys death-bedde,
    Al under the wyllowe tree.

---

[1] there
[2] that
[3] no saint in cell, but
[4] tear
[5] useless member,—i.
   e., Adam's rib
[6] nature
[7] mates
[8] savage species,—i. e.,
   wild beasts
[9] often
[10] dowered with
[11] they

[12] quickly
[13] cursed
[14] highly
[15] accompany me in my
   song
[16] holiday
[17] running
[18] hair
[19] "complexion"—
   Chatterton.
[20] ruddy
[21] cold

[1] sweet
[2] skilful (he was) in
   playing the tabor
   (a stringed instru-
   ment similar to the
   guitar)
[3] his cudgel was stout
[4] they
[5] than
[6] there is not one holy

   saint who can save
   a maid from the
   coldness that comes
   from watching at
   her lover's grave (?)
[7] fasten
[8] grow
[9] elfin
[10] by night

Waterre wytches, crownede wythe reytes,[1]
Bere mee to yer leathalle[2] tyde.
I die! I comme! mie true love waytes.
60 Thos the damselle spake, and dyed.

AN EXCELENTE BALADE OF CHARITIE:

AS WROTEN BIE THE GODE PRIESTE THOMAS
ROWLEIE, 1464
1770   1777

In Virgyne[3] the sweltrie sun gan[4]
        sheene,
And hotte upon the mees[5] did caste
        his raie;
The apple rodded[6] from its palie
        greene,
And the mole[7] peare did bende the
        leafy spraie;
5 The peede chelandri[8] sunge the live-
        long daie;
'Twas nowe the pride, the manhode
        of the yeare,
And eke the grounde was dighte[9] in its
        most defte aumere.[10]

The sun was glemeing in the middle
        of daie,
Deadde still the aire, and eke the
        welken blue,
10 When from the sea arist[11] in drear
        arraie
A hepe of cloudes of sable sullen hue,
The which full fast unto the wood-
        lande drewe,
Hiltring attenes the sunnis fetyve
        face,[12]
And the blacke tempeste swolne[13] and
        gatherd up apace.

15 Beneathe an holme,[14] by a pathwaie
        side
Which dyde unto Seyncte Godwine's
        covent[15] lede,
A hapless pilgrim moneynge[16] dyd
        abide,

Pore in his viewe,[1] ungentle[2] in his
        weede,[3]
Longe bretful[4] of the miseries of
        neede:
20 Where from the hailstone coulde the
        almer[5] flie?
He had no housen theere, ne anie covent
        nie.

Look in his glommèd[6] face, his spright
        there scanne:
Howe woe-be-gone, how withered, for-
        wynd,[7] deade!
Haste to thie church-glebe-house,[8]
        asshrewed[9] manne;
25 Haste to thie kiste,[10] thie onlie dor-
        toure[11] bedde:
Cale[12] as the claie whiche will gre[13] on
        thie hedde
Is Charitie and Love aminge[14] highe
        elves;[15]
Knightis and Barons live for pleasure and
        themselves.

The gatherd storme is rype; the bigge
        drops falle;
30 The forswat[16] meadowes smethe,[17] and
        drenche[18] the raine;
The comyng ghastness[19] do the cattle
        pall,[20]
And the full flockes are drivynge ore
        the plaine;
Dashde from the cloudes, the waters
        flott[21] againe;
The welkin opes, the yellow levynne[22]
        flies,
35 And the hot fierie smothe[17] in the wide
        lowings[23] dies.

Liste! now the thunder's rattling clym-
        mynge[24] sound
Cheves[25] slowlie on, and then embollen[26]
        clangs,
Shakes the hie spyre, and, losst, dis-
        pended, drown'd,
Still on the gallard[27] eare of terroure
        hanges;
40 The windes are up, the lofty elmen
        swanges;[28]

1 water-flags
2 lethal; deadly
3 In the Virgin, that part of the zodiac which the sun enters in August.
4 did
5 meadows
6 reddened
7 soft
8 variegated or pied goldfinch
9 clothed
10 neat mantle
11 arose
12 hiding at once the sun's festive face
13 swelled
14 A kind of oak.
15 "It would have been *charitable* if the author had not pointed at personal characters in this 'Ballad of Charity.' The abbot of St. Godwin's at the time of writing of this was Ralph de Bellomont, a great stickler for the Lancastrian family. Rowley was a York-ist."—Chatterton.
16 moaning

1 appearance
2 beggarly; not like a gentleman
3 dress
4 brimful
5 beggar of alms
6 gloomy; dejected
7 dry; withered
8 the grave
9 accursed
10 chest; coffin
11 sleeping
12 cold
13 grow
14 among
15 personages
16 sunburnt
17 steam
18 drink
19 terror
20 appal; frighten
21 fly
22 lightning
23 flashings
24 noisy
25 moves
26 swelled
27 frighted
28 elm sways

Again the levynne and the thunder
  poures,
And the full cloudes are braste[1] attenes[2]
  in stonen[3] showers.

Spurreynge his palfrie oere the watrie
  plaine,
The Abbote of Seyncte Godwynes convente came:
45 His chapournette[4] was drented with the
  reine,
And his pencte[5] gyrdle met with mickle
  shame,[6]
He aynewarde tolde his bederoll[7] at the
  same.[8]
The storme encreasen, and he drew
  aside
With the mist[9] almes-craver neere[10] to the
  holme to bide.

50 His cope[11] was all of Lyncolne clothe
  so fyne,
With a gold button fasten'd neere his
  chynne;
His autremete[12] was edged with golden
  twynne,[13]
And his shoone[14] pyke[15] a loverds[16]
  mighte have binne;
Full well it shewn he thoughten coste
  no sinne;
55 The trammels[17] of the palfrye pleasde
  his sighte,
For the horse-millanare[18] his head with
  roses dighte.

"An almes, sir prieste!" the droppynge[19] pilgrim saide;
"O! let me waite within your convente
  dore,
Till the sunne sheneth hie above our
  heade,
60 And the loude tempeste of the aire is
  oer.
Helpless and ould am I, alas! and
  poor;
No house, ne friend, ne moneie in my
  pouche;
All yatte[20] I calle my owne is this my silver
  crouche."[21]

65 "Varlet," replyd the Abbatte, "cease
  your dinne!
This is no season almes and prayers to
  give.
Mie porter never lets a faitour[1] in;
None touch mie rynge[2] who not in
  honour live."
And now the sonne with the blacke
  cloudes did stryve,
And shettynge[3] on the grounde his
  glairie raie:[4]
70 The Abbatte spurrde his steede, and eft-
  soones roadde awaie.

Once moe the skie was blacke, the
  thounder rolde:
Faste reyneynge oer the plaine a prieste
  was seen,
Ne dighte[5] full proude, ne buttoned up
  in golde;
His cope and jape[6] were graie, and eke
  were clene;
75 A Limitoure he was of order seene.[7]
And from the pathwaie side then turnèd
  hee,
Where the pore almer laie binethe the
  holmen tree.

"An almes, sir priest!" the droppynge
  pilgrim sayde,
"For sweete Seyncte Marie and your
  order sake."
80 The Limitoure then loosen'd his pouche
  threade,
And did thereoute a groate[8] of silver
  take;
The mister[9] pilgrim dyd for halline[10]
  shake.
Here take this silver, it maie eathe[11]
  thie care;
We are Goddes stewards all, nete[12] of
  oure owne we bare.

85 But ah! unhailie[13] pilgrim, lerne of
  me,
Scathe[14] anie give a rentrolle,[15] to their
  Lorde.
Here take my semecope,[16] thou arte
  bare I see;

---

[1] burst
[2] at once
[3] stony
[4] A small round hat.
[5] painted
[6] much soil
[7] "He told his beads backwards; a figurative expression to signify cursing." — Chatterton.
[8] then; at the same time
[9] poor
[10] nearer
[11] cloak
[12] a loose white robe
[13] twine
[14] shoes
[15] peaked
[16] lord's
[17] shackles, used to make a horse amble
[18] one who decks out horses
[19] drooping
[20] that
[21] cross

[1] vagabond
[2] hammer of the door-knocker
[3] shooting
[4] shining ray
[5] dressed; adorned
[6] A short surplice.
[7] as to his order, he was seen to be a limiter, — i. e., a friar licensed to beg within a certain limited area
[8] A small coin, worth four pence.
[9] poor
[10] joy
[11] ease
[12] naught
[13] unhappy
[14] scarcely
[15] rental, account of rents
[16] under-cloak

Tis thyne; the Seynctes will give me
mie rewarde.''
He left the pilgrim, and his waie
aborde.[1]
90 Virgynne and hallie Seyncte, who sitte
yn gloure,[2]
Or give the mittee[3] will, or give the gode
man power!

EPITAPH ON ROBERT CANYNGE
1770   1777

Thys mornynge starre of Radcleves
rysynge raie,
A true manne good of mynde and
Canynge hyghte,[4]
Benethe thys stone lies moltrynge[5] ynto
claie,
Untylle the dark tombe sheene an[6]
eterne lyghte.
5 Thyrde from hys loynes the present
Canynge came;
Houton[7] are wordes for to telle hys
doe;[8]
For aye shall lyve hys heaven-recorded
name,
Ne shall yt dye whanne tyme shalle
bee no moe;[9]
Whanne Mychael's trumpe shall sounde
to rise the solle,
10 He'll wynge to heaven with kynne,[10] and
happie bee hys dolle.[11]

William Beckford 1759-1844

From THE HISTORY OF THE CALIPH[12]
VATHEK
1783   1786

Vathek, ninth Caliph of the race of the
Abassides, was the son of Motassem, and
the grandson of Haroun Al Raschid. From
an early accession to the throne, and
5 the talents he possessed to adorn it, his
subjects were induced to expect that his
reign would be long and happy. His
figure was pleasing and majestic; but when
he was angry one of his eyes became so
10 terrible, that no person could bear to
behold it, and the wretch upon whom it
was fixed instantly fell backward, and

sometimes expired. For fear, however, of
depopulating his dominions and making
his palace desolate, he but rarely gave way
to his anger.

Being much addicted to women and the
5 pleasures of the table, he sought by his affability to procure agreeable companions; and
he succeeded the better as his generosity
was unbounded, and his indulgences unre-
10 strained, for he was by no means scrupulous,
nor did he think with the Caliph Omar Ben
Abdalaziz, that it was necessary to make
a hell of this world to enjoy Paradise in
the next.

He surpassed in magnificence all his pred-
15 ecessors. The palace of Alkoremmi, which
his father Motassem had erected on the hill
of Pied Horses, and which commanded the
whole city of Samarah, was in his idea far
20 too scanty; he added, therefore, five wings,
or rather other palaces, which he destined
for the particular gratification of each of
his senses.

In the first of these were tables con-
25 tinually covered with the most exquisite
dainties, which were supplied both by
night and by day according to their constant consumption, whilst the most delicious wines and the choicest cordials
30 flowed forth from a hundred fountains
that were never exhausted. This palace
was called ''The Eternal or Unsatiating
Banquet.''

The second was styled ''The Temple of
35 Melody, or the Nectar of the Soul.'' It
was inhabited by the most skilful musicians
and admired poets of the time, who not
only displayed their talents within, but, dis-
persing in bands without, caused every sur-
40 rounding scene to reverberate their songs,
which were continually varied in the most
delightful succession.

The palace named ''The Delight of the
Eyes, or the Support of Memory,'' was
45 one entire enchantment. Rarities collected
from every corner of the earth were there
found in such profusion as to dazzle and
confound, but for the order in which they
were arranged. One gallery exhibited the
50 pictures of the celebrated Mani, and statues
that seemed to be alive. Here a well-man-
aged perspective attracted the sight, there
the magic of optics agreeably deceived it;
whilst the naturalist on his part exhibited,
55 in their several classes, the various gifts
that Heaven had bestowed on our globe.
In a word, Vathek omitted nothing in this
palace that might gratify the curiosity of
those who resorted to it, although he was

[1] went on	[10] his kinsmen
[2] glory	[11] lot
[3] mighty	[12] A title of the suc-
[4] named	cessors of Moham-
[5] moldering	med, now claimed
[6] shine in	by the Sultan of
[7] empty	Turkey. It com-
[8] deeds	prehends the char-
[9] more	acter of prophet,
	priest, and king.

not able to satisfy his own, for he was of all men the most curious.

"The Palace of Perfumes," which was termed likewise "The Incentive to Pleasure," consisted of various halls where the different perfumes which the earth produces were kept perpetually burning in censers of gold. Flambeaus and aromatic lamps were here lighted in open day. But the too powerful effects of this agreeable delirium might be avoided by descending into an immense garden, where an assemblage of every fragrant flower diffused through the air the purest odors.

The fifth palace, denominated "The Retreat of Joy, or the Dangerous," was frequented by troops of young females beautiful as the houris[1] and not less seducing, who never failed to receive with caresses all whom the Caliph allowed to approach them; for he was by no means disposed to be jealous, as his own women were secluded within the palace he inhabited himself.

Notwithstanding the sensuality in which Vathek indulged, he experienced no abatement in the love of his people, who thought that a sovereign immersed in pleasure was not less tolerable to his subjects than one that employed himself in creating them foes. But the unquiet and impetuous disposition of the Caliph would not allow him to rest there; he had studied so much for his amusement in the lifetime of his father, as to acquire a great deal of knowledge, though not a sufficiency to satisfy himself; for he wished to know everything, even sciences that did not exist. He was fond of engaging in disputes with the learned, but liked them not to push their opposition with warmth; he stopped the mouths of those with presents whose mouths could be stopped, whilst others, whom his liberality was unable to subdue, he sent to prison to cool their blood, a remedy that often succeeded.

Vathek discovered also a predilection for theological controversy, but it was not with the orthodox that he usually held. By this means he induced the zealots to oppose him, and then persecuted them in return; for he resolved at any rate to have reason on his side.

The great prophet Mahomet, whose vicars the caliphs are, beheld with indignation from his abode in the seventh heaven the irreligious conduct of such a viceregent. "Let

us leave him to himself," said he to the Genii,[1] who are always ready to receive his commands; "let us see to what lengths his folly and impiety will carry him; if he runs into excess we shall know how to chastise him. Assist him, therefore, to complete the tower which, in imitation of Nimrod, he hath begun, not, like that great warrior, to escape being drowned, but from the insolent curiosity of penetrating the secrets of Heaven; he will not divine the fate that awaits him."

The Genii obeyed, and when the workmen had raised their structure a cubit in the day time, two cubits more were added in the night. The expedition with which the fabric arose was not a little flattering to the vanity of Vathek. He fancied that even insensible matter showed a forwardness to subserve his designs, not considering that the successes of the foolish and wicked form the first rod of their chastisement.

His pride arrived at its height when, having ascended for the first time the eleven thousand stairs of his tower, he cast his eyes below and beheld men not larger than pismires, mountains than shells, and cities than beehives. The idea which such an elevation inspired of his own grandeur completely bewildered him; he was almost ready to adore himself, till, lifting his eyes upward, he saw the stars as high above him as they appeared when he stood on the surface of the earth. He consoled himself, however, for this transient perception of his littleness, with the thought of being great in the eyes of others, and flattered himself that the light of his mind would extend beyond the reach of his sight, and transfer to the stars the decrees of his destiny.

With this view the inquisitive Prince passed most of his nights at the summit of his tower, till he became an adept in the mysteries of astrology, and imagined that the planets had disclosed to him the most marvellous adventures, which were to be accomplished by an extraordinary personage from a country altogether unknown. Prompted by motives of curiosity he had always been courteous to strangers, but from this instant he redoubled his attention, and ordered it to be announced by sound of

[1] Beautiful virgins of the Mohammedan Paradise.

[1] In Oriental mythology, the genii are of a higher order than man, but lower than the angels. They are said to have governed the world before the creation of Adam. They were noted for their architectural skill, the Egyptian pyramids having been ascribed to them. The Persians called them peris and dives.

trumpet, through all the streets of Samarah that no one of his subjects, on peril of displeasure, should either lodge or detain a traveller, but forthwith bring him to the palace.

Not long after this proclamation there arrived in his metropolis a man so hideous that the very guards who arrested him were forced to shut their eyes as they led him along. The Caliph himself appeared startled at so horrible a visage, but joy succeeded to this emotion of terror when the stranger displayed to his view such rarities as he had never before seen, and of which he had no conception.

In reality nothing was ever so extraordinary as the merchandize this stranger produced; most of his curiosities, which were not less admirable for their workmanship than splendor, had besides, their several virtues described on a parchment fastened to each. There were slippers which enabled the feet to walk; knives that cut without the motion of a hand; sabres which dealt the blow at the person they were wished to strike, and the whole enriched with gems that were hitherto unknown.

The sabres, whose blades emitted a dazzling radiance, fixed more than all the Caliph's attention, who promised himself to decipher at his leisure the uncouth characters engraven on their sides. Without, therefore, demanding their price, he ordered all the coined gold to be brought from his treasury, and commanded the merchant to take what he pleased; the stranger complied with modesty and silence.

Vathek, imagining that the merchant's taciturnity was occasioned by the awe which his presence inspired, encouraged him to advance, and asked him, with an air of condescension, who he was, whence he came, and where he obtained such beautiful commodities. The man, or rather monster, instead of making a reply, thrice rubbed his forehead, which, as well as his body, was blacker than ebony, four times clapped his paunch, the projection of which was enormous, opened wide his huge eyes, which glowed like firebrands, began to laugh with a hideous noise, and discovered his long amber-colored teeth bestreaked with green.

The Caliph, though a little startled, renewed his inquiries, but without being able to procure a reply; at which, beginning to be ruffled, he exclaimed: "Knowest thou, varlet, who I am? and at whom thou art aiming thy gibes?" Then, addressing his guards, "Have ye heard him speak? is he dumb?"

"He hath spoken," they replied, "though but little."

"Let him speak again then," said Vathek, "and tell me who he is, from whence he came, and where he procured these singular curiosities, or I swear by the ass of Balaam[1] that I will make him rue his pertinacity."

The menace was accompanied by the Caliph with one of his angry and perilous glances, which the stranger sustained without the slightest emotion, although his eyes were fixed on the terrible eye of the Prince.

No words can describe the amazement of the courtiers when they beheld this rude merchant withstand the encounter unshocked. They all fell prostrate with their faces on the ground to avoid the risk of their lives, and continued in the same abject posture till the Caliph exclaimed in a furious tone: "Up, cowards! seize the miscreant! see that he be committed to prison and guarded by the best of my soldiers! Let him, however, retain the money I gave him; it is not my intent to take from him his property; I only want him to speak."

No sooner had he uttered these words than the stranger was surrounded, pinioned with strong fetters, and hurried away to the prison of the great tower, which was encompassed by seven empalements of iron bars, and armed with spikes in every direction longer and sharper than spits.

The Caliph, nevertheless, remained in the most violent agitation; he sat down indeed to eat, but of the three hundred covers that were daily placed before him could taste of no more than thirty-two. A diet to which he had been so little accustomed was sufficient of itself to prevent him from sleeping; what then must be its effect when joined to the anxiety that preyed upon his spirits? At the first glimpse of dawn he hastened to the prison, again to importune this intractable stranger; but the rage of Vathek exceeded all bounds on finding the prison empty, the gates burst asunder, and his guards lying lifeless around him. In the paroxysm of his passion he fell furiously on the poor carcasses, and kicked them till evening without intermission. His courtiers and vizirs exerted their efforts to soothe his extravagance, but finding every expedient ineffectual they all united in one vociferation: "The Caliph is

---

[1] See *Numbers,* 22-24. Mohammedans believed that all animals would be raised again, and that many of them, including the ass of Balaam, were admitted into Paradise.

gone mad! the Caliph is out of his senses!"

This outcry, which soon resounded through the streets of Samarah, at length reaching the ears of Carathis, his mother, she flew in the utmost consternation to try her ascendancy on the mind of her son. Her tears and caresses called off his attention, and he was prevailed upon by her entreaties to be brought back to the palace.

Carathis, apprehensive of leaving Vathek to himself, caused him to be put to bed, and seating herself by him, endeavored by her conversation to heal and compose him. Nor could any one have attempted it with better success, for the Caliph not only loved her as a mother, but respected her as a person of superior genius; it was she who had induced him, being a Greek herself, to adopt all the sciences and systems of her country, which good Mussulmans hold in such thorough abhorrence. Judicial astrology[1] was one of those systems in which Carathis was a perfect adept; she began, therefore, with reminding her son of the promise which the stars had made him, and intimated an intention of consulting them again.

"Alas!" sighed the Caliph, as soon as he could speak, "what a fool have I been! not for the kicks bestowed on my guards who so tamely submitted to death, but for never considering that this extraordinary man was the same the planets had foretold, whom, instead of ill-treating, I should have conciliated by all the arts of persuasion."

"The past," said Carathis, "cannot be recalled, but it behooves us to think of the future; perhaps you may again see the object you so much regret; it is possible the inscriptions on the sabres will afford information. Eat, therefore, and take thy repose, my dear son; we will consider, tomorrow, in what manner to act."

Vathek yielded to her counsel as well as he could, and arose in the morning with a mind more at ease. The sabres he commanded to be instantly brought, and poring upon them through a green glass, that their glittering might not dazzle, he set himself in earnest to decipher the inscriptions; but his reiterated attempts were all of them nugatory; in vain did he beat his head and bite his nails, not a letter of the whole was he able to ascertain. So unlucky a disappointment would have undone him again, had not Carathis by good fortune entered the apartment.

"Have patience, son!" said she; "you certainly are possessed of every important science, but the knowledge of languages is a trifle at best, and the accomplishment of none but a pedant. Issue forth a proclamation that you will confer such rewards as become your greatness upon any one that shall interpret what you do not understand, and what it is beneath you to learn, you will soon find your curiosity gratified."

"That may be," said the Caliph; "but in the meantime I shall be horribly disgusted by a crowd of smatterers, who will come to the trial as much for the pleasure of retailing their jargon as from the hope of gaining the reward. To avoid this evil, it will be proper to add that I will put every candidate to death who shall fail to give satisfaction; for, thank heaven! I have skill enough to distinguish between one that translates and one that invents."

"Of that I have no doubt," replied Carathis; "but to put the ignorant to death is somewhat severe, and may be productive of dangerous effects; content yourself with commanding their beards to be burnt,[1]—beards in a state are not quite so essential as men."

The Caliph submitted to the reasons of his mother, and sending for Morakanabad, his prime vizir, said: "Let the common criers proclaim, not only in Samarah, but throughout every city in my empire, that whosoever will repair hither and decipher certain characters which appear to be inexplicable, shall experience the liberality for which I am renowned; but that all who fail upon trial shall have their beards burnt off to the last hair. Let them add also that I will bestow fifty beautiful slaves, and as many jars of apricots from the isle of Kirmith, upon any man that shall bring me intelligence of the stranger."

The subjects of the Caliph, like their sovereign, being great admirers of women and apricots from Kirmith, felt their mouths water at these promises, but were totally unable to gratify their hankering, for no one knew which way the stranger had gone.

As to the Caliph's other requisition, the result was different. The learned, the half-learned, and those who were neither, but fancied themselves equal to both, came boldly to hazard their beards, and all shamefully lost them.

The exaction of these forfeitures, which

---

[1] A pseudo-science concerned with foretelling the future of nations and individuals, from observation of the stars.

[1] From the earliest times, among the Mohammedans, the loss of the beard was regarded as highly disgraceful.

found sufficient employment for the eunuchs, gave them such a smell of singed hair as greatly to disgust the ladies of the seraglio, and make it necessary that this new occupation of their guardians should be transferred into other hands.

At length, however, an old man presented himself whose beard was a cubit and a half longer than any that had appeared before him. The officers of the palace whispered to each other, as they ushered him in, "What a pity such a beard should be burnt!" Even the Caliph, when he saw it, concurred with them in opinion, but his concern was entirely needless. This venerable personage read the characters with facility, and explained them verbatim as follows: "We were made where every thing good is made; we are the least of the wonders of a place where all is wonderful, and deserving the sight of the first potentate on earth."

"You translate admirably!" cried Vathek; "I know to what these marvellous characters allude. Let him receive as many robes of honor and thousands of sequins[1] of gold, as he hath spoken words. I am in some measure relieved from the perplexity that embarrassed me!"

Vathek invited the old man to dine, and even to remain some days in the palace. Unluckily for him he accepted the offer; for the Caliph, having ordered him next morning to be called, said: "Read again to me what you have read already; I cannot hear too often the promise that is made me, the completion of which I languish to obtain."

The old man forthwith put on his green spectacles, but they instantly dropped from his nose on perceiving the characters he had read the day preceding had given place to others of different import.

"What ails you?" asked the Caliph; "and why these symptoms of wonder?"

"Sovereign of the world," replied the old man, "these sabres hold another language today from that they yesterday held."

"How say you?" returned Vathek—"but it matters not! tell me, if you can, what they mean."

"It is this, my Lord," rejoined the old man: "Woe to the rash mortal who seeks to know that of which he should remain ignorant, and to undertake that which surpasseth his power!"

"And woe to thee!" cried the Caliph, in a burst of indignation; "today thou art void of understanding; begone from my presence, they shall burn but the half of thy

[1] A gold coin, worth about $2.25.

beard, because thou wert yesterday fortunate in guessing;—my gifts I never resume."

The old man, wise enough to perceive he had luckily escaped, considering the folly of disclosing so disgusting a truth, immediately withdrew and appeared not again.

But it was not long before Vathek discovered abundant reason to regret his precipitation; for though he could not decipher the characters himself, yet by constantly poring upon them he plainly perceived that they every day changed, and unfortunately no other candidate offered to explain them. This perplexing occupation inflamed his blood, dazzled his sight, and brought on a giddiness and debility that he could not support. He failed not, however, though in so reduced a condition, to be often carried to his tower, as he flattered himself that he might there read in the stars which he went to consult something more congenial to his wishes: but in this his hopes were deluded; for his eyes, dimmed by the vapors of his head, began to subserve his curiosity so ill, that he beheld nothing but a thick dun cloud, which he took for the most direful of omens.

Agitated with so much anxiety, Vathek entirely lost all firmness; a fever seized him, and his appetite failed. Instead of being one of the greatest eaters he became as distinguished for drinking. So insatiable was the thirst which tormented him, that his mouth, like a funnel, was always open to receive the various liquors that might be poured into it, and especially cold water, which calmed him more than every other.

This unhappy prince being thus incapacitated for the enjoyment of any pleasure, commanded the palaces of the five senses to be shut up, forbore to appear in public, either to display his magnificence or administer justice, and retired to the inmost apartment of his harem. As he had ever been an indulgent husband, his wives, overwhelmed with grief at his deplorable situation, incessantly offered their prayers for his health and unremittingly supplied him with water.

In the meantime the Princess Carathis, whose affliction no words can describe, instead of restraining herself to sobbing and tears, was closeted daily with the Vizir Morakanabad, to find out some cure or mitigation of the Caliph's disease. Under the persuasion that it was caused by enchantment, they turned over together, leaf by leaf, all the books of magic that might point out a remedy, and caused the horrible stranger, whom they accused as the enchanter, to be everywhere sought for with the strictest diligence.

At the distance of a few miles from Samarah stood a high mountain, whose sides were swarded with wild thyme and basil, and its summit overspread with so delightful a plain, that it might be taken for the paradise destined for the faithful. Upon it grew a hundred thickets of eglantine and other fragrant shrubs, a hundred arbors of roses, jessamine, and honeysuckle, as many clumps of orange trees, cedar, and citron, whose branches, interwoven with the palm, the pomegranate, and the vine, presented every luxury that could regale the eye or the taste. The ground was strewed with violets, harebells, and pansies, in the midst of which sprung forth tufts of jonquils, hyacinths, and carnations, with every other perfume that impregnates the air. Four fountains, not less clear than deep, and so abundant as to slake the thirst of ten armies, seemed profusely placed here to make the scene more resemble the garden of Eden, which was watered by the four sacred rivers.[1] Here the nightingale sang the birth of the rose, her well-beloved, and at the same time lamented its short-lived beauty; whilst the turtle[2] deplored the loss of more substantial pleasures, and the wakeful lark hailed the rising light that reanimates the whole creation. Here more than anywhere the mingled melodies of birds expressed the various passions they inspired, as if the exquisite fruits which they pecked at pleasure had given them a double energy.

To this mountain Vathek was sometimes brought for the sake of breathing a purer air, and especially to drink at will of the four fountains, which were reputed in the highest degree salubrious and sacred to himself. His attendants were his mother, his wives, and some eunuchs, who assiduously employed themselves in filling capacious bowls of rock crystal, and emulously presenting them to him; but it frequently happened that his avidity exceeded their zeal, insomuch that he would prostrate himself upon the ground to lap up the water, of which he could never have enough.

One day when this unhappy prince had been long lying in so debasing a posture, a voice hoarse but strong, thus addressed him: "Why assumest thou the function of a dog, O Caliph, so proud of thy dignity and power?"

At this apostrophe he raised his head and beheld the stranger that had caused him so much affliction. Inflamed with anger at the sight, he exclaimed: "Accursed Giaour![1] what comest thou hither to do? is it not enough to have transformed a prince remarkable for his agility into one of those leather barrels which the Bedouin Arabs carry on their camels when they traverse the deserts? Perceivest thou not that I may perish by drinking to excess no less than by a total abstinence?"

"Drink then this draught," said the stranger, as he presented to him a phial of a red and yellow mixture; "and, to satiate the thirst of thy soul as well as of thy body, know that I am an Indian, but from a region of India which is wholly unknown."

The Caliph, delighted to see his desires accomplished in part, and flattering himself with the hope of obtaining their entire fulfilment, without a moment's hesitation swallowed the potion, and instantaneously found his health restored, his thirst appeased, and his limbs as agile as ever.

In the transports of his joy Vathek leaped upon the neck of the frightful Indian, and kissed his horrid mouth and hollow cheeks as though they had been the coral lips, and the lilies and roses of his most beautiful wives; whilst they, less terrified than jealous at the sight, dropped their veils to hide the blush of mortification that suffused their foreheads.

Nor would the scene have closed here, had not Carathis, with all the art of insinuation, a little repressed the raptures of her son. Having prevailed upon him to return to Samarah, she caused a herald to precede him, whom she commanded to proclaim as loudly as possible: "The wonderful stranger hath appeared again, he hath healed the Caliph, he hath spoken! he hath spoken!"

Forthwith all the inhabitants of this vast city quitted their habitations, and ran together in crowds to see the procession of Vathek and the Indian, whom they now blessed as much as they had before execrated, incessantly shouting: "He hath healed our sovereign, he hath spoken! he hath spoken!" Nor were these words forgotten in the public festivals which were celebrated the same evening, to testify the general joy; for the poets applied them as a chorus to all the songs they composed.

.   .   .   .   .

The Caliph, fired with the ambition of pre-

---

[1] Pishon, Gihon, Hiddekel, and Euphrates.—*Genesis*, 2:10-14.
[2] turtledove

[1] A term applied to all persons not of the Mohammedan faith.

scribing laws to the Intelligences of Darkness, was but little embarrassed at this dereliction; the impetuosity of his blood prevented him from sleeping, nor did he encamp any more as before. Nouronihar, whose impatience if possible exceeded his own, importuned him to hasten his march, and lavished on him a thousand caresses to beguile all reflection; she fancied herself already more potent than Balkis, and pictured to her imagination the Genii falling prostrate at the foot of her throne. In this manner they advanced by moonlight, till they came within view of the two towering rocks that form a kind of portal to the valley, at whose extremity rose the vast ruins of Istakhar. Aloft on the mountain glimmered the fronts of various royal mausoleums, the horror of which was deepened by the shadows of night. They passed through two villages almost deserted, the only inhabitants remaining being a few feeble old men, who, at the sight of horses and litters, fell upon their knees and cried out:

"O heaven! is it then by these phantoms that we have been for six months tormented? Alas! it was from the terror of these spectres and the noise beneath the mountains, that our people have fled, and left us at the mercy of maleficent spirits!"

The Caliph, to whom these complaints were but unpromising auguries, drove over the bodies of these wretched old men, and at length arrived at the foot of the terrace of black marble; there he descended from his litter, handing down Nouronihar; both with beating hearts stared wildly around them, and expected with an apprehensive shudder the approach of the Giaour; but nothing as yet announced his appearance.

A deathlike stillness reigned over the mountain and through the air; the moon dilated on a vast platform the shades of the lofty columns, which reached from the terrace almost to the clouds; the gloomy watch-towers, whose numbers could not be counted, were veiled by no roof, and their capitals, of an architecture unknown in the records of the earth, served as an asylum for the birds of darkness, which, alarmed at the approach of such visitants, fled away croaking.

The chief of the eunuchs, trembling with fear, besought Vathek that a fire might be kindled.

"No!" replied he, "there is no time left to think of such trifles; abide where thou art, and expect my commands."

Having thus spoken he presented his hand to Nouronihar, and, ascending the steps of a vast staircase, reached the terrace, which was flagged with squares of marble, and resembled a smooth expanse of water, upon whose surface not a leaf ever dared to vegetate; on the right rose the watch-towers, ranged before the ruins of an immense palace, whose walls were embossed with various figures; in front stood forth the colossal forms of four creatures, composed of the leopard and the griffin; and, though but of stone, inspired emotions of terror; near these were distinguished by the splendor of the moon, which streamed full on the place, characters like those on the sabres of the Giaour, that possessed the same virtue of changing every moment; these, after vacillating for some time, at last fixed in Arabic letters, and prescribed to the Caliph the following words:

"Vathek! thou hast violated the conditions of my parchment, and deservest to be sent back; but, in favor to thy companion, and as the meed for what thou hast done to obtain it, Eblis permitteth that the portal of his palace shall be opened, and the subterranean fire will receive thee into the number of its adorers."

He scarcely had read these words before the mountain against which the terrace was reared trembled, and the watch-towers were ready to topple headlong upon them; the rock yawned, and disclosed within it a staircase of polished marble that seemed to approach the abyss; upon each stair were planted two large torches, like those Nouronihar had seen in her vision, the camphorated vapor ascending from which gathered into a cloud under the hollow of the vault.

This appearance, instead of terrifying, gave new courage to the daughter of Fakreddin. Scarcely deigning to bid adieu to the moon and the firmament, she abandoned without hesitation the pure atmosphere to plunge into these infernal exhalations. The gait of those impious personages was haughty and determined; as they descended by the effulgence of the torches they gazed on each other with mutual admiration, and both appeared so resplendent, that they already esteemed themselves spiritual Intelligences; the only circumstance that perplexed them was their not arriving at the bottom of the stairs; on hastening their descent with an ardent impetuosity, they felt their steps accelerated to such a degree, that they seemed not walking, but falling from a precipice. Their progress, however, was at length impeded by a vast portal of ebony, which the Caliph without difficulty recognized; here the Giaour awaited them with the key in his hand.

"Ye are welcome," said he to them with a ghastly smile, "in spite of Mahomet and all his dependants. I will now admit you into that palace where you have so highly merited a place."

Whilst he was uttering these words he touched the enamelled lock with his key, and the doors at once expanded, with a noise still louder than the thunder of mountains, and as suddenly recoiled the moment they had entered.

The Caliph and Nouronihar beheld each other with amazement, at finding themselves in a place which, though roofed with a vaulted ceiling, was so spacious and lofty that at first they took it for an immeasurable plain. But their eyes at length growing familiar to the grandeur of the objects at hand, they extended their view to those at a distance, and discovered rows of columns and arcades, which gradually diminished till they terminated in a point, radiant as the sun when he darts his last beams athwart the ocean; the pavement, strewed over with gold dust and saffron, exhaled so subtle an odor as almost overpowered them; they, however, went on, and observed an infinity of censers, in which ambergris and the wood of aloes were continually burning; between the several columns were placed tables, each spread with a profusion of viands, and wines of every species sparkling in vases of crystal. A throng of Genii and other fantastic spirits of each sex danced lasciviously in troops, at the sound of music which issued from beneath.

In the midst of this immense hall a vast multitude was incessantly passing, who severally kept their right hands on their hearts, without once regarding anything around them; they had all the livid paleness of death; their eyes, deep sunk in their sockets, resembled those phosphoric meteors that glimmer by night in places of interment. Some stalked slowly on, absorbed in profound reveries; some, shrieking with agony, ran furiously about, like tigers wounded with poisoned arrows; whilst others, grinding their teeth in rage, foamed along, more frantic than the wildest maniac. They all avoided each other, and, though surrounded by a multitude that no one could number, each wandered at random, unheedful of the rest, as if alone on a desert which no foot had trodden.

Vathek and Nouronihar, frozen with terror at a sight so baleful, demanded of the Giaour what these appearances might mean, and why these ambulating spectres never withdrew their hands from their hearts.

"Perplex not yourselves," replied he bluntly, "with so much at once, you will soon be acquainted with all; let us haste and present you to Eblis."

They continued their way through the multitude, but, notwithstanding their confidence at first, they were not sufficiently composed to examine with attention the various perspectives of halls and of galleries that opened on the right hand and left, which were all illuminated by torches and braziers, whose flames rose in pyramids to the centre of the vault. At length they came to a place where long curtains, brocaded with crimson and gold, fell from all parts in striking confusion; here the choirs and dances were heard no longer, the light which glimmered came from afar.

After some time Vathek and Nouronihar perceived a gleam brightening through the drapery, and entered a vast tabernacle carpeted with the skins of leopards; an infinity of elders with streaming beards, and Afrits[1] in complete armor, had prostrated themselves before the ascent of a lofty eminence, on the top of which, upon a globe of fire, sat the formidable Eblis. His person was that of a young man, whose noble and regular features seemed to have been tarnished by malignant vapors; in his large eyes appeared both pride and despair; his flowing hair retained some resemblance to that of an angel of light; in his hand, which thunder had blasted, he swayed the iron sceptre that causes the monster Ouranabad, the Afrits, and all the powers of the abyss to tremble; at his presence the heart of the Caliph sunk within him, and for the first time, he fell prostrate on his face. Nouronihar, however, though greatly dismayed, could not help admiring the person of Eblis; for she expected to have seen some stupendous Giant. Eblis, with a voice more mild than might be imagined, but such as transfused through the soul the deepest melancholy, said:

"Creatures of clay, I receive you into mine empire; ye are numbered amongst my adorers; enjoy whatever this palace affords; the treasures of the pre-adamite Sultans, their bickering[2] sabres, and those talismans that compel the Dives to open the subterranean expanses of the mountain of Kaf, which communicate with these; there, insatiable as your curiosity may be, shall you

[1] Powerful evil demons in Arabic mythology.
[2] clashing

find sufficient to gratify it; you shall possess the exclusive privilege of entering the fortress of Aherman, and the halls of Argenk, where are portrayed all creatures endowed with intelligence, and the various animals that inhabited that earth prior to the creation of that contemptible being, whom ye denominate the Father of Mankind.''

Vathek and Nouronihar, feeling themselves revived and encouraged by this harangue, eagerly said to the Giaour:

''Bring us instantly to the place which contains these precious talismans.''

''Come!'' answered this wicked Dive, with his malignant grin, ''come! and possess all that my Sovereign hath promised, and more.''

He then conducted them into a long aisle adjoining the tabernacle, preceding them with hasty steps, and followed by his disciples with the utmost alacrity. They reached, at length, a hall of great extent, and covered with a lofty dome, around which appeared fifty portals of bronze, secured with as many fastenings of iron; a funereal gloom prevailed over the whole scene; here, upon two beds of incorruptible cedar, lay recumbent the fleshless forms of the Pre-adamite Kings, who had been monarchs of the whole earth; they still possessed enough of life to be conscious of their deplorable condition; their eyes retained a melancholy motion; they regarded each other with looks of the deepest dejection, each holding his right hand motionless on his heart; at their feet were inscribed the events of their several reigns, their power, their pride, and their crimes; Soliman Raad, Soliman Daki, and Soliman Di Gian Ben Gian, who, after having chained up the Dives in the dark caverns of Kaf, became so presumptuous as to doubt of the Supreme Power; all these maintained great state, though not to be compared with the eminence of Soliman Ben Daoud.

This king, so renowned for his wisdom, was on the loftiest elevation, and placed immediately under the dome; he appeared to possess more animation than the rest; though from time to time he labored with profound sighs, and, like his companions, kept his right hand on his heart; yet his countenance was more composed, and he seemed to be listening to the sullen roar of a vast cataract, visible in part through the grated portals; this was the only sound that intruded on the silence of these doleful mansions. A range of brazen vases surrounded the elevation.

''Remove the covers from these cabalistic depositaries,'' said the Giaour to Vathek, ''and avail thyself of the talismans, which will break asunder all these gates of bronze; and not only render thee master of the treasures contained within them, but also of the spirits by which they are guarded.''

The Caliph, whom this ominous preliminary had entirely disconcerted, approached the vases with faltering footsteps, and was ready to sink with terror when he heard the groans of Soliman. As he proceeded, a voice from the livid lips of the Prophet articulated these words:

''In my life-time I filled a magnificent throne, having on my right hand twelve thousand seats of gold, where the patriarchs and the prophets heard my doctrines; on my left the sages and doctors, upon as many thrones of silver, were present at all my decisions. Whilst I thus administered justice to innumerable multitude, the birds of the air librating[1] over me served as a canopy from the rays of the sun; my people flourished, and my palace rose to the clouds; I erected a temple to the Most High, which was the wonder of the universe; but I basely suffered myself to be seduced by the love of women, and a curiosity that could not be restrained by sublunary things; I listened to the counsels of Aherman and the daughter of Pharaoh, and adored fire and the hosts of heaven; I forsook the holy city, and commanded the Genii to rear the stupendous palace of Istakhar, and the terrace of the watch-towers, each of which was consecrated to a star; there for a while I enjoyed myself in the zenith of glory and pleasure; not only men, but supernatural existences were subject also to my will. I began to think, as these unhappy monarchs around had already thought, that the vengeance of Heaven was asleep; when at once the thunder burst my structures asunder and precipitated me hither; where, however, I do not remain, like the other inhabitants, totally destitute of hope, for an angel of light hath revealed that, in consideration of the piety of my early youth, my woes shall come to an end when this cataract shall forever cease to flow; till then I am in torments, ineffable torments! an unrelenting fire preys on my heart.''

Having uttered this exclamation Soliman raised his hands towards Heaven, in token of supplication, and the Caliph discerned through his bosom, which was transparent as crystal, his heart enveloped in flames. At a sight so full of horror Nouronihar fell

[1] balancing

back, like one petrified, into the arms of Vathek, who cried out with a convulsive sob: "O Giaour! whither hast thou brought us? Allow us to depart, and I will relinquish all thou hast promised. O Mahomet! remains there no more mercy?"

"None! none!" replied the malicious Dive. "Know, miserable prince! thou art now in the abode of vengeance and despair; thy heart also will be kindled, like those of the other votaries of Eblis. A few days are allotted thee previous to this fatal period; employ them as thou wilt; recline on these heaps of gold; command the Infernal Potentates; range at thy pleasure through these immense subterranean domains; no barrier shall be shut against thee; as for me, I have fulfilled my mission; I now leave thee to thyself." At these words he vanished.

The Caliph and Nouronihar remained in the most abject affliction; their tears unable to flow, scarcely could they support themselves. At length, taking each other despondingly by the hand, they went faltering from this fatal hall, indifferent which way they turned their steps; every portal opened at their approach; the Dives fell prostrate before them; every reservoir of riches was disclosed to their view; but they no longer felt the incentives of curiosity, pride, or avarice. With like apathy they heard the chorus of Genii, and saw the stately banquets prepared to regale them; they went wandering on from chamber to chamber, hall to hall, and gallery to gallery, all without bounds or limit, all distinguishable by the same lowering gloom, all adorned with the same awful grandeur, all traversed by persons in search of repose and consolation, but who sought them in vain; for, every one carried within him a heart tormented in flames: shunned by these various sufferings, who seemed by their looks to be upbraiding the partners of their guilt, they withdrew from them to wait in direful suspense the moment which should render them to each other the like objects of terror.

"What!" exclaimed Nouronihar; "will the time come when I shall snatch my hand from thine?"

"Ah!" said Vathek; "and shall my eyes ever cease to drink from thine long draughts of enjoyment! Shall the moments of our reciprocal ecstasies be reflected on with horror! It was not thou that broughtest me hither; the principles by which Carathis perverted my youth, have been the sole cause of my perdition!" Having given vent to these painful expressions, he called to an Afrit, who was stirring up one of the braziers, and bade him fetch the Princess Carathis from the palace of Samarah.

After issuing these orders, the Caliph and Nouronihar continued walking amidst the silent crowd, till they heard voices at the end of the gallery; presuming them to proceed from some unhappy beings, who like themselves were awaiting their final doom, they followed the sound, and found it to come from a small square chamber, where they discovered sitting on sofas five young men of goodly figure, and a lovely female, who were all holding a melancholy conversation by the glimmering of a lonely lamp; each had a gloomy and forlorn air, and two of them were embracing each other with great tenderness. On seeing the Caliph and the daughter of Fakreddin enter, they arose, saluted and gave them place; then he who appeared the most considerable of the group addressed himself thus to Vathek.

"Strangers! who doubtless are in the same state of suspense with ourselves, as you do not yet bear your hand on your heart, if you are come hither to pass the interval allotted previous to the infliction of our common punishment, condescend to relate the adventures that have brought you to this fatal place, and we in return will acquaint you with ours, which deserve but too well to be heard; we will trace back our crimes to their source; though we are not permitted to repent, this is the only employment suited to wretches like us!"

The Caliph and Nouronihar assented to the proposal, and Vathek began, not without tears and lamentations, a sincere recital of every circumstance that had passed. When the afflicting narrative was closed, the young man entered on his own. Each person proceeded in order, and when the fourth prince had reached the midst of his adventures, a sudden noise interrupted him, which caused the vault to tremble and to open.

Immediately a cloud descended, which gradually dissipating, discovered Carathis on the back of an Afrit, who grievously complained of his burden. She, instantly springing to the ground, advanced towards her son and said:

"What dost thou here in this little square chamber? As the Dives are become subject to thy beck, I expected to have found thee on the throne of the Pre-adamite Kings."

"Execrable woman!" answered the Caliph; "cursed be the day thou gavest me birth! go, follow this Afrit, let him conduct thee to the hall of the Prophet Soliman;

there thou wilt learn to what these palaces are destined, and how much I ought to abhor the impious knowledge thou hast taught me."

"The height of power, to which thou art arrived, has certainly turned thy brain," answered Carathis; "but I ask no more than permission to show my respect for the Prophet. It is, however, proper thou shouldest know, that (as the Afrit has informed me neither of us shall return to Samarah) I requested his permission to arrange my affairs, and he politely consented; availing myself, therefore, of the few moments allowed me, I set fire to the tower, and consumed in it the mutes, negresses, and serpents which have rendered me so much good service; nor should I have been less kind to Morakanabad, had he not prevented me, by deserting at last to thy brother. As for Bababalouk, who had the folly to return to Samarah, and all the good brotherhood to provide husbands for thy wives, I undoubtedly would have put them to the torture, could I but have allowed them the time; being, however, in a hurry, I only hung him after having caught him in a snare with thy wives, whilst them I buried alive by the help of my negresses, who thus spent their last moments greatly to their satisfaction. With respect to Dilara, who ever stood high in my favor, she hath evinced the greatness of her mind by fixing herself near in the service of one of the Magi, and I think will soon be our own."

Vathek, too much cast down to express the indignation excited by such a discourse, ordered the Afrit to remove Carathis from his presence, and continued immersed in thought, which his companion durst not disturb.

Carathis, however, eagerly entered the dome of Soliman, and, without regarding in the least the groans of the Prophet, undauntedly removed the covers of the vases, and violently seized on the talismans; then, with a voice more loud than had hitherto been heard within these mansions, she compelled the Dives to disclose to her the most secret treasures, the most profound stores, which the Afrit himself had not seen; she passed by rapid descents known only to Eblis and his most favored potentates, and thus penetrated the very entrails of the earth, where breathes the Sansar, or icy wind of death; nothing appalled her dauntless soul; she perceived, however, in all the inmates who bore their hands on their heart a little singularity, not much to her taste. As she was emerging from one of the abysses,

Eblis stood forth to her view, but, notwithstanding he displayed the full effulgence of his infernal majesty, she preserved her countenance unaltered, and even paid her compliments with considerable firmness.

This superb Monarch thus answered: "Princess, whose knowledge and whose crimes have merited a conspicuous rank in my empire, thou dost well to employ the leisure that remains; for the flames and torments, which are ready to seize on thy heart, will not fail to provide thee with full employment." He said this, and was lost in the curtains of his tabernacle.

Carathis paused for a moment with surprise; but, resolved to follow the advice of Eblis, she assembled all the choirs of Genii, and all the Dives, to pay her homage; thus marched she in triumph through a vapor of perfumes, amidst the acclamations of all the malignant spirits, with most of whom she had formed a previous acquaintance; she even attempted to dethrone one of the Solimans for the purpose of usurping his place, when a voice, proceeding from the abyss of Death, proclaimed, "All is accomplished!" Instantaneously, the haughty forehead of the intrepid Princess was corrugated with agony; she uttered a tremendous yell, and fixed, no more to be withdrawn, her right hand upon her heart, which was become a receptacle of eternal fire.

In this delirium, forgetting all ambitious projects and her thirst for that knowledge which should ever be hidden from mortals, she overturned the offerings of the Genii and, having execrated the hour she was begotten and the womb that had borne her, glanced off in a whirl that rendered her invisible, and continued to revolve without intermission.

At almost the same instant the same voice announced to the Caliph, Nouronihar, the five princes, and the princess, the awful and irrevocable decree. Their hearts immediately took fire, and they at once lost the most precious of the gifts of heaven—Hope. These unhappy beings recoiled with looks of the most furious distraction; Vathek beheld in the eyes of Nouronihar nothing but rage and vengeance, nor could she discern aught in his but aversion and despair. The two princes who were friends, and till that moment had preserved their attachment, shrunk back, gnashing their teeth with mutual and unchangeable hatred. Kalilah and his sister made reciprocal gestures of imprecation, whilst the two other princes testified their horror for each other by the most ghastly convulsions, and screams that could not be smothered. All severally plunged themselves into the accursed multitude, there to wander in an eternity of unabating anguish.

5 Such was, and such should be, the punishment of unrestrained passions and atrocious actions! Such is, and such should be, the chastisement of blind ambition, that would transgress those bounds which the Creator 10 hath prescribed to human knowledge; and, by aiming at discoveries reserved for pure Intelligence, acquire that infatuated pride, which perceives not the condition appointed to man is to be ignorant and humble.

15 Thus the Caliph Vathek, who, for the sake of empty pomp and forbidden power, had sullied himself with a thousand crimes, became a prey to grief without end, and remorse without mitigation; whilst the humble 20 and despised Gulchenrouz passed whole ages in undisturbed tranquillity, and the pure happiness of childhood.

William Cowper 1731-1800

From OLNEY HYMNS
1763-73   1779

LOVEST THOU ME?[1]

Hark, my soul! it is the Lord;
'Tis thy Savior, hear his word;
Jesus speaks, and speaks to thee;
"Say, poor sinner, lov'st thou me?

5 I deliver'd thee when bound,
And, when bleeding, heal'd thy wound;
Sought thee wand'ring, set thee right,
Turn'd thy darkness into light.

Can a woman's tender care
10 Cease towards the child she bare?
Yes, she may forgetful be,
Yet will I remember thee.

Mine is an unchanging love,
Higher than the heights above;
15 Deeper than the depths beneath,
Free and faithful, strong as death.

Thou shalt see my glory soon,
When the work of grace is done;
Partner of my throne shalt be;
20 Say, poor sinner, lov'st thou me?"

Lord, it is my chief complaint,
That my love is weak and faint;
Yet I love thee and adore,
Oh! for grace to love thee more!

[1] *John,* 21:16.

LIGHT SHINING OUT OF DARKNESS[1]

God moves in a mysterious way,
His wonders to perform;
He plants his footsteps in the sea,
And rides upon the storm.

5 Deep in unfathomable mines
Of never-failing skill;
He treasures up his bright designs,
And works his sovereign will.

Ye fearful saints, fresh courage take,
10 The clouds ye so much dread
Are big with mercy, and shall break
In blessings on your head.

Judge not the Lord by feeble sense,
But trust him for his grace;
15 Behind a frowning providence,
He hides a smiling face.

His purposes will ripen fast,
Unfolding ev'ry hour;
The bud may have a bitter taste,
20 But sweet will be the flow'r.

Blind unbelief is sure to err,
And scan his work in vain;
God is his own interpreter,
And he will make it plain.

THE TASK
1783-1784   1785

From BOOK I. THE SOFA

         Scenes that sooth'd
Or charm'd me young, no longer young,
   I find
Still soothing and of pow'r to charm me
   still.
And witness, dear companion of my
   walks,[2]
145 Whose arm this twentieth winter I perceive
Fast lock'd in mine, with pleasure such
   as love,
Confirm'd by long experience of thy
   worth
And well-tried virtues, could alone inspire—
Witness a joy that thou hast doubled
   long.
150 Thou know'st my praise of nature most
   sincere,

[1] *John,* 13:7.
[2] Mrs. Mary Unwin, the friend and companion of Cowper for thirty-four years. See Cowper's *To Mary,* p. 153.

And that my raptures are not conjur'd
  up
To serve occasions of poetic pomp,
But genuine, and art partner of them
  all.
How oft upon yon eminence our pace
155 Has slacken'd to a pause, and we have
  borne
The ruffling wind, scarce conscious that
  it blew,
While admiration, feeding at the eye,
And still unsated, dwelt upon the scene.
Thence with what pleasure have we just
  discern'd
160 The distant plough slow moving, and
  beside
His lab'ring team, that swerv'd not
  from the track,
The sturdy swain diminish'd to a boy!
Here Ouse, slow winding through a level
  plain
Of spacious meads with cattle sprinkled
  o'er,
165 Conducts the eye along his sinuous
  course
Delighted. There, fast rooted in their
  bank,
Stand, never overlook'd, our fav'rite
  elms,
That screen the herdsman's solitary hut;
While far beyond, and overthwart the
  stream
170 That, as with molten glass, inlays the
  vale,
The sloping land recedes into the clouds;
Displaying on its varied side the grace
Of hedge-row beauties numberless,
  square tow'r,
Tall spire, from which the sound of
  cheerful bells
175 Just undulates upon the list'ning ear;
Groves, heaths, and smoking villages,
  remote.
Scenes must be beautiful, which, daily
  view'd,
Please daily, and whose novelty survives
Long knowledge and the scrutiny of
  years—
180 Praise justly due to those that I describe.
  Nor rural sights alone, but rural sounds,
Exhilarate the spirit, and restore
The tone of languid Nature. Mighty
  winds,
That sweep the skirt of some far-spread-
  ing wood
185 Of ancient growth, make music not unlike

The wash of Ocean on his winding
  shore,
And lull the spirit while they fill the
  mind;
Unnumber'd branches waving in the
  blast,
And all their leaves fast flutt'ring, all
  at once.
190 Nor less composure waits upon the
  roar
Of distant floods, or on the softer
  voice
Of neighb'ring fountain, or of rills that
  slip
Through the cleft rock, and, chiming as
  they fall
Upon loose pebbles, lose themselves at
  length
195 In matted grass, that with a livelier
  green
Betrays the secret of their silent course.
Nature inanimate employs sweet sounds,
But animated nature sweeter still,
To sooth and satisfy the human ear.
200 Ten thousand warblers cheer the day,
  and one
The livelong night: nor these alone, whose
  notes
Nice-finger'd art must emulate in vain,
But cawing rooks, and kites that swim
  sublime
In still repeated circles, screaming loud,
205 The jay, the pie, and ev'n the boding
  owl
That hails the rising moon, have charms
  for me.
Sounds inharmonious in themselves and
  harsh,
Yet heard in scenes where peace forever
  reigns,
And only there, please highly for their
  sake.

  . . . .

  God made the country, and man made
  the town.
750 What wonder then that health and virtue, gifts
That can alone make sweet the bitter
  draught
That life holds out to all, should most
  abound
And least be threaten'd in the fields
  and groves?
Possess ye, therefore, ye who, borne
  about
755 In chariots and sedans, know no fatigue
But that of idleness, and taste no
  scenes

But such as art contrives, possess ye
   still
Your element; there only ye can shine,
There only minds like your's can do no
   harm.
760 Our groves were planted to console at
   noon
The pensive wand'rer in their shades.
   At eve
The moonbeam, sliding softly in between
The sleeping leaves, is all the light they
   wish,
Birds warbling all the music. We can
   spare
765 The splendor of your lamps; they but
   eclipse
Our softer satellite. Your songs confound
Our more harmonious notes: the thrush
   departs
Scar'd, and th' offended nightingale is
   mute.
There is a public mischief in your mirth;
770 It plagues your country. Folly such as
   your's,
Grac'd with a sword, and worthier of a
   fan,
Has made, what enemies could ne'er
   have done,
Our arch of empire, stedfast but for
   you,
A mutilated structure, soon to fall.

From Book II. The Time-Piece

Oh for a lodge in some vast wilderness,
Some boundless contiguity of shade,
Where rumor of oppression and deceit,
Of unsuccessful or successful war,
5 Might never reach me more! My ear is
   pain'd,
My soul is sick, with ev'ry day's report
Of wrong and outrage with which earth
   is fill'd.
There is no flesh in man's obdurate
   heart,
It does not feel for man; the nat'ral
   bond
10 Of brotherhood is sever'd as the flax
That falls asunder at the touch of fire.
He finds his fellow guilty of a skin
Not color'd like his own; and, having
   pow'r
T' enforce the wrong, for such a worthy
   cause
15 Dooms and devotes him as his lawful
   prey.

Lands intersected by a narrow frith
Abhor each other. Mountains interpos'd
Make enemies of nations, who had else,
Like kindred drops, been mingled into
   one.
20 Thus man devotes his brother, and destroys;
And, worse than all, and most to be
   deplor'd,
As human nature's broadest, foulest
   blot,
Chains him, and tasks him, and exacts
   his sweat
With stripes, that Mercy, with a bleeding heart,
25 Weeps when she sees inflicted on a
   beast.
Then what is man? And what man,
   seeing this,
And having human feelings, does not
   blush,
And hang his head, to think himself a
   man?
I would not have a slave to till my
   ground,
30 To carry me, to fan me while I sleep,
And tremble when I wake, for all the
   wealth
That sinews bought and sold have ever
   earn'd.
No: dear as freedom is, and in my
   heart's
Just estimation priz'd above all price,
35 I had much rather be myself the slave,
And wear the bonds, than fasten them
   on him.
We have no slaves at home.—Then why
   abroad?
And they themselves, once ferried o'er
   the wave
That parts us, are emancipate and loos'd.
40 Slaves cannot breathe in England;[1] if
   their lungs
Receive our air, that moment they are
   free;
They touch our country, and their shackles fall.
That's noble, and bespeaks a nation
   proud
And jealous of the blessing. Spread it
   then,
45 And let it circulate through ev'ry vein
Of all your empire; that where Britain's
   pow'r
Is felt, mankind may feel her mercy too.
. . . .

---

[1] The court decision that "slaves cannot breathe
in England" was given by Lord Mansfield in
1772. The slave trade was abolished in 1807.

From Book VI. The Winter Walk
at Noon

560 I would not enter on my list of friends
(Tho' grac'd with polish'd manners and
    fine sense,
Yet wanting sensibility) the man
Who needlessly sets foot upon a worm.
An inadvertent step may crush the snail
565 That crawls at ev'ning in the public
    path;
But he that has humanity, forewarn'd,
Will tread aside, and let the reptile live.
The creeping vermin, loathsome to the
    sight,
And charg'd perhaps with venom, that
    intrudes,
570 A visitor unwelcome, into scenes
Sacred to neatness and repose—th' al-
    cove,
The chamber, or refectory—may die:
A necessary act incurs no blame.
Not so when, held within their proper
    bounds,
575 And guiltless of offence, they range the
    air,
Or take their pastime in the spacious
    field:
There they are privileg'd; and he that
    hunts
Or harms them there is guilty of a wrong,
Disturbs th' economy of Nature's realm,
580 Who, when she form'd, design'd them
    an abode.
The sum is this.—If man's convenience,
    health,
Or safety interfere, his rights and
    claims
Are paramount, and must extinguish
    their's.
Else they are all—the meanest things
    that are—
585 As free to live, and to enjoy that life,
As God was free to form them at the
    first,
Who, in his sov'reign wisdom, made them
    all.
Ye, therefore, who love mercy, teach
    your sons
To love it too. The spring-time of our
    years
590 Is soon dishonor'd and defil'd in most
By budding ills, that ask a prudent hand
To check them. But, alas! none sooner
    shoots,
If unrestrain'd, into luxuriant growth,
Than cruelty, most dev'lish of them all.
595 Mercy to him that shows it, is the
    rule
And righteous limitation of its act,

By which Heav'n moves in pard'ning
    guilty man;
And he that shows none, being ripe in
    years,
And conscious of the outrage he com-
    mits,
600 Shall seek it, and not find it, in his turn.

.   .   .   .   .   .

THE POPLAR-FIELD
1784   1785

The poplars are fell'd; farewell to the
    shade
And the whispering sound of the cool
    colonnade;
The winds play no longer and sing in
    the leaves,
Nor Ouse on his bosom their image re-
    ceives.

5 Twelve years have elaps'd since I first
    took a view
Of my favorite field and the bank where
    they grew;
And now in the grass behold they are
    laid,
And the tree is my seat that once lent
    me a shade.

The blackbird has fled to another retreat,
10 Where the hazels afford him a screen
    from the heat,
And the scene where his melody charm'd
    me before,
Resounds with his sweet-flowing ditty
    no more.

My fugitive years are all hasting away,
And I must ere long lie as lowly as they,
15 With a turf on my breast, and a stone
    at my head,
Ere another such grove shall arise in its
    stead.

'Tis a sight to engage me, if anything
    can,
To muse on the perishing pleasures of
    man;
Though his life be a dream, his enjoy-
    ments, I see,
20 Have a being less durable even than he.

THE NEGRO'S COMPLAINT
1788   1793

Forc'd from home and all its pleasures,
    Afric's coast I left forlorn,
To increase a stranger's treasures,
    O'er the raging billows borne.

⁵ Men from England bought and sold me,
  Paid my price in paltry gold;
But, though slave they have enroll'd me,
  Minds are never to be sold.

Still in thought as free as ever,
¹⁰ What are England's rights, I ask,
Me from my delights to sever,
  Me to torture, me to task?
Fleecy locks and black complexion
  Cannot forfeit nature's claim;
¹⁵ Skins may differ, but affection
  Dwells in white and black the same.

Why did all-creating Nature
  Make the plant for which we toil?
Sighs must fan it, tears must water,
²⁰ Sweat of ours must dress the soil.
Think, ye masters, iron-hearted,
  Lolling at your jovial boards,
Think how many backs have smarted
  For the sweets your cane affords.

²⁵ Is there, as ye sometimes tell us,
  Is there one who reigns on high?
Has he bid you buy and sell us,
  Speaking from his throne, the sky?
Ask him if your knotted scourges,
³⁰ Matches, blood-extorting screws,
Are the means which duty urges
  Agents of his will to use?

Hark! he answers!—Wild tornadoes,
  Strewing yonder sea with wrecks;
³⁵ Wasting towns, plantations, meadows,
  Are the voice with which he speaks.
He, foreseeing what vexations
  Afric's sons should undergo,
Fix'd their tyrants' habitations
⁴⁰ Where his whirlwinds answer—No.

By our blood in Afric wasted,
  Ere our necks receiv'd the chain;
By the mis'ries that we tasted,
  Crossing in your barks the main;
⁴⁵ By our suff'rings since ye brought us
  To the man-degrading mart;
All sustain'd by patience, taught us
  Only by a broken heart:

Deem our nation brutes no longer
⁵⁰ Till some reason ye shall find
Worthier of regard and stronger
  Than the color of our kind.
Slaves of gold, whose sordid dealings
  Tarnish all your boasted pow'rs,
⁵⁵ Prove that you have human feelings,
  Ere you proudly question ours!

ON THE RECEIPT OF MY MOTHER'S PICTURE OUT OF NORFOLK

THE GIFT OF MY COUSIN ANN BODHAM
1790   1798

Oh that those lips had language! Life
      has pass'd
With me but roughly since I heard thee
      last.
Those lips are thine—thy own sweet
      smile I see,
The same that oft in childhood solaced
      me;
⁵ Voice only fails, else, how distinct they
      say,
"Grieve not, my child, chase all thy
      fears away!"
The meek intelligence of those dear eyes
(Blest be the art that can immortalize,
The art that baffles Time's tyrannic claim
¹⁰ To quench it) here shines on me still the
      same.
  Faithful remembrancer of one so dear,
O welcome guest, though unexpected,
      here!
Who bidd'st me honor with an artless
      song,
Affectionate, a mother lost so long,[1]
¹⁵ I will obey, not willingly alone,
But gladly, as the precept were her own;
And, while that face renews my filial
      grief,
Fancy shall weave a charm for my re-
      lief—
Shall steep me in Elysian reverie,
²⁰ A momentary dream, that thou art she.
  My mother! when I learn'd that thou
      wast dead,
Say, wast thou conscious of the tears I
      shed?
Hover'd thy spirit o'er thy sorrowing
      son,
Wretch even then, life's journey just
      begun?
²⁵ Perhaps thou gav'st me, though unfelt,
      a kiss;
Perhaps a tear, if souls can weep in
      bliss—
Ah, that maternal smile! it answers—
      Yes.
I heard the bell toll'd on thy burial day,
I saw the hearse that bore thee slow
      away,
³⁰ And, turning from my nurs'ry window,
      drew
A long, long sigh, and wept a last adieu!
But was it such?—It was.—Where thou
      art gone

[1] Cowper's mother died in 1737.

Adieus and farewells are a sound un-
    known.
May I but meet thee on that peaceful
    shore,
35 The parting word shall pass my lips no
    more!
Thy maidens griev'd themselves at my
    concern,
Oft gave me promise of thy quick return.
What ardently I wish'd, I long believ'd,
And, disappointed still, was still de-
    ceiv'd;
40 By expectation every day beguil'd,
Dupe of *tomorrow* even from a child.
Thus many a sad tomorrow came and
    went,
Till, all my stock of infant sorrow spent,
I learn'd at last submission to my lot;
45 But, though I less deplor'd thee, ne'er
    forgot.
    Where once we dwelt our name is
    heard no more,
Children not thine have trod my nurs'ry
    floor;
And where the gard'ner Robin, day by
    day,
Drew me to school along the public way,
50 Delighted with my bauble coach, and
    wrapt
In scarlet mantle warm, and velvet capt,
'Tis now become a history little known,
That once we call'd the past'ral house
    our own.
Short-liv'd possession! but the record
    fair
55 That mem'ry keeps of all thy kindness
    there,
Still outlives many a storm that has
    effac'd
A thousand other themes less deeply
    trac'd,
Thy nightly visits to my chamber made,
That thou might'st know me safe and
    warmly laid;
60 Thy morning bounties ere I left my home,
The biscuit, or confectionary plum;
The fragrant waters on my cheeks be-
    stow'd
By thy own hand, till fresh they shone
    and glow'd;
All this, and more endearing still than
    all,
65 Thy constant flow of love, that knew no
    fall,
Ne'er roughen'd by those cataracts and
    brakes
That humor interpos'd too often makes;
All this still legible in mem'ry's page,
And still to be so, to my latest age,

70 Adds joy to duty, makes me glad to pay
Such honors to thee as my numbers may;
Perhaps a frail memorial, but sincere,
Not scorn'd in heav'n, though little no-
    tic'd here.
    Could Time, his flight revers'd, restore
    the hours,
75 When, playing with thy vesture's tissued
    flow'rs,
The violet, the pink, and jessamine,
I prick'd them into paper with a pin,
(And thou wast happier than myself the
    while,
Would'st softly speak, and stroke my
    head, and smile)
80 Could those few pleasant hours again
    appear,
Might one wish bring them, would I wish
    them here?
I would not trust my heart—the dear
    delight
Seems so to be desir'd, perhaps I might.—
But no—what here we call our life is
    such,
85 So little to be lov'd, and thou so much,
That I should ill requite thee to constrain
Thy unbound spirit into bonds again.
    Thou, as a gallant bark from Albion's
    coast
(The storms all weather'd and the ocean
    cross'd)
90 Shoots into port at some well-haven'd
    isle,
Where spices breathe, and brighter sea-
    sons smile,
There sits quiescent on the floods that
    show
Her beauteous form reflected clear below,
While airs impregnated with incense play
95 Around her, fanning light her streamers
    gay;
So thou, with sails how swift! hast
    reach'd the shore
"Where tempests never beat nor billows
    roar,"[1]
And thy lov'd consort on the dang'rous
    tide
Of life, long since, has anchor'd at thy
    side.[2]
100 But me, scarce hoping to attain that rest,
Always from port withheld, always dis-
    tress'd—
Me howling blasts drive devious, tempest
    toss'd,
Sails ript, seams op'ning wide, and com-
    pass lost,

[1] Garth, *The Dispensary*, 3, 226,—"Where billows never break, nor tempests roar."
[2] Cowper's father died in 1756.

And day by day some current's thwart-
     ing force
105 Sets me more distant from a pros'prous
     course.
Yet, oh, the thought that thou art safe,
     and he!
That thought is joy, arrive what may to
     me.
My boast is not that I deduce my birth
From loins enthron'd, and rulers of the
     earth;[1]
110 But higher far my proud pretensions
     rise—
The son of parents pass'd into the skies.
And now, farewell—Time, unrevok'd, has
     run
His wonted course, yet what I wish'd is
     done
By contemplation's help, not sought in
     vain,
115 I seem t' have liv'd my childhood o'er
     again;
To have renew'd the joys that once were
     mine,
Without the sin of violating thine:
And, while the wings of Fancy still are
     free,
And I can view this mimic show of thee,
120 Time has but half succeeded in his
     theft—
Thyself remov'd, thy power to sooth me
     left.

YARDLEY OAK
1791   1804

Survivor sole, and hardly such, of all
That once liv'd here thy brethren!—at my
     birth
(Since which I number three-score win-
     ters past)
A shatter'd veteran, hollow-trunk'd per-
     haps
5 As now, and with excoriate[2] forks de-
     form,
Relics of ages! Could a mind, imbued
With truth from heav'n, created thing
     adore,
I might with rev'rence kneel and worship
     thee.
It seems idolatry with some excuse
10 When our forefather Druids in their oaks
Imagin'd sanctity. The conscience yet
Unpurified by an authentic act
Of amnesty, the meed of blood divine,
Lov'd not the light, but, gloomy, into
     gloom

15 Of thickest shades, like Adam after taste
Of fruit proscrib'd, as to a refuge, fled.
Thou wast a bauble once; a cup and
     ball,
Which babes might play with; and the
     thievish jay
Seeking her food, with ease might have
     purloin'd
20 The auburn nut that held thee, swallow-
     ing down
Thy yet close-folded latitude of boughs
And all thine embryo vastness, at a gulp.
But Fate thy growth decreed: autumnal
     rains
Beneath thy parent tree mellow'd the
     soil,
25 Design'd thy cradle; and a skipping
     deer,
With pointed hoof dibbling the glebe,[1]
     prepared
The soft receptacle, in which, secure,
Thy rudiments should sleep the winter
     through.
So Fancy dreams.—Disprove it, if ye can,
30 Ye reas'ners broad awake, whose busy
     search
Of argument, employ'd too oft amiss,
Sifts half the pleasures of short life
     away.
Thou fell'st mature, and in the loamy
     clod
Swelling, with vegetative force instinct
35 Didst burst thine egg, as theirs the fabled
     Twins
Now stars;[2] two lobes, protruding, pair'd
     exact;
A leaf succeeded, and another leaf,
And all the elements thy puny growth
Fost'ring propitious, thou becam'st a
     twig.
40 Who liv'd when thou wast such? Oh,
     couldst thou speak,
As in Dodona once thy kindred trees
Oracular,[3] I would not curious ask
The future, best unknown, but at thy
     mouth
Inquisitive, the less ambiguous past.
45 By thee I might correct, erroneous oft,
The clock of history, facts and events
Timing more punctual, unrecorded facts
Recov'ring, and misstated setting right—
Desp'rate attempt, till trees shall speak
     again!

---

[1] On his mother's side, Cowper traced his an-
     cestry to Henry III.
[2] bark-removing

[1] making holes in the sod or ground
[2] Castor and Pollux, who, according to one tra-
     dition, were born of an egg.
[3] The responses of the oracle at Dodona, in
     Epirus, were given by the rustling of the oak
     trees in the wind. The sounds were inter-
     preted by priests.

50 Time made thee what thou wast—King
        of the woods;
And Time hath made thee what thou
        art—a cave
For owls to roost in. Once thy spread-
        ing boughs
O'erhung the champaign;[1] and the nu-
        merous flocks
That graz'd it stood beneath that ample
        cope
55 Uncrowded, yet safe-shelter'd from the
        storm.
No flock frequents thee now. Thou hast
        outliv'd
Thy popularity and art become
(Unless verse rescue thee awhile) a thing
Forgotten, as the foliage of thy youth.
60   While thus through all the stages thou
        hast push'd
Of treeship, first a seedling hid in grass,
Then twig, then sapling, and, as century
        roll'd
Slow after century, a giant bulk
Of girth enormous, with moss-cushion'd
        root
65 Upheav'd above the soil, and sides em-
        boss'd
With prominent wens globose,[2] till at
        the last
The rottenness, which Time is charg'd
        t' inflict
On other mighty ones, found also thee.
What exhibitions various hath the world
70 Witness'd of mutability in all
That we account most durable below!
Change is the diet on which all subsist,
Created changeable, and change at last
Destroys them. Skies uncertain, now the
        heat
75 Transmitting cloudless, and the solar
        beam
Now quenching in a boundless sea of
        clouds;
Calm and alternate storm, moisture and
        drought,
Invigorate by turns the springs of life
In all that live,—plant, animal, and
        man,—
80 And in conclusion mar them. Nature's
        threads,
Fine passing thought, ev'n in her coars-
        est works,
Delight in agitation, yet sustain
The force, that agitates not unimpair'd,
But, worn by frequent impulse, to the
        cause
85 Of their best tone their dissolution owe.

¹ field
² growths in the shape of globes

Thought cannot spend itself, compar-
        ing still
The great and little of thy lot, thy
        growth
From almost nullity into a state
Of matchless grandeur, and declension
        thence,
90 Slow, into such magnificent decay.
Time was when, settling on thy leaf, a
        fly
Could shake thee to the root; and time
        has been
When tempests could not. At thy firmest
        age
Thou hadst within thy bole solid contents
95 That might have ribb'd the sides and
        plank'd the deck
Of some flagg'd admiral; and tortuous
        arms,
The shipwright's darling treasure, didst
        present
To the four-quarter'd winds, robust and
        bold,
Warp'd into tough knee-timber, many a
        load.
100 But the axe spared thee; in those
        thriftier days
Oaks fell not, hewn by thousands, to
        supply
The bottomless demands of contest wag'd
For senatorial honors. Thus to Time
The task was left to whittle thee away
105 With his sly scythe, whose ever-nibbling
        edge,
Noiseless, an atom, and an atom more,
Disjoining from the rest, has, unobserv'd,
Achiev'd a labor, which had, far and
        wide,
(By man perform'd) made all the forest
        ring.
110   Embowell'd now, and of thy ancient
        self
Possessing nought but the scoop'd rind,
        that seems
An huge throat calling to the clouds for
        drink,
Which it would give in riv'lets to thy
        root,
Thou temptest none, but rather much
        forbid'st
115 The feller's toil, which thou couldst ill
        requite.
Yet is thy root sincere, sound as the
        rock,
A quarry of stout spurs and knotted fangs,
Which, crook'd into a thousand whim-
        sies, clasp
The stubborn soil, and hold thee still
        erect.

120 So stands a kingdom, whose founda-
tion yet
Fails not, in virtue and in wisdom laid,
Though all the superstructure, by the
tooth
Pulveriz'd of venality, a shell
Stands now, and semblance only of itself.
125 Thine arms have left thee. Winds have
rent them off
Long since, and rovers of the forest wild
With bow and shaft have burnt them.
Some have left
A splinter'd stump, bleach'd to a snowy
white;
And some memorial none, where once they
grew.
130 Yet life still lingers in thee, and puts
forth
Proof not contemptible of what she can,
Even where death predominates. The
Spring
Finds thee not less alive to her sweet
force
Than yonder upstart of the neighboring
wood,
135 So much thy juniors, who their birth
receiv'd
Half a millennium since the date of
thine.
But since, although well qualified by
age
To teach, no spirit dwells in thee, nor
voice
May be expected from thee, seated here
140 On thy distorted root, with hearers none
Or prompter, save the scene, I will per-
form
Myself the oracle, and will discourse
In my own ear such matter as I may.
One man alone, the Father of us all,
145 Drew not his life from woman; never
gaz'd,
With mute unconsciousness of what he
saw,
On all around him; learn'd not by degrees,
Nor owed articulation to his ear;
But, moulded by his Maker into man
150 At once, upstood intelligent, survey'd
All creatures, with precision understood
Their purport, uses, properties, assign'd
To each his name significant, and, fill'd
With love and wisdom, render'd back to
heav'n
155 In praise harmonious the first air he drew.
He was excus'd the penalties of dull
Minority. No tutor charg'd his hand
With the thought-tracing quill, or task'd
his mind
With problems; history, not wanted yet,

160 Lean'd on her elbow, watching Time, whose
course,
Eventful, should supply her with a theme.

*   *   *   *   *   *

TO MARY
1793   1803

The twentieth year is well-nigh past,
Since our first sky was overcast;[1]
Ah, would that this might be the last!
     My Mary!

5 Thy spirits have a fainter flow,
I see thee daily weaker grow—
'Twas my distress that brought thee low,
     My Mary!

Thy needles, once a shining store,
10 For my sake restless heretofore,
Now rust disus'd, and shine no more,
     My Mary!

For though thou gladly wouldst fulfil
The same kind office for me still,
15 Thy sight now seconds not thy will,
     My Mary!

But well thou play'd'st the housewife's
part,
And all thy threads with magic art
Have wound themselves about this heart,
20   My Mary!

Thy indistinct expressions seem
Like language utter'd in a dream;
Yet me they charm, whate'er the theme,
     My Mary!

25 Thy silver locks, once auburn bright,
Are still more lovely in my sight
Than golden beams of orient light,
     My Mary!

For, could I view nor them nor thee,
30 What sight worth seeing could I see?
The sun would rise in vain for me,
     My Mary!

Partakers of thy sad decline,
Thy hands their little force resign;
35 Yet, gently prest, press gently mine,
     My Mary!

And then I feel that still I hold
A richer store ten thousandfold
Than misers fancy in their gold,
40   My Mary!

Such feebleness of limbs thou prov'st,
That now at every step thou mov'st

[1] A reference to Cowper's violent attack of insanity in 1773.

Upheld by two; yet still thou lov'st,
    My Mary!

45 And still to love, though prest with ill,
In wintry age to feel no chill,
With me is to be lovely still,
    My Mary!

But ah! by constant heed I know,
50 How oft the sadness that I show
Transforms thy smiles to looks of woe,
    My Mary!

And should my future lot be cast
With much resemblance of the past,
55 Thy worn-out heart will break at last,
    My Mary!

THE CASTAWAY
1799   1803

Obscurest night involv'd the sky,
 Th' Atlantic billows roar'd,
When such a destin'd wretch as I,
 Wash'd headlong from on board,
5 Of friends, of hope, of all bereft,
 His floating home forever left.

No braver chief could Albion boast
 Than he with whom he went,
Nor ever ship left Albion's coast,
10 With warmer wishes sent.
He loved them both, but both in vain,
Nor him beheld, nor her again.

Not long beneath the whelming brine,
 Expert to swim, he lay;
15 Nor soon he felt his strength decline,
 Or courage die away;
But wag'd with death a lasting strife,
Supported by despair of life.

He shouted: nor his friends had fail'd
20 To check the vessel's course,
But so the furious blast prevail'd,
 That, pitiless perforce,
They left their outcast mate behind,
And scudded still before the wind.

25 Some succor yet they could afford;
 And, such as storms allow,
The cask, the coop, the floated cord,
 Delay'd not to bestow.
But he (they knew) nor ship, nor shore,
30 Whate'er they gave, should visit more.

Nor, cruel as it seem'd, could he
 Their haste himself condemn,
Aware that flight, in such a sea,
 Alone could rescue them;

35 Yet bitter felt it still to die
Deserted, and his friends so nigh.

He long survives, who lives an hour
 In ocean, self-upheld;
And so long he, with unspent pow'r,
40 His destiny repell'd;
And ever, as the minutes flew,
Entreated help, or cried—"Adieu!"

At length, his transient respite past,
 His comrades, who before
45 Had heard his voice in ev'ry blast,
 Could catch the sound no more.
For then, by toil subdued, he drank
The stifling wave, and then he sank.

No poet wept him: but the page
50 Of narrative sincere,
That tells his name, his worth, his age,
 Is wet with Anson's tear.[1]
And tears by bards or heroes shed
Alike immortalize the dead.

55 I therefore purpose not, or dream,
 Descanting[2] on his fate,
To give the melancholy theme
 A more enduring date:
But misery still delights to trace
60 Its semblance in another's case.

No voice divine the storm allay'd,
 No light propitious shone,
When, snatch'd from all effectual aid,
 We perish'd, each alone:
65 But I beneath a rougher sea,
And whelm'd in deeper gulfs than he.[3]

George Crabbe 1754-1832

From THE VILLAGE
1780-1783   1783

BOOK I

The village life, and every care that
  reigns
O'er youthful peasants and declining
  swains;
What labor yields, and what, that labor
  past,
Age, in its hour of languor, finds at last;
5 What form the real picture of the poor,
Demand a song—the Muse can give no
  more.

---

[1] The poem is founded on an incident in Lord George Anson's *Voyage Round the World* (1748).
[2] commenting freely
[3] Cowper had a delusion that he had lost the favor of God. See his letter to Newton, written April 11, 1799.

Fled are those times, when, in harmonious strains,
The rustic poet praised his native plains:
No shepherds now, in smooth alternate verse,
10 Their country's beauty or their nymphs' rehearse;
Yet still for these we frame the tender strain,
Still in our lays fond Corydons complain,
And shepherds' boys their amorous pains reveal,
The only pains, alas! they never feel.
15 On Mincio's banks, in Cæsar's bounteous reign,
If Tityrus found the Golden Age again,
Must sleepy bards the flattering dream prolong,
Mechanic echoes of the Mantuan song?
From Truth and Nature shall we widely stray,
20 Where Virgil, not where Fancy, leads the way?
Yes, thus the Muses sing of happy swains,
Because the Muses never knew their pains:
They boast their peasants' pipes; but peasants now
Resign their pipes and plod behind the plough;
25 And few, amid the rural-tribe, have time
To number syllables, and play with rhyme;
Save honest Duck, what son of verse could share
The poet's rapture, and the peasant's care?
Or the great labors of the field degrade,
30 With the new peril of a poorer trade?
From this chief cause these idle praises spring,
That themes so easy few forbear to sing;
For no deep thought the trifling subjects ask;
To sing of shepherds is an easy task:
35 The happy youth assumes the common strain,
A nymph his mistress, and himself a swain;
With no sad scenes he clouds his tuneful prayer,
But all, to look like her, is painted fair.
I grant indeed that fields and flocks have charms
40 For him that grazes or for him that farms;
But when amid such pleasing scenes I trace

The poor laborious natives of the place,
And see the mid-day sun, with fervid ray,
On their bare heads and dewy temples play;
45 While some, with feebler heads and fainter hearts,
Deplore their fortune, yet sustain their parts:
Then shall I dare these real ills to hide
In tinsel trappings of poetic pride?
No; cast by Fortune on a frowning coast,
50 Which neither groves nor happy valleys boast,
Where other cares than those the Muse relates,
And other shepherds dwell with other mates,
By such examples taught, I paint the cot,
As Truth will paint it, and as bards will not:
55 Nor you, ye poor, of letter'd scorn complain,
To you the smoothest song is smooth in vain;
O'ercome by labor, and bow'd down by time,
Feel you the barren flattery of a rhyme?
Can poets soothe you, when you pine for bread,
60 By winding myrtles round your ruin'd shed?
Can their light tales your weighty griefs o'erpower,
Or glad with airy mirth the toilsome hour?
Lo! where the heath with withering brake grown o'er,
Lends the light turf that warms the neighboring poor;
65 From thence a length of burning sand appears,
Where the thin harvest waves its wither'd ears;
Rank weeds, that every art and care defy,
Reign o'er the land, and rob the blighted rye:
There thistles stretch their prickly arms afar,
70 And to the ragged infant threaten war;
There poppies nodding, mock the hope of toil;
There the blue bugloss[1] paints the sterile soil;
Hardy and high, above the slender sheaf,
The slimy mallow[1] waves her silky leaf;

[1] A kind of plant.

75 O'er the young shoot the charlock[1] throws
  a shade,
And clasping tares[1] cling round the sickly
  blade;
With mingled tints the rocky coasts
  abound,
And a sad splendor vainly shines around.
So looks the nymph whom wretched arts
  adorn,
80 Betray'd by man, then left for man to
  scorn;
Whose cheek in vain assumes the mimic
  rose,
While her sad eyes the troubled breast
  disclose;
Whose outward splendor is but folly's
  dress,
Exposing most, when most it gilds distress.
85 Here joyless roam a wild amphibious
  race,
With sullen wo display'd in every face;
Who, far from civil arts and social fly,
And scowl at strangers with suspicious
  eye.
  Here too the lawless merchant of the
  main[2]
90 Draws from his plough th' intoxicated
  swain;[3]
Want only claim'd the labor of the day,
But vice now steals his nightly rest
  away.
  Where are the swains, who, daily labor
  done,
With rural games play'd down the setting sun;
95 Who struck with matchless force the
  bounding ball,
Or made the pond'rous quoit obliquely
  fall;
While some huge Ajax, terrible and
  strong,
Engaged some artful stripling of the
  throng,
And fell beneath him, foil'd, while far
  around
100 Hoarse triumph rose, and rocks return'd
  the sound?
Where now are these?—Beneath yon cliff
  they stand,
To show the freighted pinnace where to
  land;[4]

To load the ready steed with guilty
  haste,
To fly in terror o'er the pathless waste,
105 Or, when detected, in their straggling
  course,
To foil their foes by cunning or by
  force;
Or, yielding part (which equal knaves
  demand),
To gain a lawless passport through the
  land.
  Here, wand'ring long, amid these frowning fields,
110 I sought the simple life that Nature
  yields;
Rapine and Wrong and Fear usurp'd her
  place,
And a bold, artful, surly, savage race,
Who, only skill'd to take the finny tribe,
The yearly dinner, or septennial bribe,[1]
115 Wait on the shore, and, as the waves run
  high,
On the tost vessel bend their eager eye,
Which to their coast directs its vent'rous
  way,
Theirs, or the ocean's, miserable prey.
  As on their neighboring beach yon
  swallows stand,
120 And wait for favoring winds to leave
  the land,
While still for flight the ready wing is
  spread,
So waited I the favoring hour, and fled—
Fled from these shores where guilt and
  famine reign,
And cried, Ah! hapless they who still
  remain;
125 Who still remain to hear the ocean roar,
Whose greedy waves devour the lessening
  shore;
Till some fierce tide, with more imperious
  sway,
Sweeps the low hut and all it holds away;
When the sad tenant weeps from door to
  door,
130 And begs a poor protection from the
  poor!
But these are scenes where Nature's niggard hand
Gave a spare portion to the famish'd
  land;
Hers is the fault, if here mankind complain
Of fruitless toil and labor spent in vain;
135 But yet in other scenes more fair in view,
Where Plenty smiles—alas! she smiles
  for few—

---

[1] A kind of plant.
[2] The smuggler.
[3] He became intoxicated on smuggled brandy.
[4] So enormous was the smuggling business that
agriculture, in some places, was seriously impeded by the constant employment of farmers'
horses in carrying goods to a distance from
the shore.

[1] bribe given at the septennial elections of members of Parliament

And those who taste not, yet behold her
 store,
Are as the slaves that dig the golden
 ore,—
The wealth around them makes them
 doubly poor.
140 Or will you deem them amply paid in
 health,
Labor's fair child, that languishes with
 wealth?
Go then! and see them rising with the
 sun,
Through a long course of daily toil to
 run;
See them beneath the dog-star's raging
 heat,
145 When the knees tremble and the temples
 beat;
Behold them, leaning on their scythes,
 look o'er
The labor past, and toils to come explore;
See them alternate suns and showers engage,
And hoard up aches and anguish for
 their age;
150 Through fens and marshy moors their
 steps pursue,
When their warm pores imbibe the evening dew;
Then own that labor may as fatal be
To these thy slaves, as thine excess to
 thee.
 Amid this tribe too oft a manly pride
155 Strives in strong toil the fainting heart
 to hide;
There may you see the youth of slender
 frame
Contend with weakness, weariness, and
 shame;
Yet, urged along, and proudly loth to
 yield,
He strives to join his fellows of the field,
160 Till long-contending nature droops at
 last,
Declining health rejects his poor repast,
His cheerless spouse the coming danger
 sees,
And mutual murmurs urge the slow disease.
 Yet grant them health, 'tis not for us
 to tell,
165 Though the head droops not, that the
 heart is well;
Or will you praise that homely, healthy
 fare,
Plenteous and plain, that happy peasants share!
Oh! trifle not with wants you cannot
 feel,

170 Nor mock the misery of a stinted meal;
Homely, not wholesome, plain, not plenteous, such
As you who praise would never deign to
 touch.
 Ye gentle souls, who dream of rural
 ease,
Whom the smooth stream and smoother
 sonnet please;
Go! if the peaceful cot your praises
 share,
175 Go look within, and ask if peace be there;
If peace be his—that drooping weary
 sire,
Or theirs, that offspring round their
 feeble fire;
Or hers, that matron pale, whose trembling hand
Turns on the wretched hearth th' expiring brand!
180 Nor yet can Time itself obtain for these
Life's latest comforts, due respect and
 ease;
For yonder see that hoary swain, whose
 age
Can with no cares except his own engage;
Who, propp'd on that rude staff, looks
 up to see
185 The bare arms broken from the withering
 tree,
On which, a boy, he climb'd the loftiest
 bough,
Then his first joy, but his sad emblem
 now.
 He once was chief in all the rustic
 trade;
His steady hand the straightest furrow
 made;
190 Full many a prize he won, and still is
 proud
To find the triumphs of his youth allow'd;
A transient pleasure sparkles in his eyes,
He hears and smiles, then thinks again
 and sighs:
For now he journeys to his grave in pain;
195 The rich disdain him; nay, the poor disdain:
Alternate masters now their slave command,
Urge the weak efforts of his feeble hand,
And, when his age attempts its task in
 vain,
With ruthless taunts, of lazy poor complain.
200 Oft may you see him, when he tends
 the sheep,
His winter-charge, beneath the hillock
 weep;

Oft hear him murmur to the winds that
    blow
O'er his white locks and bury them in
    snow,
When, roused by rage and muttering in
    the morn,
205 He mends the broken hedge with icy
    thorn:—
"Why do I live, when I desire to be
At once from life and life's long labor
    free?
Like leaves in spring, the young are
    blown away,
Without the sorrows of a slow decay;
210 I, like yon wither'd leaf, remain behind,
Nipp'd by the frost, and shivering in
    the wind;
There it abides till younger buds come on,
As I, now all my fellow-swains are gone;
Then, from the rising generation thrust,
215 It falls, like me, unnoticed, to the dust.
    "These fruitful fields, these numerous
    flocks I see,
Are others' gain, but killing cares to me;
To me the children of my youth are
    lords,
Cool in their looks, but hasty in their
    words:
220 Wants of their own demand their care;
    and who
Feels his own want and succors others
    too?
A lonely, wretched man, in pain I go,
None need my help, and none relieve my
    wo;
Then let my bones beneath the turf be
    laid,
225 And men forget the wretch they would
    not aid."
    Thus groan the old, till, by disease
    oppress'd,
They taste a final wo, and then they rest.
Theirs is yon house that holds the
    parish-poor,
Whose walls of mud scarce bear the
    broken door;
230 There, where the putrid vapors, flagging,
    play,
And the dull wheel[1] hums doleful through
    the day;—
There children dwell who know no par-
    ents' care;
Parents who know no children's love,
    dwell there!
Heartbroken matrons on their joyless
    bed,
235 Forsaken wives, and mothers never wed,

Dejected widows with unheeded tears,
And crippled age with more than child-
    hood fears;
The lame, the blind, and, far the hap-
    piest they!
The moping idiot and the madman gay.
240 Here too the sick their final doom receive,
Here brought, amid the scenes of grief,
    to grieve,
Where the loud groans from some sad
    chamber flow,
Mix'd with the clamors of the crowd
    below;
Here, sorrowing, they each kindred sor-
    row scan,
245 And the cold charities of man to man:
Whose laws indeed for ruin'd age pro-
    vide,
And strong compulsion plucks the scrap
    from pride;
But still that scrap is bought with many
    a sigh,
And pride embitters what it can't deny.
250 Say ye, oppress'd by some fantastic
    woes,
Some jarring nerve that baffles your re-
    pose;
Who press the downy couch, while slaves
    advance
With timid eye, to read the distant
    glance;
Who with sad prayers the weary doctor
    tease,
255 To name the nameless ever-new disease;
Who with mock patience dire complaints
    endure,
Which real pain and that alone can cure;
How would ye bear in real pain to lie,
Despised, neglected, left alone to die?
260 How would ye bear to draw your latest
    breath,
Where all that's wretched paves the way
    for death?
    Such is that room which one rude
    beam divides,
And naked rafters form the sloping
    sides;
Where the vile bands that bind the
    thatch are seen,
265 And lath and mud are all that lie be-
    tween,
Save one dull pane, that, coarsely
    patch'd, gives way
To the rude tempest, yet excludes the
    day:
Here, on a matted flock,[1] with dust o'er-
    spread,

[1] The spinning-wheel.

[1] A bed filled with flocks of coarse wool.

The drooping wretch reclines his languid
head;
270 For him no hand the cordial cup applies,
Or wipes the tear that stagnates in his
eyes;
No friends with soft discourse his pain
beguile,
Or promise hope till sickness wears a
smile.
But soon a loud and hasty summons
calls,
275 Shakes the thin roof, and echoes round
the walls;
Anon, a figure enters, quaintly neat,
All pride and business, bustle and conceit;
With looks unalter'd by these scenes of
wo,
With speed that, entering, speaks his
haste to go,
280 He bids the gazing throng around him
fly,
And carries fate and physic in his eye:
A potent quack, long versed in human ills,
Who first insults the victim whom he
kills;
Whose murd'rous hand a drowsy Bench[1]
protect,
285 And whose most tender mercy is neglect.
Paid by the parish for attendance here,
He wears contempt upon his sapient sneer;
In haste he seeks the bed where Misery
lies,
Impatience mark'd in his averted eyes;
290 And, some habitual queries hurried o'er,
Without reply, he rushes on the door:
His drooping patient, long inured to
pain,
And long unheeded, knows remonstrance
vain;
He ceases now the feeble help to crave
295 Of man; and silent sinks into the grave.
But ere his death some pious doubts
arise,
Some simple fears, which "bold bad" men
despise;
Fain would he ask the parish-priest to
prove
His title certain to the joys above:
300 For this he sends the murmuring nurse,
who calls
The holy stranger to these dismal walls:
And doth not he, the pious man, appear,
He, "passing rich with forty pounds a
year"?[2]
Ah! no; a shepherd of a different stock,
305 And far unlike him, feeds this little flock:

[1] The local body of Justices of the Peace.
[2] Goldsmith. *The Deserted Village*, 142.

A jovial youth, who thinks his Sunday's
task
As much as God or man can fairly ask;
The rest he gives to loves and labors
light,
To fields the morning, and to feasts the
night;
310 None better skill'd the noisy pack to
guide,
To urge their chase, to cheer them or to
chide;
A sportsman keen, he shoots through half
the day,
And, skill'd at whist, devotes the night
to play:
Then, while such honors bloom around
his head,
315 Shall he sit sadly by the sick man's
bed,
To raise the hope he feels not, or with
zeal
To combat fears that e'en the pious feel?
Now once again the gloomy scene explore,
Less gloomy now; the bitter hour is o'er,
320 The man of many sorrows sighs no more.
Up yonder hill, behold how sadly slow
The bier moves winding from the vale
below;
There lie the happy dead, from trouble
free,
And the glad parish pays the frugal fee:
325 No more, O Death! thy victim starts to
hear
Churchwarden stern, or kingly overseer;
No more the farmer claims his humble
bow,
Thou art his lord, the best of tyrants
thou!
Now to the church behold the mourn-
ers come,
330 Sedately torpid and devoutly dumb;
The village children now their games
suspend,
To see the bier that bears their ancient
friend;
For he was one in all their idle sport,
And like a monarch ruled their little
court.
335 The pliant bow he form'd, the flying ball,
The bat, the wicket, were his labors all;
Him now they follow to his grave, and
stand
Silent and sad, and gazing, hand in hand;
While bending low, their eager eyes explore
340 The mingled relics of the parish poor:
The bell tolls late, the moping owl flies
round,

Fear marks the flight and magnifies the
     sound;
The busy priest, detain'd by weightier
     care,
Defers his duty till the day of prayer;
345 And, waiting long, the crowd retire
     distress'd,
To think a poor man's bones should lie
     unbless'd.

From THE BOROUGH
1810
LETTER I. GENERAL DESCRIPTION

"Describe the Borough"—though our
     idle tribe
May love description, can we so describe,
That you shall fairly streets and build-
     ings trace,
And all that gives distinction to a place?
5 This cannot be; yet, moved by your re-
     quest,
A part I paint—let fancy form the rest.
     Cities and towns, the various haunts
     of men,
Require the pencil; they defy the pen:
Could he, who sang so well the Grecian
     fleet,[1]
10 So well have sung of alley, lane, or street?
Can measured lines these various build-
     ings show,
The Town-Hall Turning, or the Prospect
     Row?
Can I the seats of wealth and want ex-
     plore,
And lengthen out my lays from door to
     door?
15   Then let thy fancy aid me—I repair
From this tall mansion of our last-year's
     mayor,
Till we the outskirts of the Borough
     reach,
And these half-buried buildings next the
     beach,
Where hang at open doors the net and
     cork,
20 While squalid sea-dames mend the meshy
     work,
Till comes the hour, when fishing through
     the tide,
The weary husband throws his freight
     aside,
A living mass, which now demands the
     wife,
Th' alternate labors of their humble life.
25   Can scenes like these withdraw thee from
     thy wood,
Thy upland forest or thy valley's flood?

[1] Homer, *Iliad*, 2.

Seek then thy garden's shrubby bound,
     and look,
As it steals by, upon the bordering
     brook;
That winding streamlet, limpid, linger-
     ing, slow,
30 Where the reeds whisper when the zeph-
     yrs blow;
Where in the midst, upon her throne of
     green,
Sits the large lily as the water's queen;
And makes the current, forced awhile
     to stay,
Murmur and bubble as it shoots away;
35 Draw then the strongest contrast to
     that stream,
And our broad river will before thee
     seem.
     With ceaseless motion comes and goes
     the tide,
Flowing, it fills the channel vast and
     wide;
Then back to sea, with strong majestic
     sweep
40 It rolls, in ebb yet terrible and deep;
Here sampire-banks[1] and salt-wort[1] bound
     the flood;
There stakes and sea-weeds withering on
     the mud;
And higher up, a ridge of all things
     base,
Which some strong tide has roll'd upon
     the place.
45   Thy gentle river boasts its pigmy
     boat,
Urged on by pains, half grounded, half
     afloat,
While at her stern an angler takes his
     stand,
And marks the fish he purposes to land,
From that clear space, where, in the
     cheerful ray
50 Of the warm sun, the scaly people play.
     Far other craft our prouder river shows,
Hoys, pinks, and sloops; brigs, brigan-
     tines, and snows:[2]
Nor angler we on our wide stream de-
     scry,
But one poor dredger where his oysters
     lie:
55 He, cold and wet, and driving with the
     the tide,
Beats his weak arms against his tarry
     side,
Then drains the remnant of diluted gin,
To aid the warmth that languishes within,
Renewing oft his poor attempts to beat

[1] A kind of sea shrub.
[2] Kinds of small coasting vessels.

60 His tingling fingers into gathering heat.
He shall again be seen when evening
comes,
And social parties crowd their favorite
rooms:
Where on the table pipes and papers lie,
The steaming bowl or foaming tankard by;
65 'Tis then, with all these comforts spread
around,
They hear the painful dredger's welcome
sound;
And few themselves the savory boon
deny,
The food that feeds, the living luxury.
Yon is our quay! those smaller hoys
from town,
70 Its various wares, for country-use, bring
down;
Those laden wagons, in return, impart
The country-produce to the city mart;
Hark to the clamor in that miry road,
Bounded and narrow'd by yon vessels'
load,
75 The lumbering wealth she empties round
the place,
Package and parcel, hogshead, chest, and
case.
While the loud seaman and the angry
hind,
Mingling in business, bellow to the wind.
Near these a crew amphibious, in the
docks,
80 Rear, for the sea, those castles on the
stocks,
See! the long keel, which soon the waves
must hide;
See! the strong ribs which form the
roomy side;
Bolts yielding slowly to the sturdiest
stroke,
And planks which curve and crackle in
the smoke.
85 Around the whole rise cloudy wreaths,
and far
Bear the warm pungence of o'er-boiling
tar.
Dabbling on shore half-naked sea-boys
crowd,
Swim round a ship, or swing upon the
shroud;
Or in a boat purloin'd, with paddles play,
90 And grow familiar with the watery way:
Young though they be, they feel whose
sons they are,
They know what British seamen do and
dare,
Proud of that fame, they raise and they
enjoy
The rustic wonder of the village-boy.

95 Before you bid these busy scenes adieu,
Behold the wealth that lies in public
view,
Those far-extended heaps of coal and
coke,
Where fresh-fill'd lime-kilns breathe
their stifling smoke.
This shall pass off, and you behold, instead,
100 The night-fire gleaming on its chalky bed;
When from the light-house brighter
beams will rise,
To show the shipman where the shallow
lies.
Thy walks are ever pleasant; every scene
Is rich in beauty, lively, or serene—
105 Rich—is that varied view with woods
around,
Seen from thy seat, within the shrubb'ry
bound;
Where shines the distant lake, and
where appear
From ruins bolting, unmolested deer;
Lively—the village-green, the inn, the
place,
110 Where the good widow schools her infant
race,
Shops, whence are heard the hammer
and the saw,
And village-pleasures unreproved by law;
Then how serene! when in your favorite
room,
Gales from your jasmines soothe the
evening gloom;
115 When from your upland paddock[1] you
look down,
And just perceive the smoke which hides
the town;
When weary peasants at the close of day
Walk to their cots, and part upon the way;
When cattle slowly cross the shallow
brook,
120 And shepherds pen their folds, and rest
upon their crook.
We prune our hedges, prime our slender trees,
And nothing looks untutor'd and at ease;
On the wide heath, or in the flow'ry vale,
We scent the vapors of the sea-born gale;
125 Broad-beaten paths lead on from stile
to stile,
And sewers from streets, the road-side
banks defile;
Our guarded fields a sense of danger show,
Where garden-crops with corn and clover
grow;
Fences are form'd of wreck and placed
around,

[1] small pasture; field

130 (With tenters[1] tipp'd) a strong repul-
    sive bound;
Wide and deep ditches by the gardens run,
And there in ambush lie the trap and gun;
Or yon broad board, which guards each
    tempting prize,
"Like a tall bully, lifts its head and lies."[2]
135   There stands a cottage with an open
    door,
Its garden undefended blooms before:
Her wheel is still, and overturn'd her stool,
While the lone widow seeks the neigh-
    b'ring pool:
This gives us hope, all views of town to
    shun—
140 No! here are tokens of the sailor-son;
That old blue jacket, and that shirt of
    check,
And silken kerchief for the seaman's neck;
Sea-spoils and shells from many a dis-
    tant shore,
And furry robe from frozen Labrador.
145   Our busy streets and sylvan-walks be-
    tween,
Fen, marshes, bog, and heath all intervene;
Here pits of crag, with spongy, plashy base,
To some enrich th' uncultivated space:
For there are blossoms rare, and curious
    rush,
150 The gale's[3] rich balm, and sun-dew's[3]
    crimson blush,
Whose velvet leaf with radiant beauty
    dress'd,
Forms a gay pillow for the plover's
    breast.
    Not distant far, a house commodious
    made,
(Lonely yet public stands) for Sunday-
    trade;
155 Thither, for this day free, gay parties go,
Their tea-house walk, their tippling ren-
    dezvous;
There humble couples sit in corner-
    bowers,
Or gaily ramble for th' allotted hours;
Sailors and lasses from the town attend,
160 The servant-lover, the apprentice-friend;
With all the idle social tribes who seek,
And find their humble pleasures once a
    week.
    Turn to the watery world!—but who
    to thee
(A wonder yet unview'd) shall paint—
    the sea?
165 Various and vast, sublime in all its forms,
When lull'd by zephyrs, or when roused
    by storms,

[1] sharp hooked nails   Epistle 1, 340.
[2] Pope, *Moral Essays,*   [3] A kind of plant.

Its colors changing, when from clouds
    and sun
Shades after shades upon the surface run;
Embrown'd and horrid[1] now, and now
    serene,
170 In limpid blue, and evanescent green;
And oft the foggy banks on ocean lie,
Lift the fair sail, and cheat th' expe-
    rienced eye.
    Be it the summer-noon: a sandy space
The ebbing tide has left upon its place;
175 Then just the hot and stony beach above,
Light twinkling streams in bright con-
    fusion move;
(For heated thus, the warmer air
    ascends,
And with the cooler in its fall con-
    tends)—
Then the broad bosom of the ocean keeps
180 An equal motion; swelling as it sleeps,
Then slowly sinking; curling to the strand,
Faint, lazy waves o'ercreep the ridgy sand,
Or tap the tarry boat with gentle blow,
And back return in silence, smooth and
    slow.
185 Ships in the calm seem anchor'd; for
    they glide
On the still sea, urged solely by the tide;
Art thou not present, this calm scene
    before,
Where all beside is pebbly length of shore,
And far as eye can reach, it can discern
    no more?
190   Yet sometimes comes a ruffling cloud
    to make
The quiet surface of the ocean shake,
As an awaken'd giant with a frown
Might show his wrath, and then to sleep
    sink down.
    View now the winter-storm! above, one
    cloud,
195 Black and unbroken, all the skies o'er-
    shroud;
Th' unwieldy porpoise through the day
    before
Had roll'd in view of boding men on shore;
And sometimes hid and sometimes
    show'd his form,
Dark as the cloud, and furious as the
    storm.
200 All where the eye delights, yet dreads
    to roam,
The breaking billows cast the flying foam
Upon the billows rising—all the deep
Is restless change; the waves so swell'd
    and steep,
Breaking and sinking, and the sunken
    swells,

[1] rough (a Latinism)

205 Nor one, one moment, in its station dwells:
But nearer land you may the billows trace,
As if contending in their watery chase;
May watch the mightiest till the shoal
they reach,
Then break and hurry to their utmost
stretch;
210 Curl'd as they come, they strike with
furious force,
And then re-flowing, take their grating
course,
Raking the rounded flints, which ages past
Roll'd by their rage, and shall to ages last.
Far off the petrel in the troubled way
215 Swims with her brood, or flutters in the
spray;
She rises often, often drops again,
And sports at ease on the tempestuous
main.
High o'er the restless deep, above the
reach
Of gunner's hope, vast flights of wild-
ducks stretch;
220 Far as the eye can glance on either side,
In a broad space and level line they glide;
All in their wedge-like figures from the
north,
Day after day, flight after flight go forth.
In-shore their passage tribes of sea-
gulls urge,
225 And drop for prey within the sweeping
surge;
Oft in the rough opposing blast they fly
Far back, then turn, and all their force
apply,
While to the storm they give their weak
complaining cry;
Or clap the sleek white pinion to the
breast,
230 And in the restless ocean dip for rest.
Darkness begins to reign; the louder
wind
Appals the weak and awes the firmer
mind;
But frights not him, whom evening and
the spray
In part conceal—yon prowler on his way:
235 Lo! he has something seen; he runs apace,
As if he fear'd companion in the chase;
He sees his prize, and now he turns again,
Slowly and sorrowing — "Was your
search in vain?"
Gruffly he answers, " 'Tis a sorry sight!
240 A seaman's body: there'll be more tonight!"
Hark! to those sounds! they're from
distress at sea:
How quick they come! What terrors
may there be!

Yes, 'tis a driven vessel: I discern
Lights, signs of terror, gleaming from
the stern;
245 Others behold them too, and from the town
In various parties seamen hurry down;
Their wives pursue, and damsels urged
by dread,
Lest men so dear be into danger led;
Their head the gown has hooded, and
their call
250 In this sad night is piercing like the squall;
They feel their kinds of power, and when
they meet,
Chide, fondle, weep, dare, threaten, or
entreat.
See one poor girl, all terror and alarm,
Has fondly seized upon her lover's arm;
255 "Thou shalt not venture;" and he answers, "No!
I will not"—still she cries, "Thou shalt
not go."
No need of this; not here the stoutest
boat
Can through such breakers, o'er such
billows float;
Yet may they view these lights upon the
beach,
260 Which yield them hope, whom help can
never reach.
From parted clouds the moon her
radiance throws
On the wild waves, and all the danger
shows;
But shows them beaming in her shining
vest,
Terrific splendor! gloom in glory dress'd!
265 This for a moment, and then clouds again
Hide every beam, and fear and darkness
reign.
But hear we now those sounds? Do
lights appear?
I see them not! the storm alone I hear:
And lo! the sailors homeward take their
way;
270 Man must endure—let us submit and pray.
Such are our winter-views; but night
comes on—
Now business sleeps, and daily cares are
gone;
Now parties form, and some their friends
assist
To waste the idle hours at sober whist;
275 The tavern's pleasure or the concert's
charm
Unnumber'd moments of their sting dis-
arm;
Play-bills and open doors a crowd invite,
To pass off one dread portion of the night;
And show and song and luxury combined,

280 Lift off from man this burthen of mankind.
      Others advent'rous walk abroad and
        meet
    Returning parties pacing through the
      street;
    When various voices, in the dying day,
    Hum in our walks, and greet us in our
      way;
285 When tavern-lights flit on from room to
      room,
    And guide the tippling sailor staggering
      home.
    There as we pass, the jingling bells betray
    How business rises with the closing day:
    Now walking silent, by the river's side,
290 The ear perceives the rippling of the tide;
    Or measured cadence of the lads who tow
    Some enter'd hoy, to fix her in her row;
    Or hollow sound, which from the parish-
      bell
    To some departed spirit bids farewell!
295   Thus shall you something of our Borough
      know,
    Far as a verse, with Fancy's aid, can show;
    Of sea or river, of a quay or street,
    The best description must be incomplete;
    But when a happier theme succeeds, and
      when
300 Men are our subjects and the deeds of men;
    Then may we find the Muse in happier
      style,
    And we may sometimes sigh and some-
      times smile.

William Lisle Bowles 1762-1850
AT TYNEMOUTH PRIORY
1789

As slow I climb the cliff's ascending side,
Much musing on the track of terror past,
When o'er the dark wave rode the howling
  blast,
Pleased I look back, and view the tranquil
  tide
5 That laves the pebbled shore: and now the
    beam
Of evening smiles on the gray battlement,
And yon forsaken tower that time has rent;
The lifted oar far off with transient gleam
Is touched, and hushed is all the billowy
  deep!
10 Soothed by the scene, thus on tired Na-
    ture's breast
A stillness slowly steals, and kindred rest,
While sea-sounds lull her, as she sinks to
  sleep,
Like melodies that mourn upon the lyre,
Waked by the breeze, and, as they mourn,
  expire!

THE BELLS, OSTEND
1787   1789

How sweet the tuneful bells' responsive
  peal!
As when, at opening morn, the fragrant
  breeze
Breathes on the trembling sense of pale
  disease,
So piercing to my heart their force I feel!
5 And hark! with lessening cadence now they
    fall!
And now, along the white and level tide,
They fling their melancholy music wide,
Bidding me many a tender thought recall
Of summer days, and those delightful years
10 When from an ancient tower, in life's fair
    prime,
The mournful magic of their mingling
  chime
First waked my wondering childhood into
  tears!
But seeming now, when all those days are
  o'er,
The sounds of joy once heard, and heard no
  more.

BEREAVEMENT
1789

Whose was that gentle voice, that, whisper-
  ing sweet,
Promised, methought, long days of bliss
  sincere!
Soothing it stole on my deluded ear,
Most like soft music, that might sometimes
  cheat
5 Thoughts dark and drooping. 'Twas the
    voice of Hope.
Of love, and social scenes, it seemed to
  speak,
Of truth, of friendship, of affection meek;
That oh! poor friend, might to life's downward slope
Lead us in peace, and bless our latest hours.
10 Ah me! the prospect saddened as she sung;
Loud on my startled ear the death-bell
  rung;
Chill darkness wrapt the pleasurable
  bowers,
Whilst Horror pointing to yon breathless
  clay,
"No peace be thine," exclaimed, "away,
  away!"

BAMBOROUGH CASTLE
1789

Ye holy towers that shade the wave-worn
  steep,
Long may ye rear your aged brows sublime,
Though, hurrying silent by, relentless Time

Assail you, and the winds of winter sweep
5 Round your dark battlements; for far
from halls
Of Pride, here Charity hath fixed her seat,
Oft listening, tearful, when the tempests
beat
With hollow bodings round your ancient
walls;
And Pity, at the dark and stormy hour
10 Of midnight, when the moon is hid on high,
Keeps her lone watch upon the topmost
tower,
And turns her ear to each expiring cry;
Blessed if her aid some fainting wretch may
save,
And snatch him cold and speechless from
the wave.

HOPE
1789

As one who, long by wasting sickness worn,
Weary has watched the lingering night, and
heard
Unmoved the carol of the matin bird
Salute his lonely porch; now first at morn
5 Goes forth, leaving his melancholy bed;
He the green slope and level meadow views,
Delightful bathed with slow-ascending
dews;
Or marks the clouds, that o'er the moun-
tain's head
In varying forms fantastic wander white;
10 Or turns his ear to every random song,
Heard the green river's winding marge
along,
The whilst each sense is steeped in still
delight.
So o'er my breast young Summer's breath
I feel,
Sweet Hope! thy fragrance pure and heal-
ing incense steal!

INFLUENCE OF TIME ON GRIEF
1789

O Time! who know'st a lenient hand to lay
Softest on sorrow's wounds, and slowly
thence,
Lulling to sad repose the weary sense,
The faint pang stealest unperceived away:
5 On thee I rest my only hope at last,
And think, when thou hast dried the bitter
tear
That flows in vain o'er all my soul held
dear,
I may look back on every sorrow past,
And meet life's peaceful evening with a
smile;—
10 As some lone bird, at day's departing hour,

Sings in the sunbeam, of the transient
shower
Forgetful, though its wings are wet the
while;—
Yet ah! how much must that poor heart
endure,
Which hopes from thee, and thee alone, a
cure.

APPROACH OF SUMMER
1789

How shall I meet thee, Summer, wont to fill
My heart with gladness, when thy pleasant
tide
First came, and on the Coomb's romantic
side
Was heard the distant cuckoo's hollow
bill![1]
5 Fresh flowers shall fringe the margin of the
stream,
As with the songs of joyance and of hope
The hedge-rows shall ring loud, and on the
slope
The poplars sparkle in the passing beam;
The shrubs and laurels that I loved to tend,
10 Thinking their May-tide fragrance would
delight,
With many a peaceful charm, thee, my
poor friend,
Shall put forth their green shoots, and
cheer the sight!
But I shall mark their hues with sadder
eyes,
And weep the more for one who in the cold
earth lies!

ABSENCE
1793

There is strange music in the stirring wind,
When lowers the autumnal eve, and all
alone
To the dark wood's cold covert thou art
gone,
Whose ancient trees on the rough slope reclined
5 Rock, and at times scatter their tresses sere.
If in such shades, beneath their murmuring,
Thou late hast passed the happier hours of
spring,
With sadness thou wilt mark the fading
year;
Chiefly if one, with whom such sweets at
morn
10 Or evening thou hast shared, afar shall
stray.
O Spring, return! return, auspicious May!

[1] bell; boom

But sad will be thy coming, and forlorn,
If she return not with thy cheering ray,
Who from these shades is gone, far, far
away.

William Blake 1757-1827

From POETICAL SKETCHES

1783

TO SPRING

O thou, with dewy locks, who lookest down
Thro' the clear windows of the morning,
turn
Thine angel eyes upon our western isle,
Which in full choir hails thy approach,
O Spring!

5 The hills tell each other, and the list'ning
Vallies hear; all our longing eyes are
turned
Up to thy bright pavillions: issue forth,
And let thy holy feet visit our clime.

Come o'er the eastern hills, and let our
winds
10 Kiss thy perfumed garments; let us taste
Thy morn and evening breath; scatter
thy pearls
Upon our love-sick land that mourns for
thee.

O deck her forth with thy fair fingers; pour
Thy soft kisses on her bosom; and put
15 Thy golden crown upon her languish'd
head,
Whose modest tresses were bound up for
thee!

TO THE EVENING STAR

Thou fair-hair'd angel of the evening,
Now, whilst the sun rests on the mountains, light
Thy bright torch of love; thy radiant
crown
Put on, and smile upon our evening bed!
5 Smile on our loves, and, while thou draw-
est the
Blue curtains of the sky, scatter thy silver
dew
On every flower that shuts its sweet eyes
In timely sleep. Let thy west wind sleep on
The lake; speak silence with thy glimmering eyes,
10 And wash the dusk with silver. Soon, full
soon,
Dost thou withdraw; then the wolf rages
wide,
And the lion glares thro' the dun forest:

The fleeces of our flocks are cover'd with
Thy sacred dew: protect them with thine
influence.

SONG

How sweet I roam'd from field to field,
And tasted all the summer's pride,
'Till I the prince of love beheld,
Who in the sunny beams did glide!

5 He shew'd me lillies for my hair,
And blushing roses for my brow;
He led me through his gardens fair,
Where all his golden pleasures grow.

With sweet May dews my wings were wet,
10 And Phœbus fir'd my vocal rage;
He caught me in his silken net,
And shut me in his golden cage.

He loves to sit and hear me sing,
Then, laughing, sports and plays with
me;
15 Then stretches out my golden wing,
And mocks my loss of liberty.

SONG

My silks and fine array,
My smiles and languish'd air,
By love are driv'n away;
And mournful lean Despair
5 Brings me yew to deck my grave:
Such end true lovers have.

His face is fair as heav'n,
When springing buds unfold;
O why to him was't giv'n,
10 Whose heart is wintry cold?
His breast is love's all worship'd tomb,
Where all love's pilgrims come.

Bring me an axe and spade,
Bring me a winding sheet;
15 When I my grave have made,
Let winds and tempests beat:
Then down I'll lie, as cold as clay.
True love doth pass away!

SONG

Love and harmony combine,
And around our souls intwine,
While thy branches mix with mine,
And our roots together join.

5 Joys upon our branches sit,
Chirping loud and singing sweet;
Like gentle streams beneath our feet,
Innocence and virtue meet.

Thou the golden fruit dost bear,
10 I am clad in flowers fair;
Thy sweet boughs perfume the air,
And the turtle buildeth there.

There she sits and feeds her young,
Sweet I hear her mournful song;
15 And thy lovely leaves among,
There is love: I hear his tongue.

There his charming nest doth lay,
There he sleeps the night away;
There he sports along the day,
20 And doth among our branches play.

SONG

I love the jocund dance,
The softly-breathing song,
Where innocent eyes do glance,
And where lisps the maiden's tongue.

5 I love the laughing vale,
I love the echoing hill,
Where mirth does never fail,
And the jolly swain laughs his fill.

I love the pleasant cot,
10 I love the innocent bow'r,
Where white and brown[1] is our lot,
Or fruit in the mid-day hour.

I love the oaken seat,
Beneath the oaken tree,
15 Where all the old villagers meet,
And laugh our sports to see.

I love our neighbours all,
But, Kitty, I better love thee;
And love them I ever shall;
20 But thou art all to me.

SONG

Memory, hither come,
And tune your merry notes;
And, while upon the wind
Your music floats,
5 I'll pore upon the stream,
Where sighing lovers dream,
And fish for fancies as they pass
Within the watery glass.

I'll drink of the clear stream,
10 And hear the linnet's song;
And there I'll lie and dream
The day along:

[1] Probably white bread and brown ale; possibly white milk and brown bread.

And when night comes, I'll go
To places fit for woe,
15 Walking along the darken'd valley
With silent Melancholy.

MAD SONG

The wild winds weep,
And the night is a-cold;
Come hither, Sleep,
And my griefs unfold:
5 But lo! the morning peeps
Over the eastern steeps,
And the rustling birds of dawn
The earth do scorn.

Lo! to the vault
10 Of paved heaven,
With sorrow fraught
My notes are driven:
They strike the ear of night,
Make weep the eyes of day;
15 They make mad the roaring winds,
And with tempests play.

Like a fiend in a cloud,
With howling woe,
After night I do croud,
20 And with night will go;
I turn my back to the east
From whence comforts have increas'd;
For light doth seize my brain
With frantic pain.

SONG

Fresh from the dewy hill, the merry year
Smiles on my head, and mounts his flaming
car;
Round my young brows the laurel wreathes
a shade,
And rising glories beam around my head.

5 My feet are wing'd, while o'er the dewy
lawn
I meet my maiden, risen like the morn:
Oh bless those holy feet, like angels' feet;
Oh bless those limbs, beaming with heav'nly
light!

Like as an angel glitt'ring in the sky
10 In times of innocence and holy joy;
The joyful shepherd stops his grateful song
To hear the music of an angel's tongue.

So when she speaks, the voice of Heaven
I hear:
So when we walk, nothing impure comes
near;

¹⁵ Each field seems Eden, and each calm
        retreat;
   Each village seems the haunt of holy feet.

   But that sweet village, where my black-ey'd
        maid
   Closes her eyes in sleep beneath night's
        shade,
   Whene'er I enter, more than mortal fire
²⁰ Burns in my soul, and does my song in-
        spire.

TO THE MUSES

   Whether on Ida's shady brow,
     Or in the chambers of the East,
   The chambers of the sun, that now
     From antient melody have ceas'd;

⁵ Whether in Heav'n ye wander fair,
     Or the green corners of the earth,
   Or the blue regions of the air,
     Where the melodious winds have birth;

   Whether on chrystal rocks ye rove,
¹⁰   Beneath the bosom of the sea
   Wand'ring in many a coral grove,
     Fair Nine, forsaking Poetry!

   How have you left the antient love
     That bards of old enjoy'd in you!
¹⁵ The languid strings do scarcely move!
     The sound is forc'd, the notes are few!

From SONGS OF INNOCENCE
1789
INTRODUCTION

   Piping down the valleys wild,
   Piping songs of pleasant glee,
   On a cloud I saw a child,
   And he laughing said to me:

⁵ "Pipe a song about a Lamb!"
   So I piped with merry chear.
   "Piper, pipe that song again;"
   So I piped: he wept to hear.

   "Drop thy pipe, thy happy pipe;
¹⁰ Sing thy songs of happy chear:"
   So I sung the same again,
   While he wept with joy to hear.

   "Piper, sit thee down, and write
   In a book, that all may read."
¹⁵ So he vanish'd from my sight,
   And I pluck'd a hollow reed,

   And I made a rural pen,
   And I stain'd the water clear,

The Author & Printer W Blake

   And I wrote my happy songs
²⁰ Every child may joy to hear.

A DREAM

   Once a dream did weave a shade
   O'er my Angel-guarded bed,
   That an Emmet¹ lost its way
   Where on grass methought I lay.

⁵ Troubled, 'wilder'd, and forlorn,
   Dark, benighted, travel-worn,
   Over many a tangled spray,
   All heart-broke I heard her say:

   "O, my children! do they cry?
¹⁰ Do they hear their father sigh?
   Now they look abroad to see:
   Now return and weep for me."

   Pitying, I drop'd a tear;
   But I saw a glow-worm near,
¹⁵ Who replied: "What wailing wight
   Calls the watchman of the night?

¹ ant

"I am set to light the ground,
While the beetle goes his round:
Follow now the beetle's hum;
20 Little wanderer, hie thee home!"

THE LAMB

Little Lamb, who made thee?
Dost thou know who made thee?
Gave thee life, & bid thee feed
By the stream & o'er the mead;
5 Gave thee clothing of delight,
Softest clothing, wooly, bright;
Gave thee such a tender voice,
Making all the vales rejoice?
Little Lamb, who made thee?
10 Dost thou know who made thee?

Little Lamb, I'll tell thee,
Little Lamb, I'll tell thee:
He is called by thy name,
For He calls himself a Lamb.
15 He is meek, & he is mild;
He became a little child.
I a child, & thou a lamb,
We are called by his name.
Little Lamb, God bless thee!
20 Little Lamb, God bless thee!

THE ECCHOING GREEN

The Sun does arise,
And make happy the skies;
The merry bells ring
To welcome the Spring;
5 The skylark and thrush,
The birds of the bush,
Sing louder around
To the bells' chearful sound,
While our sports shall be seen
10 On the Ecchoing Green.

Old John, with white hair,
Does laugh away care,
Sitting under the oak,
Among the old folk.
15 They laugh at our play,
And soon they all say:
"Such, such were the joys
When we all, girls & boys,
In our youth time were seen
20 On the Ecchoing Green."

Till the little ones, weary,
No more can be merry;
The sun does descend,
And our sports have an end.
25 Round the laps of their mothers
Many sisters and brothers,
Like birds in their nest,
Are ready for rest,
And sport no more seen
30 On the darkening Green.

THE DIVINE IMAGE

To Mercy, Pity, Peace, and Love
All pray in their distress;
And to these virtues of delight
Return their thankfulness.

5 For Mercy, Pity, Peace, and Love
Is God, our father dear;
And Mercy, Pity, Peace, and Love
Is Man, his child and care.

For Mercy has a human heart,
10 Pity a human face,
And love, the human form divine;
And Peace, the human dress.

Then every man, of every clime,
That prays in his distress,
15 Prays to the human form divine,
Love, Mercy, Pity, Peace.

And all must love the human form,
In heathen, turk, or jew;

Where Mercy, Love, & Pity dwell
20   There God is dwelling too.

THE CHIMNEY SWEEPER

When my mother died I was very young,
And my father sold me while yet my
  tongue
Could scarcely cry " 'weep! 'weep! 'weep!
  'weep!"
So your chimneys I sweep, & in soot I
  sleep.

5 There's little Tom Dacre, who cried when
  his head,
That curl'd like a lamb's back, was
  shav'd: so I said
"Hush, Tom! never mind it, for when your
  head's bare
You know that the soot cannot spoil your
  white hair."

And so he was quiet, & that very night,
10 As Tom was a-sleeping, he had such a
  sight!
That thousands of sweepers, Dick, Joe,
  Ned, & Jack,
Were all of them lock'd up in coffins of
  black.

And by came an Angel who had a bright
  key,
And he open'd the coffins & set them all
  free;
15 Then down a green plain leaping, laughing, they run,
And wash in a river, and shine in the Sun.

Then naked & white, all their bags left
  behind,
They rise upon clouds and sport in the
  wind;
And the Angel told Tom, if he'd be a good
  boy,
20 He'd have God for his father, & never
  want joy.

And so Tom awoke; and we rose in the
  dark,
And got with our bags & our brushes to
  work.
Tho' the morning was cold, Tom was
  happy & warm;
So if all do their duty they need not fear
  harm.

INFANT JOY

"I have no name:
I am but two days old."
What shall I call thee?
"I happy am,
5 Joy is my name."
Sweet joy befall thee!

Pretty joy!
Sweet joy but two days old.
Sweet joy I call thee:
10 Thou dost smile,
I sing the while,
Sweet joy befall thee!

THE SHEPHERD

How sweet is the Shepherd's sweet lot!
From the morn to the evening he strays;
He shall follow his sheep all the day,
And his tongue shall be filled with praise.

5 For he hears the lamb's innocent call,
And he hears the ewe's tender reply;
He is watchful while they are in peace,
For they know when their Shepherd is nigh.

A CRADLE SONG

Sweet dreams, form a shade
O'er my lovely infant's head;
Sweet dreams of pleasant streams
By happy, silent, moony beams.

5 Sweet sleep, with soft down
Weave thy brows an infant crown.
Sweet sleep, Angel mild,
Hover o'er my happy child.

Sweet smiles, in the night
10 Hover over my delight;
Sweet smiles, Mother's smiles,
All the livelong night beguiles.

Sweet moans, dovelike sighs,
Chase not slumber from thy eyes.
15 Sweet moans, sweeter smiles,
All the dovelike moans beguiles.

Sleep, sleep, happy child,
All creation slept and smil'd;
Sleep, sleep, happy sleep,
20 While o'er thee thy mother weep.

Sweet babe, in thy face
Holy image I can trace.
Sweet babe, once like thee,
Thy maker lay and wept for me,

25 Wept for me, for thee, for all,
When he was an infant small.
Thou his image ever see,
Heavenly face that smiles on thee,

Smiles on thee, on me, on all;
30 Who became an infant small.
Infant smiles are his own smiles;
Heaven & earth to peace beguiles.

NURSE'S SONG

When the voices of children are heard on
the green
And laughing is heard on the hill,
My heart is at rest within my breast
And everything else is still.

5 "Then come home, my children, the sun is
gone down
And the dews of night arise;
Come, come, leave off play, and let us
away
Till the morning appears in the skies."

"No, no, let us play, for it is yet day
10 And we cannot go to sleep;
Besides, in the sky the little birds fly
And the hills are all cover'd with sheep."

"Well, well, go & play till the light fades
away
And then go home to bed."
15 The little ones leaped & shouted & laugh'd
And all the hills eechoed.

✳ HOLY THURSDAY

'Twas on a Holy Thursday, their innocent
faces clean,
The children walking two & two, in red &
blue & green,
Grey-headed beadles walk'd before, with
wands as white as snow,
Till into the high dome of Paul's they like
Thames' waters flow.

5 O what a multitude they seem'd, these
flowers of London town!
Seated in companies they sit with radiance
all their own.
The hum of multitudes was there, but
multitudes of lambs,
Thousands of little boys & girls raising
their innocent hands.

Now like a mighty wind they raise to
heaven the voice of song,
10 Or like harmonious thunderings the seats
of Heaven among.
Beneath them sit the aged men, wise
guardians of the poor;
Then cherish pity, lest you drive an angel
from your door.

ON ANOTHER'S SORROW

Can I see another's woe,
And not be in sorrow too?
Can I see another's grief,
And not seek for kind relief?

5 Can I see a falling tear,
And not feel my sorrow's share?
Can a father see his child
Weep, nor be with sorrow fill'd?

Can a mother sit and hear
10 An infant groan an infant fear?
No, no! never can it be!
Never, never can it be!

And can he who smiles on all
Hear the wren with sorrows small,
15 Hear the small bird's grief & care,
Hear the woes that infants bear,

And not sit beside the nest,
Pouring pity in their breast;
And not sit the cradle near,
20 Weeping tear on infant's tear;

And not sit both night & day,
Wiping all our tears away?
O, no! never can it be!
Never, never can it be!

25 He doth give his joy to all;
 He becomes an infant small;
 He becomes a man of woe;
 He doth feel the sorrow too.

 Think not thou canst sigh a sigh
30 And thy maker is not by;
 Think not thou canst weep a tear
 And thy maker is not near.

 O! he gives to us his joy
 That our grief he may destroy;
35 Till our grief is fled & gone
 He doth sit by us and moan.

LAUGHING SONG

When the green woods laugh with the
 voice of joy,
And the dimpling stream runs laughing
 by;
When the air does laugh with our merry
 wit,
And the green hill laughs with the noise
 of it;

5 When the meadows laugh with lively
 green,
And the grasshopper laughs in the merry
 scene,
When Mary and Susan and Emily
With their sweet round mouths sing
 "Ha, Ha, He!"

When the painted birds laugh in the shade,
10 Where our table with cherries and nuts
 is spread,
Come live & be merry, and join with me,
To sing the sweet chorus of "Ha, Ha, He!"

· THE LITTLE BLACK BOY

My mother bore me in the southern wild,
And I am black, but O! my soul is white;
White as an angel is the English child,
But I am black, as if bereav'd of light.

5 My mother taught me underneath a tree,
And, sitting down before the heat of day,
She took me on her lap and kissed me,
And, pointing to the east, began to say:

"Look on the rising sun: there God does
 live,
10 And gives his light, and gives his heat
 away;
And flowers and trees and beasts and men
 receive
Comfort in morning, joy in the noonday.

"And we are put on earth a little space,
That we may learn to bear the beams
 of love;
15 And these black bodies and this sunburnt
 face
Is but a cloud, and like a shady grove.

"For when our souls have learn'd the heat
 to bear,
The cloud will vanish; we shall hear his
 voice,
Saying: 'Come out from the grove, my
 love & care,
20 And round my golden tent like lambs
 rejoice.' "

Thus did my mother say, and kissed me;
And thus I say to little English boy.
When I from black and he from white
 cloud free,
And round the tent of God like lambs
 we joy,

25 I'll shade him from the heat till he can
 bear
To lean in joy upon our father's knee;

And then I'll stand and stroke his silver
hair,
And be like him, and he will then love me.

THE BOOK OF THEL
1789

THEL'S MOTTO

Does the Eagle know what is in the pit,
Or wilt thou go ask the Mole?
Can Wisdom be put in a silver rod?
Or Love in a golden bowl?

I

The Daughters of Mne Seraphim led round
their sunny flocks,
All but the youngest: she in paleness
sought the secret air,
To fade away like morning beauty from
her mortal day:
Down by the river of Adona her soft voice
is heard,
5 And thus her gentle lamentation falls
like morning dew:

"O life of this our spring! why fades
the lotus of the water,
Why fade these children of the spring,
born but to smile & fall?
Ah! Thel is like a wat'ry bow, and like a
parting cloud;
Like a reflection in a glass; like shadows
in the water;
10 Like dreams of infants, like a smile upon
an infant's face;
Like the dove's voice; like transient day;
like music in the air.
Ah! gentle may I lay me down, and
gentle rest my head,
And gentle sleep the sleep of death, and
gentle hear the voice
Of him that walketh in the garden in the
evening time."[1]

15 The Lilly of the valley, breathing in the
humble grass,
Answer'd the lovely maid and said: "I
am a wat'ry weed,
And I am very small and love to dwell
in lowly vales;
So weak, the gilded butterfly scarce
perches on my head.
Yet I am visited from heaven, and he
that smiles on all
20 Walks in the valley and each morn over
me spreads his hand,
Saying, 'Rejoice, thou humble grass, thou
new-born lilly flower,

[1] See *Genesis*, 3:8.

Thou gentle maid of silent valleys and
of modest brooks;
For thou shalt be clothed in light, and
fed with morning manna,
Till summer's heat melts thee beside the
fountains and the springs
25 To flourish in eternal vales.' Then why
should Thel complain?
Why should the mistress of the vales of
Har utter a sigh?"

She ceas'd & smil'd in tears, then sat
down in her silver shrine.

Thel answer'd: "O thou little virgin of
the peaceful valley,
Giving to those that cannot crave, the
voiceless, the o'ertired;
30 Thy breath doth nourish the innocent
lamb, he smells thy milky garments,
He crops thy flowers while thou sittest
smiling in his face,
Wiping his mild and meekin[1] mouth from
all contagious taints.
Thy wine doth purify the golden honey;
thy perfume,
Which thou dost scatter on every little
blade of grass that springs,
35 Revives the milked cow, & tames the fire-
breathing steed.
But Thel is like a faint cloud kindled at
the rising sun:
I vanish from my pearly throne, and who
shall find my place?"

"Queen of the vales," the Lilly answer'd,
"ask the tender cloud,
And it shall tell thee why it glitters in
the morning sky,
40 And why it scatters its bright beauty
thro' the humid air.
Descend, O little Cloud, & hover before
the eyes of Thel."

The Cloud descended, and the Lilly bow'd
her modest head
And went to mind her numerous charge
among the verdant grass.

II

"O little Cloud," the virgin said, "I charge
thee tell to me
45 Why thou complainest not when in one
hour thou fade away:
Then we shall seek thee, but not find. Ah!
Thel is like to thee:
I pass away: yet I complain, and no one
hears my voice."

[1] gentle

The Cloud then shew'd his golden head
   & his bright form emerg'd,
Hovering and glittering on the air before
   the face of Thel.

50 "O virgin, know'st thou not our steeds
   drink of the golden springs
Where Luvah doth renew his horses?
   Look'st thou on my youth,
And fearest thou, because I vanish and
   am seen no more,
Nothing remains? O maid, I tell thee,
   when I pass away
It is to tenfold life, to love, to peace
   and raptures holy:
55 Unseen descending, weigh my light wings
   upon balmy flowers,
And court the fair-eyed dew to take me
   to her shining tent:
The weeping virgin, trembling kneels before the risen sun,
Till we arise link'd in a golden band
   and never part,
But walk united, bearing food to all our
   tender flowers."

60 "Dost thou, O little Cloud? I fear that
   I am not like thee,
For I walk thro' the vales of Har, and
   smell the sweetest flowers,
But I feed not the little flowers; I hear
   the warbling birds,
But I feed not the warbling birds; they
   fly and seek their food:
But Thel delights in these no more, because I fade away;
65 And all shall say, 'Without a use this
   shining woman liv'd,
Or did she only live to be at death the
   food of worms?'"

The Cloud reclin'd upon his airy throne
   and answer'd thus:

"Then if thou art the food of worms, O
   virgin of the skies,
How great thy use, how great thy blessing! Every thing that lives
70 Lives not alone nor for itself.[1] Fear not,
   and I will call
The weak worm from its lowly bed, and
   thou shalt hear its voice.
Come forth, worm of the silent valley,
   to thy pensive queen."

The helpless worm arose, and sat upon
   the Lilly's leaf,

[1] See *Romans*, 14 :7.

And the bright Cloud sail'd on, to find
   his partner in the vale.

III

75 Then Thel astonish'd view'd the Worm
   upon its dewy bed.

"Art thou a Worm? Image of weakness,
   art thou but a Worm?
I see thee like an infant wrapped in the
   Lilly's leaf.
Ah! weep not, little voice, thou canst
   not speak, but thou canst weep.
Is this a Worm? I see thee lay helpless
   & naked, weeping,
80 And none to answer, none to cherish thee
   with mother's smiles."

The Clod of Clay heard the Worm's voice
   & rais'd her pitying head:
She bow'd over the weeping infant, and
   her life exhal'd
In milky fondness: then on Thel she fix'd
   her humble eyes.

"O beauty of the vales of Har! we live
   not for ourselves.
85 Thou seest me the meanest thing, and so
   I am indeed.
My bosom of itself is cold, and of itself
   is dark;
But he, that loves the lowly, pours his oil
   upon my head,
And kisses me, and binds his nuptial bands
   around my breast,
And says: 'Thou mother of my children,
   I have loved thee
90 And I have given thee a crown that none
   can take away.'
But how this is, sweet maid, I know not,
   and I cannot know;
I ponder, and I cannot ponder; yet I
   live and love."

The daughter of beauty wip'd her pitying tears with her white veil,
And said: "Alas! I knew not this, and
   therefore did I weep.
95 That God would love a Worm I knew,
   and punish the evil foot
That wilful bruis'd its helpless form;[1]
   but that he cherish'd it
With milk and oil I never knew, and
   therefore did I weep;
And I complain'd in the mild air, because
   I fade away,
And lay me down in thy cold bed, and
   leave my shining lot."

[1] See Cowper's *The Task*, 6, 560 ff. (p. 148).

100 "Queen of the vales," the matron Clay
    answer'd, "I heard thy sighs,
And all thy moans flew o'er my roof,
    but I have call'd them down.
Wilt thou, O Queen, enter my house?
    'Tis given thee to enter
And to return: fear nothing, enter with
    thy virgin feet."

IV

The eternal gates' terrific porter lifted the
    northern bar:
105 Thel enter'd in & saw the secrets of the
    land unknown.
She saw the couches of the dead, & where
    the fibrous roots
Of every heart on earth infixes deep its
    restless twists:
A land of sorrows & of tears where never
    smile was seen.

She wander'd in the land of clouds thro'
    valleys dark, list'ning
110 Dolours & lamentations; waiting oft be-
    side a dewy grave
She stood in silence, list'ning to the voices
    of the ground,
Till to her own grave plot she came, &
    there she sat down,
And heard this voice of sorrow breathed
    from the hollow pit.

"Why cannot the Ear be closed to its own
    destruction?
115 Or the glist'ning Eye to the poison of a
    smile?
Why are Eyelids stor'd with arrows ready
    drawn,
Where a thousand fighting men in am-
    bush lie?
Or an Eye of gifts & graces show'ring
    fruits & coined gold?
Why a Tongue impress'd with honey from
    every wind?
120 Why an Ear, a whirlpool fierce to draw
    creations in?
Why a Nostril wide inhaling terror, trem-
    bling, & affright?
Why a tender curb upon the youthful
    burning boy?
Why a little curtain of flesh on the bed
    of our desire?"

The Virgin started from her seat, & with
    a shriek
125 Fled back unhinder'd till she came into
    the vales of Har.

From THE MARRIAGE OF HEAVEN AND HELL

1790   c1790

THE VOICE OF THE DEVIL

All Bibles or sacred codes have been the causes of the following Errors:

1. That Man has two real existing prin-ciples: Viz: a Body & a Soul.
5   2. That Energy, call'd Evil, is alone from the Body; & that Reason, call'd Good, is alone from the Soul.

3. That God will torment Man in Eter-nity for following his Energies.

10   But the following Contraries to these are True:

1. Man has no Body distinct from his Soul; for that call'd Body is a portion of Soul discern'd by the five Senses, the chief 15 inlets of Soul in this age.

2. Energy is the only life, and is from the Body; and Reason is the bound or out-ward circumference of Energy.

3. Energy is Eternal Delight.

     . . . . . .

A MEMORABLE FANCY

As I was walking among the fires of hell, delighted with the enjoyments of Genius, which to Angels look like torment and in-sanity, I collected some of their Proverbs; 5 thinking that as the sayings used in a na-tion mark its character, so the Proverbs of Hell show the nature of Infernal wisdom better than any description of buildings or garments.

10   When I came home: on the abyss of the five senses, where a flat sided steep frowns over the present world, I saw a mighty Devil folded in black clouds, hovering on the sides of the rock: with corroding fires 15 he wrote the following sentence now per-cieved by the minds of men, & read by them on earth:

How do you know but ev'ry Bird that
    cuts the airy way,
Is an immense world of delight, clos'd
    by your senses five?

PROVERBS OF HELL

In seed time learn, in harvest teach, in
    winter enjoy.
Drive your cart and your plow over the
    bones of the dead.
The road of excess leads to the palace of
    wisdom.
Prudence is a rich, ugly old maid courted
    by Incapacity.

5 He who desires but acts not, breeds pestilence.

The cut worm forgives the plow.

Dip him in the river who loves water.

A fool sees not the same tree that a wise man sees.

He whose face gives no light, shall never become a star.

10 Eternity is in love with the productions of time.

The busy bee has no time for sorrow.

The hours of folly are measur'd by the clock; but of wisdom, no clock can measure.

All wholesome food is caught without a net or a trap.

Bring out number, weight & measure in a year of dearth.

15 No bird soars too high, if he soars with his own wings.

A dead body revenges not injuries.

The most sublime act is to set another before you.

If the fool would persist in his folly he would become wise.

Folly is the cloke of knavery.

20 Shame is Pride's cloke.

Prisons are built with stones of Law, Brothels with bricks of Religion.

The pride of the peacock is the glory of God.

The lust of the goat is the bounty of God.

The wrath of the lion is the wisdom of God.

25 The nakedness of woman is the work of God.

Excess of sorrow laughs. Excess of joy weeps.

The roaring of lions, the howling of wolves, the raging of the stormy sea, and the destructive sword, are portions of eternity, too great for the eye of man.

The fox condemns the trap, not himself.

Joys impregnate. Sorrows bring forth.

30 Let man wear the fell of the lion, woman the fleece of the sheep.

The bird a nest, the spider a web, man friendship.

The selfish, smiling fool, & the sullen, frowning fool shall be both thought wise, that they may be a rod.

What is now proved was once only imagin'd.

The rat, the mouse, the fox, the rabbet watch the roots; the lion, the tyger, the horse, the elephant watch the fruits.

35 The cistern contains: the fountain overflows.

One thought fills immensity.

Always be ready to speak your mind, and a base man will avoid you.

Every thing possible to be believ'd is an image of truth.

The eagle never lost so much time as when he submitted to learn of the crow.

40 The fox provides for himself, but God provides for the lion.

Think in the morning. Act in the noon. Eat in the evening. Sleep in the night.

He who has suffer'd you to impose on him, knows you.

As the plow follows words, so God rewards prayers.

The tygers of wrath are wiser than the horses of instruction.

45 Expect poison from the standing water.

You never know what is enough unless you know what is more than enough.

Listen to the fool's reproach! it is a kingly title!

The eyes of fire, the nostrils of air, the mouth of water, the beard of earth.

The weak in courage is strong in cunning.

50 The apple tree never asks the beech how he shall grow; nor the lion, the horse, how he shall take his prey.

The thankful receiver bears a plentiful harvest.

If others had not been foolish, we should be so.

The soul of sweet delight can never be defil'd.

When thou seest an Eagle, thou seest a portion of Genius; lift up thy head!

55 As the caterpiller chooses the fairest leaves to lay her eggs on, so the priest lays his curse on the fairest joys.

To create a little flower is the labour of ages.

Damn braces. Bless relaxes.

The best wine is the oldest, the best water the newest.

Prayers plow not! Praises reap not!

60 Joys laugh not! Sorrows weep not!

The head Sublime, the heart Pathos, the genitals Beauty, the hands & feet Proportion.

As the air to a bird or the sea to a fish, so is contempt to the contemptible.

The crow wish'd every thing was black, the owl that every thing was white.

Exuberance is Beauty.

65 If the lion was advised by the fox, he would be cunning.

Improve[me]nt makes strait roads; but the crooked roads without Improvement are roads of Genius.

Sooner murder an infant in its cradle than nurse unacted desires.

Where man is not, nature is barren.

Truth can never be told so as to be understood, and not be believ'd.

70 Enough! or Too much.

A MEMORABLE FANCY

The Prophets Isaiah and Ezekiel dined with me, and I asked them how they dared so roundly to assert that God spoke to them; and whether they did not think at the time that they would be misunderstood, & so be the cause of imposition.

Isaiah answer'd: "I saw no God, nor heard any, in a finite organical perception; but my senses discover'd the infinite in every thing, and as I was then perswaded, & remain confirm'd, that the voice of honest indignation is the voice of God, I cared not for consequences, but wrote."

Then I asked: "Does a firm perswasion that a thing is so, make it so?"

He replied: "All poets believe that it does, & in ages of imagination this firm perswasion removed mountains; but many are not capable of a firm perswasion of any thing."

Then Ezekiel said: "The philosophy of the east taught the first principles of human perception: some nations held one principle for the origin, and some another: we of Israel taught that the Poetic Genius (as you now call it) was the first principle and all the others merely derivative, which was the cause of our despising the Priests & Philosophers of other countries, and prophecying that all Gods would at last be proved to originate in ours & to be the tributaries of the Poetic Genius; it was this that our great poet, King David, desired so fervently & invokes so pathetic'ly, saying by this he conquers enemies & governs kingdoms; and we so loved our God, that we cursed in his name all the deities of surrounding nations, and asserted that they had rebelled: from these opinions the vulgar came to think that all nations would at last be subject to the jews."

"This," said he, "like all firm perswasions, is come to pass; for all nations believe the jews' code and worship the jews' god, and what greater subjection can be?"

I heard this with some wonder, & must confess my own conviction. . . .

A MEMORABLE FANCY

An Angel came to me and said: "O pitiable foolish young man! O horrible! O dreadful state! consider the hot burning dungeon thou art preparing for thyself to 5 all eternity, to which thou art going in such career."[1]

I said: "Perhaps you will be willing to shew me my eternal lot, & we will contemplate together upon it, & see whether your 10 lot or mine is most desirable."

So he took me thro' a stable & thro' a church & down into the church vault, at the end of which was a mill: thro' the mill we went, and came to a cave: down the winding 15 cavern we groped our tedious way, till a void boundless as a nether sky appear'd beneath us, & we held by the roots of trees and hung over this immensity; but I said: "if you please, we will commit ourselves 20 to this void, and see whether providence is here also: if you will not, I will:" but he answer'd: "do not presume, O young man, but as we here remain, behold thy lot which will soon appear when the darkness passes 25 away."

So I remain'd with him, sitting in the twisted root of an oak; he was suspended in a fungus, which hung with the head downward into the deep.

By degrees we beheld the infinite Abyss, fiery as the smoke of a burning city; beneath us, at an immense distance, was the sun, black but shining; round it were fiery tracks on which revolv'd vast spiders, crawling after their prey, which flew, or rather swum, in the infinite deep, in the most terrific shapes of animals sprung from corruption; & the air was full of them, & seem'd composed of them: these are Devils, 40 and are called Powers of the air. I now asked my companion which was my eternal lot? he said: "between the black & white spiders."

But now, from between the black & white 45 spiders, a cloud and fire burst and rolled thro' the deep, black'ning all beneath, so that the nether deep grew black as a sea, & rolled with a terrible noise; beneath us was nothing now to be seen but a black 50 tempest, till looking east between the clouds & the waves, we saw a cataract of blood mixed with fire, and not many stones' throw from us appear'd and sunk again the scaly fold of a monstrous serpent; at last, to the 55 east, distant about three degrees, appear'd a fiery crest above the waves; slowly it

[1] speed

reared like a ridge of golden rocks, till we discover'd two globes of crimson fire, from which the sea fled away in clouds of smoke; and now we saw it was the head of Leviathan; his forehead was divided into streaks of green & purple like those on a tyger's forehead: soon we saw his mouth & red gills hang just above the raging foam, tinging the black deep with beams of blood, advancing toward us with all the fury of a spiritual existence.

My friend the Angel climb'd up from his station into the mill: I remain'd alone; & then this appearance was no more, but I found myself sitting on a pleasant bank beside a river by moonlight, hearing a harper, who sung to the harp; & his theme was: "The man who never alters his opinion is like standing water, & breeds reptiles of the mind."

But I arose and sought for the mill, & there I found my Angel, who, surprised, asked me how I escaped?

I answered: "All that we saw was owing to your metaphysics; for when you ran away, I found myself on a bank by moonlight, hearing a harper." . . . .

A MEMORABLE FANCY

Once I saw a Devil in a flame of fire, who arose before an Angel that sat on a cloud, and the Devil utter'd these words: "The worship of God is: Honouring his gifts in other men, each according to his genius, and loving the greatest men best: those who envy or calumniate great men hate God; for there is no other God."

The Angel hearing this became almost blue; but mastering himself he grew yellow, & at last white, pink, & smiling, and then replied:

"Thou Idolater! is not God One? & is not he visible in Jesus Christ? and has not Jesus Christ given his sanction to the law of ten commandments? and are not all other men fools, sinners, & nothings?"

The Devil answer'd: "bray a fool in a morter with wheat, yet shall not his folly be beaten out of him; if Jesus Christ is the greatest man, you ought to love him in the greatest degree; now hear how he has given his sanction to the law of ten commandments: did he not mock at the sabbath, and so mock the sabbath's God? murder those who were murder'd because of him? turn away the law from the woman taken in adultery? steal the labor of others to support him? bear false witness when he omitted making a defence before Pilate? covet when he pray'd for his disciples, and when he bid them shake off the dust of their feet against such as refused to lodge them? I tell you, no virtue can exist without breaking these ten commandments. Jesus was all virtue, and acted from impulse, not from rules."

When he had so spoken, I beheld the Angel, who stretched out his arms, embracing the flame of fire, & he was consumed and arose as Elijah.

Note: This Angel, who is now become a Devil, is my particular friend; we often read the Bible together in its infernal or diabolical sense, which the world shall have if they behave well.

I have also The Bible of Hell, which the world shall have whether they will or no.

A SONG OF LIBERTY
c. 1790

1. The Eternal Female groan'd! it was heard over all the Earth.

2. Albion's[1] coast is sick, silent; the American meadows faint!

3. Shadows of Prophecy shiver along by the lakes and the rivers, and mutter across the ocean. France, rend down thy dungeon!

4. Golden Spain, burst the barriers of old Rome!

5. Cast thy keys, O Rome, into the deep, down falling, even to eternity down falling,

6. And weep!

7. In her trembling hands she took the new born terror, howling.

8. On those infinite mountains of light, now barr'd out by the atlantic sea, the new born fire stood before the starry king!

9. Flag'd with grey brow'd snows and thunderous visages, the jealous wings wav'd over the deep.

10. The speary hand burned aloft, unbuckled was the shield; forth went the hand of jealousy among the flaming hair, and hurl'd the new born wonder thro' the starry night.

11. The fire, the fire is falling!

12. Look up! look up! O citizen of London, enlarge thy countenance! O Jew, leave counting gold! return to thy oil and wine. O African! black African! (go, winged thought, widen his forehead.)

13. The fiery limbs, the flaming hair, shot like the sinking sun into the western sea.

---

[1] In the usual poetic sense; see Glossary.

14. Wak'd from his eternal sleep, the hoary element roaring fled away.

15. Down rush'd, beating his wings in vain, the jealous king; his grey brow'd
5 councellors, thunderous warriors, curl'd veterans, among helms, and shields, and chariots, horses, elephants, banners, castles, slings, and rocks,

16. Falling, rushing, ruining! buried in
10 the ruins, on Urthona's dens;

17. All night beneath the ruins; then, their sullen flames faded, emerge round the gloomy King.

18. With thunder and fire, leading his
15 starry hosts thro' the waste wilderness, he promulgates his ten commands, glancing his beamy eyelids over the deep in dark dismay,

19. Where the son of fire in his eastern
20 cloud, while the morning plumes her golden breast,

20. Spurning the clouds written with curses, stamps the stony law to dust, loosing the eternal horses from the dens of night,
25 crying: EMPIRE IS NO MORE! AND NOW THE LION & WOLF SHALL CEASE.

CHORUS

Let the Priests of the Raven of dawn no longer, in deadly black, with hoarse note curse the sons of joy. Nor his accepted brethren—whom, tyrant, he calls free—lay the bound or build the roof. Nor pale religious lechery call that virginity that wishes but acts not!

For everything that lives is Holy.

From VISIONS OF THE DAUGHTERS OF ALBION[1]

The Eye sees more than the Heart knows
1793

"With what sense is it that the chicken shuns the ravenous hawk?
With what sense does the tame pigeon measure out the expanse?
65 With what sense does the bee form cells? have not the mouse & frog
Eyes and ears and sense of touch? yet are their habitations
And their pursuits as different as their forms and as their joys.
Ask the wild ass why he refuses burdens, and the meek camel
Why he loves man: is it because of eye, ear, mouth, or skin,

---

[1] Mankind. Blake's own mystic sense of the word.

70 Or breathing nostrils? No, for these the wolf and tyger have.
Ask the blind worm the secrets of the grave, and why her spires
Love to curl round the bones of death; and ask the rav'nous snake
Where she gets poison, & the wing'd eagle why he loves the sun;
And then tell me the thoughts of man, that have been hid of old.

75 "Silent I hover all the night, and all day could be silent,
If Theotormon once would turn his loved eyes upon me.
How can I be defil'd when I reflect thy image pure?
Sweetest the fruit that the worm feeds on, & the soul prey'd on by woe,
The new wash'd lamb ting'd with the village smoke, & the bright swan
80 By the red earth of our immortal river. I bathe my wings,
And I am white and pure to hover round Theotormon's breast."

Then Theotormon broke his silence, and he answered—

"Tell me what is the night or day to one o'erflow'd with woe?
Tell me what is a thought, & of what substance is it made?
85 Tell me what is a joy, & in what gardens do joys grow?
And in what rivers swim the sorrows? and upon what mountains
Wave shadows of discontent? and in what houses dwell the wretched,
Drunken with woe forgotten, and shut up from cold despair?

"Tell me where dwell the thoughts forgotten till thou call them forth?
90 Tell me where dwell the joys of old? & where the ancient loves,
And when will they renew again, & the night of oblivion past,
That I might traverse times & spaces far remote, and bring
Comforts into a present sorrow and a night of pain?
Where goest thou, O thought? to what remote land is thy flight?
95 If thou returnest to the present moment of affliction
Wilt thou bring comforts on thy wings, and dews and honey and balm,
Or poison from the desart wilds, from the eyes of the envier?"

. . . .

Fiery the Angels rose, & as they rose deep thunder roll'd
Around their shores: indignant burning with the fires of Orc
And Bostons Angel cried aloud as they flew thro' the dark
                                                    night.

He cried: Why trembles honesty and like a murderer,
Why seeks he refuge from the frowns of his immortal station,
Must the generous tremble & leave his joy, to the idle: to
        the pestilence!
That mock him? who commanded this? what God! what Angel!
To keep the gen'rous from experience till the ungenerous
Are unrestraind performers of the energies of nature:
Till pity is become a trade, and generosity a science.
That men get rich by, & the sandy desert is givn to the strong
What God is he, writes laws of peace, & clothes him in a tempest
What pitying Angel lusts for tears, and fans himself with sighs
What crawling villain preaches abstinence & wraps himself
In fat of lambs? no more I follow, no more obedience pay.

This exact reproduction of page 11 (lines 115-129) of "America" is especially representative of Blake's illustrations.

205 "Does the sun walk in glorious raiment on
         the secret floor
Where the cold miser spreads his gold; or
         does the bright cloud drop
On his stone threshold? does his eye behold
         the beam that brings
Expansion to the eye of pity? or will he
         bind himself
Beside the ox to thy hard furrow? does not
         that mild beam blot
210 The bat, the owl, the glowing tyger, and
         the king of night?
The sea fowl takes the wintry blast for a
         cov'ring to her limbs,
And the wild snake the pestilence to adorn
         him with gems & gold;
And trees & birds & beasts & men behold
         their eternal joy.
Arise, you little glancing wings, and sing
         your infant joy!
215 Arise, and drink your bliss, for everything
         that lives is holy!"

Thus every morning wails Oothoon; but
         Theotormon sits
Upon the margin'd ocean conversing with
         shadows dire.

The Daughters of Albion hear her woes, &
         eccho back her sighs.

From AMERICA: A PROPHECY
1793

"The morning comes, the night decays, the
         watchmen leave their stations;
The grave is burst, the spices shed, the
         linen wrapped up.
The bones of death, the cov'ring clay, the
         sinews shrunk & dry'd
40 Reviving shake, inspiring move, breathing,
         awakening,
Spring like redeemed captives when their
         bonds & bars are burst.
Let the slave grinding at the mill run out
         into the field,
Let him look up into the heavens & laugh
         in the bright air;
Let the inchained soul, shut up in dark-
         ness and in sighing,
45 Whose face has never seen a smile in
         thirty weary years,
Rise and look out; his chains are loose,
         his dungeon doors are open;
And let his wife and children return from
         the oppressor's scourge.
They look behind at every step & believe
         it is a dream,
Singing: 'The Sun has left his blackness &
         has found a fresher morning,

50 And the fair Moon rejoices in the clear &
         cloudless night;
For Empire is no more; and now the Lion
         & Wolf shall cease.' "

From SONGS OF EXPERIENCE
1794

INTRODUCTION

Hear the voice of the Bard!
Who Present, Past, & Future, sees;
Whose ears have heard
The Holy Word
5 That walk'd among the ancient trees,

Calling the lapsed Soul,
And weeping in the evening dew;
That might controll
The starry pole,
10 And fallen, fallen light renew!

"O Earth, O Earth, return!
Arise from out the dewy grass;
Night is worn,
And the morn
15 Rises from the slumberous mass.

"Turn away no more;
Why wilt thou turn away?
The starry floor,
The wat'ry shore,
20 Is giv'n thee till the break of day."

EARTH'S ANSWER

Earth rais'd up her head
From the darkness dread & drear.
Her light fled,
Stony dread!
5 And her locks cover'd with grey despair.

"Prison'd on wat'ry shore,
Starry Jealousy does keep my den:
Cold and hoar,
Weeping o'er,
10 I hear the father of the ancient men.

"Selfish father of men!
Cruel, jealous, selfish fear!
Can delight,
Chain'd in night,
15 The virgins of youth and morning bear?

"Does spring hide its joy
When buds and blossoms grow?
Does the sower
Sow by night,
20 Or the plowman in darkness plow?

"Break this heavy chain
That does freeze my bones around.
Selfish! vain!
Eternal bane!
25 That free Love with bondage bound."

THE CLOD AND THE PEBBLE

"Love seeketh not Itself to please,
Nor for itself hath any care,
But for another gives its ease,
And builds a Heaven in Hell's despair."

5 So sung a little Clod of Clay,
Trodden with the cattle's feet,
But a Pebble of the brook
Warbled out these metres meet: *suggesting of regularity of convention*

"Love seeketh only Self to please,
10 To bind another to Its delight,
Joys in another's loss of ease,
And builds a Hell in Heaven's despite."

HOLY THURSDAY

Is this a holy thing to see
In a rich and fruitful land,
Babes reduc'd to misery,
Fed with cold and usurous hand?

5 Is that trembling cry a song?
Can it be a song of joy?
And so many children poor?
It is a land of poverty!

And their sun does never shine,
10 And their fields are bleak & bare,
And their ways are fill'd with thorns:
It is eternal winter there.

For where-e'er the sun does shine,
And where-e'er the rain does fall,
15 Babe can never hunger there,
Nor poverty the mind appall.

THE CHIMNEY SWEEPER

A little black thing among the snow,
Crying " 'weep! 'weep!" in notes of woe!
"Where are thy father & mother? say?"
"They are both gone up to the church to
        pray.

5 "Because I was happy upon the heath,
And smil'd among the winter's snow,
They clothed me in the clothes of death,
And taught me to sing the notes of woe.

"And because I am happy & dance & sing,
10 They think they have done me no injury,
And are gone to praise God & his Priest
        & King,
Who make up a heaven of our misery."

NURSE'S SONG

When the voices of children are heard on
        the green,
And whisp'rings are in the dale,
The days of my youth rise fresh in my
        mind,
My face turns green and pale.

5 Then come home, my children, the sun is
        gone down,
And the dews of night arise;
Your spring & your day are wasted in
        play,
And your winter and night in disguise.

THE SICK ROSE

O Rose, thou art sick!
The invisible worm
That flies in the night,
In the howling storm,

5 Has found out thy bed
Of crimson joy,
And his dark secret love
Does thy life destroy.

THE FLY

Little Fly,
Thy summer's play
My thoughtless hand
Has brush'd away.

5 Am not I
A fly like thee?
Or art not thou
A man like me?

For I dance,
10 And drink, & sing,
Till some blind hand
Shall brush my wing.

If thought is life
And strength & breath,
15 And the want
Of thought is death;

Then am I
A happy fly,
If I live
20 Or if I die.

THE ANGEL

I dreamt a Dream! what can it mean?
And that I was a maiden Queen,
Guarded by an Angel mild:
Witless woe was ne'er beguil'd!

5 And I wept both night and day,
And he wip'd my tears away,
And I wept both day and night,
And hid from him my heart's delight.

So he took his wings and fled;
10 Then the morn blush'd rosy red;
I dried my tears, & armed my fears
With ten thousand shields and spears.

Soon my Angel came again:
I was arm'd, he came in vain;
15 For the time of youth was fled,
And grey hairs were on my head.

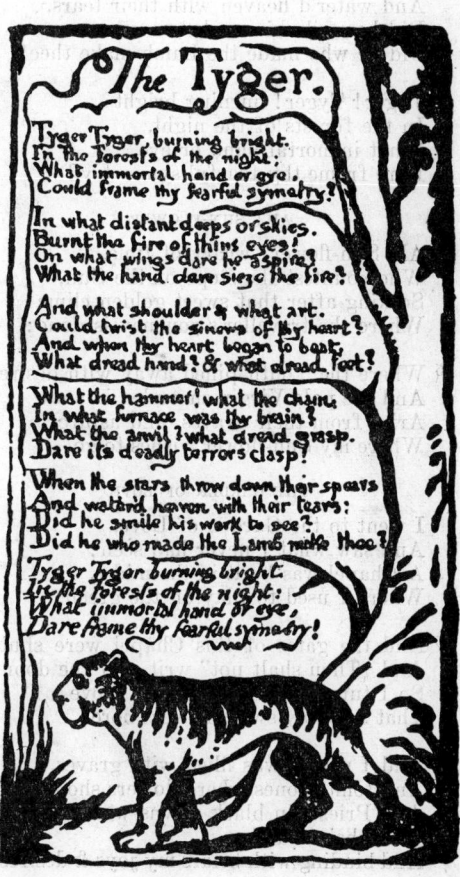

THE TYGER

Tyger! Tyger! burning bright
In the forests of the night,
What immortal hand or eye
Could frame thy fearful symmetry?

5 In what distant deeps or skies
Burnt the fire of thine eyes?
On what wings dare he aspire?
What the hand dare sieze the fire?

And what shoulder, & what art,
10 Could twist the sinews of thy heart?
And when thy heart began to beat,
What dread hand? & what dread feet?

What the hammer? what the chain?
In what furnace was thy brain?
15 What the anvil? what dread grasp
Dare its deadly terrors clasp?

When the stars threw down their spears,
And water'd heaven with their tears,
Did he smile his work to see?
20 Did he who made the Lamb make thee?

Tyger! Tyger! burning bright
In the forests of the night,
What immortal hand or eye,
Dare frame thy fearful symmetry?

AH! SUN-FLOWER

Ah, Sun-flower! weary of time,
Who countest the steps of the Sun,
Seeking after that sweet golden clime
Where the traveller's journey is done:

5 Where the Youth pined away with desire,
And the pale Virgin shrouded in snow
Arise from their graves, and aspire
Where my Sun-flower wishes to go.

THE GARDEN OF LOVE

I went to the Garden of Love,
And saw what I never had seen:
A Chapel was built in the midst,
Where I used to play on the green.

5 And the gates of this Chapel were shut,
And "Thou shalt not" writ over the door;
So I turn'd to the Garden of Love
That so many sweet flowers bore;

And I saw it was filled with graves,
10 And tomb-stones where flowers should be;
And Priests in black gowns were walking
    their rounds,
And binding with briars my joys & desires.

LONDON

I wander thro' each charter'd street,
Near where the charter'd Thames does
    flow,
And mark in every face I meet
Marks of weakness, marks of woe.

5 In every cry of every Man,
In every Infant's cry of fear,
In every voice, in every ban,
The mind-forg'd manacles I hear.

How the Chimney-sweeper's cry
10 Every black'ning Church appalls;
And the hapless Soldier's sigh
Runs in blood down Palace walls.

But most thro' midnight streets I hear
How the youthful Harlot's curse
15 Blasts the new born Infant's tear,
And blights with plagues the Marriage
    hearse.

THE HUMAN ABSTRACT

Pity would be no more
If we did not make somebody Poor;

And Mercy no more could be
If all were as happy as we.

5 And mutual fear brings peace,
Till the selfish loves increase:
Then Cruelty knits a snare,
And spreads his baits with care.

He sits down with holy fears,
10 And waters the ground with tears;
Then Humility takes its root
Underneath his foot.

Soon spreads the dismal shade
Of Mystery over his head;
15 And the Catterpiller and Fly
Feed on the Mystery.

And it bears the fruit of Deceit,
Ruddy and sweet to eat;
And the Raven his nest has made
20 In its thickest shade.

The Gods of the earth and sea
Sought thro' Nature to find this Tree;
But their search was all in vain:
There grows one in the Human Brain.

INFANT SORROW

My mother groan'd! my father wept.
Into the dangerous world I leapt:
Helpless, naked, piping loud:
Like a fiend hid in a cloud.

5 Struggling in my father's hands,
Striving against my swadling bands,
Bound and weary I thought best
To sulk upon my mother's breast.

A POISON TREE

I was angry with my friend:
I told my wrath, my wrath did end.
I was angry with my foe:
I told it not, my wrath did grow.

5 And I water'd it in fears,
Night & morning with my tears;
And I sunned it with smiles,
And with soft deceitful wiles.

And it grew both day and night,
10 Till it bore an apple bright;
And my foe beheld it shine,
And he knew that it was mine,

And into my garden stole
When the night had veil'd the pole:
15 In the morning glad I see
My foe outstretch'd beneath the tree.

A LITTLE BOY LOST

"Nought loves another as itself,
Nor venerates another so,
Nor is it possible to Thought
A greater than itself to know:

5 "And Father, how can I love you
Or any of my brothers more?
I love you like the little bird
That picks up crumbs around the door."

The Priest sat by and heard the child,
10 In trembling zeal he siez'd his hair:
He led him by his little coat,
And all admir'd the Priestly care.

And standing on the altar high,
"Lo! what a fiend is here!" said he,
15 "One who sets reason up for judge
Of our most holy Mystery."

The weeping child could not be heard,
The weeping parents wept in vain;
They strip'd him to his little shirt,
20 And bound him in an iron chain;

And burn'd him in a holy place,
Where many had been burn'd before:
The weeping parents wept in vain.
Are such things done on Albion's shore?

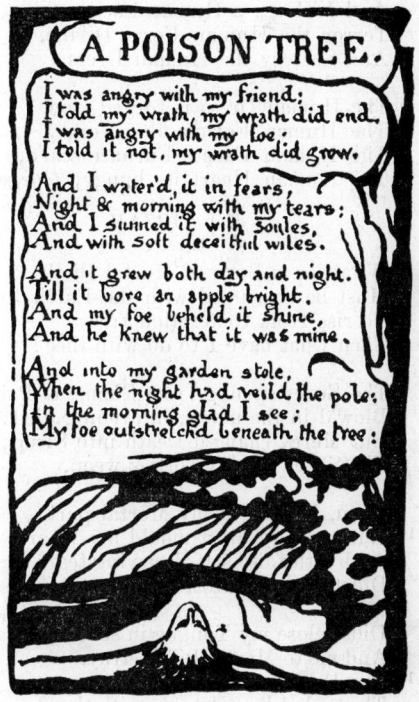

A CRADLE SONG
1794

Sleep, Sleep, beauty bright,
Dreaming o'er the joys of night.
Sleep, Sleep: in thy sleep
Little sorrows sit & weep.

5 Sweet Babe, in thy face
Soft desires I can trace,
Secret joys & secret smiles,
Little pretty infant wiles.

As thy softest limbs I feel,
10 Smiles as of the morning steal
O'er thy cheek & o'er thy breast
Where thy little heart does rest.

O, the cunning wiles that creep
In thy little heart asleep.
15 When thy little heart does wake,
Then the dreadful lightnings break.

From thy cheek & from thy eye,
O'er the youthful harvests nigh
Infant wiles & infant smiles
20 Heaven & Earth of peace beguiles.

A DIVINE IMAGE
c. 1794

Cruelty has a Human Heart,
And Jealousy a Human Face;
Terror the Human Form Divine,
And Secrecy the Human Dress.

5 The Human Dress is forged iron,
The Human Form a fiery Forge,
The Human Face a Furnace seal'd,
The Human Heart its hungry Gorge.

TO TIRZAH
c. 1801

Whate'er is Born of Mortal Birth
Must be consumed with the Earth
To rise from Generation free:
Then what have I to do with thee?

5 The Sexes sprung from Shame & Pride,
Blow'd in the morn; in evening died;
But Mercy chang'd Death into Sleep;
The Sexes rose to work & weep.

Thou, Mother of my Mortal part,
10 With cruelty didst mould my Heart,
And with false self-decieving tears
Didst bind my Nostrils, Eyes, & Ears:

Didst close my Tongue in senseless clay,
And me to Mortal Life betray.
15 The Death of Jesus set me free:
Then what have I to do with thee?

LOVE'S SECRET

Never pain to tell thy love,
Love that never told can be;
For the gentle wind does move
Silently, invisibly.

5 I told my love, I told my love,
I told her all my heart;
Trembling, cold, in ghastly fears,
Ah! she doth depart.

Soon as she was gone from me
10 A traveller came by;
Silently, invisibly
He took her with a sigh.

COUPLET

Great things are done when Men & Mountains meet;
This is not done by Jostling in the Street.

✓ From THE FOUR ZOAS
1797-1804

FROM NIGHT II

For Los & Enitharmon walk'd forth on
the dewy Earth
Contracting or expanding their all flexible
senses
505 At will to murmur in the flowers small as
the honey bee,
At will to stretch across the heavens &
step from star to star,
Or standing on the Earth erect, or on the
stormy waves
Driving the storms before them, or delighting in sunny beams,
While round their heads the Elemental
Gods kept harmony.

510 And Los said: "Lo! the Lilly pale & the
rose redd'ning fierce
Reproach thee, & the beamy gardens
sicken at thy beauty;
I grasp thy vest in my strong hands in
vain, like water springs
In the bright sands of Los evading my
embrace; then I alone
Wander among the virgins of the summer.
Look! they cry,
515 The poor forsaken Los, mock'd by the
worm, the shelly snail,
The Emmet & the beetle, hark! they laugh,
& mock at Los."

Enitharmon answer'd:
"Secure now from the smitings of thy
Power, demon of fury,
If the God enraptur'd me infold

In clouds of sweet obscurity my beauteous
    form dissolving,
520 Howl thou over the body of death; 'tis
    thine. But if among the virgins
Of summer I have seen thee sleep & turn
    thy cheek delighted
Upon the rose or lilly pale, or on a bank
    where sleep
The beamy daughters of the light, start-
    ing, they rise, they flee
From thy fierce love, for tho' I am dis-
    solv'd in the bright God,
525 My spirit still pursues thy false love over
    rocks & valleys."

Los answer'd: "Therefore fade I thus dis-
    solv'd in raptur'd trance.
Thou canst repose on clouds of secrecy,
    while o'er my limbs
Cold dews & hoary frost creep tho' I lie
    on banks of summer
Among the beauties of the World. Cold &
    repining Los
530 Still dies for Enitharmon, nor a spirit
    springs from my dead corse;
Then I am dead till thou revivest me with
    thy sweet song,
Now taking on Ahania's form & now the
    form of Enion,
I know thee not as once I knew thee in
    those blessed fields
Where memory wishes to repose among
    the flocks of Tharmas."

535 Enitharmon answer'd, "Wherefore didst
    thou throw thine arms around
Ahania's Image? I deciev'd thee & will
    still decieve.
Urizen saw thy sin & hid his beams in
    dark'ning clouds.
I still keep watch altho' I tremble & wither
    across the heavens
In strong vibrations of fierce jealousy; for
    thou art mine,
540 Created for my will, my slave, tho' strong,
    tho' I am weak.
Farewell, the God calls me away. I de-
    part in my sweet bliss."

She fled, vanishing on the wind, And left
    a dead cold corse
In Los's arms; howlings began over the
    body of death.
Los spoke. "Thy God in vain shall call
    thee if by my strong power
545 I can infuse my dear revenge into his
    glowing breast.
Then jealousy shall shadow all his moun-
    tains & Ahania
Curse thee, thou plague of woful Los, &
    seek revenge on thee."

So saying in deep sobs he languish'd till
    dead he also fell.
Night pass'd, & Enitharmon e'er the dawn
    return'd in bliss,
550 She sang O'er Los reviving him to Life:
    his groans were terrible;
But thus she sang:
"I sieze the sphery harp. I strike the
    strings!

"At the first Sound the Golden sun arises
    from the deep
And shakes his awful hair,
The Eccho wakes the moon to unbind her
    silver locks,
555 The golden sun bears on my song
And nine bright spheres of harmony rise
    round the fiery king.

"The joy of woman is the death of her
    most best beloved
Who dies for Love of her
In torments of fierce jealousy & pangs of
    adoration.
560 The Lovers' night bears on my song
And the nine spheres rejoice beneath my
    powerful controll.

"They sing unceasing to the notes of my
    immortal hand.
The solemn, silent moon
Reverberates the living harmony upon my
    limbs,
565 The birds & beasts rejoice & play,
And every one seeks for his mate to prove
    his inmost joy.

"Furious & terrible they sport & red the
    nether deep;
The deep lifts up its rugged head,
And lost in infinite humming wings
    vanishes with a cry.
570 The fading cry is ever dying,
The living voice is ever living in its in-
    most joy.

"Arise, you little glancing wings & sing
    your infant joy!
Arise & drink your bliss!
For every thing that lives is holy; for the
    source of life
575 Descends to be a weeping babe;
For the Earthworm renews the moisture
    of the sandy plain.

"Now my left hand I stretch to earth
    beneath,
And strike the terrible string.

I wake sweet joy in dens of sorrow, & I
    plant a smile
580 In forests of affliction,
And wake the bubbling springs of life in
    regions of dark death.

"O, I am weary! lay thy hand upon me or
    I faint,
I faint beneath these beams of thine,
For thou hast touched my five Senses &
    they answer'd thee.
585 Now I am nothing, & I sink
And on the bed of silence sleep till thou
    awakest me."

Thus sang the Lovely one in Rapturous
    delusive trance.
Los heard, reviving; he siez'd her in his
    arms; delusive hopes
Kindling, she led him into shadows &
    thence fled outstretch'd
590 Upon the immense like a bright rainbow,
    weeping & smiling & fading.

Thus liv'd Los, driving Enion far into the
    deathful infinite,
That he may also draw Ahania's spirit
    into her Vortex.
Ah, happy blindness! Enion sees not the
    terrors of the uncertain,
And thus she wails from the dark deep;
    the golden heavens tremble:

595 "I am made to sow the thistle for wheat,
    the nettle for a nourishing dainty.
I have planted a false oath in the earth;
    it has brought forth a poison tree.
I have chosen the serpent for a councellor,
    & the dog
For a schoolmaster to my children.
I have blotted out from light & living the
    dove & nightingale,
600 And I have caused the earth worm to beg
    from door to door.
I have taught the thief a secret path into
    the house of the just.
I have taught pale artifice to spread his
    nets upon the morning.
My heavens are brass, my earth is iron, my
    moon a clod of clay,
My sun a pestilence burning at noon & a
    vapour of death in night.

605 "What is the price of Experience? do
    men buy it for a song?
Or wisdom for a dance in the street? No,
    it is bought with the price
Of all that a man hath, his house, his wife,
    his children.

Wisdom is sold in the desolate market
    where none come to buy,
And in the wither'd field where the farmer
    plows for bread in vain.

610 "It is an easy thing to triumph in the
    summer's sun
And in the vintage & to sing on the
    waggon loaded with corn.
It is an easy thing to talk of patience to
    the afflicted,
To speak the laws of prudence to the
    houseless wanderer,
To listen to the hungry raven's cry in
    wintry season
615 When the red blood is fill'd with wine &
    with the marrow of lambs.

"It is an easy thing to laugh at wrathful
    elements,
To hear the dog howl at the wintry door,
    the ox in the slaughter house moan;
To see a god on every wind & a blessing
    on every blast;
To hear sounds of love in the thunder
    storm that destroys our enemies
    house;
620 To rejoice in the blight that covers his
    field, & the sickness that cuts off his
    children,
While our olive & vine sing & laugh round
    our door, & our children bring fruits
    & flowers.

"Then the groan & the dolor are quite for-
    gotten, & the slave grinding at the
    mill,
And the captive in chains, & the poor in
    the prison, & the soldier in the field
When the shatter'd bone hath laid him
    groaning among the happier dead.

625 "It is an easy thing to rejoice in the tents
    of prosperity:
Thus could I sing & thus rejoice: but it
    is not so with me."

Ahania heard the Lamentation, & a swift
    Vibration
Spread thro' her Golden frame. She rose
    up e'er the dawn of day
When Urizen slept on his couch: drawn
    thro' unbounded space
630 On to the margin of Non Entity the bright
    Female came.
There she beheld the *Spectrous* form of
    Enion in the Void,
And never from that moment could she
    rest upon her pillow.

✓ AUGURIES OF INNOCENCE
1801-3   1863

To see a World in a Grain of Sand
And a Heaven in a Wild Flower,
Hold Infinity in the palm of your hand
And Eternity in an hour.
5 A Robin Red breast in a Cage
Puts all Heaven in a Rage.
A dove house fill'd with doves & Pigeons
Shudders Hell thro' all its regions.
A dog starv'd at his Master's Gate
10 Predicts the ruin of the State.
A Horse misus'd upon the Road
Calls to Heaven for Human blood.
Each outcry of the hunted Hare
A fibre from the Brain does tear.
15 A Skylark wounded in the wing,
A Cherubim does cease to sing.
The Game Cock clip'd & arm'd for fight
Does the Rising Sun affright.
Every Wolf's & Lion's howl
20 Raises from Hell a Human Soul.
The wild deer, wand'ring here & there,
Keeps the Human Soul from Care.
The Lamb misus'd breeds Public strife
And yet forgives the Butcher's Knife.
25 The Bat that flits at close of Eve
Has left the Brain that won't Believe.
The Owl that calls upon the Night
Speaks the Unbeliever's fright.
He who shall hurt the little Wren
30 Shall never be belov'd by Men.
He who the Ox to wrath has mov'd
Shall never be by Woman lov'd.
The wanton Boy that kills the Fly
Shall feel the Spider's enmity.
35 He who torments the Chafer's sprite
Weaves a Bower in endless Night.
The Catterpiller on the Leaf
Repeats to thee thy Mother's grief.
Kill not the Moth nor Butterfly,
40 For the Last Judgment draweth nigh.
He who shall train the Horse to War
Shall never pass the Polar Bar.
The Begger's Dog & Widow's Cat,
Feed them & thou wilt grow fat.
45 The Gnat that sings his Summer's song
Poison gets from Slander's tongue.
The poison of the Snake & Newt
Is the sweat of Envy's Foot.
The Poison of the Honey Bee
50 Is the Artist's Jealousy.
The Prince's Robes & Beggar's Rags
Are Toadstools on the Miser's Bags.
A truth that's told with bad intent
Beats all the Lies you can invent.
55 It is right it should be so;
Man was made for Joy & Woe;
And when this we rightly know

Thro' the World we safely go.
Joy & Woe are woven fine,
60 A Clothing for the Soul divine;
Under every grief & pine
Runs a joy with silken twine.
The Babe is more than swadling Bands;
Throughout all these Human Lands
65 Tools were made, & Born were hands,
Every Farmer Understands.
Every Tear from Every Eye
Becomes a Babe in Eternity;
This is caught by Females bright
70 And return'd to its own delight.
The Bleat, the Bark, Bellow & Roar
Are Waves that Beat on Heaven's Shore.
The Babe that weeps the Rod beneath
Writes Revenge in realms of death.
75 The Beggar's Rags, fluttering in Air,
Does to Rags the Heavens tear.
The Soldier, arm'd with Sword & Gun,
Palsied strikes the Summer's Sun.
The poor Man's Farthing is worth more
80 Than all the Gold on Afric's Shore.
One Mite wrung from the Labrer's hands
Shall buy & sell the Miser's Lands:
Or, if protected from on high,
Does that whole Nation sell & buy.
85 He who mocks the Infant's Faith
Shall be mock'd in Age & Death.
He who shall teach the Child to Doubt
The rotting Grave shall ne'er get out.
He who respects the Infant's faith
90 Triumphs over Hell & Death.
The Child's Toys & the Old Man's Reasons
Are the Fruits of the Two seasons.
The Questioner, who sits so sly,
Shall never know how to Reply.
95 He who replies to words of Doubt
Doth put the Light of Knowledge out.
The Strongest Poison ever known
Came from Caesar's Laurel Crown.
Nought can deform the Human Race
100 Like to the Armour's iron brace.
When Gold & Gems adorn the Plow
To peaceful Arts shall Envy Bow.
A Riddle or the Cricket's Cry
Is to Doubt a fit Reply.
105 The Emmet's Inch & Eagle's Mile
Make Lame Philosophy to smile.
He who Doubts from what he sees
Will ne'er Believe, do what you Please.
If the Sun & Moon should doubt,
110 They'd immediately Go out.
To be in a Passion you Good may do,
But no Good if a Passion is in you.
The Whore & Gambler, by the State
Licenc'd, build that Nation's Fate.
115 The Harlot's cry from Street to Street
Shall weave Old England's winding Sheet.

The Winner's Shout, the Loser's Curse,
Dance before dead England's Hearse.
Every Night & every Morn
120 Some to Misery are Born.
Every Morn & every Night
Some are Born to sweet delight.
Some are Born to sweet delight,
Some are Born to Endless Night.
125 We are led to Believe a Lie
When we see not Thro' the Eye
Which was Born in a Night to perish in a
   Night
When the Soul Slept in Beams of Light.
God Appears & God is Light
130 To those poor Souls who dwell in Night,
But does a Human Form Display
To those who Dwell in Realms of day.

THE MENTAL TRAVELLER
1801   1863

I travel'd thro' a Land of Men,
A Land of Men & Women too,
And heard & saw such dreadful things
As cold Earth wanderers never knew.

5 For there the Babe is born in joy
That was begotten in dire woe;
Just as we Reap in joy the fruit
Which we in bitter tears did sow.

And if the Babe is born a Boy
10 He's given to a Woman Old,
Who nails him down upon a rock,
Catches his shrieks in cups of gold.

She binds iron thorns around his head,
She pierces both his hands & feet,
15 She cuts his heart out at his side
To make it feel both cold & heat.

Her fingers number every Nerve,
Just as a Miser counts his gold;
She lives upon his shrieks & cries,
20 And she grows young as he grows old.

Till he becomes a bleeding youth,
And she becomes a Virgin bright;
Then he rends up his Manacles
And binds her down for his delight.

25 He plants himself in all her Nerves,
Just as a Husbandman his mould;
And she becomes his dwelling place
And Garden fruitful seventy fold.

An aged Shadow, soon he fades,
30 Wand'ring round an Earthly Cot,
Full filled all with gems & gold
Which he by industry had got.

And these are the gems of the Human
   Soul,
The rubies & pearls of a lovesick eye,
35 The countless gold of the akeing heart,
The martyr's groan & the lover's sigh.

They are his meat, they are his drink;
He feeds the Beggar & the Poor
And the wayfaring Traveller:
40 For ever open is his door.

His grief is their eternal joy;
They make the roofs & walls to ring;
Till from the fire on the hearth
A little Female Babe does spring.

45 And she is all of solid fire
And gems & gold, that none his hand
Dares stretch to touch her Baby form,
Or wrap her in his swaddling-band.

But she comes to the Man she loves,
50 If young or old, or rich or poor;
They soon drive out the aged Host,
A Beggar at another's door.

He wanders weeping far away,
Until some other take him in;
55 Oft blind & age-bent, sore distrest,
Untill he can a Maiden win.

And to allay his freezing Age
The Poor Man takes her in his arms;
The Cottage fades before his sight,
60 The Garden & its lovely Charms.

The Guests are scatter'd thro' the land,
For the Eye altering alters all;
The Senses roll themselves in fear,
And the flat Earth becomes a Ball;

65 The stars, sun, Moon, all shrink away,
A desart vast without a bound,
And nothing left to eat or drink,
And a dark desart all around.

The honey of her Infant lips,
70 The bread & wine of her sweet smile,
The wild game of her roving Eye,
Does him to Infancy beguile;

For as he eats & drinks he grows
Younger & younger every day;
75 And on the desart wild they both
Wander in terror & dismay.

Like the wild Stag she flees away,
Her fear plants many a thicket wild;

While he pursues her night & day,
80 By various arts of Love beguil'd,

By various arts of Love & Hate,
Till the wide desart planted o'er
With Labyrinths of wayward Love,
Where roam the Lion, Wolf & Boar.

85 Till he becomes a wayward Babe,
And she a weeping Woman Old.
Then many a Lover wanders here;
The Sun & Stars are nearer roll'd.

The trees bring forth sweet Extacy
90 To all who in the desart roam;
Till many a City there is Built,
And many a pleasant Shepherd's home.

But when they find the frowning Babe,
Terror strikes thro' the region wide:
95 They cry "The Babe! the Babe is Born!"
And flee away on Every side.

For who dare touch the frowning form,
His arm is wither'd to its root;
Lions, Boars, Wolves, all howling flee,
100 And every Tree does shed its fruit.

And none can touch that frowning form,
Except it be a Woman Old;
She nails him down upon the Rock,
And all is done as I have told.

✓ From MILTON
1804

PREFACE

The Stolen and Perverted Writings of
Homer & Ovid, of Plato & Cicero, which all
Men ought to contemn, are set up by artifice
against the Sublime of the Bible; but when
5 the New Age is at leisure to Pronounce, all
will be set right, & those Grand Works of
the more ancient & consciously & professedly
Inspired Men will hold their proper rank,
& the Daughters of Memory shall become
10 the Daughters of Inspiration. Shakespeare
& Milton were both curb'd by the general
malady & infection from the silly Greek &
Latin slaves of the Sword.
   Rouze up, O Young Men of the New Age!
15 set your foreheads against the ignorant
Hirelings! For we have Hirelings in the
Camp, the Court & the University, who
would, if they could, for ever depress
Mental & prolong Corporeal War. Painters!
20 on you I call. Sculptors! Architects! Suffer
not the fashionable Fools to depress your

powers by the prices they pretend to give
for contemptible works, or the expensive
advertizing boasts that they make of such
25 works: believe Christ & His Apostles that
there is a Class of Men whose whole delight
is in Destroying. We do not want either
Greek or Roman Models if we are but
just & true to our own Imaginations, those
30 Worlds of Eternity in which we shall live
for ever in JESUS OUR LORD.

And did those feet in ancient time
Walk upon England's mountains green?
And was the holy Lamb of God
On England's pleasant pastures seen?

5 And did the Countenance Divine
Shine forth upon our clouded hills?
And was Jerusalem builded here
Among these dark Satanic Mills?

Bring me my Bow of burning gold:
10 Bring me my Arrows of desire:
Bring me my Spear: O clouds, unfold!
Bring me my Chariot of fire.

I will not cease from Mental Fight,
Nor shall my Sword sleep in my hand
15 Till we have built Jerusalem
In England's green & pleasant Land.

   "Would to God that all the Lord's people
were Prophets." NUMBERS, XI. ch., 29 v.

FROM BOOK THE SECOND

Thou hearest the Nightingale begin the
   Song of Spring.
The Lark sitting upon his earthy bed, just
   as the morn
Appears, listens silent; then springing
   from the waving Cornfield, loud
He leads the Choir of Day: trill, trill,
   trill, trill,
65 Mounting upon the wings of light into the
   Great Expanse,
Reecchoing against the lovely blue & shin-
   ing heavenly Shell.
His little throat labours with inspiration;
   every feather
On throat & breast & wings vibrates with
   the effluence Divine.
All Nature listens silent to him, & the
   awful Sun
70 Stands still upon the Mountain looking
   on this little Bird
With eyes of soft humility & wonder, love
   & awe.
Then loud from their green covert all the
   Birds begin their Song:

The Thrush, the Linnet and the Goldfinch,
    Robin & the Wren
Awake the Sun from his sweet reverie
    upon the Mountain.
75 The nightingale again assays his song, &
    thro' the day
And thro' the night warbles luxuriant,
    every Bird of Song
Attending his loud harmony with admira-
    tion & love.
This is a Vision of the lamentation of
    Beulah over Ololon.

.Thou percievest the Flowers put forth
    their precious Odours,
80 And none can tell how from so small a
    center comes such sweets,
Forgetting that within that Center Eternity
    expands
Its ever during doors that Og & Anak
    fiercely guard.
First, e'er the morning breaks, joy opens
    in the flowery bosoms,
Joy even to tears, which the Sun rising
    dries: first the Wild Thyme
85 And Meadow-sweet, downy & soft waving
    among the reeds,
Light springing on the air, lead the sweet
    Dance: they wake
The Honeysuckle sleeping on the Oak; the
    flaunting beauty
Revels along upon the wind; the White-
    thorn, lovely May,
Opens her many lovely eyes; listening the
    Rose still sleeps,
90 None dare to wake her; soon she bursts
    her crimson curtain'd bed
And comes forth in the majesty of beauty;
    every Flower,
The Pink, the Jessamine, the Wall-flower,
    the Carnation,
The Jonquil, the mild Lilly opes her
    heavens; every Tree
And Flower & Herb soon fill the air with
    an innumerable Dance,
95 Yet all in order sweet & lovely. Men are
    sick with Love.
Such is a Vision of the lamentation of
    Beulah over Ololon.
    . . . . . .
But turning toward Ololon in terrible
    majesty Milton
Replied: "Obey thou the Words of the
    Inspired Man.
All that can be (can be) annihilated must
    be annihilated
500 That the Children of Jerusalem may be
    saved from slavery.
There is a Negation, & there is a Contrary:

The Negation must be destroy'd to redeem
    the Contraries.
The Negation is the Spectre, the Reason-
    ing Power in Man:
This is a false Body, an Incrustation over
    my immortal
505 Spirit, a Selfhood which must be put off
    & annihilated alway.
To cleanse the Face of my Spirit by Self-
    examination,

"To bathe in the Waters of Life, to wash
    off the Not Human,
I come in Self-annihilation & the grandeur
    of Inspiration,
To cast off Rational Demonstration by
    Faith in the Saviour,
510 To cast off the rotten rags of Memory by
    Inspiration,
To cast off Bacon,[1] Locke & Newton from
    Albion's covering,
To take off his filthy garments & clothe
    him with Imagination,
To cast aside from Poetry all that is not
    Inspiration,
That it no longer shall dare to mock with
    the aspersion of Madness
515 Cast on the Inspired by the tame high
    finisher of paltry Blots
Indefinite, or paltry Rhymes, or paltry
    Harmonies,
Who creeps into State Government like a
    catterpiller to destroy;
To cast off the idiot Questioner who is
    always questioning
But never capable of answering, who sits
    with a sly grin
520 Silent plotting when to question, like a
    thief in a cave,
Who publishes doubt & calls it knowledge,
    whose Science is Despair,
Whose pretence to knowledge is Envy,
    whose whole Science is
To destroy the Wisdom of ages to gratify
    ravenous Envy
That rages round him like a Wolf day &
    night without rest:
525 He smiles with condescension, he talks of
    Benevolence & Virtue,
And those who act with Benevolence &
    Virtue they murder time on time.
These are the destroyers of Jerusalem,
    these are the murderers
Of Jesus, who deny the Faith & mock at
    Eternal Life,
Who pretend to Poetry that they may de-
    stroy Imagination,

[1] Cf. *Annotations to Sir Joshua Reynolds's Dis-courses*, (p. 198a, l. 46ff.).

530 By imitation of Nature's Images drawn
    from Remembrance.
These are the Sexual Garments, the
    Abomination of Desolation,
Hiding the Human Lineaments as with an
    Ark & Curtains
Which Jesus rent & now shall wholly
    purge away with Fire
Till Generation is swallow'd up in Re-
    generation." . . .

From JERUSALEM

1804-1820

From TO THE PUBLIC

We who dwell on Earth can do nothing of
ourselves; every thing is conducted by
Spirits, no less than Digestion or Sleep . . .
When this Verse was first dictated to
me, I consider'd a Monotonous Cadence, like
that used by Milton & Shakespeare & all
writers of English Blank Verse, derived
from the modern bondage of Rhyming, to be
a necessary and indispensable part of Verse.
But I soon found that in the mouth of
a true Orator such monotony was not only
awkward, but as much a bondage as rhyme
itself. I therefore have produc'd a variety
in every line, both of cadences & number of
syllables. Every word and every letter is
studied and put into its fit place; the terrific
numbers are reserved for the terrific parts,
the mild & gentle for the mild & gentle
parts, and the prosaic for inferior parts;
all are necessary to each other. Poetry Fetter'd Fetters the Human Race. Nations are
Destroy'd or Flourish in proportion as
Their Poetry, Painting and Music are Destroy'd or Flourish! The Primeval State of
Man was Wisdom, Art and Science.

From TO THE DEISTS

He never can be a Friend to the Human
Race who is the Preacher of Natural Mo-
rality or Natural Religion; he is a flatterer
who means to betray, to perpetuate Tyrant
Pride & the Laws of that Babylon which,
he foresees shall shortly be destroyed, with
the Spiritual and not the Natural Sword.
He is in the State named Rahab, which
State must be put off before he can be the
Friend of Man.

You, O Deists, profess yourselves the
Enemies of Christianity, and you are so:
you are also the Enemies of the Human
Race & of Universal Nature. Man is born a
Spectre or Satan & is altogether an Evil,

& requires a New Selfhood continually, &
must continually be changed into his direct
Contrary. But your Greek Philosophy
(which is a remnant of Druidism) teaches
that Man is Righteous in his Vegetated
Spectre: an Opinion of fatal & accursed
consequence to Man, as the Ancients saw
plainly by Revelation, to the intire abroga-
tion of Experimental Theory; and many
believed what they saw and Prophecied of
Jesus.

Man must & will have Some Religion: if
he has not the Religion of Jesus, he will
have the Religion of Satan & will erect the
Synagogue of Satan, calling the Prince of
this World, God, and destroying all who
do not worship Satan under the Name of
God. Will any one say, "Where are those
who worship Satan under the Name of
God?" Where are they? Listen! Every Religion that Preaches Vengeance for Sin is
the Religion of the Enemy & Avenger and
not of the Forgiver of Sin, and their God is
Satan, Named by the Divine Name. Your
Religion, O Deists! Deism, is the Worship
of the God of this World by the means of
what you call Natural Religion and Natural
Philosophy, and of Natural Morality or
Self-Righteousness, the Selfish Virtues of
the Natural Heart. This was the Religion
of the Pharisees who murder'd Jesus. Deism
is the same & ends in the same.

Voltaire, Rousseau, Gibbon, Hume, charge
the Spiritually Religious with Hypocrisy;
but how a Monk, or a Methodist either, can
be a Hypocrite, I cannot concieve. We are
Men of like passions with others & pretend
not to be holier than others; therefore, when
a Religious Man falls into Sin, he ought not
to be call'd a Hypocrite; this title is more
properly to be given to a Player who falls
into Sin, whose profession is Virtue & Morality, & the making Men Self-Righteous.
Foote in calling Whitefield, Hypocrite, was
himself one; for Whitefield pretended not
to be holier than others, but confessed his
Sins before all the World. Voltaire! Rousseau! You cannot escape my charge that you
are Pharisees & Hypocrites, for you are
constantly talking of the Virtues of the
Human Heart and particularly of your own,
that you may accuse others, & especially
the Religious, whose errors you, by this
display of pretended Virtue, chiefly design
to expose. Rousseau thought Men Good by
Nature: he found them Evil & found no
friend. Friendship cannot exist without
Forgiveness of Sins continually. The Book
written by Rousseau call'd his Confessions,

is an apology & cloke for his sin & not a
confession.

But you also charge the poor Monks &
Religious with being the causes of War,
while you acquit & flatter the Alexanders 5
& Caesars, the Lewis's & Fredericks, who
alone are its causes & its actors. But the
Religion of Jesus, Forgiveness of Sin, can
never be the cause of a War nor of a single
Martyrdom.

Those who Martyr others or who cause
War are Deists, but never can be Forgivers
of Sin. The Glory of Christianity is To Conquer by Forgiveness. All the Destruction,
therefore, in Christian Europe has arisen 15
from Deism, which is Natural Religion.

    I saw a Monk of Charlemaine
Arise before my sight:
    I talk'd with the Grey Monk as we stood 20
In beams of infernal light.

    Gibbon arose with a lash of steel,
And Voltaire with a wracking wheel:
    The Schools, in clouds of learning roll'd, 25
Arose with War in iron & gold.

    "Thou lazy Monk," they sound afar,
"In vain condemning glorious War;
    And in your Cell you shall ever dwell: 30
Rise, War, & bind him in his Cell!"

    The blood red ran from the Grey Monk's
      side,
His hands & feet were wounded wide, 35
    His body bent, his arms & knees
Like to the roots of ancient trees.

    When Satan first the black bow bent
And the Moral Law from the Gospel rent, 40
    He forg'd the Law into a Sword
And spill'd the blood of mercy's Lord.

    Titus! Constantine! Charlemaine!
O Voltaire! Rousseau! Gibbon! Vain 45
    Your Grecian Mocks & Roman Sword
Against this image of his Lord!

    For a Tear is an Intellectual thing;
And a Sigh is the Sword of an Angel 50
    King,
    And the bitter groan of a Martyr's woe
Is an Arrow from the Almightie's Bow.

FROM TO THE CHRISTIANS   55

Devils are False Religions.
"Saul, Saul, why persecutest thou me?"

I give you the end of a golden string,
    Only wind it into a ball,
It will lead you in at Heaven's gate,
    Built in Jerusalem's wall.

    We are told to abstain from fleshly de-
sires that we may lose no time from the
Work of the Lord. Every moment lost is a
moment that cannot be redeemed; every
pleasure that intermingles with the duty of
our station is a folly unredeemable, & is
planted like the seed of a wild flower among
our wheat. All the tortures of repentance
are tortures of self-reproach on account of
our leaving the Divine Harvest to the
Enemy: the struggles of intanglement with
incoherent roots. I know of no other
Christianity and of no other Gospel than
the liberty both of the body & mind to exercise the Divine Arts of Imagination,
Imagination, the real & eternal World of
which this Vegetable Universe is but a faint
shadow, & in which we shall live in our
Eternal or Imaginative Bodies when these
Vegetable Mortal Bodies are no more. The
Apostles knew of no other Gospel. What
were all their spiritual gifts? What is the
Divine Spirit? is the Holy Ghost any other
than an Intellectual Fountain? What is the
harvest of the Gospel & its Labours? What
is that Talent which it is a curse to hide?
What are the Treasures of Heaven which
we are to lay up for ourselves, are they
any other than Mental Studies & Per-
formances? What are all the Gifts of the
Gospel, are they not all Mental Gifts? Is
God a Spirit who must be worshipped in
Spirit & in Truth, and are not the Gifts
of the Spirit Every-thing to Man? O ye
Religious, discountenance every one among
you who shall pretend to despise Art &
Science! I call upon you in the Name of
Jesus! What is the Life of Man but Art
& Science? is it Meat & Drink? is not the
Body more than Raiment? What is Mortality but the things relating to the Body
which Dies? What is Immortality but the
things relating to the Spirit which Lives
Eternally? What is the Joy of Heaven
but Improvement in the things of the
Spirit? What are the Pains of Hell but
Ignorance, Bodily Lust, Idleness & devastation of the things of the Spirit? Answer
this to yourselves, & expel from among
you those who pretend to despise the
labours of Art & Science, which alone are
the labours of the Gospel. Is not this plain
& manifest to the thought? Can you think

at all & not pronounce heartily That to
Labour in Knowledge is to Build up Jerusalem, and to Despise Knowledge is to Despise
Jerusalem & her Builders. And remember:
He who despises & mocks a Mental Gift 5
in another, calling it pride & selfishness
& sin, mocks Jesus the giver of every
Mental Gift, which always appear to the
ignorance-loving Hypocrite as Sins; but
that which is a Sin in the sight of cruel 10
Man is not so in the sight of our kind God.
Let every Christian, as much as in him
lies, engage himself openly & publicly
before all the World in some Mental pursuit for the Building up of Jerusalem. 15

. . . . . .

England! awake! awake! awake!
  Jerusalem thy Sister calls!
Why wilt thou sleep the sleep of death
  And close her from thy ancient walls?

5 Thy hills & valleys felt her feet
  Gently upon their bosoms move:
Thy gates beheld sweet Zion's ways:
  Then was a time of joy and love.

And now the time returns again:
10 Our souls exult, & London's towers
Recieve the Lamb of God to dwell
  In England's green & pleasant bowers.

DEDICATION OF THE ILLUSTRATIONS
TO BLAIR'S *THE GRAVE*
1806-7   1808

TO THE QUEEN

The Door of Death is made of Gold,
That Mortal Eyes cannot behold;
But, when the Mortal Eyes are clos'd,
And cold and pale the Limbs repos'd,
5 The Soul awakes; and, wond'ring, sees
In her mild Hand the golden Keys:
The Grave is Heaven's golden Gate,
And rich and poor around it wait;
O Shepherdess of England's Fold,
10 Behold this Gate of Pearl and Gold!

To dedicate to England's Queen
The Visions that my Soul has seen,
And, by Her kind permission, bring
What I have borne on solemn Wing
15 From the vast regions of the Grave,
Before Her Throne my Wings I wave;
Bowing before my Sov'reign's Feet,
"The Grave produc'd these Blossoms sweet,
In mild repose from Earthly strife;
20 The Blossoms of Eternal Life!"

From THE LETTERS

TO THE REV^D DR. TRUSLER

13 Hercules Buildings,
Lambeth, *August 23, 1799*

REV^D SIR,

  I really am sorry that you are fall'n out
with the Spiritual World, Especially if I
should have to answer for it. I feel very
sorry that your Ideas & Mine on Moral
Painting differ so much as to have made
you angry with my method of study. If I
am wrong, I am wrong in good company.
I had hoped your plan comprehended All
Species of this Art, & Especially that you
would not regret that Species which gives
Existence to Every other, namely, Visions
of Eternity. You say that I want somebody
to Elucidate my Ideas. But you ought to
know that What is Grand is necessarily
obscure to Weak men. That which can be
made Explicit to the Idiot is not worth
my care. The wisest of the Ancients consider'd what is not too Explicit as the fittest
for Instruction, because it rouzes the faculties to act. I name Moses, Solomon, Esop,
Homer, Plato.
  But as you have favor'd me with your
remarks on my Design, permit me in return
to defend it against a mistaken one, which
is, That I have supposed Malevolence without a Cause. Is not Merit in one a Cause of
Envy in another, & Serenity & Happiness
& Beauty a Cause of Malevolence? But
Want of Money & the Distress of A Thief
can never be alledged as the Cause of his
Thieving, for many honest people endure
greater hardships with Fortitude. We must
therefore seek the Cause elsewhere than
in want of Money, for that is the Miser's
passion, not the Thief's.
  I have therefore proved your Reasonings
Ill proportion'd, which you can never prove
my figures to be; they are those of Michael
Angelo, Rafael & the Antique, & of the best
living Models. I percieve that your Eye is
perverted by Caricature Prints, which ought
not to abound so much as they do. Fun I
love, but too much Fun is of all things the
most loathsom. Mirth is better than Fun,
& Happiness is better than Mirth. I feel
that a Man may be happy in This World.
And I know that This World Is a World
of Imagination & Vision. I see Every thing
I paint In This World, but Every body
does not see alike. To the Eyes of a Miser

a Guinea is far more beautiful than the Sun, & a bag worn with the use of Money has more beautiful proportions than a Vine filled with Grapes. The tree which moves some to tears of joy is in the Eyes of others only a Green thing which stands in the way. Some see Nature all Ridicule & Deformity, & by these I shall not regulate my proportions; & some scarce see Nature at all. But to the Eyes of the Man of Imagination, Nature is Imagination itself. As a man is, so he sees. As the Eye is formed, such are its Powers. You certainly Mistake, when you say that the Visions of Fancy are not to be found in This World. To Me This World is all One continued Vision of Fancy or Imagination, & I feel Flatter'd when I am told so. What is it sets Homer, Virgil & Milton in so high a rank of Art? Why is the Bible more Entertaining & Instructive than any other book? Is it not because they are addressed to the Imagination, which is Spiritual Sensation, & but mediately to the Understanding or Reason? Such is True Painting, and such was alone valued by the Greeks & the best modern Artists. Consider what Lord Bacon says: "Sense sends over to Imagination before Reason have judged, & Reason sends over to Imagination before the Decree can be acted." See Advancem^t of Learning, Part 2, P. 47 of first Edition.

But I am happy to find a Great Majority of Fellow Mortals who can Elucidate My Visions, & Particularly they have been Elucidated by Children, who have taken a greater delight in contemplating my Pictures than I even hoped. Neither Youth nor Childhood is Folly or Incapacity. Some Children are Fools & so are some Old Men. But There is a vast Majority on the side of Imagination or Spiritual Sensation.

To Engrave after another Painter is infinitely more laborious than to Engrave one's own Inventions. And of the size you require my price has been Thirty Guineas, & I cannot afford to do it for less. I had Twelve for the Head I sent you as a specimen; but after my own designs I could do at least Six times the quantity of labour in the same time, which will account for the difference of price, as also that Chalk Engraving is at least six times as laborious as Aqua tinta. I have no objection to Engraving after another Artist. Engraving is the profession I was apprenticed to, & should never have attempted to live by anything else, If orders had not come in for my Designs & Paintings, which I have the pleasure

to tell you are Increasing Every Day. Thus If I am a Painter it is not to be attributed to seeking after. But I am contented whether I live by Painting or Engraving.
I am, Revd Sir, your very obedient servant,

WILLIAM BLAKE.

TO JOHN FLAXMAN

Felpham,
Septr 21, 1800, Sunday Morning.

DEAR SCULPTOR OF ETERNITY,

We are safe arrived at our Cottage, which is more beautiful than I thought it, & more convenient. It is a perfect Model for Cottages &, I think, for Palaces of Magnificence, only Enlarging, not altering its proportions, & adding ornaments & not principals. Nothing can be more Grand than its Simplicity & Usefulness. Simple without Intricacy, it seems to be the Spontaneous Effusion of Humanity, congenial to the wants of Man. No other formed House can ever please me so well; nor shall I ever be perswaded, I believe, that it can be improved either in Beauty or Use.

Mr. Hayley recieved us with his usual brotherly affection. I have begun to work. Felpham is a sweet place for Study, because it is more Spiritual than London. Heaven opens here on all sides her golden Gates; her windows are not obstructed by vapours; voices of Celestial inhabitants are more distinctly heard, & their forms more distinctly seen; & my Cottage is also a Shadow of their houses. My Wife & Sister are both well, courting Neptune for an embrace.

Our Journey was very pleasant; & tho' we had a great deal of Luggage, No Grumbling; All was Chearfulness & Good Humour on the Road, & yet we could not arrive at our Cottage before half past Eleven at night, owing to the necessary shifting of our Luggage from one Chaise to another; for we had Seven Different Chaises, & as many different drivers. We set out between Six & Seven in the Morning of Thursday, with Sixteen heavy boxes & portfolios full of prints. And Now Begins a New life, because another covering of Earth is shaken off. I am more famed in Heaven for my works than I could well conceive. In my Brain are studies & Chambers filled with books & pictures of old, which I wrote & painted in ages of Eternity before my mortal life; & these works are the delight & Study of Archangels. Why, then, should I be anxious about the riches or fame of mortality? The Lord our father will do for us & with us according to his divine will for our Good.

You, O dear Flaxman, are a Sublime Archangel, my Friend & Companion from Eternity; in the Divine bosom is our dwelling place. I look back into the regions of Reminiscence & behold our ancient days before this Earth appear'd in its vegetated mortality to my mortal vegetated eyes. I see our houses of Eternity, which can never be separated, tho' our Mortal vehicles should stand at the remotest corners of heaven from each other.

Farewell, My Best Friend! Remember Me & My Wife in Love & Friendship to our Dear Mrs. Flaxman, whom we ardently desire to Entertain beneath our thatched roof of rusted gold, & believe me for ever to remain

> Your Grateful & Affectionate,
> WILLIAM BLAKE.

From ANNOTATIONS TO SIR JOSHUA REYNOLDS'S DISCOURSES
LONDON 1798
1808

This Man was Hired to Depress Art.

This is the Opinion of Will Blake: my Proofs of this Opinion are given in the following Notes . . . .

The Arts & Sciences are the Destruction of Tyrannies or Bad Governments. Why should A Good Government endeavour to Depress what is its Chief & only Support?

The Foundation of Empire is Art & Science. Remove them or Degrade them, & the Empire is No More. Empire follows Art & Not Vice Versa as Englishmen suppose . . . .

Liberality! we want not Liberality. We want a Fair Price & Proportionate Value & a General Demand for Art.

Let not that Nation where Less than Nobility is the Reward, Pretend that Art is Encouraged by that Nation. Art is First in Intellectuals & Ought to be First in Nations . . . .

To Generalize is to be an Idiot. To Particularize is the Alone Distinction of Merit. General Knowledges are those Knowledges that Idiots possess . . . .

I consider Reynolds's Discourses to the Royal Academy as the Simulations of the Hypocrite who smiles particularly where he means to Betray. His Praise of Rafael is like the Hysteric Smile of Revenge. His Softness & Candour, the hidden trap & the poisoned feast. He praises Michel Angelo for Qualities which Michel Angelo abhorr'd, & He blames Rafael for the only Qualities which Rafael Valued. Whether Reynolds knew what he was doing is nothing to me: the Mischief is just the same whether a Man does it Ignorantly or Knowingly. I always consider'd True Art & True Artists to be particularly Insulted & Degraded by the Reputation of these Discourses, As much as they were Degraded by the Reputation of Reynolds's Paintings, & that Such Artists as Reynolds are at all times Hired by the Satans for the Depression of Art— A Pretence of Art, To destroy Art.

The Neglect of Fuseli's Milton in a Country pretending to the Encouragement of Art is a Sufficient Apology for My Vigorous Indignation, if indeed the Neglect of My own Powers had not been. Ought not the Employers of Fools to be Execrated in future Ages? They Will and Shall! Foolish Men, your own real Greatness depends on your Encouragement of the Arts, & your Fall will depend on their Neglect & Depression. What you Fear is your true Interest. Leo X was advised not to Encourage the Arts; he was too Wise to take this Advice.

The Rich Men of England form themselves into a Society to Sell & Not to Buy Pictures. The Artist who does not throw his Contempt on such Trading Exhibitions, does not know either his own Interest or his Duty.

> When Nations grow Old, The Arts grow
>   Cold
> And Commerce settles on every Tree,
> And the Poor & the Old can live upon
>   Gold,
> For all are Born Poor, Aged Sixty Three.

Reynolds's Opinion was that Genius May be Taught & that all Pretence to Inspiration is a Lie & a Deceit, to say the least of it. For if it is a Deceit, the whole Bible is Madness. This Opinion originates in the Greeks' calling the Muses Daughters of Memory.

The Enquiry in England is not whether a Man has Talents & Genius, But whether he is Passive & Polite & a Virtuous Ass & obedient to Noblemen's Opinions in Art & Science. If he is, he is a Good Man. If Not, he must be Starved.

Minute Discrimination is Not Accidental. All Sublimity is founded on Minute Discrimination.

I do not believe that Rafael taught Mich. Angelo, or that Mich. Angelo taught Rafael, any more than I believe that the Rose teaches the Lilly how to grow, or the Apple tree teaches the Pear tree how to bear Fruit. I do not believe the tales of Anecdote writers when they militate against Individual Character . . . .

Mechanical Excellence is the Only Vehicle of Genius.

Execution is the Chariot of Genius . . .

Reynolds Depreciates the Efforts of Inventive Genius. Trifling Conceits are better than Colouring without any meaning at all . . . .

Without Minute Neatness of Execution The Sublime cannot Exist! Grandeur of Ideas is founded on Precision of Ideas . . . .

The Man who never in his Mind & Thoughts travel'd to Heaven Is No Artist.

Artists who are above a plain Understanding are Mock'd & Destroy'd by this President of Fools.

It is Evident that Reynolds Wish'd none but Fools to be in the Arts & in order to this, he calls all others Vague Enthusiasts or Madmen.

What has Reasoning to do with the Art of Painting? . . .

Singular & Particular Detail is the Foundation of the Sublime. . . .

Knowledge of Ideal Beauty is Not to be Acquired. It is Born with us. Innate Ideas are in Every Man, Born with him; they are truly Himself. The Man who says that we have No Innate Ideas must be a Fool & Knave, Having No Con-Science or Innate Science.

One Central Form composed of all other Forms being Granted, it does not therefore follow that all other Forms are Deformity.

All Forms are Perfect in the Poet's Mind, but these are not Abstracted nor compounded from Nature, but are from Imagination.

The Great Bacon[1]—he is Call'd: I call him the Little Bacon—says that Every thing must be done by Experiment; his first principle is Unbelief, and yet here he says that Art must be produc'd Without such Method. He is like S[r] Joshua, full of Self-Contradiction & Knavery . . . .

Bacon's Philosophy has Destroy'd Art & Science. The Man who says that Genius is not Born, but Taught—Is a Knave.

O Reader, behold the Philosopher's Grave!

[1] Cf. *Milton* (p. 192, 1. 511ff.).

He was born quite a Fool, but he died quite a Knave.

How ridiculous it would be to see the Sheep Endeavouring to walk like the Dog, or the Ox striving to trot like the Horse; just as Ridiculous it is to see One Man Striving to Imitate Another. Man varies from Man more than Animal from Animal of different Species . . . .

Obscurity is Neither the Source of the Sublime nor of any Thing Else. . . .

The Ancients did not mean to Impose when they affirm'd their belief in Vision & Revelation. Plato was in Earnest: Milton was in Earnest. They believ'd that God did Visit Man Really & Truly & not as Reynolds pretends.

How very Anxious Reynolds is to Disprove & Contemn Spiritual Perception!

He states Absurdities in Company with Truths & calls both Absurd . . . .

It is not in Terms that Reynolds & I disagree. Two Contrary Opinions can never by any Language be made alike. I say, Taste & Genius are Not Teachable or Acquirable, but are born with us. Reynolds says the Contrary. . . .

Demonstration, Similitude & Harmony are Objects of Reasoning. Invention, Identity & Melody are Objects of Intuition.

God forbid that Truth should be Confined to Mathematical Demonstration!

He who does not Know Truth at Sight is unworthy of Her Notice . . . .

If you Endeavour to Please the Worst, you will never Please the Best. To please All is Impossible. . . .

Bad Pictures are always S[r] Joshua's Friends.

From ANNOTATIONS TO "POEMS" BY WILLIAM WORDSWORTH

VOL. I, LONDON 1815

1826

I see in Wordsw. the Natural Man rising up agst. the spiritual man continually, & then he is no poet but a heathen philosopher at Enmity agst. all true poetry or inspiration.

There is no such thing as natural piety because the natural man is at enmity with God. . . .

I cannot think that real poets have any competition. None are greatest in the Kingdom of God. It is so in Poetry.

Natural objects always did & now do weaken, deaden & obliterate Imagination in me. W. must know that what he writes valuable is not to be found in Nature. . . .

I Believe both Macpherson & Chatterton,
that what they say is Ancient is so.
  I own myself an admirer of Ossian
equally with any other poet whatever, Rowley & Chatterton also.
. . . Imagination has nothing to do with
memory.

Robert Burns 1759-1796

O, ONCE I LOV'D A BONIE[1] LASS
1774   1786

O, once I lov'd a bonie lass,
  Ay, and I love her still!
And whilst that virtue warms my breast,
  I'll love my handsome Nell.

5 As bonie lasses I hae[2] seen,
  And monie full as braw;[3]
But for a modest, gracefu' mien,
  The like I never saw.

A bonie lass, I will confess,
10 Is pleasant to the e'e,
But without some better qualities
  She's no a lass for me.

But Nelly's looks are blythe and sweet,
  And what is best of a',
15 Her reputation is complete,
  And fair without a flaw.

She dresses ay sae clean and neat,
  Both decent and genteel:
And then there's something in her gait
20 Gars[4] onie dress look weel.

A gaudy dress and gentle air
  May slightly touch the heart;
But it's innocence and modesty
  That polishes the dart.

25 'Tis this in Nelly pleases me,
  'Tis this enchants my soul;
For absolutely in my breast
  She reigns without control.

A PRAYER IN THE PROSPECT OF DEATH
1781   1786

O Thou unknown, Almighty Cause
  Of all my hope and fear!
In whose dread presence, ere an hour,
  Perhaps I must appear!

5 If I have wander'd in those paths
  Of life I ought to shun,—

As something, loudly, in my breast,
  Remonstrates I have done,—

Thou know'st that Thou hast formèd me
10 With passions wild and strong;
And list'ning to their witching voice
  Has often led me wrong.

Where human weakness has come short,
  Or frailty stept aside,
15 Do Thou, All-Good—for such Thou art—
  In shades of darkness hide.

Where with intention I have err'd,
  No other plea I have,
But, Thou art good; and Goodness still
20 Delighteth to forgive.

MARY MORISON
1781   1800

O Mary, at thy window be!
  It is the wish'd, the trysted hour.
Those smiles and glances let me see,
  That make the miser's treasure poor:
5 How blithely wad I bide[1] the stoure,[2]
  A weary slave frae[3] sun to sun;
Could I the rich reward secure,
  The lovely Mary Morison!

Yestreen,[4] when to the trembling string
10 The dance gaed[5] thro' the lighted ha',
To thee my fancy took its wing,
  I sat, but neither heard or saw:
Tho' this was fair, and that was braw,[6]
  And yon the toast of a' the town,
15 I sigh'd, and said, amang them a':
  "Ye are na Mary Morison!"

O Mary, canst thou wreck his peace
  Wha for thy sake wad gladly die?
Or canst thou break that heart of his
20 Whase only faut[7] is loving thee?
If love for love thou wilt na gie,[8]
  At least be pity to me shown;
A thought ungentle canna be
  The thought o' Mary Morison.

MY NANIE, O
1782   1787

Behind yon hills, where Lugar flows,
  'Mang moors an' mosses many, O
The wintry sun the day has clos'd,
  And I'll awa to Nanie, O.

5 The westlin wind blaws loud an' shill;[9]
  The night's baith mirk and rainy, O;

[1] pretty
[2] have
[3] gaily dressed
[4] makes

[1] await; endure
[2] dust; conflict
[3] from
[4] last night
[5] went
[6] fine; handsome
[7] fault
[8] not give
[9] shrill

But I'll get my plaid, an' out I'll steal,
　　An' owre the hill to Nanie, O.

My Nanie's charming, sweet, an' young;
10　Nae artfu' wiles to win ye, O:
May ill befa' the flattering tongue
　　That wad beguile my Nanie, O.

Her face is fair, her heart is true;
　　As spotless as she's bonie, O:
15 The op'ning gowan,[1] wat wi' dew,
　　Nae purer is than Nanie, O.

A country lad is my degree,
　　An' few there be that ken me, O;
But what care I how few they be?
20　I'm welcome ay to Nanie, O.

My riches a's my penny-fee,[2]
　　An' I maun[3] guide it cannie,[4] O;
But warl's gear[5] ne'er troubles me,
　　My thoughts are a'—my Nanie, O.

25 Our auld guidman[6] delights to view
　　His sheep an' kye thrive bonie, O;
But I'm as blythe that hauds[7] his pleugh,
　　An' has nae care but Nanie, O.

Come weel, come woe, I care na by,[8]
30　I'll tak what Heav'n will send me, O;
Nae ither care in life have I,
　　But live, an' love my Nanie, O.

POOR MAILIE'S ELEGY
1782　　　　　1786

Lament in rhyme, lament in prose,
Wi' saut tears tricklin down your nose;
Our bardie's[9] fate is at a close,
　　　　Past a' remead;[10]
5 The last, sad cape-stane[11] of his woes;
　　　　Poor Mailie's dead!

It's no the loss o' warl's gear,[12]
That could sae bitter draw the tear,
Or mak our bardie, dowie,[13] wear
10　　　　The mourning weed:
He's lost a friend an' neebor dear
　　　　In Mailie dead.

Thro' a' the toun she trotted by him;
A lang half-mile she could descry him;
15 Wi' kindly bleat, when she did spy him,
　　　　She ran wi' speed:

A friend mair faithfu' ne'er cam nigh
　　him,
　　　　Than Mailie dead.

I wat[1] she was a sheep o' sense,
20 An' could behave hersel wi' mense:[2]
I'll say 't, she never brak a fence,
　　　　Thro' thievish greed.
Our bardie, lanely,[3] keeps the spence[4]
　　　　Sin' Mailie's dead.

25 Or, if he wanders up the howe,[5]
Her living image in her yowe[6]
Comes bleatin till him, owre the knowe,[7]
　　　　For bits o' bread;
An' down the briny pearls rowe[8]
30　　　　For Mailie dead.

She was nae get[9] o' moorlan tips,[10]
Wi' tawted[11] ket,[12] an' hairy hips;
For her forbears were brought in ships
　　　　Frae 'yont[13] the Tweed:
35 A bonier fleesh ne'er cross'd the clips[14]
　　　　Than Mailie's dead.

Wae worth the man wha first did shape
That vile, wanchancie[15] thing—a rape![16]
It maks guid fellows girn[17] an' gape,
40　　　　Wi' chokin dread;
An' Robin's bonnet wave wi' crape,
　　　　For Mailie dead.

O, a' ye bards on bonie Doon!
An' wha on Ayr your chanters[18] tune!
45 Come, join the melancholious croon[19]
　　　　O' Robin's reed!
His heart will never get aboon[20]
　　　　His Mailie's dead!

GREEN GROW THE RASHES,[21] O
1783　　　　　1803
Chorus

Green grow the rashes, O!
Green grow the rashes, O!
The sweetest hours that e'er I spend
Are spent amang the lasses, O.

5 There's nought but care on ev'ry han',
In every hour that passes, O:
What signifies the life o' man,
　　An' 'twere nae for the lasses, O?

[1] daisy	[8] I care nothing
[2] wages paid in money	[9] bard's; poet's
[3] must	[10] remedy
[4] carefully	[11] cope-stone (figurative for finishing touch)
[5] world's goods	
[6] master	[12] world's goods
[7] holds	[13] gloomy

[1] know	[11] matted
[2] discretion; good manners	[12] fleece
	[13] beyond
[3] lonely	[14] shears
[4] inner room	[15] unlucky; dangerous
[5] glen	[16] rope
[6] ewe	[17] grin
[7] knoll	[18] bagpipes
[8] roll	[19] mournful tune
[9] no issue	[20] above
[10] rams	[21] rushes

The war'ly[1] race may riches chase,
10 An' riches still may fly them, O;
An' tho' at last they catch them fast,
    Their hearts can ne'er enjoy them, O.

But gie me a cannie[2] hour at e'en,
    My arms about my dearie, O:
15 An' war'ly cares, an' war'ly men,
    May a' gae tapsalteerie,[3] O.

For you sae douce,[4] ye sneer at this,
    Ye're nought but senseless asses, O:
The wisest man the warl' e'er saw,
20 He dearly lov'd the lasses, O.

Auld Nature swears the lovely dears
    Her noblest work she classes, O:
Her prentice han' she tried on man,
    An' then she made the lasses, O.

Chorus

Green grow the rashes, O!
Green grow the rashes, O!
The sweetest hours that e'er I spend
Are spent amang the lasses, O.

TO DAVIE
SECOND EPISTLE
1784   1789

AULD NEEBOR,

I'm three times doubly o'er your debtor,
For your auld-farrant[5] frien'ly letter:
Tho' I maun[6] say 't, I doubt ye flatter,
    Ye speak sae fair,
5 For my puir, silly, rhymin clatter
    Some less maun sair.[7]

Hale be your heart, hale be your fiddle;
Lang may your elbuck[8] jink[9] an' diddle,[10]
To cheer you thro' the weary widdle[11]
10   O' war'ly cares,
Till bairns' bairns[12] kindly cuddle
    Your auld gray hairs!

But Davie, lad, I'm red[13] ye 're glaikit;[14]
I'm tauld the Muse ye hae negleckit;
15 An' gif it's sae,[15] ye sud be licket[16]
        Until ye fyke;[17]
Sic han's[18] as you sud ne'er be faiket,[19]
    Be hain't wha like.[20]

For me, I'm on Parnassus' brink,[1]
20 Rivin[2] the words to gar them clink;[3]
Whyles daez't[4] wi' love, whyles daez't
    wi' drink,
        Wi' jads[5] or Masons;
An' whyles, but ay owre[6] late, I think
    Braw[7] sober lessons.

25 Of a' the thoughtless sons o' man,
Commen' me to the Bardie clan;
Except it be some idle plan
        O' rhymin clink[8]—
The devil-haet that I sud ban![9]—
30   They never think.

Nae thought, nae view, nae scheme o'
    livin,
Nae cares to gie us joy or grievin;
But just the pouchie[10] put the nieve[11] in,
    An' while ought's there
35 Then hiltie-skiltie,[12] we gae scrievin,[13]
        An' fash nae mair.[14]

Leeze me on rhyme![15] it's aye a treasure,
My chief, amaist[16] my only pleasure;
At hame, a-fiel', at wark or leisure,
40   The Muse, poor hizzie![17]
Tho' rough an' raploch[18] be her measure,
    She's seldom lazy.

Haud[19] to the Muse, my dainty Davie:
The warl' may play you monie a shavie;[20]
45 But for the Muse, she'll never leave ye,
        Tho' e'er sae puir,[21]
Na, even tho' limpin wi' the spavie[22]
    Frae door to door!

EPISTLE TO J. LAPRAIK
AN OLD SCOTTISH BARD, APRIL 1, 1785
1785   1786

While briers an' woodbines budding green,
And paitricks[23] scraichin[24] loud at e'en,
An' morning poussie[25] whiddin[26] seen,
    Inspire my Muse,
5 This freedom in an unknown frien'
    I pray excuse.

1 That is, beginning to write poetry; or, perhaps, about to publish.
2 splitting; cleaving
3 make them jingle, or rhyme
4 dazed
5 jades; wenches
6 all too
7 fine
8 jingle
9 the devil have my soul that I should curse them
10 pocket
11 fist
12 helter-skelter
13 reeling
14 and worry no more
15 blessings on rhyme (from *leis me*, dear is to me)
16 almost
17 hussy
18 homespun
19 hold
20 bad turn
21 poor
22 spavin
23 partridges
24 calling hoarsely
25 hare
26 scudding

1 worldly
2 quiet
3 topsy-turvy
4 so solemn
5 old-favoring; sagacious
6 must
7 serve
8 elbow
9 dance
10 shake
11 struggle
12 children's children
13 afraid
14 thoughtless; foolish
15 if it's so
16 beaten
17 squirm
18 such hands
19 let off
20 be spared who like— *i. e.*, whoever may be spared

On Fasten-e'en[1] we had a rockin,[2]
To ca' the crack[3] and weave our
          stockin;
And there was muckle[4] fun and jokin,
10   Ye need na doubt.
At length we had a hearty yokin[5]
          At "sang about."[6]

There was ae sang,[7] amang the rest,
Aboon[8] them a' it pleas'd me best,
15 That some kind husband had addrest
          To some sweet wife:
It thirl'd[9] the heart-strings thro' the
          breast,
          A' to the life.

I've scarce heard ought describ'd sae weel,
20 What gen'rous, manly bosoms feel;
Thought I, "Can this be Pope, or Steele,
          Or Beattie's wark?"
They tauld me 'twas an odd kind chiel[10]
          About Muirkirk.

25 It pat me fidgin-fain[11] to hear't,
An' sae about him there I spier't,[12]
Then a' that ken't[13] him round declar'd
          He had ingíne,[14]
That nane excell'd it, few cam near't,
30   It was sae fine.

That set him to a pint of ale,
An' either douce[15] or merry tale,
Or rhymes an' sangs he'd made himsel,
          Or witty catches:[16]
35 'Tween Inverness an' Teviotdale,
          He had few matches.

Then up I gat, an' swoor an aith,[17]
Tho' I should pawn my pleugh an'
          graith,[18]
Or die a cadger pownie's[19] death,
40   At some dyke-back,[20]
A pint an' gill I'd gie them baith,
          To hear your crack.[21]

But, first an' foremost, I should tell,
Amaist as soon as I could spell,

45 I to the crambo-jingle[1] fell;
          Tho' rude an' rough—
Yet crooning to a body's sel,
          Does weel eneugh.

I am nae poet, in a sense,
50 But just a rhymer like by chance,
An' hae to learning nae pretence;
          Yet, what the matter?
Whene'er my Muse does on me glance,
          I jingle at her.

55 Your critic-folk may cock their nose,
And say, "How can you e'er propose,
You, wha ken[2] hardly verse frae prose,
          To mak a sang?"
But, by your leaves, my learned foes,
60   Ye're maybe wrang.

What's a' your jargon o' your schools,
Your Latin names for horns[3] an' stools?
If honest Nature made you fools,
          What sairs[4] your gram-
                    mers?
65 Ye'd better ta'en up spades and shools,[5]
          Or knappin-hammers.[6]

A set o' dull, conceited hashes[7]
Confuse their brains in college classes;
They gang[8] in stirks,[9] and come out
          asses,
70   Plain truth to speak;
An' syne[10] they think to climb Parnassus
          By dint o' Greek!

Gie me ae spark o' Nature's fire!
That's a' the learning I desire;
75 Then, tho' I drudge thro' dub[11] an' mire
          At pleugh or cart,
My Muse, tho' hamely in aïtire,
          May touch the heart.

O for a spunk[12] o' Allan's[13] glee,
80 Or Fergusson's, the bauld an' slee,[14]
Or bright Lapraik's, my friend to be,
          If I can hit it!
That would be lear[15] eneugh for me,
          If I could get it!

85 Now, sir, if ye hae friends enow,
Tho' real friends, I b'lieve, are few,
Yet, if your catalogue be fow,[16]

---

[1] the evening before Lent
[2] social meeting
[3] have a chat
[4] much
[5] time; spell (literally the word means as much work as is done by the draught animals at one time)
[6] A game in which each participant sings a song
[7] one song
[8] above
[9] thrilled
[10] fellow
[11] put me tingling with pleasure
[12] asked
[13] knew
[14] genius
[15] serious
[16] three-part songs, each part sung in turn
[17] oath
[18] tools
[19] hawker pony's
[20] back of a fence
[21] chat

[1] rhyming
[2] knows
[3] ink-horns
[4] serves
[5] shovels
[6] hammers for breaking stone
[7] fools
[8] go
[9] yearling steers
[10] afterwards
[11] puddle
[12] spark
[13] Allan Ramsay's
[14] bold and ingenious
[15] lore; learning
[16] full

I'se no[1] insist;
But gif ye want ae friend that's true,
90   I'm on your list.

I winna[2] blaw about mysel,
As ill I like my fauts[3] to tell;
But friends an' folks that wish me well,
          They sometimes roose[4]
               me;
95 Tho', I maun[5] own, as monie still
          As far abuse me.

There's ae wee faut they whyles lay to
          me—
I like the lasses—Gude forgie me!
For monie a plack[6] they wheedle frae[7]
          me,
100   At dance or fair;
Maybe some ither thing they gie me
          They weel can spare.

But Mauchline Race, or Mauchline Fair,
I should be proud to meet you there;
105 We'se[8] gie ae night's discharge to care,
          If we forgather;
And hae a swap o' rhymin-ware
          Wi' ane anither.

The four-gill chap, we'se gar him clat-
          ter,[9]
110 An' kirsen[10] him wi' reekin[11] water;
Syne we'll sit down an' tak our whit-
          ter,[12]
               To cheer our heart;
An' faith, we'se be acquainted better
          Before we part.

115 Awa, ye selfish warly race,
Wha think that havins,[13] sense, an'
          grace,
Ev'n love an' friendship, should give
          place
          To Catch-the-Plack![14]
I dinna like to see your face,
120   Nor hear your crack.

But ye whom social pleasure charms,
Whose hearts the tide of kindness warms,
Who hold your being on the terms,
          "Each aid the others,"
125 Come to my bowl, come to my arms,
          My friends, my brothers!

But, to conclude my lang epistle,
As my auld pen's worn to the grissle;
Twa lines frae you wad gar me fissle,[1]
130   Who am most fervent,
While I can either sing or whistle,
          Your friend and servant.

EPISTLE TO THE REV. JOHN M'MATH

INCLOSING A COPY OF HOLY WILLIE'S PRAYER
WHICH HE HAD REQUESTED
1785   1808

While at the stook[2] the shearers cow'r
To shun the bitter blaudin[3] show'r,
Or in gulravage, rinnin, scowr[4]
          To pass the time,
5 To you I dedicate the hour
          In idle rhyme.

My Musie, tir'd wi' monie a sonnet
On gown an' ban,[5] an' douse[6] black-bonnet,
Is grown right eerie[7] now she's done it,
10   Lest they should blame
               her,
An' rouse their holy thunder on it,
          And anathém[8] her.

I own 'twas rash, an' rather hardy,
That I, a simple, countra bardie,
15 Should meddle wi' a pack sae sturdy,
          Wha, if they ken[9] me,
Can easy, wi' a single wordie,
          Louse[10] Hell upon me.

But I gae[11] mad at their grimaces,
20 Their sighin, cantin,[12] grace-proud faces,
Their three-mile prayers, an' hauf-mile
          graces,
               Their raxin[13] conscience,
Whase[14] greed, revenge, an' pride dis-
          graces
               Waur nor[15] their non-
               sense.

25 There's Gau'n,[16] misca'd[17] waur than a
          beast,
Wha has mair honor in his breast
Than monie scores as guid's the priest
          Wha sae abus't him.
And may a bard no crack his jest
30   What way they've use't
               him?

---

1 I shall not
2 will not
3 faults
4 praise; flatter
5 must
6 A coin worth about
   one cent.
7 from

8 we shall
9 we shall cause h i m
   to make a noise
10 christen
11 steaming
12 hearty draught
13 good manners
14 h u n t the coin (a
   game)

1 tingle with delight
2 shock of sheaves
3 pelting
4 run and chase about
   in horse-play
5 band (worn by clergy-
   men)
6 sedate
7 concerned; fearful
8 pronounce a c u r s e
   upon

9 know
10 loose
11 go
12 hypocritical
13 elastic
14 whose
15 worse than
16 Gavin H a m i l t o n
   (See Glossary.)
17 miscalled; abused

See him, the poor man's friend, in need,
The gentleman in word an' deed—
An' shall his fame an' honor bleed
      By worthless skellums,[1]
35 An' not a Muse erect her head
      To cowe the blellums?[2]

O Pope, had I thy satire's darts,
To gie the rascals their deserts,
I'd rip their rotten, hollow hearts,
40   An' tell aloud
Their jugglin hocus-pocus arts
      To cheat the crowd!

God knows, I'm no the thing I should be,
Nor am I even the thing I could be,
45 But twenty times I rather would be
      An atheist clean
Than under gospel colors hid be,
      Just for a screen.

An honest man may like a glass,
50 An honest man may like a lass;
But mean revenge, an' malice fause[3]
      He'll still disdain,
An' then cry zeal for gospel laws,
      Like some we ken.

55 They take religion in their mouth;
They talk o' mercy, grace, an' truth,
For what? to gie their malice skouth[4]
      On some puir wight,
An' hunt him down, o'er right an' ruth,
60   To ruin streight.

All hail, Religion! Maid divine!
Pardon a Muse sae mean as mine,
Who, in her rough imperfect line,
      Thus daurs to name thee,
65 To stigmatise false friends of thine
      Can ne'er defame thee.

Tho' blotch't an' foul wi' monie a stain,
An' far unworthy of thy train,
With trembling voice I tune my strain
70   To join with those
Who boldly dare thy cause maintain
      In spite of foes:

In spite o' crowds, in spite o' mobs,
In spite of undermining jobs,
75 In spite o' dark banditti stabs
      At worth an' merit,
By scoundrels, even wi' holy robes,
      But hellish spirit!

O Ayr! my dear, my native ground,
80 Within thy presbyterial bound,
A candid lib'ral band is found
      Of public teachers,
As men, as Christians too, renown'd,
      An' manly preachers.

85 Sir, in that circle you are nam'd;
Sir, in that circle you are fam'd;
An' some, by whom your doctrine's blam'd
      (Which gies ye honor),
Ev'n, sir, by them your heart's esteem'd,
90   An' winning manner.

Pardon this freedom I have taen,
An' if impertinent I've been,
Impute it not, good sir, in ane
      Whase heart ne'er
      wrang'd ye,
95 But to his utmost would befriend
      Ought that belang'd ye.

THE JOLLY BEGGARS

A CANTATA
1785   1799

RECITATIVO

When lyart[1] leaves bestrow the yird,
Or, wavering like the bauckie-bird,[2]
      Bedim cauld Boreas' blast;
When hailstanes drive wi' bitter skyte,[3]
5 And infant frosts begin to bite,
      In hoary cranreuch[4] drest;
Ae night at e'en a merry core[5]
      O' randie,[6] gangrel[7] bodies,
In Poosie-Nansie's held the splore,[8]
10   To drink their orra duddies;[9]
      Wi' quaffing and laughing,
      They ranted[10] an' they sang;
      Wi' jumping an' thumping,
      The vera girdle[11] rang.

15 First, niest[12] the fire, in auld red rags,
Ane sat, weel brac'd wi' mealy bags[13]
      And knapsack a' in order;
His doxy[14] lay within his arm;
Wi' usquebae[15] an' blankets warm,
20   She blinket on her sodger.[16]
An' ay he gies the tozie drab[17]

[1] good-for-nothings   [3] false
[2] blusterers   [4] vent

[1] gray
[2] bat
[3] dash
[4] frost
[5] corps; group
[6] lawless
[7] vagrant
[8] carousal
[9] spare rags or clothes
[10] were jovial in a noisy way
[11] A plate of metal for frying cakes.
[12] next
[13] The meal-bag was the chief equipment of the beggar. It usually contained oatmeal, which might be used as food, or traded, or sold. See l. 48.
[14] wench
[15] whisky
[16] soldier
[17] gives the tipsy wench

The tither skelpin kiss,[1]
While she held up her greedy gab
Just like an aumous[2] dish:
    Ilk[3] smack still did crack still
5   Like onie a cadger's whup,[4]
Then, swaggering an' staggering,
He roar'd this ditty up:—

AIR
TUNE—*Soldier's Joy*

I am a son of Mars, who have been in
    many wars,
30   And show my cuts and scars wherever
      I come;
This here was for a wench, and that
    other in a trench,
    When welcoming the French at the
      sound of the drum.
                Lal de daudle, etc.

My prenticeship I past, where my leader
    breath'd his last,
35   When the bloody die was cast on the
      heights of Abrám;
I serv'd out my trade when the gallant
    game was play'd,
    And the Moro low was laid at the
      sound of the drum.

I lastly was with Curtis, among the float-
    ing batt'ries,
    And there I left for witness an arm
      and a limb;
40 Yet let my country need me, with Eliott
    to head me,
    I'd clatter on my stumps at the sound
      of the drum.

And now, tho' I must beg with a wooden
    arm and leg,
    And many a tatter'd rag hanging over
      my bum,
I'm as happy with my wallet, my bottle,
    and my callet,[5]
45   As when I us'd in scarlet to follow
    a drum.

What tho' with hoary locks I must stand
    the winter shocks,
    Beneath the woods and rocks often-
      times for a home?
When the tother bag I sell,[6] and the
    tother bottle tell,[7]
    I could meet a troop of hell at the
      sound of a drum.
                Lal de daudle, etc.

RECITATIVO

50 He ended; and the kebars sheuk[1]
    Aboon[2] the chorus roar;
While frighted rattons[3] backward
    leuk,
    An' seek the benmost bore;[4]
55 A fairy fiddler frae the neuk,[5]
    He skirl'd[6] out *Encore!*
But up arose the martial chuck,[7]
    An' laid the loud uproar:—

AIR
TUNE—*Sodger Laddie*

I once was a maid, tho' I cannot tell
    when,
And still my delight is in proper young
    men.
60 Some one of a troop of dragoons was my
    daddie;
No wonder I'm fond of a sodger laddie!
             Sing, lal de dal, etc.

The first of my loves was a swaggering
    blade;
To rattle the thundering drum was his
    trade;
65 His leg was so tight,[8] and his cheek was
    so ruddy,
Transported I was with my sodger laddie.

But the godly old chaplain left him in the
    lurch;
The sword I forsook for the sake of the
    church;
He risk'd the soul, and I ventur'd the
    body:
70 'Twas then I prov'd false to my sodger
    laddie.

Full soon I grew sick of my sanctified
    sot;
The regiment at large for a husband I
    got;
From the gilded spontoon[9] to the fife I
    was ready;
I ask'd no more but a sodger laddie.

75 But the peace it reduc'd me to beg in
    despair,
Till I met my old boy in a Cunningham
    Fair;
His rags regimental they flutter'd so
    gaudy,
My heart it rejoic'd at a sodger laddie.

1 another sounding kiss   5 wench
2 alms   6 See l. 16.
3 each   7 count another bottle
4 hawker's whip

1 rafters shook   6 cried; yelled
2 above   7 hen
3 rats   8 trim; comely
4 inmost chink   9 A weapon carried by
5 nook   military officers.

And now I have liv'd—I know not how
     long!
80 And still I can join in a cup and a song;
And whilst with both hands I can hold
     the glass steady,
Here's to thee, my hero, my sodger
     laddie!
           Sing, lal de dal, etc.

RECITATIVO

Poor Merry-Andrew in the neuk,
85   Sat guzzling wi' a tinkler-hizzie,[1]
They mind't na wha the chorus teuk,
    Between themselves they were sae busy.
At length with drink and courting dizzy,
He stoiter'd[2] up an' made a face;
90 Then turn'd, an' laid a smack on Grizzie,
Syne[3] tun'd his pipes wi' grave gri-
    mace:—

AIR

TUNE—*Auld Sir Symon*

Sir Wisdom's a fool when he's fou;[4]
   Sir Knave is a fool in a session;[5]
He's there but a prentice I trow,
95   But I am a fool by profession.

My grannie she bought me a beuk,
   An' I held awa to the school;
I fear I my talent misteuk,
   But what will ye hae[6] of a fool?
100 For drink I wad venture my neck;
   A hizzie's the half of my craft;
But what could ye other expect
   Of ane that's avowedly daft?

I ance was tyed up like a stirk,[7]
105   For civilly swearing and quaffing;
I ance was abus'd in the kirk,
   For towsing a lass i' my daffin.[8]

Poor Andrew that tumbles for sport,
   Let naebody name wi' a jeer:
110 There's even, I'm taul, i' the Court
   A tumbler ca'd the Premier.

Observ'd ye yon reverend lad
   Mak faces to tickle the mob?
He rails at our mountebank squad—
115   It's rivalship just i' the job.

And now my conclusion I'll tell,
   For faith! I'm confoundedly dry;
The chiel that's a fool for himsel,
   Guid Lord! he's far dafter than I.

RECITATIVO

120 Then niest outspak a raucle carlin,[1]
Wha kent fu' weel to cleek the sterlin,[2]
For monie a pursie she had hookèd,
An' had in monie a well been doukèd.
Her love had been a Highland laddie,
125 But weary fa' the waefu' woodie![3]
Wi' sighs an' sobs she thus began
To wail her braw[4] John Highlandman:—

AIR

TUNE—*O An' Ye Were Dead, Guidman*

A Highland lad my love was born,
The Lalland[5] laws he held in scorn,
130 But he still was faithfu' to his clan,
My gallant, braw John Highlandman.

Chorus

Sing hey my braw John Highlandman!
Sing ho my braw John Highlandman!
There's not a lad in a' the lan'
135 Was match for my John Highlandman!

With his philibeg[6] an' tartan plaid,[7]
An' guid claymore[8] down his side,
The ladies' hearts he did trepan,[9]
My gallant, braw John Highlandman.

140 We rangèd a' from Tweed to Spey,[10]
An' liv'd like lords an' ladies gay;
For a Lalland face he fearèd none,
My gallant, braw John Highlandman.

They banish'd him beyond the sea,
145 But ere the bud was on the tree,
Adown my cheeks the pearls ran,
Embracing my John Highlandman.

But, Och! they catch'd him at the last,
And bound him in a dungeon fast;
150 My curse upon them every one—
They've hang'd my braw John Highland-
    man!

And now a widow, I must mourn
The pleasures that will ne'er return;
No comfort but a hearty can
155 When I think on John Highlandman.

Chorus

Sing hey my braw John Highlandman!
Sing ho my braw John Highlandman!
There's not a lad in a' the lan'
Was match for my John Highlandman!

---

1 tinker-wench
2 staggered
3 then
4 full; drunk
5 court-session
6 have
7 tied up like a young bullock or heifer,— i. e., punished with a sort of iron collar
8 fun

1 sturdy old woman
2 pinch the ready cash
3 gallows (on which her love had been hanged)
4 handsome; fine
5 Lowland
6 A kind of short plaited petticoat, reaching from the waist to the knees, worn by Highlanders
7 shawl or scarf
8 A kind of broad-sword.
9 ensnare
10 That is, from one end of the country to the other.

RECITATIVO

160 A pigmy scraper on a fiddle,
   Wha us'd to trystes an' fairs[1] to driddle,[2]
   Her strappin limb an' gawsie[3] middle
              (He reach'd nae higher)
   Had hol'd[4] his heartie like a riddle,[5]
165   An' blawn't on fire.

   Wi' hand on hainch,[6] and upward e'e,
   He croon'd[7] his gamut, one, two, three,
   Then in an *arioso*[8] key,
              The wee Apollo
170 Set off wi' *allegretto*[9] glee
              His *giga*[10] solo:—

AIR

TUNE—*Whistle Owre the Lave*[11] *O't*

   Let me ryke up to dight[12] that tear;
   An' go wi' me an' be my dear,
   An' then your every care an' fear
175 May whistle owre the lave o't.

Chorus

   I am a fiddler to my trade,
   And a' the tunes that e'er I play'd,
   The sweetest still to wife or maid,
   Was *Whistle Owre the Lave O't.*

180 At kirns[13] an' weddings we'se be there
   An' O! sae nicely's we will fare!
   We'll bowse[14] about till Daddie Care
   Sings *Whistle Owre the Lave O't.*

   Sae merrily the banes we'll pyke,[15]
185 An' sun oursels about the dyke,[16]
   An' at our leisure, when ye like,
   We'll—whistle owre the lave o't!

   But bless me wi' your heav'n o' charms,
   An' while I kittle hair on thairms,[17]
190 Hunger, cauld, an' a' sic harms,[18]
   May whistle owre the lave o't.

Chorus

   I am a fiddler to my trade,
   And a' the tunes that e'er I play'd,
   The sweetest still to wife or maid,
195 Was *Whistle Owre the Lave O't.*

RECITATIVO

   Her chairms had struck a sturdy caird,[1]
   As weel as poor gut-scraper;
   He taks the fiddler by the beard,
   And draws a roosty rapier;
200 He swoor by a' was swearing worth,
   To speet him like a pliver,[2]
   Unless he would from that time forth
   Relinquish her forever.

   Wi' ghastly e'e, poor Tweedle-Dee
205 Upon his hunkers[3] bended,
   An' pray'd for grace wi' ruefu' face,
   An' sae the quarrel ended.
   But tho' his little heart did grieve
   When round the tinkler prest her,
210 He feign'd to snirtle[4] in his sleeve,
   When thus the caird address'd her:—

AIR

TUNE—*Clout*[5] *the Cauldron*

   My bonie lass, I work in brass,
   A tinkler is my station;
   I've travell'd round all Christian ground,
215 In this my occupation.
   I've taen the gold,[6] an' been enrolled
   In many a noble squadron;
   But vain they search'd, when off I march'd
   To go an' clout the cauldron.

220 Despise that shrimp, that wither'd imp,
   Wi' a' his noise an' cap'rin,
   An' take a share wi' those that bear
   The budget[7] and the apron!
   And by that stowp,[8] my faith an' houpe!
225 And by that dear Kilbaigie![9]
   If e'er ye want, or meet wi' scant,
   May I ne'er weet my craigie.[10]

RECITATIVO

   The caird prevail'd: th' unblushing fair
   In his embraces sunk,
230 Partly wi' love o'ercome sae sair,[11]
   An' partly she was drunk.
   Sir Violino, with an air
   That show'd a man o' spunk,
   Wish'd unison between the pair,
235 An' made the bottle clunk[12]
              To their health that night.

---

[1] cattle-markets and markets for hiring servants and farm laborers
[2] toddle
[3] buxom
[4] pierced
[5] sieve
[6] haunch
[7] hummed
[8] smooth; melodious
[9] quick; spirited
[10] A lively dance.

[11] r e m a i n d e r (See Burns's poem of this title, p. 220.)
[12] reach up to wipe
[13] harvest homes
[14] booze
[15] bones we'll pick
[16] stone or turf fence
[17] tickle hair on catgut,—*i. e.,* play on the violin
[18] all such harms

[1] tinker
[2] spit him l i k e a plover
[3] hams
[4] snicker
[5] mend
[6] enlisted
[7] A tinker's bag of tools.
[8] jug

[9] A kind of whiskey, named from a noted distillery.
[10] wet my throat
[11] so sorely
[12] g u r g l e (from the sound of emptying a narrow-necked bottle)

But hurchin[1] Cupid shot a shaft,
    That play'd a dame a shavie;[2]
The fiddler rak'd her fore and aft,
240   Behint the chicken cavie.[3]
Her lord, a wight of Homer's craft,[4]
    Tho' limping wi' the spavie,[5]
He hirpl'd[6] up, an' lap like daft,[7]
    An' shor'd[8] them "Dainty Davie"[9]
245   O' boot[10] that night.

He was a care-defying blade
    As ever Bacchus listed![11]
Tho' Fortune sair upon him laid,
    His heart she ever miss'd it.
250 He had nae wish but—to be glad,
    Nor want but—when he thirsted;
He hated nought but—to be sad,
    An' thus the Muse suggested
        His sang that night.

AIR

TUNE—*For A' That, An' A' That*

255 I am a bard of no regard
    Wi' gentle folks, an' a' that;
But Homer-like, the glowrin byke,[12]
    Frae town to town I draw that.

Chorus

    For a' that, an' a' that,
260   An' twice as muckle's[13] a' that,
    I've lost but ane, I've twa behin',
    I've wife eneugh for a' that.

I never drank the Muses' stank,[14]
    Castalia's burn,[15] an' a' that;
265 But there it streams, and richly reams[16]—
    My Helicon I ca' that.

Great love I bear to a' the fair,
    Their humble slave, an' a' that;
But lordly will, I hold it still
270   A mortal sin to thraw[17] that.

In raptures sweet, this hour we meet,
    Wi' mutual love, an' a' that;
But for how lang the flie may stang,[1]
    Let inclination law[2] that!

275 Their tricks an' craft hae put me daft,[3]
    They've taen me in, an' a' that;
But clear your decks, an' here's the sex!
    I like the jads for a' that.

Chorus

    For a' that, an' a' that,
280   An' twice as muckle's a' that;
    My dearest bluid, to do them guid,
    They're welcome till't[4] for a' that!

RECITATIVO

So sang the bard, and Nansie's wa's
Shook with a thunder of applause,
285   Re-echo'd from each mouth!
They toom'd their pocks,[5] an' pawn'd
        their duds,
They scarcely left to coor their fuds,[6]
    To quench their lowin drouth.[7]
Then owre again the jovial thrang,
290   The poet did request
To lowse his pack an' wale a sang,[8]
    A ballad o' the best;
He, rising, rejoicing,
        Between his twa Deborahs,[9]
295   Looks round him, an' found them
        Impatient for the chorus:—

AIR

TUNE—*Jolly Mortals, Fill Your Glasses*

See the smoking bowl before us!
    Mark our jovial ragged ring!
Round and round take up the chorus,
300   And in raptures let us sing.

Chorus

    A fig for those by law protected!
    Liberty's a glorious feast!
    Courts for cowards were erected,
        Churches built to please the priest!

305 What is title? what is treasure?
    What is reputation's care?
If we lead a life of pleasure,
    'Tis no matter how or where!

With the ready trick and fable,
310   Round we wander all the day;

---

[1] urchin
[2] trick
[3] coop
[4] a person of Homer's profession,—*i. e.*, a poet ("Homer is allowed to be the oldest ballad singer on record."—Burns.)
[5] spavin
[6] hobbled
[7] leaped like mad
[8] offered
[9] The name of a popular song which celebrated an amorous adventure of Mass David Williamson, a seventeenth century blade, who became known as Dainty Davy. This song is printed in *The Merry Muses of Caledonia*

(1911), p. 81, and *The Ancient and Modern Scots Songs* (1791), Vol. 2, p. 283. The adventure is related in C r e i c h t o n's *M e m o i r s* (Swift ed.), 12, 19-20. (From H e n l e y's note in the Cambridge ed. of Burns, p. 335.)
[10] to boot
[11] enlisted, or enrolled, as a follower
[12] staring crowd
[13] as much as
[14] pool; ditch
[15] rivulet
[16] foams (He refers to ale as his source of inspiration.)
[17] thwart

[1] how long the fly may sting
[2] govern; rule
[3] have made me foolish
[4] to it
[5] emptied their wallets
[6] cover their bodies
[7] raging thirst
[8] open his pack and choose a song
[9] See *Judges*, 4-5.

And at night, in barn or stable,
   Hug our doxies on the hay.

Does the train-attended carriage
   Thro' the country lighter rove?
315 Does the sober bed of marriage
   Witness brighter scenes of love?

Life is all a variorum,
   We regard not how it goes;
Let them cant about decorum
320 Who have character to lose.

Here's to budgets, bags, and wallets!
Here's to all the wandering train!
Here's our ragged brats and callets!
One and all, cry out, Amen!

Chorus

325 A fig for those by law protected!
   Liberty's a glorious feast!
Courts for cowards were erected,
   Churches built to please the priest!

THE HOLY FAIR[1]
1785   1786

A robe of seeming truth and trust
   Hid crafty observation;
And secret hung, with poison'd crust,
   The dirk of defamation:
A mask that like the gorget show'd,
   Dye-varying on the pigeon;
And for a mantle large and broad
   He wrapt him in Religion.
        —*Hypocrisy à-la-mode.*

Upon a simmer Sunday morn,
   When Nature's face is fair,
I walkèd forth to view the corn,
   An' snuff the caller[2] air.
5 The rising sun owre Galston Muirs
   Wi' glorious light was glintin;
The hares were hirplin[3] down the furs,[4]
   The lav'rocks[5] they were chantin
        Fu' sweet that day.

10 As lightsomely I glowr'd[6] abroad,
   To see a scene sae gay,
Three hizzies,[7] early at the road,
   Cam skelpin[8] up the way;
Twa had manteeles o' dolefu' black,
15   But ane wi' lyart[9] lining;
The third, that gaed a wee a-back,
   Was in the fashion shining
        Fu' gay that day.

The twa appear'd like sisters twin,
20   In feature, form, an' claes;[1]
Their visage wither'd, lang, an' thin,
   An' sour as onie slaes:[2]
The third cam up, hap-step-an'-lowp,[3]
   As light as onie lambie,
25 An' wi' a curchie[4] low did stoop,
   As soon as e'er she saw me,
        Fu' kind that day.

Wi' bonnet aff, quoth I, "Sweet lass,
   I think ye seem to ken me;
30 I'm sure I've seen that bonie face,
   But yet I canna name ye."
Quo' she, an' laughin as she spak,
   An' taks me by the han's,
"Ye, for my sake, hae gi'en the feck[5]
35   Of a' the Ten Comman's
        A screed[6] some day.

"My name is Fun—your cronie dear,
   The nearest friend ye hae;
An' this is Superstition here,
40   An' that's Hypocrisy.
I'm gaun to Mauchline Holy Fair,
   To spend an hour in daffin:[7]
Gin[8] ye'll go there, yon runkl'd[9] pair,
   We will get famous laughin
45   At them this day."

Quoth I, "Wi' a' my heart, I'll do 't;
   I'll get my Sunday's sark[10] on,
An' meet you on the holy spot;
   Faith, we'se hae[11] fine remarkin!"
50 Then I gaed hame at crowdie-time,[12]
   An' soon I made me ready;
For roads were clad, frae side to side,
   Wi' monie a wearie body,
        In droves that day.

55 Here, farmers gash,[13] in ridin graith;[14]
   Gaed hoddin by their cotters;[15]
There swankies[16] young, in braw braid-
     claith,[17]
   Are springin owre the gutters.
The lasses, skelpin barefit,[18] thrang,[19]
60   In silks an' scarlets glitter;
Wi' sweet-milk cheese, in monie a
     whang,[20]
   An' farls,[21] bak'd wi' butter,
        Fu' crump[22] that day.

1 " 'Holy Fair' is a common phrase in the West of Scotland for a sacramental occasion."—Burns.
2 fresh
3 limping
4 furrows
5 larks
6 stared
7 women
8 clattering
9 gray

12 porridge time
13 self-complacent
14 attire
15 jogging by their cotagers
16 strapping fellows
17 fine broadcloth
18 hastening barefoot
19 crowded
20 thick slice
21 coarse cake
22 crisp

1 clothes
2 sloe berries
3 hop-step-and-leap
4 curtsy
5 have given the substance
6 rent
7 fun; larking
8 if
9 wrinkled
10 shirt
11 we shall have

When by the plate we set our nose,
65   Weel heapèd up wi' ha'pence,
A greedy glowr,[1] black-bonnet[2] throws,
  An' we maun draw our tippence.
Then in we go to see the show:
  On ev'ry side they're gath'rin;
70 Some carryin dails,[3] some chairs an'
     stools,
  An' some are busy bleth'rin[4]
        Right loud that day.

Here stands a shed to fend the show'rs,
  An' screen our countra gentry;
75 There Racer Jess, and twa-three whores,
  Are blinkin at the entry.
Here sits a raw of tittlin' jads,[5]
  Wi' heavin breasts an' bare neck;
An' there a batch o' wabster[6] lads,
80   Blackguardin frae Kilmarnock,
        For fun this day.

Here some are thinkin on their sins,
  An' some upo' their claes;
Ane curses feet that fyl'd[7] his shins,
85   Anither sighs an' prays:
On this hand sits a chosen swatch,[8]
  Wi' screw'd-up, grace-proud faces;
On that a set o' chaps, at watch,
  Thrang winkin on the lasses
90   To chairs that day.

O happy is that man an' blest![9]
  Nae wonder that it pride him!
Whase ain dear lass that he likes best,
  Comes clinkin[10] down beside him!
95 Wi' arm repos'd on the chair-back,
  He sweetly does compose him;
Which, by degrees, slips round her neck,
  An's loof[11] upon her bosom,
        Unkend that day.

100 Now a' the congregation o'er
  Is silent expectation:
For Moodie speels[12] the holy door,
  Wi' tidings o' damnation.
Should Hornie, as in ancient days,
105   'Mang sons o' God present him,
The vera sight o' Moodie's face
  To's ain het hame[13] had sent him
        Wi' fright that day.

Hear how he clears the points o' faith
110   Wi' rattlin an' thumpin!
Now meekly calm, now wild in wrath,
  He's stampin and he's jumpin!
His lengthen'd chin, his turn'd-up snout,
  His eldritch[1] squeel an' gestures,
115 Oh, how they fire the heart devout,
  Like cantharidian[2] plaisters,
        On sic[3] a day!

But hark! the tent has chang'd its
     voice;
  There's peace an' rest nae langer:
120 For a' the real judges rise,
  They canna sit for anger.
Smith opens out his cauld harangues
  On practice and on morals;
An' aff the godly pour in thrangs,
125   To gie the jars an' barrels
        A lift that day.

What signifies his barren shine,
  Of moral pow'rs an' reason?
His English style, an' gesture fine,
130   Are a' clean out o' season.
Like Socrates or Antonine,
  Or some auld pagan heathen,
The moral man he does define,
  But ne'er a word o' faith in
135   That's right that day.

In guid time comes an antidote
  Against sic poison'd nostrum;[4]
For Peebles, frae the water-fit,[5]
  Ascends the holy rostrum:
140 See, up he's got the word o' God,
  An' meek an' mim[6] has view'd it,
While Common Sense[7] has taen the road,
  An' aff, an' up the Cowgate
        Fast, fast, that day.

145 Wee Miller niest[8] the guard relieves,
  An' orthodoxy raibles,[9]
Tho' in his heart he weel believes
  An' thinks it auld wives' fables:
But faith! the birkie[10] wants a manse;
150   So, cannilie he hums them;[11]
Altho' his carnal wit an' sense
  Like hafflins-wise o'ercomes him[12]
        At times that day.

---

[1] look
[2] The elder who held the collection plate at the entrance usually wore a black bonnet.
[3] boards
[4] chattering
[5] row of whispering jades
[6] weaver
[7] soiled
[8] sample
[9] Psalms, 146:2 (Scotch metrical version).
[10] dropping quickly
[11] and his hand
[12] climbs,—i. e., enters (Probably a caricature of his personal appearance and style of oratory.)
[13] to his own hot home
[1] unearthly
[2] made of cantharides, a preparation of dried blister beetles
[3] such
[4] doctrine (used figuratively)
[5] from the water foot, or river's mouth,— i. e., from Newton, situated at the mouth of the River Ayr
[6] prim; affectedly meek
[7] Supposed to refer to Burns's friend, Dr. Mackenzie.
[8] next
[9] rattles off
[10] smart young fellow
[11] so cunningly he humbugs them
[12] nearly half o'ercomes him

155 Now butt an' ben[1] the change-house[2] fills,
    Wi' yill-caup[3] commentators;
    Here's crying out for bakes[4] an' gills,[5]
    And there the pint-stowp[6] clatters;
    While thick an' thrang, an' loud an' lang,
    Wi' logic an' wi' Scripture,
160 They raise a din, that in the end,
    Is like to breed a rupture
                O' wrath that day.

    Leeze me on[7] drink! it gies us mair
    Than either school or college;
165 It kindles wit, it waukens lear,[8]
    It pangs us fou[9] o' knowledge.
    Be't whisky-gill, or penny wheep,[10]
    Or onie stronger potion,
    It never fails, on drinkin deep,
170 To kittle[11] up our notion,
                By night or day.

    The lads an' lasses, blythely bent
    To mind baith saul an' body,
    Sit round the table, weel content,
175 An' steer about the toddy.
    On this ane's dress, an' that ane's leuk,
    They're makin observations;
    While some are cozie i' the neuk,[12]
    An' forming assignations
180   To meet some day.

    But now the Lord's ain trumpet touts,
    Till a' the hills are rairin,[13]
    And echoes back return the shouts;
    Black Russell is na spairin:
185 His piercin words, like Highlan' swords,
    Divide the joints an' marrow;
    His talk o' hell, whare devils dwell,
    Our verra "sauls does harrow"[14]
                Wi' fright that day!

190 A vast, unbottom'd, boundless pit,
    Fill'd fou o' lowin brunstane,[15]
    Whase ragin flame, an' scorchin heat,
    Wad melt the hardest whun-stane![16]
    The half-asleep start up wi' fear,
195 An' think they hear it roarin,
    When presently it does appear
    'Twas but some neebor snorin
                Asleep that day.

    'Twad be owre lang a tale to tell,
200 How monie stories past;

An' how they crouded to the yill,[1]
    When they were a' dismist;
How drink gaed round, in cogs[2] an'
    caups,[3]
    Amang the furms[4] an' benches;
205 An' cheese an' bread, frae women's laps,
    Was dealt about in lunches
                An' dawds[5] that day

In comes a gawsie,[6] gash[7] guidwife,
    An' sits down by the fire,
210 Syne[8] draws her kebbuck[9] an' her
        knife;
    The lasses they are shyer.
The auld guidmen, about the grace,
    Frae side to side they bother,
Till some ane by his bonnet lays,
215 An' gies them't like a tether,[10]
                Fu' lang that day.

Waesucks![11] for him that gets nae lass,
    Or lasses that hae naething!
Sma' need has he to say a grace,
220 Or melvie[12] his braw claithing!
    O wives, be mindfu' ance yoursel
    How bonie lads ye wanted,
An' dinna for a kebbuck-heel[13]
    Let lasses be affronted
225   On sic a day!

Now, Clinkumbell, wi' rattlin tow,[14]
    Begins to jow[15] an' croon;[16]
Some swagger hame the best they dow,[17]
    Some wait the afternoon.
230 At slaps[18] the billies[19] halt a blink,
    Till lasses strip their shoon;[20]
Wi' faith an' hope, an' love an' drink,
    They're a' in famous tune
                For crack[21] that day.

235 How monie hearts this day converts
    O' sinners and o' lasses!
Their hearts o' stane, gin night, are gane,
    As saft as onie flesh is.
There's some are fou o' love divine;
240   There's some are fou o' brandy;
An' monie jobs that day begin,
    May end in houghmagandie[22]
                Some ither day.

THE COTTER'S[1] SATURDAY NIGHT

INSCRIBED TO ROBERT AIKEN, ESQ.
1785　　　　　1786

Let not Ambition mock their useful toil,
　Their homely joys, and destiny obscure;
Nor Grandeur hear, with a disdainful smile,
　The short and simple annals of the poor.
　　　　　　　—GRAY'S *Elegy.*

My lov'd, my honor'd, much respected
　　friend!
No mercenary bard his homage pays;
With honest pride, I scorn each selfish end:
My dearest meed a friend's esteem and
　　praise.
5 To you I sing, in simple Scottish lays,
The lowly train in life's sequester'd scene;
The native feelings strong, the guileless
　　ways;
What Aiken in a cottage would have been;
Ah! tho' his worth unknown, far hap-
　　pier there, I ween!

10 November chill blaws loud wi' angry sugh,[2]
The short'ning winter day is near a close;
The miry beasts retreating frae the pleugh,
The black'ning trains o' craws[3] to their
　　repose;
The toil-worn cotter frae his labor goes,—
15 This night his weekly moil is at an end,—
Collects his spades, his mattocks, and his
　　hoes,
Hoping the morn in ease and rest to spend,
And weary, o'er the moor, his course
　　does hameward bend.

At length his lonely cot appears in view,
20 Beneath the shelter of an aged tree;
Th' expectant wee-things, toddlin, stacher[4]
　　through
To meet their dad, wi' flichterin'[5] noise
　　and glee.
His wee bit ingle,[6] blinkin bonilie,[7]
His clean hearth-stane, his thrifty wifie's
　　smile,
25 The lisping infant, prattling on his knee,
Does a' his weary kiaugh[8] and care be-
　　guile,
An' makes him quite forget his labor
　　and his toil.

Belyve,[9] the elder bairns come drapping in,
At service out, amang the farmers roun';
30 Some ca[10] the pleugh, some herd, some
　　tentie[11] rin

A cannie[1] errand to a neebor town:[2]
Their eldest hope, their Jenny, woman
　　grown,
In youthfu' bloom, love sparkling in her
　　e'e,
Comes hame; perhaps, to shew a braw[3]
　　new gown,
35 Or deposite her sair-won penny-fee,[4]
　To help her parents dear, if they in hard-
　　ship be.

With joy unfeign'd, brothers and sisters
　　meet,
And each for other's weelfare kindly
　　spiers:[5]
The social hours, swift-wing'd, unnotic'd
　　fleet;
40 Each tell the uncos[6] that he sees or hears.
The parents, partial, eye their hopeful
　　years;
Anticipation forward points the view;
The mother, wi' her needle and her
　　sheers,
Gars[7] auld claes look amaist as weel's the
　　new;
45　The father mixes a' wi' admonition due.

Their master's and their mistress's com-
　　mand
The younkers a' are warnèd to obey;
And mind their labors wi' an eydent[8]
　　hand,
And ne'er, tho' out o' sight, to jauk[9] or
　　play:
50 "And O! be sure to fear the Lord alway,
And mind your duty, duly, morn and night!
Lest in temptation's path ye gang astray,
Implore His counsel and assisting might:
　They never sought in vain that sought
　　the Lord aright!"

55 But hark! a rap comes gently to the door;
Jenny, wha kens[10] the meaning o' the same,
Tells how a neebor lad came o'er the moor
To do some errands, and convoy her
　　hame.
The wily mother sees the conscious flame
60 Sparkle in Jenny's e'e, and flush her
　　cheek;
With heart-struck, anxious care, enquires
　　his name,
While Jenny hafflins[11] is afraid to speak:
　Weel-pleas'd the mother hears it's na
　　wild, worthless rake.

1 cottager's	7 shining prettily
2 sound	8 anxiety
3 crows	9 presently
4 stagger	10 drive
5 fluttering	11 heedful
6 fire-place; **fire**	

1 careful	6 news
2 farm (with its collec-	7 makes
tion of buildings)	8 diligent
3 fine	9 trifle
4 hard-won wages	10 who knows
5 asks	11 partly

With kindly welcome, Jenny brings him ben;[1]
65 A strappin' youth, he takes the mother's eye;
Blythe Jenny sees the visit's no ill taen;
The father cracks[2] of horses, pleughs, and kye.[3]
The youngster's artless heart o'erflows wi' joy,
But, blate[4] and laithfu',[5] scarce can weel behave;
70 The mother, wi' a woman's wiles, can spy
What makes the youth sae bashfu' and sae grave,
Weel-pleas'd to think her bairn's respected like the lave.[6]

O happy love! where love like this is found!
O heart-felt raptures! bliss beyond compare!
75 I've pacèd much this weary, mortal round,
And sage experience bids me this declare:—
"If Heaven a draught of heavenly pleasure spare,
One cordial in this melancholy vale,
'Tis when a youthful, loving, modest pair,
80 In other's arms, breathe out the tender tale
Beneath the milk-white thorn that scents the ev'ning gale."

Is there, in human form, that bears a heart,
A wretch! a villain! lost to love and truth!
That can, with studied, sly, ensnaring art,
85 Betray sweet Jenny's unsuspecting youth?
Curse on his perjur'd arts! dissembling, smooth!
Are honor, virtue, conscience, all exil'd?
Is there no pity, no relenting ruth,
Points to the parents fondling o'er their child?
90 Then paints the ruin'd maid, and their distraction wild?

But now the supper crowns their simple board,
The healsome parritch,[7] chief of Scotia's food;
The soupe[8] their only hawkie[9] does afford,
That 'yont[10] the hallan[11] snugly chows her cood;
95 The dame brings forth, in complimental mood,

To grace the lad, her weel-hain'd kebbuck,[1] fell;[2]
And aft[3] he's prest, and aft he ca's it guid;
The frugal wifie, garrulous, will tell,
How 'twas a towmond[4] auld, sin' lint[5] was i' the bell.[6]

100 The cheerfu' supper done, wi' serious face,
They, round the ingle, form a circle wide;
The sire turns o'er, with patriarchal grace,
The big ha'-Bible,[7] ance his father's pride.
His bonnet rev'rently is laid aside,
105 His lyart haffets[8] wearing thin and bare;
Those strains that once did sweet in Zion glide,
He wales[9] a portion with judicious care,
And, "Let us worship God!" he says, with solemn air.

They chant their artless notes in simple guise;
110 They tune their hearts, by far the noblest aim;
Perhaps *Dundee's*[10] wild-warbling measures rise,
Or plaintive *Martyrs*,[10] worthy of the name.
Or noble *Elgin*[10] beets[11] the heavenward flame,
The sweetest far of Scotia's holy lays.
115 Compar'd with these, Italian trills are tame;
The tickl'd ear no heart-felt raptures raise;
Nae unison hae they with our Creator's praise.

The priest-like father reads the sacred page,—
How Abram was the friend of God on high;
120 Or Moses bade eternal warfare wage
With Amalek's ungracious progeny;
Or how the royal bard[12] did groaning lie
Beneath the stroke of Heaven's avenging ire;
Or Job's pathetic plaint, and wailing cry;
125 Or rapt Isaiah's wild, seraphic fire;
Or other holy seers that tune the sacred lyre.

Perhaps the Christian volume is the theme:
How guiltless blood for guilty man was shed;
How He, who bore in Heaven the second name,

---

1 in
2 talks
3 cows
4 shy
5 bashful
6 rest ; others

7 wholesome porridge ; oatmeal
8 milk
9 white-faced cow
10 beyond
11 partition

sembly r o o m in large houses.)
8 gray locks or temples
9 chooses
10 A sacred melody.
11 kindles
12 David.

1 well-saved cheese
2 strong
3 often
4 twelve-month
5 since flax
6 blossom
7 hall-Bible (The hall was the general as-

130 Had not on earth whereon to lay His head;
How His first followers and servants sped;
The precepts sage they wrote to many a
land;
How he,[1] who lone in Patmos banishèd,
Saw in the sun a mighty angel stand,
135 And heard great Bab'lon's doom pro-
nounc'd by Heaven's command.

Then kneeling down to Heaven's Eternal
King,
The saint, the father, and the husband
prays:
Hope "springs exulting on triumphant
wing,"[2]
That thus they all shall meet in future days;
140 There, ever bask in uncreated rays,
No more to sigh or shed the bitter tear,
Together hymning their Creator's praise,
In such society, yet still more dear,
While circling Time moves round in an
eternal sphere.

145 Compar'd with this, how poor Religion's
pride,
In all the pomp of method and of art;
When men display to congregations wide
Devotion's ev'ry grace, except the heart,
The Power, incens'd, the pageant will de-
sert,
150 The pompous strain, the sacerdotal stole;[3]
But haply, in some cottage far apart,
May hear, well-pleas'd, the language of the
soul,
And in His Book of Life the inmates
poor enroll.

Then homeward all take off their sev'ral
way;
155 The youngling cottagers retire to rest;
The parent-pair their secret homage pay,
And proffer up to Heaven the warm re-
quest,
That He, who stills the raven's clam'rous
nest,[4]
And decks the lily fair in flow'ry pride,[5]
160 Would, in the way His wisdom sees the
best,
For them and for their little ones provide;
But, chiefly, in their hearts with Grace
Divine preside.

From scenes like these, old Scotia's grandeur springs,
That makes her lov'd at home, rever'd
abroad:

165 Princes and lords are but the breath of
kings,
"An honest man's the noblest work of
God."[1]
And certes, in fair Virtue's heavenly road,
The cottage leaves the palace far behind:
What is a lordling's pomp? a cumbrous
load,
170 Disguising oft the wretch of human kind,
Studied in arts of Hell, in wickedness
refin'd!

O Scotia! my dear, my native soil!
For whom my warmest wish to Heaven is
sent!
Long may thy hardy sons of rustic toil
175 Be blest with health, and peace, and sweet
content!
And O! may Heaven their simple lives prevent
From Luxury's contagion, weak and vile!
Then, howe'er crowns and coronets be rent,
A virtuous populace may rise the while,
180 And stand a wall of fire around their
much-lov'd Isle.

O Thou, who pour'd the patriotic tide
That stream'd thro' Wallace's undaunted
heart,
Who dar'd to nobly stem tyrannic pride,
Or nobly die, the second glorious part!
185 (The patriot's God, peculiarly Thou art,
His friend, inspirer, guardian, and re-
ward!)
O never, never Scotia's realm desert;
But still the patriot and the patriot-bard
In bright succession raise, her ornament
and guard!

TO A MOUSE

ON TURNING HER UP IN HER NEST WITH
THE PLOUGH, NOVEMBER, 1785
1785   1786

Wee, sleekit,[2] cowrin, tim'rous beastie,
O, what a panic's in thy breastie!
Thou need na start awa sae hasty,
Wi' bickering brattle![3]
5 I wad be laith[4] to rin an' chase thee,
Wi' murdering pattle![5]

I'm truly sorry man's dominion
Has broken Nature's social union,
An' justifies that ill opinion
10   Which makes thee startle
At me, thy poor, earth-born companion,
An' fellow mortal!

---

[1] John.
[2] Pope, *Windsor Forest*, 112.
[3] priestly vestment
[4] See *Psalms*, 147:9.
[5] See *Matthew*, 6:28-29.

[1] Pope, *Essay on Man*, 4, 248.
[2] sleek
[3] sudden scamper
[4] would be loath
[5] paddle for cleaning the plow

I doubt na, whyles,[1] but thou may thieve;
What then? poor beastie, thou maun
    live!
15 A daimen icker in a thrave[2]
      'S a sma' request:
I'll get a blessin wi' the lave,[3]
      And never miss't!

Thy wee bit housie, too, in ruin!
20 Its silly wa's the win's are strewin!
An' naething, now, to big[4] a new ane,
      O' foggage[5] green!
An' bleak December's win's ensuin,
      Baith snell[6] an' keen!

25 Thou saw the fields laid bare an' waste,
An' weary winter comin fast,
An' cozie here, beneath the blast,
      Thou thought to dwell,
Till crash! the cruel coulter[7] past
30   Out thro' thy cell.

That wee bit heap o' leaves an' stibble
Has cost thee monie a weary nibble!
Now thou's turned out, for a' thy
    trouble,
      But[8] house or hald,[9]
35 To thole[10] the winter's sleety dribble,
      An' cranreuch[11] cauld!

But, Mousie, thou art no thy lane,[12]
In proving foresight may be vain:
The best-laid schemes o' mice an' men,
40   Gang aft agley,[13]
An' lea'e us nought but grief an' pain
      For promis'd joy!

Still thou art blest, compared wi' me!
The present only toucheth thee:
45 But och! I backward cast my e'e,
      On prospects drear!
An' forward, tho' I canna see,
      I guess an' fear!

ADDRESS TO THE DEIL
1785   1786

O Prince! O Chief of many thronèd pow'rs!
That led th' embattl'd seraphim to war!
          —MILTON.[14]

O thou! whatever title suit thee—
Auld Hornie, Satan, Nick, or Clootie[15]
Wha in yon cavern grim an' sootie,

      Clos'd under hatches,
5 Spairges[1] about the brunstane cootie,[2]
      To scaud[3] poor wretches!

Hear me, Auld Hangie,[4] for a wee,[5]
An' let poor damnèd bodies be;
I'm sure sma' pleasure it can gie,
10   Ev'n to a deil,
To skelp[6] an' scaud poor dogs like me,
      An' hear us squeel.

Great is thy pow'r, an' great thy fame;
Far kend an' noted is thy name:
15 An' tho' yon lowin heugh's[7] thy hame,
      Thou travels far;
An' faith! thou's neither lag,[8] nor lame,
      Nor blate, nor scaur.[9]

Whyles,[10] ranging like a roarin lion,
20 For prey, a' holes an' corners trying;
Whyles, on the strong-wing'd tempest
    flyin,
      Tirlin the kirks;[11]
Whyles, in the human bosom pryin,
      Unseen thou lurks.

25 I've heard my rev'rend graunie say,
In lanely[12] glens ye like to stray;
Or where auld ruin'd castles gray
      Nod to the moon,
Ye fright the nightly wand'rer's way
30   Wi' eldritch croon.[13]

When twilight did my graunie summon,
To say her pray'rs, douce,[14] honest
    woman!
Aft yont[15] the dyke she's heard you
    bummin,[16]
      Wi' eerie drone;[17]
35 Or, rustlin thro' the boortrees[18] comin,
      Wi' heavy groan.

Ae dreary, windy, winter night,
The stars shot down wi' sklentin[19]
    light,
Wi' you mysel I gat a fright:
40   Ayont the lough,[20]
Ye, like a rash-buss,[21] stood in sight,
      Wi' waving sugh.[22]

---

[1] at times
[2] an occasional ear in a shock (of twenty-four sheaves)
[3] remainder
[4] build
[5] rank grass
[6] sharp
[7] cutter attached to the beam of a plow to cut the sward
[8] without
[9] abode
[10] endure
[11] hoar-frost
[12] not alone
[13] awry
[14] *Paradise Lost*, 1, 128-9.
[15] A clootie is a little hoof.

[1] splashes
[2] brimstone ladle
[3] scald
[4] old hangman
[5] moment
[6] slap
[7] flaming cavern
[8] slow
[9] shy nor timid
[10] sometimes
[11] unroofing the churches
[12] lonely
[13] unearthly moan
[14] sober
[15] often beyond
[16] humming
[17] ghostly sound
[18] elders
[19] slanting
[20] beyond the lake
[21] bush of rushes
[22] a sound as of the wind

The cudgel in my nieve[1] did shake,
Each bristl'd hair stood like a stake,
45 When wi' an eldritch, stoor[2] "quaick,
        quaick,"
            Amang the springs,
Awa ye squatter'd like a drake,
        On whistling wings.

Let warlocks[3] grim, an' wither'd hags,
50 Tell how wi' you, on ragweed nags,[4]
They skim the muirs an' dizzy crags,
            Wi' wicked speed;
And in kirk-yards renew their leagues[5]
        Owre howkit[6] dead.

55 Thence, countra wives, wi' toil an' pain,
May plunge an' plunge the kirn[7] in vain;
For O! the yellow treasure's taen
            By witching skill;
An' dawtit,[8] twal-pint hawkie's[9] gaen
60   As yell's the bill.[10]

Thence, mystic knots mak great abuse
On young guidmen,[11] fond, keen, an'
        croose;[12]
When the best wark-lume[13] i' the house,
            By cantraip[14] wit,
65 Is instant made no worth a louse,
        Just at the bit.[15]

When thowes[16] dissolve the snawy hoord,[17]
An' float the jinglin icy-boord,[18]
Then, water-kelpies[19] haunt the foord,
70   By your direction,
An' nighted trav'llers are allur'd
        To their destruction.

And aft[20] your moss-traversing spunkies[21]
Decoy the wight that late an' drunk is:
75 The bleezin,[22] curst, mischievous monkies
            Delude his eyes,
Till in some miry slough he sunk is,
        Ne'er mair to rise.

When Masons' mystic word an' grip
80 In storms an' tempests raise you up,
Some cock or cat your rage maun stop,[23]
        Or, strange to tell!
The youngest brother ye wad whip
        Aff straight to hell.

85 Lang syne,[1] in Eden's bonie yard,
When youthfu' lovers first were pair'd,
An' all the soul of love they shar'd,
            The raptur'd hour,
Sweet on the fragrant, flow'ry swaird,
90   In shady bow'r:

Then you, ye auld, snick-drawing[2] dog!
Ye cam to Paradise incog,
An' play'd on man a cursed brogue[3]
        (Black be your fa'![4]),
95 An' gied the infant warld a shog,[5]
        'Maist ruin'd a'.

D' ye mind that day when in a bizz,[6]
Wi' reekit[7] duds, an' reestit gizz,[8]
Ye did present your smoutie phiz
100   'Mang better folk,
An' sklented[9] on the man of Uzz[10]
        Your spitefu' joke?

An' how ye gat him i' your thrall,
An' brak him out o' house an' hal',
105 While scabs an' botches did him gall,
            Wi' bitter claw,
And lows'd[11] his ill-tongu'd, wicked
        scaul,[12]
        Was warst ava?[13]

But a' your doings to rehearse,
110 Your wily snares an fechtin[14] fierce,
Sin' that day Michael did you pierce,[15]
            Down to this time,
Wad ding a Lallan tongue, or Erse,[16]
        In prose or rhyme.

115 An' now, Auld Cloots, I ken ye're thinkin,
A certain Bardie's rantin, drinkin,
Some luckless hour will send him linkin[17]
            To your black pit:
But, faith! he'll turn a corner jinkin,[18]
120   An' cheat you yet.

But, fare you weel, Auld Nickie-ben!
O, wad ye tak a thought an' men'!
Ye aiblins[19] might—I dinna ken—
            Still hae a stake:[20]
125 I'm wae[21] to think upo' yon den,
        Ev'n for your sake!

[1] fist	[13] work-loom
[2] harsh	[14] magic
[3] wizards	[15] at the time when
[4] rag-weed stems used	most needed
instead of broom-	[16] thaws
sticks, for horses	[17] snowy hoard
[5] covenants	[18] surface of ice
[6] dug-up	[19] river-demons (usu-
[7] churn	ally in the form of
[8] petted	horses)
[9] twelve-pint white-	[20] often
faced cow's	[21] will-o'-the-wisps
[10] as dry as the bull	[22] blazing
[11] newly-married men	[23] That is, by being of-
[12] bold; sure	fered as a sacrifice.

[1] long since	[14] fighting
[2] latch-lifting; intrud-	[15] See *Paradise Lost*,
ing	6, 325.
[3] trick	[16] would baffle a Low-
[4] lot	land tongue or
[5] shock	Gaelic
[6] flurry	[17] skipping; tripping
[7] smoky	[18] dodging
[8] singed face	[19] perhaps
[9] squinted; directed	[20] have a position (cf.
[10] Job.	"to have a stake in
[11] let loose	the country.")
[12] scold	[21] sad
[13] worst of all	

A BARD'S EPITAPH
1786　　1786

Is there a whim-inspirèd fool,
Owre fast for thought, owre hot for
　　rule,
Owre blate[1] to seek, owre proud to
　　snool?[2]—
　　　　　Let him draw near;
5 And owre this grassy heap sing dool,[3]
　　　　　And drap a tear.

Is there a bard of rustic song,
Who, noteless, steals the crowds among,
That weekly this aréa throng?—
10　　　　O, pass not by!
But with a frater-feeling strong,
　　　　　Here heave a sigh.

Is there a man whose judgment clear
Can others teach the course to steer,
15 Yet runs himself life's mad career
　　　　　Wild as the wave?—
Here pause—and thro' the starting tear
　　　　　Survey this grave.

The poor inhabitant below
20 Was quick to learn and wise to know,
And keenly felt the friendly glow
　　　　　And softer flame;
But thoughtless follies laid him low,
　　　　　And stain'd his name.

25 Reader, attend! whether thy soul
Soars fancy's flights beyond the pole,
Or darkling grubs this earthly hole
　　　　　In low pursuit;
Know, prudent, cautious self-control
　　　　　Is wisdom's root.

ADDRESS TO THE UNCO GUID; OR, THE RIGIDLY RIGHTEOUS
1786　　1787

My Son, these maxims make a rule,
　An' lump them ay thegither:
The Rigid Righteous is a fool,
　The Rigid Wise anither:
The cleanest corn that e'er was dight[4]
　May hae some pyles o' caff[5] in;
So ne'er a fellow-creature slight
　For random fits o' daffin.[6]
　　　　SOLOMON.—*Eccles.*, 7:16.

O ye who are sae guid yoursel,
　Sae pious and sae holy,
Ye've nought to do but mark and tell
　Your neebors' fauts[7] and folly;
5 Whase life is like a weel-gaun[8] mill,

Supplied wi' store o' water;
The heapet happer's[1] ebbing still,
　An' still the clap[2] plays clatter!

Hear me, ye venerable core,[3]
10　As counsel for poor mortals
That frequent pass douce[4] Wisdom's door
　For glaikit[5] Folly's portals;
I, for their thoughtless, careless sakes,
　Would here propone[6] defences—
15 Their donsie[7] tricks, their black mistakes,
　Their failings and mischances.

Ye see your state wi' theirs compared,
　And shudder at the niffer;[8]
But cast a moment's fair regard,
20　What makes the mighty differ?[9]
Discount what scant occasion gave,
　That purity ye pride in,
And (what's aft[10] mair than a' the lave[11])
　Your better art o' hidin.

25 Think, when your castigated pulse
　Gies now and then a wallop,[12]
What ragings must his veins convulse,
　That still eternal gallop!
Wi' wind and tide fair i' your tail,
30　Right on ye scud your sea-way;
But in the teeth o' baith[13] to sail,
　It makes an unco[14] lee-way.

See Social-life and Glee sit down,
　All joyous and unthinking,
35 Till, quite transmogrify'd,[15] they're
　　grown
Debauchery and Drinking:
O, would they stay to calculate
　Th' eternal consequences,
Or—your more dreadful hell to state—
40　Damnation of expenses!

Ye high, exalted, virtuous dames,
　Tied up in godly laces,
Before ye gie poor Frailty names,
　Suppose a change o' cases;
45 A dear-lov'd lad, convenience snug,
　A treach'rous inclination—
But, let me whisper i' your lug,[16]
　Ye're aiblins[17] nae temptation.

Then gently scan your brother man,
50　Still gentler sister woman;
Tho' they may gang a kennin[18] wrang,
　To step aside is human:

[1] shy	[5] grains of chaff
[2] cringe; crawl	[6] fun
[3] sorrow	[7] faults
[4] winnowed	[8] well-going

[1] heaped-up hopper's	[10] often
[2] clapper	[11] remainder
[3] corps; company	[12] quick jerk
[4] grave	[13] both
[5] giddy	[14] wonderful
[6] propose	[15] transformed
[7] restless	[16] ear
[8] exchange	[17] perhaps
[9] difference	[18] trifle

One point must still be greatly dark,
    The moving *why* they do it;
55 And just as lamely can ye mark
    How far, perhaps, they rue it.

Who made the heart, 'tis He alone
    Decidedly can try us;
He knows each chord, its various tone,
60   Each spring, its various bias:
Then at the balance let's be mute,
    We never can adjust it;
What's done we partly may compute,
    But know not what's resisted.

TO A MOUNTAIN DAISY

ON TURNING ONE DOWN WITH THE
PLOUGH IN APRIL, 1786
1786   1786

Wee, modest, crimson-tippèd flow'r,
Thou's met me in an evil hour;
For I maun[1] crush amang the stoure[2]
    Thy slender stem:
5 To spare thee now is past my pow'r,
    Thou bonie gem.

Alas! it's no thy neebor sweet,
The bonie lark, companion meet,
Bending thee 'mang the dewy weet,
10   Wi' spreckl'd breast!
When upward-springing, blythe, to greet
    The purpling east.

Cauld blew the bitter-biting north
Upon thy early, humble birth;
15 Yet cheerfully thou glinted forth
    Amid the storm,
Scarce rear'd above the parent-earth
    Thy tender form.

The flaunting flow'rs our gardens yield,
20 High shelt'ring woods and wa's[3] maun
    shield;
But thou, beneath the random bield[4]
    O' clod or stane,
Adorns the histie[5] stibble-field,
    Unseen, alane.

25 There, in thy scanty mantle clad,
Thy snawie bosom sun-ward spread,
Thou lifts thy unassuming head
    In humble guise;
But now the share uptears thy bed,
30   And low thou lies!

[1] must
[2] dust
[3] walls
[4] shelter
[5] dry; bare

Such is the fate of artless maid,
Sweet flow'ret of the rural shade!
By love's simplicity betray'd,
    And guileless trust;
35 Till she, like thee, all soil'd, is laid
    Low i' the dust.

Such is the fate of simple bard,
On life's rough ocean, luckless starr'd!
Unskilful he to note the card[1]
40   Of prudent lore,
Till billows rage, and gales blow hard,
    And whelm him o'er!

Such fate to suffering Worth is giv'n,
Who long with wants and woes has
    striv'n,
45 By human pride or cunning driv'n
    To mis'ry's brink;
Till, wrench'd of ev'ry stay but Heav'n,
    He, ruin'd, sink!

Ev'n thou who mourn'st the Daisy's fate,
50 That fate is thine—no distant date;
Stern Ruin's ploughshare drives elate,
    Full on thy bloom,
Till crush'd beneath the furrow's weight
    Shall be thy doom!

TO A LOUSE

ON SEEING ONE ON A LADY'S BONNET AT
CHURCH
1786   1786

Ha! whare ye gaun, ye crowlin[2] ferlie?[3]
Your impudence protects you sairly:[4]
I canna say but ye strunt[5] rarely
    Owre gauze and lace;
5 Tho', faith! I fear ye dine but sparely
    On sic a place.

Ye ugly, creepin, blastit wonner,[6]
Detested, shunn'd by saunt an' sinner,
How daur ye set your fit[7] upon her—
10   Sae fine a lady!
Gae somewhere else, and seek your dinner
    On some poor body.

Swith![8] in some beggar's hauffet[9] squat-
    tle;[10]
There ye may creep, and sprawl, and
    sprattle,[11]
15 Wi' ither kindred, jumping cattle,

[1] compass-card
[2] crawling
[3] wonder
[4] greatly
[5] strut
[6] blasted marvel (used
   contemptuously)
[7] foot
[8] quick
[9] side of the head
[10] sprawl
[11] struggle

In shoals and nations;
Whare horn[1] nor bane[2] ne'er daur un-
    settle
      Your thick plantations.

Now haud[3] you there! ye're out o' sight,
20 Below the fatt'rils,[4] snug an' tight;
Na, faith ye yet![5] ye'll no be right
      'Till ye've got on it—
The vera tapmost, tow'ring height
      O' Miss's bonnet.

25 My sooth! right bauld ye set your nose out,
As plump an' gray as onie grozet;[6]
O for some rank, mercurial rozet,[7]
      Or fell, red smeddum,[8]
I'd gie you sic a hearty dose o't,
30   Wad dress your droddum.[9]

I wad na been surpris'd to spy
You on an auld wife's flainen toy;[10]
Or aiblins[11] some bit duddie[12] boy,
      On's wyliecoat;[13]
35 But Miss's fine Lunardi![14] fye!
      How daur ye do't?

O Jenny, dinna toss your head,
An' set your beauties a' abroad![15]
Ye little ken what cursèd speed
40   The blastie's makin![16]
Thae winks an' finger-ends, I dread,
      Are notice takin!

O wad some Power the giftie[17] gie us
To see oursels as ithers see us!
45 It wad frae monie a blunder free us,
      An' foolish notion:
What airs in dress an' gait wad lea'e us,
      An' ev'n devotion!

THE SILVER TASSIE[18]
1788   1790

Go, fetch to me a pint o' wine,
    And fill it in a silver tassie,
That I may drink, before I go,
    A service to my bonie lassie!
5 The boat rocks at the pier o' Leith,
    Fu' loud the wind blaws frae the
      ferry,
The ship rides by the Berwick-Law,
    And I maun leave my bonie Mary.

The trumpets sound, the banners fly,
10   The glittering spears are rankèd
      ready;
The shouts o' war are heard afar,
    The battle closes deep and bloody.
It's not the roar o' sea or shore
    Wad make me langer wish to tarry;
15 Nor shouts o' war that's heard afar—
    It's leaving thee, my bonie Mary.

OF A' THE AIRTS[1]
1788   1790

Of a' the airts the wind can blaw,
    I dearly like the west,
For there the bonie lassie lives,
    The lassie I lo'e best.
5 There wild woods grow, and rivers row,[2]
    And monie a hill between;
But day and night my fancy's flight
    Is ever wi' my Jean.

I see her in the dewy flowers,
10   I see her sweet and fair:
I hear her in the tunefu' birds,
    I hear her charm the air.
There's not a bonie flower that springs
    By fountain, shaw,[3] or green,
15 There's not a bonie bird that sings,
    But minds me o' my Jean.

AULD LANG SYNE[4]
1788   1796
Chorus

For auld lang syne, my dear,
    For auld lang syne,
We'll tak a cup o' kindness yet
    For auld lang syne!

5 Should auld acquaintance be forgot,
    And never brought to mind?
Should auld acquaintance be forgot,
    And auld lang syne?

And surely ye'll be your pint-stowp,[5]
10   And surely I'll be mine;
And we'll tak a cup o' kindness yet
    For auld lang syne!

We twa hae run about the braes,[6]
    And pou'd[7] the gowans[8] fine;
15 But we've wandered monie a weary fit[9]
    Sin' auld lang syne.

---

[1] horn-comb
[2] bone-comb
[3] hold
[4] ribbon-ends
[5] A reiteration of the exclamation in l. 5.
[6] gooseberry
[7] rosin
[8] powder
[9] breech
[10] flannel cap
[11] perhaps
[12] small ragged

[13] flannel vest
[14] balloon - bonnet (named after Lunardi, a famous aeronaut)
[15] abroad
[16] blasted, — *i. e.*, dwarfed, creature is making (or, possibly, damned creature)
[17] small gift
[18] goblet

[1] directions
[2] roll
[3] wood
[4] old long since (old times)
[5] be good for your three-pint measure
[6] hill-sides
[7] pulled
[8] daisies
[9] foot

We twa hae paidl'd[1] in the burn,[2]
    Frae morning sun till dine;[3]
But seas between us braid[4] hae roar'd
20 Sin' auld lang syne.

And there's a hand, my trusty fiere,[5]
    And gie's a hand o' thine;
And we'll tak a right guid-willie waught[6]
    For auld lang syne.

Chorus

25   For auld lang syne, my dear,
        For auld lang syne,
        We'll tak a cup o' kindness yet
        For auld lang syne!

WHISTLE O'ER THE LAVE O'T[7]
1789   1790

First when Maggie was my care,
Heav'n, I thought, was in her air;
Now we're married—spier nae mair[8]—
    But—whistle o'er the lave o't!
5 Meg was meek, and Meg was mild,
Sweet and harmless as a child:
Wiser men than me's beguil'd—
    Whistle o'er the lave o't!

How we live, my Meg and me,
10 How we love, and how we gree,[9]
I care na by[10] how few may see—
    Whistle o'er the lave o't!
Wha I wish were maggots' meat,
Dish'd up in her winding-sheet,
15 I could write—but Meg wad see't—
    Whistle o'er the lave o't!

MY HEART'S IN THE HIGHLANDS
1789   1790
Chorus

My heart's in the Highlands, my heart
    is not here;
My heart's in the Highlands, a-chasing
    the deer;
A-chasing the wild deer, and following
    the roe—
My heart's in the Highlands, wherever
    I go.

5 Farewell to the Highlands, farewell to the
    North,
The birthplace of valor, the country of
    worth;
Wherever I wander, wherever I rove,
The hills of the Highlands forever I
    love.

Farewell to the mountains, high-cover'd
    with snow;
10 Farewell to the straths[1] and green val-
    leys below;
Farewell to the forests and wild-hanging
    woods;
Farewell to the torrents and loud-
    pouring floods.

Chorus

My heart's in the Highlands, my heart
    is not here;
My heart's in the Highlands, a-chasing
    the deer;
15 A-chasing the wild deer, and following
    the roe—
My heart's in the Highlands, wherever
    I go.

JOHN ANDERSON MY JO[2]
1789   1790

John Anderson my jo, John,
    When we were first acquent,
Your locks were like the raven,
    Your bonie brow was brent;[3]
5 But now your brow is beld,[4] John,
    Your locks are like the snaw;
But blessings on your frosty pow,[5]
    John Anderson my jo!

John Anderson my jo, John,
10 We clamb the hill thegither;
And monie a cantie[6] day, John,
    We've had wi' ane anither;
Now we maun totter down, John,
    And hand in hand we'll go,
15 And sleep thegither at the foot,
    John Anderson my jo!

SWEET AFTON
1789   1789

Flow gently, sweet Afton, among thy
    green braes;[7]
Flow gently, I'll sing thee a song in thy
    praise;
My Mary's asleep by thy murmuring
    stream—
Flow gently, sweet Afton, disturb not
    her dream.

5 Thou stock-dove, whose echo resounds
    thro' the glen,
Ye wild whistling blackbirds in yon
    thorny den,

Thou green-crested lapwing, thy scream-
    ing forbear—
I charge you, disturb not my slumbering
    fair.

How lofty, sweet Afton, thy neighbor-
    ing hills,
10 Far mark'd with the courses of clear,
    winding rills!
There daily I wander as noon rises high,
My flocks and my Mary's sweet cot in
    my eye.

How pleasant thy banks and green val-
    leys below,
Where wild in the woodlands the prim-
    roses blow;
15 There oft, as mild Ev'ning weeps over
    the lea,
The sweet-scented birk[1] shades my Mary
    and me.

Thy crystal stream, Afton, how lovely
    it glides,
And winds by the cot where my Mary
    resides!
How wanton thy waters her snowy feet
    lave,
20 As gathering sweet flowerets she stems
    thy clear wave!

Flow gently, sweet Afton, among thy
    green braes;
Flow gently, sweet river, the theme of
    my lays;
My Mary's asleep by thy murmuring
    stream—
Flow gently, sweet Afton, disturb not
    her dream.

WILLIE BREW'D A PECK OF MAUT[2]
1789   1790
Chorus

We are na fou,[3] we're nae that fou,
    But just a drappie[4] in our e'e!
The cock may craw, the day may daw,
    And ay we'll taste the barley-bree![5]

5 O, Willie brew'd a peck o' maut,
    And Rob and Allan cam to see;
Three blyther hearts, that lee-lang[6]
    night,
    Ye wad na found in Christendie.

Here are we met, three merry boys,
10   Three merry boys, I trow, are we;

And monie a night we've merry been,
    And monie mae[1] we hope to be!

It is the moon, I ken her horn,
    That's blinkin in the lift[2] sae hie;
15 She shines sae bright to wyle[3] us hame,
    But, by my sooth, she'll wait a wee!

Wha first shall rise to gang awa,
    A cuckold, coward loun is he!
Wha first beside his chair shall fa',
20   He is the king amang us three!

Chorus

We are na fou, we're nae that fou,
    But just a drappie in our e'e!
The cock may craw, the day may daw,
    And ay we'll taste the barley-bree!

TAM GLEN
1789   1789

My heart is a-breaking, dear tittie![4]
Some counsel unto me come len'.
To anger them a' is a pity,
    But what will I do wi' Tam Glen?

5 I'm thinking, wi' sic a braw[5] fellow,
    In poortith[6] I might mak a fen'.[7]
What care I in riches to wallow,
    If I mauna[8] marry Tam Glen?

There's Lowrie, the laird o' Drumeller,
10   "Guid day to you"—brute! he comes
    ben:[9]
He brags and he blaws o' his siller,
    But when will he dance like Tam Glen?

My minnie[10] does constantly deave[11] me,
    And bids me beware o' young men;
15 They flatter, she says, to deceive me—
    But wha can think sae o' Tam Glen?

My daddie says, gin[12] I'll forsake him,
    He'll gie me guid hunder marks[13] ten:
But, if it's ordain'd I maun take him,
20   O, wha will I get but Tam Glen?

Yestreen at the valentines' dealing,
    My heart to my mou[14] gied a sten,[15]
For thrice I drew ane without failing,
    And thrice it was written, "Tam Glen"!

---

[1] birch
[2] malt
[3] full; drunk
[4] small drop
[5] brew
[6] live-long

[8] in
[9] mother
[10] deafen
[11] if
[12] Scotch coins, worth 26 cents each.
[13] mouth
[14] gave a leap

[1] more
[2] sky
[3] entice
[4] sister
[5] such a fine
[6] poverty
[7] shift
[8] may not

²⁵ The last Halloween I was waukin
     My droukit sark-sleeve,[1] as ye ken;
His likeness cam up the house staukin,[3]
And the very gray breeks[4] o' Tam Glen!

Come, counsel, dear tittie, don't tarry!
30   I'll gie you my bonie black hen,
Gif ye will advise me to marry
     The lad I lo'e dearly, Tam Glen.

THOU LING'RING STAR
1789   1790

Thou ling'ring star with less'ning ray,
     That lov'st to greet the early morn,
Again thou usher'st in the day
     My Mary from my soul was torn.
⁵ O Mary, dear departed shade!
     Where is thy place of blissful rest?
See'st thou thy lover lowly laid?
     Hear'st thou the groans that rend his
        breast?

That sacred hour can I forget,
10   Can I forget the hallow'd grove,
Where, by the winding Ayr, we met
     To live one day of parting love?
Eternity cannot efface
     Those records dear of transports past,
¹⁵ Thy image at our last embrace—
     Ah! little thought we 'twas our last!

Ayr, gurgling, kiss'd his pebbl'd shore,
     O'erhung with wild woods, thickening
        green;
The fragrant birch and hawthorn hoar
20   Twin'd amorous round the raptur'd
        scene;
The flowers sprang wanton to be prest,
     The birds sang love on every spray,
Till too, too soon, the glowing west
     Proclaim'd the speed of wingèd day.

²⁵ Still o'er these scenes my mem'ry wakes
     And fondly broods with miser-care.
Time but th' impression stronger makes,
     As streams their channels deeper wear.

O Mary, dear departed shade!
30   Where is thy place of blissful rest?
See'st thou thy lover lowly laid?
     Hear'st thou the groans that rend his
        breast?

✓ TAM O' SHANTER
A TALE
1790   1791

Of Brownyis and of Bogillis[1] full is this Buke.
           —GAWIN DOUGLAS.[2]

When chapman billies[3] leave the street,
And drouthy[4] neebors, neebors meet;
As market-days are wearin late,
An' folk begin to tak the gate;[5]
⁵ While we sit bousing at the nappy,[6]
An' gettin' fou[7] and unco[8] happy,
We think na on the lang Scots miles,[9]
The mosses, waters, slaps,[10] and styles,
That lie between us and our hame,
10 Whare sits our sulky, sullen dame,
Gathering her brows like gathering
        storm,
Nursing her wrath to keep it warm.

This truth fand[11] honest Tam o'
        Shanter,
As he frae Ayr ae night did canter:
¹⁵ (Auld Ayr, wham ne'er a town surpasses,
For honest men and bonie lasses).

O Tam, hadst thou but been sae wise,
As taen thy ain wife Kate's advice!
She tauld thee weel thou was a skellum.[12]
20 A blethering,[13] blustering, drunken blel-
        lum;[14]
That frae November till October,
Ae market-day thou was na sober;
That ilka melder[15] wi' the miller,
Thou sat as lang as thou had siller;
²⁵ That ev'ry naig was ca'd[16] a shoe on,
The smith and thee gat roaring fou on;
That at the Lord's house, even on Sunday,
Thou drank wi' Kirkton Jean till Mon-
        day.
She prophesied that, late or soon,
30 Thou would be found deep drown'd in
        Doon,
Or catch'd wi' warlocks[17] in the mirk[18]
By Alloway's auld, haunted kirk.

---

[1] watching my drenched shirt-sleeve
[2] "You go out, one or more (for this is a social spell), to a south-running spring, or rivulet, where 'three lairds' lands meet,' and dip your left shirt-sleeve. Go to bed in sight of a fire, and hang your wet sleeve before it to dry. Lie awake; and some time near midnight, an apparition, having the exact figure of the grand object in question [future husband], will come and turn the sleeve, as if to dry the other side."—Burns's note on Halloween, st. 24.
[3] stalking
[4] breeches

[1] hobgoblins
[2] Translation of the Æneid, Prologue 6, 15.
[3] peddler fellows
[4] thirsty
[5] take the way,—i. e., go home
[6] drinking ale
[7] full: drunk
[8] very
[9] The old Scotch mile was 216 yards longer than the English mile.
[10] gaps; openings in fences
[11] found
[12] scamp
[13] idly-talking
[14] babbler
[15] every grist or grinding
[16] driven
[17] wizards
[18] dark

Ah, gentle dames! it gars me greet[1]
To think how monie counsels sweet,
35 How monie lengthen'd, sage advices,
The husband frae the wife despises!

But to our tale:—Ae market-night,
Tam had got planted unco right;
Fast by an ingle,[2] bleezing finely,
40 Wi' reaming swats,[3] that drank di-
    vinely;
And at his elbow, Souter[4] Johnie,
His ancient, trusty, drouthy cronie;
Tam lo'ed him like a very brither;
They had been fou for weeks thegither!
45 The night drave on wi' sangs and clatter;
And ay the ale was growing better:
The landlady and Tam grew gracious
Wi' secret favors, sweet and precious;
The Souter tauld his queerest stories;
50 The landlord's laugh was ready chorus:
The storm without might rair and rustle,
Tam did na mind the storm a whistle.

Care, mad to see a man sae happy,
E'en drown'd himsel amang the nappy.
55 As bees flee hame wi' lades o' treasure,
The minutes wing'd their way wi'
    pleasure:
Kings may be blest, but Tam was glorious,
O'er a' the ills o' life victorious!

But pleasures are like poppies spread;
60 You seize the flow'r, its bloom is shed;
Or like the snow falls in the river,
A moment white—then melts forever;
Or like the borealis race,
That flit ere you can point their place;
65 Or like the rainbow's lovely form,
Evanishing amid the storm.
Nae man can tether time nor tide;
The hour approaches Tam maun ride:
That hour, o' night's black arch the key-
    stane,
70 That dreary hour Tam mounts his beast
    in;
And sic a night he taks the road in,
As ne'er poor sinner was abroad in.

The wind blew as 'twad blawn its last;
The rattling showers rose on the blast;
75 The speedy gleams the darkness swal-
    low'd;
Loud, deep, and lang, the thunder bel-
    low'd:
That night, a child might understand,
The Deil had business on his hand.

Weel-mounted on his gray mare, Mcg—
80 A better never lifted leg—
Tam skelpit[1] on thro' dub[2] and mire,
Despising wind, and rain, and fire;
Whiles holding fast his guid blue bonnet;
Whiles crooning[3] o'er some auld Scots
    sonnet;[4]
85 Whiles glow'ring round wi' prudent cares,
Lest bogles[5] catch him unawares;
Kirk-Alloway was drawing nigh,
Where ghaists and houlets[6] nightly cry.

By this time he was cross the ford,
90 Whare in the snaw the chapman
    smoor'd;[7]
And past the birks[8] and meikle[9] stane,
Whare drunken Charlie brak's neckbane;
And thro' the whins,[10] and by the cairn,[11]
Where hunters fand the murder'd bairn;[12]
95 And near the thorn, aboon the well,
Whare Mungo's mither hang'd hersel.
Before him Doon pours all his floods;
The doubling storm roars thro' the woods;
The lightnings flash from pole to pole;
100 Near and more near the thunders roll;
When, glimmering thro' the groaning
    trees,
Kirk-Alloway seem'd in a bleeze;[13]
Thro' ilka bore[14] the beams were glancing;
And loud resounded mirth and dancing.

105 Inspiring bold John Barleycorn,
What dangers thou canst make us scorn!
Wi' tippenny,[15] we fear nae evil;
Wi' usquabae,[16] we'll face the devil!
The swats sae ream'd[17] in Tammie's noddle,
110 Fair play, he car'd na deils a boddle.[18]
But Maggie stood, right sair astonish'd,
Till, by the heel and hand admonish'd,
She ventur'd forward on the light;
And, vow! Tam saw an unco[19] sight!

115 Warlocks[20] and witches in a dance;
Nae cotillion, brent-new[21] frae France,
But hornpipes, jigs, strathspeys, and
    reels,[22]
Put life and mettle in their heels.
A winnock-bunker[23] in the east,
120 There sat Auld Nick, in shape o' beast;
A tousie tyke,[24] black, grim, and large,

---

[1] clattered
[2] puddle
[3] humming
[4] song
[5] goblins
[6] owls
[7] smothered
[8] birches
[9] great
[10] furze
[11] stone-heap
[12] child
[13] blaze
[14] every crevice
[15] two-penny ale
[16] whiskey
[17] ale so foamed
[18] copper
[19] strange
[20] wizards
[21] brand-new
[22] Names of Scottish dances.
[23] window-seat
[24] touseled, shaggy cur

---

[1] makes me grieve
[2] fire-side
[3] foaming ale
[4] cobbler

To gie them music was his charge;
He screw'd the pipes and gart them
    skirl,[1]
Till roof and rafters a' did dirl.[2]
125 Coffins stood round, like open presses,
That shaw'd the dead in their last
    dresses;
And, by some devilish cantraip sleight,[3]
Each in its cauld hand held a light,
By which heroic Tam was able
130 To note upon the haly[4] table,
A murderer's banes in gibbet-airns;[5]
Twa span-lang, wee, unchristen'd bairns;
A thief, new-cutted frae a rape,[6]
Wi' his last gasp his gab[7] did gape;
135 Five tomahawks, wi' bluid red-rusted;
Five scymitars, wi' murder crusted;
A garter, which a babe had strangled;
A knife, a father's throat had mangled,
Whom his ain son o' life bereft—
140 The gray hairs yet stack to the heft;
Wi' mair o' horrible an' awefu',
Which even to name wad be unlawfu'.

As Tammie glowr'd,[8] amaz'd, and
    curious,
The mirth and fun grew fast and furious:
145 The piper loud and louder blew,
The dancers quick and quicker flew;
They reel'd, they set, they cross'd, they
    cleekit,[9]
Till ilka carlin[10] swat and reekit,[11]
And coost her duddies to the wark,[12]
150 And linket at it in her sark![13]

Now Tam! O Tam! had thae been
    queans[14]
A' plump and strapping in their teens!
Their sarks, instead o' creeshie[15] flannen,
Been snaw-white seventeen hunder linen![16]
155 Thir breeks[17] o' mine, my only pair,
That ance were plush, o' guid blue hair,
I wad hae gi'en them aff my hurdies,[18]
For ae blink o' the bonie burdies![19]

But wither'd beldams, auld and droll,
160 Rigwoodie[20] hags wad spean[21] a foal,
Louping and flinging on a crummock,[22]
I wonder did na turn thy stomach!

But Tam kend what was what fu'
    brawlie:[1]
There was ae winsome wench and wawlie,[2]
165 That night enlisted in the core,[3]
Lang after kend on Carrick shore
(For monie a beast to dead she shot,
An' perish'd monie a bonie boat,
And shook baith meikle corn and bear,[4]
170 And kept the country-side in fear);
Her cutty sark,[5] o' Paisley harn,[6]
That while a lassie she had worn,
In longitude tho' sorely scanty,
It was her best, and she was vauntie.[7]
175 Ah! little kend thy reverend grannie,
That sark she coft[8] for her wee Nannie,
Wi' twa pund Scots[9] ('twas a' her riches),
Wad ever grac'd a dance of witches!

But here my Muse her wing maun
    cour;[10]
180 Sic flights are far beyond her power;
To sing how Nannie lap and flang[11]
(A souple jade she was, and strang),
And how Tam stood like ane bewitch'd,
And thought his very een enrich'd;
185 Even Satan glowr'd, and fidg'd fu' fain,[12]
And hotched[13] and blew wi' might and
    main:
Till first ae caper, syne anither,
Tam tint[14] his reason a' thegither,
And roars out: "Weel done, Cutty-sark!"
190 And in an instant all was dark;
And scarcely had he Maggie rallied,
When out the hellish legion sallied.

As bees bizz out wi' angry fyke,[15]
When plundering herds[16] assail their
    byke;[17]
195 As open[18] pussie's[19] mortal foes,
When, pop! she starts before their nose;
As eager runs the market-crowd,
When "Catch the thief!" resounds
    aloud;
So Maggie runs, the witches follow,
200 Wi' monie an eldritch[20] skriech and hollo.

Ah, Tam! ah, Tam! thou'lt get thy
    fairin![21]
In hell they'll roast thee like a herrin!
In vain thy Kate awaits thy comin!

[1] made them shriek
[2] ring
[3] magic trick
[4] holy
[5] b o n e s in gibbet
    irons
[6] rope
[7] mouth
[8] stared
[9] linked arms
[10] each old woman
[11] sweated and steamed
[12] cast her clothes to
    the work

[13] went at it in her
    shirt
[14] wenches
[15] greasy
[16] very fine linen, with
    1700 threads to a
    width
[17] these breeches
[18] hips
[19] lasses
[20] lean; skinny
[21] wean (by disgust)
[22] leaping and caper-
    ing on a crooked
    staff

[1] full well
[2] vigorous
[3] company
[4] wheat and barley
[5] short shirt
[6] coarse linen
[7] proud
[8] bought
[9] A pound Scots is
    worth about forty
    cents.
[10] must stoop

[11] leaped and kicked
[12] fidgeted with eager-
    ness
[13] hitched; jerked
[14] lost
[15] fuss
[16] herders of cattle
[17] hive
[18] begin to bark
[19] the hare's
[20] unearthly
[21] reward (literally, a
    present from a fair)

Kate soon will be a woefu' woman!
205 Now, do thy speedy utmost, Meg,
And win the key-stane of the brig;[1]
There, at them thou thy tail may toss,
A running stream they dare na cross;
But ere the key-stane she could make,
210 The fient[2] a tail she had to shake;
For Nannie, far before the rest,
Hard upon noble Maggie prest,
And flew at Tam wi' furious ettle;[3]
But little wist[4] she Maggie's mettle—
215 Ae spring brought off her master hale,
But left behind her ain gray tail:
The carlin claught[5] her by the rump,
And left poor Maggie scarce a stump.

Now, wha this tale o' truth shall read,
220 Ilk man and mother's son take heed:
Whene'er to drink you are inclin'd,
Or cutty sarks run in your mind,
Think! ye may buy the joys o'er dear;
Remember Tam o' Shanter's mare.

✓ YE FLOWERY BANKS
1791   1808

Ye flowery banks o' bonie Doon,
How can ye blume sae fair?
How can ye chant, ye little birds,
And I sae fu' o' care?

5 Thou'll break my heart, thou bonie bird,
That sings upon the bough;
Thou minds me o' the happy days
When my fause[6] luve was true.

Thou'll break my heart, thou bonie bird,
10 That sings beside thy mate;
For sae I sat, and sae I sang,
And wist na[7] o' my fate.

Aft[8] hae I rov'd by bonie Doon,
To see the woodbine twine,
15 And ilka[9] bird sang o' its luve,
And sae did I o' mine.

Wi' lightsome heart I pu'd a rose,
Frae aff its thorny tree;
And my fause luver staw[10] my rose,
20 But left the thorn wi' me.

AE[11] FOND KISS
1791   1792

Ae fond kiss, and then we sever;
Ae farewell, and then, forever!
Deep in heart-wrung tears I'll pledge thee,

Warring sighs and groans I'll wage[1] thee.
5 Who shall say that Fortune grieves him,
While the star of hope she leaves him?
Me, nae cheerfu' twinkle lights me;
Dark despair around benights me.

I'll ne'er blame my partial fancy;
10 Naething could resist my Nancy;
But to see her was to love her;
Love but her, and love forever.
Had we never lov'd sae kindly,
Had we never lov'd sae blindly,
15 Never met—or never parted—
We had ne'er been broken-hearted.

Fare-thee-weel, thou first and fairest!
Fare-thee-weel, thou best and dearest!
Thine be ilka[2] joy and treasure,
20 Peace, enjoyment, love, and pleasure!
Ae fond kiss, and then we sever;
Ae farewell, alas, forever!
Deep in heart-wrung tears I'll pledge
thee,
Warring sighs and groans I'll wage thee!

THE DEIL'S AWA WI' TH'
EXCISEMAN
1792   1792

Chorus

The deil's awa, the deil's awa,
The deil's awa wi' th' Exciseman;
He's danc'd awa, he's danc'd awa,
He's danc'd awa wi' th' Exciseman!

5 The deil cam fiddlin thro' the town
And danc'd awa wi' th' Exciseman,
And ilka[2] wife cries: "Auld Mahoun,[3]
I wish you luck o' the prize, man!

"We'll mak our maut,[4] we'll brew our
drink,
10 We'll laugh, sing, and rejoice, man;
And monie braw[5] thanks to the meikle[6]
black deil,
That danc'd awa wi' th' Exciseman."

There's threesome reels,[7] there's foursome
reels,
There's hornpipes and strathspeys,[8]
man;
15 But the ae best dance e'er cam to the
land
Was *The Deil's Awa wi' th' Exciseman.*

---

[1] bridge
[2] devil
[3] intention; aim
[4] knew
[5] seized
[6] false
[7] knew
[8] often
[9] every
[10] stole
[11] one

[1] pledge
[2] every
[3] Old Mahomet (an ancient name for the devil)
[4] malt
[5] many fine
[6] great
[7] reels in which three take part
[8] Lively Scottish dances.

Chorus

The deil's awa, the deil's awa,
   The deil's awa wi' th' Exciseman;
He's danc'd awa, he's danc'd awa,
20   He's danc'd awa wi' th' Exciseman!

SAW YE BONIE LESLEY
1792   1798

O, saw ye bonie Lesley,
  As she gaed o'er the border?
She's gane, like Alexander,
  To spread her conquests farther.

5 To see her is to love her,
  And love but her forever;
For Nature made her what she is,
  And never made anither!

Thou art a queen, fair Lesley—
10 Thy subjects we, before thee:
Thou art divine, fair Lesley—
  The hearts o' men adore thee.

The deil he could na skaith[1] thee,
  Nor aught that wad belang thee;
15 He'd look into thy bonie face,
  And say: "I canna wrang thee."

The Powers aboon will tent[2] thee;
  Misfortune sha' na steer[3] thee:
Thou'rt like themsel' sae lovely,
20 That ill they'll ne'er let near thee.

Return again, fair Lesley,
  Return to Caledonie!
That we may brag we hae a lass
  There's nane again sae bonie.

HIGHLAND MARY
1792   1799

Ye banks and braes[4] and streams
    around
  The castle o' Montgomery,
Green be your woods, and fair your
    flowers,
  Your waters never drumlie![5]
5 There Summer first unfald her robes,
  And there the langest tarry;
For there I took the last fareweel,
  O' my sweet Highland Mary.

How sweetly bloom'd the gay, green birk,[6]
10 How rich the hawthorn's blossom,
As underneath their fragrant shade
  I clasp'd her to my bosom!

The golden hours, on angel wings,
  Flew o'er me and my dearie;
15 For dear to me as light and life,
  Was my sweet Highland Mary.

Wi' monie a vow and lock'd embrace
  Our parting was fu' tender;
And, pledging aft[1] to meet again,
20 We tore oursels asunder.
But O, fell Death's untimely frost,
  That nipt my flower sae early!
Now green's the sod, and cauld's the
    clay,
  That wraps my Highland Mary!

25 O, pale, pale now, those rosy lips
  I aft hae kiss'd sae fondly;
And clos'd for ay, the sparkling glance,
  That dwalt on me sae kindly;
And mouldering now in silent dust,
30 That heart that lo'ed me dearly!
But still within my bosom's core
  Shall live my Highland Mary.

LAST MAY A BRAW[2] WOOER
1794   1799

Last May a braw wooer cam down the
    lang glen,
  And sair[3] wi' his love he did deave[4] me.
I said there was naething I hated like men:
  The deuce gae wi'm[5] to believe me, be-
    lieve me—
5 The deuce gae wi'm to believe me!

He spak o' the darts in my bonie black een,
  And vow'd for my love he was dyin.
I said he might die when he liket[6] for Jean:
  The Lord forgie me for lyin, for lyin—
10 The Lord forgie me for lyin!

A weel-stocket mailen,[7] himsel for the
    laird,
  And marriage aff-hand were his prof-
    fers:
I never loot on that I kenn'd it or car'd,
  But thought I might hae waur offers,[8]
    waur offers—
15 But thought I might hae waur offers.

But what wad ye think? In a fortnight or
    less
  (The Deil tak his taste to gae near her!)
He up the Gate-Slack to my black cousin,
    Bess!

---

[1] injure
[2] take care of
[3] molest
[4] slopes
[5] muddy
[6] birch

[1] often
[2] fine; handsome
[3] sorely
[4] deafen
[5] with him
[6] liked; pleased
[7] farm
[8] have worse offers

Guess ye how, the jad! I could bear her,
    could bear her—
20 Guess ye how, the jad! I could bear her.

But a' the niest[1] week, as I petted[2] wi'
    care,
    I gaed to the tryste[3] o' Dalgarnock,
And wha but my fine fickle lover was there?
    I glowr'd as I'd seen a warlock,[4] a war-
      lock—
25   I glowr'd as I'd seen a warlock.

But owre my left shouther I gae him a
    blink,
    Lest neebors might say I was saucy.
My wooer he caper'd as he'd been in
    drink,
    And vow'd I was his dear lassie, dear
      lassie—
30   And vow'd I was his dear lassie.

I spier'd[5] for my cousin fu' couthy and
    sweet,
    Gin[6] she had recover'd her hearin,
And how her new shoon fit her auld,
    shachl'd[7] feet—
    But heavens! how he fell a swearin, a
      swearin—
35   But heavens! how he fell a swearin!

He begg̀ed, for Gudesake, I wad be his
    wife,
    Or else I wad kill him wi' sorrow;
So, e'en to preserve the poor body in life,
    I think I maun[8] wed him tomorrow, to-
      morrow—
40   I think I maun wed him tomorrow!

SCOTS, WHA HAE
1793   1794

Scots, wha hae wi' Wallace bled,
Scots, wham Bruce has aften led;
Welcome to your gory bed,
    Or to Victorie!

5 Now's the day, and now's the hour;
See the front o' battle lour;
See approach proud Edward's[9] power—
    Chains and slaverie!

Wha will be a traitor knave?
10 Wha can fill a coward's grave?
Wha sae base as be a slave?—
    Let him turn and flee!

Wha for Scotland's king and law
Freedom's sword will strongly draw,
15 Freeman stand, or freeman fa';
    Let him follow me!

By Oppression's woes and pains,
By your sons in servile chains;
We will drain our dearest veins,
20   But they shall be free!

Lay the proud usurpers low!
Tyrants fall in every foe!
Liberty's in every blow!—
    Let us do or die!

A RED, RED ROSE
1794   1796

O, my luve is like a red, red rose,
    That's newly sprung in June:
O, my luve is like the melodie
    That's sweetly played in tune.

5 As fair art thou, my bonie lass,
    So deep in luve am I;
And I will luve thee still, my dear,
    Till a' the seas gang dry.

Till a' the seas gang dry, my dear,
10   And the rocks melt wi' the sun;
And I will luve thee still, my dear,
    While the sands o' life shall run.

And fare thee weel, my only luve!
    And fare thee well a while!
15 And I will come again, my luve,
    Tho' it were ten thousand mile!

MY NANIE'S AWA
1794   1799

Now in her green mantle blythe Nature
    arrays,
And listens the lambkins that bleat o'er
    the braes,[1]
While birds warble welcomes in ilka
    green shaw;[2]
But to me it's delightless—my Nanie's
    awa!

5 The snawdrap and primrose our wood-
    lands adorn,
And violets bathe in the weet[3] o' the
    morn;
They pain my sad bosom, sae sweetly
    they blaw;
They mind me o' Nanie—and Nanie's awa!

Thou lav'rock,[4] that springs frae the
    dews of the lawn
10 The shepherd to warn o' the gray-breaking
    dawn,

[1] next
[2] was vexed
[3] went to the fair
[4] wizard
[5] asked
[6] whether
[7] shapeless
[8] must
[9] Edward II, of Eng-
land.

[1] slopes
[2] every green wood
[3] wet
[4] lark

And thou mellow mavis,[1] that hails the
    night-fa,
Give over for pity—my Nanie's awa!

Come autumn, sae pensive, in yellow and
    gray,
And soothe me wi' tidings o' Nature's
    decay:
15 The dark, dreary winter, and wild-driving
    snaw,
Alane can delight me—now Nanie's awa.

CONTENTED WI' LITTLE
1794   1799

Contented wi' little, and cantie[2] wi' mair,
Whene'er I forgather wi' Sorrow and
    Care,
I gie them a skelp,[3] as they're creepin
    alang,
Wi' a cog[4] o' guid swats[5] and an auld
    Scottish sang.

5 I whyles[6] claw[7] the elbow o' troublesome-
    Thought;
But man is a soger,[8] and life is a
    faught;[9]
My mirth and guid humor are coin in
    my pouch,
And my Freedom's my lairdship nae
    monarch daur touch.

A towmond[10] o' trouble, should that be
    my fa',[11]
10 A night o' guid fellowship sowthers[12]
    it a':
When at the blythe end o' our journey
    at last,
Wha the deil ever thinks o' the road he
    has past?

Blind Chance, let her snapper and
    stoyte[13] on her way;
Be 't to me, be 't frae me, e'en let the
    jade gae:
15 Come Ease, or come Travail, come Pleas-
    ure or Pain,
My warst word is, "Welcome, and wel-
    come again!"

LASSIE WI' THE LINT-WHITE[14] LOCKS
1794   1800
Chorus

Lassie wi' the lint-white locks,
Bonie lassie, artless lassie,

Wilt thou wi' me tent[1] the flocks?
    Wilt thou be my dearie, O?

5 Now Nature cleeds[2] the flowery lea,
And a' is young and sweet like thee;
O wilt thou share its joy wi' me,
    And say thou'lt be my dearie, O?

The primrose bank, the wimpling burn,[3]
10 The cuckoo on the milk-white thorn,
The wanton lambs at early morn,
    Shall welcome thee, my dearie, O.

And when the welcome simmer shower
Has cheer'd ilk drooping little flower,
15 We'll to the breathing woodbine bower
    At sultry noon, my dearie, O.

When Cynthia lights, wi' silver ray,
The weary shearer's hameward way,
Thro' yellow waving fields we'll stray,
20   And talk o' love, my dearie, O.

And when the howling wintry blast
Disturbs my lassie's midnight rest,
Enclaspèd to my faithfu' breast,
    I'll comfort thee, my dearie, O.

Chorus

25   Lassie wi' the lint-white locks,
    Bonie lassie, artless lassie,
  Wilt thou wi' me tent the flocks?
    Wilt thou be my dearie, O?

IS THERE FOR HONEST POVERTY
1794   1795

Is there for honest poverty,
    That hings his head, an' a' that?
The coward slave, we pass him by—
    We dare be poor for a' that!
5 For a' that, an' a' that,
    Our toils obscure, an' a' that,
The rank is but the guinea's stamp;
    The man's the gowd[4] for a' that.

What though on hamely fare we dine,
10   Wear hoddin gray[5] an' a' that?
Gie fools their silks, and knaves their
    wine—
    A man's a man for a' that!
For a' that, an' a' that,
    Their tinsel show, an' a' that,
15 The honest man, tho' e'er sae poor,
    Is king o' men for a' that.

Ye see yon birkie,[6] ca'd "a lord,"
    Wha struts, an' stares, an' a' that?

---

1 thrush   9 fight
2 merry   10 twelve-month
3 slap   11 lot
4 cup   12 solders ; mends
5 ale   13 stumble and stagger
6 sometimes   14 flax-colored (a pale
7 scratch   yellow)
8 soldier

1 care for   4 gold
2 clothes   5 coarse gray cloth
3 meandering brook 6 young fellow

Tho' hundreds worship at his word,
20 He's but a cuif[1] for a' that:
For a' that, an' a' that,
His ribband, star, an' a' that,
The man o' independent mind,
He looks an' laughs at a' that.

25 A prince can mak a belted knight,
A marquis, duke, an' a' that;
But an honest man's aboon[2] his might—
Guid faith, he mauna fa'[3] that!
For a' that, an' a' that,
30 Their dignities, an' a' that,
The pith o' sense, and pride o' worth,
Are higher rank than a' that.

Then let us pray that come it may,
As come it will for a' that,
35 That sense and worth, o'er a' the earth,
Shall bear the gree[4] an' a' that;
For a' that, an' a' that,
It's comin yet for a' that,
That man to man, the world o'er,
40 Shall brithers be for a' that!

O, WERT THOU IN THE CAULD BLAST
1796   1800

O, wert thou in the cauld blast
On yonder lea, on yonder lea,
My plaidie to the angry airt,[5]
I'd shelter thee, I'd shelter thee.
5 Or did misfortune's bitter storms
Around thee blaw, around thee blaw,
Thy bield[6] should be my bosom,
To share it a', to share it a'.

Or were I in the wildest waste,
10 Sae black and bare, sae black and bare,
The desert were a paradise,
If thou wert there, if thou wert there.
Or were I monarch of the globe,
Wi' thee to reign, wi' thee to reign,
15 The brightest jewel in my crown
Wad be my queen, wad be my queen.

O, LAY THY LOOF[7] IN MINE, LASS
1796   1803
Chorus

O, lay thy loof in mine, lass,
In mine, lass, in mine, lass,
And swear on thy white hand, lass,
That thou wilt be my ain.

5 A slave to Love's unbounded sway,
He aft has wrought me meikle wae;[8]

But now he is my deadly fae,[1]
Unless thou be my ain.

There's monie a lass has broke my rest,
10 That for a blink I hae lo'ed best;
But thou art queen within my breast,
Forever to remain.

Chorus

O, lay thy loof in mine, lass,
In mine, lass, in mine, lass,
15 And swear on thy white hand, lass,
That thou wilt be my ain.

PREFACE TO THE FIRST, OR KILMAR-
NOCK EDITION OF BURNS'S POEMS
1786   1786

The following trifles are not the production of the poet, who, with all the advantages of learned art, and, perhaps,
amid the elegancies and idlenesses of
5 upper life, looks down for a rural theme,
with an eye to Theocritus or Virgil. To
the author of this, these and other celebrated names (their countrymen) are, at
least in their original language, "a foun-
10 tain shut up, and a book sealed." Unacquainted with the necessary requisites
for commencing poet[2] by rule, he sings the
sentiments and manners he felt and saw
in himself and his rustic compeers around
15 him, in his and their native language.
Though a rhymer from his earliest years,
at least from the earliest impulses of the
softer passions, it was not till very lately
that the applause, perhaps the partiality,
20 of friendship, wakened his vanity so far
as to make him think any thing of his was
worth showing; and none of the following
works were composed with a view to the
press. To amuse himself with the little
25 creations of his own fancy, amid the toil
and fatigues of a laborious life; to transcribe the various feelings, the loves, the
griefs, the hopes, the fears, in his own
breast; to find some kind of counterpoise
30 to the struggles of a world, always an
alien scene, a task uncouth to the poetical
mind; these were his motives for courting
the Muses, and in these he found poetry
to be its own reward.
35 Now that he appears in the public character of an author, he does it with fear
and trembling. So dear is fame to the
rhyming tribe, that even he, an obscure,
nameless bard, shrinks aghast at the
40 thought of being branded as "An imper-

---

[1] fool
[2] above
[3] may not claim
[4] prize
[5] windy quarter
[6] shelter
[7] palm of the hand
[8] much woe

[1] foe
[2] for beginning the vocation of a poet

tinent blockhead, obtruding his nonsense on the world; and, because he can make shift to jingle a few doggerel Scotch rhymes together, looks upon himself as a poet of no small consequence forsooth.''

It is an observation of that celebrated poet,[1] whose divine Elegies do honor to our language, our nation, and our species— that "Humility has depressed many a genius to a hermit, but never raised one to fame." If any critic catches at the word *genius*, the author tells him, once for all, that he certainly looks upon himself as possessed of some poetic abilities, otherwise his publishing in the manner he has done would be a maneuver below the worst character which, he hopes, his worst enemy will ever give him. But to the genius of a Ramsay, or the glorious dawnings of the poor, unfortunate Fergusson, he, with equal unaffected sincerity, declares that, even in his highest pulse of vanity, he has not the most distant pretensions. These two justly admired Scotch poets he has often had in his eye in the following pieces; but rather with a view to kindle at their flame, than for servile imitation.

To his subscribers the author returns his most sincere thanks. Not the mercenary bow over a counter, but the heart-throbbing gratitude of the bard, conscious how much he is indebted to benevolence and friendship for gratifying him, if he deserves it, in that dearest wish of every poetic bosom—to be distinguished. He begs his readers, particularly the learned and the polite, who may honor him with a perusal, that they will make every allowance for education and circumstances of life; but if, after a fair, candid, and impartial criticism, he shall stand convicted of dulness and nonsense, let him be done by as he would in that case do by others —let him be condemned without mercy, to contempt and oblivion.

DEDICATION TO THE SECOND, OR EDINBURGH EDITION OF BURNS'S POEMS
1787   1787

TO THE NOBLEMEN AND GENTLEMEN OF THE CALEDONIAN HUNT[2]

My Lords and Gentlemen:

A Scottish bard, proud of the name, and whose highest ambition is to sing in his country's service—where shall he so

[1] Shenstone
[2] An association of Scottish huntsmen.

properly look for patronage as to the illustrious names of his native land; those who bear the honors and inherit the virtues of their ancestors? The poetic genius of my country found me, as the prophetic bard Elijah did Elisha—at the plough;[1] and threw her inspiring mantle over me. She bade me sing the loves, the joys, the rural scenes and rural pleasures of my native soil, in my native tongue: I tuned my wild, artless notes, as she inspired. She whispered me to come to this ancient metropolis of Caledonia and lay my songs under your honored protection: I now obey her dictates.

Though much indebted to your goodness, I do not approach you, my Lords and Gentlemen, in the usual style of dedication, to thank you for past favors: that path is so hackneyed by prostituted learning that honest rusticity is ashamed of it. Nor do I present this address with the venal soul of a servile author, looking for a continuation of those favors: I was bred to the plough, and am independent. I come to claim the common Scottish name with you, my illustrious countrymen; and to tell the world that I glory in the title. I come to congratulate my country, that the blood of her ancient heroes still runs uncontaminated; and that from your courage, knowledge, and public spirit, she may expect protection, wealth, and liberty. In the last place, I come to proffer my warmest wishes to the great fountain of honor, the monarch of the universe, for your welfare and happiness.

When you go forth to waken the echoes, in the ancient and favorite amusement of your forefathers, may pleasure ever be of your party: and may social joy await your return! When harassed in courts or camps with the jostlings of bad men and bad measures, may the honest consciousness of injured worth attend your return to your native seats; and may domestic happiness, with a smiling welcome, meet you at your gates! May corruption shrink at your kindling, indignant glance; and may tyranny in the ruler, and licentiousness in the people, equally find you an inexorable foe!

I have the honor to be, with the sincerest gratitude and highest respect,
My Lords and Gentlemen,
Your most devoted humble Servant,
Robert Burns.
Edinburgh, *April* 4, 1787.

[1] See *1 Kings*, 19:19.

Mirth and Her Companions.   An illustration to Milton's "L'Allegro," by William Blake

Nineteenth Century Romanticists

Samuel Rogers 1763-1855

THE PLEASURES OF MEMORY
1792   1792

From Part I

Twilight's soft dews steal o'er the village
    green,
With magic tints to harmonize the scene.
Stilled is the hum that thro' the hamlet
    broke,
When round the ruins of their ancient oak
5 The peasants flocked to hear the minstrel
    play,
And games and carols closed the busy day.
Her wheel at rest, the matron thrills no
    more
With treasured tales, and legendary lore.
All, all are fled; nor mirth nor music flows
10 To chase the dreams of innocent repose.
All, all are fled; yet still I linger here!
What secret charms this silent spot en-
    dear!
    Mark yon old mansion frowning thro'
    the trees,
Whose hollow turret woos the whistling
    breeze.
15 That casement, arched with ivy's brownest
    shade,
First to these eyes the light of heaven con-
    veyed.
The mouldering gateway strews the grass-
    grown court,
Once the calm scene of many a simple
    sport;
When all things pleased, for life itself was
    new,
20 And the heart promised what the fancy
    drew.

    .   .   .   .   .   .

As thro' the garden's desert paths I
    rove,
70 What fond illusions swarm in every
    grove!
How oft, when purple evening tinged
    the west,

We watched the emmet[1] to her grainy
    nest;
Welcomed the wild bee home on weary
    wing,
Laden with sweets, the choicest of the
    spring!
75 How oft inscribed, with Friendship's
    votive rhyme,
The bark now silvered by the touch of
    Time;
Soared in the swing, half pleased and
    half afraid,
Thro' sister elms that waved their sum-
    mer shade;
Or strewed with crumbs yon root-inwoven
    seat,
80 To lure the redbreast from his lone
    retreat!
    Childhood's loved group revisits every
    scene;
The tangled wood-walk and the tufted
    green!
Indulgent Memory wakes, and lo, they live !
Clothed with far softer hues than Light
    can give.
85 Thou first, best friend that Heaven
    assigns below
To sooth and sweeten all the cares we
    know;
Whose glad suggestions still each vain
    alarm,
When nature fades and life forgets to
    charm;
Thee would the Muse invoke!—to thee
    belong
90 The sage's precept and the poet's song.
What softened views thy magic glass
    reveals,
When o'er the landscape Time's meek
    twilight steals!
As when in ocean sinks the orb of day,
Long on the wave reflected lustres play;
95 Thy tempered gleams of happiness re-
    signed
Glance on the darkened mirror of the
    mind.

[1] ant

The school's lone porch, with reverend
    mosses gray,
Just tells the pensive pilgrim where it lay.
Mute is the bell that rung at peep of dawn,
100 Quickening my truant feet across the
    lawn;
Unheard the shout that rent the noon-
    tide air,
When the slow dial gave a pause to care.
Up springs, at every step, to claim a
    tear,
Some little friendship formed and cher-
    ished here,
105 And not the lightest leaf, but trembling
    teems
With golden visions and romantic
    dreams!
    Down by yon hazel copse, at evening,
    blazed
The Gipsy's fagot—there we stood and
    gazed;
Gazed on her sun-burnt face with silent
    awe,
110 Her tattered mantle, and her hood of
    straw;
Her moving lips, her caldron brimming
    o'er;
The drowsy brood that on her back she
    bore,
Imps, in the barn with mousing owlet
    bred,
From rifled roost at nightly revel fed;
115 Whose dark eyes flashed thro' locks of
    blackest shade,
When in the breeze the distant watch-
    dog bayed:—
And heroes fled the Sibyl's muttered call,
Whose elfin prowess scaled the orchard-
    wall.
As o'er my palm the silver piece she
    drew,
120 And traced the line of life with search-
    ing view,
How throbbed my fluttering pulse with
    hopes and fears,
To learn the color of my future years!
    Ah, then, what honest triumph flushed
    my breast;
This truth once known—To bless is to
    be blest!
125 We led the bending beggar on his way,
(Bare were his feet, his tresses silver-
    gray)
Soothed the keen pangs his aged spirit
    felt,
And on his tale with mute attention dwelt.
As in his scrip we dropt our little store,
130 And sighed to think that little was no
    more,

He breathed his prayer, "Long may such
    goodness live!"
'Twas all he gave, 'twas all he had to
    give.
Angels, when Mercy's mandate winged
    their flight,
Had stopt to dwell with pleasure on the
    sight.
135   But hark! thro' those old firs, with
    sullen swell,
The church-clock strikes! ye tender
    scenes, farewell!
It calls me hence, beneath their shade,
    to trace
The few fond lines that Time may soon
    efface.
    On yon gray stone, that fronts the
    chancel door,
140 Worn smooth by busy feet now seen no
    more,
Each eve we shot the marble thro' the ring,
When the heart danced, and life was in
    its spring,
Alas! unconscious of the kindred earth,
That faintly echoed to the voice of mirth.
145   The glow-worm loves her emerald-light
    to shed
Where now the sexton rests his hoary
    head.
Oft, as he turned the greensward with
    his spade,
He lectured every youth that round him
    played;
And, calmly pointing where our fathers
    lay,
150 Roused us to rival each, the hero of his
    day.
    Hush, ye fond flutterings, hush! while
    here alone
I search the records of each mouldering
    stone.
Guides of my life! Instructors of my
    youth!
Who first unveiled the hallowed form of
    Truth!
155 Whose every word enlightened and
    endeared;
In age beloved, in poverty revered;
In Friendship's silent register ye live,
Nor ask the vain memorial Art can give.
    But when the sons of peace, of pleas-
    ure sleep,
160 When only Sorrow wakes, and wakes
    to weep,
What spells entrance my visionary mind
With sighs so sweet, with transports so
    refined?

.   .   .   .   .

AN ITALIAN SONG
1793

Dear is my little native vale,
The ring-dove builds and murmurs there;
Close by my cot she tells her tale
To every passing villager.
5 The squirrel leaps from tree to tree
And shells his nuts at liberty.

In orange groves and myrtle bowers,
That breathe a gale of fragrance round,
I charm the fairy-footed hours
10 With my loved lute's romantic sound;
Or crowns of living laurel weave,
For those that win the race at eve.

The shepherd's horn at break of day,
The ballet danced in twilight glade,
15 The canzonet[1] and roundelay[2]
Sung in the silent green-wood shade:
These simple joys, that never fail,
Shall bind me to my native vale.

WRITTEN AT MIDNIGHT
1806

While thro' the broken pane the tempest sighs.
And my step falters on the faithless floor,
Shades of departed joys around me rise,
With many a face that smiles on me no more,
5 With many a voice that thrills of transport gave,
Now silent as the grass that tufts their grave!

WRITTEN IN THE HIGHLANDS OF SCOTLAND
1812

Blue was the loch,[3] the clouds were gone,
Ben-Lomond in his glory shone,
When, Luss, I left thee; when the breeze
Bore me from thy silver sands,
5 Thy kirk-yard wall among the trees,
Where gray with age, the dial stands;
That dial so well known to me!
—Tho' many a shadow it had shed,
Beloved sister,[4] since with thee
10 The legend on the stone was read.
The fairy isles fled far away;
That with its woods and uplands green,
Where shepherd huts are dimly seen,
And songs are heard at close of day;
15 That too, the deer's wild covert, fled,
And that, the asylum of the dead:

[1] A short song, light and graceful.
[2] A song with a recurring word, phrase, or line.
[3] lake
[4] His sister Sarah.

While, as the boat went merrily,
Much of Rob Roy the boat-man told;
His arm that fell below his knee,
20 His cattle-ford and mountain-hold.
Tarbat, thy shore I climbed at last;
And, thy shady region passed,
Upon another shore I stood,
And looked upon another flood;
25 Great Ocean's self! ('Tis He who fills
That vast and awful depth of hills;)
Where many an elf was playing round,
Who treads unshod his classic ground;
And speaks, his native rocks among,
30 As Fingal spoke, and Ossian sung.
Night fell; and dark and darker grew
That narrow sea, that narrow sky,
As o'er the glimmering waves we flew;
The sea-bird rustling, wailing by.
35 And now the grampus, half-descried,
Black and huge above the tide;
The cliffs and promontories there,
Front to front, and broad and bare;
Each beyond each, with giant feet
40 Advancing as in haste to meet;
The shattered fortress, whence the Dane
Blew his shrill blast, nor rushed in vain,
Tyrant of the drear domain;
All into midnight shadow sweep—
45 When day springs upward from the deep
Kindling the waters in its flight,
The prow wakes splendor; and the oar,
That rose and fell unseen before,
Flashes in a sea of light!
50 Glad sign, and sure! for now we hail
Thy flowers, Glenfinnart, in the gale;
And bright indeed the path should be,
That leads to friendship and to thee!
Oh blest retreat, and sacred too!
55 Sacred as when the bell of prayer
Tolled duly on the desert air,
And crosses decked thy summits blue.
Oft, like some loved romantic tale,
Oft shall my weary mind recall,
60 Amid the hum and stir of men,
Thy beechen grove and waterfall,
Thy ferry with its gliding sail,
And her—the Lady of the Glen!

AN INSCRIPTION IN THE CRIMEA
1812

Shepherd, or huntsman, or worn mariner,
Whate'er thou art, who wouldst allay thy thirst,
Drink and be glad. This cistern of white stone,
Arched, and o'erwrought with many a sacred verse,
5 This iron cup chained for the general use,

And these rude seats of earth within the
  grove,
Were given by Fatima. Borne hence a
  bride,
'Twas here she turned from her beloved
  sire,
To see his face no more. Oh, if thou
  canst,
10 ('Tis not far off) visit his tomb with
  flowers;
And with a drop of this sweet water
  fill
The two small cells scooped in the
  marble there,
That birds may come and drink upon
  his grave,
Making it holy[1] *   *   *   *

THE BOY OF EGREMOND
1819   1819

"Say, what remains when Hope is fled?"
She answered, "Endless weeping!"
For in the herdsman's eye she read,
Who in his shroud lay sleeping.
5   At Embsay rung the matin bell,
The stag was roused on Barden fell;
The mingled sounds were swelling, dying,
And down the Wharfe a hern[2] was flying;
When near the cabin in the wood,
10 In tartan clad and forest-green,
With hound in leash and hawk in hood,
The Boy of Egremond was seen.
Blithe was his song, a song of yore;
But where the rock is rent in two,
15 And the river rushes through,
His voice was heard no more!
'Twas but a step! the gulf he passed;
But that step—it was his last!
As through the mist he winged his way,
20 (A cloud that hovers night and day,)
The hound hung back, and back he drew
The master and his merlin[3] too.
That narrow place of noise and strife
Received their little all of life!
25   There now the matin bell is rung;
The "Miserere" duly sung;
And holy men in cowl and hood
Are wandering up and down the wood.
But what avail they? Ruthless Lord,
30 Thou didst not shudder when the sword
Here on the young its fury spent,
The helpless and the innocent.
Sit now and answer, groan for groan.
The child before thee is thy own.
35 And she who wildly wanders there,
The mother in her long despair,

---

[1] A Turkish superstition.
[2] heron
[3] small European falcon

Shall oft remind thee, waking, sleeping,
Of those who by the Wharfe were
  weeping;
Of those who would not be consoled
40 When red with blood the river rolled.

From ITALY
1819-1834   1822-34
THE LAKE OF GENEVA

Day glimmered in the east, and the white
  moon
Hung like a vapor in the cloudless sky,
Yet visible, when on my way I went,
Glad to be gone, a pilgrim from the North,
5 Now more and more attracted as I drew
Nearer and nearer. Ere the artisan
Had from his window leant, drowsy,
  half-clad,
To snuff the morn, or the caged lark
  poured forth,
From his green sod upspringing as to
  heaven,
10 (His tuneful bill o'erflowing with a song
Old in the days of Homer, and his wings
With transport quivering) on my way I
  went,
Thy gates, Geneva, swinging heavily,
Thy gates so slow to open, swift to shut;
15 As on that Sabbath eve when he arrived,[1]
Whose name is now thy glory, now by thee,
Such virtue dwells in those small syllables,
Inscribed to consecrate the narrow street,
His birth-place,—when, but one short
  step too late,
20 In his despair, as though the die were cast,
He flung him down to weep, and wept till
  dawn;
Then rose to go, a wanderer through the
  world.

  'Tis not a tale that every hour brings
    with it.
Yet at a city gate, from time to time,
25 Much may be learnt; nor, London, least
    at thine,
Thy hive the busiest, greatest of them all,
Gathering, enlarging still. Let us stand by,
And note who passes. Here comes one,
    a youth,
Glowing with pride, the pride of con-
    scious power,
30 A Chatterton—in thought admired, ca-
    ressed,
And crowned like Petrarch in the Capitol;
Ere long to die, to fall by his own hand,
And fester with the vilest. Here come two,

---

[1] Jean Jacques Rousseau, who visited Geneva,
his birthplace, in 1754. He had left there in
1728, when sixteen years of age.

Less feverish, less exalted—soon to part,
35 A Garrick and a Johnson; Wealth and
      Fame
Awaiting one, even at the gate; Neglect
And Want the other. But what multi-
      tudes,
Urged by the love of change, and, like
      myself,
Adventurous, careless of tomorrow's fare,
40 Press on—though but a rill entering the sea,
Entering and lost! Our task would never
      end.

Day glimmered and I went, a gentle
      breeze
Ruffling the Leman Lake. Wave after
      wave,
If such they might be called, dashed as
      in sport,
45 Not anger, with the pebbles on the beach
Making wild music, and far westward
      caught
The sunbeam—where, alone and as en-
      tranced,
Counting the hours, the fisher in his skiff
Lay with his circular and dotted line
50 On the bright waters. When the heart
      of man
Is light with hope, all things are sure to
      please;
And soon a passage-boat swept gaily by,
Laden with peasant girls and fruits and
      flowers
And many a chanticleer and partlet[1] caged
55 For Vevey's market place—a motley group
Seen through the silvery haze. But soon
      'twas gone.
The shifting sail flapped idly to and fro,
Then bore them off. I am not one of
      those
So dead to all things in this visible world,
60 So wondrously profound, as to move on
In the sweet light of heaven, like him of
      old[2]
(His name is justly in the Calendar[3]),
Who through the day pursued this pleas-
      ant path
That winds beside the mirror of all
      beauty,
65 And, when at eve his fellow pilgrims sate,
Discoursing of the lake, asked where it was.
They marvelled as they might; and so
      must all,
Seeing what now I saw: for now 'twas day,
And the bright sun was in the firmament,
70 A thousand shadows of a thousand hues

Chequering the clear expanse. Awhile
      his orb
Hung o'er thy trackless fields of snow,
      Mont Blanc,
Thy seas of ice and ice-built promon-
      tories,
That change their shapes forever as in
      sport;
75 Then travelled onward and went down
      behind
The pine-clad heights of Jura, lighting up
The woodman's casement, and perchance
      his axe
Borne homeward through the forest in
      his hand;
And, on the edge of some o'erhanging cliff,
80 That dungeon-fortress[1] never to be named,
Where, like a lion taken in the toils,
Toussaint breathed out his brave and
      generous spirit.
Little did he,[2] who sent him there to die,
Think, when he gave the word, that he
      himself,
85 Great as he was, the greatest among men,
Should in like manner be so soon conveyed
Athwart the deep,—and to a rock so small
Amid the countless multitude of waves,
That ships have gone and sought it, and
      returned,
90 Saying it was not!

THE GONDOLA

Boy, call the Gondola; the sun is set.
It came, and we embarked; but instantly,
As at the waving of a magic wand,
Though she had stept on board so light
      of foot,
5 So light of heart, laughing she knew not
      why,
Sleep overcame her; on my arm she slept.
From time to time I waked her; but the
      boat
Rocked her to sleep again. The moon
      was now
Rising full-orbed, but broken by a cloud.
10 The wind was hushed, and the sea
      mirror-like.
A single zephyr, as enamored, played
With her loose tresses, and drew more
      and more
Her veil across her bosom. Long I lay
Contemplating that face so beautiful,
15 That rosy mouth, that cheek dimpled
      with smiles,
That neck but half-concealed, whiter
      than snow.

[1] cock and hen
[2] Bernard, Abbot of Clairvaux (1091-1153).
[3] list of saints

[1] The Castle of Joux in Franche-Comté.
[2] Napoleon, who sent Toussaint L'Ouverture to
    prison, and who was later banished to St.
    Helena.

'Twas the sweet slumber of her early age.
I looked and looked, and felt a flush of joy
I would express but cannot. Oft I wished
20 Gently—by stealth—to drop asleep myself,
And to incline yet lower that sleep might
come;
Oft closed my eyes as in forgetfulness.
'Twas all in vain. Love would not let
me rest.
But how delightful when at length she
waked!
25 When, her light hair adjusting, and her veil
So rudely scattered, she resumed her place
Beside me; and, as gaily as before,
Sitting unconsciously nearer and nearer,
Poured out her innocent mind!
So, nor long since,
30 Sung a Venetian; and his lay of love,
Dangerous and sweet, charmed Venice.
For myself,
(Less fortunate, if love be happiness)
No curtain drawn, no pulse beating alarm,
I went alone beneath the silent moon;
35 Thy square, St. Mark, thy churches,
palaces,
Glittering and frost-like, and, as day
drew on,
Melting away, an emblem of themselves.
Those porches passed, thro' which the
water-breeze
Plays, though no longer on the noble forms
40 That moved there, sable-vested—and the
quay,
Silent, grass-grown—adventurer-like I
launched
Into the deep, ere long discovering
Isles such as cluster in the southern seas,
All verdure. Everywhere, from bush and
brake,
45 The musky odor of the serpents came;
Their slimy tract across the woodman's
path
Bright in the moonshine; and, as round
I went,
Dreaming of Greece, whither the waves
were gliding,
I listened to the venerable pines
50 Then in close converse, and, if right I
guessed,
Delivering many a message to the winds,
In secret, for their kindred on Mount Ida.
Nor when again in Venice, when again
In that strange place, so stirring and so
still,
55 Where nothing comes to drown the
human voice
But music, or the dashing of the tide,
Ceased I to wander. Now a Jessica
Sung to her lute, her signal as she sate

At her half-open window. Then, me-
thought,
60 A serenade broke silence, breathing hope
Thro' walls of stone, and torturing the
proud heart
Of some Priuli. Once, we could not err,
(It was before an old Palladian house,
As between night and day we floated by)
65 A gondolier lay singing; and he sung,
As in the time when Venice was herself,
Of Tancred and Erminia. On our oars
We rested; and the verse was verse divine!
We could not err—perhaps he was the
last—
70 For none took up the strain, none an-
swered him;
And, when he ceased, he left upon my ear
A something like the dying voice of
Venice!
The moon went down; and nothing
now was seen
Save where the lamp of a Madonna shone
75 Faintly—or heard, but when he spoke,
who stood
Over the lantern at the prow and cried,
Turning the corner of some reverend pile,
Some school or hospital of old renown,
Tho' haply none were coming, none were
near,
80 "Hasten or slacken." But at length
Night fled;
And with her fled, scattering, the sons of
Pleasure.
Star after star shot by, or, meteor-like,
Crossed me and vanished—lost at once
among
Those hundred isles that tower majes-
tically,
85 That rise abruptly from the water-mark,
Not with rough crag, but marble, and the
work
Of noblest architects. I lingered still;
Nor sought my threshold, till the hour
was come
And past, when, flitting home in the gray
light,
90 The young Bianca found her father's door,
That door so often with a trembling hand,
So often—then so lately left ajar,
Shut; and, all terror, all perplexity,
Now by her lover urged, now by her love,
95 Fled o'er the waters to return no more.

THE FOUNTAIN[1]

It was a well
Of whitest marble, white as from the
quarry;

[1] "The place here described is near Mola di
Gaëta, in the kingdom of Naples."—Rogers.

And richly wrought with many a high
    relief,
Greek sculpture—in some earlier day
    perhaps
5 A tomb, and honored with a hero's ashes.
The water from the rock filled and o'er-
    flowed;
Then dashed away, playing the prodigal,
And soon was lost—stealing unseen, un-
    heard,
Thro' the long grass, and round the
    twisted roots
10 Of aged trees, discovering[1] where it ran
By the fresh verdure. Overcome with heat,
I threw me down, admiring, as I lay,
That shady nook, a singing-place for birds,
That grove so intricate, so full of flowers,
15 More than enough to please a child
    a-Maying.

    The sun had set, a distant convent-bell
Ringing the *Angelus*;[2] and now ap-
    proached
The hour for stir and village-gossip there,
The hour Rebekah came, when from the
    well
20 She drew with such alacrity to serve
The stranger and his camels.[3] Soon I
    heard
Footsteps; and lo, descending by a path
Trodden for ages, many a nymph ap-
    peared,
Appeared and vanished, bearing on her
    head
25 Her earthen pitcher. It called up the day
Ulysses landed there;[4] and long I gazed,
Like one awaking in a distant time.

    At length there came the loveliest of
    them all,
Her little brother dancing down before her;
30 And ever as he spoke, which he did ever,
Turning and looking up in warmth of
    heart
And brotherly affection. Stopping there,
She joined her rosy hands, and, filling
    them
With the pure element, gave him to drink;
35 And, while he quenched his thirst, stand-
    ing on tip-toe,
Looked down upon him with a sister's
    smile,
Nor stirred till he had done, fixed as a
    statue.

[1] disclosing
[2] That is, the summons to the Angelus, a service
  commemorating the incarnation of Christ.
[3] See *Genesis*, 24 :15-20.
[4] A tradition, recorded in Strabo's *Geographica*,
  V, 4, 5. See the *Odyssey*, 11.

Then hadst thou seen them as they
    stood, Canova,
Thou hadst endowed them with immortal
    youth;
40 And they had evermore lived undivided,
Winning all hearts—of all thy works the
    fairest.

William Godwin 1756-1836

ENQUIRY CONCERNING POLITICAL JUSTICE
1793   1793

From Book I. Of the Powers of Man Considered in His Social Capacity

CHAPTER III. SPIRIT OF POLITICAL INSTITUTIONS

Additional perspicuity will be communicated to our view of the evils of political
society, if we reflect with farther and
closer attention upon what may be called
5 its interior and domestic history.

Two of the greatest abuses relative to
the interior policy of nations, which at this
time prevail in the world, consist in the
irregular transfer of property, either first
10 by violence, or secondly by fraud. If
among the inhabitants of any country,
there existed no desire in one individual
to possess himself of the substance of another, or no desire so vehement and rest-
15 less as to prompt him to acquire it by
means inconsistent with order and justice,
undoubtedly in that country guilt could
scarcely be known but by report. If every
man could with perfect facility obtain the
20 necessaries of life, and, obtaining them,
feel no uneasy craving after its superfluities, temptation would lose its power.
Private interest would visibly accord with
public good; and civil society become what
25 poetry has feigned of the golden age. Let
us enquire into the principles to which
these evils are indebted for their existence.

First, then, it is to be observed that in
the most refined states of Europe, the in-
30 equality of property has arisen to an
alarming height. Vast numbers of their
inhabitants are deprived of almost every
accommodation that can render life tolerable or secure. Their utmost industry
35 scarcely suffices for their support. The
women and children lean with an insupportable weight upon the efforts of the
man, so that a large family has in the
lower orders of life become a proverbial
40 expression for an uncommon degree of
poverty and wretchedness. If sickness or
some of those casualties which are per-

petually incident to an active and laborious life be added to these burdens, the distress is yet greater.

It seems to be agreed that in England there is less wretchedness and distress than in most of the kingdoms of the continent. In England, the poor's rates[1] amount to the sum of two millions sterling *per annum*. It has been calculated that one person in seven of the inhabitants of this country derives at some period of his life assistance from this fund. If to this we add the persons who, from pride, a spirit of independence, or the want of a legal settlement, though in equal distress, receive no such assistance, the proportion will be considerably increased.

I lay no stress upon the accuracy of this calculation; the general fact is sufficient to give us an idea of the greatness of the abuse. The consequences that result are placed beyond the reach of contradiction. A perpetual struggle with the evils of poverty, if frequently ineffectual, must necessarily render many of the sufferers desperate. A painful feeling of their oppressed situation will itself deprive them of the power of surmounting it. The superiority of the rich, being thus unmercifully exercised, must inevitably expose them to reprisals; and the poor man will be induced to regard the state of society as a state of war, an unjust combination, not for protecting every man in his rights and securing to him the means of existence, but for engrossing all its advantages to a few favored individuals, and reserving for the portion of the rest want, dependence, and misery.

A second source of those destructive passions by which the peace of society is interrupted is to be found in the luxury, the pageantry, and magnificence with which enormous wealth is usually accompanied. Human beings are capable of encountering with cheerfulness considerable hardships, when those hardships are impartially shared with the rest of the society, and they are not insulted with the spectacle of indolence and ease in others, no way deserving of greater advantages than themselves. But it is a bitter aggravation of their own calamity to have the privileges of others forced on their observation, and, while they are perpetually and vainly endeavoring to secure for themselves and their families the poorest conveniences, to find others reveling in

[1] Taxes levied for the relief of the poor.

the fruits of their labors. This aggravation is assiduously administered to them under most of the political establishments at present in existence. There is a numerous class of individuals who, though rich, have neither brilliant talents nor sublime virtues; and however highly they may prize their education, their affability, their superior polish, and the elegance of their manners, have a secret consciousness that they possess nothing by which they can so securely assert their preeminence and keep their inferiors at a distance as the splendor of their equipage, the magnificence of their retinue, and the sumptuousness of their entertainments. The poor man is struck with this exhibition; he feels his own miseries; he knows how unwearied are his efforts to obtain a slender pittance of this prodigal waste; and he mistakes opulence for felicity. He cannot persuade himself that an embroidered garment may frequently cover an aching heart.

A third disadvantage that is apt to connect poverty with discontent consists in the insolence and usurpation of the rich. If the poor man would in other respects compose himself in philosophic indifference, and, conscious that he possesses everything that is truly honorable to man as fully as his rich neighbor, would look upon the rest as beneath his envy, his neighbor would not permit him to do so. He seems as if he could never be satisfied with his possessions unless he can make the spectacle of them grating to others; and that honest self-esteem, by which his inferior might otherwise arrive at apathy, is rendered the instrument of galling him with oppression and injustice. In many countries justice is avowedly made a subject of solicitation, and the man of the highest rank and most splendid connections almost infallibly carries his cause against the unprotected and friendless. In countries where this shameless practice is not established, justice is frequently a matter of expensive purchase, and the man with the longest purse is proverbially victorious. A consciousness of these facts must be expected to render the rich little cautious of offence in his dealings with the poor, and to inspire him with a temper, overbearing, dictatorial, and tyrannical. Nor does this indirect oppression satisfy his despotism. The rich are in all such countries, directly or indirectly, the legislators of the state; and of consequence are perpetually reducing oppression into a system, and depriving the poor of that little commonage of nature, as it were, which might otherwise still have remained to them.

The opinions of individuals, and of consequence their desires, for desire is nothing but opinion maturing for action, will always be in a great degree regulated by the opinions of the community. But the manners prevailing in many countries are accurately calculated to impress a conviction that integrity, virtue, understanding, and industry are nothing, and that opulence is everything. Does a man whose exterior denotes indigence expect to be well received in society, and especially by those who would be understood to dictate to the rest? Does he find or imagine himself in want of their assistance and favor? He is presently taught that no merits can atone for a mean appearance. The lesson that is read to him is, "Go home; enrich yourself by whatever means; obtain those superfluities which are alone regarded as estimable; and you may then be secure of an amicable reception." Accordingly, poverty in such countries is viewed as the greatest of demerits. It is escaped from with an eagerness that has no leisure for the scruples of honesty. It is concealed as the most indelible disgrace. While one man chooses the path of undistinguishing accumulation, another plunges into expenses which are to impose him upon the world as more opulent than he is. He hastens to the reality of that penury, the appearance of which he dreads; and, together with his property, sacrifices the integrity, veracity, and character, which might have consoled him in his adversity.

Such are the causes that, in different degrees under the different governments of the world, prompt mankind openly or secretly to encroach upon the property of each other. Let us consider how far they admit either of remedy or aggravation from political institution. Whatever tends to decrease the injuries attendant upon poverty, decreases, at the same time, the inordinate desire and the enormous accumulation of wealth. Wealth is not pursued for its own sake, and seldom for the sensual gratification it can purchase, but for the same reasons that ordinarily prompt men to the acquisition of learning, eloquence, and skill, for the love of distinction and fear of contempt. How few would prize the possession of riches if they were condemned to enjoy their equi-

page, their palaces, and their entertainments in solitude, with no eye to wonder at their magnificence, and no sordid observer ready to convert that wonder into an adulation of the owner! If admiration were not generally deemed the exclusive property of the rich, and contempt the constant lackey of poverty, the love of gain would cease to be an universal passion. Let us consider in what respects political institution is rendered subservient to this passion.

First, then, legislation is in almost every country grossly the favorer of the rich against the poor. Such is the character of the game laws, by which the industrious rustic is forbidden to destroy the animal that preys upon the hopes of his future subsistence, or to supply himself with the food that unsought thrusts itself in his path. Such was the spirit of the late revenue laws of France, which in several of their provisions fell exclusively upon the humble and industrious, and exempted from their operation those who are best able to support it. Thus, in England, the land tax at this moment produces half a million less than it did a century ago, while the taxes on consumption have experienced an addition of thirteen millions *per annum* during the same period. This is an attempt, whether effectual or no, to throw the burden from the rich upon the poor, and as such is an exhibition of the spirit of legislation. Upon the same principle, robbery and other offences, which the wealthier part of the community have no temptation to commit, are treated as capital crimes, and attended with the most rigorous, often the most inhuman punishments. The rich are encouraged to associate for the execution of the most partial and oppressive positive laws; monopolies and patents are lavishly dispensed to such as are able to purchase them; while the most vigilant policy is employed to prevent combinations of the poor to fix the price of labor, and they are deprived of the benefit of that prudence and judgment which would select the scene of their industry.

Secondly, the administration of law is not less iniquitous than the spirit in which it is framed. Under the late government of France,[1] the office of judge was a matter of purchase, partly by an open price advanced to the crown, and partly by a secret *douceur*[2] paid to the minister. He

[1] Before the Revolution.   [2] gift; bribe

who knew best how to manage this market in the retail trade of justice, could afford to purchase the good will of its functions at the highest price. To the client, justice was avowedly made an object of personal solicitation, and a powerful friend, a handsome woman, or a proper present, were articles of a much greater value than a good cause. In England, the criminal law is administered with greater impartiality so far as regards the trial itself; but the number of capital offences, and of consequence the frequency of pardons, open a wide door to favor and abuse. In causes relating to property, the practice of law is arrived at such a pitch as to render all justice ineffectual. The length of our chancery suits, the multiplied appeals from court to court, the enormous fees of counsel, attorneys, secretaries, clerks, the drawing of briefs, bills, replications, and rejoinders, and what has sometimes been called the glorious uncertainty of the law, render it frequently more advisable to resign a property than to contest it, and particularly exclude the impoverished claimant from the faintest hope of redress.

Thirdly, the inequality of conditions usually maintained by political institution is calculated greatly to enhance the imagined excellence of wealth. In the ancient monarchies of the East, and in Turkey at the present day, an eminent station could scarcely fail to excite implicit deference. The timid inhabitant trembled before his superior; and would have thought it little less than blasphemy to touch the veil drawn by the proud satrap over his inglorious origin. The same principles were extensively prevalent under the feudal system. The vassal, who was regarded as a sort of live stock upon the estate, and knew of no appeal from the arbitrary fiat of his lord, would scarcely venture to suspect that he was of the same species. This, however, constituted an unnatural and violent situation. There is a propensity in man to look farther than the outside; and to come with a writ of enquiry into the title of the upstart and the successful. By the operation of these causes, the insolence of wealth has been in some degree moderated. Meantime, it cannot be pretended that even among ourselves the inequality is not strained, so as to give birth to very unfortunate consequences. If, in the enormous degree in which it prevails in some parts of the world, it wholly debilitate and emasculate the human race, we shall see

some reason to believe that, even in the milder state in which we are accustomed to behold it, it is still pregnant with the most mischievous effects.

From CHAPTER V. THE VOLUNTARY ACTIONS OF MEN ORIGINATE IN THEIR OPINIONS

．　．　．　．　．　．

The corollaries respecting political truth, deducible from the simple proposition, which seems clearly established by the reasonings of the present chapter, that the voluntary actions of men are in all instances conformable to the deductions of their understanding, are of the highest importance. Hence, we may infer what are the hopes and prospects of human improvement. The doctrine which may be founded upon these principles may, perhaps, best be expressed in the five following propositions: sound reasoning and truth, when adequately communicated, must always be victorious over error; sound reasoning and truth are capable of being so communicated; truth is omnipotent; the vices and moral weakness of man are not invincible; man is perfectible, or, in other words, susceptible of perpetual improvement.

These propositions will be found in part synonymous with each other. But the time of the enquirer will not be unprofitably spent in copiously clearing up the foundations of moral and political system. It is extremely beneficial that truth should be viewed on all sides, and examined under different aspects. The propositions are even little more than so many different modes of stating the principal topic of this chapter. But if they will not admit each of a distinct train of arguments in its support, it may not, however, be useless to bestow upon each a short illustration.

The first of these propositions is so evident that it needs only be stated in order to the being universally admitted. Is there any one who can imagine that when sound argument and sophistry are fairly brought into comparison, the victory can be doubtful? Sophistry may assume a plausible appearance, and contrive to a certain extent to bewilder the understanding. But it is one of the prerogatives of truth to follow it in its mazes and strip it of disguise. Nor does any difficulty from this consideration interfere with the establishment of the present proposition. We suppose truth not merely to be exhibited, but adequately communicated; that is, in other words, distinctly apprehended by the person to whom it is addressed. In this case the victory is too sure to admit of being controverted by the most inveterate skepticism.

The second proposition is that sound reasoning and truth are capable of being adequately communicated by one man to another. This proposition may be understood of such communication, either as it affects the individual or the species. First of the individual.

In order to its due application in this point of view, opportunity for the communication must necessarily be supposed. The incapacity of human intellect at present requires that this opportunity should be of long duration or repeated recurrence. We do not always know how to communicate all the evidence we are capable of communicating, in a single conversation, and much less in a single instant. But if the communicator be sufficiently master of his subject, and if the truth be altogether on his side, he must ultimately succeed in his undertaking. We suppose him to have sufficient urbanity to conciliate the good will, and sufficient energy to engage the attention of the party concerned. In that case there is no prejudice, no blind reverence for established systems, no false fear of the inferences to be drawn, that can resist him. He will encounter these one after the other, and he will encounter them with success. Our prejudices, our undue reverence and imaginary fears flow out of some views the mind has been induced to entertain; they are founded in the belief of some propositions. But every one of these propositions is capable of being refuted. The champion we describe proceeds from point to point; if in any his success have been doubtful, that he will retrace and put out of the reach of mistake; and it is evidently impossible that with such qualifications and such perseverance he should not ultimately accomplish his purpose.

Such is the appearance which this proposition assumes when examined in a loose and practical view. In strict consideration, it will not admit of debate. Man is a rational being. If there be any man who is incapable of making inferences for himself, or understanding, when stated in the most explicit terms, the inferences of another, him we consider as an abortive production, and not in strictness belonging to the human species. It is absurd, therefore, to say that sound reasoning and truth cannot be communicated by one man to another. Whenever in any case he fails, it is that he is not sufficiently laborious, patient, and clear. We suppose, of course, the person who undertakes to communicate the truth really to possess it, and be master of his subject; for it is scarcely worth an observation to say that that which he has not himself he cannot communicate to another.

If truth, therefore, can be brought home to the conviction of the individual, let us see how it stands with the public or the world. Now in the first place, it is extremely clear that if no individual can resist the force of truth, it can only be necessary to apply this proposition from individual to individual and we shall at length comprehend the whole. Thus the affirmation in its literal sense is completely established.

With respect to the chance of success, this will depend, first, upon the precluding all extraordinary convulsions of nature, and after this upon the activity and energy of those to whose hands the sacred cause of truth may be intrusted. It is apparent that if justice be done to its merits, it includes in it the indestructible germ of ultimate victory. Every new convert that is made to its cause, if he be taught its excellence as well as its reality, is a fresh apostle to extend its illuminations through a wider sphere. In this respect it resembles the motion of a falling body, which increases its rapidity in proportion to the squares of the distances. Add to which, that when a convert to truth has been adequately informed, it is barely possible that he should ever fail in his adherence; whereas error contains in it the principle of its own mortality. Thus the advocates of falsehood and mistake must continually diminish, and the well-informed adherents of truth incessantly multiply.

It has sometimes been affirmed that whenever a question is ably brought forward for examination, the decision of the human species must ultimately be on the right side. But this proposition is to be understood with allowances. Civil policy, magnificent emoluments, and sinister motives may upon many occasions, by distracting the attention, cause the worse reason to pass as if it were the better. It is not absolutely certain that in the controversy brought forward by Clarke and Wilson against the doctrine of the Trinity, or by Collins and Woolston against the Christian revelation, the innovators had altogether the worst of the argument. Yet fifty years after the agitation of these controversies, their effects could scarcely be traced, and things appeared on all sides as if the controversies had never existed. Perhaps it will be said that though the effects of truth may be obscured for a time, they will break out in the sequel with double lustre. But this, at least, depends upon circumstances. No comet must come in the meantime and sweep away the human species; no Attila must have it in his power once again to lead back the flood of barbarism to deluge the civilized world; and the disciples, or at least the books, of the original champions must remain, or their discoveries and demonstrations must be nearly lost upon the world.

The third of the propositions enumerated is that truth is omnipotent. This proposition, which is convenient for its brevity, must be understood with limitations. It would be absurd to affirm that truth unaccompanied by the evidence which proves it to be such, or when that evidence is partially and imperfectly stated, has any such property. But it has sufficiently appeared from the arguments already adduced, that truth, when adequately communicated, is, so far as relates to the conviction of the understanding, irresistible. There may, indeed, be propositions which, though true in themselves, may be beyond the sphere of human knowledge, or respecting which human beings have not yet discovered sufficient arguments for their support. In that case, though true in themselves, they are not truths to us. The reasoning by which they are attempted to be established, is not sound reasoning. It may, perhaps, be found that the human mind is not capable of arriving at absolute certainty upon any subject of enquiry; and it must be admitted that human science is attended with all degrees of certainty, from the highest moral evidence to the slightest balance of probability. But human beings are capable of apprehending and weighing all these degrees; and to know the exact quantity of probability which I ought to ascribe to any proposition, may be said to be in one sense the possessing certain knowledge. It would farther be absurd, if we regard truth in relation to its empire over our

conduct, to suppose that it is not limited in its operations by the faculties of our frame. It may be compared to a connoisseur, who, however consummate be his talents, can extract from a given instrument only such tones as that instrument will afford. But within these limits the deduction which forms the principal substance of this chapter, proves to us that whatever is brought home to the conviction of the understanding, so long as it is present to the mind, possesses an undisputed empire over the conduct. Nor will he who is sufficiently conversant with the science of intellect be hasty in assigning the bounds of our capacity. There are some things which the structure of our bodies will render us forever unable to effect; but in many cases the lines which appear to prescribe a term to our efforts will, like the mists that arise from a lake, retire farther and farther, the more closely we endeavor to approach them.

Fourthly, the vices and moral weakness of man are not invincible. This is the preceding proposition with a very slight variation in the statement. Vice and weakness are founded upon ignorance and error; but truth is more powerful than any champion that can be brought into the field against it; consequently, truth has the faculty of expelling weakness and vice, and placing nobler and more beneficent principles in their stead.

Lastly, man is perfectible. This proposition needs some explanation.

By perfectible it is not meant that he is capable of being brought to perfection. But the word seems sufficiently adapted to express the faculty of being continually made better and receiving perpetual improvement; and in this sense it is here to be understood. The term perfectible, thus explained, not only does not imply the capacity of being brought to perfection, but stands in express opposition to it. If we could arrive at perfection, there would be an end of our improvement. There is, however, one thing of great importance that it does imply; every perfection or excellence that human beings are competent to conceive, human beings, unless in cases that are palpably and unequivocally excluded by the structure of their frame, are competent to attain.

This is an inference which immediately follows from the omnipotence of truth. Every truth that is capable of being communicated is capable of being brought home to the conviction of the mind. Every principle which can be brought home to the conviction of the mind will infallibly produce a correspondent effect upon the conduct. If there were not something in the nature of man incompatible with absolute perfection, the doctrine of the omnipotence of truth would afford no small probability that he would one day reach it. Why is the perfection of man impossible?

The idea of absolute perfection is scarcely within the grasp of human understanding. If science were more familiarized to speculations of this sort, we should perhaps discover that the notion itself was pregnant with absurdity and contradiction.

It is not necessary in this argument to dwell upon the limited nature of human faculties. We can neither be present to all places nor to all times. We cannot penetrate into the essences of things; or rather, we have no sound and satisfactory knowledge of things external to ourselves, but merely of our own sensations. We cannot discover the causes of things, or ascertain that in the antecedent which connects it with the consequent, and discern nothing but their contiguity. With what pretence can a being thus shut in on all sides lay claim to absolute perfection?

But not to insist upon these considerations, there is one principle in the human mind which must forever exclude us from arriving at a close of our acquisitions, and confine us to perpetual progress. The human mind, so far as we are acquainted with it, is nothing else but a faculty of perception. All our knowledge, all our ideas, every thing we possess as intelligent beings, comes from impression. All the minds that exist set out from absolute ignorance. They received first one impression, and then a second. As the impressions became more numerous, and were stored by the help of memory, and combined by the faculty of association; so the experience increased, and with the experience, the knowledge, the wisdom, every thing that distinguishes man from what we understand by a "clod of the valley."[1] This seems to be a simple and incontrovertible history of intellectual beings; and if it be true, then as our accumulations have been incessant in the time that is gone; so, as long as we continue to perceive, to remember or reflect, they must perpetually increase.

[1] See *Job*, 21:33.

From BOOK V. OF LEGISLATIVE AND EXECUTIVE POWER

CHAPTER IV. OF A VIRTUOUS DESPOTISM

There is a principle frequently maintained upon this subject, which is well entitled to our impartial consideration. It is granted by those who espouse it, "that absolute monarchy, from the imperfection of those by whom it is administered, is most frequently attended with evil;" but they assert, "that it is the best and most desirable of all forms under a good and virtuous prince. It is exposed," say they, "to the fate of all excellent natures, and from the best thing frequently, if corrupted, becomes the worst." This remark is certainly not very decisive of the general question, so long as any weight shall be attributed to the arguments which have been adduced to evince, what sort of character and disposition may be ordinarily expected in princes. It may, however, be allowed, if true, to create in the mind a sort of partial retrospect to this happy and perfect despotism; and if it can be shown to be false, it will render the argument for the abolition of monarchy, so far as it is concerned, more entire and complete.

Now, whatever dispositions any man may possess in favor of the welfare of others, two things are necessary to give them validity: discernment and power. I can promote the welfare of a few persons, because I can be sufficiently informed of their circumstances. I can promote the welfare of many in certain general articles, because for this purpose it is only necessary that I should be informed of the nature of the human mind as such, not of the personal situation of the individuals concerned. But for one man to undertake to administer the affairs of millions, to supply, not general principles and perspicuous reasoning, but particular application, and measures adapted to the necessities of the moment, is of all undertakings the most extravagant and absurd.

The most simple and obvious of all proceedings is for each man to be the sovereign arbiter of his own concerns. If the imperfection, the narrow views, and the mistakes of human beings render this in certain cases inexpedient and impracticable, the next resource is to call in the opinion of his peers, persons who from their vicinity may be presumed to have some general knowledge of the case, and who have leisure and means minutely to investigate the merits of the question. It cannot reasonably be doubted that the same expedient which men employed in their civil and criminal concerns, would by uninstructed mortals be adopted in the assessment of taxes, in the deliberations of commerce, and in every other article in which their common interests were involved, only generalizing the deliberative assembly or panel in proportion to the generality of the question to be decided.

Monarchy, instead of referring every question to the persons concerned or their neighbors, refers it to a single individual placed at the greatest distance possible from the ordinary members of the society. Instead of distributing the causes to be judged into as many parcels as they would conveniently admit for the sake of providing leisure and opportunities of examination, it draws them to a single centre, and renders enquiry and examination impossible. A despot, however virtuously disposed, is obliged to act in the dark, to derive his knowledge from other men's information, and to execute his behests by other men's instrumentality. Monarchy seems to be a species of government proscribed by the nature of man; and those persons who furnished their despot with integrity and virtue forgot to add omniscience and omnipotence, qualities not less necessary to fit him for the office they have provided.

Let us suppose this honest and incorruptible despot to be served by ministers, avaricious, hypocritical, and interested. What will the people gain by the good intentions of their monarch? He will mean them the greatest benefits, but he will be altogether unacquainted with their situation, their character, and their wants. The information he receives will frequently be found the very reverse of the truth. He will be taught that one individual is highly meritorious and a proper subject of reward, whose only merit is the profligate cruelty with which he has served the purposes of his administration. He will be taught that another is the pest of the community, who is indebted for this report to the steady virtue with which he has traversed and defeated the wickedness of government. He will mean the greatest benefits to his people; but when he prescribes something calculated for their advantage, his servants under pretence of complying shall in reality perpetrate dia-

metrically the reverse. Nothing will be more dangerous than to endeavor to remove the obscurity with which his ministers surround him. The man who attempts so hardy a task will become the incessant object of their hatred. However unalterable may be the justice of the sovereign, the time will come when his observation will be laid asleep, while malice and revenge are ever vigilant. Could he unfold the secrets of his prison houses of state,[1] he would find men committed in his name whose crimes he never knew, whose names he never heard of, perhaps men whom he honored and esteemed. Such is the history of the benevolent and philanthropic despots whom memory has recorded; and the conclusion from the whole is, that wherever despotism exists, there it will always be attended with the evils of despotism,—capricious measures and arbitrary infliction.

"But will not a wise king take care to provide himself with good and virtuous servants?" Undoubtedly he will effect a part of this, but he cannot supersede the essential natures of things. He that executes any office as a deputy will never discharge it in the same perfection as if he were the principal. Either the minister must be the author of the plans which he carries into effect, and then it is of little consequence, except so far as relates to his integrity in the choice of his servants, what sort of mortal the sovereign shall be found; or he must play a subordinate part, and then it is impossible to transfuse into his mind the perspicacity and energy of his master. Wherever despotism exists, it cannot remain in a single hand, but must be transmitted whole and entire through all the progressive links of authority. To render depotism auspicious and benign it is necessary, not only that the sovereign should possess every human excellence, but that all his officers should be men of penetrating genius and unspotted virtue. If they fall short of this, they will, like the ministers of Elizabeth, be sometimes specious profligates,[2] and sometimes men who, however admirably adapted for the technical emergencies of business, consult on many occasions exclusively their private advantage, worship the rising sun, enter into vindictive cabals, and cuff down new-fledged merit.[3] Wherever the continuity is

---

[1] *Hamlet*, I, 5, 14.
[2] "Dudley, Earl of Leicester."—Godwin.
[3] "Cecil, Earl of Salisbury, Lord Treasurer; Howard, Earl of Nottingham, Lord Admiral."—Godwin.

broken, the flood of vice will bear down all before it. One weak or disingenuous man will be the source of unbounded mischief. It is the nature of monarchy under all its forms to confide greatly in the discretion of individuals. It provides no resource for maintaining and diffusing the spirit of justice. Everything rests upon the permanence and extent of personal virtue.

Another position, not less generally asserted than that of the desirableness of a virtuous despotism, is, "that republicanism is a species of government, practicable only in a small state, while monarchy is best fitted to embrace the concerns of a vast and flourishing empire." The reverse of this, so far at least as relates to monarchy, appears at first sight to be the truth. The competence of any government cannot be measured by a purer standard than the extent and accuracy of its information. In this respect monarchy appears in all cases to be wretchedly deficient; but if it can ever be admitted, it must surely be in those narrow and limited instances where an individual can, with least absurdity, be supposed to be acquainted with the affairs and interests of the whole.

CHAPTER XI. MORAL EFFECTS OF ARISTOCRACY

There is one thing, more than all the rest, of importance to the well-being of mankind,—justice. Can there be any thing problematical or paradoxical in this fundamental principle,—that all injustice is injury; and a thousand times more injurious by its effects in perverting the understanding and overturning our calculations of the future, than by the immediate calamity it may produce?

All moral science may be reduced to this one head,—calculation of the future. We cannot reasonably expect virtue from the multitude of mankind if they be induced by the perverseness of the conductors of human affairs to believe that it is not their interest to be virtuous. But this is not the point upon which the question turns. Virtue is nothing else but the pursuit of general good. Justice is the standard which discriminates the advantage of the many and of the few, of the whole and a part. If this first and most important of all subjects be involved in obscurity, how shall the well-being of mankind be substantially promoted? The most benevolent of our species will be engaged in crusades of error; while the cooler and more phleg-

matic spectators, discerning no evident clue that should guide them amidst the labyrinth, sit down in selfish neutrality, and leave the complicated scene to produce its own *dénouement*.

It is true that human affairs can never be reduced to that state of depravation as to reverse the nature of justice. Virtue will always be the interest of the individual as well as of the public. Immediate virtue will always be beneficial to the present age, as well as to their posterity. But though the depravation cannot rise to this excess, it will be abundantly sufficient to obscure the understanding and mislead the conduct. Human beings will never be so virtuous as they might easily be made, till justice be the spectacle perpetually presented to their view, and injustice be wondered at as a prodigy.

Of all the principles of justice there is none so material to the moral rectitude of mankind as this: that no man can be distinguished but by his personal merit. Why not endeavor to reduce to practice so simple and sublime a lesson? When a man has proved himself a benefactor to the public, when he has already by laudable perseverance cultivated in himself talents which need only encouragement and public favor to bring them to maturity, let that man be honored. In a state of society where fictitious distinctions are unknown, it is impossible he should not be honored. But that a man should be looked up to with servility and awe because the king has bestowed on him a spurious name, or decorated him with a ribband; that another should wallow in luxury because his ancestor three centuries ago bled in the quarrel of Lancaster or York;—do we imagine that these iniquities can be practiced without injury?

Let those who entertain this opinion converse a little with the lower orders of mankind. They will perceive that the unfortunate wretch, who with unremitted labor finds himself incapable adequately to feed and clothe his family, has a sense of injustice rankling at his heart.

One whom distress has spited with the world,
Is he whom tempting fiends would pitch upon
To do such deeds as make the prosperous men
Lift up their hands and wonder who could do them.[1]

Such is the education of the human species. Such is the fabric of political society.

[1] John Home, *Douglas*, III, 109-13.

But let us suppose that their sense of injustice were less acute than it is here described. What favorable inference can be drawn from that? Is not the injustice real? If the minds of men be so withered and stupified by the constancy with which it is practiced, that they do not feel the rigor that grinds them into nothing, how does that improve the picture?

Let us for a moment give the reins to reflection, and endeavor accurately to conceive the state of mankind where justice should form the public and general principle. In that case our moral feelings would assume a firm and wholesome tone, for they would not be perpetually counteracted by examples that weakened their energy and confounded their clearness. Men would be fearless because they would know that there were no legal snares lying in wait for their lives. They would be courageous because no man would be pressed to the earth that another might enjoy immoderate luxury, because every one would be secure of the just reward of his industry and prize of his exertions. Jealousy and hatred would cease, for they are the offspring of injustice. Every man would speak truth with his neighbor, for there would be no temptation to falsehood and deceit. Mind would find its level, for there would be everything to encourage and to animate. Science would be unspeakably improved, for understanding would convert into a real power, no longer an *ignis fatuus,* shining and expiring by turns, and leading us into sloughs of sophistry, false science, and specious mistake. All men would be disposed to avow their dispositions and actions; none would endeavor to suppress the just eulogium of his neighbor, for so long as there were tongues to record, the suppression would be impossible; none fear to detect the misconduct of his neighbor, for there would be no laws converting the sincere expression of our convictions into a libel.

Let us fairly consider for a moment what is the amount of injustice included in the institution of aristocracy. I am born, suppose, a Polish prince, with an income of £300,000 *per annum.* You are born a manorial serf or a Creolian negro, attached to the soil and transferable by barter or otherwise to twenty successive lords. In vain shall be your most generous efforts and your unwearied industry to free yourself from the intolerable yoke. Doomed by the law of your birth, to wait at the gates of the palace you must never enter, to sleep under a ruined weatherbeaten roof while your master sleeps under canopies of state, to feed on putrified offals while the world is ransacked for delicacies for his table, to labor without moderation or limit under a parching sun while he basks in perpetual sloth, and to be rewarded at last with contempt, reprimand, stripes, and mutilation. In fact the case is worse than this. I could endure all that injustice or caprice could inflict, provided I possessed in the resource of a firm mind the power of looking down with pity on my tyrant, and of knowing that I had that within, that sacred character of truth, virtue, and fortitude, which all his injustice could not reach. But a slave and a serf are condemned to stupidity and vice as well as to calamity.

Is all things nothing? Is all this necessary for the maintainance of civil order? Let it be recollected that, for this distinction, there is not the smallest foundation, in the nature of things; that, as we have already said, there is no particular mould for the construction of lords; and that they are born neither better nor worse than the poorest of their dependents. It is this structure of aristocracy in all its sanctuaries and fragments against which reason and philosophy have declared war. It is alike unjust, whether we consider it in the castes of India, the villainage of feudal system, or the despotism of the patricians of ancient Rome dragging their debtors into personal servitude to expiate loans they could not repay. Mankind will never be in an eminent degree virtuous and happy till each man shall possess that portion of distinction, and no more, to which he is entitled by his personal merits. The dissolution of aristocracy is equally the interest of the oppressor and the oppressed. The one will be delivered from the listlessness of tyranny, and the other from the brutalizing operation of servitude. How long shall we be told in vain, "that mediocrity of fortune is the true rampart of personal happiness?"

William Wordsworth
1770-1850
EXTRACT

FROM THE CONCLUSION OF A POEM, COMPOSED
IN ANTICIPATION OF LEAVING SCHOOL
1786   1815

Dear native regions, I foretell,
From what I feel at this farewell,
That, wheresoe'er my steps may tend,
And whensoe'er my course shall end,
5 If in that hour a single tie
Survive of local sympathy,
My soul will cast the backward view,
The longing look alone on you.

Thus, while the sun sinks down to rest
10 Far in the regions of the west,
Though to the vale no parting beam
Be given, not one memorial gleam,
A lingering light he fondly throws
On the dear hills where first he rose.

WRITTEN IN VERY EARLY YOUTH
1786   1802

Calm is all nature as a resting wheel.
The kine are couched upon the dewy grass;
The horse alone, seen dimly as I pass,
Is cropping audibly his later meal:
5 Dark is the ground; a slumber seems to
    steal
O'er vale, and mountain, and the star-
    less sky.
Now, in this blank of things, a harmony,
Home-felt, and home-created, comes to heal
That grief for which the senses still
    supply
10 Fresh food; for only then, when memory
Is hushed, am I at rest. My friends! restrain
Those busy cares that would allay my pain;
Oh! leave me to myself, nor let me feel
The officious touch that makes me droop
    again.

From AN EVENING WALK
1787-89   1793

Dear Brook, farewell! Tomorrow's
    noon again
Shall hide me, wooing long thy wild-
    wood strain;
But now the sun has gained his western
    road,
And eve's mild hour invites my steps
    abroad.

90 While, near the midway cliff, the silvered
    kite
In many a whistling circle wheels her
    flight;
Slant watery lights, from parting clouds,
    apace
Travel along the precipice's base;
Cheering its naked waste of scattered stone,
95 By lichens gray, and scanty moss, o'er-
    grown;
Where scarce the foxglove peeps, or
    thistle's beard;
And restless stone-chat,[1] all day long, is
    heard.

How pleasant, as the sun declines, to
    view
The spacious landscape change in form
    and hue!
100 Here, vanish, as in mist, before a flood
Of bright obscurity, hill, lawn, and wood;
There, objects, by the searching beams
    betrayed,
Come forth, and here retire in purple
    shade;
Even the white stems of birch, the cot-
    tage white,
105 Soften their glare before the mellow light;
The skiffs, at anchor where with um-
    brage wide
Yon chestnuts half the latticed boat-
    house hide,
Shed from their sides, that face the
    sun's slant beam,
Strong flakes of radiance on the trem-
    ulous stream:
110 Raised by yon travelling flock, a dusty
    cloud
Mounts from the road, and spreads its
    moving shroud;
The shepherd, all involved in wreaths of
    fire,
Now shows a shadowy speck, and now is
    lost entire.

. . . .

LINES

LEFT UPON A SEAT IN A YEW-TREE WHICH
STANDS NEAR THE LAKE OF ESTHWAITE,
ON A DESOLATE PART OF THE SHORE,
COMMANDING A BEAUTIFUL PROSPECT
1795   1798

Nay, traveller! rest. This lonely yew-tree
    stands
Far from all human dwelling: what if here
No sparkling rivulet spread the verdant
    herb?

[1] A common European singing bird.

What if the bee love not these barren
    boughs?
5 Yet, if the wind breathe soft, the curling
    waves,
That break against the shore, shall lull
    thy mind
By one soft impulse saved from vacancy.
             Who he was
That piled these stones and with the
    mossy sod
10 First covered, and here taught this aged
    tree
With its dark arms to form a circling
    bower,
I well remember.[1]—He was one who
    owned
No common soul. In youth by science
    nursed,
And led by Nature into a wild scene
15 Of lofty hopes, he to the world went forth
A favored Being, knowing no desire
Which genius did not hallow; 'gainst
    the taint
Of dissolute tongues, and jealousy, and
    hate,
And scorn,—against all enemies prepared,
20 All but neglect. The world, for so it
    thought,
Owed him no service; wherefore he at once
With indignation turned himself away,
And with the food of pride sustained his
    soul
In solitude.— Stranger! these gloomy
    boughs
25 Had charms for him; and here he loved
    to sit,
His only visitants a straggling sheep,
The stone-chat,[2] or the glancing sand-
    piper
And on these barren rocks, with fern
    and heath,
And juniper and thistle, sprinkled o'er,
30 Fixing his downcast eye, he many an hour
A morbid pleasure nourished, tracing here
An emblem of his own unfruitful life:
And, lifting up his head, he then would
    gaze
On the more distant scene,—how lovely 'tis
35 Thou seest,—and he would gaze till it
    became
Far lovelier, and his heart could not
    sustain
The beauty, still more beauteous! Nor,
    that time,

[1] "He was a gentleman of the neighborhood, a
man of talent and learning, who had been
educated at one of our universities, and returned to pass his time in seclusion on his
own estate."—Wordsworth.
[2] A common European singing bird.

When Nature had subdued him to her-
    self,
Would he forget those Beings to whose
    minds,
40 Warm from the labors of benevolence,
The world and human life appeared a
    scene
Of kindred loveliness: then he would sigh,
Inly disturbed, to think that others felt
What he must never feel: and so, lost
    Man!
45 On visionary views would fancy feed,
Till his eye streamed with tears. In this
    deep vale
He died,—this seat his only monument.

If thou be one whose heart the holy
    forms
Of young imagination have kept pure,
50 Stranger! henceforth be warned; and
    know that pride,
Howe'er disguised in its own majesty,
Is littleness; that he who feels contempt
For any living thing, hath faculties
Which he has never used; that thought
    with him
55 Is in its infancy. The man whose eye
Is ever on himself doth look on one,
The least of Nature's works, one who
    might move
The wise man to that scorn which wis-
    dom holds
Unlawful, ever. O be wiser, thou!
60 Instructed that true knowledge leads to
    love;
True dignity abides with him alone
Who, in the silent hour of inward thought,
Can still suspect, and still revere himself,
In lowliness of heart.

THE REVERIE OF POOR SUSAN
1797   1800

At the corner of Wood Street, when
    daylight appears,
Hangs a thrush that sings loud, it has
    sung for three years:
Poor Susan has passed by the spot, and
    has heard
In the silence of morning the song of
    the bird.

5 'Tis a note of enchantment; what ails
    her? She sees
A mountain ascending, a vision of
    trees;
Bright volumes of vapor through Loth-
    bury glide,
And a river flows on through the vale of
    Cheapside.

Green pastures she views in the midst of the dale,
10 Down which she so often has tripped with her pail;
And a single small cottage, a nest like a dove's,
The one only dwelling on earth that she loves.

She looks, and her heart is in heaven: but they fade,
The mist and the river, the hill and the shade:
15 The stream will not flow, and the hill will not rise,
And the colors have all passed away from her eyes!

WE ARE SEVEN
1798   *1798*

—A simple child,
That lightly draws its breath,
And feels its life in every limb,
What should it know of death?

5 I met a little cottage girl:
She was eight years old, she said;
Her hair was thick with many a curl
That clustered round her head.

She had a rustic, woodland air,
10 And she was wildly clad:
Her eyes were fair, and very fair;
—Her beauty made me glad.

"Sisters and brothers, little maid,
How many may you be?"
15 "How many? Seven in all," she said,
And wondering looked at me.

"And where are they? I pray you tell."
She answered, "Seven are we;
And two of us at Conway dwell,
20 And two are gone to sea.

"Two of us in the churchyard lie,
My sister and my brother;
And, in the churchyard cottage, I
Dwell near them with my mother."

25 "You say that two at Conway dwell,
And two are gone to sea,
Yet ye are seven! I pray you tell,
Sweet maid, how this may be."

Then did the little maid reply,
30 "Seven boys and girls are we;
Two of us in the churchyard lie,
Beneath the churchyard tree."

"You run about, my little maid,
Your limbs they are alive;
35 If two are in the churchyard laid,
Then ye are only five."

"Their graves are green, they may be seen,"
The little maid replied,
"Twelve steps or more from my mother's door,
40 And they are side by side.

"My stockings there I often knit,
My kerchief there I hem;
And there upon the ground I sit,
And sing a song to them.

45 "And often after sunset, sir,
When it is light and fair,
I take my little porringer,
And eat my supper there.

"The first that died was sister Jane;
50 In bed she moaning lay,
Till God released her of her pain;
And then she went away.

"So in the churchyard she was laid;
And, when the grass was dry,
55 Together round her grave we played,
My brother John and I.

"And when the ground was white with snow,
And I could run and slide,
My brother John was forced to go,
60 And he lies by her side."

"How many are you, then," said I,
"If they two are in heaven?"
Quick was the little maid's reply,
"O master! we are seven."

65 But they are dead; those two are dead!
Their spirits are in heaven!"
'Twas throwing words away; for still
The little maid would have her will,
And said, "Nay, we are seven!"

THE THORN
1798   *1798*

"There is a Thorn—it looks so old,
In truth, you'd find it hard to say
How it could ever have been young,
It looks so old and gray.
5 Not higher than a two years' child
It stands erect, this aged Thorn;
No leaves it has, no prickly points;
It is a mass of knotted joints,

A wretched thing forlorn.
10 It stands erect, and like a stone
With lichens is it overgrown.

"Like rock or stone, it is o'ergrown,
With lichens to the very top,
And hung with heavy tufts of moss,
15 A melancholy crop:
Up from the earth these mosses creep,
And this poor Thorn they clasp it round
So close, you'd say that they are bent
With plain and manifest intent
20 To drag it to the ground;
And all have joined in one endeavor
To bury this poor Thorn forever.

"High on a mountain's highest ridge,
Where oft the stormy winter gale
25 Cuts like a scythe, while through the clouds
It sweeps from vale to vale;
Not five yards from the mountain path,
This Thorn you on your left espy;
And to the left, three yards beyond,
30 You see a little muddy pond
Of water—never dry,
Though but of compass small, and bare
To thirsty suns and parching air.

"And, close beside this aged Thorn,
35 There is a fresh and lovely sight,
A beauteous heap, a hill of moss,
Just half a foot in height.
All lovely colors there you see,
All colors that were ever seen;
40 And mossy network too is there,
As if by hand of lady fair
The work had woven been;
And cups, the darlings of the eye,
So deep is their vermilion dye.

45 "Ah me! what lovely tints are there
Of olive green and scarlet bright,
In spikes, in branches, and in stars,
Green, red, and pearly white!
This heap of earth o'ergrown with moss,
50 Which close beside the Thorn you see,
So fresh in all its beauteous dyes,
Is like an infant's grave in size,
As like as like can be:
But never, never anywhere,
55 An infant's grave was half so fair.

"Now would you see this aged Thorn,
This pond, and beauteous hill of moss,
You must take care and choose your time
The mountain when to cross.
60 For oft there sits between the heap,
So like an infant's grave in size,
And that same pond of which I spoke,

A woman in a scarlet cloak,
And to herself she cries,
65 'Oh misery! oh misery!
Oh woe is me! oh misery!'

"At all times of the day and night
This wretched woman thither goes;
And she is known to every star,
70 And every wind that blows;
And there, beside the Thorn, she sits
When the blue daylight's in the skies,
And when the whirlwind's on the hill,
Or frosty air is keen and still,
75 And to herself she cries,
'Oh misery! oh misery!
Oh woe is me! oh misery!'"

"Now wherefore, thus, by day and night,
In rain, in tempest, and in snow,
80 Thus to the dreary mountain-top
Does this poor woman go?
And why sits she beside the Thorn
When the blue daylight's in the sky
Or when the whirlwind's on the hill,
85 Or frosty air is keen and still,
And wherefore does she cry?—
O wherefore? wherefore? tell me why
Does she repeat that doleful cry?"

"I cannot tell; I wish I could;
90 For the true reason no one knows:
But would you gladly view the spot,
The spot to which she goes;
The hillock like an infant's grave,
The pond—and Thorn, so old and gray;
95 Pass by her door—'tis seldom shut—
And if you see her in her hut—
Then to the spot away!
I never heard of such as dare
Approach the spot when she is there."

100 "But wherefore to the mountain-top
Can this unhappy woman go,
Whatever star is in the skies,
Whatever wind may blow?"
"Full twenty years are past and gone
105 Since she (her name is Martha Ray)
Gave with a maiden's true good-will
Her company to Stephen Hill;
And she was blithe and gay,
While friends and kindred all approved
110 Of him whom tenderly she loved.

"And they had fixed the wedding day,
The morning that must wed them both;
But Stephen to another maid
Had sworn another oath;
115 And, with this other maid, to church
Unthinking Stephen went—

Poor Martha! on that woeful day
A pang of pitiless dismay
Into her soul was sent;
120 A fire was kindled in her breast,
Which might not burn itself to rest.

"They say, full six months after this,
While yet the summer leaves were green,
She to the mountain-top would go,
125 And there was often seen.
What could she seek?—or wish to hide?
Her state to any eye was plain;
She was with child, and she was mad;
Yet often was she sober sad
130 From her exceeding pain.
O guilty father—would that death
Had saved him from that breach of faith!

"Sad case for such a brain to hold
Communion with a stirring child!
135 Sad case, as you may think, for one
Who had a brain so wild!
Last Christmas-eve we talked of this,
And gray-haired Wilfred of the glen
Held that the unborn infant wrought
140 About its mother's heart, and brought
Her senses back again:
And, when at last her time drew near,
Her looks were calm, her senses clear.

"More know I not, I wish I did,
145 And it should all be told to you;
For what became of this poor child
No mortal ever knew;
Nay—if a child to her was born
No earthly tongue could ever tell;
150 And if 'twas born alive or dead,
Far less could this with proof be said;
But some remember well
That Martha Ray about this time
Would up the mountain often climb.

155 "And all that winter, when at night
The wind blew from the mountain-peak,
'Twas worth your while, though in the dark,
The churchyard path to seek:
For many a time and oft were heard
160 Cries coming from the mountain head:
Some plainly living voices were;
And others, I've heard many swear,
Were voices of the dead:
I cannot think, whate'er they say,
165 They had to do with Martha Ray.

"But that she goes to this old Thorn,
The Thorn which I described to you,
And there sits in a scarlet cloak,
I will be sworn is true.

170 For one day with my telescope,
To view the ocean wide and bright,
When to this country first I came,
Ere I had heard of Martha's name,
I climbed the mountain's height:—
175 A storm came on, and I could see
No object higher than my knee.

" 'Twas mist and rain, and storm and rain
No screen, no fence could I discover;
And then the wind! in sooth, it was
180 A wind full ten times over.
I looked around, I thought I saw
A jutting crag,—and off I ran,
Head-foremost, through the driving rain,
The shelter of the crag to gain;
185 And, as I am a man,
Instead of jutting crag I found
A woman seated on the ground.

"I did not speak—I saw her face;
Her face!—it was enough for me;
190 I turned about and heard her cry,
'Oh misery! oh misery!'
And there she sits, until the moon
Through half the clear blue sky will go;
And when the little breezes make
195 The waters of the pond to shake,
As all the country know,
She shudders, and you hear her cry,
'Oh misery! oh misery!' "

"But what's the Thorn? and what the pond?
200 And what the hill of moss to her?
And what the creeping breeze that comes
The little pond to stir?"
"I cannot tell; but some will say
She hanged her baby on the tree;
205 Some say she drowned it in the pond,
Which is a little step beyond:
But all and each agree,
The little babe was buried there,
Beneath that hill of moss so fair.

210 "I've heard, the moss is spotted red
With drops of that poor infant's blood;
But kill a new-born infant thus,
I do not think she could;
Some say if to the pond you go,
215 And fix on it a steady view,
The shadow of a babe you trace,
A baby and a baby's face,
And that it looks at you;
Whene'er you look on it, 'tis plain
220 The baby looks at you again.

"And some had sworn an oath that she
Should be to public justice brought;

And for the little infant's bones
With spades they would have sought.
225 But instantly the hill of moss
Before their eyes began to stir!
And, for full fifty yards around,
The grass—it shook upon the ground!
Yet all do still aver
230 The little babe lies buried there,
Beneath that hill of moss so fair.

"I cannot tell how this may be,
But plain it is the Thorn is bound
With heavy tufts of moss that strive
235 To drag it to the ground;
And this I know, full many a time,
When she was on the mountain high,
By day, and in the silent night,
When all the stars shone clear and bright,
240 That I have heard her cry,
'Oh misery! oh misery!
Oh woe is me! oh misery!'"

GOODY BLAKE AND HARRY GILL

A TRUE STORY
1798　　　*1798*

Oh! what's the matter? what's the matter?
What is't that ails young Harry Gill?
That evermore his teeth they chatter,
Chatter, chatter, chatter still!
5 Of waistcoats Harry has no lack,
Good duffle[1] gray, and flannel fine;
He has a blanket on his back,
And coats enough to smother nine.

In March, December, and in July,
10 'Tis all the same with Harry Gill;
The neighbors tell, and tell you truly,
His teeth they chatter, chatter still.
At night, at morning, and at noon,
'Tis all the same with Harry Gill;
15 Beneath the sun, beneath the moon,
His teeth they chatter, chatter still!

Young Harry was a lusty drover,
And who so stout of limb as he?
His cheeks were red as ruddy clover;
20 His voice was like the voice of three.
Old Goody Blake was old and poor;
Ill fed she was, and thinly clad;
And any man who passed her door
Might see how poor a hut she had.

25 All day she spun in her poor dwelling:
And then her three hours' work at night,
Alas! 'twas hardly worth the telling,
It would not pay for candle-light.
Remote from sheltered village-green,
30 On a hill's northern side she dwelt,

---

[1] A kind of coarse woolen cloth having a thick nap.

Where from sea-blasts the hawthorns lean,
And hoary dews are slow to melt.

By the same fire to boil their pottage,
Two poor old dames, as I have known,
35 Will often live in one small cottage;
But she, poor woman! housed alone.
'Twas well enough, when summer came,
The long, warm, lightsome summer-day,
Then at her door the canty[1] dame
40 Would sit, as any linnet, gay.

But when the ice our streams did fetter,
Oh then how her old bones would shake!
You would have said, if you had met her,
'Twas a hard time for Goody Blake.
45 Her evenings then were dull and dead:
Sad case it was, as you may think,
For very cold to go to bed;
And then for cold not sleep a wink.

O joy for her! whene'er in winter
50 The winds at night had made a rout;
And scattered many a lusty splinter
And many a rotten bough about.
Yet never had she, well or sick,
As every man who knew her says,
55 A pile beforehand, turf or stick,
Enough to warm her for three days.

Now, when the frost was past enduring,
And made her poor old bones to ache,
Could anything be more alluring
60 Than an old hedge to Goody Blake?
And, now and then, it must be said,
When her old bones were cold and chill,
She left her fire, or left her bed,
To seek the hedge of Harry Gill.

65 Now Harry he had long suspected
This trespass of old Goody Blake;
And vowed that she should be detected—
That he on her would vengeance take.
And oft from his warm fire he'd go,
70 And to the fields his road would take;
And there, at night, in frost and snow,
He watched to seize old Goody Blake.

And once, behind a rick of barley,
Thus looking out did Harry stand:
75 The moon was full and shining clearly,
And crisp with frost the stubble land.
—He hears a noise—he's all awake—
Again?—on tip-toe down the hill
He softly creeps—'tis Goody Blake;
80 She's at the hedge of Harry Gill!

Right glad was he when he beheld her:
Stick after stick did Goody pull:

---

[1] cheerful

He stood behind a bush of elder,
Till she had filled her apron full.
85 When with her load she turned about,
The by-way back again to take;
He started forward, with a shout,
And sprang upon poor Goody Blake.

And fiercely by the arm he took her,
90 And by the arm he held her fast,
And fiercely by the arm he shook her,
And cried, "I've caught you then at last!"
Then Goody, who had nothing said,
Her bundle from her lap let fall;
95 And, kneeling on the sticks, she prayed
To God that is the judge of all.

She prayed, her withered hand uprearing,
While Harry held her by the arm—
"God! who art never out of hearing,
100 O may he never more be warm!"
The cold, cold moon above her head,
Thus on her knees did Goody pray;
Young Harry heard what she had said:
And icy cold he turned away.

105 He went complaining all the morrow
That he was cold and very chill:
His face was gloom, his heart was sorrow,
Alas! that day for Harry Gill!
That day he wore a riding-coat,
110 But not a whit the warmer he:
Another was on Thursday brought,
And ere the Sabbath he had three.

'Twas all in vain, a useless matter,
And blankets were about him pinned;
115 Yet still his jaws and teeth they clatter,
Like a loose casement in the wind.
And Harry's flesh it fell away;
And all who see him say, 'tis plain,
That, live as long as live he may,
120 He never will be warm again.

No word to any man he utters,
A-bed or up, to young or old;
But ever to himself he mutters,
"Poor Harry Gill is very cold."
125 A-bed or up, by night or day;
His teeth they chatter, chatter still.
Now think, ye farmers all, I pray,
Of Goody Blake and Harry Gill!

HER EYES ARE WILD
1798   1798

Her eyes are wild, her head is bare,
The sun has burnt her coal-black hair;
Her eyebrows have a rusty stain,
And she came far from over the main.
5 She had a baby on her arm,

Or else she were alone:
And underneath the hay-stack warm,
And on the greenwood stone,
She talked and sung the woods among,
10 And it was in the English tongue.

"Sweet babe! they say that I am mad,
But nay, my heart is far too glad;
And I am happy when I sing
Full many a sad and doleful thing:
15 Then, lovely baby, do not fear!
I pray thee have no fear of me;
But safe as in a cradle, here,
My lovely baby! thou shalt be:
To thee I know too much I owe;
20 I cannot work thee any woe.

"A fire was once within my brain;
And in my head a dull, dull pain;
And fiendish faces, one, two, three,
Hung at my breast, and pulled at me;
25 But then there came a sight of joy;
It came at once to do me good;
I waked, and saw my little boy,
My little boy of flesh and blood;
Oh joy for me that sight to see!
30 For he was here, and only he.

"Suck, little babe, oh suck again!
It cools my blood; it cools my brain;
Thy lips I feel them, baby! they
Draw from my heart the pain away.
35 Oh! press me with thy little hand;
It loosens something at my chest;
About that tight and deadly band
I feel thy little fingers prest.
The breeze I see is in the tree:
40 It comes to cool my babe and me.

"Oh! love me, love me, little boy!
Thou art thy mother's only joy;
And do not dread the waves below,
When o'er the sea-rock's edge we go;
45 The high crag cannot work me harm,
Nor leaping torrents when they howl;
The babe I carry on my arm,
He saves for me my precious soul;
Then happy lie; for blest am I;
50 Without me my sweet babe would die.

"Then do not fear, my boy! for thee
Bold as a lion will I be;
And I will always be thy guide,
Through hollow snows and rivers wide.
55 I'll build an Indian bower; I know
The leaves that make the softest bed:
And if from me thou wilt not go,
But still be true till I am dead,
My pretty thing! then thou shalt sing
60 As merry as the birds in spring.

"Thy father cares not for my breast,
'Tis thine, sweet baby, there to rest;
'Tis all thine own!—and if its hue
Be changed, that was so fair to view,
65 'Tis fair enough for thee, my dove!
My beauty, little child, is flown,
But thou wilt live with me in love;
And what if my poor cheek be brown?
'Tis well for me thou canst not see
70 How pale and wan it else would be.

"Dread not their taunts, my little life;
I am thy father's wedded wife;
And underneath the spreading tree
We two will live in honesty.
75 If his sweet boy he could forsake,
With me he never would have stayed:
From him no harm my babe can take;
But he, poor man! is wretched made;
And every day we two will pray
80 For him that's gone and far away.

"I'll teach my boy the sweetest things:
I'll teach him how the owlet sings.
My little babe! thy lips are still,
And thou hast almost sucked thy fill.
85 —Where art thou gone, my own dear child?
What wicked looks are those I see?
Alas! Alas! that look so wild,
It never, never came from me:
If thou art mad, my pretty lad,
90 Then I must be forever sad.

"Oh! smile on me, my little lamb!
For I thy own dear mother am:
My love for thee has well been tried:
I've sought thy father far and wide.
95 I know the poisons of the shade;
I know the earth-nuts fit for food:
Then, pretty dear, be not afraid:
We'll find thy father in the wood.
Now laugh and be gay, to the woods away!
100 And there, my babe, we'll live for aye."

SIMON LEE

THE OLD HUNTSMAN; WITH AN INCIDENT IN
WHICH HE WAS CONCERNED
1798   1798

In the sweet shire of Cardigan,
Not far from pleasant Ivor-hall,
An old man dwells, a little man,—
'Tis said he once was tall.
5 Full five and thirty years he lived
A running huntsman merry;
And still the centre of his cheek
Is red as a ripe cherry.

No man like him the horn could sound,
10 And hill and valley rang with glee

When Echo bandied, round and round,
The halloo of Simon Lee.

In those proud days, he little cared
For husbandry or tillage;
15 To blither tasks did Simon rouse
The sleepers of the village.

He all the country could outrun,
Could leave both man and horse behind;
And often, ere the chase was done,
20 He reeled, and was stone-blind.
And still there's something in the world
At which his heart rejoices;
For when the chiming hounds are out,
He dearly loves their voices!

25 But, oh the heavy change!—bereft
Of health, strength, friends, and kin-
dred, see!
Old Simon to the world is left
In liveried poverty.
His master's dead,—and no one now
30 Dwells in the Hall of Ivor;
Men, dogs, and horses, all are dead;
He is the sole survivor.

And he is lean, and he is sick;
His body, dwindled and awry,
35 Rests upon ankles swoln and thick;
His legs are thin and dry.
One prop he has, and only one,
His wife, an aged woman,
Lives with him, near the waterfall,
40 Upon the village common.

Beside their moss-grown hut of clay,
Not twenty paces from the door,
A scrap of land they have, but they
Are poorest of the poor.
45 This scrap of land he from the heath
Enclosed when he was stronger;
But what to them avails the land
Which he can till no longer?

Oft, working by her husband's side,
50 Ruth does what Simon cannot do;
For she, with scanty cause for pride,
Is stouter of the two.
And, though you with your utmost skill
From labor could not wean them,
55 'Tis little, very little—all
That they can do between them.

Few months of life has he in store
As he to you will tell,
For still, the more he works, the more
60 Do his weak ankles swell.
My gentle reader, I perceive

How patiently you've waited,
And now I fear that you expect
Some tale will be related.

65 O reader! had you in your mind
Such stores as silent thought can bring,
O gentle reader! you would find
A tale in every thing.
What more I have to say is short,
70 And you must kindly take it:
It is no tale; but, should you think,
Perhaps a tale you'll make it.

One summer-day I chanced to see
This old man doing all he could
75 To unearth the root of an old tree,
A stump of rotten wood.
The mattock tottered in his hand;
So vain was his endeavor,
That at the root of the old tree
80 He might have worked forever.

"You're overtasked, good Simon Lee,
Give me your tool," to him I said;
And at the word right gladly he
Received my proffered aid.
85 I struck, and with a single blow
The tangled root I severed,
At which the poor old man so long
And vainly had endeavored.

The tears into his eyes were brought.
90 And thanks and praises semed to run
So fast out of his heart, I thought
They never would have done.
—I've heard of hearts unkind, kind deeds
With coldness still returning;
95 Alas! the gratitude of men
Hath oftener left me mourning.

LINES WRITTEN IN EARLY SPRING
1798   1798

I heard a thousand blended notes,
While in a grove I sate reclined,
In that sweet mood when pleasant thoughts
Bring sad thoughts to the mind.

5 To her fair works did Nature link
The human soul that through me ran;
And much it grieved my heart to think
What man has made of man.

Through primrose tufts, in that green
  bower,
10 The periwinkle trailed its wreaths;
And 'tis my faith that every flower
Enjoys the air it breathes.

The birds around me hopped and played,
Their thoughts I cannot measure:—
15 But the least motion which they made,
It seemed a thrill of pleasure.

The budding twigs spread out their fan,
To catch the breezy air;
And I must think, do all I can,
20 That there was pleasure there.

If this belief from heaven be sent,
If such be Nature's holy plan,
Have I not reason to lament
What man has made of man?

TO MY SISTER[1]
1798   1798

It is the first mild day of March:
Each minute sweeter than before,
The redbreast sings from the tall larch
That stands beside our door.

5 There is a blessing in the air,
Which seems a sense of joy to yield
To the bare trees, and mountains bare,
And grass in the green field.

My sister! ('tis a wish of mine)
10 Now that our morning meal is done,
Make haste, your morning task resign;
Come forth and feel the sun.

Edward will come with you;—and, pray,
Put on with speed your woodland dress;
15 And bring no book: for this one day
We'll give to idleness.

No joyless forms shall regulate
Our living calendar:
We from today, my friend, will date
20 The opening of the year.

Love, now a universal birth,
From heart to heart is stealing,
From earth to man, from man to earth:
—It is the hour of feeling.

25 One moment now may give us more
Than years of toiling reason:
Our minds shall drink at every pore
The spirit of the season.

Some silent laws our hearts will make,
30 Which they shall long obey:
We for the year to come may take
Our temper from today.

[1] Dorothy Wordsworth.

And from the blessed power that rolls
About, below, above,
35 We'll frame the measure of our souls:
They shall be tuned to love.

Then come, my sister! come, I pray,
With speed put on your woodland dress;
And bring no book: for this one day
40 We'll give to idleness.

A WHIRL-BLAST FROM BEHIND THE HILL
1798   1800

A whirl-blast from behind the hill
Rush'd o'er the wood with startling sound;
Then—all at once the air was still,
And showers of hailstones pattered round.
5 Where leafless oaks towered high above,
I sat within an undergrove
Of tallest hollies, tall and green;
A fairer bower was never seen.
From year to year the spacious floor
10 With withered leaves is covered o'er,
And all the year the bower is green.
But see! where'er the hailstones drop
The withered leaves all skip and hop;
There's not a breeze—no breath of air—
15 Yet here, and there, and everywhere
Along the floor, beneath the shade
By those embowering hollies made,
The leaves in myriads jump and spring,
As if with pipes and music rare
20 Some Robin Good-fellow were there,
And all those leaves, in festive glee,
Were dancing to the minstrelsy.

EXPOSTULATION AND REPLY
1798   1798

"Why, William, on that old gray stone,
Thus for the length of half a day,
Why, William, sit you thus alone,
And dream your time away?

5 "Where are your books?—that light bequeathed
To beings else forlorn and blind!
Up! up! and drink the spirit breathed
From dead men to their kind.

"You look round on your Mother Earth,
10 As if she for no purpose bore you;
As if you were her first-born birth,
And none had lived before you!"

One morning thus, by Esthwaite lake,
When life was sweet, I knew not why,

15 To me my good friend Matthew[1] spake,
And thus I made reply:

"The eye—it cannot choose but see;
We cannot bid the ear be still;
Our bodies feel, where'er they be,
20 Against or with our will.

"Nor less I deem that there are Powers
Which of themselves our minds impress;
That we can feed this mind of ours
In a wise passiveness.

25 "Think you, 'mid all this mighty sum
Of things forever speaking,
That nothing of itself will come,
But we must still be seeking?

"—Then ask not wherefore, here, alone,
30 Conversing as I may,
I sit upon this old gray stone,
And dream my time away."

THE TABLES TURNED
AN EVENING SCENE ON THE SAME SUBJECT
1798   1798

Up! up! my friend, and quit your books;
Or surely you'll grow double:
Up! up! my friend, and clear your looks;
Why all this toil and trouble?

5 The sun, above the mountain's head,
A freshening lustre mellow
Through all the long green fields has spread,
His first sweet evening yellow.

Books! 'tis a dull and endless strife:
10 Come, hear the woodland linnet,
How sweet his music! on my life,
There's more of wisdom in it.

And hark! how blithe the throstle sings!
He, too, is no mean preacher:
15 Come forth into the light of things,
Let Nature be your teacher.

She has a world of ready wealth,
Our minds and hearts to bless—
Spontaneous wisdom breathed by health,
20 Truth breathed by cheerfulness.

One impulse from a vernal wood
May teach you more of man,
Of moral evil and of good,
Than all the sages can.

[1] "A friend who was somewhat unreasonably attached to modern books of moral philosophy."
—Wordsworth.

25 Sweet is the lore which Nature brings;
Our meddling intellect
Misshapes the beauteous forms of
things:—
We murder to dissect.

Enough of Science and of Art;
30 Close up those barren leaves;
Come forth, and bring with you a heart
That watches and receives.

LINES

COMPOSED A FEW MILES ABOVE TINTERN
ABBEY, ON REVISITING THE BANKS OF THE
WYE DURING A TOUR, JULY 13, 1798
            1798   *1798*

Five years have past; five summers, with
the length
Of five long winters! and again I hear
These waters, rolling from their moun-
tain-springs
With a soft inland murmur.—Once again
5 Do I behold these steep and lofty cliffs,
That on a wild secluded scene impress
Thoughts of more deep seclusion; and
connect
The landscape with the quiet of the sky.
The day is come when I again repose
10 Here, under this dark sycamore, and view
These plots of cottage-ground, these
orchard-tufts,
Which at this season, with their unripe
fruits,
Are clad in one green hue, and lose
themselves
'Mid groves and copses. Once again I see
15 These hedgerows, hardly hedgerows, little
lines
Of sportive wood run wild: these pas-
toral farms,
Green to the very door; and wreaths of
smoke
Sent up, in silence, from among the trees!
With some uncertain notice, as might seem
20 Of vagrant dwellers in the houseless woods,
Or of some hermit's cave, where by his fire
The hermit sits alone.

              These beauteous forms,
Through a long absence, have not been
to me
25 As is a landscape to a blind man's eye:
But oft, in lonely rooms, and 'mid the din
Of towns and cities, I have owed to them,
In hours of weariness, sensations sweet,
Felt in the blood, and felt along the heart;
And passing even into my purer mind,
30 With tranquil restoration:—feelings too
Of unremembered pleasure: such, perhaps,
As have no slight or trivial influence

On that best portion of a good man's life,
His little, nameless, unremembered acts
35 Of kindness and of love. Nor less, I trust,
To them I may have owed another gift,
Of aspect more sublime; that blessed mood,
In which the burthen of the mystery,
In which the heavy and the weary weight
40 Of all this unintelligible world,
Is lightened:—that serene and blessed
mood,
In which the affections gently lead us on,—
Until, the breath of this corporeal frame
And even the motion of our human blood
45 Almost suspended, we are laid asleep
In body, and become a living soul:
While with an eye made quiet by the power
Of harmony, and the deep power of joy,
We see into the life of things.
                                If this
50 Be but a vain belief, yet, oh! how oft—
In darkness and amid the many shapes
Of joyless daylight; when the fretful
stir
Unprofitable, and the fever of the world,
Have hung upon the beatings of my
heart—
55 How oft, in spirit, have I turned to thee,
O sylvan Wye! thou wanderer thro' the
woods,
How often has my spirit turned to thee!

And now, with gleams of half-extin-
guished thought,
With many recognitions dim and faint,
60 And somewhat of a sad perplexity,
The picture of the mind revives again:
While here I stand, not only with the sense
Of present pleasure, but with pleasing
thoughts
That in this moment there is life and food
65 For future years. And so I dare to hope,
Though changed, no doubt, from what I
was when first
I came among these hills; when like a roe
I bounded o'er the mountains, by the sides
Of the deep rivers, and the lonely streams,
70 Wherever nature led: more like a man
Flying from something that he dreads
than one
Who sought the thing he loved. For
nature then
(The coarser pleasures of my boyish days,
And their glad animal movements all
gone by)
75 To me was all in all.—I cannot paint
What then I was. The sounding cataract
Haunted me like a passion: the tall rock,
The mountain, and the deep and gloomy
wood,

Their colors and their forms, were then
 to me
30 An appetite; a feeling and a love,
That had no need of a remoter charm,
By thought supplied, nor any interest
Unborrowed from the eye.—That time is
 past,
And all its aching joys are now no more,
85 And all its dizzy raptures. Not for this
Faint I, nor mourn nor murmur; other
 gifts
Have followed; for such loss, I would
 believe,
Abundant recompense. For I have learned
To look on nature, not as in the hour
90 Of thoughtless youth; but hearing often-
 times
The still, sad music of humanity,
Nor harsh nor grating, though of ample
 power
To chasten and subdue. And I have felt
A presence that disturbs me with the joy
95 Of elevated thoughts; a sense sublime
Of something far more deeply interfused,
Whose dwelling is the light of setting suns,
And the round ocean and the living air,
And the blue sky, and in the mind of man:
100 A motion and a spirit, that impels
All thinking things, all objects of all
 thought,
And rolls through all things. Therefore
 am I still
A lover of the meadows and the woods,
And mountains; and of all that we behold
105 From this green earth; of all the mighty
 world
Of eye, and ear,—both what they half
 create,
And what perceive; well pleased to rec-
 ognize
In nature and the language of the sense
The anchor of my purest thoughts, the
 nurse,
110 The guide, the guardian of my heart,
 and soul
Of all my moral being.
     Nor perchance,
If I were not thus taught, should I the more
Suffer my genial spirits to decay:
For thou art with me here upon the banks
115 Of this fair river; thou my dearest friend,
My dear, dear friend; and in thy voice
 I catch
The language of my former heart, and read
My former pleasures in the shooting lights
Of thy wild eyes. Oh! yet a little while
120 May I behold in thee what I was once,
My dear, dear sister! and this prayer
 I make,

Knowing that Nature never did betray
The heart that loved her; 'tis her privilege,
Through all the years of this our life,
 to lead
125 From joy to joy: for she can so inform
The mind that is within us, so impress
With quietness and beauty, and so feed
With lofty thoughts, that neither evil
 tongues,
Rash judgments, nor the sneers of selfish
 men,
130 Nor greetings where no kindness is, nor all
The dreary intercourse of daily life,
Shall e'er prevail against us, or disturb
Our cheerful faith, that all which we
 behold
Is full of blessings. Therefore let the moon
135 Shine on thee in thy solitary walk;
And let the misty mountain-winds be free
To blow against thee: and, in after years,
When these wild ecstasies shall be matured
Into a sober pleasure; when thy mind
140 Shall be a mansion for all lovely forms,
Thy memory be as a dwelling-place
For all sweet sounds and harmonies;
 oh! then,
If solitude, or fear, or pain, or grief,
Should be thy portion, with what heal-
 ing thoughts
145 Of tender joy wilt thou remember me,
And these my exhortations! Nor, per-
 chance—
If I should be where I no more can hear
Thy voice, nor catch from thy wild eyes
 these gleams
Of past existence—wilt thou then forget
150 That on the banks of this delightful stream
We stood together; and that I, so long
A worshipper of Nature, hither came
Unwearied in that service: rather say
With warmer love—oh! with far deeper
 zeal
155 Of holier love. Nor wilt thou then forget
That after many wanderings, many years
Of absence, these steep woods and lofty
 cliffs,
And this green pastoral landscape, were
 to me
More dear, both for themselves and for
 thy sake!

THE OLD CUMBERLAND BEGGAR
1798   1800

I saw an aged beggar in my walk;
And he was seated, by the highway side,
On a low structure of rude masonry
Built at the foot of a huge hill, that they
5 Who lead their horses down the steep
 rough road

May thence remount at ease. The aged man
Had placed his staff across the broad smooth stone
That overlays the pile; and, from a bag
All white with flour, the dole of village dames,
10 He drew his scraps and fragments, one by one;
And scanned them with a fixed and serious look
Of idle computation. In the sun,
Upon the second step of that small pile,
Surrounded by those wild unpeopled hills,
15 He sat, and ate his food in solitude:
And ever scattered from his palsied hand,
That, still attempting to prevent the waste,
Was baffled still, the crumbs in little showers
Fell on the ground; and the small mountain birds,
20 Not venturing yet to peck their destined meal,
Approached within the length of half his staff.

Him from my childhood have I known; and then
He was so old, he seems not older now;
He travels on, a solitary man,
25 So helpless in appearance, that for him
The sauntering horseman throws not with a slack
And careless hand his alms upon the ground,
But stops,—that he may safely lodge the coin
Within the old man's hat; nor quits him so,
30 But still, when he has given his horse the rein,
Watches the aged beggar with a look
Sidelong, and half-reverted. She who tends
The toll-gate, when in summer at her door
She turns her wheel, if on the road she sees
35 The aged beggar coming, quits her work,
And lifts the latch for him that he may pass.
The post-boy, when his rattling wheels o'ertake
The aged beggar in the woody lane,
Shouts to him from behind; and, if thus warned
40 The old man does not change his course, the boy
Turns with less noisy wheels to the roadside,
And passes gently by, without a curse
Upon his lips or anger at his heart.

He travels on, a solitary man;
45 His age has no companion. On the ground
His eyes are turned, and, as he moves along,
They move along the ground; and, evermore,
Instead of common and habitual sight
Of fields with rural works, of hill and dale,
50 And the blue sky, one little span of earth
Is all his prospect. Thus, from day to day,
Bow-bent, his eyes forever on the ground,
He plies his weary journey; seeing still,
And seldom knowing that he sees, some straw,
55 Some scattered leaf, or marks which, in one track,
The nails of cart or chariot-wheel have left
Impressed on the white road,—in the same line,
At distance still the same. Poor traveller!
His staff trails with him; scarcely do his feet
60 Disturb the summer dust; he is so still
In look and motion, that the cottage curs,
Ere he has passed the door, will turn away,
Weary of barking at him. Boys and girls,
The vacant and the busy, maids and youths,
65 And urchins newly breeched—all pass him by:
Him even the slow-paced wagon leaves behind.

But deem not this man useless.—Statesmen! ye
Who are so restless in your wisdom, ye
Who have a broom still ready in your hands
70 To rid the world of nuisances; ye proud,
Heart-swoln, while in your pride ye contemplate
Your talents, power, or wisdom, deem him not
A burthen of the earth! 'Tis Nature's law
That none, the meanest of created things,
75 Of forms created the most vile and brute,
The dullest or most noxious, should exist
Divorced from good—a spirit and pulse of good,
A life and soul, to every mode of being
Inseparably linked. Then be assured
80 That least of all can aught—that ever owned
The heaven-regarding eye and front sublime
Which man is born to—sink, howe'er depressed,
So low as to be scorned without a sin;
Without offence to God cast out of view;

85 Like the dry remnant of a garden flower
Whose seeds are shed, or as an implement
Worn out and worthless. While from
    door to door,
This old man creeps, the villagers in him
Behold a record which together binds
90 Past deeds and offices of charity,
Else unremembered, and so keeps alive
The kindly mood in hearts which lapse
    of years,
And that half-wisdom half-experience
    gives,
Make slow to feel, and by sure steps resign
95 To selfishness and cold oblivious cares.
Among the farms and solitary huts,
Hamlets and thinly-scattered villages,
Where'er the aged beggar takes his rounds,
The mild necessity of use compels
100 To acts of love; and habit does the work
Of reason; yet prepares that after-joy
Which reason cherishes. And thus the soul,
By that sweet taste of pleasure unpursued,
Doth find herself insensibly disposed
105 To virtue and true goodness.
                    Some there are,
By their good works exalted, lofty minds,
And meditative, authors of delight
And happiness, which to the end of time
Will live, and spread, and kindle: even
    such minds
110 In childhood, from this solitary being,
Or from like wanderer haply have received
(A thing more precious far than all that
    books
Or the solicitudes of love can do!)
That first mild touch of sympathy and
    thought,
115 In which they found their kindred with
    a world
Where want and sorrow were. The easy
    man
Who sits at his own door,—and, like the
    pear
That overhangs his head from the green
    wall,
Feeds in the sunshine; the robust and
    young,
120 The prosperous and unthinking, they
    who live
Sheltered, and flourish in a little grove
Of their own kindred;—all behold in him
A silent monitor, which on their minds
Must needs impress a transitory thought
125 Of self-congratulation, to the heart
Of each recalling his peculiar boons,
His charters and exemptions; and, per-
    chance,
Though he to no one give the fortitude
And circumspection needful to preserve

130 His present blessings, and to husband up
The respite of the season, he, at least,
And 'tis no vulgar service, makes them felt.

        Yet further.—Many, I believe, there are
Who live a life of virtuous decency,
135 Men who can hear the Decalogue and feel
No self-reproach; who of the moral law
Established in the land where they abide
Are strict observers; and not negligent
In acts of love to those with whom they
    dwell,
140 Their kindred, and the children of their
    blood.
Praise be to such, and to their slumbers
    peace!
—But of the poor man ask, the abject
    poor;
Go, and demand of him, if there be here
In this cold abstinence from evil deeds,
145 And these inevitable charities,
Wherewith to satisfy the human soul?
No—man is dear to man; the poorest poor
Long for some moments in a weary life
When they can know and feel that they
    have been,
150 Themselves, the fathers and the dealers-out
Of some small blessings; have been kind
    to such
As needed kindness, for this single cause,
That we have all of us one human heart.
—Such pleasure is to one kind being
    known,
155 My neighbor, when with punctual care,
    each week,
Duly as Friday comes, though pressed
    herself
By her own wants, she from her store of
    meal
Takes one unsparing handful for the scrip
Of this old mendicant, and, from her door
160 Returning with exhilarated heart,
Sits by her fire, and builds her hope in
    heaven.

    Then let him pass, a blessing on his head!
And while in that vast solitude to which
The tide of things has borne him, he
    appears
165 To breathe and live but for himself alone,
Unblamed, uninjured, let him bear about
The good which the benignant law of
    Heaven
Has hung around him: and, while life
    is his,
Still let him prompt the unlettered villagers
170 To tender offices and pensive thoughts.
—Then let him pass, a blessing on his head!
And, long as he can wander, let him breathe

The freshness of the valleys; let his blood
Struggle with frosty air and winter snows;
175 And let the chartered[1] wind that sweeps
the heath
Beat his gray locks against his withered
face.
Reverence the hope whose vital anxiousness
Gives the last human interest to his heart.
May never House, misnamed of Industry,[2]
180 Make him a captive!—for that pent-up
din,
Those life-consuming sounds that clog
the air,
Be his the natural silence of old age!
Let him be free of mountain solitudes;
And have around him, whether heard
or not,
185 The pleasant melody of woodland birds.
Few are his pleasures: if his eyes have now
Been doomed so long to settle upon earth
That not without some effort they behold
The countenance of the horizontal sun,
190 Rising or setting, let the light at least
Find a free entrance to their languid orbs,
And let him, where and when he will,
sit down
Beneath the trees, or on a grassy bank
Of highway side, and with the little birds
195 Share his chance-gathered meal; and,
finally,
As in the eye of Nature he has lived,
So in the eye of Nature let him die!

NUTTING
1799   1800

It seems a day
(I speak of one from many singled out)
One of those heavenly days that cannot
die;
When, in the eagerness of boyish hope,
5 I left our cottage threshold, sallying forth
With a huge wallet o'er my shoulders
slung,
A nutting crook in hand; and turned my
steps
Tow'rd some far-distant wood, a figure
quaint,
Tricked out in proud disguise of cast-off
weeds[3]
10 Which for that service had been hus-
banded,
By exhortation of my frugal dame—
Motley accoutrement, of power to smile
At thorns, and brakes, and brambles,—
and in truth
More ragged than need was! O'er pathless rocks,

15 Through beds of matted fern, and tangled
thickets,
Forcing my way, I came to one dear nook
Unvisited, where not a broken bough
Drooped with its withered leaves, un-
gracious sign
Of devastation; but the hazels rose
20 Tall and erect, with tempting clusters
hung,
A virgin scene!—A little while I stood,
Breathing with such suppression of the
heart
As joy delights in; and with wise restraint
Voluptuous, fearless of a rival, eyed
25 The banquet;—or beneath the trees I sate
Among the flowers, and with the flowers
I played;
A temper known to those who, after long
And weary expectation, have been blest
With sudden happiness beyond all hope.
30 Perhaps it was a bower beneath whose
leaves
The violets of five seasons reappear
And fade, unseen by any human eye;
Where fairy water-breaks[1] do murmur on
Forever; and I saw the sparkling foam,
35 And—with my cheek on one of those
green stones
That, fleeced with moss, under the shady
trees,
Lay round me, scattered like a flock of
sheep—
I heard the murmur and the murmuring
sound,
In that sweet mood when pleasure loves
to pay
40 Tribute to ease; and, of its joy secure,
The heart luxuriates with indifferent
things,
Wasting its kindliness on stocks and stones,
And on the vacant air. Then up I rose,
And dragged to earth both branch and
bough, with crash
45 And merciless ravage: and the shady nook
Of hazels, and the green and mossy bower,
Deformed and sullied, patiently gave up
Their quiet being: and unless I now
Confound my present feelings with the
past,
50 Ere from the mutilated bower I turned
Exulting, rich beyond the wealth of kings,
I felt a sense of pain when I beheld
The silent trees, and saw the intruding
sky.—
Then, dearest maiden, move along these
shades
55 In gentleness of heart; with gentle hand
Touch—for there is a spirit in the woods.

---

[1] privileged   [3] garments
[2] The poorhouse.
[1] ripples

STRANGE FITS OF PASSION HAVE I KNOWN
1799   1800

Strange fits of passion have I known:
And I will dare to tell,
But in the lover's ear alone,
What once to me befell.

5 When she I loved looked every day
Fresh as a rose in June,
I to her cottage bent my way,
Beneath an evening moon.

Upon the moon I fixed my eye,
10 All over the wide lea;
With quickening pace my horse drew nigh
Those paths so dear to me.

And now we reached the orchard-plot;
And, as we climbed the hill,
15 The sinking moon to Lucy's cot
Came near, and nearer still.

In one of those sweet dreams I slept,
Kind Nature's gentlest boon!
And all the while my eyes I kept
20 On the descending moon.

My horse moved on; hoof after hoof
He raised, and never stopped:
When down behind the cottage roof,
At once, the bright moon dropped.

25 What fond and wayward thoughts will slide
Into a lover's head!
"O mercy!" to myself I cried,
"If Lucy should be dead!"

SHE DWELT AMONG THE UNTRODDEN WAYS
1799   1800

She dwelt among the untrodden ways
Beside the springs of Dove,
A maid whom there were none to praise
And very few to love:

5 A violet by a mossy stone
Half hidden from the eye!
—Fair as a star, when only one
Is shining in the sky.

She lived unknown, and few could know
10 When Lucy ceased to be;
But she is in her grave, and, oh,
The difference to me!

I TRAVELLED AMONG UNKNOWN MEN
1799   1807

I travelled among unknown men,
In lands beyond the sea;
Nor, England! did I know till then
What love I bore to thee.

5 'Tis past, that melancholy dream!
Nor will I quit thy shore
A second time; for still I seem
To love thee more and more.

Among thy mountains did I feel
10 The joy of my desire;
And she I cherished turned her wheel
Beside an English fire.

Thy mornings showed, thy nights concealed,
The bowers where Lucy played;
15 And thine too is the last green field
That Lucy's eyes surveyed.

THREE YEARS SHE GREW IN SUN AND SHOWER
1799   1800

Three years she grew in sun and shower,
Then Nature said, "A lovelier flower
On earth was never sown;
This child I to myself will take;
5 She shall be mine, and I will make
A lady of my own.

"Myself will to my darling be
Both law and impulse: and with me
The girl, in rock and plain,
10 In earth and heaven, in glade and bower,
Shall feel an overseeing power
To kindle or restrain.

"She shall be sportive as the fawn
That wild with glee across the lawn
15 Or up the mountain springs;
And hers shall be the breathing balm,
And hers the silence and the calm
Of mute insensate things.

"The floating clouds their state shall lend
20 To her; for her the willow bend;
Nor shall she fail to see
Even in the motions of the storm
Grace that shall mould the maiden's form
By silent sympathy.

25 "The stars of midnight shall be dear
To her; and she shall lean her ear
In many a secret place
Where rivulets dance their wayward round,
And beauty born of murmuring sound
30 Shall pass into her face.

"And vital feelings of delight
Shall rear her form to stately height,
Her virgin bosom swell;
Such thoughts to Lucy I will give
35 While she and I together live
Here in this happy dell.''

Thus Nature spake—The work was done—
How soon my Lucy's race was run!
She died, and left to me
40 This heath, this calm, and quiet scene;
The memory of what has been,
And never more will be.

A SLUMBER DID MY SPIRIT SEAL
1799   1800

A slumber did my spirit seal;
I had no human fears:
She seemed a thing that could not feel
The touch of earthly years.

5 No motion has she now, no force;
She neither hears nor sees;
Rolled round in earth's diurnal course,
With rocks, and stones, and trees.

A POET'S EPITAPH
1799   1800

Art thou a statist in the van
Of public conflicts trained and bred?
—First learn to love one living man;
Then may'st thou think upon the dead.

5 A lawyer art thou?—draw not nigh!
Go, carry to some fitter place
The keenness of that practiced eye,
The hardness of that sallow face.

Art thou a man of purple cheer?
10 A rosy man, right plump to see?
Approach; yet, doctor,[1] not too near,
This grave no cushion is for thee.

Or art thou one of gallant pride,
A soldier and no man of chaff?
15 Welcome!—but lay thy sword aside,
And lean upon a peasant's staff.

Physician art thou?—one, all eyes,
Philosopher!—a fingering slave,
One that would peep and botanize
20 Upon his mother's grave?

Wrapt closely in thy sensual fleece,
O turn aside,—and take, I pray,
That he below may rest in peace,
Thy ever-dwindling soul, away!

[1] A divine.

25 A moralist[1] perchance appears;
Led, Heaven knows how! to this poor sod
And he has neither eyes nor ears;
Himself his world, and his own God;

One to whose smooth-rubbed soul can cling
30 Nor form, nor feeling, great or small;
A reasoning, self-sufficing thing,
An intellectual all-in-all!

Shut close the door; press down the latch;
Sleep in thy intellectual crust;
35 Nor lose ten tickings of thy watch
Near this unprofitable dust.

But who is he, with modest looks,
And clad in homely russet brown?
He murmurs near the running brooks
40 A music sweeter than their own.

He is retired as noontide dew,
Or fountain in a noon-day grove;
And you must love him, ere to you
He will seem worthy of your love.

45 The outward shows of sky and earth,
Of hill and valley, he has viewed;
And impulses of deeper birth
Have come to him in solitude.

In common things that round us lie
50 Some random truths he can impart,—
The harvest of a quiet eye
That broods and sleeps on his own heart.

But he is weak; both man and boy,
Hath been an idler in the land;
55 Contented if he might enjoy
The things which others understand.

—Come hither in thy hour of strength;
Come, weak as is a breaking wave!
Here stretch thy body at full length;
60 Or build thy house upon this grave.

MATTHEW
1799   1800

If Nature, for a favorite child,
In thee hath tempered so her clay,
That every hour thy heart runs wild,
Yet never once doth go astray,

5 Read o'er these lines; and then review
This tablet, that thus humbly rears
In such diversity of hue
Its history of two hundred years.

—When through this little wreck of fame,
10 Cipher and syllable! thine eye

[1] One who teaches moral duties.

Has travelled down to Matthew's name,
Pause with no common sympathy.

And if a sleeping tear should wake,
Then be it neither checked nor stayed:
15 For Matthew a request I make
Which for himself he had not made.

Poor Matthew, all his frolics o'er,
Is silent as a standing pool;
Far from the chimney's merry roar,
20 And murmur of the village school.

The sighs which Matthew heaved were sighs
Of one tired out with fun and madness;
The tears which came to Matthew's eyes
Were tears of light, the dew of gladness.

25 Yet sometimes, when the secret cup
Of still and serious thought went round,
It seemed as if he drank it up—
He felt with spirit so profound.

—Thou soul of God's best earthly mould!
30 Thou happy Soul! and can it be
That these two words of glittering gold
Are all that must remain of thee?

THE TWO APRIL MORNINGS
1799   1800

We walked along, while bright and red
Uprose the morning sun;
And Matthew stopped, he looked, and said,
"The will of God be done!"

5 A village schoolmaster was he,
With hair of glittering gray;
As blithe a man as you could see
On a spring holiday.

And on that morning, through the grass,
10 And by the steaming rills,
We travelled merrily, to pass
A day among the hills.

"Our work," said I, "was well begun,
Then from thy breast what thought,
15 Beneath so beautiful a sun,
So sad a sigh has brought?"

A second time did Matthew stop;
And fixing still his eye
Upon the eastern mountain-top,
20 To me he made reply:

"Yon cloud with that long purple cleft
Brings fresh into my mind
A day like this which I have left
Full thirty years behind.

25 "And just above yon slope of corn
Such colors, and no other,
Were in the sky, that April morn,
Of this the very brother.

"With rod and line I sued[1] the sport
30 Which that sweet season gave,
And, to the churchyard come, stopped short,
Beside my daughter's grave.

"Nine summers had she scarcely seen,
The pride of all the vale;
35 And then she sang;—she would have been
A very nightingale.

"Six feet in earth my Emma lay;
And yet I loved her more,
For so it seemed, than till that day
40 I e'er had loved before.

"And, turning from her grave, I met,
Beside the churchyard yew,
A blooming girl, whose hair was wet
With points of morning dew.

45 "A basket on her head she bare;
Her brow was smooth and white:
To see a child so very fair,
It was a pure delight!

"No fountain from its rocky cave
50 E'er tripped with foot so free;
She seemed as happy as a wave
That dances on the sea.

"There came from me a sigh of pain
Which I could ill confine;
55 I looked at her, and looked again:
And did not wish her mine!"

Matthew is in his grave, yet now,
Methinks, I see him stand,
As at that moment, with a bough
60 Of wilding in his hand.

THE FOUNTAIN

A CONVERSATION
1799   1800

We talked with open heart, and tongue
Affectionate and true,
A pair of friends, though I was young,
And Matthew seventy-two.

5 We lay beneath a spreading oak,
Beside a mossy seat;
And from the turf a fountain broke,
And gurgled at our feet.
[1] pursued

"Now, Matthew!" said I, "let us match
10 This water's pleasant tune
With some old border-song, or catch
That suits a summer's noon;

"Or of the church-clock and the chimes
Sing here beneath the shade,
15 That half-mad thing of witty rhymes
Which you last April made!"

In silence Matthew lay, and eyed
The spring beneath the tree;
And thus the dear old man replied,
20 The gray-haired man of glee:

"No check, no stay, this streamlet fears;
How merrily it goes!
'Twill murmur on a thousand years,
And flow as now it flows.

25 "And here, on this delightful day,
I cannot choose but think
How oft, a vigorous man, I lay
Beside this fountain's brink.

"My eyes are dim with childish tears,
30 My heart is idly stirred,
For the same sound is in my ears
Which in those days I heard.

"Thus fares it still in our decay:
And yet the wiser mind
35 Mourns less for what age takes away
Than what it leaves behind.

"The blackbird amid leafy trees,
The lark above the hill,
Let loose their carols when they please,
40 Are quiet when they will.

"With Nature never do *they* wage
A foolish strife; they see
A happy youth, and their old age
Is beautiful and free:

45 "But we are pressed by heavy laws;
And often, glad no more,
We wear a face of joy, because
We have been glad of yore.

"If there be one who need bemoan
50 His kindred laid in earth,
The household hearts that were his own;
It is the man of mirth.

"My days, my friend, are almost gone,
My life has been approved,
55 And many love me! but by none
Am I enough beloved."

"Now both himself and me he wrongs,
The man who thus complains!
I live and sing my idle songs
60 Upon these happy plains;

"And, Matthew, for thy children dead
I'll be a son to thee!"
At this he grasped my hand, and said,
"Alas! that cannot be."

65 We rose up from the fountain-side;
And down the smooth descent
Of the green sheep-track did we glide;
And through the wood we went;

And, ere we came to Leonard's rock,
70 He sang those witty rhymes
About the crazy old church-clock,
And the bewildered chimes.

LUCY GRAY

OR, SOLITUDE
1799   1800

Oft I had heard of Lucy Gray:
And, when I crossed the wild,
I chanced to see at break of day
The solitary child.

5 No mate, no comrade Lucy knew;
She dwelt on a wide moor,
—The sweetest thing that ever grew
Beside a human door!

You yet may spy the fawn at play,
10 The hare upon the green;
But the sweet face of Lucy Gray
Will never more be seen.

"Tonight will be a stormy night—
You to the town must go;
15 And take a lantern, child, to light
Your mother through the snow."

"That, father! will I gladly do:
'Tis scarcely afternoon—
The minster-clock has just struck two,
20 And yonder is the moon!"

At this the father raised his hook,
And snapped a faggot-band;
He plied his work;—and Lucy took
The lantern in her hand.

25 Not blither is the mountain roe:
With many a wanton stroke
Her feet disperse the powdery snow,
That rises up like smoke.

The storm came on before its time:
30 She wandered up and down;
And many a hill did Lucy climb:
But never reached the town.

The wretched parents all that night
Went shouting far and wide;
35 But there was neither sound nor sight
To serve them for a guide.

At daybreak on a hill they stood
That overlooked the moor;
And thence they saw the bridge of wood,
40 A furlong from their door.

They wept—and, turning homeward, cried,
"In heaven we all shall meet;"
—When in the snow the mother spied
The print of Lucy's feet.

45 Then downwards from the steep hill's edge
They tracked the footmarks small;
And through the broken hawthorn hedge,
And by the long stone wall;

And then an open field they crossed:
50 The marks were still the same;
They tracked them on, nor ever lost;
And to the bridge they came.

They followed from the snowy bank
Those footmarks, one by one,
55 Into the middle of the plank;
And further there were none!

—Yet some maintain that to this day
She is a living child;
That you may see sweet Lucy Gray
60 Upon the lonesome wild.

O'er rough and smooth she trips along,
And never looks behind;
And sings a solitary song
That whistles in the wind.

THE PRELUDE
1795–1805   1850

From BOOK I. INTRODUCTION—CHILDHOOD
AND SCHOOL-TIME

Fair seed-time had my soul, and I grew up
Fostered alike by beauty and by fear:
Much favored in my birthplace, and no less
In that belovèd Vale[1] to which erelong
305 We were transplanted—there were we let
loose
For sports of wider range. Ere I had told

Ten birthdays, when among the mountain
slopes
Frost, and the breath of frosty wind, had
snapped
The last autumnal crocus, 'twas my joy
310 With store of springes[1] o'er my shoulder
hung
To range the open heights where wood-
cocks run
Among the smooth green turf. Through
half the night,
Scudding away from snare to snare, I plied
That anxious visitation;—moon and stars
315 Were shining o'er my head. I was alone,
And seemed to be a trouble to the peace
That dwelt among them. Sometimes it
befell
In these night wanderings, that a strong
desire
O'erpowered my better reason, and the bird
320 Which was the captive of another's toil
Became my prey; and when the deed was
done
I heard among the solitary hills
Low breathings coming after me, and
sounds
Of undistinguishable motion, steps
325 Almost as silent as the turf they trod.

Nor less when spring had warmed the
cultured Vale,[2]
Moved we as plunderers where the mother-
bird
Had in high places built her lodge; though
mean
Our object and inglorious, yet the end
330 Was not ignoble. Oh! when I have hung
Above the raven's nest, by knots of grass
And half-inch fissures in the slippery rock
But ill-sustained, and almost (so it seemed)
Suspended by the blast that blew amain,
335 Shouldering the naked crag, oh, at that time
While on the perilous ridge I hung alone,
With what strange utterance did the loud
dry wind
Blow through my ear! the sky seemed not
a sky
Of earth—and with what motion moved
the clouds!

340 Dust as we are, the immortal spirit grows
Like harmony in music; there is a dark
Inscrutable workmanship that reconciles
Discordant elements, makes them cling to-
gether
In one society. How strange that all
345 The terrors, pains, and early miseries,

---

[1] Esthwaite Lancashire, in which the village of
Hawkshead, where Wordsworth attended
school, was situated.

[1] snares; traps
[2] Yewdale, a vale near Hawkshead.

Regrets, vexations, lassitudes interfused
Within my mind, should e'er have borne
    a part,
And that a needful part, in making up
The calm existence that is mine when I
350 Am worthy of myself! Praise to the end!
Thanks to the means which Nature deigned
    to employ;
Whether her fearless visitings, or those
That came with soft alarm, like hurtless
    light
Opening the peaceful clouds; or she may
    use
355 Severer interventions, ministry
More palpable, as best might suit her aim.

One summer evening (led by her) I found
A little boat tied to a willow tree
Within a rocky cove, its usual home.
360 Straight I unloosed her chain, and stepping
    in
Pushed from the shore. It was an act
    of stealth
And troubled pleasure, nor without the
    voice
Of mountain echoes did my boat move on;
Leaving behind her still, on either side,
365 Small circles glittering idly in the moon,
Until they melted all into one track
Of sparkling light. But now, like one
    who rows,
Proud of his skill, to reach a chosen point
With an unswerving line, I fixed my view
370 Upon the summit of a craggy ridge,
The horizon's utmost boundary; far above
Was nothing but the stars and the gray sky.
 She was an elfin pinnace; lustily
I dipped my oars into the silent lake,
375 And, as I rose upon the stroke, my boat
Went heaving through the water like a
    swan;
When, from behind that craggy steep till
    then
The horizon's bound, a huge peak, black
    and huge,
As if with voluntary power instinct
380 Upreared its head. I struck and struck
    again,
And growing still in stature the grim shape
Towered up between me and the stars,
    and still,
For so it seemed, with purpose of its own
And measured motion like a living thing,
385 Strode after me. With trembling oars
    I turned,
And through the silent water stole my way
Back to the covert of the willow tree;
There in her mooring-place I left my
    bark,—

And through the meadows homeward went,
    in grave
390 And serious mood; but after I had seen
That spectacle, for many days, my brain
Worked with a dim and undetermined sense
Of unknown modes of being; o'er my
    thoughts
There hung a darkness, call it solitude
395 Or blank desertion. No familiar shapes
Remained, no pleasant images of trees,
Of sea or sky, no colors of green fields;
But huge and mighty forms, that do not live
Like living men, moved slowly through the
    mind
400 By day, and were a trouble to my dreams.

Wisdom and Spirit of the universe!
Thou Soul that art the eternity of thought,
That givest to forms and images a breath
And everlasting motion, not in vain
405 By day or star-light thus from my first
    dawn
Of childhood didst thou intertwine for me
The passions that build up our human soul;
Not with the mean and vulgar works of
    man,
But with high objects, with enduring
    things—
410 With life and nature—purifying thus
The elements of feeling and of thought,
And sanctifying, by such discipline,
Both pain and fear, until we recognize
A grandeur in the beatings of the heart.
415 Nor was this fellowship vouchsafed to me
With stinted kindness. In November days,
When vapors rolling down the valley made
A lonely scene more lonesome, among
    woods,
At noon and 'mid the calm of summer
    nights,
420 When, by the margin of the trembling lake,
Beneath the gloomy hills homeward I went
In solitude, such intercourse was mine;
Mine was it in the fields both day and night,
And by the waters, all the summer long.

425 And in the frosty season, when the sun
Was set, and visible for many a mile
The cottage windows blazed through twi-
    light gloom,
I heeded not their summons: happy time
It was indeed for all of us—for me
430 It was a time of rapture! Clear and loud
The village clock tolled six,—I wheeled
    about,
Proud and exulting like an untired horse
That cares not for his home. All shod
    with steel,
We hissed along the polished ice in games

435 Confederate, imitative of the chase
And woodland pleasures,—the resounding horn,
The pack loud chiming, and the hunted hare.
So through the darkness and the cold we flew,
And not a voice was idle; with the din
440 Smitten, the precipices rang aloud;
The leafless trees and every icy crag
Tinkled like iron; while far distant hills
Into the tumult sent an alien sound
Of melancholy not unnoticed, while the stars
445 Eastward were sparkling clear, and in the west
The orange sky of evening died away.
Not seldom from the uproar I retired
Into a silent bay, or sportively
Glanced sideway, leaving the tumultuous throng,
450 To cut across the reflex of a star
That fled, and, flying still before me, gleamed
Upon the glassy plain; and oftentimes,
When we had given our bodies to the wind,
And all the shadowy banks on either side
455 Came sweeping through the darkness, spinning still
The rapid line of motion, then at once
Have I, reclining back upon my heels,
Stopped short; yet still the solitary cliffs
Wheeled by me—even as if the earth had rolled
460 With visible motion her diurnal round!
Behind me did they stretch in solemn train,
Feebler and feebler, and I stood and watched
Till all was tranquil as a dreamless sleep.

Ye Presences of Nature in the sky
465 And on the earth! Ye Visions of the hills!
And Souls of lonely places! can I think
A vulgar hope was yours when ye employed
Such ministry, when ye through many a year
Haunting me thus among my boyish sports,
470 On caves and trees, upon the woods and hills,
Impressed upon all forms the characters
Of danger or desire; and thus did make
The surface of the universal earth
With triumph and delight, with hope and fear,
475 Work like a sea?
          Not uselessly employed,
Might I pursue this theme through every change

Of exercise and play, to which the year
Did summon us in his delightful round.

. . . .

Nor, sedulous as I have been to trace
545 How Nature by extrinsic passion first
Peopled the mind with forms sublime or fair,
And made me love them, may I here omit
How other pleasures have been mine, and joys
Of subtler origin; how I have felt,
550 Not seldom even in that tempestuous time,
Those hallowed and pure motions of the sense
Which seem, in their simplicity, to own
An intellectual charm; that calm delight
Which, if I err not, surely must belong
555 To those first-born affinities that fit
Our new existence to existing things,[1]
And, in our dawn of being, constitute
The bond of union between life and joy.

Yes, I remember when the changeful earth,
560 And twice five summers on my mind had stamped
The faces of the moving year, even then
I held unconscious intercourse with beauty
Old as creation, drinking in a pure
Organic pleasure from the silver wreaths
565 Of curling mist, or from the level plain
Of waters colored by impending clouds.

The sands of Westmoreland, the creeks and bays
Of Cumbria's rocky limits, they can tell
How, when the Sea threw off his evening shade
570 And to the shepherd's hut on distant hills
Sent welcome notice of the rising moon,
How I have stood, to fancies such as these
A stranger, linking with the spectacle
No conscious memory of a kindred sight,
575 And bringing with me no peculiar sense
Of quietness or peace; yet have I stood,
Even while mine eye hath moved o'er many a league
Of shining water, gathering as it seemed,
Through every hair-breadth in that field of light,
580 New pleasure like a bee among the flowers.

Thus oft amid those fits of vulgar joy
Which, through all seasons, on a child's pursuits
Are prompt attendants, 'mid that giddy bliss
Which, like a tempest, works along the blood

[1] See Ode: Intimations of Immortality (p. 329).

585 And is forgotten; even then I felt
Gleams like the flashing of a shield;—
    the earth
And common face of Nature spake to me
Remdemberable things; sometimes, 'tis true,
By chance collisions and quaint accidents
590 (Like those ill-sorted unions, work sup-
    posed
Of evil-minded fairies), yet not vain
Nor profitless, if haply they impressed
Collateral objects and appearances,
Albeit lifeless then, and doomed to sleep
595 Until maturer seasons called them forth
To impregnate and to elevate the mind.
—And if the vulgar joy by its own weight
Wearied itself out of the memory,
The scenes which were a witness of that joy
600 Remained in their substantial lineaments
Depicted on the brain, and to the eye
Were visible, a daily sight; and thus
By the impressive discipline of fear,
By pleasure and repeated happiness,
605 So frequently repeated, and by force
Of obscure feelings representative
Of things forgotten, these same scenes so
    bright,
So beautiful, so majestic in themselves,
Though yet the day was distant, did become
610 Habitually dear, and all their forms
And changeful colors by invisible links
Were fastened to the affections.

.   .   .   .

From BOOK II. SCHOOL-TIME

265   From early days,
Beginning not long after that first time
In which, a babe, by intercourse of touch
I held mute dialogues with my mother's
    heart,
I have endeavored to display the means
270 Whereby this infant sensibility,
Great birthright of our being, was in me
Augmented and sustained. Yet is a path
More difficult before me; and I fear
That in its broken windings we shall need
275 The chamois' sinews, and the eagle's wing:
For now a trouble came into my mind
From unknown causes. I was left alone
Seeking the visible world, nor knowing why.
The props of my affections were removed,
280 And yet the building stood, as if sustained
By its own spirit! All that I beheld
Was dear, and hence to finer influxes
The mind lay open, to a more exact
And close communion. Many are our joys
285 In youth, but oh! what happiness to live
When every hour brings palpable access
Of knowledge, when all knowledge is de-
    light.

And sorrow is not there! The seasons came,
And every season wheresoe'er I moved
290 Unfolded transitory qualities,
Which, but for this most watchful power
    of love,
Had been neglected; left a register
Of permanent relations, else unknown,
Hence life, and change, and beauty, soli-
    tude
295 More active even than ''best society''—
Society made sweet as solitude
By silent inobtrusive sympathies,
And gentle agitations of the mind
From manifold distinctions, difference
300 Perceived in things, where, to the unwatch-
    ful eye,
No difference is, and hence, from the same
    source,
Sublimer joy! for I would walk alone,
Under the quiet stars, and at that time
Have felt whate'er there is of power in
    sound
305 To breathe an elevated mood, by form
Or image unprofaned; and I would stand,
If the night blackened with a coming storm,
Beneath some rock, listening to notes that
    are
The ghostly language of the ancient earth,
310 Or make their dim abode in distant winds.
Thence did I drink the visionary power;
And deem not profitless those fleeting
    moods
Of shadowy exultation: not for this,
That they are kindred to our purer mind
315 And intellectual life; but that the soul,
Remembering how she felt, but what she
    felt
Remembering not, retains an obscure sense
Of possible sublimity, whereto
With growing faculties she doth aspire,
320 With faculties still growing, feeling still
That whatsoever point they gain, they yet
Have something to pursue.
                    And not alone,
'Mid gloom and tumult, but no less 'mid
    fair
And tranquil scenes, that universal power
325 And fitness in the latent qualities
And essences of things, by which the mind
Is moved with feelings of delight, to me
Came strengthened with a superadded soul,
A virtue not its own.

.   .   .   .

346 How shall I seek the origin? where find
Faith in the marvellous things which then
    I felt?
Oft in these moments such a holy calm
Would overspread my soul, that bodily eyes
350 Were utterly forgotten, and what I saw

Appeared like something in myself, a dream,
A prospect in the mind.
             'Twere long to tell
What spring and autumn, what the winter snows,
And what the summer shade, what day and night,
355 Evening and morning, sleep and waking, thought
From sources inexhaustible, poured forth
To feed the spirit of religious love
In which I walked with Nature. But let this
Be not forgotten, that I still retained
360 My first creative sensibility;
That by the regular action of the world
My soul was unsubdued. A plastic power
Abode with me; a forming hand, at times
Rebellious, acting in a devious mood;
365 A local spirit of his own, at war
With general tendency, but, for the most,
Subservient strictly to external things
With which it communed. An auxiliar light
Came from my mind, which on the setting sun
370 Bestowed new splendor; the melodious birds,
The fluttering breezes, fountains that run on
Murmuring so sweetly in themselves, obeyed
A like dominion, and the midnight storm
375 Grew darker in the presence of my eye:
Hence my obeisance, my devotion hence,
And hence my transport.
             Nor should this, perchance,
Pass unrecorded, that I still had loved
The exercise and produce of a toil,
Than analytic industry to me
380 More pleasing, and whose character I deem
Is more poetic as resembling more
Creative agency. The song would speak
Of that interminable building reared
By observation of affinities
385 In objects where no brotherhood exists
To passive minds. My seventeenth year was come;
And, whether from this habit rooted now
So deeply in my mind, or from excess
In the great social principle of life
390 Coercing all things into sympathy,
To unorganic natures were transferred
My own enjoyments; or the power of truth
Coming in revelation, did converse
With things that really are; I, at this time,
395 Saw blessings spread around me like a sea.
Thus while the days flew by, and years passed on,
From Nature and her overflowing soul

I had received so much, that all my thoughts
Were steeped in feeling; I was only then
400 Contented, when with bliss ineffable
I felt the sentiment of Being spread
O'er all that moves and all that seemeth still;
O'er all that, lost beyond the reach of thought
And human knowledge, to the human eye
405 Invisible, yet liveth to the heart;
O'er all that leaps and runs, and shouts and sings,
Or beats the gladsome air; o'er all that glides
Beneath the wave, yea, in the wave itself,
And mighty depth of waters. Wonder not
410 If high the transport, great the joy I felt
Communing in this sort through earth and heaven
With every form of creature, as it looked
Towards the Uncreated with a countenance
Of adoration, with an eye of love.
415 One song they sang, and it was audible,
Most audible, then, when the fleshly ear,
O'ercome by humblest prelude of that strain,
Forgot her functions, and slept undisturbed.

If this be error, and another faith
420 Find easier access to the pious mind,
Yet were I grossly destitute of all
Those human sentiments that make this earth
So dear, if I should fail with grateful voice
To speak of you, ye mountains, and ye lakes
425 And sounding cataracts, ye mists and winds
That dwell among the hills where I was born.
If in my youth I have been pure in heart,
If, mingling with the world, I am content
With my own modest pleasures, and have lived
430 With God and Nature communing, removed
From little enmities and low desires,
The gift is yours; if in these times of fear[1]
This melancholy waste of hopes o'erthrown,
If, 'mid indifference and apathy,
435 And wicked exultation when good men
On every side fall off, we know not how,
To selfishness, disguised in gentle names
Of peace and quiet and domestic love,

[1] During the War of the Second Coalition, 1799-1801, when England feared an invasion by Napoleon. See Coleridge's *Fears in Solitude* (p. 379).

Yet mingled not unwillingly with sneers
440 On visionary minds; if, in this time
Of dereliction and dismay, I yet
Despair not of our nature, but retain
A more than Roman confidence, a faith
That fails not, in all sorrow my support,
445 The blessing of my life; the gift is yours,
Ye winds and sounding cataracts! 'tis yours
Ye mountains! thine, O Nature! Thou
hast fed
My lofty speculations; and in thee,
For this uneasy heart of ours, I find
450 A never-failing principle of joy
And purest passion.

. . . . . .

From Book III. Residence at Cambridge

90 Oft when the dazzling show no longer new
Had ceased to dazzle, ofttimes did I quit
My comrades, leave the crowd, buildings
and groves,
And as I paced alone the level fields
Far from those lovely sights and sounds
sublime
95 With which I had been conversant, the mind
Drooped not; but there into herself re-
turning,
With prompt rebound seemed fresh as
heretofore.
At least I more distinctly recognized
Her native instincts: let me dare to speak
100 A higher language, say that now I felt
What independent solaces were mine,
To mitigate the injurious sway of place
Or circumstance, how far soever changed
In youth, or to be changed in after years.
105 As if awakened, summoned, roused, con-
strained,
I looked for universal things; perused
The common countenance of earth and sky:
Earth, nowhere unembellished by some
trace
Of that first Paradise whence man was
driven;
110 And sky, whose beauty and bounty are
expressed
By the proud name she bears—the name
of Heaven.
I called on both to teach me what they
might;
Or turning the mind in upon herself,
Pored, watched, expected, listened, spread
my thoughts
115 And spread them with a wider creeping;
felt
Incumbencies more awful, visitings
Of the Upholder of the tranquil soul,
That tolerates the indignities of Time,
And, from the centre of Eternity

120 All finite motions overruling, lives
In glory immutable. But peace! enough
Here to record that I was mounting now
To such community with highest truth—
A track pursuing, not untrod before,
125 From strict analogies by thought supplied
Or consciousnesses not to be subdued.
To every natural form, rock, fruit, or
flower,
Even the loose stones that cover the high-
way,
I gave a moral life: I saw them feel,
130 Or linked them to some feeling: the great
mass
Lay bedded in a quickening soul, and all
That I beheld respired with inward mean-
ing.
Add that whate'er of Terror or of Love
Or Beauty, Nature's daily face put on
135 From transitory passion, unto this
I was as sensitive as waters are
To the sky's influence in a kindred mood
Of passion; was obedient as a lute
That waits upon the touches of the wind.
140 Unknown, unthought of, yet I was most
rich—
I had a world about me—'twas my own;
I made it, for it only lived to me,
And to the God who sees into the heart.

. . . . . .

From Book IV. Summer Vacation

'Mid a throng
310 Of maids and youths, old men, and matrons staid,
A medley of all tempers, I had passed
The night in dancing, gaiety, and mirth,
With din of instruments and shuffling
feet,
And glancing forms, and tapers glittering,
315 And unaimed prattle flying up and down;
Spirits upon the stretch, and here and there
Slight shocks of young love-liking inter-
spersed,
Whose transient pleasure mounted to the
head,
And tingled through the veins. Ere we
retired,
320 The cock had crowed, and now the east-
ern sky
Was kindling, not unseen, from humble
copse
And open field, through which the path-
way wound,
And homeward led my steps. Magnificent
The morning rose, in memorable pomp,
325 Glorious as e'er I had beheld—in front,
The sea lay laughing at a distance; near,

The solid mountains shone, bright as the
    clouds,
Grain-tinctured,[1] drenched in empyrean
    light;
And in the meadows and the lower grounds
330 Was all the sweetness of a common dawn—
Dews, vapors, and the melody of birds,
And laborers going forth to till the fields.
Ah! need I say, dear friend! that to the
    brim
My heart was full; I made no vows, but
    vows
335 Were then made for me; bond unknown
    to me
Was given, that I should be, else sinning
    greatly,
A dedicated Spirit. On I walked
In thankful blessedness, which yet survives.

.   .   .   .   .

From BOOK V. BOOKS

These mighty workmen of our later age,
Who, with a broad highway, have over-
    bridged
The froward chaos of futurity,
350 Tamed to their bidding; they who have
    the skill
To manage books, and things, and make
    them act
On infant minds as surely as the sun
Deals with a flower; the keepers of our
    time,
The guides and wardens of our faculties,
355 Sages who in their prescience would control
All accidents, and to the very road
Which they have fashioned would con-
    fine us down,
Like engines; when will their presumption
    learn,
That in the unreasoning progress of the
    world
360 A wiser spirit is at work for us,
A better eye than theirs, most prodigal
Of blessings, and most studious of our
    good,
Even in what seem our most unfruitful
    hours?

There was a Boy: ye knew him well,
    ye cliffs
365 And islands of Winander!—many a time
At evening, when the earliest stars began
To move along the edges of the hills,
Rising or setting, would he stand alone
Beneath the trees or by the glimmering
    lake,
370 And there, with fingers interwoven, both
    hands

Pressed closely palm to palm, and to his
    mouth
Uplifted, he, as through an instrument,
Blew mimic hootings to the silent owls,
That they might answer him; and they
    would shout
375 Across the watery vale, and shout again,
Responsive to his call, with quivering peals,
And long halloos and screams, and echoes
    loud,
Redoubled and redoubled, concourse wild
Of jocund din; and, when a lengthened
    pause
380 Of silence came and baffled his best skill,
Then sometimes, in that silence while he
    hung
Listening, a gentle shock of mild surprise
Has carried far into his heart the voice
Of mountain torrents; or the visible scene
385 Would enter unawares into his mind,
With all its solemn imagery, its rocks,
Its woods, and that uncertain heaven, re-
    ceived
Into the bosom of the steady lake.

This Boy was taken from his mates,
    and died
390 In childhood, ere he was full twelve years
    old.
Fair is the spot, most beautiful the vale
Where he was born;[1] the grassy church-
    yard hangs
Upon a slope above the village school,[2]
And through that churchyard when my
    way has led
395 On summer evenings, I believe that there
A long half hour together I have stood
Mute, looking at the grave in which he lies!
Even now appears before the mind's clear
    eye
That self-same village church; I see her sit
400 (The thronèd Lady whom erewhile we
    hailed)
On her green hill, forgetful of this Boy
Who slumbers at her feet,—forgetful, too,
Of all her silent neighborhood of graves,
And listening only to the gladsome sounds
405 That, from the rural school ascending, play
Beneath her and about her. May she long
Behold a race of young ones like to those
With whom I herded!—(easily, indeed,
We might have fed upon a fatter soil
410 Of arts and letters—but be that for-
    given)—
A race of real children; not too wise,
Too learned, or too good; but wanton,
    fresh,

---

[1] dyed scarlet

[1] Esthwaite.   [2] At Hawkshead

And bandied up and down by love and
hate;
Not unresentful where self-justified;
415 Fierce, moody, patient, venturous, modest,
shy;
Mad at their sports like withered leaves
in winds;
Though doing wrong and suffering, and
full oft
Bending beneath our life's mysterious
weight
Of pain, and doubt, and fear, yet yielding
not
420 In happiness to the happiest upon earth.
Simplicity in habit, truth in speech,
Be these the daily strengtheners of their
minds;
May books and Nature be their early joy!
And knowledge, rightly honored with that
name—
425 Knowledge not purchased by the loss of
power!

. . . .

A gracious spirit o'er this earth pre-
sides,
And o'er the heart of man: invisibly
It comes, to works of unreproved delight,
And tendency benign, directing those
495 Who care not, know not, think not what
they do.
The tales that charm away the wakeful
night
In Araby, romances; legends penned
For solace by dim light of monkish lamps;
Fictions, for ladies of their love, devised
500 By youthful squires; adventures endless,
spun
By the dismantled warrior in old age,
Out of the bowels of those very schemes
In which his youth did first extravagate;[1]
These spread like day, and something in
the shape
505 Of these will live till man shall be no more.
Dumb yearnings, hidden appetites, are
ours,
And *they must* have their food. Our
childhood sits,
Our simple childhood, sits upon a throne
That hath more power than all the ele-
ments.
510 I guess not what this tells of being past,
Nor what it augurs of the life to come;
But so it is, and, in that dubious hour,
That twilight when we first begin to see
This dawning earth, to recognize, expect,
515 And, in the long probation that ensues,
The time of trial, ere we learn to live
In reconcilement with our stinted powers;

[1] wander about

To endure this state of meagre vassalage,
Unwilling to forego, confess, submit
520 Uneasy and unsettled, yoke-fellows
To custom, mettlesome, and not yet tamed
And humbled down;—oh! then we feel,
we feel,
We know where we have friends. Ye
dreamers, then,
Forgers of daring tales! we bless you then,
525 Impostors, drivellers, dotards, as the ape
Philosophy will call you; *then* we feel
With what, and how great might ye are in
league,
Who make our wish, our power, our
thought a deed,
An empire, a possession,—ye whom time
530 And seasons serve; all Faculties to whom
Earth crouches, the elements are potter's
clay,
Space like a heaven filled up with northern
lights,
Here, nowhere, there, and everywhere at
once.

. . . .

From Book VI. Cambridge and the Alps

The poet's soul was with me at that time;
Sweet meditations, the still overflow
Of present happiness, while future years
45 Lacked not anticipations, tender dreams,
No few of which have since been realized;
And some remain, hopes for my future
life.
Four years and thirty, told this very week,
Have I been now a sojourner on earth,
50 By sorrow not unsmitten; yet for me
Life's morning radiance hath not left the
hills,
Her dew is on the flowers. Those were the
days
Which also first emboldened me to trust
With firmness, hitherto but slightly touched
55 By such a daring thought, that I might
leave
Some monument behind me which pure
hearts
Should reverence. The instinctive humble-
ness,
Maintained even by the very name and
thought
Of printed books and authorship, began
60 To melt away; and further, the dread awe
Of mighty names was softened down and
seemed
Approachable, admitting fellowship
Of modest sympathy. Such aspect now,
Though not familiarly, my mind put on,
65 Content to observe, to achieve, and to
enjoy.

All winter long, whenever free to choose,
Did I by night frequent the College groves
And tributary walks; the last, and oft
The only one, who had been lingering there
70 Through hours of silence, till the porter's
    bell,
A punctual follower on the stroke of nine,
Rang with its blunt unceremonious voice,
Inexorable summons! Lofty elms,
Inviting shades of opportune recess,
75 Bestowed composure on a neighborhood
Unpeaceful in itself. A single tree
With sinuous trunk, boughs exquisitely
    wreathed,
Grew there; an ash which Winter for him-
    self
Decked as in pride, and with outlandish
    grace:
80 Up from the ground, and almost to the
    top,
The trunk and every master branch were
    green
With clustering ivy, and the lightsome
    twigs
And outer spray profusely tipped with
    seeds
That hung in yellow tassels, while the air
85 Stirred them, not voiceless. Often have I
    stood
Foot-bound uplooking at this lovely tree
Beneath a frosty moon. The hemisphere
Of magic fiction, verse of mine perchance
May never tread; but scarcely Spenser's
    self
90 Could have more tranquil visions in his
    youth,
Or could more bright appearances create
Of human forms with superhuman powers,
Than I beheld loitering on calm clear nights
Alone, beneath this fairy work of earth.
   .   .   .   .   .

Imagination—here the Power so called
Through sad incompetence of human
    speech,
That awful Power rose from the mind's
    abyss
595 Like an unfathered vapor that enwraps,
At once, some lonely traveller. I was lost;
Halted without an effort to break through;
But to my conscious soul I now can say—
"I recognize thy glory:" in such strength
600 Of usurpation, when the light of sense
Goes out, but with a flash that has revealed
The invisible world, doth greatness make
    abode,
There harbors; whether we be young or old,
Our destiny, our being's heart and home,
605 Is with infinitude, and only there;
With hope it is, hope that can never die,

Effort, and expectation, and desire,
And something evermore about to be.
Under such banners militant, the soul
610 Seeks for no trophies, struggles for no
    spoils
That may attest her prowess, blest in
    thoughts
That are their own perfection and reward,
Strong in herself and in beatitude
That hides her, like the mighty flood of
    Nile
615 Poured from his fount of Abyssinian
    clouds
To fertilize the whole Egyptian plain.

The melancholy slackening that ensued
Upon those tidings by the peasant given
Was soon dislodged. Downwards we hur-
    ried fast,
620 And with the half-shaped road which we
    had missed,
Entered a narrow chasm. The brook and
    road
Were fellow-travellers in this gloomy
    strait,
And with them did we journey several
    hours
At a slow pace. The immeasurable height
625 Of woods decaying, never to be decayed, *paradox*
The stationary blasts of waterfalls,
And in the narrow rent at every turn
Winds thwarting winds, bewildered and
    forlorn,
The torrent shooting from the clear blue
    sky,
630 The rocks that muttered close upon our
    ears,
Black drizzling crags that spake by the
    way-side
As if a voice were in them, the sick sight
And giddy prospect of the raving stream,
The unfettered clouds and region of the
    heavens,
635 Tumult and peace, the darkness and the
    light—
Were all like workings of one mind, the
    features
Of the same face, blossoms upon one tree;
Characters of the great Apocalypse,
The types and symbols of Eternity,
640 Of first, and last, and midst, and without
    end.
   .   .   .   .   .

BOOK VIII. RETROSPECT—LOVE OF NATURE
    LEADING TO LOVE OF MAN

What sounds are those, Helvellyn, that are
    heard
Up to thy summit, through the depth of air
Ascending, as if distance had the power

To make the sounds more audible? What crowd
5 Covers, or sprinkles o'er, yon village green?
Crowd seems it, solitary hill! to thee,
Though but a little family of men,
Shepherds and tillers of the ground—betimes
Assembled with their children and their wives,
10 And here and there a stranger interspersed.
They hold a rustic fair—a festival,
Such as, on this side now, and now on that,
Repeated through his tributary vales,
Helvellyn, in the silence of his rest,
15 Sees annually, if clouds towards either ocean
Blown from their favorite resting-place, or mists
Dissolved, have left him an unshrouded head.
Delightful day it is for all who dwell
In this secluded glen, and eagerly
20 They give it welcome. Long ere heat of noon,
From byre[1] or field the kine were brought; the sheep
Are penned in cotes; the chaffering is begun.
The heifer lows, uneasy at the voice
Of a new master; bleat the flocks aloud.
25 Booths are there none; a stall or two is here;
A lame man or a blind, the one to beg,
The other to make music; hither, too,
From far, with basket, slung upon her arm,
Of hawker's wares — books, pictures, combs, and pins—
30 Some aged woman finds her way again,
Year after year, a punctual visitant!
There also stands a speech-maker by rote,
Pulling the strings of his boxed raree-show;[2]
And in the lapse of many years may come
35 Prouder itinerant, mountebank, or he
Whose wonders in a covered wain lie hid.
But one there is, the loveliest of them all,
Some sweet lass of the valley, looking out
For gains, and who that sees her would not buy?
40 Fruits of her father's orchard are her wares,
And with the ruddy produce she walks round
Among the crowd, half pleased with, half ashamed
Of her new office, blushing restlessly.
The children now are rich, for the old today
45 Are generous as the young; and, if content

With looking on, some ancient wedded pair
Sit in the shade together, while they gaze,
"A cheerful smile unbends the wrinkled brow,
The days departed start again to life,
50 And all the scenes of childhood reappear,
Faint, but more tranquil, like the changing sun
To him who slept at noon and wakes at eve.'"[1]
Thus gaiety and cheerfulness prevail,
Spreading from young to old, from old to young,
55 And no one seems to want his share.—Immense
Is the recess, the circumambient world
Magnificent, by which they are embraced:
They move about upon the soft green turf:
How little they, they and their doings, seem,
60 And all that they can further or obstruct!
Through utter weakness pitiably dear,
As tender infants are: and yet how great!
For all things serve them; them the morning light
Loves, as it glistens on the silent rocks;
65 And them the silent rocks, which now from high
Look down upon them; the reposing clouds;
The wild brooks prattling from invisible haunts;
And old Helvellyn, conscious of the stir
Which animates this day their calm abode.

70 With deep devotion, Nature, did I feel,
In that enormous City's turbulent world
Of men and things, what benefit I owed
To thee, and those domains of rural peace,
Where to the sense of beauty first my heart
75 Was opened; tract more exquisitely fair
Than that famed paradise of ten thousand trees,
Or Gehol's matchless gardens,[2] for delight
Of the Tartarian dynasty composed
(Beyond that mighty wall, not fabulous,
80 China's stupendous mound) by patient toil
Of myriads and boon Nature's lavish help;
There, in a clime from widest empire chosen,
Fulfilling (could enchantment have done more?)
A sumptuous dream of flowery lawns, with domes
85 Of pleasure sprinkled over, shady dells
For eastern monasteries, sunny mounts

---

[1] cow barn   [2] cheap street-show

[1] Joseph Cottle, *Malvern Hills*, 952-56.
[2] Of Jehol, an imperial palace in inner Mongolia.

With temples crested, bridges, gondolas,
Rocks, dens, and groves of foliage taught 130
    to melt
Into each other their obsequious hues,
90 Vanished and vanishing in subtle chase,
Too fine to be pursued; or standing forth
In no discordant opposition, strong
And gorgeous as the colors side by side
Bedded among rich plumes of tropic birds; 135
95 And mountains over all, embracing all;
And all the landscape, endlessly enriched
With waters running, falling, or asleep.

    But lovelier far than this, the paradise
Where I was reared; in Nature's primi-
    tive gifts
100 Favored no less, and more to every sense 140
Delicious, seeing that the sun and sky,
The elements, and seasons as they change,
Do find a worthy fellow-laborer there—
Man free, man working for himself, with
    choice
105 Of time, and place, and object; by his
    wants,
His comforts, native occupations, cares, 145
Cheerfully led to individual ends
Or social, and still followed by a train
Unwooed, unthought-of even—simplicity,
110 And beauty, and inevitable grace.

    Yea, when a glimpse of those imperial
    bowers
Would to a child be transport over-great,
When but a half-hour's roam through 150
    such a place
Would leave behind a dance of images,
115 That shall break in upon his sleep for
    weeks;
Even then the common haunts of the green
    earth,
And ordinary interests of man,
Which they embosom, all without regard
As both may seem, are fastening on the 155
    heart
120 Insensibly, each with the other's help.
For me, when my affections first were led
From kindred, friends, and playmates, to
    partake
Love for the human creature's absolute self,
That noticeable kindliness of heart 160
125 Sprang out of fountains, there abounding
    most,
Where sovereign Nature dictated the tasks
And occupations which her beauty adorned,
And shepherds were the men that pleased 165
    me first;[1]

---

[1] These shepherds lived close to Nature and were
intensely real. They appealed to Wordsworth's imagination infinitely more than the
artificial shepherds in the pastoral literature
of the ancients and of Shakespeare and Spenser.

Not such as Saturn ruled 'mid Latian wilds,
With arts and laws so tempered, that
    their lives
Left, even to us toiling in this late day,
A bright tradition of the golden age;
Not such as, 'mid Arcadian fastnesses
Sequestered, handed down among them-
    selves
Felicity, in Grecian song renowned;[1]
Nor such as—when an adverse fate had
    driven,
From house and home, the courtly band
    whose fortunes
Entered, with Shakspeare's genius, the
    wild woods
Of Arden—amid sunshine or in shade
Culled the best fruits of Time's uncounted
    hours,
Ere Phœbe sighed for the false Gany-
    mede;[2]
Or there where Perdita and Florizel
Together danced, Queen of the feast, and
    King;[3]
Nor such as Spenser fabled.[4] True it is,
That I had heard (what he perhaps had
    seen)
Of maids at sunrise bringing in from far
Their May-bush, and along the street in
    flocks
Parading with a song of taunting rhymes,
Aimed at the laggards slumbering within
    doors;
Had also heard, from those who yet re-
    membered,
Tales of the May-pole dance, and wreaths
    that decked
Porch, doorway, or kirk pillar; and of
    youths,
Each with his maid, before the sun was up,
By annual custom, issuing forth in troops,
To drink the waters of some sainted well,
And hang it round with garlands. Love
    survives;
But, for such purpose, flowers no longer
    grow:
The times, too sage, perhaps too proud,
    have dropped
These lighter graces; and the rural ways
And manners which my childhood looked
    upon
Were the unluxuriant produce of a life
Intent on little but substantial needs,
Yet rich in beauty, beauty that was felt.
But images of danger and distress,
Man suffering among awful Powers and
    Forms;

---

[1] Polybius, *Historiæ*, 4, 20-21.
[2] *As You Like It*, III and IV.
[3] *The Winter's Tale*, IV, 4.
[4] *The Shepheardes Calender.*

Of this I heard, and saw enough to make
Imagination restless; nor was free
Myself from frequent perils; nor were
tales
Wanting,—the tragedies of former times,
170 Hazards and strange escapes, of which the
rocks
Immutable, and everflowing streams,
Where'er I roamed, were speaking monu-
ments.

Smooth life had flock and shepherd in
old time,
Long springs and tepid winters, on the
banks
175 Of delicate Galesus; and no less
Those scattered along Adria's myrtle
shores:
Smooth life had herdsman, and his snow-
white herd
To triumphs and to sacrificial rites
Devoted, on the inviolable stream
180 Of rich Clitumnus; and the goat-herd lived
As calmly, underneath the pleasant brows
Of cool Lucretilis, where the pipe was
heard
Of Pan, invisible god, thrilling the rocks
With tutelary music, from all harm
185 The fold protecting. I myself, mature
In manhood then, have seen a pastoral
tract[1]
Like one of these, where Fancy might run
wild,
Though under skies less generous, less
serene:
There, for her own delight had Nature
framed
190 A pleasure-ground, diffused a fair expanse
Of level pasture, islanded with groves
And banked with woody risings; but the
plain
Endless, here opening widely out, and there
Shut up in lesser lakes or beds of lawn
195 And intricate recesses, creek or bay
Sheltered within a shelter, where at large
The shepherd strays, a rolling hut his
home.
Thither he comes with spring-time, there
abides
All summer, and at sunrise ye may hear
200 His flageolet to liquid notes of love
Attuned, or sprightly fife resounding far.
Nook is there none, nor tract of that vast
space
Where passage opens, but the same shall
have
In turn its visitant, telling there his hours

[1] At Goslar, near the Hartz Mountains.

205 In unlaborious pleasure, with no task
More toilsome than to carve a beechen bowl
For spring or fountain, which the traveller
finds,
When through the region he pursues at
will
His devious course. A glimpse of such
sweet life
210 I saw when, from the melancholy walls
Of Goslar, once imperial, I renewed
My daily walk along that wide cham-
paign,[1]
That, reaching to her gates, spreads east
and west,
And northwards, from beneath the moun-
tainous verge
215 Of the Hercynian forest. Yet, hail to you
Moors, mountains, headlands, and ye hol-
low vales,
Ye long deep channels for the Atlantic's
voice,
Powers of my native region! Ye that seize
The heart with firmer grasp! Your snows
and streams
220 Ungovernable, and your terrifying winds,
That howl so dismally for him who treads
Companionless your awful solitudes!
There, 'tis the shepherd's task the winter
long
To wait upon the storms: of their approach
225 Sagacious, into sheltering coves he drives
His flock, and thither from the homestead
bears
A toilsome burden up the craggy ways,
And deals it out, their regular nourishment
Strewn on the frozen snow. And when the
spring
230 Looks out, and all the pastures dance with
lambs,
And when the flock, with warmer weather,
climbs
Higher and higher, him his office leads
To watch their goings, whatsoever track
The wanderers choose. For this he quits
his home
235 At day-spring, and no sooner doth the sun
Begin to strike him with a fire-like heat,
Than he lies down upon some shining rock,
And breakfasts with his dog. When they
have stolen,
As is their wont, a pittance from strict
time,
240 For rest not needed or exchange of love,
Then from his couch he starts; and now
his feet
Crush out a livelier fragrance from the
flowers

[1] level field

Of lowly thyme, by Nature's skill enwrought
In the wild turf: the lingering dews of
morn
245 Smoke round him, as from hill to hill he
hies,
His staff protending like a hunter's spear,
Or by its aid leaping from crag to crag,
And o'er the brawling beds of unbridged
streams.
Philosophy, methinks, at Fancy's call,
250 Might deign to follow him through what
he does
Or sees in his day's march; himself he
feels,
In those vast regions where his service lies,
A freeman, wedded to his life of hope
And hazard, and hard labor interchanged
255 With that majestic indolence so dear
To native man. A rambling schoolboy, thus
I felt his presence in his own domain,
As of a lord and master, or a power,
Or genius, under Nature, under God,
260 Presiding; and severest solitude
Had more commanding looks when he was
there.
When up the lonely brooks on rainy days
Angling I went, or trod the trackless hills
By mists bewildered, suddenly mine eyes
265 Have glanced upon him distant a few steps,
In size a giant, stalking through thick fog,
His sheep like Greenland bears; or, as he
stepped
Beyond the boundary line of some hill
shadow,
His form hath flashed upon me, glorified
270 By the deep radiance of the setting sun:
Or him have I descried in distant sky,
A solitary object and sublime,
Above all height! like an aerial cross
Stationed alone upon a spiry rock
275 Of the Chartreuse, for worship. Thus was
man
Ennobled outwardly before my sight,
And thus my heart was early introduced
To an unconscious love and reverence
Of human nature; hence the human form
280 To me became an index of delight,
Of grace and honor, power and worthiness.
Meanwhile this creature—spiritual almost
As those of books, but more exalted far;
Far more of an imaginative form
285 Than the gay Corin of the groves, who lives
For his own fancies, or to dance by the
hour,
In coronal, with Phyllis in the midst—
Was, for the purposes of kind, a man
With the most common; husband, father;
learned,

290 Could teach, admonish; suffered with the
rest
From vice and folly, wretchedness and
fear;
Of this I little saw, cared less for it,
But something must have felt.
　　　　　Call ye these appearances—
Which I beheld of shepherds in my youth,
295 This sanctity of Nature given to man—
A shadow, a delusion, ye who pore
On the dead letter, miss the spirit of
things;
Whose truth is not a motion or a shape
Instinct with vital functions, but a block
300 Or waxen image which yourselves have
made,
And ye adore! But blessèd be the God
Of Nature and of Man that this was so;
That men before my inexperienced eyes
Did first present themselves thus purified,
305 Removed, and to a distance that was fit:
And so we all of us in some degree
Are led to knowledge, wheresoever led,
And howsoever; were it otherwise,
And we found evil fast as we find good
310 In our first years, or think that it is found,
How could the innocent heart bear up and
live!
But doubly fortunate my lot; not here
Alone, that something of a better life
Perhaps was round me than it is the
privilege
315 Of most to move in, but that first I
looked
At man through objects that were great or
fair;
First communed with him by their help.
And thus
Was founded a sure safeguard and de-
fence
Against the weight of meanness, selfish
cares,
320 Coarse manners, vulgar passions, that
beat in
On all sides from the ordinary world
In which we traffic. Starting from this
point,
I had my face turned toward the truth;
began
With an advantage furnished by that kind
325 Of prepossession, without which the soul
Receives no knowledge that can bring forth
good,
No genuine insight ever comes to her.
From the restraint of over-watchful eyes
Preserved, I moved about, year after year,
330 Happy, and now most thankful that my
walk
Was guarded from too early intercourse

With the deformities of crowded life,
And those ensuing laughters and con-
    tempts,
Self-pleasing, which, if we would wish to
    think
335 With a due reverence on earth's rightful
    lord,
Here placed to be the inheritor of heaven,
Will not permit us; but pursue the mind,
That to devotion willingly would rise,
Into the temple and the temple's heart.

340   Yet deem not, friend! that human kind
    with me
Thus early took a place pre-eminent;
Nature herself was, at this unripe time,
But secondary to my own pursuits
And animal activities, and all
345 Their trivial pleasures; and when these
    had drooped
And gradually expired, and Nature, prized
For her own sake, became my joy, even
    then—
And upwards through late youth, until not
    less
Than two-and-twenty summers had been
    told—
350 Was Man in my affections and regards
Subordinate to her, her visible forms
And viewless agencies: a passion, she,
A rapture often, and immediate love
Ever at hand; he, only a delight
355 Occasional, an accidental grace,
His hour being not yet come. Far less had
    then
The inferior creatures, beast or bird, at-
    tuned
My spirit to that gentleness of love
(Though they had long been carefully
    observed),
360 Won from me those minute obeisances
Of tenderness, which I may number now
With my first blessings. Nevertheless, on
    these
The light of beauty did not fall in vain,
Or grandeur circumfuse them to no end.

365   But when that first poetic faculty
Of plain Imagination and severe,
No longer a mute influence of the soul,
Ventured, at some rash muse's earnest call,
To try her strength among harmonious
    words,
370 And to book-notions and the rules of art
Did knowingly conform itself; there came
Among the simple shapes of human life
A wilfulness of fancy and conceit:
And Nature and her objects beautified
375 These fictions, as in some sort, in their turn,

They burnished her. From touch of this
    new power
Nothing was safe: the elder-tree that grew
Beside the well-known charnel-house had
    then
A dismal look; the yew-tree had its ghost,
380 That took his station there for ornament:
The dignities of plain occurrence then
Were tasteless, and truth's golden mean, a
    point
Where no sufficient pleasure could be
    found.
Then, if a widow, staggering with the blow
385 Of her distress, was known to have turned
    her steps
To the cold grave in which her husband
    slept,
One night, or haply more than one,
    through pain
Or half-insensate impotence of mind,
The fact was caught at greedily, and there
390 She must be visitant the whole year
    through,
Wetting the turf with never-ending tears.

    Through quaint obliquities[1] I might
    pursue
These cravings; when the foxglove, one
    by one,
Upwards through every stage of the tall
    stem,
395 Had shed beside the public way its bells,
And stood of all dismantled, save the last
Left at the tapering ladder's top, that
    seemed
To bend as doth a slender blade of grass
Tipped with a rain-drop, Fancy loved to
    seat,
400 Beneath the plant despoiled, but crested
    still
With this last relic, soon itself to fall,
Some vagrant mother, whose arch little
    ones,
All unconcerned by her dejected plight,
Laughed as with rival eagerness their hands
405 Gathered the purple cups that round them
    lay,
Strewing the turf's green slope.
             A diamond light
(Whene'er the summer sun, declining,
    smote
A smooth rock wet with constant springs)
    was seen
Sparkling from out a copse-clad bank that
    rose
410 Fronting our cottage. Oft beside the hearth
Seated, with open door, often and long
Upon this restless lustre have I gazed,
[1] deviations

That made my fancy restless as itself.
'Twas now for me a burnished silver shield
415 Suspended over a knight's tomb, who lay
Inglorious, buried in the dusky wood:
An entrance now into some magic cave
Or palace built by fairies of the rock;
Nor could I have been bribed to disenchant
420 The spectacle by visiting the spot.
Thus wilful Fancy, in no hurtful mood,
Engrafted far-fetched shapes on feelings
bred
By pure Imagination: busy Power
She was, and with her ready pupil turned
425 Instinctively to human passions, then
Least understood. Yet, 'mid the fervent
swarm
Of these vagaries, with an eye so rich
As mine was through the bounty of a grand
And lovely region, I had forms distinct
430 To steady me: each airy thought revolved
Round a substantial centre, which at once
Incited it to motion, and controlled.
I did not pine like one in cities bred,
As was thy melancholy lot, dear friend!
435 Great Spirit as thou art, in endless dreams[1]
Of sickliness, disjoining, joining, things
Without the light of knowledge. Where
the harm,
If, when the woodman languished with
disease
Induced by sleeping nightly on the ground
440 Within his sod-built cabin, Indian-wise,
I called the pangs of disappointed love,
And all the sad etcetera of the wrong,
To help him to his grave? Meanwhile the
man,
If not already from the woods retired
445 To die at home, was haply as I knew,
Withering by slow degrees, 'mid gentle
airs,
Birds, running streams, and hills so beauti-
ful
On golden evenings, while the charcoal pile
Breathed up its smoke, an image of his
ghost
450 Or spirit that full soon must take her
flight.
Nor shall we not be tending towards that
point
Of sound humanity to which our tale
Leads, though by sinuous ways, if here I
show
How Fancy, in a season when she wove
455 Those slender cords, to guide the unconscious Boy
For the Man's sake, could feed at Nature's call

[1] See Coleridge's *Frost at Midnight*, 51-53 (p. 376).

Some pensive musings which might well
beseem
Maturer years.
          A grove there is whose boughs
Stretch from the western marge of Thurston-mere,
460 With length of shade so thick, that whoso
glides
Along the line of low-roofed water, moves
As in a cloister. Once—while, in that shade
Loitering, I watched the golden beams of
light
Flung from the setting sun, as they reposed
465 In silent beauty on the naked ridge
Of a high eastern hill—thus flowed my
thoughts
In a pure stream of words fresh from the
heart:
Dear native Regions,[1] whereso'er shall
close
My mortal course, there will I think on you
470 Dying, will cast on you a backward look;
Even as this setting sun (albeit the vale
Is nowhere touched by one memorial
gleam)
Doth with the fond remains of his last
power
Still linger, and a farewell lustre sheds
475 On the dear mountain-tops where first he
rose.

          Enough of humble arguments; recall,
My song! those high emotions which thy
voice
Has heretofore made known; that burst-
ing forth
Of sympathy, inspiring and inspired,
480 When everywhere a vital pulse was felt,
And all the several frames of things, like
stars,
Through every magnitude distinguishable,
Shone mutually indebted, or half lost
Each in the other's blaze, a galaxy
485 Of life and glory. In the midst stood Man,
Outwardly, inwardly contemplated,
As, of all visible natures, crown, though
born
Of dust, and kindred to the worm; a
Being,
Both in perception and discernment, first
490 In every capability of rapture,
Through the divine effect of power and
love;
As, more than anything we know, instinct
With godhead, and, by reason and by will,
Acknowledging dependency sublime.

[1] Lines 468-476 are recast from the *Extract*, p. 249.

495   Ere long, the lonely mountains left, I
      moved,
   Begirt, from day to day, with temporal
      shapes
   Of vice and folly thrust upon my view,
   Objects of sport, and ridicule, and scorn,
   Manners and characters discriminate,
500 And little bustling passions that eclipse,
   As well they might, the impersonated
      thought,
   The idea, or abstraction of the kind.

    An idler among academic bowers,
   Such was my new condition, as at large
505 Has been set forth; yet here the vulgar
      light
   Of present, actual, superficial life,
   Gleaming, through coloring of other times,
   Old usages and local privilege,
   Was welcome, softened, if not solemnized.
510 This notwithstanding, being brought more
      near
   To vice and guilt, forerunning wretched-
      ness,
   I trembled,—thought, at times, of human
      life
   With an indefinite terror and dismay,
   Such as the storms and angry elements
515 Had bred in me; but gloomier far, a dim
   Analogy to uproar and misrule,
   Disquiet, danger, and obscurity.

    It might be told (but wherefore speak
      of things
   Common to all?) that, seeing, I was led
520 Gravely to ponder—judging between good
   And evil, not as for the mind's delight
   But for her guidance—one who was to
      act,
   As sometimes to the best of feeble means
   I did, by human sympathy impelled;
525 And, through dislike and most offensive
      pain,
   Was to the truth conducted; of this faith
   Never forsaken, that, by acting well,
   And understanding, I should learn to love
   The end of life, and everything we know.

530   Grave teacher, stern preceptress! for at
      times
   Thou canst put on an aspect most severe;
   London, to thee I willingly return.
   Erewhile my verse played idly with the
      flowers
   Enwrought upon thy mantle; satisfied
535 With that amusement, and a simple look
   Of child-like inquisition now and then
   Cast upwards on thy countenance, to detect

   Some inner meanings which might harbor
      there.
   But how could I in mood so light indulge,
540 Keeping such fresh remembrance of the
      day,
   When, having thridded the long labyrinth
   Of the suburban villages, I first
   Entered thy vast dominion? On the roof
   Of an itinerant vehicle I sate,
545 With vulgar men about me, trivial forms
   Of houses, pavement, streets, of men and
      things,—
   Mean shapes on every side: but, at the
      instant,
   When to myself it fairly might be said,
   The threshold now is overpast, (how
      strange
550 That aught external to the living mind
   Should have such mighty sway! yet so it
      was),
   A weight of ages did at once descend
   Upon my heart; no thought embodied, no
   Distinct remembrances, but weight and
      power,—
555 Power growing under weight: alas! I feel
   That I am trifling: 'twas a moment's
      pause,—
   All that took place within me came and
      went
   As in a moment; yet with Time it dwells,
   And grateful memory, as a thing divine.

560   The curious traveller, who, from open
      day,
   Hath passed with torches into some huge
      cave,
   The Grotto of Antiparos, or the den[1]
   In old time haunted by that Danish witch,
   Yordas; he looks around and sees the vault
565 Widening on all sides; sees, or thinks he
      sees,
   Erelong, the massy roof above his head,
   That instantly unsettles and recedes,—
   Substance and shadow, light and darkness,
      all
   Commingled, making up a canopy
570 Of shapes and forms and tendencies to
      shape
   That shift and vanish, change and inter-
      change
   Like spectres,—ferment silent and sub-
      lime!
   That after a short space works less and less,
   Till, every effort, every motion gone,
575 The scene before him stands in perfect view
   Exposed, and lifeless as a written book!—
   But let him pause awhile, and look again,
   And a new quickening shall succeed, at first

[1] A cavern in Yorkshire.

Beginning timidly, then creeping fast,
580 Till the whole cave, so late a senseless mass,
Busies the eye with images and forms
Boldly assembled,—here is shadowed forth
From the projections, wrinkles, cavities,
A variegated landscape,—there the shape
585 Of some gigantic warrior clad in mail,
The ghostly semblance of a hooded monk,
Veiled nun, or pilgrim resting on his staff:
Strange congregation! yet not slow to meet
Eyes that perceive through minds that can
      inspire.

590   Even in such sort had I at first been
            moved,
Nor otherwise continued to be moved,
As I explored the vast metropolis,
Fount of my country's destiny and the
            world's;
That great emporium, chronicle at once
595 And burial-place of passions, and their
            home
Imperial, their chief living residence.

      With strong sensations teeming as it did
Of past and present, such a place must
            needs
Have pleased me, seeking knowledge at
            that time
600 Far less than craving power; yet knowl-
            edge came,
Sought or unsought, and influxes of power
Came, of themselves, or at her call derived
In fits of kindliest apprehensiveness,
From all sides, when whate'er was in itself
605 Capacious found, or seemed to find, in me
A correspondent amplitude of mind;
Such is the strength and glory of our
            youth!
The human nature unto which I felt
That I belonged, and reverenced with love,
610 Was not a punctual presence, but a spirit
Diffused through time and space, with aid
            derived
Of evidence from monuments, erect,
Prostrate, or leaning towards their com-
            mon rest
In earth, the widely scattered wreck sub-
            lime
615 Of vanished nations, or more clearly drawn
From books and what they picture and
      record.

      'Tis true, the history of our native land,
With those of Greece compared and popu-
            lar Rome,
And in our high-wrought modern narra-
            tives

620 Stript of their harmonizing soul, the life
Of manners and familiar incidents,
Had never much delighted me. And less
Than other intellects had mine been used
To lean upon extrinsic circumstance
625 Of record or tradition; but a sense
Of what in the great City had been done
And suffered, and was doing, suffering,
            still,
Weighed with me, could support the test
            of thought;
And, in despite of all that had gone by,
630 Or was departing never to return,
There I conversed with majesty and power
Like independent natures. Hence the
            place
Was thronged with impregnations like the
            wilds
In which my early feelings had been
            nursed—
635 Bare hills and valleys, full of caverns,
            rocks,
And audible seclusions, dashing lakes,
Echoes and waterfalls, and pointed crags
That into music touch the passing wind.
Here then my young imagination found
640 No uncongenial element; could here
Among new objects serve or give com-
            mand,
Even as the heart's occasions might re-
            quire,
To forward reason's else too scrupulous
            march.
The effect was, still more elevated views
645 Of human nature. Neither vice nor guilt,
Debasement undergone by body or mind,
Nor all the misery forced upon my sight,
Misery not lightly passed, but sometimes
            scanned
Most feelingly, could overthrow my trust
650 In what we may become; induce belief
That I was ignorant, had been falsely
            taught,
A solitary, who with vain conceits
Had been inspired, and walked about in
            dreams.
From those sad scenes when meditation
            turned,
655 Lo! everything that was indeed divine
Retained its purity inviolate,
Nay brighter shone, by this portentous
            gloom
Set off; such opposition as aroused
The mind of Adam, yet in Paradise
660 Though fallen from bliss, when in the
            east he saw
Darkness ere day's mid course, and morn-
            ing light
More orient in the western cloud, that drew

O'er the blue firmament a radiant white,
Descending slow with something heavenly
    fraught.

665   Add also, that among the multitudes
Of that huge city, oftentimes was seen
Affectingly set forth, more than elsewhere
Is possible, the unity of man,
One spirit over ignorance and vice
670 Predominant in good and evil hearts;
One sense for moral judgments, as one eye
For the sun's light. The soul when smit-
    ten thus
By a sublime idea, whencesoe'er
Vouchsafed for union or communion, feeds
675 On the pure bliss, and takes her rest with
    God.

    Thus from a very early age, O friend!
My thoughts by slow gradations had been
    drawn
To human-kind, and to the good and ill
Of human life: Nature had led me on;
680 And oft amid the "busy hum" I seemed
To travel independent of her help,
As if I had forgotten her; but no,
The world of human-kind outweighed not
    hers
In my habitual thoughts; the scale of love,
685 Though filling daily, still was light, com-
    pared
With that in which *her* mighty objects lay.

From Book XI. France

105 O pleasant exercise of hope and joy![1]
For mighty were the auxiliars which then
    stood
Upon our side, us who were strong in love!
Bliss was it in that dawn to be alive,
But to be young was very Heaven! O
    times,
110 In which the meagre, stale, forbidding ways
Of custom, law, and statute, took at once
The attraction of a country in romance!
When Reason seemed the most to assert her
    rights
When most intent on making of herself
115 A prime enchantress—to assist the work,
Which then was going forward in her
    name!
Not favored spots alone, but the whole
    Earth,
The beauty wore of promise—that which
    sets
(As at some moments might not be unfelt
120 Among the bowers of Paradise itself)
The budding rose above the rose full blown.

[1] To "Meditate with ardor on the rule and management of nations."—l. 99.

What temper at the prospect did not wake
To happiness unthought of? The inert
Were roused, and lively natures rapt away!
125 They who had fed their childhood upon
    dreams,
The play-fellows of fancy, who had made
All powers of swiftness, subtilty, and
    strength
Their ministers,—who in lordly wise had
    stirred
Among the grandest objects of the sense,
130 And dealt with whatsoever they found
    there
As if they had within some lurking right
To wield it;—they, too, who of gentle mood
Had watched all gentle motions, and to
    these
Had fitted their own thoughts, schemers
    more mild,
135 And in the region of their peaceful
    selves;—
Now was it that *both* found, the meek and
    lofty
Did both find, helpers to their hearts' de-
    sire,
And stuff at hand, plastic as they could
    wish,—
Were called upon to exercise their skill,
140 Not in Utopia,—subterranean fields,—
Or some secreted island,[1] Heaven knows
    where!
But in the very world, which is the world
Of all of us,—the place where, in the end,
We find our happiness, or not at all!

145   Why should I not confess that Earth
    was then
To me, what an inheritance, new-fallen,
Seems, when the first time visited, to one
Who thither comes to find in it his home?
He walks about and looks upon the spot
150 With cordial transport, moulds it and re-
    moulds,
And is half-pleased with things that are
    amiss,
'Twill be such joy to see them disappear.

    An active partisan, I thus convoked
From every object pleasant circumstance
155 To suit my ends; I moved among mankind
With genial feelings still predominant;
When erring, erring on the better part,
And in the kinder spirit; placable,
Indulgent, as not uninformed that men
160 See as they have been taught—Antiquity
Gives rights to error; and aware, no less,
That throwing off oppression must be work
As well of License as of Liberty;
And above all—for this was more than all—

[1] Such as Bacon's *New Atlantis.*

165 Not caring if the wind did now and then
Blow keen upon an eminence that gave
Prospect so large into futurity;
In brief, a child of Nature, as at first,
Diffusing only those affections wider
170 That from the cradle had grown up with
me,
And losing, in no other way than light
Is lost in light, the weak in the more strong.

In the main outline, such it might be said
Was my condition, till with open war
175 Britain opposed the liberties of France.[1]
This threw me first out of the pale of love;
Soured and corrupted, upwards to the
source,
My sentiments; was not, as hitherto,
A swallowing up of lesser things in great,
180 But change of them into their contraries;
And thus a way was opened for mistakes
And false conclusions, in degree as gross,
In kind more dangerous. What had been
a pride,
Was now a shame; my likings and my loves
185 Ran in new channels, leaving old ones
dry;
And hence a blow that, in maturer age,
Would but have touched the judgment,
struck more deep
Into sensations near the heart: meantime,
As from the first, wild theories were afloat,
190 To whose pretensions, sedulously urged,
I had but lent a careless ear, assured
That time was ready to set all things right,
And that the multitude, so long oppressed,
Would be oppressed no more.
But when events
195 Brought less encouragement, and unto these
The immediate proof of principles no more
Could be entrusted, while the events them-
selves,
Worn out in greatness, stripped of novelty,
Less occupied the mind, and sentiments
200 Could through my understanding's natural
growth
No longer keep their ground, by faith
maintained
Of inward consciousness, and hope that
laid
Her hand upon her object—evidence
Safer, of universal application, such
205 As could not be impeached, was sought
elsewhere.

But now, become oppressors in their
turn,
Frenchmen had changed a war of self-
defense
For one of conquest, losing sight of all
[1] In 1793.

Which they had struggled for: up
mounted now,
210 Openly in the eye of earth and heaven,
The scale of liberty. I read her doom,
With anger vexed, with disappointment
sore,
But not dismayed, nor taking to the shame
Of a false prophet. While resentment rose
215 Striving to hide, what nought could heal,
the wounds
Of mortified presumption, I adhered
More firmly to old tenets, and, to prove
Their temper, strained them more; and
thus, in heat
Of contest, did opinions every day
220 Grow into consequence, till round my mind
They clung, as if they were its life, nay
more,
The very being of the immortal soul.

. . . .

A strong shock
270 Was given to old opinions; all men's
minds
Had felt its power, and mine was both let
loose,
Let loose and goaded. After what hath been
Already said of patriotic love,
275 Suffice it here to add, that, somewhat stern
In temperament, withal a happy man,
And therefore bold to look on painful
things,
Free likewise of the world, and thence
more bold,
I summoned my best skill, and toiled, intent
280 To anatomize the frame of social life;
Yea, the whole body of society
Searched to its heart. Share with me,
friend! the wish
That some dramatic tale, endued with
shapes
Livelier, and flinging out less guarded
words
285 Than suit the work we fashion, might set
forth
What then I learned, or think I learned,
of truth,
And the errors into which I fell, betrayed
By present objects, and by reasonings false
From their beginnings, inasmuch as drawn
290 Out of a heart that had been turned aside
From Nature's way by outward accidents,
And which was thus confounded, more
and more
Misguided, and misguiding. So I fared,
Dragging all precepts, judgments, maxims,
creeds,
295 Like culprits to the bar; calling the mind,
Suspiciously, to establish in plain day

Her titles and her honors; now believing,
Now disbelieving; endlessly perplexed
With impulse, motive, right and wrong,
    the ground
300 Of obligation, what the rule and whence
The sanction; till, demanding formal
    proof,
And seeking it in everything, I lost
All feeling of conviction, and, in fine,
Sick, wearied out with contrarieties,
305 Yielded up moral questions in despair.

.   .   .   .   .   .

                    Then it was—
Thanks to the bounteous Giver of all
    good!—
335 That the belovèd sister[1] in whose sight
Those days were passed, now speaking in
    a voice
Of sudden admonition—like a brook
That did but cross a lonely road, and now
Is seen, heard, felt, and caught at every
    turn,
340 Companion never lost through many a
    league—
Maintained for me a saving intercourse
With my true self; for, though bedimmed
    and changed
Much, as it seemed, I was no further
    changed
Than as a clouded and a waning moon:
345 She whispered still that brightness would
    return,
She, in the midst of all, preserved me still
A poet, made me seek beneath that name,
And that alone, my office upon earth;
And, lastly, as hereafter will be shown,
350 If willing audience fail not, Nature's self,
By all varieties of human love
Assisted, led me back through opening day
To those sweet counsels between head and
    heart
Whence grew that genuine knowledge,
    fraught with peace,
355 Which, through the later sinkings of this
    cause,
Hath still upheld me, and upholds me now.

.   .   .   .   .   .

From Book XII. Imagination and Taste,
    How Impaired and Restored

Long time have human ignorance and
    guilt
Detained us, on what spectacles of woe
Compelled to look, and inwardly oppressed
With sorrow, disappointment, vexing
    thoughts,
5 Confusion of the judgment, zeal decayed,

[1] Wordsworth joined his sister Dorothy at Halifax in the winter of 1794.

And, lastly, utter loss of hope itself
And things to hope for! Not with these
    began
Our song, and not with these our song
    must end.—
Ye motions of delight, that haunt the sides
10 Of the green hills; ye breezes and soft airs,
Whose subtle intercourse with breathing
    flowers,
Feelingly watched, might teach Man's
    haughty race
How without injury to take, to give
Without offence; ye who, as if to show
15 The wondrous influence of power gently
    used,
Bend the complying heads of lordly pines,
And, with a touch, shift the stupendous
    clouds
Through the whole compass of the sky;
    ye brooks,
Muttering along the stones, a busy noise
20 By day, a quiet sound in silent night;
Ye waves, that out of the great deep steal
    forth
In a calm hour to kiss the pebbly shore,
Not mute, and then retire, fearing no
    storm;
And you, ye groves, whose ministry it is
25 To interpose the covert of your shades,
Even as a sleep, between the heart of man
And outward troubles, between man him-
    self,
Not seldom, and his own uneasy heart:
Oh! that I had a music and a voice
30 Harmonious as your own, that I might tell
What ye have done for me. The morn-
    ing shines,
Nor heedeth Man's perverseness; Spring
    returns,—
I saw the Spring return, and could rejoice,
In common with the children of her love,
35 Piping on boughs, or sporting on fresh
    fields,
Or boldly seeking pleasure nearer heaven
On wings that navigate cerulean skies.
So neither were complacency, nor peace,
Nor tender yearnings, wanting for my good
40 Through these distracted times; in Na-
    ture still
Glorying, I found a counterpoise in her,
Which, when the spirit of evil reached
    its height,
Maintained for me a secret happiness.

.   .   .   .   .   .

                    Before I was called forth
175 From the retirement of my native hills,
I loved whate'er I saw: nor lightly loved,
But most intensely; never dreamt of aught

More grand, more fair, more exquisitely
    framed
Than those few nooks to which my happy
    feet
180 Were limited. I had not at that time
Lived long enough, nor in the least survived
The first diviner influence of this world,
As it appears to unaccustomed eyes.
Worshipping then among the depth of
    things,
185 As piety ordained; could I submit
To measured admiration, or to aught
That should preclude humility and love?
I felt, observed, and pondered; did not
    judge,
Yea, never thought of judging; with the
    gift
190 Of all this glory filled and satisfied.
And afterwards, when through the gor-
    geous Alps
Roaming, I carried with me the same heart:
In truth, the degradation—howsoe'er
Induced, effect, in whatsoe'er degree,
195 Of custom that prepares a partial scale
In which the little oft outweighs the great;
Or any other cause that hath been named;
Or lastly, aggravated by the times
And their impassioned sounds, which well
    might make
200 The milder minstrelsies of rural scenes
Inaudible—was transient; I had known
Too forcibly, too early in my life,
Visitings of imaginative power
For this to last: I shook the habit off
205 Entirely and forever, and again
In Nature's presence stood, as now I stand,
A sensitive being, a *creative* soul.

. . . . . .

BOOK XIII. IMAGINATION AND TASTE, How
    IMPAIRED AND RESTORED—
      (*Concluded*)

From Nature doth emotion come; and
    moods
Of calmness equally are Nature's gift:
This is her glory; these two attributes
Are sister horns that constitute her
    strength.
5 Hence Genius, born to thrive by inter-
    change
Of peace and excitation, finds in her
His best and purest friend; from her
    receives
That energy by which he seeks the truth,
From her that happy stillness of the mind
10 Which fits him to receive it when unsought.

Such benefit the humblest intellects
Partake of, each in their degree; 'tis mine

To speak what I myself have known and
    felt;
Smooth task! for words find easy way,
    inspired
15 By gratitude, and confidence in truth.
Long time in search of knowledge did I
    range
The field of human life, in heart and mind
Benighted; but, the dawn beginning now
To reappear, 'twas proved that not in vain
20 I had been taught to reverence a Power
That is the visible quality and shape
And image of right reason; that matures
Her processes by steadfast laws; gives
    birth
To no impatient or fallacious hopes,
25 No heat of passion or excessive zeal,
No vain conceits; provokes to no quick
    turns
Of self-applauding intellect; but trains
To meekness, and exalts by humble faith;
Holds up before the mind intoxicate
30 With present objects, and the busy dance
Of things that pass away, a temperate show
Of objects that endure; and by this course
Disposes her, when over-fondly set
On throwing off incumbrances, to seek
35 In man, and in the frame of social life,
Whate'er there is desirable and good
Of kindred permanence, unchanged in
    form
And function, or, through strict vicissitude
Of life and death, revolving. Above all
40 Were re-established now those watchful
    thoughts
Which, seeing little worthy or sublime
In what the historian's pen so much de-
    lights
To blazon—power and energy detached
From moral purpose—early tutored me
45 To look with feelings of fraternal love
Upon the unassuming things that hold
A silent station in this beauteous world.

Thus moderated, thus composed, I found
Once more in Man an object of delight,
50 Of pure imagination, and of love;
And, as the horizon of my mind enlarged,
Again I took the intellectual eye
For my instructor, studious more to see
Great truths, than touch and handle little
    ones.
55 Knowledge was given accordingly; my
    trust
Became more firm in feelings that had stood
The test of such a trial; clearer far
My sense of excellence—of right and
    wrong:
The promise of the present time retired

⁶⁰ Into its true proportion; sanguine
      schemes,
Ambitious projects, pleased me less; I
      sought
For present good in life's familiar face,
And built thereon my hopes of good to
      come.

With settling judgments now of what
      would last
⁶⁵ And what would disappear; prepared to
      find
Presumption, folly, madness, in the men
Who thrust themselves upon the passive
      world
As Rulers of the world; to see in these,
Even when the public welfare is their aim,
⁷⁰ Plans without thought, or built on theories
Vague and unsound; and having brought
      the books
Of modern statists to their proper test,
Life, human life, with all its sacred claims
Of sex and age, and heaven-descended
      rights,
⁷⁵ Mortal, or those beyond the reach of
      death;
And having thus discerned how dire a thing
Is worshipped in that idol proudly named
"The Wealth of Nations,"¹ where alone
      that wealth
Is lodged, and how increased; and having
      gained
⁸⁰ A more judicious knowledge of the worth
And dignity of individual man,
No composition of the brain, but man
Of whom we read, the man whom we be-
      hold
With our own eyes—I could not but en-
      quire—
⁸⁵ Not with less interest than heretofore,
But greater, though in spirit more sub-
      dued—
Why is this glorious creature to be found
One only in ten thousand? What one is,
Why may not millions be? What bars
      are thrown
⁹⁰ By Nature in the way of such a hope?
Our animal appetites and daily wants,
Are these obstructions insurmountable?
If not, then others vanish into air.
"Inspect the basis of the social pile:
⁹⁵ Enquire," said I, "how much of mental
      power
And genuine virtue they possess who live

By bodily toil, labor exceeding far
Their due proportion, under all the weight
Of that injustice which upon ourselves
¹⁰⁰ Ourselves entail.'' Such estimate to frame
I chiefly looked (what need to look
      beyond?)
Among the natural abodes of men,
Fields with their rural works; recalled
      to mind
My earliest notices; with these compared
¹⁰⁵ The observations made in later youth,
And to that day continued.—For, the time
Had never been when throes of mighty
      Nations
And the world's tumult unto me could
      yield,
How far soe'er transported and possessed,
¹¹⁰ Full measure of content; but still I craved
An intermingling of distinct regards
And truths of individual sympathy
Nearer ourselves. Such often might be
      gleaned
From the great City, else it must have
      proved
¹¹⁵ To me a heart-depressing wilderness;
But much was wanting: therefore did I
      turn
To you, ye pathways, and ye lonely roads;
Sought you enriched with everything I
      prized,
With human kindnesses and simple joys.

¹²⁰   Oh! next to one dear state of bliss,
      vouchsafed
Alas! to few in this untoward world,
The bliss of walking daily in life's prime
Through field or forest with the maid we
      love,
While yet our hearts are young, while yet
      we breathe
¹²⁵ Nothing but happiness, in some lone nook,
Deep vale, or anywhere, the home of both,
From which it would be misery to stir:
Oh! next to such enjoyment of our youth,
In my esteem, next to such dear delight,
¹³⁰ Was that of wandering on from day to day
Where I could meditate in peace, and cull
Knowledge that step by step might lead
      me on
To wisdom; or, as lightsome as a bird
Wafted upon the wind from distant lands,
¹³⁵ Sing notes of greeting to strange fields
      or groves,
Which lacked not voice to welcome me in
      turn:
And, when that pleasant toil had ceased
      to please,
Converse with men, where if we meet a face
We almost meet a friend, on naked heaths

---

¹ A reference to the works of Adam Smith, the
famous political economist, who was charged
with treating man, in his *Wealth of Nations*,
as merely a wealth-seeking animal devoid of
altruistic motives.

140 With long long ways before, by cottage
    bench,
Or well-spring where the weary traveller
    rests.

    Who doth not love to follow with his eye
The windings of a public way? the sight,
Familiar object as it is, hath wrought
145 On my imagination since the morn
Of childhood, when a disappearing line,
One daily present to my eyes, that crossed
The naked summit of a far-off hill
Beyond the limits that my feet had trod,
150 Was like an invitation into space
Boundless, or guide into eternity.
Yes, something of the grandeur which
    invests
The mariner who sails the roaring sea
Through storm and darkness, early in my
    mind
155 Surrounded, too, the wanderers of the
    earth;
Grandeur as much, and loveliness far more.
Awed have I been by strolling Bedlamites;
From many other uncouth vagrants
    (passed
In fear) have walked with quicker step;
    but why
160 Take note of this? When I began to
    enquire,
To watch and question those I met, and
    speak
Without reserve to them, the lonely roads
Were open schools in which I daily read
With most delight the passions of mankind,
165 Whether by words, looks, sighs, or tears,
    revealed;
There saw into the depth of human souls,
Souls that appear to have no depth at all
To careless eyes. And—now convinced
    at heart
How little those formalities, to which
170 With overweening trust alone we give
The name of Education, have to do
With real feeling and just sense; how vain
A correspondence with the talking world
Proves to the most; and called to make
    good search
175 If man's estate, by doom of Nature yoked
With toil, be therefore yoked with igno-
    rance;
If virtue be indeed so hard to rear,
And intellectual strength so rare a boon—
I prized such walks still more, for there
    I found
180 Hope to my hope, and to my pleasure
    peace
And steadiness, and healing and repose
To every angry passion. There I heard,

From mouths of men obscure and lowly,
    truths
Replete with honor; sounds in unison
185 With loftiest promises of good and fair.

    There are who think that strong affec-
    tion, love
Known by whatever name, is falsely
    deemed
A gift, to use a term which they would use,
Of vulgar nature; that its growth requires
190 Retirement, leisure, language purified
By manners studied and elaborate;
That whoso feels such passion in its
    strength
Must live within the very light and air
Of courteous usages refined by art.
195 True is it, where oppression worse than
    death
Salutes the being at his birth, where grace
Of culture hath been utterly unknown,
And poverty and labor in excess
From day to day preoccupy the ground
200 Of the affections, and to Nature's self
Oppose a deeper nature; there, indeed,
Love cannot be; nor does it thrive with
    ease
Among the close and overcrowded haunts
Of cities, where the human heart is sick,
205 And the eye feeds it not, and cannot feed.
—Yes, in those wanderings deeply did I
    feel
How we mislead each other; above all,
How books mislead us, seeking their re-
    ward
From judgments of the wealthy Few, who
    see
210 By artificial lights; how they debase
The Many for the pleasure of those Few;
Effeminately level down the truth
To certain general notions, for the sake
Of being understood at once, or else
215 Through want of better knowledge in the
    heads
That framed them; flattering self-conceit
    with words,
That, while they most ambitiously set forth
Extrinsic differences, the outward marks
Whereby society has parted man
220 From man, neglect the universal heart.

    Here, calling up to mind what then I
    saw,
A youthful traveller, and see daily now
In the familiar circuit of my home,
Here might I pause, and bend in reverence
225 To Nature, and the power of human minds,
To men as they are men within themselves.
How oft high service is performed within,

When all the external man is rude in
  show,—
Not like a temple rich with pomp and gold,
230 But a mere mountain chapel, that protects
Its simple worshippers from sun and
  shower.
Of these, said I, shall be my song; of these,
If future years mature me for the task,
Will I record the praises, making verse
235 Deal boldly with substantial things; in
  truth
And sanctity of passion, speak of these,
That justice may be done, obeisance paid
Where it is due: thus haply shall I teach,
Inspire; through unadulterated ears
240 Pour rapture, tenderness, and hope,—my
  theme
No other than the very heart of man,
As found among the best of those who
  live—
Not unexalted by religious faith,
Nor uninformed by books, good books,
  though few—
245 In Nature's presence: thence may I
  select
Sorrow, that is not sorrow, but delight;
And miserable love, that is not pain
To hear of, for the glory that redounds
Therefrom to human kind, and what we
  are.
250 Be mine to follow with no timid step
Where knowledge leads me: it shall be
  my pride
That I have dared to tread this holy
  ground,
Speaking no dream, but things oracular;
Matter not lightly to be heard by those
255 Who to the letter of the outward promise
Do read the invisible soul; by men adroit
In speech, and for communion with the
  world
Accomplished; minds whose faculties are
  then
Most active when they are most eloquent,
260 And elevated most when most admired.
Men may be found of other mould than
  these,
Who are their own upholders, to them-
  selves
Encouragement, and energy, and will,
Expressing liveliest thoughts in lively
  words
265 As native passion dictates. Others, too,
There are among the walks of homely
  life
Still higher, men for contemplation
  framed,
Shy, and unpractised in the strife of
  phrase;

Meek men, whose very souls perhaps
  would sink
270 Beneath them, summoned to such inter-
  course:
Theirs is the language of the heavens, the
  power,
The thought, the image, and the silent joy:
Words are but under-agents in their souls;
When they are grasping with their great-
  est strength,
275 They do not breathe among them: this
  I speak
In gratitude to God, Who feeds our hearts
For His own service; knoweth, loveth us,
When we are unregarded by the world.

Also, about this time did I receive
280 Convictions still more strong than hereto-
  fore,
Not only that the inner frame is good,
And graciously composed, but that, no less,
Nature for all conditions wants not power
To consecrate, if we have eyes to see,
285 The outside of her creatures, and to
  breathe
Grandeur upon the very humblest face
Of human life. I felt that the array
Of act and circumstance, and visible form,
Is mainly to the pleasure of the mind
290 What passion makes them; that mean-
  while the forms
Of Nature have a passion in themselves,
That intermingles with those works of man
To which she summons him; although the
  works
Be mean, have nothing lofty of their own;
295 And that the Genius of the poet hence
May boldly take his way among mankind
Wherever Nature leads; that he hath stood
By Nature's side among the men of old,
And so shall stand forever.   Dearest
  friend!
300 If thou partake the animating faith
That poets, even as prophets, each with
  each
Connected in a mighty scheme of truth,
Have each his own peculiar faculty,
Heaven's gift, a sense that fits him to
  perceive
305 Objects unseen before, thou wilt not
  blame
The humblest of this band who dares to
  hope
That unto him hath also been vouchsafed
An insight that in some sort he possesses,
A privilege whereby a work of his,
310 Proceeding from a source of untaught
  things,
Creative and enduring, may become

A power like one of Nature's. To a hope
Not less ambitious once among the wilds
Of Sarum's Plain,[1] my youthful spirit
    was raised;
315 There, as I ranged at will the pastoral
    downs
Trackless and smooth, or paced the bare
    white roads
Lengthening in solitude their dreary line,
Time with his retinue of ages fled
Backwards, nor checked his flight until I
    saw
320 Our dim ancestral Past in vision clear;
Saw multitudes of men, and, here and
    there,
A single Briton clothed in wolf-skin vest,
With shield and stone-axe, stride across
    the wold;
The voice of spears was heard, the rattling
    spear
325 Shaken by arms of mighty bone, in
    strength,
Long mouldered, of barbaric majesty.
I called on Darkness—but before the word
Was uttered, midnight darkness seemed
    to take
All objects from my sight; and lo! again
330 The Desert visible by dismal flames;
It is the sacrificial altar, fed
With living men—how deep the groans! the
    voice
Of those that crowd the giant wicker[2]
    thrills
The monumental hillocks, and the pomp
335 Is for both worlds, the living and the dead.
At other moments—(for through that
    wide waste
Three summer days I roamed) where'er
    the Plain
Was figured o'er with circles, lines, or
    mounds,
That yet survive, a work, as some divine,
340 Shaped by the Druids, so to represent
Their knowledge of the heavens, and image
    forth
The constellations—gently was I charmed
Into a waking dream, a reverie
That, with believing eyes, where'er I
    turned,
345 Beheld long-bearded teachers, with white
    wands
Uplifted, pointing to the starry sky,

Alternately, and plain below, while breath
Of music swayed their motions, and the
    waste
Rejoiced with them and me in those sweet
    sounds.

350 This for the past, and things that may
    be viewed
Or fancied in the obscurity of years
From monumental hints: and thou, O
    friend!
Pleased with some unpremeditated strains[1]
That served those wanderings to beguile,
    hast said
355 That then and there my mind had exercised
Upon the vulgar forms of present things,
The actual world of our familiar days,
Yet higher power; had caught from them
    a tone,
An image, and a character, by books
360 Not hitherto reflected. Call we this
A partial judgment—and yet why? for
    then
We were as strangers;[2] and I may not
    speak
Thus wrongfully of verse, however rude,
Which on thy young imagination, trained
365 In the great City, broke like light from far.
Moreover, each man's Mind is to herself
Witness and judge; and I remember well
That in life's every-day appearances
I seemed about this time to gain clear sight
370 Of a new world—a world, too, that was fit
To be transmitted, and to other eyes
Made visible; as ruled by those fixed laws
Whence spiritual dignity originates,
Which do both give it being and maintain
375 A balance, an ennobling interchange
Of action from without and from within;
The excellence, pure function, and best
    power
Both of the object seen, and eye that sees.

MICHAEL

A PASTORAL POEM
1800   1800

If from the public way you turn your steps
Up the tumultuous brook of Green-head
    Ghyll,[3]
You will suppose that with an upright path
Your feet must struggle; in such bold
    ascent

[1] In 1793, Wordsworth roamed over Salisbury Plain with his friend, William Calvert. See Wordsworth's *Guilt and Sorrow*.
[2] The ancient Druids in Britain imprisoned human beings in giant idols of wickerwork and burned them alive as sacrifices to the gods. (See Holmes's *Cæsar's Conquest of Gaul*, 2nd ed., 33, 523; and *Cæsar's Gallic Wars*, 6, 16.)

[1] The *Descriptive Sketches*, praised by Coleridge as the work of "a great and original poetic genius."
[2] They did not meet until September 1795.
[3] "A Ghyll is a short, and, for the most part, a steep, narrow valley, with a stream running through it."—Wordsworth.

5 The pastoral mountains front you, face to
    face.
But courage; for around that boisterous
    brook
The mountains have all opened out them-
    selves,
And made a hidden valley of their own.
No habitation can be seen; but they
10 Who journey thither find themselves alone
With a few sheep, with rocks and stones,
    and kites
That overhead are sailing in the sky.
It is in truth an utter solitude;
Nor should I have made mention of this
    dell
15 But for one object which you might pass
    by,
Might see and notice not. Beside the brook
Appears a straggling heap of unhewn
    stones!
And to that simple object appertains
A story—unenriched with strange events,
20 Yet not unfit, I deem, for the fireside,
Or for the summer shade. It was the first
Of those domestic tales that spake to me
Of shepherds, dwellers in the valleys, men
Whom I already loved;—not verily
25 For their own sakes, but for the fields and
    hills
Where was their occupation and abode.
And hence this tale, while I was yet a boy
Careless of books, yet having felt the power
Of Nature, by the gentle agency
30 Of natural objects, led me on to feel
For passions that were not my own, and
    think
(At random and imperfectly indeed)
On man, the heart of man, and human life.
Therefore, although it be a history
35 Homely and rude, I will relate the same
For the delight of a few natural hearts;
And, with yet fonder feeling, for the sake
Of youthful poets, who among these hills
Will be my second self when I am gone.

40   Upon the forest-side in Grasmere Vale
There dwelt a shepherd, Michael was his
    name;
An old man, stout of heart, and strong of
    limb.
His bodily frame had been from youth to
    age
Of an unusual strength: his mind was keen,
45 Intense, and frugal, apt for all affairs,
And in his shepherd's calling he was
    prompt
And watchful more than ordinary men.
Hence had he learned the meaning of all
    winds,

Of blasts of every tone; and oftentimes,
50 When others heeded not, he heard the south
Make subterraneous music, like the noise
Of bagpipers on distant Highland hills.
The shepherd, at such warning, of his flock
Bethought him, and he to himself would
    say,
55 "The winds are now devising work for
    me!"
And, truly, at all times, the storm, that
    drives
The traveller to a shelter, summoned him
Up to the mountains: he had been alone
Amid the heart of many thousand mists,
60 That came to him, and left him, on the
    heights.
So lived he till his eightieth year was past.
And grossly that man errs, who should
    suppose
That the green valleys, and the streams
    and rocks,
Were things indifferent to the shepherd's
    thoughts.
65 Fields, where with cheerful spirits he had
    breathed
The common air; hills, which with vigor-
    ous step
He had so often climbed; which had im-
    pressed
So many incidents upon his mind
Of hardship, skill or courage, joy or fear;
70 Which, like a book, preserved the memory
Of the dumb animals, whom he had saved,
Had fed or sheltered, linking to such acts
The certainty of honorable gain;
Those fields, those hills—what could they
    less?—had laid
75 Strong hold on his affections, were to him
A pleasurable feeling of blind love,
The pleasure which there is in life itself.

  His days had not been passed in single-
    ness.
His helpmate was a comely matron, old—
80 Though younger than himself full twenty
    years.
She was a woman of a stirring life,
Whose heart was in her house: two wheels
    she had
Of antique form; this large, for spinning
    wool;
That small, for flax; and, if one wheel
    had rest,
85 It was because the other was at work.
The pair had but one inmate in their
    house,
An only child, who had been born to them
When Michael, telling o'er his years,
    began

To deem that he was old,—in shepherd's
phrase,
90 With one foot in the grave. This only son,
With two brave sheep-dogs tried in many
a storm,
The one of an inestimable worth,
Made all their household. I may truly say,
That they were as a proverb in the vale
95 For endless industry. When day was gone,
And from their occupations out of doors
The son and father were come home, even
then,
Their labor did not cease; unless when all
Turned to the cleanly supper-board, and
there,
100 Each with a mess of pottage and skimmed
milk,
Sat round the basket piled with oaten
cakes,
And their plain home-made cheese. Yet
when the meal
Was ended, Luke (for so the son was
named)
And his old father both betook themselves
105 To such convenient work as might employ
Their hands by the fireside; perhaps to
card
Wool for the housewife's spindle, or re-
pair
Some injury done to sickle, flail, or scythe,
Or other implement of house or field.

110 Down from the ceiling, by the chim-
ney's edge,
That in our ancient uncouth country style
With huge and black projection over-
browed
Large space beneath, as duly as the light
Of day grew dim the housewife hung a
lamp;
115 An aged utensil, which had performed
Service beyond all others of its kind.
Early at evening did it burn—and late,
Surviving comrade of uncounted hours,
Which, going by from year to year, had
found,
120 And left, the couple neither gay perhaps
Nor cheerful, yet with objects and with
hopes,
Living a life of eager industry.
And now, when Luke had reached his
eighteenth year,
There by the light of this old lamp they
sate,
125 Father and son, while far into the night
The housewife plied her own peculiar work,
Making the cottage through the silent hours
Murmur as with the sound of summer
flies.

This light was famous in its neighborhood,
130 And was a public symbol of the life
That thrifty pair had lived. For, as it
chanced,
Their cottage on a plot of rising ground
Stood single, with large prospect, north
and south,
High into Easedale, up to Dunmail-Raise,
135 And westward to the village near the lake;
And from this constant light, so regular,
And so far seen, the house itself, by all
Who dwelt within the limits of the vale,
Both old and young, was named THE
EVENING STAR.

140 Thus living on through such a length
of years,
The shepherd, if he loved himself, must
needs
Have loved his helpmate; but to Mi-
chael's heart
This son of his old age was yet more
dear—
Less from instinctive tenderness, the same
145 Fond spirit that blindly works in the
blood of all—
Than that a child, more than all other gifts
That earth can offer to declining man,
Brings hope with it, and forward-looking
thoughts,
And stirrings of inquietude, when they
150 By tendency of nature needs must fail.
Exceeding was the love he bare to him,
His heart and his heart's joy! For often-
times
Old Michael, while he was a babe in arms,
Had done him female service, not alone
155 For pastime and delight, as is the use
Of fathers, but with patient mind enforced
To acts of tenderness; and he had rocked
His cradle, as with a woman's gentle hand.

And in a later time, ere yet the boy
160 Had put on boy's attire, did Michael love,
Albeit of a stern unbending mind,
To have the young one in his sight, when
he
Wrought in the field, or on his shepherd's
stool
Sate with a fettered sheep before him
stretched
165 Under the large old oak, that near his door
Stood single, and, from matchless depth
of shade,
Chosen for the shearer's covert from the
sun,
Thence in our rustic dialect was called
THE CLIPPING TREE, a name which yet it
bears.

¹⁷⁰ There, while they two were sitting in the
        shade,
With others round them, earnest all and
        blithe,
Would Michael exercise his heart with looks
Of fond correction and reproof bestowed
Upon the child, if he disturbed the sheep
¹⁷⁵ By catching at their legs, or with his shouts
Scared them, while they lay still beneath
        the shears.

And when by Heaven's good grace the
        boy grew up
A healthy lad, and carried in his cheek
Two steady roses that were five years old;
¹⁸⁰ Then Michael from a winter coppice cut
With his own hand a sapling, which he
        hooped
With iron, making it throughout in all
Due requisites a perfect shepherd's staff,
And gave it to the boy; wherewith equipt
¹⁸⁵ He as a watchman oftentimes was placed
At gate or gap, to stem or turn the flock;
And, to his office prematurely called,
There stood the urchin, as you will divine,
Something between a hindrance and a
        help;
¹⁹⁰ And for this cause not always, I believe,
Receiving from his father hire of praise;
Though nought was left undone which
        staff, or voice,
Or looks, or threatening gestures, could
        perform.

But soon as Luke, full ten years old,
        could stand
¹⁹⁵ Against the mountain blasts; and to the
        heights,
Not fearing toil, nor length of weary ways,
He with his father daily went, and they
Were as companions, why should I relate
That objects which the shepherd loved
        before
²⁰⁰ Were dearer now? that from the boy
        there came
Feelings and emanations—things which
        were
Light to the sun and music to the wind;
And that the old man's heart seemed born
        again?

Thus in his father's sight the boy grew
        up:
²⁰⁵ And now, when he had reached his eigh-
        teenth year,
He was his comfort and his daily hope.

While in this sort the simple household
        lived

From day to day, to Michael's ear there
        came
Distressful tidings. Long before the time
²¹⁰ Of which I speak, the shepherd had been
        bound
In surety for his brother's son, a man
Of an industrious life, and ample means;
But unforeseen misfortunes suddenly
Had prest upon him; and old Michael now
²¹⁵ Was summoned to discharge the forfeiture,
A grievous penalty, but little less
Than half his substance. This unlooked-
        for claim,
At the first hearing, for a moment took
More hope out of his life than he sup-
        posed
²²⁰ That any old man ever could have lost.
As soon as he had armed himself with
        strength
To look his trouble in the face, it seemed
The shepherd's sole resource to sell at once
A portion of his patrimonial fields.
²²⁵ Such was his first resolve; he thought
        again,
And his heart failed him. "Isabel," said
        he,
Two evenings after he had heard the news,
"I have been toiling more than seventy
        years,
And in the open sunshine of God's love
²³⁰ Have we all lived; yet, if these fields
        of ours
Should pass into a stranger's hand, I think
That I could not lie quiet in my grave.
Our lot is a hard lot; the sun himself
Has scarcely been more diligent than I;
²³⁵ And I have lived to be a fool at last
To my own family. An evil man
That was, and made an evil choice, if he
Were false to us; and, if he were not false,
There are ten thousand to whom loss like
        this
²⁴⁰ Had been no sorrow. I forgive him;—but
'Twere better to be dumb than to talk thus.

"When I began, my purpose was to
        speak
Of remedies and of a cheerful hope.
Our Luke shall leave us, Isabel; the land
²⁴⁵ Shall not go from us, and it shall be free;
He shall possess it, free as is the wind
That passes over it. We have, thou
        know'st,
Another kinsman—he will be our friend
In this distress. He is a prosperous man,
²⁵⁰ Thriving in trade—and Luke to him shall
        go,
And with his kinsman's help and his own
        thrift

He quickly will repair this loss, and then
He may return to us. If here he stay,
What can be done? Where every one is
poor,
What can be gained?''
255   At this the old man paused,
And Isabel sat silent, for her mind
Was busy, looking back into past times.
''There's Richard Bateman,'' thought she
to herself,
''He was a parish-boy—at the church-door
260 They made a gathering for him, shillings,
pence,
And halfpennies, wherewith the neighbors
bought
A basket, which they filled with pedlar's
wares;
And, with this basket on his arm, the lad
Went up to London, found a master there,
265 Who, out of many, chose the trusty boy
To go and overlook his merchandise
Beyond the seas; where he grew won-
drous rich,
And left estates and monies to the poor,
And, at his birth-place, built a chapel
floored
270 With marble, which he sent from foreign
lands.''
These thoughts, and many others of like
sort,
Passed quickly through the mind of
Isabel,
And her face brightened. The old man
was glad,
And thus resumed:—''Well, Isabel! this
scheme
275 These two days has been meat and drink
to me.
Far more than we have lost is left us yet.
—We have enough—I wish indeed that I
Were younger;—but this hope is a good
hope.
Make ready Luke's best garments, of the
best
280 Buy for him more, and let us send him
forth
Tomorrow, or the next day, or tonight:
—If he *could* go, the boy should go tonight.''

  Here Michael ceased, and to the fields
went forth
With a light heart. The housewife for
five days
285 Was restless morn and night, and all day
long
Wrought on with her best fingers to prepare
Things needful for the journey of her son.

But Isabel was glad when Sunday came
To stop her in her work: for, when she lay
290 By Michael's side, she through the last
two nights
Heard him, how he was troubled in his
sleep:
And when they rose at morning she could
see
That all his hopes were gone. That day
at noon
She said to Luke, while they two by them-
selves
295 Were sitting at the door, ''Thou must not
go:
We have no other child but thee to lose,
None to remember—do not go away,
For if thou leave thy father he will die.''
The youth made answer with a jocund
voice;
300 And Isabel, when she had told her fears,
Recovered heart. That evening her best
fare
Did she bring forth, and all together sat
Like happy people round a Christmas fire.

  With daylight Isabel resumed her work;
305 And all the ensuing week the house appeared
As cheerful as a grove in spring: at length
The expected letter from their kinsman
came,
With kind assurances that he would do
His utmost for the welfare of the boy;
310 To which, requests were added, that forthwith
He might be sent to him. Ten times or
more
The letter was read over; Isabel
Went forth to show it to the neighbors
round;
Nor was there at that time on English
land
315 A prouder heart than Luke's. When Isabel
Had to her house returned, the old man
said,
''He shall depart tomorrow.'' To this
word
The housewife answered, talking much of
things
Which, if at such short notice he should go,
320 Would surely be forgotten. But at length
She gave consent, and Michael was at ease.

  Near the tumultuous brook of Green-
head Ghyll,
In that deep valley, Michael had designed
To build a sheepfold; and, before he heard
325 The tidings of his melancholy loss,
For this same purpose he had gathered up

A heap of stones, which by the streamlet's
   edge
Lay thrown together, ready for the work.
With Luke that evening hitherward he
   walked:
330 And soon as they had reached the place
   he stopped,
And thus the old man spake to him:—
   "My son,
Tomorrow thou wilt leave me: with full
   heart
I look upon thee, for thou art the same
That wert a promise to me ere thy birth,
335 And all thy life hast been my daily joy.
I will relate to thee some little part
Of our two histories; 'twill do thee good
When thou art from me, even if I should
   touch
On things thou canst not know of.—After
   thou
340 First cam'st into the world—as oft befalls
To new-born infants—thou didst sleep
   away
Two days, and blessings from thy father's
   tongue
Then fell upon thee. Day by day passed
   on,
And still I loved thee with increasing love.
345 Never to living ear came sweeter sounds
Than when I heard thee by our own fireside
First uttering, without words, a natural
   tune;
While thou, a feeding babe, didst in thy
   joy
Sing at thy mother's breast. Month followed month,
350 And in the open fields my life was passed
And on the mountains; else I think that
   thou
Hadst been brought up upon thy father's
   knees.
But we were playmates, Luke: among
   these hills,
As well thou knowest, in us the old and
   young
355 Have played together, nor with me didst
   thou
Lack any pleasure which a boy can
   know."
Luke had a manly heart; but at these
   words
He sobbed aloud. The old man grasped
   his hand,
And said, "Nay, do not take it so—I see
360 That these are things of which I need not
   speak.
—Even to the utmost I have been to thee
A kind and a good father: and herein
I but repay a gift which I myself

Received at others' hands; for, though
   now old
365 Beyond the common life of man, I still
Remember them who loved me in my
   youth.
Both of them sleep together: here they
   lived,
As all their forefathers had done; and,
   when
At length their time was come, they were
   not loth
370 To give their bodies to the family mould.
I wished that thou shouldst live the life
   they lived,
But 'tis a long time to look back, my son,
And see so little gain from threescore years.
These fields were burthened when they
   came to me;
375 Till I was forty years of age, not more
Than half of my inheritance was mine.
I toiled and toiled; God blessed me in
   my work,
And till these three weeks past the land
   was free.
—It looks as if it never could endure
380 Another master. Heaven forgive me,
   Luke,
If I judge ill for thee, but it seems good
That thou shouldst go."
            At this the old man paused;
Then, pointing to the stones near which
   they stood,
Thus, after a short silence, he resumed:
385 "This was a work for us; and now, my son,
It is a work for me. But, lay one stone—
Here, lay it for me, Luke, with thine own
   hands.
Nay, boy, be of good hope;—we both may
   live
To see a better day. At eighty-four
390 I still am strong and hale;—do thou thy
   part;
I will do mine.—I will begin again
With many tasks that were resigned to
   thee:
Up to the heights, and in among the
   storms,
Will I without thee go again, and do
395 All works which I was wont to do alone,
Before I knew thy face.—Heaven bless
   thee, boy!
Thy heart these two weeks has been beating fast
With many hopes; it should be so—yes—
   yes—
I knew that thou couldst never have a
   wish
400 To leave me, Luke: thou hast been bound
   to me

Only by links of love: when thou art gone,
What will be left to us!—But I forget
My purposes. Lay now the corner-stone,
As I requested; and hereafter, Luke,
405 When thou art gone away, should evil men
Be thy companions, think of me, my son,
And of this moment; hither turn thy
    thoughts,
And God will strengthen thee: amid all fear
And all temptation, Luke, I pray that thou
410 May'st bear in mind the life thy fathers
    lived,
Who, being innocent, did for that cause
Bestir them in good deeds. Now, fare
    thee well—
When thou return'st, thou in this place
    wilt see
A work which is not here: a covenant
415 'Twill be between us, but, whatever fate
Befall thee, I shall love thee to the last,
And bear thy memory with me to the
    grave.''

The shepherd ended here; and Luke
    stooped down,
And, as his father had requested, laid
420 The first stone of the sheepfold. At the
    sight
The old man's grief broke from him; to
    his heart
He pressed his son, he kissèd him and
    wept;
And to the house together they returned.
—Hushed was that house in peace, or
    seeming peace,
425 Ere the night fell:—with morrow's dawn
    the boy
Began his journey, and, when he had
    reached
The public way, he put on a bold face;
And all the neighbors, as he passed their
    doors,
Came forth with wishes and with farewell
    prayers,
430 That followed him till he was out of sight.

A good report did from their kinsman
    come,
Of Luke and his well-doing: and the boy
Wrote loving letters, full of wondrous
    news,
Which, as the housewife phrased it, were
    throughout,
435 ''The prettiest letters that were ever
    seen.''
Both parents read them with rejoicing
    hearts.
So, many months passed on: and once
    again

The shepherd went about his daily work
With confident and cheerful thoughts; and
    now
440 Sometimes when he could find a leisure
    hour
He to that valley took his way, and there
Wrought at the sheepfold. Meantime
    Luke began
To slacken in his duty; and, at length,
He in the dissolute city gave himself
445 To evil courses: ignominy and shame
Fell on him, so that he was driven at last
To seek a hiding place beyond the seas.

There is a comfort in the strength of
    love;
'Twill make a thing endurable, which else
450 Would overset the brain, or break the
    heart:
I have conversed with more than one who
    well
Remember the old man, and what he was
Years after he had heard this heavy news.
His bodily frame had been from youth to
    age
455 Of an unusual strength. Among the rocks
He went, and still looked up to sun and
    cloud,
And listened to the wind; and, as before,
Performed all kinds of labor for his sheep,
And for the land, his small inheritance.
460 And to that hollow dell from time to time
Did he repair, to build the fold of which
His flock had need. 'Tis not forgotten
    yet
The pity which was then in every heart
For the old man—and 'tis believed by all
465 That many and many a day he thither went,
And never lifted up a single stone.

There, by the sheepfold, sometimes was
    he seen
Sitting alone, or with his faithful dog,
Then old, beside him, lying at his feet.
470 The length of full seven years, from time
    to time,
He at the building of this sheepfold
    wrought,
And left the work unfinished when he died.
Three years, or little more, did Isabel
Survive her husband: at her death the
    estate
475 Was sold, and went into a stranger's hand.
The cottage which was named THE EVE-
    NING STAR
Is gone—the ploughshare has been through
    the ground
On which it stood; great changes have
    been wrought

In all the neighborhood:—yet the oak is
   left
480 That grew beside their door; and the
   remains
Of the unfinished sheepfold may be seen
Beside the boisterous brook of Green-head
   Ghyll.

IT WAS AN APRIL MORNING
1800   1800

It was an April morning: fresh and clear
The rivulet, delighting in its strength,
Ran with a young man's speed; and yet
   the voice
Of waters which the winter had supplied
5 Was softened down into a vernal tone.
The spirit of enjoyment and desire,
And hopes and wishes, from all living
   things
Went circling, like a multitude of sounds.
The budding groves seemed eager to urge
   on
10 The steps of June; as if their various hues
Were only hindrances that stood between
Them and their object: but, meanwhile,
   prevailed
Such an entire contentment in the air
That every naked ash, and tardy tree
15 Yet leafless, showed as if the countenance
With which it looked on this delightful day
Were native to the summer.—Up the brook
I roamed in the confusion of my heart,
Alive to all things and forgetting all.
20 At length I to a sudden turning came
In this continuous glen, where down a rock
The stream, so ardent in its course before,
Sent forth such sallies of glad sound, that
   all
Which I till then had heard appeared the
   voice
25 Of common pleasure; beast and bird, the
   lamb,
The shepherd's dog, the linnet and the
   thrush,
Vied with this waterfall, and made a song
Which, while I listened, seemed like the
   wild growth
Or like some natural produce of the air,
30 That could not cease to be. Green leaves
   were here;
But 'twas the foliage of the rocks—the
   birch,
The yew, the holly, and the bright green
   thorn,
With hanging islands of resplendent furze:
And on a summit, distant a short space,
35 By any who should look beyond the dell
A single mountain-cottage might be seen.
I gazed and gazed, and to myself I said,

"Our thoughts at least are ours; and this
   wild nook,
My Emma,[1] I will dedicate to thee."
40 ——Soon did the spot become my other
   home,
My dwelling, and my out-of-doors abode.
And of the shepherds who have seen me
   there,
To whom I sometimes in our idle talk
Have told this fancy, two or three, perhaps,
45 Years after we are gone and in our graves,
When they have cause to speak of this
   wild place,
May call it by the name of EMMA'S DELL.

'TIS SAID THAT SOME HAVE DIED
FOR LOVE
1800   1800

'Tis said that some have died for love:
And here and there a churchyard grave
   is found
In the cold north's unhallowed ground,
Because the wretched man himself had
   slain,
5 His love was such a grievous pain.
And there is one whom I five years have
   known;
He dwells alone
Upon Helvellyn's side:
He loved—the pretty Barbara died;
10 And thus he makes his moan:
Three years had Barbara in her grave been
   laid
When thus his moan he made:

"Oh, move, thou Cottage, from behind that
   oak!
Or let the aged tree uprooted lie,
15 That in some other way yon smoke
May mount into the sky!
The clouds pass on; they from the heavens
   depart:
I look—the sky is empty space;
I know not what I trace;
20 But when I cease to look, my hand is on
   my heart.

"O! what a weight is in these shades!
   Ye Leaves,
That murmur once so dear, when will it
   cease?
Your sound my heart of rest bereaves,
It robs my heart of peace.
25 Thou Thrush, that singest loud—and loud
   and free,
Into yon row of willows flit,
Upon that alder sit;
Or sing another song, or choose another
   tree.

[1] A name given to Wordsworth's sister Dorothy.

"Roll back, sweet Rill! back to thy
  mountain-bounds,
30 And there forever be thy waters chained!
For thou dost haunt the air with sounds
That cannot be sustained;
If still beneath that pine-tree's ragged
  bough
Headlong yon waterfall must come,
35 Oh let it then be dumb!
Be anything, sweet Rill, but that which
  thou art now.

"Thou Eglantine, so bright with sunny
  showers,
Proud as a rainbow spanning half the vale,
Thou one fair shrub, oh! shed thy flowers,
40 And stir not in the gale.
For thus to see thee nodding in the air,
To see thy arch thus stretch and bend,
Thus rise and thus descend,—
Disturbs me till the sight is more than I
  can bear."

45 The man who makes this feverish complaint
Is one of giant stature, who could dance
Equipped from head to foot in iron mail.
Ah gentle Love! if ever thought was thine
To store up kindred hours for me, thy face
50 Turn from me, gentle Love! nor let me
  walk
Within the sound of Emma's voice, nor
  know
Such happiness as I have known today.

THE EXCURSION
1795-1814   1814

From Book I. The Wanderer
1795-1801   1814

'Twas summer, and the sun had mounted
  high:
Southward the landscape indistinctly
  glared
Through a pale steam; but all the northern
  downs,
In clearest air ascending, showed far off
5 A surface dappled o'er with shadows flung
From brooding clouds; shadows that lay
  in spots
Determined and unmoved, with steady
  beams
Of bright and pleasant sunshine interposed;
To him most pleasant who on soft cool
  moss
10 Extends his careless limbs along the front
Of some huge cave, whose rocky ceiling
  casts
A twilight of its own, an ample shade,

Where the wren warbles, while the dreaming man,
Half conscious of the soothing melody,
15 With side-long eye looks out upon the
  scene,
By power of that impending covert,
  thrown
To finer distance. Mine was at that hour
Far other lot, yet with good hope that soon
Under a shade as grateful I should find
20 Rest, and be welcomed there to livelier joy.
Across a bare, wide Common I was toiling
With languid steps that by the slippery
  turf
Were baffled; nor could my weak arm disperse
The host of insects gathering round my
  face,
25 And ever with me as I paced along.

Upon that open moorland stood a grove,
The wished-for port to which my course
  was bound.
Thither I came, and there, amid the
  gloom
Spread by a brotherhood of lofty elms,
30 Appeared a roofless hut; four naked walls
That stared upon each other!—I looked
  round,
And to my wish and to my hope espied
The friend I sought; a man of reverend
  age,
But stout and hale, for travel unimpaired.
35 There was he seen upon the cottage-bench,
Recumbent in the shade, as if asleep;
An iron-pointed staff lay at his side.

. . . . . .

    Supine the Wanderer lay,
His eyes as if in drowsiness half shut,
440 The shadows of the breezy elms above
Dappling his face. He had not heard the
  sound
Of my approaching steps, and in the shade
Unnoticed did I stand some minutes' space.
At length I hailed him, seeing that his hat
445 Was moist with water-drops, as if the
  brim
Had newly scooped a running stream. He
  rose,
And ere our lively greeting into peace
Had settled, " 'Tis," said I, "a burning
  day:
My lips are parched with thirst, but you,
  it seems,
450 Have somewhere found relief." He, at
  the word,
Pointing towards a sweet-briar, bade me
  climb

The fence where that aspiring shrub
        looked out
Upon the public way. It was a plot
Of garden ground run wild, its matted
        weeds
455 Marked with the steps of those, whom,
        as they passed,
The gooseberry trees that shot in long lank
        slips,
Or currants, hanging from their leafless
        stems,
In scanty strings, had tempted to o'erleap
The broken wall. I looked around, and
        there,
460 Where two tall hedge-rows of thick alder
        boughs
Joined in a cold damp nook, espied a well
Shrouded with willow-flowers and plumy
        fern.
My thirst I slaked, and, from the cheerless
        spot
Withdrawing, straightway to the shade re-
        turned
465 Where sate the old man on the cottage-
        bench;
And, while, beside him, with uncovered
        head,
I yet was standing, freely to respire,
And cool my temples in the fanning air,
Thus did he speak. "I see around me
        here
470 Things which you cannot see: we die, my
        friend,
Nor we alone, but that which each man
        loved
And prized in his peculiar nook of earth
Dies with him, or is changed; and very
        soon
Even of the good is no memorial left.
475 —The poets, in their elegies and songs
Lamenting the departed, call the groves,
They call upon the hills and streams to
        mourn,
And senseless rocks; nor idly; for they
        speak,
In these their invocations, with a voice
480 Obedient to the strong creative power
Of human passion. Sympathies there are
More tranquil, yet perhaps of kindred
        birth,
That steal upon the meditative mind,
And grow with thought. Beside yon
        spring I stood,
485 And eyed its waters till we seemed to feel
One sadness, they and I. For them a bond
Of brotherhood is broken: time has **been**
When, every day, the touch of human hand
Dislodged the natural sleep that binds
        them up

490 In mortal stillness; and they ministered
To human comfort. Stooping down to
        drink,
Upon the slimy foot-stone I espied
The useless fragment of a wooden bowl,
Green with the moss of years, and subject
        only
495 To the soft handling of the elements:
There let it lie—how foolish are such
        thoughts!
Forgive them;—never—never did my steps
Approach this door but she who dwelt
        within
A daughter's welcome gave me, and I loved
        her
500 As my own child. Oh, sir! the good die
        first,
And they whose hearts are dry as summer
        dust
Burn to the socket. Many a passenger
Hath blessed poor Margaret for her gentle
        looks,
When she upheld the cool refreshment
        drawn
505 From that forsaken spring; and no one
        came
But he was welcome; no one went away
But that it seemed she loved him. She is
        dead,
The light extinguished of her lonely hut,
The hut itself abandoned to decay,
510 And she forgotten in the quiet grave.

    "I speak," continued he, "of one whose
        stock
Of virtues bloomed beneath this lowly roof.
She was a woman of a steady mind,
Tender and deep in her excess of love;
515 Not speaking much, pleased rather with
        the joy
Of her own thoughts: by some especial
        care
Her temper had been framed, as if to make
A being, who by adding love to peace
Might live on earth a life of happiness.
520 Her wedded partner lacked not on his side
The humble worth that satisfied her heart:
Frugal, affectionate, sober, and withal
Keenly industrious. She with pride would
        tell
That he was often seated at his loom,
525 In summer, ere the mower was abroad
Among the dewy grass,—in early spring,
Ere the last star had vanished.—They who
        passed
At evening, from behind the garden fence
Might hear his busy spade, which he would
        ply,
530 After his daily work, until the light

Had failed, and every leaf and flower were
    lost
In the dark hedges. So their days were
    spent
In peace and comfort; and a pretty boy
Was their best hope, next to the God in
    heaven.

535   "Not twenty years ago, but you I think
Can scarcely bear it now in mind, there
    came
Two blighting seasons, when the fields were
    left
With half a harvest. It pleased Heaven to
    add
A worse affliction in the plague of war:
540 This happy land was stricken to the heart!
A wanderer then among the cottages,
I, with my freight of winter raiment, saw
The hardships of that season: many rich
Sank down, as in a dream, among the poor;
545 And of the poor did many cease to be,
And their place knew them not. Mean-
    while, abridged
Of daily comforts, gladly reconciled
To numerous self-denials, Margaret
Went struggling on through those calami-
    tous years
550 With cheerful hope, until the second
    autumn,
When her life's helpmate on a sick-bed lay,
Smitten with perilous fever. In disease
He lingered long; and, when his strength
    returned,
He found the little he had stored, to meet
555 The hour of accident or crippling age,
Was all consumed. A second infant now
Was added to the troubles of a time
Laden, for them and all of their degree,
With care and sorrow: shoals of artisans
560 From ill-requited labor turned adrift
Sought daily bread from public charity,
They, and their wives and children—hap-
    pier far
Could they have lived as do the little birds
That peck along the hedge-rows, or the
    kite
565 That makes her dwelling on the mountain
    rocks!

    "A sad reverse it was for him who long
Had filled with plenty, and possessed in
    peace,
This lonely cottage. At the door he stood,
And whistled many a snatch of merry tunes
570 That had no mirth in them; or with his
    knife
Carved uncouth figures on the heads of
    sticks—

Then, not less idly, sought, through every
    nook
In house or garden, any casual work
Of use or ornament; and with a strange,
575 Amusing, yet uneasy, novelty,
He mingled, where he might, the various
    tasks
Of summer, autumn, winter, and of spring.
But this endured not; his good humor soon
Became a weight in which no pleasure was:
580 And poverty brought on a petted mood
And a sore temper: day by day he drooped,
And he would leave his work—and to the
    town
Would turn without an errand his slack
    steps;
Or wander here and there among the fields.
585 One while he would speak lightly of his
    babes,
And with a cruel tongue: at other times
He tossed them with a false unnatural joy:
And 'twas a rueful thing to see the looks
Of the poor innocent children. 'Every
    smile,'
590 Said Margaret to me, here beneath these
    trees,
'Made my heart bleed.'"
                At this the Wanderer paused;
And, looking up to those enormous elms,
He said, " 'Tis now the hour of deepest
    noon.
At this still season of repose and peace,
595 This hour when all things which are not at
    rest
Are cheerful; while this multitude of flies
With tuneful hum is filling all the air;
Why should a tear be on an old man's
    cheek?
Why should we thus, with an untoward
    mind,
600 And in the weakness of humanity,
From natural wisdom turn our hearts
    away;
To natural comforts shut our eyes and
    ears;
And, feeding on disquiet, thus disturb
The calm of nature with our restless
    thoughts?"

605 He spake with somewhat of a solemn tone:
But, when he ended, there was in his face
Such easy cheerfulness, a look so mild,
That for a little time it stole away
All recollection; and that simple tale
610 Passed from my mind like a forgotten
    sound.
A while on trivial things we held discourse,
To me soon tasteless. In my own despite,
I thought of that poor woman as of one

Whom I had known and loved. He had rehearsed
615 Her homely tale with such familiar power,
With such an active countenance, an eye
So busy, that the things of which he spake
Seemed present; and, attention now relaxed,
A heart-felt chilliness crept along my veins.
620 I rose; and, having left the breezy shade,
Stood drinking comfort from the warmer sun,
That had not cheered me long—ere, looking round
Upon that tranquil ruin, I returned,
And begged of the old man that, for my sake,
625 He would resume his story.
             He replied,
"It were a wantonness, and would demand
Severe reproof, if we were men whose hearts
Could hold vain dalliance with the misery
Even of the dead; contented thence to draw
630 A momentary pleasure, never marked
By reason, barren of all future good.
But we have known that there is often found
In mournful thoughts, and always might be found,
A power to virtue friendly; were 't not so,
635 I am a dreamer among men, indeed
An idle dreamer! 'Tis a common tale,
An ordinary sorrow of man's life,
A tale of silent suffering, hardly clothed
In bodily form.—But without further bidding
640 I will proceed.
            While thus it fared with them,
To whom this cottage, till those hapless years,
Had been a blessèd home, it was my chance
To travel in a country far remote;
And when these lofty elms once more appeared
645 What pleasant expectations lured me on
O'er the flat Common!—With quick step I reached
The threshold, lifted with light hand the latch;
But, when I entered, Margaret looked at me
A little while; then turned her head away
650 Speechless,—and, sitting down upon a chair,
Wept bitterly. I wist not what to do,
Nor how to speak to her. Poor wretch! at last
She rose from off her seat, and then,—O sir!

I cannot *tell* how she pronounced my name:—
655 With fervent love, and with a face of grief
Unutterably helpless, and a look
That seemed to cling upon me, she enquired
If I had seen her husband. As she spake
A strange surprise and fear came to my heart,
660 Nor had I power to answer ere she told
That he had disappeared—not two months gone.
He left his house: two wretched days had past,
And on the third, as wistfully she raised
Her head from off her pillow, to look forth,
665 Like one in trouble, for returning light,
Within her chamber casement she espied
A folded paper, lying as if placed
To meet her waking eyes. This tremblingly
She opened—found no writing, but beheld
670 Pieces of money carefully enclosed,
Silver and gold. 'I shuddered at the sight,'
Said Margaret, 'for I knew it was his hand
That must have placed it there; and ere that day
Was ended, that long anxious day, I learned,
675 From one who by my husband had been sent
With the sad news, that he had joined a troop
Of soldiers, going to a distant land.
—He left me thus—he could not gather heart
To take a farewell of me; for he feared
680 That I should follow with my babes, and sink
Beneath the misery of that wandering life.'

"This tale did Margaret tell with many tears:
And, when she ended, I had little power
To give her comfort, and was glad to take
685 Such words of hope from her own mouth as served
To cheer us both. But long we had not talked
Ere we built up a pile of better thoughts,
And with a brighter eye she looked around
As if she had been shedding tears of joy.
690 We parted.—'Twas the time of early spring;
I left her busy with her garden tools;
And well remember, o'er that fence she looked,
And, while I paced along the foot-way path,
Called out, and sent a blessing after me,
695 With tender cheerfulness, and with a voice
That seemed the very sound of happy thoughts.

"I roved o'er many a hill and many a
  dale,
With my accustomed load; in heat and cold,
Through many a wood and many an open
  ground,
700 In sunshine and in shade, in wet and fair,
Drooping or blithe of heart, as might be-
  fall;
My best companions now the driving winds,
And now the 'trotting brooks'[1] and whis-
  pering trees,
And now the music of my own sad steps,
705 With many a short-lived thought that
  passed between,
And disappeared.
                    I journeyed back this way,
When, in the warmth of midsummer, the
  wheat
Was yellow; and the soft and bladed grass,
Springing afresh, had o'er the hay-field
  spread
710 Its tender verdure. At the door arrived.
I found that she was absent. In the shade,
Where now we sit, I waited her return.
Her cottage, then a cheerful object, wore
Its customary look,—only, it seemed,
715 The honeysuckle, crowding round the
  porch,
Hung down in heavier tufts; and that
  bright weed,
The yellow stone-crop, suffered to take root
Along the window's edge, profusely grew,
Blinding the lower panes. I turned aside,
720 And strolled into her garden. It appeared
To lag behind the season, and had lost
Its pride of neatness. Daisy-flowers and
  thrift
Had broken their trim border-lines, and
  straggled
O'er paths they used to deck: carnations,
  once
725 Prized for surpassing beauty, and no less
For the peculiar pains they had required,
Declined their languid heads, wanting sup-
  port.
The cumbrous bind-weed, with its wreaths
  and bells,
Had twined about her two small rows of
  peas,
730 And dragged them to the earth.
                    Ere this an hour
Was wasted.—Back I turned my restless
  steps;
A stranger passed; and, guessing whom I
  sought,
He said that she was used to ramble far.—
The sun was sinking in the west; and now
735 I sat with sad impatience. From within

[1] Burns, *To William Simpson*, 87.

Her solitary infant cried aloud;
Then, like a blast that dies away self-
  stilled,
The voice was silent. From the bench I
  rose;
But neither could divert nor soothe my
  thoughts.
740 The spot, though fair, was very desolate—
The longer I remained, more desolate:
And, looking round me, now I first observed
The corner stones, on either side the porch,
With dull red stains discolored, and stuck
  o'er
745 With tufts and hairs of wool, as if the
  sheep,
That fed upon the Common, thither came
Familiarly, and found a couching-place
Even at her threshold. Deeper shadows
  fell
From these tall elms; the cottage-clock
  struck eight;—
750 I turned, and saw her distant a few steps.
Her face was pale and thin—her figure,
  too,
Was changed. As she unlocked the door,
  she said,
'It grieves me you have waited here so long,
But, in good truth, I've wandered much of
  late;
755 And, sometimes—to my shame I speak—
  have need
Of my best prayers to bring me back
  again.'
While on the board she spread our evening
  meal,
She told me—interrupting not the work
Which gave employment to her listless
  hands—
760 That she had parted with her elder child;
To a kind master on a distant farm
Now happily apprenticed.—'I perceive
You look at me, and you have cause; today
I have been travelling far; and many days
765 About the fields I wander, knowing this
Only, that what I seek I cannot find;
And so I waste my time: for I am changed;
And to myself,' said she, 'have done much
  wrong
And to this helpless infant. I have slept
770 Weeping, and weeping have I waked; my
  tears
Have flowed as if my body were not such
As others are; and I could never die.
But I am now in mind and in my heart
More easy; and I hope,' said she, 'that God
775 Will give me patience to endure the things
Which I behold at home.'
                    It would have grieved
Your very soul to see her. Sir, I feel

The story linger in my heart; I fear
'Tis long and tedious; but my spirit clings
780 To that poor woman:—so familiarly
Do I perceive her manner, and her look,
And presence; and so deeply do I feel
Her goodness, that, not seldom, in my
walks
A momentary trance comes over me;
785 And to myself I seem to muse on one
By sorrow laid asleep; or borne away,
A human being destined to awake
To human life, or something very near
To human life, when he shall come again
790 For whom she suffered. Yes, it would have
grieved
Your very soul to see her: evermore
Her eyelids drooped, her eyes downward
were cast;
And, when she at her table gave me food,
She did not look at me. Her voice was low,
795 Her body was subdued. In every act
Pertaining to her house-affairs, appeared
The careless stillness of a thinking mind
Self-occupied; to which all outward things
Are like an idle matter. Still she sighed,
800 But yet no motion of the breast was seen,
No heaving of the heart. While by the fire
We sate together, sighs came on my ear,
I knew not why, and hardly whence they
came.

"Ere my departure, to her care I gave,
805 For her son's use, some tokens of regard,
Which with a look of welcome she received;
And I exhorted her to place her trust
In God's good love, and seek his help by
prayer.
I took my staff, and, when I kissed her
babe,
810 The tears stood in her eyes. I left her then
With the best hope and comfort I could
give:
She thanked me for my wish;—but for my
hope
It seemed she did not thank me.
I returned,
And took my rounds along this road again
815 When on its sunny bank the primrose
flower
Peeped forth, to give an earnest of the
spring.
I found her sad and drooping: she had
learned
No tidings of her husband; if he lived,
She knew not that he lived; if he were
dead,
820 She knew not he was dead. She seemed the
same
In person and appearance; but her house

Bespake a sleepy hand of negligence;
The floor was neither dry nor neat, the
hearth
Was comfortless, and her small lot of
books,
825 Which, in the cottage-window, heretofore
Had been piled up against the corner panes
In seemly order, now, with straggling
leaves,
Lay scattered here and there, open or shut,
As they had chanced to fall. Her infant
babe
830 Had from its mother caught the trick of
grief,
And sighed among its playthings. I withdrew,
And once again entering the garden saw,
More plainly still, that poverty and grief
Were now come nearer to her: weeds defaced
835 The hardened soil, and knots of withered
grass;
No ridges there appeared of clear black
mould,
No winter greenness; of her herbs and
flowers,
It seemed the better part were gnawed
away
Or trampled into earth; a chain of straw,
840 Which had been twined about the slender
stem
Of a young apple-tree, lay at its root;
The bark was nibbled round by truant
sheep.
—Margaret stood near, her infant in her
arms,
And, noting that my eye was on the tree,
845 She said, 'I fear it will be dead and gone
Ere Robert come again.' When to the
house
We had returned together, she enquired
If I had any hope:—but for her babe
And for her little orphan boy, she said,
850 She had no wish to live, that she must die
Of sorrow. Yet I saw the idle loom
Still in its place; his Sunday garments
hung
Upon the self-same nail; his very staff
Stood undisturbed behind the door.
And when,
855 In bleak December, I retraced this way,
She told me that her little babe was dead,
And she was left alone. She now, released
From her maternal cares, had taken up
The employment common through these
wilds, and gained,
860 By spinning hemp, a pittance for herself;
And for this end had hired a neighbor's
boy

To give her needful help. That very time
Most willingly she put her work aside,
And walked with me along the miry road,
865 Heedless how far; and, in such piteous sort
That any heart had ached to hear her,
begged
That, wheresoe'er I went, I still would ask
For him whom she had lost. We parted
then—
Our final parting; for from that time forth
870 Did many seasons pass ere I returned
Into this tract again.
              Nine tedious years;
From their first separation, nine long years,
She lingered in unquiet widowhood;
A wife and widow. Needs must it have
been
875 A sore heart-wasting! I have heard, my
friend,
That in yon arbor oftentimes she sate
Alone, through half the vacant Sabbath
day;
And, if a dog passed by, she still would quit
The shade, and look abroad. On this old
bench
880 For hours she sate; and evermore her eye
Was busy in the distance, shaping things
That made her heart beat quick. You see
that path,
Now faint,—the grass has crept o'er its
gray line;
There, to and fro, she paced through many
a day
885 Of the warm summer, from a belt of hemp
That girt her waist, spinning the long-
drawn thread
With backward steps. Yet ever as there
passed
A man whose garments showed the soldier's
red,
Or crippled mendicant in soldier's garb,
890 The little child who sate to turn the
wheel
Ceased from his task; and she with faltering voice
Made many a fond enquiry; and when
they,
Whose presence gave no comfort, were
gone by,
Her heart was still more sad. And by yon
gate,
895 That bars the traveller's road, she often
stood,
And when a stranger horseman came, the
latch
Would lift, and in his face look wistfully:
Most happy, if, from aught discovered
there
Of tender feeling, she might dare repeat

900 The same sad question. Meanwhile her
poor hut
Sank to decay; for he was gone, whose
hand,
At the first nipping of October frost,
Closed up each chink, and with fresh bands
of straw
Chequered the green-grown thatch. And
so she lived
905 Through the long winter, reckless and
alone;
Until her house by frost, and thaw, and
rain,
Was sapped; and while she slept, the
nightly damps
Did chill her breast; and in the stormy day
Her tattered clothes were ruffled by the
wind,
910 Even at the side of her own fire. Yet still
She loved this wretched spot, nor would for
worlds
Have parted hence; and still that length of
road,
And this rude bench, one torturing hope
endeared,
Fast rooted at her heart: and here, my
friend,—
915 In sickness she remained; and here she
died;
Last human tenant of these ruined walls!''

    The old man ceased: he saw that I was
moved;
From that low bench, rising instinctively
I turned aside in weakness, nor had power
920 To thank him for the tale which he had
told.
I stood, and leaning o'er the garden wall
Reviewed that woman's sufferings; and it
seemed
To comfort me while with a brother's love
I blessed her in the impotence of grief.
925 Then towards the cottage I returned; and
traced
Fondly, though with an interest more mild,
That secret spirit of humanity
Which, 'mid the calm oblivious tendencies
Of nature, 'mid her plants, and weeds, and
flowers,
930 And silent overgrowings, still survived.
The old man, noting this, resumed, and
said,
"My friend! enough to sorrow you have
given,
The purposes of wisdom ask no more:
Nor more would she have craved as due to
one
935 Who, in her worst distress, had ofttimes
felt

The unbounded might of prayer; and
    learned, with soul
Fixed on the Cross, that consolation
    springs,
From sources deeper far than deepest pain,
For the meek sufferer. Why then should
    we read
940 The forms of things with an unworthy eye?
She sleeps in the calm earth, and peace is
    here.
I well remember that those very plumes,
Those weeds, and the high spear-grass on
    that wall,
By mist and silent rain-drops silvered o'er,
945 As once I passed, into my heart conveyed
So still an image of tranquillity,
So calm and still, and looked so beautiful
Amid the uneasy thoughts which filled my
    mind,
That what we feel of sorrow and despair
950 From ruin and from change, and all the
    grief
That passing shows of being leave behind,
Appeared an idle dream, that could main-
    tain,
Nowhere, dominion o'er the enlightened
    spirit
Whose meditative sympathies repose
955 Upon the breast of Faith. I turned away,
And walked along my road in happiness."

    He ceased. Ere long the sun declining
      shot
A slant and mellow radiance, which began
To fall upon us, while, beneath the trees,
960 We sate on that low bench: and now we
    felt,
Admonished thus, the sweet hour coming
    on.
A linnet warbled from those lofty elms,
A thrush sang loud, and other melodies,
At distance heard, peopled the milder air.
965 The old man rose, and, with a sprightly
    mien
Of hopeful preparation, grasped his staff;
Together casting then a farewell look
Upon those silent walls, we left the shade;
And, ere the stars were visible, had reached
970 A village-inn,—our evening resting-place.

PELION AND OSSA
1801   1815

Pelion and Ossa flourish side by side,
Together in immortal books enrolled:
His ancient dower Olympus hath not sold;
And that inspiring hill,[1] which "did
    divide
5 Into two ample horns his forehead wide,"[2]

[1] Parnassus.
[2] See Spenser's *Virgil's Gnat,* 21-22.

Shines with poetic radiance as of old;
While not an English mountain we behold
By the celestial Muses glorified.
Yet round our sea-girt shore they rise in
    crowds:
10 What was the great Parnassus' self to thee,
Mount Skiddaw? In his natural sovereignty
Our British hill is nobler far; he shrouds
His double front among Atlantic clouds
And pours forth streams more sweet than
    Castaly.

THE SPARROW'S NEST
1801   1807

Behold, within the leafy shade,
Those bright blue eggs together laid!
On me the chance-discovered sight
Gleamed like a vision of delight.
5 I started—seeming to espy
The home and sheltered bed,
The sparrow's dwelling, which, hard by
My father's house, in wet or dry
My sister Emmeline[1] and I
10   Together visited.

She looked at it and seemed to fear it;
Dreading, tho' wishing, to be near it:
Such heart was in her, being then
A little prattler among men.
15 The blessing of my later years
Was with me when a boy:
She gave me eyes, she gave me ears;
And humble cares, and delicate fears;
A heart, the fountain of sweet tears;
20   And love, and thought, and joy.

TO A BUTTERFLY
1802   1807

Stay near me—do not take thy flight!
A little longer stay in sight!
Much converse do I find in thee,
Historian of my infancy!
5 Float near me; do not yet depart!
Dead times revive in thee:
Thou bring'st, gay creature as thou art!
A solemn image to my heart,
My father's family!

10 Oh! pleasant, pleasant were the days,
The time, when in our childish plays,
My sister Emmeline[1] and I
Together chased the butterfly!
A very hunter did I rush
15 Upon the prey;—with leaps and springs
I followed on from brake to bush;
But she, God love her! feared to brush
The dust from off its wings.

[1] A name given to Wordsworth's sister Dorothy.

MY HEART LEAPS UP
1802 1807

My heart leaps up when I behold
  A rainbow in the sky:
So was it when my life began;
So is it now I am a man;
5 So be it when I shall grow old,
  Or let me die!
The Child is father of the Man;
And I could wish my days to be
Bound each to each by natural piety.

WRITTEN IN MARCH

WHILE RESTING ON THE BRIDGE AT THE FOOT
OF BROTHER'S WATER
1802 1807

  The cock is crowing,
  The stream is flowing,
  The small birds twitter,
  The lake doth glitter,
5 The green field sleeps in the sun;
  The oldest and youngest
  Are at work with the strongest;
  The cattle are grazing,
  Their heads never raising;
10 There are forty feeding like one!

  Like an army defeated
  The snow hath retreated,
  And now doth fare ill
  On the top of the bare hill;
15 The ploughboy is whooping—anon—anon:
  There's joy in the mountains;
  There's life in the fountains;
  Small clouds are sailing,
  Blue sky prevailing;
20 The rain is over and gone!

TO A BUTTERFLY
1802 1807

I've watched you now a full half-hour,
Self-poised upon that yellow flower;
And, little Butterfly! indeed
I know not if you sleep or feed.
5 How motionless!—not frozen seas
More motionless! and then
What joy awaits you, when the breeze
Hath found you out among the trees,
And calls you forth again!

10 This plot of orchard-ground is ours;
My trees they are, my sister's flowers:
Here rest your wings when they are weary;
Here lodge as in a sanctuary!
Come often to us, fear no wrong;
15 Sit near us on the bough!

We'll talk of sunshine and of song,
And summer days, when we were young;
Sweet childish days, that were as long
As twenty days are now.

TO THE SMALL CELANDINE
1802 1807

Pansies, lilies, kingcups, daisies,
Let them live upon their praises;
Long as there's a sun that sets,
Primroses will have their glory;
5 Long as there are violets,
They will have a place in story:
There's a flower that shall be mine,
'Tis the little Celandine.

Eyes of some men travel far
10 For the finding of a star;
Up and down the heavens they go,
Men that keep a mighty rout!
I'm as great as they, I trow,
Since the day I found thee out,
15 Little Flower—I'll make a stir,
Like a sage astronomer.

Modest, yet withal an Elf
Bold, and lavish of thyself;
Since we needs must first have met
20 I have seen thee, high and low,
Thirty years or more, and yet
'Twas a face I did not know:
Thou hast now, go where I may,
Fifty greetings in a day.

25 Ere a leaf is on a bush,
In the time before the thrush
Has a thought about her nest,
Thou wilt come with half a call,
Spreading out thy glossy breast
30 Like a careless Prodigal;
Telling tales about the sun,
When we've little warmth, or none.

Poets, vain men in their mood!
Travel with the multitude:
35 Never heed them; I aver
That they all are wanton wooers;
But the thrifty cottager,
Who stirs little out of doors,
Joys to spy thee near her home;
40 Spring is coming, thou art come!

Comfort have thou of thy merit,
Kindly, unassuming Spirit!
Careless of thy neighborhood,
Thou dost show thy pleasant face
45 On the moor, and in the wood,
In the lane;—there's not a place,
Howsoever mean it be,
But 'tis good enough for thee.

Ill befall the yellow flowers,
50 Children of the flaring hours!
Buttercups, that will be seen,
Whether we will see or no;
Others, too, of lofty mien;
They have done as worldlings do,
55 Taken praise that should be thine,
Little, humble Celandine.

Prophet of delight and mirth,
Ill-requited upon earth;
Herald of a mighty band,
60 Of a joyous train ensuing,
Serving at my heart's command,
Tasks that are no tasks renewing,
I will sing, as doth behove,
Hymns in praise of what I love!

TO THE SAME FLOWER
1802   1807

Pleasures newly found are sweet
When they lie about our feet:
February last, my heart
First at sight of thee was glad;
5 All unheard of as thou art,
Thou must needs, I think, have had,
Celandine! and long ago,
Praise of which I nothing know.

I have not a doubt but he,
10 Whosoe'er the man might be,
Who the first with pointed rays
(Workman worthy to be sainted)
Set the sign-board in a blaze,
When the rising sun he painted,
15 Took the fancy from a glance
At thy glittering countenance.

Soon as gentle breezes bring
News of winter's vanishing,
And the children build their bowers,
20 Sticking 'kerchief-plots[1] of mould
All about with full-blown flowers,
Thick as sheep in shepherd's fold!
With the proudest thou art there,
Mantling in the tiny square.

25 Often have I sighed to measure
By myself a lonely pleasure,
Sighed to think I read a book
Only read, perhaps, by me;
Yet I long could overlook
30 Thy bright coronet and thee,
And thy arch and wily ways,
And thy store of other praise.

Blithe of heart, from week to week
Thou dost play at hide-and-seek;
35 While the patient primrose sits

[1] Plots of the size of a handkerchief.

Like a beggar in the cold,
Thou, a flower of wiser wits,
Slip'st into thy sheltering hold;
Liveliest of the vernal train
40 When ye all are out again.

Drawn by what peculiar spell,
By what charm of sight or smell,
Does the dim-eyed curious bee,
Laboring for her waxen cells,
45 Fondly settle upon thee
Prized above all buds and bells
Opening daily at thy side,
By the season multiplied?

Thou art not beyond the moon,
50 But a thing "beneath our shoon:"[1]
Let the bold discoverer thrid
In his bark the polar sea;
Rear who will a pyramid;
Praise it is enough for me,
55 If there be but three or four
Who will love my little Flower.

RESOLUTION AND INDEPENDENCE
1802   1807

There was a roaring in the wind all night;
The rain came heavily and fell in floods;
But now the sun is rising calm and bright;
The birds are singing in the distant woods;
5 Over his own sweet voice the stock-dove
      broods;
The jay makes answer as the magpie
      chatters;
And all the air is filled with pleasant .
      noise of waters.

All things that love the sun are out of
      doors;
The sky rejoices in the morning's birth;
10 The grass is bright with rain-drops;—on
      the moors
The hare is running races in her mirth;
And with her feet she from the plashy
      earth
Raises a mist, that, glittering in the sun,
Runs with her all the way, wherever she
      doth run.

15 I was a traveller then upon the moor;
I saw the hare that raced about with joy;
I heard the woods and distant waters roar;
Or heard them not, as happy as a boy:
The pleasant season did my heart employ:
20 My old remembrances went from me
      wholly;
And all the ways of men, so vain and
      melancholy.

[1] shoes (See *Comus,* 634.)

But, as it sometimes chanceth, from the
    might
Of joy in minds that can no further go,
As high as we have mounted in delight
25 In our dejection do we sink as low;
To me that morning did it happen so;
And fears and fancies thick upon me came;
Dim sadness—and blind thoughts, I knew
    not, nor could name.

I heard the skylark warbling in the sky;
30 And I bethought me of the playful hare:
Even such a happy child of earth am I;
Even as these blissful creatures do I fare;
Far from the world I walk, and from all
    care;
But there may come another day to me—
35 Solitude, pain of heart, distress, and
    poverty.

My whole life I have lived in pleasant
    thought,
As if life's business were a summer mood;
As if all needful things would come un-
    sought
To genial faith, still rich in genial good;
40 But how can he expect that others should
Build for him, sow for him, and at his call
Love him, who for himself will take no
    heed at all?

I thought of Chatterton, the marvellous
    Boy,
The sleepless Soul that perished in his
    pride;
45 Of him who walked in glory and in joy
Following his plough, along the mountain-
    side:[1]
By our own spirits are we deified:
We poets in our youth begin in gladness;
But thereof come in the end despondency
    and madness.

50 Now, whether it were by peculiar grace,
A leading from above, a something given,
Yet it befell that, in this lonely place,
When I with these untoward thoughts had
    striven,
Beside a pool bare to the eye of heaven
55 I saw a man before me unawares:
The oldest man he seemed that ever wore
    gray hairs.

As a huge stone is sometimes seen to lie
Couched on the bald top of an eminence;
Wonder to all who do the same espy,
60 By what means it could thither come, and
    whence;

[1] Burns.

So that it seems a thing endued with sense:
Like a sea-beast crawled forth, that on a
    shelf
Of rock or sand reposeth, there to sun
    itself;

Such seemed this man, not all alive nor
    dead,
65 Nor all asleep—in his extreme old age:
His body was bent double, feet and head
Coming together in life's pilgrimage;
As if some dire constraint of pain, or rage
Of sickness felt by him in times long past,
70 A more than human weight upon his frame
    had cast.

Himself he propped, limbs, body, and pale
    face,
Upon a long gray staff of shaven wood:
And, still as I drew near with gentle pace,
Upon the margin of that moorish[1] flood
75 Motionless as a cloud the old man stood,
That heareth not the loud winds when
    they call;
And moveth all together, if it move at all.

At length, himself unsettling, he the pond
Stirred with his staff, and fixedly did look
80 Upon the muddy water, which he conned,
As if he had been reading in a book:
And now a stranger's privilege I took;
And, drawing to his side, to him did say,
"This morning gives us promise of a glo-
    rious day."

85 A gentle answer did the old man make,
In courteous speech which forth he slowly
    drew:
And him with further words I thus be-
    spake,
"What occupation do you there pursue?
This is a lonesome place for one like you."
90 Ere he replied, a flash of mild surprise
Broke from the sable orbs of his yet-vivid
    eyes.

His words came feebly, from a feeble chest,
But each in solemn order followed each,
With something of a lofty utterance
    drest—
95 Choice word and measured phrase, above
    the reach
Of ordinary men; a stately speech;
Such as grave livers do in Scotland use,
Religious men, who give to God and man
    their dues.

[1] marshy

He told, that to these waters he had come
100 To gather leeches, being old and poor:
Employment hazardous and wearisome!
And he had many hardships to endure:
From pond to pond he roamed, from moor
to moor;
Housing, with God's good help, by choice
or chance;
105 And in this way he gained an honest
maintenance.

The old man still stood talking by my side;
But now his voice to me was like a stream
Scarce heard; nor word from word could
I divide;
And the whole body of the man did seem
110 Like one whom I had met with in a dream;
Or like a man from some far region sent,
To give me human strength, by apt ad-
monishment.

My former thoughts returned: the fear
that kills;
And hope that is unwilling to be fed;
115 Cold, pain, and labor, and all fleshly ills;
And mighty poets in their misery dead.
—Perplexed, and longing to be comforted,
My question eagerly did I renew,
"How is it that you live, and what is it
you do?"

120 He with a smile did then his words repeat;
And said that, gathering leeches, far and
wide
He travelled, stirring thus about his feet
The waters of the pools where they abide.
"Once I could meet with them on every
side;
125 But they have dwindled long by slow
decay;
Yet still I persevere, and find them where
I may."

While he was talking thus, the lonely
place,
The old man's shape, and speech—all
troubled me:
In my mind's eye I seemed to see him pace
130 About the weary moors continually,
Wandering about alone and silently.
While I these thoughts within myself pursued,
He, having made a pause, the same discourse renewed.

And soon with this he other matter
blended,
135 Cheerfully uttered, with demeanor kind,

But stately in the main; and, when he
ended,
I could have laughed myself to scorn to
find
In that decrepit man so firm a mind.
"God," said I, "be my help and stay
secure;
140 I'll think of the leech-gatherer on the
lonely moor!"

I GRIEVED FOR BUONAPARTÉ
1802   1802

I grieved for Buonaparté, with a vain
And an unthinking grief! The tenderest
mood
Of that Man's mind—what can it be?
what food
Fed his first hopes? what knowledge could
he gain?
5 'Tis not in battles that from youth we
train
The Governor who must be wise and good,
And temper with the sternness of the brain
Thoughts motherly, and meek as womanhood.
Wisdom doth live with children round her
knees:
10 Books, leisure, perfect freedom, and the
talk
Man holds with week-day man in the
hourly walk
Of the mind's business: these are the
degrees
By which true Sway doth mount; this is
the stalk
True Power doth grow on; and her rights
are these.

COMPOSED UPON WESTMINSTER
BRIDGE, SEPTEMBER 3, 1803
1802   1807

Earth has not anything to show more fair:
Dull would he be of soul who could pass by
A sight so touching in its majesty:
This City now doth, like a garment, wear
5 The beauty of the morning; silent, bare,
Ships, towers, domes, theatres, and tem-
ples lie
Open unto the fields, and to the sky;
All bright and glittering in the smokeless
air.
Never did sun more beautifully steep
10 In his first splendor, valley, rock, or hill;
Ne'er saw I, never felt, a calm so deep!
The river glideth at his own sweet will:
Dear God! the very houses seem asleep;
And all that mighty heart is lying still!

COMPOSED BY THE SEA-SIDE, NEAR CALAIS, AUGUST, 1802
1802   1807

Fair Star of evening, Splendor of the
    west,
Star of my Country!—on the horizon's
    brink
Thou hangest, stooping, as might seem, to
    sink
On England's bosom; yet well pleased to
    rest,
5 Meanwhile, and be to her a glorious
    crest
Conspicuous to the Nations. Thou, I
    think
Shouldst be my Country's emblem; and
    shouldst wink,
Bright Star! with laughter on her ban-
    ners, drest
In thy fresh beauty. There! that dusky
    spot
10 Beneath thee, that is England; there she
    lies.
Blessings be on you both! one hope, one
    lot,
One life, one glory!—I, with many a
    fear
For my dear Country, many heartfelt
    sighs,
Among men who do not love her, linger
    here.

IT IS A BEAUTEOUS EVENING, CALM AND FREE
1802   1807

It is a beauteous evening, calm and free,
The holy time is quiet as a Nun
Breathless with adoration; the broad sun
Is sinking down in its tranquillity;
5 The gentleness of heaven broods o'er the
    Sea:
Listen! the mighty Being is awake,
And doth with his eternal motion make
A sound like thunder—everlastingly.
Dear Child![1] dear Girl; that walkest with
    me here,[2]
10 If thou appear untouched by solemn
    thought,
Thy nature is not therefore less divine:
Thou liest in Abraham's bosom[3] all the
    year;
And worshipp'st at the temple's inner
    shrine,
God being with thee when we know it
    not.

[1] Wordsworth's daughter Caroline.
[2] On Calais Beach.
[3] In the presence of God. See *Luke,* 16:22.

ON THE EXTINCTION OF THE VENETIAN REPUBLIC[1]
1802   1807

Once did She hold the gorgeous East in
    fee;
And was the safeguard of the West: the
    worth
Of Venice did not fall below her birth,
Venice, the eldest child of Liberty.
5 She was a maiden City, bright and free;
No guile seduced, no force could violate;
And, when she took unto herself a Mate,
She must espouse the everlasting Sea.[2]
And what if she had seen those glories
    fade,
10 Those titles vanish, and that strength
    decay;
Yet shall some tribute of regret be paid
When her long life hath reached its final
    day:
Men are we, and must grieve when even
    the Shade
Of that which once was great is passed
    away.

TO TOUSSAINT L'OUVERTURE
1802   1803

Toussaint, the most unhappy man of
    men!
Whether the whistling rustic tend his
    plough
Within thy hearing, or thy head be now
Pillowed in some deep dungeon's earless
    den;—
5 O miserable chieftain! where and when
Wilt thou find patience! Yet die not; do
    thou
Wear rather in thy bonds a cheerful
    brow:
Though fallen thyself, never to rise again,
Live, and take comfort. Thou hast left
    behind
10 Powers that will work for thee; air, earth,
    and skies;
There's not a breathing of the common
    wind
That will forget thee; thou hast great
    allies;
Thy friends are exultations, agonies,
And love, and man's unconquerable mind.

[1] Venice was an independent republic, with extensive possessions in the East, from the ninth century until conquered by Napoleon, in 1797.
[2] In 1177, the Venetians defeated the Germans in a naval battle in defense of Pope Alexander III, who gave the Doge a ring and bade him wed the Adriatic with it, as a sign of dominion over the sea. An annual ceremony was observed in which a ring was thrown into the Adriatic in token of this espousal.

COMPOSED IN THE VALLEY NEAR DOVER, ON THE DAY OF LANDING[1]
1802   1807

Here, on our native soil, we breathe once
    more.
The cock that crows, the smoke that curls,
    that sound
Of bells;—those boys who in yon meadow-
    ground
In white-sleeved shirts are playing; and
    the roar
5 Of the waves breaking on the chalky
    shore;—
All, all are English. Oft have I looked
    round
With joy in Kent's green vales; but never
    found
Myself so satisfied in heart before.
Europe is yet in bonds;[2] but let that pass,
10 Thought for another moment. Thou art
    free,
My Country! and 'tis joy enough and pride
For one hour's perfect bliss, to tread the
    grass
Of England once again, and hear and see,
With such a dear companion at my side.

NEAR DOVER, SEPTEMBER, 1802
1802   1807

Inland, within a hollow vale, I stood;
And saw, while sea was calm and air was
    clear,
The coast of France—the coast of France
    how near!
Drawn almost into frightful neighborhood.
5 I shrunk; for verily the barrier flood
Was like a lake, or river bright and fair,
A span of waters; yet what power is there!
What mightiness for evil and for good!
Even so doth God protect us if we be
10 Virtuous and wise. Winds blow, and
    waters roll,
Strength to the brave, and Power, and
    Deity;
Yet in themselves are nothing! One decree
Spake laws to *them,* and said that by the
    soul
Only, the Nations shall be great and free.

WRITTEN IN LONDON, SEPTEMBER, 1802
1802   1807

O friend![3] I know not which way I must
    look
For comfort, being, as I am, opprest,

---

[1] Wordsworth and his sister Dorothy returned from Calais, France, on August 30, 1802.
[2] That is, to Napoleon, who had forced the Peace of Amiens in March, 1802.
[3] Coleridge.

To think that now our life is only drest
For show; mean handiwork of craftsman,
    cook,
5 Or groom!—We must run glittering like
    a brook
In the open sunshine, or we are unblest:
The wealthiest man among us is the best:
No grandeur now in nature or in book
Delights us. Rapine, avarice, expense,
10 This is idolatry; and these we adore:
Plain living and high thinking are no
    more:
The homely beauty of the good old cause
Is gone; our peace, our fearful innocence,
And pure religion breathing household
    laws.

LONDON, 1802
1802   1807

Milton! thou shouldst be living at this
    hour:
England hath need of thee: she is a fen
Of stagnant waters: altar, sword, and pen,
Fireside, the heroic wealth of hall and
    bower,[1]
5 Have forfeited their ancient English dower
Of inward happiness. We are selfish men;
Oh! raise us up, return to us again;
And give us manners, virtue, freedom,
    power.
Thy soul was like a star, and dwelt apart;
10 Thou hadst a voice whose sound was like
    the sea:
Pure as the naked heavens, majestic, free,
So didst thou travel on life's common way,
In cheerful godliness; and yet thy heart
The lowliest duties on herself did lay.

GREAT MEN HAVE BEEN AMONG US
1802   1807

Great men have been among us; hands
    that penned
And tongues that uttered wisdom—better
    none:
The later Sidney, Marvel, Harrington,
Young Vane, and others who called Milton
    friend.
5 These moralists could act and comprehend:
They knew how genuine glory was put on;
Taught us how rightly a nation shone
In splendor: what strength was, that
    would not bend
But in magnanimous meekness. France,
    'tis strange,
10 Hath brought forth no such souls as we
    had then.

---

[1] The hall was the public dwelling of the Teutonic chieftain, and the bower the private apartments, especially of the women.

Perpetual emptiness! unceasing change!
No single volume paramount, no code,
No master spirit, no determined road;
But equally a want of books and men!

IT IS NOT TO BE THOUGHT OF THAT
THE FLOOD
1802   1803

It is not to be thought of that the Flood
Of British freedom, which, to the open sea
Of the world's praise, from dark antiquity
Hath flowed, "with pomp of waters, un-
    withstood,"[1]
5 Roused though it be full often to a mood
Which spurns the check of salutary bands,
That this most famous Stream in bogs and
    sands
Should perish; and to evil and to good
Be lost forever. In our halls is hung
10 Armory of the invincible Knights of old:
We must be free or die, who speak the
    tongue
That Shakspeare spake; the faith and
    morals hold
Which Milton held.—In everything we are
    sprung
Of Earth's first blood, have titles mani-
    fold.

WHEN I HAVE BORNE IN MEMORY
1802   1803

When I have borne in memory what has
    tamed
Great Nations, how ennobling thoughts
    depart
When men change swords for ledgers, and
    desert
The student's bower for gold, some fears
    unnamed
5 I had, my Country—am I to be blamed?
Now, when I think of thee, and what thou
    art,
Verily, in the bottom of my heart,
Of those unfilial fears I am ashamed.
For dearly must we prize thee; we who find
10 In thee a bulwark for the cause of men;
And I by my affection was beguiled:
What wonder if a poet now and then,
Among the many movements of his mind,
Felt for thee as a lover or a child.

TO H. C.[2]
SIX YEARS OLD
1802   1807

O thou! whose fancies from afar are
    brought;
Who of thy words dost make a mock
    apparel,

[1] Daniel, *The History of the Civil War*, 2, 53.
[2] Hartley Coleridge, son of S. T. Coleridge.

And fittest to unutterable thought
The breeze-like motion and the self-born
    carol;
5 Thou faery voyager! that dost float
In such clear water, that thy boat
May rather seem
To brood on air than on an earthly
    stream;
Suspended in a stream as clear as sky,
10 Where earth and heaven do make one
    imagery;
O blessèd vision! happy child!
Thou art so exquisitely wild,
I think of thee with many fears
For what may be thy lot in future years.

15   I thought of times when Pain might be
    thy guest,
Lord of thy house and hospitality;
And Grief, uneasy lover! never rest
But when she sate within the touch of thee.
O too industrious folly!
20 O vain and causeless melancholy!
Nature will either end thee quite;
Or, lengthening out thy season of delight,
Preserve for thee, by individual right,
A young lamb's heart among the full-
    grown flocks.
25 What hast thou to do with sorrow,
Or the injuries of tomorrow?
Thou art a dewdrop, which the morn
    brings forth,
Ill fitted to sustain unkindly shocks,
Or to be trailed along the soiling earth;
30 A gem that glitters while it lives,
And no forewarning gives;
But, at the touch of wrong, without a strife
Slips in a moment out of life.

TO THE DAISY
1802   1807

In youth from rock to rock I went,
From hill to hill in discontent
Of pleasure high and turbulent,
    Most pleased when most uneasy;
5 But now my own delights I make,—
My thirst at every rill can slake,
And gladly Nature's love partake
    Of thee, sweet Daisy!

Thee, Winter in the garland wears
10 That thinly decks his few gray hairs;
Spring parts the clouds with softest airs,
    That she may sun thee;
Whole Summer-fields are thine by right;
And Autumn, melancholy wight!
15 Doth in thy crimson head delight
    When rains are on thee.

In shoals and bands, a morrice train,[1]
Thou greet'st the traveller in the lane;
Pleased at his greeting thee again;
20   Yet nothing daunted,
Nor grieved if thou be set at nought:
And oft alone in nooks remote
We meet thee, like a pleasant thought,
   When such are wanted.

25 Be violets in their secret mews[2]
The flowers the wanton Zephyrs choose;
Proud be the rose, with rains and dews
   Her head impearling,
Thou liv'st with less ambitious aim,
30 Yet hast not gone without thy fame;
Thou art indeed by many a claim
   The poet's darling.

If to a rock from rains he fly,
Or, some bright day of April sky,
35 Imprisoned by hot sunshine lie
   Near the green holly,
And wearily at length should fare;
He needs but look about, and there
Thou art!—a friend at hand, to scare
40   His melancholy.

A hundred times, by rock or bower,
Ere thus I have lain couched an hour,
Have I derived from thy sweet power
   Some apprehension;
45 Some steady love; some brief delight;
Some memory that had taken flight;
Some chime of fancy wrong or right;
   Or stray invention.

If stately passions in me burn,
50 And one chance look to thee should turn,
I drink out of an humbler urn
   A lowlier pleasure;
The homely sympathy that heeds
The common life our nature breeds;
55 A wisdom fitted to the needs
   Of hearts at leisure.

Fresh-smitten by the morning ray,
When thou art up, alert and gay,
Then, cheerful Flower! my spirits play
60   With kindred gladness:
And when, at dusk, by dews opprest
Thou sink'st, the image of thy rest
Hath often eased my pensive breast
   Of careful sadness.

65 And all day long-I number yet,
All seasons through, another debt,
Which I, wherever thou art met,
   To thee am owing;
An instinct call it, a blind sense;
70 A happy, genial influence,
Coming one knows not how, nor whence,
   Nor whither going.

Child of the Year! that round dost run
Thy pleasant course,—when day's begun
75 As ready to salute the sun
   As lark or leveret,[1]
Thy long-lost praise thou shalt regain;
Nor be less dear to future men
Than in old time;—thou not in vain
80   Art Nature's favorite.

TO THE SAME FLOWER
1802   1807

With little here to do or see
Of things that in the great world be,
Daisy! again I talk to thee,
   For thou art worthy,
5 Thou unassuming Commonplace
Of Nature, with that homely face,
And yet with something of a grace
   Which love makes for thee!

Oft on the dappled turf at ease
10 I sit, and play with similes,
Loose types of things through all degrees,
   Thoughts of thy raising:
And many a fond and idle name
I give to thee, for praise or blame,
15 As is the humor of the game,
   While I am gazing.

A nun demure of lowly port;
Or sprightly maiden, of Love's court,
In thy simplicity the sport
20   Of all temptations;
A queen in crown of rubies drest;
A starveling in a scanty vest;
Are all, as seems to suit thee best,
   Thy appellations.

25 A little Cyclops with one eye
Staring to threaten and defy,
That thought comes next—and instantly
   The freak is over,
The shape will vanish—and behold
30 A silver shield with boss of gold,
That spreads itself, some faery bold
   In fight to cover!

---

[1] A train of Morris dancers. A Morris was a kind of rustic dance, which originated with the Moors.
[2] enclosure (literally a coop or similar place for moulting birds)

[1] young hare

I see thee glittering from afar—
And then thou art a pretty star;
35 Not quite so fair as many are
   In heaven above thee!
Yet like a star, with glittering crest,
Self-poised in air thou seem'st to rest;—
May peace come never to his nest,
40   Who shall reprove thee!

Bright *Flower!* for by that name at last,
When all my reveries are past,
I call thee, and to that cleave fast,
   Sweet silent creature!
45 That breath'st with me in sun and air,
Do thou, as thou art wont, repair
My heart with gladness, and a share
   Of thy meek nature!

TO THE DAISY
1802   1807

Bright Flower! whose home is every-
      where,
Bold in maternal Nature's care,
And, all the long year through, the heir
   Of joy and sorrow;
5 Methinks that there abides in thee
Some concord with humanity,
Given to no other flower I see
   The forest thorough!

Is it that Man is soon deprest?
10 A thoughtless Thing! who, once unblest,
Does little on his memory rest,
   Or on his reason,
And thou wouldst teach him how to find
A shelter under every wind,
15 A hope for times that are unkind
   And every season?

Thou wander'st the wide world about,
Unchecked by pride or scrupulous doubt,
With friends to greet thee, or without,
20   Yet pleased and willing;
Meek, yielding to the occasion's call,
And all things suffering from all,
Thy function apostolical
   In peace fulfilling.

THE GREEN LINNET
1803   1807

Beneath these fruit-tree boughs that shed
Their snow-white blossoms on my head,
With brightest sunshine round me spread
   Of spring's unclouded weather,
5 In this sequestered nook how sweet
To sit upon my orchard-seat!
And birds and flowers once more to greet,
   My last year's friends together.

One have I marked, the happiest guest
10 In all this covert of the blest:
Hail to thee, far above the rest
   In joy of voice and pinion!
Thou, Linnet! in thy green array,
Presiding Spirit here today,
15 Dost lead the revels of the May;
   And this is thy dominion.

While birds, and butterflies, and flowers,
Make all one band of paramours,
Thou, ranging up and down the bowers,
20   Art sole in thy employment:
A Life, a Presence like the Air,
Scattering thy gladness without care,
Too blest with any one to pair;
   Thyself thy own enjoyment.

25 Amid yon tuft of hazel trees,
That twinkle to the gusty breeze,
Behold him perched in ecstasies,
   Yet seeming still to hover;
There! where the flutter of his wings
30 Upon his back and body flings
Shadows and sunny glimmerings,
   That cover him all over.

My dazzled sight he oft deceives,
A brother of the dancing leaves;
35 Then flits, and from the cottage eaves
   Pours forth his song in gushes;
As if by that exulting strain
He mocked and treated with disdain
The voiceless Form he chose to feign,
40   While fluttering in the bushes.

YEW-TREES
1803   1815

There is a Yew-tree, pride of Lorton Vale,
Which to this day stands single, in the
      midst
Of its own darkness, as it stood of yore:
Not loth to furnish weapons for the bands
5 Of Umfraville or Percy ere they marched
To Scotland's heaths; or those that
      crossed the sea
And drew their sounding bows at Azin-
      cour,
Perhaps at earlier Crecy, or Poictiers.
Of vast circumference and gloom profound
10 This solitary Tree! a living thing
Produced too slowly ever to decay;
Of form and aspect too magnificent
To be destroyed. But worthier still of
      note
Are those fraternal Four of Borrowdale,
15 Joined in one solemn and capacious grove;
Huge trunks! and each particular trunk **a**
      growth

Of intertwisted fibres serpentine
Up-coiling, and inveterately[1] convolved;
Nor uninformed with Phantasy, and looks
20 That threaten the profane; a pillared
    shade,
Upon whose grassless floor of red-brown
    hue,
By sheddings from the pining[2] umbrage
    tinged
Perennially—beneath whose sable roof
Of boughs, as if for festal purpose decked
25 With unrejoicing berries—ghostly Shapes
May meet at noontide; Fear and trem-
    bling Hope,
Silence and Foresight; Death the Skeleton
And Time the Shadow;—there to cele-
    brate,
As in a natural temple scattered o'er
30 With altars undisturbed of mossy stone,
United worship; or in mute repose
To lie, and listen to the mountain flood
Murmuring from Glaramara's inmost
    caves.

AT THE GRAVE OF BURNS

SEVEN YEARS AFTER HIS DEATH
1803   1845

I shiver, Spirit fierce and bold,
At thought of what I now behold:
As vapors breathed from dungeons cold
    Strike pleasure dead,
5 So sadness comes from out the mould
    Where Burns is laid.

And have I then thy bones so near,
And thou forbidden to appear?
As if it were thyself that's here
10   I shrink with pain;
And both my wishes and my fear
    Alike are vain.

Off weight—nor press on weight!—away
Dark thoughts!—they came, but not to
    stay;
15 With chastened feelings would I pay
    The tribute due
To him, and aught that hides his clay
    From mortal view.

Fresh as the flower, whose modest worth
20 He sang, his genius "glinted"[3] forth,
Rose like a star that touching earth,
    For so it seems,
Doth glorify its humble birth
    With matchless beams.

25 The piercing eye, the thoughtful brow,
The struggling heart, where be they now?—
Full soon the Aspirant of the plough,
    The prompt, the brave,
Slept, with the obscurest, in the low
30   And silent grave.

I mourned with thousands, but as one
More deeply grieved, for he was gone
Whose light I hailed when first it shone,
    And showed my youth
35 How Verse may build a princely throne
    On humble truth.

Alas! where'er the current tends,
Regret pursues and with it blends,—
Huge Criffel's hoary top ascends
40   By Skiddaw seen,—
Neighbors we were, and loving friends
    We might have been;

True friends though diversely inclined;
But heart with heart and mind with mind,
45 Where the main fibres are entwined,
    Through Nature's skill,
May even by contraries be joined
    More closely still.

The tear will start, and let it flow;
50 Thou "poor Inhabitant below,"[1]
At this dread moment—even so—
    Might we together
Have sate and talked where gowans[2] blow,[3]
    Or on wild heather.

55 What treasures would have then been
    placed
Within my reach; of knowledge graced
By fancy what a rich repast!
    But why go on?—
Oh! spare to sweep, thou mournful blast,
60   His grave grass-grown.

There, too, a son, his joy and pride,
(Not three weeks past the stripling died,)
Lies gathered to his father's side,
    Soul-moving sight!
65 Yet one to which is not denied
    Some sad delight.

For *he* is safe, a quiet bed
Hath early found among the dead,
Harbored where none can be misled,
70   Wronged, or distrest;
And surely here it may be said
    That such are blest.

---

[1] by virtue of old habit
[2] decaying
[3] Burns, *To a Mountain Daisy,* 15 (p. 218).

[1] Burns, *A Bard's Epitaph,* 19 (p. 217).   [2] daisies   [3] bloom

And oh for thee, by pitying grace
Checked oft-times in a devious race,
75 May He, who halloweth the place
    Where Man is laid,
Receive thy spirit in the embrace
    For which it prayed![1]

Sighing I turned away; but ere
80 Night fell I heard, or seemed to hear,
Music that sorrow comes not near,
    A ritual hymn,
Chanted in love that casts out fear
    By Seraphim.

TO A HIGHLAND GIRL

AT INVERSNEYDE, UPON LOCH LOMOND
1803   1807

Sweet Highland Girl, a very shower
Of beauty is thy earthly dower!
Twice seven consenting years have shed
Their utmost bounty on thy head:
5 And these gray rocks; that household
    lawn;
Those trees, a veil just half withdrawn;
This fall of water that doth make
A murmur near the silent lake;
This little bay; a quiet road
10 That holds in shelter thy abode—
In truth together do ye seem
Like something fashioned in a dream;
Such Forms as from their covert peep
When earthly cares are laid asleep!
15 But, O fair creature! in the light
Of common day, so heavenly bright,
I bless thee, vision as thou art,
I bless thee with a human heart;
God shield thee to thy latest years!
20 Thee, neither know I, nor thy peers;
And yet my eyes are filled with tears.

With earnest feeling I shall pray
For thee when I am far away:
For never saw I mien, or face,
25 In which more plainly I could trace
Benignity and home-bred sense
Ripening in perfect innocence.
Here scattered, like a random seed,
Remote from men, thou dost not need,
30 The embarrassed look of shy distress,
And maidenly shamefacedness:
Thou wear'st upon thy forehead clear
The freedom of a mountaineer:
A face with gladness overspread!
35 Soft smiles, by human kindness bred!
And seemliness complete, that sways
Thy courtesies, about thee plays;

[1] See Burns's *To Ruin*, st. 2.

With no restraint, but such as springs
From quick and eager visitings
40 Of thoughts that lie beyond the reach
Of thy few words of English speech:
A bondage sweetly brooked, a strife
That gives thy gestures grace and life!
So have I, not unmoved in mind,
45 Seen birds of tempest-loving kind—
Thus beating up against the wind.

What hand but would a garland cull
For thee who art so beautiful?
O happy pleasure! here to dwell
50 Beside thee in some heathy dell;
Adopt your homely ways, and dress,
A shepherd, thou a shepherdess!
But I could frame a wish for thee
More like a grave reality:
55 Thou art to me but as a wave
Of the wild sea; and I would have
Some claim upon thee, if I could,
Though but of common neighborhood.
What joy to hear thee, and to see!
60 Thy elder brother I would be,
Thy father—anything to thee!

Now thanks to Heaven! that of its grace
Hath led me to this lonely place.
Joy have I had; and going hence
65 I bear away my recompense.
In spots like these it is we prize
Our Memory, feel that she hath eyes:
Then, why should I be loth to stir?
I feel this place was made for her;
70 To give new pleasure like the past,
Continued long as life shall last.
Nor am I loth, though pleased at heart,
Sweet Highland Girl! from thee to part;
For I, methinks, till I grow old,
75 As fair before me shall behold,
As I do now, the cabin small,
The lake, the bay, the waterfall;
And thee, the Spirit of them all!

STEPPING WESTWARD
1803   1807

"What, you are stepping westward?"—
    "Yea."
—'Twould be a *wildish* destiny,
If we, who thus together roam
In a strange land, and far from home,
5 Were in this place the guests of Chance:
Yet who would stop, or fear to advance,
Though home or shelter he had none,
With such a sky to lead him on?

The dewy ground was dark and cold;
10 Behind, all gloomy to behold;
And stepping westward seemed to be

A kind of *heavenly* destiny:
I liked the greeting; 'twas a sound
Of something without place or bound;
15 And seemed to give me spiritual right
To travel through that region bright.
The voice was soft, and she who spake
Was walking by her native lake:
The salutation had to me
20 The very sound of courtesy:
Its power was felt; and while my eye
Was fixed upon the glowing sky,
The echo of the voice enwrought
A human sweetness with the thought
25 Of travelling through the world that lay
Before me in my endless way.

THE SOLITARY REAPER
1803   1807

Behold her, single in the field,
Yon solitary Highland lass!
Reaping and singing by herself;
Stop here, or gently pass!
5 Alone she cuts and binds the grain,
And sings a melancholy strain;
O listen! for the vale profound
Is overflowing with the sound.

No nightingale did ever chaunt
10 More welcome notes to weary bands
Of travellers in some shady haunt,
Among Arabian sands:
A voice so thrilling ne'er was heard
In springtime from the cuckoo-bird,
15 Breaking the silence of the seas
Among the farthest Hebrides.

Will no one tell me what she sings?—
Perhaps the plaintive numbers flow
For old, unhappy, far-off things,
20 And battles long ago;
Or is it some more humble lay,
Familiar matter of today?
Some natural sorrow, loss, or pain,
That has been, and may be again?

25 Whate'er the theme, the maiden sang
As if her song could have no ending;
I saw her singing at her work,
And o'er the sickle bending;—
I listened, motionless and still;
30 And, as I mounted up the hill,
The music in my heart I bore,
Long after it was heard no more.

YARROW UNVISITED
1803   1807

From Stirling castle we[1] had seen
The mazy Forth unravelled;
Had trod the banks of Clyde, and Tay,

[1] Wordsworth and his sister Dorothy.

And with the Tweed had travelled;
5 And when we came to Clovenford,
Then said my "winsome marrow,"[1]
"Whate'er betide, we'll turn aside,
And see the Braes of Yarrow.'[2]

"Let Yarrow folk, frae Selkirk town,
10 Who have been buying, selling,
Go back to Yarrow, 'tis their own;
Each maiden to her dwelling!
On Yarrow's banks let herons feed,
Hares couch, and rabbits burrow!
15 But we will downward with the Tweed,
Nor turn aside to Yarrow.

"There's Galla Water, Leader Haughs,
Both lying right before us;
And Dryborough, where with chiming
        Tweed
20 The lintwhites[3] sing in chorus;
There's pleasant Tiviot-dale, a land
Made blithe with plough and harrow:
Why throw away a needful day
To go in search of Yarrow?

25 "What's Yarrow but a river bare,
That glides the dark hills under?
There are a thousand such elsewhere
As worthy of your wonder."
—Strange words they seemed of slight
        and scorn;
30 My true-love sighed for sorrow;
And looked me in the face, to think
I thus could speak of Yarrow!

"Oh! green," said I, "are Yarrow's
        holms,[4]
And sweet is Yarrow flowing!
35 Fair hangs the apple frae the rock,[5]
But we will leave it growing.
O'er hilly path, and open strath,[6]
We'll wander Scotland thorough;
But, though so near, we will not turn
40 Into the dale of Yarrow.

"Let beeves and home-bred kine partake
The sweets of Burn-mill meadow;
The swan on still St. Mary's Lake
Float double, swan and shadow!
45 We will not see them; will not go,
Today, nor yet tomorrow;
Enough if in our hearts we know
There's such a place as Yarrow.

[1] companion (See Hamilton's *The Braes of Yarrow*, p. 13.)
[2] the banks of the River Yarrow
[3] linnets
[4] lowlands

[5] Hamilton, *The Braes of Yarrow*, 51-2. The apple is probably the red berry of the mountain-ash.
[6] A valley through which a river flows.

"Be Yarrow stream unseen, unknown!
50 It must, or we shall rue it:
We have a vision of our own;
Ah! why should we undo it?
The treasured dreams of times long past,
We'll keep them, winsome marrow!
55 For when we're there, although 'tis fair,
'Twill be another Yarrow!

"If Care with freezing years should come,
And wandering seem but folly,—
Should we be loth to stir from home,
60 And yet be melancholy;
Should life be dull, and spirits low,
'Twill soothe us in our sorrow,
That earth hath something yet to show,
The bonny holms of Yarrow!"

OCTOBER, 1803
1803   1807

When, looking on the present face of
    things,
I see one man,[1] of men the meanest too!
Raised up to sway the world, to do, undo,
With mighty Nations for his underlings,
5 The great events with which old story rings
Seem vain and hollow; I find nothing
    great:
Nothing is left which I can venerate;
So that a doubt almost within me springs
Of Providence, such emptiness at length
10 Seems at the heart of all things. But,
    great God!
I measure back the steps which I have
    trod;
And tremble, seeing whence proceeds the
    strength
Of such poor Instruments, with thoughts
    sublime
I tremble at the sorrow of the time.

TO THE MEN OF KENT
1803   1807

Vanguard of Liberty, ye men of Kent,
Ye children of a Soil that doth advance[2]
Her haughty brow against the coast of
    France,
Now is the time to prove your hardiment!
5 To France be words of invitation sent!
They from their fields can see the coun-
    tenance
Of your fierce war, may ken the glittering
    lance,
And hear you shouting forth your brave
    intent.
Left single, in bold parley, ye, of yore,

10 Did from the Norman win a gallant
    wreath;[1]
Confirmed the charters that were yours
    before;—
No parleying now. In Britain is one
    breath;
We all are with you now from shore to
    shore;—
Ye men of Kent, 'tis victory or death!

ANTICIPATION, OCTOBER, 1803
1803   1803

Shout, for a mighty victory is won!
On British ground the invaders are laid
    low;
The breath of Heaven has drifted them
    like snow,
And left them lying in the silent sun,
5 Never to rise again!—the work is done.
Come forth, ye old men, now in peaceful
    show
And greet your sons! drums beat and
    trumpets blow!
Make merry, wives! ye little children,
    stun
Your grandame's ears with pleasure of
    your noise!
10 Clap, infants, clap your hands! Divine
    must be
That triumph, when the very worst, the
    pain,
And even the prospect of our brethren
    slain,
Hath something in it which the heart
    enjoys:—
In glory will they sleep and endless sanc-
    tity.

TO THE CUCKOO
1804   1807

O blithe Newcomer! I have heard,
I hear thee and rejoice.
O Cuckoo! shall I call thee Bird,
Or but a wandering Voice?

5 While I am lying on the grass
Thy twofold shout I hear;
From hill to hill it seems to pass
At once far off, and near.

Though babbling only to the Vale,
10 Of sunshine and of flowers,
Thou bringest unto me a tale
Of visionary hours.

---

[1] Napoleon.   [2] lift up

[1] The men of the southern part of Kent were never subdued in the Norman invasion, and when they surrendered they had their charters confirmed.

Thrice welcome, darling of the Spring!
Even yet thou art to me
15 No bird, but an invisible thing,
A voice, a mystery;

The same whom in my schoolboy days
I listened to; that Cry
Which made me look a thousand ways
20 In bush, and tree, and sky.

To seek thee did I often rove
Through woods and on the green;
And thou wert still a hope, a love;
Still longed for, never seen.

25 And I can listen to thee yet;
Can lie upon the plain
And listen, till I do beget
That golden time again.

O blessèd Bird! the earth we pace
30 Again appears to be
An unsubstantial, faery place;
That is fit home for thee!

SHE WAS A PHANTOM OF DELIGHT
1804   1807

She was a phantom of delight
When first she gleamed upon my sight;
A lovely apparition, sent
To be a moment's ornament;
5 Her eyes as stars of twilight fair;
Like twilight's, too, her dusky hair;
But all things else about her drawn
From Maytime and the cheerful dawn;
A dancing shape, an image gay,
10 To haunt, to startle, and waylay.

I saw her upon nearer view,
A spirit, yet a woman too!
Her household motions light and free,
And steps of virgin liberty;
15 A countenance in which did meet
Sweet records, promises as sweet;
A creature not too bright or good
For human nature's daily food;
For transient sorrows, simple wiles,
20 Praise, blame, love, kisses, tears, and
smiles.

And now I see with eye serene
The very pulse of the machine;[1]
A being breathing thoughtful breath,
A traveller between life and death;
25 The reason firm, the temperate will,
Endurance, foresight, strength, and skill;

[1] body

A perfect woman, nobly planned,
To warn, to comfort, and command;
And yet a spirit still, and bright
30 With something of angelic light.

I WANDERED LONELY AS A CLOUD
1804   1807

I wandered lonely as a cloud
That floats on high o'er vales and hills,
When all at once I saw a crowd,
A host, of golden daffodils;
5 Beside the lake, beneath the trees,
Fluttering and dancing in the breeze.

Continuous as the stars that shine
And twinkle on the Milky Way,
They stretched in never-ending line
10 Along the margin of a bay:
Ten thousand saw I at a glance,
Tossing their heads in sprightly dance.

The waves beside them danced; but they
Outdid the sparkling waves in glee:
15 A poet could not but be gay,
In such a jocund company:
I gazed—and gazed—but little thought
What wealth the show to me had brought:

For oft, when on my couch I lie
20 In vacant or in pensive mood,
They flash upon that inward eye
Which is the bliss of solitude;
And then my heart with pleasure fills,
And dances with the daffodils.

THE AFFLICTION OF MARGARET
1804   1807

Where art thou, my beloved son,
Where art thou, worse to me than dead?
Oh find me, prosperous or undone!
Or, if the grave be now thy bed,
5 Why am I ignorant of the same
That I may rest; and neither blame
Nor sorrow may attend thy name?

Seven years, alas! to have received
No tidings of an only child;
10 To have despaired, have hoped, believed,
And been for evermore beguiled;
Sometimes with thoughts of very bliss!
I catch at them, and then I miss;
Was ever darkness like to this?

15 He was among the prime in worth,
An object beauteous to behold;
Well born, well bred; I sent him forth
Ingenuous, innocent, and bold;
If things ensued that wanted grace,
20 As hath been said, they were not base;
And never blush was on my face.

Ah! little doth the young one dream,
When full of play and childish cares,
What power is in his wildest scream,
25 Heard by his mother unawares!
He knows it not, he cannot guess;
Years to a mother bring distress;
But do not make her love the less.

Neglect me! no, I suffered long
30 From that ill thought; and, being blind,
Said, "Pride shall help me in my wrong:
Kind mother have I been, as kind
As ever breathed:" and that is true;
I've wet my path with tears like dew,
35 Weeping for him when no one knew.

My son, if thou be humbled, poor,
Hopeless of honor and of gain,
Oh! do not dread thy mother's door;
Think not of me with grief and pain:
40 I now can see with better eyes;
And worldly grandeur I despise,
And fortune with her gifts and lies.

Alas! the fowls of heaven have wings,
And blasts of heaven will aid their flight;
45 They mount—how short a voyage brings
The wanderers back to their delight!
Chains tie us down by land and sea;
And wishes, vain as mine, may be
All that is left to comfort thee.

50 Perhaps some dungeon hears thee groan,
Maimed, mangled by inhuman men;
Or thou upon a desert thrown
Inheritest the lion's den;
Or hast been summoned to the deep,
55 Thou, thou and all thy mates, to keep
An incommunicable sleep.

I look for ghosts; but none will force
Their way to me: 'tis falsely said
That there was ever intercourse
60 Between the living and the dead;
For, surely, then I should have sight
Of him I wait for day and night,
With love and longings infinite.

My apprehensions come in crowds;
65 I dread the rustling of the grass;
The very shadows of the clouds
Have power to shake me as they pass:
I question things and do not find
One that will answer to my mind;
70 And all the world appears unkind.

Beyond participation lie
My troubles, and beyond relief:
If any chance to heave a sigh,

They pity me, and not my grief.
75 Then come to me, my son, or send
Some tidings that my woes may end;
I have no other earthly friend!

※ ODE TO DUTY
1805   1807

Stern Daughter of the Voice of God!
O Duty! if that name thou love
Who art a light to guide, a rod
To check the erring, and reprove;
5 Thou, who art victory and law
When empty terrors overawe;
From vain temptations dost set free;
And calm'st the weary strife of frail
      humanity!

There are who ask not if thine eye
10 Be on them; who, in love and truth,
Where no misgiving is, rely
Upon the genial sense of youth:
Glad Hearts! without reproach or blot;
Who do thy work, and know it not:
15 Oh! if through confidence misplaced
They fail, thy saving arms, dread Power,
      around them cast.

Serene will be our days and bright,
And happy will our nature be,
When love is an unerring light,
20 And joy its own security.
And they a blissful course may hold
Even now, who, not unwisely bold,
Live in the spirit of this creed;
Yet seek thy firm support, according to
      their need.

25 I, loving freedom, and untried;
No sport of every random gust,
Yet being to myself a guide,
Too blindly have reposed my trust:
And oft, when in my heart was heard
30 Thy timely mandate, I deferred
The task, in smoother walks to stray;
But thee I now would serve more strictly,
      if I may.

Through no disturbance of my soul,
Or strong compunction in me wrought,
35 I supplicate for thy control;
But in the quietness of thought:
Me this unchartered freedom tires;
I feel the weight of chance-desires:
My hopes no more must change their name,
40 I long for a repose that ever is the same.

Stern Lawgiver! yet thou dost wear
The Godhead's most benignant grace;
Nor know we anything so fair

As is the smile upon thy face:
45 Flowers laugh before thee on their beds
And fragrance in thy footing treads;
Thou dost preserve the stars from wrong;
And the most ancient heavens, through
    Thee, are fresh and strong.

To humbler functions, awful Power!
50 I call thee: I myself commend
Unto thy guidance from this hour;
Oh, let my weakness have an end!
Give unto me, made lowly wise,
The spirit of self-sacrifice;
55 The confidence of reason give;
And in the light of truth thy bondman
    let me live!

TO A SKYLARK
1805   1807

Up with me! up with me into the clouds!
    For thy song, Lark, is strong;
Up with me, up with me into the clouds!
    Singing, singing,
5 With clouds and sky about thee ringing,
    Lift me, guide me, till I find
That spot which seems so to thy mind!

I have walked through wildernesses dreary,
And today my heart is weary;
10 Had I now the wings of a Faery,
    Up to thee would I fly.
There is madness about thee, and joy
    divine
In that song of thine;
Lift me, guide me, high and high
15 To thy banqueting place in the sky.

    Joyous as morning,
Thou art laughing and scorning;
Thou hast a nest for thy love and thy
    rest,
And, though little troubled with sloth,
20 Drunken Lark! thou wouldst be loth
To be such a traveller as I.
Happy, happy Liver,
With a soul as strong as a mountain river
Pouring out praise to the almighty Giver,
25   Joy and jollity be with us both!

Alas! my journey, rugged and uneven,
Through prickly moors or dusty ways must
    wind;
But hearing thee, or others of thy kind,
As full of gladness and as free of heaven,
30 I, with my fate contented, will plod on,
And hope for higher raptures, when life's
    day is done.

☀ ELEGIAC STANZAS

SUGGESTED BY A PICTURE OF PEELE CASTLE, IN
A STORM, PAINTED BY SIR GEORGE BEAUMONT
1805   1807

I was thy neighbor once, thou rugged Pile!
Four summer weeks I dwelt in sight of
    thee:
I saw thee every day; and all the while
Thy Form was sleeping on a glassy sea.

5 So pure the sky, so quiet was the air!
So like, so very like, was day to day!
Whene'er I looked, thy Image still was
    there;
It trembled, but it never passed away.

How perfect was the calm! it seemed no
    sleep;
10 No mood, which season takes away, or
    brings:
I could have fancied that the mighty Deep
Was even the gentlest of all gentle Things.

Ah! then, if mine had been the painter's
    hand,
To express what then I saw; and add the
    gleam,
15 The light that never was, on sea or land,
The consecration, and the poet's dream;

I would have planted thee, thou hoary Pile,
Amid a world how different from this![1]
Beside a sea that could not cease to smile;
20 On tranquil land, beneath a sky of bliss.

Thou shouldst have seemed a treasure-
    house divine
Of peaceful years; a chronicle of
    heaven;—
Of all the sunbeams that did ever shine
The very sweetest had to thee been given.

25 A picture had it been of lasting ease,
Elysian quiet, without toil or strife;
No motion but the moving tide, a breeze,
Or merely silent Nature's breathing life.

Such, in the fond illusion of my heart,
30 Such picture would I at that time have
    made:
And seen the soul of truth in every part,
A steadfast peace that might not be be-
    trayed.

So once it would have been,—'tis so no
    more;
I have submitted to a new control:

[1] That is, the world of the picture.

35 A power is gone, which nothing can re-
          store;
   A deep distress hath humanized my soul.

   Not for a moment could I now behold
   A smiling sea, and be what I have been:
   The feeling of my loss will ne'er be old;
40 This, which I know, I speak with mind
          serene.

   Then, Beaumont, friend! who would have
          been the friend,
   If he had lived, of him whom I deplore,[1]
   This work of thine I blame not, but com-
          mend;
   This sea in anger, and that dismal shore.

45 O 'tis a passionate Work!—yet wise and
          well,
   Well chosen is the spirit that is here;
   That Hulk which labors in the deadly swell,
   This rueful sky, this pageantry of fear!

   And this huge Castle, standing here sub-
          lime,
50 I love to see the look with which it braves,
   Cased in the unfeeling armor of old time,
   The lightning, the fierce wind, and tramp-
          ling waves.

   Farewell, farewell the heart that lives
          alone,
   Housed in a dream, at distance from the
          Kind![2]
55 Such happiness, wherever it be known,
   Is to be pitied; for 'tis surely blind.

   But welcome fortitude, and patient cheer,
   And frequent sights of what is to be borne!
   Such sights, or worse, as are before me
          here.—
60 Not without hope we suffer and we mourn.

TO A YOUNG LADY[3]

WHO HAD BEEN REPROACHED FOR TAKING
LONG WALKS IN THE COUNTRY
          1805   1807

   Dear child of Nature, let them rail!
   —There is a nest in a green dale,
   A harbor and a hold;
   Where thou, a wife and friend, shalt see
5 Thy own heart-stirring days, and be
   A light to young and old.

   There, healthy as a shepherd boy,
   And treading among flowers of joy

---

[1] Wordsworth's brother, Capt. John Wordsworth, who was drowned Feb. 5, 1805.
[2] The human race.
[3] Wordsworth's sister Dorothy.

   Which at no season fade,
10 Thou, while thy babes around thee cling,
   Shalt show us how divine a thing
   A woman may be made.

   Thy thoughts and feelings shall not die,
   Nor leave thee, when gray hairs are nigh,
15 A melancholy slave;
   But an old age serene and bright,
   And lovely as a Lapland night,
   Shall lead thee to thy grave.

CHARACTER OF THE HAPPY WARRIOR
          1806   1807

   Who is the happy warrior? Who is he
   That every man in arms should wish to be?
   —It is the generous Spirit, who, when
          brought
   Among the tasks of real life, hath
          wrought
5 Upon the plan that pleased his boyish
          thought:
   Whose high endeavors are an inward light
   That makes the path before him always
          bright:
   Who, with a natural instinct to discern
   What knowledge can perform, is diligent
          to learn;
10 Abides by this resolve, and stops not there,
   But makes his moral being his prime care;
   Who, doomed to go in company with Pain,
   And Fear, and Bloodshed, miserable train!
   Turns his necessity to glorious gain;
15 In face of these doth exercise a power
   Which is our human nature's highest
          dower;
   Controls them and subdues, transmutes,
          bereaves
   Of their bad influence, and their good
          receives:
   By objects, which might force the soul to
          abate
20 Her feeling, rendered more compassionate;
   Is placable—because occasions rise
   So often that demand such sacrifice;
   More skilful in self-knowledge, even more
          pure,
   As tempted more; more able to endure,
25 As more exposed to suffering and distress;
   Thence, also, more alive to tenderness.
   —'Tis he whose law is reason; who depends
   Upon that law as on the best of friends;
   Whence, in a state where men are tempted
          still
30 To evil for a guard against worse ill,
   And what in quality or act is best
   Doth seldom on a right foundation rest,
   He labors good on good to fix, and owes
   To virtue every triumph that he knows:

35 —Who, if he rise to station of command,
Rises by open means; and there will stand
On honorable terms, or else retire,
And in himself possess his own desire;
Who comprehends his trust, and to the
same
40 Keeps faithful with a singleness of aim;
And therefore does not stoop, nor lie in
wait
For wealth, or honors, or for worldly
state;
Whom they must follow; on whose head
must fall,
Like showers of manna, if they come at
all:
45 Whose powers shed round him in the com-
mon strife,
Or mild concerns of ordinary life,
A constant influence, a peculiar grace;
But who, if he be called upon to face
Some awful moment to which Heaven has
joined
50 Great issues, good or bad for human
kind,
Is happy as a lover; and attired
With sudden brightness, like a man in-
spired;
And, through the heat of conflict, keeps
the law
In calmness made, and sees what he fore-
saw;
55 Or if an unexpected call succeed,
Come when it will, is equal to the need:
—He who, though thus endued as with a
sense
And faculty for storm and turbulence,
Is yet a Soul whose master-bias leans
60 To homefelt pleasures and to gentle
scenes;
Sweet images! which, wheresoe'er he be,
Are at his heart; and such fidelity
It is his darling passion to approve;
More brave for this, that he hath much
to love:—
65 'Tis, finally, the man, who, lifted high,
Conspicuous object in a nation's eye,
Or left unthought-of in obscurity,—
Who, with a toward or untoward lot,
Prosperous or adverse, to his wish or not—
70 Plays, in the many games of life, that one
Where what he most doth value must be
won:
Whom neither shape of danger can dis-
may,
Nor thought of tender happiness betray;
Who, not content that former worth stand
fast,
75 Looks forward, persevering to the last,
From well to better, daily self-surpast:

Who, whether praise of him must walk the
earth
Forever, and to noble deeds give birth,
Or he must fall, to sleep without his fame,
80 And leave a dead unprofitable name—
Finds comfort in himself and in his cause;
And, while the mortal mist is gathering,
draws
His breath in confidence of Heaven's
applause:
This is the happy warrior; this is he
85 That every man in arms should wish to be.

POWER OF MUSIC
1806   1807

An Orpheus! an Orpheus! yes, Faith may
grow bold,
And take to herself all the wonders of
old;—
Near the stately Pantheon you'll meet
with the same
In the street that from Oxford hath borrowed its name.

5 His station is there; and he works on the
crowd,
He sways them with harmony merry and
loud;
He fills with his power all their hearts to
the brim—
Was aught ever heard like his fiddle and
him?

What an eager assembly! what an empire
is this!
10 The weary have life, and the hungry have
bliss;
The mourner is cheered, and the anxious
have rest;
And the guilt-burthened soul is no longer
opprest.

As the Moon brightens round her the
clouds of the night,
So he, where he stands, is a centre of
light;
15 It gleams on the face, there, of dusky-
browed Jack,
On the pale-visaged baker's, with basket
on back.

That errand-bound 'prentice was passing
in haste—
What 'matter! he's caught—and his time
runs to waste;
The newsman is stopped, though he stops
on the fret;
20 And the half-breathless lamplighter—he's
in the net!

The porter sits down on the weight which
    he bore;
The lass with her barrow wheels hither
    her store;—
If a thief could be here he might pilfer
    at ease;
She sees the musician, 'tis all that she
    sees!

25 He stands, backed by the wall;—he abates
    not his din;
His hat gives him vigor, with boons drop-
    ping in,
From the old and the young, from the
    poorest; and there!
The one-pennied boy has his penny to
    spare.

O blest are the hearers, and proud be the
    hand
30 Of the pleasure it spreads through so
    thankful a band;
I am glad for him, blind as he is!—all the
    while
If they speak 'tis to praise, and they
    praise with a smile.

That tall man, a giant in bulk and in
    height,
Not an inch of his body is free from
    delight;
35 Can he keep himself still, if he would?
    oh, not he!
The music stirs in him like wind through
    a tree.

Mark that cripple who leans on his
    crutch; like a tower
That long has leaned forward, leans hour
    after hour!—
That mother, whose spirit in fetters is
    bound,
40 While she dandles the babe in her arms
    to the sound.

Now, coaches and chariots! roar on like
    a stream;
Here are twenty souls happy as souls in
    a dream;
They are deaf to your murmurs—they
    care not for you,
Nor what ye are flying, nor what ye
    pursue!

YES, IT WAS THE MOUNTAIN ECHO
1806   1807

Yes, it was the mountain Echo,
Solitary, clear, profound,
Answering to the shouting Cuckoo,
Giving to her sound for sound!

5 Unsolicited reply
To a babbling wanderer sent;
Like her ordinary cry,
Like—but oh, how different!

Hears not also mortal Life?
10 Hear not we, unthinking creatures!
Slaves of folly, love, or strife—
Voices of two different natures?

Have not we too?—yes, we have
Answers, and we know not whence;
15 Echoes from beyond the grave,
Recognized intelligence!

Such rebounds our inward ear
Catches sometimes from afar—
Listen, ponder, hold them dear;
20 For of God,—of God they are.

NUNS FRET NOT AT THEIR CON-VENT'S NARROW ROOM
1806   1807

Nuns fret not at their convent's narrow
    room;
And hermits are contented with their cells;
And students with their pensive citadels;
Maids at the wheel, the weaver at his loom,
5 Sit blithe and happy; bees that soar for
    bloom,
High as the highest Peak of Furness-fells,
Will murmur by the hour in foxglove bells:
In truth the prison, unto which we doom
Ourselves, no prison is: and hence for me,
10 In sundry moods, 'twas pastime to be
    bound
Within the Sonnet's scanty plot of
    ground;
Pleased if some Souls (for such there
    needs must be)
Who have felt the weight of too much
    liberty,
Should find brief solace there, as I have
    found.

PERSONAL TALK
1806   1807
I

I am not one who much or oft delight
To season my fireside with personal talk,—
Of friends, who live within an easy walk,
Or neighbors, daily, weekly, in my sight:
5 And, for my chance acquaintance, ladies
    bright,
Sons, mothers, maidens withering on the
    stalk,
These all wear out of me, like forms with
    chalk

Painted on rich men's floors,[1] for one
  feast-night.
Better than such discourse doth silence
  long,
10 Long, barren silence, square with my
  desire;
To sit without emotion, hope, or aim,
In the loved presence of my cottage fire,
And listen to the flapping of the flame,
Or kettle whispering its faint under-song.

II

15 "Yet life," you say, "is life; we have
  seen and see,
And with a living pleasure we describe;
And fits of sprightly malice do but bribe
The languid mind into activity.
Sound sense, and love itself, and mirth
  and glee
20 Are fostered by the comment and the
  gibe."
Even be it so: yet still among your tribe,
Our daily world's true worldlings, rank
  not me!
Children are blest, and powerful; their
  world lies
More justly balanced; partly at their feet,
25 And part far from them:—sweetest mel-
  odies
Are those that are by distance made more
  sweet;
Whose mind is but the mind of his own
  eyes,
He is a slave; the meanest we can meet!

III

Wings have we,—and as far as we can go
30 We may find pleasure: wilderness and
  wood,
Blank ocean and mere sky, support that
  mood
Which with the lofty sanctifies the low.
Dreams, books, are each a world; and
  books, we know,
Are a substantial world, both pure and
  good:
35 Round these, with tendrils strong as flesh
  and blood,
Our pastime and our happiness will grow.
There find I personal themes, a plenteous
  store,
Matter wherein right voluble I am,
To which I listen with a ready ear;
40 Two shall be named, pre-eminently dear,—
The gentle Lady[2] married to the Moor;
And heavenly Una with her milk-white
  Lamb.[3]

---
[1] To guide the dancers.
[2] Desdemona, wife of Othello.
[2] *The Faerie Queene*, I, 1, 4-5.

IV

Nor can I not believe but that hereby
Great gains are mine; for thus I live
  remote
45 From evil speaking; rancor, never sought,
Comes to me not; malignant truth, or lie.
Hence have I genial seasons, hence have I
Smooth passions, smooth discourse, and
  joyous thought;
And thus from day to day my little boat
50 Rocks in its harbor, lodging peaceably.
Blessings be with them—and eternal
  praise,
Who gave us nobler loves, and nobler
  cares—
The poets, who on earth have made us heirs
Of truth and pure delight by heavenly
  lays!
55 Oh! might my name be numbered among
  theirs,
Then gladly would I end my mortal days.

ADMONITION
1806   1807

Well may'st thou halt—and gaze with
  brightening eye!
The lovely Cottage in the guardian nook
Hath stirred thee deeply; with its own
  dear brook,
Its own small pasture, almost its own sky!
5 But covet not the Abode;—forbear to sigh,
As many do, repining while they look;
Intruders—who would tear from Nature's
  book
This precious leaf, with harsh impiety.
Think what the Home must be if it were
  thine,
10 Even thine, though few thy wants!—
  Roof, window, door,
The very flowers are sacred to the Poor,
The roses to the porch which they en-
  twine:
Yea, all, that now enchants thee, from
  the day
On which it should be touched, would
  melt away.

HOW SWEET IT IS, WHEN MOTHER
FANCY ROCKS
1806   1807

How sweet it is, when Mother Fancy rocks
The wayward brain, to saunter through a
  wood!
An old place, full of many a lovely brood,
Tall trees, green arbors, and ground-
  flowers in flocks;
5 And wild rose tip-toe upon hawthorn
  stocks,

Like a bold girl, who plays her agile pranks
At wakes and fairs with wandering
    mountebanks,—
When she stands cresting the clown's
    head, and mocks
The crowd beneath her. Verily I think,
10 Such place to me is sometimes like a dream
Or map of the whole world: thoughts,
    link by link,
Enter through ears and eyesight, with
    such gleam
Of all things, that at last in fear I shrink,
And leap at once from the delicious stream.

COMPOSED BY THE SIDE OF
GRASMERE LAKE
1806   1820

Clouds, lingering yet, extend in solid bars
Through the gray west; and lo! these
    waters, steeled
By breezeless air to smoothest polish, yield
A vivid repetition of the stars;
5 Jove, Venus, and the ruddy crest of Mars
Amid his fellows beauteously revealed
At happy distance from earth's groaning
    field,
Where ruthless mortals wage incessant
    wars.
Is it a mirror?—or the nether sphere
10 Opening to view the abyss in which she
    feeds
Her own calm fires?—But list! a voice is
    near;
Great Pan himself low-whispering through
    the reeds,
"Be thankful, thou; for, if unholy deeds
Ravage the world, tranquillity is here!"

THE WORLD IS TOO MUCH WITH US;
LATE AND SOON
1806   1807

The world is too much with us; late and
    soon,
Getting and spending, we lay waste our
    powers:
Little we see in Nature that is ours;
We have given our hearts away, a sordid
    boon!
5 This sea that bares her bosom to the
    moon;
The winds that will be howling at all hours,
And are up-gathered now like sleeping
    flowers;
For this, for everything, we are out of
    tune;
It moves us not.—Great God! I'd rather be
10 A Pagan suckled in a creed outworn;
So might I, standing on this pleasant lea,

Have glimpses that would make me less
    forlorn;
Have sight of Proteus rising from the sea;
Or hear old Triton blow his wreathèd horn.

TO SLEEP
1806   1807

A flock of sheep that leisurely pass by,
One after one; the sound or rain, and
    bees
Murmuring; the fall of rivers, winds and
    seas,
Smooth fields, white sheets of water, and
    pure sky;
5 I have thought of all by turns, and yet
    do lie
Sleepless! and soon the small birds'
    melodies
Must hear, first uttered from my orchard
    trees;
And the first cuckoo's melancholy cry.
Even thus last night, and two nights more,
    I lay
10 And could not win thee, Sleep! by any
    stealth:
So do not let me wear tonight away:
Without thee what is all the morning's
    wealth?
Come, blessed barrier between day and
    day,
Dear mother of fresh thoughts and joyous
    health!

NOVEMBER, 1806
1806   1807

Another year!—another deadly blow!
Another mighty Empire overthrown![1]
And we are left, or shall be left, alone;
The last that dare to struggle with the foe.
5 'Tis well! from this day forward we shall
    know
That in ourselves our safety must be
    sought;
That by our own right hands it must be
    wrought;
That we must stand unpropped, or be
    laid low.
O dastard whom such foretaste doth not
    cheer!
10 We shall exult, if they who rule the land
Be men who hold its many blessings dear,
Wise, upright, valiant; not a servile band,
Who are to judge of danger which they
    fear,
And honor which they do not understand.

[1] A reference to the French victories over the
Germans, October and November, 1806.

ODE

INTIMATIONS OF IMMORTALITY FROM RECOL-
LECTIONS OF EARLY CHILDHOOD
1802-6   1807

"The Child is father of the Man;
And I could wish my days to be
Bound each to each by natural piety."[1]

I

There was a time when meadow, grove,
        and stream,
The earth, and every common sight,
        To me did seem
        Apparelled in celestial light,
The glory and the freshness of a dream.
It is not now as it hath been of yore;—
        Turn wheresoe'er I may,
        By night or day,
The things which I have seen I now can
        see no more.

II

10   The Rainbow comes and goes,
        And lovely is the Rose,
        The Moon doth with delight
Look round her when the heavens are bare,
        Waters on a starry night
15   Are beautiful and fair;
        The sunshine is a glorious birth;
        But yet I know, where'er I go,
That there hath past away a glory from
        the earth.

III

Now, while the birds thus sing a joyous
        song,
20   And while the young lambs bound
        As to the tabor's sound,
To me alone there came a thought of grief:
A timely utterance gave that thought relief.
        And I again am strong:
25 The cataracts blow their trumpets from
        the steep;
No more shall grief of mine the season
        wrong;
I hear the Echoes through the mountains
        throng,
The Winds come to me from the fields of
        sleep,
        And all the earth is gay;
30   Land and sea
        Give themselves up to jollity,
        And with the heart of May
        Doth every beast keep holiday;—
        Thou Child of Joy,
35 Shout round me, let me hear thy shouts,
        thou happy Shepherd-boy!

¹ Wordsworth, *My Heart Leaps Up*, 7-10 (p. 308).

IV

Ye blessèd Creatures, I have heard the call
        Ye to each other make; I see
The heavens laugh with you in your
        jubilee;
        My heart is at your festival,
40   My head hath its coronal,
The fulness of your bliss, I feel—I feel
        it all.
        Oh evil day! if I were sullen
        While Earth herself is adorning,
        This sweet May-morning,
45   And the children are culling
        On every side,
        In a thousand valleys far and wide,
        Fresh flowers; while the sun shines
        warm,
And the Babe leaps up on his mother's
        arm:—
50   I hear, I hear, with joy I hear!
        —But there's a Tree, of many, one,
A single Field which I have looked upon,
Both of them speak of something that is
        gone:
        The Pansy at my feet
55   Doth the same tale repeat:
Whither is fled the visionary gleam?
Where is it now, the glory and the dream?

V

Our birth is but a sleep and a forgetting:
The Soul that rises with us, our life's Star,
60   Hath had elsewhere its setting,
            And cometh from afar:
        Not in entire forgetfulness,
        And not in utter nakedness,
But trailing clouds of glory do we come
65   From God, who is our home:
Heaven lies about us in our infancy!
Shades of the prison-house begin to close
        Upon the growing Boy,
But he beholds the light, and whence it
        flows,
70   He sees it in his joy;
The Youth, who daily farther from the east
        Must travel, still is Nature's priest,
        And by the vision splendid
        Is on his way attended;
75 At length the Man perceives it die away,
And fade into the light of common day.

VI

Earth fills her lap with pleasures of her
        own;
Yearnings she hath in her own natural
        kind,
And, even with something of a mother's
        mind,

80   And no unworthy aim,
    The homely nurse doth all she can
To make her Foster-child, her inmate Man,
    Forget the glories he hath known,
And that imperial palace whence he came.

VII

85 Behold the Child among his new-born
        blisses,
A six years' darling of a pigmy size!
See, where 'mid work of his own hand he
        lies,
Fretted by sallies of his mother's kisses,
With light upon him from his father's
        eyes!
90 See, at his feet, some little plan or chart,
Some fragment from his dream of human
        life,
Shaped by himself with newly-learned art;
    A wedding or a festival,
    A mourning or a funeral;
95   And this hath now his heart,
    And unto this he frames his song:
    Then will he fit his tongue
To dialogues of business, love, or strife;
    But it will not be long
100   Ere this be thrown aside,
    And with new joy and pride
The little Actor cons another part;
Filling from time to time his "humorous
        stage"[1]
With all the Persons, down to palsied Age,
105 That Life brings with her in her equipage;
    As if his whole vocation
    Were endless imitation.

VIII

Thou, whose exterior semblance doth belie
    Thy soul's immensity;
110 Thou best philosopher, who yet dost keep
Thy heritage, thou eye among the blind,
That, deaf and silent, read'st the Eternal
        Deep,[2]
Haunted forever by the Eternal Mind,—
    Mighty prophet! seer blest!
115   On whom those truths do rest,
Which we are toiling all our lives to find,
In darkness lost, the darkness of the grave;
Thou, over whom thy Immortality
Broods like the Day, a master o'er a slave,
120 A Presence which is not to be put by;
Thou little Child, yet glorious in the might
Of heaven-born freedom on thy being's
        height,

---

[1] See *As You Like It*, II, 7, 139 ff. *Humorous*
    refers to dominant moods.
[2] Deep mysteries of eternity.

Why with such earnest pains dost thou
        provoke
The years to bring the inevitable yoke,
125 Thus blindly with thy blessedness at strife?
Full soon thy Soul shall have her earthly
        freight,
And custom lie upon thee with a weight,
Heavy as frost, and deep almost as life!

IX

    O joy! that in our embers
    Is something that doth live,
130   That nature yet remembers
    What was so fugitive!
The thought of our past years in me doth
        breed
Perpetual benediction: not indeed
For that which is most worthy to be
        blest;
135 Delight and liberty, the simple creed
Of childhood, whether busy or at rest,
With new-fledged hope still fluttering in
        his breast:—
    Not for these I raise
    The song of thanks and praise;
140 But for those obstinate questionings
    Of sense and outward things,
    Fallings from us, vanishings;
    Blank misgivings of a Creature
145 Moving about in worlds not realized,
High instincts before which our mortal
        nature
Did tremble like a guilty thing surprised:
    But for those first affections,
    Those shadowy recollections,
150   Which, be they what they may,
Are yet the fountain-light of all our
        day,
Are yet a master-light of all our seeing;
    Uphold us, cherish, and have power
        to make
Our noisy years seem moments in the being
155 Of the Eternal Silence: truths that wake,
        To perish never:
Which neither listlessness, nor mad en-
        deavor,
    Nor man nor boy,
Nor all that is at enmity with joy,
160 Can utterly abolish or destroy!
    Hence in a season of calm weather
    Though inland far we be,
Our souls have sight of that immortal sea
    Which brought us hither,
165   Can in a moment travel thither,
And see the children sport upon the
        shore,
And hear the mighty waters rolling ever-
        more.

X

Then sing, ye Birds, sing, sing a joyous
        song!
    And let the young Lambs bound
170   As to the tabor's sound!
We in thought will join your throng,
    Ye that pipe and ye that play,
    Ye that through your hearts to-
        day
    Feel the gladness of the May!
175 What though the radiance which was
        once so bright
Be now forever taken from my sight,
    Though nothing can bring back the
        hour
Of splendor in the grass, of glory in the
        flower;
    We will grieve not, rather find
180   Strength in what remains behind;
    In the primal sympathy
    Which having been must ever be;
    In the soothing thoughts that spring
    Out of human suffering;
185   In the faith that looks through
        death,
In years that bring the philosophic mind.

XI

And O, ye Fountains, Meadows, Hills,
        and Groves,
Forebode not any severing of our loves!
Yet in my heart of hearts I feel your
        might;
190 I only have relinquished one delight
To live beneath your more habitual
        sway.
I love the Brooks which down their chan-
        nels fret,
Even more than when I tripped lightly
        as they;
The innocent brightness of a new-born
        Day
195   Is lovely yet;
The Clouds that gather round the setting
        sun
Do take a sober coloring from an eye
That hath kept watch o'er man's mor-
        tality;
Another race hath been, and other palms
        are won.
200 Thanks to the human heart by which we
        live,
Thanks to its tenderness, its joys, and
        fears,
To me the meanest flower that blows can
        give
Thoughts that do often lie too deep for
        tears.

THOUGHT OF A BRITON ON THE SUB-
JUGATION OF SWITZERLAND[1]
1807   1807

Two Voices are there; one is of the sea,[2]
One of the mountains;[3] each a mighty
        Voice:
In both from age to age thou didst rejoice,
They were thy chosen music, Liberty!
5 There came a tyrant, and with holy glee
Thou fought'st against him; but hast
        vainly striven:
Thou from thy Alpine holds at length art
        driven,
Where not a torrent murmurs heard by
        thee.
Of one deep bliss thine ear hath been
        bereft:
10 Then cleave, O cleave to that which still
        is left;
For, high-souled Maid, what sorrow would
        it be
That mountain Floods should thunder as
        before,
And Ocean bellow from his rocky shore,
And neither awful Voice be heard by thee!

CHARACTERISTICS OF A CHILD
THREE YEARS OLD[4]
1811   1815

Loving she is, and tractable, though wild;
And Innocence hath privilege in her
To dignify arch looks and laughing eyes;
And feats of cunning; and the pretty
        round
5 Of trespasses, affected to provoke
Mock-chastisement and partnership in
        play.
And, as a faggot sparkles on the hearth,
Not less if unattended and alone
Than when both young and old sit gathered
        round
10 And take delight in its activity;
Even so this happy creature of herself
Is all-sufficient; solitude to her
Is blithe society, who fills the air
With gladness and involuntary songs.
15 Light are her sallies as the tripping fawn's
Forth-startled from the fern where she
        lay couched;
Unthought-of, unexpected, as the stir
Of the soft breeze ruffling the meadow-
        flowers,
Or from before it chasing wantonly
20 The many-colored images imprest
Upon the bosom of a placid lake.

---

[1] Switzerland was con-   [2] England.
quered by the French   [3] Switzerland.
in 1798. By 1807,   [4] W o r d s w o r t h 's
Napoleon had made   daughter Catharine.
himself master of
Europe.

HERE PAUSE: THE POET CLAIMS AT LEAST THIS PRAISE
1811   1815

Here pause: the poet claims at least this
    praise,
That virtuous Liberty hath been the scope
Of his pure song, which did not shrink
    from hope
In the worst moment of these evil days;
5 From hope, the paramount duty that
    Heaven lays,
For its own honor, on man's suffering
    heart.
Never may from our souls one truth de-
    part—
That an accursed thing it is to gaze
On prosperous tyrants with a dazzled
    eye;
10 Nor—touched with due abhorrence of
    their guilt
For whose dire ends tears flow, and blood
    is spilt,
And justice labors in extremity—
Forget thy weakness, upon which is built,
O wretched man, the throne of tyranny!

LAODAMÍA
1814   1815

"With sacrifice before the rising morn
Vows have I made by fruitless hope in-
    spired;
And from the infernal gods, 'mid shades
    forlorn
Of night, my slaughtered lord have I
    required:
5 Celestial pity I again implore;—
Restore him to my sight—great Jove, re-
    store!"

So speaking, and by fervent love endowed
With faith, the suppliant heavenward lifts
    her hands;
While, like the sun emerging from a
    cloud,
10 Her countenance brightens—and her eye
    expands;
Her bosom heaves and spreads, her stature
    grows;
And she expects the issue in repose.

O terror! what hath she perceived?—O
    joy!
What doth she look on?—whom doth she
    behold?
15 Her hero slain upon the beach of Troy?
His vital presence? his corporeal mould?
It is—if sense deceive her not—'tis he!
And a god leads him, wingèd Mercury!

Mild Hermes spake—and touched her with
    his wand
20 That calms all fear; "Such grace hath
    crowned thy prayer,
Laodamía! that at Jove's command
Thy husband walks the paths of upper air:
He comes to tarry with thee three hours'
    space;
Accept the gift, behold him face to face!"

25 Forth sprang the impassioned Queen her
    lord to clasp;
Again that consummation she essayed;
But unsubstantial Form eludes her grasp
As often as that eager grasp was made.
The Phantom parts—but parts to reunite,
30 And reassume his place before her sight.

"Protesiláus, lo! thy guide is gone!
Confirm, I pray, the vision with thy voice:
This is our palace,—yonder is thy throne;
Speak, and the floor thou tread'st on will
    rejoice.
35 Not to appal me have the gods bestowed
This precious boon; and blest a sad
    abode."

"Great Jove, Laodamía! doth not leave
His gifts imperfect:—Spectre though I be,
I am not sent to scare thee or deceive;
40 But in reward of thy fidelity.
And something also did my worth obtain;
For fearless virtue bringeth boundless
    gain.

"Thou knowest, the Delphic oracle fore-
    told
That the first Greek who touched the
    Trojan strand
45 Should die; but me the threat could not
    withhold:
A generous cause a victim did demand;
And forth I leapt upon the sandy plain;
A self-devoted chief—by Hector slain."

"Supreme of heroes—bravest, noblest,
    best!
50 Thy matchless courage I bewail no more,
Which then, when tens of thousands were
    deprest
By doubt, propelled thee to the fatal
    shore;
Thou found'st—and I forgive thee—here
    thou art—
A nobler counsellor than my poor heart.

55 "But thou, though capable of sternest
    deed,
Wert kind as resolute, and good as brave;

And he, whose power restores thee, hath decreed
Thou shouldst elude the malice of the grave:
Redundant are thy locks, thy lips as fair
60 As when their breath enriched Thessalian air.

"No spectre greets me,—no vain shadow this;
Come, blooming hero, place thee by my side!
Give, on this well-known couch, one nuptial kiss
To me, this day, a second time thy bride!"
65 Jove frowned in heaven: the conscious Parcæ threw
Upon those roseate lips a Stygian hue.

"This visage tells thee that my doom is past:
Nor should the change be mourned, even if the joys
Of sense were able to return as fast
70 And surely as they vanish. Earth destroys
Those raptures duly—Erebus disdains:
Calm pleasures there abide—majestic pains.

"Be taught, O faithful consort, to control
Rebellious passion: for the gods approve
75 The depth, and not the tumult, of the soul;
A fervent, not ungovernable, love.
Thy transports moderate; and meekly mourn
When I depart, for brief is my sojourn—"

"Ah wherefore?—Did not Hercules by force
80 Wrest from the guardian Monster of the tomb[1]
Alcestis, a reanimated corse,
Given back to dwell on earth in vernal bloom?[2]
Medea's spells dispersed the weight of years,
And Æson stood a youth 'mid youthful peers.[3]

85 "The gods to us are merciful—and they
Yet further may relent: for mightier far
Than strength of nerve and sinew, or the sway
Of magic potent over sun and star,
Is love, though oft to agony distrest,
90 And though his favorite seat be feeble woman's breast.

[1] Cerberus, the guard at the entrance to Hades.
[2] See Euripides's *Alcestis* and Browning's *Balaustion's Adventure*.
[3] See Ovid's *Metamorphoses*, 7, 159 ff.

"But if thou goest, I follow—" "Peace!" he said,—
She looked upon him and was calmed and cheered;
The ghastly color from his lips had fled;
In his deportment, shape, and mien, appeared
95 Elysian beauty, melancholy grace,
Brought from a pensive though a happy place.

He spake of love, such love as Spirits feel
In worlds whose course is equable and pure;
No fears to beat away—no strife to heal—
100 The past unsighed for, and the future sure;
Spake of heroic arts in graver mood
Revived, with finer harmony pursued;

Of all that is most beauteous—imaged there
In happier beauty; more pellucid streams,
105 An ampler ether, a diviner air,
And fields invested with purpureal gleams;
Climes which the sun, who sheds the brightest day
Earth knows, is all unworthy to survey.

Yet there the Soul shall enter which hath earned
That privilege by virtue.—"Ill," said he,
"The end of man's existence I discerned,
Who from ignoble games and revelry
Could draw, when we had parted, vain delight
While tears were thy best pastime, day and night;

115 "And while my youthful peers before my eyes
(Each hero following his peculiar bent)
Prepared themselves for glorious enterprise
By martial sports,—or, seated in the tent,
Chieftains and kings in council were detained;
120 What time the fleet at Aulis lay enchained.

"The wished-for wind was given:—I then revolved
The oracle, upon the silent sea;
And, if no worthier led the way, resolved
That, of a thousand vessels, mine should be
125 The foremost prow in pressing to the strand,—
Mine the first blood that tinged the Trojan sand.

"Yet bitter, oft-times bitter, was the pang
When of thy loss I thought, belovèd wife!
On thee too fondly did my memory hang,

130 And on the joys we shared in mortal life,—
The paths which we had trod—these foun-
    tains, flowers;
My new-planned cities, and unfinished
    towers.

"But should suspense permit the foe to
    cry,
'Behold they tremble!—haughty their
    array,
135 Yet of their number no one dares to die?'
In soul I swept the indignity away:
Old frailties then recurred:—but lofty
    thought,
In act embodied, my deliverance wrought.

"And thou, though strong in love, art all
    too weak
140 In reason, in self-government too slow;
I counsel thee by fortitude to seek
Our blest reunion in the shades below.
The invisible world with thee hath sym-
    pathized;
Be thy affections raised and solemnized.

145 "Learn, by a mortal yearning, to ascend—
Seeking a higher object. Love was given,
Encouraged, sanctioned, chiefly for that
    end;
For this the passion to excess was driven—
That self might be annulled: her bondage
    prove
150 The fetters of a dream opposed to love.''

Aloud she shrieked! for Hermes re-
    appears!
Round the dear Shade she would have
    clung—'tis vain:
The hours are past—too brief had they
    been years;
And him no mortal effort can detain:
155 Swift, toward the realms that know not
    earthly day,
He through the portal takes his silent way,
And on the palace floor a lifeless corse
    she lay.

Thus, all in vain exhorted and reproved,
She perished; and, as for a wilful crime,
160 By the just gods whom no weak pity
    moved,
Was doomed to wear out her appointed
    time,
Apart from happy ghosts, that gather
    flowers
Of blissful quiet 'mid unfading bowers.

—Yet tears to human suffering are due;
165 And mortal hopes defeated and o'er-
    thrown

Are mourned by man, and not by man
    alone,
As fondly he believes.—Upon the side
Of Hellespont (such faith was enter-
    tained)
170 A knot of spiry trees[1] for ages grew
From out the tomb of him for whom she
    died;
And ever, when such stature they had
    gained
That Ilium's walls were subject to their
    view,
The trees' tall summits withered at the
    sight;
A constant interchange of growth and
    blight!

YARROW VISITED

SEPTEMBER, 1814
1814   1815

And is this—Yarrow?—*This* the stream
Of which my fancy cherished,
So faithfully, a waking dream?
An image that hath perished!
5 O that some minstrel's harp were near,
To utter notes of gladness,
And chase this silence from the air,
That fills my heart with sadness!

Yet why?—a silvery current flows
10 With uncontrolled meanderings;
Nor have these eyes by greener hills
Been soothed, in all my wanderings.
And, through her depths, Saint Mary's
    Lake
Is visibly delighted;
15 For not a feature of those hills
Is in the mirror slighted.

A blue sky bends o'er Yarrow vale,
Save where that pearly whiteness
Is round the rising sun diffused,
20 A tender hazy brightness;
Mild dawn of promise! that excludes
All profitless dejection;
Though not unwilling here to admit
A pensive recollection.

25 Where was it that the famous Flower
Of Yarrow Vale lay bleeding?[2]
His bed perchance was yon smooth mound
On which the herd is feeding:
And haply from this crystal pool,

---

[1] See Pliny's *Natural History*, 16, 44.
[2] The Flower of Yarrow was Mary Scott of Dryhope; but Wordsworth is probably following
Logan's *Braes of Yarrow*, in which the lady
mourns over the lover whom she calls "the
flower of Yarrow."

30 Now peaceful as the morning,
The water-wraith[1] ascended thrice—
And gave his doleful warning.

Delicious is the lay that sings
The haunts of happy lovers,
35 The path that leads them to the grove,
The leafy grove that covers:
And Pity sanctifies the verse
That paints, by strength of sorrow,
The unconquerable strength of love;
40 Bear witness, rueful Yarrow!

But thou, that didst appear so fair
To fond imagination,
Dost rival in the light of day
Her delicate creation:
45 Meek loveliness is round thee spread,
A softness still and holy;
The grace of forest charms decayed,
And pastoral melancholy.

That region left, the vale unfolds
50 Rich groves of lofty stature,
With Yarrow winding through the pomp
Of cultivated nature;
And, rising from those lofty groves,
Behold a Ruin hoary!
55 The shattered front of Newark's Towers,
Renowned in Border story.

Fair scenes for childhood's opening bloom.
For sportive youth to stray in:
For manhood to enjoy his strength;
60 And age to wear away in!
Yon cottage seems a bower of bliss,
A covert for protection
Of tender thoughts, that nestle there—
The brood of chaste affection.

65 How sweet, on this autumnal day.
The wild-wood fruits to gather,
And on my True-love's forehead plant
A crest of blooming heather!
And what if I enwreathed my own!
70 'Twere no offence to reason;
The sober Hills thus deck their brows
To meet the wintry season.

I see—but not by sight alone,
Loved Yarrow, have I won thee;
75 A ray of fancy still survives—
Her sunshine plays upon thee!
Thy ever-youthful waters keep
A course of lively pleasure;
And gladsome notes my lips can breathe,
80 Accordant to the measure.

1 A spirit thought to preside over waters. Lines
31-32 are taken from Logan's poem.

The vapors linger round the heights,
They melt, and soon must vanish;
One hour is theirs, nor more is mine—
Sad thought, which I would banish,
85 But that I know, where'er I go,
Thy genuine image, Yarrow!
Will dwell with me—to heighten joy,
And cheer my mind in sorrow.

HAST THOU SEEN, WITH FLASH INCESSANT
1818   *1820*

Hast thou seen, with flash incessant,
Bubbles gliding under ice,
Bodied forth and evanescent,
No one knows by what device?

5 Such are thoughts!—A wind-swept
     meadow
Mimicking a troubled sea,
Such is life; and death a shadow
From the rock eternity!

COMPOSED UPON AN EVENING OF EXTRAORDINARY SPLENDOR AND BEAUTY
1818   *1820*

Had this effulgence disappeared
With flying haste, I might have sent,
Among the speechless clouds, a look
Of blank astonishment;
5 But 'tis endued with power to stay,
And sanctify one closing day,
That frail Mortality may see—
What is?—ah no, but what can be!
Time was when field and watery cove
10 With modulated echoes rang,
While choirs of fervent angels sang
Their vespers in the grove;
Or, crowning, star-like, each some sov-
     ereign height,
Warbled, from heaven above and earth
     below,
15 Strains suitable to both.—Such holy rite,
Methinks, if audibly repeated now
From hill or valley, could not move
Sublimer transport, purer love,
Than doth this silent spectacle—the
     gleam—
20 The shadow—and the peace supreme!

No sound is uttered,—but a deep
And solemn harmony pervades
The hollow vale from steep to steep,
And penetrates the glades.
25 Far-distant images draw nigh,
Called forth by wondrous potency
Of beamy radiance, that imbues
Whate'er it strikes with gem-like hues!

In vision exquisitely clear,
30 Herds range along the mountain side;
And glistening antlers are descried;
And gilded flocks appear.
Thine is the tranquil hour, purpureal eve!
But long as god-like wish, or hope divine,
35 Informs my spirit, ne'er can I believe
That this magnificence is wholly thine!
—From worlds not quickened by the sun
A portion of the gift is won;
An intermingling of Heaven's pomp is
    spread
40 On ground which British shepherds tread!

And if there be whom broken ties
Afflict, or injuries assail,
Yon hazy ridges to their eyes
Present a glorious scale,
45 Climbing suffused with sunny air,
To stop—no record hath told where!
And tempting Fancy to ascend,
And with immortal spirits blend!
—Wings at my shoulders seem to play;
50 But, rooted here, I stand and gaze
On those bright steps that heavenward raise
Their practicable way.[1]
Come forth, ye drooping old men, look
    abroad,
And see to what fair countries ye are
    bound!
55 And if some traveller, weary of his road,
Hath slept since noon-tide on the grassy
    ground,
Ye Genii! to his covert speed;
And wake him with such gentle heed
As may attune his soul to meet the dower
60 Bestowed on this transcendent hour!

Such hues from their celestial urn
Were wont to stream before mine eye,
Where'er it wandered in the morn
Of blissful infancy.
65 This glimpse of glory, why renewed?
Nay, rather speak with gratitude;
For, if a vestige of those gleams
Survived, 'twas only in my dreams.
Dread Power! whom peace and calmness
    serve
70 No less than Nature's threatening voice,
If aught unworthy be my choice,
From thee if I would swerve;
Oh, let thy grace remind me of the light
Full early lost, and fruitlessly deplored;
75 Which, at this moment, on my waking sight
Appears to shine, by miracle restored;
My soul, though yet confined to earth,
Rejoices in a second birth!
—Tis past, the visionary splendor fades;
80 And night approaches with her shades.

[1] A ladder that may be climbed.

TO A SNOWDROP
1819   1819

Lone Flower, hemmed in with snows, and
    white as they
But hardier far, once more I see thee bend
Thy forehead as if fearful to offend,
Like an unbidden guest. Though day by
    day
5 Storms, sallying from the mountain-tops,
    waylay
The rising sun, and on the plains descend;
Yet art thou welcome, welcome as a friend
Whose zeal outruns his promise! Blue-
    eyed May
Shall soon behold this border thickly set
10 With bright jonquils, their odors lavishing
On the soft west-wind and his frolic
    peers;
Nor will I then thy modest grace forget,
Chaste Snowdrop, venturous harbinger of
    Spring,
And pensive monitor of fleeting years!

THERE IS A LITTLE UNPRETENDING RILL
1820   1820

There is a little unpretending rill
Of limpid water, humbler far than aught
That ever among men or naiads sought
Notice or name!—It quivers down the hill,
5 Furrowing its shallow way with dubious
    will;
Yet to my mind this scanty stream is
    brought
Oftener than Ganges or the Nile; a
    thought
Of private recollection sweet and still!
Months perish with their moons; year
    treads on year;
10 But, faithful Emma![1] thou with me canst
    say
That, while ten thousand pleasures dis-
    appear,
And flies their memory fast almost as
    they;
The immortal Spirit of one happy day
Lingers beside that rill, in vision clear.

BETWEEN NAMUR AND LIEGE
1820   1822

What lovelier home could gentle Fancy
    choose?
Is this the stream, whose cities, heights,
    and plains,
War's favorite playground, are with crim-
    son stains
Familiar, as the Morn with pearly dews?
5 The Morn, that now, along the silver
    Meuse,

[1] A name given to Wordsworth's sister Dorothy.

Spreading her peaceful ensigns, calls the
    swains
To tend their silent boats and ringing
    wains,
Or strip the bough whose mellow fruit
    bestrews
The ripening corn beneath it. As mine
    eyes
10 Turn from the fortified and threatening
    hill,
How sweet the prospect of yon watery
    glade,
With its gray rocks clustering in pensive
    shade—
That, shaped like old monastic turrets, rise
From the smooth meadow-ground, serene
    and still!

COMPOSED IN ONE OF THE CATHOLIC CANTONS
1820   1822

Doomed as we are our native dust
To wet with many a bitter shower,
It ill befits us to disdain
The altar, to deride the fane,
5 Where simple sufferers bend, in trust
To win a happier hour.

I love, where spreads the village lawn,
Upon some knee-worn cell to gaze:
Hail to the firm unmoving cross,
10 Aloft, where pines their branches toss!
And to the chapel far withdrawn,
That lurks by lonely ways!

Where'er we roam—along the brink
Of Rhine—or by the sweeping Po,
15 Through Alpine vale, or champaign wide,
Whate'er we look on, at our side
Be Charity!—to bid us think,
And feel, if we would know.

From THE RIVER DUDDON
1820   1820
SOLE LISTENER, DUDDON

Sole listener, Duddon! to the breeze that
    played
With thy clear voice, I caught the fitful
    sound
Wafted o'er sullen moss and craggy
    mound—
Unfruitful solitudes, that seemed to up-
    braid
5 The sun in heaven!—but now, to form a
    shade
For thee, green alders have together wound
Their foliage; ashes flung their arms
    around;

And birch trees risen in silver colonnade.
And thou hast also tempted here to rise,
10 'Mid sheltering pines, this cottage rude
    and gray;
Whose ruddy children, by the mother's
    eyes
Carelessly watched, sport through the
    summer day,
Thy pleased associates:—light as endless
    May
On infant bosoms lonely Nature lies.

AFTER-THOUGHT

I thought of thee, my partner and my
    guide,
As being past away.—Vain sympathies!
For, backward, Duddon! as I cast my
    eyes,
I see what was, and is, and will abide;
5 Still glides the Stream, and shall forever
    glide;
The Form remains, the Function never
    dies;
While we, the brave, the mighty, and the
    wise,
We Men, who in our morn of youth defied
The elements, must vanish;—be it so!
10 Enough, if something from our hands
    have power
To live, and act, and serve the future hour;
And if, as toward the silent tomb we go,
Through love, through hope, and faith's
    transcendent dower,
We feel that we are greater than we know.[1]

From ECCLESIASTICAL SONNETS
1821   1822
MUTABILITY

From low to high doth dissolution climb,
And sink from high to low, along a scale
Of awful notes, whose concord shall not
    fail;
A musical but melancholy chime,
5 Which they can hear who meddle not with
    crime,
Nor avarice, nor over-anxious care.
Truth fails not; but her outward forms
    that bear
The longest date do melt like frosty rime,
That in the morning whitened hill and plain
10 And is no more; drop like the tower
    sublime
Of yesterday, which royally did wear
His crown of weeds, but could not even
    sustain
Some casual shout that broke the silent air,
Or the unimaginable touch of Time.

[1] See *Paradise Lost*, 8, 282.

INSIDE OF KING'S COLLEGE CHAPEL, CAMBRIDGE

Tax not the royal saint[1] with vain expense,
With ill-matched aims the architect who
planned—
Albeit laboring for a scanty band
Of white-robed scholars only—this immense
5 And glorious work of fine intelligence!
Give all thou canst; high Heaven rejects
the lore
Of nicely-calculated less or more;
So deemed the man who fashioned for the
sense
These lofty pillars, spread that branching
roof
10 Self-poised, and scooped into ten thousand cells,
Where light and shade repose, where music
dwells
Lingering—and wandering on as loth to
die;
Like thoughts whose very sweetness yield-
eth proof
That they were born for immortality.

TO A SKYLARK
1825   1827

Ethereal minstrel! pilgrim of the sky!
Dost thou despise the earth where cares
abound?
Or, while the wings aspire, are heart and
eye
Both with thy nest upon the dewy ground?
5 Thy nest which thou canst drop into at will,
Those quivering wings composed, that
music still!

Leave to the nightingale her shady wood;
A privacy of glorious light is thine;
Whence thou dost pour upon the world a
flood
10 Of harmony, with instinct more divine;
Type of the wise who soar, but never roam;
True to the kindred points of Heaven and
Home!

SCORN NOT THE SONNET
1827   1827

Scorn not the Sonnet; Critic, you have
frowned,
Mindless of its just honors; with this key
Shakspeare unlocked his heart; the melody
Of this small lute gave ease to Petrarch's
wound;[2]
5 A thousand times this pipe did Tasso
sound;

With it Camoens soothed an exile's grief;[1]
The Sonnet glittered a gay myrtle leaf[2]
Amid the cypress with which Dante
crowned
His visionary brow: a glow-worm lamp,
10 It cheered mild Spenser, called from
Faery-land
To struggle through dark ways; and
when a damp
Fell round the path of Milton, in his hand
The Thing became a trumpet; whence he
blew
Soul-animating strains—alas, too few!

TO THE CUCKOO
1827   1827

Not the whole warbling grove in concert
heard
When sunshine follows shower, the breast
can thrill
Like the first summons, Cuckoo! of thy bill,
With its twin notes inseparably paired.
5 The captive 'mid damp vaults unsunned,
unaired,
Measuring the periods of his lonely doom,
That cry can reach; and to the sick man's
room
Sends gladness, by no languid smile declared.
The lordly eagle-race through hostile search
10 May perish; time may come when never
more
The wilderness shall hear the lion roar;
But, long as cock shall crow from house-
hold perch
To rouse the dawn, soft gales shall speed
thy wing,
And thy erratic[3] voice be faithful to the
spring!

YARROW REVISITED
1831   1835

The gallant youth, who may have gained,
Or seeks a "winsome marrow,"[4]
Was but an infant in the lap
When first I looked on Yarrow;[5]
5 Once more, by Newark's Castle-gate
Long left without a warder,
I stood, looked, listened, and with thee,
Great Minstrel of the Border![6]

---

[1] Henry VI, who founded King's College in 1441.
[2] His love for Laura, the inspiration of many of
his sonnets.

[1] Camoens was banished from Lisbon partly because of his passion for Donna Caterina.
After her death, he lamented her in his
Rimas.
[2] The myrtle was a symbol of love; the cypress,
of mourning. A reference to Dante's love
sonnets (found in his *Vita Nuova*) and *Divine Comedy*.
[3] wandering
[4] companion (See Hamilton's *The Braes of Yarrow*, p. 13.)
[5] In 1814. See *Yarrow Visited* (p. 334).
[6] Scott (a reference to his *Minstrelsy of the
Scottish Border*).

Grave thoughts ruled wide on that sweet
day,
10   Their dignity installing
In gentle bosoms, while sere leaves
  Were on the bough, or falling;
But breezes played, and sunshine
gleamed—
  The forest to embolden;
15 Reddened the fiery hues, and shot
  Transparence through the golden.

For busy thoughts the Stream flowed on
  In foamy agitation;
And slept in many a crystal pool
20   For quiet contemplation:
No public and no private care
  The freeborn mind enthralling,
We made a day of happy hours,
  Our happy days recalling.

25 Brisk Youth appeared, the Morn of
Youth,
  With freaks of graceful folly,—
Life's temperate Noon, her sober Eve,
  Her Night not melancholy;
Past, present, future, all appeared
30   In harmony united,
Like guests that meet, and some from far,
  By cordial love invited.

And if, as Yarrow, through the woods
  And down the meadow ranging,
35 Did meet us with unaltered face,
  Though we were changed and changing;
If, then, some natural shadows spread
  Our inward prospect over,
The soul's deep valley was not slow
40   Its brightness to recover.

Eternal blessings on the Muse,
  And her divine employment!
The blameless Muse, who trains her sons
  For hope and calm enjoyment;
45 Albeit sickness, lingering yet,
  Has o'er their pillow brooded;
And Care waylays their steps—a sprite
  Not easily eluded.

For thee, O Scott! compelled to change
50   Green Eildon-hill and Cheviot
For warm Vesuvio's vine-clad slopes;
  And leave thy Tweed and Tiviot
For mild Sorento's breezy waves;
  May classic Fancy, linking
55 With native Fancy her fresh aid,
  Preserve thy heart from sinking!

Oh! while they minister to thee,
  Each vying with the other,

May Health return to mellow Age,
60   With Strength, her venturous brother;
And Tiber, and each brook and rill
  Renowned in song and story,
With unimagined beauty shine,
  Nor lose one ray of glory!

65 For thou, upon a hundred streams,
  By tales of love and sorrow,
Of faithful love, undaunted truth,
  Hast shed the power of Yarrow;
And streams unknown, hills yet unseen,
70   Wherever they invite thee,
At parent Nature's grateful call,
  With gladness must requite thee.

A gracious welcome shall be thine,
  Such looks of love and honor
75 As thy own Yarrow gave to me
  When first I gazed upon her;
Beheld what I had feared to see,
  Unwilling to surrender
Dreams treasured up from early days,
80   The holy and the tender.

And what, for this frail world, were all
  That mortals do or suffer,
Did no responsive harp, no pen,
  Memorial tribute offer?
85 Yea, what were mighty Nature's self?
  Her features, could they win us,
Unhelped by the poetic voice
  That hourly speaks within us?

Nor deem that localized Romance
90   Plays false with our affections;
Unsanctifies our tears—made sport
  For fanciful dejections:
Ah, no! the visions of the past
  Sustain the heart in feeling
95 Life as she is—our changeful Life,
  With friends and kindred dealing.

Bear witness, ye, whose thoughts that day
  In Yarrow's groves were centred;
Who through the silent portal arch
100   Of mouldering Newark entered;
And clomb the winding stair that once
  Too timidly was mounted
By the "last Minstrel"[1] (not the last!)
  Ere he his tale recounted.

105 Flow on forever, Yarrow Stream!
  Fulfil thy pensive duty,
Well pleased that future bards should
chant
  For simple hearts thy beauty;

[1] A reference to Scott's *The Lay of the Last Minstrel,* Introduction, 31-2.

To dream-light dear while yet unseen,
110   Dear to the common sunshine,
And dearer still, as now I feel,
   To memory's shadowy moonshine!

ON THE DEPARTURE OF SIR WALTER SCOTT FROM ABBOTSFORD, FOR NAPLES
1831   1835

A trouble, not of clouds, or weeping rain,
Nor of the setting sun's pathetic light
Engendered, hangs o'er Eildon's triple height:
Spirits of Power, assembled there, complain
5 For kindred Power, departing from their sight;
While Tweed, best pleased in chanting a blithe strain,
Saddens his voice again, and yet again.
Lift up your hearts, ye Mourners! for the might
Of the whole world's good wishes with him goes;
10 Blessings and prayers in nobler retinue
Than sceptred king or laurelled conqueror knows,
Follow this wondrous Potentate. Be true,
Ye winds of ocean, and the midland sea,[1]
Wafting your Charge to soft Parthenope!

THE TROSACHS
1831   1835

There's not a nook within this solemn Pass
But were an apt confessional for One
Taught by his summer spent, his autumn gone,
That Life is but a tale of morning grass
5 Withered at eve. From scenes of art which chase
That thought away, turn, and with watchful eyes
Feed it 'mid Nature's old felicities,
Rocks, rivers, and smooth lakes more clear than glass
Untouched, unbreathed upon. Thrice happy quest,
10 If from a golden perch of aspen spray
(October's workmanship to rival May)
The pensive warbler of the ruddy breast
That moral sweeten by a heaven-taught lay,
Lulling the year, with all its cares, to rest!

IF THOU INDEED DERIVE THY LIGHT FROM HEAVEN
1832   1836

If thou indeed derive thy light from Heaven,

[1] The Mediterranean.

Then, to the measure of that heaven-born light,
Shine, Poet! in thy place, and be content:—
The stars pre-eminent in magnitude,
5 And they that from the zenith dart their beams,
(Visible though they be to half the earth,
Though half a sphere be conscious of their brightness)
Are yet of no diviner origin,
No purer essence, than the one that burns,
10 Like an untended watch-fire, on the ridge
Of some dark mountain; or than those which seem
Humbly to hang, like twinkling winter lamps,
Among the branches of the leafless trees;
All are the undying offspring of one sire:
15 Then, to the measure of the light vouchsafed,
Shine, Poet, in thy place, and be content.

IF THIS GREAT WORLD OF JOY AND PAIN
1833   1835

If this great world of joy and pain
   Revolve in one sure track;
If freedom, set, will rise again,
   And virtue, flown, come back;
5 Woe to the purblind crew who fill
   The heart with each day's care;
Nor gain, from past or future, skill
   To bear, and to forbear!

"THERE!" SAID A STRIPLING, POINTING WITH MEET PRIDE
1833   1835

"There!" said a stripling, pointing with meet pride
Towards a low roof with green trees half concealed,
"Is Mosgiel Farm; and that's the very field
Where Burns ploughed up the daisy." Far and wide
5 A plain below stretched seaward, while, descried
Above sea-clouds, the Peaks of Arran rose;
And, by that simple notice, the repose
Of earth, sky, sea, and air, was vivified.
Beneath "the random bield[1] of clod or stone"
10 Myriads of daisies have shone forth in flower
Near the lark's nest, and in their natural hour

[1] shelter (Burns, *To a Mountain Daisy*, 21, p. 218)

Have passed away; less happy than the
  One
That, by the unwilling ploughshare, died
  to prove
The tender charm of poetry and love.

MOST SWEET IT IS WITH UN-
UPLIFTED EYES
1833   1835

Most sweet it is with unuplifted eyes
To pace the ground, if path be there or
  none,
While a fair region round the traveller lies
Which he forbears again to look upon;
5 Pleased rather with some soft ideal scene,
The work of Fancy, or some happy tone
Of meditation, slipping in between
The beauty coming and the beauty gone.
If Thought and Love desert us, from that
  day
10 Let us break off all commerce with the
  Muse:
With Thought and Love companions of
  our way,
Whate'er the senses take or may refuse,
The Mind's internal heaven shall shed her
  dews
Of inspiration on the humblest lay.

TO A CHILD[1]

WRITTEN IN HER ALBUM
1834   1835

Small service is true service while it lasts:
Of humblest friends, bright creature!
  scorn not one:
The daisy, by the shadow that it casts,
Protects the lingering dewdrop from the
  sun.

EXTEMPORE EFFUSION UPON THE
DEATH OF JAMES HOGG
1835   1836

When first, descending from the moor-
  lands,
I saw the Stream of Yarrow glide
Along a bare and open valley,
The Ettrick Shepherd[2] was my guide.

5 When last along its banks I wandered,
Through groves that had begun to shed
Their golden leaves upon the pathways,
My steps the Border-minstrel[3] led.

The mighty Minstrel breathes no longer,
10 'Mid mouldering ruins low he lies;
And death upon the braes[1] of Yarrow,
Has closed the Shepherd-poet's eyes:

Nor has the rolling year twice measured,
From sign to sign, its steadfast course,
15 Since every mortal power of Coleridge
Was frozen at its marvellous source;

The rapt One, of the godlike forehead,[2]
The heaven-eyed creature sleeps in
  earth:
And Lamb, the frolic and the gentle,
20 Has vanished from his lonely hearth.

Like clouds that rake the mountain-
  summits,
Or waves that own no curbing hand,
How fast has brother followed brother,
From sunshine to the sunless land!

25 Yet I, whose lids from infant slumber
Were earlier raised, remain to hear
A timid voice, that asks in whispers,
"Who next will drop and disappear?"

Our haughty life is crowned with darkness,
30 Like London with its own black wreath,
On which with thee, O Crabbe! forth-
  looking,
I gazed from Hampstead's breezy heath.

As if but yesterday departed,
Thou too art gone before; but why,
35 O'er ripe fruit, seasonably gathered,[3]
Should frail survivors heave a sigh?

Mourn rather for that holy Spirit,
Sweet as the spring, as ocean deep;
For her[4] who, ere her summer faded,
40 Has sunk into a breathless sleep.

No more of old romantic sorrows,[5]
For slaughtered youth or love-lorn
  maid!
With sharper grief is Yarrow smitten,
And Ettrick mourns with her their Poet
  dead.

---

[1] banks
[2] Coleridge, who died in 1834. See Hazlitt's
  My First Acquaintance with Poets (p. 1055b,
  l. 22).
[3] Crabbe died in 1832, at the age of 78.
[4] Felicia Hemans, who died in 1835, at the age
  of 42.
[5] A reference to the ballads of Yarrow, by Hamilton, Logan, and others.

---

[1] Wordsworth's goddaughter, Rotha Quillinan.
[2] Hogg, who died in 1835. A reference to
  Wordsworth's tour in Scotland in 1814. See
  Yarrow Visited (p. 334).
[3] Scott, who died in 1832. A reference to Wordsworth's visit at Abbotsford in 1831. See *Yarrow Revisited* (p. 338).

HARK! 'TIS THE THRUSH
1838   1838

Hark! 'tis the Thrush, undaunted, un-
    deprest,
By twilight premature of cloud and rain;
Nor does that roaring wind deaden his
    strain
Who carols thinking of his Love and nest,
5 And seems, as more incited, still more
    blest.
Thanks; thou hast snapped a fireside
    Prisoner's chain,
Exulting Warbler! eased a fretted brain,
And in a moment charmed my cares to
    rest.
Yes, I will forth, bold Bird! and front
    the blast,
10 That we may sing together, if thou wilt,
So loud, so clear, my Partner through
    life's day,
Mute in her nest love-chosen, if not love-
    built
Like thine, shall gladden, as in seasons
    past,
Thrilled by loose snatches of the social Lay.

A POET!—HE HATH PUT HIS HEART TO SCHOOL
1842   1842

A Poet!—He hath put his heart to school,
Nor dares to move unpropped upon the
    staff
Which Art hath lodged within his hand—
    must laugh
By precept only, and shed tears by rule.
5 Thy Art be Nature; the live current quaff,
And let the groveller sip his stagnant pool,
In fear that else, when Critics grave and
    cool
Have killed him, Scorn should write his
    epitaph.
How does the meadow flower its bloom
    unfold?
10 Because the lovely little flower is free
Down to its root, and, in that freedom,
    bold;
And so the grandeur of the forest tree
Comes not by casting in a formal mould,
But from its *own* divine vitality.

SO FAIR, SO SWEET, WITHAL SO SENSITIVE
1844   1845

So fair, so sweet, withal so sensitive,
Would that the little Flowers were born
    to live,
Conscious of half the pleasure which they
    give;

That to this mountain-daisy's self were
    known
5 The beauty of its star-shaped shadow,
    thrown
On the smooth surface of this naked
    stone!
And what if hence a bold desire should
    mount
High as the Sun, that he could take
    account
Of all that issues from his glorious fount!

10 So might he ken how by his sovereign aid
These delicate companionships are made;
And how he rules the pomp of light and
    shade;

And were the Sister-power that shines by
    night
So privileged, what a countenance of de-
    light
15 Would through the clouds break forth on
    human sight!

Fond fancies! wheresoe'er shall turn thine
    eye
On earth, air, ocean, or the starry sky,
Converse with Nature in pure sympathy;

All vain desires, all lawless wishes quelled,
20 Be thou to love and praise alike impelled,
Whatever boon is granted or withheld.

THE UNREMITTING VOICE OF NIGHTLY STREAMS
1846   1850

The unremitting voice of nightly streams
That wastes so oft, we think, its tuneful
    powers,
If neither soothing to the worm that
    gleams
Through dewy grass, nor small birds
    hushed in bowers,
5 Nor unto silent leaves and drowsy
    flowers,—
That voice of unpretending harmony
(For who what is shall measure by what
    seems
To be, or not to be,
Or tax high Heaven with prodigality?)
10 Wants not a healing influence that can
    creep
Into the human breast, and mix with sleep
To regulate the motion of our dreams
For kindly issues—as through every clime
Was felt near murmuring brooks in
    earliest time;

15 As, at this day, the rudest swains who
    dwell
Where torrents roar, or hear the tinkling
    knell
Of water-breaks[1] with grateful heart could
    tell.

PREFACE

TO THE SECOND EDITION OF SEVERAL OF THE
FOREGOING POEMS, PUBLISHED, WITH AN
ADDITIONAL VOLUME, UNDER THE TITLE
OF ''LYRICAL BALLADS''
1800   1800

The first volume of these poems has
already been submitted to general perusal.
It was published as an experiment, which,
I hoped, might be of some use to ascertain,
how far, by fitting to metrical arrangement
a selection of the real language of men in
a state of vivid sensation, that sort of
pleasure and that quantity of pleasure may
be imparted, which a poet may rationally
endeavor to impart.

I had formed no very inaccurate estimate
of the probable effect of those poems: I
flattered myself that they who should be
pleased with them would read them with
more than common pleasure; and, on the
other hand, I was well aware, that by those
who should dislike them, they would be read
with more than common dislike. The result
has differed from my expectation in this
only, that a greater number have been
pleased than I ventured to hope I should
please.

Several of my friends are anxious for
the success of these poems from a belief
that, if the views with which they were composed were indeed realized, a class of poetry
would be produced well adapted to interest
mankind permanently, and not unimportant
in the quality and in the multiplicity of its
moral relations: and on this account they
have advised me to add a systematic defense of the theory upon which the poems
were written. But I was unwilling to undertake the task, because I knew that on this
occasion the reader would look coldly upon
my arguments, since I might be suspected
of having been principally influenced by
the selfish and foolish hope of *reasoning*
him into an approbation of these particular
poems: and I was still more unwilling to
undertake the task, because, adequately to
display my opinions, and fully to enforce
my arguments, would require a space wholly
disproportionate to a preface. For to treat
the subject with the clearness and coherence

[1] ripples

of which it is susceptible, it would be necessary to give a full account of the present
state of the public taste in this country, and
to determine how far this taste is healthy
or depraved; which, again, could not be
determined, without pointing out, in what
manner language and the human mind act
and react on each other, and without retracing the revolutions, not of literature
alone, but likewise of society itself. I have
therefore altogether declined to enter regularly upon this defense; yet I am sensible
that there would be some impropriety in
abruptly obtruding upon the public, without a few words of introduction, poems so
materially different from those upon which
general approbation is at present bestowed.

It is supposed that by the act of writing
in verse an author makes a formal engagement that he will gratify certain known
habits of association; that he not only thus
apprises the reader that certain classes of
ideas and expressions will be found in his
book, but that others will be carefully excluded. This exponent or symbol held forth
by metrical language must in different eras
of literature have excited very different
expectations: for example, in the age of
Catullus, Terence, and Lucretius, and that
of Statius or Claudian; and in our own
country, in the age of Shakspeare and Beaumont and Fletcher, and that of Donne and
Cowley, or Dryden, or Pope. I will not
take upon me to determine the exact import
of the promise which by the act of writing
in verse an author, in the present day,
makes to his reader; but it will undoubtedly appear to many persons that I have
not fulfilled the terms of an engagement
thus voluntarily contracted. They who have
been accustomed to the gaudiness and inane
phraseology of many modern writers, if
they persist in reading this book to its conclusion, will, no doubt, frequently have to
struggle with feelings of strangeness and
awkwardness: they will look round for
poetry, and will be induced to inquire by
what species of courtesy these attempts can
be permitted to assume that title. I hope,
therefore, the reader will not censure me for
attempting to state what I have proposed
to myself to perform; and also (as far as
the limits of a preface will permit) to explain some of the chief reasons which have
determined me in the choice of my purpose:
that at least he may be spared any unpleasant feeling of disappointment, and that I
myself may be protected from one of the
most dishonorable accusations which can be

brought against an author; namely, that of an indolence which prevents him from endeavoring to ascertain what is his duty, or, when his duty is ascertained, prevents him from performing it.

The principal object, then, proposed in these poems was to choose incidents and situations from common life, and to relate or describe them throughout, as far as was possible, in a selection of language really used by men, and, at the same time, to throw over them a certain coloring of imagination, whereby ordinary things should be presented to the mind in an unusual aspect; and, further, and above all, to make these incidents and situations interesting by tracing in them, truly though not ostentatiously, the primary laws of our nature: chiefly, as far as regards the manner in which we associate ideas in a state of excitement. Humble and rustic life was generally chosen, because, in that condition, the essential passions of the heart find a better soil in which they can attain their maturity, are less under restraint, and speak a plainer and more emphatic language; because in that condition of life our elementary feelings coexist in a state of greater simplicity, and, consequently, may be more accurately contemplated, and more forcibly communicated; because the manners of rural life germinate from those elementary feelings, and, from the necessary character of rural occupations, are more easily comprehended, and are more durable; and, lastly, because in that condition the passions of men are incorporated with the beautiful and permanent forms of nature. The language, too, of these men has been adopted (purified indeed from what appear to be its real defects, from all lasting and rational causes of dislike or disgust) because such men hourly communicate with the best objects from which the best part of language is originally derived; and because, from their rank in society and the sameness and narrow circle of their intercourse, being less under the influence of social vanity, they convey their feelings and notions in simple and unelaborated expressions. Accordingly, such a language, arising out of repeated experience and regular feelings, is a more permanent, and a far more philosophical language, than that which is frequently substituted for it by poets, who think that they are conferring honor upon themselves and their art, in proportion as they separate themselves from the sympathies of men, and indulge in arbitrary and capricious

habits of expression, in order to furnish food for fickle tastes and fickle appetites of their own creation.

I cannot, however, be insensible to the present outcry against the triviality and meanness, both of thought and language, which some of my contemporaries[1] have occasionally introduced into their metrical compositions; and I acknowledge that this defect, where it exists, is more dishonorable to the writer's own character than false refinement or arbitrary innovation, though I should contend at the same time, that it is far less pernicious in the sum of its consequences. From such verses the poems in these volumes will be found distinguished at least by one mark of difference, that each of them has a worthy *purpose*. Not that I always began to write with a distinct purpose formally conceived; but habits of meditation have, I trust, so prompted and regulated my feelings, that my descriptions of such objects as strongly excite those feelings, will be found to carry along with them a *purpose*. If this opinion be erroneous, I can have little right to the name of a poet. For all good poetry is the spontaneous overflow of powerful feelings: and though this be true, poems to which any value can be attached were never produced on any variety of subjects but by a man who, being possessed of more than usual organic sensibility, had also thought long and deeply. For our continued influxes of feeling are modified and directed by our thoughts, which are indeed the representatives of all our past feelings; and as by contemplating the relation of these general representatives to each other, we discover what is really important to men, so, by the repetition and continuance of this act, our feelings will be connected with important subjects, till at length, if we be originally possessed of much sensibility, such habits of mind will be produced that, by obeying blindly and mechanically the impulses of those habits, we shall describe objects, and utter sentiments, of such a nature, and in such connection with each other, that the understanding of the reader must necessarily be in some degree enlightened, and his affections strengthened and purified.

It has been said that each of these poems has a purpose. Another circumstance must be mentioned which distinguishes these poems from the popular poetry of the day; it is this, that the feeling therein developed

---

[1] Wordsworth may refer to Southey and Crabbe.

gives importance to the action and situation, and not the action and situation to the feeling.

A sense of false modesty shall not prevent me from asserting that the reader's attention is pointed to this mark of distinction far less for the sake of these particular poems than from the general importance of the subject. The subject is indeed important! For the human mind is capable of being excited without the application of gross and violent stimulants; and he must have a very faint perception of its beauty and dignity who does not know this, and who does not further know that one being is elevated above another, in proportion as he possesses this capability. It has therefore appeared to me that to endeavor to produce or enlarge this capability is one of the best services in which, at any period, a writer can be engaged; but this service, excellent at all times, is especially so at the present day. For a multitude of causes, unknown to former times, are now acting with a combined force to blunt the discriminating powers of the mind, and, unfitting it for all voluntary exertion, to reduce it to a state of almost savage torpor. The most effective of these causes are the great national events which are daily taking place,[1] and the increasing accumulation of men in cities, where the uniformity of their occupations produces a craving for extraordinary incident, which the rapid communication of intelligence hourly gratifies. To this tendency of life and manners the literature and theatrical exhibitions of the country have conformed themselves. The invaluable works of our elder writers, I had almost said the works of Shakspeare and Milton, are driven into neglect by frantic novels,[2] sickly and stupid German tragedies,[3] and deluges of idle and extravagant stories in verse.[4] When I think upon this degrading thirst after outrageous stimulation, I am almost ashamed to have spoken of the feeble endeavor made in these volumes to counteract it; and, reflecting upon the magnitude of the general evil, I should be oppressed with no dishonorable melancholy,

[1] Possibly a reference to the war with France, the Irish Rebellion, the passage of labor laws, etc.
[2] Such as *The Castle of Otranto, Vathek, The Mysteries of Udolpho*, and other Gothic romances.
[3] Such as Kotzebue's *Misanthropy and Repentance*, known in England as *The Stranger*.
[4] Wordsworth may refer to such poems as Gifford's *Mœviad* and *Baviad*, Landor's *Gebir*, and Scott's translations of Bürger's *Lenore* and *The Wild Huntsman*.

had I not a deep impression of certain inherent and indestructible qualities of the human mind, and likewise of certain powers in the great and permanent objects that act upon it, which are equally inherent and indestructible; and were there not added to this impression a belief, that the time is approaching when the evil will be systematically opposed by men of greater powers, and with far more distinguished success.

Having dwelt thus long on the subjects and aim of these poems, I shall request the reader's permission to apprise him of a few circumstances relating to their *style*, in order, among other reasons, that he may not censure me for not having performed what I never attempted. The reader will find that personifications of abstract ideas rarely occur in these volumes; and are utterly rejected, as an ordinary device to elevate the style and raise it above prose. My purpose was to imitate, and, as far as is possible, to adopt the very language of men; and assuredly such personifications do not make any natural or regular part of that language. They are, indeed, a figure of speech occasionally prompted by passion, and I have made use of them as such; but have endeavored utterly to reject them as a mechanical device of style, or as a family language which writers in metre seem to lay claim to by prescription. I have wished to keep the reader in the company of flesh and blood, persuaded that by so doing I shall interest him. Others who pursue a different track will interest him likewise; I do not interfere with their claim, but wish to prefer a claim of my own. There will also be found in these volumes little of what is usually called poetic diction; as much pains has been taken to avoid it as is ordinarily taken to produce it; this has been done for the reason already alleged, to bring my language near to the language of men; and further, because the pleasure which I have proposed to myself to impart, is of a kind very different from that which is supposed by many persons to be the proper object of poetry. Without being culpably particular, I do not know how to give my reader a more exact notion of the style in which it was my wish and intention to write, than by informing him that I have at all times endeavored to look steadily at my subject; consequently, there is, I hope, in these poems little falsehood of description, and my ideas are expressed in language fitted to their respective importance. Something must have been gained by this practice, as it is friendly to one property of all good poetry, namely, good sense: but it has necessarily cut me off from a large portion of phrases and figures of speech which from father to son have long been regarded as the common inheritance of poets. I have also thought it expedient to restrict myself still further, having abstained from the use of many expressions, in themselves proper and beautiful, but which have been foolishly repeated by bad poets, till such feelings of disgust are connected with them as it is scarcely possible by any art of association to overpower.

If in a poem there should be found a series of lines, or even a single line, in which the language, though naturally arranged, and according to the strict laws of metre, does not differ from that of prose, there is a numerous class of critics, who, when they stumble upon these prosaisms, as they call them, imagine that they have made a notable discovery, and exult over the poet as over a man ignorant of his own profession. Now these men would establish a canon of criticism which the reader will conclude he must utterly reject, if he wishes to be pleased with these volumes. And it would be a most easy task to prove to him that not only the language of a large portion of every good poem, even of the most elevated character, must necessarily, except with reference to the metre, in no respect differ from that of good prose, but likewise that some of the most interesting parts of the best poems will be found to be strictly the language of prose when prose is well written. The truth of this assertion might be demonstrated by innumerable passages from almost all the poetical writings, even of Milton himself. To illustrate the subject in a general manner, I will here adduce a short composition of Gray, who was at the head of those who, by their reasonings, have attempted to widen the space of separation betwixt prose and metrical composition, and was more than any other man curiously elaborate in the structure of his own poetic diction.

> In vain to me the smiling mornings shine,
> And reddening Phoebus lifts his golden fire;
> The birds in vain their amorous descant join,
> Or cheerful fields resume their green attire.
> These ears, alas! for other notes repine;
> *A different object do these eyes require;*
> *My lonely anguish melts no heart but mine;*
> *And in my breast the imperfect joys expire;*
> Yet morning smiles the busy race to cheer,
> And new-born pleasure brings to happier men;
> The fields to all their wonted tribute bear;

> To warm their little loves the birds complain.
> *I fruitless mourn to him that cannot hear,*
> *And weep the more because I weep in vain.*

It will easily be perceived that the only part of this sonnet which is of any value is the lines printed in italics; it is equally obvious that, except in the rhyme, and in the use of the single word "fruitless" for "fruitlessly," which is so far a defect, the language of these lines does in no respect differ from that of prose.

By the foregoing quotation it has been shown that the language of prose may yet be well adapted to poetry; and it was previously asserted, that a large portion of the language of every good poem can in no respect differ from that of good prose. We will go further. It may be safely affirmed, that there neither is nor can be any *essential* difference between the language of prose and metrical composition. We are fond of tracing the resemblance between poetry and painting, and, accordingly, we call them sisters: but where shall we find bonds of connection sufficiently strict to typify the affinity betwixt metrical and prose composition? They both speak by and to the same organs; the bodies in which both of them are clothed may be said to be of the same substance, their affections are kindred and almost identical, not necessarily differing even in degree; poetry sheds no tears "such as angels weep," but natural and human tears; she can boast of no celestial ichor[1] that distinguishes her vital juices from those of prose; the same human blood circulates through the veins of them both.

If it be affirmed that rhyme and metrical arrangement of themselves constitute a distinction which overturns what has just been said on the strict affinity of metrical language with that of prose, and paves the way for other artificial distinctions which the mind voluntarily admits, I answer that the language of such poetry as is here recommended is, as far as is possible, a selection of the language really spoken by men; that this selection, wherever it is made with true taste and feeling, will of itself form a distinction far greater than would at first be imagined, and will entirely separate the composition from the vulgarity and meanness of ordinary life; and, if metre be superadded thereto, I believe that a dissimilitude will be produced altogether sufficient for the gratification of a rational mind. What other distinction would we

[1] fluid that flowed in the veins of the gods

have? Whence is it to come? And where is it to exist? Not, surely, where the poet speaks through the mouths of his characters: it cannot be necessary here, either for elevation of style, or any of its supposed ornaments; for, if the poet's subject be judiciously chosen, it will naturally, and upon fit occasion, lead him to passions, the language of which, if selected truly and judiciously, must necessarily be dignified and variegated, and alive with metaphors and figures. I forbear to speak of an incongruity which would shock the intelligent reader, should the poet interweave any foreign splendor of his own with that which the passion naturally suggests: it is sufficient to say that such addition is unnecessary. And, surely, it is more probable that those passages, which with propriety abound with metaphors and figures, will have their due effect, if, upon other occasions where the passions are of a milder character, the style also be subdued and temperate.

But, as the pleasure which I hope to give by the poems now presented to the reader must depend entirely on just notions upon this subject, and, as it is in itself of high importance to our taste and moral feelings, I cannot content myself with these detached remarks. And if, in what I am about to say, it shall appear to some that my labor is unnecessary, and that I am like a man fighting a battle without enemies, such persons may be reminded that, whatever be the language outwardly holden by men, a practical faith in the opinions which I am wishing to establish is almost unknown. If my conclusions are admitted, and carried as far as they must be carried if admitted at all, our judgments concerning the works of the greatest poets, both ancient and modern, will be far different from what they are at present, both when we praise and when we censure: and our moral feelings influencing and influenced by these judgments will, I believe, be corrected and purified.

Taking up the subject, then, upon general grounds, let me ask, what is meant by the word poet? What is a poet? To whom does he address himself? And what language is to be expected from him?—He is a man speaking to men; a man, it is true, endowed with more lively sensibility, more enthusiasm and tenderness, who has a greater knowledge of human nature, and a more comprehensive soul, than are supposed to be common among mankind; a man pleased with his own passions and

volitions, and who rejoices more than other men in the spirit of life that is in him; delighting to contemplate similar volitions and passions as manifested in the goings-on of the universe, and habitually impelled to create them where he does not find them. To these qualities he has added a disposition to be affected more than other men by absent things as if they were present; an ability of conjuring up in himself passions, which are indeed far from being the same as those produced by real events, yet (especially in those parts of the general sympathy which are pleasing and delightful) do more nearly resemble the passions produced by real events than anything which, from the motions of their own minds merely, other men are accustomed to feel in themselves:—whence, and from practice, he has acquired a greater readiness and power in expressing what he thinks and feels, and especially those thoughts and feelings which, by his own choice, or from the structure of his own mind, arise in him without immediate external excitement.

But whatever portion of this faculty we may suppose even the greatest poet to possess, there cannot be a doubt that the language which it will suggest to him, must often, in liveliness and truth, fall short of that which is uttered by men in real life, under the actual pressure of those passions, certain shadows of which the poet thus produces, or feels to be produced, in himself.

However exalted a notion we would wish to cherish of the character of a poet, it is obvious that, while he describes and imitates passions, his employment is in some degree mechanical, compared with the freedom and power of real and substantial action and suffering. So that it will be the wish of the poet to bring his feelings near to those of the persons whose feelings he describes, nay, for short spaces of time, perhaps, to let himself slip into an entire delusion, and even confound and identify his own feelings with theirs; modifying only the language which is thus suggested to him by a consideration that he describes for a particular purpose, that of giving pleasure. Here, then, he will apply the principle of selection which has been already insisted upon. He will depend upon this for removing what would otherwise be painful or disgusting in the passion; he will feel that there is no necessity to trick out or to elevate nature: and, the more industriously he applies this principle, the deeper will be his faith that no words, which *his* fancy or imagination can suggest, will be to be compared with those which are the emanations of reality and truth.

But it may be said by those who do not object to the general spirit of these remarks, that, as it is impossible for the poet to produce upon all occasions language as exquisitely fitted for the passion as that which the real passion itself suggests, it is proper that he should consider himself as in the situation of a translator, who does not scruple to substitute excellencies of another kind for those which are unattainable by him; and endeavors occasionally to surpass his original, in order to make some amends for the general inferiority to which he feels that he must submit. But this would be to encourage idleness and unmanly despair. Further, it is the language of men who speak of what they do not understand; who talk of poetry, as of a matter of amusement and idle pleasure; who will converse with us as gravely about a *taste* for poetry, as they express it, as if it were a thing as indifferent as a taste for rope-dancing, or Frontiniac or Sherry.[1] Aristotle, I have been told, has said that poetry is the most philosophic of all writing:[2] it is so: its object is truth, not individual and local, but general and operative; not standing upon external testimony, but carried alive into the heart by passion; truth which is its own testimony, which gives competence and confidence to the tribunal to which it appeals, and receives them from the same tribunal. Poetry is the image of man and nature. The obstacles which stand in the way of the fidelity of the biographer and historian, and of their consequent utility, are incalculably greater than those which are to be encountered by the poet who comprehends the dignity of his art. The poet writes under one restriction only, namely, the necessity of giving immediate pleasure to a human being possessed of that information which may be expected from him, not as a lawyer, a physician, a mariner, an astronomer, or a natural philosopher, but as a man. Except this one restriction, there is no object standing between the poet and the image of things; between this, and the biographer and historian, there are a thousand.

Nor let this necessity of producing immediate pleasure be considered as a degrada-

tion of the poet's art. It is far otherwise. It is an acknowledgment of the beauty of the universe, an acknowledgment the more sincere because not formal, but indirect; it is a task light and easy to him who looks at the world in the spirit of love: further, it is a homage paid to the native and naked dignity of man, to the grand elementary principle of pleasure, by which he knows, and feels, and lives, and moves. We have no sympathy but what is propagated by pleasure: I would not be misunderstood; but wherever we sympathize with pain, it will be found that the sympathy is produced and carried on by subtle combinations with pleasure. We have no knowledge, that is, no general principles drawn from the contemplation of particular facts, but what has been built up by pleasure, and exists in us by pleasure alone. The man of science, the chemist and mathematician, whatever difficulties and disgusts they may have had to struggle with, know and feel this. However painful may be the objects with which the anatomist's knowledge is connected, he feels that his knowledge is pleasure; and where he has no pleasure he has no knowledge. What then does the poet? He considers man and the objects that surround him as acting and reacting upon each other, so as to produce an infinite complexity of pain and pleasure; he considers man in his own nature and in his own ordinary life as contemplating this with a certain quantity of immediate knowledge, with certain convictions, intuitions, and deductions, which from habit acquire the quality of intuitions; he considers him as looking upon this complex scene of ideas and sensations, and finding everywhere objects that immediately excite in him sympathies which, from the necessities of his nature, are accompanied by an overbalance of enjoyment.

To this knowledge which all men carry about with them, and to these sympathies in which, without any other discipline than that of our daily life, we are fitted to take delight, the poet principally directs his attention. He considers man and nature as essentially adapted to each other, and the mind of man as naturally the mirror of the fairest and most interesting properties of nature. And thus the poet, prompted by this feeling of pleasure, which accompanies him through the whole course of his studies, converses with general nature, with affections akin to those which, through labor and length of time, the man of

---

[1] Kinds of wine.
[2] *Poetics,* 9 :3.—"Poetry is more philosophical and more serious than history."

science has raised up in himself, by conversing with those particular parts of nature which are the objects of his studies. The knowledge both of the poet and the man of science is pleasure; but the knowledge of the one cleaves to us as a necessary part of our existence, our natural and unalienable inheritance; the other is a personal and individual acquisition, slow to come to us, and by no habitual and direct sympathy connecting us with our fellow-beings. The man of science seeks truth as a remote and unknown benefactor; he cherishes and loves it in his solitude: the poet, singing a song in which all human beings join with him, rejoices in the presence of truth as our visible friend and hourly companion. Poetry is the breath and finer spirit of all knowledge; it is the impassioned expression which is in the countenance of all science. Emphatically may it be said of the poet, as Shakspeare hath said of man, "that he looks before and after."[1] He is the rock of defense for human nature; an upholder and preserver, carrying everywhere with him relationship and love. In spite of difference of soil and climate, of language and manners, of laws and customs: in spite of things silently gone out of mind, and things violently destroyed; the poet binds together by passion and knowledge the vast empire of human society, as it is spread over the whole earth, and over all time. The objects of the poet's thoughts are everywhere; though the eyes and senses of man are, it is true, his favorite guides, yet he will follow wheresoever he can find an atmosphere of sensation in which to move his wings. Poetry is the first and last of all knowledge—it is as immortal as the heart of man. If the labors of men of science should ever create any material revolution, direct or indirect, in our condition, and in the impressions which we habitually receive, the poet will sleep then no more than at present; he will be ready to follow the steps of the man of science, not only in those general indirect effects, but he will be at his side, carrying sensation into the midst of the objects of the science itself. The remotest discoveries of the chemist, the botanist, or mineralogist, will be as proper objects of the poet's art as any upon which it can be employed, if the time should ever come when these things shall be familiar to us, and the relations under which they are contemplated by the followers of these respective sciences shall

[1] *Hamlet,* IV, 4, 37.

be manifestly and palpably material to us as enjoying and suffering beings. If the time should ever come when what is now called science, thus familiarized to men, shall be ready to put on, as it were, a form of flesh and blood, the poet will lend his divine spirit to aid the transfiguration, and will welcome the being thus produced, as a dear and genuine inmate of the household of man. It is not, then, to be supposed that any one who holds that sublime notion of poetry which I have attempted to convey, will break in upon the sanctity and truth of his pictures by transitory and accidental ornaments, and endeavor to excite admiration of himself by arts, the necessity of which must manifestly depend upon the assumed meanness of his subject.

What has been thus far said applies to poetry in general, but especially to those parts of composition where the poet speaks through the mouths of his characters; and upon this point it appears to authorize the conclusion that there are few persons of good sense who would not allow that the dramatic parts of composition are defective, in proportion as they deviate from the real language of nature, and are colored by a diction of the poet's own, either peculiar to him as an individual poet or belonging simply to poets in general; to a body of men who, from the circumstance of their compositions being in metre, it is expected will employ a particular language.

It is not, then, in the dramatic parts of composition that we look for this distinction of language; but still it may be proper and necessary where the poet speaks to us in his own person and character. To this I answer by referring the reader to the description before given of a poet. Among the qualities there enumerated as principally conducing to form a poet, is implied nothing differing in kind from other men, but only in degree. The sum of what was said is, that the poet is chiefly distinguished from other men by a greater promptness to think and feel without immediate external excitement, and a greater power in expressing such thoughts and feelings as are produced in him in that manner. But these passions and thoughts and feelings are the general passions and thoughts and feelings of men. And with what are they connected? Undoubtedly with our moral sentiments and animal sensations, and with the causes which excite these; with the operations of the elements, and the appearances of the visible universe; with storm and sunshine, with the revolutions of the seasons, with cold and heat, with loss of friends and kindred, with injuries and resentments, gratitude and hope, with fear and sorrow. These, and the like, are the sensations and objects which the poet describes, as they are the sensations of other men, and the objects which interest them. The poet thinks and feels in the spirit of human passions. How, then, can his language differ in any material degree from that of all other men who feel vividly and see clearly? It might be *proved* that it is impossible. But supposing that this were not the case, the poet might then be allowed to use a peculiar language when expressing his feelings for his own gratification, or that of men like himself. But poets do not write for poets alone, but for men. Unless, therefore, we are advocates for that admiration which subsists upon ignorance, and that pleasure which arises from hearing what we do not understand, the poet must descend from this supposed height; and, in order to excite rational sympathy, he must express himself as other men express themselves. To this it may be added that while he is only selecting from the real language of men, or, which amounts to the same thing, composing accurately in the spirit of such selection, he is treading upon safe ground, and we know what we are to expect from him. Our feelings are the same with respect to metre; for, as it may be proper to remind the reader, the distinction of metre is regular and uniform, and not, like that which is produced by what is usually called poetic diction, arbitrary, and subject to infinite caprices upon which no calculation whatever can be made. In the one case, the reader is utterly at the mercy of the poet, respecting what imagery or diction he may choose to connect with the passion; whereas, in the other, the metre obeys certain laws, to which the poet and reader both willingly submit because they are certain, and because no interference is made by them with the passion but such as the concurring testimony of ages has shown to heighten and improve the pleasure which co-exists with it.

It will now be proper to answer an obvious question, namely, Why, professing these opinions, have I written in verse? To this, in addition to such answer as is included in what has been already said, I reply, in the first place, because, however I may have restricted myself, there is still left open to me what confessedly constitutes the most valuable object of all writing, whether in prose or verse; the great and universal passions of men, the most general and interesting of their occupations, and the entire world of nature before me— to supply endless combinations of forms and imagery. Now, supposing for a moment that whatever is interesting in these objects may be as vividly described in prose, why should I be condemned for attempting to superadd to such description the charm which, by the consent of all nations, is acknowledged to exist in metrical language? To this, by such as are yet unconvinced, it may be answered that a very small part of the pleasure given by poetry depends upon the metre, and that it is injudicious to write in metre, unless it be accompanied with the other artificial distinctions of style with which metre is usually accompanied, and that, by such deviation, more will be lost from the shock which will thereby be given to the reader's associations than will be counterbalanced by any pleasure which he can derive from the general power of numbers.[1] In answer to those who still contend for the necessity of accompanying metre with certain appropriate colors of style in order to the accomplishment of its appropriate end, and who also, in my opinion, greatly underrate the power of metre in itself, it might, perhaps, as far as relates to these volumes, have been almost sufficient to observe that poems are extant, written upon more humble subjects, and in a still more naked and simple style, which have continued to give pleasure from generation to generation. Now, if nakedness and simplicity be a defect, the fact here mentioned affords a strong presumption that poems somewhat less naked and simple are capable of affording pleasure at the present day; and, what I wished *chiefly* to attempt, at present, was to justify myself for having written under the impression of this belief.

But various causes might be pointed out why, when the style is manly, and the subjects of some importance, words metrically arranged will long continue to impart such a pleasure to mankind as he who proves the extent of that pleasure will be desirous to impart. The end of poetry is to produce excitement in co-existence with an overbalance of pleasure; but, by the supposition, excitement is an unusual and irregular state of the mind; ideas and feel-

[1] That is, the mechanics of verse; or, verse itself.

ings do not, in that state, succeed each other in accustomed order. If the words, however, by which this excitement is produced be in themselves powerful, or the images and feelings have an undue proportion of pain connected with them, there is some danger that the excitement may be carried beyond its proper bounds. Now the co-presence of something regular, something to which the mind has been accustomed in various moods and in a less excited state, cannot but have great efficacy in tempering and restraining the passion by an inter-texture of ordinary feeling, and of feeling not strictly and necessarily connected with the passion. This is unquestionably true; and hence, though the opinion will at first appear paradoxical, from the tendency of metre to divest language, in a certain degree, of its reality, and thus to throw a sort of half-consciousness of unsubstantial existence over the whole composition, there can be little doubt but that more pathetic situations and sentiments, that is, those which have a greater proportion of pain connected with them, may be endured in metrical composition, especially in rhyme, than in prose. The metre of the old ballads is very artless; yet they contain many passages which would illustrate this opinion; and, I hope, if the following poems be attentively perused, similar instances will be found in them. This opinion may be further illustrated by appealing to the reader's own experience of the reluctance with which he comes to the re-perusal of the distressful parts of *Clarissa Harlowe,* or *The Gamester;* while Shakspeare's writings, in the most pathetic scenes, never act upon us, as pathetic, beyond the bounds of pleasure —an effect which, in a much greater degree than might at first be imagined, is to be ascribed to small, but continual and regular impulses of pleasurable surprise from the metrical arrangement.—On the other hand (what it must be allowed will much more frequently happen) if the poet's words should be incommensurate with the passion, and inadequate to raise the reader to a height of desirable excitement, then (unless the poet's choice of his metre has been grossly injudicious) in the feelings of pleasure which the reader has been accustomed to connect with metre in general, and in the feeling, whether cheerful or melancholy, which he has been accustomed to connect with that particular movement of metre, there will be found something which will greatly contribute to impart passion to the words, and to effect the complex end which the poet proposes to himself.

If I had undertaken a systematic defense of the theory here maintained, it would have been my duty to develop the various causes upon which the pleasure received from metrical language depends. Among the chief of these causes is to be reckoned a principle which must be well known to those who have made any of the arts the object of accurate reflection; namely, the pleasure which the mind derives from the perception of similitude in dissimilitude. This principle is the great spring of the activity of our minds, and their chief feeder. From this principle the direction of the sexual appetite, and all the passions connected with it, take their origin: it is the life of our ordinary conversation; and upon the accuracy with which similitude in dissimilitude, and dissimilitude in similitude are perceived, depend our taste and our moral feelings. It would not be a useless employment to apply this principle to the consideration of metre, and to show that metre is hence enabled to afford much pleasure, and to point out in what manner that pleasure is produced. But my limits will not permit me to enter upon this subject, and I must content myself with a general summary.

I have said that poetry is the spontaneous overflow of powerful feelings; it takes its origin from emotion recollected in tranquillity; the emotion is contemplated till, by a species of reaction, the tranquillity gradually disappears, and an emotion, kindred to that which was before the subject of contemplation, is gradually produced, and does itself actually exist in the mind. In this mood successful composition generally begins, and in a mood similar to this it is carried on; but the emotion, of whatever kind, and in whatever degree, from various causes, is qualified by various pleasures, so that in describing any passions whatsoever, which are voluntarily described, the mind will, upon the whole, be in a state of enjoyment. If Nature be thus cautious to preserve in a state of enjoyment a being so employed, the poet ought to profit by the lesson held forth to him, and ought especially to take care that, whatever passions he communicates to his reader, those passions, if his reader's mind be sound and vigorous, should always be accompanied with an overbalance of pleasure. Now the music of harmonious metrical language, the sense of difficulty overcome, and the blind association of pleasure which has been previously received from works of rhyme or metre of the same or similar construction, an indistinct perception perpetually renewed of language closely resembling that of real life, and yet, in the circumstance of metre, differing from it so widely—all these imperceptibly make up a complex feeling of delight, which is of the most important use in tempering the painful feeling always found intermingled with powerful descriptions of the deeper passions. This effect is always produced in pathetic and impassioned poetry; while, in lighter compositions, the ease and gracefulness with which the poet manages his numbers are themselves confessedly a principal source of the gratification of the reader. All that it is *necessary* to say, however, upon this subject, may be effected by affirming, what few persons will deny, that of two descriptions, either of passions, manners, or characters, each of them equally well executed, the one in prose and the other in verse, the verse will be read a hundred times where the prose is read once.

Having thus explained a few of my reasons for writing in verse, and why I have chosen subjects from common life, and endeavored to bring my language near to the real language of men, if I have been too minute in pleading my own cause, I have at the same time been treating a subject of general interest; and for this reason a few words shall be added with reference solely to these particular poems, and to some defects which will probably be found in them. I am sensible that my associations must have sometimes been particular instead of general, and that, consequently, giving to things a false importance, I may have sometimes written upon unworthy subjects; but I am less apprehensive on this account, than that my language may frequently have suffered from those arbitrary connections of feelings and ideas with particular words and phrases, from which no man can altogether protect himself. Hence I have no doubt that, in some instances, feelings, even of the ludicrous, may be given to my readers by expressions which appeared to me tender and pathetic. Such faulty expressions, were I convinced they were faulty at present, and that they must necessarily continue to be so, I would willingly take all reasonable pains to correct. But it is dangerous to make these alterations on the simple authority of a few individuals, or even of certain classes of men; for where the understanding of an author is not convinced, or his feelings altered, this cannot be done without great injury to himself: for his own feelings are his stay and support; and, if he set them aside in one instance, he may be induced to repeat this act till his mind shall lose all confidence in itself, and become utterly debilitated. To this it may be added, that the reader ought never to forget that he is himself exposed to the same errors as the poet, and, perhaps, in a much greater degree: for there can be no presumption in saying of most readers that it is not probable they will be so well acquainted with the various stages of meaning through which words have passed, or with the fickleness or stability of the relations of particular ideas to each other; and, above all, since they are so much less interested in the subject, they may decide lightly and carelessly.

Long as the reader has been detained, I hope he will permit me to caution him against a mode of false criticism which has been applied to poetry, in which the language closely resembles that of life and nature. Such verses have been triumphed over in parodies, of which Dr. Johnson's stanza is a fair specimen:—

> I put my hat upon my head
> And walked into the Strand,
> And there I met another man
> Whose hat was in his hand.

Immediately under these lines I will place one of the most justly-admired stanzas of *The Babes in the Wood.*

> These pretty babes with hand in hand
> Went wandering up and down;
> But never more they saw the Man
> Approaching from the Town.

In both these stanzas the words, and the order of the words, in no respect differ from the most unimpassioned conversation. There are words in both, for example, "the Strand," and "the Town," connected with none but the most familiar ideas; yet the one stanza we admit as admirable, and the other as a fair example of the superlatively contemptible. Whence arises this difference? Not from the metre, not from the language, not from the order of the words; but the *matter* expressed in Dr. Johnson's stanza is contemptible. The proper method of treating trivial and simple verses, to which Dr. Johnson's stanza would be a fair parallelism, is not to say, This is a bad kind of poetry, or, This is not poetry; but, This wants sense; it is neither interesting in itself, nor can *lead* to anything interesting; the images neither originate in that sane state of feeling which arises out of thought, nor can excite thought or feeling in the reader. This is the only sensible manner of dealing with such verses. Why trouble yourself about the species till you have previously decided upon the genus? Why take pains to prove that an ape is not a Newton, when it is self-evident that he is not a man?

I must make one request of my reader, which is, that in judging these poems he would decide by his own feelings genuinely, and not by reflection upon what will probably be the judgment of others. How common is it to hear a person say, "I myself do not object to this style of composition, or this or that expression, but to such and such classes of people, it will appear mean or ludicrous!" This mode of criticism, so destructive of all sound unadulterated judgment, is almost universal: let the reader then abide independently by his own feelings, and if he finds himself affected, let him not suffer such conjectures to interfere with his pleasure.

If an author, by any single composition, has impressed us with respect for his talents, it is useful to consider this as affording a presumption, that on other occasions where we have been displeased, he, nevertheless, may not have written ill or absurdly; and, further, to give him so much credit for this one composition as may induce us to review what has displeased us, with more care than we should otherwise have bestowed upon it. This is not only an act of justice, but, in our decisions upon poetry especially, may conduce, in a high degree, to the improvement of our own taste: for an *accurate* taste in poetry, and in all the other arts, as Sir Joshua Reynolds has observed, is an *acquired* talent, which can only be produced by thought and a long-continued intercourse with the best models of composition. This is mentioned, not with so ridiculous a purpose as to prevent the most inexperienced reader from judging for himself (I have already said that I wish him to judge for himself), but merely to temper the rashness of decision, and to suggest that, if poetry be a subject on which much time has not been bestowed, the judgment may be erroneous; and that, in many cases, it necessarily will be so.

Nothing would, I know, have so effectually contributed to further the end which I have in view, as to have shown of what kind the pleasure is, and how that pleasure is produced, which is confessedly produced by metrical composition essentially different from that which I have here endeavored to recommend: for the reader will say that he has been pleased by such composition; and what more can be done for him? The power of any art is limited; and he will suspect that, if it be proposed to furnish him with new friends, that can be only upon condition of his abandoning his old friends. Besides, as I have said, the reader is himself conscious of the pleasure which he has received from such composition, composition to which he has peculiarly attached the endearing name of poetry; and all men feel an habitual gratitude, and something of an honorable bigotry for the objects which have long continued to please them; we not only wish to be pleased, but to be pleased in that particular way in which we have been accustomed to be pleased. There is in these feelings enough to resist a host of arguments; and I should be the less able to combat them successfully, as I am willing to allow that, in order entirely to enjoy the poetry which I am recommending, it would be necessary to give up much of what is ordinarily enjoyed. But, would my limits have permitted me to point out how this pleasure is produced, many obstacles might have been removed, and the reader assisted in perceiving that the powers of language are not so limited as he may suppose; and that it is possible for poetry to give other enjoyments, of a purer, more lasting, and more exquisite nature. This part of the subject has not been altogether neglected; but it has not been so much my present aim to prove, that the interest excited by some other kinds of poetry is less vivid, and less worthy of the nobler powers of the mind, as to offer reasons for presuming that, if my purpose were fulfilled, a species of poetry would be produced, which is genuine poetry; in its nature well adapted to interest mankind permanently, and likewise important in the multiplicity and quality of its moral relations.

From what has been said, and from a perusal of the poems, the reader will be able clearly to perceive the object which I had in view; he will determine how far it has been attained; and, what is a much more important question, whether it be worth attaining; and upon the decision of these two questions will rest my claim to the approbation of the public.

Samuel T. Coleridge 1772-1834

LIFE
1789   1834

As late I journey'd o'er the extensive plain
Where native Otter sports his scanty
    stream,
Musing in torpid woe a sister's pain,
The glorious prospect woke me from
    the dream.

5 At every step it widen'd to my sight—
Wood, meadow, verdant hill, and dreary
    steep,
Following in quick succession of delight,—
Till all—at once—did my eye ravish'd
    sweep!

May this (I cried) my course through
    life portray!
10 New scenes of wisdom may each step
    display,
And knowledge open as my days ad-
    vance!
Till what time Death shall pour the un-
    darken'd ray,
My eye shall dart thro' infinite ex-
    panse,
And thought suspended lie in rapture's
    blissful trance.

PANTISOCRACY[1]
1794   1849

No more my visionary soul shall dwell
On joys that were; no more endure to
    weigh
The shame and anguish of the evil day,
Wisely forgetful! O'er the ocean swell
5 Sublime of Hope, I seek the cottag'd
    dell
Where Virtue calm with careless step
    may stray,
And dancing to the moonlight roundelay,
The wizard Passions weave an holy spell.
Eyes that have ach'd with sorrow! Ye
    shall weep
10 Tears of doubt-mingled joy, like theirs
    who start
From precipices of distemper'd sleep,
On which the fierce-eyed fiends their
    revels keep,
And see the rising sun, and feel it dart
New rays of pleasance trembling to the
    heart.

[1] The name given to a scheme for an ideal community which Coleridge and Southey planned
in 1794 to establish in America.

TO A YOUNG ASS
ITS MOTHER BEING TETHERED NEAR IT
1794   1794

Poor little foal of an oppressèd race!
I love the languid patience of thy face:
And oft with gentle hand I give thee bread,
And clap thy ragged coat, and pat thy
    head.
5 But what thy dulled spirits hath dismay'd,
That never thou dost sport along the glade?
And (most unlike the nature of things
    young)
That earthward still thy moveless head is
    hung?
Do thy prophetic fears anticipate,
10 Meek child of Misery! thy future fate?
The starving meal, and all the thousand
    aches
"Which patient merit of the unworthy
    takes"?[1]
Or is thy sad heart thrill'd with filial pain
To see thy wretched mother's shorten'd
    chain?
15 And truly, very piteous is her lot—
Chain'd to a log within a narrow spot,
Where the close-eaten grass is scarcely
    seen,
While sweet around her waves the tempt-
    ing green!

Poor Ass! thy master should have learnt
    to show
20 Pity—best taught by fellowship of Woe!
For much I fear me that he lives like thee,
Half famish'd in a land of Luxury!
How askingly its **footsteps hither bend**!
It seems to say, "And have I then one
    friend?"
25 Innocent foal! thou poor despis'd for-
    lorn!
I hail thee brother—spite of the fool's
    scorn!
And fain would take thee with me, in the
    Dell
Of Peace and mild Equality to dwell,
Where Toil shall call the charmer Health
    his bride,
30 And Laughter tickle Plenty's ribless side!
How thou wouldst toss thy heels in game-
    some play,
And frisk about, as lamb or kitten gay!
Yea! and more musically sweet to me
Thy dissonant harsh bray of joy would be,
35 Than warbled melodies that soothe to rest
The aching of pale Fashion's vacant
    breast!

[1] *Hamlet*, III, 1, 74.

LA FAYETTE
1794   1794

As when far off the warbled strains are
    heard
  That soar on Morning's wing the vales
    among;
  Within his cage the imprison'd matin
    bird[1]
Swells the full chorus with a generous
    song:

5 He bathes no pinion in the dewy light,
  No father's joy, no lover's bliss he
    shares,
  Yet still the rising radiance cheers his
    sight—
His fellows' freedom soothes the captive's
    cares!

Thou, Fayette! who didst wake with
    startling voice
10 Life's better sun from that long wintry
    night,
  Thus in thy Country's triumphs shalt
    rejoice
And mock with raptures high the dun-
    geon's might:

For lo! the morning struggles into day,
And Slavery's spectres shriek and vanish
    from the ray!

KOSKIUSKO
1794   1794

O what a loud and fearful shriek was
    there,
  As though a thousand souls one death-
    groan pour'd!
  Ah me! they saw beneath a hireling's
    sword
Their Koskiusko fall! Through the swart
    air

5 (As pauses the tir'd Cossac's barbarous
    yell
  Of triumph) on the chill and midnight
    gale
  Rises with frantic burst or sadder swell
The dirge of murder'd Hope! while Free-
    dom pale

Bends in such anguish o'er her destin'd
    bier,
10 As if from eldest time some Spirit meek
  Had gather'd in a mystic urn each tear
  That ever on a patriot's furrow'd cheek

[1] The lark.

Fit channel found; and she had drain'd
    the bowl
In the mere wilfulness, and sick despair
    of soul!

TO THE REVEREND W. L. BOWLES
1794   1794

My heart has thank'd thee, Bowles! for
    those soft strains
  Whose sadness soothes me, like the
    murmuring
  Of wild-bees in the sunny showers of
    spring!
For hence not callous to the mourner's
    pains

5 Through Youth's gay prime and thorn-
    less paths I went:
  And when the mightier Throes of mind
    began,
  And drove me forth, a thought-bewil-
    der'd man,
Their mild and manliest melancholy lent

A mingled charm, such as the pang con-
    sign'd
10 To slumber, though the big tear it
    renew'd;
  Bidding a strange mysterious Pleasure
    brood
Over the wavy and tumultuous mind,

As the great Spirit erst with plastic sweep
Mov'd on the darkness of the unform'd
    deep.[1]

THE EOLIAN HARP
COMPOSED AT CLEVEDON, SOMERSETSHIRE
1795   1796

My pensive Sara![2] thy soft cheek reclined
Thus on mine arm, most soothing sweet it is
To sit beside our cot, our cot o'ergrown
With white-flower'd jasmin, and the
    broad-leav'd myrtle,
5 (Meet emblems they of innocence and
    love!)
And watch the clouds, that late were rich
    with light,
Slow saddening round, and mark the star
    of eve
Serenely brilliant (such should wisdom be)
Shine opposite! How exquisite the scents
10 Snatch'd from yon bean-field! and the
    world so hush'd!
The stilly murmur of the distant sea
Tells us of silence.

[1] See *Genesis*, 1:2.
[2] Sara Fricker, whom Coleridge married, in October, 1795, before taking up his residence at
Clevedon.

And that simplest lute,
Placed length-ways in the clasping case-
    ment, hark!
15 How by the desultory breeze caress'd,
Like some coy maid half yielding to her
    lover,
It pours such sweet upbraiding, as must
    needs
Tempt to repeat the wrong! And now,
    its strings
Boldlier swept, the long sequacious[1] notes
Over delicious surges sink and rise,
20 Such a soft floating witchery of sound
As twilight Elfins make, when they at eve
Voyage on gentle gales from Fairy-Land,
Where Melodies round honey-dropping
    flowers,
Footless and wild, like birds of Paradise,
25 Nor pause, nor perch, hovering on
    untam'd wing!
O! the one life within us and abroad,
Which meets all motion and becomes its
    soul,
A light in sound, a sound-like power in
    light,
Rhythm in all thought, and joyance every
    where—
30 Methinks, it should have been impossible
Not to love all things in a world so fill'd;
Where the breeze warbles, and the mute
    still air
Is Music slumbering on her instrument.

And thus, my love! as on the midway
    slope
35 Of yonder hill I stretch my limbs at noon,
Whilst through my half-clos'd eye-lids I
    behold
The sunbeams dance, like diamonds, on
    the main,
And tranquil muse upon tranquillity;
Full many a thought uncall'd and unde-
    tain'd,
40 And many idle flitting phantasies,
Traverse my indolent and passive brain,
As wild and various as the random gales
That swell and flutter on this subject lute!

And what if all of animated nature
45 Be but organic harps diversely fram'd,
That tremble into thought, as o'er them
    sweeps
Plastic and vast, one intellectual breeze,
At once the soul of each, and God of all?
But thy more serious eye a mild reproof
50 Darts, O belovéd woman! nor such thoughts
Dim and unhallow'd dost thou not reject,

[1] successive

And biddest me walk humbly with my God.
Meek daughter in the family of Christ!
Well hast thou said and holily disprais'd
55 These shapings of the unregenerate mind;
Bubbles that glitter as they rise and break
On vain Philosophy's aye-babbling spring.
For never guiltless may I speak of him,
The Incomprehensible! save when with awe
60 I praise him, and with faith that inly feels;
Who with his saving mercies heal'd me,
A sinful and most miserable man,
Wilder'd and dark, and gave me to possess
Peace, and this cot, and thee, heart-
    honor'd maid!

REFLECTIONS ON HAVING LEFT A PLACE OF RETIREMENT[1]
1795   1796

Low was our pretty cot: our tallest rose
Peep'd at the chamber-window. We
    could hear
At silent noon, and eve, and early morn,
The sea's faint murmur. In the open air
5 Our myrtles blossom'd; and across the
    porch
Thick jasmins twined: the little land-
    scape round
Was green and woody, and refresh'd the
    eye.
It was a spot which you might aptly call
The Valley of Seclusion! Once I saw
10 (Hallowing his Sabbath-day by quietness)
A wealthy son of commerce saunter by,
Bristowa's citizen: methought, it calm'd
His thirst of idle gold, and made him muse
With wiser feelings: for he paus'd, and
    look'd
15 With a pleas'd sadness, and gaz'd all
    around,
Then eyed our cottage, and gaz'd round
    again,
And sigh'd, and said, it was a blesséd
    place.
And we were bless'd. Oft with patient ear
Long-listening to the viewless sky-lark's
    note
20 (Viewless, or haply for a moment seen
Gleaming on sunny wings) in whisper'd
    tones
I've said to my belovéd, "Such, sweet
    girl!
The inobtrusive song of happiness,
Unearthly minstrelsy! then only heard
25 When the soul seeks to hear; when all is
    hush'd,
And the heart listens!"

[1] Clevedon, near Bristol. See *The Eolian Harp*,
and note 2 (p. 355).

But the time, when first
From that low dell, steep up the stony
  mount
I climb'd with perilous toil and reach'd
  the top,
Oh! what a goodly scene! Here the bleak
  mount,
30 The bare bleak mountain speckled thin
  with sheep;
Gray clouds, that shadowing spot the
  sunny fields;
And river, now with bushy rocks o'er-
  brow'd,
Now winding bright and full, with naked
  banks;
And seats, and lawns, the abbey and the
  wood,
35 And cots, and hamlets, and faint city-
  spire;
The Channel there, the Islands and white
  sails,
Dim coasts, and cloud-like hills, and shoreless Ocean—
It seem'd like Omnipresence! God, methought,
Had built Him there a temple: the whole
  world
40 Seem'd imag'd in its vast circumference:
No wish profan'd my overwhelmèd heart.
Blest hour! It was a luxury,—to be!

Ah! quiet dell! dear cot, and mount
  sublime!
I was constrain'd to quit you. Was it
  right,
45 While my unnumber'd brethren toil'd
  and bled,
That I should dream away the entrusted
  hours
On rose-leaf beds, pampering the coward
  heart
With feelings all too delicate for use?
Sweet is the tear that from some Howard's
  eye
50 Drops on the cheek of one he lifts from
  earth:
And he that works me good with unmov'd face,
Does it but half: he chills me while he aids,
My benefactor, not my brother man!
Yet even this, this cold beneficence
55 Praise, praise it, O my Soul! oft as thou
  scann'st
The sluggard Pity's vision-weaving tribe!
Who sigh for wretchedness, yet shun the
  wretched,
Nursing in some delicious solitude
Their slothful loves and dainty sympa-
  thies!

60 I therefore go, and join head, heart, and
  hand,
Active and firm, to fight the bloodless
  fight
Of science, freedom, and the truth in
  Christ.

Yet oft when after honorable toil
Rests the tir'd mind, and waking loves to
  dream,
65 My spirit shall revisit thee, dear cot!
Thy jasmin and thy window-peeping rose,
And myrtles fearless of the mild sea-air.
And I shall sigh fond wishes—sweet
  abode!
Ah!—had none greater! And that all
  had such!
70 It might be so—but the time is not yet.
Speed it, O Father! Let thy Kingdom
  come!

SONNET

TO A FRIEND[1] WHO ASKED HOW I FELT WHEN
THE NURSE FIRST PRESENTED MY
INFANT TO ME
1796   *1797*

Charles! my slow heart was only sad,
  when first
  I scann'd that face of feeble infancy:
For dimly on my thoughtful spirit burst
  All I had been, and all my child might
  be!
5 But when I saw it on its mother's arm,
  And hanging at her bosom (she the
  while
  Bent o'er its features with a tearful
  smile)
Then I was thrill'd and melted, and most
  warm
Impress'd a father's kiss: and all
  beguil'd
10 Of dark remembrance and presageful
  fear,
  I seem'd to see an angel-form appear—
'Twas even thine, belovèd woman mild!
  So for the mother's sake the child was
  dear,
And dearer was the mother for the child.

ODE ON THE DEPARTING YEAR
1796   *1796*

I

Spirit who sweepest the wild harp of
  Time!
  It is most hard, with an untroubled ear
  Thy dark inwoven harmonies to hear!

[1] Charles Lamb.

Yet, mine eye fix'd on Heaven's unchanging clime
5 Long had I listen'd, free from mortal
 fear,
 With inward stillness, and a bowéd
  mind;
 When lo! its folds far waving on the
  wind,
 I saw the train of the Departing Year!
 Starting from my silent sadness
10 Then with no unholy madness,
 Ere yet the enter'd cloud foreclos'd my
  sight,
 I rais'd the impetuous song, and solem-
  niz'd his flight.

II

 Hither, from the recent tomb,
 From the prison's direr gloom,
15 From Distemper's midnight anguish;
 And thence, where Poverty doth waste
  and languish;
 Or where, his two bright torches
  blending,
 Love illumines Manhood's maze;
 Or where o'er cradled infants bend-
  ing,
20 Hope has fix'd her wishful gaze;
 Hither, in perpléxéd dance,
 Ye Woes! ye young-eyed Joys! ad-
  vance!
 By Time's wild harp, and by the hand
 Whose indefatigable sweep
25 Raises its fateful strings from
  sleep,
 I bid you haste, a mix'd tumultuous
  band!
 From every private bower,
 And each domestic hearth,
 Haste for one solemn hour;
30 And with a loud and yet a louder
  voice,
 O'er Nature struggling in portentous
  birth,
 Weep and rejoice!
 Still echoes the dread Name[1] that o'er the
  earth
 Let slip the storm, and woke the brood of
  Hell:
35 And now advance in saintly Jubilee
 Justice and Truth! They too have heard
  thy spell,
 They too obey thy name, divinest
  Liberty!

III

 I mark'd Ambition in his war-array!
  I heard the mailéd Monarch's troub-
   lous cry—
40 "Ah! wherefore does the Northern Con-
   queress[1] stay!
 Groans not her chariot on its onward
   way?"
  Fly, mailéd Monarch, fly!
  Stunn'd by Death's twice mortal
   mace,
 No more on Murder's lurid face
45 The insatiate hag shall gloat with drunken
   eye!
  Manes of the unnumber'd slain!
 Ye that gasp'd on Warsaw's plain![2]
 Ye that erst at Ismail's tower,[3]
 When human ruin choked the streams,
50 Fell in Conquest's glutted hour,
 Mid women's shrieks and infants' screams!
 Spirits of the uncoffin'd slain,
 Sudden blasts of triumph swelling,
 Oft, at night, in misty train,
55 Rush around her narrow dwelling!
 The exterminating fiend is fled—
 (Foul her life, and dark her doom)
 Mighty armies of the dead
 Dance, like death-fires, round her tomb!
60 Then with prophetic song relate,
 Each some Tyrant-Murderer's fate!

IV

 Departing Year! 'twas on no earthly
  shore
 My soul beheld thy Vision![4] Where
  alone,
 Voiceless and stern, before the cloudy
  throne,
65 Aye Memory sits: thy robe inscrib'd with
  gore,
 With many an unimaginable groan
 Thou storied'st thy sad hours! Silence
  ensued,
 Deep silence o'er the ethereal multitude,
 Whose locks with wreaths, whose wreaths
  with glories shone.
70 Then, his eye wild ardors glancing,
 From the choiréd gods advancing,
 The Spirit of the Earth made reverence
  meet,
 And stood up, beautiful, before the cloudy
  seat.

---

[1] "The name of Liberty, which at the commencement of the French Revolution was both the
occasion and the pretext of unnumbered
crimes and horrors."—Coleridge.

[1] The Empress of Russia.
[2] In the wars for Polish independence, 1772-95.
[3] Over 40,000 persons were killed in the Russian
siege of the Turkish stronghold at Ismail, in
1793.
[4] "Thy image in a vision."—Coleridge.

V

Throughout the blissful throng,
75   Hush'd were harp and song:
Till wheeling round the throne the Lampads[1] seven,
(The mystic Words of Heaven)
Permissive signal make:
The fervent Spirit bow'd, then spread his
    wings and spake!
80   "Thou in stormy blackness throning
    Love and uncreated Light,
By the Earth's unsolaced groaning,
    Seize thy terrors, Arm of might!
By Peace with proffer'd insult scared,
85   Masked Hate and envying Scorn!
    By years of Havoc yet unborn!
And Hunger's bosom to the frost-winds
    bared!
    But chief by Afric's wrongs,
    Strange, horrible, and foul!
90   By what deep guilt belongs
To the deaf Synod, 'full of gifts and
    lies!'
By Wealth's insensate laugh! by Torture's howl!
    Avenger, rise!
Forever shall the thankless Island scowl,
95   Her quiver full, and with unbroken bow?
Speak! from thy storm-black Heaven, O
    speak aloud!
    And on the darkling foe
Open thine eye of fire from some uncertain cloud!
O dart the flash! O rise and deal the
    blow!
100 The Past to thee, to thee the Future cries!
Hark! how wide Nature joins her groans
    below!
    Rise, God of Nature, rise!"

VI

The voice had ceas'd, the Vision fled;
    Yet still I gasp'd and reel'd with dread.
105 And ever, when the dream of night
Renews the phantom to my sight,
Cold sweat-drops gather on my limbs;
    My ears throb hot; my eye-balls start;
My brain with horrid tumult swims;
110   Wild is the tempest of my heart;
And my thick and struggling breath
Imitates the toil of death!
No stranger agony confounds
    The soldier on the war-field spread,
115 When all foredone with toil and wounds,
    Death-like he dozes among heaps of
    dead!

(The strife is o'er, the day-light fled,
    And the night-wind clamors hoarse!
See! the starting wretch's head
120 Lies pillow'd on a brother's corse!)

VII

Not yet enslaved, not wholly vile,
O Albion! O my mother Isle!
Thy valleys, fair as Eden's bowers
Glitter green with sunny showers;
125 Thy grassy uplands' gentle swells
    Echo to the bleat of flocks;
(Those grassy hills, those glittering dells
    Proudly ramparted with rocks)
And Ocean mid his uproar wild
130 Speaks safety to his Island-child!
Hence for many a fearless age
Has social Quiet lov'd thy shore;
Nor ever proud Invader's rage
Or sack'd thy towers, or stain'd thy fields
    with gore.

VIII

135 Abandon'd of Heaven![1] mad Avarice thy
    guide,
At cowardly distance, yet kindling with
    pride—
Mid thy herds and thy corn-fields secure
    thou hast stood,
And join'd the wild yelling of Famine
    and Blood!
The nations curse thee! They with eager
    wondering
140 Shall hear Destruction, like a vulture,
    scream!
Strange-eyed Destruction! who with
    many a dream
Of central fires through nether seas upthundering
Soothes her fierce solitude; yet as she lies
    By livid fount, or red volcanic stream,
145 If ever to her lidless dragon-eyes,
O Albion! thy predestin'd ruins rise,
The fiend-hag on her perilous couch doth
    leap,
Muttering distemper'd triumph in her
    charméd sleep.

IX

Away, my soul, away!
150 In vain, in vain the birds of warning
    sing—
And hark! I hear the famish'd brood of
    prey

---

[1] lamps; candlesticks (Seven is a sacred number. See *Revelation*, 4:5.)

[1] "Of the 107 last years, 50 have been years of war."—Coleridge. The year 1796 was a period of great distress for the people of England.

Flap their lank pennons on the groaning
wind!
Away, my soul, away!
I unpartaking of the evil thing,
155   With daily prayer and daily toil
Soliciting for food my scanty soil,
Have wail'd my country with a loud
lament.
Now I recentre my immortal mind
In the deep Sabbath of meek self-
content;
160 Cleans'd from the vaporous passions that
bedim
God's Image, sister of the Seraphim.[1]

THIS LIME-TREE BOWER MY PRISON

ADDRESSED TO CHARLES LAMB, OF THE
INDIA HOUSE, LONDON
1797   1800

Well, they are gone, and here must I
remain,
This lime-tree bower my prison! I have
lost
Beauties and feelings, such as would have
been
Most sweet to my remembrance even when
age
5 Had dimm'd mine eyes to blindness!
They, meanwhile,
Friends, whom I never more may meet
again,
On springy heath, along the hill-top edge,
Wander in gladness, and wind down, perchance,
To that still roaring dell, of which I
told;
10 The roaring dell, o'erwooded, narrow,
deep,
And only speckled by the mid-day sun;
Where its slim trunk the ash from rock to
rock
Flings arching like a bridge;—that branchless ash,
Unsunn'd and damp, whose few poor
yellow leaves
15 Ne'er tremble in the gale, yet tremble
still,
Fann'd by the waterfall! and there my
friends
Behold the dark green file of long, lank
weeds,
That all at once (a most fantastic sight!)
Still nod and drip beneath the dripping
edge
20 Of the blue clay-stone.

[1] The Seraphim were angels of purification by
fire, and guardians of the throne of Jehovah.

Now, my friends emerge
Beneath the wide, wide Heaven—and view
again
The many-steepled tract magnificent
Of hilly fields and meadows, and the sea,
With some fair bark, perhaps, whose sails
light up
25 The slip of smooth clear blue betwixt two
isles
Of purple shadow! Yes! they wander on
In gladness all; but thou, methinks, most
glad,
My gentle-hearted Charles! for thou hast
pined
And hunger'd after Nature, many a year,
30 In the great City pent, winning thy way
With sad yet patient soul, through evil
and pain
And strange calamity! Ah! slowly sink
Behind the western ridge, thou glorious
Sun!
Shine in the slant beams of the sinking orb,
35 Ye purple heath-flowers! richlier burn, ye
clouds!
Live in the yellow light, ye distant groves!
And kindle, thou blue Ocean! So my friend
Struck with deep joy may stand, as I
have stood,
Silent with swimming sense; yea, gazing
round
40 On the wide landscape, gaze till all doth
seem
Less gross than bodily; and of such hues
As veil the Almighty Spirit, when yet he
makes
Spirits perceive his presence.

A delight
Comes sudden on my heart, and I am glad
45 As I myself were there! Nor in this bower,
This little lime-tree bower, have I not
mark'd
Much that has sooth'd me. Pale beneath
the blaze
Hung the transparent foliage; and I
watch'd
Some broad and sunny leaf, and lov'd to
see
50 The shadow of the leaf and stem above
Dappling its sunshine! And that walnut-
tree
Was richly ting'd, and a deep radiance lay
Full on the ancient ivy, which usurps
Those fronting elms, and now, with blackest mass
55 Makes their dark branches gleam a lighter
hue
Through the late twilight: and though
now the bat

Wheels silent by, and not a swallow
    twitters,
Yet still the solitary humble-bee
Sings in the bean-flower! Henceforth I
    shall know
60 That Nature ne'er deserts the wise and
    pure;
No plot so narrow, be but Nature there,
No waste so vacant, but may well employ
Each faculty of sense, and keep the heart
Awake to Love and Beauty! and sometimes
65 'Tis well to be bereft of promis'd good,
That we may lift the soul, and contem-
    plate
With lively joy the joys we cannot share.
My gentle-hearted Charles! when the last
    rook
Beat its straight path along the dusky air
70 Homewards, I blest it! deeming its black
    wing
(Now a dim speck, now vanishing in light)
Had cross'd the mighty orb's dilated glory,
While thou stood'st gazing; or, when all
    was still,
Flew creeking o'er thy head, and had a
    charm
75 For thee, my gentle-hearted Charles, to
    whom
No sound is dissonant which tells of life.

THE DUNGEON
1797   1798

And this place our forefathers made for
    man!
This is the process of our love and wisdom,
To each poor brother who offends against
    us—
Most innocent, perhaps — and what if
    guilty?
5 Is this the only cure? Merciful God!
Each pore and natural outlet shrivell'd up
By Ignorance and parching Poverty,
His energies roll back upon his heart,
And stagnate and corrupt; till chang'd to
    poison,
10 They break out on him, like a loathsome
    plague-spot;
Then we call in our pamper'd mounte-
    banks—
And this is their best cure! uncomforted
And friendless solitude, groaning and
    tears,
And savage faces, at the clanking hour,
15 Seen through the steams and vapors of his
    dungeon,
By the lamp's dismal twilight! So he lies
Circled with evil, till his very soul
Unmoulds its essence, hopelessly deform'd
By sights of ever more deformity!

20 With other ministrations thou, O Nature!
Healest thy wandering and distemper'd
    child:
Thou pourest on him thy soft influences,
Thy sunny hues, fair forms, and breath-
    ing sweets,
Thy melodies of woods, and winds, and
    waters,
25 Till he relent, and can no more endure
To be a jarring and a dissonant thing,
Amid this general dance and minstrelsy;
But, bursting into tears, wins back his way,
His angry spirit heal'd and harmoniz'd
30 By the benignant touch of Love and
    Beauty.

THE RIME OF THE ANCIENT MARINER
IN SEVEN PARTS
1797-98   1798
ARGUMENT

How a Ship having passed the Line was driven
by storms to the cold Country towards the South
Pole; and how from thence she made her course
to the tropical Latitude of the Great Pacific
Ocean; and of the strange things that befell;
and in what manner the Ancyent Marinere came
back to his own Country.

PART I

It is an ancient Mariner,
And he stoppeth one of three.
"By thy long gray beard and glittering
    eye,
Now wherefore stopp'st thou me?

5 The Bridegroom's doors are opened wide,
And I am next of kin;
The guests are met, the feast is set:
May'st hear the merry din."

He holds him with his skinny hand,
10 "There was a ship," quoth he.
"Hold off! unhand me, gray-beard loon!"
Eftsoons his hand dropt he.

He holds him with his glittering eye—
The Wedding-Guest stood still,
15 And listens like a three years' child:
The Mariner hath his will.

The Wedding-Guest sat on a stone:
He cannot choose but hear;
And thus spake on that ancient man,
20 The bright-eyed Mariner.

1-12. An ancient Mariner meeteth three Gallants bidden to a wedding-feast, and detaineth
one.
13-21. The Wedding-Guest is spell-bound by
the eye of the old seafaring man, and constrained
to hear his tale.

"The ship was cheered, the harbor cleared,
  Merrily did we drop
Below the kirk, below the hill,
  Below the lighthouse top.

25 The Sun came up upon the left,
  Out of the sea came he!
And he shone bright, and on the right
  Went down into the sea.

Higher and higher every day,
30 Till over the mast at noon—"
The Wedding-Guest here beat his breast,
  For he heard the loud bassoon.

The bride hath paced into the hall,
  Red as a rose is she;
35 Nodding their heads before her goes
  The merry minstrelsy.

The Wedding-Guest he beat his breast,
  Yet he cannot choose but hear;
And thus spake on that ancient man,
40 The bright-eyed Mariner.

"And now the Storm-blast came, and he
  Was tyrannous and strong:
He struck with his o'ertaking wings,
  And chased us south along.

45 With sloping masts and dipping prow,
As who pursued with yell and blow
  Still treads the shadow of his foe,
  And forward bends his head,
The ship drove fast, loud roared the blast,
50 And southward aye we fled.

And now there came both mist and snow,
  And it grew wondrous cold:
And ice, mast-high, came floating by,
  As green as emerald.

55 And through the drifts the snowy clifts
  Did send a dismal sheen:
Nor shapes of men nor beasts we ken—
  The ice was all between.

The ice was here, the ice was there,
60 The ice was all around:
It cracked and growled, and roared and
    howled,
  Like noises in a swound![1]

At length did cross an Albatross,
  Thorough the fog it came;
65 As if it had been a Christian soul,
  We hailed it in God's name.

It ate the food it ne'er had eat,
  And round and round it flew.
The ice did split with a thunder-fit;
70 The helmsman steered us through!

And a good south wind sprung up behind;
  The Albatross did follow,
And every day, for food or play,
  Came to the mariners' hollo!

75 In mist or cloud, on mast or shroud,
  It perched for vespers nine;
Whiles all the night, through fog-smoke
    white,
  Glimmered the white moon-shine."

"God save thee, ancient Mariner!
80 From the fiends, that plague thee thus!—
Why look'st thou so?"—"With my cross-
    bow
I shot the Albatross!"

PART II

"The Sun now rose upon the right:
  Out of the sea came he,
85 Still hid in mist, and on the left
  Went down into the sea.

And the good south wind still blew behind,
  But no sweet bird did follow,
Nor any day for food or play
90 Came to the mariners' hollo!

And I had done a hellish thing,
  And it would work 'em woe:
For all averred, I had killed the bird
  That made the breeze to blow.
95 'Ah wretch!' said they, 'the bird to slay,
  That made the breeze to blow!'

Nor dim nor red, like God's own head,
  The glorious Sun uprist:
Then all averred, I had killed the bird
100 That brought the fog and mist.
''Twas right,' said they, 'such birds to slay,
  That bring the fog and mist.'

21-30. The Mariner tells how the ship sailed southward with a good wind and fair weather, till it reached the Line.
31-40. The Wedding-Guest heareth the bridal music; but the Mariner continueth his tale.
41-50. The ship driven by a storm toward the south pole.
51-62. The land of ice, and of fearful sounds, where no living thing was to be seen.

[1] swoon; dream

63-70. Till a great sea-bird, called the Albatross, came through the snow-fog, and was received with great joy and hospitality.
71-78. And lo! the Albatross proveth a bird of good omen, and followeth the ship as it returned northward through fog and floating ice.
79-82. The ancient Mariner inhospitably killeth the pious bird of good omen.
83-96. His shipmates cry out against the ancient Mariner, for killing the bird of good luck.
97-102. But when the fog cleared off, they justify the same, and thus make themselves accomplices in the crime.

The fair breeze blew, the white foam flew,
The furrow followed free;
105 We were the first that ever burst
Into that silent sea.

Down dropt the breeze, the sails dropt down,
'Twas sad as sad could be;
And we did speak only to break
110 The silence of the sea!

All in a hot and copper sky,
The bloody Sun, at noon,
Right up above the mast did stand,
No bigger than the Moon.

115 Day after day, day after day,
We stuck, nor breath nor motion;
As idle as a painted ship
Upon a painted ocean.

Water, water, everywhere,
120 And all the boards did shrink;
Water, water, everywhere,
Nor any drop to drink.

The very deep did rot: O Christ!
That ever this should be!
125 Yea, slimy things did crawl with legs
Upon the slimy sea.

Envy ǝver slimy life [handwritten]

About, about, in reel and rout
The death-fires[1] danced at night;
The water, like a witch's oils,
130 Burnt green, and blue, and white.

And some in dreams assuréd were
Of the Spirit that plagued us so;
Nine fathom deep he had followed us
From the land of mist and snow.

135 And every tongue, through utter drought,
Was withered at the root;
We could not speak, no more than if
We had been choked with soot.

103-106. The fair breeze continues; the ship enters the Pacific Ocean, and sails northward, even till it reaches the Line.
107-118. The ship hath been suddenly becalmed.
119-130. And the Albatross begins to be avenged.
131-138. A Spirit had followed them; one of the invisible inhabitants of this planet, neither departed souls nor angels; concerning whom the learned Jew, Josephus, and the Platonic Constantinopolitan, Michael Psellus, may be consulted. They are very numerous, and there is no climate or element without one or more.

[1] phosphorescent lights (supposed to forebode death)

Ah! well-a-day! what evil looks
140 Had I from old and young!
Instead of the cross, the Albatross
About my neck was hung.

some religious equation [handwritten]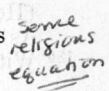

PART III

"There passed a weary time. Each throat
Was parched, and glazed each eye.
145 A weary time! a weary time!
How glazed each weary eye,
When looking westward, I beheld
A something in the sky.

At first it seemed a little speck,
150 And then it seemed a mist;
It moved and moved, and took at last
A certain shape, I wist.[1]

A speck, a mist, a shape, I wist!
And still it neared and neared:
155 As if it dodged a water-sprite,
It plunged and tacked and veered.

With throats unslaked, with black lips baked,
We could nor laugh nor wail;
Through utter drought all dumb we stood!
160 I bit my arm, I sucked the blood,
And cried, A sail! a sail!

With throats unslaked, with black lips baked,
Agape they heard me call:
Gramercy![2] they for joy did grin,
165 And all at once their breath drew in,
As they were drinking all.

See! see! (I cried) she tacks no more!
Hither to work us weal;
Without a breeze, without a tide,
170 She steadies with upright keel!

The western wave was all a-flame.
The day was well nigh done!
Almost upon the western wave
Rested the broad bright Sun;
175 When that strange shape drove suddenly
Betwixt us and the Sun.

Sun — hard inexorable retribution — justice for sin. [handwritten]

139-142. The shipmates, in their sore distress, would fain throw the whole guilt on the ancient Mariner; in sign whereof they hang the dead sea-bird round his neck.
143-156. The ancient Mariner beholdeth a sign in the element afar off.
157-163. At its nearer approach, it seemeth him to be a ship; and at a dear ransom he freeth his speech from the bonds of thirst.
164-166. A flash of joy.
167-176. And horror follows. For can it be a ship that comes onward without wind or tide?

[1] thought, knew   [2] great thanks

And straight the Sun was flecked with bars,
(Heaven's Mother send us grace!)
As if through a dungeon-grate he peered
180 With broad and burning face.

Alas! (thought I, and my heart beat loud)
How fast she nears and nears!
Are those her sails that glance in the Sun,
Like restless gossameres?[1]

185 Are those her ribs through which the Sun
Did peer, as through a grate?
And is that Woman all her crew?
Is that a Death? and are there two?
Is Death that woman's mate?

190 Her lips were red, her looks were free,
Her locks were yellow as gold:
Her skin was as white as leprosy,
The Nightmare Life-in-Death was she,
Who thicks man's blood with cold.

195 The naked hulk alongside came,
And the twain were casting dice;
'The game is done! I've won! I've won!'
Quoth she, and whistles thrice.

she wins the mariner — death wins the crew — she is the more terrible.

200 The Sun's rim dips; the stars rush out:
At one stride comes the dark;
With far-heard whisper, o'er the sea,
Off shot the spectre-bark.

We listened and looked sideways up!
Fear at my heart, as at a cup,
205 My life-blood seemed to sip!
The stars were dim, and thick the night,
The steersman's face by his lamp gleamed
     white;
From the sails the dew did drip—
210 Till clomb above the eastern bar
The hornéd Moon, with one bright star
Within the nether tip.

imagination which may yet redeem the mariner

One after one, by the star-dogged Moon,
Too quick for groan or sigh,
Each turned his face with a ghastly pang,
215 And cursed me with his eye.

Four times fifty living men,
(And I heard nor sigh nor groan)

177-186. It seemeth him but the skeleton of a ship. And its ribs are seen as bars on the face of the setting Sun.
187-194. The Spectre-Woman and her Death-mate, and no other on board the skeleton-ship. Like vessel, like crew!
195-198. Death and Life-in-Death have diced for the ship's crew, and she (the latter) winneth the ancient Mariner.
199-202. No twilight within the courts of the Sun.
203-223. At the rising of the Moon, one after another his shipmates drop down dead. But Life-in-Death begins her work on the ancient Mariner.

[1] fine spider-webs

With heavy thump, a lifeless lump,
They dropped down one by one.
220 The souls did from their bodies fly,—
They fled to bliss or woe!
And every soul, it passed me by,
Like the whizz of my cross-bow!''

PART IV

''I fear thee, ancient Mariner!
225 I fear thy skinny hand!
And thou art long, and lank, and brown,
As is the ribbed sea-sand.

I fear thee and thy glittering eye,
And thy skinny hand, so brown.''—
230 ''Fear not, fear not, thou Wedding-Guest!
This body dropt not down.

Alone, alone, all, all alone,
Alone on a wide, wide sea!
And never a saint took pity on
235 My soul in agony.

total isolation from nature + life — self will against law of life + love —

The many men, so beautiful!
And they all dead did lie:
And a thousand thousand slimy things
Lived on; and so did I.

240 I looked upon the rotting sea,
And drew my eyes away;
I looked upon the rotting deck,
And there the dead men lay.

I looked to heaven, and tried to pray;
245 But or ever a prayer had gusht,
A wicked whisper came, and made
My heart as dry as dust.

I closed my lids, and kept them close,
And the balls like pulses beat;
250 For the sky and the sea, and the sea and
     the sky
Lay like a load on my weary eye,
And the dead were at my feet.

The cold sweat melted from their limbs,
Nor rot nor reek did they:
255 The look with which they looked on me
Had never passed away.

An orphan's curse would drag to hell
A spirit from on high;
But oh! more horrible than that
260 Is the curse in a dead man's eye!
Seven days, seven nights, I saw that curse,
And yet I could not die.

224-235. The Wedding-Guest feareth that a Spirit is talking to him; but the ancient Mariner assureth him of his bodily life, and proceedeth to relate his horrible penance.
236-252. He despiseth the creatures of the calm, and envieth that they should live, and so many lie dead.
253-262. But the curse liveth for him in the eye of the dead men.

The moving moon went up the sky,
And nowhere did abide:
265 Softly she was going up,
And a star or two beside—

[handwritten: order + pattern of nature + life.]

Her beams bemocked the sultry main,
Like April hoar-frost spread;
But where the ship's huge shadow lay,
270 The charméd water burnt alway
A still and awful red.

Beyond the shadow of the ship,
I watched the water-snakes:
They moved in tracks of shining white,
275 And when they reared, the elfish light
Fell off in hoary flakes.

Within the shadow of the ship
I watched their rich attire:
Blue, glossy green, and velvet black
280 They coiled and swam; and every track
Was a flash of golden fire.

O happy living things! no tongue
Their beauty might declare:
A spring of love gushed from my heart,
285 And I blessed them unaware:
Sure my kind saint took pity on me,
And I blessed them unaware.

[handwritten: The moon constitues makes The herefore detested creatures lovely + lovable,]

The self-same moment I could pray;
And from my neck so free
290 The Albatross fell off, and sank
Like lead into the sea.

[handwritten: + with love, the mariner is somewhat freed from the spell.]

PART V

"Oh sleep! it is a gentle thing,
Beloved from pole to pole!
To Mary Queen the praise be given!
295 She sent the gentle sleep from Heaven,
That slid into my soul.

[handwritten: blessed - medieval (touched by God)]

The silly[1] buckets on the deck,
That had so long remained,
I dreamt that they were filled with dew;
300 And when I awoke, it rained.

[handwritten: water of regeneration]

263-271. In his loneliness and fixedness he
yearneth towards the journeying Moon, and the
stars that still sojourn, yet still move onward;
and everywhere the blue sky belongs to them,
and is their appointed rest, and their native
country and their own natural homes, which
they enter unannounced as lords that are certainly expected, and yet there is a silent joy at
their arrival.
272-281. By the light of the Moon he beholdeth God's creatures of the great calm.
282-283. Their beauty and their happiness.
284-287. He blesseth them in his heart.
288-291. The spell begins to break.
292-308. By grace of the holy Mother, the
ancient Mariner is refreshed with rain.

[1] innocent (or, possibly, useless)

My lips were wet, my throat was cold,
My garments all were dank;
Sure I had drunken in my dreams,
And still my body drank.

305 I moved, and could not feel my limbs:
I was so light—almost
I thought that I had died in sleep,
And was a blesséd ghost.

And soon I heard a roaring wind:
310 It did not come anear;
But with its sound it shook the sails,
That were so thin and sere.

The upper air burst into life!
And a hundred fire-flags sheen,[1]
315 To and fro they were hurried about!
And to and fro, and in and out,
The wan stars danced between.

And the coming wind did roar more loud,
And the sails did sigh like sedge;
320 And the rain poured down from one black
        cloud;
The Moon was at its edge.

[handwritten: moon accompanying regeneration—]

The thick black cloud was cleft, and still
The Moon was at its side:
Like water shot from some high crag,
325 The lightning fell with never a jag,
A river steep and wide.

The loud wind never reached the ship,
Yet now the ship moved on!
Beneath the lightning and the Moon
330 The dead men gave a groan.

They groaned, they stirred, they all uprose,
Nor spake, nor moved their eyes;
It had been strange, even in a dream,
To have seen those dead men rise.

335 The helmsman steered, the ship moved on;
Yet never a breeze up-blew;
The mariners all 'gan work the ropes,
Where they were wont to do;
They raised their limbs like lifeless tools—
340 We were a ghastly crew.

309-326. He heareth sounds and seeth strange
sights and commotions in the sky and the element.
327-376. The bodies of the ship's crew are inspired, and the ship moves on; but not by the
souls of the men, nor by demons of earth or
middle air, but by a blessed troop of angelic
spirits, sent down by the invocation of the
guardian saint.

[1] bright

The body of my brother's son
Stood by me, knee to knee:
The body and I pulled at one rope,
But he said nought to me.''—

345 "I fear thee, ancient Mariner!''
"Be calm, thou Wedding-Guest!
'Twas not those souls that fled in pain,
Which to their corses came again,
But a troop of spirits blest:

350 For when it dawned—they dropped their
    arms,
And clustered round the mast;
Sweet sounds rose slowly through their
    mouths,
And from their bodies passed.

Around, around, flew each sweet sound,
355 Then darted to the Sun;
Slowly the sounds came back again,
Now mixed, now one by one.

Sometimes a-dropping from the sky
I heard the skylark sing;
360 Sometimes all little birds that are,
How they seemed to fill the sea and air
With their sweet jargoning!

And now 'twas like all instruments,
Now like a lonely flute;
365 And now it is an angel's song,
That makes the heavens be mute.

It ceased; yet still the sails made on
A pleasant noise till noon,
A noise like of a hidden brook
370 In the leafy month of June,
That to the sleeping woods all night
Singeth a quiet tune.

Till noon we quietly sailed on,
Yet never a breeze did breathe:
375 Slowly and smoothly went the ship,
Moved onward from beneath.

Under the keel nine fathom deep,
From the land of mist and snow,
The spirit slid: and it was he
380 That made the ship to go.
The sails at noon left off their tune,
And the ship stood still also.

The Sun, right up above the mast,
Had fixed her to the ocean:
385 But in a minute she 'gan stir,

With a short uneasy motion—
Backwards and forwards half her length
With a short uneasy motion.

Then like a pawing horse let go,
390 She made a sudden bound:
It flung the blood into my head,
And I fell down in a swound.

How long in that same fit I lay,
I have not[1] to declare;
395 But ere my living life returned,
I heard and in my soul discerned
Two voices in the air.

'Is it he?' quoth one, 'Is this the man?
By him who died on cross,
400 With his cruel bow he laid full low
The harmless Albatross.

The spirit who bideth by himself
In the land of mist and snow,
He loved the bird that loved the man
405 Who shot him with his bow.'

The other was a softer voice,
As soft as honey-dew:
Quoth he, 'The man hath penance done,
And penance more will do.'

PART VI

FIRST VOICE

410 " 'But tell me, tell me! speak again,
Thy soft response renewing—
What makes that ship drive on so fast?
What is the ocean doing?'

SECOND VOICE

'Still as a slave before his lord,
415 The ocean hath no blast;
His great bright eye most silently
Up to the Moon is cast—

If he may know which way to go;
For she guides him smooth or grim.
420 See, brother, see! how graciously
She looketh down on him.'

393-409. The Polar Spirit's fellow-demons, the
invisible inhabitants of the element, take part in
his wrong; and two of them relate one to the
other, that penance long and heavy for the ancient Mariner hath been accorded to the Polar
Spirit, who returneth southward.
410-429. The Mariner hath been cast into a
trance; for the angelic power causeth the vessel
to drive northward faster than human life could
endure.

377-392. The lonesome Spirit from the south-
pole carries on the ship as far as the Line, in
obedience to the angelic troop, but still requireth
vengeance.

[1] have not the power

FIRST VOICE

'But why drives on that ship so fast,
Without or wave or wind?'

SECOND VOICE

'The air is cut away before,
425 And closes from behind.

Fly, brother, fly! more high, more high!
Or we shall be belated:
For slow and slow that ship will go,
When the Mariner's trance is abated.'

430 I woke, and we were sailing on
As in a gentle weather:
'Twas night, calm night, the moon was
     high;
The dead men stood together.

All stood together on the deck,
435 For a charnel-dungeon fitter:
All fixed on me their stony eyes,
That in the Moon did glitter.

The pang, the curse, with which they died,
Had never passed away:
440 I could not draw my eyes from theirs,
Nor turn them up to pray.

And now this spell was snapt: once more
I viewed the ocean green,
And looked far forth, yet little saw
445 Of what had else been seen—

Like one, that on a lonesome road
Doth walk in fear and dread,
And having once turned round walks on,
And turns no more his head;
450 Because he knows, a frightful fiend
Doth close behind him tread.

But soon there breathed a wind on me,
Nor sound nor motion made:
Its path was not upon the sea,
455 In ripple or in shade.

It raised my hair, it fanned my cheek
Like a meadow-gale of spring—
It mingled strangely with my fears,
Yet it felt like a welcoming.

460 Swiftly, swiftly flew the ship,
Yet she sailed softly too:
Sweetly, sweetly blew the breeze—
On me alone it blew.

Oh! dream of joy! is this indeed
465 The light-house top I see?
Is this the hill? is this the kirk?
Is this mine own countree?

We drifted o'er the harbor-bar,
And I with sobs did pray—
470 O let me be awake, my God!
Or let me sleep alway.

The harbor-bay was clear as glass,
So smoothly it was strewn!
And on the bay the moonlight lay,
475 And the shadow of the Moon.

The rock shone bright, the kirk no less,
That stands above the rock:
The moonlight steeped in silentness
The steady weathercock.

480 And the bay was white with silent light,
Till rising from the same,
Full many shapes, that shadows were,
In crimson colors came.

A little distance from the prow
485 Those crimson shadows were:
I turned my eyes upon the deck—
Oh, Christ! what saw I there!

Each corse lay flat, lifeless and flat,
And, by the holy rood![1]
490 A man all light, a seraph-man,
On every corse there stood.

This seraph-band, each waved his hand:
It was a heavenly sight!
They stood as signals to the land,
495 Each one a lovely light;

This seraph-band, each waved his hand,
No voice did they impart—
No voice; but oh! the silence sank
Like music on my heart.

500 But soon I heard the dash of oars,
I heard the Pilot's cheer;
My head was turned perforce away
And I saw a boat appear.

The Pilot and the Pilot's boy,
505 I heard them coming fast:
Dear Lord in Heaven! it was a joy
The dead men could not blast.

464-479. And the ancient Mariner beholdeth
his native country.
480-499. The angelic spirits leave the dead
bodies and appear in their own forms of light.

430-441. The supernatural motion is retarded;
the Mariner awakes, and his penance begins
anew.
442-463. The curse is finally expiated.

[1] cross

I saw a third—I heard his voice:
It is the Hermit good!
510 He singeth loud his godly hymns
That he makes in the wood.
He'll shrieve my soul, he'll wash away
The Albatross's blood.

PART VII

"This Hermit good lives in that wood
515 Which slopes down to the sea.
How loudly his sweet voice he rears!
He loves to talk with marineres
That come from a far countree.

He kneels at morn, and noon, and eve—
520 He hath a cushion plump:
It is the moss that wholly hides
The rotted old oak-stump.

The skiff-boat neared: I heard them talk,
'Why this is strange, I trow!
525 Where are those lights so many and fair,
That signal made but now?'

'Strange, by my faith!' the Hermit said—
'And they answered not our cheer!
The planks look warped! and see those
 sails,
530 How thin they are and sere!
I never saw aught like to them,
Unless perchance it were

Brown skeletons of leaves that lag
My forest-brook along;
535 When the ivy-tod[1] is heavy with snow,
And the owlet whoops to the wolf below,
That eats the she-wolf's young.'

'Dear Lord! it hath a fiendish look'—
(The Pilot made reply)
540 'I am a-feared'—'Push on, push on!'
Said the Hermit cheerily.

The boat came closer to the ship,
But I nor spake nor stirred;
The boat came close beneath the ship,
545 And straight a sound was heard.

Under the water it rumbled on,
Still louder and more dread:
It reached the ship, it split the bay;
The ship went down like lead.

550 Stunned by that loud and dreadful sound,
Which sky and ocean smote,

513-545. The Hermit of the Wood approacheth the ship with wonder.
546-549. The ship suddenly sinketh.

[1] ivy-bush

Like one that hath been seven days drowned
My body lay afloat;
But swift as dreams, myself I found
555 Within the Pilot's boat.

Upon the whirl, where sank the ship,
The boat spun round and round;
And all was still, save that the hill
Was telling of the sound.

560 I moved my lips—the Pilot shrieked
And fell down in a fit;
The holy Hermit raised his eyes,
And prayed where he did sit.

I took the oars: the Pilot's boy,
565 Who now doth crazy go,
Laughed loud and long, and all the while
His eyes went to and fro.
'Ha! ha!' quoth he, 'full plain I see,
The Devil knows how to row.'

570 And now, all in my own countree,
I stood on the firm land!
The Hermit stepped forth from the boat,
And scarcely he could stand.

'Oh shrieve me, shrieve me, holy man!'
575 The Hermit crossed his brow.[1]
'Say quick,' quoth he, 'I bid thee say—
What manner of man art thou?'

Forthwith this frame of mine was wrenched
With a woful agony,
580 Which forced me to begin my tale;
And then it left me free.

Since then, at an uncertain hour,
That agony returns:
And till my ghastly tale is told,
585 This heart within me burns.

I pass, _like night, from land to land;_ *equated with legendary figure of wandering Jew in western European stories*
I have strange power of speech;
That moment that his face I see,
I know the man that must hear me:
590 To him my tale I teach.

What loud uproar bursts from that door!
The wedding-guests are there:
But in the garden-bower the bride

550-573. The ancient Mariner is saved in the Pilot's boat.
574-581. The ancient Mariner earnestly entreateth the Hermit to shrieve him; and the penance of life falls on him.
582-625. And ever and anon throughout his future life an agony constraineth him to travel from land to land and to teach, by his own example, love and reverence to all things that God made and loveth.

[1] made the sign of the cross on his forehead

And bride-maids singing are:
595 And hark the little vesper bell,
Which biddeth me to prayer!

O Wedding-Guest! this soul hath been
Alone on a wide, wide sea:
So lonely 'twas, that God himself
600 Scarce seeméd there to be.

O sweeter than the marriage-feast,
'Tis sweeter far to me,
To walk together to the kirk
With a goodly company!—

605 To walk together to the kirk,
And all together pray,
While each to his great Father bends,
Old men, and babes, and loving friends
And youths and maidens gay!

610 Farewell, farewell! but this I tell
To thee, thou Wedding-Guest!
He prayeth well, who loveth well
Both man and bird and beast.

He prayeth best, who loveth best
615 All things both great and small;
For the dear God who loveth us,
He made and loveth all.''

The Mariner, whose eye is bright,
Whose beard with age is hoar,
620 Is gone: and now the Wedding-Guest
Turned from the bridegroom's door.

He went like one that hath been stunned,
And is of sense forlorn:[1]
A sadder and a wiser man,
625 He rose the morrow morn.

CHRISTABEL
1797-1800   1816

PART I
1797   1816

'Tis the middle of night by the castle clock,
And the owls have awakened the crowing
        cock;
Tu—whit!——Tu—whoo!
And hark, again! the crowing cock,
5 How drowsily it crew.

Sir Leoline, the Baron rich,
Hath a toothless mastiff bitch;
From her kennel beneath the rock
She maketh answer to the clock,
10 Four for the quarters, and twelve for the
        hour;

[1] deprived

Ever and aye, by shine and shower,
Sixteen short howls, not over loud;
Some say, she sees my lady's shroud.

Is the night chilly and dark?
15 The night is chilly, but not dark.
The thin gray cloud is spread on high,
It covers but not hides the sky.
The moon is behind, and at the full;
And yet she looks both small and dull.
20 The night is chill, the cloud is gray:
'Tis a month before the month of May,
And the Spring comes slowly up this way.

The lovely lady, Christabel,
Whom her father loves so well,
25 What makes her in the wood so late,
A furlong from the castle gate?
She had dreams all yesternight
Of her own betrothéd knight;
And she in the midnight wood will pray
30 For the weal of her lover that's far away.

She stole along, she nothing spoke,
The sighs she heaved were soft and low,
And naught was green upon the oak
But moss and rarest mistletoe:
35 She kneels beneath the huge oak tree,
And in silence prayeth she.

The lady sprang up suddenly,
The lovely lady, Christabel!
It moaned as near, as near can be,
40 But what it is she cannot tell.—
On the other side it seems to be,
Of the huge, broad-breasted, old oak tree.

The night is chill; the forest bare;
Is it the wind that moaneth bleak?
45 There is not wind enough in the air
To move away the ringlet curl
From the lovely lady's cheek—
There is not wind enough to twirl
The one red leaf, the last of its clan,
50 That dances as often as dance it can,
Hanging so light, and hanging so high,
On the topmost twig that looks up at the
        sky.

Hush, beating heart of Christabel!
Jesu, Maria, shield her well!
55 She folded her arms beneath her cloak,
And stole to the other side of the oak.
        What sees she there?

There she sees a damsel bright,
Drest in a silken robe of white,
60 That shadowy in the moonlight shone:
The neck that made that white robe wan,

Her stately neck, and arms were bare;
Her blue-veined feet unsandal'd were,
And wildly glittered here and there
65 The gems entangled in her hair.
I guess, 'twas frightful there to see
A lady so richly clad as she—
Beautiful exceedingly!

"Mary Mother, save me now!"
70 Said Christabel; "and who art thou?"

The lady strange made answer meet,
And her voice was faint and sweet:—
"Have pity on my sore distress,
I scarce can speak for weariness:
75 Stretch forth thy hand, and have no
      fear!"
Said Christabel, "How camest thou
      here?"
And the lady, whose voice was faint and
      sweet,
Did thus pursue her answer meet:—

"My sire is of a noble line,
80 And my name is Geraldine:
Five warriors seized me yestermorn,
Me, even me, a maid forlorn:
They choked my cries with force and
      fright,
And tied me on a palfrey white.
85 The palfrey was as fleet as wind,
And they rode furiously behind.
They spurred amain, their steeds were
      white:
And once we crossed the shade of night.
As sure as Heaven shall rescue me,
90 I have no thought what men they be;
Nor do I know how long it is
(For I have lain entranced I wis)
Since one, the tallest of the five,
Took me from the palfrey's back,
95 A weary woman, scarce alive.
Some muttered words his comrades spoke:
He placed me underneath this oak;
He swore they would return with haste;
Whither they went I cannot tell—
100 I thought I heard, some minutes past,
Sounds as of a castle bell.
Stretch forth thy hand"—thus ended
      she—
"And help a wretched maid to flee."

Then Christabel stretched forth her hand,
105 And comforted fair Geraldine:
"O well, bright dame! may you command
The service of Sir Leoline;
And gladly our stout chivalry
Will he send forth and friends withal

110 To guide and guard you safe and free
Home to your noble father's hall."

She rose: and forth with steps they passed
That strove to be, and were not, fast.
Her gracious stars the lady blest,
115 And thus spake on sweet Christabel:
"All our household are at rest,
The hall is silent as the cell;
Sir Leoline is weak in health,
And may not well awakened be,
120 But we will move as if in stealth,
And I beseech your courtesy,
This night, to share your couch with me."

They crossed the moat, and Christabel
Took the key that fitted well;
125 A little door she opened straight,
All in the middle of the gate;
The gate that was ironed within and with-
      out,
Where an army in battle array had
      marched out.
- The lady sank, belike through pain,[1]
130 And Christabel with might and main
Lifted her up, a weary weight,
Over the threshold of the gate:
Then the lady rose again,
And moved, as she were not in pain.

135 So free from danger, free from fear,
They crossed the court: right glad they
      were.
And Christabel devoutly cried
To the lady by her side,
"Praise we the Virgin all divine
140 Who hath rescued thee from thy dis-
      tress!"
"Alas, alas!" said Geraldine,
"I cannot speak for weariness."
So free from danger, free from fear,
They crossed the court: right glad they
      were.

145 Outside her kennel, the mastiff old
Lay fast asleep, in moonshine cold.
The mastiff old did not awake,
Yet she an angry moan did make!
And what can ail the mastiff bitch?
150 Never till now she uttered yell
Beneath the eye of Christabel.
Perhaps it is the owlet's scritch:
For what can ail the mastiff bitch?[2]

---

[1] Geraldine was an evil spirit and was unable
      without aid to cross the threshold, which had
      been blessed to keep evil spirits away.
[2] Animals were supposed to know when super-
      natural beings were near.

They passed the hall, that echoes still,
155 Pass as lightly as you will!
The brands were flat, the brands were
  dying,
Amid their own white ashes lying;
But when the lady passed, there came
A tongue of light, a fit of flame;
160 And Christabel saw the lady's eye,
And nothing else saw she thereby,
Save the boss of the shield of Sir Leoline
  tall,
Which hung in a murky old niche in the
  wall.
"O softly tread," said Christabel,
165 "My father seldom sleepeth well."

Sweet Christabel her feet doth bare,
And jealous of the listening air
They steal their way from stair to stair,
Now in glimmer, and now in gloom,
170 And now they pass the Baron's room,
As still as death, with stifled breath!
And now have reached her chamber door;
And now doth Geraldine press down
The rushes of the chamber floor.

175 The moon shines dim in the open air,
And not a moonbeam enters here.
But they without its light can see
The chamber carved so curiously,
Carved with figures strange and sweet,
180 All made out of the carver's brain,
For a lady's chamber meet:
The lamp with twofold silver chain
Is fastened to an angel's feet.

The silver lamp burns dead and dim;
185 But Christabel the lamp will trim.
She trimmed the lamp, and made it bright,
And left it swinging to and fro,
While Geraldine, in wretched plight,
Sank down upon the floor below.

190 "O weary lady, Geraldine,
I pray you, drink this cordial wine!
It is a wine of virtuous powers;
My mother made it of wild flowers."

"And will your mother pity me,
195 Who am a maiden most forlorn?"
Christabel answered: "Woe is me!
She died the hour that I was born.
I have heard the gray-haired friar tell
How on her death-bed she did say,
200 That she should hear the castle-bell
Strike twelve upon my wedding-day.
O mother dear! that thou wert here!"
"I would," said Geraldine, "she were!"

But soon with altered voice, said she:
205 "Off, wandering mother! Peak and pine!
I have power to bid thee flee."
Alas! what ails poor Geraldine?
Why stares she with unsettled eye?
Can she the bodiless dead espy?
210 And why with hollow voice cries she,
"Off, woman, off! this hour is mine—
Though thou her guardian spirit be,
Off, woman, off! 'tis given to me"?

Then Christabel knelt by the lady's side,
215 And raised to heaven her eyes so blue—
"Alas!" said she, "this ghastly ride—
Dear lady! it hath wildered you!"
The lady wiped her moist cold brow,
And faintly said, " 'Tis over now!"

220 Again the wild-flower wine she drank:
Her fair large eyes 'gan glitter bright,
And from the floor whereon she sank,
The lofty lady stood upright:
She was most beautiful to see,
225 Like a lady of a far countrée.

And thus the lofty lady spake:
"All they who live in the upper sky,
Do love you, holy Christabel!
And you love them, and for their sake
230 And for the good which me befel,
Even I in my degree will try,
Fair maiden, to requite you well.
But now unrobe yourself; for I
Must pray, ere yet in bed I lie."

235 Quoth Christabel, "So let it be!"
And as the lady bade, did she.
Her gentle limbs did she undress,
And lay down in her loveliness.

But through her brain of weal and woe
240 So many thoughts moved to and fro,
That vain it were her lids to close;
So half-way from the bed she rose,
And on her elbow did recline
To look at the lady Geraldine.

245 Beneath the lamp the lady bowed,
And slowly rolled her eyes around;
Then drawing in her breath aloud,
Like one that shuddered, she unbound
The cincture from beneath her breast:
250 Her silken robe, and inner vest,
Dropt to her feet, and full in view,
Behold! her bosom and half her side——
A sight to dream of, not to tell!
O shield her! shield sweet Christabel!

255 Yet Geraldine nor speaks nor stirs;
   Ah! what a stricken look was hers!
Deep from within she seems half-way
To lift some weight with sick assay,
And eyes the maid and seeks delay;
260 Then suddenly, as one defied,
Collects herself in scorn and pride,
And lay down by the maiden's side!—
And in her arms the maid she took,
   Ah wel-a-day!
265 And with low voice and doleful look
These words did say:
"In the touch of this bosom there worketh
   a spell,
Which is lord of thy utterance, Chris-
   tabel!
Thou knowest tonight, and wilt know to-
   morrow,
270 This mark of my shame, this seal of my
   sorrow;
   But vainly thou warrest,
     For this is alone in
   Thy power to declare,
     That in the dim forest
275   Thou heard'st a low moaning,
And found'st a bright lady, surpassingly
   fair;
And didst bring her home with thee in
   love and in charity,
To shield her and shelter her from the
   damp air."

THE CONCLUSION TO PART I

It was a lovely sight to see
280 The lady Christabel, when she
Was praying at the old oak tree.
   Amid the jaggèd shadows
   Of mossy leafless boughs,
   Kneeling in the moonlight,
285   To make her gentle vows;
Her slender palms together prest,
Heaving sometimes on her breast;

Her face resigned to bliss or bale—
Her face, oh, call it fair not pale,
290 And both blue eyes more bright than clear,
   Each about to have a tear.

With open eyes (ah, woe is me!)
Asleep, and dreaming fearfully,
Fearfully dreaming, yet, I wis,
295 Dreaming that alone, which is—
O sorrow and shame! Can this be she,
The lady, who knelt at the old oak tree?
And lo! the worker of these harms,
That holds the maiden in her arms,
300 Seems to slumber still and mild,
As a mother with her child.

A star hath set, a star hath risen,
O Geraldine! since arms of thine
Have been the lovely lady's prison.
305 O Geraldine! one hour was thine—
Thou'st had thy will! By tairn and rill,
The night-birds all that hour were still.
But now they are jubilant anew,
From cliff and tower, tu—whoo! tu—
   whoo!
310 Tu—whoo! tu—whoo! from wood and
   fell!

And see! the lady Christabel
Gathers herself from out her trance;
Her limbs relax, her countenance
Grows sad and soft; the smooth thin lids
315 Close o'er her eyes; and tears she sheds—
Large tears that leave the lashes bright!
And oft the while she seems to smile
As infants at a sudden light!
Yea, she doth smile, and she doth weep,
320 Like a youthful hermitess,
Beauteous in a wilderness,
Who, praying always, prays in sleep.
And, if she move unquietly,
Perchance, 'tis but the blood so free
325 Comes back and tingles in her feet.
No doubt, she hath a vision sweet.
What if her guardian spirit 'twere,
What if she knew her mother near?
But this she knows, in joys and woes,
330 That saints will aid if men will call:
For the blue sky bends over all!

PART II
1800   1816

Each matin bell, the Baron saith,
Knells us back to a world of death.
These words Sir Leoline first said,
335 When he rose and found his lady dead:
These words Sir Leoline will say
Many a morn to his dying day!

And hence the custom and law began
That still at dawn the sacristan,
340 Who duly pulls the heavy bell,
Five and forty beads must tell
Between each stroke—a warning knell,
Which not a soul can choose but hear
From Bratha Head to Wyndermere.

345 Saith Bracy the bard, "So let it knell!
And let the drowsy sacristan
Still count as slowly as he can!"
There is no lack of such, I ween,
As well fill up the space between.
350 In Langdale Pike[1] and Witch's Lair,
And Dungeon-ghyll[2] so foully rent,

    [1] peak   [2] valley

With ropes of rock and bells of air
Three sinful sextons' ghosts are pent,
Who all give back, one after t'other,
355 The death-note to their living brother;
And oft too, by the knell offended,
Just as their one! two! three! is ended,
The devil mocks the doleful tale
With a merry peal from Borodale.

360 The air is still! through mist and cloud
That merry peal comes ringing loud;
And Geraldine shakes off her dread,
And rises lightly from the bed;
Puts on her silken vestments white,
365 And tricks her hair in lovely plight,[1]
And nothing doubting of her spell
Awakens the lady Christabel.
"Sleep you, sweet lady Christabel?
I trust that you have rested well."

370 And Christabel awoke and spied
The same who lay down by her side—
O rather say, the same whom she
Raised up beneath the old oak tree!
Nay, fairer yet! and yet more fair!
375 For she belike hath drunken deep
Of all the blessedness of sleep!
And while she spake, her looks, her air
Such gentle thankfulness declare,
That (so it seemed) her girded vests
380 Grew tight beneath her heaving breasts.
"Sure I have sinn'd!" said Christabel,
"Now heaven be praised if all be well!"
And in low faltering tones, yet sweet,
Did she the lofty lady greet
385 With such perplexity of mind
As dreams too lively leave behind.

So quickly she rose, and quickly arrayed
Her maiden limbs, and having prayed
That He, who on the cross did groan,
390 Might wash away her sins unknown,
She forthwith led fair Geraldine
To meet her sire, Sir Leoline.

The lovely maid and the lady tall
Are pacing both into the hall,
395 And pacing on through page and groom,
Enter the Baron's presence-room.

The Baron rose, and while he prest
His gentle daughter to his breast,
With cheerful wonder in his eyes
400 The lady Geraldine espies,
And gave such welcome to the same,
As might beseem so bright a dame!

But when he heard the lady's tale,
And when she told her father's name,

1 fold or plait

405 Why waxed Sir Leoline so pale,
Murmuring o'er the name again,
Lord Roland de Vaux of Tryermaine?

Alas! they had been friends in youth;
But whispering tongues can poison truth;
410 And constancy lives in realms above;
And life is thorny; and youth is vain;
And to be wroth with one we love
Doth work like madness in the brain.
And thus it chanced, as I divine,
415 With Roland and Sir Leoline.
Each spake words of high disdain
And insult to his heart's best brother:
They parted—ne'er to meet again!
But never either found another
420 To free the hollow heart from paining—
They stood aloof, the scars remaining,
Like cliffs which had been rent asunder;
A dreary sea now flows between;—
But neither heat, nor frost, nor thunder,
425 Shall wholly do away, I ween,
The marks of that which once hath been.

Sir Leoline, a moment's space,
Stood gazing on the damsel's face:
And the youthful Lord of Tryermaine
430 Came back upon his heart again.

O then the Baron forgot his age,
His noble heart swelled high with rage;
He swore by the wounds in Jesu's side
He would proclaim it far and wide,
435 With trump and solemn heraldry,
That they, who thus had wronged the dame,
Were base as spotted infamy!
"And if they dare deny the same,
My herald shall appoint a week,
440 And let the recreant traitors seek
My tourney court—that there and then
I may dislodge their reptile souls
From the bodies and forms of men!"

He spake: his eye in lightning rolls!
445 For the lady was ruthlessly seized; and
      he kenned
In the beautiful lady the child of his
      friend!

And now the tears were on his face,
And fondly in his arms he took
Fair Geraldine, who met the embrace,
450 Prolonging it with joyous look.
Which when she viewed, a vision fell
Upon the soul of Christabel,
The vision of fear, the touch and pain!
She shrunk and shuddered, and saw
      again—
455 (Ah, woe is me! Was it for thee,
Thou gentle maid! such sights to see?)

Again she saw that bosom old,
Again she felt that bosom cold,
And drew in her breath with a hissing
    sound:
460 Whereat the Knight turned wildly round,
And nothing saw, but his own sweet maid
With eyes upraised, as one that prayed.

The touch, the sight, had passed away,
And in its stead that vision blest,
465 Which comforted her after-rest
While in the lady's arms she lay,
Had put a rapture in her breast,
And on her lips and o'er her eyes
Spread smiles like light!
                With new surprise,
470 "What ails then my belovéd child?"
The Baron said.—His daughter mild
Made answer, "All will yet be well!"
I ween, she had no power to tell
Aught else: so mighty was the spell.

475 Yet he, who saw this Geraldine,
Had deemed her sure a thing divine.
Such sorrow with such grace she blended,
As if she feared she had offended
Sweet Christabel, that gentle maid!
480 And with such lowly tones she prayed
She might be sent without delay
Home to her father's mansion.
                    "Nay!
Nay, by my soul!" said Leoline.
"Ho! Bracy the bard, the charge be thine!
485 Go thou, with music sweet and loud,
And take two steeds with trappings proud,
And take the youth whom thou lov'st best
To bear thy harp, and learn thy song,
Ad clothe you both in solemn vest,
490 And over the mountains haste along,
Lest wandering folk, that are abroad,
Detain you on the valley road.

"And when he has crossed the Irthing
    flood,
My merry bard! he hastes, he hastes
495 Up Knorren Moor, through Halegarth
    Wood,
And reaches soon that castle good
Which stands and threatens Scotland's
    wastes.

"Bard Bracy! bard Bracy! your horses
    are fleet,
Ye must ride up the hall, your music so
    sweet,
500 More loud than your horses' echoing feet!
And loud and loud to Lord Roland call,
Thy daughter is safe in Langdale hall!
Thy beautiful daughter is safe and free—

Sir Leoline greets thee thus through me!
505 He bids thee come without delay
With all thy numerous array
And take thy lovely daughter home:
And he will meet thee on the way
With all his numerous array
510 White with their panting palfreys' foam:
And, by mine honor! I will say,
That I repent me of the day
When I spake words of fierce disdain
To Roland de Vaux of Tryermaine!—
515 —For since that evil hour hath flown,
Many a summer's sun hath shone;
Yet ne'er found I a friend again
Like Roland de Vaux of Tryermaine."

The lady fell, and clasped his knees,
520 Her face upraised, her eyes o'erflowing;
And Bracy replied, with faltering voice,
His gracious Hail on all bestowing!—
"Thy words, thou sire of Christabel,
Are sweeter than my harp can tell;
525 Yet might I gain a boon of thee,
This day my journey should not be,
So strange a dream hath come to me,
That I had vowed with music loud
To clear yon wood from thing unblest,
530 Warned by a vision in my rest!
For in my sleep I saw that dove,
That gentle bird, whom thou dost love,
And call'st by thy own daughter's name—
Sir Leoline! I saw the same
535 Fluttering, and uttering fearful moan,
Among the green herbs in the forest alone.
Which when I saw and when I heard,
I wonder'd what might ail the bird;
For nothing near it could I see,
540 Save the grass and green herbs under-
    neath the old tree.

"And in my dream methought I went
To search out what might there be found;
And what the sweet bird's trouble meant,
That thus lay fluttering on the ground.
545 I went and peered, and could descry
No cause for her distressful cry;
But yet for her dear lady's sake
I stooped, methought, the dove to take,
When lo! I saw a bright green snake
550 Coiled around its wings and neck.
Green as the herbs on which it couched,
Close by the dove's its head it crouched;
And with the dove it heaves and stirs,
Swelling its neck as she swelled hers!
555 I woke; it was the midnight hour,
The clock was echoing in the tower;
But though my slumber was gone by,
This dream it would not pass away—
It seems to live upon my eye!

560 And thence I vowed this self-same day
With music strong and saintly song
To wander through the forest bare,
Lest aught unholy loiter there.''

Thus Bracy said: the Baron, the while,
565 Half-listening heard him with a smile;
Then turned to Lady Geraldine,
His eyes made up of wonder and love;
And said in courtly accents fine:
''Sweet maid, Lord Roland's beauteous
      dove,
570 With arms more strong than harp or song,
Thy sire and I will crush the snake!''
He kissed her forehead as he spake,
And Geraldine in maiden wise
Casting down her large bright eyes,
575 With blushing cheek and courtesy fine
She turned her from Sir Leoline;
Softly gathering up her train,
That o'er her right arm fell again;
And folded her arms across her chest,
580 And couched her head upon her breast,
And looked askance at Christabel——
Jesu, Maria, shield her well!

A snake's small eye blinks dull and shy;
And the lady's eyes they shrunk in her
      head,
585 Each shrunk up to a serpent's eye,
And with somewhat of malice, and more
      of dread,
At Christabel she looked askance!—
One moment—and the sight was fled!
But Christabel in dizzy trance
590 Stumbling on the unsteady ground
Shuddered aloud, with a hissing sound;
And Geraldine again turned round,
And like a thing, that sought relief,
Full of wonder and full of grief,
595 She rolled her large bright eyes divine
Wildly on Sir Leoline.

The maid, alas! her thoughts are gone,
She nothing sees—no sight but one!
The maid, devoid of guile and sin,
600 I know not how, in fearful wise,
So deeply had she drunken in
That look, those shrunken serpent eyes,
That all her features were resigned
To this sole image in her mind:
605 And passively did imitate
That look of dull and treacherous hate!
And thus she stood, in dizzy trance,
Still picturing that look askance
With forced unconscious sympathy
610 Full before her father's view——
As far as such a look could be
In eyes so innocent and blue!

And when the trance was o'er, the maid
Paused awhile, and inly prayed:
615 Then falling at the Baron's feet,
''By my mother's soul do I entreat
That thou this woman send away!''
She said: and more she could not say:
For what she knew she could not tell,
620 O'er-mastered by the mighty spell.

Why is thy cheek so wan and wild,
Sir Leoline? Thy only child
Lies at thy feet, thy joy, thy pride,
So fair, so innocent, so mild;
625 The same, for whom thy lady died!
O, by the pangs of her dear mother
Think thou no evil of thy child!
For her, and thee, and for no other,
She prayed the moment ere she died:
630 Prayed that the babe for whom she died,
Might prove her dear lord's joy and
      pride!
That prayer her deadly pangs beguiled,
      Sir Leoline!
And wouldst thou wrong thy only child,
635   Her child and thine?

Within the Baron's heart and brain
If thoughts, like these, had any share,
They only swelled his rage and pain,
And did but work confusion there.
640 His heart was cleft with pain and rage,
His cheeks they quivered, his eyes were wild,
Dishonored thus in his old age;
Dishonored by his only child,
And all his hospitality
645 To the wronged daughter of his friend
By more than woman's jealousy
Brought thus to a disgraceful end—
He rolled his eye with stern regard
Upon the gentle minstrel bard,
650 And said in tones abrupt, austere—
''Why, Bracy! dost thou loiter here?
I bade thee hence!'' The bard obeyed;
And turning from his own sweet maid,
The agéd knight, Sir Leoline,
655 Led forth the lady Geraldine!

THE CONCLUSION TO PART II

A little child, a limber elf,
Singing, dancing to itself,
A fairy thing with red round cheeks,
That always finds, and never seeks,
660 Makes such a vision to the sight
As fills a father's eyes with light;
And pleasures flow in so thick and fast
Upon his heart, that he at last
Must needs express his love's excess
665 With words of unmeant bitterness.

Perhaps 'tis pretty to force together
Thoughts so all unlike each other;
To mutter and mock a broken charm,
To dally with wrong that does no harm.
670 Perhaps 'tis tender too and pretty
At each wild word to feel within
A sweet recoil of love and pity.
And what, if in a world of sin
(O sorrow and shame should this be true!)
675 Such giddiness of heart and brain
Comes seldom save from rage and pain,
So talks as it's most used to do.

*   *   *   *   *   *

FROST AT MIDNIGHT
1798   1798

The frost performs its secret ministry,
Unhelped by any wind. The owlet's cry
Came loud—and hark, again! loud as
    before.
The inmates of my cottage, all at rest,
5 Have left me to that solitude, which suits
Abstruser musings: save that at my side
My cradled infant slumbers peacefully.
'Tis calm indeed! so calm, that it disturbs
And vexes meditation with its strange
10 And extreme silentness. Sea, hill, and wood,
This populous village! Sea, and hill, and
    wood,
With all the numberless goings-on of life,
Inaudible as dreams! the thin blue flame
Lies on my low-burnt fire, and quivers not;
15 Only that film, which fluttered on the
    grate,[1]
Still flutters there, the sole unquiet thing.
Methinks, its motion in this hush of nature
Gives it dim sympathies with me who live,
Making it a companionable form,
20 Whose puny flaps and freaks the idling
    spirit
By its own moods interprets, everywhere
Echo or mirror seeking of itself,
And makes a toy of thought.

             But O! how oft,
How oft, at school, with most believing
    mind,
25 Presageful, have I gazed upon the bars,
To watch that fluttering stranger! and as
    oft
With unclosed lids, already had I dreamt
Of my sweet birth-place, and the old
    church-tower,
Whose bells, the poor man's only music,
    rang
30 From morn to evening, all the hot Fair-day,
So sweetly, that they stirred and haunted
    me

[1] "In all parts of the kingdom, these films are called strangers and supposed to portend the arrival of some absent friend."—Coleridge.

With a wild pleasure, falling on mine ear
Most like articulate sounds of things to
    come!
So gazed I, till the soothing things, I
    dreamt,
35 Lulled me to sleep, and sleep prolonged
    my dreams!
And so I brooded all the following morn,
Awed by the stern preceptor's face, mine
    eye
Fixed with mock study on my swimming
    book:
Save if the door half opened, and I
    snatched
40 A hasty glance, and still my heart leaped
    up,
For still I hoped to see the stranger's face,
Townsman, or aunt, or sister more beloved,
My play-mate when we both were clothed
    alike!

    Dear babe, that sleepest cradled by my
    side,
45 Whose gentle breathings, heard in this
    deep calm,
Fill up the interspersèd vacancies
And momentary pauses of the thought!
My babe so beautiful! it thrills my heart
With tender gladness, thus to look at thee,
50 And think that thou shalt learn far other
    lore,
And in far other scenes! For I was reared
In the great city, pent 'mid cloisters dim,
And saw nought lovely but the sky and
    stars.[1]
But thou, my babe! shalt wander like a
    breeze
55 By lakes and sandy shores, beneath the
    crags
Of ancient mountain, and beneath the
    clouds,
Which image in their bulk both lakes and
    shores
And mountain crags: so shalt thou see
    and hear
The lovely shapes and sounds intelligible
60 Of that eternal language, which thy God
Utters, who from eternity doth teach
Himself in all, and all things in himself.
Great universal Teacher! he shall mould
Thy spirit, and by giving make it ask.

65   Therefore all seasons shall be sweet to
    thee,
Whether the summer clothe the general
    earth
With greenness, or the redbreast sit and
    sing

[1] See Wordsworth's *The Prelude*, 8, 433-37 (p. 282).

Betwixt the tufts of snow on the bare
    branch
Of mossy apple-tree, while the nigh thatch
70 Smokes in the sun-thaw; whether the
    eave-drops fall
Heard only in the trances of the blast,
Or if the secret ministry of frost
Shall hang them up in silent icicles,
Quietly shining to the quiet moon.

FRANCE: AN ODE
1798   1798

Ye Clouds! that far above me float and
    pause,
    Whose pathless march no mortal may
        control!
    Ye Ocean-Waves! that, wheresoe'er ye
        roll,
    Yield homage only to eternal laws!
5 Ye Woods! that listen to the night-birds
        singing,
    Midway the smooth and perilous slope
        reclined,
    Save when your own imperious branches
        swinging,
    Have made a solemn music of the wind!
Where, like a man beloved of God,
10 Through glooms, which never woodman
        trod,
    How oft, pursuing fancies holy,
My moonlight way o'er flowering weeds I
        wound,
    Inspired, beyond the guess of folly,
By each rude shape and wild unconquer-
        able sound!
15 O ye loud Waves! and O ye Forests high!
    And O ye Clouds that far above me
        soared!
    Thou rising Sun! thou blue rejoicing
        Sky!
    Yea, everything that is and will be
        free!
    Bear witness for me, wheresoe'er ye be,
20 With what deep worship I have still
        adored
    The spirit of divinest Liberty.

When France in wrath her giant-limbs
        upreared,
    And with that oath, which smote air,
        earth, and sea,
    Stamped her strong foot and said she
        would be free,
25 Bear witness for me, how I hoped and
        feared!
With what a joy my lofty gratulation
    Unawed I sang, amid a slavish band:
And when to whelm the disenchanted
    nation,

Like fiends embattled by a wizard's
    wand,
30   The Monarchs marched in evil day,
    And Britain joined the dire array;[1]
Though dear her shores and circling
    ocean,
Though many friendships, many youth-
    ful loves
    Had swoln the patriot emotion
35 And flung a magic light o'er all her hills
        and groves;
Yet still my voice, unaltered, sang defeat
    To all that braved the tyrant-quelling
        lance,
And shame too long delayed and vain
    retreat!
For ne'er, O Liberty! with partial aim
40 I dimmed thy light or damped thy holy
        flame;
    But blessed the paeans of delivered
        France,
And hung my head and wept at Britain's
    name.

"And what," I said, "though Blas-
        phemy's loud scream
    With that sweet music of deliverance
        strove!
45 Though all the fierce and drunken
        passions wove
A dance more wild than e'er was maniac's
    dream![2]
Ye storms, that round the dawning
    East assembled,
The Sun[3] was rising, though ye hid his
    light!"
And when, to soothe my soul, that
    hoped and trembled,
50 The dissonance ceased, and all seemed
    calm and bright;
When France her front deep-scarr'd
    and gory
Concealed with clustering wreaths of
    glory;
When, insupportably advancing,
    Her arm made mockery of the war-
        rior's ramp;[4]
55   While timid looks of fury glancing,
Domestic treason, crushed beneath her
    fatal stamp,
Writhed like a wounded dragon in his
    gore;
Then I reproached my fears that would
    not flee;

[1] France declared war
upon Prussia and
Austria in 1792,
and upon Holland
and England in
1793.

[2] A reference to the
excesses of the
French Revolution.
[3] Liberty.
[4] act of advancing in
warlike posture

"And soon," I said, "shall Wisdom
        teach her lore
60 In the low huts of them that toil and
        groan!
And, conquering by her happiness alone,
        Shall France compel the nations to be
        free,
Till Love and Joy look round, and call
        the Earth their own."

Forgive me, Freedom! O forgive those
        dreams!
65 I hear thy voice, I hear thy loud
        lament,
From bleak Helvetia's icy caverns
        sent—
I hear thy groans upon her blood-stained
        streams!
Heroes, that for your peaceful country
        perished,
And ye that, fleeing, spot your mountain-
        snows
70 With bleeding wounds; forgive me,
        that I cherished
One thought that ever blessed your cruel
        foes!
To scatter rage, and traitorous guilt,
Where Peace her jealous home had
        built;
A patriot-race to disinherit
75 Of all that made their stormy wilds so
        dear;
And with inexpiable spirit
To taint the bloodless freedom of the
        mountaineer—
O France, that mockest Heaven, adulter-
        ous, blind,
And patriot only in pernicious toils!
80 Are these thy boasts, Champion of human
        kind?
To mix with Kings in the low lust of
        sway,
Yell in the hunt, and share the murderous
        prey;
To insult the shrine of Liberty with spoils
From freemen torn; to tempt and to
        betray?

85   The Sensual and the Dark rebel in
        vain,
        Slaves by their own compulsion! In
        mad game
        They burst their manacles and wear the
        name
        Of Freedom, graven on a heavier
        chain!
O Liberty! with profitless endeavor
90 Have I pursued thee, many a weary hour;

But thou nor swell'st the victor's
        strain, nor ever
Didst breathe thy soul in forms of hu-
        man power.
        Alike from all, howe'er they praise
        thee,
        (Nor prayer, nor boastful name delays
        thee)
95   Alike from Priestcraft's harpy min-
        ions,
        And factious Blasphemy's obscener
        slaves,
Thou speedest on thy subtle pinions,
The guide of homeless winds, and play-
        mate of the waves!
And there I felt thee!—on that sea-
        cliff's verge,
100 Whose pines, scarce travelled by the
        breeze above,
Had made one murmur with the distant
        surge!
Yes, while I stood and gazed, my temples
        bare,
And shot my being through earth, sea,
        and air,
Possessing all things with intensest love,
105 O Liberty! my spirit felt thee there.

LEWTI

OR THE CIRCASSIAN LOVE-CHANT
1798   1798

At midnight by the stream I roved,
To forget the form I loved.
Image of Lewti! from my mind
Depart; for Lewti is not kind.

5 The moon was high, the moonlight gleam
    And the shadow of a star
Heaved upon Tamaha's stream;
    But the rock shone brighter far,
    The rock half sheltered from my view
10 By pendent boughs of tressy yew.—
So shines my Lewti's forehead fair,
Gleaming through her sable hair,
Image of Lewti! from my mind
Depart; for Lewti is not kind.

15 I saw a cloud of palest hue,
    Onward to the moon it passed;
    Still brighter and more bright it grew,
    With floating colors not a few,
    Till it reach'd the moon at last:
20 Then the cloud was wholly bright,
    With a rich and amber light!
And so with many a hope I seek
    And with such joy I find my Lewti;
And even so my pale wan cheek
25   Drinks in as deep a flush of beauty!

Nay, treacherous image! leave my mind,
If Lewti never will be kind.

The little cloud—it floats away,
  Away it goes; away so soon!
30 Alas! it has no power to stay:
Its hues are dim, its hues are gray—
Away it passes from the moon!
How mournfully it seems to fly,
  Ever fading more and more,
35 To joyless regions of the sky—
And now 'tis whiter than before!
As white as my poor cheek will be,
  When, Lewti! on my couch I lie,
A dying man for love of thee.
40 Nay, treacherous image! leave my mind—
And yet, thou didst not look unkind.

I saw a vapor in the sky,
Thin, and white, and very high;
I ne'er beheld so thin a cloud:
45   Perhaps the breezes that can fly
  Now below and now above,
Have snatched aloft the lawny shroud
Of Lady fair—that died for love.
For maids, as well as youths, have perished
50 From fruitless love too fondly cherished.
Nay, treacherous image! leave my mind—
For Lewti never will be kind.

Hush! my heedless feet from under
  Slip the crumbling banks forever:
55 Like echoes to a distant thunder,
  They plunge into the gentle river.
The river-swans have heard my tread,
And startle from their reedy bed.
O beauteous birds! methinks ye measure
60   Your movements to some heavenly tune!
O beauteous birds! 'tis such a pleasure
  To see you move beneath the moon,
I would it were your true delight
To sleep by day and wake all night.

65 I know the place where Lewti lies,
When silent night has closed her eyes:
  It is a breezy jasmine-bower,
The nightingale sings o'er her head:
  Voice of the Night! had I the power
70 That leafy labyrinth to thread,
And creep, like thee, with soundless tread,
I then might view her bosom white
Heaving lovely to my sight,
As these two swans together heave
75 On the gently-swelling wave.

Oh! that she saw me in a dream,
  And dreamt that I had died for care;
All pale and wasted I would seem,
  Yet fair withal, as spirits are!

80 I'd die indeed, if I might see
Her bosom heave, and heave for me!
Soothe, gentle image! soothe my mind!
Tomorrow Lewti may be kind.

FEARS IN SOLITUDE

WRITTEN IN APRIL, 1798, DURING THE ALARM
OF AN INVASION[1]
1798   *1798*

A green and silent spot, amid the hills,
A small and silent dell! O'er stiller place
No singing skylark ever poised himself.
The hills are heathy, save that swelling
    slope,
5 Which hath a gay and gorgeous covering
    on,
All golden with the never-bloomless furze,
Which now blooms most profusely: but
    the dell,
Bathed by the mist, is fresh and delicate
As vernal corn-field,[2] or the unripe flax,
10 When, through its half-transparent stalks,
    at eve,
The level sunshine glimmers with green
    light.
Oh! 'tis a quiet spirit-healing nook!
Which all, methinks, would love; but
    chiefly he,
The humble man, who, in his youthful
    years,
15 Knew just so much of folly, as had made
His early manhood more securely wise!
Here he might lie on fern or withered
    heath,
While from the singing lark (that sings
    unseen
The minstrelsy that solitude loves best),
20 And from the sun, and from the breezy
    air,
Sweet influences trembled o'er his frame;
And he, with many feelings, many
    thoughts,
Made up a meditative joy, and found
Religious meanings in the forms of Na-
    ture!
25 And so, his senses gradually wrapt
In a half sleep, he dreams of better
    worlds,
And dreaming hears thee still, O singing
    lark,
That singest like an angel in the clouds!

My God! it is a melancholy thing
30 For such a man, who would full fain
    preserve

[1] The French planned to invade both England
   and Ireland early in 1798.
[2] wheat-field

His soul in calmness, yet perforce must
     feel
For all his human brethren—O my God!
It weighs upon the heart, that he must
     think
What uproar and what strife may now
     be stirring
35 This way or that way o'er these silent
     hills—
Invasion, and the thunder and the shout,
And all the crash of onset; fear and rage,
And undetermined conflict—even now,
Even now, perchance, and in his native
     isle:
40 Carnage and groans beneath this blessed
     sun!
We have offended, Oh! my countrymen!
We have offended very grievously,
And been most tyrannous. From east to
     west
A groan of accusation pierces Heaven!
45 The wretched plead against us; multitudes
Countless and vehement, the sons of God,
Our brethren! Like a cloud that travels
     on,
Steamed up from Cairo's swamps of pes-
     tilence,
Even so, my countrymen! have we gone
     forth
50 And borne to distant tribes slavery and
     pangs,
And, deadlier far, our vices, whose deep
     taint
With slow perdition murders the whole
     man,
His body and his soul! Meanwhile, at
     home,
All individual dignity and power
55 Engulfed in Courts, Committees, Institu-
     tions,
Associations and Societies,
A vain, speech-mouthing, speech-reporting
     Guild,
One Benefit-Club for mutual flattery,
We have drunk up, demure as at a grace,
60 Pollutions from the brimming cup of
     wealth;
Contemptuous of all honorable rule,
Yet bartering freedom and the poor man's
     life
For gold, as at a market! The sweet words
Of Christian promise, words that even yet
65 Might stem destruction, were they wisely
     preached,
Are muttered o'er by men, whose tones
     proclaim
How flat and wearisome they feel their
     trade:
Rank scoffers some, but most too indolent

To deem them falsehoods or to know their
     truth.
70 Oh! blasphemous! the Book of Life is
     made
A superstitious instrument, on which
We gabble o'er the oaths we mean to
     break;
For all must swear—all and in every place,
College and wharf, council and justice-
     court;
75 All, all must swear, the briber and the
     bribed,
Merchant and lawyer, senator and priest,
The rich, the poor, the old man and the
     young;
All, all make up one scheme of perjury,
That faith doth reel; the very name of God
80 Sounds like a juggler's charm; and, bold
     with joy,
Forth from his dark and lonely hiding-
     place,
(Portentous sight!) the owlet Atheism,
Sailing on obscene wings athwart the noon,
Drops his blue-fringéd lids, and holds
     them close,
85 And hooting at the glorious sun in
     Heaven,
Cries out, "Where is it?"

          Thankless too for peace,
(Peace long preserved by fleets and per-
     ilous seas)
Secure from actual warfare, we have loved
To swell the war-whoop, passionate for
     war!
90 Alas! for ages ignorant of all
Its ghastlier workings, (famine or blue
     plague,
Battle, or siege, or flight through wintry
     snows,)
We, this whole people, have been clam-
     orous
For war and bloodshed; animating sports,
95 The which we pay for as a thing we talk of,
Spectators and not combatants! No guess
Anticipative of a wrong unfelt,
No speculation on contingency,
However dim and vague, too vague and
     dim
100 To yield a justifying cause; and forth,
(Stuffed out with big preamble, holy
     names,
And adjurations of the God in Heaven,)
We send our mandates for the certain
     death
Of thousands and ten thousands! Boys
     and girls,
105 And women, that would groan to see a
     child

Pull off an insect's leg, all read of war,
The best amusement for our morning meal!
The poor wretch, who has learnt his only
    prayers
From curses, who knows scarcely words
    enough
110 To ask a blessing from his Heavenly
    Father,
Becomes a fluent phraseman, absolute
And technical in victories and defeats,
And all our dainty terms for fratricide;
Terms which we trundle smoothly o'er our
    tongues
115 Like mere abstractions, empty sounds to
    which
We join no feeling and attach no form!
As if the soldier died without a wound;
As if the fibres of this godlike frame
Were gored without a pang; as if the
    wretch,
120 Who fell in battle, doing bloody deeds,
Passed off to Heaven, translated and not
    killed;
As though he had no wife to pine for him,
No God to judge him! Therefore, evil days
Are coming on us, O my countrymen!
125 And what if all-avenging Providence,
Strong and retributive, should make us
    know.
The meaning of our words, force us to feel
The desolation and the agony
Of our fierce doings?

               Spare us yet awhile,
130 Father and God! Oh! spare us yet awhile!
Oh! let not English women drag their flight
Fainting beneath the burthen of their
    babes,
Of the sweet infants, that but yesterday
Laughed at the breast! Sons, brothers,
    husbands, all
135 Who ever gazed with fondness on the
    forms
Which grew up with you round the same
    fire-side,
And all who ever heard the Sabbath-bells
Without the infidel's scorn, make your-
    selves pure!
Stand forth! be men! repel an impious foe,
140 Impious and false, a light yet cruel race,
Who laugh away all virtue, mingling mirth
With deeds of murder; and still promising
Freedom, themselves too sensual to be free,
Poison life's amities, and cheat the heart
145 Of faith and quiet hope, and all that
    soothes,
And all that lifts the spirit! Stand we
    forth;
Render them back upon the insulted ocean,

And let them toss as idly on its waves
As the vile sea-weed, which some moun-
    tain-blast
150 Swept from our shores! And oh! may
    we return
Not with a drunken triumph, but with fear,
Repenting of the wrongs with which we
    stung
So fierce a foe to frenzy!

                  I have told,
O Britons, O my brethren! I have told
155 Most bitter truth, but without bitterness.
Nor deem my zeal or factious or mis-
    timed;
For never can true courage dwell with
    them,
Who, playing tricks with conscience, dare
    not look
At their own vices. We have been too long
160 Dupes of a deep delusion! Some, belike,
Groaning with restless enmity, expect
All change from change of constituted
    power;
As if a government had been a robe,
On which our vice and wretchedness were
    tagged
165 Like fancy-points and fringes, with the
    robe
Pulled off at pleasure. Fondly these attach
A radical causation to a few
Poor drudges of chastising Providence,
Who borrow all their hues and qualities
170 From our own folly and rank wickedness,
Which gave them birth and nursed them.
    Others, meanwhile,
Dote with a mad idolatry; and all
Who will not fall before their images,
And yield them worship, they are enemies
Even of their country!

               Such have I been deemed.—
175 But, O dear Britain! O my Mother Isle!
Needs must thou prove a name most dear
    and holy
To me, a son, a brother, and a friend,
A husband, and a father! who revere
180 All bonds of natural love, and find them all
Within the limits of thy rocky shores.
O native Britain! O my Mother Isle!
How shouldst thou prove aught else but
    dear and holy
To me, who from thy lakes and mountain-
    hills,
185 Thy clouds, thy quiet dales, thy rocks
    and seas,
Have drunk in all my intellectual life,
All sweet sensations, all ennobling
    thoughts,

All adoration of the God in nature,
All lovely and all honorable things,
190 Whatever makes this mortal spirit feel
The joy and greatness of its future being?
There lives nor form nor feeling in my soul
Unborrowed from my country! O divine
And beauteous Island! thou hast been my
　　sole
195 And most magnificent temple, in the which
I walk with awe, and sing my stately songs,
Loving the God that made me!—

　　　　　　　　　　May my fears,
My filial fears, be vain! and may the
　　vaunts
And menace of the vengeful enemy
200 Pass like the gust, that roared and died
　　away
In the distant tree: which heard, and only
　　heard
In this low dell, bowed not the delicate
　　grass.

　　But now the gentle dew-fall sends
　　abroad
The fruit-like perfume of the golden furze:
205 The light has left the summit of the hill,
Though still a sunny gleam lies beautiful,
Aslant the ivied beacon. Now farewell,
Farewell, awhile, O soft and silent spot!
On the green sheep-track, up the heathy
　　hill,
210 Homeward I wind my way; and lo! recalled
From bodings that have well-nigh wearied
　　me,
I find myself upon the brow, and pause
Startled! And after lonely sojourning
In such a quiet and surrounded nook,
215 This burst of prospect, here the shadowy
　　main,
Dim-tinted, there the mighty majesty
Of that huge amphitheatre of rich
And elmy fields, seems like society—
Conversing with the mind, and giving it
220 A livelier impulse and a dance of thought!
And now, belovèd Stowey! I behold
Thy church-tower, and, methinks, the four
　　huge elms
Clustering, which mark the mansion of my
　　friend;[1]
And close behind them, hidden from my
　　view,
225 Is my own lowly cottage, where my babe
And my babe's mother dwell in peace!
　　With light
And quickened footsteps thitherward I
　　tend,

[1] Thomas Poole.

Remembering thee, O green and silent
　　dell!
And grateful, that by nature's quietness
230 And solitary musings, all my heart
Is softened, and made worthy to indulge
Love, and the thoughts that yearn for
　　human kind.

THE NIGHTINGALE
1798　　　　1798

No cloud, no relique of the sunken day
Distinguishes the west, no long thin slip
Of sullen light, no obscure trembling hues.
Come, we will rest on this old mossy
　　bridge!
5 You see the glimmer of the stream be-
　　neath,
But hear no murmuring: it flows silently,
O'er its soft bed of verdure. All is still,
A balmy night! and though the stars be
　　dim,
Yet let us think upon the vernal showers
10 That gladden the green earth, and we shall
　　find
A pleasure in the dimness of the stars.
And hark! the Nightingale begins its song,
"Most musical, most melancholy"[1] bird!
A melancholy bird? Oh! idle thought!
15 In Nature there is nothing melancholy.
But some night-wandering man whose
　　heart was pierced
With the remembrance of a grievous
　　wrong,
Or slow distemper, or neglected love,
(And so, poor wretch! filled all things
　　with himself,
20 And made all gentle sounds tell back the
　　tale
Of his own sorrow) he, and such as he,
First named these notes a melancholy
　　strain.
And many a poet echoes the conceit;
Poet who hath been building up the rhyme
25 When he had better far have stretched his
　　limbs
Beside a brook in mossy forest-dell,
By sun or moon-light, to the influxes
Of shapes and sounds and shifting ele-
　　ments
Surrendering his whole spirit, of his song
30 And of his fame forgetful! so his fame
Should share in Nature's immortality,
A venerable thing! and so his song
Should make all Nature lovelier, and itself
Be loved like Nature! But 'twill not be so;
35 And youths and maidens most poetical,

[1] *Il Penseroso,* 61.

Who lose the deepening twilights of the
    spring
In ball-rooms and hot theatres, they still
Full of meek sympathy must heave their
    sighs
O'er Philomela's pity-pleading strains.

40 My friend, and thou, our sister![1] we have
    learnt
A different lore: we may not thus profane
Nature's sweet voices, always full of love
And joyance! 'Tis the merry Nightingale
That crowds, and hurries, and precipitates
45 With fast thick warble his delicious notes,
As he were fearful that an April night
Would be too short for him to utter forth
His love-chant, and disburthen his full soul
Of all its music!
        And I know a grove
50 Of large extent, hard by a castle huge,
Which the great lord inhabits not; and so
This grove is wild with tangling under-
    wood,
And the trim walks are broken up, and
    grass,
Thin grass and king-cups grow within the
    paths.
55 But never elsewhere in one place I knew
So many nightingales; and far and near,
In wood and thicket, over the wide grove,
They answer and provoke each other's
    song,
With skirmish and capricious passagings,
60 And murmurs musical and swift jug jug,
And one low piping sound more sweet
    than all—
Stirring the air with such a harmony,
That should you close your eyes, you
    might almost
Forget it was not day! On moonlight
    bushes,
65 Whose dewy leaflets are but half-disclosed,
You may perchance behold them on the
    twigs,
Their bright, bright eyes, their eyes both
    bright and full,
Glistening, while many a glow-worm in
    the shade
Lights up her love-torch.

        A most gentle maid,
70 Who dwelleth in her hospitable home
Hard by the castle, and at latest eve
(Even like a lady vowed and dedicate
To something more than Nature in the
    grove)
Glides through the pathways; she knows
    all their notes,

[1] Wordsworth and his sister Dorothy.

75 That gentle maid! and oft, a moment's
    space,
What time the moon was lost behind a
    cloud,
Hath heard a pause of silence; till the
    moon
Emerging, hath awakened earth and sky
With one sensation, and those wakeful
    birds
80 Have all burst forth in choral minstrelsy,
As if some sudden gale had swept at once
A hundred airy harps! And she hath
    watched
Many a nightingale perch giddily
On blossomy twig still swinging from the
    breeze,
85 And to that motion tune his wanton song
Like tipsy Joy that reels with tossing
    head.

Farewell, O Warbler! till tomorrow eve,
And you, my friends! farewell, a short
    farewell!
We have been loitering long and pleasantly,
90 And now for our dear homes. — That
    strain again![1]
Full fain it would delay me! My dear babe,
Who, capable of no articulate sound,
Mars all things with his imitative lisp,
How he would place his hand beside his
    ear,
95 His little hand, the small forefinger up,
And bid us listen! And I deem it wise
To make him Nature's play-mate. He
    knows well
The evening-star; and once, when he
    awoke
In most distressful mood (some inward
    pain
100 Had made up that strange thing, an in-
    fant's dream—)
I hurried with him to our orchard-plot,
And he beheld the moon, and, hushed at
    once,
Suspends his sobs, and laughs most silently,
While his fair eyes, that swam with un-
    dropped tears,
105 Did glitter in the yellow moon-beam!
    Well!—
It is a father's tale: But if that Heaven
Should give me life, his childhood shall
    grow up
Familiar with these songs, that with the
    night
He may associate joy.—Once more, fare-
    well,
110 Sweet Nightingale! once more, my friends!
    farewell.

[1] See *Twelfth Night*, I, 1, 1-7.

THE BALLAD OF THE DARK LADIE

A FRAGMENT
1798   1834

Beneath yon birch with silver bark,
And boughs so pendulous and fair,
The brook falls scatter'd down the rock:
And all is mossy there!

5 And there upon the moss she sits,
The Dark Ladié in silent pain;
The heavy tear is in her eye,
And drops and swells again.

Three times she sends her little page
10 Up the castled mountain's breast,
If he might find the Knight that wears
The Griffin for his crest.

The sun was sloping down the sky,
And she had linger'd there all day,
15 Counting moments, dreaming fears—
Oh wherefore can he stay?

She hears a rustling o'er the brook,
She sees far off a swinging bough!
"'Tis he! 'Tis my betrothéd Knight!
20   Lord Falkland, it is thou!"

She springs, she clasps him round the neck,
She sobs a thousand hopes and fears,
Her kisses glowing on his cheeks
She quenches with her tears.

* * * * * *

25 "My friends with rude ungentle words
They scoff and bid me fly to thee!
O give me shelter in thy breast!
O shield and shelter me!

"My Henry, I have given thee much,
30 I gave what I can ne'er recall,
I gave my heart, I gave my peace,
O Heaven! I gave thee all."

The Knight made answer to the maid,
While to his heart he held her hand,
35 "Nine castles hath my noble sire,
None statelier in the land.

"The fairest one shall be my love's,
The fairest castle of the nine!
Wait only till the stars peep out,
40   The fairest shall be thine:

"Wait only till the hand of eve
Hath wholly closed yon western bars,
And through the dark we two will steal
Beneath the twinkling stars!"—

45 The dark? the dark? No! not the dark?
The twinkling stars? How, Henry? How?
O God! 'twas in the eye of noon
He pledged his sacred vow!

"And in the eye of noon my love
50 Shall lead me from my mother's door,
Sweet boys and girls all clothed in white
Strewing flowers before:

"But first the nodding minstrels go
With music meet for lordly bowers,
55 The children next in snow-white vests,
Strewing buds and flowers!

"And then my love and I shall pace,
My jet black hair in pearly braids,
Between our comely bachelors
And blushing bridal maids."

* * * * * *

KUBLA KHAN

1798   1816

In Xanadu did Kubla Khan
A stately pleasure-dome decree:
Where Alph, the sacred river, ran
Through caverns measureless to man
5   Down to a sunless sea.
So twice five miles of fertile ground
With walls and towers were girdled round:
And there were gardens bright with sin-
uous rills,
Where blossomed many an incense-bearing
tree;
10 And here were forests ancient as the
hills,
Enfolding sunny spots of greenery.

But oh! that deep romantic chasm which
slanted
Down the green hill athwart a cedarn
cover!
A savage place! as holy and enchanted
15 As e'er beneath a waning moon was
haunted
By woman wailing for her demon-lover!
And from this chasm, with ceaseless turmoil seething,
As if this earth in fast thick pants were
breathing,
A mighty fountain momently was forced:
20 Amid whose swift half-intermitted burst
Huge fragments vaulted like rebounding
hail,
Or chaffy grain beneath the thresher's
flail:
And 'mid these dancing rocks at once and
ever

It flung up momently the sacred river.
25 Five miles meandering with a mazy motion
Through wood and dale the sacred river
        ran,
Then reached the caverns measureless to
        man,
And sank in tumult to a lifeless ocean:
And 'mid this tumult Kubla heard from
        far
30 Ancestral voices prophesying war!
    The shadow of the dome of pleasure
    Floated midway on the waves;
    Where was heard the mingled measure
    From the fountain and the caves.
35 It was a miracle of rare device,
    A sunny pleasure-dome with caves of ice!

    A damsel with a dulcimer *— muse of poetry*
    In a vision once I saw:
    It was an Abyssinian maid,
40 And on her dulcimer she played,
    Singing of Mount Abora.
    Could I revive within me
    Her symphony and song,
    To such a deep delight 'twould win me,
45 That with music loud and long,
    I would build that dome in air,
    That sunny dome! those caves of ice!
    And all who heard should see them there,
    And all should cry, Beware! Beware!
50 His flashing eyes, his floating hair!
    Weave a circle round him thrice,
    And close your eyes with holy dread,
    For he on honey-dew hath fed,
    And drunk the milk of Paradise.
        *   *   *   *   *   *
                any poet

LINES

WRITTEN IN THE ALBUM AT ELBINGERODE, IN
THE HARTZ FOREST
1799   1799

I stood on Brocken's sovran height, and
        saw
Woods crowding upon woods, hills over
        hills,
A surging scene, and only limited
By the blue distance. Heavily my way
5 Downward I dragged through fir groves
        evermore,
Where bright green moss heaves in sepul-
        chral forms
Speckled with sunshine; and, but seldom
        heard,
The sweet bird's song became a hollow
        sound;
And the breeze, murmuring indivisibly,
10 Preserved its solemn murmur most distinct
From many a note of many a waterfall,

And the brook's chatter; 'mid whose islet-
        stones
The dingy kidling with its tinkling bell
Leaped frolicsome, or old romantic goat
15 Sat, his white beard slow waving. I
        moved on
In low and languid mood: for I had found
That outward forms, the loftiest, still re-
        ceive
Their finer influence from the life with-
        in;—
Fair cyphers else: fair, but of import
        vague
20 Or unconcerning, where the heart not finds
History or prophecy of friend, or child,
Or gentle maid, our first and early love,
Or father, or the venerable name
Of our adoréd country! O thou Queen,
25 Thou delegated Deity of Earth,
O dear, dear England! how my longing
        eye
Turned westward, shaping in the steady
        clouds
Thy sands and high white cliffs!

                        My native land!
Filled with the thought of thee this heart
        was proud,
30 Yea, mine eye swam with tears: that all
        the view
From sovran Brocken, woods and woody
        hills,
Floated away, like a departing dream,
Feeble and dim! Stranger, these impulses
Blame thou not lightly; nor will I pro-
        fane,
35 With hasty judgment or injurious doubt,
That man's sublimer spirit, who can feel
That God is everywhere! the God who
        framed
Mankind to be one mighty family,
Himself our Father, and the world our
        home.

LOVE
1799   1799

All thoughts, all passions, all delights,
Whatever stirs this mortal frame,
All are but ministers of Love,
    And feed his sacred flame.

5 Oft in my waking dreams do I
Live o'er again that happy hour,
When midway on the mount I lay,
    Beside the ruined tower.

The moonshine, stealing o'er the scene
10 Had blended with the lights of eve;
And she was there, my hope, my joy,
    My own dear Genevieve!

She leant against the arméd man,
The statue of the arméd knight;
15 She stood and listened to my lay,
    Amid the lingering light.

Few sorrows hath she of her own,
My hope! my joy! my Genevieve!
She loves me best, whene'er I sing
20   The songs that make her grieve.

I played a soft and doleful air,
I sang an old and moving story—
An old rude song, that suited well
    That ruin wild and hoary.

25 She listened with a flitting blush,
With downcast eyes and modest grace;
For well she knew, I could not choose
    But gaze upon her face.

I told her of the Knight that wore
30 Upon his shield a burning brand;
And that for ten long years he wooed
    The Lady of the Land.

I told her how he pined: and ah!
The deep, the low, the pleading tone
35 With which I sang another's love,
    Interpreted my own.

She listened with a flitting blush,
With downcast eyes, and modest grace;
And she forgave me that I gazed
40   Too fondly on her face!

But when I told the cruel scorn
That crazed that bold and lovely Knight,
And that he crossed the mountain-woods,
    Nor rested day nor night;

45 That sometimes from the savage den,
And sometimes from the darksome shade,
And sometimes starting up at once
    In green and sunny glade,—

There came and looked him in the face
50 An angel beautiful and bright;
And that he knew it was a fiend,
    This miserable Knight!

And that unknowing what he did,
He leaped amid a murderous band,
55 And saved from outrage worse than death
    The Lady of the Land!

And how she wept, and clasped his knees;
And how she tended him in vain—
And ever strove to expiate
60   The scorn that crazed his brain;—

And that she nursed him in a cave;
And how his madness went away,
When on the yellow forest-leaves
    A dying man he lay;—

65 His dying words—but when I reached
That tenderest strain of all the ditty,
My faltering voice and pausing harp
    Disturbed her soul with pity!

All impulses of soul and sense
70 Had thrilled my guileless Genevieve;
The music and the doleful tale,
    The rich and balmy eve;

And hopes, and fears that kindle hope,
An undistinguishable throng,
75 And gentle wishes long subdued,
    Subdued and cherished long!

She wept with pity and delight,
She blushed with love, and virgin-shame;
And like the murmur of a dream,
80   I heard her breathe my name.

Her bosom heaved—she stepped aside,
As conscious of my look she stepped—
Then suddenly, with timorous eye
    She fled to me and wept.

85 She half enclosed me with her arms,
She pressed me with a meek embrace;
And bending back her head, looked up,
    And gazed upon my face.

'Twas partly love, and partly fear,
90 And partly 'twas a bashful art,
That I might rather feel, than see,
    The swelling of her heart.

I calmed her fears, and she was calm,
And told her love with virgin pride;
95 And so I won my Genevieve,
    My bright and beauteous bride.

DEJECTION: AN ODE
1802   1802

Late, late yestreen I saw the new Moon,
With the old Moon in her arms:
And I fear, I fear, my Master dear!
We shall have a deadly storm.
    Ballad of Sir Patrick Spence.

Well! If the bard was weather-wise, who
    made
The grand old ballad of *Sir Patrick
    Spence,*
This night, so tranquil now, will not go
    hence
Unroused by winds, that ply a busier trade

⁵ Than those which mould yon cloud in lazy
    flakes,
Or the dull sobbing draft, that moans and
    rakes
Upon the strings of this Æolian lute,
    Which better far were mute.
    For lo! the New-moon winter-bright!
¹⁰ And overspread with phantom light,
    (With swimming phantom light o'er-
      spread
    But rimmed and circled by a silver
      thread)
I see the old Moon in her lap, foretelling
    The coming-on of rain and squally blast.
¹⁵ And oh! that even now the gust were
    swelling,
    And the slant night-shower driving loud
      and fast!
Those sounds which oft have raised me,
    whilst they awed,
    And sent my soul abroad,
Might now perhaps their wonted impulse
    give,
²⁰ Might startle this dull pain, and make it
    move and live!

A grief without a pang, void, dark, and
    drear,
    A stifled, drowsy, unimpassioned grief,
    Which finds no natural outlet, no relief,
      In word, or sigh, or tear—
²⁵ O Lady! in this wan and heartless mood,
To other thoughts by yonder throstle woo'd,
    All this long eve, so balmy and serene,
Have I been gazing on the western sky,
    And its peculiar tint of yellow green:
³⁰ And still I gaze—and with how blank an
    eye!
And those thin clouds above, in flakes and
    bars,
That give away their motion to the stars;
Those stars, that glide behind them or
    between,
Now sparkling, now bedimmed, but always
    seen:
³⁵ Yon crescent Moon, as fixed as if it grew
In its own cloudless, starless lake of blue;
I see them all so excellently fair,
I see, not feel, how beautiful they are!

    My genial spirits fail;
⁴⁰   And what can these avail
To lift the smothering weight from off my
    breast?
    It were a vain endeavor,
    Though I should gaze forever
On that green light that lingers in the west:
⁴⁵ I may not hope from outward forms to win
The passion and the life, whose fountains
    are within.

O Lady! we receive but what we give,
And in our life alone does Nature live:
Ours is her wedding garment, ours her
    shroud!
⁵⁰   And would we aught behold, of higher
    worth,
Than that inanimate cold world allowed
To the poor loveless ever-anxious crowd,
    Ah! from the soul itself must issue forth
A light, a glory, a fair luminous cloud
⁵⁵   Enveloping the earth—
And from the soul itself must there be sent
    A sweet and potent voice, of its own
    birth,
Of all sweet sounds the life and element!

O pure of heart! thou need'st not ask of
    me
⁶⁰ What this strong music in the soul may
    be!
What, and wherein it doth exist,
This light, this glory, this fair luminous
    mist,
This beautiful and beauty-making power.
    Joy, virtuous Lady! Joy that ne'er was
    given,
⁶⁵ Save to the pure, and in their purest hour,
Life, and life's effluence, cloud at once
    and shower,
Joy, Lady! is the spirit and the power,
Which wedding Nature to us gives in dower
    A new earth and new heaven,
⁷⁰ Undreamt of by the sensual and the
    proud—
Joy is the sweet voice, Joy the luminous
    cloud—
    We in ourselves rejoice!
And thence flows all that charms or ear
    or sight,
All melodies the echoes of that voice,
⁷⁵ All colors a suffusion from that light.

There was a time when, though my path
    was rough,
This joy within me dallied with distress,
And all misfortunes were but as the stuff
    Whence Fancy made me dreams of
    happiness:
⁸⁰ For hope grew round me, like the twining
    vine,
And fruits, and foliage, not my own,
    seemed mine.
But now afflictions bow me down to earth:
Nor care I that they rob me of my mirth;
    But oh! each visitation
⁸⁵ Suspends what nature gave me at my
    birth,
    My shaping spirit of Imagination.
For not to think of what I needs must feel,
    But to be still and patient, all I can;

And haply by abstruse research to steal
90 　From my own nature all the natural
　　　man—
　This was my sole resource, my only
　　　plan:
　Till that which suits a part infects the
　　　whole,
　And now is almost grown the habit of my
　　　soul.

Hence, viper thoughts, that coil around
　　　my mind,
95 　　Reality's dark dream!
I turn from you, and listen to the wind,
　Which long has raved unnoticed.　What
　　　a scream
Of agony by torture lengthened out
That lute sent forth!　Thou Wind, that
　　　rav'st without,
100 Bare crag, or mountain-tairn, or blasted
　　　tree,
　Or pine-grove whither woodman never
　　　clomb,
　Or lonely house, long held the witches'
　　　home,
　　Methinks were fitter instruments for
　　　thee,
　Mad lutanist! who in this month of
　　　showers,
105 Of dark-brown gardens, and of peeping
　　　flowers,
　Mak'st Devils' yule, with worse than win-
　　　try song,
　The blossoms, buds, and timorous leaves
　　　among.
　　Thou actor, perfect in all tragic sounds!
　　Thou mighty poet, e'en to frenzy bold!
110 　　What tell'st thou now about?
　　'Tis of the rushing of an host in rout,
　With groans, of trampled men, with
　　　smarting wounds—
　At once they groan with pain, and shud-
　　　der with the cold!
　But hush! there is a pause of deepest
　　　silence!
115 And all that noise, as of a rushing
　　　crowd,
　With groans, and tremulous shudderings—
　　　all is over—
　It tells another tale, with sounds less
　　　deep and loud!
　　A tale of less affright,
　　And tempered with delight,
120 As Otway's self had framed the tender
　　　lay,—
　　'Tis of a little child
　　Upon a lonesome wild,
　Not far from home, but she hath lost her
　　　way:

And now moans low in bitter grief and
　　　fear,
125 And now screams loud, and hopes to make
　　　her mother hear.[1]

'Tis midnight, but small thoughts have I
　　　of sleep:
Full seldom may my friend such vigils
　　　keep!
Visit her, gentle Sleep! with wings of
　　　healing,
　And may this storm be but a mountain-
　　　birth,
130 May all the stars hang bright above her
　　　dwelling,
　Silent as though they watched the sleep-
　　　ing earth!
　　With light heart may she rise,
　　Gay fancy, cheerful eyes,
　Joy lift her spirit, joy attune her voice;
135 To her may all things live, from pole to
　　　pole,
　Their life the eddying of her living soul!
　O simple spirit, guided from above,
　Dear Lady! friend devoutest of my choice,
Thus mayest thou ever, evermore rejoice.

HYMN BEFORE SUNRISE, IN THE VALE OF CHAMOUNI
1802　　　　1802

Hast thou a charm to stay the morning-star
In his steep course? So long he seems to
　　　pause
On thy bald awful head, O sovran Blanc,
The Arve and Arveiron at thy base
5 Rave ceaselessly; but thou, most awful
　　　Form!
Risest from forth thy silent sea of pines,
How silently! Around thee and above
Deep is the air and dark, substantial, black,
An ebon mass: methinks thou piercest it,
10 As with a wedge! But when I look again,
It is thine own calm home, thy crystal
　　　shrine,
Thy habitation from eternity!
O dread and silent Mount! I gazed upon
　　　thee,
Till thou, still present to the bodily sense,
15 Didst vanish from my thought: entranced
　　　in prayer
I worshipped the Invisible alone.

　Yet, like some sweet beguiling melody,
So sweet, we know not we are listening
　　　to it,

[1] A reference to Wordsworth's *Lucy Gray*. In
the first version of the poem, "William's" appeared in l. 120 instead of "Otway's."

Thou, the meanwhile, wast blending with
    my thought,
20 Yea, with my life and life's own secret joy:
Till the dilating Soul, enrapt, transfused,
Into the mighty vision passing—there
As in her natural form, swelled vast to
    Heaven!

    Awake, my soul! not only passive praise
25 Thou owest! not alone these swelling tears,
Mute thanks and secret ecstasy! Awake,
Voice of sweet song! Awake, my heart,
    awake!
Green vales and icy cliffs, all join my
    hymn.

    Thou first and chief, sole sovereign of
    the Vale!
30 O struggling with the darkness all the
    night,
And visited all night by troops of stars,
Or when they climb the sky or when they
    sink:
Companion of the morning-star at dawn,
Thyself Earth's rosy star, and of the
    dawn
35 Co-herald: wake, O wake, and utter praise!
Who sank thy sunless pillars deep in
    Earth?
Who filled thy countenance with rosy
    light?
Who made thee parent of perpetual
    streams?

    And you, ye five wild torrents fiercely
    glad!
40 Who called you forth from night and
    utter death,
From dark and icy caverns called you
    forth,
Down those precipitous, black, jaggéd
    rocks,
Forever shattered and the same forever?
Who gave you your invulnerable life,
45 Your strength, your speed, your fury, and
    your joy,
Unceasing thunder and eternal foam?
And who commanded (and the silence
    came),
Here let the billows stiffen, and have rest?

    Ye ice-falls! ye that from the moun-
    tain's brow
50 Adown enormous ravines slope amain—
Torrents, methinks, that heard a mighty
    voice,
And stopped at once amid their maddest
    plunge!
Motionless torrents! silent cataracts!

Who made you glorious as the gates of
    Heaven
55 Beneath the keen full moon? Who bade
    the sun
Clothe you with rainbows? Who, with
    living flowers
Of loveliest blue, spread garlands at your
    feet?—
God! let the torrents, like a shout of
    nations,
Answer! and let the ice-plains echo, God!
60 God! sing ye meadow-streams with glad-
    some voice!
Ye pine-groves, with your soft and soul-
    like sounds!
And they too have a voice, yon piles of
    snow,
And in their perilous fall shall thunder,
    God!

    Ye living flowers that skirt the eternal
    frost!
65 Ye wild goats sporting round the eagle's
    nest!
Ye eagles, play-mates of the mountain-
    storm!
Ye lightnings, the dread arrows of the
    clouds!
Ye signs and wonders of the element!
Utter forth God, and fill the hills with
    praise!

70   Thou too, hoar Mount! with thy sky-
    pointing peaks,
Oft from whose feet the avalanche, un-
    heard,
Shoots downward, glittering through the
    pure serene
Into the depth of clouds, that veil thy
    breast—
Thou too again, stupendous Mountain!
    thou
75 That as I raise my head, awhile bowed
    low
In adoration, upward from thy base
Slow travelling with dim eyes suffused
    with tears,
Solemnly seemest, like a vapory cloud,
To rise before me—Rise, O ever rise,
80 Rise like a cloud of incense from the
    Earth!
Thou kingly Spirit throned among the
    hills,
Thou dread ambassador from Earth to
    Heaven,
Great Hierarch! tell thou the silent sky,
And tell the stars, and tell yon rising sun
85 Earth, with her thousand voices, praises
    God.

INSCRIPTION FOR A FOUNTAIN ON A HEATH
1802 1802

This sycamore, oft musical with bees,
Such tents the patriarchs loved. O long
unharmed
May all its agèd boughs o'er-canopy
The small round basin, which this jutting
stone
5 Keeps pure from falling leaves. Long
may the spring,
Quietly as a sleeping infant's breath,
Send up cold waters to the traveller
With soft and even pulse; nor ever
cease
Yon tiny cone of sand its soundless
dance,
10 Which at the bottom, like a fairy's
page,
As merry and no taller, dances still,
Nor wrinkles the smooth surface of the
fount.
Here twilight is, and coolness; here is
moss,
A soft seat, and a deep and ample shade.
15 Thou may'st toil far and find no second
tree.
Drink, pilgrim, here! Here rest! And if
thy heart
Be innocent, here too shalt thou refresh
Thy spirit, listening to some gentle sound,
Or passing gale or hum of murmuring
bees.

ANSWER TO A CHILD'S QUESTION
1802 1802

Do you ask what the birds say? The
Sparrow, the Dove,
The Linnet and Thrush say, "I love and
I love!"
In the winter they're silent—the wind is
so strong;
What it says, I don't know, but it sings a
loud song.
5 But green leaves, and blossoms, and sunny
warm weather,
And singing, and loving—all come back
together.
But the Lark is so brimful of gladness
and love,
The green fields below him, the blue sky
above,
That he sings, and he sings; and forever
sings he—
10 "I love my Love, and my Love loves
me!"

THE PAINS OF SLEEP
1803 1816

Ere on my bed my limbs I lay,
It hath not been my use to pray
With moving lips or bended knees;
But silently, by slow degrees,
5 My spirit I to Love compose,
In humble trust mine eye-lids close,
With reverential resignation,
No wish conceived, no thought exprest,
Only a sense of supplication;
10 A sense o'er all my soul imprest
That I am weak, yet not unblest,
Since in me, round me, everywhere
Eternal Strength and Wisdom are.

But yester-night I prayed aloud
15 In anguish and in agony,
Up-starting from the fiendish crowd
Of shapes and thoughts that tortured me
A lurid light, a trampling throng,
Sense of intolerable wrong,
20 And whom I scorned, those only strong!
Thirst of revenge, the powerless will
Still baffled, and yet burning still!
Desire with loathing strangely mixed
On wild or hateful objects fixed.
25 Fantastic passions! maddening brawl!
And shame and terror over all!
Deeds to be hid which were not hid,
Which all confused I could not know
Whether I suffered, or I did:
30 For all seemed guilt, remorse, or woe,
My own or other still the same
Life-stifling fear, soul-stifling shame.

So two nights passed: the night's dis-
may
Saddened and stunned the coming day.
35 Sleep, the wide blessing, seemed to me
Distemper's worst calamity.
The third night, when my own loud
scream
Had waked me from the fiendish dream,
O'ercome with sufferings strange and
wild,
40 I wept as I had been a child;
And having thus by tears subdued
My anguish to a milder mood,
Such punishments, I said, were due
To natures deepliest stained with sin,—
45 For aye entempesting anew
The unfathomable hell within,
The horror of their deeds to view,
To know and loathe, yet wish and do!
Such griefs with such men well agree,
50 But wherefore, wherefore fall on me?
To be beloved is all I need,
And whom I love, I love indeed.

TO A GENTLEMAN[1]
COMPOSED ON THE NIGHT AFTER HIS RECI-
TATION OF A POEM ON THE GROWTH
OF AN INDIVIDUAL MIND
1806 1817

Friend of the wise! and teacher of the
    good!
Into my heart have I received that lay
More than historic, that prophetic lay
Wherein (high theme by thee first sung
    aright)
5 Of the foundations and the building up
Of a human spirit thou hast dared to tell
What may be told, to the understanding
    mind
Revealable; and what within the mind
By vital breathings secret as the soul
10 Of vernal growth, oft quickens in the heart
Thoughts all too deep for words![2]—

           Theme hard as high!
Of smiles spontaneous, and mysterious
    fears
(The first-born they of Reason and twin-
    birth),
Of tides obedient to external force,
15 And currents self-determined, as might
    seem,
Or by some inner Power; of moments
    awful,
Now in thy inner life, and now abroad,
When power streamed from thee, and thy
    soul received
The light reflected, as a light bestowed—
20 Of fancies fair, and milder hours of youth,
Hyblean[3] murmurs of poetic thought
Industrious in its joy, in vales and glens
Native or outland, lakes and famous hills!
Or on the lonely high-road, when the stars
25 Were rising; or by secret mountain-
    streams,
The guides and the companions of thy
    way!

Of more than Fancy, of the Social Sense
Distending wide, and man beloved as man,
Where France in all her towns lay vibrating
30 Like some becalmèd bark beneath the burst
Of Heaven's immediate thunder, when no
    cloud
Is visible, or shadow on the main.
For thou wert there, thine own brows gar-
    landed,
Amid the tremor of a realm aglow,
35 Amid a mighty nation jubilant,

[1] Wordsworth. The poem referred to in the sub-
    title is *The Prelude*.
[2] See Wordsworth's *Ode: Intimations of Im-
    mortality*, 200-4 (p. 331).
[3] smooth; sweet (Hybla was an ancient town of
    Sicily famous for its honey.)

When from the general heart of human
    kind
Hope sprang forth like a full-born Deity!
——Of that dear Hope afflicted and
    struck down,
So summoned homeward, thenceforth calm
    and sure
40 From the dread watch-tower of man's
    absolute self,
With light unwaning on her eyes, to look
Far on—herself a glory to behold,
The Angel of the vision! Then (last
    strain)
Of Duty, chosen Laws controlling choice,
45 Action and joy!—An Orphic[1] song indeed,
A song divine of high and passionate
    thoughts
To their own music chanted!

           O great bard!
Ere yet that last strain dying awed the air,
With stedfast eye I viewed thee in the
    choir
50 Of ever-enduring men. The truly great
Have all one age, and from one visible
    space
Shed influence! They, both in power and
    act,
Are permanent, and Time is not with them,
Save as it worketh for them, they in it.
55 Nor less a sacred roll, than those of old,
And to be placed, as they, with gradual
    fame
Among the archives of mankind, thy work
Makes audible a linkèd lay of Truth,
Of Truth profound a sweet continuous lay,
60 Not learnt, but native, her own natural
    notes!
Ah! as I listened with a heart forlorn,
The pulses of my being beat anew:
And even as life returns upon the
    drowned,
Life's joy rekindling roused a throng of
    pains—
65 Keen pangs of Love, awakening as a babe
Turbulent, with an outcry in the heart;
And fears self-willed, that shunned the
    eye of Hope;
And Hope that scarce would know itself
    from Fear;
Sense of past Youth, and Manhood come
    in vain,
70 And Genius given, and Knowledge won
    in vain;
And all which I had culled in wood-walks
    wild,
And all which patient toil had reared, and
    all,

[1] entrancing, like the music ascribed to Orpheus

Commune with thee had opened out—but flowers
Strewed on my corse, and borne upon my bier
75 In the same coffin, for the self-same grave!

    That way no more! and ill beseems it me,
Who came a welcomer in herald's guise,
Singing of Glory, and Futurity,
To wander back on such unhealthful road,
80 Plucking the poisons of self-harm! And ill
Such intertwine beseems triumphal wreaths
Strew'd before thy advancing!

              Nor do thou,
Sage bard! impair the memory of that hour
Of thy communion with my nobler mind
85 By pity or grief, already felt too long!
Nor let my words import more blame than needs.
The tumult rose and ceased: for Peace is nigh
Where Wisdom's voice has found a listening heart.
Amid the howl of more than wintry storms,
90 The halcyon[1] hears the voice of vernal hours
Already on the wing.

           Eve following eve,
Dear tranquil time, when the sweet sense of home
Is sweetest! moments for their own sake hailed
And more desired, more precious, for thy song,
95 In silence listening, like a devout child,
My soul lay passive, by thy various strain
Driven as in surges now beneath the stars,
With momentary stars of my own birth,
Fair constellated foam, still darting off
100 Into the darkness; now a tranquil sea,
Outspread and bright, yet swelling to the moon.

And when—O friend! my comforter and guide!
Strong in thyself, and powerful to give strength!—
Thy long sustainéd song finally closed,
105 And thy deep voice had ceased—yet thou thyself
Wert still before my eyes, and round us both

---

[1] A bird which was fabled to nest at sea about the time of the winter solstice.

That happy vision of belovéd faces—
Scarce conscious, and yet conscious of its close
I sate, my being blended in one thought
110 (Thought was it? or aspiration? or resolve?)
Absorbed, yet hanging still upon the sound—
And when I rose, I found myself in prayer.

TIME REAL AND IMAGINARY

AN ALLEGORY
1812 (?)   1817

On the wide level of a mountain's head,
(I knew not where, but 'twas some faery place)
Their pinions, ostrich-like, for sails outspread,
Two lovely children run an endless race,
5   A sister and a brother!
   This far outstript the other;
Yet ever runs she with reverted face,
And looks and listens for the boy behind:
   For he, alas! is blind!
10 O'er rough and smooth with even step he passed,
And knows not whether he be first or last.

From REMORSE

HEAR, SWEET SPIRIT, HEAR THE SPELL
1812   1813

Hear, sweet spirit, hear the spell,
Lest a blacker charm compel!
So shall the midnight breezes swell
With thy deep long-lingering knell.

5 And at evening evermore,
In a chapel on the shore,
Shall the chanters sad and saintly,
Yellow tapers burning faintly,
Doleful masses chant for thee,
10 *Miserere Domine!*[1]

Hark! the cadence dies away
  On the quiet moonlight sea:
The boatmen rest their oars and say,
Miserere Domine!

               Act III, 1, 69-82.

From ZAPOLYA

A SUNNY SHAFT DID I BEHOLD
1815   1817

A sunny shaft did I behold,
  From sky to earth it slanted:
And poised therein a bird so bold—
  Sweet bird, thou wert enchanted!

[1] Lord, have mercy

5 He sank, he rose, he twinkled, he trolled
   Within that shaft of sunny mist;
His eyes of fire, his beak of gold,
   All else of amethyst!

And thus he sang: "Adieu! adieu!
10 Love's dreams prove seldom true.
The blossoms they make no delay:
The sparkling dew-drops will not stay.
   Sweet month of May,
     We must away;
15   Far, far away!
       Today! today!"

               Act II, 1, 65-80.

THE KNIGHT'S TOMB
1817 (?)   1834

Where is the grave of Sir Arthur
   O'Kellyn?
Where may the grave of that good man
   be?—
By the side of a spring, on the breast of
   Helvellyn,
Under the twigs of a young birch tree!
5 The oak that in summer was sweet to hear,
And rustled its leaves in the fall of the
   year,
And whistled and roared in the winter
   alone,
Is gone,—and the birch in its stead is
   grown.—
The Knight's bones are dust,
10 And his good sword rust;—
His soul is with the saints, I trust.

TO NATURE
1820 (?)   1836

It may indeed be phantasy, when I
   Essay to draw from all created things
   Deep, heartfelt, inward joy that closely
      clings;
And trace in leaves and flowers that round
   me lie
5 Lessons of love and earnest piety.
   So let it be; and if the wide world
      rings
   In mock of this belief, it brings
Nor fear, nor grief, nor vain perplexity.
So will I build my altar in the fields,
10   And the blue sky my fretted dome
      shall be,
   And the sweet fragrance that the wild
      flower yields
   Shall be the incense I will yield to Thee,
Thee only God! and Thou shalt not de-
      spise
Even me, the priest of this poor sacrifice.

YOUTH AND AGE
1823-32   1828-32

Verse, a breeze mid blossoms straying,
Where Hope clung feeding, like a bee—
Both were mine! Life went a-maying
   With Nature, Hope and Poesy,
5   When I was young!

When I was young?—Ah, woful When!
Ah! for the change 'twixt Now and Then!
This breathing house not built with hands,[1]
This body that does me grievous wrong,
10 O'er aery cliffs and glittering sands,
How lightly *then* it flashed along:—
Like those trim skiffs, unknown of yore,
On winding lakes and rivers wide,
That ask no aid of sail or oar,
15 That fear no spite of wind or tide!
Nought cared this body for wind or weather
When Youth and I lived in't together.

Flowers are lovely; love is flower-like;
Friendship is a sheltering tree;
20 O! the joys, that came down shower-
   like,
Of friendship, love, and liberty,
       Ere I was old!

Ere I was old? Ah, woful Ere,
Which tells me, Youth's no longer here!
25 O Youth! for years so many and sweet,
'Tis known that thou and I were one,
I'll think it but a fond conceit—
It cannot be that thou art gone!
Thy vesper-bell hath not yet toll'd:—
30 And thou wert aye a masker bold!
What strange disguise hast now put on,
To make believe that thou art gone?
I see these locks in silvery slips,
This drooping gait, this altered size:
35 But spring-tide blossoms on thy lips,
And tears take sunshine from thine eyes!
Life is but thought: so think I will
That Youth and I are house-mates still.

Dew-drops are the gems of morning,
40 But the tears of mournful eve!
Where no hope is, life's a warning
That only serves to make us grieve,
      When we are old:

That only serves to make us grieve
45 With oft and tedious taking-leave,
Like some poor nigh-related guest,
That may not rudely be dismist;
Yet hath outstay'd his welcome while,
And tells the jest without the smile.

[1] See *2 Corinthians,* 5:1.

WORK WITHOUT HOPE
1825　　*1828*

All Nature seems at work. Slugs leave
　　their lair—
The bees are stirring—birds are on the
　　wing—
And Winter slumbering in the open air,
Wears on his smiling face a dream of
　　Spring!
5 And I the while, the sole unbusy thing,
Nor honey make, nor pair, nor build, nor
　　sing.

Yet well I ken the banks where ama-
　　ranths blow,
Have traced the fount whence streams of
　　nectar flow.
Bloom, O ye amaranths! bloom for whom
　　ye may,
10 For me ye bloom not! Glide, rich streams,
　　away!
With lips unbrightened, wreathless brow,
　　I stroll:
And would you learn the spells that
　　drowse my soul?
Work without Hope draws nectar in a
　　sieve,
And Hope without an object cannot live.

THE GARDEN OF BOCCACCIO
1828　　*1829*

Of late, in one of those most weary hours,
When life seems emptied of all genial
　　powers,
A dreary mood, which he who ne'er has
　　known
May bless his happy lot, I sate alone;
5 And, from the numbing spell to win relief,
Call'd on the Past for thought of glee or
　　grief.
In vain! bereft alike of grief and glee,
I sate and cow'r'd o'er my own vacancy!
And as I watch'd the dull continuous
　　ache,
10 Which, all else slumb'ring, seemed alone to
　　wake;
O friend![1] long wont to notice yet conceal,
And soothe by silence what words cannot
　　heal,
I but half saw that quiet hand of thine
Place on my desk this exquisite design.[2]
15 Boccaccio's Garden and its faery,
The love, the joyaunce, and the gallantry!
An idyll, with Boccaccio's spirit warm,
Framed in the silent poesy of form.

[1] Mrs. Gillman. Coleridge spent the later years
of his life at the home of the Gillmans.
[2] Stothard's engraving, *The Garden of Boccaccio.*

Like flocks adown a newly-bathéd steep
20 　Emerging from a mist: or like a stream
Of music soft that not dispels the sleep,
　　But casts in happier moulds the slum-
　　berer's dream,
Gazed by an idle eye with silent might
The picture stole upon my inward sight.
25 A tremulous warmth crept gradual o'er
　　my chest,
As though an infant's finger touch'd my
　　breast.
And one by one (I know not whence)
　　were brought
All spirits of power that most had stirr'd
　　my thought
In selfless boyhood, on a new world tost
30 Of wonder, and in its own fancies lost;
Or charm'd my youth, that, kindled from
　　above,
Loved ere it loved, and sought a form for
　　love;
Or lent a lustre to the earnest scan
Of manhood, musing what and whence is
　　man!
35 Wild strain of scalds,[1] that in the sea-
　　worn caves
Rehearsed their war-spell to the winds
　　and waves;
Or fateful hymn of those prophetic
　　maids,[2]
That call'd on Hertha in deep forest
　　glades;
Or minstrel lay, that cheer'd the baron's
　　feast;
40 Or rhyme of city pomp, of monk and
　　priest,
Judge, mayor, and many a guild in long
　　array,
To high-church pacing on the great saint's
　　day:
And many a verse which to myself I sang,
That woke the tear, yet stole away the pang
45 Of hopes, which in lamenting I renew'd:
And last, a matron now, of sober mien,
Yet radiant still and with no earthly sheen,
Whom as a faery child my childhood woo'd
Even in my dawn of thought—Philosophy;
50 Though then unconscious of herself,
　　pardie,[3]
She bore no other name than Poesy;
And, like a gift from Heaven, in lifeful
　　glee,
That had but newly left a mother's knee,
Prattled and play'd with bird and flower,
　　and stone,
55 As if with elfin playfellows well known,
And life reveal'd to innocence alone.

[1] Norse singers of heroic songs.
[2] The Scandinavian norns, or Sisters of Destiny.
[3] certainly (originally an oath, *par Dieu*, by God)

Thanks, gentle artist! now I can descry
Thy fair creation with a mastering eye,
And all awake! And now in fix'd gaze
   stand,
60 Now wander through the Eden of thy
   hand;
Praise the green arches, on the fountain
   clear
See fragment shadows of the crossing
   deer;
And with that serviceable nymph I stoop,
The crystal, from its restless pool, to
   scoop.
65 I see no longer! I myself am there,
Sit on the ground-sward, and the banquet
   share.
'Tis I, that sweep that lute's love-echoing
   strings,
And gaze upon the maid who gazing
   sings:
Or pause and listen to the tinkling bells
70 From the high tower, and think that there
   she dwells.
With old Boccaccio's soul I stand possest,
And breathe an air like life, that swells
   my chest.
The brightness of the world, O thou once
   free,
And always fair, rare land of courtesy!
75 O Florence! with the Tuscan fields and
   hills
And famous Arno, fed with all their
   rills;
Thou brightest star of star-bright Italy!
Rich, ornate, populous,— all treasures
   thine,
The golden corn, the olive, and the vine.
80 Fair cities, gallant mansions, castles old,
And forests, where beside his leafy hold
The sullen boar hath heard the distant
   horn,
And whets his tusks against the gnarléd
   thorn;
Palladian[1] palace with its storied halls;
85 Fountains, where Love lies listening to
   their falls;
Gardens, where flings the bridge its airy
   span,
And Nature makes her happy home with
   man;
Where many a gorgeous flower is duly
   fed
With its own rill, on its own spangled
   bed,
90 And wreathes the marble urn, or leans its
   head,
A mimic mourner, that with veil withdrawn

[1] See Glossary of Proper Names, p. 1499.

Weeps liquid gems, the presents of the
   dawn;—
Thine all delights, and every muse is
   thine;
And more than all, the embrace and
   intertwine
95 Of all with all in gay and twinkling
   dance!
Mid gods of Greece and warriors of romance,
See! Boccace sits, unfolding on his knees
The new-found roll of old Mæonides;[1]
But from his mantle's fold, and near the
   heart,
100 Peers Ovid's Holy Book of Love's sweet
   smart![2]

O all-enjoying and all-blending sage,
Long be it mine to con thy mazy page,
Where, half conceal'd, the eye of fancy
   views
Fauns, nymphs, and wingéd saints, all
   gracious to thy muse!

105 Still in thy garden let me watch their
   pranks,
And see in Dian's vest between the ranks
Of the trim vines, some maid that half
   believes
The vestal fires, of which her lover grieves,
With that sly satyr peeping through the
   leaves!

PHANTOM OR FACT

A DIALOGUE IN VERSE
1830   1834

AUTHOR

A lovely form there sate beside my bed,
And such a feeding calm its presence
   shed,
A tender love so pure from earthly leaven,
That I unnethe[3] the fancy might control,
5 'Twas my own spirit newly come from
   heaven,
Wooing its gentle way into my soul!
But ah! the change—It had not stirr'd,
   and yet—
Alas! that change how fain would I forget!
That shrinking back, like one that had
   mistook!
10 That weary, wandering, disavowing look!

[1] "Boccaccio claimed for himself the glory of having first introduced the works of Homer to his countrymen."—Coleridge.
[2] The *Amores*.
[3] with difficulty

'Twas all another, feature, look, and
frame,
And still, methought, **I knew it** was the
same!

FRIEND

This riddling tale, to what does it belong?
Is't history? vision? or an idle song?
15 Or rather say at once, within what space
Of time this wild disastrous change took
place?

AUTHOR

Call it a moment's work (and such it
seems)
This tale's a fragment from the life of
dreams;
But say, that years matur'd the silent
strife,
20 And 'tis a record from the dream of life.

EPITAPH
1833   1834

Stop, Christian passer-by!—Stop, child
of God,
And read with gentle breast. Beneath this
sod
A poet lies, or that which once seem'd he.
O, lift one thought in prayer for S. T. C.;
5 That he who many a year with toil of
breath
Found death in life, may here find life in
death!
Mercy for praise—to be forgiven for fame
He ask'd, and hoped, through Christ. Do
thou the same!

THE WANDERINGS OF CAIN
1798   1828
CANTO II

"A little further, O my father, yet a little
further, and we shall come into the open
moonlight." Their road was through a
forest of fir-trees; at its entrance the trees
stood at distances from each other, and the
path was broad, and the moonlight and the
moonlight shadows reposed upon it, and
appeared quietly to inhabit that solitude.
But soon the path winded and became narrow; the sun at high noon sometimes
speckled, but never illumined it, and now
it was dark as a cavern.

"It is dark, O my father!" said Enos,
"but the path under our feet is smooth
and soft, and we shall soon come out into
the open moonlight."

"Lead on, my child!" said Cain, "guide
me, little child!" And the innocent little
child clasped a finger of the hand which
had murdered the righteous Abel, and he
guided his father. "The fir branches drip
5 upon thee, my son." "Yea, pleasantly,
father, for I ran fast and eagerly to bring
thee the pitcher and the cake, and my body
is not yet cool. How happy the squirrels
are that feed on these fir-trees! they leap
10 from bough to bough, and the old squirrels play round their young ones in the
nest. I clomb a tree yesterday at noon, O
my father, that I might play with them,
but they leaped away from the branches,
15 even to the slender twigs did they leap,
and in a moment I beheld them on another
tree. Why, O my father, would they not
play with me? I would be good to them
as thou art good to me: and I groaned to
20 them even as thou groanest when thou
givest me to eat, and when thou coverest
me at evening, and as often as I stand at
thy knee and thine eyes look at me."
Then Cain stopped, and stifling his groans
25 he sank to the earth, and the child Enos
stood in the darkness beside him.

And Cain lifted up his voice and cried
bitterly, and said, "The Mighty One that
persecuteth me is on this side and on that;
30 he pursueth my soul like the wind, like the
sand-blast he passeth through me; he is
around me even as the air! O that I might
be utterly no more! I desire to die—yea,
the things that never had life, neither move
35 they upon the earth—behold! they seem
precious to mine eyes. O that a man might
live without the breath of his nostrils. So
I might abide in darkness, and blackness,
and an empty space! Yea, I would lie
40 down, I would not rise, neither would I
stir my limbs till I became as the rock in
the den of the lion, on which the young lion
resteth his head whilst he sleepeth. For
the torrent that roareth far off hath a
45 voice: and the clouds in heaven look terribly on me; the Mighty One who is against
me speaketh in the wind of the cedar grove;
and in silence am I dried up." Then Enos
spake to his father, "Arise, my father,
50 arise; we are but a little way from the place
where I found the cake and the pitcher."
And Cain said, "How knowest thou?"
and the child answered—"Behold the bare
rocks are a few of thy strides distant from
55 the forest; and while even now thou wert
lifting up thy voice, I heard the echo."
Then the child took hold of his father, as
if he would raise him: and Cain being
faint and feeble rose slowly on his knees

and pressed himself against the trunk of a fir, and stood upright and followed the child.

The path was dark till within three strides' length of its termination, when it turned suddenly; the thick black trees formed a low arch, and the moonlight appeared for a moment like a dazzling portal. Enos ran before and stood in the open air; and when Cain, his father, emerged from the darkness, the child was affrighted. For the mighty limbs of Cain were wasted as by fire; his hair was as the matted curls on the bison's forehead, and so glared his fierce and sullen eye beneath: and the black abundant locks on either side, a rank and tangled mass, were stained and scorched, as though the grasp of a burning iron hand had striven to rend them; and his countenance told in a strange and terrible language of agonies that had been, and were, and were still to continue to be.

The scene around was desolate; as far as the eye could reach it was desolate: the bare rocks faced each other, and left a long and wide interval of thin white sand. You might wander on and look round and round, and peep into the crevices of the rocks and discover nothing that acknowledged the influence of the seasons. There was no spring, no summer, no autumn: and the winter's snow, that would have been lovely, fell not on these hot rocks and scorching sands. Never morning lark had poised himself over this desert; but the huge serpent often hissed there beneath the talons of the vulture, and the vulture screamed, his wings imprisoned within the coils of the serpent. The pointed and shattered summits of the ridges of the rocks made a rude mimicry of human concerns, and seemed to prophesy mutely of things that then were not; steeples, and battlements, and ships with naked masts. As far from the wood as a boy might sling a pebble of the brook, there was one rock by itself at a small distance from the main ridge. It had been precipitated there perhaps by the groan which the Earth uttered when our first father fell. Before you approached, it appeared to lie flat on the ground, but its base slanted from its point, and between its point and the sands a tall man might stand upright. It was here that Enos had found the pitcher and cake, and to this place he led his father. But ere they had reached the rock they beheld a human shape: his back was towards them, and they were advancing unperceived, when

they heard him smite his breast and cry aloud, "Woe is me! woe is me! I must never die again, and yet I am perishing with thirst and hunger."

Pallid, as the reflection of the sheeted lightning on the heavy-sailing night-cloud, became the face of Cain; but the child Enos took hold of the shaggy skin, his father's robe, and raised his eyes to his father, and listening whispered, "Ere yet I could speak, I am sure, O my father, that I heard that voice. Have not I often said that I remembered a sweet voice? O my father! this is it:" and Cain trembled exceedingly. The voice was sweet indeed, but it was thin and querulous, like that of a feeble slave in misery, who despairs altogether, yet cannot refrain himself from weeping and lamentation. And, behold! Enos glided forward, and creeping softly round the base of the rock, stood before the stranger, and looked up into his face. And the Shape shrieked, and turned round, and Cain beheld him, that his limbs and his face were those of his brother Abel whom he had killed! And Cain stood like one who struggles in his sleep because of the exceeding terribleness of a dream.

Thus as he stood in silence and darkness of soul, the Shape fell at his feet, and embraced his knees, and cried out with a bitter outcry, "Thou eldest born of Adam, whom Eve, my mother, brought forth, cease to torment me! I was feeding my flocks in green pastures by the side of quiet rivers,[1] and thou killedst me; and now I am in misery." Then Cain closed his eyes, and hid them with his hands; and again he opened his eyes, and looked around him, and said to Enos, "What beholdest thou? Didst thou hear a voice, my son?" "Yes, my father, I beheld a man in unclean garments, and he uttered a sweet voice, full of lamentation." Then Cain raised up the Shape that was like Abel, and said: "The Creator of our father, who had respect unto thee, and unto thy offering, wherefore hath he forsaken thee?" Then the Shape shrieked a second time, and rent his garment, and his naked skin was like the white sands beneath their feet; and he shrieked yet a third time, and threw himself on his face upon the sand that was black with the shadow of the rock, and Cain and Enos sate beside him; the child by his right hand, and Cain by his left. They were all three under the rock, and within the shadow. The Shape that was like Abel raised him-

[1] See *Psalms*. 23 :2.

self up, and spake to the child, "I know where the cold waters are, but I may not drink, wherefore didst thou then take away my pitcher?" But Cain said, "Didst thou not find favor in the sight of the Lord thy God?" The Shape answered, "The Lord is God of the living only, the dead have another God." Then the child Enos lifted up his eyes and prayed; but Cain rejoiced secretly in his heart. "Wretched shall they be all the days of their mortal life," exclaimed the Shape, "who sacrifice worthy and acceptable sacrifices to the God of the dead; but after death their toil ceaseth. Woe is me, for I was well beloved by the God of the living, and cruel wert thou, O my brother, who didst snatch me away from his power and his dominion." Having uttered these words, he rose suddenly, and fled over the sands: and Cain said in his heart, "The curse of the Lord is on me; but who is the God of the dead?" and he ran after the Shape, and the Shape fled shrieking over the sands, and the sands rose like white mists behind the steps of Cain, but the feet of him that was like Abel disturbed not the sands. He greatly outrun Cain, and turning short, he wheeled round, and came again to the rock where they had been sitting, and where Enos still stood; and the child caught hold of his garment as he passed by, and he fell upon the ground. And Cain stopped, and beholding him not, said, "He has passed into the dark woods," and he walked slowly back to the rocks; and when he reached it the child told him that he had caught hold of his garment as he passed by, and that the man had fallen upon the ground: and Cain once more sate beside him, and said, "Abel, my brother, I would lament for thee, but that the spirit within me is withered, and burnt up with extreme agony. Now, I pray thee, by thy flocks, and by thy pastures, and by the quiet rivers which thou lovedst, that thou tell me all that thou knowest. Who is the God of the dead? where doth he make his dwelling? what sacrifices are acceptable unto him? for I have offered, but have not been received; I have prayed, and have not been heard; and how can I be afflicted more than I already am?" The Shape arose and answered, "O that thou hadst had pity on me as I will have pity on thee. Follow me, Son of Adam! and bring thy child with thee!"

And they three passed over the white sands between the rocks, silent as the shadows.

From BIOGRAPHIA LITERARIA
1815-16   1817
CHAPTER XIV

Occasion of the *Lyrical Ballads,* and the objects originally proposed—Preface to the second edition—The ensuing controversy, its causes and acrimony—Philosophic definitions of a Poem and Poetry with scholia.

During the first year that Mr. Wordsworth and I were neighbors,[1] our conversations turned frequently on the two cardinal points of poetry, the power of exciting the sympathy of the reader by a faithful adherence to the truth of nature, and the power of giving the interest of novelty by the modifying colors of imagination. The sudden charm, which accidents of light and shade, which moonlight or sunset diffused over a known and familiar landscape, appeared to represent the practicability of combining both. These are the poetry of nature. The thought suggested itself (to which of us I do not recollect) that a series of poems might be composed of two sorts. In the one, the incidents and agents were to be, in part at least, supernatural; and the excellence aimed at was to consist in the interesting of the affections by the dramatic truth of such emotions, as would naturally accompany such situations, supposing them real. And real in this sense they have been to every human being who, from whatever source of delusion, has at any time believed himself under supernatural agency. For the second class, subjects were to be chosen from ordinary life; the characters and incidents were to be such as will be found in every village and its vicinity, where there is a meditative and feeling mind to seek after them, or to notice them, when they present themselves.

In this idea originated the plan of the *Lyrical Ballads;* in which it was agreed, that my endeavors should be directed to persons and characters supernatural, or at least romantic; yet so as to transfer from our inward nature a human interest and a semblance of truth sufficient to procure for these shadows of imagination that willing suspension of disbelief for the moment, which constitutes poetic faith. Mr. Wordsworth, on the other hand, was to propose to himself as his object, to give the charm of novelty to things of every day, and to excite a feeling analogous to the supernatural, by awakening the mind's attention to the lethargy of custom, and directing it to the loveliness and the wonders of the

[1] 1797.

world before us; an inexhaustible treasure, but for which, in consequence of the film of familiarity and selfish solicitude, we have eyes, yet see not, ears that hear not, and hearts that neither feel nor understand.[1]

With this view I wrote *The Ancient Mariner,* and was preparing, among other poems, *The Dark Ladie,* and the *Christabel,* in which I should have more nearly realized my ideal, than I had done in my first attempt. But Mr. Wordsworth's industry had proved so much more successful, and the number of his poems so much greater, that my compositions, instead of forming a balance, appeared rather an interpolation of heterogeneous matter. Mr. Wordsworth added two or three poems written in his own character, in the impassioned, lofty, and sustained diction, which is characteristic of his genius. In this form the *Lyrical Ballads* were published; and were presented by him, as an experiment, whether subjects, which from their nature rejected the usual ornaments and extra-colloquial style of poems in general, might not be so managed in the language of ordinary life as to produce the pleasurable interest, which it is the peculiar business of poetry to impart. To the second edition he added a preface of considerable length, in which, notwithstanding some passages of apparently a contrary import, he was understood to contend for the extension of this style to poetry of all kinds, and to reject as vicious and indefensible all phrases and forms of speech that were not included in what he (unfortunately, I think, adopting an equivocal expression) called the language of real life. From this preface, prefixed to poems in which it was impossible to deny the presence of original genius, however mistaken its direction might be deemed, arose the whole long-continued controversy.[2] For from the conjunction of perceived power with supposed heresy, I explain the inveteracy and in some instances, I grieve to say, the acrimonious passions, with which the controversy has been conducted by the assailants.

Had Mr. Wordsworth's poems been the silly, the childish things, which they were for a long time described as being; had they been really distinguished from the compositions of other poets merely by meanness of language and inanity of thought; had they indeed contained nothing more than what is found in the parodies and pretended imitations of them; they must have sunk at once, a dead weight, into the slough of oblivion, and have dragged the preface along with them. But year after year increased the number of Mr. Wordsworth's admirers. They were found, too, not in the lower classes of the reading public, but chiefly among young men of strong sensibility and meditative minds; and their admiration (inflamed perhaps in some degree by opposition) was distinguished by its intensity, I might almost say, by its religious fervor. These facts, and the intellectual energy of the author, which was more or less consciously felt, where it was outwardly and even boisterously denied, meeting with sentiments of aversion to his opinions, and of alarm at their consequences, produced an eddy of criticism, which would of itself have borne up the poems by the violence with which it whirled them round and round. With many parts of this preface in the sense attributed to them and which the words undoubtedly seem to authorize, I never concurred; but on the contrary objected to them as erroneous in principle, and as contradictory (in appearance at least) both to other parts of the same preface, and to the author's own practice in the greater part of the poems themselves. Mr. Wordsworth in his recent collection has, I find, degraded this prefatory disquisition to the end of his second volume, to be read or not at the reader's choice. But he has not, as far as I can discover, announced any change in his poetic creed. At all events, considering it as the source of a controversy, in which I have been honored more than I deserve by the frequent conjunction of my name with his, I think it expedient to declare once for all, in what points I coincide with the opinions supported in that preface, and in what points I altogether differ. But in order to render myself intelligible I must previously, in as few words as possible, explain my ideas, first, of a poem; and secondly, of poetry itself, in kind and in essence.

The office of philosophical disquisition consists in just distinction; while it is the privilege of the philosopher to preserve himself constantly aware that distinction is not division. In order to obtain adequate notions of any truth, we must intellectually separate its distinguishable parts; and this is the technical process of philosophy. But having so done, we must then restore them in our conceptions to the unity, in which

---

[1] See *Isaiah,* 6 :9-10.
[2] Over Wordsworth's theory and practice of poetic art.

they actually coexist; and this is the result of philosophy. A poem contains the same elements as a prose composition; the difference, therefore, must consist in a different combination of them, in consequence of a different object being proposed. According to the difference of the object will be the difference of the combination. It is possible that the object may be merely to facilitate the recollection of any given facts or observations by artificial arrangement; and the composition will be a poem, merely because it is distinguished from prose by metre, or by rhyme, or by both conjointly. In this, the lowest sense, a man might attribute the name of a poem to the well-known enumeration of the days in the several months:

Thirty days hath September,
April, June, and November, &c.

and others of the same class and purpose. And as a particular pleasure is found in anticipating the recurrence of sounds and quantities, all compositions that have this charm superadded, whatever be their contents, *may* be entitled poems.

So much for the superficial form. A difference of object and contents supplies an additional ground of distinction. The immediate purpose may be the communication of truths; either of truth absolute and demonstrable, as in works of science; or of facts experienced and recorded, as in history. Pleasure, and that of the highest and most permanent kind, may result from the attainment of the end; but it is not itself the immediate end. In other works the communication of pleasure may be the immediate purpose; and though truth, either moral or intellectual, ought to be the ultimate end, yet this will distinguish the character of the author, not the class to which the work belongs. Blest indeed is that state of society, in which the immediate purpose would be baffled by the perversion of the proper ultimate end; in which no charm of diction or imagery could exempt the *Bathyllus* even of an Anacreon, or the *Alexis* of Virgil, from disgust and aversion!

But the communication of pleasure may be the immediate object of a work not metrically composed; and that object may have been in a high degree attained, as in novels and romances. Would then the mere superaddition of metre, with or without rhyme, entitle these to the name of poems? The answer is, that nothing can permanently please, which does not contain in itself the

reason why it is so, and not otherwise. If metre be superadded, all other parts must be made consonant with it. They must be such as to justify the perpetual and distinct attention to each part, which an exact correspondent recurrence of accent and sound are calculated to excite. The final definition then, so deduced, may be thus worded. A poem is that species of composition, which is opposed to works of science, by proposing for its immediate object pleasure, not truth; and from all other species (having this object in common with it) it is discriminated by proposing to itself such delight from the whole, as is compatible with a distinct gratification from each component part.

Controversy is not seldom excited in consequence of the disputants attaching each a different meaning to the same word; and in few instances has this been more striking, than in disputes concerning the present subject. If a man chooses to call every composition a poem, which is rhyme, or measure, or both, I must leave his opinion uncontroverted. The distinction is at least competent to characterize the writer's intention. If it were subjoined, that the whole is likewise entertaining or affecting, as a tale, or as a series of interesting reflections, I of course admit this as another fit ingredient of a poem, and an additional merit. But if the definition sought for be that of a legitimate poem, I answer, it must be one the parts of which mutually support and explain each other; all in their proportion harmonizing with, and supporting the purpose and known influences of metrical arrangement. The philosophic critics of all ages coincide with the ultimate judgment of all countries, in equally denying the praises of a just poem, on the one hand, to a series of striking lines or distiches, each of which, absorbing the whole attention of the reader to itself, disjoins it from its context, and makes it a separate whole, instead of a harmonizing part; and on the other hand, to an unsustained composition, from which the reader collects rapidly the general result unattracted by the component parts. The reader should be carried forward, not merely or chiefly by the mechanical impulse of curiosity, or by a restless desire to arrive at the final solution; but by the pleasurable activity of mind excited by the attractions of the journey itself. Like the motion of a serpent, which the Egyptians made the emblem of intellectual power; or like the path of sound through the air; at every step he pauses and half recedes, and from the retrogressive move-ment collects the force which again carries him onward. *Præcipitandus est liber spiri-tus,*[1] says Petronius Arbiter most happily. The epithet, *liber,* here balances the preceding verb; and it is not easy to conceive more meaning condensed in fewer words.

But if this should be admitted as a satisfactory character of a poem, we have still to seek for a definition of poetry. The writings of Plato, and Bishop Taylor, and the *Theoria Sacra* of Burnet, furnish undeniable proofs that poetry of the highest kind may exist without metre, and even without the contradistinguishing objects of a poem. The first chapter of *Isaiah* (indeed a very large portion of the whole book) is poetry in the most emphatic sense; yet it would be not less irrational than strange to assert, that pleasure, and not truth, was the immediate object of the prophet. In short, whatever specific import we attach to the word, poetry, there will be found involved in it, as a necessary consequence, that a poem of any length neither can be, nor ought to be, all poetry.[2] Yet if an harmonious whole is to be produced, the remaining parts must be preserved in keeping with the poetry; and this can be no otherwise effected than by such a studied selection and artificial arrangement as will partake of one, though not a peculiar property of poetry. And this again can be no other than the property of exciting a more continuous and equal attention than the language of prose aims at, whether colloquial or written.

My own conclusions on the nature of poetry, in the strictest use of the word, have been in part anticipated in the preceding disquisition on the fancy and imagination.[3] What is poetry? is so nearly the same question with, What is a poet? that the answer to the one is involved in the solution of the other. For it is a distinction resulting from the poetic genius itself, which sustains and modifies the images, thoughts, and emotions of the poet's own mind.

The poet, described in ideal perfection, brings the whole soul of man into activity, with the subordination of its faculties to each other according to their relative worth and dignity. He diffuses a tone and

spirit of unity, that blends, and (as it were) fuses, each into each, by that synthetic and magical power, to which I would exclusively appropriate the name of imagination. This power, first put in action by the will and understanding, and retained under their irremissive, though gentle and unnoticed, control (*laxis effertur habenis*[1]) reveals itself in the balance or reconcilement of opposite or discordant qualities: of sameness, with difference; of the general, with the concrete; the idea, with the image; the individual, with the representative; the sense of novelty and freshness, with old and familiar objects; a more than usual state of emotion, with more than usual order; judgment ever awake and steady self-possession, with enthusiasm and feeling profound or vehement; and while it blends and harmonizes the natural and the artificial, still subordinates art to nature; the manner to the matter; and our admiration of the poet to our sympathy with the poetry. "Doubtless," as Sir John Davies observes of the soul[2] (and his words may with slight alteration be applied, and even more appropriately, to the poetic imagination),—

Doubtless this could not be, but that she turns
  Bodies to spirit by sublimation strange,
As fire converts to fire the things it burns,
  As we our food into our nature change.

From their gross matter she abstracts their forms,
  And draws a kind of quintessence from things;
Which to her proper nature she transforms
  To bear them light on her celestial wings.

Thus does she, when from individual states
  She doth abstract the universal kinds:
Which then re-clothed in divers names and fates
  Steal access through the senses to our minds.

Finally, good sense is the body of poetic genius, fancy its drapery, motion its life, and imagination the soul that is everywhere, and in each; and forms all into one graceful and intelligent whole.

CHAPTER XVII

Examination of the tenets peculiar to Mr. Words-worth—Rustic life (above all, low and rustic life) especially unfavorable to the formation of a human diction—The best parts of language the product of philosophers, not of clowns or shepherds—Poetry essentially ideal and generic —The language of Milton as much the language of real life, yea, incomparably more so than that of the cottager.

As far, then, as Mr. Wordsworth in his preface contended, and most ably contended, for a reformation in our poetic diction; as

---

[1] The free spirit ought to be urged onward. *Satyric,* p. 63.
[2] See Poe's *The Poetic Principle,* in which is set forth the doctrine that there is no such thing as a long poem.
[3] *Biographia Literaria,* 4.

[1] is borne along with loose reins
[2] In his poem, *Of the Soul of Man,* 4, 45-56.

far as he has evinced the truth of passion, and the dramatic propriety of those figures and metaphors in the original poets, which, stripped of their justifying reasons and converted into mere artifices of connection or ornament, constitute the characteristic falsity in the poetic style of the moderns; and as far as he has, with equal acuteness and clearness, pointed out the process by which this change was effected, and the resemblances between that state into which the reader's mind is thrown by the pleasurable confusion of thought from an unaccustomed train of words and images, and that state which is induced by the natural language of impassioned feeling; he undertook a useful task, and deserves all praise, both for the attempt and for the execution. The provocations to this remonstrance in behalf of truth and nature were still of perpetual recurrence before and after the publication of this preface. I cannot likewise but add, that the comparison of such poems of merit, as have been given to the public within the last ten or twelve years, with the majority of those produced previously to the appearance of that preface, leave no doubt on my mind, that Mr. Wordsworth is fully justified in believing his efforts to have been by no means ineffectual. Not only in the verses of those who have professed their admiration of his genius, but even of those who have distinguished themselves by hostility to his theory, and depreciation of his writings, are the impressions of his principles plainly visible. It is possible that with these principles others may have been blended, which are not equally evident; and some which are unsteady and subvertible from the narrowness or imperfection of their basis. But it is more than possible that these errors of defect or exaggeration, by kindling and feeding the controversy, may have conduced not only to the wider propagation of the accompanying truths, but that, by their frequent presentation to the mind in an excited state, they may have won for them a more permanent and practical result. A man will borrow a part from his opponent the more easily, if he feels himself justified in continuing to reject a part. While there remain important points in which he can still feel himself in the right, in which he still finds firm footing for continued resistance, he will gradually adopt those opinions, which were the least remote from his own convictions, as not less congruous with his own theory than with that

which he reprobates. In like manner with a kind of instinctive prudence, he will abandon by little and little his weakest posts, till at length he seems to forget that they had ever belonged to him, or affects to consider them at most as accidental and "petty annexments," the removal of which leaves the citadel unhurt and unendangered.

My own differences from certain supposed parts of Mr. Wordsworth's theory ground themselves on the assumption that his words had been rightly interpreted, as purporting that the proper diction for poetry in general consists altogether in a language taken, with due exceptions, from the mouths of men in real life, a language which actually constitutes the natural conversation of men under the influence of natural feelings. My objection is, first, that in any sense this rule is applicable only to certain classes of poetry; secondly, that even to these classes it is not applicable, except in such a sense, as hath never by any one (as far as I know or have read) been denied or doubted; and lastly, that as far as, and in that degree in which it is practicable, it is yet, as a rule, useless, if not injurious, and, therefore, either need not or ought not to be practised. The poet informs his reader that he had generally chosen low and rustic life; but not *as* low and rustic, or in order to repeat that pleasure of doubtful moral effect, which persons of elevated rank and of superior refinement oftentimes derive from a happy imitation of the rude unpolished manners and discourse of their inferiors. For the pleasure so derived may be traced to three exciting causes. The first is the naturalness, in fact, of the things represented. The second is the apparent naturalness of the representation, as raised and qualified by an imperceptible infusion of the author's own knowledge and talent, which infusion does, indeed, constitute it an imitation as distinguished from a mere copy. The third cause may be found in the reader's conscious feeling of his superiority, awakened by the contrast presented to him; even as for the same purpose the kings and great barons of yore retained sometimes actual clowns and fools but more frequently shrewd and witty fellows in that character. These, however, were not Mr. Wordsworth's objects. He chose low and rustic life, "because in that condition the essential passions of the heart find a better soil, in which they can attain their maturity, are less under restraint, and speak a plainer and more emphatic language; because in that condition of life our elementary feelings coexist in a state of greater simplicity, and consequently may be more accurately contemplated, and more forcibly communicated; because the manners of rural life germinate from those elementary feelings; and from the necessary character of rural occupations are more easily comprehended, and are more durable; and, lastly, because in that condition the passions of men are incorporated with the beautiful and permanent forms of nature.''

Now it is clear to me that in the most interesting of the poems, in which the author is more or less dramatic, as *The Brothers, Michael, Ruth, The Mad Mother*,[1] etc., the persons introduced are by no means taken from low or rustic life in the common acceptation of those words; and it is not less clear that the sentiments and language, as far as they can be conceived to have been really transferred from the minds and conversation of such persons, are attributable to causes and circumstances not necessarily connected with ''their occupations and abode.'' The thoughts, feelings, language, and manners of the shepherd-farmers in the vales of Cumberland and Westmoreland, as far as they are actually adopted in those poems, may be accounted for from causes, which will and do produce the same results in every state of life, whether in town or country. As the two principal I rank that independence which raises a man above servitude, or daily toil for the profit of others, yet not above the necessity of industry and a frugal simplicity of domestic life; and the accompanying unambitious, but solid and religious, education which has rendered few books familiar but the Bible and the liturgy or hymn book. To this latter cause, indeed, which is so far accidental that it is the blessing of particular countries and a particular age, not the product of particular places or employments, the poet owes the show of probability, that his personages might really feel, think, and talk with any tolerable resemblance to his representation. It is an excellent remark of Dr. Henry More's, that ''a man of confined education, but of good parts, by constant reading of the Bible, will naturally form a more winning and commanding rhetoric than those that are learned, the intermixture of tongues and of artificial phrases debasing their style.''[2]

It is, moreover, to be considered that to the formation of healthy feelings, and a reflecting mind, negations involve impediments not less formidable than sophistication and vicious intermixture. I am convinced that for the human soul to prosper in rustic life a certain vantage-ground is prerequisite. It is not every man that is likely to be improved by a country life or by country labors. Education, or original sensibility, or both, must pre-exist, if the changes, forms, and incidents of nature are to prove a sufficient stimulant. And where these are not sufficient, the mind contracts and hardens by want of stimulants; and the man becomes selfish, sensual, gross, and hard-hearted. Let the management of the Poor Laws in Liverpool, Manchester, or Bristol be compared with the ordinary dispensation of the poor rates[1] in agricultural villages, where the farmers are the overseers and guardians of the poor. If my own experience have not been particularly unfortunate, as well as that of the many respectable country clergymen with whom I have conversed on the subject, the result would engender more than skepticism concerning the desirable influences of low and rustic life in and for itself. Whatever may be concluded on the other side, from the stronger local attachments and enterprising spirit of the Swiss, and other mountaineers, applies to a particular mode of pastoral life, under forms of property that permit and beget manners truly republican, not to rustic life in general, or to the absence of artificial cultivation. On the contrary, the mountaineers, whose manners have been so often eulogized, are in general better educated and greater readers than men of equal rank elsewhere. But where this is not the case, as among the peasantry of North Wales, the ancient mountains, with all their terrors and all their glories, are pictures to the blind, and music to the deaf.

I should not have entered so much into detail upon this passage, but here seems to be the point to which all the lines of difference converge as to their source and centre— I mean, as far as, and in whatever respect, my poetic creed *does* differ from the doctrines promulgated in this preface. I adopt with full faith the principle of Aristotle, that poetry, as poetry, is essentially ideal,[2] that it avoids and excludes all accident; that its apparent individualities of rank, character, or occupation must be representative of a class; and that the persons of

---

[1] In later editions entitled *Her Eyes are Wild.*
[2] *Enthusiasmus Triumphatus*, sec. 35.

[1] Taxes levied for the relief of the poor.
[2] See *Poetics*, 9, 1-4.

poetry must be clothed with generic attributes, with the common attributes of the class; not with such as one gifted individual might possibly possess, but such as from his situation it is most probable before-hand that he would possess. If my premises are right and my deductions legitimate, it follows that there can be no poetic medium between the swains of Theocritus and those of an imaginary golden age.[1]

The characters of the vicar and the shepherd-mariner in the poem of *The Brothers*, and that of the shepherd of Green-head Ghyll[2] in the *Michael*, have all the verisimilitude and representative quality that the purposes of poetry can require. They are persons of a known and abiding class, and their manners and sentiments the natural product of circumstances common to the class. Take Michael for instance:

An old man, stout of heart and strong of limb.
His bodily frame had been from youth to age
Of an unusual strength : his mind was keen,
Intense, and frugal, apt for all affairs,
And in his shepherd's calling he was prompt
And watchful more than ordinary men.
Hence he had learned the meaning of all winds,
Of blasts of every tone ; and oftentimes
When others heeded not, he heard the South
Make subterraneous music, like the noise
Of bagpipers on distant Highland hills.
The shepherd, at such warning, of his flock
Bethought him, and he to himself would say,
"The winds are now devising work for me !"
And truly, at all times, the storm, that drives
The traveller to a shelter, summoned him
Up to the mountains : he had been alone
Amid the heart of many thousand mists,
That came to him and left him on the heights.
So lived he, until his eightieth year was past.
And grossly that man errs, who should suppose
That the green valleys, and the streams and rocks,
Were things indifferent to the shepherd's thoughts.
Fields, where with cheerful spirits he had breathed
The common air ; the hills, which he so oft
Had climbed with vigorous steps ; which had impressed
So many incidents upon his mind
Of hardship, skill or courage, joy or fear ;
Which, like a book, preserved the memory
Of the dumb animals, whom he had saved,
Had fed or sheltered, linking to such acts,
So grateful in themselves, the certainty
Of honorable gain ; these fields, these hills
Which were his living Being, even more
Than his own blood—what could they less? had laid
Strong hold on his affections, were to him
A pleasurable feeling of blind love,
The pleasure which there is in life itself.[3]

On the other hand, in the poems which are pitched in a lower key, as the *Harry Gill,* and *The Idiot Boy,* etc., the feelings are those of human nature in general; though the poet has judiciously laid the scene in the country, in order to place himself in the vicinity of interesting images, without the necessity of ascribing a senti-

mental perception of their beauty to the persons of his drama. In *The Idiot Boy,* indeed, the mother's character is not so much the real and native product of a "situation where the essential passions of the heart find a better soil, in which they can attain their maturity and speak a plainer and more emphatic language," as it is an impersonation of an instinct abandoned by judgment. Hence the two following charges seems to me not wholly groundless; at least, they are the only plausible objections which I have heard to that fine poem. The one is, that the author has not, in the poem itself, taken sufficient care to preclude from the reader's fancy the disgusting images of ordinary, morbid idiocy, which yet it was by no means his intention to represent. He was even by the "burr, burr, burr,"[1] uncounteracted by any preceding description of the boy's beauty, assisted in recalling them. The other is, that the idiocy of the boy is so evenly balanced by the folly of the mother, as to present to the general reader rather a laughable burlesque on the blindness of anile[2] dotage, than an analytic display of maternal affection in its ordinary workings.

In *The Thorn,* the poet himself acknowledges in a note the necessity of an introductory poem, in which he should have portrayed the character of the person from whom the words of the poem are supposed to proceed: a superstitious man moderately imaginative, of slow faculties and deep feelings, "a captain of a small trading vessel, for example, who, being past the middle age of life, had retired upon an annuity, or small independent income, to some village or country town of which he was not a native, or in which he had not been accustomed to live. Such men having nothing to do become credulous and talkative from indolence." But in a poem, still more in a lyric poem (and the Nurse in *Romeo and Juliet* alone prevents me from extending the remark even to dramatic poetry, if indeed even the Nurse can be deemed altogether a case in point) it is not possible to imitate truly a dull and garrulous discourser, without repeating the effects of dullness and garrulity. However this may be, I dare assert that the parts (and these form the far larger portion of the whole) which might as well or still better have proceeded from the poet's own imagi-

---

[1] The swains of Theocritus were taken from real life.
[2] valley
[3] ll. 42-77.

[1] Johnnie, the idiot boy, spoke with a burr,—*i. e.,* a trilled pronunciation of the letter *r.* See *The Idiot Boy,* 97, 105.
[2] old-womanish

nation, and have been spoken in his own character, are those which have given, and which will continue to give, universal delight; and that the passages exclusively appropriate to the supposed narrator, such as the last couplet of the third stanza, the seven last lines of the tenth, and the five following stanzas, with the exception of the four admirable lines at the commencement of the fourteenth, are felt by many unprejudiced and unsophisticated hearts, as sudden and unpleasant sinkings from the height to which the poet had previously lifted them, and to which he again re-elevates both himself and his reader.

If then I am compelled to doubt the theory, by which the choice of characters was to be directed, not only *a priori,* from grounds of reason, but both from the few instances in which the poet himself need be supposed to have been governed by it, and from the comparative inferiority of these instances; still more must I hesitate in my assent to the sentence which immediately follows the former citation, and which I can neither admit as particular fact, nor as general rule. ''The language, too, of these men has been adopted (purified indeed from what appear to be its real defects, from all lasting and rational causes of dislike or disgust) because such men hourly communicate with the best objects from which the best part of language is originally derived; and because, from their rank in society and the sameness and narrow circle of their intercourse, being less under the action of social vanity, they convey their feelings and notions in simple and unelaborated expressions.'' To this I reply that a rustic's language, purified from all provincialism and grossness, and so far reconstructed as to be made consistent with the rules of grammar (which are in essence no other than the laws of universal logic, applied to psychological materials) will not differ from the language of any other man of common sense, however learned or refined he may be, except as far as the notions, which the rustic has to convey, are fewer and more indiscriminate. This will become still clearer, if we add the consideration (equally important though less obvious) that the rustic, from the more imperfect development of his faculties, and from the lower state of their cultivation, aims almost solely to convey insulated facts, either those of his scanty experience or his traditional belief; while the educated man chiefly seeks to discover and express those connections of things, or those relative bearings of fact to fact, from which some more or less general law is deducible. For facts are valuable to a wise man, chiefly as they lead to the discovery of the indwelling law, which is the true being of things, the sole solution of their modes of existence, and in the knowledge of which consists our dignity and our power.

As little can I agree with the assertion that from the objects with which the rustic hourly communicates, the best part of language is formed. For first, if to communicate with an object implies such an acquaintance with it as renders it capable of being discriminately reflected on, the distinct knowledge of an uneducated rustic would furnish a very scanty vocabulary. The few things and modes of action requisite for his bodily conveniences would alone be individualized; while all the rest of nature would be expressed by a small number of confused general terms. Secondly, I deny that the words and combinations of words derived from the objects with which the rustic is familiar, whether with distinct or confused knowledge, can be justly said to form the best part of language. It is more than probable that many classes of the brute creation possess discriminating sounds, by which they can convey to each other notices of such objects as concern their food, shelter, or safety. Yet we hesitate to call the aggregate of such sounds a language, otherwise than metaphorically. The best part of human language, properly so called, is derived from reflection on the acts of the mind itself. It is formed by a voluntary appropriation of fixed symbols to internal acts, to processes and results of imagination, the greater part of which have no place in the consciousness of uneducated man; though in civilized society, by imitation and passive remembrance of what they hear from their religious instructors and other superiors, the most uneducated share in the harvest which they neither sowed nor reaped. If the history of the phrases in hourly currency among our peasants were traced, a person not previously aware of the fact would be surprised at finding so large a number which three or four centuries ago were the exclusive property of the universities and the schools, and at the commencement of the Reformation had been transferred from the school to the pulpit, and thus gradually passed into common life. The extreme difficulty, and often the impossibility, of finding words for the simplest moral and intellectual processes of the languages of uncivilized tribes has proved perhaps the weightiest obstacle to the progress of our most zealous and adroit missionaries. Yet these tribes are surrounded by the same nature as our peasants are, but in still more impressive forms; and they are, moreover, obliged to particularize many more of them. When, therefore, Mr. Wordsworth adds, "accordingly, such a language" (meaning, as before, the language of rustic life purified from provincialism) "arising out of repeated experience and regular feelings, is a more permanent, and a far more philosophical language, than that which is frequently substituted for it by poets, who think that they are conferring honor upon themselves and their art in proportion as they indulge in arbitrary and capricious habits of expression," it may be answered that the language which he has in view can be attributed to rustics with no greater right than the style of Hooker or Bacon to Tom Brown or Sir Roger L'Estrange.[1] Doubtless, if what is peculiar to each were omitted in each, the result must needs be the same. Further, that the poet who uses an illogical diction, or a style fitted to excite only the low and changeable pleasure of wonder by means of groundless novelty, substitutes a language of folly and vanity, not for that of the rustic, but for that of good sense and natural feeling.

Here let me be permitted to remind the reader that the positions which I controvert are contained in the sentences—"a selection of the real language of men;"— "the language of these men" (that is, men in low and rustic life) "has been adopted; I have proposed to myself to imitate, and, as far as is possible, to adopt the very language of men." "Between the language of prose and that of metrical composition, there neither is nor can be any essential difference." It is against these exclusively that my opposition is directed.

I object, in the very first instance, to an equivocation in the use of the word "real." Every man's language varies according to the extent of his knowledge, the activity of his faculties, and the depth or quickness of his feelings. Every man's language has, first, its individualities; secondly, the common properties of the class to which he belongs; and thirdly, words and phrases of universal use. The language of Hooker,

Bacon, Bishop Taylor, and Burke differs from the common language of the learned class only by the superior number and novelty of the thoughts and relations which they had to convey. The language of Algernon Sidney differs not at all from that which every well-educated gentleman would wish to write, and (with due allowances for the undeliberateness, and less connected train, of thinking natural and proper to conversation) such as he would wish to talk. Neither one nor the other differ half as much from the general language of cultivated society, as the language of Mr. Wordsworth's homeliest composition differs from that of a common peasant. For "real," therefore, we must substitute ordinary, or *lingua communis.* And this, we have proved, is no more to be found in the phraseology of low and rustic life than in that of any other class. Omit the peculiarities of each, and the result of course must be common to all. And assuredly the omissions and changes to be made in the language of rustics, before it could be transferred to any species of poem, except the drama or other professed imitation, are at least as numerous and weighty as would be required in adapting to the same purpose the ordinary language of tradesmen or manufacturers. Not to mention that the language so highly extolled by Mr. Wordsworth varies in every county, nay, in every village, according to the accidental character of the clergyman, the existence or nonexistence of schools; or even, perhaps, as the exciseman, publican, and barber happen to be, or not to be, zealous politicians and readers of the weekly newspaper *pro bono publico.* Anterior to cultivation the *lingua communis* of every country, as Dante has well observed,[1] exists everywhere in parts, and nowhere as a whole.

Neither is the case rendered at all more tenable by the addition of the words, "in a state of excitement." For the nature of a man's words, where he is strongly affected by joy, grief, or anger, must necessarily depend on the number and quality of the general truths, conceptions, and images, and of the words expressing them, with which his mind had been previously stored. For the property of passion is not to create, but to set in increased activity. At least, whatever new connections of thoughts or images, or (which is equally, if not more than equally, the appropriate effect of

---

[1] Brown's writings are almost entirely valueless imitations of the ancient writers; L'Estrange's writings are noted for their vulgarity.

[1] See *De Vulgari Eloquentia (Concerning Vernacular Speech),* 1, 19.

strong excitement) whatever generalizations of truth or experience the heat of passion may produce, yet the terms of their conveyance must have pre-existed in his former conversations, and are only collected and [5] crowded together by the unusual stimulation. It is indeed very possible to adopt in a poem the unmeaning repetitions, habitual phrases, and other blank counters, which an unfurnished or confused understanding [10] interposes at short intervals, in order to keep hold of his subject, which is still slipping from him, and to give him time for recollection; or, in mere aid of vacancy, as in the scanty companies of a country [15] stage the same player pops backwards and forwards, in order to prevent the appearance of empty spaces, in the processions of *Macbeth*, or *Henry VIII*. But what assistance to the poet, or ornament to the poem, [20] these can supply, I am at a loss to conjecture. Nothing assuredly can differ either in origin or in mode more widely from the apparent tautologies of intense and turbulent feeling, in which the passion is greater [25] and of longer endurance than to be exhausted or satisfied by a single representation of the image or incident exciting it. Such repetitions I admit to be a beauty of the highest kind, as illustrated by Mr. [30] Wordsworth himself from the song of Deborah. *"At her feet he bowed, he fell, he lay down: at her feet he bowed, he fell: where he bowed, there he fell down dead."*[1]

From CHAPTER XVIII

. . . .

I conclude, therefore, that the attempt is impracticable; and that, were it not impracticable, it would still be useless. For [40] the very power of making the selection implies the previous possession of the language selected. Or where can the poet have lived? And by what rules could he direct his choice, which would not have enabled [45] him to select and arrange his words by the light of his own judgment? We do not adopt the language of a class by the mere adoption of such words exclusively as that class would use, or at least understand; but [50] likewise by following the order in which the words of such men are wont to succeed each other. Now this order, in the intercourse of uneducated men, is distinguished from the diction of their superiors in [55] knowledge and power, by the greater disjunction and separation in the component parts of that, whatever it be, which they

[1] *Judges*, 5 :27.

wish to communicate. There is a want of that prospectiveness of mind, that surview, which enables a man to foresee the whole of what he is to convey, appertaining to any one point; and by this means so to subordinate and arrange the different parts according to their relative importance, as to convey it at once, and as an organized whole.

Now I will take the first stanza, on which I have chanced to open, in the *Lyrical Ballads*. It is one of the most simple and the least peculiar in its language:

> In distant countries have I been,
> And yet I have not often seen
> A healthy man, a man full grown,
> Weep in the public roads, alone.
> But such a one, on English ground,
> And in the broad highway, I met;
> Along the broad highway he came,
> His cheeks with tears were wet:
> Sturdy he seemed, though he was sad;
> And in his arms a lamb he had.[1]

The words here are doubtless such as are current in all ranks of life; and of course not less so in the hamlet and cottage than in the shop, manufactory, college, or palace. But is this the order in which the rustic would have placed the words? I am grievously deceived, if the following less compact mode of commencing the same tale be not a far more faithful copy. "I have been in a many parts, far and near, and I don't know that I ever saw before a man crying by himself in the public road; a grown man I mean, that was neither sick nor hurt," etc., etc. But when I turn to the following [35] stanza in *The Thorn*:

> At all times of the day and night
> This wretched woman thither goes;
> And she is known to every star,
> And every wind that blows:
> And there, beside the thorn, she sits,
> When the blue day-light's in the skies,
> And when the whirlwind's on the hill,
> Or frosty air is keen and still,
> And to herself she cries,
> "Oh misery! Oh misery!
> Oh woe is me! Oh misery!"

and compare this with the language of ordinary men, or with that which I can conceive at all likely to proceed, in real life, from such a narrator as is supposed in the note to the poem—compare it either in the succession of the images or of the sentences—I [50] am reminded of the sublime prayer and hymn of praise which Milton, in opposition to an established liturgy, presents as a fair specimen of common extemporary devotion, and such as we might expect to hear from [55] every self-inspired minister of a conventicle![2]

[1] *The Last of the Flock*, 1-10.
[2] See *Paradise Lost*, 5, 152-208; also, *Eikonoklastes*, 16.

And I reflect with delight, how little a mere theory, though of his own workmanship, interferes with the processes of genuine imagination in a man of true poetic genius, who possesses, as Mr. Wordsworth, if ever man did, most assuredly does possess,

The Vision and the Faculty divine.[1]

. . . . . .

Chapter XXII

The characteristic defects of Wordsworth's poetry, with the principles from which the judgment that they are defects, is deduced—Their proportion to the beauties—For the greatest part characteristic of his theory only.

If Mr. Wordsworth have set forth principles of poetry which his arguments are insufficient to support, let him and those who have adopted his sentiments be set right by the confutation of those arguments, and by the substitution of more philosophical principles. And still let the due credit be given to the portion and importance of the truths which are blended with his theory; truths, the too exclusive attention to which had occasioned its errors by tempting him to carry those truths beyond their proper limits. If his mistaken theory have at all influenced his poetic compositions, let the effects be pointed out, and the instances given. But let it likewise be shown, how far the influence has acted; whether diffusively, or only by starts; whether the number and importance of the poems and passages thus infected be great or trifling compared with the sound portion; and lastly, whether they are inwoven into the texture of his works, or are loose and separable. The result of such a trial would evince beyond a doubt, what it is high time to announce decisively and aloud, that the *supposed* characteristics of Mr. Wordsworth's poetry, whether admired or reprobated; whether they are simplicity or simpleness; faithful adherence to essential nature, or wilful selections from human nature of its meanest forms and under the least attractive associations; are as little the *real* characteristics of his poetry at large, as of his genius and the constitution of his mind.

In a comparatively small number of poems, he chose to try an experiment; and this experiment we will suppose to have failed. Yet even in these poems it is impossible not to perceive that the natural tendency of the poet's mind is to great objects and elevated conceptions. The poem entitled *Fidelity* is for the greater part written in language as unraised and naked as any per-

[1] *The Excursion,* I, 79.

haps in the two volumes. Yet take the following stanza and compare it with the preceding stanzas of the same poem.

There sometimes doth a leaping fish
Send through the tarn a lonely cheer;
The crags repeat the raven's croak,
In symphony austere;
Thither the rainbow comes—the cloud—
And mists that spread the flying shroud;
And sun-beams; and the sounding blast,
That, if it could, would hurry past;
But that enormous barrier holds it fast.

Or compare the four last lines of the concluding stanza with the former half.

Yes, proof was plain that, since the day
On which the traveller thus had died,
The dog had watched about the spot,
Or by his master's side:
How nourish'd there through such long time
He knows, who gave that love sublime,
And gave that strength of feeling, great
Above all human estimate!

Can any candid and intelligent mind hesitate in determining which of these best represents the tendency and native character of the poet's genius? Will he not decide that the one was written because the poet *would* so write, and the other because he could not so entirely repress the force and grandeur of his mind, but that he must in some part or other of every composition write otherwise? In short, that his only disease is the being out of his element; like the swan, that, having amused himself, for a while, with crushing the weeds on the river's bank, soon returns to his own majestic movements on its reflecting and sustaining surface. Let it be observed that I am here supposing the imagined judge, to whom I appeal, to have already decided against the poet's theory, as far as it is different from the principles of the art, generally acknowledged.

I cannot here enter into a detailed examination of Mr. Wordsworth's works; but I will attempt to give the main results of my own judgment, after an acquaintance of many years, and repeated perusals. And though to appreciate the defects of a great mind it is necessary to understand previously its characteristic excellences, yet I have already expressed myself with sufficient fulness to preclude most of the ill effects that might arise from my pursuing a contrary arrangement. I will therefore commence with what I deem the prominent *defects* of his poems hitherto published.

The first characteristic, though only occasional defect, which I appear to myself to find in these poems is the *inconstancy* of the style. Under this name I refer to the sudden and unprepared transitions from lines or sentences of peculiar felicity (at all events striking and original) to a style, not only unimpassioned but undistinguished. He sinks too often and too abruptly to that style which I should place in the second division of language, dividing it into the three species; first, that which is peculiar to poetry; second, that which is only proper in prose; and third, the neutral or common to both. There have been works, such as Cowley's *Essay on Cromwell,* in which prose and verse are intermixed (not as in the *Consolation* of Boetius, or the *Argenis* of Barclay, by the insertion of poems supposed to have been spoken or composed on occasions previously related in prose, but) the poet passing from one to the other, as the nature of the thoughts or his own feelings dictated. Yet this mode of composition does not satisfy a cultivated taste. There is something unpleasant in the being thus obliged to alternate states of feeling so dissimilar, and this too in a species of writing, the pleasure from which is in part derived from the preparation and previous expectation of the reader. A portion of that awkwardness is felt which hangs upon the introduction of songs in our modern comic operas; and to prevent which the judicious Metastasio (as to whose exquisite taste there can be no hesitation, whatever doubts may be entertained as to his poetic genius) uniformly placed the *aria*[1] at the end of the scene, at the same time that he almost always raises and impassions the style of the recitative immediately preceding. Even in real life, the difference is great and evident between words used as the arbitrary marks of thought, our smooth marketcoin of intercourse, with the image and superscription worn out by currency; and those which convey pictures either borrowed from one outward object to enliven and particularize some other; or used allegorically to body forth the inward state of the person speaking; or such as are at least the exponents of his peculiar turn and unusual extent of faculty. So much so indeed, that in the social circles of private life we often find a striking use of the latter put a stop to the general flow of conversation, and by the excitement arising from concentered attention produce a sort of damp and interruption for some minutes after. But in the perusal of works of literary art, we prepare ourselves for such language; and the business of the writer, like that of a painter whose subject requires unusual splendor and prominence, is so to raise the lower and neutral tints, that

what in a different style would be the commanding colors, are here used as the means of that gentle *degradation* requisite in order to produce the effect of a whole. Where this is not achieved in a poem, the metre merely reminds the reader of his claims in order to disappoint them; and where this defect occurs frequently, his feelings are alternately startled by anticlimax and hyperclimax.

I refer the reader to the exquisite stanzas cited for another purpose[1] from *The Blind Highland Boy;* and then annex, as being in my opinion instances of this *disharmony* in style, the two following:

And one, the rarest, was a shell,
Which he, poor child, had studied well:
The shell of a green turtle, thin
And hollow;—you might sit therein,
    It was so wide, and deep.

Our Highland Boy oft visited
The house which held this prize; and, led
By choice or chance, did thither come
One day, when no one was at home,
    And found the door unbarred.

Or page 172, vol. I.[2]

'Tis gone—forgotten—*let me do
My best.* There was a smile or two—
I can remember them, I see
The smiles worth all the world to me.
Dear Baby, I must lay thee down:
Thou troublest me with strange alarms;
Smiles hast thou, sweet ones of thine own;
I cannot keep thee in my arms;
For they confound me: *as it is,*
I have forgot those smiles of his!

Or page 269, vol. I.[3]

Thou hast a nest, for thy love and thy rest,
And though little troubled with sloth,
Drunken lark! thou would'st be loth
To be such a traveller as I.
    Happy, happy liver!
*With a soul as strong as a mountain river
Pouring out praise to th' Almighty Giver;*
Joy and jollity be with us both!
Hearing thee or else some other,
    As merry a brother
I on the earth will go plodding on
By myself cheerfully till the day is done.

The incongruity which I appear to find in this passage, is that of the two noble lines in italics with the preceding and following. So vol. II, page 30.[4]

Close by a pond, upon the further side,
He stood alone; a minute's space I guess,
I watch'd him, he continuing motionless:
To the pool's further margin then I drew;
He being all the while before me full in view.

Compare this with the repetition of the same image, in the next stanza but two.

---

[1] An elaborate melody sung by a single voice.

[1] To illustrate Wordsworth's style and diction in simple narrative.—*Biographia Literaria,* 20.
[2] *The Emigrant Mother.*
[3] *To a Skylark* (p. 323).
[4] *Resolution and Independence* (p. 309).

And still as I drew near with gentle pace,
Beside the little pond or moorish flood
Motionless as a cloud the old man stood,
That heareth not the loud winds when they call;
And moveth altogether, if it move at all.

Or lastly, the second of the three following
stanzas, compared both with the first and the
third.

My former thoughts returned; the fear that kills;
And hope that is unwilling to be fed;
Cold, pain, and labor, and all fleshly ills;
And mighty poets in their misery dead.
But now, perplex'd by what the old man had said,
My question eagerly did I renew,
"How is it that you live, and what is it you do?"

He with a smile did then his words repeat;
And said, that gathering leeches far and wide
He travell'd; stirring thus about his feet
The waters of the ponds where they abide.
"Once I could meet with them on every side,
But they have dwindled long by slow decay;
Yet still I persevere, and find them where I may."

While he was talking thus, the lonely place,
The old man's shape, and speech, all troubled me:
In my mind's eye I seemed to see him pace
About the weary moors continually,
Wandering about alone and silently.

Indeed this fine poem is *especially* characteristic of the author. There is scarce a defect or excellence in his writings of which it
would not present a specimen. But it would
be unjust not to repeat that this defect is
only occasional. From a careful reperusal
of the two volumes of poems, I doubt
whether the objectionable passages would
amount in the whole to one hundred lines;
not the eighth part of the number of pages.
In *The Excursion* the feeling of incongruity
is seldom excited by the diction of any passage considered in itself, but by the sudden
superiority of some other passage forming
the context.

The second defect I can generalize with
tolerable accuracy, if the reader will pardon
an uncouth and new-coined word. There is,
I should say, not seldom a *matter-of-factness*
in certain poems. This may be divided into,
first, a laborious minuteness and fidelity in
the representation of objects, and their positions, as they appeared to the poet himself;
secondly, the insertion of accidental circumstances, in order to the full explanation of
his living characters, their dispositions and
actions, which circumstances might be necessary to establish the probability of a statement in real life, where nothing is taken for
granted by the hearer, but appear superfluous in poetry, where the reader is willing
to believe for his own sake. To this *acciden-
tality* I object, as contravening the essence
of poetry, which Aristotle pronounces to be
σπουδαιότατον καὶ φιλοσοφώτατον γένος,[1] the

[1] The most serious and most philosophical kind
(*Poetics*, 9, 3).

most intense, weighty and philosophical
product of human art; adding, as the reason, that it is the most catholic and abstract.
The following passage from Davenant's
prefatory letter to Hobbes well expresses
this truth. "When I considered the actions
which I meant to describe (those inferring
the persons), I was again persuaded rather
to choose those of a former age, than the
present; and in a century so far removed,
as might preserve me from their improper
examinations, who know not the requisites
of a poem, nor how much pleasure they lose
(and even the pleasures of heroic poesy are
not unprofitable) who take away the liberty
of a poet, and fetter his feet in the shackles
of an historian. For why should a poet
doubt in story to mend the intrigues of fortune by more delightful conveyances of
probable fictions, because austere historians
have entered into bond to truth? An obligation, which were in poets as foolish and
unnecessary, as is the bondage of false martyrs, who lie in chains for a mistaken
opinion. *But by this I would imply that
truth, narrative and past, is the idol of historians (who worship a dead thing), and
truth operative, and by effects continually
alive, is the mistress of poets, who hath not
her existence in matter, but in reason.*"
For this minute accuracy in the painting
of local imagery, the lines in *The Excursion*,
pp. 96, 97, and 98,[1] may be taken, if not as
a striking instance, yet as an illustration of
my meaning. It must be some strong motive
(as, for instance, that the description was
necessary to the intelligibility of the tale)
which could induce me to describe in a number of verses what a draughtsman could present to the eye with incomparably greater
satisfaction by half a dozen strokes of his
pencil, or the painter with as many touches
of his brush. Such descriptions too often
occasion in the mind of a reader, who is determined to understand his author, a feeling
of labor not very dissimilar to that with
which he would construct a diagram, line by
line, for a long geometrical proposition. It
seems to be like taking the pieces of a dissected map out of its box. We first look at
one part, and then at another, then join and
dovetail them; and when the successive acts
of attention have been completed, there is a
retrogressive effort of mind to behold it as
a whole. The poet should paint to the imagination, not to the fancy; and I know no
happier case to exemplify the distinction
between these two faculties. Masterpieces of

[1] Book 3, 50 ff.

the former mode of poetic painting abound in the writings of Milton, for example:

The fig-tree ; not that kind for fruit renown'd,
But such as at this day, to Indians known,
In Malabar or Decan spreads her arms
Branching so broad and long, that in the ground
The bended twigs take root, *and daughters grow
About the mother tree, a pillar'd shade
High over-arch'd and* ECHOING WALKS BETWEEN :
*There oft the Indian herdsman, shunning heat,
Shelters in cool, and tends his pasturing herds
At loopholes cut through thickest shade.*[1]

This is creation rather than painting, or if painting, yet such, and with such co-presence of the whole picture flashed at once upon the eye, as the sun paints in a camera obscura. But the poet must likewise understand and command what Bacon calls the *vestigia communia*[2] of the senses, the latency of all in each, and more especially as by a magical *penna duplex*,[3] the excitement of vision by sound and the exponents of sound. Thus, "The echoing walks between," may be almost said to reverse the fable in tradition of the head of Memnon, in the Egyptian statue.[4] Such may be deservedly entitled the *creative words* in the world of imagination.

The second division respects an apparent minute adherence to *matter-of-fact* in character and incidents; *a biographical* attention to probability, and an *anxiety* of explanation and retrospect. Under this head I shall deliver, with no feigned diffidence, the results of my best reflection on the great point of controversy between Mr. Wordsworth and his objectors; namely, on *the choice of his characters*. I have already declared and, I trust, justified, my utter dissent from the mode of argument which his critics have hitherto employed. To *their* question, Why did you choose such a character, or a character from such a rank of life? the poet might, in my opinion, fairly retort: Why with the conception of my character did you make wilful choice of mean or ludicrous associations not furnished by me, but supplied from your own sickly and fastidious feelings? How was it, indeed, probable that such arguments could have any weight with an author whose plan, whose guiding principle, and main object it was to attack and subdue that state of association which leads us to place the chief value on those things on which man differs from man, and to forget or disregard the high dignities, which belong to Human Nature, the sense

and the feeling, which may be, and ought to be, found in all ranks? The feelings with which, as Christians, we contemplate a mixed congregation rising or kneeling before their common Maker, Mr. Wordsworth would have us entertain at all times, as men, and as readers; and by the excitement of this lofty, yet prideless impartiality in poetry, he might hope to have encouraged its continuance in real life. The praise of good men be his! In real life, and, I trust, even in my imagination, I honor a virtuous and wise man, without reference to the presence or absence of artificial advantages. Whether in the person of an armed baron, a laurelled bard, or of an old pedlar, or still older leech-gatherer, the same qualities of head and heart must claim the same reverence. And even in poetry I am not conscious that I have ever suffered my feelings to be disturbed or offended by any thoughts or images which the poet himself has not presented.

But yet I object, nevertheless, and for the following reasons. First, because the object in view, as an *immediate* object, belongs to the moral philosopher, and would be pursued, not only more appropriately, but in my opinion with far greater probability of success, in sermons or moral essays, than in an elevated poem. It seems, indeed, to destroy the main fundamental distinction, not only between a poem and prose, but even between philosophy and works of fiction, inasmuch as it proposes *truth* for its immediate object, instead of *pleasure*. Now till the blessed time shall come, when truth itself shall be pleasure, and both shall be so united, as to be distinguishable in words only, not in feeling, it will remain the poet's office to proceed upon that state of association, which actually exists as general; instead of attempting first to make it what it ought to be, and then to let the pleasure follow. But here is unfortunately a small *hysteron-proteron*.[1] For the communication of pleasure is the introductory means by which alone the poet must expect to moralize his readers. Secondly: though I were to admit, for a moment, *this* argument to be groundless: yet how is the moral effect to be produced, by merely attaching the name of some low profession to powers which are *least* likely, and to qualities which are assuredly not *more* likely, to be found in it? The poet, speaking in his own person, may at once delight and improve us by sentiments which teach us the independence of goodness, of wisdom, and even of genius, on the favors of fortune.

[1] An inversion of the logical order.

---

[1] *Paradise Lost*, 9, 1101 ff.
[2] common tokens
[3] double feather
[4] The statue of Memnon, when struck by the first rays of the sun, was s a i d to give forth a sound like the snapping of a musical string.

And having made a due reverence before the
throne of Antonine, he may bow with equal
awe before Epictetus among his fellow-
slaves—

and rejoice
In the plain presence of his dignity.[1]

Who is not at once delighted and improved,
when the Poet Wordsworth himself exclaims,

O, many are the poets that are sown
By Nature; men endowed with highest gifts,
The vision and the faculty divine,
Yet wanting the accomplishment of verse,
Nor having e'er, as life advanced, been led
By circumstance to take unto the height
The measure of themselves, these favored beings,
All but a scattered few, live out their time,
Husbanding that which they possess within,
And go to the grave, unthought of. Strongest minds
Are often those of whom the noisy world
Hears least.[2]

To use a colloquial phrase, such sentiments,
in such language, do one's heart good;
though I, for my part, have not the fullest
faith in the *truth* of the observation. On
the contrary, I believe the instances to be
exceedingly rare; and should feel almost as
strong an objection to introduce such a character in a poetic fiction, as a pair of black
swans on a lake, in a fancy landscape. When
I think how many, and how much better
books than Homer, or even than Herodotus,
Pindar, or Æschylus, could have read, are
in the power of almost every man, in a country where almost every man is instructed to
read and write; and how restless, how diffi-
cultly hidden, the powers of genius are; and
yet find even in situations the most favorable, according to Mr. Wordsworth, for the
formation of a pure and poetic language—
in situations which ensure familiarity with
the grandest objects of the imagination—but
one Burns, among the shepherds of Scotland,
and not a single poet of humble life among
those of English lakes and mountains, I conclude, that Poetic Genius is not only a very
delicate, but a very rare plant.

But be this as it may; the feelings with
which

I think of Chatterton, the marvellous boy,
The sleepless soul, that perished in his pride;
Of Burns, that walk'd in glory and in joy
Behind his plough, upon the mountain-side,[3]—

are widely different from those with which
I should read a *poem*, where the author, having occasion for the character of a poet and
a philosopher in the fable of his narration,
has chosen to make him a chimney-sweeper;
and then, in order to remove all doubts on

the subject, had *invented* an account of his
birth, parentage, and education, with all the
strange and fortunate accidents which had
concurred in making him at once poet, philosopher, and sweep! Nothing but biography can justify this. If it be admissible
even in a novel, it must be one in the manner
of De Foe's, that were meant to pass for
histories, not in the manner of Fielding's:
in *The Life of Moll Flanders,* or *Colonel
Jack,* not in a *Tom Jones,* or even a *Joseph
Andrews.* Much less, then, can it be legiti-
mately introduced in a poem, the characters
of which, amid the strongest individualiza-
tion, must still remain representative. The
precepts of Horace,[1] on this point, are
grounded on the nature both of poetry and
of the human mind. They are not more peremptory, than wise and prudent. For, in the
first place, a deviation from them perplexes
the reader's feelings, and all the circumstances which are feigned in order to make
such accidents less improbable, divide and
disquiet his faith, rather than aid and support it. Spite of all attempts, the fiction will
appear, and unfortunately not as fictitious
but as false. The reader not only knows that
the sentiments and language are the poet's
own, and his own, too, in his artificial character, as poet; but by the fruitless endeavors
to make him think the contrary, he is not
even suffered to forget it. The effect is similar to that produced by an epic poet, when
the fable and the characters are *derived* from
Scripture history, as in *The Messiah* of
Klopstock, or in Cumberland's *Calvary;*
and not merely *suggested* by it as in the
Paradise Lost of Milton. That illusion,
contradistinguished from delusion, that negative faith, which simply permits the images
presented to work by their own force, without either denial or affirmation of their real
existence by the judgment, is rendered impossible by their immediate neighborhood to
words and facts of known and absolute
truth. A faith which transcends even historic belief must absolutely *put out* this
mere poetic *analogon*[2] of faith, as the summer sun is said to extinguish our household
fires, when it shines full upon them. What
would otherwise have been yielded to as
pleasing fiction, is repelled as revolting falsehood. The effect produced in this latter case
by the solemn belief of the reader, is in a
less degree brought about in the instances to
which I have been objecting, by the baffled
attempts of the author to *make* him believe.

[1] *The Excursion,* 1, 76.
[2] *The Excursion,* 1, 77 ff.
[3] *Resolution and Independence,* 43 ff. (p. 310).

[1] See his *Ars Poetica (Poetic Art),* 148 ff.
[2] analogue

Add to all the foregoing the seeming uselessness both of the project and of the anecdotes from which it is to derive support. Is there one word, for instance, attributed to the pedlar in *The Excursion,* characteristic of a pedlar? one sentiment that might not more plausibly, even without the aid of any previous explanation, have proceeded from any wise and beneficent old man, of a rank or profession in which the language of learning and refinement are natural and to be expected? Need the rank have been at all particularized, where nothing follows which the knowledge of that rank is to explain or illustrate? when on the contrary this information renders the man's language, feelings, sentiments, and information a riddle, which must itself be solved by episodes of anecdote? Finally, when this, and this alone, could have induced a genuine poet to inweave in a poem of the loftiest style, and on subjects the loftiest and of most universal interest, such minute matters of fact, (not unlike those furnished for the obituary of a magazine by the friends of some obscure "ornament of society lately deceased" in some obscure town,) as

Among the hills of Athol he was born;
There, on a small hereditary farm,
An unproductive slip of rugged ground,
His father dwelt; and died in poverty;
While he, whose lowly fortune I retrace,
The youngest of three sons, was yet a babe,
A little one—unconscious of their loss.
But ere he had outgrown his infant days
His widowed mother, for a second mate,
Espoused the teacher of the village-school;
Who on her offspring zealously bestowed
Needful instruction.

From his sixth year, the boy of whom I speak,
In summer tended cattle on the hills;
But, through the inclement and the perilous days
Of long-continuing winter, he repaired
To his step-father's school,[1] etc.

For all the admirable passages interposed in this narration, might, with trifling alterations, have been far more appropriately, and with far greater verisimilitude, told of a poet in the character of a poet; and without incurring another defect which I shall now mention, and a sufficient illustration of which will have been here anticipated.

Third; an undue predilection for the *dramatic* form in certain poems, from which one or other of two evils result. Either the thoughts and diction are different from that of the poet, and then there arises an incongruity of style; or they are the same and indistinguishable, and then it presents a species of ventriloquism, where two are represented as talking, while in truth one man only speaks.

[1] *The Excursion,* 1, 108 ff.

The fourth class of defects is closely connected with the former; but yet are such as arise likewise from an intensity of feeling disproportionate to such knowledge and value of the objects described, as can be fairly anticipated of men in general, even of the most cultivated classes; and with which therefore few only, and those few particularly circumstanced, can be supposed to sympathize. In this class, I comprise occasional prolixity, repetition, and an eddying, instead of progression, of thought. As instances, see pages 27, 28,[1] and 62[2] of the Poems, Vol. I., and the first eighty lines of the Sixth Book of *The Excursion.*

Fifth and last; thoughts and images too great for the subject. This is an approximation to what might be called mental bombast, as distinguished from verbal: for, as in the latter there is a disproportion of the expressions to the thoughts, so in this there is a disproportion of thought to the circumstance and occasion. This, by the bye, is a fault of which none but a man of genius is capable. It is the awkwardness and strength of Hercules with the distaff of Omphale.

It is a well-known fact that bright colors in motion both make and leave the strongest impressions on the eye. Nothing is more likely too, than that a vivid image or visual spectrum, thus originated, may become the link of association in recalling the feelings and images that had accompanied the original impression. But if we describe this in such lines as

They flash upon that inward eye,
Which is the bliss of solitude![3]

in what words shall we describe the joy of retrospection, when the images and virtuous actions of a whole well-spent life pass before that conscience which is indeed the *inward* eye: which is indeed "*the bliss of solitude?*" Assuredly we seem to sink most abruptly, not to say burlesquely, and almost as in a medley, from this couplet to—

And then my heart with pleasure fills,
And dances with the daffodils.
Vol. I, p. 320

The second instance is from Vol. II., page 12,[4] where the poet, having gone out for a day's tour of pleasure, meets early in the morning with a knot of Gipsies, who had pitched their blanket-tents and straw-beds, together with their children and asses, in

[1] *Anecdote for Fathers.*
[2] This page of vol. I is blank.
[3] *I Wandered Lonely As a Cloud,* 21-22 (p. 321).
[4] *Gipsies.*

some field by the roadside. At the close of
the day on his return our tourist found them
in the same place. "Twelve hours," says he,

> Twelve hours, twelve bounteous hours are gone, while I
> Have been a traveller under open sky,
> Much witnessing of change and cheer,
> Yet as I left I find them here!

Whereat the poet, without seeming to reflect that the poor tawny wanderers might
probably have been tramping for weeks together through road and lane, over moor and
mountain, and consequently must have been
right glad to rest themselves, their children
and cattle, for one whole day; and overlooking the obvious truth, that such repose might
be quite as necessary for them, as a walk of
the same continuance was pleasing or healthful for the more fortunate poet; expresses
his indignation in a series of lines, the diction and imagery of which would have been
rather above, than below the mark, had they
been applied to the immense empire of
China improgressive for thirty centuries:

> The weary Sun betook himself to rest:—
> —Then issued Vesper from the fulgent west,
> Outshining, like a visible God,
> The glorious path in which he trod!
> And now, ascending, after one dark hour,
> And one night's diminution of her power,
> Behold the mighty Moon! this way
> She looks, as if at them—but they
> Regard not her:—oh, better wrong and strife,
> Better vain deeds or evil than such life!
> The silent Heavens have goings on:
> The stars have tasks!—But these have none!

The last instance of this defect (for I
know no other than these already cited) is
from the Ode,[1] page 351, Vol. II, where,
speaking of a child, "a six years' darling
of a pigmy size," he thus addresses him:

> Thou best philosopher, who yet dost keep
> Thy heritage! Thou eye among the blind,
> That, deaf and silent, read'st the eternal deep,
> Haunted forever by the Eternal Mind,—
> Mighty Prophet! Seer blest!
> On whom those truths do rest,
> Which we are toiling all our lives to find!
> Thou, over whom thy immortality
> Broods like the day, a master o'er a slave,
> A presence which is not to be put by!

Now here, not to stop at the daring spirit
of metaphor which connects the epithets
"deaf and silent," with the apostrophized
eye: or (if we are to refer it to the preceding word, "philosopher") the faulty and
equivocal syntax of the passage; and without examining the propriety of making a
"master brood o'er a slave," or "the day"
brood at all; we will merely ask, What does
all this mean? In what sense is a child of

[1] Intimations of Immortality (p. 329).

that age a philosopher? In what sense does
he read "the eternal deep?" In what sense
is he declared to be "forever haunted" by
the Supreme Being? or so inspired as to
deserve the splendid titles of a mighty
prophet, a blessed seer? By reflection? by
knowledge? by conscious intuition? or by
any form or modification of consciousness?
These would be tidings indeed; but such as
would presuppose an immediate revelation
to the inspired communicator, and require
miracles to authenticate his inspiration.
Children at this age give us no such information of themselves; and at what time
were we dipped in the Lethe, which has produced such utter oblivion of a state so godlike? There are many of us that still possess
some remembrances, more or less distinct,
respecting themselves at six years old; pity
that the worthless straws only should float,
while treasures, compared with which all the
mines of Golconda and Mexico were but
straws, should be absorbed by some unknown
gulf into some unknown abyss.

But if this be too wild and exorbitant to
be suspected as having been the poet's meaning; if these mysterious gifts, faculties, and
operations, are not accompanied with consciousness; who else is conscious of them?
or how can it be called the child, if it be no
part of the child's conscious being? For
aught I know, the thinking Spirit within me
may be substantially one with the principle
of life, and of vital operation. For aught
I know, it might be employed as a secondary
agent in the marvellous organization and
organic movements of my body. But, surely,
it would be strange language to say that I
construct my heart! or that I propel the
finer influences through my nerves! or that
I compress my brain, and draw the curtains
of sleep round my own eyes! Spinoza and
Behmen were, on different systems, both
Pantheists; and among the ancients there
were philosophers, teachers of the EN KAI
πAN,[1] who not only taught that God was
All, but that this All constituted God. Yet
not even these would confound the part, as a
part, with the whole, as the whole. Nay, in
no system is the distinction between the individual and God, between the modification,
and the one only substance, more sharply
drawn, than in that of Spinoza. Jacobi indeed relates of Lessing, that, after a conversation with him at the house of the poet
Gleim (the Tyrtæus and Anacreon of the
German Parnassus) in which conversation
Lessing had avowed privately to Jacobi his

[1] one and the whole (pantheism)

reluctance to admit any *personal* existence of the Supreme Being, or the *possibility* of personality except in a finite Intellect, and while they were sitting at table, a shower of rain came on unexpectedly. Gleim expressed his regret at the circumstance, because they had meant to drink their wine in the garden: upon which Lessing, in one of his half-earnest, half-joking moods, nodded to Jacobi, and said, "It is *I*, perhaps, that am doing *that*," *i.e., raining!*—and Jacobi answered, "or perhaps I;" Gleim contented himself with staring at them both, without asking for any explanation.

So with regard to this passage. In what sense can the magnificent attributes, above quoted, be appropriated to a *child,* which would not make them equally suitable to a *bee*, or a *dog*, or a *field of corn;* or even to a ship, or to the wind and waves that propel it? The omnipresent Spirit works equally in them, as in the child; and the child is equally unconscious of it as they. It cannot surely be that the four lines immediately following are to contain the explanation?

> To whom the grave
> Is but a lonely bed without the sense or sight
> Of day or the warm light,
> A place of thought where we in waiting lie.[1]

Surely, it cannot be that this wonder-rousing apostrophe is but a comment on the little poem *We are Seven?* that the whole meaning of the passage is reducible to the assertion that a child, who, by the bye, at six years old would have been better instructed in most Christian families, has no other notion of death than that of lying in a dark, cold place? And still, I hope, not as in a *place of thought!* not the frightful notion of lying *awake* in his grave! The analogy between death and sleep is too simple, too natural, to render so horrid a belief possible for children; even had they not been in the habit, as all Christian children are, of hearing the latter term used to express the former. But if the child's belief be only that "he is not dead, but sleepeth,"[2] wherein does it differ from that of his father and mother, or any other adult and instructed person? To form an idea of a thing's becoming nothing; or of nothing becoming a thing; is impossible to all finite beings alike, of whatever age, and however educated or uneducated. Thus it is with splendid paradoxes in general. If the words are taken in the common sense, they convey an absurd-

ity; and if, in contempt of dictionaries and custom, they are so interpreted as to avoid the absurdity, the meaning dwindles into some bald truism. Thus you must at once understand the words *contrary* to their common import, in order to arrive at any *sense;* and *according* to their common import, if you are to receive from them any feeling of *sublimity* or *admiration.*

Though the instances of this defect in Mr. Wordsworth's poems are so few that for themselves it would have been scarcely just to attract the reader's attention toward them, yet I have dwelt on it, and perhaps the more for this very reason. For being so very few, they cannot sensibly detract from the reputation of an author who is even characterized by the number of profound truths in his writings, which will stand the severest analysis; and yet few as they are, they are exactly those passages which his *blind* admirers would be most likely, and best able, to imitate. But Wordsworth, where he is indeed Wordsworth, may be mimicked by copyists, he may be plundered by plagiarists; but he cannot be imitated, except by those who are not born to be imitators. For without his depth of feeling and his imaginative power his *sense* would want its vital warmth and peculiarity; and without his strong sense, his *mysticism* would become *sickly*—mere fog, and dimness!

To these defects which, as appears by the extracts, are only occasional, I may oppose, with far less fear of encountering the dissent of any candid and intelligent reader, the following (for the most part correspondent) excellencies. First, an austere purity of language both grammatically and logically; in short a perfect appropriateness of the words to the meaning. Of how high value I deem this, and how particularly estimable I hold the example at the present day, has been already stated:[1] and in part, too, the reasons on which I ground both the moral and intellectual importance of habituating ourselves to a strict accuracy of expression. It is noticeable how limited an acquaintance with the masterpieces of art will suffice to form a correct and even a sensitive taste, where none but masterpieces have been seen and admired: while, on the other hand, the most correct notions, and the widest acquaintance with the works of excellence of all ages and countries, will not perfectly secure us against the contagious familiarity with the far more numerous offspring of

---

[1] These lines are found only in the editions of 1807 and 1815.
[2] *Matthew,* 9 :24.

[1] *Biographia Literaria,* 2.

tastelessness or of a perverted taste. If this be the case, as it notoriously is, with the arts of music and painting, much more difficult will it be to avoid the infection of multiplied and daily examples in the practice of an art which uses words, and words only, as its instruments. In poetry, in which every line, every phrase, may pass the ordeal of deliberation and deliberate choice, it is possible, and barely possible, to attain that ultimatum which I have ventured to propose as the infallible test of a blameless style,—namely, its *untranslatableness* in words of the same language without injury to the meaning. Be it observed, however, that I include in the *meaning* of a word not only its correspondent object, but likewise all the associations which it recalls. For language is framed to convey not the object alone, but likewise the character, mood, and intentions of the person who is representing it. In poetry it *is* practicable to preserve the diction uncorrupted by the affections and misappropriations which promiscuous authorship, and reading not promiscuous only because it is disproportionately most conversant with the compositions of the day, have rendered general. Yet even to the poet, composing in his own province, it is an arduous work: and as the result and pledge of a watchful good sense, of fine and luminous distinction, and of complete self-possession, may justly claim all the honor which belongs to an attainment equally difficult and valuable, and the more valuable for being rare. It is at *all* times the proper food of the understanding; but in an age of corrupt eloquence it is both food and antidote.

In prose I doubt whether it be even possible to preserve our style wholly unalloyed by the vicious phraseology which meets us everywhere, from the sermon to the newspaper, from the harangue of the legislator to the speech from the convivial chair, announcing a *toast* or sentiment. Our chains rattle, even while we are complaining of them. The poems of Boetius rise high in our estimation when we compare them with those of his contemporaries, as Sidonius Apollinarius, &c. They might even be referred to a purer age, but that the prose in which they are set, as jewels in a crown of lead or iron, betrays the true age of the writer. Much, however, may be effected by education. I believe not only from grounds of reason, but from having in great measure assured myself of the fact by actual though limited experience, that, to a youth led from his first boyhood to investigate the meaning of every word and the reason of its choice and position, logic presents itself as an old acquaintance under new names.

On some future occasion, more especially demanding such disquisition, I shall attempt to prove the close connection between veracity and habits of mental accuracy; the beneficial after-effects of verbal precision in the preclusion of fanaticism, which masters the feelings more especially by indistinct watch-words; and to display the advantages which language alone, at least which language with incomparably greater ease and certainty than any other means, presents to the instructor of impressing modes of intellectual energy so constantly, so imperceptibly, and, as it were, by such elements and atoms, as to secure in due time the formation of a second nature. When we reflect that the cultivation of the judgment is a positive command of the moral law, since the reason can give the *principle* alone, and the conscience bears witness only to the *motive,* while the application and effects must depend on the judgment: when we consider that the greater part of our success and comfort in life depends on distinguishing the similar from the same, that which is peculiar in each thing from that which it has in common with others, so as still to select the most probable, instead of the merely possible or positively unfit, we shall learn to value earnestly and with a practical seriousness a mean, already prepared for us by nature and society, of teaching the young mind to think well and wisely by the same unremembered process and with the same never-forgotten results, as those by which it is taught to speak and converse. Now how much warmer the interest is, how much more genial the feelings of reality and practicability, and thence how much stronger the impulses to imitation are, which a *contemporary* writer, and especially a contemporary *poet,* excites in youth and commencing manhood, has been treated of in the earlier pages of these sketches.[1] I have only to add that all the praise which is due to the exertion of such influence for a purpose so important, joined with that which must be claimed for the infrequency of the same excellence in the same perfection, belongs in full right to Mr. Wordsworth. I am far, however, from denying that we have poets whose *general* style possesses the same excellence, as Mr. Moore, Lord Byron, Mr. Bowles, and, in all his later and more im-

[1] In discussing the influence of Bowles.—Chapter 1.

portant works, our laurel-honoring Laureate.[1] But there are none in whose works I do not appear to myself to find *more* exceptions than in those of Wordsworth. Quotations or specimens would here be wholly out of place, and must be left for the critic who doubts and would invalidate the justice of this eulogy so applied.

The second characteristic excellence of Mr. Wordsworth's work is: a correspondent weight and sanity of the thoughts and sentiments, won, not from books, but from the poet's own meditative observation. They are *fresh* and have the dew upon them. His muse, at least when in her strength of wing, and when she hovers aloft in her proper element,

> Makes audible a linkèd lay of truth,
> Of truth profound a sweet continuous lay,
> Not learnt, but native, her own natural notes![2]

Even throughout his smaller poems there is scarcely one which is not rendered valuable by some just and original reflection.

See page 25, vol. II[3]: or the two following passages in one of his humblest compositions.[4]

> O reader! had you in your mind
> Such stores as silent thought can bring,
> O gentle reader! you would find
> A tale in every thing;

and

> I've heard of hearts unkind, kind deeds
> With coldness still returning;
> Alas! the gratitude of men
> Has oftener left me mourning;

or in a still higher strain the six beautiful quatrains, page 134.[5]

> Thus fares it still in our decay:
> And yet the wiser mind
> Mourns less for what age takes away
> Than what it leaves behind.
>
> The blackbird in the summer trees,
> The lark upon the hill,
> Let loose their carols when they please,
> Are quiet when they will.
>
> With Nature never do *they* wage
> A foolish strife; they see
> A happy youth, and their old age
> Is beautiful and free!
>
> But we are pressed by heavy laws;
> And often glad no more,
> We wear a face of joy, because
> We have been glad of yore.
>
> If there is one who need bemoan
> His kindred laid in earth,
> The household hearts that were his own,
> It is the man of mirth.
>
> My days, my friend, are almost gone,
> My life has been approved,

> And many love me; but by none
> Am I enough beloved;

or the sonnet on Buonaparté,[1] page 202, vol. II; or finally (for a volume would scarce suffice to exhaust the instances), the last stanza of the poem on the withered Celandine,[2] vol. II, p. 312.

> To be a prodigal's favorite—then, worse truth,
> A miser's pensioner—behold our lot!
> O man! that from thy fair and shining youth
> Age might but take the things youth needed
> not.

Both in respect of this and of the former excellence, Mr. Wordsworth strikingly resembles Samuel Daniel, one of the golden writers of our golden Elizabethan age, now most causelessly neglected: Samuel Daniel, whose diction bears no mark of time, no distinction of age, which has been, and as long as our language shall last, will be so far the language of the today and forever, as that it is more intelligible to us than the transitory fashions of our own particular age. A similar praise is due to his sentiments. No frequency of perusal can deprive them of their freshness. Nor though they are brought into the full daylight of every reader's comprehension, yet are they drawn up from depths which few in any age are privileged to visit, into which few in any age have courage or inclination to descend. If Mr. Wordsworth is not equally with Daniel alike intelligible to all readers of average understanding in all passages of his works, the comparative difficulty does not arise from the greater impurity of the ore, but from the nature and uses of the metal. A poem is not necessarily obscure because it does not aim to be popular. It is enough if a work be perspicuous to those for whom it is written, and

> Fit audience find, though few.[3]

To the *Ode on the Intimations of Immortality from Recollections of Early Childhood* the poet might have prefixed the lines which Dante addresses to one of his own Canzoni—

> Canzone, i' credo, che saranno radi
> Color, che tua ragione intendan bene,
> Tanto lor sei faticoso ed alto.[4]
>
> O lyric song, there will be few, I think,
> Who may thy import understand aright:
> Thou art for *them* so arduous and so high!

But the ode was intended for such readers only as had been accustomed to watch the

---

[1] Southey.
[2] Coleridge, *To a Gentleman*, 58-60 (p. 391).
[3] *Star-Gazers*, st. 3-6.
[4] *Simon Lee* (p. 256).
[5] *The Fountain* (p. 266).

[1] *I Grieved for Buonaparté* (p. 311).
[2] *The Small Celandine*.
[3] *Paradise Lost*, 7, 31.
[4] *Il Convivio*, 2, Canzone Prima.

flux and reflux of their inmost nature, to
venture at times into the twilight realms of
consciousness, and to feel a deep interest in
modes of inmost being, to which they know
that the attributes of time and space are
inapplicable and alien, but which yet can
not be conveyed, save in symbols of time and
space. For such readers the sense is sufficiently plain, and they will be as little disposed to charge Mr. Wordsworth with believing the Platonic pre-existence, in the
ordinary interpretation of the words, as I
am to believe that Plato himself ever meant
or taught it.

Πολλά δι ὑπ᾽ ἀγκῶ-
νος ὠκέα βέλη
ἔνδον ἐντὶ φαρέτρας
φωνᾶντα συνετοῖσιν· ἐς
δὲ τὸ πᾶν ἑρμηνέων
χατίζει. σοφὸς ὁ πολ-
λα εἰδὼς φυᾷ.
μαθόντες δὲ λάβροι
παγγλωσσια, κόρακες ὣς,
ἄκραντα γαρύετον
Διὸς πρὸς ὄρνιχα θεῖον.[1]

Third (and wherein he soars far above
Daniel), the sinewy strength and originality
of single lines and paragraphs: the frequent
curiosa felicitas[2] of his diction, of which I
need not here give specimens, having anticipated them in a preceding page. This
beauty, and as eminently characteristic of
Wordsworth's poetry, his rudest assailants
have felt themselves compelled to acknowledge and admire.

Fourth, the perfect truth of nature in
his images and descriptions as taken immediately from nature, and proving a long and
genial intimacy with the spirit which gives
the physiognomic expression to all the works
of nature. Like a green field reflected in a
calm and perfectly transparent lake, the
image is distinguished from the reality only
by its greater softness and lustre. Like the
moisture or the polish on a pebble, genius
neither distorts nor false-colors its objects;
but on the contrary brings out many a vein
and many a tint, which escape the eye of
common observation, thus raising to the
rank of gems what had been often kicked
away by the hurrying foot of the traveller
on the dusty high road of custom.

Let me refer to the whole description of
skating, vol. I, page 42 to 47,[1] especially to
the lines

So through the darkness and the cold we flew,
And not a voice was idle: with the din
Meanwhile the precipices rang aloud;
The leafless trees and every icy crag
Tinkled like iron; while the distant hills
Into the tumult sent an alien sound
Of melancholy, not unnoticed, while the stars
Eastward were sparkling clear, and in the west
The orange sky of evening died away.

Or to the poem on *The Green Linnet,* vol.
I, page 244. What can be more accurate
yet more lovely than the two concluding
stanzas?

Upon yon tuft of hazel trees,
That twinkle to the gusty breeze,
Behold him perched in ecstasies,
    Yet seeming still to hover;
There! where the flutter of his wings
Upon his back and body flings
Shadows and sunny glimmerings,
    That cover him all over.

While thus before my eyes he gleams,
A brother of the leaves he seems;
When in a moment forth he teems
    His little song in gushes:
As if it pleased him to disdain
And mock the form which he did feign
While he was dancing with the train
    Of leaves among the bushes.

Or the description of the blue-cap, and
of the noontide silence, page 284;[2] or the
poem to the cuckoo, page 299;[3] or, lastly,
though I might multiply the references to
ten times the number, to the poem, so completely Wordsworth's, commencing

Three years she grew in sun and shower—

Fifth, a meditative pathos, a union of
deep and subtle thought with sensibility;
a sympathy with man as man; the sympathy
indeed of a contemplator, rather than a
fellow-sufferer or co-mate (*spectator, haud
particeps*[4]), but of a contemplator, from
whose view no difference of rank conceals
the sameness of the nature; no injuries of
wind or weather, or toil, or even of ignorance, wholly disguise the human face divine. The superscription and the image of
the Creator still remain legible to *him* under
the dark lines with which guilt or calamity
had cancelled or cross-barred it. Here the
man and the poet lose and find themselves
in each other, the one as glorified, the latter
as substantiated. In this mild and philosophic pathos, Wordsworth appears to me
without a compeer. Such as he *is:* so he

[1] "I have many swift missiles within the quiver
under my arm that speak to those who understand; but for the multitude they need inter-
preters. Wise is he who knows many things by
nature; but those who have learned, ravenous
in their loquacity, like crows chatter idly
against the divine bird of Zeus."—Pindar,
Olympian Odes, 2, 91 ff. (Teuberg ed.).
[2] painstaking happiness

[1] *Influence of Natural Objects* (*The Prelude,* 1,
401-63, p. 269).
[2] *The Kitten and Fallen Leaves.*
[3] The one written in 1804 (p. 320)
[4] a looker-on, not a partaker

writes. See vol. I, pages 134 to 136,[1] or that most affecting composition, *The Affliction of Margaret —— of ——*, pages 165 to 168, which no mother, and, if I may judge by my own experience, no parent can read without a tear. Or turn to that genuine lyric, in the former edition, entitled *The Mad Mother,*[2] pages 174 to 178, of which I cannot refrain from quoting two of the stanzas, both of them for their pathos, and the former of the fine transition in the two concluding lines of the stanza, so expressive of that deranged state in which, from the increased sensibility, the sufferer's attention is abruptly drawn off by every trifle, and in the same instant plucked back again by the one despotic thought, bringing home with it, by the blending, *fusing* power of Imagination and Passion, the alien object to which it had been so abruptly diverted, no longer an alien but an ally and an inmate.

> Suck, little babe, oh suck again!
> It cools my blood; it cools my brain;
> Thy lips, I feel them, baby! they
> Draw from my heart the pain away.
> Oh! press me with thy little hand;
> It loosens something at my chest;
> About that tight and deadly band
> I feel thy little fingers prest.
> The breeze I see is in the tree!
> It comes to cool my babe and me.
>
> Thy father cares not for my breast,
> 'Tis thine, sweet baby, there to rest;
> 'Tis all thine own—and if its hue
> Be changed, that was so fair to view,
> 'Tis fair enough for thee, my dove!
> My beauty, little child, is flown,
> But thou wilt live with me in love;
> And what if my poor cheek be brown?
> 'Tis well for me, thou canst not see
> How pale and wan it else would be.

Last, and pre-eminently, I challenge for this poet the gift of Imagination in the highest and strictest sense of the word. In the play of *fancy,* Wordsworth, to my feelings, is not always graceful, and sometimes recondite. The *likeness* is occasionally too strange, or demands too peculiar a point of view, or is such as appears the creature of predetermined research, rather than spontaneous presentation. Indeed, his fancy seldom displays itself as mere and unmodified fancy. But in imaginative power he stands nearest of all modern writers to Shakespeare and Milton; and yet in a kind perfectly unborrowed and his own. To employ his own words, which are at once an instance and an illustration, he does indeed to all thoughts and to all objects—

> add the gleam,
> The light that never was, on sea or land,
> The consecration, and the poet's dream.[3]

[1] *'Tis Said That Some Have Died for Love* (p. 299).
[2] Later entitled *Her Eyes are Wild* (p. 255).
[3] *Elegiac Stanzas Suggested by a Picture of Peele Castle,* 14-16 (p. 323).

I shall select a few examples as most obviously manifesting this faculty; but if I should ever be fortunate enough to render my analysis of Imagination, its origin and characters, thoroughly intelligible to the reader, he will scarcely open on a page of this poet's works without recognizing, more or less, the presence and the influences of this faculty.

From the poem on the *Yew Trees,* vol. I, page 303, 304.

> But worthier still of note
> Are those fraternal four of Borrowdale,
> Joined in one solemn and capacious grove;
> Huge trunks!—and each particular trunk a
>   growth
> Of intertwisted fibres serpentine
> Up-coiling, and inveterately convolved,—
> Not uninformed with phantasy, and looks
> That threaten the profane;—a pillared shade,
> Upon whose grassless floor of red-brown hue,
> By sheddings from the pinal umbrage tinged
> Perennially—beneath whose sable roof
> Of boughs, as if for festal purpose, decked
> With unrejoicing berries, ghostly shapes
> May meet at noontide: Fear and trembling Hope,
> Silence and Foresight; Death, the skeleton,
> And Time, the shadow; there to celebrate,
> As in a natural temple scattered o'er
> With altars undisturbed of mossy stone,
> United worship; or in mute repose
> To lie, and listen to the mountain flood
> Murmuring from Glaramara's inmost caves.

The effect of the old man's figure in the poem of *Resolution and Independence,* vol. II, page 33.

> While he was talking thus, the lonely place,
> The old man's shape, and speech, all troubled
>   me:
> In my mind's eye I seemed to see him pace
> About the weary moors continually,
> Wandering about alone and silently.

Or the 8th,[1] 9th,[2] 19th,[3] 26th,[4] 31st,[5] and 33rd,[6] in the collection of miscellaneous sonnets—the sonnet on the subjugation of Switzerland,[7] page 210, or the last ode,[8] from which I especially select the two following stanzas or paragraphs, pages 349 to 350.

> Our birth is but a sleep and a forgetting;
> The soul that rises with us, our life's star,
> Hath had elsewhere its setting,
>   And cometh from afar.
> Not in entire forgetfulness,
> And not in utter nakedness,
> But trailing clouds of glory do we come
> From God, who is our home:
> Heaven lies about us in our infancy!
> Shades of the prison-house begin to close
>   Upon the growing boy;
> But he beholds the light, and whence it flows,
>   He sees it in his joy!

[1] *Where Lies the Land?*
[2] *Even as a Dragon's Eye.*
[3] *O Mountain Stream.*
[4] *Composed Upon Westminster Bridge* (p. 311).
[5] *Methought I Saw the Footsteps of a Throne.*
[6] *It is a Beauteous Evening, Calm and Free* (p. 312).
[7] *Thought of a Briton on the Subjugation of Switzerland* (p. 331).
[8] *Intimations of Immortality* (p. 329).

The youth who daily further from the East
Must travel, still is Nature's priest,
    And by the vision splendid
    Is on his way attended ;
At length the man perceives it die away,
And fade into the light of common day.

And pages 352 to 354 of the same ode.

O joy ! that in our embers
Is something that doth live,
That nature yet remembers
What was so fugitive !
The thought of our past years in me doth breed
Perpetual benedictions : not indeed
For that which is most worthy to be blest ;
Delight and liberty, the simple creed
Of childhood, whether busy or at rest,
With new-fledged hope still fluttering in his
        breast :—
Not for these I raise
The song of thanks and praise ;
But for those obstinate questionings
Of sense and outward things,
Fallings from us, vanishings ;
Blank misgivings of a creature
Moving about in worlds not realized,
High instincts, before which our mortal nature
Did tremble like a guilty thing surprised !
But for those first affections,
Those shadowy recollections,
Which, be they what they may,
Are yet the fountain light of all our day,
Are yet a master light of all our seeing ;
Uphold us—cherish—and have power to make
Our noisy years seem moments in the being
Of the eternal silence ; truths that wake
        To perish never ;
Which neither listlessness, nor mad endeavor,
Nor man nor boy,
Nor all that is at enmity with joy,
Can utterly abolish or destroy !
Hence, in a season of calm weather,
Though inland far we be,
Our souls have sight of that immortal sea
Which brought us hither,
Can in a moment travel thither,—
And see the children sport upon the shore,
And hear the mighty waters rolling evermore.

And since it would be unfair to conclude
with an extract which, though highly characteristic, must yet, from the nature of the
thoughts and the subject, be interesting or
perhaps intelligible, to but a limited number of readers, I will add, from the poet's
last published work, a passage equally
Wordsworthian, of the beauty of which, and
of the imaginative power displayed therein,
there can be but one opinion, and one feeling. See *White Doe*, page 5.

Fast the church-yard fills :—anon
Look again and they all are gone ;
The cluster round the porch, and the folk
Who sate in the shade of the Prior's Oak !
And scarcely have they disappeared
Ere the prelusive hymn is heard :—
With one consent the people rejoice,
Filling the church with a lofty voice !
They sing a service which they feel :
For 'tis the sun-rise now of zeal ;
And faith and hope are in their prime
In great Eliza's golden time.

A moment ends the fervent din.
And all is hushed, without and within ;
For though the priest, more tranquilly,
Recites the holy liturgy,
The only voice which you can hear
Is the river murmuring near.
When soft !—the dusky trees between,

And down the path through the open green,
Where is no living thing to be seen ;
And through yon gateway, where is found,
Beneath the arch with ivy bound,
Free entrance to the church-yard ground ;
And right across the verdant sod,
Towards the very house of God ;
Comes gliding in with lovely gleam,
Comes gliding in serene and slow,
Soft and silent as a dream.
A solitary doe !
White she is as lily of June,
And beauteous as the silver moon
When out of sight the clouds are driven
And she is left alone in heaven !
Or like a ship some gentle day
In sunshine sailing far away—
A glittering ship that hath the plain
Of ocean for her own domain.

        *   *   *   *   *

What harmonious pensive changes
Wait upon her as she ranges
Round and through this pile of state
Overthrown and desolate !
Now a step or two her way
Is through space of open day.
Where the enamored sunny light
Brightens her that was so bright ;
Now doth a delicate shadow fall,
Falls upon her like a breath,
From some lofty arch or wall,
As she passes underneath.[1]

The following analogy will, I am apprehensive, appear dim and fantastic, but in
reading Bartram's *Travels* I could not help
transcribing the following lines as a sort of
allegory, or connected simile and metaphor
of Wordsworth's intellect and genius.—
"The soil is a deep, rich, dark mould, on
a deep stratum of tenacious clay ; and that
on a foundation of rocks, which often
break through both strata, lifting their backs
above the surface. The trees which chiefly
grow here are the gigantic black oak, magnolia grandiflora, fraximus excelsior, pla-
tane, and a few stately tulip trees."[2] What
Mr. Wordsworth *will* produce, it is not for
me to prophesy : but I could pronounce
with the liveliest convictions what he is
capable of producing. It is the FIRST
GENUINE PHILOSOPHIC POEM.

The preceding criticism will not, I am
aware, avail to overcome the prejudices of
those who have made it a business to attack
and ridicule Mr. Wordsworth's compositions.

Truth and prudence might be imagined as
concentric circles. The poet may perhaps
have passed beyond the latter, but he has
confined himself far within the bounds of
the former, in designating these critics as
too petulant to be passive to a genuine poet,
and too feeble to grapple with him ; "men
of palsied imaginations, in whose minds all
healthy action is languid ;—who, therefore,
feed as the many direct them, or with the

---

[1] *The White Doe of Rylstone*, 1, 31-66 ; 79-90.
[2] *Travels thro' North and South Carolina and the
    Cherokee Country* (1792), p. 36.

many are greedy after vicious provocatives."[1]

Let not Mr. Wordsworth be charged with having expressed himself too indignantly, till the wantonness and the systematic and malignant perseverance of the aggressions have been taken into fair consideration. I myself heard the commander-in-chief[2] of this manly warfare make a boast of his private admiration of Wordsworth's genius. I have heard him declare that whoever came into his room would probably find the *Lyrical Ballads* lying open on his table, and that (speaking exclusively of those written by Mr. Wordsworth himself) he could nearly repeat the whole of them by heart. *But* a Review, in order to be a saleable article, must be *personal, sharp,* and *pointed:* and, *since then,* the poet has made himself, and with himself all who were, or were supposed to be, his friends and admirers, the object of the critic's revenge—how? by having spoken of a work so conducted in the terms which it deserved! I once heard a clergyman in boots and buckskin avow that he would cheat his own father *in a horse.* A moral system of a similar nature seems to have been adopted by too many anonymous critics. As we used to say at school, in reviewing they *make* being rogues: and he who complains is to be laughed at for his ignorance of the *game.* With the pen out of their hand they are *honorable men.* They exert indeed power (which is to that of the injured party who should attempt to expose their glaring perversions and misstatements, as twenty to one) to write down, and (where the author's circumstances permit) to *impoverish* the man, whose learning and genius they themselves in private have repeatedly admitted. They knowingly strive to make it impossible for the man even to publish any future work without exposing himself to all the wretchedness of debt and embarrassment. But this is all *in their vocation;* and, bating what they do in their *vocation, "who can say that black is the white of their eye?"*

So much for the detractors from Wordsworth's merits. On the other hand, much as I might wish for their fuller sympathy, I dare not flatter myself that the freedom with which I have declared my opinions concerning both his theory and his defects. most of which are more or less connected with his theory, either as cause or effect, will be satisfactory or pleasing to *all* the poet's admirers and advocates. More indiscriminate than mine their admiration may be: deeper and more sincere it cannot be. But I have advanced no opinion either for praise or censure, other than as texts introductory to the reasons which compel me to form it. Above all, I was fully convinced that such a criticism was not only wanted; but that, if executed with adequate ability, it must conduce, in no mean degree, to Mr. Wordsworth's *reputation.* His *fame* belongs to another age, and can neither be accelerated nor retarded. How small the proportion of the defects are to the beauties, I have repeatedly declared; and that no one of them originates in deficiency of poetic genius. Had they been more and greater, I should still, as a friend to his literary character in the present age, consider an analytic display of them as *pure gain;* if only it removed, as surely to all reflecting minds even the foregoing analysis must have removed, the strange mistake, so slightly grounded, yet so widely and industriously propagated, of Mr. Wordsworth's turn for *simplicity!* I am not half as much irritated by hearing his enemies abuse him for vulgarity of style, subject, and conception, as I am disgusted with the gilded side of the same meaning, as displayed by some affected admirers, with whom he is, forsooth, a "sweet, simple poet!" and *so* natural, that little master Charles and his younger sister are *so* charmed with them, that they play at "Goody Blake," or at "Johnny and Betty Foy!"

Were the collection of poems, published with these biographical sketches, important enough (which I am not vain enough to believe) to deserve such a distinction, *even as I have done, so would I be done unto.*

CHARACTERISTICS OF SHAKSPEARE'S DRAMAS
1813-1818 1836

In lectures of which amusement forms a large part of the object, there are some peculiar difficulties. The architect places his foundation out of sight, and the musician tunes his instrument before he makes his appearance; but the lecturer has to try his chords in the presence of the assembly, an operation not likely, indeed, to produce much pleasure, but yet indispensably necessary to a right understanding of the subject to be developed.

Poetry in essence is as familiar to barbarous as to civilized nations. The Laplander and the savage Indian are cheered by

---

[1] *Essay, Supplementary to the Preface.*
[2] Jeffrey.

it as well as the inhabitants of London and Paris; its spirit takes up and incorporates surrounding materials, as a plant clothes itself with soil and climate, whilst it exhibits the working of a vital principle within independent of all accidental circumstances. And to judge with fairness of an author's works, we ought to distinguish what is inward and essential from what is outward and circumstantial. It is essential to poetry that it be simple, and appeal to the elements and primary laws of our nature; that it be sensuous, and by its imagery elicit truth at a flash; that it be impassioned, and be able to move our feelings and awaken our affections. In comparing different poets with each other, we should inquire which have brought into the fullest play our imagination and our reason, or have created the greatest excitement and produced the completest harmony. If we consider great exquisiteness of language and sweetness of metre alone, it is impossible to deny to Pope the character of a delightful writer; but whether he be a poet, must depend upon our definition of the word; and, doubtless, if every thing that pleases be poetry, Pope's satires and epistles must be poetry. This I must say, that poetry, as distinguished from other modes of composition, does not rest in metre, and that it is not poetry, if it make no appeal to our passions or our imagination. One character belongs to all true poets, that they write from a principle within, not originating in any thing without; and that the true poet's work in its form, its shapings, and its modifications, is distinguished from all other works that assume to belong to the class of poetry, as a natural from an artificial flower, or as the mimic garden of a child from an enamelled meadow. In the former the flowers are broken from their stems and stuck into the ground; they are beautiful to the eye and fragrant to the sense, but their colors soon fade, and their odor is transient as the smile of the planter; while the meadow may be visited again and again with renewed delight; its beauty is innate in the soil, and its bloom is of the freshness of nature.

The next ground of critical judgment, and point of comparison, will be as to how far a given poet has been influenced by accidental circumstances. As a living poet must surely write, not for the ages past, but for that in which he lives, and those which are to follow, it is, on the one hand, natural that he should not violate, and on the other,

necessary that he should not depend on, the mere manners and modes of his day. See how little does Shakspeare leave us to regret that he was born in his particular age! The great era in modern times was what is called the Restoration of Letters; the ages preceding it are called the dark ages; but it would be more wise, perhaps, to call them the ages in which we were in the dark. It is usually overlooked that the supposed dark period was not universal, but partial and successive, or alternate; that the dark age of England was not the dark age of Italy, but that one country was in its light and vigor, whilst another was in its gloom and bondage. But no sooner had the Reformation sounded through Europe like the blast of an archangel's trumpet, than from king to peasant there arose an enthusiasm for knowledge; the discovery of a manuscript became the subject of an embassy; Erasmus read by moonlight, because he could not afford a torch, and begged a penny, not for the love of charity, but for the love of learning. The three great points of attention were religion, morals, and taste; men of genius as well as men of learning, who in this age need to be so widely distinguished, then alike became copyists of the ancients; and this, indeed, was the only way by which the taste of mankind could be improved, or their understandings informed. Whilst Dante imagined himself a humble follower of Virgil, and Ariosto of Homer, they were both unconscious of that greater power working within them, which in many points carried them beyond their supposed originals. All great discoveries bear the stamp of the age in which they are made; hence we perceive the effects of the purer religion of the moderns, visible for the most part in their lives; and in reading their works we should not content ourselves with the mere narratives of events long since passed, but should learn to apply their maxims and conduct to ourselves.

Having intimated that times and manners lend their form and pressure[1] to genius, let me once more draw a slight parallel between the ancient and modern stage, the stages of Greece and of England. The Greeks were polytheists; their religion was local; almost the only object of their knowledge, art, and taste, was their gods; and, accordingly, their productions were, if the expression may be allowed, statuesque, whilst those of the moderns are picturesque.

[1] impression (See *Hamlet,* III, 2, 27.)

The Greeks reared a structure which in its parts, and as a whole, filled the mind with the calm and elevated impression of perfect beauty, and symmetrical proportion. The moderns also produced a whole, a more striking whole; but it was by blending materials and fusing the parts together. And as the Pantheon is to York Minster or Westminster Abbey, so is Sophocles compared with Shakspeare; in the one a completeness, a satisfaction, an excellence, on which the mind rests with complacency; in the other a multitude of interlaced materials, great and little, magnificent and mean, accompanied, indeed, with the sense of a falling short of perfection, and yet, at the same time, so promising of our social and individual progression, that we would not, if we could, exchange it for that repose of the mind which dwells on the forms of symmetry in the acquiescent admiration of grace. This general characteristic of the ancient and modern drama might be illustrated by a parallel of the ancient and modern music, the one consisting of melody arising from a succession only of pleasing sounds, the modern embracing harmony also, the result of combination and the effect of a whole.

I have said, and I say it again, that great as was the genius of Shakspeare, his judgment was at least equal to it. Of this any one will be convinced, who attentively considers those points in which the dramas of Greece and England differ, from the dissimilitude of circumstances by which each was modified and influenced. The Greek stage had its origin in the ceremonies of a sacrifice, such as of the goat to Bacchus, whom we most erroneously regard as merely the jolly god of wine; for among the ancients he was venerable, as the symbol of that power which acts without our consciousness in the vital energies of nature,— the *vinum mundi*,[1]—as Apollo was that of the conscious agency of our intellectual being. The heroes of old under the influences of this Bacchic enthusiasm performed more than human actions; hence tales of the favorite champions soon passed into dialogue. On the Greek stage the chorus was always before the audience; the curtain was never dropped, as we should say; and change of place being therefore, in general, impossible, the absurd notion of condemning it merely as improbable in itself was never entertained by any one. If we can believe ourselves at Thebes in one act, we

may believe ourselves at Athens in the next. If a story lasts twenty-four hours or twenty-four years, it is equally improbable. There seems to be no just boundary but what the feelings prescribe. But on the Greek stage where the same persons were perpetually before the audience, great judgment was necessary in venturing on any such change. The poets never, therefore, attempted to impose on the senses by bringing places to men, but they did bring men to places, as in the well known instance in the *Eumenides*,[1] where during an evident retirement of the chorus from the orchestra, the scene is changed to Athens, and Orestes is first introduced in the temple of Minerva, and the chorus of Furies come in afterwards in pursuit of him.

In the Greek drama there were no formal divisions into scenes and acts; there were no means, therefore, of allowing for the necessary lapse of time between one part of the dialogue and another, and unity of time in a strict sense was, of course, impossible. To overcome that difficulty of accounting for time, which is effected on the modern stage by dropping a curtain, the judgment and great genius of the ancients supplied music and measured motion, and with the lyric ode filled up the vacuity. In the story of the *Agamemnon* of Æschylus, the capture of Troy is supposed to be announced by a fire lighted on the Asiatic shore, and the transmission of the signal by successive beacons to Mycenæ. The signal is first seen at the 21st line, and the herald from Troy itself enters at the 486th, and Agamemnon himself at the 783rd line. But the practical absurdity of this was not felt by the audience, who, in imagination stretched minutes into hours, while they listened to the lofty narrative odes of the chorus which almost entirely filled up the interspace. Another fact deserves attention here, namely, that regularly on the Greek stage a drama, or acted story, consisted in reality of three dramas, called together a trilogy, and performed consecutively in the course of one day. Now you may conceive a tragedy of Shakspeare's as a trilogy connected in one single representation. Divide *Lear* into three parts, and each would be a play with the ancients; or take the three Æschylean dramas of *Agamemnon*,[2] and divide them into, or call them, as many acts, and they together would be one play. The first act would comprise

[1] wine of the world

[1] V, 230-239.
[2] *Agamemnon, Chœphorai*, and *Eumenides*.

the usurpation of Ægisthus, and the murder of Agamemnon; the second, the revenge of Orestes, and the murder of his mother; and the third, the penance and absolution of Orestes;—occupying a period of twenty-two years.

The stage in Shakspeare's time was a naked room with a blanket for a curtain; but he made it a field for monarchs. That law of unity, which has its foundations, not in the factitious necessity of custom, but in nature itself, the unity of feeling, is everywhere and at all times observed by Shakspeare in his plays. Read *Romeo and Juliet:* all is youth and spring; youth with its follies, its virtues, its precipitancies; spring with its odors, its flowers, and its transciency. It is one and the same feeling that commences, goes through, and ends the play. The old men, the Capulets and the Montagues, are not common old men; they have an eagerness, a heartiness, a vehemence, the effect of spring; with Romeo, his change of passion, his sudden marriage, and his rash death, are all the effects of youth; whilst in Juliet, love has all that is tender and melancholy in the nightingale, all that is voluptuous in the rose, with whatever is sweet in the freshness of spring; but it ends with a long deep sigh like the last breeze of the Italian evening. This unity of feeling and character pervades every drama of Shakspeare.

It seems to me that his plays are distinguished from those of all other dramatic poets by the following characteristics:

1. Expectation in preference to surprise. It is like the true reading of the passage: "God said, Let there be light, and there was *light;*" not there *was* light. As the feeling with which we startle at a shooting star compared with that of watching the sunrise at the pre-established moment, such and so low is surprise compared with expectation.

2. Signal adherence to the great law of nature, that all opposites tend to attract and temper each other. Passion in Shakspeare generally displays libertinism, but involves morality; and if there are exceptions to this, they are, independently of their intrinsic value, all of them indicative of individual character, and, like the farewell admonitions of a parent, have an end beyond the parental relation. Thus the Countess's beautiful precepts to Bertram, by elevating her character, raise that of Helena her favorite, and soften down the point in her which Shakspeare does not mean us not to see, but to see and to for-give, and at length to justify. And so it is in Polonius, who is the personified memory of wisdom no longer actually possessed. This admirable character is always misrepresented on the stage. Shakspeare never intended to exhibit him as a buffoon; for although it was natural that Hamlet (a young man of fire and genius, detesting formality, and disliking Polonius on political grounds, as imagining that he had assisted his uncle in his usurpation) should express himself satirically; yet this must not be taken as exactly the poet's conception of him. In Polonius a certain induration of character had arisen from long habits of business; but take his advice to Laertes, and Ophelia's reverence for his memory, and we shall see that he was meant to be represented as a statesman somewhat past his faculties,—his recollections of life all full of wisdom, and showing a knowledge of human nature, whilst what immediately takes place before him, and escapes from him, is indicative of weakness.

But as in Homer all the deities are in armor, even Venus, so in Shakspeare all the characters are strong. Hence real folly and dulness are made by him the vehicles of wisdom. There is no difficulty for one being a fool to imitate a fool; but to be, remain, and speak like a wise man and a great wit, and yet so as to give a vivid representation of a veritable fool,—*hic labor, hoc opus est.*[1] A drunken constable is not uncommon, nor hard to draw; but see and examine what goes to make up a Dogberry.

3. Keeping at all times in the high road of life. Shakspeare has no innocent adulteries, no interesting incests, no virtuous vice; he never renders that amiable which religion and reason alike teach us to detest, or clothe impurity in the garb of virtue, like Beaumont and Fletcher, the Kotzebues of the day.[2] Shakspeare's fathers are roused by ingratitude, his husbands stung by unfaithfulness; in him, in short, the affections are wounded in those points in which all may, nay, must, feel. Let the morality of Shakspeare be contrasted with that of the writers of his own, or the succeeding, age, or of those of the present day, who boast their superiority in this respect. No one can dispute that the result of such a comparison is altogether in favor of Shak-

---

[1] this is the labor, this is the work (*Æneid,* 6, 129)
[2] Kotzebue (1761-1819) was a prolific German writer of emotional and immoral plays, for many years popular in England.

speare; even the letters of women of high rank in his age were often coarser than his writings. If he occasionally disgusts a keen sense of delicacy, he never injures the mind; he neither excites nor flatters passion in order to degrade the subject of it; he does not use the faulty thing for a faulty purpose, nor carries on warfare against virtue, by causing wickedness to appear as no wickedness, through the medium of a morbid sympathy with the unfortunate. In Shakspeare vice never walks as in twilight; nothing is purposely out of its place; he inverts not the order of nature and propriety, does not make every magistrate a drunkard or glutton, nor every poor man meek, humane, and temperate; he has no benevolent butchers, nor any sentimental rat-catchers.

4. Independence of the dramatic interest on the plot. The interest in the plot is always in fact on account of the characters, not *vice versa*, as in almost all other writers; the plot is a mere canvass and no more. Hence arises the true justification of the same stratagem being used in regard to Benedict and Beatrice, the vanity in each being alike. Take away from the *Much Ado About Nothing* all that which is not indispensable to the plot, either as having little to do with it, or, at best, like Dogberry and his comrades, forced into the service, when any other less ingeniously absurd watchmen and night-constables would have answered the mere necessities of the action; take away Benedict, Beatrice, Dogberry, and the reaction of the former on the character of Hero, and what will remain? In other writers the main agent of the plot is always the prominent character; in Shakspeare it is so, or is not so, as the character is in itself calculated, or not calculated, to form the plot. Don John is the main-spring of the plot of this play; but he is merely shown and then withdrawn.

5. Independence of the interest on the story as the ground-work of the plot. Hence Shakspeare never took the trouble of inventing stories. It was enough for him to select from those that had been already invented or recorded such as had one or other, or both, of two recommendations, namely, suitableness to his particular purpose, and their being parts of popular tradition,—names of which we had often heard, and of their fortunes, and as to which all we wanted was, to see the man himself. So it is just the man himself, the Lear, the Shylock, the Richard, that Shak-

speare makes us for the first time acquainted with. Omit the first scene in *Lear,* and yet every thing will remain; so the first and second scenes in *The Merchant of Venice.* Indeed it is universally true.

6. Interfusion of the lyrical (that which in its very essence is poetical) not only with the dramatic, as in the plays of Metastasio, where at the end of the scenes comes the *aria*[1] as the *exit* speech of the character, but also in and through the dramatic. Songs in Shakspeare are introduced as songs only, just as songs are in real life, beautifully as some of them are characteristic of the person who has sung or called for them, as Desdemona's "Willow," and Ophelia's wild snatches, and the sweet carollings in *As You Like It.* But the whole of the *Midsummer Night's Dream* is one continued specimen of the dramatized lyrical. And observe how exquisitely the dramatic of Hotspur:—

> Marry, and I'm glad on't with all my heart;
> I'd rather be a kitten and cry mew, &c.

melts away into the lyric of Mortimer:—

> I understand thy looks · that pretty Welsh
> Which thou pourest down from these swelling
>   heavens,
> I am too perfect in, &c.
>   *Henry IV,* Part 1, Act iii, sc. i.

7. The characters of the *dramatis personæ,* like those in real life, are to be inferred by the reader; they are not told to him. And it is well worth remarking that Shakspeare's characters, like those in real life, are very commonly misunderstood, and almost always understood by different persons in different ways. The causes are the same in either case. If you take only what the friends of the character say, you may be deceived, and still more so, if that which his enemies say; nay, even the character himself sees through the medium of his character, and not exactly as he is. Take all together, not omitting a shrewd hint from the clown, or the fool, and perhaps your impression will be right; and you may know whether you have in fact discovered the poet's own idea, by all the speeches receiving light from it, and attesting its reality by reflecting it.

Lastly, in Shakspeare the heterogeneous is united, as it is in nature. You must not suppose a pressure or passion always acting on or in the character. Passion in Shakspeare is that by which the individual is distinguished from others, not that which makes a different kind of him. Shakspeare

---

[1] An elaborate melody sung by a single voice in operas, cantatas, etc.

followed the main march of the human affections. He entered into no analysis of the passions or faiths of men, but assured himself that such and such passions and
5 faiths were grounded in our common nature, and not in the mere accidents of ignorance or disease. This is an important consideration, and constitutes our Shakspeare the morning star, the guide and the pioneer, of
10 true philosophy.

Robert Southey 1774-1843

SONNET

CONCERNING THE SLAVE TRADE
1794   1795

Why dost thou beat thy breast, and rend
    thine hair,
And to the deaf sea pour thy frantic cries?
Before the gale, the laden vessel flies;
The heavens all-favoring smile, the breeze
    is fair.
5 Hark to the clamors of the exulting crew!
Hark, how their cannon mock the patient
    skies!
Why dost thou shriek, and strain thy red-
    swoln eyes,
As the white sail is lessening from thy
    view?
Go, pine in want and anguish and despair:
10 There is no mercy found in human-kind.
Go, widow, to thy grave, and rest thee
    there!
But may the God of justice bid the wind
Whelm that cursed bark beneath the
    mountain-wave,
And bless with liberty and death the Slave!

THE BATTLE OF BLENHEIM
1798   1798

It was a summer evening,
  Old Kaspar's work was done,
And he before his cottage door
  Was sitting in the sun,
5 And by him sported on the green
His little grandchild Wilhelmine.

She saw her brother Peterkin
  Roll something large and round,
Which he beside the rivulet
10   In playing there had found;
He came to ask what he had found,
That was so large, and smooth, and round.

Old Kaspar took it from the boy,
  Who stood expectant by;
15 And then the old man shook his head,
  And, with a natural sigh,

" 'Tis some poor fellow's skull," said he,
"Who fell in the great victory.

"I find them in the garden,
20   For there's many here about;
And often when I go to plough,
  The ploughshare turns them out!
For many a thousand men," said he,
"Were slain in that great victory."

25 "Now tell us what 'twas all about,
  Young Peterkin, he cries;
And little Wilhelmine looks up
  With wonder-waiting eyes;
"Now tell us all about the war,
30 And what they fought each other for."

"It was the English," Kaspar cried,
  "Who put the French to rout;
But what they fought each other for,
  I could not well make out;
35 But everybody said," quoth he,
  "That 'twas a famous victory.

"My father lived at Blenheim then,
  Yon little stream hard by;
They burnt his dwelling to the ground,
40   And he was forced to fly;
So with his wife and child he fled,
Nor had he where to rest his head.[1]

"With fire and sword the country round
  Was wasted far and wide,
45 And many a childing mother then,
  And new-born baby died;
But things like that, you know, must be
At every famous victory.

"They say it was a shocking sight
50   After the field was won;
For many thousand bodies here
  Lay rotting in the sun;
But things like that, you know, must be
After a famous victory.

55 "Great praise the Duke of Marlbro' won,
  And our good Prince Eugene."
"Why 'twas a very wicked thing!"
  Said little Wilhelmine.
"Nay, nay, my little girl," quoth he,
60 "It was a famous victory.

"And everybody praised the Duke
  Who this great fight did win."
"But what good came of it at last?"
  Quoth little Peterkin.
65 "Why that I cannot tell," said he,
"But 'twas a famous victory."

[1] See *Matthew*, 8:20.

THE HOLLY TREE
1798   1799

O reader! hast thou ever stood to see
  The Holly Tree?
The eye that contemplates it well perceives
  Its glossy leaves
5 Order'd by an intelligence so wise,
As might confound the Atheist's sophis-
    tries.

Below, a circling fence, its leaves are seen
  Wrinkled and keen;
No grazing cattle through their prickly
  round
10   Can reach to wound;
But as they grow where nothing is to fear,
Smooth and unarm'd the pointless leaves
    appear.

I love to view these things with curious
  eyes,
  And moralize:
15 And in this wisdom of the Holly Tree
  Can emblems see
Wherewith perchance to make a pleasant
  rhyme,
One which may profit in the after time.

Thus, though abroad perchance I might
  appear
20   Harsh and austere,
To those who on my leisure would intrude
  Reserved and rude,
Gentle at home amid my friends I'd be
Like the high leaves upon the Holly Tree.

25 And should my youth, as youth is apt I
  know,
  Some harshness show,
All vain asperities I day by day
  Would wear away,
Till the smooth temper of my age should
  be
30 Like the high leaves upon the Holly Tree.

And as when all the summer trees are seen
  So bright and green,
The Holly leaves a sober hue display
  Less bright than they,
35 But when the bare and wintry woods we
  see,
What then so cheerful as the Holly Tree?

So serious should my youth appear among
  The thoughtless throng,
So would I seem amid the young and gay
40   More grave than they,
That in my age as cheerful I might be
As the green winter of the Holly Tree.

THE OLD MAN'S COMFORTS
AND HOW HE GAINED THEM
1799   1799

"You are old, Father William," the
  young man cried,
"The few locks which are left you are
  gray;
You are hale, Father William, a hearty
  old man,
  Now tell me the reason, I pray."

5 "In the days of my youth," Father
  William replied,
"I remembered that youth would fly
  fast,
And abused not my health, and my vigor
  at first,
That I never might need them at last."

"You are old, Father William," the
  young man cried,
10 "And pleasures with youth pass away;
And yet you lament not the days that are
  gone,
  Now tell me the reason, I pray."

"In the days of my youth," Father
  William replied,
"I remembered that youth could not
  last;
15 I thought of the future, whatever I did,
That I never might grieve for the past."

"You are old, Father William, the
  young man cried,
"And life must be hastening away;
You are cheerful, and love to converse
  upon death,
20   Now tell me the reason, I pray."

"I am cheerful, young man," Father
  William replied,
"Let the cause thy attention engage;
In the days of my youth I remember'd
  my God!
And He hath not forgotten my age."

GOD'S JUDGMENT ON A WICKED BISHOP
1799   1799

The summer and autumn had been so wet,
That in winter the corn was growing yet,
'Twas a piteous sight to see all around
The grain lie rotting on the ground.

5 Every day the starving poor
Crowded around Bishop Hatto's door,
For he had a plentiful last-year's store,

And all the neighborhood could tell
His granaries were furnish'd well.

10 At last Bishop Hatto appointed a day
To quiet the poor without delay;
He bade them to his great barn repair,
And they should have food for the winter
   there.

Rejoiced such tidings good to hear,
15 The poor folk flock'd from far and near;
The great barn was full as it could hold
Of women and children, and young and
   old.

Then when he saw it could hold no more,
Bishop Hatto he made fast the door;
20 And while for mercy on Christ they call,
He set fire to the barn and burnt them all.

I 'faith 'tis an excellent bonfire!'' quoth he,
''And the country is greatly obliged to me,
For ridding it in these times forlorn,
25 Of rats that only consume the corn.''

So then to his palace returned he,
And he sat down to supper merrily,
And he slept that night like an innocent
   man;
But Bishop Hatto never slept again.

30 In the morning as he enter'd the hall
Where his picture hung against the wall,
A sweat like death all over him came,
For the rats had eaten it out of the frame.

As he look'd there came a man from his
   farm—
35 He had a countenance white with alarm;
''My Lord, I open'd your granaries this
   morn,
And the rats had eaten all your corn.''

Another came running presently,
And he was pale as pale could be,
40 ''Fly! my Lord Bishop, fly,'' quoth he,
''Ten thousand rats are coming this
   way,—
The Lord forgive you for yesterday!''

''I'll go to my tower on the Rhine,''
   replied he,
'' 'Tis the safest place in Germany;
45 The walls are high and the shores are
   steep,
And the stream is strong and the water
   deep.''

Bishop Hatto fearfully hasten'd away,
And he crost the Rhine without delay,

And reach'd his tower, and barr'd with
   care
50 All the windows, doors, and loop-holes
   there.

He laid him down and closed his eyes;
But soon a scream made him arise,
He started and saw two eyes of flame
On his pillow from whence the screaming
   came.

55 He listen'd and look'd;—it was only the
   cat;
But the Bishop he grew more fearful for
   that,
For she sat screaming, mad with fear
At the army of rats that were drawing
   near.

For they have swum over the river so
   deep,
60 And they have climb'd the shores so steep,
And up the tower their way is bent,
To do the work for which they were
   sent.

They are not to be told by the dozen or
   score,
By thousands they come, and by myriads
   and more,
65 Such numbers had never been heard of
   before,
Such a judgment had never been witness'd
   of yore.

Down on his knees the Bishop fell,
And faster and faster his beads did he
   tell,
As louder and louder drawing near
70 The gnawing of their teeth he could hear.

And in at the windows and in at the door,
And through the walls helter-skelter they
   pour,
And down from the ceiling and up through
   the floor,
From the right and the left, from behind
   and before,
75 From within and without, from above and
   below,
And all at once to the Bishop they go.

They have whetted their teeth against the
   stones,
And now they pick the Bishop's bones;
They gnaw'd the flesh from every limb,
80 For they were sent to do judgment on
   him!

From THE CURSE OF KEHAMA
1801-09   1810

I. THE FUNERAL

Midnight, and yet no eye
Through all the Imperial City closed in
    sleep!
Behold her streets a-blaze
With light that seems to kindle the red sky,
5   Her myriads swarming through the
        crowded ways!
Master and slave, old age and infancy,
    All, all abroad to gaze;
House-top and balcony
Clustered with women, who throw back
        their veils
10 With unimpeded and insatiate sight
To view the funeral pomp which passes by,
    As if the mournful rite
Were but to them a scene of joyance and
    delight.

Vainly, ye blessed twinklers of the night,
15   Your feeble beams ye shed,
Quench'd in the unnatural light which
        might out-stare
Even the broad eye of day;
    And thou from thy celestial way
Pourest, O Moon, an ineffectual ray!
20 For lo! ten thousand torches flame and
        flare
    Upon the midnight air,
    Blotting the lights of heaven
    With one portentous glare.
Behold the fragrant smoke in many a fold
25 Ascending, floats along the fiery sky,
    And hangeth visible on high,
    A dark and waving canopy.

Hark! 'tis the funeral trumpet's breath!
    'Tis the dirge of death!
30 At once ten thousand drums begin,
With one long thunder-peal the ear assail-
        ing;
    Ten thousand voices then join in,
    And with one deep and general din
        Pour their wild wailing.
35   The song of praise is drown'd
    Amid the deafening sound;
You hear no more the trumpet's tone,
You hear no more the mourner's moan,
Though the trumpet's breath, and the
        dirge of death,
40 Swell with commingled force the funeral
        yell.
    But rising over all in one acclaim
Is heard the echoed and re-echoed name,
    From all that countless rout;
        Arvalan! Arvalan!

45   Arvalan! Arvalan!
    Ten times ten thousand voices in one
        shout
Call Arvalan! The overpowering sound,
    From house to house repeated rings
        about,
    From tower to tower rolls round.

50   The death-procession moves along;
Their bald heads shining to the torches'
        ray,
    The Bramins lead the way,
    Chanting the funeral song.
And now at once they shout,
55   Arvalan! Arvalan!
    With quick rebound of sound,
    All in accordance cry,
        Arvalan! Arvalan!
    The universal multitude reply.
60 In vain ye thunder on his ear the name;
    Would ye awake the dead?
Borne upright in his palankeen,[1]
    There Arvalan is seen!
A glow is on his face, a lively red;
65   It is the crimson canopy
Which o'er his cheek a reddening shade
        hath shed;
    He moves, he nods his head,
But the motion comes from the bearers'
        tread,
    As the body, borne aloft in state,
70 Sways with the impulse of its own dead
        weight.

Close following his dead son, Kehama
        came,
    Nor joining in the ritual song,
    Nor calling the dear name;
    With head deprest and funeral vest,
75   And arms enfolded on his breast,
Silent and lost in thought he moves along.
King of the World, his slaves, unenvying
        now,
Behold their wretched Lord; rejoiced they
        see
    The mighty Rajah's misery;
80 That Nature in his pride hath dealt the
        blow,
    And taught the Master of Mankind to
        know
Even he himself is man, and not exempt
        from woe.

O sight of grief! the wives of Arvalan,
Young Azla, young Nealliny, are seen!
85   Their widow-robes of white,
    With gold and jewels bright,
    Each like an Eastern queen.
Woe! woe! around their palankeen,

[1] A conveyance borne on the shoulders of men.

As on a bridal day,
90 With symphony, and dance, and song,
Their kindred and their friends come on.
The dance of sacrifice! the funeral song!
And next the victim slaves in long array,
Richly bedight to grace the fatal day,
95   Move onward to their death;
The clarions' stirring breath
Lifts their thin robes in every flowing fold,
And swells the woven gold,
That on the agitated air
100 Flutters and glitters to the torch's glare.

A man and maid of aspect wan and wild,
Then, side by side, by bowmen guarded,
came;
O wretched father! O unhappy child!
Them were all eyes of all the throng
exploring.
105   Is this the daring man
Who raised his fatal hand at Arvalan?
Is this the wretch condemn'd to feel
Kehama's dreadful wrath?
Then were all hearts of all the throng
deploring;
110 For not in that innumerable throng
Was one who loved the dead; for who
could know
What aggravated wrong
Provoked the desperate blow!

Far, far behind, beyond all reach of
sight,
115 In order'd files the torches flow along,
One ever-lengthening line of gliding
light:
Far, far behind,
Rolls on the undistinguishable clamor,
Of horn, and trump, and tambour;
120   Incessant as the roar
Of streams which down the wintry
mountain pour,
And louder than the dread commotion
Of breakers on a rocky shore,
When the winds rage over the waves,
125   And Ocean to the Tempest raves.

And now toward the bank they go,
Where winding on their way below,
Deep and strong the waters flow.
Here doth the funeral pile appear
130   With myrrh and ambergris bestrew'd,
And built of precious sandal wood.
They cease their music and their outcry
here,
Gently they rest the bier;
They wet the face of Arvalan,
135 No sign of life the sprinkled drops ex-
cite;

They feel his breast,—no motion there;
They feel his lips,—no breath;
For not with feeble, nor with erring hand,
The brave avenger dealt the blow of
death.
140 Then with a doubling peal and deeper
blast,
The tambours and the trumpets sound on
high,
And with a last and loudest cry,
They call on Arvalan.

Woe! woe! for Azla takes her seat
145 Upon the funeral pile!
Calmly she took her seat,
Calmly the whole terrific pomp survey'd;
As on her lap the while
The lifeless head of Arvalan was laid.

150   Woe! woe! Nealliny,
The young Nealliny!
They strip her ornaments away,
Bracelet and anklet, ring, and chain, and
zone;[1]
Around her neck they leave
155   The marriage knot alone,—
That marriage band, which when
Yon waning moon was young,
Around her virgin neck
With bridal joy was hung.
160 Then with white flowers, the coronal of
death,
Her jetty locks they crown.

O sight of misery!
You cannot hear her cries; their sound
In that wild dissonance is drown'd;
165   But in her face you see
The supplication and the agony,
See in her swelling throat the desperate
strength
That with vain effort struggles yet for
life;
Her arms contracted now in fruitless
strife,
170   Now wildly at full length
Towards the crown in vain for pity
spread,
They force her on, they bind her to the
dead.

Then all around retire;
Circling the pile, the ministering Bra-
mins stand,
175 Each lifting in his hand a torch on fire.
Alone the father of the dead advanced
And lit the funeral pyre.

1 girdle

At once on every side
The circling torches drop,
180   At once on every side
The fragrant oil is pour'd,
At once on every side
The rapid flames rush up.
Then hand in hand the victim band
185 Roll in the dance around the funeral pyre;
Their garments' flying folds
Float inward to the fire;
In drunken whirl they wheel around;
One drops, another plunges in;
190   And still with overwhelming din
The tambours and the trumpets sound;
And clap of hand, and shouts, and cries,
From all the multitude arise;
While round and round, in giddy wheel,
195   Intoxicate they roll and reel,
Till one by one whirl'd in they fall,
And the devouring flames have swallow'd all.

Then all was still; the drums and clarions ceased;
The multitude were hush'd in silent awe;
200 Only the roaring of the flames was heard.

THE MARCH TO MOSCOW
1813   1814

The Emperor Nap[1] he would set off
On a summer excursion to Moscow;
The fields were green, and the sky was blue,
Morbleu! Parbleu![2]
5 What a pleasant excursion to Moscow!

Four hundred thousand men and more
Must go with him to Moscow:
There were Marshals by the dozen,
And Dukes by the score;
10 Princes a few, and Kings one or two;
While the fields are so green, and the sky so blue,
Morbleu! Parbleu!
What a pleasant excursion to Moscow!

There was Junot and Augereau,
15   Heigh-ho for Moscow!
Dombrowsky and Poniatowsky,
Marshal Ney, lack-a-day!
General Rapp and the Emperor Nap;
Nothing would do
20 While the fields were so green, and the sky so blue,
Morbleu! Parbleu!
Nothing would do
For the whole of this crew,
But they must be marching to Moscow.

25 The Emperor Nap he talk'd so big
That he frighten'd Mr. Roscoe.
John Bull, he cries, if you'll be wise,
Ask the Emperor Nap if he will please
To grant you peace upon your knees,
30   Because he is going to Moscow.
He'll make all the Poles come out of their holes,
And beat the Russians and eat the Prussians,
For the fields are green, and the sky is blue,
Morbleu! Parbleu!
35 And he'll certainly march to Moscow!

And Counsellor Brougham was all in a fume
At the thought of the march to Moscow:
The Russians, he said, they were undone,
And the great Fee-Faw-Fum
40   Would presently come
With a hop, step, and jump unto London.
For as for his conquering Russia,
However some persons might scoff it,
Do it he could, and do it he would,
45 And from doing it nothing would come but good,
And nothing could call him off it.
Mr. Jeffrey said so, who must certainly know,
For he was the Edinburgh Prophet.
They all of them knew Mr. Jeffrey's *Review*,
50   Which with Holy Writ ought to be reckon'd:
It was through thick and thin to its party true;
Its back was buff, and its sides were blue,[1]
Morbleu! Parbleu!
It served them for Law and for Gospel too.

55 But the Russians stoutly they turned-to
Upon the road to Moscow.
Nap had to fight his way all through;
They could fight, though they could not parlez-vous,[2]
But the fields were green, and the sky was blue,
60   Morbleu! Parbleu!
And so he got to Moscow.

He found the place too warm for him,
For they set fire to Moscow.
To get there had cost him much ado,
65   And then no better course he knew,

---

[1] Napoleon, who invaded Russia with disastrous results to his army, in 1812.
[2] French oaths.

[1] *The Edinburgh Review* was bound in buff and blue, the colors of the Whig party.
[2] speak French (a humorous expression)

While the fields were green, and the sky
was blue,
    Morbleu! Parbleu!
But to march back again from Moscow.

The Russians they stuck close to him
70   All on the road from Moscow.
There was Tormazow and Jemalow
And all the others that end in ow;
    Milarodovitch and Jaladovitch
      And Karatschkowitch,
75 And all the others that end in itch;
    Schamscheff, Souchosaneff,
      And Schepaleff,
And all the others that end in eff;
    Wasiltschikoff, Kostomaroff,
80   And Tchoglokoff,
And all the others that end in off;
    Rajeffsy and Novereffsy,
      And Rieffsky,
And all the others that end in effsky;
35   Oscharoffsky and Rostoffsky,
And all the others that end in offsky;
    And Platoff he play'd them off,
    And Shouvaloff he shovell'd them off,
    And Markoff he mark'd them off,
90   And Krosnoff he cross'd them off,
    And Tuchkoff he touch'd them off,
    And Boroskoff he bored them off,
    And Kutousoff he cut them off,
    And Parenzoff he pared them off,
95   And Worronzoff he worried them off,
    And Doctoroff he doctor'd them off,
    And Rodionoff he flogg'd them off.
    And last of all an Admiral came,
    A terrible man with a terrible name,
100 A name which you all know by sight very
well;
But which no one can speak, and no one
can spell.
They stuck close to Nap with all their
might,
They were on the left and on the right,
Behind and before, and by day and by
night,
105 He would rather parlez-vous than fight;
    But he look'd white and he look'd blue,
      Morbleu! Parbleu!
When parlez-vous no more would do,
For they remember'd Moscow.

110 And then came on the frost and snow
    All on the road from Moscow.
The wind and the weather he found in
that hour
Cared nothing for him nor for all his
power;
For him who, while Europe crouch'd
under his rod,

115 Put his trust in his fortune, and not in
his God,
Worse and worse every day the ele-
ments grew,
The fields so white and the sky so blue,
    Sacrebleu! Ventrebleu![1]
What a horrible journey from Moscow!

120 What then thought the Emperor Nap
    Upon the road from Moscow?
Why, I ween he thought it small delight
To fight all day, and to freeze all night:
And he was besides in a very great fright,
125   For a whole skin he liked to be in;
    And so, not knowing what else to do,
When the fields were so white and the sky
so blue,
      Morbleu! Parbleu!
    He stole away, I tell you true,
130   Upon the road from Moscow.
'Tis myself, quoth he, I must mind most;
So the Devil may take the hindmost.

    Too cold upon the road was he,
    Too hot had he been at Moscow;
135   But colder and hotter he may be,
    For the grave is colder than Muscovy:
    And a place there is to be kept in view
Where the fire is red and the brimstone
blue,
      Morbleu! Parbleu!
140   Which he must go to,
    If the Pope say true,
If he does not in time look about him;
    Where his namesake almost
    He may have for his Host,
145 He has reckon'd too long without him;
If that host get him in Purgatory,
He won't leave him there alone with his
glory;
    But there he must stay for a very long
day.
For from thence there is no stealing
away
150 As there was on the road from Moscow.

ODE

WRITTEN DURING THE NEGOTIATIONS WITH
BUONAPARTE, IN JANUARY, 1814
1814   1814

Who counsels peace at this momentous
hour,
    When God hath given deliverance to
the oppress'd,
    And to the injured power?[2]

---

[1] French oaths.
[2] After being successful in a number of engagements against Napoleon in the winter of 1813-
14, the allies made proposals for peace.

Who counsels peace, when Vengeance
like a flood
5 Rolls on, no longer now to be repress'd;
When innocent blood
From the four corners of the world
cries out
For justice upon one accursed head;
When Freedom hath her holy banners
spread
10 Over all nations, now in one just
cause
United; when with one sublime accord
Europe throws off the yoke abhorr'd,
And Loyalty and Faith and Ancient Laws
Follow the avenging sword!

15 Woe, woe to England! woe and endless
shame,
If this heroic land,
False to her feelings and unspotted fame,
Hold out the olive to the tyrant's hand!
Woe to the world, if Buonaparte's throne
20 Be suffer'd still to stand!
For by what names shall right and
wrong be known,
What new and courtly phrases must
we feign
For falsehood, murder, and all mon-
strous crimes,
If that perfidious Corsican maintain
25 Still his detested reign,
And France, who yearns even now to
break her chain,
Beneath his iron rule be left to groan?
No! by the innumerable dead
Whose blood hath for his lust of power
been shed,
30 Death only can for his foul deeds atone;
That peace which Death and Judgment
can bestow,
That peace be Buonaparte's, that alone!

For sooner shall the Ethiop change his
skin,
Or from the leopard shall her spots
depart,[1]
35 Than this man change his old flagitious
heart.
Have ye not seen him in the balance
weigh'd,
And there found wanting?[2] On the
stage of blood
Foremost the resolute adventurer stood;
And when, by many a battle won,
40 He placed upon his brow the crown,
Curbing delirious France beneath his
sway,
Then, like Octavius in old time,

[1] See *Jeremiah*, 13 :23.
[2] See *Daniel*, 5 :27.

Fair name might he have handed down,
Effacing many a stain of former crime.
45 Fool! should he cast away that
bright renown!
Fool! the redemption proffer'd should he
lose!
When Heaven such grace vouchsafed
him that the way
To good and evil lay
Before him, which to choose.

50 But evil was his good,[1]
For all too long in blood had he been
nurst,
And ne'er was earth with verier tyrant
curst.
Bold man and bad,
Remorseless, godless, full of fraud
and lies,
55 And black with murders and with
perjuries,
Himself in Hell's whole panoply he clad;
No law but his own headstrong will
he knew,
No counsellor but his own wicked heart.
From evil thus portentous strength
he drew,
60 And trampled under foot all human ties,
All holy laws, all natural charities.

O France! beneath this fierce barbarian's sway
Disgraced thou art to all succeeding
times;
Rapine, and blood, and fire have mark'd
thy way,
65 All loathsome, all unutterable crimes.
A curse is on thee, France! from far
and wide
It hath gone up to Heaven. All lands
have cried
For vengeance upon thy detested head!
All nations curse thee, France! for
wheresoe'er
70 In peace or war thy banner hath
been spread,
All forms of human woe have follow'd
there.
The living and the dead
Cry out alike against thee! They who bear,
Crouching beneath its weight, thine
iron yoke,
75 Join in the bitterness of secret prayer
The voice of that innumerable throng,
Whose slaughter'd spirits day and
night invoke
The Everlasting Judge of right and
wrong.

[1] See *Paradise Lost*, 4, 108.

How long, O Lord! Holy and Just,
    how long!

80 A merciless oppressor hast thou been,
    Thyself remorselessly oppress'd
        meantime;
    Greedy of war, when all that thou
        couldst gain
Was but to dye thy soul with deeper crime,
And rivet faster round thyself the chain.
85 O blind to honor, and to interest blind,
When thus in abject servitude resign'd
    To this barbarian upstart, thou
        couldst brave
God's justice, and the heart of human
        kind!
    Madly thou thoughtest to enslave the
        world,
90   Thyself the while a miserable slave.
Behold the flag of vengeance is unfurl'd!
    The dreadful armies of the North
        advance;
While England, Portugal, and Spain
        combined,
Give their triumphant banners to the wind,
95   And stand victorious in the fields of
        France.

One man hath been for ten long
        wretched years
The cause of all this blood and all these
        tears;
One man in this most awful point
        of time
Draws on thy danger, as he caused thy
        crime.
100   Wait not too long the event,
For now whole Europe comes against thee
        bent,
His wiles and their own strength the
        nations know:
Wise from past wrongs, on future peace
        intent,
The people and the princes, with one
        mind,
105 From all parts move against the general
        foe:
One act of justice, one atoning blow,
    One execrable head laid low,
    Even yet, O France! averts thy
        punishment.
Open thine eyes! too long hast thou been
        blind;
110   Take vengeance for thyself, and for
        mankind!

France! if thou lovest thine ancient
        fame,

Revenge thy sufferings and thy shame!
By the bones which bleach on Jaffa's
        beach;
By the blood which on Domingo's shore
115   Hath clogg'd the carrion-birds with
        gore;
By the flesh which gorged the wolves of
        Spain,
    Or stiffen'd on the snowy plain
        Of frozen Moscovy;
By the bodies which lie all open to the sky,
120 Tracking from Elbe to Rhine the
        tyrant's flight;
By the widow's and the orphan's cry;
    By the childless parent's misery;
    By the lives which he hath shed;
      By the ruin he hath spread;
125 By the prayers which rise for curses on
        his head;
    Redeem, O France! thine ancient fame,
    Revenge thy sufferings and thy shame,
Open thine eyes! too long hast thou been
        blind;
    Take vengeance for thyself, and for
        mankind!

130   By those horrors which the night
    Witness'd, when the torches' light
    To the assembled murderers show'd
    Where the blood of Condé flow'd;
    By thy murder'd Pichegru's fame;
135 By murder'd Wright, an English name;
    By murder'd Palm's atrocious doom;
    By murder'd Hofer's martyrdom;
Oh! by the virtuous blood thus vilely spilt,
The villain's own peculiar private guilt,
140 Open thine eyes! too long has thou been
        blind!
    Take vengeance for thyself and for
        mankind!

MY DAYS AMONG THE DEAD ARE PAST
1818   1823

My days among the dead are past;
    Around me I behold,
Where'er these casual eyes are cast,
    The mighty minds of old;
5 My never-failing friends are they,
With whom I converse day by day.

With them I take delight in weal,
    And seek relief in woe;
And while I understand and feel
10   How much to them I owe,
My cheeks have often been bedew'd
With tears of thoughtful gratitude.

My thoughts are with the dead, with
    them
  I live in long-past years,
15 Their virtues love, their faults condemn,
  Partake their hopes and fears,
And from their lessons seek and find
Instruction with an humble mind.

My hopes are with the dead, anon
20 My place with them will be,
And I with them shall travel on
  Through all futurity;
Yet leaving here a name, I trust,
That will not perish in the dust.

From A VISION OF JUDGMENT
1820   1821
VII. THE BEATIFICATION

When the Spirit withdrew, the Monarch[1]
  around the assembly
Looked, but none else came forth; and
  he heard the voice of the Angel,—
"King of England! speak for thyself;
  here is none to arraign thee."
"Father," he replied, "from whom no
  secrets are hidden,
5 What should I say? Thou knowest that
  mine was an arduous station,
Full of cares, and with perils beset. How
  heavy the burden,
Thou alone canst tell! Short-sighted and
  frail hast Thou made us;
And Thy judgments who can abide? But,
  as surely Thou knowest
The desire of my heart hath been alway
  the good of my people,
10 Pardon my errors, O Lord! and in mercy
  accept the intention:
As in Thee I have trusted, so let me not
  now be confounded."

Bending forward, he spake with earnest
  humility. "Well done,
Good and faithful servant!" then said a
  Voice from the Brightness;
"Enter thou into the joy of thy Lord."[2]
  The ministering Spirits
15 Clapped their pennons therewith, and
  from that whole army of Angels
Songs of thanksgiving and joy resounded,
  and loud hallelujahs;
While, on the wings of Winds upraised,
  the pavilion of splendor,
Where inscrutable light enveloped the
  Holy of Holies,
Moved, and was borne away, through the
  empyrean ascending.

[1] George III.
[2] See *Matthew*, 25:21.

20 Beautiful then on its hill appeared the
  Celestial City,
Softened, like evening suns, to a mild and
  bearable lustre.
Beautiful was the ether above; and the
  sapphire beneath us,
Beautiful was its tone, to the dazzled sight
  as refreshing
As the fields with their loveliest green at
  the coming of summer,
25 When the mind is at ease, and the eye
  and the heart are contented.

Then methought we approached the
  gate. In front of the portal,
From a rock where the standard of man's
  redemption was planted,
Issued the Well of Life, where whosoever
  would enter—
So it was written—must drink, and put
  away all that is earthly.
30 Earth among its gems, its creations of
  art and of nature,
Offers not aught whereto that marvellous
  Cross may be likened
Even in dim similitude, such was its wonderful substance.
Pure it was and diaphanous. It had no
  visible lustre;
Yet from it alone whole Heaven was
  illuminate alway:
35 Day and night being none in the upper
  firmament, neither
Sun nor moon nor stars; but from that
  Cross, as a fountain,
Flowed the Light uncreated; light all-
  sufficing, eternal;
Light which was, and which is, and which
  will be forever and ever;[1]
Light of light, which, if daringly gazed
  on, would blind an Archangel,
40 Yet the eye of weak man may behold,
  and beholding is strengthened;
Yea, while we wander below, oppressed
  with our bodily burden,
And in the shadow of death, this Light is
  in mercy vouchsafed us;
So we seek it with humble heart; and the
  soul that receives it
Hath with it healing and strength, peace,
  love, and life everlasting.

45 Thither the King drew nigh, and kneeling he drank of the water.
Oh, what a change was wrought! In the
  semblance of age he had risen,
Such as at last he appeared, with the
  traces of time and affliction

[1] See *Revelation*, 22:5.

Deep on his faded form, when the burden
    of years was upon him.
Oh, what a change was wrought! For
    now the corruptible put on
50 Incorruption;[1] the mortal put off mortal-
    ity. Rising
Rejuvenescent, he stood in a glorified body,
    obnoxious[2]
Never again to change, nor to evil and
    trouble and sorrow,
But for eternity formed, and to bliss ever-
    lasting appointed.

. . . . . .

THE CATARACT OF LODORE

DESCRIBED IN RHYMES FOR THE NURSERY
1820   1823

"How does the water
    Come down at Lodore?"
My little boy ask'd me
Thus, once on a time;
5 And moreover he task'd me
    To tell him in rhyme.
    Anon at the word,
There first came one daughter
And then came another,
10   To second and third
The request of their brother,
And to hear how the water
    Comes down at Lodore,
With its rush and its roar,
15   As many a time
They had seen it before.
So I told them in rhyme,
For of rhymes I had store:
And 'twas in my vocation
20   For their recreation
That so I should sing;
Because I was Laureate
    To them and the King.[3]

From its sources which well
25   In the tarn[4] on the fell;[5]
    From its fountains
    In the mountains,
Its rills and its gills;[6]
Through moss and through brake,
30   It runs and it creeps
    For awhile, till it sleeps
    In its own little lake.
And thence at departing,
    Awakening and starting,
35   It runs through the reeds
    And away it proceeds,
Through meadow and glade,

---

[1] See *1 Corinthians,*   laureate in 1813.
  15:53.   [4] small lake
[2] subject; liable   [5] moor
[3] George IV. Southey [6] brooks
  was appointed poet

    In sun and in shade,
And through the wood-shelter,
40 Among crags in its flurry,
    Helter-skelter,
    Hurry-scurry.
Here it comes sparkling,
And there it lies darkling;
45 Now smoking and frothing
Its tumult and wrath in,
Till in this rapid race
    On which it is bent,
    It reaches the place
50   Of its steep descent.

    The cataract strong
    Then plunges along,
Striking and raging
As if a war waging
55 Its caverns and rocks among:
    Rising and leaping,
    Sinking and creeping,
    Swelling and sweeping,
    Showering and springing,
60   Flying and flinging,
    Writhing and ringing,
    Eddying and whisking,
    Spouting and frisking,
    Turning and twisting,
65   Around and around
    With endless rebound!
    Smiting and fighting,
    A sight to delight in;
Confounding, astounding,
70 Dizzying and deafening the ear with its
    sound.

Collecting, projecting,
Receding and speeding,
And shocking and rocking,
And darting and parting,
75 And threading and spreading,
And whizzing and hissing,
And dripping and skipping,
And hitting and splitting,
And shining and twining,
80 And rattling and battling,
And shaking and quaking,
And pouring and roaring,
And waving and raving,
And tossing and crossing,
85 And flowing and going,
And running and stunning,
And foaming and roaming,
And dinning and spinning,
And dropping and hopping,
90 And working and jerking,
And guggling and struggling,
And heaving and cleaving,
And moaning and groaning;

And glittering and frittering,
95 And gathering and feathering,
And whitening and brightening,
And quivering and shivering,
And hurrying and skurrying,
And thundering and floundering;
100 Dividing and gliding and sliding,
And falling and brawling and sprawling,
And driving and riving and striving,
And sprinkling and twinkling and wrinkling,
And sounding and bounding and rounding,
105 And bubbling and troubling and doubling,
And grumbling and rumbling and tumbling,
And clattering and battering and shattering;

Retreating and beating and meeting and sheeting,
Delaying and straying and playing and spraying,
110 Advancing and prancing and glancing and dancing,
Recoiling, turmoiling and toiling and boiling,
And gleaming and streaming and steaming and beaming,
And rushing and flushing and brushing and gushing,
And flapping and rapping and clapping and slapping,
115 And curling and whirling and purling and twirling,
And thumping and plumping and bumping and jumping,
And dashing and flashing and splashing and clashing;
And so never ending, but always descending,
Sounds and motions forever and ever are blending,
120 All at once and all o'er, with a mighty uproar;
And this way the water comes down at Lodore.

From THE LIFE OF NELSON
1808-13   1813

THE BATTLE OF TRAFALGAR

Unremitting exertions were made to equip the ships which he had chosen,[1] and especially to refit the *Victory*, which was once more to bear his flag. Before he left Lon-don he called at his upholsterer's, where the coffin which Captain Hallowell had given him was deposited, and desired that its history[1] might be engraven upon the lid, [5] saying it was highly probable he might want it on his return. He seemed, indeed, to have been impressed with an expectation that he should fall in the battle. In a letter to his brother, written immediately [10] after his return,[2] he had said: "We must not talk of Sir Robert Calder's battle.[3] I might not have done so much with my small force. If I had fallen in with them, you might probably have been a lord before I [15] wished, for I know they meant to make a dead set at the *Victory*." Nelson had once regarded the prospect of death with gloomy satisfaction; it was when he anticipated the upbraidings of his wife and the displeasure of his venerable father.[4] The state of his feelings now was expressed in his private journal in these words: "Friday night (Sept. 13th), at half-past ten, I drove from dear, dear Merton, where I left all [25] which I hold dear in this world, to go to serve my king and country. May the great God whom I adore enable me to fulfil the expectations of my country! And if it is His good pleasure that I should return, [30] my thanks will never cease being offered up to the throne of His mercy. If it is His good providence to cut short my days upon earth, I bow with the greatest submission; relying that He will protect those so dear [35] to me, whom I may leave behind! His will be done! Amen! Amen! Amen!"

Early on the following morning he reached Portsmouth; and, having despatched his business on shore, endeavored [40] to elude the populace by taking a byway to the beach; but a crowd collected in his train, pressing forward to obtain a sight of his face;—many were in tears, and many knelt down before him, and blessed [45] him as he passed. England has had many heroes, but never one who so entirely possessed the love of his fellow-countrymen as Nelson. All men knew that his heart was as humane as it was fearless; that there [50] was not in his nature the slightest alloy of selfishness or cupidity; but that, with per-

---

[1] That is, which Nelson had chosen to engage the combined fleets of France and Spain, under the French admiral Villeneuve.

[1] It had been made from the mainmast of the French ship. *L'Orient*, destroyed by Nelson in the Battle of the Nile, Aug. 1, 1798.
[2] From his search for the French fleet in September, 1805.
[3] An engagement with the French and Spanish fleets, which was fought without a victory for either side, on July 22, 1805.
[4] On account of his relations with Lady Hamilton, a noted adventuress.

fect and entire devotion, he served his country with all his heart, and with all his soul, and with all his strength;[1] and, therefore, they loved him as truly and as fervently as he loved England. They pressed upon the parapet to gaze after him when his barge pushed off, and he was returning their cheers by waving his hat. The sentinels, who endeavored to prevent them from trespassing upon this ground, were wedged among the crowd; and an officer, who, not very prudently upon such an occasion, ordered them to drive the people down with their bayonets, was compelled speedily to retreat; for the people would not be debarred from gazing, till the last moment, upon the hero, the darling hero of England. . . .

About half-past nine in the morning of the 19th, the *Mars,* being the nearest to the fleet of the ships which formed the line of communication with the frigates in shore, repeated the signal that the enemy were coming out of port.[2] The wind was at this time very light, with partial breezes, mostly from the S.S.W. Nelson ordered the signal to be made for a chase in the south-east quarter. About two, the repeating ships announced that the enemy were at sea. All night the British fleet continued under all sail, steering to the south-east. At daybreak[3] they were in the entrance of the Straits,[4] but the enemy were not in sight. About seven, one of the frigates made signal that the enemy were bearing north. Upon this the *Victory* hove-to, and shortly afterwards Nelson made sail again to the northward. In the afternoon the wind blew fresh from the south-west, and the English began to fear that the foe might be forced to return to port.

A little before sunset, however, Blackwood, in the *Euryalus,* telegraphed that they appeared determined to go to the westward. "And that," said the Admiral in his diary, "they shall not do, if it is in the power of Nelson and Bronte to prevent them." Nelson had signified to Blackwood that he depended upon him to keep sight of the enemy. They were observed so well that all their motions were made known to him, and, as they wore twice, he inferred that they were aiming to keep the port of Cadiz open, and would retreat there as soon as they saw the British fleet; for this reason he was very careful not to approach near enough to be seen by them during the

night. At daybreak the combined fleets were distinctly seen from the *Victory's* deck, formed in a close line of battle ahead, on the starboard tack, about twelve miles to leeward, and standing to the south. Our fleet consisted of twenty-seven sail of the line[1] and four frigates; theirs of thirty-three and seven large frigates. Their superiority was greater in size and weight of metal than in numbers. They had four thousand troops on board; and the best riflemen who could be procured, many of them Tyrolese, were dispersed through the ships. Little did the Tyrolese, and little did the Spaniards at that day, imagine what horrors the wicked tyrant whom they served was preparing for their country.[2]

Soon after daylight Nelson came upon deck. The 21st of October was a festival in his family, because on that day his uncle, Captain Suckling, in the *Dreadnought,* with two other line-of-battle ships, had beaten off a French squadron of four sail of the line and three frigates. Nelson, with that sort of superstition from which few persons are entirely exempt, had more than once expressed his persuasion that this was to be the day of his battle also; and he was well pleased at seeing his prediction about to be verified. The wind was now from the west,—light breezes, with a long heavy swell. Signal was made to bear down upon the enemy in two lines; and the fleet set all sail. Collingwood, in the *Royal Sovereign,* led the lee-line of thirteen ships; the *Victory* led the weather-line of fourteen. Having seen that all was as it should be, Nelson retired to his cabin, and wrote this prayer:—

"May the Great God, whom I worship, grant to my country, and for the benefit of Europe in general, a great and glorious victory; and may no misconduct in any one tarnish it; and may humanity after victory be the predominant feature in the British fleet. For myself individually, I commit my life to Him that made me, and may His blessing alight on my endeavors for serving my country faithfully! To Him I resign myself, and the just cause which is intrusted to me to defend. Amen, Amen, Amen."

. . . . . .

[1] See *Luke,* 10:27.
[2] That is, Cadiz.
[3] Oct. 21, 1805.
[4] That is, of Gibraltar.

[1] The sail of the line carried much heavier armament than did the frigates.
[2] When the Tyrolese were fighting for freedom from the Bavarians in 1809, Napoleon aided the Bavarians. In 1808, he made his brother Joseph king of Spain.

Blackwood went on board the *Victory* about six. He found him in good spirits, but very calm; not in that exhilaration which he had felt upon entering into battle at Aboukir and Copenhagen; he knew that his own life would be particularly aimed at, and seems to have looked for death with almost as sure an expectation as for victory. His whole attention was fixed upon the enemy. They tacked to the northward, and formed their line on the larboard tack; thus bringing the shoals of Trafalgar and St. Pedro under the lee of the British, and keeping the port of Cadiz open for themselves. This was judiciously done: and Nelson, aware of all the advantages which it gave them, made signal to prepare to anchor.

Villeneuve was a skilful seaman, worthy of serving a better master and a better cause. His plan of defence was as well conceived, and as original, as the plan of attack. He formed the fleet in a double line, every alternate ship being about a cable's length[1] to windward of her second ahead and astern. Nelson, certain of a triumphant issue to the day, asked Blackwood what he should consider as a victory. That officer answered that, considering the handsome way in which battle was offered by the enemy, their apparent determination for a fair trial of strength, and the situation of the land, he thought it would be a glorious result if fourteen were captured. He replied: "I shall not be satisfied with less than twenty." Soon afterwards he asked him if he did not think there was a signal wanting. Captain Blackwood made answer that he thought the whole fleet seemed very clearly to understand what they were about. These words were scarcely spoken before that signal was made which will be remembered as long as the language or even the memory of England shall endure—Nelson's last signal: "ENGLAND EXPECTS EVERY MAN TO DO HIS DUTY!" It was received throughout the fleet with a shout of answering acclamation, made sublime by the spirit which it breathed and the feeling which it expressed. "Now," said Lord Nelson, "I can do no more. We must trust to the great Disposer of all events and the justice of our cause. I thank God for this great opportunity of doing my duty."

He wore that day, as usual, his Admiral's frock-coat, bearing on the left breast four stars of the different orders with which he was invested. Ornaments which rendered

[1] Six hundred feet.

him so conspicuous a mark for the enemy were beheld with ominous apprehensions by his officers. It was known that there were riflemen on board the French ships, and it could not be doubted but that his life would be particularly aimed at. They communicated their fears to each other, and the surgeon, Mr. Beatty, spoke to the chaplain, Dr. Scott, and to Mr. Scott, the public secretary, desiring that some person would entreat him to change his dress or cover the stars; but they knew that such a request would highly displease him. "In honor I gained them," he had said when such a thing had been hinted to him formerly, "and in honor I will die with them." Mr. Beatty, however, would not have been deterred by any fear of exciting his displeasure from speaking to him himself upon a subject in which the weal of England, as well as the life of Nelson, was concerned; but he was ordered from the deck before he could find an opportunity. This was a point upon which Nelson's officers knew that it was hopeless to remonstrate or reason with him; but both Blackwood and his own captain, Hardy, represented to him how advantageous to the fleet it would be for him to keep out of action as long as possible; and he consented at last to let the *Leviathan* and the *Téméraire*, which were sailing abreast of the *Victory*, be ordered to pass ahead. Yet even here the last infirmity of this noble mind[1] was indulged; for these ships could not pass ahead if the *Victory* continued to carry all her sail; and so far was Nelson from shortening sail, that it was evident he took pleasure in pressing on, and rendering it impossible for them to obey his own orders. A long swell was setting into the Bay of Cadiz: our ships, crowding all sail, moved majestically before it, with light winds from the south-west. The sun shone on the sails of the enemy; and their well-formed line, with their numerous three-deckers, made an appearance which any other assailants would have thought formidable; but the British sailors only admired the beauty and the splendor of the spectacle; and, in full confidence of winning what they saw, remarked to each other, what a fine sight yonder ships would make at Spithead!

The French admiral, from the *Bucentaure*, beheld the new manner in which his enemy was advancing, Nelson and Collingwood each leading his line; and, pointing them out to his officers, he is said to have

[1] That is, ambition. See *Lycidas*, 71.

exclaimed that such conduct could not fail to be successful. Yet Villeneuve had made his own dispositions with the utmost skill, and the fleets under his command waited for the attack with perfect coolness. Ten minutes before twelve they opened their fire. Eight or nine of the ships immediately ahead of the *Victory,* and across her bows, fired single guns at her, to ascertain whether she was yet within their range. As soon as Nelson perceived that their shot passed over him, he desired Blackwood and Captain Prowse, of the *Sirius,* to repair to their respective frigates, and on their way to tell all the captains of the line-of-battle ships that he depended on their exertions, and that, if by the prescribed mode of attack they found it impracticable to get into action immediately, they might adopt whatever they thought best, provided it led them quickly and closely alongside an enemy. As they were standing on the front of the poop, Blackwood took him by the hand, saying he hoped soon to return and find him in possession of twenty prizes. He replied, "God bless you, Blackwood; I shall never see you again."

Nelson's column was steered about two points more to the north than Collingwood's, in order to cut off the enemy's escape into Cadiz. The lee line, therefore, was first engaged. "See," cried Nelson, pointing to the *Royal Sovereign,* as she steered right for the centre of the enemy's line, cut through it astern of the *Santa Anna,* three-decker, and engaged her at the muzzle of her guns on the starboard side; "see how that noble fellow Collingwood carries his ship into action!" Collingwood, delighted at being first in the heat of the fire, and knowing the feelings of his Commander and old friend, turned to his captain and exclaimed, "Rotherham, what would Nelson give to be here!" Both these brave officers perhaps at this moment thought of Nelson with gratitude for a circumstance which had occurred on the preceding day. Admiral Collingwood, with some of the captains, having gone on board the *Victory* to receive instructions, Nelson inquired of him where his captain was, and was told in reply that they were not upon good terms with each other. "Terms!" said Nelson, "good terms with each other!" Immediately he sent a boat for Captain Rotherham, led him, as soon as he arrived, to Collingwood, and saying, "Look, yonder are the enemy!" bade them shake hands like Englishmen.

The enemy continued to fire a gun at a time at the *Victory* till they saw that a shot had passed through her main-topgallant sail; then they opened their broadsides, aiming chiefly at her rigging, in the hope of disabling her before she could close with them. Nelson, as usual, had hoisted several flags, lest one should be shot away. The enemy showed no colors till late in the action, when they began to feel the necessity of having them to strike. For this reason the *Santissima Trinidad*—Nelson's old acquaintance, as he used to call her—was distinguishable only by her four decks; and to the bow of this opponent he ordered the *Victory* to be steered. Meantime an incessant raking fire was kept up upon the *Victory.* The admiral's secretary was one of the first who fell: he was killed by a cannon-shot, while conversing with Hardy. Captain Adair, of the marines, with the help of a sailor, endeavored to remove the body from Nelson's sight, who had a great regard for Mr. Scott; but he anxiously asked, "Is that poor Scott that's gone?" and being informed that it was indeed so, exclaimed, "Poor fellow!" Presently a double-headed shot struck a party of marines, who were drawn up on the poop, and killed eight of them: upon which Nelson immediately desired Captain Adair to disperse his men round the ship, that they might not suffer so much from being together. A few minutes afterwards a shot struck the forebrace bits on the quarter-deck, and passed between Nelson and Hardy, a splinter from the bit tearing off Hardy's buckle and bruising his foot. Both stopped, and looked anxiously at each other, each supposing the other to be wounded. Nelson then smiled, and said, "This is too warm work, Hardy, to last long."

The *Victory* had not yet returned a single gun: fifty of her men had been by this time killed or wounded, and her main-topmast, with all her studding sails and their booms, shot away. Nelson declared that, in all his battles, he had seen nothing which surpassed the cool courage of his crew on this occasion. At four minutes after twelve she opened her fire from both sides of her deck. It was not possible to break the enemy's line without running on board one of their ships: Hardy informed him of this, and asked which he would prefer. Nelson replied: "Take your choice, Hardy, it does not signify much." The master was then ordered to put the helm to port.

and the *Victory* ran on board the *Redoubtable,* just as her tiller ropes were shot away. The French ship received her with a broadside, then instantly let down her lower-deck ports for fear of being boarded through them, and never afterwards fired a great gun during the action. Her tops, like those of all the enemy's ships, were filled with riflemen. Nelson never placed musketry in his tops; he had a strong dislike to the practice, not merely because it endangers setting fire to the sails, but also because it is a murderous sort of warfare, by which individuals may suffer, and a commander now and then be picked off, but which never can decide the fate of a general engagement.

Captain Harvey, in the *Téméraire,* fell on board the *Redoubtable* on the other side; another enemy was in like manner on board the *Téméraire;* so that these four ships formed as compact a tier as if they had been moored together, their heads all lying the same way. The lieutenants of the *Victory,* seeing this, depressed their guns of the middle and lower decks, and fired with a diminished charge, lest the shot should pass through and injure the *Téméraire;* and because there was danger that the *Redoubtable* might take fire from the lower-deck guns, the muzzles of which touched her side when they were run out, the fireman of each gun stood ready with a bucket of water, which, as soon as the gun was discharged, he dashed into the hole made by the shot. An incessant fire was kept up from the *Victory* from both sides; her larboard guns playing upon the *Bucentaure* and the huge *Santissima Trinidad.*

It had been part of Nelson's prayer that the British fleet might be distinguished by humanity in the victory which he expected. Setting an example himself, he twice gave orders to cease firing upon the *Redoubtable,* supposing that she had struck, because her great guns were silent; for, as she carried no flag, there was no means of instantly ascertaining the fact. From this ship, which he had thus twice spared, he received his death. A ball fired from her mizzen-top, which, in the then situation of the two vessels, was not more than fifteen yards from that part of the deck where he was standing, struck the epaulette on his left shoulder,—about a quarter after one, just in the heat of the action. He fell upon his face, on the spot which was covered with his poor secretary's blood. Hardy, who was a few steps from him, turning round, saw three men raising him up. "They have done for me at last, Hardy," said he. "I hope not!" cried Hardy. "Yes," he replied; "my back bone is shot through." Yet even now, not for a moment losing his presence of mind, he observed, as they were carrying him down the ladder, that the tiller ropes, which had been shot away, were not yet replaced, and ordered that new ones should be rove immediately:— then, that he might not be seen by the crew, he took out his handkerchief, and covered his face and his stars.—Had he but concealed these badges of honor from the enemy, England, perhaps, would not have had cause to receive with sorrow the news of the battle of Trafalgar.

The cockpit was crowded with wounded and dying men, over whose bodies he was with some difficulty conveyed, and laid upon a pallet in the midshipmen's berth. It was soon perceived, upon examination, that the wound was mortal. This, however, was concealed from all, except Captain Hardy, the chaplain, and the medical attendants. He himself being certain, from the sensation in his back, and the gush of blood which he felt momently within his breast, that no human care could avail him, insisted that the surgeon should leave him, and attend to those to whom he might be useful; "for," said he, "you can do nothing for me." All that could be done was to fan him with paper, and frequently to give him lemonade to alleviate his intense thirst. He was in great pain, and expressed much anxiety for the event of the action, which now began to declare itself. As often as a ship struck, the crew of the *Victory* hurraed, and at every hurra a visible expression of joy gleamed in the eyes and marked the countenance of the dying hero. But he became impatient to see Captain Hardy; and as that officer, though often sent for, could not leave the deck, Nelson feared that some fatal cause prevented him, and repeatedly cried: "Will no one bring Hardy to me? He must be killed! He is surely dead!" An hour and ten minutes elapsed from the time when Nelson received his wound before Hardy could come to him They shook hands in silence; Hardy in vain struggling to suppress the feelings of that most painful and yet sublimest moment. "Well, Hardy," said Nelson, "how goes the day with us?"—"Very well," replied Hardy, "ten ships have struck, but five of the van have tacked, and show an intention to bear down upon the *Victory.* I have called two or three of our fresh ships round, and have no doubt of giving them a drubbing."—"I hope," said Nelson, "none of our ships have struck?" Hardy answered, "There was no fear of that." Then, and not till then, Nelson spoke of himself. "I am a dead man, Hardy," said he; "I am going fast; it will be all over with me soon. Come nearer to me. Let my dear Lady Hamilton have my hair and all other things belonging to me." Hardy observed that he hoped Mr. Beatty could yet hold out some prospect of life. "Oh no!" he replied, "it is impossible; my back is shot through. Beatty will tell you so." Captain Hardy then once more shook hands with him, and with a heart almost bursting hastened upon deck.

By this time all feeling below the breast was gone; and Nelson, having made the surgeon ascertain this, said to him: "You know I am gone. I know it. I feel something rising in my breast"—putting his hand on his left side—"which tells me so." And upon Beatty's inquiring whether his pain was very great, he replied, "So great that he wished he was dead. Yet," said he in a lower voice, "one would like to live a little longer too!" And after a few minutes, in the same under-tone, he added: "What would become of poor Lady Hamilton if she knew my situation?" Next to his country she occupied his thoughts. Captain Hardy, some fifty minutes after he had left the cockpit, returned, and again taking the hand of his dying friend and Commander, congratulated him on having gained a complete victory. How many of the enemy were taken he did not know, as it was impossible to perceive them distinctly, but fourteen or fifteen at least. "That's well!" cried Nelson, "but I bargained for twenty." And then in a stronger voice he said: "Anchor, Hardy, anchor." Hardy upon this hinted that Admiral Collingwood would take upon himself the direction of affairs. "Not while I live, Hardy," said the dying Nelson, ineffectually endeavoring to raise himself from the bed. "Do you anchor." His previous order for preparing to anchor had shown how clearly he foresaw the necessity of this. Presently, calling Hardy back, he said to him, in a low voice, "Don't throw me overboard"; and he desired that he might be buried by his parents, unless it should please the king to order otherwise. Then, reverting to private feelings: "Take care of my dear Lady Hamilton, Hardy; take care

of poor Lady Hamilton.—Kiss me, Hardy," said he. Hardy knelt down, and kissed his cheek: and Nelson said, "Now I am satisfied. Thank God, I have done my duty." Hardy stood over him in silence for a moment or two, then knelt again, and kissed his forehead. "Who is that?" said Nelson; and being informed, he replied, "God bless you, Hardy." And Hardy then left him—forever.

Nelson now desired to be turned upon his right side, and said: "I wish I had not left the deck; for I shall soon be gone." Death was, indeed, rapidly approaching. He said to the chaplain: "Doctor, I have *not* been a *great* sinner"; and, after a short pause, "Remember that I leave Lady Hamilton, and my daughter, Horatia, as a legacy to my country." His articulation now became difficult; but he was distinctly heard to say, "Thank God, I have done my duty!" These words he had repeatedly pronounced; and they were the last words he uttered. He expired at thirty minutes after four,—three hours and a quarter after he had received his wound.

. . . . . .

Once, amidst his sufferings, Nelson had expressed a wish that he were dead; but immediately the spirit subdued the pains of death, and he wished to live a little longer; doubtless that he might hear the completion of the victory which he had seen so gloriously begun. That consolation—that joy—that triumph, was afforded him. He lived to know that the victory was decisive; and the last guns which were fired at the flying enemy were heard a minute or two before he expired.

. . . . . .

It is almost superfluous to add that all the honors which a grateful country could bestow were heaped upon the memory of Nelson. His brother was made an earl, with a grant of £6,000 per year; £10,000 were voted to each of his sisters; and £100,000 for the purchase of an estate. A public funeral was decreed, and a public monument. Statues and monuments also were voted by most of our principal cities. The leaden coffin, in which he was brought home, was cut in pieces, which were distributed as relics of Saint Nelson,—so the gunner of the *Victory* called them,—and when, at his interment, his flag was about to be lowered into the grave, the sailors who assisted at the ceremony, with one accord rent it in pieces, that each might preserve a fragment while he lived.

The death of Nelson was felt in England as something more than a public calamity: men started at the intelligence, and turned pale, as if they had heard of the loss of a dear friend. An object of our admiration and affection, of our pride and of our hopes, was suddenly taken from us; and it seemed as if we had never, till then, known how deeply we loved and reverenced him. What the country had lost in its great naval hero—the greatest of our own, and of all former times—was scarcely taken into the account of grief. So perfectly, indeed, had he performed his part, that the maritime war, after the battle of Trafalgar, was considered at an end; the fleets of the enemy were not merely defeated, but destroyed; new navies must be built, and a new race of seamen reared for them, before the possibility of their invading our shores could again be contemplated. It was not, therefore, from any selfish reflection upon the magnitude of our loss that we mourned for him: the general sorrow was of a higher character. The people of England grieved that funeral ceremonies, public monuments, and posthumous rewards, were all which they could now bestow upon him, whom the king, the legislature, and the nation, would alike have delighted to honor; whom every tongue would have blessed; whose presence in every village through which he might have passed would have wakened the church bells, have given school-boys a holiday, have drawn children from their sports to gaze upon him, and "old men from the chimney corner,"[1] to look upon Nelson ere they died. The victory of Trafalgar was celebrated, indeed, with the usual forms of rejoicing, but they were without joy; for such already was the glory of the British navy, through Nelson's surpassing genius, that it scarcely seemed to receive any addition from the most signal victory that ever was achieved upon the seas; and the destruction of this mighty fleet, by which all the maritime schemes of France were totally frustrated, hardly appeared to add to our security or strength; for while Nelson was living, to watch the combined squadrons of the enemy, we felt ourselves as secure as now, when they were no longer in existence.

There was reason to suppose, from the appearances upon opening the body, that in the course of nature he might have attained, like his father, to a good old age.

[1] Sidney, *The Defense of Poesy*, 23, 27 (Ath. Press ed.).

Yet he cannot be said to have fallen prematurely whose work was done, nor ought he to be lamented who died so full of honors and at the height of human fame. The most triumphant death is that of the martyr; the most awful that of the martyred patriot; the most splendid that of the hero in the hour of victory; and if the chariot and the horses of fire had been vouchsafed for Nelson's translation,[1] he could scarcely have departed in a brighter blaze of glory. He has left us, not indeed his mantle of inspiration,[2] but a name and an example which are at this hour inspiring thousands of the youth of England—a name which is our pride, and an example which will continue to be our shield and our strength. Thus it is that the spirits of the great and the wise continue to live and to act after them, verifying in this sense the language of the old mythologist:

Τοί μεν δαίμονες εἰσί, Διός μεγάλου διὰ βουλὰς
'Εσθλοί, ἐπιχθόνιοι, φύλακες θνητῶν ἀνθρώπων.[3]

Thomas Campbell 1777-1844

THE PLEASURES OF HOPE
1796-99   1799
From PART I

At summer eve, when Heaven's ethereal
　　bow
Spans with bright arch the glittering hills
　　below,
Why to yon mountain turns the musing
　　eye,
Whose sunbright summit mingles with the
　　sky?
5 Why do those cliffs of shadowy tint
　　appear
More sweet than all the landscape smiling
　　near?
'Tis distance lends enchantment to the
　　view,
And robes the mountain in its azure hue.
Thus, with delight, we linger to survey
10 The promised joys of life's unmeasured
　　way;
Thus, from afar, each dim-discover'd
　　scene
More pleasing seems than all the past
　　hath been,
And every form, that Fancy can repair
From dark oblivion, glows divinely there.

[1] As they had been for Elijah (*2 Kings*, 2 :11-13).
[2] Which Elijah left for Elisha (*2 Kings*, 2 :8, 13, 35).
[3] Shining spirits there are, that dwell upon earth among mortals,
Prompting illustrious deeds, and fulfilling the counsels of Zeus.
　—Hesiod, *The Works and Days*, 122.

15   What potent spirit guides the raptured
        eye
    To pierce the shades of dim futurity?
    Can Wisdom lend, with all her heavenly
        power,
    The pledge of Joy's anticipated hour?
    Ah, no! she darkly sees the fate of man—
20   Her dim horizon bounded to a span;
    Or, if she hold an image to the view,
    'Tis Nature pictured too severely true.
    With thee, sweet Hope! resides the heav-
        enly light,
    That pours remotest rapture on the sight:
25   Thine is the charm of life's bewilder'd
        way,
    That calls each slumbering passion into
        play.
    Waked by thy touch, I see the sister band,
    On tiptoe watching, start at thy com-
        mand,
    And fly where'er thy mandate bids them
        steer,
30   To Pleasure's path or Glory's bright
        career.
      Primeval Hope, the Aönian Muses say,
    When Man and Nature mourn'd their
        first decay;
    When every form of death, and every woe,
    Shot from malignant stars to earth below;
35   When Murder bared her arm, and ram-
        pant War
    Yoked the red dragons of her iron car;
    When Peace and Mercy, banish'd from
        the plain,
    Sprung on the viewless winds to Heaven
        again;
    All, all forsook the friendless, guilty mind,
40   But Hope, the charmer, linger'd still
        behind.[1]

      .   .   .   .   .   .

    Where barbarous hordes on Scythian
        mountains roam,
340   Truth, Mercy, Freedom, yet shall find a
        home;
    Where'er degraded Nature bleeds and
        pines,
    From Guinea's coast to Sibir's dreary
        mines,
    Truth shall pervade th' unfathom'd dark-
        ness there,
    And light the dreadful features of De-
        spair.—
345   Hark! the stern captive spurns his heavy
        load,

And asks the image back that Heaven
    bestow'd!
Fierce in his eye the fire of valor burns,
And, as the slave departs, the man returns.
    Oh! sacred Truth! thy triumph ceased
    a while,
350 And Hope, thy sister, ceased with thee to
    smile,
When leagued Oppression[1] pour'd to
    Northern wars
Her whiskered pandoors and her fierce
    hussars,[2]
Waved her dread standard to the breeze
    of morn,
Peal'd her loud drum, and twang'd her
    trumpet horn;
355 Tumultuous horror brooded o'er her
    van,
Presaging wrath to Poland—and to man!
    Warsaw's last champion[3] from her
    height survey'd,
Wide o'er the fields, a waste of ruin laid,—
"Oh! Heaven!" he cried, "my bleeding
    country save!—
360 Is there no hand on high to shield the
    brave?
Yet, though destruction sweep those lovely
    plains,
Rise, fellow-men! our country yet re-
    mains!
By that dread name, we wave the sword
    on high!
And swear for her to live!—with her to
    die!"
365   He said, and on the rampart-heights
    array'd
His trusty warriors, few, but undismay'd;
Firm-paced and slow, a horrid front they
    form,
Still as the breeze, but dreadful as the
    storm;
Low murmuring sounds along their ban-
    ners fly,
370 Revenge, or death,—the watchword and
    reply;
Then peal'd the notes, omnipotent to
    charm,
And the loud tocsin toll'd their last
    alarm!—
    In vain, alas! in vain, ye gallant few!
From rank to rank your volley'd thunder
    flew:—
375 Oh, bloodiest picture in the book of Time,

---

[1] See the story of Pandora, from whose box all
the blessings but hope escaped; also the story
of the Iron Age, in which the vices took possession of the earth after the virtues had departed.

[1] In 1792 and 1794 when Russia, Prussia, and
Austria united in wars for the partition of
Poland.
[2] The pandoors were members of a regiment in
the Austrian army, noted for its courage and
cruelty. The hussars were light cavalrymen.
[3] Thaddeus Kosciusko: he was defeated and
taken prisoner, Oct. 10, 1794.

Sarmatia fell, unwept, without a crime;
Found not a generous friend, a pitying foe,
Strength in her arms, nor mercy in her woe!
Dropp'd from her nerveless grasp the shatter'd spear,
380 Closed her bright eye, and curb'd her high career;—
Hope, for a season, bade the world farewell,
And Freedom shriek'd as Kosciusko fell!
The sun went down, nor ceased the carnage there,
Tumultuous Murder shook the midnight air—
385 On Prague's proud arch the fires of ruin glow,
His blood-dyed waters murmuring far below;
The storm prevails, the rampart yields a way,
Bursts the wild cry of horror and dismay!
Hark, as the smouldering piles with thunder fall,
390 A thousand shrieks for hopeless mercy call!
Earth shook—red meteors flash'd along the sky,
And conscious Nature shudder'd at the cry!
Oh! righteous Heaven; ere Freedom found a grave,
Why slept the sword, omnipotent to save?
395 Where was thine arm, O Vengeance! where thy rod,
That smote the foes of Zion and of God;[1]
That crush'd proud Ammon, when his iron car
Was yoked in wrath, and thunder'd from afar?[2]
Where was the storm that slumber'd till the host
400 Of blood-stain'd Pharaoh left their trembling coast;
Then bade the deep in wild commotion flow,
And heaved an ocean on their march below?[3]
Departed spirits of the mighty dead!
Ye that at Marathon and Leuctra bled!
405 Friends of the world! restore your swords to man,
Fight in his sacred cause, and lead the van!
Yet for Sarmatia's tears of blood atone,
And make her arm puissant as your own!
Oh! once again to Freedom's cause return
410 The patriot Tell—the Bruce of Bannockburn!
Yes! thy proud lords, unpitied land, shall see

[1] See *Isaiah*, 51:7-10.
[2] See *Judges*, 11:8-33; *Ezekiel*, 25:1-7.
[3] See *Exodus*, 14.

That man hath yet a soul—and dare be free!
A little while, along thy saddening plains,
The starless night of Desolation reigns;
415 Truth shall restore the light by Nature given,
And, like Prometheus, bring the fire of Heaven!
Prone to the dust Oppression shall be hurl'd,
Her name, her nature, wither'd from the world!

YE MARINERS OF ENGLAND

A NAVAL ODE
1799-1800   1801

Ye mariners of England,
That guard our native seas;
Whose flag has braved, a thousand years,
The battle and the breeze!
5 Your glorious standard launch again
To match another foe,[1]
And sweep through the deep,
While the stormy winds do blow;
While the battle rages loud and long,
10 And the stormy winds do blow.

The spirits of your fathers
Shall start from every wave!
For the deck it was their field of fame,
And Ocean was their grave.
15 Where Blake and mighty Nelson fell,
Your manly hearts shall glow,
As ye sweep through the deep,
While the stormy winds do blow;
While the battle rages loud and long,
20 And the stormy winds do blow.

Britannia needs no bulwarks,
No towers along the steep;
Her march is o'er the mountain-waves,
Her home is on the deep.
25 With thunders from her native oak,
She quells the floods below,
As they roar on the shore,
When the stormy winds do blow;
When the battle rages loud and long,
30 And the stormy winds do blow.

The meteor flag of England
Shall yet terrific burn,
Till danger's troubled night depart,
And the star of peace return.
35 Then, then, ye ocean-warriors!
Our song and feast shall flow

[1] England had won naval victories over the French in the battles of Cape St. Vincent (1797) and of the Nile (1798).

To the fame of your name,
When the storm has ceased to blow;
When the fiery fight is heard no more,
40 And the storm has ceased to blow.

HOHENLINDEN
1802　　　1802

On Linden, when the sun was low,
All bloodless lay th' untrodden snow,
And dark as winter was the flow
Of Iser, rolling rapidly.

5 But Linden saw another sight,
When the drum beat at dead of night,
Commanding fires of death to light
The darkness of her scenery.

By torch and trumpet fast array'd,
10 Each horseman drew his battle-blade,
And furious every charger neigh'd,
To join the dreadful revelry.

Then shook the hills with thunder riven,
Then rush'd the steed to battle driven,
15 And louder than the bolts of heaven,
Far flash'd the red artillery.

But redder yet that light shall glow
On Linden's hills of stainèd snow,
And bloodier yet the torrent flow
20 Of Iser, rolling rapidly.

'Tis morn; but scarce yon level sun
Can pierce the war-clouds, rolling dun,
Where furious Frank and fiery Hun,
Shout in their sulphurous canopy.

25 The combat deepens. On, ye brave,
Who rush to glory, or the grave!
Wave, Munich! all thy banners wave,
And charge with all thy chivalry!

Few, few, shall part where many meet!
30 The snow shall be their winding-sheet,
And every turf beneath their feet
Shall be a soldier's sepulchre.

LOCHIEL'S WARNING
1802　　　1802

WIZARD

Lochiel, Lochiel! beware of the day
When the lowlands shall meet thee in
　　battle array!
For a field of the dead rushes red on my
　　sight,
And the clans of Culloden are scatter'd
　　in fight.

5 They rally, they bleed, for their kingdom
　　and crown;
Woe, woe to the riders that trample them
　　down!
Proud Cumberland prances, insulting the
　　slain,
And their hoof-beaten bosoms are trod
　　to the plain.
But hark! through the fast-flashing light-
　　ning of war,
10 What steed to the desert flies frantic and
　　far?
'Tis thine, oh Glenullin! whose bride shall
　　await,
Like a love-lighted watch-fire, all night at
　　the gate.
A steed comes at morning: no rider is
　　there;
But its bridle is red with the sign of
　　despair.
15 Weep, Albin! to death and captivity led!
Oh weep, but thy tears cannot number
　　the dead:
For a merciless sword on Culloden shall
　　wave,
Culloden! that reeks with the blood of the
　　brave.

LOCHIEL

Go, preach to the coward, thou death-
　　telling seer!
20 Or, if gory Culloden so dreadful appear,
Draw, dotard, around thy old wavering
　　sight
This mantle, to cover the phantoms of
　　fright.

WIZARD

Ha! laugh'st thou, Lochiel, my vision to
　　scorn?
Proud bird of the mountain, thy plume
　　shall be torn!
25 Say, rush'd the bold eagle exultingly
　　forth,
From his home, in the dark, rolling clouds
　　of the north?
Lo! the death-shot of foemen outspeeding,
　　he rode
Companionless, bearing destruction
　　abroad;
But down let him stoop from his havoc
　　on high!
Ah! home let him speed, for the spoiler
　　is nigh.
Why flames the far summit? Why shoot
　　to the blast
Those embers, like stars from the firma-
　　ment cast?
'Tis the fire-shower of ruin, all dread-
　　fully driven

From his eyrie, that beacons the darkness of heaven.

35 Oh, crested Lochiel! the peerless in might,
Whose banners arise on the battlements' height,
Heaven's fire is around thee, to blast and to burn;
Return to thy dwelling! all lonely return!
For the blackness of ashes shall mark where it stood,
40 And a wild mother scream o'er her famishing brood.

LOCHIEL

False Wizard, avaunt! I have marshall'd my clan,
Their swords are a thousand, their bosoms are one!
They are true to the last of their blood and their breath,
And like reapers descend to the harvest of death.
45 Then welcome be Cumberland's steed to the shock!
Let him dash his proud foam like a wave on the rock!
But woe to his kindred, and woe to his cause,
When Albin her claymore[1] indignantly draws;
When her bonneted chieftains to victory crowd,
50 Clanronald the dauntless, and Moray the proud,
All plaided and plumed in their tartan[2] array——

WIZARD

Lochiel, Lochiel! beware of the day;
For, dark and despairing, my sight I may seal,
But man cannot cover what God would reveal;
55 'Tis the sunset of life gives me mystical lore,
And coming events cast their shadows before.
I tell thee, Culloden's dread echoes shall ring
With the bloodhounds that bark for thy fugitive king.
Lo! anointed by Heaven with the vials of wrath,
60 Behold, where he flies on his desolate path!
Now in darkness and billows, he sweeps from my sight:

[1] A large two-edged sword.
[2] Woolen cloth checkered with narrow bands of various colors; the characteristic dress of the Highland clans.

Rise, rise! ye wild tempests, and cover his flight!
'Tis finish'd. Their thunders are hush'd on the moors:
Culloden is lost, and my country deplores.
65 But where is the iron-bound prisoner? Where?
For the red eye of battle is shut in despair.
Say, mounts he the ocean-wave, banish'd, forlorn,
Like a limb from his country cast bleeding and torn?
Ah no! for a darker departure is near;
70 The war-drum is muffled, and black is the bier;
His death-bell is tolling: oh! mercy, dispel
Yon sight, that it freezes my spirit to tell!
Life flutters convulsed in his quivering limbs,
And his blood-streaming nostril in agony swims.
75 Accursed be the fagots, that blaze at his feet,
Where his heart shall be thrown, ere it ceases to beat,
With the smoke of its ashes to poison the gale——

LOCHIEL

Down, soothless insulter! I trust not the tale:
For never shall Albin a destiny meet,
80 So black with dishonor, so foul with retreat.
Tho' my perishing ranks should be strew'd in their gore,
Like ocean-weeds heap'd on the surf-beaten shore,
Lochiel, untainted by flight or by chains,
While the kindling of life in his bosom remains,
85 Shall victor exult, or in death be laid low,
With his back to the field, and his feet to the foe!
And leaving in battle no blot on his name,
Look proudly to Heaven from the death-bed of fame.

LORD ULLIN'S DAUGHTER
1804-05   1809

A chieftain, to the Highlands bound,
Cries, "Boatman, do not tarry!
And I'll give thee a silver pound,
To row us o'er the ferry."

5 "Now who be ye, would cross Lochgyle,
This dark and stormy water?"

"O, I'm the chief of Ulva's isle,
And this, Lord Ullin's daughter.

"And fast before her father's men
10   Three days we've fled together,
For should he find us in the glen,
  My blood would stain the heather.

"His horsemen hard behind us ride;
  Should they our steps discover,
15 Then who will cheer my bonny bride
  When they have slain her lover?"

Out spoke the hardy Highland wight,
  "I'll go, my chief; I'm ready:
It is not for your silver bright;
20   But for your winsome lady.

"And by my word! the bonny bird
  In danger shall not tarry;
So though the waves are raging white,
  I'll row you o'er the ferry."

25 By this the storm grew loud apace,
  The water wraith[1] was shrieking;
And in the scowl of heaven each face
  Grew dark as they were speaking.

But still as wilder blew the wind,
30   And as the night grew drearer,
Adown the glen rode armed men—
  Their trampling sounded nearer.

"O haste thee, haste!" the lady cries,
  "Though tempests round us gather;
35 I'll meet the raging of the skies,
  But not an angry father."

The boat has left a stormy land,
  A stormy sea before her,—
When, oh! too strong for human hand,
40   The tempest gathered o'er her.

And still they row'd amidst the roar
  Of waters fast prevailing:
Lord Ullin reach'd that fatal shore—
  His wrath was changed to wailing.

45 For sore dismay'd, through storm and
    shade,
  His child he did discover:
One lovely hand she stretch'd for aid,
  And one was round her lover.

"Come back! come back!" he cried in
    grief,
50   "Across this stormy water;
And I'll forgive your Highland chief,
  My daughter! oh, my daughter!"

[1] spirit supposed to preside over the waters.

'Twas vain;—the loud waves lash'd the
  shore,
  Return or aid preventing:
55 The waters wild went o'er his child,
  And he was left lamenting.

BATTLE OF THE BALTIC
1804-05   1809

Of Nelson and the North,
Sing the glorious day's renown,
When to battle fierce came forth
All the might of Denmark's crown,
5 And her arms along the deep proudly
    shone;
By each gun and lighted brand,
In a bold determined hand,
And the Prince of all the land
Led them on.

10 Like leviathans afloat,
Lay their bulwarks on the brine,
While the sign of battle flew
On the lofty British line;
It was ten of April morn by the chime.
15 As they drifted on their path,
There was silence deep as death;
And the boldest held his breath,
For a time.

But the might of England flush'd
20 To anticipate the scene;
And her van the fleeter rush'd
O'er the deadly space between.
"Hearts of oak!" our captain cried, when
    each gun
From its adamantine lips
25 Spread a death-shade round the ships,
Like the hurricane eclipse
Of the sun.

Again! again! again!
And the havoc did not slack,
30 Till a feeble cheer the Dane
To our cheering sent us back;
Their shots along the deep slowly boom—
Then ceased—and all is wail,
As they strike the shatter'd sail,
35 Or in conflagration pale
Light the gloom.

Out spoke the victor then,
As he hail'd them o'er the wave;
"Ye are brothers! ye are men!
40 And we conquer but to save;
So peace instead of death let us bring.
But yield, proud foe, thy fleet,
With the crews, at England's feet,
And make submission meet
45 To our King."

Then Denmark bless'd our chief,
That he gave her wounds repose;
And the sounds of joy and grief
From her people wildly rose,
50 As Death withdrew his shades from the day.
While the sun look'd smiling bright
O'er a wide and woful sight,
Where the fires of funeral light
Died away.

55 Now joy, old England, raise!
For the tidings of thy might,
By the festal cities' blaze,
Whilst the wine-cup shines in light;
And yet amidst that joy and uproar,
60 Let us think of them that sleep,
Full many a fathom deep,
By thy wild and stormy steep,
Elsinore!

Brave hearts! to Britain's pride
65 Once so faithful and so true,
On the deck of fame that died,
With the gallant good Riou;
Soft sigh the winds of Heaven o'er their grave!
While the billow mournful rolls,
70 And the mermaid's song condoles,
Singing glory to the souls
Of the brave!

THE LAST MAN
1823

All worldly shapes shall melt in gloom,
  The Sun himself must die,
Before this mortal shall assume
  Its immortality!
5 I saw a vision in my sleep,
That gave my spirit strength to sweep
  Adown the gulf of Time!
I saw the last of human mould
That shall Creation's death behold,
10 As Adam saw her prime!

The Sun's eye had a sickly glare,
  The Earth with age was wan,
The skeletons of nations were
  Around that lonely man!
15 Some had expired in fight,—the brands
Still rusted in their bony hands,
  In plague and famine some!
Earth's cities had no sound nor tread;
And ships were drifting with the dead
20 To shores where all was dumb!

Yet, prophet-like, that lone one stood,
  With dauntless words and high,
That shook the sere leaves from the wood

As if a storm pass'd by,
25 Saying, ''We are twins in death, proud Sun!
Thy face is cold, thy race is run,
  'Tis Mercy bids thee go;
For thou ten thousand thousand years
Hast seen the tide of human tears,
30 That shall no longer flow.

''What though beneath thee man put forth
  His pomp, his pride, his skill;
And arts that made fire, flood, and earth,
  The vassals of his will?
35 Yet mourn I not thy parted sway,
Thou dim discrowned king of day;
  For all those trophied arts
And triumphs that beneath thee sprang,
Heal'd not a passion or a pang
40 Entail'd on human hearts.

Go, let oblivion's curtain fall
  Upon the stage of men,
Nor with thy rising beams recall
  Life's tragedy again:
45 Its piteous pageants bring not back,
Nor waken flesh, upon the rack
  Of pain anew to writhe;
Stretch'd in disease's shapes abhorr'd,
Or mown in battle by the sword,
50 Like grass beneath the scythe.

Ev'n I am weary in yon skies
  To watch thy fading fire;
Test of all sumless agonies,
  Behold not me expire.
55 My lips that speak thy dirge of death
Their rounded gasp and gurgling breath
  To see thou shalt not boast.
The eclipse of Nature spreads my pall,
The majesty of Darkness shall
60 Receive my parting ghost!

This spirit shall return to Him
  Who gave its heavenly spark;
Yet think not, Sun, it shall be dim
  When thou thyself art dark!
65 No! it shall live again, and shine
In bliss unknown to beams of thine.
  By him recall'd to breath,
Who captive led captivity,
Who robb'd the grave of Victory,
70 And took the sting from Death![1]

Go, Sun, while Mercy holds me up
  On Nature's awful waste
To drink this last and bitter cup
  Of grief that man shall taste—
75 Go, tell the night that hides thy face,
Thou saw'st the last of Adam's race.

[1] See *1 Corinthians*, 15:55.

On Earth's sepulchral clod,
The darkening universe defy
To quench his immortality,
80   Or shake his trust in God!

THE DEATH-BOAT OF HELIGOLAND
1828

Can restlessness reach the cold sepulchred
   head?
Ay, the quick have their sleep-walkers, so
   have the dead.
There are brains, though they moulder,
   that dream in the tomb,
And that maddening forehear the last
   trumpet of doom,
5 Till their corses start sheeted to revel on
   earth,
Making horror more deep by the semblance of mirth:
By the glare of new-lighted volcanoes they
   dance,
Or at mid-sea appall the chill'd mariner's
   glance.
Such, I wot, was the band of cadaverous
   smile
10 Seen ploughing the night-surge of Heli-
   go's isle.

The foam of the Baltic had sparkled like
   fire,
And the red moon look'd down with an
   aspect of ire;
But her beams on a sudden grew sick-like
   and gray,
And the mews[1] that had slept clang'd and
   shriek'd far away;
15 And the buoys and the beacons extinguish'd their light,
As the boat of the stony-eyed dead came
   in sight,
High bounding from billow to billow;
   each form
Had its shroud like a plaid flying loose
   to the storm;
With an oar in each pulseless and icy-cold
   hand,
20 Fast they plough'd by the lee-shore of
   Heligoland,
Such breakers as boat of the living ne'er
   cross'd;
Now surf-sunk for minutes again they
   uptoss'd;
And with livid lips shouted reply o'er the
   flood
To the challenging watchman, that curdled
   his blood:
25 "We are dead—we are bound from our
   graves in the west,

[1] gulls

First to Hecla, and then to——'' Unmeet
   was the rest
For man's ear. The old abbey bell thunder'd its clang,
And their eyes gleam'd with phosphorus
   light as it rang:
Ere they vanish'd, they stopp'd, and
   gazed silently grim,
30 Till the eye could define them, garb, feature, and limb.

Now who were those roamers? of gallows
   or wheel[1]
Bore they marks, or the mangling anatomist's steel?
No, by magistrates' chains 'mid their
   grave-clothes you saw
They were felons too proud to have perish'd by law:
35 But a ribbon that hung where a rope
   should have been,
'Twas the badge of their faction, its hue
   was not green,
Show'd them men who had trampled and
   tortured and driven
To rebellion the fairest Isle breathed on
   by Heaven,—
Men whose heirs would yet finish the
   tyrannous task,
40 If the Truth and the Time had not
   dragg'd off their mask,
They parted—but not till the sight might
   discern
A scutcheon distinct at their pinnace's
   stern,
Where letters emblazon'd in blood-color'd
   flame,
Named their faction—I blot not my page
   with its name.

Thomas Moore 1779-1852
THE LAKE OF THE DISMAL SWAMP
WRITTEN AT NORFOLK IN VIRGINIA
1804   1806

"They made her a grave, too cold and
   damp
   For a soul so warm and true;
And she's gone to the Lake of the Dismal
   Swamp,
Where, all night long, by a fire-fly lamp,
5   She paddles her white canoe.

"And her fire-fly lamp I soon shall see,
   And her paddle I soon shall hear;
Long and loving our life shall be,
And I'll hide the maid in a cypress tree,
10   When the footstep of death is near."

[1] wheel of torture

Away to the Dismal Swamp he speeds—
  His path was rugged and sore,
Through tangled juniper, beds of reeds,
Through many a fen, where the serpent
    feeds,
15   And man never trod before.

And when on the earth he sunk to sleep,
  If slumber his eyelids knew,
He lay where the deadly vine doth weep
Its venomous tear and nightly steep
20   The flesh with blistering dew!

And near him the she-wolf stirr'd the
    brake,[1]
  And the copper-snake breath'd in his
    ear,
Till he starting cried, from his dream
    awake,
"Oh! when shall I see the dusky Lake,
25   And the white canoe of my dear?"

He saw the Lake, and a meteor bright
  Quick over its surface play'd—
"Welcome," he said, "my dear one's
    light!"
And the dim shore echoed, for many a
    night,
30   The name of the death-cold maid.

Till he hollow'd a boat of the birchen bark,
  Which carried him off from shore;
Far, far he follow'd the meteor spark,
The wind was high and the clouds were
    dark,
35   And the boat return'd no more.

But oft, from the Indian hunter's camp,
  This lover and maid so true
Are seen at the hour of midnight damp
To cross the Lake by a fire-fly lamp,
40   And paddle their white canoe!

A CANADIAN BOAT SONG

WRITTEN ON THE RIVER ST. LAWRENCE
1804   1806

Faintly as tolls the evening chime,
Our voices keep tune and our oars keep
    time.
Soon as the woods on shore look dim,
We'll sing at St. Ann's our parting hymn.
5 Row, brothers, row, the stream runs fast,
The rapids are near and the daylight's
    past.

Why should we yet our sail unfurl?
There is not a breath the blue wave to
    curl;
But, when the wind blows off the shore,

[1] thicket

10 Oh! sweetly we'll rest our weary oar.
Blow, breezes, blow, the stream runs fast,
The rapids are near and the daylight's
    past.

Utawas' tide! this trembling moon
Shall see us float over thy surges soon.
15 Saint of this green isle! hear our prayers,
Oh, grant us cool heavens and favoring
    airs.
Blow, breezes, blow, the stream runs fast,
The rapids are near and the daylight's
    past.

From IRISH MELODIES

1807 28   1808-34
OH, BREATHE NOT HIS NAME!

Oh, breathe not his name! let it sleep in
    the shade,
Where cold and unhonored his relics are
    laid;
Sad, silent, and dark be the tears that we
    shed,
As the night-dew that falls on the grass
    o'er his head.

5 But the night-dew that falls, though in
    silence it weeps,
Shall brighten with verdure the grave
    where he sleeps;
And the tear that we shed, though in secret
    it rolls,
Shall long keep his memory green in our
    souls.

WHEN HE WHO ADORES THEE

When he who adores thee has left but the
    name
  Of his fault and his sorrows behind,
Oh! say wilt thou weep, when they darken
    the fame
  Of a life that for thee was resign'd?
5 Yes, weep, and however my foes may con-
    demn,
  Thy tears shall efface their decree;
For Heaven can witness, though guilty to
    them,
  I have been but too faithful to thee.

With thee were the dreams of my earliest
    love;
10   Every thought of my reason was thine;
In my last humble prayer to the Spirit
    above,
  Thy name shall be mingled with mine.
Oh! blest are the lovers and friends who
    shall live
  The days of thy glory to see;
15 But the next dearest blessing that Heaven
    can give
  Is the pride of thus dying for thee.

THE HARP THAT ONCE THROUGH TARA'S HALLS

The harp that once through Tara's halls
  The soul of music shed,
Now hangs as mute on Tara's walls
  As if that soul were fled.
5 So sleeps the pride of former days,
  So glory's thrill is o'er,
And hearts that once beat high for praise
  Now feel that pulse no more!

No more to chiefs and ladies bright
10   The harp of Tara swells;
The chord alone that breaks at night
  Its tale of ruin tells.
Thus Freedom now so seldom wakes,
  The only throb she gives
15 Is when some heart indignant breaks,
  To show that still she lives.

OH! BLAME NOT THE BARD

Oh! blame not the bard, if he fly to the
  bowers,
  Where Pleasure lies, carelessly smiling
    at Fame;
He was born for much more, and in hap-
  pier hours
  His soul might have burn'd with a
    holier flame.
5 The string, that now languishes loose o'er
  the lyre,
  Might have bent a proud bow to the
    warrior's dart;
And the lip, which now breathes but the
  song of desire,
  Might have pour'd the full tide of a
    patriot's heart.

But alas for his country!—her pride is
  gone by,
10   And that spirit is broken, which never
    would bend;
O'er the ruin her children in secret must
  sigh,
  For 'tis treason to love her, and death
    to defend.
Unpriz'd are her sons, till they've learn'd
  to betray;
  Undistinguish'd they live, if they shame
    not their sires;
15 And the torch, that would light them
  thro' dignity's way,
  Must be caught from the pile, where
    their country expires.

Then blame not the bard, if in pleasure's
  soft dream,
  He should try to forget what he never
    can heal:

Oh! give but a hope—let a vista but
  gleam
20   Through the gloom of his country, and
    mark how he'll feel!
That instant, his heart at her shrine would
  lay down
  Every passion it nurs'd, every bliss it
    ador'd;
While the myrtle, now idly entwin'd with
  his crown,
  Like the wreath of Harmodius, should
    cover his sword.

25 But tho' glory be gone, and tho' hope
  fade away,
  Thy name, lov'd Erin, shall live in his
    songs;
Not ev'n in the hour, when his heart is
  most gay,
  Will he lose the resemblance of thee
    and thy wrongs.
The stranger shall hear thy lament on his
  plains;
30   The sigh of thy harp shall be sent o'er
    the deep,
Till thy masters themselves, as they rivet
  thy chains,
  Shall pause at the song of their captive,
    and weep.

LESBIA HATH A BEAMING EYE

Lesbia hath a beaming eye,
  But no one knows for whom it beameth;
Right and left its arrows fly,
  But what they aim at no one dreameth.
5 Sweeter 'tis to gaze upon
  My Nora's lid that seldom rises;
Few its looks, but every one,
  Like unexpected light, surprises!
    Oh, my Nora Creina,[1] dear,
10   My gentle, bashful Nora Creina,
    Beauty lies
    In many eyes,
  But Love in yours, my Nora Creina.

Lesbia wears a robe of gold,
15   But all so close the nymph hath lac'd it,
Not a charm of beauty's mould
  Presumes to stay where nature plac'd it.
Oh! my Nora's gown for me,
  That floats as wild as mountain breezes,
20 Leaving every beauty free
  To sink or swell as Heaven pleases.
    Yes, my Nora Creina, dear,
  My simple, graceful Nora Creina,
    Nature's dress
25   Is loveliness—
  The dress you wear, my Nora Creina.

[1] darling

Lesbia, hath a wit refin'd,
  But, when its points are gleaming round
      us,
Who can tell if they're design'd
30 To dazzle merely, or to wound us?
Pillow'd on my Nora's heart,
  In safer slumber Love reposes—
Bed of peace! whose roughest part
  Is but the crumpling of the roses.
35   Oh! my Nora Creina, dear,
    My mild, my artless Nora Creina!
      Wit, though bright,
      Hath no such light,
  As warms your eyes, my Nora Creina.

THE YOUNG MAY MOON

The young May moon is beaming, love,
The glow-worm's lamp is gleaming, love,
    How sweet to rove
    Through Morna's grove,
5 When the drowsy world is dreaming, love!
Then awake!—the heavens look bright,
  my dear,
'Tis never too late for delight, my dear,
    And the best of all ways
    To lengthen our days,
10 Is to steal a few hours from the night, my
  dear!

Now all the world is sleeping, love,
But the sage, his star-watch keeping, love,
    And I, whose star,
    More glorious far,
15 Is the eye from that casement peeping,
  love.
Then awake!—till rise of sun, my dear,
The sage's glass we'll shun, my dear,
    Or, in watching the flight
    Of bodies of light,
20 He might happen to take thee for one,
  my dear.

THE MINSTREL BOY

The Minstrel Boy to the war is gone,
  In the ranks of death you'll find him;
His father's sword he has girded on,
  And his wild harp slung behind him.—
5 "Land of song!" said the warrior-bard,
  "Though all the world betray thee,
One sword, at least, thy rights shall guard,
  One faithful harp shall praise thee!"

The Minstrel fell!—but the foeman's
  chain
10 Could not bring his proud soul under;
The harp he lov'd ne'er spoke again,
  For he tore its chords asunder;

And said, "No chains shall sully thee,
  Thou soul of love and bravery!
15 Thy songs were made for the pure and
    free,
  They shall never sound in slavery."

FAREWELL!—BUT WHENEVER YOU WELCOME THE HOUR

Farewell!—but whenever you welcome the
  hour
That awakens the night-song of mirth in
  your bower,
Then think of the friend who once welcom'd it too,
And forgot his own griefs to be happy
  with you.
5 His griefs may return, not a hope may
  remain
Of the few that have brighten'd his pathway of pain,
But he ne'er will forget the short vision
  that threw
Its enchantment around him, while lin-
  g'ring with you.

And still on that evening, when pleasure
  fills up
10 To the highest top sparkle each heart and
  each cup,
Where'er my path lies, be it gloomy or
  bright,
My soul, happy friends, shall be with you
  that night;
Shall join in your revels, your sports, and
  your wiles,
And return to me, beaming all o'er with
  your smiles—
15 Too blest, if it tells me that, 'mid the gay
  cheer,
Some kind voice had murmur'd, "I wish
  he were here!"

Let Fate do her worst, there are relics of
  joy,
Bright dreams of the past, which she cannot destroy;
Which come in the night-time of sorrow
  and care,
20 And bring back the features that joy used
  to wear.
Long, long be my heart with such memories fill'd!
Like the vase, in which roses have once
  been distilled—
You may break, you may shatter the vase,
  if you will,
But the scent of the roses will hang round
  it still.

The Time I've Lost in Wooing

The time I've lost in wooing,
In watching and pursuing
    The light that lies
    In woman's eyes,
5 Has been my heart's undoing.
Though Wisdom oft has sought me,
I scorn'd the lore she brought me,
    My only books
    Were woman's looks,
10 And folly's all they've taught me.

Her smile when Beauty granted,
I hung with gaze enchanted,
    Like him, the Sprite,
    Whom maids by night
15 Oft meet in glen that's haunted.
Like him, too, Beauty won me,
But while her eyes were on me;
    If once their ray
    Was turn'd away,
20 Oh, winds could not outrun me.

And are those follies going?
And is my proud heart growing
    Too cold or too wise
    For brilliant eyes
25 Again to set it glowing?
No, vain, alas! th' endeavor
From bonds so sweet to sever;
    Poor Wisdom's chance
    Against a glance
30 Is now as weak as ever.

Dear Harp of My Country

Dear Harp of my Country! in darkness
    I found thee,
The cold chain of silence had hung o'er
    thee long,
When proudly, my own Island Harp, I
    unbound thee,
And gave all thy chords to light, free-
    dom, and song!
5 The warm lay of love and the light note
    of gladness
Have waken'd thy fondest, thy liveliest
    thrill;
But, so oft hast thou echo'd the deep sigh
    of sadness,
That ev'n in thy mirth it will steal from
    thee still.

Dear Harp of my Country! farewell to
    thy numbers,
10   This sweet wreath of song is the last we
    shall twine!
Go, sleep with the sunshine of Fame on
    thy slumbers,

Till touch'd by some hand less unworthy
    than mine;
If the pulse of the patriot, soldier, or
    lover,
Have throbb'd at our lay, 'tis thy glory
    alone;
15 I was but as the wind, passing heedlessly
    over,
And all the wild sweetness I wak'd was
    thy own.

From NATIONAL AIRS
1815
Oh, Come to Me When Daylight Sets
Venetian Air

Oh, come to me when daylight sets;
    Sweet! then come to me,
When smoothly go our gondolets
    O'er the moonlight sea.
5 When Mirth's awake, and Love begins,
    Beneath that glancing ray,
With sounds of lutes and mandolins,
    To steal young hearts away.
Then, come to me when daylight sets;
10   Sweet! then come to me,
When smoothly go our gondolets
    O'er the moonlight sea.

Oh, then's the hour for those who love,
    Sweet! like thee and me;
15 When all's so calm below, above,
    In heav'n and o'er the sea.
When maidens sing sweet barcarolles[1]
    And Echo sings again
So sweet, that all with ears and souls
20   Should love and listen then.
So, come to me when daylight sets;
    Sweet! then come to me,
When smoothly go our gondolets
    O'er the moonlight sea.

Oft, in the Stilly Night
Scotch Air

Oft, in the stilly night,
    Ere Slumber's chain has bound me,
Fond Memory brings the light
    Of other days around me;
5   The smiles, the tears,
     Of boyhood's years,
The words of love then spoken;
     The eyes that shone,
     Now dimmed and gone,
10   The cheerful hearts now broken!
Thus, in the stilly night,
    Ere Slumber's chain has bound me,

_____
[1] Popular songs sung by Venetian gondoliers.

Sad Memory brings the light
  Of other days around me.

15 When I remember all
    The friends, so linked together,
  I've seen around me fall,
    Like leaves in wintry weather;
    I feel like one
20   Who treads alone
  Some banquet-hall deserted,
    Whose lights are fled,
    Whose garlands dead,
  And all but he departed!
25 Thus, in the stilly night,
  Ere Slumber's chain has bound me,
Sad Memory brings the light
  Of other days around me.

LALLA ROOKH
1814-17   1817

From THE LIGHT OF THE HARAM

Who has not heard of the Vale of Cash-
    mere,
  With its roses the brightest that earth
    ever gave,
Its temples, and grottos, and fountains as
    clear
  As the love-lighted eyes that hang over
    their wave?

5 Oh! to see it at sunset, when warm o'er
    the lake
  Its splendor at parting a summer eve
    throws,
Like a bride, full of blushes, when
    ling'ring to take
  A last look of her mirror at night ere
    she goes!
When the shrines through the foliage are
    gleaming half shown,
10 And each hallows the hour by some rites
    of its own.
Here the music of pray'r from a minaret[1]
    swells,
  Here the Magian[2] his urn, full of per-
    fume, is swinging,
And here, at the altar, a zone[3] of sweet
    bells
  Round the waist of some fair Indian
    dancer is ringing.
15 Or to see it by moonlight, when mellowly
    shines
  The light o'er its palaces, gardens, and
    shrines;
When the water-falls gleam, like a quick
    fall of stars,

[1] slender tower of a mosque or temple, surrounded by one or more projecting balconies
[2] priest
[3] girdle

And the nightingale's hymn from the Isle
    of Chenars
  Is broken by laughs and light echoes of
    feet
20 From the cool, shining walks where the
    young people meet:
  Or at morn, when the magic of daylight
    awakes
A new wonder each minute, as slowly it
    breaks,—
Hills, cupolas, fountains, call'd forth
    every one
  Out of darkness, as if but just born of
    the Sun.
25 When the Spirit of Fragrance is up with
    the day,
  From his Haram of night-flowers stealing
    away;
And the wind, full of wantonness, woos
    like a lover
The young aspen-trees, till they tremble
    all over.
When the East is as warm as the light of
    first hopes,
30   And Day, with his banner of radiance
    unfurl'd,
Shines in through the mountainous portal
    that opes,
  Sublime, from that valley of bliss to the
    world!

But never yet, by night or day,
In dew of spring or summer's ray,
35 Did the sweet valley shine so gay
As now it shines—all love and light,
Visions by day and feasts by night!
A happier smile illumes each brow,
  With quicker spread each heart un-
    closes,
40 And all its ecstasy, for now
  The valley holds its Feast of Roses;
The joyous time, when pleasures pour
Profusely round and, in their shower,
Hearts open, like the season's rose,—
45   The flow'ret of a hundred leaves,
Expanding while the dew-fall flows,
  And every leaf its balm receives.

'Twas when the hour of evening came
Upon the lake, serene and cool,
50 When Day had hid his sultry flame
  Behind the palms of Baramoule,
When maids began to lift their heads,
Refresh'd from their embroider'd beds,
Where they had slept the sun away,
55 And wak'd to moonlight and to play.
All were abroad—the busiest hive
On Bela's hills is less alive,
When saffron beds are full in flow'r,

Than look'd the valley in that hour.
60 A thousand restless torches play'd
Through every grove and island shade;
A thousand sparkling lamps were set
On every dome and minaret;
And fields and pathways, far and near,
65 Were lighted by a blaze so clear,
That you could see, in wand'ring round,
The smallest rose-leaf on the ground.
Yet did the maids and matrons leave
Their veils at home, that brilliant eve;
70 And there were glancing eyes about,
And cheeks, that would not dare shine out
    In open day, but thought they might
    Look lovely then, because 'twas night.
And all were free, and wandering,
75   And all exclaim'd to all they met,
    That never did the summer bring
    So gay a Feast of Roses yet;
    The moon had never shed a light
    So clear as that which bless'd them
    there;
80 The roses ne'er shone half so bright,
    Nor they themselves look'd half so
    fair.

And what a wilderness of flow'rs!
It seem'd as though from all the bow'rs
And fairest fields of all the year,
85 The mingled spoil were scatter'd here.
The lake, too, like a garden breathes,
    With the rich buds that o'er it lie,—
    As if a shower of fairy wreaths
    Had fall'n upon it from the sky!
90 And then the sound of joy:—the beat
Of tabors and of dancing feet;
The minaret-crier's chant of glee
Sung from his lighted gallery,
And answer'd by a ziraleet[1]
95 From neighboring Haram, wild and
    sweet;
The merry laughter, echoing
From gardens, where the silken swing
Wafts some delighted girl above
The top leaves of the orange-grove;
100 Or, from those infant groups at play
Among the tents that line the way,
Flinging, unaw'd by slave or mother,
Handfuls of roses at each other.
Then the sounds from the lake:—the low
    whisp'ring in boats,
105   As they shoot through the moonlight;
    the dipping of oars;
And the wild, airy warbling that ev'ry-
    where floats,
    Through the groves, round the islands,
    as if all the shores,

1 joyous chorus

Like those of Kathay, utter'd music,
    and gave
An answer in song to the kiss of each
    wave.
110 But the gentlest of all are those sounds,
    full of feeling,
That soft from the lute of some lover
    are stealing,
Some lover, who knows all the heart-
    touching power
Of a lute and a sigh in this magical
    hour.
Oh! best of delights as it ev'rywhere is
115 To be near the lov'd *One*,—what a rap-
    ture is his
Who in moonlight and music thus
    sweetly may glide
O'er the Lake of Cashmere, with that
    One by his side!
If woman can make the worst wilder-
    ness dear,
Think, think what a heav'n she must
    make of Cashmere!

. . . .

From FABLES FOR THE HOLY
ALLIANCE
1823

I. THE DISSOLUTION OF THE HOLY ALLIANCE

A DREAM

I've had a dream that bodes no good
Unto the Holy Brotherhood.
I may be wrong, but I confess—
    As far as it is right or lawful
5 For one, no conjurer, to guess—
    It seems to me extremely awful.

Methought upon the Neva's flood
A beautiful ice palace stood,
A dome of frost-work, on the plan
10 Of that once built by Empress Anne,[1]
Which shone by moonlight—as the tale is—
Like an Aurora Borealis.

In this said palace, furnish'd all
    And lighted as the best on land are,
15 I dreamt there was a splendid ball,
    Given by the Emperor Alexander,[2]
To entertain with all due zeal,
    Those holy gentlemen, who've shown a
Regard so kind for Europe's weal,
20   At Troppau, Laybach, and Verona.

The thought was happy—and design'd
To hint how thus the human mind

---

[1] The ice-palace of St. Petersburg was built by
the Empress Anna in the winter of 1740.
See Cowper's *The Task*, 5, 126 ff; also *The
Penny Magazine*, 1837, p. 459.
[2] Alexander I, Emperor of Russia, 1801-25.

May, like the stream imprison'd there,
Be check'd and chill'd, till it can bear
25 The heaviest kings, that ode or sonnet
E'er yet be-prais'd, to dance upon it.

And all were pleas'd, and cold, and
stately,
Shivering in grand illumination—
Admir'd the superstructure greatly,
30 Nor gave one thought to the foundation.
Much too the Czar himself exulted,
To all plebeian fears a stranger,
For, Madame Krudener, when consulted,
Had pledg'd her word there was no
danger.
35 So, on he caper'd, fearless quite,
Thinking himself extremely clever,
And waltz'd away with all his might,
As if the frost would last forever.

Just fancy how a bard like me,
40 Who reverence monarchs, must have
trembled,
To see that goodly company,
At such a ticklish sport assembled.

Nor were the fears, that thus astounded
My loyal soul, at all unfounded—
45 For, lo! ere long, those walls so massy
Were seiz'd with an ill-omen'd dripping,
And o'er the floors, now growing glassy,
Their Holinesses took to slipping.
The Czar, half through a polonaise[1]
50 Could scarce get on for downright stum-
bling;
And Prussia, though to slippery ways
Well used, was cursedly near tumbling.

Yet still 'twas, who could stamp the floor
most,
Russia and Austria 'mong the foremost.—
55 And now, to an Italian air,
This precious brace would, hand in
hand, go;
Now—while old Louis,[2] from his chair,
Intreated them his toes to spare—
Call'd loudly out for a fandango.[3]

60 And a fandango, 'faith, they had,
At which they all set to, like mad!
Never were kings (though small the
expense is
Of wit among their Excellencies)
So out of all their princely senses.
65 But, ah, that dance—that Spanish dance—

Scarce was the luckless strain begun,
When, glaring red, as 'twere a glance
Shot from an angry southern sun,
A light through all the chambers flam'd,
70 Astonishing old Father Frost,
Who, bursting into tears, exclaim'd,
"A thaw, by Jove—we're lost, we're
lost;
Run, France—a second *Waterloo*
Is come to drown you—*sauve qui peut!*"[1]

75 Why, why will monarchs caper so
In palaces without foundations?—
Instantly all was in a flow,
Crowns, fiddles, sceptres, decorations—
Those royal arms, that look'd so nice,
80 Cut out in the resplendent ice—
Those eagles, handsomely provided
With double heads for double dealings—
How fast the globes and sceptres glided
Out of their claws on all the ceilings!
85 Proud Prussia's double bird of prey
Tame as a spatchcock,[2] slunk away;
While—just like France herself, when
she
Proclaims how great her naval skill is—
Poor Louis' drowning fleurs-de-lys
90 Imagin'd themselves *water*-lilies.

And not alone rooms, ceilings, shelves,
But—still more fatal execution—
The Great Legitimates themselves
Seem'd in a state of dissolution.
95 The indignant Czar—when just about
To issue a sublime ukase,[3]
"Whereas all light must be kept out"—
Dissolv'd to nothing in its blaze.
Next Prussia took his turn to melt,
100 And, while his lips illustrious felt
The influence of this southern air,
Some word, like "constitution"—long
Congeal'd in frosty silence there—
Came slowly thawing from his tongue.
105 While Louis, lapsing by degrees,
And sighing out a faint adieu
To truffles,[4] salmis,[5] toasted cheese
And smoking fondus,[6] quickly grew,
Himself, into a fondu too;—
110 Or like that goodly king they make
Of sugar for a Twelfth-night cake,[7]
When, in some urchin's mouth, alas,
It melts into a shapeless mass!

---

[1] A stately Polish dance.
[2] Louis XVIII, King of France (1814-24).
[3] A lively Spanish dance.

[1] save himself who can
[2] A fowl killed and im-
mediately broiled.
[3] proclamation
[4] A kind of edible
fungus.
[5] Roasted game stewed
with sauce, wine,
bread, etc.
[6] Dishes made of
cheese, eggs, butter,
etc., melted together.
[7] A cake made for the
festival held on the
twelfth night after
Christmas. It usu-
ally contained a
bean or a coin.

In short, I scarce could count a minute,
115 Ere the bright dome, and all within it,
Kings, fiddlers, emperors, all were gone—
And nothing now was seen or heard
But the bright river, rushing on,
Happy as an enfranchis'd bird,
120 And prouder of that natural ray,
Shining along its chainless way—
More proudly happy thus to glide
In simple grandeur to the sea,
Than when, in sparkling fetters tied,
125 'Twas deck'd with all that kingly pride
Could bring to light its slavery!

Such is my dream—and, I confess,
I tremble at its awfulness.
That Spanish dance—that southern beam—
130 But I say nothing—there's my dream—
And Madame Krudener, the she-prophet,
May make just what she pleases of it.

Charles Wolfe 1791-1823

THE BURIAL OF SIR JOHN MOORE
AT CORUNNA
1817

Not a drum was heard, not a funeral note,
As his corse to the rampart we hurried;
Not a soldier discharged his farewell shot
O'er the grave where our hero we
buried.

5 We buried him darkly at dead of night,
The sods with our bayonets turning;
By the struggling moonbeam's misty light,
And the lantern dimly burning.

No useless coffin enclosed his breast,
10 Not in sheet nor in shroud we wound
him,
But he lay like a warrior taking his rest
With his martial cloak around him.

Few and short were the prayers we said,
And we spoke not a word of sorrow;
15 But we steadfastly gazed on the face that
was dead,
And we bitterly thought of the morrow.

We thought as we hollowed his narrow bed,
And smoothed down his lonely pillow,
That the foe and the stranger would tread
o'er his head,
20 And we far away on the billow!

Lightly they'll talk of the spirit that's
gone,
And o'er his cold ashes upbraid him,—
But little he'll reck, if they let him sleep on
In the grave where a Briton has laid him.

25 But half of our weary task was done
When the clock struck the hour for
retiring;
And we heard the distant and random gun
That the foe was sullenly firing.

Slowly and sadly we laid him down,
30 From the field of his fame fresh and
gory;
We carved not a line, and we raised not
a stone—
But we left him alone with his glory.

SONNET
1900

My spirit's on the mountains, where the
birds
In wild and sportive freedom wing the
air,
Amidst the heath flowers and the browsing
herds,
Where nature's altar is, my spirit's
there.
5 It is my joy to tread the pathless hills,
Though but in fancy—for my mind is
free
And walks by sedgy ways and trickling
rills,
While I'm forbid the use of liberty.
This is delusion—but it is so sweet
10 That I could live deluded. Let me be
Persuaded that my springing soul may
meet
The eagle on the hills—and I am free.
Who'd not be flattered by a fate like this?
To fancy is to feel our happiness.

OH SAY NOT THAT MY HEART IS
COLD
1825

Oh say not that my heart is cold
To aught that once could warm it—
That Nature's form so dear of old
No more has power to charm it;
5 Or that th' ungenerous world can chill
One glow of fond emotion
For those who made it dearer still,
And shared my wild devotion.

Still oft those solemn scenes I view
10 In rapt and dreamy sadness;
Oft look on those who loved them too
With fancy's idle gladness;
Again I longed to view the light
In Nature's features glowing;
15 Again to tread the mountain's height,
And taste the soul's o'erflowing.

Stern Duty rose, and frowning flung
  His leaden chain around me;
With iron look and sullen tongue
20 He muttered as he bound me—
"The mountain breeze, the boundless
    heaven,
Unfit for toil the creature;
These for the free alone are given,—
  But what have slaves with Nature?"

Sir Walter Scott 1771-1832

WILLIAM AND HELEN
1795   1796

From heavy dreams fair Helen rose,
  And eyed the dawning red:
"Alas, my love, thou tarriest long!
  O art thou false or dead?"

5 With gallant Fred'rick's princely power
  He sought the bold crusade;[1]
But not a word from Judah's wars
  Told Helen how he sped.

With Paynim and with Saracen
10 At length a truce was made,
And every knight return'd to dry
  The tears his love had shed.

Our gallant host was homeward bound
  With many a song of joy;
15 Green waved the laurel in each plume,
  The badge of victory.

And old and young, and sire and son,
  To meet them crowd the way,
With shouts, and mirth, and melody,
20 The debt of love to pay.

Full many a maid her true-love met,
  And sobb'd in his embrace,
And flutt'ring joy in tears and smiles
  Array'd full many a face.

25 Nor joy nor smile for Helen sad;
  She sought the host in vain;
For none could tell her William's fate,
  If faithless or if slain.

The martial band is past and gone;
30 She rends her raven hair,
And in distraction's bitter mood
  She weeps with wild despair.

"O rise, my child," her mother said,
  "Nor sorrow thus in vain;
35 A perjured lover's fleeting heart
  No tears recall again."

[1] He went on the Third Crusade, in 1189-92,
with Frederick Barbarossa.

"O mother, what is gone, is gone,
  What's lost forever lorn:
Death, death alone can comfort me;
40 O had I ne'er been born!

"O break, my heart—O break at once!
  Drink my life-blood, Despair!
No joy remains on earth for me,
  For me in heaven no share."

45 "O enter not in judgment, Lord!"
  The pious mother prays;
"Impute not guilt to thy frail child!
  She knows not what she says.

"O say thy pater noster, child!
50 O turn to God and grace!
His will, that turn'd thy bliss to bale,
  Can change thy bale to bliss."

"O mother, mother, what is bliss?
  O mother, what is bale?
My William's love was heaven on earth,
56 Without it earth is hell.

"Why should I pray to ruthless Heaven,
  Since my loved William's slain?
I only pray'd for William's sake,
60 And all my prayers were vain."

"O take the sacrament, my child,
  And check these tears that flow;
By resignation's humble prayer,
  O hallow'd be thy woe!"

65 "No sacrament can quench this fire,
  Or slake this scorching pain;
No sacrament can bid the dead
  Arise and live again.

"O break, my heart—O break at once!
70 Be thou my god, Despair!
Heaven's heaviest blow has fallen on me,
  And vain each fruitless prayer."

"O enter not in judgment, Lord,
  With thy frail child of clay!
75 She knows not what her tongue has spoke;
  Impute it not, I pray!

"Forbear, my child, this desperate woe,
  And turn to God and grace;
Well can devotion's heavenly glow
80 Convert thy bale to bliss."

"O mother, mother, what is bliss?
  O mother, what is bale?
Without my William what were heaven,
  Or with him what were hell?"

85 Wild she arraigns the eternal doom,
    Upbraids each sacred power,
Till, spent, she sought her silent room,
    All in the lonely tower.

She beat her breast, she wrung her hands,
90   Till sun and day were o'er,
And through the glimmering lattice shone
    The twinkling of the star.

Then, crash! the heavy drawbridge fell
    That o'er the moat was hung;
95 And, clatter! clatter! on its boards
    The hoof of courser rung.

The clank of echoing steel was heard
    As off the rider bounded;
And slowly on the winding stair
100   A heavy footstep sounded.

And hark! and hark! a knock—tap! tap!
    A rustling stifled noise;
Door-latch and tinkling staples ring;
    At length a whispering voice:

105 "Awake, awake, arise, my love!
    How, Helen, dost thou fare?
Wak'st thou, or sleep'st? laugh'st thou,
    or weep'st?
Hast thought on me, my fair?"

"My love! my love!—so late by night!
110   I waked, I wept for thee:
Much have I borne since dawn of morn;
    Where, William, couldst thou be?"

"We saddle late—from Hungary
    I rode since darkness fell;
115 And to its bourne we both return
    Before the matin-bell."[1]

"O rest this night within my arms,
    And warm thee in their fold!
Chill howls through hawthorn bush the
    wind:—
120   My love is deadly cold."

"Let the wind howl through hawthorn
    bush!
This night we must away;
The steed is wight,[2] the spur is bright;
    I cannot stay till day.

125 "Busk, busk, and boune![3] thou mount'st
    behind
    Upon my black barb[4] steed:

[1] bell summoning to early morning worship
[2] powerful
[3] dress and prepare for the journey
[4] Barbary horse (noted for speed and endurance)

O'er stock[1] and stile, a hundred miles,
    We haste to bridal bed."

"Tonight—tonight a hundred miles?
130   O dearest William, stay!
The bell strikes twelve—dark, dismal
    hour!
O wait, my love, till day!"

"Look here, look here—the moon shines
    clear—
    Full fast I ween[2] we ride;
135 Mount and away! for ere the day
    We reach our bridal bed.

"The black barb snorts, the bridle rings;
    Haste, busk, and boune, and seat thee!
The feast is made, the chamber spread,
140   The bridal guests await thee."

Strong love prevail'd. She busks, she
    bounes,
    She mounts the barb behind,
And round her darling William's waist
    Her lily arms she twined.

145 And, hurry! hurry! off they rode,
    As fast as fast might be;
Spurn'd from the courser's thundering
    heels
    The flashing pebbles flee.

And on the right, and on the left,
150   Ere they could snatch a view,
Fast, fast each mountain, mead, and plain,
    And cot, and castle flew.

"Sit fast—dost fear? The moon shines
    clear;
    Fleet goes my barb—keep hold!
155 Fear'st thou?"—"O no!" she faintly said;
    "But why so stern and cold?

"What yonder rings? what yonder sings?
    Why shrieks the owlet gray?"
" 'Tis death-bells' clang, 'tis funeral song,
160   The body to the clay.

"With song and clang, at morrow's dawn,
    Ye may inter the dead:
Tonight I ride, with my young bride,
    To deck our bridal bed.

165 "Come with thy choir, thou coffin'd guest,
    To swell our nuptial song!
Come, priest, to bless our marriage feast!
    Come all, come all along!"

[1] stump
[2] think

Ceased clang and song; down sunk the
    bier;
170 The shrouded corpse arose:
And, hurry! hurry! all the train
    The thundering steed pursues.

And, forward! forward! on they go;
    High snorts the straining steed;
175 Thick pants the rider's laboring breath,
    As headlong on they speed.

"O William, why this savage haste?
    And where thy bridal bed?"
" 'Tis distant far, low, damp, and chill,
180   And narrow, trustless maid."

"No room for me?"—"Enough for both;
    Speed, speed, my barb, thy course!"
O'er thundering bridge, through boiling
    surge
He drove the furious horse.

185 Tramp! tramp! along the land they rode,
    Splash! splash! along the sea;
The scourge is wight, the spur is bright,
    The flashing pebbles flee.

Fled past on right and left how fast
190   Each forest, grove, and bower!
On right and left fled past how fast
    Each city, town, and tower!

"Dost fear? dost fear? The moon shines
    clear,
    Dost fear to ride with me?
195 Hurrah! hurrah! the dead can ride!"—
    "O William, let them be!

"See there, see there! What yonder
    swings,
    And creaks 'mid whistling rain?"—
"Gibbet and steel, th' accursed wheel;[1]
200   A murderer in his chain.

"Hollo! thou felon, follow here:
    To bridal bed we ride;
And thou shalt prance a fetter dance
    Before me and my bride."

205 And, hurry! hurry! clash! clash! clash!
    The wasted form descends;
And fleet as wind through hazel bush
    The wild career[2] attends.

Tramp! tramp! along the land they rode,
210   Splash! splash! along the sea;
The scourge is red, the spur drops blood,
    The flashing pebbles flee.

[1] wheel of torture   [2] gallop; ride

How fled what moonshine faintly show'd!
    How fled what darkness hid!
215 How fled the earth beneath their feet,
    The heaven above their head!

"Dost fear? dost fear? The moon shines
    clear,
    And well the dead can ride;
Does faithful Helen fear for them?"—
220   "O leave in peace the dead!"

"Barb! barb! methinks I hear the cock;
    The sand will soon be run:
Barb! barb! I smell the morning air;
    The race is wellnigh done."

225 Tramp! tramp! along the land they rode,
    Splash! splash! along the sea;
The scourge is red, the spur drops blood,
    The flashing pebbles flee.

"Hurrah! hurrah! well ride the dead;
230   The bride, the bride is come;
And soon we reach the bridal bed,
    For, Helen, here's my home."

Reluctant on its rusty hinge
    Revolved an iron door,
235 And by the pale moon's setting beam
    Were seen a church and tower.

With many a shriek and cry, whiz round
    The birds of midnight, scared;
And rustling like autumnal leaves
240   Unhallow'd ghosts were heard.

O'er many a tomb and tombstone pale
    He spurr'd the fiery horse,
Till sudden at an open grave
    He check'd the wondrous course.

245 The falling gauntlet quits the rein,
    Down drops the casque of steel,
The cuirass leaves his shrinking side,
    The spur his gory heel.

The eyes desert the naked skull,
250   The mould'ring flesh the bone,
Till Helen's lily arms entwine
    A ghastly skeleton.

The furious barb snorts fire and foam,
    And, with a fearful bound,
255 Dissolves at once in empty air,
    And leaves her on the ground.

Half seen by fits, by fits half heard,
    Pale spectres flit along,
Wheel round the maid in dismal dance,
260   And howl the funeral song;

"E'en when the heart's with anguish
   cleft,
Revere the doom of Heaven!
Her soul is from her body reft;
   Her spirit be forgiven!"

THE VIOLET
1797   1810

The violet in her greenwood bower,
   Where birchen boughs with hazels
     mingle,
May boast itself the fairest flower
   In glen, or copse, or forest dingle.[1]

5 Though fair her gems of azure hue,
   Beneath the dewdrop's weight reclining;
I've seen an eye of lovelier blue,
   More sweet through wat'ry lustre
     shining.

The summer sun that dew shall dry,
10   Ere yet the day be past its morrow;
Nor longer in my false love's eye
   Remain'd the tear of parting sorrow.

TO A LADY
WITH FLOWERS FROM THE ROMAN WALL[2]
1797

Take these flowers which, purple waving,
   On the ruin'd rampart grew,
Where, the sons of freedom braving,
   Rome's imperial standards flew.

5 Warriors from the breach of danger
   Pluck no longer laurels there;
They but yield the passing stranger
   Wild-flower wreaths for Beauty's hair.

GLENFINLAS; OR
LORD RONALD'S CORONACH[3]
1799   1801

For them the viewless forms of air obey,
   Their bidding heed, and at their beck repair;
They know what spirit brews the stormful day,
   And heartless oft, like moody madness stare,
To see the phantom-train their secret work pre-
   pare.   COLLINS.[4]

O hone a rie'![5] O hone a rie'!
   The pride of Albin's line is o'er,
And fall'n Glenartney's stateliest tree;
   We ne'er shall see Lord Ronald more!

5 O! sprung from great Macgillianore,
   The chief that never fear'd a foe,

How matchless was thy broad claymore,[1]
   How deadly thine unerring bow!

Well can the Saxon widows tell,
10   How on the Teith's resounding shore
The boldest Lowland warriors fell,
   As down from Lenny's pass you bore.

But o'er his hills, in festal day,
   How blazed Lord Ronald's beltane tree,[2]
15 While youths and maids the light strath-
     spey[3]
   So nimbly danced with Highland glee!

Cheer'd by the strength of Ronald's
   shell,[4]
   E'en age forgot his tresses hoar;
But now the loud lament we swell,
20   O, ne'er to see Lord Ronald more!

From distant isles a chieftain came,
   The joys of Ronald's halls to find,
And chase with him the dark-brown game,
   That bounds o'er Albin's hills of wind.

25 'Twas Moy, whom in Columba's isle[5]
   The seer's prophetic spirit found,
As, with a minstrel's fire the while,
   He waked his harp's harmonious sound.

Full many a spell to him was known,
30   Which wandering spirits shrink to hear;
And many a lay of potent tone,
   Was never meant for mortal ear.

For there, 'tis said, in mystic mood,
   High converse with the dead they hold,
35 And oft espy the fated shroud,
   That shall the future corpse enfold.

O, so it fell that on a day,
   To rouse the red deer from their den,
The Chiefs have ta'en their distant way,
40   And scour'd the deep Glenfinlas glen.

No vassals wait their sports to aid,
   To watch their safety, deck their board;
Their simple dress the Highland plaid,
   Their trusty guard the Highland sword.

45 Three summer days, through brake[6] and
   dell,
   Their whistling shafts successful flew;

---

[1] narrow dell
[2] The wall of Hadrian,
   in Cumberland.
[3] lament; dirge

[4] *Ode on the Popular
   Superstitions of the
   Highlands of Scot-
   land*, 65-69 (p. 54).
[5] alas for the chief

[1] A l a r g e two-edged
   sword.
[2] tree burned in con-
   nection with the
   celebration on May-
   day
[3] A lively Scottish
   dance.

[4] The first lyre is said
   to have been made
   from a t o r t o i s e
   shell. The word is
   here used for *harp.*
[5] Icolmkill, or Iona.
[6] thicket

And still, when dewy evening fell,
The quarry[1] to their hut they drew.

In gray Glenfinlas' deepest nook
50 The solitary cabin stood,
Fast by Moneira's sullen brook,
Which murmurs through that lonely
wood.

Soft fell the night, the sky was calm,
When three successive days had flown;
55 And summer mist in dewy balm
Steep'd heathy bank and mossy stone.

The moon, half-hid in silvery flakes,
Afar her dubious radiance shed,
Quivering on Katrine's distant lakes,
60 And resting on Benledi's head.

Now in their hut, in social guise,
Their silvan fare the Chiefs enjoy;
And pleasure laughs in Ronald's eyes,
As many a pledge he quaffs to Moy.

65 "What lack we here to crown our bliss,
While thus the pulse of joy beats high?
What, but fair woman's yielding kiss,
Her panting breath and melting eye?

"To chase the deer of yonder shades,
70 This morning left their father's pile[2]
The fairest of our mountain maids,
The daughters of the proud Glengyle.

"Long have I sought sweet Mary's heart,
And dropp'd the tear, and heaved the
sigh:
75 But vain the lover's wily art,
Beneath a sister's watchful eye.

"But thou mayst teach that guardian fair,
While far with Mary I have flown,
Of other hearts to cease her care,
80 And find it hard to guard her own.

"Touch but thy harp—thou soon shalt see
The lovely Flora of Glengyle,
Unmindful of her charge and me,
Hang on thy notes 'twixt tear and smile.

85 "Or, if she choose a melting tale,
All underneath the greenwood bough,
Will good Saint Oran's rule[3] prevail,
Stern huntsman of the rigid brow?"

"Since Enrick's fight, since Morna's
death,
90 No more on me shall rapture rise,
Responsive to the panting breath,
Or yielding kiss, or melting eyes.

"E'en then, when o'er the heath of woe,
Where sunk my hopes of love and fame,
95 I bade my harp's wild wailings flow,
On me the Seer's sad spirit came.

"The last dread curse of angry heaven,
With ghastly sights and sounds of woe,
To dash each glimpse of joy, was given;
100 The gift—the future ill to know.

"The bark thou saw'st yon summer morn
So gaily part from Oban's bay,
My eye beheld her dash'd and torn,
Far on the rocky Colonsay.

105 "Thy Fergus too, thy sister's son,—
Thou saw'st with pride the gallant's
power,
As marching 'gainst the Lord of Downe
He left the skirts of huge Benmore.

"Thou only saw'st their tartans[1] wave,
110 As down Benvoirlich's side they wound,
Heard'st but the pibroch[2] answering brave
To many a target[3] clanking round.

"I heard the groans, I mark'd the tears,
I saw the wound his bosom bore,
115 When on the serried Saxon spears
He pour'd his clans's resistless roar.

"And thou who bidst me think of bliss,
And bidst my heart awake to glee,
And court like thee the wanton kiss—
120 That heart, O Ronald, bleeds for thee!

"I see the death-damps chill thy brow;
I hear thy Warning Spirit cry;
The corpse-lights dance! they're gone!
and now—
No more is given to gifted eye!"

125 "Alone enjoy thy dreary dreams,
Sad prophet of the evil hour!
Say, should we scorn joy's transient
beams,
Because tomorrow's storm may lour?

"Or false or sooth thy words of woe,
130 Clangillian's Chieftain ne'er shall fear;

---

[1] game
[2] castle
[3] That no woman
should pay her de-
votions in St. Oran's
chapel in Icolmkill,
or be buried in the
cemetery there.

[1] garments made of
checkered woolen
cloth
[2] A kind of Highland
bagpipe music, usu-
ally martial.
[3] A kind of small
shield.

His blood shall bound at rapture's glow,
Though doom'd to stain the Saxon spear.

"E'en now, to meet me in yon dell,
My Mary's buskins[1] brush the dew."
135 He spoke, nor bade the Chief farewell,
But called his dogs, and gay withdrew.

Within an hour return'd each hound;
In rush'd the rousers of the deer;
They howl'd in melancholy sound,
140 Then closely couch'd beside the Seer.

No Ronald yet—though midnight came,
And sad were Moy's prophetic dreams,
As, bending o'er the dying flame,
He fed the watch-fire's quivering gleams.

145 Sudden the hounds erect their ears,
And sudden cease their moaning howl;
Close press'd to Moy, they mark their fears
By shivering limbs and stifled growl.

Untouch'd, the harp began to ring,
150 As softly, slowly, oped the door;
And shook responsive every string,
As, light, a footstep press'd the floor.

And by the watch-fire's glimmering light,
Close by the minstrel's side was seen
155 An huntress maid in beauty bright,
All dropping wet her robes of green.

All dropping wet her garments seem;
Chill'd was her cheek, her bosom bare,
As, bending o'er the dying gleam,
160 She wrung the moisture from her hair.

With maiden blush, she softly said,
"O gentle huntsman, hast thou seen,
In deep Glenfinlas' moonlight glade,
A lovely maid in vest[2] of green:

165 "With her a Chief in Highland pride;
His shoulders bear the hunter's bow,
The mountain dirk adorns his side,
Far on the wind his tartans flow?"

"And who art thou? and who are they?"
170 All ghastly gazing, Moy replied:
"And why, beneath the moon's pale ray,
Dare ye thus roam Glenfinlas' side?"

"Where wild Loch Katrine pours her tide,
Blue, dark and deep, round many an isle,

175 Our father's towers o'erhang her side,
The castle of the bold Glengyle.

"To chase the dun Glenfinlas deer
Our woodland course this morn we bore,
And haply met, while wandering here,
180 The son of great Macgillianore.

"O, aid me, then, to seek the pair,
Whom, loitering in the woods, I lost;
Alone, I dare not venture there,
Where walks, they say, the shrieking ghost."

185 "Yes, many a shrieking ghost walks there;
Then, first, my own sad vow to keep,
Here will I pour my midnight prayer,
Which still must rise when mortals sleep."

"O, first, for pity's gentle sake,
190 Guide a lone wanderer on her way!
For I must cross the haunted brake,
And reach my father's towers ere day."

"First, three times tell each Ave-bead,[1]
And thrice a Paternoster[2] say,
195 Then kiss with me the holy rede;[3]
So shall we safely wend our way."

"O shame to knighthood, strange and foul!
Go, doff the bonnet from thy brow,
And shroud thee in the monkish cowl,
200 Which best befits thy sullen vow.

"Not so, by high Dunlathmon's fire,
Thy heart was froze to love and joy,
When gaily rung thy raptured lyre
To wanton Morna's melting eye."

205 Wild stared the minstrel's eyes of flame,
And high his sable locks arose,
And quick his color went and came,
As fear and rage alternate rose.

"And thou! when by the blazing oak
210 I lay, to her and love resign'd,
Say, rode ye on the eddying smoke.
Or sail'd ye on the midnight wind?

"Not thine a race of mortal blood,
Nor old Glengyle's pretended line;
215 Thy dame, the Lady of the Flood—
Thy sire, the Monarch of the Mine."

---

[1] coverings for the feet; half-boots   [2] dress; robe

[1] One of the beads of a rosary which are counted as the prayers to the Virgin Mary are uttered. A rosary contains 150 Ave Marias, 15 Paternosters, and 15 Gloria Patris.   [2] The Lord's Prayer.   [3] cross

He mutter'd thrice Saint Oran's rhyme,
    And thrice Saint Fillan's powerful
        prayer;
Then turn'd him to the eastern clime,
220 And sternly shook his coal-black hair.

And, bending o'er his harp, he flung
    His wildest witch-notes on the wind;
And loud and high and strange they rung,
    As many a magic change they find.

225 Tall wax'd the Spirit's altering form
    Till to the roof her stature grew;
Then, mingling with the rising storm,
    With one wild yell away she flew.

Rain beats, hail rattles, whirlwinds tear:
230 The slender hut in fragments flew;
But not a lock of Moy's loose hair
    Was waved by wind, or wet by dew.

Wild mingling with the howling gale,
    Loud bursts of ghastly laughter rise;
235 High o'er the minstrel's head they sail,
    And die amid the northern skies.

The voice of thunder shook the wood,
    As ceased the more than mortal yell;
And, spattering foul, a shower of blood
240 Upon the hissing firebrands fell.

Next dropp'd from high a mangled arm;
    The fingers strain'd at half-drawn
        blade;
And last, the life-blood streaming warm,
    Torn from the trunk, a gasping head.

245 Oft o'er that head, in battling field,
    Stream'd the proud crest of high Ben-
        more;
That arm the broad claymore could wield,
    Which dyed the Teith with Saxon gore.

Woe to Moneira's sullen rills!
250 Woe to Glenfinlas' dreary glen!
There never son of Albin's hills
    Shall draw the hunter's shaft agen!

E'en the tired pilgrim's burning feet
    At noon shall shun that sheltering den,
255 Lest, journeying in their rage, he meet
    The wayward Ladies of the Glen.

And we—behind the Chieftain's shield
    No more shall we in safety dwell;
None leads the people to the field—
260 And we the loud lament must swell.

O hone a rie'! O hone a rie'!
    The pride of Albin's line is o'er!
And fall'n Glenartney's stateliest tree;
    We ne'er shall see Lord Ronald more!

CADYOW CASTLE
1801   1803

When princely Hamilton's abode
    Ennobled Cadyow's Gothic towers,
The song went round, the goblet flow'd,
    And revel sped the laughing hours.

5 Then, thrilling to the harp's gay sound,
    So sweetly rung each vaulted wall,
And echoed light the dancer's bound,
    As mirth and music cheer'd the hall.

But Cadyow's towers, in ruins laid,
10 And vaults by ivy mantled o'er,
Thrill to the music of the shade,
    Or echo Evan's hoarser roar.

Yet still of Cadyow's faded fame
    You bid me tell a minstrel tale,
15 And tune my harp of Border frame
    On the wild banks of Evandale.

For thou, from scenes of courtly pride,
    From pleasure's lighter scenes, canst
        turn,
To draw oblivion's pall aside,
20 And mark the long-forgotten urn.

Then, noble maid![1] at thy command,
    Again the crumbled halls shall rise;
Lo! as on Evan's banks we stand,
    The past returns—the present flies.

25 Where with the rock's wood-cover'd side
    Were blended late the ruins green,
Rise turrets in fantastic pride,
    And feudal banners flaunt between.

Where the rude torrent's brawling course
30 Was shagg'd with thorn and tangling
        sloe,[2]
The ashler[3] buttress braves its force,
    And ramparts frown in 'battled row.

'Tis night: the shade of keep and spire
    Obscurely dance on Evan's stream;
35 And on the wave the warder's fire
    Is chequering the moonlight beam.

Fades slow their light—the east is gray;
    The weary warder leaves his tower;

[1] Lady Anne Hamilton, to whom the poem was addressed.   [2] blackthorn   [3] hewn stone

Steeds snort, uncoupled stag-hounds bay,
40   And merry hunters quit the bower.

The drawbridge falls—they hurry out—
   Clatters each plank and swinging chain,
As, dashing o'er, the jovial rout
   Urge the shy steed, and slack the rein.

45 First of his troop the Chief rode on;
   His shouting merry-men throng behind;
The steed of princely Hamilton
   Was fleeter than the mountain wind.

From the thick copse the roebucks bound,
50   The startled red-deer scuds the plain,
For the hoarse bugle's warrior-sound
   Has roused their mountain haunts again.

Through the huge oaks of Evandale,
   Whose limbs a thousand years have
     worn,
55 What sullen roar comes down the gale
   And drowns the hunter's pealing horn?

Mightiest of all the beasts of chase
   That roam in woody Caledon,
Crashing the forest in his race,
60   The Mountain Bull comes thundering on.

Fierce on the hunter's quiver'd band
   He rolls his eyes of swarthy glow,
Spurns with black hoof and horn the
     sand,
   And tosses high his mane of snow.

65 Aim'd well the Chieftain's lance has
     flown—
   Struggling in blood the savage lies;
His roar is sunk in hollow groan—
   Sound, merry huntsmen! sound the
     pryse.[1]

'Tis noon: against the knotted oak
70   The hunters rest the idle spear;
Curls through the trees the slender smoke,
   Where yeomen dight[2] the woodland
     cheer.

Proudly the Chieftain mark'd his clan,
   On greenwood lap all careless thrown,
75 Yet miss'd his eye the boldest man
   That bore the name of Hamilton.

"Why fills not Bothwellhaugh his place,
   Still wont our weal and woe to share?
Why comes he not our sport to grace?
80   Why shares he not our hunter's fare?"

[1] The note blown at the death of the game.
[2] prepare

Stern Claud replied with darkening face—
   Gray Paisley's haughty lord was he—
"At merry feast or buxom chase
   No more the warrior wilt thou see.

85 "Few suns have set since Woodhouselee
   Saw Bothwellhaugh's bright goblets
     foam,
When to his hearths in social glee
   The war-worn soldier turn'd him home.

"There, wan from her maternal throes,
90   His Margaret, beautiful and mild,
Sate in her bower, a pallid rose,
   And peaceful nursed her new-born
     child.

"O change accursed! past are those days;
   False Murray's ruthless spoilers came,
95 And, for the hearth's domestic blaze,
   Ascends destruction's volumed flame.

"What sheeted phantom wanders wild,
   Where mountain Eske through wood-
     land flows,
Her arms enfold a shadowy child—
100   Oh! is it she, the pallid rose?

"The wilder'd traveller sees her glide,
   And hears her feeble voice with awe;
'Revenge,' she cries, 'on Murray's pride!
   And woe for injured Bothwellhaugh!'"

105 He ceased; and cries of rage and grief
   Burst mingling from the kindred band,
And half arose the kindling Chief,
   And half unsheathed his Arran brand.

But who, o'er bush, o'er stream and rock,
110   Rides headlong, with resistless speed,
Whose bloody poniard's frantic stroke
   Drives to the leap his jaded steed;

Whose cheek is pale, whose eyeballs glare,
   As one some vision'd sight that saw,
115 Whose hands are bloody, loose his hair?—
   'Tis he! 'tis he! 'tis Bothwellhaugh.

From gory selle,[1] and reeling steed,
   Sprung the fierce horseman with a
     bound,
And, reeking from the recent deed,
120   He dash'd his carbine on the ground.

Sternly he spoke: "'Tis sweet to hear
   In good greenwood the bugle blown,
But sweeter to Revenge's ear,
   To drink a tyrant's dying groan.

[1] saddle

125 "Your slaughter'd quarry[1] proudly trode,
　　At dawning morn, o'er dale and down,
But prouder base-born Murray rode
　　Through old Linlithgow's crowded town.

"From the wild Border's humbled side,
130 　In haughty triumph marchèd he,
While Knox relax'd his bigot pride
　　And smiled the traitorous pomp to see.

"But can stern Power, with all his vaunt,
　　Or Pomp, with all her courtly glare
135 The settled heart of Vengeance daunt,
　　Or change the purpose of Despair?

"With hackbut bent,[2] my secret stand,
　　Dark as the purposed deed, I chose,
And mark'd where, mingling in his band,
140 　Troop'd Scottish pikes and English
　　　　bows.

"Dark Morton, girt with many a spear,
　　Murder's foul minion, led the van;
And clash'd their broadswords in the rear
　　The wild Macfarlanes' plaided clan.

145 "Glencairn and stout Parkhead were
　　　　nigh,
　　Obsequious at their Regent's[3] rein,
And haggard Lindesay's iron eye,
　　That saw fair Mary weep in vain.[4]

" 'Mid pennon'd spears, a steely grove,
150 　Proud Murray's plumage floated
　　　　high;
Scarce could his trampling charger move,
　　So close the minions crowded nigh.

"From the raised vizor's shade, his eye
　　Dark-rolling glanced the ranks along,
155 And his steel truncheon,[5] waved on high,
　　Seem'd marshalling the iron throng.

"But yet his sadden'd brow confess'd
　　A passing shade of doubt and awe;
Some fiend was whispering in his breast;
160 　'Beware of injured Bothwellhaugh!'

"The death-shot parts! the charger
　　　　springs,
　　Wild rises tumult's startling roar,
And Murray's plumy helmet rings—
　　Rings on the ground, to rise no more.

165 "What joy the raptured youth can feel
　　To hear her love the loved one tell!
Or he who broaches[1] on his steel
　　The wolf by whom his infant fell!

"But dearer to my injured eye
170 　To see in dust proud Murray roll;
And mine was ten times trebled joy,
　　To hear him groan his felon soul.

"My Margaret's spectre glided near,
　　With pride her bleeding victim saw,
175 And shriek'd in his death-deafen'd ear
　　'Remember injured Bothwellhaugh!'

"Then speed thee, noble Chatlerault!
　　Spread to the wind thy banner'd tree![2]
Each warrior bend his Clydesdale bow!—
180 　Murray is fall'n, and Scotland free!"

Vaults every warrior to his steed;
　　Loud bugles join their wild acclaim:
"Murray is fall'n, and Scotland freed!
　　Couch,[3] Arran! couch thy spear of
　　　　flame!"

185 But, see! the minstrel vision fails—
　　The glimmering spears are seen no more;
The shouts of war die on the gales,
　　Or sink in Evan's lonely roar.

For the loud bugle, pealing high,
190 　The blackbird whistles down the vale,
And sunk in ivied ruins lie
　　The banner'd towers of Evandale.

For chiefs, intent on bloody deed,
　　And Vengeance shouting o'er the slain,
195 Lo! high-born Beauty rules the steed,
　　Or graceful guides the silken rein.

And long may Peace and Pleasure own
　　The maids who list the minstrel's tale;
Nor e'er a ruder guest be known
200 　On the fair banks of Evandale!

From THE MINSTRELSY OF THE SCOTTISH BORDER
1802-03

KINMONT WILLIE

O have ye na heard o the fause[4] Sakelde?
O have ye na heard o the keen Lord
　　Scroop?
How they hae taen bauld[5] Kinmont Willie,
　　On Hairibee to hang him up?

---

[1] prey
[2] with gun cocked
[3] Murray's.
[4] Lord Lindsay, who was sent to extort Queen Mary's sig-

nature to the deed of resignation, was unmoved by Mary's weeping as she signed the deed.
[5] staff of authority

[1] pierces
[2] A half-sawed oak was the emblem of the Hamilton family.

[3] lower for the charge
[4] false
[5] have taken bold

5 Had Willie had but twenty men,
  But twenty men as stout as he,
Fause Sakelde had never the Kinmont
    taen,
  Wi eight score in his companie.

They band his legs beneath the steed,
10 They tied his hands behind his back;
They guarded him, fivesome[1] on each side,
  And they brought him ower the Liddel-
    rack.[2]

They led him thro the Liddel-rack,
  And also thro the Carlisle sands;
15 They brought him to Carlisle castell,
  To be at my Lord Scroope's commands.

"My hands are tied, but my tongue is free,
  And whae will dare this deed avow?
Or answer by the Border law?
20 Or answer to the bauld Buccleuch?''

"Now haud[3] thy tongue, thou rank
    reiver![4]
There's never a Scot shall set ye free;
Before ye cross my castle-yate,[5]
  I trow ye shall take farewell o me.''

25 "Fear na ye that, my lord,'' quo Willie;
  "By the faith o my bodie, Lord
    Scroop,'' he said,
"I never yet lodged in a hostelrie
  But I paid my lawing before I gaed.''[6]

Now word is gane[7] to the bauld Keeper,
30 In Branksome Ha[8] where that he lay,
That Lord Scroope has taen the Kinmont
    Willie,
  Between the hours of night and day.

He has taen[9] the table wi his hand,
  He garrd[10] the red wine spring on hie;
35 "Now Christ's curse on my head,'' he
    said,
  "But avenged of Lord Scroop I'll be!

"O is my basnet[11] a widow's curch?[12]
  Or my lance a wand of the willow-tree?
Or my arm a ladye's lilye hand?
40 That an English lord should lightly
    me.[13]

"And have they taen him Kinmont Willie,
  Against the truce of Border tide,

And forgotten that the bauld Bacleuch
  Is keeper here on the Scottish side?

45 "And have they een taen him Kinmont
    Willie,
  Withouten either dread or fear,
And forgotten that the bauld Bacleuch
  Can back a steed, or shake a spear?

"O were there war between the lands,
50 As well I wot that there is none,
I would slight[1] Carlisle castell high,
  Tho it were builded of marble-stone.

"I would set that castell in a low,[2]
  And sloken[3] it with English blood;
55 There's nevir a man in Cumberland
  Should ken where Carlisle castell stood.

"But since nae war's between the lands,
  And there is peace, and peace should be,
I'll neither harm English lad or lass,
60 And yet the Kinmont freed shall be!''

He has calld him forty marchmen bauld,
  I trow they were of his ain name,
Except Sir Gilbert Elliot, calld
  The Laird of Stobs, I mean the same.

65 He has calld him forty marchmen bauld,
  Were kinsmen to the bauld Buccleuch,
With spur on heel, and splent on spauld,[4]
  And gleuves[5] of green, and feathers
    blue.

There were five and five before them a',
70 Wi hunting-horns and bugles bright;
And five and five came wi Buccleuch,
  Like Warden's men, arrayed for fight.

And five and five like a mason-gang,
  That carried the ladders lang and hie;
75 And five and five like broken men;[6]
  And so they reached the Woodhouselee.

And as we crossed the Bateable Land,
  When to the English side we held,
The first o men that we met wi,
80 Whae sould it be but fause Sakelde!

"Where be ye gaun, ye hunters keen?''
  Quo fause Sakelde; "come tell to me!''
"We go to hunt an English stag,
  Has trespassed on the Scots countrie.''

---

[1] five together
[2] ford
[3] hold
[4] robber
[5] castle-gate
[6] reckoning before I went
[7] gone
[8] hall
[9] struck
[10] made
[11] helmet
[12] head-covering
[13] treat me with contempt

[1] demolish
[2] flame
[3] quench
[4] armor on shoulder
[5] gloves
[6] outlaws

85 "Where be ye gaun, ye marshal-men?"
 Quo false Sakelde; "come tell me true!"
"We go to catch a rank reiver,
 Has broken faith wi the bauld Buccleuch."

"Where are ye gaun, ye mason-lads,
90 Wi a' your ladders lang and hie?"
"We gang to herry a corbie's nest,[1]
 That wons[2] not far frae Woodhouse-lee."

"Where be ye gaun, ye broken men?"
 Quo false Sakelde; "come tell to me!"
95 Now Dickie of Dryhope led that band,
 And the never a word o lear[3] had he.

"Why trespass ye on the English side?
 Row-footed[4] outlaws, stand!" quo he;
The neer[5] a word had Dickie to say,
100 Sae he thrust the lance thro his fause bodie.

Then on we held for Carlisle toun,
 And at Staneshaw-bank the Eden we crossd;
The water was great, and meikle of spait,[6]
 But the nevir a horse nor man we lost.

105 And when we reachd the Stanshaw-bank,
 The wind was rising loud and hie;
And there the laird garrd leave[7] our steeds,
 For fear that they should stamp and nie.[8]

And when we left the Staneshaw-bank,
110 The wind began full loud to blaw;
But 'twas wind and weet, and fire and sleet,
 When we came beneath the castel-wa.

We crept on knees, and held our breath,
 Till we placed the ladders against the wa;
115 And sae ready was Buccleuch himsell
 To mount the first before us a'.

He has taen the watchman by the throat,
 He flung him down upon the lead:[9]
"Had there not been peace between our lands,
120 Upon the other side thou hadst gaed."

"Now sound out, trumpets!" quo Buccleuch;
 "Let's waken Lord Scroope right merrilie!"
Then loud the Warden's trumpets blew
 "O whae dare meddle wi me?"[1]

125 Then speedilie to wark we gaed,
 And raised the slogan ane and a',
And cut a hole thro a sheet of lead,
 And so we wan[2] to the castel-ha.

They thought King James and a' his men
130 Had won the house wi bow and speir:
It was but twenty Scots and ten
 That put a thousand in sic a stear![3]

Wi coulters[4] and wi forehammers,[5]
 We garrd the bars bang merrilie,
135 Untill we came to the inner prison,
 Where Willie o Kinmont he did lie.

And when we came to the lower prison,
 Where Willie o Kinmont he did lie,
"O sleep ye, wake ye, Kinmont Willie,
140 Upon the morn that thou's to die?"

"O I sleep saft, and I wake aft,[6]
 It's lang since sleeping was fleyd[7] frae me;
Gie my service back to my wyfe and bairns,
 And a' gude fellows that speer[8] for me."

145 Then Red Rowan has hente[9] him up,
 The starkest men in Teviotdale:
"Abide, abide now, Red Rowan,
 Till of my Lord Scroope I take farewell.

"Farewell, farewell, my gude Lord Scroope!
150 My gude Lord Scroope, farewell!" he cried;
"I'll pay you for my lodging-maill[10]
 When first we meet on the border-side."

Then shoulder high, with shout and cry,
 We bore him down the ladder lang;
155 At every stride Red Rowan made,
 I wot the Kinmont's airns playd clang.[11]

---

[1] A famous Liddesdale song.
[2] came
[3] such a fright
[4] The coulter is an iron blade attached to the front of a plow to cut the sod, etc.
[5] sledge hammers
[6] often
[7] frightened
[8] ask
[9] seized
[10] rent for lodging
[11] irons rattled

[1] plunder a crow's nest
[2] dwells
[3] word of learning
[4] rough-footed
[5] never
[6] great of flood; overflooded
[7] made us leave
[8] neigh
[9] leaden roof

"O mony a time," quo Kinmont Willie,
"I have ridden horse baith wild and
    wood;[1]
But a rougher beast than Red Rowan
160 I ween my legs have neer bestrode.

"And mony a time," quo Kinmont
    Willie,
"I've pricked a horse out oure the
    furs;[2]
But since the day I backed a steed
I nevir wore sic cumbrous spurs."

165 We scarce had won the Staneshaw-bank,
When a' the Carlisle bells were rung,
And a thousand men, in horse and foot,
Cam wi the keen Lord Scroope along.

Buccleuch has turned to Eden Water,
170 Even where it flowd frae bank to brim,
And he has plunged in wi a' his band,
And safely swam them thro the stream.

He turned him on the other side,
And at Lord Scroope his glove flung
    he:[3]
175 "If ye like na my visit in merry England,
In fair Scotland come visit me!"

All sore astonished stood Lord Scroope,
He stood as still as rock of stane;
He scarcely dared to trew[4] his eyes
180 When thro the water they had gane.

"He is either himsell a devil frae hell,
Or else his mother a witch maun be;[5]
I wad na have ridden that wan water
For a' the gowd in Christentie."[6]

LORD RANDAL

"O where hae ye been, Lord Randal, my
    son?
O where hae ye been, my handsome young
    man?"
"I hae been to the wild wood; mother,
    make my bed soon,
For I'm weary wi hunting, and fain wald
    lie down."

5 "Where gat ye your dinner, Lord Randal,
    my son?
Where gat ye your dinner, my handsome
    young man?"

"I din'd wi my true-love; mother, make
    my bed soon,
For I'm weary wi hunting, and fain wald
    lie down."

"What gat ye to your dinner, Lord Ran-
    dal, my son?
What gat ye to your dinner, my handsome
    young man?"
10 "I gat eels boiled in broo;[1] mother, make
    my bed soon,
For I'm weary wi hunting, and fain wald
    lie down."

"What became of your bloodhounds, Lord
    Randal, my son?
What became of your bloodhounds, my
    handsome young man?"
"O they swelld and they died; mother,
    make my bed soon,
15 For I'm weary wi hunting, and fain wald
    lie down."

"O I fear ye are poisond, Lord Randal,
    my son!
O I fear ye are poisond, my handsome
    young man!"
"O yes! I am poisond; mother, make my
    bed soon,
For I'm sick at the heart and I fain wald
    lie down."

THE LAY OF THE LAST MINSTREL
1802-04   1805
From CANTO VI

Breathes there the man, with soul so dead,
Who never to himself hath said,
  This is my own, my native land!
Whose heart hath ne'er within him burn'd,
5 As home his footsteps he hath turn'd,
  From wandering on a foreign strand!
If such there breathe, go, mark him well;
For him no minstrel raptures swell;
High though his titles, proud his name,
10 Boundless his wealth as wish can claim,—
Despite those titles, power, and pelf,
The wretch, concentred all in self,
Living, shall forfeit fair renown,
And, doubly dying, shall go down
15 To the vile dust, from whence he sprung.
Unwept, unhonor'd, and unsung.

O Caledonia! stern and wild,
Meet nurse for a poetic child!
Land of brown heath and shaggy wood,
20 Land of the mountain and the flood,

---

[1] both wild and mad
[2] over the furrows, or ground
[3] As the sign of a challenge.
[4] trust
[5] must be
[6] gold in Christendom

[1] broth

Land of my sires! what mortal hand
Can e'er untie the filial band,
That knits me to thy rugged strand!
Still as I view each well-known scene,
25 Think what is now, and what hath been,
Seems as to me, of all bereft,
Sole friends thy woods and streams were
        left;
And thus I love them better still,
Even in extremity of ill.
30 By Yarrow's stream still let me stray,
Though none should guide my feeble way;
Still feel the breeze down Ettrick break,
Although it chill my wither'd cheek;
Still lay my head by Teviot Stone,
35 Though there, forgotten and alone,
The bard may draw his parting groan.

Not scorn'd like me, to Branksome Hall
The minstrels came at festive call;
Trooping they came, from near and far,
40 The jovial priests of mirth and war;
Alike for feast and fight prepar'd,
Battle and banquet both they shar'd.
Of late, before each martial clan,
They blew their death-note in the van,
45 But now, for every merry mate,
Rose the portcullis' iron grate;
They sound the pipe, they strike the string,
They dance, they revel, and they sing,
Till the rude turrets shake and ring.

. . . .

And much of wild and wonderful
In these rude isles might fancy cull;
For thither came, in times afar,
325 Stern Lochlin's sons of roving war,
The Norsemen, train'd to spoil and blood,
Skill'd to prepare the raven's food;
Kings of the main their leaders brave,
Their barks the dragons of the wave.
330 And there, in many a stormy vale,
The Scald[1] had told his wondrous tale;
And many a runic[2] column high
Had witness'd grim idolatry.
And thus had Harold in his youth
335 Learn'd many a Saga's rhyme uncouth—
Of that Sea-Snake,[3] tremendous curl'd,
Whose monstrous circle girds the world;
Of those dread Maids,[4] whose hideous yell
Maddens the battle's bloody swell;
340 Of Chiefs, who, guided through the gloom
By the pale death-lights of the tomb,

Ransack'd the graves of warriors old,[1]
Their falchions wrench'd from corpses'
        hold,
Wak'd the deaf tomb with war's alarms,
345 And bade the dead arise to arms!
With war and wonder all on flame,
To Roslin's bowers young Harold came,
Where, by sweet glen and greenwood tree,
He learn'd a milder minstrelsy;
350 Yet something of the Northern spell
Mix'd with the softer numbers well.

HAROLD

O listen, listen, ladies gay!
    No haughty feat of arms I tell;
Soft is the note, and sad the lay,
355   That mourns the lovely Rosabelle.

—"Moor, moor the barge, ye gallant crew!
    And, gentle ladye, deign to stay!
Rest thee in Castle Ravensheuch,
    Nor tempt the stormy firth today.

360 "The blackening wave is edg'd with white:
    To inch[2] and rock the sea-mews fly;
The fishers have heard the water-sprite,
    Whose screams forebode that wreck is nigh.

"Last night the gifted seer did view
365   A wet shroud swathed round ladye gay;
Then stay thee, fair, in Ravensheuch:
    Why cross the gloomy firth today?"

" 'Tis not because Lord Lindesay's heir
    Tonight at Roslin leads the ball,
370 But that my ladye-mother there
    Sits lonely in her castle-hall.

" 'Tis not because the ring they ride,[3]
    And Lindesay at the ring rides well,
But that my sire the wine will chide,
375   If 'tis not fill'd by Rosabelle."

O'er Roslin all that dreary night
    A wondrous blaze was seen to gleam;
'Twas broader than the watch-fire's light,
    And redder than the bright moonbeam.

380 It glar'd on Roslin's castled rock,
    It ruddied all the copse-wood glen;
'Twas seen from Dryden's groves of oak,
    And seen from cavern'd Hawthornden.

Seem'd all on fire that chapel proud,
385   Where Roslin's chiefs uncoffin'd lie,
Each Baron, for a sable shroud,
    Sheath'd in his iron panoply.

---

[1] Norse singer of heroic poems.
[2] carved with runes (characters used in writing
    by the early Germanic peoples)
[3] The *jormungandr*, or Snake of the Ocean, which
    in Norse mythology encircles the earth.
[4] The *Valkyriur*, or Choosers of the Slain, who
    directed the course of battle. See Gray's *The
    Fatal Sisters* (p. 66).

[1] Northern warriors were buried with their
    weapons and treasures. These were said to be
    guarded by the spirits of the dead warriors.
[2] island
[3] A favorite sport in which a horseman rides past
    a suspended ring and tries to carry it off on
    the point of a lance.

Seem'd all on fire within, around,
Deep sacristy and altar's pale;[1]
390 Shone every pillar foliage-bound,
And glimmer'd all the dead men's mail.

Blaz'd battlement and pinnet[2] high,
Blaz'd every rose-carved buttress fair—
So still they blaze when fate is nigh
395 The lordly line of high St. Clair.

There are twenty of Roslin's barons bold
Lie buried within that proud chapelle;
Each one the holy vault doth hold—
But the sea holds lovely Rosabelle!

400 And each St. Clair was buried there,
With candle, with book, and with knell;
But the sea-caves rung, and the wild winds
sung,
The dirge of lovely Rosabelle.

. . . .

THE MAID OF NEIDPATH
1806

O, lovers' eyes are sharp to see,
And lovers' ears in hearing;
And love, in life's extremity,
Can lend an hour of cheering.
5 Disease had been in Mary's bower,
And slow decay from mourning,
Though now she sits on Neidpath's tower,
To watch her love's returning.

All sunk and dim her eyes so bright,
10 Her form decay'd by pining,
Till through her wasted hand, at night,
You saw the taper shining;
By fits, a sultry hectic hue
Across her cheek was flying;
15 By fits, so ashy pale she grew,
Her maidens thought her dying.

Yet keenest powers to see and hear
Seem'd in her frame residing;
Before the watch-dog prick'd his ear
20 She heard her lover's riding;
Ere scarce a distant form was ken'd,[3]
She knew, and waved to greet him;
And o'er the battlement did bend,
As on the wing to meet him.

25 He came—he pass'd—an heedless gaze,
As o'er some stranger glancing;
Her welcome, spoke in faltering phrase,
Lost in the courser's prancing.
The castle arch, whose hollow tone
30 Returns each whisper spoken,
Could scarcely catch the feeble moan
Which told her heart was broken.

HUNTING SONG
1808

Waken, lords and ladies gay,
On the mountain dawns the day,
All the jolly chase is here,
With hawk, and horse, and hunting-spear!
5 Hounds are in their couples[1] yelling,
Hawks are whistling, horns are knelling,
Merrily, merrily, mingle they,
"Waken, lords and ladies gay."

Waken, lords and ladies gay,
10 The mist has left the mountain gray,
Springlets in the dawn are steaming,
Diamonds on the brake[2] are gleaming:
And foresters have busy been,
To track the buck in thicket green;
15 Now we come to chant our lay,
"Waken, lords and ladies gay."

Waken, lords and ladies gay,
To the greenwood haste away;
We can show you where he lies,
20 Fleet of foot, and tall of size;
We can show the marks he made,
When 'gainst the oak his antlers fray'd;
You shall see him brought to bay,
"Waken, lords and ladies gay."

25 Louder, louder chant the lay,
Waken, lords and ladies gay!
Tell them youth, and mirth, and glee,
Run a course as well as we;
Time, stern huntsman! who can baulk,
30 Stanch as hound, and fleet as hawk:
Think of this, and rise with day,
Gentle lords and ladies gay.

From MARMION
1806   1808
WHERE SHALL THE LOVER REST

Where shall the lover rest,
Whom the fates sever
From his true maiden's breast,
Parted forever?
5 Where, through groves deep and high,
Sounds the far billow,
Where early violets die,
Under the willow.

Chorus

Eleu loro, etc.   Soft shall be his pillow.

10 There, through the summer day,
Cool streams are laving;
There, while the tempests sway,
Scarce are boughs waving;

---

[1] inclosure
[2] pinnacle
[3] recognized

[1] leashes
[2] brushwood; thicket

There thy rest shalt thou take,
15 Parted forever,
Never again to wake,
Never, O never!

Chorus

Eleu loro, etc. Never, O never!

Where shall the traitor rest,
20   He the deceiver,
Who could win maiden's breast,
Ruin and leave her?
In the lost battle,
Borne down by the flying,
25 Where mingles war's rattle
With groans of the dying.

Chorus

Eleu loro, etc. There shall he be lying.

Her wing shall the eagle flap
O'er the false-hearted:
30 His warm blood the wolf shall lap,
Ere life be parted.
Shame and dishonor sit
By his grave ever;
Blessing shall hallow it,—
35   Never, O never!

Chorus

Eleu loro, etc. Never, O never!

LOCHINVAR

O, young Lochinvar is come out of the
    west!
Through all the wide Border his steed was
    the best;
And save his good broadsword he weapons
    had none;
He rode all unarmed, and he rode all
    alone.
5 So faithful in love, and so dauntless in
    war,
There never was knight like the young
    Lochinvar.

He stayed not for brake,[1] and he stopped
    not for stone;
He swam the Eske river where ford there
    was none;
But ere he alighted at Netherby gate,
10 The bride had consented, the gallant came
    late:
For a laggard in love, and a dastard in
    war,
Was to wed the fair Ellen of brave Loch-
    invar.

[1] brushwood; thicket

So boldly he entered the Netherby Hall,
Among bride'smen, and kinsmen, and
    brothers, and all.
15 Then spoke the bride's father, his hand
    on his sword,
(For the poor craven bridegroom said
    never a word):
"O come ye in peace here, or come ye in
    war,
Or to dance at our bridal, young Lord
    Lochinvar?"

"I long wooed your daughter; my suit
    you denied;
20 Love swells like the Solway, but ebbs like
    its tide;
And now am I come, with this lost love of
    mine
To lead but one measure, drink one cup
    of wine.
There are maidens in Scotland more lovely
    by far,
That would gladly be bride to the young
    Lochinvar."

25 The bride kissed the goblet; the knight
    took it up,
He quaffed off the wine, and he threw
    down the cup.
She looked down to blush, and she looked
    up to sigh,
With a smile on her lips, and a tear in
    her eye.
He took her soft hand, ere her mother
    could bar,—
30 "Now tread we a measure!" said young
    Lochinvar.

So stately his form, and so lovely her face,
That never a hall such a galliard[1] did
    grace;
While her mother did fret, and her
    father did fume,
And the bridegroom stood dangling his
    bonnet and plume;
35 And the bride-maidens whispered,
    " 'Twere better by far
To have matched our fair cousin with
    young Lochinvar."

One touch to her hand, and one word in
    her ear,
When they reached the hall-door, and the
    charger stood near;
So light to the croupe[2] the fair lady he
    swung,
40 So light to the saddle before her he
    sprung!

[1] A spirited dance. [2] place behind the saddle

"She is won! we are gone, over bank,
    bush, and scaur!"[1]
They'll have fleet steeds that follow!" 20
    quoth young Lochinvar.

There was mounting 'mong Graemes of
    the Netherby clan;
Forsters, Fenwicks, and Musgraves, they
    rode and they ran;
45 There was racing and chasing, on Can-
    nobie Lee,
But the lost bride of Netherby ne'er did
    they see.
So daring in love and so dauntless in war,
Have ye e'er heard of gallant like young
    Lochinvar?

From THE LADY OF THE LAKE
1809-10   1810

Canto I. The Chase

Harp of the North![2] that mouldering long
    hast hung
On the witch-elm[3] that shades Saint
    Fillan's spring,
And down the fitful breeze thy numbers[4]
    flung,
    Till envious ivy did around thee cling,
5 Muffling with verdant ringlet every
    string,—
    O minstrel Harp, still must thine ac-
    cents sleep?
'Mid rustling leaves and fountains mur-
    muring,
    Still must thy sweeter sounds their
    silence keep,
Nor bid a warrior smile, nor teach a maid
    to weep?

10 Not thus, in ancient days of Caledon,
    Was thy voice mute amid the festal
    crowd,
When lay of hopeless love, or glory
    won,
    Aroused the fearful, or subdued the
    proud.
At each according pause was heard aloud
15 Thine ardent symphony sublime and
    high!
Fair dames and crested chiefs attention
    bow'd;
    For still the burden of thy minstrelsy
Was Knighthood's dauntless deed, and
    Beauty's matchless eye.

O wake once more! how rude soe'er the
    hand
    That ventures o'er thy magic maze to
    stray;
O wake once more! though scarce my skill
    command
Some feeble echoing of thine earlier lay:
Though harsh and faint, and soon to die
    away,
    And all unworthy of thy nobler strain,
25 Yet if one heart throb higher at its sway,
    The wizard note has not been touch'd
    in vain.
Then silent be no more! Enchantress,
    wake again!

The stag at eve had drunk his fill,
Where danced the moon on Monan's rill,
30 And deep his midnight lair had made
In lone Glenartney's hazel shade;
But, when the sun his beacon red
Had kindled on Benvoirlich's head,
The deep-mouth'd bloodhound's heavy bay
35 Resounded up the rocky way,
And faint, from farther distance borne,
Were heard the clanging hoof and horn.

As chief, who hears his warder call,
"To arms! the foemen storm the wall,"
40 The antler'd monarch of the waste
Sprung from his heathery couch in haste,
But, ere his fleet career he took,
The dew-drops from his flanks he shook;
Like crested leader proud and high,
45 Toss'd his beam'd frontlet to the sky;
A moment gazed adown the dale,
A moment snuff'd the tainted gale,
A moment listen'd to the cry,
That thicken'd as the chase drew nigh;
50 Then, as the headmost foes appear'd,
With one brave bound the copse he clear'd,
And, stretching forward free and far,
Sought the wild heaths of Uam-Var.

Yell'd on the view the opening pack;
55 Rock, glen, and cavern, paid them back;
To many a mingled sound at once
The awaken'd mountain gave response.
A hundred dogs bay'd deep and strong,
Clatter'd a hundred steeds along,
60 Their peal the merry horns rung out,
A hundred voices join'd the shout;
With hark and whoop and wild halloo,
No rest Benvoirlich's echoes knew.
Far from the tumult fled the roe,
65 Close in her covert cower'd the doe;
The falcon, from her cairn[1] on high,

---

[1] rock
[2] An invocation to an-
cient Scottish min-
strelsy. The harp
was the national
musical instrument.
[3] The broad-leafed elm.
[4] verses

[1] crag; peak (literally, a heap of stones)

Cast on the rout a wondering eye,
Till far beyond her piercing ken
The hurricane had swept the glen.
70 Faint and more faint, its failing din
Return'd from cavern, cliff, and linn,[1]
And silence settled, wide and still,
On the lone wood and mighty hill.

Less loud the sounds of silvan war
75 Disturb'd the heights of Uam-Var,
And roused the cavern, where, 'tis told,
A giant made his den of old;
For ere that steep ascent was won,
High in his pathway hung the sun,
80 And many a gallant, stay'd perforce,
Was fain to breathe his faltering horse,
And of the trackers of the deer,
Scarce half the lessening pack was near;
So shrewdly[2] on the mountain side
85 Had the bold burst their mettle tried.

The noble stag was pausing now
Upon the mountain's southern brow,
Where broad extended, far beneath,
The varied realms of fair Menteith.
90 With anxious eye he wander'd o'er
Mountain and meadow, moss and moor,
And ponder'd refuge from his toil
By far Lochard or Aberfoyle.
But nearer was the copsewood gray,
95 That waved and wept on Loch-Achray,
And mingled with the pine-trees blue
On the bold cliffs of Benvenue.
Fresh vigor with the hope return'd,
With flying foot the heath he spurn'd,
100 Held westward with unwearied race,
And left behind the panting chase.

'Twere long to tell what steeds gave o'er,
As swept the hunt through Cambusmore:
What reins were tighten'd in despair;
105 When rose Benledi's ridge in air;
Who flagg'd upon Bochastle's heath,
Who shunn'd to stem the flooded Teith,—
For twice that day, from shore to shore,
The gallant stag swam stoutly o'er.
110 Few were the stragglers, following far,
That reach'd the lake of Vennachar;
And when the Brigg of Turk was won,
The headmost horseman rode alone.

Alone, but with unbated zeal,
115 That horseman plied the scourge and steel;
For jaded now, and spent with toil,
Emboss'd with foam, and dark with soil,
While every gasp with sobs he drew,
The laboring stag strain'd full in view.

120 Two dogs of black Saint Hubert's breed,[1]
Unmatch'd for courage, breath, and speed,
Fast on his flying traces came,
And all but won that desperate game;
For, scarce a spear's length from his haunch,
125 Vindictive toil'd the bloodhounds stanch;
Nor nearer might the dogs attain,
Nor farther might the quarry[2] strain.
Thus up the margin of the lake,
Between the precipice and brake,[3]
130 O'er stock and rock their race they take.

The hunter mark'd that mountain high,
The lone lake's western boundary,
And deem'd the stag must turn to bay,
Where that huge rampart barr'd the way;
135 Already glorying in the prize,
Measured his antlers with his eyes;
For the death-wound and death-halloo,
Muster'd his breath, his whinyard[4] drew;—
But thundering as he came prepared,
140 With ready arm and weapon bared,
The wily quarry shunn'd the shock,
And turn'd him from the opposing rock;
Then, dashing down a darksome glen,
Soon lost to hound and hunter's ken,
145 In the deep Trosachs' wildest nook
His solitary refuge took.
There, while close couch'd, the thicket shed
Cold dews and wild-flowers on his head,
He heard the baffled dogs in vain
150 Rave through the hollow pass amain,
Chiding the rocks that yell'd again.

Close on the hounds the hunter came,
To cheer them on the vanish'd game;
But, stumbling in the rugged dell,
155 The gallant horse exhausted fell.
The impatient rider strove in vain
To rouse him with the spur and rein,
For the good steed, his labors o'er,
Stretch'd his stiff limbs, to rise no more;
160 Then, touch'd with pity and remorse,
He sorrow'd o'er the expiring horse:
"I little thought, when first thy rein
I slack'd upon the banks of Seine,
That Highland eagle e'er should feed
165 On thy fleet limbs, my matchless steed!
Woe worth[5] the chase, woe worth the day,
That costs thy life, my gallant gray!"

Then through the dell his horn resounds,
From vain pursuit to call the hounds.
170 Back limp'd, with slow and crippled pace,

<hr/>

¹ steep ravine   ² keenly; severely

¹ Black hounds. Hu-
bert was the patron
saint of hunting.
² prey
³ brushwood; thicket
⁴ A kind of short
sword.
⁵ woe be to

The sulky leaders of the chase;
Close to their master's side they press'd,
With drooping tail and humbled crest;
But still the dingle's[1] hollow throat
175 Prolong'd the swelling bugle-note.
The owlets started from their dream,
The eagles answer'd with their scream,
Round and around the sounds were cast,
Till echo seem'd an answering blast;
180 And on the hunter hied his way,
To join some comrades of the day;
Yet often paused, so strange the road,
So wondrous were the scenes it show'd.

The western waves of ebbing day
185 Roll'd o'er the glen their level way;
Each purple peak, each flinty spire,
Was bathed in floods of living fire.
But not a setting beam could glow
Within the dark ravines below,
190 Where twined the path in shadow hid,
Round many a rocky pyramid,
Shooting abruptly from the dell
Its thunder-splinter'd pinnacle;
Round many an insulated mass,
195 The native bulwarks of the pass,
Huge as the tower which builders vain
Presumptuous piled on Shinar's plain.[2]
The rocky summits, split and rent,
Form'd turret, dome, or battlement,
200 Or seem'd fantastically set
With cupola or minaret,[3]
Wild crests as pagod[4] ever deck'd,
Or mosque of Eastern architect.
Nor were these earth-born castles bare,
205 Nor lack'd they many a banner fair;
For, from their shiver'd brows display'd,
Far o'er the unfathomable glade,
All twinkling with the dewdrop sheen,
The brier-rose fell in streamers green,
210 And creeping shrubs, of thousand dyes,
Waved in the west-wind's summer sighs.

Boon[5] nature scatter'd, free and wild,
Each plant or flower, the mountain's child.
Here eglantine embalm'd the air,
215 Hawthorn and hazel mingled there;
The primrose pale, and violet flower,
Found in each cliff a narrow bower;
Fox-glove and night-shade, side by side,
Emblems of punishment and pride,
220 Group'd their dark hues with every stain
The weather-beaten crags retain.
With boughs that quaked at every breath,

Gray birch and aspen wept beneath;
Aloft, the ash and warrior oak
225 Cast anchor in the rifted rock;
And, higher yet, the pine-tree hung
His shatter'd trunk, and frequent flung,
Where seem'd the cliffs to meet on high,
His boughs athwart the narrow'd sky.
230 Highest of all, where white peaks glanced,
Where glist'ning streamers[1] waved and
     danced,
The wanderer's eye could barely view
The summer heaven's delicious blue;
So wondrous wild, the whole might seem
235 The scenery of a fairy dream.

Onward, amid the copse 'gan peep
A narrow inlet, still and deep,
Affording scarce such breadth of brim
As served the wild duck's brood to swim.
240 Lost for a space, through thickets veer-
     ing,
But broader when again appearing,
Tall rocks and tufted knolls their face
Could on the dark-blue mirror trace;
And farther as the hunter stray'd,
245 Still broader sweep its channels made.
The shaggy mounds no longer stood,
Emerging from entangled wood,
But, wave-encircled, seem'd to float,
Like castle girdled with its moat;
250 Yet broader floods extending still
Divide them from their parent hill,
Till each, retiring, claims to be
An islet in an inland sea.

And now, to issue from the glen,
255 No pathway meets the wanderer's ken.
Unless he climb, with footing nice,
A far projecting precipice.
The broom's[2] tough roots his ladder made,
The hazel saplings lent their aid;
260 And thus an airy point he won,
Where, gleaming with the setting sun,
One burnish'd sheet of living gold,
Loch Katrine lay beneath him roll'd;
In all her length far winding lay,
265 With promontory, creek, and bay,
And islands that, empurpled bright,
Floated amid the livelier light,
And mountains, that like giants stand,
To sentinel enchanted land.
270 High on the south, huge Benvenue
Down to the lake in masses threw
Crags, knolls, and mountains, confusedly
     hurl'd,
The fragments of an earlier world;
A wildering forest feather'd o'er

---

[1] narrow dell's
[2] See *Genesis*, 11:1-9.
[3] lofty tower of a temple, surrounded by one or more projecting balconies
[4] pagoda, a towerlike structure with several stories; usually a temple
[5] bountiful

[1] Of ivy or other vines.
[2] A kind of shrub.

275 His ruin'd sides and summit hoar,
While on the north, through middle air,
Ben-an heaved high his forehead bare.

From the steep promontory gazed
The stranger, raptured and amazed.
280 And, "What a scene were here," he cried,
"For princely pomp, or churchman's
pride!
On this bold brow, a lordly tower;
In that soft vale, a lady's bower;
On yonder meadow, far away,
285 The turrets of a cloister gray;
How blithely might the bugle-horn
Chide, on the lake, the lingering morn!
How sweet, at eve, the lover's lute
Chime, when the groves were still and
mute!
290 And, when the midnight moon should lave
Her forehead in the silver wave,
How solemn on the ear would come
The holy matins'[1] distant hum,
While the deep peal's commanding tone
295 Should wake, in yonder islet lone,
A sainted hermit from his cell,
To drop a bead with every knell—
And bugle, lute, and bell, and all,
Should each bewilder'd stranger call
300 To friendly feast, and lighted hall.

"Blithe were it then to wander here!
But now,—beshrew yon nimble deer,—
Like that same hermit's, thin and spare,
The copse must give my evening fare;
305 Some mossy bank my couch must be,
Some rustling oak my canopy.
Yet pass we that; the war and chase
Give little choice of resting-place;—
A summer night, in greenwood spent,
310 Were but tomorrow's merriment:
But hosts may in these wilds abound,
Such as are better miss'd than found;
To meet with Highland plunderers here
Were worse than loss of steed or deer.-
315 I am alone;—my bugle-strain
May call some straggler of the train;
Or, fall the worst that may betide,
Ere now this falchion[2] has been tried."

But scarce again his horn he wound,
320 When lo! forth starting at the sound,
From underneath an aged oak,
That slanted from the islet rock,
A damsel guider of its way,
A little skiff shot to the bay,
325 That round the promontory steep

Led its deep line in graceful sweep,
Eddying, in almost viewless wave,
The weeping willow-twig to lave,
And kiss, with whispering sound and slow,
330 The beach of pebbles bright as snow.
The boat had touch'd this silver strand,
Just as the hunter left his stand,
And stood conceal'd amid the brake,
To view this Lady of the Lake.
335 The maiden paused, as if again
She thought to catch the distant strain.
With head up-raised, and look intent,
And eye and ear attentive bent,
And locks flung back, and lips apart,
340 Like monument of Grecian art,
In listening mood, she seem'd to stand,
The guardian Naiad of the strand.

And ne'er did Grecian chisel trace
A Nymph, a Naiad, or a Grace
345 Of finer form, or lovelier face!
What though the sun, with ardent frown,
Had slightly tinged her cheek with brown;
The sportive toil, which, short and light,
Had dyed her glowing hue so bright,
350 Served too in hastier swell to show
Short glimpses of a breast of snow:
What though no rule of courtly grace
To measured mood had train'd her pace;
A foot more light, a step more true,
355 Ne'er from the heath-flower dash'd the
dew;
E'en the slight harebell raised its head,
Elastic from her airy tread:
What though upon her speech there hung
The accents of the mountain tongue;
360 Those silver sounds, so soft, so dear,
The listener held his breath to hear!

A chieftain's daughter seemed the maid;
Her satin snood,[1] her silken plaid,
Her golden brooch, such birth betray'd.
365 And seldom was a snood amid
Such wild luxuriant ringlets hid,
Whose glossy black to shame might bring
The plumage of the raven's wing;
And seldom o'er a breast so fair,
370 Mantled a plaid with modest care,
And never brooch the folds combin'd
Above a heart more true and kind.
Her kindness and her worth to spy,
You need but gaze on Ellen's eye;
375 Not Katrine, in her mirror blue,
Gives back the shaggy banks more true,
Than every free-born glance confess'd
The guileless movements of her breast;
Whether joy danced in her dark eye,

---

[1] A prayer service for the morning, properly said at midnight, but sometimes at daybreak. [2] sword

[1] band worn around the hair

380 Or woe or pity claim'd a sigh,
Or filial love was glowing there,
Or meek devotion pour'd a prayer,
Or tale of injury call'd forth
The indignant spirit of the North.
385 One only passion unreveal'd,
With maiden pride the maid conceal'd,
Yet not less purely felt the flame;—
O need I tell that passion's name?

Impatient of the silent horn,
390 Now on the gale her voice was borne:—
"Father!" she cried; the rocks around
Loved to prolong the gentle sound.
Awhile she paused, no answer came;
"Malcolm, was thine the blast?" the name
395 Less resolutely utter'd fell;
The echoes could not catch the swell.
"A stranger I," the huntsman said,
Advancing from the hazel shade.
The maid, alarm'd, with hasty oar,

400 Push'd her light shallop[1] from the shore,
And when a space was gain'd between,
Closer she drew her bosom's screen;
(So forth the startled swan would swing,
So turn to prune his ruffled wing.)
405 Then safe, though flutter'd and amazed,
She paused, and on the stranger gazed.
Not his the form, nor his the eye,
That youthful maidens wont to fly.

On his bold visage middle age
410 Had slightly press'd its signet sage,
Yet had not quench'd the open truth
And fiery vehemence of youth;
Forward and frolic glee was there,
The will to do, the soul to dare,
415 The sparkling glance, soon blown to fire,
Of hasty love, or headlong ire.
His limbs were cast in manly mould,
For hardy sports or contest bold;
And though in peaceful garb array'd,
420 And weaponless, except his blade,
His stately mien as well implied
A high-born heart, a martial pride,
As if a baron's crest he wore,
And sheathed in armor trode the shore.
425 Slighting the petty need he show'd,
He told of his benighted road;
His ready speech flow'd fair and free,
In phrase of gentlest courtesy;
Yet seem'd that tone, and gesture bland,
430 Less used to sue than to command.

Awhile the maid the stranger eyed,
And, reassured, at length replied,
That Highland halls were open still

[1] A kind of small open boat.

To wilder'd wanderers of the hill.
435 "Nor think you unexpected come
To yon lone isle, our desert home;
Before the heath had lost the dew,
This morn, a couch was pull'd for you;
On yonder mountain's purple head
440 Have ptarmigan[1] and heath-cock[1] bled,
And our broad nets have swept the mere,[2]
To furnish forth your evening cheer."
"Now, by the rood,[3] my lovely maid,
Your courtesy has err'd," he said;
445 "No right have I to claim, misplaced,
The welcome of expected guest.
A wanderer, here by fortune tost,
My way, my friends, my courser lost,
I ne'er before, believe me, fair,
450 Have ever drawn your mountain air,
Till on this lake's romantic strand
I found a fay in fairy land!"

"I well believe," the maid replied,
As her light skiff approach'd the side,
455 "I well believe that ne'er before
Your foot has trod Loch Katrine's shore;
But yet, as far as yesternight,
Old Allan-Bane foretold your plight,—
A gray-hair'd sire, whose eye intent
460 Was on the vision'd future bent.
He saw your steed, a dappled gray,
Lie dead beneath the birchen way;
Painted exact your form and mien,
Your hunting suit of Lincoln green,
465 That tassell'd horn so gaily gilt,
That falchion's crooked blade and hilt,
That cap with heron plumage trim,
And yon two hounds so dark and grim.
He bade that all should ready be
470 To grace a guest of fair degree;[4]
But light I held his prophecy,
And deem'd it was my father's horn
Whose echoes o'er the lake were borne."

The stranger smiled: "Since to your home
475 A destined errant-knight I come,
Announced by prophet sooth and old,
Doom'd, doubtless, for achievement bold,
I'll lightly front each high emprise
For one kind glance of those bright eyes.
480 Permit me, first, the task to guide
Your fairy frigate o'er the tide."
The maid, with smile suppress'd and sly,
The toil unwonted saw him try;
For seldom sure, if e'er before,
485 His noble hand had grasp'd an oar:
Yet with main strength his strokes he drew
And o'er the lake the shallop flew;
With heads erect, and whimpering cry,

[1] A kind of grouse.
[2] lake
[3] by the cross
[4] high rank

The hounds behind their passage ply.
490 Nor frequent does the bright oar break
The dark'ning mirror of the lake,
Until the rocky isle they reach,
And moor their shallop on the beach.

The stranger view'd the shore around;
495 'Twas all so close with copseweed bound,
Nor track nor pathway might declare
That human foot frequented there,
Until the mountain-maiden show'd
A clambering unsuspected road,
500 That winded through the tangled screen
And open'd on a narrow green,
Where weeping birch and willow round
With their long fibres swept the ground.
Here, for retreat in dangerous hour,
505 Some chief had framed a rustic bower.

It was a lodge of ample size,
But strange of structure and device;
Of such materials, as around
The workman's hand had readiest found;
510 Lopp'd off their boughs, their hoar trunks
bared,
And by the hatchet rudely squared.
To give the walls their destined height
The sturdy oak and ash unite;
While moss and clay and leaves combin'd
515 To fence each crevice from the wind.
The lighter pine-trees, over-head,
Their slender length for rafters spread,
And wither'd heath and rushes dry
Supplied a russet canopy.
520 Due westward, fronting to the green,
A rural portico was seen,
Aloft on native pillars borne,
Of mountain fir, with bark unshorn,
Where Ellen's hand had taught to twine
525 The ivy and Idaean vine,[1]
The clematis, the favor'd flower
Which boasts the name of virgin-bower,
And every hardy plant could bear
Loch Katrine's keen and searching air.
530 An instant in this porch she staid,
And gaily to the stranger said,
"On heaven and on thy lady call,
And enter the enchanted hall!"

"My hope, my heaven, my trust must be,
535 My gentle guide, in following thee."
He cross'd the threshold—and a clang
Of angry steel that instant rang.
To his bold brow his spirit rush'd,
But soon for vain alarm he blush'd
540 When on the floor he saw display'd,
Cause of the din, a naked blade

Dropp'd from the sheath, that careless
flung,
Upon a stag's huge antlers swung;
For all around, the walls to grace,
545 Hung trophies of the fight or chase:
A target[1] there, a bugle here,
A battle-axe, a hunting-spear,
And broadswords, bows, and arrows store,[2]
With the tusk'd trophies of the boar.
550 Here grins the wolf as when he died,
And there the wild-cat's brindled hide
The frontlet of the elk adorns,
Or mantles o'er the bison's horns;
Pennons and flags defaced and stain'd,
555 That blackening streaks of blood retain'd
And deer-skins, dappled, dun, and white,
With otter's fur and seal's unite,
In rude and uncouth tapestry all,
To garnish forth the silvan hall.

560 The wondering stranger round him gazed,
And next the fallen weapon raised:
Few were the arms whose sinewy strength
Sufficed to stretch it forth at length;
And as the brand he poised and sway'd,
565 "I never knew but one," he said,
"Whose stalwart arms might brook to
wield
A blade like this in battle-field."
She sigh'd, then smiled and took the word:
"You see the guardian champion's sword;
570 As light it trembles in his hand,
As in my grasp a hazel wand;
My sire's tall form might grace the part
Of Ferragus or Ascabart;
But in the absent giant's hold
575 Are women now, and menials old."

The mistress of the mansion came,
Mature of age, a graceful dame;
Whose easy step and stately port
Had well become a princely court;
580 To whom, though more than kindred knew,[3]
Young Ellen gave a mother's due.
Meet welcome to her guest she made,
And every courteous rite was paid
That hospitality could claim,
585 Though all unask'd his birth and name.
Such then the reverence to a guest,
That fellest foe might join the feast,
And from his deadliest foeman's door
Unquestion'd turn, the banquet o'er.
590 At length his rank the stranger names,
"The Knight of Snowdoun, James Fitz-
James;

[1] The red whortleberry. Mt Ida, in Crete, was famous for its vines.

[1] A kind of small shield.
[2] in plenty
[3] She was the maternal aunt of Ellen, who loved her more than was usual in such a relationship.

Lord of a barren heritage
Which his brave sires, from age to age,
By their good swords have held with toil;
595 His sire had fallen in such turmoil,
And he, God wot, was forced to stand
Oft for his right with blade in hand.
This morning, with Lord Moray's train,
He chased a stalwart stag in vain,
600 Outstripp'd his comrades, miss'd the deer,
Lost his good steed, and wander'd here.''

Fain would the Knight in turn require
The name and state of Ellen's sire.
Well show'd the elder lady's mien,
605 That courts and cities she had seen;
Ellen, though more her looks display'd
The simple grace of silvan maid,
In speech and gesture, form and face,
Show'd she was come of gentle race.
610 'Twere strange, in ruder rank to find
Such looks, such manners, and such mind.
Each hint the Knight of Snowdoun gave,
Dame Margaret heard with silence grave;
Or Ellen, innocently gay,
615 Turn'd all inquiry light away—
"Weird women[1] we! by dale and down[2]
We dwell, afar from tower and town.
We stem the flood, we ride the blast,
On wandering knights our spells we cast;
620 While viewless minstrels touch the string,
'Tis thus our charmed rhymes we sing.''
She sung, and still a harp unseen
Fill'd up the symphony between.

SONG

Soldier rest! thy warfare o'er,
625　Sleep the sleep that knows not breaking;
Dream of battled fields no more,
　Days of danger, nights of waking.
In our isle's enchanted hall,
　Hands unseen thy couch are strewing,
630 Fairy strains of music fall,
　Every sense in slumber dewing.
Soldier, rest! thy warfare o'er,
Dream of fighting fields no more;
Sleep the sleep that knows not breaking,
635 Morn of toil, nor night of waking.

No rude sound shall reach thine ear,
　Armor's clang, or war-steed champing,
Trump[3] nor pibroch[4] summon here
　Mustering clan, or squadron tramping.
640 Yet if the lark's shrill fife may come
　At the daybreak from the fallow,[5]
And the bittern sound his drum,
　Booming from the sedgy shallow.
Ruder sounds shall none be near,
645 Guards nor warders challenge here;

[1] women skilled in witchcraft, or gifted with prophecy
[2] valley and hill
[3] sound of trumpet
[4] A kind of Highland bagpipe music.
[5] uncultivated land

Here's no war-steed's neigh and champing,
Shouting clans or squadron's stamping.

She paused—then, blushing, led the lay
To grace the stranger of the day.
650 Her mellow notes awhile prolong
The cadence of the flowing song,
Till to her lips in measured frame
The minstrel verse spontaneous came:—

SONG CONTINUED

Huntsman, rest! thy chase is done,
655　While our slumbrous spells assail ye,
Dream not, with the rising sun,
　Bugles here shall sound reveille,[1]
Sleep! the deer is in his den;
　Sleep! thy hounds are by thee lying;
660 Sleep! nor dream in yonder glen
　How thy gallant steed lay dying.
Huntsman, rest! thy chase is done;
Think not of the rising sun,
For, at dawning to assail ye,
665 Here no bugles sound reveille.

The hall was cleared—the stranger's
　bed
Was there of mountain heathers spread,
Where oft a hundred guests had lain,
And dream'd their forest sports again.
670 But vainly did the heath-flower shed
Its moorland fragrance round his head;
Not Ellen's spell had lull'd to rest
The fever of his troubled breast.
In broken dreams the image rose
675 Of varied perils, pains, and woes:
His steed now flounders in the brake,
Now sinks his barge upon the lake;
Now leader of a broken host,
His standard falls, his honor's lost.
680 Then,—from my couch may heavenly
　might
Chase that worst phantom of the night!—
Again return'd the scenes of youth,
Of confident undoubting truth;
Again his soul he interchanged
685 With friends whose hearts were long
　estranged.
They come, in dim procession led,
The cold, the faithless, and the dead;
As warm each hand, each brow as gay,
As if they parted yesterday.
690 And doubt distracts him at the view—
O were his senses false or true?
Dream'd he of death, or broken vow,
Or is it all a vision now?

At length, with Ellen in a grove
695 He seem'd to walk, and speak of love;

[1] morning signal summoning soldiers to the duties of the day

She listen'd with a blush and sigh,
His suit was warm, his hopes were high.
He sought her yielded hand to clasp,
And a cold gauntlet met his grasp:
700 The phantom's sex had changed and
     gone,
Upon its head a helmet shone;
Slowly enlarged to giant size,
With darken'd cheek and threatening
     eyes,
The grisly visage, stern and hoar,
705 To Ellen still a likeness bore.
He woke, and, panting with affright,
Recall'd the vision of the night.
The hearth's decaying brands were red,
And deep and dusky lustre shed,
710 Half showing, half concealing, all
The uncouth trophies of the hall.
'Mid those the stranger fix'd his eye,
Where that huge falchion hung on high,
And thoughts on thoughts, a countless
     throng,
715 Rush'd, chasing countless thoughts along
Until, the giddy whirl to cure,
He rose, and sought the moonshine pure.

The wild-rose, eglantine, and broom,
Wasted around their rich perfume;
720 The birch-trees wept in fragrant balm,
The aspens slept beneath the calm;
The silver light, with quivering glance,
Play'd on the water's still expanse:
Wild were the heart whose passion's
     sway
725 Could rage beneath the sober ray!
He felt its calm, that warrior guest,
While thus he communed with his breast:
"Why is it, at each turn I trace
Some memory of that exiled race?[1]
730 Can I not mountain-maiden spy,
But she must bear the Douglas eye?
Can I not view a Highland brand,
But it must match the Douglas hand?
Can I not frame a fever'd dream,
735 But still the Douglas is the theme?
I'll dream no more; by manly mind
Not even in sleep is will resign'd.
My midnight orisons[2] said o'er,
I'll turn to rest, and dream no more."
740 His midnight orisons he told,
A prayer with every bead of gold,
Consign'd to heaven his cares and woes,
And sunk in undisturb'd repose;
Until the heath-cock shrilly crew,
745 And morning dawn'd on Benvenue.

[1] The Douglases, hated by James V because the Earl of Angus, who had married James's mother, had sought to make himself King of Scotland.
[2] prayers

From Canto II

BOAT SONG

Hail to the chief who in triumph advances!
     Honor'd and bless'd be the evergreen
     pine!
Long may the tree, in his banner that
     glances,
     Flourish, the shelter and grace of our
     line!
5   Heaven send it happy dew,
     Earth lend it sap anew,
Gayly to bourgeon,[1] and broadly to grow,
     While every Highland glen
     Sends our shout back agen,
10 Roderigh Vich Alpine dhu,[2] ho, ieroe!

Ours is no sapling, chance-sown by the
     fountain,
     Blooming at Beltane,[3] in winter to fade;
When the whirlwind has stripp'd every
     leaf on the mountain,
     The more shall Clan-Alpine exult in her
     shade.
15   Moor'd in the rifted rock,
     Proof to the tempest's shock,
Firmer he roots him the ruder it blow;
     Menteith and Breadalbane, then,
     Echo his praise again,
20 Roderigh Vich Alpine dhu, ho! ieroe!

Proudly our pibroch has thrill'd in Glen
     Fruin,
     And Bannochar's groans to our slogan
     replied;
Glen Luss and Ross-dhu, they are smoking
     in ruin,
     And the best of Loch Lomond lie dead
     on her side.
25   Widow and Saxon maid
     Long shall lament our raid,
Think of Clan-Alpine with fear and with
     woe;
     Lennox and Leven-glen
     Shake when they hear again,
30 Roderigh Vich Alpine dhu, ho! ieroe!

Row, vassals, row, for the pride of the
     Highlands!
     Stretch to your oars, for the evergreen
     pine!
O! that the rose-bud that graces yon
     islands
     Were wreathed in a garland around him
     to twine!

[1] put forth buds
[2] "Black Roderick, the descendant of Alpine."—Scott. The epithet belonged to Roderick as head of the clan.
[3] May-day

35   O that some seedling gem,
          Worthy such noble stem,
      Honor'd and bless'd in their shadow
          might grow!
          Loud should Clan-Alpine then
          Ring from her deepmost glen,
40 Roderigh Vich Alpine dhu, ho! ieroe!

From Canto III

CORONACH[1]

      He is gone on the mountain,
      He is lost to the forest,
      Like a summer-dried fountain,
      When our need was the sorest.
5   The font, reappearing,
      From the rain-drops shall borrow,
      But to us comes no cheering,
      To Duncan no morrow!

      The hand of the reaper
10   Takes the ears that are hoary,
      But the voice of the weeper
      Wails manhood in glory.
      The autumn winds rushing
      Waft the leaves that are searest,
15 But our flower was in flushing,
      When blighting was nearest.

      Fleet foot on the correi,[2]
      Sage counsel in cumber,[3]
      Red hand in the foray,
20   How sound is thy slumber!
      Like the dew on the mountain,
      Like the foam on the river,
      Like the bubble on the fountain,
      Thou art gone, and forever!

CANTO VI.   THE GUARD-ROOM

      The sun, awakening, through the smoky air
      Of the dark city casts a sullen glance,
      Rousing each caitiff to his task of care,
      Of sinful men the sad inheritance;
5   Summoning the revellers from the lagging
          dance,
      Scaring the prowling robber to his den;
      Gilding on battled tower the warder's
          lance,
      And warning student pale to leave his
          pen,
      And yield his drowsy eyes to the kind
          nurse of men.

10 What various scenes, and, O! what scenes
          of woe,
          Are witness'd by that red and strug-
          gling beam!

1 lament
2 hollow in a hill, the resort of game
3 trouble

      The fever'd patient, from his pallet low,
          Through crowded hospital beholds its
          stream;
      The ruin'd maiden trembles at its gleam,
15   The debtor wakes to thought of gyve
          and jail,
      The love-lorn wretch starts from torment-
          ing dream;
          The wakeful mother, by the glimmering
          pale,
      Trims her sick infant's couch, and soothes
          his feeble wail.

      At dawn the towers of Stirling rang
20   With soldier-step and weapon-clang,
      While drums, with rolling note, foretell
      Relief to weary sentinel.
      Through narrow loop and casement barr'd,
      The sunbeams sought the Court of Guard,
25   And, struggling with the smoky air,
      Deaden'd the torches' yellow glare.
      In comfortless alliance shone
      The lights through arch of blacken'd stone,
      And show'd wild shapes in garb of war,
30 Faces deform'd with beard and scar,
      All haggard from the midnight watch,
      And fever'd with the stern debauch;
      For the oak table's massive board,
      Flooded with wine, with fragments stored,
35   And beakers drain'd, and cups o'er-
          thrown,
      Show'd in what sport the night had
          flown.
      Some, weary, snored on floor and bench;
      Some labor'd still their thirst to quench;
      Some, chill'd with watching, spread their
          hands
40 O'er the huge chimney's dying brands,
      While round them, or beside them flung,
      At every step their harness rung.

      These drew not for their fields the sword,
      Like tenants of a feudal lord,
45 Nor own'd the patriarchal claim
      Of chieftain in their leader's name;
      Adventurers they, from far who roved,
      To live by battle which they loved.
      There the Italian's clouded face,
50   The swarthy Spaniard's there you trace;
      The mountain-loving Switzer there
      More freely breathed in mountain-air;
      The Fleming there despised the soil,
      That paid so ill the laborer's toil;
55   Their rolls show'd French and German
          name;
      And merry England's exiles came,
      To share, with ill conceal'd disdain,
      Of Scotland's pay the scanty gain.
      All brave in arms, well train'd to wield

60 The heavy halberd,[1] brand, and shield;
　In camps licentious, wild, and bold;
　In pillage fierce and uncontroll'd;
　And now, by holytide[2] and feast,
　From rules of discipline released.

65 They held debate of bloody fray,
　Fought 'twixt Loch Katrine and Achray.
　Fierce was their speech, and, 'mid their
　　　words,
　Their hands oft grappled to their swords;
　Nor sunk their tone to spare the ear
70 Of wounded comrades groaning near,
　Whose mangled limbs, and bodies gored,
　Bore token of the mountain sword,
　Though, neighboring to the Court of
　　　Guard,
　Their prayers and feverish wails were
　　　heard;
75 Sad burden to the ruffian joke,
　And savage oath by fury spoke!
　At length up-started John of Brent,
　A yeoman from the banks of Trent;
　A stranger to respect or fear,
80 In peace a chaser of the deer,
　In host[3] a hardy mutineer,
　But still the boldest of the crew,
　When deed of danger was to do.
　He grieved, that day, their games cut
　　　short,
85 And marr'd the dicer's brawling sport,
　And shouted loud, ''Renew the bowl!
　And, while a merry catch I troll,[4]
　Let each the buxom chorus bear,
　Like brethren of the brand and spear:—

SOLDIER'S SONG

90 Our vicar still preaches that Peter and Poule
　Laid a swinging long curse on the bonny
　　　brown bowl,
　That there's wrath and despair in the jolly
　　　black-jack,[5]
　And the seven deadly sins[6] in a flagon of
　　　sack;[7]
　Yet whoop, Barnaby! off with thy liquor,
95 Drink upsees out,[8] and a fig for the vicar.

　Our vicar he calls it damnation to sip
　The ripe ruddy dew of a woman's dear lip,
　Says, that Beelzebub lurks in her kerchief
　　　so sly,
　And Apollyon shoots darts from her merry
　　　black eye;
100 Yet whoop, Jack! kiss Gillian the quicker,
　Till she bloom like a rose, and a fig for the
　　　vicar!

　Our vicar thus preaches—and why should he
　　　not?
　For the dues of his cure are the placket and
　　　pot;[1]
　And 'tis right of his office poor laymen to
　　　lurch,[2]
105 Who infringe the domains of our good
　　　Mother Church.
　Yet whoop, bully-boys! off with your liquor,
　Sweet Marjorie's the word, and a fig for the
　　　vicar!

　The warder's challenge, heard without,
　Staid in mid-roar the merry shout.
110 A soldier to the portal went,—
　''Here is old Bertram, sirs, of Ghent;
　And, beat for jubilee the drum!
　A maid and minstrel with him come.''
　Bertram, a Fleming, gray and scarr'd,
115 Was entering now the Court of Guard,
　A harper with him, and in plaid
　All muffled close, a mountain maid,
　Who backward shrunk to 'scape the view
　Of the loose scene and boisterous crew.
120 ''What news?'' they roar'd. ''I only
　　　know,
　From noon till eve we fought with foe,
　As wild and as untameable
　As the rude mountains where they dwell;
　On both sides store of blood is lost,
125 Nor much success can either boast.''
　''But whence thy captives, friend? such
　　　spoil
　As theirs must needs reward thy toil.
　Old dost thou wax, and wars grow sharp;
　Thou now hast glee-maiden[3] and harp!
130 Get thee an ape, and trudge the land,
　The leader of a juggler band.''

　''No, comrade; no such fortune mine.
　After the fight these sought our line,
　That aged harper and the girl,
135 And, having audience of the Earl,
　Mar bade I should purvey them steed,
　And bring them hitherward with speed.
　Forbear your mirth and rude alarm,
　For none shall do them shame or harm.''
140 ''Hear ye his boast?'' cried John of
　　　Brent,
　Ever to strife and jangling bent;
　''Shall he strike doe beside our lodge,
　And yet the jealous niggard grudge
　To pay the forester his fee?
145 I'll have my share, howe'er it be,
　Despite of Moray, Mar, or thee.''
　Bertram his forward step withstood;
　And, burning in his vengeful mood,
　Old Allan, though unfit for strife,

---

[1] A kind of long-
　handled battle-axe.
[2] holiday
[3] An army.
[4] sing loudly
[5] black leather pitcher

[6] Pride, idleness, glut-
　tony, lust, avarice,
　envy, and wrath.
[7] wine
[8] deeply; to the bottom
　of the tankard

[1] A cant phrase for
　"women and wine."
[2] swindle; rob
[3] dancing-girl

150 Laid hand upon his dagger-knife;
But Ellen boldly stepp'd between,
And dropp'd at once the tartan screen:
So, from his morning cloud, appears
The sun of May, through summer tears.
155 The savage soldiery, amazed,
As on descended angel gazed;
Even hardy Brent, abash'd and tamed,
Stood half admiring, half ashamed.

Boldly she spoke, "Soldiers, attend!
160 My father was the soldier's friend;
Cheer'd him in camps, in marches led,
And with him in the battle bled.
Not from the valiant, or the strong,
Should exile's daughter suffer wrong."
165 Answer'd De Brent, most forward still
In every feat or good or ill—
"I shame me of the part I play'd:
And thou an outlaw's child, poor maid!
An outlaw I by forest laws,
170 And merry Needwood knows the cause.
Poor Rose—if Rose be living now"—
He wiped his iron eye and brow—
"Must bear such age, I think, as thou.
Hear ye, my mates;—I go to call
175 The captain of our watch to hall:
There lies my halberd on the floor:
And he that steps my halberd o'er,
To do the maid injurious part,
My shaft shall quiver in his heart!
180 Beware loose speech, or jesting rough:
Ye all know John de Brent. Enough."

Their captain came, a gallant young,
(Of Tullibardine's house he sprung,)
Nor wore he yet the spurs of knight;
185 Gay was his mien, his humor light,
And, though by courtesy controll'd,
Forward his speech, his bearing bold,
The high-born maiden ill could brook
The scanning of his curious look
190 And dauntless eye;—and yet, in sooth,
Young Lewis was a generous youth:
But Ellen's lovely face and mien,
Ill suited to the garb and scene,
Might lightly bear construction strange,
195 And give loose fancy scope to range.
"Welcome to Stirling towers, fair maid!
Come ye to seek a champion's aid,
On palfrey white, with harper hoar,
Like errant[1] damosel of yore?
200 Does thy high quest a knight require,
Or may the venture suit a squire?"
Her dark eye flash'd; she paused and
 sigh'd,
"O what have I to do with pride!

Through scenes of sorrow, shame, and
 strife,
205 A suppliant for a father's life,
I crave an audience of the King.
Behold, to back my suit, a ring,
The royal pledge of grateful claims,
Given by the Monarch to Fitz-James."

210 The signet-ring young Lewis took,
With deep respect and alter'd look;
And said, "This ring our duties own;
And pardon, if to worth unknown,
In semblance mean obscurely veil'd,
215 Lady, in aught my folly fail'd.
Soon as the day flings wide his gates,
The King shall know what suitor waits.
Please you, meanwhile, in fitting bower,
Repose you till his waking hour;
220 Female attendance shall obey
Your hest, for service or array.
Permit I marshall you the way."
But, ere she followed, with the grace
And open bounty of her race,
225 She bade her slender purse be shared
Among the soldiers of the guard.
The rest with thanks their guerdon took;
But Brent, with shy and awkward look,
On the reluctant maiden's hold
230 Forced bluntly back the proffer'd gold—
"Forgive a haughty English heart,
And O forget its ruder part!
The vacant purse shall be my share,
Which in my barret-cap[1] I'll bear,
235 Perchance, in jeopardy of war,
Where gayer crests may keep afar."
With thanks ('twas all she could) the maid
His rugged courtesy repaid.

When Ellen forth with Lewis went,
240 Allan made suit to John of Brent:
"My lady safe, O let your grace
Give me to see my master's face!
His minstrel I; to share his doom
Bound from the cradle to the tomb;
245 Tenth in descent, since first my sires
Waked for his noble house their lyres;
Nor one of all the race was known
But prized its weal above their own.
With the chief's birth begins our care;
250 Our harp must soothe the infant heir,
Teach the youth tales of fight, and grace
His earliest feat of field or chase;
In peace, in war, our rank we keep,
We cheer his board, we soothe his sleep,
255 Nor leave him till we pour our verse,
A doleful tribute! o'er his hearse.
Then let me share his captive lot;

---

[1] wandering on missions of chivalry

[1] A kind of small cap formerly worn by soldiers.

It is my right, deny it not!''
"Little we reck," said John of Brent,
260 "We Southern men, of long descent;
Nor wot[1] we how a name, a word,
Makes clansmen vassals to a lord:
Yet kind my noble landlord's part,—
God bless the house of Beaudesert!
265 And, but I loved to drive the deer,
More than to guide the laboring steer,
I had not dwelt an outcast here.
Come, good old Minstrel, follow me;
Thy lord and chieftain shalt thou see.''

270 Then, from a rusted iron hook,
A bunch of ponderous keys he took,
Lighted a torch, and Allan led
Through grated arch and passage dread;
Portals they pass'd, where, deep within,
275 Spoke prisoner's moan, and fetters' din;
Through rugged vaults, where, loosely
stored,
Lay wheel, and axe, and headsman's sword,
And many an hideous engine[2] grim,
For wrenching joint, and crushing limb,
280 By artist form'd, who deem'd it shame
And sin to give their work a name.
They halted at a low-brow'd porch,
And Brent to Allan gave the torch,
While bolt and chain he backward roll'd,
285 And made the bar unhasp its hold.
They enter'd: 'twas a prison-room
Of stern security and gloom,
Yet not a dungeon; for the day
Through lofty gratings found its way,
290 And rude and antique garniture
Deck'd the sad walls and oaken floor;
Such as the rugged days of old
Deem'd fit for captive noble's hold.
"Here," said De Brent, "thou mayst
remain
295 Till the leech visit him again.
Strict is his charge, the warders tell,
To tend the noble prisoner well.''
Retiring then, the bolt he drew,
And the lock's murmurs growl'd anew.
300 Roused at the sound, from lowly bed
A captive feebly raised his head;
The wondering Minstrel look'd, and knew
Not his dear lord, but Roderick Dhu!
For, come from where Clan-Alpine fought,
305 They, erring, deem'd the Chief he sought.

As the tall ship, whose lofty prore[3]
Shall never stem the billows more,
Deserted by her gallant band,
Amid the breakers lies astrand,
510 So, on his couch, lay Roderick Dhu!

And oft his fever'd limbs he threw
In toss abrupt, as when her sides
Lie rocking in the advancing tides,
That shake her frame with ceaseless beat,
315 Yet cannot heave her from her seat;
O! how unlike her course at sea!
Or his free step on hill and lea!
Soon as the Minstrel he could scan,
"What of thy lady? of my clan?
320 My mother? Douglas? tell me all?
Have they been ruin'd in my fall?
Ah, yes! or wherefore art thou here?
Yet speak, speak boldly, do not fear.''
(For Allan, who his mood well knew,
325 Was choked with grief and terror too.)—
''Who fought—who fled? Old man, be
brief;
Some might—for they had lost their chief.
Who basely live? who bravely died?''
"O, calm thee, Chief!" the Minstrel cried,
330 "Ellen is safe.'' — "For that, thank
Heaven!''
"And hopes are for the Douglas given;
The Lady Margaret, too, is well;
And, for thy clan,—on field or fell,
Has never harp of minstrel told,
335 Of combat fought so true and bold.
Thy stately pine is yet unbent,
Though many a goodly bough is rent.''

The Chieftain rear'd his form on high,
And fever's fire was in his eye;
340 But ghastly, pale, and livid streaks
Chequer'd his swarthy brow and cheeks.
—''Hark, Minstrel! I have heard thee play,
With measure bold, on festal day,
In yon lone isle,—again where ne'er
345 Shall harper play, or warrior hear!—
That stirring air that peals on high,
O'er Dermid's race[1] our victory.
Strike it! and then (for well thou canst)
Free from thy minstrel-spirit glanced,
350 Fling me the picture of the fight
When met my clan the Saxon might.
I'll listen, till my fancy hears
The clang of swords, the crash of spears!
These grates, these walls, shall vanish then,
355 For the fair field of fighting men,
And my free spirit burst away
As if it soar'd from battle fray.''
The trembling Bard with awe obey'd,
Slow on the harp his hand he laid;
360 But soon remembrance of the sight
He witness'd from the mountain's height,
With what old Bertram told at night,
Awaken'd the full power of song,
And bore him in career along—

[1] know   [2] contrivance   [3] prow   [1] The Campbells.

365 As shallop launch'd on river's tide,
    That slow and fearful leaves the side,
    But, when it feels the middle stream,
    Drives downward swift as lightning's
        beam:

BATTLE OF BEAL' AN DUINE

    The Minstrel came once more to view
370 The eastern ridge of Benvenue,
    For, ere he parted, he would say
    Farewell to lovely Loch Achray:
    Where shall he find, in foreign land,
    So lone a lake, so sweet a strand!
375   There is no breeze upon the fern,
      Nor ripple on the lake;
    Upon her eyry[1] nods the erne,[2]
      The deer has sought the brake;
    The small birds will not sing aloud,
380   The springing trout lies still,
    So darkly glooms yon thunder cloud,
    That swathes, as with a purple shroud,
      Benledi's distant hill.
    Is it the thunder's solemn sound
385   That mutters deep and dread,
    Or echoes from the groaning ground
      The warrior's measured tread?
    Is it the lightning's quivering glance
    That on the thicket streams,
390 Or do they flash on spear and lance
      The sun's retiring beams?
    I see the dagger-crest of Mar,
    I see the Moray's silver star
    Wave o'er the cloud of Saxon war,
395 That up the lake comes winding far!
    To hero bound for battle-strife,
      Or bard of martial lay,
    'Twere worth ten years of peaceful life,
      One glance at their array!

400   Their light-arm'd archers far and near
      Survey'd the tangled ground;
    Their centre ranks, with pike and spear,
      A twilight forest frown'd;
    Their barded[3] horsemen, in the rear,
405   The stern battalia[4] crown'd.
    No cymbal clash'd, no clarion rang,
      Still were the pipe and drum;
    Save heavy tread, and armor's clang,
      The sullen march was dumb.
410 There breathed no wind their crests to
      shake,
      Or wave their flags abroad;
    Scarce the frail aspen seem'd to quake,
      That shadow'd o'er their road.
    Their vaward[5] scouts no tidings bring,
415   Can rouse no lurking foe,
      Nor spy a trace of living thing,
      Save when they stirr'd the roe;
    The host moves like a deep-sea wave,
    Where rise no rocks its pride to brave,
420   High-swelling, dark, and slow.
    The lake is pass'd, and now they gain

A narrow and a broken plain,
Before the Trosachs' rugged jaws;
And here the horse and spearmen pause,
425 While, to explore the dangerous glen,
Dive through the pass the archer-men.

    At once there rose so wild a yell
    Within that dark and narrow dell,
    As all the fiends, from heaven that fell,
430 Had peal'd the banner-cry of hell!
      Forth from the pass in tumult driven,
      Like chaff before the wind of heaven,
        The archery appear;
    For life! for life! their flight they ply—
435   And shriek, and shout, and battle-cry,
    And plaids and bonnets waving high,
    And broadswords flashing to the sky,
      Are maddening in the rear.
    Onward they drive, in dreadful race,
440   Pursuers and pursued;
    Before that tide of flight and chase,
    How shall it keep its rooted place,
      The spearmen's twilight wood?
    "Down, down," cried Mar, "your lances
      down!
445   Bear back both friend and foe!"
    Like reeds before the tempest's frown,
    That serried grove of lances brown
      At once lay levell'd low;
    And closely shouldering side to side,
450   The bristling ranks the onset bide.
    "We'll quell the savage mountaineer,
      As their Tinchel[1] cows the game!
    They come as fleet as forest deer,
    We'll drive them back as tame."

455 Bearing before them, in their course,
    The relics of the archer force,
    Like wave with crest of sparkling foam,
    Right onward did Clan-Alpine come.
    Above the tide, each broadsword bright
460 Was brandishing like beam of light,
      Each targe[2] was dark below;
    And with the ocean's mighty swing,
    When heaving to the tempest's wing,
      They hurl'd them on the foe.
465 I heard the lance's shivering crash,
    As when the whirlwind rends the ash,
    I heard the broadsword's deadly clang,
    As if a hundred anvils rang!
    But Moray wheel'd his rearward rank
470 Of horsemen on Clan-Alpine's flank,
      "My banner-man, advance!
    I see," he cried, "their column shake.
    Now, gallants! for your ladies' sake,
      Upon them with the lance!"
475   The horsemen dash'd among the rout,
      As deer break through the broom;
    Their steeds are stout, their swords are out,
    They soon make lightsome room.
    Clan-Alpine's best are backward borne!
480   Where, where was Roderick then?
    One blast upon his bugle-horn
    Were worth a thousand men!

---

[1] nest   [4] battle array
[2] eagle   [5] vanward
[3] armored

[1] A circle of hunters surrounding game.
[2] shield

And refluent through the pass of fear,
The battle's tide was pour'd;
485 Vanish'd the Saxon's struggling spear,
Vanish'd the mountain-sword.
As Bracklinn's chasm, so black and steep,
Receives her roaring linn,[1]
As the dark caverns of the deep
490 Suck the wild whirlpool in,
So did the deep and darksome pass
Devour the battle's mingled mass:
None linger now upon the plain,
Save those who ne'er shall fight again.

495 Now westward rolls the battle's din,
That deep and doubling pass within.
Minstrel, away, the work of fate
Is bearing on: its issue wait,
Where the rude Trosachs' dread defile
500 Opens on Katrine's lake and isle.
Gray Benvenue I soon repass'd,
Loch Katrine lay beneath me cast.
The sun is set; the clouds are met,
The lowering scowl of heaven
505 An inky hue of livid blue
To the deep lake has given;
Strange gusts of wind from mountain-glen
Swept o'er the lake, then sunk again.
I heeded not the eddying surge,
510 Mine eye but saw the Trosachs' gorge,
Mine ear but heard the sullen sound,
Which like an earthquake shook the ground,
And spoke the stern and desperate strife
That parts not but with parting life,
515 Seeming, to minstrel ear, to toll
The dirge of many a passing soul.
Nearer it comes; the dim-wood glen
The martial flood disgorged again,
But not in mingled tide;
520 The plaided warriors of the North
High on the mountain thunder forth
And overhang its side;
While by the lake below appears
The dark'ning cloud of Saxon spears.
525 At weary bay each shatter'd band,
Eyeing their foemen, sternly stand;
Their banners stream like tatter'd sail,
That flings its fragments to the gale,
And broken arms and disarray
530 Mark'd the fell havoc of the day.

Viewing the mountain's ridge askance
The Saxons stood in sullen trance,
Till Moray pointed with his lance,
And cried—"Behold yon isle!
535 See! none are left to guard its strand,
But women weak, that wring the hand:
'Tis there of yore the robber band
Their booty wont to pile;
My purse, with bonnet-pieces store,[2]
540 To him will swim a bow-shot o'er,
And loose a shallop from the shore.
Lightly we'll tame the war-wolf then,
Lords of his mate, and brood, and den."
Forth from the ranks a spearman sprung,

545 On earth his casque and corslet rung,
He plunged him in the wave:
All saw the deed, the purpose knew,
And to their clamors Benvenue
A mingled echo gave;
550 The Saxons shout, their mate to cheer,
The helpless females scream for fear,
And yells for rage the mountaineer.
'Twas then, as by the outcry riven,
Pour'd down at once the lowering heaven:
555 A whirlwind swept Loch Katrine's breast,
Her billows rear'd their snowy crest,
Well for the swimmer swell'd they high,
To mar the Highland marksman's eye;
For round him shower'd, 'mid rain and hail,
560 The vengeful arrows of the Gael.
In vain; he nears the isle, and lo!
His hand is on a shallop's bow.
Just then a flash of lightning came,
It tinged the waves and strand with flame;
565 I mark'd Duncraggan's widow'd dame,[1]
Behind an oak I saw her stand,
A naked dirk gleamed in her hand:
It darken'd; but, amid the moan
Of waves, I heard a dying groan;
570 Another flash!—the spearman floats
A weltering corse beside the boats,
And the stern matron o'er him stood,
Her hand and dagger streaming blood.

"Revenge! revenge!" the Saxons cried,
575 The Gaels' exulting shout replied.
Despite the elemental rage,
Again they hurried to engage;
But, ere they closed in desperate fight,
Bloody with spurring came a knight,
580 Sprung from his horse, and, from a crag,
Waved 'twixt the hosts a milk-white flag.
Clarion and trumpet by his side
Rung forth a truce-note high and wide,
While, in the Monarch's name, afar
585 An herald's voice forbade the war,
For Bothwell's lord,[2] and Roderick bold,
Were both, he said, in captive hold.

But here the lay made sudden stand!
The harp escaped the Minstrel's hand!
590 Oft had he stolen a glance, to spy
How Roderick brook'd his minstrelsy:
At first, the Chieftain, to the chime,
With lifted hand, kept feeble time;
That motion ceased, yet feeling strong
595 Varied his look as changed the song;
At length, no more his deafen'd ear
The minstrel melody can hear;
His face grows sharp, his hands are
clench'd,
As if some pang his heart-strings
wrench'd;
600 Set are his teeth, his fading eye
Is sternly fix'd on vacancy;
Thus, motionless, and moanless, drew

---

[1] cataract: waterfall
[2] filled with gold coins embossed with the King's
head wearing a bonnet instead of a crown

[1] The widow of the Duncan lamented in the
Coronach (p. 482).
[2] Ellen's father.

His parting breath, stout Roderick Dhu!
Old Allan-bane look'd on aghast,
605 While grim and still his spirit pass'd:
But when he saw that life was fled,
He pour'd his wailing o'er the dead:

LAMENT

And art thou cold and lowly laid,
Thy foeman's dread, thy people's aid,
610 Breadalbane's boast, Clan-Alpine's shade!
For thee shall none a requiem say?
For thee, who loved the minstrel's lay,
For thee, of Bothwell's house the stay,
The shelter of her exiled line,
615 E'en in this prison-house of thine,
I'll wail for Alpine's honor'd pine!

What groans shall yonder valleys fill!
What shrieks of grief shall rend yon hill!
What tears of burning rage shall thrill,
620 When mourns thy tribe thy battles done,
Thy fall before the race was won,
Thy sword ungirt ere set of sun!
There breathes not clansman of thy line,
But would have given his life for thine.
625 O, woe for Alpine's honor'd pine!

Sad was thy lot on mortal stage!
The captive thrush may brook the cage,
The prison'd eagle dies for rage.
Brave spirit, do not scorn my strain!
630 And, when its notes awake again,
Even she, so long beloved in vain,
Shall with my harp her voice combine,
And mix her woe and tears with mine,
To wail Clan-Alpine's honor'd pine.

635 Ellen the while with bursting heart
Remain'd in lordly bower apart,
Where play'd with many-color'd gleams,
Through storied pane[1] the rising beams.
In vain on gilded roof they fall,
640 And lighten'd up a tapestried wall,
And for her use a menial train
A rich collation spread in vain.
The banquet proud, the chamber gay,
Scarce drew one curious glance astray;
645 Or, if she look'd, 'twas but to say,
With better omen dawn'd the day
In that lone isle, where waved on high
The dun-deer's hide for canopy;
Where oft her noble father shared
650 The simple meal her care prepared,
While Lufra, crouching by her side
Her station claim'd with jealous pride,
And Douglas, bent on woodland game,
Spoke of the chase to Malcolm Graeme,
655 Whose answer, oft at random made,
The wandering of his thoughts betray'd.
Those who such simple joys have known,

Are taught to prize them when they're
    gone.
But sudden, see, she lifts her head!
660 The window seeks with cautious tread.
What distant music has the power
To win her in this woful hour!
'Twas from a turret that o'erhung
Her latticed bower, the strain was sung:

LAY OF THE IMPRISONED HUNTSMAN

665 My hawk is tired of perch and hood,
My idle greyhound loathes his food,
My horse is weary of his stall,
And I am sick of captive thrall.

I wish I were, as I have been,
670 Hunting the hart in forest green,
With bended bow and bloodhound free,
For that's the life is meet for me.

I hate to learn the ebb of time
From yon dull steeple's drowsy chime,
675 Or mark it as the sunbeams crawl,
Inch after inch, along the wall.

The lark was wont my matins ring,
The sable rook my vespers sing;
These towers, although a king's they be,
680 Have not a hall of joy for me.

No more at dawning morn I rise,
And sun myself in Ellen's eyes,
Drive the fleet deer the forest through,
And homeward wend with evening dew;

685 A blithesome welcome blithely meet,
And lay my trophies at her feet,
While fled the eve on wing of glee:
That life is lost to love and me!

The heart-sick lay was hardly said,
690 The list'ner had not turn'd her head,
It trickled still, the starting tear,
When light a footstep struck her ear,
And Snowdoun's graceful knight was near.
She turn'd the hastier, lest again
695 The prisoner should renew his strain,
"O welcome, brave Fitz-James!" she said;
"How may an almost orphan maid
Pay the deep debt"—"O say not so!
To me no gratitude you owe.
700 Not mine, alas! the boon to give,
And bid thy noble father live;
I can but be thy guide, sweet maid,
With Scotland's king thy suit to aid.
No tyrant he, though ire and pride
705 May lay his better mood aside.
Come, Ellen, come! 'tis more than time,
He holds his court at morning prime."[1]
With beating heart, and bosom wrung,
As to a brother's arm she clung.

---

[1] windows decorated with historical scenes (See
  Il Penseroso, 159.)

[1] dawn (It is literally the first hour of prayer,
  or 6 A. M.)

710 Gently he dried the falling tear,
And gently whisper'd hope and cheer;
Her faltering steps half led, half stayed,
Through gallery fair, and high arcade,
Till, at his touch, its wings of pride
715 A portal arch unfolded wide.

Within 'twas brilliant all and light,
A thronging scene of figures bright;
It glow'd on Ellen's dazzled sight,
As when the setting sun has given
720 Ten thousand hues to summer even,
And from their tissue fancy frames
Aërial knights and fairy dames.
Still by Fitz-James her footing stayed;
A few faint steps she forward made,
725 Then slow her drooping head she raised,
And fearful round the presence gazed;
For him she sought, who own'd this state,
The dreaded prince whose will was fate.
She gazed on many a princely port,
730 Might well have ruled a royal court;
On many a splendid garb she gazed,
Then turn'd bewilder'd and amazed,
For all stood bare; and, in the room,
Fitz-James alone wore cap and plume.
735 To him each lady's look was lent;
On him each courtier's eye was bent;
Midst furs, and silks, and jewels sheen,
He stood, in simple Lincoln green,[1]
The centre of the glittering ring.
740 And Snowdoun's Knight is Scotland's
King!

As wreath of snow, on mountain-breast,
Slides from the rock that gave it rest,
Poor Ellen glided from her stay,
And at the Monarch's feet she lay;
745 No word her choking voice commands;
She show'd the ring, she clasp'd her hands.
O! not a moment could he brook,
The generous prince, that suppliant look!
Gently he raised her; and, the while,
750 Check'd with a glance the circle's smile;
Graceful, but grave, her brow he kiss'd,
And bade her terrors be dismiss'd:
"Yes, fair, the wandering poor Fitz-James
The fealty of Scotland claims.
755 To him thy woes, thy wishes, bring;
He will redeem his signet ring.
Ask nought for Douglas; yester even,
His prince and he have much forgiven.
Wrong hath he had from slanderous
tongue,
760 I, from his rebel kinsmen, wrong.
We would not, to the vulgar crowd,
Yield what they craved with clamor loud;
Calmly we heard and judged his cause,

Our council aided, and our laws.
765 I stanch'd thy father's death-feud stern
With stout De Vaux and Gray Glencairn;
And Bothwell's Lord henceforth we own
The friend and bulwark of our throne.
But, lovely infidel, how now?
770 What clouds thy misbelieving brow?
Lord James of Douglas, lend thine aid;
Thou must confirm this doubting maid.''

Then forth the noble Douglas sprung,
And on his neck his daughter hung.
775 The Monarch drank, that happy hour,
The sweetest, holiest draught of Power,
When it can say, with godlike voice,
Arise, sad Virtue, and rejoice!
Yet would not James the general eye
780 On Nature's raptures long should pry;
He stepp'd between—"Nay, Douglas, nay,
Steal not my proselyte away!
The riddle 'tis my right to read,
That brought this happy chance to speed.[1]
785 Yes, Ellen, when disguised I stray
In life's more low but happier way,
'Tis under name which veils my power,
Nor falsely veils, for Stirling's tower
Of yore the name of Snowdoun claims,
790 And Normans call me James Fitz-James.
Thus watch I o'er insulted laws,
Thus learn to right the injured cause."
Then, in a tone apart and low,—
"Ah, little traitress! none must know
795 What idle dream, what lighter thought,
What vanity full dearly bought,
Join'd to thine eye's dark witchcraft, drew
My spell-bound steps to Benvenue,
In dangerous hour, and all but gave
800 Thy Monarch's life to mountain glaive!''[2]
—Aloud he spoke—"Thou still dost hold
That little talisman of gold,
Pledge of my faith, Fitz-James's ring;
What seeks fair Ellen of the King?"

805 Full well the conscious maiden guess'd
He probed the weakness of her breast;
But, with that consciousness, there came
A lightening of her fears for Græme,
And more she deem'd the Monarch's ire
810 Kindl'd 'gainst him, who, for her sire,
Rebellious broadsword boldly drew;
And, to her generous feeling true,
She craved the grace of Roderick Dhu.
"Forbear thy suit: the King of kings
815 Alone can stay life's parting wings:
I know his heart, I know his hand,
Have shared his cheer, and proved his
brand:

---

[1] A cloth made in Lincoln, worn by huntsmen.

[1] to a successful issue   [2] broadsword

My fairest earldom would I give
To bid Clan-Alpine's Chieftain live!
820 Hast thou no other boon to crave?
No other captive friend to save?"
Blushing, she turn'd her from the King,
And to the Douglas gave the ring,
As if she wish'd her sire to speak
825 The suit that stain'd her glowing cheek.—
"Nay, then, my pledge has lost its force,
And stubborn justice holds her course.
Malcolm, come forth!" And at the word,
Down kneel'd the Græme to Scotland's
Lord.
830 "For thee, rash youth, no suppliant sues,
From thee may Vengeance claim her dues,
Who, nurtured underneath our smile,
Hast paid our care by treacherous wile,
And sought, amid thy faithful clan,
835 A refuge for an outlaw'd man,
Dishonoring thus thy loyal name.
Fetters and warder for the Græme!"
His chain of gold the King unstrung,
The links o'er Malcolm's neck he flung,
840 Then gently drew the glittering band,
And laid the clasp on Ellen's hand.

Harp of the North, farewell! The hills
grow dark,
On purple peaks a deeper shade descending;
In twilight copse the glow-worm lights
her spark,
845 The deer, half-seen, are to the covert
wending.
Resume thy wizard elm! the fountain
lending,
And the wild breeze, thy wilder minstrelsy;
Thy numbers sweet with nature's vespers
blending,
With distant echo from the fold and lea,
850 And herd-boy's evening pipe, and hum
of housing bee.

Yet once again farewell, thou Minstrel
harp!
Yet once again forgive my feeble sway,
And little reck I of the censure sharp
May idly cavil at an idle lay.
855 Much have I owed thy strains on life's
long way,
Through secret woes the world has
never known,
When on the weary night dawn'd wearier
day,
And bitterer was the grief devour'd
alone.
That I o'erlive such woes, Enchantress!
is thine own.

860 Hark! as my lingering footsteps slow
retire,
Some Spirit of the Air has waked thy
string!
'Tis now a seraph bold, with touch of fire,
'Tis now the brush of Fairy's frolic
wing.
Receding now, the dying numbers ring
865 Fainter and fainter down the rugged
dell,
And now the mountain breezes scarcely
bring
A wandering witch-note of the distant
spell—
And now, 'tis silent all!—Enchantress,
fare thee well!

From ROKEBY
1812   1813

BRIGNALL BANKS

O, Brignall banks are wild and fair,
And Greta woods are green,
And you may gather garlands there
Would grace a summer queen.
5 And as I rode by Dalton-hall,
Beneath the turrets high,
A maiden on the castle wall
Was singing merrily:—
"O Brignall banks are fresh and fair,
10 And Greta woods are green;
I'd rather rove with Edmund there,
Than reign our English queen."

"If, maiden, thou wouldst wend with me,
To leave both tower and town,
15 Thou first must guess what life lead we,
That dwell by dale and down.[1]
And if thou canst that riddle read,
As read full well you may,
Then to the greenwood shalt thou speed,
20 As blithe as Queen of May."
Yet sung she, "Brignall banks are fair,
And Greta woods are green;
I'd rather rove with Edmund there,
Than reign our English queen.

25 "I read you, by your bugle-horn,
And by your palfrey good,
I read you for a ranger sworn,
To keep the king's greenwood."
"A ranger, lady, winds his horn,
30 And 'tis at peep of light;
His blast is heard at merry morn,
And mine at dead of night."
Yet sung she, "Brignall banks are fair,
And Greta woods are gay;
35 I would I were with Edmund there,
To reign his Queen of May!

[1] valley and hill.

"With burnish'd brand and musketoon,[1]
  So gallantly you come,
I read you for a bold dragoon,
40   That lists the tuck[2] of drum."
"I list no more the tuck of drum,
  No more the trumpet hear;
But when the beetle sounds his hum,
  My comrades take the spear.
45 And O! though Brignall banks be fair,
  And Greta woods be gay,
Yet mickle[3] must the maiden dare,
  Would reign my Queen of May!

"Maiden! a nameless life I lead,
50 A nameless death I'll die;
The fiend, whose lantern lights the mead,
  Were better mate than I!
And when I'm with my comrades met
  Beneath the greenwood bough,
55 What once we were we all forget,
  Nor think what we are now.
Yet Brignall banks are fresh and fair,
  And Greta woods are green,
And you may gather garlands there
60 Would grace a summer queen."

ALLEN-A-DALE

Allen-a-Dale has no fagot for burning,
Allen-a-Dale has no furrow for turning,
Allen-a-Dale has no fleece for the spin-
  ning,
Yet Allen-a-Dale has red gold for the
  winning.
Come, read me my riddle! come, hearken
  my tale!
And tell me the craft[4] of bold Allen-a-
  Dale.

The Baron of Ravensworth prances in
  pride,
And he views his domains upon Arkin-
  dale side;
The mere[5] for his net, and the land for
  his game,
The chase for the wild, and the park for
  the tame;
Yet the fish of the lake, and the deer of
  the vale,
Are less free to Lord Dacre than Allen-
  a-Dale!

Allen-a-Dale was ne'er belted a knight,
Though his spur be as sharp, and his blade
  be as bright;
15 Allen-a-Dale is no baron or lord,
Yet twenty tall yeomen will draw at his
  word;

[1] short musket   [4] trade
[2] beat   [5] lake
[3] much

And the best of our nobles his bonnet will
  vail,[1]
Who at Rere-cross on Stanmore meets
  Allen-a-Dale.

Allen-a-Dale to his wooing is come;
20 The mother, she ask'd of his household
  and home:
"Though the castle of Richmond stand
  fair on the hill,
My hall," quoth bold Allen, "shows gal-
  lanter still;
'Tis the blue vault of heaven, with its
  crescent so pale,
And with all its bright spangles," said
  Allen-a-Dale.

25 The father was steel, and the mother was
  stone;
They lifted the latch, and they bade him
  be gone;
But loud, on the morrow, their wail and
  their cry:
He had laugh'd on the lass with his bonny
  black eye,
And she fled to the forest to hear a love-
  tale,
30 And the youth it was told by was
  Allen-a-Dale!

From WAVERLEY
1805-14   1814
HIE AWAY, HIE AWAY

Hie away, hie away,
Over bank and over brae,[2]
Where the copsewood is the greenest,
Where the fountains glisten sheenest,
5 Where the lady-fern grows strongest,
Where the morning dew lies longest,
Where the black-cock sweetest sips it,
Where the fairy latest trips it:
Hie to haunts right seldom seen,
10 Lovely, lonesome, cool, and green,
Over bank and over brae,
Hie away, hie away.

From GUY MANNERING
1814-15   1815
TWIST YE, TWINE YE

Twist ye, twine ye! even so
Mingle shades of joy and woe,
Hope, and fear, and peace, and strife,
In the thread of human life.

5 While the mystic twist is spinning,
And the infant's life beginning,

[1] take off   [2] hillside

Dimly seen through twilight bending,
Lo, what varied shapes attending!
Passions wild, and follies vain,
10 Pleasures soon exchanged for pain;
Doubt, and jealousy, and fear,
In the magic dance appear.

Now they wax, and now they dwindle,
Whirling with the whirling spindle.
15 Twist ye, twine ye! even so
Mingle human bliss and woe.

WASTED, WEARY, WHEREFORE STAY

Wasted, weary, wherefore stay,
Wrestling thus with earth and clay?
From the body pass away;—
Hark! the mass is singing.

5 From thee doff thy mortal weed,
Mary Mother be thy speed,[1]
Saints to help thee at thy need;—
Hark! the knell is ringing.

Fear not snowdrift driving fast,
10 Sleet, or hail, or levin[2] blast;
Soon the shroud shall lap thee fast,
And the sleep be on thee cast
That shall ne'er know waking.

Haste thee, haste thee, to be gone,
15 Earth flits fast, and time draws on,—
Gasp thy gasp, and groan thy groan,
Day is near the breaking.

LINES

ON THE LIFTING OF THE BANNER OF THE HOUSE
OF BUCCLEUCH, AT A GREAT FOOTBALL
MATCH ON CARTERHAUGH
1815 1815

From the brown crest of Newark its
summons extending,
Our signal is waving in smoke and in
flame;
And each forester blithe, from his mountain descending,
Bounds light o'er the heather to join
in the game.

Chorus

5 Then up with the Banner, let forest winds
fan her,
She has blazed over Ettrick eight ages
and more;

In sport we'll attend her, in battle defend
her,
With heart and with hand, like our
fathers before.

When the Southern invader spread waste
and disorder,
10 At the glance of her crescents he paused
and withdrew,
For round them were marshall'd the pride
of the Border,
The Flowers of the Forest, the Bands
of Buccleuch.

A stripling's weak hand to our revel has
borne her,
15 No mail-glove has grasp'd her, no
spearmen surround;
But ere a bold foeman should scathe or
should scorn her,
A thousand true hearts would be cold
on the ground.

We forget each contention of civil dissension,
20 And hail, like our brethren, Home,
Douglas, and Car;
And Elliot and Pringle in pastime shall
mingle,
As welcome in peace as their fathers in
war.

Then strip, lads, and to it, though sharp
be the weather,
25 And if, by mischance, you should happen to fall,
There are worse things in life than a
tumble on heather,
And life is itself but a game of football.

And when it is over, we'll drink a blithe
measure
30 To each Laird and each Lady that witness'd our fun,
And to every blithe heart that took part
in our pleasure,
To the lads that have lost and the lads
that have won.

May the Forest still flourish, both Borough
and Landward,[1]
35 From the hall of the Peer to the Herd's
ingle-nook;
And huzza! my brave hearts, for Buccleuch and his standard,
For the King and the Country, the Clan
and the Duke!

[1] help   [2] lightning

[1] town and country

Chorus

Then up with the Banner, let forest winds
    fan her,
  She has blazed over Ettrick eight ages
      and more;
40 In sport we'll attend her, in battle defend
      her,
  With heart and with hand, like our
      fathers before.

JOCK OF HAZELDEAN
1816   1816

"Why weep ye by the tide, ladie?
  Why weep ye by the tide?
I'll wed ye to my youngest son,
  And ye sall be his bride:
5 And ye sall be his bride, ladie,
  Sae comely to be seen"—
But aye she loot the tears down fa'
  For Jock of Hazeldean.

"Now let this wilfu' grief be done,
10 And dry that cheek so pale;
Young Frank is chief of Errington,
  And lord of Langley-dale;
His step is first in peaceful ha',
  His sword in battle keen"—
15 But aye she loot the tears down fa'
  For Jock of Hazeldean.

"A chain of gold ye sall not lack,
  Nor braid to bind your hair;
Nor mettled hound, nor managed[1] hawk,
20 Nor palfrey fresh and fair;
And you, the foremost o' them a',
  Shall ride our forest queen"—
But aye she loot the tears down fa'
  For Jock of Hazeldean.

25 The kirk was deck'd at morning-tide,
  The tapers glimmer'd fair;
The priest and bridegroom wait the bride,
  And dame and knight are there.
They sought her baith by bower and ha';[2]
30 The ladie was not seen!
She's o'er the Border, and awa'
  Wi' Jock of Hazeldean.

PIBROCH[3] OF DONUIL DHU
1816   1816

Pibroch of Donuil Dhu,
  Pibroch of Donuil,
Wake thy wild voice anew,
  Summon Clan-Conuil.

5 Come away, come away,
  Hark to the summons!
Come in your war array,
  Gentles and commons.

Come from deep glen, and
10 From mountain so rocky,
The war-pipe and pennon
  Are at Inverlochy.
Come every hill-plaid, and
  True heart that wears one,
15 Come every steel blade, and
  Strong hand that bears one.

Leave untended the herd,
  The flock without shelter;
Leave the corpse uninterr'd,
20 The bride at the altar;
Leave the deer, leave the steer,
  Leave nets and barges:
Come with your fighting gear,
  Broadswords and targes.[1]

25 Come as the winds come, when
  Forests are rended,
Come as the waves come, when
  Navies are stranded:
Faster come, faster come,
30 Faster and faster,
Chief, vassal, page and groom,
  Tenant and master.

Fast they come, fast they come;
  See how they gather!
35 Wide waves the eagle plume,
  Blended with heather.
Cast your plaids, draw your blades,
  Forward, each man, set!
Pibroch of Donuil Dhu,
40 Knell for the onset!

From THE ANTIQUARY
1815-16   1816

Why Sitt'st Thou by that Ruin'd Hall?

"Why sitt'st thou by that ruin'd hall,
  Thou aged carle[2] so stern and gray?
Dost thou its former pride recall,
  Or ponder how it pass'd away?"—

5 "Know'st thou not me?" the Deep Voice
      cried;
  "So long enjoy'd, so oft misused—
Alternate, in thy fickle pride,
  Desired, neglected, and accused!

---

[1] trained
[2] The hall was the public dwelling of the Teu-
    tonic chieftain, and the bower the private
    apartments, especially of the women. See
    Wordsworth's *London*, 4 (p. 313).
[3] A kind of Highland bagpipe music.

[1] shields
[2] churl; peasant

"Before my breath, like blazing flax,
10 Man and his marvels pass away!
And changing empires wane and wax,
  Are founded, flourish, and decay.

"Redeem mine hours—the space is brief—
  While in my glass the sand-grains
    shiver,
15 And measureless thy joy or grief
  When Time and thou shall part for-
    ever!''

From OLD MORTALITY
1816   1816

AND WHAT THOUGH WINTER WILL PINCH SEVERE

And what though winter will pinch severe
  Through locks of gray and a cloak
    that's old,
Yet keep up thy heart, bold cavalier,
  For a cup of sack[1] shall fence the cold.

5 For time will rust the brightest blade,
  And years will break the strongest bow;
Was never wight so starkly made,[2]
  But time and years would overthrow.

CLARION

Sound, sound the clarion, fill the fife!
  To all the sensual world proclaim,
One crowded hour of glorious life
  Is worth an age without a name.

THE DREARY CHANGE
1817   1817

The sun upon the Weirdlaw Hill,
  In Ettrick's vale, is sinking sweet;
The westland wind is hush and still,
  The lake lies sleeping at my feet.
5 Yet not the landscape to mine eye
  Bears those bright hues that once it
    bore;
Though evening, with her richest dye,
  Flames o'er the hills of Ettrick's shore.

With listless look along the plain,
10 I see Tweed's silver current glide,
And coldly mark the holy fane
  Of Melrose rise in ruin'd pride.
The quiet lake, the balmy air,
  The hill, the stream, the tower, the
    tree,—

15 Are they still such as once they were?
  Or is the dreary change in me?

Alas, the warp'd and broken board,
  How can it bear the painter's dye!
The harp of strain'd and tuneless chord,
20 How to the minstrel's skill reply!
To aching eyes each landscape lowers,
  To feverish pulse each gale blows chill;
And Araby's or Eden's bowers
  Were barren as this moorland hill.

From ROB ROY
1817   1817

FAREWELL TO THE LAND

Farewell to the land where the clouds love
    to rest,
Like the shroud of the dead on the moun-
    tain's cold breast;
To the cataract's roar where the eagles
    reply,
And the lake her lone bosom expands to
    the sky.

From THE HEART OF MIDLOTHIAN
1818   1818

PROUD MAISIE

Proud Maisie is in the wood,
  Walking so early;
Sweet Robin sits on the bush,
  Singing so rarely.

5 "Tell me, thou bonny bird,
  When shall I marry me?''
"When six braw[1] gentlemen
  Kirkward shall carry ye.''

"Who makes the bridal bed,
10 Birdie, say truly?''
"The gray-headed sexton
  That delves the grave duly.

"The glow-worm o'er grave and stone
  Shall light thee steady;
15 The owl from the steeple sing,
  'Welcome, proud lady.' ''

From IVANHOE
1819   1819

THE BAREFOOTED FRIAR

I'll give thee, good fellow, a twelvemonth
    or twain,
To search Europe through from Byzan-
    tium to Spain;

---

[1] wine
[2] person made so strong

[1] fine; handsome

But ne'er shall you find, should you search
   till you tire,
So happy a man as the Barefooted
   Friar.

5 Your knight for his lady pricks forth in
   career,
And is brought home at even-song prick'd
   through with a spear;
I confess him in haste—for his lady de-
   sires
No comfort on earth save the Barefooted
   Friar's.

Your monarch?—Pshaw! many a prince
   has been known
10 To barter his robes for our cowl and our
   gown;
But which of us e'er felt the idle desire
To exchange for a crown the gray hood of
   a Friar?

The Friar has walk'd out, and where'er he
   has gone,
The land and its fatness is mark'd for his
   own;
15 He can roam where he lists, he can stop
   when he tires,
For every man's house is the Barefooted
   Friar's.

He's expected at noon, and no wight,[1] till
   he comes,
May profane the great chair, or the porridge of plums;
For the best of the cheer, and the seat by
   the fire,
20 Is the undenied right of the Barefooted
   Friar.

He's expected at night, and the pasty's
   made hot,
They broach[2] the brown ale, and they fill
   the black pot;
And the goodwife would wish the good-
   man in the mire,
Ere he lack'd a soft pillow, the Barefooted Friar.

Long flourish the sandal, the cord, and the
   cope,
The dread of the devil and trust of the
   Pope!
For to gather life's roses, unscathed by
   the brier,
Is granted alone to the Barefooted Friar.

1 person   2 open

REBECCA'S HYMN

When Israel, of the Lord beloved,
   Out from the land of bondage came,
Her fathers' God before her moved,
   An awful guide in smoke and flame.[1]
5 By day, along the astonish'd lands
   The cloudy pillar glided slow;
By night, Arabia's crimson'd sands
   Return'd the fiery column's glow.

There rose the choral hymn of praise,
10   And trump and timbrel[2] answer'd keen,
And Zion's daughters pour'd their lays,
   With priest's and warrior's voice be-
      tween.
No portents now our foes amaze,
   Forsaken Israel wanders lone:
15 Our fathers would not know Thy ways,
   And Thou hast left them to their own.

But present still, though now unseen!
   When brightly shines the prosperous
      day,
Be thoughts of Thee a cloudy screen
20   To temper the deceitful ray.
And oh, when stoops on Judah's path
   In shade and storm the frequent night,
Be Thou, long-suffering, slow to wrath,
   A burning and a shining light!

25 Our harps we left by Babel's streams,
   The tyrant's jest, the Gentile's scorn;
No censer round our altar beams,
   And mute our timbrel, harp, and horn.
But Thou hast said, The blood of goat,
30   The flesh of rams I will not prize;
A contrite heart, a humble thought,
   Are mine accepted sacrifice.[3]

From THE MONASTERY
1819-20   1820
BORDER MARCH

March, march, Ettrick and Teviot-dale,
   Why the deil dinna ye march forward
      in order?
March, march, Eskdale and Liddesdale,
   All the Blue Bonnets are bound for the
      Border.
5   Many a banner spread,
   Flutters above your head,
Many a crest that is famous in story.
   Mount and make ready then,
   Sons of the mountain glen,
10 Fight for the Queen[4] and the old Scot-
   tish glory.

1 See Exodus, 13 :21-22.   3 See Psalms, 51 :17.
2 trumpet and tambou-   4 Mary, Queen of Scots.
   rine

Come from the hills where your hirsels[1]
    are grazing,
  Come from the glen of the buck and
    the roe;
Come to the crag where the beacon is
    blazing,
  Come with the buckler, the lance, and
    the bow.
15   Trumpets are sounding,
    War-steeds are bounding,
  Stand to your arms then, and march in
    good order;
    England shall many a day
    Tell of the bloody fray,
20 When the Blue Bonnets came over the
    Border.

From THE PIRATE
1821   1821

THE SONG OF THE REIM-KENNAR[2]

Stern eagle of the far north-west,
Thou that bearest in thy grasp the
    thunderbolt,
Thou whose rushing pinions stir ocean to
    madness,
Thou the destroyer of herds, thou the
    scatterer of navies,
5 Amidst the scream of thy rage,
Amidst the rushing of thy onward wings,
Though thy scream be as loud as the cry
    of a perishing nation,
Though the rushing of thy wings be like
    the roar of ten thousand waves,
Yet hear, in thine ire and thy haste,
10 Hear thou the voice of the Reim-kennar.

Thou hast met the pine-trees of Dront-
    heim,
Their dark-green heads lie prostrate be-
    side their up-rooted stems;
Thou hast met the rider of the ocean,
The tall, the strong bark of the fearless
    rover,
15 And she has struck to thee the topsail
That she had not veil'd[3] to a royal armada.
Thou has met the tower that bears its crest
    among the clouds,
The battled massive tower of the Jarl[4] of
    former days,
And the cope-stone of the turret
20 Is lying upon its hospitable hearth;
But thou too shalt stoop, proud compeller
    of clouds,

[1] herds; flocks
[2] sorceress; one who knows magic rhymes or spells
[3] lowered
[4] The title of a Norse chieftain.

When thou hearest the voice of the Reim-
    kennar.

There are verses that can stop the stag in
    the forest,
Ay, and when the dark-color'd dog is
    opening on his track;
25 There are verses can make the wild hawk
    pause on the wing,
Like the falcon that wears the hood and
    the jesses,[1]
And who knows the shrill whistle of the
    fowler.
Thou who canst mock at the scream of the
    drowning mariner,
And the crash of the ravaged forest,
30 And the groan of the overwhelmed crowds,
When the church hath fallen in the mo-
    ment of prayer;
There are sounds which thou also must
    list,
When they are chanted by the voice of the
    Reim-kennar.

Enough of woe hast thou wrought on the
    ocean,
35 The widows wring their hands on the
    beach;
Enough of woe hast thou wrought on the
    land,
The husbandman folds his arms in de-
    spair;
Cease thou the waving of thy pinions,
Let the ocean repose in her dark strength;
40 Cease thou the flashing of thine eye,
Let the thunderbolt sleep in the armory
    of Odin;
Be thou still at my bidding, viewless racer
    of the north-western heaven,—
Sleep thou at the voice of Norna the
    Reim-kennar.

Eagle of the far north-western waters,
45 Thou hast heard the voice of the Reim-
    kennar,
Thou hast closed thy wide sails at her
    bidding,
And folded them in peace by thy side.
My blessing be on thy retiring path;
When thou stoopest from thy place on
    high,
50 Soft be thy slumbers in the caverns of the
    unknown ocean,
Rest till destiny shall again awaken thee;
Eagle of the north-west, thou hast heard
    the voice of the Reim-kennar.

[1] short straps secured around the legs of falcons, for attaching the leash

FAREWELL TO THE MUSE
1822

Enchantress, farewell, who so oft hast
    decoy'd me,
  At the close of the evening through
    woodlands to roam,
Where the forester, 'lated, with wonder
    espied me
  Explore the wild scenes he was quitting
    for home.
5 Farewell, and take with thee thy numbers
    wild speaking
  The language alternate of rapture and
    woe:
Oh! none but some lover, whose heart-
    strings are breaking,
  The pang that I feel at our parting can
    know.

Each joy thou couldst double, and when
    there came sorrow,
10 Or pale disappointment to darken my
    way,
What voice was like thine, that could sing
    of tomorrow,
  Till forgot in the strain was the grief of
    today!
But when friends drop around us in life's
    weary waning,
  The grief, Queen of Numbers, thou
    canst not assuage;
15 Nor the gradual estrangement of those yet
    remaining,
  The languor of pain, and the chillness
    of age.

'Twas thou that once taught me, in accents
    bewailing,
  To sing how a warrior[1] lay stretch'd on
    the plain,
And a maiden hung o'er him with aid
    unavailing,
20 And held to his lips the cold goblet in
    vain;
As vain thy enchantments, O Queen of
    wild Numbers,
  To a bard when the reign of his fancy
    is o'er,
And the quick pulse of feeling in apathy
    slumbers—
  Farewell, then, Enchantress! I meet
    thee no more!

From QUENTIN DURWARD
1823   1823
COUNTY GUY

Ah! County Guy, the hour is nigh,
  The sun has left the lea,
The orange flower perfumes the bower,

[1] Marmion.

The breeze is on the sea.
5 The lark, his lay who thrill'd[1] all day,
  Sits hush'd his partner nigh;
Breeze, bird, and flower, confess the hour,
  But where is County Guy?

The village maid steals through the shade,
10 Her shepherd's suit to hear;
To beauty shy, by lattice high,
  Sings high-born Cavalier.
The star of Love, all stars above,
  Now reigns o'er earth and sky;
15 And high and low the influence know—
  But where is County Guy?

From THE TALISMAN
1825   1825
WHAT BRAVE CHIEF

What brave chief shall head the forces
  Where the red-cross[2] legions gather?
Best of horsemen, best of horses,
  Highest head and fairest feather.

5 Ask not Austria, why 'mid princes
  Still her banner rises highest;
Ask as well the strong-wing'd eagle
  Why to heaven he soars the nighest.

From THE DOOM OF DEVERGOIL
1825   1830
ROBIN HOOD

O, Robin Hood was a bowman good,
  And a bowman good was he,
And he met with a maiden in merry
    Sherwood,
  All under the greenwood tree.

5 Now give me a kiss, quoth bold Robin
    Hood,
  Now give me a kiss, said he,
For there never came maid into merry
    Sherwood,
  But she paid the forester's fee.

BONNY DUNDEE

To the Lords of Convention 'twas Claver'se
    who spoke,
"Ere the King's crown shall fall there
    are crowns to be broke;
So let each Cavalier who loves honor and
    me,
Come follow the bonnet of Bonny Dundee.

5 "Come fill up my cup, come fill up my
    can,
  Come saddle your horses, and call up
    your men;

[1] trilled
[2] The red cross is the national emblem of England.

Come open the West Port, and let me
gang free,
And it's room for the bonnets of Bonny
Dundee!''

Dundee he is mounted, he rides up the
street,
10 The bells are rung backward,[1] the drums
they are beat;
But the Provost,[2] douce[3] man, said, ''Just
e'en let him be,
The Gude Town is weel quit of that Deil
of Dundee.''

Come fill up my cup, etc.

As he rode down the sanctified bends of
the Bow,[4]
15 Ilk carline[5] was flyting[6] and shaking her
pow;[7]
But the young plants of grace they look'd
couthie and slee,[8]
Thinking, ''Luck to thy bonnet, thou
Bonny Dundee!''

Come fill up my cup, etc.

With sour-featured Whigs the Grass-
market was cramm'd
20 As if half the West had set tryst to be
hang'd;
There was spite in each look, there was
fear in each e'e,
As they watch'd for the bonnets of Bonny
Dundee.

Come fill up my cup, etc.

These cowls of Kilmarnock[9] had spits[10]
and had spears,
25 And lang-hafted gullies[11] to kill Cavaliers;
But they shrunk to close-heads,[12] and the
causeway was free,
At the toss of the bonnet of Bonny
Dundee.

Come fill up my cup, etc.

He spurr'd at the foot of the proud Castle
rock,[13]
30 And with the gay Gordon he gallantly
spoke;

''Let Mons Meg[1] and her marrows[2] speak
twa words or three,
For the love of the Bonnet of Bonny
Dundee.''

Come fill up my cup, etc.

The Gordon demands of him which way
he goes—
35 ''Where'er shall direct me the shade of
Montrose!
Your Grace in short space shall hear
tidings of me,
Or that low lies the bonnet of Bonny
Dundee.

Come fill up my cup, etc.

''There are hills beyond Pentland, and
lands beyond Forth,
40 If there's lords in the Lowlands, there's
chiefs in the North;
There are wild Duniewassals,[3] three thousand times three,
Will cry *hoigh!* for the bonnet of Bonny
Dundee.

Come fill up my cup, etc.

''There's brass on the target[4] of barken'd[5]
bull-hide;
45 There's steel in the scabbard that dangles
beside;
The brass shall be burnish'd, the steel
shall flash free,
At a toss of the bonnet of Bonny Dundee.

Come fill up my cup, etc.

''Away to the hills, to the caves, to the
rocks—
50 Ere I own an usurper, I'll couch with the
fox;
And tremble, false Whigs, in the midst of
your glee,
You have not seen the last of my bonnet
and me!''

Come fill up my cup, etc.

He waved his proud hand, and the trumpets were blown,
55 The kettle-drums clash'd, and the horsemen rode on,
Till on Ravelston's cliffs and on Clermis-
ton's lee,
Died away the wild war-notes of Bonny
Dundee.

---

[1] The chimes are sounded in reverse order as an alarm.
[2] Mayor
[3] sedate; prudent
[4] windings of Bow Street (It was inhabited chiefly by Covenanters.)
[5] each old woman
[6] scolding
[7] head
[8] loving and sly

[9] hooded garments made at Kilmarnock (Here used for the Presbyterians, who wore them.)
[10] swords
[11] long-handled knives
[12] upper ends of narrow passages leading from the street
[13] The site of Edinburgh Castle, then held by the Duke of Gordon.

[1] The nickname of a great cannon, supposed to have been made in Mons, Belgium.
[2] mates; companions
[3] Highland gentlemen of secondary rank.
[4] shield
[5] tanned with bark

Come fill up my cup, come fill up my
    can,
Come saddle the horses, and call up the
    men,
60 Come open your gates, and let me gae
    free,
For it's up with the bonnets of Bonny
    Dundee!

When Friends Are Met

When friends are met o'er merry cheer,
And lovely eyes are laughing near,
And in the goblet's bosom clear
    The cares of day are drown'd;
5 When puns are made, and bumpers
    quaff'd,
And wild Wit shoots his roving shaft,
And Mirth his jovial laugh has laugh'd,
    Then is our banquet crown'd,
        Ah gay,
10   Then is our banquet crown'd.

When glees[1] are sung, and catches troll'd,[2]
And bashfulness grows bright and bold,
And beauty is no longer cold,
    And age no longer dull;
15 When chimes are brief, and cocks do crow,
To tell us it is time to go,
Yet how to part we do not know,
    Then is our feast at full,
        Ah gay,
20   Then is our feast at full.

From WOODSTOCK
1826   1826

Glee for King Charles

Bring the bowl which you boast,
    Fill it up to the brim;
'Tis to him we love most,
    And to all who love him.
5 Brave gallant, stand up,
    And avaunt ye, base carles![3]
Were there death in the cup,
    Here's a health to King Charles!

Though he wanders through dangers,
10   Unaided, unknown,
Dependent on strangers,
    Estranged from his own;
Though 'tis under our breath,
    Amidst forfeits and perils,

---

[1] A glee is an unaccompanied song for several
    solo voices, and usually in contrasted move-
    ments. A catch differs in that each of several
    persons sings a part to one continuous melody.
[2] sung loudly
[3] churls; peasants

15 Here's to honor and faith,
    And a health to King Charles!

Let such honors abound
    As the time can afford,
The knee on the ground,
20   And the hand on the sword;
But the time shall come round
    When, 'mid Lords, Dukes, and Earls,
The loud trumpet shall sound,
    Here's a health to King Charles!

THE FORAY
1830

The last of our steers on the board has
    been spread,
And the last flask of wine in our goblet is
    red;
Up, up, my brave kinsmen! belt swords
    and begone,
There are dangers to dare, and there's
    spoil to be won.

The eyes, that so lately mix'd glances
    with ours,
For a space must be dim, as they gaze
    from the towers,
And strive to distinguish through tempest
    and gloom
The prance of the steed and the toss of
    the plume.

The rain is descending; the wind rises
    loud;
10 And the moon her red beacon has veil'd
    with a cloud;
'Tis the better, my mates! for the
    warder's dull eye
Shall in confidence slumber, nor dream
    we are nigh.

Our steeds are impatient! I hear my
    blithe gray!
There is life in his hoof-clang, and hope
    in his neigh;
15 Like the flash of a meteor, the glance of
    his mane
Shall marshal your march through the
    darkness and rain.

The drawbridge has dropp'd, the bugle
    has blown;
One pledge is to quaff yet—then mount
    and begone!—
To their honor and peace, that shall rest
    with the slain;
20 To their health and their glee, that see
    Teviot again!

Joanna Baillie 1762-1851

From THE BEACON
1812

FISHERMAN'S SONG

No fish stir in our heaving net,
And the sky is dark and the night is wet;
And we must ply the lusty oar,
For the tide is ebbing from the shore;
5 And sad are they whose faggots burn,
So kindly stored for our return.

Our boat is small, and the tempest raves,
And naught is heard but the lashing waves
And the sullen roar of the angry sea
10 And the wild winds piping drearily;
Yet sea and tempest rise in vain,
We'll bless our blazing hearths again.

Push bravely, mates! Our guiding star
Now from its towerlet streameth far,
15 And now along the nearing strand,
See, swiftly moves yon flaming brand:
Before the midnight watch be past
We'll quaff our bowl and mock the blast.

WOO'D AND MARRIED AND A'
1822

The bride she is winsome and bonny,
Her hair it is snooded[1] sae sleek,
And faithfu' and kind is her Johnny,
Yet fast fa' the tears on her cheek.
5 New pearlins[2] are cause of her sorrow,
New pearlins and plenishing[3] too;
The bride that has a' to borrow
Has e'en right mickle ado.
Woo'd and married and a'!
10 Woo'd and married and a'!
Is na' she very weel aff
To be woo'd and married at a'?

Her mither then hastily spak,
"The lassie is glaikit[4] wi' pride;
15 In my pouch I had never a plack[5]
On the day when I was a bride.
E'en tak to your wheel and be clever,
And draw out your thread in the sun;
The gear[6] that is gifted[7] it never
20 Will last like the gear that is won.
Woo'd and married and a'!
Wi' havins and tocher[8] sae sma'!
I think ye are very weel aff
To be woo'd and married at a'."

25 "Toot, toot," quo' her gray-headed faither,
"She's less o' a bride than a bairn,

She's ta'en like a cout[1] frae the heather,
Wi' sense and discretion to learn.
Half husband, I trow, and half daddy,
30 As humor inconstantly leans,
The chiel[2] maun[3] be patient and steady
That yokes wi' a mate in her teens.
A kerchief sae douce[4] and sae neat
O'er her locks that the wind used to blaw!
35 I'm baith like to laugh and to greet
When I think of her married at a'!"

Then out spak the wily bridegroom,
Weel waled[5] were his wordies, I ween,
"I'm rich, though my coffer be toom,[6]
40 Wi' the blinks o' your bonny blue e'en.
I'm prouder o' thee by my side,
Though thy ruffles or ribbons be few,
Than if Kate o' the Croft were my bride
Wi' purfles[7] and pearlins enow.
45 Dear and dearest of ony!
Ye're woo'd and buikit[8] and a'!
And do ye think scorn o' your Johnny,
And grieve to be married at a'?"

She turn'd, and she blush'd, and she smiled,
50 And she looked sae bashfully down;
The pride o' her heart was beguiled,
And she played wi' the sleeves o' her gown.
She twirled the tag o' her lace,
And she nipped her boddice sae blue,
55 Syne[9] blinkit sae sweet in his face,
And aff like a maukin[10] she flew.
Woo'd and married and a'!
Wi' Johnny to roose[11] her and a'!
She thinks hersel very weel aff
60 To be woo'd and married at a'!

A SCOTCH SONG
1822

The gowan[12] glitters on the sward,
The lavrock's[13] in the sky,
And collie on my plaid keeps ward,
And time is passing by.
5 Oh no! sad and slow
And lengthened on the ground,
The shadow of our trysting bush,
It wears so slowly round!

My sheep-bell tinkles frae the west,
10 My lambs are bleating near,
But still the sound that I lo'e best,

---

1 bound up in a riband
2 finery; laces
3 furnishings
4 foolish
5 A small coin, worth about one cent.
6 clothing and property
7 given
8 goods and dowry

1 colt
2 fellow
3 must
4 tidy
5 chosen
6 empty
7 trimmings
8 registered as intending to marry
9 then
10 hare
11 praise
12 daisy
13 lark's

Alack! I canna' hear.
    Oh no! sad and slow,
    The shadow lingers still,
15 And like a lonely ghaist I stand
    And croon[1] upon the hill.

I hear below the water roar,
    The mill wi' clacking din,
And Lucky scolding frae her door,
20   To ca' the bairnies in.
    Oh no! sad and slow,
    These are na' sounds for me,
    The shadow of our trysting bush,
    It creeps sae drearily.

25 I coft yestreen frae Chapman Tam,[2]
    A snood[3] of bonny blue,
And promised when our trysting cam',
    To lie it round her brow.
    Oh no! sad and slow,
30   The mark it winna' pass;
    The shadow of that weary thorn
    Is tethered on the grass.

O now I see her on the way,
    She's past the witch's knowe,[4]
35 She's climbing up the Browny's brae,[5]
    My heart is in a lowe![6]
    Oh no! 'tis no' so,
    'Tis glam'rie[7] I have seen;
    The shadow of that hawthorne bush
40   Will move na' mair till e'en.

My book o' grace I'll try to read,
    Though conned wi' little skill,
When collie barks I'll raise my head,
    And find her on the hill;
45   Oh no! sad and slow,
    The time will ne'er be gane,
    The shadow of the trysting bush
    Is fixed like ony stane.

Allan Cunningham 1784-1842

THE LOVELY LASS OF PRESTON MILL
1807   1813

The lark had left the evening cloud,
    The dew fell saft, the wind was lowne,[8]
Its gentle breath amang the flowers,
    Scarce stirred the thistle's tap o' down;
5 The dappled swallow left the pool
    The stars were blinking owre the hill,
As I met, amang the hawthornes green,
    The lovely lass of Preston Mill.

Her naked feet, amang the grass,
10   Shone like twa dew-gemmed lilies fair;
Her brow shone comely 'mang her locks,
    Dark curling owre her shoulders bare;
Her cheeks were rich wi' bloomy youth;
    Her lips had words and wit at will;
15 And heaven seemed looking through her
      een,—
    The lovely lass of Preston Mill.

Quo' I, "Sweet lass, will ye gang wi' me,
    Where blackcocks craw, and plovers
      cry?
Six hills are woolly wi' my sheep,
20   Six vales are lowing wi' my kye:
I hae looked lang for a weel-faur'd[1] lass,
    By Nithsdale's holmes[2] an' monie a
      hill;"
She hung her head like a dew-bent rose,—
    The lovely lass of Preston Mill.

25 Quo' I, "Sweet maiden, look nae down,
    But gie's a kiss, and gang wi' me:"
A lovelier face, O, never looked up,
    And the tears were drapping frae her ee:
"I hae a lad, wha's far awa',
30   That weel could win a woman's will;
My heart's already fu' o' love,"
    Quo' the lovely lass of Preston Mill.

"Now wha is he wha could leave sic a lass,
    To seek for love in a far countree?"—
35 Her tears drapped down like simmer dew;
    I fain wad kissed them frae her ee.
I took but ane o' her comely cheek;
    "For pity's sake, kind sir, be still!
My heart is fu' o' other love,"
40   Quo' the lovely lass of Preston Mill.

She stretched to heaven her twa white
      hands,
    And lifted up her watery ee:
"Sae lang's my heart kens aught o' God,
    Or light is gladsome to my ee;
45 While woods grow green, and burns[3] rin
      clear,
    Till my last drap o' blood be still,
My heart shall haud nae other love,"
    Quo' the lovely lass of Preston Mill.

There's comely maids on Dee's wild banks
50   And Nith's romantic vale is fu';
By lanely Cluden's hermit stream
    Dwells monie a gentle dame, I trow!
O, they are lights of a gladsome kind,
    As ever shone on vale or hill;
55 But there's a light puts them a' out,—
    The lovely lass of Preston Mill!

---

[1] wail with low monotonous sounds
[2] bought yesterday evening from Peddler Tam
[3] band worn around the hair
[4] knoll
[5] slope
[6] flame
[7] enchantment
[8] calm

[1] well-favored; handsome
[2] low lands
[3] brooks

GANE WERE BUT THE WINTER CAULD
1813

Gane were but the winter cauld,
    And gane were but the snaw,
I could sleep in the wild woods,
    Where primroses blaw.

5 Cauld's the snaw at my head,
    And cauld at my feet,
And the finger o' death's at my een,
    Closing them to sleep.

Let nane tell my father,
10   Or my mither sae dear:
I'll meet them baith in heaven
    At the spring o' the year.

A WET SHEET AND A FLOWING SEA
1825

A wet sheet and a flowing sea,
    A wind that follows fast,
And fills the white and rustling sail
    And bends the gallant mast;
5 And bends the gallant mast, my boys,
    While, like the eagle free,
Away the good ship flies, and leaves
    Old England on the lee.

"O for a soft and gentle wind!"
10   I heard a fair one cry;
But give to me the snoring breeze
    And white waves heaving high;
And white waves heaving high, my lads,
    The good ship tight and free,—
15 The world of waters is our home,
    And merry men are we.

There's tempest in yon hornéd moon,
    And lightning in yon cloud;
But hark the music, mariners!
20   The wind is piping loud;
The wind is piping loud, my boys,
    The lightning flashes free,—
While the hollow oak our palace is,
    Our heritage the sea.

James Hogg 1770-1835

WHEN THE KYE COMES HAME
1810

Come, all ye jolly shepherds
    That whistle through the glen,
I'll tell ye of a secret
    That courtiers dinna ken:[1]
5 What is the greatest bliss
    That the tongue o'man can name?
'Tis to woo a bonnie lassie
    When the kye comes hame,

10   When the kye comes hame,
    When the kye comes hame,
  'Tween the gloaming and the mirk,[1]
    When the kye comes hame.

'Tis not beneath the coronet,
    Nor canopy of state,
15 'Tis not on couch of velvet,
    Nor arbor of the great—
'Tis beneath the spreading birk,[2]
    In the glen without the name,
Wi' a bonnie, bonnie lassie,
20   When the kye comes hame.
    When the kye comes hame, etc.

There the blackbird bigs[3] her nest
    For the mate he lo'es to see,
And on the topmost bough,
25   Oh, a happy bird is he;
Where he pours his melting ditty,
    And love is a' the theme,
And he'll woo his bonnie lassie
    When the kye comes hame.
30   When the kye comes hame, etc.

When the blewart[4] bears a pearl,
    And the daisy turns a pea,
And the bonnie lucken-gowan[5]
    Has fauldit[6] up her ee,
35 Then the laverock[7] frae the blue lift[8]
    Drops down, an' thinks nae shame
To woo his bonnie lassie
    When the kye comes hame,
    When the kye comes hame, etc.

40 See yonder pawkie[9] shepherd,
    That lingers on the hill,
His ewes are in the fauld,
    An' his lambs are lying still;
Yet he downa gang[10] to bed,
45   For his heart is in a flame
To meet his bonnie lassie
    When the kye comes hame.
    When the kye comes hame, etc.

When the little wee bit heart
50   Rises high in the breast,
An' the little wee bit starn[11]
    Rises red in the east,
Oh there's a joy sae dear,
    That the heart can hardly frame,
55 Wi' a bonnie, bonnie lassie,
    When the kye comes hame!
    When the kye comes hame, etc.

[1] do not know

[1] dark	[7] lark
[2] birch	[8] sky
[3] builds	[9] sly ; artful
[4] A kind of shrub.	[10] cannot go
[5] globeflower	[11] star
[6] folded : closed	

Then since all nature joins
  In this love without alloy,
60 Oh, wha wad prove a traitor
  To Nature's dearest joy?
Or wha wad choose a crown,
  Wi' its perils and its fame,
And *miss* his bonnie lassie
65   When the kye comes hame,
  When the kye comes hame,
  When the kye comes hame,
  'Tween the gloaming and the mirk,
  When the kye comes hame!

THE SKYLARK
1810

Bird of the wilderness,
  Blithesome and cumberless,
Sweet be thy matin[1] o'er moorland and
    lea!
  Emblem of happiness,
5   Blest is thy dwelling-place—
Oh, to abide in the desert with thee!

Wild is thy lay and loud,
  Far in the downy cloud,
Love gives it energy, love gave it birth.
10   Where, on thy dewy wing,
  Where art thou journeying?
Thy lay is in heaven, thy love is on earth.

O'er fell[2] and fountain sheen,
  O'er moor and mountain green,
15 O'er the red streamer that heralds the
    day,
  Over the cloudlet dim,
  Over the rainbow's rim,
Musical cherub, soar, singing, away!

Then, when the gloaming comes,
20   Low in the heather blooms
Sweet will thy welcome and bed of love
    be!
  Emblem of happiness,
  Blest is thy dwelling-place—
Oh, to abide in the desert with thee!

WHEN MAGGY GANGS AWAY
1810

Oh, what will a' the lads do
  When Maggy gangs away?
Oh, what will a' the lads do
  When Maggy gangs away?
5 There's no a heart in a' the glen
  That disna[3] dread the day:
Oh, what will a' the lads do
  When Maggy gangs away?

Young Jock has ta'en the hill for't—
10   A waefu' wight[1] is he;
Poor Harry's ta'en the bed for't,
  An' laid him down to dee;
An' Sandy's gane into the kirk,
  An' learnin' fast to pray;
15 And oh, what will the lads do
  When Maggy gangs away?

The young laird o' the Lang-Shaw
  Has drunk her health in wine;
The priest has said—in confidence—
20   The lassie was divine,
And that is mair in maiden's praise
  Than ony priest should say:
But oh, what will the lads do
  When Maggy gangs away?

25 The wailing in our green glen
  That day will quaver high;
Twill draw the redbreast frae the wood,
  The laverock frae the sky;
The fairies frae their beds o' dew
30   Will rise an' join the lay:
An' hey! what a day will be
  When Maggy gangs away!

From THE QUEEN'S WAKE
1813
KILMENY

Bonnie Kilmeny gaed up the glen;
But it wasna to meet Duneira's men,
Nor the rosy monk of the isle to see,
For Kilmeny was pure as pure could be.
5 It was only to hear the yorlin[2] sing,
And pu' the cress-flower round the spring;
The scarlet hypp[3] and the hind-berrye,[4]

And the nest that hung frae the hazel
    tree;
For Kilmeny was pure as pure could be.
10 But lang may her minny[5] look o'er the
    wa';
And lang may she seek i' the greenwood
    shaw;[6]
Lang the laird o' Duneira blame,
And lang lang greet[7] or Kilmeny come
    hame!

When many lang day had come and fled,
15 When grief grew calm, and hope was
    dead,
When mass for Kilmeny's soul had been
    sung,

---

[1] morning song
[2] moor; elevated wild field
[3] does not

[1] woeful fellow
[2] yellow-hammer
[3] ripened fruit, or berry, of the dog-rose
[4] European raspberry, or bramble-berry.
[5] mother
[6] thicket
[7] weep

When the bedesman[1] had pray'd and the
    dead-bell rung,
Late, late in a gloaming, when all was still,
When the fringe was red on the westlin
    hill,
20 The wood was sere, the moon i' the wane,
The reek o' the cot hung o'er the plain,
Like a wee cloud in the world its lane;[2]
When the ingle lowed wi' an eiry leme[3]—
Late, late in the gloaming Kilmeny came
    hame!

25   "Kilmeny, Kilmeny, where have you
    been?
Lang hae we sought baith holt and dean;[4]
By burn,[5] by ford, by greenwood tree,
Yet you are halesome and fair to see.
Where gat ye that joup[6] o' the lily sheen?
30 That bonnie snood[7] o' the birk[8] sae
    green?
And those roses, the fairest that ever
    were seen?
Kilmeny, Kilmeny, where have you
    been?''

Kilmeny look'd up wi' a lovely grace,
But nae smile was seen on Kilmeny's
    face;
35 As still was her look, and as still was her
    ee,
As the stillness that lay on the emerant[9]
    lea,
Or the mist that sleeps on a waveless sea.
For Kilmeny had been, she kenned not
    where,

And Kilmeny had seen what she could not
    declare;
40 Kilmeny had been where the cock never
    crew,
Where the rain never fell, and the wind
    never blew.
But it seemed as the harp of the sky had
    rung,
And the airs of heaven played round her
    tongue,
When she spoke of the lovely forms she
    had seen,
45 And a land where sin had never been;
A land of love and a land of light,
Withouten sun, or moon, or night;
Where the river swa'd[10] a living stream,
And the light a pure and cloudless beam;

50 The land of vision, it would seem,
A still, an everlasting dream.

In yon green wood there is a waik,[1]
And in that waik there is a wene,[2]
And in that wene there is a maike;[3]
55 That neither has flesh, nor blood, nor
    bane;
And down in yon greenwood he walks his
    lane.[4]

In that green wene Kilmeny lay,
Her bosom hap'd[5] wi' flowerets gay;
But the air was soft, and the silence deep,
60 And bonny Kilmeny fell sound asleep.
She kenned nae mair, nor open'd her ee,
Till wak'd by the hymns of a far coun-
    trye.

She woke on a couch of silk sae slim,
All striped wi' the bars of the rainbow's
    rim;
65 And lovely beings round were rife,
Who erst had travelled mortal life;
And aye they smiled and 'gan to speer,[6]
''What spirit has brought this mortal
    here?''

''Lang have I rang'd the world wide,''
70 A meek and reverend fere[7] replied;
''Baith night and day I have watched the
    fair,
Eident[8] a thousand years and mair.
Yes, I have watched o'er ilk degree,[9]
Wherever blooms feminitye;
75 And sinless virgin, free of stain
In mind and body, found I nane.
Never since the banquet of time
Found I a virgin in her prime,
Till late this bonnie maiden I saw,
80 As spotless as the morning snaw;
Full twenty years she has lived as free
As the spirits that sojourn in this coun-
    trye:
I have brought her away from the snares
    of men,
That sin or death she never may ken.''

85   They clasped her waist, and her hands
    sae fair,
They kissed her cheeks, and they kemmed
    her hair;
And round came many a blooming fere,
Saying, ''Bonnie Kilmeny, ye're welcome
    here!

---

[1] A poor man required
  to pray for his bene-
  factor.
[2] alone
[3] fire-place blazed with
  an uncanny gleam
[4] wood and valley
[5] brook
[6] coat; tunic
[7] band worn around
  the hair
[8] birch
[9] emerald
[10] swayed; surged

[1] pasture; park
[2] bower; cave
[3] being; mate
[4] alone
[5] covered
[6] inquire
[7] fellow; companion
[8] diligent; attentive
[9] every rank

Women are freed of the littand scorn,[1]
90 O blessed be the day Kilmeny was born!
Now shall the land of the spirits see,
Now shall it ken what a woman may be!
Many lang year, in sorrow and pain,
Many lang year through the world we've
      gane,
95 Commissioned to watch fair woman-kind,
For it's they who nurse the immortal mind.
We have watched their steps as the dawn-
      ing shone,
And deep in the greenwood walks alone;
By lily bower and silken bed,
100 The viewless tears have been o'er them
      shed;
Have soothed their ardent minds to sleep,
Or left the couch of love to weep.
We have seen, we have seen! but the time
      maun[2] come,
And the angels will weep at the day of
      doom!

105   "O would the fairest of mortal kind
Aye keep these holy truths in mind,
That kindred spirits their motions see,
Who watch their ways with anxious ee,
And grieve for the guilt of humanitye!
110 O, sweet to Heaven the maiden's prayer,
And the sigh that heaves a bosom sae fair!
And dear to Heaven the words of truth
And the praise of virtue frae beauty's
      mouth!
And dear to the viewless forms of air,
115 The mind that kythes[3] as the body fair!

      "O, bonny Kilmeny! free frae stain,
If ever you seek the world again,
That world of sin, of sorrow, and fear,
O tell of the joys that are waiting here;
120 And tell of the signs you shall shortly
      see;
Of the times that are now, and the times
      that shall be."

      They lifted Kilmeny, they led her away,
And she walked in the light of a sunless
      day;
The sky was a dome of crystal bright,
125 The fountain of vision, and fountain of
      light;
The emerant fields were of dazzling glow,
And the flowers of everlasting blow.[4]
Then deep in the stream her body they laid,
That her youth and her beauty never might
      fade;
130 And they smil'd on Heaven, when they
      saw her lie

In the stream of life that wandered by.
And she heard a song, she heard it sung,
She ken'd not where, but sae sweetly it
      rung,
It fell on the ear like a dream of the
      morn,—
135 "O blest be the day Kilmeny was born!
Now shall the land of the spirits see,
Now shall it ken what a woman may be!
The sun that shines on the world sae
      bright,
A borrowed gleid[1] frae the fountain of
      light;
140 And the moon that sleeks[2] the sky sae dun,
Like a gouden[3] bow or a beamless sun,
Shall wear away and be seen nae mair,
And the angels shall miss them travelling
      the air.
But lang, lang after, baith nicht and day,
145 When the sun and the world have fled
      away;
When the sinner has gane to his waesome
      doom,
Kilmeny shall smile in eternal bloom!''

      They bore her away, she wist not how,
For she felt not arm nor rest below;
150 But so swift they wained[4] her through the
      light,
'Twas like the motion of sound or sight;
They seemed to split the gales of air,
And yet nor gale nor breeze was there.
Unnumbered groves below them grew,
155 They came, they passed, and backward
      flew,
Like floods of blossoms gliding on,
A moment seen, in a moment gone.
Ah! never vales to mortal view
Appeared like those o'er which they flew,
160 That land to human spirits given,
The lowermost vales of the storied heaven;
From thence they can view the world be-
      low,
And heaven's blue gates with sapphires
      glow.
More glory yet unmeet to know .

165   They bore her far to a mountain green,
To see what mortal never had seen,
And they seated her high on a purple
      sward,
And bade her heed what she saw and
      heard,
And note the changes the spirits wrought,
170 For now she lived in the land of thought.
She looked, and she saw nor sun nor skies,
But a crystal dome of a thousand dyes:

---

1 blushing scorn;   3 shows itself
   scorn of guilt   4 bloom
2 must

1 ray; spark   3 golden
2 glides over   4 conveyed

She looked, and she saw nae land aright,
But an endless whirl of glory and light,
175 And radiant beings went and came,
Far swifter than wind, or the linkèd flame.
She hid her een frae the dazzling view;
She looked again, and the scene was new.

She saw a sun in a summer sky,
180 And clouds of amber sailing by;
A lovely land beneath her lay,
And that land had lakes and mountains
gray;
And that land had valleys and hoary piles,
And marled[1] seas and a thousand isles.
185 Its fields were speckled, its forests green,
And its lakes were all of the dazzling sheen,
Like magic mirrors, where shining lay
The sun, and the sky, and the cloudlet
gray;
Which heaved and trembled and gently
swung,
190 On every shore they seemed to be hung:
For there they were seen on their down-
ward plain
A thousand times and a thousand again;
In winding lake and placid firth,
Little peaceful heavens in the bosom of
earth.

195 Kilmeny sighed and seemed to grieve,
For she found her heart to that land did
cleave;
She saw the corn[2] wave on the vale;
She saw the deer run down the dale;
She saw the plaid and the broad claymore,[3]
200 And the brows that the badge of freedom
bore,—
And she thought she had seen the land
before.

She saw a lady sit on a throne,
The fairest that ever the sun shone on:
A lion licked her hand of milk,
205 And she held him in a leish of silk;
And a leifu'[4] maiden stood at her knee,
With a silver wand and melting ee;
Her sovereign shield till love stole in,
And poisoned all the fount within.

210 Then a gruff, untoward bedesman came,
And hundit[5] the lion on his dame;
And the guardian maid wi' the dauntless
ee,
She dropped a tear, and left her knee;
And she saw till the queen frae the lion
fled,

215 Till the bonniest flower o' the world lay
dead;
A coffin was set on a distant plain,
And she saw the red blood fall like rain;
Then bonnie Kilmeny's heart grew sair,
And she turned away, and could look nae
mair.

220 Then the gruff, grim carle[1] girned[2]
amain,
And they trampled him down, but he rose
again;
And he baited[3] the lion to deeds of weir,[4]
Till he lapped the blood to the kingdom
dear;
And weening[5] his head was danger preef,[6]
225 When crowned with the rose and clover
leaf,
He gowled[7] at the carle, and chased him
away,
To feed wi' the deer on the mountain gray.
He gowled at the carle, and he gecked[8] at
heaven,
But his mark was set and his arles given.[9]
230 Kilmeny a while her een withdrew;
She looked again, and the scene was new.

She saw before her fair unfurled
One-half of all the glowing world,
Where oceans rolled, and rivers ran,
235 To bound the aims of sinful man.
She saw a people, fierce and fell,
Burst frae their bounds like fiends of hell;
There lilies grew, and the eagle flew;
And she herkèd[10] on her ravening crew,
240 Till the cities and towers were wrapt in a
blaze,
And the thunder it roared o'er the lands
and the seas.
The widows wailed, and the red blood ran,
And she threatened an end to the race of
man;
She never lened,[11] nor stood in awe,
245 Till caught by the lion's deadly paw.
Oh! then the eagle swinked[12] for life,
And brainzelled[13] up a mortal strife;
But flew she north, or flew she south,
She met wi' the gowl[14] o' the lion's
mouth.

250 With a mooted[15] wing and waefu'
maen,[16]

1 variegated
2 wheat
3 A large two-edged sword.
4 loyal
5 hounded; incited

1 fellow
2 grinned
3 set on
4 dread
5 thinking
6 proof
7 howled
8 scorned; mocked
9 his limit or course
   was determined,
   and his earnest
money given,—i. e.,
he had got his
wages, his desert.
10 urged on
11 rested; ceased
12 struggled; toiled
13 stirred
14 howl
15 moulted
16 woeful mien

The eagle sought her eiry again;
But lang may she cower in her bloody nest,
And lang, lang sleek her wounded breast,
Before she sey[1] another flight,
255 To play wi' the norland lion's might.

But to sing the sights Kilmeny saw,
So far surpassing nature's law,
The singer's voice wad sink away,
And the string of his harp wad cease to play.
260 But she saw till the sorrows of man were by,
And all was love and harmony;—
Till the stars of heaven fell calmly away,
Like flakes of snaw on a winter day.

Then Kilmeny begged again to see
265 The friends she had left in her ain countrie,
To tell of the place where she had been,
And the glories that lay in the land unseen;
To warn the living maidens fair,
The loved of heaven, the spirits' care,
270 That all whose minds unmeled[2] remain
Shall bloom in beauty when time is gane.

With distant music, soft and deep,
They lulled Kilmeny sound asleep;
And when she awakened, she lay her lane,[3]
275 All happed with flowers, in the greenwood wene.
When seven long years had come and fled,
When grief was calm, and hope was dead,
Whence scarce was remembered Kilmeny's name,
Late, late in a gloamin' Kilmeny came hame.
280 And O, her beauty was fair to see,
But still and steadfast was her ee!
Such beauty bard may never declare,
For there was no pride nor passion there;
And the soft desire of maiden's een
285 In that mild face could never be seen.
Her seymar[4] was the lily flower,
And her cheek the moss-rose in the shower;
And her voice like the distant melodye,
That floats along the twilight sea.
290 But she loved to raike[5] the lanely glen,
And keep afar frae the haunts of men,
Her holy hymns unheard to sing,
To suck the flowers, and drink the spring;

But wherever her peaceful form appeared,
295 The wild beasts of the hill were cheered;
The wolf played blythely round the field,
The lordly byson lowed, and kneeled;
The dun deer wooed with manner bland,
And cowered beneath her lily hand.
300 And when at eve the woodlands rung,
When hymns of other worlds she sung
In ecstasy of sweet devotion,
O, then the glen was all in motion!
The wild beasts of the forest came,
305 Broke from their boughts and faulds[1] the tame,
And goved[2] around, charmed and amazed;
Even the dull cattle crooned and gazed,
And murmured, and looked with anxious pain
For something the mystery to explain.
310 The buzzard came with the throstle-cock;[3]
The corby left her houf[4] in the rock;
The blackbird alang wi' the eagle flew;
The hind came tripping o'er the dew;
The wolf and the kid their raike[5] began,
315 And the kid and the lamb and the leveret[6] ran;
The hawk and the hern attour them hung,[7]
And the merle and the mavis[8] forhooyed[9] their young;
And all in a peaceful ring were hurled—
It was like an eve in a sinless world!

320 When a month and a day had come and gane,
Kilmeny sought the greenwood wene;
There laid her down on the leaves sae green,
And Kilmeny on earth was never mair seen.
But O! the words that fell frae her mouth
325 Were words of wonder, and words of truth!
But all the land were in fear and dread,
For they kendna[10] whether she was living or dead.
It wasna her hame, and she couldna remain;
She left this world of sorrow and pain,
330 And returned to the land of thought again.

THE WITCH O' FIFE
1813

Hurray, hurray, the jade's away,
Like a rocket of air with her bandalet![11]

[1] essay; try	[4] robe
[2] unmixed; pure	[5] roam
[3] alone	

[1] pens and folds	[7] heron hung over them
[2] stared	
[3] male mistlethrush	[8] blackbird and thrush
[4] raven left her haunt	[9] abandoned
[5] running	[10] knew not
[6] young hare	[11] small band or ribbon

I'm up in the air on my bonnie gray
   mare,
   But I see her yet, I see her yet.
5 I'll ring the skirts o' the gowden wain[1]
   Wi' curb an' bit, wi' curb an' bit:
   An' catch the Bear by the frozen mane—
   An' I see her yet, I see her yet.

Away, away, o'er mountain an' main,
10   To sing at the morning's rosy yett;[2]
   An' water my mare at its fountain clear—
   But I see her yet, I see her yet.
   Away, thou bonnie witch o' Fife,
   On foam of the air to heave an' flit,
15 An' little reck thou of a poet's life,
   For he sees thee yet, he sees thee yet!

A BOY'S SONG
1840

Where the pools are bright and deep,
Where the gray trout lies asleep,
Up the river and o'er the lea,
That's the way for Billy and me.

5 Where the blackbird sings the latest,
Where the hawthorn blooms the sweetest,
Where the nestlings chirp and flee,
That's the way for Billy and me.

Where the mowers mow the cleanest,
10 Where the hay lies thick and greenest;
There to trace the homeward bee,
That's the way for Billy and me.

Where the hazel bank is steepest,
Where the shadow falls the deepest,
15 Where the clustering nuts fall free,
That's the way for Billy and me.

Why the boys should drive away
Little maidens from their play,
Or love to banter and fight so well,
20 That's the thing I never could tell.

But this I know, I love to play,
Through the meadow, among the hay:
Up the water and o'er the lea,
That's the way for Billy and me.

M'KIMMAN
1840

Is your war-pipe asleep, and forever,
   M'Kimman?
   Is your war-pipe asleep, and forever?
Shall the pibroch[3] that welcomed the foe
   to Ben-Aer

---

[1] golden wagon (a con-
   stellation)
[2] gate

[3] A kind of Highland
   bagpipe music.

Be hushed when we seek the red wolf in
   his lair,
5   To give back our wrongs to the giver?
To the raid and the onslaught our chieftains have gone—
Like the course of the fire-flaught[1] their
   clansmen pass'd on;
With the lance and the shield 'gainst the
   foe they have bound them,
And have taken the field with their vassals
   around them.
10   Then raise the wild slogan-cry, On
      to the foray!
      Sons of the heather-hill, pine-
      wood, and glen;
   Shout for M'Pherson, M'Leod, and
      the Moray,
      Till the Lomonds re-echo the chal-
      lenge again.

Youth of the daring heart, bright be thy
   doom
15   As the bodings which light up thy bold
      spirit now;
But the fate of M'Kimman is closing in
   gloom,
   And the breath of the gray wraith[2] hath
      pass'd o'er his brow.
Victorious in joy thou'lt return to Ben-
   Aer,
And be clasp'd to the hearts of thy best
   beloved there;
20 But M'Kimman, M'Kimman, M'Kimman
      shall never—
   O never—never—never—never!

Wilt thou shrink from the doom thou can
   shun not, M'Kimman?
   Wilt thou shrink from the doom thou
      can shun not?
If thy course must be brief, let the proud
   Saxon know
25 That the soul of M'Kimman ne'er quail'd
   when a foe
   Bared his blade in a land he had won
      not.
Where the light-footed roe leaves the wild
   breeze behind,
And the red heather-bloom gives its sweets
   to the wind—
There our broad pennon flies, and our
   keen steeds are prancing
30 'Mid the startling war-cries, and the
   bright weapons glancing!
      Then raise the wild slogan-cry, On
      to the foray!

---

[1] lightning
[2] specter (supposed to foreshadow death)

Sons of the heather-hill, pinewood, and glen;
Shout for M'Pherson, M'Leod, and
the Moray,
Till the Lomonds re-echo the
challenge again!

LOCK THE DOOR, LARISTON
1840

"Lock the door, Lariston, lion of Liddesdale;
Lock the door, Lariston, Lowther comes
on;
The Armstrongs are flying,
The widows are crying,
5 The Castletown's burning, and Oliver's
gone!

"Lock the door, Lariston—high on the
weather-gleam
See how the Saxon plumes bob on the
sky—
Yeomen[1] and carbineer,[2]
Billman[3] and halberdier,[4]
10 Fierce is the foray, and far is the cry!

"Bewcastle brandishes high his broad
scimitar;
Ridley is riding his fleet-footed gray;
Hidley and Howard there,
Wandale and Windermere;
15 Lock the door, Lariston; hold them at bay.

"Why dost thou smile, noble Elliot of
Lariston?
Why does the joy-candle gleam in thine
eye?
Thou bold Border ranger,
Beware of thy danger;
20 Thy foes are relentless, determined, and
nigh."

Jack Elliot raised up his steel bonnet and
lookit,
His hand grasp'd the sword with a nervous embrace;
"Ah, welcome, brave foemen,
On earth there are no men
25 More gallant to meet in the foray or
chase!

"Little know you of the hearts I have
hidden here;

Little know you of our moss-troopers'[1]
might—
Linhope and Sorbie true,
Sundhope and Milburn too,
30 Gentle in manner, but lions in fight!

"I have Mangerton, Ogilvie, Raeburn,
and Netherbie,
Old Sim of Whitram, and all his array;
Come all Northumberland,
Teesdale and Cumberland,
35 Here at the Breaken tower end shall the
fray!"

Scowled the broad sun o'er the links[2] of
green Liddesdale,
Red as the beacon-light tipped he the
wold;[3]
Many a bold martial eye
Mirror'd that morning sky,
40 Never more oped on his orbit of gold.

Shrill was the bugle's note, dreadful the
warrior's shout,
Lances and halberds in splinters were
borne;
Helmet and hauberk[4] then
Braved the claymore[5] in vain,
45 Buckler and armlet in shivers were shorn.

See how they wane—the proud files of the
Windermere!
Howard! ah, woe to thy hopes of the
day!
Hear the wide welkin rend,
While the Scots' shouts ascend—
50 "Elliot of Lariston, Elliot for aye!"

THE MAID OF THE SEA
1840

Come from the sea,
Maiden, to me,
Maiden of mystery, love, and pain!
Wake from thy sleep,
5 Low in the deep,
Over thy green waves sport again!
Come to this sequestered spot, love,
Death's where thou art, as where thou art
not, love;
Then come unto me,
10 Maid of the Sea,
Rise from the wild and stormy main;
Wake from thy sleep,
Calm in the deep,
Over thy green waves sport again!

---

[1] cavalrymen of the yeomanry class
[2] cavalry soldier armed with a carbine, a short
rifle
[3] soldier armed with a bill, a hook-shaped blade
attached to the end of a long staff
[4] soldier armed with a halberd, a long-handled
weapon with a sharp point and several sharp
edges

[1] freebooters infesting the border country between England and Scotland
[2] windings   [4] coat of mail
[3] hill   [5] A large two-edged sword.

15   Is not the wave
    Made for the slave,
Tyrant's chains, and stern control;
    Land for the free
    Spirit like thee?
20 Thing of delight to a minstrel's soul,
Come, with thy song of love and of sad-
    ness,
Beauty of face and rapture of madness;
    O, come unto me,
    Maid of the Sea,
25 Rise from the wild and surging main;
    Wake from thy sleep,
    Calm in the deep,
Over thy green waves sport again!

George Noel Gordon, Lord Byron *1788-1824*

LACHIN Y GAIR
1807

Away, ye gay landscapes, ye gardens of
    roses!
In you let the minions of luxury rove;
Restore me the rocks, where the snow-
    flake reposes,
Though still they are sacred to freedom
    and love:
5 Yet, Caledonia, beloved are thy mountains,
Round their white summits though ele-
    ments war;
Though cataracts foam 'stead of smooth-
    flowing fountains,
I sigh for the valley of dark Loch na
    Garr.

Ah! there my young footsteps in infancy
    wander'd;
10 My cap was the bonnet, my cloak was
    the plaid;
On chieftains long perish'd my memory
    ponder'd,
As daily I strode through the pine-
    cover'd glade;
I sought not my home till the day's dying
    glory
Gave place to the rays of the bright
    polar star;

15 For fancy was cheer'd by traditional
    story,
Disclosed by the natives of dark Loch
    na Garr.

"Shades of the dead! have I not heard
    your voices
Rise on the night-rolling breath of the
    gale?"
Surely the soul of the hero rejoices,

20 And rides on the wind, o'er his own
    Highland vale.
Round Loch na Garr while the stormy
    mist gathers,
Winter presides in his cold icy car:
Clouds there encircle the forms of my
    fathers;
They dwell in the tempests of dark
    Loch na Garr.

25 "Ill-starr'd, though brave, did no visions
    foreboding
Tell you that fate had forsaken your
    cause?"[1]
Ah! were you destined to die at Culloden,
Victory crown'd not your fall with
    applause:
Still were you happy in death's earthly
    slumber,
30 You rest with your clan in the caves of
    Braemar;
The pibroch[2] resounds, to the piper's loud
    number,
Your deeds on the echoes of dark Loch
    na Garr.

Years have roll'd on, Loch na Garr, since
    I left you,
Years must elapse ere I tread you again:
35 Nature of verdure and flow'rs has be-
    reft you,
Yet still are you dearer than Albion's
    plain.
England! thy beauties are tame and do-
    mestic
To one who has roved o'er the moun-
    tains afar:
Oh for the crags that are wild and majes-
    tic!
40 The steep frowning glories of dark
    Loch na Garr.

FAREWELL! IF EVER FONDEST PRAYER
1808   1814

Farewell! if ever fondest prayer
    For other's weal avail'd on high,
Mine will not all be lost in air,
    But waft thy name beyond the sky.
5 'Twere vain to speak, to weep, to sigh:
    Oh! more than tears of blood can tell,
When wrung from guilt's expiring eye,
    Are in that word—Farewell!—Fare-
    well!

---

[1] "I allude here to my maternal ancestors, the
Gordons, many of whom fought for the unfortunate Prince Charles, better known by
the name of Pretender."—Byron.
[2] A kind of Highland bagpipe music.

These lips are mute, these eyes are dry;
10   But in my breast and in my brain,
Awake the pangs that pass not by,
    The thought that ne'er shall sleep again.
My soul nor deigns nor dares complain,
    Though grief and passion there rebel;
15 I only know we loved in vain—
    I only feel—Farewell!—Farewell!

BRIGHT BE THE PLACE OF THY SOUL!
1808   1815

Bright be the place of thy soul!
    No lovelier spirit than thine
E'er burst from its mortal control,
    In the orbs of the blessed to shine.

5 On earth thou wert all but divine,
    As thy soul shall immortally be;
And our sorrow may cease to repine
    When we know that thy God is with
      thee.

Light be the turf of thy tomb!
10   May its verdure like emeralds be!
There should not be the shadow of gloom
    In aught that reminds us of thee.

Young flowers and an evergreen tree
    May spring from the spot of thy rest:
15 But nor cypress nor yew[1] let us see;
    For why should we mourn for the blest?

WHEN WE TWO PARTED
1808   1816

When we two parted
    In silence and tears,
Half broken-hearted
    To sever for years,
5 Pale grew thy cheek and cold,
    Colder thy kiss;
Truly that hour foretold
    Sorrow to this.

The dew of the morning
10   Sunk chill on my brow—
It felt like the warning
    Of what I feel now.
Thy vows are all broken,
    And light is thy fame:
15 I hear thy name spoken,
    And share in its shame.

They name thee before me,
    A knell to mine ear;
A shudder comes o'er me—
20   Why wert thou so dear?
They know not I knew thee,
    Who knew thee too well:—

[1] The cypress and the yew are common trees in graveyards.

Long, long shall I rue thee,
    Too deeply to tell.

25 In secret we met—
    In silence I grieve,
That thy heart could forget,
    Thy spirit deceive.
If I should meet thee
30   After long years,
How should I greet thee?—
    With silence and tears.

From ENGLISH BARDS AND SCOTCH REVIEWERS
1807-09   1809

Still must I hear?—shall hoarse Fitz-
    gerald bawl
His creaking couplets in a tavern hall,
And I not sing, lest, haply, Scotch reviews
Should dub me scribbler, and denounce my
    muse?
5 Prepare for rhyme—I'll publish, right or
    wrong:
Fools are my theme, let satire be my
    song.

Oh! nature's noblest gift—my gray
    goose-quill!
Slave of my thoughts, obedient to my
    will,
Torn from thy parent bird to form a pen,
10 That mighty instrument of little men!
The pen! foredoom'd to aid the mental
    throes
Of brains that labor, big with verse or
    prose,
Though nymphs forsake, and critics may
    deride,
The lover's solace, and the author's pride.
15 What wits, what poets dost thou daily
    raise!
How frequent is thy use, how small thy
    praise!
Condemn'd at length to be forgotten quite,
With all the pages which 'twas thine to
    write.
But thou, at least, mine own especial pen!
20 Once laid aside, but now assumed again,
Our task complete, like Hamet's shall be
    free;
Though spurn'd by others, yet beloved by
    me:
Then let us soar today; no common theme,
No eastern vision, no distemper'd dream
25 Inspires—our path, though full of thorns,
    is plain;
Smooth be the verse, and easy be the
    strain.

When Vice triumphant holds her sov'-
reign sway,
Obey'd by all who nought beside obey;
When Folly, frequent harbinger of crime,
30 Bedecks her cap with bells of every
clime;
When knaves and fools combined o'er all
prevail,
And weigh their justice in a golden scale;
E'en then the boldest start from public
sneers,
Afraid of shame, unknown to other fears,
35 More darkly sin, by satire kept in awe,
And shrink from ridicule, though not from
law.

Such is the force of wit! but not be-
long
To me the arrows of satiric song;
The royal vices of our age demand
40 A keener weapon, and a mightier hand.
Still there are follies, e'en for me to
chase,
And yield at least amusement in the race:
Laugh when I laugh, I seek no other
fame;
The cry is up, and scribblers are my game.
45 Speed, Pegasus!—ye strains of great
and small,
Ode, epic, elegy, have at you all!
I too can scrawl, and once upon a time
I pour'd along the town a flood of rhyme,
A school boy freak, unworthy praise or
blame;
50 I printed—older children do the same.
'Tis pleasant, sure, to see one's name in
print;
A book's a book, although there's nothing
in 't.
Not that a title's sounding charm can save
Or scrawl or scribbler from an equal
grave:
55 This Lambe must own, since his patrician
name
Fail'd to preserve the spurious farce from
shame.
No matter, George continues still to write,
Though now the name is veil'd from public sight.
Moved by the great example, I pursue
60 The self-same road, but make my own
review:
Not seek great Jeffrey's, yet, like him, will
be
Self-constituted judge of poesy.

A man must serve his time to every
trade
Save censure—critics all are ready made.

65 Take hackney'd jokes from Miller, got
by rote,
With just enough of learning to misquote;
A mind well skill'd to find or forge a
fault;
A turn for punning, call it Attic salt;[1]
To Jeffrey go, be silent and discreet,
70 His pay is just ten sterling pounds per
sheet:
Fear not to lie, 'twill seem a sharper hit;
Shrink not from blasphemy, 'twill pass
for wit;
Care not for feeling—pass your proper
jest,
And stand a critic, hated yet caress'd.

75 And shall we own such judgment? no
—as soon
Seek roses in December—ice in June;
Hope constancy in wind, or corn in chaff;
Believe a woman or an epitaph,
Or any other thing that's false, before
80 You trust in critics, who themselves are
sore;
Or yield one single thought to be misled
By Jeffrey's heart, or Lambe's Bœotian
head.[2]
To these young tyrants, by themselves
misplaced,
Combined usurpers on the throne of taste;
85 To these, when authors bend in humble
awe,
And hail their voice as truth, their word
as law—
While these are censors, 'twould be sin
to spare;
While such are critics, why should I forbear?
But yet, so near all modern worthies
run,
90 'Tis doubtful whom to seek, or whom to
shun;
Nor know we when to spare, or where to
strike,
Our bards and censors are so much alike.

Then should you ask me, why I venture
o'er
The path which Pope and Gifford trod
before;
95 If not yet sicken'd, you can still proceed:
Go on; my rhyme will tell you as you
read.
"But hold!" exclaims a friend, "here's
some neglect:
This—that—and t'other line seem incorrect."

[1] That is, wit.
[2] The Bœotians were proverbial for dullness.

What then? the self-same blunder Pope
   has got,
100 And careless Dryden—"Ay, but Pye has
   not:"—
Indeed!—'tis granted, faith!—but what
   care I?
Better to err with Pope, than shine with
   Pye.

   Time was, ere yet in these degenerate
   days,
Ignoble themes obtain'd mistaken praise,
105 When sense and wit with poesy allied,
No fabled graces, flourish'd side by side;
From the same fount their inspiration
   drew,
And, rear'd by taste, bloom'd fairer as
   they grew.
Then, in this happy isle, a Pope's pure
   strain
110 Sought the rapt soul to charm, nor sought
   in vain;
A polish'd nation's praise aspired to
   claim,
And raised the people's, as the poet's
   fame.
Like him great Dryden pour'd the tide of
   song,
In stream less smooth, indeed, yet doubly
   strong.
115 Then Congreve's scenes could cheer, or
   Otway's melt—
For nature then an English audience felt.
But why these names, or greater still, retrace,
When all to feebler bards resign their
   place?
Yet to such times our lingering looks are
   cast,
120 When taste and reason with those times
   are past.
Now look around, and turn each trifling
   page,
Survey the precious works that please the
   age;
This truth at least let satire's self allow,
No dearth of bards can be complain'd of
   now.
125 The loaded press beneath her labor groans,
And printers' devils shake their weary
   bones;
While Southey's epics cram the creaking
   shelves,
And Little's lyrics shine in hot-press'd
   twelves.[1]
Thus saith the Preacher: "Nought beneath the sun

130 Is new;"[1] yet still from change to change
   we run:
What varied wonders tempt us as they
   pass!
The cow-pox,[2] tractors,[3] galvanism,[4] and
   gas,[5]
In turns appear, to make the vulgar stare,
Till the swoln bubble bursts—and all is
   air!
135 Nor less new schools of Poetry arise,
Where dull pretenders grapple for the
   prize:
O'er taste awhile these pseudo-bards pre-
   vail;
Each country book-club bows the knee to
   Baal,
And, hurling lawful genius from the
   throne,
140 Erects a shrine and idol of its own;
Some leaden calf—but whom it matters
   not,
From soaring Southey down to grovelling
   Stott.

   Behold! in various throngs the scrib-
   bling crew,
For notice eager, pass in long review:
145 Each spurs his jaded Pegasus apace,
And rhyme and blank maintain an equal
   race;
Sonnets on sonnets crowd, and ode on ode;
And tales of terror[6] jostle on the road;
Immeasurable measures move along;[7]
150 For simpering folly loves a varied song,
To strange mysterious dulness still the
   friend,
Admires the strain she cannot comprehend.
Thus Lays of Minstrels—may they be the
   last![8]—
On half-strung harps whine mournful to
   the blast.
155 While mountain spirits prate to river
   sprites,
That dames may listen to the sound at
   nights;

---

[1] A reference to the size of the volume—a duo-
   decimo—and to the process of imparting
   smoothness to the printed sheets by passing
   them between hot rollers.

[1] *Ecclesiastes*, 1:9.
[2] A disease of cows which, when communicated
   to the human system by vaccination, protects from the small-pox.
[3] Metal rods used in treating rheumatism, etc.
[4] The use of electric currents for curative purposes.
[5] Laughing gas. All of these "wonders" were
   quack panaceas of the early 19th century.
[6] A reference to Lewis's *Tales of Terror* (1799)
   and *Tales of Wonder* (1800).
[7] A thrust at the new anapestic meters, introduced by Cowper, Coleridge, Southey, Moore,
   and others.
[8] A reference to Scott's *The Lay of the Last
   Minstrel* (1805), which grew out of a suggestion for a ballad on the Border legend of
   Gilpin Horner.

And goblin brats, of Gilpin Horner's
    brood,
Decoy young border-nobles through the
    wood,
And skip at every step, Lord knows how
    high,
160 And frighten foolish babes, the Lord
    knows why;
While high-born ladies in their magic cell,
Forbidding knights to read who cannot
    spell,
Despatch a courier to a wizard's grave,
And fight with honest men to shield a
    knave.

165   Next view in state, proud prancing on
    his roan,
The golden-crested haughty Marmion,
Now forging scrolls, now foremost in the
    fight,
Not quite a felon, yet but half a knight,
The gibbet or the field prepare to grace;
170 A mighty mixture of the great and base.
And think'st thou, Scott! by vain conceit
    perchance,
On public taste to foist thy stale romance,
Though Murray with his Miller may com-
    bine
To yield thy muse just half-a-crown per
    line?
175 No! when the sons of song descend to
    trade,
Their bays[1] are sear, their former laurels
    fade.
Let such forego the poet's sacred name,
Who rack their brains for lucre, not for
    fame:
Still for stern Mammon may they toil in
    vain!
180 And sadly gaze on gold they cannot gain!
Such be their meed, such still the just
    reward
Of prostituted muse and hireling bard!
For this we spurn Apollo's venal son,[2]
And bid a long "good night to Marmion."[3]

185   These are the themes that claim our
    plaudits now;
These are the bards to whom the muse
    must bow;
While Milton, Dryden, Pope, alike forgot,
Resign their hallow'd bays to Walter
    Scott.

    The time has been, when yet the muse
    was young,
190 When Homer swept the lyre, and Maro
    sung,

---

[1] Wreaths of honor made from leaves of the
    bay-tree, a kind of laurel.
[2] Scott, who received £1,000 for *Marmion*.
[3] *Marmion*, 6, 869.

An epic scarce ten centuries could claim,
While awe-struck nations hail'd the magic
    name:
The work of each immortal bard appears
The single wonder of a thousand years.
195 Empires have moulder'd from the face of
    earth,
Tongues have expired with those who gave
    them birth,
Without the glory such a strain can give,
As even in ruin bids the language live.
Not so with us, though minor bards, con-
    tent,
200 On one great work a life of labor spent:
With eagle pinion soaring to the skies,
Behold the ballad-monger Southey rise!
To him let Camoëns, Milton, Tasso yield,
Whose annual strains, like armies, take the
    field.
205 First in the ranks see Joan of Arc ad-
    vance,[1]
The scourge of England and the boast of
    France!
Though burnt by wicked Bedford for a
    witch,
Behold her statue placed in glory's niche;
Her fetters burst, and just released from
    prison,
210 A virgin phœnix from her ashes risen.
Next see tremendous Thalaba come on,
Arabia's monstrous, wild, and wondrous
    son;
Domdaniel's dread destroyer, who o'er-
    threw
More mad magicians than the world e'er
    knew.
215 Immortal hero! all thy foes o'ercome,
Forever reign—the rival of Tom Thumb!
Since startled metre fled before thy face,
Well wert thou doom'd the last of all thy
    race!
Well might triumphant genii bear thee
    hence,
220 Illustrious conqueror of common sense!
Now, last and greatest, Madoc spreads his
    sails,
Cacique[2] in Mexico, and prince in Wales;
Tells us strange tales, as other travellers
    do,
More old than Mandeville's, and not so
    true.
225 Oh! Southey! Southey! cease thy varied
    song!
A bard may chant too often and too long:
As thou art strong in verse, in mercy,
    spare!

---

[1] Southey's *Joan of Arc*, *Thalaba*, and *Madoc*
    appeared in 1796, 1801, and 1805, respec-
    tively.
[2] chief; petty king

A fourth, alas! were more than we could 265
    bear.
But if, in spite of all the world can say,
230 Thou still wilt verseward plod thy weary
    way;[1]
If still in Berkley ballads most uncivil,
Thou wilt devote old women to the devil,[2]
The babe unborn thy dread intent may
    rue:
"God help thee,"[3] Southey, and thy 270
    readers too.

235   Next comes the dull disciple of thy
    school,
That mild apostate from poetic rule,
The simple Wordsworth, framer of a lay
As soft as evening in his favorite May,
Who warns his friend "to shake off toil 275
    and trouble,
240 And quit his books for fear of growing
    double;"[4]
Who, both by precept and example, shows
That prose is verse, and verse is merely
    prose;
Convincing all, by demonstration plain,
Poetic souls delight in prose insane;
245 And Christmas stories tortured into rhyme 280
Contain the essence of the true sublime.
Thus, when he tells the tale of Betty Foy,[5]
The idiot mother of "an idiot boy;"
A moon-struck, silly lad, who lost his way,
250 And, like his bard, confounded night with
    day;
So close on each pathetic part he dwells,
And each adventure so sublimely tells,
That all who view the "idiot in his glory"
Conceive the bard the hero of the story.

255   Shall gentle Coleridge pass unnoticed
    here,
To turgid ode and tumid stanza dear?
Though themes of innocence amuse him
    best,
Yet still obscurity's a welcome guest.
If Inspiration should her aid refuse
260 To him who takes a pixy for a muse,[6]
Yet none in lofty numbers can surpass
The bard who soars to elegize an ass.[7]
So well the subject suits his noble mind,
He brays the laureat of the long-ear'd
    kind.

Oh! wonder-working Lewis! monk, or
    bard,
Who fain wouldst make Parnassus a
    churchyard!
Lo! wreaths of yew,[1] not laurel, bind thy
    brow,
Thy muse a sprite, Apollo's sexton thou!
Whether on ancient tombs thou tak'st thy
    stand,
By gibb'ring spectres hail'd, thy kindred
    band;
Or tracest chaste descriptions on thy page,
To please the females of our modest age;[2]
All hail, M. P.![3] from whose infernal
    brain
Thin-sheeted phantoms glide, a grisly
    train;
At whose command "grim women" throng
    in crowds,
And kings of fire, of water, and of clouds,
With "small gray men," "wild ya-
    gers,"[4] and what not,
To crown with honor thee and Walter
    Scott;[5]
Again all hail! if tales like thine may
    please,
St. Luke alone can vanquish the disease;[6]
Even Satan's self with thee might dread
    to dwell,
And in thy skull discern a deeper hell.

  Who in soft guise, surrounded by a
    choir
Of virgins melting, not to Vesta's fire,
285 With sparkling eyes, and cheek by pas-
    sion flush'd,
Strikes his wild lyre, whilst listening
    dames are hush'd?
'Tis Little! young Catullus of his day,
As sweet, but as immoral, in his lay!
Grieved to condemn, the muse must still
    be just,
290 Nor spare melodious advocates of lust.
Pure is the flame which o'er her altar
    burns;
From grosser incense with disgust she
    turns:
Yet kind to youth, this expiation o'er,
She bids thee "mend thy line and sin no
    more."

---

[1] See Gray's *Elegy Written in a Country Church-
    yard*, 3 (p. 59).
[2] In Southey's ballad *The Old Woman of Berke-
    ley*, the old woman is carried away by the
    devil.
[3] Quoted from the last line of a poem written by
    Gifford as a parody on Southey's dactylics
    and published in *Poetry of the Anti-Jacobin*,
    32 (1854 ed.). Southey had used the phrase
    in his *The Soldier's Wife*, 3.
[4] *The Tables Turned*, 1-4 (p. 258).
[5] In *The Idiot Boy*.
[6] A reference to Coleridge's *Songs of the Pixies*
    (Devonshire fairies).
[7] A reference to Coleridge's *To a Young Ass* (p.
    354).

[1] The yew is an emblem of mourning; it is a
    common tree in graveyards.
[2] Lewis's *The Monk* was condemned for its in-
    decency.
[3] Lewis was a Member of Parliament from 1796
    to 1802.
[4] huntsmen
[5] Scott contributed *The Fire King*, *Glenfinlas*,
    The Wild Huntsman, and other poems to
    Lewis's *Tales of Wonder*. Southey contrib-
    uted *The Old Woman of Berkeley* and other
    poems. H. Bunbury contributed *The Little
    Gray Man*.
[6] St. Luke was traditionally regarded as a phy-
    sician.

295 For thee, translator of the tinsel song,
To whom such glittering ornaments be-
    long,
Hibernian Strangford! with thine eyes of
    blue,
And boasted locks of red or auburn hue,
Whose plaintive strain each love-sick miss
    admires,
300 And o'er harmonious fustian half expires,
Learn, if thou canst, to yield thine au-
    thor's sense,
Nor vend thy sonnets on a false pretence.
Think'st thou to gain thy verse a higher
    place,
By dressing Camoëns in a suit of lace?
305 Mend, Strangford! mend thy morals and
    thy taste;
Be warm, but pure; be amorous, but be
    chaste;
Cease to deceive; thy pilfer'd harp re-
    store,
Nor teach the Lusian bard[1] to copy Moore.

Behold—ye tarts![2]—one moment spare
    the text—
310 Hayley's last work, and worst—until his
    next;
Whether he spin poor couplets into plays,
Or damn the dead with purgatorial praise,
His style in youth or age is still the same,
Forever feeble and forever tame.
315 Triumphant first see *Temper's Triumphs*
    shine!
At least I'm sure they triumph'd over
    mine.
Of *Music's Triumphs,* all who read may
    swear
That luckless music never triumph'd there.

Moravians, rise! bestow some meet re-
    ward
320 On dull devotion—Lo! the Sabbath bard,
Sepulchral Grahame, pours his notes sub-
    lime
In mangled prose, nor e'en aspires to
    rhyme;
Breaks into blank the Gospel of St. Luke,
And boldly pilfers from the Pentateuch;
325 And, undisturb'd by conscientious qualms,
Perverts the Prophets, and purloins the
    Psalms.

Hail, Sympathy! thy soft idea brings
A thousand visions of a thousand things,

And shows, still whimpering through
    three-score of years,
330 The maudlin prince of mournful son-
    neteers.
And art thou not their prince, harmonious
    Bowles!
Thou first, great oracle of tender souls?
Whether thou sing'st with equal ease, and
    grief,
The fall of empires, or a yellow leaf;
335 Whether thy muse most lamentably tells
What merry sounds proceed from Oxford
    bells,
Or, still in bells delighting, finds a friend
In every chime that jingled from Ostend;[1]
Ah! how much juster were thy muse's
    hap,
340 If to thy bells thou wouldst but add a
    cap![2]
Delightful Bowles! still blessing and still
    blest,
All love thy strain, but children like it
    best.
'Tis thine, with gentle Little's moral song,
To soothe the mania of the amorous
    throng!
345 With thee our nursery damsels shed their
    tears,
Ere miss as yet completes her infant
    years:
But in her teens thy whining powers are
    vain;
She quits poor Bowles for Little's purer
    strain.
Now to soft themes thou scornest to con-
    fine
350 The lofty numbers of a harp like thine;
"Awake a louder and a loftier strain,"[3]
Such as none heard before, or will again!
Where all Discoveries jumbled from the
    flood,
Since first the leaky ark reposed in mud,
355 By more or less, are sung in every book,
From Captain Noah down to Captain
    Cook.
Nor this alone; but, pausing on the road,
The bard sighs forth a gentle episode;[4]
And gravely tells—attend, each beauteous
    miss!—
360 When first Madeira trembled to a kiss.
Bowles! in thy memory let this precept
    dwell,

---

[1] Camoëns, whose *Lusiad* is the national epic of Portugal.
[2] The pastry cooks used the pages of unsold books to line tins for cooking. See Rostand's *Cyrano de Bergerac*, II, 1, 23 ff.; also Byron's *The Blues*, 1, 14-21, and Pope's *The Dunciad*, 1, 155-56.

[1] Among the poems of Bowles are *The Fall of Empires, To a Withered Leaf, At Oxford,* and *The Bells; Ostend* (p. 164).
[2] A cap and bells constituted the head-dress worn by court fools and professional jesters.
[3] Bowles, *The Spirit of Discovery by Sea,* 1.
[4] A reference to the story of two lovers in *The Spirit of Discovery by Sea,* whose kiss made the woods of Madeira tremble.

Stick to thy sonnets, man!—at least they
   sell.
But if some new-born whim, or larger
   bribe,
Prompt thy crude brain, and claim thee
   for a scribe;
365 If chance some bard, though once by
   dunces fear'd,
Now, prone in dust, can only be revered;
If Pope, whose fame and genius, from the
   first,
Have foil'd the best of critics, needs the
   worst,
Do thou essay: each fault, each failing
   scan;
370 The first of poets was, alas! but man.
Rake from each ancient dunghill every
   pearl,
Consult Lord Fanny, and confide in Curll;
Let all the scandals of a former age
Perch on thy pen, and flutter o'er thy
   page;
375 Affect a candor which thou canst not feel,
Clothe envy in the garb of honest zeal;
Write, as if St. John's soul could still
   inspire,
And do from hate what Mallet did for
   hire.[1]
Oh! hadst thou lived in that congenial
   time,
380 To rave with Dennis, and with Ralph to
   rhyme;
Throng'd with the rest around his living
   head,
Not raised thy hoof against the lion dead;
A meet reward had crown'd thy glorious
   gains,
And link'd thee to *The Dunciad* for thy
   pains.

385   Another epic! Who inflicts again
More books of blank upon the sons of
   men?
Bœotian Cottle, rich Bristowa's boast,
Imports old stories from the Cambrian
   coast.
And sends his goods to market—all alive!
390 Lines forty thousand, cantos twenty-five?
Fresh fish from Hippocrene! who'll buy,
   who'll buy?
The precious bargain's cheap—in faith,
   not I.
Your turtle-feeder's verse must needs be
   flat,

Though Bristol bloat him with the ver-
   dant fat;
395 If Commerce fills the purse, she clogs the
   brain,
And Amos Cottle strikes the lyre in vain.
In him an author's luckless lot behold,
Condemn'd to make the books which once
   he sold.
Oh, Amos Cottle!—Phœbus! what a name
400 To fill the speaking trump of future
   fame!
Oh, Amos Cottle! for a moment think
What meagre profits spring from pen
   and ink!
When thus devoted to poetic dreams,
Who will peruse thy prostituted reams?
405 Oh! pen perverted! paper misapplied!—
Had Cottle still adorn'd the counter's
   side,
Bent o'er the desk, or, born to useful
   toils,
Been taught to make the paper which he
   soils,
Plough'd, delved, or plied the oar with
   lusty limb,
410 He had not sung of Wales, nor I of him.

   As Sīsyphus against the infernal steep
Rolls the huge rock whose motions ne'er
   may sleep,
So up thy hill, ambrosial Richmond,
   heaves
Dull Maurice all his granite weight of
   leaves:
415 Smooth, solid monuments of mental pain!
The petrifactions of a plodding brain,
That, ere they reach the top, fall lumbering back again.

   With broken lyre and cheek serenely
   pale,
Lo! sad Alcæus wanders down the vale;
420 Though fair they rose, and might have
   bloom'd at last,
His hopes have perish'd by the northern
   blast:
Nipp'd in the bud by Caledonian gales,
His blossoms wither as the blast prevails!
O'er his lost works let *classic* Sheffield
   weep;
425 May no rude hand disturb their early
   sleep!

   Yet say! why should the bard at once
   resign
His claim to favor from the sacred nine?[1]
Forever startled by the mingled howl
Of northern wolves, that still in darkness
   prowl;

[1] The Muses.

---

[1] Mallet was hired by Henry St. John, Lord Bolingbroke, to defame Pope, after his death, because he had kept some copies of *The Patriot King*, a work by Bolingbroke, which Bolingbroke himself had ordered destroyed.

430 A coward brood, which mangle as they
    prey,
By hellish instinct, all that cross their
    way;
Aged or young, the living or the dead,
No mercy find—these harpies must be fed.
Why do the injured unresisting yield
435 The calm possession of their native field?
Why tamely thus before their fangs re-
    treat,
Nor hunt the blood-hounds back to Ar-
    thur's Seat?

    Health to immortal Jeffrey! once, in
    name,
England could boast a judge almost the
    same;[1]
440 In soul so like, so merciful, yet just,
Some think that Satan has resign'd his
    trust,
And given the spirit to the world again,
To sentence letters, as he sentenced men.
With hand less mighty, but with heart
    as black,
445 With voice as willing to decree the rack;
Bred in the courts betimes, though all that
    law
As yet hath taught him is to find a flaw;
Since well instructed in the patriot school
To rail at party, though a party tool;
450 Who knows, if chance his patrons should
    restore
Back to the sway they forfeited before,
His scribbling toils some recompense may
    meet,
And raise this Daniel to the judgment-
    seat?[2]
Let Jeffreys' shade indulge the pious hope,
455 And greeting thus, present him with a
    rope:
"Heir to my virtues! man of equal mind!
Skill'd to condemn as to traduce man-
    kind,
This cord receive, for thee reserved with
    care,
To wield in judgment, and at length to
    wear."

460   Health to great Jeffrey! Heaven pre-
    serve his life,
To flourish on the fertile shores of Fife,
And guard it sacred in its future wars,
Since authors sometimes seek the field of
    Mars!
Can none remember that eventful day

465 That ever-glorious, almost fatal fray,
When Little's leadless pistol met his eye,[1]
And Bow-Street myrmidons[2] stood laugh-
    ing by?
Oh, day disastrous! on her firm-set rock,
Dunedin's castle felt a secret shock;
470 Dark roll'd the sympathetic waves of
    Forth,
Low groan'd the startled whirlwinds of
    the north;
Tweed ruffled half his waves to form a
    tear,
The other half pursued its calm career;
Arthur's steep summit nodded to its base,
475 The surly Tolbooth scarcely kept her place.
The Tolbooth felt—for marble sometimes
    can,
On such occasions, feel as much as man—
The Tolbooth felt defrauded of his
    charms,
If Jeffrey died, except within her arms:
480 Nay last, not least, on that portentous
    morn,
The sixteenth story, where himself was
    born,
His patrimonial garret, fell to ground,
And pale Edina shudder'd at the sound:
Strew'd were the streets around with milk-
    white reams,
485 Flow'd all the Canongate with inky
    streams;
This of his candor seem'd the sable dew,
That of his valor show'd the bloodless
    hue;
And all with justice deem'd the two com-
    bined
The mingled emblems of his mighty mind.
490 But Caledonia's goddess hover'd o'er
The field, and saved him from the wrath
    of Moore;
From either pistol snatch'd the vengeful
    lead,
And straight restored it to her favorite's
    head;
That head, with greater than magnetic
    power,
495 Caught it, as Danaë caught the golden
    shower,
And, though the thickening dross will
    scarce refine,
Augments its ore, and is itself a mine.
"My son," she cried, "ne'er thirst for
    gore again,
Resign the pistol and resume the pen;

---

[1] The infamous judge, George Jeffreys, of the "Bloody Assizes," in 1685.
[2] See *The Merchant of Venice*, IV, 1, 223, and *The History of Susanna*, 45 ff., in the Apocrypha of the Bible.

[1] Jeffrey and Moore met in 1806 to engage in a duel, but were prevented by the magistrates. It was Jeffrey's pistol that was found to be empty.
[2] officers from the Bow street police court (London)

500 O'er politics and poesy preside,
Boast of thy country, and Britannia's
guide!
For long as Albion's heedless sons submit,
Or Scottish taste decides on English wit,
So long shall last thine unmolested reign,
505 Nor any dare to take thy name in vain.
Behold, a chosen band shall aid thy plan,
And own thee chieftain of the critic clan.
First in the oat-fed phalanx shall be seen
The travell'd thane, Athenian Aberdeen.
510 Herbert shall wield Thor's hammer, and
sometimes,
In gratitude, thou'lt praise his rugged
rhymes.
Smug Sidney too thy bitter page shall
seek,
And classic Hallam, much renown'd for
Greek;
Scott may perchance his name and in-
fluence lend,
515 And paltry Pillans shall traduce his
friend;
While gay Thalia's luckless votary,
Lambe,
Damn'd like the devil, devil-like will
damn.
Known be thy name, unbounded be thy
sway!
Thy Holland's banquets shall each toil
repay;
520 While grateful Britain yields the praise
she owes
To Holland's hirelings and to learning's
foes.
Yet mark one caution ere thy next *Review*
Spread its light wings of saffron and of
blue,[1]
Beware lest blundering Brougham destroy
the sale,
525 Turn beef to bannocks,[2] cauliflowers to
kail.''[3]
Thus having said, the kilted goddess
kiss'd
Her son, and vanish'd in a Scottish mist.

Then prosper, Jeffrey! pertest of the
train
Whom Scotland pampers with her fiery
grain!
530 Whatever blessing wait a genuine Scot,
In double portion swells thy glorious lot;
For thee Edina culls her evening sweets,
And showers their odors on thy candid
sheets,

[1] The colors in which the volumes of *The Edinburgh Review* were bound.
[2] A kind of unleavened oatmeal cake.
[3] A kind of cabbage. Bannocks and kail were
common articles of Scotch diet.

Whose hue and fragrance to thy work
adhere—
535 This scents its pages, and that gilds its
rear.
Lo! blushing Itch, coy nymph, enamor'd
grown,
Forsakes the rest, and cleaves to thee
alone;
And, too unjust to other Pictish men,
Enjoys thy person, and inspires thy pen!

·   ·   ·   ·   ·

To the famed throng now paid the
tribute due,
800 Neglected genius! let me turn to you.
Come forth, oh Campbell! give thy talents
scope;
Who dares aspire if thou must cease to
hope?[1]
And thou, melodious Rogers! rise at last,
Recall the pleasing memory of the past;[2]
805 Arise! let blest remembrance still inspire,
And strike to wonted tones thy hallow'd
lyre;
Restore Apollo to his vacant throne,
Assert thy country's honor and thine own.
What! must deserted Poesy still weep
810 Where her last hopes with pious Cowper
sleep?
Unless, perchance, from his cold bier she
turns,
To deck the turf that wraps her minstrel,
Burns!
No! though contempt hath mark'd the
spurious brood,
The race who rhyme from folly, or for
food,
815 Yet still some genuine sons 'tis hers to
boast,
Who, least affecting, still affect the most:
Feel as they write, and write but as they
feel—
Bear witness Gifford, Sotheby, Macneil.

"Why slumbers Gifford?" once was
ask'd in vain;
820 Why slumbers Gifford? let us ask again.[3]
Are there no follies for his pen to purge?
Are there no fools whose backs demand
the scourge?
Are there no sins for satire's bard to
greet?
Stalks not gigantic Vice in every street?
825 Shall peers or princes tread pollution's
path,

[1] A reference to Campbell's *The Pleasures of
Hope* (p. 443).
[2] A reference to Rogers's *The Pleasures of Memory* (p. 233).
[3] Gifford had announced that *The Baviad*
(1794) and *The Mœviad* (1795) would not be
his last original works.

And 'scape alike the law's and muse's
    wrath?
Nor blaze with guilty glare through future
    time,
Eternal beacons of consummate crime?
Arouse thee, Gifford! be thy promise
    claim'd,
830 Make bad men better, or at least ashamed.

    Unhappy White! while life was in its
      spring,
And thy young muse just waved her joy-
    ous wing,
The spoiler swept that soaring lyre away,
Which else had sounded an immortal lay.
835 Oh! what a noble heart was here undone,[1]
When Science' self destroy'd her favorite
    son!
Yes, she too much indulged thy fond pur-
    suit,
She sow'd the seeds, but death has reap'd
    the fruit.
'Twas thine own genius gave the final
    blow,
840 And help'd to plant the wound that laid
    thee low:
So the struck eagle, stretch'd upon the
    plain,
No more through rolling clouds to soar
    again,
View'd his own feather on the fatal
    dart,
And wing'd the shaft that quiver'd in his
    heart;
845 Keen were his pangs, but keener far to
    feel
He nursed the pinion which impell'd the
    steel;
While the same plumage that had warm'd
    his nest
Drank the last life-drop of his bleeding
    breast.

    There be who say, in these enlighten'd
      days,
850 That splendid lies are all the poet's
    praise;
That strain'd invention, ever on the wing,
Alone impels the modern bard to sing:
'Tis true, that all who rhyme—nay, all
    who write,
Shrink from that fatal word to genius—
    trite;
855 Yet Truth sometimes will lend her noblest
    fires,
And decorate the verse herself inspires:
This fact in Virtue's name let Crabbe
    attest;
[1] See *Hamlet*, III, 1. 158.

Though nature's sternest painter, yet the
    best.

  . . . . .

    Yet let them[1] not to vulgar Wordsworth
    stoop,
The meanest object of the lowly group,
905 Whose verse, of all but childish prattle
    void,
Seems blessed harmony to Lamb and
    Lloyd:
Let them—but hold, my muse, nor dare
    to teach
A strain far, far beyond thy humble
    reach:
The native genius with their being given
910 Will point the path, and peal their notes
    to heaven.

    And thou, too, Scott! resign to min-
      strels rude
The wilder slogan of a Border feud:
Let others spin their meagre lines for hire;
Enough for genius, if itself inspire!
915 Let Southey sing, although his teeming
    muse,
Prolific every spring, be too profuse;
Let simple Wordsworth chime his childish
    verse,
And brother Coleridge lull the babe at
    nurse;[2]
Let spectre-mongering Lewis aim, at most,
920 To rouse the galleries, or to raise a ghost;
Let Moore still sigh; let Strangford steal
    from Moore,
And swear that Camoëns sang such notes
    of yore;
Let Hayley hobble on, Montgomery rave,
And godly Grahame chant a stupid stave:
925 Let sonneteering Bowles his strains refine,
And whine and whimper to the fourteenth
    line;
Let Stott, Carlisle, Matilda, and the rest
Of Grub Street, and of Grosvenor Place
    the best,
Scrawl on, till death release us from the
    strain,
930 Or Common Sense assert her rights again.
But thou, with powers that mock the aid
    of praise,
Shouldst leave to humbler bards ignoble
    lays:
Thy country's voice, the voice of all the
    nine,

[1] A band of mediocre English poets who translated and published, in 1806, *Translations
chiefly from the Greek Anthology, with Tales
and Miscellaneous Poems.*
[2] See Coleridge's *Frost at Midnight*, 10, 44 (p.
376), and *Sonnet to a Friend* (p. 357).

Demand a hallow'd harp—that harp is
   thine.
935 Say! will not Caledonia's annals yield
The glorious record of some nobler field,
Than the wild foray of a plundering clan,
Whose proudest deeds disgrace the name
   of man?
Or Marmion's acts of darkness, fitter food
940 For Sherwood's outlaw tales of Robin
   Hood?
Scotland! still proudly claim thy native
   bard,
And be thy praise his first, his best re-
   ward!
Yet not with thee alone his name should
   live,
But own the vast renown a world can give:
945 Be known, perchance, when Albion is no
   more,
And tell the tale of what she was before;
To future times her faded fame recall,
And save her glory, though his country
   fall.

. . . .

For me, who, thus unask'd, have dared
   to tell
My country what her sons should know
   too well,
Zeal for her honor bade me here engage
The host of idiots that infest her age;
995 No just applause her honor'd name shall
   lose,
As first in freedom, dearest to the muse.
Oh! would thy bards but emulate thy
   fame,
And rise more worthy, Albion, of thy
   name!
What Athens was in science, Rome in
   power,
1000 What Tyre appear'd in her meridian hour,
'Tis thine at once, fair Albion! to have
   been—
Earth's chief dictatress, ocean's lovely
   queen:
But Rome decay'd, and Athens strew'd
   the plain,
And Tyre's proud piers lie shatter'd in
   the main;
1005 Like these, thy strength may sink, in ruin
   hurl'd,
And Britain fall, the bulwark of the
   world.
But let me cease, and dread Cassandra's
   fate,
With warning ever scoff'd at, till too late;
To themes less lofty still my lay confine,
1010 And urge thy bards to gain a name like
   thine.

Then, hapless Britain! be thy rulers
   blest,
The senate's oracles, the people's jest!
Still hear thy motley orators dispense
The flowers of rhetoric, though not of
   sense,
1015 While Canning's colleagues hate him for
   his wit,
And old dame Portland fills the place of
   Pitt.

Yet once again, adieu! ere this the sail
That wafts me hence is shivering in the
   gale;
And Afric's coast, and Calpe's adverse
   height,
1020 And Stamboul's minarets[1] must greet my
   sight:
Thence shall I stray through beauty's native clime,
Where Kaff is clad in rocks, and crown'd
   with snows sublime.
But should I back return, no tempting
   press
Shall drag my journal from the desk's
   recess;
1025 Let coxcombs, printing as they come from
   far,
Snatch his own wreath of ridicule from
   Carr;
Let Aberdeen and Elgin still pursue
The shade of fame through regions of
   virtù;
Waste useless thousands on their Phidian
   freaks,
1030 Misshapen monuments and maim'd an-
   tiques;
And make their grand saloons a general
   mart
For all the mutilated blocks of art:
Or Dardan[2] tours let dilettanti tell,
I leave topography to rapid Gell;
1035 And, quite content, no more shall interpose
To stun the public ear—at least with
   prose.

Thus far I've held my undisturb'd
   career,
Prepared for rancor, steel'd 'gainst selfish fear:
This thing of rhyme I ne'er disdain'd to
   own—
1040 Though not obtrusive, yet not quite unknown:[3]

[1] towers attached to mosques, and surrounded
   by projecting balconies
[2] Trojan
[3] Byron's *Hours of Idleness* was published
   anonymously, but the author was known.

My voice was heard again, though not so
 loud,
My page, though nameless, never disavow'd;
And now at once I tear the veil away:[1]—
Cheer on the pack! the quarry[2] stands at
 bay,
1045 Unscared by all the din of Melbourne
 House,
By Lambe's resentment, or by Holland's
 spouse,
By Jeffrey's harmless pistol, Hallam's
 rage,
Edina's brawny sons and brimstone page.
Our men in buckram[3] shall have blows
 enough,
1050 And feel they too are "penetrable
 stuff:"[4]
And though I hope not hence unscathed
 to go,[5]
Who conquers me shall find a stubborn
 foe.
The time hath been, when no harsh sound
 would fall
From lips that now may seem imbued
 with gall;
1055 Nor fools nor follies tempt me to despise
The meanest thing that crawl'd beneath
 my eyes:
But now, so callous grown, so changed
 since youth,
I've learned to think, and sternly speak
 the truth;
Learn'd to deride the critic's starch decree,
1060 And break him on the wheel he meant
 for me;
To spurn the rod a scribbler bids me kiss,
Nor care if courts and crowds applaud or
 hiss:
Nay more, though all my rival rhyme-
 sters frown,
I too can hunt a poetaster down;
1065 And, arm'd in proof, the gauntlet cast
 at once
To Scotch marauder, and to southern
 dunce.
Thus much I've dared; if my incondite[6]
 lay
Hath wrong'd these righteous times, let
 others say;

This, let the world, which knows not how
 to spare,
1070 Yet rarely blames unjustly, now declare.

MAID OF ATHENS,[1] ERE WE PART
1810   1812

Ζώη μοῦ, σᾶς ἀγαπῶ.[2]

Maid of Athens, ere we part,
Give, oh give me back my heart!
Or, since that has left my breast,
Keep it now, and take the rest!
5 Hear my vow before I go,
Ζώη μοῦ, σᾶς ἀγαπῶ.

By those tresses unconfined,
Woo'd by each Ægean wind;
By those lids whose jetty fringe
10 Kiss thy soft cheeks' blooming tinge;
By those wild eyes like the roe,
Ζώη μοῦ, σᾶς ἀγαπῶ.

By that lip I long to taste;
By that zone-encircled[3] waist;
15 By all the token-flowers that tell
What words can never speak so well;
By love's alternate joy and woe,
Ζώη μοῦ, σᾶς ἀγαπῶ.

Maid of Athens, I am gone:
20 Think of me, sweet! when alone.
Though I fly to Istambol,
Athens holds my heart and soul:
Can I cease to love thee? No!
Ζώη μοῦ, σᾶς ἀγαπῶ.

THE BRIDE OF ABYDOS
A TURKISH TALE
1813   1813

Had we never loved sae kindly,
Had we never loved sae blindly,
Never met or never parted,
We had ne'er been broken-hearted.
    —Burns.[4]

Canto the First

Know ye the land where the cypress and
 myrtle[5]
Are emblems of deeds that are done in
 their clime?
Where the rage of the vulture, the love of
 the turtle,[6]
 Now melt into sorrow, now madden to
 crime!
5 Know ye the land of the cedar and vine,

[1] The first edition of *English Bards and Scotch Reviewers* was published anonymously. Lines 1037 ff. were added in the second edition, published in October, 1809.

[2] game; prey

[3] An allusion to the volumes of *The Edinburgh Review,* bound in buckram. See 1 *Henry IV,* I, 2, 180 ff., and II, 4, 126 ff.

[4] *Hamlet,* III, 4, 36.

[5] See *Marmion,* 6, 434.

[6] ill-composed; crude

[1] Supposed to be Theresa Macri, who later became the wife of an English-man named Black.

[2] my life, I love you

[3] girdle-encircled.

[4] *Ae Fond Kiss,* 13-16 (p. 225).

[5] The cypress is an emblem of mourning; the myrtle, of love.

[6] turtledove

Where the flowers ever blossom, the beams
    ever shine;
Where the light wings of Zephyr, op-
    press'd with perfume,
Wax faint o'er the gardens of Gúl[1] in
    her bloom;
Where the citron and olive are fairest of
    fruit,
10 And the voice of the nightingale never
    is mute:
Where the tints of the earth, and the hues
    of the sky,
In color though varied, in beauty may vie,
And the purple of ocean is deepest in dye;
Where the virgins are soft as the roses
    they twine,
15 And all, save the spirit of man, is divine?
'Tis the clime of the East; 'tis the land
    of the Sun—
Can he smile on such deeds as his chil-
    dren have done?
Oh! wild as the accents of lovers' farewell
Are the hearts which they bear, and the
    tales which they tell.

20 Begirt with many a gallant slave,
Apparell'd as becomes the brave,
Awaiting each his lord's behest
To guide his steps, or guard his rest,
Old Giaffir sate in his Divan:[2]
25   Deep thought was in his aged eye;
And though the face of Mussulman
    Not oft betrays to standers by
The mind within, well skill'd to hide
All but unconquerable pride,
30 His pensive cheek and pondering brow
Did more than he was wont avow.

"Let the chamber be clear'd."—The train
    disappear'd.—
"Now call me the chief of the Haram
    guard."
With Giaffir is none but his only son,
35 And the Nubian awaiting the sire's
    award.
"Haroun—when all the crowd that wait
Are pass'd beyond the outer gate,
(Woe to the head whose eye beheld
My child Zuleika's face unveil'd!)
40 Hence, lead my daughter from her
    tower;
Her fate is fix'd this very hour:
Yet not to her repeat my thought;
By me alone be duty taught!"

"Pacha! to hear is to obey."
45 No more must slave to despot say—

Then to the tower had ta'en his way,
But here young Selim silence brake,
    First lowly rendering reverence meet;
And downcast look'd, and gently spake,
    Still standing at the Pacha's feet:
For son of Moslem must expire,
Ere dare to sit before his sire!

"Father! for fear that thou shouldst
    chide
My sister, or her sable guide,
Know—for the fault, if fault there be,
Was mine, then fall thy frowns on
    me—
So lovelily the morning shone,
    That—let the old and weary sleep—
I could not; and to view alone
    The fairest scenes of land and deep,
With none to listen and reply
To thoughts with which my heart beat
    high
Were irksome—for whate'er my mood,
In sooth I love not solitude;
I on Zuleika's slumber broke,
    And, as thou knowest that for me
    Soon turns the Haram's grating key,
Before the guardian slaves awoke
We to the cypress groves had flown,
And made earth, main, and heaven our
    own!
There linger'd we, beguiled too long
With Mejnoun's tale, or Sadi's song;
Till I, who heard the deep tambour[1]
Beat thy Divan's approaching hour,
To thee, and to my duty true,
Warn'd by the sound, to greet thee
    flew:
But there Zuleika wanders yet—
Nay, father, rage not—nor forget
That none can pierce that secret bower
But those who watch the women's
    tower."

"Son of a slave"—the Pacha said—
"From unbelieving mother bred,
Vain were a father's hope to see
Aught that beseems a man in thee.
Thou, when thine arm should bend the
    bow,
    And hurl the dart, and curb the steed,
    Thou, Greek in soul if not in creed,
Must pore where babbling waters flow,
And watch unfolding roses blow.
Would that yon orb, whose matin glow
Thy listless eyes so much admire,
Would lend thee something of his fire!
Thou, who wouldst see this battlement

---

[1] the rose
[2] royal court; council of state

[1] A large kettledrum which was sounded at
sunrise, noon, and twilight.

By Christian cannon piecemeal rent;
95 Nay, tamely view old Stambol's wall
Before the dogs of Moscow fall,
Nor strike one stroke for life and death
Against the curs of Nazareth!
Go—let thy less than woman's hand
100 Assume the distaff—not the brand.
But, Haroun!—to my daughter speed;
And hark—of thine own head take
    heed—
If thus Zuleika oft takes wing—
Thou see'st yon bow—it hath a string!"

105 No sound from Selim's lip was heard,
    At least that met old Giaffir's ear,
But every frown and every word
Pierced keener than a Christian's sword.
"Son of a slave!—reproach'd with
    fear!
110   Those gibes had cost another dear.
Son of a slave!—and *who* my sire?"
    Thus held his thoughts their dark
    career;
And glances ev'n of more than ire
Flash forth, then faintly disappear.
115 Old Giaffir gazed upon his son
    And started; for within his eye
He read how much his wrath had done;
He saw rebellion there begun:
    "Come hither, boy—what, no reply?
120 I mark thee—and I know thee too;
But there be deeds thou dar'st not do:
But if thy beard had manlier length,
And if thy hand had skill and strength,
I'd joy to see thee break a lance,
125 Albeit against my own perchance."

As sneeringly these accents fell,
On Selim's eye he fiercely gazed:
    That eye return'd him glance for
    glance,
And proudly to his sire's was raised,
130   Till Giaffir's quail'd and shrunk
    askance—
And why—he felt, but durst not tell.
"Much I misdoubt this wayward boy
Will one day work me more annoy:
I never loved him from his birth,
135 And—but his arm is little worth,
And scarcely in the chase could cope
With timid fawn or antelope,
Far less would venture into strife
Where man contends for fame and
    life—
140 I would not trust that look or tone:
No—nor the blood so near my own.
That blood—he hath not heard—no
    more—
I'll watch him closer than before.

He is an Arab to my sight,[1]
145 Or Christian crouching in the fight—
But hark!—I hear Zuleika's voice;
Like Houris' hymn it meets mine ear:
She is the offspring of my choice;
    Oh! more than ev'n her mother dear,
150 With all to hope, and nought to fear—
My Peri! ever welcome here!
Sweet, as the desert fountain's wave
To lips just cool'd in time to save—
    Such to my longing sight art thou;
155 Nor can they waft to Mecca's shrine
More thanks for life, than I for thine,
    Who blest thy birth and bless thee
    now."

Fair, as the first that fell of womankind,[2]
    When on that dread yet lovely serpent
    smiling,
160 Whose image then was stamp'd upon her
    mind—
    But once beguil'd—and ever more be-
    guiling;
Dazzling, as that, oh! too transcendent
    vision
    To Sorrow's phantom-peopled slumber
    given,
When heart meets heart again in dreams
    Elysian,
165   And paints the lost on Earth revived
    in Heaven;
Soft, as the memory of buried love;
Pure, as the prayer which Childhood
    wafts above,
Was she—the daughter of that rude old
    Chief,
Who met the maid with tears—but not
    of grief.

170 Who hath not proved how feebly words
    essay
To fix one spark of Beauty's heavenly
    ray?
Who doth not feel, until his failing sight
Faints into dimness with its own delight,
His changing cheek, his sinking heart
    confess
175 The might, the majesty of Loveliness?
Such was Zuleika, such around her shone
The nameless charms unmark'd by her
    alone—
The light of love, the purity of grace,
The mind, the Music breathing from her
    face,
180 The heart whose softness harmonized the
    whole,
And oh! that eye was in itself a Soul!

---

[1] The Arabs are more despised by the Turks
than are the Christians.
[2] Eve. See *Genesis*, 3.

Her graceful arms in meekness bending
  Across her gently-budding breast;
At one kind word those arms extending 235
185   To clasp the neck of him who blest
His child caressing and carest,
Zuleika came—and Giaffir felt
His purpose half within him melt:
  Not that against her fancied weal 240
190   His heart though stern could ever feel;
Affection chain'd her to that heart;
Ambition tore the links apart.

"Zuleika! child of gentleness!
  How dear this very day must tell,
195 When I forget my own distress, 245
In losing what I love so well,
To bid thee with another dwell:
Another! and a braver man
Was never seen in battle's van.
200 We Moslem reck not much of blood; 250
  But yet the line of Carasman
Unchanged, unchangeable hath stood
First of the bold Timariot bands[1]
That won and well can keep their lands.
205 Enough that he who comes to woo
Is kinsman of the Bey Oglou:
His years need scarce a thought employ; 255
I would not have thee wed a boy.
And thou shalt have a noble dower:
210 And his and my united power
Will laugh to scorn the death-firman,[2]
Which others tremble but to scan, 260
And teach the messenger what fate
The bearer of such boon may wait.
215 And now thou know'st thy father's
    will:
  All that thy sex hath need to know:
'Twas mine to teach obedience still— 265
  The way to love, thy lord may
    show."

In silence bow'd the virgin's head;
220   And if her eye was fill'd with tears
That stifled feeling dare not shed,
And changed her cheek from pale to red, 270
  And red to pale, as though her ears
Those winged words like arrows sped,
225   What could such be but maiden fears?
So bright the tear in Beauty's eye,
Love half regrets to kiss it dry;
So sweet the blush of Bashfulness, 275
Even Pity scarce can wish it less!

230 Whate'er it was the sire forgot;
Or if remember'd, mark'd it not;
Thrice clapp'd his hands, and call'd his
  steed,

Resign'd his gem-adorned chibouque,[1]
And mounting featly[2] for the mead,
  With Maugrabee[3] and Mamaluke,[4]
His way amid his Delis[5] took,
To witness many an active deed
With sabre keen, or blunt jerreed.[6]
The Kislar[7] only and his Moors
Watch well the Haram's massy doors.

His head was leant upon his hand,
  His eye look'd o'er the dark blue water
That swiftly glides and gently swells
Between the winding Dardanelles;
But yet he saw nor sea nor strand,
Nor even his Pacha's turban'd band
  Mix in the game of mimic slaughter,
Careering cleave the folded felt,
With sabre stroke right sharply dealt;
Nor mark'd the javelin-darting crowd
Nor heard their Ollahs[8] wild and loud—
  He thought but of old Giaffir's daugh-
    ter!

No word from Selim's bosom broke;
One sigh Zuleika's thought bespoke;
Still gazed he through the lattice grate,
Pale, mute, and mournfully sedate.
To him Zuleika's eye was turn'd,
But little from his aspect learn'd:
Equal her grief, yet not the same;
Her heart confess'd a gentler flame:
But yet that heart, alarm'd or weak,
She knew not why, forbade to speak.
Yet speak she must—but when essay?
"How strange he thus should turn
  away!
Not thus we e'er before have met;
Nor thus shall be our parting yet."
Thrice paced she slowly through the
  room,
  And watch'd his eye—it still was fix'd:
She snatch'd the urn wherein was
  mix'd
The Persian Atar-gul's perfume,[9]
And sprinkled all its odors o'er
The pictured roof and marble floor:
The drops, that through his glittering
  vest
The playful girl's appeal address'd,
Unheeded o'er his bosom flew,
As if that breast were marble too.
"What, sullen yet? it must not be—

[1] One of the groups of   of Turkey.
  the feudal cavalry   [2] death-warrant

[1] A kind of Turkish   [5] Cavalrymen who be-
  pipe.   gin the action.
[2] nimbly   [6] A kind of javelin.
[3] Moorish mercenaries. [7] The head of the black
[4] A body of soldiers re-   eunuchs.
  cruited from slaves.   [8] battle-cries
                [9] attar of roses

Oh! gentle Selim, this from thee!''
She saw in curious order set
280   The fairest flowers of eastern land—
"He loved them once; may touch them yet,
    If offer'd by Zuleika's hand.''
The childish thought was hardly breathed
Before the rose was pluck'd and wreathed;
285 The next fond moment saw her seat
Her fairy form at Selim's feet:
"This rose to calm my brother's cares
A message from the bulbul[1] bears;
It says tonight he will prolong
290 For Selim's ear his sweetest song;
And though his note is somewhat sad,
He'll try for once a strain more glad,
With some faint hope his alter'd lay
May sing these gloomy thoughts away.

295   "What! not receive my foolish flower?
Nay then I am indeed unblest:
On me can thus thy forehead lower?
    And know'st thou not who loves thee best?
Oh, Selim dear! oh, more than dearest!
300 Say, is it me thou hat'st or fearest?
Come, lay thy head upon my breast,
And I will kiss thee into rest,
Since words of mine, and songs must fail,
Ev'n from my fabled nightingale.
305 I knew our sire at times was stern,
But this from thee had yet to learn:
Too well I know he loves thee not;
But is Zuleika's love forgot?
Ah! deem I right? the Pacha's plan—
310 This kinsman Bey of Carasman
Perhaps may prove some foe of thine.
If so, I swear by Mecca's shrine,—
If shrines that ne'er approach allow
To woman's step admit her vow,—
315 Without thy free consent, command,
The Sultan should not have my hand!
Think'st thou that I could bear to part
With thee, and learn to halve my heart?
Ah! were I sever'd from thy side,
320 Where were thy friend—and who my guide?
Years have not seen, Time shall not see,
The hour that tears my soul from thee:
Ev'n Azrael, from his deadly quiver
When flies that shaft, and fly it must,
325 That parts all else, shall doom forever
Our hearts to undivided dust!''

¹ The Turkish nightingale.

He lived—he breathed—he moved—he felt;
He raised the maid from where she knelt;
His trance was gone—his keen eye shone
330 With thoughts that long in darkness dwelt;
With thoughts that burn—in rays that melt.
As the stream late conceal'd
    By the fringe of its willows,
When it rushes reveal'd
335   In the light of its billows;
As the bolt bursts on high
    From the black cloud that bound it,
Flash'd the soul of that eye
    Through the long lashes round it.
340 A war-horse at the trumpet's sound,
A lion roused by heedless hound,
A tyrant waked to sudden strife
By graze of ill-directed knife,
Starts not to more convulsive life
345 Than he, who heard that vow, display'd,
And all, before repress'd, betray'd:
"Now thou art mine, forever mine,
With life to keep, and scarce with life resign;
Now thou art mine, that sacred oath,
350 Though sworn by one, hath bound us both.
Yes, fondly, wisely hast thou done;
That vow hath saved more heads than one:
But blench not thou—thy simplest tress
Claims more from me than tenderness;
355 I would not wrong the slenderest hair
That clusters round thy forehead fair,
For all the treasures buried far
Within the caves of Istakar.
This morning clouds upon me lower'd,
360 Reproaches on my head were shower'd,
And Giaffir almost call'd me coward!
Now I have motive to be brave;
The son of his neglected slave,
Nay, start not, 'twas the term he gave,
365 May show, though little apt to vaunt,
A heart his words nor deeds can daunt.
His son, indeed!—yet, thanks to thee,
Perchance I am, at least shall be;
But let our plighted secret vow
370 Be only known to us as now.
I know the wretch who dares demand
From Giaffir thy reluctant hand;
More ill-got wealth, a meaner soul
Holds not a Musselim's[1] control:
375 Was he not bred in Egripo?
A viler race let Israel show!
But let that pass—to none be told

¹ A governor, next in rank to a Pasha.

Our oath; the rest shall time unfold.
To me and mine leave Osman Bey;
380 I've partisans for peril's day:
Think not I am what I appear;
I've arms, and friends, and vengeance
    near.''

"Think not thou art what thou appear-
    est!
    My Selim, thou art sadly changed:
385 This morn I saw thee gentlest, dearest;
But now thou'rt from thyself es-
    tranged.
My love thou surely knew'st before,
It ne'er was less, nor can be more.
To see thee, hear thee, near thee stay,
390   And hate the night I know not
    why,
Save that we meet not but by day;
    With thee to live, with thee to die,
I dare not to my hope deny:
Thy cheek, thine eyes, thy lips to kiss,
395 Like this—and this—no more than this;
For, Allah! sure thy lips are flame:
    What fever in thy veins is flushing?
My own have nearly caught the same,
    At least I feel my cheek, too, blush-
    ing.
400 To soothe thy sickness, watch thy health,
Partake, but never waste thy wealth,
Or stand with smiles unmurmuring by,
And lighten half thy poverty;
Do all but close thy dying eye,
405 For that I could not live to try;
To these alone my thoughts aspire:
More can I do? or thou require?
But, Selim, thou must answer why
We need so much of mystery?
410 The cause I cannot dream nor tell,
But be it, since thou say'st 'tis well;
Yet what thou mean'st by 'arms' and
    'friends,'
Beyond my weaker sense extends.
I meant that Giaffir should have heard
415   The very vow I plighted thee;
His wrath would not revoke my word:
    But surely he would leave me free.
Can this fond wish seem strange in
    me,
To be what I have ever been?
420 What other hath Zuleika seen
From simple childhood's earliest hour?
    What other can she seek to see
Than thee, companion of her bower,
    The partner of her infancy?
425 These cherish'd thoughts with life
    begun,
    Say, why must I no more avow?
What change is wrought to make me
    shun

    The truth; my pride, and thine till
    now?
430 To meet the gaze of stranger's eyes
Our law, our creed, our God denies;
Nor shall one wandering thought of
    mine
At such, our Prophet's will, repine:
No! happier made by that decree,
He left me all in leaving thee.
435 Deep were my anguish, thus compell'd
To wed with one I ne'er beheld:
This wherefore should I not reveal?
Why wilt thou urge me to conceal?
I know the Pacha's haughty mood
440 To thee hath never boded good;
And he so often storms at nought,
Allah! forbid that e'er he ought!
And why I know not, but within
My heart concealment weighs like sin.
445 If then such secrecy be crime,
    And such it feels while lurking here;
Oh, Selim! tell me yet in time,
    Nor leave me thus to thoughts of fear.
Ah! yonder see the Tchocadar,[1]
450 My father leaves the mimic war;
I tremble now to meet his eye—
Say, Selim, canst thou tell me why?''

"Zuleika—to thy tower's retreat
Betake thee—Giaffir I can greet:
455 And now with him I fain must prate
Of firmans,[2] imposts, levies, state.
There's fearful news from Danube's
    banks,
Our Vizier[3] nobly thins his ranks,
For which the Giaour[4] may give him
    thanks!
460 Our Sultan hath a shorter way
Such costly triumph to repay.
But, mark me, when the twilight drum
    Hath warn'd the troops to food and
    sleep,
Unto thy cell will Selim come:
465 Then softly from the Haram creep
Where we may wander by the deep:
Our garden battlements are steep;
Nor these will rash intruder climb
To list our words, or stint our time;
470 And if he doth, I want not steel
Which some have felt, and more may
    feel.
Then shalt thou learn of Selim more
Than thou hast heard or thought be-
    fore:

[1] An attendant who precedes a man of au-
    thority.
[2] royal decrees
[3] A title of various high officials in Moham-
    medan countries, especially of the chief
    ministers of state.
[4] A term applied to all persons not of the Mo-
    hammedan faith, especially Christians.

Trust me, Zuleika—fear not me!
475 Thou know'st I hold a Haram key.''
"Fear thee, my Selim! ne'er till now
Did word like this——''
        "Delay not thou;
I keep the key—and Haroun's guard
Have *some,* and hope of *more* reward.
480 Tonight, Zuleika, thou shalt hear
My tale, my purpose, and my fear:
I am not, love! what I appear.''

CANTO THE SECOND

The winds are high on Helle's wave,
  As on that night of stormy water
When Love, who sent, forgot to save
The young, the beautiful, the brave,
5   The lonely hope of Sestos' daughter.[1]
Oh! when alone along the sky
Her turret-torch was blazing high,
Though rising gale, and breaking foam,
And shrieking sea-birds warn'd him
  home;
10 And clouds aloft and tides below,
With signs and sounds, forbade to go,
He could not see, he would not hear,
Or sound or sign foreboding fear;
His eye but saw that light of love,
15 The only star it hail'd above;
His ear but rang with Hero's song,
"Ye waves, divide not lovers long!''—
That tale is old, but love anew
May nerve young hearts to prove as
  true.

20 The winds are high, and Helle's tide
  Rolls darkly heaving to the main;
And Night's descending shadows hide
  That field with blood bedew'd in vain,
The desert of old Priam's pride;
25   The tombs, sole relics of his reign,
All—save immortal dreams that could be-
  guile
The blind old man of Scio's rocky isle!

Oh! yet—for there my steps have been;
These feet have press'd the sacred
  shore,
30 These limbs that buoyant wave hath
  borne[2]—
Minstrel! with thee to muse, to mourn,
To trace again those fields of yore,
Believing every hillock green
Contains no fabled hero's ashes,

35 And that around the undoubted scene
  Thine own "broad Hellespont'' still
  dashes,
Be long my lot! and cold were he
Who there could gaze denying thee!

The night hath closed on Helle's stream,
40   Nor yet hath risen on Ida's hill
That moon, which shone on his high
  theme:
No warrior chides her peaceful beam,
  But conscious shepherds bless it still.
Their flocks are grazing on the mound
45   Of him[1] who felt the Dardan's arrow:
That mighty heap of gather'd ground
Which Ammon's son[2] ran proudly round,
By nations raised, by monarchs crown'd,
  Is now a lone and nameless barrow!
50 Within—thy dwelling-place how nar-
  row!
Without—can only strangers breathe
The name of him that *was* beneath:
Dust long outlasts the storied stone;
But thou—thy very dust is gone!

55 Late, late tonight will Dian cheer
The swain, and chase the boatman's
  fear;
Till then—no beacon on the cliff
May shape the course of struggling
  skiff;
The scatter'd lights that skirt the bay,
60 All, one by one, have died away;
The only lamp of this lone hour
Is glimmering in Zuleika's tower.
Yes! there is light in that lone chamber,
  And o'er her silken ottoman[3]
65 Are thrown the fragrant beads of
  amber,[4]
  O'er which her fairy fingers ran;
Near these, with emerald rays beset,
(How could she thus that gem forget?)
Her mother's sainted amulet,
70 Whereon engraved the Koorsee text,
Could smooth this life, and win the
  next;
And by her comboloio[5] lies
A Koran of illumined dyes;
And many a bright emblazon'd rhyme
75 By Persian scribes redeem'd from time;
And o'er those scrolls, not oft so mute,
Reclines her now neglected lute;

---

[1] Hero, a native of the city of Sestos. A reference to the classical story of Hero and Leander, told by Ovid (*Heroïdes,* 18-19) and
others.
[2] Byron swam across the Hellespont to test
Homer's use of the adjective ἄπειρος, broad
or boundless. See Byron's *Don Juan,* 2, 105
and n. 1 (p. 615).

[1] Achilles, whom Paris, the Trojan, wounded in
the heel with an arrow and then killed.
[2] Alexander, who ran naked to the tomb of
Achilles after placing a garland upon it and
anointing himself with oil. See Plutarch's
Life of Alexander, 15.
[3] stuffed seat without a back
[4] "When rubbed, the amber is susceptible of a
perfume, which is slight, but *not* disagreeable."—Byron.
[5] A Turkish rosary.

And round her lamp of fretted gold
Bloom flowers in urns of China's mould;
80 The richest work of Iran's loom,
And Sheeraz' tribute of perfume;
All that can eye or sense delight
Are gather'd in that gorgeous room:
But yet it hath an air of gloom.
85 She, of this Peri cell the sprite,
What doth she hence, and on so rude a
    night?

Wrapt in the darkest sable vest,
    Which none save noblest Moslem
    wear,
To guard from winds of heaven the
    breast
90 As heaven itself to Selim dear,
With cautious steps the thicket thread-
    ing,
    And starting oft, as through the glade
    The gust its hollow moaning made,
Till on the smoother pathway treading,
95 More free her timid bosom beat,
    The maid pursued her silent guide;
And though her terror urged retreat,
    How could she quit her Selim's side?
    How teach her tender lips to chide?

100 They reach'd at length a grotto, hewn
    By nature, but enlarged by art,
Where oft her lute she wont to tune,
    And oft her Koran conn'd apart;
And oft in youthful reverie
105 She dream'd what Paradise might be:
Where woman's parted soul shall go
Her Prophet had disdain'd to show;[1]
But Selim's mansion was secure,
Nor deem'd she, could he long endure
110 His bower in other worlds of bliss
Without _her,_ most beloved in this!
Oh! who so dear with him could dwell?
What Houri soothe him half so well?

Since last she visited the spot
115 Some change seem'd wrought within
    the grot:
It might be only that the night
Disguised things seen by better light:
That brazen lamp but dimly threw
A ray of no celestial hue;
120 But in a nook within the cell
Her eye on stranger objects fell.
There arms were piled, not such as wield
The turban'd Delis in the field;
But brands of foreign blade and hilt,
125 And one was red—perchance with guilt!
Ah! how without can blood be spilt?

1 "The Koran allots at least a third of Paradise
to well-behaved women."—Byron.

A cup too on the board was set
That did not seem to hold sherbet.
130 What may this mean? she turn'd to see
Her Selim—"Oh! can this be he?"

His robe of pride was thrown aside,
    His brow no high-crown'd turban
    bore,
But in its stead a shawl of red,
135 Wreathed lightly round, his temples
    wore:
That dagger, on whose hilt the gem
Were worthy of a diadem,
No longer glitter'd at his waist,
Where pistols unadorn'd were braced;
140 And from his belt a sabre swung,
And from his shoulder loosely hung
The cloak of white, the thin capote[1]
That decks the wandering Candiote;[2]
Beneath—his golden plated vest
145 Clung like a cuirass to his breast;
The greaves below his knee that wound
With silvery scales were sheathed and
    bound.
But were it not that high command
Spake in his eye, and tone, and hand,
150 All that a careless eye could see
In him was some young Galiongée.[3]

"I said I was not what I seem'd;
    And now thou see'st my words were
    true:
I have a tale thou hast not dream'd,
155 If sooth—its truth must others rue.
My story now 'twere vain to hide,
I must not see thee Osman's bride:
But had not thine own lips declared
How much of that young heart I shared,
160 I could not, must not, yet have shown
The darker secret of my own.
In this I speak not now of love;
That, let time, truth, and peril prove:
But first—Oh! never wed another—
Zuleika! I am not thy brother!"

165 "Oh! not my brother!—yet unsay—
    God! am I left alone on earth
To mourn—I dare not curse—the day
    That saw my solitary birth?
Oh! thou wilt love me now no more!
170 My sinking heart forboded ill;
But know _me_ all I was before,
    Thy sister—friend—Zuleika still.
Thou led'st me here perchance to kill;
    If thou hast cause for vengeance, see!
175 My breast is offer'd—take thy fill!
    Far better with the dead to be

1 A kind of long outer   2 Cretan
garment.   3 Turkish sailor

Than live thus nothing now to thee!
Perhaps far worse, for now I know
Why Giaffir always seem'd thy foe;
180 And I, alas! am Giaffir's child,
For whom thou wert contemn'd, reviled.
If not thy sister—wouldst thou save
My life, oh! bid me be thy slave!''

"My slave, Zuleika!—nay, I'm thine:
185 But, gentle love, this transport calm.
Thy lot shall yet be link'd with mine;
I swear it by our Prophet's shrine,
And be that thought thy sorrow's
balm.
So may the Koran verse display'd
190 Upon its steel direct my blade,
In danger's hour to guard us both,
As I preserve that awful oath!
The name in which thy heart hath prided
Must change; but, my Zuleika, know,
195 That tie is widen'd, not divided,
Although thy sire's my deadliest foe.
My father was to Giaffir all
That Selim late was deem'd to thee:
That brother wrought a brother's fall,
200 But spared, at least, my infancy;
And lull'd with me a vain deceit
That yet a like return may meet.
He rear'd me, not with tender help,
But like the nephew of a Cain;
205 He watch'd me like a lion's whelp,
That gnaws and yet may break his
chain.
My father's blood in every vein
Is boiling; but for thy dear sake
No present vengeance will I take;
210 Though here I must no more remain.
But first, beloved Zuleika! hear
How Giaffir wrought this deed of fear.

"How first their strife to rancor grew,
If love or envy made them foes,
215 It matters little if I knew;
In fiery spirits, slights, though few
And thoughtless, will disturb repose.
In war Abdallah's arm was strong,
Remember'd yet in Bosniac song,
220 And Paswan's rebel hordes attest
How little love they bore such guest:
His death is all I need relate,
The stern effect of Giaffir's hate;
And how my birth disclosed to me,
225 Whate'er beside it makes, hath made
me free.

"When Paswan, after years of strife,
At last for power, but first for life,
In Widdin's walls too proudly sate,
Our Pachas rallied round the state;

230 Nor last nor least in high command,
Each brother led a separate band;
They gave their horse-tails[1] to the wind,
And mustering in Sophia's plain
Their tents were pitch'd, their post
assign'd;
235 To one, alas! assign'd in vain!
What need of words! the deadly bowl,
By Giaffir's order drugged and given,
With venom subtle as his soul,
Dismiss'd Abdallah's hence to heaven.
240 Reclined and feverish in the bath,
He, when the hunter's sport was up,
But little deem'd a brother's wrath
To quench his thirst had such a cup:
The bowl a bribed attendant bore;
245 He drank one draught, nor needed
more!
If thou my tale, Zuleika, doubt,
Call Haroun—he can tell it out.

"The deed once done, and Paswan's
feud
In part suppress'd, though ne'er sub-
dued,
250 Abdallah's Pachalick[2] was gain'd:—
Thou know'st not what in our Divan
Can wealth procure for worse than
man—
Abdallah's honors were obtain'd—
By him a brother's murder stain'd;
255 'Tis true, the purchase nearly drain'd
His ill got treasure, soon replaced.
Wouldst question whence? Survey the
waste,
And ask the squalid peasant how
His gains repay his broiling brow!—
260 Why me the stern usurper spared,
Why thus with me his palace shared,
I know not. Shame, regret, remorse,
And little fear from infant's force;
Besides, adoption as a son
265 By him whom Heaven accorded none,
Or some unknown cabal, caprice,
Preserved me thus;—but not in peace:
He cannot curb his haughty mood,
Nor I forgive a father's blood.

270 "Within thy father's house are foes;
Not all who break his bread are true:
To these should I my birth disclose,
His days, his very hours were few:
They only want a heart to lead,
275 A hand to point them to the deed.
But Haroun only knows, or knew,
This tale, whose close is almost nigh:
He in Abdallah's palace grew,

---

[1] A horse tail is the standard of a Pasha.
[2] The territory governed by a Pasha.

And held that post in his Serai[1]
280   Which holds he here—he saw him die: 330
But what could single slavery do?
Avenge his lord? alas! too late;
Or save his son from such a fate?
He chose the last, and when elate
285   With foes subdued, or friends be-
            tray'd,
Proud Giaffir in high triumph sate,   335
He led me helpless to his gate,
And not in vain it seems essay'd
To save the life for which he pray'd.
290 The knowledge of my birth secured
        From all and each, but most from me;
Thus Giaffir's safety was insured.   340
    Removed he too from Roumelie
To this our Asiatic side,
295 Far from our seats by Danube's tide,
With none but Haroun, who retains
Such knowledge—and that Nubian feels 345
    A tyrant's secrets are but chains,
From which the captive gladly steals,
300 And this and more to me reveals:
Such still to guilt just Alla sends—
Slaves, tools, accomplices—no friends! 350

"All this, Zuleika, harshly sounds;
    But harsher still my tale must be:
305 Howe'er my tongue thy softness wounds,
    Yet I must prove all truth to thee.
I saw thee start this garb to see,
Yet is it one I oft have worn,   355
    And long must wear: this Galiongée,
310 To whom thy plighted vow is sworn,
    Is leader of those pirate hordes,
    Whose laws and lives are on their
            swords;
To hear whose desolating tale   360
Would make thy waning cheek more
            pale:
315 Those arms thou see'st my band have
            brought,
The hands that wield are not remote;
This cup too for the rugged knaves   365
    Is fill'd—once quaff'd, they ne'er re-
            pine:
Our Prophet might forgive the slaves;
320   They're only infidels in wine.

"What could I be? Proscribed at 370
        home,
And taunted to a wish to roam;
And listless left—for Giaffir's fear
Denied the courser and the spear—
325 Though oft—Oh, Mahomet! how oft!—
In full Divan the despot scoff'd,   375
As if *my* weak unwilling hand
Refused the bridle or the brand:

[1] harem

He ever went to war alone,
And pent me here untried—unknown;
To Haroun's care with women left,
By hope unblest, of fame bereft,
While thou—whose softness long en-
        dear'd,
Though it unmann'd me, still had
        cheer'd—
To Brusa's walls for safety sent,
Awaited'st there the field's event.
Haroun, who saw my spirit pining
    Beneath inaction's sluggish yoke,
His captive, though with dread resign-
        ing,
    My thraldom for a season broke,
On promise to return before
The day when Giaffir's charge was o'er.
'Tis vain—my tongue cannot impart
My almost drunkenness of heart,
When first this liberated eye
Survey'd Earth, Ocean, Sun, and Sky,
As if my spirit pierced them through,
And all their inmost wonders knew!
One word alone can paint to thee
That more than feeling—I was Free!
E'en for thy presence ceased to pine;
The World—nay, Heaven itself was
        mine!

"The shallop of a trusty Moor
Convey'd me from this idle shore;
I long'd to see the isles that gem
Old Ocean's purple diadem:
I sought by turns, and saw them all;
    But when and where I join'd the
            crew,
With whom I'm pledged to rise or fall,
    When all that we design to do
Is done, 'twill then be time more meet
To tell thee, when the tale's complete.

" 'Tis true, they are a lawless brood,
But rough in form, nor mild in mood;
And every creed, and every race,
With them hath found—may find a
        place;
But open speech, and ready hand,
Obedience to their chief's command;
A soul for every enterprise,
That never sees with terror's eyes;
Friendship for each, and faith to all,
And vengeance vow'd for those who
        fall,
Have made them fitting instruments
For more than ev'n my own intents.
And some—and I have studied all
    Distinguish'd from the vulgar rank,
But chiefly to my council call
    The wisdom of the cautious Frank—

And some to higher thoughts aspire,
380   The last of Lambro's patriots there
Anticipated freedom share;
And oft around the cavern fire
On visionary schemes debate,
To snatch the Rayahs[1] from their fate.
385 So let them ease their hearts with prate
Of equal rights, which man ne'er knew;
I have a love for freedom too.
Ay! let me like the ocean-Patriarch roam,
Or only know on land the Tartar's home!
390 My tent on shore, my galley on the sea,
Are more than cities and serais to me:
Borne by my steed, or wafted by my sail,
Across the desert, or before the gale,
Bound where thou wilt, my barb![2] or
glide, my prow!
395 But be the star that guides the wanderer,
thou!
Thou, my Zuleika, share and bless my
bark;
The dove of peace and promise to mine
ark![3]
Or, since that hope denied in worlds of
strife,
Be thou the rainbow to the storms of life!
400 The evening beam that smiles the clouds
away,
And tints tomorrow with prophetic ray!
Blest—as the Muezzin's strain from Mec-
ca's wall
To pilgrims pure and prostrate at his call;
Soft—as the melody of youthful days,
405 That steals the trembling tear of speechless praise;
Dear—as his native song to exile's ears,
Shall sound each tone thy long-loved voice
endears.
For thee in those bright isles is built a
bower
Blooming as Aden[4] in its earliest hour.
110 A thousand swords, with Selim's heart
and hand,
Wait—wave—defend—destroy—at thy
command!
Girt by my band, Zuleika at my side,
The spoil of nations shall bedeck my bride.
The Haram's languid years of listless ease
415 Are well resign'd for cares—for joys like
these:
Not blind to fate, I see, where'er I rove,
Unnumber'd perils—but one only love!
Yet well my toils shall that fond breast
repay,

Though fortune frown, or falser friends
betray.
420 How dear the dream in darkest hours of
ill,
Should all be changed, to find thee faithful still!
Be but thy soul, like Selim's, firmly
shown;
To thee be Selim's tender as thine own;
To soothe each sorrow, share in each delight,
425 Blend every thought, do all—but disunite!
Once free, 'tis mine our horde again to
guide;
Friends to each other, foes to aught be-
side:
Yet there we follow but the bent assign'd
By fatal Nature to man's warring kind:
430 Mark! where his carnage and his conquests cease!
He makes a solitude, and calls it—peace!
I, like the rest, must use my skill or
strength,
But ask no land beyond my sabre's length:
Power sways but by division—her resource
435 The blessed alternative of fraud or force!
Ours be the last; in time deceit may come
When cities cage us in a social home:
There ev'n thy soul might err—how oft
the heart
Corruption shakes which peril could not
part!
440 And woman, more than man, when death
or woe,
Or even Disgrace, would lay her lover
low,
Sunk in the lap of Luxury will shame—
Away suspicion!—not Zuleika's name!
But life is hazard at the best; and here
445 No more remains to win, and much to
fear:
Yes, fear! the doubt, the dread of losing
thee,
By Osman's power, and Giaffir's stern
decree.
That dread shall vanish with the favoring
gale,
Which Love tonight hath promised to my
sail:
450 No danger daunts the pair his smile hath
blest,
Their steps still roving, but their hearts
at rest.
With thee all toils are sweet, each clime
hath charms;
Earth—sea alike—our world within our
arms!
Ay—let the loud winds whistle o'er the
deck,

---

[1] Those who pay the capitation tax levied upon
male unbelievers.
[2] Barbary horse (noted for speed and endurance).
[3] See *Genesis*, 8:11.
[4] The Mohammedan paradise.

455 So that those arms cling closer round my
    neck:
The deepest murmur of this lip shall be,
No sigh for safety, but a prayer for thee!
The war of elements no fears impart
To Love, whose deadliest bane is human
    Art:
460 *There* lie the only rocks our course can
    check;
Here moments menace—*there* are years of
    wreck!
But hence ye thoughts that rise in Hor-
    ror's shape!
This hour bestows, or ever bars escape.
Few words remain of mine my tale to
    close;
465 Of thine but *one* to waft us from our foes;
Yea—foes—to me will Giaffir's hate de-
    cline?
And is not Osman, who would part us,
    thine?

  "His head and faith from doubt and
    death
    Return'd in time my guard to save;
470   Few heard, none told, that o'er the
    wave
From isle to isle I roved the while;
And since, though parted from my band
Too seldom now I leave the land,
No deed they've done, nor deed shall do,
475 Ere I have heard and doom'd it too:
I form the plan, decree the spoil,
'Tis fit I oftener share the toil.
But now too long I've held thine ear;
Time presses, floats my bark, and here
480 We leave behind but hate and fear.
Tomorrow Osman with his train
Arrives—tonight must break thy chain:
And wouldst thou save that haughty
    Bey,—
  Perchance *his* life who gave thee
    thine,—
485 With me this hour away—away!
  But yet, though thou art plighted
    mine,
Wouldst thou recall thy willing vow,
Appall'd by truths imparted now,
Here rest I—not to see thee wed:
490 But be that peril on *my* head!"

Zuleika, mute and motionless,
Stood like that statue of distress,
When, her last hope forever gone,
The mother harden'd into stone:
495 All in the maid that eye could see
Was but a younger Niobé.
But ere her lip, or even her eye,
Essay'd to speak, or look reply,

Beneath the garden's wicket porch
500 Far flash'd on high a blazing torch!
Another—and another—and another—
"Oh! fly—no more—yet now my more
    than brother!"
Far, wide, through every thicket spread
505 The fearful lights are gleaming red;
Nor these alone—for each right hand
Is ready with a sheathless brand.
They part, pursue, return, and wheel
With searching flambeau,[1] shining steel;
510 And last of all, his sabre waving,
Stern Giaffir in his fury raving:
And now almost they touch the cave—
Oh! must that grot be Selim's grave?

Dauntless he stood—"'Tis come—soon
    past—
One kiss, Zuleika—'tis my last:
515   But yet my band not far from shore
May hear this signal, see the flash;
Yet now too few—the attempt were rash:
  No matter—yet one effort more."
Forth to the cavern mouth he stept;
520   His pistol's echo rang on high,
Zuleika started not, nor wept,
  Despair benumb'd her breast and
    eye!—
"They hear me not, or if they ply
Their oars, 'tis but to see me die;
525 That sound hath drawn my foes more
    nigh.

Then forth my father's scimitar,
Thou ne'er hast seen less equal war!
Farewell, Zuleika!—sweet! retire:
  Yet stay within—here linger safe,
530 At thee his rage will only chafe.
Stir not—lest even to thee perchance
Some erring blade or ball should glance.
Fear'st thou for him?—may I expire
If in this strife I seek thy sire!
535 No—though by him that poison pour'd;
No—though again he call me coward!
But tamely shall I meet their steel?
No—as each crest save *his* may feel!"

One bound he made, and gain'd the
    sand:
540   Already at his feet hath sunk
The foremost of the prying band,
  A gasping head, a quivering trunk:
Another falls—but round him close
A swarming circle of his foes;
545 From right to left his path he cleft,
  And almost met the meeting wave:
His boat appears — not five oars'
    length—

[1] flaming torch

His comrades strain with desperate
strength—
Oh! are they yet in time to save?
550 His feet the foremost breakers lave;
His band are plunging in the bay,
Their sabres glitter through the spray;
Wet—wild—unwearied to the strand
They struggle—now they touch the land!
555 They come—'tis but to add to slaugh-
ter—
His heart's best blood is on the water.

Escaped from shot, unharm'd by steel,
Or scarcely grazed its force to feel,
Had Selim won, betray'd, beset,
560 To where the strand and billows met;
There as his last step left the land—
And the last death-blow dealt his hand—
Ah! wherefore did he turn to look
For her his eye but sought in vain?
565 That pause, that fatal gaze he took,
Hath doom'd his death, or fix'd his
chain.
Sad proof, in peril and in pain,
How late will lover's hope remain!
His back was to the dashing spray;
570 Behind, but close, his comrades lay,
When, at the instant, hiss'd the ball—
"So may the foes of Giaffir fall!"
Whose voice is heard? whose carbine
rang?
Whose bullet through the night-air sang,
575 Too nearly, deadly aim'd to err?
'Tis thine—Abdallah's murderer!
The father slowly rued thy hate,
The son hath found a quicker fate:
Fast from his breast the blood is bub-
bling,
580 The whiteness of the sea-foam troub-
ling—
If aught his lips essay'd to groan,
The rushing billows choked the tone!

Morn slowly rolls the clouds away;
Few trophies of the fight are there:
585 The shouts that shook the midnight-bay
Are silent; but some signs of fray
That strand of strife may bear,
And fragments of each shiver'd brand;
Steps stamp'd; and dash'd into the
sand
590 The print of many a struggling hand
May there be mark'd; nor far remote
A broken torch, an oarless boat;
And tangled on the weeds that heap
The beach where shelving to the deep
595 There lies a white capote!
'Tis rent in twain—one dark-red stain
The wave yet ripples o'er in vain;

But where is he who wore?
Ye! who would o'er his relics weep,
600 Go, seek them where the surges sweep
Their burthen round Sigæum's steep
And cast on Lemnos' shore:
The sea-birds shriek above the prey,
O'er which their hungry beaks delay,
605 As shaken on his restless pillow,
His head heaves with the heaving bil-
low;
That hand, whose motion is not life,
Yet feebly seems to menace strife,
Flung by the tossing tide on high,
610 Then levell'd with the wave—
What recks it, though that corse shall
lie
Within a living grave?
The bird that tears that prostrate form
Hath only robb'd the meaner worm;
615 The only heart, the only eye
Had bled or wept to see him die,
Had seen those scatter'd limbs com-
posed,
And mourn'd above his turban-stone,
That heart hath burst—that eye was
closed—
620 Yea—closed before his own!

By Helle's stream there is a voice of wail!
And woman's eye is wet—man's cheek is
pale:
Zuleika! last of Giaffir's race,
Thy destined lord is come too late:
625 He sees not—ne'er shall see thy face!
Can he not hear
The loud Wul-wulleh[1] warn his distant
ear?
Thy handmaids weeping at the gate,
The Koran-chanters of the hymn of
fate,
630 The silent slaves with folded arms that
wait,
Sighs in the hall, and shrieks upon the
gale,
Tell him thy tale!
Thou didst not view thy Selim fall!
That fearful moment when he left the
cave
635 Thy heart grew chill:
He was thy hope—thy joy—thy love—
thine all,
And that last thought on him thou couldst
not save
Sufficed to kill;
Burst forth in one wild cry—and all was
still.
640 Peace to thy broken heart, and virgin
grave!

[1] The death song of the Turkish women.

Ah! happy! but of life to lose the worst!
That grief—though deep—though fatal—
    was thy first!
Thrice happy ne'er to feel nor fear the
    force
Of absence, shame, pride, hate, revenge,
    remorse!
645 And, oh! that pang where more than mad-
    ness lies!
The worm that will not sleep—and never
    dies;
Thought of the gloomy day and ghastly
    night,
That dreads the darkness, and yet loathes
    the light,
That winds around, and tears the quiver-
    ing heart!
650 Ah! wherefore not consume it—and de-
    part!
Woe to thee, rash and unrelenting chief!
  Vainly thou heap'st the dust upon thy
    head,
  Vainly the sackcloth o'er thy limbs dost
    spread:
  By that same hand Abdallah—Selim
    bled.
655 Now let it tear thy beard in idle grief:
  Thy pride of heart, thy bride for Osman's
    bed,
  She, whom thy sultan had but seen to wed,
    Thy daughter's dead!
  Hope of thine age, thy twilight's
    lonely beam,
660   The star hath set that shone on Helle's
    stream.
What quench'd its ray?—the blood that
    thou hast shed!
Hark! to the hurried question of Despair:
"Where is my child?"—an Echo an-
    swers—"Where?"

Within the place of thousand tombs
665   That shine beneath, while dark above
The sad but living cypress blooms
And withers not, though branch and leaf
Are stamp'd with an eternal grief,
  Like early unrequited Love,
670 One spot exists, which ever blooms,
  Ev'n in that deadly grove—
A single rose is shedding there
  Its lonely lustre, meek and pale:
It looks as planted by Despair:
675   So white—so faint—the slightest gale
Might whirl the leaves on high;
  And yet, though storms and blight
    assail,
And hands more rude than wintry sky
  May wring it from the stem—in
    vain—

680 Tomorrow sees it bloom again:
The stalk some spirit gently rears,
And waters with celestial tears;
  For well may maids of Helle deem
That this can be no earthly flower,
685 Which mocks the tempest's withering
    hour,
And buds unshelter'd by a bower;
Nor droops though Spring refuse her
    shower,
  Nor woos the summer beam:
To it the livelong night there sings
690   A bird unseen—but not remote:
Invisible his airy wings,
But soft as harp that Houri strings
  His long entrancing note!
It were the bulbul; but his throat,
695   Though mournful, pours not such a
    strain:
For they who listen cannot leave
The spot, but linger there and grieve,
  As if they loved in vain!
And yet so sweet the tears they shed,
700 'Tis sorrow so unmix'd with dread,
They scarce can bear the morn to break
  That melancholy spell,
And longer yet would weep and wake,
  He sings so wild and well!
705 But when the day-blush bursts from
    high
  Expires that magic melody.
And some have been who could believe,
(So fondly youthful dreams deceive,
  Yet harsh be they that blame,)
710 That note so piercing and profound
Will shape and syllable its sound
  Into Zuleika's name.
'Tis from her cypress summit heard,
That melts in air the liquid word:
'Tis from her lowly virgin earth
That white rose takes its tender birth.
There late was laid a marble stone;
Eve saw it placed—the Morrow gone!
It was no mortal arm that bore
720 That deep-fix'd pillar to the shore;
For there, as Helle's legends tell,
Next morn 'twas found where Selim
    fell;
Lash'd by the tumbling tide, whose wave
Denied his bones a holier grave:
725 And there by night, reclined, 'tis said,
Is seen a ghastly turban'd head:
  And hence extended by the billow,
  'Tis named the "Pirate-phantom's
    pillow!"
  Where first it lay that mourning
    flower
730 Hath flourish'd; flourisheth this
    hour,

Alone and dewy, coldly pure and pale;
　As weeping Beauty's cheek at Sorrow's
　　tale!

ODE TO NAPOLEON BUONAPARTE
1814　　　　　1814

'Tis done—but yesterday a king!
　And arm'd with kings to strive—
And now thou art a nameless thing:
　So abject—yet alive!
5 Is this the man of thousand thrones,
Who strew'd our earth with hostile bones,
　And can he thus survive?
Since he, miscall'd the Morning Star,[1]
Nor man nor field hath fallen so far.

10 Ill-minded man! why scourge thy kind
　Who bow'd so low the knee?
By gazing on thyself grown blind,
　Thou taught'st the rest to see.
With　might　unquestion'd,—power　to
　save,—
15 Thine only gift hath been the grave,
　To those that worshipp'd thee;
Nor till thy fall could mortals guess
Ambition's less than littleness!

Thanks for that lesson—It will teach
20 　To after-warriors more,
Than high Philosophy can preach,
　And vainly preach'd before.
That spell upon the minds of men
Breaks never to unite again,
25 　That led them to adore
Those Pagod things[2] of sabre sway
With fronts of brass, and feet of clay.

The triumph and the vanity,
　The rapture of the strife—
30 The earthquake voice of Victory,
　To thee the breath of life;
The sword, the sceptre, and that sway
Which man seem'd made but to obey,
　Wherewith renown was rife—
35 All quell'd!—Dark Spirit! what must be
The madness of thy memory!

The desolator desolate!
　The victor overthrown!
The arbiter of others' fate
40 　A suppliant for his own!
Is it some yet imperial hope
That with such change can calmly cope?
　Or dread of death alone?
To die a prince—or live a slave—
45 Thy choice is most ignobly brave!

[1] Lucifer. See *Isaiah*, 14:12.
[2] idols

He who of old would rend the oak
　Dream'd not of the rebound:[1]
Chain'd by the trunk he vainly broke—
　Alone—how look'd he round?
50 Thou, in the sternness of thy strength,
An equal deed hast done at length,
　And darker fate hast found:[2]
He fell, the forest prowlers' prey;
But thou must eat thy heart away!

55 The Roman,[3] when his burning heart
　Was slaked with blood of Rome,
Threw down the dagger—dared depart,
　In savage grandeur, home—
He dared depart in utter scorn
60 Of men that such a yoke had borne,
　Yet left him such a doom!
His only glory was that hour
Of self-upheld abandon'd power.

The Spaniard,[4] when the lust of sway
65 　Had lost its quickening spell,
Cast crowns for rosaries away,
　An empire for a cell;
A strict accountant of his beads,
A subtle disputant on creeds,
70 　His dotage trifled well:
Yet better had he neither known
A bigot's shrine—nor despot's throne.

But thou—from thy reluctant hand
　The thunderbolt is wrung—
75 Too late thou leav'st the high command
　To which thy weakness clung;
All Evil Spirit as thou art,
It is enough to grieve the heart
　To see thine own unstrung;
80 To think that God's fair world hath been
The footstool of a thing so mean;

And Earth hath spilt her blood for him,
　Who thus can hoard his own!
And monarchs bow'd the trembling limb,
85 　And thank'd him for a throne!
Fair Freedom! we may hold thee dear,
When thus thy mightiest foes their fear
　In humblest guise have shown.

[1] Milo, a famous Greek athlete (6th cent. B. C.), who is said to have been eaten by wolves while his hands were caught in the cleft of a tree which he had tried to pull apart. See Valerius Maximus's *Factorum et Dictorum Memorabilium*, IX. 12, 2, 9.
[2] After Napoleon abdicated the throne on April 3, 1814, he was banished to the Island of Elba.
[3] Sulla, the great Roman general, who made himself dictator, revenged himself on his foes, and then, in the height of his power (79 B. C.), retired to private life.
[4] Charles V, King of Spain and Emperor of the Holy Roman Empire, who abdicated his throne in 1556, and spent the rest of his life in a monastery.

Oh! ne'er may tyrant leave behind
90 A brighter name to lure mankind!

Thine evil deeds are writ in gore,
    Nor written thus in vain—
Thy triumphs tell of fame no more,
    Or deepen every stain:
95 If thou hadst died as honor dies,
Some new Napoleon might arise,
    To shame the world again—
But who would soar the solar height,
To set in such a starless night?

100 Weigh'd in the balance, hero dust
    Is vile as vulgar clay;
Thy scales, Mortality! are just
    To all that pass away:
But yet methought the living great
105 Some higher sparks should animate,
    To dazzle and dismay:
Nor deem'd Contempt could thus make
        mirth
Of these, the conquerors of the earth.

And she, proud Austria's mournful flower,
110   Thy still imperial bride;[1]
How bears her breast the torturing hour?
    Still clings she to thy side?
Must she too bend, must she too share
Thy late repentance, long despair,
115   Thou throneless homicide?
If still she loves thee, hoard that gem,—
    'Tis worth thy vanish'd diadem!

Then haste thee to thy sullen isle,
    And gaze upon the sea;
120 That element may meet thy smile—
    It ne'er was ruled by thee!
Or trace with thine all idle hand
In loitering mood upon the sand
    That Earth is now as free!
125 That Corinth's pedagogue[2] hath now
Transferr'd his by-word to thy brow.

Thou Timour! in his captive's cage[3]
    What thoughts will there be thine,
While brooding in thy prison'd rage?
130   But one—"The world was mine!"
Unless, like he of Babylon,[4]
All sense is with thy sceptre gone,

Life will not long confine
That spirit pour'd so widely forth—
135 So long obey'd—so little worth!

Or, like the thief of fire from heaven,[1]
    Wilt thou withstand the shock?
And share with him, the unforgiven,
    His vulture and his rock!
140 Foredoom'd by God—by man accurst,
And that last act, though not thy worst,
    The very Fiend's arch mock;[2]
He in his fall preserved his pride,
And, if a mortal, had as proudly died!

145 There was a day—there was an hour,
    While earth was Gaul's—Gaul thine—
When that immeasurable power
    Unsated to resign
Had been an act of purer fame
150 Than gathers round Marengo's name,
    And gilded thy decline,
Through the long twilight of all time,
Despite some passing clouds of crime.

But thou forsooth must be a king,
155   And don the purple vest,
As if that foolish robe could wring
    Remembrance from thy breast.
Where is that faded garment? where
The gewgaws thou wert fond to wear,
160   The star, the string,[3] the crest?
Vain froward child of empire! say,
Are all thy playthings snatched away?

Where may the wearied eye repose
    When gazing on the Great;
165 Where neither guilty glory glows,
    Nor despicable state?
Yes—one—the first—the last—the best—
The Cincinnatus of the West,
    Whom envy dared not hate,
170 Bequeath'd the name of Washington,
To make man blush there was but one!

SHE WALKS IN BEAUTY[4]
1814   1815

She walks in beauty, like the night
    Of cloudless climes and starry skies;
And all that's best of dark and bright
    Meet in her aspect and her eyes:
5 Thus mellow'd to that tender light
    Which heaven to gaudy day denies.

---

[1] Maria Louisa, daughter of Francis I, Emperor of Austria (1804-35).
[2] Dionysius the Younger, who opened a school for boys at Corinth (344 B. C.) after he was banished from Syracuse.
[3] Napoleon is likened to Timur (Tamerlane), the Mongolian conqueror, who in 1402 defeated and captured Bajazet I, Sultan of Turkey, and is said to have carried him about in an iron cage. See Marlowe's *Tamburlaine the Great*, IV, 2; also Rowe's *Tamerlane*.
[4] Nebuchadnezzar, King of Babylon (604-561 B. C.). He was insane for seven years. See *Daniel*, 4.

[1] Prometheus.
[2] A reference to the story that Napoleon was engaged in an unworthy love affair at the time of his abdication. See *Othello*, IV, 1, 69.
[3] The chain of enameled eagles.
[4] Lady Wilmot Horton, whom Byron had seen at a ball, attired in mourning with spangles on her dress.

One shade the more, one ray the less,
  Had half impaired the nameless grace
Which waves in every raven tress,
10 Or softly lightens o'er her face;
Where thoughts serenely sweet express
  How pure, how dear their dwelling-
    place.

And on that cheek, and o'er that brow,
So soft, so calm, yet eloquent,
15 The smiles that win, the tints that glow,
  But tell of days in goodness spent,
A mind at peace with all below,
  A heart whose love is innocent!

OH! SNATCH'D AWAY IN BEAUTY'S BLOOM[1]
1814   1815

Oh! snatch'd away in beauty's bloom,
On thee shall press no ponderous tomb;
But on thy turf shall roses rear
  Their leaves, the earliest of the year;
5 And the wild cypress[2] wave in tender
  gloom: *too facile, + trite*

And oft by yon blue gushing stream
  Shall Sorrow lean her drooping head,
And feed deep thought with many a
  dream,
  And lingering pause and lightly tread;
10 Fond wretch! as if her step disturb'd
  the dead!

Away! we know that tears are vain,
  That death nor heeds nor hears distress:
Will this unteach us to complain?
  Or make one mourner weep the less?
15 And thou—who tell'st me to forget,
Thy looks are wan, thine eyes are wet.

MY SOUL IS DARK
1814   1815

My soul is dark—Oh! quickly string
  The harp I yet can brook to hear;[3]
And let thy gentle fingers fling
  Its melting murmurs o'er mine ear.
5 If in this heart a hope be dear,
  That sound shall charm it forth again:
If in these eyes there lurk a tear,
  'Twill flow, and cease to burn my brain.

But bid the strain be wild and deep,
10 Nor let thy notes of joy be first:

---

[1] It has been surmised that this poem refers to the unidentified Thyrza. See Byron's *To Thyrza.*
[2] The cypress is an emblem of mourning; it is a common tree in graveyards.
[3] See Macpherson's *Oina Morul* (p. 92a, 32). Byron was a great admirer of the Ossianic poems.

I tell thee, minstrel, I must weep,
  Or else this heavy heart will burst;
For it hath been by sorrow nursed,
  And ach'd in sleepless silence long;
15 And now 'tis doom'd to know the worst,
  And break at once—or yield to song.

SONG OF SAUL BEFORE HIS LAST BATTLE[1]
1815   1815

Warriors and chiefs! should the shaft or
  the sword
Pierce me in leading the host of the Lord,
Heed not the corse, though a king's, in
  your path:
Bury your steel in the bosoms of Gath!

5 Thou who art bearing my buckler and
  bow,
Should the soldiers of Saul look away
  from the foe,
Stretch me that moment in blood at thy
  feet!
Mine be the doom which they dared not to
  meet.

Farewell to others, but never we part,
10 Heir to my royalty, son of my heart!
Bright is the diadem, boundless the sway,
Or kingly the death, which awaits us
  today!

HEROD'S LAMENT FOR MARIAMNE
1815   1815

Oh, Mariamne! now for thee
  The heart for which thou bled'st is
    bleeding;
Revenge is lost in agony,
  And wild remorse to rage succeeding.
5 Oh, Mariamne! where art thou?
  Thou canst not hear my bitter pleading:
Ah! could'st thou—thou would'st pardon
  now,
  Though Heaven were to my prayer un-
    heeding.

And is she dead?—and did they dare
10 Obey my frenzy's jealous raving?
My wrath but doom'd my own despair:
  The sword that smote her's o'er me
    waving.—
But thou art cold, my murder'd love!
  And this dark heart is vainly craving
15 For her who soars alone above,
  And leaves my soul unworthy saving.

She's gone, who shared my diadem;
  She sunk, with her my joys entombing;

---

[1] See *1 Samuel*, 31.

I swept that flower from Judah's stem,
20   Whose leaves for me alone were blooming;
And mine's the guilt, and mine the hell,
  This bosom's desolation dooming;
And I have earn'd those tortures well,
  Which unconsumed are still consuming!

THE DESTRUCTION OF SENNACHERIB[1]
1815   1815

The Assyrian came down like the wolf on
  the fold,
And his cohorts were gleaming in purple
  and gold;
And the sheen of their spears was like
  stars on the sea,
When the blue wave rolls nightly on deep
  Galilee.

5 Like the leaves of the forest when summer
  is green,
That host with their banners at sunset
  were seen:
Like the leaves of the forest when autumn
  hath blown,
That host on the morrow lay wither'd and
  strown.

For the Angel of Death spread his wings
  on the blast,
10 And breathed in the face of the foe as he
  pass'd;
And the eyes of the sleepers wax'd deadly
  and chill,
And their hearts but once heaved, and forever
  grew still!

And there lay the steed with his nostril all
  wide,
But through it there roll'd not the breath
  of his pride;
15 And the foam of his gasping lay white on
  the turf,
And cold as the spray of the rock-beating
  surf.

And there lay the rider distorted and pale,
With the dew on his brow, and the rust on
  his mail:
And the tents were all silent, the banners
  alone,
20 The lances unlifted, the trumpet unblown.

And the widows of Ashur are loud in
  their wail,
And the idols are broke in the temple of
  Baal;

[1] See *2 Kings*, 18-19.

And the might of the Gentile, unsmote by
  the sword,
Hath melted like snow in the glance of the
  Lord!

STANZAS FOR MUSIC
1815   1816

There's not a joy the world can give like
  that it takes away,
When the glow of early thought declines
  in feeling's dull decay;
'Tis not on youth's smooth cheek the blush
  alone, which fades so fast,
But the tender bloom of heart is gone, ere
  youth itself be past.

5 Then the few whose spirits float above the
  wreck of happiness
Are driven o'er the shoals of guilt or ocean
  of excess:
The magnet of their course is gone, or
  only points in vain
The shore to which their shiver'd sail shall
  never stretch again.

Then the mortal coldness of the soul like
  death itself comes down;
10 It cannot feel for others' woes, it dare
  not dream its own;
That heavy chill has frozen o'er the fountain
  of our tears,
And though the eye may sparkle still, 'tis
  where the ice appears.

Though wit may flash from fluent lips,
  and mirth distract the breast,
Through midnight hours that yield no
  more their former hope of rest;
15 'Tis but as ivy-leaves around the ruin'd
  turret wreath,
All green and wildly fresh without, but
  worn and gray beneath.

Oh could I feel as I have felt,—or be what
  I have been,
Or weep as I could once have wept o'er
  many a vanish'd scene;
As springs in deserts found seem sweet,
  all brackish though they be,
20 So, midst the wither'd waste of life, those
  tears would flow to me.

FARE THEE WELL[1]
1816   1816

"Alas! they had been friends in youth;
But whispering tongues can poison truth;
And constancy lives in realms above;
And life is thorny; and youth is vain;
And to be wroth with one we love,
Doth work like madness in the brain;
     *   *   *   *

[1] Addressed to Byron's wife, shortly after their
separation.

> But never either found another
> To free the hollow heart from paining—
> They stood aloof, the scars remaining,
> Like cliffs which had been rent asunder;
> A dreary sea now flows between,
> But neither heat, nor frost, nor thunder,
> Shall wholly do away, I ween,
> The marks of that which once hath been."
> —COLERIDGE'S *Christabel*.[1]

Fare thee well! and if forever,
   Still forever, fare *thee well:*
Even though unforgiving, never
   'Gainst thee shall my heart rebel.

5 Would that breast were bared before thee
   Where thy head so oft hath lain,
While that placid sleep came o'er thee
   Which thou ne'er canst know again:

Would that breast, by thee glanced over,
10   Every inmost thought could show!
Then thou wouldst at last discover
   'Twas not well to spurn it so.

Though the world for this commend thee—
   Though it smile upon the blow,
15 Even its praises must offend thee,
   Founded on another's woe:

Though my many faults defaced me,
   Could no other arm be found,
Than the one which once embraced me,
20   To inflict a cureless wound?

Yet, oh yet, thyself deceive not;
   Love may sink by slow decay,
But by sudden wrench, believe not
   Hearts can thus be torn away:

25 Still thine own its life retaineth,
   Still must mine, though bleeding, beat;
And the undying thought which paineth
   Is—that we no more may meet.

These are words of deeper sorrow
30   Than the wail above the dead;
Both shall live, but every morrow
   Wakes us from a widow'd bed.

And when thou wouldst solace gather,
   When our child's first accents flow,
35 Wilt thou teach her to say "Father!"[2]
   Though his care she must forego?

When her little hands shall press thee,
   When her lip to thine is press'd,
Think of him whose prayer shall bless thee,
40   Think of him thy love had bless'd!

---

[1] Lines 408-13; 419-26 (p. 373).
[2] Lady Byron kept Byron's relationship concealed from their daughter Ada.

Should her lineaments resemble
   Those thou never more may'st see,
Then thy heart will softly tremble
   With a pulse yet true to me.

45 All my faults perchance thou knowest,
   All my madness none can know;
All my hopes, where'er thou goest,
   Wither, yet with *thee* they go.

Every feeling hath been shaken;
50   Pride, which not a world could bow,
Bows to thee—by thee forsaken,
   Even my soul forsakes me now:

But 'tis done—all words are idle—
   Words from me are vainer still;
55 But the thoughts we cannot bridle
   Force their way without the will.

Fare thee well! thus disunited,
   Torn from every nearer tie,
Sear'd in heart, and lone, and blighted,
60   More than this I scarce can die.

STANZAS FOR MUSIC
1816   1816

There be none of Beauty's daughters
   With a magic like thee;
And like music on the waters
   Is thy sweet voice to me:
5 When, as if its sound were causing
   The charmed ocean's pausing,
The waves lie still and gleaming,
   And the lull'd winds seem dreaming:

And the midnight moon is weaving
10   Her bright chain o'er the deep;
Whose breast is gently heaving,
   As an infant's asleep:
So the spirit bows before thee,
   To listen and adore thee;
15 With a full but soft emotion,
   Like the swell of Summer's ocean.

SONNET ON CHILLON
1816   1816

Eternal Spirit of the chainless Mind!
Brightest in dungeons, Liberty! thou art,
For there thy habitation is the heart—
The heart which love of thee alone can
   bind;
5 And when thy sons to fetters are consign'd—
To fetters, and the damp vault's dayless
   gloom,
Their country conquers with their martyrdom,

And Freedom's fame finds wings on every
     wind.
Chillon! thy prison is a holy place,
10 And thy sad floor an altar—for 'twas trod,
Until his very steps have left a trace
Worn, as if thy cold pavement were a sod,
By Bonnivard! May none those marks
     efface!
For they appeal from tyranny to God.

THE PRISONER OF CHILLON
1816   1816

My hair is gray, but not with years,
     Nor grew it white
     In a single night,
As men's have grown from sudden fears:[1]
5 My limbs are bow'd, though not with toil,
     But rusted with a vile repose,
For they have been a dungeon's spoil,
     And mine has been the fate of those
To whom the goodly earth and air
10 Are bann'd, and barr'd—forbidden fare:
But this was for my father's faith
I suffer'd chains and courted death;
That father perish'd at the stake
For tenets he would not forsake;
15 And for the same his lineal race
In darkness found a dwelling-place;
We were seven—who now are one,
     Six in youth, and one in age,
Finish'd as they had begun,
20   Proud of Persecution's rage;
One in fire, and two in field,
Their belief with blood have seal'd,
Dying as their father died,
For the God their foes denied;
25 Three were in a dungeon cast,
Of whom this wreck is left the last.

There are seven pillars of Gothic mould,
In Chillon's dungeons deep and old,
There are seven columns, massy and gray,
30 Dim with a dull imprison'd ray,
A sunbeam which hath lost its way,
And through the crevice and the cleft
Of the thick wall is fallen and left;
Creeping o'er the floor so damp,
35 Like a marsh's meteor lamp:
And in each pillar there is a ring,
     And in each ring there is a chain;
That iron is a cankering thing,
     For in these limbs its teeth remain,
40 With marks that will not wear away,
Till I have done with this new day,
Which now is painful to these eyes,
Which have not seen the sun so rise

1 Byron cites, in a note, the cases of Ludovico
Sforza (1451-1508) and others.

For years—I cannot count them o'er,
45 I lost their long and heavy score,
When my last brother droop'd and died,
And I lay living by his side.

They chain'd us each to a column stone,
And we were three—yet, each alone;
50 We could not move a single pace,
We could not see each other's face,
But with that pale and livid light
That made us strangers in our sight:
And thus together—yet apart,
55 Fetter'd in hand, but join'd in heart,
'Twas still some solace, in the dearth
Of the pure elements of earth,
To hearken to each other's speech,
And each turn comforter to each
60 With some new hope, or legend old,
Or song heroically bold;
But even these at length grew cold.
Our voices took a dreary tone,
An echo of the dungeon stone,
65   A grating sound, not full and free
     As they of yore were wont to be:
     It might be fancy, but to me
They never sounded like our own.

I was the eldest of the three,
70   And to uphold and cheer the rest
     I ought to do—and did my best;
And each did well in his degree.
     The youngest, whom my father loved,
Because our mother's brow was given
75 To him, with eyes as blue as heaven—
     For him my soul was sorely moved;
And truly might it be distress'd
To see such bird in such a nest;
For he was beautiful as day
80   (When day was beautiful to me
     As to young eagles, being free)—
A polar day, which will not see
A sunset till its summer's gone,
     Its sleepless summer of long light,
85 The snow-clad offspring of the sun:
     And thus he was as pure and bright,
And in his natural spirit gay,
With tears for nought but others' ills,
And then they flow'd like mountain rills,
90 Unless he could assuage the woe
Which he abhorr'd to view below.

The other was as pure of mind,
But form'd to combat with his kind;
Strong in his frame, and of a mood
95 Which 'gainst the world in war had stood,
And perish'd in the foremost rank
     With joy:—but not in chains to pine:
His spirit wither'd with their clank,
     I saw it silently decline—

100 And so perchance in sooth did mine:
But yet I forced it on to cheer
Those relics of a home so dear.
He was a hunter of the hills,
Had follow'd there the deer and wolf;
105 To him his dungeon was a gulf,
And fetter'd feet the worst of ills.

Lake Leman lies by Chillon's walls:
A thousand feet in depth below,
Its massy waters meet and flow;
110 Thus much the fathom-line was sent
From Chillon's snow-white battlement,
Which round about the wave inthrals:
A double dungeon wall and wave
Have made—and like a living grave.
115 Below the surface of the lake[1]
The dark vault lies wherein we lay;
We heard it ripple night and day;
Sounding o'er our heads it knock'd;
And I have felt the winter's spray
120 Wash through the bars when winds were high
And wanton in the happy sky;
And then the very rock hath rock'd,
And I have felt it shake, unshock'd,
Because I could have smiled to see
125 The death that would have set me free.

I said my nearer brother pined,
I said his mighty heart declined,
He loathed and put away his food;
It was not that 'twas coarse and rude,
130 For we were used to hunters' fare,
And for the like had little care:
The milk drawn from the mountain goat
Was changed for water from the moat,
Our bread was such as captives' tears
135 Have moisten'd many a thousand years,
Since man first pent his fellow men
Like brutes within an iron den;
But what were these to us or him?
These wasted not his heart or limb;
140 My brother's soul was of that mould
Which in a palace had grown cold,
Had his free breathing been denied
The range of the steep mountain's side;
But why delay the truth?—he died.
145 I saw, and could not hold his head,
Nor reach his dying hand—nor dead,—
Though hard I strove, but strove in vain,
To rend and gnash my bonds in twain.
He died—and they unlock'd his chain,
150 And scoop'd for him a shallow grave
Even from the cold earth of our cave.
I begg'd them, as a boon, to lay
His corse in dust whereon the day

[1] The dungeon is not below the surface of the lake.

Might shine—it was a foolish thought,
155 But then within my brain it wrought,
That even in death his freeborn breast
In such a dungeon could not rest.
I might have spared my idle prayer—
They coldly laugh'd, and laid him there:
160 The flat and turfless earth above
The being we so much did love;
His empty chain above it leant,
Such murder's fitting monument!

But he, the favorite and the flower,
165 Most cherish'd since his natal hour,
His mother's image in fair face,
The infant love of all his race,
His martyr'd father's dearest thought,
My latest care, for whom I sought
170 To hoard my life, that his might be
Less wretched now, and one day free;
He, too, who yet had held untired
A spirit natural or inspired—
He, too, was struck, and day by day
175 Was wither'd on the stalk away.
Oh, God! it is a fearful thing
To see the human soul take wing
In any shape, in any mood:
I've seen it rushing forth in blood,
180 I've seen it on the breaking ocean
Strive with a swoln convulsive motion,
I've seen the sick and ghastly bed
Of Sin delirious with its dread;
But these were horrors—this was woe
185 Unmix'd with such—but sure and slow:
He faded, and so calm and meek,
So softly worn, so sweetly weak,
So tearless, yet so tender—kind,
And grieved for those he left behind;
190 With all the while a cheek whose bloom
Was as a mockery of the tomb,
Whose tints as gently sunk away
As a departing rainbow's ray;
An eye of most transparent light,
195 That almost made the dungeon bright,
And not a word of murmur, not
A groan o'er his untimely lot,—
A little talk of better days,
A little hope my own to raise,
200 For I was sunk in silence—lost
In this last loss, of all the most;
And then the sighs he would suppress
Of fainting nature's feebleness,
More slowly drawn, grew less and less:
205 I listen'd, but I could not hear;
I call'd, for I was wild with fear;
I knew 'twas hopeless, but my dread
Would not be thus admonished;
I call'd, and thought I heard a sound—
210 I burst my chain with one strong bound,
And rush'd to him:—I found him not,

I only stirr'd in this black spot,
I only lived, *I* only drew
The accursed breath of dungeon-dew;
215 The last, the sole, the dearest link
Between me and the eternal brink,
Which bound me to my failing race,
Was broken in this fatal place.
One on the earth, and one beneath—
220 My brothers—both had ceased to breathe:
I took that hand which lay so still,
Alas! my own was full as chill;
I had not strength to stir, or strive,
But felt that I was still alive—
225 A frantic feeling, when we know
That what we love shall ne'er be so.
    I know not why
    I could not die,
I had no earthly hope—but faith,
230 And that forbade a selfish death.

What next befell me then and there
    I know not well—I never knew;
First came the loss of light, and air,
    And then of darkness too:
235 I had no thought, no feeling—none;
Among the stones I stood a stone,
And was, scarce conscious what I wist,
As shrubless crags within the mist;
For all was blank, and bleak, and gray;
240 It was not night, it was not day;
It was not even the dungeon-light,
So hateful to my heavy sight,
But vacancy absorbing space,
And fixedness—without a place;
245 There were no stars, no earth, no time,
No check, no change, no good, no crime—
But silence, and a stirless breath
Which neither was of life nor death;
A sea of stagnant idleness,
250 Blind, boundless, mute, and motionless!

A light broke in upon my brain,—
    It was the carol of a bird;
It ceased, and then it came again,
    The sweetest song ear ever heard,
255 And mine was thankful till my eyes
Ran over with the glad surprise,
And they that moment could not see
I was the mate of misery;
But then by dull degrees came back
260 My senses to their wonted track;
I saw the dungeon walls and floor
Close slowly round me as before;
I saw the glimmer of the sun
Creeping as it before had done,
265 But through the crevice where it came
That bird was perch'd, as fond and tame,
    And tamer than upon the tree;
A lovely bird, with azure wings,

And song that said a thousand things,
270   And seem'd to say them all for me!
I never saw its like before,
I ne'er shall see its likeness more:
It seem'd like me to want a mate,
But was not half so desolate,
275 And it was come to love me when
None lived to love me so again,
And cheering from my dungeon's brink,
Had brought me back to feel and think.
I know not if it late were free,
280   Or broke its cage to perch on mine,
But knowing well captivity,
    Sweet bird! I could not wish for thine!
Or if it were, in winged guise,
A visitant from Paradise,
285 For—Heaven forgive that thought! the while
Which made me both to weep and smile—
I sometimes deem'd that it might be
My brother's soul come down to me;
But then at last away it flew,
290 And then 'twas mortal—well I knew,
For he would never thus have flown,
And left me twice so doubly lone,—
Lone—as the corse within its shroud,
Lone—as a solitary cloud,
295   A single cloud on a sunny day,
While all the rest of heaven is clear,
A frown upon the atmosphere,
That hath no business to appear
    When skies are blue, and earth is gay.

300 A kind of change came in my fate,
My keepers grew compassionate;
I know not what had made them so,
They were inured to sights of woe,
But so it was:—my broken chain
305 With links unfasten'd did remain,
And it was liberty to stride
Along my cell from side to side,
And up and down, and then athwart,
And tread it over every part;
310 And round the pillars one by one,
Returning where my walk begun,
Avoiding only, as I trod,
My brothers' graves without a sod;
For if I thought with heedless tread
315 My step profaned their lowly bed,
My breath came gaspingly and thick,
And my crush'd heart fell blind and sick.

I made a footing in the wall,
    It was not therefrom to escape,
320 For I had buried one and all
    Who loved me in a human shape;
And the whole earth would henceforth be
A wider prison unto me:
No child, no sire, no kin had I,

325 No partner in my misery;
      I thought of this, and I was glad,
      For thought of them had made me mad;
      But I was curious to ascend
      To my barr'd windows, and to bend
330 Once more, upon the mountains high,
      The quiet of a loving eye.

      I saw them—and they were the same,
      They were not changed like me in frame;
      I saw their thousand years of snow
335 On high—their wide long lake below,
      And the blue Rhone in fullest flow;
      I heard the torrents leap and gush
      O'er channell'd rock and broken bush;
      I saw the white-wall'd distant town,[1]
340 And whiter sails go skimming down;
      And then there was a little isle,
      Which in my very face did smile,
        The only one in view;
      A small green isle, it seem'd no more,
345 Scarce broader than my dungeon floor,
      But in it there were three tall trees,
      And o'er it blew the mountain breeze,
      And by it there were waters flowing,
      And on it there were young flowers
        growing,
350 Of gentle breath and hue.
      The fish swam by the castle wall,
      And they seem'd joyous each and all;
      The eagle rode the rising blast,
      Methought he never flew so fast
355 As then to me he seem'd to fly;
      And then new tears came in my eye,
      And I felt troubled—and would fain
      I had not left my recent chain;
      And when I did descend again,
360 The darkness of my dim abode
      Fell on me as a heavy load;
      It was as in a new-dug grave,
      Closing o'er one we sought to save,—
      And yet my glance, too much opprest,
365 Had almost need of such a rest.

      It might be months, or years, or days—
        I kept no count, I took no note,
      I had no hope my eyes to raise,
        And clear them of their dreary mote;
370 At last men came to set me free;
        I ask'd not why, and reck'd not where;
      It was at length the same to me,
      Fetter'd or fetterless to be,
        I learn'd to love despair.
375 And thus when they appear'd at last,
      And all my bonds aside were cast,
      These heavy walls to me had grown
      A hermitage—and all my own!
      And half I felt as they were come
      [1] Villeneuve.

380 To tear me from a second home:
      With spiders I had friendship made,
      And watch'd them in their sullen trade,
      Had seen the mice by moonlight play,
      And why should I feel less than they?
385 We were all inmates of one place,
      And I, the monarch of each race,
      Had power to kill—yet, strange to tell!
      In quiet we had learn'd to dwell;
      My very chains and I grew friends,
390 So much a long communion tends
      To make us what we are:—even I
      Regain'd my freedom with a sigh.

STANZAS TO AUGUSTA
1816   1816

      Though the day of my destiny's over,
        And the star of my fate hath declined,
      Thy soft heart refused to discover
        The faults which so many could find;[1]
5   Though thy soul with my grief was ac-
          quainted,
        It shrunk not to share it with me,
      And the love which my spirit hath painted
        It never hath found but in *thee*.
      Then when nature around me is smiling,
10   The last smile which answers to mine,
      I do not believe it beguiling,
        Because it reminds me of thine;
      And when winds are at war with the
          ocean,
        As the breasts I believed in with me,
15 If their billows excite an emotion,
        It is that they bear me from *thee*.

      Though the rock of my last hope is
          shiver'd,
        And its fragments are sunk in the wave,
      Though I feel that my soul is deliver'd
20   To pain—it shall not be its slave.
      There is many a pang to pursue me:
        They may crush, but they shall not
            contemn;
      They may torture, but shall not subdue
            me;
        'Tis of *thee* that I think—not of them.

25 Though human, thou didst not deceive
            me,
        Though woman, thou didst not forsake,
      Though loved, thou forborest to grieve
            me,
        Though slander'd, thou never couldst
            shake;
      Though trusted, thou didst not disclaim
            me,

      [1] Throughout all his domestic troubles, Byron
      was loyally supported by his sister Augusta.
      See *Childe Harold's Pilgrimage*, III, 53-55 (p.
      557).

30 Though parted, it was not to fly,
  Though watchful, 'twas not to defame
      me,
  Nor, mute, that the world might belie.

  Yet I blame not the world, nor despise it,
  Nor the war of the many with one;
35 If my soul was not fitted to prize it,
    'Twas folly not sooner to shun:
  And if dearly that error hath cost me,
    And more than I once could foresee,
  I have found that, whatever it lost me,
40   It could not deprive me of *thee*.

  From the wreck of the past, which hath
      perish'd,
    Thus much I at least may recall,
  It hath taught me that what I most
      cherish'd
    Deserved to be dearest of all:
45 In the desert a fountain is springing,
    In the wide waste there still is a tree,
  And a bird in the solitude singing,
    Which speaks to my spirit of *thee*.

EPISTLE TO AUGUSTA
1816   1830

  My sister! my sweet sister! if a name
  Dearer and purer were, it should be
      thine;
  Mountains and seas divide us, but I
      claim
  No tears, but tenderness to answer
      mine:
5 Go where I will, to me thou art the
      same—
  A loved regret which I would not re-
      sign.
  There yet are two things in my des-
      tiny,—
  A world to roam through, and a home
      with thee.

  The first were nothing—had I still the
      last,
10 It were the haven of my happiness;
  But other claims and other ties thou
      hast,
  And mine is not the wish to make them
      less.
  A strange doom is thy father's son's,
      and past
  Recalling, as it lies beyond redress;
15 Reversed for him our grandsire's fate
      of yore,—
  He had no rest at sea,[1] nor I on shore.

  [1] Admiral John Byron (1723-86), who was said
  to have encountered a storm on every voyage.
  He was known to the sailors as "Foulweather
  Jack."

  If my inheritance of storms hath been
  In other elements, and on the rocks
  Of perils, overlook'd or unforeseen,
20 I have sustain'd my share of worldly
      shocks,
  The fault was mine; nor do I seek to
      screen
  My errors with defensive paradox;
  I have been cunning in mine over-
      throw,
  The careful pilot of my proper[1] woe.

25 Mine were my faults, and mine be their
      reward.
  My whole life was a contest, since the
      day
  That gave me being, gave me that which
      marr'd
  The gift,—a fate, or will, that walk'd
      astray;
  And I at times have found the struggle
      hard,
30 And thought of shaking off my bonds
      of clay:
  But now I fain would for a time sur-
      vive,
  If but to see what next can well arrive.

  Kingdoms and empires in my little day
  I have outlived, and yet I am not old;
35 And when I look on this, the petty
      spray
  Of my own years of trouble, which have
      roll'd
  Like a wild bay of breakers, melts
      away:
  Something—I know not what—does
      still uphold
  A spirit of slight patience;—not in vain,
40 Even for its own sake, do we purchase
      pain.

  Perhaps the workings of defiance stir
  Within me,—or perhaps a cold despair,
  Brought on when ills habitually recur,—
  Perhaps a kinder clime, or purer air
45 (For even to this may change of soul
      refer,
  And with light armor we may learn to
      bear),
  Have taught me a strange quiet, which
      was not
  The chief companion of a calmer lot.

  I feel almost at times as I have felt
50 In happy childhood; trees, and flowers,
      and brooks,

  [1] own

Which do remember me of where I
    dwelt
Ere my young mind was sacrificed to
    books,
Come as of yore upon me, and can melt
My heart with recognition of their
    looks;
55 And even at moments I could think I
    see
Some living thing to love—but none like
    thee.

Here are the Alpine landscapes which
    create
A fund for contemplation;—to admire
Is a brief feeling of a trivial date;
60 But something worthier do such scenes
    inspire:
Here to be lonely is not desolate,
For much I view which I could most
    desire,
And, above all, a lake I can behold[1]
Lovelier, not dearer, than our own of old.[2]

65 Oh that thou wert but with me!—but
    I grow
The fool of my own wishes, and forget
The solitude, which I have vaunted so,
Has lost its praise in this but one re-
    gret;
There may be others which I less may
    show;—
70 I am not of the plaintive mood, and yet
I feel an ebb in my philosophy,
And the tide rising in my alter'd eye.

I did remind thee of our own dear lake,
By the old hall which may be mine no
    more.
75 Leman's is fair; but think not I for-
    sake
The sweet remembrance of a dearer
    shore:
Sad havoc Time must with my memory
    make,
Ere *that* or *thou* can fade these eyes
    before;
Though, like all things which I have
    loved, they are
80 Resign'd forever, or divided far.

The world is all before me; I but ask
Of Nature that with which she will
    comply—
It is but in her summer's sun to bask,
To mingle with the quiet of her sky,

85 To see her gentle face without a mask,
And never gaze on it with apathy.
She was my early friend, and now
    shall be
My sister—till I look again on thee.

I can reduce all feelings but this one;
90 And that I would not;—for at length
    I see
Such scenes as those wherein my life
    begun,
The earliest—even the only paths for
    me;
Had I but sooner learnt the crowd to
    shun,
I had been better than I now can be;
95 The passions which have torn me would
    have slept;
I had not suffer'd, and *thou* hadst not
    wept.

With false Ambition what had I to do?
Little with Love, and least of all with
    Fame;
And yet they came unsought, and with
    me grew,
100 And made me all which they can make
    —a name.
Yet this was not the end I did pursue;
Surely I once beheld a nobler aim.
But all is over—I am one the more
To baffled millions which have gone be-
    fore.

105 And for the future, this world's future
    may
From me demand but little of my care;
I have outlived myself by many a day,
Having survived so many things that
    were;
My years have been no slumber, but
    the prey
110 Of ceaseless vigils; for I had the share
Of life which might have fill'd a cen-
    tury,
Before its fourth in time had pass'd me
    by.

And for the remnant which may be to
    come
I am content; and for the past I feel
115 Not thankless,—for within the crowded
    sum
Of struggles, happiness at times would
    steal;
And for the present, I would not be-
    numb
My feelings further.—Nor shall I con-
    ceal

---

[1] Lake Leman (Geneva).
[2] The lake of Newstead Abbey. For a description of it, see *Don Juan*, XIII, 57.

That with all this I still can look around,
120 And worship Nature with a thought profound.

For thee, my own sweet sister, in thy heart
I know myself secure, as thou in mine;
We were and are—I am, even as thou art—
Beings who ne'er each other can resign;
125 It is the same, together or apart,
From life's commencement to its slow decline
We are entwined—let death come slow or fast,
The tie which bound the first endures the last!

DARKNESS
1816   1816

I had a dream, which was not all a dream.
The bright sun was extinguish'd, and the stars
Did wander darkling in the eternal space,
Rayless, and pathless, and the icy earth
5 Swung blind and blackening in the moonless air;
Morn came and went—and came, and brought no day,
And men forgot their passions in the dread
Of this their desolation; and all hearts
Were chill'd into a selfish prayer for light:
10 And they did live by watchfires—and the thrones,
The palaces of crowned kings—the huts,
The habitations of all things which dwell,
Were burnt for beacons; cities were consumed,
And men were gather'd round their blazing homes
15 To look once more into each other's face;
Happy were those who dwelt within the eye
Of the volcanos, and their mountain-torch:
A fearful hope was all the world contain'd;
Forests were set on fire—but hour by hour
200 They fell and faded—and the crackling trunks
Extinguish'd with a crash—and all was black.
The brows of men by the despairing light
Wore an unearthly aspect, as by fits
The flashes fell upon them; some lay down

25 And hid their eyes and wept; and some did rest
Their chins upon their clenched hands, and smiled;
And others hurried to and fro, and fed
Their funeral piles with fuel, and look'd up
With mad disquietude on the dull sky,
30 The pall of a past world; and then again
With curses cast them down upon the dust,
And gnash'd their teeth and howl'd: the wild birds shriek'd
And, terrified, did flutter on the ground,
And flap their useless wings; the wildest brutes
35 Came tame and tremulous; and vipers crawl'd
And twined themselves among the multitude,
Hissing, but stingless—they were slain for food!
And War, which for a moment was no more,
Did glut himself again:—a meal was bought
40 With blood, and each sate sullenly apart
Gorging himself in gloom: no love was left;
All earth was but one thought—and that was death
Immediate and inglorious; and the pang
Of famine fed upon all entrails—men
45 Died, and their bones were tombless as their flesh;
The meagre by the meagre were devour'd,
Even dogs assail'd their masters, all save one,
And he was faithful to a corse, and kept
The birds and beasts and famish'd men at bay,
50 Till hunger clung them,[1] or the dropping dead
Lured their lank jaws; himself sought out no food,
But with a piteous and perpetual moan,
And a quick desolate cry, licking the hand
Which answer'd not with a caress—he died.
55 The crowd was famish'd by degrees; but two
Of an enormous city did survive,
And they were enemies: they met beside
The dying embers of an altar-place,
Where had been heap'd a mass of holy things
60 For an unholy usage; they raked up,

[1] dried them up (See *Macbeth*, V, 5, 40.)

And shivering scraped with their cold
 skeleton hands
The feeble ashes, and their feeble breath
Blew for a little life, and made a flame
65 Which was a mockery; then they lifted up
Their eyes as it grew lighter, and beheld
Each other's aspects—saw, and shriek'd,
 and died—
Even of their mutual hideousness they
 died,
Unknowing who he was upon whose brow
Famine had written Fiend. The world
 was void,
70 The populous and the powerful was a
 lump
Seasonless, herbless, treeless, manless,
 lifeless—
A lump of death—a chaos of hard clay.
The rivers, lakes, and ocean all stood still,
And nothing stirr'd within their silent
 depths;
75 Ships sailorless lay rotting on the sea,
And their masts fell down piecemeal: as
 they dropp'd
They slept on the abyss without a surge—
The waves were dead; the tides were in
 their grave,
The Moon, their mistress, had expired before;
80 The winds were wither'd in the stagnant
 air,
And the clouds perish'd; Darkness had
 no need
Of aid from them—She was the Universe.

PROMETHEUS
1816   1816

Titan! to whose immortal eyes
 The sufferings of mortality,
 Seen in their sad reality,
Were not as things that gods despise;
5 What was thy pity's recompense?
A silent suffering, and intense;
The rock, the vulture, and the chain,
All that the proud can feel of pain,
The agony they do not show,
10 The suffocating sense of woe,
 Which speaks but in its loneliness,
And then is jealous lest the sky
Should have a listener, nor will sigh
 Until its voice is echoless.

15 Titan! to thee the strife was given
 Between the suffering and the will,
 Which torture where they cannot kill;
And the inexorable Heaven,
And the deaf tyranny of Fate,
20 The ruling principle of Hate,
Which for its pleasure doth create

The things it may annihilate,
Refused thee even the boon to die:
The wretched gift eternity
25 Was thine—and thou hast borne it well.[1]
All that the Thunderer[2] wrung from thee
Was but the menace which flung back
On him the torments of thy rack;
The fate thou didst so well foresee,
30 But would not to appease him tell;[3]
And in thy silence was his sentence,
And in his soul a vain repentance,
And evil dread so ill dissembled,
That in his hand the lightnings trembled.

35 Thy Godlike crime was to be kind,
 To render with thy precepts less
 The sum of human wretchedness,
And strengthen man with his own mind;
But baffled as thou wert from high,
40 Still in thy patient energy,
In the endurance, and repulse
 Of thine impenetrable spirit,
Which Earth and Heaven could not con-
 vulse,
 A mighty lesson we inherit:
45 Thou art a symbol and a sign
 To mortals of their fate and force;
Like thee, man is in part divine,
 A troubled stream from a pure source;
And man in portions can foresee
50 His own funereal destiny;
His wretchedness, and his resistance,
And his sad unallied existence:
To which his spirit may oppose
Itself—and equal to all woes,
55 And a firm will, and a deep sense,
Which even in torture can descry
 Its own concenter'd recompense,
Triumphant where it dares defy,
And making death a victory.

SONNET TO LAKE LEMAN
1816   1816

Rousseau, Voltaire, our Gibbon, and De
 Staël—
Leman! these names are worthy of thy
 shore,
Thy shore of names likes these!—Wert
 thou no more
Their memory thy remembrance would
 recall:
5 To them thy banks were lovely as to all,
But they have made them lovelier, for the
 lore
Of mighty minds doth hallow in the core

[1] See the legend of Tithonus, and Tennyson's
 Tithonus.
[2] Jupiter.
[3] Prometheus knew that Jupiter and his dynasty
 would be overthrown. See Shelley's *Prome-*
 theus Unbound, I, 371-74 (p. 693).

Of human hearts the ruin of a wall
Where dwelt the wise and wondrous; but
  by *thee*
10 How much more, Lake of Beauty! do we
  feel,
In sweetly gliding o'er thy crystal sea,
The wild glow of that not ungentle zeal,
Which of the heirs of immortality
Is proud, and makes the breath of glory
  real!

STANZAS FOR MUSIC
1816   1829

They say that Hope is happiness;
  But genuine Love must prize the past,
And Memory wakes the thoughts that
    bless:
  They rose the first—they set the last;
5 And all that Memory loves the most
  Was once our only Hope to be,
And all that Hope adored and lost
Hath melted into Memory.

Alas! it is delusion all:
10   The future cheats us from afar,
Nor can we be what we recall,
  Nor dare we think on what we are.

From

CHILDE HAROLD'S PILGRIMAGE
1809-17   1812-18
CANTO III
1816   1816

1 Is thy face like thy mother's, my fair
    child!
  Ada! sole daughter of my house and
    heart?
  When last I saw thy young blue eyes
    they smiled,
  And then we parted,—not as now we
    part,
  But with a hope.—[1]
            A waking with a start,
  The waters heave around me; and on
    high
  The winds lift up their voices: I depart,
  Whither I know not; but the hour's
    gone by,
  When Albion's lessening shores could
    grieve or glad mine eye.

2 Once more upon the waters! yet once
    more!
  And the waves bound beneath me as a
    steed

That knows his rider. Welcome to their
  roar!
Swift be their guidance, wheresoe'er it
  lead!
Though the strain'd mast should quiver
  as a reed,
And the rent canvas fluttering strew the
  gale,
Still must I on; for I am as a weed,
Flung from the rock, on Ocean's foam
  to sail
Where'er the surge may sweep, the tempest's breath prevail.

3 In my youth's summer I did sing of one,[1]
  The wandering outlaw of his own dark
    mind:
  Again I seize the theme, then but begun,
  And bear it with me, as the rushing
    wind
  Bears the cloud onwards: in that tale I
    find
  The furrows of long thought, and dried-
    up tears,
  Which, ebbing, leave a sterile track be-
    hind,
  O'er which all heavily the journeying
    years
  Plod the last sands of life,—where not a
    flower appears.

4 Since my young days of passion—
    joy, or pain,
  Perchance my heart and harp have lost
    a string,
  And both may jar: it may be, that in
    vain
  I would essay as I have sung to sing.
  Yet, though a dreary strain, to this I
    cling;
  So that it wean me from the weary
    dream
  Of selfish grief or gladness—so it fling
  Forgetfulness around me — it shall
    seem
  To me, though to none else, a not un-
    grateful theme.

5 He, who grown aged in this world of
    woe,
  In deeds, not years, piercing the depths
    of life,
  So that no wonder waits him; nor be-
    low
  Can love or sorrow, fame, ambition,
    strife,

---

[1] Lady Byron left her husband in January, 1816.
Ada was then only five weeks old. Byron
never saw her again.

[1] The First Canto of *Childe Harold's Pilgrimage*
was written in 1809, when Byron was 21
years of age.

Cut to his heart again with the keen
  knife
Of silent, sharp endurance: he can tell
Why thought seeks refuge in lone caves,
  yet rife
With airy images, and shapes which
  dwell
Still unimpair'd, though old, in the soul's
  haunted cell.

6 'Tis to create, and in creating live
A being more intense that we endow
With form our fancy, gaining as we
  give
The life we image, even as I do now.
What am I? Nothing: but not so art
  thou,
Soul of my thought! with whom I
  traverse earth,
Invisible, but gazing, as I glow
Mix'd with thy spirit, blended with thy
  birth,
And feeling still with thee in my crush'd
  feelings' dearth.

7 Yet must I think less wildly:—I *have*
  thought
Too long and darkly, till my brain
  became,
In its own eddy boiling and o'erwrought,
A whirling gulf of phantasy and flame:
And thus, untaught in youth my heart
  to tame,
My springs of life were poison'd. 'Tis
  too late!
Yet am I changed; though still enough
  the same
In strength to bear what time cannot
  abate,
And feed on bitter fruits without accus-
  ing Fate.

8 Something too much of this:[1]—but now
  'tis past,
And the spell closes with its silent
  seal.[2]
Long absent Harold reappears at last;
He of the breast which fain no more
  would feel,
Wrung with the wounds which kill not,
  but ne'er heal;
Yet Time, who changes all, had alter'd
  him
In soul and aspect as in age: years
  steal

---

[1] See *Hamlet*, III, 2, 79.
[2] On the story of his own tragedy is set the seal
of silence.

Fire from the mind as vigor from the
  limb;
And life's enchanted cup but sparkles
  near the brim.

9 His had been quaff'd too quickly, and
  he found
The dregs were wormwood; but he
  fill'd again,
And from a purer fount, on holier
  ground,
And deem'd its spring perpetual; but
  in vain!
Still round him clung invisible a chain
Which gall'd forever, fettering though
  unseen,
And heavy though it clank'd not; worn
  with pain,
Which pined although it spoke not, and
  grew keen,
Entering with every step he took through
  many a scene.

10 Secure in guarded coldness, he had mix'd
Again in fancied safety with his kind,
And deem'd his spirit now so firmly fix'd
And sheath'd with an invulnerable mind,
That, if no joy, no sorrow lurk'd behind;
And he, as one, might 'midst the many
  stand
Unheeded, searching through the crowd
  to find
Fit speculation; such as in strange land
He found in wonder-works of God and
  Nature's hand.

11 But who can view the ripen'd rose, nor[1]
  seek
To wear it? who can curiously behold
The smoothness and the sheen of
  beauty's cheek,
Nor feel the heart can never all grow
  old?
Who can contemplate Fame through
  clouds unfold
The star which rises o'er her steep, nor
  climb?
Harold, once more within the vortex,
  roll'd
On with the giddy circle, chasing Time,
Yet with a nobler aim than in his youth's
  fond[2] prime.

12 But soon he knew himself the most unfit
Of men to herd with man; with whom
  he held
Little in common; untaught to submit

---

[1] and not   [2] foolish

His thoughts to others, though his soul
was quell'd
In youth by his own thoughts; still
uncompell'd,
He would not yield dominion of his
mind
To spirits against whom his own re-
bell'd;
Proud though in desolation; which
could find
A life within itself, to breathe without
mankind.

13 Where rose the mountains, there to him
were friends;
Where roll'd the ocean, thereon was his
home;
Where a blue sky, and glowing clime,
extends,
He had the passion and the power to
roam,
The desert, forest, cavern, breaker's
foam,
Were unto him companionship; they
spake
A mutual language, clearer than the
tome
Of his land's tongue, which he would
oft forsake
For Nature's pages glass'd by sunbeams
on the lake.

14 Like the Chaldean, he could watch the
stars,[1]
Till he had peopled them with beings
bright
As their own beams; and earth, and
earth-born jars,
And human frailties, were forgotten
quite:
Could he have kept his spirit to that
flight
He had been happy; but this clay will
sink
Its spark immortal, envying it the light
To which it mounts, as if to break the
link
That keeps us from yon heaven which
woos us to its brink.

15 But in man's dwellings he became a
thing
Restless and worn, and stern and wearisome,
Droop'd as a wild-born falcon with
clipt wing,
To whom the boundless air alone were
home:

[1] The Chaldeans were especially versed in
astrology.

Then came his fit again,[1] which to o'ercome,
As eagerly the barr'd-up bird will beat
His breast and beak against his wiry
dome
Till the blood tinge his plumage, so
the heat
Of his impeded soul would through his
bosom eat.

16 Self-exiled Harold wanders forth again,
With nought of hope left, but with less
of gloom;
The very knowledge that he lived in
vain,
That all was over on this side the tomb,
Had made Despair a smilingness as-
sume,
Which, though 'twere wild,—as on the
plunder'd wreck
When mariners would madly meet their
doom
With draughts intemperate on the sink-
ing deck,—
Did yet inspire a cheer, which he forbore
to check.

17 Stop!—for thy tread is on an empire's
dust!
An earthquake's spoil is sepulchred be-
low!
Is the spot mark'd with no colossal
bust?
Nor column trophied for triumphal
show?
None; but the moral's truth tells sim-
pler so,
As the ground was before, thus let it
be;—
How that red rain hath made the har-
vest grow!
And is this all the world has gain'd by
thee,
Thou first and last of fields! king-making
Victory?[2]

18 And Harold stands upon this place of
skulls,
The grave of France, the deadly Waterloo!
How in an hour the power which gave
annuls
Its gifts, transferring fame as fleeting
too!
In "pride of place"[3] here last the eagle
flew,

[1] See *Macbeth*, III, 4, 21.
[2] The Battle of Waterloo made the thrones of
the European kings more secure.
[3] *Macbeth*, II, 4, 12. This is a term in falconry,
and means *the highest point of flight*.

Then tore with bloody talon the rent
plain,
Pierced by the shaft of banded nations
through;
Ambition's life and labors all were
vain;
He wears the shatter'd links of the
world's broken chain.

19 Fit retribution! Gaul may champ the
bit
And foam in fetters;—but is Earth
more free?
Did nations combat to make *one* submit;
Or league to teach all kings true sovereignty?
What! shall reviving Thraldom again be
The patch'd-up idol of enlighten'd
days?[1]
Shall we, who struck the Lion[2] down,
shall we
Pay the Wolf[3] homage? proffering
lowly gaze
And servile knees to thrones? No; *prove*
before ye praise!

20 If not, o'er one fallen despot boast no
more!
In vain fair cheeks were furrow'd with
hot tears
For Europe's flowers long rooted up
before
The trampler of her vineyards; in vain,
years
Of death, depopulation, bondage, fears,
Have all been borne, and broken by
the accord
Of roused-up millions; all that most
endears
Glory, is when the myrtle wreathes a
sword
Such as Harmodius drew on Athens'
tyrant lord.

21 There was a sound of revelry by night,[4]
And Belgium's capital had gather'd
then
Her Beauty and her Chivalry, and
bright
The lamps shone o'er fair women and
brave men;

A thousand hearts beat happily; and
when
Music arose with its voluptuous swell,
Soft eyes look'd love to eyes which
spake again,
And all went merry as a marriage bell;
But hush! hark! a deep sound strikes
like a rising knell!

22 Did ye not hear it?—No; 'twas but the
wind,
Or the car rattling o'er the stony street;
On with the dance! let joy be uncon-
fined;
No sleep till morn, when Youth and
Pleasure meet
To chase the glowing Hours with flying
feet—
But hark!—that heavy sound breaks in
once more,
As if the clouds its echo would repeat;
And nearer, clearer, deadlier than be-
fore!
Arm! Arm! it is—it is—the cannon's
opening roar!

23 Within a window'd niche of that high
hall
Sate Brunswick's fated chieftain;[1] he
did hear
That sound the first amidst the festival,
And caught its tone with Death's
prophetic ear;
And when they smiled because he
deem'd it near,
His heart more truly knew that peal too
well
Which stretch'd his father on a bloody
bier,
And roused the vengeance blood alone
could quell;
He rush'd into the field, and, foremost
fighting, fell.

24 Ah! then and there was hurrying to
and fro,
And gathering tears, and tremblings of
distress,
And cheeks all pale, which but an hour
ago
Blush'd at the praise of their own loveliness;
And there were sudden partings, such
as press
The life from out young hearts, and
choking sighs

---

[1] The Holy Alliance aimed at the restoration of
pre-Revolutionary conditions.
[2] Napoleon.
[3] Such a poor imitation of imperial strength as
the Austrian emperor and others.
[4] A ball was given at Brussels on the evening
before the battle of Quatre-Bras, which occurred two days before the Battle of Waterloo.

[1] Frederick William, Duke of Brunswick. His
father was killed in the Battle of Auerstädt,
in 1806.

Which ne'er might be repeated; who
  could guess
If ever more should meet those mutual
  eyes,
Since upon night so sweet such awful
  morn could rise!

25 And there was mounting in hot haste:
      the steed,
    The mustering squadron, and the clat-
      tering car,
    Went pouring forward with impetuous
      speed,
    And swiftly forming in the ranks of
      war;
    And the deep thunder peal on peal
      afar;
    And near, the beat of the alarming
      drum
    Roused up the soldier ere the morning
      star;
    While throng'd the citizens with terror
      dumb,
    Or whispering, with white lips—"The
      foe! they come! they come!"

26 And wild and high the *Cameron's Gather-
      ing*[1] rose!
    The war-note of Lochiel, which Albyn's
      hills
    Have heard, and heard, too, have her
      Saxon foes:—[2]
    How in the noon of night that pibroch[3]
      thrills,
    Savage and shrill! But with the breath
      which fills
    Their mountain-pipe, so fill the moun-
      taineers
    With the fierce native daring which
      instils
    The stirring memory of a thousand
      years,
    And Evan's, Donald's fame rings in each
      clansman's ears!

27 And Ardennes waves above them her
      green leaves,
    Dewy with Nature's tear-drops, as they
      pass,
    Grieving, if aught inanimate e'er
      grieves,
    Over the unreturning brave,—alas!
    Ere evening to be trodden like the grass
    Which now beneath them, but above
      shall grow

In its next verdure, when this fiery
  mass
Of living valor, rolling on the foe
And burning with high hope shall moulder cold and low.

28 Last noon beheld them full of lusty
      life,
    Last eve in Beauty's circle proudly gay,
    The midnight brought the signal-sound
      of strife,
    The morn the marshalling in arms,—
      the day
    Battle's magnificently stern array!
    The 'thunder-clouds close o'er it, which
      when rent
    The earth is cover'd thick with other
      clay,
    Which her own clay shall cover, heap'd
      and pent,
  Rider and horse,—friend, foe,—in one
      red burial blent!

29 Their praise is hymn'd by loftier harps
      than mine:[1]
    Yet one I would select from that proud
      throng,[2]
    Partly because they blend me with his
      line,
    And partly that I did his sire some
      wrong,
    And partly that bright names will hal-
      low song;
    And this was of the bravest, and when
      shower'd
    The death-bolts deadliest the thinn'd
      files along,
    Even where the thickest of war's tem-
      pest lower'd,
  They reach'd no nobler breast than thine,
      young gallant Howard!

30 There have been tears and breaking
      hearts for thee,
    And mine were nothing, had I such to
      give;
    But when I stood beneath the fresh
      green tree,
    Which living waves where thou didst
      cease to live,
    And saw around me the wide field
      revive

[1] The war song which summoned the Cameron
    clan.
[2] The English.
[3] A kind of Highland bagpipe music.

[1] See Scott's *The Field of Waterloo*, and Words-
    worth's *Character of the Happy Warrior* (p.
    324); also Tennyson's *Ode on the Death of
    the Duke of Wellington.*
[2] Frederick Howard, whose father, the fifth
    Earl of Carlisle, Byron's second cousin, had
    been satirized in *English Bards and Scotch
    Reviewers*, 725 ff.

With fruits and fertile promise, and
the Spring
Came forth her work of gladness to
contrive,
With all her reckless birds upon the
wing,
I turn'd from all she brought to those
she could not bring.

31   I turn'd to thee, to thousands, of whom
each
And one as all a ghastly gap did make
In his own kind and kindred, whom to
teach
Forgetfulness were mercy for their
sake;
The Archangel's trump, not Glory's,
must awake
Those whom they thirst for; though the
sound of Fame
May for a moment soothe, it cannot
slake
The fever of vain longing, and the
name
So honor'd but assumes a stronger, bitterer
claim.

32   They mourn, but smile at length; and,
smiling, mourn
The tree will wither long before it fall;
The hull drives on, though mast and
sail be torn;
The roof-tree sinks, but moulders on
the hall
In massy hoariness; the ruin'd wall
Stands when its wind-worn battlements
are gone;
The bars survive the captive they en-
thral;
The day drags through, though storms
keep out the sun;
And thus the heart will break, yet brokenly
live on:

33   Even as a broken mirror, which the
glass
In every fragment multiplies; and
makes
A thousand images of one that was,
The same, and still the more, the more
it breaks;
And thus the heart will do which not
forsakes,
Living in shatter'd guise; and still, and
cold,
And bloodless, with its sleepless sor-
row aches,
Yet withers on till all without is old,
Showing no visible sign, for such things
are untold.

34   There is a very life in our despair,
Vitality of poison,—a quick root
Which feeds these deadly branches; for
it were
As nothing did we die; but Life will
suit
Itself to Sorrow's most detested fruit,
Like to the apples on the Dead Sea's
shore,
All ashes to the taste.[1] Did man com-
pute
Existence by enjoyment, and count o'er
Such hours 'gainst years of life,—say,
would he name threescore?

35   The Psalmist number'd out the years
of man:[2]
They are enough; and if thy tale be
true,
Thou, who didst grudge him even that
fleeting span,
More than enough,[3] thou fatal Waterloo!
Millions of tongues record thee, and
anew
Their children's lips shall echo them,
and say—
"Here, where the sword united nations
drew,
Our countrymen were warring on that
day!"
And this is much, and all which will not
pass away.

36   There sunk the greatest, nor the worst
of men,
Whose spirit, antithetically mixt,
One moment of the mightiest, and again
On little objects with like firmness fixt;
Extreme in all things! hadst thou been
betwixt,
Thy throne had still been thine, or
never been;
For daring made thy rise as fall: thou
seek'st
Even now to re-assume the imperial
mien,
And shake again the world, the Thun-
derer of the scene!

37   Conqueror and captive of the earth art
thou!
She trembles at thee still, and thy wild
name

[1] "The (fabled) apples on the brink of the lake
Asphaltes were said to be fair without, and
within, ashes.—*Vide* Tacitus, *Histor.* 5, 7."—
Byron.
[2] See *Psalms,* 90 :10.
[3] If Waterloo really means what is seems to
mean to mankind, the fleeting span of three
score years and ten allowed by the Psalmist
is more than enough to immortalize human
achievement.

Was ne'er more bruited[1] in men's
   minds than now
That thou art nothing, save the jest of
   Fame,
Who woo'd thee once, thy vassal, and
   became
The flatterer of thy fierceness, till thou
   wert
A god unto thyself! nor less the same
To the astounded kingdoms all inert,
Who deem'd thee for a time whate'er
   thou didst assert.

38   Oh, more or less than man—in high or
     low,
   Battling with nations, flying from the
     field;
   Now making monarchs' necks thy foot-
     stool, now
   More than thy meanest soldier taught
     to yield;
   An empire thou couldst crush, com-
     mand, rebuild,
   But govern not thy pettiest passion,
     nor,
   However deeply in men's spirits skill'd,
   Look through thine own, nor curb the
     lust of war,
   Nor learn that tempted Fate will leave
     the loftiest star.

39   Yet well thy soul hath brook'd the
     turning tide
   With that untaught innate philosophy,
   Which, be it wisdom, coldness, or deep
     pride,
   Is gall and wormwood to an enemy.
   When the whole host of hatred stood
     hard by,
   To watch and mock thee shrinking, thou
     hast smiled
   With a sedate and all-enduring eye;—
   When Fortune fled her spoil'd and
     favorite child,
   He stood unbow'd beneath the ills upon
     him piled.

40   Sager than in thy fortunes; for in them
   Ambition steel'd thee on too far to
     show
   That just habitual scorn, which could
     contemn
   Men and their thoughts; 'twas wise to
     feel, not so
   To wear it ever on thy lip and brow,
   And spurn the instruments thou wert
     to use[2]

Till they were turn'd unto thine overthrow:
'Tis but a worthless world to win or
   lose;
So hath it proved to thee, and all such lot
   who choose.

41   If, like a tower upon a headland rock,
   Thou hadst been made to stand or fall
     alone,
   Such scorn of man had help'd to brave
     the shock;
   But men's thoughts were the steps
     which paved thy throne,
   Their admiration thy best weapon
     shone;
   The part of Philip's son[1] was thine,
     not then
   (Unless aside thy purple had been
     thrown)
   Like stern Diogenes to mock at men;
   For sceptred cynics earth were far too
     wide a den.

42   But quiet to quick bosoms is a hell,
   And *there* hath been thy bane; there is
     a fire
   And motion of the soul which will not
     dwell
   In its own narrow being, but aspire
   Beyond the fitting medium of desire;
   And, but once kindled, quenchless ever-
     more,
   Preys upon high adventure, nor can
     tire
   Of aught but rest; a fever at the core,
   Fatal to him who bears, to all who ever
     bore.

43   This makes the madmen who have made
     men mad
   By their contagion; conquerors and
     kings,
   Founders of sects and systems, to whom
     add
   Sophists, bards, statesmen, all unquiet
     things
   Which stir too strongly the soul's secret
     springs,
   And are themselves the fools to those
     they fool;
   Envied, yet how unenviable! what
     stings
   Are theirs! One breast laid open were
     a school
   Which would unteach mankind the lust to
     shine or rule:

---

[1] noised abroad
[2] See *Macbeth,* II, 1, 43.

[1] Alexander, who should have been his model
   instead of the cynic Diogenes.

44   Their breath is agitation, and their life
    A storm whereon they ride, to sink at
        last,
    And yet so nursed and bigoted to strife,
    That should their days, surviving perils
        past,
    Melt to calm twilight, they feel over-
        cast
    With sorrow and supineness, and so
        die;
    Even as a flame unfed, which runs to
        waste
    With its own flickering, or a sword laid
        by,
Which eats into itself, and rusts inglo-
        riously.

45   He who ascends to mountain-tops, shall
        find
    The loftiest peaks most wrapt in clouds
        and snow;
    He who surpasses or subdues mankind,
    Must look down on the hate of those
        below.
    Though high *above* the sun of glory
        glow,
    And far *beneath* the earth and ocean
        spread,
    Round him are icy rocks, and loudly
        blow
    Contending tempests on his naked head,
    And thus reward the toils which to those
        summits led.

46   Away with these! true Wisdom's world
        will be
    Within its own creation, or in thine,
    Maternal Nature! for who teems like
        thee,
    Thus on the banks of thy majestic
        Rhine?
    There Harold gazes on a work divine,
    A blending of all beauties; streams and
        dells,
    Fruit, foliage, crag, wood, cornfield,
        mountain, vine,
    And chiefless castles breathing stern
        farewells
From gray but leafy walls, where Ruin
        greenly dwells.

47   And there they stand, as stands a lofty
        mind,
    Worn, but unstooping to the baser
        crowd,
    All tenantless, save to the crannying
        wind,
    Or holding dark communion with the
        cloud.

There was a day when they were young
    and proud;
Banners on high, and battles[1] pass'd
    below;
But they who fought are in a bloody
    shroud,
And those which waved are shredless
    dust ere now,
And the bleak battlements shall bear no
    future blow.

48   Beneath these battlements, within those
        walls,
    Power dwelt amidst her passions; in
        proud state
    Each robber chief upheld his armed
        halls,
    Doing his evil will, nor less elate
    Than mightier heroes of a longer date.
    What want these outlaws conquerors
        should have[2]
    But history's purchased page to call
        them great?
    A wider space, an ornamented grave?
Their hopes were not less warm, their
        souls were full as brave.

49   In their baronial feuds and single fields,
    What deeds of prowess unrecorded
        died!
    And Love, which lent a blazon to their
        shields,
    With emblems well devised by amorous
        pride,
    Through all the mail of iron hearts
        would glide;
    But still their flame was fierceness, and
        drew on
    Keen contest and destruction near
        allied,
    And many a tower for some fair mis-
        chief won,
Saw the discolor'd Rhine beneath its ruin
        run.

50   But thou, exulting and abounding river!
    Making thy waves a blessing as they
        flow
    Through banks whose beauty would
        endure forever
    Could man but leave thy bright crea-
        tion so,
    Nor its fair promise from the surface
        mow
    With the sharp scythe of conflict,—
        then to see

---

[1] battalions

[2] In Ramsay's version of the ballad *Johnie Arm-
strong,* the King asks Johnie :—
"What wants that knave that a king suld haif
But the sword of honor and the crown?"

Thy valley of sweet waters, were to
  know
Earth paved like heaven; and to seem
  such to me,
Even now what wants thy stream?—that
  it should Lethe be.

51   A thousand battles have assail'd thy
       banks,
     But these and half their fame have
       pass'd away,
     And Slaughter heap'd on high his wel-
       tering ranks;
     Their very graves are gone, and what
       are they?
     Thy tide wash'd down the blood of yes-
       terday,
     And all was stainless, and on thy clear
       stream
     Glass'd, with its dancing light, the
       sunny ray;
     But o'er the blacken'd memory's
       blighting dream
Thy waves would vainly roll, all sweep-
       ing as they seem.

52   Thus Harold inly said, and pass'd
       along,
     Yet not insensible to all which here
     Awoke the jocund birds to early
       song
     In glens which might have made even
       exile dear:
     Though on his brow were graven lines
       austere,
     And tranquil sternness, which had ta'en
       the place
     Of feelings fierier far but less severe,
     Joy was not always absent from his
       face,
But o'er it in such scenes would steal with
       transient trace.

53   Nor was all love shut from him, though
       his days
     Of passion had consumed themselves to
       dust.
     It is in vain that we would coldly
       gaze
     On such as smile upon us; the heart
       must
     Leap kindly back to kindness, though
       disgust
     Hath wean'd it from all worldlings:
       thus he felt,
     For there was soft remembrance, and
       sweet trust
     In one fond breast, to which his own
       would melt,

And in its tenderer hour on that his
  bosom dwelt.[1]

54   And he had learn'd to love,—I know
       not why,
     For this in such as him seems strange
       of mood,—
     The helpless looks of blooming infancy,
     Even in its earliest nurture; what sub-
       dued,
     To change like this, a mind so far
       imbued
     With scorn of man, it little boots to
       know;
     But thus it was; and though in solitude
     Small power the nipp'd affections have
       to grow,
In him this glow'd when all beside had
       ceased to glow.

55   And there was one soft breast, as hath
       been said,
     Which unto his was bound by stronger
       ties
     Than the church links withal; and,
       though unwed,
     That love was pure, and, far above
       disguise,
     Had stood the test of mortal enmities
     Still undivided, and cemented more
     By peril, dreaded most in female eyes;
     But this was firm, and from a foreign
       shore
Well to that heart might his these absent
       greetings pour!

1

The castled crag of Drachenfels
Frowns o'er the wide and winding Rhine,
Whose breast of waters broadly swells
Between the banks which bear the vine,
And hills all rich with blossom'd trees,
And fields that promise corn[2] and wine,
And scatter'd cities crowning these,
Whose far white walls along them shine,
Have strew'd a scene, which I should see
With double joy wert *thou*[3] with me.

2

And peasant girls, with deep blue eyes,
And hands which offer early flowers,
Walk smiling o'er this paradise;
Above, the frequent feudal towers
Through green leaves lift their walls of gray;
And many a rock which steeply lowers,
And noble arch in proud decay,

[1] A reference to Byron's sister Augusta, who
  was steadfast in her love for Byron when he
  was under the ban of society. See stanza 55;
  also Byron's *Stanzas to Augusta* and *Epistle
  to Augusta* (pp. 544-45).
[2] grain
[3] Byron's sister Augusta.

Look o'er this vale of vintage-bowers;
But one thing want these banks of Rhine,—
Thy gentle hand to clasp in mine!

3

I send the lilies given to me;
Though long before thy hand they touch,
I know that they must wither'd be,
But yet reject them not as such;
For I have cherish'd them as dear,
Because they yet may meet thine eye,
And guide thy soul to mine even here,
When thou behold'st them drooping nigh,
And know'st them gather'd by the Rhine,
And offer'd from my heart to thine!

4

The river nobly foams and flows,
The charm of this enchanted ground,
And all its thousand turns disclose
Some fresher beauty varying round:
The haughtiest breast its wish might bound
Through life to dwell delighted here;
Nor could on earth a spot be found
To nature and to me so dear,
Could thy dear eyes in following mine
Still sweeten more these banks of Rhine;

56 By Coblentz, on a rise of gentle ground,
There is a small and simple pyramid,
Crowning the summit of the verdant
mound;
Beneath its base are heroes' ashes hid,
Our enemy's—but let not that forbid
Honor to Marceau! o'er whose early
tomb
Tears, big tears, gush'd from the rough
soldier's lid,
Lamenting and yet envying such a
doom,
Falling for France, whose rights he bat-
tled to resume.

57 Brief, brave, and glorious was his
young career,—
His mourners were two hosts, his
friends and foes;
And fitly may the stranger lingering
here
Pray for his gallant spirit's bright
repose;
For he was Freedom's champion, one
of those,
The few in number, who had not o'er-
stept
The charter to chastise which she bestows
On such as wield her weapons; he had
kept
The whiteness of his soul, and thus men
o'er him wept.

58 Here Ehrenbreitstein, with her shatter'd wall
Black with the miner's blast, upon her
height
Yet shows of what she was, when shell
and ball
Rebounding idly on her strength did
light:
A tower of victory! from whence the
flight
Of baffled foes was watch'd along the
plain:
But Peace destroy'd what War could
never blight,
And laid those proud roofs bare to summer's rain—
On which the iron shower for years had
pour'd in vain.

59 Adieu to thee, fair Rhine! How long
delighted
The stranger fain would linger on his
way!
Thine is a scene alike where souls
united
Or lonely Contemplation thus might
stray;
And could the ceaseless vultures cease
to prey
On self-condemning bosoms, it were
here,
Where Nature, nor too sombre nor too
gay,
Wild but not rude, awful yet not austere,
Is to the mellow earth as autumn to the
year.

60 Adieu to thee again! a vain adieu!
There can be no farewell to scene like
thine;
The mind is color'd by thy every hue;
And if reluctantly the eyes resign
Their cherish'd gaze upon thee, lovely
Rhine!
'Tis with the thankful heart of parting
praise;
More mighty spots may rise, more glar-
ing shine,
But none unite in one attaching maze
The brilliant, fair, and soft,—the glories
of old days.

61 The negligently grand, the fruitful
bloom
Of coming ripeness, the white city's
sheen,
The rolling stream, the precipice's
gloom,

The forest's growth, and Gothic walls
 between,
The wild rocks shaped as they had turrets been,
In mockery of man's art; and these
 withal
A race of faces happy as the scene,
Whose fertile bounties here extend to
 all,
Still springing o'er thy banks, though
 empires near them fall.

62 But these recede. Above me are the
  Alps,
The palaces of Nature, whose vast
 walls
Have pinnacled in clouds their snowy
 scalps,
And throned Eternity in icy halls
Of cold sublimity, where forms and
 falls
The avalanche — the thunderbolt of
 snow!
All that expands the spirit, yet appals,
Gather around these summits, as to
 show
How earth may pierce to heaven, yet
 leave vain man below.

63 But ere these matchless heights I dare
  to scan,
There is a spot should not be pass'd in
 vain,—
Morat! the proud, the patriot field!
 where man
May gaze on ghastly trophies of the
 slain,
Nor blush for those who conquer'd on
 that plain;
Here Burgundy bequeath'd his tomb-
 less host,
A bony heap, through ages to remain,
Themselves their monument; — the
 Stygian coast
Unsepulchred they roam'd, and shriek'd
 each wandering ghost.[1]

64 While Waterloo with Cannæ's carnage
  vies,
Morat and Marathon twin names shall
 stand;
They were true Glory's stainless victories,
Won by the unambitious heart and
 hand

[1] An allusion to the superstition that the spirits
of unburied men could not pass the river
Styx, which bounded Hades.

Of a proud, brotherly, and civic band,
All unbought champions in no princely
 cause
Of vice-entail'd Corruption; they no
 land
Doom'd to bewail the blasphemy of
 laws
Making kings' rights divine, by some
 Draconic clause.[1]

65 By a lone wall a lonelier column rears
A gray and grief-worn aspect of old
 days;
'Tis the last remnant of the wreck of
 years,
And looks as with the wild-bewilder'd
 gaze
Of one to stone converted by amaze,
Yet still with consciousness; and there
 it stands
Making a marvel that it not decays,
When the coeval pride of human hands,
Levell'd Aventicum, hath strew'd her
 subject lands.

66 And there—oh! sweet and sacred be
  the name!—
Julia—the daughter, the devoted—gave
Her youth to Heaven; her heart, beneath a claim
Nearest to Heaven's, broke o'er a
 father's grave.[2]
Justice is sworn 'gainst tears, and hers
 would crave
The life she lived in; but the judge
 was just,
And then she died on him she could not
 save.
Their tomb was simple, and without a
 bust,
And held within their urn one mind, one
 heart, one dust.

67 But these are deeds which should not
  pass away,
And names that must not wither, though
 the earth
Forgets her empires with a just decay,
The enslavers and the enslaved, their
 death and birth;
The high, the mountain-majesty of worth

[1] The code of Draco, an Athenian lawgiver of
the seventh century, was noted for its free
use of the death penalty.

[2] A reference to the story of Julia Alpinula,
who was thought to have died after vainly
trying to save the life of her father, who was
condemned to death as a traitor by Aulus
Cæcinia. Byron's information was derived
from an inscription on a monument, since
proved to be forged.

Should be, and shall, survivor of its
woe,
And from its immortality look forth
In the sun's face, like yonder Alpine
snow,
Imperishably pure beyond all things below.

68   Lake Leman woos me with its crystal
face,
The mirror where the stars and mountains view
The stillness of their aspect in each
trace
Its clear depth yields of their far height
and hue:
There is too much of man here, to look
through
With a fit mind the might which I
behold;
But soon in me shall Loneliness renew
Thoughts hid, but not less cherish'd
than of old,
Ere mingling with the herd had penn'd
me in their fold.

69   To fly from, need not be to hate, man-
kind:
All are not fit with them to stir and
toil,
Nor is it discontent to keep the mind
Deep in its fountain, lest it overboil
In the hot throng, where we become
the spoil
Of our infection, till too late and long
We may deplore and struggle with the
coil,
In wretched interchange of wrong for
wrong
Midst a contentious world, striving where
none are strong.

70   There, in a moment we may plunge our
years
In fatal penitence, and in the blight
Of our own soul turn all our blood to
tears,
And color things to come with hues of
Night;
The race of life becomes a hopeless
flight
To those that walk in darkness: on the
sea
The boldest steer but where their ports
invite;
But there are wanderers o'er Eternity[1]
Whose bark drives on and on, and
anchor'd ne'er shall be.

[1] See Shelley's *Adonais*, 30 :3 ff. (p. 760).

71   Is it not better, then, to be alone,
And love Earth only for its earthly
sake?
By the blue rushing of the arrowy
Rhone,
Or the pure bosom of its nursing lake,
Which feeds it as a mother who doth
make
A fair but froward infant her own
care,
Kissing its cries away as these awake;—
Is it not better thus our lives to wear,
Than join the crushing crowd, doom'd to
inflict or bear?

72   I live not in myself, but I become
Portion of that around me; and to me
High mountains are a feeling,[1] but the
hum
Of human cities torture: I can see
Nothing to loathe in nature, save to be
A link reluctant in a fleshly chain,
Class'd among creatures, when the soul
can flee,
And with the sky, the peak, the heav-
ing plain
Of ocean, or the stars, mingle, and not in
vain.

73   And thus I am absorb'd, and this is
life:
I look upon the peopled desert past,
As on a place of agony and strife,
Where, for some sin, to sorrow I was
cast,
To act and suffer, but remount at last
With a fresh pinion; which I feel to
spring,
Though young, yet waxing vigorous as
the blast
Which I would cope with, on delighted
wing,
Spurning the clay-cold bonds which round
our being cling.

74   And when, at length, the mind shall be
all free
From what it hates in this degraded
form,
Reft of its carnal life, save what shall
be
Existent happier in the fly and worm,—
When elements to elements conform,
And dust is as it should be, shall I not
Feel all I see, less dazzling, but more
warm?

[1] See Wordsworth's *Lines Composed a Few Miles Above Tintern Abbey*, 76 ff. (p. 259).

The bodiless thought? the spirit of
each spot?
Of which, even now, I share at times the
immortal lot?

75 Are not the mountains, waves, and
skies, a part
Of me and of my soul, as I of them?
Is not the love of these deep in my
heart
With a pure passion? should I not con-
temn
All objects, if compared with these?
and stem
A tide of suffering, rather than forego
Such feelings for the hard and worldly
phlegm
Of those whose eyes are only turn'd
below,
Gazing upon the ground, with thoughts
which dare not glow?

76 But this is not my theme; and I return
To that which is immediate, and require
Those who find contemplation in the
urn,
To look on one,[1] whose dust was once all
fire,
A native of the land where I respire
The clear air for a while—a passing
guest,
Where he became a being,—whose desire
Was to be glorious; 'twas a foolish
quest,
The which to gain and keep, he sacrificed
all rest.

77 Here the ~~self-torturing sophist,~~ wild
Rousseau,
The apostle of affliction, he who threw
Enchantment over passion, and from
woe
Wrung overwhelming eloquence, first
drew
The breath which made him wretched;
yet he knew
How to make madness beautiful, and
cast
O'er erring deeds and thoughts a heav-
enly hue
Of words, like sunbeams, dazzling as
they past
The eyes, which o'er them shed tears
feelingly and fast.

78 His love was passion's essence:—as a
tree
On fire by lightning, with ethereal flame

[1] Jean Jacques Rousseau (1712-78), who was
born in Geneva.

Kindled he was, and blasted; for to be
Thus, and enamor'd, were to him the
same.
But his was not the love of living dame,
Nor of the dead who rise upon our
dreams,
But of ideal beauty, which became
In him existence, and o'erflowing teems
Along his burning page, distemper'd
though it seems.

79 *This* breathed itself to life in Julie, *this*
Invested her with all that's wild and
sweet;
This hallow'd, too, the memorable kiss
Which every morn his fever'd lip would
greet,
From hers, who but with friendship
his would meet;[1]
But to that gentle touch through brain
and breast
Flash'd the thrill'd spirit's love-devour-
ing heat;
In that absorbing sigh perchance more
blest
Than vulgar minds may be with all they
seek possest.

80 His life was one long war with self-
sought foes,
Or friends by him self-banish'd; for
his mind
Had grown Suspicion's sanctuary, and
chose,
For its own cruel sacrifice, the kind,
'Gainst whom he raged with fury
strange and blind.
But he was phrensied,—wherefore, who
may know?
Since cause might be which skill could
never find;
But he was phrensied by disease or woe,
To that worst pitch of all, which wears a
reasoning show.

81 For then he was inspired, and from
him came,
As from the Pythian's mystic cave of
yore,
Those oracles which set the world in
flame,
Nor ceased to burn till kingdoms were
no more:
Did he not this for France? which lay
before

[1] In his *Confessions* (Bk. 9), Rousseau gives an
account of his passion for Madame D'Hel-
bach, whom he met every morning for the
kiss which was the common salutation of
French acquaintances.

Bow'd to the inborn tyranny of years?
Broken and trembling to the yoke she
   bore,
Till by the voice of him and his compeers
Roused up to too much wrath, which follows o'ergrown fears?

82   They made themselves a fearful monu-
     ment!
The wreck of old opinions — things
   which grew,
Breathed from the birth of time: the
   veil they rent,
And what behind it lay, all earth shall
   view.
But good with ill they also overthrew,
Leaving but ruins, wherewith to rebuild
Upon the same foundation, and renew
Dungeons and thrones, which the same
   hour refill'd,
As heretofore, because ambition was self-
   will'd.

83   But this will not endure, nor be en-
     dured!
Mankind have felt their strength, and
   made it felt.
They might have used it better, but
   allured
By their new vigor, sternly have they
   dealt
On one another; pity ceased to melt
With her once natural charities. But
   they,
Who in oppression's darkness caved
   had dwelt,
They were not eagles, nourish'd with
   the day;
What marvel then, at times, if they mis-
   took their prey?

84   What deep wounds ever closed without
     a scar?
The heart's bleed longest, and but heal
   to wear
That which disfigures it; and they who
   war
With their own hopes, and have been
   vanquish'd, bear
Silence, but not submission: in his lair
Fix'd Passion holds his breath, until
   the hour
Which shall atone for years; none need
   despair:
It came, it cometh, and will come,—
   the power
To punish or forgive—in *one* we shall be
   slower.

85   Clear, placid Leman! thy contrasted
     lake,
With the wild world I dwelt in, is a
   thing
Which warns me, with its stillness, to
   forsake
Earth's troubled waters for a purer
   spring.
This quiet sail is as a noiseless wing
To waft me from distraction; once I
   loved
Torn Ocean's roar, but thy soft mur-
   muring
Sounds sweet as if a sister's voice re-
   proved,
That I with stern delights should e'er
   have been so moved.

86   It is the hush of night, and all between
Thy margin and the mountains, dusk,
   yet clear,
Mellow'd and mingling, yet distinctly
   seen,
Save darken'd Jura, whose capt heights
   appear
Precipitously steep; and drawing near,
There breathes a living fragrance from
   the shore,
Of flowers yet fresh with childhood; on
   the ear
Drops the light drip of the suspended
   oar,
Or chirps the grasshopper one good-night
   carol more;—

87   He is an evening reveller, who makes
His life an infancy, and sings his fill;
At intervals, some bird from out the
   brakes
Starts into voice a moment, then is
   still.
There seems a floating whisper on the
   hill,
But that is fancy, for the starlight
   dews
All silently their tears of love instil,
Weeping themselves away, till they in-
   fuse
Deep into Nature's breast the spirit of
   her hues.

88   Ye stars! which are the poetry of
     heaven!
If in your bright leaves we would read
   the fate
Of men and empires,—'t is to be for-
   given,
That in our aspirations to be great,
Our destinies o'erleap their mortal state,

And claim a kindred with you; for ye are
A beauty and a mystery, and create
In us such love and reverence from afar,
That fortune, fame, power, life, have named themselves a star.

89 All heaven and earth are still—though not in sleep,[1]
But breathless, as we grow when feeling most;
And silent, as we stand in thoughts too deep:—
All heaven and earth are still. From the high host
Of stars, to the lull'd lake and mountain-coast,
All is concenter'd in a life intense,
Where not a beam, nor air, nor leaf is lost,
But hath a part of being, and a sense
Of that which is of all Creator and Defence.

90 Then stirs the feeling infinite, so felt
In solitude, where we are *least* alone;
A truth, which through our being then doth melt,
And purifies from self: it is a tone,
The soul and source of music, which makes known
Eternal harmony, and sheds a charm
Like to the fabled Cytherea's zone,[2]
Binding all things with beauty; — 'twould disarm
The spectre Death, had he substantial power to harm.

91 Not vainly did the early Persian make
His altar the high places, and the peak
Of earth-o'ergazing mountains, and thus take
A fit and unwall'd temple, there to seek
The Spirit, in whose honor shrines are weak,
Uprear'd of human hands. Come, and compare
Columns and idol-dwellings, Goth or Greek,
With Nature's realms of worship, earth and air,
Nor fix on fond abodes to circumscribe thy pray'r!

92 Thy sky is changed!—and such a change! Oh night,
And storm, and darkness, ye are wondrous strong,
Yet lovely in your strength, as is the light
Of a dark eye in woman! Far along,
From peak to peak, the rattling crags among
Leaps the live thunder! Not from one lone cloud,
But every mountain now hath found a tongue,
And Jura answers, through her misty shroud,
Back to the joyous Alps, who call to her aloud!

93 And this is in the night:—Most glorious night!
Thou wert not sent for slumber! let me be
A sharer in thy fierce and far delight,—
A portion of the tempest and of thee!
How the lit lake shines, a phosphoric sea,
And the big rain comes dancing to the earth!
And now again 'tis black,—and now, the glee
Of the loud hills shakes with its mountain-mirth,
As if they did rejoice o'er a young earthquake's birth.

94 Now, where the swift Rhone cleaves his way between
Heights which appear as lovers who have parted[1]
In hate, whose mining depths so intervene,
That they can meet no more, though broken-hearted;
Though in their souls, which thus each other thwarted,
Love was the very root of the fond rage
Which blighted their life's bloom, and then departed:
Itself expired, but leaving them an age
Of years all winters,—war within themselves to wage.

95 Now, where the quick Rhone thus hath cleft his way,
The mightiest of the storms hath ta'en his stand:

---

[1] See Wordsworth's *It Is a Beauteous Evening, Calm and Free* (p. 312).
[2] The girdle of Venus, which inspired love.

[1] See Coleridge's *Christabel*, 408-26 (p. 373).

For here, not one, but many, make their
   play,
And fling their thunder-bolts from hand
   to hand,
Flashing and cast around; of all the
   band,
The brightest through these parted hills **99**
   hath fork'd
His lightnings,—as if he did understand
That in such gaps as desolation work'd,
There the hot shaft should blast whatever
   therein lurk'd.

96   Sky, mountains, rivers, winds, lake,
     lightning! ye!
With night, and clouds, and thunder,
   and a soul
To make these felt and feeling, well
   may be
Things that have made me watchful;
   the far roll
Of your departing voices, is the knoll[1]
Of what in me is sleepless,—if I rest.
But where of ye, O tempests! is the
   goal?
Are ye like those within the human
   breast?
Or do ye find, at length, like eagles, some
   high nest?

97   Could I embody and unbosom now
That which is most within me,—could
   I wreak
My thoughts upon expression, and thus
   throw
Soul, heart, mind, passions, feelings,
   strong or weak,
All that I would have sought, and all
   I seek,
Bear, know, feel, and yet breathe—into
   one word,
And that one word were Lightning, I
   would speak;
But as it is, I live and die unheard,
With a most voiceless thought, sheathing
   it as a sword.

98   The morn is up again, the dewy morn,
With breath all incense, and with cheek
   all bloom,
Laughing the clouds away with play-
   ful scorn,
And living as if earth contain'd no
   tomb,—
And glowing into day: we may resume
The march of our existence: and thus I,

[1] knell

Still on thy shores, fair Leman! may
   find room
And food for meditation, nor pass by
Much, that may give us pause, if ponder'd fittingly.

Clarens! sweet Clarens, birthplace of
   deep Love!
Thine air is the young breath of passionate thought;
Thy trees take root in Love; the snows
   above
The very glaciers have his colors caught,
And sun-set into rose-hues sees them
   wrought
By rays which sleep there lovingly: the
   rocks,
The permanent crags, tell here of Love,
   who sought
In them a refuge from the worldly
   shocks,
Which stir and sting the soul with hope
   that woos, then mocks.

100 Clarens! by heavenly feet thy paths are
   trod,—
Undying Love's, who here ascends a
   throne
To which the steps are mountains;
   where the god
Is a pervading life and light,—so shown
Not on those summits solely, nor alone
In the still cave and forest; o'er the
   flower
His eye is sparkling, and his breath
   hath blown,
His soft and summer breath, whose ten-
   der power
Passes the strength of storms in their most
   desolate hour.

101 All things are here of *him;* from the
   black pines,
Which are his shade on high, and the
   loud roar
Of torrents, where he listeneth, to the
   vines
Which slope his green path downward
   to the shore,
Where the bow'd waters meet him, and
   adore,
Kissing his feet with murmurs; and the
   wood,
The covert of old trees, with trunks all
   hoar,
But light leaves, young as joy, stands
   where it stood,
Offering to him, and his, a populous
   solitude.

102   A populous solitude of bees and birds,
And fairy-form'd and many-color'd
  things,
Who worship him with notes more sweet
  than words,
And innocently open their glad wings,
Fearless and full of life: the gush of
  springs,
And fall of lofty fountains, and the
  bend
Of stirring branches, and the bud which
  brings
The swiftest thought of beauty, here
  extend,
Mingling, and made by Love, unto one
  mighty end.

103   He who hath loved not, here would learn
  that lore,
And make his heart a spirit; he who
  knows
That tender mystery, will love the more;
For this is Love's recess, where vain
  men's woes,
And the world's waste, have driven him
  far from those,
For 'tis his nature to advance or die;
He stands not still, but or decays, or
  grows
Into a boundless blessing, which may
  vie
With the immortal lights, in its eternity!

104   'T was not for fiction chose Rousseau
  this spot,
Peopling it with affections; but he
  found
It was the scene which Passion must
  allot
To the mind's purified beings; 't was
  the ground
Where early Love his Psyche's zone
  unbound,[1]
And hallow'd it with loveliness; 'tis
  lone,
And wonderful, and deep, and hath a
  sound,
And sense, and sight of sweetness; here
  the Rhone
Hath spread himself a couch, the Alps
  have rear'd a throne.

105   Lausanne! and Ferney! ye have been
  the abodes
Of names which unto you bequeath'd a
  name;[2]

106   Mortals, who sought and found, by
  dangerous roads,
A path to perpetuity of fame:
They were gigantic minds, and their
  steep aim
Was, Titan-like, on daring doubts to
  pile
Thoughts which should call down thunder, and the flame
Of Heaven again assail'd, if Heaven the
  while
On man and man's research could deign
  do more than smile.

107   The one was fire and fickleness,[1] a child,
Most mutable in wishes, but in mind
A wit as various,—gay, grave, sage, or
  wild,—
Historian, bard, philosopher, combined;
He multiplied himself among mankind,
The Proteus of their talents; but his own
Breathed most in ridicule,—which, as
  the wind,
Blew where it listed,[2] laying all things
  prone,—
Now to o'erthrow a fool, and now to
  shake a throne. *Popeian II*

108   The other, deep and slow, exhausting
  thought,
And hiving wisdom with each studious
  year,
In meditation dwelt, with learning
  wrought,
And shaped his weapon with an edge
  severe,
Sapping a solemn creed with solemn
  sneer; *P.*
The lord of irony,—that master-spell,
Which stung his foes to wrath, which
  grew from fear,
And doom'd him to the zealot's ready
  Hell,
Which answers to all doubts so eloquently
  well.

  Yet, peace be with their ashes,—for by
  them,
If merited, the penalty is paid;
It is not ours to judge,—far less con-
  demn;
The hour must come when such things
  shall be made
Known unto all, or hope and dread
  allay'd
By slumber, on one pillow, in the dust,

---

[1] A reference to the legend of Cupid and Psyche.
[2] Voltaire (1694-1778) and Gibbon (1737-94).

[1] Voltaire. Stanza 107 refers to Gibbon. Both
of these men were skeptics. See stanza 105;
also Gibbon's *The History of the Decline and
Fall of the Roman Empire*, chapters 15-16.
[2] See *John*, 3 :8.

Which, thus much we are sure, must lie
    decay'd;
And when it shall revive, as is our trust,
'Twill be to be forgiven, or suffer what is
    just.

109   But let me quit man's works, again to
    read
His Maker's, spread around me, and
    suspend
This page, which from my reveries I
    feed,
Until it seems prolonging without end.
The clouds above me to the white Alps 113
    tend,
And I must pierce them, and survey
    whate'er
May be permitted, as my steps I bend
To their most great and growing region,
    where
The earth to her embrace compels the
    powers of air.

110   Italia! too, Italia! looking on thee,
Full flashes on the soul the light of ages,
Since the fierce Carthaginian[1] almost
    won thee,
To the last halo of the chiefs and sages
Who glorify thy consecrated pages;
Thou wert the throne and grave of em-
    pires; still
The fount at which the panting mind
    assuages
Her thirst of knowledge, quaffing there
    her fill,
Flows from the eternal source of Rome's
    imperial hill.

111   Thus far have I proceeded in a theme
Renew'd with no kind auspices:—to feel
We are not what we have been, and to
    deem
We are not what we should be, and to
    steel
The heart against itself; and to conceal,
With a proud caution, love, or hate, or
    aught,—
Passion or feeling, purpose, grief or
    zeal,—
Which is the tyrant spirit of our
    thought,
Is a stern task of soul:—no matter,—it is
    taught.

112   And for these words, thus woven into
    song,
It may be that they are a harmless
    wile,—

[1] Hannibal, in the Second Punic War. 216 B. C.

The coloring of the scenes which fleet
    along,
Which I would seize, in passing, to be-
    guile
My breast, or that of others, for a while.
Fame is the thirst of youth, but I am
    not
So young as to regard men's frown or
    smile,
As loss or guerdon of a glorious lot;
I stood and stand alone,—remember'd or
    forgot.

113   I have not loved the world, nor the
    world me;[1]
I have not flatter'd its rank breath, nor
    bow'd
To its idolatries a patient knee,
Nor coin'd my cheek to smiles, nor cried
    aloud
In worship of an echo; in the crowd
They could not deem me one of such;
    I stood
Amongst them, but not of them; in a
    shroud
Of thoughts which were not their
    thoughts, and still could,
Had I not filed[2] my mind, which thus
    itself subdued.

114   I have not loved the world, nor the
    world me,—
But let us part fair foes; I do believe,
Though I have found them not, that
    there may be
Words which are things, hopes which
    will not deceive,
And virtues which are merciful, nor
    weave
Snares for the failing; I would also
    deem
O'er others' griefs that some sincerely
    grieve;
That two, or one, are almost what they
    seem,
That goodness is no name, and happiness
    no dream.

115   My daughter! with thy name this song
    begun;
My daughter! with thy name thus much
    shall end;
I see thee not, I hear thee not, but none
Can be so wrapt in thee; thou art the
    friend
To whom the shadows of far years ex-
    tend:

[1] See *Manfred*, II, 2, 50 ff. (p. 583).
[2] defiled (See *Macbeth*, III, 1, 64.)

Albeit my brow thou never shouldst
behold,
My voice shall with thy future visions
blend,
And reach into thy heart, when mine is
cold,
A token and a tone, even from thy father's
mould.

116   To aid thy mind's development, to watch
Thy dawn of little joys, to sit and see
Almost thy very growth, to view thee
catch
Knowledge of objects,—wonders yet to
thee!
To hold thee lightly on a gentle knee,
And print on thy soft cheek a parent's
kiss,—
This, it should seem, was not reserved
for me;
Yet this was in my nature: as it is,
I know not what is there, yet something
like to this.

117   Yet, though dull hate as duty should be
taught,
I know that thou wilt love me; though
my name
Should be shut from thee, as a spell still
fraught
With desolation, and a broken claim:
Though the grave closed between us,—
'twere the same,
I know that thou wilt love me; though
to drain
My blood from out thy being were an
aim,
And an attainment,—all would be in
vain,—
Still thou wouldst love me, still that more
than life retain.

118   The child of love, though born in bitter-
ness,
And nurtured in convulsion,—of thy sire
These were the elements, and thine no
less.
As yet such are around thee, but thy fire
Shall be more temper'd, and thy hope
far higher.
Sweet be thy cradled slumbers! O'er
the sea
And from the mountains where I now
respire,
Fain would I waft such blessing upon
thee,
As, with a sigh, I deem thou might'st
have been to me.

From Canto IV
1817   1818

1   I stood in Venice, on the Bridge of
Sighs;
A palace and a prison on each hand:
I saw from out the wave her structures
rise
As from the stroke of the enchanter's
wand:
A thousand years their cloudy wings
expand
Around me, and a dying Glory smiles
O'er the far times, when many a subject
land
Look'd to the winged Lion's marble
piles,[1]
Where Venice sate in state, throned on
her hundred isles!

2   She looks a sea Cybele, fresh from
ocean,
Rising with her tiara of proud towers
At airy distance, with majestic motion,
A ruler of the waters and their powers:
And such she was;—her daughters had
their dowers
From spoils of nations, and the exhaust-
less East
Pour'd in her lap all gems in sparkling
showers.
In purple was she robed, and of her
feast
Monarchs partook, and deem'd their dig-
nity increased.

3   In Venice Tasso's echoes are no more,
And silent rows the songless gondolier;[2]
Her palaces are crumbling to the shore,
And music meets not always now the
ear:
Those days are gone—but Beauty still
is here.
States fall, arts fade—but Nature doth
not die,
Nor yet forget how Venice once was
dear,
The pleasant place of all festivity,
The revel of the earth, the masque of
Italy!

4   But unto us she hath a spell beyond
Her name in story, and her long array
Of mighty shadows, whose dim forms
despond

---

[1] The winged Lion of St. Mark stands on a
column near the Ducal Palace.
[2] Before the capture of Venice by Napoleon, in
1797, the gondoliers were accustomed to sing
stanzas of Tasso's *Jerusalem Delivered*. See
Rogers's *The Gondola* (p. 237).

Above the dogeless city's vanish'd
sway;[1]
Ours is a trophy which will not decay
With the Rialto; Shylock and the Moor,
And Pierre, cannot be swept or worn
away—
The keystones of the arch! though all
were o'er,
For us repeopled were the solitary shore.

5   The beings of the mind are not of clay;
Essentially immortal, they create
And multiply in us a brighter ray
And more beloved existence: that which
Fate
Prohibits to dull life, in this our state
Of mortal bondage, by these spirits
supplied,
First exiles, then replaces what we hate;
Watering the hearts whose early flowers
have died,
And with a fresher growth replenishing
the void.

.   .   .   .   .   .

13   Before St. Mark still glow his steeds of
brass,[2]
Their gilded collars glittering in the
sun;
But is not Doria's menace come to pass?
Are they not *bridled?*—Venice, lost and
won,
Her thirteen hundred years of freedom
done,
Sinks, like a seaweed, into whence she
rose!
Better be whelm'd beneath the waves,
and shun,
Even in destruction's depth, her foreign
foes,
From whom submission wrings an infamous repose.

14   In youth she was all glory,—a new
Tyre;
Her very by-word sprung from victory,
The "Planter of the Lion,"[3] which
through fire
And blood she bore o'er subject earth
and sea;

Though making many slaves, herself
still free,
And Europe's bulwark 'gainst the Ottomite;[1]
Witness Troy's rival, Candia! Vouch
it, ye
Immortal waves that saw Lepanto's
fight!
For ye are names no time nor tyranny can
blight.

15   Statues of glass—all shiver'd—the long
file
Of her dead Doges are declined to dust;
But where they dwelt, the vast and
sumptuous pile
Bespeaks the pageant of their splendid
trust;
Their sceptre broken, and their sword
in rust,
Have yielded to the stranger: empty
halls,
Thin streets, and foreign aspects, such
as must
Too oft remind her who and what
enthrals,
Have flung a desolate cloud o'er Venice'
lovely walls.

16   When Athens' armies fell at Syracuse,[2]
And fetter'd thousands bore the yoke of
war,
Redemption rose up in the Attic Muse,
Her voice their only ransom from afar:
See! as they chant the tragic hymn, the
car
Of the o'ermaster'd victor stops, the
reins
Fall from his hands, his idle scimitar
Starts from its belt—he rends his cap-
tive's chains,
And bids him thank the bard for freedom
and his strains.

17   Thus, Venice, if no stronger claim were
thine,
Were all thy proud historic deeds forgot,
Thy choral memory of the Bard divine,
Thy love of Tasso, should have cut the
knot

---

[1] The territory of Venice was taken by France
and Austria in 1797. See Wordsworth's *On
the Extinction of the Venetian Republic* (p.
312).
[2] The famous bronze steeds of St. Mark's
Church, which the Genoese commander Doria
said in 1379, he should bridle before giving
the Venetians peace.
[3] The Lion of St. Mark was the emblem of the
Republic of Venice.

[1] The Venetians defended Candia, in Crete,
against the Turks for 24 years. Troy was besieged 10 years by the Greeks.
[2] Plutarch relates, in his *Life of Nicias*, that
after the Athenians had been defeated and
captured at Syracuse (5th cent. B. C.), those
who could recite passages from the works of
Euripides were set free. See Browning's
Balaustion's Adventure, 125 ff.

Which ties thee to thy tyrants; and thy
  lot
Is shameful to the nations,—most of all,
Albion! to thee: the Ocean queen
  should not
Abandon Ocean's children; in the fall
Of Venice, think of thine, despite thy
  watery wall.

18 I loved her from my boyhood; she to
      me
    Was as a fairy city of the heart,
    Rising like water-columns from the sea,
    Of joy the sojourn, and of wealth the
      mart;
    And Otway, Radcliffe, Schiller, Shak-
      speare's art,[1]
    Had stamp'd her image in me, and
      even so,
    Although I found her thus, we did not
      part;
    Perchance even dearer in her day of
      woe,
    Than when she was a boast, a marvel, and
      a show.

19 I can repeople with the past—and of
    The present there is still for eye and
      thought,
    And meditation chasten'd down, enough;
    And more, it may be, than I hoped or
      sought;
    And of the happiest moments which
      were wrought
    Within the web of my existence, some
    From thee, fair Venice! have their
      colors caught:
    There are some feelings Time cannot
      benumb,
    Nor Torture shake, or mine would now be
      cold and dumb.

            .   .   .   .   .   .

25 But my soul wanders; I demand it
      back
    To meditate amongst decay, and stand
    A ruin amidst ruins; there to track
    Fall'n states and buried greatness, o'er
      a land
    Which *was* the mightiest in its old com-
      mand,
    And *is* the loveliest, and must ever be
    The master-mould of Nature's heavenly
      hand;

---

[1] Otway in *Venice Preserved*, Mrs. Radcliffe in
The Mysteries of Udolpho, Schiller in *The
Ghost-Seer*, Shakespeare in *The Merchant of
Venice* and *Othello*.

Wherein were cast the heroic and the
  free,
The beautiful, the brave, the lords of earth
  and sea,

26 The commonwealth of kings, the men of
      Rome!
    And even since, and now, fair Italy!
    Thou art the garden of the world, the
      home
    Of all Art yields, and Nature can de-
      cree;
    Even in thy desert, what is like to thee?
    Thy very weeds are beautiful, thy waste
    More rich than other climes' fertility;
    Thy wreck a glory, and thy ruin graced
    With an immaculate charm which cannot
      be defaced.

27 The moon is up, and yet it is not night;
    Sunset divides the sky with her; a sea
    Of glory streams along the Alpine
      height
    Of blue Friuli's mountains; Heaven is
      free
    From clouds, but of all colors seems to
      be,—
    Melted to one vast Iris of the West,—
    Where the Day joins the past Eternity,
    While, on the other hand, meek Dian's
      crest
    Floats through the azure air—an island of
      the blest!

28 A single star is at her side, and reigns
    With her o'er half the lovely heaven;
      but still
    Yon sunny sea heaves brightly, and re-
      mains
    Roll'd o'er the peak of the far Rhætian
      hill,
    As Day and Night contending were,
      until
    Nature reclaim'd her order:—gently
      flows
    The deep-dyed Brenta, where their hues
      instil
    The odorous purple of a new-born rose,
    Which streams upon her stream, and
      glass'd within it glows,

29 Fill'd with the face of Heaven, which,
      from afar,
    Comes down upon the waters; all its
      hues,
    From the rich sunset to the rising star,
    Their magical variety diffuse:
    And now they change; a paler shadow
      strews

Its mantle o'er the mountains; parting
    day
Dies like the dolphin, whom each pang
    imbues
With a new color as it gasps away,
The last still loveliest,—till—'tis gone—
    and all is gray.

. . . .

78 Oh Rome! my country! city of the soul!
The orphans of the heart must turn to
    thee,
Lone mother of dead empires! and con-
    trol
In their shut breasts their petty misery.
What are our woes and sufferance?
    Come and see
The cypress,[1] hear the owl, and plod
    your way
O'er steps of broken thrones and tem-
    ples, Ye!
Whose agonies are evils of a day—
A world is at our feet as fragile as our
    clay.

79 The Niobe of nations! there she stands,
Childless and crownless, in her voiceless
    woe;
An empty urn within her wither'd
    hands,
Whose holy dust was scatter'd long
    ago;
The Scipios' tomb contains no ashes
    now;
The very sepulchres lie tenantless
Of their heroic dwellers: dost thou
    flow,
Old Tiber! through a marble wilder-
    ness?
Rise, with thy yellow waves, and mantle
    her distress.

80 The Goth, the Christian, Time, War,
    Flood, and Fire,
Have dealt upon the seven-hill'd city's
    pride;
She saw her glories star by star
    expire,
And up the steep barbarian monarchs
    ride,
Where the car climb'd the Capitol; far
    and wide
Temple and tower went down, nor left
    a site:
Chaos of ruins! who shall trace the
    void,

[1] The cypress is an emblem of mourning; it is a common tree in graveyards.

O'er the dim fragments cast a lunar
    light,
And say, "here was, or is," where all is
    doubly night?

. . . . . .

95 I speak not of men's creeds—they rest
    between
Man and his Maker—but of things al-
    low'd,
Averr'd, and known, and daily, hourly
    seen:—
The yoke that is upon us doubly bow'd,
And the intent of tyranny avow'd,
The edict of Earth's rulers, who are
    grown
The apes of him[1] who humbled once the
    proud,
And shook them from their slumbers on
    the throne—
Too glorious, were this all his mighty arm
    had done.

96 Can tyrants but by tyrants conquer'd be,
And Freedom find no champion and no
    child
Such as Columbia saw arise when she
Sprung forth a Pallas, arm'd and unde-
    filed?
Or must such minds be nourish'd in the
    wild,
Deep in the unpruned forest, 'midst the
    roar
Of cataracts, where nursing Nature
    smiled
On infant Washington? Has Earth no
    more
Such seeds within her breast, or Europe no
    such shore?

97 But France got drunk with blood to
    vomit crime,
And fatal have her Saturnalia been
To Freedom's cause, in every age and
    clime;
Because the deadly days which we have
    seen,[2]
And vile Ambition, that built up between
Man and his hopes an adamantine wall,
And the base pageant last upon the
    scene,
Are grown the pretext for the eternal
    thrall
Which nips life's tree, and dooms man's
    worst—his second fall.

[1] Napoleon.
[2] The days of the Congress of Vienna, of the Holy Alliance, and of the Second Treaty of Paris (Sept.-Nov., 1815). These constitute the "base pageant" of l. 6. 7.

98 Yet, Freedom! yet thy banner, torn but
flying,
Streams like the thunder-storm *against*
the wind;
Thy trumpet voice, though broken now
and dying,
The loudest still the tempest leaves be-
hind;
Thy tree hath lost its blossoms, and the
rind,
Chopp'd by the axe, looks rough and lit-
tle worth,
But the sap lasts, and still the seed we
find
Sown deep, even in the bosom of the
North:[1]
So shall a better Spring less bitter fruit
bring forth.

.   .   .   .   .   .

128 Arches on arches! as it were that Rome,
Collecting the chief trophies of her line,
Would build up all her triumphs in one
dome,
Her Coliseum stands; the moonbeams
shine
As 'twere its natural torches, for divine
Should be the light which streams here
to illume
This long-explored but still exhaustless
mine
Of contemplation; and the azure gloom
Of an Italian night, where the deep skies
assume

129 Hues which have words, and speak to
ye of heaven,
Floats o'er this vast and wondrous
monument,
And shadows forth its glory. There is
given
Unto the things of earth, which Time
hath bent,
A spirit's feeling, and where he hath
leant
His hand, but broke his scythe, there is
a power
And magic in the ruin'd battlement,
For which the palace of the present
hour
Must yield its pomp, and wait till ages
are its dower.

130 Oh Time! the beautifier of the dead,
Adorner of the ruin, comforter
And only healer when the heart hath
bled;

[1] England.

Time! the corrector when our judg-
ments err,
The test of truth, love—sole philoso-
pher,
For all beside are sophists—from thy
thrift,
Which never loses though it doth defer—
Time, the avenger! unto thee I lift
My hands, and eyes, and heart, and crave
of thee a gift:

131 Amidst this wreck, where thou hast made
a shrine
And temple more divinely desolate,
Among thy mightier offerings here are
mine,
Ruins of years, though few, yet full of
fate:
If thou hast ever seen me too elate,
Hear me not; but if calmly I have borne
Good, and reserved my pride against the
hate
Which shall not whelm me, let me not
have worn
This iron in my soul in vain—shall *they*
not mourn?

132 And thou, who never yet of human
wrong
Left the unbalanced scale, great Nemesis!
Here, where the ancient paid thee
homage long—
Thou who didst call the Furies from the
abyss,
And round Orestes bade them howl and
hiss
For that unnatural retribution[1]—just,
Had it but been from hands less near—
in this
Thy former realm, I call thee from the
dust!
Dost thou not hear my heart?—Awake!
thou shalt, and must.

133 It is not that I may not have incurr'd
For my ancestral faults or mine the
wound
I bleed withal, and, had it been con-
ferr'd
With a just weapon, it had flow'd un-
bound;
But now my blood shall not sink in the
ground;
To thee I do devote it—*thou* shalt take
The vengeance, which shall yet be
sought and found,

[1] The slaying of his mother and her lover, who
together had killed his father, Agamemnon.

Which if *I* have not taken for the sake——
But let that pass—I sleep, but thou shalt yet awake.

134 And if my voice break forth, 'tis not that now
I shrink from what is suffer'd: let him speak
Who hath beheld decline upon my brow,
Or seen my mind's convulsion leave it weak;
But in this page a record will I seek.
Not in the air shall these my words disperse,
Though I be ashes; a far hour shall wreak
The deep prophetic fulness of this verse,
And pile on human heads the mountain of my curse!

135 That curse shall be Forgiveness.—Have I not—
Hear me, my mother Earth! behold it, Heaven!
Have I not had to wrestle with my lot?
Have I not suffer'd things to be forgiven?
Have I not had my brain sear'd, my heart riven,
Hopes sapp'd, name blighted, Life's life lied away?
And only not to desperation driven,
Because not altogether of such clay
As rots into the souls of those whom I survey.

136 From mighty wrongs to petty perfidy
Have I not seen what human things could do?
From the loud roar of foaming calumny
To the small whisper of the as paltry few,
And subtler venom of the reptile crew,
The Janus glance of whose significant eye,
Learning to lie with silence, would *seem* true,
And without utterance, save the shrug or sigh,
Deal round to happy fools its speechless obloquy.

137 But I have lived, and have not lived in vain:
My mind may lose its force, my blood its fire,
And my frame perish even in conquering pain;

But there is that within me which shall tire
Torture and Time, and breathe when I expire;
Something unearthly, which they deem not of,
Like the remember'd tone of a mute lyre,
Shall on their soften'd spirits sink, and move
In hearts all rocky now the late remorse of love.

138 The seal is set.—Now welcome, thou dread power!
Nameless, yet thus omnipotent, which here
Walk'st in the shadow of the midnight hour
With a deep awe, yet all distinct from fear;
Thy haunts are ever where the dead walls rear
Their ivy mantles, and the solemn scene
Derives from thee a sense so deep and clear
That we become a part of what has been,
And grow unto the spot, all-seeing but unseen.

139 And here the buzz of eager nations ran,
In murmur'd pity, or loud-roar'd applause,
As man was slaughter'd by his fellow-man.
And wherefore slaughter'd? wherefore, but because
Such were the bloody Circus' genial laws,
And the imperial pleasure.—Wherefore not?
What matters where we fall to fill the maws
Of worms—on battle-plains or listed spot?[1]
Both are but theatres where the chief actors rot.

140 I see before me the Gladiator lie:[2]
He leans upon his hand—his manly brow
Consents to death, but conquers agony,
And his droop'd head sinks gradually low—

---

[1] That is, field of the list, or tournament.
[2] Suggested by the statue formerly called *The Dying Gladiator*, but now thought to represent a wounded warrior, and hence called *The Dying Gaul*. It is in the Museum of the Capitol.

And through his side the last drops,
   ebbing slow
From the red gash, fall heavy, one by
   one,
Like the first of a thunder-shower; and
   now
The arena swims around him—he is
   gone,
Ere ceased the inhuman shout which hail'd
   the wretch who won.

141 He heard it, but he heeded not—his eyes
   Were with his heart, and that was far
     away;
  He reck'd not of the life he lost nor
    prize,
  But where his rude hut by the Danube
    lay,
  There were his young barbarians all at
    play,
  There was their Dacian mother[1]—he,
    their sire,
  Butcher'd to make a Roman holiday—
  All this rush'd with his blood—Shall he
    expire
  And unavenged? Arise, ye Goths, and
    glut your ire!

142 But here, where Murder breathed her
    bloody stream;
  And here, where buzzing nations choked
    the ways,
  And roar'd or murmur'd like a moun-
    tain stream
  Dashing or winding as its torrent strays;
  Here, where the Roman million's blame
    or praise,
  Was death or life, the playthings of a
    crowd,
  My voice sounds much—and fall the
    stars' faint rays
  On the arena void—seats crush'd—walls
    bow'd—
And galleries, where my steps seem echoes
    strangely loud.

143 A ruin—yet what ruin! from its mass
   Walls, palaces, half-cities, have been
    rear'd;
  Yet oft the enormous skeleton ye pass,
  And marvel where the spoil could have
    appear'd.
  Hath it indeed been plunder'd, or but
    clear'd?
  Alas! developed, opens the decay,

When the colossal fabric's form is
   near'd:
It will not bear the brightness of the
   day,
Which streams too much on all years, man,
   have reft away.

144 But when the rising moon begins to
    climb
  Its topmost arch, and gently pauses
    there;
  When the stars twinkle through the
    loops of time,
  And the low night-breeze waves along
    the air
  The garland-forest, which the gray
    walls wear,
  Like laurels on the bald first Cæsar's
    head;[1]
  When the light shines serene but doth
    not glare,
  Then in this magic circle raise the dead:
Heroes have trod this spot—'tis on their
    dust ye tread.

145 "While stands the Coliseum, Rome shall
    stand;
  When falls the Coliseum, Rome shall
    fall;
  And when Rome falls—the World."[2]
    From our own land
  Thus spake the pilgrims o'er this mighty
    wall
  In Saxon times, which we are wont to
    call
  Ancient; and these three mortal things
    are still
  On their foundations, and unalter'd all;
  Rome and her Ruin past Redemption's
    skill,
  The World, the same wide den — of
    thieves, or what ye will.

    .   .   .   .   .   .

175 But I forget.—My pilgrim's shrine is
    won,
  And he and I must part,—so let it be,—
  His task and mine alike are nearly done;

---

[1] "Suetonius informs us that Julius Cæsar was particularly gratified by that decree of the senate which enabled him to wear a wreath of laurel on all occasions. He was anxious, not to show that he was the conqueror of the world, but to hide that he was bald."—Byron. See Suetonius's *Lives of the Cæsars,* 1, 45.

[2] "This is quoted in *The Decline and Fall of the Roman Empire* as a proof that the Coliseum was entire when seen by the Anglo-Saxon pilgrims at the end of the seventh, or the beginning of the eighth century."—Byron. See Gibbon's *The History of the Decline and Fall of the Roman Empire,* ch. 71 (1862 ed., p. 533); Gibbon gives the source of his quotation in a foot-note,—namely, Bede's *Glossarium* (ed. Basil), 2, 407.

---

[1] After Trajan had conquered the region north of the Lower Danube and had made it into the Roman province of Dacia (101 B. C.), he carried 10,000 captives to Rome and exhibited them in combats for the amusement of the people.

Yet once more let us look upon the sea;
The midland ocean[1] breaks on him and
  me,
And from the Alban Mount we now
  behold
Our friend of youth, that Ocean, which,
  when we
Beheld it last by Calpe's rock[2] unfold
Those waves, we follow'd on till the dark
  Euxine roll'd

176   Upon the blue Symplegades. Long
  years—
Long, though not very many—since
  have done
Their work on both; some suffering and
  some tears
Have left us nearly where we had
  begun:
Yet not in vain our mortal race hath
  run;
We have our own reward, and it is
  here,—
That we can yet feel gladden'd by the
  sun,
And reap from earth, sea, joy almost
  as dear
As if there were no man to trouble what
  is clear.

177   Oh! that the desert were my dwelling-
  place,
With one fair Spirit for my minister,[3]
That I might all forget the human race,
And, hating no one, love but only her!
Ye elements!—in whose ennobling stir
I feel myself exalted—Can ye not
Accord me such a being? Do I err
In deeming such inhabit many a spot?
Though with them to converse can rarely
  be our lot.

178   There is a pleasure in the pathless
  woods,
There is a rapture on the lonely shore,
There is society, where none intrudes,
By the deep sea, and music in its roar:
I love not man the less, but Nature more,
From these our interviews, in which I
  steal
From all I may be, or have been before,
To mingle with the Universe,[4] and feel
What I can ne'er express, yet cannot all
  conceal.

179   Roll on, thou deep and dark blue
  Ocean—roll!
Ten thousand fleets sweep over thee in
  vain;
Man marks the earth with ruin—his
  control
Stops with the shore; upon the watery
  plain
The wrecks are all thy deed, nor doth
  remain
A shadow of man's ravage, save his
  own,
When, for a moment, like a drop of
  rain,
He sinks into thy depths with bubbling
  groan,
Without a grave, unknell'd, uncoffin'd,
  and unknown.[1]

180   His steps are not upon thy paths,—thy
  fields
Are not a spoil for him,—thou dost rise
And shake him from thee; the vile
  strength he wields
For earth's destruction thou dost all
  despise,
Spurning him from thy bosom to the
  skies,
And send'st him, shivering in thy playful spray
And howling, to his gods, where haply
  lies
His petty hope in some near port or
  bay,
And dashest him again to earth:—there
  let him lay.

181   The armaments which thunderstrike the
  walls
Of rock-built cities, bidding nations
  quake,
And monarchs tremble in their capitals,
The oak leviathans, whose huge ribs
  make
Their clay creator the vain title take
Of lord of thee, and arbiter of war—
These are thy toys, and, as the snowy
  flake,
They melt into thy yeast of waves,
  which mar
Alike the Armada's pride or spoils of
  Trafalgar.[2]

---

[1] The Mediterranean.
[2] Gibraltar. Byron had last seen the Mediterranean on his return journey to England in
  1811. See *Childe Harold's Pilgrimage*, II,
  22, 1.
[3] Byron's sister Augusta. See *Epistle to Augusta*, 1-10 (p. 545).
[4] See Canto III, 72, 8-9 (p. 560); also *Epistle
  to Augusta*, 81 ff. (p. 546).

[1] See Scott's *The Lay of the Last Minstrel*, 6,
  14-16 (p. 470).
[2] Over half of the Spanish fleet which sailed
  against England in 1588 was destroyed in a
  sea-storm, as were also most of the French
  ships captured by Nelson at Trafalgar, in
  1805.

182 Thy shores are empires, changed in all
    save thee—
Assyria, Greece, Rome, Carthage, what
    are they?
Thy waters wash'd them power while
    they were free,
And many a tyrant since; their shores
    obey
The stranger, slave, or savage; their
    decay
Has dried up realms to deserts:—not so
    thou;—
Unchangeable, save to thy wild waves'
    play,
Time writes no wrinkle on thine azure
    brow:
Such as creation's dawn beheld, thou
    rollest now.

183 Thou glorious mirror, where the Al-
    mighty's form
Glasses itself in tempests; in all time,—
Calm or convulsed, in breeze, or gale, or
    storm,
Icing the pole, or in the torrid clime
Dark-heaving—boundless, endless, and
    sublime,
The image of Eternity, the throne
Of the Invisible; even from out thy
    slime
The monsters of the deep are made;
    each zone
Obeys thee; thou goest forth, dread,
    fathomless, alone.

184 And I have loved thee, Ocean! and my
    joy
Of youthful sports was on thy breast
    to be
Borne, like thy bubbles, onward: from
    a boy
I wanton'd with thy breakers—they to
    me
Were a delight; and if the freshening
    sea
Made them a terror—'twas a pleasing
    fear,
For I was as it were a child of thee,
And trusted to thy billows far and near,
And laid my hand upon thy mane—as I do
    here.

185 My task is done, my song hath ceased,
    my theme
Has died into an echo; it is fit
The spell should break of this pro-
    tracted dream.
The torch shall be extinguish'd which
    hath lit

My midnight lamp—and what is writ,
    is writ;
Would it were worthier! but I am not
    now
That which I have been—and my visions
    flit
Less palpably before me—and the glow
Which in my spirit dwelt is fluttering,
    faint, and low.

186 Farewell! a word that must be, and
    hath been—
A sound which makes us linger;—yet—
    farewell!
Ye! who have traced the pilgrim to the
    scene
Which is his last, if in your memories
    dwell
A thought which once was his, if on ye
    swell
A single recollection, not in vain
He wore his sandal-shoon and scallop-
    shell;[1]
Farewell! with *him* alone may rest the
    pain,
If such there were—with *you*, the moral
    of his strain.

MANFRED

A DRAMATIC POEM
1816-17   1817

There are more things in heaven and earth,
    Horatio,
Than are dreamt of in your philosophy.[2]

DRAMATIS PERSONÆ

MANFRED	WITCH OF THE ALPS
CHAMOIS HUNTER	ARIMANES
ABBOT OF ST. MAURICE	NEMESIS
MANUEL	THE DESTINIES
HERMAN	SPIRITS, &c

The SCENE of the Drama is amongst the
Higher Alps—partly in the Castle of Manfred,
and partly in the Mountains.

ACT I

SCENE I

MANFRED *alone.—Scene, a Gothic Gallery.*
    Time, Midnight.

Man. The lamp must be replenish'd,
    but even then
It will not burn so long as I must watch:
My slumbers—if I slumber—are not sleep,
But a continuance of enduring thought,
5 Which then I can resist not: in my heart
There is a vigil, and these eyes but close
To look within; and yet I live, and bear

[1] The sandals indicated travel by land; the
scallop-shell, which was worn in the hat,
travel by sea.
[2] *Hamlet*, I, 5, 166-7.

The aspect and the form of breathing men.
But grief should be the instructor of the wise;
10 Sorrow is knowledge: they who know the most
Must mourn the deepest o'er the fatal truth, 50
The Tree of Knowledge is not that of Life.
Philosophy and science, and the springs
Of wonder, and the wisdom of the world,
15 I have essay'd, and in my mind there is
A power to make these subject to itself—
But they avail not: I have done men good,
And I have met with good even among men—
But this avail'd not: I have had my foes,
20 And none have baffled, many fallen before me—
But this avail'd not:—Good, or evil, life,
Powers, passions, all I see in other beings,
Have been to me as rain unto the sands,
Since that all-nameless hour. I have no dread,
25 And feel the curse to have no natural fear,
Nor fluttering throb, that beats with hopes or wishes,
Or lurking love of something on the earth.
Now to my task.—
　　　　　　Mysterious agency!
Ye spirits of the unbounded Universe!
30 Whom I have sought in darkness and in light—
Ye, who do compass earth about, and dwell
In subtler essence—ye, to whom the tops
Of mountains inaccessible are haunts,
And earth's and ocean's caves familiar things—
35 I call upon ye by the written charm
Which gives me power upon you—Rise!
　　Appear!　　　　　　[A pause.
They come not yet.—Now by the voice of him
Who is the first among you—by this sign,
Which makes you tremble—by the claims of him
40 Who is undying, — Rise! Appear!——
　　Appear!　　　　　　[A pause.
If it be so—Spirits of earth and air,
Ye shall not thus elude me: by a power,
Deeper than all yet urged, a tyrant-spell,
Which had its birthplace in a star con-demn'd,
45 The burning wreck of a demolish'd world,
A wandering hell in the eternal space;
By the strong curse which is upon my soul,
The thought which is within me and around me,
I do compel ye to my will—Appear!

[A star is seen at the darker end of the gallery: it is stationary; and a voice is heard singing.

First Spirit

50 Mortal! to thy bidding bow'd,
From my mansion in the cloud,
Which the breath of twilight builds,
And the summer's sunset gilds
With the azure and vermilion,
55 Which is mix'd for my pavilion;
Though thy quest may be forbidden,
On a star-beam I have ridden:
To thine adjuration bow'd,
Mortal—be thy wish avow'd!

Voice of the Second Spirit

60 Mont Blanc is the monarch of moun-tains;
They crown'd him long ago
On a throne of rocks, in a robe of clouds,
With a diadem of snow.
Around his waist are forests braced,
65 The avalanche in his hand;
But ere it fall, that thundering ball
Must pause for my command.
The glacier's cold and restless mass
Moves onward day by day;
70 But I am he who bids it pass,
Or with its ice delay.
I am the spirit of the place,
Could make the mountain bow
And quiver to his cavern'd base—
75 And what with me would *thou?*

Voice of the Third Spirit

In the blue depth of the waters,
Where the wave hath no strife,
Where the wind is a stranger,
And the sea-snake hath life,
80 Where the mermaid is decking
Her green hair with shells,
Like the storm on the surface
Came the sound of thy spells;
O'er my calm Hall of Coral
85 The deep echo roll'd—
To the Spirit of Ocean
Thy wishes unfold!

Fourth Spirit

Where the slumbering earthquake
Lies pillow'd on fire,
90 And the lakes of bitumen
Rise boilingly higher;
Where the roots of the Andes
Strike deep in the earth,
As their summits to heaven

95 Shoot soaringly forth;
I have quitted my birthplace,
Thy bidding to bide—
Thy spell hath subdued me,
Thy will be my guide!

Fifth Spirit

100 I am the rider of the wind,
The stirrer of the storm;
The hurricane I left behind
Is yet with lightning warm;
To speed to thee, o'er shore and sea
105 I swept upon the blast:
The fleet I met sail'd well, and yet
'Twill sink ere night be past.

Sixth Spirit

My dwelling is the shadow of the night,
Why doth thy magic torture me with
light?

Seventh Spirit

110 The star which rules thy destiny
Was ruled, ere earth began, by me:
It was a world as fresh and fair
As e'er revolved round sun in air;
Its course was free and regular,
115 Space bosom'd not a lovelier star.
The hour arrived—and it became
A wandering mass of shapeless flame,
A pathless comet, and a curse,
The menace of the universe;
120 Still rolling on with innate force,
Without a sphere, without a course,
A bright deformity on high,
The monster of the upper sky!
And thou! beneath its influence born—
125 Thou worm! whom I obey and scorn—
Forced by a power (which is not
thine,
And lent thee but to make thee mine)
For this brief moment to descend,
Where these weak spirits round thee
bend
130 And parley with a thing like thee—
What wouldst thou, child of Clay! with
me?

The Seven Spirits

Earth, ocean, air, night, mountains,
winds, thy star,
Are at thy beck and bidding, child of
Clay!
Before thee at thy quest their spirits
are—
135 What wouldst thou with us, son of
mortals—say?

Man. Forgetfulness—
First Spirit. Of what—of whom—and
why?
Man. Of that which is within me; read
it there—
Ye know it, and I cannot utter it.
Spirit. We can but give thee that which
we possess:
140 Ask of us subjects, sovereignty, the power
O'er earth—the whole, or portion—or a
sign
Which shall control the elements, whereof
We are the dominators,—each and all,
These shall be thine.
Man.   Oblivion, self-oblivion!
145 Can ye not wring from out the hidden
realms
Ye offer so profusely what I ask?
Spirit. It is not in our essence, in our
skill;
But—thou may'st die.
Man.   Will death bestow it on me?
Spirit. We are immortal, and do not
forget;
150 We are eternal; and to us the past
Is, as the future, present. Art thou an-
swer'd?
Man. Ye mock me—but the power which
brought ye here
Hath made you mine. Slaves, scoff not at
my will!
The mind, the spirit, the Promethean
spark,
155 The lightning of my being, is as bright,
Pervading, and far darting as your own,
And shall not yield to yours, though
coop'd in clay! *Byron's version of*
Answer, or I will teach you what I am. *neo-*
Spirit. We answer as we answer'd; our *Platonic*
reply   *limitation*
160 Is even in thine own words.
Man.   Why say ye so?
Spirit. If, as thou say'st, thine essence
be as ours,
We have replied in telling thee, the thing
Mortals call death hath nought to do with
us.
Man. I then have call'd ye from your
realms in vain;
165 Ye cannot, or ye will not, aid me.
Spirit.   Say,
What we possess we offer; it is thine:
Bethink ere thou dismiss us; ask again—
Kingdom, and sway, and strength, and
length of days—
Man. Accursed! what have I to do with
days?
170 They are too long already.—Hence—be-
gone!

Spirit. Yet pause: being here, our will 210
  would do thee service;
Bethink thee, is there then no other gift
Which we can make not worthless in thine
  eyes?
  Man. No, none: yet stay—one moment,
  ere we part, 215
175 I would behold ye face to face. I hear
Your voices, sweet and melancholy sounds,
As music on the waters; and I see
The steady aspect of a clear large star;
But nothing more. Approach me as ye 220
  are,
180 Or one, or all, in your accustom'd forms.
  Spirit. We have no forms, beyond the
    elements
Of which we are the mind and principle:
But choose a form—in that we will appear. 225
  Man. I have no choice; there is no
    form on earth
185 Hideous or beautiful to me. Let him,
  Who is most powerful of ye, take such
    aspect 230
As unto him may seem most fitting—Come!
Seventh Spirit (*appearing in the shape
  of a beautiful female figure*). Be-
  hold!
  Man. Oh God! if it be thus, and *thou*
Art not a madness and a mockery, 235
190 I yet might be most happy, I will clasp
  thee,
And we again will be—
                [*The figure vanishes.*
          My heart is crush'd!
                [MANFRED *falls senseless.*
                                        240

(*A voice is heard in the Incantation which
  follows.*)
When the moon is on the wave,
  And the glow-worm in the grass,
And the meteor on the grave,
195   And the wisp on the morass; 245
When the falling stars are shooting,
And the answer'd owls are hooting,
And the silent leaves are still
  In the shadow of the hill,
200   Shall my soul be upon thine,
  With a power and with a sign. 250

Though thy slumber may be deep,
Yet thy spirit shall not sleep;
There are shades that will not vanish,
205   There are thoughts thou canst not
    banish; 255
By a power to thee unknown,
Thou canst never be alone;
Thou art wrapt as with a shroud,
Thou art gather'd in a cloud;

And forever shalt thou dwell
In the spirit of this spell.

Though thou seest me not pass by,
Thou shalt feel me with thine eye
As a thing that, though unseen,
Must be near thee, and hath been;
And when in that secret dread
Thou hast turn'd around thy head,
Thou shalt marvel I am not
As thy shadow on the spot,
And the power which thou dost feel
Shall be what thou must conceal.

And a magic voice and verse
Hath baptized thee with a curse;
And a spirit of the air
Hath begirt thee with a snare;
In the wind there is a voice
Shall forbid thee to rejoice;
And to thee shall night deny
All the quiet of her sky;
And the day shall have a sun,
Which shall make thee wish it done.

From thy false tears I did distil
An essence which hath strength to kill;
From thy own heart I then did wring
The black blood in its blackest spring;
From thy own smile I snatch'd the
  snake,
For there it coil'd as in a brake;[1]
From thy own lip I drew the charm
Which gave all these their chiefest
  harm;
In proving every poison known,
I found the strongest was thine own.

By thy cold breast and serpent smile,
By thy unfathom'd gulfs of guile,
By that most seeming virtuous eye,
By thy shut soul's hypocrisy;
By the perfection of thine art
Which pass'd for human thine own
  heart;
By thy delight in others' pain,
And by thy brotherhood of Cain,
I call upon thee! and compel
Thyself to be thy proper hell!

And on thy head I pour the vial
Which doth devote thee to this trial;
Nor to slumber, nor to die,
Shall be in thy destiny;
Though thy death shall still seem near
To thy wish, but as a fear;
Lo! the spell now works around thee,

---
[1] thicket

And the clankless chain hath bound
    thee;
260 O'er thy heart and brain together
    Hath the word been pass'd—now wither!

SCENE II

The Mountain of the Jungfrau.—Time,
    *Morning.—*MANFRED *alone upon*
        the Cliffs.

    Man. The spirits I have raised abandon
    me,
The spells which I have studied baffle me,
The remedy I reck'd of tortured me;
I lean no more on superhuman aid;
5 It hath no power upon the past, and for
The future, till the past be gulf'd in
    darkness,
It is not of my search.—My mother Earth!
And thou fresh breaking day, and you, ye
    mountains,
Why are ye beautiful? I cannot love ye.
10 And thou, the bright eye of the universe,
That openest over all, and unto all
Art a delight—thou shin'st not on my
    heart.
And you, ye crags, upon whose extreme
    edge
I stand, and on the torrent's brink beneath
15 Behold the tall pines dwindled as to shrubs
In dizziness of distance; when a leap,
A stir, a motion, even a breath, would
    bring
My breast upon its rocky bosom's bed
To rest forever—wherefore do I pause?
20 I feel the impulse—yet I do not plunge;
I see the peril—yet do not recede;
And my brain reels—and yet my foot is
    firm:
There is a power upon me which with-
    holds,
And makes it my fatality to live;
25 If it be life to wear within myself
This barrenness of spirit, and to be
My own soul's sepulchre, for I have ceased
To justify my deeds unto myself—
The last infirmity of evil. Ay,
30 Thou winged and cloud-cleaving minister,
        [*An eagle passes.*
Whose happy flight is highest into heaven,
Well may'st thou swoop so near me—I
    should be
Thy prey, and gorge thine eaglets; thou
    art gone
Where the eye cannot follow thee; but
    thine
35 Yet pierces downward, onward, or above,
With a pervading vision.—Beautiful!
How beautiful is all this visible world![1]
[1] See *Hamlet,* II, 2, 286 ff.

How glorious in its action and itself!
But we, who name ourselves its sovereigns,
    we,
40 Half dust, half deity, alike unfit
To sink or soar, with our mix'd essence
    make
A conflict of its elements, and breathe
The breath of degradation and of pride,
Contending with low wants and lofty will,
45 Till our mortality predominates,
And men are—what they name not to
    themselves,
And trust not to each other. Hark! the
    note,   [*The Shepherd's pipe in*
        the distance is heard.
The natural music of the mountain reed—
For here the patriarchal days are not
50 A pastoral fable—pipes in the liberal air,
Mix'd with the sweet bells of the saunter-
    ing herd;
My soul would drink those echoes. Oh,
    that I were
The viewless spirit of a lovely sound,—
A living voice, a breathing harmony,
55 A bodiless enjoyment[1]—born and dying
With the blest tone which made me!

Enter from below a CHAMOIS HUNTER.
    Chamois Hunter.   Even so
This way the chamois leapt: her nimble
    feet
Have baffled me; my gains today will
    scarce
Repay my break-neck travail.—What is
    here?
60 Who seems not of my trade, and yet hath
    reach'd
A height which none even of our moun-
    taineers,
Save our best hunters, may attain: his
    garb
Is goodly, his mien manly, and his air
Proud as a free-born peasant's, at this
    distance:
65 I will approach him nearer.
    Man. (*not perceiving the other*). To be
    thus—
Gray-hair'd with anguish, like these blasted
    pines,
Wrecks of a single winter, barkless,
    branchless,
A blighted trunk upon a cursed root,
Which but supplies a feeling to decay—
70 And to be thus, eternally but thus,
Having been otherwise! Now furrow'd
    o'er
With wrinkles, plough'd by moments,—
    not by years,—
[1] See Shelley's *To a Skylark,* 15 (p. 730).

And hours, all tortured into ages—hours
Which I outlive!—Ye toppling crags of
   ice!
75 Ye avalanches, whom a breath draws down
In mountainous o'erwhelming, come and
   crush me!
I hear ye momently above, beneath,
Crash with a frequent conflict; but ye
   pass,
And only fall on things that still would
   live;
80 On the young flourishing forest, or the hut
And hamlet of the harmless villager.
   C. Hun. The mists begin to rise from
      up the valley;
I'll warn him to descend, or he may chance
To lose at once his way and life together.
85 *Man.* The mists boil up around the
      glaciers; clouds
Rise curling fast beneath me, white and
   sulphury,
Like foam from the roused ocean of deep
   hell,
Whose every wave breaks on a living
   shore,
Heap'd with the damn'd like pebbles.—
   I am giddy.
90 *C. Hun.* I must approach him cau-
      tiously; if near,
A sudden step will startle him, and he
Seems tottering already.
   Man.   Mountains have fallen,
Leaving a gap in the clouds, and with the
   shock
Rocking their Alpine brethren; filling
   up
95 The ripe green valleys with destruction's
   splinters;
Damming the rivers with a sudden dash,
Which crush'd the waters into mist and
   made
Their fountains find another channel—
   thus,
Thus, in its old age, did Mount Rosenberg—
100 Why stood I not beneath it?
   C. Hun.   Friend! have a care,
Your next step may be fatal!—for the
   love
Of him who made you, stand not on that
   brink!
   Man. (*not hearing him*). Such would
      have been for me a fitting tomb;
My bones had then been quiet in their
   depth;
105 They had not then been strewn upon the
   rocks
For the wind's pastime—as thus—thus
   they shall be—

In this one plunge.—Farewell, ye opening
   heavens!
Look not upon me thus reproachfully—
Ye were not meant for me—Earth! take
   these atoms!
      [*As* MANFRED *is in act to spring
      from the cliff, the* CHAMOIS
      HUNTER *seizes and retains
      him with a sudden grasp.*[1]
110 *C. Hun.*   Hold, madman! — though
      aweary of thy life,
Stain not our pure vales with thy guilty
   blood:
Away with me—I will not quit my hold.
   Man. I am most sick at heart—nay,
      grasp me not—
I am all feebleness—the mountains whirl
115 Spinning around me—I grow blind—
      What art thou?
   C. Hun. I'll answer that anon. Away
      with me!
The clouds grow thicker—there—now lean
   on me—
Place your foot here—here, take this staff,
   and cling
A moment to that shrub—now give me
   ' your hand,
120 And hold fast by my girdle—softly—
   well—
The Chalet will be gain'd within an hour:
Come on, we'll quickly find a surer footing,
And something like a pathway, which the
   torrent
Hath wash'd since winter.—Come, 'tis
   bravely done—
125 You should have been a hunter.—Follow
   me. [*As they descend the rocks with
      difficulty, the scene closes.*

ACT II

SCENE I

A Cottage amongst the Bernese Alps.

MANFRED *and the* CHAMOIS HUNTER.

   C. Hun. No, no—yet pause—thou must
      not yet go forth:
Thy mind and body are alike unfit
To trust each other, for some hours, at
   least;
When thou art better, I will be thy guide—
5 But whither?
   Man.   It imports not: I do know
My route full well, and need no further
   guidance.

---

[1] See *King Lear*, IV, 6. In Tate's adaptation of
   King Lear, Edgar seizes Gloster, his blind
   father, as he is about to leap from what he
   thinks is Dover Cliff.

C. Hun. Thy garb and gait bespeak
thee of high lineage—
One of the many chiefs, whose castled
crags
Look o'er the lower valleys—which of
these
10 May call thee lord? I only know their
portals;
My way of life leads me but rarely down
To bask by the huge hearths of those old
halls,
Carousing with the vassals; but the paths,
Which step from out our mountains to
their doors,
15 I know from childhood—which of these is
thine?
  Man. No matter.
C. Hun.   Well, sir, pardon me
the question,
And be of better cheer. Come, taste my
wine;
'T is of an ancient vintage; many a day
'T has thaw'd my veins among our glaciers, now
20 Let it do thus for thine. Come, pledge me
fairly.
  Man. Away, away! there's blood upon
the brim!
Will it then never—never sink in the
earth?
  C. Hun. What dost thou mean? thy
senses wander from thee.
  Man. I say 'tis blood—my blood! the
pure warm stream
25 Which ran in the veins of my fathers, and
in ours
When we were in our youth, and had one
heart,
And loved each other as we should not
love,
And this was shed: but still it rises up,
Coloring the clouds, that shut me out from
heaven,
30 Where thou art not—and I shall never be.
  C. Hun. Man of strange words, and
some half-maddening sin,
Which makes thee people vacancy, what-
e'er
Thy dread and sufferance be, there's comfort yet—
The aid of holy men, and heavenly patience—
35   *Man.* Patience and patience! Hence—
that word was made
For brutes of burthen, not for birds of
prey;
Preach it to mortals of a dust like thine,—
I am not of thine order.
  C. Hun.   Thanks to heaven!

I would not be of thine for the free fame
40 Of William Tell; but whatsoe'er thine ill,
It must be borne, and these wild starts are
useless.
  Man. Do I not bear it?—Look on me—
I live.
  C. Hun. This is convulsion, and no
healthful life.
  Man. I tell thee, man! I have lived
many years,
45 Many long years, but they are nothing
now
To those which I must number: ages—
ages—
Space and eternity—and consciousness,
With the fierce thirst of death—and still
unslaked!
  C. Hun. Why, on thy brow the seal of
middle age
50 Hath scarce been set; I am thine elder far.
  Man. Think'st thou existence doth depend on time?
It doth; but actions are our epochs: mine
Have made my days and nights imperishable,
Endless, and all alike, as sands on the
shore,
55 Innumerable atoms; and one desert,
Barren and cold, on which the wild waves
break,
But nothing rests, save carcasses and
wrecks,
Rocks, and the salt-surf weeds of bitterness.
  C. Hun. Alas! he's mad—but yet I
must not leave him.
60   *Man.* I would I were—for then the
things I see
Would be but a distemper'd dream.
  C. Hun.   What is it
That thou dost see, or think thou look'st
upon?
  Man. Myself, and thee—a peasant of
the Alps—
Thy humble virtues, hospitable home,
65 And spirit patient, pious, proud, and free;
Thy self-respect, grafted on innocent
thoughts;
Thy days of health, and nights of sleep;
thy toils,
By danger dignified, yet guiltless; hopes
Of cheerful old age and a quiet grave,
70 With cross and garland over its green turf,
And thy grandchildren's love for epitaph;
This do I see—and then I look within—
It matters not—my soul was scorch'd
already!
  C. Hun. And wouldst thou then ex-
change thy lot for mine?

75 *Man.* No, friend! I would not wrong
　　thee, nor exchange
My lot with living being: I can bear—
However wretchedly, 'tis still to bear—
In life what others could not brook to
　　dream,
But perish in their slumber.
　　C. Hun. And with this—
80 This cautious feeling for another's pain,
Canst thou be black with evil?—say not
　　so.
Can one of gentle thoughts have wreak'd
　　revenge
Upon his enemies?
　　Man. Oh! no, no, no!
My injuries came down on those who loved
　　me—
85 On those whom I best loved: I never
　　quell'd[1]
An enemy, save in my just defence—
But my embrace was fatal.
　　C. Hun. Heaven give thee rest!
And penitence restore thee to thyself;
My prayers shall be for thee.
　　Man. I need them not—
90 But can endure thy pity. I depart—
'Tis time—farewell!—Here's gold, and
　　thanks for thee;
No words—it is thy due. Follow me not—
I know my path—the mountain peril's
　　past:
And once again I charge thee, follow not!
　　　　　　　　　　　　[*Exit* MANFRED.

SCENE II

A lower Valley in the Alps.—A Cataract.

Enter MANFRED.

It is not noon—the sunbow's rays still
　　arch
The torrent with the many hues of heaven,
And roll the sheeted silver's waving column
O'er the crag's headlong perpendicular,
5 And fling its lines of foaming light along,
And to and fro, like the pale courser's
　　tail,
The giant steed, to be bestrode by Death,
As told in the Apocalypse.[2] No eyes
But mine now drink this sight of loveli-
　　ness;
10 I should be sole in this sweet solitude,
And with the Spirit of the place divide
The homage of these waters.—I will call
　　her.
　　　[MANFRED *takes some of the water
　　　　into the palm of his hand, and
　　　　flings it into the air, muttering
　　　　the adjuration. After a pause,
　　　　the* WITCH OF THE ALPS *rises*

　　*beneath the arch of the sunbow
　　　　of the torrent.*
Beautiful Spirit! with thy hair of light,
And dazzling eyes of glory, in whose form
15 The charms of earth's least mortal daugh-
　　ters grow
To an unearthly stature, in an essence
Of purer elements; while the hues of
　　youth,—
Carnation'd like a sleeping infant's cheek,
Rock'd by the beating of her mother's
　　heart,
20 Or the rose tints, which summer's twilight
　　leaves
Upon the lofty glacier's virgin snow,
The blush of earth embracing with her
　　heaven,—
Tinge thy celestial aspect, and make tame
The beauties of the sunbow which bends
　　o'er thee.
25 Beautiful Spirit! in thy calm clear brow,
Wherein is glass'd serenity of soul,
Which of itself shows immortality,
I read that thou wilt pardon to a son
Of Earth, whom the abstruser powers
　　permit
30 At times to commune with them—if that
　　he
Avail him of his spells—to call thee thus,
And gaze on thee a moment.
　　Witch. Son of Earth!
I know thee, and the powers which give
　　thee power;
I know thee for a man of many thoughts,
35 And deeds of good and ill, extreme in
　　both,
Fatal and fated in thy sufferings.
I have expected this—what wouldst thou
　　with me?
　　Man. To look upon thy beauty—nothing
　　further.
The face of the earth hath madden'd me,
　　and I
40 Take refuge in her mysteries, and pierce
To the abodes of those who govern her—
But they can nothing aid me. I have
　　sought
From them what they could not bestow,
　　and now
I search no further.
　　Witch. What could be the quest
45 Which is not in the power of the most
　　powerful,
The rulers of the invisible?
　　Man. A boon;
But why should I repeat it? 'twere in
　　vain.
　　Witch. I know not that; let thy lips
　　utter it.

---

[1] killed　　　　[2] *Revelation*, 6 :8.

Man. Well, though it torture me, 'tis
  but the same;
50 My pangs shall find a voice. From my
  youth upwards
My spirit walk'd not with the souls of
  men,
Nor look'd upon the earth with human
  eyes;[1]
The thirst of their ambition was not mine,
The aim of their existence was not mine;
55 My joys, my griefs, my passions, and my
  powers,
Made me a stranger; though I wore the
  form
I had no sympathy with breathing flesh,
Nor midst the creatures of clay that girded
  me
Was there but one who—but of her anon.
60 I said with men, and with the thoughts of
  men,
I held but slight communion; but instead,
My joy was in the wilderness,—to breathe
The difficult air of the iced mountain's top,
Where the birds dare not build, nor in-
  sect's wing
65 Flit o'er the herbless granite; or to plunge
Into the torrent, and to roll along
On the swift whirl of the new breaking
  wave
Of river-stream, or ocean, in their flow.
In these my early strength exulted; or
70 To follow through the night the moving
  moon,
The stars and their development; or catch
The dazzling lightnings till my eyes grew
  dim;
Or to look, list'ning, on the scatter'd
  leaves,
While autumn winds were at their evening
  song.
75 These were my pastimes, and to be alone;
For if the beings, of whom I was one,—
Hating to be so,—cross'd me in my path,
I felt myself degraded back to them,
And was all clay again. And then I dived,
80 In my lone wanderings, to the caves of
  death,
Searching its cause in its effect; and drew
From wither'd bones, and skulls, and
  heap'd up dust,
Conclusions most forbidden. Then I pass'd
The nights of years in sciences untaught,
85 Save in the old time; and with time and
  toil,
And terrible ordeal, and such penance
As in itself hath power upon the air,
And spirits that do compass air and earth,

90 Space, and the peopled infinite, I made
Mine eyes familiar with Eternity,
Such as, before me, did the Magi, and
He who from out their fountain dwellings
  raised
Eros and Anteros, at Gadara,[1] *(Milton)*
As I do thee;—and with my knowledge
  grew
95 The thirst of knowledge, and the power
  and joy
Of this most bright intelligence, until—
Witch. Proceed.
  Man. Oh! I but thus prolong'd my
  words,
Boasting these idle attributes, because
As I approach the core of my heart's
  grief—
100 But to my task. I have not named to thee
Father, or mother, mistress, friend, or
  being,
With whom I wore the chain of human
  ties;
If I had such, they seem'd not such to me;
Yet there was one—
  Witch.   Spare not thyself—proceed.
105 *Man.* She was like me in lineaments;
  her eyes,
Her hair, her features, all, to the very tone
Even of her voice, they said were like to
  mine;
But soften'd all, and temper'd into beauty:
She had the same lone thoughts and wan-
  derings,
110 The quest of hidden knowledge, and a
  mind
To comprehend the universe: nor these
Alone, but with them gentler powers than
  mine,
Pity, and smiles, and tears—which I had
  not;
And tenderness—but that I had for her;
115 Humility—and that I never had.
Her faults were mine—her virtues were
  her own—
I loved her, and destroy'd her!
  Witch.   With thy hand?
  Man. Not with my hand, but heart—
  which broke her heart;
It gazed on mine, and wither'd. I have
  shed
120 Blood, but not hers—and yet her blood
  was shed;
I saw—and could not stanch it.

---

[1] See *Childe Harold's Pilgrimage*, III, 113
  (p. 566).

[1] While Jamblicus, a Neo-Platonic philosopher
of the fourth century, was bathing with his
scholars in the hot baths of Gadara, in Syria,
he called up the love-gods Eros and Anteros
from the springs which bore their names, in
order to explain why the springs were so
called.

Witch.   And for this—
A being of the race thou dost despise,
The order, which thine own would rise
    above,
Mingling with us and ours,—thou dost
    forego
125 The gifts of our great knowledge, and
    shrink'st back
To recreant mortality—Away!
    Man. Daughter of Air! I tell thee,
    since that hour—
But words are breath—look on me in my
    sleep,
Or watch my watchings—Come and sit by
    me!
130 My solitude is solitude no more,
But peopled with the Furies;—I have
    gnash'd
My teeth in darkness till returning morn,
Then cursed myself till sunset;—I have
    pray'd
For madness as a blessing—'tis denied
    me.
135 I have affronted death—but in the war
Of elements the waters shrunk from me,
And fatal things pass'd harmless; the
    cold hand
Of an all-pitiless demon held me back,
Back by a single hair, which would not
    break.
140 In fantasy, imagination, all
The affluence of my soul—which one day
    was
A Crœsus in creation—I plunged deep,
But, like an ebbing wave, it dash'd me
    back
Into the gulf of my unfathom'd thought.
145 I plunged amidst mankind—Forgetfulness
I sought in all, save where 'tis to be found,
And that I have to learn; my sciences,
My long-pursued and superhuman art,
Is mortal here: I dwell in my despair—
150 And live—and live forever.
    Witch.   It may be
That I can aid thee.
    Man.   To do this thy power
Must wake the dead, or lay me low with
    them.
Do so—in any shape—in any hour—
With any torture—so it be the last.
155   *Witch.* That is not in my province;
    but if thou
Wilt swear obedience to my will, and do
My bidding, it may help thee to thy wishes.
    Man. I will not swear—Obey! and
    whom? the spirits
Whose presence I command, and be the
    slave
160 Of those who served me—Never!

Witch.   Is this all?
Hast thou no gentler answer?—Yet be-
    think thee,
And pause ere thou rejectest.
    Man.   I have said it.
    Witch. Enough! I may retire then—
    say!
    Man. Retire!
                [*The* WITCH *disappears.*
Man (*alone*). We are the fools of time
    and terror. Days
165 Steal on us, and steal from us; yet we
    live,
Loathing our life, and dreading still to
    die.
In all the days of this detested yoke—
This vital weight upon the struggling
    heart,
Which sinks with sorrow, or beats quick
    with pain,
170 Or joy that ends in agony or faintness—
In all the days of past and future, for
In life there is no present, we can number
How few—how less than few—wherein
    the soul
Forbears to pant for death, and yet draws
    back
175 As from a stream in winter, though the
    chill
Be but a moment's. I have one resource
Still in my science—I can call the dead,
And ask them what it is we dread to be:
The sternest answer can but be the Grave,
180 And that is nothing. If they answer
    not—
The buried prophet[1] answered to the Hag
Of Endor; and the Spartan Monarch
    drew
From the Byzantine maid's unsleeping
    spirit
An answer and his destiny[2]—he slew
185 That which he loved, unknowing what he
    slew,
And died unpardon'd—though he call'd
    in aid
The Phyxian Jove, and in Phigalia roused
The Arcadian Evocators to compel
The indignant shadow to depose her
    wrath,
190 Or fix her term of vengeance—she replied

---

[1] Samuel. See *1 Samuel,* 28 :9 ff.
[2] Pausanias, King of Sparta (479-470 B. C.),
    being enamored of the Byzantine maiden
    Cleonice, demanded her as his mistress. One
    night as she entered his room, he mistook
    her for an enemy and killed her. He was
    haunted by her image until in the temple at
    Heraclea he invoked her spirit and gained
    the information that he would soon be de-
    livered from all his troubles. The oracle
    was fulfilled by his death. The story is told
    in Plutarch's *Life of Cimon,* 6. See also
    Bulwer-Lytton's *Pausanias the Spartan.*

In words of dubious import, but fulfill'd.
If I had never lived, that which I love
Had still been living; had I never loved,
That which I love would still be beautiful,
195 Happy and giving happiness. What is
    she?
What is she now?—a sufferer for my
    sins—
A thing I dare not think upon—or nothing.
Within few hours I shall not call in vain—
Yet in this hour I dread the thing I dare:
200 Until this hour I never shrunk to gaze
On spirit, good or evil—now I tremble,
And feel a strange cold thaw upon my
    heart.
But I can act even what I most abhor,
And champion human fears.—The night
    approaches.   [*Exit.*

SCENE III

The Summit of the Jungfrau Mountain.
Enter FIRST DESTINY.

The moon is rising broad, and round, and
    bright;
And here on snows, where never human
    foot
Of common mortal trod, we nightly tread,
And leave no traces: o'er the savage sea,
5 The glassy ocean of the mountain ice,
We skim its rugged breakers, which put on
The aspect of a tumbling tempest's foam,
Frozen in a moment—a dead whirlpool's
    image:
And this most steep fantastic pinnacle,
10 The fretwork of some earthquake—where
    the clouds.
Pause to repose themselves in passing
    by—
Is sacred to our revels, or our vigils;
Here do I wait my sisters, on our way
To the Hall of Arimanes, for tonight
15 Is our great festival—'tis strange they
    come not.

A Voice without, singing

The captive usurper,
    Hurl'd down from the throne,
Lay buried in torpor,
    Forgotten and lone;
20 I broke through his slumbers,
    I shiver'd his chain,
I leagued him with numbers—
    He's tyrant again!
With the blood of a million he'll answer
    my care,
25 With a nation's destruction—his flight
    and despair.

Second Voice, without

The ship sail'd on, the ship sail'd fast,
But I left not a sail, and I left not a mast;
There is not a plank of the hull or the deck,
And there is not a wretch to lament o'er
    his wreck;
30 Save one, whom I held, as he swam, by
    the hair,
And he was a subject, well worthy my
    care;
A traitor on land, and a pirate at sea—[1]
But I saved him to wreak further havoc
    for me!

First Destiny, answering

The city lies sleeping;
    The morn, to deplore it,
May dawn on it weeping:
    Sullenly, slowly,
The black plague flew o'er it—
    Thousands lie lowly;
40 Tens of thousands shall perish;
    The living shall fly from
The sick they should cherish;
    But nothing can vanquish
The touch that they die from.
45   Sorrow and anguish,
And evil and dread,
    Envelop a nation;
The blest are the dead,
    Who see not the sight
50 Of their own desolation;
    This work of a night—
This wreck of a realm—this deed of my
    doing—
For ages I've done, and shall still be
    renewing!

Enter the SECOND *and* THIRD DESTINIES.
The Three

Our hands contain the hearts of men,
    Our footsteps are their graves;
We only give to take again
    The spirits of our slaves!

First Des. Welcome!—Where's Nemesis?
Second Des.   At some great work;
But what I know not, for my hands were
    full.
Third Des. Behold she cometh.

Enter NEMESIS.
60 *First Des.*   Say, where hast thou been?
My sisters and thyself are slow tonight.
    Nem. I was detain'd repairing shat-
    ter'd thrones,

[1] Byron may refer to Thomas Lord Cochrane
(1775-1860). See Glossary.

Marrying fools, restoring dynasties,
Avenging men upon their enemies,
65 And making them repent their own revenge;
Goading the wise to madness; from the
  dull
Shaping out oracles to rule the world
Afresh, for they were waxing out of date,
And mortals dared to ponder for themselves,
70 To weigh kings in the balance, and to
  speak
Of freedom, the forbidden fruit.—Away!
We have outstay'd the hour—mount we
  our clouds.   [*Exeunt.*

SCENE IV

The Hall of Arimanes.[1]—*Arimanes on his
Throne, a Globe of Fire, surrounded by
the Spirits.*

Hymn of the Spirits

Hail to our Master!—Prince of Earth and
  Air!
Who walks the clouds and waters—in
  his hand
The sceptre of the elements, which tear
  Themselves to chaos at his high com-
  mand!
5 He breatheth—and a tempest shakes the
  sea;
He speaketh—and the clouds reply in
  thunder;
He gazeth—from his glance the sunbeams
  flee;
He moveth—earthquakes rend the world
  asunder.
Beneath his footsteps the volcanoes rise;
10 His shadow is the Pestilence; his path
The comets herald through the crackling
  skies;
And planets turn to ashes at his wrath.
To him War offers daily sacrifice;
  To him Death pays his tribute; Life is
  his,
15 With all its infinite of agonies—
And his the spirit of whatever is!

Enter the DESTINIES *and* NEMESIS.

First Des. Glory to Arimanes! on the
  earth
His power increaseth—both my sisters did
His bidding, nor did I neglect my duty!
20 *Second Des.* Glory to Arimanes! we
  who bow

[1] Cp. the description of the Hall of Eblis in
Beckford's *Vathek* (p. 141b, 22 ff.).

The necks of men, bow down before his
  throne!
  Third Des. Glory to Arimanes! we await
His nod!
  Nem.   Sovereign of sovereigns! we
  are thine,
And all that liveth, more or less, is ours,
25 And most things wholly so; still to in-
  crease
Our power, increasing thine, demands our
  care,
And we are vigilant. Thy late commands
Have been fulfill'd to the utmost.

Enter MANFRED.

  A Spirit.   What is here?
A mortal!—Thou most rash and fatal
  wretch,
Bow down and worship!
30 *Second Spirit.*   I do know the man—
A Magian of great power, and fearful
  skill!
  Third Spirit. Bow down and worship,
  slave!—
What, know'st thou not
Thine and our Sovereign?—Tremble, and
  obey!
  All the Spirits. Prostrate thyself, and
  thy condemned clay,
35 Child of the Earth! or dread the worst.
  Man.   I know it;
And yet ye see I kneel not.
  Fourth Spirit.   'Twill be taught thee.
  Man. 'Tis taught already;—many a
  night on the earth,
On the bare ground, have I bow'd down
  my face,
And strew'd my head with ashes; I have
  known
40 The fulness of humiliation, for
I sunk before my vain despair, and knelt
To my own desolation.
  Fifth Spirit.   Dost thou dare
Refuse to Arimanes on his throne
What the whole earth accords, beholding
  not
45 The terror of his glory?—Crouch, I say.
  Man. Bid *him* bow down to that which
  is above him,
The overruling Infinite—the Maker
Who made him not for worship—let him
  kneel,
And we will kneel together.
  The Spirits.   Crush the worm!
50 Tear him in pieces!—
  First Des. Hence! avaunt!—he's mine.
Prince of the Powers invisible! This man
Is of no common order, as his port
And presence here denote; his sufferings

Have been of an immortal nature, like
55 Our own; his knowledge, and his powers
    and will,
As far as is compatible with clay,
Which clogs the ethereal essence, have been
    such
As clay hath seldom borne; his aspirations
Have been beyond the dwellers of the
    earth,
60 And they have only taught him what we
    know—
That knowledge is not happiness, and
    science
But an exchange of ignorance for that
Which is another kind of ignorance.
This is not all—the passions, attributes
65 Of earth and heaven, from which no
    power, nor being,
Nor breath from the worm upwards is
    exempt,
Have pierced his heart, and in their conse-
    quence
Made him a thing which I, who pity not,
Yet pardon those who pity. He is mine,
70 And thine, it may be; be it so, or not,
No other Spirit in this region hath
A soul like his—or power upon his soul.
    Nem. What doth he here then?
    First Des. Let him answer that.
    Man. Ye know what I have known;
        and without power
75 I could not be amongst ye: but there are
Powers deeper still beyond—I come in
    quest
Of such, to answer unto what I seek.
    Nem. What wouldst thou?
    Man. Thou canst not reply to me.
Call up the dead—my question is for them.
80 *Nem.* Great Arimanes, doth thy will
        avouch
The wishes of this mortal?
    Ari. Yea.
    Nem. Whom wouldst thou
Uncharnel?
    Man. One without a tomb—call up
Astarte.

Nemesis

Shadow! or Spirit!
85   Whatever thou art,
    Which still doth inherit
        The whole or a part
    Of the form of thy birth,
        Of the mould of thy clay,
90   Which return'd to the earth,—
        Reappear to the day!
    Bear what thou borest,
        The heart and the form,
    And the aspect thou worest

95   Redeem from the worm.
    Appear!—Appear!—Appear!
    Who sent thee there requires thee here!
    [*The Phantom of* ASTARTE *rises
        and stands in the midst.*
    Man. Can this be death? there's bloom
        upon her cheek;
But now I see it is no living hue,
100 But a strange hectic—like the unnatural
    red
Which Autumn plants upon the perish'd
    leaf.
It is the same! Oh, God! that I should
    dread
To look upon the same—Astarte!—No,
I cannot speak to her—but bid her speak—
105 Forgive me or condemn me.

Nemesis

    By the power which hath broken
        The grave which enthrall'd thee,
    Speak to him who hath spoken,
        Or those who have call'd thee!
    Man. She is silent,
110 And in that silence I am more than an-
    swer'd.
    Nem. My power extends no further.
        Prince of Air!
It rests with thee alone—command her
    voice.
    Ari. Spirit—obey this sceptre!
    Nem. Silent still!
She is not of our order, but belongs
115 To the other powers. Mortal! thy quest is
    vain,
And we are baffled also.
    Man. Hear me, hear me—
Astarte! my beloved! speak to me:
I have so much endured—so much endure—
Look on me! the grave hath not changed
    thee more
120 Than I am changed for thee. Thou lovedst
    me
Too much, as I loved thee: we were not
    made
To torture thus each other, though it were
The deadliest sin to love as we have loved.
Say that thou loath'st me not—that I do
    bear
125 This punishment for both—that thou wilt
    be
One of the blessed—and that I shall die;
For hitherto all hateful things conspire
To bind me in existence—in a life
Which makes me shrink from immortal-
    ity—
130 A future like the past. I cannot rest.
I know not what I ask, nor what I seek:
I feel but what thou art, and what I am;

And I would hear yet once before I perish
The voice which was my music—Speak to 165
   me!
135 For I have call'd on thee in the still night,
Startled the slumbering birds from the
   hush'd boughs,
And woke the mountain wolves, and made
   the caves
Acquainted with thy vainly echoed name,
Which answer'd me—many things an-
   swer'd me—
140 Spirits and men—but thou wert silent all.
Yet speak to me! I have outwatch'd the
   stars,
And gazed o'er heaven in vain in search
   of thee.
Speak to me! I have wander'd o'er the
   earth,
And never found thy likeness—Speak to
   me!
145 Look on the fiends around—they feel for
   me:
I fear them not, and feel for thee alone—
Speak to me! though it be in wrath;—
   but say—
I reck not what—but let me hear thee
   once—
This once—once more!
   Phantom of Astarte. Manfred!
   Man.   Say on, say on—
150 I live but in the sound—it is thy voice!
   Phan. Manfred! Tomorrow ends thine
      earthly ills.
Farewell!
   Man.   Yet one word more—am I for-
      given?
   Phan. Farewell!
   Man.   Say, shall we meet again?
   Phan. Farewell!
   Man.   One word for mercy!
Say, thou lovest me.
   Phan. Manfred!
   [*The Spirit of* ASTARTE *disappears.*
155   *Nem.* She's gone, and will not be re-
      call'd;
Her words will be fulfill'd. Return to the
   earth.
   A Spirit. He is convulsed.—This is to
   be a mortal
And seek the things beyond mortality.
   Another Spirit. Yet, see, he mastereth
      himself, and makes
160 His torture tributary to his will.
Had he been one of us, he would have
   made
An awful spirit.
   Nem.   Hast thou further question
Of our great sovereign, or his worshippers?
   Man. None.

   Nem.   Then for a time farewell.
   Man. We meet then! Where? On the
      earth?—
Even as thou wilt: and for the grace
   accorded
I now depart a debtor. Fare ye well!
               [*Exit* MANFRED.
   (*Scene closes.*)

ACT III

SCENE I

A Hall in the Castle of Manfred.

MANFRED *and* HERMAN.

   Man. What is the hour?
   Her.   It wants but one till sunset,
And promises a lovely twilight.
   Man.   Say,
Are all things so disposed of in the tower
As I directed?
   Her.   All, my lord, are ready:
5 Here is the key and casket.
   Man.   It is well:
Thou may'st retire.   [*Exit* HERMAN.
   Man. (*alone.*) There is a calm upon me—
Inexplicable stillness! which till now
Did not belong to what I knew of life.
If that I did not know philosophy
10 To be of all our vanities the motliest,
The merest word that ever fool'd the ear
From out the schoolman's jargon, I should
   deem
The golden secret, the sought "Kalon,"[1]
   found,
And seated in my soul. It will not last,
15 But it is well to have known it, though but
   once:
It hath enlarged my thoughts with a new
   sense,
And I within my tablets would note down
That there is such a feeling. Who is there?

   Re-enter HERMAN.

   Her. My lord, the abbot of St. Maurice
   craves
20 To greet your presence.

   Enter the ABBOT OF ST. MAURICE.

   Abbot.   Peace be with Count Manfred!
   Man. Thanks, holy father! welcome to
      these walls;
Thy presence honors them, and blesseth
   those
Who dwell within them.
   Abbot.   Would it were so, Count!—
But I would fain confer with thee alone.

[1] The beautiful; the best of human existence.

25 *Man.* Herman, retire.—What would my
        reverend guest?
    Abbot. Thus, without prelude: — Age
        and zeal, my office,
    And good intent, must plead my privilege;
    Our near, though not acquainted neigh-
        borhood,
    May also be my herald. Rumors strange,
30 And of unholy nature, are abroad,
    And busy with thy name; a noble name
    For centuries: may he who bears it now
    Transmit it unimpair'd!
    Man.   Proceed,—I listen.
    Abbot. 'Tis said thou holdest converse
        with the things
35 Which are forbidden to the search of man;
    That with the dwellers of the dark abodes,
    The many evil and unheavenly spirits
    Which walk the valley of the shade of
        death,
    Thou communest. I know that with man-
        kind,
40 Thy fellows in creation, thou dost rarely
    Exchange thy thoughts, and that thy soli-
        tude
    Is as an anchorite's, were it but holy.
    Man. And what are they who do avouch
        these things?
    Abbot. My pious brethren—the scared
        peasantry—
45 Even thy own vassals—who do look on
        thee
    With most unquiet eyes. Thy life's in peril.
    Man. Take it.
    Abbot. I come to save, and not destroy:
    I would not pry into thy secret soul;
    But if these things be sooth, there still is
        time
50 For penitence and pity: reconcile thee
    With the true church, and through the
        church to heaven.
    Man. I hear thee. This is my reply:
        whate'er
    I may have been, or am, doth rest between
    Heaven and myself. I shall not choose a
        mortal
55 To be my mediator. Have I sinn'd
    Against your ordinances? prove and
        punish!
    Abbot. My son! I did not speak of
        punishment,
    But penitence and pardon;—with thyself
    The choice of such remains—and for the
        last,
60 Our institutions and our strong belief
    Have given me power to smooth the path
        from sin
    To higher hope and better thoughts; the
        first

I leave to heaven,—"Vengeance is mine
    alone!"[1]
So saith the Lord, and with all humbleness
65 His servant echoes back the awful word.
    Man. Old man! there is no power in
        holy men,
    Nor charm in prayer, nor purifying form
    Of penitence, nor outward look, nor fast,
    Nor agony—nor, greater than all these,
70 The innate tortures of that deep despair,
    Which is remorse without the fear of hell,
    But all in all sufficient to itself
    Would make a hell of heaven[2]—can exor-
        cise
    From out the unbounded spirit the quick
        sense
75 Of its own sins, wrongs, sufferance, and
        revenge
    Upon itself; there is no future pang
    Can deal that justice on the self-condemn'd
    He deals on his own soul.
    Abbot.   All this is well;
    For this will pass away, and be succeeded
80 By an auspicious hope, which shall look
        up
    With calm assurance to that blessed place,
    Which all who seek may win, whatever be
    Their earthly errors, so they be atoned:
    And the commencement of atonement is
85 The sense of its necessity. Say on—
    And all our church can teach thee shall be
        taught;
    And all we can absolve thee shall be par-
        don'd.
    Man. When Rome's sixth emperor[3] was
        near his last,
    The victim of a self-inflicted wound,
90 To shun the torments of a public death
    From senates once his slaves, a certain
        soldier,
    With show of loyal pity, would have
        stanch'd
    The gushing throat with his officious robe;
    The dying Roman thrust him back, and
        said—
95 Some empire still in his expiring glance—
    "It is too late—is this fidelity?"
    Abbot. And what of this?
    Man.   I answer with the Roman—
    "It is too late!"
    Abbot.   It never can be so,
    To reconcile thyself with thy own soul,
100 And thy own soul with heaven. Hast thou
        no hope?
    'Tis strange—even those who do despair
        above,

[1] *Romans*, 12:19.
[2] See *Paradise Lost*, 1, 254-55.
[3] Nero, Emperor of Rome (54-68). See Sueto-
    nius's *Lives of the Cæsars*, 6, 49.

Yet shape themselves some fantasy on earth,
To which frail twig they cling, like drowning men.
    Man. Ay—father! I have had those earthly visions,
105 And noble aspirations in my youth,
To make my own the mind of other men,
The enlightener of nations; and to rise
I knew not whither—it might be to fall;
But fall, even as the mountain-cataract,
110 Which, having leapt from its more dazzling height,
Even in the foaming strength of its abyss
(Which casts up misty columns that become
Clouds raining from the re-ascended skies),
Lies low but mighty still.—But this is past,
115 My thoughts mistook themselves.
    Abbot. And wherefore so?
    Man. I could not tame my nature down; for he
Must serve who fain would sway; and soothe, and sue,
And watch all time, and pry into all place,
And be a living lie, who would become
120 A mighty thing amongst the mean, and such
The mass are; I disdain'd to mingle with
A herd, though to be leader—and of wolves.
The lion is alone, and so am I.
    Abbot. And why not live and act with other men?
125   *Man.* Because my nature was averse from life;
And yet not cruel; for I would not make,
But find a desolation. Like the wind,
The red-hot breath of the most lone simoom,
Which dwells but in the desert, and sweeps o'er
130 The barren sands which bear no shrubs to blast,
And revels o'er their wild and arid waves,
And seeketh not, so that it is not sought,
But being met is deadly,—such hath been
The course of my existence; but there came
135 Things in my path which are no more.
    Abbot. Alas!
I 'gin to fear that thou art past all aid
From me and from my calling; yet so young,
I still would—
    Man. Look on me! there is an order
Of mortals on the earth, who do become
140 Old in their youth, and die ere middle age,

Without the violence of warlike death;
Some perishing of pleasure, some of study,
Some worn with toil, some of mere weariness,
Some of disease, and some insanity,
145 And some of wither'd or of broken hearts;
For this last is a malady which slays
More than are number'd in the lists of Fate,
Taking all shapes, and bearing many names.
Look upon me! for even of all these things
150 Have I partaken; and of all these things,
One were enough; then wonder not that I
Am what I am, but that I ever was,
Or having been, that I am still on earth.
    Abbot. Yet, hear me still—
    Man. Old man! I do respect
155 Thine order, and revere thine years; I deem
Thy purpose pious, but it is in vain:
Think me not churlish; I would spare thyself,
Far more than me, in shunning at this time
All further colloquy; and so—farewell.
    [*Exit* MANFRED.
160   *Abbot.* This should have been a noble creature: he
Hath all the energy which would have made
A goodly frame of glorious elements,
Had they been wisely mingled; as it is,
It is an awful chaos—light and darkness,
165 And mind and dust, and passions and pure thoughts
Mix'd, and contending without end or order,—
All dormant or destructive; he will perish,
And yet he must not; I will try once more.
For such are worth redemption; and my duty
170 Is to dare all things for a righteous end.
I'll follow him—but cautiously, though surely.
    [*Exit* ABBOT.

SCENE II

Another Chamber.

MANFRED *and* HERMAN.

    Her. My lord, you bade me wait on you at sunset:
He sinks behind the mountain.
    Man. Doth he so?
I will look on him.
    [MANFRED *advances to the Window of the Hall.*
    Glorious orb! the idol
Of early nature, and the vigorous race

5 Of undiseased mankind, the giant sons
Of the embrace of angels,[1] with a sex
More beautiful than they, which did draw
  down
The erring spirits who can ne'er return.—
Most glorious orb! that wert a worship, ere
10 The mystery of thy making was reveal'd!
Thou earliest minister of the Almighty,
Which gladden'd, on their mountain tops,
  the hearts
Of the Chaldean shepherds,[2] till they
  pour'd
Themselves in orisons! Thou material God!
15 And representative of the Unknown—
Who chose thee for his shadow! Thou
  chief star!
Centre of many stars! which mak'st our
  earth
Endurable, and temperest the hues
And hearts of all who walk within thy
  rays!
20 Sire of the seasons! Monarch of the
  climes,
And those who dwell in them! for near or
  far,
Our inborn spirits have a tint of thee
Even as our outward aspects;—thou dost
  rise,
And shine, and set in glory. Fare thee
  well!
25 I ne'er shall see thee more. As my first
  glance
Of love and wonder was for thee, then
  take
My latest look; thou wilt not beam on one
To whom the gifts of life and warmth
  have been
Of a more fatal nature. He is gone:
30 I follow.   [Exit MANFRED.

SCENE III

*The Mountains—The Castle of Manfred
at some distance—A Terrace before a
Tower.—Time, Twilight.*

HERMAN, MANUEL, and other Dependants
of MANFRED.

Her. 'Tis strange enough; night after
  night, for years,
He hath pursued long vigils in this tower,
Without a witness. I have been within it,—
So have we all been ofttimes; but from it,
5 Or its contents, it were impossible
To draw conclusions absolute, of aught
His studies tend to. To be sure, there is
One chamber where none enter: I would
  give

[1] See *Genesis*, 6:2-4.
[2] The Chaldeans were especially versed in
  astrology.

The fee of[1] what I have to come these
  three years,
10 To pore upon its mysteries.
Manuel.   'Twere dangerous:
Content thyself with what thou know'st
  already.
  Her. Ah! Manuel! thou art elderly
  and wise,
And couldst say much; thou hast dwelt
  within the castle—
How many years is 't?
  Manuel.   Ere Count Manfred's birth,
15 I served his father, whom he nought re-
  sembles.
  Her. There be more sons in like pre-
  dicament.
But wherein do they differ?
  Manuel.   I speak not
Of features or of form, but mind and
  habits;
Count Sigismund was proud, but gay and
  free,—
20 A warrior and a reveller; he dwelt not
With books and solitude, nor made the
  night
A gloomy vigil, but a festal time,
Merrier than day; he did not walk the
  rocks
And forests like a wolf, nor turn aside
25 From men and their delights.
  Her.   Beshrew the hour,
But those were jocund times! I would
  that such
Would visit the old walls again; they look
As if they had forgotten them.
  Manuel.   These walls
Must change their chieftain first. Oh! I
  have seen
30 Some strange things in them, Herman.
  Her.   Come, be friendly,
Relate me some to while away our watch:
I've heard thee darkly speak of an event
Which happen'd hereabouts, by this same
  tower.
  Manuel. That was a night indeed! I
  do remember
35 'Twas twilight, as it may be now, and
  such
Another evening;—yon red cloud, which
  rests
On Eigher's pinnacle, so rested then,—
So like that it might be the same; the wind
Was faint and gusty, and the mountain
  snows
40 Began to glitter with the climbing moon;
Count Manfred was, as now, within his
  tower,—
How occupied, we knew not, but with him

[1] title to

The sole companion of his wanderings
And watchings—her, whom of all earthly
    things
45 That lived, the only thing he seem'd to
    love,—
As he, indeed, by blood was bound to do,
The lady Astarte, his—
            Hush! who comes here?

Enter the ABBOT.

Abbot. Where is your master?
Her.   Yonder in the tower.
Abbot. I must speak with him.
Manuel.   'T is impossible;
50 He is most private, and must not be thus
Intruded on.
Abbot.   Upon myself I take
The forfeit of my fault, if fault there
    be—
But I must see him.
Her.   Thou hast seen him once
This eve already.
Abbot.   Herman! I command thee,
55 Knock, and apprize the Count of my
    approach.
Her. We dare not.
Abbot.   Then it seems I must be herald
Of my own purpose.
Manuel.   Reverend father, stop—
I pray you pause.
Abbot.   Why so?
Manuel.   But step this way,
And I will tell you further.   [*Exeunt.*

SCENE IV

Interior of the Tower.

MANFRED *alone.*

The stars are forth, the moon above the
    tops
Of the snow-shining mountains.—Beauti-
    ful!
I linger yet with Nature, for the night
Hath been to me a more familiar face
5 Than that of man; and in her starry shade
Of dim and solitary loveliness,
I learn'd the language of another world.[1]
I do remember me, that in my youth,
When I was wandering,—upon such a
    night
10 I stood within the Coliseum's wall,
'Midst the chief relics of almighty Rome;
The trees which grew along the broken
    arches
Waved dark in the blue midnight, and the
    stars

[1] See *Childe Harold's Pilgrimage*, III, 86-90 (pp. 562-63).

Shone through the rents of ruin; **from**
    afar
15 The watch-dog bay'd beyond the Tiber;
    and
More near from out the Cæsar's palace
    came
The owl's long cry, and, interruptedly,
Of distant sentinels the fitful song
Begun and died upon the gentle wind.
20 Some cypresses beyond the time-worn
    breach
Appear'd to skirt the horizon, yet they
    stood
Within a bowshot. Where the Cæsars
    dwelt,
And dwell the tuneless birds of night,
    amidst
A grove which springs through levell'd
    battlements,
25 And twines its roots with the imperial
    hearths,
Ivy usurps the laurel's place of growth;
But the gladiator's bloody Circus stands,
A noble wreck in ruinous perfection,
While Cæsar's chambers, and the Augus-
    tan halls,
30 Grovel on earth in indistinct decay.
And thou didst shine, thou rolling moon,
    upon
All this, and cast a wide and tender light,
Which soften'd down the hoar austerity
Of rugged desolation, and fill'd up,
35 As 't were anew, the gaps of centuries;
Leaving that beautiful which still was
    so,
And making that which was not, till the
    place
Became religion, and the heart ran o'er
With silent worship of the great of old,—
40 The dead but sceptred sovereigns, who still
    rule
Our spirits from their urns.
              'Twas such a night!
'Tis strange that I recall it at this time;
But I have found our thoughts take wild-
    est flight
Even at the moment when they should
    array
45 Themselves in pensive order.

Enter the ABBOT.

Abbot.   My good lord!
I crave a second grace for this approach;
But yet let not my humble zeal offend
By its abruptness—all it hath of ill
Recoils on me; its good in the effect
50 May light upon your head—could I say
    heart—

Could I touch *that,* with words or prayers,
    I should
Recall a noble spirit which hath wander'd;
But is not yet all lost.
    Man.   Thou know'st me not;
My days are number'd, and my deeds
    recorded;
55 Retire, or 't will be dangerous—Away!
    Abbot. Thou dost not mean to menace
    me?
    Man.   Not I;
I simply tell thee peril is at hand,
And would preserve thee.
    Abbot.   What dost thou mean?
    Man.   Look there!
What dost thou see?
    Abbot.   Nothing.
    Man.   Look there, I say,
60 And steadfastly;—now tell me what thou
    seest.
    Abbot. That which should shake me,
    but I fear it not:
I see a dusk and awful figure rise,
Like an infernal god, from out the earth;
His face wrapt in a mantle, and his
    form
65 Robed as with angry clouds: he stands
    between
Thyself and me—but I do fear him not.
    Man. Thou hast no cause; he shall not
    harm thee, but
His sight may shock thine old limbs into
    palsy.
I say to thee—Retire!
    Abbot.   And I reply—
70 Never—till I have battled with this fiend:—
What doth he here?
    Man.   Why—ay—what doth he here?
I did not send for him,—he is unbidden.
    Abbot. Alas! lost mortal! what with
    guests like these
Hast thou to do? I tremble for thy sake:
75 Why doth he gaze on thee, and thou on
    him?
Ah! he unveils his aspect: on his brow
The thunder-scars are graven: from his
    eye
Glares forth the immortality of hell—
Avaunt!—
    Man. Pronounce—what is thy mission?
    Spirit.   Come!
80 *Abbot.* What art thou, unknown being?
    answer!—speak!
    Spirit. The genius of this mortal.—
    Come! 'tis time.
    Man. I am prepared for all things, but
    deny
The power which summons me. Who sent
    thee here?

    Spirit. Thou 'lt know anon — Come!
    come!
    Man.   I have commanded
85 Things of an essence greater far than
    thine,
And striven with thy masters. Get thee
    hence!
    Spirit. Mortal! thine hour is come—
    Away! I say.
    Man. I knew, and know my hour is
    come, but not
To render up my soul to such as thee:
90 Away! I'll die as I have lived—alone.
    Spirit. Then I must summon up my
    brethren.—Rise!
                 [*Other Spirits rise up.*
    Abbot. Avaunt! ye evil ones!—Avaunt!
    I say;
Ye have no power where piety hath power,
And I do charge ye in the name—
    Spirit.   Old man!
95 We know ourselves, our mission, and thine
    order;
Waste not thy holy words on idle uses,
It were in vain: this man is forfeited.
Once more I summon him—Away! Away!
    Man. I do defy ye,—though I feel my
    soul
100 Is ebbing from me, yet I do defy ye;
Nor will I hence, while I have earthly
    breath
To breathe my scorn upon ye—earthly
    strength
To wrestle, though with spirits; what ye
    take
Shall be ta'en limb by limb.
    Spirit.   .   Reluctant mortal!
105 Is this the Magian who would so pervade
The world invisible, and make himself
Almost our equal? Can it be that thou
Art thus in love with life? the very life
Which made thee wretched!
    Man.   Thou false fiend, thou liest!
110 My life is in its last hour,—*that* I know,
Nor would redeem a moment of that hour;
I do not combat against death, but thee
And thy surrounding angels; my past
    power,
Was purchased by no compact with thy
    crew,
115 But by superior science—penance, daring,
And length of watching, strength of mind,
    and skill
In knowledge of our fathers—when the
    earth
Saw men and spirits walking side by side,
And gave ye no supremacy: I stand
120 Upon my strength—I do defy—deny—
Spurn back, and scorn ye!—

Spirit.   But thy many crimes
Have made thee—
Man.   What are they to such as thee?
Must crimes be punish'd but by other
    crimes,
And greater criminals?—Back to thy
    hell!
125 Thou hast no power upon me, *that* I feel;
Thou never shalt possess me, *that* I know:
What I have done is done; I bear within
A torture which could nothing gain from
    thine:
The mind which is immortal makes itself
130 Requital for its good or evil thoughts,—
Is its own origin of ill and end
And its own place and time;[1] its innate
    sense,
When stripp'd of this mortality, de-
    rives
No color from the fleeting things with-
    out,
135 But is absorb'd in sufferance or in joy,
Born from the knowledge of its own
    desert.
Thou didst not tempt me, and thou couldst
    not tempt me;
I have not been thy dupe, nor am thy
    prey—
But was my own destroyer, and will be
140 My own hereafter.—Back, ye baffled
    fiends!—
The hand of death is on me—but not
    yours.   [*The Demons disappear.*
Abbot. Alas! how pale thou art—thy
    lips are white—
And thy breast heaves—and in thy gasp-
    ing throat
The accents rattle: Give thy prayers to
    heaven—
145 Pray—albeit but in thought,—but die not
    thus.
Man. 'Tis over—my dull eyes can fix
    thee not;
But all things swim around me, and the
    earth
Heaves as it were beneath me. Fare thee
    well!
Give me thy hand.
Abbot.   Cold—cold—even to the
    heart—
150 But yet one prayer—Alas! how fares it
    with thee?
Man. Old man! 't is not so difficult to
    die.   [MANFRED *expires.*
Abbot. He's gone—his soul hath ta'en
    its earthless flight;
Whither? I dread to think—but he is gone.

[1] See *Paradise Lost*, 1, 254-55.

SO, WE'LL GO NO MORE A-ROVING
1817   1830

So, we'll go no more a-roving
    So late into the night,
Though the heart be still as loving,
    And the moon be still as bright.

5 For the sword outwears its sheath,
    And the soul outwears the breast,
And the heart must pause to breathe,
    And love itself have rest.

Though the night was made for loving,
10   And the day returns too soon,
Yet we'll go no more a-roving
    By the light of the moon.

MY BOAT IS ON THE SHORE
1817   1821

My boat is on the shore,
    And my bark is on the sea;
But, before I go, Tom Moore,
    Here's a double health to thee!

5 Here's a sigh to those who love me,
    And a smile to those who hate;
And, whatever sky 's above me,
    Here's a heart for every fate.

Though the ocean roar around me,
10   Yet it still shall bear me on;
Though a desert should surround me,
    It hath springs that may be won.

Were 't the last drop in the well,
    As I gasp'd upon the brink,
15 Ere my fainting spirit fell,
    'T is to thee that I would drink.

With that water, as this wine,
    The libation I would pour
Should be—peace with thine and mine,
20   And a health to thee, Tom Moore.

STRAHAN, TONSON, LINTOT OF THE TIMES
1818   1830

Strahan, Tonson, Lintot of the times,
Patron and publisher of rhymes,
For thee the bard up Pindus climbs,
        My Murray.

5 To thee, with hope and terror dumb,
The unfledged MS. authors come;
Thou printest all—and sellest some—
        My Murray.

Upon thy table's baize so green
10 The last new *Quarterly* is seen;
But where is thy new Magazine,
        My Murray?

Along thy sprucest bookshelves shine
The works thou deemest most divine—
15 The *Art of Cookery*, and mine,
     My Murray.

Tours, Travels, Essays, too, I wist,
And Sermons, to thy mill bring grist;
And then thou hast the *Navy List*,
20   My Murray.

And Heaven forbid I should conclude
Without "the Board of Longitude,"
Although this narrow paper would,
    My Murray.

MAZEPPA
1818   1819

'T was after dread Pultowa's day,
   When fortune left the royal Swede,[1]
Around a slaughter'd army lay,
   No more to combat and to bleed.
5 The power and glory of the war,
   Faithless as their vain votaries, men,
Had pass'd to the triumphant Czar,
   And Moscow's walls were safe again,
Until a day more dark and drear,[2]
10 And a more memorable year,
Should give to slaughter and to shame
A mightier host and haughtier name;
A greater wreck, a deeper fall,
A shock to one—a thunderbolt to all.

15 Such was the hazard of the die;
The wounded Charles was taught to fly
By day and night through field and flood,
Stain'd with his own and subjects' blood;
For thousands fell that flight to aid:
20 And not a voice was heard t' upbraid
Ambition in his humbled hour,
When truth had nought to dread from
     power.
His horse was slain, and Gieta gave
His own—and died the Russians' slave.
25 This too sinks after many a league
Of well sustain'd but vain fatigue;
And in the depth of forests darkling,
The watch-fires in the distance sparkling—
The beacons of surrounding foes—
30 A king must lay his limbs at length.
Are these the laurels and repose
For which the nations strain their strength?
They laid him by a savage tree,
In outworn nature's agony;
35 His wounds were stiff, his limbs were stark;

[1] Charles XII, King of Sweden (1697-1718), whose forces were almost annihilated by those of Peter the Great of Russia, in the Battle of Poltáva, July 8, 1709.
[2] A reference to Napoleon's Russian campaign of 1812, in which Moscow was burned and the French army almost destroyed by hunger and cold on the return march.

The heavy hour was chill and dark;
The fever in his blood forbade
A transient slumber's fitful aid:
And thus it was; but yet through all,
40 Kinglike the monarch bore his fall,
And made, in this extreme of ill,
His pangs the vassals of his will:
All silent and subdued were they,
As once the nations round him lay.

45 A band of chiefs!—alas! how few,
   Since but the fleeting of a day
Had thinn'd it; but this wreck was true
   And chivalrous: upon the clay
Each sate him down, all sad and mute,
50   Beside his monarch and his steed;
For danger levels man and brute,
   And all are fellows in their need.
Among the rest, Mazeppa made
His pillow in an old oak's shade—
55 Himself as rough, and scarce less old,
The Ukraine's Hetman,[1] calm and bold;
But first, outspent with this long course,
The Cossack prince rubb'd down his horse,
And made for him a leafy bed,
60   And smooth'd his fetlocks and his mane,
   And slack'd his girth, and stripp'd his
     rein,
And joy'd to see how well he fed;
For until now he had the dread
His wearied courser might refuse
65 To browse beneath the midnight dews:
But he was hardy as his lord,
And little cared for bed and board;
But spirited and docile, too,
Whate'er was to be done, would do.
70 Shaggy and swift, and strong of limb,
All Tartar-like he carried him;
Obey'd his voice, and came to call,
And knew him in the midst of all:
Though thousands were around, — and
    Night,
75 Without a star, pursued her flight,—
That steed from sunset until dawn
His chief would follow like a fawn.

This done, Mazeppa spread his cloak
And laid his lance beneath his oak,
80 Felt if his arms in order good
The long day's march had well withstood—
If still the powder fill'd the pan,
   And flints unloosen'd kept their lock—
His sabre's hilt and scabbard felt,
85 And whether they had chafed his belt;
And next the venerable man,
From out his haversack and can
   Prepared and spread his slender stock;

[1] The Cossack chief from Ukraine, a district in Russia lying in the valley of the river Dnieper. Mazeppa had deserted from the Russians and joined the Swedes.

And to the monarch and his men
90 The whole or portion offer'd then
With far less of inquietude
Than courtiers at a banquet would.
And Charles of this his slender share
With smiles partook a moment there,
95 To force of cheer a greater show,
And seem above both wounds and woe;
And then he said—"Of all our band,
Though firm of heart and strong of hand,
In skirmish, march, or forage, none
100 Can less have said or more have done
Than thee, Mazeppa! on the earth
So fit a pair had never birth,
Since Alexander's days till now,
As thy Bucephalus and thou:
105 All Scythia's fame to thine should yield
For pricking on o'er flood and field.''
Mazeppa answer'd—''Ill betide
The school wherein I learn'd to ride!''
Quoth Charles—''Old Hetman, wherefore so,
110 Since thou hast learn'd the art so well?''
Mazeppa said—'' 'T were long to tell;
And we have many a league to go,
With every now and then a blow,
And ten to one at least the foe,
115 Before our steeds may graze at ease
Beyond the swift Borysthenes:
And, Sire, your limbs have need of rest,
And I will be the sentinel
Of this your troop.''—''But I request,''
120   Said Sweden's monarch, ''thou wilt tell
This tale of thine, and I may reap,
Perchance, from this the boon of sleep;
For at this moment from my eyes
The hope of present slumber flies.''

125 ''Well, Sire, with such a hope, I'll track
My seventy years of memory back:
I think 't was in my twentieth spring,—
Ay, 't was,—when Casimir was king[1]—
John Casimir,—I was his page
130 Six summers, in my earlier age:
A learned monarch, faith! was he,
And most unlike your majesty;
He made no wars, and did not gain
New realms to lose them back again;
135 And (save debates in Warsaw's diet)
He reign'd in most unseemly quiet;
Not that he had no cares to vex;
He loved the muses and the sex;
And sometimes these so froward are,
140 They made him wish himself at war;
But soon his wrath being o'er, he took
Another mistress—or new book:
And then he gave prodigious fêtes—

All Warsaw gather'd round his gates
145 To gaze upon his splendid court,
And dames, and chiefs, of princely port:
He was the Polish Solomon,
So sung his poets, all but one,
Who, being unpension'd, made a satire,
150 And boasted that he could not flatter.
It was a court of jousts and mimes,
Where every courtier tried at rhymes;
Even I for once produced some verses,
And sign'd my odes 'Despairing Thyrsis.'
155 There was a certain Palatine,
   A count of far and high descent,
Rich as a salt[1] or silver mine;
   And he was proud, ye may divine,
As if from heaven he had been sent:
160 He had such wealth in blood and ore
   As few could match beneath the throne;
And he would gaze upon his store,
And o'er his pedigree would pore,
Until by some confusion led,
165 Which almost look'd like want of head,
   He thought their merits were his own.
His wife was not of his opinion;
   His junior she by thirty years,
Grew daily tired of his dominion;
170   And, after wishes, hopes, and fears,
   To virtue a few farewell tears,
A restless dream or two, some glances
At Warsaw's youth, some songs, and dances,
Awaited but the usual chances,
175 Those happy accidents which render
The coldest dames so very tender,
To deck her Count with titles given,
'T is said, as passports into heaven;
But, strange to say, they rarely boast
180 Of these, who have deserved them most.

''I was a goodly stripling then;
   At seventy years I so may say,
That there were few, or boys or men,
   Who, in my dawning time of day,
185 Of vassal or of knight's degree,
   Could vie in vanities with me;
For I had strength, youth, gaiety,
A port, not like to this ye see,
But smooth, as all is rugged now;
190   For time, and care, and war, have plough'd
My very soul from out my brow;
   And thus I should be disavow'd
By all my kind and kin, could they
Compare my day and yesterday;
195 This change was wrought, too, long ere age
Had ta'en my features for his page;
With years, ye know, have not declined

---

[1] John Casimir was King of Poland from 1649 to 1668.

[1] The wealth of Poland consists largely in salt mines.

My strength, my courage, or my mind,
Or at this hour I should not be
200 Telling old tales beneath a tree,
With starless skies my canopy
But let me on: Theresa's form—
Methinks it glides before me now,
Between me and yon chestnut's bough,
205 The memory is so quick and warm;
And yet I find no words to tell
The shape of her I loved so well:
She had the Asiatic eye,
Such as our Turkish neighborhood
210 Hath mingled with our Polish blood,
Dark as above us is the sky;
But through it stole a tender light,
Like the first moonrise of midnight;
Large, dark, and swimming in the stream,
215 Which seem'd to melt to its own beam;
All love, half languor, and half fire,
Like saints that at the stake expire,
And lift their raptured looks on high,
As though it were a joy to die.
220 A brow like a midsummer lake,
Transparent with the sun therein,
When waves no murmur dare to make,
And heaven beholds her face within.
A cheek and lip—but why proceed?
225 I loved her then, I love her still;
And such as I am, love indeed
In fierce extremes—in good and ill.
But still we love even in our rage,
And haunted to our very age
230 With the vain shadow of the past,
As is Mazeppa to the last.

"We met—we gazed—I saw, and sigh'd;
She did not speak, and yet replied;
There are ten thousand tones and signs
235 We hear and see, but none defines—
Involuntary sparks of thought,
Which strike from out the heart o'er-
wrought,
And form a strange intelligence,
Alike mysterious and intense,
240 Which link the burning chain that binds,
Without their will, young hearts and minds;
Conveying, as the electric wire,
We know not how, the absorbing fire.
I saw, and sigh'd—in silence wept,
245 And still reluctant distance kept,
Until I was made known to her,
And we might then and there confer
Without suspicion—then, even then,
I long'd, and was resolved to speak;
250 But on my lips they died again,
The accents tremulous and weak,
Until one hour.—There is a game,
A frivolous and foolish play,
Wherewith we while away the day;

255 It is—I have forgot the name—
And we to this, it seems, were set,
By some strange chance, which I forget:
I reck'd not if I won or lost,
It was enough for me to be
260 So near to hear, and oh! to see
The being whom I loved the most.
I watch'd her as a sentinel,
(May ours this dark night watch as well!)
Until I saw, and thus it was,
265 That she was pensive, nor perceived
Her occupation, nor was grieved
Nor glad to lose or gain; but still
Play'd on for hours, as if her will
Yet bound her to the place, though not
270 That hers might be the winning lot.
Then through my brain the thought did
pass
Even as a flash of lightning there,
That there was something in her air
Which would not doom me to despair;
275 And on the thought my words broke forth,
All incoherent as they were;
Their eloquence was little worth,
But yet she listen'd—'t is enough—
Who listens once will listen twice;
280 Her heart, be sure, is not of ice,
And one refusal no rebuff.

"I loved, and was beloved again—
They tell me, Sire, you never knew
Those gentle frailties; if 't is true,
285 I shorten all my joy or pain;
To you 't would seem absurd as vain;
But all men are not born to reign,
Or o'er their passions, or as you
Thus o'er themselves and nations too.
290 I am—or rather was—a prince,
A chief of thousands, and could lead
Them on where each would foremost
bleed;
But could not o'er myself evince
The like control—But to resume:
295 I loved, and was beloved again;
In sooth, it is a happy doom,
But yet where happiest ends in pain.
We met in secret, and the hour
Which led me to that lady's bower
300 Was fiery Expectation's dower.
My days and nights were nothing—all
Except that hour, which doth recall,
In the long lapse from youth to age,
No other like itself: I'd give
305 The Ukraine back again to live
It o'er once more, and be a page,
The happy page, who was the lord
Of one soft heart, and his own sword,
And had no other gem nor wealth
310 Save nature's gift of youth and health.

We met in secret—doubly sweet,
Some say, they find it so to meet;
I know not that—I would have given
My life but to have call'd her mine
315 In the full view of earth and heaven;
For I did oft and long repine
That we could only meet by stealth.

"For lovers there are many eyes,
And such there were on us; the devil
320 On such occasions should be civil—
The devil!—I'm loth to do him wrong,
It might be some untoward saint,
Who would not be at rest too long,
But to his pious bile gave vent—
325 But one fair night, some lurking spies
Surprised and seized us both.
The Count was something more than
  wroth—
I was unarm'd; but if in steel,
All cap-à-pie from head to heel,
330 What 'gainst their numbers could I do?
'T was near his castle, far away
From city or from succor near,
And almost on the break of day;
I did not think to see another,
335 My moments seem'd reduced to few;
And with one prayer to Mary Mother,
And, it may be, a saint or two,
As I resign'd me to my fate,
They led me to the castle gate:
340 Theresa's doom I never knew,
Our lot was henceforth separate.
An angry man, ye may opine,
Was he, the proud Count Palatine;
And he had reason good to be,
345 But he was most enraged lest such
An accident should chance to touch
Upon his future pedigree;
Nor less amazed, that such a blot
His noble 'scutcheon should have got,
350 While he was highest of his line;
Because unto himself he seem'd
The first of men, nor less he deem'd
In others' eyes, and most in mine.
'Sdeath![1] with a *page*—perchance a king
355 Had reconciled him to the thing;
But with a stripling of a page—
I felt, but cannot paint his rage.

" 'Bring forth the horse!'—the horse was
  brought;
In truth, he was a noble steed,
360 A Tartar of the Ukraine breed,
Who look'd as though the speed of thought
Were in his limbs; but he was wild,
Wild as the wild deer, and untaught,
With spur and bridle undefiled—

[1] God's death.

365 'T was but a day he had been caught;
And snorting, with erected mane,
And struggling fiercely, but in vain,
In the full foam of wrath and dread
To me the desert-born was led:
370 They bound me on, that menial throng;
Upon his back with many a thong;
Then loosed him with a sudden lash—
Away!—away!—and on we dash!
Torrents less rapid and less rash.

375 "Away!—away! My breath was gone,
I saw not where he hurried on:
'T was scarcely yet the break of day,
And on he foam'd—away!—away!
The last of human sounds which rose,
380 As I was darted from my foes,
Was the wild shout of savage laughter,
Which on the wind came roaring after
A moment from that rabble rout:
With sudden wrath I wrench'd my head,
385 And snapp'd the cord, which to the mane
Had bound my neck in lieu of rein,
And, writhing half my form about,
Howl'd back my curse; but 'midst the
  tread,
The thunder of my courser's speed,
390 Perchance they did not hear nor heed:
It vexes me—for I would fain
Have paid their insult back again.
I paid it well in after days:
There is not of that castle gate,
395 Its drawbridge and portcullis' weight,
Stone, bar, moat, bridge, or barrier left;
Nor of its fields a blade of grass,
Save what grows on a ridge of wall,
Where stood the hearth-stone of the
  hall;
400 And many a time ye there might pass,
Nor dream that e'er that fortress was.
I saw its turrets in a blaze,
Their crackling battlements all cleft,
And the hot lead pour down like rain
405 From off the scorch'd and blackening roof,
Whose thickness was not vengeance-proof.
They little thought that day of pain,
When launch'd, as on the lightning's flash,
They bade me to destruction dash,
410 That one day I should come again,
With twice five thousand horse, to thank
The Count for his uncourteous ride.
They play'd me then a bitter prank,
When, with the wild horse for my guide,
415 They bound me to his foaming flank:
At length I play'd them one as frank—
For time at last sets all things even—
And if we do but watch the hour,
There never yet was human power
420 Which could evade, if unforgiven,

The patient search and vigil long
Of him who treasures up a wrong.

"Away, away, my steed and I,
 Upon the pinions of the wind,
425 All human dwellings left behind;
We sped like meteors through the sky,
When with its crackling sound the night
Is chequer'd with the Northern light.
Town—village—none were on our track,
430 But a wild plain of far extent,
And bounded by a forest black;
 And, save the scarce seen battlement
On distant heights of some strong hold,
Against the Tartars built of old,
435 No trace of man. The year before
A Turkish army had march'd o'er;
And where the Spahi's[1] hoof hath trod,
The verdure flies the bloody sod:
The sky was dull, and dim, and gray,
440 And a low breeze crept moaning by—
I could have answer'd with a sigh—
But fast we fled, away, away—
And I could neither sigh nor pray;
And my cold sweat-drops fell like rain
445 Upon the courser's bristling mane;
But, snorting still with rage and fear,
He flew upon his far career:
At times I almost thought, indeed,
He must have slacken'd in his speed;
450 But no—my bound and slender frame
 Was nothing to his angry might,
And merely like a spur became:
Each motion which I made to free
My swoln limbs from their agony
455 Increased his fury and affright:
I tried my voice,—'t was faint and low—
But yet he swerved as from a blow;
And, starting to each accent, sprang
As from a sudden trumpet's clang:
460 Meantime my cords were wet with gore,
Which, oozing through my limbs, ran o'er;
And in my tongue the thirst became
A something fierier far than flame.

"We near'd the wild wood—'t was so wide,
465 I saw no bounds on either side;
'T was studded with old sturdy trees,
That bent not to the roughest breeze
Which howls down from Siberia's waste,
And strips the forest in its haste,—
470 But these were few and far between,
Set thick with shrubs more young and
  green,
Luxuriant with their annual leaves,
Ere strown by those autumnal eves
That nip the forest's foliage dead,
475 Discolor'd with a lifeless red,

[1] A Turkish cavalryman.

Which stands thereon like stiffen'd gore
Upon the slain when battle's o'er,
And some long winter's night hath shed
Its frost o'er every tombless head,
480 So cold and stark the raven's beak
May peck unpierced each frozen cheek:
'T was a wild waste of underwood,
And here and there a chestnut stood,
The strong oak, and the hardy pine;
485 But far apart—and well it were,
Or else a different lot were mine—
 The boughs gave way, and did not tear
My limbs; and I found strength to bear
My wounds, already scarr'd with cold;
490 My bonds forbade to loose my hold.
We rustled through the leaves like wind,
Left shrubs, and trees, and wolves behind;
By night I heard them on the track,
Their troop came hard upon our back,
495 With their long gallop, which can tire
The hound's deep hate, and hunter's fire:
Where'er we flew they follow'd on,
Nor left us with the morning sun;
Behind I saw them, scarce a rood,
500 At day-break winding through the wood,
And through the night had heard their feet
Their stealing, rustling step repeat.
Oh! how I wish'd for spear or sword,
At least to die amidst the horde,
505 And perish—if it must be so—
At bay, destroying many a foe!
When first my courser's race begun,
I wish'd the goal already won;
But now I doubted strength and speed:
510 Vain doubt! his swift and savage breed
Had nerved him like the mountain-roe;
Nor faster falls the blinding snow
Which whelms the peasant near the door
Whose threshold he shall cross no more,
515 Bewilder'd with the dazzling blast,
Than through the forest-paths he pass'd—
Untired, untamed, and worse than wild;
All furious as a favor'd child
Balk'd of its wish; or fiercer still—
520 A woman piqued—who has her will!

"The wood was past; 't was more than
  noon,
But chill the air, although in June;
Or it might be my veins ran cold—
Prolong'd endurance tames the bold;
525 And I was then not what I seem,
But headlong as a wintry stream,
And wore my feelings out before
I well could count their causes o'er:
And what with fury, fear, and wrath,
530 The tortures which beset my path,
Cold, hunger, sorrow, shame, distress,
Thus bound in nature's nakedness

(Sprung from a race whose rising blood,
When stirr'd beyond its calmer mood,
535 And trodden hard upon, is like
The rattle-snake's, in act to strike),
What marvel if this worn-out trunk
Beneath its woes a moment sunk?
The earth gave way, the skies roll'd round,
540 I seem'd to sink upon the ground;
But err'd, for I was fastly bound.
My heart turn'd sick, my brain grew sore,
And throbb'd awhile, then beat no more:
The skies spun like a mighty wheel;
545 I saw the trees like drunkards reel,
And a slight flash sprang o'er my eyes,
Which saw no farther: he who dies
Can die no more than then I died,
O'ertortured by that ghastly ride.
550 I felt the blackness come and go,
   And strove to wake; but could not make
My senses climb up from below:
I felt as on a plank at sea,
When all the waves that dash o'er thee,
555 At the same time upheave and whelm,
And hurl thee towards a desert realm.
My undulating life was as
The fancied lights that flitting pass
Our shut eyes in deep midnight, when
560 Fever begins upon the brain;
But soon it pass'd, with little pain,
   But a confusion worse than such:
   I own that I should deem it much,
Dying, to feel the same again;
565 And yet I do suppose we must
Feel far more ere we turn to dust:
No matter; I have bared my brow
Full in Death's face—before—and now.

"My thoughts came back; where was I?
   Cold,
570   And numb, and giddy: pulse by pulse
Life reassumed its lingering hold,
And throb by throb,—till grown a pang
   Which for a moment would convulse,
My blood reflow'd, though thick and
   chill;
575 My ear with uncouth noises rang,
   My heart began once more to thrill;
My sight return'd, though dim; alas!
And thicken'd, as it were, with glass.
Methought the dash of waves was nigh;
580 There was a gleam too of the sky,
Studded with stars;—it is no dream;
The wild horse swims the wilder stream!
The bright broad river's gushing tide
Sweeps, winding onward, far and wide,
585 And we are half-way, struggling o'er
To yon unknown and silent shore.
The waters broke my hollow trance,
And with a temporary strength

My stiffen'd limbs were rebaptized.
590 My courser's broad breast proudly braves,
And dashes off the ascending waves,
And onward we advance!
We reach the slippery shore at length,
   A haven I but little prized,
595 For all behind was dark and drear,
And all before was night and fear.
How many hours of night or day
In those suspended pangs I lay,
I could not tell; I scarcely knew
600 If this were human breath I drew.

"With glossy skin, and dripping mane,
   And reeling limbs, and reeking flank,
The wild steed's sinewy nerves still strain
   Up the repelling bank.
605 We gain the top: a boundless plain
Spreads through the shadow of the night,
   And onward, onward, onward, seems,
   Like precipices in our dreams,
To stretch beyond the sight;
610 And here and there a speck of white,
Or scatter'd spot of dusky green,
In masses broke into the light,
As rose the moon upon my right:
But nought distinctly seen
615 In the dim waste would indicate
The omen of a cottage gate;
No twinkling taper from afar
Stood like a hospitable star;
Not even an ignis-fatuus rose
620 To make him merry with my woes:
   That very cheat had cheer'd me then!
Although detected, welcome still,
Reminding me, through every ill,
   Of the abodes of men.

625 "Onward we went—but slack and slow;
   His savage force at length o'erspent,
The drooping courser, faint and low,
   All feebly foaming went:
A sickly infant had had power
630 To guide him forward in that hour;
But, useless all to me,
His new-born tameness nought avail'd—
My limbs were bound; my force had fail'd,
Perchance, had they been free.
635 With feeble effort still I tried
To rend the bonds so starkly tied,
   But still it was in vain;
My limbs were only wrung the more,
And soon the idle strife gave o'er,
640   Which but prolong'd their pain.
The dizzy race seem'd almost done,
Although no goal was nearly won:
Some streaks announced the coming sun—
   How slow, alas! he came!
645 Methought that mist of dawning gray

Would never dapple into day;
How heavily it roll'd away—
　Before the eastern flame
Rose crimson, and deposed the stars,
650 And call'd the radiance from their cars,
And fill'd the earth, from his deep throne,
With lonely lustre, all his own.

"Up rose the sun; the mists were curl'd
Back from the solitary world
655 Which lay around, behind, before.
What booted it to traverse o'er
Plain, forest, river? Man nor brute,
Nor dint of hoof, nor print of foot,
Lay in the wild luxuriant soil;
660 No sign of travel, none of toil;
The very air was mute;
And not an insect's shrill small horn,
Nor matin bird's[1] new voice was borne
From herb nor thicket. Many a werst,[2]
665 Panting as if his heart would burst,
The weary brute still stagger'd on;
And still we were—or seem'd—alone.
At length, while reeling on our way,
Methought I heard a courser neigh,
670 From out yon tuft of blackening firs.
Is it the wind those branches stirs?
No, no! from out the forest prance
　A trampling troop; I see them come!
In one vast squadron they advance!
675 　I strove to cry—my lips were dumb!
The steeds rush on in plunging pride;
But where are they the reins to guide?
A thousand horse—and none to ride!
With flowing tail, and flying mane,
680 Wide nostrils never stretch'd by pain,
Mouths bloodless to the bit or rein,
And feet that iron never shod,
And flanks unscarr'd by spur or rod,
A thousand horse, the wild, the free,
685 Like waves that follow o'er the sea,
　Came thickly thundering on,
As if our faint approach to meet.
The sight re-nerved my courser's feet,
A moment staggering, feebly fleet,
690 A moment, with a faint low neigh,
　He answer'd, and then fell;
With gasps and glazing eyes he lay,
And reeking limbs immovable—
His first and last career is done!
695 On came the troop—they saw him stoop,
They saw me strangely bound along
His back with many a bloody thong.
They stop—they start—they snuff the air,
Gallop a moment here and there,
700 Approach, retire, wheel round and round,
Then plunging back with sudden bound,

[1] lark's
[2] A Russian measure equal to 3,500 feet.

Headed by one black mighty steed,
Who seem'd the patriarch of his breed,
　Without a single speck or hair
705 Of white upon his shaggy hide;
They snort—they foam—neigh—swerve
　aside,
And backward to the forest fly,
By instinct, from a human eye.
They left me there to my despair,
710 Link'd to the dead and stiffening wretch,
Whose lifeless limbs beneath me stretch,
Relieved from that unwonted weight,
From whence I could not extricate
Nor him nor me—and there we lay,
715 　The dying on the dead!
I little deem'd another day
　Would see my houseless, helpless head.

"And there from morn to twilight bound,
I felt the heavy hours toil round,
720 With just enough of life to see
My last of suns go down on me,
In hopeless certainty of mind,
That makes us feel at length resign'd
To that which our foreboding years
725 Present the worst and last of fears:
Inevitable—even a boon,
Nor more unkind for coming soon,
Yet shunn'd and dreaded with such care,
As if it only were a snare
730 　That Prudence might escape:
At times both wish'd for and implored,
At times sought with self-pointed sword,
Yet still a dark and hideous close
To even intolerable woes,
735 　And welcome in no shape.
And, strange to say, the sons of pleasure,
They who have revell'd beyond measure
In beauty, wassail, wine, and treasure,
Die calm, or calmer, oft than he
740 Whose heritage was misery.
For he who hath in turn run through
All that was beautiful and new,
　Hath nought to hope, and nought to
　　leave;
And, save the future (which is view'd
745 Not quite as men are base or good,
But as their nerves may be endued),
　With nought perhaps to grieve:
The wretch still hopes his woes must end,
And Death, whom he should deem his
　　friend,
750 Appears, to his distemper'd eyes,
Arrived to rob him of his prize,
The tree of his new Paradise.
Tomorrow would have given him all,
Repaid his pangs, repair'd his fall;
755 Tomorrow would have been the first
Of days no more deplored or curst,

But bright, and long, and beckoning years,
Seen dazzling through the mist of tears,
Guerdon of many a painful hour;
760 Tomorrow would have given him power
To rule, to shine, to smite, to save—
And must it dawn upon his grave?

"The sun was sinking—still I lay
Chain'd to the chill and stiffening steed;
765 I thought to mingle there our clay,
And my dim eyes of death had need;
No hope arose of being freed.
I cast my last looks up the sky,
And there between me and the sun
770 I saw the expecting raven fly,
Who scarce would wait till both should die,
Ere his repast begun;
He flew, and perch'd, then flew once more,
And each time nearer than before;
775 I saw his wing through twilight flit,
And once so near me he alit
I could have smote, but lack'd the strength;
But the slight motion of my hand,
And feeble scratching of the sand,
780 The exerted throat's faint struggling noise,
Which scarcely could be called a voice,
Together scared him off at length.—
I know no more—my latest dream
Is something of a lovely star
785 Which fix'd my dull eyes from afar,
And went and came with wandering beam,
And of the cold, dull, swimming, dense
Sensation of recurring sense,
And then subsiding back to death,
790 And then again a little breath,
A little thrill, a short suspense,
An icy sickness curdling o'er
My heart, and sparks that cross'd my brain—
A gasp, a throb, a start of pain,
795 A sigh, and nothing more.

"I woke—where was I?—Do I see
A human face look down on me?
And doth a roof above me close?
Do these limbs on a couch repose?
800 Is this a chamber where I lie?
And is it mortal yon bright eye,
That watches me with gentle glance?
I closed my own again once more,
As doubtful that my former trance
805 Could not as yet be o'er.
A slender girl, long-hair'd, and tall,
Sate watching by the cottage wall;
The sparkle of her eye I caught,

Even with my first return of thought;
810 For ever and anon she threw
A prying, pitying glance on me
With her black eyes so wild and free:
I gazed, and gazed, until I knew
No vision it could be,—
815 But that I lived, and was released
From adding to the vulture's feast:
And when the Cossack maid beheld
My heavy eyes at length unseal'd,
She smiled—and I essay'd to speak,
820 But fail'd—and she approach'd, and made
With lip and finger signs that said,
I must not strive as yet to break
The silence, till my strength should be
Enough to leave my accents free;
825 And then her hand on mine she laid;
And smooth'd the pillow for my head,
And stole along on tiptoe tread,
And gently oped the door, and spake
In whispers—ne'er was voice so sweet!
830 Even music follow'd her light feet:
But those she call'd were not awake,
And she went forth; but, ere she pass'd,
Another look on me she cast,
Another sign she made, to say,
835 That I had nought to fear, that all
Were near, at my command or call,
And she would not delay
Her due return:—while she was gone,
Methought I felt too much alone.

840 "She came with mother and with sire—
What need of more?—I will not tire
With long recital of the rest,
Since I became the Cossack's guest.
They found me senseless on the plain,
845 They bore me to the nearest hut,
They brought me into life again—
Me—one day o'er their realm to reign!
Thus the vain fool who strove to glut
His rage, refining on my pain,
850 Sent me forth to the wilderness,
Bound, naked, bleeding, and alone,
To pass the desert to a throne,—
What mortal his own doom may guess?
Let none despond, let none despair!
855 Tomorrow the Borysthenes
May see our coursers graze at ease
Upon his Turkish bank, and never
Had I such welcome for a river
As I shall yield when safely there.
860 Comrades, good night!"—The Hetman threw
His length beneath the oak-tree shade,
With leafy couch already made,
A bed nor comfortless nor new
To him, who took his rest whene'er

865 The hour arrived, no matter where:
His eyes the hastening slumbers steep.
And if ye marvel Charles forgot
To thank his tale, *he* wonder'd not,—
The king had been an hour asleep.

From DON JUAN
1818-23   1819-24
DEDICATION
1818   1833

1 Bob Southey! You're a poet — Poet-
laureate,
And representative of all the race;
Although 'tis true that you turn'd out a
Tory at
Last, yours has lately been a common
case;[1]
And now, my Epic Renegade! what are
ye at?
With all the Lakers,[2] in and out of
place?
A nest of tuneful persons, to my eye
Like "four and twenty Blackbirds in a
pye;

2 "Which pye being open'd they began to
sing"
(This old song and new simile holds
good),
"A dainty dish to set before the King,"
Or Regent,[3] who admires such kind of
food;—
And Coleridge, too, has lately taken wing,
But like a hawk encumbered with his
hood,—
Explaining metaphysics to the nation—
I wish he would explain his Explanation.[4]

3 You, Bob! are rather insolent, you know,
At being disappointed in your wish
To supersede all warblers here below,
And be the only Blackbird in the dish;
And then you overstrain yourself, or so,
And tumble downward like the flying
fish
Gasping on deck, because you soar too
high, Bob,
And fall, for lack of moisture, quite a-dry,
Bob!

[1] Southey, like Wordsworth and Coleridge, was
at one time an ardent Republican, but the
excesses and the failures of the French Revolution led him finally to become a Tory.
[2] Wordsworth, Coleridge, and others, so called
because of their residence in the Lake District.
[3] The Prince of Wales, afterwards George IV,
who was appointed Regent when his father,
George III, became insane in 1811. Southey
was made poet laureate in 1813.
[4] A reference to Coleridge's *Biographia Literaria*, which appeared in 1817.

4 And Wordsworth, in a rather long *Excur-
sion*
(I think the quarto holds five hundred
pages),
Has given a sample from the vasty version
Of his new system to perplex the sages;
'Tis poetry—at least by his assertion,
And may appear so when the dog-star
rages—
And he who understands it would be
able
To add a story to the Tower of Babel.

5 You—Gentlemen! by dint of long seclu-
sion
From better company, have kept your
own
At Keswick,[1] and, through still continued
fusion
Of one another's minds, at last have
grown
To deem as a most logical conclusion,
That Poesy has wreaths for you alone:
There is a narrowness in such a notion,
Which makes me wish you'd change your
lakes for ocean.

6 I would not imitate the petty thought,
Nor coin my self-love to so base a
vice,
For all the glory your conversion brought,
Since gold alone should not have been
its price.
You have your salary: was 't for that
you wrought?
And Wordsworth has his place in the
Excise.[2]
You're shabby fellows—true—but poets
still,
And duly seated on the immortal hill.

7 Your bays[3] may hide the baldness of your
brows—
Perhaps some virtuous blushes;—let
them go—
To you I envy neither fruit nor boughs—
And for the fame you would engross
below,
The field is universal, and allows
Scope to all such as feel the inherent
glow:
Scott, Rogers, Campbell, Moore, and
Crabbe will try
'Gainst you the question with posterity.

[1] Southey joined Coleridge at Keswick, in the
Lake District, in 1803.
[2] Wordsworth was appointed Distributor of
Stamps for Westmoreland in 1813, but he
never had any connection with the excise.
[3] Wreaths of honor made from leaves of the
bay-tree, a kind of laurel.

8 For me, who, wandering with pedestrian
    Muses,
    Contend not with you on the winged
      steed,
I wish your fate may yield ye, when she
    chooses,
    The fame you envy, and the skill you
      need;
And recollect a poet nothing loses
    In giving to his brethren their full meed
Of merit, the complaint of present days
Is not the certain path to future praise.

9 He that reserves his laurels for posterity
    (Who does not often claim the bright
      reversion)
Has generally no great crop to spare it, he
    Being only injured by his own asser-
      tion;
And although here and there some glo-
      rious rarity
    Arise like Titan from the sea's immer-
      sion,
The major part of such appellants go
To—God knows where—for no one else
    can know.

10 If, fallen in evil days on evil tongues,[1]
    Milton appealed to the Avenger, Time,
If Time, the Avenger, execrates his
      wrongs,
    And makes the word "Miltonic" mean
      "*sublime*,"
He deign'd not to belie his soul in songs,
    Nor turn his very talent to a crime;
He did not loathe the Sire to laud the Son,
But closed the tyrant-hater he begun.[2]

11 Think'st thou, could he—the blind Old
      Man—arise,
    Like Samuel from the grave,[3] to freeze
      once more
The blood of monarchs with his prophe-
      cies,
    Or be alive again—again all hoar
With time and trials, and those helpless
      eyes,
    And heartless daughters[4]—worn—and
      pale—and poor;
Would *he* adore a sultan? *he* obey
The intellectual eunuch Castlereagh?

12 Cold-blooded, smooth-faced, placid mis-
      creant!
    Dabbling its sleek young hands in
      Erin's gore,

---

[1] See *Paradise Lost*, 7, 26.
[2] Byron here contrasts Milton and Southey.
[3] See *1 Samuel*, 28 :7 ff.
[4] A reference to the shameful treatment which
    Milton is said to have received from his eld-
    est daughters.

And thus for wider carnage taught to
      pant,
    Transferr'd to gorge upon a sister
      shore,
The vulgarest tool that Tyranny could
      want,
    With just enough of talent, and no
      more,
To lengthen fetters by another fix'd,
And offer poison long already mix'd.

13 An orator of such set trash of phrase
    Ineffably—legitimately vile,
That even its grossest flatterers dare not
      praise,
    Nor foes—all nations—condescend to
      smile;
Not even a sprightly blunder's spark can
      blaze
    From that Ixion grindstone's ceaseless
      toil,
That turns and turns to give the world a
      notion
Of endless torments and perpetual motion.

14 A bungler even in its disgusting trade,
    And botching, patching, leaving still
      behind
Something of which its masters are afraid,
    States to be curb'd, and thoughts to be
      confined,
Conspiracy or Congress to be made—
    Cobbling at manacles for all mankind—
A tinkering slave-maker, who mends old
      chains,
With God's and man's abhorrence for its
      gains.

15 If we may judge of matter by the mind,
    Emasculated to the marrow *It*
Hath but two objects, how to serve, and
      bind,
    Deeming the chain it wears even men
      may fit,
Eutropius of its many masters,—blind
    To worth as freedom, wisdom as to wit,
Fearless—because *no* feeling dwells in ice,
Its very courage stagnates to a vice.

16 Where shall I turn me not to *view* its
      bonds,
    For I will never *feel* them?—Italy!
Thy late reviving Roman soul desponds
    Beneath the lie this State-thing breathed
      o'er thee—
Thy clanking chain, and Erin's yet green
      wounds,
    Have voices—tongues to cry aloud for
      me.

Europe has slaves, allies, kings, armies still,
And Southey lives to sing them very ill.

17 Meantime, Sir Laureate, I proceed to dedicate,
In honest simple verse, this song to you.
And, if in flattering strains I do not predicate,
'Tis that I still retain my "buff and blue;"[1]
My politics as yet are all to educate:
Apostasy's so fashionable, too,
To keep *one* creed's a task grown quite Herculean:
Is it not so, my Tory, Ultra-Julian?[2]

From CANTO I
1818   1819

1 I want a hero: an uncommon want,
When every year and month sends forth a new one,
Till, after cloying the gazettes with cant,
The age discovers he is not the true one:
Of such as these I should not care to vaunt,
I'll therefore take our ancient friend Don Juan—
We all have seen him, in the pantomime,[3]
Sent to the devil somewhat ere his time.

. . . .

5 Brave men were living before Agamemnon
And since, exceeding valorous and sage,
A good deal like him too, though quite the same none;
But then they shone not on the poet's page,
And so have been forgotten:—I condemn none,
But can't find any in the present age
Fit for my poem (that is, for my new one);
So, as I said, I'll take my friend Don Juan.

6 Most epic poets plunge "in medias res"[4]
(Horace makes this the heroic turnpike road),

And then your hero tells, whene'er you please,
What went before—by way of episode,
While seated after dinner at his ease,
Beside his mistress in some soft abode,
Palace, or garden, paradise or cavern,
Which serves the happy couple for a tavern.

7 That is the usual method, but not mine—
My way is to begin with the beginning;
The regularity of my design
Forbids all wandering as the worst of sinning,
And therefore I shall open with a line
(Although it cost me half an hour in spinning)
Narrating somewhat of Don Juan's father,
And also of his mother, if you'd rather.

8 In Seville was he born, a pleasant city,
Famous for oranges and women—he
Who has not seen it will be much to pity,
So says the proverb—and I quite agree;
Of all the Spanish towns is none more pretty,
Cadiz, perhaps—but that you soon may see;
Don Juan's parents lived beside the river,
A noble stream, and call'd the Guadalquivir.

9 His father's name was Jóse—*Don*, of course,—
A true Hidalgo,[1] free from every stain
Of Moor or Hebrew blood, he traced his source
Through the most Gothic gentlemen of Spain;[2]
A better cavalier ne'er mounted horse,
Or, being mounted, e'er got down again,
Than Jóse, who begot our hero, who
Begot—but that's to come—Well, to renew:

10 His mother was a learned lady,[3] famed
For every branch of every science known—
In every Christian language ever named,
With virtues equall'd by her wit alone:
She made the cleverest people quite ashamed,

---

[1] The colors of the uniform adopted by members of the Whig Club; hence, the binding of *The Edinburgh Review*, the Whig organ.
[2] "I allude not to our friend Landor's hero, the traitor Count Julian, but to Gibbon's hero, vulgarly yclept 'The Apostate.'"—Byron.
[3] A short version of Shadwell's *Libertine*, acted under the title of *Don Juan; or, The Libertine Destroyed*. At the conclusion of the last Act, Don Juan is thrown into the flames by the Furies.
[4] into the middle of things (Horace, *Ars Poetica*, 148)

[1] A title denoting a Spanish nobleman of the lower class.
[2] That is, of the purest Spanish stock. The Goths established the Visigothic kingdom in Spain and southern France in the fifth century, and were the ancestors of the later Spanish nobility.
[3] Stanzas 10-29 are said to refer to Byron's wife.

And even the good with inward envy
     groan,
Finding themselves so very much exceeded
In their own way by all the things that
     she did.

11 Her memory was a mine: she knew by
     heart
    All Calderon and greater part of Lopé,
So that if any actor miss'd his part
    She could have served him for the
     prompter's copy;
For her Feinagle's were an useless art,
    And he himself obliged to shut up
     shop—he
Could never make a memory so fine as
That which adorn'd the brain of Donna
     Inez.

12 Her favorite science was the mathemat-
     ical,
    Her noblest virtue was her magna-
     nimity;
Her wit (she sometimes tried at wit) was
     Attic[1] all,
    Her serious saying darken'd to sub-
     limity;
In short, in all things she was fairly what
     I call
    A prodigy—her morning dress was
     dimity,
    Her evening silk, or, in the summer,
     muslin,
And other stuffs, with which I won't stay
     puzzling.

13 She knew the Latin—that is, "the Lord's
     prayer,"
    And Greek—the alphabet—I'm nearly
     sure;
She read some French romances here and
     there,
    Although her mode of speaking was not
     pure;
For native Spanish she had no great care,
    At least her conversation was obscure;
Her thoughts were theorems, her words a
     problem.
As if she deem'd that mystery would
     ennoble 'em.

14 She liked the English and the Hebrew
     tongue,
    And said there was analogy between
     'em;
She proved it somehow out of sacred song,
    But I must leave the proofs to those
     who've seen 'em,

[1] delicate; poignant

But this I heard her say, and can't be
     wrong,
    And all may think which way their
     judgments lean 'em,
" 'Tis strange—the Hebrew noun which
     means 'I am,'
The English always use to govern d—n.''

15 Some women use their tongues—she *look'd*
     a lecture,
    Each eye a sermon, and her brow a
     homily,
An all-in-all sufficient self-director,
    Like the lamented late Sir Samuel
     Romilly,
The Law's expounder, and the State's
     corrector,
    Whose suicide was almost an anomaly—
One sad example more, that "All is
     vanity,"—[1]
(The jury brought their verdict in "In-
     sanity.")

16 In short, she was a walking calculation,
    Miss Edgeworth's novels stepping from
     their covers,
Or Mrs. Trimmer's books on education,
    Or "Cœlebs' Wife" set out in quest of
     lovers,
Morality's prim personification,
    In which not Envy's self a flaw dis-
     covers;
To others' share let "female errors fall,"[2]
For she had not even one—the worst of
     all.

17 Oh! she was perfect past all parallel—
    Of any modern female saint's compari-
     son;
So far above the cunning powers of hell,
    Her guardian angel had given up his
     garrison;
Even her minutest motions went as well
    As those of the best time-piece made by
     Harrison:
In virtues nothing earthly could surpass
     her,
Save thine "incomparable oil," Macas-
     sar![3]

18 Perfect she was, but as perfection is
    Insipid in this naughty world of ours,
Where our first parents never learn'd to
     kiss

[1] *Ecclesiastes*, 1:2.
[2] Pope, *The Rape of the Lock*, 2, 17.
[3] A description of the virtues of the "incomparable oil of Macassar" was included in Alexander Rowland's *An Historical, Philosophical,
and Practical Essay on the Human Hair*
(1816).

Till they were exiled from their earlier
    bowers,
Where all was peace, and innocence, and
    bliss
(I wonder how they got through the
    twelve hours),
Don Jóse, like a lineal son of Eve,
Went plucking various fruit without her
    leave.

19 He was a mortal of the careless kind,
    With no great love for learning, or the
      learn'd,
Who chose to go where'er he had a mind,
And never dream'd his lady was con-
    cern'd;
The world, as usual, wickedly inclined
    To see a kingdom or a house o'er-
      turn'd,
Whisper'd he had a mistress, some said
    two,
But for domestic quarrels *one* will do.

20 Now Donna Inez had, with all her merit,
    A great opinion of her own good quali-
      ties;
Neglect, indeed, requires a saint to bear it,
    And such, indeed, she was in her moral-
      ities;
But then she had a devil of a spirit,
    And sometimes mix'd up fancies with
      realities,
And let few opportunities escape
Of getting her liege lord into a scrape.

21 This was an easy matter with a man
    Oft in the wrong, and never on his
      guard;
And even the wisest, do the best they can,
    Have moments, hours, and days, so un-
      prepared,
That you might "brain them with their
    lady's fan;"[1]
    And sometimes ladies hit exceeding
      hard,
And fans turn into falchions in fair
    hands,
And why and wherefore no one under-
    stands.

22 'Tis pity learned virgins ever wed
    With persons of no sort of education,
Or gentlemen, who, though well born and
    bred,
    Grow tired of scientific conversation;
I don't choose to say much upon this
    head,
I'm a plain man, and in a single station,

[1] 1 *Henry IV*, II, 3, 19.

But—Oh! ye lords of ladies intellectual,
Inform us truly, have they not hen-peck'd
    you all?

23 Don Jóse and his lady quarrell'd—*why,*
    Not any of the many could divine,
Though several thousand people chose to
    try,
    'Twas surely no concern of theirs nor
      mine;
I loathe that low vice—curiosity;
    But if there's anything in which I shine,
'Tis in arranging all my friends' affairs,
Not having, of my own, domestic cares.

24 And so I interfered, and with the best
    Intentions, but their treatment was not
      kind;
I think the foolish people were possess'd,
    For neither of them could I ever find,
Although their porter afterwards con-
    fess'd—
But that's no matter, and the worst's
    behind,
For little Juan o'er me threw, down stairs,
A pail of housemaid's water unawares.

25 A little curly-headed, good-for-nothing,
    And mischief-making monkey from his
      birth;
His parents ne'er agreed except in doting
    Upon the most unquiet imp on earth;
Instead of quarrelling, had they been but
    both in
    Their senses, they'd have sent young
      master forth
To school, or had him soundly whipp'd at
    home,
To teach him manners for the time to
    come.

26 Don Jóse and the Donna Inez led
    For some time an unhappy sort of life,
Wishing each other, not divorced, but
    dead;
    They lived respectably as man and wife,
Their conduct was exceedingly well-bred,
    And gave no outward signs of inward
      strife,
Until at length the smother'd fire broke
    out,
And put the business past all kind of
    doubt.

27 For Inez call'd some druggists and physi-
    cians,
    And tried to prove her loving lord was
      mad,[1]

[1] 1 Lady Byron consulted physicians in regard to her husband's supposed insanity.

But as he had some lucid intermissions,
  She next decided he was only *bad;*
Yet when they ask'd her for her deposi-
    tions,
No sort of explanation could be had,
  Save that her duty both to man and God
Required this conduct—which seem'd very
    odd.

28 She kept a journal, where his faults were
    noted,
  And open'd certain trunks of books and
    letters,
All which might, if occasion served, be
    quoted;
  And then she had all Seville for abet-
    tors,
Besides her good old grandmother (who
    doted);
  The hearers of her case became repeat-
    ers,
Then advocates, inquisitors, and judges,
  Some for amusement, others for old
    grudges.

29 And then this best and meekest woman
    bore
  With such serenity her husband's woes,
Just as the Spartan ladies did of yore,
  Who saw their spouses kill'd, and nobly
    chose
Never to say a word about them more—
  Calmly she heard each calumny that
    rose,
And saw *his* agonies with such sublimity,
That all the world exclaim'd, ''What
    magnanimity!''

30 No doubt this patience, when the world is
    damning us,
  Is philosophic in our former friends;
'Tis also pleasant to be deem'd magnani-
    mous,
  The more so in obtaining our own ends;
And what the lawyers call a *''malus
    animus''* [1]
  Conduct like this by no means compre-
    hends:
Revenge in person's certainly no virtue,
But then 'tis not *my* fault, if *others* hurt
    you.

31 And if our quarrels should rip up old
    stories,
  And help them with a lie or two addi-
    tional,
I'm not to blame, as you well know—no
    more is

[1] malice aforethought

Any one else—they were become tradi-
    tional;
Besides, their resurrection aids our glories
  By contrast, which is what we just were
    wishing all:
And science profits by this resurrection—
  Dead scandals form good subjects for dis-
    section.

32 Their friends had tried at reconciliation,
  Then their relations, who made matters
    worse,
('Twere hard to tell upon a like occasion
  To whom it may be best to have re-
    course—
I can't say much for friend or yet rela-
    tion):
  The lawyers did their utmost for di-
    vorce,
But scarce a fee was paid on either side
Before, unluckily, Don Jóse died.

33 He died: and most unluckily, because
  According to all hints I could collect
From counsel learned in those kinds of
    laws
  (Although their talk's obscure and cir-
    cumspect),
His death contrived to spoil a charming
    cause;
  A thousand pities also with respect
To public feeling, which on this occasion
Was manifested in a great sensation.

34 But ah! he died; and buried with him lay
  The public feeling and the lawyers'
    fees:
His house was sold, his servants sent away,
  A Jew took one of his two mistresses,
A priest the other—at least so they say:
  I ask'd the doctors after his disease—
He died of the slow fever called the
    tertian,
And left his widow to her own aversion.

35 Yet Jóse was an honorable man,
  That I must say, who knew him very
    well;
Therefore his frailties I'll no further
    scan,
  Indeed there were not many more to
    tell:
And if his passions now and then out-
    ran
  Discretion, and were not so peaceable
As Numa's (who was also named Pom-
    pilius),
He had been ill brought up, and was born
    bilious.

36 Whate'er might be his worthlessness or
worth,
Poor fellow! he had many things to
wound him,
Let's own—since it can do no good on
earth—
It was a trying moment that which
found him
Standing alone beside his desolate hearth,
Where all his household gods lay shiver'd round him:
No choice was left his feelings or his
pride,
Save death or Doctors' Commons[1]—so he
died.

37 Dying intestate, Juan was sole heir
To a chancery suit, and messuages[2] and
lands,
Which, with a long minority and care,
Promised to turn out well in proper
hands:
Inez became sole guardian, which was fair,
And answer'd but to nature's just demands;
An only son left with an only mother
Is brought up much more wisely than
another.

38 Sagest of women, even of widows, she
Resolved that Juan should be quite a
paragon,
And worthy of the noblest pedigree:
(His sire was of Castile, his dam from
Aragon).
Then for accomplishments of chivalry,
In case our lord the king should go to
war again,
He learn'd the arts of riding, fencing,
gunnery,
And how to scale a fortress—or a nunnery.

39 But that which Donna Inez most desired,
And saw into herself each day before all
The learned tutors whom for him she
hired,
Was, that his breeding should be strictly
moral:
Much into all his studies she inquired,
And so they were submitted first to her,
all,
Arts, sciences, no branch was made a mystery
To Juan's eyes, excepting natural history.

40 The languages, especially the dead,
The sciences, and most of all the abstruse,
The arts, at least all such as could be said
To be the most remote from common
use,
In all these he was much and deeply read:
But not a page of anything that's loose,
Or hints continuation of the species,
Was ever suffer'd, lest he should grow
vicious.

41 His classic studies made a little puzzle,
Because of filthy loves of gods and goddesses,
Who in the earlier ages raised a bustle,
But never put on pantaloons or bodices;
His reverend tutors had at times a tussle,
And for their Æneids, Iliads, and
Odysseys,
Were forced to make an odd sort of
apology,
For Donna Inez dreaded the Mythology.

42 Ovid's a rake, as half his verses show him,
Anacreon's morals are a still worse
sample,
Catullus scarcely has a decent poem,
I don't think Sappho's Ode a good
example,
Although Longinus tells us there is no
hymn
Where the sublime soars forth on wings
more ample;[1]
But Virgil's songs are pure, except that
horrid one
Beginning with "Formosum Pastor Corydon."[2]

43 Lucretius' irreligion is too strong
For early stomachs, to prove wholesome food;
I can't help thinking Juvenal was wrong,
Although no doubt his real intent was
good,
For speaking out so plainly in his song,
So much indeed as to be downright
rude;
And then what proper person can be partial
To all those nauseous epigrams of Martial?

44 Juan was taught from out the best edition,
Expurgated by learned men, who place,

[1] That is, divorce. The Doctor's Commons, originally a common dining hall of the Association of Doctors of Civil Law, in London, consisted of a number of buildings which were used by courts having jurisdiction over marriage licenses, divorces, etc.
[2] dwelling houses, with adjacent buildings and lands

[1] See his essay *On the Sublime*, 10. The ode referred to is entitled *To a Loved One*.
[2] Handsome Shepherd Corydon.—*Eclogues*, 2.

Judiciously, from out the schoolboy's
　　vision,
The grosser parts; but, fearful to deface
Too much their modest bard by this omis-
　　sion,
And pitying sore this mutilated case,
They only add them all in an appendix,
Which saves, in fact, the trouble of an
　　index;

45 For there we have them all "at one fell
　　swoop,"[1]
　　Instead of being scatter'd through the
　　　pages;
　　They stand forth marshall'd in a hand-
　　　some troop,
　　To meet the ingenuous youth of future
　　　ages,
　　Till some less rigid editor shall stoop
　　　To call them back into their separate
　　　　cages,
　　Instead of standing staring all together,
　　Like garden gods—and not so decent
　　　either.

46 The Missal too (it was the family Missal)
　　　Was ornamented in a sort of way
　　Which ancient mass-books often are, and
　　　this all
　　　Kinds of grotesques illumined; and how
　　　　they,
　　Who saw those figures on the margin kiss
　　　all,
　　　Could turn their optics to the text and
　　　　pray,
　　Is more than I know—But Don Juan's
　　　mother
　　Kept this herself, and gave her son an-
　　　other.

47 Sermons he read, and lectures he endured,
　　　And homilies, and lives of all the saints;
　　To Jerome and to Chrysostom inured,
　　　He did not take such studies for re-
　　　　straints;
　　But how faith is acquired, and then in-
　　　sured,
　　　So well not one of the aforesaid paints
　　As Saint Augustine in his fine *Confes-
　　　sions*,[2]
　　Which make the reader envy his trans-
　　　gressions.

48 This, too, was a seal'd book to little
　　　Juan—
　　I can't but say that his mamma was
　　　right,

1 *Macbeth*, IV, 3, 219.
2 See especially Bk. 1, ch. 9, and Bk. 2, ch. 2

If such an education was the true one.
　　She scarcely trusted him from out her
　　　sight;
　　Her maids were old, and if she took a
　　　new one,
　　　You might be sure she was a perfect
　　　　fright,
　　She did this during even her husband's
　　　life—
　　I recommend as much to every wife.

49 Young Juan wax'd in godliness and grace;
　　　At six a charming child, and at eleven
　　With all the promise of as fine a face
　　　As e'er to man's maturer growth was
　　　　given.
　　He studied steadily and grew apace,
　　　And seem'd, at least, in the right road
　　　　to heaven,
　　For half his days were pass'd at church,
　　　the other
　　Between his tutors, confessor, and mother.

50 At six, I said, he was a charming child,
　　　At twelve he was a fine, but quiet boy;
　　Although in infancy a little wild,
　　　They tamed him down amongst them:
　　　　to destroy
　　His natural spirit not in vain they toil'd,
　　　At least it seem'd so; and his mother's
　　　　joy
　　Was to declare how sage, and still, and
　　　steady,
　　Her young philosopher was grown al-
　　　ready.

51 I had my doubts, perhaps I have them still,
　　　But what I say is neither here nor there:
　　I knew his father well, and have some
　　　skill
　　　In character—but it would not be fair
　　From sire to son to augur good or ill:
　　　He and his wife were an ill sorted pair—
　　But scandal's my aversion—I protest
　　Against all evil speaking, even in jest.

52 For my part I say nothing—nothing—but
　　　This I will say—my reasons are my
　　　　own—
　　That if I had an only son to put
　　　To school (as God be praised that I
　　　　have none),
　　'Tis not with Donna Inez I would shut
　　　Him up to learn his catechism alone,
　　No—no—I'd send him out betimes to
　　　college,
　　For there it was I pick'd up my own
　　　knowledge.

53 For there one learns—'tis not for me to
boast,
Though I acquired—but I pass over
that,
As well as all the Greek I since have lost:
I say that there's the place — but
"*Verbum sat,*"[1]
I think I pick'd up too, as well as most,
Knowledge of matters—but no matter
what—
I never married—but, I think, I know
That sons should not be educated so.

. . . . . .

200 My poem's epic, and is meant to be
Divided in twelve books; each book con-
taining,
With love, and war, a heavy gale at sea,
A list of ships, and captains, and kings
reigning,
New characters; the episodes are three:
A panoramic view of hell's in training,
After the style of Virgil and of Homer,
So that my name of Epic's no misnomer.

201 All these things will be specified in time,
With strict regard to Aristotle's rules,[2]
The *Vade Mecum*[3] of the true sublime,
Which makes so many poets, and some
fools:
Prose poets like blank-verse, I'm fond of
rhyme,
Good workmen never quarrel with their
tools;
I've got new mythological machinery,
And very handsome supernatural scenery.

202 There's only one slight difference between
Me and my epic brethren gone before,
And here the advantage is my own, I ween
(Not that I have not several merits more,
But this will more peculiarly be seen);
They so embellish, that 'tis quite a bore
Their labyrinth of fables to thread through,
Whereas this story's actually true.

203 If any person doubt it, I appeal
To history, tradition, and to facts,
To newspapers, whose truth all know and
feel,
To plays in five, and operas in three
acts;
All these confirm my statement a good
deal,
But that which more completely faith
exacts

Is, that myself, and several now in Seville,
Saw Juan's last elopement with the devil.

204 If ever I should condescend to prose,
I'll write poetical commandments, which
Shall supersede beyond all doubt all those
That went before; in these I shall en-
rich
My text with many things that no one
knows,
And carry precept to the highest pitch:
I'll call the work "Longinus o'er a Bottle,
Or, Every Poet his *own* Aristotle."

205 Thou shalt believe in Milton, Dryden,
Pope;
Thou shalt not set up Wordsworth,
Coleridge, Southey;
Because the first is crazed beyond all hope,
The second drunk, the third so quaint
and mouthy:
With Crabbe it may be difficult to cope,
And Campbell's Hippocrene is some-
what drouthy:
Thou shalt not steal from Samuel Rogers,
nor
Commit — flirtation with the muse of
Moore.

206 Thou shalt not covet Mr. Sotheby's Muse,
His Pegasus, nor anything that's his;
Thou shalt not bear false witness like "the
Blues"[1]—
(There's one, at least, is very fond of
this);
Thou shalt not write, in short, but what I
choose;
This is true criticism, and you may kiss—
Exactly as you please, or not,—the rod;
But if you don't, I'll lay it on, by G—d!

207 If any person should presume to assert
This story is not moral, first, I pray,
That they will not cry out before they're
hurt,
Then that they'll read it o'er again, and
say
(But, doubtless, nobody will be so pert),
That this is not a moral tale, though gay;
Besides, in Canto Twelfth, I mean to show
The very place where wicked people go.

208 If, after all, there should be some so blind
To their own good this warning to de-
spise,

[1] a word to the wise is sufficient
[2] Regarding epic and narrative poetry
[3] handbook (literally, go with me)

[1] The Bluestockings, a name applied to a society
of women affecting an interest in literature
and politics. The idea originated about 1750,
but the name here given was first used about
1790. See Byron's *The Blues;* also Ethel R.
Wheeler's *Famous Blue-Stockings* (London,
1910).

Led by some tortuosity of mind,
　Not to believe my verse and their own
　　eyes,
And cry that they "the moral cannot
　　find,"
　I tell him, if a clergyman, he lies;
Should captains the remark, or critics,
　　make,
　They also lie too—under a mistake.

209　The public approbation I expect,
　And beg they'll take my word about the
　　moral,
Which I with their amusement will connect
　(So children cutting teeth receive a
　　coral);
Meantime they'll doubtless please to recol-
　　lect
　My epical pretensions to the laurel:
For fear some prudish readers should grow
　　skittish,
　I've bribed my grandmother's review—the
　　British.

210　I sent it in a letter to the Editor,
　Who thank'd me duly by return of
　　post—
I'm for a handsome article his creditor;
　Yet, if my gentle Muse he please to
　　roast,
And break a promise after having made it
　　her,
　Denying the receipt of what it cost,
And smear his page with gall instead of
　　honey,
　All I can say is—that he had the money.

211　I think that with this holy new alliance
　I may ensure the public, and defy
All other magazines of art or science,
　Daily, or monthly, or three monthly; I
Have not essay'd to multiply their clients,
　Because they tell me 'twere in vain to
　　try,
And that *The Edinburgh Review* and
　Quarterly
Treat a dissenting author very martyrly.[1]

212　"*Non ego hoc ferrem calidâ juventâ
　Consule Planco,*"[2] Horace said, and so
Say I; by which quotation there is meant a
　Hint that some six or seven good years
　　ago

---

[1] Both of these journals were hostile to Byron.
See *English Bards and Scotch Reviewers* (p.
511), which was inspired by an attack upon
Byron published in *The Edinburgh Review*,
Jan., 1808 (Vol. 11, pp. 285-89).
[2] I should not have endured this in my passion-
ate youth in the consulship of Plancus.—
Horace, *Odes*, III, 14, 27.

　(Long ere I dreamt of dating from the
　　Brenta)
　I was most ready to return a blow,
And would not brook at all this sort of
　　thing
In my hot youth—when George the Third
　　was King.

213　But now at thirty years my hair is gray
　(I wonder what it will be like at forty?
I thought of a peruke the other day)—
　My heart is not much greener; and, in
　　short, I
Have squander'd my whole summer while
　　'twas May,
　And feel no more the spirit to retort; I
Have spent my life, both interest and prin-
　　cipal,
　And deem not, what I deem'd, my soul
　　invincible.

214　No more—no more—Oh! never more on me
　The freshness of the heart can fall like
　　dew,
Which out of all the lovely things we see
　Extracts emotions beautiful and new;
Hived in our bosoms like the bag o' the
　　bee.
　Think'st thou the honey with those ob-
　　jects grew?
Alas! 'twas not in them, but in thy power
To double even the sweetness of a flower.

215　No more—no more—Oh! never more, my
　　heart,
　Canst thou be my sole world, my uni-
　　verse!
Once all in all, but now a thing apart,
　Thou canst not be my blessing or my
　　curse:
The illusion's gone forever, and thou art
　Insensible, I trust, but none the worse,
And in thy stead I've got a deal of judg-
　　ment,
　Though heaven knows how it ever found a
　　lodgment.

216　My days of love are over; me no more
　The charms of maid, wife, and still less
　　of widow,
Can make the fool of which they made
　　before,—
　In short, I must not lead the life I did do;
The credulous hope of mutual minds is
　　o'er,
　The copious use of claret is forbid too,
So for a good old-gentlemanly vice
I think I must take up with avarice.

217 Ambition was my idol, which was broken
    Before the shrines of Sorrow, and of
        Pleasure;
And the two last have left me many a token
    O'er which reflection may be made at
        leisure;
Now, like Friar Bacon's brazen head, I've
        spoken,
    "Time is, Time was, Time's past:"[1]—
        a chymic[2] treasure
Is glittering youth, which I have spent
        betimes—
My heart in passion, and my head on
        rhymes.

218 What is the end of fame? 'tis but to fill
    A certain portion of uncertain paper:
Some liken it to climbing up a hill,[3]
    Whose summit, like all hills, is lost in
        vapor;
For this men write, speak, preach, and
        heroes kill,
    And bards burn what they call their
        "midnight taper,"
To have, when the original is dust,
A name, a wretched picture, and worse
        bust.

219 What are the hopes of man? Old Egypt's
        King
    Cheops erected the first pyramid
And largest, thinking it was just the thing
    To keep his memory whole, and mummy
        hid:
But somebody or other rummaging,
    Burglariously broke his coffin's lid.
Let not a monument give you or me hopes,
Since not a pinch of dust remains of
        Cheops.

220 But I, being fond of true philosophy,
    Say very often to myself, "Alas!
All things that have been born were born
        to die,
    And flesh (which Death mows down to
        hay) is grass;[4]
You've pass'd your youth not so un-
        pleasantly,
    And if you had it o'er again—'twould
        pass—
So thank your stars that matters are no
        worse,
And read your Bible, sir, and mind your
        purse."

---

[1] The speech of the Brazen Head in Greene's
   *The Honorable History of Friar Bacon and
   Friar Bungay*, 11, 58 ff.
[2] of alchemic metal,—*i. e.*, counterfeit gold
[3] See Beattie's *The Minstrel*, 1, 1-2 (p. 120).
[4] See *Psalms*, 37 :2 ; and *Isaiah*, 40 :6.

221 But for the present, gentle reader! and
    Still gentler purchaser! the bard—that's
        I—
Must, with permission, shake you by the
        hand,
    And so "Your humble servant, and
        good-bye!"
We meet again, if we should understand
    Each other; and if not, I shall not try
Your patience further than by this short
        sample—
'Twere well if others follow'd my example.

222 "Go, little book, from this my solitude!
    I cast thee on the waters—go thy ways!
And if, as I believe, thy vein be good,
    The world will find thee after many
        days."[1]
When Southey's read, and Wordsworth
        understood,
    I can't help putting in my claim to
        praise—
The four first rhymes are Southey's, every
        line:
For God's sake, reader! take them not for
        mine!

From Canto II
1818-19   1819

44 The ship was evidently settling now[2]
    Fast by the head; and, all distinction
        gone,
Some went to prayers again, and made a
        vow
    Of candles to their saints—but there
        were none
To pay them with; and some look'd o'er
        the bow;
    Some hoisted out the boats; and there
        was one
That begg'd Pedrillo for an absolution,
Who told him to be damn'd—in his con-
        fusion.

45 Some lash'd them in their hammocks; some
        put on
    Their best clothes, as if going to a fair;
Some cursed the day on which they saw
        the sun,
    And gnash'd their teeth, and howling,
        tore their hair;
And others went on as they had begun,
    Getting the boats out, being well aware
That a tight boat will live in a rough sea,
Unless with breakers close beneath her lee.

---

[1] Southey, *Carmen Nuptiale,—The Lay of the
   Laureate*, L'Envoy, 1-4.
[2] The ship in which Juan and his tutor Pedrillo
   left Spain for Italy was wrecked in a storm.

46 The worst of all was, that in their condition,
    Having been several days in great distress,
'Twas difficult to get out such provision
    As now might render their long suffering less:
Men, even when dying, dislike inanition;
    Their stock was damaged by the weather's stress:
Two casks of biscuit, and a keg of butter,
Were all that could be thrown into the cutter.

47 But in the long-boat they contrived to stow
    Some pounds of bread, though injured by the wet;
Water, a twenty-gallon cask or so;
    Six flasks of wine: and they contrived to get
A portion of their beef up from below,
    And with a piece of pork, moreover, met,
But scarce enough to serve them for a luncheon—
Then there was rum, eight gallons in a puncheon.[1]

48 The other boats, the yawl and pinnace, had
    Been stove in the beginning of the gale;
And the long-boat's condition was but bad,
    As there were but two blankets for a sail,
And one oar for a mast, which a young lad
    Threw in by good luck over the ship's rail;
And two boats could not hold, far less be stored,
To save one half the people then on board.

49 'Twas twilight, and the sunless day went down
    Over the waste of waters; like a veil,
Which, if withdrawn, would but disclose the frown
    Of one whose hate is mask'd but to assail.
Thus to their hopeless eyes the night was shown,
    And grimly darkled o'er the faces pale,
And the dim desolate deep: twelve days had Fear
Been their familiar,[2] and now Death was here.

50 Some trial had been making at a raft,
    With little hope in such a rolling sea,
A sort of thing at which one would have laugh'd,
    If any laughter at such times could be,
Unless with people who too much have quaff'd,
    And have a kind of wild and horrid glee,
Half epileptical, and half hysterical:—
Their preservation would have been a miracle.

51 At half-past eight o'clock, booms, hencoops, spars,
    And all things, for a chance, had been cast loose
That still could keep afloat the struggling tars,
    For yet they strove, although of no great use:
There was no light in heaven but a few stars,
    The boats put off o'ercrowded with their crews;
She gave a heel, and then a lurch to port,
And, going down head foremost—sunk, in short.

52 Then rose from sea to sky the wild farewell—
    Then shriek'd the timid, and stood still the brave—
Then some leap'd overboard with dreadful yell,
    As eager to anticipate their grave;
And the sea yawn'd around her like a hell,
    And down she suck'd with her the whirling wave,
Like one who grapples with his enemy,
And strives to strangle him before he die.

53 And first one universal shriek there rush'd,
    Louder than the loud ocean, like a crash
Of echoing thunder; and then all was hush'd,
    Save the wild wind and the remorseless dash
Of billows; but at intervals there gush'd,
    Accompanied with a convulsive splash,
A solitary shriek, the bubbling cry
Of some strong swimmer in his agony.

54 The boats, as stated, had got off before,
    And in them crowded several of the crew;
And yet their present hope was hardly more
    Than what it had been, for so strong it blew
There was slight chance of reaching any shore;
    And then they were too many, though so few—

[1] A kind of large cask.   [2] attendant spirit

Nine in the cutter, thirty in the boat,
Were counted in them when they got afloat.

. . . . . .

103 As they drew nigh the land, which now was
    seen
    Unequal in its aspect here and there,
They felt the freshness of its growing
    green,
    That waved in forest-tops, and smooth'd
    the air,
And fell upon their glazed eye like a screen
    From glistening waves, and skies so hot
    and bare—
Lovely seem'd any object that should sweep
Away the vast, salt, dread, eternal deep.

104 The shore look'd wild, without a trace of
    man,
    And girt by formidable waves; but they
Were mad for land, and thus their course
    they ran,
    Though right ahead the roaring breakers
    lay:
A reef between them also now began
    To show its boiling surf and bounding
    spray,
But finding no place for their landing
    better,
They ran the boat for shore,—and overset
    her.

105 But in his native stream, the Guadalquivir,
    Juan to lave his youthful limbs was
    wont;
And having learnt to swim in that sweet
    river,
    Had often turn'd the art to some ac-
    count:
A better swimmer you could scarce see ever,
    He could, perhaps, have pass'd the
    Hellespont,
As once (a feat on which ourselves we
    prided)
Leander, Mr. Ekenhead, and I did.[1]

106 So here, though faint, emaciated, and
    stark,
    He buoy'd his boyish limbs, and strove
    to ply
With the quick wave, and gain, ere it was
    dark,
    The beach which lay before him, high
    and dry:
The greatest danger here was from a shark,

[1] Byron and Ekenhead, an officer in the British
navy, swam across the Hellespont on May 3,
1810. See Byron's poem, *Written After Swimming from Sestos to Abydos.*

That carried off his neighbor by the
    thigh;
As for the other two, they could not swim,
So nobody arrived on shore but him.

107 Nor yet had he arrived but for the oar,
    Which, providentially for him, was
    wash'd
Just as his feeble arms could strike no
    more,
    And the hard wave o'erwhelmed him as
    'twas dash'd
Within his grasp; he clung to it, and sore
    The waters beat while he thereto was
    lash'd;
At last, with swimming, wading, scram-
    bling, he
Roll'd on the beach, half senseless, from
    the sea:

108 There, breathless, with his digging nails he
    clung
    Fast to the sand, lest the returning wave,
From whose reluctant roar his life he
    wrung,
    Should suck him back to her insatiate
    grave:
And there he lay, full length, where he was
    flung,
    Before the entrance of a cliff-worn cave,
With just enough of life to feel its pain,
And deem that it was saved, perhaps in
    vain.

109 With slow and staggering effort he arose,
    But sunk again upon his bleeding knee
And quivering hand; and then he look'd
    for those
    Who long had been his mates upon the
    sea;
But none of them appear'd to share his
    woes,
    Save one, a corpse, from out the fam-
    ish'd three,
Who died two days before, and now had
    found
An unknown barren beach for burial-
    ground.

110 And as he gazed, his dizzy brain spun fast,
    And down he sunk; and as he sunk, the
    sand
Swam round and round, and all his senses
    pass'd:
    He fell upon his side, and his stretch'd
    hand
Droop'd dripping on the oar (their jury-
    mast),[1]

[1] temporary mast

And, like a wither'd lily, on the land
His slender frame and pallid aspect lay,
As fair a thing as e'er was form'd of clay.

111 How long in his damp trance young Juan
　　lay
　　He knew not, for the earth was gone for
　　　him,
　　And time had nothing more of night nor
　　　day
　　For his congealing blood, and senses
　　　dim;
　　And how this heavy faintness pass'd away
　　He knew not, till each painful pulse and
　　　limb,
　　And tingling vein, seem'd throbbing back
　　　to life,
　　For Death, though vanquish'd, still retired
　　　with strife.

112 His eyes he open'd, shut, again unclosed,
　　For all was doubt and dizziness; he
　　　thought
　　He still was in the boat, and had but dozed,
　　And felt again with his despair o'er-
　　　wrought,
　　And wish'd it death in which he had re-
　　　posed,
　　And then once more his feelings back
　　　were brought,
　　And slowly by his swimming eyes was seen
　　A lovely female face of seventeen.

113 'Twas bending close o'er his, and the small
　　mouth
　　Seem'd almost prying into his for
　　　breath;
　　And chafing him, the soft warm hand of
　　　youth
　　Recall'd his answering spirits back from
　　　death;
　　And, bathing his chill temples, tried to
　　　soothe
　　Each pulse to animation, till beneath
　　Its gentle touch and trembling care, a sigh
　　To these kind efforts made a low reply.

114 Then was the cordial pour'd, and mantle
　　flung
　　Around his scarce-clad limbs; and the
　　　fair arm
　　Raised higher the faint head which o'er it
　　　hung;
　　And her transparent cheek, all pure and
　　　warm,
　　Pillow'd his death-like forehead; then she
　　　wrung
　　His dewy curls, long drench'd by every
　　　storm;

And watch'd with eagerness each throb
　　that drew
A sigh from his heaved bosom—and hers,
　　too.

115 And lifting him with care into the cave,
　　The gentle girl, and her attendant,—one
　　Young, yet her elder, and of brow less
　　　grave,
　　And more robust of figure—then begun
　　To kindle fire, and as the new flames gave
　　Light to the rocks that roof'd them,
　　　which the sun
　　Had never seen, the maid, or whatsoe'er
　　She was, appear'd distinct, and tall, and
　　　fair.

116 Her brow was overhung with coins of
　　　gold,
　　That sparkled o'er the auburn of her
　　　hair,
　　Her clustering hair, whose longer locks
　　　were roll'd
　　In braids behind; and though her stature
　　　were
　　Even of the highest for a female mould,
　　They nearly reach'd her heel; and in her
　　　air
　　There was a something which bespoke com-
　　　mand,
　　As one who was a lady in the land.

117 Her hair, I said, was auburn; but her eyes
　　Were black as death, their lashes the
　　　same hue,
　　Of downcast length, in whose silk shadow
　　　lies
　　Deepest attraction; for when to the view
　　Forth from its raven fringe the full glance
　　　flies,
　　Ne'er with such force the swiftest arrow
　　　flew;
　　'Tis as the snake late coil'd, who pours his
　　　length,
　　And hurls at once his venom and his
　　　strength.

118 Her brow was white and low, her cheek's
　　pure dye
　　Like twilight rosy still with the set sun;
　　Short upper lip—sweet lips! that make us
　　　sigh
　　Ever to have seen such; for she was one
　　Fit for the model of a statuary
　　(A race of mere impostors, when all's
　　　done—
　　I've seen much finer women, ripe and real,
　　Than all the nonsense of their stone ideal).

119 I'll tell you why I say so, for 'tis just
   One should not rail without a decent
      cause:
There was an Irish lady, to whose bust
   I ne'er saw justice done, and yet she was
A frequent model; and if e'er she must
   Yield to stern Time and Nature's wrin-
      kling laws,
They will destroy a face which mortal
      thought
Ne'er compass'd, nor less mortal chisel
   wrought.

120 And such was she, the lady of the cave:
   Her dress was very different from the
      Spanish,
Simpler, and yet of colors not so grave;
   For, as you know, the Spanish women
      banish
Bright hues when out of doors, and yet,
   while wave
   Around them (what I hope will never
      vanish)
The basquina[1] and the mantilla,[2] they
Seem at the same time mystical and gay.

121 But with our damsel this was not the case:
   Her dress was many-color'd, finely spun;
Her locks curl'd negligently round her
   face,
   But through them gold and gems pro-
      fusely shone:
Her girdle sparkled, and the richest lace
   Flow'd in her veil, and many a precious
      stone
Flash'd on her little hand; but, what was
   shocking,
Her small snow feet had slippers, but no
   stocking.

122 The other female's dress was not unlike,
   But of inferior materials: she
Had not so many ornaments to strike,
   Her hair had silver only, bound to be
Her dowry; and her veil, in form alike,
   Was coarser; and her air, though firm,
      less free;
Her hair was thicker, but less long; her
   eyes
As black, but quicker, and of smaller size.

123 And these two tended him, and cheer'd him
      both
   With food and raiment, and those soft
      attentions,
Which are—(as I must own)—of female
   growth,

[1] A rich outer petticoat.
[2] A kind of veil, covering the head and shoulders.

And have ten thousand delicate inven-
      tions:
They made a most superior mess of broth,
   A thing which poesy but seldom men-
      tions,
But the best dish that e'er was cook'd
      since Homer's
Achilles order'd dinner for new comers.[1]

124 I'll tell you who they were, this female
      pair,
   Lest they should seem princesses in dis-
      guise;
Besides, I hate all mystery, and that air
   Of clap-trap, which your recent poets
      prize;
And so, in short, the girls they really were
   They shall appear before your curious
      eyes,
Mistress and maid; the first was only
      daughter
Of an old man, who lived upon the water.

125 A fisherman he had been in his youth,
   And still a sort of fisherman was he;
But other speculations were, in sooth,
   Added to his connection with the sea,
Perhaps not so respectable, in truth:
   A little smuggling, and some piracy,
Left him, at last, the sole of many masters
Of an ill-gotten million of piastres.[2]

126 A fisher, therefore, was he,—though of
      men,
   Like Peter the Apostle,[3]—and he fish'd
For wandering merchant vessels, now and
      then,
   And sometimes caught as many as he
      wish'd;
The cargoes he confiscated, and gain
   He sought in the slave-market too, and
      dish'd
Full many a morsel for that Turkish trade,
By which, no doubt, a good deal may be
   made.

127 He was a Greek, and on his isle had built
   (One of the wild and smaller Cyclades)
A very handsome house from out his guilt,
   And there he lived exceedingly at ease;
Heaven knows what cash he got, or blood
      he spilt,
   A sad old fellow was he, if you please;
But this I know, it was a spacious building,
Full of barbaric carving, paint, and gild-
   ing.

[1] Ajax, Ulysses, and Phœnix are brought before
   Achilles, who then leads them into the tent
   and sets meat and wine before them. See the
   Iliad, 9, 193 ff.
[2] A coin worth about a dollar.
[3] See *Matthew*, 4 :18-19.

128 He had an only daughter, call'd Haidée.
    The greatest heiress of the Eastern Isles;
Besides, so very beautiful was she,
    Her dowry was as nothing to her smiles:
Still in her teens, and like a lovely tree
    She grew to womanhood, and between
        whiles
Rejected several suitors, just to learn
How to accept a better in his turn.

129 And walking out upon the beach, below
    The cliff, towards sunset, on that day she
        found,
Insensible,—not dead, but nearly so,—
    Don Juan, almost famish'd, and half
        drown'd;
But being naked, she was shock'd, you
        know,
    Yet deem'd herself in common pity
        bound,
As far as in her lay, "to take him in,
A stranger,"[1] dying, with so white a skin.

130 But taking him into her father's house
    Was not exactly the best way to save,
But like conveying to the cat the mouse,
    Or people in a trance into their grave;
Because the good old man had so much
    "*vous*,"[2]
Unlike the honest Arab thieves so brave,
He would have hospitably cured the
    stranger
And sold him instantly when out of danger.

131 And therefore, with her maid, she thought
    it best
    (A virgin always on her maid relies)
To place him in the cave for present rest:
    And when, at last, he open'd his black
        eyes,
Their charity increased about their guest;
    And their compassion grew to such a
        size,
It open'd half the turnpike gates to
    heaven—
(St. Paul says, 'tis the toll which must
    be given).[3]

132 They made a fire,— but such a fire as they
    Upon the moment could contrive with
        such
Materials as were cast up round the bay,—
    Some broken planks, and oars, that to
        the touch
Were nearly tinder, since so long they lay
    A mast was almost crumbled to a crutch;
But, by God's grace, here wrecks were in
    such plenty,

That there was fuel to have furnish'd
    twenty.

133 He had a bed of furs, and a pelisse,[1]
    For Haidée stripp'd her sables off to
    make
His couch; and, that he might be more at
    ease,
    And warm, in case by chance he should
    awake,
They also gave a petticoat apiece,
    She and her maid,—and promised by
    daybreak
To pay him a fresh visit, with a dish
For breakfast, of eggs, coffee, bread, and
    fish.

134 And thus they left him to his lone repose:
    Juan slept like a top, or like the dead,
Who sleep at last, perhaps (God only
    knows),
    Just for the present; and in his lull'd
    head
Not even a vision of his former woes
    Throbb'd in accursed dreams, which
    sometimes spread
Unwelcome visions of our former years,
Till the eye, cheated, opens thick with
    tears.

135 Young Juan slept all dreamless:—but the
    maid,
    Who smooth'd his pillow, as she left
    the den
Look'd back upon him, and a moment staid,
    And turn'd, believing that he call'd
    again.
He slumber'd; yet she thought, at least
    she said
    (The heart will slip, even as the tongue
    and pen),
He had pronounced her name—but she
    forgot
That at this moment Juan knew it not.

136 And pensive to her father's house she
    went,
    Enjoining silence strict to Zoe, who
Better than her knew what, in fact, she
    meant,
    She being wiser by a year or two:
A year or two's an age when rightly spent,
    And Zoe spent hers, as most women do,
In gaining all that useful sort of knowl-
    edge
Which is acquired in Nature's good old
    college.

    .   .   .   .   .

---

[1] See *Matthew*, 25:35.   [3] See *Hebrews*, 10:34.
[2] intellect

[1] A kind of long outer garment.

174 And thus a moon roll'd on, and fair
    Haidée
  Paid daily visits to her boy, and took
Such plentiful precautions, that still he
  Remain'd unknown within his craggy
    nook;
At last her father's prows put out to sea,
  For certain merchantmen upon the look,
Not as of yore to carry off an Io,
  But three Ragusan vessels bound for Scio.

175 Then came her freedom, for she had no
    mother,
  So that, her father being at sea, she was
Free as a married woman, or such other
  Female, as where she likes may freely
    pass,
Without even the encumbrance of a
  brother,
  The freest she that ever gazed on glass:
I speak of Christian lands in this com-
    parison,
  Where wives, at least, are seldom kept in
    garrison.

176 Now she prolonged her visits and her
    talk
  (For they must talk), and he had learnt
    to say
So much as to propose to take a walk,—
  For little had he wander'd since the day
On which, like a young flower snapp'd
  from the stalk,
  Drooping and dewy on the beach he
    lay,—
And thus they walk'd out in the afternoon,
And saw the sun set opposite the moon.

177 It was a wild and breaker-beaten coast,
  With cliffs above, and a broad sandy
    shore,
Guarded by shoals and rocks as by an
  host,
  With here and there a creek, whose
    aspect wore
A better welcome to the tempest-tost;
  And rarely ceased the haughty billow's
    roar,
Save on the dead long summer days, which
  make
  The outstretch'd ocean glitter like a lake.

178 And the small ripple spilt upon the beach
  Scarcely o'erpass'd the cream of your
    champagne,
When o'er the brim the sparkling bumpers
  reach,
  That spring-dew of the spirit! the
    heart's rain!

Few things surpass old wine; and they
  may preach
Who please,—the more because they
  preach in vain,—
Let us have wine and women, mirth and
  laughter,
Sermons and soda-water the day after.

179 Man, being reasonable, must get drunk;
  The best of life is but intoxication:
Glory, the grape, love, gold, in these are
  sunk
  The hopes of all men, and of every
    nation;
Without their sap, how branchless were
  the trunk
  Of life's strange tree, so fruitful on
    occasion!
But to return,—Get very drunk, and when
You wake with headache, you shall see
  what then.

180 Ring for your valet—bid him quickly
    bring
  Some hock and soda-water, then you'll
    know
A pleasure worthy Xerxes the great king;
  For not the blest sherbet, sublimed with
    snow,
Nor the first sparkle of the desert spring,
  Nor Burgundy in all its sunset glow,
After long travel, ennui, love, or slaughter,
Vie with that draught of hock and soda-
  water.

181 The coast—I think it was the coast that I
  Was just describing—Yes, it *was* the
    coast—
Lay at this period quiet as the sky,
  The sands untumbled, the blue waves
    untost,
And all was stillness, save the sea-bird's
  cry,
  And dolphin's leap, and little billow
    crost
By some low rock or shelve, that made it
  fret
Against the boundary it scarcely wet.

182 And forth they wander'd, her sire being
  gone,
  As I have said, upon an expedition;
And mother, brother, guardian, she had
  none,
  Save Zoe, who, although with due pre-
    cision
She waited on her lady with the sun,
  Thought daily service was her only mis-
    sion,

Bringing warm water, wreathing her long
    tresses,
And asking now and then for cast-off
    dresses.

183 It was the cooling hour, just when the
    rounded
    Red sun sinks down behind the azure
      hill,
Which then seems as if the whole earth it
    bounded,
    Circling all nature, hush'd, and dim, and
      still,
With the far mountain-crescent half sur-
    rounded
    On one side, and the deep sea calm and
      chill,
Upon the other, and the rosy sky,
    With one star sparkling through it like
      an eye.

184 And thus they wander'd forth, and hand
    in hand,
    Over the shining pebbles and the shells,
Glided along the smooth and harden'd
    sand,
And in the worn and wild receptacles
Work'd by the storms, yet work'd as it
    were plann'd,
    In hollow halls, with sparry roofs and
      cells,
They turn'd to rest; and, each clasp'd by
    an arm,
Yielded to the deep twilight's purple
    charm.

185 They look'd up to the sky, whose floating
    glow
    Spread like a rosy ocean, vast and
      bright;
They gazed upon the glittering sea below,
    Whence the broad moon rose circling
      into sight;
They heard the waves splash, and the
    wind so low,
    And saw each other's dark eyes darting
      light
Into each other—and, beholding this,
Their lips drew near, and clung into a kiss;

186 A long, long kiss, a kiss of youth, and
    love,
    And beauty, all concentrating like rays
Into one focus, kindled from above;
    Such kisses as belong to early days,
Where heart, and soul, and sense, in con-
    cert move,
    And the blood's lava, and the pulse
      a blaze,

Each kiss a heart-quake,—for a kiss's
    strength,
I think it must be reckon'd by its length.

187 By length I mean duration; theirs en-
    dured
    Heaven knows how long—no doubt they
      never reckon'd;
And if they had, they could not have se-
    cured
    The sum of their sensations to a second:
They had not spoken; but they felt al-
    lured,
    As if their souls and lips each other
      beckon'd,
Which, being join'd, like swarming bees
    they clung—
Their hearts the flowers from whence the
    honey sprung.

188 They were alone, but not alone as they
    Who shut in chambers think it loneli-
      ness;
The silent ocean, and the starlight bay,
    The twilight glow, which momently grew
      less,
The voiceless sands, and dropping caves,
    that lay
    Around them, made them to each other
      press,
As if there were no life beneath the sky
Save theirs, and that their life could never
    die.

189 They fear'd no eyes nor ears on that lone
    beach,
    They felt no terrors from the night;
      they were
All in all to each other; though their
    speech
    Was broken words, they *thought* a
      language there,—
And all the burning tongues the passions
    teach
    Found in one sigh the best interpreter
Of nature's oracle—first love,—that all
Which Eve has left her daughters since
    her fall.

    .   .   .   .   .   .

199 Alas! the love of women! it is known
    To be a lovely and a fearful thing;
For all of theirs upon that die is thrown,
    And if 'tis lost, life hath no more to
      bring
To them but mockeries of the past alone,
    And their revenge is as the tiger's
      spring,

Deadly, and quick, and crushing; yet, as
 real
Torture is theirs, what they inflict they
 feel.

200 They are right; for man, to man so oft
 unjust,
　Is always so to women; one sole bond
Awaits them, treachery is all their trust;
　Taught to conceal, their bursting hearts
　 despond
Over their idol, till some wealthier lust
　Buys them in marriage—and what rests
　 beyond?
A thankless husband, next a faithless
 lover,
Then dressing, nursing, praying, and all's
 over.

201 Some take a lover, some take drams or
 prayers,
　Some mind their household, others dis-
　 sipation,
Some run away, and but exchange their
 cares,
　Losing the advantage of a virtuous sta-
　 tion;
Few changes e'er can better their affairs,
　Theirs being an unnatural situation,
From the dull palace to the dirty hovel:
Some play the devil, and then write a
 novel.

202 Haidée was Nature's bride, and knew not
 this:
　Haidée was Passion's child, born where
　 the sun
Showers triple light, and scorches even the
 kiss
　Of his gazelle-eyed daughters; she was
　 one
Made but to love, to feel that she was
 his
　Who was her chosen: what was said or
　 done
Elsewhere was nothing. She had nought
 to fear,
Hope, care, nor love beyond,—her heart
 beat *here*.

203 And oh! that quickening of the heart, that
 beat!
　How much it costs us! yet each rising
　 throb
Is in its cause as its effect so sweet,
　That Wisdom, ever on the watch to rob
Joy of its alchemy, and to repeat
　Fine truths; even Conscience, too, has
　 a tough job

To make us understand each good old
 maxim,
So good—I wonder Castlereagh don't tax
 'em.

204 And now 'twas done—on the lone shore
 were plighted
　Their hearts; the stars, their nuptial
　 torches, shed
Beauty upon the beautiful they lighted:
　Ocean their witness, and the cave their
　 bed,
By their own feelings hallow'd and united,
　Their priest was Solitude, and they were
　 wed:
And they were happy, for to their young
 eyes
Each was an angel, and earth paradise.

· · · · · · ·

From CANTO III
1819-20　　　1821

78 And now they[1] were diverted by their
 suite,
　Dwarfs, dancing-girls, black eunuchs,
　 and a poet,[2]
Which made their new establishment com-
 plete;
　The last was of great fame, and liked to
　 show it;
His verses rarely wanted their due feet—
　And for his theme—he seldom sung be-
　 low it,
He being paid to satirize or flatter,
As the psalm says, "inditing a good mat-
 ter."[3]

79 He praised the present, and abused the
 past,
　Reversing the good custom of old days,
An Eastern anti-jacobin[4] at last
　He turn'd, preferring pudding to *no*
　 praise—
For some few years his lot had been o'er-
 cast
　By his seeming independent in his lays,
But now he sung the Sultan and the Pacha
With truth like Southey, and with verse
 like Crashaw.

80 He was a man who had seen many changes,
　And always changed as true as any
　 needle;

[1] Haidée and Juan, who hold a feast during the absence of Haidée's father.
[2] The poet represents Southey.
[3] *Psalms*, 45 :1.
[4] The "Lakers," Wordsworth, Coleridge, and Southey, became anti-Jacobins after the excesses and failures of the French Revolution. See *Don Juan*, Dedication, 1 (p. 603).

His polar star being one which rather
   ranges,
And not the fix'd—he knew the way to
   wheedle:
So vile he 'scaped the doom which oft
   avenges;
   And being fluent (save indeed when
      fee'd ill),
He lied with such a fervor of intention—
There was no doubt he earn'd his laureate
   pension.

81 But he had genius,—when a turncoat has
     it,
   The "Vates irritabilis"[1] takes care
That without notice few full moons shall
   pass it;
   Even good men like to make the public
     stare:—
But to my subject—let me see—what was
   it?—
Oh!—the third canto—and the pretty
   pair—
   Their loves, and feasts, and house, and
     dress, and mode
Of living in their insular abode.

82 Their poet, a sad trimmer,[2] but no less
   In company a very pleasant fellow,
Had been the favorite of full many a mess
   Of men, and made them speeches when
     half mellow;
   And though his meaning they could rarely
     guess,
   Yet still they deign'd to hiccup or to
     bellow
The glorious meed of popular applause,
Of which the first ne'er knows the second
   cause.

83 But now being lifted into high society,
   And having pick'd up several odds and
     ends
Of free thoughts in his travels, for variety,
   He deem'd, being in a lone isle, among
     friends,
That without any danger of a riot, he
   Might for long lying make himself
     amends;
And singing as he sung in his warm youth,
Agree to a short armistice with truth.

84 He had travell'd 'mongst the Arabs,
   Turks, and Franks,
   And knew the self-loves of the different
     nations;

And having lived with people of all ranks,
   Had something ready upon most occa-
     sions—
Which got him a few presents and some
   thanks.
   He varied with some skill his adulations;
To "do at Rome as Romans do,"[1] a piece
Of conduct was which he observed in
   Greece.

85 Thus, usually, when he was asked to sing,
   He gave the different nations something
     national;
'Twas all the same to him—"God save
   the king,"
   Or "Ca ira,"[2] according to the fashion
     all:
His muse made increment of anything,
   From the high lyric down to the low
     rational:[3]
If Pindar sang horse-races, what should
   hinder
Himself from being as pliable as Pindar?

86 In France, for instance, he would write a
   chanson;[4]
In England a six canto quarto tale;
In Spain he'd make a ballad or romance
   on
   The last war—much the same in Por-
     tugal;
In Germany, the Pegasus he'd prance on
   Would be old Goethe's— (see what says
     De Staël);[5]
In Italy he'd ape the "Trecentisti"[6];
In Greece, he'd sing some sort of hymn
   like this t' ye:

1

The isles of Greece, the isles of Greece!
   Where burning Sappho loved and sung,
Where grew the arts of war and peace,
   Where Delos rose, and Phœbus sprung!
Eternal summer gilds them yet,
But all, except their sun, is set.

2

The Scian and the Teian muse,[7]
   The hero's harp, the lover's lute,
Have found the fame your shores refuse;

---

[1] irritable soothsayer (Chapter 2 of Coleridge's *Biographia Literaria* is on "The Supposed Irritability of Men of Genius.")
[2] One who does not adhere to one set of opinions in politics.
[1] St. Augustine, *Epistles*, 36, 14.
[2] it will succeed (A song of the French Revolutionists.)
[3] A reference to Coleridge's praise of Southey in his *Biographia Literaria*, 1.
[4] song
[5] Madame De Staël had recently published a book on Germany, in which she said that Goethe represented the entire literature of Germany.
[6] Writers in the Italian style of the 14th century.
[7] Homer, of the island of Scio, and Anacreon, of Teos, Asia Minor.

Their place of birth alone is mute
To sounds which echo further west
Than your sires' "Islands of the Blest."[1]

3

The mountains look on Marathon —
　And Marathon looks on the sea;
And musing there an hour alone,
　I dream'd that Greece might still be free;
For standing on the Persians' grave,
I could not deem myself a slave.

4

A king[2] sate on the rocky brow
　Which looks o'er sea-born Salamis;
And ships, by thousands, lay below,
　And men in nations;—all were his!
He counted them at break of day—
And when the sun set where were they?

5

And where are they? and where art thou,
　My country? On thy voiceless shore
The heroic lay is tuneless now—
　The heroic bosom beats no more!
And must thy lyre, so long divine,
Degenerate into hands like mine?

6

'Tis something, in the dearth of fame,
　Though link'd among a fetter'd race,
To feel at least a patriot's shame,
　Even as I sing, suffuse my face;
For what is left the poet here?
For Greeks a blush—for Greece a tear.

7

Must *we* but weep o'er days more blest?
　Must *we* but blush?—Our fathers bled.
Earth! render back from out thy breast
　A remnant of our Spartan dead!
Of the three hundred grant but three,
To make a new Thermopylæ!

8

What, silent still? and silent all?
　Ah! no;—the voices of the dead
Sound like a distant torrent's fall,
　And answer, "Let one living head,
But one arise,—we come, we come!"
'Tis but the living who are dumb.

9

In vain—in vain; strike other chords;
　Fill high the cup with Samian wine!
Leave battles to the Turkish hordes,
　And shed the blood of Scio's vine!
Hark, rising to the ignoble call—
How answers each bold Bacchanal!

10

You have the Pyrrhic dance[1] as yet;
　Where is the Pyrrhic phalanx[2] gone?
Of two such lessons, why forget
　The nobler and the manlier one?
You have the letters Cadmus gave—
Think ye he meant them for a slave?

11

Fill high the bowl with Samian wine!
　We will not think of themes like these!
It made Anacreon's song divine:
　He served—but served Polycrates—
A tyrant; but our masters then
Were still, at least, our countrymen.

12

The tyrant of the Chersonese
　Was freedom's best and bravest friend;
That tyrant was Miltiades!
　Oh! that the present hour would lend
Another despot of the kind!
Such chains as his were sure to bind.

13

Fill high the bowl with Samian wine!
　On Suli's rock, and Parga's shore,
Exists the remnant of a line
　Such as the Doric mothers bore;
And there, perhaps, some seed is sown,
The Heracleidan[3] blood might own.

14

Trust not for freedom to the Franks—
　They have a king who buys and sells;
In native swords, and native ranks,
　The only hope of courage dwells;
But Turkish force, and Latin fraud,
Would break your shield, however broad.

15

Fill high the bowl with Samian wine!
　Our virgins dance beneath the shade—
I see their glorious black eyes shine;
　But gazing on each glowing maid,
My own the burning tear-drop laves,
To think such breasts must suckle slaves.

16

Place me on Sunium's marbled steep,
　Where nothing, save the waves and I,
May hear our mutual murmurs sweep;
　There, swan-like, let me sing and die:[4]
A land of slaves shall ne'er be mine—
Dash down yon cup of Samian wine!

87 Thus sung, or would, or could, or should
　　　have sung,
　The modern Greek, in tolerable verse;
If not like Orpheus quite, when Greece was
　　　young,

---

[1] Mythical islands said to lie in the Western Ocean, where the favorites of the gods dwell after death, in eternal joy. See Hesiod's *Works and Days*, 169.
[2] Xerxes, King of Persia (486-465 B. C.).

[1] An ancient war-dance in quick time.
[2] The phalanx as used by Pyrrhus, the great Greek general (3rd cent. B. C.).
[3] tracing back to Hercules,—*i. e.*, ancient Greek
[4] The swan was said to sing melodiously when about to die.

Yet in these times he might have done
　　much worse:
His strain display'd some feeling—right
　　or wrong;
And feeling, in a poet, is the source
Of others' feeling; but they are such liars,
And take all colors—like the hands of
　　dyers.

88 But words are things, and a small drop of
　　ink,
　　Falling like dew, upon a thought, pro-
　　　　duces
That which makes thousands, perhaps mil-
　　lions, think;
　　'Tis strange, the shortest letter which
　　　　man uses
Instead of speech, may form a lasting link
　　Of ages; to what straits old Time re-
　　　　duces
Frail man, when paper—even a rag like
　　this,
　　Survives himself, his tomb, and all that's
　　　　his!

89 And when his bones are dust, his grave a
　　blank,
　　His station, generation, even his nation,
Become a thing, or nothing, save to rank
　　In chronological commemoration,
Some dull MS. oblivion long has sank,
　　Or graven stone found in a barrack's
　　　　station
In digging the foundation of a closet,
May turn his name up, as a rare deposit.

90 And glory long has made the sages smile;
　　'Tis something, nothing, words, illusion,
　　　　wind—
Depending more upon the historian's style
　　Than on the name a person leaves be-
　　　　hind:
Troy owes to Homer what whist owes to
　　Hoyle:
　　The present century was growing blind
To the great Marlborough's skill in giving
　　knocks,[1]
Until his late Life by Archdeacon Coxe.

91 Milton's the prince of poets—so we say;
　　A little heavy, but no less divine:
An independent being in his day—
　　Learn'd, pious, temperate in love and
　　　　wine;
But his life falling into Johnson's way[2]

---

[1] He defeated the French in the Battle of Blenheim, in 1704. See Southey's *The Battle of Blenheim* (p. 426); also Addison's *The Campaign*.
[2] Johnson wrote a Life of Milton, published in his *Lives of the English Poets*, 1779-80.

We're told this great high priest of all
　　the Nine[1]
Was whipt at college—a harsh sire—odd
　　spouse,
For the first Mrs. Milton left his house.

92 All these are, *certes,* entertaining facts,
　　Like Shakspeare's stealing deer,[2] Lord
　　　　Bacon's bribes;[3]
Like Titus' youth,[4] and Cæsar's earliest
　　acts;
　　Like Burns (whom Doctor Currie well
　　　　describes);
Like Cromwell's pranks;[5]—but although
　　truth exacts
　　These amiable descriptions from the
　　　　scribes,
As most essential to their hero's story,
They do not much contribute to his glory.

93 All are not moralists, like Southey, when
　　He prated to the world of "Pantisoc-
　　　　rasy;"[6]
Or Wordsworth unexcised,[7] unhired, who
　　then
　　Season'd his pedlar poems[8] with democ-
　　　　racy;
Or Coleridge, long before his flighty pen
　　Let to *The Morning Post* its aristocracy;[9]
When he and Southey, following the same
　　path,
Espoused two partners (milliners of
　　Bath.)[10]

94 Such names at present cut a convict figure,
　　The very Botany Bay in moral geog-
　　　　raphy;
Their loyal treason, renegado rigor,
　　Are good manure for their more bare
　　　　biography,
Wordsworth's last quarto, by the way, is
　　bigger
　　Than any since the birthday of typog-
　　　　raphy;

[1] The nine Muses.
[2] A fictitious anecdote popularly associated with Shakespeare's youth.
[3] Bacon was charged with accepting bribes, and was therefore excluded from Parliament.
[4] The youth of Titus Vespasianus, Roman Emperor (79-81), like that of Julius Cæsar and that of Burns, was noted for its voluptuousness.
[5] The youthful Cromwell was noted for robbing orchards.
[6] The name given to a scheme for an ideal community which Southey, Coleridge, and others planned in 1794 to establish in America.
[7] Wordsworth was appointed Distributor of Stamps, but he never had any connection with the excise.
[8] A reference to Wordsworth's *Peter Bell*, the hero of which is a pedlar.
[9] Coleridge began his contributions to *The Morning Post* in 1798.
[10] Coleridge married Sarah Fricker; Southey, her sister Edith. They were not milliners at the time of their marriage in 1795.

A drowsy frowzy poem, call'd *The Excur-*
sion,[1]
Writ in a manner which is my aversion.

95 He there builds up a formidable dyke
Between his own and others' intellect:
But Wordsworth's poem, and his follow-
ers, like
Joanna Southcote's Shiloh,[2] and her
sect,
Are things which in this century don't
strike
The public mind,—so few are the elect;
And the new births of both their stale
virginities
Have proved but dropsies, taken for divin-
ities.

96 But let me to my story: I must own,
If I have any fault, it is digression—
Leaving my people to proceed alone,
While I soliloquize beyond expression:
But these are my addresses from the
throne,
Which put off business to the ensuing
session:
Forgetting each omission is a loss to
The world, not quite so great as Ariosto.

97 I know that what our neighbors call
"longueurs"[3]
(We've not so good a *word,* but have
the *thing,*
In that complete perfection which insures
An epic from Bob Southey every
spring),
Form not the true temptation which allures
The reader; but 'twould not be hard to
bring
Some fine examples of the *epopée,*[4]
To prove its grand ingredient is *ennui.*[5]

98 We learn from Horace, "Homer sometimes
sleeps;"[6]
We feel without him, Wordsworth
sometimes wakes,—
To show with what complacency he creeps,
With his dear *"Waggoners,"* around
his lakes.
He wishes for *"a boat"* to sail the deeps—
Of ocean?—No, of air; and then he
makes
Another outcry for a *"a little boat,"*[7]
And drivels seas to set it well afloat.

99 If he must fain sweep o'er the ethereal
plain,
And Pegasus runs restive in his "Wag-
gon,"
Could he not beg the loan of Charles's
Wain?[1]
Or pray Medea for a single dragon?
Or if, too classic for his vulgar brain,
He fear'd his neck to venture such a
nag on,
And he must needs mount nearer to the
moon,
Could not the blockhead ask for a balloon?

100 "Pedlars," and "Boats," and "Wag-
gons!" Oh! ye shades
Of Pope and Dryden, are we come to
this?
That trash of such sort not alone evades
Contempt, but from the bathos' vast
abyss
Floats scumlike uppermost, and these
Jack Cades
Of sense and song above your graves
may hiss—
The "little boatman" and his "Peter
Bell"
Can sneer at him who drew "Achito-
phel!"[2]

101 T' our tale.—The feast was over, the slaves
gone,
The dwarfs and dancing girls had all
retired;
The Arab lore and poet's song were done,
And every sound of revelry expired;
The lady and her lover, left alone,
The rosy flood of twilight's sky ad-
mired;—
Ave Maria! o'er the earth and sea,
That heavenliest hour of Heaven is
worthiest thee!

102 Ave Maria! blessed be the hour!
The time, the clime, the spot, where I
so oft
Have felt that moment in its fullest power
Sink o'er the earth so beautiful and
soft,
While swung the deep bell in the distant
tower,
Or the faint dying day-hymn stole aloft,
And not a breath crept through the rosy
air,
And yet the forest leaves seem'd stirr'd
with prayer.

---

[1] See p. 300.
[2] Joanna Southcott was a visionary who prophesied that she would give birth to a second
Shiloh, or Messiah, on Oct. 19, 1814. When
that time came, she fell into a trance and
died ten days later.
[3] tedious passages [4] epic [5] languid weariness
[6] *Ars Poetica,* 359 [7] *Peter Bell,* st. 1

[1] Charles's Wagon, the constellation known as
the Dipper.
[2] Dryden, of whom Wordsworth was not fond.
See Wordsworth's *Essay, Supplementary to
the Preface.*

103 Ave Maria! 'tis the hour of prayer!
    Ave Maria! 'tis the hour of love!
    Ave Maria! may our spirits dare
    Look up to thine and to thy Son's above!
    Ave Maria! oh that face so fair!
      Those downcast eyes beneath the Almighty dove—
    What though 'tis but a pictured image?—strike—
    That painting is no idol,—'tis too like.

104 Some kinder casuists are pleased to say,
    In nameless print—that I have no devotion;
    But set those persons down with me to pray,
    And you shall see who has the properest notion
    Of getting into heaven the shortest way;
    My altars are the mountains and the ocean,
    Earth, air, stars,—all that springs from the great Whole,
    Who hath produced, and will receive the soul.

105 Sweet hour of twilight!—in the solitude
    Of the pine forest, and the silent shore
    Which bounds Ravenna's immemorial wood,
    Rooted where once the Adrian wave flow'd o'er,
    To where the last Cæsarean fortress[1] stood,
    Evergreen forest! which Boccaccio's lore
    And Dryden's lay[2] made haunted ground to me,
    How have I loved the twilight hour and thee!

106 The shrill cicalas,[3] people of the pine,
    Making their summer lives one ceaseless song,
    Were the sole echoes, save my steed's and mine,
    And vesper bell's that rose the boughs along;
    The spectre huntsman of Onesti's line,[4]
    His hell-dogs, and their chase, and the fair throng
    Which learn'd from this example not to fly

[1] In Ravenna.
[2] *Theodore and Honoria*, a tale of a specter huntsman who haunted the region of Ravenna, adapted from Boccaccio's *The Decameron*, 5, 8.
[3] locusts
[4] Dryden's Theodore is Boccaccio's Onesti. The specter merely appeared to Onesti; it was not of his line.

    From a true lover,—shadow'd my mind's eye.

107 Oh, Hesperus! thou bringest all good things—
    Home to the weary, to the hungry cheer,
    To the young bird the parent's brooding wings,
    The welcome stall to the o'erlabor'd steer;
    Whate'er of peace about our hearthstone clings,
    Whate'er our household gods protect of dear,
    Are gather'd round us by thy look of rest;
    Thou bring'st the child, too, to the mother's breast.

108 Soft hour! which wakes the wish and melts the heart
    Of those who sail the seas, on the first day
    When they from their sweet friends are torn apart;
    Or fills with love the pilgrim on his way
    As the far bell of vesper makes him start,
    Seeming to weep the dying day's decay;
    Is this a fancy which our reason scorns?
    Ah! surely nothing dies but something mourns!

109 When Nero perish'd by the justest doom
    Which ever the destroyer yet destroy'd,
    Amidst the roar of liberated Rome,
    Of nations freed, and the world over-joy'd,
    Some hands unseen strew'd flowers upon his tomb:
    Perhaps the weakness of a heart not void
    Of feeling for some kindness done, when power
    Had left the wretch an uncorrupted hour.

110 But I'm digressing; what on earth has Nero,
    Or any such like sovereign buffoons,
    To do with the transactions of my hero,
    More than such madmen's fellow man—the moon's?
    Sure my invention must be down at zero,
    And I grown one of many "wooden spoons"
    Of verse (the name with which we Cantabs[1] please
    To dub the last of honors in degrees).

[1] Cantabrigians—*i. e.*, those associated with the University of Cambridge.

111 I feel this tediousness will never do—
  'Tis being *too* epic, and I must cut down
(In copying) this long canto into two;
  They'll never find it out, unless I own,
The fact, excepting some experienced few;
  And then as an improvement 'twill be
    shown:
I'll prove that such the opinion of the
    critic is
From Aristotle *passim.*—See Ποιητικῆς.[1]

From Canto IV
1819-20   1821

1 Nothing so difficult as a beginning
  In poesy, unless perhaps the end;
For oftentimes when Pegasus seems win-
    ning
  The race, he sprains a wing, and down
    we tend,
Like Lucifer when hurl'd from heaven for
    sinning;[2]
  Our sin the same, and hard as his to
    mend,
Being pride, which leads the mind to soar
    too far,
  Till our own weakness shows us what we
    are.

2 But Time, which brings all beings to their
    level,
  And sharp Adversity, will teach at last
Man,—and, as we would hope,—perhaps
    the devil,
  That neither of their intellects are vast:
While youth's hot wishes in our red veins
    revel,
  We know not this—the blood flows on
    too fast:
But as the torrent widens toward the
    ocean,
We ponder deeply on each past emotion.

3 As boy, I thought myself a clever fellow,
  And wish'd that others held the same
    opinion;
They took it up when my days grew more
    mellow,
  And other minds acknowledged my do-
    minion:
Now my sere fancy "falls into the yellow
  Leaf,"[3] and Imagination droops her
    pinion,
And the sad truth which hovers o'er my
    desk
Turns what was once romantic to bur-
    lesque.

[1] Τὰ περὶ Ποιητικῆς (*Poetics*).
[2] See *Paradise Lost*, 4, 40.
[3] *Macbeth*, V, 3, 23.

4 And if I laugh at any mortal thing,
  'Tis that I may not weep; and if I weep,
'Tis that our nature cannot always bring
  Itself to apathy, for we must steep
Our hearts first in the depths of Lethe's
    spring,
  Ere what we least wish to behold will
    sleep:
Thetis baptized her mortal son in Styx;
A mortal mother would on Lethe fix.[1]

5 Some have accused me of a strange design
  Against the creed and morals of the
    land,
And trace it in this poem every line;
  I don't pretend that I quite understand
My own meaning when I would be *very*
    fine;
  But the fact is that I have nothing
    plann'd,
Unless it were to be a moment merry,
A novel word in my vocabulary.

6 To the kind reader of our sober clime
  This way of writing will appear exotic;
Pulci was sire of the half-serious rhyme,
  Who sang when chivalry was more Quix-
    otic,
And revell'd in the fancies of the time,
  True knights, chaste dames, huge giants,
    kings despotic:
But all these, save the last, being obsolete,
I chose a modern subject as more meet.

7 How I have treated it, I do not know;
  Perhaps no better than they have
    treated me,
Who have imputed such designs as show
  Not what they saw, but what they
    wish'd to see;
But if it gives them pleasure, be it so,
  This is a liberal age, and thoughts are
    free:
Meantime Apollo plucks me by the ear,
And tells me to resume my story here.

8 Young Juan and his lady-love were left
  To their own hearts' most sweet society;
Even Time the pitiless in sorrow cleft
  With his rude scythe such gentle bosoms;
    he
Sigh'd to behold them of their hours
    bereft,
  Though foe to love; and yet they could
    not be
Meant to grow old, but die in happy spring,
Before one charm or hope had taken wing.

[1] would choose Lethe

9 Their faces were not made for wrinkles,
    their
  Pure blood to stagnate, their great hearts
    to fail!
The blank gray was not made to blast their
    hair,
  But like the climes that know nor snow
    nor hail,
  They were all summer; lightning might
    assail
And shiver them to ashes, but to trail
A long and snake-like life of dull decay
Was not for them—they had too little clay.

10 They were alone once more; for them to be
  Thus was another Eden; they were never
Weary, unless when separate: the tree
  Cut from its forest root of years—the
    river
Damm'd from its fountain—the child from
    the knee
  And breast maternal wean'd at once for-
    ever,—
Would wither less than these two torn
    apart;
Alas! there is no instinct like the heart—

11 The heart—which may be broken: happy
    they!
  Thrice fortunate! who of that fragile
    mould,
The precious porcelain of human clay,
  Break with the first fall: they can ne'er
    behold
The long year link'd with heavy day on
    day,
  And all which must be borne, and never
    told;
While life's strange principle will often lie
Deepest in those who long the most to die.

12 "Whom the gods love die young" was said
    of yore,[1]
  And many deaths do they escape by this·
The death of friends, and that which slays
    even more—
  The death of friendship, love, youth, all
    that is,
Except mere breath; and since the silent
    shore
  Awaits at last even those who longest
    miss
The old archer's shafts, perhaps the early
    grave

[1] By Menander, in *Dis Exapaton*, Fragment 4;
by Plautus, in *Bacchides*, IV, 7, 18-19 ; and by
Hypsæus, quoted by Stobæus, in *Florilegium*,
120, 13. See Wordsworth's *The Excursion*, 1,
500 (p. 301). For an illustration of this sentiment, see the story of Cleobis and Bito, in
Herodotus's *Historiæ*, 1, 31.

Which men weep over may be meant to
    save!

13 Haidée and Juan thought not of the dead—
  The heavens, and earth, and air seem'd
    made for them:
They found no fault with Time, save that
    he fled;
  They saw not in themselves aught to con-
    demn;
Each was the other's mirror, and but read
  Joy sparkling in their dark eyes like a
    gem,
And knew such brightness was but the re-
    flection
Of their exchanging glances of affection.

14 The gentle pressure, and the thrilling
    touch,
  The least glance better understood than
    words,
Which still said all, and ne'er could say too
    much;
  A language, too, but like to that of birds,
Known but to them, at least appearing
    such
  As but to lovers a true sense affords;
Sweet playful phrases, which would seem
    absurd
To those who have ceased to hear such, or
    ne'er heard,—

15 All these were theirs, for they were chil-
    dren still,
  And children still they should have ever
    been;
They were not made in the real world to fill
  A busy character in the dull scene,
But like two beings born from out a rill,
  A nymph and her beloved, all unseen
To pass their lives in fountains and on
    flowers,
And never know the weight of human
    hours.

16 Moons changing had roll'd on, and change-
    less found
  Those their bright rise had lighted to
    such joys
As rarely they beheld throughout their
    round;
  And these were not of the vain kind
    which cloys,
For theirs were buoyant spirits, never
    bound
  By the mere senses; and that which de-
    stroys
Most love, possession, unto them appear'd
A thing which each endearment more en-
    dear'd.

17 Oh beautiful! and rare as beautiful!
　　But theirs was love in which the mind
　　　　delights
　　To lose itself, when the old world grows
　　　　dull,
　　And we are sick of its hack sounds and
　　　　sights,
　　Intrigues, adventures of the common
　　　　school,
　　Its petty passions, marriages, and flights,
　　Where Hymen's torch but brands one
　　　　strumpet more,
　　Whose husband only knows her not a
　　　　whore.

18 Hard words; harsh truth; a truth which
　　　　many know.
　　Enough.—The faithful and the fairy
　　　　pair,
　　Who never found a single hour too slow,
　　　　What was it made them thus exempt
　　　　　from care?
　　Young innate feelings all have felt below,
　　　　Which perish in the rest, but in them
　　　　　were
　　Inherent—what we mortals call romantic,
　　And always envy, though we deem it
　　　　frantic.

19 This is in others a factitious state,
　　An opium dream[1] of too much youth
　　　　and reading,
　　But was in them their nature or their fate:
　　No novels e'er had set their young hearts
　　　　bleeding,
　　For Haidée's knowledge was by no means
　　　　great,
　　And Juan was a boy of saintly breeding;
　　So that there was no reason for their loves
　　More than for those of nightingales or
　　　　doves.

20 They gazed upon the sunset; 'tis an hour
　　Dear unto all, but dearest to *their* eyes,
　　For it had made them what they were: the
　　　　power
　　Of love had first o'erwhelm'd them from
　　　　such skies,
　　When happiness had been their only dower,
　　　　And twilight saw them link'd in pas-
　　　　　sion's ties;
　　Charm'd with each other, all things
　　　　charm'd that brought
　　The past still welcome as the present
　　　　thought.

21 I know not why, but in that hour tonight,
　　Even as they gazed, a sudden tremor
　　　　came,

[1] Possibly Byron refers to Coleridge's *Kubla Khan* (p. 384).

And swept, as t'were, across their hearts'
　　delight,
　　Like the wind o'er a harp-string, or a
　　　　flame,
　　When one is shook in sound, and one in
　　　　sight:
　　And thus some boding flash'd through
　　　　either frame,
　　And call'd from Juan's breast a faint low
　　　　sigh,
　　While one new tear arose in Haidée's eye.

22 That large black prophet eye seem'd to
　　　　dilate
　　And follow far the disappearing sun,
　　As if their last day of a happy date
　　　　With his broad, bright, and dropping
　　　　　orb were gone;
　　Juan gazed on her as to ask his fate—
　　　　He felt a grief, but knowing cause for
　　　　　none,
　　His glance inquired of hers for some
　　　　excuse
　　For feelings causeless, or at least abstruse.

23 She turn'd to him, and smiled, but in that
　　　　sort
　　　　Which makes not others smile; then
　　　　　turn'd aside:
　　Whatever feeling shook her, it seem'd
　　　　short,
　　　　And master'd by her wisdom or her
　　　　　pride;
　　When Juan spoke, too—it might be in
　　　　sport—
　　　　Of this their mutual feeling, she re-
　　　　　plied—
　　"If it should be so,—but—it cannot be—
　　Or I at least shall not survive to see."

24 Juan would question further, but she
　　　　press'd
　　　　His lips to hers, and silenced him with
　　　　　this,
　　And then dismiss'd the omen from her
　　　　breast,
　　　　Defying augury with that fond kiss;
　　And no doubt of all methods 'tis the best:
　　　　Some people prefer wine—'tis not
　　　　　amiss;
　　I have tried both; so those who would a
　　　　part take
　　May choose between the headache and the
　　　　heartache.

25 One of the two according to your choice,
　　Woman or wine, you'll have to undergo;
　　Both maladies are taxes on our joys:

But which to choose, I really hardly
    know;
And if I had to give a casting voice,
    For both sides I could many reasons
      show,
And then decide, without great wrong to
    either,
It were much better to have both than
    neither.

26 Juan and Haidée gazed upon each other
    With swimming looks of speechless ten-
      derness,
Which mix'd all feelings—friend, child,
    lover, brother—,
All that the best can mingle and express
When two pure hearts are pour'd in one
    another,
And love too much, and yet cannot love
    less;
But almost sanctify the sweet excess
By the immortal wish and power to bless.

27 Mix'd in each other's arms, and heart in
    heart,
Why did they not then die?—they had
    lived too long
Should an hour come to bid them breathe
    apart;
    Years could but bring them cruel things
    or wrong;
The world was not for them, nor the
    world's art
    For beings passionate as Sappho's song;
Love was born *with* them, *in* them, so in-
    tense,
It was their very spirit—not a sense.

28 They should have lived together deep in
    woods,
Unseen as sings the nightingale;[1] they
    were
Unfit to mix in these thick solitudes
    Call'd social, haunts of Hate, and Vice,
    and Care;
How lonely every freeborn creature
    broods!
    The sweetest song-birds nestle in a pair;
The eagle soars alone; the gull and crow
Flock o'er their carrion, just like men
    below.

29 Now pillow'd cheek to cheek, in loving
    sleep,
Haidée and Juan their siesta took,
A gentle slumber, but it was not deep,
    For ever and anon a something shook

[1] See *The Two Gentlemen of Verona*, V, 4, 2-6.

Juan, and shuddering o'er his frame would
    creep;
    And Haidée's sweet lips murmur'd like
    a brook
A worldless music, and her face so fair
Stirr'd with her dream, as rose-leaves with
    the air;

30 Or as the stirring of a deep clear stream
    Within an Alpine hollow, when the wind
Walks o'er it, was she shaken by the dream,
    The mystical usurper of the mind—
O'erpowering us to be whate'er may seem
    Good to the soul which we no more can
    bind:
Strange state of being! (for 'tis still to be),
Senseless to feel, and with seal'd eyes to
    see.

31 She dream'd of being alone on the sea-
    shore,
    Chain'd to a rock; she knew not how,
    but stir
She could not from the spot, and the loud
    roar
    Grew, and each wave rose roughly,
    threatening her;
And o'er her upper lip they seem'd to
    pour,
Until she sobb'd for breath, and soon
    they were
Foaming o'er her lone head, so fierce and
    high—
Each broke to drown her, yet she could not
    die.

32 Anon—she was released, and then she
    stray'd
    O'er the sharp shingles with her bleeding
    feet,
And stumbled almost every step she made;
    And something roll'd before her in a
    sheet,
Which she must still pursue howe'er
    afraid:
    'Twas white and indistinct, nor stopp'd
    to meet
Her glance nor grasp, for still she gazed
    and grasp'd,
And ran, but it escaped her as she clasp'd.

33 The dream changed:—in a cave she stood,[1]
    its walls
    Were hung with marble icicles; the work
Of ages on its water-fretted halls,
    Where waves might wash, and seals
    might breed and lurk;

[1] See the description of the cave in Byron's
    The Island, 4, 121 ff.

Her hair was dripping, and the very
    balls
  Of her black eyes seem'd turn'd to tears,
    and mirk
The sharp rocks look'd below each drop
    they caught,
Which froze to marble as it fell,—she
    thought.

34 And wet, and cold, and lifeless at her feet,
    Pale as the foam that froth'd on his dead
    brow,
  Which she assay'd in vain to clear (how
    sweet
  Were once her cares, how idle seem'd
    they now!),
Lay Juan, nor could aught renew the beat
    Of his quench'd heart; and the sea
    dirges low
Rang in her sad ears like a mermaid's
    song,
And that brief dream appear'd a life too
    long.

35 And gazing on the dead, she thought his
    face
  Faded, or alter'd into something new—
Like to her father's features, till each trace
    More like and like to Lambro's aspect
    grew—
With all his keen worn look and Grecian
    grace;
  And starting, she awoke, and what to
    view?
Oh! Powers of Heaven! what dark eye
    meets she there
'Tis—'tis her father's—fixed upon the
    pair!

36 Then shrieking, she arose, and shrieking
    fell,
  With joy and sorrow, hope and fear, to
    see
Him whom she deem'd a habitant where
    dwell
  The ocean-buried, risen from death, to be
Perchance the death of one she loved too
    well;
  Dear as her father had been to Haidée,
It was a moment of that awful kind—
I have seen such—but must not call to
    mind.

37 Up Juan sprang to Haidée's bitter shriek,
    And caught her falling, and from off the
    wall
Snatch'd down his sabre, in hot haste to
    wreak

Vengeance on him who was the cause of
    all:
Then Lambro who till now forebore to
    speak,
  Smiled scornfully, and said, "Within
    my call,
A thousand scimitars await the word;
Put up, young man, put up your silly
    sword."

38 And Haidée clung around him; "Juan,
    'tis—
  'Tis Lambro—'tis my father! Kneel
    with me—
He will forgive us—yes—it must be—yes.
    Oh! dearest father, in this agony
Of pleasure and of pain—even while I kiss
    Thy garment's hem[1] with transport, can
    it be
That doubt should mingle with my filial
    joy?
Deal with me as thou wilt, but spare this
    boy."

39 High and inscrutable the old man stood,
    Calm in his voice, and calm within his
    eye—
  Not always signs with him of calmest
    mood:
  He look'd upon her, but gave no reply;
Then turn'd to Juan, in whose cheek the
    blood
  Oft came and went, as there resolved to
    die;
In arms, at least, he stood, in act to spring
On the first foe whom Lambro's call might
    bring.

40 "Young man, your sword;" so Lambro
    once more said:
  Juan replied, "Not while this arm is
    free."
The old man's cheek grew pale, but not
    with dread,
  And drawing from his belt a pistol, he
Replied, "Your blood be then on your own
    head."
  Then look'd close at the flint, as if to see
'Twas fresh—for he had lately used the
    lock—
And next proceeded quietly to cock.

41 It has a strange quick jar upon the ear,
    That cocking of a pistol, when you know
A moment more will bring the sight to bear

---

[1] To kiss the garments was a means of expressing veneration for the person who wore them.
See *Matthew.* 14 :36.

Upon your person, twelve yards off,
or so;
A gentlemanly distance, not too near,
If you have got a former friend for foe;
But after being fired at once or twice,
The ear becomes more Irish, and less nice.

42 Lambro presented, and one instant more
Had stopp'd this Canto, and Don Juan's
breath,
When Haidée threw herself her boy be-
fore;
Stern as her sire: "On me," she cried,
"let death
Descend—the fault is mine; this fatal
shore
He found—but sought not. I have
pledged my faith;
I love him—I will die with him: I knew
Your nature's firmness—know your daugh-
ter's too."

43 A minute past, and she had been all tears,
And tenderness, and infancy; but now
She stood as one who champion'd human
fears—
Pale, statue-like, and stern, she woo'd
the blow;
And tall beyond her sex, and their com-
peers,
She drew up to her height, as if to show
A fairer mark; and with a fix'd eye
scann'd
Her father's face—but never stopp'd his
hand.

44 He gazed on her, and she on him; 'twas
strange
How like they look'd! the expression was
the same;
Serenely savage, with a little change
In the large dark eye's mutual-darted
flame;
For she, too, was as one who could avenge,
If cause should be—a lioness, though
tame;
Her father's blood before her father's face
Boil'd up, and proved her truly of his race.

45 I said they were alike, their features and
Their stature, differing but in sex and
years:
Even to the delicacy of their hand
There was resemblance, such as true
blood wears;
And now to see them, thus divided, stand
In fix'd ferocity, when joyous tears,
And sweet sensations, should have wel-
comed both,

Show what the passions are in their full
growth.

46 The father paused a moment, then with-
drew
His weapon, and replaced it; but stood
still,
And looking on her, as to look her through,
"Not I," he said, "have sought this
stranger's ill;
Not I have made this desolation: few
Would bear such outrage, and forbear to
kill;
But I must do my duty—how thou hast
Done thine, the present vouches for the
past.

47 "Let him disarm; or, by my father's head,
His own shall roll before you like a
ball!"
He raised his whistle as the word he said,
And blew; another answer'd to the call,
And rushing in disorderly, though led,
And arm'd from boot to turban, one and
all,
Some twenty of his train came, rank on
rank;
He gave the word, "Arrest or slay the
Frank."

48 Then, with a sudden movement, he with-
drew
His daughter; while compress'd within
his clasp,
'Twixt her and Juan interposed the crew;
In vain she struggled in her father's
grasp—
His arms were like a serpent's coil: then
flew
Upon their prey, as darts an angry asp,
The file of pirates: save the foremost, who
Had fallen, with his right shoulder half cut
through.

49 The second had his cheek laid open; but
The third, a wary, cool old sworder, took
The blows upon his cutlass, and then put
His own well in; so well, ere you could
look,
His man was floor'd, and helpless at his
foot,
With the blood running like a little brook
From two smart sabre gashes, deep and
red—
One on the arm, the other on the head.

50 And then they bound him where he fell,
and bore
Juan from the apartment: with a sign

Old Lambro bade them take him to the
  shore,
  Where lay some ships which were to sail
    at nine.
They laid him in a boat, and plied the oar
  Until they reach'd some galliots,[1] placed
    in line;
On board of one of these, and under
    hatches,
  They stow'd him, with strict orders to the
    watches.

51 The world is full of strange vicissitudes,
  And here was one exceedingly unpleas-
    ant:
A gentleman so rich in the world's goods,
  Handsome and young, enjoying all the
    present,
Just at the very time when he least broods
  On such a thing, is suddenly to sea sent,
Wounded and chain'd, so that he cannot
    move,
  And all because a lady fell in love.

52 Here I must leave him, for I grow pathetic,
  Moved by the Chinese nymph of tears,
    green tea!
Than whom Cassandra was not more pro-
    phetic;
  For if my pure libations exceed three,
I feel my heart become so sympathetic,
  That I must have recourse to black
    Bohea:[2]
'Tis pity wine should be so deleterious,
  For tea and coffee leave us much more
    serious,

53 Unless when qualified with thee, Cogniac![3]
  Sweet Naïad of the Phlegethontic rill![4]
Ah! why the liver wilt thou thus attack,
  And make, like other nymphs, thy lovers
    ill?
I would take refuge in weak punch, but
    rack
  (In each sense[5] of the word), whene'er
    I fill
My mild and midnight beakers to the brim,
  Wakes me next morning with its syno-
    nym.[6]

54 I leave Don Juan for the present, safe—
  Not sound, poor fellow, but severely
    wounded;

[1] A small, swift galley moved by sails and oars.
[2] An inferior kind of black tea.
[3] A kind of French brandy.
[4] Phlegethon, the river of fire in Hades.
[5] That is, *punch* and *disorder*.
[6] That is, a headache.

Yet could his corporal pangs amount to
    half
  Of those with which his Haidée's bosom
    bounded!
She was not one to weep, and rave, and
    chafe,
  And then give way, subdued because sur-
    rounded;
Her mother was a Moorish maid from Fez,
  Where all is Eden, or a wilderness.

55 There the large olive rains its amber store
  In marble fonts; there grain, and flour,
    and fruit,
Gush from the earth until the land runs
    o'er;
  But there, too, many a poison-tree has
    root,
And midnight listens to the lion's roar,
  And long, long deserts scorch the camel's
    foot,
Or heaving whelm the helpless caravan;
  And as the soil is, so the heart of man.

56 Afric is all the sun's, and as her earth
  Her human clay is kindled; full of
    power
For good or evil, burning from its birth,
  The Moorish blood partakes the planet's
    hour,
And like the soil beneath it will bring
    forth:
  Beauty and love were Haidée's mother's
    dower;
But her large dark eye show'd deep Pas-
    sion's force,
  Though sleeping like a lion near a source.

57 Her daughter, temper'd with a milder ray,
  Like summer clouds all silvery, smooth,
    and fair,
Till slowly charged with thunder they dis-
    play
  Terror to earth, and tempest to the air,
Had held till now her soft and milky way,
  But overwrought with passion and des-
    pair,
The fire burst forth from her Numidian
    veins,
  Even as the Simoom sweeps the blasted
    plains.

58 The last sight which she saw was Juan's
    gore,
  And he himself o'ermaster'd and cut
    down;
His blood was running on the very floor
  Where late he trod, her beautiful, her
    own;

Thus much she view'd an instant and no
    more,—
  Her struggles ceased with one convulsive
    groan;
On her sire's arm, which until now scarce
    held
  Her writhing, fell she like a cedar fell'd.

59 A vein had burst, and her sweet lips' pure
    dyes
  Were dabbled with the deep blood which
    ran o'er;
And her head droop'd, as when the lily lies
  O'ercharged with rain: her summon'd
    handmaids bore
Their lady to her couch with gushing eyes;
  Of herbs and cordials they produced
    their store,
But she defied all means they could employ,
Like one life could not hold, nor death de-
    stroy.

60 Days lay she in that state unchanged,
    though chill—
  With nothing livid, still her lips were
    red;
She had no pulse, but death seem'd absent
    still;
  No hideous sign proclaim'd her surely
    dead;
Corruption came not in each mind to kill
  All hope; to look upon her sweet face
    bred
New thoughts of life, for it seem'd full of
    soul—
She had so much, earth could not claim the
    whole

61 The ruling passion, such as marble shows
  When exquisitely chisell'd, still lay there,
But fix'd as marble's unchanged aspect
    throws
  O'er the fair Venus, but forever fair;
O'er the Laocoön's all eternal throes,
  And ever-dying Gladiator's air,[1]
Their energy like life forms all their fame,
Yet looks not life, for they are still the
    same.

62 She woke at length, but not as sleepers
    wake,
  Rather the dead, for life seem'd some-
    thing new,
A strange sensation which she must par-
    take
  Perforce, since whatsoever met her view
Struck not on memory, though a heavy
    ache

[1] See *Childe Harold's Pilgrimage*, 4, 140 (p. 572).

Lay at her heart, whose earliest beat still
    true
Brought back the sense of pain without the
    cause,
For, for a while, the furies made a pause.

63 She look'd on many a face with vacant eye,
  On many a token without knowing what;
She saw them watch her without asking
    why,
  And reck'd not who around her pillow
    sat;
Not speechless, though she spoke not; **not**
    a sigh
  Relieved her thoughts; dull silence and
    quick chat
Were tried in vain by those who served;
    she gave
No sign, save breath, of having left the
    grave.

64 Her handmaids tended, but she heeded not;
  Her father watch'd, she turn'd her eyes
    away;
She recognized no being, and no spot,
  However dear or cherish'd in their **day**;
They changed from room to room—but all
    forgot—
  Gentle, but without memory she lay;
At length those eyes, which they would
    fain be weaning
Back to old thoughts, wax'd full of fearful
    meaning.

65 And then a slave bethought her of a harp;
  The harper came, and tuned his instru-
    ment;
At the first notes, irregular and sharp,
  On him her flashing eyes a moment **bent,**
Then to the wall she turn'd as if to warp
  Her thoughts from sorrow through her
    heart re-sent;
And he began a long low island song
Of ancient days, ere tyranny grew strong.[1]

66 Anon her thin wan fingers beat the wall
  In time to his old tune; he changed the
    theme,
And sung of love; the fierce name struck
    through all
  Her recollection; on her flash'd the
    dream
Of what she was, and is, if ye could call
  To be so being; in a gushing stream
The tears rush'd forth from her o'er-
    clouded brain,
Like mountain mists at length dissolved in
    rain.

[1] Cf. David's playing before Saul, *1 Samuel*,
16:16-23. See also Browning's *Saul*.

67 Short solace, vain relief!—thought came
    too quick,
    And whirl'd her brain to madness; she
    arose
As one who ne'er had dwelt among the sick,
    And flew at all she met, as on her foes;
But no one ever heard her speak or shriek,
    Although her paroxysm drew towards its
    close;—
Hers was a frenzy which disdain'd to rave,
Even when they smote her, in the hope to
save.

68 Yet she betray'd at times a gleam of sense;
    Nothing could make her meet her father's
    face,
Though on all other things with looks in-
    tense
    She gazed, but none she ever could
    retrace;
Food she refused, and raiment; no pretence
    Avail'd for either; neither change of
    place,
Nor time, nor skill, nor remedy, could give
    her
Senses to sleep—the power seem'd gone
    forever.

69 Twelve days and nights she wither'd thus;
    at last,
    Without a groan, or sigh, or glance, to
    show
A parting pang, the spirit from her passed:
    And they who watch'd her nearest could
    not know
The very instant, till the change that cast
    Her sweet face into shadow, dull and
    slow,
Glazed o'er her eyes—the beautiful, the
    black—
Oh! to possess such lustre—and then lack!

70 She died, but not alone; she held within
    A second principle of life, which might
Have dawn'd a fair and sinless child of
    sin;
    But closed its little being without light,
And went down to the grave unborn,
    wherein
    Blossom and bough lie wither'd with one
    blight;
In vain the dews of Heaven descend above
The bleeding flower and blasted fruit of
    love.

71 Thus lived—thus died she; never more on
    her
    Shall sorrow light, or shame. She was
    not made

Through years or moons the inner weight
    to bear,
    Which colder hearts endure till they are
    laid
By age in earth: her days and pleasures
    were
    Brief, but delightful—such as had not
    staid
Long with her destiny; but she sleeps
    well[1]
By the sea-shore, whereon she loved to
    dwell.

72 That isle is now all desolate and bare,
    Its dwellings down, its tenants pass'd
    away;
None but her own and father's grave is
    there,
    And nothing outward tells of human
    clay;
Ye could not know where lies a thing so
    fair,
    No stone is there to show, no tongue to
    say,
What was; no dirge, except the hollow
    sea's,
Mourns o'er the beauty of the Cyclades.

73 But many a Greek maid in a loving song
    Sighs o'er her name; and many an
    islander
With her sire's story makes the night less
    long;
    Valor was his, and beauty dwelt with
    her:
If she loved rashly, her life paid for
    wrong—
    A heavy price must all pay who thus err,
In some shape; let none think to fly the
    danger,
For soon or late Love is his own avenger.

•   •   •   •   •

From CANTO XI
1822-23   1823

53 Juan knew several languages—as well
    He might—and brought them up with
    skill, in time
To save his fame with each accomplish'd
    belle,
    Who still regretted that he did not
    rhyme.
There wanted but this requisite to swell
    His qualities (with them) into sublime:
Lady Fitz-Frisky, and Miss Mævia Man-
    nish,
Both long'd extremely to be sung in
    Spanish.

[1] See *Macbeth*, III, 2, 23.

54 However, he did pretty well, and was
    Admitted as an aspirant to all
The coteries, and, as in Banquo's glass,[1]
    At great assemblies or in parties small,
He saw ten thousand living authors pass,
    That being about their average numeral;
Also the eighty "greatest living poets,"
As every paltry magazine can show *its*.

55 In twice five years the "greatest living
    poet,"
    Like to the champion in the fisty ring,
Is call'd on to support his claim, or show
    it,
    Although 'tis an imaginary thing.
Even I—albeit I'm sure I did not know it,
    Nor sought of foolscap subjects to be
    king—
Was reckon'd, a considerable time,
    The grand Napoleon of the realms of
    rhyme.

56 But Juan was my Moscow, and Faliero
    My Leipsic, and my Mont Saint Jean
    seems Cain:[2]
"La Belle Alliance"[3] of dunces down at
    zero,
    Now that the Lion's fall'n, may rise
    again:
But I will fall at least as fell my hero;
    Nor reign at all, or as a *monarch* reign;
Or to some lonely isle of gaolers go,
    With turncoat Southey for my turnkey
    Lowe.

57 Sir Walter reign'd before me; Moore and
    Campbell
    Before and after: but now grown more
    holy,
The Muses upon Sion's hill must ramble
    With poets almost clergymen, or wholly:
And Pegasus has a psalmodic amble
    Beneath the very Reverend Rowley
    Powley,
Who shoes the glorious animal with stilts,
    A modern Ancient Pistol—by the hilts![4]

58 Still he excels that artificial hard
    Laborer[5] in the same vineyard, though
    the vine

[1] The glass in which Macbeth saw Banquo and his descendants as kings of Scotland.—*Macbeth*, IV, 1, 119-20.

[2] That is, Byron's heroes, Juan, Faliero, and Cain, were great literary disasters for him, as the battles mentioned were disasters for Napoleon.

[3] The handsome Alliance. A reference to the Lake poets—Wordsworth, Coleridge, and Southey.

[4] See 1 *Henry IV*, II, 4, 197.

[5] Henry Hart Milman (1791-1868), who Byron mistakenly thought wrote the critique which "killed John Keats." See st. 60 and n. 5.

Yields him but vinegar for his reward,—
    That neutralized dull Dorus of the Nine;
That swarthy Sporus, neither man nor
    bard;
    That ox of verse,[1] who *ploughs* for
    every line:—
Cambyses' roaring Romans[2] beat at least
    The howling Hebrews of Cybele's priest.—

59 Then there's my gentle Euphues,[3] who,
    they say,
    Sets up for being a sort of *moral me;*
He'll find it rather difficult some day
    To turn out both, or either, it may be.
Some persons think that Coleridge hath
    the sway;
    And Wordsworth has supporters, two
    or three;
And that deep-mouth'd Bœotian[4] "Sav-
    age Landor"
Has taken for a swan rogue Southey's
    gander

60 John Keats, who was kill'd off by one
    critique,[5]
    Just as he really promised something
    great,
If not intelligible, without Greek
    Contrived to talk about the gods of
    late,
Much as they might have been supposed
    to speak.
    Poor fellow! His was an untoward fate;
'Tis strange the mind, that very fiery
    particle,[6]
    Should let itself be snuff'd out by an
    article.

61 The list grows long of live and dead pre-
    tenders
    To that which none will gain—or none
    will know

[1] Milman recently had been appointed Professor of Poetry at Oxford.

[2] The shouting soldiers in Croly's *Cataline*, V, 2. Croly is Powley of st. 57.

[3] Bryan Waller Procter (Barry Cornwall), who had been said by Jeffrey, in *The Edinburgh Review*, Jan., 1820 (Vol. 33, p. 153), to possess the better qualities of Byron—elegance, delicacy, and tenderness—without the profligacy, horror, mocking of virtue and of honor, and mixture of buffoonery and grandeur.

[4] The Bœotians were proverbial for dullness. Landor had recently published a volume of Latin poems as the work of Savagius Landor. Savage was his middle name.

[5] A reference to the article on *Endymion* in *The Quarterly Review*, April, 1818 (Vol. 19, pp. 204-08). See Byron's *Who Kill'd John Keats?* (p. 639) and Shelley's Preface to *Adonais* (see Critical Note on Shelley's *Adonais*) and stanzas 36-37 (p. 761). The article referred to was written by J. W. Croker (p. 939), but it did not kill Keats. See Keats's letter to George and Georgiana Keats, October, 1818 (p. 890).

[6] See Horace's *Satires*, II, 2, 79.

The conqueror at least; who, ere Time renders
  His last award, will have the long grass grow
Above his burnt-out brain, and sapless cinders.
  If I might augur, I should rate but low
Their chances;—they're too numerous, like the thirty
Mock tyrants, when Rome's annals wax'd but dirty.[1]

62 This is the literary *lower* empire,
  Where the prætorian bands[2] take up the matter;—
A "dreadful trade," like his who "gathers samphire,"[3]
  The insolent soldiery to soothe and flatter,
With the same feelings as you'd coax a vampire.
  Now, were I once at home, and in good satire,
I'd try conclusions with those Janizaries,[4]
And show them *what* an intellectual war is.

63 I think I know a trick or two, would turn
  Their flanks;—but it is hardly worth my while
With such small gear to give myself concern:
  Indeed I've not the necessary bile;
My natural temper's really aught but stern,
  And even my Muse's worst reproof's a smile;
And then she drops a brief and modern curtsy,
And glides away, assured she never hurts ye.

64 My Juan, whom I left in deadly peril
  Amongst live poets and blue ladies,[5] pass'd
With some small profit through that field so sterile,

Being tired in time, and neither least nor last,
  Left it before he had been treated very ill;
And henceforth found himself more gaily class'd
  Amongst the higher spirits of the day,
The sun's true son, no vapor, but a ray.

65 His morns he pass'd in business—which dissected,
  Was like all business, a laborious nothing
That leads to lassitude, the most infected
  And Centaur Nessus garb of mortal clothing,
And on our sofas makes us lie dejected,
  And talk in tender horrors of our loathing
All kinds of toil, save for our country's good—
Which grows no better, though 'tis time it should.

66 His afternoons he pass'd in visits, luncheons,
  Lounging, and boxing; and the twilight hour
In riding round those vegetable puncheons
  Call'd "Parks," where there is neither fruit nor flower
Enough to gratify a bee's slight munchings;
  But after all it is the only "bower"[1]
(In Moore's phrase) where the fashionable fair
Can form a slight acquaintance with fresh air.

67 Then dress, then dinner, then awakes the world!
  Then glare the lamps, then whirl the wheels, then roar
Through street and square fast flashing chariots hurl'd
  Like harness'd meteors; then along the floor
Chalk mimics painting; then festoons are twirl'd;
  Then roll the brazen thunders of the door,
Which opens to the thousand happy few
An earthly Paradise of "Or Molu."[2]

68 There stands the noble hostess, nor shall sink
  With the three-thousandth curtsy; there the waltz,
The only dance which teaches girls to think,

[1] For an account of the body of pretenders to the Roman Empire, in the 3rd century, popularly called "The Thirty Tyrants," see Gibbon's *The History of the Decline and Fall of the Roman Empire*, ch. 10.
[2] The prætorian cohorts, a body of troops stationed just outside the walls of Rome and acting as a special guard of the Emperor. At times they controlled the selection of Emperor. See Gibbon's *History*, ch. 5.
[3] *King Lear*, IV, 6, 15.
[4] A former body of Turkish infantry constituting the Sultan's guard and the main part of the standing army. Before it was abolished in 1826, it became very powerful and turbulent.
[5] Literary pedants. See p. 611b, n. 1.

[1] In Moore's "phrase," a bower is a secret place for two.
[2] Gilded Bronze.

Makes one in love even with its very
    faults.
Saloon, room, hall, o'erflow beyond their
    brink,
And long the latest of arrivals halts,
    'Midst royal dukes and dames condemn'd
    to climb,
And gain an inch of staircase at a time.

69 Thrice happy he who, after a survey
    Of the good company, can win a corner,
A door that's *in* or boudoir *out* of the
    way,
    Where he may fix himself like small
      "Jack Horner,"
And let the Babel round run as it may,
    And look on as a mourner, or a scorner,
Or an approver, or a mere spectator,
Yawning a little as the night grows later.

70 But this won't do, save by and by; and he
    Who, like Don Juan, takes an active
    share,
Must steer with care through all that glit-
    tering sea
    Of gems and plumes and pearls and
    silks, to where
He deems it is his proper place to be;
    Dissolving in the waltz to some soft air,
Or proudlier prancing with mercurial skill,
Where Science marshals forth her own
    quadrille.

71 Or, if he dance not, but hath higher views
    Upon an heiress or his neighbor's bride,
Let him take care that that which he pur-
    sues
    Is not at once too palpably descried.
Full many an eager gentleman oft rues
    His haste; impatience is a blundering
    guide,
Amongst a people famous for reflection,
Who like to play the fool with circum-
    spection.

72 But, if you can contrive, get next at sup-
    per;
    Or if forestall'd, get opposite and
    ogle:—
Oh, ye ambrosial moments! always upper
    In mind, a sort of sentimental bogle,[1]
Which sits for ever upon memory's crup-
    per,
    The ghost of vanish'd pleasures once in
    vogue! Ill
Can tender souls relate the rise and fall
Of hopes and fears which shake a single
    ball.

73 But these precautionary hints can touch
    Only the common run, who must pursue,

[1] goblin

And watch, and ward;[1] whose plans a
    word too much
    Or little overturns; and not the few
Or many (for the number's sometimes
    such)
    Whom a good mien, especially if new,
Or fame, or name, for wit, war, sense,
    or nonsense,
Permits whate'er they please, or *did* not
    long since.

74 Our hero, as a hero, young and handsome,
    Noble, rich, celebrated, and a stranger,
Like other slaves of course must pay his
    ransom,
    Before he can escape from so much
    danger
As will environ a conspicuous man. Some
    Talk about poetry, and "rack and man-
    ger,"[2]
And ugliness, disease, as toil and trouble;—
I wish they knew the life of a young noble.

    .   .   .   .   .

86 But "carpe diem,"[3] Juan, "carpe,
    carpe!"
    Tomorrow sees another race as gay
And transient, and devour'd by the same
    harpy.
"Life's a poor player,"[4]—then "play out
    the play,
Ye villains!"[5] and above all keep a sharp
    eye
Much less on what you do than what you
    you say:
Be hypocritical, be cautious, be
Not what you *seem*, but always what you
    see.

87 But how shall I relate in other cantos
    Of what befell our hero in the land,
Which 'tis the common cry and lie to
    vaunt as
    A moral country? But I hold my
    hand—
For I disdain to write an Atalantis;
    But 'tis well at once to understand
You are *not* a moral people, and you
    know it
Without the aid of too sincere a poet.

88 What Juan saw and underwent shall be
    My topic, with of course the due restric-
    tion
Which is required by proper courtesy;
    And recollect the work is only fiction,

[1] guard
[2] The phrase means *waste, disorder*.
[3] "Carpe diem, quam minimum credulo postero."
    —Horace, *Odes*, I, 11, 8. (Seize the **day**,
    trust the future as little as possible.)
[4] *Macbeth*, V, 5, 24.
[5] 1 *Henry IV*, II, 4, 463.

And that I sing of neither mine nor me,
　Though every scribe, in some slight turn
　　of diction,
Will hint allusions never *meant*. Ne'er
　doubt
This—when I speak, I *don't hint*, but *speak
　out*.

89 Whether he married with the third or
　　fourth
　Offspring of some sage husband-hunting
　　countess,
Or whether with some virgin of more
　　worth
　(I mean in Fortune's matrimonial
　　bounties)
He took to regularly peopling Earth,
　Of which your lawful, awful wedlock
　　fount is—
Or whether he was taken in for damages,
For being too excursive in his homages,—

90 Is yet within the unread events of time.
　Thus far, go forth, thou lay, which I
　　will back
Against the same given quantity of rhyme,
　For being as much the subject of attack
As ever yet was any work sublime,
　By those who love to say that white is
　　black.
So much the better!—I may stand alone,
But would not change my free thoughts for
　a throne.

. . . .

WHEN A MAN HATH NO FREEDOM TO FIGHT FOR AT HOME
1820 　　　 1824

When a man hath no freedom to fight for
　at home,
　Let him combat for that of his neigh-
　　bors;
Let him think of the glories of Greece and
　of Rome,
　And get knock'd on his head for his
　　labors.

5 To do good to mankind is the chivalrous
　plan,
　And is always as nobly requited;
Then battle for freedom wherever you can,
　And, if not shot or hang'd, you'll get
　　knighted.

THE WORLD IS A BUNDLE OF HAY
1821 　　　 1830

The world is a bundle of hay,
　Mankind are the asses who pull;
Each tugs it a different way.
　And the greatest of all is John Bull.

WHO KILL'D JOHN KEATS[1]
1821 　　　 1830

"Who kill'd John Keats?"
　"I," says *The Quarterly*,
So savage and Tartarly;
　" 'Twas one of my feats."

5 "Who shot the arrow?"
　"The poet-priest Milman
(So ready to kill man),
　Or Southey, or Barrow."

FOR ORFORD AND FOR WALDEGRAVE
1821 　　　 1830

For Orford and for Waldegrave
You give much more than me you *gave;*
Which is not fairly to behave,
　　　　My Murray!

5 Because if a live dog, 'tis said,
Be worth a lion fairly sped,
A *live lord* must be worth *two* dead,
　　　　My Murray!

And if, as the opinion goes,
10 Verse hath a better sale than prose,—
Certes, I should have more than those,
　　　　My Murray!

But now this sheet is nearly cramm'd,
So, if *you will, I* shan't be shamm'd,
15 And if you *won't,—you* may be damn'd,
　　　　My Murray.

THE VISION OF JUDGMENT[2]
1821 　　　 1822

1 Saint Peter sat by the celestial gate:
　His keys were rusty, and the lock was
　　dull,
So little trouble had been given of late;
　Not that the place by any means was
　　full,
But since the Gallic era "eighty-eight"[3]
　The devils had ta'en a longer, stronger
　　pull,
And "a pull all together," as they say
At sea—which drew most souls another
　way.

2 The angels all were singing out of tune,
　And hoarse with having little else to do,
Excepting to wind up the sun and moon,
　Or curb a runaway young star or two,
Or wild colt of a comet, which too soon
　Broke out of bounds o'er the ethereal
　　blue,

[1] See Byron's *Don Juan*, XI, 60 and n. 5 (p. 636b).
[2] See Southey's *A Vision of Judgment* (p. 435).
[3] The French Revolution, which began in 1788.

Splitting some planet with its playful tail,
As boats are sometimes by a wanton whale.

3 The guardian seraphs had retired on high,
    Finding their charges past all care be-
       low;
Terrestrial business fill'd nought in the
       sky
Save the recording angel's black bureau;
Who found, indeed, the facts to multiply
    With such rapidity of vice and woe,
That he had stripp'd off both his wings in
       quills,
And yet was in arrear of human ills.

4 His business so augmented of late years,
    That he was forced, against his will no
       doubt
(Just like those cherubs, earthly minis-
       ters),
    For some resource to turn himself about,
And claim the help of his celestial peers,
    To aid him ere he should be quite worn
       out
By the increased demand for his remarks:
Six angels and twelve saints were named
       his clerks.

5 This was a handsome board—at least for
       heaven;
    And yet they had even then enough to
       do,
So many conquerors' cars were daily
       driven,
    So many kingdoms fitted up anew;
Each day too slew its thousands six or
       seven,
Till at the crowning carnage, Waterloo,
They threw their pens down in divine
       disgust—
The page was so besmear'd with blood and
       dust.

6 This by the way; 'tis not mine to record
    What angels shrink from: even the very
       devil
On this occasion his own work abhorr'd,
    So surfeited with the infernal revel:
Though he himself had sharpen'd every
       sword,
    It almost quench'd his innate thirst of
       evil.
(Here Satan's sole good work deserves
       insertion—
'Tis, that he has both generals[1] in rever-
       sion.)[2]

7 Let's skip a few short years of hollow
       peace,
    Which peopled earth no better, hell as
       wont,
And heaven none—they form the tyrant's
       lease,
    With nothing but new names sub-
       scribed upon 't;
'Twill one day finish: meantime they in-
       crease,
    "With seven heads and ten horns,"
       and all in front,
Like Saint John's foretold beast;[1] but ours
       are born
Less formidable in the head than horn.

8 In the first year of freedom's second
       dawn[2]
    Died George the Third; although no
       tyrant, one
Who shielded tyrants, till each sense with-
       drawn
    Left him nor mental nor external sun:
A better farmer ne'er brush'd dew from
       lawn,
    A worse king never left a realm undone!
He died—but left his subjects still behind,
One half as mad—and t'other no less blind.

9 He died!—his death made no great stir on
       earth:
    His burial made some pomp; there was
       profusion
Of velvet, gilding, brass, and no great
       dearth
    Of aught but tears—save those shed by
       collusion.
For these things may be bought at their
       true worth;
    Of elegy there was the due infusion—
Bought also; and the torches, cloaks, and
       banners,
Heralds, and relics of old Gothic manners,[3]

10 Form'd a sepulchral melodrame. Of all
    The fools who flock'd to swell or see the
       show,
Who cared about the corpse? The funeral
Made the attraction, and the black the
       woe.
There throbb'd not there a thought which
       pierced the pall;
    And when the gorgeous coffin was laid
       low,

---

[1] Wellington and Napoleon.
[2] That is, his by right of future possession.

[1] See *Revelation*. 13.
[2] The year 1820, in which the revolutionary
   spirit broke out all over southern Europe.
[3] That is, of the Age of Chivalry, which was
   noted for its display.

It seem'd the mockery of hell to fold
The rottenness of eighty years in gold.

11 So mix his body with the dust! It might
    Return to what it *must* far sooner, were
The natural compound left alone to fight
    Its way back into earth, and fire, and
      air;
But the unnatural balsams merely blight
    What nature made him at his birth, as
      bare
As the mere million's base unmummied
    clay—
Yet all his spices but prolong decay.

12 He's dead—and upper earth with him has
    done;
    He's buried; save the undertaker's bill,
Or lapidary scrawl,[1] the world is gone
    For him, unless he left a German will:[2]
But where's the proctor who will ask his
    son?[3]
In whom his qualities are reigning still,
    Except that household virtue, most un-
      common,
Of constancy to a bad, ugly woman.

13 "God save the king!" It is a large
    economy
    In God to save the like; but if he will
Be saving, all the better; for not one am I
    Of those who think damnation better
      still:
I hardly know too if not quite alone am I
    In this small hope of bettering future ill
By circumscribing, with some slight re-
    striction,
The eternity of hell's hot jurisdiction.

14 I know this is unpopular; I know
    'Tis blasphemous; I know one may be
      damn'd
For hoping no one else may e'er be so;
    I know my catechism; I know we're
      cramm'd
With the best doctrine till we quite o'er-
    flow;
    I know that all save England's church
      have shamm'd,
And that the other twice two hundred
    churches
And synagogues have made a *damn'd* bad
    purchase.

15 God help us all! God help me too! I am,
    God knows, as helpless as the devil can
      wish,
And not a whit more difficult to damn,
    Than is to bring to land a late-hook'd
      fish,
Or to the butcher to purvey the lamb;
    Not that I'm fit for such a noble dish,
As one day will be that immortal fry
Of almost everybody born to die.

16 Saint Peter sat by the celestial gate,
    And nodded o'er his keys; when, lo!
      there came
A wondrous noise he had not heard of
    late—
    A rushing sound of wind, and stream,
      and flame;
In short, a roar of things extremely
    great,
    Which would have made aught save a
      saint exclaim;
But he, with first a start and then a wink,
Said, "There's another star gone out, I
    think!"

17 But ere he could return to his repose,
    A cherub flapp'd his right wing o'er his
      eyes—
At which St. Peter yawn'd, and rubb'd his
    nose:
    "Saint porter," said the angel, "prithee
      rise!"
Waving a goodly wing, which glow'd, as
    glows
    An earthly peacock's tail, with heavenly
      dyes:
To which the saint replied, "Well, what's
    the matter?
"Is Lucifer come back with all this
    clatter?"

18 "No," quoth the cherub; "George the
    Third is dead."
    "And who *is* George the Third?" re-
      plied the apostle:
"*What George? what Third?*"—"The
    king of England," said
The angel. "Well! he won't find kings
    to jostle
Him on his way; but does he wear his
    head?
    Because the last we saw here had a
      tussle,
And ne'er would have got into heaven's
    good graces,
Had he not flung his head in all our
    faces.

---

[1] Inscription on a tombstone
[2] The Georges belonged to the German house of Hanover. Byron frequently sneered at the Germans.
[3] A thrust at George IV, who was thought capable of following the example of George II in concealing his father's will. See *Don Juan*, XI, 78, 3. The proctor was a special officer of the court.

19 "He was, if I remember, king of France;[1]
 That head of his, which could not keep
  a crown
On earth, yet ventured in my face to ad-
  vance
 A claim to those of martyrs—like my
  own:
If I had had my sword, as I had once
 When I cut ears off, I had cut him down;
But having but my *keys,* and not my brand,
I only knock'd his head from out his hand.

20 "And then he set up such a headless howl,
 That all the saints came out and took
  him in;
And there he sits by St. Paul, cheek by
  jowl;
 That fellow Paul—the parvenù![2] The
  skin
Of St. Bartholomew, which makes his cowl
 In heaven, and upon earth redeem'd his
  sin,
So as to make a martyr, never sped
Better than did this weak and wooden head.

21 "But had it come up here upon its shoul-
  ders,
 There would have been a different tale to
  tell:
The fellow-feeling in the saint's beholders
 Seems to have acted on them like a spell,
And so this very foolish head heaven
  solders
 Back on its trunk: it may be very well,
And seems the custom here to overthrow
Whatever has been wisely done below."

22 The angel answer'd, "Peter! do not pout:
 The king who comes has head and all
  entire,
And never knew much what it was about;
 He did as doth the puppet—by its wire,
And will be judged like all the rest, no
  doubt:
 My business and your own is not to
  inquire
Into such matters, but to mind our cue—
Which is to act as we are bid to do."

23 While thus they spake, the angelic caravan,
 Arriving like a rush of mighty wind,
Cleaving the fields of space, as doth the
  swan
 Some silver stream (say Ganges, Nile,
  or Inde,
Or Thames, or Tweed), and 'midst them
  an old man

[1] Louis XVI, who was guillotined in January, 1793.
[2] upstart

With an old soul, and both **extremely**
 blind,
Halted before the gate, and in his shroud
Seated their fellow traveller on a cloud.

24 But bringing up the rear of this bright host
 A Spirit of a different aspect waved
His wings, like thunder-clouds above some
  coast
 Whose barren beach with frequent
  wrecks is paved;
His brow was like the deep when tempest-
  toss'd;
 Fierce and unfathomable thoughts en-
  graved
Eternal wrath on his immortal face,
And *where* he gazed a gloom pervaded
  space.

25 As he drew near, he gazed upon the gate
 Ne'er to be enter'd more by him or sin,
With such a glance of supernatural hate,
 As made Saint Peter wish himself with-
  in;
He patter'd with his keys at a great rate,
 And sweated through his apostolic skin:
Of course his perspiration was but ichor,[1]
Or some such other spiritual liquor.

26 The very cherubs huddled all together,
 Like birds when soars the falcon; and
  they felt
A tingling to the tip of every feather,
 And form'd a circle like Orion's belt
Around their poor old charge; who scarce
  knew whither
 His guards had led him, though they
  gently dealt
With royal manes (for by many stories,
And true, we learn the angels are all
  Tories).

27 As things were in this posture, the gate
  flew
 Asunder, and the flashing of its hinges
Flung over space an universal hue
 Of many-color'd flame, until its tinges
Reach'd even our speck of earth, and made
  a new
 Aurora borealis spread its fringes
O'er the North Pole; the same seen, when
  ice-bound,
By Captain Parry's crew, in "Melville's
  Sound."

28 And from the gate thrown open issued
  beaming
 A beautiful and mighty Thing of Light,

[1] ethereal fluid that flowed in the veins of the gods

Radiant with glory, like a banner stream-
    ing
Victorious from some world-o'erthrow-
    ing fight:
My poor comparisons must needs be
    teeming
    With earthly likenesses, for here the
      night
Of clay obscures our best conceptions,
    saving
    Johanna Southcote,[1] or Bob Southey
      raving.

29 'Twas the archangel Michael; all men
    know
    The make of angels and archangels, since
There's scarce a scribbler has not one to
    show,
    From the fiends' leader to the angels'
      prince;
There also are some altar-pieces, though
    I really can't say that they much evince
One's inner notions of immortal spirits;
But let the connoisseurs explain *their*
    merits.

30 Michael flew forth in glory and in good;
    A goodly work of him from whom all
      glory
And good arise; the portal past—he stood;
    Before him the young cherubs and saints
      hoary—
(I say *young,* begging to be understood
    By looks, not years; and should be very
      sorry
To state, they were not older than St. Peter,
But merely that they seem'd a little
      sweeter).

31 The cherubs and the saints bow'd down
    before
    That arch-angelic hierarch, the first
Of essences angelical, who wore
    The aspect of a god; but this ne'er
      nursed
Pride in his heavenly bosom, in whose core
No thought, save for his Maker's serv-
    ice, durst
Intrude, however glorified and high;
He knew him but the viceroy of the sky.

32 He and the sombre, silent Spirit met—
    They knew each other both for good and
      ill;
Such was their power, that neither could
    forget
    His former friend and future foe; but
      still

There was a high, immortal, proud regret
    In either's eye, as if 'twere less their will
Than destiny to make the eternal years
Their date of war, and their "champ
    clos"[1] the spheres.

33 But here they were in neutral space: we
    know
    From Job, that Satan hath the power to
      pay
A heavenly visit thrice a year or so;
    And that the "sons of God,"[2] like those
      of clay,
Must keep him company; and we might
    show
    From the same book, in how polite a way
The dialogue is held between the Powers
Of Good and Evil—but 'twould take up
    hours.

34 And this is not a theologic tract,
    To prove with Hebrew and with Arabic,
If Job be allegory or a fact,
    But a true narrative; and thus I pick
From out the whole but such and such an
    act
    As sets aside the slightest thought of
      trick.
'Tis every tittle true, beyond suspicion,
And accurate as any other vision.

35 The spirits were in neutral space, before
    The gate of heaven; like eastern thres-
      holds is
The place where Death's grand cause is
    argued o'er,
    And souls despatch'd to that world or to
      this;
And therefore Michael and the other wore
    A civil aspect; though they did not kiss,
Yet still between his Darkness and his
    Brightness
There pass'd a mutual glance of great
    politeness.

36 The Archangel bow'd, not like a modern
    beau,
    But with a graceful Oriental bend,
Pressing one radiant arm just where below
    The heart in good men is supposed to
      tend;
He turn'd as to an equal, not too low,
    But kindly; Satan met his ancient friend
With more hauteur, as might an old Cas-
    tilian
Poor noble meet a mushroom rich civilian.

---

[1] She believed that she was to give birth to a new
Messiah. See Byron's *Don Juan,* III, 95, 4,
and n. 2 (p. 625).

[1] closed field for combat at a tourney
[2] *Job.* 1:6.

37 He merely bent his diabolic brow
    An instant; and then raising it, he stood
In act to assert his right or wrong, and
    show
    Cause why King George by no means
      could or should
Make out a case to be exempt from woe
    Eternal, more than other kings, endued
With better sense and hearts, whom his-
    tory mentions,
Who long have "paved hell with their good
    intentions."[1]

38 Michael began: "What wouldst thou with
    this man,
    Now dead, and brought before the Lord?
      What ill
Hath he wrought since his mortal race
    began,
    That thou canst claim him? Speak!
      and do thy will,
If it be just: if in this earthly span
    He hath been greatly failing to fulfil
His duties as a king and mortal, say,
And he is thine; if not, let him have way."

39 "Michael!" replied the Prince of Air,
    "even here
Before the gate of him thou servest, must
    I claim my subject: and will make appear
    That as he was my worshipper in dust,
So shall he be in spirit, although dear
    To thee and thine, because nor wine nor
      lust
Were of his weaknesses; yet on the throne
He reign'd o'er millions to serve me alone.

40 "Look to *our* earth, or rather *mine;* it was,
    Once, more thy master's: but I triumph
      not
In this poor planet's conquest; nor, alas!
    Need he thou servest envy me my lot:
With all the myriads of bright worlds
    which pass
    In worship round him, he may have
      forgot
Yon weak creation of such paltry things:
I think few worth damnation save their
    kings,—

41 "And these but as a kind of quit-rent,[2] to
    Assert my right as lord; and even had
I such an inclination, 'twere (as you
    Well know) superfluous; they are grown
    so bad,

That hell has nothing better left to do
    Than leave them to themselves: so much
      more mad
And evil by their own internal curse,
Heaven cannot make them better, nor I
    worse.

42 "Look to the earth, I said, and say again:
    When this old, blind, mad, helpless,
      weak, poor worm
Began in youth's first bloom and flush to
    reign,
    The world and he both wore a different
      form,
And much of earth and all the watery plain
    Of ocean call'd him king: through many
      a storm
His isles had floated on the abyss of time;
For the rough virtues chose them for their
    clime.

43 "He came to his sceptre young; he leaves
    it old:[1]
    Look to the state in which he found his
      realm,
And left it; and his annals too behold,
    How to a minion first he gave the helm;[2]
How grew upon his heart a thirst for
    gold,
    The beggar's vice, which can but over-
      whelm
The meanest hearts; and for the rest, but
    glance
Thine eye along America and France.

44 'Tis true, he was a tool from first to last
    (I have the workmen safe); but as a
      tool
So let him be consumed. From out the
    past
    Of ages, since mankind have known the
      rule
Of monarchs—from the bloody rolls
    amass'd
    Of sin and slaughter—from the Cæsar's
      school,
Take the worst pupil; and produce a reign
More drench'd with gore, more cumber'd
    with the slain.

45 "He ever warr'd with freedom and the
    free:
    Nations as men, home subjects, foreign
      foes,
So that they utter'd the word 'Liberty!'

---

[1] A proverb found in most modern languages.
It was a saying of Samuel Johnson's. See
Boswell's *The Life of Samuel Johnson* (Oxford ed., 1904), 1, 591.
[2] fixed rent paid by a tenant in commutation of
services

[1] George III reigned from 1760 to 1820.
[2] John Stuart, Earl of Bute (1713-92), who as
Secretary of State and as Prime Minister exercised a considerable influence upon George
III.

Found George the Third their first oppo-
nent. Whose
History was ever stain'd as his will be
With national and individual woes?
I grant his household abstinence; I grant
His neutral virtues, which most monarchs
want;

46 "I know he was a constant consort; own
He was a decent sire, and middling lord.
All this is much, and most upon a throne;
As temperance, if at Apicius' board,
Is more than at an anchorite's supper
shown.
I grant him all the kindest can accord;
And this was well for him, but not for those
Millions who found him what oppression
chose.

47 "The New World shook him off; the Old
yet groans
Beneath what he and his prepared, if not
Completed; he leaves heirs on many
thrones
To all his vices, without what begot
Compassion for him—his tame virtues;
drones
Who sleep, or despots who have now
forgot
A lesson which shall be re-taught them,
wake
Upon the thrones of earth; but let them
quake!

48 "Five millions of the primitive, who hold
The faith which makes ye great on
earth,[1] implored
A *part* of that vast *all* they held of old,—
Freedom to worship—not alone your
Lord,
Michael, but you, and you, Saint Peter!
Cold
Must be your souls, if you have not
abhorr'd
The foe to Catholic participation
In all the license of a Christian nation.

49 "True! he allow'd them to pray God;
but as
A consequence of prayer, refused the
law
Which would have placed them upon the
same base
With those who did not hold the saints
in awe."
But here Saint Peter started from his
place,

[1] Roman Catholics, whom George III refused to
admit to political office.

And cried, "You may the prisoner with-
draw:
Ere heaven shall ope her portals to this
Guelph,[1]
While I am guard, may I be damn'd my-
self!

50 "Sooner will I with Cerberus exchange
My office (and *his* is no sinecure)
Than see this royal Bedlam bigot range
The azure fields of heaven, of that be-
sure!"
"Saint!" replied Satan, "you do well to
avenge
The wrongs he made your satellites en-
dure;
And if to this exchange you should be
given,
I'll try to coax *our* Cerberus up to
heaven!"

51 Here Michael interposed: "Good saint!
and devil!
Pray, not so fast; you both outrun dis-
cretion.
Saint Peter! you were wont to be more
civil!
Satan! excuse this warmth of his ex-
pression,
And condescension to the vulgar's level:
Even saints sometimes forget themselves
in session.
Have you got more to say?"—"No."—
"If you please,
I'll trouble you to call your witnesses."

52 Then Satan turn'd and waved his swarthy
hand,
Which stirr'd with its electric qualities
Clouds farther off than we can understand,
Although we find him sometimes in our
skies.
Infernal thunder shook both sea and land
In all the planets, and hell's batteries
Let off the artillery, which Milton mentions
As one of Satan's most sublime inven-
tions.[2]

53 This was a signal unto such damn'd souls
As have the privilege of their damnation
Extended far beyond the mere controls
Of worlds past, present, or to come; no
station
Is theirs particularly in the rolls
Of hell assign'd; but where their in-
clination

[1] The House of Hanover was descended from the
Guelphs.
[2] See *Paradise Lost*, 6, 484 ff.

Or business carries them in search of
   game,
They may range freely—being damn'd the
   same.

54 They're proud of this—as very well they
   may,
   It being a sort of knighthood, or gilt
     key
Stuck in their loins;[1] or like to an
   "entré"[2]
Up the back stairs, or such free-masonry.
I borrow my comparisons from clay,
   Being clay myself. Let not those spirits
     be
Offended with such base low likenesses;
We know their posts are nobler far than
   these.

55 When the great signal ran from heaven to
   hell—
   About ten million times the distance
     reckon'd
From our sun to its earth, as we can tell
   How much time it takes up, even to a
     second,
For every ray that travels to dispel
   The fogs of London, through which,
     dimly beacon'd,
The weathercocks are gilt some thrice a
   year,
If that the *summer* is not too severe:

56 I say that I can tell—'twas half a minute;
   I know the solar beams take up more
     time
Ere, pack'd up for their journey, they
   begin it;
But then their telegraph is less sublime,
And if they ran a race, they would not
   win it
'Gainst Satan's couriers bound for their
   own clime.
The sun takes up some years for every ray
To reach its goal—the devil not half a day.

57 Upon the verge of space, about the size
   Of half-a-crown, a little speck appear'd
(I've seen a something like it in the skies
   In the Ægean, ere a squall); it near'd,
And, growing bigger, took another guise;
   Like an aërial ship it tack'd, and steer'd,
Or *was* steer'd (I am doubtful of the
   grammar
Of the last phrase, which makes the stanza
   stammer;—

58 But take your choice); and then it grew a
   cloud;
And so it was—a cloud of witnesses.
But such a cloud! No land e'er saw a
   crowd
   Of locusts numerous as the heavens saw
     these;
They shadow'd with their myriads space;
   their loud
   And varied cries were like those of wild
     geese
(If nations may be liken'd to a goose),
And realized the phrase of "hell broke
   loose."[1]

59 Here crash'd a sturdy oath of stout John
   Bull,
   Who damn'd away his eyes as hereto-
     fore:
There Paddy brogued "By Jasus!"—
   "What's your wull?"
   The temperate Scot exclaim'd: the
     French ghost swore
In certain terms I shan't translate in full,
   As the first coachman will; and 'midst
     the war,
The voice of Jonathan was heard to ex-
   press,
"*Our* president is going to war, I guess."

60 Besides there were the Spaniard, Dutch,
   and Dane;
   In short, an universal shoal of shades,
From Otaheite's isle to Salisbury Plain,
   Of all climes and professions, years and
     trades,
Ready to swear against the good king's
   reign,
   Bitter as clubs in cards are against
     spades:
All summon'd by this grand "subpœna,"
   to
Try if kings mayn't be damn'd like me or
   you.

61 When Michael saw this host, he first grew
   pale,
   As angels can; next, like Italian twi-
     light,
He turn'd all colors—as a peacock's tail,
   Or sunset streaming through a Gothic
     skylight
In some old abbey, or a trout not stale,
   Or distant lightning on the horizon *by*
     night,
Or a fresh rainbow, or a grand review
Of thirty regiments in red, green, and blue.

---

[1] A gold key is an insignia of the office of Lord
   Chamberlain and of other court officials.
[2] right of entry

[1] See *Paradise Lost*, 4, 918. Other references
   are cited in Murray's *A New English Dictionary* under *hell*, 10.

62 Then he address'd himself to Satan:
    "Why—
  My good old friend, for such I deem you,
    though
  Our different parties make us fight so shy,
  I ne'er mistake you for a *personal* foe;
  Our difference is *political*, and I
    Trust that, whatever may occur below,
  You know my great respect for you: and
    this
  Makes me regret whate'er you do amiss—

63 "Why, my dear Lucifer, would you abuse
    My call for witnesses? I did not mean
  That you should half of earth and hell
    produce;
  'Tis even superfluous, since two honest,
    clean,
  True testimonies are enough: we lose
    Our time, nay, our eternity, between
  The accusation and defence: if we
  Hear both, 'twill stretch our immortality."

64 Satan replied, "To me the matter is
    Indifferent, in a personal point of view:
  I can have fifty better souls than this
    With far less trouble than we have gone
    through
  Already; and I merely argued his
    Late majesty of Britain's case with you
  Upon a point of form: you may dispose
  Of him; I've kings enough below, God
    knows!"

65 Thus spoke the Demon (late call'd "multi-
    faced"[1]
  By multo-scribbling Southey). "Then
    we'll call
  One or two persons of the myriads placed
    Around our congress, and dispense with
    all
  The rest," quoth Michael: "Who may be
    so graced
  As to speak first? there's choice enough
    —who shall
  It be?" Then Satan answer'd, "There
    are many;
  But you may choose Jack Wilkes as well as
    any."

66 A merry, cock-eyed, curious-looking sprite
    Upon the instant started from the
    throng,
  Dress'd in a fashion now forgotten quite;
    For all the fashions of the flesh stick
    long
  By people in the next world; where unite

[1] Southey, *A Vision of Judgment*, 5, 70.

All the costumes since Adam's, right or
    wrong,
  From Eve's fig-leaf down to the petticoat,
  Almost as scanty, of days less remote.

67 The spirit look'd around upon the crowds
    Assembled, and exclaim'd, "My friends
    of all
  The spheres, we shall catch cold amongst
    these clouds;
  So let's to business: why this general
    call?
  If those are freeholders I see in shrouds,
    And 'tis for an election that they bawl,
  Behold a candidate with unturn'd coat![1]
  Saint Peter, may I count upon your vote?"

68 "Sir," replied Michael, "you mistake;
    these things
  Are of a former life, and what we do
  Above is more august; to judge of kings
    Is the tribunal met: so now you know."
  "Then I presume those gentlemen with
    wings,"
    Said Wilkes, "are cherubs; and that
    soul below
  Looks much like George the Third, but to
    my mind
  A good deal older—Bless me! is he blind?"

69 "He is what you behold him, and his doom
    Depends upon his deeds," the Angel
    said;
  "If you have aught to arraign in him, the
    tomb
    Gives license to the humblest beggar's
    head
  To lift itself against the loftiest."—
    "Some,"
    Said Wilkes, "don't wait to see them
    laid in lead,
  For such a liberty—and I, for one,
  Have told them what I thought beneath the
    sun."

70 "*Above* the sun repeat, then, what thou
    hast
    To urge against him," said the Arch-
    angel. "Why,"
  Replied the spirit, "since old scores are
    past,
    Must I turn evidence? In faith, not I.
  Besides, I beat him hollow at the last,[2]

[1] Byron called Southey a turncoat and a renegade
for transferring his allegiance to the Tory
party. See st. 97; also *Don Juan*, Dedication,
1 (p. 603).
[2] In 1782 Wilkes had been successful as a Member
of Parliament in passing a motion to expunge from the records the resolution under
which he had been expelled from the House in
1764.

With all his Lords and Commons: in the
   sky
I don't like ripping up old stories, since
His conduct was but natural in a prince.

71 "Foolish, no doubt, and wicked, to oppress
   A poor unlucky devil without a shilling;
But then I blame the man himself much
   less
   Than Bute and Grafton, and shall be
      unwilling
To see him punish'd here for their excess,
   Since they were both damn'd long ago,
      and still in
Their place below: for me, I have for-
   given,
And vote his 'habeas corpus' into heaven.''

72 "Wilkes," said the Devil, "I understand
   all this;
   You turn'd to half a courtier ere you
      died,
And seem to think it would not be amiss
   To grow a whole one on the other side
Of Charon's ferry; you forget that *his*
   Reign is concluded; whatsoe'er betide,
He won't be sovereign more: you've lost
   your labor,
For at the best he will be but your neigh-
   bor.

73 "However, I knew what to think of it,
   When I beheld you in your jesting way,
Flitting and whispering round about the
   spit
Where Belial, upon duty for the day,
With Fox's lard[1] was basting William
   Pitt,
   His pupil; I knew what to think, I say:
That fellow even in hell breeds farther ills;
I'll have him *gagg'd*—'twas one of his own
   bills.[2]

74 "Call Junius!" From the crowd a shadow
   stalk'd,
   And at the name there was a general
      squeeze,
So that the very ghosts no longer walk'd
   In comfort, at their own aërial ease,
But were all ramm'd, and jamm'd (but to
   be balk'd,
   As we shall see), and jostled hands and
      knees,
Like wind compress'd and pent within a
   bladder,
Or like a human colic, which is sadder.

[1] A reference to the corpulence of Fox.
[2] A reference to the Treason and Sedition bills of 1795, known as the Pitt and Grenville Acts, which aimed at restricting the liberty of the press and the liberty of speech.

75 The shadow came—a tall, thin, gray-hair'd
   figure,
   That look'd as it had been a shade on
      earth;
Quick in its motions, with an air of vigor,
   But nought to mark its breeding or its
      birth;
Now it wax'd little, then again grew
   bigger,
   With now an air of gloom, or savage
      mirth;
But as you gazed upon its features, they
Changed every instant—to *what,* none
   could say.

76 The more intently the ghosts gazed, the less
   Could they distinguish whose the fea-
      tures were;[1]
The Devil himself seem'd puzzled even to
   guess;
   They varied like a dream—now here, now
      there;
And several people swore from out the
   press,
   They knew him perfectly; and one could
      swear
He was his father; upon which another
Was sure he was his mother's cousin's
   brother:

77 Another, that he was a duke, or knight,
   An orator, a lawyer, or a priest,
A nabob,[2] a man-midwife; but the wight
   Mysterious changed his countenance at
      least
As oft as they their minds; though in full
   sight
   He stood, the puzzle only was increased;
The man was a phantasmagoria in
Himself—he was so volatile and thin.

78 The moment that you had pronounced him
   one,
   Presto! his face changed, and he was
      another;
And when that change was hardly well
   put on,
   It varied, till I don't think his own
      mother
(If he had a mother) would her son
   Have known, he shifted so from one to
      t'other;
Till guessing from a pleasure grew a task,
At this epistolary "Iron Mask."

[1] More than fifty persons have been suggested as the possible authors of the Letters of Junius. The list includes Burke, Francis, Tooke, Wilmot, and others. The authorship has not yet been determined.
[2] governor of a Hindu province; man of great wealth

79 For sometimes he like Cerberus would
    seem—
    "Three gentlemen at once"[1] (as sagely
      says
Good Mrs. Malaprop); then you might
    deem
    That he was not even *one;* now many
      rays
Were flashing round him; and now a thick
    steam
    Hid him from sight—like fogs on Lon-
      don days:
Now Burke, now Tooke, he grew to peo-
    ple's fancies,
And certes[2] often like Sir Philip Francis.

80 I've an hypothesis—'tis quite my own;
    I never let it out till now, for fear
Of doing people harm about the throne,
    And injuring some minister or peer,
On whom the stigma might perhaps be
    blown;
    It is—my gentle public, lend thine ear!
'Tis, that what Junius we are wont to call
Was *really, truly,* nobody at all.

81 I don't see wherefore letters should not be
    Written without hands, since we daily
      view
Them written without heads; and books,
    we see,
    Are fill'd as well without the latter
    too:
And really till we fix on somebody
    For certain sure to claim them as his
      due,
Their author, like the Niger's mouth, will
    bother
The world to say if *there* be mouth or
    author.

82 "And who and what art thou?" the Arch-
    angel said.
    "For *that* you may consult my title-
      page,"[3]
Replied this mighty shadow of a shade:
    "If I have kept my secret half an age,
I scarce shall tell it now."—"Canst thou
    upbraid,"
    Continued Michael, "George Rex, or
    allege
Aught further?" Junius answer'd, "You
    had better
First ask him for *his* answer to my letter:

[1] Sheridan, *The Rivals*, IV, 2, 298.
[2] certainly
[3] The title-page read: *Letters of Junius, Stat Nominis Umbra.* [He stands the shadow of a name.] See Lucan's *Pharsalia*, 1, 135.

83 "My charges upon record will outlast
    The brass of both his epitaph and
      tomb."
    "Repent'st thou not," said Michael, "of
      some past
Exaggeration? something which may
    doom
Thyself if false, as him if true? Thou
      wast
Too bitter—is it not so?—in thy gloom
Of passion?"—"Passion!" cried the
    phantom dim,
    "I loved my country, and I hated him.

84 "What I have written, I have written:[1] let
    The rest be on his head or mine!" So
      spoke
Old "Nominis Umbra;" and while speak-
    ing yet,
    Away he melted in celestial smoke.
Then Satan said to Michael, "Don't forget
    To call George Washington, and John
      Horne Tooke,
And Franklin;"—but at this time there
    was heard
A cry for room, though not a phantom
    stirr'd.

85 At length with jostling, elbowing, and the
    aid
    Of cherubim appointed to that post,
The devil Asmodeus to the circle made
    His way, and look'd as if his journey
      cost
Some trouble. When his burden down he
    laid,
    "What's this?" cried Michael; "why,
      'tis not a ghost?"
"I know it," quoth the incubus;[2] "but he
Shall be one, if you leave the affair to me.

86 "Confound the renegado! I have sprain'd
    My left wing, he's so heavy; one would
      think
Some of his works about his neck were
    chain'd.
But to the point; while hovering o'er
    the brink
Of Skiddaw (where as usual it still rain'd),
    I saw a taper, far below me, wink,
And stooping, caught this fellow at a
    libel—
No less on history than the Holy Bible.

87 "The former is the devil's scripture, and
    The latter yours, good Michael: so the
      affair
Belongs to all of us, you understand.

[1] See *John*, 19:22.
[2] evil spirit

I snatch'd him up just as you see him there,
And brought him off for sentence out of hand:
I've scarcely been ten minutes in the air—
At least a quarter it can hardly be:
I dare say that his wife is still at tea.''

88 Here Satan said, ''I know this man of old,
And have expected him for some time here;
A sillier fellow you will scarce behold,
Or more conceited in his petty sphere:
But surely it was not worth while to fold
Such trash below your wing, Asmodeus dear:
We had the poor wretch safe (without being bored
With carriage) coming of his own accord.

89 ''But since he's here, let's see what he has done.''
''Done!'' cried Asmodeus, ''he anticipates
The very business you are now upon,
And scribbles as if head clerk to the Fates.
Who knows to what his ribaldry may run,
When such an ass as this, like Balaam's, prates?''[1]
''Let's hear,'' quoth Michael, ''what he has to say:
You know we're bound to that in every way.''

90 Now the bard, glad to get an audience, which
By no means often was his case below,
Began to cough, and hawk, and hem, and pitch
His voice into that awful note of woe
To all unhappy hearers within reach
Of poets when the tide of rhyme's in flow;
But stuck fast with his first hexameter,[2]
Not one of all whose gouty feet would stir.

91 But ere the spavin'd dactyls could be spurr'd
Into recitative, in great dismay
Both cherubim and seraphim were heard
To murmur loudly through their long array;
And Michael rose ere he could get a word
Of all his founder'd verses under way,
And cried, ''For God's sake, stop, my friend! 'twere best—

Non Di, non homines[1]—you know the rest.''

92 A general bustle spread throughout the throng,
Which seem'd to hold all verse in detestation;
The angels had of course enough of song
When upon service; and the generation
Of ghosts had heard too much in life, not long
Before, to profit by a new occasion:
The monarch, mute till then, exclaim'd, ''What! what!
Pye come again? No more—no more of that!''

93 The tumult grew; an universal cough
Convulsed the skies, as during a debate,
When Castlereagh has been up long enough
(Before he was first minister of state,
I mean—the slaves hear now); some cried ''Off! off!''
As at a farce; till, grown quite desperate,
The bard Saint Peter pray'd to interpose
(Himself an author) only for his prose.

94 The varlet was not an ill-favor'd knave;
A good deal like a vulture in the face,
With a hook nose and a hawk's eye, which gave
A smart and sharper-looking sort of grace
To his whole aspect, which, though rather grave,
Was by no means so ugly as his case;
But that, indeed, was hopeless as can be,
Quite a poetic felony ''de se.''[2]

95 Then Michael blew his trump, and still'd the noise
With one still greater, as is yet the mode
On earth besides; except some grumbling voice,
Which now and then will make a slight inroad
Upon decorous silence, few will twice
Lift up their lungs when fairly over-crow'd;
And now the bard could plead his own bad cause,
With all the attitudes of self-applause.

96 He said (I only give the heads)—he said,
He meant no harm in scribbling; 'twas his way
Upon all topics; 'twas, besides, his bread,

---

[1] See Numbers, 22 :28.
[2] Southey's A Vision of Judgment was written in dactylic hexameter measure. See p. 435.

[1] neither gods nor men nor booksellers have granted to poets to be mediocre.—Horace, Ars Poetica, 372.
[2] felony upon himself,—i. e., suicide

Of which he butter'd both sides; 'twould
delay
Too long the assembly (he was pleased to
dread),
 And take up rather more time than a
day,
To name his works—he would but cite a
few—
*Wat Tyler—Rhymes on Blenheim—Water-
loo.*

97 He had written praises of a regicide;[1]
 He had written praises of all kings what-
ever;
He had written for republics far and wide,
 And then against them bitterer than
ever;[2]
For pantisocracy[3] he once had cried
 Aloud, a scheme less moral than 'twas
clever;
Then grew a hearty anti-jacobin[4]—
 Had turn'd his coat—and would have
turn'd his skin.

98 He had sung against all battles, and again
 In their high praise and glory; he had
call'd
Reviewing "the ungentle craft,"[5] and
then
 Become as base a critic as e'er crawl'd—
Fed, paid, and pamper'd by the very men
 By whom his muse and morals had been
maul'd:[6]
He had written much blank verse, and
blanker prose,
 And more of both than anybody knows.

99 He had written Wesley's life:—here turning round
 To Satan, "Sir, I'm ready to write
yours,
In two octavo volumes, nicely bound,

---

[1] One of Southey's early poems is entitled *Inscription for the Apartment in Chepstow
Castle, where Henry Martin, the Regicide,
Was Imprisoned Thirty Years.*
[2] In *Wat Tyler,* written in 1794, Southey expressed strong republican ideas; in *The Poet's
Pilgrimage to Waterloo,* written in 1816, he
rejoiced over the downfall of the French Republic.
[3] The name given to a scheme for an ideal community which Southey, Coleridge, and others
planned in 1794 to establish in America. It
was perfectly moral.
[4] One opposed to democratic, or revolutionary,
principles.
[5] Southey, *The Life of Henry Kirke White*
(1808), 1, 23. The term *gentle craft* is now
frequently applied to the sport of angling;
formerly it was applied to the trade of shoe-
making. See Dekker's *The Shoemaker's Holiday, or a Pleasant Comedy of the Gentle Craft*
(1599).
[6] Southey became a regular contributor to *The
Quarterly Review* in 1809.

With notes and preface, all that most
allures
 The pious purchaser; and there's no
ground
For fear, for I can choose my own re-
viewers:
So let me have the proper documents,
 That I may add you to my other saints."

100 Satan bow'd, and was silent. "Well, if
you,
 With amiable modesty, decline
My offer, what says Michael? There are
few
 Whose memoirs could be render'd more
divine.
Mine is a pen of all work; not so new
 As it was once, but I would make you
shine
Like your own trumpet. By the way, my
own
 Has more of brass in it, and is as well
blown.

101 "But talking about trumpets, here's my
Vision![1]
 Now you shall judge, all people; yes,
you shall
Judge with my judgment, and by my deci-
sion
 Be guided who shall enter heaven or fall.
I settle all these things by intuition,
 Times present, past, to come, heaven,
hell, and all,
Like King Alphonso.[2] When I thus see
double,
 I save the Deity some worlds of trouble."

102 He ceased, and drew forth an MS.; and no
 Persuasion on the part of devils, saints,
Or angels, now could stop the torrent; so
 He read the first three lines of the con-
tents;
But at the fourth, the whole spiritual show
 Had vanish'd, with variety of scents,
Ambrosial and sulphureous, as they
sprang,
 Like lightning, off from his "melodious
twang."[3]

103 Those grand heroics acted as a spell:
 The angels stopp'd their ears and plied
their pinions;

---

[1] His *A Vision of Judgment.* See p. 435.
[2] "King Alphonso, speaking of the Ptolomean
system, said that had he been consulted at the
creation of the world, he would have spared
the Maker some absurdities."—Byron.
[3] John Aubrey (1626-97), *Miscellanies Upon
Various Subjects* (1857), 81. The passage in
which the expression occurs is quoted in
Scott's *The Antiquary,* ch. 9.

The devils ran howling, deafen'd, down to
    hell;
  The ghosts fled, gibbering, for their own
    dominions
(For 'tis not yet decided where they dwell,
  And I leave every man to his opinions);
Michael took refuge in his trump—but, lo!
His teeth were set on edge, he could not
    blow!

104 Saint Peter, who has hitherto been known
  For an impetuous saint, upraised his
    keys,
And at the fifth line knock'd the poet
    down;
  Who fell like Phaeton, but more at ease,
Into his lake, for there he did not drown;
  A different web being by the Destinies
Woven for the Laureate's final wreath,
    whene'er
Reform shall happen either here or there.

105 He first sank to the bottom—like his works,
  But soon rose to the surface—like him-
    self;
For all corrupted things are buoy'd like
    corks,
  By their own rottenness, light as an elf,
Or wisp that flits o'er a morass: he lurks,
  It may be, still, like dull books on a
    shelf,
In his own den, to scrawl some "Life" or
    "Vision,"
As Welborn says—"the devil turn'd pre-
    cisian."[1]

106 As for the rest, to come to the conclusion
  Of this true dream, the telescope is gone
Which kept my optics free from all delu-
    sion,
  And show'd me what I in my turn have
    shown;
All I saw farther, in the last confusion,
  Was, that King George slipp'd into
    heaven for one;
And when the tumult dwindled to a calm,
I left him practicing the hundredth psalm.

STANZAS WRITTEN ON THE ROAD BETWEEN FLORENCE AND PISA
1821   1830

Oh, talk not to me of a name great in
    story;
The days of our youth are the days of our
    glory;

---

[1] Massinger, *A New Way to Pay Old Debts*, I,
1. 6.

And the myrtle and ivy[1] of sweet two-and-
    twenty
Are worth all your laurels, though ever so
    plenty.

5 What are garlands and crowns to the brow
    that is wrinkled?
'Tis but as a dead-flower with May-dew
    besprinkled.
Then away with all such from the head
    that is hoary!
What care I for the wreaths that can *only*
    give glory!

Oh Fame!—if I e'er took delight in thy
    praises,
10 'Twas less for the sake of thy high-
    sounding phrases,
Than to see the bright eyes of the dear one
    discover,
She thought that I was not unworthy to
    love her.

There chiefly I sought thee, *there* only I
    found thee;
Her glance was the best of the rays that
    surround thee;
15 When it sparkled o'er aught that was
    bright in my story,
I knew it was love, and I felt it was glory.

ON THIS DAY I COMPLETE MY THIRTY-SIXTH YEAR
1824   1824

'Tis time this heart should be unmoved,
  Since others it hath ceased to move:
Yet, though I cannot be beloved,
    Still let me love!

5 My days are in the yellow leaf;[2]
  The flowers and fruits of love are gone;
The worm, the canker, and the grief
    Are mine alone!

The fire that on my bosom preys
10   Is lone as some volcanic isle;
No torch is kindled at its blaze—
    A funeral pile.

The hope, the fear, the jealous care,
  The exalted portion of the pain
15 And power of love, I cannot share,
    But wear the chain.

But 'tis not *thus*—and 'tis not *here*—
  Such thoughts should shake my soul, nor
    now,

---

[1] The myrtle was a symbol of love; the ivy, of
constancy in friendship.
[2] See *Macbeth*, V, 2, 22.

Where glory decks the hero's bier,
20   Or binds his brow.

The sword, the banner, and the field,
    Glory and Greece, around me see!
The Spartan, borne upon his shield,[1]
    Was not more free.

25 Awake! (not Greece—she *is* awake!)
    Awake, my spirit! Think through *whom*
Thy life-blood tracks its parent lake,[2]
    And then strike home!

Tread those reviving passions down,
30   Unworthy manhood!—unto thee
Indifferent should the smile or frown
    Of beauty be.

If thou regrett'st thy youth, *why live?*
    The land of honorable death
35 Is here:—up to the field, and give
    Away thy breath!

Seek out—less often sought than found—
    A soldier's grave, for thee the best;
Then look around, and choose thy ground,
40   And take thy rest.

Percy Bysshe Shelley 1792-1822

QUEEN MAB
1812   1813

From SECTION II

If solitude hath ever led thy steps
    To the wild ocean's echoing shore,
    And thou hast lingered there,
    Until the sun's broad orb
5 Seemed resting on the burnished wave,
    Thou must have marked the lines
    Of purple gold that motionless
    Hung o'er the sinking sphere:
Thou must have marked the billowy
        clouds,
10 Edged with intolerable radiancy,
    Towering like rocks of jet
    Crowned with a diamond wreath.
    And yet there is a moment,
    When the sun's highest point
15 Peeps like a star o'er ocean's western edge.
    When those far clouds of feathery gold,
    Shaded with deepest purple, gleam
    Like islands on a dark blue sea;

[1] The killed or wounded Spartan was carried from the battle-field on his shield.
[2] Byron's mother was a descendant of James I; his father traced his ancestry to heroes of the time of the Norman Conquest.

Then has thy fancy soared above the earth,
20   And furled its wearied wing
    Within the Fairy's fane.

Yet not the golden islands
    Gleaming in yon flood of light,
    Nor the feathery curtains
25 Stretching o'er the sun's bright couch,
    Nor the burnished ocean-waves
    Paving that gorgeous dome,
So fair, so wonderful a sight
As Mab's ethereal palace could afford.
30 Yet likest evening's vault, that faëry Hall!
As Heaven, low resting on the wave, it
        spread
    Its floors of flashing light,
    Its vast and azure dome,
    Its fertile golden islands
35   Floating on a silver sea;
Whilst suns their mingling beamings darted
Through clouds of circumambient darkness,
    And pearly battlements around
    Looked o'er the immense of Heaven.

The magic car no longer moved.
40   The Fairy and the Spirit
    Entered the Hall of Spells.
    Those golden clouds
    That rolled in glittering billows
45   Beneath the azure canopy
With the ethereal footsteps trembled not;
    The light and crimson mists,
Floating to strains of thrilling melody
    Through that unearthly dwelling,
50 Yielded to every movement of the will;
Upon their passive swell the Spirit leaned,
And, for the varied bliss that pressed
        around,
    Used not the glorious privilege
    Of virtue and of wisdom.

55   "Spirit!" the Fairy said,
    And pointed to the gorgeous dome,
    "This is a wondrous sight
    And mocks all human grandeur;
But, were it virtue's only meed to dwell
60 In a celestial palace, all resigned
To pleasurable impulses, immured
Within the prison of itself, the will
Of changeless Nature would be unfulfilled.
Learn to make others happy. Spirit, come!
65 This is thine high reward:—the past shall
        rise;
Thou shalt behold the present; I will teach
    The secrets of the future."

The Fairy and the Spirit
Approached the overhanging battlement.—
70   Below lay stretched the universe!

There, far as the remotest line
That bounds imagination's flight,
Countless and unending orbs
In mazy motion intermingled,
75 Yet still fulfilled immutably
    Eternal Nature's law.
    Above, below, around,
    The circling systems formed
    A wilderness of harmony;
80   Each with undeviating aim,
In eloquent silence, through the depths of
    space
    Pursued its wondrous way.

    There was a little light
That twinkled in the misty distance:
    None but a spirit's eye,
    Might ken that rolling orb;
    None but a spirit's eye
    And in no other place
But that celestial dwelling, might behold
90 Each action of this earth's inhabitants.
    But matter, space, and time
In those aërial mansions cease to act;
And all-prevailing wisdom, when it reaps
The harvest of its excellence, o'erbounds
95 Those obstacles of which an earthly soul
    Fears to attempt the conquest.

    The Fairy pointed to the earth.
    The Spirit's intellectual eye
    Its kindred beings recognized.
100 The thronging thousands, to a passing
    view,
    Seemed like an ant-hill's citizens.
    How wonderful! that even
    The passions, prejudices, interests,
That sway the meanest being—the weak
    touch
105   That moves the finest nerve,
    And in one human brain
Causes the faintest thought, becomes a
    link
In the great chain of Nature!

. . . .

    "Spirit! ten thousand years
    Have scarcely passed away,
Since, in the waste where now the savage
    drinks
185 His enemy's blood, and, aping Europe's
    sons,
    Wakes the unholy song of war,
    Arose a stately city,
Metropolis of the western continent.
    There, now, the mossy column-stone,
190 Indented by Time's unrelaxing grasp,
    Which once appeared to brave

All, save its country's ruin,—
    There the wide forest scene,
Rude in the uncultivated loveliness
195   Of gardens long run wild,—
Seems, to the unwilling sojourner, whose
    steps
    Chance in that desert has delayed,
Thus to have stood since earth was what
    it is.
Yet once it was the busiest haunt,
200 Whither, as to a common centre, flocked
    Strangers, and ships, and merchan-
    dise:
    Once peace and freedom blessed
    The cultivated plain:
    But wealth, that curse of man,
205 Blighted the bud of its prosperity:
Virtue and wisdom, truth and liberty,
Fled, to return not, until man shall know
    That they alone can give the bliss
    Worthy a soul that claims
210   Its kindred with eternity.

    "There's not one atom of yon earth
    But once was living man;
    Nor the minutest drop of rain,
    That hangeth in its thinnest cloud,
215   But flowed in human veins:
    And from the burning plains
    Where Libyan monsters yell,
    From the most gloomy glens
    Of Greenland's sunless clime,
220   To where the golden fields
    Of fertile England spread
    Their harvest to the day,
    Thou canst not find one spot
    Whereon no city stood.

225   "How strange is human pride!
I tell thee that those living things,
To whom the fragile blade of grass,
    That springeth in the morn
    And perisheth ere noon,
    Is an unbounded world;
I tell thee that those viewless beings,
Whose mansion is the smallest particle
    Of the impassive atmosphere,
    Think, feel, and live like man;
235 That their affections and antipathies,
    Like his, produce the laws
    Ruling their moral state;
    And the minutest throb
That through their frame diffuses
240   The slightest, faintest motion,
    Is fixed and indispensable
    As the majestic laws
    That rule yon rolling orbs."

. . . .

From Section V

"Hence commerce springs, the venal inter-
  change
Of all that human art or Nature yield;
40 Which wealth should purchase not, but
  want demand,
And natural kindness hasten to supply
From the full fountain of its boundless
  love,
Forever stifled, drained, and tainted now.
Commerce! beneath whose poison-breath-
  ing shade
45 No solitary virtue dares to spring,
But poverty and wealth with equal hand
Scatter their withering curses, and un-
  fold
The doors of premature and violent death
To pining famine and full-fed disease,
50 To all that shares the lot of human life,
Which, poisoned body and soul, scarce
  drags the chain
That lengthens as it goes and clanks be-
  hind.

"Commerce has set the mark of selfishness,
The signet of its all-enslaving power
55 Upon a shining ore, and called it gold:
Before whose image bow the vulgar
  great,
The vainly rich, the miserable proud,
The mob of peasants, nobles, priests, and
  kings,
And with blind feelings reverence the
  power
60 That grinds them to the dust of misery.
But in the temple of their hireling hearts
Gold is a living god, and rules in scorn
All earthly things but virtue.

"Since tyrants, by the sale of human life,
65 Heap luxuries to their sensualism, and
  fame
To their wide-wasting and insatiate pride,
Success has sanctioned to a credulous world
The ruin, the disgrace, the woe of war.
His hosts of blind and unresisting dupes
70 The despot numbers; from his cabinet
These puppets of his schemes he moves at
  will,
Even as the slaves by force or famine
  driven,
Beneath a vulgar master, to perform
A task of cold and brutal drudgery;—
75 Hardened to hope, insensible to fear,
Scarce living pulleys of a dead machine,
Mere wheels of work and articles of trade,
That grace the proud and noisy pomp of
  wealth!

"The harmony and happiness of man
80 Yields to the wealth of nations; that which
  lifts
His nature to the heaven of its pride,
Is bartered for the poison of his soul;
The weight that drags to earth his towering
  hopes,
Blighting all prospect but of selfish gain,
85 Withering all passion but of slavish fear,
Extinguishing all free and generous love
Of enterprise and daring, even the pulse
That fancy kindles in the beating heart
To mingle with sensation, it destroys,—
90 Leaves nothing but the sordid lust of self,
The grovelling hope of interest and gold,
Unqualified, unmingled, unredeemed
Even by hypocrisy.

                        And statesmen boast
Of wealth! The wordy eloquence, that
  lives
95 After the ruin of their hearts, can gild
The bitter poison of a nation's woe,
Can turn the worship of the servile mob
To their corrupt and glaring idol, fame,
From virtue, trampled by its iron tread,
100 Although its dazzling pedestal be raised
Amid the horrors of a limb-strewn field,
With desolated dwellings smoking round.
The man of ease, who, by his warm fireside,
To deeds of charitable intercourse,
105 And bare fulfilment of the common laws
Of decency and prejudice, confines
The struggling nature of his human heart,
Is duped by their cold sophistry; he sheds
A passing tear perchance upon the wreck
110 Of earthly peace, when near his dwelling's
  door
The frightful waves are driven,—when his
  son
Is murdered by the tyrant, or religion
Drives his wife raving mad. But the poor
  man,
Whose life is misery, and fear, and care;
115 Whom the morn wakens but to fruitless
  toil;
Who ever hears his famished offspring's
  scream,
Whom their pale mother's uncomplaining
  gaze
Forever meets, and the proud rich man's
  eye
Flashing command, and the heart-breaking
  scene
120 Of thousands like himself;—he little heeds
The rhetoric of tyranny; his hate
Is quenchless as his wrongs; he laughs to
  scorn
The vain and bitter mockery of words,

Feeling the horror of the tyrant's deeds,
125 And unrestrained but by the arm of power,
That knows and dreads his enmity.

"The iron rod of penury still compels
Her wretched slaves to bow the knee to
wealth,
And poison, with unprofitable toil,
130 A life too void of solace to confirm
The very chains that bind him to his doom.
Nature, impartial in munificence,
Has gifted man with all-subduing will.
Matter, with all its transitory shapes,
135 Lies subjected and plastic at his feet,
That, weak from bondage, tremble as they
tread.
How many a rustic Milton has passed by,
Stifling the speechless longings of his
heart,
In unremitting drudgery and care!
140 How many a vulgar Cato has compelled
His energies, no longer tameless then,
To mould a pin, or fabricate a nail!
How many a Newton, to whose passive ken
Those mighty spheres that gem infinity
145 Were only specks of tinsel, fixed in Heaven
To light the midnights of his native town!

"Yet every heart contains perfection's
germ:[1]
The wisest of the sages of the earth,
That ever from the stores of reason drew
150 Science and truth, and virtue's dreadless
tone,
Were but a weak and inexperienced boy,
Proud, sensual, unimpassioned, unimbued
With pure desire and universal love,
Compared to that high being, of cloudless
brain,
155 Untainted passion, elevated will,
Which Death (who even would linger long
in awe
Within his noble presence, and beneath
His changeless eyebeam) might alone sub-
due.
Him, every slave now dragging through
the filth
160 Of some corrupted city his sad life,
Pining with famine, swoln with luxury,
Blunting the keenness of his spiritual
sense
With narrow schemings and unworthy
cares,
Or madly rushing through all violent
crime,
165 To move the deep stagnation of his soul,—
Might imitate and equal.

[1] See Godwin's *An Enquiry Concerning Political
Justice*, 1, 5 (p. 244b, 35 ff.)

But mean lust
Has bound its chains so tight about the
earth,
That all within it but the virtuous man
Is venal: gold or fame will surely reach
170 The price prefixed by Selfishness, to all
But him of resolute and unchanging
will;
Whom, nor the plaudits of a servile crowd,
Nor the vile joys of tainting luxury,
Can bribe to yield his elevated soul
175 To Tyranny or Falsehood, though they
wield
With blood-red hand the sceptre of the
world.

. . . . . .

"There is a nobler glory, which survives
215 Until our being fades, and, solacing
All human care, accompanies its change;
Deserts not virtue in the dungeon's gloom,
And, in the precincts of the palace, guides
Its footsteps through that labyrinth of
crime;
220 Imbues his lineaments with dauntlessness,
Even when, from Power's avenging hand,
he takes
Its sweetest, last, and noblest title—death;
—The consciousness of good, which neither
gold,
Nor sordid fame, nor hope of heavenly
bliss
225 Can purchase; but a life of resolute good,
Unalterable will, quenchless desire
Of universal happiness, the heart
That beats with it in unison, the brain
Whose ever wakeful wisdom toils to
change
Reason's rich stores for its eternal weal.

. . . . . .

"But hoary-headed Selfishness has felt
250 Its death-blow, and is tottering to the
grave:
A brighter morn awaits the human day,
When every transfer of earth's natural
gifts
Shall be a commerce of good words and
works;
When poverty and wealth, the thirst of
fame,
255 The fear of infamy, disease and woe,
War with its million horrors, and fierce
hell
Shall live but in the memory of Time,
Who, like a penitent libertine, shall start,
Look back, and shudder at his younger
years."

Section VIII

"The present and the past thou hast
    beheld:
It was a desolate sight. Now, Spirit,
    learn
    The secrets of the future.—Time!
Unfold the brooding pinion of thy gloom,
5 Render thou up thy half-devoured babes,
And from the cradles of eternity,
Where millions lie lulled to their portioned
    sleep
By the deep murmuring stream of passing
    things,
Tear thou that gloomy shroud.—Spirit,
    behold
10   Thy glorious destiny!"

Joy to the Spirit came.
Through the wide rent in Time's eternal
    veil,
Hope was seen beaming through the mists
    of fear:
    Earth was no longer Hell;
15   Love, freedom, health, had given
Their ripeness to the manhood of its prime,
    And all its pulses beat
Symphonious to the planetary spheres:[1]
    Then dulcet music swelled
20 Concordant with the life-strings of the
    soul;
It throbbed in sweet and languid beatings
    there,
Catching new life from transitory death,—
Like the vague sighings of a wind at even,
That wakes the wavelets of the slumbering
    sea
25 And dies on the creation of its breath,
And sinks and rises, fails and swells by
    fits:
    Was the pure stream of feeling
    That sprung from these sweet notes,
And o'er the Spirit's human sympathies
30 With mild and gentle motion calmly
    flowed.

Joy to the Spirit came,—
Such joy as when a lover sees
The chosen of his soul in happiness,
    And witnesses her peace
35 Whose woe to him were bitterer than death,
    Sees her unfaded cheek
Glow mantling in first luxury of health,
    Thrills with her lovely eyes,
Which like two stars amid the heaving
    main
40   Sparkle through liquid bliss.

[1] The ancients believed that the movement of the
celestial spheres produced music.

Then in her triumph spoke the Fairy
    Queen:
"I will not call the ghost of ages gone
To unfold the frightful secrets of its lore;
    The present now is past,
45 And those events that desolate the earth
Have faded from the memory of Time,
Who dares not give reality to that
Whose being I annul. To me is given
The wonders of the human world to keep,
50 Space, matter, time, and mind. Futurity
Exposes now its treasure; let the sight
Renew and strengthen all thy failing hope.
O human Spirit! spur thee to the goal
Where virtue fixes universal peace,
55 And 'midst the ebb and flow of human
    things,
Show somewhat stable, somewhat certain
    still,
A lighthouse o'er the wild of dreary waves.

"The habitable earth is full of bliss;
Those wastes of frozen billows that were
    hurled
60 By everlasting snowstorms round the
    poles,
Where matter dared not vegetate or live,
But ceaseless frost round the vast solitude
Bound its broad zone of stillness, are un-
    loosed;
And fragrant zephyrs there from spicy
    isles
65 Ruffle the placid ocean-deep, that rolls
Its broad, bright surges to the sloping
    sand,
Whose roar is wakened into echoings sweet
To murmur through the Heaven-breathing
    groves
And melodize with man's blest nature
    there.

70 "Those deserts of immeasurable sand,
Whose age-collected fervors scarce allowed
A bird to live, a blade of grass to spring,
Where the shrill chirp of the green lizard's
    love
Broke on the sultry silentness alone,
75 Now teem with countless rills and shady
    woods,
Cornfields and pastures and white cot-
    tages;
And where the startled wilderness beheld
A savage conqueror stained in kindred
    blood,
A tigress sating with the flesh of lambs
80 The unnatural famine of her toothless
    cubs,
Whilst shouts and howlings through the
    desert rang,

Sloping and smooth the daisy-spangled
   lawn,
Offering sweet incense to the sunrise, smiles
To see a babe before his mother's door,
85   Sharing his morning's meal
With the green and golden basilisk[1]
That comes to lick his feet.

"Those trackless deeps, where many a
   weary sail
Has seen above the illimitable plain,
90 Morning on night, and night on morning
   rise,
Whilst still no land to greet the wanderer
   spread
Its shadowy mountains on the sun-bright
   sea,
Where the loud roarings of the tempest-
   waves
So long have mingled with the gusty wind
95 In melancholy loneliness, and swept
The desert of those ocean solitudes
But vocal to the sea-bird's harrowing
   shriek,
The bellowing monster, and the rushing
   storm,
Now to the sweet and many-mingling
   sounds
100 Of kindliest human impulses respond.
Those lonely realms bright garden-isles
   begem,
With lightsome clouds and shining seas
   between,
And fertile valleys, resonant with bliss,
Whilst green woods overcanopy the wave,
105 Which like a toil-worn laborer leaps to
   shore,
To meet the kisses of the flow'rets there.

"All things are recreated, and the flame
Of consentaneous[2] love inspires all life:
The fertile bosom of the earth gives
   suck
110 To myriads, who still grow beneath her
   care,
Rewarding her with their pure perfectness:
The balmy breathings of the wind inhale
Her virtues, and diffuse them all abroad:
Health floats amid the gentle atmosphere,
115 Glows in the fruits, and mantles on the
   stream:
No storms deform the beaming brow of
   Heaven,
Nor scatter in the freshness of its pride
The foliage of the ever-verdant trees;
But fruits are ever ripe, flowers ever fair,

120 And Autumn proudly bears her matron
   grace,
Kindling a flush on the fair cheek of
   Spring,
Whose virgin bloom beneath the ruddy
   fruit
Reflects its tint, and blushes into love.

"The lion now forgets to thirst for blood:
125 There might you see him sporting in the
   sun
Beside the dreadless kid;[1] his claws are
   sheathed,
His teeth are harmless, custom's force has
   made
His nature as the nature of a lamb.
Like passion's fruit, the nightshade's
   tempting bane
130 Poisons no more the pleasure it bestows:
All bitterness is past; the cup of joy
Unmingled mantles to the goblet's brim,[2]
And courts the thirsty lips it fled before.

"But chief, ambiguous man, he that can
   know
135 More misery, and dream more joy than all;
Whose keen sensations thrill within his
   breast
To mingle with a loftier instinct there,
Lending their power to pleasure and to
   pain,
Yet raising, sharpening, and refining each;
140 Who stands amid the ever-varying world,
The burthen or the glory of the earth;
He chief perceives the change, his being
   notes
The gradual renovation, and defines
Each movement of its progress on his
   mind.

145 "Man, where the gloom of the long polar
   night
Lowers o'er the snow-clad rocks and
   frozen soil,
Where scarce the hardiest herb that braves
   the frost
Basks in the moonlight's ineffectual glow,
Shrank with the plants, and darkened with
   the night;
150 His chilled and narrow energies, his heart,
Insensible to courage, truth, or love,
His stunted stature and imbecile frame,
Marked him for some abortion of the earth,
Fit compeer of the bears that roamed
   around,
155 Whose habits and enjoyments were his
   own:

---

[1] A fabulous serpent, or lizard, whose breath or
   look was fatal.
[2] harmonious

[1] See *Isaiah*, 11 :6-9.   [2] See *Psalms*, 23 :5.

His life a feverish dream of stagnant woe,
Whose meagre wants, but scantily fulfilled,
Apprised him ever of the joyless length
Which his short being's wretchedness had
  reached;
160 His death a pang which famine, cold and
  toil
Long on the mind, whilst yet the vital
  spark
Clung to the body stubbornly, had brought:
All was inflicted here that Earth's revenge
Could wreak on the infringers of her law;
165 One curse alone was spared—the name
  of God.

"Nor where the tropics bound the realms
  of day
With a broad belt of mingling cloud and
  flame,
Where blue mists through the unmoving
  atmosphere
Scattered the seeds of pestilence, and fed
170 Unnatural vegetation, where the land
Teemed with all earthquake, tempest and
  disease,
Was man a nobler being; slavery
Had crushed him to his country's blood-
  stained dust;
Or he was bartered for the fame of power,
175 Which, all internal impulses destroying,
Makes human will an article of trade;
Or he was changed with Christians for
  their gold,
And dragged to distant isles, where to the
  sound
Of the flesh-mangling scourge, he does the
  work
180 Of all-polluting luxury and wealth,
Which doubly visits on the tyrants' heads
The long-protracted fulness of their woe;
Or he was led to legal butchery,
To turn to worms beneath that burning
  sun,
185 Where kings first leagued against the rights
  of men,
And priests first traded with the name of
  God.[1]

"Even where the milder zone afforded
  man
A seeming shelter, yet contagion there,
Blighting his being with unnumbered ills,
190 Spread like a quenchless fire; nor truth
  till late
Availed to arrest its progress, or create
That peace which first in bloodless victory
  waved

[1] In Africa, the source of the British slave trade.

Her snowy standard o'er this favored
  clime:
There man was long the train-bearer of
  slaves,
195 The mimic of surrounding misery,
The jackal of ambition's lion-rage,
The bloodhound of religion's hungry zeal.

"Here now the human being stands adorn-
  ing
This loveliest earth with taintless body
  and mind;
200 Blessed from his birth with all bland im-
  pulses,
Which gently in his noble bosom wake
All kindly passions and all pure desires.
Him, still from hope to hope the bliss
  pursuing
Which from the exhaustless lore of human
  weal
205 Dawns on the virtuous mind, the thoughts
  that rise
In time-destroying infiniteness, gift
With self-enshrined eternity, that mocks
The unprevailing hoariness of age;
And man, once fleeting o'er the transient
  scene
210 Swift as an unremembered vision, stands
Immortal upon earth: no longer now
He slays the lamb that looks him in the
  face,
And horribly devours his mangled flesh,
Which, still avenging Nature's broken
  law,
215 Kindled all putrid humors in his frame,
All evil passions, and all vain belief,
Hatred, despair, and loathing in his mind,
The germs of misery, death, disease, and
  crime.
No longer now the wingèd habitants,
220 That in the woods their sweet lives sing
  away,
Flee from the form of man; but gather
  round,
And prune their sunny feathers on the
  hands
Which little children stretch in friendly
  sport
Towards these dreadless partners of their
  play.
225 All things are void of terror. Man has
  lost
His terrible prerogative, and stands
An equal amidst equals: happiness
And science dawn, though late, upon the
  earth;
Peace cheers the mind, health renovates
  the frame;
230 Disease and pleasure cease to mingle here,

Reason and passion cease to combat there;
Whilst each unfettered o'er the earth extend
Their all-subduing energies, and wield
The sceptre of a vast dominion there;
235 Whilst every shape and mode of matter lends
Its force to the omnipotence of mind,
Which from its dark mine drags the gem of truth
To decorate its paradise of peace."

MUTABILITY
1815   1816

We are as clouds that veil the midnight moon;
How restlessly they speed, and gleam, and quiver,
Streaking the darkness radiantly!—yet soon
Night closes round, and they are lost forever:

5 Or like forgotten lyres, whose dissonant strings
Give various response to each varying blast,
To whose frail frame no second motion brings
One mood or modulation like the last.

We rest—a dream has power to poison sleep;
10 We rise—one wandering thought pollutes the day;
We feel, conceive or reason, laugh or weep;
Embrace fond woe, or cast our cares away:

It is the same!—For, be it joy or sorrow,
The path of its departure still is free:
15 Man's yesterday may ne'er be like his morrow;
Nought may endure but Mutability.

TO ———1
1815   1816

Oh! there are spirits of the air,
And genii of the evening breeze,
And gentle ghosts, with eyes as fair
As star-beams among twilight trees:—
5 Such lovely ministers to meet
Oft hast thou turned from men thy lonely feet.

1 This poem is thought to be addressed to Shelley's own spirit, although Mrs. Shelley states that it is addressed to Coleridge.

With mountain winds, and babbling springs,
And moonlight seas, that are the voice
Of these inexplicable things,
10 Thou didst hold commune, and rejoice
When they did answer thee; but they
Cast, like a worthless boon, thy love away.

And thou hast sought in starry eyes
Beams that were never meant for thine,
15 Another's wealth:—tame sacrifice
To a fond faith! still dost thou pine?
Still dost thou hope that greeting hands,
Voice, looks, or lips, may answer thy demands?

Ah! wherefore didst thou build thine hope
20 On the false earth's inconstancy?
Did thine own mind afford no scope
Of love, or moving thoughts to thee,
That natural scenes or human smiles
Could steal the power to wind thee in their wiles?

25 Yes, all the faithless smiles are fled
Whose falsehood left thee brokenhearted;
The glory of the moon is dead;
Night's ghosts and dreams have now departed;
Thine own soul still is true to thee,
30 But changed to a foul fiend through misery.

This fiend, whose ghastly presence ever
Beside thee like thy shadow hangs,
Dream not to chase;—the mad endeavor
Would scourge thee to severer pangs.
35 Be as thou art. Thy settled fate,
Dark as it is, all change would aggravate.

TO WORDSWORTH
1815   1816

Poet of Nature, thou hast wept to know
That things depart which never may return:
Childhood and youth, friendship and love's first glow,
Have fled like sweet dreams, leaving thee to mourn.
5 These common woes I feel. One loss is mine
Which thou too feel'st, yet I alone deplore.
Thou wert as a lone star, whose light did shine
On some frail bark in winter's midnight roar:
Thou hast like to a rock-built refuge stood
10 Above the blind and battling multitude:
In honored poverty thy voice did weave

Songs consecrate to truth and liberty,—
Deserting these, thou leavest me to grieve,
Thus having been, that thou shouldst cease
   to be.

FEELINGS OF A REPUBLICAN ON THE FALL OF BONAPARTE
1815   1816

I hated thee, fallen tyrant! I did groan
To think that a most unambitious slave,
Like thou, shouldst dance and revel on the
   grave
Of Liberty. Thou mightst have built thy
   throne
5 Where it had stood even now: thou didst
   prefer
A frail and bloody pomp which Time has
   swept
In fragments towards oblivion. Massacre,
For this I prayed, would on thy sleep have
   crept,
Treason and Slavery, Rapine, Fear, and
   Lust,
10 And stifled thee, their minister. I know
Too late, since thou and France are in the
   dust,
That Virtue owns a more eternal foe
Than Force or Fraud: old Custom, legal
   Crime,
And bloody Faith the foulest birth of Time.

ALASTOR
OR
THE SPIRIT OF SOLITUDE
1815   1816

Earth, Ocean, Air, belovèd brotherhood!
If our great Mother[2] has imbued my soul
With aught of natural piety to feel
Your love, and recompense the boon with
   mine;
5 If dewy morn, and odorous noon, and
   even,
With sunset and its gorgeous ministers,
And solemn midnight's tingling silentness;
If Autumn's hollow sighs in the sere wood,
And Winter robing with pure snow and
   crowns
10 Of starry ice the gray grass and bare
   boughs;
If Spring's voluptuous pantings when she
   breathes
Her first sweet kisses, have been dear to
   me;
If no bright bird, insect, or gentle beast
I consciously have injured, but still loved

---

[1] *Alastor* is a Greek word meaning *evil genius*; it is here made synonymous with the spirit of solitude.
[2] Nature.

15 And cherished these my kindred; then
   forgive
This boast, belovèd brethren, and withdraw
No portion of your wonted favor now!

Mother of this unfathomable world!
Favor my solemn song, for I have loved
20 Thee ever, and thee only; I have watched
Thy shadow, and the darkness of thy
   steps,
And my heart ever gazes on the depth
Of thy deep mysteries. I have made my
   bed
In charnels and on coffins,[1] where black
   death
25 Keeps record of the trophies won from
   thee,
Hoping to still these obstinate question-
   ings
Of thee and thine, by forcing some lone
   ghost,
Thy messenger, to render up the tale
Of what we are. In lone and silent hours,
30 When night makes a weird sound of its
   own stillness,
Like an inspired and desperate alchemist
Staking his very life on some dark hope,
Have I mixed awful talk and asking looks
With my most innocent love, until strange
   tears
35 Uniting with those breathless kisses, made
Such magic as compels the charmèd night
To render up thy charge: and, though
   ne'er yet
Thou hast unveiled thy inmost sanctuary,
Enough from incommunicable dream,
40 And twilight phantasms, and deep noon-
   day thought,
Has shone within me, that serenely now
And moveless, as a long-forgotten lyre
Suspended in the solitary dome
Of some mysterious and deserted fane,
45 I wait thy breath, Great Parent, that my
   strain
May modulate with murmurs of the air,
And motions of the forests and the sea,
And voice of living beings, and woven
   hymns
Of night and day, and the deep heart of
   man.

50 There was a Poet whose untimely tomb
No human hands with pious reverence
   reared,
But the charmed eddies of autumnal winds
Built o'er his mouldering bones a pyramid
Of mouldering leaves in the waste wilder-
   ness:—

---

[1] Shelley is said to have done this.

55 A lovely youth,—no mourning maiden
  decked
With weeping flowers, or votive cypress
  wreath,[1]
The lone couch of his everlasting sleep:—
Gentle, and brave, and generous,—no lorn
  bard
Breathed o'er his dark fate one melodious
  sigh:
60 He lived, he died, he sung, in solitude.
Strangers have wept to hear his passionate
  notes,
And virgins, as unknown he passed, have
  pined
And wasted for fond love of his wild
  eyes.
The fire of those soft orbs has ceased to
  burn,
65 And Silence, too enamored of that voice,
Locks its mute music in her rugged cell.

By solemn vision, and bright silver
  dream,
His infancy was nurtured. Every sight
And sound from the vast earth and am-
  bient air,
70 Sent to his heart its choicest impulses.
The fountains of divine philosophy
Fled not his thirsting lips, and all of great,
Or good, or lovely, which the sacred past
In truth or fable consecrates, he felt
75 And knew. When early youth had passed,
  he left
His cold fireside and alienated home
To seek strange truths in undiscovered
  lands.
Many a wide waste and tangled wilderness
Has lured his fearless steps; and he
  has bought
80 With his sweet voice and eyes, from savage
  men,
His rest and food. Nature's most secret
  steps
He like her shadow has pursued, where'er
The red volcano overcanopies
Its fields of snow and pinnacles of ice
85 With burning smoke, or where bitumen
  lakes
On black bare pointed islets ever beat
With sluggish surge, or where the secret
  caves
Rugged and dark, winding among the
  springs
Of fire and poison, inaccessible
90 To avarice or pride, their starry domes
Of diamond and of gold expand above
Numberless and immeasurable halls,

Frequent[1] with crystal column, and clear
  shrines
Of pearl, and thrones radiant with chryso-
  lite.
95 Nor had that scene of ampler majesty
Than gems or gold, the varying roof of
  heaven
And the green earth, lost in his heart its
  claims
To love and wonder; he would linger long
In lonesome vales, making the wild his
  home,
100 Until the doves and squirrels would partake
From his innocuous hand his bloodless
  food,
Lured by the gentle meaning of his looks,
And the wild antelope, that starts when-
  e'er
The dry leaf rustles in the brake,[2] suspend
105 Her timid steps to gaze upon a form
More graceful than her own.

His wandering step
Obedient to high thoughts, has visited
The awful ruins of the days of old:
Athens, and Tyre, and Balbec, and the
  waste
110 Where stood Jerusalem, the fallen towers
Of Babylon, the eternal pyramids,
Memphis and Thebes, and whatsoe'er of
  strange,
Sculptured on alabaster obelisk,
Or jasper tomb, or mutilated sphynx,
115 Dark Æthiopia in her desert hills
Conceals. Among the ruined temples
  there,
Stupendous columns, and wild images
Of more than man, where marble dae-
  mons[3] watch
The Zodiac's brazen mystery,[4] and dead
  men
120 Hang their mute thoughts on the mute
  walls around,
He lingered, poring on memorials
Of the world's youth; through the long
  burning day
Gazed on those speechless shapes, nor,
  when the moon
Filled the mysterious halls with floating
  shades
125 Suspended he that task, but ever gazed

---

[1] The cypress is an emblem of mourning; it is a
  common tree in graveyards.

[1] crowded; thronged
[2] thicket
[3] Supernatural beings of Greek mythology conceived as holding a position between gods and
  men.
[4] Mythological figures arranged in the fashion of
  the zodiac, on the walls, columns, etc., of the
  temple of Denderah, a city in Upper Egypt.

And gazed, till meaning on his vacant
mind
Flashed like strong inspiration, and he
saw
The thrilling secrets of the birth of time.

Meanwhile an Arab maiden brought his
food,
130 Her daily portion, from her father's
tent,
And spread her matting for his couch,
and stole
From duties and repose to tend his
steps—
Enamored, yet not daring for deep awe
To speak her love—and watched his nightly
sleep,
135 Sleepless herself, to gaze upon his lips
Parted in slumber, whence the regular
breath
Of innocent dreams arose; then, when
red morn
Made paler the pale moon, to her cold
home
Wildered, and wan, and panting, she returned.

140 The Poet, wandering on, through Arabie
And Persia, and the wild Carmanian
waste,
And o'er the aërial mountains which pour
down
Indus and Oxus from their icy caves,
In joy and exultation held his way;
145 Till in the vale of Cashmire, far within
Its loneliest dell, where odorous plants
entwine
Beneath the hollow rocks a natural bower,
Beside a sparkling rivulet he stretched
His languid limbs. A vision on his sleep
150 There came, a dream of hopes that never
yet
Had flushed his cheek. He dreamed a
veilèd maid
Sate near him, talking in low solemn
tones.
Her voice was like the voice of his own
soul
Heard in the calm of thought; its music
long,
155 Like woven sounds of streams and breezes,
held
His inmost sense suspended in its web
Of many-colored woof and shifting hues.
Knowledge and truth and virtue were her
theme,
And lofty hopes of divine liberty,
160 Thoughts the most dear to him, and poesy,
Herself a poet. Soon the solemn mood

Of her pure mind kindled through all her
frame
A permeating fire: wild numbers then
She raised, with voice stifled in tremulous
sobs
165 Subdued by its own pathos: her fair hands
Were bare alone, sweeping from some
strange harp
Strange symphony, and in their branching
veins
The eloquent blood told an ineffable tale.
The beating of her heart was heard to
fill
170 The pauses of her music, and her breath
Tumultuously accorded with those fits
Of intermitted song. Sudden she rose,
As if her heart impatiently endured
Its bursting burthen: at the sound he
turned,
175 And saw by the warm light of their own
life
Her glowing limbs beneath the sinuous
veil
Of woven wind, her outspread arms now
bare,
Her dark locks floating in the breath of
night,
Her beamy bending eyes, her parted lips
180 Outstretched, and pale, and quivering
eagerly.
His strong heart sunk and sickened with
excess
Of love. He reared his shuddering limbs
and quelled
His gasping breath, and spread his arms
to meet
Her panting bosom: she drew back awhile,
185 Then, yielding to the irresistible joy,
With frantic gesture and short breathless
cry
Folded his frame in her dissolving arms.
Now blackness veiled his dizzy eyes, and
night
Involved and swallowed up the vision;
sleep,
190 Like a dark flood suspended in its course,
Rolled back its impulse on his vacant
brain.

Roused by the shock he started from
his trance—
The cold white light of morning, the blue
moon
Low in the west, the clear and garish hills,
195 The distinct valley and the vacant woods,
Spread round him where he stood.
Whither have fled
The hues of heaven that canopied his
bower

Of yesternight? The sounds that soothed
    his sleep,
The mystery and the majesty of Earth,
200 The joy, the exultation? His wan eyes
Gaze on the empty scene as vacantly
As ocean's moon looks on the moon in
    heaven.
The spirit of sweet human love has sent
A vision to the sleep of him who spurned
205 Her choicest gifts. He eagerly pursues
Beyond the realms of dream that fleeting
    shade;
He overleaps the bounds. Alas! Alas!
Were limbs, and breath, and being inter-
    twined
Thus treacherously? Lost, lost, forever
    lost,
210 In the wide pathless desert of dim sleep,
That beautiful shape! Does the dark gate
    of death
Conduct to thy mysterious paradise,
O Sleep? Does the bright arch of rain-
    bow clouds
And pendent mountains seen in the calm
    lake
215 Lead only to a black and watery depth,
While death's blue vault, with loathliest
    vapors hung,
Where every shade which the foul grave
    exhales
Hides its dead eye from the detested day,
Conducts, O Sleep, to thy delightful
    realms?
220 This doubt with sudden tide flowed on his
    heart;
The insatiate hope which it awakened,
    stung
His brain even like despair.

           While daylight held
The sky, the Poet kept mute conference
With his still soul. At night the passion
    came,
225 Like the fierce fiend of a distempered
    dream,
And shook him from his rest, and led him
    forth
Into the darkness.—As an eagle grasped
In folds of the green serpent, feels her
    breast
Burn with the poison, and precipitates
230 Through night and day, tempest, and
    calm, and cloud,
Frantic with dizzying anguish, her blind
    flight
O'er the wide aëry wilderness: thus driven
By the bright shadow of that lovely dream,
Beneath the cold glare of the desolate
    night,

235 Through tangled swamps and deep pre-
    cipitous dells,
Startling with careless step the moonlight
    snake,
He fled. Red morning dawned upon his
    flight,
Shedding the mockery of its vital hues
Upon his cheek of death. He wandered on
240 Till vast Aornos seen from Petra's steep
Hung o'er the low horizon like a cloud;
Through Balk, and where the desolated
    tombs
Of Parthian kings scatter to every wind
Their wasting dust,[1] wildly he wandered
    on,
245 Day after day a weary waste of hours,
Bearing within his life the brooding care
That ever fed on its decaying flame.
And now his limbs were lean; his scat-
    tered hair,
Sered by the autumn of strange suffering,
250 Sung dirges in the wind; his listless hand
Hung like dead bone within its withered
    skin;
Life, and the lustre that consumed it,
    shone,
As in a furnace burning secretly,
From his dark eyes alone. The cottagers,
255 Who ministered with human charity
His human wants, beheld with wondering
    awe
Their fleeting visitant. The mountaineer,
Encountering on some dizzy precipice
That spectral form, deemed that the
    Spirit of Wind
260 With lightning eyes, and eager breath,
    and feet
Disturbing not the drifted snow had
    paused
In its career: the infant would conceal
His troubled visage in his mother's robe
In terror at the glare of those wild eyes,
265 To remember their strange light in many
    a dream
Of aftertimes; but youthful maidens,
    taught
By nature, would interpret half the woe
That wasted him, would call him with false
    names
Brother, and friend, would press his pallid
    hand
270 At parting, and watch, dim through tears,
    the path
Of his departure from their father's door.

    At length upon the lone Chorasmian
    shore
He paused, a wide and melancholy waste

[1] At Arbela, a city in Assyria.

Of putrid marshes. A strong impulse urged
275 His steps to the sea-shore. A swan was there,
Beside a sluggish stream among the reeds.
It rose as he approached, and, with strong wings
Scaling the upward sky, bent its bright course
High over the immeasurable main.
280 His eyes pursued its flight.—"Thou hast a home,
Beautiful bird; thou voyagest to thine home,
Where thy sweet mate will twine her downy neck
With thine, and welcome thy return with eyes
Bright in the lustre of their own fond joy.
285 And what am I that I should linger here,
With voice far sweeter than thy dying notes,[1]
Spirit more vast than thine, frame more attuned
To beauty, wasting these surpassing powers
In the deaf air, to the blind earth, and heaven
290 That echoes not my thoughts?" A gloomy smile
Of desperate hope wrinkled his quivering lips.
For sleep, he knew, kept most relentlessly
Its precious charge, and silent death exposed,
Faithless perhaps as sleep, a shadowy lure,
295 With doubtful smile mocking its own strange charms.

Startled by his own thoughts, he looked around.
There was no fair fiend near him, not a sight
Or sound of awe but in his own deep mind.
A little shallop floating near the shore
300 Caught the impatient wandering of his gaze.
It had been long abandoned, for its sides
Gaped wide with many a rift, and its frail joints
Swayed with the undulations of the tide.
A restless impulse urged him to embark
305 And meet lone Death on the drear ocean's waste;
For well he knew that mighty Shadow loves
The slimy caverns of the populous deep.

[1] The swan was said to sing melodiously when about to die.

The day was fair and sunny; sea and sky
Drank its inspiring radiance, and the wind
310 Swept strongly from the shore, blackening the waves.
Following his eager soul, the wanderer
Leaped in the boat; he spread his cloak aloft
On the bare mast, and took his lonely seat,
And felt the boat speed o'er the tranquil sea
315 Like a torn cloud before the hurricane.

As one that in a silver vision floats
Obedient to the sweep of odorous winds
Upon resplendent clouds, so rapidly
Along the dark and ruffled waters fled
320 The straining boat. A whirlwind swept it on,
With fierce gusts and precipitating force,
Through the white ridges of the chafèd sea.
The waves arose. Higher and higher still
Their fierce necks writhed beneath the tempest's scourge
325 Like serpents struggling in a vulture's grasp.
Calm and rejoicing in the fearful war
Of wave ruining on wave, and blast on blast
Descending, and black flood on whirlpool driven
With dark obliterating course, he sate:
330 As if their genii were the ministers
Appointed to conduct him to the light
Of those belovèd eyes, the Poet sate,
Holding the steady helm. Evening came on;
The beams of sunset hung their rainbow hues
335 High 'mid the shifting domes of sheeted spray
That canopied his path o'er the waste deep;
Twilight, ascending slowly from the east,
Entwined in duskier wreaths her braided locks
O'er the fair front and radiant eyes of Day;
340 Night followed, clad with stars. On every side
More horribly the multitudinous streams
Of ocean's mountainous waste to mutual war
Rushed in dark tumult thundering, as to mock
The calm and spangled sky. The little boat
345 Still fled before the storm; still fled, like foam
Down the steep cataract of a wintry river;

Now pausing on the edge of the riven
    wave;
Now leaving far behind the bursting mass
That fell, convulsing ocean: safely fled—
350 As if that frail and wasted human form,
Had been an elemental god.

        At midnight
The moon arose: and lo! the ethereal cliffs
Of Caucasus, whose icy summits shone
Among the stars like sunlight, and around
355 Whose caverned base the whirlpools and
    the waves
Bursting and eddying irresistibly
Rage and resound forever.—Who shall
    save?—
The boat fled on,—the boiling torrent
    drove,—
The crags closed round with black and
    jagg`ed arms,
360 The shattered mountain overhung the sea,
And faster still, beyond all human speed,
Suspended on the sweep of the smooth
    wave,
The little boat was driven. A cavern there
Yawned, and amid its slant and winding
    depths
365 Ingulfed the rushing sea. The boat fled
    on
With unrelaxing speed.—"Vision and
    Love!"
The Poet cried aloud, "I have beheld
The path of thy departure. Sleep and
    death
Shall not divide us long!"

        The boat pursued
370 The windings of the cavern. Daylight
    shone
At length upon that gloomy river's flow;
Now, where the fiercest war among the
    waves
Is calm, on the unfathomable stream
The boat moved slowly. Where the moun-
    tain, riven,
375 Exposed those black depths to the azure
    sky,
Ere yet the flood's enormous volume fell
Even to the base of Caucasus, with sound
That shook the everlasting rocks, the mass
Filled with one whirlpool all that ample
    chasm;
380 Stair above stair the eddying waters rose,
Circling immeasurably fast, and laved
With alternating dash the gnarl`ed roots
Of mighty trees, that stretched their giant
    arms
In darkness over it. I' the midst was left,
385 Reflecting, yet distorting every cloud,

A pool of treacherous and tremendous
    calm.
Seized by the sway of the ascending
    stream,
With dizzy swiftness, round, and round,
    and round,
Ridge after ridge the straining boat arose,
390 Till on the verge of the extremest curve,
Where, through an opening of the rocky
    bank,
The waters overflow, and a smooth spot
Of glassy quiet mid those battling tides
Is left, the boat paused shuddering.—
    Shall it sink
395 Down the abyss? Shall the reverting
    stress
Of that resistless gulf embosom it?
Now shall it fall?—A wandering stream
    of wind,
Breathed from the west, has caught the
    expanded sail,
And, lo! with gentle motion, between
    banks
400 Of mossy slope, and on a placid stream,
Beneath a woven grove it sails, and, hark!
The ghastly torrent mingles its far roar,
With the breeze murmuring in the musical
    woods.
Where the embowering trees recede, and
    leave
405 A little space of green expanse, the cove
Is closed by meeting banks, whose yellow
    flowers
Forever gaze on their own drooping eyes,
Reflected in the crystal calm. The wave
Of the boat's motion marred their pensive
    task,
410 Which nought but vagrant bird, or wanton
    wind,
Or falling spear-grass, or their own decay
Had e'er disturbed before. The Poet
    longed
To deck with their bright hues his withered
    hair,
But on his heart its solitude returned,
415 And he forbore. Not the strong impulse
    hid
In those flushed cheeks, bent eyes, and
    shadowy frame
Had yet performed its ministry: it hung
Upon his life, as lightning in a cloud
Gleams, hovering ere it vanish, ere the
    floods
420 Of night close over it.

        The noonday sun
Now shone upon the forest, one vast mass
Of mingling shade, whose brown magnifi-
    cence

A narrow vale embosoms. There, huge
  caves,
Scooped in the dark base of their aëry
  rocks,
425 Mocking its moans, respond and roar for-
  ever.
The meeting boughs and implicated[1] leaves
Wove twilight o'er the Poet's path, as led
By love, or dream, or god, or mightier
  Death,
He sought in Nature's dearest haunt, some
  bank,
430 Her cradle and his sepulchre. More dark
And dark the shades accumulate. The oak,
Expanding its immense and knotty arms,
Embraces the light beech. The pyramids
Of the tall cedar overarching, frame
435 Most solemn domes within, and far below,
Like clouds suspended in an emerald sky,
The ash and the acacia floating hang
Tremulous and pale. Like restless ser-
  pents, clothed
In rainbow and in fire, the parasites,
440 Starred with ten thousand blossoms, flow
  around
The gray trunks, and, as gamesome in-
  fants' eyes,
With gentle meanings, and most innocent
  wiles,
Fold their beams round the hearts of those
  that love,
These twine their tendrils with the wedded
  boughs,
445 Uniting their close union; the woven leaves
Make net-work of the dark blue light of
  day,
And the night's noontide clearness, mutable
As shapes in the weird clouds. Soft mossy
  lawns
Beneath these canopies extend their swells,
450 Fragrant with perfumed herbs, and eyed
  with blooms
Minute yet beautiful. One darkest glen
Sends from its woods of musk-rose, twined
  with jasmine,
A soul-dissolving odor, to invite
To some more lovely mystery. Through
  the dell,
455 Silence and Twilight here, twin-sisters,
  keep
Their noonday watch, and sail among the
  shades,
Like vaporous shapes half-seen; beyond, a
  well,
Dark, gleaming, and of most translucent
  wave,
Images all the woven boughs above,

1 interwoven

460 And each depending leaf, and every speck
Of azure sky darting between their chasms;
Nor aught else in the liquid mirror laves
Its portraiture, but some inconstant star
Between one foliaged lattice twinkling fair,
465 Or painted bird, sleeping beneath the moon,
Or gorgeous insect floating motionless,
Unconscious of the day, ere yet his wings
Have spread their glories to the gaze of
  noon.

Hither the Poet came. His eyes beheld
470 Their own wan light through the reflected
  lines
Of his thin hair, distinct in the dark depth
Of that still fountain; as the human heart,
Gazing in dreams over the gloomy grave,
Sees its own treacherous likeness there.
  He heard
475 The motion of the leaves—the grass that
  sprung
Startled and glanced and trembled even to
  feel
An unaccustomed presence—and the sound
Of the sweet brook that from the secret
  springs
Of that dark fountain rose. A Spirit
  seemed
480 To stand beside him—clothed in no bright
  robes
Of shadowy silver or enshrining light,
Borrowed from aught the visible world
  affords
Of grace, or majesty, or mystery;—
But, undulating woods, and silent well,
485 And leaping rivulet, and evening gloom
Now deepening the dark shades, for speech
  assuming,
Held commune with him, as if he and it
Were all that was; only—when his regard
Was raised by intense pensiveness—two
  eyes,
490 Two starry eyes, hung in the gloom of
  thought,
And seemed with their serene and azure
  smiles
To beckon him.

          Obedient to the light
That shone within his soul, he went, pursuing
The windings of the dell.—The rivulet
495 Wanton and wild, through many a green
  ravine
Beneath the forest flowed. Sometimes it
  fell
Among the moss with hollow harmony
Dark and profound. Now on the polished
  stones

It danced, like childhood laughing as it
    went:
500 Then, through the plain in tranquil wan-
    derings crept,
Reflecting every herd and drooping bud
That overhung its quietness.—"O stream!
Whose source is inaccessibly profound,
Whither do thy mysterious waters tend?
505 Thou imagest my life. Thy darksome still-
    ness,
Thy dazzling waves, thy loud and hollow
    gulfs,
Thy searchless fountain, and invisible
    course
Have each their type in me: and the wide
    sky,
And measureless ocean may declare as soon
510 What oozy cavern or what wandering cloud
Contains thy waters, as the universe
Tell where these living thoughts reside,
    when stretched
Upon thy flowers my bloodless limbs shall
    waste
I' the passing wind!"

        Beside the grassy shore
515 Of the small stream he went; he did im-
    press
On the green moss his tremulous step, that
    caught
Strong shuddering from his burning limbs.
    As one
Roused by some joyous madness from the
    couch
Of fever, he did move; yet, not like
    him,
520 Forgetful of the grave, where, when the
    flame
Of his frail exultation shall be spent,
He must descend. With rapid steps he
    went
Beneath the shade of trees, beside the flow
Of the wild babbling rivulet; and now
525 The forest's solemn canopies were changed
For the uniform and lightsome evening
    sky.
Gray rocks did peep from the spare moss,
    and stemmed
The struggling brook: tall spires of
    windlestrae[1]
Threw their thin shadows down the rugged
    slope,
530 And nought but gnarlèd roots of ancient
    pines
Branchless and blasted, clenched with
    grasping roots
The unwilling soil. A gradual change was
    here,

[1] A grass stalk used for making ropes.

Yet ghastly. For, as fast years flow away,
The smooth brow gathers, and the hair
    grows thin
535 And white, and where irradiate dewy eyes
Had shone, gleam stony orbs: so from
    his steps
Bright flowers departed, and the beautiful
    shade
Of the green groves, with all their odorous
    winds
And musical motions. Calm, he still pur-
    sued
540 The stream, that with a larger volume
    now
Rolled through the labyrinthine dell; and
    there
Fretted a path through its descending
    curves
With its wintry speed. On every side now
    rose
Rocks, which, in unimaginable forms,
545 Lifted their black and barren pinnacles
In the light of evening, and, its precipice
Obscuring the ravine, disclosed above,
Mid toppling stones, black gulfs and yawn-
    ing caves,
Whose windings gave ten thousand various
    tongues
550 To the loud stream. Lo! where the pass
    expands
Its stony jaws, the abrupt mountain
    breaks,
And seems, with its accumulated crags,
To overhang the world: for wide expand
Beneath the wan stars and descending
    moon
555 Islanded seas, blue mountains, mighty
    streams,
Dim tracts and vast, robed in the lustrous
    gloom
Of leaden-colored even, and fiery hills
Mingling their flames with twilight, on the
    verge
Of the remote horizon. The near scene,
560 In naked and severe simplicity,
Made contrast with the universe. A pine,
Rock-rooted, stretched athwart the vacancy
Its swinging boughs, to each inconstant
    blast
Yielding one only response, at each pause
565 In most familiar cadence, with the howl
The thunder and the hiss of homeless
    streams
Mingling its solemn song, whilst the broad
    river,
Foaming and hurrying o'er its rugged
    path,
Fell into that immeasurable void
570 Scattering its waters to the passing winds.

Yet the gray precipice and solemn pine
And torrent were not all;—one silent nook
Was there. Even on the edge of that vast
    mountain,
Upheld by knotty roots and fallen rocks,
575 It overlooked in its serenity
The dark earth, and the bending vault of
    stars.
It was a tranquil spot, that seemed to smile
Even in the lap of horror. Ivy clasped
The fissured stones with its entwining arms,
580 And did embower with leaves forever green,
And berries dark, the smooth and even
    space
Of its inviolated floor; and here
The children of the autumnal whirlwind
    bore,
In wanton sport, those bright leaves whose
    decay,
585 Red, yellow, or ethereally pale,
Rivals the pride of summer. 'Tis the haunt
Of every gentle wind, whose breath can
    teach
The wilds to love tranquillity. One step,
One human step alone, has ever broken
590 The stillness of its solitude:—one voice
Alone inspired its echoes;—even that voice
Which hither came, floating among the
    winds,
And led the loveliest among human forms
To make their wild haunts the depository
595 Of all the grace and beauty that endued
Its motions, render up its majesty,
Scatter its music on the unfeeling storm,
And to the damp leaves and blue cavern
    mould,
Nurses of rainbow flowers, and branching
    moss,
600 Commit the colors of that varying cheek,
That snowy breast, those dark and droop-
    ing eyes.

The dim and hornèd moon hung low, and
    poured
A sea of lustre on the horizon's verge
That overflowed its mountains. Yellow
    mist
605 Filled the unbounded atmosphere, and
    drank
Wan moonlight even to fulness: not a star
Shone, not a sound was heard; the very
    winds,
Danger's grim playmates, on that precipice
Slept, clasped in his embrace.—O, storm of
    death!
610 Whose sightless speed divides this sullen
    night:
And thou, colossal Skeleton,[1] that, still

[1] Death.

Guiding its irresistible career
In thy devastating omnipotence,
Art king of this frail world, from the red
    field
615 Of slaughter, from the reeking hospital,
The patriot's sacred couch, the snowy bed
Of innocence, the scaffold and the throne,
A mighty voice invokes thee. Ruin calls
His brother Death. A rare and regal prey
620 He hath prepared, prowling around the
    world;
Glutted with which thou mayst repose, and
    men
Go to their graves like flowers or creeping
    worms,
Nor ever more offer at thy dark shrine
The unheeded tribute of a broken heart.

625 When on the threshold of the green
    recess
The wanderer's footsteps fell, he knew
    that death
Was on him. Yet a little, ere it fled,
Did he resign his high and holy soul
To images of the majestic past,
630 That paused within his passive being now,
Like winds that bear sweet music, when
    they breathe
Through some dim latticed chamber. He
    did place
His pale lean hand upon the rugged trunk
Of the old pine. Upon an ivied stone
635 Reclined his languid head; his limbs did
    rest,
Diffused and motionless, on the smooth
    brink
Of that obscurest chasm;—and thus he lay,
Surrendering to their final impulses
The hovering powers of life. Hope and
    Despair,
640 The torturers, slept; no mortal pain or
    fear
Marred his repose, the influxes of sense,
And his own being unalloyed by pain,
Yet feebler and more feeble, calmly fed
The stream of thought, till he lay breathing
    there
645 At peace, and faintly smiling. His last
    sight
Was the great moon, which o'er the west-
    ern line
Of the wide world her mighty horn sus-
    pended,
With whose dun beams inwoven darkness
    seemed
To mingle. Now upon the jaggèd hills
650 It rests, and still as the divided frame
Of the vast meteor sunk, the Poet's blood,
That ever beat in mystic sympathy

With Nature's ebb and flow, grew feebler
   still:
And when two lessening points of light
   alone
655 Gleamed through the darkness, the alter-
   nate gasp
Of his faint respiration scarce did stir
The stagnate night:—till the minutest ray
Was quenched, the pulse yet lingered in his
   heart.
It paused—it fluttered. But when heaven
   remained
660 Utterly black, the murky shades involved
An image, silent, cold, and motionless,
As their own voiceless earth and vacant air.
Even as a vapor fed with golden beams
That ministered on sunlight, ere the west
665 Eclipses it, was now that wondrous frame—
No sense, no motion, no divinity—
A fragile lute, on whose harmonious strings
The breath of heaven did wander—a bright
   stream
Once fed with many-voicèd waves—a dream
670 Of youth, which night and time have
   quenched forever—
Still, dark, and dry, and unremembered
   now.

Oh, for Medea's wondrous alchemy,
Which wheresoe'er it fell made the earth
   gleam
With bright flowers, and the wintry boughs
   exhale
675 From vernal blooms fresh fragrance! Oh,
   that God,
Profuse of poisons, would concede the
   chalice[1]
Which but one living man has drained,[2]
   who now,
Vessel of deathless wrath,[3] a slave that
   feels
No proud exemption in the blighting curse
680 He bears, over the world wanders forever,
Lone as incarnate death! Oh, that the
   dream[4]
Of dark magician in his visioned cave,
Raking the cinders of a crucible
For life and power, even when his feeble
   hand
685 Shakes in its last decay, were the true law
Of this so lovely world! But thou art fled
Like some frail exhalation, which the dawn

---

[1] That is, of immortality.
[2] A Jew who refused to allow Christ to rest at
his house on the way to Calvary, and was
therefore condemned to wander upon earth
until Christ's second coming. For a full account of the widespread legend of the Wandering Jew, see *The Encyclopædia Britannica*
(11th ed.).
[3] See *Romans*, 9:22.
[4] Of immortal youth.

Robes in its golden beams,—ah! thou hast
   fled!
The brave, the gentle, and the beautiful,
690 The child of grace and genius. Heartless
   things
Are done and said i' the world, and many
   worms
And beasts and men live on, and mighty
   Earth
From sea and mountain, city and wilder-
   ness,
In vesper low or joyous orison,
695 Lifts still its solemn voice:—but thou art
   fled—
Thou canst no longer know or love the
   shapes
Of this phantasmal scene, who have to thee
Been purest ministers, who are, alas!
Now thou art not. Upon those pallid lips
700 So sweet even in their silence, on those
   eyes,
That image sleep in death, upon that form
Yet safe from the worm's outrage, let no
   tear
Be shed—not even in thought. Nor, when
   those hues
Are gone, and those divinest lineaments,
705 Worn by the senseless wind, shall live alone
In the frail pauses of this simple strain,
Let not high verse, mourning the memory
Of that which is no more, or painting's woe
Or sculpture, speak in feeble imagery
710 Their own cold powers. Art and eloquence,
And all the shows o' the world, are frail
   and vain
To weep a loss that turns their lights to
   shade.
It is a woe too "deep for tears,"[1] when all
Is reft at once, when some surpassing
   Spirit,
715 Whose light adorned the world around it,
   leaves
Those who remain behind, not sobs or
   groans,
The passionate tumult of a clinging hope;
But pale despair and cold tranquillity,
Nature's vast frame, the web of human
   things,
720 Birth and the grave, that are not as they
   were.

HYMN TO INTELLECTUAL BEAUTY
1816   1817

The awful shadow of some unseen Power
Floats though unseen among us, visiting
This various world with as inconstant
   wing

---

[1] Wordsworth, *Ode: Intimations of Immortality*,
203 (p. 331).

As summer winds that creep from flower to
flower;
5 Like moonbeams that behind some piny
mountain shower,
It visits with inconstant glance
Each human heart and countenance;
Like hues and harmonies of evening,—
Like clouds in starlight widely
spread,—
10 Like memory of music fled,—
Like aught that for its grace may be
Dear, and yet dearer for its mystery.

Spirit of Beauty, that dost consecrate
With thine own hues all thou dost shine
upon
15 Of human thought or form, where art
thou gone?
Why dost thou pass away and leave our
state,
This dim vast vale of tears, vacant and
desolate?
Ask why the sunlight not forever
Weaves rainbows o'er yon mountain-
river;
20 Why aught should fail and fade that once
is shown;
Why fear and dream and death and
birth
Cast on the daylight of this earth
Such gloom; why man has such a
scope
For love and hate, despondency and hope?

25 No voice from some sublimer world hath
ever
To sage or poet these responses[1] given;
Therefore the names of Demon,[2] Ghost,
and Heaven,
Remain the records of their vain endeavor—
Frail spells, whose uttered charm might
not avail to sever,
30 From all we hear and all we see,
Doubt, chance, and mutability.
Thy light alone, like mist o'er mountains
driven,
Or music by the night wind sent
Through strings of some still instrument,
35 Or moonlight on a midnight stream,
Gives grace and truth to life's unquiet
dream.

Love, Hope, and Self-esteem, like clouds
depart

[1] Responses to these questions.
[2] A supernatural being of Greek mythology conceived as holding a position between gods and
men.

And come, for some uncertain moments
lent.
Man were immortal, and omnipotent,
40 Didst thou, unknown and awful as thou
art,
Keep with thy glorious train firm state
within his heart.
Thou messenger of sympathies
That wax and wane in lovers' eyes—
Thou, that to human thought art nourish-
ment,
45 Like darkness to a dying flame,
Depart not as thy shadow came!
Depart not, lest the grave should be,
Like life and fear, a dark reality.

While yet a boy I sought for ghosts, and
sped
50 Through many a listening chamber, cave
and ruin,
And starlight wood, with fearful steps
pursuing
Hopes of high talk with the departed dead.
I called on poisonous names with which our
youth is fed;
I was not heard—I saw them not—
55 When, musing deeply on the lot
Of life, at that sweet time when winds are
wooing
All vital things that wake to bring
News of birds and blossoming,—
Sudden, thy shadow fell on me;
60 I shrieked, and clasped my hands in
ecstasy!

I vowed that I would dedicate my powers
To thee and thine—have I not kept the
vow?
With beating heart and streaming eyes,
even now
I call the phantoms of a thousand hours
65 Each from his voiceless grave: they have
in visioned bowers
Of studious zeal or love's delight
Outwatched with me the envious
night—
They know that never joy illumed my brow
Unlinked with hope that thou wouldst
free
70 This world from its dark slavery,—
That thou, O awful Loveliness,
Wouldst give whate'er these words cannot
express.

The day becomes more solemn and serene
When noon is past; there is a harmony
75 In autumn, and a lustre in its sky,
Which through the summer is not heard or
seen,

As if it could not be, as if it had not been!
   Thus let thy power, which like the
       truth
   Of nature on my passive youth
80 Descended, to my onward life supply
   Its calm—to one who worships thee,
   And every form containing thee,
   Whom, Spirit fair, thy spells did bind
To fear himself, and love all human kind.

MONT BLANC

LINES WRITTEN IN THE VALE OF CHAMOUNI
    1816   **1817**

The everlasting universe of things
Flows through the mind, and rolls its rapid
   waves,
Now dark—now glittering—now reflecting
   gloom—
Now lending splendor, where from secret
   springs
5 The source of human thought its tribute
   brings
Of waters,—with a sound but half its own,
Such as a feeble brook will oft assume
In the wild woods, among the mountains
   lone,
Where waterfalls around it leap forever,
10 Where woods and winds contend, and a
   vast river
Over its rocks ceaselessly bursts and raves.

Thus thou, Ravine of Arve—dark, deep
   Ravine—
Thou many-colored, many-voicèd vale,
Over whose pines, and crags, and caverns
   sail
15 Fast cloud-shadows and sunbeams: awful
   scene,
Where Power in likeness of the Arve comes
   down
From the ice-gulfs that gird his secret
   throne,
Bursting through these dark mountains like
   the flame
Of lightning through the tempest! thou
   dost lie,—
20 Thy giant brood of pines around thee
   clinging,
Children of elder time, in whose devotion
The chainless winds still come and ever
   came
To drink their odors, and their mighty
   swinging
To hear—an old and solemn harmony;
25 Thine earthly rainbows stretched across the
   sweep
Of the ethereal waterfall, whose veil

Robes some unsculptured image; the
   strange sleep
Which when the voices of the desert fail
Wraps all in its own deep eternity;—
30 Thy caverns echoing to the Arve's commo-
   tion,
A loud, lone sound no other sound can
   tame;
Thou art pervaded with that ceaseless mo-
   tion,
Thou art the path of that unresting sound,
Dizzy Ravine! and when I gaze on thee
35 I seem as in a trance sublime and strange
To muse on my own separate fantasy,
My own, my human mind, which passively
Now renders and receives fast influencings,
Holding an unremitting interchange
40 With the clear universe of things around;
One legion of wild thoughts, whose wan-
   dering wings
Now float above thy darkness, and now rest
Where that or thou art no unbidden guest,
In the still cave of the witch Poesy,
45 Seeking among the shadows that pass by—
Ghosts of all things that are—some shade
   of thee,
Some phantom, some faint image; till the
   breast
From which they fled recalls them, thou art
   there!

Some say that gleams of a remoter world
50 Visit the soul in sleep,—that death is
   slumber,
And that its shapes the busy thoughts out-
   number
Of those who wake and live.—I look on
   high;
Has some unknown Omnipotence unfurled
The veil of life and death? or do I lie
55 In dream, and does the mightier world of
   sleep
Spread far around and inaccessibly
Its circles? For the very spirit fails,
Driven like a homeless cloud from steep to
   steep
That vanishes among the viewless gales!
60 Far, far above, piercing the infinite sky,
Mont Blanc appears,—still, snowy, and
   serene—
Its subject mountains their unearthly
   forms
Pile around it, ice and rock; broad vales
   between
Of frozen floods, unfathomable deeps,
65 Blue as the overhanging heaven, that
   spread
And wind among the accumulated steeps;
A desert peopled by the storms alone.

Save when the eagle brings some hunter's
bone,
And the wolf tracks her there. How hid-
eously
70 Its shapes are heaped around! rude, bare,
and high,
Ghastly, and scarred, and riven.—Is this
the scene
Where the old Earthquake-dæmon taught
her young
Ruin? Were these their toys? or did a sea
Of fire envelop once this silent snow?
75 None can reply—all seems eternal now.
The wilderness has a mysterious tongue
Which teaches awful doubt, or faith so
mild,
So solemn, so serene, that man may be,
But for such faith, with nature reconciled;
80 Thou hast a voice, great Mountain, to
repeal
Large codes of fraud and woe; not under-
stood
By all, but which the wise, and great, and
good
Interpret, or make felt, or deeply feel.

The fields, the lakes, the forests, and the
streams,
85 Ocean, and all the living things that dwell
Within the dædal¹ earth; lightning, and
rain,
Earthquake, and fiery flood, and hurricane;
The torpor of the year when feeble dreams
Visit the hidden buds, or dreamless sleep
90 Holds every future leaf and flower, the
bound
With which from that detested trance they
leap;
The works and ways of men, their death
and birth,
And that of him and all that his may be;—
All things that move and breathe with toil
and sound
95 Are born and die, revolve, subside, and
swell.
Power dwells apart in its tranquillity,
Remote, serene, and inaccessible:
And *this*, the naked countenance of earth,
On which I gaze, even these primeval
mountains
100 Teach the adverting mind. The glaciers
creep
Like snakes that watch their prey, from
their far fountains,
Slow rolling on; there, many a precipice,
Frost and the Sun in scorn of mortal power
Have piled—dome, pyramid, and pinnacle,
105 A city of death, distinct with many a tower

¹ marvelously formed

And wall impregnable of beaming ice.
Yet not a city, but a flood of ruin
Is there, that from the boundaries of the
sky
Rolls its perpetual stream; vast pines are
strewing
110 Its destined path, or in the mangled soil
Branchless and shattered stand; the rocks,
drawn down
From yon remotest waste, have overthrown
The limits of the dead and living world,
Never to be reclaimed. The dwelling-place
115 Of insects, beasts, and birds, becomes its
spoil,
Their food and their retreat forever gone;
So much of life and joy is lost. The race
Of man flies far in dread; his work and
dwelling
Vanish, like smoke before the tempest's
stream,
120 And their place is not known. Below, vast
caves
Shine in the rushing torrents' restless
gleam,
Which from those secret chasms in tumult
welling
Meet in the vale, and one majestic river,
The breath and blood of distant lands, forever
125 Rolls its loud waters to the ocean waves,
Breathes its swift vapors to the circling air.

Mont Blanc yet gleams on high:—the
power is there,
The still and solemn power of many sights,
And many sounds, and much of life and
death.
130 In the calm darkness of the moonless
nights,
In the lone glare of day, the snows descend
Upon that mountain; none beholds them
there,
Nor when the flakes burn in the sinking
sun,
Or the star-beams dart through them;
winds contend
135 Silently there, and heap the snow, with
breath
Rapid and strong, but silently! Its home
The voiceless lightning in these solitudes
Keeps innocently, and like vapor broods
Over the snow. The secret strength of things
140 Which governs thought, and to the infinite
dome
Of Heaven is as a law, inhabits thee!
And what were thou, and earth, and stars,
and sea,
If to the human mind's imaginings
Silence and solitude were vacancy?

LINES[1]
1816　　　　1823

The cold earth slept below;
　Above the cold sky shone;
And all around, with a chilling sound,
　From caves of ice and fields of snow,
5　The breath of night like death did flow
　Beneath the sinking moon.

The wintry hedge was black;
　The green grass was not seen;
The birds did rest on the bare thorn's
　　breast,
10　Whose roots, beside the pathway track,
　Had bound their folds o'er many a crack
　Which the frost had made between.

Thine eyes glowed in the glare
　Of the moon's dying light;
15　As a fen-fire's beam on a sluggish stream
Gleams dimly—so the moon shone there,
And it yellowed the strings of thy
　　tangled hair,
　That shook in the wind of night.

The moon made thy lips pale, belovèd;
20　The wind made thy bosom chill;
The night did shed on thy dear head
　Its frozen dew, and thou didst lie
Where the bitter breath of the naked
　　sky
　Might visit thee at will.

TO MARY[2]　——　——

DEDICATION TO THE REVOLT OF ISLAM
1817　　　　1818

So now my summer task is ended, Mary,
　And I return to thee, mine own heart's
　　home;
As to his Queen some victor Knight of
　　Faëry,
　Earning bright spoils for her enchanted
　　dome;
5　Nor thou disdain, that ere my fame become
A star among the stars of mortal night,
If it indeed may cleave its natal gloom,
　Its doubtful promise thus I would unite
With thy beloved name, thou child of love
　　and light.

10　The toil which stole from thee so many an
　　hour,
　Is ended,—and the fruit is at thy feet!
No longer where the woods to frame a
　　bower

With interlacèd branches mix and meet,
　Or where with sound like many voices
　　sweet,
15　Waterfalls leap among wild islands green,
　Which framed for my lone boat a lone
　　retreat
Of moss-grown trees and weeds, shall I be
　　seen:
　But beside thee, where still my heart has
　　ever been.

Thoughts of great deeds were mine, dear
　　friend, when first
20　The clouds which wrap this world from
　　youth did pass.
I do remember well the hour which burst
　My spirit's sleep. A fresh May-dawn it
　　was,
When I walked forth upon the glittering
　　grass,
And wept, I knew not why; until there rose
25　From the near schoolroom, voices, that,
　　alas!
Were but one echo from a world of woes—
　The harsh and grating strife of tyrants
　　and of foes.

And then I clasped my hands and looked
　　around,
　But none was near to mock my streaming
　　eyes,
30　Which poured their warm drops on the
　　sunny ground—
So, without shame, I spake:—"I will be
　　wise,
And just, and free, and mild, if in me lies
Such power, for I grow weary to behold
The selfish and the strong still tyrannize
35　Without reproach or check." I then con-
　　trolled
My tears, my heart grew calm, and I was
　　meek and bold.

And from that hour did I with earnest
　　thought
Heap knowledge from forbidden mines of
　　lore;
Yet nothing that my tyrants knew or
　　taught
40　I cared to learn, but from that secret store
Wrought linkèd armor for my soul, before
It might walk forth to war among man-
　　kind;
Thus power and hope were strengthened
　　more and more
Within me, till there came upon my mind
45　A sense of loneliness, a thirst with which I
　　pined.

[1] This poem is thought to refer to the death of
Shelley's first wife, Harriet, who drowned
herself in November, 1816.
[2] Mary Wollstonecraft Godwin, Shelley's second
wife

Alas, that love should be a blight and snare
To those who seek all sympathies in one!
Such once I sought in vain; then black despair,
The shadow of a starless night, was thrown
50 Over the world in which I moved alone:[1]—
Yet never found I one not false to me,
Hard hearts, and cold, like weights of icy stone
Which crushed and withered mine, that could not be
Aught but a lifeless clod, until revived by thee.

55 Thou friend, whose presence on my wintry heart
Fell, like bright spring upon some herbless plain;
How beautiful and calm and free thou wert
In thy young wisdom, when the mortal chain
Of Custom thou didst burst and rend in twain,[2]
60 And walked as free as light the clouds among,
Which many an envious slave then breathed in vain
From his dim dungeon, and my spirit sprung
To meet thee from the woes which had begirt it long!

No more alone through the world's wilderness,
65 Although I trod the paths of high intent,
I journeyed now: no more companionless,
Where solitude is like despair, I went.
There is the wisdom of a stern content
When Poverty can blight the just and good,
70 When Infamy dares mock the innocent,
And cherished friends turn with the multitude
To trample: this was ours, and we unshaken stood!

Now has descended a serener hour,
And with inconstant fortune, friends return;
75 Though suffering leaves the knowledge and the power
Which says:—Let scorn be not repaid with scorn.
And from thy side two gentle babes are born

To fill our homes with smiles, and thus are we
Most fortunate beneath life's beaming morn;
80 And these delights, and thou, have been to me
The parents of the song I consecrate to thee.

Is it that now my inexperienced fingers
But strike the prelude of a loftier strain?
Or must the lyre on which my spirit lingers
85 Soon pause in silence, ne'er to sound again,
Though it might shake the Anarch Custom's reign,[1]
And charm the minds of men to Truth's own sway
Holier than was Amphion's? I would fain
Reply in hope—but I am worn away,
90 And Death and Love are yet contending for their prey.

And what art thou? I know, but dare not speak:
Time may interpret to his silent years.
Yet in the paleness of thy thoughtful cheek,
And in the light thine ample forehead wears,
95 And in thy sweetest smiles, and in thy tears,
And in thy gentle speech, a prophecy
Is whispered, to subdue my fondest fears:
And through thine eyes, even in thy soul I see
A lamp of vestal fire burning internally.

100 They say that thou wert lovely from thy birth,
Of glorious parents,[2] thou aspiring child.
I wonder not—for one then left this earth
Whose life was like a setting planet mild,
Which clothed thee in the radiance undefiled
105 Of its departing glory; still her fame
Shines on thee, through the tempests dark and wild
Which shake these latter days; and thou canst claim
The shelter, from thy sire, of an immortal name.

One voice[3] came forth from many a mighty spirit,
110 Which was the echo of three thousand years;

---

[1] A reference to the year before he met Mary.
[2] She and Shelley eloped on July 28, 1814, disregarding Shelley's marriage to Harriet Westbrook.

[1] Custom is here conceived as the destroyer of true relations between men.
[2] William Godwin and Mary Wollstonecraft, each the author of political and social writings of importance.
[3] The voice of Truth.

And the tumultuous world stood mute to
    hear it,
As some lone man who in a desert hears
The music of his home:—unwonted fears
Fell on the pale oppressors of our race,
115 And Faith, and Custom, and low-thoughted
    cares,
Like thunder-stricken dragons, for a space
Left the torn human heart, their food and
    dwelling-place

Truth's deathless voice pauses among man-
    kind!
If there must be no response to my cry—
120 If men must rise and stamp with fury
    blind
On his pure name who loves them,—thou
    and I,
Sweet friend! can look from our tran-
    quillity
Like lamps into the world's tempestuous
    night,—
Two tranquil stars, while clouds are pass-
    ing by
125 Which wrap them from the foundering
    seaman's sight,
That burn from year to year with unextin-
    guished light.

DEATH
1817   1824

They die—the dead return not. Misery
    Sits near an open grave and calls them
      over,
A Youth with hoary hair and haggard
    eye.
    They are the names of kindred, friend,
      and lover,
5 Which he so feebly calls; they all are
    gone—
Fond wretch, all dead! those vacant names
    alone,
This most familiar scene, my pain,
These tombs,—alone remain.

Misery, my sweetest friend, oh, weep no
    more!
10   Thou wilt not be consoled—I wonder
    not!
For I have seen thee from thy dwelling's
    door
    Watch the calm sunset with them, and
    this spot
Was even as bright and calm, but transi-
    tory,—
And now thy hopes are gone, thy hair is
    hoary;
15   This most familiar scene, my pain,
    These tombs,—alone remain.

LINES TO A CRITIC
1817   1823

Honey from silkworms who can gather,
    Or silk from the yellow bee?
The grass may grow in winter weather
    As soon as hate in me.

5 Hate men who cant, and men who pray,
    And men who rail like thee;
An equal passion to repay
    They are not coy like me.

Or seek some slave of power and gold,
10   To be thy dear heart's mate;
Thy love will move that bigot cold
    Sooner than me, thy hate.

A passion like the one I prove
    Cannot divided be;
15 I hate thy want of truth and love—
    How should I then hate thee?

OZYMANDIAS
1817   1818

I met a traveller from an antique land
Who said: "Two vast and trunkless legs
    of stone
Stand in the desert. Near them, on the
    sand,
Half sunk, a shattered visage lies, whose
    frown,
5 And wrinkled lip, and sneer of cold com-
    mand,
Tell that its sculptor well those passions
    read
Which yet survive, stamped on these life-
    less things,
The hand[1] that mocked them, and the
    heart[2] that fed:
And on the pedestal these words appear:
10 'My name is Ozymandias, king of kings:
Look on my works, ye Mighty, and de-
    spair!'
Nothing beside remains. Round the decay
Of that colossal wreck, boundless and bare
The lone and level sands stretch far away."

THE PAST
1818   1824

Wilt thou forget the happy hours
Which we buried in Love's sweet bowers,
Heaping over their corpses cold
Blossoms and leaves, instead of mould?
5   Blossoms which were the joys that fell,
    And leaves, the hopes that yet remain.

Forget the dead, the past? Oh, yet
There are ghosts that may take revenge
    for it;

1 Of the sculptor.   2 Of Ozymandias.

Memories that make the heart a tomb,
10 Regrets which glide through the spirit's
    gloom,
And with ghastly whispers tell
That joy, once lost, is pain.

ON A FADED VIOLET
1818   1821

The odor from the flower is gone,
  Which like thy kisses breathed on me;
The color from the flower is flown,
  Which glowed of thee, and only thee!

5 A shrivelled, lifeless, vacant form,
  It lies on my abandoned breast,
And mocks the heart, which yet is warm,
  With cold and silent rest.

I weep,—my tears revive it not!
10 I sigh,—it breathes no more on me;
Its mute and uncomplaining lot
  Is such as mine should be.

LINES WRITTEN AMONG THE
EUGANEAN HILLS
1818   1819

Many a green isle needs must be
In the deep, wide sea of misery,
Or the mariner, worn and wan,
Never thus could voyage on
5 Day and night, and night and day,
Drifting on his dreary way,
With the solid darkness black
Closing round his vessel's track;
Whilst above, the sunless sky,
10 Big with clouds, hangs heavily,
And behind, the tempest fleet
Hurries on with lightning feet,
Riving sail, and cord, and plank,
Till the ship has almost drank
15 Death from the o'er-brimming deep,
And sinks down, down, like that sleep
When the dreamer seems to be
Weltering through eternity;
And the dim low line before
20 Of a dark and distant shore
Still recedes, as ever still
Longing with divided will
But no power to seek or shun,
He is ever drifted on
25 O'er the unreposing wave
To the haven of the grave.
What, if there no friends will greet?
What, if there no heart will meet
His with love's impatient beat?
30 Wander wheresoe'er he may,
Can he dream before that day
To find refuge from distress
In friendship's smile, in love's caress?

Then 'twill wreak him little woe
35 Whether such there be or no;
Senseless is the breast, and cold,
Which relenting love would fold;
Bloodless are the veins, and chill,
Which the pulse of pain did fill;
40 Every little living nerve
That from bitter words did swerve
Round the tortured lips and brow,
Are like sapless leaflets now
Frozen upon December's bough.

45 On the beach of a northern sea
Which tempests shake eternally,
As once the wretch there lay to sleep,
Lies a solitary heap,
One white skull and seven dry bones,
50 On the margin of the stones,
Where a few gray rushes stand,
Boundaries of the sea and land:
Nor is heard one voice of wail
But the sea-mews, as they sail
55 O'er the billows of the gale;
Or the whirlwind up and down
Howling, like a slaughtered town,
When a king in glory rides
Through the pomp of fratricides:
60 Those unburied bones around
There is many a mournful sound;
There is no lament for him,
Like a sunless vapor, dim,
Who once clothed with life and thought
65 What now moves nor murmurs not.

Ay, many flowering islands lie
In the waters of wide agony:
To such a one this morn was led
My bark by soft winds piloted:
70 'Mid the mountains Euganean
I stood listening to the pæan
With which the legioned rooks did hail
The sun's uprise majestical;
Gathering round with wings all hoar,
75 Through the dewy mist they soar
Like gray shades, till the eastern heaven
Bursts, and then, as clouds of even,
Flecked with fire and azure, lie
In the unfathomable sky,
80 So their plumes of purple grain,[1]
Starred with drops of golden rain,
Gleam above the sunlight woods,
As in silent multitudes
On the morning's fitful gale
85 Through the broken mist they sail,
And the vapors cloven and gleaming
Follow, down the dark steep streaming,
Till all is bright, and clear, and still,
Round the solitary hill.
1 color

⁹⁰ Beneath is spread like a green sea
    The waveless plain of Lombardy,
    Bounded by the vaporous air,
    Islanded by cities fair;
    Underneath Day's azure eyes
⁹⁵ Ocean's nursling, Venice lies,
    A peopled labyrinth of walls,
    Amphitrite's destined halls.
    Which her hoary sire[1] now paves
    With his blue and beaming waves.
¹⁰⁰ Lo! the sun upsprings behind,
    Broad, red, radiant, half-reclined
    On the level quivering line
    Of the waters crystalline;
    And before that chasm of light,
¹⁰⁵ As within a furnace bright,
    Column, tower, and dome, and spire,
    Shine like obelisks of fire,
    Pointing with inconstant motion
    From the altar of dark ocean
¹¹⁰ To the sapphire-tinted skies;
    As the flames of sacrifice
    From the marble shrines did rise,
    As to pierce the dome of gold
    Where Apollo spoke of old.

¹¹⁵ Sun-girt City, thou hast been
    Ocean's child, and then his queen;[2]
    Now is come a darker day,[3]
    And thou soon must be his prey,
    If the power that raised thee here
¹²⁰ Hallow so thy watery bier.
    A less drear ruin then than now,
    With thy conquest-branded brow
    Stooping to the slave of slaves
    From thy throne among the waves,
¹²⁵ Wilt thou be, when the sea-mew
    Flies, as once before it flew,[4]
    O'er thine isles depopulate,
    And all is in its ancient state,
    Save where many a palace gate
¹³⁰ With green sea-flowers overgrown
    Like a rock of Ocean's own,
    Topples o'er the abandoned sea
    As the tides change sullenly.
    The fisher on his watery way,
¹³⁵ Wandering at the close of day,
    Will spread his sail and seize his oar
    Till he pass the gloomy shore,
    Lest thy dead should, from their sleep
    Bursting o'er the starlight deep,
¹⁴⁰ Lead a rapid masque of death

[1] Oceanus.
[2] A reference to the old annual custom of throwing a ring into the ocean in representation of the marriage of Venice and the Sea. See Wordsworth's *On the Extinction of the Venetian Republic* (p. 312).
[3] At this time, 1818, the greater part of northern Italy, including the old free cities, was under the oppressive domination of Austria, the "Celtic Anarch" of l. 152.
[4] Before the founding of the city.

    O'er the waters of his path.
    Those who alone thy towers behold
    Quivering through aërial gold,
    As I now behold them here,
¹⁴⁵ Would imagine not they were
    Sepulchres, where human forms,
    Like pollution-nourished worms,
    To the corpse of greatness cling,
    Murdered, and now mouldering:
¹⁵⁰ But if Freedom should awake
    In her omnipotence, and shake
    From the Celtic[1] Anarch's hold
    All the keys of dungeons cold,
    Where a hundred cities lie
¹⁵⁵ Chained like thee, ingloriously,
    Thou and all thy sister band
    Might adorn this sunny land,
    Twining memories of old time
    With new virtues more sublime;
¹⁶⁰ If not, perish thou and they!—
    Clouds which stain truth's rising day
    By her sun consumed away—
    Earth can spare ye: while like flowers,
    In the waste of years and hours,
¹⁶⁵ From your dust new nations spring
    With more kindly blossoming.

    Perish! let there only be
    Floating o'er thy heartless sea,
    As the garment of thy sky
¹⁷⁰ Clothes the world immortally,
    One remembrance, more sublime
    Than the tattered pall of time,
    Which scarce hides thy visage wan;—
    That a tempest-cleaving swan[2]
¹⁷⁵ Of the songs of Albion,
    Driven from his ancestral streams
    By the might of evil dreams,
    Found a nest in thee; and Ocean
    Welcomed him with such emotion
¹⁸⁰ That its joy grew his, and sprung
    From his lips like music flung
    O'er a mighty thunder-fit,
    Chastening terror. What though yet
    Poesy's unfailing river,
¹⁸⁵ Which through Albion winds forever
    Lashing with melodious wave
    Many a sacred poet's grave,
    Mourn its latest nursling fled?
    What though thou with all thy dead
¹⁹⁰ Scarce can for this fame repay
    Aught thine own? oh, rather say
    Though thy sins and slaveries foul
    Overcloud a sunlike soul?
    As the ghost of Homer clings
¹⁹⁵ Round Scamander's wasting springs;
    As divinest Shakespeare's might

[1] *Celtic* is here applied to northern barbarians not natives of Italy.
[2] A reference to Byron.

Fills Avon and the world with light
Like omniscient power which he
Imaged 'mid mortality;
200 As the love from Petrarch's urn,
Yet amid yon hills doth burn,
A quenchless lamp, by which the heart
Sees things unearthly;—so thou art,
Mighty spirit! so shall be
205 The city that did refuge thee.

Lo, the sun floats up the sky
Like thought-wingèd Liberty,
Till the universal light
Seems to level plain and height;
210 From the sea a mist has spread,
And the beams of morn lie dead
On the towers of Venice now,
Like its glory long ago.
By the skirts of that gray cloud
215 Many-domèd Padua proud
Stands, a peopled solitude,
'Mid the harvest-shining plain,
Where the peasant heaps his grain
In the garner of his foe,
220 And the milk-white oxen slow
With the purple vintage strain,
Heaped upon the creaking wain,[1]
That the brutal Celt may swill
Drunken sleep with savage will;
225 And the sickle to the sword
Lies unchanged, though many a lord,
Like a weed whose shade is poison,
Overgrows this region's foison,[2]
Sheaves of whom are ripe to come
230 To destruction's harvest-home:
Men must reap the things they sow,[3]
Force from force must ever flow,
Or worse; but 'tis a bitter woe
That love or reason cannot change
235 The despot's rage, the slave's revenge.
Padua, thou within whose walls
Those mute guests at festivals,
Son and mother, Death and Sin,
Played at dice for Ezzelin,
240 Till Death cried, "I win, I win!"[4]
And Sin cursed to lose the wager,
But Death promised, to assuage her,
That he would petition for
Her to be made vice-emperor,
245 When the destined years were o'er,
Over all between the Po
And the eastern Alpine snow,
Under the mighty Austrian.[5]
Sin smiled so as Sin only can,
250 And since that time, ay, long before,

[1] wagon
[2] plenty; rich harvest
[3] See *Galatians*, 6:7.
[4] See Coleridge's *The Rime of the Ancient Mariner*, 197 (p. 364).
[5] Francis I, Emperor of Austria (1804-35).

Both have ruled from shore to shore,—
That incestuous pair, who follow
Tyrants as the sun the swallow,
As Repentance follows Crime,
255 And as changes follow Time.

In thine halls the lamp of learning,
Padua, now no more is burning;
Like a meteor, whose wild way
Is lost over the grave of day,
260 It gleams betrayed and to betray:
Once remotest nations came
To adore that sacred flame,
When it lit not many a hearth
On this cold and gloomy earth:
265 Now new fires from antique light
Spring beneath the wide world's might;
But their spark lies dead in thee,
Trampled out by Tyranny.
As the Norway woodman quells,
270 In the depth of piny dells,
One light flame among the brakes,[1]
While the boundless forest shakes,
And its mighty trunks are torn
By the fire thus lowly born:
275 The spark beneath his feet is dead,
He starts to see the flames it fed
Howling through the darkened sky
With a myriad tongues victoriously,
And sinks down in fear: so thou,
280 O Tyranny, beholdest now
Light around thee, and thou hearest
The loud flames ascend, and fearest:
Grovel on the earth; ay, hide
In the dust thy purple pride!

285 Noon descends around me now:
'Tis the noon of autumn's glow,
When a soft and purple mist
Like a vaporous amethyst,
Or an air-dissolvèd star
290 Mingling light and fragrance, far
From the curved horizon's bound
To the point of heaven's profound,[2]
Fills the overflowing sky;
And the plains that silent lie
295 Underneath, the leaves unsodden
Where the infant Frost has trodden
With his morning-wingèd feet,
Whose bright print is gleaming yet;
And the red and golden vines,
300 Piercing with their trellised lines
The rough, dark-skirted wilderness;
The dun and bladed grass no less,
Pointing from this hoary tower
In the windless air; the flower
305 Glimmering at my feet; the line

[1] thickets   [2] That is, to the zenith.

Of the olive-sandalled[1] Apennine
In the south dimly islanded;
And the Alps, whose snows are spread
High between the clouds and sun;
310 And of living things each one;
And my spirit, which so long
Darkened this swift stream of song,—
Interpenetrated lie
By the glory of the sky:
315 Be it love, light, harmony,
Odor, or the soul of all
Which from heaven like dew doth fall,
Or the mind which feeds this verse
Peopling the lone universe.

320 Noon descends, and after noon
Autumn's evening meets me soon,
Leading the infantine moon,
And that one star, which to her
Almost seems to minister
325 Half the crimson light she brings
From the sunset's radiant springs:
And the soft dreams of the morn
(Which like wingèd winds had borne
To that silent isle, which lies
330 Mid remembered agonies,
The frail bark of this lone being)
Pass, to other sufferers fleeing,
And its ancient pilot, Pain,
Sits beside the helm again.

335 Other flowering isles must be
In the sea of life and agony:
Other spirits float and flee
O'er that gulf: even now, perhaps,
On some rock the wild wave wraps,
340 With folded wings they waiting sit
For my bark, to pilot it
To some calm and blooming cove,
Where for me, and those I love,
May a windless bower be built,
345 Far from passion, pain, and guilt,
In a dell mid lawny hills,
Which the wild sea-murmur fills,
And soft sunshine, and the sound
Of old forests echoing round,
350 And the light and smell divine
Of all flowers that breathe and shine:
We may live so happy there,
That the spirits of the air,
Envying us, may even entice
355 To our healing paradise
The polluting multitude;
But their rage would be subdued
By that clime divine and calm,
And the winds whose wings rain balm
360 On the uplifted soul, and leaves
Under which the bright sea heaves;
[1] covered with olive trees at the base

While each breathless interval
In their whisperings musical
The inspired soul supplies
365 With its own deep melodies;
And the love which heals all strife,
Circling, like the breath of life,
All things in that sweet abode
With its own mild brotherhood,
370 They, not it, would change; and soon
Every sprite beneath the moon
Would repent its envy vain,
And the earth grow young again.

STANZAS

WRITTEN IN DEJECTION, NEAR NAPLES
1818   1824

The sun is warm, the sky is clear,
  The waves are dancing fast and
    bright;
Blue isles and snowy mountains wear
  The purple noon's transparent might;
5   The breath of the moist earth is light
Around its unexpanded buds;
  Like many a voice of one delight,
The winds, the birds, the ocean floods,
The City's voice itself, is soft like Soli-
    tude's.

10   I see the Deep's untrampled floor
  With green and purple seaweeds
    strown;
I see the waves upon the shore,
  Like light dissolved in star-showers,
    thrown:
  I sit upon the sands alone,—
15   The lightning of the noontide ocean
Is flashing round me, and a tone
Arises from its measured motion,
How sweet! did any heart now share in
    my emotion.

Alas! I have nor hope nor health,
20   Nor peace within nor calm around,
Nor that content surpassing wealth
  The sage in meditation found,[1]
  And walked with inward glory
    crowned—
Nor fame, nor power, nor love, nor
    leisure.
25   Others I see whom these surround—
Smiling they live, and call life pleas-
    ure;—
To me that cup has been dealt in another
    measure.

[1] Numerous poets and philosophers have found
consolation in solitude. See Cowper's *The
Task*, 2 (p. 147); Byron's *Childe Harold's
Pilgrimage*, 4, 177-8 (p. 574); Keats's *Sonnet
to Solitude* (p. 780); also, De Quincey's *The
Affliction of Childhood* (p. 1115).

Yet now despair itself is mild,
    Even as the winds and waters are;
30 I could lie down like a tired child,
    And weep away the life of care
    Which I have borne and yet must
        bear,
    Till death like sleep might steal on me,
    And I might feel in the warm air
35 My cheek grow cold, and hear the sea
    Breathe o'er my dying brain its last
        monotony.

    Some might lament that I were cold,
    As I, when this sweet day is gone,
    Which my lost heart, too soon grown
        old,
40 Insults with this untimely moan;
    They might lament—for I am one
    Whom men love not,—and yet regret,
    Unlike this day, which, when the sun
    Shall on its stainless glory set,
45 Will linger, though enjoyed, like joy in
        memory yet.

LINES WRITTEN DURING THE CASTLEREAGH ADMINIS-TRATION
1819   *1832*

    Corpses are cold in the tomb—
    Stones on the pavement are dumb—
    Abortions are dead in the womb,
    And their mothers look pale, like the death-
        white shore
5   Of Albion, free no more.

    Her sons are as stones in the way—
    They are masses of senseless clay—
    They are trodden, and move not away—
    The abortion with which *she* travaileth
10   Is Liberty, smitten to death.

    Then trample and dance, thou Oppres-
        sor!
    For thy victim is no redresser—
    Thou art sole lord and possessor
    Of her corpses, and clods, and abortions—
        they pave
15   Thy path to the grave.

    Hearest thou the festival din
    Of Death and Destruction and Sin,
    And Wealth crying Havoc! within?
    'Tis the Bacchanal triumph that makes
        Truth dumb,—
20   Thine Epithalamium.

    Ay, marry thy ghastly wife!
    Let Fear and Disquiet and Strife
    Spread thy couch in the chamber of
        Life;

    Marry Ruin, thou Tyrant! and Hell be
        thy guide
25   To the bed of the bride!

THE MASK OF ANARCHY
WRITTEN ON THE OCCASION OF THE MASSACRE
AT MANCHESTER[1]
1819   *1832*

    As I lay asleep in Italy,
    There came a voice from over the sea,
    And with great power it forth led me
    To walk in the visions of Poesy.

5   I met Murder on the way—
    He had a mask like Castlereagh;
    Very smooth he looked, yet grim;
    Seven bloodhounds followed him.

    All were fat; and well they might
10 Be in admirable plight,
    For one by one, and two by two,
    He tossed them human hearts to chew,
    Which from his wide cloak he drew.

    Next came Fraud, and he had on,
15 Like Eldon, an ermined gown;
    His big tears, for he wept well,
    Turned to mill-stones as they fell;

    And the little children, who
    Round his feet played to and fro,
20 Thinking every tear a gem,
    Had their brains knocked out by them.

    Clothed with the Bible as with light,
    And the shadows of the night,
    Like Sidmouth, next Hypocrisy
25 On a crocodile rode by.

    And many more Destructions played
    In this ghastly masquerade,
    All disguised, even to the eyes,
    Like bishops, lawyers, peers, or spies.

30 Last came Anarchy; he rode
    On a white horse splashed with blood;
    He was pale even to the lips,
    Like Death in the Apocalypse.[2]

    And he wore a kingly crown;
35 In his hand a sceptre shone;
    On his brow this mark I saw—
    "I AM GOD, AND KING, AND LAW!"

    With a pace stately and fast,
    Over English land he passed,
40 Trampling to a mire of blood
    The adoring multitude.

[1] A mass-meeting of citizens who were eager for parliamentary reforms was attacked by soldiers in St. Peter's Field, on Aug. 16, 1819. A few persons were killed and several hundred injured.
[2] See *Revelation*, 6:8.

And a mighty troop around
With their trampling shook the ground,
Waving each a bloody sword
45 For the service of their Lord.

And, with glorious triumph, they
Rode through England, proud and gay,
Drunk as with intoxication
Of the wine of desolation.

50 O'er fields and towns, from sea to sea,
Passed that pageant swift and free,
Tearing up, and trampling down,
Till they came to London town.

And each dweller, panic-stricken,
55 Felt his heart with terror sicken,
Hearing the tempestuous cry
Of the triumph of Anarchy.

For with pomp to meet him came,
Clothed in arms like blood and flame,
60 The hired murderers, who did sing
"Thou art God, and Law, and King.

"We have waited, weak and lone
For thy coming, Mighty One!
Our purses are empty, our swords are cold,
65 Give us glory, and blood, and gold."

Lawyers and priests, a motley crowd,
To the earth their pale brows bowed;
Like a bad prayer not over loud,
Whispering—"Thou art Law and God!"

70 Then all cried with one accord,
"Thou art King, and God, and Lord;
Anarchy, to thee we bow,
Be thy name made holy now!"

And Anarchy, the Skeleton,
75 Bowed and grinned to every one,
As well as if his education
Had cost ten millions to the nation.

For he knew the palaces
Of our kings were rightly his;
80 His the sceptre, crown, and globe,
And the gold-inwoven robe.

So he sent his slaves before
To seize upon the Bank and Tower,
And was proceeding with intent
85 To meet his pensioned Parliament,

When one fled past, a maniac maid,
And her name was Hope, she said;
But she looked more like Despair,
And she cried out in the air:

90 "My father Time is weak and gray
With waiting for a better day;
See how idiot-like he stands,
Fumbling with his palsied hands!

"He has had child after child,
95 And the dust of death is piled
Over every one but me.
Misery, oh, Misery!"

Then she lay down in the street,
Right before the horses' feet,
100 Expecting, with a patient eye,
Murder, Fraud, and Anarchy;

When between her and her foes
A mist, a light, an image rose,—
Small at first, and weak, and frail
105 Like the vapor of a vale;

Till as clouds grow on the blast,
Like tower-crowned giants striding fast,
And glare with lightnings as they fly,
And speak in thunder to the sky,

110 It grew—a Shape arrayed in mail
Brighter than the viper's scale,
And upborne on wings whose grain[1]
Was as the light of sunny rain.

On its helm, seen far away,
115 A planet, like the Morning's, lay;
And those plumes its light rained through,
Like a shower of crimson dew.

With step as soft as wind it passed
O'er the heads of men—so fast
120 That they knew the presence there,
And looked—but all was empty air.

As flowers beneath May's footstep waken,
As stars from Night's loose hair are shaken,
As waves arise when loud winds call,
125 Thoughts sprung wher'er that step did
fall.

And the prostrate multitude
Looked—and ankle-deep in blood,
Hope, that maiden most serene,
Was walking with a quiet mien;

130 And Anarchy, the ghastly birth,
Lay dead earth upon the earth;
The Horse of Death, tameless as wind,
Fled, and with his hoofs did grind
To dust the murderers thronged behind.

135 A rushing light of clouds and splendor,
A sense, awakening and yet tender,

1 color

Was heard and felt, and at its close
These words of joy and fear arose,

As if their own indignant Earth,
140 Which gave the sons of England birth,
Had felt their blood upon her brow,
And, shuddering with a mother's throe.

Had turnèd every drop of blood,
By which her face had been bedewed,
145 To an accent unwithstood,
As if her heart had cried aloud:

"Men of England, heirs of glory,
Heroes of unwritten story,
Nurslings of one mighty Mother,
150 Hopes of her, and one another:

"Rise like lions after slumber,
In unvanquishable number;
Shake your chains to earth like dew
Which in sleep had fallen on you—
155 Ye are many, they are few.

"What is Freedom?—Ye can tell
That which Slavery is too well,
For its very name has grown
To an echo of your own.

160 " 'Tis to work, and have such pay
As just keeps life from day to day
In your limbs, as in a cell,
For the tyrants' use to dwell,—

"So that ye for them are made
165 Loom, and plough, and sword, and spade
With or without your own will, bent
To their defence and nourishment.

" 'Tis to see your children weak
With their mothers pine and peak,[1]
170 When the winter winds are bleak—
They are dying whilst I speak.

" 'Tis to hunger for such diet
As the rich man in his riot
Casts to the fat dogs that lie
175 Surfeiting beneath his eye.

" 'Tis to let the Ghost of Gold
Take from toil a thousandfold
More than e'er its substance could
In the tyrannies of old;

180 "Paper coin[2]—that forgery
Of the title-deeds which ye

[1] See *Macbeth*, I, 3, 23.
[2] Paper currency in England was worth considerably less than gold, but was declared to be of equal value by the House of Commons in 1810. See Cobbett's *Rural Rides*, Kensington, Jan. 4, 1822 (p. 1028).

Hold to something from the **worth**
Of the inheritance of Earth.

" 'Tis to be a slave in soul,
185 And to hold no strong control
Over your own wills, but be
All that others make of ye.

"And at length when ye complain
With a murmur weak and vain,
190 'Tis to see the Tyrant's crew
Ride over your wives and you—
Blood is on the grass like dew!

"Then it is to feel revenge,
Fiercely thirsting to exchange
195 Blood for blood—and wrong for wrong:
Do not thus when ye are strong!

"Birds find rest in narrow nest,
When weary of their wingèd quest;
Beasts find fare in woody lair,
200 When storm and snow are in the air.

"Horses, oxen, have a home,
When from daily toil they come;
Household dogs, when the wind roars,
Find a home within warm doors.

205 "Asses, swine, have litter spread,
And with fitting food are fed;
All things have a home but one—
Thou, O Englishman, hast none!

"This is Slavery; savage men,
210 Or wild beasts within a den,
Would endure not as ye do—
But such ills they never knew.

"What art thou, Freedom? Oh, could slaves
Answer from their living graves
215 This demand, tyrants would flee
Like a dream's dim imagery.

"Thou art not, as impostors say,
A shadow soon to pass away,
A superstition, and a name
220 Echoing from the cave of Fame.

"For the laborer thou art bread
And a comely table spread,
From his daily labor come
In a neat and happy home.

225 "Thou art clothes, and fire, and food
For the trampled multitude;
No—in countries that are free
Such starvation cannot be
As in England now we see.

230 "To the rich thou art a check;
When his foot is on the neck
Of his victim, thou dost make
That he treads upon a snake.

"Thou art Justice—ne'er for gold
235 May thy righteous laws be sold,
As laws are in England; thou
Shield'st alike the high and low.

"Thou art Wisdom—freemen never
Dream that God will damn forever
240 All who think those things untrue
Of which priests make such ado.

"Thou art Peace—never by thee
Would blood and treasure wasted be,
As tyrants wasted them, when all
245 Leagued to quench thy flame in Gaul.[1]

"What if English toil and blood
Was poured forth, even as a flood?
It availed, O Liberty!
To dim, but not extinguish thee.

250 "Thou art Love—the rich have kissed
Thy feet, and like him[2] following Christ,
Give their substance to the free
And through the rough world follow thee;

"Or turn their wealth to arms, and make
255 War for thy belovèd sake
On wealth and war and fraud, whence they
Drew the power which is their prey.

"Science, Poetry, and Thought
Are thy lamps; they make the lot
260 Of the dwellers in a cot
Such they curse their Maker not.

"Spirit, Patience, Gentleness,
All that can adorn and bless
Art thou—let deeds, not words, express
265 Thine exceeding loveliness.

"Let a great Assembly be
Of the fearless and the free,
On some spot of English ground
Where the plains stretch wide around.

270 "Let the blue sky overhead,
The green earth on which ye tread,
All that must eternal be,
Witness the solemnity.

"From the corners uttermost
275 Of the bounds of English coast;

From every hut, village, and town,
Where those, who live and suffer, moan
For others' misery or their own;

"From the workhouse and the prison,
280 Where, pale as corpses newly risen,
Women, children, young and old,
Groan for pain, and weep for cold;

"From the haunts of daily life,
Where is waged the daily strife
285 With common wants and common cares,
Which sows the human heart with tares;

"Lastly, from the palaces,
Where the murmur of distress
Echoes, like the distant sound
290 Of a wind alive, around

"Those prison-halls of wealth and fashion,
Where some few feel such compassion,
For those who groan, and toil, and wail,
As must make their brethren pale;—

295 "Ye who suffer woes untold,
Or to feel or to behold
Your lost country bought and sold
With a price of blood and gold:

"Let a vast Assembly be,
300 And with great solemnity
Declare with measured words that ye
Are, as God has made ye, free!

"Be your strong and simple words
Keen to wound as sharpened swords;
305 And wide as targes[1] let them be,
With their shade to cover ye.

"Let the tyrants pour around
With a quick and startling sound,
Like the loosening of a sea,
310 Troops of armed emblazonry.[2]

"Let the charged artillery drive,
Till the dead air seems alive
With the clash of clanging wheels
And the tramp of horses' heels.

315 "Let the fixèd bayonet
Gleam with sharp desire to wet
Its bright point in English blood,
Looking keen as one for food.

"Let the horsemen's scimitars
320 Wheel and flash, like sphereless stars

---

[1] A reference to the French Revolution and to
the union of the powers against France.
[2] See *Luke*, 18:18-22

[1] shields
[2] with shields, standards, etc., decorated with
brilliant figures or pictures

Thirsting to eclipse their burning
In a sea of death and mourning.

"Stand ye calm and resolute,
Like a forest close and mute,
325 With folded arms, and looks which are
Weapons of unvanquished war.

"And let Panic, who outspeeds
The career of armèd steeds,
Pass, a disregarded shade,
330 Through your phalanx undismayed.

"Let the laws of your own land,
Good or ill, between ye stand,
Hand to hand, and foot to foot,
Arbiters of the dispute:—

335 "The old laws of England—they
Whose reverend heads with age are gray,
Children of a wiser day,
And whose solemn voice must be
Thine own echo—Liberty!

340 "On those who first should violate
Such sacred heralds in their state,
Rest the blood that must ensue;
And it will not rest on you.

"And if then the tyrants dare,
345 Let them ride among you there,
Slash, and stab, and maim, and hew:
What they like, that let them do.

"With folded arms and steady eyes,
And little fear, and less surprise,
350 Look upon them as they slay,
Till their rage has died away.

"Then they will return with shame
To the place from which they came;
And the blood thus shed will speak
355 In hot blushes on their cheek.

"Every woman in the land
Will point at them as they stand;
They will hardly dare to greet
Their acquaintance in the street.

360 "And the bold, true warriors
Who have hugged Danger in wars,
Will turn to those who would be free,
Ashamed of such base company.

"And that slaughter to the Nation
365 Shall steam up like inspiration,
Eloquent, oracular;
A volcano heard afar.

"And these words shall then become
Like Oppression's thundered doom
370 Ringing through each heart and brain,
Heard again—again—again!

"Rise like lions after slumber
In unvanquishable number!
Shake your chains to earth, like dew
375 Which in sleep had fallen on you—
Ye are many, they are few!''

SONG TO THE MEN OF ENGLAND
1819   1839

Men of England, wherefore plough
For the lords who lay ye low?
Wherefore weave with toil and care
The rich robes your tyrants wear?

5 Wherefore feed, and clothe, and save,
From the cradle to the grave,
Those ungrateful drones who would
Drain your sweat—nay, drink your blood?

Wherefore, bees of England, forge
10 Many a weapon, chain, and scourge,
That these stingless drones may spoil
The forced produce of your toil.

Have ye leisure, comfort, calm,
Shelter, food, love's gentle balm?
15 Or what is it ye buy so dear
With your pain and with your fear?

The seed ye sow, another reaps;
The wealth ye find, another keeps;
The robes ye weave, another wears;
20 The arms ye forge, another bears.

Sow seed,—but let no tyrant reap;
Find wealth,—let no impostor heap;
Weave robes,—let not the idle wear;
Forge arms,—in your defence to bear.

25 Shrink to your cellars, holes, and cells;
In halls ye deck, another dwells.
Why shake the chains ye wrought? Ye see
The steel ye tempered glance on ye.

With plough and spade, and hoe and loom,
30 Trace your grave, and build your tomb,
And weave your winding-sheet, till fair
England be your sepulchre.

ENGLAND IN 1819
1819   1839

An old, mad, blind, despised, and dying
king;[1]
Princes, the dregs of their dull race, who
flow

[1] George III, King of England (1760-1820).

Through public scorn—mud from a muddy
 spring;
Rulers who neither see, nor feel, nor know,
5 But leech-like to their fainting country
 cling,
Till they drop, blind in blood, without a
 blow;
A people starved and stabbed in the un-
 tilled field;
An army, which liberticide and prey
Makes as a two-edged sword to all who
 wield;
10 Golden and sanguine laws which tempt
 and slay;
Religion Christless, Godless — a book
 sealed;
A Senate—Time's worst statute unre-
 pealed,—
Are graves, from which a glorious Phantom may
Burst to illumine our tempestuous day.

ODE TO THE WEST WIND
1819 1820

I

O wild West Wind, thou breath of Autumn's being,
Thou, from whose unseen presence the
 leaves dead
Are driven, like ghosts from an enchanter
 fleeing,

Yellow, and black, and pale, and hectic
 red,
5 Pestilence-stricken multitudes: O thou,
Who chariotest to their dark wintry bed

The wingèd seeds, where they lie cold
 and low,
Each like a corpse within its grave, until
Thine azure sister of the Spring shall
 blow

10 Her clarion o'er the dreaming earth, and
 fill
(Driving sweet buds like flocks to feed in
 air)
With living hues and odors plain and hill:

Wild Spirit, which art moving everywhere;
Destroyer and preserver; hear! oh, hear!

II

15 Thou on whose stream, mid the steep
 sky's commotion,
Loose clouds like earth's decaying leaves
 are shed,

Shook from the tangled boughs of Heaven
 and Ocean,

Angels of rain and lightning: there are
 spread
On the blue surface of thine airy surge,
20 Like the bright hair uplifted from the
 head

Of some fierce Mænad, even from the dim
 verge
Of the horizon to the zenith's height,
The locks of the approaching storm. Thou
 dirge

Of the dying year, to which this closing
 night[1]
25 Will be the dome of a vast sepulchre,
Vaulted with all thy congregated might

Of vapors, from whose solid atmosphere
Black rain, and fire, and hail will burst:
 oh, hear!

III

Thou who didst waken from his summer
 dreams
30 The blue Mediterranean, where he lay,
Lulled by the coil of his crystàlline
 streams,

Beside a pumice[2] isle in Baiæ's bay,
And saw in sleep old palaces and towers
Quivering within the wave's intenser day,

35 All overgrown with azure moss and flowers
So sweet, the sense faints picturing them!
 thou
For whose path the Atlantic's level
 powers

Cleave themselves into chasms, while far
 below
The sea-blooms and the oozy woods which
 wear
40 The sapless foliage of the ocean, know

Thy voice, and suddenly grow gray with
 fear,
And tremble and despoil themselves: oh,
 hear!

IV

If I were a dead leaf thou mightest bear;
If I were a swift cloud to fly with thee;
45 A wave to pant beneath thy power, and
 share

[1] night sky closing down over the earth
[2] A light, porous, volcanic substance.

The impulse of thy strength, only less
    free   10
Than thou, O uncontrollable! If even
I were as in my boyhood, and could be

The comrade of thy wanderings over
    heaven,   15
50 As then, when to outstrip thy skyey speed
Scarce seemed a vision; I would ne'er
    have striven

As thus with thee in prayer in my sore
    need.   20
Oh, lift me as a wave, a leaf, a cloud!
I fall upon the thorns of life! I bleed!

55 A heavy weight of hours has chained and
    bowed
One too like thee: tameless, and swift, and
    proud.

V

Make me thy lyre, even as the forest is:
What if my leaves are falling like its
    own!
The tumult of thy mighty harmonies

60 Will take from both a deep, autumnal
    tone,
Sweet though in sadness. Be thou, Spirit
    fierce,
My spirit! Be thou me, impetuous one!

Drive my dead thoughts over the universe
Like withered leaves to quicken a new
    birth!
65 And, by the incantation of this verse,

Scatter, as from an unextinguished hearth
Ashes and sparks, my words among man-
    kind!
Be through my lips to unawakened earth

The trumpet of a prophecy! O Wind,
70 If Winter comes, can Spring be far be-
    hind?

THE INDIAN SERENADE
1819   *1822*

I arise from dreams of thee
  In the first sweet sleep of night,
When the winds are breathing low,
  And the stars are shining bright:
5 I arise from dreams of thee,
  And a spirit in my feet
Hath led me—who knows how?
  To thy chamber window, sweet!

The wandering airs, they faint
  On the dark, the silent stream;
The champak[1] odors fail
  Like sweet thoughts in a dream;
The nightingale's complaint,
  It dies upon her heart,
15 As I must die on thine,
  Oh, belovèd as thou art!

Oh, lift me from the grass!
  I die! I faint! I fail!
Let thy love in kisses rain
  On my lips and eyelids pale.
My cheek is cold and white, alas!
  My heart beats loud and fast;—
Oh! press it close to thine again,
  Where it will break at last.

LOVE'S PHILOSOPHY
1819   *1819*

The fountains mingle with the river
  And the rivers with the ocean;
The winds of heaven mix forever
  With a sweet emotion;
5 Nothing in the world is single;
  All things by a law divine
In one spirit meet and mingle.
  Why not I with thine?

See the mountains kiss high heaven,
10   And the waves clasp one another;
No sister-flower would be forgiven
  If it disdained its brother;
And the sunlight clasps the earth,
  And the moonbeams kiss the sea:
15 What are all these kissings worth
  If thou kiss not me?

THE POET'S LOVER
1819   *1862*

I am as a spirit who has dwelt
Within his heart of hearts, and I have felt
His feelings, and have thought his thoughts,
  and known
The inmost converse of his soul, the tone
5 Unheard but in the silence of his blood,
When all the pulses in their multitude
Image the trembling calm of summer seas.
I have unlocked the golden melodies
Of his deep soul, as with a master-key,
10 And loosened them and bathed myself
  therein—
Even as an eagle in a thunder-mist
Clothing his wings with lightning.

[1] An Indian tree of the magnolia family

PROMETHEUS UNBOUND

A LYRICAL DRAMA IN FOUR ACTS
1818-19   1820

DRAMATIS PERSONÆ

PROMETHEUS	ASIA
DEMOGORGON	PANTHEA }Oceanides.
JUPITER	IONE
THE EARTH	THE PHANTASM OF JUPITER
OCEAN	THE SPIRIT OF THE EARTH
APOLLO	THE SPIRIT OF THE MOON
MERCURY	SPIRITS OF THE HOURS
HERCULES	SPIRITS ECHOES
	FAUNS FURIES

ACT I

SCENE.—*A Ravine of Icy Rocks in the
Indian Caucasus.* PROMETHEUS *is dis-
covered bound to the Precipice.* PAN-
THEA *and* IONE *are seated at his feet.
Time, night. During the Scene, morn-
ing slowly breaks.*

Prometheus. Monarch of Gods and
  Dæmons,[1] and all Spirits
But One,[2] who throng those bright and
  rolling worlds
Which Thou and I alone of living things
Behold with sleepless eyes! regard this
  Earth
5 Made multitudinous with thy slaves, whom
  thou
Requitest for knee-worship, prayer, and
  praise,
And toil, and hecatombs[3] of broken hearts,
With fear and self-contempt and barren
  hope.
Whilst me, who am thy foe, eyeless in
  hate,
10 Hast thou made reign and triumph, to thy
  scorn,
O'er mine own misery and thy vain revenge.
Three thousand years of sleep-unsheltered
  hours,
And moments aye divided by keen pangs
Till they seemed years, torture and solitude,
15 Scorn and despair,—these are mine empire:—
More glorious far than that which thou
  surveyest
From thine unenvied throne, O Mighty
  God!
Almighty, had I deigned to share the
  shame
Of thine ill tyranny, and hung not here
20 Nailed to this wall of eagle-baffling mountain,

[1] Supernatural beings of Greek mythology conceived as holding a position between gods
and men.
[2] Prometheus himself. See l. 265.
[3] sacrifices of great numbers

Black, wintry, dead, unmeasured; without
  herb,
Insect, or beast, or shape or sound of life.
Ah me! alas, pain, pain ever, forever!

No change, no pause, no hope! Yet I
  endure.
25 I ask the Earth, have not the mountains
  felt?
I ask yon Heaven, the all-beholding Sun,
Has it not seen? The Sea, in storm or
  calm,
Heaven's ever-changing shadow, spread
  below,
Have its deaf waves not heard my agony?
30 Ah me! alas, pain, pain ever, forever!

The crawling glaciers pierce me with the
  spears
Of their moon-freezing crystals; the bright
  chains
Eat with their burning cold into my bones.
Heaven's wingèd hound,[1] polluting from
  thy lips
35 His beak in poison not his own, tears up
My heart; and shapeless sights come wandering by,
The ghastly people of the realm of dream,
Mocking me: and the Earthquake-fiends
  are charged
To wrench the rivets from my quivering
  wounds
40 When the rocks split and close again
  behind:
While from their loud abysses howling
  throng
The genii of the storm, urging the rage
Of whirlwind, and afflict me with keen
  hail.
And yet to me welcome is day and night,
45 Whether one breaks the hoar-frost of the
  morn,
Or starry, dim, and slow, the other climbs
The leaden-colored east; for then they
  lead
The wingless, crawling hours, one among
  whom—
As some dark priest hales the reluctant
  victim—
50 Shall drag thee, cruel King, to kiss the
  blood
From these pale feet, which then might
  trample thee
If they disdained not such a prostrate
  slave.
Disdain! Ah, no! I pity thee. What ruin

[1] The vulture, which, according to ancient story,
daily tore the entrails of Prometheus.

Will hunt thee undefended through the wide Heaven!
55 How will thy soul, cloven to its depth with terror,
Gape like a hell within! I speak in grief,
Not exultation, for I hate no more,
As then ere misery made me wise. The curse
Once breathed on thee I would recall. Ye Mountains,
60 Whose many-voicèd Echoes, through the mist
Of cataracts, flung the thunder of that spell!
Ye icy Springs, stagnant with wrinkling frost,
Which vibrated to hear me, and then crept
Shuddering through India! Thou serenest Air,
65 Through which the Sun walks burning without beams!
And ye swift Whirlwinds, who on poisèd wings
Hung mute and moveless o'er yon hushed abyss,
As thunder, louder than your own, made rock
The orbèd world! If then my words had power,
70 Though I am changed so that aught evil wish
Is dead within; although no memory be
Of what is hate, let them not lose it now!
What was that curse? for ye all heard me speak.

First Voice (from the Mountains)

Thrice three hundred thousand years
75 O'er the Earthquake's couch we stood:
Oft, as men convulsed with fears,
We trembled in our multitude.

Second Voice (from the Springs)

Thunderbolts had parched our water,
We had been stained with bitter blood,
80 And had run mute, 'mid shrieks of slaughter,
Thro' a city and a solitude.

Third Voice (from the Air)

I had clothed, since Earth uprose,
Its wastes in colors not their own,
And oft had my serene repose
85 Been cloven by many a rending groan.

Fourth Voice (from the Whirlwinds)

We had soared beneath these mountains
Unresting ages; nor had thunder,
Nor yon volcano's flaming fountains,
Nor any power above or under
90 Ever made us mute with wonder.

First Voice

But never bowed our snowy crest
As at the voice of thine unrest.

Second Voice

Never such a sound before
To the Indian waves we bore.
95 A pilot asleep on the howling sea
Leaped up from the deck in agony,
And heard, and cried, "Ah, woe is me!"
And died as mad as the wild waves be.

Third Voice

By such dread words from Earth to Heaven
100 My still realm was never riven:
When its wound was closed, there stood
Darkness o'er the day like blood.

Fourth Voice

And we shrank back: for dreams of ruin
To frozen caves our flight pursuing
105 Made us keep silence—thus—and thus—
Though silence is as hell to us.

The Earth. The tongueless Caverns of the craggy hills
Cried "Misery!" then; the hollow Heaven replied
"Misery!" And the Ocean's purple waves,
110 Climbing the land, howled to the lashing winds,
And the pale nations heard it, "Misery!"
Prometheus. I heard a sound of voices: not the voice
Which I gave forth. Mother, thy sons and thou
Scorn him, without whose all-enduring will
115 Beneath the fierce omnipotence of Jove,
Both they and thou had vanished, like thin mist
Unrolled on the morning wind. Know ye not me,
The Titan? He who made his agony
The barrier to your else all-conquering foe?
120 O rock-embosomed lawns, and snow-fed streams,
Now seen athwart frore[1] vapors, deep below,
Through whose o'ershadowing woods I wandered once
With Asia, drinking life from her lovèd eyes;

[1] frozen

Why scorns the spirit which informs[1] ye,
now
125 To commune with me? me alone, who
checked,
As one who checks a fiend-drawn charioteer,
The falsehood and the force of him who
reigns
Supreme, and with the groans of pining
slaves
Fills your dim glens and liquid wilder-
nesses:
130 Why answer ye not, still? Brethren!
 The Earth.   They dare not.
Prometheus. Who dares? for I would
hear that curse again.
Ha, what an awful whisper rises up!
'Tis scarce like sound: it tingles through
the frame
135 As lightning tingles, hovering ere it strike.
Speak, Spirit! from thine inorganic voice
I only know that thou are moving near
And love. How cursed I him?
 The Earth.   How canst thou hear
Who knowest not the language of the dead?
 Prometheus. Thou art a living spirit;
speak as they.
140 *The Earth*. I dare not speak like life,
lest Heaven's fell King
Should hear, and link me to some wheel of
pain
More torturing than the one whereon I roll.
Subtle thou art and good, and though the
Gods
Hear not this voice, yet thou art more than
God,
145 Being wise and kind: earnestly hearken
now.
 Prometheus. Obscurely through my
brain, like shadows dim,
Sweep awful thoughts, rapid and thick.
I feel
Faint, like one mingled in entwining love;
Yet 'tis not pleasure.
 The Earth. No, thou canst not hear:
150 Thou art immortal, and this tongue is
known
Only to those who die.
 Prometheus. And what are thou,
O melancholy Voice?
 The Earth. I am the Earth,
Thy mother; she within whose stony veins,
To the last fibre of the loftiest tree
155 Whose thin leaves trembled in the frozen
air,
Joy ran, as blood within a living frame,
When thou didst from her bosom, like a
cloud
Of glory, arise, a spirit of keen joy!
[1] animates

160 And at thy voice her pining sons uplifted
Their prostrate brows from the polluting
dust,
And our almighty Tyrant with fierce dread
Grew pale, until his thunder chained thee
here.
Then—see those million worlds which burn
and roll
Around us—their inhabitants beheld
165 My spherèd light wane in wide Heaven;
the sea
Was lifted by strange tempest, and new
fire
From earthquake-rifted mountains of
bright snow
Shook its portentous hair beneath Heav-
en's frown;
Lightning and Inundation vexed the plains;
170 Blue thistles bloomed in cities; foodless
toads
Within voluptuous chambers panting
crawled:
When Plague had fallen on man and beast
and worm,
And Famine; and black blight on herb
and tree;
And in the corn, and vines, and meadow-
grass,
175 Teemed ineradicable poisonous weeds
Draining their growth; for my wan breast
was dry
With grief; and the thin air, my breath,
was stained
With the contagion of a mother's hate
Breathed on her child's destroyer; ay, I
heard
180 Thy curse, the which, if thou rememberest
not,
Yet my innumerable seas and streams,
Mountains, and caves, and winds, and yon
wide air,
And the inarticulate people of the dead,
Preserve, a treasured spell. We meditate
185 In secret joy and hope those dreadful
words,
But dare not speak them.
 Prometheus. Venerable mother!
All else who live and suffer take from
thee
Some comfort; flowers, and fruits, and
happy sounds,
And love, though fleeting; these may not
be mine.
190 But mine own words, I pray, deny me not.
 The Earth. They shall be told. Ere
Babylon was dust,
The Magus Zoroaster, my dead child,
Met his own image walking in the garden.
That apparition, sole of men, he saw.

195 For know there are two worlds of life and
    death:
One that which thou beholdest; but the
    other
Is underneath the grave, where do inhabit
The shadows of all forms that think and
    live,
Till death unite them and they part no
    more;
200 Dreams and the light imaginings of men,
And all that faith creates or love desires,
Terrible, strange, sublime, and beauteous
    shapes.
There thou art, and dost hang, a writhing
    shade,
'Mid whirlwind-peopled mountains; all
    the gods
205 Are there, and all the powers of nameless
    worlds,
Vast, sceptred phantoms; heroes, men, and
    beasts;
And Demogorgon, a tremendous gloom;
And he, the supreme Tyrant, on his throne
Of burning gold. Son, one of these shall
    utter
210 The curse which all remember. Call at will
Thine own ghost, or the ghost of Jupiter,
Hades or Typhon, or what mightier Gods
From all-prolific Evil, since thy ruin
Have sprung, and trampled on my pros-
    trate sons.
215 Ask, and they must reply: so the revenge
Of the Supreme may sweep through vacant
    shades,
As rainy wind through the abandoned gate
Of a fallen palace.
    Prometheus. Mother, let not aught
Of that which may be evil, pass again
220 My lips, or those of aught resembling me.
Phantasm of Jupiter, arise, appear!

Ione

My wings are folded o'er mine ears:
    My wings are crossèd o'er mine eyes:
Yet through their silver shade appears,
225   And through their lulling plumes arise,
A Shape, a throng of sounds;
    May it be no ill to thee
    O thou of many wounds!
Near whom, for our sweet sister's sake,
230 Ever thus we watch and wake.

Panthea

The sound is of whirlwind underground,
    Earthquake, and fire, and mountains
    cloven;
The shape is awful like the sound,
    Clothed in dark purple, star-inwoven.

235 A sceptre of pale gold
    To stay steps proud, o'er the slow
    cloud
His veinèd hand doth hold.
Cruel he looks, but calm and strong,
Like one who does, not suffers wrong.

240 *Phantasm of Jupiter.* Why have the
    secret powers of this strange world
Driven me, a frail and empty phantom,
    hither
On direst storms? What unaccustomed
    sounds
Are hovering on my lips, unlike the voice
With which our pallid race hold ghastly
    talk
245 In darkness? And, proud sufferer, who
    art thou?
    Prometheus. Tremendous Image, as thou
    art must be
He whom thou shadowest forth. I am his
    foe,
The Titan. Speak the words which I would
    hear,
Although no thought inform thine empty
    voice.
250   *The Earth.* Listen! And though your
    echoes must be mute,
Gray mountains, and old woods, and
    haunted springs,
Prophetic caves, and isle - surrounding
    streams,
Rejoice to hear what yet ye cannot speak.
    Phantasm. A spirit seizes me and speaks
    within:
255 It tears me as fire tears a thunder-cloud.
    Panthea. See how he lifts his mighty
    looks! the Heaven
Darkens above.
    Ione.   He speaks! O shelter me!
    Prometheus. I see the curse on gestures
    proud and cold,
And looks of firm defiance, and calm hate,
260 And such despair as mocks itself with
    smiles,
Written as on a scroll: yet speak: Oh,
    speak!

Phantasm

Fiend, I defy thee! with a calm, fixed
    mind,
    All that thou canst inflict I bid thee
    do;
Foul Tyrant both of Gods and human-
    kind,
265   One only being shalt thou not subdue.
    Rain then thy plagues upon me here,
    Ghastly disease, and frenzying fear;
    And let alternate frost and fire

Eat into me, and be thine ire
270 Lightning, and cutting hail, and legioned
forms
Of furies, driving by upon the wounding
storms.

Ay, do thy worst. Thou art omnipotent.
O'er all things but thyself I gave thee
power,
And my own will. Be thy swift mis-
chiefs sent
275 To blast mankind, from yon ethereal
tower.
Let thy malignant spirit move
In darkness over those I love:
On me and mine I imprecate
The utmost torture of thy hate;
280 And thus devote to sleepless agony,
This undeclining head while thou must
reign on high.

But thou, who art the God and Lord:
O thou
Who fillest with thy soul this world of
woe,
To whom all things of Earth and Heaven
do bow
285 In fear and worship—all-prevailing
foe!
I curse thee! let a sufferer's curse
Clasp thee, his torturer, like remorse;
Till thine Infinity shall be
A robe of envenomed agony;[1]
290 And thine Omnipotence a crown of pain,
To cling like burning gold round thy dis-
solving brain.

Heap on thy soul, by virtue of this Curse,
Ill deeds, then be thou damned, be-
holding good;
Both infinite as is the universe,
295 And thou, and thy self-torturing soli-
tude.
An awful image of calm power
Though now thou sittest, let the hour
Come, when thou must appear to be
That which thou art internally;
300 And after many a false and fruitless crime
Scorn track thy lagging fall through
boundless space and time.

Prometheus. Were these my words, O
Parent?
The Earth. They were thine.
Prometheus. It doth repent me: words
are quick and vain;
Grief for awhile is blind, and so was mine.
305 I wish no living thing to suffer pain.

[1] A reference to the shirt of Nessus which
poisoned Hercules.

The Earth
Misery, Oh, misery to me,
That Jove at length should vanquish
thee.
Wail, howl aloud, Land and Sea,
The Earth's rent heart shall answer ye.
310 Howl, Spirits of the living and the dead,
Your refuge, your defence lies fallen and
vanquishèd!

First Echo
Lies fallen and vanquishèd!

Second Echo
Fallen and vanquishèd!

Ione
Fear not: 'tis but some passing spasm,
The Titan is unvanquished still.
315 But see, where through the azure chasm
Of yon forked and snowy hill
Trampling the slant winds on high
With golden-sandalled feet, that glow
320 Under plumes of purple dye,
Like rose-ensanguined ivory,
A Shape comes now,
Stretching on high from his right hand
A serpent-cinctured wand.[1]

Panthea
325 'Tis Jove's world-wandering herald,
Mercury.

Ione
And who are those with hydra tresses
And iron wings that climb the wind,
Whom the frowning God represses,—
Like vapors steaming up behind,
330 Clanging loud, an endless crowd?

Panthea
These are Jove's tempest-walking hounds,
Whom he gluts with groans and blood,
When charioted on sulphurous cloud
He bursts Heaven's bounds.

Ione
335 Are they now led from the thin dead
On new pangs to be fed?

Panthea
The Titan looks as ever, firm, not proud.

First Fury. Ha! I scent life!
Second Fury. Let me but look into
his eyes!

[1] The rod entwined with two serpents and carried by Mercury.

Third Fury. The hope of torturing him
    smells like a heap
340 Of corpses, to a death-bird after battle.
    First Fury. Darest thou delay, O Her-
    ald! take cheer, Hounds
Of Hell: what if the Son of Maia[1] soon
Should make us food and sport—who can
    please long
The Omnipotent?
    Mercury. Back to your towers of iron,
345 And gnash, beside the streams of fire, and
    wail,
Your foodless teeth. Geryon, arise! and
    Gorgon,
Chimæra, and thou Sphinx, subtlest of
    fiends
Who ministered to Thebes Heaven's poi-
    soned wine,[2]
Unnatural love, and more unnatural
    hate:
350 These shall perform your task.
    First Fury. Oh, mercy! mercy!
We die with our desire: drive us not back!
    Mercury. Crouch then in silence.
             Awful Sufferer!
To thee unwilling, most unwillingly
I come, by the great Father's will driven
    down,
355 To execute a doom of new revenge.
Alas! I pity thee, and hate myself
That I can do no more: aye from thy
    sight
Returning, for a season, Heaven seems
    Hell,
So thy worn form pursues me night and
    day,
360 Smiling reproach. Wise art thou, firm and
    good,
But vainly wouldst stand forth alone in
    strife
Against the Omnipotent; as yon clear
    lamps
That measure and divide the weary years
From which there is no refuge, long have
    taught
365 And long must teach. Even now thy Tor-
    turer arms
With the strange might of unimagined
    pains
The powers who scheme slow agonies in
    Hell,
And my commission is to lead them
    here,
Or what more subtle, foul, or savage fiends
370 People the abyss, and leave them to their
    task.

[1] Mercury.
[2] The Sphinx propounded a riddle to the Thebans,
and killed all passers-by who could not solve
it. See DeQuincey's *The Sphinx's Riddle.*

Be it not so! there is a secret known
To thee, and to none else of living things,[1]
Which may transfer the sceptre of wide
    Heaven,
The fear of which perplexes the Supreme:
375 Clothe it in words, and bid it clasp his
    throne
In intercession; bend thy soul in prayer,
And like a suppliant in some gorgeous
    fane,
Let the will kneel within thy haughty
    heart:
For benefits and meek submission tame
380 The fiercest and the mightiest.
    Prometheus. Evil minds
Change good to their own nature. I gave
    all
He has; and in return he chains me here
Years, ages, night and day: whether the
    Sun
Split my parched skin, or in the moony
    night
385 The crystal-wingèd snow cling round my
    hair:
Whilst my belovèd race is trampled down
By his thought-executing ministers.[2]
Such is the tyrant's recompense. 'Tis just.
He who is evil can receive no good;
390 And for a world bestowed, or a friend lost,
He can feel hate, fear, shame; not grati-
    tude:
He but requites me for his own misdeed.
Kindness to such is keen reproach, which
    breaks
With bitter stings the light sleep of Re-
    venge.
395 Submission, thou dost know I cannot try:
For what submission but that fatal word,
The death-seal of mankind's captivity,
Like the Sicilian's hair-suspended sword,[3]
Which trembles o'er his crown, would he
    accept,
400 Or could I yield? Which yet I will not
    yield.
Let others flatter Crime where it sits
    throned
In brief Omnipotence: secure are they:
For Justice, when triumphant, will weep
    down
Pity, not punishment, on her own wrongs,
405 Too much avenged by those who err. I
    wait,

[1] Prometheus knew that Jupiter would be overthrown. See Byron's *Prometheus,* 30-31 (p.
548).
[2] See *King Lear,* III, 2, 4.
[3] The sword which was suspended on a single
hair over the head of Damocles while he was
seated at a royal banquet, to rebuke him for
his constant praises of the happiness of
kings.

Enduring thus, the retributive hour
Which since we spake is even nearer now.
But hark, the hell-hounds clamor: fear
    delay:
Behold! Heaven lowers under thy Fa-
    ther's frown.
410 *Mercury.* Oh, that we might be spared:
    I to inflict
And thou to suffer! Once more answer me:
Thou knowest not the period of Jove's
    power?
    Prometheus. I know but this, that it
      must come.
    Mercury. Alas!
Thou canst not count thy years to come of
    pain!
415 *Prometheus.* They last while Jove must
      reign: nor more, nor less
Do I desire or fear.
    Mercury. Yet pause, and plunge
Into Eternity, where recorded time,
Even all that we imagine, age on age,
Seems but a point, and the reluctant mind
420 Flags wearily in its unending flight,
Till it sink, dizzy, blind, lost, shelterless;
Perchance it has not numbered the slow
    years
Which thou must spend in torture, un-
    reprieved?
    Prometheus. Perchance no thought can
      count them, yet they pass.
425 *Mercury.* If thou might'st dwell among
      the Gods the while
Lapped in voluptuous joy?
    Prometheus. I would not quit
This bleak ravine, these unrepentant pains.
    Mercury. Alas! I wonder at, yet pity
    thee.
    Prometheus. Pity the self-despising
      slaves of Heaven,
430 Not me, within whose mind sits peace
    serene,
As light in the sun, throned. How vain is
    talk!
Call up the fiends.
    Ione. Oh, sister, look! White fire
Has cloven to the roots yon huge snow-
    loaded cedar;
How fearfully God's thunder howls be-
    hind!
435 *Mercury.* I must obey his words and
    thine. Alas!
Most heavily remorse hangs at my heart!
    Panthea. See where the child of Heav-
    en, with wingèd feet,
Runs down the slanted sunlight of the
    dawn.
    Ione. Dear sister, close thy plumes over
    thine eyes.

440 Lest thou behold and die: they come—they
    come—
Blackening the birth of day with countless
    wings,
And hollow underneath, like death.
    First Fury. Prometheus!
    Second Fury. Immortal Titan!
    Third Fury. Champion of Heaven's
      slaves!
    Prometheus. He whom some dreadful
      voice invokes is here,
445 Prometheus, the chained Titan. Horrible
    forms,
What and who are ye? Never yet there
    came
Phantasms so foul through monster-teem-
    ing Hell
From the all-miscreative brain of Jove;
Whilst I behold such execrable shapes,
450 Methinks I grow like what I contemplate,
And laugh and stare in loathsome sym-
    pathy.
    First Fury. We are the ministers of
      pain, and fear,
And disappointment, and mistrust, and
    hate,
And clinging crime; and as lean dogs
    pursue
455 Through wood and lake some struck and
    sobbing fawn,
We track all things that weep, and bleed,
    and live,
When the great King betrays them to our
    will.
    Prometheus. O many fearful natures in
      one name,
I know ye; and these lakes and echoes
    know
460 The darkness and the clangor of your
    wings.
But why more hideous than your loathèd
    selves
Gather ye up in legions from the deep?
    Second Fury. We knew not that. Sis-
      ters, rejoice, rejoice!
    Prometheus. Can aught exult in its de-
      formity?
465 *Second Fury.* The beauty of delight
      makes lovers glad,
Gazing on one another: so are we.
As from the rose which the pale priestess
    kneels
To gather for her festal crown of flowers
The aërial crimson falls, flushing her
    cheek,
470 So from our victim's destined agony
The shade which is our form invests us
    round;
Else we are shapeless as our mother Night.

Prometheus. I laugh your power, and his who sent you here,
To lowest scorn.[1] Pour forth the cup of pain.

475 *First Fury.* Thou thinkest we will rend thee bone from bone,
And nerve from nerve, working like fire within?

Prometheus. Pain is my element, as hate is thine;
Ye rend me now: I care not.

Second Fury. Dost imagine
We will but laugh into thy lidless eyes?

480 *Prometheus.* I weigh not what ye do, but what ye suffer,
Being evil. Cruel was the power which called
You, or aught else so wretched, into light.

Third Fury. Thou think'st we will live through thee, one by one,
Like animal life, and though we can obscure not

485 The soul which burns within, that we will dwell
Beside it, like a vain loud multitude
Vexing the self-content of wisest men:
That we will be dread thought beneath thy brain,
And foul desire round thine astonished heart,

490 And blood within thy labyrinthine veins
Crawling like agony?

Prometheus. Why, ye are thus now;
Yet am I king over myself, and rule
The torturing and conflicting throngs within,
As Jove rules you when Hell grows mutinous.

Chorus of Furies

495 From the ends of the earth, from the ends of the earth,
Where the night has its grave and the morning its birth,
Come, come, come!
Oh, ye who shake hills with the scream of your mirth,
When cities sink howling in ruin; and ye

500 Who with wingless footsteps trample the sea,
And close upon Shipwreck and Famine's track,
Sit chattering with joy on the foodless wreck;
Come, come, come!
Leave the bed, low, cold, and red,

505 Strewed beneath a nation dead;

[1] See *Macbeth*, IV, 1, 79-80.

Leave the hatred, as in ashes
Fire is left for future burning:
It will burst in bloodier flashes
When ye stir it, soon returning:

510 Leave the self-contempt implanted
In young spirits, sense-enchanted,
Misery's yet unkindled fuel:
Leave Hell's secrets half unchanted
To the maniac dreamer; cruel

515 More than ye can be with hate
Is he with fear.
Come, come, come!
We are steaming up from Hell's wide gate
And we burthen the blasts of the atmosphere,

520 But vainly we toil till ye come here.

Ione. Sister, I hear the thunder of new wings.
Panthea. These solid mountains quiver with the sound
Even as the tremulous air: their shadows make
The space within my plumes more black than night.

First Fury

525 Your call was as a wingèd car
Driven on whirlwinds fast and far;
It rapped us from red gulfs of war.

Second Fury

From wide cities, famine-wasted;

Third Fury

Groans half heard, and blood untasted;

Fourth Fury

530 Kingly conclaves stern and cold,
Where blood with gold is bought and sold;

Fifth Fury

From the furnace, white and hot,
In which—

A Fury

Speak not: whisper not:
I know all that ye would tell,

535 But to speak might break the spell
Which must bend the Invincible,
The stern of thought;
He yet defies the deepest power of Hell.

A Fury

Tear the veil!

Another Fury

It is torn.

Chorus

The pale stars of the morn
540 Shine on a misery, dire to be borne.
Dost thou faint, mighty Titan? We laugh
    thee to scorn.
Dost thou boast the clear knowledge thou
    waken'dst for man?
Then was kindled within him a thirst which
    outran
Those perishing waters; a thirst of fierce
    fever,
545 Hope, love, doubt, desire, which consume
    him forever.
One came forth of gentle worth[1]
Smiling on the sanguine earth;
His words outlived him, like swift poison
Withering up truth, peace, and pity.
550 Look! where round the wide horizon
Many a million-peopled city
Vomits smoke in the bright air.
Mark that outcry of despair!
'Tis his mild and gentle ghost
555   Wailing for the faith he kindled:
Look again! the flames almost
    To a glow-worm's lamp have dwin-
    dled:
The survivors round the embers
    Gather in dread.
560   Joy, joy, joy!
Past ages crowd on thee, but each one
    remembers,
And the future is dark, and the present is
    spread
Like a pillow of thorns for thy slumberless
    head.

Semichorus I

Drops of bloody agony flow
565 From his white and quivering brow.
Grant a little respite now:
See! a disenchanted nation
Springs like day from desolation;
To Truth its state is dedicate,
570 And Freedom leads it forth, her mate;
A legioned band of linkèd brothers
Whom Love calls children—

Semichorus II

'Tis another's:
See how kindred murder kin!
'Tis the vintage-time for Death and Sin:
575 Blood, like new wine, bubbles within:
Till Despair smothers
The struggling world, which slaves and
    tyrants win.

[All the FURIES vanish, except one.

[1] A reference to Christ.

Ione. Hark, sister! what a low yet
    dreadful groan
Quite unsuppressed is tearing up the heart
580 Of the good Titan, as storms tear the deep,
And beasts hear the sea moan in inland
    caves.
Darest thou observe how the fiends torture
    him?
Panthea. Alas! I looked forth twice,
    but will no more.
Ione. What didst thou see?
Panthea.   A woful sight: a youth
585 With patient looks nailed to a crucifix.
Ione. What next?
Panthea.   The heaven around,
    the earth below,
Was peopled with thick shapes of human
    death,
All horrible, and wrought by human hands;
And some appeared the work of human
    hearts,
590 For men were slowly killed by frowns and
    smiles:
And other sights too foul to speak and live
Were wandering by. Let us not tempt
    worse fear
By looking forth: those groans are grief
    enough.
Fury. Behold an emblem: those who do
    endure
595 Deep wrongs for man, and scorn, and
    chains, but heap
Thousandfold torment on themselves and
    him.
Prometheus. Remit the anguish of that
    lighted stare;
Close those wan lips; let that thorn-
    wounded brow
Stream not with blood; it mingles with
    thy tears!
600 Fix, fix those tortured orbs in peace and
    death,
So thy sick throes shake not that crucifix,
So those pale fingers play not with thy
    gore.
Oh, horrible! Thy name I will not speak—
It hath become a curse. I see, I see
605 The wise, the mild, the lofty, and the
    just,
Whom thy slaves hate for being like to
    thee,
Some hunted by foul lies from their heart's
    home,
An early-chosen, late-lamented home,
As hooded ounces cling to the driven
    hind;[1]

[1] The ounce is the cheetah, or leopard, which is
used in Southern Asia for hunting deer. It
is kept hooded, or blindfolded, until the game
is sighted.

610 Some linked to corpses in unwholesome
    cells:
Some—hear I not the multitude laugh
    loud?—
Impaled in lingering fire: and mighty
    realms
Float by my feet, like sea-uprooted isles,
Whose sons are kneaded down in common
    blood
615 By the red light of their own burning
    homes.
    Fury. Blood thou canst see, and fire;
        and canst hear groans;
Worse things, unheard, unseen, remain be-
    hind.
    Prometheus. Worse?
    Fury. In each human heart terror
        survives
The ruin it has gorged: the loftiest fear
620 All that they would disdain to think were
    true:
Hypocrisy and custom make their minds
The fanes of many a worship, now out-
    worn.
They dare not devise good for man's estate,
And yet they know not that they do not
    dare.
625 The good want power, but to weep barren
    tears.
The powerful goodness want: worse need
    for them.
The wise want love; and those who love
    want wisdom;
And all best things are thus confused to ill.
Many are strong and rich, and would be
    just,
630 But live among their suffering fellow-men
As if none felt: they know not what they
    do.
    Prometheus. Thy words are like a cloud
        of wingèd snakes;
And yet I pity those they torture not.
    Fury. Thou pitiest them? I speak no
        more! [*Vanishes.*
    Prometheus. Ah woe!
635 Ah woe! Alas! pain, pain ever, forever!
I close my tearless eyes, but see more
    clear
Thy works within my woe-illumèd mind,
Thou subtle tyrant! Peace is in the grave.
The grave hides all things beautiful and
    good:
640 I am a God and cannot find it there,
Nor would I seek it: for, though dread
    revenge,
This is defeat, fierce King, not victory.
The sights with which thou torturest gird
    my soul
With new endurance, till the hour arrives

645 When they shall be no types of things
    which are.
    Panthea. Alas! what sawest thou?
    Prometheus. There are two woes—
To speak, and to behold; thou spare me
    one.
Names are there, Nature's sacred watch-
    words, they
Were borne aloft in bright emblazonry;
650 The nations, thronged around, and cried
    aloud,
As with one voice, Truth, Liberty, and
    Love!
Suddenly fierce confusion fell from heaven
Among them: there was strife, deceit, and
    fear:
Tyrants rushed in, and did divide the spoil.
655 This was the shadow of the truth I saw.
    The Earth. I felt thy torture, son, with
        such mixed joy
As pain and virtue give. To cheer thy state
I bid ascend those subtle and fair spirits,
Whose homes are the dim caves of human
    thought,
660 And who inhabit, as birds wing the wind,
Its world-surrounding ether: they behold
Beyond that twilight realm, as in a glass,
The future: may they speak comfort to
    thee!
    Panthea. Look, sister, where a troop of
        spirits gather,
665 Like flocks of clouds in spring's delight-
    ful weather,
Thronging in the blue air!
    Ione. And see! more come,
Like fountain-vapors when the winds are
    dumb,
That climb up the ravine in scattered lines.
And hark! is it the music of the pines?
670 Is it the lake? Is it the waterfall?
    Panthea. 'Tis something sadder, sweeter
        far than all.

Chorus of Spirits

From unremembered ages we
Gentle guides and guardians be
Of heaven-oppressed mortality;
And we breathe, and sicken not,
675 The atmosphere of human thought:
Be it dim, and dank, and gray,
Like a storm-extinguished day,
Travell'd o'er by dying gleams;
Be it bright as all between
680 Cloudless skies and windless streams,
Silent, liquid, and serene;
As the birds within the wind,
As the fish within the wave,
As the thoughts of man's own mind
685 Float through all above the grave;

We make there our liquid lair,
Voyaging cloudlike and unpent
Through the boundless element:
690   Thence we bear the prophecy
Which begins and ends in thee!

Ione. More yet come, one by one: the
    air around them
Looks radiant as the air around a star.

First Spirit

On a battle-trumpet's blast
695   I fled hither, fast, fast, fast,
'Mid the darkness upward cast.
From the dust of creeds outworn,
From the tyrant's banner torn,
Gathering 'round me, onward borne,
700   There was mingled many a cry—
Freedom! Hope! Death! Victory!
Till they faded through the sky;
And one sound, above, around,
One sound beneath, around, above,
705   Was moving; 'twas the soul of love;
'Twas the hope, the prophecy,
Which begins and ends in thee.

Second Spirit

A rainbow's arch stood on the sea,
Which rocked beneath, immovably;
710   And the triumphant storm did flee,
Like a conqueror, swift and proud,
Between,[1] with many a captive cloud,
A shapeless, dark and rapid crowd,
Each by lightning riven in half:
715   I heard the thunder hoarsely laugh:
Mighty fleets were strewn like chaff
And spread beneath a hell of death
O'er the white waters. I alit
On a great ship lightning-split,
720   And speeded hither on the sigh
Of one who gave an enemy
His plank, then plunged aside to die.

Third Spirit

I sate beside a sage's bed,
And the lamp was burning red
725   Near the book where he had fed,
When a Dream with plumes of flame,
To his pillow hovering came,
And I knew it was the same
Which had kindled long ago
730   Pity, eloquence, and woe;
And the world awhile below
Wore the shade, its lustre made.
It has borne me here as fleet
As Desire's lightning feet:

---

[1] Between arch and sea.

735   I must ride it back ere morrow,
Or the sage will wake in sorrow.

Fourth Spirit

On a poet's lips I slept
Dreaming like a love-adept
740   In the sound his breathing kept;
Nor seeks nor finds he mortal blisses,
But feeds on the aërial kisses
Of shapes that haunt thought's
    wilderness.
He will watch from dawn to gloom
The lake-reflected sun illume
745   The yellow bees in the ivy-bloom,
Nor heed nor see, what things they be;
But from these create he can
Forms more real than living man,
Nurslings of immortality!
750   One of these awakened me,
And I sped to succor thee.

Ione

Behold'st thou not two shapes from the
    east and west
Come, as two doves to one belovèd nest,
Twin nurslings of the all-sustaining air
755   On swift still wings glide down the
    atmosphere?
And, hark! their sweet, sad voices! 'tis
    despair
Mingled with love and then dissolved in
    sound.
Panthea. Canst thou speak, sister? all
    my words are drowned.
Ione. Their beauty gives me voice. See
    how they float
760 On their sustaining wings of skyey grain,[1]
Orange and azure deepening into gold:
Their soft smiles light the air like a star's
    fire.

Chorus of Spirits

Hast thou beheld the form of Love?

Fifth Spirit

          As over wide dominions
I sped, like some swift cloud that wings
    the wide air's wildernesses,
765 That planet-crested Shape swept by on
    lightning-braided pinions,
Scattering the liquid joy of life from
    his ambrosial[2] tresses:
His footsteps paved the world with light;
    but as I passed 'twas fading,
And hollow Ruin yawned behind: great
    sages bound in madness,

---

[1] color   [2] divinely beautiful

And headless patriots, and pale youths
   who perished, unupbraiding,
770 Gleamed in the night. I wandered o'er,
   till thou, O King of sadness,
Turned by thy smile the worst I saw to
   recollected gladness.

Sixth Spirit

Ah, sister! Desolation is a delicate thing:
   It walks not on the earth, it floats not on
      the air,
But treads with lulling footstep, and fans
   with silent wing
775 The tender hopes which in their hearts
   the best and gentlest bear;
Who, soothed to false repose by the fanning plumes above
And the music-stirring motion of its soft
   and busy feet,
Dream visions of aërial joy, and call the
   monster, Love,
And wake, and find the shadow Pain, as
   he whom now we greet.

Chorus

780 Though Ruin now Love's shadow be,
Following him, destroyingly,
   On Death's white and wingèd steed,[1]
Which the fleetest cannot flee,
   Trampling down both flower and weed,
785 Man and beast, and foul and fair,
Like a tempest through the air;
Thou shalt quell[2] this horseman grim,
Woundless though in heart or limb.

   Prometheus. Spirits! how know ye this
      shall be?

Chorus

790 In the atmosphere we breathe,
As buds grow red when the snow-storms
   flee,
From Spring gathering up beneath,
Whose mild winds shake the elder-brake,[3]
And the wandering herdsmen know
795 That the white-thorn soon will blow:
   Wisdom, Justice, Love, and Peace,
   When they struggle to increase,
   Are to us as soft winds be
   To shepherd boys, the prophecy
800   Which begins and ends in thee.

   Ione. Where are the Spirits fled?
   Panthea.   Only a sense
Remains of them, like the omnipotence
Of music, when the inspired voice and lute

Languish, ere yet the responses are mute,
805 Which through the deep and labyrinthine
   soul,
Like echoes through long caverns, wind
   and roll.
   Prometheus. How fair these airborn
      shapes! and yet I feel
Most vain all hope but love; and thou art
   far,
Asia! who, when my being overflowed,
810 Wert like a golden chalice to bright wine
Which else had sunk into the thirsty dust.
All things are still. Alas! how heavily
This quiet morning weighs upon my heart;
Though I should dream I could even sleep
   with grief
815 If slumber were denied not. I would fain
Be what it is my destiny to be,
The savior and the strength of suffering
   man,
Or sink into the original gulf of things:
There is no agony, and no solace left;
820 Earth can console, Heaven can torment no
   more.
   Panthea. Hast thou forgotten one who
      watches thee
The cold dark night, and never sleeps but
   when
The shadow of thy spirit falls on her?
   Prometheus. I said all hope was vain
      but love: thou lovest.
825   *Panthea.* Deeply in truth; but the east-
      ern star looks white,
And Asia waits in that far Indian vale,
The scene of her sad exile; rugged once
And desolate and frozen, like this ravine;
But now invested with fair flowers and
   herbs,
830 And haunted by sweet airs and sounds,
   which flow
Among the woods and waters, from the
   ether
Of her transforming presence, which
   would fade
If it were mingled not with thine. Farewell!

ACT II

Scene I.—*Morning. A lovely Vale in the
   Indian Caucasus.* Asia *alone.*

   Asia. From all the blasts of heaven thou
      hast descended:
Yes, like a spirit, like a thought, which
   makes
Unwonted tears throng to the horny eyes,
And beatings haunt the desolated heart,
5 Which should have learnt repose: thou
   hast descended

---

[1] See *Revelation*, 6:8.   [3] elder-thicket
[2] kill

Cradled in tempests; thou dost wake, O
   Spring!
O child of many winds! As suddenly
Thou comest as the memory of a dream,
Which now is sad because it hath been
   sweet;
10 Like genius, or like joy which riseth up
As from the earth, clothing with golden
   clouds
The desert of our life.
This is the season, this the day, the hour;
At sunrise thou shouldst come, sweet sister
   mine,[1]
15 Too long desired, too long delaying, come!
How like death-worms the wingless mo-
   ments crawl!
The point of one white star is quivering
   still
Deep in the orange light of widening morn
Beyond the purple mountains: through a
   chasm
20 Of wind-divided mist the darker lake
Reflects it: now it wanes: it gleams again
As the waves fade, and as the burning
   threads
Of woven cloud unravel in pale air:
'Tis lost! and through yon peaks of cloud-
   like snow
25 The roseate sunlight quivers: hear I not
The Æolian music of her sea-green plumes
Winnowing the crimson dawn?
              [PANTHEA enters.
              I feel, I see
Those eyes which burn through smiles that
   fade in tears,
Like stars half-quenched in mists of silver
   dew.
30 Belovèd and most beautiful, who wearest
The shadow of that soul[2] by which I
   live,
How late thou art! the spherèd sun had
   climbed
The sea; my heart was sick with hope,
   before
The printless air felt thy belated plumes.
35   *Panthea.* Pardon, great sister! but my
   wings were faint
With the delight of a remembered dream,
As are the noontide plumes of summer
   winds
Satiate with sweet flowers. I was wont to
   sleep
Peacefully, and awake refreshed and calm
40 Before the sacred Titan's fall and thy
Unhappy love had made, through use and
   pity,
Both love and woe familiar to my heart

As they had grown to thine: erewhile I
   slept
Under the glaucous[1] caverns of old Ocean
45 Within dim bowers of green and purple
   moss,
Our young Ione's soft and milky arms
Locked then, as now, behind my dark, moist
   hair,
While my shut eyes and cheek were pressed
   within
The folded depth of her life-breathing
   bosom:
50 But not as now, since I am made the wind
Which fails beneath the music that I bear
Of thy most wordless converse; since dissolved
Into the sense with which love talks, my
   rest
Was troubled and yet sweet; my waking
   hours
55 Too full of care and pain.
    Asia.   Lift up thine eyes,
And let me read thy dream.
    Panthea.   As I have said
With our sea-sister at his feet I slept.
The mountain mists, condensing at our
   voice
Under the moon, had spread their snowy
   flakes,
60 From the keen ice shielding our linkèd
   sleep.
Then two dreams came. One, I remember
   not.
But in the other his pale wound-worn limbs
Fell from Prometheus, and the azure night
Grew radiant with the glory of that form
65 Which lives unchanged within, and his
   voice fell
Like music which makes giddy the dim
   brain,
Faint with intoxication of keen joy:
"Sister of her whose footsteps pave the
   world
With loveliness—more fair than aught but
   her,
70 Whose shadow thou art—lift thine eyes on
   me."
I lifted them: the overpowering light
Of that immortal shape was shadowed
   o'er
By love; which, from his soft and flowing
   limbs,
And passion-parted lips, and keen, faint
   eyes,
75 Steamed forth like vaporous fire; an atmosphere

---

[1] Panthea.
[2] The soul of Prometheus.

[1] bluish green (Glaucus was a sea god, originally a fisherman, who became immortal by
   tasting magic grass.)

Which wrapped me in its all-dissolving
  power,
As the warm ether of the morning sun
Wraps ere it drinks some cloud of wander-
  ing dew.
I saw not, heard not, moved not, only felt
80 His presence flow and mingle through my
  blood
Till it became his life, and his grew mine,
And I was thus absorbed, until it passed,
And like the vapors when the sun sinks
  down,
Gathering again in drops upon the pines,
85 And tremulous as they, in the deep night
My being was condensed; and as the rays
Of thought were slowly gathered, I could
  hear
His voice, whose accents lingered ere they
  died
Like footsteps of weak melody: thy name
90 Among the many sounds alone I heard
Of what might be articulate; though still
I listened through the night when sound
  was none.
Ione wakened then, and said to me:
"Canst thou divine what troubles me to-
  night?
95 I always knew what I desired before,
Nor ever found delight to wish in vain.
But now I cannot tell thee what I seek;
I know not; something sweet, since it is
  sweet
Even to desire; it is thy sport, false sister;
100 Thou hast discovered some enchantment
  old,
Whose spells have stolen my spirit as I
  slept
And mingled it with thine: for when just
  now
We kissed, I felt within thy parted lips
The sweet air that sustained me, and the
  warmth
105 Of the life-blood, for loss of which I faint,
Quivered between our intertwining arms."
I answered not, for the Eastern star grew
  pale,
But fled to thee.
  Asia.   Thou speakest, but thy words
Are as the air: I feel them not. Oh, lift
110 Thine eyes, that I may read his written
  soul!
  Panthea. I lift them though they droop
  beneath the load
Of that they would express; what canst
  thou see
But thine own fairest shadow imaged
  there?
  Asia. Thine eyes are like the deep, blue,
  boundless heaven

115 Contracted to two circles underneath
Their long, fine lashes; dark, far, measureless,
Orb within orb, and line through line inwoven.
  Panthea. Why lookest thou as if a spirit
  passed?
  Asia. There is a change; beyond their
  inmost depth
120 I see a shade, a shape: 'tis he, arrayed
In the soft light of his own smiles, which
  spread
Like radiance from the cloud-surrounded
  moon.
Prometheus, it is thine! depart not yet!
Say not those smiles that we shall meet
  again
125 Within that bright pavilion which their
  beams
Shall build on the waste world? The
  dream is told.
What shape is that between us? Its rude
  hair
Roughens the wind that lifts it, its regard[1]
Is wild and quick, yet 'tis a thing of air,
130 For through its gray robe gleams the
  golden dew
Whose stars the noon has quenched not.
  Dream.   Follow! Follow!
  Panthea. It is mine other dream.
  Asia.   It disappears.
  Panthea. It passes now into my mind.
  Methought
As we sate here, the flower-infolding
  buds
135 Burst on yon lightning-blasted almond-
  tree,
When swift from the white Scythian wil-
  derness
A wind swept forth wrinkling the Earth
  with frost:
I looked, and all the blossoms were blown
  down;
But on each leaf was stamped, as the blue
  bells
140 Of Hyacinth tell Apollo's written grief,[2]
Oh, follow, follow!
  Asia. As you speak, your words
Fill, pause by pause, my own forgotten
  sleep
With shapes. Methought among these
  lawns together
We wandered, underneath the young gray
  dawn,
145 And multitudes of dense white fleecy clouds

[1] look; aspect
[2] The interjection *Ai* (woe), thought to be
  visible on the petals of the hyacinth, which
  sprang from the blood of Hyacinthus, accidentally killed by Apollo.

Were wandering in thick flocks along the
　　mountains
Shepherded by the slow, unwilling wind;
And the white dew on the new-bladed
　　grass,
Just piercing the dark earth, hung silently;
150 And there was more which I remember
　　not:
But on the shadows of the morning clouds,
Athwart the purple mountain slope, was
　　written
FOLLOW, OH, FOLLOW! as they vanished
　　by;
And on each herb, from which Heaven's
　　dew had fallen,
155 The like was stamped, as with a withering
　　fire;
A wind arose among the pines; it shook
The clinging music from their boughs, and
　　then
Low, sweet, faint sounds, like the farewell
　　of ghosts,
Were heard: OH, FOLLOW, FOLLOW, FOL-
　　LOW ME!
160 And then I said: "Panthea, look on me."
But in the depth of those belovèd eyes
Still I saw, FOLLOW, FOLLOW!
　　Echo.　　　　　Follow, follow!
　　Panthea.　The crags, this clear spring
　　　morning, mock our voices
As they were spirit-tongued.
　　Asia.　　　　　It is some being
165 Around the crags. What fine clear sounds!
　　Oh list!

Echoes (unseen)

Echoes we: listen!
　　We cannot stay:
　　As dew-stars glisten
　　Then fade away—
170 　　Child of Ocean!

Asia. Hark! Spirits speak. The liquid
　　responses
Of their aërial tongues yet sound.
　Panthea.　　　　　　　I hear.

Echoes

Oh, follow, follow,
　　As our voice recedeth
175 Through the caverns hollow,
　　Where the forest spreadeth;

(More distant)

Oh, follow, follow!
Through the caverns hollow,
As the song floats thou pursue,
180 Where the wild bee never flew,

Through the noontide darkness deep,
By the odor-breathing sleep
Of faint night-flowers, and the waves
At the fountain-lighted caves,
185 While our music, wild and sweet,
Mocks thy gently falling feet,
　　Child of Ocean!

Asia. Shall we pursue the sound? It
grows more faint and distant.
Panthea. List! the strain floats nearer
　　now.

Echoes

190 In the world unknown
　　Sleeps a voice unspoken;
By thy step alone
　　Can its rest be broken;
　　Child of Ocean!

195 *Asia.* How the notes sink upon the
　　ebbing wind!

Echoes

Oh, follow, follow!
Through the caverns hollow,
As the song floats thou pursue,
200 By the woodland noontide dew;
By the forest, lakes, and fountains,
Through the many-folded mountains;
To the rents, and gulfs, and chasms,
Where the Earth reposed from spasms,
On the day when he and thou
205 Parted, to commingle now;
　　Child of Ocean!

Asia. Come, sweet Panthea, link thy
　　hand in mine,
And follow, ere the voices fade away.

SCENE II.—*A Forest, intermingled with
Rocks and Caverns.* ASIA *and* PANTHEA
*pass into it. Two young Fauns are sit-
ting on a Rock listening.*

Semichorus I of Spirits

The path through which that lovely twain
Have passed, by cedar, pine, and yew,
And each dark tree that ever grew,
Is curtained out from Heaven's wide
　　blue;
5 Nor sun, nor moon, nor wind, nor rain,
　　Can pierce its interwoven bowers,
Nor aught, save where some cloud of
　　dew,
Drifted along the earth-creeping breeze,
Between the trunks of the hoar trees,

10   Hangs each a pearl in the pale
       flowers
     Of the green laurel, blown anew;
And bends, and then fades silently,
One frail and fair anemone:
Or when some star of many a one
15 That climbs and wanders through steep
       night,
Has found the cleft through which alone
Beams fall from high those depths upon
Ere it is borne away, away,
By the swift Heavens that cannot stay,
20 It scatters drops of golden light,
Like lines of rain that ne'er unite:
And the gloom divine is all around,
And underneath is the mossy ground.

Semichorus II

There the voluptuous nightingales,
25   Are awake through all the broad noon-
       day.
When one with bliss or sadness fails,
     And through the windless ivy-
       boughs,
     Sick with sweet love, droops dying
       away
On its mate's music-panting bosom;
30 Another from the swinging blossom,
     Watching to catch the languid close
Of the last strain, then lifts on high
The wings of the weak melody,
Till some new strain of feeling bear
35   The song, and all the woods are mute;
When there is heard through the dim
       air
The rush of wings, and rising there
Like many a lake-surrounded flute,
Sounds overflow the listener's brain
40 So sweet, that joy is almost pain.

Semichorus I

There those enchanted eddies play
Of echoes, music-tongued, which draw,
By Demogorgon's mighty law,
With melting rapture, or sweet awe,
45 All spirits on that secret way;
As inland boats are driven to Ocean
Down streams made strong with moun-
       tain-thaw:
     And first there comes a gentle sound
     To those in talk or slumber bound,
50   And wakes the destined soft emo-
       tion,—
Attracts, impels them; those who saw
Say from the breathing earth behind
There steams a plume-uplifting wind
Which drives them on their path, while
       they

55 Believe their own swift wings and feet
The sweet desires within obey:
And so they float upon their way,
Until, still sweet, but loud and strong,
The storm of sound is driven along,
60   Sucked up and hurrying: as they fleet
     Behind, its gathering billows meet
And to the fatal mountain[1] bear
Like clouds amid the yielding air.

First Faun.   Canst thou imagine where
     those spirits live
65 Which make such delicate music in the
       woods?
We haunt within the least frequented caves
And closest coverts, and we know these
       wilds,
Yet never meet them, though we hear them
       oft:
Where may they hide themselves?
     Second Faun.   'Tis hard to tell:
70 I have heard those more skilled in spirits
       say,
The bubbles, which the enchantment of the
       sun
Sucks from the pale faint water-flowers
       that pave
The oozy bottom of clear lakes and pools,
Are the pavilions where such dwell and
       float
75 Under the green and golden atmosphere
Which noontide kindles through the woven
       leaves;
And when these burst, and the thin fiery
       air,
The which they breathed within those
       lucent domes,
Ascends to flow like meteors through the
       night,
80 They ride on them, and rein their headlong
       speed,
And bow their burning crests, and glide in
       fire
Under the waters of the earth again.
     First Faun.   If such live thus, have
     others other lives,
Under pink blossoms or within the bells
85 Of meadow flowers, or folded violets deep,
Or on their dying odors, when they die,
Or in the sunlight of the spherèd dew?
     Second Faun.   Ay, many more which
     we may well divine.
But, should we stay to speak, noontide
     would come,
90 And thwart[2] Silenus find his goats un-
       drawn,

---

[1] The mountain at which Asia and Panthea arrive in the next scene.
[2] perverse; stubborn

And grudge to sing those wise and lovely
   songs
Of Fate, and Chance, and God, and Chaos
   old,
And Love, and the chained Titan's woful
   doom,
And how he shall be loosed, and make the
   earth
95 One brotherhood: delightful strains which
   cheer
Our solitary twilights, and which charm
To silence the unenvying nightingales.

SCENE III.—*A Pinnacle of Rock among
Mountains.* ASIA *and* PANTHEA.

Panthea. Hither the sound has borne
   us—to the realm
Of Demogorgon, and the mighty portal,
Like a volcano's meteor-breathing chasm,
Whence the oracular vapor is hurled up
5 Which lonely men drink wandering in
   their youth,
And call truth, virtue, love, genius, or joy,
That maddening wine of life, whose dregs
   they drain
To deep intoxication; and uplift,
Like Mænads who cry loud, Evoe! Evoe![1]
10 The voice which is contagion to the world.
  Asia. Fit throne for such a Power!
   Magnificent!
How glorious art thou, Earth! And if
   thou be
The shadow of some spirit lovelier still,
Though evil stain its work, and it should
   be
15 Like its creation, weak yet beautiful,
I could fall down and worship that and
   thee.
Even now my heart adoreth. Wonderful!
Look, sister, ere the vapor dim thy brain:
Beneath is a wide plain of billowy mist,
20 As a lake, paving in the morning sky,
With azure waves which burst in silver
   light,
Some Indian vale. Behold it, rolling on
Under the curdling winds, and islanding
The peak whereon we stand, midway,
   around,
25 Encinctured by the dark and blooming
   forests,
Dim twilight-lawns, and stream-illumined
   caves,
And wind-enchanted shapes of wander-
   ing mist;
And far on high the keen sky-cleaving
   mountains
From icy spires of sun-like radiance fling

[1] A Bacchanalian exclamation.

30 The dawn, as lifted Ocean's dazzling
   spray,
From some Atlantic islet scattered up,
Spangles the wind with lamp-like water-
   drops.
The vale is girdled with their walls, a
   howl
Of cataracts from their thaw-cloven ravines,
35 Satiates the listening wind, continuous,
   vast,
Awful as silence. Hark! the rushing
   snow!
The sun-awakened avalanche! whose mass,
Thrice sifted by the storm, had gathered
   there
Flake after flake, in heaven-defying
   minds
40 As thought by thought is piled, till some
   great truth
Is loosened, and the nations echo round,
Shaken to their roots, as do the mountains now.
  Panthea. Look how the gusty sea of
   mist is breaking
In crimson foam, even at our feet! it
   rises
45 As Ocean at the enchantment of the moon
Round foodless men wrecked on some
   oozy isle.
  Asia. The fragments of the cloud are
   scattered up;
The wind that lifts them disentwines my
   hair;
Its billows now sweep o'er mine eyes; my
   brain
50 Grows dizzy; I see shapes within the mist.
  Panthea. A countenance with beckoning smiles: there burns
An azure fire within its golden locks!
Another and another: hark! they speak!

Song of Spirits

To the deep, to the deep,
   Down, down!
55
Through the shade of sleep,
Through the cloudy strife
Of Death and of Life;
Through the veil and the bar
60
Of things which seem and are
Even to the steps of the remotest throne,
   Down, down!

While the sound whirls around,
   Down, down!
65
As the fawn draws the hound,
As the lightning the vapor,
As the weak moth the taper;
Death, despair; love, sorrow;

Time both; today, tomorrow;
70 As steel obeys the spirit of the stone,
   Down, down!

Through the gray, void abysm,
   Down, down!
Where the air is no prism,
75 And the moon and stars are not,
And the cavern-crags wear not
The radiance of Heaven,
Nor the gloom to Earth given,
Where there is one pervading, one
 alone,
80   Down, down!

In the depth of the deep,
   Down, down!
Like veiled lightning asleep,
Like the spark nursed in embers,
85 The last look Love remembers,
Like a diamond, which shines
On the dark wealth of mines,
A spell is treasured but for thee alone.
   Down, down!

90 We have bound thee, we guide thee;
   Down, down!
With the bright form beside thee;
Resist not the weakness,
Such strength is in meekness
95 That the Eternal, the Immortal,
Must unloose through life's portal
The snake-like Doom coiled underneath
 his throne
   By that alone.

* SCENE IV.—*The Cave of Demogorgon.*
   ASIA *and* PANTHEA.

Panthea. What veiled form sits on
 that ebon throne?
Asia. The veil has fallen.
Panthea.   I see a mighty darkness
Filling the seat of power, and rays of
 gloom
Dart round, as light from the meridian
 sun.
5 Ungazed upon and shapeless; neither limb,
Nor form, nor outline; yet we feel it is
A living Spirit.
Demogorgon. Ask what thou wouldst
 know.
Asia. What canst thou tell?
Demogorgon. All things thou dar'st
 demand.
Asia. Who made the living world?
Demogorgon.   God.
Asia.   Who made all
10 That it contains? thought, passion, reason,
 will,

Imagination?
Demogorgon. God: Almighty God.
Asia. Who made that sense which,
 when the winds of spring
In rarest visitation, or the voice
Of one beloved heard in youth alone,
15 Fills the faint eyes with falling tears
 which dim
The radiant looks of unbewailing flowers,
And leaves this peopled earth a solitude
When it returns no more?
Demogorgon.   Merciful God.
Asia. And who made terror, madness,
 crime, remorse,
20 Which from the links of the great chain
 of things,
To every thought within the mind of man
Sway and drag heavily, and each one reels
Under the load towards the pit of death:
Abandoned hope, and love that turns to
 hate;
25 And self-contempt, bitterer to drink than
 blood;
Pain, whose unheeded and familiar speech
Is howling, and keen shrieks, day after
 day;
And Hell, or the sharp fear of Hell?
Demogorgon.   He reigns.
Asia. Utter his name; a world pining
 in pain
30 Asks but his name; curses shall drag him
 down.
Demogorgon. He reigns.
Asia.   I feel, I know it: who?
Demogorgon.   He reigns.
Asia. Who reigns? There was the
 Heaven and Earth at first,
And Light and Love; then Saturn, from
 whose throne
Time fell, an envious shadow: such the
 state
35 Of the earth's primal spirits beneath his
 sway,
As the calm joy of flowers and living
 leaves
Before the wind or sun has withered them
And semivital worms; but he refused
The birthright of their being, knowledge,
 power,
40 The skill which wields the elements, the
 thought
Which pierces this dim universe like light,
Self-empire, and the majesty of love;
For thirst of which they fainted. Then
 Prometheus
Gave wisdom, which is strength, to Jupiter,
45 And with this law alone, "Let man be
 free,"

Clothed him with the dominion of wide
   Heaven.
To know nor faith, nor love, nor law; to be
Omnipotent but friendless, is to reign;
And Jove now reigned; for on the race
   of man
50 First famine, and then toil, and then dis-
   ease,
Strife, wounds, and ghastly death unseen
   before,
Fell; and the unseasonable seasons drove
With alternating shafts of frost and
   fire,
Their shelterless, pale tribes to mountain
   caves:
55 And in their desert hearts fierce wants he
   sent,
And mad disquietudes, and shadows idle
Of unreal good, which levied mutual war,
So ruining the lair wherein they raged.
Prometheus saw, and waked the legioned
   hopes
60 Which sleep within folded Elysian flowers,
Nepenthe, Moly, Amaranth,[1] fadeless
   blooms,
That they might hide with thin and rainbow wings
The shape of Death; and Love he sent to
   bind
The disunited tendrils of that vine
65 Which bears the wine of life, the human
   heart;
And he tamed fire which, like some beast
   of prey,
Most terrible, but lovely, played beneath
The frown of man; and tortured to his
   will
Iron and gold, the slaves and signs of
   power,
70 And gems and poisons, and all subtlest
   forms
Hidden beneath the mountains and the
   waves.
He gave man speech, and speech created
   thought,
Which is the measure of the universe;
And Science struck the thrones of earth
   and heaven,
75 Which shook, but fell not; and the harmonious mind
Poured itself forth in all-prophetic song;
And music lifted up the listening spirit
Until it walked, exempt from mortal care,

Godlike, o'er the clear billows of sweet
   sound;
80 And human hands first mimicked and then
   mocked,
With moulded limbs more lovely than its
   own,
The human form, till marble grew divine;
And mothers, gazing, drank the love men
   see
Reflected in their race, behold, and perish.
85 He told the hidden power of herbs and
   springs,
And Disease drank and slept. Death
   grew like sleep.
He taught the implicated[1] orbits woven
Of the wide-wandering stars; and how
   the sun
Changes his lair, and by what secret spell
90 The pale moon is transformed, when her
   broad eye
Gazes not on the interlunar[2] sea:
He taught to rule, as life directs the limbs,
The tempest-wingèd chariots of the Ocean,
And the Celt knew the Indian. Cities then
95 Were built, and through their snow-like
   columns flowed
The warm winds, and the azure ether
   shone,
And the blue sea and shadowy hills were
   seen.
Such, the alleviations of his state,
Prometheus gave to man, for which he
   hangs
100 Withering in destined pain: but who rains
   down
Evil, the immedicable plague, which, while
Man looks on his creation like a God
And sees that it is glorious, drives him on,
The wreck of his own will, the scorn of
   earth,
105 The outcast, the abandoned, the alone?
Not Jove: while yet his frown shook
   heaven, ay, when
His adversary from adamantine chains
Cursed him, he trembled like a slave.
   Declare
Who is his master? Is he too a slave?
110   *Demogorgon.* All spirits are enslaved
   which serve things evil:
Thou knowest if Jupiter be such or no.
   Asia. Whom calledst thou God?
   Demogorgon. I spoke but as ye speak,
For Jove is the supreme of living things.
   Asia. Who is the master of the slave?
   Demogorgon.   If the abysm
115 Could vomit forth its secrets—but a voice

---

[1] Nepenthe was a magic drug which caused forgetfulness of sorrow (*Odyssey*, 4, 221). Moly
was the herb given by Hermes to Odysseus
to counteract the spells of Circe (*Odyssey*,
10, 302 ff.). Amaranth was an imaginary
flower supposed never to fade (*Paradise
Lost*, 3, 353 ff.).

[1] interwoven
[2] That is, in the interval between the old moon
and the new.

Is wanting, the deep truth is imageless;
For what would it avail to bid thee gaze
On the revolving world? (What to bid
    speak
Fate, Time, Occasion, Chance, and Change?
    To these
120 All things are subject but eternal Love.)
    Asia. So much I asked before, and
        my heart gave
The response thou hast given; and of such
    truths
Each to himself must be the oracle.
One more demand; and do thou answer
    me
125 As mine own soul would answer, did it
        know
That which I ask. Prometheus shall arise
Henceforth the sun of this rejoicing world:
When shall the destined hour arrive?
    Demogorgon.   Behold!
    Asia. The rocks are cloven, and
        through the purple night
130 I see cars drawn by rainbow-wingèd
        steeds
Which trample the dim winds; in each
    there stands
A wild-eyed charioteer urging their flight.
Some look behind, as fiends pursued them
    there,
And yet I see no shapes but the keen
    stars:
135 Others, with burning eyes, lean forth,
        and drink
With eager lips the wind of their own
    speed,
As if the thing they loved fled on before,
And now, even now, they clasped it.
    Their bright locks
Stream like a comet's flashing hair; they
    all
Sweep onward.
140   *Demogorgon.* These are the immortal
        Hours,
Of whom thou didst demand. One waits
    for thee.
    Asia. A spirit with a dreadful coun-
        tenance
Checks its dark chariot by the craggy
    gulf.
Unlike thy brethren, ghastly charioteer,
145 Who art thou? Whither wouldst thou
        bear me? Speak!
    Spirit. I am the Shadow of a destiny
More dread than is my aspect; ere yon
    planet
Has set, the darkness which ascends with
    me
Shall wrap in lasting night heaven's
    kingless throne.

150   *Asia.* What meanest thou?
    Panthea.   That terrible Shadow floats
Up from its throne, as may the lurid
    smoke
Of earthquake-ruined cities o'er the sea.
Lo! it ascends the car; the coursers fly
Terrified; watch its path among the stars
Blackening the night!
155   *Asia.*   Thus I am answered: strange!
    Panthea. See, near the verge, another
        chariot stays;
An ivory shell inlaid with crimson fire,
Which comes and goes within its sculp-
    tured rim
Of delicate strange tracery; the young
    Spirit
160 That guides it has the dove-like eyes of
        hope;
How its soft smiles attract the soul! as
    light
Lures wingèd insects through the lampless
    air.

Spirit

My coursers are fed with the lightning,
    They drink of the whirlwind's stream,
165 And when the red morning is bright-
        'ning
    They bathe in the fresh sunbeam;
    They have strength for their swift-
        ness I deem,
Then ascend with me, daughter of
    Ocean.

I desire—and their speed makes night
    kindle;
    I fear—they outstrip the typhoon;
170 Ere the cloud piled on Atlas can
        dwindle,
    We encircle the earth and the moon.
    We shall rest from long labors at
        noon:
Then ascend with me, daughter of
    Ocean.

SCENE V.—*The Car pauses within a Cloud
on the top of a snowy Mountain.* ASIA,
PANTHEA, *and the* SPIRIT OF THE HOUR.

Spirit

On the brink of the night and the
    morning
    My coursers are wont to respire;
But the Earth has just whispered a
    warning
    That their flight must be swifter than
        fire:
5   They shall drink the hot speed of
        desire!

Asia. Thou breathest on their nostrils,
  but my breath
Would give them swifter speed.
  Spirit.   Alas! it could not.
  Panthea. O Spirit! pause, and tell
    whence is the light
Which fills this cloud? the sun is yet
    unrisen.
10 *Spirit.* The sun will rise not until
    noon. Apollo
Is held in heaven by wonder; and the light
Which fills this vapor, as the aërial hue
Of fountain-gazing roses fills the water,
Flows from thy mighty sister.
  Panthea.   Yes, I feel—
15 *Asia.* What is it with thee, sister?
    Thou art pale.
  Panthea. How thou art changed! I
    dare not look on thee;
I feel but see thee not. I scarce endure
The radiance of thy beauty. Some good
    change
Is working in the elements, which suffer
20 Thy presence thus unveiled. The Nereids
    tell
That on the day when the clear hyaline[1]
Was cloven at thine uprise, and thou
    didst stand
Within a veinèd shell, which floated on
Over the calm floor of the crystal sea,
25 Among the Ægean isles, and by the shores
Which bear thy name,—love, like the at-
    mosphere
Of the sun's fire filling the living world,
Burst from thee, and illumined earth and
    heaven
And the deep ocean and the sunless caves
30 And all that dwells within them; till grief
    cast
Eclipse upon the soul from which it
    came:
Such art thou now; nor is it I alone,
Thy sister, thy companion, thine own
    chosen one,
But the whole world which seeks thy
    sympathy.
35 Hearest thou not sounds i' the air which
    speak the love
Of all articulate beings? Feelest thou not
The inanimate winds enamoured of thee?
    List!   [*Music.*
  Asia. Thy words are sweeter than
    aught else but his
Whose echoes they are: yet all love is
    sweet,
40 Given or returned. Common as light is
    love,
And its familiar voice wearies not ever.
  [1] sea (a poetic term)

Like the wide heaven, the all-sustaining
    air,
It makes the reptile equal to the God:
They who inspire it most are fortunate,
45 As I am now; but those who feel it most
Are happier still, after long sufferings,
As I shall soon become.
  Panthea.   List! Spirits speak.

Voice in the Air, singing

Life of Life! thy lips enkindle
  With their love the breath between
    them;
50 And thy smiles before they dwindle
  Make the cold air fire; then screen
    them
In those looks, where whoso gazes
Faints, entangled in their mazes.

Child of Light! thy limbs are burning
55 Through the vest which seems to hide
    them;
As the radiant lines of morning
  Through the clouds ere they divide
    them;
And this atmosphere divinest
Shrouds thee wheresoe'er thou shinest.

60 Fair are others; none beholds thee,
  But thy voice sounds low and tender
Like the fairest, for it folds thee
  From the sight, that liquid splendor,
And all feel, yet see thee never,
65 As I feel now, lost forever!

Lamp of Earth! where'er thou movest
  Its dim shapes are clad with bright-
    ness,
And the souls of whom thou lovest
  Walk upon the winds with lightness,
70 Till they fail, as I am failing,
Dizzy, lost, yet unbewailing!

Asia

My soul is an enchanted boat,
  Which, like a sleeping swan, doth float
Upon the silver waves of thy sweet singing;
75 And thine doth like an angel sit
  Beside a helm conducting it.
Whilst all the winds with melody are
    ringing.
  It seems to float ever, forever,
  Upon that many-winding river,
80 Between mountains, woods, abysses,
  A paradise of wildernesses!
Till, like one in slumber bound,
Borne to the ocean, I float down, around,
Into a sea profound, of ever-spreading
    sound:

85 Meanwhile thy spirit lifts its pinions
In music's most serene dominions;
Catching the winds that fan that happy
heaven.
And we sail on, away, afar,
Without a course, without a star,
90 But, by the instinct of sweet music driven;
Till through Elysian garden islets
By thee, most beautiful of pilots,
Where never mortal pinnace glided,
The boat of my desire is guided:
95 Realms where the air we breathe is love,
Which in the winds and on the waves doth
move,
Harmonizing this earth with what we feel
above.

We have passed Age's icy caves,
And Manhood's dark and tossing waves,
100 And Youth's smooth ocean, smiling to
betray:
Beyond the glassy gulfs we flee
Of shadow-peopled Infancy,
Through Death and Birth, to a diviner
day;
A paradise of vaulted bowers,
105 Lit by downward-gazing flowers,
And watery paths that wind between
Wildernesses calm and green,
Peopled by shapes too bright to see,
And rest, having beheld; somewhat like
thee;
110 Which walk upon the sea, and chant
melodiously!

ACT III

SCENE I.—*Heaven.* JUPITER *on his
Throne;* THETIS *and the other
Deities assembled.*

Jupiter. Ye congregated powers of
heaven, who share
The glory and the strength of him ye
serve,
Rejoice! henceforth I am omnipotent.
All else had been subdued to me; alone
5 The soul of man, like unextinguished fire,
Yet burns towards heaven with fierce re-
proach and doubt,
And lamentation, and reluctant prayer,
Hurling up insurrection, which might
make
Our antique empire insecure, though built
10 On eldest faith, and hell's coeval, fear;
And though my curses through the pen-
dulous air,
Like snow on herbless peaks, fall flake by
flake,

And cling to it; though under my wrath's
night
It climb the crags of life, step after
step,
15 Which wound it, as ice wounds unsan-
dalled feet,
It yet remains supreme o'er misery,
Aspiring, unrepressed, yet soon to fall:
Even now have I begotten a strange
wonder,
That fatal child, the terror of the earth,
20 Who waits but till the destined hour ar-
rive,
Bearing from Demogorgon's vacant throne
The dreadful might of ever-living limbs
Which clothed that awful spirit unbeheld,
To redescend, and trample out the
spark.
25 Pour forth heaven's wine, Idæan Gany-
mede,
And let it fill the dædal[1] cups like fire,
And from the flower-inwoven soil divine,
Ye all-triumphant harmonies, arise,
As dew from earth under the twilight
stars:
30 Drink! be the nectar circling through your
veins
The soul of joy, ye ever-living Gods,
Till exultation burst in one wide voice
Like music from Elysian winds.
                                   And thou
Ascend beside me, veilèd in the light
35 Of the desire which makes thee one with
me,
Thetis, bright image of eternity!
When thou didst cry, "Insufferable might!
God! Spare me! I sustain not the quick
flames,
The penetrating presence; all my being,
40 Like him whom the Numidian seps did
thaw
Into a dew with poison,[2] is dissolved,
Sinking through its foundations," even
then
Two mighty spirits, mingling, made a
third
Mightier than either, which, unbodied
now,
45 Between us floats, felt, although unbeheld,
Waiting the incarnation, which ascends.
(Hear ye the thunder of the fiery wheels
Griding[3] the winds?) from Demogorgon's
throne.
Victory! victory! Feel'st thou not, O
world,

---

[1] marvelously formed
[2] The soldier Sabellus, who died from the bite of
a seps, a kind of poisonous serpent. See Lucan's *Pharsalia*, 9, 763 ff.
[3] piercing

50 The earthquake of his chariot thundering
    up
Olympus?
    [*The Car of the* HOUR *arrives.*
    DEMOGORGON *descends, and moves*
    towards the Throne of JUPITER.

    Awful shape, what art thou? Speak!
Demogorgon.   Eternity. Demand no
    direr name.
Descend, and follow me down the abyss.
I am thy child, as thou wert Saturn's
    child;
55 Mightier than thee: and we must dwell
    together
Henceforth in darkness. Lift thy light-
    nings not.
The tyranny of heaven none may retain,
Or reassume, or hold, succeeding thee:
Yet if thou wilt, as 'tis the destiny
60 Of trodden worms to writhe till they are
    dead,
Put forth thy might.
    Jupiter.   Detested prodigy!
Even thus beneath the deep Titanian
    prisons[1]
I trample thee! Thou lingerest?
                    Mercy! mercy!
No pity, no release, no respite! Oh,
65 That thou wouldst make mine enemy my
    judge,
Even where he hangs, seared by my long
    revenge,
On Caucasus! he would not doom me thus.
Gentle, and just, and dreadless, is he not
The monarch of the world? What then
    art thou?
No refuge! no appeal!
70   Sink with me then,
We two will sink on the wide waves of
    ruin,
Even as a vulture and a snake outspent
Drop, twisted in inextricable fight,
Into a shoreless sea. Let hell unlock
75 Its mounded oceans of tempestuous fire,
And whelm on them into the bottomless
    void
This desolated world, and thee, and me,
The conqueror and the conquered, and the
    wreck
Of that for which they combated.
                    Ai! Ai![2]
80 The elements obey me not. I sink
Dizzily down, ever, forever, down.
And, like a cloud, mine enemy above
Darkens my fall with victory! Ai, Ai!

[1] When the Titans were overcome by Jupiter,
    they were imprisoned in an abyss below Tar-
    tarus, the lowest portion of Hades.
[2] woe! woe!

SCENE II.—*The Mouth of a great River*
in the Island Atlantis. OCEAN *is dis-*
covered reclining near the shore;
APOLLO *stands beside him.*

    Ocean. He fell, thou sayest, beneath
        his conqueror's frown?
    Apollo. Ay, when the strife was ended
        which made dim
The orb I rule, and shook the solid stars,
The terrors of his eye illumined heaven
5 With sanguine light, through the thick
        ragged skirts
Of the victorious darkness, as he fell:
Like the last glare of day's red agony,
Which, from a rent among the fiery
        clouds,
Burns far along the tempest-wrinkled
        deep.
10   *Ocean.* He sunk to the abyss? To the
        dark void?
    Apollo. An eagle so caught in some
        bursting cloud
On Caucasus, his thunder-baffled wings
Entangled in the whirlwind, and his eyes
Which gazed on the undazzling sun, now
        blinded
15 By the white lightning, while the pon-
        derous hail
Beats on his struggling form, which sinks
        at length
Prone, and the aërial ice clings over it.
    Ocean. Henceforth the fields of heaven-
        reflecting sea
Which are my realm, will heave, unstained
        with blood,
20 Beneath the uplifting winds, like plains
        of corn[1]
Swayed by the summer air; my streams
        will flow
Round many-peopled continents, and
        round
Fortunate isles; and from their glassy
        thrones
Blue Proteus and his humid nymphs shall
        mark
25 The shadow of fair ships, as mortals see
The floating bark of the light-laden moon
With that white star, its sightless pilot's
        crest,
Borne down the rapid sunset's ebbing sea,
Tracking their path no more by blood and
        groans,
30 And desolation, and the mingled voice
Of slavery and command; but by the
        light
Of wave-reflected flowers, and floating
        odors,

[1] wheat

And music soft, and mild, free, gentle
    voices,
And sweetest music, such as spirits love.
35   *Apollo.* And I shall gaze not on the
    deeds which make
My mind obscure with sorrow, as eclipse
Darkens the sphere I guide; but list, I
    hear
The small, clear, silver lute of the young
    Spirit
That sits i' the morning star.
    Ocean.   Thou must away;
40 Thy steeds will pause at even, till when
    farewell:
The loud deep calls me home even now to
    feed it
With azure calm out of the emerald urns
Which stand forever full beside my throne.
Behold the Nereids under the green sea,
45 Their wavering limbs borne on the wind-
    like stream,
Their white arms lifted o'er their stream-
    ing hair
With garlands pied and starry sea-flower
    crowns,
Hastening to grace their mighty sister's
    joy.   [*A sound of waves is heard.*
It is the unpastured sea hungering for
    calm.
50 Peace, monster; I come now. Farewell.
    Apollo.   Farewell.

SCENE III. — *Caucasus.* PROMETHEUS,
HERCULES, IONE, *the* EARTH, SPIRITS,
ASIA, *and* PANTHEA, *borne in the Car
with the* SPIRIT OF THE HOUR. HERCU-
LES *unbinds* PROMETHEUS, *who descends.*

    Hercules. Most glorious among Spirits,
    thus doth strength
To wisdom, courage, and long-suffering
    love,
And thee, who art the form they animate,
Minister like a slave.
    Prometheus.   Thy gentle words
5 Are sweeter even than freedom long de-
    sired
And long delayed.
             Asia, thou light of life,
Shadow of beauty unbeheld; and ye,
Fair sister nymphs, who made long years
    of pain
Sweet to remember, through your love and
    care:
10 Henceforth we will not part. There is a
    cave,
All overgrown with trailing odorous plants,
Which curtain out the day with leaves and
    flowers,

And paved with veinèd emerald, and a
    fountain
Leaps in the midst with an awakening
    sound.
15 From its curved roof the mountain's
    frozen tears
Like snow, or silver, or long diamond spires,
Hang downward, raining forth a doubtful
    light;
And there is heard the ever-moving air,
Whispering without from tree to tree, and
    birds,
20 And bees; and all around are mossy seats,
And the rough walls are clothed with long
    soft grass;
A simple dwelling, which shall be our own;
Where we will sit and talk of time and
    change,
As the world ebbs and flows, ourselves un-
    changed.
25 What can hide man from mutability?
And if ye sigh, then I will smile; and thou,
Ione, shalt chant fragments of sea-music,
Until I weep, when ye shall smile away
The tears she brought, which yet were
    sweet to shed.
30 We will entangle buds and flowers and
    beams
Which twinkle on the fountain's brim, and
    make
Strange combinations out of common
    things,
Like human babes in their brief innocence;
And we will search, with looks and words
    of love,
35 For hidden thoughts, each lovelier than the
    last,
Our unexhausted spirits; and like lutes
Touched by the skill of the enamored wind,
Weave harmonies divine, yet ever new,
From difference sweet where discord can-
    not be;
40 And hither come, sped on the charmèd
    winds,
Which meet from all the points of heaven,
    as bees
From every flower aërial Enna feeds,
At their known island-homes in Himera,
The echoes of the human world, which tell
45 Of the low voice of love, almost unheard,
And dove-eyed pity's murmured pain, and
    music,
Itself the echo of the heart, and all
That tempers or improves man's life, now
    free;
And lovely apparitions—dim at first,
50 Then radiant, as the mind arising bright
From the embrace of beauty (whence the
    forms

Of which these are the phantoms) casts on
them
The gathered rays which are reality—
Shall visit us, the progeny immortal
55 Of Painting, Sculpture, and rapt Poesy,
And arts, though unimagined, yet to be.
The wandering voices and the shadows
these
Of all that man becomes, the mediators
Of that best worship love, by him and us
60 Given and returned; swift shapes and
sounds, which grow
More fair and soft as man grows wise and
kind,
And, veil by veil, evil and error fall.
Such virtue has the cave and place around.
[*Turning to the* SPIRIT OF THE HOUR.
For thee, fair Spirit, one toil remains.
Ione,
65 Give her that curvèd shell,[1] which Proteus
old
Made Asia's nuptial boon, breathing with-
in it
A voice to be accomplished, and which thou
Didst hide in grass under the hollow rock.
Ione. Thou most desired Hour, more
loved and lovely
70 Than all thy sisters, this is the mystic shell;
See the pale azure fading into silver
Lining it with a soft yet glowing light.
Looks it not like lulled music sleeping
there?
Spirit. It seems in truth the fairest shell
of Ocean:
75 Its sound must be at once both sweet and
strange.
Prometheus. Go, borne over the cities of
mankind
On whirlwind-footed coursers; once again
Outspeed the sun around the orbèd world;
And as thy chariot cleaves the kindling
air,
80 Thou breathe into the many-folded shell,
Loosening its mighty music; it shall be
As thunder mingled with clear echoes: then
Return; and thou shalt dwell beside our
cave.
And thou, O Mother Earth!—
The Earth.   I hear, I feel;
85 Thy lips are on me, and their touch runs
down
Even to the adamantine central gloom
Along these marble nerves; 'tis life, 'tis
joy,
And through my withered, old, and icy
frame
The warmth of an immortal youth shoots
down

[1] trumpet

90 Circling. Henceforth the many children
fair
Folded in my sustaining arms; all plants,
And creeping forms, and insects rainbow-
winged,
And birds, and beasts, and fish, and human
shapes,
Which drew disease and pain from my wan
bosom,
95 Draining the poison of despair, shall take
And interchange sweet nutriment; to me
Shall they become like sister-antelopes
By one fair dam, snow-white and swift as
wind,
Nursed among lilies near a brimming
stream.
100 The dew-mists of my sunless sleep shall
float
Under the stars like balm; night-folded
flowers
Shall suck unwithering hues in their repose;
And men and beasts in happy dreams shall
gather
Strength for the coming day, and all its
joy;
105 And death shall be the last embrace of
her
Who takes the life she gave, even as a
mother
Folding her child, says, "Leave me not
again."
Asia. Oh, mother! wherefore speak the
name of death?
Cease they to love, and move, and breathe,
and speak,
110 Who die?
The Earth. It would avail not to reply;
Thou art immortal, and this tongue is
known
But to the uncommunicating dead.
Death is the veil which those who live call
life;
They sleep, and it is lifted: and meanwhile
115 In mild variety the seasons mild
With rainbow-skirted showers, and odorous
winds,
And long blue meteors cleansing the dull
night,
And the life-kindling shafts of the keen
sun's
All-piercing bow, and the dew-mingled rain
120 Of the calm moonbeams, a soft influence
mild,
Shall clothe the forests and the fields, ay,
even
The crag-built deserts of the barren deep,
With ever-living leaves, and fruits, and
flowers.

And thou! there is a cavern where my spirit
125 Was panted forth in anguish whilst thy pain
Made my heart mad, and those who did inhale it
Became mad too, and built a temple there,
And spoke, and were oracular, and lured
The erring nations round to mutual war,
130 And faithless faith, such as Jove kept with thee;
Which breath now rises, as amongst tall weeds
A violet's exhalation, and it fills
With a serener light and crimson air
Intense, yet soft, the rocks and woods around;
135 It feeds the quick growth of the serpent vine,
And the dark linkèd ivy tangling wild,
And budding, blown, or odor-faded blooms
Which star the winds with points of colored light,
As they rain through them, and bright golden globes
140 Of fruit, suspended in their own green heaven,
And through their veinèd leaves and amber stems
The flowers whose purple and translucid bowls
Stand ever mantling with aërial dew,
The drink of spirits; and it circles round,
145 Like the soft waving wings of noonday dreams,
Inspiring calm and happy thoughts, like mine,
Now thou art thus restored. This cave is thine.
Arise! Appear!

[*A* SPIRIT *rises in the likeness of a winged child.*

This is my torch-bearer;
Who let his lamp out in old time with gazing
150 On eyes from which he kindled it anew
With love, which is as fire, sweet daughter mine,
For such is that within thine own. Run, wayward,
And guide this company beyond the peak
Of Bacchic Nysa, Mænad-haunted mountain,
155 And beyond Indus and its tribute rivers,
Trampling the torrent streams and glassy lakes
With feet unwet, unwearied. undelaying,
And up the green ravine, across the vale,

160 Beside the windless and crystalline pool,
Where ever lies, on unerasing waves,
The image of a temple, built above,
Distinct with column, arch, and architrave,
And palm-like capital, and over-wrought,
And populous most with living imagery,
165 Praxitelean shapes,[1] whose marble smiles
Fill the hushed air with everlasting love.
It is deserted now, but once it bore
Thy name, Prometheus; there the emulous youths
Bore to thy honor through the divine gloom
170 The lamp which was thine emblem; even as those
Who bear the untransmitted torch of hope
Into the grave, across the night of life,
As thou hast borne it most triumphantly
To this far goal of Time. Depart, farewell.
175 Beside that temple is the destined cave.

SCENE IV.—*A Forest. In the Background a Cave.* PROMETHEUS, ASIA, PANTHEA, IONE, *and the* SPIRIT OF THE EARTH.

Ione. Sister, it is not earthly; how it glides
Under the leaves! how on its head there burns
A light, like a green star, whose emerald beams
Are twined with its fair hair! how, as it moves,
5 The splendor drops in flakes upon the grass!
Knowest thou it?
Panthea. It is the delicate spirit
That guides the earth through heaven. From afar
The populous constellations call that light
The loveliest of the planets; and sometimes
10 It floats along the spray of the salt sea,
Or makes its chariot of a foggy cloud,
Or walks through fields or cities while men sleep,
Or o'er the mountain tops, or down the rivers,
Or through the green waste wilderness, as now,
15 Wondering at all it sees. Before Jove reigned
It loved our sister Asia, and it came
Each leisure hour to drink the liquid light
Out of her eyes, for which it said it thirsted
As one bit by a dipsas,[2] and with her

[1] That is, shapes as perfect as the statues of Praxiteles, the famous Greek sculptor (5th cent. B. C.).
[2] A kind of serpent; its bite caused intense thirst. See Lucan's *Pharsalia*, 9, 610.

20 It made a childish confidence, and told her
All it had known or seen, for it saw much,
Yet idly reasoned what it saw; and called
 her—
For whence it sprung it knew not, nor
 do I—
Mother, dear mother.
 The Spirit of the Earth (running to
 ASIA). Mother, dearest mother;
25 May I then talk with thee as I was wont?
May I then hide my eyes in thy soft arms,
After thy looks have made them tired of
 joy?
May I then play beside thee the long noons,
When work is none in the bright silent air?
30 *Asia.* I love thee, gentlest being, and
 henceforth
Can cherish thee unenvied. Speak, I pray;
Thy simple talk once solaced, now delights.
 Spirit of the Earth. Mother, I am grown
 wiser, though a child
Cannot be wise like thee, within this day;
35 And happier too; happier and wiser both.
Thou knowest that toads, and snakes, and
 loathly worms,
And venomous and malicious beasts, and
 boughs
That bore ill berries in the woods, were ever
An hindrance to my walks o'er the green
 world;
40 And that, among the haunts of humankind,
Hard-featured men, or with proud, angry
 looks,
Or cold, staid gait, or false and hollow
 smiles,
Or the dull sneer of self-loved ignorance,
Or other such foul masks, with which ill
 thoughts
45 Hide that fair being whom we spirits call
 man;
And women too, ugliest of all things evil
(Though fair, even in a world where thou
 art fair,
When good and kind, free and sincere like
 thee),
When false or frowning made me sick at
 heart
50 To pass them, though they slept, and I
 unseen.
Well, my path lately lay through a great
 city
Into the woody hills surrounding it;
A sentinel was sleeping at the gate;
When there was heard a sound,[1] so loud,
 it shook
55 The towers amid the moonlight, yet more
 sweet

Than any voice but thine, sweetest of all;
A long, long sound, as it would never end;
And all the inhabitants leaped suddenly
Out of their rest, and gathered in the
 streets,
60 Looking in wonder up to Heaven, while yet
The music pealed along. I hid myself
Within a fountain in the public square
Where I lay like the reflex of the moon
Seen in a wave under green leaves; and
 soon
65 Those ugly human shapes and visages
Of which I spoke as having wrought me
 pain,
Passed floating through the air, and fading
 still
Into the winds that scattered them; and
 those
From whom they passed seemed mild and
 lovely forms
70 After some foul disguise had fallen, and
 all
Were somewhat changed, and after brief
 surprise
And greetings of delighted wonder, all
Went to their sleep again: and when the
 dawn
Came, wouldst thou think that toads, and
 snakes, and efts,[1]
75 Could e'er be beautiful? yet so they were,
And that with little change of shape or
 hue:
All things had put their evil nature off:
I cannot tell my joy, when o'er a lake,
Upon a drooping bough with nightshade
 twined,
80 I saw two azure halcyons[2] clinging downward
And thinning one bright bunch of amber
 berries,
With quick long beaks, and in the deep
 there lay
Those lovely forms imaged as in a sky;
So, with my thoughts full of these happy
 changes,
85 We meet again, the happiest change of all.
 Asia. And never will we part, till thy
 chaste sister,[3]
Who guides the frozen and inconstant
 moon,
Will look on thy more warm and equal
 light
Till her heart thaw like flakes of April
 snow
90 And love thee.
 Spirit of the Earth. What! as Asia
 loves Prometheus?

---

[1] The sound of the shell. See sc. 3, 64 ff. (p.
712).

[1] lizards   [2] kingfishers
[3] Diana (Artemis), goddess of the moon.

Asia. Peace, wanton, thou art yet not old enough.
Think ye by gazing on each other's eyes
To multiply your lovely selves, and fill
With spherèd fire the interlunar air?
95 *Spirit of the Earth.* Nay, mother, while my sister trims her lamp
'Tis hard I should go darkling.[1]
Asia. Listen; look!

[*The* SPIRIT OF THE HOUR *enters.*

Prometheus. We feel what thou hast heard and seen: yet speak.
Spirit of the Hour. Soon as the sound had ceased whose thunder filled
The abysses of the sky and the wide earth,
100 There was a change; the impalpable thin air
And the all-circling sunlight were transformed,
As if the sense of love dissolved in them
Had folded itself round the spherèd world.
My vision then grew clear, and I could see
105 Into the mysteries of the universe,[2]
Dizzy as with delight I floated down;
Winnowing the lightsome air with languid plumes,
My coursers sought their birthplace in the sun,
Where they henceforth will live exempt from toil,
110 Pasturing flowers of vegetable fire;
And where my moonlike car will stand within
A temple, gazed upon by Phidian forms
Of thee, and Asia, and the Earth, and me,
And you fair nymphs looking the love we feel,—
115 In memory of the tidings it has borne,—
Beneath a dome fretted with graven flowers,
Poised on twelve columns of resplendent stone,
And open to the bright and liquid sky.
Yoked to it by an amphisbænic[3] snake
120 The likeness of those wingèd steeds will mock
The flight from which they find repose.
Alas,
Whither has wandered now my partial tongue
When all remains untold which ye would hear?
As I have said, I floated to the earth;
125 It was, as it is still, the pain of bliss

To move, to breathe, to be; I wandering went
Among the haunts and dwellings of mankind,
And first was disappointed not to see
Such mighty change as I had felt within
130 Expressed in outward things; but soon I looked,
And behold, thrones were kingless, and men walked
One with the other even as spirits do—
None fawned, none trampled; hate, disdain, or fear,
Self-love or self-contempt, on human brows
135 No more inscribed, as o'er the gate of hell,
"All hope abandon ye who enter here;"[1]
None frowned, none trembled, none with eager fear
Gazed on another's eye of cold command,
Until the subject of a tyrant's will
140 Became, worse fate, the abject of his own,
Which spurred him, like an outspent horse, to death.
None wrought his lips in truth-entangling lines
Which smiled the lie his tongue disdained to speak;
None, with firm sneer, trod out in his own heart
145 The sparks of love and hope till there remained
Those bitter ashes, a soul self-consumed,
And the wretch crept a vampire among men,
Infecting all with his own hideous ill;
None talked that common, false, cold, hollow talk
150 Which makes the heart deny the *yes* it breathes,
Yet question that unmeant hypocrisy
With such a self-mistrust as has no name.
And women, too, frank, beautiful, and kind
As the free heaven which rains fresh light and dew
155 On the wide earth, passed; gentle, radiant forms,
From custom's evil taint exempt and pure;
Speaking the wisdom once they could not think,
Looking emotions once they feared to feel,
And changed to all which once they dared not be,
160 Yet being now, made earth like heaven: nor pride,
Nor jealousy, nor envy, nor ill shame,
The bitterest of those drops of treasured gall,

---

[1] in the dark
[2] See Wordsworth's *Lines Composed a Few Miles Above Tintern Abbey*, 35 ff. (p. 259).
[3] having a head at each end and capable of moving forward and backward

[1] The inscription on the gate of Hell, in Dante's *Inferno*, 3, 9.

Spoiled the sweet taste of the nepenthe,
    love.

Thrones, altars, judgment-seats, and pris-
    ons, wherein,
165 And beside which, by wretched men were
    borne
Sceptres, tiaras, swords, and chains, and
    tomes
Of reasoned wrong, glozed on by igno-
    rance,
Were like those monstrous and barbaric
    shapes,
The ghosts of a no-more-remembered fame,
170 Which, from their unworn obelisks, look
    forth
In triumph o'er the palaces and tombs
Of those who were their conquerors;
    mouldering round,
These imaged to the pride of kings and
    priests
A dark yet mighty faith, a power as wide
175 As is the world it wasted, and are now
But an astonishment; even so the tools
And emblems of its last captivity,
Amid the dwellings of the peopled earth,
Stand, not o'erthrown, but unregarded
    now.
180 And those foul shapes, abhorred by god
    and man,—
Which, under many a name and many a
    form
Strange, savage, ghastly, dark, and exe-
    crable,
Were Jupiter, the tyrant of the world,
And which the nations, panic-stricken,
    served
185 With blood, and hearts broken by long
    hope, and love
Dragged to his altars soiled and garland-
    less,
And slain amid men's unreclaiming tears,
Flattering the thing they feared, which
    fear was hate,—
Frown, mouldering fast, o'er their aban-
    doned shrines.
190 The painted veil, by those who were, called
    life,
Which mimicked, as with colors idly spread,
All men believed or hoped, is torn aside;
The loathsome mask has fallen, the man
    remains
Sceptreless, free, uncircumscribed, but man
195 Equal, unclassed, tribeless, and nationless,
Exempt from awe, worship, degree, the
    king
Over himself; just, gentle, wise; but man
Passionless—no, yet free from guilt or
    pain,

Which were, for his will made or suffered
    them;
200 Nor yet exempt, though ruling them like
    slaves,
From chance, and death, and mutability,
The clogs of that which else might oversoar
The loftiest star of unascended heaven,
Pinnacled dim in the intense inane.

ACT IV

Scene.—*A Part of the Forest near the
Cave of* Prometheus. Panthea *and*
Ione *are sleeping: they awaken grad-
ually during the first Song.*

Voice of unseen Spirits

The pale stars are gone!
For the sun, their swift shepherd,
To their folds them compelling,
In the depths of the dawn,
5 Hastes, in meteor-eclipsing array, and
    they flee
Beyond his blue dwelling,
As fawns flee the leopard.
But where are ye?

*A Train of dark Forms and Shadows
passes by confusedly, singing.*

Here, oh here!
10 We bear the bier
Of the Father of many a cancelled year!
Spectres we
Of the dead Hours be,
We bear Time to his tomb in Eternity.

15 Strew, oh, strew
Hair, not yew![1]
Wet the dusty pall with tears, not dew!
Be the faded flowers
Of Death's bare bowers
20 Spread on the corpse of the King of
    Hours!

Haste, oh, haste!
As shades are chased,
Trembling, by day, from heaven's blue
    waste.
We melt away,
25 Like dissolving spray,
From the children of a diviner day,
With the lullaby
Of winds that die
On the bosom of their own harmony!

Ione

30 What dark forms were they?

[1] The yew is an emblem of mourning; it is a
common tree in graveyards.

Panthea

The past Hours weak and gray,
With the spoil which their toil
  Raked together
From the conquest but One[1] could foil.

Ione

35 Have they passed?

Panthea

      They have passed;
They outspeeded the blast,
While 'tis said, they are fled:

Ione

Whither, oh, whither?

Panthea

To the dark, to the past, to the dead.

Voice of unseen Spirits

40 Bright clouds float in heaven,
Dew-stars gleam on earth,
Waves assemble on ocean,
They are gathered and driven
By the storm of delight, by the panic of
  glee!
45 They shake with emotion,
They dance in their mirth.
    But where are ye?

The pine boughs are singing
Old songs with new gladness,
50 The billows and fountains
Fresh music are flinging,
Like the notes of a spirit from land and
  from sea;
The storms mock the mountains
With the thunder of gladness.
55   But where are ye?

Ione. What charioteers are these?
Panthea.   Where are their chariots?

Semichorus of Hours

The voice of the Spirits of Air and of
  Earth
Have drawn back the figured curtain of
  sleep
Which covered our being and darkened our
  birth
60 In the deep.

A Voice

In the deep?

[1] Prometheus.

Semichorus II

Oh! below the deep.

Semichorus I

An hundred ages we had been kept
  Cradled in visions of hate and care,
And each one who waked as his brother
  slept,
  Found the truth—

Semichorus II

Worse than his visions were!

Semichorus I

65 We have heard the lute of Hope in sleep;
We have known the voice of Love in
  dreams;
We have felt the wand of Power, and
  leap—

Semichorus II

As the billows leap in the morning
  beams!

Chorus

Weave the dance on the floor of the breeze,
70   Pierce with song heaven's silent light,
Enchant the Day that too swiftly flees,
  To check its flight ere the cave of Night.

Once the hungry Hours were hounds
  Which chased the Day like a bleeding
    deer,
75 And it limped and stumbled with many
    wounds
  Through the nightly dells of the desert
    year.

But now, oh, weave the mystic measure
  Of music, and dance, and shapes of light,
Let the Hours, and the Spirits of might
  and pleasure,
80   Like the clouds and sunbeams, unite—

A Voice

      Unite!
Panthea. See, where the Spirits of the
  human mind,
Wrapped in sweet sounds, as in bright
  veils, approach.

Chorus of Spirits

  We join the throng
  Of the dance and the song,
85 By the whirlwind of gladness borne along;
  As the flying-fish leap
  From the Indian deep,
And mix with the sea-birds, half asleep.

Chorus of Hours

Whence come ye, so wild and so fleet,
90 For sandals of lightning are on your feet,
And your wings are soft and swift as
thought,
. And your eyes are as love which is veilèd
not?

Chorus of Spirits

We come from the mind
Of human kind,
95 Which was late so dusk, and obscene, and
blind;
Now 'tis an ocean
Of clear emotion,
A heaven of serene and mighty motion.

From that deep abyss
100 Of wonder and bliss,
Whose caverns are crystal palaces;
From those skyey towers
Where Thought's crowned powers
Sit watching your dance, ye happy Hours!

105 From the dim recesses
Of woven caresses,
Where lovers catch ye by your loose tresses;
From the azure isles,
Where sweet Wisdom smiles,
110 Delaying your ships with her siren wiles.

From the temples high
Of Man's ear and eye,
Roofed over Sculpture and Poesy;
From the murmurings
115 Of the unsealed springs
Where Science bedews her dædal wings.

Years after years,
Through blood, and tears,
And a thick hell of hatreds, and hopes, and
fears;
120 We waded and flew,
And the islets were few
Where the bud-blighted flowers of happi-
ness grew.

Our feet now, every palm,
Are sandalled with calm, .
125 And the dew of our wings is a rain of balm;
And, beyond our eyes,
The human love lies,
Which makes all it gazes on, Paradise.

Chorus of Spirits and Hours

Then weave the web of the mystic
measure;
130 From the depths of the sky and the ends
of the earth,

Come, swift Spirits of might and of
pleasure,
Fill the dance and the music of mirth,
As the waves of a thousand streams rush
by
To an ocean of splendor and harmony!

Chorus of Spirits

135 Our spoil is won,
Our task is done,
We are free to dive, or soar, or run;
Beyond and around,
Or within the bound
140 Which clips[1] the world with darkness
round.

We'll pass the eyes
Of the starry skies
Into the hoar deep to colonize:
Death, Chaos, and Night,
145 From the sound of our flight,
Shall flee, like mist from a tempest's might.

And Earth, Air, and Light,
And the Spirit of Might,
Which drives round the stars in their fiery
flight;
150 And Love, Thought, and Breath,
The powers that quell Death,
Wherever we soar shall assemble beneath.

And our singing shall build
In the void's loose field
155 A world for the Spirit of Wisdom to wield;
We will take our plan
From the new world of man,
And our work shall be called the Prome-
thean.

Chorus of Hours

Break the dance, and scatter the song;
160 Let some depart, and some remain.

Semichorus I

We, beyond heaven, are driven along:

Semichorus II

Us the enchantments of earth retain:

Semichorus I

Ceaseless, and rapid, and fierce, and free,
With the Spirits which build a new earth
and sea,
165 And a heaven where yet heaven could never
be;

---

[1] embraces; encompasses

Semichorus II

Solemn, and slow, and serene, and bright,
Leading the Day and outspeeding the
    Night,
With the powers of a world of perfect
    light;

Semichorus I

We whirl, singing loud, round the gather-
    ing sphere,
170 Till the trees, and the beasts, and the clouds
    appear
From its chaos made calm by love, not fear.

Semichorus II

We encircle the ocean and mountains of
    earth,
And the happy forms of its death and birth
Change to the music of our sweet mirth.

Chorus of Hours and Spirits

175 Break the dance, and scatter the song;
    Let some depart, and some remain;
    Wherever we fly we lead along
    In leashes, like starbeams, soft yet strong,
      The clouds that are heavy with love's
      sweet rain.

180   *Panthea.* Ha! they are gone!
    Ione.   Yet feel you no delight
From the past sweetness?
    Panthea.   As the bare green hill
When some soft cloud vanishes into rain,
Laughs with a thousand drops of sunny
    water
To the unpavilioned sky!
    Ione.   Even whilst we speak
185 New notes arise. What is that awful
    sound?
    Panthea. 'Tis the deep music of the
    rolling world[1]
Kindling within the strings of the waved
    air
Æolian modulations.
    Ione.   Listen too,
How every pause is filled with under-notes,
190 Clear, silver, icy, keen awakening tones,
Which pierce the sense, and live within the
    soul,
As the sharp stars pierce winter's crystal
    air
And gaze upon themselves within the sea.
    Panthea. But see where, through two
    openings in the forest
195 Which hanging branches overcanopy,

[1] The ancients believed that the movement of
the celestial spheres produced music.

And where two runnels of a rivulet,
Between the close moss violet-inwoven,
Have made their path of melody, like
    sisters
Who part with sighs that they may meet in
    smiles,
200 Turning their dear disunion to an isle
Of lovely grief, a wood of sweet sad
    thoughts;
Two visions of strange radiance float upon
The ocean-like enchantment of strong
    sound,
Which flows intenser, keener, deeper yet,
205 Under the ground and through the wind-
    less air.
    Ione. I see a chariot like that thinnest
    boat,
In which the Mother of the Months[1] is
    borne
By ebbing light into her western cave,
When she upsprings from interlunar
    dreams;
210 O'er which is curved an orblike canopy
Of gentle darkness, and the hills and woods,
Distinctly seen through that dusk aery veil,
Regard[2] like shapes in an enchanter's
    glass;
Its wheels are solid clouds, azure and gold,
215 Such as the genii of the thunderstorm
Pile on the floor of the illumined sea
When the sun rushes under it; they roll
And move and grow as with an inward
    wind;
Within it sits a wingèd infant, white
220 Its countenance, like the whiteness of
    bright snow,
Its plumes are as feathers of sunny frost,
Its limbs gleam white, through the wind-
    flowing folds
Of its white robe, woof of ethereal pearl.
Its hair is white, the brightness of white
    light
225 Scattered in strings; yet its two eyes are
    heavens
Of liquid darkness, which the Deity
Within seems pouring, as a storm is poured
From jaggèd clouds, out of their arrowy
    lashes,
Tempering the cold and radiant air around,
230 With fire that is not brightness; in its
    hand
It sways a quivering moonbeam, from
    whose point
A guiding power directs the chariot's prow
Over its wheelèd clouds, which as they roll
Over the grass, and flowers, and waves,
    wake sounds,
235 Sweet as a singing rain of silver dew.

[1] Diana (Artemis).   [2] appear

Panthea. And from the other opening
    in the wood
Rushes, with loud and whirlwind harmony,
A sphere,[1] which is as many thousand
    spheres,
Solid as crystal, yet through all its mass
240 Flow, as through empty space, music and
    light;
Ten thousand orbs involving and involved,
Purple and azure, white, green, and golden,
Sphere within sphere; and every space
    between
Peopled with unimaginable shapes,
245 Such as ghosts dream dwell in the lampless
    deep,
Yet each inter-transpicuous;[2] and they
    whirl
Over each other with a thousand motions,
Upon a thousand sightless axles spinning,
And with the force of self-destroying
    swiftness,
250 Intensely, slowly, solemnly roll on,
Kindling with mingled sounds, and many
    tones,
Intelligible words and music wild.
With mighty whirl the multitudinous orb
Grinds the bright brook into an azure
    mist
255 Of elemental subtlety, like light;
And the wild odor of the forest flowers,
The music of the living grass and air,
The emerald light of leaf-entangled beams
Round its intense yet self-conflicting speed,
260 Seem kneaded into one aërial mass
Which drowns the sense. Within the orb
    itself,
Pillowed upon its alabaster arms,
Like to a child o'erwearied with sweet toil,
On its own folded wings, and wavy hair,
265 The Spirit of the Earth is laid asleep,
And you can see its little lips are moving,
Amid the changing light of their own
    smiles,
Like one who talks of what he loves in
    dream.
    Ione. 'Tis only mocking the orb's har-
    mony.
270   *Panthea.* And from a star upon its fore-
    head, shoot,
Like swords of azure fire, or golden spears
With tyrant-quelling myrtle[3] overtwined,
Embleming heaven and earth united now,
Vast beams like spokes of some invisible
    wheel

275 Which whirl as the orb whirls, swifter
    than thought,
Filling the abyss with sun-like lightnings,
And perpendicular now, and now trans-
    verse,
Pierce the dark soil, and as they pierce and
    pass,
Make bare the secrets of the earth's deep
    heart;
280 Infinite mines of adamant and gold,
Valueless[1] stones, and unimagined gems,
And caverns on crystalline columns poised
With vegetable silver overspread;
Wells of unfathomed fire, and water-
    springs
285 Whence the great sea, even as a child, is
    fed,
Whose vapors clothe earth's monarch
    mountain-tops
With kingly, ermine snow. The beams
    flash on
And make appear the melancholy ruins
Of cancelled cycles; anchors, beaks of
    ships;
290 Planks turned to marble; quivers, helms,
    and spears,
And gorgon-headed targes,[2] and the wheels
Of scythèd chariots, and the emblazonry
Of trophies, standards, and armorial
    beasts,
Round which death laughed, sepulchred
    emblems
295 Of dead destruction, ruin within ruin!
The wrecks beside of many a city vast,
Whose population which the earth grew
    over
Was mortal, but not human; see, they lie,
Their monstrous works, and uncouth skele-
    tons,
300 Their statues, homes, and fanes; prodi-
    gious shapes
Huddled in gray annihilation, split,
Jammed in the hard, black deep; and over
    these,
The anatomies of unknown wingèd things,
And fishes which were isles of living scale,
305 And serpents, bony chains, twisted around
The iron crags, or within heaps of dust
To which the tortuous strength of their last
    pangs
Had crushed the iron crags; and over these
The jaggèd alligator, and the might
310 Of earth-convulsing behemoth,[3] which once
Were monarch beasts, and on the slimy
    shores,

---

[1] The earth.
[2] transparent within
[3] A reference to the story of Harmodius and Aristogeiton, Athenian heroes who hid their swords under myrtle branches at the time of their attack upon Hipparchus, the tyrant of Athens, in 514 B. C.

[1] priceless
[2] shields bearing the image of the head of Medusa, one of the Gorgons
[3] A very large animal, probably the hippopotamus.

And weed-overgrown continents of earth,
Increased and multiplied like summer
    worms
On an abandoned corpse, till the blue
    globe[1]
315 Wrapped deluge round it like a cloak, and
    they
Yelled, gasped, and were abolished; or
    some God
Whose throne was in a comet, passed, and
    cried,
"Be not!" And like my words they were
    no more.

The Earth

The joy, the triumph, the delight, the
    madness!
320 The boundless, overflowing, bursting
    gladness,
The vaporous exultation not to be con-
    fined!
Ha! ha! the animation of delight
Which wraps me, like an atmosphere of
    light,
And bears me as a cloud is borne by its own
    wind.

The Moon

325 Brother mine, calm wanderer,
Happy globe of land and air,
Some Spirit is darted like a beam from
    thee,
Which penetrates my frozen frame,
And passes with the warmth of flame,
330 With love, and odor, and deep melody
Through me, through me!

The Earth

Ha! ha! the caverns of my hollow
    mountains,
My cloven fire-crags, sound-exulting
    fountains,
Laugh with a vast and inextinguishable
    laughter.
335 The oceans, and the deserts, and the
    abysses,
And the deep air's unmeasured wilder-
    nesses,
Answer from all their clouds and billows,
    echoing after.

They cry aloud as I do. Sceptred curse,[2]
Who all our green and azure universe
340 Threatenedst to muffle round with black
    destruction, sending
A solid cloud to rain hot thunderstones,

And splinter and knead down my chil-
    dren's bones,
All I bring forth, to one void mass batter-
    ing and blending,—

Until each crag-like tower, and storied
    column,
345 Palace, and obelisk, and temple solemn,
My imperial mountains crowned with
    cloud, and snow, and fire,
My sea-like forests, every blade and
    blossom
Which finds a grave or cradle in my
    bosom,
Were stamped by thy strong hate into a
    lifeless mire:

350 How art thou sunk, withdrawn, covered,
    drunk up
By thirsty nothing, as the brackish cup
Drained by a desert-troop, a little drop for
    all;
And from beneath, around, within,
    above,
Filling thy void annihilation, love
355 Burst in like light on coves cloven by the
    thunder-ball.

The Moon

The snow upon my lifeless mountains
Is loosened into living fountains,
My solid oceans flow, and sing, and shine:
A spirit from my heart bursts forth,
360 It clothes with unexpected birth
My cold bare bosom. Oh! it must be thine
On mine, on mine!

Gazing on thee I feel, I know,
Green stalks burst forth, and bright
    flowers grow,
365 And living shapes upon my bosom move:
Music is in the sea and air,
Wingèd clouds soar here and there,
Dark with the rain new buds are dreaming
    of:
'Tis love, all love!

The Earth

370 It interpenetrates my granite mass,
Through tangled roots and trodden clay
    doth pass
Into the utmost leaves and delicatest
    flowers;
Upon the winds, among the clouds 'tis
    spread,
It wakes a life in the forgotten dead,—
375 They breathe a spirit up from their ob-
    scurest bowers;

----

[1] The sea.   [2] Jupiter.

And like a storm bursting its cloudy
    prison
With thunder, and with whirlwind, has
    arisen
Out of the lampless caves of unimagined
    being:
With earthquake shock and swiftness
    making shiver
380 Thought's stagnant chaos, unremoved
    forever,
Till hate, and fear, and pain, light-van-
    quished shadows, fleeing,

Leave Man, who was a many-sided
    mirror,
Which could distort to many a shape of
    error,
This true fair world of things, a sea re-
    flecting love;
385 Which over all his kind, as the sun's
    heaven
Gliding o'er ocean, smooth, serene, and
    even,
Darting from starry depths radiance and
    life, doth move:

Leave Man, even as a leprous child is
    left,
Who follows a sick beast to some warm
    cleft
390 Of rocks, through which the might of
    healing springs is poured;
Then when it wanders home with rosy
    smile,
Unconscious, and its mother fears awhile
It is a spirit, then, weeps on her child
    restored.

Man, oh, not men! a chain of linkèd
    thought,
395 Of love and might to be divided not,
Compelling the elements with adamantine
    stress;
As the sun rules, even with a tyrant's
    gaze,
The unquiet republic of the maze
Of planets, struggling fierce towards heav-
    en's free wilderness.

400 Man, one harmonious soul of many a
    soul,
Whose nature is its own divine control,
Where all things flow to all, as rivers to
    the sea;
Familiar acts are beautiful through love;
Labor, and pain, and grief, in life's
    green grove
405 Sport like tame beasts; none knew how
    gentle they could be!

His will, with all mean passions, bad
    delights,
And selfish cares, its trembling satellites,
A spirit ill to guide, but mighty to obey,
    410 Is as a tempest-wingèd ship, whose
    helm
Love rules, through waves which dare
    not overwhelm,
Forcing life's wildest shores to own its
    sovereign sway.

All things confess his strength. Through
    the cold mass
Of marble and of color his dreams
    pass—
Bright threads whence mothers weave the
    robes their children wear;
415 Language is a perpetual Orphic[1] song,
Which rules with dædal harmony a
    throng
Of thoughts and forms, which else sense-
    less and shapeless were.

The lightning is his slave; heaven's ut-
    most deep
Gives up her stars, and like a flock of
    sheep
420 They pass before his eye, are numbered,
    and roll on!
The tempest is his steed, he strides the
    air;
And the abyss shouts from her depth
    laid bare,
"Heaven, hast thou secrets? Man unveils
    me; I have none."

The Moon

The shadow of white death has passed
425 From my path in heaven at last,
A clinging shroud of solid frost and
    sleep;
And through my newly-woven bowers,
Wander happy paramours,[2]
Less mighty, but as mild as those who keep
    430 Thy vales more deep.

The Earth

As the dissolving warmth of dawn may
    fold
A half unfrozen dew-globe, green, and
    gold,
And crystalline, till it becomes a wingèd
    mist,
And wanders up the vault of the blue
    day,

[1] entrancing (from Orpheus, the famous Greek
poet and musician)
[2] Used here in the innocent sense of *lovers*.

435   Outlives the moon, and on the sun's last
       ray
    Hangs o'er the sea, a fleece of fire and
       amethyst.

The Moon

    Thou art folded, thou art lying
    In the light which is undying
    Of thine own joy, and heaven's smile
       divine;
440   All suns and constellations shower
    On thee a light, a life, a power,
    Which doth array thy sphere; thou pour-
       est thine
    On mine, on mine!

The Earth

    I spin beneath my pyramid of night,
445   Which points into the heavens dreaming
       delight,
    Murmuring victorious joy in my enchanted
       sleep;
    As a youth lulled in love-dreams faintly
       sighing,
    Under the shadow of his beauty lying,
    Which round his rest a watch of light and
       warmth doth keep.

The Moon

450   As in the soft and sweet eclipse,
    When soul meets soul on lovers' lips,
    High hearts are calm, and brightest eyes
       are dull;
    So when thy shadow falls on me,
    Then am I mute and still, by thee
455   Covered; of thy love, Orb most beautiful,
       Full, oh, too full!

    Thou art speeding round the sun
    Brightest world of many a one;
    Green and azure sphere which shinest
460   With a light which is divinest
    Among all the lamps of Heaven
    To whom life and light is given;
    I, thy crystal paramour
    Borne beside thee by a power
465   Like the polar Paradise,
    Magnet-like of lovers' eyes;
    I, a most enamored maiden
    Whose weak brain is overladen
    With the pleasure of her love,
470   Maniac-like around thee move
    Gazing, an insatiate bride,
    On thy form from every side
    Like a Mænad, round the cup
    Which Agave lifted up
475   In the weird Cadmæan forest.
    Brother, wheresoe'er thou soarest
    I must hurry, whirl, and follow

    Through the heavens wide and hollow,
    Sheltered by the warm embrace
480   Of thy soul from hungry space,
    Drinking from thy sense and sight
    Beauty, majesty, and might,
    As a lover or a chameleon
    Grows like what it looks upon,
485   As a violet's gentle eye
    Gazes on the azure sky
    Until its hue grows like what it beholds,
    As a gray and watery mist
    Glows like solid amethyst
490   Athwart the western mountain it enfolds,
    When the sunset sleeps
      Upon its snow—

The Earth

    And the weak day weeps
      That it should be so.
495 O gentle Moon, the voice of thy delight
    Falls on me like thy clear and tender light
    Soothing the seaman, borne the summer
       night,
    Through isles forever calm;
    O gentle Moon, thy crystal accents pierce
500 The caverns of my pride's deep universe,
    Charming the tiger joy, whose tramplings
       fierce
    Made wounds which need thy balm.

    Panthea.   I rise as from a bath of
       sparkling water,
    A bath of azure light, among dark rocks,
505 Out of the stream of sound.
    Ione.   Ah me! sweet sister,
    The stream of sound has ebbed away from
       us,
    And you pretend to rise out of its wave,
    Because your words fall like the clear, soft
       dew
    Shaken from a bathing wood-nymph's
       limbs and hair.
510   *Panthea.* Peace! peace! A mighty
       Power, which is as darkness,
    Is rising out of Earth, and from the sky
    Is showered like night, and from within the
       air
    Bursts, like eclipse which had been gath-
       ered up
    Into the pores of sunlight: the bright
       visions,
515 Wherein the singing Spirits rode and
       shone,
    Gleam like pale meteors through a watery
       night.
    Ione. There is a sense of words upon
       mine ear.
    Panthea. An universal sound like words:
       Oh, list!

Demogorgon

Thou, Earth, calm empire of a happy soul,
520 Sphere of divinest shapes and har-
    monies,
Beautiful orb! gathering as thou dost roll
The love which paves thy path along the
    skies:

The Earth

I hear: I am as a drop of dew that dies.

Demogorgon

Thou, Moon, which gazest on the nightly
    Earth
525 With wonder, as it gazes upon thee;
Whilst each to men, and beasts, and the
    swift birth
Of birds, is beauty, love, calm, harmony:

The Moon

I hear: I am a leaf shaken by thee!

Demogorgon

Ye Kings of suns and stars, Dæmons and
    Gods,
530 Etherial Dominations,[1] who possess
Elysian, windless, fortunate abodes
Beyond Heaven's constellated wilder-
    ness:

A Voice from above

Our great Republic hears: we are blest,
    and bless.

Demogorgon

Ye happy dead, whom beams of brightest
    verse
535 Are clouds to hide, not colors to portray,
Whether your nature is that universe
Which once ye saw and suffered—

A Voice from beneath

               Or, as they
Whom we have left, we change and pass
    away.

Demogorgon

Ye elemental Genii, who have homes
540 From man's high mind even to the cen-
    tral stone
Of sullen lead; from Heaven's star-
    fretted domes
To the dull weed some sea-worm battens
    on:

---

[1] A high order of angels. See *Paradise Lost*, 3,
392; 5, 601, 772, etc.

A confused Voice

We hear: thy words waken Oblivion.

Demogorgon

Spirits, whose homes are flesh: ye beasts
    and birds,
545 Ye worms, and fish; ye living leaves and
    buds;
Lightning and wind; and ye untameable
    herds,
Meteors and mists, which throng air's
    solitudes:—

A Voice

Thy voice to us is wind among still woods.

Demogorgon

Man, who wert once a despot and a slave,
550 A dupe and a deceiver, a decay,
A traveller from the cradle to the grave[1]
Through the dim night of this immortal
    day:

All

Speak: thy strong words may never
    pass away.

Demogorgon

This is the day which down the void abysm
555 At the Earth-born's spell[2] yawns for
    Heaven's despotism,
    And Conquest is dragged captive
    through the deep:
Love, from its awful throne of patient
    power
In the wise heart, from the last giddy hour
    Of dread endurance, from the slippery,
    steep,
560 And narrow verge of crag-like agony,
    springs
And folds over the world its healing wings.

Gentleness, Virtue, Wisdom, and Endur-
    ance,—
These are the seals of that most firm
    assurance
Which bars the pit over Destruction's
    strength;
565 And if, with infirm hand, Eternity,
Mother of many acts and hours, should
    free
The serpent that would clasp her with
    his length,
These are the spells by which to reassume
An empire o'er the disentangled doom.

---

[1] See Wordsworth's *She Was a Phantom of Delight*, 24 (p. 321).
[2] The spell of Prometheus.

570 To suffer woes which Hope thinks infinite;
To forgive wrongs darker than death or
night;
To defy Power, which seems omnipotent;
To love, and bear; to hope till Hope
creates
From its own wreck the thing it contem-
plates;
575 Neither to change, nor falter, nor re-
pent;—
This, like thy glory, Titan, is to be
Good, great and joyous, beautiful and free;
This is alone Life, Joy, Empire, and
Victory!

THE SENSITIVE PLANT
1820   1820
PART FIRST

A Sensitive Plant in a garden grew,
And the young winds fed it with silver dew,
And it opened its fan-like leaves to the
light,
And closed them beneath the kisses of
Night.

5 And the Spring arose on the garden fair,
Like the Spirit of Love felt everywhere;
And each flower and herb on Earth's dark
breast
Rose from the dreams of its wintry rest.

But none ever trembled and panted with
bliss
10 In the garden, the field, or the wilderness,
Like a doe in the noontide with love's
sweet want,
As the companionless Sensitive Plant.

The snowdrop, and then the violet,
Arose from the ground with warm rain
wet,
15 And their breath was mixed with fresh
odor, sent
From the turf, like the voice and the
instrument.

Then the pied wind-flowers[1] and the tulip
tall,
And narcissi, the fairest among them all,
Who gaze on their eyes in the stream's
recess,
20 Till they die of their own dear loveliness;

And the Naiad-like lily of the vale,
Whom youth makes so fair, and passion
so pale,

[1] anemones (from Greek ἄνεμος, wind)

That the light of its tremulous bells is
seen
Through their pavilions of tender green;

25 And the hyacinth purple, and white, and
blue,
Which flung from its bells a sweet peal
anew
Of music so delicate, soft, and intense,
It was felt like an odor within the sense;

And the rose like a nymph to the bath addressed,
30 Which unveiled the depth of her glowing
breast,
Till, fold after fold, to the fainting air
The soul of her beauty and love lay bare;

And the wand-like lily, which lifted up,
As a Mænad, its moonlight-colored cup,
35 Till the fiery star, which is its eye,
Gazed through clear dew on the tender sky;

And the jessamine faint, and the sweet
tuberose,
The sweetest flower for scent that blows;
And all rare blossoms from every clime
40 Grew in that garden in perfect prime.

And on the stream whose inconstant bosom
Was pranked, under boughs of embower-
ing blossom,
With golden and green light, slanting
through
Their heaven of many a tangled hue,

45 Broad water-lilies lay tremulously,
And starry river-buds glimmered by,
And around them the soft stream did
glide and dance
With a motion of sweet sound and radi-
ance.

And the sinuous paths of lawn and of
moss,
50 Which led through the garden along and
across,
Some open at once to the sun and the
breeze,
Some lost among bowers of blossoming
trees,

Were all paved with daisies and delicate
bells,
As fair as the fabulous asphodels,[1]
55 And flow'rets which, drooping as day
drooped too,

[1] Asphodels (daffodils) were said to cover the
fields of Elysium, the abode of the blessed
after death.

Fell into pavilions, white, purple, and
    blue,
To roof the glow-worm from the evening
    dew.

And from this undefiled Paradise
The flowers (as an infant's awakening
    eyes
60 Smile on its mother, whose singing sweet
Can first lull, and at last must awaken it),

When Heaven's blithe winds had unfolded
    them,
As mine-lamps enkindle a hidden gem,
Shone smiling to Heaven, and every one
65 Shared joy in the light of the gentle sun;

For each one was interpenetrated
With the light and the odor its neighbor
    shed,
Like young lovers whom youth and love
    make dear
Wrapped and filled by their mutual atmos-
    phere.

70 But the Sensitive Plant which could give
    small fruit
Of the love which it felt from the leaf to
    the root,
Received more than all, it loved more than
    ever,
Where none wanted but it, could belong
    to the giver,—

For the Sensitive Plant has no bright
    flower;
75 Radiance and odor are not its dower;
It loves, even like Love, its deep heart is
    full,
It desires what it has not, the beautiful!

The light winds which from unsustaining
    wings
Shed the music of many murmurings;
80 The beams which dart from many a star
Of the flowers whose hues they bear afar;

The plumèd insects swift and free,
Like golden boats on a sunny sea,
Laden with light and odor, which pass
85 Over the gleam of the living grass;

The unseen clouds of the dew, which lie
Like fire in the flowers till the sun rides
    high,
Then wander like spirits among the
    spheres,
Each cloud faint with the fragrance it
    bears;

90 The quivering vapors of dim noontide,
Which like a sea o'er the warm earth glide,
In which every sound, and odor, and beam,
Move, as reeds in a single stream;

Each and all like ministering angels were
95 For the Sensitive Plant sweet joy to bear,
Whilst the lagging hours of the day went
    by
Like windless clouds o'er a tender sky.

And when evening descended from Heaven
    above,
And the Earth was all rest, and the air was
    all love,
100 And delight, though less bright, was far
    more deep,
And the day's veil fell from the world of
    sleep,

And the beasts, and the birds, and the in-
    sects were drowned
In an ocean of dreams without a sound,
Whose waves never mark, though they ever
    impress
105 The light sand which paves it, conscious-
    ness;

(Only overhead the sweet nightingale
Ever sang more sweet as the day might
    fail,
And snatches of its Elysian chant
Were mixed with the dreams of the Sensi-
    tive Plant);—

110 The Sensitive Plant was the earliest
Upgathered into the bosom of rest;
A sweet child weary of its delight,
The feeblest and yet the favorite,
Cradled within the embrace of Night.

PART SECOND

There was a Power in this sweet place,
An Eve in this Eden; a ruling Grace
Which to the flowers, did they waken or
    dream,
Was as God is to the starry scheme.

5 A lady, the wonder of her kind,
Whose form was upborne by a lovely
    mind
Which, dilating, had moulded her mien
    and motion
Like a sea-flower unfolded beneath the
    ocean,

Tended the garden from morn to even:
10 And the meteors of that sublunar Heaven,

Like the lamps of the air when Night
walks forth,
Laughed round her footsteps up from the
Earth!

She had no companion of mortal race,
But her tremulous breath and her flushing
face
15 Told, whilst the morn kissed the sleep
from her eyes,
That her dreams were less slumber than
Paradise:

As if some bright Spirit for her sweet sake
Had deserted Heaven while the stars were
awake,
As if yet around her he lingering were,
20 Though the veil of daylight concealed him
from her.

Her steps seemed to pity the grass it
pressed;
You might hear, by the heaving of her
breast,
That the coming and going of the wind
Brought pleasure there and left passion
behind.

25 And wherever her airy footstep trod,
Her trailing hair from the grassy sod
Erased its light vestige, with shadowy
sweep,
Like a sunny storm o'er the dark green
deep.

I doubt not the flowers of that garden sweet
30 Rejoiced in the sound of her gentle feet;
I doubt not they felt the spirit that came
From her glowing fingers through all their
frame.

She sprinkled bright water from the
stream
On those that were faint with the sunny
beam;
35 And out of the cups of the heavy flowers
She emptied the rain of the thunder-
showers.

She lifted their heads with her tender
hands,
And sustained them with rods and osier-
bands;[1]
If the flowers had been her own infants,
she
40 Could never have nursed them more tenderly.

[1] willow-bands

And all killing insects and gnawing worms,
And things of obscene and unlovely forms,
She bore in a basket of Indian woof,
Into the rough woods far aloof,—

45 In a basket, of grasses and wild-flowers
full,
The freshest her gentle hands could pull
For the poor banished insects, whose in-
tent,
Although they did ill, was innocent.

But the bee, and the beamlike ephemeris[1]
50 Whose path is the lightning's, and soft
moths that kiss
The sweet lips of the flowers, and harm
not, did she
Make her attendant angels be.

And many an antenatal tomb,
Where butterflies dream of the life to
come,
55 She left clinging round the smooth and
dark
Edge of the odorous cedar bark.

This fairest creature from earliest spring
Thus moved through the garden ministering
All the sweet season of summertide,
60 And ere the first leaf looked brown—she
died!

PART THIRD

Three days the flowers of the garden fair,
Like stars when the moon is awakened,
were,
Or the waves of Baiæ, ere luminous
She floats up through the smoke of Vesu-
vius.

5 And on the fourth, the Sensitive Plant
Felt the sound of the funeral chant,
And the steps of the bearers, heavy and
slow,
And the sobs of the mourners, deep and
low;

The weary sound and the heavy breath,
10 And the silent motions of passing death,
And the smell, cold, oppressive, and dank,
Sent through the pores of the coffin plank;

The dark grass, and the flowers among the
grass,
Were bright with tears as the crowd did
pass;

[1] A delicate insect with net-veined wings.

¹⁵ From their sighs the wind caught a mournful tone,
And sate in the pines, and gave groan for groan.

The garden, once fair, became cold and foul,
Like the corpse of her who had been its soul,
Which at first was lovely as if in sleep,
²⁰ Then slowly changed, till it grew a heap
To make men tremble who never weep.

Swift summer into the autumn flowed,
And frost in the mist of the morning rode,
Though the noonday sun looked clear and bright,
²⁵ Mocking the spoil of the secret night.

The rose-leaves, like flakes of crimson snow,
Paved the turf and the moss below.
The lilies were drooping, and white, and wan,
Like the head and the skin of a dying man.

³⁰ And Indian plants, of scent and hue
The sweetest that ever were fed on dew,
Leaf by leaf, day after day,
Were massed into the common clay.

And the leaves, brown, yellow, and gray, and red,
³⁵ And white with the whiteness of what is dead,
Like troops of ghosts on the dry wind passed;
Their whistling noise made the birds aghast.

And the gusty winds waked the wingèd seeds,
Out of their birthplace of ugly weeds,
⁴⁰ Till they clung round many a sweet flower's stem,
Which rotted into the earth with them.

The water-blooms under the rivulet
Fell from the stalks on which they were set;
And the eddies drove them here and there,
⁴⁵ As the winds did those of the upper air.

Then the rain came down, and the broken stalks
Were bent and tangled across the walks;
And the leafless network of parasite bowers
Massed into ruin, and all sweet flowers.

⁵⁰ Between the time of the wind and the snow
All loathliest weeds began to grow,
Whose coarse leaves were splashed with many a speck,
Like the water-snake's belly and the toad's back.

And thistles, and nettles, and darnels[1] rank,
⁵⁵ And the dock, and henbane, and hemlock dank,
Stretched out its long and hollow shank,
And stifled the air till the dead wind stank.

And plants, at whose names the verse feels loath,
Filled the place with a monstrous undergrowth,
⁶⁰ Prickly, and pulpous, and blistering, and blue,
Livid, and starred with a lurid dew.

And agarics,[2] and fungi, with mildew and mould,
Started like mist from the wet ground cold;
Pale, fleshy, as if the decaying dead
⁶⁵ With a spirit of growth had been animated!

Their moss rotted off them, flake by flake,
Till the thick stalk stuck like a murderer's stake,
Where rags of loose flesh yet tremble on high,
Infecting the winds that wander by.

⁷⁰ Spawn, weeds, and filth, a leprous scum,
Made the running rivulet thick and dumb,
And at its outlet flags huge as stakes
Dammed it up with roots knotted like water-snakes.

And hour by hour, when the air was still,
⁷⁵ The vapors arose which have strength to kill;
At morn they were seen, at noon they were felt,
At night they were darkness no star could melt.

And unctuous meteors from spray to spray
Crept and flitted in broad noonday
⁸⁰ Unseen; every branch on which they alit
By a venomous blight was burned and bit.

[1] A kind of grass weed.
[2] A kind of fungus.

The Sensitive Plant, like one forbid,[1]
Wept, and the tears within each lid
Of its folded leaves, which together grew,
85 Were changed to a blight of frozen glue.

For the leaves soon fell, and the branches soon
By the heavy axe of the blast were hewn;
The sap shrank to the root through every pore
As blood to a heart that will beat no more.

90 For Winter came: the wind was his whip:
One choppy finger was on his lip:[2]
He had torn the cataracts from the hills
And they clanked at his girdle like manacles;

His breath was a chain which without a sound
95 The earth, and the air, and the water bound;
He came, fiercely driven, in his chariot-throne
By the tenfold blasts of the Arctic zone.

Then the weeds which were forms of living death
Fled from the frost to the earth beneath.
100 Their decay and sudden flight from frost
Was but like the vanishing of a ghost!

And under the roots of the Sensitive Plant
The moles and the dormice died for want:
The birds dropped stiff from the frozen air
105 And were caught in the branches naked and bare.

First there came down a thawing rain
And its dull drops froze on the boughs again;
Then there steamed up a freezing dew
Which to the drops of the thaw-rain grew;

110 And a northern whirlwind, wandering about,
Like a wolf that had smelt a dead child out,
Shook the boughs thus laden, and heavy, and stiff,
And snapped them off with his rigid griff.[3]

When Winter had gone and Spring came back,
115 The Sensitive Plant was a leafless wreck;

[1] accursed (See *Macbeth*, I, 3, 21.)
[2] See *Macbeth*, I, 3, 44-45.
[3] claw

But the mandrakes, and toadstools, and docks, and darnels,
Rose like the dead from their ruined charnels.

CONCLUSION

Whether the Sensitive Plant, or that
Which within its boughs like a spirit sat,
Ere its outward form had known decay,
Now felt this change, I cannot say.

5 Whether that lady's gentle mind,
No longer with the form combined
Which scattered love, as stars do light,
Found sadness, where it left delight,

I dare not guess; but in this life
10 Of error, ignorance, and strife,
Where nothing is, but all things seem,
And we the shadows of the dream,

It is a modest creed, and yet
Pleasant if one considers it,
15 To own that death itself must be,
Like all the rest, a mockery.

That garden sweet, that lady fair,
And all sweet shapes and odors there,
In truth have never passed away:
20 'Tis we, 'tis ours, are changed; not they.

For love, and beauty, and delight,
There is no death nor change: their might
Exceeds our organs, which endure
No light, being themselves obscure.

THE CLOUD
1820   1820

I bring fresh showers for the thirsting flowers,
From the seas and the streams;
I bear light shade for the leaves when laid
In their noonday dreams.
5 From my wings are shaken the dews that waken
The sweet buds every one,
When rocked to rest on their mother's breast,
As she dances about the sun.
I wield the flail of the lashing hail,
10 And whiten the green plains under,
And then again I dissolve it in rain,
And laugh as I pass in thunder.

I sift the snow on the mountains below,
And their great pines groan aghast;
15 And all the night 'tis my pillow white,
While I sleep in the arms of the blast.

Sublime on the towers of my skyey bowers,
  Lightning my pilot sits;
In a cavern under is fettered the thunder,
20 It struggles and howls at fits;
Over earth and ocean, with gentle motion,
  This pilot is guiding me,
Lured by the love of the genii that move
  In the depths of the purple sea;
25 Over the rills, and the crags, and the hills,
  Over the lakes and the plains,
Wherever he dream, under mountain or
    stream,
  The Spirit he loves remains;
And I all the while bask in heaven's blue
    smile,
30 Whilst he is dissolving in rains.

The sanguine sunrise, with his meteor
    eyes,
  And his burning plumes outspread,
Leaps on the back of my sailing rack,[1]
  When the morning star shines dead;
35 As on the jag of a mountain crag,
  Which an earthquake rocks and swings,
An eagle alit one moment may sit
  In the light of its golden wings.
And when sunset may breathe, from the
    lit sea beneath,
40 Its ardors of rest and of love,
And the crimson pall of eve may fall
  From the depth of heaven above,
With wings folded I rest, on mine airy
    nest,
  As still as a brooding dove.

45 That orbèd maiden with white fire laden,
  Whom mortals call the Moon,
Glides glimmering o'er my fleece-like
    floor,
  By the midnight breezes strewn;
And wherever the beat of her unseen feet,
50 Which only the angels hear,
May have broken the woof of my tent's
    thin roof,
  The stars peep behind her and peer;
And I laugh to see them whirl and flee,
  Like a swarm of golden bees,
55 When I widen the rent in my wind-built
    tent,
  Till the calm rivers, lakes, and seas,
Like strips of the sky fallen through me
    on high,
  Are each paved with the moon and these.[2]

I bind the sun's throne with a burning
    zone,[3]
60 And the moon's with a girdle of pearl;

[1] flying broken cloud   [3] girdle
[2] The stars.

The volcanos are dim, and the stars reel
    and swim,
  When the whirlwinds my banner unfurl.
From cape to cape, with a bridge-like
    shape,
  Over a torrent sea,
65 Sunbeam-proof, I hang like a roof,—
  The mountains its columns be.
The triumphal arch through which I
    march
  With hurricane, fire, and snow,
When the powers of the air are chained to
    my chair,
70 Is the million-colored bow;
The sphere-fire above its soft colors wove,
  While the moist earth was laughing be-
    low.

I am the daughter of earth and water,
  And the nursling of the sky;
75 I pass through the pores of the ocean and
    shores;
  I change, but I cannot die.
For after the rain when with never a stain
  The pavilion of heaven is bare,
And the winds and sunbeams with their
    convex gleams
80 Build up the blue dome of air,
I silently laugh at my own cenotaph,[1]
  And out of the caverns of rain,
Like a child from the womb, like a ghost
    from the tomb,
  I arise and unbuild it again.

TO A SKYLARK
1820   1820

Hail to thee, blithe spirit!
  Bird thou never wert,
That from heaven, or near it,
  Pourest thy full heart
5 In profuse strains of unpremeditated art.

Higher still and higher
  From the earth thou springest
Like a cloud of fire;
  The blue deep thou wingest,
10 And singing still dost soar, and soaring
    ever singest.

In the golden lightning
  Of the sunken sun,
O'er which clouds are bright'ning,
  Thou dost float and run;
15 Like an unbodied joy[2] whose race is just
    begun.

[1] empty tomb (the blue dome of air)
[2] See Byron's *Manfred*, I, 2, 55 (p. 579).

The pale purple even
  Melts around thy flight;
Like a star of heaven,
  In the broad daylight
20 Thou art unseen, but yet I hear thy shrill
     delight,

Keen as are the arrows
  Of that silver sphere,
Whose intense lamp narrows
  In the white dawn clear
25 Until we hardly see—we feel that it is
     there.

All the earth and air
  With thy voice is loud,
As, when night is bare,
  From one lonely cloud
30 The moon rains out her beams, and heaven
     is overflowed.

What thou art we know not;
  What is most like thee?
From rainbow clouds there flow not
  Drops so bright to see
35 As from thy presence showers a rain of
     melody.

Like a poet hidden
  In the light of thought,
Singing hymns unbidden,
  Till the world is wrought
40 To sympathy with hopes and fears it
     heeded not:

Like a high-born maiden
  In a palace tower,
Soothing her love-laden
  Soul in secret hour
45 With music sweet as love, which overflows
     her bower:

Like a glow-worm golden
  In a dell of dew,
Scattering unbeholden
  Its aërial hue
50 Among the flowers and grass, which screen
     it from the view!

Like a rose embowered
  In its own green leaves,
By warm winds deflowered,
  Till the scent it gives
55 Makes faint with too much sweet those
     heavy-wingèd thieves:

Sound of vernal showers
  On the twinkling grass,

Rain-awakened flowers,
  All that ever was
60 Joyous, and clear, and fresh, thy music
     doth surpass:

Teach us, sprite or bird,
  What sweet thoughts are thine:
I have never heard
  Praise of love or wine
65 That panted forth a flood of rapture so
     divine.

Chorus hymeneal,
  Or triumphal chant,
Matched with thine would be all
  But an empty vaunt,
70 A thing wherein we feel there is some
     hidden want.

What objects are the fountains
  Of thy happy strain?
What fields, or waves, or mountains?
  What shapes of sky or plain?
75 What love of thine own kind? what igno-
     rance of pain?

With thy clear keen joyance
  Languor cannot be:
Shadow of annoyance
  Never came near thee:
80 Thou lovest—but ne'er knew love's sad
     satiety.

Waking or asleep,
  Thou of death must deem
Things more true and deep
  Than we mortals dream,
85 Or how could thy notes flow in such a
     crystal stream?

We look before and after,
  And pine for what is not:
Our sincerest laughter
  With some pain is fraught;
90 Our sweetest songs are those that tell of
     saddest thought.

Yet if we could scorn
  Hate, and pride, and fear;
If we were things born
  Not to shed a tear,
95 I know not how thy joy we ever should
     come near.

Better than all measures
  Of delightful sound,
Better than all treasures

That in books are found,
100 Thy skill to poet were, thou scorner of
          the ground!

Teach me half the gladness
     That thy brain must know,
Such harmonious madness
     From my lips would flow
105 The world should listen then—as I am
     listening now.

TO ——
1820   1824

I fear thy kisses, gentle maiden,
     Thou needest not fear mine;
My spirit is too deeply laden
     Ever to burthen thine.

5 I fear thy mien, thy tones, thy motion,
     Thou needest not fear mine;
Innocent is the heart's devotion
     With which I worship thine.

ARETHUSA
1820   1824

Arethusa arose
     From her couch of snows
In the Acroceraunian mountains,
     From cloud and from crag,
5   With many a jag,
. Shepherding her bright fountains.
     She leapt down the rocks,
     With her rainbow locks
Streaming among the streams;—
10   Her steps paved with green
     The downward ravine
Which slopes to the western gleams;
     And gliding and springing
     She went, ever singing
15 In murmurs as soft as sleep;
     The Earth seemed to love her,
     And Heaven smiled above her,
As she lingered towards the deep.

     Then Alpheus bold,
20   On his glacier cold,
With his trident the mountains strook;
     And opened a chasm
     In the rocks—with the spasm
All Erymanthus shook.
25   And the black south wind
     It unsealed behind
The urns of the silent snow,
     And earthquake and thunder
     Did rend in sunder
30 The bars of the springs below.
     And the beard and the hair
     Of the River-god were
Seen through the torrent's sweep,

     As he followed the light
35   Of the fleet nymph's flight
To the brink of the Dorian deep.
     "Oh, save me! Oh, guide me!
     And bid the deep hide me,
For he grasps me now by the hair!"
40   The loud Ocean heard,
     To its blue depth stirred,
And divided at her prayer;
     And under the water
     The Earth's white daughter
45 Fled like a sunny beam;
     Behind her descended
     Her billows, unblended
With the brackish Dorian stream:—
     Like a gloomy stain
50   On the emerald main
Alpheus rushed behind,—
     As an eagle pursuing
     A dove to its ruin
Down the streams of the cloudy wind.

55   Under the bowers
     Where the Ocean Powers
Sit on their pearlèd thrones;
     Through the coral floods
     Of the weltering floods,
60 Over heaps of unvalued stones;
     Through the dim beams
     Which amid the streams
Weave a network of colored light;
     And under the caves,
65   Where the shadowy waves
Are as green as the forest's night:—
     Outspeeding the shark.
     And the swordfish dark,
Under the ocean foam,
70   And up through the rifts
     Of the mountain clifts
They passed to their Dorian home.

     And now from their fountains
     In Enna's mountains,
75 Down one vale where the morning basks,
     Like friends once parted
     Grown single-hearted,
They ply their watery tasks.
     At sunrise they leap
80   From their cradles steep
In the cave of the shelving hill;
     At noontide they flow
     Through the woods below
And the meadows of asphodel;[1]
85   And at night they sleep
     In the rocking deep
Beneath the Ortygian shore;—
     Like spirits that lie
     In the azure sky
90 When they love but live no more.
     [1] daffodils

HYMN OF APOLLO
1820   1824

The sleepless Hours who watch me as I lie,
  Curtained with star-inwoven tapestries
From the broad moonlight of the sky,
    Fanning the busy dreams from my dim
     eyes,
5 Waken me when their mother, the gray
     Dawn,
  Tells them that dreams and that the moon
     is gone.

Then I arise, and climbing Heaven's blue
     dome,
I walk over the mountains and the waves,
Leaving my robe upon the ocean foam;
10 My footsteps pave the clouds with fire;
     the caves
Are filled with my bright presence, and the
     air
Leaves the green Earth to my embraces
     bare.

The sunbeams are my shafts, with which I
     kill
  Deceit, that loves the night and fears the
     day;
15 All men who do or even imagine ill
  Fly me, and from the glory of my ray
Good minds and open actions take new
     might,
Until diminished by the reign of Night.

I feed the clouds, the rainbows, and the
     flowers
20 With their ethereal colors; the moon's
     globe
And the pure stars in their eternal bowers
  Are cinctured with my power as with a
     robe;
Whatever lamps on Earth or Heaven may
     shine
Are portions of one power, which is mine.

25 I stand at noon upon the peak of Heaven,
  Then with unwilling steps I wander
     down
Into the clouds of the Atlantic even;
  For grief that I depart they weep and
     frown.
What look is more delightful than the
     smile
30 With which I soothe them from the west-
     ern isle?

I am the eye with which the Universe
  Beholds itself and knows itself divine;
All harmony of instrument or verse,
  All prophecy, all medicine are mine,

35 All light of Art or Nature;—to my song
  Victory and praise in its own right belong.

HYMN OF PAN
1820   1824

From the forests and highlands
  We come, we come;
From the river-girt islands,
  Where loud waves are dumb
5   Listening to my sweet pipings.
The wind in the reeds and the rushes,
  The bees on the bells of thyme,
The birds on the myrtle bushes,
  The cicale[1] above in the lime,
10 And the lizards below in the grass,
  Were as silent as ever old Tmolus was,
    Listening to my sweet pipings.

Liquid Peneus was flowing,
  And all dark Tempe lay
15 In Pelion's shadow, outgrowing
  The light of the dying day,
    Speeded by my sweet pipings.
The Sileni, and Sylvans, and Fauns,
  And the Nymphs of the woods and the
    waves,
20 To the edge of the moist river-lawns,
  And the brink of the dewy caves,
And all that did then attend and follow,
Were silent with love, as you now, Apollo,
  With envy of my sweet pipings.

25 I sang of the dancing stars,
  I sang of the dædal[2] Earth,
And of Heaven—and the giant wars,
  And Love, and Death, and Birth;—
    And then I changed my pipings,—
30 Singing how down the vale of Mænalus
  I pursued a maiden and clasped a reed.[3]
Gods and men, we are all deluded thus!
  It breaks in our bosom and then we bleed.
All wept, as I think both ye now would,
35 If envy or age had not frozen your blood,
  At the sorrow of my sweet pipings.

THE QUESTION
1820   1822

I dreamed that, as I wandered by the way,
  Bare winter suddenly was changed to
    spring,
And gentle odors led my steps astray,
  Mixed with a sound of waters murmur-
    ing
5 Along a shelving bank of turf, which lay

---

[1] cicadas; locusts   [2] marvelously formed
[3] As Pan was about to embrace the nymph
  Syrinx, who was fleeing from him, she was
  transformed into reeds. Pan named his flute
  after her. See Ovid's *Metamorphoses*, 1,
  691 ff.

Under a copse, and hardly dared to
fling
Its green arms round the bosom of the
stream,
But kissed it and then fled, as thou mightest in dream.

There grew pied wind-flowers[1] and violets,
10   Daisies, those pearled Arcturi of the
earth,
The constellated flower that never sets;
  Faint oxslips; tender bluebells, at whose
birth
The sod scarce heaved; and that tall
flower[2] that wets—
Like a child, half in tenderness and
mirth—
15 Its mother's face with heaven-collected
tears,
When the low wind, its playmate's voice,
it hears.

And in the warm hedge grew lush eglantine,
  Green cowbind[3] and the moonlight-
colored may,[4]
And cherry-blossoms, and white cups,
whose wine
20   Was the bright dew, yet drained not by
the day;
And wild roses, and ivy serpentine,
  With its dark buds and leaves, wandering astray;
And flowers, azure, black, and streaked
with gold,
Fairer than any wakened eyes behold.

25 And nearer to the river's trembling edge
  There grew broad flag-flowers, purple
pranked with white;
And starry river buds among the sedge;
  And floating water-lilies, broad and
bright,
Which lit the oak that overhung the hedge
30   With moonlight beams of their own
watery light;
And bulrushes and reeds of such deep
green
As soothed the dazzled eye with sober
sheen.

Methought that of these visionary flowers
I made a nosegay, bound in such a way
35 That the same hues, which in their natural
bowers
Were mingled or opposed, the like array

1 anemones (from Greek ἄνεμος, wind)
2 Probably, the tulip. See Shelley's *The Sensitive Plant*, 1, 17 (p. 725).
3 bryony   4 hawthorn

Kept these imprisoned children of the
Hours
Within my hand,—and then, elate and
gay,
I hastened to the spot whence I had come,
40 That I might there present it!—Oh, to
whom?

THE TWO SPIRITS: AN ALLEGORY
1820   1824

First Spirit

O thou, who plumed with strong desire
  Wouldst float above the earth, beware!
A Shadow tracks thy flight of fire—
  Night is coming!
5   Bright are the regions of the air,
And among the winds and beams
  It were delight to wander there—
  Night is coming!

Second Spirit

The deathless stars are bright above;
10   If I would cross the shade of night,
Within my heart is the lamp of love,
  And that is day!
And the moon will smile with gentle light
On my golden plumes where'er they move;
15   The meteors will linger round my flight,
  And make night day.

First Spirit

But if the whirlwinds of darkness waken
  Hail, and lightning, and stormy rain?
See, the bounds of the air are shaken—
20   Night is coming!
The red swift clouds of the hurricane
Yon declining sun have overtaken,
  The clash of the hail sweeps over the
plain—
  Night is coming!

Second Spirit

25 I see the light, and I hear the sound;
  I'll sail on the flood of the tempest dark,
With the calm within and the light around
  Which makes night day;
And thou, when the gloom is deep and
stark,
30 Look from thy dull earth, slumber-bound,
  My moon-like flight thou then mayst
mark
  On high, far away.

———

Some say there is a precipice
  Where one vast pine is frozen to ruin
35 O'er piles of snow and chasms of ice

Mid Alpine mountains;
And that the languid storm pursuing
That wingèd shape, forever flies
Round those hoar branches, aye renew-
    ing
40   Its aëry fountains.
Some say when nights are dry and clear,
And the death-dews sleep on the morass,
Sweet whispers are heard by the traveller,
    Which make night day;
45 And a silver shape like his early love
        doth pass,
Upborne by her wild and glittering hair,
And, when he awakes on the fragrant
        grass,
        He finds night day.

AUTUMN: A DIRGE
1820   1824

The warm sun is failing, the bleak wind is
        wailing,
The bare boughs are sighing, the pale flow-
    ers are dying,
    And the Year
On the earth, her death-bed, in a shroud of
        leaves dead,
5   Is lying.
Come, Months, come away,
From November to May,
In your saddest **array**;
Follow the bier
10 Of the dead cold Year,
And like dim shadows watch by her sep-
        ulchre.

The chill rain is falling, the nipped worm is
        crawling,
The rivers are swelling, the thunder is
        knelling
    For the Year;
15 The blithe swallows are flown, and the liz-
        ards each gone
    To his dwelling;
Come, Months, come away;
Put on white, black, and gray;
Let your light sisters play—
20 Ye, follow the bier
Of the dead cold Year,
And make her grave green with tear on
        tear.

THE WANING MOON
1820   1824

And like a dying lady, lean and pale,
Who totters forth, wrapped in a gauzy
        veil,
Out of her chamber, led by the insane
And feeble wanderings of her fading brain,

5 The moon arose up in the murky East,
A white and shapeless mass.

* * * * * *

TO THE MOON
1820   1824

Art thou pale for weariness
Of climbing heaven and gazing on the
        earth,
Wandering companionless
Among the stars that have a different
        birth,—
5 And ever changing, like a joyless eye
That finds no object worth its constancy?

Thou chosen sister of the spirit,
That gazes on thee till in thee it pities

* * * * * *

DEATH
1820.   1824

Death is here, and death is there,
Death is busy everywhere,
All around, within, beneath,
Above, is death—and we are death.

5 Death has set his mark and seal
On all we are and all we feel,
On all we know and all we fear,

* * * * * *

First our pleasures die—and then
10 Our hopes, and then our fears—and when
These are dead, the debt is due,
Dust claims dust—and we die too.

All things that we love and cherish,
Like ourselves must fade and perish;
15 Such is our rude mortal lot—
Love itself would, did they not.

THE WORLD'S WANDERERS
1820   1824

Tell me, thou star, whose wings of light
Speed thee in thy fiery flight,
In what cavern of the night
        Will thy pinions close now?

5 Tell me, moon, thou pale and gray
Pilgrim of heaven's homeless way,
In what depth of night or day
        Seekest thou repose now?

Weary wind, who wanderest
10 Like the world's rejected guest,
Hast thou still some secret nest
        On the tree or billow?

TIME LONG PAST
1820   1870

Like the ghost of a dear friend dead
  Is Time long past.
A tone which is now forever fled,
A hope which is now forever past,
5 A love so sweet it could not last,
  Was Time long past.

There were sweet dreams in the night
  Of Time long past:
And, was it sadness or delight,
10 Each day a shadow onward cast
Which made us wish it yet might last—
  That Time long past.

There is regret, almost remorse,
  For Time long past.
15 'Tis like a child's belovèd corse
A father watches, till at last
Beauty is like remembrance, cast
  From Time long past.

AN ALLEGORY
1820   1824

A portal as of shadowy adamant
  Stands yawning on the highway of the life
Which we all tread, a cavern huge and gaunt;
  Around it rages an unceasing strife
5 Of shadows, like the restless clouds that haunt
The gap of some cleft mountain, lifted high
Into the whirlwinds of the upper sky.

And many pass it by with careless tread,
  Not knowing that a shadowy [   ]
10 Tracks every traveler even to where the dead
  Wait peacefully for their companion new;
But others, by more curious humor led,
  Pause to examine;—these are very few,
And they learn little there, except to know
15 That shadows follow them where'er they go.

THE WITCH OF ATLAS
1820   1824
To Mary[1]

ON HER OBJECTING TO THE FOLLOWING POEM,
UPON THE SCORE OF ITS CONTAIN-
ING NO HUMAN INTEREST

How, my dear Mary, are you critic-bitten
  (For vipers kill, though dead) by some review,

[1] Shelley's wife.

That you condemn these verses I have written,
  Because they tell no story, false or true!
5 What, though no mice are caught by a young kitten,
  May it not leap and play as grown cats do,
Till its claws come? Prithee, for this one time,
Content thee with a visionary rhyme.

What hand would crush the silken-wingèd fly,
10   The youngest of inconstant April's minions,
Because it cannot climb the purest sky,
  Where the swan sings, amid the sun's dominions?
Not thine. Thou knowest 'tis its doom to die,
  When Day shall hide within her twilight pinions
15 The lucent eyes, and the eternal smile,
Serene as thine, which lent it life awhile.

To thy fair feet a wingèd Vision[1] came,
  Whose date should have been longer than a day,
And o'er thy head did beat its wings for fame,
20   And in thy sight its fading plumes display;
The watery bow burned in the evening flame,
  But the shower fell, the swift Sun went his way—
And that is dead. Oh, let me not believe
That anything of mine is fit to live!

25 Wordsworth informs us he was nineteen years
  Considering and retouching *Peter Bell*;
Watering his laurels with the killing tears
  Of slow, dull care, so that their roots to Hell
Might pierce, and their wide branches blot the spheres
30   Of heaven with dewy leaves and flowers; this well
May be, for Heaven and Earth conspire to foil
The over-busy gardener's blundering toil.

My Witch indeed is not so sweet a creature
  As Ruth or Lucy,[2] whom his graceful praise
35 Clothes for our grandsons—but she matches Peter,
  Though he took nineteen years, and she three days
In dressing. Light the vest of flowing metre
  She wears; he, proud as dandy with his stays,
Has hung upon his wiry limbs a dress
40 Like King Lear's "looped and windowed raggedness."[3]

[1] *The Revolt of Islam*, which also was dedicated to Shelley's wife.
[2] See Wordsworth's *Ruth* and *Lucy Gray* (p. 267).
[3] *King Lear*, III, 4, 31.

If you strip Peter, you will see a fellow
 Scorched by Hell's hyperequatorial climate
Into a kind of sulphureous yellow:
 A lean mark, hardly fit to fling a rhyme at;
45 In shape a Scaramouch, in hue Othello.
 If you unveil my Witch, no priest nor primate
Can shrive you of that sin,—if sin there be
In love, when it becomes idolatry.

---

1 Before those cruel Twins, whom at one birth
 Incestuous Change bore to her father Time,
Error and Truth, had hunted from the Earth
 All those bright natures which adorned its prime,
And left us nothing to believe in, worth
 The pains of putting into learnèd rhyme,
A Lady-Witch there lived on Atlas' mountain
Within a cavern, by a secret fountain.

2 Her mother was one of the Atlantides:
 The all-beholding Sun had ne'er beholden
In his wide voyage o'er continents and seas
 So fair a creature, as she lay enfolden
In the warm shadow of her loveliness;
 He kissed her with his beams, and made all golden
The chamber of gray rock in which she lay—
She, in that dream of joy, dissolved away.

3 'Tis said, she first was changed into a vapor,
 And then into a cloud, such clouds as flit,
Like splendor-wingèd moths about a taper,
 Round the red west when the sun dies in it:
And then into a meteor, such as caper
 On hill-tops when the moon is in a fit:
Then, into one of those mysterious stars
Which hide themselves between the Earth and Mars.

4 Ten times the Mother of the Months[1] had bent
 Her bow beside the folding-star,[2] and bidden
With that bright sign the billows to indent
 The sea-deserted sand — like children chidden,
At her command they ever came and went—

[1] Diana (Artemis), goddess of the moon.
[2] An evening star which appears about folding time.

Since in that cave a dewy splendor hidden
 Took shape and motion: with the living form
Of this embodied Power, the cave grew warm.

5 A lovely lady garmented in light
 From her own beauty; deep her eyes as are
Two openings of unfathomable night
 Seen through a temple's cloven roof; her hair
Dark; the dim brain whirls dizzy with delight,
 Picturing her form; her soft smiles shone afar,
And her low voice was heard like love, and drew
All living things towards this wonder new.

6 And first the spotted camelopard[1] came
 And then the wise and fearless elephant;
Then the sly serpent, in the golden flame
 Of his own volumes intervolved.   All gaunt
And sanguine beasts her gentle looks made tame;
 They drank before her at her sacred fount;
And every beast of beating heart grew bold,
Such gentleness and power even to behold.

7 The brinded lioness led forth her young,
 That she might teach them how they should forego
Their inborn thirst of death; the pard[2] unstrung
 His sinews at her feet, and sought to know
With looks whose motions spoke without a tongue
 How he might be as gentle as the doe.
The magic circle of her voice and eyes
All savage natures did imparadise.

8 And old Silenus, shaking a green stick
 Of lilies, and the wood-gods in a crew
Came, blithe, as in the olive copses thick
 Cicadæ[3] are, drunk with the noonday dew;
And Dryope and Faunus followed quick,
 Teasing the god to sing them something new;
Till in this cave they found the Lady lone,
Sitting upon a seat of emerald stone.

[1] giraffe [2] leopard [3] locusts

9 And universal Pan, 'tis said, was there;
 And, though none saw him, through the
  adamant
Of the deep mountains, through the track-
  less air,
 And through those living spirits, like a
  want,
He passed out of his everlasting lair
 Where the quick heart of the great world
  doth pant,
And felt that wondrous Lady all alone,—
 And she felt him, upon her emerald throne.

10 And every nymph of stream and spreading tree,
 And every shepherdess of Ocean's
  flocks,
Who drives her white waves over the green
  sea,
 And Ocean with the brine on his gray
  locks,
And quaint Priapus with his company,
 All came, much wondering how the en-
  wombèd rocks
Could have brought forth so beautiful a
  birth;
 Her love subdued their wonder and their
  mirth.

11 The herdsmen and the mountain maidens
  came,
 And the rude kings of pastoral Gara-
  mant;
Their spirits shook within them, as a flame
 Stirred by the air under a cavern gaunt:
Pigmies and Polyphemes, by many a
  name,
 Centaurs, and Satyrs, and such shapes
  as haunt
Wet clefts, and lumps neither alive nor
  dead,
Dog-headed, bosom-eyed, and bird-footed.

12 For she was beautiful; her beauty made
 The bright world dim, and everything
  beside
Seemed like the fleeting image of a shade;
 No thought of living spirit could abide,
Which to her looks had ever been betrayed,
 On any object in the world so wide,
On any hope within the circling skies,
But on her form, and in her inmost eyes.

13 Which when the Lady knew, she took her
  spindle
 And twined three threads of fleecy mist,
  and three
Long lines of light, such as the dawn may
  kindle

 The clouds and waves and mountains
  with; and she
As many star-beams, ere their lamps could
  dwindle
 In the belated moon, wound skilfully;
And with these threads a subtle veil she
  wove—
A shadow for the splendor of her love.

14 The deep recesses of her odorous dwelling
 Were stored with magic treasures—
  sounds of air,
Which had the power all spirits of com-
  pelling,
 Folded in cells of crystal silence there;
Such as we hear in youth, and think the
  feeling
 Will never die—yet ere we are aware,
The feeling and the sound are fled and
  gone,
And the regret they leave remains alone.

15 And there lay Visions swift, and sweet,
  and quaint,
 Each in its thin sheath, like a chrysalis;
Some eager to burst forth, some weak and
  faint
 With the soft burden of intensest bliss.
It is its work to bear to many a saint
 Whose heart adores the shrine which
  holiest is,
Even Love's; and others white, green,
  gray, and black,
And of all shapes—and each was at her
  beck.

16 And odors in a kind of aviary
 Of ever-blooming Eden-trees she kept,
Clipped in a floating net, a love-sick Fairy
 Had woven from dew-beams while the
  moon yet slept;
As bats at the wired window of a dairy,
 They beat their vans; and each was an
  adept,
When loosed and missioned, making wings
  of winds,
To stir sweet thoughts or sad, in destined
  minds.

17 And liquors clear and sweet, whose health-
  ful might
 Could medicine the sick soul to happy
  sleep,
And change eternal death into a night
 Of glorious dreams,—or, if eyes needs
  must weep,
Could make their tears all wonder and de-
  light,—
 She in her crystal vials did closely keep:

If men could drink of those clear vials,
    'tis said,
The living were not envied of the dead.

18 Her cave was stored with scrolls of
    strange device,
    The works of some Saturnian Archi-
      mage,[1]
Which taught the expiations at whose price
    Men from the gods might win that
      happy age
Too lightly lost, redeeming native vice;
    And which might quench the earth-con-
      suming rage
Of gold and blood, till men should live
    and move
Harmonious as the sacred stars above;

19 And how all things that seem untamable,
    Not to be checked and not to be con-
      fined,
Obey the spells of Wisdom's wizard skill;
    Time, earth, and fire, the ocean and the
      wind,
And all their shapes, and man's imperial
    will;
    And other scrolls whose writings did
      unbind
The inmost lore of Love—let the profane
Tremble to ask what secrets they contain.

20 And wondrous works of substances un-
    known,
    To which the enchantment of her
      father's power
Had changed those ragged blocks of sav-
    age stone,
    Were heaped in the recesses of her
      bower;
Carved lamps and chalices, and vials which
    shone
    In their own golden beams—each like a
      flower
Out of whose depth a fire-fly shakes his
    light
Under a cypress[2] in a starless night.

21 At first she lived alone in this wild home,
    And her own thoughts were each a min-
      ister,
Clothing themselves, or with the ocean
    foam,
    Or with the wind, or with the speed of
      fire,
To work whatever purposes might come

[1] wizard; enchanter (See Spenser's *The Faerie
    Queene*, I, 1, 29 ff.)
[2] The cypress is a common tree in graveyards.

Into her mind; such power her mighty
    sire
Had girt them with, whether to fly or run,
Through all the regions which he shines
    upon.

22 The Ocean-nymphs and Hamadryades,
    Oreads and Naiads with long weedy
      locks,
Offered to do her bidding through the seas,
    Under the earth, and in the hollow
      rocks,
And far beneath the matted roots of trees,
    And in the gnarlèd heart of stubborn
      oaks,
So they might live forever in the light
Of her sweet presence—each a satellite.

23 "This may not be," the Wizard Maid re-
    plied;
    "The fountains where the Naiades be-
      dew
Their shining hair, at length are drained
    and dried;
    The solid oaks forget their strength, and
      strew
Their latest leaf upon the mountains wide;
    The boundless ocean, like a drop of dew,
Will be consumed—the stubborn centre
    must
Be scattered, like a cloud of summer dust.

24 "And ye with them will perish, one by
    one;—
    If I must sigh to think that this shall be,
If I must weep when the surviving Sun
    Shall smile on your decay—oh, ask not
      me
To love you till your little race is run;
    I cannot die as ye must—over me
Your leaves shall glance—the streams in
    which ye dwell
Shall be my paths henceforth, and so—
    farewell!"

25 She spoke and wept; the dark and azure
    well
    Sparkled beneath the shower of her
      bright tears,
And every little circlet where they fell
    Flung to the cavern-roof inconstant
      spheres
And intertangled lines of light; a knell
    Of sobbing voices came upon her ears
From those departing Forms, o'er the
    serene
Of the white streams and of the forest
    green.

26 All day the Wizard Lady sate aloof,
    Spelling out scrolls of dread antiquity,
Under the cavern's fountain-lighted roof;
    Or broidering the pictured poesy
Of some high tale upon her growing woof,
    Which the sweet splendor of her smiles
        could dye
In hues outshining Heaven—and ever she
Added some grace to the wrought poesy.

27 While on her hearth lay blazing many a
        piece
    Of sandal wood, rare gums, and cin-
        namon;
Men scarcely know how beautiful fire is;
    Each flame of it is as a precious stone
Dissolved in ever-moving light, and this
Belongs to each and all who gaze upon.
The Witch beheld it not, for in her hand
She held a woof that dimmed the burning
        brand.

28 This Lady never slept, but lay in trance
    All night within the fountain, as in
        sleep.
Its emerald crags glowed in her beauty's
        glance;
    Through the green splendor of the
        water deep
She saw the constellations reel and dance
    Like fire-flies, and withal did ever keep
The tenor of her contemplations calm,
With open eyes, closed feet, and folded
        palm.

29 And when the whirlwinds and the clouds
        descended
    From the white pinnacles of that cold
        hill,
She passed at dewfall to a space extended,
    Where, in a lawn of flowering asphodel[1]
Amid a wood of pines and cedars blended,
    There yawned an inextinguishable well
Of crimson fire, full even to the brim,
And overflowing all the margin trim;

30 Within the which she lay when the fierce
        war
    Of wintry winds shook that innocuous
        liquor
In many a mimic moon and bearded star
    O'er woods and lawns; the serpent heard
        it flicker
In sleep, and, dreaming still, he crept afar;
    And when the windless snow descended
        thicker
Than autumn leaves, she watched it as it
        came
Melt on the surface of the level flame.

[1] daffodils

31 She had a boat which some say Vulcan
        wrought
    For Venus as the chariot of her star;
But it was found too feeble to be fraught
    With all the ardors in that sphere
        which are,
And so she sold it, and Apollo bought
    And gave it to this daughter; from a car
Changed to the fairest and the lightest boat
Which ever upon mortal stream did float.

32 And others say that, when but three hours
        old,
    The first-born Love out of his cradle
        leapt,
And clove dun Chaos with his wings of
        gold,
    And like a horticultural adept,
Stole a strange seed, and wrapped it up in
        mould,
    And sowed it in his mother's star, and
        kept
Watering it all the summer with sweet dew,
And with his wings fanning it as it grew.

33 The plant grew strong and green; the
        snowy flower
    Fell, and the long and gourd-like fruit
        began
To turn the light and dew by inward power
    To its own substance; woven tracery
        ran
Of light firm texture, ribbed and branch-
        ing, o'er
    The solid rind, like a leaf's veinèd fan,
Of which Love scooped this boat, and with
        soft motion
Piloted it round the circumfluous ocean.

34 This boat she moored upon her fount, and
        lit
    A living spirit within all its frame,
Breathing the soul of swiftness into it.
    Couched on the fountain, like a panther
        tame,—
One of the twain at Evan's feet that sit—
    Or as on Vesta's sceptre a swift flame,
Or on blind Homer's heart a wingèd
        thought,—
In joyous expectation lay the boat.

35 Then by strange art she kneaded <u>fire and</u>
        <u>snow</u>
    Together, tempering the repugnant mass
With liquid love — all things together
        grow
    Through which the harmony of love
        can pass;

And a fair Shape out of her hands did
    flow,
  A living Image, which did far surpass
In beauty that bright shape of vital stone
Which drew the heart out of Pygmalion.[1] 40

36 A sexless thing it was, and in its growth
    It seemed to have developed no defect
Of either sex, yet all the grace of both;
  In gentleness and strength its limbs were
    decked;
The bosom swelled lightly with its full
    youth,
  The countenance was such as might se-
    lect
Some artist that his skill should never die,
Imaging forth such perfect purity.

37 From its smooth shoulders hung two rapid
    wings,
  Fit to have borne it to the seventh
    sphere,
Tipped with the speed of liquid lighten-
    ings,
  Dyed in the ardors of the atmosphere.
She led her creature to the boiling springs
  Where the light boat was moored, and
    said, "Sit here!"
And pointed to the prow, and took her
    seat
Beside the rudder, with opposing feet.

38 And down the streams which clove those
    mountains vast,
  Around their inland islets, and amid
The panther-peopled forests, whose shade
    cast
Darkness and odors, and a pleasure hid
In melancholy gloom, the pinnace passed;
  By many a star-surrounded pyramid
Of icy crag cleaving the purple sky,
And caverns yawning round unfathom-
    ably.

39 The silver noon into that winding dell,
  With slanted gleam athwart the forest
    tops,
Tempered like golden evening, feebly fell;
  A green and glowing light, like that
    which drops
From folded lilies in which glow-worms
    dwell,
  When Earth over her face Night's man-
    tle wraps;

[1] Pygmalion fell in love with the statue of a
woman which he had carved, and which came
to life. See Morris's *Pygmalion and the
Image* in *The Earthly Paradise* (1868-70)
and Gilbert's *Pygmalion and Galatea* (1871).

Between the severed mountains lay on
    high,
Over the stream, a narrow rift of sky.

40 And ever as she went, the Image lay
  With folded wings and unawakened
    eyes;
And o'er its gentle countenance did play
  The busy dreams, as thick as summer
    flies,
Chasing the rapid smiles that would not
    stay,
  And drinking the warm tears, and the
    sweet sighs
Inhaling, which, with busy murmur vain,
They had aroused from that full heart
    and brain.

41 And ever down the prone vale, like a cloud
  Upon a stream of wind, the pinnace
    went:
Now lingering on the pools, in which
    abode
  The calm and darkness of the deep con-
    tent
In which they paused; now o'er the shal-
    low road
  Of white and dancing waters, all be-
    sprent
With sand and polished pebbles: mortal
    boat
In such a shallow rapid could not float.

42 And down the earthquaking cataracts,
    which shiver
  Their snow-like waters into golden air,
Or under chasms unfathomable ever
  Sepulchre them, till in their rage they
    tear
A subterranean portal for the river,
  It fled—the circling sunbows did upbear
Its fall down the hoar precipice of spray,
Lighting it far upon its lampless way.

43 And when the Wizard-Lady would ascend
  The labyrinth of some many-winding
    vale,
Which to the inmost mountain upward
    tend,
  She called "Hermaphroditus!"; and
    the pale
And heavy hue which slumber could extend
  Over its lips and eyes, as on the gale
A rapid shadow from a slope of grass,
Into the darkness of the stream did pass.

44 And it unfurled its heaven-colored pinions,
  With stars of fire spotting the stream
    below;

And from above into the Sun's dominions
Flinging a glory, like the golden glow
In which Spring clothes her emerald-
winged minions,
All interwoven with fine feathery snow
And moonlight splendor of intensest rime,[1]
With which frost paints the pines in winter
time.

45 And then it winnowed the Elysian air
Which ever hung about that lady bright,
With its ethereal vans; and speeding there,
Like a star upon the torrent of the night,
Or a swift eagle in the morning glare
Breasting the whirlwind with impetuous
flight,
The pinnace, oared by those enchanted
wings,
Clove the fierce streams towards their
upper springs.

46 The water flashed, like sunlight by the
prow
Of a noon-wandering meteor flung to
Heaven;
The still air seemed as if its waves did flow
In tempest down the mountains; loosely
driven
The Lady's radiant hair streamed to and
fro;
Beneath, the billows having vainly
striven
Indignant and impetuous, roared to feel
The swift and steady motion of the keel.

47 Or, when the weary moon was in the wane,
Or in the noon of interlunar[2] night,
The Lady-Witch in visions could not chain
Her spirit; but sailed forth under the
light
Of shooting stars, and bade extend amain
Its storm-outspeeding wings, the Her-
maphrodite;
She to the Austral waters took her way,
Beyond the fabulous Thamondocana,

48 Where, like a meadow which no scythe has
shaven,
Which rain could never bend, or whirl-
blast shake,
With the Antarctic constellations paven,
Canopus and his crew, lay the Austral
lake;
There she would build herself a windless
haven
Out of the clouds whose moving turrets
make

[1] hoarfrost
[2] That is, in the interval between the old moon
and the new.

The bastions of the storm, when through
the sky
The spirits of the tempest thundered by;

49 A haven, beneath whose translucent floor
The tremulous stars sparkled unfathom-
ably,
And around which the solid vapors hoar,
Based on the level waters, to the sky
Lifted their dreadful crags, and, like a
shore
Of wintry mountains, inaccessibly
Hemmed in, with rifts and precipices gray
And hanging crags, many a cove and bay.

50 And whilst the outer lake beneath the lash
Of the wind's scourge, foamed like a
wounded thing,
And the incessant hail with stony clash
Ploughed up the waters, and the flagging
wing
Of the roused cormorant in the lightning
flash
Looked like the wreck of some wind-
wandering
Fragment of inky thunder-smoke—this
haven
Was as a gem to copy Heaven engraven;

51 On which that Lady played her many
pranks,
Circling the image of a shooting star,
Even as a tiger on Hydaspes' banks
Outspeeds the antelopes which speediest
are,
In her light boat; and many quips and
cranks[1]
She played upon the water, till the car
Of the late moon, like a sick matron wan,
To journey from the misty east began.

52 And then she called out of the hollow
turrets
Of those high clouds, white, golden, and
vermilion,
The armies of her ministering spirits;
In mighty legions, million after million,
They came, each troop emblazoning its
merits
On meteor flags; and many a proud
pavilion
Of the intertexture of the atmosphere
They pitched upon the plain of the calm
mere.

53 They framed the imperial tent of their
great Queen
Of woven exhalations, underlaid
[1] See L'Allegro, 27.

With lambent lightning-fire, as may be
  seen
A dome of thin and open ivory inlaid
With crimson, silk; cressets[1] from the
  serene
Hung there, and on the water for her
  tread
A tapestry of fleece-like mist was strewn,
Dyed in the beams of the ascending moon.

54 And on a throne o'erlaid with starlight,
  caught
Upon those wandering isles of aëry dew,
Which highest shoals of mountain ship-
  wreck not,
She sate, and heard all that had hap-
  pened new
Between the earth and moon, since they
  had brought
The last intelligence; and now she grew
Pale as that moon lost in the watery night,
And now she wept, and now she laughed
  outright.

55 These were tame pleasures. She would
  often climb
The steepest ladder of the crudded rack[2]
Up to some beakèd cape of cloud sublime,
And like Arion on the dolphin's back
Ride singing through the shoreless air;
  oft-time
Following the serpent lightning's wind-
  ing track,
She ran upon the platforms of the wind,
And laughed to hear the fire-balls roar
  behind.

56 And sometimes to those streams of upper
  air,
Which whirl the earth in its diurnal
  round,
She would ascend, and win the spirits there
To let her join their chorus. Mortals
  found
That on those days the sky was calm and
  fair,
And mystic snatches of harmonious
  sound
Wandered upon the earth where'er she
  passed,
And happy thoughts of hope, too sweet to
  last.

57 But her choice sport was, in the hours of
  sleep,
  To glide adown old Nilus, where he
  threads

Egypt and Æthiopia, from the steep
  Of utmost Axumé, until he spreads,
Like a calm flock of silver-fleecèd sheep,
  His waters on the plain,—and crested
  heads
Of cities and proud temples gleam amid,
And many a vapor-belted pyramid.

58 By Mœris and the Mareotid lakes,
  Strewn with faint blooms, like bridal
  chamber floors,
Where naked boys bridling tame water-
  snakes,
  Or charioteering ghastly alligators,
Had left on the sweet waters mighty wakes
  Of those huge forms—within the brazen
  doors
Of the great Labyrinth slept both boy and
  beast,
Tired with the pomp of their Osirian feast.

59 And where within the surface of the river
  The shadows of the massy temples lie,
And never are erased—but tremble ever
  Like things which every cloud can doom
  to die;
Through lotus-paven canals, and whereso-
  ever
  The works of man pierced that serenest
  sky
With tombs, and towers, and fanes,— 'twas
  her delight
To wander in the shadow of the night.

60 With motion like the spirit of that wind
  Whose soft step deepens slumber, her
  light feet
Passed through the peopled haunts of
  humankind,
  Scattering sweet visions from her presence sweet;
Through fane and palace-court, and labyrinth mined
  With many a dark and subterranean
  street
Under the Nile, through chambers high and
  deep
She passed, observing mortals in their
  sleep.

61 A pleasure sweet doubtless it was to see
  Mortals subdued in all the shapes of
  sleep.
Here lay two sister-twins in infancy;
  There, a lone youth who in his dreams
  did weep;
Within, two lovers linkèd innocently
  In their loose locks which over both did
  creep

Like ivy from one stem; and there lay
calm
Old age with snow-bright hair and folded
palm.

62 But other troubled forms of sleep she saw,
Not to be mirrored in a holy song;
Distortions foul of supernatural awe,
And pale imaginings of visioned wrong;
And all the code of Custom's lawless law
Written upon the brows of old and
young:
"This," said the Wizard-Maiden, "is the
strife
Which stirs the liquid surface of man's
life."

63 And little did the sight disturb her soul.
We, the weak mariners of that wide lake,
Where'er its shores extend or billows roll,
Our course unpiloted and starless make
O'er its wild surface to an unknown goal;
But she in the calm depths her way could
take,
Where in bright bowers immortal forms
abide
Beneath the weltering of the restless tide.

64 And she saw princes couched under the
glow
Of sunlike gems; and round each temple-
court
In dormitories ranged, row after row,
She saw the priests asleep—all of one
sort—
For all were educated to be so.—
The peasants in their huts, and in the
port
The sailors she saw cradled on the waves,
And the dead lulled within their dreamless
graves.

65 And all the forms in which those spirits lay
Were to her sight like the diaphanous
Veils, in which those sweet ladies oft array
Their delicate limbs, who would conceal
from us
Only their scorn of all concealment; they
Move in the light of their own beauty
thus.
But these and all now lay with sleep upon
them,
And little thought a witch was looking on
them.

66 She all those human figures breathing there
Beheld as living spirits; to her eyes
The naked beauty of the soul lay bare,

And often through a rude and worn
disguise
She saw the inner form most bright and
fair;
And then she had a charm of strange
device,
Which, murmured on mute lips with tender
tone,
Could make that spirit mingle with her
own.

67 Alas, Aurora! what wouldst thou have
given
For such a charm when Tithon became
gray?
Or how much, Venus, of thy silver Heaven
Wouldst thou have yielded, ere Proser-
pina
Had half (oh! why not all?) the debt
forgiven
Which dear Adonis had been doomed to
pay,
To any witch who would have taught you
it?
The Heliad doth not know its value yet.

68 'Tis said in after times her spirit free
Knew what love was, and felt itself
alone;
But holy Dian could not chaster be
Before she stooped to kiss Endymion,
Than now this lady—like a sexless bee
Tasting all blossoms, and confined to
none;
Among those mortal forms, the Wizard-
Maiden
Passed with an eye serene and heart un-
laden.

69 To those she saw most beautiful, she gave
Strange panacea in a crystal bowl;
They drank in their deep sleep of that
sweet wave,
And lived thenceforward as if some con-
trol,
Mightier than life, were in them; and the
grave
Of such, when death oppressed the
weary soul,
Was as a green and overarching bower
Lit by the gems of many a starry flower.

70 For on the night when they were buried,
she
Restored the embalmers' ruining, and
shook
The light out of the funeral lamps, to be
A mimic day within that deathy nook;
And she unwound the woven imagery

Of second childhood's swaddling bands,
and took
The coffin, its last cradle, from its niche,
And threw it with contempt into a ditch.

71 And there the body lay, age after age,
Mute, breathing, beating, warm, and un-
decaying,
Like one asleep in a green hermitage,
With gentle smiles about its eyelids
playing,
And living in its dreams beyond the rage
Of death or life, while they were still
arraying
In liveries ever new, the rapid, blind,
And fleeting generations of mankind.

72 And she would write strange dreams upon
the brain
Of those who were less beautiful, and
make
All harsh and crooked purposes more vain
Than in the desert is the serpent's wake
Which the sand covers; all his evil gain
The miser in such dreams would rise and
shake
Into a beggar's lap; the lying scribe
Would his own lies betray without a bribe.

73 The priests would write an explanation
full,
Translating hieroglyphics into Greek,
How the god Apis really was a bull,
And nothing more; and bid the herald
stick
The same against the temple doors, and
pull
The old cant down; they licensed all to
speak
Whate'er they thought of hawks, and cats,
and geese,
By pastoral letters to each diocese.[1]

74 The king would dress an ape up in his
crown
And robes, and seat him on his glorious
seat,
And on the right hand of the sunlike throne
Would place a gaudy mock-bird to re-
peat
The chatterings of the monkey. Every one
Of the prone courtiers crawled to kiss
the feet
Of their great Emperor, when the morning
came,
And kissed—alas, how many kiss the same.

75 The soldiers dreamed that they were black-
smiths, and
Walked out of quarters in somnam-
bulism;
Round the red anvils you might see them
stand
Like Cyclopses in Vulcan's sooty abysm,
Beating their swords to ploughshares;[1] in
a band
The gaolers sent those of the liberal
schism
Free through the streets of Memphis,
much, I wis,[2]
To the annoyance of king Amasis.

76 And timid lovers who had been so coy
They hardly knew whether they loved or
not,
Would rise out of their rest, and take sweet
joy,
To the fulfilment of their inmost
thought;
And when next day the maiden and the
boy
Met one another, both, like sinners
caught,
Blushed at the thing which each believed
was done
Only in fancy—till the tenth moon shone;

77 And then the Witch would let them take
no ill;
Of many thousand schemes which lovers
find,
The Witch found one,—and so they took
their fill
Of happiness in marriage, warm and
kind.
Friends who, by practice of some envious
skill,
Were torn apart—a wide wound, mind
from mind—
She did unite again with visions clear
Of deep affection and of truth sincere.

78 These were the pranks she played among
the cities
Of mortal men, and what she did to
sprites
And gods, entangling them in her sweet
ditties
To do her will, and show their subtle
sleights,
I will declare another time; for it is
A tale more fit for the weird winter
nights[3]

---

[1] A satirical reference to Egyptian beast worship, and to modern theology.

[1] See *Isaiah*, 2:4.   [2] I think.
[3] See *The Winter's Tale*, II, 1, 25.

Than for these garish summer days, when
   we
Scarcely believe much more than we can
   see.

EPIPSYCHIDION

VERSES ADDRESSED TO THE NOBLE AND UN-
FORTUNATE LADY, EMILIA V——, NOW IM-
PRISONED IN THE CONVENT OF ——
1821   1821

Sweet Spirit! sister of that orphan
   one,[1]
Whose empire is the name[2] thou weepest
   on,
In my heart's temple I suspend to thee
These votive wreaths of withered memory.

5   Poor captive bird! who, from thy nar-
   row cage,
Pourest such music, that it might assuage
The rugged hearts of those who prisoned
   thee,
Were they not deaf to all sweet melody,—
This song shall be thy rose: its petals pale
10 Are dead, indeed, my adored nightingale!
But soft and fragrant is the faded blossom,
And it has no thorn left to wound thy
   bosom.

High, spirit-wingèd Heart! who dost
   forever
Beat thine unfeeling bars with vain endeavor,
15 Till those bright plumes of thought, in
   which arrayed
It over-soared this low and worldly shade,
Lie shattered; and thy panting, wounded
   breast
Stains with dear blood its unmaternal nest!
I weep vain tears; blood would less bitter
   be,
20 Yet poured forth gladlier, could it profit
   thee.

Seraph of Heaven! too gentle to be
   human,
Veiling beneath that radiant form of
   Woman
All that is insupportable in thee
Of light, and love, and immortality!
25 Sweet Benediction in the eternal Curse!
Veiled Glory of this lampless Universe!
Thou Moon beyond the clouds! Thou liv-
   ing Form
Among the Dead! Thou Star above the
   Storm!

[1] Mary Shelley, whose mother died in giving
   birth to her.
[2] Shelley.

Thou Wonder, and thou Beauty, and thou
   Terror!
30 Thou Harmony of Nature's art! Thou
   Mirror
In whom, as in the splendor of the Sun,
All shapes look glorious which thou gazest
   on!
Ay, even the dim words which obscure thee
   now
Flash, lightning-like, with unaccustomed
   glow;
35 I pray thee that thou blot from this sad
   song
All of its much mortality and wrong,
With those clear drops, which start like
   sacred dew
From the twin lights thy sweet soul dark-
   ens through,
Weeping, till sorrow becomes ecstasy—
40 Then smile on it, so that it may not die.

I never thought before my death to see
Youth's vision[1] thus made perfect. Emily,
I love thee; though the world by no thin
   name
Will hide that love from its unvalued
   shame.[2]
45 Would we two had been twins of the same
   mother!
Or, that the name my heart lent to another
Could be a sister's bond for her and thee,
Blending two beams of one eternity!
Yet were one lawful[3] and the other true,[4]
50 These names,[5] though dear, could paint
   not, as is due,
How beyond refuge I am thine. Ah me!
I am not thine—I am a part of *thee.*

Sweet Lamp! my moth-like Muse has
   burned its wings,
Or, like a dying swan who soars and
   sings,[6]
55 Young Love should teach Time, in his own
   gray style,
All that thou art. Art thou not void of
   guile,
A lovely soul formed to be blessed and
   bless?
A well of sealed and secret happiness,
Whose waters like blithe light and music
   are,
60 Vanquishing dissonance and gloom? a star

[1] The ideal which Shelley had formed in his
   youth. See *Alastor*, 203 ff. (p. 664).
[2] The contempt to which Shelley is indifferent.
[3] That Emily and Mary should both be married
   to him.
[4] That he and Emily were brother and sister.
[5] Sister and wife.
[6] The swan was said to sing melodiously when
   about to die.

love of ideal becomes love Emilia because unattainable— of the unattainable— like Dante 4 levels

Which moves not in the moving heavens,
alone?
A smile amid dark frowns? a gentle tone
Amid rude voices? a belovèd light?
A solitude, a refuge, a delight?
65 A lute, which those whom Love has taught
to play
Make music on, to soothe the roughest day
And lull fond Grief asleep? a buried
treasure?
A cradle of young thoughts of wingless
pleasure?
A violet-shrouded grave of woe?—I meas-
ure
70 The world of fancies, seeking one like thee,
And find—alas! mine own infirmity.

metaphor language

She met me, stranger, upon life's rough
way,
And lured me towards sweet death; as
Night by Day,
Winter by Spring, or Sorrow by swift
Hope,
75 Led into light, life, peace.[1] An antelope,
In the suspended impulse of its lightness,
Were less ethereally light; the brightness
Of her divinest presence trembles through
Her limbs, as underneath a cloud of
dew
80 Embodied in the windless heaven of June
Amid the splendor-wingèd stars, the Moon
Burns, inextinguishably beautiful;
And from her lips, as from a hyacinth full
Of honey-dew, a liquid murmur drops,
85 Killing the sense with passion, sweet as
stops
Of planetary music[2] heard in trance.
In her mild lights the starry spirits dance,
The sunbeams of those wells which ever
leap
Under the lightnings of the soul—too deep
90 For the brief fathom-line of thought or
sense.
The glory of her being, issuing thence,
Stains the dead, blank, cold air with a
warm shade
Of unentangled intermixture, made
By Love, of light and motion; one intense
95 Diffusion, one serene Omnipresence,
Whose flowing outlines mingle in their
flowing,
Around her cheeks and utmost fingers
glowing,
With the unintermitted blood, which there
Quivers (as in a fleece of snow-like air

[1] *Light, life, peace,* refer respectively to *Day, Spring, Hope.*
[2] The ancients believed that the movement of the celestial spheres produced music.

100 The crimson pulse of living morning
quiver)
Continuously prolonged, and ending never,
Till they are lost, and in that Beauty furled
Which penetrates and clasps and fills the
world;
Scarce visible from extreme loveliness.
105 Warm fragrance seems to fall from her
light dress
And her loose hair; and where some heavy
tress
The air of her own speed has disentwined,
The sweetness seems to satiate the faint
wind;
And in the soul a wild odor is felt,
110 Beyond the sense, like fiery dews that melt
Into the bosom of a frozen bud.—
See where she stands! a mortal shape in-
dued
With love and life and light and deity,
And motion which may change but cannot
die;
115 An image of some bright Eternity;
A shadow of some golden dream; a Splen-
dor
Leaving the third sphere[1] pilotless; a
tender
Reflection of the eternal Moon of Love
Under whose motions life's dull billows
move;
120 A metaphor of Spring and Youth and
Morning;
A vision like incarnate April, warning,
With smiles and tears, Frost the Anatomy
Into his summer grave.

Ah, woe is me!
What have I dared? where am I lifted?
how
125 Shall I descend, and perish not? I know
That Love makes all things equal; I have
heard
By mine own heart this joyous truth
averred:
The spirit of the worm beneath the sod
In love and worship, blends itself with
God.

130 Spouse! Sister! Angel! Pilot of the Fate
Whose course has been so starless! Oh, too
late
Belovèd! Oh, too soon adored, by me!
For in the fields of immortality
My spirit should at first have worshiped
thine,
135 A divine presence in a place divine;
Or should have moved beside it on this
earth,

[1] The sphere of Venus, goddess of love.

A shadow of that substance,[1] from its
    birth;
But not as now. I love thee; yes, I feel
That on the fountain of my heart a seal
140 Is set, to keep its waters pure and bright
For thee, since in those *tears* thou hast de-
    light.
We—are we not formed, as notes of music
    are,
For one another, though dissimilar;
Such difference without discord as can
    make
145 Those sweetest sounds, in which all spirits
    shake
As trembling leaves in a continuous air?

Thy wisdom speaks in me, and bids me
    dare
Beacon the rocks on which high hearts are
    wrecked.
I never was attached to that great sect,
150 Whose doctrine is, that each one should
    select
Out of the crowd a mistress or a friend,
And all the rest, though fair and wise,
    commend
To cold oblivion, though 'tis in the code
Of modern morals, and the beaten road
155 Which those poor slaves with weary foot-
    steps tread
Who travel to their home among the dead
By the broad highway of the world, and so
With one chained friend, perhaps a jealous
    foe,
The dreariest and the longest journey go.

160 True love in this differs from gold and
    clay,
That to divide is not to take away.
Love is like understanding, that grows
    bright
Gazing on many truths; 'tis like thy light,
Imagination! which, from earth and sky,
165 And from the depths of human fantasy,
As from a thousand prisms and mirrors,
    fills
The Universe with glorious beams, and
    kills
Error, the worm, with many a sun-like
    arrow
Of its reverberated lightning. Narrow
170 The heart that loves, the brain that con-
    templates,
The life that wears, the spirit that creates
One object, and one form, and builds
    thereby
A sepulchre for its eternity.

[1] Her spirit.

175 Mind from its object differs most in this;
Evil from good; misery from happiness;
The baser from the nobler; the impure
And frail, from what is clear and must
    endure:
If you divide suffering and dross, you may
Diminish till it is consumed away;
180 If you divide pleasure and love and
    thought,
Each part exceeds the whole; and we know
    not
How much, while any yet remains un-
    shared,
Of pleasure may be gained, of sorrow
    spared:
This truth is that deep well, whence sages
    draw
185 The unenvied light of hope; the eternal
    law
By which those live, to whom this world of
    life
Is as a garden ravaged, and whose strife
Tills for the promise of a later birth
The wilderness of this Elysian earth.

190 There was a Being[1] whom my spirit oft
Met on its visioned wanderings, far aloft,
In the clear golden prime of my youth's
    dawn,
Upon the fairy isles of sunny lawn,
Amid the enchanted mountains, and the
    caves
195 Of divine sleep, and on the air-like waves
Of wonder-level dream, whose tremulous
    floor
Paved her light steps. On an imagined
    shore,
Under the gray beak of some promontory
She met me, robed in such exceeding glory
200 That I beheld her not. In solitudes
Her voice came to me through the whisper-
    ing woods,
And from the fountains and the odors
    deep
Of flowers, which, like lips murmuring in
    their sleep
Of the sweet kisses which had lulled them
    there,
205 Breathed but of *her* to the enamored air;
And from the breezes whether low or loud,
And from the rain of every passing cloud,
And from the singing of the summer-birds,
And from all sounds, all silence. In the
    words
210 Of antique verse and high romance, in
    form,

[1] The ideal described in *Alastor*, 150-80 (p. 663)
and in *Hymn to Intellectual Beauty* (p. 670).

Sound, color, in whatever checks that storm
Which with the shattered present chokes
  the past;[1]
And in that best philosophy, whose taste
Makes this cold common hell, our life, a
  doom
215 As glorious as a fiery martyrdom—
Her Spirit was the harmony of truth.

Then from the caverns of my dreamy
  youth
I sprang, as one sandalled with plumes of
  fire,
And towards the lodestar of my one desire
220 I flitted, like a dizzy moth, whose flight
Is as a dead leaf's in the owlet[2] light,
When it would seek in Hesper's setting
  sphere
A radiant death, a fiery sepulchre,
As if it were a lamp of earthly flame.
225 But She, whom prayers or tears then could
  not tame,
Passed, like a God throned on a wingèd
  planet,
Whose burning plumes to tenfold swift-
  ness fan it,
Into the dreary cone of our life's shade;
And as a man with mighty loss dismayed,
230 I would have followed, though the grave
  between
Yawned like a gulf whose spectres are
  unseen:
When a voice said:—"O thou of hearts
  the weakest,
The phantom is beside thee whom thou
  seekest."
Then I—"Where?"—the world's echo
  answered "Where?"
235 And in that silence, and in my despair,
I questioned every tongueless wind that
  flew
Over my tower of mourning, if it knew
Whither 'twas fled, this soul out of my
  soul;
And murmured names and spells which
  have control
240 Over the sightless tyrants of our fate;
But neither prayer nor verse could dissipate
The night which closed on her; nor un-
  create
That world within this Chaos, mine and
  me,
Of which she was the veiled Divinity,—

245 The world I say of thoughts that worshiped her;
And therefore I went forth, with hope and
  fear
And every gentle passion sick to death,
Feeding my course with expectation's
  breath,
Into the wintry forest of our life;
250 And struggling through its error[1] with
  vain strife,
And stumbling in my weakness and my
  haste,
And half bewildered by new forms, I
  passed,
Seeking among those untaught foresters
If I could find one form resembling hers,
255 In which she might have masked herself
  from me.
There,—One, whose voice was venomed
  melody
Sate by a well, under blue nightshade
  bowers;
The breath of her false mouth was like
  faint flowers;
Her touch was as electric poison,—flame
260 Out of her looks into my vitals came,
And from her living cheeks and bosom flew
A killing air, which pierced like honey-dew
Into the core of my green heart, and lay
Upon its leaves; until, as hair grown gray
265 O'er a young brow, they hid its unblown
  prime
With ruins of unseasonable time.

In many mortal forms I rashly sought
The shadow of that idol of my thought.
And some were fair—but beauty dies
  away;
270 Others were wise—but honeyed words be-
  tray;
And one was true—oh! why not true to
  me?
Then, as a hunted deer that could not flee,
I turned upon my thoughts, and stood at
  bay,
Wounded and weak and panting; the cold
  day
275 Trembled, for pity of my strife and pain,
When, like a noonday dawn, there shone
  again
Deliverance. One stood on my path who
  seemed
As like the glorious shape which I had
  dreamed
As is the Moon, whose changes ever run
280 Into themselves, to the eternal Sun;
The cold chaste Moon, the Queen of
  Heaven's bright isles,

---

[2] In whatever survives death, and is immortal
  in works of art.
[2] That is, in the dim, uncanny light which the
  moth leaves for the brighter light of Hesperus, the evening star.

[1] irregular course

Who makes all beautiful on which she
    smiles,
That wandering shrine of soft yet icy flame
Which ever is transformed, yet still the
    same,
285 And warms not but illumines. Young and
    fair
As the descended Spirit of that sphere,
She hid me, as the Moon may hide the night
From its own darkness, until all was bright
Between the Heaven and Earth of my calm
    mind,
290 And, as a cloud charioted by the wind,
She led me to a cave in that wild place,
And sate beside me, with her downward
    face
Illumining my slumbers, like the Moon
Waxing and waning o'er Endymion.
295 And I was laid asleep, spirit and limb,
And all my being became bright or dim
As the Moon's image in a summer sea,
According as she smiled or frowned on
    me;
And there I lay, within a chaste cold bed.
300 Alas, I then was nor alive nor dead;
For at her silver voice came Death and
    Life,
Unmindful each of their accustomed strife,
Masked like twin babes, a sister and a
    brother,
The wandering hopes of one abandoned
    mother,
305 And through the cavern without wings
    they flew,
And cried, "Away, he is not of our crew."
I wept, and though it be a dream, I weep.

    What storms then shook the ocean of
    my sleep,
Blotting that Moon, whose pale and waning
    lips
310 Then shrank as in the sickness of eclipse;
And how my soul was as a lampless sea,
And who was then its Tempest; and when
    She,
The Planet of that hour, was quenched,
    what frost
Crept o'er those waters, till from coast to
    coast
315 The moving billows of my being fell
Into a death of ice, immovable;
And then what earthquakes made it gape
    and split,
The white Moon smiling all the while
    on it,
These words conceal; if not, each word
    would be
320 The key of staunchless tears. Weep not
    for me!

At length, into the obscure forest came
The Vision I had sought through grief and
    shame.
Athwart that wintry wilderness of thorns
Flashed from her motion splendor like the
    Morn's,
325 And from her presence life was radiated
Through the gray earth and branches bare
    and dead;
So that her way was paved, and roofed
    above
With flowers as soft as thoughts of bud-
    ding love;
And music from her respiration spread
330 Like light,—all other sounds were pene-
    trated
By the small, still, sweet spirit of that
    sound,
So that the savage winds hung mute
    around;
And odors warm and fresh fell from her
    hair
Dissolving the dull cold in the frore[1] air:
335 Soft as an Incarnation of the Sun,
When light is changed to love, this glorious
    One
Floated into the cavern where I lay,
And called my Spirit, and the dreaming
    clay
Was lifted by the thing that dreamed below
340 As smoke by fire, and in her beauty's glow
I stood, and felt the dawn of my long night
Was penetrating me with living light:
I knew it was the Vision veiled from me
So many years—that it was Emily.

345   Twin Spheres of light[2] who rule this
    passive Earth,
This world of love, this *me;* and into birth
Awaken all its fruits and flowers, and dart
Magnetic might into its central heart;
And lift its billows and its mists, and guide
350 By everlasting laws, each wind and tide
To its fit cloud, and its appointed cave;
And lull its storms, each in the craggy
    grave
Which was its cradle, luring to faint
    bowers
The armies of the rainbow-wingèd showers;
355 And, as those married lights, which from
    the towers
Of Heaven look forth and fold the wander-
    ing globe
In liquid sleep and splendor, as a robe;
And all their many-mingled influence
    blend,
If equal, yet unlike, to one sweet end;—

[1] frozen
[2] Emily and Mary as the sun and the moon.

360 So ye, bright regents, with alternate sway
Govern my sphere of being, night and day!
Thou, not disdaining even a borrowed
    might;
Thou, not eclipsing a remoter light;
And, through the shadow of the seasons
    three,
365 From Spring to Autumn's sere maturity,
Light it into the Winter of the tomb,
Where it may ripen to a brighter bloom.
Thou too, O Comet beautiful and fierce,
Who drew the heart[1] of this frail Uni-
    verse
370 Towards thine own; till, wrecked in that
    convulsion,
Alternating attraction and repulsion,
Thine went astray, and that was rent in
    twain;
Oh, float into our azure heaven again!
Be there Love's folding-star[2] at thy re-
    turn;
375 The living Sun will feed thee from its urn
Of golden fire; the Moon will veil her horn
In thy last smiles; adoring Even and Morn
Will worship thee with incense of calm
    breath
And lights and shadows, as the star of
    Death
380 And Birth is worshiped by those sisters
    wild
Called Hope and Fear—upon the heart are
    piled
Their offerings,—of this sacrifice divine
A world shall be the altar.

                        Lady mine,
Scorn not these flowers of thought, the
    fading birth
385 Which from its heart of hearts that plant
    puts forth
Whose fruit, made perfect by thy sunny
    eyes,
Will be as of the trees of Paradise.

    The day is come, and thou wilt fly with
        me.
To whatsoe'er of dull mortality
390 Is mine, remain a vestal sister[3] still;
To the intense, the deep, the imperishable,
Not mine but me, henceforth be thou united
Even as a bride, delighting and delighted.
The hour is come:—the destined Star has
    risen
395 Which shall descend upon a vacant prison.
The walls are high, the gates are strong,
    thick set

The sentinels—but true love never yet
Was thus constrained; it overleaps all
    fence:
Like lightning, with invisible violence
400 Piercing its continents;[1] like Heaven's
    free breath,
Which he who grasps can hold not; liker
    Death,
Who rides upon a thought, and makes his
    way
Through temple, tower, and palace, and
    the array
Of arms: more strength has Love than he
    or they;
405 For it can burst his charnel, and make free
The limbs in chains, the heart in agony,
The soul in dust and chaos.

                            Emily,
A ship is floating in the harbor now,
A wind is hovering o'er the mountain's
    brow;
410 There is a path on the sea's azure floor—
No keel has ever ploughed that path be-
    fore;
The halcyons brood around the foamless
    isles;[2]
The treacherous Ocean has forsworn its
    wiles;
The merry mariners are bold and free:
415 Say, my heart's sister, wilt thou sail with
    me?
Our bark is as an albatross, whose nest
Is a far Eden of the purple East;
And we between her wings will sit, while
    Night,
And Day, and Storm, and Calm, pursue
    their flight,
420 Our ministers, along the boundless Sea,
Treading each other's heels, unheededly.
It is an isle under Ionian skies,
Beautiful as a wreck of Paradise,
And, for the harbors are not safe and good,
425 This land would have remained a solitude
But for some pastoral people native there,
Who from the Elysian, clear, and golden
    air
Draw the last spirit of the age of gold,[3]
Simple and spirited, innocent and bold.
430 The blue Ægean girds this chosen home
With ever-changing sound and light and
    foam,
Kissing the sifted sands, and caverns hoar;
And all the winds wandering along the
    shore

---

[1] Shelley's heart.
[2] An evening star which appears about folding
    time.
[3] nun; virgin

[1] things holding or containing it
[2] Halcyons, or kingfishers, were said to make
    their nests at sea, and to calm the waves.
[3] The first period of the history of the world,
    the era of perfect happiness.

Undulate with the undulating tide;
435 There are thick woods where sylvan forms
abide;
And many a fountain, rivulet, and pond,
As clear.as elemental diamond,
Or serene morning air; and far beyond,
The mossy tracks made by the goats and
deer
440 (Which the rough shepherd treads but
once a year)
Pierce into glades, caverns, and bowers,
and halls
Built round with ivy, which the waterfalls
Illumining, with sound that never fails
Accompany the noonday nightingales;
445 And all the place is peopled with sweet
airs;
The light clear element which the isle wears
Is heavy with the scent of lemon-flowers,
Which floats like mist laden with unseen
showers,
And falls upon the eyelids like faint sleep;
450 And from the moss violets and jonquils
peep,
And dart their arrowy odor through the
brain
Till you might faint with that delicious
pain.
And every motion, odor, beam, and tone,
With that deep music is in unison,
455 Which is a soul within the soul—they seem
Like echoes of an antenatal dream.
It is an isle 'twixt Heaven, Air, Earth, and
Sea,
Cradled, and hung in clear tranquillity;
Bright as that wandering Eden, Lucifer,
460 Washed by the soft blue oceans of young
air.
It is a favored place. Famine or Blight,
Pestilence, War, and Earthquake, never
light
Upon its mountain-peaks; blind vultures,
they
Sail onward far upon their fatal way;
465 The wingèd storms, chanting their thunder-
psalm
To other lands, leave azure chasms of calm
Over this isle, or weep themselves in dew,
From which its fields and woods ever renew
Their green and golden immortality.
470 And from the sea there rise, and from the
sky
There fall, clear exhalations, soft and
bright,
Veil after veil, each hiding some delight,
Which Sun or Moon or zephyr draws aside,
Till the isle's beauty, like a naked bride
475 Glowing at once with love and loveliness,
Blushes and trembles at its own excess;

Yet, like a buried lamp, a Soul no less
Burns in the heart of this delicious isle,
An atom of the Eternal, whose own smile
480 Unfolds itself, and may be felt, not seen,
O'er the gray rocks, blue waves, and for-
ests green,
Filling their bare and void interstices.
But the chief marvel of the wilderness
Is a lone dwelling, built by whom or how
485 None of the rustic island-people know;
'Tis not a tower of strength, though with
its height
It overtops the woods; but, for delight,
Some wise and tender ocean-king, ere crime
Had been invented, in the world's young
prime,
490 Reared it, a wonder of that simple time,
An envy of the isles, a pleasure-house
Made sacred to his sister and his spouse.
It scarce seems now a wreck of human art,
But, as it were, Titanic; in the heart
495 Of Earth having assumed its form, then
grown
Out of the mountains, from the living
stone,
Lifting itself in caverns light and high;
For all the antique and learnèd imagery
Has been erased, and in the place of it
500 The ivy and the wild vine interknit
The volumes of their many-twining stems;
Parasite flowers illume with dewy gems
The lampless halls, and when they fade, the
sky
Peeps through their winter-woof of tracery
505 With moonlight patches, or star-atoms
keen,
Or fragments of the day's intense serene,
Working mosaic on their Parian floors.
And, day and night, aloof, from the high
towers
And terraces, the Earth and Ocean seem
510 To sleep in one another's arms, and dream
Of waves, flowers, clouds, woods, rocks,
and all that we
Read in their smiles, and call reality.

This isle and house are mine, and I have
vowed
Thee to be lady of the solitude.
515 And I have fitted up some chambers there
Looking towards the golden Eastern air,
And level with the living winds, which flow
Like waves above the living waves below.
I have sent books and music there, and
all
520 Those instruments with which high spirits
call
The future from its cradle, and the past
Out of its grave, and make the present last

In thoughts and joys which sleep, but can-
not die,
Folded within their own eternity.
525 Our simple life wants little, and true taste
Hires not the pale drudge Luxury to waste
The scene it would adorn, and therefore
still,
Nature with all her children haunts the
hill.
The ring-dove, in the embowering ivy, yet
530 Keeps up her love-lament, and the owls flit
Round the evening tower, and the young
stars glance
Between the quick bats in their twilight
dance;
The spotted deer bask in the fresh moon-
light
Before our gate, and the slow, silent night
535 Is measured by the pants of their calm
sleep.
Be this our home in life, and when years
heap
Their withered hours, like leaves, on our
decay,
Let us become the overhanging day,
The living soul of this Elysian isle,
540 Conscious, inseparable, one. Meanwhile
We two will rise, and sit, and walk to-
gether,
Under the roof of blue Ionian weather,
And wander in the meadows, or ascend
The mossy mountains, where the blue heav-
ends bend
545 With lightest winds, to touch their para-
mour;
Or linger, where the pebble-paven shore,
Under the quick, faint kisses of the sea
Trembles and sparkles as with ecstasy,—
Possessing and possessed by all that is
550 Within that calm circumference of bliss,
And by each other, till to love and live
Be one; or, at the noontide hour, arrive
Where some old cavern hoar seems yet to
keep
The moonlight of the expired night asleep,
555 Through which the awakened day can
never peep;
A veil for our seclusion, close as Night's,
Where secure sleep may kill thine innocent
lights;[1]
Sleep, the fresh dew of languid love, the
rain
Whose drops quench kisses till they burn
again.
560 And we will talk, until thought's melody
Become too sweet for utterance, and it die
In words, to live again in looks, which dart
With thrilling tone into the voiceless heart,

[1] eyes

Harmonizing silence without a sound.
565 Our breath shall intermix, our bosoms
bound,
And our veins beat together; and our lips
With other eloquence than words, eclipse
The soul that burns between them, and the
wells
Which boil under our being's inmost
cells,
570 The fountains of our deepest life, shall be
Confused in passion's golden purity,
As mountain-springs under the morning
sun.
We shall become the same, we shall be one
Spirit within two frames, oh! wherefore
two?
575 One passion in twin-hearts, which grows
and grew,
Till like two meteors of expanding flame,
Those spheres instinct with it become the
same,
Touch, mingle, are transfigured; ever still
Burning, yet ever inconsumable;
580 In one another's substance finding food,
Like flames too pure and light and un-
imbued
To nourish their bright lives with baser
prey,
Which point to Heaven and cannot pass
away:
One hope within two wills, one will beneath
585 Two overshadowing minds, one life, one
death,
One Heaven, one Hell, one immortality,
And one annihilation. Woe is me!
The wingèd words on which my soul would
pierce
Into the height of love's rare Universe,
590 Are chains of lead around its flight of
fire.
I pant, I sink, I tremble, I expire!

———

Weak verses, go, kneel at your Sovereign's feet,
And say:—"We are the masters of thy
slave;
What wouldest thou with us and ours and
thine?"
595 Then call your sisters from Oblivion's
cave,
All singing loud: "Love's very pain is
sweet,
But its reward is in the world divine
Which, if not here, it builds beyond the
grave."
So shall ye live when I am there. Then
haste
600 Over the hearts of men, until ye meet

Marina, Vanna, Primus,[1] and the rest,
And bid them love each other and be
   blessed;
And leave the troop which errs, and which
   reproves,
And come and be my guest,—for I am
   Love's.

SONG
1820   1824

Rarely, rarely, comest thou,
   Spirit of Delight!
Wherefore hast thou left me now
   Many a day and night?
5 Many a weary night and day
'Tis since thou art fled away.

How shall ever one like me
   Win thee back again?
With the joyous and the free
10   Thou wilt scoff at pain.
Spirit false! thou hast forgot
All but those who need thee not.

As a lizard with the shade
   Of a trembling leaf,
15 Thou with sorrow art dismayed;
   Even the sighs of grief
Reproach thee, that thou art not near,
And reproach thou wilt not hear.

Let me set my mournful ditty
20   To a merry measure;
Thou wilt never come for pity,
   Thou wilt come for pleasure;
Pity then will cut away
Those cruel wings, and thou wilt stay.

25 I love all that thou lovest,
   Spirit of Delight!
The fresh Earth in new leaves dressed,
   And the starry night;
Autumn evening, and the morn
30 When the golden mists are born.

I love snow, and all the forms
   Of the radiant frost;
I love waves, and winds, and storms,
   Everything almost
35 Which is Nature's, and may be
Untainted by man's misery.

I love tranquil solitude,
   And such society

---

[1] Mary Shelley, Jane Williams, Edward Williams.
The Williamses were warm friends of the
Shelleys. See Shelley's *To Edward Williams*
(p. 766), *With a Guitar: To Jane* (p. 768),
and *To Jane* (p. 768).

As is quiet, wise, and good;
40   Between thee and me
What difference? but thou dost possess
The things I seek, not love them less.

I love Love—though he has wings,
   And like light can flee,
45 But above all other things,
   Spirit, I love thee—
Thou art love and life! Oh, come,
Make once more my heart thy home.

TO NIGHT
1821   1824

Swiftly walk o'er the western wave,
   Spirit of Night!
Out of the misty eastern cave,
Where, all the long and lone daylight,
5 Thou wovest dreams of joy and fear,
Which make thee terrible and dear,—
   Swift be thy flight!

Wrap thy form in a mantle gray,
   Star-inwrought!
10 Blind with thine hair the eyes of Day;
Kiss her until she be wearied out;
Then wander o'er city, and sea, and land,
Touching all with thine opiate wand—
   Come, long-sought!

15 When I arose and saw the dawn,
   I sighed for thee;
When light rode high, and the dew was
   gone,
And noon lay heavy on flower and tree,
And the weary Day turned to his rest,
20 Lingering like an unloved guest,
   I sighed for thee.

Thy brother Death came, and cried,
   Wouldst thou me?
Thy sweet child Sleep, the filmy-eyed,
25 Murmured like a noontide bee,
Shall I nestle near thy side?
Wouldst thou me?—And I replied,
   No, not thee!

Death will come when thou art dead,
30   Soon, too soon;
Sleep will come when thou art fled;
Of neither would I ask the boon
I ask of thee, belovèd Night,—
Swift be thine approaching flight,
35   Come, soon, soon!

TIME
1821   1824

Unfathomable Sea! whose waves are
   years,
   Ocean of Time, whose waters of deep
   woe

Are brackish with the salt of human
    tears!
  Thou shoreless flood, which in thy ebb
    and flow
5 Claspest the limits of mortality,
And sick of prey, yet howling on for
    more,
Vomitest thy wrecks on its inhospitable
    shore;
Treacherous in calm, and terrible in
    storm,
    Who shall put forth on thee,
10   Unfathomable Sea?

TO EMILIA VIVIANI
1821   1824

Madonna,[1] wherefore hast thou sent to me
  Sweet-basil and mignonette?
  Embleming love and health, which never
    yet
In the same wreath might be.
5   Alas, and they are wet!
Is it with thy kisses or thy tears?
    For never rain or dew
    Such fragrance drew
From plant or flower—the very doubt en-
    dears
10   My sadness ever new,
The sighs I breathe, the tears I shed for
    thee.

Send the stars light, but send not love to me,
  In whom love ever made
Health like a heap of embers soon to fade.
*   *   *   *   *   *

TO ――
1821   1824

Music, when soft voices die,
Vibrates in the memory;
Odors, when sweet violets sicken,
Live within the sense they quicken.

5 Rose leaves, when the rose is dead,
Are heaped for the belovèd's bed;
And so thy thoughts, when thou art gone,
Love itself shall slumber on.

TO ――
1821   1824

When passion's trance is overpast,
If tenderness and truth could last,
Or live, whilst all wild feelings keep
Some mortal slumber, dark and deep,
6 I should not weep, I should not weep!

It were enough to feel, to see
Thy soft eyes gazing tenderly,

[1] An Italian term of address equivalent to
madame: it means *my lady*.

And dream the rest—and burn and **be**
The secret food of fires unseen,
10 Couldst thou but be as thou hast been.

After the slumber of the year
The woodland violets reappear;
All things revive in field or grove,
And sky and sea, but two, which move
15 And form all others, life and love.

MUTABILITY
1821   1824

The flower that smiles today
    Tomorrow dies;
All that we wish to stay
    Tempts and then flies.
5 What is this world's delight?
Lightning that mocks the night,
    Brief even as bright.

Virtue, how frail it is!
    Friendship how rare!
10 Love, how it sells poor bliss
    For proud despair!
But we, though soon they fall,
Survive their joy, and all
    Which ours we call.

15 Whilst skies are blue and bright,
    Whilst flowers are gay,
Whilst eyes that change ere night
    Make glad the day;
Whilst yet the calm hours creep,
20 Dream thou—and from thy sleep
    Then wake to weep.

A LAMENT
1821   1824

O world! O life! O time!
On whose last steps I climb,
  Trembling at that where I had stood
    before;
When will return the glory of your prime?
5   No more—oh, never more!

Out of the day and night
A joy has taken flight;
  Fresh spring, and summer, and winter
    hoar,
Move my faint heart with grief, but with
    delight
10   No more—oh, never more!

SONNET: POLITICAL GREATNESS
1821   1824

Nor happiness, nor majesty, nor fame,
Nor peace, nor strength, nor skill in arms
    or arts,
Shepherd those herds whom tyranny makes
    tame;

Verse echoes not one beating of their
    hearts,
5 History is but the shadow of their shame,
Art veils her glass, or from the pageant
    starts
As to oblivion their blind millions fleet,
Staining that Heaven with obscene imagery
Of their own likeness. What are numbers
    knit
10 By force or custom? Man who man would
    be,
Must rule the empire of himself; in it
Must be supreme, establishing his throne
On vanquished will, quelling the anarchy
Of hopes and fears, being himself alone.

ADONAIS

AN ELEGY ON THE DEATH OF JOHN KEATS
1821   1821

1 I weep for Adonais—he is dead!
Oh weep for Adonais! though our tears
Thaw not the frost which binds so dear a
    head!
And thou, sad Hour, selected from all years
To mourn our loss, rouse thy obscure
    compeers,[1]
And teach them thine own sorrow! Say:
    "With me
Died Adonais; till the Future dares
Forget the Past, his fate and fame shall be
An echo and a light unto Eternity!"

2 Where wert thou, mighty Mother,[2] when
    he lay,
When thy son lay, pierced by the shaft
    which flies
In darkness? where was lorn Urania
When Adonais died? With veilèd eyes,
'Mid listening Echoes, in her paradise
She sate, while one,[3] with soft enamored
    breath,
Rekindled all the fading melodies,
With which, like flowers that mock the
    corse beneath,
He had adorned and hid the coming bulk
    of death.

3 Oh, weep for Adonais—he is dead!
Wake, melancholy Mother, wake and weep!
Yet wherefore? Quench within their
    burning bed
Thy fiery tears, and let thy loud heart keep
Like his, a mute and uncomplaining sleep;

---

[1] Hours less memorable than the one which
    marked the death of Keats.
[2] Urania, the muse of astronomy. Probably
    Shelley identifies her with the highest spirit
    of lyrical poetry.
[3] One echo.

For he is gone, where all things wise and
    fair
Descend. Oh, dream not that the amorous
    Deep
Will yet restore him to the vital air;
Death feeds on his mute voice, and laughs
    at our despair.

4 Most musical of mourners, weep again!
Lament anew, Urania!—He died,[1]
Who was the sire of an immortal strain,
Blind, old, and lonely, when his country's
    pride,
The priest, the slave, and the liberticide,
Trampled and mocked with many a
    loathèd rite
Of lust and blood;[2] he went, unterrified,
Into the gulf of death; but his clear Sprite
Yet reigns o'er earth, the third among the
    sons of light.[3]

5 Most musical of mourners, weep anew!
Not all to that bright station dared to
    climb;
And happier they their happiness who
    knew,
Whose tapers yet burn through that night
    of time
In which suns perished; others more sub-
    lime,
Struck by the envious wrath of man or
    God,
Have sunk, extinct in their refulgent
    prime;
And some yet live, treading the thorny
    road,
Which leads, through toil and hate, to
    Fame's serene abode.

6 But now, thy youngest, dearest one has
    perished,
The nursling of thy widowhood, who
    grew,
Like a pale flower by some sad maiden
    cherished,
And fed with true-love tears, instead of
    dew;[4]
Most musical of mourners, weep anew!
Thy extreme[5] hope, the loveliest and the
    last,
The bloom, whose petals nipped before
    they blew,

---

[1] Milton.
[2] An accurate characterization of the Restora-
    tion period.
[3] The other two may be Homer and Shakespeare;
    or, if epic poets are meant, Homer and Dante.
    See Shelley's *A Defense of Poetry* (ed. Cook,
    p. 31).
[4] A reference to Keats's *Isabella* (p. 844).
[5] last

Died on the promise of the fruit, is waste;
The broken lily lies—the storm is overpast.

7 To that high Capital,[1] where kingly Death
Keeps his pale court in beauty and decay,
He came; and bought, with price of pur-
est breath,
A grave among the eternal.—Come away!
Haste, while the vault of blue Italian day
Is yet his fitting charnel-roof! while still
He lies, as if in dewy sleep he lay;
Awake him not! surely he takes his fill
Of deep and liquid rest, forgetful of all ill.

8 He will awake no more, oh, never more!
Within the twilight chamber spreads apace
The shadow of white Death, and at the
door
Invisible Corruption waits to trace
His extreme way[2] to her dim dwelling-
place;
The eternal Hunger[3] sits, but pity and awe
Soothe her pale rage, nor dares she to
deface.
So fair a prey, till darkness, and the law
Of change, shall o'er his sleep the mortal
curtain draw.

9 Oh, weep for Adonais!—The quick Dreams,
The passion-wingèd ministers of thought,
Who were his flocks, whom near the living
streams
Of his young spirit he fed, and whom he
taught
The love which was its music, wander
not,—
Wander no more, from kindling brain to
brain,
But droop there, whence they sprung; and
mourn their lot
Round the cold heart, where, after their
sweet pain,[4]
They ne'er will gather strength, or find a
home again.

10 And one with trembling hands clasps his
cold head,
And fans him with her moonlight wings,
and cries;
"Our love, our hope, our sorrow, is not
dead;
See, on the silken fringe of his faint eyes,
Like dew upon a sleeping flower, there
lies
A tear some Dream has loosened from his
brain."

[1] Rome, where Keats had gone for his health.
[2] to mark out Keats's last path
[3] Corruption.
[4] Birth pangs.

Lost Angel of a ruined paradise!
She knew not 'twas her own; as with no
stain
She faded, like a cloud which had out-
wept its rain.

11 One from a lucid urn of starry dew
Washed his light limbs as if embalming
them;
Another clipped her profuse locks, and
threw
The wreath upon him, like an anadem,[1]
Which frozen tears instead of pearls
begem;
Another in her wilful grief would break
Her bow and winged reeds, as if to stem
A greater loss with one which was more
weak;
And dull the barbèd fire against his frozen
cheek.

12 Another Splendor on his mouth alit,
That mouth, whence it was wont to draw
the breath
Which gave it strength to pierce the
guarded wit,
And pass into the panting heart beneath
With lightning and with music: the damp
death
Quenched its caress upon his icy lips;
And, as a dying meteor stains a wreath
Of moonlight vapor, which the cold night
clips,[2]
It flushed through his pale limbs, and
passed to its eclipse.

13 And others came—Desires and Adorations,
Wingèd Persuasions and veiled Destinies,
Splendors, and Glooms, and glimmering
Incarnations
Of hopes and fears, and twilight Fan-
tasies;
And Sorrow, with her family of Sighs,
And Pleasure, blind with tears, led by the
gleam
Of her own dying smile instead of eyes,
Came in slow pomp;—the moving pomp
might seem
Like pageantry of mist on an autumnal
stream.

14 All he had loved, and moulded into
thought,
From shape, and hue, and odor, and sweet
sound,
Lamented Adonais. Morning sought

[1] wreath for the head　　[2] embraces

Her eastern watch-tower, and her hair
    unbound,
Wet with the tears which should adorn
    the ground,
Dimmed the aëreal eyes that kindle day;
Afar the melancholy thunder moaned,
Pale Ocean in unquiet slumber lay,
And the wild winds flew round, sobbing in
    their dismay.

15 Lost Echo sits amid the voiceless moun-
    tains,
And feeds her grief with his remembered
    lay,
And will no more reply to winds or foun-
    tains,
Or amorous birds perched on the young
    green spray,
Or herdsman's horn, or bell at closing
    day;
Since she can mimic not his lips, more
    dear
Than those for whose disdain she pined
    away
Into a shadow of all sounds:[1]—a drear
Murmur, between their songs, is all the
    woodmen hear.

16 Grief made the young Spring wild, and
    she threw down
Her kindling buds, as if she Autumn were,
Or they dead leaves; since her delight is
    flown,
For whom should she have waked the
    sullen year?
To Phœbus was not Hyacinth so dear
Nor to himself Narcissus, as to both
Thou, Adonais: wan they stand and sere
Amid the faint companions of their youth,
With dew all turned to tears; odor, to
    sighing ruth.

17 Thy spirit's sister, the lorn nightingale[2]
Mourns not her mate with such melodious
    pain;
Not so the eagle, who like thee could scale
Heaven, and could nourish in the sun's
    domain
Her mighty youth with morning, doth
    complain,
Soaring and screaming round her empty
    nest,
As Albion wails for thee: the curse of
    Cain
Light on his head who pierced thy inno-
    cent breast,

[1] Narcissus, for whose love Echo pined away
into a mere voice.
[2] A reference to Keats's *Ode to a Nightingale*
(p. 857), and to the melody of his verse.

And scared the angel soul that was its
    earthly guest![1]

18 Ah, woe is me! Winter is come and gone,
But grief returns with the revolving year;
The airs and streams renew their joyous
    tone;
The ants, the bees, the swallows reappear;
Fresh leaves and flowers deck the dead
    Seasons' bier;
The amorous birds now pair in every
    brake,[2]
And build their mossy homes in field and
    brere;[3]
And the green lizard, and the golden
    snake,
Like unimprisoned flames, out of their
    trance awake.

19 Through wood and stream and field and
    hill and ocean
A quickening life from the Earth's heart
    has burst
As it has ever done, with change and mo-
    tion,
From the great morning of the world
    when first
God dawned on Chaos; in its stream im-
    mersed,
The lamps of Heaven flash with a softer
    light;
All baser things pant with life's sacred
    thirst;
Diffuse themselves; and spend in love's
    delight,
The beauty and the joy of their renewèd
    might.

20 The leprous corpse, touched by this spirit
    tender,
Exhales itself in flowers of gentle breath;
Like incarnations of the stars, when
    splendor
Is changed to fragrance, they illumine
    death
And mock the merry worm that wakes
    beneath;
Nought we know dies. Shall that alone
    which knows
Be as a sword consumed before the sheath

[1] Shelley wrongly believed that the death of
Keats was due to hostile attacks upon his
poetry. Keats's *Endymion* had been severely
criticized in an unsigned article published in
The Quarterly Review, April, 1818 (Vol. 19,
pp. 204-8). This article was written by J.
W. Croker. See p. 939. See also. Byron's
Don Juan, XI, 60, 1, and n. 5 (p. 636), and
Who Killed John Keats? (p. 639).
[2] thicket
[3] briar

By sightless lightning?—the intense atom glows
A moment, then is quenched in a most cold repose.

21 Alas! that all we loved of him should be,
But for our grief, as if it had not been,
And grief itself be mortal! Woe is me!
Whence are we, and why are we? of what scene
The actors or spectators? Great and mean
Meet massed in death, who lends what life must borrow.
As long as skies are blue, and fields are green,
Evening must usher night, night urge the morrow,
Month follow month with woe, and year wake year to sorrow.

22 *He* will awake no more, oh, never more!
"Wake thou," cried Misery, "childless Mother, rise
Out of thy sleep, and slake, in thy heart's core,
A wound more fierce than his, with tears and sighs."
And all the Dreams that watched Urania's eyes,
And all the Echoes whom their sister's song
Had held in holy silence, cried: "Arise!"
Swift as a Thought by the snake Memory stung,
From her ambrosial rest the fading Splendor sprung.

23 She rose like an autumnal Night, that springs
Out of the East, and follows wild and drear
The golden Day, which, on eternal wings,
Even as a ghost abandoning a bier,
Had left the Earth a corpse;—sorrow and fear
So struck, so roused, so rapt Urania;
So saddened round her like an atmosphere
Of stormy mist; so swept her on her way
Even to the mournful place where Adonais lay.

24 Out of her secret paradise she sped,
Through camps and cities rough with stone, and steel,
And human hearts, which to her airy tread
Yielding not, wounded the invisible
Palms of her tender feet where'er they fell:

And barbèd tongues, and thoughts more sharp than they,
Rent the soft Form they never could repel,
Whose sacred blood, like the young tears of May,
Paved with eternal flowers that undeserving way.

25 In the death-chamber for a moment Death,
Shamed by the presence of that living Might,
Blushed to annihilation, and the breath
Revisited those lips, and Life's pale light
Flashed through those limbs, so late her dear delight.
"Leave me not wild and drear and comfortless,
As silent lightning leaves the starless night!
Leave me not!" cried Urania: her distress
Roused Death: Death rose and smiled, and met her vain caress.

26 "Stay yet awhile! speak to me once again;
Kiss me, so long but as a kiss may live;
And in my heartless[1] breast and burning brain
That word, that kiss, shall all thoughts else survive,
With food of saddest memory kept alive,
Now thou art dead, as if it were a part
Of thee, my Adonais! I would give
All that I am to be as thou now art!
But I am chained to Time, and cannot thence depart!

27 "O gentle child, beautiful as thou wert,
Why didst thou leave the trodden paths of men
Too soon, and with weak hands though mighty heart
Dare the unpastured dragon[2] in his den?
Defenceless as thou wert, oh, where was then
Wisdom the mirrored shield,[3] or scorn the spear?
Or hadst thou waited the full cycle when
Thy spirit should have filled its crescent sphere,[4]
The monsters of life's waste had fled from thee like deer.

[1] Her heart had been given to Adonais.
[2] The unfed and ravenous critic. See Scott's *Marmion*, 6, 432.
[3] A reference to the shield which protected Perseus from the fatal gaze of the Gorgons, and which enabled him to cut off the head of Medusa as he saw it by reflection.
[4] Attained maturity of power.

28 "The herded wolves,[1] bold only to pursue;
The obscene ravens, clamorous o'er the
   dead;
The vultures to the conqueror's banner
   true
Who feed where Desolation first has fed,
And whose wings rain contagion;—how
   they fled,
When, like Apollo, from his golden bow
The Pythian of the age[2] one arrow sped
And smiled!—The spoilers tempt no sec-
   ond blow,
They fawn on the proud feet that spurn
   them lying low.

29 "The sun comes forth, and many reptiles
   spawn;
He sets, and each ephemeral insect then
Is gathered into death without a dawn,
And the immortal stars awake again;
So is it in the world of living men:
A godlike mind soars forth, in its delight
Making earth bare and veiling heaven, and
   when
It sinks, the swarms that dimmed or shared
   its light
Leave to its kindred lamps the spirit's
   awful night."

30 Thus ceased she: and the mountain shep-
   herds came,
Their garlands sere, their magic mantles
   rent;[3]
The Pilgrim of Eternity,[4] whose fame
Over his living head like Heaven is bent,
An early but enduring monument,
Came, veiling all the lightnings of his song
In sorrow; from her wilds Ierne sent
The sweetest lyrist of her saddest wrong,[5]
And love taught grief to fall like music
   from his tongue.

31 Midst others of less note, came one frail
   Form,[6]
A phantom among men; companionless
As the last cloud of an expiring storm
Whose thunder is its knell; he, as I guess,
Had gazed on Nature's naked loveliness,
Actæon-like, and now he fled astray
With feeble steps o'er the world's wilder-
   ness,

And his own thoughts, along that rugged
   way,
Pursued, like raging hounds, their father
   and their prey.

32 A pardlike[1] Spirit beautiful and swift—
A Love in desolation masked;—a Power
Girt round with weakness;—it can scarce
   uplift
The weight of the superincumbent hour;
It is a dying lamp, a falling shower,
A breaking billow;—even whilst we speak
Is it not broken? On the withering flower
The killing sun smiles brightly: on a cheek
The life can burn in blood, even while the
   heart may break.

33 His head was bound with pansies[2] over-
   blown,
And faded violets, white, and pied, and
   blue;
And a light spear topped with a cypress
   cone,
Round whose rude shaft dark ivy-tresses
   grew
Yet dripping with the forest's noonday
   dew,
Vibrated, as the ever-beating heart
Shook the weak hand that grasped it; of
   that crew
He came the last, neglected and apart;
A herd-abandoned deer struck by the hunt-
   er's dart.[3]

34 All stood aloof, and at his partial moan
Smiled through their tears; well knew that
   gentle band
Who in another's fate now wept his own,
As in the accents of an unknown land[4]
He sung new sorrow; sad Urania scanned
The stranger's mien, and murmured:
   "Who art thou?"
He answered not, but with a sudden hand
Made bare his branded and ensanguined
   brow,
Which was like Cain's or Christ's—oh!
   that it should be so![5]

35 What softer voice is hushed over the dead?
Athwart what brow is that dark mantle
   thrown?

---

[1] The banded critics.
[2] Byron in his *English Bards and Scotch Reviewers* (p. 511), by allusion to the Pythian
Apollo, slayer of the Python.
[3] See *The Tempest*, I, 2, 24.
[4] Byron. A reference to his *Childe Harold's Pilgrimage* (p. 549).
[5] Thomas Moore. A reference to his *Irish Melodies* (p. 451), and probably to the suppression
of the insurrection of 1803 and to the execution of the Irish leader, Robert Emmet.
[6] Shelley himself.

[1] leopard-like
[2] The pansy is a symbol of thought; the violet,
of modesty; the cypress, of mourning; the
ivy, of constancy in friendship.
[3] See Shelley's *Epipsychidion*, 272 ff. (p. 749);
also, Cowper's *The Task*, 3, 108 ff.
[4] That is, he wrote in the language of England,
a land unknown to the Greek muse, Urania.
[5] Shelley means that he bore marks of cruel
treatment such as the world gave to Cain, an
enemy of the race, or to Christ, a benefactor.

What form leans sadly o'er the white
 death-bed,
In mockery of monumental stone,
The heavy heart heaving without a moan?
If it be he, who, gentlest of the wise,[1]
Taught, soothed, loved, honored the de-
 parted one,
Let me not vex, with inharmonious sighs,
The silence of that heart's accepted sacri-
 fice.

36 Our Adonais has drunk poison—oh,
What deaf and viperous murderer could
 crown
Life's early cup with such a draught of
 woe?
The nameless worm[2] would now itself dis-
 own:
It felt, yet could escape, the magic tone
Whose prelude held all envy, hate, and
 wrong,
But what was howling in one breast alone,[3]
Silent with expectation of the song,
Whose master's hand is cold, whose silver
 lyre unstrung.

37 Live thou,[4] whose infamy is not thy fame!
Live! fear no heavier chastisement from
 me,
Thou noteless blot on a remembered name!
But be thyself, and know thyself to be!
And ever at thy season be thou free
To spill the venom when thy fangs o'er-
 flow:
Remorse and Self-Contempt shall cling to
 thee;
Hot Shame shall burn upon thy secret
 brow,
And like a beaten hound tremble thou
 shalt—as now.

38 Nor let us weep that our delight is fled
Far from these carrion kites that scream
 below;
He wakes or sleeps with the enduring
 dead;
Thou canst not soar where he is sitting
 now.[5]—
Dust to the dust! but the pure spirit shall
 flow
Back to the burning fountain whence it
 came,

A portion of the Eternal, which must glow
Through time and change, unquenchably
 the same,
Whilst thy cold embers choke the sordid
 hearth of shame.

39 Peace, peace! he is not dead, he doth not
 sleep—
He hath awakened from the dream of
 life—
'Tis we, who, lost in stormy visions, keep
With phantoms an unprofitable strife,
And in mad trance, strike with our spirit's
 knife
Invulnerable nothings. *We* decay
Like corpses in a charnel; fear and grief
Convulse us and consume us day by day,
And cold hopes swarm like worms within
 our living clay.

40 He has outsoared the shadow of our night;
Envy and calumny and hate and pain,
And that unrest which men miscall delight,
Can touch him not and torture not again;
From the contagion of the world's slow
 stain
He is secure, and now can never mourn
A heart grown cold, a head grown gray in
 vain;
Nor, when the spirit's self has ceased to
 burn,
With sparkless ashes load an unlamented
 urn.

41 He lives, he wakes—'tis Death is dead,
 not he;
Mourn not for Adonais.—Thou young
 Dawn,
Turn all thy dew to splendor, for from
 thee
The spirit thou lamentest is not gone;
Ye caverns and ye forests, cease to moan!
Cease, ye faint flowers and fountains, and
 thou air,
Which like a mourning veil thy scarf hadst
 thrown
O'er the abandoned Earth, now leave it
 bare
Even to the joyous stars which smile on
 its despair!

42 He is made one with Nature:[1] there is heard
His voice in all her music, from the moan
Of thunder, to the song of night's sweet
 bird;
He is a presence to be felt and known

---

[1] Leigh Hunt, Keats's close friend and patron.
[2] The criticism of *Endymion* in *The Quarterly Review* was unsigned.
[3] In the breast of the writer of the article in *The Quarterly Review*. A harsher criticism, however, appeared in *Blackwood's Magazine*, August, 1818 (Vol. 3, p. 519).
[4] The reviewer.
[5] See *Paradise Lost*, 4, 829.

[1] See Shelley's *Prometheus Unbound*, IV, 534-38 (p. 724).

In darkness and in light, from herb and
    stone,
Spreading itself where'er that Power may
    move
Which has withdrawn his being to its own;
Which wields the world with never-wearied
    love,
Sustains it from beneath, and kindles it
    above.

43 He is a portion of the loveliness
    Which once he made more lovely: he doth
        bear
His part, while the one Spirit's plastic[1]
    stress
Sweeps through the dull dense world, com-
    pelling there,
All new successions to the forms they
    wear,[2]
Torturing the unwilling dross that checks
    its flight
To its own likeness, as[3] each mass may
    bear;
And bursting in its beauty and its might
From trees and beasts and men into the
    Heaven's light.

44 The splendors of the firmament of time
May be eclipsed, but are extinguished not;
Like stars to their appointed height they
    climb,
And death is a low mist which cannot blot
The brightness it may veil. When lofty
    thought
Lifts a young heart above its mortal lair,
And love and life contend in it for what
Shall be its earthly doom, the dead live
    there
And move like winds of light on dark and
    stormy air.

45 The inheritors of unfulfilled renown
Rose from their thrones, built beyond mor-
    tal thought,
Far in the Unapparent. Chatterton
Rose pale,—his solemn agony had not
Yet faded from him; Sidney, as he fought
And as he fell and as he lived and loved
Sublimely mild, a Spirit without spot,
Arose; and Lucan, by his death approved:
Oblivion as they rose shrank like a thing
    reproved.

[1] shaping; molding
[2] The spirit of Love and Beauty is thought of as
    permeating all matter and as molding every-
    thing into its proper form. See Wordsworth's
    *Lines Composed a Few Miles Above Tintern
    Abbey*, 93-102 (p. 260).
[3] according as

46 And many more, whose names on earth are
    dark,
But whose transmitted effluence cannot
    die
So long as fire outlives the parent spark,
Rose, robed in dazzling immortality.
"Thou art become as one of us," they
    cry,
"It was for thee yon kingless sphere has
    long
Swung blind in unascended majesty,
Silent alone amid an heaven of song.
Assume thy wingèd throne, thou Vesper of
    our throng!"

47 Who mourns for Adonais? Oh, come
    forth,
Fond wretch! and know thyself and him
    aright.
Clasp with thy panting soul the pendulous
    earth;
As from a centre, dart thy spirit's light
Beyond all worlds, until its spacious might
Satiate the void circumference: then shrink
Even to a point within our day and night;
And keep thy heart light lest it make thee
    sink
When hope has kindled hope, and lured
    thee to the brink.

48 Or go to Rome, which is the sepulchre,
Oh, not of him, but of our joy: 'tis nought
That ages, empires, and religions there
Lie buried in the ravage they have
    wrought;
For such as he can lend,—they borrow not
Glory from those who made the world their
    prey;
And he is gathered to the kings of thought
Who waged contention with their time's
    decay,
And of the past are all that cannot pass
    away.[1]

49 Go thou to Rome,—at once the Paradise,
The grave, the city, and the wilderness;
And where its wrecks like shattered moun-
    tains rise,
And flowering weeds and fragrant copses
    dress
The bones of Desolation's nakedness,
Pass, till the Spirit of the spot shall lead
Thy footsteps to a slope of green access[2]
Where, like an infant's smile, over the
    dead
A light of laughing flowers along the grass
    is spread;

[1] See Shelley's *Epipsychidion*, 209-12 (p. 748-49).
[2] The Protestant cemetery at Rome.

50 And gray walls moulder round, on which
    dull Time
Feeds, like slow fire, upon a hoary brand;
And one keen pyramid[1] with wedge sub-
    lime,
Pavilioning the dust of him who planned
This refuge for his memory, doth stand
Like flame transformed to marble; and
    beneath,
A field is spread, on which a newer band
Have pitched in Heaven's smile their camp
    of death,
Welcoming him we lose with scarce extin-
    guished breath.

51 Here pause: these graves are all too
    young[2] as yet
To have outgrown the sorrow which con-
    signed
Its charge to each; and if the seal is set,
Here, on one fountain of a mourning mind,
Break it not thou! too surely shalt thou
    find
Thine own well full, if thou returnest
    home,
Of tears and gall. From the world's bitter
    wind
Seek shelter in the shadow of the tomb.
What Adonais is, why fear we to become?

52 The One remains, the many change and
    pass;
Heaven's light forever shines, Earth's
    shadows fly;
Life, like a dome of many-colored glass,
Stains the white radiance of Eternity,
Until Death tramples it to fragments.—
    Die,
If thou wouldst be with that which thou
    dost seek![3]
Follow where all is fled!—Rome's azure
    sky,
Flowers, ruins, statues, music, words, are
    weak
The glory they transfuse with fitting truth
    to speak.

53 Why linger, why turn back, why shrink,
    my heart?
Thy hopes are gone before: from all things
    here
They have departed; thou shouldst now
    depart!
A light is passed from the revolving year,

And man, and woman; and what still is
    dear
Attracts to crush, repels to make thee
    wither.
The soft sky smiles,—the low wind whis-
    pers near:
'Tis Adonais calls! oh, hasten thither,
No more let Life divide what Death can
    join together.

54 That Light whose smile kindles the Uni-
    verse,
That Beauty in which all things work and
    move,
That Benediction which the eclipsing Curse
Of birth can quench not, that sustaining
    Love
Which through the web of being blindly
    wove
By man and beast and earth and air and
    sea,
Burns bright or dim, as[1] each are mir-
    rors of
The fire for which all thirst; now beams
    on me,
Consuming the last clouds of cold mor-
    tality.

55 The breath whose might I have invoked in
    song
Descends on me; my spirit's bark is driven,
Far from the shore, far from the trem-
    bling throng
Whose sails were never to the tempest
    given;
The massy earth and spherèd skies are
    riven!
I am borne darkly, fearfully, afar:
Whilst, burning through the inmost veil
    of Heaven,
The soul of Adonais, like a star,
Beacons from the abode where the Eternal
    are.

From HELLAS
1821   1822

LIFE MAY CHANGE, BUT IT MAY FLY NOT

Life may change, but it may fly not;
Hope may vanish, but can die not;
Truth be veiled, but still it burneth;
Love repulsed,—but it returneth!

5 Yet were life a charnel where
Hope lay coffined with Despair;
Yet were truth a sacred lie.
Love were lust—

[1] The tomb of Caius Cestius, built in the time of
    Augustus.
[2] Shelley's son William, who died in 1819, was
    buried there.
[3] Absolute Beauty.

[1] according as

If Liberty
Lent not life its soul of light,
10 Hope its iris of delight,
Truth its prophet's robe to wear,
Love its power to give and bear.

WORLDS ON WORLDS ARE ROLLING EVER

Worlds on worlds are rolling ever
    From creation to decay,
Like the bubbles on a river
    Sparkling, bursting, borne away.
5   But they are still immortal
    Who, through birth's orient portal
And death's dark chasm hurrying to and
        fro,
    Clothe their unceasing flight
    In the brief dust and light
10 Gathered around their chariots as they go;
    New shapes they still may weave,
    New gods, new laws receive,
Bright or dim are they as the robes they
        last
    On Death's bare ribs had cast.

15   A power from the unknown God,
    A Promethean conqueror, came;
Like a triumphal path he trod
    The thorns of death and shame.
    A mortal shape to him
20   Was like the vapor dim
Which the orient planet animates with
        light;
    Hell, Sin, and Slavery came,
    Like bloodhounds mild and tame,
Nor preyed, until their lord had taken
        flight;
25   The moon of Mahomet
    Arose, and it shall set:
While blazoned as on Heaven's immortal
        noon
    The cross leads generations on.

Swift as the radiant shapes of sleep
30   From one whose dreams are Paradise,
Fly, when the fond wretch wakes to
        weep,
    And Day peers forth with her blank
        eyes;
    So fleet, so faint, so fair,
    The Powers of earth and air
35 Fled from the folding-star[1] of Bethle-
        hem:
    Apollo, Pan, and Love,
    And even Olympian Jove

[1] An evening star which appears about folding
    time.

Grew weak, for killing Truth had glared
        on them;
    Our hills and seas and streams,
    Dispeopled of their dreams,
40 Their waters turned to blood, their dew to
        tears,
    Wailed for the golden years.

DARKNESS HAS DAWNED IN THE EAST

Darkness has dawned in the east
    On the noon of time:
The death-birds descend to their feast
    From the hungry clime.
5 Let Freedom and Peace flee far
    To a sunnier strand,
And follow Love's folding-star
    To the Evening land!

    The young moon has fed
        Her exhausted horn
10 With the sunset's fire:
    The weak day is dead,
        But the night is not born;
And, like loveliness panting with wild de-
        sire
15   While it trembles with fear and delight,
Hesperus flies from awakening night,
And pants in its beauty and speed with
        light
    Fast-flashing, soft, and bright.
Thou beacon of love! thou lamp of the
        free!
20   Guide us far, far away,
To climes where now veiled by the ardor
        of day
        Thou art hidden
    From waves on which weary Noon
    Faints in her summer swoon,
25   Between kingless continents sinless as
        Eden,
    Around mountains and islands in-
        violably
    Pranked on the sapphire sea.

    Through the sunset of hope,
    Like the shapes of a dream,
30 What Paradise islands of glory
        gleam!
    Beneath Heaven's cope,
    Their shadows more clear float by—
The sound of their oceans, the light of their
        sky,
The music and fragrance their solitudes
        breathe
35 Burst, like morning on dream, or like
        Heaven on death,
    Through the walls of our prison;
    And Greece, which was dead, is
        arisen!

The World's Great Age Begins Anew

The world's great age begins anew,
  The golden years return,
The earth doth like a snake renew
  Her winter weeds[1] outworn:
5 Heaven smiles, and faiths and empires
    gleam,
  Like wrecks of a dissolving dream.

A brighter Hellas rears its mountains
  From waves serener far;
A new Peneus rolls his fountains
10 Against the morning star.
Where fairer Tempes bloom, there sleep
Young Cyclads on a sunnier deep.

A loftier Argo cleaves the main,
  Fraught with a later prize;
15 Another Orpheus sings again,
  And loves, and weeps, and dies.
A new Ulysses leaves once more
Calypso for his native shore.

Oh, write no more the tale of Troy,
20 If earth Death's scroll must be!
Nor mix with Laian rage the joy
  Which dawns upon the free:
Although a subtler Sphinx renew
Riddles of death Thebes never knew.[2]

25 Another Athens shall arise,
  And to remoter time
Bequeath, like sunset to the skies,
  The splendor of its prime;
And leave, if nought so bright may live,
30 All earth can take or Heaven can give.

Saturn and Love their long repose
  Shall burst, more bright and good
Than all who fell,[3] than One who rose,
  Than many unsubdued:
35 Not gold, not blood, their altar dowers,
But votive tears and symbol flowers.

Oh, cease! must hate and death return?
  Cease! must men kill and die?
Cease! drain not to its dregs the urn
40 Of bitter prophecy.
The world is weary of the past,
Oh, might it die or rest at last!

---

1 garments
2 The Sphinx propounded a riddle to the Thebans, and killed all passers-by who could not
solve it. When the riddle was finally solved
by Œdipus, the Sphinx slew herself. See De
Quincey's *The Sphinx's Riddle.*
3 The gods of Greece, Asia, and Egypt. The
"One who rose" is Christ; the "many unsubdued" are the objects of the idolatry of
China, India, etc.

EVENING

PONTE AL MARE, PISA
1821   1824

The sun is set; the swallows are asleep;
  The bats are flitting fast in the gray air;
The slow soft toads out of damp corners
    creep,
  And evening's breath, wandering here
    and there
5 Over the quivering surface of the stream,
Wakes not one ripple from its summer
    dream.

There is no dew on the dry grass tonight,
  Nor damp within the shadow of the
    trees;
The wind is intermitting, dry, and light;
10 And in the inconstant motion of the
    breeze
The dust and straws are driven up and
    down,
And whirled about the pavement of the
    town.

Within the surface of the fleeting river
  The wrinkled image of the city lay,
15 Immovably unquiet, and forever
  It trembles, but it never fades away;
Go to the [   ]
You, being changed, will find it then as
    now.

The chasm in which the sun has sunk is
    shut
20 By darkest barriers of enormous cloud,
Like mountain over mountain huddled—
    but
  Growing and moving upwards in a
    crowd,
And over it a space of watery blue,
Which the keen evening star is shining
    through.

TO ——

1821   1824

One word is too often profaned
  For me to profane it,
One feeling too falsely disdained
  For thee to disdain it;
5 One hope is too like despair
  For prudence to smother,
And pity from thee more dear
  Than that from another.

I can give not what men call love,
10 But wilt thou accept not

The worship the heart lifts above
    And the Heavens reject not,—
The desire of the moth for the star,
    Of the night for the morrow,
15 The devotion to something afar
    From the sphere of our sorrow?

ON KEATS

WHO DESIRED THAT ON HIS TOMB
SHOULD BE INSCRIBED—
1821   1822

"Here lieth One whose name was writ on
    water."
But, ere the breath that could erase it
    blew,
Death, in remorse for that fell slaughter,—
Death, the immortalizing winter, flew
5   Athwart the stream,—and time's print-
    less torrent grew
A scroll of crystal, blazoning the name
    Of Adonais!

   *   *   *   *   *   *

TOMORROW
1821   1824

Where art thou, belovèd Tomorrow?
    When young and old, and strong and
    weak,
Rich and poor, through joy and sorrow,
    Thy sweet smiles we ever seek,—
5 In thy place—ah! well-a-day!
We find the thing we fled—Today.

REMEMBRANCE
1821   1824

Swifter far than summer's flight,
Swifter far than youth's delight,
Swifter far than happy night,
    Art thou come and gone.
5 As the wood when leaves are shed,
As the night when sleep is fled,
As the heart when joy is dead,
    I am left lone, alone.

The swallow summer comes again,
10 The owlet night[1] resumes his reign,
But the wild-swan youth is fain
    To fly with thee, false as thou.
My heart each day desires the morrow;
Sleep itself is turned to sorrow;
15 Vainly would my winter borrow
    Sunny leaves from any bough.

Lilies for a bridal bed,
Roses for a matron's head,

[1] The dim, uncanny night.

Violets for a maiden dead—
20   Pansies[1] let *my* flowers be;
On the living grave I bear,
    Scatter them without a tear—
Let no friend, however dear,
    Waste one hope, one fear for me.

TO EDWARD WILLIAMS
1821   1834

The serpent is shut out from Paradise.[2]
    The wounded deer[3] must seek the herb
    no more
    In which its heart-cure lies:
    The widowed dove must cease to
    haunt a bower
5 Like that from which its mate with feignèd
    sighs
    Fled in the April hour.
I too must seldom seek again
Near happy friends a mitigated pain.

Of hatred I am proud,—with scorn con-
    tent;
10   Indifference, that once hurt me, now is
    grown
    Itself indifferent;
But, not to speak of love, pity alone
Can break a spirit already more than bent.
    The miserable one
15   Turns the mind's poison into food,—
Its medicine is tears,—its evil good.

Therefore, if now I see you seldomer,
    Dear friends, dear *friend*! know that
    I only fly
    Your looks, because they stir
20   Griefs that should sleep, and hopes
    that cannot die:
The very comfort that they minister
    I scarce can bear, yet I,
    So deeply is the arrow gone,
Should quickly perish if it were withdrawn.

25 When I return to my cold home, you ask
    Why I am not as I have ever been.
    You spoil me for the task
    Of acting a forced part in life's dull
    scene,
Of wearing on my brow the idle mask
30   Of author, great or mean,
    In the world's carnival. I sought
Peace thus, and but in you I found it not.

[1] The lily is a symbol of purity; the rose, of
constancy; the violet, of modesty; the pansy,
of thought, or remembrance. See Shelley's
    Adonais, 33 (p. 760).
[2] Shelley had been named "The Snake" by Byron.
[3] See Shelley's *Epipsychidion*, 272 ff. (p. 749).

Full half an hour, today, I tried my lot
  With various flowers, and every one
     still said,
35   "She loves me—loves me not."
And if this meant a vision long since
     fled—
If it meant fortune, fame, or peace of
     thought—
     If it meant,—but I dread
To speak what you may know too
     well:
40 Still there was truth in the sad oracle.

The crane o'er seas and forests seeks her
     home;[1]
  No bird so wild but has its quiet nest,
     When it no more would roam;
  The sleepless billows on the ocean's
     breast
45 Break like a bursting heart, and die in
     foam,
     And thus at length find rest:
Doubtless there is a place of peace
Where *my* weak heart and all its throbs
     will cease.

I asked her, yesterday, if she believed
50   That I had resolution. One who
     had
  Would ne'er have thus relieved
His heart with words,—but what his
     judgment bade
Would do, and leave the scorner unre-
     lieved.
     These verses are too sad
55   To send to you, but that I know,
Happy yourself, you feel another's woe.

MUSIC
1821   1824

I pant for the music which is divine,
  My heart in its thirst is a dying flower;
Pour forth the sound like enchanted
     wine,
  Loosen the notes in a silver shower;
5 Like a herbless plain for the gentle rain,
I gasp, I faint, till they wake again.
Let me drink of the spirit of that sweet
     sound,
  More, oh more,—I am thirsting yet;
It loosens the serpent which care has
     bound
10 Upon my heart to stifle it;
  The dissolving strain, through every
     vein,
Passes into my heart and brain.

[1] See Shelley's *Alastor,* 280-84 (p. 665).

As the scent of a violet withered up,
  Which grew by the brink of a silver
     lake,
15 When the hot noon has drained its dewy
     cup,
  And mist there was none its thirst to
     slake—
And the violet lay dead while the odor flew
On the wings of the wind o'er the waters
     blue—

As one who drinks from a charmèd cup
20 Of foaming, and sparkling, and mur-
     muring wine,
Whom, a mighty Enchantress filling up,
  Invites to love with her kiss divine

*   *   *   *   *   *

LINES
1822   1824

When the lamp is shattered,
The light in the dust lies dead;
When the cloud is scattered,
The rainbow's glory is shed;
5 When the lute is broken,
Sweet tones are remembered not;
  When the lips have spoken,
Loved accents are soon forgot.

  As music and splendor
10 Survive not the lamp and the lute,
  The heart's echoes render
No song when the spirit is mute:—
  No song but sad dirges,
Like the wind through a ruined cell,
15 Or the mournful surges
That ring the dead seaman's knell.

  When hearts have once mingled,
Love first leaves the well-built nest;
  The weak one is singled
20 To endure what it once possessed.
  O Love! who bewailest
The frailty of all things here,
  Why choose you the frailest
For your cradle, your home, and your bier?

25 Its passions will rock thee,
As the storms rock the ravens on high;
  Bright reason will mock thee,
Like the sun from a wintry sky.
  From thy nest every rafter
30 Will rot, and thine eagle home
  Leave thee naked to laughter,
When leaves fall and cold winds come.

WITH A GUITAR: TO JANE[1]
1822   1832

Ariel to Miranda:—Take
This slave of Music, for the sake
Of him who is the slave of thee,
And teach it all the harmony
5 In which thou canst, and only thou,
Make the delighted spirit glow,
Till joy denies itself again,
And, too intense, is turned to pain;
For by permission and command
10 Of thine own Prince Ferdinand
Poor Ariel sends this silent token
Of more than ever can be spoken;
Your guardian spirit, Ariel, who,
From life to life, must still pursue
15 Your happiness,—for thus alone
Can Ariel ever find his own.
From Prospero's enchanted cell,
As the mighty verses tell,
To the throne of Naples, he
20 Lit you o'er the trackless sea,
Flitting on, your prow before,
Like a living meteor.
When you die, the silent Moon,
In her interlunar[2] swoon,
25 Is not sadder in her cell
Than deserted Ariel.
When you live again on earth,
Like an unseen star of birth,
Ariel guides you o'er the sea
30 Of life from your nativity.
Many changes have been run
Since Ferdinand and you begun
Your course of love, and Ariel still
Has tracked your steps, and served your
will;
35 Now, in humbler, happier lot,
This is all remembered not;
And now, alas! the poor sprite is
Imprisoned, for some fault of his,
In a body like a grave.
40 From you he only dares to crave,
For his service and his sorrow,
A smile today, a song tomorrow.

The artist who this idol wrought
To echo all harmonious thought,
45 Felled a tree, while on the steep
The woods were in their winter sleep,
Rocked in that repose divine
On the wind-swept Apennine;
And dreaming, some of autumn past,
50 And some of spring approaching fast,
And some of April buds and showers,
And some of songs in July bowers,
And all of love; and so this tree—
Oh, that such our death may be!—
55 Died in sleep, and felt no pain,
To live in happier form again:
From which, beneath Heaven's fairest
star,
The artist wrought this loved guitar,
And taught it justly to reply,
60 To all who question skilfully,
In language gentle as thine own;
Whispering in enamored tone
Sweet oracles of woods and dells,
And summer winds in sylvan cells;
65 For it had learned all harmonies
Of the plains and of the skies,
Of the forests and the mountains,
And the many-voicèd fountains;
The clearest echoes of the hills,
70 The softest notes of falling rills,
The melodies of birds and bees,
The murmuring of summer seas,
And pattering rain, and breathing dew,
And airs of evening; and it knew
75 That seldom-heard mysterious sound,
Which, driven on its diurnal round,
As it floats through boundless day,
Our world enkindles on its way.—
All this it knows but will not tell
80 To those who cannot question well
The Spirit that inhabits it;
It talks according to the wit
Of its companions; and no more
Is heard than has been felt before,
85 By those who tempt it to betray
These secrets of an elder day:
But, sweetly as its answers will
Flatter hands of perfect skill,
It keeps its highest, holiest tone
90 For our belovèd Jane alone.

TO JANE[1]
1822   1832-39

The keen stars were twinkling,
And the fair moon was rising among them,
Dear Jane!
The guitar was tinkling,
5 But the notes were not sweet till you sung
them
Again.

As the moon's soft splendor
O'er the faint cold starlight of heaven
Is thrown,

[1] Jane Williams, the wife of Edward Williams.
Both were warm friends of the Shelleys.
[2] That is, in the interval between the old moon
and the new.

[1] See previous poem and n. 1.

10 So your voice most tender
　To the strings without soul had then given
　　Its own.

The stars will awaken,
Though the moon sleep a full hour later,
15 　Tonight;
No leaf will be shaken
Whilst the dews of your melody scatter
　　Delight.

Though the sound overpowers,
20 Sing again, with your dear voice revealing
　A tone
Of some world far from ours,
Where music and moonlight and feeling
　　Are one.

From CHARLES THE FIRST
1822　　　1824

A Widow Bird Sate Mourning for Her Love

A widow bird sate mourning for her love
Upon a wintry bough;
The frozen wind crept on above,
The freezing stream below.

5 There was no leaf upon the forest bare,
No flower upon the ground,
And little motion in the air
Except the mill-wheel's sound.

A DIRGE
1822　　　1824

Rough wind, that moanest loud
　Grief too sad for song;
Wild wind, when sullen cloud
　Knells all the night long;
5 Sad storm, whose tears are vain,
Bare woods, whose branches strain,
Deep caves and dreary main,—
　Wail, for the world's wrong!

LINES
1822　　　1862

We meet not as we parted,
　We feel more than all may see;
My bosom is heavy-hearted,
　And thine full of doubt for me:—
5 　One moment has bound the free.

That moment is gone forever,
　Like lightning that flashed and died,
Like a snowflake upon the river,

Like a sunbeam upon the tide,
10 　Which the dark shadows hide.[1]

That moment from time was singled
　As the first of a life of pain;
The cup of its joy was mingled—
　Delusion too sweet though vain!
15 Too sweet to be mine again.

Sweet lips, could my heart have hidden
　That its life was crushed by you,
Ye would not have then forbidden
　The death which a heart so true
20 Sought in your briny dew.

*　*　*　*　*　*

Methinks too little cost
For a moment so found, so lost!

THE ISLE
1822　　　1824

There was a little lawny islet
By anemone and violet,
　Like mosaic, paven;
And its roof was flowers and leaves
5 Which the summer's breath enweaves,
Where nor sun nor showers nor breeze
Pierce the pines and tallest trees,
　Each a gem engraven;—
Girt by many an azure wave
10 With which the clouds and mountains pave
A lake's blue chasm.

From A DEFENSE OF POETRY
1821　　　1840

According to one mode of regarding those
two classes of mental action which are called
reason and imagination, the former may be
considered as mind contemplating the rela-
5 tions borne by one thought to another, however produced, and the latter as mind acting
upon those thoughts so as to color them with
its own light, and composing from them, as
from elements, other thoughts, each contain-
10 ing within itself the principle of its own
integrity. The one is the τὸ ποιεῖν, or the
principle of synthesis, and has for its object
those forms which are common to universal
nature and existence itself; the other is the
15 τὸ λογίζειν, or principle of analysis, and its
action regards the relations of things simply
as relations; considering thoughts not in
their integral unity, but as the algebraical
representations which conduct to certain

[1] See Burns's *Tam O'Shanter*, 59-66 (p. 223).

general results. Reason is the enumeration of quantities already known; imagination is the perception of the value of those quantities, both separately and as a whole. Reason respects the differences, and imagination the similitudes of things. Reason is to imagination as the instrument to the agent, as the body to the spirit, as the shadow to the substance.

Poetry, in a general sense, may be defined to be "the expression of the imagination"; and poetry is connate with the origin of man. Man is an instrument over which a series of external and internal impressions are driven, like the alternations of an ever-changing wind over an Æolian lyre, which move it by their motion to ever-changing melody. But there is a principle within the human being, and perhaps within all sentient beings, which acts otherwise than in a lyre, and produces not melody alone, but harmony, by an internal adjustment of the sounds and motions thus excited to the impressions which excite them. It is as if the lyre could accommodate its chords to the motions of that which strikes them, in a determined proportion of sound; even as the musician can accommodate his voice to the sound of the lyre. A child at play by itself will express its delight by its voice and motions; and every inflection of tone and every gesture will bear exact relation to a corresponding antitype in the pleasurable impressions which awakened it; it will be the reflected image of that impression; and as the lyre trembles and sounds after the wind has died away, so the child seeks, by prolonging in its voice and motions, the duration of the effect, to prolong also a consciousness of the cause. In relation to the objects which delight a child, these expressions are what poetry is to higher objects. The savage (for the savage is to ages what the child is to years) expresses the emotions produced in him by surrounding objects in a similar manner; and language and gesture, together with plastic or pictorial imitation, become the image of the combined effect of those objects and his apprehension of them. Man in society, with all his passions and his pleasures, next becomes the object of the passions and pleasures of man; an additional class of emotions produces an augmented treasure of expression; and language, gesture, and the imitative arts become at once the representation and the medium, the pencil and the picture, the chisel and the statue, the chord and the harmony. The social sympathies, or those laws from which, as from its elements, so-

ciety results, begin to develop themselves from the moment that two human beings co-exist; the future is contained within the present as the plant within the seed; and equality, diversity, unity, contrast, mutual dependence, become the principles alone capable of affording the motives according to which the will of a social being is determined to action, inasmuch as he is social; and constitute pleasure in sensation, virtue in sentiment, beauty in art, truth in reasoning, and love in the intercourse of kind. Hence men, even in the infancy of society, observe a certain order in their words and actions, distinct from that of the objects and the impressions represented by them, all expression being subject to the laws of that from which it proceeds. But let us dismiss those more general considerations which might involve an inquiry into the principles of society itself, and restrict our view to the manner in which the imagination is expressed upon its forms.

In the youth of the world, men dance and sing and imitate natural objects, observing in these actions, as in all others, a certain rhythm or order. And, although all men observe a similar, they observe not the same order in the motions of the dance, in the melody of the song, in the combinations of language, in the series of their imitations of natural objects. For there is a certain order or rhythm belonging to each of these classes of mimetic representation, from which the hearer and the spectator receive an intenser and purer pleasure than from any other; the sense of an approximation to this order has been called taste by modern writers. Every man, in the infancy of art, observes an order which approximates more or less closely to that from which this highest delight results; but the diversity is not sufficiently marked as that its gradations should be sensible, except in those instances where the predominance of this faculty of approximation to the beautiful (for so we may be permitted to name the relation between this highest pleasure and its cause) is very great. Those in whom it exists to excess are poets, in the most universal sense of the word; and the pleasure resulting from the manner in which they express the influence of society or nature upon their own minds, communicates itself to others, and gathers a sort of reduplication from the community. Their language is vitally metaphorical; that is, it marks the before unapprehended relations of things and perpetuates their apprehension, until words, which represent them, become, through time, signs for portions or classes of thought instead of pictures of integral thoughts; and then, if no new poets should arise to create afresh the associations which have been thus disorganized, language will be dead to all the nobler purposes of human intercourse. These similitudes or relations are finely said by Lord Bacon to be "the same footsteps of nature impressed upon the various subjects of the world"[1]—and he considers the faculty which perceives them as the storehouse of axioms common to all knowledge. In the infancy of society every author is necessarily a poet, because language itself is poetry; and to be a poet is to apprehend the true and the beautiful, in a word, the good which exists in the relation subsisting, first between existence and perception, and secondly between perception and expression. Every original language near to its source is in itself the chaos of a cyclic poem;[2] the copiousness of lexicography and the distinctions of grammar are the works of a later age, and are merely the catalogue and the forms of the creations of poetry.

But poets, or those who imagine and express this indestructible order, are not only the authors of language and of music, of the dance, and architecture, and statuary, and painting: they are the institutors of laws, and the founders of civil society, and the inventors of the arts of life, and the teachers who draw into a certain propinquity with the beautiful and the true that partial apprehension of the agencies of the invisible world which is called religion. Hence all original religions are allegorical, or susceptible of allegory, and, like Janus, have a double face of false and true. Poets, according to the circumstances of the age and nation in which they appeared, were called, in the earlier epochs of the world, legislators or prophets; a poet essentially comprises and unites both these characters. For he not only beholds intensely the present as it is, and discovers those laws according to which present things ought to be ordered, but he beholds the future in the present, and his thoughts are the germs of the flower and the fruit of latest time. Not that I assert poets to be prophets in the gross sense of the word, or that they can foretell the form as surely as they foreknow the spirit of events; such is the pretence of superstition, which would make poetry an attribute of prophecy,

rather than prophecy an attribute of poetry. A poet participates in the eternal, the infinite, and the one; as far as relates to his conceptions, time and place and number are not. The grammatical forms which express the moods of time, and the difference of persons, and the distinction of place, are convertible with respect to the highest poetry without injuring it as poetry; and the choruses of Æschylus, and the *Book of Job,* and Dante's *Paradise,* would afford, more than any other writings, examples of this fact, if the limits of this essay did not forbid citation. The creations of music, sculpture, and painting are illustrations still more decisive.

Language, color, form, and religious and civil habits of action, are all the instruments and materials of poetry; they may be called poetry by that figure of speech which considers the effect as a synonym of the cause. But poetry in a more restricted sense expresses those arrangements of language, and especially metrical language, which are created by that imperial faculty whose throne is curtained within the invisible nature of man. And this springs from the nature itself of language, which is a more direct representation of the actions and passions of our internal being, and is susceptible of more various and delicate combinations, than color, form, or motion, and is more plastic and obedient to the control of that faculty of which it is the creation. For language is arbitrarily produced by the imagination, and has relation to thoughts alone; but all other materials, instruments, and conditions of art have relations among each other, which limit and interpose between conception and expression. The former is as a mirror which reflects, the latter as a cloud which enfeebles, the light of which both are mediums of communication. Hence the fame of sculptors, painters, and musicians, although the intrinsic powers of the great masters of these arts may yield in no degree to that of those who have employed language as the hieroglyphic of their thoughts, has never equalled that of poets in the restricted sense of the term; as two performers of equal skill will produce unequal effects from a guitar and a harp. The fame of legislators and founders of religions, so long as their institutions last, alone seem to exceed that of poets in the restricted sense; but it can scarcely be a question, whether, if we deduct the celebrity which their flattery of the gross opinions of the vulgar usually conciliates, together with that which

---

[1] *"De Augment. Scient.,* cap. 1, lib. iii"—Shelley. See *The Advancement of Learning,* 2, 5, 3.

[2] A poem relating to an epic cycle.

belonged to them in their higher character of poets, any excess will remain.

We have thus circumscribed the word *poetry* within the limits of that art which is the most familiar and the most perfect expression of the faculty itself. It is necessary, however, to make the circle still narrower, and to determine the distinction between measured and unmeasured language; for the popular division into prose and verse is inadmissible in accurate philosophy.

Sounds as well as thoughts have relation both between each other and towards that which they represent, and a perception of the order of those relations has always been found connected with a perception of the order of the relations of thoughts. Hence the language of poets has ever affected a sort of uniform and harmonious recurrence of sound, without which it were not poetry, and which is scarcely less indispensable to the communication of its influence than the words themselves without reference to that peculiar order. Hence the vanity of translation; it were as wise to cast a violet into a crucible that you might discover the formal principles of its color and odor, as to seek to transfuse from one language into another the creations of a poet. The plant must spring again from its seed, or it will bear no flower—and this is the burthen of the curse of Babel.[1]

An observation of the regular mode of the recurrence of harmony in the language of poetical minds, together with its relation to music, produced metre, or a certain system of traditional forms of harmony and language. Yet it is by no means essential that a poet should accommodate his language to this traditional form, so that the harmony, which is its spirit, be observed. The practice is indeed convenient and popular, and to be preferred especially in such composition as includes much action; but every great poet must inevitably innovate upon the example of his predecessors in the exact structure of his peculiar versification. The distinction between poets and prose writers is a vulgar error. The distinction between philosophers and poets has been anticipated. Plato was essentially a poet—the truth and splendor of his imagery, and the melody of his language, are the most intense that it is possible to conceive. He rejected the harmony of the epic, dramatic, and lyrical forms, because he sought to kindle a harmony in thoughts divested of shape and action, and he forebore to invent any

* See *Genesis,* 11:6-9.

regular plan of rhythm which would include, under determinate forms, the varied pauses of his style. Cicero sought to imitate the cadence of his periods, but with little success. Lord Bacon was a poet.[1] His language has a sweet and majestic rhythm which satisfies the sense, no less than the almost superhuman wisdom of his philosophy satisfies the intellect; it is a strain which distends and then bursts the circumference of the reader's mind, and pours itself forth together with it into the universal element with which it has perpetual sympathy. All the authors of revolutions in opinion are not only necessarily poets as they are inventors, nor even as their words unveil the permanent analogy of things by images which participate in the life of truth; but as their periods are harmonious and rhythmical, and contain in themselves the elements of verse, being the echo of the eternal music. Nor are those supreme poets, who have employed traditional forms of rhythm on account of the form and action of their subjects, less capable of perceiving and teaching the truth of things, than those who have omitted that form. Shakespeare, Dante, and Milton (to confine ourselves to modern writers) are philosophers of the very loftiest power.

A poem is the very image of life expressed in its eternal truth. There is this difference between a story and a poem, that a story is a catalogue of detached facts, which have no other connection than time, place, circumstance, cause, and effect; the other is the creation of actions according to the unchangeable forms of human nature, as existing in the mind of the creator, which is itself the image of all other minds. The one is partial, and applies only to a definite period of time, and a certain combination of events which can never again recur; the other is universal, and contains within itself the germ of a relation to whatever motives or actions have place in the possible varieties of human nature. Time, which destroys the beauty and the use of the story of particular facts, stripped of the poetry which should invest them, augments that of poetry, and forever develops new and wonderful applications of the eternal truth which it contains. Hence epitomes have been called the moths of just history;[2] they eat out the poetry of it. A story of particular facts is

---

[1] "See the *Filum Labyrinthi,* and the *Essay on Death,* particularly."—Shelley.
[2] See Bacon's *De Augmentis Scientiarum,* 2, 6; and *The Advancement of Learning,* 2, 2, 4.

as a mirror which obscures and distorts that which should be beautiful; poetry is a mirror which makes beautiful that which is distorted.

The parts of a composition may be poetical, without the composition as a whole being a poem. A single sentence may be considered as a whole, though it may be found in the midst of a series of unassimilated portions; a single word even may be a spark of inextinguishable thought. And thus all the great historians, Herodotus, Plutarch, Livy, were poets; and although the plan of these writers, especially that of Livy, restrained them from developing this faculty in its highest degree, they made copious and ample amends for their subjection, by filling all the interstices of their subjects with living images.

Having determined what is poetry, and who are poets, let us proceed to estimate its effects upon society.

Poetry is ever accompanied with pleasure: all spirits on which it falls open themselves to receive the wisdom which is mingled with its delight. In the infancy of the world, neither poets themselves nor their auditors are fully aware of the excellency of poetry, for it acts in a divine and unapprehended manner, beyond and above consciousness; and it is reserved for future generations to contemplate and measure the mighty cause and effect in all the strength and splendor of their union. Even in modern times, no living poet ever arrived at the fulness of his fame; the jury which sits in judgment upon a poet, belonging as he does to all time, must be composed of his peers; it must be impanelled by Time from the selectest of the wise of many generations. A poet is a nightingale, who sits in darkness and sings to cheer its own solitude with sweet sounds; his auditors are as men entranced by the melody of an unseen musician, who feel that they are moved and softened, yet know not whence or why. The poems of Homer and his contemporaries were the delight of infant Greece; they were the elements of that social system which is the column upon which all succeeding civilization has reposed. Homer embodied the ideal perfection of his age in human character; nor can we doubt that those who read his verses were awakened to an ambition of becoming like to Achilles, Hector, and Ulysses; the truth and beauty of friendship, patriotism, and persevering devotion to an object, were unveiled to their depths in these immortal creations; the sentiments of the auditors must have

been refined and enlarged by a sympathy with such great and lovely impersonations, until from admiring they imitated, and from imitation they identified themselves with the objects of their admiration. Nor let it be objected that these characters are remote from moral perfection, and that they are by no means to be considered as edifying patterns for general imitation. Every epoch, under names more or less specious, has deified its peculiar errors; Revenge is the naked idol of the worship of a semi-barbarous age; and Self-Deceit is the veiled image of unknown evil, before which luxury and satiety lie prostrate. But a poet considers the vices of his contemporaries as the temporary dress in which his creations must be arrayed, and which cover without concealing the eternal proportions of their beauty. An epic or dramatic personage is understood to wear them around his soul, as he may the ancient armor or modern uniform around his body, whilst it is easy to conceive a dress more graceful than either. The beauty of the internal nature can not be so far concealed by its accidental vesture, but that the spirit of its form shall communicate itself to the very disguise, and indicate the shape it hides from the manner in which it is worn. A majestic form and graceful motions will express themselves through the most barbarous and tasteless costume. Few poets of the highest class have chosen to exhibit the beauty of their conceptions in its naked truth and splendor; and it is doubtful whether the alloy of costume, habit, etc. be not necessary to temper this planetary music[1] for mortal ears.

The whole objection, however, of the immorality of poetry rests upon a misconception of the manner in which poetry acts to produce the moral improvement of man. Ethical science arranges the elements which poetry has created, and propounds schemes and proposes examples of civil and domestic life; nor is it for want of admirable doctrines that men hate, and despise, and censure, and deceive, and subjugate one another. But poetry acts in another and diviner manner. It awakens and enlarges the mind itself by rendering it the receptacle of a thousand unapprehended combinations of thought. Poetry lifts the veil from the hidden beauty of the world, and makes familiar objects be as if they were not familiar; it reproduces all that it represents, and

[1] A reference to the belief of the ancients that the movement of the celestial spheres produced music too ethereal for human ears.

the impersonations clothed in its Elysian light stand thenceforward in the minds of those who have once contemplated them, as memorials of that gentle and exalted content which extends itself over all thoughts and actions with which it co-exists. The great secret of morals is love; or a going out of our own nature, and an identification of ourselves with the beautiful which exists in thought, action, or person, not our own. A man, to be greatly good, must imagine intensely and comprehensively; he must put himself in the place of another and of many others; the pains and pleasures of his species must become his own. The great instrument of moral good is the imagination; and poetry administers to the effect by acting upon the cause. Poetry enlarges the circumference of the imagination by replenishing it with thoughts of ever new delight, which have the power of attracting and assimilating to their own nature all other thoughts, and which form new intervals and interstices whose void forever craves fresh food. Poetry strengthens the faculty which is the organ of the moral nature of man, in the same manner as exercise strengthens a limb. A poet therefore would do ill to embody his own conceptions of right and wrong, which are usually those of his place and time, in his poetical creations, which participate in neither. By this assumption of the inferior office of interpreting the effect, in which perhaps after all he might acquit himself but imperfectly, he would resign a glory in the participation of the cause. There was little danger that Homer, or any of the eternal poets, should have so far misunderstood themselves as to have abdicated this throne of their widest dominion. Those in whom the poetical faculty, though great, is less intense, as Euripides, Lucan, Tasso, Spenser, have frequently affected a moral aim, and the effect of their poetry is diminished in exact proportion to the degree in which they compel us to advert to this purpose.

. . . . . .

The functions of the poetical faculty are two-fold: by one it creates new materials of knowledge, and power, and pleasure; by the other it engenders in the mind a desire to reproduce and arrange them according to a certain rhythm and order which may be called the beautiful and the good. The cultivation of poetry is never more to be desired than at periods when, from an excess of the selfish and calculating principle, the accumulation of the materials of external life exceed the quantity of the power of assimilating them to the internal laws of human nature. The body has then become too unwieldy for that which animates it.

Poetry is indeed something divine. It is at once the centre and circumference of knowledge; it is that which comprehends all science, and that to which all science must be referred. It is at the same time the root and blossom of all other systems of thought; it is that from which all spring, and that which adorns all; and that which, if blighted, denies the fruit and the seed, and withholds from the barren world the nourishment and the succession of the scions of the tree of life. It is the perfect and consummate surface and bloom of all things; it is as the odor and the color of the rose to the texture of the elements which compose it, as the form and splendor of unfaded beauty to the secrets of anatomy and corruption. What were virtue, love, patriotism, friendship; what were the scenery of this beautiful universe which we inhabit; what were our consolations on this side of the grave, and what were our aspirations beyond it,— if poetry did not ascend to bring light and fire from those eternal regions where the owl-winged faculty of calculation dare not ever soar? Poetry is not like reasoning, a power to be exerted according to the determination of the will. A man cannot say, "I will compose poetry." The greatest poet even cannot say it; for the mind in creation is as a fading coal, which some invisible influence, like an inconstant wind, awakens to transitory brightness; this power arises from within, like the color of a flower which fades and changes as it is developed, and the conscious portions of our nature are unprophetic either of its approach or its departure. Could this influence be durable in its original purity and force, it is impossible to predict the greatness of the results; but when composition begins, inspiration is already on the decline, and the most glorious poetry that has ever been communicated to the world is probably a feeble shadow of the original conceptions of the poet. I appeal to the greatest poets of the present day whether it is not an error to assert that the finest passages of poetry are produced by labor and study. The toil and the delay recommended by critics can be justly interpreted to mean no more than a careful observation of the inspired moments, and an artificial connection of the spaces between their suggestions by the intertexture of conventional expressions—a necessity only imposed by the limitedness of the poetical faculty itself; for Milton conceived the *Paradise Lost* as a whole before he executed it in portions. We have his own authority also for the muse having "dictated" to him the "unpremeditated song."[1] And let this be an answer to those who would allege the fifty-six various readings of the first line of the *Orlando Furioso*. Compositions so produced are to poetry what mosaic is to painting. The instinct and intuition of the poetical faculty is still more observable in the plastic and pictorial arts: a great statue or picture grows under the power of the artist as a child in the mother's womb; and the very mind which directs the hands in formation, is incapable of accounting to itself for the origin, the gradations, or the media of the process.

Poetry is the record of the best and happiest moments of the happiest and best minds. We are aware of evanescent visitations of thought and feeling, sometimes associated with place or person, sometimes regarding our own mind alone, and always arising unforeseen and departing unbidden, but elevating and delightful beyond all expression; so that even in the desire and the regret they leave, there cannot but be pleasure, participating as it does in the nature of its object. It is, as it were, the interpenetration of a diviner nature through our own; but its footsteps are like those of a wind over the sea, which the morning calm erases, and whose traces remain only, as on the wrinkled sand which paves it. These and corresponding conditions of being are experienced principally by those of the most delicate sensibility and the most enlarged imagination; and the state of mind produced by them is at war with every base desire. The enthusiasm of virtue, love, patriotism, and friendship is essentially linked with such emotions; and whilst they last, self appears as what it is, an atom to a universe. Poets are not only subject to these experiences as spirits of the most refined organization, but they can color all that they combine with the evanescent hues of this ethereal world; a word, a trait in the representation of a scene or a passion will touch the enchanted chord, and reanimate, in those who have ever experienced these emotions, the sleeping, the cold, the buried image of the past. Poetry thus makes immortal all that is best and most beautiful in the world; it arrests the vanishing appa-

ritions which haunt the interlunations[1] of life, and veiling them or in language or in form, sends them forth among mankind, bearing sweet news of kindred joy to those with whom their sisters abide—abide, because there is no portal of expression from the caverns of the spirit which they inhabit into the universe of things. Poetry redeems from decay the visitations of the divinity in man.

Poetry turns all things to loveliness; it exalts the beauty of that which is most beautiful, and it adds beauty to that which is most deformed; it marries exultation and horror, grief and pleasure, eternity and change; it subdues to union under its light yoke all irreconcilable things. It transmutes all that it touches, and every form moving within the radiance of its presence is changed by wondrous sympathy to an incarnation of the spirit which it breathes; its secret alchemy turns to potable[2] gold the poisonous waters which flow from death through life; it strips the veil of familiarity from the world, and lays bare the naked and sleeping beauty which is the spirit of its forms.

All things exist as they are perceived: at least in relation to the percipient.

The mind is its own place, and in itself
Can make a Heaven of Hell, a Hell of Heaven.[3]

But poetry defeats the curse which binds us to be subjected to the accident of surrounding impressions. And whether it spreads its own figured curtain, or withdraws life's dark veil from before the scene of things, it equally creates for us a being within our being. It makes us the inhabitant of a world to which the familiar world is a chaos. It reproduces the common universe of which we are portions and percipients, and it purges from our inward sight the film of familiarity which obscures from us the wonder of our being. It compels us to feel that which we perceive, and to imagine that which we know. It creates anew the universe, after it has been annihilated in our minds by the recurrence of impressions blunted by reiteration. It justifies the bold and true words of Tasso: *Non merita nome di creatore, se non Iddio ed il Poeta*.[4]

A poet, as he is the author to others of the

---

[1] *Paradise Lost*, 9, 21-24. See also Shelley's *To a Skylark*, 5 (p. 730).

[1] dark periods (literally, the interval between the old moon and the new)
[2] suitable for drinking
[3] *Paradise Lost*, 1, 254-5.
[4] None merits the name of creator, except God and the poet.

highest wisdom, pleasure, virtue, and glory, so he ought personally to be the happiest, the best, the wisest, and the most illustrious of men. As to his glory, let time be challenged to declare whether the fame of any other institutor of human life be comparable to that of a poet. That he is the wisest, the happiest, and the best, inasmuch as he is a poet, is equally incontrovertible; the greatest poets have been men of the most spotless virtue, of the most consummate prudence, and, if we would look into the interior of their lives, the most fortunate of men; and the exceptions, as they regard those who possessed the poetic faculty in a high yet inferior degree, will be found on consideration to confirm rather than destroy the rule. Let us for a moment stoop to the arbitration of popular breath, and usurping and uniting in our own persons the incompatible characters of accuser, witness, judge, and executioner, let us decide without trial, testimony, or form, that certain motives of those who are "there sitting where we dare not soar,"[1] are reprehensible. Let us assume that Homer was a drunkard, that Virgil was a flatterer, that Horace was a coward, that Tasso was a madman, that Lord Bacon was a peculator, that Raphael was a libertine, that Spenser was a poet laureate. It is inconsistent with this division of our subject to cite living poets, but posterity has done ample justice to the great names now referred to. Their errors have been weighed and found to have been dust in the balance;[2] if their sins were as scarlet, they are now white as snow,[3] they have been washed in the blood of the mediator and redeemer,[4] Time. Observe in what a ludicrous chaos the imputations of real or fictitious crime have been confused in the contemporary calumnies against poetry and poets; consider how little is as it appears—or appears as it is; look to your own motives, and judge not, lest ye be judged.[5]

Poetry, as has been said, differs in this respect from logic, that it is not subject to the control of the active powers of the mind, and that its birth and recurrence have no necessary connection with the consciousness or will. It is presumptuous to determine that these are the necessary conditions of all mental causation, when mental conditions are experienced insusceptible of being referred to them. The frequent recurrence of the poetical power, it is obvious to suppose, may produce in the mind a habit of order and harmony correlative with its own nature and with its effects upon other minds. But in the intervals of inspiration—and they may be frequent without being durable—a poet becomes a man, and is abandoned to the sudden reflux of the influences under which others habitually live. But as he is more delicately organized than other men, and sensible to pain and pleasure, both his own and that of others, in a degree unknown to them, he will avoid the one and pursue the other with an ardor proportioned to this difference. And he renders himself obnoxious to calumny when he neglects to observe the circumstances under which these objects of universal pursuit and flight have disguised themselves in one another's garments.

But there is nothing necessarily evil in this error, and thus cruelty, envy, revenge, avarice, and the passions purely evil, have never formed any portion of the popular imputations on the lives of poets.

I have thought it most favorable to the cause of truth to set down these remarks according to the order in which they were suggested to my mind, by a consideration of the subject itself, instead of observing the formality of a polemical reply;[1] but if the view which they contain be just, they will be found to involve a refutation of the arguers against poetry, so far at least as regards the first division of the subject. I can readily conjecture what should have moved the gall of some learned and intelligent writers who quarrel with certain versifiers; I, like them, confess myself unwilling to be stunned by the Theseids of the hoarse Codri of the day. Bavius and Mævius undoubtedly are, as they ever were, insufferable persons. But it belongs to a philosophical critic to distinguish rather than confound.

The first part of these remarks has related to poetry in its elements and principles; and it has been shown, as well as the narrow limits assigned them would permit, that what is called poetry in a restricted sense, has a common source with all other forms of order and of beauty according to which the materials of human life are susceptible of being arranged, and which is poetry in a universal sense.

The second part[2] will have for its object an application of these principles to the present state of the cultivation of poetry,

---

[1] *Paradise Lost*, 4, 829.
[2] See *Daniel*, 5 :27 ; and *Isaiah*, 40 :15.
[3] See *Isaiah*, 1 :18.
[4] See *Hebrews*, 9 :15.
[5] See *Matthew*, 7 :1.

[1] To Peacock's *The Four Ages of Poetry*, which contained a rather narrow view of what constitutes poetry.
[2] This was never written.

and a defense of the attempt to idealize the modern forms of manners and opinions, and compel them into a subordination to the imaginative and creative faculty. For the literature of England, an energetic development of which has ever preceded or accompanied a great and free development of the national will, has arisen as it were from a new birth. In spite of the low-thoughted envy which would undervalue contemporary merit, our own will be a memorable age in intellectual achievements, and we live among such philosophers and poets as surpass beyond comparison any who have appeared since the last national struggle for civil and religious liberty. The most unfailing herald, companion, and follower of the awakening of a great people to work a beneficial change in opinion or institution, is poetry. At such periods there is an accumulation of the power of communicating and receiving intense and impassioned conceptions respecting man and nature. The persons in whom this power resides may often, as far as regards many portions of their nature, have little apparent correspondence with that spirit of good of which they are the ministers. But even whilst they deny and abjure, they are yet compelled to serve the power which is seated on the throne of their own soul. It is impossible to read the compositions of the most celebrated writers of the present day without being startled with the electric life which burns within their words. They measure the circumference and sound the depths of human nature with a comprehensive and all-penetrating spirit, and they are themselves perhaps the most sincerely astonished at its manifestations; for it is less their spirit than the spirit of the age. Poets are the hierophants[1] of an unapprehended inspiration; the mirrors of the gigantic shadows which futurity casts upon the present; the words which express what they understand not; the trumpets which sing to battle and feel not what they inspire; the influence which is moved not, but moves. Poets are the unacknowledged legislators of the world.

John Keats 1795-1821

IMITATION OF SPENSER
1814   1817

Now Morning from her orient chamber
came,
And her first footsteps touch'd a verdant hill;

[1] high priests

Crowning its lawny crest with amber
flame,
Silv'ring the untainted gushes of its
rill;
5 Which, pure from mossy beds, did down
distill,
And after parting beds of simple flowers,
By many streams a little lake did fill,
Which round its marge reflected woven
bowers,
And, in its middle space, a sky that never
lowers.

10 There the kingfisher saw his plumage
bright
Vying with fish of brilliant dye below;
Whose silken fins, and golden scales'
light
Cast upward, through the waves, a ruby
glow:
There saw the swan his neck of arched
snow,
15 And oar'd himself along with majesty;
Sparkled his jetty eyes; his feet did
show
Beneath the waves like Afric's ebony,
And on his back a fay reclined voluptuously.

Ah! could I tell the wonders of an isle
20 That in that fairest lake had placed
been,
I could e'en Dido of her grief[1] beguile;
Or rob from aged Lear his bitter teen:[2]
For sure so fair a place was never seen,

Of all that ever charm'd romantic eye:
25 It seem'd an emerald in the silver sheen
Of the bright waters; or as when on
high,
Through clouds of fleecy white, laughs the
cœrulean sky.

And all around it dipp'd luxuriously
Slopings of verdure through the glossy
tide,
30 Which, as it were in gentle amity,
Rippled delighted up the flowery side;
As if to glean the ruddy tears, it tried,
Which fell profusely from the rose-tree
stem!
Haply it was the workings of its pride,
35 In strife to throw upon the shore a gem
Outvying all the buds in Flora's diadem.

*   *   *   *   *   *

[1] For Æneas, when he left her for the new home which the gods had promised him. See the *Æneid*, 4, 279 ff.
[2] sorrow; pain

TO BYRON
1814   1848

Byron! how sweetly sad thy melody!
Attuning still the soul to tenderness,
As if soft Pity, with unusual stress,
Had touch'd her plaintive lute, and thou,
    being by,
5 Hadst caught the tones, nor suffer'd them
    to die.
O'ershadowing sorrow doth not make thee
    less
Delightful: thou thy griefs dost dress
With a bright halo, shining beamily,
As when a cloud the golden moon doth
    veil,
10 Its sides are ting'd with a resplendent
    glow,
Through the dark robe oft amber rays
    prevail,
And like fair veins in sable marble flow;
Still warble, dying swan![1] still tell the tale,
The enchanting tale, the tale of pleasing
    woe.

TO CHATTERTON
1815   1848

O Chatterton! how very sad thy fate![2]
Dear child of sorrow—son of misery!
How soon the film of death obscur'd that
    eye,
Whence Genius mildly flash'd, and high
    debate.
5 How soon that voice, majestic and elate,
Melted in dying numbers! Oh! how nigh
Was night to thy fair morning. Thou didst
    die
A half-blown flow'ret which cold blasts
    amate.[3]
But this is past: thou art among the stars
10 Of highest Heaven: to the rolling spheres
Thou sweetly singest: naught thy hymning
    mars,
Above the ingrate world and human fears.
On earth the good man base detraction bars
From thy fair name, and waters it with
    tears.

WOMAN! WHEN I BEHOLD THEE
FLIPPANT, VAIN
1816   1817

Woman! when I behold thee flippant, vain,
Inconstant, childish, proud, and full of
    fancies;
Without that modest softening that en-
    hances

---

[1] The swan was said to sing melodiously when
    about to die.
[2] Chatterton committed suicide in a fit of
    despondency, when seventeen years of age.
    See Shelley's *Adonais*, 45 (p. 762).
[3] subdue; dishearten

The downcast eye, repentant of the pain
5 That its mild light creates to heal again:
    E'en then, elate, my spirit leaps, and
        prances,
    E'en then my soul with exultation
        dances
For that to love, so long, I've dormant
    lain:
But when I see thee meek, and kind, and
    tender,
10   Heavens! how desperately do I adore
Thy winning graces;—to be thy defender
I hotly burn—to be a Calidore
A very Red Cross Knight—a stout Lean-
    der—
    Might I be loved by thee like these of
        yore.

15 Light feet, dark violet eyes, and parted
    hair;
    Soft dimpled hands, white neck, and
        creamy breast,
    Are things on which the dazzled senses
        rest
Till the fond, fixed eyes, forget they stare.
From such fine pictures, heavens! I can-
    not dare
20   To turn my admiration, though unpos-
        sess'd
    They be of what is worthy,—though not
        drest
In lovely modesty, and virtues rare.
Yet these I leave as thoughtless as a
    lark;
    These lures I straight forget,—e'en ere
        I dine,
25 Or thrice my palate moisten: but when I
    mark
    Such charms with mild intelligences
        shine,
My ear is open like a greedy shark,
    To catch the tunings of a voice divine.

Ah! who can e'er forget so fair a being?
30   Who can forget her half-retiring sweets?
    God! she is like a milk-white lamb that
        bleats
For man's protection. Surely the All-
    seeing,
Who joys to see us with his gifts agreeing,
    Will never give him pinions, who in-
        treats
35   Such innocence to ruin,—who vilely
        cheats
A dove-like bosom. In truth there is no
    freeing
One's thoughts from such a beauty; when
    I hear
A lay that once I saw her hand awake,

Her form seems floating palpable, and
   near;
10 Had I e'er seen her from an arbor take
A dewy flower, oft would that hand appear,
And o'er my eyes the trembling moisture shake.

WRITTEN ON THE DAY THAT MR. LEIGH HUNT LEFT PRISON[1]
1815   1817

What though, for showing truth to flatter'd
   state,
Kind Hunt was shut in prison, yet has he,
In his immortal spirit, been as free
As the sky-searching lark, and as elate.
5 Minion of grandeur! think you he did
   wait?
Think you he naught but prison walls did
   see,
Till, so unwilling, thou unturn'dst the key?
Ah, no! far happier, nobler was his fate!
In Spenser's halls he stray'd, and bowers
   fair,
10 Culling enchanted flowers; and he flew
With daring Milton through the fields of
   air:
To regions of his own his genius true
Took happy flights. Who shall his fame
   impair
When thou art dead, and all thy wretched
   crew?

TO A YOUNG LADY WHO SENT ME A LAUREL CROWN
1816   1848

Fresh morning gusts have blown away all
   fear
From my glad bosom,—now from gloomi-
   ness
I mount forever—not an atom less
Than the proud laurel shall content my
   bier.
5 No! by the eternal stars! or why sit here
In the Sun's eye, and 'gainst my temples
   press
Apollo's very leaves,[2] woven to bless
By thy white fingers and thy spirit clear.
Lo! who dares say, "Do this?" Who
   dares call down
10 My will from its high purpose? Who say,
   "Stand,"
Or "Go"? This mighty moment I would
   frown

[1] Hunt had been imprisoned for an unfriendly characterization of the Prince Regent, published in *The Examiner*, 1812. He was released on Feb. 3, 1815. See Hunt's *To Hampstead* (p. 893).
[2] The laurel, which was sacred to Apollo.

On abject Cæsars—not the stoutest band
Of mailed heroes should tear off my crown:
Yet would I kneel and kiss thy gentle
   hand!

HOW MANY BARDS GILD THE LAPSES OF TIME
1816   1817

How many bards gild the lapses of time!
A few of them have ever been the food
Of my delighted fancy,—I could brood
Over their beauties, earthly, or sublime:
5 And often, when I sit me down to rhyme,
These will in throngs before my mind in-
   trude:
But no confusion, no disturbance rude
Do they occasion; 'tis a pleasing chime.
So the unnumber'd sounds that evening
   store;
10 The songs of birds—the whisp'ring of the
   leaves—
The voice of waters—the great bell that
   heaves
With solemn sound,—and thousand others
   more,
That distance of recognizance bereaves,
Make pleasing music, and not wild uproar.

KEEN, FITFUL GUSTS ARE WHISP'RING HERE AND THERE
1816   1817

Keen, fitful gusts are whisp'ring here and
   there
Among the bushes half leafless, and dry;
The stars look very cold about the sky,
And I have many miles on foot to fare.
5 Yet feel I little of the cool bleak air,
Or of the dead leaves rustling drearily,
Or of these silver lamps that burn on high,
Or of the distance from home's pleasant
   lair:
For I am brimful of the friendliness
10 That in a little cottage[1] I have found;
Of fair-hair'd Milton's eloquent distress,
And all his love for gentle Lycid drown'd;
Of lovely Laura in her light green dress,
And faithful Petrarch gloriously crown'd.

ON FIRST LOOKING INTO CHAPMAN'S HOMER
1816   1816

Much have I travell'd in the realms of
   gold,
And many goodly states and kingdoms
   seen;
Round many western islands have I been
Which bards in fealty to Apollo hold.

[1] Leigh Hunt's home at Hampstead Heath.

5 Oft of one wide expanse had I been told
That deep-brow'd Homer ruled as his
    demesne;
Yet did I never breathe its pure serene
Till I heard Chapman speak out loud and
    bold:
Then felt I like some watcher of the skies
10 When a new planet swims into his ken;
Or like stout Cortez when with eagle eyes
He star'd at the Pacific[1]—and all his men
Look'd at each other with a wild surmise—
Silent, upon a peak in Darien.

AS FROM THE DARKENING GLOOM A
SILVER DOVE
1816   1876

As from the darkening gloom a silver dove
Upsoars, and darts into the eastern light,
On pinions that naught moves but pure
    delight,
So fled thy soul into the realms above,
5 Regions of peace and everlasting love;
Where happy spirits, crown'd with cir-
    clets bright
Of starry beam, and gloriously bedight,[2]
Taste the high joy none but the blest can
    prove.
There thou or joinest the immortal quire
10 In melodies that even Heaven fair
Fill with superior bliss, or, at desire
Of the omnipotent Father, cleav'st the air
On holy message sent — What pleasures
    higher?
Wherefore does any grief our joy impair?

SONNET TO SOLITUDE
1816   1816

O Solitude! if I must with thee dwell,
Let it not be among the jumbled heap
Of murky buildings; climb with me the
    steep,—
Nature's observatory,—whence the dell,
5 Its flowery slopes, its river's crystal swell
May seem a span; let me thy vigils keep
'Mongst boughs pavilion'd where the
    deer's swift leap
Startles the wild bee from the fox-glove
    bell.
But though I'll gladly trace[3] these scenes
    with thee,
10 Yet the sweet converse of an innocent
    mind,
Whose words are images of thoughts
    refin'd,
Is my soul's pleasure; and it sure must be

[1] Balboa, not Cortez, discovered the Pacific
    Ocean in 1513.
[2] adorned
[3] wander over

Almost the highest bliss of human-kind,
When to thy haunts two kindred spirits
    flee.

TO ONE WHO HAS BEEN LONG IN
CITY PENT[1]
1816   1817

To one who has been long in city pent,
'Tis very sweet to look into the fair
And open face of heaven,—to breathe a
    prayer
Full in the smile of the blue firmament.
5 Who is more happy, when, with heart's
    content,
Fatigued he sinks into some pleasant lair
Of wavy grass, and reads a debonair
And gentle tale of love and languishment?
Returning home at evening, with an ear
10 Catching the notes of Philomel,—an eye
Watching the sailing cloudlet's bright
    career,
He mourns that day so soon has glided by:
E'en like the passage of an angel's tear
That falls through the clear ether silently.

OH! HOW I LOVE ON A FAIR SUM-
MER'S EVE
1816   1848

Oh! how I love, on a fair summer's eve,
When streams of light pour down the
    golden west,
And on the balmy zephyrs tranquil rest
The silver clouds, far—far away to leave
5 All meaner thoughts, and take a sweet re-
    prieve
From little cares; to find, with easy quest,
A fragrant wild, with Nature's beauty
    drest,
And there into delight my soul deceive.
There warm my breast with patriotic lore,
10 Musing on Milton's fate—on Sydney's
    bier—
Till their stern forms before my mind
    arise:
Perhaps on wing of Poesy upsoar,
Full often dropping a melodious tear,
When some melodious sorrow spells mine
    eyes.

I STOOD TIPTOE UPON A LITTLE HILL
1816   1817

    Places of nestling green for Poets made
      —Leigh Hunt, *The Story of Rimini.*[2]

I stood tiptoe upon a little hill,
The air was cooling, and so very still
That the sweet buds which with a modest
    pride

[1] See *Paradise Lost,* 9, 445; also **Coleridge's**
    Frost at Midnight, 52 (p. 376).
[2] Canto 3, 290 (p. 893).

Pull droopingly, in slanting curve aside,
5 Their scantly-leav'd, and finely-tapering
    stems,
Had not yet lost those starry diadems
Caught from the early sobbing of the
    morn.
The clouds were pure and white as flocks
    new shorn,
And fresh from the clear brook; sweetly
    they slept
10 On the blue fields of heaven, and then
    there crept
A little noiseless noise among the leaves,
Born of the very sigh that silence heaves:
For not the faintest motion could be seen
Of all the shades that slanted o'er the
    green.
15 There was wide wand'ring for the greed-
    iest eye,
To peer about upon variety;
Far round the horizon's crystal air to
    skim,
And trace the dwindled edgings of its
    brim;
To picture out the quaint and curious
    bending
20 Of a fresh woodland alley, never ending;
Or by the bowery clefts, and leafy shelves,
Guess where the jaunty streams refresh
    themselves.
I gazed awhile, and felt as light and free
As though the fanning wings of Mercury
25 Had play'd upon my heels: I was light-
    hearted,
And many pleasures to my vision started;
So I straightway began to pluck a posey
Of luxuries bright, milky, soft, and rosy.

A bush of May flowers with the bees
    about them;
30 Ah, sure no tasteful nook would be with-
    out them;
And let a lush laburnum oversweep them,
And let long grass grow round the roots
    to keep them
Moist, cool, and green; and shade the vio-
    lets,
That they may bind the moss in leafy nets.

35 A filbert hedge with wild briar over-
    twined,
And clumps of woodbine taking the soft
    wind
Upon their summer thrones; there too
    should be
The frequent chequer of a youngling tree,
That with a score of light green brethren
    shoots
40 From the quaint mossiness of aged roots;

Round which is heard a spring-head of
    clear waters
Babbling so wildly of its lovely daughters
The spreading blue-bells: it may haply
    mourn
That such fair clusters should be rudely
    torn
45 From their fresh beds, and scattered
    thoughtlessly
By infant hands, left on the path to die.

Open afresh your round of starry folds,
Ye ardent marigolds!
Dry up the moisture from your golden
    lids,
50 For great Apollo bids
That in these days your praises should be
    sung
On many harps, which he has lately strung;
And when again your dewiness he kisses,
Tell him, I have you in my world of blisses:
55 So haply when I rove in some far vale,
His mighty voice may come upon the gale.

Here are sweet peas, on tiptoe for a
    flight,
With wings of gentle flush o'er delicate
    white,
And taper fingers catching at all things,
60 To bind them all about with tiny rings.

Linger awhile upon some bending planks
That lean against a streamlet's rushy
    banks,
And watch intently Nature's gentle doings;
They will be found softer than ring-dove's
    cooings.
65 How silent comes the water round that
    bend;
Not the minutest whisper does it send
To the o'erhanging sallows:[1] blades of
    grass
Slowly across the chequer'd shadows pass.
Why, you might read two sonnets, ere
    they reach.
70 To where the hurrying freshnesses aye
    preach
A natural sermon o'er their pebbly beds;
Where swarms of minnows show their little
    heads,
Staying their wavy bodies 'gainst the
    streams,
To taste the luxury of sunny beams
75 Temper'd with coolness. How they ever
    wrestle
With their own sweet delight, and ever
    nestle
Their silver bellies on the pebbly sand.
1 willows

If you but scantily hold out the hand,
That very instant not one will remain;
80 But turn your eye, and they are there
      again.
The ripples seem right glad to reach those
      cresses,
And cool themselves among the em'rald
      tresses;
The while they cool themselves, they fresh-
      ness give,
And moisture, that the bowery green may
      live:
85 So keeping up an interchange of favors,
Like good men in the truth of their be-
      haviors.
Sometimes goldfinches one by one will drop
From low-hung branches; little space they
      stop;
But sip, and twitter, and their feathers
      sleek;
90 Then off at once, as in a wanton freak:
Or perhaps, to show their black, and golden
      wings,
Pausing upon their yellow flutterings.
Were I in such a place, I sure should pray
That naught less sweet, might call my
      thoughts away,
95 Than the soft rustle of a maiden's gown
Fanning away the dandelion's down;
Than the light music of her nimble toes
Patting against the sorrel as she goes.
How she would start, and blush, thus to
      be caught
100 Playing in all her innocence of thought.
O let me lead her gently o'er the brook,
Watch her half-smiling lips, and down-
      ward look;
O let me for one moment touch her wrist;
Let me one moment to her breathing list;
105 And as she leaves me may she often turn
Her fair eyes looking through her locks
      aubùrne.
What next? A tuft of evening prim-
      roses,
O'er which the mind may hover till it
      dozes;
O'er which it well might take a pleasant
      sleep,
110 But that 'tis ever startled by the leap
Of buds into ripe flowers; or by the flit-
      ting
Of diverse moths, that aye their rest are
      quitting;
Or by the moon lifting her silver rim
Above a cloud, and with a gradual swim
115 Coming into the blue with all her light.
O Maker of sweet poets, dear delight
Of this fair world, and all its gentle livers;
Spangler of clouds, halo of crystal rivers,

Mingler with leaves, and dew and tumbling
      streams,
120 Closer of lovely eyes to lovely dreams,
Lover of loneliness, and wandering,
Of upcast eye, and tender pondering!
Thee must I praise above all other glories
That smile us on to tell delightful stories.
125 For what has made the sage or poet write
But the fair paradise of Nature's light?
In the calm grandeur of a sober line,
We see the waving of the mountain pine;
And when a tale is beautifully staid,
130 We feel the safety of a hawthorn glade:
When it is moving on luxurious wings,
The soul is lost in pleasant smotherings:
Fair dewy roses brush against our faces,
And flowering laurels spring from dia-
      mond vases;
135 O'er head we see the jasmine and sweet
      briar,
And bloomy grapes laughing from green
      attire;
While at our feet, the voice of crystal
      bubbles
Charms us at once away from all our
      troubles:
So that we feel uplifted from the world,
140 Walking upon the white clouds wreath'd
      and curl'd.
So felt he who first told how Psyche went
On the smooth wind to realms of wonder-
      ment;
What Psyche felt, and Love, when their
      full lips
First touch'd; what amorous and fondling
      nips
145 They gave each other's cheeks; with all
      their sighs,
And how they kist each other's tremulous
      eyes:
The silver lamp,—the ravishment,—the
      wonder—
The darkness, — loneliness, — the fearful
      thunder;
Their woes gone by, and both to heaven
      upflown,
150 To bow for gratitude before Jove's
      throne.
So did he feel, who pull'd the boughs aside,
That we might look into a forest wide,
To catch a glimpse of Fauns, and Dryades
Coming with softest rustle through the
      trees;
155 And garlands woven of flowers wild, and
      sweet,
Upheld by ivory wrists, or sporting feet:
Telling us how fair, trembling Syrinx
      fled
Arcadian Pan, with such a fearful dread.

Poor nymph,—poor Pan,—how he did
    weep to find,
160 Nought but a lovely sighing of the wind
Along the reedy stream; a half-heard
    strain,
Full of sweet desolation—balmy pain.

    What first inspired a bard of old to sing
Narcissus pining o'er the untainted
    spring?
165 In some delicious ramble, he had found
A little space, with boughs all woven
    round;
And in the midst of all, a clearer pool
Than e'er reflected in its pleasant cool,
The blue sky here, and there, serenely
    peeping
170 Through tendril wreaths fantastically
    creeping.
And on the bank, a lonely flower he spied,
A meek and forlorn flower, with naught of
    pride,
Drooping its beauty o'er the watery clear-
    ness,
To woo its own sad image into nearness:
175 Deaf to light Zephyrus it would not move;
But still would seem to droop, to pine, to
    love.
So while the poet stood in this sweet spot,
Some fainter gleamings o'er his fancy
    shot;
Nor was it long ere he had told the tale
180 Of young Narcissus, and sad Echo's bale.

    Where had he been, from whose warm
    head outflew
That sweetest of all songs, that ever new,
That aye refreshing, pure deliciousness,
Coming ever to bless
185 The wanderer by moonlight? to him bring-
    ing
Shapes from the invisible world, unearthly
    singing
From out the middle air, from flowery
    nests,
And from the pillowy silkiness that rests
Full in the speculation of the stars.
190 Ah! surely he had burst our mortal bars;
Into some wond'rous region he had gone,
To search for thee, divine Endymion!

    He was a poet, sure a lover too,
Who stood on Latmus' top, what time there
    blew
195 Soft breezes from the myrtle vale below;
And brought in faintness solemn, sweet,
    and slow
A hymn from Dian's temple; while up-
    swelling,

The incense went to her own starry dwell-
    ing.
But though her face was clear as infant's
    eyes,
200 Though she stood smiling o'er the sacri-
    fice,
The poet wept at her so piteous fate,
Wept that such beauty should be desolate:
So in fine wrath some golden sounds he
    won,
And gave meek Cynthia her Endymion.

205   Queen of the wide air; thou most lovely
    queen
Of all the brightness that mine eyes have
    seen!
As thou exceedest all things in thy shine,
So every tale, does this sweet tale of thine.
O for three words of honey, that I might
210 Tell but one wonder of thy bridal night!

    Where distant ships do seem to show
    their keels,
Phœbus awhile delay'd his mighty wheels,
And turn'd to smile upon thy bashful eyes,
Ere he his unseen pomp would solemnize.
215 The evening weather was so bright, and
    clear,
That men of health were of unusual cheer;
Stepping like Homer at the trumpet's call,
Or young Apollo on the pedestal:[1]
And lovely women were as fair and warm
220 As Venus looking sideways in alarm.[2]
The breezes were ethereal, and pure,
And crept through half-closed lattices to
    cure
The languid sick; it cool'd their fever'd
    sleep,
And soothed them into slumbers full and
    deep.
225 Soon they awoke clear-eyed: nor burnt
    with thirsting,
Nor with hot fingers, nor with temples
    bursting:
And springing up, they met the wond'ring
    sight
Of their dear friends, nigh foolish with
    delight;
Who feel their arms and breasts, and kiss
    and stare,
230 And on their placid foreheads part the
    hair.
Young men and maidens at each other
    gaz'd
With hands held back, and motionless,
    amaz'd
To see the brightness in each other's eyes;

[1] Probably the statue *Apollo Belvedere.*
[2] Probably the statue *Venus de Medici.*

And so they stood, fill'd with a sweet surprise,
235 Until their tongues were loos'd in poesy.
Therefore no lover did of anguish die:
But the soft numbers,[1] in that moment
   spoken,
Made silken ties, that never may be broken.
Cynthia! I cannot tell the greater blisses,
240 That follow'd thine, and thy dear shepherd's kisses:
Was there a poet born?—but now no more,
My wand'ring spirit must no further
   soar.—

SLEEP AND POETRY
1816   1817

As I lay in my bed slepe full unmete[2]
Was unto me, but why that I ne might
Rest I ne wist,[3] for there n'as erthly wight[4]
[As I suppose] had more of hertis ese[5]
Than I, for I n'ad[6] sicknesse nor disese.
                     CHAUCER.[7]

What is more gentle than a wind in
   summer?
What is more soothing than the pretty
   hummer
That stays one moment in an open flower,
And buzzes cheerily from bower to bower?
5 What is more tranquil than a musk-rose
   blowing
In a green island, far from all men's
   knowing?
More healthful than the leafiness of dales?
More secret than a nest of nightingales?
More serene than Cordelia's countenance?
10 More full of visions than a high romance?
What but thee, Sleep? Soft closer of our
   eyes!
Low murmurer of tender lullabies!
Light hoverer around our happy pillows!
Wreather of poppy buds, and weeping
   willows!
15 Silent entangler of a beauty's tresses!
Most happy listener! when the morning
   blesses
Thee for enlivening all the cheerful eyes
That glance so brightly at the new sun-rise.

But what is higher beyond thought than
   thee?
20 Fresher than berries of a mountain tree?
More strange, more beautiful, more smooth,
   more regal,
Than wings of swans, than doves, than
   dim-seen eagle?
What is it? And to what shall I compare
   it?

[1] verses   [2] immeasurable   [3] knew not
[4] was no earthly person
[5] heart's ease   [6] had not
[7] *The Floure and the Lefe,* 17-21. This poem for
a long time was accredited to Chaucer. Its
authorship is unknown.

It has a glory, and naught else can share
   it:
25 The thought thereof is awful, sweet, and
   holy,
Chasing away all worldliness and folly;
Coming sometimes like fearful claps of
   thunder,
Or the low rumblings earth's regions
   under;
And sometimes like a gentle whispering
30 Of all the secrets of some wond'rous thing
That breathes about us in the vacant air;
So that we look around with prying stare,
Perhaps to see shapes of light, aerial
   limning,[1]
And catch soft floatings from a faint-
   heard hymning;
35 To see the laurel wreath, on high suspended,
That is to crown our name when life is
   ended.
Sometimes it gives a glory to the voice,
And from the heart up-springs, rejoice!
   rejoice!
Sounds which will reach the Framer of all
   things,
40 And die away in ardent mutterings.

No one who once the glorious sun has
   seen,
And all the clouds, and felt his bosom clean
For his great Maker's presence, but must
   know
What 'tis I mean, and feel his being glow:
45 Therefore no insult will I give his spirit,
By telling what he sees from native merit.

O Poesy! for thee I hold my pen,
That am not yet a glorious denizen
Of thy wide heaven.—Should I rather kneel
50 Upon some mountain-top until I feel
A glowing splendor round about me hung,
And echo back the voice of thine own
   tongue?
O Poesy! for thee I grasp my pen,
That am not yet a glorious denizen
55 Of thy wide heaven; yet, to my ardent
   prayer,
Yield from thy sanctuary some clear air,
Smooth'd for intoxication by the breath
Of flowering bays,[2] that I may die a death
Of luxury, and my young spirit follow
60 The morning sun-beams to the great Apollo
Like a fresh sacrifice; or, if I can bear
The o'erwhelming sweets, 'twill bring to
   me the fair
Visions of all places: a bowery nook
Will be Elysium—an eternal book
65 Whence I may copy many a lovely saying

[1] painting   [2] A kind of laurel tree.

About the leaves, and flowers—about the
    playing
Of nymphs in woods, and fountains; and
    the shade
Keeping a silence round a sleeping maid;
And many a verse from so strange influ-
    ence
70 That we must ever wonder how, and whence
It came. Also imaginings will hover
Round my fire-side, and haply there dis-
    cover
Vistas of solemn beauty, where I'd wander
In happy silence, like the clear Meander
75 Through its lone vales; and where I found
    a spot
Of awfuller shade, or an enchanted grot,
Or a green hill o'erspread with chequer'd
    dress
Of flowers, and fearful from its loveliness,
Write on my tablets all that was permitted,
80 All that was for our human senses fitted.
Then the events of this wide world I'd seize
Like a strong giant, and my spirit teaze
Till at its shoulders it should proudly see
Wings to find out an immortality.

85   Stop and consider! life is but a day;
A fragile dew-drop on its perilous way
From a tree's summit; a poor Indian's
    sleep
While his boat hastens to the monstrous
    steep
Of Montmorenci. Why so sad a moan?
90 Life is the rose's hope while yet unblown;
The reading of an ever-changing tale;
The light uplifting of a maiden's veil;
A pigeon tumbling in clear summer air;
A laughing school-boy, without grief or
    care,
95 Riding the springy branches of an elm.

O for ten years, that I may overwhelm
Myself in Poesy; so I may do the deed
That my own soul has to itself decreed.
Then will I pass the countries that I see
100 In long perspective, and continually
Taste their pure fountains. First the
    realm I'll pass
Of Flora and old Pan: sleep in the grass,
Feed upon apples red, and strawberries,
And choose each pleasure that my fancy
    sees;
105 Catch the white-handed nymphs in shady
    places,
To woo sweet kisses from averted faces,—
Play with their fingers, touch their shoul-
    ders white
Into a pretty shrinking with a bite
As hard as lips can make it: till agreed,

110 A lovely tale of human life we'll read.
And one will teach a tame dove how it best
May fan the cool air gently o'er my rest;
Another, bending o'er her nimble tread,
Will set a green robe floating round her
    head,
115 And still will dance with ever varied ease,
Smiling upon the flowers and the trees:
Another will entice me on, and on
Through almond blossoms and rich cinna-
    mon;
Till in the bosom of a leafy world
120 We rest in silence, like two gems upcurl'd
In the recesses of a pearly shell.

And can I ever bid these joys farewell?
Yes, I must pass them for a nobler life,
Where I may find the agonies, the strife
125 Of human hearts: for lo! I see afar,
O'ersailing the blue cragginess, a car
And steeds with streamy manes—the
    charioteer
Looks out upon the winds with glorious
    fear:
And now the numerous tramplings quiver
    lightly
130 Along a huge cloud's ridge; and now with
    sprightly
Wheel downward come they into fresher
    skies,
Tipt round with silver from the sun's
    bright eyes.
Still downward with capacious whirl they
    glide;
And now I see them on a green-hill's side
135 In breezy rest among the nodding stalks.
The charioteer with wond'rous gesture
    talks
To the trees and mountains; and there
    soon appear
Shapes of delight, of mystery, and fear,
Passing along before a dusky space
140 Made by some mighty oaks: as they would
    chase
Some ever-fleeting music on they sweep.
Lo! how they murmur, laugh, and smile,
    and weep:
Some with upholden hand and mouth
    severe;
Some with their faces muffled to the ear
145 Between their arms; some, clear in youth-
    ful bloom,
Go glad and smilingly athwart the gloom;
Some looking back, and some with upward
    gaze;
Yes, thousands in a thousand different
    ways
Flit onward—now a lovely wreath of girls
150 Dancing their sleek hair into tangled curls;

And now broad wings. Most awfully in-
tent
The driver of those steeds is forward bent,
And seems to listen: O that I might know
All that he writes with such a hurrying
glow.

155   The visions all are fled—the car is fled
Into the light of heaven, and in their stead
A sense of real things comes doubly strong,
And, like a muddy stream, would bear
along
My soul to nothingness: but I will strive
160 Against all doubtings, and will keep alive
The thought of that same chariot, and the
strange
Journey it went.

Is there so small a range
In the present strength of manhood, that
the high
Imagination cannot freely fly
165 As she was wont of old? prepare her
steeds,
Paw up against the light, and do strange
deeds
Upon the clouds? Has she not shown us
all?
From the clear space of ether, to the small
Breath of new buds unfolding? From the
meaning
170 Of Jove's large eye-brow,[1] to the tender
greening
Of April meadows? Here her altar shone,
E'en in this isle; and who could paragon
The fervid choir[2] that lifted up a noise
Of harmony, to where it aye will poise
175 Its mighty self of convoluting sound,
Huge as a planet, and like that roll round,
Eternally around a dizzy void?
Ay, in those days the Muses were nigh
cloy'd
With honors; nor had any other care
180 Than to sing out and sooth their wavy hair.

Could all this be forgotten? Yes, a schism
Nurtured by foppery and barbarism,
Made great Apollo blush for this his land.[3]
Men were thought wise who could not
understand
185 His glories: with a puling infant's force
They sway'd about upon a rocking horse,
And thought it Pegasus. Ah, dismal soul'd!
The winds of heaven blew, the ocean roll'd
Its gathering waves—ye felt it not. The
blue

190 Bared its eternal bosom, and the dew
Of summer nights collected still to make
The morning precious: beauty was awake!
Why were ye not awake? But ye were dead
To things ye knew not of,—were closely
wed
195 To musty laws lined out with wretched rule
And compass vile: so that ye taught a
school
Of dolts to smooth, inlay, and clip, and fit,
Till, like the certain wands of Jacob's
wit,[1]
Their verses tallied. Easy was the task:
200 A thousand handicraftsmen wore the mask
Of Poesy. Ill-fated, impious race!
That blasphemed the bright Lyrist to his
face,
And did not know it,—no, they went about,
Holding a poor, decrepid standard out,
205 Mark'd with most flimsy mottoes, and in
large
The name of one Boileau!

O ye whose charge
It is to hover round our pleasant hills!
Whose congregated majesty so fills
My boundly[2] reverence, that I cannot
trace
210 Your hallowed names, in this unholy place,
So near those common folk; did not their
shames
Affright you? Did our old lamenting
Thames
Delight you? Did ye never cluster round
Delicious Avon, with a mournful sound,
215 And weep? Or did ye wholly bid adieu
To regions where no more the laurel grew?
Or did ye stay to give a welcoming
To some lone spirits who could proudly
sing
Their youth away, and die? 'Twas even
so:
220 But let me think away those times of
woe:
Now 'tis a fairer season; ye have breathed
Rich benedictions o'er us; ye have wreathed
Fresh garlands: for sweet music has been
heard
In many places;—some has been upstirr'd
225 From out its crystal dwelling in a lake,
By a swan's ebon bill;[3] from a thick
brake,[4]
Nested and quiet in a valley mild,
Bubbles a pipe; fine sounds are floating
wild
About the earth: happy are ye and glad.

---

[1] A reference to Jove's irrevocable nod, in connection with which the eye-brow is promi-
nently mentioned. See the *Iliad,* 1, 528.
[2] The Elizabethan poets.
[3] A reference to eighteenth century poets.

[1] See *Genesis,* 30:37-
39.
[2] bounden
[3] Supposed to refer to
Wordsworth.
[4] thicket

230 These things are, doubtless: yet in truth
    we've had
Strange thunders from the potency of
    song;
Mingled indeed with what is sweet and
    strong
From majesty: but in clear truth the
    themes
Are ugly clubs, the Poets Polyphemes
235 Disturbing the grand sea. A drainless
    shower
Of light is Poesy; 'tis the supreme of
    power;
'Tis might half slumb'ring on its own
    right arm.
The very archings of her eye-lids charm
A thousand willing agents to obey,
240 And still she governs with the mildest
    sway:
But strength alone though of the Muses
    born
Is like a fallen angel: trees uptorn,
Darkness, and worms, and shrouds, and
    sepulchres
Delight it; for it feeds upon the burrs,
245 And thorns of life; forgetting the great
    end
Of Poesy, that it should be a friend
To soothe the cares, and lift the thoughts
    of man.

    Yet I rejoice: a myrtle fairer than
E'er grew in Paphos, from the bitter weeds
250 Lifts its sweet head into the air, and feeds
A silent space with ever sprouting green.
All tenderest birds there find a pleasant
    screen,
Creep through the shade with jaunty
    fluttering,
Nibble the little cupped flowers and sing.
255 Then let us clear away the choking thorns
From round its gentle stem; let the young
    fawns,
Yeaned[1] in aftertimes, when we are flown,
Find a fresh sward beneath it, overgrown
With simple flowers: let there nothing
    be
260 More boisterous than a lover's bended
    knee;
Nought more ungentle than the placid look
Of one who leans upon a closed book;
Nought more untranquil than the grassy
    slopes
Between two hills. All hail, delightful
    hopes!
265 As she was wont, th' imagination
Into most lovely labyrinths will be gone,
And they shall be accounted poet kings
    ¹ born

Who simply tell the most heart-easing
    things.
O may these joys be ripe before I die.

270 Will not some say that I presump-
    tuously
Have spoken? that from hastening dis-
    grace
'Twere better far to hide my foolish face?
That whining boyhood should with rever-
    ence bow
Ere the dread thunderbolt could reach?
    How!
275 If I do hide myself, it sure shall be
In the very fane, the light of Poesy:
If I do fall, at least I will be laid
Beneath the silence of a poplar shade;
And over me the grass shall be smooth
    shaven;
280 And there shall be a kind memorial graven.
But off, Despondence! miserable bane!
They should not know thee, who athirst to
    gain
A noble end, are thirsty every hour.
What though I am not wealthy in the
    dower
285 Of spanning wisdom; though I do not
    know
The shiftings of the mighty winds that
    blow
Hither and thither all the changing
    thoughts
Of man: though no great minist'ring rea-
    son sorts
Out the dark mysteries of human souls
290 To clear conceiving: yet there ever rolls
A vast idea before me, and I glean
Therefrom my liberty; thence too I've seen
The end and aim of Poesy. 'Tis clear
As anything most true; as that the year
295 Is made of the four seasons—manifest
As a large cross, some old cathedral's crest,
Lifted to the white clouds. Therefore
    should I
Be but the essence of deformity,
A coward, did my very eyelids wink
300 At speaking out what I have dared to
    think.
Ah! rather let me like a madman run
Over some precipice; let the hot sun
Melt my Dædalian wings, and drive me
    down
Convuls'd and headlong! Stay! an in-
    ward frown
305 Of conscience bids me be more calm awhile.
An ocean dim, sprinkled with many an isle,
Spreads awfully before me. How much
    toil!
How many days! what desperate turmoil!

Ere I can have explored its widenesses.
310 Ah, what a task! upon my bended knees,
I could unsay those—no, impossible!
Impossible!

For sweet relief I'll dwell
On humbler thoughts, and let this strange
    assay
Begun in gentleness die so away.
315 E'en now all tumult from my bosom fades:
I turn full-hearted to the friendly aids
That smooth the path of honor; brother-
    hood,
And friendliness, the nurse of mutual good.
The hearty grasp that sends a pleasant
    sonnet[1]
320 Into the brain ere one can think upon it;
The silence when some rhymes are coming
    out;
And when they're come, the very pleasant
    rout:
The message certain to be done tomorrow.
'Tis perhaps as well that it should be to
    borrow
325 Some precious book from out its snug re-
    treat,
To cluster round it when we next shall
    meet.
Scarce can I scribble on; for lovely airs
Are fluttering round the room like doves
    in pairs;
Many delights of that glad day recalling,
330 When first my senses caught their tender
    falling.
And with these airs come forms of elegance
Stooping their shoulders o'er a horse's
    prance,
Careless, and grand — fingers soft and
    round
Parting luxuriant curls;—and the swift
    bound
335 Of Bacchus from his chariot, when his eye
Made Ariadne's cheek look blushingly.
Thus I remember all the pleasant flow
Of words at opening a portfolio.

Things such as these are ever harbingers
340 To trains of peaceful images: the stirs
Of a swan's neck unseen among the rushes;
A linnet starting all about the bushes;
A butterfly, with golden wings broad
    parted,
Nestling a rose, convuls'd as though it
    smarted
345 With over pleasure—many, many more,
Might I indulge at large in all my store
Of luxuries; yet I must not forget
Sleep, quiet with his poppy coronet:

[1] song

For what there may be worthy in these
    rhymes
350 I partly owe to him: and thus, the chimes
Of friendly voices had just given place
To as sweet a silence, when I 'gan retrace
The pleasant day, upon a couch at ease.
It was a poet's house[1] who keeps the keys
355 Of pleasure's temple. Round about were
    hung
The glorious features of the bards who
    sung
In other ages—cold and sacred busts
Smiled at each other. Happy he who trusts
To clear Futurity his darling fame!
360 Then there were fauns and satyrs taking
    aim
At swelling apples with a frisky leap
And reaching fingers, 'mid a luscious heap
Of vine-leaves. Then there rose to view a
    fane
Of liny[2] marble, and thereto a train
365 Of nymphs approaching fairly o'er the
    sward:
One, loveliest, holding her white hand
    toward
The dazzling sunrise; two sisters sweet
Bending their graceful figures till they
    meet
Over the trippings of a little child;
370 And some are hearing, eagerly, the wild
Thrilling liquidity of dewy piping.
See, in another picture, nymphs are wiping
Cherishingly Diana's timorous limbs;—
A fold of lawny mantle dabbling swims
375 At the bath's edge, and keeps a gentle
    motion
With the subsiding crystal: as when ocean
Heaves calmly its broad swelling smooth-
    ness o'er
Its rocky marge, and balances once more
The patient weeds; that now unshent by
    foam
380 Feel all about their undulating home.

Sappho's meek head was there half
    smiling down
At nothing; just as though the earnest
    frown
Of over-thinking had that moment gone
From off her brow, and left her all alone.

385 Great Alfred's too, with anxious, pity-
    ing eyes,
As if he always listened to the sighs
Of the goaded world; and Kosciusko's
    worn
By horrid sufferance—mightily forlorn.

[1] Leigh Hunt's. The lines following describe
    the room in which the poem was written.
[2] marked with lines

Petrarch, outstepping from the shady
green,
390 Starts at the sight of Laura; nor can wean
His eyes from her sweet face. Most happy
they!
For over them was seen a free display
Of outspread wings, and from between
them shone
The face of Poesy: from off her throne
395 She overlook'd things that I scarce could
tell.
The very sense of where I was might well
Keep Sleep aloof: but more than that
there came
Thought after thought to nourish up the
flame
Within my breast; so that the morning
light
400 Surprised me even from a sleepless night;
And up I rose refresh'd, and glad, and gay,
Resolving to begin that very day
These lines; and howsoever they be done,
I leave them as a father does his son.

ADDRESSED TO BENJAMIN ROBERT HAYDON
1816 1817

Great spirits now on earth are sojourning;
He of the cloud, the cataract, the lake,[1]
Who on Helvellyn's summit, wide awake,
Catches his freshness from Archangel's
wing:
5 He of the rose, the violet, the spring,[2]
The social smile, the chain for Freedom's
sake:
And lo!—whose steadfastness would never
take
A meaner sound than Raphael's whisper-
ing.[3]
And other spirits there are standing apart
10 Upon the forehead of the age to come;
These, these will give the world another
heart,
And other pulses. Hear ye not the hum
Of mighty workings in the human mart?
Listen awhile ye nations, and be dumb.

TO G. A. W.[4]
1816 1817

Nymph of the downward smile and sidelong glance,
In what diviner moments of the day
Art thou most lovely?—when gone far
astray
Into the labyrinths of sweet utterance,
5 Or when serenely wand'ring in a trance

Of sober thought?—or when starting away
With careless robe to meet the morning ray
Thou spar'st the flowers in thy mazy
dance?
Haply 'tis when thy ruby lips part sweetly,
10 And so remain, because thou listenest:
But thou to please wert nurtured so com-
pletely
That I can never tell what mood is best.
I shall as soon pronounce which Grace
more neatly
Trips it before Apollo than the rest.

STANZAS
1817 1829

In a drear-nighted December,
Too happy, happy tree,
Thy branches ne'er remember
Their green felicity:
5 The north cannot undo them,
With a sleety whistle through them;
Nor frozen thawings glue them
From budding at the prime.

In a drear-nighted December,
10 Too happy, happy brook,
Thy bubblings ne'er remember
Apollo's summer look;
But with a sweet forgetting,
They stay their crystal fretting,
15 Never, never petting[1]
About the frozen time.

Ah! would 'twere so with many
A gentle girl and boy!
But were there ever any
20 Writh'd not at passed joy?
To know the change and feel it,
When there is none to heal it,
Nor numbed sense to steel it,
Was never said in rhyme.

HAPPY IS ENGLAND
1816 1817

Happy is England! I could be content
To see no other verdure than its own;
To feel no other breezes than are blown
Through its tall woods with high romances
blent:
5 Yet do I sometimes feel a languishment
For skies Italian, and an inward groan
To sit upon an Alp as on a throne,
And half forget what world or worldling
meant.
Happy is England, sweet her artless
daughters;
10 Enough their simple loveliness for me,

---

[1] Wordsworth. [2] Leigh Hunt. [3] Haydon.
[4] Georgiana Augusta Wylie, afterward the wife
of Keats's brother George.

[1] complaining

Enough their whitest arms in silence clinging:
Yet do I often warmly burn to see
Beauties of deeper glance, and hear their
  singing,
And float with them about the summer
  waters.

ON THE GRASSHOPPER AND CRICKET
1816   1817

The poetry of earth is never dead:
When all the birds are faint with the hot
  sun,
And hide in cooling trees, a voice will run
From hedge to hedge about the new-mown
  mead;
5 That is the Grasshopper's—he takes the
  lead
In summer luxury,—he has never done
With his delights; for when tired out with
  fun
He rests at ease beneath some pleasant
  weed.
The poetry of earth is ceasing never:
10 On a lone winter evening, when the frost
Has wrought a silence, from the stove there
  shrills
The Cricket's song, in warmth increasing
  ever,
And seems to one, in drowsiness half lost,
The Grasshopper's among some grassy
  hills.

AFTER DARK VAPORS HAVE
OPPRESS'D OUR PLAINS
1817   1817

After dark vapors have oppress'd our
  plains
For a long dreary season, comes a day
Born of the gentle South, and clears away
From the sick heavens all unseemly stains.
5 The anxious month, relieved of its pains,
Takes as a long-lost right the feel of May;
The eyelids with the passing coolness
  play
Like rose leaves with the drip of summer
  rains.
The calmest thoughts come round us; as
  of leaves
10 Budding—fruit ripening in stillness—au-
  tumn suns
Smiling at eve upon the quiet sheaves—
Sweet Sappho's cheek—a smiling infant's
  breath—
The gradual sand that through an hour-
  glass runs—
A woodland rivulet—a Poet's death.

WRITTEN ON THE BLANK SPACE AT
THE END OF CHAUCER'S TALE OF
"THE FLOURE AND THE LEFE"[1]
1817   1817

This pleasant tale is like a little copse:
The honied lines do freshly interlace
To keep the reader in so sweet a place,
So that he here and there full-hearted
  stops;
5 And oftentimes he feels the dewy drops
Come cool and suddenly against his face,
And by the wandering melody may trace
Which way the tender-legged linnet hops.
Oh! what a power has white simplicity!
10 What mighty power has this gentle story!
I that forever feel athirst for glory
Could at this moment be content to lie
Meekly upon the grass, as those whose sob-
  bings
Were heard of none beside the mournful
  robins.

ON A PICTURE OF LEANDER
1817   1829

Come hither, all sweet maidens, soberly,
Down-looking aye, and with a chasten'd
  light
Hid in the fringes of your eyelids white,
And meekly let your fair hands joined be,
5 As if so gentle that ye could not see,
Untouch'd, a victim of your beauty bright,
Sinking away to his young spirit's night,—
Sinking bewilder'd 'mid the dreary sea:
'Tis young Leander toiling to his death;
10 Nigh swooning, he doth purse his weary
  lips
For Hero's cheek, and smiles against her
  smile.
O horrid dream! see how his body dips
Dead-heavy; arms and shoulders gleam
  awhile:
He's gone: up bubbles all his amorous
  breath!

TO LEIGH HUNT, ESQ.
1817   1817

Glory and loveliness have pass'd away;
For if we wander out in early morn,
No wreathed incense do we see upborne
Into the east, to meet the smiling day:
5 No crowd of nymphs soft-voic'd, and
  young, and gay,
In woven baskets bringing ears of corn,[2]
Roses, and pinks, and violets, to adorn
The shrine of Flora in her early May.
But there are left delights as high as these,
10 And I shall ever bless my destiny,
That in a time, when under pleasant trees

[1] Chaucer's authorship of this poem is now discredited.   [2] wheat

Pan is no longer sought, I feel a free,
A leafy luxury, seeing I could please
With these poor offerings,[1] a man like
    thee.

ON SEEING THE ELGIN MARBLES[2]
1817   1817

My spirit is too weak—mortality
Weighs heavily on me like unwilling sleep,
And each imagin'd pinnacle and steep
Of godlike hardship, tells me I must die
5 Like a sick eagle looking at the sky.
Yet 'tis a gentle luxury to weep
That I have not the cloudy winds to keep
Fresh for the opening of the morning's
    eye.
Such dim-conceived glories of the brain
10 Bring round the heart an undescribable
    feud;
So do these wonders a most dizzy pain,
That mingles Grecian grandeur with the
    rude
Wasting of old Time—with a billowy
    main—
A sun—a shadow of a magnitude.

ON THE SEA
1817   1848

It keeps eternal whisperings around
Desolate shores, and with its mighty swell
Gluts twice ten thousand caverns, till the
    spell
Of Hecate leaves them their old shadowy
    sound.
5 Often 'tis in such gentle temper found,
That scarcely will the very smallest shell
Be mov'd for days from where it some-
    time fell,
When last the winds of heaven were un-
    bound.
Oh ye! who have your eye-balls vex'd and
    tir'd,
10 Feast them upon the wideness of the sea;
Oh ye! whose ears are dinn'd with uproar
    rude,
Or fed too much with cloying melody—
Sit ye near some old cavern's mouth, and
    brood
Until ye start, as if the sea-nymphs quir'd!

LINES
1817   1848

Unfelt, unheard, unseen,
I've left my little queen,
Her languid arms in silver slumber lying:

[1] Keats's first volume of poems, dedicated to
    Hunt.
[2] Sculptures from the Parthenon which were
    taken to London from Athens by Lord Elgin
    in 1803.

Ah! through their nestling touch,
5   Who—who could tell how much
There is for madness—cruel, or comply-
    ing?

Those faery lids how sleek!
Those lips how moist!—they speak,
In ripest quiet, shadows of sweet sounds:
10   Into my fancy's ear
  Melting a burden dear,
How "Love doth know no fulness and no
    bounds."

True!—tender monitors!
  I bend unto your laws:
15 This sweetest day for dalliance was born!
  So, without more ado,
  I'll feel my heaven anew,
For all the blushing of the hasty morn.

ON LEIGH HUNT'S POEM "THE
STORY OF RIMINI"[1]
1817   1848

Who loves to peer up at the morning sun,
With half-shut eyes and comfortable
    cheek,
Let him, with this sweet tale, full often
    seek
For meadows where the little rivers run;
5 Who loves to linger with that brightest one
Of heaven — Hesperus — let him lowly
    speak
These numbers to the night, and starlight
    meek,
Or moon, if that her hunting be begun.
He who knows these delights, and too is
    prone
10 To moralize upon a smile or tear,
Will find at once a region of his own,
A bower for his spirit, and will steer
To alleys where the fir-tree drops its cone,
Where robins hop, and fallen leaves are
    sear.

WHEN I HAVE FEARS THAT I MAY
CEASE TO BE
1818   1848

When I have fears that I may cease to be
Before my pen has glean'd my teeming
    brain,
Before high-piled books, in charactry,[2]
Hold like rich garners the full ripen'd
    grain;
5 When I behold, upon the night's starr'd
    face,
Huge cloudy symbols of a high romance,
And think that I may never live to trace

[1] See p. 892.   [2] characters; letters

Their shadows, with the magic hand of
    chance;
And when I feel, fair creature of an hour,
10 That I shall never look upon thee more,
Never have relish in the faery power
Of unreflecting love;—then on the shore
Of the wide world I stand alone, and think
Till love and fame to nothingness do sink.

ON SITTING DOWN TO READ "KING LEAR" ONCE AGAIN
1818   *1848*

O golden-tongued Romance, with serene
    lute!
Fair-plumed Syren, Queen of far-away!
Leave melodizing on this wintry day,
Shut up thine olden pages, and be mute:
5 Adieu; for, once again, the fierce dispute
Betwixt damnation and impassion'd clay
Must I burn through; once more humbly
    assay
The bitter-sweet of this Shakespearian
    fruit:
Chief poet! and ye clouds of Albion,[1]
10 Begetters of our deep eternal theme!
When through the old oak forest I am
    gone,
Let me not wander in a barren dream,
But, when I am consumed in the fire,
Give me new phœnix-wings[2] to fly at my
    desire.

LINES ON THE MERMAID TAVERN
1818   *1820*

Souls of Poets dead and gone,
What Elysium have ye known,
Happy field or mossy cavern,
Choicer than the Mermaid Tavern?

5 Have ye tippled drink more fine
Than mine host's Canary wine?
Or are fruits of Paradise
Sweeter than those dainty pies
Of venison? O generous food!
10 Drest as though bold Robin Hood
Would, with his Maid Marian,
Sup and bowse[3] from horn and can.

I have heard that on a day
Mine host's sign-board flew away,
15 Nobody knew whither, till
An astrologer's old quill
To a sheepskin gave the story,
Said he saw you in your glory,
Underneath a new-old sign

[1] The story of Lear belongs to British legend.
[2] The phœnix was a mythical bird said to be consumed in fire and to rise in youthful freshness from its own ashes.
[3] drink

20 Sipping beverage divine,
And pledging with contented smack
The Mermaid in the Zodiac.

Souls of Poets dead and gone,
What Elysium have ye known,
25 Happy field or mossy cavern,
Choicer than the Mermaid Tavern?

ROBIN HOOD

TO A FRIEND[1]
1818   *1820*

No! those days are gone away,
And their hours are old and gray,
And their minutes buried all
Under the down-trodden pall
5 Of the leaves of many years:
Many times have Winter's shears,
Frozen North, and chilling East,
Sounded tempests to the feast
Of the forest's whispering fleeces,
10 Since men knew nor rent nor leases.

No, the bugle sounds no more,
And the twanging bow no more;
Silent is the ivory shrill
Past the heath and up the hill;
15 There is no mid-forest laugh,
Where lone Echo gives the half
To some wight,[2] amaz'd to hear
Jesting, deep in forest drear.

On the fairest time of June
20 You may go, with sun or moon,
Or the seven stars[3] to light you,
Or the polar ray to right you;
But you never may behold
Little John, or Robin bold;
25 Never one, of all the clan,
Thrumming on an empty can
Some old hunting ditty, while
He doth his green way beguile
To fair hostess Merriment,
30 Down beside the pasture Trent;
For he left the merry tale
Messenger for spicy ale.

Gone, the merry morris[4] din;
Gone, the song of Gamelyn;
35 Gone, the tough-belted outlaw
Idling in the "grenè shawe";
All are gone away and past!
And if Robin should be cast

[1] J. H. Reynolds, who had sent Keats two sonnets which he had written on Robin Hood. See Keats's letter to Reynolds (p. 888).
[2] person   [3] The Pleiades.
[4] A popular dance in which the dancers often took the parts of Robin Hood, Maid Marian, and other fictitious characters.

Sudden from his turfed grave,
40 And if Marian should have
Once again her forest days,
She would weep, and he would craze:
He would swear, for all his oaks,
Fall'n beneath the dockyard strokes,
45 Have rotted on the briny seas;
She would weep that her wild bees
Sang not to her—strange! that honey
Can't be got without hard money!

So it is: yet let us sing,
50 Honor to the old bow-string!
Honor to the bugle-horn!
Honor to the woods unshorn!
Honor to the Lincoln green![1]
Honor to the archer keen!
55 Honor to tight[2] Little John,
And the horse he rode upon!
Honor to bold Robin Hood,
Sleeping in the underwood!
Honor to Maid Marian,
60 And to all the Sherwood-clan!
Though their days have hurried by
Let us two a burden[3] try.

TO THE NILE
1818   1848

Son of the old moon-mountains African!
Chief of the Pyramid and Crocodile!
We call thee fruitful, and, that very while,
A desert fills our seeing's inward span;
5 Nurse of swart nations[4] since the world began,
Art thou so fruitful? or dost thou beguile
Such men to honor thee, who, worn with toil,
Rest for a space 'twixt Cairo and Decan?
O may dark fancies err! They surely do;
10 'Tis ignorance that makes a barren waste
Of all beyond itself, thou dost bedew
Green rushes like our rivers, and dost taste
The pleasant sun-rise. Green isles hast thou too,
And to the sea as happily dost haste.

TO SPENSER
1818   1848

Spenser! a jealous honorer of thine,
A forester deep in thy midmost trees,
Did last eve ask my promise to refine
Some English that might strive thine ear to please.
5 But, elfin poet, 'tis impossible
For an inhabitant of wintry earth
To rise like Phœbus with a golden quill

---

[1] A cloth made in Lincoln, worn by huntsmen.
[2] well-formed; trim
[3] chorus   [4] The Negro races.

Fire-wing'd and make a morning in his mirth.
It is impossible to escape from toil
10 O' the sudden and receive thy spiriting:
The flower must drink the nature of the soil
Before it can put forth its blossoming:
Be with me in the summer days and I
Will for thine honor and his pleasure try.

THE HUMAN SEASONS
1818   1819

Four seasons fill the measure of the year;
There are four seasons in the mind of man;
He has his lusty spring, when fancy clear
Takes in all beauty with an easy span:
5 He has his summer, when luxuriously
Spring's honied cud of youthful thought he loves
To ruminate, and by such dreaming high
Is nearest unto heaven: quiet coves
His soul has in its autumn, when his wings
10 He furleth close; contented so to look
On mists in idleness—to let fair things
Pass by unheeded as a threshold brook.
He has his winter too of pale misfeature,
Or else he would forego his mortal nature.

ENDYMION
1817-18   1818

BOOK I

A thing of beauty is a joy forever:
Its loveliness increases; it will never
Pass into nothingness; but still will keep
A bower quiet for us, and a sleep
5 Full of sweet dreams, and health, and quiet breathing.
Therefore, on every morrow, are we wreathing
A flowery band to bind us to the earth,
Spite of despondence, of the inhuman dearth
Of noble natures, of the gloomy days,
10 Of all the unhealthy and o'er-darkened ways
Made for our searching: yes, in spite of all,
Some shape of beauty moves away the pall
From our dark spirits. Such the sun, the moon,
Trees old, and young, sprouting a shady boon
15 For simple sheep; and such are daffodils
With the green world they live in; and clear rills
That for themselves a cooling covert make

'Gainst the hot season; the mid-forest
    brake,[1]
Rich with a sprinkling of fair musk-rose
    blooms:
20 And such too is the grandeur of the dooms[2]
We have imagined for the mighty dead;
All lovely tales that we have heard or read:
An endless fountain of immortal drink,
Pouring unto us from the heaven's brink.

25   Nor do we merely feel these essences
For one short hour; no, even as the trees
That whisper round a temple become soon
Dear as the temple's self, so does the moon,
The passion Poesy, glories infinite,
30 Haunt us till they become a cheering light
Unto our souls, and bound to us so fast,
That, whether there be shine, or gloom
    o'ercast,
They always must be with us, or we die.

    Therefore, 'tis with full happiness that I
35 Will trace the story of Endymion.
The very music of the name has gone
Into my being, and each pleasant scene
Is growing fresh before me as the green
Of our own valleys: so I will begin
40 Now while I cannot hear the city's din;
Now while the early budders are just new,
And run in mazes of the youngest hue
About old forests; while the willow trails
Its delicate amber; and the dairy pails
45 Bring home increase of milk. And, as the
    year
Grows lush in juicy stalks, I'll smoothly
    steer
My little boat, for many quiet hours,
With streams that deepen freshly into
    bowers.
Many and many a verse I hope to write,
50 Before the daisies, vermeil rimm'd and
    white,
Hide in deep herbage; and ere yet the bees
Hum about globes of clover and sweet
    peas,
I must be near the middle of my story.
O may no wintry season, bare and hoary,
55 See it half finish'd: but let Autumn bold,
With universal tinge of sober gold,
Be all about me when I make an end.
And now at once, adventuresome, I send
My herald thought into a wilderness:
60 There let its trumpet blow, and quickly
    dress
My uncertain path with green, that I may
    speed
Easily onward, thorough flowers and weed.

    Upon the sides of Latmos was outspread
A mighty forest; for the moist earth fed
65 So plenteously all weed-hidden roots
Into o'er-hanging boughs, and precious
    fruits.
And it had gloomy shades, sequestered
    deep,
Where no man went; and if from shep-
    herd's keep
A lamb stray'd far a-down those inmost
    glens,
70 Never again saw he the happy pens
Whither his brethren, bleating with con-
    tent,
Over the hills at every nightfall went.
Among the shepherds, 'twas believed ever,
That not one fleecy lamb which thus did
    sever
75 From the white flock, but pass'd un-
    worried
By angry wolf, or pard[1] with prying head,
Until it came to some unfooted plains
Where fed the herds of Pan: aye great his
    gains
Who thus one lamb did lose. Paths there
    were many,
80 Winding through palmy fern, and rushes
    fenny,
And ivy banks; all leading pleasantly
To a wide lawn, whence one could only see
Stems thronging all around between the
    swell
Of turf and slanting branches: who could
    tell
85 The freshness of the space of heaven
    above,
Edg'd round with dark tree tops, through
    which a dove
Would often beat its wings, and often too
A little cloud would move across the blue?

    Full in the middle of this pleasantness
90 There stood a marble altar, with a tress
Of flowers budded newly; and the dew
Had taken fairy phantasies to strew
Daisies upon the sacred sward last eve,
And so the dawned light in pomp receive.
95 For 'twas the morn: Apollo's upward fire
Made every eastern cloud a silvery pyre
Of brightness so unsullied, that therein
A melancholy spirit well might win
Oblivion, and melt out his essence fine
100 Into the winds: rain-scented eglantine
Gave temperate sweets to that well-wooing
    sun;
The lark was lost in him; cold springs had
    run
To warm their chilliest bubbles in the grass;

---

[1] thicket   [2] destinies   [1] leopard

Man's voice was on the mountains; and the mass
105 Of nature's lives and wonders puls'd tenfold,
To feel this sunrise and its glories old.

Now while the silent workings of the dawn
Were busiest, into that self-same lawn
All suddenly, with joyful cries, there sped
110 A troop of little children garlanded;
Who gathering round the altar, seem'd to pry
Earnestly round as wishing to espy
Some folk of holiday: nor had they waited
For many moments, ere their ears were sated
115 With a faint breath of music, which ev'n then
Fill'd out its voice, and died away again.
Within a little space again it gave
Its airy swellings, with a gentle wave,
To light-hung leaves, in smoothest echoes breaking
120 Through copse-clad valleys,—ere their death, o'ertaking
The surgy murmurs of the lonely sea.

And now, as deep into the wood as we
Might mark a lynx's eye, there glimmer'd light
Fair faces and a rush of garments white,
125 Plainer and plainer showing, till at last
Into the widest alley they all past,
Making directly for the woodland altar.
O kindly muse! let not my weak tongue faulter
In telling of this goodly company,
130 Of their old piety, and of their glee:
But let a portion of ethereal dew
Fall on my head, and presently unmew[1]
My soul; that I may dare, in wayfaring,
To stammer where old Chaucer us'd to sing.

135　Leading the way, young damsels danced along,
Bearing the burden of a shepherd song;
Each having a white wicker overbrimm'd
With April's tender younglings: next, well trimm'd,
A crowd of shepherds with as sunburnt looks
140 As may be read of in Arcadian books;
Such as sat listening round Apollo's pipe,
When the great deity, for earth too ripe,
Let his divinity o'erflowing die

[1] release

In music, through the vales of Thessaly:[1]
145 Some idly trail'd their sheep-hooks on the ground,
And some kept up a shrilly mellow sound
With ebon-tipped flutes: close after these,
Now coming from beneath the forest trees,
A venerable priest full soberly,
150 Begirt with minist'ring looks: alway his eye
Steadfast upon the matted turf he kept,
And after him his sacred vestments swept.
From his right hand there swung a vase, milk-white,
Of mingled wine, out-sparkling generous light;
155 And in his left he held a basket full
Of all sweet herbs that searching eye could cull:
Wild thyme, and valley-lilies whiter still
Than Leda's love,[2] and cresses from the rill.
His aged head, crowned with beechen wreath,
160 Seem'd like a poll[3] of ivy in the teeth
Of winter hoar. Then came another crowd
Of shepherds, lifting in due time aloud
Their share of the ditty. After them appear'd,
Up-follow'd by a multitude that rear'd
165 Their voices to the clouds, a fair wrought car,
Easily rolling so as scarce to mar
The freedom of three steeds of dapple brown:
Who stood therein did seem of great renown
Among the throng. His youth was fully blown,
170 Showing like Ganymede to manhood grown;
And, for those simple times, his garments were
A chieftain king's: beneath his breast, half bare,
Was hung a silver bugle, and between
His nervy knees there lay a boar-spear keen.
175 A smile was on his countenance; he seem'd,
To common lookers-on, like one who dream'd
Of idleness in groves Elysian:

[1] A reference to Apollo's service with King Admetus. Æsculapius. Apollo's son, had been killed by a bolt of lightning forged by the Cyclops. Apollo killed the Cyclops, and was compelled to undergo human service as punishment. See Lowell's *The Shepherd of King Admetus*; also Meredith's *Phœbus with Admetus*.
[2] Jove, in the form of a swan. [3] head

But there were some who feelingly could
    scan
A lurking trouble in his nether lip,
180 And see that oftentimes the reins would
    slip
Through his forgotten hands: then would
    they sigh,
And think of yellow leaves, of owlet's cry,
Of logs piled solemnly.—Ah, well-a-day,
Why should our young Endymion pine
    away?

185   Soon the assembly, in a circle rang'd,
Stood silent round the shrine: each look
    was chang'd
To sudden veneration: women meek
Beckon'd their sons to silence; while each
    cheek
Of virgin bloom paled gently for slight
    fear.
190 Endymion too, without a forest peer,
Stood, wan and pale, and with an awed
    face,
Among his brothers of the mountain chace.
In midst of all, the venerable priest
Eyed them with joy from greatest to the
    least,
195 And, after lifting up his aged hands,
Thus spake he: ''Men of Latmos! shep-
    herd bands!
Whose care it is to guard a thousand flocks:
Whether descended from beneath the rocks
That overtop your mountains; whether
    come
200 From valleys where the pipe is never
    dumb;
Or from your swelling downs, where sweet
    air stirs
Blue harebells lightly, and where prickly
    furze
Buds lavish gold; or ye, whose precious
    charge
Nibble their fill at ocean's very marge,
205 Whose mellow reeds are touch'd with
    sounds forlorn
By the dim echoes of old Triton's horn:
Mothers and wives! who day by day pre-
    pare
The scrip,[1] with needments, for the moun-
    tain air;
And all ye gentle girls who foster up
210 Udderless lambs, and in a little cup
Will put choice honey for a favor'd youth:
Yea, every one attend! for in good truth
Our vows are wanting to our great god
    Pan.
Are not our lowing heifers sleeker than

215 Night-swollen mushrooms? Are not our
    wide plains
Speckled with countless fleeces? Have not
    rains
Green'd over April's lap? No howling sad
Sickens our fearful ewes; and we have had
Great bounty from Endymion our lord.
220 The earth is glad: the merry lark has
    pour'd
His early song against yon breezy sky
That spreads so clear o'er our solemnity.''

    Thus ending, on the shrine he heap'd a
    spire
Of teeming sweets, enkindling sacred fire;
225 Anon he stain'd the thick and spongy sod
With wine, in honor of the shepherd-god.
Now while the earth was drinking it, and
    while
Bay leaves were cracking in the fragrant
    pile,
And gummy frankincense was sparkling
    bright
230 'Neath smothering parsley, and a hazy
    light
Spread grayly eastward, thus a chorus
    sang:

    ''O thou, whose mighty palace roof doth
    hang
From jagged trunks, and overshadoweth
Eternal whispers, glooms, the birth, life,
    death
235 Of unseen flowers in heavy peacefulness;
Who lov'st to see the hamadryads[1] dress
Their ruffled locks where meeting hazels
    darken;
And through whole solemn hours dost sit,
    and hearken
The dreary melody of bedded reeds—
240 In desolate places, where dank moisture
    breeds
The pipy hemlock to strange overgrowth;
Bethinking thee, how melancholy loth
Thou wast to lose fair Syrinx—do thou now,
By thy love's milky brow!
245 By all the trembling mazes that she ran,
Hear us, great Pan!

    ''O thou, for whose soul-soothing quiet,
    turtles[2]
Passion their voices cooingly 'mong myrtles,
What time thou wanderest at eventide
250 Through sunny meadows, that outskirt the
    side
Of thine enmossed realms: O thou, to whom
Broad-leaved fig trees even now foredoom[3]
Their ripen'd fruitage; yellow girted bees
Their golden honeycombs; our village leas
255 Their fairest blossom'd beans and poppied
    corn;[4]

---

[1] A small bag for food. See Spenser's *The Faerie Queene*, I, 6, 35.

[1] tree nymphs   [3] predestinate; decree
[2] turtledoves   [4] wheat filled with poppies

The chuckling linnet its five young unborn,
To sing for thee; low creeping strawberries
Their summer coolness; pent up butterflies
Their freckled wings; yea, the fresh-bud-
ding year
260 All its completions—be quickly near,
By every wind that nods the mountain pine,
O Forester divine!

"Thou, to whom every faun and satyr
flies
For willing service; whether to surprise
265 The squatted hare while in half-sleeping
fit;
Or upward ragged precipices flit
To save poor lambkins from the eagle's
maw;
Or by mysterious enticement draw
Bewilder'd shepherds to their path again;
270 Or to tread breathless round the frothy main,
And gather up all fancifullest shells
For thee to tumble into Naiads' cells,
And, being hidden, laugh at their out-peep-
ing;
Or to delight thee with fantastic leaping,
275 The while they pelt each other on the crown
With silvery oak-apples, and fir-cones
brown,—
By all the echoes that about thee ring,
Hear us, O satyr king!

"O hearkener to the loud-clapping shears
280 While ever and anon to his shorn peers
A ram goes bleating: winder of the horn,
When snouted wild-boars routing tender corn
Anger our huntsmen: breather round our
farms,
To keep off mildews, and all weather harms:
285 Strange ministrant of undescribed sounds,
That come a-swooning over hollow grounds,
And wither drearily on barren moors:
Dread opener of the mysterious doors
Leading to universal knowledge,—see,
290 Great son of Dryope,
The many that are come to pay their vows
With leaves about their brows!

"Be still the unimaginable lodge
For solitary thinking; such as dodge
295 Conception to the very bourne of heaven,
Then leave the naked brain: be still the
leaven,
That spreading in this dull and clodded
earth
Gives it a touch ethereal—a new birth:
Be still a symbol of immensity;
300 A firmament reflected in a sea;
An element filling the space between;
An unknown—but no more; we humbly
screen
With uplift hands our foreheads, lowly bend-
ing,
And giving out a shout most heaven-rending,
305 Conjure thee to receive our humble Pæan,[1]
Upon thy Mount Lycean!''

[1] song of praise

Even while they brought the burden to a
close,
A shout from the whole multitude arose,
That linger'd in the air like dying rolls
310 Of abrupt thunder, when Ionian shoals
Of dolphins bob their noses through the
brine.
Meantime, on shady levels, mossy fine,
Young companies nimbly began dancing
To the swift treble pipe, and humming
string.
315 Aye, those fair living forms swam heav-
enly
To tunes forgotten—out of memory:
Fair creatures! whose young children's
children bred
Thermopylæ its heroes—not yet dead,
But in old marbles ever beautiful.
320 High genitors,[1] unconscious did they cull
Time's sweet first-fruits—they danc'd to
weariness,
And then in quiet circles did they press
The hillock turf, and caught the latter end
Of some strange history, potent to send
325 A young mind from its bodily tenement.
Or they might watch the quoit-pitchers,
intent
On either side; pitying the sad death
Of Hyacinthus, when the cruel breath
Of Zephyr slew him,—Zephyr penitent,
330 Who now, ere Phœbus mounts the firma-
ment,
Fondles the flower amid the sobbing rain.
The archers too, upon a wider plain,
Beside the feathery whizzing of the shaft,
And the dull twanging bowstring, and the
raft[2]
335 Branch down sweeping from a tall ash top,
Call'd up a thousand thoughts to envelope
Those who would watch. Perhaps, the
trembling knee
And frantic gape of lonely Niobe,
Poor, lonely Niobe! when her lovely young
340 Were dead and gone, and her caressing
tongue
Lay a lost thing upon her paly lip,
And very, very deadliness did nip
Her motherly cheeks. Arous'd from this
sad mood
By one, who at a distance loud halloo'd,
345 Uplifting his strong bow into the air,
Many might after brighter visions stare:
After the Argonauts, in blind amaze
Tossing about on Neptune's restless ways,
Until, from the horizon's vaulted side,
350 There shot a golden splendor far and wide,
Spangling those million poutings of the
brine

[1] ancestors   [2] broken

With quivering ore: 'twas even an awful
    shine
From the exaltation of Apollo's bow;
A heavenly beacon in their dreary woe.
355 Who thus were ripe for high contemplat-
    ing,
Might turn their steps towards the sober
    ring
Where sat Endymion and the aged priest
'Mong shepherds gone in eld, whose looks
    increas'd
The silvery setting of their mortal star.
360 There they discours'd upon the fragile bar
That keeps us from our homes ethereal;
And what our duties there: to nightly call
Vesper, the beauty - crest of summer
    weather;
To summon all the downiest clouds to-
    gether
365 For the sun's purple couch; to emulate
In minist'ring the potent rule of fate
With speed of fire-tail'd exhalations;[1]
To tint her pallid cheek with bloom, who
    cons
Sweet poesy by moonlight: besides these,
370 A world of other unguess'd offices.
Anon they wander'd, by divine converse,
Into Elysium; vying to rehearse
Each one his own anticipated bliss.
One felt heart-certain that he could not
    miss
375 His quick-gone love, among fair blossom'd
    boughs,
Where every zephyr-sigh pouts, and en-
    dows
Her lips with music for the welcoming.
Another wish'd, 'mid that eternal spring,
To meet his rosy child, with feathery sails,
380 Sweeping, eye-earnestly, through almond
    vales:
Who, suddenly, should stoop through the
    smooth wind,
And with the balmiest leaves his temples
    bind;
And, ever after, through those regions be
His messenger, his little Mercury.
385 Some were athirst in soul to see again
Their fellow huntsmen o'er the wide cham-
    paign[2]
In times long past; to sit with them, and
    talk
Of all the chances in their earthly walk;
Comparing, joyfully, their plenteous stores
390 Of happiness, to when upon the moors,
Benighted, close they huddled from the
    cold,

And shar'd their famish'd scrips. Thus
    all out-told
Their fond imaginations,—saving him
Whose eyelids curtain'd up their jewels
    dim,
395 Endymion: yet hourly had he striven
To hide the cankering venom, that had
    riven
His fainting recollections. Now indeed
His senses had swoon'd off: he did not
    heed
The sudden silence, or the whispers low,
400 Or the old eyes dissolving at his woe,
Or anxious calls, or close of trembling
    palms,
Or maiden's sigh, that grief itself em-
    balms:
But in the self-same fixed trance he kept,
Like one who on the earth had never stept.
405 Aye, even as dead-still as a marble man,
Frozen in that old tale Arabian.[1]

Who whispers him so pantingly and
    close?
Peona, his sweet sister: of all those,
His friends, the dearest. Hushing signs
    she made,
410 And breath'd a sister's sorrow to persuade
A yielding up, a cradling on her care.
Her eloquence did breathe away the curse:
She led him, like some midnight spirit
    nurse
Of happy changes in emphatic dreams,
415 Along a path between two little streams,—
Guarding his forehead, with her round
    elbow,
From low-grown branches, and his foot-
    steps slow
From stumbling over stumps and hillocks
    small;
Until they came to where these streamlets
    fall,
420 With mingled bubblings and a gentle rush,
Into a river, clear, brimful, and flush
With crystal mocking of the trees and sky.
A little shallop, floating there hard by,
Pointed its beak over the fringed bank;
425 And soon it lightly dipt, and rose, and
    sank,
And dipt again, with the young couple's
    weight,—
Peona guiding, through the water straight,
Towards a bowery island opposite;
Which gaining presently, she steered light
430 Into a shady, fresh, and ripply cove,
Where nested was an arbor, overwove
By many a summer's silent fingering;
To whose cool bosom she was used to bring

---

[1] Shooting stars, or meteors, which were supposed to exhale fire.
[2] level field

[1] *The Arabian Nights' Entertainments.*

Her playmates, with their needle broidery,
435 And minstrel memories of times gone by.

So she was gently glad to see him laid
Under her favorite bower's quiet shade,
On her own couch, new made of flower
    leaves,
Dried carefully on the cooler side of
    sheaves
440 When last the sun his autumn tresses
    shook,
And the tann'd harvesters rich armfuls
    took.
Soon was he quieted to slumbrous rest:
But, ere it crept upon him, he had prest
Peona's busy hand against his lips,
445 And still, a-sleeping, held her finger-tips
In tender pressure. And as a willow keeps
A patient watch over the stream that
    creeps
Windingly by it, so the quiet maid
Held her in peace: so that a whispering
    blade
450 Of grass, a wailful gnat, a bee bustling
Down in the blue-bells, or a wren light-
    rustling
Among sere leaves and twigs, might all be
    heard.

O magic sleep! O comfortable bird,
That broodest o'er the troubled sea of the
    mind
455 Till it is hush'd and smooth! O uncon-
    fin'd
Restraint! imprison'd liberty! great key
To golden palaces, strange minstrelsy,
Fountains grotesque, new trees, bespangled
    caves,
Echoing grottoes, full of tumbling waves
460 And moonlight; aye, to all the mazy world
Of silvery enchantment!—who, upfurl'd
Beneath thy drowsy wing a triple hour,
But renovates and lives?—Thus, in the
    bower,
Endymion was calm'd to life again.
465 Opening his eyelids with a healthier brain,
He said: "I feel this thine endearing
    love
All through my bosom: thou art as a dove
Trembling its closed eyes and sleeked wings
About me; and the pearliest dew not
    brings
470 Such morning incense from the fields of
    May,
As do those brighter drops that twinkling
    stray
From those kind eyes,—the very home and
    haunt
Of sisterly affection. Can I want

Aught else, aught nearer heaven, than
    such tears?
475 Yet dry them up, in bidding hence all fears
That, any longer, I will pass my days
Alone and sad. No, I will once more raise
My voice upon the mountain-heights; once
    more
Make my horn parley from their foreheads
    hoar:
480 Again my trooping hounds their tongues
    shall loll
Around the breathed boar: again I'll poll[1]
The fair-grown yew tree, for a chosen
    bow:
And, when the pleasant sun is getting
    low,
Again I'll linger in a sloping mead
485 To hear the speckled thrushes, and see
    feed
Our idle sheep. So be thou cheered, sweet,
And, if thy lute is here, softly intreat
My soul to keep in its resolved course."

Hereat Peona, in their silver source,
490 Shut her pure sorrow-drops with glad ex-
    claim,
And took a lute, from which there pulsing
    came
A lively prelude, fashioning the way
In which her voice should wander. 'Twas
    a lay
More subtle cadenced, more forest wild
495 Than Dryope's lone lulling of her child;
And nothing since has floated in the air
So mournful strange. Surely some influ-
    ence rare
Went, spiritual, through the damsel's
    hand;
For still, with Delphic emphasis,[2] she
    spann'd
500 The quick invisible strings, even though
    she saw
Endymion's spirit melt away and thaw
Before the deep intoxication.
But soon she came, with sudden burst,
    upon
Her self-possession — swung the lute
    aside,
505 And earnestly said: "Brother, 'tis vain
    to hide
That thou dost know of things mysterious,
Immortal, starry; such alone could thus
Weigh down thy nature. Hast thou sinn'd
    in aught
Offensive to the heavenly powers? Caught
510 A Paphian dove[3] upon a message sent?

[1] cut the top from
[2] That is, with frenzied passion, like that of
the inspired priestess at Delphi.
[3] A dove sent by Venus from Paphos.

Thy deathful bow against some deer-herd
    bent
Sacred to Dian? Haply, thou hast seen
Her naked limbs among the alders green;
And that, alas! is death.[1] No, I can trace
515 Something more high perplexing in thy
    face!''

    Endymion look'd at her, and press'd
      her hand,
And said, ''Art thou so pale, who wast so
    bland
And merry in our meadows? How is this?
Tell me thine ailment: tell me all amiss!—
520 Ah! thou hast been unhappy at the change
Wrought suddenly in me. What indeed
    more strange?
Or more complete to overwhelm surmise?
Ambition is so sluggard: 'tis no prize,
That toiling years would put within my
    grasp,
525 That I have sigh'd for: with so deadly
    gasp
No man e'er panted for a mortal love.
So all have set my heavier grief above
These things which happen. Rightly have
    they done:
I, who still saw the horizontal sun
530 Heave his broad shoulder o'er the edge of
    the world,
Out-facing Lucifer, and then had hurl'd
My spear aloft, as signal for the chase—
I, who for very sport of heart, would race
With my own steed from Araby; pluck
    down
535 A vulture from his towery perching;
    frown
A lion into growling, loth retire—
To lose, at once, all my toil-breeding fire,
And sink thus low! but I will ease my
    breast
Of secret grief, here in this bowery nest.

540 ''This river does not see the naked sky,
Till it begin to progress silverly
Around the western border of the wood,
Whence, from a certain spot, its winding
    flood
Seems at the distance like a crescent moon:
545 And in that nook, the very pride of June,
Had I been used to pass my weary eves;
The rather for the sun unwilling leaves
So dear a picture of his sovereign power,
And I could witness his most kingly hour,
550 When he doth tighten up the golden reins,
And paces leisurely down amber plains

His snorting four. Now when his chariot
    last
Its beam against the zodiac-lion cast,[1]
There blossom'd suddenly a magic bed
555 Of sacred ditamy,[2] and poppies red:
At which I wondered greatly, knowing well
That but one night had wrought this flow-
    ery spell;
And, sitting down close by, began to muse
What it might mean. Perhaps, thought I,
    Morpheus,
560 In passing here, his owlet pinions shook;
Or, it may be, ere matron Night uptook
Her ebon urn, young Mercury, by stealth,
Had dipt his rod in it: such garland
    wealth
Came not by common growth. Thus on I
    thought,
565 Until my head was dizzy and distraught.
Moreover, through the dancing poppies
    stole
A breeze, most softly lulling to my soul;
And shaping visions all about my sight
Of colors, wings, and bursts of spangly
    light;
570 The which became more strange, and
    strange, and dim,
And then were gulf'd in a tumultuous
    swim:
And then I fell asleep. Ah, can I tell
The enchantment that afterwards befell?
Yet it was but a dream: yet such a dream
575 That never tongue, although it overteem
With mellow utterance, like a cavern
    spring,
Could figure out and to conception bring
All I beheld and felt. Methought I lay
Watching the zenith, where the milky way
580 Among the stars in virgin splendor pours;
And travelling my eye, until the doors
Of heaven appear'd to open for my flight,
I became loth and fearful to alight
From such high soaring by a downward
    glance:
585 So kept me stedfast in that airy trance,
Spreading imaginary pinions wide.
When, presently, the stars began to glide,
And faint away, before my eager view:
At which I sigh'd that I could not pursue,
590 And dropt my vision to the horizon's
    verge;
And lo! from opening clouds, I saw emerge
The loveliest moon, that ever silver'd o'er
A shell for Neptune's goblet: she did soar
So passionately bright, my dazzled soul

---

[1] A reference to Actæon, who saw Diana bathing, and who was transformed into a stag
and killed by his own hounds.

[1] The sun is in the sign of the lion from July
22 to August 22.
[2] dittany, a plant famous for supposed medicinal
virtues

595 Commingling with her argent spheres did
    roll
Through clear and cloudy, even when she
    went
At last into a dark and vapory tent—
Whereat, methought, the lidless-eyed train
Of planets all were in the blue again.
600 To commune with those orbs, once more I
    rais'd
My sight right upward: but it was quite
    daz'd
By a bright something, sailing down apace,
Making me quickly veil my eyes and face:
Again I look'd, and, O ye deities,
605 Who from Olympus watch our destinies!
Whence that completed form of all com-
    pleteness?
Whence came that high perfection of all
    sweetness?
Speak, stubborn earth, and tell me where,
    O where
Hast thou a symbol of her golden hair?
610 Not oat-sheaves drooping in the western
    sun;
Not—thy soft hand, fair sister! let me
    shun
Such follying before thee—yet she had,
Indeed, locks bright enough to make me
    mad;
And they were simply gordian'd up[1] and
    braided,
615 Leaving, in naked comeliness, unshaded,
Her pearl round ears, white neck, and
    orbed brow;
The which were blended in, I know not
    how,
With such a paradise of lips and eyes,
Blush-tinted cheeks, half smiles, and
    faintest sighs,
620 That, when I think thereon, my spirit
    clings
And plays about its fancy, till the stings
Of human neighborhood envenom all.
Unto what awful power shall I call?
To what high fane?—Ah! see her hovering
    feet,
625 More bluely vein'd, more soft, more
    whitely sweet
Than those of sea-born Venus,[2] when she
    rose
From out her cradle shell. The wind out-
    blows
Her scarf into a fluttering pavilion;
'Tis blue, and over-spangled with a million
630 Of little eyes, as though thou wert to shed,

Over the darkest, lushest blue-bell bed,
Handfuls of daisies.''—''Endymion, how
    strange!
Dream within dream!''—''She took an
    airy range,
And then, towards me, like a very maid,
635 Came blushing, waning, willing, and
    afraid,
And press'd me by the hand: Ah! 'twas
    too much;
Methought I fainted at the charmed
    touch,
Yet held my recollection, even as one
Who dives three fathoms where the waters
    run
640 Gurgling in beds of coral: for anon,
I felt upmounted in that region
Where falling stars dart their artillery
    forth,
And eagles struggle with the buffeting
    north
That balances the heavy meteor-stone;[1]—
645 Felt too, I was not fearful, nor alone,
But lapp'd and lull'd along the dangerous
    sky.
Soon, as it seem'd, we left our journeying
    high,
And straightway into frightful eddies
    swoop'd;
Such as aye muster where gray time has
    scoop'd
650 Huge dens and caverns in a mountain's
    side:
There hollow sounds arous'd me, and I
    sigh'd
To faint once more by looking on my
    bliss—
I was distracted; madly did I kiss
The wooing arms which held me, and did
    give
655 My eyes at once to death: but 'twas to
    live,
To take in draughts of life from the gold
    fount
Of kind and passionate looks; to count,
    and count
The moments, by some greedy help that
    seem'd
A second self, that each might be redeem'd
660 And plunder'd of its load of blessedness.
Ah, desperate mortal! I e'en dar'd to
    press
Her very cheek against my crowned lip,
And, at that moment, felt my body dip
Into a warmer air: a moment more,
665 Our feet were soft in flowers. There was
    store

[1] made into an intricate knot
[2] According to Hesiod, Venus arose from the
    foam of the sea, and was called, by the
    Greeks, Aphrodite, *the foam born.*

[1] the north wind which checks the flying meteor

Of newest joys upon that alp.[1] Some-
　　times
A scent of violets, and blossoming limes,[2]
Loiter'd around us; then of honey cells,
Made delicate from all white-flower bells;
670 And once, above the edges of our nest,
An arch face peep'd,—an Oread as I
　　guess'd.

　　"Why did I dream that sleep o'er-
　　　power'd me
In midst of all this heaven? Why not see,
Far off, the shadows of his pinions dark,
675 And stare them from me? But no, like
　　a spark
That needs must die, although its little
　　beam
Reflects upon a diamond, my sweet dream
Fell into nothing—into stupid sleep.
And so it was, until a gentle creep,
680 A careful moving caught my waking ears,
And up I started: Ah! my sighs, my
　　tears,
My clenched hands;—for lo! the poppies
　　hung
Dew-dabbled on their stalks, the ouzel[3]
　　sung
A heavy ditty, and the sullen day
685 Had chidden herald Hesperus away,
With leaden looks: the solitary breeze
Bluster'd, and slept, and its wild self did
　　teaze
With wayward melancholy; and I thought,
Mark me, Peona! that sometimes it
　　brought
690 Faint fare-thee-wells, and sigh-shrilled
　　adieus!—
Away I wander'd—all the pleasant hues
Of heaven and earth had faded: deepest
　　shades
Were deepest dungeons; heaths and sunny
　　glades
Were full of pestilent light; our taintless
　　rills
695 Seem'd sooty, and o'er-spread with up-
　　turn'd gills
Of dying fish; the vermeil rose had blown
In frightful scarlet, and its thorns out-
　　grown
Like spiked aloe. If an innocent bird
Before my heedless footsteps stirr'd, and
　　stirr'd
700 In little journeys, I beheld in it
A disguis'd demon, missioned to knit
My soul with under darkness; to entice
My stumblings down some monstrous
　　precipice:

Therefore I eager follow'd, and did curse
705 The disappointment. Time, that aged
　　nurse,
Rock'd me to patience. Now, thank gentle
　　heaven!
These things, with all their comfortings,
　　are given
To my down-sunken hours, and with thee,
Sweet sister, help to stem the ebbing sea
Of weary life."

710 　　　　Thus ended he, and both
Sat silent: for the maid was very loth
To answer; feeling well that breathed
　　words
Would all be lost, unheard, and vain as
　　swords
Against the enchased[1] crocodile, or leaps
715 Of grasshoppers against the sun. She
　　weeps,
And wonders; struggles to devise some
　　blame;
To put on such a look as would say, *Shame
On this ·poor weakness!* but, for all her
　　strife
She could as soon have crush'd away the
　　life
720 From a sick dove. At length, to break the
　　pause,
She said with trembling chance: "Is this
　　the cause?
This all? Yet it is strange, and sad,
　　alas!
That one who through this middle earth
　　should pass
Most like a sojourning demi-god, and leave
725 His name upon the harp-string, should
　　achieve
No higher bard than simple maidenhood,
Singing alone, and fearfully,—how the
　　blood
Left his young cheek; and how he used to
　　stray
He knew not where; and how he would say,
　　nay,
730 If any said 'twas love: and yet 'twas love;
What could it be but love? How a ring-
　　dove
Let fall a sprig of yew tree in his path;
And how he died: and then, that love doth
　　scathe,
The gentle heart, as northern blasts do
　　roses;
735 And then the ballad of his sad life closes
With sighs, and an alas!—Endymion!
Be rather in the trumpet's mouth,—anon
Among the winds at large—that all may
　　hearken!

[1] high mountain　　　[3] European blackbird
[2] lindens

[1] incased

Although, before the crystal heavens
darken,
740 I watch and dote upon the silver lakes
Pictur'd in western cloudiness, that takes
The semblance of gold rocks and bright
gold sands,
Islands, and creeks, and amber-fretted
strands
With horses prancing o'er them, palaces
745 And towers of amethyst,—would I so
tease
My pleasant days, because I could not
mount
Into those regions? The Morphean fount
Of that fine element that visions, dreams,
And fitful whims of sleep are made of,
streams
750 Into its airy channels with so subtle,
So thin a breathing, not the spider's
shuttle,
Circled a million times within the space
Of a swallow's nest-door, could delay a
trace,
A tinting of its quality: how light
755 Must dreams themselves be; seeing they're
more slight
Than the mere nothing that engenders
them!
Then wherefore sully the entrusted gem
Of high and noble life with thoughts so
sick?
Why pierce high-fronted honor to the quick
760 For nothing but a dream?" Hereat the
youth
Look'd up: a conflicting of shame and
ruth
Was in his plaited brow: yet, his eyelids
Widened a little, as when Zephyr bids
A little breeze to creep between the fans
765 Of careless butterflies: amid his pains
He seem'd to taste a drop of manna-dew,
Full palatable; and a color grew
Upon his cheek, while thus he lifeful spake.

"Peona! ever have I long'd to slake
770 My thirst for the world's praises: nothing
base,
No merely slumberous phantasm, could
unlace
The stubborn canvas for my voyage prepar'd—
Though now 'tis tatter'd; leaving my bark
bar'd
And sullenly drifting: yet my higher hope
775 Is of too wide, too rainbow-large a scope,
To fret at myriads of earthly wrecks.
Wherein lies happiness? In that which
becks
Our ready minds to fellowship divine,

A fellowship with essence; till we shine,
780 Full alchemiz'd,[1] and free of space. Be-
hold
The clear religion of heaven! Fold
A rose leaf round thy finger's taperness,
And soothe thy lips: hist, when the airy
stress
Of music's kiss impregnates the free
winds,
785 And with a sympathetic touch unbinds
Æolian magic from their lucid wombs:
Then old songs waken from enclouded
tombs;
Old ditties sigh above their father's
grave;
Ghosts of melodious prophesyings rave
790 Round every spot where trod Apollo's
foot;
Bronze clarions awake, and faintly bruit,[2]
Where long ago a giant battle was;
And, from the turf, a lullaby doth pass
In every place where infant Orpheus slept.
795 Feel we these things?—that moment have
we stept
Into a sort of oneness, and our state
Is like a floating spirit's. But there are
Richer entanglements, enthralments far
More self-destroying, leading, by degrees,
800 To the chief intensity: the crown of these
Is made of love and friendship, and sits
high
Upon the forehead of humanity.
All its more ponderous and bulky worth
Is friendship, whence there ever issues
forth
805 A steady splendor; but at the tip-top,
There hangs by unseen film, an orbed drop
Of light, and that is love: its influence,
Thrown in our eyes, genders a novel sense,
At which we start and fret; till in the end,
810 Melting into its radiance, we blend,
Mingle, and so become a part of it,—
Nor with aught else can our souls interknit
So wingedly: when we combine therewith,
Life's self is nourish'd by its proper pith,
815 And we are nurtured like a pelican brood.
Aye, so delicious is the unsating food,
That men, who might have tower'd in the
van
Of all the congregated world, to fan
And winnow from the coming step of
time
820 All chaff of custom, wipe away all slime
Left by men-slugs and human serpentry,
Have been content to let occasion die,
Whilst they did sleep in love's Elysium.
And, truly, I would rather be struck dumb,

[1] changed to a higher nature
[2] sound

825 Than speak against this ardent listlessness:
For I have ever thought that it might bless
The world with benefits unknowingly;
As does the nightingale, upperched high,
And cloister'd among cool and bunched
leaves—
830 She sings but to her love, nor e'er con-
ceives
How tiptoe Night holds back her dark-
gray hood.
Just so may love, although 'tis understood
The mere commingling of passionate
breath,
Produce more than our searching wit-
nesseth:
835 What I know not: but who, of men, can
tell
That flowers would bloom, or that green
fruit would swell
To melting pulp, that fish would have
bright mail,
The earth its dower of river, wood, and
vale,
The meadows runnels, runnels pebble-
stones,
840 The seed its harvest, or the lute its tones,
Tones ravishment, or ravishment its sweet,
If human souls did never kiss and greet.

"Now, if this earthly love has power to
make
Men's being mortal, immortal; to shake
845 Ambition from their memories, and brim
Their measure of content: what merest
whim,
Seems all this poor endeavor after fame,
To one, who keeps within his stedfast aim
A love immortal, an immortal too.
850 Look not so wilder'd; for these things are
true,
And never can be born of atomies
That buzz about our slumbers, like brain-
flies,
Leaving us fancy-sick. No, no, I'm sure,
My restless spirit never could endure
855 To brood so long upon one luxury,
Unless it did, though fearfully, espy
A hope beyond the shadow of a dream.
My sayings will the less obscured seem,
When I have told thee how my waking
sight
860 Has made me scruple whether that same
night
Was pass'd in dreaming. Hearken, sweet
Peona!
Beyond the matron-temple of Latona,
Which we should see but for these darken-
ing boughs,

Lies a deep hollow, from whose ragged
brows
865 Bushes and trees do lean all round athwart
And meet so nearly, that with wings
outraught,[1]
And spreaded tail, a vulture could not glide
Past them, but he must brush on every
side.
Some moulder'd steps lead into this cool
cell,
870 Far as the slabbed margin of a well,
Whose patient level peeps its crystal eye
Right upward, through the bushes, to the
sky.
Oft have I brought thee flowers, on their
stalks set
Like vestal primroses, but dark velvet
875 Edges them round, and they have golden
pits:
'Twas there I got them, from the gaps and
slits
In a mossy stone, that sometimes was my
seat,
When all above was faint with mid-day
heat.
And there in strife no burning thoughts to
heed,
880 I'd bubble up the water through a reed;
So reaching back to boyhood: make me
ships
Of moulted feathers, touchwood,[2] alder
chips,
With leaves stuck in them; and the Neptune be
Of their pretty ocean. Oftener, heavily,
885 When lovelorn hours had left me less a
child,
I sat contemplating the figures wild
Of o'er-head clouds melting the mirror
through.
Upon a day, while thus I watch'd, by flew
A cloudy Cupid, with his bow and quiver;
890 So plainly character'd, no breeze would
shiver
The happy chance: so happy, I was fain
To follow it upon the open plain,
And, therefore, was just going, when, be-
hold!
A wonder, fair as any I have told—
895 The same bright face I tasted in my
sleep,
Smiling in the clear well. My heart did
leap
Through the cool depth.—It moved as if to
flee—
I started up, when lo! refreshfully,
There came upon my face, in plenteous
showers,

---

[1] outreached   [2] decayed wood

900 Dew-drops, and dewy buds, and leaves,
    and flowers,
Wrapping all objects from my smother'd
    sight,
Bathing my spirit in a new delight.
Aye, such a breathless honey-feel of bliss
Alone preserved me from the drear abyss
905 Of death, for the fair form had gone
    again.
Pleasure is oft a visitant; but pain
Clings cruelly to us, like the gnawing
    sloth
On the deer's tender haunches: late, and
    loth,
'Tis scar'd away by slow returning pleas-
    ure.
910 How sickening, how dark the dreadful
    leisure
Of weary days, made deeper exquisite,
By a foreknowledge of unslumbrous night!
Like sorrow came upon me, heavier still,
Than when I wander'd from the poppy
    hill:
915 And a whole age of lingering moments
    crept
Sluggishly by, ere more contentment swept
Away at once the deadly yellow spleen.
Yes, thrice have I this fair enchantment
    seen;
Once more been tortured with renewed
    life.
920 When last the wintry gusts gave over strife
With the conquering sun of spring, and
    left the skies
Warm and serene, but yet with moisten'd
    eyes
In pity of the shatter'd infant buds,—
That time thou didst adorn, with amber
    studs,
925 My hunting cap, because I laugh'd and
    smil'd,
Chatted with thee, and many days exil'd
All torment from my breast;—'twas even
    then,
Straying about, yet, coop'd up in the
    den
Of helpless discontent,—hurling my lance
930 From place to place, and following at
    chance,
At last, by hap, through some young trees
    it struck,
And, plashing among bedded pebbles,
    stuck
In the middle of a brook,—whose silver
    ramble
Down twenty little falls, through reeds and
    bramble,
935 Tracing[1] along, it brought me to a cave,
    [1] wandering

Whence it ran brightly forth, and white
    did lave
The nether sides of mossy stones and
    rock,—
'Mong which it gurgled blythe adieus, to
    mock
Its own sweet grief at parting. Overhead,
940 Hung a lush screen of drooping weeds,
    and spread
Thick, as to curtain up some wood-
    nymph's home.
"Ah! impious mortal, whither do I
    roam?"
Said I, low-voic'd: "Ah, whither! 'Tis
    the grot
Of Proserpine, when Hell, obscure and hot,
945 Doth her resign; and where her tender
    hands
She dabbles, on the cool and sluicy sands:
Or 'tis the cell of Echo, where she sits,
And dabbles thorough silence, till her wits
Are gone in tender madness, and anon,
950 Faints into sleep, with many a dying tone
Of sadness. O that she would take my
    vows,
And breathe them sighingly among the
    boughs,
To sue her gentle ears for whose fair head,
Daily, I pluck sweet flowerets from their
    bed,
955 And weave them dyingly—send honey-
    whispers
Round every leaf, that all those gentle
    lispers
May sigh my love unto her pitying!
O charitable Echo! hear, and sing
This ditty to her!—tell her"—So I stay'd
960 My foolish tongue, and listening, half-
    afraid,
Stood stupefied with my own empty folly.
And blushing for the freaks of melan-
    choly.
Salt tears were coming, when I heard my
    name
Most fondly lipp'd, and then these accents
    came:
965 "Endymion! the cave is secreter
Than the isle of Delos. Echo hence shall stir
No sighs but sigh-warm kisses, or light
    noise
Of thy combing hand, the while it travel-
    ling cloys
And trembles through my labyrinthine
    hair."
970 At that oppress'd I hurried in.—Ah!
    where
Are those swift moments? Whither are
    they fled?
I'll smile no more, Peona; nor will wed

Sorrow the way to death; but patiently
Bear up against it: so farewell, sad sigh;
975 And come instead demurest meditation,
To occupy me wholly, and to fashion
My pilgrimage for the world's dusky
    brink.
No more will I count over, link by link,
My chain of grief: no longer strive to find
980 A half-forgetfulness in mountain wind
Blustering about my ears: aye, thou shalt
    see,
Dearest of sisters, what my life shall be;
What a calm round of hours shall make
    my days.
There is a paly flame of hope that plays
985 Where'er I look: but yet, I'll say 'tis
    naught—
And here I bid it die. Have not I caught,
Already, a more healthy countenance?
By this the sun is setting; we may chance
Meet some of our near-dwellers with my
    car.''

990   This said, he rose, faint-smiling like a
    star
Through autumn mists, and took Peona's
    hand:
They stept into the boat, and launch'd
    from land.

Book II

O sovereign power of love! O grief! O
    balm!
All records, saving thine, come cool, and
    calm,
And shadowy, through the mist of passed
    years:
For others, good or bad, hatred and tears
5 Have become indolent; but touching thine,
One sigh doth echo, one poor sob doth pine,
One kiss brings honey-dew from buried
    days.
The woes of Troy, towers smothering o'er
    their blaze,
Stiff-holden shields, far-piercing spears,
    keen blades,
10 Struggling, and blood, and shrieks—all
    dimly fades
Into some backward corner of the brain;
Yet, in our very souls, we feel amain
The close[1] of Troïlus and Cressid sweet.
Hence, pageant history! hence, gilded
    cheat!
15 Swart[2] planet in the universe of deeds!
Wide sea, that one continuous murmur
    breeds
Along the pebbled shore of memory!
Many old rotten-timber'd boats there be

Upon thy vaporous bosom, magnified
20 To goodly vessels; many a sail of pride,
And golden-keel'd, is left unlaunch'd and
    dry.
But wherefore this? What care, though
    owl did fly
About the great Athenian admiral's mast.[1]
What care, though striding Alexander past
25 The Indus with his Macedonian numbers?
Though old Ulysses tortured from his slum-
    bers
The glutted Cyclops, what care?—Juliet
    leaning
Amid her window-flowers, — sighing, —
    weaning
Tenderly her fancy from its maiden snow,
30 Doth more avail than these: the silver flow
Of Hero's tears, the swoon of Imogen,
Fair Pastorella in the bandit's den,
Are things to brood on with more ardency
Than the death-day of empires. Fearfully
35 Must such conviction come upon this head,
Who, thus far, discontent, has dared to
    tread,
Without one muse's smile, or kind behest,
The path of love and poesy.[2] But rest,[3]
In chafing restlessness, is yet more drear
40 Than to be crush'd, in striving to uprear
Love's standard on the battlements of song.
So once more days and nights aid me along,
Like legion'd soldiers.

                Brain-sick shepherd-prince,
What promise hast thou faithful guarded
    since
45 The day of sacrifice? Or, have new sorrows
Come with the constant dawn upon thy
    morrows?
Alas! 'tis his old grief. For many days,
Has he been wandering in uncertain ways:
Through wilderness, and woods of mossed
    oaks;
50 Counting his woe-worn minutes, by the
    strokes
Of the lone woodcutter; and listening still,
Hour after hour, to each lush-leav'd rill.
Now he is sittting by a shady spring,
And elbow-deep with feverous fingering
55 Stems the upbursting cold: a wild rose tree
Pavilions him in bloom, and he doth see
A bud which snares his fancy: lo! but now

---

[1] As Themistocles was presenting to his followers his plan of a naval attack against the
Persians at the Battle of Salamis (480 B.C.),
an owl alighted in the rigging of his ship.
As the owl was sacred to Athena, the patroness of Athens, the incident was regarded as a
good omen, and the plan was approved. See
Plutarch's *Life of Themistocles*, 12.
[2] A reference to the poor success of Keats's first
volume of poetry, published in 1817.
[3] inactivity

[1] embrace   [2] evil; causing blight

He plucks it, dips its stalk in the water:
 how!
It swells, it buds, it flowers beneath his
 sight;
60 And, in the middle, there is softly pight[1]
A golden butterfly; upon whose wings
There must be surely character'd strange
 things,
For with wide eye he wonders, and smiles
 oft.

 Lightly this little herald flew aloft,
65 Follow'd by glad Endymion's clasped
 hands:
Onward it flies. From languor's sullen
 bands
His limbs are loos'd, and eager, on he hies
Dazzled to trace it in the sunny skies.
It seem'd he flew, the way so easy was;
70 And like a new-born spirit did he pass
Through the green evening quiet in the
 sun,
O'er many a heath, through many a wood-
 land dun,
Through buried paths, where sleepy twi-
 light dreams
The summer time away. One track un-
 seams
75 A wooded cleft, and, far away, the blue
Of ocean fades upon him; then, anew,
He sinks adown a solitary glen,
Where there was never sound of mortal
 men,
Saving, perhaps, some snow-light cadences
80 Melting to silence, when upon the breeze
Some holy bark let forth an anthem sweet,
To cheer itself to Delphi. Still his feet
Went swift beneath the merry-winged
 guide,
Until it reach'd a splashing fountain's side
85 That, near a cavern's mouth, forever
 pour'd
Unto the temperate air: then high it soar'd,
And, downward, suddenly began to dip,
As if, athirst with so much toil, 'twould sip
The crystal spout-head: so it did, with
 touch
90 Most delicate, as though afraid to smutch
Even with mealy gold the waters clear.
But, at that very touch, to disappear
So fairy-quick, was strange! Bewildered,
Endymion sought around, and shook each
 bed
95 Of covert flowers in vain; and then he
 flung
Himself along the grass. What gentle
 tongue,
What whisperer, disturb'd his gloomy
 rest?

[1] pitched

It was a nymph uprisen to the breast
In the fountain's pebbly margin, and she
 stood
100 'Mong lilies, like the youngest of the brood.
To him her dripping hand she softly kist,
And anxiously began to plait and twist
Her ringlets round her fingers, saying:
 "Youth!
Too long, alas, hast thou starv'd on the
 ruth,
105 The bitterness of love: too long indeed,
Seeing thou art so gentle. Could I weed
Thy soul of care, by heavens, I would offer
All the bright riches of my crystal coffer
To Amphitrite; all my clear-eyed fish,
10 Golden, or rainbow-sided, or purplish,
Vermilion-tail'd, or finn'd with silvery
 gauze;
Yea, or my veined pebble-floor, that draws
A virgin light to the deep; my grotto-sands
Tawny and gold, ooz'd slowly from far
 lands
15 By my diligent springs; my level lilies,
 shells,
My charming rod, my potent river spells;
Yes, everything, even to the pearly cup
Meander gave me,—for I bubbled up
To fainting creatures in a desert wild.
120 But woe is me, I am but as a child
To gladden thee; and all I dare to say,
Is, that I pity thee; that on this day
I've been thy guide; that thou must wan-
 der far
In other regions, past the scanty bar
125 To mortal steps, before thou canst be ta'en
From every wasting sigh, from every pain,
Into the gentle bosom of thy love.
Why it is thus, one knows in heaven above:
But, a poor Naiad, I guess not. Farewell!
130 I have a ditty for my hollow cell.''

 Hereat, she vanish'd from Endymion's
 gaze,
Who brooded o'er the water in amaze:
The dashing fount pour'd on, and where
 its pool
Lay, half-asleep, in grass and rushes cool,
135 Quick waterflies and gnats were sporting
 still,
And fish were dimpling, as if good nor ill
Had fallen out that hour. The wanderer,
Holding his forehead, to keep off the burr
Of smothering fancies, patiently sat down;
140 And, while beneath the evening's sleepy
 frown
Glowworms began to trim their starry
 lamps,
Thus breath'd he to himself: "Whoso en-
 camps
To take a fancied city of delight,

O what a wretch is he! and when 'tis his,
145 After long toil and travelling, to miss
The kernel of his hopes, how more than
   vile:
Yet, for him there's refreshment even in
   toil;
Another city doth he set about,
Free from the smallest pebble-bead of
   doubt
150 That he will seize on trickling honeycombs:
Alas, he finds them dry; and then he foams,
And onward to another city speeds.
But this is human life: the war, the deeds,
The disappointment, the anxiety,
155 Imagination's struggles, far and nigh,
All human; bearing in themselves this
   good,
That they are still the air, the subtle food,
To make us feel existence, and to show
How quiet death is. Where soil is, men
   grow,
160 Whether to weeds or flowers; but for me,
There is no depth to strike in: I can see
Naught earthly worth my compassing; so
   stand
Upon a misty, jutting head of land—
Alone? No, no; and by the Orphean lute,
165 When mad Eurydice is listening to 't;
I'd rather stand upon this misty peak,
With not a thing to sigh for, or to seek,
But the soft shadow of my thrice-seen[1]
   love,
Than be—I care not what. O meekest dove
170 Of heaven! O Cynthia, ten-times bright
   and fair!
From thy blue throne, now filling all the
   air,
Glance but one little beam of temper'd
   light
Into my bosom, that the dreadful might
And tyranny of love be somewhat scar'd!
175 Yet do not so, sweet queen; one torment
   spar'd,
Would give a pang to jealous misery,
Worse than the torment's self: but rather
   tie
Large wings upon my shoulders, and point
   out
My love's far dwelling. Though the play-
   ful rout
180 Of Cupids shun thee, too divine art thou,
Too keen in beauty, for thy silver prow
Not to have dipp'd in love's most gentle
   stream.
O be propitious, nor severely deem
My madness impious; for, by all the stars
185 That tend thy bidding, I do think the bars
That kept my spirit in are burst—that I

[1] See Book 1, ll. 600 ff.; 896 ff., and 971.

Am sailing with thee through the dizzy
   sky!
How beautiful thou art! The world how
   deep!
How tremulous-dazzlingly the wheels
   sweep
190 Around their axle! Then these gleaming
   reins,
How lithe! When this thy chariot attains
Its airy goal, haply some bower veils
Those twilight eyes? Those eyes!—my
   spirit fails—
Dear goddess, help! or the wide-gaping air
195 Will gulf me—help!''—At this with madden'd stare,
And lifted hands, and trembling lips, he
   stood;
Like old Deucalion mountain'd o'er the
   flood,
Or blind Orion hungry for the morn.
And, but from the deep cavern there was
   borne
200 A voice, he had been froze to senseless
   stone;
Nor sigh of his, nor plaint, nor passion'd
   moan
Had more been heard. Thus swell'd it
   forth: ''Descend,
Young mountaineer! descend where alleys
   bend
Into the sparry[1] hollows of the world!
205 Oft hast thou seen bolts of the thunder
   hurl'd
As from thy threshold; day by day hast
   been
A little lower than the chilly sheen
Of icy pinnacles, and dipp'dst thine arms
Into the deadening ether that still charms
210 Their marble being: now, as deep pro-
   found
As those are high, descend! He ne'er is
   crown'd
With immortality, who fears to follow
Where airy voices lead: so through the
   hollow,
The silent mysteries of earth, descend!''

215 He heard but the last words, nor could
   contend
One moment in reflection: for he fled
Into the fearful deep, to hide his head
From the clear moon, the trees, and coming
   madness.

'Twas far too strange, and wonderful
   for sadness;
220 Sharpening, by degrees, his appetite

[1] abounding with spar,—i. e., non-metallic min-
erals

To dive into the deepest. Dark, nor light,
The region; nor bright, nor sombre wholly,
But mingled up; a gleaming melancholy;
A dusky empire and its diadems;
225 One faint eternal eventide of gems.
Aye, millions sparkled on a vein of gold,
Along whose track the prince quick foot-
    steps told,
With all its lines abrupt and angular:
Out-shooting sometimes, like a meteor-star,
230 Through a vast antre;[1] then the metal
    woof,
Like Vulcan's rainbow, with some mon-
    strous roof
Curves hugely: now, far in the deep abyss,
It seems an angry lightning, and doth hiss
Fancy into belief: anon it leads
235 Through winding passages, where same-
    ness breeds
Vexing conceptions of some sudden
    change;
Whether to silver grots, or giant range
Of sapphire columns, or fantastic bridge
Athwart a flood of crystal. On a ridge
240 Now fareth he, that o'er the vast beneath
Towers like an ocean-cliff, and whence he
    seeth
A hundred waterfalls, whose voices come
But as the murmuring surge. Chilly and
    numb
His bosom grew, when first he, far away
245 Descried an orbed diamond, set to fray[2]
Old darkness from his throne: 'twas like
    the sun
Uprisen o'er chaos: and with such a stun
Came the amazement, that, absorb'd in it,
He saw not fiercer wonders—past the wit
250 Of any spirit to tell, but one of those
Who, when this planet's sphering time
    doth close,
Will be its high remembrancers: who they?
The mighty ones who have made eternal
    day
For Greece and England. While astonish-
    ment
255 With deep-drawn sighs was quieting, he
    went
Into a marble gallery, passing through
A mimic temple, so complete and true
In sacred custom, that he well-nigh fear'd
To search it inwards; whence far off ap-
    pear'd,
260 Through a long pillar'd vista, a fair shrine,
And just beyond, on light tiptoe divine,
A quiver'd Dian. Stepping awfully,
The youth approach'd, oft turning his
    veil'd eye
Down sidelong aisles, and into niches old.

[1] cavern   [2] frighten

265 And when, more near against the marble
    cold
He had touch'd his forehead, he began to
    thread
All courts and passages, where silence dead
Rous'd by his whispering footsteps mur-
    mur'd faint:
And long he travers'd to and fro, to ac-
    quaint
270 Himself with every mystery, and awe;
Till, weary, he sat down before the maw
Of a wide outlet, fathomless and dim,
To wild uncertainty and shadows grim.
There, when new wonders ceas'd to float
    before,
275 And thoughts of self came on, how crude
    and sore
The journey homeward to habitual self!
A mad-pursuing of the fog-born elf,
Whose flitting lantern, through rude nettle-
    briar,
Cheats us into a swamp, into a fire,
280 Into the bosom of a hated thing.

What misery most drowningly doth sing
In lone Endymion's ear, now he has
    raught[1]
The goal of consciousness? Ah, 'tis the
    thought,
The deadly feel of solitude: for lo!
285 He cannot see the heavens, nor the flow
Of rivers, nor hill-flowers running wild
In pink and purple chequer, nor, up-pil'd,
The cloudy rack slow journeying in the
    west,
Like herded elephants; nor felt, nor prest
290 Cool grass, nor tasted the fresh slumberous
    air;
But far from such companionship to wear
An unknown time, surcharg'd with grief,
    away,
Was now his lot. And must he patient stay,
Tracing fantastic figures with his spear?
295 "No!" exclaim'd he, "why should I tarry
    here?"
No! loudly echoed times innumerable.
At which he straightway started, and 'gan
    tell
His paces back into the temple's chief;
Warming and glowing strong in the belief
300 Of help from Dian: so that when again
He caught her airy form, thus did he
    plain,[2]
Moving more near the while: "O Haunter
    chaste
Of river sides, and woods, and heathy
    waste,
Where with thy silver bow and arrows keen

[1] reached   [2] lament

305 Art thou now forested? O woodland
    Queen,
What smoothest air thy smoother forehead
    woos?
Where dost thou listen to the wide halloos
Of thy disparted nymphs? Through what
    dark tree
Glimmers thy crescent? Wheresoe'er it be,
310 'Tis in the breath of heaven: thou dost
    taste
Freedom as none can taste it, nor dost
    waste
Thy loveliness in dismal elements;
But, finding in our green earth sweet con-
    tents,
There livest blissfully. Ah, if to thee
315 It feels Elysian, how rich to me,
An exil'd mortal, sounds its pleasant
    name!
Within my breast there lives a choking
    flame—
O let me cool 't the zephyr-boughs among!
A homeward fever parches up my tongue—
320 O let me slake it at the running springs!
Upon my ear a noisy nothing rings—
O let me once more hear the linnet's note!
Before mine eyes thick films and shadows
    float—
O let me 'noint them with the heaven's
    light!
325 Dost thou now lave thy feet and ankles
    white?
O think how sweet to me the freshening
    sluice!
Dost thou now please thy thirst with berry-
    juice?
O think how this dry palate would rejoice!
If in soft slumber thou dost hear my voice,
330 O think how I should love a bed of
    flowers!—
Young goddess! let me see my native
    bowers!
Deliver me from this rapacious deep!''

Thus ending loudly, as he would o'erleap
His destiny, alert he stood: but when
335 Obstinate silence came heavily again,
Feeling about for its old couch of space
And airy cradle, lowly bow'd his face
Desponding, o'er the marble floor's cold
    thrill.
But 'twas not long; for, sweeter than the
    rill
340 To its old channel, or a swollen tide
To margin sallows,[1] were the leaves he
    spied,
And flowers, and wreaths, and ready myr-
    tle crowns

[1] willows

Upheaping through the slab: refreshment
    drowns
Itself, and strives its own delights to hide—
345 Nor in one spot alone; the floral pride
In a long whispering birth enchanted grew
Before his footsteps; as when heav'd anew
Old ocean rolls a lengthen'd wave to the
    shore,
Down whose green back the short-liv'd
    foam, all hoar,
350 Bursts gradual, with a wayward indolence.

Increasing still in heart, and pleasant
    sense,
Upon his fairy journey on he hastes;
So anxious for the end, he scarcely wastes
One moment with his hand among the
    sweets:
355 Onward he goes—he stops—his bosom
    beats
As plainly in his ear, as the faint charm
Of which the throbs were born. This still
    alarm,
This sleepy music, forc'd him walk tiptoe:
For it came more softly than the east could
    blow
360 Arion's magic to the Atlantic isles;
Or than the west, made jealous by the
    smiles
Of thron'd Apollo, could breathe back the
    lyre
To seas Ionian and Tyrian.

O did he ever live, that lonely man,
365 Who lov'd—and music slew not? 'Tis the
    pest
Of love, that fairest joys give most unrest;
That things of delicate and tenderest worth
Are swallow'd all, and made a seared
    dearth,
By one consuming flame: it doth immerse
370 And suffocate true blessings in a curse.
Half-happy, by comparison of bliss,
Is miserable. 'Twas even so with this
Dew-dropping melody, in the Carian's
    ear;[1]
First heaven, then hell, and then forgotten
    clear,
375 Vanish'd in elemental passion.

And down some swart abysm he had
    gone,
Had not a heavenly guide benignant led
To where thick myrtle branches, 'gainst his
    head
Brushing, awakened: then the sounds again
380 Went noiseless as a passing noontide rain

[1] That is, in the ear of Endymion, who was
said to reside in Caria, Asia Minor.

Over a bower, where little space he stood;
For as the sunset peeps into a wood
So saw he panting light, and towards it went
Through winding alleys; and lo, wonderment!
385 Upon soft verdure saw, one here, one there,
Cupids a-slumbering on their pinions fair.[1]

After a thousand mazes overgone,
At last, with sudden step, he came upon
A chamber, myrtle wall'd, embower'd high,
390 Full of light, incense, tender minstrelsy,
And more of beautiful and strange beside:
For on a silken couch of rosy pride,
In midst of all, there lay a sleeping youth
Of fondest beauty; fonder, in fair sooth,
395 Than sighs could fathom, or contentment reach:
And coverlids gold-tinted like the peach,
Or ripe October's faded marigolds,
Fell sleek about him in a thousand folds—
Not hiding up an Apollonian curve
400 Of neck and shoulder, nor the tenting swerve[2]
Of knee from knee, nor ankles pointing light;
But rather, giving them to the fill'd sight
Officiously. Sideway his face repos'd
On one white arm, and tenderly unclos'd,
405 By tenderest pressure, a faint damask mouth
To slumbery pout; just as the morning south
Disparts a dew-lipp'd rose. Above his head,
Four lily stalks did their white honors wed
To make a coronal; and round him grew
410 All tendrils green, of every bloom and hue,
Together intertwin'd and trammel'd fresh:
The vine of glossy sprout; the ivy mesh,
Shading its Ethiop berries; and woodbine,
Of velvet-leaves and bugle-blooms divine;
415 Convolvulus in streaked vases flush;
The creeper, mellowing for an autumn blush;
And virgin's bower, trailing airily;
With others of the sisterhood. Hard by,
Stood serene Cupids watching silently.
420 One, kneeling to a lyre, touch'd the strings,
Muffling to death the pathos with his wings;
And, ever and anon, uprose to look
At the youth's slumber; while another took
A willow-bough, distilling odorous dew,
425 And shook it on his hair; another flew

[1] See Spenser's description of the garden of Adonis, in *The Faerie Queene*, III, 6, 44-47.
[2] Keats defines this as a swerve in the form of the top of a tent.

In through the woven roof, and flutteringwise
Rain'd violets upon his sleeping eyes.

At these enchantments, and yet many more,
The breathless Latmian[1] wonder'd o'er and o'er;
430 Until, impatient in embarrassment,
He forthright pass'd, and lightly treading went
To that same feather'd lyrist, who straightway,
Smiling, thus whisper'd: "Though from upper day
Thou art a wanderer, and thy presence here
435 Might seem unholy, be of happy cheer!
For 'tis the nicest touch of human honor,
When some ethereal and high-favoring donor
Presents immortal bowers to mortal sense;
As now 'tis done to thee, Endymion. Hence
440 Was I in no wise startled. So recline
Upon these living flowers. Here is wine,
Alive with sparkles—never, I aver,
Since Ariadne was a vintager,
So cool a purple: taste these juicy pears,
445 Sent me by sad Vertumnus, when his fears
Were high about Pomona: here is cream,
Deepening to richness from a snowy gleam;
Sweeter than that nurse Amalthea skimm'd
For the boy Jupiter: and here, undimm'd
450 By any touch, a bunch of blooming plums
Ready to melt between an infant's gums:
And here is manna pick'd from Syrian trees,
In starlight, by the three Hesperides.
Feast on, and meanwhile I will let thee know
455 Of all these things around us." He did so,
Still brooding o'er the cadence of his lyre;
And thus: "I need not any hearing tire
By telling how the sea-born goddess pin'd
For a mortal youth,[2] and how she strove to bind
460 Him all in all unto her doting self.
Who would not be so prison'd? but, fond elf,
He was content to let her amorous plea
Faint through his careless arms; content to see

[1] Endymion, who resided on Mt. Latmus, in Caria.
[2] A reference to the story of Venus and Adonis. See *Endymion*, 1, 626 (p. 801). Adonis was killed by a wild boar. As a result of Venus's grief the gods required Adonis to spend only a part of each year in Hades. See ll. 475-76.

An unseiz'd heaven dying at his feet;
465 Content, O fool! to make a cold retreat,
When on the pleasant grass such love, love-
    lorn,
Lay sorrowing; when every tear was born
Of diverse passion; when her lips and eyes
Were closed in sullen moisture, and quick
    sighs
470 Came vex'd and pettish through her nos-
    trils small.
Hush! no exclaim—yet, justly mightst
    thou call
Curses upon his head.—I was half glad,
But my poor mistress went distract and
    mad,
When the boar tusk'd him: so away she
    flew
475 To Jove's high throne, and by her plain-
    ings[1] drew
Immortal tear-drops down the thunder-
    er's[2] beard;
Whereon, it was decreed he should be
    rear'd
Each summer time to life. Lo! this is he,
That same Adonis, safe in the privacy
480 Of this still region all his winter-sleep.
Aye, sleep; for when our love-sick queen
    did weep
Over his waned corse, the tremulous shower
Heal'd up the wound, and, with a balmy
    power,
Medicin'd death to a lengthen'd drowsi-
    ness:
485 The which she fills with visions, and doth
    dress
In all this quiet luxury; and hath set
Us young immortals, without any let,[3]
To watch his slumber through. 'Tis well
    nigh pass'd,
Even to a moment's filling up, and fast
490 She scuds with summer breezes, to pant
    through
The first long kiss, warm firstling, to renew
Embower'd sports in Cytherea's isle.[4]
Look! how those winged listeners all this
    while
Stand anxious: see! behold!''—This
    clamant[5] word
495 Broke through the careful silence; for
    they heard
A rustling noise of leaves, and out there
    flutter'd
Pigeons and doves:[6] Adonis something
    mutter'd

The while one hand, that erst upon his
    thigh
Lay dormant, mov'd convuls'd and grad-
    ually
500 Up to his forehead. Then there was a hum
Of sudden voices, echoing, ''Come! come!
Arise! awake! Clear summer has forth
    walk'd
Unto the clover-sward, and she has talk'd
Full soothingly to every nested finch:
505 Rise, Cupids! or we'll give the blue-bell
    pinch
To your dimpled arms.[1] Once more sweet
    life begin!''
At this, from every side they hurried in,
Rubbing their sleepy eyes with lazy wrists,
And doubling over head their little fists
510 In backward yawns. But all were soon
    alive:
For as delicious wine doth, sparkling, dive
In nectar'd clouds and curls through water
    fair,
So from the arbor roof down swell'd an
    air
Odorous and enlivening; making all
515 To laugh, and play, and sing, and loudly
    call
For their sweet queen: when lo! the
    wreathed green
Disparted, and far upward could be seen
Blue heaven, and a silver car, air-borne,
Whose silent wheels, fresh wet from clouds
    of morn,
520 Spun off a drizzling dew,—which falling
    chill
On soft Adonis' shoulders, made him still
Nestle and turn uneasily about.
Soon were the white doves plain, with neck
    stretch'd out,
And silken traces lighten'd in descent;
525 And soon, returning from love's banish-
    ment,
Queen Venus leaning downward open-
    arm'd:
Her shadow fell upon his breast, and
    charm'd
A tumult to his heart, and a new life
Into his eyes. Ah, miserable strife,
530 But for her comforting! unhappy sight,
But meeting her blue orbs! Who, who can
    write
Of these first minutes? The unchariest
    muse
To embracements warm as theirs makes coy
    excuse.

---

[1] lamentings; sorrow-
ings.
[2] Jove's.
[3] hindrance
[4] Cyprus.
[5] clamorous; loud

[6] Pigeons and doves
were sacred to
Venus. Her car
was drawn by
doves. See ll. 523-
4.

[1] That is, we'll pinch them blue. In Keats's
first draft of *Endymion*, these lines read:
Cupids awake! or black and blue we'll pinch
Your dimpled arms.

O it has ruffled every spirit there,
535 Saving Love's self, who stands superb to
share
The general gladness: awfully he stands;
A sovereign quell[1] is in his waving hands;
No sight can bear the lightning of his bow;
His quiver is mysterious, none can know
540 What themselves think of it; from forth
his eyes
There darts strange light of varied hues
and dyes:
A scowl is sometimes on his brow, but who
Look full upon it feel anon the blue
Of his fair eyes run liquid through their
souls.
545 Endymion feels it, and no more controls
The burning prayer within him; so, bent
low,
He had begun a plaining of his woe.
But Venus, bending forward, said: "My
child,
Favor this gentle youth; his days are wild
550 With love—he—but alas! too well I see
Thou know'st the deepness of his misery.
Ah, smile not so, my son: I tell thee true,
That when through heavy hours I used to
rue
The endless sleep of this new-born Adon',
555 This stranger aye I pitied. For upon
A dreary morning once I fled away
Into the breezy clouds, to weep and pray
For this my love: for vexing Mars had
teas'd
Me even to tears: thence, when a little
eas'd,
560 Down-looking, vacant, through a hazy
wood,
I saw this youth as he despairing stood:
Those same dark curls blown vagrant in
the wind;
Those same full fringed lids a constant
blind
Over his sullen eyes: I saw him throw
565 Himself on wither'd leaves, even as though
Death had come sudden; for no jot he
mov'd,
Yet mutter'd wildly. I could hear he lov'd
Some fair immortal, and that his embrace
Had zoned[2] her through the night. There
is no trace
570 Of this in heaven: I have mark'd each
cheek,
And find it is the vainest thing to seek;
And that of all things 'tis kept secretest.
Endymion! one day thou wilt be blest:
So still obey the guiding hand that fends
575 Thee safely through these wonders for
sweet ends.

[1] power of subduing   [2] encircled

'Tis a concealment needful in extreme:
And if I guess'd not so, the sunny beam
Thou shouldst mount up to with me. Now
adieu!
Here must we leave thee.''—At these words
upflew
580 The impatient doves, uprose the floating
car,
Up went the hum celestial. High afar
The Latmian saw them minish into naught;
And, when all were clear vanish'd, still he
caught
A vivid lightning from that dreadful bow.
585 When all was darken'd, with Ætnean throe
The earth clos'd—gave a solitary moan—
And left him once again in twilight lone.

He did not rave, he did not stare aghast,
For all those visions were o'ergone, and
past,
590 And he in loneliness: he felt assur'd
Of happy times, when all he had endur'd
Would seem a feather to the mighty prize.
So, with unusual gladness, on he hies
Through caves, and palaces of mottled ore,
595 Gold dome, and crystal wall, and turquois
floor,
Black polish'd porticos of awful shade,
And, at the last, a diamond balustrade,
Leading afar past wild magnificence,
Spiral through ruggedest loopholes, and
thence
600 Stretching across a void, then guiding o'er
Enormous chasms, where, all foam and
roar,
Streams subterranean tease their granite
beds;
Then heighten'd just above the silvery
heads
Of a thousand fountains, so that he could
dash
605 The waters with his spear; but at the
splash,
Done heedlessly, those spouting columns
rose
Sudden a poplar's height, and 'gan to
enclose
His diamond path with fretwork, streaming round
Alive, and dazzling cool, and with a sound,
610 Haply, like dolphin tumults, when sweet
shells
Welcome the float of Thetis. Long he
dwells
On this delight; for, every minute's space,
The streams with changed magic interlace:
Sometimes like delicatest lattices,
615 Cover'd with crystal vines; then weeping
trees,

Moving about as in a gentle wind,
Which, in a wink, to watery gauze refin'd,
Pour'd into shapes of curtain'd canopies,
Spangled, and rich with liquid broideries
620 Of flowers, peacocks, swans, and naiads
        fair.
Swifter than lightning went these wonders
        rare;
    And then the water, into stubborn
        streams
Collecting, mimick'd the wrought oaken
        beams,
Pillars, and frieze, and high fantastic roof,
625 Of those dusk places in times far aloof
Cathedrals call'd. He bade a loth farewell
To these founts Protean, passing gulf, and
        dell,
And torrent, and ten thousand jutting
        shapes,
Half seen through deepest gloom, and
        griesly gapes,
630 Blackening on every side, and overhead
A vaulted dome like Heaven's, far be-
        spread
With starlight gems: aye, all so huge and
        strange,
The solitary felt a hurried change
Working within him into something
        dreary,—
635 Vex'd like a morning eagle, lost, and
        weary,
And purblind amid foggy, midnight
        wolds.[1]
But he revives at once: for who beholds
New sudden things, nor casts his mental
        slough?
Forth from a rugged arch, in the dusk
        below,
640 Came mother Cybele! alone—alone—
In sombre chariot; dark foldings thrown
About her majesty, and front death-pale,
With turrets crown'd. Four maned lions
        hale
The sluggish wheels; solemn their toothed
        maws,
645 Their surly eyes brow-hidden, heavy paws
Uplifted drowsily, and nervy tails
Cowering their tawny brushes. Silent sails
This shadowy queen athwart, and faints
        away
In another gloomy arch.

        Wherefore delay,
650 Young traveller, in such a mournful place?
Art thou wayworn, or canst not further
        trace
The diamond path? And does it indeed end
Abrupt in middle air? Yet earthward bend

[1] open country

Thy forehead, and to Jupiter cloud-borne
655 Call ardently! He was indeed wayworn;
Abrupt, in middle air, his way was lost;
To cloud-borne Jove he bowed, and there
        crost
Towards him a large eagle,[1] 'twixt whose
        wings,
Without one impious word, himself he
        flings,
660 Committed to the darkness and the gloom:
Down, down, uncertain to what pleasant
        doom,
Swift as a fathoming plummet down he
        fell
Through unknown things; till exhaled
        asphodel,[2]
And rose, with spicy fannings inter-
        breath'd,
665 Came swelling forth where little caves
        were wreath'd
So thick with leaves and mosses, that they
        seem'd
Large honey-combs of green, and freshly
        teem'd[3]
With airs delicious. In the greenest nook
The eagle landed him, and farewell took.

670 It was a jasmine bower, all bestrown
With golden moss. His every sense had
        grown
Ethereal for pleasure; 'bove his head
Flew a delight half-graspable; his tread
Was Hesperean; to his capable ears
675 Silence was music from the holy spheres;[4]
A dewy luxury was in his eyes;
The little flowers felt his pleasant sighs
And stirr'd them faintly. Verdant cave
        and cell
He wander'd through, oft wondering at
        such swell
680 Of sudden exaltation: but, "Alas,"
Said he, "will all this gush of feeling pass
Away in solitude? And must they wane,
Like melodies upon a sandy plain,
Without an echo? Then shall I be left
685 So sad, so melancholy, so bereft!
Yet still I feel immortal! O my love,
My breath of life, where art thou? High
        above,
Dancing before the morning gates of
        heaven?
Or keeping watch among those starry
        seven,
690 Old Atlas' children? Art a maid of the
        waters,

[1] The eagle was Jove's special messenger.
[2] daffodil   [3] abounded
[4] The ancients believed that the movement of
    the celestial spheres produced music.

One of shell-winding Triton's bright-
   hair'd daughters?
Or art, impossible! a nymph of Dian's,
Weaving a coronal of tender scions
For very idleness? Where'er thou art,
695 Methinks it now is at my will to start
Into thine arms; to scare Aurora's train,
And snatch thee from the morning; o'er
   the main
To scud like a wild bird, and take thee off
From thy sea-foamy cradle; or to doff
700 Thy shepherd vest, and woo thee 'mid fresh
   leaves.
No, no, too eagerly my soul deceives
Its powerless self: I know this cannot be.
O let me then by some sweet dreaming flee
To her entrancements: hither sleep awhile!
705 Hither most gentle sleep! and soothing foil
For some few hours the coming solitude.''

   Thus spake he, and that moment felt
      endued
With power to dream deliciously; so wound
Through a dim passage, searching till he
   found
710 The smoothest mossy bed and deepest,
      where
He threw himself, and just into the air
Stretching his indolent arms, he took, O
   bliss!
A naked waist: ''Fair Cupid, whence is
   this?''
A well-known voice sigh'd, ''Sweetest,
   here am I!''
715 At which soft ravishment, with doting cry
They trembled to each other.—Helicon!
O fountain'd hill! Old Homer's Helicon!
That thou wouldst spout a little streamlet
   o'er
These sorry pages; then the verse would
   soar
720 And sing above this gentle pair, like lark
Over his nested young: but all is dark
Around thine aged top, and thy clear fount
Exhales in mists to heaven. Aye, the count
Of mighty Poets is made up; the scroll
725 Is folded by the Muses; the bright roll
Is in Apollo's hand: our dazed eyes
Have seen a new tinge in the western skies:
The world has done its duty. Yet, oh yet,
Although the sun of Poesy is set,
730 These lovers did embrace, and we must
   weep
That there is no old power left to steep
A quill immortal in their joyous tears.
Long time ere silence did their anxious
   fears
Question that thus it was; long time they
   lay

735 Fondling and kissing every doubt away;
Long time ere soft caressing sobs began
To mellow into words, and then there ran
Two bubbling springs of talk from their
   sweet lips.
''O known Unknown! from whom my
   being sips
740 Such darling essence, wherefore may I not
Be ever in these arms? in this sweet spot
Pillow my chin forever? ever press
These toying hands and kiss their smooth
   excess?
Why not forever and forever feel
745 That breath about my eyes? Ah, thou wilt
   steal
Away from me again, indeed, indeed—
Thou wilt be gone away, and wilt not heed
My lonely madness. Speak, delicious fair!
Is—is it to be so? No! Who will dare
750 To pluck thee from me? And, of thine
   own will,
Full well I feel thou wouldst not leave me.
   Still
Let me entwine thee surer, surer—now
How can we part? Elysium: who art
   thou?
Who, that thou canst not be forever here,
755 Or lift me with thee to some starry sphere?
Enchantress! tell me by this soft embrace,
By the most soft completion[1] of thy face,
Those lips, O slippery blisses, twinkling
   eyes,
And by these tenderest, milky sovereign-
   ties—
760 These tenderest, and by the nectar-wine,
The passion''———''O dov'd Ida the di-
   vine!
Endymion! dearest! Ah, unhappy me!
His soul will 'scape us—O felicity!
How he does love me! His poor temples
   beat
765 To the very tune of love—how sweet, sweet,
   sweet.
Revive, dear youth, or I shall faint and die;
Revive, or these soft hours will hurry by
In tranced dulness; speak, and let that
   spell
Affright this lethargy! I cannot quell
770 Its heavy pressure, and will press at least
My lips to thine, that they may richly feast
Until we taste the life of love again.
What! dost thou move? dost kiss? O bliss!
   O pain!
I love thee, youth, more than I can con-
   ceive;
775 And so long absence from thee doth bereave
My soul of any rest: yet must I hence:
Yet, can I not to starry eminence
   ¹ perfection

Uplift thee; nor for very shame can
    own
Myself to thee. Ah, dearest, do not groan
780 Or thou wilt force me from this secrecy,
And I must blush in heaven. O that I
Had done 't already; that the dreadful
    smiles
At my lost brightness, my impassion'd
    wiles,
Had waned from Olympus' solemn height,
785 And from all serious Gods; that our de-
    light
Was quite forgotten, save of us alone!
And wherefore so ashamed? 'Tis but to
    atone
For endless pleasure, by some coward
    blushes:
Yet must I be a coward!—Honor rushes
790 Too palpable before me—the sad look
Of Jove—Minerva's start—no bosom
    shook
With awe of purity—no Cupid pinion
In reverence veil'd—my crystalline do-
    minion
Half lost, and all old hymns made nullity!
795 But what is this to love? O I could fly
With thee into the ken of heavenly powers,
So thou wouldst thus, for many sequent
    hours,
Press me so sweetly. Now I swear at once
That I am wise, that Pallas is a dunce—
800 Perhaps her love like mine is but un-
    known—
O I do think that I have been alone
In chastity: yes, Pallas has been sighing,
While every eve saw me my hair uptying
With fingers cool as aspen leaves. Sweet
    love,
805 I was as vague as solitary dove,
Nor knew that nests were built. Now a
    soft kiss—
Aye, by that kiss, I vow an endless bliss,
An immortality of passion's thine:
Ere long I will exalt thee to the shine
810 Of heaven ambrosial; and we will shade
Ourselves whole summers by a river glade;
And I will tell thee stories of the sky,
And breathe thee whispers of its min-
    strelsy.
My happy love will overwing all bounds!
815 O let me melt into thee; let the sounds
Of our close voices marry at their birth;
Let us entwine hoveringly—O dearth
Of human words! roughness of mortal
    speech!
Lispings empyrean will I sometime teach
820 Thine honied tongue — lute-breathings,
    which I gasp
To have thee understand, now while I clasp

Thee thus, and weep for fondness—I am
    pain'd,
Endymion: woe! woe! is grief contain'd
In the very deeps of pleasure, my sole
    life?''—
825 Hereat, with many sobs, her gentle strife
Melted into a languor. He return'd
Entranced vows and tears.

              Ye who have yearn'd
With too much passion, will here stay and
    pity,
For the mere sake of truth; as 'tis a ditty
830 Not of these days, but long ago 'twas told
By a cavern wind unto a forest old;[1]
And then the forest told it in a dream
To a sleeping lake, whose cool and level
    gleam
A poet caught as he was journeying
835 To Phœbus' shrine: and in it he did fling
His weary limbs, bathing an hour's space,
And after, straight in that inspired place
He sang the story up into the air,
Giving it universal freedom. There
840 Has it been ever sounding for those ears
Whose tips are glowing hot. The legend
    cheers
Yon sentinel stars; and he who listens to it
Must surely be self-doom'd or he will rue
    it:
For quenchless burnings come upon the
    heart,
845 Made fiercer by a fear lest any part
Should be engulfed in the eddying wind.
As much as here is penn'd doth always find
A resting-place, thus much comes clear
    and plain;
Anon the strange voice is upon the wane—
850 And 'tis but echo'd from departing sound,
That the fair visitant at last unwound
Her gentle limbs, and left the youth
    asleep.—
Thus the tradition of the gusty deep.

    Now turn we to our former chroniclers.—
855 Endymion awoke, that grief of hers
Sweet paining on his ear: he sickly guess'd
How lone he was once more, and sadly
    press'd
His empty arms together, hung his head,
And most forlorn upon that widow'd bed
860 Sat silently. Love's madness he had known:
Often with more than tortured lion's groan
Moanings had burst from him; but now
    that rage
Had pass'd away: no longer did he wage

[1] *Cf.* the means by which Midas's secret concerning the ass's ears on his head became
known. See Ovid's *Metamorphoses,* II, 174-
93.

A rough-voic'd war against the dooming
    stars.
865 No, he had felt too much for such harsh
    jars:
The lyre of his soul Æolian tun'd
Forgot all violence, and but commun'd
With melancholy thought: O he had
    swoon'd
Drunken from pleasure's nipple; and his
    love
870 Henceforth was dove-like.—Loth was he to
    move
From the imprinted couch, and when he
    did,
'Twas with slow, languid paces, and face
    hid
In muffling hands. So temper'd, out he
    stray'd
Half seeing visions that might have dis-
    may'd
875 Alecto's serpents; ravishments more keen
Than Hermes' pipe,[1] when anxious he did
    lean
Over eclipsing eyes: and at the last
It was a sounding grotto, vaulted, vast,
O'erstudded with a thousand, thousand
    pearls,
880 And crimson mouthed shells with stubborn
    curls,
Of every shape and size, even to the bulk
In which whales arbor close, to brood and
    sulk
Against an endless storm. Moreover too,
Fish-semblances, of green and azure hue,
885 Ready to snort their streams. In this cool
    wonder
Endymion sat down, and 'gan to ponder
On all his life: his youth, up to the day
When 'mid acclaim, and feasts, and gar-
    lands gay,
He stept upon his shepherd throne: the
    look
890 Of his white palace in wild forest nook,
And all the revels he had lorded there:
Each tender maiden whom he once thought
    fair,
With every friend and fellow-woodlander—
Pass'd like a dream before him. Then the
    spur
895 Of the old bards to mighty deeds: his plans
To nurse the golden age 'mong shepherd
    clans:
That wondrous night: the great Pan-
    festival:[2]
His sister's sorrow; and his wanderings all,

---

[1] By playing upon his pipe, Hermes lulled
   Argus to sleep, and afterward killed him.
[2] A festival held in honor of Pan, the god of
   shepherds, and recorded in Book I.

Until into the earth's deep maw he rush'd:
900 Then all its buried magic, till it flush'd
High with excessive love. "And now,"
    thought he,
"How long must I remain in jeopardy
Of blank amazements that amaze no more?
Now I have tasted her sweet soul to the
    core
905 All other depths are shallow: essences,
Once spiritual, are like muddy lees,
Meant but to fertilize my earthly root,
And make my branches lift a golden fruit
Into the bloom of heaven: other light,
910 Though it be quick and sharp enough to
    blight
The Olympian eagle's vision, is dark,
Dark as the parentage of chaos. Hark!
My silent thoughts are echoing from these
    shells;
Or they are but the ghosts, the dying swells
915 Of noises far away?—list!"—Hereupon
He kept an anxious ear. The humming tone
Came louder, and behold, there as he lay,
On either side outgush'd, with misty spray,
A copious spring; and both together dash'd
920 Swift, mad, fantastic round the rocks, and
    lash'd
Among the conchs and shells of the lofty
    grot,
Leaving a trickling dew. At last they shot
Down from the ceiling's height, pouring
    a noise
As of some breathless racers whose hopes
    poise
925 Upon the last few steps, and with spent
    force
Along the ground they took a winding
    course.
Endymion follow'd—for it seem'd that one
Ever pursued, the other strove to shun—
Follow'd their languid mazes, till well
    nigh
930 He had left thinking of the mystery,—
And was now rapt in tender hoverings
Over the vanish'd bliss. Ah! what is it
    sings
His dream away? What melodies are
    these?
They sound as through the whispering of
    trees,
935 Not native in such barren vaults. Give ear!

"O Arethusa, peerless nymph! why fear
Such tenderness as mine? Great Dian,
    why,
Why didst thou hear her prayer? O that I
Were rippling round her dainty fairness
    now,

940 Circling about her waist, and striving how
To entice her to a dive! then stealing in
Between her luscious lips and eyelids thin.
O that her shining hair was in the sun,
And I distilling from it thence to run
945 In amorous rillets down her shrinking
      form!
To linger on her lily shoulders, warm
Between her kissing breasts, and every
      charm
Touch raptur'd!—See how painfully I
      flow:
Fair maid, be pitiful to my great woe.
950 Stay, stay thy weary course, and let me
      lead,
A happy wooer, to the flowery mead
Where all that beauty snar'd me.''—
      ''Cruel god,
Desist! or my offended mistress' nod
Will stagnate all thy fountains:—tease me
      not
955 With siren words—Ah, have I really got
Such power to madden thee? And is it
      true—
Away, away, or I shall dearly rue
My very thoughts: in mercy then away,
Kindest Alpheus, for should I obey
960 My own dear will, 'twould be a deadly
      bane.—
O, Oread-Queen![1] would that thou hadst a
      pain
Like this of mine, then would I fearless
      turn
And be a criminal. Alas, I burn,
I shudder—gentle river, get thee hence.
965 Alpheus! thou enchanter! every sense
Of mine was once made perfect in these
      woods.
Fresh breezes, bowery lawns, and innocent
      floods,
Ripe fruits, and lonely couch, contentment
      gave;
But ever since I heedlessly did lave
970 In thy deceitful stream, a panting glow
Grew strong within me: wherefore serve
      me so,
And call it love? Alas, 'twas cruelty.
Not once more did I close my happy eye
Amid the thrush's song. Away! avaunt!
975 O 'twas a cruel thing.''—''Now thou dost
      taunt
So softly, Arethusa, that I think
If thou wast playing on my shady brink,
Thou wouldst bathe once again. Innocent
      maid!
Stifle thine heart no more; nor be afraid
980 Of angry powers: there are deities

---

¹ Diana. The Oreads were nymphs of mountains and hills.

Will shade us with their wings. Those fit-
      ful sighs
'Tis almost death to hear: O let me pour
A dewy balm upon them!—fear no more,
Sweet Arethusa! Dian's self must feel
985 Sometime these very pangs. Dear maiden,
      steal
Blushing into my soul, and let us fly
These dreary caverns for the open sky.
I will delight thee all my winding course,
From the green sea up to my hidden source
990 About Arcadian forests; and will show
The channels where my coolest waters flow
Through mossy rocks; where, 'mid exuber-
      ant green,
I roam in pleasant darkness, more unseen
Than Saturn in his exile; where I brim
995 Round flowery islands, and take thence a
      skim
Of mealy sweets, which myriads of bees
Buzz from their honied wings: and thou
      shouldst please
Thyself to choose the richest, where we
      might
Be incense-pillow'd every summer night.
1000 Doff all sad fears, thou white deliciousness,
And let us be thus comforted; unless
Thou couldst rejoice to see my hopeless
      stream
Hurry distracted from Sol's temperate
      beam,
And pour to death along some hungry
      sands.''—
1005 ''What can I do, Alpheus? Dian stands
Severe before me: persecuting fate!
Unhappy Arethusa! thou wast late
A huntress free in''—At this, sudden fell
Those two sad streams adown a fearful
      dell.
1010 The Latmian listen'd, but he heard no
      more,
Save echo, faint repeating o'er and o'er
The name of Arethusa. On the verge
Of that dark gulf he wept, and said: ''I
      urge
Thee, gentle Goddess of my pilgrimage,
1015 By our eternal hopes, to soothe, to assuage,
If thou art powerful, these lovers' pains;
And make them happy in some happy
      plains.''

He turn'd—there was a whelming sound
      —he stept,
There was a cooler light; and so he kept
1020 Towards it by a sandy path, and lo!
More suddenly than doth a moment go,
The visions of the earth were gone and
      fled—
He saw the giant sea above his head.

Book III

There are who lord it o'er their fellow-
    men
With most prevailing tinsel: who unpen
Their baaing vanities, to browse away
The comfortable green and juicy hay
5 From human pastures; or, O torturing
    fact!
Who, through an idiot blink, will see un-
    pack'd
Fire-branded foxes[1] to sear up and singe
Our gold and ripe-ear'd hopes. With not
    one tinge
Of sanctuary splendor, not a sight
10 Able to face an owl's, they still are dight[2]
By the blear-eyed nations in empurpled
    vests,
And crowns, and turbans. With unladen
    breasts,
Save of blown self-applause, they proudly
    mount
To their spirit's perch, their being's high
    account,
15 Their tiptop nothings, their dull skies,
    their thrones—
Amid the fierce intoxicating tones
Of trumpets, shoutings, and belabor'd
    drums,
And sudden cannon. Ah! how all this
    hums,
In wakeful ears, like uproar past and
    gone—
20 Like thunder clouds that spake to Babylon,
And set those old Chaldeans to their
    tasks.[3]—
Are then regalities all gilded masks?
No, there are throned seats unscalable
But by a patient wing, a constant spell,
25 Or by ethereal things that, unconfin'd,
Can make a ladder of the eternal wind,
And poise about in cloudy thunder-tents
To watch the abysm-birth of elements.
Aye, 'bove the withering of old-lipp'd
    Fate
30 A thousand Powers keep religious state,
In water, fiery realm, and airy bourne;
And silent, as a consecrated urn,
Hold sphery sessions for a season due.
Yet few of these far majesties, ah, few,
35 Have bared their operations to this globe—
Few, who with gorgeous pageantry enrobe
Our piece of heaven—whose benevolence
Shakes hand with our own Ceres; every
    sense
Filling with spiritual sweets to plenitude,

40 As bees gorge full their cells. And, by
    the feud
'Twixt Nothing and Creation, I here swear,
Eterne Apollo! that thy sister fair[1]
Is of all these the gentlier-mightiest.
When thy gold breath is misting in the
    west,
45 She unobserved steals unto her throne,
And there she sits most meek and most
    alone;
As if she had not pomp subservient;
As if thine eye, high Poet! was not bent
Towards her with the Muses in thine heart;
50 As if the minist'ring stars kept not apart,
Waiting for silver-footed messages.
O Moon! the oldest shades 'mong oldest
    trees
Feel palpitations when thou lookest in:
O Moon! old boughs lisp forth a holier din
55 The while they feel thine airy fellowship.
Thou dost bless everywhere, with silver lip
Kissing dead things to life. The sleeping
    kine,
Couch'd in thy brightness, dream of fields
    divine:
Innumerable mountains rise, and rise,
60 Ambitious for the hallowing of thine eyes;
And yet thy benediction passeth not
One obscure hiding-place, one little spot
Where pleasure may be sent: the nested
    wren
Has thy fair face within its tranquil ken,
65 And from beneath a sheltering ivy leaf
Takes glimpses of thee; thou art a relief
To the poor patient oyster, where it sleeps
Within its pearly house. — The mighty
    deeps,
The monstrous sea is thine—the myriad
    sea!
70 O Moon! far-spooming[2] Ocean bows to
    thee,
And Tellus feels his forehead's cumbrous
    load.

Cynthia! where art thou now? What
    far abode
Of green or silvery bower doth enshrine
Such utmost beauty? Alas, thou dost
    pine
75 For one as sorrowful: thy cheek is pale
For one whose cheek is pale: thou dost
    bewail
His tears, who weeps for thee. Where
    dost thou sigh?
Ah! surely that light peeps from Vesper's
    eye,
Or what a thing is love! 'Tis she, but lo!

---

[1] foxes let loose with fire brands tied to their tails (See *Judges*, 15:4-5.)
[2] adorned; dressed
[3] See *Ezekiel*, 1, 4 ff.

[1] Cynthia, goddess of the moon.
[2] far-driving; far-rushing

80 How chang'd, how full of ache, how gone
    in woe!
She dies at the thinnest cloud; her loveli-
    ness
Is wan on Neptune's blue: yet there's a
    stress
Of love-spangles, just off yon cape of trees,
Dancing upon the waves, as if to please
85 The curly foam with amorous influence.
O, not so idle: for down-glancing thence
She fathoms eddies, and runs wild about
O'erwhelming water-courses; scaring out
The thorny sharks from hiding-holes, and
    fright'ning
90 Their savage eyes with unaccustom'd light-
    ning.
Where will the splendor be content to
    reach?
O Love! how potent has thou been to
    teach
Strange journeyings! Wherever beauty
    dwells,
In gulf or aerie,[1] mountains or deep dells,
95 In light, in gloom, in star or blazing
    sun,
Thou pointest out the way, and straight
    'tis won.
Amid his toil thou gav'st Leander breath;[2]
Thou leddest Orpheus through the gleams
    of death;[3]
Thou madest Pluto bear thin element;[4]
100 And now, O winged Chieftain! thou hast
    sent
A moon-beam to the deep, deep water-
    world,
To find Endymion.

          On gold sand impearl'd
With lily shells, and pebbles milky white,
Poor Cynthia greeted him, and sooth'd her
    light
105 Against his pallid face: he felt the charm
To breathlessness, and suddenly a warm
Of his heart's blood: 'twas very sweet;
    he stay'd
His wandering steps, and half-entranced
    laid
His head upon a tuft of straggling weeds,
110 To taste the gentle moon, and freshening
    beads,[5]
Lash'd from the crystal roof by fishes'
    tails.
And so he kept, until the rosy veils

Mantling the east, by Aurora's peering
    hand
Were lifted from the water's breast, and
    fann'd
115 Into sweet air; and sober'd morning came
Meekly through billows:—when like taper-
    flame
Left sudden by a dallying breath of air,
He rose in silence, and once more 'gan
    fare
Along his fated way.

          Far had he roam'd,
120 With nothing save the hollow vast, that
    foam'd,
Above, around, and at his feet; save
    things
More dead than Morpheus' imaginings:
Old rusted anchors, helmets, breastplates
    large
Of gone sea-warriors; brazen beaks[1] and
    targe;[2]
125 Rudders that for a hundred years had
    lost
The sway of human hand; gold vase em-
    boss'd
With long-forgotten story, and wherein
No reveller had ever dipp'd a chin
But those of Saturn's vintage;[3] moulder-
    ing scrolls,
130 Writ in the tongue of heaven, by those
    souls
Who first were on the earth; and sculp-
    tures rude
In ponderous stone, developing the mood
Of ancient Nox;—then skeletons of man,
Of beast, behemoth, and leviathan,
135 And elephant, and eagle, and huge jaw
Of nameless monster. A cold leaden awe
These secrets struck into him; and unless
Dian had chased away that heaviness,
He might have died: but now, with cheered
    feel,
140 He onward kept; wooing these thoughts
    to steal
About the labyrinth in his soul of love.

"What is there in thee, Moon! that thou
    shouldst move
My heart so potently? When yet a child
I oft have dried my tears when thou hast
    smil'd.
145 Thou seem'dst my sister: hand in hand we
    went
From eve to morn across the firmament.
No apples would I gather from the tree,

---

[1] nesting place of eagles and other birds of prey; mountain height
[2] When he swam the Hellespont nightly to visit Hero.
[3] When he descended to Hades to lead his wife Eurydice back to earth.
[4] When he came to earth to seek Proserpine.
[5] That is, bubbles of air.

[1] armed projections from the prows of ancient galleys
[2] shield
[3] That is, not since the age of Saturn.

Till thou hadst cool'd their cheeks deli-
    ciously:
No tumbling water ever spake romance,
150 But when my eyes with thine thereon
    could dance:
No woods were green enough, no bower
    divine,
Until thou liftedst up thine eyelids fine:
In sowing time ne'er would I dibble[1] take,
Or drop a seed, till thou wast wide awake;
155 And, in the summer tide of blossoming,
No one but thee hath heard me blithely
    sing
And mesh my dewy flowers all the night.
No melody was like a passing spright
If it went not to solemnize thy reign.
160 Yes, in my boyhood, every joy and pain
By thee were fashion'd to the self-same
    end;
And as I grew in years, still didst thou
    blend
With all my ardors: thou wast the deep
    glen;
Thou wast the mountain-top—the sage's
    pen—
165 The poet's harp—the voice of friends—
    the sun;
Thou wast the river—thou wast glory won;
Thou wast my clarion's blast—thou wast
    my steed—
My goblet full of wine—my topmost
    deed:—
Thou wast the charm of women, lovely
    Moon!
170 O what a wild and harmonized tune
My spirit struck from all the beautiful!
On some bright essence could I lean, and
    lull
Myself to immortality: I prest
Nature's soft pillow in a wakeful rest.
175 But, gentle Orb! there came a nearer
    bliss—
My strange love came—Felicity's abyss!
She came, and thou didst fade, and fade
    away—
Yet not entirely; no, thy starry sway
Has been an under-passion to this hour.
180 Now I begin to feel thine orby power
Is coming fresh upon me: O be kind,
Keep back thine influence,[2] and do not
    blind
My sovereign vision.—Dearest love, for-
    give
That I can think away from thee and
    live!—

185 Pardon me, airy planet, that I prize
One thought beyond thine argent[1] lux-
    uries!
How far beyond!'' At this a surpris'd
    start
Frosted the springing verdure of his heart;
For as he lifted up his eyes to swear
190 How his own goddess was past all things
    fair,
He saw far in the concave green of the
    sea
An old man sitting calm and peacefully.[2]
Upon a weeded rock this old man sat,
And his white hair was awful, and a mat
195 Of weeds were cold beneath his cold thin
    feet;
And, ample as the largest winding-sheet,
A cloak of blue wrapp'd up his aged
    bones,
O'erwrought with symbols by the deepest
    groans
Of ambitious magic: every ocean-form
200 Was woven in with black distinctness;
    storm,
And calm, and whispering, and hideous
    roar,
Quicksand, and whirlpool, and deserted
    shore,
Were emblem'd in the woof; with every
    shape
That skims, or dives, or sleeps, 'twixt cape
    and cape.
205 The gulfing whale was like a dot in the
    spell,
Yet look upon it, and 'twould size and
    swell
To its huge self; and the minutest fish
Would pass the very hardest gazer's wish,
And show his little eye's anatomy.
210 Then there was pictur'd the regality
Of Neptune; and the sea-nymphs round
    his state,
In beauteous vassalage, look up and wait.
Beside this old man lay a pearly wand,
And in his lap a book, the which he conn'd
215 So steadfastly, that the new denizen
Had time to keep him in amazed ken,
To mark these shadowings, and stand in
    awe.

The old man rais'd his hoary head and
    saw
The wilder'd stranger—seeming not to see,
220 His features were so lifeless. Suddenly
He woke as from a trance; his snow-white
    brows

---

[1] A pointed implement used for making holes
   in the ground for seeds or plants.
[2] The ancients believed that a stream of ethereal
   fluid flowed from the stars and affected the
   actions of men.

[1] silvery; shining
[2] Glaucus, a sea divinity, formerly a fisherman,
   who became immortal by eating a magic
   herb.

Went arching up, and like two magic
    ploughs
Furrow'd deep wrinkles in his forehead
    large,
Which kept as fixedly as rocky marge,
225 Till round his wither'd lips had gone a
    smile.
Then up he rose, like one whose tedious
    toil
Had watch'd for years in forlorn hermi-
    tage,
Who had not from mid-life to utmost
    age
Eas'd in one accent his o'er-burden'd soul,
230 Even to the trees. He rose: he grasp'd
    his stole,
With convuls'd clenches waving it abroad,
And in a voice of solemn joy, that aw'd
Echo into oblivion, he said:—

"Thou art the man! Now shall I lay
    my head
235 In peace upon my watery pillow: now
Sleep will come smoothly to my weary
    brow.
O Jove! I shall be young again, be young!
O shell-borne Neptune, I am pierc'd and
    stung
With new-born life! What shall I do?
    Where go,
240 When I have cast this serpent-skin of
    woe?—
I'll swim to the sirens,[1] and one moment
    listen
Their melodies, and see their long hair
    glisten;
Anon upon that giant's[2] arm I'll be,
That writhes about the roots of Sicily:
245 To northern seas I'll in a twinkling sail,
And mount upon the snortings of a whale
To some black cloud; thence down I'll
    madly sweep
On forked lightning, to the deepest deep,
Where through some sucking pool I will
    be hurl'd
250 With rapture to the other side of the
    world!
O, I am full of gladness! Sisters three,[3]
I bow full hearted to your old decree!
Yes, every god be thank'd, and power
    benign,
For I no more shall wither, droop, and
    pine.[4]

[1] Sea nymphs who were said to inhabit an island off the coast of Italy, and by their singing to lure mariners to destruction.
[2] Enceladus, who warred against Jupiter, and upon whom Minerva threw the island of Sicily.
[3] The three Fates.
[4] See *Macbeth*, I, 3, 23.

255 Thou art the man!" Endymion started
    back
Dismay'd; and, like a wretch from whom
    the rack
Tortures hot breath, and speech of agony,
Mutter'd: "What lonely death am I to
    die
In this cold region? Will he let me freeze,
260 And float my brittle limbs o'er polar seas?
Or will he touch me with his searing hand,
And leave a black memorial on the sand?
Or tear me piecemeal with a bony saw,
And keep me as a chosen food to draw
265 His magian[1] fish through hated fire and
    flame?
O misery of hell! resistless, tame,
Am I to be burnt up? No, I will shout,
Until the gods through heaven's blue look
    out!—
O Tartarus! but some few days agone
270 Her soft arms were entwining me, and on
Her voice I hung like fruit among green
    leaves:
Her lips were all my own, and—ah, ripe
    sheaves
Of happiness! ye on the stubble droop,
But never may be garner'd. I must stoop
275 My head, and kiss death's foot. Love!
    love, farewell!
Is there no hope from thee? This horrid
    spell
Would melt at thy sweet breath.—By
    Dian's hind[2]
Feeding from her white fingers, on the
    wind
I see thy streaming hair! and now, by Pan,
280 I care not for this old mysterious man!"

He spake, and walking to that aged
    form,
Look'd high defiance. Lo! his heart 'gan
    warm
With pity, for the gray-hair'd creature
    wept.
Had he then wrong'd a heart where sor-
    row kept?
285 Had he, though blindly contumelious,
    brought
Rheum to kind eyes, a sting to human
    thought,
Convulsion to a mouth of many years?
He had in truth; and he was ripe for tears.
The penitent shower fell, as down he knelt
290 Before that care-worn sage, who trembling
    felt
About his large dark locks, and faltering
    spake:

[1] magical
[2] The hind was Diana's favorite animal.

"Arise, good youth, for sacred Phœbus'
   sake!
I know thine inmost bosom, and I feel
A very brother's yearning for thee steal
295 Into mine own: for why? thou openest
The prison gates that have so long opprest
My weary watching. Though thou know'st
   it not,
Thou art commission'd to this fated spot
For great enfranchisement. O weep no
   more;
300 I am a friend to love, to loves of yore:
Aye, hadst thou never lov'd an unknown
   power,
I had been grieving at this joyous hour.
But even now most miserable old,
I saw thee, and my blood no longer cold
305 Gave mighty pulses: in this tottering case
Grew a new heart, which at this moment
   plays
As dancingly as thine. Be not afraid,
For thou shalt hear this secret all dis-
   play'd,
Now as we speed towards our joyous
   task."

310   So saying, this young soul in age's mask
Went forward with the Carian side by
   side:
Resuming quickly thus, while ocean's tide
Hung swollen at their backs, and jewel'd
   sands
Took silently their foot-prints.

                "My soul stands
315 Now past the midway from mortality,
And so I can prepare without a sigh
To tell thee briefly all my joy and pain.
I was a fisher once, upon this main,
And my boat danc'd in every creek and
   bay;
320 Rough billows were my home by night and
   day,—
The sea-gulls not more constant; for I had
No housing from the storm and tempests
   mad,
But hollow rocks,—and they were palaces
Of silent happiness, of slumberous ease:
325 Long years of misery have told me so.
Aye, thus it was one thousand years ago.
One thousand years!—Is it then possible
To look so plainly through them? to dispel
A thousand years with backward glance
   sublime?
330 To breathe away as 'twere all scummy
   slime
From off a crystal pool, to see its deep,
And one's own image from the bottom
   peep?

Yes: now I am no longer wretched thrall,
My long captivity and moanings all
335 Are but a slime, a thin-pervading scum,
The which I breathe away, and thronging
   come
Like things of yesterday my youthful
   pleasures.

"I touch'd no lute, I sang not, trod no
   measures:
I was a lonely youth on desert shores.
340 My sports were lonely, 'mid continuous
   roars,
And craggy isles, and sea-mew's plaintive
   cry
Plaining discrepant between sea and sky.
Dolphins were still my playmates; shapes
   unseen
Would let me feel their scales of gold
   and green,
345 Nor be my desolation; and, full oft,
When a dread waterspout had rear'd
   aloft
Its hungry hugeness, seeming ready ripe
To burst with hoarsest thunderings, and
   wipe
My life away like a vast sponge of fate,
350 Some friendly monster, pitying my sad
   state,
Has dived to its foundations, gulf'd it
   down,
And left me tossing safely. But the
   crown
Of all my life was utmost quietude:
More did I love to lie in cavern rude,
355 Keeping in wait whole days for Neptune's
   voice,
And if it came at last, hark, and rejoice!
There blush'd no summer eve but I would
   steer
My skiff along green shelving coasts, to
   hear
The shepherd's pipe come clear from aery
   steep,
360 Mingled with ceaseless bleatings of his
   sheep:
And never was a day of summer shine,
But I beheld its birth upon the brine:
For I would watch all night to see un-
   fold
Heaven's gates, and Æthon snort his
   morning gold
365 Wide o'er the swelling streams: and con-
   stantly
At brim of day-tide, on some grassy lea,
My nets would be spread out, and I at
   rest.
The poor folk of the sea-country I blest
With daily boon of fish most delicate:

370 They knew not whence this bounty, and
elate
Would strew sweet flowers on a sterile
beach.

"Why was I not contented? Wherefore
reach
At things which, but for thee, O Latmian!
Had been my dreary death? Fool! I began
375 To feel distemper'd longings: to desire
The utmost privilege that ocean's sire[1]
Could grant in benediction: to be free
Of all his kingdom. Long in misery
I wasted, ere in one extremest fit
380 I plung'd for life or death. To interknit
One's senses with so dense a breathing
stuff
Might seem a work of pain; so not enough
Can I admire how crystal-smooth it felt,
And buoyant round my limbs. At first I
dwelt
385 Whole days and days in sheer astonish-
ment;
Forgetful utterly of self-intent;
Moving but with the mighty ebb and flow.
Then, like a new fledg'd bird that first doth
show
His spreaded feathers to the morrow chill,
390 I tried in fear the pinions of my will.
'Twas freedom! and at once I visited
The ceaseless wonders of this ocean-bed.
No need to tell thee of them, for I see
That thou hast been a witness—it must be
395 For these I know thou canst not feel a
drouth,
By the melancholy corners of that mouth.
So I will in my story straightway pass
To more immediate matter. Woe, alas!
That love should be my bane! Ah, Scylla
fair!
400 Why did poor Glaucus ever—ever dare
To sue thee to his heart? Kind stranger-
youth!
I lov'd her to the very white of truth,
And she would not conceive it. Timid
thing!
She fled me swift as sea-bird on the wing,
405 Round every isle, and point, and promon-
tory,
From where large Hercules wound up his
story[2]
Far as Egyptian Nile. My passion grew
The more, the more I saw her dainty hue
Gleam delicately through the azure clear:
410 Until 'twas too fierce agony to bear;
And in that agony, across my grief

It flash'd, that Circe might find some re-
lief—
Cruel enchantress! So above the water
I rear'd my head, and look'd for Phœbus'
daughter.[1]
415 Æœa's isle was wondering at the moon:—
It seem'd to whirl around me, and a swoon
Left me dead-drifting to that fatal power.

"When I awoke, 'twas in a twilight
bower;
Just when the light of morn, with hum of
bees,
420 Stole through its verdurous matting of
fresh trees.
How sweet, and sweeter! for I heard a lyre,
And over it a sighing voice expire.
It ceased—I caught light footsteps; and
anon
The fairest face that morn e'er look'd
upon
425 Push'd through a screen of roses. Starry
Jove!
With tears, and smiles, and honey-words
she wove
A net whose thraldom was more bliss than
all
The range of flower'd Elysium. Thus did
fall
The dew of her rich speech: 'Ah! Art
awake?
430 O let me hear thee speak, for Cupid's
sake!
I am so oppress'd with joy! Why, I have
shed
An urn of tears, as though thou wert cold
dead;
And now I find thee living, I will pour
From these devoted eyes their silver store,
435 Until exhausted of the latest drop,
So it will pleasure thee, and force thee stop
Here, that I too may live: but if beyond
Such cool and sorrowful offerings, thou
art fond
Of soothing warmth, of dalliance supreme;
440 If thou art ripe to taste a long love-dream;
If smiles, if dimples, tongues for ardor
mute,
Hang in thy vision like a tempting fruit,
O let me pluck it for thee.' Thus she link'd
Her charming syllables, till indistinct
445 Their music came to my o'er-sweeten'd
soul;
And then she hover'd over me, and stole
So near, that if no nearer it had been
This furrow'd visage thou hadst never
seen.

---

[1] Poseidon (Neptune).
[2] Mt. Œta, in Greece, where the body of Hercules was burned on his funeral pyre.

[1] Circe. She was the daughter of Helios, often
identified with Phœbus Apollo.

"Young man of Latmos! thus particular
450 Am I, that thou may'st plainly see how
far
This fierce temptation went: and thou
may'st not
Exclaim, How then, was Scylla quite forgot?

"Who could resist? Who in this uni-
verse?
She did so breathe ambrosia; so immerse
455 My fine existence in a golden clime.
She took me like a child of suckling time,
And cradled me in roses. Thus con-
demn'd,
The current of my former life was
stemm'd,
And to this arbitrary queen of sense
460 I bow'd a tranced vassal: nor would thence
Have mov'd, even though Amphion's harp
had woo'd
Me back to Scylla o'er the billows rude.
For as Apollo each eve doth devise
A new apparelling for western skies;
465 So every eve, nay every spendthrift hour
Shed balmy consciousness within that
bower.
And I was free of haunts umbrageous;
Could wander in the mazy forest-house
Of squirrels, foxes shy, and antler'd deer,
470 And birds from coverts innermost and
drear
Warbling for very joy mellifluous sor-
row—
To me new-born delights!

"Now let me borrow,
For moments few, a temperament as stern
As Pluto's sceptre, that my words not burn
475 These uttering lips, while I in calm speech
tell
How specious heaven was changed to real
hell.

"One morn she left me sleeping: half
awake
I sought for her smooth arms and lips, to
slake
My greedy thirst with nectarous camel-
draughts;
480 But she was gone. Whereat the barbed
shafts
Of disappointment stuck in me so sore,
That out I ran and search'd the forest o'er.
Wandering about in pine and cedar gloom
Damp awe assail'd me; for there 'gan to
boom
485 A sound of moan, an agony of sound,

Sepulchral from the distance all around.
Then came a conquering earth-thunder,
and rumbled
That fierce complain to silence: while I
stumbled
Down a precipitous path, as if impell'd.
490 I came to a dark valley.—Groanings
swell'd
Poisonous about my ears, and louder grew,
The nearer I approach'd a flame's gaunt
blue,
That glar'd before me through a thorny
brake.[1]
This fire, like the eye of gordian[2] snake
495 Bewitch'd me towards; and I soon was
near
A sight too fearful for the feel of fear:
In thicket hid I curs'd the haggard[3]
scene—
The banquet of my arms, my arbor queen,
Seated upon an uptorn forest root;
500 And all around her shapes, wizard and
brute,
Laughing, and wailing, grovelling, serpent-
ing,
Showing tooth, tusk, and venom-bag, and
sting!
O such deformities! Old Charon's self,
Should he give up awhile his penny pelf,[4]
505 And take a dream 'mong rushes Stygian,
It could not be so phantasied. Fierce, wan,
And tyrannizing was the lady's look,
As over them a gnarled staff she shook.
Ofttimes upon the sudden she laugh'd out,
510 And from a basket emptied to the rout
Clusters of grapes, the which they
raven'd[5] quick
And roar'd for more; with many a hungry
lick
About their shaggy jaws. Avenging,
slow,
Anon she took a branch of mistletoe,
515 And emptied on't a black dull-gurgling
phial:
Groan'd one and all, as if some piercing
trial
Was sharpening for their pitiable bones.
She lifted up the charm: appealing groans
From their poor breasts went suing to
her ear
520 In vain; remorseless as an infant's bier
She whisk'd against their eyes the sooty
oil.
Whereat was heard a noise of painful toil,
Increasing gradual to a tempest rage,

---

[1] thicket   [2] knotted; twisted   [3] wild
[4] The fee which he demanded for ferrying the
spirits of the dead across the River Styx.
[5] devoured

Shrieks, yells, and groans of torture-pil-
　　grimage;
525 Until their grieved bodies 'gan to bloat
And puff from the tail's end to stifled
　　throat:
Then was appalling silence: then a sight
More wildering than all that hoarse
　　affright;
For the whole herd, as by a whirlwind
　　writhen,
530 Went through the dismal air like one huge
　　Python
Antagonizing Boreas;—and so vanish'd.
Yet there was not a breath of wind: she
　　banish'd
These phantoms with a nod. Lo! from the
　　dark
Came waggish fauns, and nymphs, and
　　satyrs stark,
535 With dancing and loud revelry,—and went
Swifter than centaurs after rapine bent.—
Sighing an elephant appear'd and bow'd
Before the fierce witch, speaking thus aloud
In human accent: 'Potent goddess! chief
540 Of pains resistless! make my being brief,
Or let me from this heavy prison fly:
Or give me to the air, or let me die!
I sue not for my happy crown again;
I sue not for my phalanx on the plain;
545 I sue not for my lone, my widow'd wife;
I sue not for my ruddy drops of life,
My children fair, my lovely girls and boys!
I will forget them; I will pass these joys;
Ask nought so heavenward, so too—too
　　high:
550 Only I pray, as fairest boon, to die,
Or be deliver'd from this cumbrous flesh,
From this gross, detestable, filthy mesh,
And merely given to the cold bleak air.
Have mercy, Goddess! Circe, feel my
　　prayer!'

555 　　"That curst magician's name fell icy
　　numb
Upon my wild conjecturing: truth had
　　come
Naked and sabre-like against my heart.
I saw a fury whetting a death-dart;
And my slain spirit, overwrought with
　　fright,
560 Fainted away in that dark lair of night.
Think, my deliverer, how desolate
My waking must have been! disgust, and
　　hate,
And terrors manifold divided me
A spoil amongst them. I prepar'd to flee
565 Into the dungeon core of that wild wood:
I fled three days—when lo! before me
　　stood

Glaring the angry witch. O Dis, even now,
A clammy dew is beading on my brow.
At mere remembering her pale laugh, and
　　curse.
570 'Ha! ha! Sir Dainty! there must be a
　　nurse
Made of rose-leaves and thistle-down, ex-
　　press,
To cradle thee, my sweet, and lull thee:
　　yes,
I am too flinty-hard for thy nice touch:
My tenderest squeeze is but a giant's
　　clutch.
575 So, fairy-thing, it shall have lullabies
Unheard of yet: and it shall still its cries
Upon some breast more lily-feminine.
Oh, no—it shall not pine, and pine, and
　　pine
More than one pretty, trifling thousand
　　years;
580 And then 'twere pity, but fate's gentle
　　shears
Cut short its immortality. Sea-flirt!
Young dove of the waters! truly I'll not
　　hurt
One hair of thine: see how I weep and
　　sigh,
That our heart-broken parting is so nigh.
585 And must we part? Ah, yes, it must be so.
Yet ere thou leavest me in utter woe,
Let me sob over thee my last adieus,
And speak a blessing. Mark me! Thou
　　hast thews
Immortal, for thou art of heavenly race:
590 But such a love is mine, that here I chase
Eternally away from thee all bloom
Of youth, and destine thee towards a tomb.
Hence shalt thou quickly to the watery
　　vast;
And there, ere many days be overpast,
595 Disabled age shall seize thee; and even
　　then
Thou shalt not go the way of aged men;
But live and wither, cripple and still
　　breathe
Ten hundred years: which gone, I then
　　bequeath
Thy fragile bones to unknown burial.
600 Adieu, sweet love, adieu!'—As shot stars
　　fall,
She fled ere I could groan for mercy.
　　Stung
And poison'd was my spirit: despair sung
A war-song of defiance 'gainst all hell.
A hand was at my shoulder to compel
605 My sullen steps; another 'fore my eyes
Moved on with pointed finger. In this
　　guise
Enforced, at the last by ocean's foam

I found me; by my fresh, my native home.
Its tempering coolness, to my life akin,
610 Came salutary as I waded in;
And, with a blind voluptuous rage, I gave
Battle to the swollen billow-ridge, and
    drave
Large froth before me, while there yet
    remain'd
Hale strength, nor from my bones all mar-
    row drain'd.

615   "Young lover, I must weep—such hell-
    ish spite
With dry cheek who can tell? Why thus
    my might
Proving upon this element, dismay'd,
Upon a dead thing's face my hand I laid;
I look'd—'twas Scylla! Cursed, cursed
    Circe!
620 O vulture-witch, hast never heard of
    mercy?
Could not thy harshest vengence be con-
    tent,
But thou must nip this tender innocent
Because I lov'd her?—Cold, O cold indeed
Were her fair limbs, and like a common
    weed
625 The sea-swell took her hair. Dead as she
    was
I clung about her waist, nor ceas'd to
    pass
Fleet as an arrow through unfathom'd
    brine,
Until there shone a fabric crystalline,
Ribb'd and inlaid with coral, pebble, and
    pearl.
630 Headlong I darted; at one eager swirl
Gain'd its bright portal, enter'd, and be-
    hold!
'Twas vast, and desolate, and icy-cold;
And all around—But wherefore this to
    thee
Who in few minutes more thyself shalt
    see?—
635 I left poor Scylla in a niche and fled.
My fever'd parchings up, my scathing
    dread
Met palsy half way: soon these limbs be-
    came
Gaunt, wither'd, sapless, feeble, cramp'd,
    and lame.

  "Now let me pass a cruel, cruel space,
640 Without one hope, without one faintest
    trace
Of mitigation, or redeeming bubble
Of color'd phantasy; for I fear 'twould
    trouble
Thy brain to loss of reason: and next tell

How a restoring chance came down to
    quell
645 One half of the witch in me.

               "On a day,
Sitting upon a rock above the spray,
I saw grow up from the horizon's brink
A gallant vessel: soon she seem'd to sink
Away from me again, as though her course
650 Had been resum'd in spite of hindering
    force—
So vanish'd: and not long, before arose
Dark clouds, and muttering of wind mo-
    rose,
Old Æolus would stifle his mad spleen,
But could not: therefore all the billows
    green
655 Toss'd up the silver spume against the
    clouds.
The tempest came: I saw that vessel's
    shrouds
In perilous bustle; while upon the deck
Stood trembling creatures. I beheld the
    wreck;
The final gulfing; the poor struggling
    souls:
660 I heard their cries amid loud thunder-
    rolls.
O they had all been sav'd but crazed eld
Annull'd my vigorous cravings: and thus
    quell'd
And curb'd, think on't, O Latmian! did I
    sit
Writhing with pity, and a cursing fit
665 Against that hell-born Circe. The crew
    had gone,
By one and one, to pale oblivion;
And I was gazing on the surges prone,
With many a scalding tear and many a
    groan,
When at my feet emerg'd an old man's
    hand,
670 Grasping this scroll, and this same slender
    wand.
I knelt with pain—reach'd out my hand—
    had grasp'd
These treasures—touch'd the knuckles—
    they unclasp'd—
I caught a finger: but the downward
    weight
O'erpowered me—it sank. Then 'gan
    abate
675 The storm, and through chill aguish gloom
    outburst
The comfortable sun. I was athirst
To search the book, and in the warming air
Parted its dripping leaves with eager care.
Strange matters did it treat of, and drew
    on

680 My soul page after page, till well-nigh
    won
Into forgetfulness; when, stupefied,
I read these words, and read again, and
    tried
My eyes against the heavens, and read
    again.
O what a load of misery and pain
685 Each Atlas-line bore off![1]—a shine of
    hope
Came gold around me, cheering me to
    cope
Strenuous with hellish tyranny. Attend!
For thou hast brought their promise to an
    end.

    "'In the wide sea there lives a forlorn
        wretch,
690 *Doom'd with enfeebled carcase to out-*
    stretch
His loath'd existence through ten centuries,
And then to die alone. Who can devise
A total opposition? No one. So
One million times ocean must ebb and
    flow,
695 *And he oppressed. Yet he shall not die,*
These things accomplish'd:—If he utterly
Scans all the depths of magic, and ex-
    pounds
The meanings of all motions, shapes, and
    sounds;
If he explores all forms and substances
700 *Straight homeward to their symbol-*
    essences;
He shall not die. Moreover, and in chief,
He must pursue this task of joy and grief
Most piously;—all lovers tempest-tost,
And in the savage overwhelming lost,
705 *He shall deposit side by side, until*
Time's creeping shall the dreary space ful-
    fil:
Which done, and all these labors ripened,
A youth, by heavenly power lov'd and
    led,
Shall stand before him; whom he shall
    direct
710 *How to consummate all. The youth elect*
Must do the thing, or both will be de-
    stroy'd.'"—

"Then," cried the young Endymion,
    overjoy'd,
"We are twin brothers in this destiny!
Say, I entreat thee, what achievement
    high
715 Is, in this restless world, for me reserv'd.

[1] The misery which each line bears is compared to the world which Atlas bore upon his shoulders.

What! if from thee my wandering feet
    had swerv'd,
Had we both perish'd?"—"Look!" the
    sage replied,
"Dost thou not mark a gleaming through
    the tide,
Of divers brilliances? 'Tis the edifice
720 I told thee of, where lovely Scylla lies;
And where I have enshrined piously
All lovers, whom fell storms have doom'd
    to die
Throughout my bondage." Thus dis-
    coursing, on
They went till unobscur'd the porches
    shone;
725 Which hurryingly they gain'd, and enter'd
    straight.
Sure never since King Neptune held his
    state
Was seen such wonder underneath the
    stars.
Turn to some level plain where haughty
    Mars
Has legion'd all his battle; and behold
730 How every soldier, with firm foot, doth
    hold
His even breast: see, many steeled squares,
And rigid ranks of iron—whence who
    dares
One step? Imagine further, line by line,
These warrior thousands on the field
    supine:—
735 So in that crystal place, in silent rows,
Poor lovers lay at rest from joys and
    woes.—
The stranger from the mountains, breath-
    less, trac'd
Such thousands of shut eyes in order
    plac'd;
Such ranges of white feet, and patient
    lips
740 All ruddy,—for here death no blossom
    nips.
He mark'd their brows and foreheads;
    saw their hair
Put sleekly on one side with nicest care;
And each one's gentle wrists, with rev-
    erence,
Put cross-wise to its heart.

        "Let us commence,"
745 Whisper'd the guide, stuttering with joy,
    "even now."
He spake, and, trembling like an aspen-
    bough,
Began to tear his scroll in pieces small,
Uttering the while some mumblings fu-
    neral.
He tore it into pieces small as snow

750 That drifts unfeather'd when bleak north-
    erns blow;
And having done it, took his dark blue
    cloak
And bound it round Endymion: then
    struck
His wand against the empty air times
    nine.—
"What more there is to do, young man, is
    thine:
755 But first a little patience; first undo
This tangled thread, and wind it to a
    clue.
Ah, gentle! 'tis as weak as spider's skein;
And shouldst thou break it—What, is it
    done so clean?
A power overshadows thee! Oh, brave!
760 The spite of hell is tumbling to its grave.
Here is a shell; 'tis pearly blank to me,
Nor mark'd with any sign or charac-
    tery[1]—
Canst thou read aught? O read for pity's
    sake!
Olympus! we are safe! Now, Carian,
    break
765 This wand against yon lyre on the ped-
    estal.''

'Twas done: and straight with sudden
    swell and fall
Sweet music breath'd her soul away, and
    sigh'd
A lullaby to silence.—"Youth! now strew
These minced leaves on me, and passing
    through
770 Those files of dead, scatter the same
    around,
And thou wilt see the issue.''—'Mid the
    sound
Of flutes and viols, ravishing his heart,
Endymion from Glaucus stood apart,
And scatter'd in his face some fragments
    light.
775 How lightning-swift the change! a youth-
    ful wight[2]
Smiling beneath a coral diadem,
Out-sparkling sudden like an upturn'd
    gem,
Appear'd, and, stepping to a beauteous
    corse,
Kneel'd down beside it, and with tenderest
    force
780 Press'd its cold hand, and wept,—and
    Scylla sigh'd!
Endymion, with quick hand, the charm
    applied—
The nymph arose: he left them to their joy,

[1] characters; letters   [2] person; being

And onward went upon his high employ,
Showering those powerful fragments on
    the dead.
785 And, as he pass'd, each lifted up its head,
As doth a flower at Apollo's touch.
Death felt it to his inwards: 'twas too
    much:
Death fell a-weeping in his charnel-house.
The Latmian persever'd along, and thus
790 All were re-animated. There arose
A noise of harmony, pulses and throes
Of gladness in the air—while many, who
Had died in mutual arms devout and true,
Sprang to each other madly; and the
    rest
795 Felt a high certainty of being blest.
They gaz'd upon Endymion. Enchant-
    ment
Grew drunken, and would have its head
    and bent.
Delicious symphonies, like airy flowers,
Budded, and swell'd, and, full-blown, shed
    full showers
800 Of light, soft, unseen leaves of sounds
    divine.
The two deliverers tasted a pure wine
Of happiness, from fairy-press ooz'd out.
Speechless they eyed each other, and
    about
The fair assembly wander'd to and fro,
805 Distracted with the richest overflow
Of joy that ever pour'd from heaven.

            ——"Away!"
Shouted the new-born God; "Follow, and
    pay
Our piety to Neptunus supreme!''—
Then Scylla, blushing sweetly from her
    dream,
810 They led on first, bent to her meek sur-
    prise,
Through portal columns of a giant size,
Into the vaulted, boundless emerald.
Joyous all follow'd as the leader call'd,
Down marble steps; pouring as easily
815 As hour-glass sand,—and fast, as you
    might see
Swallows obeying the south summer's call,
Or swans upon a gentle waterfall.

Thus went that beautiful multitude, nor
    far,
Ere from among some rocks of glittering
    spar,
820 Just within ken, they saw descending thick
Another multitude. Whereat more quick
Moved either host. On a wide sand they
    met,
And of those numbers every eye was wet;

For each their old love found. A mur-
    muring rose,
825 Like what was never heard in all the throes
Of wind and waters: 'tis past human wit
To tell; 'tis dizziness to think of it.

    This mighty consummation made, the
      host
Mov'd on for many a league; and gain'd,
    and lost
830 Huge sea-marks; vanward swelling in
    array,
And from the rear diminishing away,—
Till a faint dawn surpris'd them. Glaucus
    cried,
"Behold! behold, the palace of his pride!
God Neptune's palaces!" With noise
    increas'd,
835 They shoulder'd on towards that brighten-
    ing east.
At every onward step proud domes arose
In prospect,—diamond gleams, and golden
    glows
Of amber 'gainst their faces levelling.
Joyous, and many as the leaves in spring,
840 Still onward; still the splendor gradual
    swell'd.
Rich opal domes were seen, on high upheld
By jasper pillars, letting through their
    shafts
A blush of coral. Copious wonder-draughts
Each gazer drank; and deeper drank more
    near:
845 For what poor mortals fragment up, as
    mere[1]
As marble was there lavish, to the vast
Of one fair palace, that far, far surpass'd,
Even for common bulk, those olden three,
Memphis, and Babylon, and Nineveh.

850   As large, as bright, as color'd as the bow
Of Iris, when unfading it doth show
Beyond a silvery shower, was the arch
Through which this Paphian army took its
    march,
Into the outer courts of Neptune's state:
855 Whence could be seen, direct, a golden gate,
To which the leaders sped; but not half
    raught[2]
Ere it burst open swift as fairy thought,
And made those dazzled thousands veil
    their eyes
Like callow eagles at the first sunrise.
860 Soon with an eagle nativeness their gaze
Ripe from hue-golden swoons took all the
    blaze,
And then, behold! large Neptune on his
    throne

[1] entire : perfect   [2] reached

Of emerald deep: yet not exalt alone;
At his right hand stood winged Love, and
    on
865 His left sat smiling Beauty's paragon.[1]

Far as the mariner on highest mast
Can see all round upon the calmed vast,
So wide was Neptune's hall: and as the
    blue
Doth vault the waters, so the waters drew
870 Their doming curtains, high, magnificent,
Aw'd from the throne aloof;—and when
    storm-rent
Disclos'd the thunder-gloomings in Jove's
    air;
But sooth'd as now, flash'd sudden every-
    where,
Noiseless, sub-marine cloudlets, glittering
875 Death to a human eye: for there did spring
From natural west, and east, and south,
    and north,
A light as of four sunsets, blazing forth
A gold-green zenith 'bove the Sea-God's
    head.
Of lucid depth the floor, and far outspread
880 As breezeless lake, on which the slim canoe
Of feather'd Indian darts about, as
    through
The delicatest air: air verily,
But for the portraiture of clouds and sky:
This palace floor breath-air,—but for the
    amaze
885 Of deep-seen wonders motionless,—and
    blaze
Of the dome pomp, reflected in extremes,
Globing a golden sphere.

                They stood in dreams
Till Triton blew his horn. The palace rang;
The Nereids danc'd; the Sirens faintly
    sang;
890 And the great Sea-King bow'd his drip-
    ping head.
Then Love took wing, and from his pinions
    shed
On all the multitude a nectarous dew.
The ooze-born Goddess[2] beckoned and
    drew
Fair Scylla and her guides to conference;
895 And when they reach'd the throned emi-
    nence
She kiss'd the sea-nymph's cheek,—who
    sat her down
A-toying with the doves. Then,—"Mighty
    crown
And sceptre of this kingdom!" Venus
    said,

[1] Venus.
[2] Venus. See *Endymion*, 1, 626, and n. (p. 801).

"Thy vows were on a time to Nais paid:
900 Behold!"— Two copious tear-drops in-
stant fell
From the God's large eyes; he smil'd de-
lectable,
And over Glaucus held his blessing hands.—
"Endymion! Ah! still wandering in the
bands
Of love? Now this is cruel. Since the hour
905 I met thee in earth's bosom, all my power
Have I put forth to serve thee. What, not
yet
Escap'd from dull mortality's harsh net?
A little patience, youth! 'twill not be long,
Or I am skilless quite: an idle tongue,
910 A humid eye, and steps luxurious,
Where these are new and strange, are omi-
nous.
Aye, I have seen these signs in one of
heaven,
When others were all blind: and were I
given
To utter secrets, haply I might say
915 Some pleasant words:—but Love will have
his day.
So wait awhile expectant. Pr'ythee soon,
Even in the passing of thine honey-moon,
Visit thou my Cythera: thou wilt find
Cupid well-natur'd, my Adonis kind;
920 And pray persuade with thee—Ah, I have
done,
All blisses be upon thee, my sweet son!"—
Thus the fair Goddess: while Endymion
Knelt to receive those accents halcyon.[1]

Meantime a glorious revelry began
925 Before the Water-Monarch. Nectar ran
In courteous fountains to all cups out-
reach'd;
And plunder'd vines, teeming exhaustless,
pleach'd[2]
New growth about each shell and pendent
lyre;
The which, in disentangling for their fire,
930 Pull'd down fresh foliage and coverture
For dainty toying. Cupid, empire-sure,
Flutter'd and laugh'd, and ofttimes
through the throng
Made a delighted way. Then dance, and
song,
And garlanding grew wild; and pleasure
reign'd.
935 In harmless tendril they each other chain'd,
And strove who should be smother'd deepest in
Fresh crush of leaves.

[1] calm; peaceful (The halcyon, or kingfisher,
was said to make its nest at sea and to
calm the waves.)
[2] interwove

O 'tis a very sin
For one so weak to venture his poor verse
In such a place as this. O do not curse,
940 High Muses! let him hurry to the ending.

All suddenly were silent. A soft blend-
ing
Of dulcet instruments came charmingly;
And then a hymn.

"King of the stormy sea!
Brother of Jove, and co-inheritor
945 Of elements; Eternally before
Thee the waves awful bow. Fast, stubborn
rock,
At thy fear'd trident shrinking, doth unlock
Its deep foundations, hissing into foam.
All mountain-rivers, lost in the wide home
950 Of thy capacious bosom, ever flow.
Thou frownest, and old Æolus thy foe
Skulks to his cavern, 'mid the gruff com-
plaint
Of all his rebel tempests. Dark clouds faint
When, from thy diadem, a silver gleam
955 Slants over blue dominion. Thy bright team
Gulfs in the morning light, and scuds along
To bring thee nearer to that golden song
Apollo singeth, while his chariot
Waits at the doors of heaven. Thou art not
960 For scenes like this: an empire stern hast
thou;
And it hath furrow'd that large front: yet
now,
As newly come of heaven, dost thou sit
To blend and interknit
Subdued majesty with this glad time.
965 O shell-borne King sublime!
We lay our hearts before thee evermore—
We sing, and we adore!

"Breathe softly, flutes;
Be tender of your strings, ye soothing lutes;
970 Nor be the trumpet heard! O vain, O vain;
Not flowers budding in an April rain,
Nor breath of sleeping dove, nor river's
flow,—
No, nor the Æolian twang of Love's own
bow,
Can mingle music fit for the soft ear
975 Of goddess Cytherea!
Yet deign, white Queen of Beauty, thy fair
eyes
On our souls' sacrifice.

"Bright-winged child!
Who has another care when thou hast smil'd?
980 Unfortunates on earth, we see at last
All death-shadows, and glooms that overcast
Our spirits, fann'd away by thy light pinions.
O sweetest essence! sweetest of all minions!
God of warm pulses, and dishevell'd hair,
985 And panting bosoms bare!
Dear unseen light in darkness! eclipser
Of light in light! delicious poisoner!
Thy venom'd goblet will we quaff until

We fill—we fill!
990 And by thy mother's lips——''

          Was heard no more
For clamor, when the golden palace door
Opened again, and from without, in shone
A new magnificence. On oozy throne
Smooth-moving came Oceanus the old,
995 To take a latest glimpse at his sheep-fold,
Before he went into his quiet cave
To muse forever—then a lucid wave
Scoop'd from its trembling sisters of mid-
    sea,
Afloat, and pillowing up the majesty
1000 Of Doris, and the Ægean seer,[1] her
    spouse—
Next, on a dolphin, clad in laurel boughs,
Theban Amphion leaning on his lute:
His fingers went across it.—All were mute
To gaze on Amphitrite, queen of pearls,
1005 And Thetis pearly too.—

          The palace whirls
Around giddy Endymion, seeing he
Was there far strayed from mortality.
He could not bear it—shut his eyes in vain;
Imagination gave a dizzier pain.
1010 ''O I shall die! sweet Venus, be my stay!
Where is my lovely mistress? Well-away!
I die—I hear her voice—I feel my wing—''
At Neptune's feet he sank. A sudden ring
Of Nereids were about him, in kind strife
1015 To usher back his spirit into life:
But still he slept. At last they interwove
Their cradling arms, and purpos'd to con-
    vey
Towards a crystal bower far away.

Lo! while slow carried through the pity-
    ing crowd,
1020 To his inward senses these words spake
    aloud;
Written in starlight on the dark above:
''*Dearest Endymion! my entire love!*
How have I dwelt in fear of fate: 'tis
    done—
Immortal bliss for me too hast thou won.
1025 *Arise then! for the hen-dove shall not hatch*
Her ready eggs, before I'll kissing snatch
Thee into endless heaven. Awake! awake!''

The youth at once arose: a placid lake
Came quiet to his eyes; and forest green,
1030 Cooler than all the wonders he had seen,
Lull'd with its simple song his fluttering
    breast.
How happy once again in grassy nest!

[1] Nereus, a sea divinity who lived chiefly in the
    Ægean Sea.

Book IV

Muse of my native land! loftiest **Muse**!
O first-born on the mountains! by the hues
Of heaven on the spiritual air begot:
Long didst thou sit alone in northern grot,
5 While yet our England was a wolfish den;
Before our forests heard the talk of men;
Before the first of Druids was a child;[1]—
Long didst thou sit amid our regions wild
Rapt in a deep prophetic solitude.
10 There came an eastern voice[2] of solemn
    mood:—
Yet wast thou patient. Then sang forth the
    Nine,[3]
Apollo's garland:—yet didst thou divine
Such home-bred glory, that they cried in
    vain,
''Come hither, sister of the Island!''[4]
    Plain
15 Spake fair Ausonia;[5] and once more she
    spake
A higher summons:[6]—still didst thou be-
    take
Thee to thy native hopes. O thou hast won
A full accomplishment![7] The thing is
    done,
Which undone, these our latter days had
    risen
20 On barren souls. Great Muse, thou know'st
    what prison
Of flesh and bone curbs, and confines, and
    frets
Our spirits' wings: despondency besets
Our pillows; and the fresh tomorrow morn
Seems to give forth its light in very scorn
25 Of our dull, uninspir'd, snail-paced lives.
Long have I said, how happy he who shrives
To thee! But then I thought on poets gone,
And could not pray:—nor can I now—so
    on
I move to the end in lowliness of heart.—

30 ''Ah, woe is me! that I should fondly
    part
From my dear native land! Ah, foolish
    maid!
Glad was the hour, when, with thee, myriads
    bade
Adieu to Ganges and their pleasant fields!
To one so friendless the clear freshet yields
35 A bitter coolness; the ripe grape is sour:

[1] The Druids were said to be the first poets of
    Britain.
[2] The voice of the muse of Hebrew literature.
[3] The nine muses of Grecian song.
[4] The muse of England.
[5] A reference to Roman literature.
[6] A reference to Dante and Italian literature of
    the Renaissance.
[7] A reference to Elizabethan literature.

Yet I would have, great gods! but one
  short hour
Of native air—let me but die at home.''

Endymion to heaven's airy dome
Was offering up a hecatomb[1] of vows,
40 When these words reach'd him. Where-
  upon he bows
His head through thorny-green entangle-
  ment
Of underwood, and to the sound is bent,
Anxious as hind towards her hidden fawn.

  ''Is no one near to help me? No fair
  dawn
45 Of life from charitable voice? No sweet
  saying
To set my dull and sadden'd spirit playing?
No hand to toy with mine? No lips so
  sweet
That I may worship them? No eyelids
  meet
To twinkle on my bosom? No one dies
50 Before me, till from these enslaving eyes
Redemption sparkles!—I am sad and
  lost.''

  Thou, Carian lord, hadst better have
  been tost
Into a whirlpool. Vanish into air,
Warm mountaineer! for canst thou only
  bear
55 A woman's sigh alone and in distress?
See not her charms! Is Phœbe passion-
  less?
Phœbe is fairer far—O gaze no more:—
Yet if thou wilt behold all beauty's store,
Behold her panting in the forest grass!
60 Do not those curls of glossy jet surpass
For tenderness the arms so idly lain
Amongst them? Feelest not a kindred
  pain,
To see such lovely eyes in swimming search
After some warm delight, that seems to
  perch
65 Dovelike in the dim cell lying beyond
Their upper lids?—Hist!

           ''O for Hermes' wand,
To touch this flower into human shape!
That woodland Hyacinthus could escape
From his green prison, and here kneeling
  down
70 Call me his queen, his second life's fair
  crown!
Ah me, how I could love!—My soul doth
  melt
For the unhappy youth—Love! I have felt
¹ great number

So faint a kindness, such a meek surrender
To what my own full thoughts had made
  too tender,
75 That but for tears my life had fled away!—
Ye deaf and senseless minutes of the day,
And thou, old forest, hold ye this for true,
There is no lightning, no authentic dew
But in the eye of love: there's not a sound,
80 Melodious howsoever, can confound
The heavens and earth in one to such a
  death
As doth the voice of love: there's not a
  breath
Will mingle kindly with the meadow air,
Till it has panted round, and stolen a share
85 Of passion from the heart!''—

                 Upon a bough
He leant, wretched. He surely cannot now
Thirst for another love: O impious,
That he can ever dream upon it thus!—
Thought he, ''Why am I not as are the
  dead,
90 Since to a woe like this I have been led
Through the dark earth, and through the
  wondrous sea?
Goddess! I love thee not the less: from thee
By Juno's smile I turn not—no, no, no—
While the great waters are at ebb and
  flow.—
95 I have a triple soul! O fond pretence—
For both, for both my love is so immense,
I feel my heart is cut for them in twain.''

  And so he groan'd, as one by beauty
  slain.
The lady's heart beat quick, and he could
  see
100 Her gentle bosom heave tumultuously.
He sprang from his green covert: there
  she lay,
Sweet as a muskrose upon new-made hay;
With all her limbs on tremble, and her eyes
Shut softly up alive. To speak he tries.
105 ''Fair damsel, pity me! forgive that I
Thus violate thy bower's sanctity!
O pardon me, for I am full of grief—
Grief born of thee, young angel! fairest
  thief!
Who stolen hast away the wings wherewith
110 I was to top the heavens. Dear maid, sith
Thou art my executioner, and I feel
Loving and hatred, misery and weal,
Will in a few short hours be nothing to me,
And all my story that much passion slew
  me;
115 Do smile upon the evening of my days:
And, for my tortur'd brain begins to craze,
Be thou my nurse; and let me understand

How dying I shall kiss that lily hand.—
Dost weep for me? Then should I be content.
120 Scowl on, ye fates! until the firmament
Outblackens Erebus, and the full-cavern'd earth
Crumbles into itself. By the cloud-girth
Of Jove, those tears have given me a thirst
To meet oblivion.''—As her heart would burst
125 The maiden sobb'd awhile, and then replied:
''Why must such desolation betide
As that thou speak'st of? Are not these green nooks
Empty of all misfortune? Do the brooks
Utter a gorgon[1] voice? Does yonder thrush,
130 Schooling its half-fledg'd little ones to brush
About the dewy forest, whisper tales?—
Speak not of grief, young stranger, or cold snails
Will slime the rose tonight. Though if thou wilt,
Methinks 'twould be a guilt—a very guilt—
135 Not to companion thee, and sigh away
The light—the dusk—the dark—till break of day!''
''Dear lady,'' said Endymion, '''tis past:
I love thee! and my days can never last.
That I may pass in patience still speak:
140 Let me have music dying, and I seek
No more delight—I bid adieu to all.
Didst thou not after other climates call,
And murmur about Indian streams?''—Then she,
Sitting beneath the midmost forest tree,
145 For pity sang this roundelay—

''O Sorrow,
Why dost borrow
The natural hue of health, from vermeil lips?—
To give maiden blushes
150 To the white rose bushes?
Or is't thy dewy hand the daisy tips?

''O Sorrow,
Why dost borrow
The lustrous passion from a falcon-eye?—
155 To give the glowworm light?
Or, on a moonless night,
To tinge, on siren shores, the salt sea-spry?

''O Sorrow,
Why dost borrow
160 The mellow ditties from a mourning tongue?—

[1] killing, like a Gorgon

To give at evening pale
Unto the nightingale,
That thou mayst listen the cold dews among?

''O Sorrow,
165 Why dost borrow
Heart's lightness from the merriment of May?—
A lover would not tread
A cowslip on the head,
Though he should dance from eve till peep of day—
170 Nor any drooping flower
Held sacred for thy bower,
Wherever he may sport himself and play.

''To Sorrow,
I bade good-morrow,
175 And thought to leave her far away behind;
But cheerly, cheerly,
She loves me dearly;
She is so constant to me, and so kind;
I would deceive her
180 And so leave her,
But ah! she is so constant and so kind.

''Beneath my palm trees, by the river side,
I sat a-weeping: in the whole world wide,
There was no one to ask me why I wept,—
185 And so I kept
Brimming the water-lily cups with tears
Cold as my fears.

''Beneath my palm trees, by the river side,
I sat a-weeping: what enamor'd bride,
190 Cheated by shadowy wooer from the clouds,
But hides and shrouds
Beneath dark palm trees by a river side?

''And as I sat, over the light blue hills
There came a noise of revellers: the rills
195 Into the wide stream came of purple hue—
'Twas Bacchus and his crew!
The earnest trumpet spake, and silver thrills
From kissing cymbals made a merry din—
'Twas Bacchus and his kin!
200 Like to a moving vintage down they came,
Crown'd with green leaves, and faces all on flame;
All madly dancing through the pleasant valley,
To scare thee, Melancholy!
O then, O then, thou wast a simple name!
205 And I forgot thee, as the berried holly
By shepherds is forgotten, when, in June,
Tall chestnuts keep away the sun and moon:—
I rush'd into the folly!

''Within his car, aloft, young Bacchus stood,
210 Trifling his ivy-dart,[1] in dancing mood,
With sidelong laughing;
And little rills of crimson wine imbrued
His plump white arms, and shoulders, enough white

[1] The ivy was sacred to Bacchus.

For Venus' pearly bite:
215 And near him rode Silenus on his ass,
Pelted with flowers as he on did pass
Tipsily quaffing.

"Whence came ye, merry damsels! whence
came ye!
So many, and so many, and such glee?
220 Why have ye left your bowers desolate,
Your lutes, and gentler fate?—
'We follow Bacchus; Bacchus on the wing,
A-conquering!
Bacchus, young Bacchus! good or ill betide,
225 We dance before him thorough kingdoms
wide:—
Come hither, lady fair, and joined be
To our wild minstrelsy!'

"Whence came ye, jolly Satyrs! whence
came ye!
So many, and so many, and such glee?
230 Why have ye left your forest haunts, why
left
Your nuts in oak-tree cleft?—
'For wine, for wine we left our kernel tree;
For wine we left our heath, and yellow
brooms,
And cold mushrooms;
235 For wine we follow Bacchus through the
earth;
Great God of breathless cups and chirping
mirth!—
Come hither, lady fair, and joined be
To our mad minstrelsy!'

"Over wide streams and mountains great
we went,
240 And, save when Bacchus kept his ivy tent,
Onward the tiger and the leopard pants,
With Asian elephants:
Onward these myriads—with song and dance,
With zebras striped, and sleek Arabians'
prance,
245 Web-footed alligators, crocodiles,
Bearing upon their scaly backs, in files,
Plump infant laughers mimicking the coil
Of seamen, and stout galley-rowers' toil:
With toying oars and silken sails they glide,
250 Nor care for wind and tide.

"Mounted on panthers' furs and lions'
manes,
From rear to van they scour about the
plains;
A three days' journey in a moment done:
And always, at the rising of the sun,
255 About the wild they hunt with spear and
horn,
On spleenful unicorn.

"I saw Osirian Egypt kneel adown
Before the vine-wreath crown!
I saw parch'd Abyssinia rouse and sing
260 To the silver cymbals' ring!
I saw the whelming vintage hotly pierce
Old Tartary the fierce!

The kings of Inde their jewel-scepters vail,[1]
And from their treasures scatter pearled
hail;
265 Great Brahma from his mystic heaven
groans,
And all his priesthood moans;
Before young Bacchus' eye-wink turning
pale.—
Into these regions came I following him,
Sick-hearted, weary—so I took a whim
270 To stray away into these forests drear
Alone, without a peer:
And I have told thee all thou mayest hear.

"Young stranger!
I've been a ranger
275 In search of pleasure throughout every clime:
Alas, 'tis not for me!
Bewitch'd I sure must be,
To lose in grieving all my maiden prime.

"Come then, Sorrow!
280 Sweetest Sorrow!
Like an own babe I nurse thee on my
breast:
I thought to leave thee
And deceive thee,
But now of all the world I love thee best.

285 "There is not one,
No, no, not one
But thee to comfort a poor lonely maid;
Thou art her mother,
And her brother,
290 Her playmate, and her wooer in the shade."

O what a sigh she gave in finishing,
And look, quite dead to every worldly
thing!
Endymion could not speak, but gazed on
her;
And listened to the wind that now did stir
295 About the crisped oaks full drearily,
Yet with as sweet a softness as might be
Remember'd from its velvet summer song.
At last he said: "Poor lady, how thus long
Have I been able to endure that voice?
300 Fair Melody! kind Siren! I've no choice;
I must be thy sad servant evermore:
I cannot choose but kneel here and adore.
Alas, I must not think—by Phœbe, no!
Let me not think, soft Angel! shall it be so?
305 Say, beautifullest, shall I never think?
O thou could'st foster me beyond the brink
Of recollection! make my watchful care
Close up its bloodshot eyes, nor see despair!
Do gently murder half my soul, and I
310 Shall feel the other half so utterly!—
I'm giddy at that cheek so fair and smooth;
O let it blush so ever! let it soothe
My madness! let it mantle rosy-warm

[1] lower

With the tinge of love, panting in safe
    alarm.—
315 This cannot be thy hand, and yet it is;
And this is sure thine other softling—this
Thine own fair bosom, and I am so near!
Wilt fall asleep? O let me sip that tear!
And whisper one sweet word that I may
    know
320 This is this world—sweet dewy blossom!''
    —Woe!
*Woe! Woe to that Endymion! Where is
    he?—*
Even these words went echoing dismally
Through the wide forest—a most fearful
    tone,
Like one repenting in his latest moan;
325 And while it died away a shade pass'd by,
As of a thundercloud. When arrows fly
Through the thick branches, poor ring-
    doves sleek forth
Their timid necks and tremble; so these
    both
Leant to each other trembling, and sat so
330 Waiting for some destruction—when lo!
Foot-feather'd Mercury appear'd sublime
Beyond the tall tree tops; and in less time
Than shoots the slanted hail-storm, down
    he dropt
Towards the ground; but rested not, nor
    stopt
335 One moment from his home: only the
    sward
He with his wand light touch'd, and
    heavenward
Swifter than sight was gone—even before
The teeming earth a sudden witness bore
Of his swift magic. Diving swans appear
340 Above the crystal circlings white and clear;
And catch the cheated eye in wide surprise,
How they can dive in sight and unseen
    rise—
So from the turf outsprang two steeds jet-
    black,
Each with large dark-blue wings upon his
    back.
345 The youth of Caria plac'd the lovely dame
On one, and felt himself in spleen to tame
The other's fierceness. Through the air
    they flew,
High as the eagles. Like two drops of dew
Exhal'd to Phœbus' lips, away they are
    gone,
350 Far from the earth away—unseen, alone,
Among cool clouds and winds, but that the
    free,
The buoyant life of song can floating be
Above their heads, and follow them un-
    tir'd.—
Muse of my native land, am I inspir'd?

355 This is the giddy air, and I must spread
Wide pinions to keep here; nor do I dread
Or height, or depth, or width, or any chance
Precipitous: I have beneath my glance
Those towering horses and their mournful
    freight.
360 Could I thus sail, and see, and thus await
Fearless for power of thought, without
    thine aid?—

There is a sleepy dusk, an odorous shade
From some approaching wonder, and be-
    hold
Those winged steeds, with snorting nostrils
    bold
365 Snuff at its faint extreme, and seem to
    tire,
Dying to embers from their native fire!

There curl'd a purple mist around them;
    soon,
It seem'd as when around the pale new
    moon
Sad Zephyr droops the clouds like weeping
    willow:
370 'Twas Sleep slow journeying with head on
    pillow.
For the first time, since he came nigh dead-
    born
From the old womb of night, his cave
    forlorn
Had he left more forlorn; for the first
    time,
He felt aloof the day and morning's
    prime—
375 Because into his depth Cimmerian
There came a dream, showing how a young
    man,[1]
Ere a lean bat could plump its wintery
    skin,
Would at high Jove's empyreal footstool
    win
An immortality, and how espouse
380 Jove's daughter, and be reckon'd of his
    house.
Now was he slumbering towards heaven's
    gate,
That he might at the threshold one hour
    wait
To hear the marriage melodies, and then
Sink downward to his dusky cave again,
385 His litter of smooth semilucent mist,
Diversely ting'd with rose and amethyst,
Puzzled those eyes that for the centre
    sought;
And scarcely for one moment could be
    caught
His sluggish form reposing motionless.

[1] Endymion, beloved of Diana.

390 Those two on winged steeds, with all the
        stress
    Of vision search'd for him, as one would
        look
    Athwart the sallows of a river nook
    To catch a glance at silver-throated eels,—
    Or from old Skiddaw's top, when fog con-
        ceals
395 His rugged forehead in a mantle pale,
    With an eye-guess towards some pleasant
        vale
    Descry a favorite hamlet faint and far.

    These raven horses, though they foster'd
        are
    Of earth's splenetic fire, dully drop
400 Their full-vein'd ears, nostrils blood wide,
        and stop;
    Upon the spiritless mist have they out-
        spread
    Their ample feathers, are in slumber
        dead,—
    And on those pinions, level in mid air,
    Endymion sleepeth and the lady fair.
405 Slowly they sail, slowly as icy isle
    Upon a calm sea drifting: and meanwhile
    The mournful wanderer dreams. Behold!
        he walks
    On heaven's pavement; brotherly he talks
    To divine powers: from his hand full fain
410 Juno's proud birds[1] are pecking pearly
        grain:
    He tries the nerve of Phœbus' golden bow,
    And asketh where the golden apples grow:
    Upon his arm he braces Pallas' shield,
    And strives in vain to unsettle and wield
415 A Jovian thunderbolt: arch Hebe brings
    A full-brimm'd goblet, dances lightly, sings
    And tantalizes long; at last he drinks
    And lost in pleasure at her feet he sinks,
    Touching with dazzled lips her starlight
        hand.
420 He blows a bugle,—an ethereal band
    Are visible above: the Seasons four,—
    Green-kirtled Spring, flush Summer, gol-
        den store
    In Autumn's sickle, Winter frosty hoar,
    Join dance with shadowy Hours; while
        still the blast,
425 In swells unmitigated, still doth last
    To sway their floating morris.[2] "Whose
        is this?
    Whose bugle?" he inquires; they smile—
        "O Dis!
    Why is this mortal here? Dost thou not
        know
    Its mistress' lips? Not thou? — 'Tis
        Dian's: lo!

430 She rises crescented!'' He looks, 'tis she,
    His very goddess: good-bye earth, and sea,
    And air, and pains, and care, and suffer-
        ing;
    Good-bye to all but love! Then doth he
        spring
    Towards her, and awakes—and, strange,
        o'erhead,
435 Of those same fragrant exhalations bred,
    Beheld awake his very dream: the gods
    Stood smiling; merry Hebe laughs and
        nods;
    And Phœbe bends towards him crescented.
    O state perplexing! On the pinion bed,
440 Too well awake, he feels the panting side
    Of his delicious lady. He who died[1]
    For soaring too audacious in the sun,
    When that same treacherous wax began to
        run,
    Felt not more tongue-tied than Endymion.
445 His heart leapt up as to its rightful throne,
    To that fair-shadow'd passion puls'd its
        way—
    Ah, what perplexity! Ah, well a day!
    So fond, so beauteous was his bed-fellow,
    He could not help but kiss her: then he
        grew
450 Awhile forgetful of all beauty save
    Young Phœbe's, golden hair'd; and so
        'gan crave
    Forgiveness: yet he turn'd once more to
        look
    At the sweet sleeper,—all his soul was
        shook,—
    She press'd his hand in slumber; so once
        more
455 He could not help but kiss her and adore.
    At this the shadow wept, melting away.
    The Latmian started up: "Bright goddess,
        stay!
    Search my most hidden breast! By truth's
        own tongue,
    I have no dædale[2] heart: why is it wrung
460 To desperation? Is there nought for me,
    Upon the bourne of bliss, but misery?''

    These words awoke the stranger of dark
        tresses:
    Her dawning love-look rapt Endymion
        blesses
    With 'havior soft. Sleep yawn'd from
        underneath.
465 "Thou swan of Ganges, let us no more
        breathe
    This murky phantasm! thou contented
        seem'st
    Pillow'd in lovely idleness, nor dream'st
    What horrors may discomfort thee and me.

---

[1] Peacocks.   [2] An old popular dance.   [1] Icarus.   [2] cunning; deceptive

Ah, shouldst thou die from my heart-
 treachery!—
470 Yet did she merely weep—her gentle soul
Hath no revenge in it: as it is whole
In tenderness, would I were whole in love!
Can I prize thee, fair maid, all price above,
Even when I feel as true as innocence?
475 I do, I do.—What is this soul then?
 Whence
Came it? It does not seem my own, and I
Have no self-passion or identity.
Some fearful end must be: where, where
 is it?
By Nemesis, I see my spirit flit
480 Alone about the dark—Forgive me, sweet:
Shall we away?'' He rous'd the steeds:
 they beat
Their wings chivalrous into the clear air,
Leaving old Sleep within his vapory lair.

 The good-night blush of eve was waning
  slow,
485 And Vesper, risen star, began to throe
In the dusk heavens silverly, when they
Thus sprang direct towards the Galaxy.
Nor did speed hinder converse soft and
  strange—
Eternal oaths and vows they interchange,
490 In such wise, in such temper, so aloof
Up in the winds, beneath a starry roof,
So witless of their doom, that verily
'Tis well-nigh past man's search their
  hearts to see;
Whether they wept, or laugh'd, or griev'd,
 or toy'd—
495 Most like with joy gone mad, with sorrow
  cloy'd.

 Full facing their swift flight, from ebon
  streak,
The moon put forth a little diamond peak,
No bigger than an unobserved star,
Or tiny point of fairy scimitar;
500 Bright signal that she only stoop'd to tie
Her silver sandals, ere deliciously
She bow'd into the heavens her timid
 head.
Slowly she rose, as though she would have
 fled,
While to his lady meek the Carian turn'd,
505 To mark if her dark eyes had yet discern'd
This beauty in its birth—Despair! despair!
He saw her body fading gaunt and spare
In the cold moonshine. Straight he seiz'd
 her wrist;
It melted from his grasp: her hand he
 kiss'd,
510 And, horror! kiss'd his own—he was
 alone.

Her steed a little higher soar'd, and then
Dropt hawkwise to the earth.

     There lies a den,
Beyond the seeming confines of the space
Made for the soul to wander in and trace
515 Its own existence, of remotest glooms.
Dark regions are around it, where the
 tombs
Of buried griefs the spirit sees, but scarce
One hour doth linger weeping, for the
 pierce
Of new-born woe it feels more inly smart:
520 And in these regions many a venom'd dart
At random flies; they are the proper home
Of every ill: the man is yet to come
Who hath not journeyed in this native hell.
But few have ever felt how calm and well
525 Sleep may be had in that deep den of all.
There anguish does not sting; nor pleasure
 pall:
Woe-hurricanes beat ever at the gate,
Yet all is still within and desolate.
Beset with plainful gusts, within ye hear
530 No sound so loud as when on curtain'd bier
The death-watch tick is stifled. Enter none
Who strive therefore: on the sudden it is
 won.
Just when the sufferer begins to burn,
Then it is free to him; and from an urn,
535 Still fed by melting ice, he takes a
 draught—
Young Semele such richness never quaff'd
In her maternal longing! Happy gloom!
Dark Paradise! where pale becomes the
 bloom
Of health by due; where silence dreariest
540 Is most articulate; where hopes infest;
Where those eyes are the brightest far that
 keep
Their lids shut longest in a dreamless
 sleep.
O happy spirit-home! O wondrous soul!
Pregnant with such a den to save the whole
545 In thine own depth. Hail, gentle Carian!
For, never since thy griefs and woes began,
Hast thou felt so content: a grievous feud
Hath led thee to this Cave of Quietude
Aye, his lull'd soul was there, although
 upborne
550 With dangerous speed: and so he did not
 mourn
Because he knew not whither he was going.
So happy was he, not the aerial blowing
Of trumpets at clear parley from the east
Could rouse from that fine relish, that high
 feast.
555 They stung the feather'd horse: with fierce
 alarm

He flapp'd towards the sound. Alas, no
   charm
Could lift Endymion's head, or he had
   view'd
A skyey mask, a pinion'd multitude,—
And silvery was its passing: voices sweet
560 Warbling the while as if to lull and greet
The wanderer in his path. Thus warbled
   they,
While past the vision went in bright array.

"Who, who from Dian's feast would be
   away?
For all the golden bowers of the day
565 Are empty left? Who, who away would be
From Cynthia's wedding and festivity?
Not Hesperus: lo! upon his silver wings
He leans away for highest heaven and
   sings,
Snapping his lucid fingers merrily!—
570 Ah, Zephyrus; art here, and Flora too!
Ye tender bibbers of the rain and dew,
Young playmates of the rose and daffodil,
Be careful, ere ye enter in, to fill
   Your baskets high
575 With fennel green, and balm, and golden
   pines,
Savory, latter-mint, and columbines,
Cool parsley, basil sweet, and sunny thyme;
Yea, every flower and leaf of every clime,
All gather'd in the dewy morning: hie
580   Away! fly! fly!—
Crystalline brother of the belt of heaven,
Aquarius! to whom king Jove has given
Two liquid pulse streams 'stead of feather'd
   wings,
Two fan-like fountains,—thine illuminings
585   For Dian play:
Dissolve the frozen purity of air;
Let thy white shoulders silvery and bare
Show cold through watery pinions; make
   more bright
The Star-Queen's[1] crescent on her marriage
   night:
590   Haste, haste away!—
Castor has tamed the planet Lion, see!
And of the Bear has Pollux mastery:
A third in the race! who is the third
Speeding away swift as the eagle bird?
595   The ramping Centaur!
The Lion's mane's on end: the Bear how
   fierce!
The Centaur's arrow ready seems to pierce
Some enemy: far forth his bow is bent
Into the blue of heaven. He'll be shent,[2]
600   Pale unrelentor,
When he shall hear the wedding lutes a-
   playing.—
Andromeda! sweet woman! why delaying
So timidly among the stars: come hither!
Join this bright throng, and nimbly follow
   whither
605   They all are going.

Danaë's son,[1] before Jove newly bow'd,
Has wept for thee, calling to Jove aloud.
Thee, gentle lady, did he disenthral:
Ye shall forever live and love, for all
610   Thy tears are flowing.—
By Daphne's fright, behold Apollo!—"

               More
Endymion heard not: down his steed him
   bore,
Prone to the green head of a misty hill.

His first touch of the earth went nigh to
   kill.
615 "Alas!" said he, "were I but always
   borne
Through dangerous winds, had but my
   footsteps worn
A path in hell, forever would I bless
Horrors which nourish an uneasiness
For my own sullen conquering: to him
620 Who lives beyond earth's boundary, grief
   is dim,
Sorrow is but a shadow: now I see
The grass; I feel the solid ground—Ah,
   me!
It is thy voice—divinest! Where?—who?
   who
Left thee so quiet on this bed of dew?
625 Behold upon this happy earth we are;
Let us ay love each other; let us fare
On forest-fruits, and never, never go
Among the abodes of mortals here below,
Or be by phantoms duped. O destiny!
630 Into a labyrinth now my soul would fly,
But with thy beauty will I deaden it.
Where didst thou melt to? By thee will I
   sit
Forever: let our fate stop here—a kid
I on this spot will offer: Pan will bid
635 Us live in peace, in love and peace among
His forest wildernesses. I have clung
To nothing, lov'd a nothing, nothing seen
Or felt but a great dream! Oh, I have been
Presumptuous against love, against the
   sky,
640 Against all elements, against the tie
Of mortals each to each, against the blooms
Of flowers, rush of rivers, and the tombs
Of heroes gone! Against his proper glory
Has my own soul conspired: so my story
645 Will I to children utter, and repent.
There never liv'd a mortal man, who bent
His appetite beyond his natural sphere,
But starv'd and died. My sweetest Indian,
   here,
Here will I kneel, for thou redeemed hast

---

[1] Diana's.   [2] put to shame or confusion

[1] Perseus, who rescued Andromeda from the sea-
   monster.

650 My life from too thin breathing: gone and
    past
  Are cloudy phantasms. Caverns lone,
    farewell!
  And air of visions, and the monstrous swell
  Of visionary seas! No, never more
  Shall airy voices cheat me to the shore
655 Of tangled wonder, breathless and aghast.
  Adieu, my daintiest Dream! although so
    vast
  My love is still for thee. The hour may come
  When we shall meet in pure Elysium.
  On earth I may not love thee; and there-
    fore
660 Doves will I offer up, and sweetest store
  All through the teeming year: so thou wilt
    shine
  On me, and on this damsel fair of mine,
  And bless our simple lives. My Indian
    bliss!
  My river-lily bud! one human kiss!
665 One sign of real breath—one gentle
    squeeze,
  Warm as a dove's nest among summer
    trees,
  And warm with dew at ooze from living
    blood!
  Whither didst melt? Ah, what of that!—
    all good
  We'll talk about—no more of dreaming.—
    Now,
670 Where shall our dwelling be? Under the
    brow
  Of some steep mossy hill, where ivy dun
  Would hide us up, although spring leaves
    were none;
  And where dark yew trees, as we rustle
    through,
  Will drop their scarlet berry cups of dew?
675 O thou wouldst joy to live in such a place;
  Dusk for our loves, yet light enough to
    grace
  Those gentle limbs on mossy bed reclin'd:
  For by one step the blue sky shouldst thou
    find,
  And by another, in deep dell below,
680 See, through the trees, a little river go
  All in its mid-day gold and glimmering.
  Honey from out the gnarled hive I'll
    bring,
  And apples, wan with sweetness, gather
    thee,—
  Cresses that grow where no man may them
    see,
685 And sorrel untorn by the dew-claw'd stag:
  Pipes will I fashion of the syrinx flag,[1]

[1] A reference to the myth of the Arcadian
nymph Syrinx, who, to escape the embraces
of Pan, was changed into a tuft of reeds, out
of which Pan then made his pipes.

  That thou mayst always know whither I
    roam,
  When it shall please thee in our quiet home
  To listen and think of love. Still let me
    speak;
690 Still let me dive into the joy I seek,—
  For yet the past doth prison me. The
    rill,
  Thou haply mayst delight in, will I fill
  With fairy fishes from the mountain tarn,
  And thou shalt feed them from the squir-
    rel's barn.
695 Its bottom will I strew with amber shells,
  And pebbles blue from deep enchanted
    wells.
  Its sides I'll plant with dew-sweet eglan-
    tine,
  And honeysuckles full of clear bee-wine.
  I will entice this crystal rill to trace
700 Love's silver name upon the meadow's
    face.
  I'll kneel to Vesta, for a flame of fire;
  And to god Phœbus, for a golden lyre;
  To Empress Dian, for a hunting spear;
  To Vesper, for a taper silver-clear,
705 That I may see thy beauty through the
    night;
  To Flora, and a nightingale shall light
  Tame on thy finger; to the River-Gods,
  And they shall bring thee taper fishing-
    rods
  Of gold, and lines of Naiads' long bright
    tress.
710 Heaven shield thee for thine utter love-
    liness!
  Thy mossy footstool shall the altar be
  'Fore which I'll bend, bending, dear love,
    to thee:
  Those lips shall be my Delphos, and shall
    speak
  Laws to my footsteps, color to my cheek,
715 Trembling or steadfastness to this same
    voice,
  And of three sweetest pleasurings the
    choice:
  And that affectionate light, those diamond
    things,
  Those eyes, those passions, those supreme
    pearl springs,
  Shall be my grief, or twinkle me to
    pleasure.
720 Say, is not bliss within our perfect seizure?
  O that I could not doubt!''

                  The mountaineer
  Thus strove by fancies vain and crude to
    clear
  His briar'd path to some tranquillity.
  It gave bright gladness to his lady's eye,

725 And yet the tears she wept were tears of
    sorrow;
Answering thus, just as the golden mor-
    row
Beam'd upward from the valleys of the
    east:
"O that the flutter of this heart had ceas'd,
Or the sweet name of love had pass'd away.
730 Young feather'd tyrant! by a swift decay
Wilt thou devote this body to the earth:
And I do think that at my very birth
I lisp'd thy blooming titles inwardly;
For at the first, first dawn and thought of
    thee,
735 With uplift hands I blest the stars of
    heaven.
Art thou not cruel? Ever have I striven
To think thee kind, but ah, it will not
    do!
When yet a child, I heard that kisses drew
Favor from thee, and so I kisses gave
740 To the void air, bidding them find out love:
But when I came to feel how far above
All fancy, pride, and fickle maidenhood,
All earthly pleasure, all imagin'd good,
Was the warm tremble of a devout kiss,—
745 Even then, that moment, at the thought of
    this,
Fainting I fell into a bed of flowers,
And languish'd there three days. Ye
    milder powers,
Am I not cruelly wrong'd? Believe, be-
    lieve
Me, dear Endymion, were I to weave
750 With my own fancies garlands of sweet
    life,
Thou shouldst be one of all. Ah, bitter
    strife!
I may not be thy love: I am forbidden—
Indeed I am—thwarted, affrighted, chid-
    den,
By things I trembled at, and gorgon wrath.
755 Twice hast thou ask'd whither I went:
    henceforth
Ask me no more! I may not utter it,
Nor may I be thy love. We might commit
Ourselves at once to vengeance; we might
    die;
We might embrace and die: voluptuous
    thought!
760 Enlarge not to my hunger, or I'm caught
In trammels of perverse deliciousness.
No, no, that shall not be: thee will I bless,
And bid a long adieu.''

The Carian

No word return'd: both lovelorn, silent,
    wan,
765 Into the valleys green together went.

Far wandering, they were perforce content
To sit beneath a fair lone beechen tree;
Nor at each other gaz'd, but heavily
Por'd on its hazel cirque of shedded leaves.

770 Endymion! unhappy! it nigh grieves
Me to behold thee thus in last extreme:
Enskied ere this, but truly that I deem
Truth the best music in a first-born song.
Thy lute-voic'd brother[1] will I sing ere
    long,
775 And thou shalt aid—hast thou not aided
    me?
Yes, moonlight Emperor! felicity
Has been thy meed for many thousand
    years;
Yet often have I, on the brink of tears,
Mourn'd as if yet thou wert a forester;—
Forgetting the old tale.

780   He did not stir
His eyes from the dead leaves, or one small
    pulse
Of joy he might have felt. The spirit
    culls
Unfaded amaranth,[2] when wild it strays
Through the old garden-ground of boyish
    days.
785 A little onward ran the very stream
By which he took his first soft poppy
    dream;
And on the very bark 'gainst which he
    leant
A crescent he had carv'd, and round it
    spent
His skill in little stars. The teeming tree
790 Had swollen and green'd the pious char-
    actery,
But not ta'en out. Why, there was not a
    slope
Up which he had not fear'd the antelope;
And not a tree, beneath whose rooty shade
He had not with his tamed leopards
    play'd:
795 Nor could an arrow light, or javelin,
Fly in the air where his had never been—
And yet he knew it not.

        O treachery!
Why does his lady smile, pleasing her eye
With all his sorrowing? He sees her not.
800 But who so stares on him? His sister sure!
Peona of the woods!—Can she endure—
Impossible—how dearly they embrace!
His lady smiles; delight is in her face;
It is no treachery.

[1] A reference to Hyperion, whom Keats already
    had in mind as the subject of a poem. Hype-
    rion was not a brother of Endymion.
[2] An imaginary flower supposed never to fade.

"Dear brother mine!
805 Endymion, weep not so! Why shouldst
thou pine
When all great Latmos so exalt will be?
Thank the great gods, and look not bit-
terly;
And speak not one pale word, and sigh no
more.
Sure I will not believe thou hast such store
810 Of grief, to last thee to my kiss again.
Thou surely canst not bear a mind in pain,
Come hand in hand with one so beautiful.
Be happy both of you! for I will pull
The flowers of autumn for your coronals.
815 Pan's holy priest for young Endymion
calls;
And when he is restor'd, thou, fairest
dame,
Shalt be our queen. Now, is it not a shame
To see ye thus,—not very, very sad?
Perhaps ye are too happy to be glad:
820 O feel as if it were a common day;
Free-voic'd as one who never was away.
No tongue shall ask, Whence come ye?
but ye shall
Be gods of your own rest imperial.
Not even I, for one whole month, will pry
825 Into the hours that have pass'd us by,
Since in my arbor I did sing to thee.
O Hermes! on this very night will be
A hymning up to Cynthia, queen of light;
For the soothsayers old saw yesternight
830 Good visions in the air,—whence will befall,
As say these sages, health perpetual
To shepherds and their flocks; and fur-
thermore,
In Dian's face they read the gentle lore:
Therefore for her these vesper-carols are.
835 Our friends will all be there from nigh
and far.
Many upon thy death have ditties made;
And many, even now, their foreheads
shade
With cypress,[1] on a day of sacrifice.
New singing for our maids shalt thou de-
vise,
840 And pluck the sorrow from our hunts-
men's brows.
Tell me, my lady-queen, how to espouse
This wayward brother to his rightful joys!
His eyes are on thee bent, as thou didst
poise
His fate most goddess-like. Help me, I
pray,
845 To lure—Endymion, dear brother, say
What ails thee?" He could bear no more,
and so
Bent his soul fiercely like a spiritual bow,

[1] The cypress is an emblem of mourning.

And twang'd it inwardly, and calmly said:
"I would have thee my only friend, sweet
maid!
850 My only visitor! not ignorant though,
That those deceptions which for pleasure
go
'Mong men, are pleasures real as real may
be:
But there are higher ones I may not see,
If impiously an earthly realm I take.
855 Since I saw thee, I have been wide awake
Night after night, and day by day, until
Of the empyrean I have drunk my fill.
Let it content thee, sister, seeing me
More happy than betides mortality.
860 A hermit young, I'll live in mossy cave,
Where thou alone shalt come to me, and
lave
Thy spirit in the wonders I shall tell.
Through me the shepherd realm shall pros-
per well;
For to thy tongue will I all health confide.
865 And, for my sake, let this young maid
abide
With thee as a dear sister. Thou alone,
Peona, mayst return to me. I own
This may sound strangely: but when,
dearest girl,
Thou seest it for my happiness, no pearl
870 Will trespass down those cheeks. Com-
panion fair!
Wilt be content to dwell with her, to share
This sister's love with me?" Like one
resign'd
And bent by circumstance, and thereby
blind
In self-commitment, thus that meek un-
known:
875 "Aye, but a buzzing by my ears has flown,
Of jubilee to Dian:—truth I heard?
Well then, I see there is no little bird,
Tender soever, but is Jove's own care.[1]
Long have I sought for rest, and, unaware,
880 Behold I find it! so exalted too!
So after my own heart! I knew, I knew
There was a place untenanted in it:
In that same void white Chastity shall sit,
And monitor me nightly to lone slumber.
885 With sanest lips I vow me to the number
Of Dian's sisterhood; and, kind lady,
With thy good help, this very night shall
see
My future days to her fane consecrate."

As feels a dreamer what doth most create
890 His own particular fright, so these three
felt:
Or like one who, in after ages, knelt

[1] See *Matthew.* 10:29.

To Lucifer or Baal, when he'd pine
After a little sleep: or when in mine
Far under-ground, a sleeper meets his
  friends
895 Who know him not. Each diligently
  bends
Towards common thoughts and things for
  very fear;
Striving their ghastly malady to cheer,
By thinking it a thing of yes and no,
That housewives talk of. But the spirit-
  blow
900 Was struck, and all were dreamers. At the
  last
Endymion said: "Are not our fates all
  cast?
Why stand we here? Adieu, ye tender
  pair!
Adieu!" Whereat those maidens, with
  wild stare,
Walk'd dizzily away. Pained and hot
905 His eyes went after them, until they got
Near to a cypress grove, whose deadly
  maw,
In one swift moment, would what then he
  saw
Engulf forever. "Stay!" he cried, "ah
  stay!
Turn, damsels! hist! one word I have to
  say.
910 Sweet Indian, I would see thee once again.
It is a thing I dote on: so I'd fain,
Peona, ye should hand in hand repair
Into those holy groves, that silent are
Behind great Dian's temple. I'll be yon,
915 At Vesper's earliest twinkle—they are
  gone—
But once, once, once again—" At this he
  press'd
His hands against his face, and then did
  rest
His head upon a mossy hillock green,
And so remain'd as he a corpse had been
920 All the long day; save when he scantly
  lifted
His eyes abroad, to see how shadows
  shifted
With the slow move of time,—sluggish and
  weary
Until the poplar tops, in journey dreary,
Had reach'd the river's brim. Then up he
  rose,
925 And, slowly as that very river flows,
Walk'd towards the temple grove with this
  lament:
"Why such a golden eve? The breeze is
  sent
Careful and soft, that not a leaf may fall
Before the serene father of them all

930 Bows down his summer head below the
  west.
Now am I of breath, speech, and speed
  possest,
But at the setting I must bid adieu
To her for the last time. Night will
  strew
On the damp grass myriads of lingering
  leaves,
935 And with them shall I die; nor much it
  grieves
To die, when summer dies on the cold
  sward.
Why, I have been a butterfly, a lord
Of flowers, garlands, love-knots, silly
  posies,
Groves, meadows, melodies, and arbor
  roses;
940 My kingdom's at its death, and just it is
That I should die with it: so in all this
We miscall grief, bale, sorrow, heartbreak,
  woe,
What is there to plain of? By Titan's
  foe[1]
I am but rightly serv'd." So saying, he
945 Tripp'd lightly on, in sort of deathful
  glee;
Laughing at the clear stream and setting
  sun,
As though they jests had been: nor had
  he done
His laugh at nature's holy countenance,
Until that grove appear'd, as if perchance,
950 And then his tongue with sober seem-
  lihed[2]
Gave utterance as he enter'd: "Ha! I said,
King of the butterflies; but by this gloom,
And by old Rhadamanthus' tongue of
  doom,
This dusk religion, pomp of solitude,
955 And the Promethean clay by thief en-
  dued,[3]
By old Saturnus' forelock, by his head
Shook with eternal palsy, I did wed
Myself to things of light from infancy;
And thus to be cast out, thus lorn to die,
960 Is sure enough to make a mortal man
Grow impious." So he inwardly began
On things for which no wording can be
  found;
Deeper and deeper sinking, until drown'd
Beyond the reach of music: for the choir
965 Of Cynthia he heard not, though rough
  briar
Nor muffling thicket interpos'd to dull

[1] Jupiter
[2] seemliness
[3] Prometheus stole fire from heaven and gave it
  to man, whom he made of clay and endowed
  with life.

The vesper hymn, far swollen, soft and
full,
Through the dark pillars of those sylvan
aisles.
He saw not the two maidens, nor their
smiles,
970 Wan as primroses gather'd at midnight
By chilly-finger'd spring. "Unhappy
wight!
Endymion!" said Peona, "we are here!
What wouldst thou ere we all are laid on
bier?"
Then he embrac'd her, and his lady's hand
975 Press'd, saying: "Sister, I would have
command,
If it were heaven's will, on our sad fate."
At which that dark-eyed stranger stood
elate
And said, in a new voice, but sweet as
love,
To Endymion's amaze: "By Cupid's
dove,
980 And so thou shalt! and by the lily truth
Of my own breast thou shalt, beloved
youth!"
And as she spake, into her face there came
Light, as reflected from a silver flame:
Her long black hair swell'd ampler, in
display
985 Full golden; in her eyes a brighter day
Dawn'd blue and full of love. Aye, he
beheld
Phœbe, his passion! joyous she upheld
Her lucid bow, continuing thus: "Drear,
drear
Has our delaying been; but foolish fear
990 Withheld me first; and then decrees of
fate;
And then 'twas fit that from this mortal
state
Thou shouldst, my love, by some unlook'd-
for change
Be spiritualiz'd. Peona, we shall range
These forests, and to thee they safe shall
be
995 As was thy cradle; hither shalt thou flee
To meet us many a time." Next Cynthia
bright
Peona kiss'd, and bless'd with fair good
night:
Her brother kiss'd her too, and knelt
adown
Before his goddess, in a blissful swoon.
1000 She gave her fair hands to him, and behold,
Before three swiftest kisses he had told,
They vanish'd far away!—Peona went
Home through the gloomy wood in wonderment.

ISABELLA; OR THE POT OF BASIL[1]

A STORY FROM BOCCACCIO[2]
1818   1820

1 Fair Isabel, poor simple Isabel!
Lorenzo, a young palmer in Love's eye![3]
They could not in the self-same mansion
dwell
Without some stir of heart, some mal-
ady;
They could not sit at meals but feel how
well
It soothed each to be the other by;
They could not, sure, beneath the same roof
sleep
But to each other dream, and nightly weep.

2 With every morn their love grew tenderer,
With every eve deeper and tenderer still;
He might not in house, field, or garden stir,
But her full shape would all his seeing
fill;
And his continual voice was pleasanter
To her, than noise of trees or hidden
rill;
Her lute-string gave an echo of his name,
She spoilt her half-done broidery with the
same.

3 He knew whose gentle hand was at the
latch
Before the door had given her to his
eyes;
And from her chamber-window he would
catch
Her beauty farther than the falcon
spies;
And constant as her vespers would he
watch,
Because her face was turn'd to the same
skies;
And with sick longing all the night out-
wear,
To hear her morning-step upon the stair.

4 A whole long month of May in this sad
plight
Made their cheeks paler by the break of
June:
"Tomorrow will I bow to my delight,
Tomorrow will I ask my lady's boon."—
"O may I never see another night,
Lorenzo, if thy lips breathe not love's
tune."—
So spake they to their pillows; but, alas,
Honeyless days and days did he let pass;

[1] An aromatic shrubby plant.
[2] From *The Decameron*, 4, 5.
[3] That is, a votary of Love.

5 Until sweet Isabella's untouch'd cheek
    Fell sick within the rose's just domain,
Fell thin as a young mother's, who doth
    seek
    By every lull to cool her infant's pain:
"How ill she is," said he, "I may not
    speak;
    And yet I will, and tell my love all
    plain:
If looks speak love-laws, I will drink her
    tears,
And at the least 'twill startle off her
    cares.''

6 So said he one fair morning, and all day
    His heart beat awfully against his side;
And to his heart he inwardly did pray
    For power to speak; but still the ruddy
    tide
Stifled his voice, and puls'd resolve away—
    Fever'd his high conceit of such a bride,
Yet brought him to the meekness of a
    child:
Alas! when passion is both meek and wild!

7 So once more he had wak'd and anguished
    A dreary night of love and misery,
If Isabel's quick eye had not been wed
    To every symbol on his forehead high;
She saw it waxing very pale and dead,
    And straight all flush'd; so, lisped ten-
    derly,
"Lorenzo!"—here she ceas'd her timid
    quest,
But in her tone and look he read the rest.

8 "O Isabella, I can half perceive
    That I may speak my grief into thine
    ear;
If thou didst ever anything believe,
    Believe how I love thee, believe how near
My soul is to its doom: I would not grieve
    Thy hand by unwelcome pressing, would
    not fear
Thine eyes by gazing; but I cannot live
Another night, and not my passion shrive.

9 "Love! thou art leading me from wintry
    cold,
    Lady! thou leadest me to summer clime,
And I must taste the blossoms that unfold
    In its ripe warmth this gracious morn-
    ing time.''
So said, his erewhile timid lips grew bold,
    And poesied with hers in dewy rhyme:
Great bliss was with them, and great hap-
    piness
Grew, like a lusty flower in June's caress.

10 Parting, they seem'd to tread upon the
    air,
    Twin roses by the zephyr blown apart
Only to meet again more close, and share
    The inward fragrance of each other's
    heart.
She, to her chamber gone, a ditty fair
    Sang, of delicious love and honey'd dart;
He with light steps went up a western hill,
And bade the sun farewell, and joy'd his
    fill.

11 All close they met again, before the dusk
    Had taken from the stars its pleasant
    veil,
All close they met, all eves, before the dusk
    Had taken from the stars its pleasant
    veil,
Close in a bower of hyacinth and musk,
    Unknown of any, free from whispering
    tale.
Ah! better had it been forever so,
Than idle ears should pleasure in their woe.

12 Were they unhappy then?—It cannot be—
    Too many tears for lovers have been
    shed,
Too many sighs give we to them in fee,[1]
    Too much of pity after they are dead,
Too many doleful stories do we see,
    Whose matter in bright gold were best
    be read;
Except in such a page where Theseus'
    spouse[2]
Over the pathless waves towards him bows.

13 But, for the general award of love,
    The little sweet doth kill much bitter-
    ness;
Though Dido silent is in under-grove,
    And Isabella's was a great distress,
Though young Lorenzo in warm Indian
    clove
Was not embalm'd, this truth is not the
    less—
Even bees, the little almsmen of spring-
    bowers,
Know there is richest juice in poison-
    flowers.

14 With her two brothers this fair lady dwelt,
    Enriched from ancestral merchandize,
And for them many a weary hand did
    swelt
    In torched mines and noisy factories,

[1] pay; wages
[2] Ariadne. She aided Theseus in finding his way out of the labyrinth and fled with him to the island of Naxos, where she was abandoned. (*Odyssey*, 11, 321 ff.)

And many once proud-quiver'd loins did
melt
In blood from stinging whip;—with hol-
low eyes
Many all day in dazzling river stood,
To take the rich-ored driftings of the flood.

15 For them the Ceylon diver held his breath,
And went all naked to the hungry shark;
For them his ears gush'd blood; for them
in death
The seal on the cold ice with piteous bark
Lay full of darts; for them alone did
seethe
A thousand men in troubles wide and
dark:
Half-ignorant, they turn'd an easy wheel,
That set sharp racks at work, to pinch and
peel.

16 Why were they proud? Because their
marble founts
Gush'd with more pride than do a
wretch's tears?—
Why were they proud? Because fair
orange-mounts
Were of more soft ascent than lazar
stairs?[1]—
Why were they proud? Because red-
lin'd accounts
Were richer than the songs of Grecian
years?—
Why were they proud? again we ask aloud,
Why in the name of Glory were they
proud?

17 Yet were these Florentines as self-retired
In hungry pride and gainful cowardice,
As two close Hebrews in that land inspired,
Paled in[2] and vineyarded from beggar-
spies;
The hawks of ship-mast forests[3]—the un-
tired
And pannier'd mules for ducats and old
lies—
Quick cat's-paws on the generous stray-
away,—
Great wits in Spanish, Tuscan, and Malay.

18 How was it these same ledger-men could
spy
Fair Isabella in her downy nest?
How could they find out in Lorenzo's eye
A straying from his toil? Hot Egypt's
pest[4]

Into their vision covetous and sly!
How could these money-bags see east
and west?—
Yet so they did—and every dealer fair
Must see behind, as doth the hunted hare.

19 O eloquent and famed Boccaccio!
Of thee we now should ask forgiving
boon,
And of thy spicy myrtles as they blow,
And of thy roses amorous of the moon,
And of thy lilies, that do paler grow
Now they can no more hear thy ghit-
tern's[1] tune,
For venturing syllables that ill beseem
The quiet glooms of such a piteous theme.

20 Grant thou a pardon here, and then the
tale
Shall move on soberly, as it is meet;
There is no other crime, no mad assail
To make old prose in modern rhyme
more sweet:
But it is done—succeed the verse or fail—
To honor thee, and thy gone spirit greet;
To stead thee as a verse in English tongue,
An echo of thee in the north-wind sung.

21 These brethren having found by many
signs
What love Lorenzo for their sister had,
And how she lov'd him too, each uncon-
fines
His better thoughts to other, well nigh
mad
That he, the servant of their trade designs,
Should in their sister's love be blithe
and glad,
When 'twas their plan to coax her by
degrees
To some high noble and his olive-trees.

22 And many a jealous conference had they,
And many times they bit their lips alone,
Before they fix'd upon a surest way
To make the youngster for his crime
atone;
And at the last, these men of cruel clay
Cut Mercy with a sharp knife to the
bone;
For they resolved in some forest dim
To kill Lorenzo, and there bury him.

23 So on a pleasant morning, as he leant
Into the sunrise, o'er the balustrade
Of the garden-terrace, towards him they
bent

---

[1] hospital stairs　　　　　[2] enclosed
[3] They take advantage of trading vessels in
port.
[4] Swarms of flies. See *Exodus*, 8 :21.

[1] A stringed instrument similar to a guitar.

Their footing through the dews; and to
    him said,
"You seem there in the quiet of content,
    Lorenzo, and we are most loth to invade
Calm speculation; but if you are wise,
    Bestride your steed while cold is in the
    skies.

24 "Today we purpose, aye, this hour we
    mount
To spur three leagues towards the Apen-
    nine;
Come down, we pray thee, ere the hot sun
    count
    His dewy rosary on the eglantine."
Lorenzo, courteously as he was wont,
    Bow'd a fair greeting to these serpents'
    whine;
And went in haste, to get in readiness,
    With belt, and spur, and bracing hunts-
    man's dress.

25 And as he to the court-yard pass'd along,
    Each third step did he pause, and lis-
    ten'd oft
If he could hear his lady's matin-song,
    Or the light whisper of her footstep
    soft;
And as he thus over his passion hung,
    He heard a laugh full musical aloft;
When, looking up, he saw her features
    bright
Smile through an in-door lattice, all de-
    light.

26 "Love, Isabel!" said he, "I was in pain
    Lest I should miss to bid thee a good
    morrow:
Ah! what if I should lose thee, when so
    fain
I am to stifle all the heavy sorrow
Of a poor three hours' absence? but we'll
    gain
    Out of the amorous dark what day doth
    borrow.
Good bye! I'll soon be back."—"Good
    bye!" said she:—
And as he went she chanted merrily.

27 So the two brothers and their murder'd
    man
    Rode past fair Florence, to where Arno's
    stream
Gurgles through straiten'd banks, and still
    doth fan
    Itself with dancing bulrush, and the
    bream
Keeps head against the freshets. Sick and
    wan

The brothers' faces in the ford did seem,
Lorenzo's flush with love.—They pass'd
    the water
Into a forest quiet for the slaughter.

28 There was Lorenzo slain and buried in,
    There in that forest did his great love
    cease;
Ah! when a soul doth thus its freedom win,
    It aches in loneliness—is ill at peace
As the break-covert bloodhounds of such
    sin:
    They dipp'd their swords in the water,
    and did tease
Their horses homeward, with convulsed
    spur,
Each richer by his being a murderer.

29 They told their sister how, with sudden
    speed,
    Lorenzo had ta'en ship for foreign
    lands,
Because of some great urgency and need
    In their affairs, requiring trusty hands.
Poor girl! put on thy stifling widow's
    weed,[1]
    And 'scape at once from Hope's ac-
    cursed bands;
Today thou wilt not see him, nor to-
    morrow,
And the next day will be a day of sorrow.

30 She weeps alone for pleasures not to be;
    Sorely she wept until the night came on,
And then, instead of love, O misery!
    She brooded o'er the luxury alone:
His image in the dusk she seem'd to see,
    And to the silence made a gentle moan,
Spreading her perfect arms upon the air,
And on her couch low murmuring "Where?
    O where?"

31 But Selfishness, Love's cousin, held not
    long
    Its fiery vigil in her single breast;
She fretted for the golden hour, and hung
    Upon the time with feverish unrest—
Not long—for soon into her heart a throng
    Of higher occupants, a richer zest,
Came tragic; passion not to be subdued,
And sorrow for her love in travels rude.

32 In the mid days of autumn, on their eves
    The breath of winter comes from far
    away,
And the sick west continually bereaves
    Of some gold tinge, and plays a rounde-
    lay

[1] garment: attire

Of death among the bushes and the leaves,
To make all bare before he dares to stray
From his north cavern. So sweet Isabel
By gradual decay from beauty fell,

33 Because Lorenzo came not. Oftentimes
She ask'd her brothers, with an eye all
pale,
Striving to be itself, what dungeon climes
Could keep him off so long? They spake
a tale
Time after time, to quiet her. Their crimes
Came on them, like a smoke from Hin-
nom's vale;
And every night in dreams they groan'd
aloud,
To see their sister in her snowy shroud.

34 And she had died in drowsy ignorance,
But for a thing more deadly dark than
all;
It came like a fierce potion, drunk by
chance,
Which saves a sick man from the feath-
er'd pall
For some few gasping moments; like a
lance,
Waking an Indian from his cloudy hall
With cruel pierce, and bringing him again
Sense of the gnawing fire at heart and
brain.

35 It was a vision.—In the drowsy gloom,
The dull of midnight, at her couch's foot
Lorenzo stood, and wept: the forest tomb
Had marr'd his glossy hair which once
could shoot
Lustre into the sun, and put cold doom
Upon his lips, and taken the soft lute
From his lorn voice, and past his loamed
ears
Had made a miry channel for his tears.

36 Strange sound it was, when the pale
shadow spake;
For there was striving, in its piteous
tongue,
To speak as when on earth it was awake,
And Isabella on its music hung:
Languor there was in it, and tremulous
shake,
As in a palsied Druid's harp unstrung;
And through it moan'd a ghostly under-
song,
Like hoarse night-gusts sepulchral briars
among.

37 Its eyes, though wild, were still all dewy
bright

With love, and kept all phantom fear
aloof
From the poor girl by magic of their light,
The while it did unthread the horrid
woof
Of the late darken'd time,—the murder-
ous spite
Of pride and avarice,—the dark pine
roof
In the forest,—and the sodden turfed dell,
Where, without any word, from stabs he
fell.

38 Saying moreover, "Isabel, my sweet!
Red whortleberries droop above my
head,
And a large flint-stone weighs upon my
feet;
Around me beeches and high chestnuts
shed
Their leaves and prickly nuts; a sheep-
fold bleat
Comes from beyond the river to my bed:
Go, shed one tear upon my heather-bloom,
And it shall comfort me within the tomb.

39 "I am a shadow now, alas! alas!
Upon the skirts of human nature dwell-
ing
Alone: I chant alone the holy mass,
While little sounds of life are round me
knelling,
And glossy bees at noon do fieldward pass,
And many a chapel bell the hour is
telling,
Paining me through: these sounds grow
strange to me,
And thou art distant in Humanity.

40 "I know what was, I feel full well what is,
And I should rage, if spirits could go
mad;
Though I forget the taste of earthly bliss,
That paleness warms my grave, as
though I had
A seraph chosen from the bright abyss
To be my spouse: thy paleness makes
me glad;
Thy beauty grows upon me, and I feel
A greater love through all my essence
steal."

41 The Spirit mourn'd "Adieu!"—dissolv'd
and left
The atom darkness in a slow turmoil;
As when of healthful midnight sleep bereft,
Thinking on rugged hours and fruitless
toil,

We put our eyes into a pillowy cleft,
  And see the spangly[1] gloom froth up
  and boil:
It made sad Isabella's eyelids ache,
And in the dawn she started up awake;

42 "Ha! ha!" said she, "I knew not this
  hard life,
  I thought the worst was simple misery;
I thought some Fate with pleasure or with
  strife
  Portion'd us—happy days, or else to
  die;
But there is crime—a brother's bloody
  knife!
Sweet Spirit, thou hast school'd my in-
  fancy:
I'll visit thee for this, and kiss thine eyes,
And greet thee morn and even in the
  skies."

43 When the full morning came, she had de-
  vis'd
  How she might secret to the forest hie;
How she might find the clay, so dearly
  priz'd,
  And sing to it one latest lullaby;
How her short absence might be unsur-
  mis'd,
  While she the inmost of the dream would
  try.
Resolv'd, she took with her an aged nurse,
And went into that dismal forest-hearse.

44 See, as they creep along the river side,
  How she doth whisper to that aged dame,
And, after looking round the champaign[2]
  wide,
  Shows her a knife.—"What feverous
  hectic flame
Burns in thee, child?—What good can
  thee betide,
  That thou should'st smile again?"—
  The evening came,
And they had found Lorenzo's earthy bed;
The flint was there, the berries at his head.

45 Who hath not loiter'd in a green churchyard,
  And let his spirit, like a demon-mole,
Work through the clayey soil and gravel
  hard,
  To see skull, coffin'd bones, and funeral
  stole;
Pitying each form that hungry Death hath
  marr'd,
  And filling it once more with human
  soul?

[1] shining   [2] level field

Ah! this is holiday to what was felt
When Isabella by Lorenzo knelt.

46 She gaz'd into the fresh-thrown mould, as
  though
  One glance did fully all its secrets tell;
Clearly she saw, as other eyes would know
  Pale limbs at bottom of a crystal well;
Upon the murderous spot she seem'd to
  grow,
  Like to a native lily of the dell:
Then with her knife, all sudden, she began
To dig more fervently than misers can.

47 Soon she turn'd up a soiled glove, whereon
  Her silk had play'd in purple phan-
  tasies,
She kiss'd it with a lip more chill than
  stone,
  And put it in her bosom, where it dries
And freezes utterly unto the bone
  Those dainties made to still an infant's
  cries:
Then 'gan she work again; nor stay'd her
  care,
But to throw back at times her veiling hair.

48 That old nurse stood beside her wondering,
  Until her heart felt pity to the core
At sight of such a dismal laboring,
  And so she kneeled, with her locks all
  hoar,
And put her lean hands to the horrid thing:
  Three hours they labor'd at this travail
  sore;
At last they felt the kernel of the grave,
And Isabella did not stamp and rave.

49 Ah! wherefore all this wormy circum-
  stance?
  Why linger at the yawning tomb so long?
O for the gentleness of old Romance,
  The simple plaining[1] of a minstrel's
  song!
Fair reader, at the old tale take a glance,
  For here, in truth, it doth not well belong
To speak:—O turn thee to the very tale,
And taste the music of that vision pale.

50 With duller steel than the Perséan sword[2]
  They cut away no formless monster's
  head,
But one, whose gentleness did well accord
  With death, as life. The ancient harps
  have said,
Love never dies, but lives, immortal Lord:
  If Love impersonate was ever dead,

[1] melody
[2] The sword with which Perseus slew Medusa.

Pale Isabella kiss'd it, and low moan'd.
'Twas love; cold,—dead indeed, but not
  dethron'd.

51 In anxious secrecy they took it home,
      And then the prize was all for Isabel:
    She calm'd its wild hair with a golden
      comb,
      And all around each eye's sepulchral cell
    Pointed each fringed lash; the smeared
      loam
    With tears, as chilly as a dripping well,
    She drench'd away:—and still she comb'd,
      and kept
    Sighing all day—and still she kiss'd, and
      wept.

52 Then in a silken scarf,—sweet with the
      dews
      Of precious flowers pluck'd in Araby,
    And divine liquids come with odorous ooze
    Through the cold serpent-pipe[1] refresh-
      fully,—
    She wrapp'd it up; and for its tomb did
      choose
    A garden-pot, wherein she laid it·by,
    And cover'd it with mould, and o'er it set
    Sweet Basil, which her tears kept ever wet.

53 And she forgot the stars, the moon, and
      sun,
      And she forgot the blue above the trees,
    And she forgot the dells where waters run,
      And she forgot the chilly autumn breeze;
    She had no knowledge when the day was
      done,
      And the new morn she saw not: but in
        peace
    Hung over her sweet Basil evermore,
    And moisten'd it with tears unto the core.

54 And so she ever fed it with thin tears,
      Whence thick, and green, and beautiful
        it grew,
    So that it smelt more balmy than its peers
      Of Basil-tufts in Florence; for it drew
    Nurture besides, and life, from human
      fears,
      From the fast mouldering head there
        shut from view:
    So that the jewel, safely casketed,
    Came forth, and in perfumed leafits spread.

65 O Melancholy, linger here awhile!
      O Music, Music, breathe despondingly!
    O Echo, Echo, from some sombre isle,
      Unknown, Lethean, sigh to us—O sigh!

[1] A pipe used in distilling liquids.

Spirits in grief, lift up your heads, and
  smile;
    Lift up your heads, sweet Spirits,
      heavily,
  And make a pale light in your cypress[1]
    glooms,
  Tinting with silver wan your marble tombs.

56 Moan hither, all ye syllables of woe,
      From the deep throat of sad Melpomene!
    Through bronzed lyre in tragic order go,
      And touch the strings into a mystery;
    Sound mournfully upon the winds and
      low;
      For simple Isabel is soon to be
    Among the dead: she withers, like a palm
    Cut by an Indian for its juicy balm.

57 O leave the palm to wither by itself;
      Let not quick winter chill its dying
        hour!—
    It may not be—those Baälites of pelf,[2]
      Her brethren, noted the continual shower
    From her dead eyes; and many a curious
      elf,
      Among her kindred, wonder'd that such
        dower
    Of youth and beauty should be thrown
      aside
    By one mark'd out to be a noble's bride.

58 And, furthermore, her brethren wonder'd
      much
      Why she sat drooping by the Basil green,
    And why it flourish'd, as by magic touch;
      Greatly they wonder'd what the thing
        might mean:
    They could not surely give belief, that such
      A very nothing would have power to
        wean
    Her from her own fair youth, and pleas-
      ures gay,
    And even remembrance of her love's delay.

59 Therefore they watch'd a time when they
      might sift
      This hidden whim; and long they
        watch'd in vain;
    For seldom did she go to chapel-shrift,
      And seldom felt she any hunger-pain;
    And when she left, she hurried back, as
      swift
      As bird on wing to breast its eggs again;
    And, patient as a hen-bird, sat her there
    Beside her Basil, weeping through her hair.

[1] The cypress is an emblem of mourning. It is
a common tree in graveyards.
[2] Worshipers of pelf, as pagans worshiped Baal.

60 Yet they contriv'd to steal the Basil-pot,
    And to examine it in secret place;
The thing was vile with green and livid
    spot,
    And yet they knew it was Lorenzo's
    face:
The guerdon of their murder they had got,
    And so left Florence in a moment's
    space,
Never to turn again.—Away they went,
With blood upon their heads, to banish-
    ment.

61 O Melancholy, turn thine eyes away!
    O Music, Music, breathe despondingly!
O Echo, Echo, on some other day,
    From isles Lethean, sigh to us—O sigh!
Spirits of grief, sing not your "Well-a-
    way!"
    For Isabel, sweet Isabel, will die;
Will die a death too lone and incomplete,
Now they have ta'en away her Basil sweet.

62 Piteous she look'd on dead and senseless
    things,
    Asking for her lost Basil amorously;
And with melodious chuckle in the strings
    Of her lorn voice, she oftentimes would
    cry
After the pilgrim in his wanderings,
    To ask him where her Basil was; and
    why
'Twas hid from her: "For cruel 'tis,"
    said she,
"To steal my Basil-pot away from me."

63 And so she pined, and so she died forlorn,
    Imploring for her Basil to the last.
No heart was there in Florence but did
    mourn
    In pity of her love, so overcast.
And a sad ditty of this story born
    From mouth to mouth through all the
    country pass'd:
Still is the burthen sung — "O cruelty,
To steal my Basil-pot away from me!"

TO HOMER
1818   1848

Standing aloof in giant ignorance,
Of thee I hear and of the Cyclades,
As one who sits ashore and longs perchance
To visit dolphin-coral in deep seas.
5 So thou wast blind;—but then the veil
    was rent,
For Jove uncurtain'd Heaven to let thee
    live,
And Neptune made for thee a spumy tent,

And Pan made sing for thee his forest-
    hive;
Ay on the shores of darkness there is light,
10 And precipices show untrodden green,
There is a budding morrow in midnight,
There is a triple sight in blindness keen;
Such seeing hadst thou, as it once befel
To Dian, Queen of Earth, and Heaven,
    and Hell.

FRAGMENT OF AN ODE TO MAIA
1818   1848

Mother of Hermes! and still youthful
    Maia!
    May I sing to thee
As thou wast hymned on the shores of
    Baiæ?
    Or may I woo thee
5 In earlier Sicilian?[1] or thy smiles
Seek as they once were sought, in Grecian
    isles,
By bards who died content on pleasant
    sward,
    Leaving great verse unto a little clan?
O, give me their old vigor, and unheard
10   Save of the quiet primrose, and the span
    Of heaven and few ears,
Rounded by thee, my song should die away
    Content as theirs,
Rich in the simple worship of a day.

TO AILSA ROCK
1818   1819

Hearken, thou craggy ocean pyramid!
Give answer from thy voice, the sea-fowls'
    screams!
When were thy shoulders mantled in huge
    streams?
When, from the sun, was thy broad fore-
    head hid?
5 How long is 't since the mighty power bid
Thee heave to airy sleep from fathom
    dreams?
Sleep in the lap of thunder or sunbeams,
Or when gray clouds are thy cold cover-
    lid.
Thou answer'st not; for thou art dead
    asleep;
10 Thy life is but two dead eternities—
The last in air, the former in the deep;
First with the whales, last with the eagle-
    skies—
Drown'd wast thou till an earthquake made
    thee steep,
Another cannot wake thy giant size.

[1] Baiæ and Sicily were both Greek colonies.

FANCY
1818   1820

Ever let the Fancy roam,
Pleasure never is at home:
At a touch sweet Pleasure melteth,
Like to bubbles when rain pelteth;
5 Then let winged Fancy wander
Through the thought still spread beyond
        her:
Open wide the mind's cage-door,
She'll dart forth, and cloudward soar.
O sweet Fancy! let her loose;
10 Summer's joys are spoilt by use,
And the enjoying of the spring
Fades as does its blossoming;
Autumn's red-lipp'd fruitage too,
Blushing through the mist and dew,
15 Cloys with tasting. What do then?
Sit thee by the ingle,[1] when
The sear faggot blazes bright,
Spirit of a winter's night;
When the soundless earth is muffled,
20 And the caked snow is shuffled
From the ploughboy's heavy shoon;[2]
When the Night doth meet the Noon
In a dark conspiracy
To banish Even from her sky.
25 Sit thee there, and send abroad,
With a mind self-overaw'd,
Fancy, high-commission'd:—send her!
She has vassals to attend her:
She will bring, in spite of frost,
30 Beauties that the earth hath lost;
She will bring thee, all together,
All delights of summer weather;
All the buds and bells of May,
From dewy sward or thorny spray;
35 All the heaped autumn's wealth,
With a still, mysterious stealth:
She will mix these pleasures up
Like three fit wines in a cup,
And thou shalt quaff it:—thou shalt hear
40 Distant harvest-carols clear;
Rustle of the reaped corn;[3]
Sweet birds antheming the morn:
And, in the same moment—hark!
'Tis the early April lark,
45 Or the rooks, with busy caw,
Foraging for sticks and straw.
Thou shalt, at one glance, behold
The daisy and the marigold;
White-plum'd lilies, and the first
50 Hedge-grown primrose that hath burst;
Shaded hyacinth, alway
Sapphire queen of the mid-May;
And every leaf, and every flower
Pearled with the self-same shower.

[1] fireplace   [2] shoes   [3] wheat

55 Thou shalt see the field-mouse peep
Meagre from its celled sleep;
And the snake all winter-thin
Cast on sunny bank its skin;
Freckled nest-eggs thou shalt see
60 Hatching in the hawthorn-tree,
When the hen-bird's wing doth rest
Quiet on her mossy nest;
Then the hurry and alarm
When the bee-hive casts its swarm;
65 Acorns ripe down-pattering,
While the autumn breezes sing.

Oh, sweet Fancy! let her loose;
Every thing is spoilt by use:
Where's the cheek that doth not fade,
70 Too much gaz'd at? Where's the maid
Whose lip mature is ever new?
Where's the eye, however blue,
Doth not weary? Where's the face
One would meet in every place?
75 Where's the voice, however soft,
One would hear so very oft?
At a touch sweet Pleasure melteth
Like to bubbles when rain pelteth.
Let, then, winged Fancy find
80 Thee a mistress to thy mind:
Dulcet-eyed as Ceres' daughter,[1]
Ere the God of Torment taught her
How to frown and how to chide;
With a waist and with a side
85 White as Hebe's, when her zone[2]
Slipt its golden clasp, and down
Fell her kirtle to her feet,
While she held the goblet sweet,
And Jove grew languid.—Break the mesh
90 Of the Fancy's silken leash;
Quickly break her prison-string
And such joys as these she'll bring.—
Let the winged Fancy roam,
Pleasure never is at home.

ODE
1818   1820

Bards of Passion and of Mirth,
Ye have left your souls on earth!
Have ye souls in heaven too,
Double-lived in regions new?
5 Yes, and those of heaven commune
With the spheres of sun and moon;
With the noise of fountains wond'rous,
And the parle[3] of voices thund'rous;
With the whisper of heaven's trees
10 And one another, in soft ease
Seated on Elysian lawns

[1] Proserpine, whom Pluto carried as his bride to
  the lower world.
[2] girdle
[3] parley; discourse

Brows'd by none but Dian's fawns;[1]
Underneath large blue-bells tented,
Where the daisies are rose-scented,
15 And the rose herself has got
Perfume which on earth is not;
Where the nightingale doth sing
Not a senseless, tranced thing,
But divine melodious truth;
20 Philosophic numbers smooth;
Tales and golden histories
Of heaven and its mysteries.

Thus ye live on high, and then
On the earth ye live again;
25 And the souls ye left behind you
Teach us, here, the way to find you,
Where your other souls are joying,
Never slumber'd, never cloying.
Here, your earth-born souls still speak
30 To mortals, of their little week;
Of their sorrows and delights;
Of their passions and their spites;
Of their glory and their shame;
What doth strengthen and what maim.
35 Thus ye teach us, every day,
Wisdom, though fled far away.

Bards of Passion and of Mirth,
Ye have left your souls on earth!
Ye have souls in heaven too,
40 Double-lived in regions new!

ODE ON MELANCHOLY
1819   1820

No, no! go not to Lethe, neither twist
Wolf's-bane,[2] tight-rooted, for its poisonous wine;
Nor suffer thy pale forehead to be kiss'd
By nightshade, ruby grape of Proserpine;
5 Make not your rosary of yew-berries,[3]
Nor let the beetle,[4] nor the death-moth[5]
be
Your mournful Psyche,[6] nor the
downy owl
A partner in your sorrow's mysteries;
For shade to shade will come too
drowsily,
10   And drown the wakeful anguish of
the soul.

[1] The fawn was Diana's favorite animal.
[2] A kind of poisonous plant.
[3] The yew is an emblem of mourning.
[4] The sacred beetle of Egypt was regarded as a symbol of the resurrection of the soul, and was placed in coffins.
[5] A moth with markings which resembled the human skull.
[6] Psyche, the soul, was symbolized by the butterfly.

But when the melancholy fit shall fall
Sudden from heaven like a weeping
cloud,
That fosters the droop-headed flowers all,
And hides the green hill in an April
shroud;
15 Then glut thy sorrow on a morning rose,
Or on the rainbow of the salt sand-
wave,
Or on the wealth of globed peonies;
Or if thy mistress some rich anger shows,
Emprison her soft hand, and let her
rave,
20   And feed deep, deep upon her peerless eyes.

She dwells with Beauty — Beauty that
must die;
And Joy, whose hand is ever at his lips
Bidding adieu; and aching Pleasure nigh,
Turning to poison while the bee-mouth
sips:
25 Ay, in the very temple of Delight
Veil'd Melancholy has her sovran
shrine,
Though seen of none save him whose
strenuous tongue
Can burst Joy's grape against his palate fine;
His soul shall taste the sadness of her
might,
30   And be among her cloudy trophies
hung.

ODE ON A GRECIAN URN
1819   1820

Thou still unravish'd bride of quietness,
Thou foster-child of silence and slow
time,
Sylvan historian,[1] who canst thus express
A flowery tale more sweetly than our
rhyme:
5 What leaf-fring'd legend haunts about
thy shape
Of deities or mortals, or of both,
In Tempe or the dales of Arcady?
What men or gods are these? What
maidens loth?
What mad pursuit? What struggle to
escape?
10   What pipes and timbrels? What
wild ecstasy?

Heard melodies are sweet, but those unheard
Are sweeter; therefore, ye soft pipes,
play on;

[1] historian of scenes of the wood

Not to the sensual ear,[1] but, more en-
      dear'd,
   Pipe to the spirit ditties of no tone:
15 Fair youth, beneath the trees, thou canst
      not leave
   Thy song, nor ever can those trees be
      bare;
   Bold lover, never, never canst thou
      kiss,
   Though winning near the goal—yet, do
      not grieve;
   She cannot fade, though thou hast not
      thy bliss,
20 Forever wilt thou love, and she be fair!

   Ah, happy, happy boughs! that cannot
      shed
   Your leaves, nor ever bid the spring
      adieu;
   And, happy melodist, unwearied,
   Forever piping songs forever new;
25 More happy love! more happy, happy
      love!
   Forever warm and still to be enjoy'd,
      Forever panting, and forever young;
   All breathing human passion far above,
      That leaves a heart high-sorrowful and
      cloy'd,
30   A burning forehead, and a parching
      tongue.

   Who are these coming to the sacrifice?
      To what green altar, O mysterious
      priest,
   Lead'st thou that heifer lowing at the
      skies,
   And all her silken flanks with garlands
      drest?
35 What little town by river or sea shore,
      Or mountain-built with peaceful citadel,
      Is emptied of this folk, this pious
      morn?
   And, little town, thy streets forevermore
      Will silent be; and not a soul to tell
40   Why thou art desolate, can e'er re-
      turn.

   O Attic shape! Fair attitude! with brede[2]
   Of marble men and maidens over-
      wrought,
   With forest branches and the trodden
      weed;
   Thou, silent form, dost tease us out of
      thought
45 As doth eternity. Cold pastoral![3]
   When old age shall this generation waste,

---

[1] ear of sense
[2] embroidery
[3] pastoral story in marble.

Thou shalt remain, in midst of other
      woe
   Than ours, a friend to man, to whom
      thou say'st,
   "Beauty is truth, truth beauty,"—that is all
50 Ye know on earth, and all ye need to
      know.[1]"

ODE ON INDOLENCE
1819   1848
They toil not, neither do they spin.[2]

   One morn before me were three figures
      seen,
      With bowed necks, and joined hands,
      side-fac'd;
   And one behind the other stepp'd serene,
      In placid sandals, and in white robes
      grac'd;
5 They pass'd, like figures on a marble urn,
      When shifted round to see the other
      side;
      They came again; as when the urn
      once more
   Is shifted round, the first seen shades re-
      turn;
      And they were strange to me, as may
      betide
10   With vases, to one deep in Phidian
      lore.

   How is it, shadows! that I knew ye not?
   How came ye muffled in so hush a mask?
   Was it a silent deep-disguised plot
      To steal away, and leave without a task
15 My idle days? Ripe was the drowsy hour;
      The blissful cloud of summer-indolence
      Benumb'd my eyes; my pulse grew
      less and less;
   Pain had no sting, and pleasure's wreath
      no flower:
      O, why did ye not melt, and leave my
      sense
20   Unhaunted quite of all but—nothing-
      ness?

   A third time pass'd they by, and, passing,
      turn'd
   Each one the face a moment whiles to
      me;
   Then faded, and to follow them I burn'd
   And ach'd for wings because I knew the
      three;
25 The first was a fair maid, and Love her
      name;
      The second was Ambition, pale of cheek,

---

[1] See Keats's *Hyperion*, 2. 228-9 (p. 882); also
   his letter to Benjamin Bailey (p. 888a, 1).
[2] *Matthew*, 6:28.

And ever watchful with fatigued eye;
The last, whom I love more, the more of
    blame
    Is heap'd upon her, maiden most un-
      meek,—
30   I knew to be my demon[1] Poesy.

They faded, and, forsooth! I wanted
    wings:
O folly! What is Love? and where
    is it?
And for that poor Ambition! it springs
    From a man's little heart's short fever-
      fit;
35 For Poesy!—no,—she has not a joy,—
    At least for me,—so sweet as drowsy
      noons,
    And evenings steep'd in honied indo-
      lence;
O, for an age so shelter'd from annoy,
    That I may never know how change the
      moons,
40   Or hear the voice of busy common-
      sense!

And once more came they by;—alas!
    wherefore?
My sleep had been embroider'd with
    dim dreams;
My soul had been a lawn besprinkled o'er
    With flowers, and stirring shades, and
      baffled beams:
45 The morn was clouded, but no shower fell,
    Tho' in her lids hung the sweet tears of
      May;
    The open casement press'd a new-
      leav'd vine,
Let in the budding warmth and
    throstle's lay;
O shadows! 'twas a time to bid farewell!
50   Upon your skirts had fallen no tears
    of mine.

So, ye three ghosts, adieu! Ye cannot
    raise
My head cool-bedded in the flowery
    grass;
For I would not be dieted with praise,
A pet-lamb in a sentimental farce!
55 Fade softly from my eyes, and be once
    more
    In masque-like figures on the dreamy
      urn;
    Farewell! I yet have visions for the
      night,
And for the day faint visions there is
    store;

[1] guardian spirit

Vanish, ye phantoms! from my idle
    spright,
60 Into the clouds, and nevermore return!
   *   *   *   *   *   *

LA BELLE DAME SANS MERCI[1]
1819   1820

Ah, what can ail thee, wretched wight,[2]
  Alone and palely loitering;
The sedge is wither'd from the lake,
  And no birds sing.

5 Ah, what can ail thee, wretched wight,
  So haggard and so woe-begone?
The squirrel's granary is full,
  And the harvest's done.

I see a lily on thy brow,
10 With anguish moist and fever dew;
And on thy cheek a fading rose
  Fast withereth too.

I met a lady in the meads
  Full beautiful—a faery's child;
15 Her hair was long, her foot was light,
  And her eyes were wild.

I set her on my pacing steed,
  And nothing else saw all day long;
For sideways would she lean, and sing
20 A faery's song.

I made a garland for her head,
  And bracelets too, and fragrant zone;[3]
She look'd at me as she did love,
  And made sweet moan.

25 She found me roots of relish sweet,
  And honey wild, and manna dew;
And sure in language strange she said,
  "I love thee true."

She took me to her elfin grot,
30 And there she gaz'd and sighed deep,
And there I shut her wild, wild eyes—
  So kiss'd to sleep.

And there we slumber'd on the moss,
  And there I dream'd—ah! woe betide!—
35 The latest dream I ever dream'd
  On the cold hillside.

I saw pale kings, and princes too,
  Pale warriors, death-pale were they all;
Who cry'd—"La Belle Dame sans Merci
40 Hath thee in thrall!"

[1] The Beautiful Lady Without Pity. See Keats's
   The Eve of St. Agnes, 33 (p. 872).
[2] person; creature   [3] girdle; belt

I saw their starv'd lips in the gloam
  With horrid warning gaped wide,
And I awoke, and found me here
  On the cold hillside.

45 And this is why I sojourn here
  Alone and palely loitering,
Though the sedge is wither'd from the lake,
  And no birds sing.

ON FAME
1819   *1848*

You cannot eat your cake and have it too.
                 Proverb.

How fever'd is the man, who cannot look
Upon his mortal days with temperate
    blood,
Who vexes all the leaves of his life's book,
And robs its fair name of its maidenhood;
5 It is as if the rose should pluck herself,
Or the ripe plum finger its misty bloom,
As if a Naiad, like a meddling elf,
Should darken her pure grot with muddy
    gloom:
But the rose leaves herself upon the briar,
10 For winds to kiss and grateful bees to feed,
And the ripe plum still wears its dim attire,
The undisturbed lake has crystal space,
Why then should man, teasing the world
    for grace,
Spoil his salvation for a fierce miscreed?[1]

ANOTHER ON FAME
1819   *1848*

Fame, like a wayward girl, will still be coy
To those who woo her with too slavish
    knees,
But makes surrender to some thoughtless
    boy,
And dotes the more upon a heart at ease;
5 She is a Gipsy,—will not speak to those
Who have not learnt to be content without
    her;
A Jilt, whose ear was never whisper'd
    close,
Who thinks they scandal her who talk
    about her;
A very Gipsy is she, Nilus-born,
10 Sister-in-law to jealous Potiphar;[2]
Ye love-sick bards, repay her scorn for
    scorn,
Ye artists lovelorn, madmen that ye are!
Make your best bow to her and bid adieu,
Then, if she likes it, she will follow you.

TO SLEEP
1819   *1848*

O soft embalmer of the still midnight,
Shutting, with careful fingers and benign,
Our gloom-pleas'd eyes, embower'd from
    the light,
Enshaded in forgetfulness divine:
5 O soothest Sleep! if so it please thee,
    close
In midst of this thine hymn my willing
    eyes,
Or wait the amen, ere thy poppy throws
Around my bed its lulling charities.
Then save me, or the passed day will shine
10 Upon my pillow, breeding many woes,—
Save me from curious conscience, that still
    lords
Its strength for darkness, burrowing like a
    mole;
Turn the key deftly in the oiled wards,
And seal the hushed casket of my soul.

ODE TO PSYCHE
1819   *1820*

O Goddess! hear these tuneless numbers,
    wrung
  By sweet enforcement and remembrance
    dear,
And pardon that thy secrets should be
    sung
  Even into thine own soft-conched[1] ear:
5 Surely I dreamt today, or did I see
  The wingèd Psyche with awaken'd eyes?
I wander'd in a forest thoughtlessly,
  And, on the sudden, fainting with sur-
    prise,
Saw two fair creatures, couched side by
    side
10   In deepest grass, beneath the whis-
    p'ring roof
  Of leaves and trembled blossoms, where
    there ran
    A brooklet, scarce espied:

'Mid hush'd, cool-rooted flowers fragrant-
    eyed,
  Blue, silver-white, and budded Tyrian,[2]
15 They lay calm-breathing on the bedded
    grass;
  Their arms embraced, and their pinions
    too;
  Their lips touch'd not, but had not bade
    adieu,
As if disjoined by soft-handed slumber,
And ready still past kisses to outnumber
20   At tender eye-dawn of aurorean love:

---

[1] false creed
[2] See *Genesis*, 39.

[1] shell-shaped
[2] with buds of Tyrian purple

The winged boy I knew;
But who wast thou, O happy, happy
    dove?
His Psyche true!

O latest-born and loveliest vision far
25 Of all Olympus' faded hierarchy!
Fairer than Phœbe's sapphire-region'd
    star,
  Or Vesper, amorous glowworm of the
    sky;
Fairer than these, though temple thou
    hast none,
  Nor altar heap'd with flowers;
30 Nor virgin-choir to make delicious moan
    Upon the midnight hours;
No voice, no lute, no pipe, no incense
    sweet
  From chain-swung censer teeming;
No shrine, no grove, no oracle, no heat
35 Of pale-mouth'd prophet dreaming.

O brightest! though too late for antique
    vows,
  Too, too late for the fond believing
    lyre,
When holy were the haunted forest
    boughs,
  Holy the air, the water, and the fire;
40 Yet even in these days so far retir'd
    From happy pieties, thy lucent fans,
    Fluttering among the faint Olympians,
I see, and sing, by my own eyes inspir'd.
So let me be thy choir, and make a moan
45   Upon the midnight hours;
  Thy voice, thy lute, thy pipe, thy incense
    sweet
  From swinged censer teeming;
Thy shrine, thy grove, thy oracle, thy heat
  Of pale-mouth'd prophet dreaming.

50 Yes, I will be thy priest, and build a fane
    In some untrodden region of my mind,
Where branched thoughts, new grown
    with pleasant pain,
  Instead of pines shall murmur in the
    wind:
Far, far around shall those dark-cluster'd
    trees
55 Fledge the wild-ridged mountains steep
    by steep;
And there by zephyrs, streams, and birds,
    and bees,
  The moss-lain Dryads shall be lull'd to
    sleep;
And in the midst of this wide quietness
  A rosy sanctuary will I dress
60 With the wreath'd trellis of a working
    brain,

With buds, and bells, and stars without
    a name,
With all the gardener Fancy e'er could
    feign,
Who breeding flowers, will never breed
    the same:
And there shall be for thee all soft delight
65 That shadowy thought can win,
A bright torch, and a casement ope at
    night,
  To let the warm Love in!

ODE TO A NIGHTINGALE
1819   1819

My heart aches, and a drowsy numbness
    pains
  My sense, as though of hemlock[1] I had
    drunk,
Or emptied some dull opiate to the drains
  One minute past, and Lethe-wards had
    sunk:
5 'Tis not through envy of thy happy lot,
  But being too happy in thine happi-
    ness,—
    That thou, light-winged Dryad of the
    trees,
      In some melodious plot
  Of beechen green, and shadows number-
    less,
10   Singest of summer in full-throated
    ease.

O for a draught of vintage! that hath been
  Cool'd a long age in the deep-delved
    earth,
Tasting of Flora and the country green,
  Dance, and Provençal song, and sun-
    burnt mirth!
15 O for a beaker full of the warm South,
  Full of the true, the blushful Hippo-
    crene,
    With beaded bubbles winking at the
    brim,
    And purple-stained mouth;
That I might drink, and leave the world
    unseen,
20   And with thee fade away into the
    forest dim:

Fade far away, dissolve, and quite forget
  What thou among the leaves hast never
    known,
The weariness, the fever, and the fret
  Here, where men sit and hear each other
    groan;
25 Where palsy shakes a few, sad, last gray
    hairs,

[1] the poisonous hemlock shrub

Where youth grows pale, and spectre-
 thin, and dies;
Where but to think is to be full of
 sorrow
And leaden-eyed despairs,
Where Beauty cannot keep her lustrous
 eyes,
30 Or new Love pine at them beyond tomorrow.

Away! away! for I will fly to thee,
 Not charioted by Bacchus and his
  pards,[1]
But on the viewless[2] wings of Poesy,
 Though the dull brain perplexes and
  retards:
35 Already with thee! tender is the night,
 And haply the Queen-Moon is on her
  throne,
  Cluster'd around by all her starry
   fays;
 But here there is no light,
 Save what from heaven is with the
  breezes blown
40 Through verdurous glooms and winding mossy ways.

I cannot see what flowers are at my feet,
 Nor what soft incense hangs upon the
  boughs,
But, in embalmed[3] darkness, guess each
  sweet
Wherewith the seasonable month en-
  dows
45 The grass, the thicket, and the fruit-tree
  wild;
 White hawthorn, and the pastoral eglantine;
 Fast fading violets cover'd up in
  leaves;
 And mid-May's eldest child,
 The coming musk-rose, full of dewy
  wine,
50 The murmurous haunt of flies on
  summer eves.

Darkling I listen; and, for many a time
 I have been half in love with easeful
  Death,
Call'd him soft names in many a mused
  rhyme,
 To take into the air my quiet breath;
55 Now more than ever seems it rich to die,
 To cease upon the midnight with no
  pain,
  While thou art pouring forth thy
   soul abroad

  In such an ecstasy!
Still wouldst thou sing, and I have ears
 in vain—
60 To thy high requiem become a sod.

Thou wast not born for death, immortal
 bird!
No hungry generations tread thee down;
 The voice I hear this passing night was
  heard
 In ancient days by emperor and clown:
65 Perhaps the self-same song that found a
 path
 Through the sad heart of Ruth, when,
  sick for home,
  She stood in tears amid the alien
   corn;[1]
 The same that oft-times hath
 Charm'd magic casements, opening on
  the foam
70 Of perilous seas, in faery lands forlorn.

Forlorn! the very word is like a bell
 To toll me back from thee to my sole
  self!
Adieu! the fancy cannot cheat so well
 As she is fam'd to do, deceiving elf.
75 Adieu! adieu! thy plaintive anthem fades
 Past the near meadows, over the still
  stream,
 Up the hill-side; and now 'tis buried
  deep
 In the next valley-glades:
Was it a vision, or a waking dream?
80 Fled is that music:—do I wake or
  sleep?

LAMIA
1819   1820

PART I

Upon a time, before the faery broods
Drove Nymph and Satyr from the prosperous woods,
Before King Oberon's bright diadem,
Sceptre, and mantle, clasp'd with dewy
 gem,
5 Frighted away the Dryads and the Fauns
From rushes green, and brakes,[2] and cowslip'd lawns,
The ever-smitten Hermes empty left
His golden throne, bent warm on amorous
 theft:
From high Olympus had he stolen light,
10 On this side of Jove's clouds, to escape
 the sight

---

[1] leopards [2] invisible [3] balmy   [1] wheat (See *Ruth*, 2.) [2] thickets

Of his great summoner, and made retreat
Into a forest on the shores of Crete.
For somewhere in that sacred island dwelt
A nymph, to whom all hoofed Satyrs
knelt;
15 At whose white feet the languid Tritons
pour'd
Pearls, while on land they wither'd and
ador'd.
Fast by the springs where she to bathe was
wont,
And in those meads where sometime she
might haunt,
Were strewn rich gifts, unknown to any
Muse,
20 Though Fancy's casket were unlock'd to
choose.
Ah, what a world of love was at her feet!
So Hermes thought, and a celestial heat
Burnt from his winged heels to either ear,
That from a whiteness, as the lily clear,
25 Blush'd into roses 'mid his golden hair,
Fallen in jealous curls about his shoulders
bare.

From vale to vale, from wood to wood,
he flew,
Breathing upon the flowers his passion
new,
And wound with many a river to its head,
30 To find where this sweet nymph prepar'd
her secret bed:
In vain; the sweet nymph might nowhere
be found,
And so he rested, on the lonely ground,
Pensive, and full of painful jealousies
Of the Wood-Gods, and even the very
trees.
35 There as he stood, he heard a mournful
voice,
Such as once heard, in gentle heart, destroys
All pain but pity: thus the lone voice
spake:
"When from this wreathed tomb shall I
awake!
When move in a sweet body fit for life,
40 And love, and pleasure, and the ruddy
strife
Of hearts and lips! Ah, miserable me!"
The God, dove-footed, glided silently
Round bush and tree, soft-brushing, in
his speed,
The taller grasses and full-flowering weed,
45 Until he found a palpitating snake,
Bright, and cirque-couchant[1] in a dusky
brake.

She was a gordian shape[1] of dazzling
hue,
Vermilion-spotted, golden, green, and blue;
Strip'd like a zebra, freckled like a pard,[2]
50 Ey'd like a peacock, and all crimson
barr'd;
And full of silver moons, that, as she
breath'd,
Dissolv'd, or brighter shone, or inter-
wreath'd
Their lustres with the gloomier tapestries—
So rainbow-sided, touch'd with miseries,
55 She seem'd, at once, some penanc'd lady
elf,
Some demon's mistress, or the demon's
self.
Upon her crest she wore a wannish fire
Sprinkled with stars, like Ariadne's tiar.[3]
Her head was serpent, but ah, bitter-sweet!
60 She had a woman's mouth with all its
pearls complete:
And for her eyes—what could such eyes
do there
But weep, and weep, that they were born
so fair?
As Proserpine still weeps for her Sicilian
air.[4]
Her throat was serpent, but the words she
spake
65 Came, as through bubbling honey, for
Love's sake,
And thus; while Hermes on his pinions
lay,
Like a stoop'd falcon ere he takes his
prey.

"Fair Hermes, crown'd with feathers,
fluttering light,
I had a splendid dream of thee last night:
70 I saw thee sitting, on a throne of gold,
Among the Gods, upon Olympus old,
The only sad one; for thou didst not hear
The soft, lute-finger'd Muses chanting
clear,
Nor even Apollo when he sang alone,
75 Deaf to his throbbing throat's long, long
melodious moan.
I dreamt I saw thee, rob'd in purple flakes,
Break amorous through the clouds, as
morning breaks,
And, swiftly as a bright Phœbean dart,
Strike for the Cretan isle; and here thou
art!

---

[1] coiled

[1] That is, twisted in-
to an intricate knot.
[2] leopard
[3] crown (It became a
constellation after
Ariadne's death.)
[4] The vale of Enna,
in Sicily, from
which she was car-
ried off by Pluto to
the lower world.

80 Too gentle Hermes, hast thou found the
    maid?''
Whereat the star of Lethe[1] not delay'd
His rosy eloquence, and thus inquired:
"Thou smooth-lipp'd serpent, surely high
    inspired!
Thou beauteous wreath, with melancholy
    eyes,
85 Possess whatever bliss thou canst devise,
Telling me only where my nymph is fled,—
Where she doth breathe!''—''Bright
    planet, thou hast said,''
Return'd the snake, ''but seal with oaths,
    fair God!''
''I swear,'' said Hermes, ''by my serpent
    rod,[2]
90 And by thine eyes, and by thy starry
    crown!''
Light flew his earnest words, among the
    blossoms blown.
Then thus again the brilliance feminine:
''Too frail of heart! for this lost nymph
    of thine,
Free as the air, invisibly, she strays
95 About these thornless wilds; her pleasant
    days
She tastes unseen; unseen her nimble feet
Leave traces in the grass and flowers
    sweet;
From weary tendrils, and bow'd branches
    green,
She plucks the fruit unseen, she bathes un-
    seen:
100 And by my power is her beauty veil'd
To keep it unaffronted, unassail'd
By the love-glances of unlovely eyes,
Of Satyrs, Fauns, and blear'd Silenus'
    sighs.
Pale grew her immortality, for woe
105 Of all these lovers, and she grieved so
I took compassion on her, bade her steep
Her hair in weïrd syrups, that would keep
Her loveliness invisible, yet free
To wander as she loves, in liberty.
110 Thou shalt behold her, Hermes, thou alone,
If thou wilt, as thou swearest, grant my
    boon!''
Then, once again, the charmed God began
An oath, and through the serpent's ears
    it ran
Warm, tremulous, devout, psalterian.[3]
115 Ravish'd, she lifted her Circean head,
Blush'd a live damask, and swift-lisping
    said,
''I was a woman, let me have once more

<hr>

[1] Hermes, so called because he led souls to
    Hades.
[2] The magic rod of Hermes was entwined with
    serpents.
[3] musical

A woman's shape, and charming as before.
I love a youth of Corinth—O the bliss!
120 Give me my woman's form, and place me
    where he is.
Stoop, Hermes, let me breathe upon thy
    brow,
And thou shalt see thy sweet nymph even
    now.''
The God on half-shut feathers sank serene,
She breath'd upon his eyes, and swift was
    seen
125 Of both the guarded nymph near-smiling
    on the green.
It was no dream; or say a dream it was,
Real are the dreams of Gods, and smoothly
    pass
Their pleasures in a long immortal dream.
One warm, flush'd moment, hovering, it
    might seem
130 Dash'd by the wood-nymph's beauty, so
    he burn'd;
Then, lighting on the printless verdure,
    turn'd
To the swoon'd serpent, and with languid
    arm,
Delicate, put to proof the lithe Caducean
    charm.[1]
So done, upon the nymph his eyes he
    bent
135 Full of adoring tears and blandishment,
And towards her stept: she, like a moon
    in wane,
Faded before him, cower'd, nor could re-
    strain
Her fearful sobs, self-folding like a flower
That faints into itself at evening hour:
140 But the God fostering her chilled hand,
She felt the warmth, her eyelids open'd
    bland,
And, like new flowers at morning song of
    bees,
Bloom'd, and gave up her honey to the
    lees.
Into the green-recessed woods they flew;
145 Nor grew they pale, as mortal lovers do.

Left to herself, the serpent now began
To change; her elfin blood in madness ran,
Her mouth foam'd, and the grass, there-
    with besprent,
Wither'd at dew so sweet and virulent;
150 Her eyes in torture fix'd, and anguish
    drear,
Hot, glaz'd, and wide, with lid-lashes all
    sear,
Flash'd phosphor and sharp sparks, with-
    out one cooling tear.

<hr>

[1] He touched her with his magic rod, the cadu-
    ceus.

The colors all inflam'd throughout her train,
She writh'd about, convuls'd with scarlet pain:
155 A deep volcanian yellow took the place
Of all her milder-mooned body's grace;
And, as the lava ravishes the mead,
Spoilt all her silver mail, and golden brede;[1]
Made gloom of all her frecklings, streaks, and bars,
160 Eclips'd her crescents, and lick'd up her stars:
So that, in moments few, she was undrest
Of all her sapphires, greens, and amethyst,
And rubious-argent: of all these bereft,
Nothing but pain and ugliness were left.
165 Still shone her crown; that vanish'd, also she
Melted and disappear'd as suddenly;
And in the air, her new voice luting soft,
Cried, "Lycius! gentle Lycius!"—Borne aloft
With the bright mists about the mountains hoar
170 These words dissolv'd: Crete's forests heard no more.

Whither fled Lamia, now a lady bright,
A full-born beauty new and exquisite?
She fled into that valley they pass o'er
Who go to Corinth from Cenchreas' shore;
175 And rested at the foot of those wild hills,
The rugged founts of the Peræan rills,
And of that other ridge whose barren back
Stretches, with all its mist and cloudy rack,
South-westward to Cleone. There she stood
180 About a young bird's flutter from a wood,
Fair, on a sloping green of mossy tread,
By a clear pool, wherein she passioned
To see herself escap'd from so sore ills,
While her robes flaunted with the daffodils.

185 Ah, happy Lycius!—for she was a maid
More beautiful than ever twisted braid,
Or sigh'd, or blush'd, or on spring-flow'red lea
Spread a green kirtle to the minstrelsy:
A virgin purest lipp'd, yet in the lore
190 Of love deep learned to the red heart's core:
Not one hour old, yet of sciential[2] brain

To unperplex bliss from its neighbor pain;
Define their pettish limits, and estrange
Their points of contact, and swift counter-change;
195 Intrigue with the specious chaos, and dispart
Its most ambiguous atoms with sure art;
As though in Cupid's college she had spent
Sweet days a lovely graduate, still unshent,[1]
And kept his rosy terms[2] in idle languishment.

200 Why this fair creature chose so fairily
By the wayside to linger, we shall see;
But first 'tis fit to tell how she could muse
And dream, when in the serpent prison-house,
Of all she list, strange or magnificent:
205 How, ever, where she will'd, her spirit went;
Whether to faint Elysium, or where
Down through tress-lifting waves the Nereids fair
Wind into Thetis' bower by many a pearly stair;
Or where God Bacchus drains his cups divine,
210 Stretch'd out, at ease, beneath a glutinous pine;
Or where in Pluto's gardens palatine[3]
Mulciber's columns gleam in far piazzian line.
And sometimes into cities she would send
Her dream, with feast and rioting to blend;
215 And once, while among mortals dreaming thus,
She saw the young Corinthian Lycius
Charioting foremost in the envious race,
Like a young Jove with calm uneager face,
And fell into a swooning love of him.
220 Now on the moth-time of that evening dim
He would return that way, as well she knew,
To Corinth from the shore; for freshly blew
The eastern soft wind, and his galley now
Grated the quaystones with her brazen prow
225 In port Cenchreas, from Egina isle
Fresh anchor'd; whither he had been awhile
To sacrifice to Jove, whose temple there
Waits with high marble doors for blood and incense rare.
Jove heard his vows, and better'd his desire;

---

[1] braid; embroidery   [2] endowed with knowledge   [1] unharmed; innocent   [2] sessions   [3] palatial

230 For by some freakful chance he made
    retire
From his companions, and set forth to
    walk,
Perhaps grown wearied of their Corinth
    talk:
Over the solitary hills he fared,
Thoughtless at first, but ere eve's star
    appear'd
235 His phantasy was lost, where reason fades,
In the calm'd twilight of Platonic shades.
Lamia beheld him coming, near, more
    near—
Close to her passing, in indifference drear,
His silent sandals swept the mossy green;
240 So neighbor'd to him, and yet so unseen
She stood: he pass'd, shut up in mysteries,
His mind wrapp'd like his mantle, while
    her eyes
Follow'd his steps, and her neck regal
    white
Turn'd — syllabling thus, "Ah, Lycius
    bright,
245 And will you leave me on the hills alone?
Lycius, look back! and be some pity
    shown."
He did; not with cold wonder fearingly,
But Orpheus-like at an Eurydice;
For so delicious were the words she sung,
250 It seem'd he had lov'd them a whole sum-
    mer long:
And soon his eyes had drunk her beauty
    up,
Leaving no drop in the bewildering cup,
And still the cup was full,—while he,
    afraid
Lest she should vanish ere his lip had paid
255 Due adoration, thus began to adore;
Her soft look growing coy, she saw his
    chain so sure:
"Leave thee alone! Look back! Ah, God-
    dess, see
Whether my eyes can ever turn from thee!
For pity do not this sad heart belie—
260 Even as thou vanishest so shall I die.
Stay! though a Naiad of the rivers, stay!
To thy far wishes will thy streams obey:
Stay! though the greenest woods be thy
    domain,
Alone they can drink up the morning rain:
265 Though a descended Pleiad, will not one
Of thine harmonious sisters keep in tune
Thy spheres,[1] and as thy silver proxy
    shine?
So sweetly to these ravish'd ears of mine
Came thy sweet greeting, that if thou
    shouldst fade

[1] A reference to the ancient belief that the movement of the celestial spheres produced music.

270 Thy memory will waste me to a shade:—
For pity do not melt!"—"If I should
    stay,"
Said Lamia, "here, upon this floor of
    clay,
And pain my steps upon these flowers too
    rough,
What canst thou say or do of charm enough
275 To dull the nice remembrance of my
    home?
Thou canst not ask me with thee here to
    roam
Over these hills and vales, where no joy
    is,—
Empty of immortality and bliss!
Thou art a scholar, Lycius, and must know
280 That finer spirits cannot breathe below
In human climes, and live. Alas! poor
    youth,
What taste of purer air hast thou to soothe
My essence? What serener palaces,
Where I may all my many senses please,
285 And by mysterious sleights a hundred
    thirsts appease?
It cannot be—Adieu!" So said, she rose
Tiptoe with white arms spread. He, sick
    to lose
The amorous promise of her lone complain,
Swoon'd, murmuring of love, and pale
    with pain.
290 The cruel lady, without any show
Of sorrow for her tender favorite's woe,
But rather, if her eyes could brighter be,
With brighter eyes and slow amenity,
Put her new lips to his, and gave afresh
295 The life she had so tangled in her mesh:
And as he from one trance was wakening
Into another, she began to sing,
Happy in beauty, life, and love, and every-
    thing,
A song of love, too sweet for earthly lyres,
300 While, like held breath, the stars drew in
    their panting fires.
And then she whisper'd in such trembling
    tone,
As those who, safe together met alone
For the first time through many anguish'd
    days,
Use other speech than looks; bidding him
    raise
305 His drooping head, and clear his soul of
    doubt,
For that she was a woman, and without
Any more subtle fluid in her veins
Than throbbing blood, and that the self-
    same pains
Inhabited her frail-strung heart as his.
310 And next she wonder'd how his eyes could
    miss

Her face so long in Corinth, where, she
said,
She dwelt but half retir'd, and there had
led
Days happy as the gold coin could invent
Without the aid of love; yet in content
315 Till she saw him, as once she pass'd him
by,
Where 'gainst a column he leant thought-
fully
At Venus' temple porch, 'mid baskets
heap'd
Of amorous herbs and flowers, newly
reap'd
Late on that eve, as 'twas the night before
320 The Adonian feast;[1] whereof she saw no
more,
But wept alone those days, for why should
she adore?
Lycius from death awoke into amaze,
To see her still, and singing so sweet lays;
Then from amaze into delight he fell
325 To hear her whisper woman's lore so well;
And every word she spake entic'd him on
To unperplex'd delight and pleasure
known.
Let the mad poets say whate'er they please
Of the sweets of Fairies, Peris, Goddesses,
330 There is not such a treat among them all,
Haunters of cavern, lake, and waterfall,
As a real woman, lineal indeed
From Pyrrha's pebbles[2] or old Adam's
seed.
Thus gentle Lamia judg'd, and judg'd
aright,
335 That Lycius could not love in half a fright,
So threw the goddess off, and won his heart
More pleasantly by playing woman's part,
With no more awe than what her beauty
gave,
That, while it smote, still guaranteed to
save.
340 Lycius to all made eloquent reply,
Marrying to every word a twin-born sigh;
And last, pointing to Corinth, ask'd her
sweet,
If 'twas too far that night for her soft
feet.
The way was short, for Lamia's eagerness
345 Made, by a spell, the triple league de-
crease
To a few paces; not at all surmis'd
By blinded Lycius, so in her compris'd.
They pass'd the city gates, he knew not
how,
So noiseless, and he never thought to know.

350 As men talk in a dream, so Corinth all,
Throughout her palaces imperial,
And all her populous streets and temples
lewd,[1]
Mutter'd, like tempest in the distance
brew'd,
To the wide-spreaded night above her
towers,
355 Men, women, rich and poor, in the cool
hours,
Shuffled their sandals o'er the pavement
white,
Companion'd or alone; while many a light
Flar'd, here and there, from wealthy festivals,
And threw their moving shadows on the
walls,
360 Or found them cluster'd in the corniced
shade
Of some arch'd temple door, or dusky
colonnade.

Muffling his face, of greeting friends in
fear,
Her fingers he press'd hard, as one came
near
With curl'd gray beard, sharp eyes, and
smooth bald crown,
365 Slow-stepp'd, and rob'd in philosophic
gown:
Lycius shrank closer, as they met and past,
Into his mantle, adding wings to haste,
While hurried Lamia trembled: "Ah,"
said he,
"Why do you shudder, love, so ruefully?
370 Why does your tender palm dissolve in
dew?"—
"I'm wearied," said fair Lamia: "tell me
who
Is that old man? I cannot bring to mind
His features:—Lycius! wherefore did you
blind
Yourself from his quick eyes?" Lycius
replied,
375 " 'Tis Apollonius sage, my trusty guide
And good instructor; but tonight he seems
The ghost of folly haunting my sweet
dreams."

While yet he spake they had arriv'd
before
A pillar'd porch, with lofty portal door,
380 Where hung a silver lamp, whose phosphor
glow
Reflected in the slabbed steps below,
Mild as a star in water; for so new,

---

[1] The festival in honor of Adonis.
[2] After the deluge, Deucalion and Pyrrha repeopled the earth by casting behind them stones
which became men and women.

[1] That is, temples or buildings devoted to lewd
practices in the service of Venus, goddess of
love. Corinth was a seat of Venus worship.

And so unsullied was the marble's hue,
So through the crystal polish, liquid fine,
385 Ran the dark veins, that none but feet divine
Could e'er have touch'd there. Sounds Æolian
Breath'd from the hinges, as the ample span
Of the wide doors disclos'd a place unknown
Some time to any, but those two alone,
390 And a few Persian mutes, who that same year
Were seen about the markets: none knew where
They could inhabit; the most curious
Were foil'd, who watch'd to trace them to their house:
And but the flitter-winged verse must tell,
395 For truth's sake, what woe afterwards befel,
'Twould humor many a heart to leave them thus,
Shut from the busy world of more incredulous.

PART II

Love in a hut, with water and a crust,
Is — Love, forgive us! — cinders, ashes, dust;
Love in a palace is perhaps at last
More grievous torment than a hermit's fast:—
5 That is a doubtful tale from fairy land,
Hard for the non-elect to understand.
Had Lycius liv'd to hand his story down,
He might have given the moral a fresh frown,
Or clench'd it quite: but too short was their bliss
10 To breed distrust and hate, that make the soft voice hiss.
Besides, there, nightly, with terrific glare,
Love, jealous grown of so complete a pair,
Hover'd and buzz'd his wings, with fearful roar,
Above the lintel[1] of their chamber door,
15 And down the passage cast a glow upon the floor.

For all this came a ruin: side by side
They were enthroned, in the even tide,
Upon a couch, near to a curtaining
Whose airy texture, from a golden string,
20 Floated into the room, and let appear
Unveil'd the summer heaven, blue and clear,

[1] A horizontal piece spanning an opening.

Betwixt two marble shafts:—there they repos'd,
Where use had made it sweet, with eyelids clos'd,
Saving a tithe which love still open kept,
25 That they might see each other while they almost slept;
When from the slope side of a suburb hill,
Deafening the swallow's twitter, came a thrill
Of trumpets—Lycius started—the sounds fled,
But left a thought, a buzzing in his head.
30 For the first time, since first he harbor'd in
That purple-lined palace of sweet sin,
His spirit pass'd beyond its golden bourn
Into the noisy world almost forsworn.
The lady, ever watchful, penetrant,
35 Saw this with pain, so arguing a want
Of something more, more than her empery
Of joys; and she began to moan and sigh
Because he mus'd beyond her, knowing well
That but a moment's thought is passion's passing bell.
40 "Why do you sigh, fair creature?" whisper'd he:
"Why do you think?" return'd she tenderly:
"You have deserted me;—where am I now?
Not in your heart while care weighs on your brow:
No, no, you have dismiss'd me; and I go
45 From your breast houseless: aye, it must be so."
He answer'd, bending to her open eyes,
Where he was mirror'd small in paradise,
"My silver planet, both of eve and morn!
Why will you plead yourself so sad forlorn,
50 While I am striving how to fill my heart
With deeper crimson, and a double smart?
How to entangle, trammel up, and snare
Your soul in mine, and labyrinth you there
Like the hid scent in an unbudded rose?
55 Aye, a sweet kiss—you see your mighty woes.
My thoughts! shall I unveil them? Listen then!
What mortal hath a prize, that other men
May be confounded and abash'd withal,
But lets it sometimes pace abroad majestical,
60 And triumph, as in thee I should rejoice
Amid the hoarse alarm of Corinth's voice.
Let my foes choke, and my friends shout afar,

While through the thronged streets your
    bridal car
Wheels round its dazzling spokes.''—The
    lady's cheek
65 Trembled; she nothing said, but, pale and
    meek,
Arose and knelt before him, wept a rain
Of sorrows at his words; at last with
    pain
Beseeching him, the while his hand she
    wrung,
To change his purpose. He thereat was
    stung,
70 Perverse, with stronger fancy to reclaim
Her wild and timid nature to his aim:
Besides, for all his love, in self despite,
Against his better self, he took delight
Luxurious in her sorrows, soft and new.
75 His passion, cruel grown, took on a hue
Fierce and sanguineous as 'twas possible
In one whose brow had no dark veins to
    swell.
Fine was the mitigated fury, like
Apollo's presence when in act to strike
80 The serpent—Ha, the serpent! certes, she
Was none. She burnt, she lov'd the tyr-
    anny,
And, all subdued, consented to the hour
When to the bridal he should lead his
    paramour.
Whispering in midnight silence, said the
    youth,
85 ''Sure some sweet name thou hast, though,
    by my truth,
I have not ask'd it, ever thinking thee
Not mortal, but of heavenly progeny,
As still I do. Hast any mortal name,
Fit appellation for this dazzling frame?
90 Or friends or kinsfolk on the citied earth,
To share our marriage feast and nuptial
    mirth?''
''I have no friends,'' said Lamia, ''no, not
    one;
My presence in wide Corinth hardly
    known:
My parents' bones are in their dusty urns
95 Sepulchred, where no kindled incense
    burns,
Seeing all their luckless race are dead,
    save me,
And I neglect the holy rite for thee.
Even as you list invite your many guests;
But if, as now it seems, your vision rests
100 With any pleasure on me, do not bid
Old Apollonius—from him keep me hid.''
Lycius, perplex'd at words so blind and
    blank,
Made close inquiry; from whose touch she
    shrank,

Feigning a sleep; and he to the dull shade
105 Of deep sleep in a moment was betray'd.

It was the custom then to bring away
The bride from home at blushing shut of
    day,
Veil'd, in a chariot, heralded along
By strewn flowers, torches, and a marriage
    song,
110 With other pageants: but this fair un-
    known
Had not a friend. So being left alone,
(Lycius was gone to summon all his kin)
And knowing surely she could never win
His foolish heart from its mad pompous-
    ness,
115 She set herself, high-thoughted, how to
    dress
The misery in fit magnificence.
She did so, but 'tis doubtful how and
    whence
Came, and who were her subtle servitors.
About the halls, and to and from the doors,
120 There was a noise of wings, till in short
    space
The glowing banquet-room shone with
    wide-arched grace.
A haunting music, sole perhaps and lone
Supportress of the fairy roof, made moan
Throughout, as fearful the whole charm
    might fade.
125 Fresh carved cedar, mimicking a glade
Of palm and plantain, met from either
    side,
High in the midst, in honor of the bride:
Two palms and then two plantains, and
    so on,
From either side their stems branch'd one
    to one
130 All down the aisled place; and beneath all
There ran a stream of lamps straight on
    from wall to wall.
So canopied, lay an untasted feast
Teeming with odors. Lamia, regal drest,
Silently pac'd about, and as she went,
135 In pale contented sort of discontent,
Mission'd her viewless servants to enrich
The fretted splendor of each nook and
    niche.
Between the tree-stems, marbled plain at
    first,
Came jasper panels; then, anon, there
    burst
140 Forth creeping imagery of slighter trees,
And with the larger wove in small intrica-
    cies.
Approving all, she faded at self-will,
And shut the chamber up, close, hush'd
    and still,

Complete and ready for the revels rude,
145 When dreadful guests would come to spoil
    her solitude.

The day appear'd, and all the gossip
    rout.
O senseless Lycius! Madman! wherefore
    flout
The silent-blessing fate, warm cloister'd
    hours,
And show to common eyes these secret
    bowers?
150 The herd approach'd; each guest, with
    busy brain,
Arriving at the portal, gaz'd amain,
And enter'd marveling: for they knew the
    street,
Remember'd it from childhood all com-
    plete
Without a gap, yet ne'er before had seen
155 That royal porch, that high-built fair
    demesne;
So in they hurried all, amaz'd, curious,
    and keen:
Save one, who look'd thereon with eye
    severe.
And with calm-planted steps walk'd in
    austere;
'Twas Apollonius: something too he
    laugh'd,
160 As though some knotty problem, that had
    daft[1]
His patient thought, had now begun to
    thaw,
And solve, and melt:— 'twas just as he
    foresaw.

He met within the murmurous vestibule
His young disciple. " 'Tis no common
    rule,
165 Lycius," said he, "for uninvited guest
To force himself upon you, and infest
With an unbidden presence the bright
    throng
Of younger friends; yet must I do this
    wrong,
And you forgive me." Lycius blush'd,
    and led
170 The old man through the inner doors
    broad-spread;
With reconciling words and courteous mien
Turning into sweet milk the sophist's
    spleen.

Of wealthy lustre was the banquet-
    room,
Fill'd with pervading brilliance and per-
    fume:

[1] thrust aside

175 Before each lucid panel fuming stood
A censer fed with myrrh and spiced wood,
Each by a sacred tripod held aloft,
Whose slender feet wide-swerv'd upon the
    soft
Wool-woofed carpets: fifty wreaths of
    smoke
180 From fifty censers their light voyage took
To the high roof, still mimick'd as they
    rose
Along the mirror'd walls by twin-clouds
    odorous.
Twelve sphered tables, by silk seats in-
    spher'd,
High as the level of a man's breast rear'd
185 On libbard's[1] paws, upheld the heavy
    gold
Of cups and goblets, and the store thrice
    told
Of Ceres' horn, and, in huge vessels, wine
Come from the gloomy tun with merry
    shine.
Thus loaded with a feast the tables stood,
190 Each shrining in the midst the image of a
    God.

When in an antechamber every guest
Had felt the cold full sponge to pleasure
    press'd,
By minist'ring slaves, upon his hands and
    feet,
And fragrant oils with ceremony meet
195 Pour'd on his hair, they all mov'd to the
    feast
In white robes, and themselves in order
    plac'd
Around the silken couches, wondering
Whence all this mighty cost and blaze of
    wealth could spring.

Soft went the music the soft air along,
200 While fluent Greek a vowel'd undersong
Kept up among the guests, discoursing
    low
At first, for scarcely was the wine at flow;
But when the happy vintage touch'd their
    brains,
Louder they talk, and louder come the
    strains
205 Of powerful instruments:—the gorgeous
    dyes,
The space, the splendor of the draperies,
The roof of awful richness, nectarous
    cheer,
Beautiful slaves, and Lamia's self, appear,
Now, when the wine has done its rosy deed,
210 And every soul from human trammels
    freed,

[1] leopard's

No more so strange; for merry wine, sweet
wine,
Will make Elysian shades not too fair, too
divine.
Soon was God Bacchus at meridian height;
Flush'd were their cheeks, and bright eyes
double bright:
215 Garlands of every green, and every scent
From vales deflower'd, or forest-trees
branch-rent,
In baskets of bright osier'd gold[1] were
brought
High as the handles heap'd, to suit the
thought
Of every guest: that each, as he did please,
220 Might fancy-fit his brows, silk-pillow'd
at his ease.

What wreath for Lamia? What for
Lycius?
What for the sage, old Apollonius?
Upon her aching forehead be there hung
The leaves of willow[2] and of adder's
tongue:
225 And for the youth, quick, let us strip for
him
The thyrsus,[3] that his watching eyes may
swim
Into forgetfulness; and, for the sage,
Let spear-grass and the spiteful thistle
wage
War on his temples. Do not all charms fly
230 At the mere touch of cold philosophy?
There was an awful rainbow once in
heaven:[4]
We know her woof, her texture; she is
given
In the dull catalogue of common things.
Philosophy will clip an Angel's wings,
235 Conquer all mysteries by rule and line,
Empty the haunted air, and gnomed
mine—
Unweave a rainbow, as it erewhile made
The tender-person'd Lamia melt into a
shade.

By her glad Lycius sitting, in chief place,
240 Scarce saw in all the room another face,
Till, checking his love trance, a cup he took
Full brimm'd, and opposite sent forth a
look
'Cross the broad table, to beseech a glance
From his old teacher's wrinkled counte-
nance,

[1] willow overlaid with gold
[2] In anticipation of her death.
[3] A staff entwined with ivy and surmounted by
a pine cone; an attribute of Bacchus.
[4] Keats thought that Newton had destroyed all
the poetry of the rainbow by reducing it to
the prismatic colors.

245 And pledge him. The bald-head philoso-
pher
Had fix'd his eye, without a twinkle or stir
Full on the alarmed beauty of the bride,
Brow-beating her fair form, and troubling
her sweet pride.
Lycius then press'd her hand, with devout
touch,
250 As pale it lay upon the rosy couch:
'Twas icy, and the cold ran through his
veins;
Then sudden it grew hot, and all the pains
Of an unnatural heat shot to his heart.
"Lamia, what means this? Wherefore
dost thou start?
255 Know'st thou that man?" Poor Lamia
answer'd not.
He gaz'd into her eyes, and not a jot
Own'd they the lovelorn piteous appeal:
More, more he gaz'd: his human senses
reel:
Some hungry spell that loveliness absorbs;
260 There was no recognition in those orbs.
"Lamia!" he cried—and no soft-ton'd
reply.
The many heard, and the loud revelry
Grew hush; the stately music no more
breathes.
The myrtle[1] sicken'd in a thousand
wreaths.
265 By faint degrees, voice, lute, and pleasure
ceas'd;
A deadly silence step by step increas'd
Until it seem'd a horrid presence there,
And not a man but felt the terror in his
hair.
"Lamia!" he shriek'd; and nothing but
the shriek
270 With its sad echo did the silence break.
"Begone, foul dream!" he cried, gazing
again
In the bride's face, where now no azure
vein
Wander'd on fair-spac'd temples; no soft
bloom
Misted the cheek; no passion to illume
275 The deep-recessed vision:—all was blight;
Lamia, no longer fair, there sat a deadly
white
"Shut, shut those juggling eyes, thou
ruthless man!
Turn them aside, wretch! or the righteous
ban
Of all the Gods, whose dreadful images
280 Here represent their shadowy presences,
May pierce them on the sudden with the
thorn
Of painful blindness; leaving thee forlorn,

[1] The myrtle was sacred to Venus.

In trembling dotage to the feeblest fright
Of conscience, for their long-offended
    might,
285 For all thine impious proud-heart sophis-
    tries,
Unlawful magic, and enticing lies.
Corinthians! look upon that gray-beard
    wretch!
Mark how, possess'd, his lashless eyelids
    stretch
Around his demon eyes! Corinthians, see!
290 My sweet bride withers at their potency.''
''Fool!'' said the sophist in an under-tone
Gruff with contempt; which a death-nigh-
    ing moan
From Lycius answer'd, as heart-struck and
    lost,
He sank supine beside the aching ghost.
295 ''Fool! Fool!'' repeated he, while his eyes
    still
Relented not, nor mov'd; ''from every ill
Of life have I preserv'd thee to this day,
And shall I see thee made a serpent's
    prey?''
Then Lamia breath'd death breath; the
    sophist's eye,
300 Like a sharp spear, went through her
    utterly,
Keen, cruel, perceant,[1] stinging: she, as
    well
As her weak hand could any meaning tell,
Motion'd him to be silent; vainly so,
He look'd and look'd again a level—No!
305 ''A serpent!'' echoed he; no sooner said,
Than with a frightful scream she vanished:
And Lycius' arms were empty of delight,
As were his limbs of life, from that same
    night.
On the high couch he lay!—His friends
    came round—
310 Supported him—no pulse, or breath they
    found,
And, in its marriage robe, the heavy body
    wound.

THE EVE OF ST. AGNES
1819   1820

1   St. Agnes' Eve—Ah, bitter chill it was!
The owl, for all his feathers, was a-cold;
The hare limp'd trembling through the
    frozen grass,
And silent was the flock in woolly fold:
Numb were the beadsman's[2] fingers,
    while he told
His rosary,[3] and while his frosted breath,

[1] piercing
[2] A poor man supported in an almshouse and re-
    quired to pray for its founder.
[3] numbered the beads on his rosary

Like pious incense from a censer old,
Seem'd taking flight for heaven, without
    a death,
Past the sweet Virgin's picture, while his
    prayer he saith.

2   His prayer he saith, this patient, holy
    man;
Then takes his lamp, and riseth from his
    knees,
And back returneth, meagre, barefoot,
    wan,
Along the chapel aisle by slow degrees:
The sculptur'd dead, on each side, seem
    to freeze,
Emprison'd in black, purgatorial rails:
Knights, ladies, praying in dumb ora-
    t'ries,
He passeth by; and his weak spirit fails
To think how they may ache in icy hoods
    and mails.

3   Northward he turneth through a little
    door,
And scarce three steps, ere Music's
    golden tongue
Flatter'd to tears this aged man and
    poor;
But no—already had his deathbell rung:
The joys of all his life were said and
    sung:
His was harsh penance on St. Agnes'
    Eve:
Another way he went, and soon among
Rough ashes sat he for his soul's re-
    prieve,
And all night kept awake, for sinners'
    sake to grieve.

4   That ancient beadsman heard the prel-
    ude soft;
And so it chanc'd, for many a door was
    wide,
From hurry to and fro. Soon, up aloft,
The silver, snarling trumpets 'gan to
    chide:
The level chambers, ready with their
    pride,
Were glowing to receive a thousand
    guests:
The carved angels, ever eager-eyed,
Star'd, where upon their heads the cor-
    nice rests,
With hair blown back, and wings put
    cross-wise on their breasts.

5   At length burst in the argent[1] revelry,
With plume, tiara,[2] and all rich array,

[1] shining
[2] A crownlike head ornament.

Numerous as shadows haunting fairily
The brain, new stuff'd, in youth, with
   triumphs gay
Of old romance. These let us wish
   away,
And turn, sole-thoughted, to one lady
   there,
Whose heart had brooded, all that wintry
   day,
On love, and wing'd St. Agnes' saintly
   care,
As she had heard old dames full many
   times declare.

6   They told her how, upon St. Agnes' Eve,
Young virgins might have visions of
   delight,
And soft adorings from their loves re-
   ceive
Upon the honey'd middle of the night,
If ceremonies due they did aright;
As, supperless to bed they must retire,
And couch supine their beauties, lily
   white;
Nor look behind, nor sideways, but re-
   quire
Of Heaven with upward eyes for all that
   they desire.

7   Full of this whim was thoughtful Made-
   line:
The music, yearning like a god in pain,
She scarcely heard: her maiden eyes
   divine,
Fix'd on the floor, saw many a sweeping
   train[1]
Pass by—she heeded not at all: in vain
Came many a tiptoe, amorous cavalier,
And back retir'd; not cool'd by high
   disdain,
But she saw not: her heart was other-
   where:
She sigh'd for Agnes' dreams, the sweetest
   of the year.

8   She danc'd along with vague, regardless
   eyes,
Anxious her lips, her breathing quick
   and short:
The hallow'd hour was near at hand:
   she sighs
Amid the timbrels,[2] and the throng'd resort
Of whisperers in anger, or in sport;
'Mid looks of love, defiance, hate, and
   scorn,

Hoodwink'd[1] with faery fancy; all
   amort,[2]
Save to St. Agnes and her lambs unshorn,
And all the bliss to be before tomorrow
   morn.

9   So, purposing each moment to retire,
She linger'd still. Meantime, across the
   moors,
Had come young Porphyro, with heart
   on fire
For Madeline. Beside the portal doors,
Buttress'd from moonlight, stands he,
   and implores
All saints to give him sight of Madeline,
But for one moment in the tedious hours,
That he might gaze and worship all un-
   seen;
Perchance speak, kneel, touch, kiss—in
   sooth such things have been.

10   He ventures in: let no buzz'd whisper
   tell:
All eyes be muffled, or a hundred swords
Will storm his heart, Love's fev'rous
   citadel:
For him, those chambers held barbarian
   hordes,
Hyena foemen, and hot-blooded lords,
Whose very dogs would execrations howl
Against his lineage: not one breast
   affords
Him any mercy, in that mansion foul,
Save one old beldame, weak in body and
   in soul.

11   Ah, happy chance! the aged creature
   came,
Shuffling along with ivory-headed wand,
To where he stood, hid from the torch's
   flame,
Behind a broad hall-pillar, far beyond
The sound of merriment and chorus
   bland:
He startled her; but soon she knew his
   face,
And grasp'd his fingers in her palsied
   hand,
Saying, "Mercy, Porphyro! hie thee
   from this place:
They are all here tonight, the whole blood-
   thirsty race!

12   "Get hence! get hence! there's dwarf-
   ish Hildebrand;
He had a fever late, and in the fit

---

[1] "Skirts sweeping along the floor."—Keats.
[2] Small hand drums, or tambourines.

[1] blinded   [2] dead

He cursed thee and thine, both house
   and land:
Then there's that old Lord Maurice, not
   a whit
More tame for his gray hairs—Alas me!
   flit!
Flit like a ghost away.''—''Ah, gossip
   dear,
We're safe enough; here in this arm-
   chair sit,
And tell me how''—''Good Saints! not
   here, not here;
Follow me, child, or else these stones will
   be thy bier.''

13   He follow'd through a lowly arched way,
Brushing the cobwebs with his lofty
   plume,
And as she mutter'd ''Well-a—well-a-
   day!''
He found him in a little moonlight room,
Pale, lattic'd, chill, and silent as a tomb.
''Now tell me where is Madeline,'' said
   he,
''O tell me, Angela, by the holy loom
Which none but secret sisterhood may
   see,
When they St. Agnes' wool are weaving
   piously.''

14   ''St. Agnes! Ah! it is St. Agnes' Eve—
Yet men will murder upon holy days:
Thou must hold water in a witch's sieve,
And be liege-lord of all the elves and
   fays,
To venture so: it fills me with amaze
To see thee, Porphyro!—St. Agnes'
   Eve!
God's help! my lady fair the conjuror
   plays
This very night: good angels her de-
   ceive!
But let me laugh awhile, I've mickle[1] time
   to grieve.''

15   Feebly she laugheth in the languid moon,
While Porphyro upon her face doth
   look,
Like puzzled urchin on an aged crone
Who keepeth clos'd a wond'rous riddle-
   book,
As spectacled she sits in chimney nook.
But soon his eyes grew brilliant, when
   she told
His lady's purpose; and he scarce could
   brook
Tears, at the thought of those enchant-
   ments cold,
And Madeline asleep in lap of legends old.

[1] much; ample

16   Sudden a thought came like a full-blown
   rose,
Flushing his brow, and in his pained
   heart
Made purple riot: then doth he propose
A stratagem, that makes the beldame
   start:
''A cruel man and impious thou art:
Sweet lady, let her pray, and sleep, and
   dream
Alone with her good angels, far apart
From wicked men like thee. Go, go!—I
   deem
Thou canst not surely be the same that
   thou didst seem.''

17   ''I will not harm her, by all saints I
   swear,''
Quoth Porphyro: ''O may I ne'er find
   grace
When my weak voice shall whisper its
   last prayer,
If one of her soft ringlets I displace,
Or look with ruffian passion in her face:
Good Angela, believe me by these tears;
Or I will, even in a moment's space,
Awake, with horrid shout, my foemen's
   ears,
And beard them, though they be more
   fang'd than wolves and bears.''

18   ''Ah! why wilt thou affright a feeble
   soul?
A poor, weak, palsy-stricken, church-
   yard thing,
Whose passing-bell may ere the mid-
   night toll;
Whose prayers for thee, each morn and
   evening,
Were never miss'd.''—Thus plaining,
   doth she bring
A gentler speech from burning Por-
   phyro;
So woful, and of such deep sorrowing,
That Angela gives promise she will do
Whatever he shall wish, betide her weal or
   woe.

19   Which was, to lead him, in close secrecy,
Even to Madeline's chamber, and there
   hide
Him in a closet, of such privacy
That he might see her beauty unespied,
And win perhaps that night a peerless
   bride,
While legion'd faeries pac'd the cover-
   let,
And pale enchantment held her sleepy-
   eyed.

Never on such a night have lovers met, 23
Since Merlin paid his demon all the mon-
    strous debt.[1]

20 "It shall be as thou wishest," said the
    dame:
All cates[2] and dainties shall be stored
    there
Quickly on this feast-night: by the tam-
    bour frame[3]
Her own lute thou wilt see: no time to
    spare,
For I am slow and feeble, and scarce
    dare
On such a catering trust my dizzy head.
Wait here, my child, with patience;
    kneel in prayer
The while. Ah! thou must needs the
    lady wed,
Or may I never leave my grave among the
    dead."

21 So saying, she hobbled off with busy
    fear.
The lover's endless minutes slowly
    pass'd;
The dame return'd, and whisper'd in his
    ear
To follow her; with aged eyes aghast
From fright of dim espial. Safe at last,
Through many a dusky gallery, they
    gain
The maiden's chamber, silken, hush'd,
    and chaste;
Where Porphyro took covert, pleas'd
    amain.[4]
His poor guide hurried back with agues in
    her brain.

22 Her falt'ring hand upon the balustrade,
Old Angela was feeling for the stair,
When Madeline, St. Agnes' charmed
    maid,
Rose, like a mission'd spirit, unaware:
With silver taper's light, and pious care,
She turn'd, and down the aged gossip
    led
To a safe level matting. Now prepare,
Young Porphyro, for gazing on that
    bed;
She comes, she comes again, like ringdove
    fray'd[5] and fled.

---

[1] According to one legend, Merlin, the magician
  of Arthur's court, was begotten by demons
  and was killed by one of his own spells. See
  Tennyson's *Merlin and Vivien.*
[2] delicacies
[3] A drumlike embroidery frame.
[4] exceedingly
[5] alarmed

Out went the taper as she hurried in;
Its little smoke, in pallid moonshine,
    died:
She clos'd the door, she panted, all akin
To spirits of the air, and visions wide:
No uttered syllable, or, woe betide!
But to her heart, her heart was voluble,
Paining with eloquence her balmy side;
As though a tongueless nightingale
    should swell
Her throat in vain, and die, heart-stifled,
    in her dell.

24 A casement high and triple-arch'd there
    was,
All garlanded with carven imag'ries
Of fruits, and flowers, and bunches of
    knot-grass,
And diamonded with panes of quaint
    device,
Innumerable of stains and splendid dyes,
As are the tiger-moth's deep-damask'd
    wings;
And in the midst, 'mid thousand
    heraldries,
And twilight saints, and dim emblazon-
    ings,
A shielded scutcheon blush'd with blood of
    queens and kings.

25 Full on this casement shone the wintry
    moon,
And threw warm gules[1] on Madeline's
    fair breast,
As down she knelt for heaven's grace
    and boon;
Rose-bloom fell on her hands, together
    prest,
And on her silver cross soft amethyst,
And on her hair a glory, like a saint:
She seem'd a splendid angel, newly
    drest,
Save wings, for heaven: — Porphyro
    grew faint:
She knelt, so pure a thing, so free from
    mortal taint.

26 Anon his heart revives: her vespers
    done,
Of all its wreathed pearls her hair she
    frees;
Unclasps her warmed jewels one by one;
Loosens her fragrant bodice; by degrees
Her rich attire creeps rustling to her
    knees:
Half-hidden, like a mermaid in sea-weed,
Pensive awhile she dreams awake, and
    sees

[1] red color (a term in heraldry)

In fancy, fair St. Agnes in her bed,
But dares not look behind, or all the charm
  is fled.

27 Soon, trembling in her soft and chilly
    nest,
  In sort of wakeful swoon, perplex'd she
    lay,
  Until the poppied warmth of sleep op-
    press'd
  Her soothed limbs, and soul fatigued
    away;
  Flown, like a thought, until the morrow-
    day;
  Blissfully haven'd both from joy and
    pain;
  Clasp'd like a missal where swart Pay-
    nims pray;[1]
  Blinded alike from sunshine and from
    rain,
As though a rose should shut, and be a
  bud again.

28 Stol'n to this paradise, and so entranced,
  Porphyro gazed upon her empty dress,
  And listen'd to her breathing, if it
    chanced
  To wake into a slumberous tenderness;
  Which when he heard, that minute did
    he bless,
  And breath'd himself: then from the
    closet crept,
  Noiseless as fear[2] in a wide wilderness,
  And over the hush'd carpet, silent, stept,
And 'tween the curtain peep'd, where,
  lo!—how fast she slept.

29 Then by the bed-side, where the faded
    moon
  Made a dim, silver twilight, soft he set
  A table, and, half anguish'd, threw
    thereon
  A cloth of woven crimson, gold, and
    jet:—
  O for some drowsy Morphean amulet!
  The boisterous, midnight, festive clarion,
  The kettle-drum, and far-heard clarinet,
  Affray his ears, though but in dying
    tone:—
The hall door shuts again, and all the noise
  is gone.

30 And still she slept an azure-lidded sleep,
  In blanched linen, smooth, and laven-
    der'd,[3]

While he from forth the closet brought
    a heap
Of candied apple, quince, and plum, and
    gourd;
With jellies soother[1] than the creamy
    curd,
And lucent syrups, tinct with cinnamon;
Manna and dates, in argosy[2] transferr'd
From Fez; and spiced dainties, every
    one,
From silken Samarcand to cedar'd Leba-
  non.

31 These delicates he heap'd with glowing
    hand
  On golden dishes and in baskets bright
  Of wreathed silver: sumptuous they
    stand
  In the retired quiet of the night,
  Filling the chilly room with perfume
    light.—
  "And now, my love, my seraph fair,
    awake!
  Thou art my heaven, and I thine
    eremite:[3]
  Open thine eyes, for meek St. Agnes'
    sake,
Or I shall drowse beside thee, so my soul
  doth ache."

32 Thus whispering, his warm, unnerved
    arm
  Sank in her pillow. Shaded was her
    dream
  By the dusk curtains:—'twas a midnight
    charm
  Impossible to melt as iced stream:
  The lustrous salvers in the moonlight
    gleam;
  Broad golden fringe upon the carpet
    lies:
  It seem'd he never, never could redeem
  From such a stedfast spell his lady's
    eyes;
So mus'd awhile, entoil'd in woofed
  phantasies.

33 Awakening up, he took her hollow lute,—
  Tumultuous,—and, in chords that ten-
    derest be,
  He play'd an ancient ditty, long since
    mute,
  In Provence call'd, "La belle dame sans
    mercy:"[4]

[1] shut, unopened, like a prayer book, which
    pagans would have no occasion to unclasp
[2] That is, a person in fear.
[3] perfumed with lavender (a European mint)

[1] smoother (Cf. this banquet with that pre-
    pared by Eve for Raphael, *Paradise Lost*, 5,
    331-49.)
[2] A large merchant vessel.   [3] hermit
[4] The beautiful lady without pity; the title of a
    poem by Alain Chartier, a translation of
    which Keats found in a volume of Chaucer.
    See Keats's poem of this title (p. 855).

Close to her ear touching the melody;—
Wherewith disturb'd, she utter'd a soft
  moan:
He ceased—she panted quick—and sud-
  denly
Her blue affrayed eyes wide open shone:
Upon his knees he sank, pale as smooth-
  sculptured stone.

34   Her eyes were open, but she still beheld,
Now wide awake, the vision of her sleep:
There was a painful change, that nigh
  expell'd
The blisses of her dream so pure and
  deep
At which fair Madeline began to weep,
And moan forth witless words with
  many a sigh;
While still her gaze on Porphyro would
  keep;
Who knelt, with joined hands and pit-
  eous eye,
Fearing to move or speak, she look'd so
  dreamingly.

35   "Ah, Porphyro!" said she, "but even
  now
Thy voice was at sweet tremble in mine
  ear,
Made tuneable with every sweetest vow;
And those sad eyes were spiritual and
  clear:
How chang'd thou art! how pallid, chill,
  and drear!
Give me that voice again, my Porphyro,
Those looks immortal, those complain-
  ings dear!
Oh leave me not in this eternal woe,
For if thou diest, my love, I know not
  where to go."

36   Beyond a mortal man impassion'd far
At these voluptuous accents, he arose,
Ethereal, flush'd, and like a throbbing
  star
Seen mid the sapphire heaven's deep
  repose;
Into her dream he melted, as the rose
Blendeth its odor with the violet,—
Solution sweet: meantime the frost-
  wind blows
Like Love's alarum pattering the sharp
  sleet
Against the window-panes; St. Agnes'
  moon hath set.

37   'Tis dark: quick pattereth the flaw-
  blown sleet:
"This is no dream, my bride, my Madeline!"

'Tis dark: the iced gusts still rave and
  beat:
"No dream, alas! alas! and woe is
  mine!
Porphyro will leave me here to fade and
  pine.—
Cruel! what traitor could thee hither
  bring?
I curse not, for my heart is lost in thine,
Though thou forsakest a deceived
  thing;—
A dove forlorn and lost with sick unpruned wing."

38   "My Madeline! sweet dreamer! lovely
  bride!
Say, may I be for aye thy vassal blest?
Thy beauty's shield, heart-shap'd and
  vermeil-dyed?
Ah, silver shrine, here will I take my
  rest
After so many hours of toil and quest,
A famish'd pilgrim,—sav'd by miracle.
Though I have found, I will not rob thy
  nest
Saving of thy sweet self; if thou
  think'st well
To trust, fair Madeline, to no rude infidel.

39   "Hark! 'tis an elfin-storm from faery
  land,
Of haggard seeming,[1] but a boon indeed:
Arise—arise! the morning is at hand;—
The bloated wassaillers will never
  heed:—
Let us away, my love, with happy
  speed;
There are no ears to hear, or eyes to
  see,—
Drown'd all in Rhenish[2] and the sleepy
  mead:[3]
Awake! arise! my love, and fearless be,
For o'er the southern moors I have a home
  for thee."

40   She hurried at his words, beset with
  fears,
For there were sleeping dragons all
  around,
At glaring watch, perhaps, with ready
  spears—
Down the wide stairs a darkling way
  they found.—
In all the house was heard no human
  sound.
A chain-droop'd lamp was flickering by
  each door;

[1] wild appearance
[2] Wine from the vine-yards of the Rhine.
[2] A fermented drink made of honey, water, etc.

The arras,[1] rich with horseman, hawk,
and hound,
Flutter'd in the besieging wind's uproar;
And the long carpets rose along the gusty
floor.

41 They glide, like phantoms, into the wide
hall;
Like phantoms, to the iron porch, they
glide;
Where lay the porter in uneasy sprawl,
With a huge empty flagon by his side:
The wakeful bloodhound rose, and
shook his hide,
But his sagacious eye an inmate owns:
By one and one, the bolts full easy
slide:—
The chains **lie silent** on the footworn
stones;—
The key turns, and the door upon its
hinges groans.

42 And they are gone: aye, ages long ago
These lovers fled away into the storm.
That night the Baron dreamt of many a
woe,
And all his warrior-guests, with shade
and form
Of witch, and demon, and large coffin-
worm,
Were long be-nightmar'd. Angela the
old
Died palsy-twitch'd, with meagre face
deform;
The beadsman **after** thousand aves[2]
told,
For aye unsought-for slept among his
ashes cold.

THE EVE OF ST. MARK

A FRAGMENT
1819   1848

Upon a Sabbath-day it fell;
Twice holy was the Sabbath-bell,
That call'd the folk to evening prayer;
The city streets were clean and fair
5 From wholesome drench of April rains;
And, on the western window panes,
The chilly sunset faintly told
Of unmatur'd green valleys cold,
Of the green thorny bloomless hedge,
10 Of rivers new **with spring tide** sedge,
Of primroses by shelter'd rills,

And daisies on the aguish[1] hills,
Twice holy was the Sabbath-bell:
The silent streets were crowded well
15 With staid and pious companies,
Warm from their fire-side orat'ries;
And moving, with demurest air,
To even-song, and vesper prayer.
Each arched porch, and entry low,
20 Was fill'd with patient folk and slow,
With whispers hush, and shuffling feet,
While play'd the organ loud and sweet.

The bells had ceas'd, the prayers begun,
And Bertha had not yet half done
25 A curious volume, patch'd and torn,
That all day long, from earliest morn,
Had taken captive her two eyes,
Among its golden broideries;
Perplex'd her with a thousand things,—
30 The stars of Heaven, and angels' wings,
Martyrs in a fiery blaze,
Azure saints in silver rays,
Moses' breastplate,[2] and the seven
Candlesticks John saw in Heaven,[3]
35 The winged Lion of Saint Mark,[4]
And the Covenantal Ark,[5]
With its many mysteries,
Cherubim and golden mice.[6]

Bertha was a maiden fair,
40 Dwelling in th' old Minster-square;
From her fireside she could see,
Sidelong, its rich antiquity,
Far as the Bishop's garden-wall;
Where sycamores and elm-trees tall,
45 Full-leav'd, the forest had outstript,
By no sharp north-wind ever nipt,
So shelter'd by the mighty pile.
Bertha arose, and read awhile,
With forehead 'gainst the window-pane.
50 Again she tried, and then again,
Until the dusk eve left her dark
Upon the legend of St. Mark.
From plaited lawn-frill, fine and thin,
She lifted up her soft warm chin,
55 With aching neck and swimming eyes,
And daz'd with saintly imag'ries.

All was gloom, and silent all,
Save now and then the still foot-fall
Of one returning homewards late,
60 Past the echoing minster-gate.
The clamorous daws, that all the day
Above tree-tops and towers play,

---

[1] tapestry hung on the walls
[2] The beads of a rosary, which are counted as
the Aves, or salutations to the Virgin Mary,
are uttered.

[1] chilly
[2] See *Exodus*, 28 :15 ; 39 :8.
[3] See *Revelation*, 1 :12.
[4] A winged lion was the emblem of St. Mark,
the evangelist.
[5] See *Exodus*, 25 :10-22 ; 37 :1-9.
[6] See *1 Samuel*, 6 :1-11.

Pair by pair had gone to rest,
Each in its ancient belfry-nest,
65 Where asleep they fall betimes,
To music of the drowsy chimes.

All was silent, all was gloom,
Abroad and in the homely room:
Down she sat, poor cheated soul!
70 And struck a lamp from the dismal
    coal;
Lean'd forward, with bright drooping hair
And slant book, full against the glare.
Her shadow, in uneasy guise,
Hover'd about, a giant size,
75 On ceiling-beam and old oak chair,
The parrot's cage, and panel square;
And the warm angled winter-screen,
On which were many monsters seen,
Call'd doves of Siam, Lima mice,
80 And legless birds of Paradise,
Macaw, and tender av'davat,[1]
And silken-furr'd Angora cat.
Untir'd she read, her shadow still
Glower'd about, as it would fill
85 The room with wildest forms and shades,
As though some ghostly queen of spades
Had come to mock behind her back,
And dance, and ruffle her garments black.
Untir'd she read the legend page,
90 Of holy Mark, from youth to age,
On land, on sea, in pagan chains,
Rejoicing for his many pains.
Sometimes the learned eremite,[2]
With golden star, or dagger bright,
95 Referr'd to pious poesies
Written in smallest crow-quill size
Beneath the text; and thus the rhyme
Was parcell'd out from time to time:
—— "Als[3] writith he of swevenis,[4]
100 Men han[5] beforne they wake in bliss,
Whanne that hir[6] friendes thinke hem
    bound
In crimped[7] shroude farre under grounde;
And how a litling child mote[8] be
A saint er[9] its nativitie,[10]
105 Gif[11] that the modre[12] (God her blesse!)
Kepen in solitarinesse,
And kissen devoute the holy croce.
Of Goddes love, and Sathan's force,—
He writith; and thinges many mo:
110 Of swiche[13] thinges I may not show.
Bot I must tellen verilie
Somdel[14] of Saintè Cicilie,

[1] A small Indian song-   [8] might
   bird.   [9] before
[2] hermit   [10] birth
[3] also   [11] if
[4] dreams   [12] mother
[5] have   [13] such
[6] their   [14] something
[7] plaited; folded

And chieflie what he auctorethe[1]
Of Saintè Markis life and dethe:"
115 At length her constant eyelids come
Upon the fervent martyrdom;
Then lastly to his holy shrine,
Exalt amid the tapers' shine
At Venice,—

*   *   *   *   *   *

HYPERION earlier

A FRAGMENT
1818-19   1820

BOOK I

Deep in the shady sadness of a vale
Far sunken from the healthy breath of
    morn,
Far from the fiery noon, and eve's one
    star,
Sat gray-hair'd Saturn, quiet as a stone,
5 Still as the silence round about his lair;
Forest on forest hung about his head
Like cloud on cloud. No stir of air was
    there,
Not so much life as on a summer's day
Robs not one light seed from the feather'd
    grass,
10 But where the dead leaf fell, there did it
    rest.
A stream went voiceless by, still deadened
    more
By reason of his fallen divinity
Spreading a shade; the Naiad 'mid her
    reeds
Press'd her cold finger closer to her lips.

15   Along the margin-sand large foot-
    marks went,
No further than to where his feet had
    stray'd,
And slept there since. Upon the sodden
    ground
His old right hand lay nerveless, listless,
    dead,
Unsceptred; and his realmless eyes were
    closed;
20 While his bow'd head seem'd list'ning to
    the Earth,
His ancient mother, for some comfort yet.

It seem'd no force could wake him from
    his place;
But there came one,[2] who with a kindred
    hand

[1] writes
[2] Thea, Hyperion's sister and wife, and one of
the female Titans.

Touch'd his wide shoulders, after bending
    low
25 With reverence, though to one who knew
    it not.
She was a Goddess of the infant world;
By her in stature the tall Amazon
Had stood a pigmy's height: she would
    have ta'en
Achilles by the hair and bent his neck;
30 Or with a finger stay'd Ixion's wheel.
Her face was large as that of Memphian
    sphinx,
Pedestal'd haply in a palace court,
When sages look'd to Egypt for their
    lore.
But oh! how unlike marble was that face:
35 How beautiful, if sorrow had not made
Sorrow more beautiful than Beauty's self.
There was a listening fear in her regard,[1]
As if calamity had but begun;
As if the vanward clouds of evil days
40 Had spent their malice, and the sullen
    rear
Was with its stored thunder laboring up.
One hand she press'd upon that aching
    spot
Where beats the human heart, as if just
    there,
Though an immortal, she felt cruel pain:
45 The other upon Saturn's bended neck
She laid, and to the level of his ear
Leaning with parted lips, some words she
    spake
In solemn tenor and deep organ tone:
Some mourning words, which in our feeble
    tongue
50 Would come in these like accents; O how
    frail
To that large utterance of the early Gods!
"Saturn, look up!—though wherefore,
    poor old King?
I have no comfort for thee, no not one:
I cannot say, 'O wherefore sleepest thou?'
55 For heaven is parted from thee, and the
    earth
Knows thee not, thus afflicted, for a God;
And ocean too, with all its solemn noise,
Has from thy sceptre pass'd; and all the
    air
Is emptied of thine hoary majesty.
60 Thy thunder, conscious of the new com-
    mand,
Rumbles reluctant o'er our fallen house;
And thy sharp lightning in unpractis'd
    hands
Scorches and burns our once serene do-
    main.
O aching time! O moments big as years!
[1] look; aspect

65 All as ye pass swell out the monstrous
    truth,
And press it so upon our weary griefs
That unbelief has not a space to breathe.
Saturn, sleep on:—O thoughtless, why
    did I
70 Thus violate thy slumbrous solitude?
Why should I ope thy melancholy eyes?
Saturn, sleep on! while at thy feet I
    weep.''

    As when, upon a tranced summer-night,
Those green-rob'd senators of mighty
    woods,
Tall oaks, branch-charmed by the earnest
    stars,
75 Dream, and so dream all night without a
    stir,
Save from one gradual solitary gust
Which comes upon the silence, and dies
    off,
As if the ebbing air had but one wave;
So came these words and went; the while
    in tears
80 She touch'd her fair large forehead to the
    ground,
Just where her falling hair might be out-
    spread
A soft and silken mat for Saturn's feet.
One moon, with alteration slow, had shed
Her silver seasons four upon the night,
85 And still these two were postured motion-
    less,
Like natural sculpture in cathedral cavern;
The frozen God still couchant on the
    earth,
And the sad Goddess weeping at his feet:
Until at length old Saturn lifted up
90 His faded eyes, and saw his kingdom
    gone,
And all the gloom and sorrow of the place,
And that fair kneeling Goddess; and then
    spake,
As with a palsied tongue, and while his
    beard
Shook horrid with such aspen-malady:
95 "O tender spouse of gold Hyperion,
Thea, I feel thee ere I see thy face;
Look up, and let me see our doom in it;
Look up, and tell me if this feeble shape
Is Saturn's; tell me, if thou hear'st the
    voice
100 Of Saturn; tell me, if this wrinkling
    brow,
Naked and bare of its great diadem,
Peers like the front of Saturn. Who
    had power
To make me desolate? whence came the
    strength?

How was it nurtur'd to such bursting
    forth,
105 While Fate seem'd strangled in my nerv-
    ous grasp?
But it is so; and I am smother'd up,
And buried from all godlike exercise
Of influence benign on planets pale,
Of admonitions to the winds and seas,
110 Of peaceful sway above man's harvesting,
And all those acts which Deity supreme
Doth ease its heart of love in.—I am gone
Away from my own bosom: I have left
My strong identity, my real self,
115 Somewhere between the throne, and where
    I sit
Here on this spot of earth. Search, Thea,
    search!
Open thine eyes eterne, and sphere them
    round
Upon all space: space starr'd, and lorn of
    light;
Space region'd with life-air; and barren
    void;
120 Spaces of fire, and all the yawn of hell.—
Search, Thea, search! and tell me, if thou
    seest
A certain shape or shadow, making way
With wings or chariot fierce to repossess
A heaven he lost erewhile: it must—it
    must
125 Be of ripe progress—Saturn must be King.
Yes, there must be a golden victory;
There must be Gods thrown down, and
    trumpets blown
Of triumph calm, and hymns of festival
Upon the gold clouds metropolitan,
130 Voices of soft proclaim, and silver stir
Of strings in hollow shells; and there shall
    be
Beautiful things made new, for the sur-
    prise
Of the sky-children; I will give command:
Thea! Thea! Thea! where is Saturn?''

135   This passion lifted him upon his feet,
And made his hands to struggle in the
    air,
His Druid locks to shake and ooze with
    sweat,
His eyes to fever out, his voice to cease.
He stood, and heard not Thea's sobbing
    deep;
140 A little time, and then again he snatch'd
Utterance thus.—''But cannot I create?
Cannot I form? Cannot I fashion forth
Another world, another universe,
To overbear and crumble this to naught?
145 Where is another chaos? Where?''—
    That word

Found way unto Olympus, and made
    quake
The rebel three.[1]—Thea was startled up,
And in her bearing was a sort of hope,
As thus she quick-voic'd spake, yet full
    of awe.

150 ''This cheers our fallen house: come to
    our friends,
O Saturn! come away, and give them
    heart;
I know the covert, for thence came I
    hither.''
Thus brief; then with beseeching eyes she
    went
With backward footing through the shade
    a space:
155 He follow'd, and she turn'd to lead the
    way
Through aged boughs, that yielded like
    the mist
Which eagles cleave upmounting from
    their nest.

    Meanwhile in other realms big tears
    were shed,
More sorrow like to this, and such like
    woe,
160 Too huge for mortal tongue or pen of
    scribe:
The Titans fierce, self-hid, or prison-
    bound,
Groan'd for the old allegiance once more,
And listen'd in sharp pain for Saturn's
    voice.
But one of the whole mammoth-brood still
    kept
165 His sov'reignty, and rule, and majesty;—
Blazing Hyperion on his orbed fire
Still sat, still snuff'd the incense, teeming
    up
From man to the sun's God; yet insecure:
For as among us mortals omens drear
170 Fright and perplex, so also shuddered he—
Not at dog's howl, or gloom-bird's[2] hated
    screech,
Or the familiar visiting of one
Upon the first toll of his passing-bell,
Or prophesyings of the midnight lamp;
175 But horrors, portion'd to a giant nerve,
Oft made Hyperion ache. His palace
    bright
Bastion'd with pyramids of glowing gold,
And touch'd with shade of bronzed obe-
    lisks,
Glar'd a blood-red through all its thou-
    sand courts,

---

[1] Jupiter, Pluto, and Neptune, who had rebelled
  against their father Saturn (Cronus).
[2] owl's

¹⁸⁰ Arches, and domes, and fiery galleries;
And all its curtains of Aurorian[1] clouds
Flush'd angerly: while sometimes eagle's wings,
Unseen before by Gods or wondering men,
Darken'd the place; and neighing steeds were heard,
¹⁸⁵ Not heard before by Gods or wondering men.
Also, when he would taste the spicy wreaths
Of incense, breath'd aloft from sacred hills,
Instead of sweets, his ample palate took
Savor of poisonous brass and metal sick:
¹⁹⁰ And so, when harbor'd in the sleepy west,
After the full completion of fair day,—
For rest divine upon exalted couch
And slumber in the arms of melody,
He pac'd away the pleasant hours of ease
¹⁹⁵ With stride colossal, on from hall to hall;
While far within each aisle and deep recess,
His winged minions in close clusters stood,
Amaz'd and full of fear; like anxious men
Who on wide plains gather in panting troops,
²⁰⁰ When earthquakes jar their battlements and towers.
Even now, while Saturn, rous'd from icy trance,
Went step for step with Thea through the woods,
Hyperion, leaving twilight in the rear,
Came slope upon the threshold of the west;
²⁰⁵ Then, as was wont, his palace-door flew ope
In smoothest silence, save what solemn tubes,
Blown by the serious Zephyrs, gave of sweet
And wandering sounds, slow-breathed melodies;
And like a rose in vermeil tint and shape,
²¹⁰ In fragrance soft, and coolness to the eye,
That inlet to severe magnificence
Stood full blown, for the God to enter in.

He enter'd, but he enter'd full of wrath;
His flaming robes stream'd out beyond his heels,
²¹⁵ And gave a roar, as if of earthly fire,
That scar'd away the meek ethereal Hours
And made their dove-wings tremble. On he flared,

---

¹ pertaining to Aurora, goddess of the dawn

From stately nave to nave, from vault to vault,
Through bowers of fragrant and enwreathed light,
²²⁰ And diamond-paved lustrous long arcades,
Until he reach'd the great main cupola;
There standing fierce beneath, he stamp'd his foot,
And from the basements deep to the high towers
Jarr'd his own golden region; and before
²²⁵ The quavering thunder thereupon had ceas'd,
His voice leapt out, despite of godlike curb,
To this result: "O dreams of day and night!
O monstrous forms! O effigies of pain!
O spectres busy in a cold, cold gloom!
²³⁰ O lank-ear'd Phantoms of black-weeded pools!
Why do I know ye? why have I seen ye? why
Is my eternal essence thus distraught
To see and to behold these horrors new?
Saturn is fallen, am I too to fall?
²³⁵ Am I to leave this haven of my rest,
This cradle of my glory, this soft clime,
This calm luxuriance of blissful light,
These crystalline pavilions, and pure fanes,
Of all my lucent empire? It is left
²⁴⁰ Deserted, void, nor any haunt of mine.
The blaze, the splendor, and the symmetry,
I cannot see—but darkness, death and darkness.
Even here, into my centre of repose,
The shady visions come to domineer,
²⁴⁵ Insult, and blind, and stifle up my pomp.—
Fall!—No, by Tellus and her briny robes!
Over the fiery frontier of my realms
I will advance[1] a terrible right arm
Shall scare that infant thunderer, rebel Jove,
²⁵⁰ And bid old Saturn take his throne again."—
He spake, and ceas'd, the while a heavier threat
Held struggle with his throat but came not forth;
For as in theatres of crowded men
Hubbub increases more they call out "Hush!"
²⁵⁵ So at Hyperion's words the Phantoms pale
Bestirr'd themselves, thrice horrible and cold;
And from the mirror'd level where he stood
A mist arose, as from a scummy marsh.
At this, through all his bulk an agony

---

¹ lift up

260 Crept gradual, from the feet unto the
crown,
Like a lithe serpent vàst and muscular
Making slow way, with head and neck
convuls'd
From over-strained might. Releas'd, he
fled
To the eastern gates, and full six dewy
hours
265 Before the dawn in season due should
blush,
He breath'd fierce breath against the sleepy
portals,
Clear'd them of heavy vapors, burst them
wide
Suddenly on the ocean's chilly streams.
The planet orb of fire, whereon he rode
270 Each day from east to west the heavens
through,
Spun round in sable curtaining of clouds;
Not therefore veiled quite, blindfold, and
hid,
But ever and anon the glancing spheres,
Circles, and arcs, and broad-belting colure,[1]
275 Glow'd through, and wrought upon the
muffling dark
Sweet-shaped lightnings from the nadir[2]
deep
Up to the zenith,—hieroglyphics old
Which sages and keen-eyed astrologers
Then living on the earth, with laboring
thought
280 Won from the gaze of many centuries:
Now lost, save what we find on remnants
huge
Of stone, or marble swart; their import
gone,
Their wisdom long since fled.—Two wings
this orb
Possess'd for glory, two fair argent[3] wings,
285 Ever exalted at the God's approach:
And now, from forth the gloom their
plumes immense
Rose, one by one, till all outspreaded were;
While still the dazzling globe maintain'd
eclipse,
Awaiting for Hyperion's command.
290 Fain would he have commanded, fain took
throne
And bid the day begin, if but for change.
He might not:—No, though a primeval
God:
The sacred seasons might not be disturb'd.
Therefore the operations of the dawn

295 Stay'd in their birth, even as here 'tis told.
Those silver wings expanded sisterly,
Eager to sail their orb; the porches wide
Open'd upon the dusk demesnes of night;
And the bright Titan, frenzied with new
woes,
300 Unus'd to bend, by hard compulsion bent
His spirit to the sorrow of the time;
And all along a dismal rack of clouds,
Upon the boundaries of day and night,
He stretch'd himself in grief and radiance
faint.
305 There as he lay, the Heaven with its stars
Look'd down on him with pity, and the
voice
Of Cœlus, from the universal space,
Thus whisper'd low and solemn in his ear.
"O brightest of my children dear, earth-
born
310 And sky-engendered, Son of Mysteries
All unrevealed even to the powers
Which met at thy creating; at whose joys
And palpitations sweet, and pleasures soft,
I, Cœlus, wonder, how they came and
whence;
315 And at the fruits thereof what shapes they
be,
Distinct, and visible; symbols divine,
Manifestations of that beauteous life
Diffus'd unseen throughout eternal space:
Of these new-form'd art thou, oh brightest
child!
320 Of these, thy brethren and the Goddesses!
There is sad feud among ye, and rebellion
Of son against his sire. I saw him fall,
I saw my first-born[1] tumbled from his
throne!
To me his arms were spread, to me his voice
325 Found way from forth the thunders round
his head!
Pale wox[2] I, and in vapors hid my face.
Art thou, too, near such doom? vague fear
there is:
For I have seen my sons most unlike Gods.
Divine ye were created, and divine
330 In sad demeanor, solemn, undisturb'd,
Unruffled, like high Gods, ye liv'd and
ruled:
Now I behold in you fear, hope, and wrath;
Actions of rage and passion; even as
I see them, on the mortal world beneath,
335 In men who die.—This is the grief, O Son!
Sad sign of ruin, sudden dismay, and fall!
Yet do thou strive; as thou art capable,
As thou canst move about, an evident God;
And canst oppose to each malignant hour
340 Ethereal presence:—I am but a voice;
My life is but the life of winds and tides,

---

[1] One of the two great circles which surround the celestial sphere at right angles to each other.
[2] lowest point of the celestial sphere, directly opposite the zenith
[3] silver; shining

[1] Saturn.   [2] waxed; grew

No more than winds and tides can I
    avail:—
But thou canst.—Be thou therefore in the
    van
Of circumstance; yea, seize the arrow's
    barb
345 Before the tense string murmur.—To the
    earth!
For there thou wilt find Saturn, and his
    woes.
Meantime I will keep watch on thy bright
    sun,
And of thy seasons be a careful nurse.''—
Ere half this region-whisper had come
    down,
350 Hyperion arose, and on the stars
Lifted his curved lids, and kept them wide
Until it ceas'd; and still he kept them wide:
And still they were the same bright, patient
    stars.
Then with a slow incline of his broad
    breast,
355 Like to a diver in the pearly seas,
Forward he stoop'd over the airy shore,
And plung'd all noiseless into the deep
    night.

Book II

Just at the self-same beat of Time's wide
    wings
Hyperion slid into the rustled air,
And Saturn gain'd with Thea that sad
    place
Where Cybele and the bruis'd Titans
    mourn'd.
5 It was a den where no insulting light
Could glimmer on their tears; where their
    own groans
They felt, but heard not, for the solid roar
Of thunderous waterfalls and torrents
    hoarse,
Pouring a constant bulk, uncertain where.
10 Crag jutting forth to crag, and rocks that
    seem'd
Ever as if just rising from a sleep,
Forehead to forehead with their monstrous
    horns;
And thus in thousand hugest phantasies
Made a fit roofing to this nest of woe.
15 Instead of thrones, hard flint they sat
    upon,
Couches of rugged stone, and slaty ridge
Stubborn'd with iron. All were not as-
    sembled:
Some chain'd in torture, and some wander-
    ing.
Cœus, and Gyges, and Briareüs,
20 Typhon, and Dolor, and Porphyrion,

With many more, the brawniest in assault,
Were pent in regions of laborious breath;
Dungeon'd in opaque element, to keep
Their clenched teeth still clench'd, and all
    their limbs
25 Lock'd up like veins of metal, crampt and
    screw'd;
Without a motion, save of their big hearts
Heaving in pain, and horribly convuls'd
With sanguine, feverous, boiling gurge[1]
    of pulse.
Mnemosyne was straying in the world;
30 Far from her moon had Phœbe wandered;
And many else were free to roam abroad,
But for the main, here found they covert
    drear.
Scarce images of life, one here, one there,
Lay vast and edgeways; like a dismal
    cirque
35 Of Druid stones, upon a forlorn moor,
When the chill rain begins at shut of eve,
In dull November, and their chancel vault,
The Heaven itself, is blinded throughout
    night.
Each one kept shroud, nor to his neighbor
    gave
40 Or word, or look, or action of despair.
Creüs was one; his ponderous iron mace
Lay by him, and a shatter'd rib of rock
Told of his rage, ere he thus sank and
    pined.
Iäpetus another; in his grasp,
45 A serpent's plashy[2] neck; its barbed
    tongue
Squeez'd from the gorge, and all its un-
    curl'd length
Dead; and because the creature could not
    spit
Its poison in the eyes of conquering Jove.
Next Cottus: prone he lay, chin upper-
    most,
50 As though in pain; for still upon the flint
He ground severe his skull, with open
    mouth
And eyes at horrid working. Nearest him
Asia, born of most enormous Caf,
Who cost her mother Tellus keener pangs,
55 Though feminine, than any of her sons:
More thought than woe was in her dusky
    face,
For she was prophesying of her glory;
And in her wide imagination stood
Palm-shaded temples, and high rival fanes,
60 By Oxus or in Ganges' sacred isles.
Even as Hope upon her anchor leans,[3]
So leant she, not so fair, upon a tusk
Shed from the broadest of her elephants.

[1] whirlpool
[2] speckled

[3] See *Hebrews*, 6:19.

Above her, on a crag's uneasy shelve,
65 Upon his elbow rais'd, all prostrate else,
Shadow'd Enceladus; once tame and mild
As grazing ox unworried in the meads;
Now tiger-passion'd, lion-thoughted,
      wroth,
He meditated, plotted, and even now
70 Was hurling mountains in that second
      war,[1]
Not long delay'd, that scar'd the younger
      Gods
To hide themselves in forms of beast and
      bird.
Not far hence Atlas; and beside him prone
Phorcus, the sire of Gorgons. Neighbor'd
      close
75 Oceanus, and Tethys, in whose lap
Sobb'd Clymene among her tangled hair.
In midst of all lay Themis, at the feet
Of Ops the queen all clouded round from
      sight;
No shape distinguishable, more than when
80 Thick night confounds the pine-tops with
      the clouds:
And many else whose names may not be
      told.
For when the Muse's wings are air-ward
      spread,
Who shall delay her flight? And she must
      chant
Of Saturn, and his guide, who now had
      climb'd
85 With damp and slippery footing from a
      depth
More horrid still. Above a sombre cliff
Their heads appear'd, and up their stature
      grew
Till on the level height their steps found
      ease:
Then Thea spread abroad her trembling
      arms
90 Upon the precincts of this nest of pain,
And sidelong fix'd her eye on Saturn's
      face:
There saw she direst strife; the supreme
      God
At war with all the frailty of grief,
Of rage, or fear, anxiety, revenge,
95 Remorse, spleen, hope, but most of all
      despair.
Against these plagues he strove in vain;
      for Fate
Had pour'd a mortal oil upon his head,
A disanointing poison: so that Thea,
Affrighted, kept her still, and let him pass
00 First onwards in, among the fallen tribe.

[1] The war of the Giants against the Olympian gods. The Giants clothed themselves in the skins of beasts and birds.

As with us mortal men, the laden heart
Is persecuted more, and fever'd more,
When it is nighing to the mournful house
Where other hearts are sick of the same
      bruise;
105 So Saturn, as he walk'd into the midst,
Felt faint, and would have sunk among
      the rest,
But that he met Enceladus's eye,
Whose mightiness, and awe of him, at once
Came like an inspiration; and he shouted,
110 "Titans, behold your God!" at which
      some groan'd;
Some started on their feet; some also
      shouted;
Some wept, some wail'd,—all bow'd with
      reverence;
And Ops, uplifting her black folded veil,
Show'd her pale cheeks, and all her fore-
      head wan,
115 Her eyebrows thin and jet, and hollow
      eyes.
There is a roaring in the bleak-grown pines
When Winter lifts his voice; there is a
      noise
Among immortals when a God gives sign,
With hushing finger, how he means to load
120 His tongue with the full weight of utter-
      less thought,
With thunder, and with music, and with
      pomp:
Such noise is like the roar of bleak-grown
      pines;
Which, when it ceases in this mountain'd
      world,
No other sound succeeds; but ceasing here,
125 Among these fallen, Saturn's voice there-
      from
Grew up like organ, that begins anew
Its strain, when other harmonies, stopt
      short,
Leave the dinn'd air vibrating silverly.
Thus grew it up—"Not in my own sad
      breast,
130 Which is its own great judge and searcher
      out,
Can I find reason why ye should be thus:
Not in the legends of the first of days,
Studied from that old spirit-leaved book
Which starry Uranus with finger bright
135 Sav'd from the shores of darkness, when
      the waves
Low-ebb'd still hid it up in shallow
      gloom;—
And the which book ye know I ever kept
For my firm-based footstool.—Ah, infirm!
Not there, nor in sign, symbol, or portent
140 Of element, earth, water, air, and fire,—
At war, at peace, or inter-quarreling

One against one, or two, or three, or all
Each several one against the other three,
As fire with air loud warring when rain-
  floods
145 Drown both, and press them both against
  earth's face,
Where, finding sulphur, a quadruple wrath
Unhinges the poor world;—not in that
  strife,
Wherefrom I take strange lore, and read
  it deep,
Can I find reason why ye should be thus:
150 No, nowhere can unriddle, though I search,
And pore on Nature's universal scroll
Even to swooning, why ye, Divinities,
The first-born of all shap'd and palpable
  Gods,
Should cower beneath what, in comparison,
155 Is untremendous might. Yet ye are here,
O 'erwhelm'd, and spurn'd, and batter'd,
  ye are here!
O Titans, shall I say, 'Arise!'—Ye groan:
Shall I say 'Crouch!'—Ye groan. What
  can I then?
O Heaven wide! O unseen parent dear!
160 What can I? Tell me, all ye brethren Gods,
How we can war, how engine[1] our great
  wrath!
O speak your counsel now, for Saturn's ear
Is all a-hunger'd. Thou, Oceanus,
Ponderest high and deep; and in thy face
165 I see, astonied, that severe content
Which comes of thought and musing: give
  us help!''

  So ended Saturn; and the God of the
    Sea,
Sophist and sage, from no Athenian grove,
But cogitation in his watery shades,
170 Arose, with locks not oozy, and began,
In murmurs, which his first-endeavoring
  tongue
Caught infant-like from the far-foamed
  sands.
"O ye, whom wrath consumes! who,
  passion-stung,
Writhe at defeat, and nurse your agonies!
175 Shut up your senses, stifle up your ears,
My voice is not a bellows unto ire.
Yet listen, ye who will, whilst I bring proof
How ye, perforce, must be content to stoop:
And in the proof much comfort will I give,
180 If ye will take that comfort in its truth.
We fall by course of Nature's law, not
  force
Of thunder, or of Jove. Great Saturn,
  thou
Hast sifted well the atom-universe;

[1] plan; execute

But for this reason, that thou art the King,
185 And only blind from sheer supremacy,
One avenue was shaded from thine eyes,
Through which I wandered to eternal truth.
And first, as thou wast not the first of
  powers,
So art thou not the last; it cannot be:
190 Thou are not the beginning nor the end.
From chaos and parental darkness came
Light, the first fruits of that intestine broil,
That sullen ferment, which for wondrous
  ends
Was ripening in itself. The ripe hour
  came,
195 And with it light, and light, engendering
Upon its own producer, forthwith touch'd
The whole enormous matter into life.
Upon that very hour, our parentage,
The Heavens and the Earth, were mani-
  fest:
200 Then thou first-born, and we the giant-race,
Found ourselves ruling new and beauteous
  realms.
Now comes the pain of truth, to whom 'tis
  pain;
O folly! for to bear all naked truths,
And to envisage circumstance, all calm,
205 That is the top of sovereignty. Mark well!
As Heaven and Earth are fairer, fairer far
Than Chaos and blank Darkness, though
  once chiefs;
And as we show beyond that Heaven and
  Earth
In form and shape compact and beautiful,
210 In will, in action free, companionship,
And thousand other signs of purer life;
So on our heels a fresh perfection treads,
A power more strong in beauty, born of us
And fated to excel us, as we pass
215 In glory that old Darkness: nor are we
Thereby more conquer'd, than by us the
  rule
Of shapeless Chaos. Say, doth the dull soil
Quarrel with the proud forests it hath fed,
And feedeth still, more comely than itself?
220 Can it deny the chiefdom of green groves?
Or shall the tree be envious of the dove
Because it cooeth, and hath snowy wings
To wander wherewithal and find its joys?
We are such forest-trees, and our fair
  boughs
225 Have bred forth, not pale solitary doves,
But eagles golden-feather'd, who do tower
Above us in their beauty, and must reign
In right thereof; for 'tis the eternal law
That first in beauty should be first in
  might:[1]

[1] See Keats's *Ode on a Grecian Urn*, 49-50 (p.
  854); also his letter to Bailey (p. 888a, 1).

230 Yea, by that law, another race may drive
Our conquerors to mourn as we do now.
Have ye beheld the young God of the
Seas,[1]
My dispossessor? Have ye seen his face?
Have ye beheld his chariot, foam'd along
235 By noble winged creatures he hath made?
I saw him on the calmed waters scud,
With such a glow of beauty in his eyes,
That it enforc'd me to bid sad farewell
To all my empire: farewell sad I took,
240 And hither came, to see how dolorous fate
Had wrought upon ye; and how I might
best
Give consolation in this woe extreme.
Receive the truth, and let it be your balm.''

Whether through poz'd[2] conviction, or
disdain,
245 They guarded silence, when Oceanus
Left murmuring, what deepest thought can
tell?
But so it was, none answer'd for a space,
Save one whom none regarded, Clymene;
And yet she answer'd not, only com-
plain'd,
250 With hectic lips, and eyes up-looking mild,
Thus wording timidly among the fierce:
''O Father, I am here the simplest voice,
And all my knowledge is that joy is gone,
And this thing woe crept in among our
hearts,
255 There to remain forever, as I fear:
I would not bode of evil, if I thought
So weak a creature could turn off the help
Which by just right should come of mighty
Gods;
Yet let me tell my sorrow, let me tell
260 Of what I heard, and how it made me weep,
And know that we had parted from all
hope.
I stood upon a shore, a pleasant shore,
Where a sweet clime was breathed from a
land
Of fragrance, quietness, and trees, and
flowers.
265 Full of calm joy it was, as I of grief;
Too full of joy, and soft delicious warmth;
So that I felt a movement in my heart
To chide, and to reproach that solitude
With songs of misery, music of our woes;
270 And sat me down, and took a mouthed
shell[3]
And murmur'd into it, and made melody—
O melody no more! for while I sang,
And with poor skill let pass into the breeze

The dull shell's echo, from a bowery strand
275 Just opposite, an island of the sea,
There came enchantment with the shifting
wind,
That did both drown and keep alive my
ears.
I threw my shell away upon the sand,
And a wave fill'd it, as my sense was fill'd
280 With that new blissful golden melody.
A living death was in each gush of sounds,
Each family of rapturous hurried notes,
That fell, one after one, yet all at once,
Like pearl beads dropping sudden from
their string:
285 And then another, then another strain,
Each like a dove leaving its olive perch,
With music wing'd instead of silent
plumes,
To hover round my head, and make me sick
Of joy and grief at once. Grief overcame,
290 And I was stopping up my frantic ears,
When, past all hindrance of my trembling
hands,
A voice came sweeter, sweeter than all tune,
And still it cried, 'Apollo! young Apollo!
The morning-bright Apollo! young Apollo!'
295 I fled, it follow'd me, and cried 'Apollo!'
O Father, and O Brethren, had ye felt
Those pains of mine; O Saturn, hadst
thou felt,
Ye would not call this too-indulged tongue
Presumptuous, in thus venturing to be
heard.''

300 So far her voice flow'd on, like timorous
brook
That, lingering along a pebbled coast,
Doth fear to meet the sea: but sea it met,
And shudder'd; for the overwhelming
voice
Of huge Enceladus swallow'd it in wrath:
305 The ponderous syllables, like sullen waves
In the half-glutted hollows of reef-rocks,
Came booming thus, while still upon his
arm
He lean'd; not rising, from supreme con-
tempt.
''Or shall we listen to the over-wise,
310 Or to the over-foolish, giant Gods?
Not thunderbolt on thunderbolt, till all
That rebel Jove's whole armory were spent,
Not world on world upon these shoulders
piled,
Could agonize me more than baby-words
315 In midst of this dethronement horrible.
Speak! roar! shout! yell! ye sleepy Titans
all.
Do ye forget the blows, the buffets vile?
Are ye not smitten by a youngling arm?

---

[1] Neptune.　　[2] beaten; overcome
[3] lyre (The first lyre is said to have been made
from a tortoise shell.)

Dost thou forget, sham Monarch of the
 Waves,
320 Thy scalding in the seas? What! have I
 rous'd
Your spleens with so few simple words as
 these?
O joy! for now I see ye are not lost:
O joy! for now I see a thousand eyes
Wide-glaring for revenge!''—As this he
 said,
325 He lifted up his stature vast, and stood,
Still without intermission speaking thus:
''Now ye are flames, I'll tell you how to
 burn,
And purge the ether[1] of our enemies;
How to feed fierce the crooked stings of
 fire,
330 And singe away the swollen clouds of Jove,
Stifling that puny essence in its tent.
O let him feel the evil he hath done;
For though I scorn Oceanus's lore,
Much pain have I for more than loss of
 realms:
335 The days of peace and slumberous calm
 are fled;
Those days, all innocent of scathing war,
When all the fair Existences of heaven
Came open-eyed to guess what we would
 speak:—
That was before our brows were taught to
 frown,
340 Before our lips knew else but solemn
 sounds;
That was before we knew the winged thing,
Victory, might be lost, or might be won.
And be ye mindful that Hyperion,
Our brightest brother, still is undisgraced—
345 Hyperion, lo! his radiance is here!''

 All eyes were on Enceladus's face,
And they beheld, while still Hyperion's
 name
Flew from his lips up to the vaulted rocks,
A pallid gleam across his features stern:
350 Not savage, for he saw full many a God
Wroth as himself. He look'd upon them
 all,
And in each face he saw a gleam of light,
But splendider in Saturn's, whose hoar
 locks
Shone like the bubbling foam about a keel
355 When the prow sweeps into a midnight
 cove.
In pale and silver silence they remain'd,
Till suddenly a splendor, like the morn,
Pervaded all the beetling gloomy steeps,
All the sad spaces of oblivion,
360 And every gulf, and every chasm old,
[1] upper regions

And every height, and every sullen depth,
Voiceless, or hoarse with loud tormented
 streams:
And all the everlasting cataracts,
And all the headlong torrents far and
 near,
365 Mantled before in darkness and huge
 shade,
Now saw the light and made it terrible.
It was Hyperion:—a granite peak
His bright feet touch'd, and there he stay'd
 to view
The misery his brilliance had betray'd
370 To the most hateful seeing of itself.
Golden his hair of short Numidian curl,
Regal his shape majestic, a vast shade
In midst of his own brightness, like the
 bulk
Of Memnon's image at the set of sun
375 To one who travels from the dusking East:
Sighs, too, as mournful as that Memnon's
 harp,[1]
He utter'd, while his hands contemplative
He press'd together, and in silence stood.
Despondence seiz'd again the fallen Gods
380 At sight of the dejected King of Day,
And many hid their faces from the light:
But fierce Enceladus sent forth his eyes
Among the brotherhood; and, at their
 glare,
Uprose Iäpetus, and Creüs too,
385 And Phorcus, sea-born, and together strode
To where he towered on his eminence.
There those four shouted forth old Sat-
 urn's name;
Hyperion from the peak loud answered,
 ''Saturn!''
Saturn sat near the Mother of the Gods,[2]
390 In whose face was no joy, though all the
 Gods
Gave from their hollow throats the name
 of ''Saturn!''

Book III

Thus in alternate uproar and sad peace,
Amazed were those Titans utterly.
O leave them, Muse! O leave them to their
 woes;
For thou art weak to sing such tumults
 dire:
5 A solitary sorrow best befits
Thy lips, and antheming a lonely grief.
Leave them, O Muse! for thou anon wilt
 find

[1] The Egyptian statue of Memnon, when struck
 by the first rays of the sun, was said to give
 forth a sound like the snapping of a musical
 string.
[2] Ops (Rhea).

Many a fallen old Divinity
Wandering in vain about bewildered shores.
10 Meantime touch piously the Delphic harp,
And not a wind of heaven but will breathe
In aid soft warble from the Dorian flute;
For lo! 'tis for the Father of all verse.
Flush every thing that hath a vermeil hue,
15 Let the rose glow intense and warm the air,
And let the clouds of even and of morn
Float in voluptuous fleeces o'er the hills;
Let the red wine within the goblet boil,
Cold as a bubbling well; let faint-lipp'd
      shells,
20 On sands, or in great deeps, vermilion turn
Through all their labyrinths; and let the
      maid
Blush keenly, as with some warm kiss sur-
      pris'd.
Chief isle of the embowered Cyclades,
Rejoice, O Delos, with thine olives green,
25 And poplars, and lawn-shading palms, and
      beech,
In which the Zephyr breathes the loudest
      song,
And hazels thick, dark-stemm'd beneath
      the shade:
Apollo is once more the golden theme!
Where was he, when the Giant of the
      Sun[1]
30 Stood bright, amid the sorrow of his peers?
Together had he left his mother fair
And his twin-sister sleeping in their bower,
And in the morning twilight wandered
      forth
Beside the osiers[2] of a rivulet,
35 Full ankle-deep in lilies of the vale.
The nightingale had ceas'd, and a few stars
Were lingering in the heavens, while the
      thrush
Began calm-throated. Throughout all the
      isle
There was no covert, no retired cave
40 Unhaunted by the murmurous noise of
      waves,
Though scarcely heard in many a green
      recess.
He listen'd, and he wept, and his bright
      tears
Went trickling down the golden bow he
      held.
Thus with half-shut suffused eyes he stood,
45 While from beneath some cumbrous boughs
      hard by
With solemn step an awful Goddess came,
And there was purport in her looks for
      him,
Which he with eager guess began to read
Perplex'd, the while melodiously he said:

[1] Hyperion.   [2] willows

50 "How cam'st thou over the unfooted sea?
Or hath that antique mien and robed form
Mov'd in these vales invisible till now?[1]
Sure I have heard those vestments sweep-
      ing o'er
The fallen leaves, when I have sat alone
55 In cool mid-forest. Surely I have traced
The rustle of those ample skirts about
These grassy solitudes, and seen the flowers
Lift up their heads, as still the whisper
      pass'd.
Goddess! I have beheld those eyes before,
60 And their eternal calm, and all that face,
Or I have dream'd."—"Yes," said the
      supreme shape,
"Thou hast dream'd of me; and awaking
      up
Didst find a lyre all golden by thy side,
Whose strings touch'd by thy fingers, all
      the vast
65 Unwearied ear of the whole universe
Listen'd in pain and pleasure at the birth
Of such new tuneful wonder. Is't not
      strange
That thou shouldst weep, so gifted? Tell
      me, youth,
What sorrow thou canst feel; for I am sad
70 When thou dost shed a tear: explain thy
      griefs
To one who in this lonely isle hath been
The watcher of thy sleep and hours of life,
From the young day when first thy infant
      hand
Pluck'd witless the weak flowers, till thine
      arm
75 Could bend that bow heroic to all times.
Show thy heart's secret to an ancient
      Power
Who hath forsaken old and sacred thrones
For prophecies of thee, and for the sake
Of loveliness new born."—Apollo then,
80 With sudden scrutiny and gloomless eyes,
Thus answer'd, while his white melodious
      throat
Throbb'd with the syllables.—"Mnemos-
      yne!
Thy name is on my tongue, I know not
      how;
Why should I tell thee what thou so well
      seest?
85 Why should I strive to show what from thy
      lips
Would come no mystery? For me, dark,
      dark,
And painful vile oblivion seals my eyes:
I strive to search wherefore I am so sad,
Until a melancholy numbs my limbs;

[1] Possibly reminiscent of the *Odyssey*, 1. 173 ff.

90 And then upon the grass I sit, and moan,
Like one who once had wings.—O why should I
Feel curs'd and thwarted, when the liege-less air
Yields to my step aspirant? why should I
Spurn the green turf as hateful to my feet?
95 Goddess benign, point forth some unknown thing:
Are there not other regions than this isle?
What are the stars? There is the sun, the sun!
And the most patient brilliance of the moon!
And stars by thousands! Point me out the way
100 To any one particular beauteous star,
And I will fit into it with my lyre,
And make its silvery splendor pant with bliss.
I have heard the cloudy thunder: Where is power?
Whose hand, whose essence, what divinity
105 Makes this alarum in the elements,
While I here idle listen on the shores
In fearless yet in aching ignorance?
O tell me, lonely Goddess, by thy harp,
That waileth every morn and eventide,
110 Tell me why thus I rave, about these groves!
Mute thou remainest—mute! yet I can read
A wondrous lesson in thy silent face:
Knowledge enormous makes a God of me.
Names, deeds, gray legends, dire events, rebellions,
115 Majesties, sovran voices, agonies,
Creations and destroyings, all at once
Pour into the wide hollows of my brain,
And deify me, as if some blithe wine
Or bright elixir peerless I had drunk,
120 And so become immortal.''—Thus the God,
While his enkindling eyes, with level glance
Beneath his white soft temples, steadfast kept
Trembling with light upon Mnemosyne.
Soon wild commotions shook him, and made flush
125 All the immortal fairness of his limbs;
Most like the struggle at the gate of death;
Or liker still to one who should take leave
Of pale immortal death, and with a pang
As hot as death's is chill, with fierce convulse
130 Die into life: so young Apollo anguish'd:
His very hair, his golden tresses famed
Kept undulation round his eager neck.
During the pain Mnemosyne upheld
Her arms as one who prophesied. — At length

135 Apollo shriek'd;—and lo! from all his limbs
Celestial——

* * * * * *

TO AUTUMN
1819   1820

Season of mists and mellow fruitfulness,
Close bosom-friend of the maturing sun;
Conspiring with him how to load and bless
With fruit the vines that round the thatch-eaves run;
5 To bend with apples the moss'd cottage-trees,
And fill all fruit with ripeness to the core;
To swell the gourd, and plump the hazel shells
With a sweet kernel; to set budding more,
And still more, later flowers for the bees,
10 Until they think warm days will never cease,
For Summer has o'er-brimm'd their clammy cells.

Who hath not seen thee oft amid thy store?
Sometimes whoever seeks abroad may find
Thee sitting careless on a granary floor,
15 Thy hair soft-lifted by the winnowing wind;
Or on a half-reap'd furrow sound asleep,
Drows'd with the fume of poppies, while thy hook
Spares the next swath and all its twined flowers:
And sometimes like a gleaner thou dost keep
20 Steady thy laden head across a brook;
Or by a cider-press, with patient look,
Thou watchest the last oozings hours by hours.

Where are the songs of Spring? Ay, where are they?
Think not of them, thou hast thy music too,—
25 While barred clouds bloom the soft-dying day,
And touch the stubble-plains with rosy hue;
Then in a wailful choir the small gnats mourn
Among the river sallows,[1] borne aloft

[1] willows

Or sinking as the light wind lives or
dies;
30 And full-grown lambs loud bleat from
hilly bourn;[1]
Hedge-crickets sing; and now with
treble soft
The redbreast whistles from a garden-
croft;[2]
And gathering swallows twitter in
the skies.

TO FANNIE[3]
1819   1848

I cry your mercy—pity—love!—aye, love!
Merciful love that tantalizes not,
One-thoughted, never-wandering, guileless
love,
Unmask'd, and being seen—without a blot!
5 O! let me have thee whole,—all—all—be
mine!
That shape, that fairness, that sweet minor
zest
Of love, your kiss,—those hands, those eyes
divine,
That warm, white, lucent, million-pleasur'd
breast,—
Yourself—your soul—in pity give me all,
10 Withhold no atom's atom or I die,
Or living on perhaps, your wretched thrall,
Forget, in the mist of idle misery,
Life's purposes,—the palate of my mind
Losing its gust, and my ambition blind!

BRIGHT STAR, WOULD I WERE
STEADFAST AS THOU ART
1819-20   1848

Bright star, would I were steadfast as thou
art!
Not in lone splendor hung aloft the night,
And watching, with eternal lids apart,
Like Nature's patient, sleepless eremite,[4]
5 The moving waters at their priestlike task
Of pure ablution round earth's human
shores,
Or gazing on the new soft-fallen mask
Of snow upon the mountains and the
moors:
No—yet still steadfast, still unchangeable,
10 Pillow'd upon my fair love's ripening
breast,
To feel forever its soft fall and swell,
Awake forever in a sweet unrest,
Still, still to hear her tender-taken breath,
And so live ever—or else swoon to death.

[1] boundary (perhaps, region)
[2] small piece of enclosed ground
[3] Fanny Brawne, a young woman to whom Keats
was fondly devoted.
[4] hermit

From KEATS'S LETTERS
1816-20   1848-91

TO BENJAMIN BAILEY

[BURFORD BRIDGE, November 22, 1817.]

My dear Bailey—I will get over the first
part of this (*un*said) letter as soon as possible, for it relates to the affairs of poor
Cripps.—To a man of your nature such a
5 letter as Haydon's must have been extremely
cutting— What occasions the greater part
of the world's quarrels?— simply this—two
minds meet, and do not understand each
other time enough to prevent any shock or
10 surprise at the conduct of either party—
As soon as I had known Haydon three days,
I had got enough of his character not to
have been surprised at such a letter as he
has hurt you with. Nor, when I knew it, was
15 it a principle with me to drop his acquaintance; although with you it would have been
an imperious feeling.

I wish you knew all that I think about
genius and the heart—and yet I think that
20 you are thoroughly acquainted with my
innermost breast in that respect, or you
could not have known me even thus long,
and still hold me worthy to be your dear
friend. In passing, however, I must say one
25 thing that has pressed upon me lately, and
increased my humility and capability of submission—and that is this truth—men of genius are great as certain ethereal chemicals
operating on the mass of neutral intellect—
30 but they have not any individuality, any determined character—I would call the top
and head of those who have a proper self,[1]
men of power.

But I am running my head into a subject
35 which I am certain I could not do justice
to under five years' study, and 3 vols. octavo
—and, moreover, I long to be talking about
the imagination—so my dear Bailey, do not
think of this unpleasant affair, if possible
40 do not—I defy any harm to come of it—
I defy. I shall write to Cripps this week,
and request him to tell me all his goings-on
from time to time by letter wherever I may
be. It will go on well—so don't because
45 you have suddenly discovered a coldness in
Haydon suffer yourself to be teased—Do
not my dear fellow—O! I wish I was as
certain of the end of all your troubles as
that of your momentary start about the
50 authenticity of the imagination. I am certain of nothing but of the holiness of the
heart's affections, and the truth of imagination. What the imagination seizes as

[1] That is, those who have an individuality.

beauty must be truth[1]—whether it existed before or not,—for I have the same idea of all our passions as of love: they are all, in their sublime, creative of essential beauty. In a word, you may know my favorite speculation by my first Book, and the little Song[2] I sent in my last, which is a representation from the fancy of the probable mode of operating in these matters. The imagination may be compared to Adam's dream,—he awoke and found it truth:[3]—I am more zealous in this affair, because I have never yet been able to perceive how anything can be known for truth by consecutive reasoning—and yet it must be. Can it be that even the greatest philosopher ever arrived at his goal without putting aside numerous objections? However it may be, O for a life of sensations rather than of thoughts! It is "a vision in the form of youth," a shadow of reality to come—And this consideration has further convinced me,—for it has come as auxiliary to another favorite speculation of mine,—that we shall enjoy ourselves hereafter by having what we called happiness on earth repeated in a finer tone—And yet such a fate can only befall those who delight in sensation, rather than hunger as you do after truth. Adam's dream will do here, and seems to be a conviction that imagination and its empyreal reflection, is the same as human life and its spiritual repetition. But, as I was saying, the simple imaginative mind may have its reward in the repetition of its own silent working coming continually on the spirit with a fine suddenness—to compare great things with small, have you never by being surprised with an old melody, in a delicious place by a delicious voice, *felt* over again your very speculations and surmises at the time it first operated on your soul?—do you not remember forming to yourself the singer's face—more beautiful than it was possible, and yet with the elevation of the moment you did not think so? Even then you were mounted on the wings of imagination, so high that the prototype must be hereafter —that delicious face you will see. What a time! I am continually running away from the subject. Sure this cannot be exactly the case with a complex mind—one that is imaginative, and at the same time careful of its fruits,—who would exist partly on sensation, partly on thought—to whom it is necessary that years should bring the philosophic mind?[1] Such a one I consider yours, and therefore it is necessary to your eternal happiness that you not only drink this old wine of heaven, which I shall call the redigestion of our most ethereal musings upon earth, but also increase in knowledge and know all things. I am glad to hear that you are in a fair way for Easter. You will soon get through your unpleasant reading, and then!—but the world is full of troubles, and I have not much reason to think myself pestered with many. . . . . .

Your affectionate friend,
JOHN KEATS.

To John Hamilton Reynolds

HAMPSTEAD, [February 3, 1818].

My dear Reynolds—I thank you for your dish of filberts[2]—would I could get a basket of them by way of dessert every day for the sum of twopence. Would we were a sort of ethereal pigs, and turned loose to feed upon spiritual mast and acorns—which would be merely being a squirrel and feeding upon filberts, for what is a squirrel but an airy pig, or a filbert but a sort of archangelical acorn? About the nuts being worth cracking, all I can say is, that where there are a throng of delightful images ready drawn, simplicity is the only thing. The first is the best on account of the first line, and the "arrow, foil'd of its antler'd food," and moreover (and this is the only word or two I find fault with, the more because I have had so much reason to shun it as a quicksand) the last has "tender and true." We must cut this, and not be rattle-snaked into any more of the like. It may be said that we ought to read our contemporaries, that Wordsworth, etc., should have their due from us. But, for the sake of a few fine imaginative or domestic passages, are we to be bullied into a certain philosophy engendered in the whims of an egotist? Every man has his speculations, but every man does not brood and peacock over them till he makes a false coinage and deceives himself. Many a man can travel to the very bourne of heaven, and yet want confidence to put down his half-seeing. Sancho will invent a journey heavenward as well as anybody. We hate poetry that has a

---

[1] See Keats's *Ode on a Grecian Urn*, 49-50 (p. 854); also his *Hyperion*, 2, 228-9 (p. 882).
[2] Supposed to be the poem entitled *Lines* (p. 791).
[3] See *Paradise Lost*, 8, 478-84.

[1] See Wordsworth's *Ode: Intimations of Immortality*, 186 (p. 331). Keats was fond of this poem.
[2] Two sonnets which Reynolds had written on Robin Hood and which he had sent to Keats.

palpable design upon us, and, if we do not agree, seems to put its hand into its breeches pocket. Poetry should be great and unobtrusive, a thing which enters into one's soul, and does not startle or amaze it with itself—but with its subject. How beautiful are the retired flowers!—how would they lose their beauty were they to throng into the highway, crying out, "Admire me, I am a violet! Dote upon me, I am a primrose!" Modern poets differ from the Elizabethans in this: each of the moderns like an Elector of Hanover governs his petty state and knows how many straws are swept daily from the causeways in all his dominions, and has a continual itching that all the housewives should have their coppers well scoured: the ancients were emperors of vast provinces, they had only heard of the remote ones and scarcely cared to visit them. I will cut all this—I will have no more of Wordsworth or Hunt in particular—Why should we be of the tribe of Manasseh, when we can wander with Esau?[1] Why should we kick against the pricks,[2] when we can walk on roses? Why should we be owls, when we can be eagles? Why be teased with "nice-eyed wagtails," when we have in sight "the Cherub Contemplation"?[3] Why with Wordsworth's "Matthew with a bough of wilding in his hand,"[4] when we can have Jacques "under an oak,"[5] etc.? The secret of the bough of wilding will run through your head faster than I can write it. Old Matthew spoke to him some years ago on some nothing, and because he happens in an evening walk to imagine the figure of the old man, he must stamp it down in black and white, and it is henceforth sacred. I don't mean to deny Wordsworth's grandeur and Hunt's merit, but I mean to say we need not be teased with grandeur and merit when we can have them uncontaminated and unobtrusive. Let us have the old poets and Robin Hood. Your letter and its sonnets gave me more pleasure than will the Fourth Book of *Childe Harold* and the whole of anybody's

life and opinions. In return for your dish of filberts, I have gathered a few catkins,[1] I hope they'll look pretty. . . . . . .

Your sincere friend and co-scribbler,
JOHN KEATS.

TO JOHN TAYLOR

[HAMPSTEAD, February 27, 1818.]

My dear Taylor—

. . . . . . It is a sorry thing for me that any one should have to overcome prejudices in reading my verses—that affects me more than any hypercriticism on any particular passage—In *Endymion*, I have most likely but moved into the go-cart from the leading-strings—In poetry I have a few axioms, and you will see how far I am from their centre.

1st. I think poetry should surprise by a fine excess, and not by singularity; It should strike the reader as a wording of his own highest thoughts, and appear almost a remembrance.

2d. Its touches of beauty should never be half-way, thereby making the reader breathless, instead of content. The rise, the progress, the setting of imagery should, like the sun, come natural to him, shine over him, and set soberly, although in magnificence, leaving him in the luxury of twilight. But it is easier to think what poetry should be, than to write it—And this leads me to

Another axiom—That if poetry comes not as naturally as the leaves to a tree, it had better not come at all.—However it may be with me, I cannot help looking into new countries with "O for a Muse of Fire to ascend!"[2] If *Endymion* serves me as a pioneer, perhaps I ought to be content—I have great reason to be content, for thank God I can read, and perhaps understand Shakspeare to his depths; and I have I am sure many friends, who, if I fail, will attribute any change in my life and temper to humbleness rather than pride—to a cowering under the wings of great poets, rather than to a bitterness that I am not appreciated. . . . . . .

Your sincere and obliged friend,
JOHN KEATS.

---

[1] That is, why should we dwell in cities when we can roam the fields? See *Genesis*, 25 :27 ; *Numbers*, 32 :33 ff. Wordsworth's unfriendly attitude toward the paganism expressed in Keats's "Hymn to Pan," in *Endymion*, 1, 232-306 (p. 796), may account for Keats's estimate of Wordsworth expressed in this letter. Keats had recited the Hymn to Wordsworth.
[2] See *Acts*, 9 :5.
[3] *Il Penseroso*, 54.
[4] Wordsworth's *The Two April Mornings*, 59-60 (p. 266).
[5] *As You Like It*, II, 1, 31.

[1] A reference to Keats's two poems, *Lines on the Mermaid Tavern* (p. 792) and *Robin Hood* (p. 792), which accompanied the letter.
[2] *Henry V*, chorus, 1.

To James Augustus Hessey

[Hampstead, October 9, 1818.]

My dear Hessey—You are very good in sending me the letters from *The Chronicle*[1] —and I am very bad in not acknowledging such a kindness sooner—pray forgive me. It has so chanced that I have had that paper every day—I have seen today's. I cannot but feel indebted to those gentlemen who have taken my part—As for the rest, I begin to get a little acquainted with my own strength and weakness. — Praise or blame has but a momentary effect on the man whose love of beauty in the abstract makes him a severe critic on his own works. My own domestic criticism has given me pain without comparison beyond what Blackwood or *The Quarterly*[2] could possibly inflict—and also when I feel I am right, no external praise can give me such a glow as my own solitary reperception and ratification of what is fine. J. S.[3] is perfectly right in regard to the slip-shod *Endymion.* That it is so is no fault of mine. No!—though it may sound a little paradoxical. It is as good as I had power to make it—by myself—Had I been nervous about its being a perfect piece, and with that view asked advice, and trembled over every page, it would not have been written; for it is not in my nature to fumble[4]—I will write independently.—I have written independently *without judgment.* I may write independently, and *with judgment,* hereafter. The genius of poetry must work out its own salvation in a man. It cannot be matured by law and precept, but by sensation and watchfulness in itself—That which is creative must create itself—In *Endymion,* I leaped headlong into the sea, and thereby have become better acquainted with the soundings, the quicksands, and the rocks, than if I had stayed upon the green shore, and piped a silly pipe, and took tea and comfortable advice. I was never afraid of failure; for I would sooner fail than not be among the greatest—But I am nigh getting into a rant. So, with remembrances to Taylor and Woodhouse, etc., I am

Yours very sincerely,   John Keats.

[1] Two letters to the editor of *The Morning Chronicle,* a London daily, printed Oct. 3 and 8, 1818.
[2] *Blackwood's Edinburgh Magazine* and *The Quarterly Review* were both hostile to Keats. See Shelley's *Adonais,* 17, 7-9 (p. 758); Byron's *Don Juan,* 11, 60, 1, and n. 5 (p. 636); and Croker's review of *Endymion* (p. 939).
[3] John Scott, author of one of the letters to *The Morning Chronicle.*
[4] grope about perplexedly

To George and Georgiana Keats

[Hampstead, October 25, 1818.]

My dear George—

. . . . I shall in a short time write you as far as I know how I intend to pass my life—I cannot think of those things now Tom[1] is so unwell and weak. Notwithstanding your happiness and your recommendation I hope I shall never marry. Though the most beautiful creature were waiting for me at the end of a journey or a walk; though the carpet were of silk, the curtains of the morning clouds; the chairs and sofa stuffed with cygnet's[2] down; the food manna, the wine beyond claret, the window opening on Winander mere, I should not feel—or rather my happiness would not be so fine, as my solitude is sublime. Then instead of what I have described, there is a sublimity to welcome me home—The roaring of the wind is my wife and the stars through the window pane are my children. The mighty abstract idea I have of beauty in all things stifles the more divided and minute domestic happiness—an amiable wife and sweet children I contemplate as a part of that beauty, but I must have a thousand of those beautiful particles to fill up my heart. I feel more and more every day, as my imagination strengthens, that I do not live in this world alone but in a thousand worlds—No sooner am I alone than shapes of epic greatness are stationed around me, and serve my spirit the office which is equivalent to a king's bodyguard—then "Tragedy with sceptred pall comes sweeping by."[3] According to my state of mind I am with Achilles shouting in the trenches,[4] or with Theocritus in the vales of Sicily. Or I throw my whole being into Troilus, and repeating those lines, "I wander like a lost soul upon the stygian banks staying for waftage,"[5] I melt into the air with a voluptuousness so delicate that I am content to be alone. These things, combined with the opinion I have of the generality of women—who appear to me as children to whom I would rather give a sugar plum than my time, form a barrier against matrimony which I rejoice in.

I have written this that you might see I have my share of the highest pleasures, and that though I may choose to pass my days alone I shall be no solitary. You see there is nothing spleenical in all this. The only

[1] Keats's brother. He died Dec. 1, 1818.
[2] young swan's   [3] *Il Penseroso,* 98.
[4] See the *Iliad,* 18, 217 ff.
[5] *Troilus and Cressida,* III, 2, 10.

thing that can ever affect me personally for more than one short passing day, is any doubt about my powers for poetry—I seldom have any, and I look with hope to the nighing time when I shall have none. I am as happy as a man can be—that is, in myself I should be happy if Tom was well, and I knew you were passing pleasant days. Then I should be most enviable— with the yearning passion I have for the beautiful, connected and made one with the ambition of my intellect. Think of my pleasure in solitude in comparison of my commerce with the world—there I am a child—there they do not know me, not even my most intimate acquaintance—I give in to their feelings as though I were refraining from irritating a little child. Some think me middling, others silly, others foolish— every one thinks he sees my weak side against my will, when in truth it is with my will—I am content to be thought all this because I have in my own breast so great a resource. This is one great reason why they like me so; because they can all show to advantage in a room and eclipse from a certain tact one who is reckoned to be a good poet. I hope I am not here playing tricks "to make the angels weep":[1] I think not: for I have not the least contempt for my species, and though it may sound paradoxical, my greatest elevations of soul leave me every time more humbled—Enough of this—though in your love for me you will not think it enough. . . . .
Believe me, my dear brother and sister,
Your anxious and affectionate Brother,
                                         JOHN.

To John Hamilton Reynolds

WINCHESTER, August 25, [1819].

My dear Reynolds—By this post I write to Rice, who will tell you why we have left Shanklin; and how we like this place. I have indeed scarcely anything else to say, leading so monotonous a life, except I was to give you a history of sensations, and daynightmares. You would not find me at all unhappy in it, as all my thoughts and feelings which are of the selfish nature, home speculations, every day continue to make me more iron—I am convinced more and more, every day, that fine writing is, next to fine doing, the top thing in the world; the *Paradise Lost* becomes a greater wonder. The more I know what my diligence may in time probably effect, the more does

[1] *Measure for Measure*, II, 2, 117.

my heart distend with pride and obstinacy— I feel it in my power to become a popular writer—I feel it in my power to refuse the poisonous suffrage of a public. My own being which I know to be becomes of more consequence to me than the crowds of shadows in the shape of men and women that inhabit a kingdom. The soul is a world of itself, and has enough to do in its own home. Those whom I know already, and who have grown as it were a part of myself, I could not do without: but for the rest of mankind, they are as much a dream to me as Milton's Hierarchies.[1] I think if I had a free and healthy and lasting organization of heart, and lungs as strong as an ox's so as to be able to bear unhurt the shock of extreme thought and sensation without weariness, I could pass my life very nearly alone though it should last eighty years. But I feel my body too weak to support me to the height, I am obliged continually to check myself, and be nothing. It would be vain for me to endeavor after a more reasonable manner of writing to you. I have nothing to speak of but myself, and what can I say but what I feel? If you should have any reason to regret this state of excitement in me, I will turn the tide of your feelings in the right channel, by mentioning that it is the only state for the best sort of poetry—that is all I care for, all I live for. Forgive me for not filling up the whole sheet; letters become so irksome to me, that the next time I leave London I shall petition them all to be spared me. To give me credit for constancy, and at the same time waive letter writing will be the highest indulgence I can think of.
      Ever your affectionate friend,
                                   JOHN KEATS.

To Percy Bysshe Shelley

[HAMPSTEAD, August, 1820.]

My dear Shelley—I am very much gratified that you, in a foreign country, and with a mind almost over-occupied, should write to me in the strain of the letter beside me. If I do not take advantage of your invitation, it will be prevented by a circumstance I have very much at heart to prophesy. There is no doubt that an English winter would put an end to me, and do so in a lingering, hateful manner. Therefore, I must either voyage or journey to Italy, as a soldier marches up to a battery. My nerves at present are the worst part of me,

[1] The three divisions into which the nine orders of angels were divided. See *Paradise Lost*, 1, 737.

yet they feel soothed that, come what extreme may, I shall not be destined to remain
in one spot long enough to take a hatred
of any four particular bedposts. I am glad
5 you take any pleasure in my poor poem,
which I would willingly take the trouble to
unwrite, if possible, did I care so much as
I have done about reputation. I received
a copy of *The Cenci*, as from yourself, from
10 Hunt. There is only one part of it I am
judge of—the poetry and dramatic effect,
which by many spirits nowadays is considered the Mammon. A modern work, it is
said, must have a purpose, which may be
15 the God. An artist must serve Mammon;
he must have "self-concentration"—selfishness, perhaps. You, I am sure, will forgive
me for sincerely remarking that you might
curb your magnanimity, and be more of an
20 artist, and load every rift of your subject
with ore. The thought of such discipline
must fall like cold chains upon you, who
perhaps never sat with your wings furled
for six months together. And is not this
25 extraordinary talk for the writer of *Endymion*, whose mind was like a pack of
scattered cards? I am picked up and sorted
to a pip.[1] My imagination is a monastery,
and I am its monk. I am in expectation of
30 *Prometheus*[2] every day. Could I have my
own wish effected, you would have it still in
manuscript, or be but now putting an end
to the second act. I remember you advis-
ing me not to publish my first blights, on
35 Hampstead Heath. I am returning advice
upon your hands. Most of the poems in
the volume I send you have been written
above two years, and would never have been
published but for hope of gain; so you see
40 I am inclined enough to take your advice
now. I must express once more my deep
sense of your kindness, adding my sincere
thanks and respects for Mrs. Shelley.

In the hope of soon seeing you, I remain
45 most sincerely yours,

JOHN KEATS.

Leigh Hunt 1784-1859

THE STORY OF RIMINI
1812-16   1816

From CANTO III

240   A noble range it was, of many a rood,
Wall'd and tree-girt, and ending in a wood.
A small sweet house o'erlook'd it from a
nest

[1] That is, minutely. A pip is one of the spots
on laying cards.
[2] Shelley's drama, *Prometheus Unbound*.

Of pines:—all wood and garden was the
rest,
Lawn, and green lane, and covert:—and it
had
245 A winding stream about it, clear and glad,
With here and there a swan, the creature
born
To be the only graceful shape of scorn.[1]
The flower-beds all were liberal of delight:
Roses in heaps were there, both red and
white,
250 Lilies angelical, and gorgeous glooms
Of wall-flowers, and blue hyacinths, and
blooms
Hanging thick clusters from light boughs;
in short,
All the sweet cups to which the bees resort,
With plots of grass, and leafier walks between
255 Of red geraniums, and of jessamine,
And orange, whose warm leaves so finely
suit,
And look as if they shade a golden fruit;
And midst the flow'rs, turf'd round be-
neath a shade
Of darksome pines, a babbling fountain
play'd,
260 And 'twixt their shafts you saw the water
bright,
Which through the tops glimmer'd with
show'ring light.
So now you stood to think what odors best
Made the air happy in that lovely nest;
And now you went beside the flowers, with
eyes
265 Earnest as bees, restless as butterflies;
And then turn'd off into a shadier walk,
Close and continuous, fit for lovers' talk;
And then pursued the stream, and as you
trod
Onward and onward o'er the velvet sod,
270 Felt on your face an air, watery and sweet,
And a new sense in your soft-lighting feet.
At last you enter'd shades indeed, the
wood,
Broken with glens and pits, and glades
far-view'd,
Through which the distant palace now and
then
275 Look'd lordly forth with many-window'd
ken;
A land of trees,—which reaching round
about
In shady blessing stretch'd their old arms
out;
With spots of sunny openings, and with
nooks

[1] Born to express scorn and grace at the same
time.

To lie and read in, sloping into brooks,
280 Where at her drink you startled the slim
   deer,
Retreating lightly with a lovely fear.
And all about, the birds kept leafy house,
And sung and darted in and out the
   boughs;
And all about, a lovely sky of blue
285 Clearly was felt, or down the leaves
   laugh'd through.
And here and there, in ev'ry part, were
   seats,
Some in the open walks, some in retreats,—
With bow'ring leaves o'erhead, to which
   the eye
Look'd up half sweetly and half awfully,—
290 Places of nestling green, for poets made,
Where, when the sunshine struck a yellow
   shade,
The rugged trunks, to inward peeping
   sight,
Throng'd in dark pillars up the gold green
   light.

But 'twixt the wood and flowery walks,
   half-way,
295 And form'd of both, the loveliest portion
   lay,—
A spot, that struck you like enchanted
   ground:—
It was a shallow dell, set in a mound
Of sloping orchards,—fig, and almond
   trees,
Cherry and pine, and some few cypresses;
300 Down by whose roots, descending darkly
   still,
(You saw it not, but heard) there gush'd
   a rill,
Whose low sweet talking seem'd as if it
   said,
Something eternal to that happy shade.
The ground within was lawn, with fruits
   and flowers
305 Heap'd towards the centre, half of citron
   bowers;
And in the middle of those golden trees,
Half seen amidst the globy oranges,
Lurk'd a rare summer-house, a lovely
   sight,—
Small, marble, well-proportion'd, creamy
   white,
310 Its top with vine-leaves sprinkled,—but no
   more,—
And a young bay-tree either side the
   door.
The door was to the wood, forward and
   square,
The rest was domed at top, and circular;

And through the dome the only light came
   in,
315 Ting'd as it enter'd by the vine-leaves thin.

It was a beauteous piece of ancient skill,
Spar'd from the rage of war, and perfect
   still;
By some suppos'd the work of fairy
   hands,—
Fam'd for luxurious taste, and choice of
   lands,
320 Alcina or Morgana,—who from fights
And errant[1] fame inveigled amorous
   knights,
And liv'd with them in a long round of
   blisses,
Feasts, concerts, baths, and bower-en-
   shaded kisses.
But 'twas a temple, as its sculpture told,
325 Built to the Nymphs that haunted there of
   old;
For o'er the door was carv'd a sacrifice
By girls and shepherds brought, with reverent eyes,
Of sylvan drinks and foods, simple and
   sweet,
And goats with struggling horns and
   planted feet:
330 And round about ran, on a line with this,
In like relief, a world of pagan bliss,
That show'd, in various scenes, the nymphs
   themselves;
Some by the water-side, on bowery shelves
Leaning at will,—some in the stream at
   play,—
335 Some pelting the young Fauns with buds
   of May,—
Or half asleep pretending not to see
The latter in the brakes[2] come creepingly,
While from their careless urns, lying aside
In the long grass, the struggling waters
   glide.
340 Never, be sure, before or since was seen
A summer-house so fine in such a nest of
   green.

TO HAMPSTEAD

WRITTEN DURING THE AUTHOR'S IMPRISON-
   MENT,[3] AUGUST, 1813
   1813   1813

Sweet upland, to whose walks, with fond
   repair,[4]
Out of thy western slope I took my rise

[1] belonging to chivalric enterprise
[2] thickets
[3] Hunt was imprisoned for an unfriendly characterization of the Prince Regent, published
   in *The Examiner*, 1812.
[4] journey

Day after day, and on these feverish eyes
Met the moist fingers of the bathing air;—
5 If health, unearn'd of thee, I may not
   share,
Keep it, I pray thee, where my memory
   lies,
In thy green lanes, brown dells, and breezy
   skies,
Till I return, and find thee doubly fair.

Wait then my coming, on that lightsome
   land,
10 Health, and the joy that out of nature
   springs,
And Freedom's air-blown locks;—but stay
   with me,
Friendship, frank entering with the cordial hand,
And Honor, and the Muse with growing
   wings,
And Love Domestic, smiling equably.

TO THE GRASSHOPPER AND THE
CRICKET
1816   *1817*

Green little vaulter in the sunny grass,
Catching your heart up at the feel of June,
Sole voice that's heard amidst the lazy
   noon,
When even the bees lag at the summoning
   brass[1]
5 And you, warm little housekeeper, who
   class
With those who think the candles come too
   soon,
Loving the fire, and with your tricksome
   tune
Nick the glad silent moments as they pass;

Oh sweet and tiny cousins, that belong,
10 One to the fields, the other to the hearth,
Both have your sunshine; both, though
   small, are strong
At your clear hearts; and both seem given
   to earth
To ring in thoughtful ears this natural
   song—
In doors and out, summer and winter,
   mirth.

THE NILE
1818   *1818*

It flows through old hush'd Egypt and its
   sands,
Like some grave mighty thought threading
   a dream,

[1] A reference to the old custom of beating on
pans to cause swarming bees to settle so
that they can be captured.

And times and things, as in that vision,
   seem
Keeping along it their eternal stands,—
5 Caves, pillars, pyramids, the shepherd
   bands
That roamed through the young world, the
   glory extreme
Of high Sesostris, and that southern beam,
The laughing queen[1] that caught the
   world's great hands.

Then comes a mightier silence, stern and
   strong,
10 As of a world left empty of its throng,
And the void weighs on us; and then we
   wake,
And hear the fruitful stream lapsing along
'Twixt villages, and think how we shall
   take
Our own calm journey on for human sake.

MAHMOUD
1823

There came a man, making his hasty
   moan
Before the Sultan Mahmoud on his throne,
And crying out—"My sorrow is my right,
And I *will* see the Sultan, and tonight."
5 "Sorrow," said Mahmoud, "is a reverend
   thing:
I recognize its right, as king with king;
Speak on."—"A fiend has got into my
   house,"
Exclaim'd the staring man, "and tortures
   us:
One of thine officers;—he comes, the ab-
   horr'd,
10 And takes possession of my house, my
   board,
My bed:—I have two daughters and a
   wife,
And the wild villain comes, and makes me
   mad with life."
"Is he there now?" said Mahmoud.—
   "No;—he left
The house when I did, of my wits bereft;
15 And laugh'd me down the street, because
   I vow'd
I'd bring the prince himself to lay him in
   his shroud.
I'm mad with want—I'm mad with misery,
And, oh thou Sultan Mahmoud, God cries
   out for thee!"

The Sultan comforted the man, and said,
20 "Go home, and I will send thee wine and
   bread,"

[1] Cleopatra.

(For he was poor) "and other comforts.
Go;
And, should the wretch return, let Sultan
Mahmoud know."

In three days' time, with haggard eyes
and beard,
And shaken voice, the suitor reappear'd,
25 And said, "He's come."—Mahmoud said
not a word,
But rose and took four slaves, each with a
sword,
And went with the vex'd man. They reach
the place,
And hear a voice, and see a woman's face,
That to the window flutter'd in affright:
30 "Go in," said Mahmoud, "and put out
the light;
But tell the females first to leave the
room;
And when the drunkard follows them, we
come."

The man went in. There was a cry,
and hark!
A table falls, the window is struck dark;
35 Forth rush the breathless women; and
behind
With curses comes the fiend in desperate
mind.
In vain: the sabres soon cut short the
strife,
And chop the shrieking wretch, and drink
his bloody life.

"Now *light* the light," the Sultan cried
aloud.
40 'Twas done; he took it in his hand, and
bow'd
Over the corpse, and look'd upon the face;
Then turn'd, and knelt, and to the throne
of grace
Put up a prayer, and from his lips there
crept
Some gentle words of pleasure, and he
wept.

45 In reverent silence the beholders wait,
Then bring him at his call both wine and
meat;
And when he had refresh'd his noble
heart,
He bade his host be blest, and rose up to
depart.

The man amaz'd, all mildness now, and
tears,
50 Fell at the Sultan's feet with many
prayers,

And begg'd him to vouchsafe to tell his
slave
The reason first of that command he gave
About the light; then, when he saw the
face,
Why he knelt down; and, lastly, how it
was
55 That fare so poor as his detain'd him in
the place.

The Sultan said, with a benignant eye,
"Since first I saw thee come, and heard
thy cry,
I could not rid me of a dread, that one
By whom such daring villainies were done,
60 Must be some lord of mine,—aye, e'en,
perhaps, a son.
Whoe'er he was, I knew my task, but
fear'd
A father's heart, in case the worst ap-
pear'd:
For this I had the light put out; but when
I saw the face, and found a stranger slain,
65 I knelt and thank'd the sovereign Arbiter,
Whose work I had perform'd through
pain and fear;
And then I rose and was refresh'd with
food,
The first time since thy voice had marr'd
my solitude."

SONG OF FAIRIES ROBBING ORCHARD
1830   1830

We the fairies blithe and antic,
Of dimensions not gigantic,
Though the moonshine mostly keep us
Oft in orchards frisk and peep us.

5 Stolen sweets are always sweeter;
Stolen kisses much completer;
Stolen looks are nice in chapels;
Stolen, stolen be your apples.

When to bed the world are bobbing,
10 Then's the time for orchard-robbing;
Yet the fruit were scarce worth peeling
Were it not for stealing, stealing.

ABOU BEN ADHEM AND THE ANGEL
1834   1844

Abou Ben Adhem (may his tribe increase)
Awoke one night from a deep dream of
peace,
And saw, within the moonlight in his
room,
Making it rich, and like a lily in bloom,
5 An angel writing in a book of gold:—

Exceeding peace had made Ben Adhem
    bold,
And to the presence in the room he said,
"What writest thou?"—The vision rais'd
    its head,
And with a look made of all sweet accord,
10 Answer'd, "The names of those who love
    the Lord."
"And is mine one?" said Abou. "Nay,
    not so,"
Replied the angel. Abou spoke more low,
But cheerly still; and said, "I pray thee
    then,
"Write me as one that loves his fellow
    men."

15 The angel wrote, and vanish'd. The
    next night
It came again with a great wakening light,
And show'd the names whom love of God
    had bless'd,
And lo! Ben Adhem's name led all the
    rest.

THE GLOVE AND THE LIONS[1]
1836   1836

King Francis[2] was a hearty king, and
    loved a royal sport,
And one day, as his lions fought, sat look-
    ing on the court.
The nobles filled the benches, with the
    ladies in their pride,
And 'mongst them sat the Count de Lorge,
    with one for whom he sighed:
5 And truly 'twas a gallant thing to see that
    crowning show,
Valor and love, and a king above, and the
    royal beasts below.

Ramped and roared the lions, with horrid
    laughing jaws;
They bit, they glared, gave blows like
    beams, a wind went with their paws;
With wallowing might and stifled roar they
    rolled on one another,
10 Till all the pit with sand and mane was in
    a thunderous smother;
    The bloody foam above the bars came
    whisking through the air;
Said Francis then, "Faith, gentlemen,
    we're better here than there."

De Lorge's love o'erheard the King, a
    beauteous lively dame,
With smiling lips and sharp bright eyes,
    which always seemed the same;

[1] See poems by Browning and Schiller on the
    same subject.
[2] Francis I, King of France (1515-47).

15 She thought, the Count, my lover, is brave
    as brave can be;
He surely would do wondrous things to
    show his love of me;
King, ladies, lovers, all look on; the occa-
    sion is divine;
I'll drop my glove, to prove his love; great
    glory will be mine.

She dropped her glove, to prove his love,
    then looked at him and smiled;
20 He bowed, and in a moment leaped among
    the lions wild;
The leap was quick, return was quick, he
    has regained his place,
Then threw the glove, but not with love,
    right in the lady's face.
"By Heaven," said Francis, "rightly
    done!" and he rose from where he
    sat;
"No love," quoth he, "but vanity, sets
    love a task like that."

RONDEAU
1838   1838

Jenny kissed me when we met,
    Jumping from the chair she sat in;
Time, you thief, who love to get
    Sweets into your list, put that in:
5 Say I'm weary, say I'm sad,
    Say that health and wealth have
    missed me,
Say I'm growing old, but add,
    Jenny kissed me.

THE FISH, THE MAN, AND THE
SPIRIT
1857

To Fish

You strange, astonish'd-looking, angle-
    faced,
Dreary-mouth'd, gaping wretches of the
    sea,
Gulping salt-water everlastingly,
Cold-blooded, though with red your blood
    be graced,
5 And mute, though dwellers in the roaring
    waste;
And you, all shapes beside, that fishy be,—
Some round, some flat, some long, all dev-
    ilry,
Legless, unloving, infamously chaste:—

O scaly, slippery, wet, swift, staring
    wights,[1]
10 What is't ye do? what life lead? eh, dull
    goggles?

[1] creatures

How do ye vary your vile days and nights?
How pass your Sundays? Are ye still but
     joggles[1]
In ceaseless wash? Still nought but gapes
     and bites,
And drinks, and stares, diversified with
     boggles?[2]

A Fish Answers

15 Amazing monster! that, for aught I know,
With the first sight of thee didst make our
          race
Forever stare! Oh flat and shocking face,
Grimly divided from the breast below!
Thou that on dry land horribly dost go
20 With a split body and most ridiculous pace,
Prong after prong, disgracer of all grace,
Long-useless-finned, hair'd, upright, un-
     wet, slow!

O breather of unbreathable, sword-sharp
     air,
How canst exist? How bear thyself, thou
     dry
25 And dreary sloth. What particle canst
     share
Of the only blessed life, the watery?
I sometimes see of ye an actual *pair*
Go by! link'd fin by fin! most odiously.

The Fish turns into a Man, and then into a Spirit, and again speaks

Indulge thy smiling scorn, if smiling still,
30 O man! and loathe, but with a sort of
     love:
For difference must its use by difference
     prove,
And, in sweet clang, the spheres with music
     fill.[3]
One of the spirits am I, that at his will
Live in whate'er has life—fish, eagle,
     dove—
35 No hate, no pride, beneath nought, nor
     above,
A visitor of the rounds of God's sweet
     skill.

Man's life is warm, glad, sad, 'twixt loves
     and graves,
Boundless in hope, honor'd with pangs
     austere,
Heaven-gazing; and his angel-wings he
     craves:
40 The fish is swift, small-needing, vague yet
     clear,

[1] wiggling masses
[2] shyings
[3] A reference to the ancient belief that the move-
     ment of the celestial spheres produced music.

A cold, sweet, silver life, wrapp'd in round
     waves,
Quicken'd with touches of transporting
     fear.

HEARING MUSIC
1857

When lovely sounds about my ears
     Like winds in Eden's tree-tops rise,
And make me, though my spirit hears,
     For very luxury close my eyes,
5 Let none but friends be round about
     Who love the smoothing joy like me,
That so the charm be felt throughout,
     And all be harmony.

And when we reach the close divine,
10   Then let the hand of her I love
Come with its gentle palm on mine,
     As soft as snow or lighting dove;
And let, by stealth, that more than friend
     Look sweetness in my opening eyes,
15 For only so such dreams should end,
     Or wake in Paradise.

THE OLD LADY
1816

If the Old Lady is a widow and lives
alone, the manners of her condition and
time of life are so much the more apparent.
She generally dresses in plain silks, that
make a gentle rustling as she moves about
the silence of her room; and she wears a
nice cap with a lace border, that comes under
the chin. In a placket at her side is an old
enamelled watch, unless it is locked up in a
10 drawer of her toilet, for fear of accidents.
Her waist is rather tight and trim than
otherwise, as she had a fine one when young;
and she is not sorry if you see a pair of her
stockings on a table, that you may be aware
15 of the neatness of her leg and foot. Contented with these and other evident indications of a good shape, and letting her young
friends understand that she can afford to
obscure it a little, she wears pockets, and
20 uses them well too. In the one is her handkerchief, and any heavier matter that is not
likely to come out with it, such as the change
of a sixpence; in the other is a miscellaneous
assortment, consisting of a pocket-book, a
25 bunch of keys, a needle-case, a spectacle-
case, crumbs of biscuit, a nutmeg and
grater, a smelling-bottle, and, according to
the season, an orange or apple, which after
many days she draws out, warm and glossy,
30 to give some little child that has well behaved itself. She generally occupies two
rooms, in the neatest condition possible. In

the chamber is a bed with a white coverlet, built up high and round, to look well, and with curtains of a pastoral pattern, consisting alternately of large plants, and shepherds and shepherdesses. On the mantelpiece are more shepherds and shepherdesses, with dot-eyed sheep at their feet, all in colored ware: the man, perhaps, in a pink jacket and knots of ribbons at his knees and shoes, holding his crook lightly in one hand, and with the other at his breast, turning his toes out and looking tenderly at the shepherdess; the woman holding a crook, also, and modestly returning his look, with a gipsy-hat jerked up behind, a very slender waist, with petticoat and hips to counteract, and the petticoat pulled up through the pocket-holes, in order to show the trimness of her ankles. But these patterns, of course, are various. The toilet[1] is ancient, carved at the edges, and tied about with a snow-white drapery of muslin. Beside it are various boxes, mostly Japan; and the set of drawers are exquisite things for a little girl to rummage, if ever little girl be so bold,—containing ribbons and laces of various kinds; linen smelling of lavender, of the flowers of which there is always dust in the corners; a heap of pocket-books for a series of years; and pieces of dress long gone by, such as head-fronts, stomachers, and flowered satin shoes, with enormous heels. The stock of letters are under especial lock and key. So much for the bedroom. In the sitting-room is rather a spare assortment of shining old mahogany furniture, or carved arm-chairs equally old, with chintz draperies down to the ground; a folding or other screen, with Chinese figures, their round, little-eyed, meek faces perking sideways; a stuffed bird, perhaps in a glass case (a living one is too much for her); a portrait of her husband over the mantelpiece, in a coat with frog-buttons, and a delicate frilled hand lightly inserted in the waistcoat; and opposite him on the wall, is a piece of embroidered literature, framed and glazed, containing some moral distich or maxim, worked in angular capital letters, with two trees or parrots below, in their proper colors; the whole concluding with an ABC and numerals, and the name of the fair industrious, expressing it to be "her work, Jan. 14, 1762." The rest of the furniture consists of a looking-glass with carved edges, perhaps a settee, a hassock for the feet, a mat for the little dog, and a small set of shelves, in which are *The Spec-*

tator and *Guardian, The Turkish Spy,* a *Bible* and *Prayer Book,* Young's *Night Thoughts* with a piece of lace in it to flatten, Mrs. Rowe's *Devout Exercises of the Heart,* Mrs. Glasse's *Cookery,* and perhaps *Sir Charles Grandison,* and *Clarissa. John Buncle* is in the closet among the pickles and preserves. The clock is on the landing-place between the two room doors, where it ticks audibly but quietly; and the landing-place, as well as the stairs, is carpeted to a nicety. The house is most in character, and properly coeval, if it is in a retired suburb, and strongly built, with wainscot rather than paper inside, and lockers in the windows. Before the windows should be some quivering poplars. Here the Old Lady receives a few quiet visitors to tea, and perhaps an early game at cards: or you may see her going out on the same kind of visit herself, with a light umbrella running up into a stick and crooked ivory handle, and her little dog, equally famous for his love to her and captious antipathy to strangers. Her grand-children dislike him on holidays, and the boldest sometimes ventures to give him a sly kick under the table. When she returns at night, she appears, if the weather happens to be doubtful, in a calash[1]; and her servant in pattens[2], follows half behind and half at her side, with a lantern.

Her opinions are not many nor new. She thinks the clergyman a nice man. The Duke of Wellington, in her opinion, is a very great man; but she has a secret preference for the Marquis of Granby. She thinks the young women of the present day too forward, and the men not respectful enough; but hopes her grandchildren will be better; though she differs with her daughter in several points respecting their management. She sets little value on the new accomplishments; is a great though delicate connoisseur in butcher's meat and all sorts of housewifery; and if you mention waltzes, expatiates on the grace and fine breeding of the minuet. She longs to have seen one danced by Sir Charles Grandison, whom she almost considers as a real person. She likes a walk of a summer's evening, but avoids the new streets, canals, etc., and sometimes goes through the churchyard, where her children and her husband lie buried, serious, but not melancholy. She has had three great epochs in her life,—her marriage, her

---

[1] dressing table

[1] A kind of hood which can be drawn forward or thrown back.
[2] A kind of overshoe with a wooden sole.

having been at court to see the King and Queen and Royal Family, and a compliment on her figure she once received, in passing, from Mr. Wilkes, whom she describes as a sad, loose man, but engaging. His plainness she thinks much exaggerated. If anything takes her at a distance from home, it is still the court; but she seldom stirs, even for that. The last time but one that she went, was to see the Duke of Wirtemberg; and most probably for the last time of all, to see the Princess Charlotte and Prince Leopold. From this beatific vision she returned with the same admiration as ever for the fine comely appearance of the Duke of York and the rest of the family, and great delight at having had a near view of the Princess, whom she speaks of with smiling pomp and lifted mittens, clasping them as passionately as she can together, and calling her, in a transport of mixed loyalty and self-love, a fine royal young creature, and "Daughter of England."

GETTING UP ON COLD MORNINGS
1820

An Italian author, Giulio Cordara, a Jesuit, has written a poem upon insects, which he begins by insisting, that those troublesome and abominable little animals were created for our annoyance, and that they were certainly not inhabitants of Paradise. We of the North may dispute this piece of theology; but on the other hand, it is as clear as the snow on the house-tops, that Adam was not under the necessity of shaving; and that when Eve walked out of her delicious bower, she did not step upon ice three inches thick.

Some people say it is a very easy thing to get up of a cold morning. You have only, they tell you, to take the resolution; and the thing is done. This may be very true; just as a boy at school has only to take a flogging, and the thing is over. But we have not at all made up our minds upon it; and we find it a very pleasant exercise to discuss the matter, candidly, before we get up. This, at least, is not idling, though it may be lying. It affords an excellent answer to those who ask how lying in bed can be indulged in by a reasoning being,—a rational creature. How? Why, with the argument calmly at work in one's head, and the clothes over one's shoulder. Oh—it is a fine way of spending a sensible, impartial half-hour.

If these people would be more charitable they would get on with their argument better. But they are apt to reason so ill, and

to assert so dogmatically, that one could wish to have them stand round one's bed, of a bitter morning, and *lie* before their faces. They ought to hear both sides of the bed, the inside and out. If they cannot entertain themselves with their own thoughts for half-an-hour or so, it is not the fault of those who can.

Candid inquiries into one's decumbency[1], besides the greater or less privileges to be allowed a man in proportion to his ability of keeping early hours, the work given his faculties, etc., will at least concede their due merits to such representations as the following. In the first place, says the injured but calm appealer, I have been warm all night, and find my system in a state perfectly suitable to a warm-blooded animal. To get out of this state into the cold, besides the inharmonious and uncritical abruptness of the transition, is so unnatural to such a creature, that the poets, refining upon the tortures of the damned, make one of their greatest agonies consist in being suddenly transported from heat to cold, from fire to ice. They are "haled" out of their "beds," says Milton, by "harpy-footed furies,"[2]— fellows who come to call them. On my first movement towards the anticipation of getting up I find that such parts of the sheets and bolsters as are exposed to the air of the room are stone-cold. On opening my eyes, the first thing that meets them is my own breath rolling forth, as if in the open air, like smoke out of a chimney. Think of this symptom. Then I turn my eyes sideways and see the window all frozen over. Think of that. Then the servant comes in. "It is very cold this morning, is it not?"— "Very cold, sir."—"Very cold indeed, isn't it?"—"Very cold indeed, sir."—"More than usually so, isn't it, even for this weather?" (Here the servant's wit and good-nature are put to a considerable test, and the inquirer lies on thorns for the answer.) "Why, sir—I think it *is.*" (Good creature! There is not a better or more truth-telling servant going.) "I must rise, however—get me some warm water."— Here comes a fine interval between the departure of the servant and the arrival of the hot water, during which, of course, it is of "no use?" to get up. The hot water comes. "Is it quite hot?"—"Yes, sir."—"Perhaps too hot for shaving: I must wait a little?"—"No, sir; it will just do." (There is an over-nice pro-

[1] act or posture of lying down
[2] *Paradise Lost*, 2, 596.

priety sometimes, an officious zeal of virtue, a little troublesome.) "Oh—the shirt—you must air my clean shirt;—linen gets very damp this weather."—"Yes, sir." Here another delicious five minutes. A knock at the door. "Oh, the shirt—very well. My stockings—I think the stockings had better be aired too."—"Very well, sir."—Here another interval. At length everything is ready, except myself. I now, continues our incumbent (a happy word, by-the-bye, for a country vicar)—I now cannot help thinking a good deal—who can?—upon the unnecessary and villainous custom of shaving: it is a thing so unmanly (here I nestle closer)—so effeminate (here I recoil from an unlucky step into the colder part of the bed). —No wonder that the Queen of France[1] took part with the rebels against that degenerate King, her husband, who first affronted her smooth visage with a face like her own. The Emperor Julian never showed the luxuriancy of his genius to better advantage than in reviving the flowing beard. Look at Cardinal Bembo's picture—at Michael Angelo's—at Titian's—at Shakespeare's— at Fletcher's—at Spenser's—at Chaucer's —at Alfred's—at Plato's—I could name a great man for every tick of my watch.— Look at the Turks, a grave and otiose[2] people.—Think of Haroun Al Raschid and Bed-ridden Hassan.—Think of Wortley Montague, the worthy son of his mother, above the prejudice of his time.—Look at the Persian gentlemen, whom one is ashamed of meeting about the suburbs, their dress and appearance are so much finer than our own. —Lastly, think of the razor itself—how totally opposed to every sensation of bed— how cold, how edgy, how hard! how utterly different from anything like the warm and circling amplitude, which

> Sweetly recommends itself
> Unto our gentle senses.[3]

Add to this, benumbed fingers, which may help you to cut yourself, a quivering body, a frozen towel, and a ewer full of ice; and he that says there is nothing to oppose in all this, only shows that he has no merit in opposing it.

Thomson the poet, who exclaims in his *Seasons*

> Falsely luxurious! Will not man awake?[4]

[1] Eleanor of Aquitaine, wife of Louis VII of France (1137-80), and later of Henry II of England (1154-89). Louis VII had shaved off his beard in compliance with an episcopal edict.
[2] indolent   [3] *Macbeth*, I, 6, 2.   [4] *Summer*, 67.

used to lie in bed till noon, because he said he had no motive in getting up. He could imagine the good of rising; but then he could also imagine the good of lying still; and his exclamation, it must be allowed, was made upon summer-time, not winter. We must proportion the argument to the individual character. A money-getter may be drawn out of his bed by three or four pence; but this will not suffice for a student. A proud man may say, "What shall I think of myself, if I don't get up?" but the more humble one will be content to waive this prodigious notion of himself out of respect to his kindly bed. The mechanical man shall get up without any ado at all; and so shall the barometer. An ingenious lier-in-bed will find hard matter of discussion even on the score of health and longevity. He will ask us for our proofs and precedents of the ill effects of lying later in cold weather; and sophisticate much on the advantages of an even temperature of body; of the natural propensity (pretty universal) to have one's way; and of the animals that roll themselves up and sleep all the winter. As to longevity, he will ask whether the longest is of necessity the best; and whether Holborn is the handsomest street in London.[1]

From ON THE REALITIES OF IMAGINATION
1820

There is not a more unthinking way of talking than to say such and such pains and pleasures are only imaginary, and therefore to be got rid of or undervalued accordingly. There is nothing imaginary in the common acceptation of the word. The logic of Moses in *The Vicar of Wakefield* is good argument here: — "Whatever is, is."[1] Whatever touches us, whatever moves us, does touch and does move us. We recognize the reality of it, as we do that of a hand in the dark. We might as well say that a sight which makes us laugh, or a blow which brings tears into our eyes, is imaginary, as that anything else is imaginary which makes us laugh or weep. We can only judge of things by their effects. Our perception constantly deceives us, in things with which we suppose ourselves perfectly conversant; but our reception of their effect is a different matter. Whether we are materialists or immaterialists, whether things be about us or within us, whether we think the sun is a sub-

[1] Holborn was not the longest street in London, but in some districts it was very unattractive.
[2] Goldsmith, *The Vicar of Wakefield*, ch. 7.

stance, or only the image of a divine thought, an idea, a thing imaginary, we are equally agreed as to the notion of its warmth. But on the other hand, as this warmth is felt differently by different temperaments, so what we call imaginary things affect different minds. What we have to do is not to deny their effect, because we do not feel in the same proportion, or whether we even feel it at all; but to see whether our neighbors may not be moved. If they are, there is, to all intents and purposes, a moving cause. But we do not see it? No;—neither perhaps do they. They only feel it; they are only sentient,—a word which implies the sight given to the imagination by the feelings. But what do you mean, we may ask in return, by seeing? Some rays of light come in contact with the eye; they bring a sensation to it; in a word, they touch it; and the impression left by this touch we call sight. How far does this differ in effect from the impression left by any other touch, however mysterious? An ox knocked down by a butcher, and a man knocked down by a fit of apoplexy, equally feel themselves compelled to drop. The tickling of a straw and of a comedy equally move the muscles about the mouth. The look of a beloved eye will so thrill the frame, that old philosophers have had recourse to a doctrine of beams and radiant particles flying from one sight to another. In fine, what is contact itself, and why does it affect us? There is no one cause more mysterious than another, if we look into it.

Nor does the question concern us like moral causes. We may be content to know the earth by its fruits; but how to increase and improve them is a more attractive study. If, instead of saying that the causes which moved in us this or that pain or pleasure were imaginary, people were to say that the causes themselves were removable, they would be nearer the truth. When a stone trips us up, we do not fall to disputing its existence: we put it out of the way. In like manner, when we suffer from what is called an imaginary pain, our business is not to canvass the reality of it. Whether there is any cause or not in that or any other perception, or whether everything consists not in what is called effect, it is sufficient for us that the effect is real. Our sole business is to remove those second causes, which always accompany the original idea. As in deliriums, for instance, it would be idle to go about persuading the patient that he did not behold the figures he says he does. He might reasonably ask us, if he could, how we know anything about the matter; or how we can be sure that in the infinite wonders of the universe certain realities may not become apparent to certain eyes, whether diseased or not. Our business would be to put him into that state of health in which human beings are not diverted from their offices and comforts by a liability to such imaginations. The best reply to his question would be, that such a morbidity is clearly no more a fit state for a human being than a disarranged or incomplete state of works is for a watch; and that seeing the general tendency of nature to this completeness or state of comfort, we naturally conclude that the imaginations in question, whether substantial or not, are at least not of the same lasting or prevailing description.

We do not profess metaphysics. We are indeed so little conversant with the masters of that art, that we are never sure whether we are using even its proper terms. All that we may know on the subject comes to us from some reflection and some experience; and this all may be so little as to make a metaphysician smile; which, if he be a true one, he will do good-naturedly. The pretender will take occasion, from our very confession, to say that we know nothing. Our faculty, such as it is, is rather instinctive than reasoning; rather physical than metaphysical; rather sentient because it loves much, than because it knows much; rather calculated by a certain retention of boyhood, and by its wanderings in the green places of thought, to light upon a piece of the old golden world, than to tire ourselves, and conclude it unattainable, by too wide and scientific a search. We pretend to see farther than none but the worldly and the malignant. And yet those who see farther may not see so well. We do not blind our eyes with looking upon the sun in the heavens. We believe it to be there, but we find its light upon earth also; and we would lead humanity, if we could, out of misery and coldness into the shine of it. Pain might still be there; must be so, as long as we are mortal;

For oft we still must weep, since we are human;

but it should be pain for the sake of others, which is noble; not unnecessary pain inflicted by or upon them, which it is absurd not to remove. The very pains of mankind struggle towards pleasures; and such pains as are proper for them have this

inevitable accompaniment of true humanity,
—that they cannot but realize a certain gentleness of enjoyment. Thus the true bearer
of pain would come round to us; and he
would not grudge us a share of his burden,
though in taking from his trouble it might
diminish his pride. Pride is but a bad
pleasure at the expense of others. The
great object of humanity is to enrich everybody. If it is a task destined not to succeed, it is a good one from its very nature;
and fulfills at least a glad destiny of its
own. To look upon it austerely is in reality
the reverse of austerity. It is only such an
impatience of the want of pleasure as leads
us to grudge it in others; and this impatience
itself, if the sufferer knew how to use it, is
but another impulse, in the general yearning,
towards an equal wealth of enjoyment.

But we shall be getting into other discussions.—The ground-work of all happiness
is health. Take care of this ground, and
the doleful imaginations that come to warn
us against its abuse will avoid it. Take care
of this ground, and let as many glad imaginations throng to it as possible. Read the
magical works of the poets, and they will
come. If you doubt their existence, ask
yourself whether you feel pleasure at the
idea of them; whether you are moved into
delicious smiles, or tears as delicious. If
you are, the result is the same to you,
whether they exist or not. It is not mere
words to say that he who goes through a
rich man's park, and sees things in it which
never bless the mental eyesight of the possessor, is richer than he. He is richer.
More results of pleasure come home to him.
The ground is actually more fertile to him:
the place haunted with finer shapes. He has
more servants to come at his call, and administer to him with full hands. Knowledge,
sympathy, imagination, are all divining-
rods, with which he discovers treasure. Let
a painter go through the grounds, and he
will see not only the general colors of green
and brown, but their combinations and contrasts, and the modes in which they might
again be combined and contrasted. He will
also put figures in the landscape if there are
none there, flocks and herds, or a solitary
spectator, or Venus lying with her white
body among the violets and primroses. Let
a musician go through, and he will hear
"differences discreet"[1] in the notes of the
birds and the lapsing of the water-fall.
He will fancy a serenade of wind instruments in the open air at a lady's window,

[1] Spenser, *The Faerie Queene*, II, 12, 71, 7.

with a voice rising through it; or the horn
of the hunter; or the musical cry of the
hounds,

Matched in mouth-like bells,
Each under each;[1]

or a solitary voice in a bower, singing for
an expected lover; or the chapel organ,
waking up like the fountain of the winds.
Let a poet go through the grounds and he
will heighten and increase all these sounds
and images. He will bring the colors from
heaven, and put an unearthly meaning into
the voice. He will have stories of the sylvan
inhabitants; will shift the population
through infinite varieties; will put a sentiment upon every sight and sound; will be
human, romantic, supernatural; will make
all nature send tribute into that spot.[2]

. . . .

We may say of the love of nature what
Shakespeare says of another love, that it
Adds a precious seeing to the eye.[3]
And we may say also, upon the like principle, that it adds a precious hearing to the
ear. This and imagination, which ever follows upon it, are the two purifiers of our
sense, which rescue us from the deafening
babble of common cares, and enable us to
hear all the affectionate voices of earth and
heaven. The starry orbs, lapsing about in
their smooth and sparkling dance, sing to us.
The brooks talk to us of solitude. The
birds are the animal spirits of nature, carolling in the air, like a careless lass.

The gentle gales,
Fanning their odoriferous wings, dispense
Native perfumes; and whisper whence they
stole
Those balmy spoils.—*Paradise Lost*, 4, 156-9.

The poets are called creators, because with
their magical words they bring forth to our
eyesight the abundant images and beauties
of creation. They put them there, if the
reader pleases; and so are literally creators.
But whether put there or discovered, whether
created or invented (for invention means
nothing but finding out), there they are.
If they touch us, they exist to as much purpose as anything else which touches us. If
a passage in *King Lear* brings the tears into
our eyes, it is real as the touch of a sorrowful hand. If the flow of a song of Anacreon's intoxicates us, it is as true to a pulse

[1] *A Midsummer Night's Dream*, IV, 1, 127.
[2] See Jeffrey's review of Alison's *Essays on the
Nature and Principles of Taste* (p. 917a, 11 ff.).
[3] *Love's Labour's Lost*, IV, 3, 333.

within us as the wine he drank. We hear not their sounds with ears, nor see their sights with eyes; but we hear and see both so truly, that we are moved with pleasure; and the advantage, nay even the test, of seeing and hearing, at any time, is not in the seeing and hearing, but in the ideas we realize, and the pleasure we derive. Intellectual objects, therefore, inasmuch as they come home to us, are as true a part of the stock of nature as visible ones; and they are infinitely more abundant. Between the tree of a country clown and the tree of a Milton or Spenser, what a difference in point of productiveness! Between the plodding of a sexton through a church-yard and the walk of a Gray, what a difference! What a difference between the Bermudas of a ship-builder and the Bermoothes of Shakespeare! the isle

> Full of noises,
> Sounds, and sweet airs, that give delight, and
>   hurt not;[1]

the isle of elves and fairies, that chased the tide to and fro on the sea-shore; of coral-bones and the knell of sea-nymphs; of spirits dancing on the sands, and singing amidst the hushes of the wind; of Caliban, whose brute nature enchantment had made poetical; of Ariel, who lay in cowslip bells, and rode upon the bat; of Miranda, who wept when she saw Ferdinand work so hard, and begged him to let her help; telling him,

> I am your wife if you will marry me;
> If not, I'll die your maid. To be your fellow
> You may deny me; but I'll be your servant,
> Whether you will or no.[2]

Such are the discoveries which the poets make for us; worlds to which that of Columbus was but a handful of brute matter. America began to be richer for us the other day, when Humboldt came back and told us of its luxuriant and gigantic vegetation; of the myriads of shooting lights, which revel at evening in the southern sky; and of that grand constellation, at which Dante seems to have made so remarkable a guess (*Purgatorio*, cant., 1, 5, 22). The natural warmth of the Mexican and Peruvian genius, set free from despotism, will soon do all the rest of it; awaken the sleeping riches of its eyesight, and call forth the glad music of its affections.

. . . .

Imagination enriches everything. A great library contains not only books, but

[1] *The Tempest*, III, 2, 144 ff. [2] *Ibid.*, III, 1, 83 ff.

The assembled souls of all that men held wise.
>   —DAVENANT.[1]

The moon is Homer's and Shakespeare's moon, as well as the one we look at. The sun comes out of his chamber in the east, with a sparkling eye, "rejoicing like a bridegroom.''[2] The commonest thing becomes like Aaron's rod, that budded.[3] Pope called up the spirits of the cabala[4] to wait upon a lock of hair,[5] and justly gave it the honors of a constellation; for he has hung it, sparkling forever in the eyes of posterity. A common meadow is a sorry thing to a ditcher or a coxcomb; but by the help of its dues from imagination and the love of nature, the grass brightens for us, the air soothes us, we feel as we did in the daisied hours of childhood. Its verdures, its sheep, its hedge-row elms—all these, and all else which sight, and sound, and associations can give it, are made to furnish a treasure of pleasant thoughts. Even brick and mortar are vivified, as of old, at the harp of Orpheus. A metropolis becomes no longer a mere collection of houses or of trades. It puts on all the grandeur of its history, and its literature; its towers, and rivers; its art, and jewelry, and foreign wealth; its multitude of human beings all intent upon excitement, wise or yet to learn; the huge and sullen dignity of its canopy of smoke by day; the wide gleam upwards of its lighted lustre at night-time; and the noise of its many chariots, heard at the same hour, when the wind sets gently towards some quiet suburb.

A "NOW"

DESCRIPTIVE OF A HOT DAY
1820

Now the rosy- (and lazy-) fingered Aurora, issuing from her saffron house, calls up the moist vapors to surround her, and goes veiled with them as long as she can; till Phœbus, coming forth in his power, looks everything out of the sky, and holds sharp, uninterrupted empire from his throne of beams. Now the mower begins to make his sweeping cuts more slowly, and resorts oftener to the beer. Now the carter sleeps a-top of his load of hay, or plods with double slouch of shoulder, looking out with eyes winking under his shading hat, and with a hitch upward of one side of his mouth. Now the little girl at her grandmother's cottage-door watches the coaches that go by, with her hand held up over her

[1] *Gondibert*, II, 5, 146. [2] *Psalms*, 19:5.
[3] *Numbers*, 17:8. [4] mystic art
[5] See *The Rape of the Lock*.

sunny forehead. Now laborers look well resting in their white shirts at the doors of rural ale-houses. Now an elm is fine there, with a seat under it; and horses drink out of the trough, stretching their yearning necks with loosened collars; and the traveller calls for his glass of ale, having been without one for more than ten minutes; and his horse stands wincing at the flies, giving sharp shivers of his skin, and moving to and fro his ineffectual docked tail; and now Miss Betty Wilson, the host's daughter, comes streaming forth in a flowered gown and earrings, carrying with four of her beautiful fingers the foaming glass, for which, after the traveller has drank it, she receives with an indifferent eye, looking another way, the lawful twopence. Now grasshoppers "fry," as Dryden says.[1] Now cattle stand in water, and ducks are envied. Now boots, and shoes, and trees by the road-side, are thick with dust; and dogs, rolling in it, after issuing out of the water, into which they have been thrown to fetch sticks, come scattering horror among the legs of the spectators. Now a fellow who finds he has three miles further to go in a pair of tight shoes is in a pretty situation. Now rooms with the sun upon them become intolerable; and the apothecary's apprentice, with a bitterness beyond aloes, thinks of the pond he used to bathe in at school. Now men with powdered heads[2] (especially if thick) envy those that are unpowdered, and stop to wipe them up hill, with countenances that seem to expostulate with destiny. Now boys assemble round the village pump with a ladle to it, and delight to make a forbidden splash and get wet through the shoes. Now also they make suckers of leather, and bathe all day long in rivers and ponds, and make mighty fishings for "tittle-bats."[3] Now the bee, as he hums along, seems to be talking heavily of the heat. Now doors and brick-walls are burning to the hand; and a walled lane, with dust and broken bottles in it, near a brickfield, is a thing not to be thought of. Now a green lane, on the contrary, thick-set with hedge-row elms, and having the noise of a brook "rumbling in pebble-stone,"[4] is one of the pleasantest things in the world.

Now, in town, gossips talk more than ever to one another, in rooms, in door-ways, and out of window, always beginning the conversation with saying that the heat is over-

powering. Now blinds are let down, and doors thrown open, and flannel waistcoats left off, and cold meat preferred to hot, and wonder expressed why tea continues so refreshing, and people delight to sliver lettuces into bowls, and apprentices water door-ways with tin canisters that lay several atoms of dust. Now the water-cart, jumbling along the middle of the street, and jolting the showers out of its box of water, really does something. Now fruiterers' shops and dairies look pleasant, and ices are the only things to those who can get them. Now ladies loiter in baths; and people make presents of flowers; and wine is put into ice; and the after-dinner lounger recreates his head with applications of perfumed water out of long-necked bottles. Now the lounger, who cannot resist riding his new horse, feels his boots burn him. Now buck-skins are not the lawn of Cos.[1] Now jockeys, walking in great-coats to lose flesh, curse inwardly. Now five fat people in a stage-coach hate the sixth fat one who is coming in, and think he has no right to be so large. Now clerks in office do nothing but drink soda-water and spruce-beer, and read the newspaper. Now the old-clothesman drops his solitary cry more deeply into the areas on the hot and forsaken side of the street; and bakers look vicious; and cooks are aggravated; and the steam of a tavern-kitchen catches hold of us like the breath of Tartarus. Now delicate skins are beset with gnats; and boys make their sleeping companion start up, with playing a burning-glass on his hand; and blacksmiths are super-carbonated; and cobblers in their stalls almost feel a wish to be transplanted; and butter is too easy to spread; and the dragoons wonder whether the Romans liked their helmets; and old ladies, with their lappets unpinned, walk along in a state of dilapidation; and the servant maids are afraid they look vulgarly hot; and the author, who has a plate of strawberries brought him, finds that he has come to the end of his writing.

SHAKING HANDS
1820

Among the first things which we remember noticing in the manners of people, were two errors in the custom of shaking hands. Some we observed, grasped everybody's hand alike,—with an equal fervor of grip. You would have thought that Jenkins was the best friend they had in the world; but

---

[1] See Dryden's translation of Virgil's *Eclogues*, 2, 13-14.
[2] The eighteenth century habit of powdering the hair was still in practice.
[3] sticklebacks (a kind of small fish)
[4] Spenser, *Virgil's Gnat*, 163.

[1] A kind of fine linen introduced from the Island of Cos, in the Ægean Sea.

on succeeding to the squeeze, though a slight acquaintance, you found it equally flattering to yourself; and on the appearance of some-body else (whose name, it turned out, the operator had forgotten), the crush was no less complimentary:—the face was as earnest and beaming, the ''glad to see you'' as syllabical and sincere, and the shake as close, as long, and as rejoicing, as if the semi-unknown was a friend come home from the Deserts.

On the other hand, there would be a gen-tleman, now and then, as coy of his hand, as if he were a prude, or had a whitlow.[1] It was in vain that your pretensions did not go beyond the ''civil salute'' of the ordinary shake; or that being introduced to him in a friendly manner, and expected to shake hands with the rest of the company, you could not in decency omit his. His fingers, half coming out and half retreating, seemed to think that you were going to do them a mischief; and when you got hold of them, the whole shake was on your side; the other hand did but proudly or pensively acquiesce —there was no knowing which; you had to sustain it, as you might a lady's, in handing her to a seat; and it was an equal perplexity to know whether to shake or to let it go. The one seemed a violence done to the patient, the other an awkward responsibility brought upon yourself. You did not know, all the evening, whether you were not an ob-ject of dislike to the person; till, on the party's breaking up, you saw him behave like an equally ill-used gentleman to all who practiced the same unthinking civility.

Both these errors, we think, might as well be avoided; but, of the two, we must say we prefer the former. If it does not look so much like particular sincerity, it looks more like general kindness; and if those two vir-tues are to be separated (which they as-suredly need not be, if considered without spleen), the world can better afford to dis-pense with an unpleasant truth than a gratuitous humanity. Besides, it is more difficult to make sure of the one than to practice the other, and kindness itself is the best of all truths. As long as we are sure of that, we are sure of something, and of something pleasant. It is always the best end, if not in every instance the most logical means.

This manual shyness is sometimes attrib-uted to modesty, but never, we suspect, with justice, unless it be that sort of modesty whose fear of committing itself is grounded

in pride. Want of address is a better rea-son; but this particular instance of it would be grounded in the same feeling. It always implies a habit either of pride or mistrust. We have met with two really kind men[1] who evinced this soreness of hand. Neither of them, perhaps, thought himself inferior to anybody about him, and both had good reason to think highly of themselves, but both had been sanguine men contradicted in their early hopes. There was a plot to meet the hand of one of them with a fish-slice, in order to show him the disadvantage to which he put his friends by that flat mode of salutation; but the conspirator had not the courage to do it. Whether he heard of the intention we know not, but shortly afterwards he took very kindly to a shake. The other was the only man of a warm set of politicians, who remained true to his first hopes of mankind. He was impatient at the change of his companions, and at the folly and inattention of the rest; but though his manner became cold, his consistency remained warm, and this gave him a right to be as strange as he pleased.

From DREAMS ON THE BORDERS OF
THE LAND OF POETRY
1828   *1828*

I. THE DEMANDS OF POETRY

I have not been in the habit of making memorandums for my verses. Such verse as I could write I have written at once. But the older I grow, the more reverent notions I entertain of poetry; and as I cannot as-pire to put anything into verse, and pretend to call it poetry, without shaping it in the best manner of which I am capable (for poetry, without the fit sculpture of verse, is no more to be called poetry, than beauty conceived is beauty accomplished), so I have neither leisure to pay it the requisite atten-tion, nor can I afford the spirit and emotion necessary for this task above all others. The greatest of all poets (who, according to Plato,[2] is God) uttered the planets in his en-ergy, and they went singing around him,[3] perfect. Milton (not to speak it with pro-faneness,[4] after that unreachable instance) could pour forth his magnificent verses,

---

[1] An inflammation of the fingers.

[1] The second of these men was Hazlitt; the first has not been identified.
[2] See Plato's *Ion*, 534 (Jowett's translation, 1, 224). The same thought is expressed by Mrs. Browning in *Hymn to Pan*, st. 36, and by Browning in *Paracelsus*, 2, 648.
[3] A reference to the ancient belief that the move-ment of the celestial spheres produced music.
[4] See *Hamlet*, III, 3, 33.

mighty and full of music, like a procession towards a temple of glory. We conceive of Shakespeare, that he had a still easier might, and that the noblest verses to him were no greater difficulty than talking. He dispensed them as Nature does the summer showers and the thunder. Alas! to us petty men, who are not sure that we have even the right of being.

Proud to be less, but of that godlike race,

to us and our inferior natures there are sometimes toils in life less voluntary and more exhausting than poetry, in reposing from which it is not always possible for us to labor even with the minor energies necessary to throw out the forms within our capacity. We cannot wrestle to fit purpose even with that pettier god within us. We cannot condense those lighter vapors of inspiration into their most vigorous and graceful shape, and feel a right to say to the world, "Behold!"

A poet's hand should be like the energy within the oak, to make strong; and like the wind that bends its foliage, to make various. Without concentration, and without variety, there is neither strength of imagination, nor beauty of verse. Alas! I could no more look to making verses with an ambition of this sort, wearied as I am at present, than I could think of looking through burning glasses for eyes, or hewing the solid rock into a dance of the Graces.

But I have the wish to be a poet, and thoughts will arise within me as painful not to express as a lover's. I therefore write memorandums for verse;—thoughts that might perhaps be worthy of putting into that shape, if they could be properly developed;—hints and shadows of something poetical, that have the same relationship to actual poetry as the little unborn spirits that perish by the waters of Lethe have to the souls that visit us, and become immortal.

II. MY BOWER

I seek not for grand emotions when I muse. My life has had enough of them. I seek for enjoyment and repose; and, thanks to the invincible youthfulness of my heart, I find them with as much ease in my green world as giant sorrows have found me in the world of strife.

Woods and meadows are to me an enchanted ground, of which a knight-errantry of a new sort has put me in possession.

In the indulgence of these effusions I lay my head as on the pillow before I sleep, as on the grass in summer, as on the lap that soothes us. O lovers of books and of nature, lovers of one another, lovers of love, rest with me under my bowers; and the shadows of pleasant thoughts shall play upon your eyelids.

III. ON A BUST OF BACCHUS

Gigantic, earnest, luxuriant, his head a very bower of hair and ivy;[1] his look a mixture of threat, and reassurance, and the giving of pleasure; the roughness of wine in his eyes, and the sweetness of it on his lips. Annibal Caracci would have painted such a face, and grown jealous when his mistress looked at it.

To those shoulders belong the bands that lifted the satyr[2] by the nape of the neck, and played with the lion's mouth as with a dog's.[3]

Cannot you see the glow in the face, even though sculptured? a noontide of the south in its strength? with dark wells in the eyes, under shining locks and sunny leaves? The geniality of his father Jove is in it, with the impetuosity of wine: but it is the lord, not the servant, of wine; the urger of the bowl among the divinities, when the pulses of heaven are in movement with song and dance, and goddess by the side of god looks downward.

Such did he appear when Ariadne turned pale with loving him; and he said, with divine insolence in his eyes, "Am I not then better than a mortal?"

. . . . . .

OF THE SIGHT OF SHOPS

From PART II
1888

In the general glance that we have taken at shops, we found ourselves unwillingly compelled to pass some of them too quickly. It is the object, therefore, of the present article to enter into those more attractive thresholds, and look a little about us. We imagine a fine day; time, about noon; scene, any good brilliant street. The ladies are abroad in white and green; the beaux lounging, conscious of their waists and neckcloths; the busy pushing onward, conscious of their bills.

[1] The forehead of Bacchus was crowned with vine-leaves or ivy.
[2] Probably Silenus, who was a boon companion of Bacchus.
[3] A portion of the frieze of *The Monument of Lysicrates* represents Bacchus with his hand on the face of a lion.

To begin, then, where our shopping experience began, with the toy-shop—

Visions of glory, spare our aching sight!
Ye just-breech'd ages,[1] crowd not on our soul![2]

We still seem to have a lively sense of the smell of that gorgeous red paint which was on the handle of our first wooden sword! The pewter guard also—how beautifully fretted and like silver did it look! How did we hang it round our shoulder by the proud belt of an old ribbon;—then feel it well suspended; then draw it out of the sheath, eager to cut down four savage men for illusing ditto of damsels! An old muff made an excellent grenadier's cap; or one's hat and feather, with the assistance of three surreptitious large pins, became fiercely modern and military. There it is, in that corner of the window—the same identical sword, to all appearance, which kept us awake the first night behind our pillow. We still feel ourselves little boys while standing in this shop; and for that matter, so we do on other occasions. A field has as much merit in our eyes, and ginger-bread almost as much in our mouths, as at that daisy-plucking and cake-eating period of life. There is the trigger-rattling gun, fine of its kind, but not so complete a thing as the sword. Its memories are not so ancient: for Alexander or St. George did not fight with a musket. Neither is it so true a thing; it is not "like life." The trigger is too much like that of a cross-bow; and the pea which it shoots, however hard, produces, even to the imaginative faculties of boyhood, a humiliating flash of the mock-heroic. It is difficult to fancy a dragon killed with a pea: but the shape and appurtenances of the sword being genuine, the whole sentiment of massacre is as much in its wooden blade as if it were steel of Damascus. The drum is still more real, though not so heroic.—In the corner opposite are battledores and shuttle-cocks, which have their maturer beauties; balls, which possess the additional zest of the danger of breaking people's windows;—ropes, good for swinging and skipping, especially the long ones which others turn for you, while you run in a masterly manner up and down, or skip in one spot with an easy and endless exactitude of toe, looking alternately at their conscious faces;—blood-allies, with which the possessor of

a crisp finger and thumb-knuckle causes the smitten marbles to vanish out of the ring; kites, which must appear to more vital birds a ghastly kind of fowl, with their grim, long, white faces, no bodies, and endless tails;—cricket-bats, manly to handle;—trap-bats,[1] a genteel inferiority;—swimming-corks, despicable;—horses on wheels, an imposition on the infant public;—rocking-horses, too much like Pegasus, ardent yet never getting on;—Dutch toys, so like life, that they ought to be better;—Jacob's ladders, flapping down one over another with tintinnabulary[2] shutters;—dissected maps, from which the infant statesmen may learn how to dovetail provinces and kingdoms;—paper posture-makers, who hitch up their knees against their shoulder-blades, and dangle their legs like an opera dancer;—Lilliputian plates, dishes, and other household utensils, in which a grand dinner is served up out of half an apple;—boxes of paints, to color engravings with, always beyond the outline;—ditto of bricks, a very sensible and lasting toy, which we except from a grudge we have against the gravity of infant geometrics;—whips, very useful for cutting people's eyes unawares;—hoops, one of the most ancient as well as excellent of toys;—sheets of pictures, from A apple-pie up to farming, military, and zoölogical exhibitions, always taking care that the Fly is as large as the Elephant, and the letter X exclusively appropriated to Xerxes;—musical deal-boxes,[3] rather complaining than sweet, and more like a peal of bodkins than bells;—penny trumpets, awful at Bartlemy-tide;[4]—jews' harps, that thrill and breathe between the lips like a metal tongue;—carts—carriages —hobby-horses, upon which the infant equestrian prances about proudly on his own feet;—in short, not to go through the whole representative body of existence— dolls, which are so dear to the maternal instincts of little girls. We protest, however, against that abuse of them, which makes them full-dressed young ladies in body, while they remain infant in face; especially when they are of frail wax. It is cultivating finery instead of affection. We prefer good, honest, plump limbs of cotton and sawdust, dressed in baby-linen; or even our ancient young friends, with their staring dotted eyes, red varnished

---

[1] The ages at which boys begin to wear breeches. The expression is used here to indicate the time when boys first show an interest in toys.
[2] Gray, *The Bard*, 108-9 (p. 65). Hunt substitutes *just-breech'd* for *unborn*.

[1] small bats used in playing trapball
[2] jingling; rattling
[3] boxes made of pine or fir
[4] the time of the festival of St. Bartholomew, Aug. 24

faces, triangular noses, and Rosinante[1] wooden limbs—not, it must be confessed, excessively shapely or feminine, but the reverse of fragile beauty, and prepared against all disasters.

The next step is to the Pastry-cook's, where the plain bun is still the pleasantest thing in our eyes, from its respectability in those of childhood. The pastry, less patronized by judicious mothers, is only so much elegant indigestion: yet it is not easy to forget the pleasure of nibbling away the crust all around a raspberry or currant tart, in order to enjoy the three or four delicious semicircular bites at the fruity plenitude remaining. There is a custard with a wall of paste round it, which provokes a siege of this kind; and the cheese-cake has its amenities of approach. The acid flavor is a relief to the mawkishness of the biffin[2] or pressed baked apple, and an addition to the glib and quivering lightness of the jelly. Twelfth Cake,[3] which, when cut, looks like the side of a rich pit of earth covered with snow, is pleasant from warmer associations. Confectionery does not seem in the same request as of old; its paint has hurt its reputation. Yet the school-boy has still much to say for its humbler suavities. Kisses are very amiable and allegorical. Eight or ten of them, judiciously wrapped up in pieces of letter-paper, have saved many a loving heart the trouble of a less eloquent *billet-doux*. Candied citron we look upon to be the very acme and atticism[4] of confectionery grace. Preserves are too much of a good thing, with the exception of the jams that retain their fruit-skins. "Jam satis."[5] They qualify the cloying. Yet marmalade must not be passed over in these times, when it has been raised to the dignity of the peerage. The other day there was a Duke of Marmalade in Hayti, and a Count of Lemonade,[6]—so called, from places in which those eminent relishes are manufactured. After all, we must own that there is but one thing for which we care much at a pastry-cook's, except our old acquaintance the bun; especially as we can take up that and go on. It is an ice. Fancy a very hot day; the blinds down; the loungers unusually languid; the pavement burning one's feet; the sun, with a strong outline

in the street, baking one whole side of it like a brick-kiln; so that everybody is crowding on the other, except a man going to intercept a creditor bound for the Continent. Then think of a heaped-up ice, brought upon a salver with a spoon. What statesman, of any warmth of imagination, would not pardon the Neapolitans in summer, for an insurrection on account of the want of ice? Think of the first sidelong dip of the spoon in it, bringing away a well-sliced lump; then of the sweet wintry refreshment, that goes lengthening down one's throat; and lastly, of the sense of power and satisfaction resulting from having *had* the ice.

Not heaven itself can do away that slice;
But what has been, has been; and I have had
    my ice.

. . . .

PROEM TO SELECTION FROM KEATS'S POETRY
1844   1844

Keats was born a poet of the most poetical kind. All his feelings came to him through a poetical medium, or were speedily colored by it. He enjoyed a jest as heartily as any one, and sympathized with the lowliest commonplace; but the next minute his thoughts were in a garden of enchantment with nymphs, and fauns, and shapes of exalted humanity;

Elysian beauty, melancholy grace.[1]

It might be said of him that he never beheld an oak tree without seeing the Dryad. His fame may now forgive the critics who disliked his politics, and did not understand his poetry. Repeated editions of him in England, France, and America attest its triumphant survival of all obloquy; and there can be no doubt that he has taken a permanent station among the British poets, of a very high, if not thoroughly mature, description.

Keats's early poetry, indeed, partook plentifully of the exuberance of youth; and even in most of his later, his sensibility, sharpened by mortal illness, tended to a morbid excess. His region is "a wilderness of sweets"[2]—flowers of all hue, and "weeds of glorious feature,"[3]—where, as he says, the luxuriant soil brings

The pipy hemlock to strange overgrowth.[4]

---

[1] long and bony like Rosinante (the steed of Don Quixote, the hero of Cervantes's Spanish romance *Don Quixote*)
[2] An English variety of apple.
[3] A cake made for the celebration held on the twelfth night after Christmas.
[4] highest quality (characteristic of Attic Greek)
[5] already enough
[6] This is said to be a fact.

[1] Wordsworth, *Laodamia*, 95 (p. 333).
[2] *Paradise Lost*, 5, 294.
[3] Spenser, *Muiopotmus*, 213.
[4] Keats, *Endymion*, 1, 241 (p. 796).

But there also is the "rain-scented eglantine,"[1] and bushes of May-flowers, with bees, and myrtle, and bay,—and endless paths into forests haunted with the loveliest as well as gentlest beings; and the gods live in the distance, amid notes of majestic thunder. I do not need to say that no "surfeit" is ever there; but I do, that there is no end of the "nectared sweets."[2] In what other English poet (however superior to him in other respects) are you so *certain* of never opening a page without lighting upon the loveliest imagery and the most eloquent expressions? Name one. Compare any succession of their pages at random, and see if the young poet is not sure to present his stock of beauty; crude it may be, in many instances; too indiscriminate in general; never, perhaps, thoroughly perfect in cultivation; but there it is, exquisite of its kind, and filling envy with despair. He died at five-and-twenty; he had not revised his earlier works, nor given his genius its last pruning. His *Endymion*,[3] in resolving to be free from all critical trammels, had no versification; and his last noble fragment, *Hyperion*,[4] is not faultless, —but it is nearly so. *The Eve of St. Agnes*[5] betrays morbidity only in one instance (noticed in the comment).[6] Even in his earliest productions, which are to be considered as those of youth just emerging from boyhood, are to be found passages of as masculine a beauty as ever were written. Witness the *Sonnet on Reading Chapman's Homer*,[7]— epical in the splendor and dignity of its images, and terminating with the noblest Greek simplicity. Among his finished productions, however, of any length, *The Eve of St. Agnes* still appears to me the most delightful and complete specimen of his genius. It stands midway between his most sensitive ones (which, though of rare beauty, occasionally sink into feebleness) and the less generally characteristic majesty of the fragment of *Hyperion*. Doubtless his greatest poetry is to be found in *Hyperion;* and had he lived, there is as little doubt he would have written chiefly in that strain; rising superior to those languishments of love which made the critics so angry, and which they might so easily have pardoned at his time of life. But *The Eve of St. Agnes* had already bid most of them adieu, —exquisitely loving as it is. It is young, but full-grown poetry of the rarest description; graceful as the beardless Apollo; glowing and gorgeous with the colors of romance. I have therefore reprinted the whole of it in the present volume, together with the comment alluded to in the Preface; especially as, in addition to felicity of treatment, its subject is in every respect a happy one, and helps to "paint" this our bower of "poetry with delight." Melancholy, it is true, will "break in" when the reader thinks of the early death of such a writer; but it is one of the benevolent provisions of nature that all good things tend to pleasure in the recollection, when the bitterness of their loss is past, their own sweetness embalms them.

A thing of beauty is a joy forever.[1]

While writing this paragraph, a hand-organ out-of-doors has been playing one of the mournfullest and loveliest airs of Bellini—another genius who died young. The sound of music always gives a feeling either of triumph or tenderness to the state of mind in which it is heard; in this instance it seemed like one departed spirit come to bear testimony to another, and to say how true indeed may be the union of sorrowful and sweet recollections.

Keats knew the youthful faults of his poetry as well as any man, as the reader may see by the Preface to *Endymion*,[2] and its touching though manly acknowledgment of them to critical candor. I have this moment read it again, after a lapse of years, and have been astonished to think how anybody could answer such an appeal to the mercy of strength, with the cruelty of weakness. All the good for which Mr. Gifford[3] pretended to be zealous, he might have effected with pain to no one, and glory to himself; and therefore all the evil he mixed with it was of his own making. But the secret at the bottom of such unprovoked censure is exasperated inferiority. Young poets, upon the whole,—at least very young poets, —had better not publish at all. They are pretty sure to have faults; and jealousy

[1] Keats, *Endymion*, 1, 100 (p. 794).
[2] *Comus*, 479.   [3] See p. 793.
[4] See p. 875.   [5] See p. 868.
[6] The commentary which accompanied selections from Keats and other poets published in 1844 in a volume entitled *Imagination and Fancy*. The Proem here printed is from the same volume. The notes on *The Eve of St. Agnes* originally were published with the poem in Hunt's *The London Journal*, Jan. 21, 1835. The instance of morbidity which Hunt notes is in Porphyro's growing faint, st. 25, 8 (p. 871).
[7] See p. 779.

[1] Keats, *Endymion*, 1, 1 (p. 793).
[2] See Critical Note on Keats's *Endymion*.
[3] Gifford was long thought to be the author of the hostile article on Keats's *Endymion*, published in *The Quarterly Review*, April, 1818 (vol. 19, 204-08). See p. 939.

and envy are as sure to find them out, and wreak upon them their own disappointments. The critic is often an unsuccessful author, almost always an inferior one to a man of genius, and possesses his sensibility neither to beauty nor to pain. If he does,—if by any chance he is a man of genius himself (and such things have been), sure and certain will be his regret, some day, for having given pains which he might have turned into noble pleasures; and nothing will console him but that very charity towards himself, the grace of which can only be secured to us by our having denied it to no one.

Let the student of poetry observe that in all the luxury of *The Eve of St. Agnes* there is nothing of the conventional craft of artificial writers; no heaping up of words or similes for their own sakes or the rhyme's sake; no gaudy commonplaces, no borrowed airs of earnestness; no tricks of inversion; no substitution of reading or of ingenious thoughts for feeling or spontaneity; no irrelevancy or unfitness of any sort. All flows out of sincerity and passion. The writer is as much in love with the heroine as his hero is; his description of the painted window, however gorgeous, has not an untrue or superfluous word; and the only speck of fault in the whole poem arises from an excess of emotion.

Francis Jeffrey 1773-1850

From CRABBE'S POEMS[1]
1808   1808

We receive the proofs of Mr. Crabbe's poetical existence, which are contained in this volume,[2] with the same sort of feeling that would be excited by tidings of an ancient friend, whom we no longer expected to hear of in this world. We rejoice in his resurrection, both for his sake and for our own; but we feel also a certain movement of self-condemnation, for having been remiss in our inquiries after him, and somewhat too negligent of the honors which ought, at any rate, to have been paid to his memory.

It is now, we are afraid, upwards of twenty years since we were first struck with the vigor, originality, and truth of description of *The Village*;[3] and since, we regretted that an author who could write so well should have written so little. From that

[1] For text of Crabbe's poems, see pp. 154 ff.
[2] An edition of Crabbe's poems, published in Oct., 1807, and containing, besides reprints of *The Library*, *The Village*, and *The Newspaper*, some new poems, of which the most significant was *The Parish Register*.
[3] See p. 154.

time to the present, we have heard little of Mr. Crabbe; and fear that he has been in a great measure lost sight of by the public, as well as by us. With a singular, and scarcely pardonable indifference to fame, he has remained, during this long interval, in patient or indolent repose; and, without making a single movement to maintain or advance the reputation he had acquired, has permitted others to usurp the attention which he was sure of commanding, and allowed himself to be nearly forgotten by a public, which reckons upon being reminded of all the claims which the living have on its favor. His former publications, though of distinguished merit, were perhaps too small in volume to remain long the objects of general attention, and seem, by some accident, to have been jostled aside in the crowd of more clamorous competitors.

Yet, though the name of Crabbe has not hitherto been very common in the mouths of our poetical critics, we believe there are few real lovers of poetry to whom some of his sentiments and descriptions are not secretly familiar. There is a truth and force in many of his delineations of rustic life, which is calculated to sink deep into the memory; and, being confirmed by daily observation, they are recalled upon innumerable occasions, when the ideal pictures of more fanciful authors have lost all their interest. For ourselves at least, we profess to be indebted to Mr. Crabbe for many of these strong impressions; and have known more than one of our unpoetical acquaintances, who declared they could never pass by a parish workhouse without thinking of the description of it they had read at school in the *Poetical Extracts*. The volume before us will renew, we trust, and extend many such impressions. It contains all the former productions of the author, with about double their bulk of new matter, most of it in the same taste and manner of composition with the former, and some of a kind of which we had no previous example in this author. The whole, however, is of no ordinary merit, and will be found, we have little doubt, a sufficient warrant for Mr. Crabbe to take his place as one of the most original, nervous, and pathetic poets of the present century.

His characteristic, certainly, is force, and truth of description, joined for the most part to great selection and condensation of expression,—that kind of strength and originality which we meet with in Cowper, and that sort of diction and versification which we admire in *The Deserted Village* of Goldsmith, or *The Vanity of Human Wishes* of Johnson. If he can be said to have imitated the manner of any author, it is Goldsmith, indeed, who has been the object of his imitation; and yet his general train of thinking, and his views of society, are so extremely opposite, that, when *The Village* was first published, it was commonly considered as an antidote or an answer to the more captivating representations of *The Deserted Village*. Compared with this celebrated author, he will be found, we think, to have more vigor and less delicacy; and while he must be admitted to be inferior in the fine finish and uniform beauty of his composition, we cannot help considering him superior, both in the variety and the truth of his pictures. Instead of that uniform tint of pensive tenderness which overspreads the whole poetry of Goldsmith, we find in Mr. Crabbe many gleams of gaiety and humor. Though his habitual views of life are more gloomy than those of his rival, his poetical temperament seems far more cheerful; and when the occasions of sorrow and rebuke are gone by, he can collect himself for sarcastic pleasantry, or unbend in innocent playfulness. His diction, though generally pure and powerful, is sometimes harsh, and sometimes quaint; and he has occasionally admitted a couplet or two in a state so unfinished as to give a character of inelegance to the passages in which they occur. With a taste less disciplined and less fastidious than that of Goldsmith, he has, in our apprehension, a keener eye for observation, and a readier hand for the delineation of what he has observed. There is less poetical keeping in his whole performance; but the groups of which it consists are conceived, we think, with equal genius, and drawn with greater spirit as well as far greater fidelity.

It is not quite fair, perhaps, thus to draw a detailed parallel between a living poet, and one whose reputation has been sealed by death, and by the immutable sentence of a surviving generation. Yet there are so few of his contemporaries to whom Mr. Crabbe bears any resemblance that we can scarcely explain our opinion of his merit without comparing him to some of his predecessors. There is one set of writers, indeed, from whose works those of Mr. Crabbe might receive all that elucidation which results from contrast, and from an entire opposition in all points of taste and opinion. We allude now to the Wordsworths, and the Southeys, and Coleridges,

and all that ambitious fraternity, that, with good intentions and extraordinary talents, are laboring to bring back our poetry to the fantastical oddity and puling childishness of Withers, Quarles, or Marvel. These gentlemen write a great deal about rustic life, as well as Mr. Crabbe; and they even agree with him in dwelling much on its discomforts; but nothing can be more opposite than the views they take of the subject, or the manner in which they execute their representations of them.

Mr. Crabbe exhibits the common people of England pretty much as they are, and as they must appear to every one who will take the trouble of examining into their condition, at the same time that he renders his sketches in a very high degree interesting and beautiful by selecting what is most fit for description, by grouping them into such forms as must catch the attention or awake the memory, and by scattering over the whole such traits of moral sensibility, of sarcasm, and of deep reflection, as every one must feel to be natural, and own to be powerful. The gentlemen of the new school, on the other hand, scarcely ever condescend to take their subjects from any description of persons at all known to the common inhabitants of the world; but invent for themselves certain whimsical and unheard-of beings, to whom they impute some fantastical combination of feelings, and then labor to excite our sympathy for them, either by placing them in incredible situations, or by some strained and exaggerated moralization of a vague and tragical description. Mr. Crabbe, in short, shows us something which we have all seen, or may see, in real life; and draws from it such feelings and such reflections as every human being must acknowledge that it is calculated to excite. He delights us by the truth, and vivid and picturesque beauty of his representations, and by the force and pathos of the sensations with which we feel that they are connected. Mr. Wordsworth and his associates, on the other hand, introduce us to beings whose existence was not previously suspected by the acutest observers of nature; and excite an interest for them—where they do excite any interest—more by an eloquent and refined analysis of their own capricious feelings, than by any obvious or intelligible ground of sympathy in their situation.

Those who are acquainted with the *Lyrical Ballads*, or the more recent publications of Mr. Wordsworth, will scarcely deny the justice of this representation; but in order to vindicate it to such as do not enjoy that advantage, we must beg leave to make a few hasty references to the former, and by far the least exceptionable of those productions.

A village schoolmaster, for instance, is a pretty common poetical character. Goldsmith has drawn him inimitably;[1] so has Shenstone, with the slight change of sex;[2] and Mr. Crabbe, in two passages, has followed their footsteps.[3] Now, Mr. Wordsworth has a village schoolmaster also, a personage who makes no small figure in three or four of his poems.[4] But by what traits is this worthy old gentleman delineated by the new poet? No pedantry, no innocent vanity of learning, no mixture of indulgence with the pride of power, and of poverty with the consciousness of rare acquirements. Every feature which belongs to the situation, or marks the character in common apprehension, is scornfully discarded by Mr. Wordsworth, who represents his gray-haired rustic pedagogue as a sort of half crazy, sentimental person, overrun with fine feelings, constitutional merriment, and a most humorous melancholy. Here are the two stanzas in which this consistent and intelligible character is portrayed. The diction is at least as new as the conception.

The sighs which Matthew heav'd were sighs
Of one tir'd out with *fun* and *madness;*
The tears which came to Matthew's eyes
Were tears of light—*the oil of gladness.*

Yet sometimes, when the secret cup
Of still and serious thought went round
He seem'd as if he *drank it up,*
He felt with spirit so profound.
Thou *soul* of God's best *earthly mould,*[5] etc.

A frail damsel again is a character common enough in all poems, and one upon which many fine and pathetic lines have been expended. Mr. Wordsworth has written more than three hundred on the subject; but, instead of new images of tenderness, or delicate representation of intelligible feelings, he has contrived to tell us nothing whatever of the unfortunate fair one, but that her name is Martha Ray, and that she goes up to the top of a hill, in a red cloak, and cries, "O misery!" All the rest of the poem[6] is filled with a description of an old thorn and a pond, and of the silly stories which the neighboring old women told about them.

[1] See *The Deserted Village,* 193-218.
[2] See *The Schoolmistress* (p. 40).
[3] See *The Village,* 1, 296 ff. (p. 159).
[4] See *Matthew, The Two April Mornings,* and *The Fountain* (pp. 265-66).
[5] *Matthew,* 21 ff. (p. 265).   [6] *The Thorn* (p. 251).

The sports of childhood, and the untimely death of promising youth, is also a common topic of poetry. Mr. Wordsworth has made some blank verse about it; but, instead of the delightful and picturesque sketches with which so many authors of modern talents have presented us on this inviting subject, all that he is pleased to communicate of *his* rustic child is, that he used to amuse himself with shouting to the owls, and hearing them answer. To make amends for this brevity, the process of his mimicry is most accurately described.

——With fingers interwoven, both hands
Press'd closely palm to palm, and to his mouth
Uplifted, he, as through an instrument,
Blew mimic hootings to the silent owls,
That they might answer him.[1]

This is all we hear of him; and for the sake of this one accomplishment, we are told that the author has frequently stood mute, and gazed on his grave for half an hour together!

Love, and the fantasies of lovers, have afforded an ample theme to poets of all ages. Mr. Wordsworth, however, has thought fit to compose a piece, illustrating this copious subject by one single thought. A lover trots away to see his mistress one fine evening, gazing all the way on the moon; when he comes to her door,

O mercy! to myself I cried,
If Lucy should be dead![2]

And there the poem ends!

Now, we leave it to any reader of common candor and discernment to say whether these representations of character and sentiment are drawn from that eternal and universal standard of truth and nature, which every one is knowing enough to recognize, and no one great enough to depart from with impunity; or whether they are not formed, as we have ventured to allege, upon certain fantastic and affected peculiarities in the mind or fancy of the author, into which it is most improbable that many of his readers will enter, and which cannot, in some cases, be comprehended without much effort and explanation. Instead of multiplying instances of these wide and wilful aberrations from ordinary nature, it may be more satisfactory to produce the author's own admission of the narrowness of the plan upon which he writes, and of the very extraordinary circumstances which he himself

[1] *The Boy of Winander* (There Was a Boy), *The Prelude,* 5, 370 ff. (p. 274).
[2] *Strange Fits of Passion Have I Known* (p. 264).

sometimes thinks it necessary for his readers to keep in view, if they would wish to understand the beauty or propriety of his delineations.

A pathetic tale of guilt or superstition may be told, we are apt to fancy, by the poet himself, in his general character of poet, with full as much effect as by any other person. An old nurse, at any rate, or a monk or parish clerk, is always at hand to give grace to such a narration. None of these, however, would satisfy Mr. Wordsworth. He has written a long poem of this sort,[1] in which he thinks it indispensably necessary to apprise the reader, that he has endeavored to represent the language and sentiments of a particular character—of which character, he adds, "the reader will have a general notion, if he has ever known a man, *a captain of a small trading vessel,* for example, who being *past the middle age of life,* has retired upon an *annuity, or small independent income,* to some *village* or country town, of which he was *not a native,* or in which he had not been accustomed to live!''[2]

Now, we must be permitted to doubt whether, among all the readers of Mr. Wordsworth (few or many), there is a single individual who has had the happiness of knowing a person of this very peculiar description; or who is capable of forming any sort of conjecture of the particular disposition and turn of thinking such a combination of attributes would be apt to produce. To us, we will confess, the *annonce*[3] appears as ludicrous and absurd as it would be in the author of an ode or an epic to say, "Of this piece the reader will necessarily form a very erroneous judgment unless he is apprised that it was written by a pale man in a green coat—sitting cross-legged on an oaken stool—with a scratch on his nose, and a spelling dictionary on the table.''[4]

[1] *The Thorn* (p. 251). See Coleridge's *Biographia Literaria,* 18 (p. 407b, 35 ff.).
[2] Quoted from Wordsworth's note to *The Thorn* (see Critical Note on Wordsworth's *The Thorn*). See Coleridge's *Biographia Literaria,* 17 (p. 404b, 29 ff.).
[3] announcement
[4] "Some of our readers may have a curiosity to know in what manner this old annuitant captain does actually express himself in the village of his adoption. For their gratification, we annex the two first stanzas of his story, in which, with all the attention we have been able to bestow, we have been utterly unable to detect any traits that can be supposed to characterize either a seaman, an annuitant, or a stranger in a country town. It is a style, on the contrary, which we should ascribe, without hesitation, to a certain poetical fraternity in the west of England, and which, we verily believe, never was, and never will be, used by anyone out of that fraternity.

From these childish and absurd affectations, we turn with pleasure to the manly sense and correct picturing of Mr. Crabbe; and, after being dazzled and made giddy with the elaborate raptures and obscure originalities of these new artists, it is refreshing to meet again with the spirit and nature of our old masters, in the nervous pages of the author now before us.

•   •   •   •   •

From ALISON'S ESSAYS ON THE NATURE AND PRINCIPLES OF TASTE
1811   1811

•   •   •   •   •

It is unnecessary, however, to pursue these criticisms,[1] or, indeed, this hasty review of the speculation of other writers, any farther. The few observations we have already made, will enable the intelligent reader, both to understand in a general way what has been already done on the subject, and in some degree prepare him to appreciate the merits of that theory, substantially the same with Mr. Alison's, which we shall now proceed to illustrate somewhat more in detail.

The basis of it is, that the beauty which we impute to outward objects is nothing more than the reflection of our own inward emotions, and is made up entirely of certain little portions of love, pity, or other affections, which have been connected with these objects, and still adhere, as it were, to them, and move us anew whenever they are pre-

> There is a thorn—it looks so old,
>   In truth you'd find it hard to say
> How it could ever have been young!
>   It looks so old and gray.
> Not higher than a two-years' child,
>   *It stands erect,* this aged thorn;
> No leaves it has, no thorny points;
> It is a mass of knotted joints,
>   A wretched thing forlorn.
> *It stands erect;* and like a stone,
>   With lichens it is overgrown.
>
> *Like rock or stone, it is o'ergrown
>   With lichens;*—to the very top;
> And hung with heavy tufts of moss
>   A melancholy crop.
> Up from the earth these mosses creep,
>   And *this poor thorn,* they clasp it round
> So close, you'd say that they were bent
> *With plain and manifest intent!*
>   To drag it to the ground;
> And all had joined in one endeavor
> To bury *this poor thorn* forever.

And this, it seems, is Nature, and Pathos, and Poetry!''—Jeffrey.

[1] Jeffrey has pointed out the objections to the most important theories of beauty from the earliest times to his own day. He has given especial attention to the theories advanced by Dugald Stewart (1753-1828) in his *Philosophical Essays,* and by Richard Payne Knight (1750-1824) in his *Analytical Inquiry Into the Nature and Principles of Taste.*

sented to our observation. Before proceeding to bring any proof of the truth of this proposition, there are two things that it may be proper to explain a little more distinctly. First, What are the primary affections, by the suggestion of which we think the sense of beauty is produced? And, secondly, What is the nature of the connection by which we suppose that the objects we call beautiful are enabled to suggest these affections?

With regard to the first of these points, it fortunately is not necessary either to enter into any tedious details, or to have recourse to any nice distinctions. All sensations that are not absolutely indifferent, and are, at the same time, either agreeable when experienced by ourselves, or attractive when contemplated in others, may form the foundation of the emotions of sublimity or beauty. The love of *sensation* seems to be the ruling appetite of human nature; and many sensations, in which the painful may be thought to predominate, are consequently sought for with avidity, and recollected with interest, even in our own persons. In the persons of others, emotions still more painful are contemplated with eagerness and delight: and therefore we must not be surprised to find that many of the pleasing sensations of beauty or sublimity resolve themselves ultimately into recollections of feelings that may appear to have a very opposite character. The sum of the whole is, that every feeling which it is agreeable to experience, to recall, or to witness, may become the source of beauty in external objects, when it is so connected with them as that their appearance reminds us of that feeling. Now, in real life, and from daily experience and observation, we know that it is agreeable, in the first place, to recollect our own pleasurable sensations, or to be enabled to form a lively conception of the pleasures of other men, or even of sentient beings of any description. We know likewise, from the same sure authority, that there is a certain delight in the remembrance of our past, or the conception of our future emotions, even though attended with great pain, provided the pain be not forced too rudely on the mind, and be softened by the accompaniment of any milder feeling. And finally, we know, in the same manner, that the spectacle or conception of the emotions of others, even when in a high degree painful, is extremely interesting and attractive, and draws us away, not only from the consideration of indifferent objects, but even from the pursuit of

light or frivolous enjoyments. All these are plain and familiar facts, of the existence of which, however they may be explained, no one can entertain the slightest doubt—and into which, therefore, we shall have made no inconsiderable progress, if we can resolve the more mysterious fact of the emotions we receive from the contemplation of sublimity or beauty.

Our proposition then is, that these emotions are not original emotions, nor produced directly by any material qualities in the objects which excite them; but are reflections, or images, of the more radical and familiar emotions to which we have already alluded; and are occasioned, not by any inherent virtue in the objects before us, but by the accidents, if we may so express ourselves, by which these may have been enabled to suggest or recall to us our past sensations or sympathies. We might almost venture, indeed, to lay it down as an axiom, that, except in the plain and palpable case of bodily pain or pleasure, we can never be *interested* in anything but the fortunes of sentient beings;—and that everything partaking of the nature of mental emotion, must have for its object *the feelings,* past, present, or possible, of something capable of sensation. Independent, therefore, of all evidence, and without the help of any explanation, we should have been apt to conclude that the emotions of beauty and sublimity must have for their objects the sufferings or enjoyments of sentient beings;—and to reject, as intrinsically absurd and incredible, the supposition that material objects, which obviously do neither hurt nor delight the body, should yet excite, by their mere physical qualities, the very powerful emotions which are sometimes excited by the spectacle of beauty.

Of the feelings, by their connection with which external objects become beautiful, we do not think it necessary to speak more minutely;—and, therefore, it only remains, under this preliminary view of the subject, to explain the nature of that connection by which we conceive this effect to be produced. Here, also, there is but little need for minuteness, or fulness of enumeration. Almost every tie, by which two objects can be bound together in the imagination, in such a manner as that the presentment of the one shall recall the memory of the other;—or, in other words, almost every possible relation which can subsist between such objects, may serve to connect the things we call sublime and beautiful, with feelings that are interesting or delightful. It may be useful, however, to class these bonds of association between mind and matter in a rude and general way.

It appears to us, then, that objects are sublime or beautiful, *first,* when they are the natural signs and perpetual concomitants of pleasurable sensations, or, at any rate, of some lively feeling of emotion in ourselves or in some other sentient beings; or, *secondly,* when they are the arbitrary or accidental concomitants of such feelings; or, *thirdly,* when they bear some analogy or fanciful resemblance to things with which these emotions are necessarily connected. In endeavoring to illustrate the nature of these several relations, we shall be led to lay before our readers some proofs that appear to us satisfactory of the truth of the general theory.

The most obvious and the strongest association that can be established between inward feelings and external objects is where the object is necessarily and universally connected with the feeling by the law of nature, so that it is always presented to the senses when the feeling is impressed upon the mind —as the sight or the sound of laughter, with the feeling of gaiety—of weeping, with distress—of the sound of thunder, with ideas of danger and power. Let us dwell for a moment on the last instance.—Nothing, perhaps, in the whole range of nature, is more strikingly and universally sublime than the sound we have just mentioned; yet it seems obvious that the sense of sublimity is produced, not by any quality that is perceived by the ear, but altogether by the impression of power and of danger that is necessarily made upon the mind, whenever that sound is heard. That it is not produced by any peculiarity in the sound itself, is certain, from the mistakes that are frequently made with regard to it. The noise of a cart rattling over the stones, is often mistaken for thunder; and as long as the mistake lasts, this very vulgar and insignificant noise is actually felt to be prodigiously sublime. It is so felt, however, it is perfectly plain, merely because it is then associated with ideas of prodigious power and undefined danger;—and the sublimity is accordingly destroyed, the moment the association is dissolved, though the sound itself and its effect on the organ, continue exactly the same. This, therefore, is an instance in which sublimity is distinctly proved to consist, not in any physical quality of the object to which it is ascribed, but in its necessary connection with that vast and uncontrolled Power which is the natural object of awe and veneration.

．　．　．　．　．　．

Hitherto we have spoken of the beauty of external objects only. But the whole difficulty of the theory consists in its application to them. If that be once adjusted, the beauty of immaterial objects can occasion no perplexity. Poems and other compositions in words are beautiful in proportion as they are conversant with beautiful objects—or as they suggest to us, in a more direct way, the moral and social emotions on which the beauty of all objects depends. Theorems and demonstrations, again, are beautiful according as they excite in us emotions of admiration for the genius and intellectual power of their inventors, and images of the magnificent and beneficial ends to which such discoveries may be applied;—and mechanical contrivances are beautiful when they remind us of similar talents and ingenuity, and at the same time impress us with a more direct sense of their vast utility to mankind, and of the great additional conveniences with which life is consequently adorned. In all cases, therefore, there is the suggestion of some interesting conception or emotion associated with a present perception, in which it is apparently confounded and embodied— and this, according to the whole of the preceding deduction, is the distinguishing characteristic of beauty.

Having now explained, as fully as we think necessary, the grounds of that opinion as to the nature of beauty which appears to be most conformable to the truth, we have only to add a word or two as to the necessary consequences of its adoption upon several other controversies of a kindred description.

In the first place, then, we conceive that it establishes the substantial identity of the sublime, the beautiful, and the picturesque; and consequently puts an end to all controversy that is not purely verbal, as to the difference of those several qualities. Every material object that interests us, without actually hurting or gratifying our bodily feelings, must do so, according to this theory, in one and the same manner,—that is, by suggesting or recalling some emotion or affection of ourselves or some other sentient being, and presenting, to our imagination at least, some natural object of love, pity, admiration, or awe. The interest of material objects, therefore, is always *the same;* and arises, in every case, not from any physical qualities they may possess, but from their association with some idea of emotion. But though material objects have but one means of exciting emotion, the emotions they do excite are infinite. They are mirrors that reflect all shades and all colors, and, in point of fact, do seldom reflect the same hues twice. No two interesting objects, perhaps, whether known by the name of beautiful, sublime, or picturesque, ever produced exactly the same emotion in the beholder; and no object, it is most probable, ever moved any two persons to the very same conceptions. As they may be associated with all the feelings and affections of which the human mind is susceptible, so they may suggest those feelings in all their variety, and, in fact, do daily excite all sorts of emotions—running through every gradation, from extreme gaiety and elevation to the borders of horror and disgust.

Now it is certainly true that all the variety of emotions raised in this way on the single basis of association may be classed, in a rude way, under the denominations of sublime, beautiful, and picturesque, according as they partake of awe, tenderness, or admiration; and we have no other objection to this nomenclature except its extreme imperfection, and the delusions to which we know that it has given occasion. If objects that interest by their association with ideas of power and danger and terror are to be distinguished by the peculiar name of the sublime, why should there not be a separate name also for objects that interest by associations of mirth and gaiety—another for those that please by suggestions of softness and melancholy—another for such as are connected with impressions of comfort and tranquillity—and another for those that are related to pity and admiration and love and regret and all the other distinct emotions and affections of our nature? These are not in reality less distinguishable from each other than from the emotions of awe and veneration that confer the title of sublime on *their* representatives; and while all the former are confounded under the comprehensive appellation of beauty, this partial attempt at distinction is only apt to mislead us into an erroneous opinion of our accuracy, and to make us believe, both that there is a greater conformity among the things that pass under the same name, and a greater difference between those that pass under different

names, than is really the case. We have seen already that the radical error of almost all preceding inquirers has lain in supposing that everything that passed under the name of beautiful must have some real and inherent quality in common with everything else that obtained that name. And it is scarcely necessary for us to observe that it has been almost as general an opinion that sublimity was not only something radically different from beauty, but actually opposed to it; whereas the fact is, that it is far more nearly related to some sorts of beauty than many sorts of beauty are to each other; and that both are founded exactly upon the same principle of suggesting some past or possible emotion of some sentient being.

Upon this point we are happy to find our opinions confirmed by the authority of Mr. Stewart, who, in his *Essay on the Beautiful,* already referred to, has observed, not only that there appears to him to be no inconsistency or impropriety in such expressions as the *sublime beauties* of nature, or of the sacred Scriptures;—but has added in express terms that "to oppose the beautiful to the sublime or to the picturesque strikes him as something analogous to a contrast between the beautiful and the comic—the beautiful and the tragic—the beautiful and the pathetic—or the beautiful and the romantic."

The only other advantage which we shall specify as likely to result from the general adoption of the theory we have been endeavoring to illustrate is, that it seems calculated to put an end to all these perplexing and vexatious questions about the standard of taste, which have given occasion to so much impertinent and so much elaborate discussion. If things are not beautiful in themselves, but only as they serve to suggest interesting conceptions to the mind, then everything which does in point of fact suggest such a conception to any individual, *is beautiful* to that individual; and it is not only quite true that there is no room for disputing about tastes, but that all tastes are equally just and correct, in so far as each individual speaks only of his own emotions. When a man calls a thing beautiful, however, he may indeed mean to make two very different assertions;—he may mean that it gives *him* pleasure by suggesting to him some interesting emotion; and, in this sense, there can be no doubt that, if he merely speak truth, the thing is beautiful; and that it pleases him precisely in the same way that all other things please those to whom they appear beautiful. But if he mean farther to say that the thing possesses some quality which should make it appear beautiful to every other person, and that it is owing to some prejudice or defect in them if it appear otherwise, then he is as unreasonable and absurd as he would think those who should attempt to convince him that he felt no emotion of beauty.

All tastes, then, are equally just and true, in so far as concerns the individual whose taste is in question; and what a man feels distinctly to be beautiful, *is beautiful* to him, whatever other people may think of it. All this follows clearly from the theory now in question: but it does not follow, from it, that all tastes are equally good or desirable, or that there is any difficulty in describing that which is really the best, and the most to be envied. The only use of the faculty of taste is to afford an innocent delight, and to assist in the cultivation of a finer morality; and that man certainly will have the most delight from this faculty, who has the most numerous and most powerful perceptions of beauty. But, if beauty consist in the reflection of our affections and sympathies, it is plain that *he* will always see the most beauty whose affections are the warmest and most exercised—whose imagination is the most powerful, and who has most accustomed himself to attend to the objects by which he is surrounded. In so far as mere feeling and enjoyment are concerned, therefore, it seems evident that the best taste must be that which belongs to the best affections, the most active fancy, and the most attentive habits of observation. It will follow pretty exactly, too, that all men's perceptions of beauty will be nearly in proportion to the degree of their sensibility and social sympathies; and that those who have no affections towards sentient beings, will be as certainly insensible to beauty in external objects, as he, who cannot hear the sound of his friend's voice, must be deaf to its echo.[1]

In so far as the sense of beauty is regarded as a mere source of enjoyment, this seems to be the only distinction that deserves to be attended to; and the only cultivation that taste should ever receive, with a view to the gratification of the individual, should be through the indirect channel of cultivating the affections and powers of observation. If we aspire, however, to be *creators,*

[1] See Hunt's *On the Realities of Imagination* (p. 902a, 33 ff.).

as well as observers of beauty, and place any part of our happiness in ministering to the gratification of others—as artists, or poets, or authors of any sort—then, indeed, a new distinction of tastes, and a far more laborious system of cultivation, will be necessary. A man who pursues only his own delight, will be as much charmed with objects that suggest powerful emotions in consequence of personal and accidental associations, as with those that introduce similar emotions by means of associations that are universal and indestructible. To him, all objects of the former class are really as beautiful as those of the latter—and for his own gratification, the creation of that sort of beauty is just as important an occupation: but if he conceive the ambition of creating beauties for the admiration of others, he must be cautious to employ only such objects as are the *natural* signs, or the *inseparable* concomitants of emotions, of which the greater part of mankind are susceptible; and his taste will *then* deserve to be called bad and false, if he obtrude upon the public, as beautiful, objects that are not likely to be associated in common minds with any interesting impressions.

For a man himself, then, there is no taste that is either bad or false; and the only difference worthy of being attended to, is that between a great deal and a very little. Some who have cold affections, sluggish imaginations, and no habits of observation, can with difficulty discern beauty in anything; while others, who are full of kindness of sensibility, and who have been accustomed to attend to all the objects around them, feel it almost in everything. It is no matter what other people may think of the objects of their admiration; nor ought it to be any concern of theirs that the public would be astonished or offended, if they were called upon to join in that admiration. So long as no such call is made, this anticipated discrepancy of feeling need give *them* no uneasiness; and the suspicion of it should produce no contempt in any other persons. It is a strange aberration indeed of vanity that makes us despise persons for being happy—for having sources of enjoyment in which we cannot share:—and yet this is the true source of the ridicule which is so generally poured upon individuals who seek only to enjoy their peculiar tastes unmolested:— for, if there be any truth in the theory we have been expounding, no taste is bad for any other reason than because it is peculiar —as the objects in which it delights must actually serve to suggest to the individual those common emotions and universal affections upon which the sense of beauty is everywhere founded. The misfortune is, however, that we are apt to consider all persons who make known their peculiar relishes, and especially all who create any objects for their gratification, as in some measure dictating to the public, and setting up an idol for general adoration; and hence this intolerant interference with almost all peculiar perceptions of beauty, and the unsparing derision that pursues all deviations from acknowledged standards. This intolerance, we admit, is often provoked by something of a spirit of *proselytism* and arrogance, in those who mistake their own casual associations for natural or universal relations; and the consequence is, that mortified vanity ultimately dries up, even for them, the fountain of their peculiar enjoyment; and disenchants, by a new association of general contempt or ridicule, the scenes that had been consecrated by some innocent but accidental emotion.

As all men must have some peculiar associations, all men must have some peculiar notions of beauty, and, of course, to a certain extent, a taste that the public would be entitled to consider as false or vitiated. For those who make no demands on public admiration, however, it is hard to be obliged to sacrifice this source of enjoyment; and, even for those who labor for applause, the wisest course, perhaps, if it were only practicable, would be to have *two* tastes—one to enjoy, and one to work by—one founded upon universal associations, according to which they finished those performances for which they challenged universal praise— and another guided by all casual and individual association, through which they might still look fondly upon nature, and upon the objects of their secret admiration.

From WORDSWORTH'S THE EXCURSION[1]
1814   1814

This will never do! It bears no doubt the stamp of the author's heart and fancy; but unfortunately not half so visibly as that of his peculiar system. His former poems were intended to recommend that system, and to bespeak favor for it by their individual merit; but this, we suspect, must be recommended by the system, and can only expect to succeed where it has been previously estab-

[1] For text of Book 1 of *The Excursion,* see pp. 300 ff.

lished. It is longer, weaker, and tamer than any of Mr. Wordsworth's other productions, with less boldness of originality, and less even of that extreme simplicity and lowliness of tone which wavered so prettily, in the *Lyrical Ballads,* between silliness and pathos. We have imitations of Cowper, and even of Milton here, engrafted on the natural drawl of the Lakers[1]—and all diluted into harmony by that profuse and irrepressible wordiness which deluges all the blank verse of this school of poetry, and lubricates and weakens the whole structure of their style.

Though it fairly fills four hundred and twenty good quarto pages, without note, vignette, or any sort of extraneous assistance, it is stated in the title—with something of an imprudent candor—to be but "a portion" of a larger work; and in the preface, where an attempt is rather unsuccessfully made to explain the whole design, it is still more rashly disclosed that it is but "*a part of the second part,* of a *long* and laborious work"—which is to consist of three parts!

What Mr. Wordsworth's ideas of length are, we have no means of accurately judging. But we cannot help suspecting that they are liberal, to a degree that will alarm the weakness of most modern readers. As far as we can gather from the preface, the entire poem—or one of them (for we really are not sure whether there is to be one or two) is of a biographical nature, and is to contain the history of the author's mind, and of the origin and progress of his poetical powers, up to the period when they were sufficiently matured to qualify him for the great work on which he has been so long employed. Now, the quarto before us contains an account of one of his youthful rambles in the vales of Cumberland, and occupies precisely the period of three days! So that, by the use of a very powerful *calculus,* some estimate may be formed of the probable extent of the entire biography.

This small specimen, however, and the statements with which it is prefaced, have been sufficient to set our minds at rest in one particular. The case of Mr. Wordsworth, we perceive, is now manifestly hopeless; and we give him up as altogether incurable, and beyond the power of criticism. We cannot indeed altogether omit taking precautions now and then against the

[1] A name given to Wordsworth, Coleridge, and Southey because of their residence in the lake district of England.

spreading of the malady; but for himself, though we shall watch the progress of his symptoms as a matter of professional curiosity and instruction, we really think it right not to harass him any longer with nauseous remedies, but rather to throw in cordials and lenitives, and wait in patience for the natural termination of the disorder. In order to justify this desertion of our patient, however, it is proper to state why we despair of the success of a more active practice.

A man who has been for twenty years at work on such matter as is now before us, and who comes complacently forward with a whole quarto of it, after all the admonitions he has received, cannot reasonably be expected to "change his hand, or check his pride," upon the suggestion of far weightier monitors than we can pretend to be. Inveterate habits must now have given a kind of sanctity to the errors of early taste; and the very powers of which we lament the perversion, have probably become incapable of any other application. The very quantity, too, that he has written, and is at this moment working up for publication upon the old pattern, makes it almost hopeless to look for any change of it. All this is so much capital already sunk in the concern, which must be sacrificed if that be abandoned; and no man likes to give up for lost the time and talent and labor which he has embodied in any permanent production. We were not previously aware of these obstacles to Mr. Wordsworth's conversion; and, considering the peculiarities of his former writings merely as the result of certain wanton and capricious experiments on public taste and indulgence, conceived it to be our duty to discourage their repetition by all the means in our power. We now see clearly, however, how the case stands; and, making up our minds, though with the most sincere pain and reluctance, to consider him as finally lost to the good cause of poetry, shall endeavor to be thankful for the occasional gleams of tenderness and beauty which the natural force of his imagination and affections must still shed over all his productions, and to which we shall ever turn with delight, in spite of the affectation and mysticism and prolixity, with which they are so abundantly contrasted.

Long habits of seclusion, and an excessive ambition of originality, can alone account for the disproportion which seems to exist between this author's taste and his genius; or for the devotion with which he has sacrificed so many precious gifts at the shrine of those paltry idols which he has set up for himself among his lakes and his mountains. Solitary musings, amidst such scenes, might no doubt be expected to nurse up the mind to the majesty of poetical conception, (though it is remarkable that all the greater poets lived, or had lived, in the full current of society); but the collision of equal minds —the admonition of prevailing impressions —seems necessary to reduce its redundancies, and repress that tendency to extravagance or puerility, into which the self-indulgence and self-admiration of genius is so apt to be betrayed, when it is allowed to wanton, without awe or restraint, in the triumph and delight of its own intoxication. That its flights should be graceful and glorious in the eyes of men, it seems almost to be necessary that they should be made in the consciousness that men's eyes are to behold them, and that the inward transport and vigor by which they are inspired should be tempered by an occasional reference to what will be thought of them by those ultimate dispensers of glory. An habitual and general knowledge of the few settled and permanent maxims which form the canon of general taste in all large and polished societies—a certain tact, which informs us at once that many things, which we still love, and are moved by in secret, must necessarily be despised as childish, or derided as absurd, in all such societies—though it will not stand in the place of genius, seems necessary to the success of its exertions; and though it will never enable any one to produce the higher beauties of art, can alone secure the talent which does produce them from errors that must render it useless. Those who have most of the talent, however, commonly acquire this knowledge with the greatest facility; and if Mr. Wordsworth, instead of confining himself almost entirely to the society of the dalesmen and cottagers, and little children, who form the subjects of his book, had condescended to mingle a little more with the people that were to read and judge of it, we cannot help thinking that its texture might have been considerably improved. At least it appears to us to be absolutely impossible that any one who had lived or mixed familiarly with men of literature and ordinary judgment in poetry (of course we exclude the coadjutors and disciples of his own school) could ever have fallen into such gross faults, or so long mistaken them for beauties. His first essays[1] we looked

[1] attempts (A reference to Wordsworth's poems published in 1798 in a volume entitled *Lyrical Ballads.*)

upon in a good degree as poetical paradoxes,—maintained experimentally, in order to display talent, and court notoriety;—and so maintained, with no more serious belief in their truth than is usually generated by an ingenious and animated defence of other paradoxes. But when we find that he has been for twenty years exclusively employed upon articles of this very fabric, and that he has still enough of raw material on hand to keep him so employed for twenty years to come, we cannot refuse him the justice of believing that he is a sincere convert to his own system, and must ascribe the peculiarities of his composition, not to any transient affectation, or accidental caprice of imagination, but to a settled perversity of taste or understanding, which has been fostered, if not altogether created, by the circumstances to which we have alluded.

The volume before us, if we were to describe it very shortly, we should characterize as a tissue of moral and devotional ravings, in which innumerable changes are rung upon a very few simple and familiar ideas—but with such an accompaniment of long words, long sentences, and unwieldy phrases, and such a hubbub of strained raptures and fantastical sublimities, that it is often difficult for the most skilful and attentive student to obtain a glimpse of the author's meaning—and altogether impossible for an ordinary reader to conjecture what he is about. Moral and religious enthusiasm, though undoubtedly poetical emotions, are at the same time but dangerous inspirers of poetry, nothing being so apt to run into interminable dulness or mellifluous extravagance without giving the unfortunate author the slightest intimation of his danger. His laudable zeal for the efficacy of his preachments, he very naturally mistakes for the ardor of poetical inspiration; and, while dealing out the high words and glowing phrases which are so readily supplied by themes of this description, can scarcely avoid believing that he is eminently original and impressive. All sorts of commonplace notions and expressions are sanctified in his eyes by the sublime ends for which they are employed; and the mystical verbiage of the Methodist pulpit is repeated till the speaker entertains no doubt that he is the chosen organ of divine truth and persuasion. But if such be the common hazards of seeking inspiration from those potent fountains, it may easily be conceived what chance Mr. Wordsworth had of escaping their enchantment, with his natural propen-

sities to wordiness, and his unlucky habit of debasing pathos with vulgarity. The fact accordingly is, that in this production he is more obscure that a Pindaric poet[1] of the seventeenth century; and more verbose "than even himself of yore;" while the wilfulness with which he persists in choosing his examples of intellectual dignity and tenderness exclusively from the lowest ranks of society, will be sufficiently apparent, from the circumstance of his having thought fit to make his chief prolocutor[2] in this poetical dialogue, and chief advocate of Providence and Virtue, *an old Scotch Pedlar,* retired indeed from business, but still rambling about in his former haunts, and gossiping among his old customers, without his pack on his shoulders. The other persons of the drama are a retired military chaplain, who has grown half an atheist and half a misanthrope, the wife of an unprosperous weaver, a servant girl with her natural child, a parish pauper, and one or two other personages of equal rank and dignity.

The character of the work is decidedly didactic; and more than nine-tenths of it are occupied with a species of dialogue, or rather a series of long sermons or harangues which pass between the pedlar, the author, the old chaplain, and a worthy vicar, who entertains the whole party at dinner on the last day of their excursion. The incidents which occur in the course of it are as few and trifling as can well be imagined; and those which the different speakers narrate in the course of their discourses, are introduced rather to illustrate their arguments or opinions, than for any interest they are supposed to possess of their own. The doctrine which the work is intended to enforce, we are by no means certain that we have discovered. In so far as we can collect, however, it seems to be neither more nor less than the old familiar one, that a firm belief in the providence of a wise and beneficent Being must be our great stay and support under all afflictions and perplexities upon earth; and that there are indications of his power and goodness in all the aspects of the visible universe, whether living or inanimate, every part of which should therefore be regarded with love and reverence, as exponents of those great attributes. We can testify, at least, that these salutary and important truths are inculcated at far greater lengths, and with more repetitions,

---

[1] A poet, like Cowley, who writes odes in imitation of the Greek poet Pindar.
[2] spokesman

than in any ten volumes of sermons that we ever perused. It is also maintained, with equal conciseness and originality, that there is frequently much good sense, as well as much enjoyment, in the humbler conditions of life; and that, in spite of great vices and abuses, there is a reasonable allowance both of happiness and goodness in society at large. If there be any deeper or more recondite doctrines in Mr. Wordsworth's book, we must confess that they have escaped us; and, convinced as we are of the truth and soundness of those to which we have alluded, we cannot help thinking that they might have been better enforced with less parade and prolixity. His effusions on what may be called the physiognomy of external nature, or its moral and theological expression, are eminently fantastic, obscure, and affected. It is quite time, however, that we should give the reader a more particular account of this singular performance.

It opens with a picture of the author toiling across a bare common in a hot summer day, and reaching at last a ruined hut surrounded with tall trees, where he meets by appointment with a hale old man, with an iron-pointed staff lying beside him. Then follows a retrospective account of their first acquaintance — formed, it seems, when the author was at a village school, and his aged friend occupied "one room—the fifth part of a house"[1]— in the neighborhood. After this, we have the history of this reverend person at no small length. He was born, we are happy to find, in Scotland—among the hills of Athol; and his mother, after his father's death, married the parish schoolmaster— so that he was taught his letters betimes. But then, as it is here set forth with much solemnity,

From his sixth year, the boy of whom I speak, In summer tended cattle on the hills![2]

And again, a few pages after, that there may be no risk of mistake as to a point of such essential importance—

From early childhood, even, as hath been said, From his *sixth year*, he had been sent abroad, *In summer*—to tend herds! Such was his task![3]

In the course of this occupation it is next recorded that he acquired such a taste for rural scenery and the open air, that when he was sent to teach a school in a neighboring village, he found it "a misery to him,"[1] and determined to embrace the more romantic occupation of a pedlar—or, as Mr. Wordsworth more musically expresses it,

A vagrant merchant, bent beneath his load;[2]

—and in the course of his peregrinations had acquired a very large acquaintance, which, after he had given up dealing, he frequently took a summer ramble to visit.

The author, on coming up to this interesting personage, finds him sitting with his eyes half shut,—and not being quite sure whether he is asleep or awake, stands "some minutes' space"[3] in silence beside him.—"At length," says he, with his own delightful simplicity—

At length I hail'd him—*seeing that his hat Was moist* with water-drops, as if the brim Had newly scoop'd a running stream!—

* * * * * * *

—"'Tis," said I, "a burning day! My lips are parched with thirst;—but you, I guess, Have somewhere found relief!"[4]

Upon this, the benevolent old man points him out, not a running stream, but a well in a corner, to which the author repairs, and after minutely describing its situation, beyond a broken wall, and between two alders that "grew in a cold damp nook,"[5] he thus faithfully chronicles the process of his return:—

My thirst was slak'd, and from the cheerless spot Withdrawing, straightway to the shade return'd, Where sat the old man on the cottage bench.[6]

The Pedlar then gives an account of the last inhabitants of the deserted cottage beside them. These were a good industrious weaver and his wife and children. They were very happy for awhile, till sickness and want of work came upon them, and then the father enlisted as a soldier, and the wife pined in that lonely cottage— growing every year more careless and desponding, as her anxiety and fears for her absent husband, of whom no tidings ever reached her, accumulated. Her children died and left her cheerless and alone; and at last she died also; and the cottage fell to decay. We must say that there is very considerable pathos in the telling of this

---

[1] Book 1, 57. (Jeffrey's quotations are from the 1814 edition of *The Excursion*.)
[2] Book 1, 118-19.   [3] Book 1, 215-17.

[1] Book 1, 314.   [2] Book 1, 323.   [3] Book 1, 443.
[4] Book 1, 444-50.   [5] Book 1, 461.   [6] Book 1, 463-65.

simple story, and that they who can get over the repugnance excited by the triteness of its incidents, and the lowness of its objects, will not fail to be struck with the author's knowledge of the human heart, and the power he possesses of stirring up its deepest and gentlest sympathies. His prolixity, indeed, it is not so easy to get over. This little story fills about twenty-five quarto pages, and abounds, of course, with mawkish sentiment and details of preposterous minuteness. When the tale is told, the travellers take their staffs and end their first day's journey, without further adventure, at a little inn.

The Second Book sets them forward betimes in the morning. They pass by a Village Wake,[1] and as they approach a more solitary part of the mountains, the old man tells the author that he is taking him to see an old friend of his who had formerly been chaplain to a Highland regiment—had lost a beloved wife—been roused from his dejection by the first enthusiasm of the French Revolution—had emigrated, on its miscarriage, to America—and returned disgusted to hide himself in the retreat to which they were now ascending. That retreat is then most tediously described—a smooth green valley in the heart of the mountain, without trees, and with only one dwelling. Just as they get sight of it from the ridge above, they see a funeral train proceeding from the solitary abode, and hurry on with some apprehension for the fate of the amiable misanthrope, whom they find, however, in very tolerable condition at the door, and learn that the funeral was that of an aged pauper who had been boarded out by the parish in that cheap farmhouse, and had died in consequence of long exposure to heavy rain. The old chaplain, or, as Mr. Wordsworth is pleased to call him, the Solitary, tells his dull story at prodigious length, and after giving an inflated description of an effect of mountain mists in the evening sun, treats his visitors with a rustic dinner—and they walk out to the fields at the close of the Second Book.

The Third makes no progress in the excursion. It is entirely filled with moral and religious conversation and debate, and with a more ample detail of the Solitary's past life than had been given in the sketch of his friend. The conversation is, in our

[1] An annual festival of the nature of a fair or market. See Book 2, 115-51. Originally, the festival was held in commemoration of the dedication of a church.

judgment, exceedingly dull and mystical, and the Solitary's confessions insufferably diffuse. Yet there is occasionally very considerable force of writing and tenderness of sentiment in this part of the work.

The Fourth Book is also filled with dialogues, ethical and theological, and, with the exception of some brilliant and forceful expressions here and there, consists of an exposition of truisms, more cloudy, wordy, and inconceivably prolix, than anything we ever met with.

In the beginning of the Fifth Book, they leave the solitary valley, taking its pensive inhabitant along with them, and stray on to where the landscape sinks down into milder features, till they arrive at a church which stands on a moderate elevation in the centre of a wide and fertile vale. Here they meditate for awhile among the monuments, till the Vicar comes out and joins them, and recognizing the Pedlar for an old acquaintance, mixes graciously in the conversation, which proceeds in a very edifying manner till the close of the book.

The Sixth contains a choice obituary, or characteristic account of several of the persons who lie buried before this group of moralizers;—an unsuccessful lover, who had found consolation in natural history—a miner, who had worked on for twenty years, in despite of universal ridicule, and at last found the vein he had expected—two political enemies reconciled in old age to each other—an old female miser—a seduced damsel—and two widowers, one who had devoted himself to the education of his daughters, and one who had preferred marrying a prudent middle-aged woman to take care of them.

In the beginning of the Eighth Book, the worthy Vicar expresses, in the words of Mr. Wordsworth's own epitome,[1] "his apprehension that he had detained his auditors too long—invites them to his house —Solitary, disciplined to comply, rallies the Wanderer, and somewhat playfully draws a comparison between his itinerant profession and that of a knight-errant— which leads to the Wanderer giving an account of changes in the country, from the manufacturing spirit—Its favorable effects —The other side of the picture," etc., etc. After these very poetical themes are exhausted, they all go into the house, where they are introduced to the Vicar's wife and daughter; and while they sit chatting

[1] Prefixed to Book 8.

in the parlor over a family dinner, his son and one of his companions come in with a fine dish of trouts piled on a blue slate, and after being caressed by the company, they are sent to dinner in the nursery.— This ends the Eighth Book.

The Ninth and last is chiefly occupied with a mystical discourse of the Pedlar, who maintains that the whole universe is animated by an active principle, the noblest seat of which is in the human soul; and, moreover, that the final end of old age is to train and enable us

To hear the mighty stream of *Tendency*
Uttering, for elevation of our thought,
A clear sonorous voice, inaudible
To the vast multitude whose doom it is
To run the giddy round of vain delight—[1]

with other matters as luminous and emphatic. The hostess at length breaks off the harangue by proposing that they should make a little excursion on the lake,—and they embark accordingly, and after navigating for some time along its shores, and drinking tea on a little island, land at last on a remote promontory, from which they see the sun go down,—and listen to a solemn and pious, but rather long, prayer from the Vicar. Then they walk back to the parsonage door, where the author and his friend propose to spend the evening,—but the Solitary prefers walking back in the moonlight to his own valley, after promising to take another ramble with them—

If time, with free consent, be yours to give,
And season favors.[2]

—And here the publication somewhat abruptly closes.

Our abstract of the story has been so extremely concise that it is more than usually necessary for us to lay some specimens of the work itself before our readers. Its grand staple, as we have already said, consists of a kind of mystical morality: and the chief characteristics of the style are that it is prolix, and very frequently unintelligible: and though we are sensible that no great gratification is to be expected from the exhibition of those qualities, yet it is necessary to give our readers a taste of them, both to justify the sentence we have passed, and to satisfy them that it was really beyond our power to present them with any abstract or intelligible account of those long conversations which we have had so much occasion

to notice in our brief sketch of its contents. We need give ourselves no trouble, however, to select passages for this purpose. Here is the first that presents itself to us on opening the volume; and if our readers can form the slightest guess at its meaning, we must give them credit for a sagacity to which we have no pretension.

But by the storms *of circumstance* unshaken,
And subject neither to eclipse or wane,
Duty exists;—immutably survive,
For our support, the measures and the forms,
Which an abstract Intelligence supplies;
Whose kingdom is where Time and Space are not:
Of other converse, which mind, soul, and heart,
Do, with united urgency, require,
What more, that may not perish?[1]

'Tis, by comparison, an easy task
Earth to despise; but to converse with Heav'n,
This is not easy:—to relinquish all
We have, or hope, of happiness and joy,—
And stand in freedom loosen'd from this world;
I deem not arduous!—but must needs confess
That 'tis a thing impossible to frame
Conceptions equal to the Soul's desires.[2]

This is a fair sample of that rapturous mysticism which eludes all comprehension, and fills the despairing reader with painful giddiness and terror. The following, which we meet with on the very next page, is in the same general strain, though the first part of it affords a good specimen of the author's talent for enveloping a plain and trite observation in all the mock majesty of solemn verbosity. A reader of plain understanding, we suspect, could hardly recognize the familiar remark that excessive grief for our departed friends is not very consistent with a firm belief in their immortal felicity, in the first twenty lines of the following passage. In the succeeding lines we do not ourselves pretend to recognize anything.

From this infirmity of mortal kind
Sorrow proceeds, which else were not;—at least,
If grief be something hallow'd and ordain'd,
If, in proportion, it be just and meet,
Through this, 'tis able to maintain its hold,
In that excess which conscience disapproves.
For who could sink and settle to that point
Of selfishness; so senseless who could be
In framing estimates of loss and gain,
As long and perseveringly to mourn
For any object of his love, remov'd
From this unstable world, if he could fix
A satisfying view upon that state
Of pure, imperishable blessedness,
Which reason promises, and Holy Writ

[1] Book 9, 87-91.   [2] Book 9, 782-83.   [1] Book 4, 71-79.   [2] Book 4, 130-37.

Ensures to all believers?—Yet mistrust
Is of such incapacity, methinks,
No natural branch; despondency far less.
—And if there be whose tender frames have
    droop'd
Ev'n to the dust; apparently, through weight 5
Of anguish unreliev'd, and lack of power
An agonizing sorrow to *transmute;*
Infer not hence a hope from those withheld
When wanted most; a confidence impair'd
So pitiably, that, having ceas'd to see 10
With bodily eyes, they are borne down by love
Of what is lost, and perish through regret!
Oh! no, full oft the innocent Suff'rer sees
Too clearly, feels too vividly, and longs
To realize the vision with intense
And overconstant yearning.—There—there lies 15
The excess, by which the balance is destroy'd.
Too, too contracted are these walls of flesh,
This vital warmth too cold, these visual orbs,
Though inconceivably endow'd, too dim
For any passion of the soul that leads 20
To ecstasy! and, all the crooked paths
Of time and change disdaining, takes its
    course
Along the line of limitless desires.
I, speaking now from such disorder free,
Nor sleep, nor craving, but in settled peace, 25
I cannot doubt that they whom you deplore
Are glorified.''[1]

If any farther specimen be wanted of
the learned author's propensity to deal out
the most familiar truths as the oracles of
his own inspired understanding, the follow- 30
ing wordy paraphrase of the ordinary remark that the best consolation in distress
is to be found in the exercises of piety and
the testimony of a good conscience, may be
found on turning the leaf.

    ''What then remains?—To seek 35
Those helps, for his occasions ever near,
Who lacks not will to use them; vows, renew'd
On the first motion of a holy thought!
Vigils of contemplation; praise; and pray'r, 40
A stream, which, from the fountain of the
    heart,
Issuing however feebly, nowhere flows
Without access of unexpected strength.
But, above all, the victory is most sure
For him who, seeking faith by virtue strives 45
To yield entire submission to the law
Of conscience; conscience reverenc'd and
    obey'd
As God's most intimate presence in the soul,
And his most perfect image in the world.''[2] 50

. . . . . .

There is no beauty, we think, it must be
admitted, in these passages, and so little
either of interest or curiosity in the incidents they disclose, that we can scarcely 55
conceive that any man to whom they had
actually occurred should take the trouble

[1] Book 4, 146-89.   [2] Book 4, 214-27.

to recount them to his wife and children by
his idle fireside; but that man or child
should think them worth writing down in
blank verse and printing in magnificent
quarto, we should certainly have supposed
altogether impossible, had it not been for
the ample proofs which Mr. Wordsworth
has afforded to the contrary.

Sometimes their silliness is enhanced by
a paltry attempt at effect and emphasis, as
in the following account of that very touching and extraordinary occurrence of a lamb
bleating among the mountains. The poet
would actually persuade us that he thought
the mountains themselves were bleating,
and that nothing could be so grand or
impressive. ''List!'' cries the old Pedlar,
suddenly breaking off in the middle of one
of his daintiest ravings—

    —''List!—I heard,
From yon huge breast of rock, *a solemn
    bleat!*
Sent forth as if it were the mountain's voice!
As if the visible mountain made the cry!
Again!''—The effect upon the soul was such
As he express'd; for, from the mountain's
    heart
The solemn bleat appear'd to come! There
    was
No other—and the region all around
Stood silent, empty of all shape of life.
—*It was a Lamb*—left somewhere to itself![1]

What we have now quoted will give the
reader a notion of the taste and spirit in
which this volume is composed: and yet if
it had not contained something a good deal
better, we do not know how we should have
been justified in troubling him with any
account of it. But the truth is that Mr.
Wordsworth, with all his perversities, is a
person of great powers; and has frequently
a force in his moral declamations, and a
tenderness in his pathetic narratives, which
neither his prolixity nor his affectation can
altogether deprive of their effect. We shall
venture to give some extracts from the
simple tale of the Weaver's solitary cottage.[2]
Its heroine is the deserted wife, and its
chief interest consists in the picture of her
despairing despondence and anxiety after
his disappearance. The Pedlar, recurring
to the well to which he had directed his
companion, observes,

    —''As I stoop'd to drink,
Upon the slimy foot-stone I espied
The useless fragment of a wooden bowl,
Green with the moss of years! a pensive sight
That mov'd my heart!—recalling former days

[1] Book 4, 402-11.   [2] In Book 1 (pp. 300 ff.).

When I could never pass that road but she
Who liv'd within these walls, at my approach,
A daughter's welcome gave me; and I lov'd her
As my own child! O sir! the good die first!
And they whose hearts are dry as summer dust
Burn to the socket.''[1]

    —''By some especial care
Her temper had been fram'd, as if to make
A being—who by adding love to peace
Might live on earth a life of happiness.''[2]

The bliss and tranquillity of these prosperous years is well and copiously described;—but at last came sickness and want of employment;—and the effect on the kindhearted and industrious mechanic is strikingly delineated.

    —''At his door he stood,
And whistl'd many a snatch of merry tunes
That had no mirth in them! or with his knife
Carv'd uncouth figures on the heads of sticks—
Then, not less idly, sought, through every nook
In house or garden, any casual work
Of use or ornament.''[3]—

''One while he would speak lightly of his babes,
And with a cruel tongue: at other times
He toss'd them with a false unnat'ral joy;
And 'twas a rueful thing to see the looks
Of the poor innocent children.''[4]

At last he steals from his cottage and enlists as a soldier, and when the benevolent Pedlar comes, in his rounds, in hope of a cheerful welcome, he meets with a scene of despair.

    —''Having reach'd the door
I knock'd,—and, when I enter'd with the hope
Of usual greeting, Margaret look'd at me
A little while; then turn'd her head away
Speechless,—and sitting down upon a chair
Wept bitterly! I wist not what to do,
Or how to speak to her. Poor wretch! at last
She rose from off her seat, and then,—O sir!
I cannot *tell* how she pronounced my name.—
With fervent love, and with a face of grief
Unutterably helpless;''[5]

Hope, however, and native cheerfulness were not yet subdued; and her spirit still bore up against the pressure of this desertion.

    —''Long we had not talk'd
Ere we built up a pile of better thoughts,

And with a brighter eye she look'd around
As if she had been shedding tears of joy.
We parted.—'Twas the time of early spring;
I left her busy with her garden tools,
And well remember, o'er that fence she look'd,
And, while I paced along the footway path,
Called out, and sent a blessing after me,
With tender cheerfulness, and with a voice
That seem'd the very sound of happy thoughts.''[1]

The gradual sinking of the spirit under the load of continued anxiety, and the destruction of all the finer springs of the soul by a course of unvarying sadness, are very feelingly represented in the sequel of this simple narrative.

    —''I journey'd back this way
Towards the wane of summer, when the wheat
Was yellow, and the soft and bladed grass
Springing afresh had o'er the hay-field spread
Its tender verdure. At the door arriv'd,
I found that she was absent. In the shade,
Where now we sit, I waited her return.
Her cottage, then a cheerful object, wore
Its customary look,—only, I thought,
The honeysuckle, crowding round the porch,
Hung down in heavier tufts, and that bright weed,
The yellow stone-crop,[2] suffer'd to take root
Along the window's edge, profusely grew,
Blinding the lower panes. I turn'd aside
And stroll'd into her garden. It appear'd
To lag behind the season, and had lost
Its pride of neatness.''[3]

''The sun was sinking in the west; and now
I sat with sad impatience. From within
Her solitary infant cried aloud;
Then, like a blast that dies away self-still'd
The voice was silent.''[4]—

The desolate woman had now an air of still and listless, though patient, sorrow.

    —''Evermore
Her eyelids droop'd, her eyes were downward cast;
And, when she at her table gave me food,
She did not look at me! Her voice was low,
Her body was subdu'd. In ev'ry act
Pertaining to her house affairs, appear'd
The careless stillness of a thinking mind
Self-occupied, to which all outward things
Are like an idle matter. Still she sigh'd,
But yet no motion of the breast was seen,
No heaving of the heart. While by the fire
We sat together, signs came on my ear,
I know not how, and hardly whence they came.''[5]

---

[1] Book 1, 686-96.
[2] A moss-like European plant which grows on rocks or walls.
[3] Book 1, 706-22.
[4] Book 1, 734-38.
[5] Book 1, 791-803.

[1] Book 1, 491-502.
[2] Book 1, 516-19.
[3] Book 1, 568-74.
[4] Book 1, 585-89.
[5] Book 1, 646-56.

—"I return'd,
And took my rounds along this road again,
Ere on its bank the primrose flow'r
Peep'd forth, to give an earnest of the spring,
I found her sad and drooping; she had   5
    learn'd
No tidings of her husband; if he liv'd
She knew not that he liv'd; if he were dead
She knew not he was dead. She seem'd the
    same
In person and appearance, but her house   10
Bespake a sleepy hand of negligence"[1]—

—"Her infant babe
Had from its mother caught the trick of grief,   15
And sigh'd among its playthings!"[2]

Returning seasons only deepened this gloom, and confirmed this neglect. Her child died, and she spent her weary days in roaming over the country, and repeating her fond and vain inquiries to every passer-by.

"Meantime her house by frost, and thaw,
    and rain,
Was sapp'd; and while she slept, the nightly
    damps   25
Did chill her breast; and in the stormy day
Her tatter'd clothes were ruffl'd by the wind,
Ev'n at the side of her own fire. Yet still
She lov'd this wretched spot; * * * and
    here, my friend,
In sickness she remain'd; and here she died!   30
Last human tenant of these ruin'd walls."[3]

The story of the old Chaplain, though a little less lowly, is of the same mournful cast, and almost equally destitute of incidents,—for Mr. Wordsworth delineates only feelings—and all his adventures are   35
of the heart. The narrative which is given by the sufferer himself is, in my opinion, the most spirited and interesting part of the poem. He begins thus, and addressing himself, after a long pause, to his ancient   40
countryman and friend, the Pedlar—

"You never saw, your eyes did never look
On the bright form of her whom once I
    lov'd!—
Her silver voice was heard upon the earth,   45
A sound unknown to you; else, honor'd friend,
Your heart had borne a pitiable share
Of what I suffer'd, when I wept that loss!
And suffer now, not seldom, from the thought   50
That I remember—and can weep no more!"[4]

The following account of his marriage and early felicity is written with great sweetness—a sweetness like that of Massinger, in his softer, more mellifluous passages.   55

—"This fair bride—
In the devotedness of youthful love,
Preferring me to parents, and the choir
Of gay companions, to the natal roof,
And all known places and familiar sights,   5
(Resign'd with sadness gently weighing down
Her trembling expectations, but no more
Than did to her due honor, and to me
Yielded, that day, a confidence sublime
In what I had to build upon)—this bride,   10
Young, modest, meek, and beautiful, I led
To a low cottage in a sunny bay,
Where the salt sea innocuously breaks,
And the sea breeze as innocently breathes,
On Devon's leafy shores;—a shelter'd hold,   15
In a soft clime, encouraging the soil
To a luxuriant bounty!—As our steps
Approach the embower'd abode, our chosen
    seat,
See, rooted in the earth, its kindly bed,
The unendanger'd myrtle, deck'd with   20
    flowers,"[1] etc.

—"Wild were our walks upon those lonely
    downs
*   *   *   *   *   *
Whence, unmolested wanderers, we beheld   25
The shining giver of the day diffuse
His brightness, o'er a tract of sea and land
Gay as our spirits, free as our desires,
As our enjoyments boundless.—From these
    heights
We dropp'd at pleasure into sylvan combs;   30
Where arbors of impenetrable shade,
And mossy seats detain'd us, side by side
With hearts at ease, and knowledge in our
    hearts
'That all the grove and all the day was
    ours.'"[2]

There, seven years of unmolested happiness were blessed with two lovely children.

"And on these pillars rested, as on air,   40
Our solitude."[3]

Suddenly a contagious malady swept off both the infants.

"Calm as a frozen lake when ruthless winds   45
Blow fiercely, agitating earth and sky,
The mother now remain'd.[4]

—"Yet, stealing slow,
Dimness o'er this clear luminary crept
Insensibly!—The immortal and divine
Yielded to mortal reflux, her pure glory,
As from the pinnacle of worldly state
Wretched ambition drops astounded, fell
Into a gulf obscure of silent grief,
And keen heart-anguish—of itself asham'd,
Yet obstinately cherishing itself:

---

[1] Book 1, 813-22.   [3] Book 1, 906-16.
[2] Book 1, 829-31.   [4] Book 3, 480-87.

[1] Book 3, 504-23.   [3] Book 3, 597-98.
[2] Book 3, 532-49.   [4] Book 3, 650-52.

And, so consum'd, she melted from my arms!
And left me, on this earth, disconsolate.''[1]

The agony of mind into which the survivor was thrown is described with a powerful eloquence, as well as the doubts and distracting fears which the skeptical speculations of his careless days had raised in his spirit. There is something peculiarly grand and terrible to our feelings in the imagery of these three lines—

"By pain of heart, now check'd, and now impell'd,
The intellectual power, through words and things,
Went sounding on,—a dim and perilous way!''[2]

At last he is roused from his dejected mood by the glorious promises which seemed held out to human nature by the first dawn of the French Revolution;—and it indicates a fine perception of the secret springs of character and emotion, to choose a being so circumstanced as the most ardent votary of that far-spread enthusiasm.

"Thus was I reconverted to the world!
Society became my glitt'ring bride,
And airy hopes my children! * * * If busy men
In sober conclave met, to weave a web
Of amity, whose living threads should stretch
Beyond the seas, and to the farthest pole,
There did I sit assisting. If, with noise
And acclamation, crowds in open air
Express'd the tumult of their minds, my voice
There mingled, heard or not. The powers of song
I left not uninvok'd; and, in still groves,
Where mild enthusiasts tun'd a pensive lay
Of thanks and expectation, in accord
With their belief, I sang Saturnian rule
Return'd,—a progeny of golden years
Permitted to descend, and bless mankind.''[3]

On the disappearance of that bright vision, he was inclined to take part with the desperate party who still aimed at establishing universal regeneration, though by more questionable instruments than they had originally assumed. But the military despotism which ensued soon closed the scene against all such exertions; and, disgusted with men and Europe, he sought for shelter in the wilds of America. In the calm of the voyage, Memory and Conscience awoke him to a sense of his misery.

—"Feebly must they have felt
Who, in old time, attir'd with snakes and whips

[1] Book 3, 669-79.   [3] Book 3, 734-58.
[2] Book 3, 699-701.

The vengeful Furies.[1] *Beautiful* regards
Were turn'd on me—the face of her I lov'd!
The wife and mother, pitifully fixing
Tender reproaches, insupportable!''[2]

His disappointment, and ultimate seclusion in England, have been already sufficiently detailed.

.   .   .   .   .   .

Besides those more extended passages of interest or beauty, which we have quoted, and omitted to quote, there are scattered up and down the book, and in the midst of its most repulsive portions, a very great number of single lines and images, that sparkle like gems in the desert, and startle us by an intimation of the great poetic powers that lie buried in the rubbish that has been heaped around them. It is difficult to pick up these, after we have once passed them by; but we shall endeavor to light upon one or two. The beneficial effect of intervals of relaxation and pastime on youthful minds is finely expressed, we think, in a single line, when it is said to be—

Like vernal ground to Sabbath sunshine left.[3]

The following image of the bursting forth of a mountain spring seems to us also to be conceived with great elegance and beauty.

And a few steps may bring us to the spot,
Where haply crown'd with flow'rets and green herbs,
The mountain Infant to the Sun comes forth,
Like human life from darkness![4]

The ameliorating effects of song and music on the minds which most delight in them are likewise very poetically expressed.

—And when the stream
Which overflow'd the soul was pass'd away,
A consciousness remained that it had left,
Deposited upon the silent shore
Of memory, images and precious thoughts,
That shall not die, and cannot be destroy'd.[5]

Nor is anything more elegant than the representation of the graceful tranquillity occasionally put on by one of the author's favorites, who, though gay and airy, in general—

Was graceful, when it pleased him, smooth and still

As the mute swan that floats adown the stream,
Or on the waters of th' unruffled lake
Anchors her placid beauty. Not a leaf

[1] Æschylus and Euripides were the first poets to attire the Furies with snakes. See Æschylus's *Choëphori*, 1048-50; Euripides's *Iphigenia in Taurica*, 285-87, and *Orestes*, 256.
[2] Book 3, 850-55.   [4] Book 3, 32-35.
[3] Book 7, 781.   [5] Book 7, 25-30.

That flutters on the bough more light than he,
And not a flow'r that droops in the green
    shade
More winningly reserv'd.[1]

Nor are there wanting morsels of a sterner 5
and more majestic beauty, as when, assuming the weightier diction of Cowper, he says,
in language which the hearts of all readers
of modern history must have responded—
        —Earth is sick 10
And Heav'n is weary of the hollow words
Which States and Kingdoms utter when they
    speak
Of Truth and Justice.[2]

These examples, we perceive, are not very 15
well chosen—but we have not leisure to improve the selection; and, such as they are,
they may serve to give the reader a notion
of the sort of merit which we meant to illustrate by their citation. When we look back 20
to them, indeed, and to the other passages
which we have now extracted, we feel half
inclined to rescind the severe sentence which
we passed on the work at the beginning; but
when we look into the work itself, we per- 25
ceive that it cannot be rescinded. Nobody
can be more disposed to do justice to the
great powers of Mr. Wordsworth than we
are; and, from the first time that he came
before us, down to the present moment, we 30
have uniformly testified in their favor, and
assigned indeed our high sense of their value
as the chief ground of the bitterness with
which we resented their perversion. That
perversion, however, is now far more visible 35
than their original dignity; and while we
collect the fragments, it is impossible not to
mourn over the ruins from which we are
condemned to pick them. If any one should
doubt of the existence of such a perversion, 40
or be disposed to dispute about the instances
we have hastily brought forward, we would
just beg leave to refer him to the general
plan and character of the poem now before
us. Why should Mr. Wordsworth have 45
made his hero a superannuated pedlar?
What but the most wretched affectation, or
provoking perversity of taste, could induce
any one to place his chosen advocate of wisdom and virtue in so absurd and fantastic a 50
condition? Did Mr. Wordsworth really
imagine that his favorite doctrines were
likely to gain anything in point of effect or
authority by being put into the mouth of a
person accustomed to higgle about tape or 55
brass sleeve-buttons? Or is it not plain
that, independent of the ridicule and disgust which such a personification must ex-

  [1] Book 6, 292-98.   [2] Book 5, 378-81.

cite in many of his readers, its adoption
exposes his work throughout to the charge
of revolting incongruity and utter disregard
of probability or nature? For, after he has
thus wilfully debased his moral teacher by
a low occupation, is there one word that he
puts into his mouth, or one sentiment of
which he makes him the organ, that has the
most remote reference to that occupation?
Is there anything in his learned, abstract
and logical harangues that savors of the
calling that is ascribed to him? Are any of
their materials such as a pedlar could possibly have dealt in? Are the manners, the very
diction, the sentiments in any, the very
smallest degree, accommodated to a person
in that condition? or are they not eminently
and conspicuously such as could not by
possibility belong to it? A man who went
about selling flannel and pocket-handkerchiefs in this lofty diction would soon
frighten away all his customers; and would
infallibly pass either for a madman or for
some learned and affected gentleman, who,
in a frolic, had taken up a character which
he was peculiarly ill qualified for supporting.

The absurdity in this case, we think, is
palpable and glaring; but it is exactly of
the same nature with that which infects the
whole substance of the work, a puerile ambition of singularity engrafted on an unlucky predilection for truisms, and an
affected passion for simplicity and humble
life, most awkwardly combined with a taste
for mystical refinements, and all the gorgeousness of obscure phraseology. His taste
for simplicity is evinced by sprinkling up
and down his interminable declamations a
few descriptions of baby-houses, and of old
hats with wet brims; and his amiable partiality for humble life, by assuring us that
a wordy rhetorician, who talks about Thebes,
and allegorizes all the heathen mythology,
was once a pedlar—and making him break
in upon his magnificent orations with two or
three awkward notices of something that he
had seen when selling winter raiment about
the country—or of the changes in the state
of society, which had almost annihilated his
former calling.

From WORDSWORTH'S THE WHITE DOE
OF RYLSTONE
1815   *1815*

This, we think, has the merit of being the
very worst poem we ever saw imprinted in a
quarto volume; and though it was scarcely
to be expected, we confess that Mr. Words-

worth, with all his ambition, should so soon have attained to that distinction, the wonder may perhaps be diminished when we state that it seems to us to consist of a happy union of all the faults, without any of the beauties, which belong to his school of poetry. It is just such a work, in short, as some wicked enemy of that school might be supposed to have devised, on purpose to make it ridiculous; and when we first took it up we could not help suspecting that some ill-natured critic had actually taken this harsh method of instructing Mr. Words-worth, by example, in the nature of those errors against which our precepts had been so often directed in vain. We had not gone far, however, till we felt intimately that nothing in the nature of a joke could be so insupportably dull; and that this must be the work of one who earnestly believed it to be a pattern of pathetic simplicity, and gave it out as such to the admiration of all intelligent readers. In this point of view the work may be regarded as curious at least, if not in some degree interesting; and, at all events, it must be instructive to be made aware of the excesses into which superior understandings may be betrayed, by long self-indulgence, and the strange extravagances into which they may run, when under the influence of that intoxication which is produced by unrestrained admiration of themselves. This poetical intoxication, indeed, to pursue the figure a little farther, seems capable of assuming as many forms as the vulgar one which arises from wine; and it appears to require as delicate a management to make a man a good poet by the help of the one as to make him a good companion by means of the other. In both cases, a little mistake as to the dose or the quality of the inspiring fluid may make him absolutely outrageous, or lull him over into the most profound stupidity, instead of brightening up the hidden stores of his genius; and truly we are concerned to say that Mr. Wordsworth seems hitherto to have been unlucky in the choice of his liquor—or of his bottle-holder. In some of his odes and ethic exhortations he was exposed to the public in a state of incoherent rapture and glorious delirium, to which we think we have seen a parallel among the humbler lovers of jollity. In the *Lyrical Ballads* he was exhibited, on the whole, in a vein of very pretty deliration;[1] but in the poem before us he appears in a state of low and maudlin imbecility, which would not have

[1] delirium

misbecome Master Silence himself, in the close of a social day. Whether this unhappy result is to be ascribed to any adulteration of his Castalian cups,[1] or to the unlucky choice of his company over them, we cannot presume to say. It may be that he has dashed his Hippocrene with too large an infusion of lake water, or assisted its operation too exclusively by the study of the ancient historical ballads of "the north countrie."[2] That there are palpable imitations of the style and manner of those venerable compositions in the work before us is indeed undeniable; but it unfortunately happens that while the hobbling versification, the mean diction, and flat stupidity of these models are very exactly copied, and even improved upon, in this imitation, their rude energy, manly simplicity, and occasional felicity of expression have totally disappeared; and, instead of them, a large allowance of the author's own metaphysical sensibility and mystical wordiness is forced into an unnatural combination with the borrowed beauties which have just been mentioned.

The story of the poem, though not capable of furnishing out matter for a quarto volume, might yet have made an interesting ballad, and, in the hands of Mr. Scott or Lord Byron, would probably have supplied many images to be loved, and descriptions to be remembered. The incidents arise out of the short-lived Catholic insurrection of the Northern counties, in the reign of Elizabeth, which was supposed to be connected with the project of marrying the Queen of the Scots to the Duke of Norfolk; and terminated in the ruin of the Earls of Northumberland and Westmoreland, by whom it was chiefly abetted. Among the victims of this rash enterprise was Richard Norton of Rylstone, who comes to the array with a splendid banner, at the head of eight tall sons, but against the will and advice of a ninth, who, though he refused to join the host, yet follows unarmed in its rear, out of anxiety for the fate of his family; and, when the father and his gallant progeny are made prisoners, and led to execution at York, recovers the fatal banner, and is slain by a party of the Queen's horse near Bolton Priory, in

[1] That is, source of poetic inspiration. Castalia was a fountain on Mount Parnassus, sacred to Apollo and the Muses. Hippocrene was a similar fountain on Mount Helicon.
[2] The scene of many of the old ballads of England and Scotland is in "the north countrie," the traditional dwelling place of fairies, demons, giants, etc.

which place he had been ordered to deposit it by the dying voice of his father. The stately halls and pleasant bowers of Rylstone are then wasted, and fall into desolation; while the heroic daughter, and only survivor of the house, is sheltered among its faithful retainers, and wanders about for many years in its neighborhood, accompanied by a beautiful white doe, which had formerly been a pet in the family; and continues, long after the death of this sad survivor, to repair every Sunday to the churchyard of Bolton Priory, and there to feed and wander among the graves, to the wonder and delight of the rustic congregation that came there to worship.

This, we think, is a pretty subject for a ballad; and, in the author's better day, might have made a lyrical one of considerable interest. Let us see, however, how he deals with it, since he has bethought him of publishing in quarto.

The First Canto merely contains the description of the doe coming into the churchyard on Sunday, and of the congregation wondering at her. She is described as being as white as a lily—or the moon—or a ship in the sunshine; and this is the style in which Mr. Wordsworth marvels and moralizes about her through ten quarto pages.

.　.　.　.　.　.　.

The Seventh and last Canto contains the history of the desolated Emily[1] and her faithful doe; but so discreetly and cautiously written, that we will engage that the most tender-hearted reader shall peruse it without the least risk of excessive emotion. The poor lady runs about indeed for some years in a very disconsolate way, in a worsted gown and flannel nightcap; but at last the old white doe finds her out, and takes again to following her—whereupon Mr. Wordsworth breaks out into this fine and natural rapture:

Oh, moment ever blest! O pair!
Belov'd of Heaven, Heaven's choicest care!
This was for you a precious greeting,—
For both a bounteous, fruitful meeting.
Join'd are they; and the sylvan doe
Can she depart? Can she forego
The lady, once her playful peer?

*　*　*　*　*

That day, the first of a reunion
Which was to teem with high communion,
That day of balmy April weather,
They tarried in the wood together.[2]

[1] Emily Norton, whose relatives had been killed in the uprising which they had promoted.
[2] Canto 7. 115-33.

What follows is not quite so intelligible.

When Emily by morning light
Went forth, the doe was there in sight.
She shrunk:—with one frail shock of pain,
Received and followed by a prayer,
Did she behold—saw once again;
Shun will she not, she feels, will bear;—
But wheresoever she look'd round
All now was trouble-haunted ground.[1]

It certainly is not easy to guess what was in the mind of the author when he penned these four last inconceivable lines; but we are willing to infer that the lady's loneliness was cheered by this mute associate; and that the doe, in return, found a certain comfort in the lady's company—

Communication, like the ray
Of a new morning, to the nature
And prospects of the inferior creature![2]

In due time the poor lady dies, and is laid beside her mother; and the doe continues to haunt the places which they had frequented together, and especially to come and pasture every Sunday upon the fine grass in Bolton churchyard, the gate of which is never opened but on occasion of the weekly service.—In consequence of all which, we are assured by Mr. Wordsworth, that she "is approved by earth and sky, in their benignity;"[3] and moreover, that the old Priory itself takes her for a daughter of the Eternal Prime—which we have no doubt is a very great compliment, though we have not the good luck to know what it means.

And aye, methinks, this hoary pile,
Subdued by outrage and decay,
Looks down upon her with a smile,
A gracious smile that seems to say,
"Thou, thou are not a child of Time,
But daughter of the Eternal Prime!"[4]

From CHILDE HAROLD'S PILGRIMAGE,
CANTO THE THIRD[5]
1816　　　　　1816

If the finest poetry be that which leaves the deepest impression on the minds of its readers—and this is not the worst test of its excellence—Lord Byron, we think, must be allowed to take precedence of all his distinguished contemporaries. He has not the variety of Scott, nor the delicacy of Campbell, nor the absolute truth of Crabbe, nor the polished sparkling of Moore; but

[1] Canto 7, 144-51.　　　[3] Canto 7, 353-54.
[2] Canto 7, 279-81.　　　[4] Canto 7, 355-60.
[5] For text of *Childe Harold's Pilgrimage*, see pp. 549 ff.

in force of diction, and inextinguishable energy of sentiment, he clearly surpasses them all. "Words that breathe, and thoughts that burn,"[1] are not merely the ornaments, but the common staple of his poetry; and he is not inspired or impressive only in some happy passages, but through the whole body and tissue of his composition. It was an unavoidable condition, perhaps, of this higher excellence, that his scene should be narrow, and his persons few. To compass such ends as he had in view, it was necessary to reject all ordinary agents, and all trivial combinations. He could not possibly be amusing, or ingenious or playful; or hope to maintain the requisite pitch of interest by the recitation of sprightly adventures, or the opposition of common characters. To produce great effects, in short, he felt that it was necessary to deal only with the greater passions—with the exaltations of a daring fancy, and the errors of a lofty intellect—with the pride, the terrors, and the agonies of strong emotion—the fire and air alone of our human elements.[2]

In this respect, and in his general notion of the end and means of poetry, we have sometimes thought that his views fell more in with those of the Lake poets,[3] than of any other existing party in the poetical commonwealth; and, in some of his later productions especially, it is impossible not to be struck with his occasional approaches to the style and manner of this class of writers. Lord Byron, however, it should be observed, like all other persons of a quick sense of beauty, and sure enough of their own originality to be in no fear of paltry imputations, is a great mimic of styles and manners, and a great borrower of external character. He and Scott, accordingly, are full of imitations of all the writers from whom they have ever derived gratification; and the two most original writers of the age might appear, to superficial observers, to be the most deeply indebted to their predecessors. In this particular instance, we have no fault to find with Lord Byron. For undoubtedly the finer passages of Wordsworth and Southey have in them wherewithal to lend an impulse to the utmost ambition of rival genius; and their diction

and manner of writing is frequently both striking and original. But we must say that it would afford us still greater pleasure to find these tuneful gentlemen returning to compliment which Lord Byron has here paid to their talents, and forming themselves on the model rather of his imitations, than of their own originals. In those imitations they will find that, though he is sometimes abundantly mystical, he never, or at least very rarely, indulges in absolute nonsense, never takes his lofty flights upon mean or ridiculous occasions, and, above all, never dilutes his strong conceptions, and magnificent imaginations, with a flood of oppressive verbosity. On the contrary, he is, of all living writers, the most concise and condensed; and, we would fain hope, may go far, by his example, to redeem the great reproach of our modern literature—its intolerable prolixity and redundance. In his nervous and manly lines, we find no elaborate amplification of common sentiments, no ostentatious polishing of pretty expressions; and we really think that the brilliant success which has rewarded his disdain of those paltry artifices, should put to shame forever that puling and self-admiring race, who can live through half a volume on the stock of a single thought, and expatiate over divers fair quarto pages with the details of one tedious description. In Lord Byron, on the contrary, we have a perpetual stream of thick-coming fancies,[1] an eternal spring of fresh-blown images, which seem called into existence by the sudden flash of those glowing thoughts and overwhelming emotions that struggle for expression through the whole flow of his poetry, and impart to a diction that is often abrupt and irregular a force and a charm which frequently realize all that is said of inspiration.

With all these undoubted claims to our admiration, however, it is impossible to deny that the noble author before us has still something to learn, and a good deal to correct. He is frequently abrupt and careless, and sometimes obscure. There are marks, occasionally, of effort and straining after an emphasis which is generally spontaneous; and above all, there is far too great a monotony in the moral coloring of his pictures, and too much repetition of the same sentiments and maxims. He delights too exclusively in the delineation of a certain morbid exaltation of character and feeling, a sort of demoniacal sublimity, not without some traits of the ruined Arch-

[1] Gray, *The Progress of Poesy*, 110 (p. 63). *Words* and *thoughts* are here transposed.
[2] A reference to the ancient belief that all forms of physical existence were composed of earth, air, fire, and water.
[3] Wordsworth, Coleridge, and Southey, so called because they lived in the lake district of England.

[1] See *Macbeth*, V, 3, 38.

angel. He is haunted almost perpetually with the image of a being feeding and fed upon by violent passions, and the recollections of the catastrophes they have occasioned; and, though worn out by their past indulgence, unable to sustain the burden of an existence which they do not continue to animate:—full of pride, and revenge, and obduracy—disdaining life and death, and mankind and himself—and trampling, in his scorn, not only upon the falsehood and formality of polished life, but upon its tame virtues and slavish devotion; yet envying, by fits, the very beings he despises, and melting into mere softness and compassion, when the helplessness of childhood or the frailty of woman make an appeal to his generosity. Such is the person with whom we are called upon almost exclusively to sympathize in all the greater productions of this distinguished writer,—in *Childe Harold*—in *The Corsair*—in *Lara*—in *The Siege of Corinth*—in *Parisina,* and in most of the smaller pieces.

It is impossible to represent such a character better than Lord Byron has done in all these productions; or indeed to represent anything more terrible in its anger, or more attractive in its relenting. In point of effect, we readily admit that no one character can be more poetical or impressive, but it is really too much to find the scene perpetually filled by one character, not only in all the acts of each several drama, but in all the different dramas of the series; and, grand and impressive as it is, we feel at last that these very qualities make some relief more indispensable, and oppress the spirits of ordinary mortals with too deep an impression of awe and repulsion. There is too much guilt in short, and too much gloom, in the leading character; and though it be a fine thing to gaze, now and then, on stormy seas, and thunder-shaken mountains, we should prefer passing our days in sheltered valleys, and by the murmur of calmer waters.[1]

We are aware that these metaphors may be turned against us, and that, without metaphor, it may be said that men do not *pass their days* in reading poetry, and that, as they may look into Lord Byron only about as often as they look abroad upon tempests, they have no more reason to complain of him for being grand and gloomy, than to complain of the same qualities in the glaciers and volcanoes which they go so far to visit. Painters, too, it may be said,

[1] See *Psalms,* 23:2.

have often gained great reputation by their representations of tigers and other ferocious animals, or of caverns and banditti; and poets should be allowed, without reproach, to indulge in analogous exercises. We are far from thinking that there is no weight in these considerations; and feel how plausibly it may be said that we have no better reason for a great part of our complaint than that an author, to whom we are already very greatly indebted, has chosen rather to please himself than us, in the use he makes of his talents.

This, no doubt, seems both unreasonable and ungrateful. But it is nevertheless true that a public benefactor becomes a debtor to the public, and is, in some degree, responsible for the employment of those gifts which seem to be conferred upon him, not merely for his own delight, but for the delight and improvement of his fellows through all generations. Independent of this, however, we think there is a reply to the analogy. A great living poet is not like a distant volcano, or an occasional tempest. He is a volcano in the heart of our land, and a cloud that hangs over our dwellings; and we have some reason to complain, if, instead of genial warmth and grateful shade, he voluntarily darkens and inflames our atmosphere with perpetual fiery explosions and pitchy vapors. Lord Byron's poetry, in short, is too attractive and too famous to lie dormant or inoperative; and, therefore, if it produce any painful or pernicious effects, there will be murmurs, and ought to be suggestions of alteration. Now, though an artist may draw fighting tigers and hungry lions in as lively or natural a way as he can, without giving any encouragement to human ferocity, or even much alarm to human fear, the case is somewhat different when a poet represents men with tiger-like dispositions; and yet more so when he exhausts the resources of his genius to make this terrible being interesting and attractive, and to represent all the lofty virtues as the natural allies of his ferocity. It is still worse when he proceeds to show that all these precious gifts of dauntless courage, strong affection, and high imagination, are not only akin to guilt, but the parents of misery; and that those only have any chance of tranquillity or happiness in this world whom it is the object of his poetry to make us shun and despise.

These, it appears to us, are not merely errors in taste, but perversions of morality; and, as a great poet is necessarily a moral teacher, and gives forth his ethical lessons, in general with far more effect and authority than any of his graver brethren, he is peculiarly liable to the censures reserved for those who turn the means of improvement to purposes of corruption.

It may no doubt be said that poetry in general tends less to the useful than the splendid qualities of our nature, that a character poetically good has long been distinguished from one that is morally so, and that, ever since the time of Achilles, our sympathies, on such occasions, have been chiefly engrossed by persons whose deportment is by no means exemplary, and who, in many points, approach to the temperament of Lord Byron's ideal hero. There is some truth in this suggestion also. But other poets, in the *first* place, do not allow their favorites so outrageous a monopoly of the glory and interest of the piece, and sin less, therefore, against the laws either of poetical or distributive justice. In the *second* place, their heroes are not, generally, either so bad or so good as Lord Byron's, and do not indeed very much exceed the standard of truth and nature, in either of the extremes. His, however, are as monstrous and unnatural as centaurs[1] and hippogriffs,[2] and must ever figure in the eye of sober reason as so many bright and hateful impossibilities. But the most important distinction is, that the other poets who deal in peccant heroes, neither feel nor express that ardent affection for them which is visible in the whole of this author's delineations, but merely make use of them as necessary agents in the extraordinary adventures they have to detail, and persons whose mingled vices and virtues are requisite to bring about the catastrophe of their story. In Lord Byron, however, the interest of the story, where there happens to be one, which is not always the case, is uniformly postponed to that of the character itself, into which he enters so deeply, and with so extraordinary a fondness, that he generally continues to speak in its language, after it has been dismissed from the stage, and to inculcate, on his own authority, the same sentiments which had been previously recommended by its example. We do not consider it as unfair, therefore, to say that Lord Byron appears to us to be the zealous apostle of a certain fierce and magnificent misanthropy, which has already saddened

[1] Fabulous monsters, half man and half horse.
[2] Fabulous winged monsters, part man, part lion, and part eagle.

his poetry with too deep a shade, and not only led to a great misapplication of great talents, but contributed to render popular some very false estimates of the constituents of human happiness and merit. It is irksome, however, to dwell upon observations so general, and we shall probably have better means of illustrating these remarks, if they are really well founded, when we come to speak of the particular publications by which they have now been suggested.

We had the good fortune, we believe, to be among the first who proclaimed the rising of a new luminary, on the appearance of *Childe Harold* on the poetical horizon, and we pursued his course with due attention through several of the constellations. If we have lately omitted to record his progress with the same accuracy, it is by no means because we have regarded it with more indifference, or supposed that it would be less interesting to the public, but because it was so extremely conspicuous as no longer to require the notices of an official observer. In general, we do not think it necessary, nor indeed quite fair, to oppress our readers with an account of works which are as well known to them as to ourselves, or with a repetition of sentiments in which all the world is agreed. Wherever a work, therefore, is very popular, and where the general opinion of its merits appears to be substantially right, we think ourselves at liberty to leave it out of our chronicle, without incurring the censure of neglect or inattention. A very rigorous application of this maxim might have saved our readers the trouble of reading what we now write—and, to confess the truth, we write it rather to gratify ourselves, than with the hope of giving them much information. At the same time, some short notice of the progress of such a writer ought, perhaps, to appear in his contemporary journals, as a tribute due to his eminence; and a zealous critic can scarcely set about examining the merits of any work, or the nature of its reception by the public, without speedily discovering very urgent cause for his admonitions, both to the author and his admirers.

The most considerable of [the author's recent publications] is the Third Canto of *Childe Harold*, a work which has the disadvantage of all continuations, in admitting of little absolute novelty in the plan of the work or the cast of its character, and must, besides, remind all Lord Byron's readers of the extraordinary effect produced by the sudden blazing forth of his genius, upon their first introduction to that title. In spite of all this, however, we are persuaded that this Third Part of the poem will not be pronounced inferior to either of the former; and, we think, will probably be ranked above them by those who have been most delighted with the whole. The great success of this singular production, indeed, has always appeared to us an extraordinary proof of its merits; for, with all its genius, it does not belong to a sort of poetry that rises easily to popularity. It has no story or action, very little variety of character, and a great deal of reasoning and reflection of no very attractive tenor. It is substantially a contemplative and ethical work, diversified with fine description, and adorned or overshadowed by the perpetual presence of one emphatic person, who is sometimes the author, and sometimes the object, of the reflections on which the interest is chiefly rested. It required, no doubt, great force of writing, and a decided tone of originality to recommend a performance of this sort so powerfully as this has been recommended to public notice and admiration; and those high characteristics belong perhaps still more eminently to the part that is now before us, than to any of the former. There is the same stern and lofty disdain of mankind, and their ordinary pursuits and enjoyments, with the same bright gaze on nature, and the same magic power of giving interest and effect to her delineations—but mixed up, we think, with deeper and more matured reflections, and a more intense sensibility to all that is grand or lovely in the external world. Harold, in short, is somewhat older since he last appeared upon the scene;[1] and while the vigor of his intellect has been confirmed, and his confidence in his own opinions increased, his mind has also become more sensitive; and his misanthropy, thus softened over by habits of calmer contemplation, appears less active and impatient, even although more deeply rooted than before. Undoubtedly the finest parts of the poem before us are those which thus embody the weight of his moral sentiments; or disclose the lofty sympathy which binds the despiser of Man to the glorious aspects of Nature. It is in these, we think, that the great attractions of the work consist, and the strength of the author's genius is seen. The narrative and mere description are of

[1] The first and second cantos had appeared in 1812.

far inferior interest. With reference to the sentiments and opinions, however, which thus give its distinguishing character to the piece, we must say, that it seems no longer possible to ascribe them to the ideal person whose name it bears, or to any other than the author himself. Lord Byron, we think, has formerly complained of those who identified him with his hero, or supposed that Harold was but the expositor of his own feelings and opinions; and in noticing the former portions of the work, we thought it unbecoming to give any countenance to such a supposition. In this last part, however, it is really impracticable to distinguish them. Not only do the author and his hero travel and reflect together, but, in truth, we scarcely ever have any distinct intimation to which of them the sentiments so energetically expressed are to be ascribed; and in those which are unequivocally given as those of the noble author himself, there is the very same tone of misanthropy, sadness, and scorn, which we were formerly willing to regard as a part of the assumed costume of the Childe. We are far from supposing, indeed, that Lord Byron would disavow any of these sentiments; and though there are some which we must ever think it most unfortunate to entertain, and others which it appears improper to have published, the greater part are admirable, and cannot be perused without emotion, even by those to whom they may appear erroneous.

The poem opens with a burst of grand poetry and lofty and impetuous feeling, in which the author speaks undisguisedly in his own person.

[2]

Once more upon the waters! Yet once more!
And the waves bound beneath me, as a steed
That knows his rider. Welcome, to their roar!
Swift be their guidance, wheresoe'er it lead!
Though the strain'd mast should quiver as a reed,
And the rent canvas fluttering strew the gale,
Still must I on; for I am as a weed,
Flung from the rock, on Ocean's foam, to sail
Where'er the surge may sweep, the tempest's breath prevail.

[3]

In my youth's summer, did I sing of one,
The wand'ring outlaw of his own dark mind;
Again I seize the theme then but begun,
And bear it with me, as the rushing wind
Bears the cloud onwards. In that tale I find
The furrows of long thought, and dried-up tears,
Which, ebbing, leave a sterile track behind,

O'er which all heavily the journeying years
Plod the last sands of life,—where not a
    flower appears.

[4]

Since my young days of passion—joy, or pain,
Perchance my heart and harp have lost a
    string,
And both may jar. It may be that in vain
I would essay, as I have sung, to sing.
Yet, though a dreary strain, to this I cling;   10
So that it wean me from the weary dream
Of selfish grief or gladness!—so it fling
Forgetfulness around me—it shall seem,
To me, though to none else, a not ungrateful
    theme.

                         15

   After a good deal more in the same strain,
he proceeds,

[7]

Yet must I think less wildly:—I *have* thought
Too long and darkly; till my brain became   20
In its own eddy boiling and o'erwrought,
A whirling gulf of phantasy and flame:
And thus, untaught in youth my heart to tame,
My springs of life were poison'd.—
Something too much of this:—but now 'tis   25
    past,
And the spell closes with its silent seal!
Long absent Harold reappears at last.

   The character and feelings of this unjoyous personage are then depicted with   30
great force and fondness;—and at last he
is placed upon the plain of Waterloo.

[18]

In "pride of place" where late the eagle flew,   35
Then tore with bloody talon the rent plain,
Pierc'd by the shaft of branded nations
    through!

[19]

Fit retribution! Gaul may champ the bit   40
And foam in fetters;—but is earth more free?
Did nations combat to make *one* submit;
Or league to teach all kings true sovereignty?
What! shall reviving thraldom again be
The patch'd-up idol of enlighten'd days?
Shall we, who struck the lion down, shall we   45
Pay the wolf homage?—

[20]

If not, o'er *one* fall'n despot boast no more!

   There can be no more remarkable proof
of the greatness of Lord Byron's genius   50
than the spirit and interest he has contrived to communicate to his picture of the
often-drawn and difficult scene of the
breaking up from Brussels before the great
battle. It is a trite remark, that poets gen-   55
erally fail in the representation of great
events, when the interest is recent, and the
particulars are consequently clearly and
commonly known: and the reason is obvious; for as it is the object of poetry to
make us feel for distant or imaginary occurrences nearly as strongly as if they were
present and real, it is plain that there is no
scope for her enchantments where the impressive reality, with all its vast prepon-
derance of interest, is already before us,
and where the concern we take in the
gazette[1] far outgoes any emotion that can
be conjured up in us by the help of fine
descriptions. It is natural, however, for
the sensitive tribe of poets to mistake the
common interest which they then share with
the unpoetical part of their countrymen,
for a vocation to versify; and so they proceed to pour out the lukewarm distillations
of their phantasies upon the unchecked
effervescence of public feeling! All our
bards, accordingly, great and small, and
of all sexes, ages, and professions, from
Scott and Southey down to hundreds without names or additions,[2] have ventured
upon this theme—and failed in the management of it! And while they yielded to
the patriotic impulse, as if they had all
caught the inspiring summons—

Let those rhyme now who never rhym'd before,
And those who always rhyme, rhyme now the
    more—[3]

The result has been that scarcely a line to
be remembered had been produced on a
subject which probably was thought, of itself, a secure passport to immortality. It
required some courage to venture on a
theme beset with so many dangers, and
deformed with the wrecks of so many former adventurers;—and a theme, too, which,
in its general conception, appeared alien to
the prevailing tone of Lord Byron's poetry.
See, however, with what easy strength he
enters upon it, and with how much grace
he gradually finds his way back to his own
peculiar vein of sentiment and diction.

[21]

There was a sound of revelry by night;
And Belgium's capital had gather'd then
Her beauty and her chivalry; and bright
The lamps shone o'er fair women and brave
    men.
A thousand hearts beat happily; and when

---

[1] That is, the report published in an official gazette, or newspaper.
[2] titles
[3] Adapted from the refrain of Parnell's *The Vigil
   of Venus*, a translation of a Latin poem ascribed to Catullus. Jeffrey substitutes *rhyme*
   and *rhym'd* for *love* and *lov'd*.

Music arose with its voluptuous swell,
Soft eyes look'd love to eyes which spake
   again,
And all went merry as a marriage bell;
But hush! hark! a deep sound strikes like a
   rising knell!

[24]

Ah! then and there was hurrying to and fro,
And gathering tears, and tremblings of dis-
   tress,
And cheeks all pale, which but an hour ago 10
Blush'd at the praise of their own loveliness;
And there were sudden partings; such as press
The life from out young hearts; and choking
   sighs
Which ne'er might be repeated:—who could
   guess 15
If ever more should meet those mutual eyes,
Since upon nights so sweet such awful morn
   could rise?

[25]

And there was mounting in hot haste: the 20
   steed,
The must'ring squadron, and the clatt'ring
   car,
Went pouring forward with impetuous speed,
And swiftly forming in the ranks of war; 25
And the deep thunder, peal on peal afar;
And near, the beat of the alarming drum
Rous'd up the soldier ere the morning star.

[27]

And Ardennes waves above them her green 30
   leaves,
Dewy with Nature's teardrops, as they pass!
Grieving, if aught inanimate e'er grieves,
Over the unreturning brave,—alas!
Ere evening to be trodden like the grass
Which now beneath them, but *above* shall grow 35
In its next verdure! when this fiery mass
Of living valor, rolling on the foe
And burning with high hope, shall fall and
   moulder cold and low.

After some brief commemoration of the 40
worth and valor that fell in that bloody
field, the author turns to the many hopeless
mourners that survive to lament their extinction; the many broken-hearted families,
whose incurable sorrow is enhanced by the 45
national exultation that still points, with
importunate joy, to the scene of their destruction. There is a richness and energy
in the following passage which is peculiar
to Lord Byron, among all modern poets.— 50
a throng of glowing images, poured forth
at once, with a facility and profusion which
must appear mere wastefulness to more
economical writers, and a certain negligence
and harshness of diction, which can belong 55
only to an author who is oppressed with the
exuberance and rapidity of his conceptions.

[31]

The Archangel's trump, not Glory's, must
   awake
Those whom they thirst for! though the sound
   of Fame
May for a moment soothe, it cannot slake 5
The fever of vain longing; and the name
So honor'd but assumes a stronger, bitterer
   claim.

[32]

They mourn, but smile at length; and, smiling,
   mourn!
The tree will wither long before it fall;
The hull drives on, though mast and sail be
   torn!
The roof-tree sings, but moulders on the hall
In massy hoariness; the ruin'd wall 15
Stand when its wind-worn battlements are
   gone;
The bars survive the captive they enthral;
The day drags through, though storms keep
   out the sun;
And thus the heart will break, yet brokenly 20
   live on:

[33]

Even as a broken mirror, which the glass
In every fragment multiplies; and makes
A thousand images of one that was,
The same, and still the more, the more it
   breaks;
And thus the heart will do which not forsakes,
Living in shatter'd guise, and still, and cold,
And bloodless, with its sleepless sorrow aches,
Yet withers on till all without is old,
Showing no visible sign,—for such things are
   untold.

There is next an apostrophe to Napoleon,
graduating into a series of general reflections, expressed with infinite beauty and
earnestness, and illustrated by another cluster of magical images;—but breathing the
very essence of misanthropical disdain, and
embodying opinions which we conceive not
to be less erroneous than revolting. After
noticing the strange combinations of grandeur and littleness which seemed to form the
character of that greatest of all captains
and conquerors, the author proceeds,

[39]

Yet well thy soul hath brook'd the turning
   tide
With that untaught innate philosophy,
Which, be it wisdom, coldness, or deep pride,
Is gall and wormwood to an enemy.
When the whole host of hatred stood hard by,
To watch and mock thee shrinking, thou hast
   smil'd
With a sedate and all-enduring eye;—
When fortune fled her spoil'd and favorite
   child,
He stood unbow'd beneath the ills upon him
   pil'd.

[40]

Sager than in thy fortunes: For in them
Ambition steel'd thee on too far to show
That just habitual scorn which could contemn
Men and their thoughts. 'Twas wise to feel;
not so
To wear it ever on thy lip and brow,
And spurn the instruments thou wert to use
Till they were turn'd unto thine overthrow:
'Tis but a worthless world to win or lose!—
So hath it prov'd to thee, and all such lot who 10
choose.

[42]

But quiet to quick bosoms is a hell,
And *there* hath been thy bane! There is a fire
And motion of the soul which will not dwell 15
In its own narrow being, but aspire
Beyond the fitting medium of desire;
And, but once kindled, quenchless evermore,
Preys upon high adventure; nor can tire
Of aught but rest; a fever at the core, 20
Fatal to him who bears, to all who ever bore.

[43]

This makes the madmen, who have made men
mad
By their contagion; conquerors and kings, 25
Founders of sects and systems,—to whom add
Sophists, bards, statemen, all unquiet things,
Which stir too strongly the soul's secret
springs,
And are themselves the fools to those they 30
fool;
Envied, yet how unenviable! What stings
Are theirs! One breast laid open were a
school
Which would unteach mankind the lust to 35
shine or rule;

[44]

Their breath is agitation; and their life,
A storm whereupon they ride, to sink at last;
And yet so nurs'd and bigoted to strife,
That should their days, surviving perils past, 40
Melt to calm twilight, they feel overcast
With sorrow and supineness, and so die!
Even as a flame unfed, which runs to waste
With its own flickering; or a sword laid by
Which eats into itself, and rusts ingloriously. 45

[45]

He who ascends to mountain-tops, shall find
The loftiest peaks most wrapped in clouds and
snow;
He who *surpasses* or *subdues* mankind,
Must look down on the hate of those below. 50
Though high *above* the sun of glory glow,
And far *beneath* the earth and ocean spread,
Round him are icy rocks; and loudly blow
Contending tempests on his naked head,
And thus reward the toils which to those sum- 55
mits led.

This is splendidly written, no doubt—
but we trust it is not true; and as it is

delivered with much more than poetical
earnestness, and recurs, indeed, in other
forms in various parts of the volume, we
must really be allowed to enter our dissent
somewhat at large. With regard to conquerors, we wish with all our hearts that
this were as the noble author represents it:
but we greatly fear they are neither half
so unhappy, nor half so much hated as
they should be. On the contrary, it seems
plain enough that they are very commonly
idolized and admired, even by those on
whom they trample; and we suspect, moreover, that in general they actually pass their
time rather agreeably, and derive considerable satisfaction from the ruin and desolation of the world. From Macedonia's
madman[1] to the Swede[2]—from Nimrod to
Bonaparte, the hunters of men have pursued their sport with as much gaiety, and
as little remorse, as the hunters of other
animals—and have lived as cheerily in their
days of action, and as comfortably in their
repose, as the followers of better pursuits.
For this, and for the fame which they have
generally enjoyed, they are obviously indebted to the great interests connected with
their employment, and the mutual excitement which belongs to its hopes and hazards. It would be strange, therefore, if the
other active, but more innocent spirits,
whom Lord Byron has here placed in the
same predicament, and who share all *their*
sources of enjoyment, without the guilt and
the hardness which they cannot fail of contracting, should be more miserable or more
unfriended than those splendid curses of
their kind.—And it would be *passing
strange,* and pitiful,[3] if the most precious
gifts of Providence should produce only
unhappiness, and mankind regard with hostility their greatest benefactors.

We do not believe in any such prodigies.
Great vanity and ambition may indeed lead
to feverish and restless efforts—to jealousies, to hate, and to mortification—but
these are only their effects when united to
inferior abilities. It is not those, in short,
who actually surpass mankind, that are unhappy; but those who struggle in vain to
surpass them: and this moody temper,
which eats into itself from within, and provokes fair and unfair opposition from without, is generally the result of pretensions
which outgo the merits by which they are

[1] Alexander the Great, King of Macedonia (336-323 B. C.).
[2] Charles XII, King of Sweden (1697-1718). See Byron's *Mazeppa* (p. 595).
[3] See *Othello,* I, 3, 160-61.

supported—and disappointments, that may be clearly traced, not to the excess of genius, but its defect.

It will be found, we believe, accordingly, that the master spirits of their age have always escaped the unhappiness which is here supposed to be the inevitable lot of extraordinary talents; and that this strange tax upon genius has only been levied from those who held the secondary shares of it. Men of truly great powers of mind have generally been cheerful, social, and indulgent; while a tendency to sentimental whining, or fierce intolerance, may be ranked among the surest symptoms of little souls and inferior intellects. In the whole list of our English poets, we can only remember Shenstone and Savage—two, certainly, of the lowest—who were querulous and discontented. Cowley, indeed, used to call himself melancholy;—but he was not in earnest; and, at any rate, was full of conceits and affectations; and has nothing to make us proud of him. Shakespeare, the greatest of them all, was evidently of a free and joyous temperament;—and so was Chaucer, their common master. The same disposition appears to have predominated in Fletcher, Jonson, and their great contemporaries. The genius of Milton partook something of the austerity of the party to which he belonged, and of the controversies in which he was involved; but even when fallen on evil days and evil tongues,[1] his spirit seems to have retained its serenity as well as its dignity; and in his private life, as well as in his poetry, the majesty of a high character is tempered with great sweetness, genial indulgences, and practical wisdom. In the succeeding age our poets were but too gay; and though we forbear to speak of living authors, we know enough of them to speak with confidence, that to be miserable or to be hated is not now, any more than heretofore, the common lot of those who excel.

If this, however, be the case with poets, confessedly the most irritable and fantastic of all men of genius—and of poets, too, bred and born in the gloomy climate of England, it is not likely that those who have surpassed their fellows in other ways, or in other regions, have been more distinguished for unhappiness. Were Socrates and Plato, the greatest philosophers of antiquity, remarkable for unsocial or gloomy tempers?—Was Bacon, the greatest in modern times?—Was Sir Thomas More—or

[1] See *Paradise Lost*, 7, 26.

Erasmus—or Hume—or Voltaire?—Was Newton—or Fenelon?—Was Francis I., or Henry IV., the paragon of kings and conquerors?—Was Fox, the most ardent, and, in the vulgar sense, the least successful of statesmen? These, and men like these, are undoubtedly the lights and the boast of the world. Yet there was no alloy of misanthropy or gloom in their genius. They did not disdain the men they had surpassed; and neither feared nor experienced their hostility. Some detractors they might have, from envy or misapprehension; but, beyond all doubt, the prevailing sentiments in respect to them have always been those of gratitude and admiration; and the error of public judgment, where it has erred, has much oftener been to overrate than to undervalue the merits of those who had claims on their good opinion. On the whole, we are far from thinking that eminent men are actually happier than those who glide through life in peaceful obscurity: but it is their eminence, and the consequences of it, rather than the mental superiority by which it is obtained, that interferes with their enjoyment. Distinction, however won, usually leads to a passion for more distinction: and is apt to engage us in laborious efforts and anxious undertakings: and those, even when successful, seldom repay, in our judgment, at least, the ease, the leisure, and tranquillity, of which they require the sacrifice: but it really surpasses our imagination to conceive that the very highest degrees of intellectual vigor, or fancy, or sensibility, should of themselves be productive either of unhappiness or general dislike.

     .   .   .   .   .

In passing Ferney and Lausanne, there is a fine account of Voltaire and Gibbon;[1] but we have room for but one more extract, and must take it from the characteristic reflections with which the piece is concluded. These, like most of the preceding, may be thought to savor too much of egotism; but this is of the essence of such poetry, and if Lord Byron had only been happier, or even in better humor with the world, we should have been delighted with the confidence he has here reposed in his readers:—as it is, it sounds too like the last disdainful address of a man who is about to quit a world which has ceased to have any attractions—like the resolute speech of Pierre—

[1] Stanzas 105-8.

For this vile world and I have long been
jangling,
And cannot part on better terms than now.—[1]

The reckoning, however, is steadily and sternly made, and though he does not spare himself, we must say that the world comes off much the worst in the comparison. The passage is very singular, and written with much force and dignity.

[111]

Thus far I have proceeded in a theme
Renew'd with no kind auspices.—To feel
We are not what we might have been, and to
deem
We are not what we should be;—and to steel
The heart against itself; and to conceal,
With a proud caution, love, or hate, or
aught,—
Passion or feeling, purpose, grief or zeal,—
Which is the tyrant spirit of our thought,
Is a stern task of soul!—No matter!—it is
taught.

[113]

I have not lov'd the world—nor the world me!
I have not flatter'd its rank breath; nor bow'd
To its idolatries a patient knee,—
Nor coin'd my cheek to smiles,—nor cried
aloud
In worship of an echo. In the crowd
They could not deem me one of such; I stood
Among them, but not of them, etc.

[114]

I have not lov'd the world, nor the world me!
But let us part fair foes; I do believe,
Though I have found them not, that there
may be
Words which are things,—hopes which will not
deceive
And virtues which are merciful, nor weave
Snares for the failing! I would also deem
O'er others' griefs that some sincerely grieve;
That two or one, are almost what they seem,—
That goodness is no name, and happiness no
dream.

The closing stanzas of the poem are extremely beautiful,—but we are immovable in the resolution that no statement of ours shall ever give additional publicity to the subjects of which they treat.[2]

John Wilson Croker *1780-1857*

ENDYMION: A POETIC ROMANCE[3]

BY JOHN KEATS
1818   1818

Reviewers have been sometimes accused of not reading the works which they affected to criticize. On the present occasion we shall anticipate the author's complaint, and honestly confess that we have not read his work. Not that we have been wanting in our duty—far from it; indeed, we have made efforts almost as superhuman as the story itself appears to be, to get through it; but with the fullest stretch of our perseverance, we are forced to confess that we have not been able to struggle beyond the first of the four books of which this "Poetic Romance" consists. We should extremely lament this want of energy, or whatever it may be, on our parts, were it not for one consolation—namely, that we are no better acquainted with the meaning of the book through which we have so painfully toiled, than we are with that of the three which we have not looked into.

It is not that Mr. Keats (if that be his real name, for we almost doubt that any man in his senses would put his real name to such a rhapsody), it is not, we say, that the author has not powers of language, rays of fancy, and gleams of genius—he has all these; but he is unhappily a disciple of the new school of what has been somewhere called Cockney poetry,[1] which may be defined to consist of the most incongruous ideas in the most uncouth language.

Of this school, Mr. Leigh Hunt, as we observed in a former Number,[2] aspires to be the hierophant. Our readers will recollect the pleasant recipes for harmonious and sublime poetry which he gave us in his Preface to *Rimini*,[3] and the still more facetious instances of his harmony and sublimity in the verses themselves; and they will recollect above all the contempt of Pope, Johnson, and such poetasters and pseudo-critics, which so forcibly contrasted itself with Mr. Leigh Hunt's self-complacent approbation of

—all the things itself had wrote,
Of special merit though of little note.

This author is a copyist of Mr. Hunt; but he is more unintelligible, almost as rugged, twice as diffuse, and ten times more tiresome and absurd than his prototype, who, though he impudently presumed to seat himself in the chair of criticism, and to measure his own poetry by his own stand-

---

[1] Otway, *Venice Preserved*, IV, 2, 224-25.
[2] Byron's family troubles.
[3] For text of *Endymion*, see pp. 793 ff.

[1] A nickname applied by Lockhart and other English critics to the poetry of Leigh Hunt, Shelley, Keats, and others. See *Blackwood's Magazine*, Oct. and Nov., 1817 (Vol. 2, 38-41; 194-201); July and Aug., 1818 (Vol. 3, 453-56; 519-24).
[2] See *The Quarterly Review*, Jan. 1816 (Vol. 14, 473-81), and Jan., 1818 (Vol. 18, 324-35).
[3] For a selection from *The Story of Rimini*, see pp. 892 ff. For the Preface, see Critical Note on Hunt's *The Story of Rimini*.

ard, yet generally had a meaning. But Mr. Keats had advanced no dogmas which he was bound to support by examples; his nonsense, therefore, is quite gratuitous; he writes it for its own sake; and, being bitten by Mr. Leigh Hunt's insane criticism, more than rivals the insanity of his poetry.

Mr. Keats's Preface hints that his poem was produced under peculiar circumstances.[1]

"Knowing within myself (he says) the manner in which this poem has been produced, it is not without a feeling of regret that I make it public.—What manner I mean, will be *quite clear* to the reader, who must soon perceive great inexperience, immaturity, and every error denoting a feverish attempt, rather than a deed accomplished."—*Preface*, p. vii.

We humbly beg his pardon, but this does not appear to us to be *quite so clear*—we really do not know what he means—but the next passage is more intelligible.

"The two first books, and indeed the two last, I feel sensible are not of such completion[2] as to warrant their passing the press."—*Preface*, p. vii.

Thus "the two first books" are, even in his own judgment, unfit to appear, and "the two last" are, it seems, in the same condition—and as two and two make four, and as that is the whole number of books, we have a clear and, we believe, a very just estimate of the entire work.

Mr. Keats, however, deprecates criticism on this "immature and feverish work" in terms which are themselves sufficiently feverish; and we confess that we should have abstained from inflicting upon him any of the tortures of the "*fierce hell*" of criticism, which terrify his imagination, if he had not begged to be spared in order that he might write more; if we had not observed in him a certain degree of talent which deserves to be put in the right way, or which, at least, ought to be warned of the wrong; and if, finally, he had not told us that he is of an age and temper which imperiously require mental discipline.

Of the story we have been able to make out but little; it seems to be mythological, and probably relates to the loves of Diana and Endymion; but of this, as the scope of the work has altogether escaped us, we cannot speak with any degree of certainty; and must therefore content ourselves with giving some instances of its diction and versification; and here again we are perplexed and puzzled. At first it appeared to us that

Mr. Keats had been amusing himself and wearying his readers with an immeasurable game at *bouts-rimés;*[1] but, if we recollect rightly, it is an indispensable condition at this play, that the rhymes when filled up shall have a meaning; and our author, as we have already hinted, has no meaning. He seems to us to write a line at random, and then he follows not the thought excited by this line, but that suggested by the *rhyme* with which it concludes. There is hardly a complete couplet inclosing a complete idea in the whole book.[2] He wanders from one subject to another, from the association, not of ideas but of sounds, and the work is composed of hemistichs[3] which, it is quite evident, have forced themselves upon the author by the mere force of the catchwords on which they turn.

We shall select, not as the most striking instance, but as that least liable to suspicion, a passage from the opening of the poem.[4]

——Such the sun, the moon,
Trees old and young, sprouting a shady boon
For simple sheep; and such are daffodils
With the green world they live in; and clear
    rills
That for themselves a cooling covert make
'Gainst the hot season; the mid-forest brake,[5]
Rich with a sprinkling of fair musk-rose
    blooms;
And such, too, is the grandeur of the dooms
We have imagined for the mighty dead; etc.,
    etc.   —[ll. 13-21]

Here it is clear that the word, and not the idea, *moon* produces the simple sheep and their shady *boon*, and that "the *dooms* of the mighty dead" would never have intruded themselves but for the "*fair musk-rose blooms.*"

Again.

For 'twas the morn: Apollo's upward fire
Made every eastern cloud a silvery pyre
Of brightness so unsullied, that therein
A melancholy spirit well might win
Oblivion, and melt out his essence fine
Into the winds: rain-scented eglantine
Gave temperate sweets to the well-wooing sun;
The lark was lost in him; cold springs had run
To warm their chilliest bubbles in the grass;
Man's voice was on the mountains; and the
    mass
Of nature's lives and wonders puls'd tenfold,
To feel this sun-rise and its glories old.
        —[ll. 95-106]

---

[1] See Critical Note on Keats's *Endymion*.
[2] perfection

[1] rhyming words proposed to fill out verses
[2] The 18th century couplet usually expressed a complete thought.
[3] incomplete lines
[4] All of the quotations which follow are from Book 1 (pp. 793 ff.).
[5] thicket

Here Apollo's *fire* produces a *pyre,* a silvery pyre of clouds, *wherein* a spirit might *win* oblivion and melt his essence *fine,* and scented *eglantine* gives sweets to the *sun,* and cold springs had *run* into the grass, and then the pulse of the *mass* pulsed *tenfold* to feel the glories *old* of the new-born day, etc.

One example more.

Be still the unimaginable lodge
For solitary thinkings, such as dodge
Conception to the very bourne of heaven,
Then leave the naked brain: be still the leaven,
That spreading in this dull and clodded earth
Gives it a touch ethereal—a new birth.
　　　　　　　　　　　　　[ll. 293-298]

Lodge, dodge—heaven, leaven—earth, birth; such, in six words, is the sum and substance of six lines.

We come now to the author's taste in versification. He cannot indeed write a sentence, but perhaps he may be able to spin a line. Let us see. The following are specimens of his prosodial notions of our English heroic metre.

Dear as the temple's self, so does the moon,
The passion poesy, glories infinite.—[ll. 28, 29]
So plenteously all weed-hidden roots.—[l. 65]
Of some strange history, potent to send.
　　　　　　　　　　　　　　　—[l. 324]
Before the deep intoxication.—[l. 502]
Her scarf into a fluttering pavilion.—[l. 628]
The stubborn canvas for my voyage prepared.
　　　　　　　　　　　　　　　—[l. 772]

"Endymion! the cave is secreter
Than the isle of Delos. Echo hence shall stir
No sighs but sigh-warm kisses, or light noise
Of thy combing hand, the while it travelling
　　　cloys
And trembles through my labyrinthine hair."
　　　　　　　　　　　　　—[ll. 965-969]

By this time our readers must be pretty well satisfied as to the meaning of his sentences and the structure of his lines. We now present them with some of the new words with which, in imitation of Mr. Leigh Hunt, he adorns our language.

We are told that "turtles *passion* their voices" [l. 248]; that an "arbor was *nested* [l. 431]; and a lady's locks "*gordian'd up*" [l. 614]; and to supply the place of the nouns thus verbalized, Mr. Keats, with great fecundity, spawns new ones; such as "men-slugs and human *serpentry*" [l. 821]; the *honey-feel of bliss*" [l. 903]; "*wives* prepare *needments*" [l. 208]—and so forth.

Then he has formed new verbs by the process of cutting off their natural tails,

the adverbs, and affixing them to their fore-heads; thus, "the wine out-sparkled" [l. 154]; the "multitude up-followed" [l. 164]; and "night up-took" [l. 561]. "The wind up-blows" [l. 627]; and the "hours are down-sunken" [l. 708].

But if he sinks some adverbs in the verbs, he compensates the language with adverbs and adjectives which he separates from the parent stock. Thus, a lady "whispers *pantingly* and close" [l. 407], makes "*hushing* signs" [l. 409], and steers her skiff into a "*ripply* cove" [l. 430]; a shower falls "*refreshfully*" [l. 898]; and a vulture has a "*spreaded* tail" [l. 867].

But enough of Mr. Leigh Hunt and his simple neophyte. If any one should be bold enough to purchase this "Poetic Romance," and so much more patient than ourselves as to get beyond the first book, and so much more fortunate as to find a meaning, we entreat him to make us acquainted with his success; we shall then return to the task which we now abandon in despair, and endeavor to make all due amends to Mr. Keats and to our readers.

Charles Lamb 1775-1834

THE MIDNIGHT WIND
1794　　　　　　1796

O! I could laugh to hear the midnight
　　wind,
That, rushing on its way with careless
　　sweep,
Scatters the ocean waves. And I could
　　weep
Like to a child. For now to my raised mind
On wings of winds comes wild-eyed
　　Phantasy.
And her rude visions give severe delight.
O wingéd bark! how swift along the night
Pass'd thy proud keel! nor shall I let go
　　by
Lightly of that drear hour the memory,
When wet and chilly on thy deck I stood,
Unbonneted,[1] and gazed upon the flood,
Even till it seemed a pleasant thing to
　　die,—
To be resolv'd into the elemental wave,
Or take my portion with the winds that
　　rave.

WAS IT SOME SWEET DEVICE
OF FAERY
1794　　　　　　1797

Was it some sweet device of Faery
That mocked my steps with many a lonely
　　glade,

---

[1] See *King Lear,* III, 1, 14.

And fancied wanderings with a fair-hair'd
maid?[1]
Have these things been? or what rare
witchery,
5 Impregning with delights the charmèd air,
Enlighted up the semblance of a smile
In those fine eyes? methought they spake
the while
Soft soothing things, which might enforce
Despair
To drop the murdering knife, and let go by
10 His foul resolve. And does the lonely
glade
Still court the footsteps of the fair-hair'd
maid?
Still in her locks the gales of summer sigh?
While I forlorn do wander reckless where,
And 'mid my wanderings meet no Anna
there.

IF FROM MY LIPS SOME ANGRY
ACCENTS FELL
1795 *1797*

If from my lips some angry accents fell,
Peevish complaint, or harsh reproof un-
kind,
'Twas but the error of a sickly mind
And troubled thoughts, clouding the purer
well,
5 And waters clear, of Reason; and for me
Let this my verse the poor atonement be—
My verse, which thou to praise wert e'er
inclined
Too highly, and with a partial eye to see
No blemish. Thou to me didst ever show
10 Kindest affection; and would oft-times lend
An ear to the desponding love-sick lay,
Weeping my sorrows with me, who repay
But ill the mighty debt of love I owe,
Mary, to thee, my sister and my friend.

CHILDHOOD
1796 *1797*

In my poor mind it is most sweet to muse
Upon the days gone by; to act in thought
Past seasons o'er, and be again a child;
To sit in fancy on the turf-clad slope,
5 Down which the child would roll; to pluck
gay flowers,
Make posies in the sun, which the child's
hand
(Childhood offended soon, soon reconciled)
Would throw away, and straight take up
again,
Then fling them to the winds, and o'er the
lawn

---

10 Bound with so playful and so light a foot,
That the pressed daisy scarce declined her
head.

THE OLD FAMILIAR FACES
1798 1798

Where are they gone, the old familiar
faces?

I had a mother, but she died, and left me,
Died prematurely in a day of horrors[1]—
All, all are gone, the old familiar faces.

5 I have had playmates, I have had companions,
In my days of childhood, in my joyful
school-days—
All, all are gone, the old familiar faces.

I have been laughing, I have been carousing,
Drinking late, sitting late, with my bosom
cronies—
10 All, all are gone, the old familiar faces.

I loved a love once,[2] fairest among
women.
Closed are her doors on me, I must not
see her—
All, all are gone, the old familiar faces.

I have a friend,[3] a kinder friend has no
man.
15 Like an ingrate, I left my friend abruptly;
Left him, to muse on the old familiar faces.

Ghost-like, I paced round the haunts of
my childhood.
Earth seemed a desert I was bound to
traverse,
Seeking to find the old familiar faces.

20 Friend of my bosom,[4] thou more than a
brother!
Why wert not thou born in my father's
dwelling?
So might we talk of the old familiar faces.

For some they have died, and some they
have left me,
And some are taken from me; all are
departed;
25 All, all are gone, the old familiar faces.

---

[1] Ann Simmons, a Hertfordshire girl, Lamb's boyhood sweetheart. She is probably the Alice Winterton of Lamb's *Dream Children* (p. 974a, 3). See also his *New Year's Eve* and *Blakesmoor in H—shire.*

[1] Lamb's mother was killed in 1796 by his sister Mary, who was suffering an attack of insanity.
[2] Ann Simmons, referred to in *Was It Some Sweet Device of Faëry* (p. 941).
[3] Charles Lloyd (1775-1815), a minor English poet. He was a pupil of Coleridge, with whom he lived for some time.
[4] Coleridge.

HESTER[1]
1803   1818

When maidens such as Hester die,
Their place ye may not well supply,
Though ye among a thousand try,
　　With vain endeavor.

5 A month or more hath she been dead,
Yet cannot I by force be led
To think upon the wormy bed,
　　And her together.

A springy motion in her gait,
10 A rising step, did indicate
Of pride and joy no common rate,
　　That flush'd her spirit.

I know not by what name beside
I shall it call:—if 'twas not pride,
15 It was a joy to that allied,
　　She did inherit.

Her parents held the Quaker rule,
Which doth the human feeling cool,
But she was train'd in Nature's school,
20 　　Nature had blest her.

A waking eye, a prying mind,
A heart that stirs, is hard to bind,
A hawk's keen sight ye cannot blind,
　　Ye could not Hester.

25 My sprightly neighbor, gone before
To that unknown and silent shore,
Shall we not meet, as heretofore,
　　Some summer morning,

When from thy cheerful eyes a ray
30 Hath struck a bliss upon the day,
A bliss that would not go away,
　　A sweet forewarning?

THE THREE GRAVES
1820

Close by the ever-burning brimstone beds
Where Bedloe, Oates, and Judas hide
　　their heads,
I saw great Satan like a sexton stand
With his intolerable spade in hand,
5 Digging three graves. Of coffin-shape
　　they were,
For those who, coffinless, must enter there
With unblest rites. The shrouds were of
　　that cloth
Which Clotho weaveth in her blackest
　　wrath:
The dismal tinct oppress'd the eye, that
　　dwelt
10 Upon it long, like darkness to be felt.
The pillows to those baleful beds were
　　toads,

---

[1] Hester Savary, a young Quakeress with whom Lamb had fallen in love in 1800. She died in 1803.

Large, living, livid, melancholy loads,
Whose softness shock'd. Worms of all
　　monstrous size
Crawl'd round; and one, upcoil'd, which
　　never dies.
15 A doleful bell, inculcating despair,
Was always ringing in the heavy air.
And all about the detestable pit
Strange headless ghosts, and quarter'd
　　forms, did flit;
Rivers of blood, from dripping traitors
　　spilt,
20 By treachery stung from poverty to guilt.
I ask'd the fiend for whom these rites were
　　meant.
"These graves," quoth he, "when life's
　　brief oil is spent,
When the dark night comes, and they're
　　sinking bedwards,
I mean for Castles, Oliver, and Edwards.'"

THE GIPSY'S MALISON
1829

"Suck, baby, suck; mother's love grows
　　by giving;
Drain the sweet founts that only thrive by
　　wasting;
Black manhood comes, when riotous guilty
　　living
Hands thee the cup that shall be death in
　　tasting.

5 "Kiss, baby, kiss; mother's lips shine by
　　kisses;
Choke the warm breath that else would
　　fall in blessings:
Black manhood comes, when turbulent
　　guilty blisses
Tend thee the kiss that poisons 'mid
　　caressings.

"Hang, baby, hang; mother's love loves
　　such forces;
10 Strain the fond neck that bends still to
　　thy clinging:
Black manhood comes, when violent law-
　　less courses
Leave thee a spectacle in rude air swing-
　　ing.''

So sang a wither'd Beldam energetical,
And bann'd the ungiving door with lips
　　prophetical.

ON AN INFANT DYING AS SOON
AS BORN[1]
1827   1829

I saw where in the shroud did lurk
A curious frame of Nature's work.

---

[1] This poem was inspired by the death of Thomas Hood's first child.

A floweret crushed in the bud,
A nameless piece of Babyhood,
5 Was in her cradle-coffin lying;
Extinct, with scarce the sense of dying;
So soon to exchange the imprisoning
    womb
For darker closets of the tomb!
She did but ope an eye, and put
10 A clear beam forth, then straight up
    shut
For the long dark: ne'er more to see
Through glasses of mortality.
Riddle of destiny, who can show
What thy short visit meant, or know
15 What thy errand here below?
Shall we say, that Nature blind
Checked her hand, and changed her mind,
Just when she had exactly wrought
A finished pattern without fault?
20 Could she flag, or could she tire,
Or lacked she the Promethean fire[1]
(With her nine moons' long workings
    sickened)
That should thy little limbs have quick-
    ened?
Limbs so firm, they seemed to assure
25 Life of health, and days mature:
Woman's self in miniature!
Limbs so fair, they might supply
(Themselves now but cold imagery)
The sculptor to make Beauty by.
30 Or did the stern-eyed Fate descry,
That babe, or mother, one must die;
So in mercy left the stock,
And cut the branch; to save the shock
Of young years widowed; and the pain,
35 When Single State comes back again
To the lone man who, reft of wife,
Thenceforward drags a maimed life?
The economy of Heaven is dark;
And wisest clerks[2] have missed the mark,
40 Why human buds, like this, should fall,
More brief than fly ephemeral,
That has his day; while shrivelled crones
Stiffen with age to stocks and stones;
And crabbed use the conscience sears
45 In sinners of an hundred years
Mother's prattle, mother's kiss,
Baby fond, thou ne'er wilt miss.
Rites, which custom does impose,
Silver bells and baby clothes;
50 Coral redder than those lips,
Which pale death did late eclipse;
Music framed for infant's glee,
Whistle never tuned for thee;
Though thou want'st not, thou shalt have
    them,

1 According to mythology, Prometheus stole fire
  from heaven and bestowed it upon man.
2 scholars

55 Loving hearts were they which gave them.
Let not one be missing; nurse,
See them laid upon the hearse[1]
Of infant slain by doom perverse.
Why should kings and nobles have
60 Pictured trophies to their grave;
And we, churls, to thee deny
Thy pretty toys with thee to lie,
A more harmless vanity?

SHE IS GOING

For their elder sister's hair
Martha does a wreath prepare
Of bridal rose, ornate and gay:
Tomorrow is the wedding day:
5   She is going.

Mary, youngest of the three,
Laughing idler, full of glee,
Arm in arm doth fondly chain her,
Thinking, poor trifler, to detain her—
10   But she's going.

Vex not, maidens, nor regret
Thus to part with Margaret.
Charms like yours can never stay
Long within doors; and one day
15   You'll be going.

LETTER TO WORDSWORTH
January 30, 1801

Thanks for your letter and present. I
had already borrowed your second volume.[2]
What most pleases me are the *Song of
Lucy*[3]—*Simon's sickly daughter*[4] in *The
5 Sexton* made me cry. Next to these are the
description of the continuous echoes in the
story of Joanna's laugh,[5] where the mountains and all the scenery absolutely seem
alive—and that fine Shakesperian charac-
10 ter of the happy man, in *The Brothers*,

—that creeps about the fields,
Following his fancies by the hour, to bring
Tears down his cheek, or solitary smiles
Into his face, *until the setting sun*
15 *Write fool upon his forehead*.[6]

I will mention one more: the delicate
and curious feeling in the wish for the
Cumberland Beggar, that he may have
about him the melody of birds, altho' he
20 hear them not.[7] Here the mind knowingly
passes a fiction upon herself, first substi-

1 coffin
2 A copy of the second edition of *Lyrical Ballads*,
  published in two volumes in 1800.
3 *Lucy Gray* (p. 267).   4 See *To a Sexton*, 14.
5 See *To Joanna*, 51-65. This poem was addressed
  to Joanna Hutchinson, Mrs. Wordsworth's
  sister.
6 Ll. 108-12.
7 See *The Old Cumberland Beggar*, 184-5 (p.
  263).

tuting her own feelings for the Beggar's, and, in the same breath detecting the fallacy, will not part with the wish.—*The Poet's Epitaph*[1] is disfigured, to my taste, by the vulgar satire upon parsons and lawyers in the beginning, and the coarse epithet of pin-point in the 6th stanza. All the rest is eminently good, and your own. I will just add that it appears to me a fault in the Beggar that the instructions conveyed in it are too direct and like a lecture; they don't slide into the mind of the reader while he is imagining no such matter. An intelligent reader finds a sort of insult in being told: I will teach you how to think upon this subject. This fault, if I am right, is in a ten-thousandth worse degree to be found in Sterne and many, many novelists and modern poets, who continually put a sign post up to show where you are to feel. They set out with assuming their readers to be stupid. Very different from *Robinson Crusoe, The Vicar of Wakefield, Roderick Random,* and other beautiful bare narratives. There is implied an unwritten compact between author and reader: I will tell you a story, and I suppose you will understand it. Modern novels, *St. Leons* and the like, are full of such flowers as these: "Let not my reader suppose"— "Imagine, *if you can*"—modest!—etc.—I will here have done with praise and blame. I have written so much, only that you may not think I have passed over your book without observation.—I am sorry that Coleridge has christened his *Ancient Marinere*[2] "a Poet's Reverie"—it is as bad as Bottom the Weaver's declaration that he is not a lion but only the scenical representation of a lion.[3] What new idea is gained by this title, but one subversive of all credit, which the tale should force upon us, of its truth? For me, I was never so affected with any human tale. After first reading it, I was totally possessed with it for many days—I dislike all the miraculous part of it, but the feelings of the man under the operation of such scenery dragged me along like Tom Piper's magic whistle.[4] I totally differ from your idea that the Marinere should have had a character and profes-

sion.[1] This is a beauty in *Gulliver's Travels,* where the mind is kept in a placid state of little wonderments; but the Ancient Marinere undergoes such trials as overwhelm and bury all individuality or memory of what he was, like the state of a man in a bad dream, one terrible peculiarity of which is that all consciousness of personality is gone. Your other observation is, I think, as well a little unfounded: the Marinere from being conversant in supernatural events *has* acquired a supernatural and strange cast of phrase, eye, appearance, etc., which frighten the wedding-guest. You will excuse my remarks, because I am hurt and vexed that you should think it necessary with a prose apology to open the eyes of dead men that cannot see. To sum up a general opinion of the second vol.—I do not feel any one poem in it so forcibly as *The Ancient Marinere, The Mad Mother,*[2] and the *Lines at Tintern Abbey,*[3] in the first.[4]—I could, too, have wished the critical preface[5] had appeared in a separate treatise. All its dogmas are true and just, and most of them new, *as* criticism. But they associate a *diminishing* idea with the poems which follow, as having been written for *experiment* on the public taste, more than having sprung (as they must have done) from living and daily circumstances. —I am prolix, because I am gratified in the opportunity of writing to you, and I don't well know when to leave off. I ought before this to have reply'd to your very kind invitation into Cumberland. With you and your sister I could gang[6] anywhere; but I am afraid whether I shall ever be able to afford so desperate a journey. Separate from the pleasure of your company, I don't much care if I never see a mountain in my life. I have passed all my days in London, until I have formed as many and intense local attachments as

---

[1] See p. 265.
[2] See p. 361.
[3] See *A Midsummer Night's Dream,* III, 1, 40 ff.; V. 1, 222 ff.
[4] Probably a reference to the legend of the piper who by his music freed the city of Hamelin from rats, and who, because the townsmen refused to pay him for his work, enticed their children into a cavern in the side of a mountain. See Browning's *The Pied Piper of Hamelin,* and Peabody's *The Piper*

[1] In a note on *The Ancient Mariner, a Poet's Reverie,* published in the first volume of *Lyrical Ballads,* Wordsworth said: "The poem of my friend has, indeed, great defects: first, that the principal person has no distinct character, either in his profession of mariner or as a human being who, having been long under the control of supernatural impressions, might be supposed himself to partake of something supernatural; secondly, that he does not act. but is continually acted upon; thirdly, that the events, having no necessary connection, do not produce each other; and lastly, that the imagery is somewhat too laboriously accumulated."
[2] In later editions entitled *Her Eyes Are Wild,* (p. 255).
[3] See p. 259.
[4] For the contents of *Lyrical Ballads,* see Glossary.
[5] See p. 343.
[6] go

any of you mountaineers can have done with
dead Nature. The lighted shops of the
Strand and Fleet Street; the innumerable
trades, tradesmen and customers, coaches,
wagons, playhouses; all the bustle and wickedness round about Covent Garden; the
very women of the Town; the watchmen,
drunken scenes, rattles; life awake, if you
awake, at all hours of the night; the impossibility of being dull in Fleet Street; the
crowds, the very dirt and mud, the sun
shining upon houses and pavements, the
print shops, the old-book stalls, parsons
cheap'ning[1] books, coffee-houses, steams of
soups from kitchens, the pantomimes—London itself a pantomime and a masquerade—
all these things work themselves into my
mind, and feed me, without a power of
satiating me. The wonder of these sights impels me into night-walks about her crowded
streets, and I often shed tears in the motley
Strand from fulness of joy at so much life.
All these emotions must be strange to you;
so are your rural emotions to me. But consider, what must I have been doing all my
life, not to have lent great portions of my
heart with usury to such scenes?

My attachments are all local, purely
local. I have no passion (or have had none
since I was in love, and then it was the
spurious engendering of poetry and books)
to groves and valleys. The rooms where I
was born, the furniture which has been before my eyes all my life, a book-case which
has followed me about (like a faithful dog,
only exceeding him in knowledge), wherever I have moved, old chairs, old tables,
streets, squares, where I have sunned myself, my old school,—these are my mistresses. Have I not enough, without your
mountains? I do not envy you. I should
pity you, did I not know that the mind will
make friends of anything. Your sun, and
moon, and skies, and hills, and lakes, affect
me no more, or scarcely come to me in more
venerable characters, than as a gilded room
with tapestry and tapers, where I might live
with handsome visible objects. I consider
the clouds above me but as a roof beautifully painted,[2] but unable to satisfy my
mind; and at last, like the pictures of the
apartment of a connoisseur, unable to afford
him any longer a pleasure. So fading upon
me, from disuse, have been the beauties of
Nature, as they have been confinedly called;
so ever fresh, and green, and warm are all
the inventions of men, and assemblies of

[1] bargaining for
[2] See *Hamlet*, II, 2, 213.

men in this great city. I should certainly
have laughed with dear Joanna.

Give my kindest love and my sister's to
D.[1] and yourself; and a kiss from me to
little Barbara Lewthwaite.[2] Thank you for
liking my play.[3]   C. L.

From CHARACTERS OF DRAMATIC WRIT-
ERS CONTEMPORARY WITH
SHAKSPEARE[4]
1808-18

When I selected for publication, in 1808,
Specimens of English Dramatic Poets who
lived about the time of Shakspeare, the
kind of extracts which I was anxious to
give were, not so much passages of wit and
humor, though the old plays are rich in
such, as scenes of passion, sometimes of the
deepest quality, interesting situations, serious descriptions, that which is more nearly
allied to poetry than to wit, and to tragic
rather than to comic poetry. The plays
which I made choice of were, with few exceptions, such as treat of human life and
manners, rather than masques and Arcadian pastorals, with their train of abstractions, unimpassioned deities, passionate
mortals—Claius, and Medorus, and Amin-
tas, and Amarillis. My leading design was,
to illustrate what may be called the moral
sense of our ancestors. To show in what
manner they felt, when they placed themselves by the power of imagination in trying
circumstances, in the conflicts of duty and
passion, or the strife of contending duties;
what sort of loves and enmities theirs were;
how their griefs were tempered, and their
full-swoln joys abated; how much of
Shakspeare shines in the great men his
contemporaries, and how far in his divine
mind and manners he surpassed them and
all mankind. I was also desirous to bring
together some of the most admired scenes
of Fletcher and Massinger, in the estimation
of the world the only dramatic poets of that
age entitled to be considered after Shakspeare, and, by exhibiting them in the same
volume with the more impressive scenes of
old Marlowe, Heywood, Tourneur, Webster, Ford, and others, to show what we had
slighted, while beyond all proportion we
had been crying up one or two favorite
names. From the desultory criticism which

[1] Wordsworth's sister Dorothy.
[2] A child in Wordsworth's poem *The Pet Lamb.*
[3] *John Woodvil.*
[4] The following selections are Lamb's abridge-
ments of the notes to his *Specimens of English Dramatic Poets,* published in 1808.

accompanied that publication, I have selected a few which I thought would best stand by themselves, as requiring least immediate reference to the play or passage by which they were suggested.

Thomas Heywood

A Woman Killed with Kindness. Heywood is a sort of *prose* Shakspeare. His scenes are to the full as natural and affecting. But we miss *the poet,* that which in Shakspeare always appears out and above the surface of *the nature.* Heywood's characters in this play, for instance, his country gentlemen, etc., are exactly what we see, but of the best kind of what we see, in life. Shakspeare makes us believe, while we are among his lovely creations, that they are nothing but what we are familiar with, as in dreams new things seem old; but we awake, and sigh for the difference.

The English Traveller. Heywood's preface to this play is interesting, as it shows the heroic indifference about the opinion of posterity, which some of these great writers seem to have felt. There is a magnanimity in authorship as in everything else. His ambition seems to have been confined to the pleasure of hearing the players speak his lines while he lived. It does not appear that he ever contemplated the possibility of being read by after ages. What a slender pittance of fame was motive sufficient to the production of such plays as *The English Traveller, The Challenge for Beauty,* and *The Woman Killed with Kindness!* Posterity is bound to take care that a writer loses nothing by such a noble modesty.

John Webster

The Duchess of Malfy. All the several parts of the dreadful apparatus with which the death of the Duchess is ushered in, the waxen images which counterfeit death, the wild masque of madmen, the tomb-maker, the bellman, the living person's dirge, the mortification by degrees,—are not more remote from the conceptions of ordinary vengeance, than the strange character of suffering which they seem to bring upon their victim is out of the imagination of ordinary poets. As they are not like inflictions of this life, so her language seems not of this world. She has lived among horrors till she is become "native and endowed unto that element."[1] She speaks the dialect of

[1] *Hamlet,* IV. 7. 180-1.

despair; her tongue has a smatch[1] of Tartarus and the souls in bale.[2] To move a horror skilfully, to touch a soul to the quick, to lay upon fear as much as it can bear, to wean and weary a life till it is ready to drop, and then step in with mortal instruments to take its last forfeit: this only a Webster can do. Inferior geniuses may "upon horror's head horrors accumulate,"[3] but they cannot do this. They mistake quantity for quality; they "terrify babes with painted devils;"[4] but they know not how a soul is to be moved. Their terrors want dignity, their affrightments are without decorum.

John Ford

The Broken Heart. I do not know where to find, in any play, a catastrophe so grand, so solemn, and so surprising, as in this. This is indeed, according to Milton, to describe high passions and high actions.[5] The fortitude of the Spartan boy, who let a beast gnaw out his bowels till he died without expressing a groan,[6] is a faint bodily image of this dilaceration[7] of the spirit, and exenteration[8] of the inmost mind, which Calantha, with a holy violence against her nature, keeps closely covered, till the last duties of a wife and a queen are fulfilled. Stories of martyrdom are but of chains and the stake; a little bodily suffering. These torments

On the purest spirits prey,
As on the entrails, joints, and limbs,
With answerable pains, but more intense.[9]

What a noble thing is the soul in its strengths and in its weaknesses! Who would be less weak than Calantha? Who can be so strong? The expression of this transcendant scene almost bears us in imagination to Calvary and the Cross; and we seem to perceive some analogy between the scenical sufferings which we are here contemplating, and the real agonies of that final completion to which we dare no more than hint a reference. Ford was of the first order of poets. He sought for sublimity, not by parcels, in

[1] smack ; taste   [2] torment   [3] *Othello.* III. 3, 370.
[4] Webster, *The White Devil,* III, 2, 146. See, also *Macbeth.* II, 2, 55.
[5] See *Paradise Regained,* 4. 266.
[6] The story is told by Plutarch in his *Life of Lycurgus,* 18, to illustrate the power of endurance of the Spartan boys as well as their serious attitude toward stealing, training in which was a vital part of their education. A boy had stolen a fox, which he concealed under his cloak ; but rather than have the theft detected, the boy suffered death by allowing his bowels to be torn out by the fox.
[7] tearing to pieces   [8] tearing out ; disemboweling
[9] Milton, *Samson Agonistes,* 613-15.

metaphors or visible images, but directly where she has her full residence in the heart of man; in the actions and sufferings of the greatest minds. There is a grandeur of the soul above mountains, seas, and the elements. Even in the poor perverted reason of Giovanni and Annabella, in the play[1] which stands at the head of the modern collection of the works of this author, we discern traces of that fiery particle, which, in the irregular starting from out the road of beaten action, discovers something of a right line even in obliquity, and shows hints of an improvable greatness in the lowest descents and degradations of our nature.

George Chapman

Bussy D'Ambois, Byron's Conspiracy, Byron's Tragedy, etc., etc. Webster has happily characterized the "full and heightened style"[2] of Chapman, who, of all the English play-writers, perhaps approaches nearest to Shakspeare in the descriptive and didactic, in passages which are less purely dramatic. He could not go out of himself, as Shakspeare could shift at pleasure, to inform and animate other existences, but in himself he had an eye to perceive and a soul to embrace all forms and modes of being. He would have made a great epic poet, if indeed he has not abundantly shown himself to be one; for his Homer is not so properly a translation as the stories of Achilles and Ulysses rewritten. The earnestness and passion which he has put into every part of these poems, would be incredible to a reader of mere modern translations. His almost Greek zeal for the glory of his heroes can only be paralleled by that fierce spirit of Hebrew bigotry, with which Milton, as if personating one of the zealots of the old law, clothed himself when he sat down to paint the acts of Samson against the uncircumcised.[3] The great obstacle to Chapman's translations being read is their unconquerable quaintness. He pours out in the same breath the most just and natural, and the most violent and crude expressions. He seems to grasp at whatever words come first to hand while the enthusiasm is upon him, as if all other must be inadequate to the divine meaning. But passion (the all in all in poetry) is everywhere present, raising the low, dignifying the mean, and

[1] Ford's *'Tis Pity She's a Whore.*
[2] In his Remarks to the Reader, prefaced to his play *The White Devil.*
[3] In *Samson Agonistes.*

putting sense into the absurd. He makes his readers glow, weep, tremble, take any affection which he pleases, be moved by words, or in spite of them, be disgusted and overcome their disgust.

Francis Beaumont.—John Fletcher

Maid's Tragedy. One characteristic of the excellent old poets is their being able to bestow grace upon subjects which naturally do not seem susceptible of any. I will mention two instances: Zelmane in the *Arcadia* of Sidney, and Helena in the *All's Well that Ends Well* of Shakspeare. What can be more unpromising at first sight, than the idea of a young man disguising himself in women's attire, and passing himself off for a woman among women; and that for a long space of time? Yet Sir Philip has preserved so matchless a decorum, that neither does Pryocles' manhood suffer any stain for the effeminacy of Zelmane, nor is the respect due to the princesses at all diminished when the deception comes to be known. In the sweetly constituted mind of Sir Philip Sidney, it seems as if no ugly thought or unhandsome meditation could find a harbor. He turned all that he touched into images of honor and virtue. Helena in Shakspeare is a young woman seeking a man in marriage. The ordinary rules of courtship are reversed, the habitual feelings are crossed. Yet with such exquisite address this dangerous subject is handled, that Helena's forwardness loses her no honor; delicacy dispenses with its laws in her favor; and nature, in her single case, seems content to suffer a sweet violation. Aspatia, in *The Maid's Tragedy,* is a character equally difficult, with Helena, of being managed with grace. She too is a slighted woman, refused by the man who had once engaged to marry her. Yet it is artfully contrived that while we pity we respect her, and she descends without degradation. Such wonders true poetry and passion can do, to confer dignity upon subjects which do not seem capable of it. But Aspatia must not be compared at all points with Helena; she does not so absolutely predominate over her situation but she suffers some diminution, some abatement of the full lustre of the female character, which Helena never does. Her character has many degrees of sweetness, some of delicacy; but it has weakness, which, if we do not despise, we are sorry for. After all, Beaumont and Fletcher were but an inferior sort of Shakspeares and Sidneys.

From ON THE TRAGEDIES OF SHAKS-
PEARE, CONSIDERED WITH REFER-
ENCE TO THEIR FITNESS FOR
STAGE REPRESENTATION
1811 1811

.   .   .   .   .

It may seem a paradox, but I cannot help being of opinion that the plays of Shakspeare are less calculated for performance on a stage, than those of almost any other dramatist whatever. Their distinguished excellence is a reason that they should be so. There is so much in them which comes not under the province of acting, with which eye, and tone, and gesture, have nothing to do.

The glory of the scenic art is to personate passion, and the turns of passion; and the more coarse and palpable the passion is, the more hold upon the eyes and ears of the spectators the performer obviously possesses. For this reason, scolding scenes, scenes where two persons talk themselves into a fit of fury, and then in a surprising manner talk themselves out of it again, have always been the most popular upon our stage. And the reason is plain, because the spectators are here most palpably appealed to; they are the proper judges in this war of words; they are the legitimate ring that should be formed round such "intellectual prize-fighters." Talking is the direct object of the imitation here. But in all the best dramas, and in Shakspeare above all, how obvious it is that the form of *speaking*, whether it be in soliloquy or dialogue, is only a medium, and often a highly artificial one, for putting the reader or spectator into possession of that knowledge of the inner structure and workings of mind in a character, which he could otherwise never have arrived at *in that form of composition* by any gift short of intuition. We do here as we do with novels written in the *epistolary form*. How many improprieties, perfect solecisms in letter-writing, do we put up with in *Clarissa* and other books, for the sake of the delight with which that form upon the whole gives us.

But the practice of stage representation reduces everything to a controversy of elocution. Every character, from the boisterous blasphemings of Bajazet to the shrinking timidity of womanhood, must play the orator. The love-dialogues of Romeo and Juliet, their silver-sweet sounds of lovers' tongues by night; the more intimate and sacred sweetness of nuptial colloquy between an Othello or a Posthumus with their married wives, all those delicacies which are so delightful in the reading, as when we read of those youthful dalliances in Paradise—

As beseem'd
Fair couple link'd in happy nuptial league
Alone:[1]

by the inherent fault of stage representation, how are these things sullied and turned from their very nature by being exposed to a large assembly; when such speeches as Imogen addresses to her lord,[2] come drawling out of the mouth of a hired actress, whose courtship, though nominally addressed to the personated Posthumus, is manifestly aimed at the spectators, who are to judge of her endearments and her returns of love.

The character of Hamlet is perhaps that by which, since the days of Betterton, a succession of popular performers have had the greatest ambition to distinguish themselves. The length of the part may be one of their reasons. But for the character itself, we find it in a play, and therefore we judge it a fit subject of dramatic representation. The play itself abounds in maxims and reflections beyond any other, and therefore we consider it as a proper vehicle for conveying moral instruction. But Hamlet himself—what does he suffer meanwhile by being dragged forth as a public schoolmaster, to give lectures to the crowd! Why, nine parts in ten of what Hamlet does are transactions between himself and his moral sense; they are the effusions of his solitary musings, which he retires to holes and corners and the most sequestered parts of the palace to pour forth; or rather, they are the silent meditations with which his bosom is bursting, reduced to *words* for the sake of the reader, who must else remain ignorant of what is passing there. These profound sorrows, these light-and-noise-abhorring ruminations, which the tongue scarce dares utter to deaf walls and chambers, how can they be represented by a gesticulating actor, who comes and mouths them out before an audience, making four hundred people his confidants at once? I say not that it is the fault of the actor so to do; he must pronounce them *ore rotundo*,[3] he must accompany them with his eye, he must insinuate them into his auditory by some trick of the eye, tone, or gesture, or he fails. *He must be thinking all the while of his appearance, because he knows that all the while the spectators are judging of it.* And this is the way to represent the shy, negligent, retiring Hamlet.

[1] *Paradise Lost*, 4, 338-40.
[2] *Cymbeline*, I, 1.   [3] in an orotund voice

It is true that there is no other mode of conveying a vast quantity of thought and feeling to a great portion of the audience, who otherwise would never earn it for themselves by reading, and the intellectual acquisition gained this way may, for aught I know, be inestimable; but I am not arguing that Hamlet should not be acted, but how much Hamlet is made another thing by being acted. I have heard much of the wonders which Garrick performed in this part; but as I never saw him, I must have leave to doubt whether the representation of such a character came within the province of his art. Those who tell me of him, speak of his eye, of the magic of his eye, and of his commanding voice: physical properties, vastly desirable in an actor, and without which he can never insinuate meaning into an auditory,—but what have they to do with Hamlet? what have they to do with intellect? In fact, the things aimed at in theatrical representation are to arrest the spectator's eye upon the form and the gesture, and so to gain a more favorable hearing to what is spoken: it is not what the character is, but how he looks; not what he says, but how he speaks it. I see no reason to think that if the play of *Hamlet* were written over again by some such writer as Banks or Lillo, retaining the process of the story, but totally omitting all the poetry of it, all the divine features of Shakspeare, his stupendous intellect, and only taking care to give us enough of passionate dialogue, which Banks or Lillo were never at a loss to furnish,—I see not how the effect could be much different upon an audience, nor how the actor has it in his power to represent Shakspeare to us differently from his representation of Banks or Lillo. Hamlet would still be a youthful accomplished prince, and must be gracefully personated; he might be puzzled in his mind, wavering in his conduct, seemingly-cruel to Ophelia; he might see a ghost, and start at it, and address it kindly when he found it to be his father; all this in the poorest and most homely language of the servilest creeper after nature that ever consulted the palate of an audience, without troubling Shakspeare for the matter: and I see not but there would be room for all the power which an actor has, to display itself. All the passions and changes of passion might remain: for those are much less difficult to write or act than is thought; it is a trick easy to be attained; it is but rising or falling a note or two in the voice, a whisper with a significant foreboding look to announce its approach, and so contagious the counterfeit appearance of any emotion is that, let the words be what they will, the look and tone shall carry it off and make it pass for deep skill in the passions.

It is common for people to talk of Shakspeare's plays being *so natural;* that everybody can understand him. They are natural indeed; they are grounded deep in nature, so deep that the depth of them lies out of the reach of most of us. You shall hear the same persons say that *George Barnwell* is very natural, and *Othello* very natural, that they are both very deep; and to them they are the same kind of thing. At the one they sit and shed tears, because a good sort of young man is tempted by a naughty woman to commit *a trifling peccadillo,* the murder of an uncle or so,[1] that is all, and so comes to an untimely end, which is *so moving;* and at the other, because a blackamoor in a fit of jealousy kills his innocent white wife: and the odds are that ninety-nine out of a hundred would willingly behold the same catastrophe happen to both the heroes, and have thought the rope more due to Othello than to Barnwell. For of the texture of Othello's mind, the inward construction marvellously laid open with all its strengths and weaknesses, its heroic confidences and its human misgivings, its agonies of hate springing from the depths of love, they see no more than the spectators at a cheaper rate, who pay their pennies apiece to look through the man's telescope in Leicester-fields, see into the inward plot and topography of the moon. Some dim thing or other they see; they see an actor personating a passion, of grief or anger, for instance, and they recognize it as a copy of the usual external effects of such passions; or for at least as being true to *that symbol of the emotion which passes current at the theatre for it,* for it is often

[1] "If this note could hope to meet the eye of any of the managers, I would entreat and beg of them, in the name of both the galleries, that this insult upon the morality of the common people of London should cease to be eternally repeated in the holiday weeks. Why are the 'prentices of this famous and well-governed city, instead of an amusement, to be treated over and over again with the nauseous sermon of George Barnwell? Why *at the end of their vistas* are we to place the *gallows?* Were I an uncle, I should not much like a nephew of mine to have such an example placed before his eyes. It is really making uncle-murder too trivial to exhibit it as done upon the slight motives:—it is attributing too much to such characters as Millwood:—it is putting things into the heads of good young men, which they would never otherwise have dreamed of. Uncles that think anything of their lives should fairly petition the chamberlain against it."—Lamb.

no more than that: but of the grounds of the passion, its correspondence to a great or heroic nature, which is the only worthy object of tragedy,—that common auditors know anything of this, or can have any such notions dinned into them by the mere strength of an actor's lungs,—that apprehensions foreign to them should be thus infused into them by storm, I can neither believe, nor understand how it can be possible.

We talk of Shakspeare's admirable observation of life, when we should feel, that not from a petty inquisition into those cheap and every-day characters which surrounded him, as they surround us, but from his own mind, which was, to borrow a phrase of Ben Jonson's the very "sphere of humanity,"[1] he fetched those images of virtue and of knowledge, of which every one of us recognizing a part, think we comprehend in our natures the whole, and oftentimes mistake the powers which he positively creates in us, for nothing more than indigenous faculties of our own minds which only waited the application of corresponding virtues in him to return a full and clear echo of the same.

To return to Hamlet.—Among the distinguishing features of that wonderful character, one of the most interesting (yet painful) is that soreness of mind which makes him treat the intrusions of Polonius with harshness, and that asperity which he puts on in his interviews with Ophelia. These tokens of an unhinged mind (if they be not mixed in the latter case wth a profound artifice of love, to alienate Ophelia by affected discourtesies, so to prepare her mind for the breaking off of that loving intercourse, which can no longer find a place amidst business so serious as that which he has to do) are parts of his character, which to reconcile with our admiration of Hamlet, the most patient consideration of his situation is no more than necessary; they are what we *forgive afterwards*, and explain by the whole of his character, but *at the time* they are harsh and unpleasant. Yet such is the actor's necessity of giving strong blows to the audience, that I have never seen a player in this character who did not exaggerate and strain to the utmost these ambiguous features,—these temporary deformities in the character. They make him express a vulgar scorn at Polonius, which utterly degrades his gentility, and which no explanation can render palatable; they make him

[1] Jonson, *A Pindaric Ode to the Immortal Memory and Friendship of That Noble Pair, Sir Lucius Cary and Sir H. Morison*, 2, 20.

show contempt, and curl up the nose at Ophelia's father,—contempt in its very grossest and most hateful form; but they get applause by it: it is natural, people say; that is, the words are scornful, and the actor expresses scorn, and that they can judge of: but why so much scorn, and of that sort, they never think of asking.

So to Ophelia.—All the Hamlets that I have ever seen, rant and rave at her as if she had committed some great crime, and the audience are highly pleased, because the words of the part are satirical, and they are enforced by the strongest expression of satirical indignation of which the face and voice are capable. But then, whether Hamlet is likely to have put on such brutal appearances to a lady whom he loved so dearly, is never thought on. The truth is that in all such deep affections as had subsisted between Hamlet and Ophelia, there is a stock of *supererogatory love* (if I may venture to use the expression), which in any great grief of heart, especially where that which preys upon the mind cannot be communicated, confers a kind of indulgence upon the grieved party to express itself, even to its heart's dearest object, in the language of a temporary alienation; but it is not alienation, it is a distraction purely, and so it always makes itself to be felt by that object: it is not anger, but grief assuming the appearance of anger,—love awkwardly counterfeiting hate, as sweet countenances when they try to frown: but such sternness and fierce disgust as Hamlet is made to show is no counterfeit, but the real face of absolute aversion,—of irreconcilable alienation. It may be said he puts on the madman; but then he should only so far put on this counterfeit lunacy as his own real distraction will give him leave; that is, incompletely, imperfectly; not in that confirmed practiced way, like a master of his art, or, as Dame Quickly would say, "like one of those harlotry players."[1]

The truth is, the characters of Shakspeare are so much the objects of meditation rather than of interest or curiosity as to their actions, that while we are reading any of his great criminal characters,—Macbeth, Richard, even Iago,—we think not so much of the crimes which they commit, as of the ambition, the aspiring spirit, the intellectual activity, which prompts them to overleap those moral fences. Barnwell is a wretched murderer; there is a certain fitness between

[1] 1 *Henry IV*, II, 4, 437.

Standard popular 18th cent. villain.

perception of the punctual nature of the imagery

his neck and the rope; he is the legitimate heir to the gallows; nobody who thinks at all can think of any alleviating circumstances in his case to make him a fit object of mercy. Or to take an instance from the higher tragedy, what else but a mere assassin is Glenalvon! Do we think of anything but of the crime which he commits, and the rack which he deserves? That is all which we really think about him. Whereas in corresponding characters in Shakspeare so little do the actions comparatively affect us, that while the impulses, the inner mind in all its perverted greatness, solely seems real and is exclusively attended to, the crime is comparatively nothing. But when we see these things represented, the acts which they do are comparatively everything, their impulses nothing. The state of sublime emotion into which we are elevated by those images of night and horror which Macbeth is made to utter, that solemn prelude with which he entertains the time till the bell shall strike which is to call him to murder Duncan,— when we no longer read it in a book, when we have given up that vantage-ground of abstraction which reading possesses over seeing, and come to see a man in his bodily shape before our eyes actually preparing to commit a murder, if the acting be true and impressive, as I have witnessed it in Mr. K.'s[1] performance of that part, the painful anxiety about the act, the natural longing to prevent it while it yet seems unperpetrated, the too close pressing semblance of reality, give a pain and an uneasiness which totally destroy all the delight which the words in the book convey, where the deed doing never presses upon us with the painful sense of presence: it rather seems to belong to history,—to something past and inevitable, if it has anything to do with time at all. The sublime images, the poetry alone, is that which is present to our minds in the reading.

So to see Lear acted,—to see an old man tottering about the stage with a walking-stick, turned out of doors by his daughters in a rainy night, has nothing in it but what is painful and disgusting. We want to take him into shelter and relieve him. That is all the feeling which the acting of Lear ever produced in me. But the Lear of Shakspeare cannot be acted. The contemptible machinery by which they mimic the storm which he goes out in, is not more inadequate to represent the horrors of the real elements, than any actor can be to represent Lear: they might more easily propose to personate the Satan of Milton upon a stage, or one of Michael Angelo's terrible figures. The greatness of Lear is not in corporal dimension, but in intellectual: the explosions of his passion are terrible as a volcano: they are storms turning up and disclosing to the bottom that sea, his mind, with all its vast riches. It is his mind which is laid bare. This case of flesh and blood seems too insignificant to be thought on; even as he himself neglects it. On the stage we see nothing but corporal infirmities and weakness, the impotence of rage; while we read it, we see not Lear, but we are Lear,—we are in his mind, we are sustained by a grandeur which baffles the malice of daughters and storms; in the aberrations of his reason, we discover a mighty irregular power of reasoning, immethodized from the ordinary purposes of life, but exerting its powers, as the wind blows where it listeth,[1] at will upon the corruptions and abuses of mankind. What have looks, or tones, to do with that sublime identification of his age with that of the *heavens themselves*, when in his reproaches to them for conniving at the injustice of his children, he reminds them that "they themselves are old"?[2] What gesture shall we appropriate to this? What has the voice or the eye to do with such things? But the play is beyond all art, as the tamperings with it show: it is too hard and stony; it must have love-scenes, and a happy ending. It is not enough that Cordelia is a daughter; she must shine as a lover too. Tate has put his hook in the nostrils of this Leviathan, for Garrick and his followers, the showmen of the scene, to draw the mighty beast about more easily. A happy ending!—as if the living martyrdom that Lear had gone through,—the flaying of his feelings alive, did not make a fair dismissal from the stage of life the only decorous thing for him. If he is to live and be happy after, if he could sustain this world's burden after, why all this pudder and preparation,—why torment us with all this unnecessary sympathy? As if the childish pleasure of getting his gilt robes and sceptre again could tempt him to act over again his misused station,—as if at his years, and with his experience, anything was left but to die. . . .

---

[1] John Philip Kemble (1757-1823), the noted Shakespearian actor.

[1] See *John*, 3:8.   [2] *King Lear*, II, 4, 194.

THE SOUTH-SEA HOUSE
1820

Reader, in thy passage from the Bank—where thou hast been receiving thy half-yearly dividends (supposing thou art a lean annuitant[1] like myself)—to the Flower Pot, to secure a place for Dalston, or Shackle-well, or some other thy suburban retreat northerly,—didst thou never observe a melancholy looking, handsome, brick and stone edifice, to the left—where Threadneedle-street abuts upon Bishopsgate? I dare say thou hast often admired its magnificent portals ever gaping wide, and disclosing to view a grave court, with cloisters and pillars, with few or no traces of goers-in or comers-out—a desolation something like Balclutha's.[2]

This was once a house of trade,—a centre of busy interests. The throng of merchants was here—the quick pulse of gain—and here some forms of business are still kept up, though the soul be long since fled. Here are still to be seen stately porticoes; imposing staircases; offices roomy as the state apartments in palaces—deserted, or thinly peopled with a few straggling clerks; the still more sacred interiors of court and committee rooms, with venerable faces of beadles,[3] door-keepers—directors seated in form on solemn days (to proclaim a dead dividend) at long worm-eaten tables, that have been mahogany, with tarnished gilt-leather coverings, supporting massy silver inkstands long since dry;—the oaken wainscots hung with pictures of deceased governors and sub-governors, of Queen Anne, and the two first monarchs of the Brunswick dynasty;[4]—huge charts, which subsequent discoveries have antiquated;—dusty maps of Mexico, dim as dreams,—and soundings of the Bay of Panama!—The long passages hung with buckets, appended in idle rows, to walls, whose substance might defy any, short of the last, conflagration;—with vast ranges of cellarage under all, where dollars and pieces of eight[5] once lay, an "unsunned heap,"[6] for Mammon to have solaced his solitary heart withal,—long since dissipated, or scattered into air at the blast of the breaking of that famous Bubble.[7]

Such is the South-Sea House. At least, such it was forty years ago, when I knew it,—a magnificent relic! What alterations may have been made in it since, I have had no opportunities of verifying. Time, I take for granted, has not freshened it. No wind has resuscitated the face of the sleeping waters. A thicker crust by this time stagnates upon it. The moths, that were then battening upon its obsolete ledgers and day-books, have rested from their depredations, but other light generations have succeeded, making fine fretwork among their single and double entries. Layers of dust have accumulated (a superfœtation[1] of dirt!) upon the old layers, that seldom used to be disturbed, save by some curious finger, now and then, inquisitive to explore the mode of bookkeeping, in Queen Anne's reign; or, with less hallowed curiosity, seeking to unveil some of the mysteries of that tremendous hoax, whose extent the petty peculators of our day look back upon with the same expression of incredulous admiration, and hopeless ambition of rivalry, as would become the puny faces of modern conspiracy contemplating the Titan size of Vaux's superhuman plot.[2]

Peace to the manes[3] of the Bubble! Silence and destitution are upon thy walls, proud house, for a memorial!

Situated as thou art, in the very heart of stirring and living commerce,—amid the fret and fever of speculation—with the Bank, and the 'Change, and the India-house about thee, in the hey-day of present prosperity, with their important faces, as if were, insulting thee, their *poor neighbor out of business*—to the idle and merely contemplative,—to such as me, old house; there is a charm in thy quiet:—a cessation—a coolness from business—an indolence almost cloistral—which is delightful! With what reverence have I paced thy great bare rooms and courts at eventide! They spoke of the past:—the shade of some dead accountant, with visionary pen in ear, would flit by me, stiff as in life. Living accounts and accountants puzzle me. I have no skill in figuring. But thy great dead tomes, which scarce three degenerate clerks of the present day could lift from their enshrining shelves—with their old fantastic flourishes and decorative rubric interlacings[4]—their sums in

---

[1] Lamb was not an annuitant when this essay was written.
[2] "I passed by the walls of Balclutha, and they were desolate.—Ossian."—Lamb. See p. 87b, 39-40.   [3] Servants in charge of the offices.
[4] George I and George II.
[5] Spanish dollars, or *pesos*. Each coin was marked with the figure 8, which indicated its value in *reales*.   [6] Comus, 398.
[7] The failure of the South Sea Company, in which great numbers of shareholders were ruined by the dishonesty of the managers.

---

[1] second engendering,—*i. e.*, double layer
[2] The plot of Guido Vaux (Guy Fawkes) and others to blow up the Houses of Parliament in 1605.
[3] shades
[4] Flourishes after signatures were called rubrics, from being written in red ink.

triple columniations,[1] set down with formal superfluity of cyphers—with pious sentences at the beginning, without which our religious ancestors never ventured to open a book of business, or bill of lading—the costly vellum covers of some of them almost persuading us that we are got into some *better library,*—are very agreeable and edifying spectacles. I can look upon these defunct dragons with complacency. Thy heavy odd-shaped ivory-handled pen-knives (our ancestors had every thing on a larger scale than we have hearts for) are as good as anything from Herculaneum. The pounce-boxes[2] of our days have gone retrograde.

The very clerks which I remember in the South-Sea House—I speak of forty years back—had an air very different from those in the public offices that I have had to do with since. They partook of the genius of the place!

They were mostly (for the establishment did not admit of superfluous salaries) bachelors. Generally (for they had not much to do) persons of a curious and speculative turn of mind. Old-fashioned, for a reason mentioned before. Humorists,[3] for they were of all descriptions; and, not having been brought together in early life (which has a tendency to assimilate the members of corporate bodies to each other), but, for the most part, placed in this house in ripe or middle age, they necessarily carried into it their separate habits and oddities, unqualified, if I may so speak, as into a common stock. Hence they formed a sort of Noah's ark.[4] Odd fishes. A lay-monastery. Domestic retainers in a great house, kept more for show than use. Yet pleasant fellows, full of chat—and not a few among them arrived at considerable proficiency on the German flute.

The cashier at that time was one Evans, a Cambro-Briton. He had something of the choleric complexion of his countrymen stamped on his visage, but was a worthy sensible man at bottom. He wore his hair, to the last, powdered and frizzed out, in the fashion which I remember to have seen in caricatures of what were termed, in my young days, *Maccaronies.* He was the last of that race of beaux. Melancholy as a gib-cat[5] over his counter all the forenoon, I

think I see him, making up his cash (as they call it) with tremulous fingers, as if he feared every one about him was a defaulter; in his hypochondry ready to imagine himself one; haunted, at least, with the idea of the possibilities of his becoming one: his tristful visage clearing up a little over his roast neck of veal at Anderton's at two (where his picture still hangs, taken a little before his death by desire of the master of the coffee-house, which he had frequented for the last five-and-twenty years), but not attaining the meridian of its animation till evening brought on the hour of tea and visiting. The simultaneous sound of his well-known rap at the door with the stroke of the clock announcing six, was a topic of never-failing mirth in the families which this dear old bachelor gladdened with his presence. Then was his *forte,* his glorified hour! How would he chirp, and expand, over a muffin! How would he dilate into secret history! His countryman, Pennant himself, in particular, could not be more eloquent than he in relation to old and new London—the site of old theatres, churches, streets gone to decay—where Rosamond's pond stood—the Mulberry-gardens—and the Conduit in Cheap—with many a pleasant anecdote, derived from paternal tradition, of those grotesque figures which Hogarth has immortalized in his picture of *Noon,*—the worthy descendants of those historic confessors,[1] who, flying to this country, from the wrath of Louis the Fourteenth and his dragoons, kept alive the flame of pure religion in the sheltering obscurities of Hog-lane, and the vicinity of the Seven Dials!

Deputy, under Evans, was Thomas Tame. He had the air and stoop of a nobleman. You would have taken him for one, had you met him in one of the passages leading to Westminster-hall. By stoop, I mean that gentle bending of the body forwards, which, in great men, must be supposed to be the effect of an habitual condescending attention to the applications of their inferiors. While he held you in converse, you felt strained to the height[2] in the colloquy. The conference over, you were at leisure to smile at the comparative insignificance of the pretensions which had just awed you. His intellect was of the shallowest order. It did not reach to a saw or a proverb. His mind was in its original state of white paper. A sucking babe might have posed[3] him. What

[1] columns under three headings,—£., s., d.
[2] Boxes with perforated lids for sprinkling pounce, a fine powder, on manuscripts to dry the ink.
[3] eccentric persons
[4] See *Genesis,* 6:14 ff.
[5] male cat (See 1 *Henry IV,* I, 2, 83.)

[1] Huguenot refugees.
[2] See *Paradise Lost,* 8, 454.
[3] puzzled him by putting a question

was it then? Was he rich? Alas, no! Thomas Tame was very poor. Both he and his wife looked outwardly gentlefolks, when I fear all was not well at all times within. She had a neat meagre person, which it was evident she had not sinned in over-pampering; but in its veins was noble blood. She traced her descent, by some labyrinth of relationship, which I never thoroughly understood,—much less can explain with any heraldic certainty at this time of day,—to the illustrious, but unfortunate house of Derwentwater. This was the secret of Thomas's stoop. This was the thought— the sentiment—the bright solitary star of your lives,—ye mild and happy pair,— which cheered you in the night of intellect, and in the obscurity of your station! This was to you instead of riches, instead of rank, instead of glittering attainments: and it was worth them all together. You insulted none with it; but, while you wore it as a piece of defensive armor only, no insult likewise could reach you through it. *Decus et solamen*.[1]

Of quite another stamp was the then accountant, John Tipp. He neither pretended to high blood, nor in good truth cared one fig about the matter. He "thought an accountant the greatest hero in the world, and himself the greatest accountant in it."[2] Yet John was not without his hobby. The fiddle relieved his vacant hours. He sang, certainly, with other notes than to the Orphean lyre.[3] He did, indeed, scream and scrape most abominably. His fine suite of official rooms in Threadneedle-street, which without anything very substantial appended to them, were enough to enlarge a man's notions of himself that lived in them (I know not who is the occupier of them now),[4] resounded fortnightly to the notes of a concert of "sweet breasts,"[5] as our ancestors would have called them, culled from club-rooms and orchestras—chorus singers—first and second violoncellos—double basses—and clarionets—who ate his cold mutton, and

drank his punch, and praised his ear. He sate like Lord Midas among them.[1] But at the desk Tipp was quite another sort of creature. Thence all ideas, that were purely ornamental, were banished. You could not speak of any thing romantic without rebuke. Politics were excluded. A newspaper was thought too refined and abstracted. The whole duty of man consisted in writing off dividend warrants. The striking of the annual balance in the company's book (which, perhaps, differed from the balance of last year in the sum of 25*l*. 1*s*. 6*d*.) occupied his days and nights for a month previous. Not that Tipp was blind to the deadness of *things* (as they call them in the city) in his beloved house, or did not sigh for a return of the old stirring days when South Sea hopes were young— (he was indeed equal to the wielding of any the most intricate accounts of the most flourishing company in these or those days) :—but to a genuine accountant the difference of proceeds is as nothing. The fractional farthing is as dear to his heart as the thousands which stand before it. He is the true actor, who, whether his part be a prince or a peasant, must act it with like intensity. With Tipp form was everything. His life was formal. His actions seemed ruled with a ruler. His pen was not less erring than his heart. He made the best executor in the world: he was plagued with incessant executorships accordingly, which excited his spleen and soothed his vanity in equal ratios. He would swear (for Tipp swore) at the little orphans, whose rights he would guard with a tenacity like the grasp of the dying hand, that commended their interests to his protection. With all this there was about him a sort of timidity (his few enemies used to give it a worse name)—a something which, in reverence to the dead, we will place, if you please, a little on this side of the heroic. Nature certainly had been pleased to endow John Tipp with a sufficient measure of the principle of self-preservation. There is a cowardice which we do not despise, because it has nothing base or treacherous in its elements; it betrays itself, not you: it is mere temperament; the absence of the romantic and the enterprising; it sees a lion in the way,[2] and will not, with Fortinbras, "greatly find quarrel in a straw,"[3] when some supposed honor is at stake. Tipp never mounted the

[1] glory and consolation (*Æneid*, 10, 859)
[2] Adapted from Fielding's *The Adventures of Joseph Andrews*, 3, 5.
[3] See *Paradise Lost*, 3, 17.
[4] "I have since been informed that the present tenant of them is a Mr. Lamb, a gentleman who is happy in the possession of some choice pictures, and among them a rare portrait of Milton, which I mean to do myself the pleasure of going to see, and at the same time to refresh my memory with the sight of old scenes. Mr. Lamb has the character of a right courteous and communicative collector." —Lamb. (Mr. Lamb was Lamb's brother John.)
[5] musical voices (See *Twelfth Night*, II, 3, 20-21, 56.)

[1] That is, without any skill in judging music. See Glossary.
[2] See *Proverbs*, 26 :13.
[3] *Hamlet*, IV, 4, 55.

box of a stage-coach in his life; or leaned against the rails of a balcony; or walked upon the ridge of a parapet; or looked down a precipice; or let off a gun; or went upon a water-party;[1] or would willingly let you go if he could have helped it: neither was it recorded of him, that for lucre, or for intimidation, he ever forsook friend or principle.

Whom next shall we summon from the dusty dead,[2] in whom common qualities become uncommon? Can I forget thee, Henry Man, the wit, the polished man of letters, the *author,* of the South-Sea House? who never enteredst thy office in a morning, or quittedst it in mid-day (what didst *thou* in an office?)—without some quirk that left a sting! Thy gibes and thy jokes are now extinct, or survive but in two forgotten volumes,[3] which I had the good fortune to rescue from a stall in Barbican, not three days ago, and found thee terse, fresh, epigrammatic, as alive. Thy wit is a little gone by in these fastidious days—they topics are staled by the "new-born gauds"[4] of the time:—but great thou used to be in *Public Ledgers,* and in *Chronicles,* upon Chatham, and Shelburne, and Rockingham, and Howe, and Burgoyne, and Clinton, and the war which ended in the tearing from Great Britain her rebellious colonies,—and Keppel, and Wilkes, and Sawbridge, and Bull, and Dunning, and Pratt, and Richmond,—and such small politics.

A little less facetious, and a great deal more obstreperous, was fine rattling, rattle-headed Plumer. He was descended,—not in a right line, reader, (for his lineal pretensions, like his personal, favored a little of the sinister bend[5]) from the Plumers of Hertfordshire. So tradition gave him out; and certain family features not a little sanctioned the opinion. Certainly old Walter Plumer (his reputed author) had been a rake in his days, and visited much in Italy, and had seen the world. He was uncle, bachelor-uncle, to the fine old whig[6] still living, who has represented the county in so many successive parliaments, and has a fine old mansion near Ware. Walter flourished in George the Second's days, and was

the same who was summoned before the House of Commons about a business of franks,[1] with the old Duchess of Marlborough. You may read of it in Johnson's *Life of Cave.* Cave came off cleverly in that business. It is certain our Plumer did nothing to discountenance the rumor. He rather seemed pleased whenever it was, with all gentleness, insinuated. But, besides his family pretensions, Plumer was an engaging fellow, and sang gloriously.

Not so sweetly sang Plumer as thou sangest, mild, childlike, pastoral M—;[2] a flute's breathing less divinely whispering than thy Arcadian melodies, when, in tones worthy of Arden, thou didst chant that song sung by Amiens to the banished Duke,[3] which proclaims the winter wind more lenient than for a man to be ungrateful. Thy sire was old surly M—, the unapproachable churchwarden of Bishopsgate. He knew not what he did, when he begat thee, like spring, gentle offspring of blustering winter:—only fortunate in thy ending, which should have been mild, conciliatory, swan-like.[4]

Much remains to sing. Many fantastic shapes rise up, but they must be mine in private:—already I have fooled the reader to the top of his bent;[5]—else could I omit that strange creature Woollett, who existed in trying the question, and *bought litigations?*—and still stranger, inimitable solemn Hepworth, from whose gravity Newton might have deduced the law of gravitation. How profoundly would he nib[6] a pen—with what deliberation would he wet a wafer![7]

But it is time to close—night's wheels are rattling fast over me—it is proper to have done with this solemn mockery.

Reader, what if I have been playing with thee all this while—peradventure the very *names,* which I have summoned up before thee, are fantastic — insubstantial — like Henry Pimpernel, and old John Naps of Greece:—

Be satisfied that something answering to them has had a being. Their importance is from the past.

---

[1] picnic
[2] See *Macbeth,* V. 5, 22.
[3] *Miscellaneous Works in Verse and Prose of the late Henry Man* (1802).
[4] *Troilus and Cressida,* III. 3, 176.
[5] A term in heraldry signifying illegitimacy.
[6] William Plumer, for whom Lamb's grandmother, Mrs. Field, had been housekeeper.

[1] free mail service
[2] T. Maynard, a clerk who, according to Lamb, hanged himself.
[3] See *As You Like It,* II, 7.
[4] The swan was said to sing melodiously when about to die.
[5] See *Hamlet,* III, 2, 401.
[6] sharpen the point of
[7] seal

CHRIST'S HOSPITAL FIVE AND THIRTY YEARS AGO
1820

In Mr. Lamb's "Works," published a year or two since, I find a magnificent eulogy on my old school,[1] such as it was, or now appears to him to have been, between the years 1782 and 1789. It happens, very oddly, that my own standing at Christ's was nearly corresponding with his; and, with all gratitude to him for his enthusiasm for the cloisters, I think he has contrived to bring together whatever can be said in praise of them, dropping all the other side of the argument most ingeniously.

I remember L. at school; and can well recollect that he had some peculiar advantages, which I and others of his schoolfellows had not. His friends lived in town, and were near at hand; and he had the privilege of going to see them, almost as often as he wished, through some invidious distinction, which was denied to us. The present worthy sub-treasurer[2] to the Inner Temple can explain how that happened. He had his tea and hot rolls in a morning, while we were battening upon our quarter of a penny loaf—our *crug*[3]—moistened with attenuated small beer, in wooden piggins,[4] smacking of the pitched leathern jack it was poured from. Our Monday's milk porritch, blue and tasteless, and the pease soup of Saturday, coarse and choking, were enriched for him with a slice of "extraordinary bread and butter," from the hot-loaf of the Temple. The Wednesday's mess of millet, somewhat less repugnant (we had three banyan[5] to four meat days in the week), was endeared to his palate with a lump of double-refined,[6] and a smack of ginger (to make it go down the more glibly) or the fragrant cinnamon. In lieu of our *half-pickled* Sundays, or *quite fresh* boiled beef on Thursdays (strong as *caro equina*[7]), with detestable marigolds floating in the pail to poison the broth—our scanty mutton crags[8] on Fridays—and rather more savory, but grudging, portions of the same flesh, rotten-roasted or rare, on the Tuesdays (the only dish which excited our appetites, and disappointed our stomachs, in almost equal proportion)—he had his hot plate of roast veal, or the more tempting griskin[1] (exotics unknown to our palates), cooked in the paternal kitchen (a great thing), and brought him daily by his maid or aunt![2] I remember the good old relative (in whom love forbade pride) squatting down upon some odd stone in a by-nook of the cloisters, disclosing the viands (of higher regale than those cates[3] which the ravens ministered to the Tishbite[4]); and the contending passions of L. at the unfolding. There was love for the bringer; shame for the thing brought, and the manner of its bringing; sympathy for those who were too many to share in it; and, at top of all, hunger (eldest, strongest of the passions!) predominant, breaking down the stony fences of shame, and awkwardness, and a troubling over-consciousness.

I was a poor friendless boy. My parents and those who should care for me, were far away. Those few acquaintances of theirs, which they could reckon upon being kind to me in the great city, after a little forced notice, which they had the grace to take of me on my first arrival in town, soon grew tired of my holiday visits. They seemed to them to recur too often, though I thought them few enough; and one after another, they all failed me, and I felt myself alone among six hundred playmates.

O the cruelty of separating a poor lad from his early homestead! The yearnings which I used to have towards it in those unfledged years! How, in my dreams, would my native town (far in the west) come back, with its church, and trees, and faces! How I would wake weeping, and in the anguish of my heart exclaim upon sweet Calne in Wiltshire!

To this late hour of my life, I trace impressions left by the recollection of those friendless holidays. The long warm days of summer never return but they bring with them a gloom from the haunting memory of those *whole-day-leaves*, when, by some strange arrangement, we were turned out, for the live-long day, upon our own hands, whether we had friends to go to, or none. I remember those bathing-excursions to the New-River, which L. recalls with such relish, better, I think, than he can—for he was a home-seeking lad, and did not much care for such water-pastimes.

---

[1] A reference to Lamb's *Recollections of Christ's Hospital*, published in 1813.
[2] Randal Norris, a friend of Lamb.
[3] School slang for *bread*.
[4] small pails with upright staves as handles
[5] The days on which sailors have no allowance of meat.
[6] That is, sugar.   [7] horseflesh
[8] necks

[1] pork chop
[2] Lamb's Aunt Hetty, mentioned in the essay *The Decay of Beggars*.
[3] delicacies
[4] Elijah. See *1 Kings*, 17; also *Paradise Regained*, 2, 266 ff.

How merrily we would sally forth into the fields; and strip under the first warmth of the sun; and wanton like young dace[1] in the streams; getting us appetites for noon, which those of us that were pennyless (our scanty morning crust long since exhausted) had not the means of allaying—while the cattle, and the birds, and the fishes, were at feed about us, and we had nothing to satisfy our cravings—the very beauty of the day, and the exercise of the pastime, and the sense of liberty, setting a keener edge upon them!—How faint and languid, finally, we would return, towards nightfall, to our desired morsel, half-rejoicing, half-reluctant, that the hours of our uneasy liberty had expired!

It was worse in the days of winter, to go prowling about the streets objectless—shivering at cold windows of print-shops, to extract a little amusement; or haply, as a last resort, in the hope of a little novelty, to pay a fifty-times repeated visit (where our individual faces should be as well known to the warden as those of his own charges) to the Lions in the Tower—to whose levée[2] by courtesy immemorial, we had a prescriptive title to admission.

L.'s governor[3] (so we called the patron who presented us to the foundation) lived in a manner under his paternal roof. Any complaint which he had to make was sure of being attended to. This was understood at Christ's, and was an effectual screen to him against the severity of masters, or worse tyranny of the monitors. The oppressions of these young brutes are heart-sickening to call to recollection. I have been called out of my bed, and *waked for the purpose*, in the coldest winter nights—and this not once, but night after night—in my shirt, to receive the discipline of a leathern thong, with eleven other sufferers, because it pleased my callow overseer, when there has been any talking heard after we were gone to bed, to make the six last beds in the dormitory, where the youngest children of us slept, answerable for an offense they neither dared to commit, nor had the power to hinder. The same execrable tyranny drove the younger part of us from the fires, when our feet were perishing with snow; and, under the cruelest penalties, forbad the indulgence of a drink of water, when we lay in sleepless summer nights, fevered with the season, and the day's sports.

There was one H——,[1] who, I learned, in after days was seen expiating some maturer offense in the hulks.[2] (Do I flatter myself in fancying that this might be the planter of that name, who suffered—at Nevis, I think, or St. Kits,—some few years since? My friend Tobin was the benevolent instrument of bringing him to the gallows.) This petty Nero actually branded a boy, who had offended him, with a red hot iron; and nearly starved forty of us, with exacting contributions, to the one-half of our bread, to pamper a young ass, which, incredible as it may seem, with the connivance of the nurse's daughter (a young flame of his) he had contrived to smuggle in, and keep upon the leads[3] of the *ward,* as they called our dormitories. This game went on for better than a week, till the foolish beast, not able to fare well but he must cry roast meat[4]—happier than Caligula's minion,[5] could he have kept his own counsel—but, foolisher, alas! than any of his species in the fables—waxing fat, and kicking,[6] in the fulness of bread,[7] one unlucky minute would needs proclaim his good fortune to the world below; and, laying out his simple throat, blew such a ram's-horn blast, as (toppling down the walls of his own Jericho[8]) set concealment any longer at defiance. The client was dismissed, with certain attentions, to Smithfield; but I never understood that the patron underwent any censure on the occasion. This was in the stewardship of L.'s admired Perry.

Under the same *facile* administration, can L. have forgotten the cool impunity with which the nurses used to carry away openly, in open platters, for their own tables, one out of two of every hot joint, which the careful matron had been seeing scrupulously weighed out for our dinners? These things were daily practiced in that magnificent apartment, which L. (grown connoisseur since, we presume) praises so highly for the grand paintings "by Verrio, and others," with which it is "hung round and adorned."[9] But the sight of sleek well-fed

---

[1] A kind of fresh-water fish.
[2] reception (The lions were transferred to the Zoölogical Gardens in 1831.)
[3] Samuel Salt. See Glossary.

[1] Hodges.
[2] vessels used as prisons
[3] flat roofs covered with sheets of lead
[4] That is, publish his good fortune.
[5] Incitatus, a horse which the Roman Emperor Caligula made a consul and a priest. He was kept in a marble stable, and fed with wine and gilded oats.
[6] See *Deuteronomy*, 32 :15.
[7] See *Ezekiel*, 16 :49 ; *Hamlet*, III, 3, 80.
[8] See *Joshua,* 6 :5.
[9] Quoted from Lamb's essay *Recollections of Christ's Hospital.*

blue-coat[1] boys in pictures was, at that time,
I believe, little consolatory to him, or us,
the living ones, who saw the better part of
our provisions carried away before our
faces by harpies; and ourselves reduced
(with the Trojan[2] in the hall of Dido)

To feed our mind with idle portraiture.[3]

L. has recorded the repugnance of the
school to *gags,* or the fat of fresh beef
boiled; and sets it down to some superstition. But these unctuous morsels are never
grateful to young palates (children are universally fat-haters) and in strong, coarse,
boiled meats, *unsalted,* are detestable. A
gag-eater in our time was equivalent to a
goul[4] and held in equal detestation. ——[5]
suffered under the imputation:

——— 'Twas said
He ate strange flesh.[6]

He was observed, after dinner, carefully
to gather up the remnants[7] left at his table
(not many, nor very choice fragments, you
may credit me)—and, in an especial manner, these disreputable morsels, which he
would convey away and secretly stow in the
settle that stood at his bed-side. None saw
when he ate them. It was rumored that
he privately devoured them in the night.
He was watched, but no traces of such midnight practices were discoverable. Some
reported that, on leave-days, he had been
seen to carry out of the bounds a large blue
check handkerchief, full of something.
This then must be the accursed thing.[8]
Conjecture next was at work to imagine how
he could dispose of it. Some said he sold
it to the beggars. This belief generally prevailed. He went about moping. None spake
to him. No one would play with him. He
was excommunicated; put out of the pale
of the school. He was too powerful a boy
to be beaten, but he underwent every mode
of that negative punishment, which is more
grievous than many stripes. Still he per-
severed. At length he was observed by two
of his schoolfellows, who were determined
to get at the secret, and had traced him one
leave-day for that purpose, to enter a large

worn-out building, such as there exist specimens of in Chancery-lane, which are let out
to various scales of pauperism with open
door, and a common staircase. After him
they silently slunk in, and followed by
stealth up four flights, and saw him tap at
a poor wicket, which was opened by an
aged woman, meanly clad. Suspicion was
now ripened into certainty. The informers
had secured their victim. They had him in
their toils. Accusation was formally preferred, and retribution most signal was
looked for. Mr. Hathaway, the then steward (for this happened a little after my
time), with that patient sagacity which tempered all his conduct, determined to investigate the matter, before he proceeded to
sentence. The result was that the supposed
mendicants, the receivers or purchasers of
the mysterious scraps, turned out to be the
parents of ——, an honest couple come to
decay,—whom this seasonable supply had,
in all probability, saved from mendicancy;
and that this young stork, at the expense of
his own good name, had all this while been
only feeding the old birds!—The governors
on this occasion, much to their honor, voted
a present relief to the family of ——, and
presented him with a silver medal. The
lesson which the steward read upon RASH
JUDGMENT, on the occasion of publicly delivering the medal to ——, I believe, would
not be lost upon his auditory. I had left
school then, but I well remember ——. He
was a tall, shambling youth, with a cast in
his eye, not at all calculated to conciliate
hostile prejudices. I have since seen him
carrying a baker's basket. I think I heard
he did not do quite so well by himself, as
he had done by the old folks.

I was a hypochondriac lad; and the
sight of a boy in fetters, upon the day of
my first putting on the blue clothes, was
not exactly fitted to assuage the natural
terrors of initiation. I was of tender years,
barely turned of seven; and had only read
of such things in books, or seen them but
in dreams. I was told he had *run away.*
This was the punishment for the first offence. As a novice I was soon after taken
to see the dungeons. These were little,
square, Bedlam cells, where a boy could just
lie at his length upon straw and a blanket—
a mattress, I think, was afterwards substituted—with a peep of light, let in askance,
from a prison-orifice at top, barely enough
to read by. Here the poor boy was locked
in by himself all day, without sight of any
but the porter who brought him his bread

[1] Christ's Hospital was called the Blue-Coat
School from the dress of the pupils.
[2] Æneas, wrecked on the coast of Africa, went
into the newly-built Temple of Dido, but found
only pictures.
[3] Æneid, 1, 464.
[4] ghoul, an imaginary evil being who robs graves
and feeds upon the corpses
[5] It is not known to whom Lamb refers.
[6] Antony and Cleopatra, I, 4, 67.
[7] See John, 6:12.
[8] See Joshua, 6:13; 7:13.

and water—who *might not speak to him;*—or of the beadle,[1] who came twice a week to call him out to receive his periodical chastisement, which was almost welcome, because it separated him for a brief interval from solitude:—and here he was shut by himself *of nights,* out of the reach of any sound, to suffer whatever horrors the weak nerves, and superstition incident to his time of life, might subject him to.[2] This was the penalty for the second offence.—Wouldst thou like, reader, to see what became of him in the next degree?

The culprit, who had been a third time an offender, and whose expulsion was at this time deemed irreversible, was brought forth, as at some solemn *auto da fe,*[3] arrayed in uncouth and most appalling attire—all trace of his late "watchet weeds"[4] carefully effaced, he was exposed in a jacket, resembling those which London lamplighters formerly delighted in, with a cap of the same. The effect of this divestiture was such as the ingenious devisers of it could have anticipated. With his pale and frighted features, it was as if some of those disfigurements in Dante[5] had seized upon him. In this disguisement he was brought into the hall (*L.'s favorite state-room*), where awaited him the whole number of his school-fellows, whose joint lessons and sports he was thenceforth to share no more; the awful presence of the steward, to be seen for the last time; of the executioner beadle, clad in his state robe for the occasion; and of two faces more, of direr import, because never but in these extremities visible. These were governors; two of whom, by choice, or charter, were always accustomed to officiate at these *Ultima Supplicia;*[6] not to mitigate (so at least we understood it), but to enforce the uttermost stripe. Old Bamber Gascoigne, and Peter Aubert, I remember, were colleagues on one occasion, when the beadle turning rather pale, a glass of brandy was ordered to prepare him for the mysteries.[7] The scourg-

ing was, after the old Roman fashion, long and stately. The lictor[1] accompanied the criminal quite round the hall. We were generally too faint with attending to the previous disgusting circumstances, to make accurate report with our eyes of the degree of corporal punishment inflicted. Report, of course, gave out the back knotty and livid. After scourging, he was made over, in his *San Benito,*[2] to his friends, if he had any (but commonly such poor runagates were friendless), or to his parish officer, who, to enhance the effect of the scene, had his station allotted to him on the outside of the hall gate.

These solemn pageantries were not played off so often as to spoil the general mirth of the community. We had plenty of exercise and recreation *after* school hours; and, for myself, I must confess, that I was never happier, than *in* them. The Upper and Lower Grammar Schools were held in the same room; and an imaginary line only divided their bounds. Their character was as different as that of the inhabitants of the two sides of the Pyrenees. The Rev. James Boyer was the Upper Master; but the Rev. Matthew Field presided over that portion of the apartment of which I had the good fortune to be a member. We lived a life as careless as birds. We talked and did just what we pleased, and nobody molested us. We carried an accidence, or a grammar, for form; but for any trouble it gave us, we might take two years in getting through the verbs deponent, and another two in forgetting all that we had learned about them. There was now and then the formality of saying a lesson, but if you had not learned it, a brush across the shoulders (just enough to disturb a fly) was the sole remonstrance. Field never used the rod; and in truth he wielded the cane with no great good will—holding it "like a dancer."[3] It looked in his hands rather like an emblem than an instrument of authority; and an emblem, too, he was ashamed of. He was a good easy man, that did not care to ruffle his own peace, nor perhaps set any great consideration upon the value of juvenile time. He came among us, now and then, but often staid away whole days from us; and when he came, it made no difference to us—he had his private room to retire to, the short time he

---

[1] An officer who looked after the school buildings.

[2] "One or two instances of lunacy, or attempted suicide, accordingly, at length convinced the governors of the impolicy of this part of the sentence, and the midnight torture of the spirits was dispensed with. This fancy of dungeons for children was a sprout of Howard's brain, for which (saving the reverence due to Holy Paul) methinks I could willingly spit upon his statue."—Lamb.

[3] act of faith (The ceremony of executing a judgment of the Spanish Inquisition. The condemned heretics were strangled or burned.)

[4] light blue garments (Collins, *The Manners,* 68; Drayton, *Polyolbion,* 5, 13)

[5] In the *Inferno,* 28 and 30.

[6] extreme torments   [7] ceremonies

[1] A Roman officer whose duty was to punish criminals.

[2] The dress worn by persons condemned by the Inquisition.

[3] *Antony and Cleopatra,* III, 11, 36.

staid, to be out of the sound of our noise. Our mirth and uproar went on. We had classics of our own, without being beholden to "insolent Greece or haughty Rome,"[1] that passed current among us—*Peter Wilkins*—*The Adventures of the Hon. Capt. Robert Boyle*—*The Fortunate Blue Coat Boy*—and the like. Or we cultivated a turn for mechanic or scientific operations; making little sun-dials of paper; or weaving those ingenious parentheses, called *cat-cradles;* or making dry peas to dance upon the end of a tin pipe; or studying the art military over that laudable game "French and English,"[2] and a hundred other such devices to pass away the time—mixing the useful with the agreeable—as would have made the souls of Rousseau and John Locke chuckle to have seen us.[3]

Matthew Field belonged to that class of modest divines who affect to mix in equal proportion the *gentleman,* the *scholar,* and the *Christian;* but, I know not how, the first ingredient is generally found to be the predominating dose in the composition. He was engaged in gay parties, or with his courtly bow at some episcopal levée, when he should have been attending upon us. He had for many years the classical charge of a hundred children, during the four or five first years of their education; and his very highest form seldom proceeded further than two or three of the introductory fables of Phædrus. How things were suffered to go on thus, I cannot guess. Boyer, who was the proper person to have remedied these abuses, always affected, perhaps felt, a delicacy in interfering in a province not strictly his own. I have not been without my suspicions that he was not altogether displeased at the contrast we presented to his end of the school. We were a sort of Helots to his young Spartans.[4] He would sometimes, with ironic deference, send to borrow a rod of the Under Master, and then, with sardonic grin, observe to one of his upper boys, "how neat and fresh the twigs looked." While his pale students were battering their brains over Xenophon and Plato, with a silence as deep as that enjoined by the Samite,[1] we were enjoying ourselves at our ease in our little Goshen.[2] We saw a little into the secrets of his discipline, and the prospect did but the more reconcile us to our lot. His thunders rolled innocuous for us; his storms came near, but never touched us; contrary to Gideon's miracle, while all around were drenched, our fleece was dry.[3] His boys turned out the better scholars; we, I suspect, have the advantage in temper. His pupils cannot speak of him without something of terror allaying their gratitude; the remembrance of Field comes back with all the soothing images of indolence, and summer slumbers, and work like play, and innocent idleness, and Elysian exemptions, and life itself a "playing holiday."[4]

Though sufficiently removed from the jurisdiction of Boyer, we were near enough (as I have said) to understand a little of his system. We occasionally heard sounds of the *Ululantes,*[5] and caught glances of Tartarus. B. was a rabid pedant. His English style was crampt to barbarism. His Easter anthems (for his duty obliged him to those periodical flights) were grating as *scrannel*[6] *pipes.*[7] He would laugh, ay, and heartily, but then it must be at Flaccus's quibble about *Rex*[8] —— or at the *tristis severitas in vultu,*[9] or *inspicere in patinas,*[10] of Terence—thin jests, which at their first broaching could hardly have had *vis*[11]

---

[1] Jonson, *To the Memory of My Beloved Master, William Shakespeare, and What He Hath Left Us,* 39.

[2] A game in which the players,—one French and one English,—with eyes closed, draw a pencil across a piece of paper covered with dots. The player wins whose pencil strikes the most dots.

[3] Rousseau and Locke advocated a system of education which combined the practical with the theoretical.

[4] A reference to the practice of the Spartans of exhibiting to their sons, as a warning, a drunken Helot, or slave.

[1] Pythagoras (6th cent. B. C.), the Greek philosopher of Samos, who enjoined silence upon his pupils until they had listened to his lectures for five years. They were also bound to keep everything secret from the outer world.

[2] See *Genesis,* 47 :6; *Exodus,* 8 :22.

[3] Lamb cites Cowley as the source of this phrase. See Cowley's *The Complaint,* 69-74; also, *Judges,* 6 :37-38.

[4] 1 *Henry IV,* 1, 2, 227.

[5] howling sufferers (*Æneid,* 6, 557)

[6] thin; dry (See *Lycidas,* 124.)

[7] "In this and everything B. was the antipodes of his coadjutor. While the former was digging his brains for crude anthems, worth a pignut, F. would be recreating his gentlemanly fancy in the more flowery walks of the Muses. A little dramatic effusion of his, under the name of *Vertumnus and Pomona,* is not yet forgotten by the chroniclers of that sort of literature. It was accepted by Garrick, but the town did not give it their sanction. B. used to say of it, in a way of half-compliment, half-irony, that it was *too classical for representation.*"—Lamb.

[8] Flaccus,—*i. e.,* Horace, in his *Satires,* I, 7, 35, uses the word *Rex* with the double meaning of *king,* a monarch, and *King,* a surname.

[9] gloomy sternness on the countenance (A comic character in Terence's *Andria,* V, 2, 16, uses this phrase to describe a bearer of lies.)

[10] to look into the stewpans (A servant in Terence's *The Adelphi,* III, 3, 74, parodies the words of an old man to his son—"to look into the lives of men as into a mirror"—by saying that he directs his fellows to look into their stewpans as into a mirror.

[11] force

enough to move Roman muscle.—He had two wigs, both pedantic, but of differing omen. The one serene, smiling, fresh powdered, betokening a mild day. The other, an old discolored, unkempt, angry caxon,[1] denoting frequent and bloody execution. Woe to the school, when he made his morning appearance in his *passy*, or *passionate wig*. No comet expounded surer.[2]—J. B. had a heavy hand. I have known him double his knotty fist at a poor trembling child (the maternal milk hardly dry upon its lips) with a "Sirrah, do you presume to set your wits at me?"—Nothing was more common than to see him make a headlong entry into the schoolroom, from his inner recess, or library, and, with turbulent eye, singling out a lad, roar out, "Od's my life,[3] Sirrah" (his favorite adjuration), "I have a great mind to whip you,"—then, with as sudden a retracting impulse, fling back into his lair—and, after a cooling lapse of some minutes (during which all but the culprit had totally forgotten the context) drive headlong out again, piecing out his imperfect sense, as if it had been some Devil's Litany, with the expletory yell—"*and I* WILL, *too*."—In his gentler moods, when the *rabidus furor*[4] was assuaged, he had resort to an ingenious method, peculiar, for what I have heard, to himself, of whipping the boy, and reading the Debates, at the same time; a paragraph, and a lash between; which in those times, when parliamentary oratory was most at a height and flourishing in these realms, was not calculated to impress the patient with a veneration for the diffuser graces of rhetoric.

Once, and but once, the uplifted rod was known to fall ineffectual from his hand— when droll squinting W——[5] having been caught putting the inside of the master's desk to a use for which the architect had clearly not designed it, to justify himself, with great simplicity averred, that *he did not know that the thing had been forewarned*. This exquisite irrecognition of any law antecedent to the *oral* or *declaratory*, struck so irresistibly upon the fancy of all who heard it (the pedagogue himself not excepted) that remission was unavoidable.

L. has given credit to B.'s great merits as an instructor. Coleridge, in his *Literary Life*,[6] has pronounced a more intelligible

and ample encomium on them. The author of *The Country Spectator*[1] doubts not to compare him with the ablest teachers of antiquity. Perhaps we cannot dismiss him better than with the pious ejaculation of C— when he heard that his old master was on his death-bed—"Poor J. B.!—may all his faults be forgiven; and may he be wafted to bliss by little cherub boys, all head and wings, with no *bottoms* to reproach his sublunary infirmities."

Under him were many good and sound scholars bred. — First Grecian[2] of my time was Lancelot Pepys Stevens, kindest of boys and men, since Co-grammar-master (and inseparable companion) with Dr. T——e.[3] What an edifying spectacle did this brace of friends present to those who remembered the anti-socialities of their predecessors!—You never met the one by chance in the street without a wonder, which was quickly dissipated by the almost immediate sub-appearance of the other. Generally arm in arm, these kindly coadjutors lightened for each other the toilsome duties of their profession, and when, in advanced age, one found it convenient to retire, the other was not long in discovering that it suited him to lay down the fasces[4] also. Oh, it is pleasant, as it is rare, to find the same arm linked in yours at forty, which at thirteen helped it to turn over the *Cicero De Amicitia*,[5] or some tale of Antique Friendship, which the young heart even then was burning to anticipate!—Co-Grecian with S. was Th—,[6] who has since executed with ability various diplomatic functions at the Northern courts. Th— was a tall, dark, saturnine youth, sparing of speech, with raven locks. Thomas Fanshaw Middleton followed him (now Bishop of Calcutta) a scholar and a gentleman in his teens. He has the reputation of an excellent critic; and is author (besides *The Country Spectator*) of *A Treatise on the Greek Article, against Sharpe*.—M. is said to bear his mitre[7] in India, where the *regni novitas*[8] (I dare say) sufficiently justifies the bearing. A humility quite as primitive as that of Jewel or Hooker might not be

---

[1] An old kind of wig.
[2] Comets were regarded as omens of impending disaster.
[3] as God is my life
[4] raging fury (Catullus, *Carmina*, 63, 38)
[5] W— has not been identified.
[6] *Biographia Literaria*, 1.

[1] Thomas Fanshaw Middleton.
[2] A name given to the students of the first class in Christ's Hospital.
[3] Dr. Arthur William Trollope, who succeeded Boyer as headmaster of the school.
[4] Bundles of rods carried by lictors before the Roman magistrates as a symbol of authority: used here for *birch rod*.
[5] Cicero's *Essay Concerning Friendship*.
[6] Sir Edward Thornton (1766-1852).
[7] The official head-dress of a bishop.
[8] newness of rule,—*i. e.*, British rule (See the Æneid, 1, 562.)

exactly fitted to impress the minds of those Anglo-Asiatic diocesans with a reverence for home institutions, and the church which those fathers watered.[1] The manners of M. at school, though firm, were mild, and unassuming.—Next to M. (if not senior to him) was Richards, author of *The Aboriginal Britons,* the most spirited of the Oxford Prize Poems; a pale, studious Grecian.— Then followed poor S——,[2] ill-fated M——![3] of these the Muse is silent.

Finding some of Edward's race
Unhappy pass their annals by.[4]

Come back into memory, like as thou wert in the day-spring of thy fancies, with hope like a fiery column before thee[5]—the dark pillar not yet turned—Samuel Taylor Coleridge—Logician, Metaphysician, Bard!— How have I seen the casual passer through the Cloisters stand still, intranced with admiration (while he weighed the disproportion between the *speech* and the *garb* of the young Mirandula), to hear thee unfold, in thy deep and sweet intonations, the mysteries of Jamblichus, or Plotinus (for even in those years thou waxedst not pale at such philosophic draughts), or reciting Homer in his Greek, or Pindar——while the walls of the old Grey Friars re-echoed to the accents of the *inspired charity-boy!*— Many were the "wit-combats"[6] (to dally awhile with the words of old Fuller), between him and C. V. LeG——,[7] "which two I behold like a Spanish great galleon, and an English man of war; Master Coleridge, like the former, was built far higher in learning, solid, but slow in his performances. C. V. L., with the English man of war, lesser in bulk, but lighter in sailing, could turn with all tides, tack about, and take advantage of all winds, by the quickness of his wit and invention."

Nor shalt thou, their compeer, be quickly forgotten, Allen, with the cordial smile, and still more cordial laugh, with which thou wert wont to make the old Cloisters shake, in thy cognition of some poignant jest of

theirs; or the anticipation of some more material, and, peradventure, practical one, of thine own. Extinct are those smiles, with that beautiful countenance, with which (for thou wert the *Nireus formosus*[1] of the school), in the days of thy maturer waggery, thou didst disarm the wrath of infuriated town-damsel, who, incensed by provoking pinch, turning tigress-like round, suddenly converted by thy angel-look, exchanged the half-formed terrible "*bl*——," for a gentler greeting—"*bless thy handsome face!*"

Next follow two, who ought to be now alive, and the friends of Elia—the junior Le G——[2] and F——;[3] who impelled, the former by a roving temper, the latter by too quick a sense of neglect—ill capable of enduring the slights poor sizars[4] are sometimes subject to in our seats of learning— exchanged their Alma Mater for the camp; perishing, one by climate, and one on the plains of Salamanca:—Le G——, sanguine, volatile, sweet-natured; F——, dogged, faithful, anticipative of insult, warmhearted, with something of the old Roman height about him.

Fine, frank-hearted Fr——,[5] the present master of Hertford, with Marmaduke T——,[6] mildest of missionaries—and both my good friends still—close the catalogue of Grecians in my time.

THE TWO RACES OF MEN
1820

The human species, according to the best theory I can form of it, is composed of two distinct races, *the men who borrow,* and *the men who lend.* To these two original diversities may be reduced all those impertinent classifications of Gothic and Celtic tribes, white men, black men, red men. All the dwellers upon earth, "Parthians, and Medes, and Elamites,"[7] flock hither, and do naturally fall in with one or other of these primary distinctions. The infinite superiority of the former, which I choose to designate as the *great race,* is discernible in their figure, port, and a certain instinctive sovereignty. The latter are born degraded.

[1] See *1 Corinthians,* 3 :6-8.
[2] A student named Scott, who died in a hospital for the insane.
[3] A student named Maunde, who was dismissed from school.
[4] Prior, *Carmen Seculare for the Year 1700, st.* 8, 4-5. The reference is to the students of Christ's Hospital, which was founded by Edward VI in 1551.
[5] See *Exodus,* 13 :21 ; *Numbers,* 9 :15-23.
[6] Adapted from a passage in Fuller's *The History of the Worthies in England* (1662), in which is described a wit combat between Shakespeare and Ben Jonson.
[7] Charles Valentine Le Grice (1773-1858), one of the Grecians at Christ's Hospital.

[1] handsome Nireus (Nireus was the handsomest man among the Greeks before Troy. See the *Iliad,* 2, 673.)
[2] Samuel Le Grice, who became a soldier and died in the West Indies.
[3] Joseph Favell, who left Cambridge because he was ashamed of his father, a house-painter. He is the "poor W" of Lamb's *Poor Relations* (p. 981b, 45).
[4] students exempted from college fees
[5] Frederick William Franklin.
[6] Marmaduke Thompson.   [7] *Acts,* 2 :9.

"He shall serve his brethren."[1] There is something in the air of one of this cast, lean and suspicious;[2] contrasting with the open, trusting, generous manners of the other.

Observe who have been the greatest borrowers of all ages—Alcibiades—Falstaff—Sir Richard Steele—our late incomparable Brinsley—what a family likeness in all four!

What a careless, even deportment hath your borrower! what rosy gills! what a beautiful reliance on Providence doth he manifest,—taking no more thought than lilies![3] What contempt for money,—accounting it (yours and mine especially) no better than dross. What a liberal confounding of those pedantic distinctions of *meum* and *tuum*![4] or rather, what a noble simplification of language (beyond Tooke), resolving these supposed opposites into one clear, intelligible pronoun adjective!—What near approaches doth he make to the primitive *community*,[5]—to the extent of one half of the principle at least!

He is the true taxer who "calleth all the world up to be taxed";[6] and the distance is as vast between him and *one of us,* as subsisted betwixt the Augustan Majesty[7] and the poorest obolary[8] Jew that paid it tribute-pittance at Jerusalem!—His exactions, too, have such a cheerful, voluntary air! So far removed from your sour parochial or state-gatherers,—those ink-horn varlets, who carry their want of welcome in their faces! He cometh to you with a smile, and troubleth you with no receipt; confining himself to no set season. Every day is his Candlemas, or his Feast of Holy Michael.[9] He applieth the *lene tormentum*[10] of a pleasant look to your purse,—which to that gentle warmth expands her silken leaves, as naturally as the cloak of the traveler, for which sun and wind contended![11] He is the true Propontic which never ebbeth![12] The sea which taketh handsomely at each man's hand. In vain the victim, whom he delighteth to honor,[13] struggles with destiny; he is in the net. Lend therefore cheerfully, O

man ordained to lend—that thou lose not in the end, with thy worldly penny, the reversion promised.[1] Combine not preposterously in thine own person the penalties of Lazarus and of Dives![2]—but, when thou seest the proper authority coming, meet it smilingly, as it were half-way. Come, a handsome sacrifice! See how light *he* makes of it! Strain not courtesies with a noble enemy.

Reflections like the foregoing were forced upon my mind by the death of my old friend, Ralph Bigod, Esq., who departed this life on Wednesday evening, dying, as he had lived, without much trouble. He boasted himself a descendant from mighty ancestors of that name, who heretofore held ducal dignities in this realm. In his actions and sentiments he belied not the stock to which he pretended. Early in life he found himself invested with ample revenues, which, with that noble disinterestedness which I have noticed as inherent in men of the *great race,* he took almost immediate measures entirely to dissipate and bring to nothing: for there is something revolting in the idea of a king holding a private purse; and the thoughts of Bigod were all regal. Thus furnished, by the very act of disfurnishment; getting rid of the cumbersome luggage of riches, more apt (as one sings)

To slacken virtue, and abate her edge,
Than prompt her to do aught may merit praise;[3]

he set forth, like some Alexander, upon his great enterprise, "borrowing and to borrow"![4]

In his periegesis,[5] or triumphant progress throughout this island, it has been calculated that he laid a tythe[6] part of the inhabitants under contribution. I reject this estimate as greatly exaggerated:—but having had the honor of accompanying my friend, divers times, in his perambulations about this vast city, I own I was greatly struck at first with the prodigious number of faces we met who claimed a sort of respectful acquaintance with us. He was one day so obliging as to explain the phenomenon. It seems, these were his tributaries; feeders of his exchequer; gentlemen, his good friends (as he was pleased to express himself), to whom he had occasionally been beholden for a loan. Their multitudes did

---

[1] *Genesis*, 9 :25.
[2] See *Julius Cæsar*, 1, 2, 194-95.
[3] See *Matthew*, 6 :28-29.
[4] mine and thine (See Fielding's *The History of the Life of the Late Mr. Jonathan Wild the Great*, 3, 14.)
[5] See *Acts*, 2 :44.
[6] *Luke*, 2 :1.
[7] The Imperial Government.
[8] impoverished; possessing only small coins like oboli
[9] These were days on which rents fell due.
[10] gentle stimulus (Horace, *Odes*, III, 21, 13)
[11] In one of the fables of Æsop.
[12] See *Othello*, III, 3, 453.
[13] See *Esther*, 6 :6.

[1] See *Proverbs*, 19 :17.
[2] See *Luke*, 16 :19-31.
[3] *Paradise Regained*, 2, 455.
[4] See *Revelation*, 6 :2.
[5] tour   [6] tenth

no way disconcert him. He rather took a pride in numbering them; and, with Comus, seemed pleased to be "stocked with so fair a herd."[1]

With such sources, it was a wonder how he contrived to keep his treasury always empty. He did it by force of an aphorism, which he had often in his mouth, that "money kept longer than three days stinks." So he made use of it while it was fresh. A good part he drank away (for he was an excellent toss-pot), some he gave away, the rest he threw away, literally tossing and hurling it violently from him—as boys do burrs, or as if it had been infectious, —into ponds, or ditches, or deep holes,— inscrutable cavities of the earth;—or he would bury it (where he would never seek it again) by a river's side under some bank, which (he would facetiously observe) paid no interest—but out away from him it must go peremptorily, as Hagar's offspring into the wilderness,[2] while it was sweet. He never missed it. The streams were perennial which fed his fisc.[3] When new supplies became necessary, the first person that had the felicity to fall in with him, friend or stranger, was sure to contribute to the deficiency. For Bigod had an *undeniable* way with him. He had a cheerful, open exterior, a quick jovial eye, a bald forehead, just touched with gray (*cana fides*[4]). He anticipated no excuse, and found none. And, waiving for a while my theory as to the *great race,* I would put it to the most untheorizing reader, who may at times have disposable coin in his pocket, whether it is not more repugnant to the kindliness of his nature to refuse such a one as I am describing, than to say *no* to a poor petitionary rogue (your bastard borrower) who, by his mumping visnomy,[5] tells you, that he expects nothing better, and, therefore, whose preconceived notions and expectations you do in reality so much less shock in the refusal.

When I think of this man; his fiery glow of heart; his swell of feeling; how magnificent, how *ideal* he was; how great at the midnight hour; and when I compare with him the companions with whom I have associated since, I grudge the saving of a few idle ducats, and think that I am fallen into the society of *lenders,* and *little men.*

[1] *Comus,* 152.
[2] Ishmael. See *Genesis,* 16.
[3] treasury
[4] hoary fidelity (*Æneid,* 1, 292)
[5] mumbling physiognomy

To one like Elia, whose treasures are rather cased in leather covers than closed in iron coffers, there is a class of alienators more formidable than that which I have touched upon; I mean your *borrowers of books—those* mutilators of collections, spoilers of the symmetry of shelves, and creators of odd volumes. There is Comberbatch, matchless in his depredations!

That foul gap in the bottom shelf facing you, like a great eye-tooth knocked out (you are now with me in my little back study in Bloomsbury, reader!), with the huge Switzer-like[1] tomes on each side (like the Guildhall giants,[2] in their reformed posture, guardant of nothing), once held the tallest of my folios, *Opera Bonaventuræ,*[3] choice and massy divinity, to which its two supporters (school divinity also, but of a lesser calibre, — Bellarmine, and Holy Thomas), showed but as dwarfs,—itself an Ascapart!—*that* Comberbatch abstracted upon the faith of a theory he holds, which is more easy, I confess, for me to suffer by than to refute, namely, that "the title to property in a book (my Bonaventure, for instance) is in exact ratio to the claimant's powers of understanding and appreciating the same." Should he go on acting upon this theory, which of our shelves is safe?

The slight vacuum in the left-hand case— two shelves from the ceiling—scarcely distinguishable but by the quick eye of a loser —was whilom the commodious resting-place of Browne on *Urn Burial.* C. will hardly allege that he knows more about that treatise than I do, who introduced it to him, and was indeed the first (of the moderns) to discover its beauties—but so have I known a foolish lover to praise his mistress in the presence of a rival more qualified to carry her off than himself.—Just below, Dodsley's dramas want their fourth volume, where *Vittoria Corombona* is! The remainder nine are as distasteful as Priam's refuse sons, when the Fates *borrowed Hector.*[4] Here stood *The Anatomy of Melancholy,* in sober state.—There loitered *The Complete Angler,* quiet as in life, by some stream side.—In yonder nook,

[1] That is, enormous, like the giant Swiss guards formerly in the French service.
[2] Two colossal wooden figures of Gog and Magog in the council hall of London.
[3] Works of Bonaventura (1221-74), an Italian theologian.
[4] In the Trojan War, Hector, the favorite son of Priam, was slain by Achilles. With nine of his fifty sons still living, Priam begged Achilles for the body of Hector. See the *Iliad,* 24, 486 ff.

John Buncle, a widower-volume, with "eyes closed,"[1] mourns his ravished mate.

One justice I must do my friend, that if he sometimes, like the sea, sweeps away a treasure, at another time, sea-like, he throws up as rich an equivalent to match it. I have a small under-collection of this nature (my friend's gatherings in his various calls), picked up, he has forgotten at what odd places, and deposited with as little memory at mine. I take in these orphans, the twice-deserted. These proselytes of the gate are welcome as the true Hebrews.[2] There they stand in conjunction; natives, and naturalized. The latter seem as little disposed to inquire out their true lineage as I am.—I charge no warehouse-room for these deodands,[3] nor shall ever put myself to the ungentlemanly trouble of advertising a sale of them to pay expenses.

To lose a volume to C. carries some sense and meaning in it. You are sure that he will make one hearty meal on your viands, if he can give no account of the platter after it. But what moved thee, wayward, spiteful K.,[4] to be so importunate to carry off with thee, in spite of tears and adjurations to thee to forbear, the *Letters* of that princely woman, the thrice noble Margaret Newcastle?—knowing at the time, and knowing that I knew also, thou most assuredly wouldst never turn over one leaf of the illustrious folio:—what but the mere spirit of contradiction, and childish love of getting the better of thy friend?—Then, worst cut of all![5] to transport it with thee to the Gallican land—
Unworthy land to harbor such a sweetness,
A virtue in which all ennobling thoughts dwelt,
Pure thoughts, kind thoughts, high thoughts,
    her sex's wonder!

——hadst thou not thy play-books, and books of jests and fancies, about thee, to keep thee merry, even as thou keepest all companies with thy quips and mirthful tales?—Child of the Green-room,[6] it was unkindly done of thee. Thy wife, too, that part-French, better-part Englishwoman!— that *she* could fix upon no other treatise to bear away, in kindly token of remembering us, than the works of Fulke Greville, Lord Brooke — of which no Frenchman, nor woman of France, Italy, or England, was ever by nature constituted to comprehend a tittle! *Was there not Zimmerman on Solitude?*

Reader, if haply thou art blessed with a moderate collection, be shy of showing it; or if thy heart overfloweth to lend them, lend thy books; but let it be to such a one as S. T. C.[1]—he will return them (generally anticipating the time appointed) with usury; enriched with annotations, tripling their value. I have had experience. Many are these precious MSS. of his—(in *matter* oftentimes, and almost in *quantity* not unfrequently vying with the originals)—in no very clerkly hand—legible in my Daniel; in old Burton; in Sir Thomas Browne; and those abstruser cogitations of the Greville, now, alas! wandering in Pagan lands.—I counsel thee, shut not thy heart, nor thy library, against S. T. C.

MRS. BATTLE'S OPINIONS ON WHIST
1821

"A clear fire, a clean hearth,[2] and the rigor of the game." This was the celebrated *wish* of old Sarah Battle (now with God) who, next to her devotions, loved a good game at whist. She was none of your lukewarm gamesters, your half-and-half players, who have no objection to take a hand, if you want one to make up a rubber; who affirm that they have no pleasure in winning; that they like to win one game, and lose another; that they can while away an hour very agreeably at a card-table, but are indifferent whether they play or no; and will desire an adversary, who has slipt a wrong card, to take it up and play another.[3] These insufferable triflers are the curse of a table. One of these flies will spoil a whole pot. Of such it may be said, that they do not play at cards, but only play at playing at them.

Sarah Battle was none of that breed. She detested them, as I do, from her heart and soul; and would not, save upon a striking emergency, willingly seat herself at the same table with them. She loved a thorough-paced partner, a determined enemy.

[1] A reference to the statement of John Buncle, the hero of the book, that when one of his wives died he remained four days with his eyes shut.
[2] That is, the books which Lamb had purchased. Proselytes were converts to Judaism, who were not governed by such strict religious laws as were the true Hebrews. See *Leviticus,* 19 : 33-34.
[3] things given or forfeited
[4] James Kenney (1780-1849), a dramatist.
[5] See *Julius Cæsar,* III, 2, 187.
[6] The stage; literally, the dressing-room behind the scenes.

[1] Samuel Taylor Coleridge.
[2] "This was before the introduction of rugs, reader. You must remember the intolerable crash of the unswept cinders betwixt your foot and the marble."—Lamb.
[3] "As if a sportsman should tell you he liked to kill a fox one day and lose him the next."—Lamb.

She took, and gave, no concessions. She hated favors. She never made a revoke,[1] nor ever passed it over in her adversary without exacting the utmost forfeiture. She fought a good fight:[2] cut and thrust. She held not her good sword (her cards) "like a dancer."[3] She sat bolt upright; and neither showed you her cards, nor desired to see yours. All people have their blind side—their superstitions; and I have heard her declare, under the rose,[4] that Hearts was her favorite suit.

I never in my life—and I knew Sarah Battle many of the best years of it—saw her take out her snuff-box when it was her turn to play; or snuff a candle in the middle of a game; or ring for a servant, till it was fairly over. She never introduced, or connived at, miscellaneous conversation during its process. As she emphatically observed, cards were cards: and if I ever saw unmingled distaste in her fine last-century countenance, it was at the airs of a young gentleman of a literary turn, who had been with difficulty persuaded to take a hand; and who, in his excess of candor, declared that he thought there was no harm in unbending the mind now and then, after serious studies, in recreations of that kind! She could not bear to have her noble occupation, to which she wound up her faculties, considered in that light. It was her business, her duty, the thing she came into the world to do,—and she did it. She unbent her mind afterwards—over a book.

Pope was her favorite author: his *Rape of the Lock* her favorite work. She once did me the favor to play over with me (with the cards) his celebrated game of ombre in that poem; and to explain to me how far it agreed with, and in what points it would be found to differ from, tradrille. Her illustrations were apposite and poignant; and I had the pleasure of sending the substance of them to Mr. Bowles, but I suppose they came too late to be inserted among his ingenious notes upon that author.

Quadrille,[5] she has often told me, was her first love; but whist had engaged her maturer esteem. The former, she said, was showy and specious, and likely to allure young persons. The uncertainty and quick shifting of partners—a thing which the constancy of whist abhors;—the dazzling supremacy and regal investiture of Spa-

dille[1]—absurd, as she justly observed, in the pure aristocracy of whist, where his crown and garter gave him no proper power above his brother-nobility of the Aces;—the giddy vanity, so taking to the inexperienced, of playing alone:—above all, the overpowering attractions of a *Sans Prendre Vole*,[2]—to the triumph of which there is certainly nothing parallel or approaching, in the contingencies of whist;—all these, she would say, make quadrille a game of captivation to the young and enthusiastic. But whist was the *solider* game: that was her word. It was a long meal; not, like quadrille, a feast of snatches. One or two rubbers might co-extend in duration with an evening. They gave time to form rooted friendships, to cultivate steady enmities. She despised the chance-started, capricious, and ever fluctuating alliances of the other. The skirmishes of quadrille, she would say, reminded her of the petty ephemeral embroilments of the little Italian states, depicted by Machiavel;[3] perpetually changing postures and connections; bitter foes today, sugared darling tomorrow; kissing and scratching in a breath;—but the wars of whist were comparable to the long, steady, deep-rooted, rational antipathies of the great French and English nations.

A grave simplicity was what she chiefly admired in her favorite game. There was nothing silly in it, like the nob[4] in cribbage—nothing superfluous. No *flushes*—that most irrational of all pleas that a reasonable being can set up:—that any one should claim four by virtue of holding cards of the same mark and color, without reference to the playing of the game, or the individual worth or pretensions of the cards themselves! She held this to be a solecism; as pitiful an ambition at cards as alliteration is in authorship. She despised superficiality, and looked deeper than the colors of things,—Suits were soldiers, she would say, and must have a uniformity of array to distinguish them: but what should we say to a foolish squire, who should claim a merit from dressing up his tenantry in red jackets, that never were to be marshalled—never to take the field?—She even wished that whist were more simple than it is; and, in my mind, would have stript it of some appendages, which, in the state of human frailty, may be venially, and even com-

---

[1] never failed to follow suit when able
[2] See *2 Timothy*, 4:7.
[3] *Antony and Cleopatra*, III, 11, 36.
[4] in confidence
[5] ombre played by four persons

[1] The ace of spades.
[2] winning all the tricks single-handed
[3] In his *Florentine History*.
[4] The knave of the same suit as the card turned up, counting one for the holder.

mendably allowed of. She saw no reason for the deciding of the trump by the turn of the card. Why not one suit always trumps?—Why two colors, when the mark of the suits would have sufficiently distinguished them without it?—

"But the eye, my dear Madam, is agreeably refreshed with the variety. Man is not a creature of pure reason—he must have his senses delightfully appealed to. We see it in Roman Catholic countries, where the music and the paintings draw in many to worship, whom your quaker spirit of unsensualizing would have kept out.—You, yourself, have a pretty collection of paintings—but confess to me, whether, walking in your gallery at Sandham, among those clear Vandykes, or among the Paul Potters in the ante-room, you ever felt your bosom glow with an elegant delight, at all comparable to *that* you have it in your power to experience most evenings over a well-arranged assortment of the court cards? —the pretty antic habits, like heralds in a procession—the gay triumph-assuring scarlets—the contrasting deadly-killing sables —the 'hoary majesty of spades,'[1] Pam[2] in all his glory!—

"All these might be dispensed with; and, with their naked names upon the drab pasteboard, the game might go on very well, picture-less. But the *beauty* of cards would be extinguished forever. Stripped of all that is imaginative in them, they must degenerate into mere gambling.—Imagine a dull deal board,[3] or drum head, to spread them on, instead of that nice verdant carpet (next to nature's), fittest arena for those courtly combatants to play their gallant jousts and turneys in!—Exchange those delicately-turned ivory markers—(work of Chinese artist, unconscious of their symbol, —or as profanely slighting their true application as the arrantest Ephesian journeyman[4] that turned out those little shrines for the goddess[5])—exchange them for little bits of leather (our ancestors' money) or chalk and a slate!"—

The old lady, with a smile, confessed the soundness of my logic; and to her approbation of my arguments on her favorite topic that evening, I have always fancied myself indebted for the legacy of a curious cribbage board, made of the finest Sienna marble, which her maternal uncle (old Wal-

ter Plumer, whom I have elsewhere celebrated[1]) brought with him from Florence: —this, and a trifle of five hundred pounds, came to me at her death.

The former bequest (which I do not least value) I have kept with religious care; though she herself, to confess a truth, was never greatly taken with cribbage. It was an essentially vulgar game, I have heard her say,—disputing with her uncle, who was very partial to it. She could never heartily bring her mouth to pronounce *"go"*—or *"that's a go."*[2] She called it an ungrammatical game. The pegging[3] teased her. I once knew her to forfeit a rubber (a five dollar stake), because she would not take advantage of the turn-up knave, which would have given it her, but which she must have claimed by the disgraceful tenure of declaring *"two for his heels."* There is something extremely genteel in this sort of self-denial. Sarah Battle was a gentlewoman born.

Piquet she held the best game at the cards for two persons, though she would ridicule the pedantry of the terms—such as pique[4] —repique[5]—the capot[6]—they savored (she thought) of affectation. But games for two, or even three, she never greatly cared for. She loved the quadrate, or square. She would argue thus:—Cards are warfare: the ends are gain, with glory. But cards are war, in disguise of a sport: when single adversaries encounter, the ends proposed are too palpable. By themselves, it is too close a fight; with spectators, it is not much bettered. No looker-on can be interested, except for a bet, and then it is a mere affair of money; he cares not for your luck *sympathetically,* or for your play.—Three are still worse; a mere naked war of every man against every man, as in cribbage, without league or alliance; or a rotation of petty and contradictory interests, a succession of heartless leagues, and not much more hearty infractions of them, as in tradrille.—But in square games (*she meant whist*) all that is possible to be attained in card-playing is accomplished. There are the incentives of profit with honor, common to every species —though the *latter* can be but very imperfectly enjoyed in those other games, where the spectator is only feebly a participator. But the parties in whist are spectators and

[1] Pope, *The Rape of the Lock*, 3, 56.
[2] The knave of clubs.
[3] A board of pine or fir.
[4] Demetrius. See *Acts*, 19:24-41.
[5] Diana.

[1] In *The South Sea House* (p. 956a, 35 ff.).
[2] Terms used when the player is unable to play.
[3] scoring by means of pegs
[4] scoring 30 points before the other player scores
[5] scoring 30 or more points before play begins,
    thereby counting 60 points additional
[6] winning all the tricks, counting 40

principals too. They are a theatre to themselves, and a looker-on is not wanted. He is rather worse than nothing, and an impertinence. Whist abhors neutrality, or interests beyond its sphere. You glory in some surprising stroke of skill or fortune, not because a cold—or even an interested—bystander witnesses it, but because your *partner* sympathizes in the contingency. You win for two. You triumph for two. Two are exalted. Two again are mortified; which divides their disgrace, as the conjunction doubles (by taking off the invidiousness) your glories. Two losing to two are better reconciled, than one to one in that close butchery. The hostile feeling is weakened by multiplying the channels. War becomes a civil game.—By such reasonings as these the old lady was accustomed to defend her favorite pastime.

No inducement could ever prevail upon her to play at any game, where chance entered into the composition, *for nothing.* Chance, she would argue—and here again, admire the subtlety of her conclusion!—chance is nothing, but where something else depends upon it. It is obvious, that cannot be *glory.* What rational cause of exultation could it give to a man to turn up size ace[1] a hundred times together by himself? or before spectators, where no stake was depending?—Make a lottery of a hundred thousand tickets with but one fortunate number —and what possible principle of our nature, except stupid wonderment, could it gratify to gain that number as many times successively, without a prize?—Therefore she disliked the mixture of chance in backgammon, where it was not played for money. She called it foolish, and those people idiots, who were taken with a lucky hit under such circumstances. Games of pure skill were as little to her fancy. Played for a stake, they were a mere system of over-reaching. Played for glory, they were a mere setting of one man's wit,—his memory, or combination-faculty rather—against another's; like a mock-engagement at a review, bloodless and profitless.—She could not conceive a *game* wanting the spritely infusion of chance,—the handsome excuses of good fortune. Two people playing at chess in a corner of a room, whilst whist was stirring in the centre, would inspire her with insufferable horror and ennui. Those well-cut similitudes of Castles, and Knights, the *imagery* of the board, she would argue

[1] six and one (a lucky throw of dice in the game of backgammon)

(and I think in this case justly), were entirely misplaced and senseless. Those hard head-contests can in no instance ally with the fancy. They reject form and color. A pencil and dry slate (she used to say) were the proper arena for such combatants.

To those puny objectors against cards, as nurturing the bad passions, she would retort that man is a gaming animal. He must be always trying to get the better in something or other:—that this passion can scarcely be more safely expended than upon a game at cards; that cards are a temporary illusion; in truth, a mere drama; for we do but *play* at being mightily concerned, where a few idle shillings are at stake, yet, during the illusion, we *are* as mightily concerned as those whose stake is crowns and kingdoms. They are a sort of dream-fighting; much ado; great battling, and little bloodshed; mighty means for disproportioned ends; quite as diverting, and a great deal more innoxious, than many of those more serious *games* of life, which men play, without esteeming them to be such.

With great deference to the old lady's judgment on these matters, I think I have experienced some moments in my life, when playing at cards *for nothing* has even been agreeable. When I am in sickness, or not in the best spirits, I sometimes call for the cards, and play a game at piquet *for love* with my cousin Bridget—Bridget Elia.[1]

I grant there is something sneaking in it; but with a tooth-ache, or a sprained ancle, —when you are subdued and humble,—you are glad to put up with an inferior spring of action.

There is such a thing in nature, I am convinced, as *sick whist.*

I grant it is not the highest style of man —I deprecate the manes[2] of Sarah Battle— she lives not, alas! to whom I should apologize.

At such times, those *terms* which my old friend objected to, come in as something admissible.—I love to get a tierce[3] or a quatorze,[4] though they mean nothing. I am subdued to an inferior interest. Those shadows of winning amuse me.

That last game I had with my sweet cousin (I capotted[5] her)—(dare I tell thee, how foolish I am?)—I wished it might have lasted forever, though we gained nothing, and lost nothing, though it was a mere

[1] Lamb's sister Mary.
[2] shade; spirit
[3] sequence of three cards of the same suit
[4] the four aces, kings, queens, knaves, or tens
[5] won all the tricks from

shade of play: I would be content to go on in that idle folly forever. The pipkin[1] should be ever boiling, that was to prepare the gentle lenitive to my foot, which Bridget was doomed to apply after the game was over: and, as I do not much relish appliances, there it should ever bubble. Bridget and I should be ever playing.

MACKERY END, IN HERTFORDSHIRE
1821

Bridget Elia[2] has been my housekeeper for many a long year. I have obligations to Bridget, extending beyond the period of memory. We house together, old bachelor and maid, in a sort of double singleness; with such tolerable comfort, upon the whole, that I, for one, find in myself no sort of disposition to go out upon the mountains, with the rash king's offspring,[3] to bewail my celibacy. We agree pretty well in our tastes and habits—yet so, as "with a difference."[4] We are generally in harmony, with occasional bickerings—as it should be among near relations. Our sympathies are rather understood, then expressed; and once, upon my dissembling a tone in my voice more kind than ordinary, my cousin burst into tears, and complained that I was altered. We are both great readers in different directions. While I am hanging over (for the thousandth time) some passage in old Burton, or one of his strange contemporaries, she is abstracted in some modern tale, or adventure, whereof our common reading-table is daily fed 'with assiduously fresh supplies. Narrative teases me. I have little concern in the progress of events. She must have a story—well, ill, or indifferently told —so there be life stirring in it, and plenty of good or evil accidents. The fluctuations of fortune in fiction—and almost in real life— have ceased to interest, or operate but dully upon me. Out-of-the-way humors and opinions—heads with some diverting twist in them—the oddities of authorship please me most. My cousin has a native disrelish of anything that sounds odd or bizarre. Nothing goes down with her, that is quaint, irregular, or out of the road of common sympathy. She "holds Nature more clever."[5] I can pardon her blindness to the beautiful obliquities[6] of the *Religio Medici;* but she

must apologize to me for certain disrespectful insinuations, which she has been pleased to throw out latterly, touching the intellectuals of a dear favorite of mine, of the last century but one—the thrice noble, chaste, and virtuous,—but again somewhat fantastical, and original-brain'd, generous Margaret Newcastle.

It has been the lot of my cousin, oftener perhaps than I could have wished, to have had for her associates and mine, free-thinkers—leaders, and disciples, of novel philosophies and systems; but she neither wrangles with, nor accepts, their opinions. That which was good and venerable to her, when a child, retains its authority over her mind still. She never juggles or plays tricks with her understanding.

We are both of us inclined to be a little too positive; and I have observed the result of our disputes to be almost uniformly this, —that in matters of fact, dates, and circumstances, it turns out that I was in the right, and my cousin in the wrong. But where we have differed upon moral points; upon something proper to be done, or let alone; whatever heat of opposition, or steadiness of conviction, I set out with, I am sure always, in the long run, to be brought over to her way of thinking.

I must touch upon the foibles of my kinswoman with a gentle hand, for Bridget does not like to be told of her faults. She hath an awkward trick (to say no worse of it) of reading in company: at which times she will answer *yes* or *no* to a question, without fully understanding its purport—which is provoking, and derogatory in the highest degree to the dignity of the putter of the said question. Her presence of mind is equal to the most pressing trials of life, but will sometimes desert her upon trifling occasions. When the purpose requires it, and is a thing of moment, she can speak to it greatly; but in matters which are not stuff of the conscience,[1] she hath been known sometimes to let slip a word less seasonably.

Her education in youth was not much attended to; and she happily missed all that train of female garniture, which passeth by the name of accomplishments. She was tumbled early, by accident or design, into a spacious closet of good old English reading,[2] without much selection or prohibition, and browsed at will upon that fair and wholesome pasturage. Had I twenty girls, they

---

[1] A small earthen pot.
[2] Lamb's sister Mary.
[3] Jephthah's daughter. See *Judges,* 11 :31-40; also Tennyson's *A Dream of Fair Women,* 197-248.
[4] *Hamlet,* IV, 5, 183. (An heraldic term.)
[5] Gay, *Epitaph of Bywords,* 4.
[6] irregularities

[1] *Othello,* I, 2, 2.
[2] In the library of Samuel Salt of the Inner Temple. See Glossary.

should be brought up exactly in this fashion. I know not whether their chance in wedlock might not be diminished by it; but I can answer for it, that it makes (if the worst come to the worst) most incomparable old maids.

In a season of distress, she is the truest comforter; but in the teasing accidents, and minor perplexities, which do not call out the *will* to meet them, she sometimes maketh matters worse by an excess of participation. If she does not always divide your trouble, upon the pleasanter occasions of life, she is sure always to treble your satisfaction. She is excellent to be at play with, or upon a visit; but best, when she goes a journey with you.

We made an excursion together a few summers since, into Hertfordshire, to beat up the quarters of some of our less-known relations in that fine corn[1] country.

The oldest thing I remember is Mackery End; or Mackerel End, as it is spelt, perhaps more properly, in some old maps of Hertfordshire; a farm-house,—delightfully situated within a gentle walk from Wheat-hampstead. I can just remember having been there, on a visit to a great-aunt, when I was a child, under the care of Bridget, who, as I have said, is older than myself by some ten years. I wish that I could throw into a heap the remainder of our joint existences, that we might share them in equal division. But that is impossible. The house was at that time in the occupation of a substantial yeoman, who had married my grandmother's sister. His name was Gladman. My grandmother was a Bruton, married to a Field. The Gladmans and the Brutons are still flourishing in that part of the county, but the Fields are almost extinct. More than forty years had elapsed since the visit I speak of; and, for the greater portion of that period, we had lost sight of the other two branches also. Who or what sort of persons inherited Mackery End—kindred or strange folk—we were afraid almost to conjecture, but determined some day to explore.

By somewhat a circuitous route, taking the noble park at Luton in our way from Saint Alban's, we arrived at the spot of our anxious curiosity about noon. The sight of the old farm-house, though every trace of it was effaced from my recollection, affected me with a pleasure which I had not experienced for many a year. For though *I* had forgotten it, *we* had never forgotten being there together, and we had been talking

[1] wheat

about Mackery End all our lives, till memory on my part became mocked with a phantom of itself, and I thought I knew the aspect of a place, which, when present, O how unlike it was to *that*, which I had conjured up so many times instead of it!

Still the air breathed balmily about it; the season was in the "heart of June,"[1] and I could say with the poet,

> But thou, that didst appear so fair
> To fond imagination,
> Dost rival in the light of day
> Her delicate creation![2]

Bridget's was more a waking bliss[3] than mine, for she easily remembered her old acquaintance again—some altered features, of course, a little grudged at. At first, indeed, she was ready to disbelieve for joy; but the scene soon reconfirmed itself in her affections—and she traversed every out-post of the old mansion, to the wood-house, the orchard, the place where the pigeon-house had stood (house and birds were alike flown)—with a breathless impatience of recognition, which was more pardonable perhaps than decorous at the age of fifty odd. But Bridget in some things is behind her years.

The only thing left was to get into the house—and that was a difficulty which to me singly would have been insurmountable; for I am terribly shy in making myself known to strangers and out-of-date kinsfolk. Love, stronger than scruple, winged my cousin in without me; but she soon returned with a creature that might have sat to a sculptor for the image of Welcome. It was the youngest of the Gladmans; who, by marriage with a Bruton, had become mistress of the old mansion. A comely brood are the Brutons. Six of them, females, were noted as the handsomest young women in the county. But this adopted Bruton, in my mind, was better than they all—more comely. She was born too late to have remembered me. She just recollected in early life to have had her cousin Bridget once pointed out to her, climbing a stile. But the name of kindred, and of cousinship, was enough. Those slender ties, that prove slight as gossamer in the rending atmosphere of a metropolis, bind faster, as we found it, in hearty, homely, loving Hertfordshire. In five minutes we were as thoroughly acquainted as if we had been born

[1] Jonson, *Epithalamium; or a Song Celebrating the Nuptials of That Noble Gentleman, Mr. Hierome Weston*, 16.
[2] Wordsworth, *Yarrow Visited*, 41 ff. (p. 335).
[3] See *Comus*, 263.

and bred up together; were familiar, even to the calling each other by our Christian names. So Christians should call one another. To have seen Bridget, and her—it was like the meeting of the two scriptural cousins![1] There was a grace and dignity, an amplitude of form.and stature, answering to her mind, in this farmer's wife, which would have shined in a palace—or so we thought it. We were made welcome by husband and wife equally—we, and our friend that was with us—I had almost forgotten him—but B. F.[2] will not so soon forget that meeting, if peradventure he shall read this on the far distant shores where the kangaroo haunts. The fatted calf was made ready, or rather was already so, as if in anticipation of our coming;[3] and, after an appropriate glass of native wine, never let me forget with what honest pride this hospitable cousin made us proceed to Wheathampstead, to introduce us (as some new-found rarity) to her mother and sister Gladmans, who did indeed know something more of us, at a time when she almost knew nothing.—With what corresponding kindness we were received by them also—how Bridget's memory, exalted by the occasion, warmed into a thousand half-obliterated recollections of things and persons, to my utter astonishment, and her own—and to the astonishment of B. F., who sat by, almost the only thing that was not a cousin there,—old effaced images of more than half-forgotten names and circumstances still crowding back upon her, as words written in lemon come out upon exposure to a friendly warmth,—when I forget all this, then may my country cousins forget me; and Bridget no more remember, that in the days of weakling infancy I was her tender charge—as I have been her care in foolish manhood since—in those pretty pastoral walks, long ago, about Mackery End, in Hertfordshire.

DREAM-CHILDREN

A REVERIE
1822

Children love to listen to stories about their elders when *they* were children; to stretch their imagination to the conception of a traditionary great-uncle, or grandame whom they never saw. It was in this spirit that my little ones crept about me the other evening to hear about their great-grandmother Field who lived in a great house in Norfolk[1] (a hundred times bigger than that in which they and papa lived) which had been the scene—so at least it was generally believed in that part of the country—of the tragic incidents which they had lately become familiar with from the ballad of *The Children in the Wood*. Certain it is that the whole story of the children and their cruel uncle was to be seen fairly carved out in wood upon the chimney-piece of the great hall, the whole story down to the Robin Redbreasts, till a foolish rich person pulled it down to set up a marble one of modern invention in its stead, with no story upon it. Here Alice put out one of her dear mother's looks, too tender to be called upbraiding. Then I went on to say how religious and how good their great-grandmother Field was, how beloved and respected by everybody, though she was not indeed the mistress of this great house, but had only the charge of it (and yet in some respects she might be said to be the mistress of it too) committed to her by the owner, who preferred living in a newer and more fashionable mansion which he had purchased somewhere in the adjoining county; but still she lived in it in a manner as if it had been her own, and kept up the dignity of the great house in a sort while she lived, which afterwards came to decay, and was nearly pulled down, and all its old ornaments stripped and carried away to the owner's other house, where they were set up, and looked as awkward as if some one were to carry away the old tombs they had seen lately at the Abbey, and stick them up in Lady C.'s tawdry gilt drawing-room. Here John smiled, as much as to say, "that would be foolish indeed." And then I told how, when she came to die, her funeral was attended by a concourse of all the poor, and some of the gentry too, of the neighborhood for many miles round, to show their respect for her memory, because she had been such a good and religious woman; so good indeed that she knew all the Psaltery,[2] by heart, ay, and a great part of the Testament besides. Here little Alice spread her hands.[3] Then I told what a tall, upright, graceful person their great-grandmother Field once was; and how in her youth she was esteemed the best dancer—here Alice's little right foot played an involuntary movement, till, upon my looking

---

[1] Mary and Elizabeth. See *Luke,* 1:39-40.
[2] Barron Field, an English barrister.
[3] See *Luke,* 15:23.

[1] Lamb's grandmother lived in Hertfordshire. Norfolk was the scene of the legend of the children in the wood.
[2] The version of the psalms in the *Book of Common Prayer.*
[3] A sign of astonishment.

grave, it desisted—the best dancer, I was saying, in the county, till a cruel disease, called a cancer, came, and bowed her down with pain; but it could never bend her good spirits, or make them stoop, but they were still upright, because she was so good and religious. Then I told how she was used to sleep by herself in a lone chamber of the great lone house; and how she believed that an apparition of two infants[1] was to be seen at midnight gliding up and down the great staircase near where she slept, but she said "those innocents would do her no harm"; and how frightened I used to be, though in those days I had my maid to sleep with me, because I was never half so good or religious as she—and yet I never saw the infants. Here John expanded all his eye-brows and tried to look courageous. Then I told how good she was to all her grand-children, having us to the great-house in the holydays, where I in particular used to spend many hours by myself, in gazing upon the old busts of the Twelve Cæsars, that had been Emperors of Rome, till the old marble heads would seem to live again, or I to be turned into marble with them; how I never could be tired with roaming about that huge mansion, with its vast empty rooms, with their worn-out hangings, fluttering tapestry, and carved oaken panels, with the gilding almost rubbed out—sometimes in the spacious old-fashioned gardens, which I had almost to myself, unless when now and then a solitary gardening man would cross me—and how the nectarines and peaches hung upon the walls, without my ever offering to pluck them, because they were forbidden fruit, unless now and then,—and because I had more pleasure in strolling about among the old melancholy-looking yew trees, or the firs, and picking up the red berries, and the fir apples, which were good for nothing but to look at—or in lying about upon the fresh grass, with all the fine garden smells around me—or basking in the orangery, till I could almost fancy myself ripening too along with the oranges and the limes in that grateful warmth—or in watching the dace that darted to and fro in the fish-pond, at the bottom of the garden, with here and there a great sulky pike hanging midway down the water in silent state, as if it mocked at their impertinent friskings,[2]—I had more pleasure in these busy-idle diversions than in all the sweet flavors of peaches, nectarines, oranges, and such like common baits of children.

Here John slyly deposited back upon the plate a bunch of grapes, which, not unobserved by Alice, he had meditated dividing with her, and both seemed willing to relinquish them for the present as irrelevant. Then in somewhat a more heightened tone, I told how, though their great-grandmother Field loved all her grand-children, yet in an especial manner she might be said to love their uncle, John L——,[1] because he was so handsome and spirited a youth, and a king to the rest of us; and, instead of moping about in solitary corners, like some of us, he would mount the most mettlesome horse he could get, when but an imp no bigger than themselves, and make it carry him half over the county in a morning, and join the hunters when there were any out—and yet he loved the old great house and gardens too, but had too much spirit to be always pent up within their boundaries—and how their uncle grew up to man's estate as brave as he was handsome, to the admiration of every body, but of their great-grandmother Field especially; and how he used to carry me upon his back when I was a lame-footed boy—for he was a good bit older than me—many a mile when I could not walk for pain;—and how in after life he became lame-footed too, and I did not always (I fear) make allowances enough for him when he was impatient, and in pain, nor remember sufficiently how considerate he had been to me when I was lame-footed; and how when he died, though he had not been dead an hour, it seemed as if he had died a great while ago, such a distance there is betwixt life and death; and how I bore his death as I thought pretty well at first, but afterwards it haunted and haunted me; and though I did not cry or take it to heart as some do, and as I think he would have done if I had died, yet I missed him all day long, and knew not till then how much I had loved him. I missed his kindness, and I missed his crossness, and wished him to be alive again, to be quarrelling with him (for we quarrelled sometimes) rather than not have him again, and was as uneasy without him, as he their poor uncle must have been when the doctor took off his limb.[2] Here the children fell a-crying, and asked if their little mourning which they had on was not for uncle John, and they looked up, and prayed me not to go on about their uncle, but to tell them some stories about their pretty dead mother. Then I told how for seven

---

[1] An old legend of the family.
[2] The pike feeds upon dace.

[1] John Lamb.
[2] A detail of Lamb's imagination.

long years, in hope sometimes, sometimes in despair, yet persisting ever, I courted the fair Alice W—n;[1] and, as much as children could understand, I explained to them what coyness, and difficulty, and denial meant in maidens—when suddenly, turning to Alice, the soul of the first Alice looked out at her eyes with such a reality of re-presentment, that I became in doubt which of them stood there before me, or whose that bright hair was; and while I stood gazing, both the children gradually grew fainter to my view, receding, and still receding till nothing at last but two mournful features were seen in the uttermost distance, which, without speech, strangely impressed upon me the effects of speech: "We are not of Alice, nor of thee, nor are we children at all. The children of Alice called Bartrum[2] father. We are nothing; less than nothing, and dreams. We are only what might have been, and must wait upon the tedious shores of Lethe[3] millions of ages before we have existence, and a name"——and immediately awaking, I found myself quietly seated in my bachelor arm-chair, where I had fallen asleep, with the faithful Bridget unchanged by my side—but John L. (or James Elia) was gone forever.

A DISSERTATION UPON ROAST PIG
1822

Mankind, says a Chinese manuscript, which my friend M.[4] was obliging enough to read and explain to me, for the first seventy thousand ages ate their meat raw, clawing or biting it from the living animal, just as they do in Abyssinia to this day. This period is not obscurely hinted at by their great Confucius in the second chapter of his *Mundane Mutations,* where he designates a kind of golden age by the term Cho-fang, literally the Cooks' Holiday. The manuscript goes on to say, that the art of roasting, or rather broiling (which I take to be the elder brother) was accidentally discovered in the manner following. The swineherd, Ho-ti, having gone out into the woods one morning, as his manner was, to collect mast[5] for his hogs, left his cottage in the care of his eldest son Bo-bo, a great lubberly boy, who being fond of playing

[1] Winterton, a feigned name. She was probably Ann Simmons. See Lamb's *Was It Some Sweet Device of Faëry* (p. 941), and *The Old Familiar Faces,* 11-13 (p. 942).
[2] Ann Simmons married a Mr. Bartrum, a London pawnbroker.
[3] See the *Æneid,* 6, 748-51.
[4] Thomas Manning.
[5] food consisting of acorns, beechnuts, chestnuts, etc.

with fire, as younkers of his age commonly are, let some sparks escape into a bundle of straw, which kindling quickly, spread the conflagration over every part of their poor mansion till it was reduced to ashes. Together with the cottage (a sorry antediluvian make-shift of a building, you may think it), what was of much more importance, a fine litter of new-farrowed pigs, no less than nine in number, perished. China pigs have been esteemed a luxury all over the East from the remotest periods that we read of. Bo-bo was in the utmost consternation, as you may think, not so much for the sake of the tenement, which his father and he could easily build up again with a few dry branches, and the labor of an hour or two, at any time, as for the loss of the pigs. While he was thinking what he should say to his father, and wringing his hands over the smoking remnants of one of those untimely sufferers, an odor assailed his nostrils, unlike any scent which he had before experienced. What could it proceed from? —not from the burnt cottage—he had smelt that smell before—indeed this was by no means the first accident of the kind which had occurred through the negligence of this unlucky young fire-brand. Much less did it resemble that of any known herb, weed, or flower. A premonitory moistening at the same time overflowed his nether lip. He knew not what to think. He next stooped down to feel the pig, if there were any signs of life in it. He burnt his fingers, and to cool them he applied them in his booby fashion to his mouth. Some of the crumbs of the scorched skin had come away with his fingers, and for the first time in his life (in the world's life indeed, for before him no man had known it) he tasted—*crackling!*[1] Again he felt and fumbled at the pig. It did not burn him so much now, still he licked his fingers from a sort of habit. The truth at length broke into his slow understanding, that it was the pig that smelt so, and the pig that tasted so delicious; and, surrendering himself up to the new-born pleasure, he fell to tearing up whole handfuls of the scorched skin with the flesh next it, and was cramming it down his throat in his beastly fashion, when his sire entered amid the smoking rafters, armed with retributory cudgel, and finding how affairs stood, began to rain blows upon the young rogue's shoulders, as thick as hail-stones, which Bo-bo heeded not any more than if they had been flies. The tickling pleasure, which he expe-

[1] The crisp skin of roasted pork.

rienced in his lower regions, had rendered him quite callous to any inconveniences he might feel in those remote quarters. His father might lay on, but he could not beat him from his pig, till he had fairly made an end of it, when, becoming a little more sensible of his situation, something like the following dialogue ensued.

"You graceless whelp, what have you got there devouring? Is it not enough that you have burnt me down three houses with your dog's tricks, and be hanged to you, but you must be eating fire, and I know not what—what have you got there, I say?"

"O father, the pig, the pig, do come and taste how nice the burnt pig eats."

The ears of Ho-ti tingled with terror. He cursed his son, and he cursed himself that ever he should beget a son that should eat burnt pig.

Bo-bo, whose scent was wonderfully sharpened since morning, soon raked out another pig, and fairly rending it asunder, thrust the lesser half by main force into the fists of Ho-ti, still shouting out "Eat, eat, eat the burning pig, father, only taste—O Lord,"—with such-like barbarous ejaculations, cramming all the while as if he would choke.

Ho-ti trembled in every joint while he grasped the abominable thing, wavering whether he should not put his son to death for an unnatural young monster, when the crackling scorching his fingers, as it had done his son's, and applying the same remedy to them, he in his turn tasted some of its flavor, which, make what sour mouths he would for a pretence, proved not altogether displeasing to him. In conclusion (for the manuscript here is a little tedious) both father and son fairly sat down to the mess, and never left off till they had despatched all that remained of the litter.

Bo-bo was strictly enjoined not to let the secret escape, for the neighbors would certainly have stoned them for a couple of abominable wretches, who could think of improving upon the good meat which God had sent them. Nevertheless, strange stories got about. It was observed that Ho-ti's cottage was burnt down now more frequently than ever. Nothing but fires from this time forward. Some would break out in broad day, others in the night-time. As often as the sow farrowed, so sure was the house of Ho-ti to be in a blaze; and Ho-ti himself, which was the more remarkable, instead of chastising his son, seemed to grow more indulgent to him than ever. At length

they were watched, the terrible mystery discovered, and father and son summoned to take their trial at Pekin, then an inconsiderable assize town.[1] Evidence was given, the obnoxious food itself produced in court, and verdict about to be pronounced, when the foreman of the jury begged that some of the burnt pig, of which the culprits stood accused, might be handed into the box. He handled it, and they all handled it, and burning their fingers, as Bo-bo and his father had done before them, and nature prompting to each of them the same remedy, against the face of all the facts, and the clearest charge which judge had ever given—to the surprise of the whole court, townsfolk, strangers, reporters, and all present—without leaving the box, or any manner of consultation whatever, they brought in a simultaneous verdict of Not Guilty.

The judge, who was a shrewd fellow, winked at the manifest iniquity of the decision: and, when the court was dismissed, went privily, and bought up all the pigs that could be had for love or money. In a few days his Lordship's town house was observed to be on fire. The thing took wing, and now there was nothing to be seen but fires in every direction. Fuel and pigs grew enormously dear all over the district. The insurance offices one and all shut up shop. People built slighter and slighter every day, until it was feared that the very science of architecture would in no long time be lost to the world. Thus this custom of firing houses continued, till in process of time, says my manuscript, a sage arose, like our Locke, who made a discovery, that the flesh of swine, or indeed of any other animal, might be cooked (*burnt*, as they called it) without the necessity of consuming a whole house to dress it. Then first began the rude form of a gridiron. Roasting by the string, or spit, came in a century or two later; I forget in whose dynasty. By such slow degrees, concludes the manuscript, do the most useful and seemingly the most obvious arts, make their way among mankind.

Without placing too implicit faith in the account above given, it must be agreed, that if a worthy pretext for so dangerous an experiment as setting houses on fire (especially in these days) could be assigned in favor of any culinary object, that pretext and excuse might be found in ROAST PIG.

Of all the delicacies in the whole *mundus*

---

[1] A county town in which judges held court.

edibilis,[1] I will maintain it to be the most delicate—*princeps obsoniorum.*[2]

I speak not of your grown porkers—things between pig and pork—those hobbydehoys—but a young and tender suckling—under a moon old—guiltless as yet of the sty—with no original speck of the *amor immunditiæ,*[3] the hereditary failing of the first parent, yet manifest—his voice as yet not broken, but something between a childish treble, and a grumble—the mild forerunner, or *præludium,*[4] of a grunt.

He must be roasted. I am not ignorant that our ancestors ate them seethed, or boiled—but what a sacrifice of the exterior tegument!

There is no flavor comparable, I will contend, to that of the crisp, tawny, well-watched, not over-roasted, *crackling,* as it is well called—the very teeth are invited to their share of the pleasure at this banquet in overcoming the coy, brittle resistance—with the adhesive oleaginous—O call it not fat—but an indefinable sweetness growing up to it—the tender blossoming of fat—fat cropped in the bud—taken in the shoot—in the first innocence—the cream and quintessence of the child-pig's yet pure food——the lean, no lean, but a kind of animal manna—or, rather, fat and lean (if it must be so) blended and running into each other, that both together make but one ambrosial result, or common substance.

Behold him, while he is doing—it seemeth rather a refreshing warmth, than a scorching heat, that he is so passive to. How equably he twirleth round the string!—Now he is just done. To see the extreme sensibility of that tender age, he hath wept out his pretty eyes—radiant jellies—shooting stars[5]—

See him in the dish, his second cradle, how meek he lieth!—wouldst thou have had this innocent grow up to the grossness and indocility which too often accompany maturer swinehood? Ten to one he would have proved a glutton, a sloven, an obstinate, disagreeable animal—wallowing in all manner of filthy conversation[6]—from these sins he is happily snatched away—

Ere sin could blight, or sorrow fade,
Death came with timely care——[7]

his memory is odoriferous—no clown curseth, while his stomach half rejecteth, the rank bacon—no coalheaver bolteth him in reeking sausages—he hath a fair sepulchre in the grateful stomach of the judicious epicure—and for such a tomb might be content to die.

He is the best of sapors.[1] Pine-apple is great. She is indeed almost too transcendent—a delight, if not sinful, yet so like to sinning, that really a tender-conscienced person would do well to pause—too ravishing for mortal taste, she woundeth and excoriateth the lips that approach her—like lovers' kisses, she biteth—she is a pleasure bordering on pain from the fierceness and insanity of her relish—but she stoppeth at the palate—she meddleth not with the appetite—and the coarsest hunger might barter her consistently for a mutton chop.

Pig—let me speak his praise—is no less provocative of the appetite, than he is satisfactory to the criticalness of the censorious palate. The strong man may batten on him, and the weakling refuseth not his mild juices.

Unlike to mankind's mixed characters, a bundle of virtues and vices, inexplicably intertwisted, and not to be unravelled without hazard, he is—good throughout. No part of him is better or worse than another. He helpeth, as far as his little means extend, all around. He is the least envious of banquets. He is all neighbors' fare.

I am one of those who freely and ungrudgingly impart a share of the good things of this life which fall to their lot (few as mine are in this kind), to a friend. I protest I take as great an interest in my friend's pleasures, his relishes, and proper[2] satisfactions, as in mine own. "Presents," I often say, "endear Absents."[3] Hares, pheasants, partridges, snipes, barn-door chicken (those "tame villatic[4] fowl"), capons, plovers, brawn,[5] barrels of oysters, I dispense as freely as I receive them. I love to taste them, as it were, upon the tongue of my friend. But a stop must be put somewhere. One would not, like Lear, "give everything."[6] I make my stand upon pig. Methinks it is an ingratitude to the Giver of all good flavors, to extra-domiciliate, or send out of the house, slightingly, (under pretext of friendship, or I know not what)

---

[1] edible world   [2] chief of delicacies
[3] love of dirt (suggested as the original sin of pigdom)
[4] prelude
[5] A reference to the old superstition that shooting stars leave jellies where they fall.
[6] conduct (See *2 Peter,* 2 :7.)
[7] Coleridge, *Epitaph on a Young Infant,* 1-2.

[1] savors
[2] peculiar to himself
[3] those absent
[4] farm yard (Milton, *Samson Agonistes,* 1695)
[5] pickled boar's flesh
[6] *King Lear,* II, 4, 253.

a blessing so particularly adapted, predestined, I may say, to my individual taste.—It argues an insensibility.

I remember a touch of conscience in this kind at school. My good old aunt,[1] who never parted from me at the end of a holiday without stuffing a sweet-meat, or some nice thing, into my pocket, had dismissed me one evening with a smoking plum-cake, fresh from the oven. In my way to school (it was over London bridge) a gray-headed old beggar saluted me (I have no doubt at this time of day that he was a counterfeit). I had no pence to console him with, and in the vanity of self-denial, and the very coxcombry of charity, school-boy-like, I made him a present of—the whole cake! I walked on a little, buoyed up, as one is on such occasions, with a sweet soothing of self-satisfaction; but before I had got to the end of the bridge, my better feelings returned, and I burst into tears, thinking how ungrateful I had been to my good aunt, to go and give her good gift away to a stranger, that I had never seen before, and who might be a bad man for aught I knew; and then I thought of the pleasure my aunt would be taking in thinking that I—I myself, and not another—would eat her nice cake—and what should I say to her the next time I saw her—how naughty I was to part with her pretty present—and the odor of that spicy cake came back upon my recollection, and the pleasure and the curiosity I had taken in seeing her make it, and her joy when she sent it to the oven, and how disappointed she would feel that I had never had a bit of it in my mouth at last—and I blamed my impertinent spirit of alms-giving, and out-of-place hypocrisy of goodness, and above all I wished never to see the face again of that insidious, good-for-nothing, old gray impostor.

Our ancestors were nice in their methods of sacrificing these tender victims. We read of pigs whipt to death with something of a shock, as we hear of any other obsolete custom. The age of discipline[2] is gone by, or it would be curious to inquire (in a philosophical light merely) what effect this process might have towards intenerating and duleifying[3] a substance, naturally so mild and dulcet as the flesh of young pigs. It looks like refining a violet. Yet we should be cautious, while we condemn the inhumanity, how we censure the wisdom of the practice. It might impart a gusto—

I remember an hypothesis, argued upon by the young students, when I was at St. Omer's,[1] and maintained with much learning and pleasantry on both sides, "Whether, supposing that the flavor of a pig who obtained his death by whipping (*per flagellationem extremam*[2]) superadded a pleasure upon the palate of a man more intense than any possible suffering we can conceive in the animal, is man justified in using that method of putting the animal to death?" I forget the decision.

His sauce should be considered. Decidedly, a few bread crumbs, done up with his liver and brains, and a dash of mild sage. But, banish, dear Mrs. Cook, I beseech you, the whole onion tribe. Barbecue[3] your whole hogs to your palate, steep them in shalots,[4] stuff them out with plantations of the rank and guilty garlic; you cannot poison them, or make them stronger than they are—but consider, he is a weakling—a flower.

OLD CHINA
1823

I have an almost feminine partiality for old china. When I go to see any great house, I inquire for the china-closet, and next for the picture gallery. I cannot defend the order of preference, but by saying that we have all some taste or other, of too ancient a date to admit of our remembering distinctly that it was an acquired one. I can call to mind the first play, and the first exhibition, that I was taken to; but I am not conscious of a time when china jars and saucers were introduced into my imagination.

I had no repugnance then—why should I now have?—to those little, lawless, azure-tinctured grotesques, that under the notion of men and women, float about, uncircumscribed by any element, in that world before perspective—a china tea-cup.

I like to see my old friends—whom distance cannot diminish—figuring up in the air (so they appear to our optics), yet on *terra firma* still—for so we must in courtesy interpret that speck of deeper blue, which the decorous artist, to prevent absurdity, has made to spring up beneath their sandals.

I love the men with women's faces, and

---

[1] Lamb's Aunt Hetty, mentioned in *The Decay of Beggars*.
[2] The didactic practice of training the mind by engaging in hair-splitting distinctions.
[3] making tender and sweet

[1] A Jesuit college in France. Lamb was never a student there.
[2] by whipping to death
[3] roast whole after stuffing
[4] strong onions

the women, if possible, with still more womanish expressions.

Here is a young and courtly Mandarin, handing tea to a lady from a salver—two miles off. See how distance seems to set off respect! And here the same lady, or another—for likeness is identity on tea-cups—is stepping into a little fairy boat, moored on the hither side of this calm garden river, with a dainty mincing foot, which in a right angle of incidence (as angles go in our world) must infallibly land her in the midst of a flowery mead—a furlong off on the other side of the same strange stream!

Farther on—if far or near can be predicated of their world—see horses, trees, pagodas, dancing the hays.[1]

Here—a cow and rabbit couchant, and co-extensive—so objects show, seen through the lucid atmosphere of fine Cathay.

I was pointing out to my cousin last evening, over our Hyson[2] (which we are old fashioned enough to drink unmixed still of an afternoon), some of these *speciosa miracula*[3] upon a set of extraordinary old blue china (a recent purchase) which we were now for the first time using; and could not help remarking, how favorable circumstances had been to us of late years, that we could afford to please the eye sometimes with trifles of this sort—when a passing sentiment seemed to over-shade the brows of my companion.[4] I am quick at detecting these summer clouds in Bridget.

"I wish the good old times would come again," she said, "when we were not quite so rich. I do not mean that I want to be poor; but there was a middle state;"—so she was pleased to ramble on,—"in which I am sure we were a great deal happier. A purchase is but a purchase, now that you have money enough and to spare. Formerly it used to be a triumph. When we coveted a cheap luxury (and, O! how much ado I had to get you to consent in those times!) we were used to have a debate two or three days before, and to weigh the *for* and *against,* and think what we might spare it out of, and what saving we could hit upon, that should be an equivalent. A thing was worth buying then, when we felt the money that we paid for it.

"Do you remember the brown suit, which you made to hang upon you, till all your

friends cried shame upon you, it grew so thread-bare—and all because of that folio Beaumont and Fletcher, which you dragged home late at night from Barker's in Covent-garden? Do you remember how we eyed it for weeks before we could make up our minds to the purchase, and had not come to a determination till it was near ten o'clock of the Saturday night, when you set off from Islington, fearing you should be too late—and when the old bookseller with some grumbling opened his shop, and by the twinkling taper (for he was setting bedwards) lighted out the relic from his dusty treasures—and when you lugged it home, wishing it were twice as cumbersome—and when you presented it to me—and when we were exploring the perfectness of it (*collating* you called it)—and while I was repairing some of the loose leaves with paste, which your impatience would not suffer to be left till day-break—was there no pleasure in being a poor man? or can those neat black clothes which you wear now, and are so careful to keep brushed, since we have become rich and finical, give you half the honest vanity with which you flaunted it about in that over-worn suit—your old corbeau[1]—for four or five weeks longer than you should have done, to pacify your conscience for the mighty sum of fifteen—or sixteen shillings was it?—a great affair we thought it then—which you had lavished on the old folio. Now you can afford to buy any book that pleases you, but I do not see that you ever bring me home any nice old purchases now.

"When you came home with twenty apologies for laying out a less number of shillings upon that print after Lionardo, which we christened the *Lady Blanch;*[2] when you looked at the purchase, and thought of the money—and thought of the money, and looked again at the picture—was there no pleasure in being a poor man? Now, you have nothing to do but to walk into Colnaghi's, and buy a wilderness of Lionardos. Yet do you?

"Then, do you remember our pleasant walks to Enfield, and Potter's Bar, and Waltham, when we had a holyday—holydays, and all other fun, are gone, now we are rich—and the little hand-basket in which I used to deposit our day's fare of savory cold lamb and salad—and how you would pry about at noon-tide for some decent

---

[1] A country dance.
[2] green tea
[3] glorious wonders (Horace uses this phrase in *Ars Poetica*, 144, to describe the stories of the *Iliad*.)
[4] Lamb's sister Mary, whom he calls Bridget Elia.

[1] black coat
[2] See Mary Lamb's poem entitled *Lines Suggested by a Picture of Two Females by Lionardo da Vinci.*

house, where we might go in, and produce our store—only paying for the ale that you must call for—and speculate upon the looks of the landlady, and whether she was likely to allow us a table-cloth—and wish for such another honest hostess, as Izaak Walton has described[1] many a one on the pleasant banks of the Lea, when he went a-fishing— and sometimes they would prove obliging enough, and sometimes they would look grudgingly upon us—but we had cheerful looks still for one another, and would eat our plain food savorily, scarcely grudging Piscator his Trout Hall? Now, when we go out a day's pleasuring, which is seldom moreover, we *ride* part of the way—and go into a fine inn, and order the best of dinners, never debating the expense—which, after all, never has half the relish of those chance country snaps, when we were at the mercy of uncertain usage, and a precarious welcome.

"You are too proud to see a play anywhere now but in the pit.[2] Do you remember where it was we used to sit, when we saw *The Battle of Hexham,* and *The Surrender of Calais,* and Bannister and Mrs. Bland in *The Children in the Wood*—when we squeezed out our shillings a-piece to sit three or four times in a season in the one-shilling gallery—where you felt all the time that you ought not to have brought me—and more strongly I felt obligation to you for having brought me—and the pleasure was the better for a little shame—and when the curtain drew up, what cared we for our place in the house, or what mattered it where we were sitting, when our thoughts were with Rosalind in Arden, or with Viola at the Court of Illyria? You used to say that the gallery was the best place of all for enjoying a play socially—that the relish of such exhibitions must be in proportion to the infrequency of going—that the company we met there, not being in general readers of plays, were obliged to attend the more, and did attend, to what was going on, on the stage—because a word lost would have been a chasm, which it was impossible for them to fill up. With such reflections we consoled our pride then— and I appeal to you, whether, as a woman, I met generally with less attention and accommodation than I have done since in more expensive situations in the house? The getting in indeed, and the crowding up those inconvenient staircases, was bad enough,— but there was still a law of civility to women

recognized to quite as great an extent as we ever found in the other passages—and how a little difficulty overcome heightened the snug seat, and the play, afterwards! Now we can only pay our money, and walk in. You cannot see, you say, in the galleries now. I am sure we saw, and heard too, well enough then—but sight, and all, I think, is gone with our poverty.

"There was pleasure in eating strawberries, before they became quite common— in the first dish of peas, while they were yet dear—to have them for a nice supper, a treat. What treat can we have now? If we were to treat ourselves now—that is, to have dainties a little above our means, it would be selfish and wicked. It is the very little more that we allow ourselves beyond what the actual poor can get at, that makes what I call a treat—when two people living together, as we have done, now and then indulge themselves in a cheap luxury, which both like; while each apologizes, and is willing to take both halves of the blame to his single share. I see no harm in people making much of themselves in that sense of the word. It may give them a hint how to make much of others. But now—what I mean by the word—we never do make much of ourselves. None but the poor can do it. I do not mean the veriest poor of all, but persons as we were, just above poverty.

"I know what you were going to say, that it is mighty pleasant at the end of the year to make all meet—and much ado we used to have every Thirty-first Night of December to account for our exceedings—many a long face did you make over your puzzled accounts, and in contriving to make it out how we had spent so much—or that we had not spent so much—or that it was impossible we should spend so much next year— and still we found our slender capital decreasing—but then, betwixt ways, and projects, and compromises of one sort or another, and talk of curtailing this charge, and doing without that for the future—and the hope that youth brings, and laughing spirits (in which you were never poor till now), we pocketed up our loss, and in conclusion, with 'lusty brimmers'[1] (as you used to quote it out of *hearty cheerful Mr. Cotton,* as you called him),[2] we used to welcome in the 'coming guest.'[3] Now we have no reckoning at all at the end of the old

[1] In *The Complete Angler.*
[2] The best portion of the theatre.

[1] Charles Cotton, *The New Year,* 50.
[2] See Lamb's *New Year's Eve,* in which Cotton's poem is quoted.
[3] Pope, *The Odyssey,* 15, 84.

year—no flattering promises about the new year doing better for us."

Bridget is so sparing of her speech, on most occasions, that when she gets into a rhetorical vein, I am careful how I interrupt it. I could not help, however, smiling at the phantom of wealth which her dear imagination had conjured up out of a clear income of poor —— hundred pounds a year. "It is true we were happier when we were poorer, but we were also younger, my cousin. I am afraid we must put up with the excess, for if we were to shake the superflux into the sea, we should not much mend ourselves. That we had much to struggle with, as we grew up together, we have reason to be most thankful. It strengthened, and knit our compact closer. We could never have been what we have been to each other, if we had always had the sufficiency which you now complain of. The resisting power—those natural dilations of the youthful spirit, which circumstances cannot straiten—with us are long since passed away. Competence to age is supplementary youth; a sorry supplement indeed, but I fear the best that is to be had. We must ride, where we formerly walked: live better, and lie softer—and shall be wise to do so—than we had means to do in those good old days you speak of. Yet could those days return—could you and I once more walk our thirty miles a day—could Bannister and Mrs. Bland again be young, and you and I be young to see them—could the good old one-shilling gallery days return—they are dreams, my cousin, now—but could you and I at this moment, instead of this quiet argument, by our well-carpeted fire-side, sitting on this luxurious sofa—be once more struggling up those inconvenient stair-cases, pushed about, and squeezed, and elbowed by the poorest rabble of poor gallery scramblers—could I once more hear those anxious shrieks of yours—and the delicious *Thank God, we are safe*, which always followed when the topmost stair, conquered, let in the first light of the whole cheerful theatre down beneath us—I know not the fathom line that ever touched a descent so deep as I would be willing to bury more wealth in than Crœsus had, or the great Jew R——[1] is supposed to have, to purchase it. And now do just look at that merry little Chinese waiter holding an umbrella, big enough for a bed-tester,[2] over the head of that pretty insipid

[1] Nathan Meyer Rothschild (1777-1836), the founder of the English branch of the great European banking firm of the Rothschilds.
[2] bed canopy

half-Madonna-ish chit of a lady in that very blue summer-house."

POOR RELATIONS
1823

A poor relation is the most irrelevant thing in nature,—a piece of impertinent correspondency,—an odious approximation,—a haunting conscience,—a preposterous shadow, lengthening in the noontide of your prosperity,—an unwelcome remembrancer,—a perpetually recurring mortification,—a drain on your purse,—a more intolerable dun upon your pride,—a drawback upon success,—a rebuke to you rising,—a stain in your blood,—a blot on your scutcheon,—a rent in your garment,—a death's head at your banquet,[1]—Agathocles' pot,[2]—a Mordecai in your gate,[3]—a Lazarus at your door,[4]—a lion in your path,[5]—a frog in your chamber,[6]—a fly in your ointment,[7]—a mote in your eye,[8]—a triumph to your enemy,—an apology to your friends,—the one thing not needful,[9]—the hail in harvest,[10]—the ounce of sour in a pound of sweet.[11]

He is known by his knock. Your heart telleth you "That is Mr. ——." A rap, between familiarity and respect, that demands, and at the same time, seems to despair of entertainment. He entereth smiling, and—embarrassed. He holdeth out his hand to you to shake, and—draweth it back again. He casually looketh in about dinner time—when the table is full. He offereth to go away, seeing you have company—but is induced to stay. He filleth a chair, and your visitor's two children are accommodated at a side table. He never cometh upon open days, when your wife says with some complacency, "My dear, perhaps Mr. —— will drop in today." He remembereth birthdays—and professeth he is fortunate to have stumbled upon one. He declareth against fish, the turbot being small—yet suffereth himself to be importuned into a slice against his first resolution. He sticketh by the port —yet will be prevailed upon to empty the remainder glass of claret, if a stranger press

[1] A reference to the custom of the Egyptians of having a coffin containing a representation of a dead body carried through the banquet hall at the close of the feast to remind the guests of their necessary end, and to suggest that they should drink and be merry. See Herodotus's *Historiæ*, 2, 78.
[2] Agathocles, tyrant of Sicily (317-289 B. C.), hated the sight of a pot because it reminded him that he was the son of a potter.
[3] See *Esther*, 3:1-2; 5:11-13. [4] See *Luke*, 16:20.
[5] See *I Kings*, 13:24. [6] See *Exodus*, 8:3-4.
[7] See *Ecclesiastes*, 10:1. [8] See *Matthew*, 7:3-5.
[9] See *Luke*, 10:42. [10] See *Proverbs*, 26:1.
[11] See Spenser's *The Faerie Queene*, I, 3, 30, 4. This phrase was the motto of Hunt's *The Indicator*.

it upon him. He is a puzzle to the servants, who are fearful of being too obsequious, or not civil enough, to him. The guests think "they have seen him before." Every one speculateth upon his condition;[1] and the most part take him to be—a tide-waiter.[2] He calleth you by your Christian name, to imply that his other is the same with your own. He is too familiar by half, yet you wish he had less diffidence. With half the familiarity he might pass for a casual dependent; with more boldness he would be in no danger of being taken for what he is. He is too humble for a friend, yet taketh on him more state than befits a client.[3] He is a worse guest than a country tenant, inasmuch as he bringeth up no rent—yet 'tis odds, from his garb and demeanor, that your guests take him for one. He is asked to make one at the whist table; refuseth on the score of poverty, and—resents being left out. When the company breaks up, he proffereth to go for a coach—and lets the servant go. He recollects your grandfather; and will thrust in some mean, and quite unimportant anecdote of—the family. He knew it when it was not quite so flourishing as "he is blest in seeing it now." He reviveth past situations, to institute what he calleth—favorable comparisons. With a reflecting—sort of congratulation, he will inquire the price of your furniture; and insults you with a special commendation of your window-curtains. He is of opinion that the urn is the more elegant shape, but, after all, there was something more comfortable about the old tea-kettle—which you must remember. He dare say you must find a great convenience in having a carriage of your own, and appealeth to your lady if it is not so. Inquireth if you have had your arms done on vellum yet; and did not know till lately that such-and-such had been the crest of the family. His memory is unseasonable; his compliments perverse; his talk a trouble; his stay pertinacious; and when he goeth away, you dismiss his chair into a corner, as precipitately as possible, and feel fairly rid of two nuisances.

There is a worse evil under the sun, and that is—a female Poor Relation. You may do something with the other; you may pass him off tolerably well; but your indigent she-relative is hopeless. "He is an old humorist,"[4] you may say, "and affects to go threadbare. His circumstances are better than folks would take them to be. You are fond of having a Character at your table, and truly he is one." But in the indications of female poverty there can be no disguise. No woman dresses below herself from caprice. The truth must out without shuffling. "She is plainly related to the L—s; or what does she at their house?" She is, in all probability, your wife's cousin. Nine times out of ten, at least, this is the case. Her garb is something between a gentlewoman and a beggar, yet the former evidently predominates. She is most provokingly humble and ostentatiously sensible to her inferiority. He may require to be repressed sometimes—*aliquando sufflaminandus erat*[1]—but there is no raising her. You send her soup at dinner, and she begs to be helped—after the gentlemen. Mr. —— requests the honor of taking wine with her; she hesitates between port and Madeira, and chooses the former—because he does. She calls the servant *Sir;* and insists on not troubling him to hold her plate. The housekeeper patronizes her. The children's governess takes upon her to correct her, when she has mistaken the piano for a harpsichord.

Richard Amlet, Esq., in the play,[2] is a notable instance of the disadvantages, to which this chimerical notion of *affinity constituting a claim to acquaintance,* may subject the spirit of a gentleman. A little foolish blood is all that is betwixt him and a lady of great estate. His stars are perpetually crossed by the malignant maternity of an old woman, who persists in calling him "her son Dick." But she has wherewithal in the end to recompense his indignities, and float him again upon the brilliant surface, under which it had been her seeming business and pleasure all along to sink him. All men, besides, are not of Dick's temperament. I knew an Amlet in real life, who, wanting Dick's buoyancy, sank indeed. Poor W——[3] was of my own standing at Christ's, a fine classic, and a youth of promise. If he had a blemish, it was too much pride; but its quality was inoffensive; it was not of that sort which hardens the heart, and serves to keep inferiors at a distance; it only sought to ward off derogation from itself. It was the principle of self-respect carried as far as it could go, without infringing upon that re-

---

[1] social rank
[2] A minor customs official who waits for the arrival of ships and enforces the revenue laws.
[3] dependent   [4] eccentric person

[1] sometimes he had to be checked
[2] *The Confederacy,* by John Vanbrugh (1664-1726).
[3] A young man named Favell. See Lamb's *Christ's Hospital Five-and-Thirty Years Ago* (p. 963b, 16).

spect, which he would have every one else equally maintain for himself. He would have you to think alike with him on this topic. Many a quarrel have I had with him, when we were rather older boys, and our tallness[1] made us more obnoxious to observation in the blue clothes, because I would not thread the alleys and blind ways of the town with him to elude notice, when we have been out together on a holiday in the streets of this sneering and prying metropolis. W—— went, sore with these notions, to Oxford, where the dignity and sweetness of a scholar's life, meeting with the alloy of a humble introduction, wrought in him a passionate devotion to the place, with a profound aversion from the society. The servitor's gown[2] (worse than his school array) clung to him with Nessian venom.[3] He thought himself ridiculous in a garb, under which Latimer[4] would have walked erect; and in which Hooker,[5] in his young days, possibly flaunted in a vein of no discommendable vanity. In the depth of college shades, or in his lonely chamber, the poor student shrunk from observation. He found shelter among books, which insult not; and studies, that ask no questions of a youth's finances. He was lord of his library, and seldom cared for looking out beyond his domains. The healing influence of studious pursuits was upon him, to soothe and to abstract. He was almost a healthy man; when the waywardness of his fate broke out against him with a second and worse malignity. The father of W—— had hitherto exercised the humble profession of house-painter at N——, near Oxford. A supposed interest with some of the heads of the colleges had now induced him to take up his abode in that city, with the hope of being employed upon some public works which were talked of. From that moment I read in the countenance of the young man, the determination which at length tore him from academical pursuits forever. To a person unacquainted with our universities, the distance between the gownsmen and the townsmen, as they are called—the trading part of the latter especially—is carried to an excess that would appear harsh and incredible. The temperament of W——'s father was

diametrically the reverse of his own. Old W—— was a little, busy, cringing tradesman, who, with his son upon his arm, would stand bowing and scraping, cap in hand, to anything that wore the semblance of a gown—insensible to the winks and opener remonstrances of the young man, to whose chamber-fellow, or equal in standing, perhaps, he was thus obsequiously and gratuitously ducking. Such a state of things could not last. W—— must change the air of Oxford or be suffocated. He chose the former; and let the sturdy moralist, who strains the point of the filial duties as high as they can bear, censure the dereliction; he cannot estimate the struggle. I stood with W——, the last afternoon I ever saw him, under the eaves of his paternal dwelling. It was in the fine lane leading from the High-street to the back of —— College, where W—— kept his rooms. He seemed thoughtful, and more reconciled. I ventured to rally him—finding him in a better mood—upon a representation of the Artist Evangelist,[1] which the old man, whose affairs were beginning to flourish, had caused to be set up in a splendid sort of frame over his really handsome shop, either as a token of prosperity, or badge of gratitude to his saint. W—— looked up at the Luke, and, like Satan, "knew his mounted sign—and fled."[2] A letter on his father's table the next morning, announced that he had accepted a commission in a regiment about to embark for Portugal. He was among the first who perished before the walls of St. Sebastian.

I do not know how, upon a subject which I began with treating half-seriously, I should have fallen upon a recital so eminently painful; but this theme of poor relationship is replete with so much matter for tragic as well as comic associations, that it is difficult to keep the account distinct without blending. The earliest impressions which I received on this matter are certainly not attended with anything painful, or very humiliating, in the recalling. At my father's table (no very splendid one) was to be found, every Saturday, the mysterious figure of an aged gentleman, clothed in neat black, of a sad yet comely appearance. His deportment was of the essence of gravity; his words few or none; and I was not to make a noise in his presence. I had little inclination to have done so—for my cue was

---

[1] Lamb really was short of stature.

[2] The distinguishing dress of an undergraduate who was partly supported by college funds, and who waited on table at the Commons.

[3] Hercules slew Nessus with a poisoned arrow, and lost his own life by wearing a shirt dipped in the poisonous blood of Nessus.

[4] Latimer had been a sizar (same as servitor) at Cambridge.

[5] Hooker had been a servitor at Oxford.

[1] St. Luke, by tradition a painter as well as a physician.

[2] *Paradise Lost*, 4, 1013.

to admire in silence. A particular elbow chair was appropriated to him, which was in no case to be violated. A peculiar sort of sweet pudding, which appeared on no other occasion, distinguished the days of his coming. I used to think him a prodigiously rich man. All I could make out of him was, that he and my father had been school-fellows a world ago at Lincoln, and that he came from the Mint.[1] The Mint I knew to be a place where all the money was coined—and I thought he was the owner of all that money. Awful ideas of the Tower twined themselves about his presence. He seemed above human infirmities and passions. A sort of melancholy grandeur invested him. From some inexplicable doom I fancied him obliged to go about in an eternal suit of mourning; a captive—a stately being, let out of the Tower on Saturdays. Often have I wondered at the temerity of my father, who, in spite of an habitual general respect which we all in common manifested towards him, would venture now and then to stand up against him in some argument, touching their youthful days. The houses of the ancient city of Lincoln are divided (as most of my readers know) between the dwellers on the hill, and in the valley. This marked distinction formed an obvious division between the boys who lived above (however brought together in a common school) and the boys whose paternal residence was on the plain; a sufficient cause of hostility in the code of these young Grotiuses.[2] My father had been a leading Mountaineer; and would still maintain the general superiority, in skill and hardihood, of the *Above Boys* (his own faction) over the *Below Boys* (so were they called), of which party his contemporary had been a chieftain. Many and hot were the skirmishes on this topic—the only one upon which the old gentleman was ever brought out—and bad blood bred; even sometimes almost to the recommencement (so I expected) of actual hostilities. But my father, who scorned to insist upon advantages, generally contrived to turn the conversation upon some adroit by-commendation of the old Minster, in the general preference of which, before all other cathedrals in the island, the dweller on the hill, and the plain-born, could meet on a conciliating level, and lay down their less important differences. Once only I saw the old gentle-

man really ruffled, and I remember with anguish the thought that came over me: "Perhaps he will never come here again." He had been pressed to take another plate of the viand, which I have already mentioned as the indispensable concomitant of his visits. He had refused, with a resistance amounting to rigor—when my aunt, an old Lincolnian, but who had something of this, in common with my cousin Bridget, that she would sometimes press civility out of season—uttered the following memorable application—"Do take another slice, Mr. Billet, for you do not get pudding every day." The old gentleman said nothing at the time—but he took occasion in the course of the evening, when some argument had intervened between them, to utter with an emphasis which chilled the company, and which chills me now as I write it—"Woman, you are superannuated." John Billet did not survive long, after the digesting of this affront; but he survived long enough to assure me that peace was actually restored! and, if I remember aright, another pudding was discreetly substituted in the place of that which had occasioned the offence. He died at the Mint (Anno 1781) where he had long held, what he accounted, a comfortable independence; and with five pounds, fourteen shillings, and a penny, which were found in his escrutoire after his decease, left the world, blessing God that he had enough to bury him, and that he had never been obliged to any man for a sixpence. This was—a Poor Relation.

SANITY OF TRUE GENIUS
1826

So far from the position holding true, that great wit (or genius, in our modern way of speaking) has a necessary alliance with insanity, the greatest wits, on the contrary, will ever be found to be the sanest writers. It is impossible for the mind to conceive of a mad Shakspeare. The greatness of wit, by which the poetic talent is here chiefly to be understood, manifests itself in the admirable balance of all the faculties. Madness is the disproportionate straining or excess of any one of them. "So strong a wit," says Cowley, speaking of a poetical friend,

"——did Nature to him frame,
As all things but his judgment overcame,
His judgment like the heavenly moon did show,
Tempering that mighty sea below."[1]

[1] *On the Death of Mr. William Hervey,* 97-100.

---

[1] The Mint was near the Tower of London, the state prison.
[2] Law students. Hugo Grotius (1583-1645) was the great Dutch authority on international law.

The ground of the mistake is that men, finding in the raptures of the higher poetry a condition of exaltation, to which they have no parallel in their own experience, besides the spurious resemblance of it in dreams and fevers, impute a state of dreaminess and fever to the poet. But the true poet dreams being awake. He is not possessed by his subject, but has dominion over it. In the groves of Eden he walks familiar as in his native paths. He ascends the empyrean heaven, and is not intoxicated. He treads the burning marl[1] without dismay; he wins his flight without self-loss through realms of chaos "and old night."[2] Or if, abandoning himself to that severer chaos of a "human mind untuned,"[3] he is content awhile to be mad with Lear, or to hate mankind (a sort of madness) with Timon, neither is that madness, nor the misanthropy, so unchecked, but that,—never letting the reins of reason wholly go, while most he seems to do so,—he has his better genius still whispering at his ear, with the good servant Kent suggesting saner counsels,[4] or with the honest steward Flavius recommending kindlier resolutions.[5] Where he seems most to recede from humanity, he will be found the truest to it. From beyond the scope of Nature if he summon possible existences, he subjugates them to the law of her consistency. He is beautifully loyal to that sovereign directress, even when he appears most to betray and desert her. His ideal tribes submit to policy; his very monsters are tamed to his hand, even as that wild sea-brood, shepherded by Proteus. He tames, and he clothes them with attributes of flesh and blood, till they wonder at themselves, like Indian Islanders forced to submit to European vesture. Caliban, the Witches, are as true to the laws of their own nature (ours with a difference) as Othello, Hamlet, and Macbeth. Herein the great and little wits are differenced; that if the latter wander ever so little from nature or actual existence, they lose themselves and their readers. Their phantoms are lawless; their visions nightmares. They do not create, which implies shaping and consistency. Their imaginations are not active—for to be active is to call something into act and form—but passive, as men in sick dreams. For the super-natural, or something super-added to what we know of nature, they give you the plainly non-natural. And if this were all, and that these mental hallucinations were discoverable only in the treatment of subjects out of nature, or transcending it, the judgment might with some plea be pardoned if it ran riot, and a little wantonized:[1] but even in the describing of real and everyday life, that which is before their eyes, one of these lesser wits shall more deviate from nature—show more of that inconsequence, which has a natural alliance with frenzy,—than a great genius in his "maddest fits," as Withers somewhere calls them.[2] We appeal to any one that is acquainted with the common run of Lane's novels,—as they existed some twenty or thirty years back,—those scanty intellectual viands of the whole female reading public, till a happier genius[3] arose, and expelled forever the innutritious phantoms, —whether he has not found his brain more "betossed,"[4] his memory more puzzled, his sense of when and where more confounded, among the improbable events, the incoherent incidents, the inconsistent characters, or no-characters, of some third-rate love intrigue—where the persons shall be a Lord Glendamour and a Miss Rivers, and the scene only alternate between Bath and Bond-street—a more bewildering dreaminess induced upon him than he has felt wandering over all the fairy grounds of Spenser. In the productions we refer to, nothing but names and places is familiar; the persons are neither of this world nor of any other conceivable one; an endless string of activities without purpose, of purposes destitute of motive:—we meet phantoms in our known walks; *fantasques*[5] only christened. In the poet we have names which announce fiction; and we have absolutely no place at all, for the things and persons of *The Fairy Queen* prate not of their "whereabout."[6] But in their inner nature, and the law of their speech and actions, we are at home and upon acquainted ground. The one turns life into a dream; the other to the wildest dreams gives the sobrieties of everyday occurrences. By what subtile art of tracing the mental processes it is effected, we are not philosophers enough to explain, but in that wonderful episode of the cave of Mammon,[7] in which the Money God appears first in the lowest form of a miser, is then a worker

[1] earth (See *Paradise Lost*, 1, 295.)
[2] *Paradise Lost*, 1, 543.
[3] *King Lear*, IV, 7, 16-17.
[4] *King Lear*, I, 1, 146 ff.
[5] *Timon of Athens*, II, 2, 141 ff.

[1] unrestrained
[2] See *The Shepheard's Hunting*, Eclogue 4, 410.
[3] Probably Scott.
[4] *Romeo and Juliet*, V, 3, 76.
[5] whims
[6] *Macbeth*, II, 1, 58.
[7] *The Faerie Queene*, II, 7.

of metals, and becomes the god of all the treasures of the world; and has a daughter, Ambition, before whom all the world kneels for favors—with the Hesperian fruit,[1] the waters of Tantalus, with Pilate washing his hands vainly,[2] but not impertinently, in the same stream—that we should be at one moment in the cave of an old hoarder of treasures, at the next at the forge of the Cyclops, in a palace and yet in hell, all at once, with the shifting mutations of the most rambling dream, and our judgment yet all the time awake, and neither able nor willing to detect the fallacy,—is a proof of that hidden sanity which still guides the poet in his widest seeming-aberrations.

It is not enough to say that the whole episode is a copy of the mind's conceptions in sleep; it is, in some sort—but what a copy! Let the most romantic of us, that has been entertained all night with the spectacle of some wild and magnificent vision, recombine it in the morning, and try it by his waking judgment. That which appeared so shifting, and yet so coherent, while that faculty was passive, when it comes under cool examination, shall appear so reasonless and so unlinked, that we are ashamed to have been so deluded; and to have taken, though but in sleep, a monster for a god. But the transitions in this episode are every whit as violent as in the most extravagant dream, and yet the waking judgment ratifies them.

THE DEATH OF COLERIDGE

IN THE ALBUM OF MR. KEYMER
1834   1835

When I heard of the death of Coleridge, it was without grief. It seemed to me that he long had been on the confines of the next world,—that he had a hunger for eternity. I grieved then that I could not grieve. But since, I feel how great a part he was of me. His great and dear spirit haunts me. I cannot think a thought, I cannot make a criticism on men or books, without an ineffectual turning and reference to him. He was the proof and touchstone of all my cogitations. He was a Grecian[3] (or in the first form) at Christ's Hospital, where I was deputy Grecian; and the same subordination and deference to him I have pre-

served through a life-long acquaintance. Great in his writings, he was greatest in his conversation. In him was disproved that old maxim that we should allow every one his share of talk. He would talk from morn to dewy eve,[1] nor cease till far midnight, yet who ever would interrupt him,—who would obstruct that continuous flow of converse, fetched from Helicon or Zion? He had the tact of making the unintelligible seem plain. Many who read the abstruser parts of his *Friend* would complain that his words did not answer to his spoken wisdom. They were identical. But he had a tone in oral delivery, which seemed to convey sense to those who were otherwise imperfect recipients. He was my fifty-years-old friend without a dissension. Never saw I his likeness, nor probably the world can see again. I seemed to love the house he died at more passionately than when he lived. I love the faithful Gilmans[2] more than while they exercised their virtues towards him living. What was his mansion is consecrated to me a chapel.

Walter Savage Landor 1775-1864

From GEBIR
1798

BOOK I

I sing the fates of Gebir. He had dwelt
Among those mountain-caverns which retain
His labors yet, vast halls and flowing wells,
Nor have forgotten their old master's name
5 Though sever'd from his people: here, incenst
By meditating on primeval wrongs,
He blew his battle-horn, at which uprose
Whole nations; here, ten thousand of most might
He call'd aloud; and soon Charoba saw
10 His dark helm hover o'er the land of Nile.
What should the virgin do? should royal knees
Bend suppliant? or defenceless hands engage
Men of gigantic force, gigantic arms?
For 'twas reported that nor sword sufficed,
15 Nor shield immense nor coat of massive mail,

[1] Golden apples from the mythological garden of Hesperides.
[2] See *Matthew*, 27:24.
[3] A name given to students of the highest class who were preparing to enter a university; students of the second class were called deputy Grecians.

[1] See *Paradise Lost*, 1, 742-43.
[2] Coleridge was a frequent visitor at the home of the Gilmans, in Highgate. They cared for him at the time of his last illness and death.

But that upon their towering heads they
　　bore
Each a huge stone, refulgent as the stars.
This told she Dalica, then cried aloud,
"If on your bosom laying down my head
20 I sobb'd away the sorrows of a child,
If I have always, and Heav'n knows I
　　have,
Next to a mother's held a nurse's name,
Succor this one distress, recall those days,
Love me, tho' 'twere because you lov'd
　　me then."
25　　But whether confident in magic rites
Or touch'd with sexual pride to stand im-
　　plor'd,
Dalica smiled, then spake—"Away those
　　fears.
Though stronger than the strongest of his
　　kind,
He falls; on me devolve that charge; he
　　falls.
30 Rather than fly him, stoop thou to allure;
Nay, journey to his tents. A city stood
Upon that coast, they say, by Sidad built,
Whose father Gad built Gadir; on this
　　ground
Perhaps he sees an ample room for war.
35 Persuade him to restore the walls himself
In honor of his ancestors, persuade—
But wherefore this advice? young, un-
　　espoused,
Charoba want persuasions! and a queen!"
"O Dalica!" the shuddering maid ex-
　　claim'd,
40 Could I encounter that fierce frightful
　　man?
Could I speak? no, nor sigh."—"And
　　canst thou reign?"
Cried Dalica; "yield empire or comply."
Unfix'd, though seeming fix'd, her eyes
　　downcast,
The wonted buzz and bustle of the court
45 From far through sculptured galleries met
　　her ear,
Then lifting up her head, the evening sun
Pour'd a fresh splendor on her burnish'd
　　throne:
The fair Charoba, the young queen, com-
　　plied.
　　But Gebir, when he heard of her ap-
　　proach,
50 Laid by his orbed shield; his vizor-helm,
His buckler and his corset he laid by,
And bade that none attend him: at his
　　side
Two faithful dogs that urge the silent
　　course,
Shaggy, deep-chested, crouch'd; the croco-
　　diie,

55 Crying, oft made them raise their flaccid
　　ears
And push their heads within their master's
　　hand.
There was a brightening paleness in his
　　face,
Such as Diana rising o'er the rocks
Shower'd on the lonely Latmian; on his
　　brow
60 Sorrow there was, yet nought was there
　　severe.
But when the royal damsel first he saw,
Faint, hanging on her handmaid, and her
　　knees
Tottering, as from the motion of the car,
His eyes look'd earnest on her, and those
　　eyes
65 Show'd, if they had not, that they might
　　have, lov'd,
For there was pity in them at that hour.
With gentle speech, and more with gentle
　　looks,
He sooth'd her; but lest Pity go beyond
And cross'd Ambition lose her lofty aim,
70 Bending, he kiss'd her garment, and re-
　　tired.
He went, nor slumber'd in the sultry noon,
When viands, couches, generous wines,
　　persuade,
And slumber most refreshes; nor at night,
When heavy dews are laden with disease;
75 And blindness waits not there for lingering
　　age.
Ere morning dawn'd behind him, he ar-
　　rived
At those rich meadows where young
　　Tamar fed
The royal flocks entrusted to his care.
"Now," said he to himself, "will I re-
　　pose
80 At least this burthen on a brother's
　　breast."
His brother stood before him: he, amazed,
Rear'd suddenly his head, and thus began.
"Is it thou, brother! Tamar, is it thou!
Why, standing on the valley's utmost
　　verge,
85 Lookest thou on that dull and dreary shore
Where beyond sight Nile blackens all the
　　sand?
And why that sadness? When I pass'd
　　our sheep
The dew-drops were not shaken off the
　　bar,
Therefore if one be wanting, 'tis untold."
90 "Yes, one is wanting, nor is that un-
　　told,"
Said Tamar; "and this dull and dreary
　　shore

Is neither dull nor dreary at all hours.''
Whereon the tear stole silent down his
    cheek,
Silent, but not by Gebir unobserv'd:
95 Wondering he gazed awhile, and pitying
    spake.
"Let me approach thee; does the morning
    light
Scatter this wan suffusion o'er thy brow,
This faint blue lustre under both thine
    eyes?''
"O brother, is this pity or reproach?''
100 Cried Tamar, "cruel if it be reproach,
If pity, O how vain!''—"Whate'er it be
That grieves thee, I will pity, thou but
    speak,
And I can tell thee, Tamar, pang for
    pang.''
"Gebir! then more than brothers are
    we now!
105 Everything (take my hand) will I confess.
I neither feed the flock nor watch the fold;
How can I, lost in love? But, Gebir, why
That anger which has risen to your cheek?
Can other men? could you? what, no re-
    ply!
110 And still more anger, and still worse con-
    ceal'd!
Are these your promises? your pity this?''
"Tamar, I well may pity what I feel—
Mark me aright—I feel for thee—pro-
    ceed—
Relate me all.''—"Then will I all relate,
115 Said the young shepherd, gladden'd from
    his heart.
" 'Twas evening, though not sunset, and
    the tide
Level with these green meadows, seem'd
    yet higher:
'Twas pleasant; and I loosen'd from my
    neck

The pipe you gave me, and began to play.
120 O that I ne'er had learnt the tuneful art!
It always brings us enemies or love.
Well, I was playing, when above the
    waves
Some swimmer's head methought I saw
    ascend;
I, sitting still, survey'd it, with my pipe
125 Awkwardly held before my lips half-
    closed,
Gebir! it was a Nymph! a Nymph divine!
I cannot wait describing how she came,
How I was sitting, how she first assum'd
The sailor; of what happen'd there re-
    mains
130 Enough to say, and too much to forget.
The sweet deceiver stepp'd upon this bank

Before I was aware; for with surprise
Moments fly rapid as with love itself.
Stooping to tune afresh the hoarsen'd
    reed,
135 I heard a rustling, and where that arose
My glance first lighted on her nimble feet.
Her feet resembled those long shells[1] ex-
    plored
By him who to befriend his steed's dim
    sight
Would blow the pungent powder in the
    eye.
140 Her eyes too! O immortal Gods! her eyes
Resembled—what could they resemble?
    what
Ever resemble those? Even her attire
Was not of wonted woof nor vulgar art:
Her mantle show'd the yellow samphire-
    pod,
145 Her girdle the dove-color'd wave serene.
'Shepherd,' said she, 'and will you wrestle
    now,
And with the sailor's hardier race en-
    gage?'
I was rejoiced to hear it, and contrived
How to keep up contention: could I fail
150 By pressing not too strongly, yet to press?
'Whether a shepherd, as indeed you seem,
Or whether of the hardier race you boast,
I am not daunted; no; I will engage.'
'But first,' said she, 'what wager will you
    lay?'
155 'A sheep,' I answered: 'add whate'er you
    will.'
'I cannot,' she replied, 'make that return:
Our hided vessels in their pitchy round
Seldom, unless from rapine, hold a sheep.
But I have sinuous shells of pearly hue
160 Within, and they that lustre have imbibed
In the sun's palace-porch, where when
    unyoked
His chariot-wheel stands midway in the
    wave:
Shake one and it awakens, then apply
Its polish'd lips to your attentive ear,
165 And it remembers its august abodes,
And murmurs as the ocean murmurs there.
And I have others given me by the nymphs,
Of sweeter sound than any pipe you
    have;[2]
But we, by Neptune! for no pipe contend,
170 This time a sheep I win, a pipe the next.'
Now came she forward eager to engage,
But first her dress, her bosom then sur-
    vey'd,

---

[1] White shells of cuttlefish.
[2] For a similar passage, see Wordsworth's *The
    Excursion*, 4. 1132-50; and Byron's *The
    Island*, 2, 406-15.

And heav'd it, doubting if she could deceive.
Her bosom seem'd, inclos'd in haze like
heav'n,
175 To baffle touch, and rose forth undefined;
Above her knee she drew the robe suc-
cinct,[1]
Above her breast, and just below her
arms.
'This will preserve my breath when tightly
bound,
If struggle and equal strength should so
constrain.'
180 Thus, pulling hard to fasten it, she spake,
And, rushing at me, closed: I thrill'd
throughout
And seem'd to lessen and shrink up with
cold.
Again with violent impulse gush'd my
blood,
And hearing nought external, thus absorb'd,
185 I heard it, rushing through each turbid
vein,
Shake my unsteady swimming sight in air.
Yet with unyielding though uncertain
arms
I clung around her neck; the vest beneath
Rustled against our slippery limbs entwined:
190 Often mine springing with eluded force
Started aside and trembled till replaced:
And when I most succeeded, as I thought,
My bosom and my throat felt so compress'd
That life was almost quivering on my lips,
195 Yet nothing was there painful: these are
signs
Of secret arts and not of human might;
What arts I cannot tell; I only know
My eyes grew dizzy and my strength
decay'd;
I was indeed o'ercome—with what regret,
200 And more, with what confusion, when I
reach'd
The fold, and yielding up the sheep, she
cried,
'This pays a shepherd to a conquering
maid.'
She smiled, and more of pleasure than
disdain
Was in her dimpled chin and liberal lip,
205 And eyes that languish'd, lengthening, just
like love.
She went away; I on the wicker gate
Leant, and could follow with my eyes
alone.
The sheep she carried easy as a cloak;

[1] girded: tucked up

But when I heard its bleating, as I did,
210 And saw, she hastening on, its hinder
feet
Struggle, and from her snowy shoulder
slip,
One shoulder its poor efforts had unveil'd,
Then all my passions mingling fell in
tears;
Restless then ran I to the highest ground
215 To watch her; she was gone; gone down
the tide;
And the long moon-beam on the hard wet
sand
Lay like a jasper column half up-rear'd."
"But, Tamar! tell me, will she not
return?"
"She will return, yet not before the
moon
220 Again is at the full: she promis'd this,
Tho' when she promis'd I could not
reply."
"By all the Gods I pity thee! go on,
Fear not my anger, look not on my
shame,
For when a lover only hears of love
225 He finds his folly out, and is ashamed.
Away with watchful nights and lonely
days,
Contempt of earth and aspect up to
heaven,
With contemplation, with humility,
A tatter'd cloak that pride wears when
deform'd,
230 Away with all that hides me from myself,
Parts me from others, whispers I am
wise:
From our own wisdom less is to be reap'd
Than from the barest folly of our
friend.
Tamar! thy pastures, large and rich, afford
235 Flowers to thy bees and herbage to thy
sheep,
But, battened on too much, the poorest
croft
Of thy poor neighbor yields what thine
denies."
They hasten'd to the camp, and Gebir
there
Resolved his native country to forego,
240 And order'd from those ruins to the
right
They forthwith raise a city. Tamar heard
With wonder, tho' in passing 'twas half-
told,
His brother's love, and sigh'd upon his
own.

. . . . . .

ROSE AYLMER
1806

Ah, what avails the sceptred race,[1]
  Ah, what the form divine!
What every virtue, every grace!
  Rose Aylmer, all were thine.
5 Rose Aylmer, whom these wakeful eyes
  May weep, but never see,
A night of memories and of sighs
  I consecrate to thee.

CHILD OF A DAY, THOU KNOWEST NOT
1831

Child of a day, thou knowest not
  The tears that overflow thine urn,
The gushing eyes that read thy lot,
  Nor, if thou knewest, couldst return!
5 And why the wish! the pure and blest
  Watch like thy mother o'er thy sleep.
O peaceful night! O envied rest!
  Thou wilt not ever see her weep.

FOR AN EPITAPH AT FIESOLE
1831

Lo! where the four mimosas blend their
    shade
In calm repose at last is Landor laid,
For ere he slept he saw them planted here
By her his soul had ever held most dear,
5 And he had lived enough when he had
    dried her tear.

LYRICS, TO IANTHE
1806-63

HOMAGE
1831

Away, my verse; and never fear,
  As men before such beauty do;
On you she will not look severe,
  She will not turn her eyes from you.
5 Some happier graces could I lend
  That in her memory you should live,
Some little blemishes might blend,
  For it would please her to forgive.

ON THE SMOOTH BROW AND CLUSTERING HAIR
1846

On the smooth brow and clustering hair,
  Myrtle and rose![2] your wreath combine,
The duller olive I would wear,
  Its constancy, its peace, be mine.

[1] A reference to the titled Aylmer family.
[2] The myrtle and the rose are emblems of love.

HEART'S-EASE
1858

There is a flower I wish to wear,
  But not until first worn by you—
Heart's-ease—of all earth's flowers most
    rare;
  Bring it; and bring enough for two.

IT OFTEN COMES INTO MY HEAD
1846

It often comes into my head
That we may dream when we are dead,
  But I am far from sure we do.
O that it were so! then my rest
5 Would be indeed among the blest;
  I should forever dream of you.

ALL TENDER THOUGHTS THAT E'ER POSSESS'D
1831

All tender thoughts that e'er possess'd
The human brain or human breast,
  Centre in mine for thee—
Excepting one—and that must thou
5 Contribute: come, confer it now:
  Grateful I fain would be.

THOU HAST NOT RAISED, IANTHE, SUCH DESIRE
1846

Thou hast not rais'd, Ianthe, such desire
  In any breast as thou hast rais'd in mine.
No wandering meteor now, no marshy fire,
  Leads on my steps, but lofty, but divine:
5 And, if thou chillest me, as chill thou dost
  When I approach too near, too boldly
    gaze,
So chills the blushing morn, so chills the
    host
  Of vernal stars, with light more chaste
    than day's.

PLEASURE! WHY THUS DESERT THE HEART
1831

Pleasure! why thus desert the heart
  In its spring-tide?
I could have seen her, I could part,
  And but have sigh'd!

5 O'er every youthful charm to stray,
  To gaze, to touch—
Pleasure! why take so much away,
  Or give so much!

RENUNCIATION
1846

Lie, my fond heart at rest,
　She never can be ours.
Why strike upon my breast
　The slowly passing hours?
5 Ah! breathe not out the name,
　That fatal folly stay!
Conceal the eternal flame,
　And tortured ne'er betray.

YOU SMILED, YOU SPOKE, AND I BELIEVED
1846

You smiled, you spoke, and I believed,
By every word and smile deceived.
Another man would hope no more;
Nor hope I what I hoped before:
5 But let not this last wish be vain;
Deceive, deceive me once again.

SO LATE REMOVED, FROM HIM SHE SWORE
1831

So late removed from him she swore,
　With clasping arms and vows and tears,
In life and death she would adore,
　While memory, fondness, bliss, endears.

5 Can she forswear? can she forget?
　Strike, mighty Love! strike, Vengeance!
　　Soft!
Conscience must come and bring regret—
These let her feel!—nor these too oft!

I HELD HER HAND, THE PLEDGE OF BLISS
1831

I held her hand, the pledge of bliss,
　Her hand that trembled and withdrew;
She bent her head before my kiss—
　My heart was sure that hers was true.
5 Now I have told her I must part,
　She shakes my hand, she bids adieu,
Nor shuns the kiss—Alas, my heart!
　Hers never was the heart for you.

ABSENCE
1831

Ianthe! you are call'd to cross the sea;[1]
　A path forbidden *me!*
Remember, while the Sun his blessing sheds
　Upon the mountain-heads,
5 How often we have watch'd him laying
　down
　His brow, and dropp'd our own
Against each other's, and how faint and
　short

[1] In 1815, a short time after her marriage with M. de Molandé, Sophia Jane Swift, the Ianthe of these poems, went to live in Paris.

And sliding the support!
What will succeed it now? Mine is un-
　blest,
　Ianthe! nor will rest
But on the very thought that swells with
　pain.
　O bid me hope again!
O give me back what Earth, what (with-
　out you)
　Not Heaven itself can do,
15 One of the golden days that we have past;
　And let it be my last!
Or else the gift would be, however sweet,
　Fragile and incomplete.

FLOW, PRECIOUS TEARS! THUS SHALL MY RIVAL KNOW
1806

Flow, precious tears! thus shall my rival
　know
　For me, not him, ye flow.
Stay, precious tears! ah, stay! this jeal-
　ous heart
　Would bid you flow apart,
5 Lest he should see you rising o'er the brim,
　And hope you rise for him.
Your secret cells, while he is absent, keep,
　Nor, tho' I'm absent, weep.

MILD IS THE PARTING YEAR, AND SWEET
1831

Mild is the parting year, and sweet
　The odor of the falling spray;
Life passes on more rudely fleet,
　And balmless is its closing day.
5 I wait its close, I court its gloom,
　But mourn that never must there fall
Or on my breast or on my tomb
　The tear that would have sooth'd it all.

PAST RUIN'D ILION HELEN LIVES
1831

Past ruin'd Ilion Helen lives,
　Alcestis rises from the shades;
Verse calls them forth; 'tis verse that gives
　Immortal youth to mortal maids.

5 Soon shall Oblivion's deepening veil
　Hide all the peopled hills you see,
The gay, the proud, while lovers hail
　These many summers you and me.

HERE EVER SINCE YOU WENT ABROAD
1846

Here, ever since you went abroad,
　If there be change, no change I see,
I only walk our wonted road,
　The road is only walk'd by me.

5 Yes; I forgot; a change there is;
　　Was it of *that* you bade me tell?
I catch at times, at times I miss
　　The sight, the tone, I know so well.

Only two months since you stood here!
10　Two shortest months! then tell me why
Voices are harsher than they were,
　　And tears are longer ere they dry.

Years After
1846

"Do you remember me? or are you
　　proud?"
Lightly advancing thro' her star-trimm'd
　　crowd,
Ianthe said, and look'd into my eyes.
"A *yes,* a *yes,* to both: for Memory
5 Where you but once have been must ever
　　be,
And at your voice Pride from his throne
　　must rise."

She I Love (Alas in Vain!)
1846

She I love (alas in vain!)
　　Floats before my slumbering eyes:
When she comes she lulls my pain,
　　When she goes what pangs arise!
5 Thou whom love, whom memory flies,
　　Gentle Sleep! prolong thy reign!
If even thus she soothe my sighs,
　　Never let me wake again!

No, My Own Love of Other Years
1846

No, my own love of other years!
　　No, it must never be.
Much rests with you that yet endears,
　　Alas! but what with me?
5 Could those bright years o'er me revolve
　　So gay, o'er you so fair,
The pearl of life we would dissolve
　　And each the cup might share.
You show that truth can ne'er decay,
10　Whatever fate befalls;
I, that the myrtle and the bay[1]
　　Shoot fresh on ruin'd walls.

I Wonder Not That Youth Remains
1853

I wonder not that Youth remains
　　With you, wherever else she flies:
Where could she find such fair domains,
　　Where bask beneath such sunny eyes?

[1] The myrtle is an emblem of love; the bay, or laurel, an emblem of honor or victory.

Your Pleasures Spring Like Daisies in the Grass
1846

Your pleasures spring like daisies in the
　　grass,
　　Cut down, and up again as blithe as ever;
From you, Ianthe, little troubles pass
　　Like little ripples down a sunny river.

Years, Many Parti-Colored Years
1853

Years, many parti-colored years,
　　Some have crept on, and some have flown
Since first before me fell those tears
　　I never could see fall alone.
5 Years, not so many, are to come,
　　Years not so varied, when from you
One more will fall: when, carried home,
　　I see it not, nor hear *adieu.*

Well I Remember How You Smiled
1863

Well I remember how you smiled
　　To see me write your name upon
The soft sea-sand. *"O! what a child!
　　You think you're writing upon stone!"*
5 I have since written what no tide
　　Shall ever wash away, what men
Unborn shall read o'er ocean wide
　　And find Ianthe's name again.

A Fiesolan Idyl[1]
1831

Here, where precipitate Spring with one
　　light bound
Into hot Summer's lusty arms expires,
And where go forth at morn, at eve, at
　　night,
Soft airs that want the lute to play with
　　'em,
5 And softer sighs that know not what they
　　want,
Aside a wall, beneath an orange-tree,
Whose tallest flowers could tell the lowlier
　　ones
Of sights in Fiesolè right up above,
While I was gazing a few paces off
10 At what they seem'd to show me with their
　　nods,
Their frequent whispers and their pointing
　　shoots,
A gentle maid came down the garden-steps
And gathered the pure treasure in her lap.
I heard the branches rustle, and stepp'd
　　forth
15 To drive the ox away, or mule, or goat,

[1] Landor lived for some years in Fiesole, near Florence, Italy.

Such I believed it must be. How could I
Let beast o'erpower them? When hath
    wind or rain
Borne hard upon weak plant that wanted
    me,
And I (however they might bluster round)
20 Walk'd off? 'Twere most ungrateful: for
    sweet scents
Are the swift vehicles of still sweeter
    thoughts,
And nurse and pillow the dull memory
That would let drop without them her best
    stores.
They bring me tales of youth and tones
    of love,
25 And 'tis and ever was my wish and way
To let all flowers live freely, and all die
(Whene'er their Genius bids their souls
    depart)
Among their kindred in their native place.
I never pluck the rose; the violet's head
30 Hath shaken with my breath upon its bank
And not reproach'd me; the ever-sacred
    cup
Of the pure lily hath between my hands
Felt safe, unsoil'd, nor lost one grain of
    gold.
I saw the light that made the glossy leaves
35 More glossy; the fair arm, the fairer
    cheek
Warmed by the eye intent on its pursuit;
I saw the foot that, although half-erect
From its gray slipper, could not lift her
    up
To what she wanted: I held down a branch
40 And gather'd her some blossoms; since
    their hour
Was come, and bees had wounded them,
    and flies
Of harder wing were working their way
    thro'
And scattering them in fragments under
    foot.
So crisp were some, they rattled unevolved,
45 Others, ere broken off, fell into shells,
For such appear the petals when detach'd,
Unbending, brittle, lucid, white like snow,
And like snow not seen through, by eye
    or sun:
Yet every one her gown received from me
50 Was fairer than the first. I thought not so,
But so she praised them to reward my
    care.
I said, "You find the largest."
                "This indeed,"
Cried she, "is large and sweet." She held
    one forth,
Whether for me to look at or to take
55 She knew not, nor did I; but taking it

Would best have solved (and this she felt)
    her doubt.
I dared not touch it; for it seemed a part
Of her own self; fresh, full, the most
    mature
Of blossoms, yet a blossom; with a touch
60 To fall, and yet unfallen. She drew back
The boon she tender'd, and then, finding
    not
The ribbon at her waist to fix it in,
Dropp'd it, as loth to drop it, on the rest.

From THE CITATION AND EXAMINA-
TION OF WILLIAM SHAKSPEARE
1834

THE MAID'S LAMENT

I loved him not; and yet now he is gone
    I feel I am alone.
I check'd[1] him while he spoke; yet could
    he speak,
    Alas! I would not check.
5 For reasons not to love him once I sought,
    And wearied all my thought
To vex myself and him: I now would give
    My love, could he but live
Who lately lived for me, and when he
    found
10   'Twas vain, in holy ground
He hid his face amid the shades of death.
    I waste for him my breath
Who wasted his for me: but mine returns,
    And this lorn bosom burns
15 With stifling heat, heaving it up in sleep,
    And waking me to weep
Tears that had melted his soft heart: for
    years
    Wept he as bitter tears.
Merciful God! such was his latest prayer,
20   *These may she never share.*
Quieter is his breath, his breast more cold,
    Than daisies in the mould,
Where children spell, athwart the church-
    yard gate,
    His name, and life's brief date.
25 Pray for him, gentle souls, whoe'er you be,
    And, O! pray too for me.

UPON A SWEET-BRIAR

My briar that smelledst sweet
When gentle spring's first heat
  Ran through thy quiet veins,—
Thou that wouldst injure none,
5   But wouldst be left alone,
Alone thou leavest me, and nought of thine
    remains.

What! hath no poet's lyre
O'er thee, sweet-breathing briar,

1 rebuked

Hung fondly, ill or well?
10 And yet methinks with thee
A poet's sympathy,
Whether in weal or woe, in life or death,
might dwell.

Hard usage both must bear,
Few hands your youth will rear,
15 Few bosoms cherish you;
Your tender prime must bleed
Ere you are sweet, but freed
From life, you then are prized; thus prized
are poets too.

And art thou yet alive?
20 And shall the happy hive
Send out her youth to cull
Thy sweets of leaf and flower,
And spend the sunny hour
With thee, and thy faint heart with mur-
muring music lull?

25 Tell me what tender care,
Tell me what pious prayer,
Bade thee arise and live.
The fondest-favored bee
Shall whisper nought to thee
30 More loving than the song my grateful
muse shall give.

From PERICLES AND ASPASIA
1836

CORINNA TO TANAGRA
FROM ATHENS

Tanagra! think not I forget
Thy beautifully-storied streets;
Be sure my memory bathes yet
In clear Thermodon, and yet greets
5 The blithe and liberal shepherd-boy,
Whose sunny bosom swells with joy
When we accept his matted rushes
Upheav'd with sylvan fruit; away he
bounds, and blushes.

A gift I promise: one I see
10 Which thou with transport wilt re-
ceive,
The only proper gift for thee,
Of which no mortal shall bereave
In later times thy mouldering walls,
Until the last old turret falls;
15 A crown, a crown from Athens won,
A crown no God can wear, beside Latona's
son.

There may be cities who refuse
To their own child the honors due,
And look ungently on the Muse;
20 But ever shall those cities rue

The dry, unyielding, niggard breast,
Offering no nourishment, no rest,
To that young head which soon shall rise
Disdainfully, in might and glory, to the
skies.

25 Sweetly where cavern'd Dirce flows
Do white-arm'd maidens chant my lay,
Flapping the while with laurel-rose
The honey-gathering tribes away;
And sweetly, sweetly Attic tongues
30 Lisp your Corinna's early songs;
To her with feet more graceful come
The verses that have dwelt in kindred
breasts at home.

O let thy children lean aslant
Against the tender mother's knee,
35 And gaze into her face, and want
To know what magic there can be
In words that urge some eyes to dance,
While others as in holy trance
Look up to heaven: be such my praise!
40 Why linger? I must haste, or lose the
Delphic bays.[1]

I WILL NOT LOVE

I will not love!
————These sounds have often
Burst from a troubled breast;
Rarely from one no sighs could soften,
5 Rarely from one at rest.

THE DEATH OF ARTEMIDORA

Artemidora! Gods invisible,
While thou art lying faint along the couch,
Have tied the sandal to thy veined feet
And stand beside thee, ready to convey
5 Thy weary steps where other rivers flow.
Refreshing shades will waft thy weariness
Away, and voices like thy own come nigh
Soliciting nor vainly thy embrace."
Artemidora sigh'd, and would have
press'd
10 The hand now pressing hers, but was too
weak.
Fate's shears were over her dark hair
unseen
While thus Elpenor spake. He look'd into
Eyes that had given light and life ere-
while
To those above them, those now dim with
tears

[1] A crown made of leaves or twigs of the bay,
or laurel, and given as a reward to conquerors and poets. Delphi was the seat of the
oracle of Apollo, the god of poetry, to whom
the laurel was sacred.

¹⁵ And watchfulness. Again he spake of joy
Eternal.   At that word, that sad word,
    joy,
Faithful and fond her bosom heav'd once
    more:
Her head fell back; one sob, one loud deep
    sob
Swell'd through the darken'd chamber;
    'twas not hers.
²⁰ With her that old boat incorruptible,
Unwearied, undiverted in its course,
Had plash'd the water up the farther
    strand.

LIFE PASSES NOT AS SOME MEN SAY

Life passes not as some men say,
If you will only urge his stay,
    And treat him kindly all the while.
He flies the dizzy strife of towns,
⁵ Cowers before thunder-bearing frowns,
    But freshens up again at song and smile.

Ardalia! we will place him here,
And promise that nor sigh nor tear
    Shall ever trouble his repose.
¹⁰ What precious seal will you impress
To ratify his happiness?
    That rose[1] thro' which you breathe?
    Come, bring that rose.

LITTLE AGLAE
TO HER FATHER, ON HER STATUE BEING CALLED LIKE HER

Father! the little girl we see
Is not, I fancy, so like me;
    You never hold her on your knee.

When she came home, the other day,
⁵ You kiss'd her; but I cannot say
    She kiss'd you first and ran away.

WE MIND NOT HOW THE SUN IN THE MID-SKY

We mind not how the sun in the mid-sky
Is hastening on; but when the golden orb
Strikes the extreme of earth, and when the
    gulfs
Of air and ocean open to receive him,
⁵ Dampness and gloom invade us; then we
    think
Ah! thus is it with Youth. Too fast his
    feet
Run on for sight; hour follows hour; fair
    maid
Succeeds fair maid; bright eyes bestar his
    couch;
The cheerful horn awakens him; the feast,

[1] The rose is an emblem of love.

¹⁰ The revel, the entangling dance, allure,
And voices mellower than the Muse's own
Heave up his buoyant bosom on their
    wave.
A little while, and then—Ah Youth!
    dear Youth!
Listen not to my words—but stay with me!
¹⁵ When thou art gone, Life may go too:
    the sigh
That follows is for thee, and not for Life.

SAPPHO TO HESPERUS

I have beheld thee in the morning hour
A solitary star, with thankless eyes,
Ungrateful as I am! who bade thee rise
When sleep all night had wandered from
    my bower.

⁵ Can it be true that thou art he
Who shinest now above the sea
Amid a thousand, but more bright?
Ah yes! the very same art thou
That heard me then, and hearest now—
Thou seemst, star of love! to throb with
    light.

DIRCE

Stand close around, ye Stygian set,
    With Dirce in one boat conveyed,
Or Charon, seeing, may forget
    That he is old, and she a shade.

ON SEEING A HAIR OF LUCRETIA BORGIA
1837

Borgia, thou once wert almost too august
And high for adoration; now thou'rt dust;
All that remains of thee these plaits un-
    fold,
Calm hair, meandering in pellucid gold.

TO WORDSWORTH
1833   1837

Those who have laid the harp aside
    And turn'd to idler things,
From very restlessness have tried
    The loose and dusty strings,
⁵ And, catching back some favorite strain,
Run with it o'er the chords again.

But Memory is not a Muse,
    O Wordsworth! though 'tis said
They all descend from her, and use
¹⁰ To haunt her fountain-head:
That other men should work for me
In the rich mines of Poesie,

Pleases me better than the toil
  Of smoothing under hardened hand,
15 With attic[1] emery and oil,
  The shining point for Wisdom's wand,
Like those thou temperest 'mid the rills
Descending from thy native hills.
Without his governance, in vain,
20   Manhood is strong, and Youth is bold.

If oftentimes the o'er-piled strain,
  Clogs in the furnace and grows cold
Beneath his pinions deep and frore,[2]
And swells and melts and flows no more,
25 That is because the heat beneath
  Pants in its cavern poorly fed.
Life springs not from the couch of Death,
  Nor Muse nor Grace can raise the dead;
Unturn'd then let the mass remain,
30 Intractable to sun or rain.

A marsh, where only flat leaves lie,
And showing but the broken sky,
Too surely is the sweetest lay
That wins the ear and wastes the day,
35 Where youthful Fancy pouts alone
And lets not Wisdom touch her zone.[3]

He who would build his fame up high,
The rule and plummet must apply.
Nor say, "I'll do what I have plann'd,"
40 Before he try if loam or sand
Be still remaining in the place
Delved for each polish'd pillar's base.
With skilful eye and fit device
Thou raisest every edifice,
45 Whether in sheltered vale it stand,
Or overlook the Dardan[4] strand,
Amid the cypresses[5] that mourn
Laodameia's love forlorn.

We both have run o'er half the space
50 Listed for mortal's earthly race;
We both have cross'd life's fervid line,
And other stars before us shine:
May they be bright and prosperous
As those that have been stars for us!
55 Our course by Milton's light was sped,
And Shakespeare shining overhead:
Chatting on deck was Dryden too,
The Bacon of the rhyming crew;
None ever cross'd our mystic sea
60 More richly stored with thought than he;
Tho' never tender nor sublime,
He wrestles with and conquers Time.

[1] refined; of superior quality
[2] frozen
[3] girdle
[4] Trojan.
[5] The cypress is an emblem of mourning; it is a
  common tree in graveyards.

To learn my lore on Chaucer's knee,
I left much prouder company;
65 Thee gentle Spenser fondly led,
But me he mostly sent to bed.

I wish them every joy above
That highly blessed spirits prove,
Save one: and that too shall be theirs,
70 But after many rolling years,
When 'mid their light thy light appears.

TO JOSEPH ABLETT
1834   1834-37

Lord of the Celtic dells,
Where Clwyd listens as his minstrel tells
Of Arthur, or Pendragon, or perchance
  The plumes of flashy France,
5 Or, in dark region far across the main,
Far as Grenada in the world of Spain,

Warriors untold to Saxon ear,
Until their steel-clad spirits reappear;
  How happy were the hours that held
10 Thy friend (long absent from his native
    home)
Amid thy scenes with thee! how wide afield
From all past cares and all to come!

What hath Ambition's feverish grasp,
  what hath
Inconstant Fortune, panting Hope;
15   What Genius, that should cope
With the heart-whispers in that path
Winding so idly, where the idler stream
Flings at the white-hair'd poplars gleam
    for gleam?

Ablett! of all the days
20 My sixty summers ever knew,
Pleasant as there have been no few,
  Memory not one surveys
Like those we spent together. Wisely
    spent
Are they alone that leave the soul content.

25 Together we have visited the men
  Whom Pictish pirates[1] vainly would
    have drown'd;
Ah, shall we ever clasp the hand again
  That gave the British harp its truest
    sound?
Live, Derwent's guest![2] and thou by Gras-
    mere's springs!
30 Serene creators of immortal things.

[1] Jeffrey and others, who were hostile to the
  Lake School of poets—Wordsworth, Coleridge, and Southey.
[2] Southey, who lived near the river Derwent.—
  Wordsworth lived near by in Grasmere.

And live too thou for happier days
Whom Dryden's force and Spenser's fays
  Have heart and soul possess'd:[1]
Growl in grim London he who will,
35 Revisit thou Maiano's hill,[2]
    And swell with pride his sunburnt
      breast.

Old Redi in his easy-chair
With varied chant awaits thee there,
  And here are voices in the grove
40 Aside my house, that make me think
Bacchus is coming down to drink
    To Ariadne's love.

But whither am I borne away
From thee, to whom began my lay?
45   Courage! I am not yet quite lost;
I stepp'd aside to greet my friends;
Believe me, soon the greeting ends,
    I know but three or four at most.

Deem not that Time hath borne too hard
50 Upon the fortunes of thy bard,
  Leaving me only three or four:
'Tis my old number; dost thou start
At such a tale? in what man's heart
    Is there fireside for more?

55   I never courted friends or Fame;
She pouted at me long, at last she came,
And threw her arms around my neck and
    said,
"Take what hath been for years delay'd,
And fear not that the leaves will fall
60 One hour the earlier from thy coronal."

Ablett! thou knowest with what even hand
  I waved away the offer'd seat
Among the clambering, clattering, stilted
    great,
    The rulers of our land;
65 Nor crowds nor kings can lift me up,
Nor sweeten Pleasure's purer cup.

Thou knowest how, and why, are dear to
    me
My citron groves of Fiesole,[3]
My chirping Affrico, my beechwood nook,
70 My Naiads,[4] with feet only in the brook,
Which runs away and giggles in their
    faces,
Yet there they sit, nor sigh for other
    places.

'Tis not Pelasgian wall,
By him made sacred whom alone
75   'Twere not profane to call
The bard divine,[1] nor (thrown
Far under me) Valdarno, nor the crest
Of Vallombrosa in the crimson east.

Here can I sit or roam at will:
80   Few trouble me, few wish me ill,
Few come across me, few too near;
  Here all my wishes make their stand;
  Here ask I no one's voice or hand;
Scornful of favor, ignorant of fear.

85   Yon vine upon the maple bough
  Flouts at the hearty wheat below;
Away her venal wines the wise man sends,
  While those of lower stem he brings
  From inmost treasure vault, and sings
90 Their worth and age among his chosen
    friends.

Behold our Earth, most nigh the sun
Her zone[2] least opens to the genial heat,
  But farther off her veins more freely
    run:
'Tis thus with those who whirl about the
    great;
95 The nearest shrink and shiver, we remote
May open-breasted blow the pastoral oat.[3]

TO THE SISTER OF ELIA[4]
1834   1837

Comfort thee, O thou mourner, yet awhile!
  Again shall Elia's smile
Refresh thy heart, where heart can ache
    no more.
    What is it we deplore?

5 He leaves behind him, freed from griefs
    and years,
  Far worthier things than tears.
The love of friends without a single foe:
  Unequalled lot below!

His gentle soul, his genius, these are thine;
10   For these dost thou repine?
He may have left the lowly walks of men;
  Left them he has; what then?

Are not his footsteps followed by the eyes
  Of all the good and wise?
15 Tho' the warm day is over, yet they seek
  Upon the lofty peak

---

[1] Leigh Hunt.
[2] Florence, the home of Maiano (1442-97), an
  eminent Italian sculptor and architect.
[3] Landor lived for some years in Fiesole, near
  Florence. See his *A Fiesolan Idyl* (p. 991).
[4] That is, my statues of sea nymphs.

---

[1] Homer.   [2] girdle,—*i. e.*, equator
[3] A musical pipe made of oat-straw; the symbol
  of pastoral poetry.
[4] Mary Lamb. Many of Lamb's essays were
  written over the pseudonym of "Elia." Lamb
  died in 1834.

Of his pure mind the roseate light that
   glows
O'er death's perennial snows.
Behold him! from the region of the blest
20   He speaks: he bids thee rest.

ON HIS OWN AGAMEMNON AND
IPHIGENEIA
1837

From eve to morn, from morn to parting
   night,
Father and daughter stood before my sight.
I felt the looks they gave, the words they
   said,
And reconducted each serener shade.
5 Ever shall these to me be well-spent days,
Sweet fell the tears upon them, sweet the
   praise.
Far from the footstool of the tragic throne,
I am tragedian in this scene alone.

I CANNOT TELL, NOT I, WHY SHE
1846

I cannot tell, not I, why she
Awhile so gracious, now should be
So grave: I cannot tell you why
The violet hangs its head awry.
5 It shall be cull'd, it shall be worn,
In spite of every sign of scorn,
Dark look, and overhanging thorn.

YOU TELL ME I MUST COME AGAIN
1846

You tell me I must come again
   Now buds and blooms appear;
Ah! never fell one word in vain
   Of yours on mortal ear.
5 You say the birds are busy now
   In hedgerow, brake,[1] and grove,
And slant their eyes to find the bough
   That best conceals their love:
How many warble from the spray!
10   How many on the wing!
"Yet, yet," say you, "one voice away
   I miss the sound of spring."
How little could that voice express,
   Belovèd, when we met!
15 But other sounds hath tenderness,
   Which neither shall forget.

REMAIN, AH NOT IN YOUTH ALONE
1846

Remain, ah not in youth alone,
   Tho' youth, where you are, long will
   stay,
But when my summer days are gone,
   And my autumnal haste away.
5 *"Can I be always by your side?"*
   [1] thicket

No; but the hours you can, you must,
Nor rise at Death's approaching stride,
Nor go when dust is gone to dust.

"YOU MUST GIVE BACK," HER
MOTHER SAID
1846

"You must give back," her mother said
To a poor sobbing little maid,
"All the young man has given you,
Hard as it now may seem to do."
5   " 'Tis done already, mother dear!"
Said the sweet girl, "So, never fear."
  Mother. Are you quite certain? Come,
   recount
(There was not much) the whole amount.
  Girl. The locket: the kid gloves.
  Mother.   Go on.
10 *Girl.* Of the kid gloves I found but one.
  Mother. Never mind that. What else?
   Proceed.
You gave back all his trash?
  Girl.   Indeed.
  Mother. And was there nothing you
   would save?
  Girl. Everything I could give I gave.
15 *Mother.* To the last tittle?
  Girl.   Even to that.
  Mother. Freely?
  Girl. My heart went *pit-a-pat*
At giving up—ah me! ah me!
I cry so I can hardly see—
All the fond looks and words that pass'd,
20 And all the kisses, to the last.

THE MAID I LOVE NE'ER THOUGHT
OF ME
1846

The maid I love ne'er thought of me
Amid the scenes of gaiety;
But when her heart or mine sank low,
Ah then it was no longer so.
5 From the slant palm she rais'd her head,
And kiss'd the cheek whence youth had
   fled.
Angels! some future day for this,
Give her as sweet and pure a kiss.

VERY TRUE, THE LINNETS SING
1846

Very true, the linnets sing
Sweetest in the leaves of spring:
You have found in all these leaves
That which changes and deceives,
5 And, to pine by sun or star,
Left them, false ones as they are.
But there be who walk beside
Autumn's, till they all have died,
And who lend a patient ear
10 To low notes from branches sere.

TO A PAINTER
1846

Conceal not Time's misdeeds, but on my
    brow
    Retrace his mark:
Let the retiring hair be silvery now
    That once was dark:
5 Eyes that reflected images too bright
    Let clouds o'ercast,
And from the tablet be abolish'd quite
    The cheerful past.
Yet Care's deep lines should one from
    waken'd Mirth
10   Steal softly o'er,
Perhaps on me the fairest of the Earth,
    May glance once more.

DULL IS MY VERSE: NOT EVEN THOU
1846

Dull is my verse: not even thou
    Who movest many cares away
From this lone breast and weary brow,
    Canst make, as once, its fountain play;
5 No, nor those gentle words that now
    Support my heart to hear thee say:
"The bird upon its lonely bough
    Sings sweetest at the close of day."

SWEET WAS THE SONG THAT YOUTH SANG ONCE
1846

Sweet was the song that Youth sang once,
And passing sweet was the response;
But there are accents sweeter far
When Love leaps down our evening star,
5 Holds back the blighting wings of Time,
Melts with his breath the crusty rime,
And looks into our eyes, and says,
"Come, let us talk of former days."

TO SLEEP
1846

Come, Sleep! but mind ye! if you come
    without
The little girl that struck me at the rout,
By Jove! I would not give you half-a-
    crown
For all your poppy-heads and all your
    down.

WHY, WHY REPINE
1846

Why, why repine, my pensive friend,
    At pleasures slipp'd away?
Some the stern Fates will never lend,
    And all refuse to stay.

5 I see the rainbow in the sky,
    The dew upon the grass,

I see them, and I ask not why
    They glimmer or they pass.

With folded arms I linger not
10   To call them back; 'twere vain;
In this, or in some other spot,
    I know they'll shine again.

MOTHER, I CANNOT MIND MY WHEEL
1846

Mother, I cannot mind my wheel;
    My fingers ache, my lips are dry:
Oh! if you felt the pain I feel!
    But oh, who ever felt as I?
5 No longer could I doubt him true—
    All other men may use deceit;
He always said my eyes were blue,
    And often swore my lips were sweet.

TO A BRIDE,[1] FEB. 17, 1846
1846   1846

A still, serene, soft day; enough of sun
To wreathe the cottage smoke like pine-
    tree snow,
Whiter than those white flowers the bride-
    maids wore;
Upon the silent boughs the lissom[2] air
5 Rested; and, only when it went, they
    moved,
Nor more than under linnet springing off.
Such was the wedding morn: the joyous
    Year
Leapt over March and April up to May.
Regent of rising and of ebbing hearts,
10 Thyself borne on in cool serenity,
All heaven around and bending over thee,
All earth below and watchful of thy
    course!
Well hast thou chosen, after long demur
To aspirations from more realms than one.
15 Peace be with those thou leavest! peace
    with thee!
Is that enough to wish thee? not enough,
But very much: for Love himself feels
    pain,
While brighter plumage shoots, to shed
    last year's;
And one at home (how dear that one!)
    recalls
20 Thy name, and thou recallest one at home.
Yet turn not back thine eyes; the hour of
    tears
Is over; nor believe thou that Romance
Closes against pure Faith her rich domain.
Shall only blossoms flourish there? Arise,

---

[1] The daughter of Rose Aylmer's half-sister.
See Landor's *Rose Aylmer* (p. 989), and *The
Three Roses* (p. 1009).
[2] nimble

25 Far sighted bride! look forward! clearer
        views
And higher hopes lie under calmer skies.
Fortune in vain call'd out to thee; in vain
Rays from high regions darted; Wit
        pour'd out
His sparkling treasures; Wisdom laid his
        crown
30 Of richer jewels at thy reckless feet.
Well hast thou chosen. I repeat the words,
Adding as true ones, not untold before,
That incense must have fire for its ascent,
Else 'tis inert and can not reach the idol.
35 Youth is the sole equivalent of youth.
Enjoy it while it lasts; and last it will;
Love can prolong it in despite of Years.

ONE YEAR AGO MY PATH WAS GREEN
1846

One year ago my path was green,
My footstep light, my brow serene;
Alas! and could it have been so
        One year ago?

5 There is a love that is to last
When the hot days of youth are past:
Such love did a sweet maid bestow
        One year ago.

I took a leaflet from her braid
10 And gave it to another maid.
Love! broken should have been thy bow
        One year ago.

YES; I WRITE VERSES NOW AND THEN
1846

Yes; I write verses now and then,
But blunt and flaccid is my pen,
No longer talk'd of by young men
        As rather clever:
5 In the last quarter are my eyes,
You see it by their form and size;
Is it not time then to be wise?
        Or now or never.

Fairest that ever sprang from Eve!
10 While Time allows the short reprieve,
Just look at me! would you believe
        'Twas once a lover?
I cannot clear the five-bar gate,
But, trying first its timbers' state,
15 Climb stiffly up, take breath, and wait
        To trundle over.

Thro' gallopade[1] I cannot swing
The entangling blooms of Beauty's spring:
I cannot say the tender thing,

[1] A kind of lively dance.

20   Be't true or false,
And am beginning to opine
Those girls are only half-divine
Whose waists yon wicked boys entwine
        In giddy waltz.

25 I fear that arm above that shoulder,
I wish them wiser, graver, older,
Sedater, and no harm if colder
        And panting less.
Ah! people were not half so wild
30 In former days, when, starchly mild,
Upon her high-heel'd Essex smiled
        The brave Queen Bess.

THE LEAVES ARE FALLING; SO AM I
1846

The leaves are falling; so am I;
The few late flowers have moisture in the
        eye;
        So have I too.
Scarcely on any bough is heard
5 Joyous, or even unjoyous, bird
        The whole wood through.
Winter may come: he brings but nigher
His circle (yearly narrowing) to the fire
        Where old friends meet:
10 Let him; now heaven is overcast,
And spring and summer both are past,
        And all things sweet.

THE PLACE WHERE SOON I THINK TO LIE
1846

The place where soon I think to lie,
In its old creviced nook hard-by
        Rears many a weed:
If parties bring you there, will you
5 Drop slily in a grain or two
        Of wall-flower seed?

I shall not see it, and (too sure!)
I shall not ever hear that your
        Light step was there;
10 But the rich odor some fine day
Will, what I cannot do, repay
        That little care.

GIVE ME THE EYES THAT LOOK ON MINE
1846

Give me the eyes that look on mine,
And, when they see them dimly shine,
        Are moister than they were.
Give me the eyes that fain would find
5 Some relics of a youthful mind
        Amid the wrecks of care.
Give me the eyes that catch at last
A few faint glimpses of the past,

And, like the arkite dove,
10 Bring back a long-lost olive-bough,[1]
And can discover even now
    A heart that once could love.

TWENTY YEARS HENCE MY EYES MAY GROW
1846

Twenty years hence my eyes may grow
If not quite dim, yet rather so,
Still yours from others they shall know
    Twenty years hence.

5 Twenty years hence tho' it may hap
That I be call'd to take a nap
In a cool cell where thunder-clap
    Was never heard,

There breathe but o'er my arch of grass
10 A not too sadly sigh'd *Alas,*
And I shall catch, ere you can pass,
    That wingèd word.

PROUD WORD YOU NEVER SPOKE
1846

Proud word you never spoke, but you will
    speak
    Four not exempt from pride some fu-
    ture day.
Resting on one white hand a warm wet
    cheek
Over my open volume you will say,
5 "This man loved *me!*" then rise and
    trip away.

ALAS, HOW SOON THE HOURS ARE OVER
1846

Alas, how soon the hours are over
Counted us out to play the lover!
And how much narrower is the stage
Allotted us to play the sage!
5 But when we play the fool, how wide,
The theatre expands! beside,
How long the audience sits before us!
How many prompters! what a chorus!

MY HOPES RETIRE; MY WISHES AS BEFORE
1846

My hopes retire; my wishes as before
    Struggle to find their resting-place in
    vain;
The ebbing sea thus beats against the
    shore;
    The shore repels it; it returns again.

[1] See *Genesis,* 8:8-11.

VARIOUS THE ROADS OF LIFE; IN ONE
1846

Various the roads of life; in one
    All terminate, one lonely way.
We go; and "Is he gone?"
    Is all our best friends say.

IS IT NOT BETTER AT AN EARLY HOUR
1846

Is it not better at an early hour
    In its calm cell to rest the weary head,
While birds are singing and while blooms
    the bower,
    Than sit the fire out and go starv'd to
    bed?

PURSUITS! ALAS, I NOW HAVE NONE
1846

Pursuits! alas, I now have none,
    But idling where were once pursuits,
Often, all morning quite alone,
    I sit upon those twisted roots
5 Which rise above the grass, and shield
    Our harebell, when the churlish year
Catches her coming first afield,
    And she looks pale tho' spring is near;
I chase the violets, that would hide
10   Their little prudish heads away,
And argue with the rills, that chide
    When we discover them at play.

WITH AN ALBUM
1846

I know not whether I am proud,
But this I know, I hate the crowd:
Therefore pray let me disengage
My verses from the motley page,
5 Where others far more sure to please
Pour out their choral song with ease.

And yet perhaps, if some should tire
With too much froth or too much fire,
There is an ear that may incline
10 Even to words so dull as mine.

THE DAY RETURNS, MY NATAL DAY
1846

The day returns, my natal day,
    Borne on the storm and pale with snow,
And seems to ask me why I stay,
    Stricken by Time and bowed by Woe.

5 Many were once the friends who came
    To wish me joy; and there are some

Who wish it now; but not the same;
    They are whence friend can never come.

Nor are they you my love watch'd o'er
10   Cradled in innocence and sleep;
You smile into my eyes no more,
    Nor see the bitter tears they weep.

HOW MANY VOICES GAILY SING
1846

How many voices gaily sing,
  "O happy morn, O happy spring
Of life!'' Meanwhile there comes o'er me
A softer voice from Memory,
5 And says, ''If loves and hopes have flown
With years, think too what griefs are
    gone!''

TO ROBERT BROWNING
1846

There is delight in singing, tho' none hear
Beside the singer; and there is delight
In praising, tho' the praiser sit alone
And see the prais'd far off him, far above.
5 Shakespeare is not our poet, but the
    world's,
Therefore on him no speech! and brief for
    thee,
Browning! Since Chaucer was alive and
    hale,
No man hath walked along our roads with
    step
So active, so inquiring eye, or tongue
10 So varied in discourse. But warmer climes[1]
Give brighter plumage, strong wing: the
    breeze
Of Alpine heights thou playest with, borne
    on
Beyond Sorrento and Amalfi, where
The Siren waits thee, singing song for
    song.

From THE HELLENICS[2]
1846-59

ON THE HELLENICS
1847

Come back, ye wandering Muses, come
    back home,
Ye seem to have forgotten where it lies:
Come, let us walk upon the silent sands
Of Simois, where deep footmarks show
    long strides;
5 Thence we may mount, perhaps, to higher
    ground,
Where Aphroditè from Athenè won
The golden apple, and from Herè too,

[1] Browning had just married Elizabeth Barrett,
  and moved to Italy.
[2] A group of poems by Landor on Greek topics.

And happy Ares shouted far below.
  Or would ye rather choose the grassy
    vale
10 Where flows Anapos thro' anemones,
Hyacinths, and narcissuses, that bend
To show their rival beauty in the stream?
  Bring with you each her lyre, and each
    in turn
Temper a graver with a lighter song.

THRASYMEDES AND EUNÖE
1846

Who will away to Athens with me? who
Loves choral songs and maidens crown'd
    with flowers,
Unenvious? mount the pinnace; hoist the
    sail.
I promise ye, as many as are here,
5 Ye shall not, while ye tarry with me, taste
From unrinsed barrel the diluted wine
Of a low vineyard or a plant ill-pruned,
But such as anciently the Ægean isles
Pour'd in libation at their solemn feasts:
10 And the same goblets shall ye grasp, em-
    boss'd
With no vile figures of loose languid boors,
But such as gods have lived with and have
    led.
  The sea smiles bright before us. What
    white sail
Plays yonder? What pursues it? Like
    two hawks
15 Away they fly. Let us away in time
To overtake them. Are they menaces
We hear? And shall the strong repulse
    the weak,
Enraged at her defender? Hippias!
Art thou the man? 'Twas Hippias. He
    had found
20 His sister borne from the Cecropian port[1]
By Thrasymedes. And reluctantly?
Ask, ask the maiden; I have no reply.
''Brother! O brother Hippias! O, if love,
If pity, ever touch'd thy breast, forbear!
25 Strike not the brave, the gentle, the be-
    loved,
My Thrasymedes, with his cloak alone
Protecting his own head and mine from
    harm.''
''Didst thou not once before,'' cried Hip-
    pias,
Regardless of his sister, hoarse with wrath
30 At Thrasymedes, ''didst not thou, dog-
    eyed,
Dare, as she walk'd up to the Parthenon,
On the most holy of all holy days,
In sight of all the city, dare to kiss
Her maiden cheek?''

[1] Athens.

"Ay, before all the gods,
35 Ay, before Pallas, before Artemis,
Ay, before Aphroditè, before Herè,
I dared; and dare again. Arise, my
    spouse!
Arise! and let my lips quaff purity
From thy fair open brow."
                         The sword was up,
40 And yet he kiss'd her twice. Some god
    withheld
The arm of Hippias; his proud blood
    seeth'd slower
And smote his breast less angrily; he laid
His hand on the white shoulder, and spake
    thus:
"Ye must return with me. A second time
45 Offended, will our sire Pisistratos
Pardon the affront? Thou shouldst have
    ask'd thyself
This question ere the sail first flapp'd the
    mast."
"Already thou hast taken life from me;
Put up thy sword," said the sad youth,
    his eyes
50 Sparkling; but whether love or rage or
    grief
They sparkled with, the gods alone could
    see.
Piræeus they re-entered, and their ship
Drove up the little waves against the quay,
Whence was thrown out a rope from one
    above,
55 And Hippias caught it. From the virgin's
    waist
Her lover dropp'd his arm, and blush'd to
    think
He had retain'd it there in sight of rude
Irreverent men: he led her forth, nor
    spake.
Hippias walked silent too, until they
    reach'd
60 The mansion of Pisistratos her sire.
Serenely in his sternness did the prince
Look on them both awhile: they saw not
    him,
For both had cast their eyes upon the
    ground.
"Are these the pirates thou hast taken,
    son?"
65 Said he. "Worse, father! worse than
    pirates they,
Who thus abuse thy patience, thus abuse
Thy pardon, thus abuse the holy rites
Twice over."
"Well hast thou performed thy duty,"
Firmly and gravely said Pisistratos.
70 "Nothing then, rash young man! could
    turn thy heart
From Eunöe, my daughter?"

"Nothing, sir,
Shall ever turn it. I can die but once
And love but once. O Eunöe! farewell!"
"Nay, she shall see what thou canst bear
    for her."
75 "O father! shut me in my chamber, shut
    me
In my poor mother's tomb, dead or alive,
But never let me see what he can bear;
I know how much that is, when borne for
    me."
"Not yet: come on. And lag not thou
    behind,
80 Pirate of virgin and of princely hearts!
Before the people and before the goddess
Thou hadst evinced the madness of thy
    passion,
And now wouldst bear from home and
    plenteousness
To poverty and exile this my child."
85 Then shuddered Thrasymedes, and ex-
    claim'd,
"I see my crime; I saw it not before.
The daughter of Pisistratos was born
Neither for exile nor for poverty,
Ah! nor for me!" He would have wept,
    but one
90 Might see him, and weep worse. The
    prince unmoved
Strode on, and said, "Tomorrow shall the
    people,
All who beheld thy trespasses, behold
The justice of Pisistratos, the love
He bears his daughter, and the reverence
95 In which he holds the highest law of God."
He spake; and on the morrow they were
    one.

IPHIGENEIA AND AGAMEMNON
1846

Iphigeneia, when she heard her doom
At Aulis, and when all beside the King
Had gone away, took his right hand, and
    said,
"O father! I am young and very happy.
5 I do not think the pious Calchas heard
Distinctly what the goddess spake. Old-
    age
Obscures the senses. If my nurse, who
    knew
My voice so well, sometimes misunderstood
While I was resting on her knee both arms
10 And hitting it to make her mind my words,
And looking in her face, and she in mine,
Might he not also hear one word amiss,
Spoken from so far off, even from Olym-
    pus?"
The father placed his cheek upon her head,

15 And tears dropp'd down it, but the king
     of men
   Replied not. Then the maiden spake once
     more.
   "O father! sayst thou nothing? Hear'st
     thou not
   Me, whom thou ever hast, until this hour,
   Listen'd to fondly, and awaken'd me
20 To hear my voice amid the voice of birds,
   When it was inarticulate as theirs,
   And the down deadened it within the
     nest?"
   He moved her gently from him, silent
     still,
   And this, and this alone, brought tears
     from her,
25 Altho' she saw fate nearer: then with
     sighs,
   "I thought to have laid down my hair
     before
   Benignant Artemis, and not have dimmed
   Her polish'd altar with my virgin blood;
   I thought to have selected the white flowers
30 To please the Nymphs, and to have ask'd
     of each
   By name, and with no sorrowful regret,
   Whether, since both my parents will'd the
     change,
   I might at Hymen's feet bend my clipp'd
     brow;
   And (after those who mind us girls the
     most)
35 Adore our own Athena,[1] that she would
   Regard me mildly with her azure eyes,
   But father! to see you no more, and see
   Your love, O father! go ere I am gone"—
   Gently he moved her off, and drew her
     back,
40 Bending his lofty head far over hers,
   And the dark depths of nature heaved
     and burst.
   He turn'd away; not far, but silent still.
   She now first shudder'd; for in him, so
     nigh,
   So long a silence seem'd the approach of
     death,
45 And like it. Once again she rais'd her
     voice.
   "O father! if the ships are now detain'd,
   And all your vows move not the gods
     above,
   When the knife strikes me there will be
     one prayer
   The less to them: and purer can there
     be
50 Any, or more fervent than the daughter's
     prayer
   For her dear father's safety and success?"

1 Athena was the patroness of Argos.

A groan that shook him shook not his re-
     solve.
An aged man now enter'd, and without
One word, stepp'd slowly on, and took the
     wrist
55 Of the pale maiden. She look'd up and
     saw
The fillet of the priest and calm cold eyes.
Then turn'd she where her parent stood,
     and cried,
"O father! grieve no more: the ships can
     sail."

THE HAMADRYAD[1]
1846

Rhaicos was born amid the hills wherefrom
Gnidos the light of Caria is discern'd,
And small are the white-crested that play
     near,
And smaller onward are the purple waves.
5 Thence festal choirs were visible, all
     crown'd
With rose and myrtle if they were inborn;
If from Pandion sprang they, on the coast
Where stern Athenè raised her citadel,
Then olive was intwined with violets
10 Cluster'd in bosses,[2] regular and large.
For various men wore various coronals;
But one was their devotion; 'twas to her
Whose laws all follow, her whose smile
     withdraws
The sword from Ares, thunderbolt from
     Zeus,
15 And whom in his chill cave the mutable
Of mind, Poseidon, the sea-king, reveres,
And whom his brother, stubborn Dis, hath
     pray'd
To turn in pity the averted cheek
Of her he bore away,[3] with promises,
20 Nay, with loud oath before dread Styx
     itself,
To give her daily more and sweeter flowers
Than he made drop from her on Enna's
     dell.

   Rhaicos was looking from his father's
     door
At the long trains that hastened to the
     town
25 From all the valleys, like bright rivulets
Gurgling with gladness, wave outrunning
     wave,
And thought it hard he might not also go
And offer up one prayer, and press one
     hand,

1 See Lowell's *Rhœcus.*
2 raised ornaments
3 Proserpina.

He knew not whose. The father call'd
   him in,
30 And said, "Son Rhaicos! those are idle
   games;
Long enough I have lived to find them so."
And ere he ended sighed, as old men do
Always, to think how idle such games are.
"I have not yet," thought Rhaicos in his
   heart,
35 And wanted proof.
            "Suppose thou go and help
Echeion at the hill, to bark yon oak
And lop its branches off, before we delve
About the trunk and ply the root with
   axe:
This we may do in winter."
                    Rhaicos went;
40 For thence he could see farther, and see
   more
Of those who hurried to the city-gate.
Echeion he found there with naked arm
Swart-hair'd, strong-sinew'd, and his eyes
   intent
Upon the place where first the axe should
   fall:
45 He held it upright. "There are bees about,
Or wasps, or hornets," said the cautious
   eld,
"Look sharp, O son of Thallinos!" The
   youth
Inclined his ear, afar, and warily,
And cavern'd in his hand. He heard a
   buzz
50 At first, and then the sound grew soft and
   clear,
And then divided into what seem'd tune,
And there were words upon it, plaintive
   words.
He turn'd, and said, "Echeion! do not
   strike
That tree: it must be hollow; for some god
55 Speaks from within. Come thyself near."
   Again
Both turn'd toward it: and behold! there
   sat
Upon the moss below, with her two palms
Pressing it, on each side, a maid in form.
Downcast were her long eyelashes, and pale
60 Her cheek, but never mountain-ash dis-
   play'd
Berries of color like her lip so pure,
Nor were the anemones about her hair
Soft, smooth, and wavering like the face
   beneath.
"What dost thou here?" Echeion, half-
   afraid,
65 Half-angry cried. She lifted up her eyes,
But nothing spake she. Rhaicos drew one
   step

Backward, for fear came likewise over
   him,
But not such fear: he panted, gasp'd,
   drew in
His breath, and would have turn'd it into
   words,
70 But could not into one.
                    "O send away
That sad old man!" said she. The old man
   went
Without a warning from his master's
   son,
Glad to escape, for sorely he now fear'd.
And the axe shone behind him in their
   eyes.
75   *Hamad.* And wouldst thou too shed the
   most innocent
Of blood? No vow demands it; no god
   wills
The oak to bleed.
   Rhaicos.   Who art thou? whence?
   why here?
And whither wouldst thou go? Among the
   robed
In white or saffron, or the hue that most
80 Resembles dawn or the clear sky, is none
Array'd as thou art. What so beautiful
As that gray robe which clings about thee
   close,
Like moss to stones adhering, leaves to
   trees,
Yet lets thy bosom rise and fall in turn,
85 As, touch'd by zephyrs, fall and rise the
   boughs
Of graceful platan[1] by the river-side?
   Hamad. Lovest thou well thy father's
   house?
   Rhaicos.   Indeed
I love it, well I love it, yet would leave
For thine, where'er it be, my father's
   house,
90 With all the marks upon the door, that
   show
My growth at every birthday since the
   third,
And all the charms, o'erpowering evil
   eyes,
My mother nail'd for me against my bed,
And the Cydonian[2] bow (which thou shalt
   see)
95 Won in my race last spring from Euty-
   chos.
   Hamad. Bethink thee what it is to leave
   a home
Thou never yet hast left, one night, one
   day.

[1] plane tree
[2] of Cydonia (an ancient city on the coast of
   Crete, famous for its archers)

Rhaicos. No, 'tis not hard to leave it;
'tis not hard
To leave, O maiden, that paternal home,
100 If there be one on earth whom we may love
First, last, forever; one who says that she
Will love forever too. To say which word,
Only to say it, surely is enough—
It shows such kindness—if 'twere possible
105 We at the moment think she would indeed.
  Hamad. Who taught thee all this folly
at thy age?
  Rhaicos. I have seen lovers and have
learn'd to love.
  Hamad. But wilt thou spare the tree?
  Rhaicos. My father wants
The bark; the tree may hold its place
awhile.
110   *Hamad.* Awhile! thy father numbers
then my days?
  Rhaicos. Are there no others where the
moss beneath
Is quite as tufty? Who would send thee
forth
Or ask thee why thou tarriest? Is thy flock
Anywhere near?
  Hamad.   I have no flock: I kill
115 Nothing that breathes, that stirs, that feels
the air,
The sun, the dew. Why should the beautiful
(And thou art beautiful) disturb the source
Whence springs all beauty? Hast thou
never heard
Of Hamadryads?
  Rhaicos.   Heard of them I have:
120 Tell me some tale about them. May I sit
Beside thy feet? Art thou not tired? The
herbs
Are very soft; I will not come too nigh;
Do but sit there, nor tremble so, nor doubt.
Stay, stay an instant: let me first explore
125 If any acorn of last year be left
Within it; thy thin robe too ill protects
Thy dainty limbs against the harm one
small
Acorn may do. Here's none. Another day
Trust me; till then let me sit opposite.
130   *Hamad.* I seat me; be thou seated, and
content.
  Rhaicos. O sight for gods! ye men below! adore
The Aphroditè. *Is* she there below?
Or sits she here before me, as she sate
Before the shepherd on those heights that
shade
135 The Hellespont, and brought his kindred
woe?

  Hamad. Reverence the higher Powers;
nor deem amiss
Of her who pleads to thee, and would
repay—
Ask not how much—but very much. Rise
not;
No, Rhaicos, no! Without the nuptial vow
140 Love is unholy. Swear to me that none
Of mortal maids shall ever taste thy kiss,
Then take thou mine; then take it, not
before.
  Rhaicos. Hearken, all gods above! O
Aphroditè!
O Herè! Let my vow be ratified!
145 But wilt thou come into my father's house?
  Hamad. Nay; and of mine I cannot
give thee part.
  Rhaicos. Where is it?
  Hamad.   In this oak.
  Rhaicos.   Ay; now begins
The tale of Hamadryad; tell it through.
  Hamad. Pray of thy father never to
cut down
150 My tree; and promise him, as well thou
mayst,
That every year he shall receive from me
More honey than will buy him nine fat
sheep,
More wax than he will burn to all the gods.
Why fallest thou upon thy face? Some
thorn
155 May scratch it, rash young man! Rise up;
for shame!
  Rhaicos. For shame I can not rise. O
pity me!
I dare not sue for love—but do not hate!
Let me once more behold thee—not once
more,
But many days: let me love on—unloved!
160 I aimed too high: on my head the bolt
Falls back, and pierces to the very brain.
  Hamad. Go—rather go, than make me
say I love.
  Rhaicos. If happiness is immortality,
(And whence enjoy it else the gods above?)
165 I am immortal too: my vow is heard:
Hark! on the left—Nay, turn not from
me now,
I claim my kiss.
  Hamad.   Do men take first, then claim?
Do thus the seasons run their course with
them?

Her lips were seal'd, her head sank on
his breast.
170 'Tis said that laughs were heard within
the wood:
But who should hear them?—and whose
laughs? and why?

Savory was the smell, and long past noon,
Thallinos! in thy house: for marjoram,
Basil and mint, and thyme and rosemary,
175 Were sprinkled on the kid's well roasted length,
Awaiting Rhaicos. Home he came at last,
Not hungry, but pretending hunger keen,
With head and eyes just o'er the maple plate.
"Thou seest but badly, coming from the sun,
180 Boy Rhaicos!" said the father. "That oak's bark
Must have been tough, with little sap between;
It ought to run; but it and I are old."
Rhaicos, although each morsel of the bread
Increas'd by chewing, and the meat grew cold
185 And tasteless to his palate, took a draught
Of gold-bright wine, which, thirsty as he was,
He thought not of until his father fill'd
The cup, averring water was amiss,
But wine had been at all times pour'd on kid,—
190 It was religion.

He thus fortified
Said, not quite boldly, and not quite abash'd,
"Father, that oak is Zeus's own; that oak
Year after year will bring thee wealth from wax
And honey. There is one who fears the gods
195 And the gods love—that one"
(He blush'd, nor said
What one)
"Has promis'd this, and may do more.
Thou hast not many moons to wait until
The bees have done their best; if then there come
Nor wax nor honey, let the tree be hewn."
200 "Zeus hath bestow'd on thee a prudent mind,"
Said the glad sire; "but look thou often there,
And gather all the honey thou canst find
In every crevice, over and above
What has been promis'd; would they reckon that?"

205 Rhaicos went daily; but the nymph as oft,
Invisible. To play at love, she knew,
Stopping its breathings when it breathes most soft,
Is sweeter than to play on any pipe.

She play'd on his: she fed upon his sighs;
210 They pleased her when they gently waved her hair,
Cooling the pulses of her purple veins,
And when her absence brought them out, they pleased.
Even among the fondest of them all,
What mortal or immortal maid is more
215 Content with giving happiness than pain?
One day he was returning from the wood
Despondently. She pitied him, and said
"Come back!" and twined her fingers in the hem
Above his shoulder. Then she led his steps
220 To a cool rill that ran o'er level sand
Through lentisk[1] and through oleander,[2] there
Bathed she his feet, lifting them on her lap
When bathed, and drying them in both her hands.
He dared complain; for those who most are loved
225 Most dare it; but not harsh was his complaint.
"O thou inconstant!" said he, "if stern law
Bind thee, or will, stronger than sternest law,
O, let me know henceforward when to hope
The fruit of love that grows for me but here."
230 He spake; and pluck'd it from its pliant stem.
"Impatient Rhaicos! Why thus intercept
The answer I would give? There is a bee
Whom I have fed, a bee who knows my thoughts
And executes my wishes: I will send
235 That messenger. If ever thou art false,
Drawn by another, own it not, but drive
My bee away; then shall I know my fate,
And—for thou must be wretched—weep at thine.
But often as my heart persuades to lay
240 Its cares on thine and throb itself to rest,
Expect her with thee, whether it be morn
Or eve, at any time when woods are safe."

Day after day the Hours beheld them blest,
And season after season: years had past,
245 Blest were they still. He who asserts that Love
Ever is sated of sweet things, the same
Sweet things he fretted for in earlier days,
Never, by Zeus! loved he a Hamadryad.

[1] A kind of sweet shrub.
[2] A poisonous evergreen shrub with fragrant flowers.

The night had now grown longer, and perhaps
250 The Hamadryads find them lone and dull
Among their woods; one did, alas! She called
Her faithful bee: 'twas when all bees should sleep,
And all did sleep but hers. She was sent forth
To bring that light which never wintry blast
255 Blows out, nor rain nor snow extinguishes,
The light that shines from loving eyes upon
Eyes that love back, till they can see no more.

Rhaicos was sitting at his father's hearth:
Between them stood the table, not o'er-spread
260 With fruits which autumn now profusely bore,
Nor anise cakes,[1] nor odorous wine; but there
The draft-board was expanded; at which game
Triumphant sat old Thallinos; the son
Was puzzled, vex'd, discomfited, dis-traught.
265 A buzz was at his ear: up went his hand,
And it was heard no longer. The poor bee
Return'd, (but not until the morn shone bright)
And found the Hamadryad with her head
Upon her aching wrist, and showed one wing
270 Half-broken off, the other's meshes marr'd,
And there were bruises which no eye could see
Saving a Hamadryad's.
At this sight
Down fell the languid brow, both hands fell down,
A shriek was carried to the ancient hall
275 Of Thallinos: he heard it not: his son
Heard it, and ran forthwith into the wood.
No bark was on the tree, no leaf was green,
The trunk was riven through. From that day forth
Nor word nor whisper sooth'd his ear, nor sound
280 Even of insect wing; but loud laments
The woodmen and the shepherds one long year
Heard day and night; for Rhaicos would not quit

---

[1] Cakes flavored with the fruit or seed of the anise plant.

The solitary place, but moan'd and died.
Hence milk and honey wonder not, O guest,
285 To find set duly on the hollow stone.

SHAKESPEARE AND MILTON
1853

The tongue of England, that which myriads
Have spoken and will speak, were para-lyzed
Hereafter, but two mighty men stand forth
Above the flight of ages, two alone;
5 One crying out,
All nations spoke thro' me.
The other:
True; and thro' this trumpet burst
God's word; the fall of Angels, and the doom
First of immortal, then of mortal, Man.
Glory! be glory! not to me, to God.

TO YOUTH
1853

Where art thou gone, light-ankled Youth?
With wing at either shoulder,
And smile that never left thy mouth
Until the Hours grew colder:

5 Then somewhat seem'd to whisper near
That thou and I must part;
I doubted it; I felt no fear,
No weight upon the heart.

If aught befell it, Love was by
10 And roll'd it off again;
So, if there ever was a sigh,
'Twas not a sigh of pain.

I may not call thee back; but thou
Returnest when the hand
15 Of gentle Sleep waves o'er my brow
His poppy-crested wand;

Then smiling eyes bend over mine,
Then lips once press'd invite;
But sleep hath given a silent sign,
20 And both, alas! take flight.

TO AGE
1853

Welcome, old friend! These many years
Have we lived door by door:
The Fates have laid aside their shears
Perhaps for some few more.

5 I was indocile at an age
When better boys were taught,
But thou at length hast made me sage,
If I am sage in aught.

Little I know from other men,
10 Too little they from me,
But thou hast pointed well the pen
That writes these lines to thee.

Thanks for expelling Fear and Hope,
One vile, the other vain;
15 One's scourge, the other's telescope,
I shall not see again:

Rather what lies before my feet
My notice shall engage—
He who hath braved Youth's dizzy heat
20 Dreads not the frost of Age.

THE CHRYSOLITES[1] AND RUBIES BACCHUS BRINGS
1853

The chrysolites and rubies Bacchus brings
To crown the feast where swells the
broad-vein'd brow,
Where maidens blush at what the minstrel
sings,
They who have coveted may covet now.

5 Bring me, in cool alcove, the grape un-
crush'd,
The peach of pulpy cheek and down
mature,
Where every voice (but bird's or child's)
is hush'd,
And every thought, like the brook nigh,
runs pure.

SO THEN, I FEEL NOT DEEPLY!
1853

So then, I feel not deeply! if I did,
I should have seized the pen and pierced
therewith
The passive world!
            And thus thou reasonest?
Well hast thou known the lover's, not so
well
5 The poet's heart: while that heart bleeds,
the hand
Presses it close. Grief must run on and
pass
Into near Memory's more quiet shade
Before it can compose itself in song.
He who is agonized and turns to show
10 His agony to those who sit around
Seizes the pen in vain: thought, fancy,
power,
Rush back into his bosom; all the strength
Of genius can not draw them into light
From under mastering Grief; but Memory,
15 The Muse's mother, nurses, rears them up,
Informs, and keeps them with her all her
days.
1 yellow or greenish gems

ON MUSIC
1853

Many love music but for music's sake,
Many because her touches can awake
Thoughts that repose within the breast
half-dead,
And rise to follow where she loves to lead.
5 What various feelings come from days
gone by!
What tears from far-off sources dim the
eye!
Few, when light fingers with sweet voices
play
And melodies swell, pause, and melt away,
Mind how at every touch, at every tone,
10 A spark of life hath glisten'd and hath
gone.

DEATH STANDS ABOVE ME
1853

Death stands above me, whispering low
I know not what into my ear:
Of his strange language all I know
Is, there is not a word of fear.

ON HIS SEVENTY-FIFTH BIRTHDAY
1853

I strove with none; for none was worth
my strife,
Nature I loved, and next to Nature, Art;
I warmed both hands before the fire of life,
It sinks, and I am ready to depart.

I ENTREAT YOU, ALFRED TENNYSON
1853

I entreat you, Alfred Tennyson,
Come and share my haunch of venison.
I have too a bin of claret,
Good, but better when you share it.
5 Tho' 'tis only a small bin,
There's a stock of it within.
And as sure as I'm a rhymer,
Half a butt of Rudesheimer.
Come; among the sons of men is one
10 Welcomer than Alfred Tennyson?

TO E. ARUNDELL
1853

Nature! thou mayest fume and fret,
There's but one white violet;
Scatter o'er the vernal ground
Faint resemblances around,
5 Nature! I will tell thee yet
There's but one white violet.

AGE
1853

Death, tho' I see him not, is near
And grudges me my eightieth year.

Now, I would give him all these last
For one that fifty have run past.
5 Ah! he strikes all things, all alike,
But bargains: those he will not strike.

TO HIS YOUNG ROSE AN OLD MAN SAID
1853

To his young Rose an old man said,
"You will be sweet when I am dead:
Where skies are brightest we shall meet,
And there will you be yet more sweet,
5 Leaving your winged company
To waste an idle thought on me."

NAY, THANK ME NOT AGAIN FOR THOSE
1853

Nay, thank me not again for those
Camelias, that untimely rose;
But if, whence you might please the more
And win the few unwon before,
5 I sought the flowers you loved to wear,
O'erjoy'd to see them in your hair,
Upon my grave, I pray you, set
One primrose or one violet.
——Stay——I can wait a little yet.

ONE LOVELY NAME ADORNS MY SONG
1853

One lovely name adorns my song,
And, dwelling in the heart,
Forever falters at the tongue,
And trembles to depart.

SEPARATION
1853

There is a mountain and a wood between
us,
Where the lone shepherd and late bird
have seen us
Morning and noon and even-tide repass.
Between us now the mountain and the wood
Seem standing darker than last year they
stood,
And say we must not cross, alas! alas!

ALL IS NOT OVER WHILE THE SHADE
1853

All is not over while the shade
Of parting life, if now aslant,
Rests on the scene whereon it play'd
And taught a docile heart to pant.
5 Autumn is passing by; his day
Shines mildly yet on gather'd sheaves,
And, tho' the grape be plucked away,
Its color glows amid the leaves.

GOD SCATTERS BEAUTY AS HE SCATTERS FLOWERS
1853

God scatters beauty as he scatters flowers
O'er the wide earth, and tells us all are
ours.
A hundred lights in every temple burn,
And at each shrine I bend my knee in turn.

THOU NEEDST NOT PITCH UPON MY HAT
1853

Thou needst not pitch upon my hat,
Thou wither'd leaf! to show how near
Is now the winter of my year;
Alas! I want no hint of that.

5 Prythee, ah prythee, get along!
Whisper as gently in the ear,
I once could whisper in, to fear
No change, but live for dance and song.

TO A CYCLAMEN
1853

I come to visit thee again,
My little flowerless cyclamen;
To touch the hand, almost to press,
That cheer'd thee in thy loneliness.
5 What could thy careful guardian find
Of thee in form, of me in mind,
What is there in us rich or rare,
To make us claim a moment's care?
Unworthy to be so caress'd,
10 We are but withering leaves at best.

ON SOUTHEY'S DEATH
1858

Friends! hear the words my wandering
thoughts would say,
And cast them into shape some other day.
Southey, my friend of forty years, is gone,
And, shattered by the fall, I stand alone.

THE THREE ROSES[1]
1858

When the buds began to burst,
Long ago, with Rose the First,
I was walking; joyous then
Far above all other men,
5 Till before us up there stood
Britonferry's oaken wood,
Whispering, "*Happy as thou art,
Happiness and thou must part.*"
Many summers have gone by
10 Since a Second Rose and I
(Rose from that same stem) have told
This and other tales of old.

[1] Rose Aylmer (see *Rose Aylmer*, p. 989), the
daughter of her half-sister, and her grand-
niece.

She upon her wedding-day
Carried home my tenderest lay:[1]
15 From her lap I now have heard
Gleeful, chirping, Rose the Third,
Not for *her* this hand of mine
Rhyme with nuptial wreath shall twine;
Cold and torpid it must lie,
20 Mute the tongue and closed the eye.

LATELY OUR SONGSTERS LOITER'D IN GREEN LANES
1863

Lately our songsters loiter'd in green lanes,
Content to catch the ballads of the plains;
I fancied I had strength enough to climb
A loftier station at no distant time,
5 And might securely from intrusion doze,
Upon the flowers thro' which Ilissus flows.
In those pale olive grounds all voices cease,
And from afar dust fills the paths of Greece.
My slumber broken, and my doublet torn,
10 I find the laurel[2] also bears a thorn.

From HEROIC IDYLS
1863
THESEUS AND HIPPOLYTA

Hippolyta. Eternal hatred I have sworn against
The persecutor of my sisterhood;
In vain, proud son of Ægeus, hast thou snapped
Their arrows and derided them; in vain
5 Leadest thou me a captive; I can die,
And die I will.
    Theseus. Nay; many are the years
Of youth and beauty for Hippolyta.
    Hippolyta. I scorn my youth, I hate my beauty. Go!
Monster! of all the monsters in these wilds
10 Most frightful and most odious to my sight.
    Theseus. I boast not that I saved thee from the bow
Of Scythian.
    Hippolyta. And for what? To die disgraced.
Strong as thou art, yet thou art not so strong
As Death is, when we call him for support.
15   *Theseus.* Him too will I ward off; he strikes me first,
Hippolyta, long after, when these eyes
Are closed, and when the knee that supplicates
Can bend no more.

[1] *To a Bride* (p. 998).
[2] The laurel is an emblem of honor or victory.

    Hippolyta. Is the man mad?
    Theseus. He is.
    Hippolyta. So, thou canst tell one truth, however false
In other things.
20   *Theseus.* What other? Thou dost pause,
And thine eyes wander over the smooth turf
As if some gem (but gem thou wearest not)
Had fallen from the remnant of thy hair.
Hippolyta! speak plainly, answer me,
25 What have I done to raise thy fear or hate?
    Hippolyta. Fear I despise, perfidy I abhor.
Unworthy man! did Heracles delude
The maids who trusted him?
    Theseus. Did ever I?
Whether he did or not, they never told me:
30 I would have chided him.
    Hippolyta. Thou chide him! thou!
The Spartan mothers well remember thee.
    Theseus. Scorn adds no beauty to the beautiful.
Heracles was beloved by Omphale,
He never parted from her, but obey'd
35 Her slightest wish, as Theseus will Hippolyta's.
    Hippolyta. Then leave me, leave me instantly; I know
The way to my own country.
    Theseus. This command,
And only this, my heart must disobey.
My country shall be thine, and there thy state
40 Regal.
    Hippolyta. Am I a child? Give me my own,
And keep for weaker heads thy diadems.
Thermodon I shall never see again,
Brightest of rivers, into whose clear depth
My mother plunged me from her warmer breast,
45 And taught me early to divide the waves
With arms each day more strong, and soon to chase
And overtake the father swan, nor heed
His hoarser voice or his uplifted wing.
Where are my sisters? are there any left?
    Theseus. I hope it.
50   *Hippolyta.* And I fear it: theirs may be
A fate like mine; which, O ye Gods, forbid'
    Theseus. I pity thee, and would assuage thy grief.
    Hippolyta. Pity me not: thy anger I could bear.

Theseus. There is no place for anger where thou art.
55 Commiseration even men may feel
For those who want it: even the fiercer beasts
Lick the sore-wounded of a kindred race,
Hearing their cry, albeit they may not help.
 Hippolyta. This is no falsehood: and can he be false
60 Who speaks it?
 I remember not the time
When I have wept, it was so long ago.
Thou forcest tears from me, because—
because—
I cannot hate thee as I ought to do.

THEY ARE SWEET FLOWERS THAT ONLY BLOW BY NIGHT
1863

They are sweet flowers that only blow by night,
And sweet tears are there that avoid the light;
No mortal sees them after day is born,
They, like the dew, drop trembling from their thorn.

MEMORY
1863

The Mother of the Muses, we are taught,
Is Memory: she has left me; they remain,
And shake my shoulder, urging me to sing
About the summer days, my loves of old.
5 *Alas! alas!* is all I can reply.
Memory has left with me that name[1] alone,
Harmonious name, which other bards[2] may sing,
But her bright image in my darkest hour
Comes back, in vain comes back, call'd or uncall'd.
10 Forgotten are the names of visitors
Ready to press my hand but yesterday;
Forgotten are the names of earlier friends
Whose genial converse and glad countenance
Are fresh as ever to mine ear and eye;
15 To these, when I have written and besought
Remembrance of me, the word *Dear* alone
Hangs on the upper verge, and waits in vain.
A blessing wert thou, O oblivion,
If thy stream carried only weeds away,
20 But vernal and autumnal flowers alike
It hurries down to wither on the strand.

[1] Ianthe. See *Lyrics, To Ianthe* (p. 989).
[2] Byron and Shelley, both of whom had used the name *Ianthe* in their poetry,—Shelley in *Queen Mab* (1813), and Byron in the Dedication of *Childe Harold's Pilgrimage* (1812).

AN AGED MAN WHO LOVED TO DOZE AWAY
1863

An aged man who loved to doze away
An hour by daylight, for his eyes were dim,
And he had seen too many suns go down
And rise again, dreamed that he saw two forms
5 Of radiant beauty; he would clasp them both,
But both flew stealthily away. He cried
In his wild dream,
 "I never thought, O youth,
That thou, altho' so cherished, would'st return,
But I did think that he who came with thee,
10 Love, who could swear more sweetly than birds sing,
Would never leave me comfortless and lone."
A sigh broke through his slumber, not the last.

TO MY NINTH DECADE
1863

To my ninth decade I have totter'd on,
 And no soft arm bends now my steps to steady;
She, who once led me where she would, is gone,[1]
 So when he calls me, Death shall find me ready.

From IMAGINARY CONVERSATIONS
1824-52

TIBERIUS AND VIPSANIA
1828

Tiberius. Vipsania, my Vipsania, whither art thou walking?
Vipsania. Whom do I see?—my Tiberius?
Tiberius. Ah! no, no, no! but thou seest the father of thy little Drusus. Press him to thy heart the more closely for this meeting, and give him——
Vipsania. Tiberius! the altars, the gods, 10 the destinies, are all between us—I will take it from this hand; thus, thus shall he receive it.
Tiberius. Raise up thy face, my beloved! I must not shed tears. Augustus, Livia, ye 15 shall not extort them from me. Vipsania! I may kiss thy head—for I have saved it.

[1] Probably a reference to Landor's mother, who died in 1829. Landor always regarded her with the tenderest affection.

Thou sayest nothing. I have wronged thee; ay?

Vipsania. Ambition does not see the earth she treads on; the rock and the herbage are of one substance to her. Let me excuse you to my heart, O Tiberius. It has many wants; this is the first and greatest.

Tiberius. My ambition, I swear by the immortal gods, places not the bar of severance between us. A stronger hand, the hand that composes Rome and sways the world——

Vipsania. Overawed Tiberius. I know it; Augustus willed and commanded it.

Tiberius. And overawed Tiberius! Power bent, Death terrified, a Nero! What is our race, that any should look down on us and spurn us? Augustus, my benefactor, I have wronged thee! Livia, my mother, this one cruel deed was thine! To reign, forsooth, is a lovely thing. O womanly appetite! Who would have been before me, though the palace of Cæsar cracked and split with emperors, while I, sitting in idleness on a cliff of Rhodes, eyed the sun as he swung his golden censer athwart the heavens, or his image as it overstrode the sea? I have it before me; and, though it seems falling on me, I can smile on it—just as I did from my little favorite skiff, painted round with the marriage of Thetis, when the sailors drew their long shaggy hair across their eyes, many a stadium[1] away from it, to mitigate its effulgence.

These, too, were happy days: days of happiness like these I could recall and look back upon with unaching brow.

O land of Greece! Tiberius blesses thee, bidding thee rejoice and flourish.

Why cannot one hour, Vipsania, beauteous and light as we have led, return?

Vipsania. Tiberius! is it to me that you were speaking? I would not interrupt you; but I thought I heard my name as you walked away and looked up toward the East. So silent!

Tiberius. Who dared to call thee? Thou wert mine before the gods—do they deny it? Was it my fault——

Vipsania. Since we are separated, and forever, O Tiberius, let us think no more on the cause of it. Let neither of us believe that the other was to blame: so shall separation be less painful.

Tiberius. O mother! and did I not tell thee what she was?—patient in injury, proud in innocence, serene in grief!

Vipsania. Did you say that too? But I think it was so: I had felt little. One vast wave has washed away the impression of smaller from my memory. Could Livia, could your mother, could she who was so kind to me——

Tiberius. The wife of Cæsar did it. But hear me now; hear me: be calm as I am. No weaknesses are such as those of a mother who loves her only son immoderately; and none are so easily worked upon from without. Who knows what impulses she received? She is very, very kind: but she regards me only, and that which at her bidding is to encompass and adorn me. All the weak look after Power, protectress of weakness. Thou art a woman, O Vipsania! is there nothing in thee to excuse my mother? So good she ever was to me! so loving.

Vipsania. I quite forgive her: be tranquil, O Tiberius!

Tiberius. Never can I know peace— never can I pardon—anyone. Threaten me with thy exile, thy separation, thy seclusion! Remind me that another climate might endanger thy health!—There death met me and turned me round. Threaten me to take our son from us—our one boy, our helpless little one—him whom we made cry because we kissed him both together! Rememberest thou? Or dost thou not hear? turning thus away from me!

Vipsania. I hear; I hear! Oh cease, my sweet Tiberius! Stamp not upon that stone: my heart lies under it.

Tiberius. Ay, there again death, and more than death, stood before me. Oh, she maddened me, my mother did, she maddened me—she threw me to where I am at one breath. The gods cannot replace me where I was, nor atone to me, nor console me, nor restore my senses. To whom can I fly; to whom can I open my heart; to whom speak plainly? There was upon the earth a man I could converse with, and fear nothing; there was a woman, too, I could love, and fear nothing. What a soldier, what a Roman, was my father, O my young bride! How could those who never saw him have discoursed so rightly upon virtue!

Vipsania. These words cool my breast like pressing his urn against it. He was brave: shall Tiberius want courage?

Tiberius. My enemies scorn me. I am a garland dropped from a triumphal car, and taken up and looked on for the place I occupied; and tossed away and laughed at. Senators! laugh, laugh! Your merits may

---

[1] A measure of length equal to 607 ft.

be yet rewarded—be of good cheer! Counsel me, in your wisdom, what services I can render you, conscript fathers![1]

Vipsania. This seems mockery: Tiberius did not smile so, once.

Tiberius. They had not then congratulated me.

Vipsania. On what?

Tiberius. And it was not because she was beautiful, as they thought her, and virtuous, as I know she is; but because the flowers on the altar were to be tied together by my heart-string. On this they congratulated me. Their day will come. Their sons and daughters are what I would wish them to be: worthy to succeed them.

Vipsania. Where is that quietude, that resignation, that sanctity, that heart of true tenderness?

Tiberius. Where is my love?—my love?

Vipsania. Cry not thus aloud, Tiberius! there is an echo in the place. Soldiers and slaves may burst in upon us.

Tiberius. And see my tears? There is no echo, Vipsania; why alarm and shake me so? We are too high here for the echoes: the city is below us. Methinks it trembles and totters: would it did! from the marble quays of the Tiber to this rock. There is a strange buzz and murmur in my brain; but I should listen so intensely, I should hear the rattle of its roofs, and shout with joy.

Vipsania. Calm, O my life! calm this horrible transport.

Tiberius. Spake I so loud? Did I indeed then send my voice after a lost sound, to bring it back; and thou fanciedest it an echo? Wilt not thou laugh with me, as thou were wont to do, at such an error? What was I saying to thee, my tender love, when I commanded—I know not whom—to stand back, on pain of death? Why starest thou on me in such agony? Have I hurt thy fingers, child? I loose them; now let me look! Thou turnest thine eyes away from me. Oh! oh! I hear my crime! Immortal gods! I cursed them audibly, and before the sun, my mother!

MARCELLUS AND HANNIBAL
1828

Hannibal. Could a Numidian horseman ride no faster? Marcellus! oh! Marcellus! He moves not—he is dead. Did he not stir his fingers? Stand wide, soldiers—wide, forty paces—give him air—bring water—halt! Gather those broad leaves, and all the rest, growing under the brushwood—

[1] Roman senators.

unbrace his armor. Loose the helmet first—his breast rises. I fancied his eyes were fixed on me—they have rolled back again. Who presumeth to touch my shoulder? This horse? It was surely the horse of Marcellus! Let no man mount him. Ha! ha! the Romans, too, sink into luxury: here is gold about the charger.

Gaulish Chieftain. Execrable thief! The golden chain of our king under a beast's grinders! The vengeance of the gods hath overtaken the impure——

Hannibal. We will talk about vengeance when we have entered Rome, and about purity among the priests, if they will hear us. Sound for the surgeon. That arrow may be extracted from the side, deep as it is. —The conqueror of Syracuse lies before me.—Send a vessel off to Carthage. Say Hannibal is at the gates of Rome.—Marcellus, who stood alone between us, fallen. Brave man! I would rejoice and cannot. —How awfully serene a countenance! Such as we hear are in the Islands of the Blessed.[1] And how glorious a form and stature! Such too was theirs! They also once lay thus upon the earth wet with their blood—few other enter there. And what plain armor!

Gaulish Chieftain. My party slew him—indeed I think I slew him myself. I claim the chain: it belongs to my king; the glory of Gaul requires it. Never will she endure to see another take it.

Hannibal. My friend, the glory of Marcellus did not require him to wear it. When he suspended the arms of your brave king in the temple, he thought such a trinket unworthy of himself and of Jupiter. The shield he battered down, the breast-plate he pierced with his sword—these he showed to the people and to the gods; hardly his wife and little children saw this, ere his horse wore it.

Gaulish Chieftain. Hear me, O Hannibal!

Hannibal. What! when Marcellus lies before me? when his life may perhaps be recalled? when I may lead him in triumph to Carthage? when Italy, Sicily, Greece, Asia, wait to obey me? Content thee! I will give thee mine own bridle, worth ten such.

Gaulish Chieftain. For myself?

Hannibal. For thyself.

[1] Mythical islands said to lie in the Western Ocean, where the favorites of the gods dwell after death, in eternal joy. See Hesiod's *Works and Days,* 169.

Gaulish Chieftain. And these rubies and emeralds, and that scarlet——

Hannibal. Yes, yes.

Gaulish Chieftain. O glorious Hannibal! unconquerable hero! O my happy country! to have such an ally and defender. I swear eternal gratitude—yes, gratitude, love, devotion, beyond eternity.

Hannibal. In all treaties we fix the time: I could hardly ask a longer. Go back to thy station.—I would see what the surgeon is about, and hear what he thinks. The life of Marcellus! the triumph of Hannibal! what else has the world in it? Only Rome and Carthage: these follow.

Marcellus. I must die then? The gods be praised! The commander of a Roman army is no captive.

Hannibal (*to the Surgeon*). Could not he bear a sea-voyage. Extract the arrow.

Surgeon. He expires that moment.

Marcellus. It pains me: extract it.

Hannibal. Marcellus, I see no expression of pain on your countenance, and never will I consent to hasten the death of an enemy in my power. Since your recovery is hopeless, you say truly you are no captive. (*To the Surgeon.*) Is there nothing, man, that can assuage the mortal pain? for, suppress the signs of it as he may, he must feel it. Is there nothing to alleviate and allay it?

Marcellus. Hannibal, give me thy hand —thou hast found it and brought it me, compassion.

(*To the Surgeon.*) Go, friend; others want thy aid; several fell around me.

Hannibal. Recommend to your country, O Marcellus, while time permits it, reconciliation and peace with me, informing the Senate of my superiority in force, and the impossibility of resistance. The tablet is ready: let me take off this ring—try to write, to sign it, at least. Oh, what satisfaction I feel at seeing you able to rest upon the elbow, and even to smile!

Marcellus. Within an hour or less, with how severe a brow would Minos say to me, "Marcellus, is this thy writing?"

Rome loses one man: she hath lost many such, and she still hath many left.

Hannibal. Afraid as you are of falsehood, say you this? I confess in shame the ferocity of my countrymen. Unfortunately, too, the nearer posts are occupied by Gauls, infinitely more cruel. The Numidians are so in revenge: the Gauls both in revenge and in sport. My presence is required at a distance, and I apprehend the barbarity of one or other, learning, as they must do, your refusal to execute my wishes for the common good, and feeling that by this refusal you deprive them of their country, after so long an absence.

Marcellus. Hannibal, thou art not dying.

Hannibal. What then? What mean you?

Marcellus. That thou mayest, and very justly, have many things yet to apprehend: I can have none. The barbarity of thy soldiers is nothing to me: mine would not dare be cruel. Hannibal is forced to be absent; and his authority goes away with his horse. On the turf lies defaced the semblance of a general; but Marcellus is yet the regulator of his army. Dost thou abdicate a power conferred on thee by thy nation? Or wouldst thou acknowledge it to have become, by thy own sole fault, less plenary than thy adversary's?

I have spoken too much: let me rest; this mantle oppresses me.

Hannibal. I placed my mantle on your head when the helmet was first removed, and while you were lying in the sun. Let me fold it under, and then replace the ring.

Marcellus. Take it, Hannibal. It was given me by a poor woman who flew to me at Syracuse, and who covered it with her hair, torn off in desperation that she had no other gift to offer. Little thought I that her gift and her words should be mine. How suddenly may the most powerful be in the situation of the most helpless! Let that ring and the mantle under my head be the exchange of guests at parting. The time may come, Hannibal, when thou (and the gods alone know whether as conqueror or conquered) mayest sit under the roof of my children, and in either case it shall serve thee. In thy adverse fortune, they will remember on whose pillow their father breathed his last; in thy prosperous (Heaven grant it may shine upon thee in some other country!), it will rejoice thee to protect them. We feel ourselves the most exempt from affliction when we relieve it, although we are then the most conscious that it may befall us.

There is one thing here which is not at the disposal of either.

Hannibal. What?

Marcellus. This body.

Hannibal. Whither would you be lifted? Men are ready.

Marcellus. I meant not so. My strength is failing. I seem to hear rather what is within than what is without. My sight and my other senses are in confusion. I would have said—This body, when a few bubbles of air shall have left it, is no more worthy of thy notice than of mine; but thy glory will not let thee refuse it to the piety of my family.

Hannibal. You would ask something else. I perceive an inquietude not visible till now.

Marcellus. Duty and Death make us think of home sometimes.

Hannibal. Thitherward the thoughts of the conqueror and of the conquered fly together.

Marcellus. Hast thou any prisoners from my escort?

Hannibal. A few dying lie about—and let them lie—they are Tuscans. The remainder I saw at a distance, flying, and but one brave man among them—he appeared a Roman—a youth who turned back, though wounded. They surrounded and dragged him away, spurring his horse with their swords. These Etrurians measure their courage carefully, and tack it well together before they put it on, but throw it off again with lordly ease.

Marcellus, why think about them? or does aught else disquiet your thoughts?

Marcellus. I have suppressed it long enough. My son—my beloved son.

Hannibal. Where is he? Can it be? Was he with you?

Marcellus. He would have shared my fate—and has not. Gods of my country! beneficent throughout life to me, in death surpassingly beneficent: I render you, for the last time, thanks.

METELLUS AND MARIUS
1829

Metellus. Well met, Caius Marius! My orders are to find instantly a centurion who shall mount the walls; one capable of observation, acute in remark, prompt, calm, active, intrepid. The Numantians are sacrificing to the gods in secrecy; they have sounded the horn once only,—and hoarsely and low and mournfully.

Marius. Was that ladder I see yonder among the caper-bushes and purple lilies, under where the fig-tree grows out of the rampart, left for me?

Metellus. Even so, wert thou willing. Wouldst thou mount it?

Marius. Rejoicingly. If none are below or near, may I explore the state of things by entering the city?

Metellus. Use thy discretion in that.

What seest thou? Wouldst thou leap down? Lift the ladder.

Marius. Are there spikes in it where it sticks in the turf? I should slip else.

Metellus. How! bravest of the centurions, art even thou afraid? Seest thou any one by?

Marius. Ay; some hundreds close beneath me.

Metellus. Retire, then. Hasten back; I will protect thy descent.

Marius. May I speak, O Metellus, without an offence to discipline?

Metellus. Say.

Marius. Listen! Dost thou not hear?

Metellus. Shame on thee! alight, alight! my shield shall cover thee.

Marius. There is a murmur like the hum of bees in the bean-field of Cereate; for the sun is hot, and the ground is thirsty. When will it have drunk up for me the blood that has run, and is yet oozing on it, from those fresh bodies!

Metellus. How! We have not fought for many days; what bodies, then, are fresh ones?

Marius. Close beneath the wall are those of infants and of girls; in the middle of the road are youths, emaciated; some either unwounded or wounded months ago; some on their spears, others on their swords: no few have received in mutual death the last interchange of friendship; their daggers unite them, hilt to hilt, bosom to bosom.

Metellus. Mark rather the living,—what are they about?

Marius. About the sacrifice, which portends them, I conjecture, but little good,—it burns sullenly and slowly. The victim will lie upon the pyre till morning, and still be unconsumed, unless they bring more fuel.

I will leap down and walk on cautiously, and return with tidings, if death should spare me.

Never was any race of mortals so unmilitary as these Numantians; no watch, no stations, no palisades across the streets.

Metellus. Did they want, then, all the wood for the altar?

Marius. It appears so—I will return anon.

Metellus. The gods speed thee, my brave, honest Marius!

Marius (*returned*). The ladder should have been better spiked for that slippery ground. I am down again safe, however. Here a man may walk securely, and without picking his steps.

Metellus. Tell me, Caius, what thou sawest.

Marius. The streets of Numantia.

Metellus. Doubtless; but what else?

Marius. The temples and markets and places of exercise and fountains.

Metellus. Art thou crazed, centurion? what more? Speak plainly, at once, and briefly.

Marius. I beheld, then, all Numantia.

Metellus. Has terror maddened thee? has thou descried nothing of the inhabitants but those carcasses under the ramparts?

Marius. Those, O Metellus, lie scattered, although not indeed far asunder. The greater part of the soldiers and citizens—of the fathers, husbands, widows, wives, espoused—were assembled together.

Metellus. About the altar?

Marius. Upon it.

Metellus. So busy and earnest in devotion! but how all upon it?

Marius. It blazed under them, and over them, and round about them.

Metellus. Immortal gods! Art thou sane, Caius Marius? Thy visage is scorched: thy speech may wander after such an enterprise; thy shield burns my hand.

Marius. I thought it had cooled again. Why, truly, it seems hot: I now feel it.

Metellus. Wipe off those embers.

Marius. 'Twere better: there will be none opposite to shake them upon for some time.

The funereal horn, that sounded with such feebleness, sounded not so from the faint heart of him who blew it. Him I saw; him only of the living. Should I say it? there was another: there was one child whom its parent could not kill, could not part from. She had hidden it in her robe, I suspect; and, when the fire had reached it, either it shrieked or she did. For suddenly a cry pierced through the crackling pinewood, and something of round in figure fell from brand to brand, until it reached the pavement, at the feet of him who had blown the horn. I rushed toward him, for I wanted to hear the whole story, and felt the pressure of time. Condemn not my weakness, O Cæcilius! I wished an enemy to live an hour longer; for my orders were to explore and bring intelligence. When I gazed on him, in height almost gigantic, I wondered not that the blast of his trumpet was so weak; rather did I wonder that Famine, whose hand had indented every limb and feature, had left him any voice articulate. I rushed toward him, however, ere my eyes

had measured either his form or strength. He held the child against me, and staggered under it.

"Behold," he exclaimed, "the glorious ornament of a Roman triumph!"

I stood horror-stricken; when suddenly drops, as of rain, pattered down from the pyre. I looked; and many were the precious stones, many were the amulets and rings and bracelets, and other barbaric ornaments, unknown to me in form or purpose, that tinkled on the hardened and black branches, from mothers and wives and betrothed maids; and some, too, I can imagine, from robuster arms—things of joyance, won in battle. The crowd of incumbent bodies was so dense and heavy, that neither the fire nor the smoke could penetrate upward from among them; and they sank, whole and at once, into the smouldering cavern eating out below. He at whose neck hung the trumpet felt this, and started.

"There is yet room," he cried, "and there is strength enough yet, both in the element and in me."

He extended his withered arms, he thrust forward the gaunt links of his throat, and upon gnarled knees, that smote each other audibly, tottered into the civic fire. It—like some hungry and strangest beast on the innermost wild of Africa, pierced, broken, prostrate, motionless, gazed at by its hunter in the impatience of glory, in the delight of awe—panted once more, and seized him.

I have seen within this hour, O Metellus, what Rome in the cycle of her triumphs will never see, what the Sun in his eternal course can never show her, what the Earth has borne but now, and must never rear again for her, what Victory herself has envied her,—a Numantian.

Metellus. We shall feast tomorrow. Hope, Caius Marius, to become a tribune: trust in fortune.

Marius. Auguries are surer: surest of all is perseverance.

Metellus. I hope the wine has not grown vapid in my tent: I have kept it waiting, and must now report to Scipio the intelligence of our discovery. Come after me, Caius.

Marius (*alone*). The tribune is the discoverer! the centurion is the scout! Caius Marius must enter more Numantias. Light-hearted Cæcilius, thou mayest perhaps hereafter, and not with humbled but with exulting pride, take orders from this hand. If Scipio's words are fate, and to me they sound so, the portals of the Capitol may shake before my chariot, as my horses plunge back at the applauses of the people, and Jove in his high domicile[1] may welcome the citizen of Arpinum.[2]

LEOFRIC AND GODIVA[3]
1829

Godiva. There is a dearth in the land, my sweet Leofric! Remember how many weeks of drought we have had, even in the deep pastures of Leicestershire; and how many Sundays we have heard the same prayers for rain, and supplications that it would please the Lord in his mercy to turn aside his anger from the poor, pining cattle. You, my dear husband, have imprisoned more than one malefactor for leaving his dead ox in the public way; and other hinds[4] have fled before you out of the traces, in which they, and their sons and their daughters, and haply their old fathers and mothers, were dragging the abandoned wain homeward. Although we were accompanied by many brave spearmen and skilful archers, it was perilous to pass the creatures which the farm-yard dogs, driven from the hearth by the poverty of their masters, were tearing and devouring; while others, bitten and lamed, filled the air either with long and deep howls or sharp and quick barkings, as they struggled with hunger and feebleness, or were exasperated by heat and pain. Nor could the thyme from the heath, nor the bruised branches of the fir-tree, extinguish or abate the foul odor.

Leofric. And now, Godiva, my darling, thou art afraid we should be eaten up before we enter the gates of Coventry; or perchance that in the gardens there are no roses to greet thee, no sweet herbs for thy mat and pillow.

Godiva. Leofric, I have no such fears. This is the month of roses: I find them everywhere since my blessed marriage. They, and all other sweet herbs, I know not why, seem to greet me wherever I look at them, as though they knew and expected me. Surely they cannot feel that I am fond of them.

Leofric. O light, laughing simpleton! But what wouldst thou? I came not hither to pray; and yet if praying would satisfy thee, or remove the drought, I would ride

up straightway to Saint Michael's and pray until morning.

Godiva. I would do the same, O Leofric! but God hath turned away his ear from holier lips than mine. Would my own dear husband hear me, if I implored him for what is easier to accomplish,—what he can do like God?

Leofric. How! what is it?

Godiva. I would not, in the first hurry of your wrath, appeal to you, my loving lord, in behalf of these unhappy men who have offended you.

Leofric. Unhappy! is that all?

Godiva. Unhappy they must surely be, to have offended you so grievously. What a soft air breathes over us! how quiet and serene and still an evening! how calm are the heavens and the earth!—Shall none enjoy them; not even we, my Leofric? The sun is ready to set: let it never set, O Leofric, on your anger. These are not my words: they are better than mine.[1] Should they lose their virtue from my unworthiness in uttering them?

Leofric. Godiva, wouldst thou plead to me for rebels?

Godiva. They have, then, drawn the sword against you? Indeed, I knew it not.

Leofric. They have omitted to send me my dues, established by my ancestors, well knowing of our nuptials, and of the charges and festivities they require, and that in a season of such scarcity my own lands are insufficient.

Godiva. If they were starving, as they said they were——

Leofric. Must I starve too? Is it not enough to lose my vassals?

Godiva. Enough! O God! too much! too much! May you never lose them! Give them life, peace, comfort, contentment. There are those among them who kissed me in my infancy, and who blessed me at the baptismal font. Leofric, Leofric! the first old man I meet I shall think is one of those; and I shall think on the blessing he gave me, and (ah me!) on the blessing I bring back to him. My heart will bleed, will burst; and he will weep at it! he will weep, poor soul, for the wife of a cruel lord who denounces vengeance on him, who carries death into his family!

Leofric. We must hold solemn festivals.

Godiva. We must, indeed.

Leofric. Well, then?

Godiva. Is the clamorousness that succeeds the death of God's dumb creatures,

---

[1] The Temple of Jupiter, where victorious leaders offered sacrifice.
[2] Marius, whose childhood was spent near Arpinum.
[3] See Tennyson's *Godiva.*
[4] peasants

[1] See *Ephesians,* 4:26.

are crowded halls, are slaughtered cattle, festivals?—are maddening songs, and giddy dances, and hireling praises from parti-colored coats? Can the voice of a minstrel tell us better things of ourselves than our own internal one might tell us; or can his breath make our breath softer in sleep? O my beloved! let everything be a joyance to us: it will, if we will. Sad is the day, and worse must follow, when we hear the blackbird in the garden, and do not throb with joy. But, Leofric, the high festival is strown by the servant of God upon the heart of man. It is gladness, it is thanksgiving; it is the orphan, the starveling, pressed to the bosom, and bidden as its first commandment to remember its benefactor. We will hold this festival; the guests are ready; we may keep it up for weeks, and months, and years together, and always be the happier and the richer for it. The beverage of this feast, O Leofric, is sweeter than bee or flower or vine can give us:[1] it flows from heaven; and in heaven will it abundantly be poured out again to him who pours it out here unsparingly.

Leofric. Thou art wild.

Godiva. I have, indeed, lost myself. Some Power, some good kind Power, melts me (body and soul and voice) into tenderness and love. O my husband, we must obey it. Look upon me! look upon me! lift your sweet eyes from the ground! I will not cease to supplicate; I dare not.

Leofric. We may think upon it.

Godiva. Never say that! What! think upon goodness when you can be good? Let not the infants cry for sustenance! The mother of our blessed Lord will hear them; us never, never afterward.

Leofric. Here comes the Bishop: we are but one mile from the walls. Why dismountest thou? no bishop can expect it. Godiva! my honor and rank among men are humbled by this. Earl Godwin will hear of it. Up! up! the Bishop hath seen it: he urgeth his horse onward. Dost thou not hear him now upon the solid turf behind thee?

Godiva. Never, no, never will I rise, O Leofric, until you remit this most impious tax—this tax on hard labor, on hard life.

Leofric. Turn round: look how the fat nag canters, as to the tune of a sinner's psalm, slow and hard-breathing. What reason or right can the people have to complain, while their bishop's steed is so sleek

and well caparisoned? Inclination to change, desire to abolish old usages.—Up! up! for shame! They shall smart for it, idlers! Sir Bishop, I must blush for my young bride.

Godiva. My husband, my husband! will you pardon the city?

Leofric. Sir Bishop! I could not think you would have seen her in this plight. Will I pardon? Yea, Godiva, by the holy rood,[1] will I pardon the city, when thou ridest naked at noontide through the streets!

Godiva. O my dear, cruel Leofric, where is the heart you gave me? It was not so: can mine have hardened it?

Bishop. Earl, thou abashest thy spouse; she turneth pale, and weepeth. Lady Godiva, peace be with thee.

Godiva. Thanks, holy man! peace will be with me when peace is with your city. Did you hear my lord's cruel word?

Bishop. I did, lady.

Godiva. Will you remember it, and pray against it?

Bishop. Wilt *thou* forget it, daughter?

Godiva. I am not offended.

Bishop. Angel of peace and purity!

Godiva. But treasure it up in your heart: deem it an incense, good only when it is consumed and spent, ascending with prayer and sacrifice. And, now, what was it?

Bishop. Christ save us! that he will pardon the city when thou ridest naked through the streets at noon.

Godiva. Did he not swear an oath?

Bishop. He sware by the holy rood.

Godiva. My Redeemer, thou hast heard it! save the city!

Leofric. We are now upon the beginning of the pavement: these are the suburbs. Let us think of feasting: we may pray afterward; tomorrow we shall rest.

Godiva. No judgments, then, tomorrow, Leofric?

Leofric. None: we will carouse.

Godiva. The saints of heaven have given me strength and confidence; my prayers are heard; the heart of my beloved is now softened.

Leofric (*aside*). Ay, ay—they shall smart, though.

Godiva. Say, dearest Leofric, is there indeed no other hope, no other mediation?

Leofric. I have sworn. Beside, thou hast made me redden and turn my face away from thee, and all the knaves have seen it: this adds to the city's crime.

---

[1] That is, sweeter than mead, which is made of honey, nectar, and wine.

[1] cross

Godiva. I have blushed too, Leofric, and was not rash nor obdurate.

Leofric. But thou, my sweetest, art given to blushing: there is no conquering it in thee. I wish thou hadst not alighted so 5 hastily and roughly: it hath shaken down a sheaf of thy hair. Take heed thou sit not upon it, lest it anguish thee. Well done! it mingleth now sweetly with the cloth of gold upon the saddle, running here and 10 there, as if it had life and faculties and business, and were working thereupon some newer and cunninger device. O my beauteous Eve! there is a Paradise about thee! the world is refreshed as thou movest and 15 breathest on it. I cannot see or think of evil where thou art. I could throw my arms even here about thee. No signs for me! no shaking of sunbeams! no reproof or frown or wonderment—I *will* say it—now, then, 20 for worse—I could close with my kisses thy half-open lips, ay, and those lovely and loving eyes, before the people.

Godiva. Tomorrow you shall kiss me, and they shall bless you for it. I shall be 25 very pale, for tonight I must fast and pray.

Leofric. I do not hear thee; the voices of the folk are so loud under this archway.

Godiva (to herself). God help them! 30 good kind souls! I hope they will not crowd about me so tomorrow. O Leofric! could my name be forgotten, and yours alone remembered! But perhaps my innocence may save me from reproach; and how 35 many as innocent are in fear and famine! No eye will open on me but fresh from tears. What a young mother for so large a family! Shall my youth harm me? Under God's 40 hand it gives me courage. Ah! when will the morning come? Ah! when will the noon be over?

From PERICLES AND ASPASIA
1836

66. Pericles to Aspasia

There are things, Aspasia, beyond the art of Phidias. He may represent Love 50 leaning upon his bow and listening to Philosophy; but not for hours together: he may represent Love, while he is giving her a kiss for her lesson, tying her arms behind her; loosing them again must be upon 55 another marble.

69. Pericles to Aspasia

Do you love me? do you love me? Stay, reason upon it, sweet Aspasia! doubt, hesitate, question, drop it, take it up again, provide, raise obstacles, reply indirectly. Oracles are sacred, and there is a pride in being a diviner.

70. Aspasia to Pericles

I will do none of those things you tell me to do; but I will say something you forgot to say, about the insufficiency of Phidias.

He may represent a hero with unbent brows, a sage with the lyre of Poetry in his hand, Ambition with her face half-averted from the city, but he cannot represent, in the same sculpture, at the same 20 distance, Aphrodite higher than Pallas. He would be derided if he did; and a great man can never do that for which a little man may deride him.

I shall love you even more than I do, if 25 you will love yourself more than me. Did ever lover talk so? Pray tell me, for I have forgotten all they ever talked about. But, Pericles! Pericles! be careful to lose nothing of your glory, or you lose all that can be 30 lost of me; my pride, my happiness, my content; everything but my poor weak love. Keep glory, then, for my sake!

104. Pericles to Aspasia

Send me a note whenever you are idle and thinking of me, dear Aspasia! Send it always by some old slave, ill-dressed. The people will think it a petition, or something as good, and they will be sure to observe 40 the pleasure it throws into my countenance. Two winds at once will blow into my sails, each helping me onward.

If I am tired, your letter will refresh me; 45 if occupied, it will give me activity. Beside, what a deal of time we lose in business!

105. Aspasia to Pericles

Would to heaven, O Pericles! you had no business at all, but the conversation of your friends. You must always be the 50 greatest man in the city, whoever may be the most popular. I wish we could spend the whole day together; must it never be? Are you not already in possession of all you ever contended for?

It is time, methinks, that you should leave off speaking in public, for you begin to be negligent and incorrect. I am to write you a note whenever I am idle and thinking of you!

Pericles! Pericles! how far is it from idleness to think of you! We come to rest before we come to idleness.

173. ASPASIA TO PERICLES

When the war is over, as surely it must be in another year, let us sail among the islands of the Ægean, and be young as ever. O that it were permitted us to pass together the remainder of our lives in privacy and retirement! This is never to be hoped for in Athens.

I inherit from my mother a small yet beautiful house in Tenos: I remember it well. Water, clear and cold, ran before the vestibule; a sycamore shaded the whole building. I think Tenos must be nearer to Athens than to Miletus. Could we not go now for a few days? How temperate was the air, how serene the sky, how beautiful the country! the people how quiet, how gentle, how kind-hearted!

Is there any station so happy as an uncontested place in a small community, where manners are simple, where wants are few, where respect is the tribute of probity, and love is the guerdon of beneficence! O Pericles! let us go; we can return at any time.

192. ASPASIA TO PERICLES

Now the fever is raging, and we are separated, my comfort and delight is in our little Pericles. The letters you send me come less frequently, but I know you write whenever your duties will allow you, and whenever men are found courageous enough to take charge of them. Although you preserved with little care the speeches you delivered formerly, yet you promised me a copy of the latter, and as many of the earlier as you could collect among your friends. Let me have them as soon as possible. Whatever bears the traces of your hand is precious to me: how greatly more precious what is imprest with your genius, what you have meditated and spoken! I shall see your calm thoughtful face while I am reading, and will be cautious not to read aloud lest I lose the illusion of your voice.

194. ASPASIA TO PERICLES

Gratitude to the immortal gods overpowers every other impulse of my breast. You are safe.

Pericles! O my Pericles! come into this purer air! live life over again in the smiles of your child, in the devotion of your Aspasia! Why did you fear for me the plague within the city, the Spartans round it? why did you exact the vow at parting, that nothing but your command should recall me again to Athens? Why did I ever make it? Cruel! to refuse me the full enjoyment of your recovered health! crueller to keep me in ignorance of its decline! The happiest of pillows is not that which Love first presses; it is that which Death has frowned on and passed over.

231. ASPASIA TO CLEONE

Where on earth is there so much society as in a beloved child? He accompanies me in my walks, gazes into my eyes for what I am gathering from books, tells me more and better things than they do, and asks me often what neither I nor they can answer. When he is absent I am filled with reflections; when he is present I have room for none beside what I receive from him. The charms of his childhood bring me back to the delights of mine, and I fancy I hear my own words in a sweeter voice. Will he (O how I tremble at the mute oracle of futurity!), will he ever be as happy as I have been? Alas! and must he ever be as subject to fears and apprehensions? No; thanks to the gods! never, never He carries his father's heart within his breast: I see him already an orator and a leader. I try to teach him daily some of his father's looks and gestures, and I never smile but at his docility and gravity. How his father will love him! the little thunderer! the winner of cities! the vanquisher of Cleones!

233. ASPASIA TO PERICLES

Never tell me, O my Pericles! that you are suddenly changed in appearance. May every change of your figure and countenance be gradual, so that I shall not perceive it; but if you really are altered to such a degree as you describe, I must transfer my affection —from the first Pericles to the second. Are you jealous? If you are, it is I who am to be pitied, whose heart is destined to fly from the one to the other incessantly. In the end it will rest, it shall, it must, on the nearest. I would write a longer letter; but it is a sad and wearisome thing to aim at playfulness where the hand is palsied by affliction. Be well, and all is well; be happy, and Athens rises up again, alert, and blooming, and vigorous, from between war and pestilence. Love me: for love cures all but love. How can we fear to die, how can we die, while we cling or are clung to the beloved?

234. PERICLES TO ASPASIA

The pestilence has taken from me both my sons. You, who were ever so kind and affectionate to them, will receive a tardy recompense, in hearing that the least gentle and the least grateful did acknowledge it.

I mourn for Paroles, because he loved me; for Xanthippos, because he loved me not.

Preserve with all your maternal care our little Pericles. I cannot be fonder of him than I have always been; I can only fear more for him.

Is he not with my Aspasia? What fears then are so irrational as mine? But oh! I am living in a widowed house, a house of desolation; I am living in a city of tombs and torches; and the last I saw before me were for my children.

235. PERICLES TO ASPASIA

It is right and orderly, that he who has partaken so largely in the prosperity of the Athenians, should close the procession of their calamities. The fever that has depopulated our city, returned upon me last night, and Hippocrates and Acron tell me that my end is near.

When we agreed, O Aspasia! in the beginning of our loves, to communicate our thoughts by writing, even while we were both in Athens, and when we had many reasons for it, we little foresaw the more powerful one that has rendered it necessary of late. We never can meet again: the laws forbid it,[1] and love itself enforces them. Let wisdom be heard by you as imperturbably, and affection as authoritatively, as ever; and remember that the sorrow of Pericles can arise but from the bosom of Aspasia. There is only one word of tenderness we could say, which we have not said oftentimes before; and there is no consola-

[1] Because the fever was contagious.

tion in it. The happy never say, and never hear said, farewell.

Reviewing the course of my life, it appears to me at one moment as if we met but yesterday; at another as if centuries had passed within it; for within it have existed the greater part of those who, since the origin of the world, have been the luminaries of the human race. Damon called me from my music to look at Aristides on his way to exile; and my father pressed the wrist by which he was leading me along, and whispered in my ear:

"Walk quickly by; glance cautiously; it is there Miltiades is in prison."

In my boyhood Pindar took me up in his arms, when he brought to our house the dirge he had composed for the funeral of my grandfather; in my adolescence I offered the rites of hospitality to Empedocles; not long afterward I embraced the neck of Æschylus, about to abandon his country. With Sophocles I have argued on eloquence; with Euripides on polity and ethics; I have discoursed, as became an inquirer, with Protagoras and Democritus, with Anaxagoras and Meton. From Herodotus I have listened to the most instructive history, conveyed in a language the most copious and the most harmonious; a man worthy to carry away the collected suffrages of universal Greece; a man worthy to throw open the temples of Egypt, and to celebrate the exploits of Cyrus. And from Thucydides, who alone can succeed to him, how recently did my Aspasia hear with me the energetic praises of his just supremacy!

As if the festival of life were incomplete, and wanted one great ornament to crown it, Phidias placed before us, in ivory and gold, the tutelary Deity of this land, and the Zeus of Homer and Olympus.

To have lived with such men, to have enjoyed their familiarity and esteem, overpays all labors and anxieties. I were unworthy of the friendships I have commemorated, were I forgetful of the latest. Sacred it ought to be, formed as it was under the portico of Death, my friendship with the most sagacious, the most scientific, the most beneficent of philosophers, Acron and Hippocrates. If mortal could war against Pestilence and Destiny, they had been victorious. I leave them in the field: unfortunate he who finds them among the fallen!

And now, at the close of my day, when every light is dim and every guest departed, let me own that these wane before me, remembering, as I do in the pride and fulness of my heart, that Athens confided her glory, and Aspasia her happiness, to me.

Have I been a faithful guardian? do I resign them to the custody of the gods undiminished and unimpaired? Welcome then, welcome my last hour! After enjoying for so great a number of years, in my public and my private life, what I believe has never been the lot of any other, I now extend my hand to the urn,[1] and take without reluctance or hesitation what is the lot of all.

. . . . . .

THE PENTAMERON
1837

From FIFTH DAY'S INTERVIEW
THE DREAM OF BOCCACCIO

Boccaccio. In vain had I determined not only to mend in future, but to correct the past; in vain had I prayed most fervently for grace to accomplish it, with a final aspiration to Fiammetta that she would unite with your beloved Laura and that, gentle and beatified spirits as they are, they would breathe together their purer prayers on mine. See what follows.

Petrarca. Sigh not at it. Before we can see all that follows from their intercession, we must join them again. But let me hear anything in which they are concerned.

Boccaccio. I prayed; and my breast, after some few tears, grew calmer. Yet sleep did not ensue until the break of morning, when the dropping of soft rain on the leaves of the fig-tree at the window, and the chirping of a little bird, to tell another there was shelter under them, brought me repose and slumber. Scarcely had I closed my eyes, if indeed time can be reckoned any more in sleep than in heaven, when my Fiammetta seemed to have led me into the meadow. You will see it below you: turn away that branch: gently! gently! do not break it; for the little bird sat there.

Petrarca. I think, Giovanni, I can divine the place. Although this fig-tree, growing out of the wall between the cellar and us, is fantastic enough in its branches, yet that other which I see yonder, bent down and forced to crawl along the grass by the prepotency of the young shapely walnut-tree, is much more so. It forms a seat, about a cubit above the ground, level and long enough for several.

[1] A vessel used for preserving the ashes of the dead; here used figuratively for *grave.*

Boccaccio. Ha! you fancy it must be a favorite spot with me, because of the two strong forked stakes wherewith it is propped and supported!

Petrarca. Poets know the haunts of poets at first sight; and he who loved Laura —O Laura! did I say he who *loved* thee?— hath whisperings where those feet would wander which have been restless after Fiammetta.

Boccaccio. It is true, my imagination has often conducted her thither; but here in this chamber she appeared to me more visibly in a dream.

"Thy prayers have been heard, O Giovanni," said she.

I sprang to embrace her.

"Do not spill the water! Ah! you have spilt a part of it."

I then observed in her hand a crystal vase. A few drops were sparkling on the sides and running down the rim; a few were trickling from the base and from the hand that held it.

"I must go down to the brook," said she, "and fill it again as it was filled before."

What a moment of agony was this to me! Could I be certain how long might be her absence? She went: I was following: she made a sign for me to turn back: I disobeyed her only an instant: yet my sense of disobedience, increasing my feebleness and confusion, made me lose sight of her. In the next moment she was again at my side, with the cup quite full. I stood motionless: I feared my breath might shake the water over. I looked her in the face for her commands—and to see it—to see it so calm, so beneficent, so beautiful. I was forgetting what I had prayed for, when she lowered her head, tasted of the cup, and gave it me. I drank; and suddenly sprang forth before me, many groves and palaces and gardens, and their statues and their avenues, and their labyrinths of alaternus and bay, and alcoves of citron, and watchful loopholes in the retirements of impenetrable pomegranate. Farther off, just below where the fountain slipt away from its marble hall and guardian gods, arose, from their beds of moss and drosera and darkest grass, the sisterhood of oleanders, fond of tantalizing with their bosomed flowers and their moist and pouting blossoms the little shy rivulet, and of covering its face with all the colors of the dawn. My dream expanded and moved forward. I trod again the dust of Posilippo, soft as the feathers in the wings of Sleep. I emerged on Baia; I crossed her innumerable arches; I loitered in the breezy sunshine of her mole;[1] I trusted the faithful seclusion of her caverns, the keepers of so many secrets; and I reposed on the buoyancy of her tepid sea. Then Naples, and her theatres and her churches, and grottoes and dells and forts and promontories, rushed forward in confusion, now among soft whispers, now among sweetest sounds, and subsided, and sank, and disappeared. Yet a memory seemed to come fresh from every one: each had time enough for its tale, for its pleasure, for its reflection, for its pang. As I mounted with silent steps the narrow staircase of the old palace, how distinctly did I feel against the palm of my hand the coldness of that smooth stonework, and the greater of the cramps of iron in it!

"Ah me! is this forgetting?" cried I anxiously to Fiammetta.

"We must recall these scenes before us," she replied; "such is the punishment of them. Let us hope and believe that the apparition, and the compunction which must follow it, will be accepted as the full penalty, and that both will pass away almost together."

I feared to lose anything attendant on her presence: I feared to approach her forehead with my lips: I feared to touch the lily on its long wavy leaf in her hair, which filled my whole heart with fragrance. Venerating, adoring, I bowed my head at last to kiss her snow-white robe, and trembled at my presumption. And yet the effulgence of her countenance vivified while it chastened me. I loved her—I must not say *more* than ever—*better* than ever; it was Fiammetta who had inhabited the skies. As my hand opened toward her,

"Beware!" said she, faintly smiling; "beware, Giovanni! Take only the crystal; take it, and drink again."

"Must all be then forgotten?" said I sorrowfully.

"Remember your prayer and mine, Giovanni. Shall both have been granted—O how much worse than in vain!"

I drank instantly; I drank largely. How cool my bosom grew; how could it grow so cool before her! But it was not to remain in its quiescency; its trials were not yet over. I will not, Francesco! no, I may not commemorate the incidents she related to me, nor which of us said, "I blush for having loved *first;*" nor which of us replied, "Say *least,* say *least,* and blush again."

The charm of the words (for I felt not

[1] A structure serving as a pier or breakwater.

the encumbrance of the body nor the acuteness of the spirit) seemed to possess me wholly. Although the water gave me strength and comfort, and somewhat of celestial pleasure, many tears fell around the border of the vase as she held it up before me, exhorting me to take courage, and inviting me with more than exhortation to accomplish my deliverance. She came nearer, more tenderly, more earnestly; she held the dewy globe with both hands, leaning forward, and sighed and shook her head, drooping at my pusillanimity. It was only when a ringlet had touched the rim, and perhaps the water (for a sunbeam on the surface could never have given it such a golden hue), that I took courage, clasped it, and exhausted it. Sweet as was the water, sweet as was the serenity it gave me—alas! that also which it moved away from me was sweet!

"This time you can trust me alone," said she, and parted my hair, and kissed my brow. Again she went toward the brook: again my agitation, my weakness, my doubt, came over me: nor could I see her while she raised the water, nor knew I whence she drew it. When she returned, she was close to me at once: she smiled: her smile pierced me to the bones: it seemed an angel's. She sprinkled the pure water on me; she looked most fondly; she took my hand; she suffered me to press hers to my bosom; but, whether by design I cannot tell, she let fall a few drops of the chilly element between.

"And now, O my beloved!" said she, "we have consigned to the bosom of God our earthly joys and sorrows. The joys cannot return, let not the sorrows. These alone would trouble my repose among the blessed."

"Trouble thy repose! Fiammetta! Give me the chalice!" cried I—"not a drop will I leave in it, not a drop."

"Take it!" said that soft voice. "O now most dear Giovanni! I know thou hast strength enough; and there is but little—at the bottom lies our first kiss."

"Mine! didst thou say, beloved one? and is that left thee still?"

"*Mine,*" said she, pensively; and as she abased her head, the broad leaf of the lily hid her brow and her eyes; the light of heaven shone through the flower.

"O Fiammetta! Fiammetta!" cried I in agony, "God is the God of mercy, God is the God of love—can I, can I ever?" I struck the chalice against my head, unmindful that I held it; the water covered my

face and my feet. I started up, not yet
awake, and I heard the name of Fiammetta
in the curtains.

Petrarca. Love, O Giovanni, and life
[5] itself, are but dreams at best.

Thomas Love Peacock 1785-1866

BENEATH THE CYPRESS[1] SHADE
1806

I dug, beneath the cypress shade,
　　What well might seem an elfin's grave;
And every pledge in earth I laid,
　　That erst thy false affection gave.

[5] I pressed them down the sod beneath;
　　I placed one mossy stone above;
And twined the rose's fading wreath
　　Around the sepulchre of love.

Frail as thy love, the flowers were dead,
[10] 　Ere yet the evening sun was set;
But years shall see the cypress spread,
　　Immutable as my regret.

From HEADLONG HALL
1815　　　　1816

HAIL TO THE HEADLONG

Chorus

Hail to the Headlong! the Headlong
　　Ap[2]-Headlong!
All hail to the Headlong, the Headlong
　　Ap-Headlong!
The Headlong Ap-Headlong
Ap-Breakneck Ap-Headlong
[5] Ap-Cataract Ap-Pistyll Ap-Rhaiader
　　Ap-Headlong!

The bright bowl we steep in the name of
　　the Headlong:
Let the youths pledge it deep to the Head-
　　long Ap-Headlong,
And the rosy-lipped lasses
Touch the brim as it passes,
[10] And kiss the red tide for the Headlong
　　Ap-Headlong!

The loud harp resounds in the hall of the
　　Headlong:
The light step rebounds in the hall of the
　　Headlong:
Where shall the music invite us,
Or beauty delight us,
[15] If not in the hall of the Headlong Ap-
　　Headlong?

[1] The cypress is an emblem of mourning; it is a
common tree in graveyards.
[2] *Ap* is a common Welsh prefix in surnames; it
means *son of.*

Huzza! to the health of the Headlong Ap-
　　Headlong!
Fill the bowl, fill in floods, to the health
　　of the Headlong!
Till the stream ruby-glowing,
On all sides o'erflowing,
[20] Shall fall in cascades to the health of the
　　Headlong!
The Headlong Ap-Headlong
Ap-Breakneck Ap-Headlong
Ap-Cataract Ap-Pistyll Ap-Rhaiader Ap-
　　Headlong!

From NIGHTMARE ABBEY
1818　　　　1818

SEAMEN THREE! WHAT MEN BE YE?

Seamen three! what men be ye?
　　Gotham's three Wise Men we be.
Whither in your bowl so free?
　　To rake the moon from out the sea.
[5] The bowl goes trim; the moon doth shine;
　　And our ballast is old wine:
　　And your ballast is old wine.

Who art thou, so fast adrift?
　　I am he they call Old Care.
[10] Here on board we will thee lift.
　　No: I may not enter there.
Wherefore so? 'Tis Jove's decree—
　　In a bowl Care may not be:
　　In a bowl Care may not be.

[15] Fear ye not the waves that roll?
　　No: in charmed bowl we swim.
What the charm that floats the bowl?
　　Water may not pass the brim.
The bowl goes trim; the moon doth shine;
[20] 　And our ballast is old wine:
　　And your ballast is old wine.

From MAID MARIAN
1818-22　　　1822

FOR THE SLENDER BEECH AND THE SAPLING
OAK

For the slender beech and the sapling
　　oak
That grow by the shadowy rill,
You may cut down both at a single
　　stroke,
You may cut down which you will.

[5] But this you must know, that as long as
　　they grow,
Whatever change may be,
You never can teach either oak or beech
　　To be aught but a greenwood tree.

Though I Be Now a Gray, Gray Friar

Though I be now a gray, gray friar,
    Yet I was once a hale young knight:
The cry of my dogs was the only choir
    In which my spirit did take delight.
5 Little I recked of matin bell,
    But drowned its toll with my clanging
        horn;
And the only beads I loved to tell[1]
    Were the beads of dew on the spangled
        thorn.

Little I reck of matin bell,
10   But drown its toll with my clanging
        horn:
And the only beads I love to tell
    Are the beads of dew on the spangled
        thorn.

An archer keen I was withal,
    As ever did lean on greenwood tree;
15 And could make the fleetest roebuck fall,
    A good three hundred yards from me.
Though changeful time, with hand severe,
    Has made me now these joys forego,
Yet my heart bounds whene'er I hear
20   Yoicks! hark away! and tally ho![2]

Though changeful time, with hand severe,
    Has made me now these joys forego,
Yet my heart bounds whene'er I hear
    Yoicks! hark away! and tally ho!

Oh! Bold Robin Hood Is a Forester Good

Oh! bold Robin Hood is a forester good,
As ever drew bow in the merry greenwood:
At his bugle's shrill singing the echoes are
    ringing,
The wild deer are springing for many a
    rood:
5 Its summons we follow, through brake,[3]
    over hollow,
The thrice-blown shrill summons of bold
    Robin Hood.

And what eye hath e'er seen such a sweet
    Maiden Queen,
As Marian, the pride of the forester's
    green?
A sweet garden-flower, she blooms in the
    bower,
10 Where alone to this hour the wild rose
    has been:

[1] That is, count while prayers are being uttered.
[2] Cries of encouragement to the hounds.
[3] thicket

We hail her in duty the Queen of all
    beauty:
We will live, we will die, by our sweet
    Maiden Queen.

And here's a gray friar, good as heart can
    desire,
To absolve all our sins as the case may
    require:
15 Who with courage so stout, lays his oak-
    plant about,
And puts to the rout all the foes of his
    choir;
For we are his choristers, we merry for-
    esters,
Chorusing thus with our militant friar.

And Scarlet doth bring his good yew-
    bough and string,
20 Prime minister is he of Robin our King;
No mark is too narrow for Little John's
    arrow,
That hits a cock sparrow a mile on the
    wing:
Robin and Mariòn, Scarlet and Little John,
Long with their glory old Sherwood shall
    ring.

25 Each a good liver, for well-feathered
    quiver
Doth furnish brawn,[1] venison, and fowl
    of the river:
But the best game we dish up, it is a fat
    bishop:
When his angels[2] we fish up, he proves a
    free giver:
For a prelate so lowly has angels more
    holy,
30 And should this world's false angels to
    sinners deliver.

Robin and Mariòn, Scarlet and Little John,
Drink to them one by one, drink as ye sing:
Robin and Mariòn, Scarlet and Little John,
Echo to echo through Sherwood shall fling:
35 Robin and Mariòn, Scarlet and Little John,
Long with their glory old Sherwood shall
    ring.

Ye Woods, That Oft at Sultry Noon

Ye woods, that oft at sultry noon
    Have o'er me spread your massy shade:
Ye gushing streams, whose murmured tune
    Has in my ear sweet music made,
While, where the dancing pebbles show
    Deep in the restless mountain-pool
5 The gelid water's upward flow,
    My second flask was laid to cool:

[1] boar's flesh
[2] Gold coins worth about $3.42 each.

Ye pleasant sights of leaf and flower:
Ye pleasant sounds of bird and bee:
Ye sports of deer in sylvan bower:
10   Ye feasts beneath the greenwood tree:
Ye baskings in the vernal sun:
Ye slumbers in the summer dell:
Ye trophies that his arm has won:
And must you hear your friar's fare-
well?

MARGARET LOVE PEACOCK[1]
1826

Long night succeeds thy little day:
   O, blighted blossom! can it be
That this gray stone and grassy clay
   Have clos'd our anxious care of thee?

5 The half-form'd speech of artless thought,
   That spoke a mind beyond thy years,
The song, the dance by Nature taught,
   The sunny smiles, the transient tears,

The symmetry of face and form,
10   The eye with light and life replete,
The little heart so fondly warm,
   The voice so musically sweet,—

These, lost to hope, in memory yet
   Around the hearts that lov'd thee cling,
15 Shadowing with long and vain regret
   The too fair promise of thy Spring.

From THE MISFORTUNES OF ELPHIN
1829   1829

THE CIRCLING OF THE MEAD[2] HORNS

Fill the blue horn, the blue buffalo horn:
Natural is mead in the buffalo horn:
As the cuckoo in spring, as the lark in the
   morn,
So natural is mead in the buffalo horn.

5 As the cup of the flower to the bee when he
   sips,
Is the full cup of mead to the true Briton's
   lips:
From the flower-cups of summer, on field
   and on tree,
Our mead cups are filled by the vintager
   bee.

Seithenyn ap[3] Seithyn, the generous, the
   bold,
10 Drinks the wine of the stranger from vessels of gold;

[1] Peacock's daughter, who died when she was
   three years old.
[2] A fermented drink made of honey, nectar, and
   wine.
[3] son of

But we from the horn, the blue silver-
   rimmed horn,
Drink the ale and the mead in our fields
   that were born.

The ale froth is white, and the mead
   sparkles bright;
They both smile apart, and with smiles they
   unite:[1]
15 The mead from the flower, and the ale from
   the corn,[2]
Smile, sparkle, and sing in the buffalo
   horn.

The horn, the blue horn, cannot stand on
   its tip;
Its path is right on from the hand to the
   lip:
Though the bowl and the wine cup our
   tables adorn,
20 More natural the draught from the buffalo horn.

But Seithenyn ap Seithyn, the generous,
   the bold,
Drinks the bright-flowing wine from the
   far-gleaming gold:
The wine, in the bowl by his lip that is
   worn,
Shall be glorious as mead in the buffalo
   horn.

25 The horns circle fast, but their fountains
   will last,
As the stream passes ever, and never is
   past:
Exhausted so quickly, replenished so soon,
They wax and they wane like the horns of
   the moon.

Fill high the blue horn, the blue buffalo
   horn;
30 Fill high the long silver-rimmed buffalo
   horn:
While the roof of the hall by our chorus
   is torn,
Fill, fill to the brim the deep silver-rimmed
   horn.

THE WAR SONG OF DINAS VAWR

The mountain sheep are sweeter,
But the valley sheep are fatter;
We therefore deemed it meeter
To carry off the latter.
5 We made an expedition;

[1] "The mixture of ale and mead made *bradawd*,
   a favorite drink of the Ancient Britons."—
   Peacock.
[2] grain

We met an host and quelled it;
We forced a strong position
And killed the men who held it.

On Dyfed's richest valley,
10 Where herds of kine were browsing,
We made a mighty sally,
To furnish our carousing.
Fierce warriors rushed to meet us;
We met them, and o'erthrew them:
15 They struggled hard to beat us,
But we conquered them, and slew them.

As we drove our prize at leisure,
The king marched forth to catch us:
His rage surpassed all measure,
20 But his people could not match us.
He fled to his hall-pillars;
And, ere our force we led off,
Some sacked his house and cellars,
While others cut his head off.

25 We there, in strife bewildering,
Spilt blood enough to swim in:
We orphaned many children
And widowed many women.
The eagles and the ravens
30 We glutted with our foemen:
The heroes and the cravens,
The spearmen and the bowmen.

We brought away from battle,
And much their land bemoaned them,
35 Two thousand head of cattle
And the head of him who owned them:
Ednyfed, King of Dyfed,
His head was borne before us;
His wine and beasts supplied our feasts,
40 And his overthrow, our chorus.

From CROTCHET CASTLE
1831   1831

IN THE DAYS OF OLD

In the days of old
Lovers felt true passion,
Deeming years of sorrow
By a smile repaid:
5 Now the charms of gold,
Spells of pride and fashion,
Bid them say Good-morrow
To the best-loved maid.

Through the forests wild,
10 O'er the mountains lonely,
They were never weary
Honor to pursue:
If the damsel smiled
Once in seven years only,

15 All their wanderings dreary
Ample guerdon knew.

Now one day's caprice
Weighs down years of smiling,
Youthful hearts are rovers,
20 Love is bought and sold.
Fortune's gifts may cease,
Love is less beguiling:
Wiser were the lovers
In the days of old.

From GRYLL GRANGE
1859   1860

LOVE AND AGE

I played with you mid cowslips blowing,
When I was six and you were four;
When garlands weaving, flower-balls throw-
ing,
Were pleasures soon to please no more.
5 Through groves and meads, o'er grass and
heather,
With little playmates, to and fro,
We wandered hand in hand together;
But that was sixty years ago.

You grew a lovely roseate maiden,
10 And still our early love was strong;
Still with no care our days were laden,
They glided joyously along;
And I did love you very dearly,
How dearly words want power to show;
15 I thought your heart was touched as
nearly;
But that was fifty years ago.

Then other lovers came around you,
Your beauty grew from year to year.
And many a splendid circle found you
20 The centre of its glittering sphere.
I saw you then, first vows forsaking,
On rank and wealth your hand bestow;
Oh, then I thought my heart was break-
ing,—
But that was forty years ago.

25 And I lived on, to wed another;
No cause she gave me to repine;
And when I heard you were a mother,
I did not wish the children mine.
My own young flock, in fair progression
30 Made up a pleasant Christmas row:
My joy in them was past expression,—
But that was thirty years ago.

You grew a matron plump and comely,
You dwelt in fashion's brightest blaze;
35 My earthly lot was far more homely;

But I too had my festal days.
No merrier eyes have ever glistened
Around the hearth-stone's wintry glow,
Than when my youngest child was chris-
    tened,—
40 But that was twenty years ago.

Time passed. My eldest girl was married,
And I am now a grandsire gray;
One pet of four years old I've carried
Among the wild-flowered meads to play.
45 In our old fields of childish pleasure,
Where now, as then, the cowslips blow,
She fills her basket's ample measure,—
But that is not ten years ago.

But though first love's impassioned blind-
    ness
50 Has passed away in colder light,
I still have thought of you with kindness,
And shall do, till our last good-night.
The ever-rolling silent hours
Will bring a time we shall not know,
55 When our young days of gathering flowers
Will be an hundred years ago.

William Cobbett 1763-1835

From RURAL RIDES
1821-32   1830-33

KENSINGTON,
Friday, 4 Jan., 1822.

Got home from *Battle.* I had no time to
see the town, having entered the Inn on
Wednesday in the dusk of the evening, having been engaged all day yesterday in the
Inn, and having come out of it only to get
into the coach this morning. I had not time
to go even to see *Battle Abbey,* the seat of the
Webster family, now occupied by a man
of the name of *Alexander!* Thus they
replace them![1] It will take a much shorter
time than most people imagine to put out
all the ancient families. I should think that
six years will turn out all those who receive
nothing out of taxes. The greatness of the
estate is no protection to the owner; for,
great or little, it will soon yield him *no*
rents; and, when the produce is nothing in
either case, the small estate is as good as the
large one. Mr. Curteis said that the *land*
was *immovable*; yes; but the *rents are not.*
And, if freeholds cannot be seized for common contract debts, the carcass of the
owner may. But, in fact, there will be no

[1] A reference to the change taking place in the
social history of England. Cobbett's toryism,
suggested here, is in odd contrast with his
more usual radicalism.

rents; and, without these, the ownership is
an empty sound. Thus, at last, the burthen
will, as I always said it would, fall upon
the *landowner*; and, as the fault of sup-
5 porting the system has been wholly his, the
burthen will fall upon the *right back.*
Whether he will now call in the people to
help him to shake it off is more than I can
say; but, if he do not, I am sure that he must
10 sink under it. And then, will *revolution
No. I* have been accomplished; but far, and
very far indeed, will that be from being the
close of the drama!—I cannot quit Battle
without observing, that the country is very
15 pretty all about it. All hill, or valley. A
great deal of wood-land, in which the underwood is generally very fine, though the oaks
are not very fine, and a good deal covered
with *moss.* This shows that the clay ends
20 before the *tap*-root of the oak gets as deep
as it would go; for, when the clay goes the
full depth, the oaks are always fine.—The
woods are too large and too near each other
for hare-hunting; and as to coursing,[1] it
25 is out of the question here. But it is a fine
country for shooting and for harboring game
of all sorts.—It was rainy as I came home;
but the woodmen were at work. A great
many *hop-poles* are cut here, which makes
30 the coppices more valuable than in many
other parts. The women work in the coppices, shaving the bark off the hop-poles,
and, indeed, at various other parts of the
business. These poles are shaved to prevent
35 *maggots* from breeding in the bark and ac-
celerating the destruction of the pole. It is
curious that the bark of trees should gen-
erate maggots; but it has, as well as the
wood, a *sugary* matter in it. The hickory
40 wood in America sends out from the ends
of the logs when these are burning, great
quantities of the finest syrup that can be
imagined. Accordingly, that wood breeds
maggots, or worms as they are usually
45 called, surprisingly. Our *ash* breeds worms
very much. When the tree or pole is cut,
the moist matter between the outer bark
and the wood, putrifies. Thence come the
maggots, which soon begin to eat their way
50 into the wood. For this reason the bark
is shaved off the hop-poles, as it ought to be
off all our timber trees, as soon as cut,
especially the ash.—Little boys and girls
shave hop-poles and assist in other coppice
55 work very nicely. And, it is pleasant work
when the weather is dry over head. The
woods, bedded with leaves as they are, are

[1] pursuing game with dogs that follow by sight
instead of by scent

clean and dry underfoot. They are warm too, even in the coldest weather. When the ground is frozen several inches deep in the open fields, it is scarcely frozen at all in a coppice where the underwood is a good plant, and where it is nearly high enough to cut. So that the woodman's is really a pleasant life. We are apt to think that the birds have a hard time of it in winter. But, we forget the warmth of the woods, which far exceeds any thing to be found in farm yards. When Sidmouth started me from my farm, in 1817,[1] I had just planted my farm round with a pretty coppice. But, never mind, Sidmouth and I shall, I dare say, have plenty of time and occasion to talk about that coppice, and many other things, before we die. And, can I, when I think of these things now, *pity* those to whom Sidmouth *owed his power* of starting me!— But let me forget the subject for this time at any rate.—Woodland countries are interesting on many accounts. Not so much on account of their masses of green leaves, as on account of the variety of sights and sounds and incidents that they afford. Even in winter the coppices are beautiful to the eye, while they comfort the mind with the idea of shelter and warmth. In spring they change their hue from day to day during two whole months, which is about the time from the first appearance of the delicate leaves of the birch to the full expansion of those of the ash; and, even before the leaves come at all to intercept the view, what in the vegetable creation is so delightful to behold as the bed of a coppice bespangled with primroses and bluebells? The opening of the birch leaves is the signal for the pheasant to begin to crow, for the blackbird to whistle, and the thrush to sing, and, just when the oak-buds begin to look reddish, and not a day before, the whole tribe of finches burst forth in songs from every bough, while the lark, imitating them all, carries the joyous sounds to the sky. These are amongst the means which Providence has benignantly appointed to sweeten the toils by which food and raiment are produced; these the English ploughman could once hear without the sorrowful reflection that he himself was *a pauper,* and that the bounties of nature had, for him, been scattered in vain! And shall he never see an end to this state of things! Shall he never have the due reward of his labor! Shall unsparing taxation never cease to make him a miserable dejected being, a creature famishing in the midst of abundance, fainting, expiring with hunger's feeble moans, surrounded by a carolling creation! O! accursed paper-money![1] Has hell a torment surpassing the wickedness of thy inventor!

Thursley,
Wednesday, 26 Oct., 1825.

The weather has been beautiful ever since last Thursday morning; but there has been a white frost every morning, and the days have been coldish. *Here,* however, I am quite at home in a room, where there is one of my *American Fireplaces,* bought, by my host,[2] of Mr. Judson of Kensington, who has made many a score of families comfortable, instead of sitting shivering in the cold. At the house of the gentleman whose house I am now in, there is a good deal of *fuelwood;* and here I see in the parlors, those fine and cheerful fires that make a great part of the happiness of the Americans. But these fires are to be had only in this sort of fireplace. Ten times the fuel; nay, no quantity, would effect the same object, in any other fireplace. It is equally good for coal as for wood; but for *pleasure,* a woodfire is the thing. There is, round about almost every gentleman's or great farmer's house, more wood suffered to rot every year, in one shape or another, than would make (with this fireplace) a couple of rooms constantly warm, from October to June. *Here,* peat, turf, saw-dust, and wood are burnt in these fireplaces. My present host has three of the fireplaces.

Being out a-coursing today, I saw a queer-looking building upon one of the thousands of hills that nature has tossed up in endless variety of form round the skirts of the lofty Hindhead. This building is, it seems, called a *Semaphore, or Semiphare,* or

---

[1] In 1817, Henry Addington, first Viscount Sidmouth, restricted the liberty of the press because Cobbett's attacks on the government, published in his *Weekly Political Register,* caused a growing discontent among the working classes. In order to continue his attacks unmolested, Cobbett left his "Farmhouse" at Botley, Hampshire, and came to America.

[1] In 1797, the Bank of England was forbidden to make its payments in gold. The paper-money which was then issued in large quantities gradually depreciated in value until fears of a national bankruptcy became general. It was doubted whether the Bank ever could and would resume cash payments, and Cobbett announced that when that time came he would give himself up to be broiled upon a gridiron. Cash payments were resumed, however, on May 1, 1821. See Martineau's *The History of England,* 1, 294-99, and 2, 225-30; Peacock's *Paper Money Lyrics* and *Melincourt,* ch. 30, "The Paper-Mill"; also Shelley's *The Mask of Anarchy,* 180 (p. 683).

[2] John Knowles, of Thursley.

something of that sort. What this word may have been hatched out of I cannot say; but it means *a job*,[1] I am sure. To call it an *alarm-post* would not have been so convenient; for people not endued with Scotch *intellect* might have wondered why we should have to pay for alarm-posts; and might have thought that, with all our "glorious victories,"[2] we had "brought our hogs to a fine market,"[3] if our dread of the enemy were such as to induce us to have alarm-posts all over the country! Such unintellectual people might have thought that we had "conquered France by the immortal Wellington," to little purpose, if we were still in such fear as to build alarm-posts; and they might, in addition, have observed that, for many hundred of years, England stood in need of neither signal-posts nor standing army of mercenaries; but relied safely on the courage and public spirit of the people themselves. By calling the thing by an outlandish name, these reflections amongst the unintellectual are obviated. *Alarm-post* would be a nasty name; and it would puzzle people exceedingly, when they saw one of these at a place like Ashe, a little village on the north side of the chalk-ridge (called the Hog's Back) going from Guildford to Farnham! What can this be *for?* Why are these expensive things put up all over the country? Respecting the movements of *whom* is wanted this *alarm-system?* Will no member ask this in parliament? Not one: not a man: and yet it is a thing to ask about. Ah! it is in vain, THING,[4] that you thus are *making your preparations;* in vain that you are setting your trammels! The debt, the blessed debt, that best ally of the people, will break them all; will snap them, as the hornet does the cobweb; and even these very "Semaphores" contribute towards the force of that ever-blessed debt. Curious to see how things *work!* The "glorious revolution,"[5] which was made for the avowed purpose of maintaining the Protestant ascendancy, and which was followed by such terrible persecution of the Catholics; that "glorious" affair, which set aside a race of kings, because they were Catholics, served as the *precedent* for the American revolution, also called "glorious," and this second revolution compelled the successors of the makers of the first to begin to cease their persecutions of the Catholics! Then again, the debt was made to raise and keep armies on foot to prevent reform of parliament, because, as it was feared by the aristocracy, reform would have humbled them; and this debt, created for this purpose, is fast sweeping the aristocracy out of their estates, as a clown, with his foot, kicks field-mice out of their nests. There was a hope that the debt could have been reduced by stealth, as it were; that the aristocracy could have been saved in this way. That hope now no longer exists. In all likelihood the funds will keep going down. What is to prevent this, if the interest of Exchequer Bills[1] be raised, as the broadsheet[2] tells us it is to be? What! the funds fall in time of peace; and the French funds not fall in time of peace! However, it will all happen just as it ought to happen. Even the next session of parliament will bring out matters of some interest. The thing is now working in the surest possible way.

The great business of life, in the country, appertains, in some way or other, to the *game,* and especially at this time of the year. If it were not for the game, a country life would be like an *everlasting honey-moon,* which would, in about half a century, put an end to the human race. In towns, or large villages, people make a shift to find the means of rubbing the rust off from each other by a vast variety of sources of contest. A couple of wives meeting in the street, and giving each other a wry look, or a look not quite civil enough, will, if the parties be hard pushed for a ground of contention, do pretty well. But in the country, there is, alas! no such resource. Here are no walls for people to take of each other.[3] Here they are so placed as to prevent the possibility of such lucky local contact. Here is more than room of every sort, elbow, leg, horse, or carriage, for them all. Even *at church* (most of the people being in the meeting-houses) the pews are surprisingly too large. Here, therefore, where all circumstances seem calculated to cause never-ceasing concord with its accompanying dullness, there would be no relief at all, were it not for the *game.* This, happily, supplies the place of all other sources of alternate dispute and reconciliation; it keeps

---

[1] Cobbett denounced the erection of semaphores on the hills of Surrey, as a waste of public money for private gain. The semaphore consisted of towers equipped with apparatus for giving warning signals.

[2] See Southey's *The Battle of Blenheim*, 36 (p. 426).

[3] A proverb spoken in derision when an undertaking has failed.

[4] Cobbett's usual name for the Government.

[5] The Revolution of 1688, which placed William and Mary on the throne.

---

[1] Short-time bills of credit issued by the Government, and bearing interest.

[2] Any large-paged newspaper.

[3] *To take the wall* is to walk next to the wall or on the inner side of a sidewalk when walking with or meeting another person

all in life and motion, from the lord down to the hedger. When I see two men, whether in a market-room, by the way-side, in a parlor, in a churchyard, or even in the church itself, engaged in manifestly deep and most momentous discourse, I will, if it be any time between September and February, bet ten to one, that it is, in some way or other, about *the game*. The wives and daughters hear so much of it, that they inevitably get engaged in the disputes; and thus all are kept in a state of vivid animation. I should like very much to be able to take a spot, a circle of 12 miles in diameter, and take an exact amount of all the *time* spent by each individual, above the age of ten (that is the age they begin at), in talking, during the game season of one year, about the game and about sporting exploits. I verily believe that it would amount, upon an average, to six times as much as all the other talk put together; and, as to the anger, the satisfaction, the scolding, the commendation, the chagrin, the exultation, the envy, the emulation, where are there any of these in the country, unconnected with *the game?*

There is, however, an important distinction to be made between *hunters* (including coursers) and *shooters*. The latter are, as far as relates to their exploits, a disagreeable class, compared with the former; and the reason of this is, their doings are almost wholly their own; while, in the case of the others, the achievements are the property of the dogs. Nobody likes to hear another talk *much* in praise of his own acts, unless those acts have a manifest tendency to produce some good to the hearer; and shooters do talk *much* of their own exploits, and those exploits rather tend to *humiliate* the hearer. Then, a *great shooter* will, nine times out of ten, go so far as almost to *lie a little;* and, though people do not tell him of it, they do not like him the better for it; and he but too frequently discovers that they do not believe him: whereas, hunters are mere followers of the dogs, as mere spectators; their praises, if any are called for, are bestowed on the greyhounds, the hounds, the fox, the hare, or the horses. There is a little rivalship in the riding, or in the behavior of the horses; but this has so little to do with the personal merit of the sportsmen, that it never produces a want of good fellowship in the evening of the day. A shooter who has been *missing* all day, must have an uncommon share of good sense, not to feel mortified while the slaughterers are relating the adventures of that day; and this is what cannot exist in the case of the hunters. Bring me into a room, with a dozen men in it, who have been sporting all day; or, rather let me be in an adjoining room, where I can hear the sound of their voices, without being able to distinguish the words, and I will bet ten to one that I tell whether they be hunters or shooters.

I was once acquainted with a *famous shooter* whose name was William Ewing. He was a barrister of Philadelphia, who became far more renowned by his gun than by his law cases. We spent scores of days together a-shooting, and were extremely well matched. I having excellent dogs and caring little about my reputation as a shot, his dogs being good for nothing, and he caring more about his reputation as a shot than as a lawyer. The fact which I am going to relate respecting this gentleman, ought to be a warning to young men, how they become enamored of this species of vanity. We had gone about ten miles from our home, to shoot where partridges were said to be very plentiful. We found them so. In the course of a November day, he had, just before dark, shot, and sent to the farm-house, or kept in his bag, *ninety-nine* partridges. He made some few *double shots*, and he might have a *miss* or two, for he sometimes shot when out of my sight, on account of the woods. However, he said that he killed at every shot; and, as he had counted the birds, when we went to dinner at the farm-house and when he cleaned his gun, he, just before sun-set, knew that he had killed *ninety-nine* partridges, every one upon the wing, and a great part of them in woods very thickly set with largish trees. It was a grand achievement; but unfortunately, he wanted to make it *a hundred*. The sun was setting, and, in that country, darkness comes almost at once; it is more like the going out of a candle than that of a fire; and I wanted to be off, as we had a very bad road to go, and as he, being under strict petticoat government, to which he most loyally and dutifully submitted, was compelled to get home that night, taking me with him, the vehicle (horse and gig) being mine. I, therefore, pressed him to come away, and moved on myself towards the house (that of old John Brown, in Bucks county, grandfather of that General Brown, who gave some of our whiskered heroes such a rough handling last war,[1] which was waged for the purpose of "depos-

[1] The Anglo-American War of 1812, which occurred during the presidency of Madison. The idea of "deposing James Madison" is attributed to Sir Joseph Sydney Yorke (1768-1831), a British admiral.

ing James Madison''), at which house I would have stayed all night, but from which I was compelled to go by that watchful government, under which he had the good fortune to live. Therefore I was in haste to be off. No: he would kill the *hundredth* bird! In vain did I talk of the bad road and its many dangers for want of moon. The poor partridges, which we had scattered about, were *calling* all around us; and, just at this moment, up got one under his feet, in a field in which the wheat was three or four inches high. He shot and *missed*. "That's it," said he, running as if to *pick up* the bird. "What!" said I, "you don't think you *killed*, do you? Why there is the bird now, not only alive, but *calling* in that wood''; which was at about a hundred yards distance. He, in that *form of words* usually employed in such cases, asserted that he had shot the bird and saw it fall; and I, in much about the same form of words, asserted, that he had *missed*, and that I, with my own eyes, saw the bird fly into the wood. This was too much! To *miss* once out of a hundred times! To lose such a chance of immortality! He was a good-humored man; I liked him very much; and I could not help feeling for him, when he said, "Well, *Sir*, I killed the bird; and if you choose to go away and take your dog away, so as to prevent me from *finding* it, you must do it; the dog is *yours*, to be sure."—"The *dog*," said I, in a very mild tone; "why, Ewing, there is the spot; and could we not see it, upon this smooth green surface, if it were there?" However, he began to *look about*; and I called the dog, and affected to join him in the search. Pity for his weakness got the better of my dread of the bad road. After walking backward and forward many times upon about twenty yards square with our eyes to the ground, looking for what both of us knew was not there, I had passed him (he going one way and I the other), and I happened to be turning round just after I had passed him, when I saw him, putting his hand behind him, *take a partridge out of his bag and let it fall upon the ground!* I felt no temptation to detect him, but turned away my head, and kept looking about. Presently he having returned to the spot where the bird was, called out to me, in a most triumphant tone; "*Here! here!* Come here!" I went up to him, and he, pointing with his finger down to the bird, and looking hard in my face at the same time, said, "There, Cobbett; I hope that will be a *warning* to you never to be obstinate again"!—"Well," said I, "come

along": and away we went as merry as larks. When we got to Brown's, he told them the story, triumphed over me most clamorously, and, though he often repeated the story to my face, I never had the heart to let him know, that I knew of the imposition, which puerile vanity had induced so sensible and honorable a man to be mean enough to practice.

A *professed shot* is, almost always, a very disagreeable brother sportsman. He must, in the first place, have a head rather of the emptiest to *pride himself* upon so poor a talent. Then he is always out of temper, if the game fail, or if he miss it. He never participates in that great delight which all sensible men enjoy at beholding the beautiful action, the docility, the zeal, the wonderful sagacity of the pointer and the setter. He is always thinking about *himself;* always anxious to surpass his companions. I remember that, once, Ewing and I had lost our dog. We were in a wood, and the dog had gone out, and found a covey in a wheat stubble joining the wood. We had been whistling and calling him for, perhaps, half an hour, or more. When we came out of the wood we saw him pointing, with one foot up; and, soon after, he, keeping his feet and body unmoved, gently turned round his head towards the spot where he heard us, as if to bid us to come on, and, when he saw that we saw him, turned his head back again. I was so delighted that I stopped to look with admiration. Ewing, astonished at my want of alacrity, pushed on, shot one of the partridges, and thought no more about the conduct of the dog than if the sagacious creature had had nothing at all to do with the matter. When I left America, in 1800, I gave this dog to Lord Henry Stuart, who was, when he came home, a year or two afterwards, about to bring him to astonish the sportsmen even in England; but, those of Pennsylvania were resolved not to part with him, and, therefore they *stole* him the night before his Lordship came away. Lord Henry had plenty of pointers after his return, and he *saw* hundreds; but always declared that he never saw anything approaching in excellence this American dog. For the information of sportsmen I ought to say that this was a small-headed and sharp-nosed pointer, hair as fine as that of a greyhound, little and short ears, very light in the body, very long legged, and swift as a good lurcher. I had him a puppy, and he never had any *breaking*, but he pointed staunchly at once; and I am of opinion that this sort is, in all respects, better than the heavy breed. Mr. Thornton (I beg his pardon, I believe he is now a Knight of some sort), who was, and perhaps still is, our envoy in Portugal, at the time here referred to, was a sort of partner with Lord Henry in this famous dog; and gratitude (to the memory of *the dog,* I mean) will, I am sure, or, at least, I hope so, make him bear witness to the truth of my character of him; and, if one could hear an Ambassador *speak out,* I think that Mr. Thornton would acknowledge that his calling has brought him in pretty close contact with many a man who was possessed of most tremendous political power, without possessing half the sagacity, half the understanding, of this dog, and without being a thousandth part so faithful to his trust.

I am quite satisfied that there are as many *sorts* of men as there are of dogs.[1] Swift, was a man, and so is Walter the base.[2] But, is the *sort* the same? It cannot be *education* alone that makes the amazing difference that we see. Besides, we see men of the very same rank and riches and education, differing as widely as the pointer does from the pug. The name, *man,* is common to all the sorts, and hence arises very great mischief. What confusion must there be in rural affairs, if there were no names whereby to distinguish hounds, greyhounds, pointers, spaniels, terriers, and sheep dogs, from each other! And, what pretty work, if, without regard to the *sorts* of dogs, men were to attempt to *employ them!* Yet, this is done in the case of *men!* A man is always *a man;* and, without the least regard as to the *sort,* they are promiscuously placed in all kinds of situations. Now, if Mr. Brougham, Doctors Birkbeck, Macculloch and Black, and that profound personage, Lord John Russell, will, in their forthcoming "London University,"[3] teach us how to divide men *into sorts,* instead of teaching us to "augment the capital of the nation," by making paper-money, they will render us a real service. That will be *feelosofy* worth attending to. What would be said of the 'Squire who should take a fox-hound out to find partridges for him to shoot at? Yet, would this be *more* absurd than to set a man to law-making who was manifestly formed for the express purpose of sweeping the streets or digging out sewers?

[1] See *Macbeth,* III, 1, 90-100.
[2] John Walter (1739-1812), founder of *The London Times.*
[3] London University was founded in 1825, but was not chartered until 1836.

EAST EVERLEY, *Monday Morning,*
5 o'clock, 28 Aug., 1826.

A very fine morning; a man, *eighty-two years of age,* just beginning to mow the short-grass, in the garden; I thought it, even when I was young, the *hardest work* that man had to do. To *look on,* this work seems nothing; but it tries every sinew in your frame, if you go upright and do your work well. This old man never knew how to do it well, and he stoops, and he hangs his scythe wrong; but, with all this, it must be a surprising man to mow short-grass, as well as he does, at *eighty. I wish I* may be able to mow short-grass at eighty! That's all I have to say of the matter. I am just setting off for the source of the Avon, which runs from near Marlborough to Salisbury, and thence to the sea; and I intend to pursue it as far as Salisbury. In the distance of thirty miles, here are, I see by the books, more than thirty churches. I wish to see, with my own eyes, what evidence there is that those thirty churches were built without hands, without money, and without a congregation; and, thus, to find matter, if I can, to justify the mad wretches, who, from Committee-Rooms and elsewhere, are bothering this half-distracted nation to death about a "surplus popalashon, mon."[1]

My horse is ready; and the rooks are just gone off to the stubble-fields. These rooks rob the pigs; but, they have *a right* to do it. I wonder (upon my soul I do) that there is no lawyer, Scotchman, or Parson-Justice, to propose a law to punish the rooks for *trespass.*

William Hazlitt 1778-1830
From CHARACTERS OF SHAKESPEAR'S PLAYS
1817

HAMLET

This is that Hamlet the Dane, whom we read of in our youth, and whom we may be said almost to remember in our after-years; he who made that famous soliloquy on life,[2] who gave the advice to the players,[3] who thought "this goodly frame, the earth, a sterile promontory, and this brave o'erhanging firmament, the air, this majestical

[1] A reference to the political economist T. R. Malthus (1766-1834) and his followers, who held that population tends to multiply faster than does its means of subsistence, and that unless the increase can be checked, poverty and suffering will be inevitable. See Hood's *Ode to Mr. Malthus.* In spite of the census returns Cobbett persisted in believing that the population was decreasing.
[2] *Hamlet,* III, 1, 56-88.   [3] Act III, 2, 1-50.

roof fretted with golden fire, a foul and pestilent congregation of vapors;"[1] whom "man delighted not, nor woman neither;"[2] he who talked with the grave-diggers, and moralized on Yorick's skull;[3] the schoolfellow of Rosencrans and Guildenstern at Wittenberg; the friend of Horatio; the lover of Ophelia; he that was mad and sent to England;[4] the slow avenger of his father's death; who lived at the court of Horwendillus five hundred years before we were born, but all whose thoughts we seem to know as well as we do our own, because we have read them in Shakespear.

Hamlet is a name; his speeches and sayings but the idle coinage of the poet's brain. What then, are they not real? They are as real as our own thoughts. Their reality is in the reader's mind. It is we who are Hamlet. This play has a prophetic truth, which is above that of history. Whoever has become thoughtful and melancholy through his own mishaps or those of others; whoever has borne about with him the clouded brow of reflection, and thought himself "too much i' th' sun;"[5] whoever has seen the golden lamp of day dimmed by envious mists rising in his own breast, and could find in the world before him only a dull blank with nothing left remarkable in it; whoever has known "the pangs of despised love, the insolence of office, or the spurns which patient merit of the unworthy takes;"[6] he who has felt his mind sink within him, and sadness cling to his heart like a malady, who has had his hopes blighted and his youth staggered by the apparitions of strange things; who cannot be well at ease, while he sees evil hovering near him like a spectre; whose powers of action have been eaten up by thought, he to whom the universe seems infinite, and himself nothing; whose bitterness of soul makes him careless of consequences, and who goes to a play as his best resource to shove off, to a second remove, the evils of life by a mock representation of them—this is the true Hamlet.

We have been so used to this tragedy that we hardly know how to criticize it any more than we should know how to describe our own faces. But we must make such observations as we can. It is the one of Shakespear's plays that we think of the oftenest, because it abounds most in striking reflections on human life, and because the distresses of Hamlet are transferred, by the turn of his mind, to the general account of humanity. Whatever happens to him we apply to ourselves, because he applies it so himself as a means of general reasoning. He is a great moralizer; and what makes him worth attending to is that he moralizes on his own feelings and experience. He is not a common-place pedant. If *Lear* shows the greatest depth of passion, *Hamlet* is the most remarkable for the ingenuity, originality, and unstudied development of character. Shakespear had more magnanimity than any other poet, and he has shown more of it in this play than in any other. There is no attempt to force an interest: everything is left for time and circumstances to unfold. The attention is excited without effort, the incidents succeed each other as matters of course, the characters think and speak and act just as they might do, if left entirely to themselves. There is no set purpose, no straining at a point. The observations are suggested by the passing scene— the gusts of passion come and go like sounds of music borne on the wind. The whole play is an exact transcript of what might be supposed to have taken place at the court of Denmark, at the remote period of time fixed upon,[1] before the modern refinements in morals and manners were heard of. It would have been interesting enough to have been admitted as a by-stander in such a scene, at such a time, to have heard and seen something of what was going on. But here we are more than spectators. We have not only "the outward pageants and the signs of grief;" but "we have that within which passes show."[2] We read the thoughts of the heart, we catch the passions living as they rise. Other dramatic writers give us very fine versions and paraphrases of nature: but Shakespear, together with his own comments, gives us the original text, that we may judge for ourselves. This is a very great advantage.

The character of Hamlet is itself a pure effusion of genius. It is not a character marked by strength of will or even of passion, but by refinement of thought and sentiment. Hamlet is as little of the hero as a man can well be: but he is a young and princely novice, full of high enthusiasm and quick sensibility—the sport of circumstances, questioning with fortune and refining on his own feelings, and forced from the natural bias of his disposition by the strangeness of his situation. He seems in-

[1] Act II, 2, 310-15.
[2] Act II, 2, 322.
[3] Act V, 1, 127-215.
[4] Act V, 1, 161.
[5] Act I, 2, 67.
[6] Act III, 1, 72-74.

[1] The Hamlet story in its earliest form was told by Saxo Grammaticus in his Latin history of Denmark (c. 1200).
[2] Act I, 2, 85.

capable of deliberate action, and is only hurried into extremities on the spur of the occasion, when he has no time to reflect, as in the scene where he kills Polonius,[1] and again, where he alters the letters which Rosencrans and Guildenstern are taking with them to England,[2] purporting his death. At other times, when he is most bound to act, he remains puzzled, undecided, and skeptical, dallies with his purposes, till the occasion is lost, and always finds some pretence to relapse into indolence and thoughtfulness again. For this reason he refuses to kill the King when he is at his prayers,[3] and by a refinement in malice, which is in truth only an excuse for his own want of resolution, defers his revenge to some more fatal opportunity, when he shall be engaged in some act "that has no relish of salvation in it."[4]

He kneels and prays,
And now I'll do 't, and so he goes to heaven,
And so am I reveng'd; *that would be scann'd:*
He kill'd my father, and for that,
I, his sole son, send him to heaven.
Why this is reward, not revenge.
Up sword and know thou a more horrid time,
When he is drunk, asleep, or in a rage.[5]

He is the prince of philosophical speculators, and because he cannot have his revenge perfect, according to the most refined idea his wish can form, he misses it altogether. So he scruples to trust the suggestions of the Ghost, contrives the scene of the play to have surer proof of his uncle's guilt,[6] and then rests satisfied with this confirmation of his suspicions, and the success of his experiment, instead of acting upon it. Yet he is sensible of his own weakness, taxes himself with it, and tries to reason himself out of it.

How all occasions do inform against me,
And spur my dull revenge! What is a man,
If his chief good and market of his time
Be but to sleep and feed? A beast; no more.
Sure he that made us with such large discourse,
Looking before and after, gave us not
That capability and god-like reason
To rust in us unus'd: now whether it be
Bestial oblivion, or some craven scruple
Of thinking too precisely on th' event,—
A thought which quarter'd, hath but one part wisdom,
And ever three parts coward:—I do not know
Why yet I live to say, this thing's to do;
Sith I have cause, and will, and strength, and means
To do it. Examples gross as earth excite me:

Witness this army[1] of such mass and charge,
Led by a delicate and tender prince,
Whose spirit with divine ambition puff'd,
Makes mouths at the invisible event,
Exposing what is mortal and unsure
To all that fortune, death and danger dare,
Even for an egg-shell. 'Tis not to be great,
Never to stir without great argument;
But greatly to find quarrel in a straw,
When honor's at the stake. How stand I then,
That have a father kill'd, a mother stain'd,
Excitements of my reason and my blood,
And let all sleep, while to my shame I see
The imminent death of twenty thousand men,
That for a fantasy and trick of fame,
Go to their graves like beds, fight for a plot
Whereon the numbers cannot try the cause,
Which is not tomb enough and continent
To hide the slain?—O, from this time forth,
My thoughts be bloody or be nothing worth.[2]

Still he does nothing; and this very speculation on his own infirmity only affords him another occasion for indulging it. It is not for any want of attachment to his father or abhorrence of his murder that Hamlet is thus dilatory, but it is more to his taste to indulge his imagination in reflecting upon the enormity of the crime and refining on his schemes of vengeance, than to put them into immediate practice. His ruling passion is to think, not to act: and any vague pretence that flatters this propensity instantly diverts him from his previous purposes.

The moral perfection of this character has been called in question, we think, by those who did not understand it. It is more interesting than according to rules: amiable, though not faultless. The ethical delineations of "that noble and liberal casuist"[3] (as Shakespear has been well called) do not exhibit the drab-colored quakerism of morality. His plays are not copied either from *The Whole Duty of Man* or from *The Academy of Compliments!* We confess, we are a little shocked at the want of refinement in those who are shocked at the want of refinement in Hamlet. The want of punctilious exactness in his behavior either partakes of the "license of the time," or else belongs to the very excess of intellectual refinement in the character, which makes the common rules of life, as well as his own purposes, sit loose upon him.[4] He may be said to be amenable only to the tribunal of his own thoughts, and is too much taken up with the airy world

---

[1] Act III, 4, 24.
[2] Act V, 2, 13-53.
[3] Act III, 3, 73-95.
[4] Act III, 3, 92.
[5] Act III, 3, 73-79 ; 88, 89.
[6] Act II, 2, 623-34.

[1] The Norwegian army led by Fortinbras.
[2] Act IV, 4, 32-66.
[3] Lamb refers to the Elizabethan dramatists as "those noble and liberal casuists" in his *Characters of Dramatic Writers;* the expression occurs in the remarks on Thomas Middleton and William Rowley.
[4] With this passage compare Lamb's *On the Tragedies of Shakspeare* (p. 951a, 28 ff.).

of contemplation to lay as much stress as he ought on the practical consequences of things. His habitual principles of action are unhinged and out of joint with the time. His conduct to Ophelia is quite natural in his circumstances. It is that of assumed severity only. It is the effect of disappointed hope, of bitter regrets, of affection suspended, not obliterated, by the distractions of the scene around him! Amidst the natural and preternatural horrors of his situation, he might be excused in delicacy from carrying on a regular courtship When "his father's spirit was in arms,"[1] it was not a time for the son to make love in. He could neither marry Ophelia, nor wound her mind by explaining the cause of his alienation, which he durst hardly trust himself to think of. It would have taken him years to have come to a direct explanation on the point. In the harassed state of his mind, he could not have done otherwise than he did. His conduct does not contradict what he says when he sees her funeral,

I loved Ophelia: forty thousand brothers
Could not with all their quantity of love
Make up my sum.[2]

Nothing can be more affecting or beautiful than the Queen's apostrophe to Ophelia on throwing the flowers into the grave.

Sweets to the sweet, farewell.
I hop'd thou should'st have been my Hamlet's wife:
I thought thy bride-bed to have deck'd,
    sweet maid,
And not have strew'd thy grave.[3]

Shakespear was thoroughly a master of the mixed motives of human character, and he here shows us the Queen, who was so criminal in some respects, not without sensibility and affection in other relations of life. —Ophelia is a character almost too exquisitely touching to be dwelt upon. Oh, rose of May! oh, flower too soon faded! Her love, her madness, her death, are described with the truest touches of tenderness and pathos. It is a character which nobody but Shakespear could have drawn in the way that he has done, and to the conception of which there is not even the smallest approach, except in some of the old romantic ballads.[4]

[1] Act I, 2, 255.
[2] Act V, 1, 292-94.   [3] Act V, 1, 266-69.
[4] "In the account of her death, a friend has pointed out an instance of the poet's exact observation of nature:—
'There is a willow growing o'er a brook,
That shows its hoary leaves i' th' glassy stream.'
The inside of the leaves of the willow next the water, is of a whitish color, and the reflection would therefore be 'hoary.' "—Hazlitt. The lines quoted are found in Act IV, 7, 167-8.

Her brother, Laertes, is a character we do not like so well: he is too hot and choleric, and somewhat rhodomontade.[1] Polonius is a perfect character in its kind; nor is there any foundation for the objections which have been made to the consistency of this part. It is said that he acts very foolishly and talks very sensibly. There is no inconsistency in that. Again, that he talks wisely at one time and foolishly at another; that his advice to Laertes[2] is very sensible, and his advice to the King and Queen on the subject of Hamlet's madness[3] very ridiculous. But he gives the one as a father, and is sincere in it; he gives the other as a mere courtier, a busy-body, and is accordingly officious, garrulous, and impertinent. In short, Shakespear has been accused of inconsistency in this and other characters, only because he has kept up the distinction which there is in nature, between the understandings and moral habits of men, between the absurdity of their ideas and the absurdity of their motives. Polonius is not a fool, but he makes himself so. His folly, whether in his actions or speeches, comes under the head of impropriety of intention.

We do not like to see our author's plays acted, and least of all, *Hamlet.* There is no play that suffers so much in being transferred to the stage. Hamlet himself seems hardly capable of being acted. Mr. Kemble unavoidably fails in this character from a want of ease and variety. The character of Hamlet is made up of undulating lines; it has the yielding flexibility of "a wave o' th' sea."[4] Mr. Kemble plays it like a man in armor, with a determined inveteracy of purpose, in one undeviating straight line, which is as remote from the natural grace and refined susceptibility of the character, as the sharp angles and abrupt starts which Mr. Kean introduces into the part. Mr. Kean's Hamlet is as much too splenetic and rash as Mr. Kemble's is too deliberate and formal. His manner is too strong and pointed. He throws a severity, approaching to virulence, into the common observations and answers. There is nothing of this in Hamlet. He is, as it were, wrapped up in his reflections, and only *thinks aloud.* There should therefore be no attempt to impress what he says upon others by a studied exaggeration of emphasis or manner; no *talking at* his hearers. There should be as much of the gentleman and scholar as possible infused into the part, and as little of the actor. A pensive air of sadness should

[1] boastful   [2] Act I, 3, 58-81.   [3] Act II, 2, 86-151.
[4] *The Winter's Tale,* IV, 4, 141.

sit reluctantly upon his brow, but no appearance of fixed and sullen gloom. He is full of weakness and melancholy, but there is no harshness in his nature. He is the most amiable of misanthropes.

ON FAMILIAR STYLE
1821

It is not easy to write a familiar style. Many people mistake a familiar for a vulgar style, and suppose that to write without affectation is to write at random. On the contrary, there is nothing that requires more precision, and, if I may so say, purity of expression, than the style I am speaking of. It utterly rejects not only all unmeaning pomp, but all low, cant phrases, and loose, unconnected, *slipshod* allusions. It is not to take the first word that offers, but the best word in common use; it is not to throw words together in any combination we please, but to follow and avail ourselves of the true idiom of the language. To write a genuine familiar or truly English style, is to write as any one would speak in common conversation, who had a thorough command and choice of words, or who could discourse with ease, force, and perspicuity, setting aside all pedantic and oratorical flourishes. Or to give another illustration, to write naturally is the same thing in regard to common conversation, as to read naturally is in regard to common speech. It does not follow that it is an easy thing to give the true accent and inflection to the words you utter, because you do not attempt to rise above the level of ordinary life and colloquial speaking. You do not assume indeed the solemnity of the pulpit, or the tone of stage-declamation: neither are you at liberty to gabble on at a venture, without emphasis or discretion, or to resort to vulgar dialect or clownish pronunciation. You must steer a middle course. You are tied down to a given and appropriate articulation, which is determined by the habitual associations between sense and sound, and which you can only hit by entering into the author's meaning, as you must find the proper words and style to express yourself by fixing your thoughts on the subject you have to write about. Any one may mouth out a passage with a theatrical cadence, or get upon stilts to tell his thoughts: but to write or speak with propriety and simplicity is a more difficult task. Thus it is easy to affect a pompous style, to use a word twice as big as the thing you want to express: it is not so easy to pitch upon the very word that exactly fits it. Out of eight or ten words equally common, equally intelligible, with nearly equal pretensions, it is a matter of some nicety and discrimination to pick out the very one, the preferableness of which is scarcely perceptible, but decisive. The reason why I object to Dr. Johnson's style is, that there is no discrimination, no selection, no variety in it. He uses none but "tall, opaque words,"[1] taken from the "first row of the rubric:"[2]—words with the greatest number of syllables, or Latin phrases with merely English terminations. If a fine style depended on this sort of arbitrary pretension, it would be fair to judge of an author's elegance by the measurement of his words, and the substitution of foreign circumlocutions (with no precise associations) for the mother-tongue.[3] How simple it is to be dignified without ease, to be pompous without meaning! Surely, it is but a mechanical rule for avoiding what is low to be always pedantic and affected. It is clear you cannot use a vulgar English word, if you never use a common English word at all. A fine tact is shown in adhering to those which are perfectly common, and yet never falling into any expressions which are debased by disgusting circumstances, or which owe their signification and point to technical or professional allusions. A truly natural or familiar style can never be quaint or vulgar, for this reason, that it is of universal force and applicability, and that quaintness and vulgarity arise out of the immediate connection of certain words with coarse and disagreeable, or with confined ideas. The last form what we understand by cant or slang phrases. —To give an example of what is not very clear in the general statement. I should say that the phrase *To cut with a knife,* or *To cut a piece of wood,* is perfectly free from vulgarity, because it is perfectly common: but to *cut an acquaintance* is not quite unexceptionable, because it is not perfectly common or intelligible, and has hardly yet escaped out of the limits of slang phraseology. I should hardly therefore use the word in this sense without putting it in italics as a license of expression, to be received *cum*

[1] Sterne, *The Life and Opinions of Tristram Shandy*, 3, 20, The Author's Preface. Hazlitt had used this phrase in discussing Miss O'Neill's Elwina in his *A View of the English Stage*.

[2] See *Hamlet*, II, 2, 438. The rubric referred to is probably the prescribed rule of the liturgy formerly written or printed in red.

[3] "I have heard of such a thing as an author who makes it a rule never to admit a monosyllable into his vapid verse. Yet the charm and sweetness of Marlow's lines depended often on their being made up almost entirely of monosyllables."—Hazlitt.

grano salis.[1] All provincial or bye-phrases come under the same mark of reprobation—all such as the writer transfers to the page from his fireside or a particular *coterie,* or that he invents for his own sole use and convenience. I conceive that words are like money, not the worse for being common, but that it is the stamp of custom alone that gives them circulation or value. I am fastidious in this respect, and would almost as soon coin the currency of the realm as counterfeit the King's English. I never invented or gave a new and unauthorized meaning to any word but one single one (the term *impersonal* applied to feelings) and that was in an abstruse metaphysical discussion to express a very difficult distinction. I have been (I know) loudly accused of revelling in vulgarisms and broken English. I cannot speak to that point: but so far I plead guilty to the determined use of acknowledged idioms and common elliptical expressions. I am not sure that the critics in question know the one from the other, that is, can distinguish any medium between formal pedantry and the most barbarous solecism. As an author, I endeavor to employ plain words and popular modes of construction, as were I a chapman[2] and dealer, I should common weights and measures.

The proper force of words lies not in the words themselves, but in their application. A word may be a fine-sounding word, of an unusual length, and very imposing from its learning and novelty, and yet in the connection in which it is introduced, may be quite pointless and irrelevant. It is not pomp or pretension, but the adaptation of the expression to the idea that clenches a writer's meaning:—as it is not the size or glossiness of the materials, but their being fitted each to its place, that gives strength to the arch; or as the pegs and nails are as necessary to the support of the building as the larger timbers, and more so than the mere showy, unsubstantial ornaments. I hate anything that occupies more space than it is worth. I hate to see a load of band-boxes go along the street, and I hate to see a parcel of big words without anything in them. A person who does not deliberately dispose of all his thoughts alike in cumbrous draperies and flimsy disguises, may strike out twenty varieties of familiar everyday language, each coming somewhat nearer to the feeling he wants to convey, and at last not hit upon that particular and only one, which may be

said to be identical with the exact impression in his mind. This would seem to show that Mr. Cobbett is hardly right in saying that the first word that occurs is always the best.[1] It may be a very good one; and yet a better may present itself on reflection or from time to time. It should be suggested naturally, however, and spontaneously, from a fresh and lively conception of the subject. We seldom succeed by trying at improvement, or by merely substituting one word for another that we are not satisfied with, as we cannot recollect the name of a place or person by merely plaguing ourselves about it. We wander farther from the point by persisting in a wrong scent; but it starts up accidentally in the memory when we least expected it, by touching some link in the chain of previous association.

There are those who hoard up and make a cautious display of nothing but rich and rare phraseology;—ancient medals, obscure coins, and Spanish pieces of eight.[2] They are very curious to inspect; but I myself would neither offer nor take them in the course of exchange. A sprinkling of archaisms is not amiss; but a tissue of obsolete expressions is more fit *for keep than wear.* I do not say I would not use any phrase that had been brought into fashion before the middle or the end of the last century; but I should be shy of using any that had not been employed by any approved author during the whole of that time. Words, like clothes, get old-fashioned, or mean and ridiculous, when they have been for some time laid aside. Mr. Lamb is the only imitator of old English style I can read with pleasure; and he is so thoroughly imbued with the spirit of his authors, that the idea of imitation is almost done away. There is an inward unction, a marrowy vein both in the thought and feeling, an intuition, deep and lively, of his subject, that carries off any quaintness or awkwardness arising from an antiquated style and dress. The matter is completely his own, though the manner is assumed. Perhaps his ideas are altogether so marked and individual as to require their point and pungency to be neutralized by the affectation of a singular but traditional form of conveyance. Tricked out in the prevailing costume, they would probably seem more startling and out of the way. The old English authors, Burton, Fuller, Coryate, Sir Thomas

---

[1] with a grain of salt,—*i. e.,* with some allowance
[2] peddler

[1] See Cobbett's *A Grammar of the English Language,* Letter 23.
[2] Spanish dollars, or *pesos.* Each coin was marked with the figure 8, which indicated its value in *reales.*

Brown, are a kind of mediators between us and the more eccentric and whimsical modern, reconciling us to his peculiarities. I do not, however, know how far this is the case or not, till he condescends to write like one of us. I must confess that what I like best of his papers under the signature of "Elia" (still I do not presume, amidst such excellence, to decide what is most excellent) is the account of *Mrs. Battle's Opinions on Whist*,[1] which is also the most free from obsolete allusions and turns of expression—

A well of native English undefiled.[2]

To those acquainted with his admired prototypes, these *Essays* of the ingenious and highly gifted author have the same sort of charm and relish, that Erasmus's *Colloquies* or a fine piece of modern Latin have to the classical scholar. Certainly, I do not know any borrowed pencil that has more power or felicity of execution than the one of which I have here been speaking.

It is as easy to write a gaudy style without ideas, as it is to spread a pallet of showy colors, or to smear in a flaunting transparency. "What do you read?"—"Words, words, words."—"What is the matter?"[3]— "*Nothing*," it might be answered. The florid style is the reverse of the familiar. The last is employed as an unvarnished medium to convey ideas; the first is resorted to as a spangled veil to conceal the want of them. When there is nothing to be set down but words, it costs little to have them fine. Look through the dictionary, and cull out a *florilegium*,[4] rival the *tulippomania*.[5] *Rouge* high enough, and never mind the natural complexion. The vulgar, who are not in the secret, will admire the look of preternatural health and vigor; and the fashionable, who regard only appearances, will be delighted with the imposition. Keep to your sounding generalities, your tinkling phrases,[6] and all will be well. Swell out an unmeaning truism to a perfect tympany[7] of style. A thought, a distinction is the rock on which all this brittle cargo of verbiage splits at once. Such writers have merely *verbal* imaginations, that retain nothing but words. Or their puny thoughts have dragon-wings, all green and gold. They soar far above the vulgar failing

of the *Sermo humi obrepens*[1]—their most ordinary speech is never short of an hyperbole, splendid, imposing, vague, incomprehensible, magniloquent, a cento[2] of sounding commonplaces. If some of us, whose "ambition is more lowly,"[3] pry a little two narrowly into nooks and corners to pick up a number of "unconsidered trifles,"[4] they never once direct their eyes or lift their hands to seize on any but the most gorgeous, tarnished, thread-bare patch-work set of phrases, the left-off finery of poetic extravagance, transmitted down through successive generations of barren pretenders. If they criticize actors and actresses, a huddled phantasmagoria of feathers, spangles, floods of light, and oceans of sound float before their morbid sense, which they paint in the style of Ancient Pistol.[5] Not a glimpse can you get of the merits or defects of the performers: they are hidden in a profusion of barbarous epithets and wilful rhodomontade. Our hypercritics are not thinking of these little fantoccini beings—[6]

That strut and fret their hour upon the stage[7]—

but of tall phantoms of words, abstractions, *genera* and *species,* sweeping clauses, periods that unite the poles, forced alliterations, astounding antitheses—

And on their pens *Fustian* sits plumed.[8]

If they describe kings and queens, it is an Eastern pageant. The Coronation at either House is nothing to it. We get at four repeated images—a curtain, a throne, a sceptre, and a foot-stool. These are with them the wardrobe of a lofty imagination; and they turn their servile strains to servile uses. Do we read a description of pictures? It is not a reflection of tones and hues which "nature's own sweet and cunning hand laid on,"[9] but piles of precious stones, rubies, pearls, emeralds, Golconda's mines, and all the blazonry of art. Such persons are in fact besotted with words, and their brains are turned with the glittering, but empty and sterile phantoms of things. Personifications, capital letters, seas of sunbeams, visions of glory, shining inscriptions, the figures of a transparency, Britannia with her shield, or

---

[1] See p. 966.   [2] *The Faerie Queene*, IV, 2, 32.
[3] *Hamlet*, II, 2, 193-95.
[4] A descriptive list of flowers
[5] A mania for growing tulips, specifically that which raged in Holland about 1634.
[6] See *1 Corinthians*, 13 :1.
[7] inflation ; bombast (literally, kettle-drum)

[1] speech that creeps on the ground
[2] patchwork   [3] See *Julius Cæsar*, II, 1, 22.
[4] *The Winter's Tale*, IV, 3, 25.
[5] A character in Shakespeare's *Henry IV, Henry V,* and *The Merry Wives of Windsor,* noted for his bombastic speeches.
[6] puppets   [7] *Macbeth*, V, 5, 25.
[8] Adapted from *Paradise Lost*, 4, 988.
[9] *Twelfth Night*, I, 5, 258.

Hope leaning on an anchor,[1] make up their stock in trade. They may be considered as *hieroglyphical* writers. Images stand out in their minds isolated and important merely in themselves, without any ground-work of feeling—there is no context in their imaginations. Words affect them in the same way, by the mere sound, that is, by their possible, not by their actual application to the subject in hand. They are fascinated by first appearances, and have no sense of consequences. Nothing more is meant by them than meets the ear:[2] they understand or feel nothing more than meets their eye. The web and texture of the universe, and of the heart of man, is a mystery to them: they have no faculty that strikes a chord in unison with it. They cannot get beyond the daubings of fancy, the varnish of sentiment. Objects are not linked to feelings, words to things, but images revolve in splendid mockery, words represent themselves in their strange rhapsodies. The categories of such a mind are pride and ignorance—pride in outside show, to which they sacrifice everything, and ignorance of the true worth and hidden structure both of words and things. With a sovereign contempt for what is familiar and natural, they are the slaves of vulgar affectation—of a routine of high-flown phrases. Scorning to imitate realities, they are unable to invent anything, to strike out one original idea. They are not copyists of nature, it is true: but they are the poorest of all plagiarists, the plagiarists of words. All is far-fetched, dear-bought, artificial, oriental in subject and allusion: all is mechanical, conventional, vapid, formal, pedantic in style and execution. They startle and confound the understanding of the reader, by the remoteness and obscurity of their illustrations: they soothe the ear by the monotony of the same everlasting round of circuitous metaphors. They are the *mock-school* in poetry and prose. They flounder about between fustian in expression, and bathos in sentiment. They tantalize the fancy, but never reach the head nor touch the heart. Their Temple of Fame is like a shadowy structure raised by Dulness to Vanity, or like Cowper's description of the Empress of Russia's palace of ice, as "worthless as in show 'twas glittering"—

It smiled, and it was cold![3]

[1] See *Hebrews*, 6:19.   [2] See *Il Penseroso*, 120.
[3] *The Task*, 5, 176. The ice-palace of St. Petersburg was built by the Empress Anna in 1740. See Moore's *The Dissolution of the Holy Alliance* (p. 456).

THE FIGHT[1]
1822

The *fight*, the *fight's* the thing,
Wherein I'll catch the conscience of the king.[2]

Where there's a will, there's a way,—I said to myself, as I walked down Chancery-lane, about half-past six o'clock on Monday the 10th of December, to inquire at Jack Randall's where the fight the next day was to be; and I found "the proverb" nothing "musty"[3] in the present instance. I was determined to see this fight, come what would, and see it I did, in great style. It was my *first fight,* yet it more than answered my expectations. Ladies! it is to you I dedicate this description; nor let it seem out of character for the fair to notice the exploits of the brave. Courage and modesty are the old English virtues; and may they never look cold and askance on one another! Think, ye fairest of the fair, loveliest of the lovely kind, ye practicers of soft enchantment, how many more ye kill with poisoned baits than ever fell in the ring; and listen with subdued air and without shuddering, to a tale only tragic in appearance, and sacred to the FANCY.[4]

I was going down Chancery-lane, thinking to ask at Jack Randall's where the fight was to be, when looking through the glass-door of the *Hole in the Wall,* I heard a gentleman asking the same question *at* Mrs. Randall, as the author of *Waverley*[5] would express it. Now Mrs. Randall stood answering the gentleman's question, with the authenticity of the lady of the Champion of the Light Weights. Thinks I, I'll wait till this person comes out, and learn from him how it is. For to say a truth, I was not fond of going into this house of call[6] for heroes and philosophers, ever since the owner of it (for Jack is no gentleman) threatened once upon a time to kick me out of doors for wanting a mutton-chop at his hospitable board, when the conqueror in thirteen battles was more full of *blue ruin*[7] than of good manners. I was the more mortified at this repulse, inasmuch as I had heard Mr. James Simpkins, hosier in the Strand, one day when the character of the *Hole in the Wall* was brought in question, observe—"The house is a very

[1] The fight here described took place at Hungerford, Wiltshire, Dec. 11, 1821, between Tom Hickman (the Gasman) and Bill Neate, both professional prize-fighters.
[2] Adapted from *Hamlet*, II, 2, 634.
[3] *Hamlet*, III, 2, 359.
[4] The prize-fighting world.
[5] Sir Walter Scott.
[6] Meeting place; literally, a house where journeymen assemble, ready for the call of employers.
[7] Slang for *gin*.

good house, and the company quite genteel: I have been there myself!'' Remembering this unkind treatment of mine host, to which mine hostess was also a party, and not wishing to put her in unquiet thoughts at a time jubilant like the present, I waited at the door, when, who should issue forth but my friend Jo. Toms, and turning suddenly up Chancery-lane with that quick jerk and impatient stride which distinguishes a lover of the FANCY, I said, ''I'll be hanged if that fellow is not going to the fight, and is on his way to get me to go with him.'' So it proved in effect, and we agreed to adjourn to my lodgings to discuss measures with that cordiality which makes old friends like new, and new friends like old, on great occasions. We are cold to others only when we are dull in ourselves, and have neither thoughts nor feelings to impart to them. Give man a topic in his head, a throb of pleasure in his heart, and he will be glad to share it with the first person he meets. Toms and I, though we seldom meet, were an *alter idem*[1] on this memorable occasion, and had not an idea that we did not candidly impart; and ''so carelessly did we fleet the time,''[2] that I wish no better, when there is another fight, than to have him for a companion on my journey down, and to return with my friend Jack Pigott, talking of what was to happen or of what did happen, with a noble subject always at hand, and liberty to digress to others whenever they offered. Indeed, on my repeating the lines from Spenser in an involuntary fit of enthusiasm,

What more felicity can fall to creature,
Than to enjoy delight with liberty?[3]

my last-named ingenious friend stopped me by saying that this, translated into the vulgate, meant ''*Going to see a fight.*''

Jo. Toms and I could not settle about the method of going down. He said there was a caravan, he understood, to start from Tom Belcher's at two, which would go there *right out* and back again the next day. Now I never travel at night, and said I should get a cast[4] to Newbury by one of the mails. Jo. swore the thing was impossible, and I could only answer that I had made up my mind to it. In short, he seemed to me to waver, said he only came to see if I was going, had letters to write, a cause coming on the day after, and faintly said at parting (for I was bent on setting out that moment)—''Well, we

meet at Philippi!''[1] I made the best of my way to Piccadilly. The mail coach stand was bare. ''They are all gone,'' said I—''this is always the way with me—in the instant I lose the future[2]—if I had not stayed to pour that last cup of tea, I should have been just in time''—and cursing my folly and ill-luck together, without inquiring at the coach-office whether the mails were gone or not, I walked on in despite, and to punish my own dilatoriness and want of determination. At any rate I would not turn back: I might get to Hounslow, or perhaps farther, to be on my road the next morning. I passed Hyde Park Corner (my Rubicon), and trusted to fortune. Suddenly I heard the clattering of a Brentford stage, and the fight rushed full upon my fancy. I argued (not unwisely) that even a Brentford coachman was better company than my own thoughts (such as they were just then), and at his invitation mounted the box with him. I immediately stated my case to him—namely, my quarrel with myself for missing the Bath or Bristol mail, and my determination to get on in consequence as well as I could, without any disparagement or insulting comparison between longer or shorter stages. It is a maxim with me that stage-coaches, and consequently stage-coachmen, are respectable in proportion to the distance they have to travel: so I said nothing on that subject to my Brentford friend. Any incipient tendency to an abstract proposition, or (as he might have construed it) to a personal reflection of this kind, was however nipped in the bud; for I had no sooner declared indignantly that I had missed the mails, than he flatly denied that they were gone along, and lo! at the instant three of them drove by in rapid, provoking, orderly succession, as if they would devour the ground before them. Here again I seemed in the contradictory situation of the man in Dryden who exclaims,

I follow Fate, which does too hard pursue![3]

If I had stopped to inquire at the White Horse Cellar, which would not have taken me a minute, I should now have been driving down the road in all the dignified unconcern and *ideal* perfection of mechanical conveyance. The Bath mail I had set my mind upon, and I had missed it, as I missed every thing else, by my own absurdity, in putting the will for the deed, and aiming at ends without employing means. ''Sir,'' said he

---

[1] a selfsame other one
[2] *As You Like It*, I, 1, 124.
[3] Spenser, *Muiopotmos*, 209-10.
[4] lift; assistance on the way

[1] *Julius Cæsar*, IV, 3, 287.
[2] See *Macbeth*, I, 5, 58-59.
[3] Dryden. *The Indian Emperor*, IV, 3, 5.

of the Brentford, "the Bath mail will be up presently, my brother-in-law drives it, and I will engage to stop him if there is a place empty." I almost doubted my good genius; but, sure enough, up it drove like lightning, and stopped directly at the call of the Brentford Jehu.[1] I would not have believed this possible, but the brother-in-law of a mail-coach driver is himself no mean man. I was transferred without loss of time from the top of one coach to that of the other, desired the guard to pay my fare to the Brentford coachman for me as I had no change, was accommodated with a great coat, put up my umbrella to keep off a drizzling mist, and we began to cut through the air like an arrow. The milestones disappeared one after another, the rain kept off; Tom Turtle, the trainer, sat before me on the coach-box, with whom I exchanged civilities as a gentleman going to the fight; the passion that had transported me an hour before was subdued to pensive regret and conjectural musing on the next day's battle; I was promised a place inside at Reading, and upon the whole, I thought myself a lucky fellow. Such is the force of imagination! On the outside of any other coach on the 10th of December, with a Scotch mist drizzling through the cloudy moonlight air, I should have been cold, comfortless, impatient, and, no doubt, wet through; but seated on the Royal mail, I felt warm and comfortable, the air did me good, the ride did me good, I was pleased with the progress we had made, and confident that all would go well through the journey. When I got inside at Reading, I found Turtle and a stout valetudinarian, whose costume bespoke him of one of the FANCY, and who had risen from a three months' sick bed to get into the mail to see the fight. They were intimate, and we fell into a lively discourse. My friend the trainer was confined in his topics to fighting dogs and men, to bears and badgers; beyond this he was "quite chap-fallen,"[2] had not a word to throw at a dog, or indeed very wisely fell asleep, when any other game was started. The whole art of training (I, however, learnt from him) consists in two things —exercise and abstinence, abstinence and exercise, repeated alternately and without end. A yolk of an egg with a spoonful of rum in it is the first thing in the morning, and then a walk of six miles till breakfast. This meal consists of a plentiful supply of tea and toast and beefsteaks. Then another six or seven

miles till dinner-time and another supply of solid beef or mutton with a pint of porter, and perhaps, at the utmost, a couple of glasses of sherry. Martin trains on water, but this increases his infirmity on another very dangerous side. The Gas-man takes now and then a chirping glass (under the rose[1]) to console him, during a six weeks' probation, for the absence of Mrs. Hickman—an agreeable woman, with (I understand) a pretty fortune of two hundred pounds. How matter presses on me! What stubborn things are facts! How inexhaustible is nature and art! "It is well," as I once heard Mr. Richmond observe, "to see a variety." He was speaking of cock-fighting as an edifying spectacle. I cannot deny but that one learns more of what is (I do not say of what ought to be) in this desultory mode of practical study, than from reading the same book twice over, even though it should be a moral treatise. Where was I? I was sitting at dinner with the candidate for the honors of the ring, "where good digestion waits on appetite, and health on both."[2] Then follows an hour of social chat and native glee; and afterwards, to another breathing over heathy hill or dale. Back to supper, and then to bed, and up by six again—Our hero

> Follows so the ever-running sun
> With profitable ardor."[3]

to the day that brings him victory or defeat in the green fairy circle. Is not this life more sweet than mine? I was going to say; but I will not libel any life by comparing it to mine, which is (at the date of these presents) bitter as coloquintida and the dregs of aconitum!

The invalid in the Bath mail soared a pitch above the trainer, and did not sleep so sound, because he had "more figures and more fantasies."[4] We talked the hours away merrily. He had faith in surgery, for he had had three ribs set right, that had been broken in a turn-up[5] at Belcher's, but thought physicians old women, for they had no antidote in their catalogue for brandy. An indigestion is an excellent common-place for two people that never met before. By way of ingratiating myself, I told him the story of my doctor, who, on my earnestly representing to him that I thought his regimen had done me harm, assured me that the whole pharmacopeia contained nothing comparable

[1] That is, coachman. See 2 Kings, 9.
[2] Hamlet, V, 1, 212.

[1] That is, in secret.
[2] Macbeth, III, 4, 38.
[3] Henry V, IV, 1, 293.
[4] Julius Cæsar, II, 1, 231.
[5] disturbance

to the prescription he had given me; and, as a proof of its undoubted efficacy, said that "he had had one gentleman with my complaint under his hands for the last fifteen years." This anecdote made my companion shake the rough sides of his three great coats with boisterous laughter; and Turtle, starting out of his sleep, swore he knew how the fight would go, for he had had a dream about it. Sure enough the rascal told us how the three first rounds went off, but "his dream," like, others, "denoted a foregone conclusion."[1] He knew his men. The moon now rose in silver state, and I ventured, with some hesitation, to point out this object of placid beauty, with the blue serene beyond, to the man of science, to which his ear he "seriously inclined,"[2] the more as it gave promise *d'un beau jour*[3] for the morrow, and showed the ring undrenched by envious showers, arrayed in sunny smiles. Just then, all going on well, I thought of my friend Toms, whom I had left behind, and said innocently, "There was a blockhead of a fellow I left in town, who said there was no possibility of getting down by the mail, and talked of going by a caravan from Belcher's at two in the morning, after he had written some letters."—"Why," said he of the lapels, "I should not wonder if that was the very person we saw running about like mad from one coach-door to another, and asking if anyone had seen a friend of his, a gentleman going to the fight, whom he had missed stupidly enough by staying to write a note."—"Pray, Sir," said my fellow-traveller, "had he a plaid-cloak on?"—"Why, no," said I, "not at the time I left him, but he very well might afterwards, for he offered to lend me one." The plaid-cloak and the letter decided the thing. Joe, sure enough, was in the Bristol mail, which preceded us by about fifty yards. This was droll enough. We had now but a few miles to our place of destination, and the first thing I did on alighting at Newbury, both coaches stopping at the same time, was to call out, "Pray, is there a gentleman in that mail of the name of Toms?"—"No," said Joe, borrowing something of the vein of Gilpin,[4] "for I have just got out."—"Well!" says he, "this is lucky; but you don't know how vexed I was to miss you; for," added he, lowering his voice, "do you know when I left you I went to Belcher's to ask about the caravan, and Mrs. Belcher said

very obligingly, she couldn't tell about that, but there were two gentlemen who had taken places by the mail and were gone on in a landau, and she could frank us.[1] It's a pity I didn't meet with you; we could then have got down for nothing. But *mum's the word.*" It's the devil for anyone to tell me a secret, for it's sure to come out in print. I do not care so much to gratify a friend, but the public ear is too great a temptation for me.

Our present business was to get beds and supper at an inn; but this was no easy task. The public-houses were full, and where you saw a light at a private house, and people poking their heads out of the casement to see what was going on, they instantly put them in and shut the window, the moment you seemed advancing with a suspicious overture for accommodation. Our guard and coachman thundered away at the outer gate of the Crown for some time without effect—such was the greater noise within;—and when the doors were unbarred, and we got admittance, we found a party assembled in the kitchen round a good hospitable fire, some sleeping, others drinking, others talking on politics and on the fight. A tall English yeoman (something like Matthews in the face, and quite as great a wag) —

A lusty man to ben an abbot able,[2]—

was making such a prodigious noise about rents and taxes, and the price of corn[3] now and formerly, that he had prevented us from being heard at the gate. The first thing I heard him say was to a shuffling fellow who wanted to be off a bet for a shilling glass of brandy and water—"Confound it, man, don't be *insipid!*" Thinks I, that is a good phrase. It was a good omen. He kept it up so all night, nor flinched with the approach of morning. He was a fine fellow, with sense, wit, and spirit, a hearty body and a joyous mind, freespoken, frank, convivial—one of that true English breed that went with Harry the Fifth to the siege of Harfleur[4]—"standing like greyhounds in the slips,"[5] etc. We ordered tea and eggs (beds were soon found to be out of the question) and this fellow's conversation was *sauce piquante*. It did one's heart good to see him brandish his oaken towel[6] and to hear him talk. He made mince-meat of a drunken, stupid, red-

---

[1] *Othello*, III, 3, 428.
[2] *Othello*, I, 3, 146.
[3] of a fair day
[4] That is, jocosely. See Cowper's *The Diverting History of John Gilpin*.

[1] secure free passage for us
[2] Chaucer, *Prologue to the Canterbury Tales*, 167.
[3] wheat
[4] In the war with France, 1415.
[5] *Henry V*, III, 1, 31.
[6] cudgel

faced, quarrelsome, *frowsy* farmer, whose
nose "he moralized into a thousand similes,"[1] making it out a firebrand like Bar-
dolph's.[2] "I'll tell you what my friend,"
says he, "the landlady has only to keep you
here to save fire and candle. If one was to
touch your nose, it would go off like a piece
of charcoal." At this the other only grinned
like an idiot, the sole variety in his purple
face being his little peering gray eyes and
yellow teeth, called for another glass, swore
he would not stand it, and after many attempts to provoke his humorous antagonist
to single combat, which the other turned off
(after working him up to a ludicrous pitch
of choler) with great adroitness, he fell
quietly asleep with a glass of liquor in his
hand, which he could not lift to his head.
His laughing persecutor made a speech over
him, and turning to the opposite side of the
room, while they were all sleeping in the
midst of this "loud and furious fun,"[3]
said, "There's a scene, by G–d, for Hogarth
to paint. I think he and Shakspeare were
our two best men at copying life." This confirmed me in my good opinion of him. Hogarth, Shakspeare, and Nature, were just
enough for him (indeed for any man) to
know. I said, "You read Cobbett, don't you?
At least," says I, "you talk just as well as
he writes." He seemed to doubt this. But I
said, "We have an hour to spare: if you'll
get pen, ink, and paper, and keep on talking,
I'll write down what you say; and if it
doesn't make a capital *Political Register,*
I'll forfeit my head. You have kept me alive
tonight, however. I don't know what I
should have done without you." He did not
dislike this view of the thing, nor my asking
if he was not about the size of Jem Belcher;
and told me soon afterwards, in the confidence of friendship, that "the circumstance
which had given him nearly the greatest concern in his life, was Cribb's beating Jem
after he had lost his eye by racket-playing."[4]
—The morning dawns; that dim but yet
clear light appears, which weighs like solid
bars of metal on the sleepless eyelids; the
guests drop down from their chambers one
by one—but it was too late to think of going
to bed now (the clock was on the stroke of
seven), we had nothing for it but to find a
barber's (the pole that glittered in the morning sun lighted us to his shop), and then a

[1] *As You Like It,* II, 1, 45.
[2] See 1 *Henry IV,* III, 3, 48.
[3] Burns, *Tam O'Shanter,* 144 (p. 224).
[4] Cribbs defeated Jem Belcher in 1807 and again
in 1809. Belcher lost his eye while playing
rackets, in 1803.

nine miles' march to Hungerford. The day
was fine, the sky was blue, the mists were
retiring from the marshy ground, the path
was tolerably dry, the sitting-up all night
had not done us much harm—at least the
cause was good; we talked of this and that
with amicable difference, roving and sipping
of many subjects, but still invariably we
returned to the fight. At length, a mile to
the left of Hungerford, on a gentle eminence, we saw the ring surrounded by covered carts, gigs, and carriages, of which
hundreds had passed us on the road; Toms
gave a youthful shout, and we hastened down
a narrow lane to the scene of action.

Reader, have you ever seen a fight? If
not, you have a pleasure to come, at least if
it is a fight like that between the Gas-man
and Bill Neate. The crowd was very great
when we arrived on the spot; open carriages
were coming up, with streamers flying and
music playing, and the country-people were
pouring in over hedge and ditch in all directions, to see their hero beat or be beaten.
The odds were still on Gas, but only about
five to four. Gully had been down to try
Neate, and had backed him considerably,
which was a damper to the sanguine confidence of the adverse party. About two hundred thousand pounds were pending. The
Gas says he has lost 3000*l.* which were promised him by different gentlemen if he had
won. He had presumed too much on himself, which had made others presume on him.
This spirited and formidable young fellow
seems to have taken for his motto the old
maxim, that "there are three things necessary to success in life—*Impudence! Impudence! Impudence!*" It is so in matters of
opinion, but not in the FANCY, which is the
most practical of all things, though even here
confidence is half the battle, but only half.
Our friend had vapored and swaggered too
much, as if he wanted to grin and bully his
adversary out of the fight. "Alas! the Bristol man was not so tamed!"[1]—"This is *the
grave-digger*" (would Tom Hickman exclaim in the moments of intoxication from
gin and success, showing his tremendous
right hand), "this will send many of them
to their long homes; I haven't done with
them yet!" Why should he—though he had
licked four of the best men within the hour,
yet why should he threaten to inflict dishonorable chastisement on my old master Richmond, a veteran going off the stage, and who
has borne his sable honors meekly? Magnanimity, my dear Tom, and bravery, should

[1] Cowper, *The Task,* 2, 322.

be inseparable. Or why should he go up to his antagonist, the first time he ever saw him at the Fives Court, and measuring him from head to foot with a glance of contempt, as Achilles surveyed Hector, say to him, "What, are you Bill Neate? I'll knock more blood out of that great carcase of thine, this day fortnight, than you ever knock'd out of a bullock's!" It was not manly, 'twas not fighter-like. If he was sure of the victory (as he was not), the less said about it the better. Modesty should accompany the FANCY as its shadow. The best men were always the best behaved. Jem Belcher, the Game Chicken[1] (before whom the Gas-man could not have lived) were civil, silent men. So is Cribb, so is Tom Belcher, the most elegant of sparrers, and not a man for everyone to take by the nose. I enlarged on this topic in the mail (while Turtle was asleep), and said very wisely (as I thought) that impertinence was a part of no profession. A boxer was bound to beat his man, but not to thrust his fist, either actually or by implication, in everyone's face. Even a highwayman, in the way of trade, may blow out your brains, but if he uses foul language at the same time, I should say he was no gentleman. A boxer, I would infer, need not be a blackguard or a coxcomb, more than another. Perhaps I press this point too much on a fallen man— Mr. Thomas Hickman has by this time learnt that first of all lessons, "That man was made to mourn."[2] He has lost nothing by the late fight but his presumption; and that every man may do as well without! By an over-display of this quality, however, the public had been prejudiced against him, and the *knowing-ones* were taken in. Few but those who had bet on him wished Gas to win. With my own prepossessions on the subject, the result of the 11th of December appeared to me as fine a piece of poetical justice as I had ever witnessed. The difference of weight between the two combatants (14 stone to 12) was nothing to the sporting men. Great, heavy, clumsy, long-armed Bill Neate kicked the beam in the scale of the Gas-man's vanity. The amateurs were frightened at his big words, and thought that they would make up for the difference of six feet and five feet nine. Truly, the FANCY are not men of imagination. They judge of what has been, and cannot conceive of anything that is to be. The Gas-man had won hitherto; therefore he must beat a man half as big again

as himself—and that to a certainty. Besides, there are as many feuds, factions, prejudices, pedantic notions in the FANCY as in the state or in the schools. Mr. Gully is almost the only cool, sensible man among them, who exercises an unbiased discretion, and is not a slave to his passions in these matters. But enough of reflections, and to our tale. The day, as I have said, was fine for a December morning. The grass was wet, and the ground miry, and ploughed up with multitudinous feet, except that, within the ring itself, there was a spot of virgin-green closed in and unprofaned by vulgar tread, that shone with dazzling brightness in the mid-day sun. For it was now noon, and we had an hour to wait. This is the trying time. It is then the heart sickens, as you think what the two champions are about, and how short a time will determine their fate. After the first blow is struck, there is no opportunity for nervous apprehensions; you are swallowed up in the immediate interest of the scene—but

Between the acting of a dreadful thing
And the first motion, all the interim is
Like a phantasma, or a hideous dream.[1]

I found it so as I felt the sun's rays clinging to my back, and saw the white wintry clouds sink below the verge of the horizon. "So, I thought, my fairest hopes have faded from my sight!—so will the Gas-man's glory, or that of his adversary, vanish in an hour." The *swells* were parading in their white box-coats, the outer ring was cleared with some bruises on the heads and shins of the rustic assembly (for the *cockneys* had been distanced by the sixty-six miles); the time drew near, I had got a good stand; a bustle, a buzz, ran through the crowd, and from the opposite side entered Neate, between his second and bottle-holder. He rolled along, swathed in his loose great coat, his knock-knees bending under his huge bulk; and, with a modest cheerful air, threw his hat into the ring.[2] He then just looked around, and began quietly to undress; when from the other side there was a similar rush and an opening made, and the Gas-man came forward with a conscious air of anticipated triumph, too much like the cock-of-the-walk. He strutted about more than became a hero, sucked oranges with a supercilious air, and threw away the skin with a toss of his head, and went up and looked at Neate, which

---

[1] Henry Pearce (1777-1809), a well-known English pugilist.
[2] Burns, *Man Was Made to Mourn*, 24.

[1] *Julius Cæsar*, II, 1, 63-65.
[2] A signal that he was ready for the fight to begin.

was an act of supererogation. The only sensible thing he did was, as he strode away from the modern Ajax, to fling out his arms, as if he wanted to try whether they would do their work that day. By this time they had stripped, and presented a strong contrast in appearance. If Neate was like Ajax, "with Atlantean shoulders, fit to bear"[1] the pugilistic reputation of all Bristol, Hickman might be compared to Diomed, light, vigorous, elastic, and his back glistened in the sun, as he moved about, like a panther's hide. There was now a dead pause—attention was awe-struck. Who at that moment, big with a great event, did not draw his breath short—did not feel his heart throb? All was ready. They tossed up for the sun, and the Gas-man won. They were led up to the *scratch*—shook hands, and went at it.

In the first round everyone thought it was all over. After making play a short time, the Gas-man flew at his adversary like a tiger, struck five blows in as many seconds, three first, and then following him as he staggered back, two more, right and left, and down he fell, a mighty ruin. There was a shout, and I said, "There is no standing this." Neate seemed like a lifeless lump of flesh and bone, round which the Gas-man's blows played with the rapidity of electricity or lightning, and you imagined he would only be lifted up to be knocked down again. It was as if Hickman held a sword or a fire in that right hand of his, and directed it against an unarmed body. They met again, and Neate seemed, not cowed, but particularly cautious. I saw his teeth clenched together and his brows knit close against the sun. He held both his arms at full length straight before him, like two sledge-hammers, and raised his left an inch or two higher. The Gas-man could not get over this guard— they struck mutually and fell, but without advantage on either side. It was the same in the next round; but the balance of power was thus restored—the fate of the battle was suspended. No one could tell how it would end. This was the only moment in which opinion was divided; for in the next, the Gas-man aiming a mortal blow at his adversary's neck, with his right hand, and failing from the length he had to reach, the other returned it with his left at full swing, planted a tremendous blow on his cheek-bone and eyebrow, and made a red ruin of that side of his face. The Gas-man went down, and there was another shout—a roar of triumph as the waves of fortune rolled tumultuously

[1] *Paradise Lost*, 2, 306.

from side to side. This was a settler. Hickman got up, and "grinned horrible a ghastly smile,"[1] yet he was evidently dashed in his opinion of himself; it was the first time he had been so punished; all one side of his face was perfect scarlet, and his right eye was closed in dingy blackness, as he advanced to the fight, less confident, but still determined. After one or two rounds, not receiving another such remembrancer, he rallied and went at it with his former impetuosity. But in vain. His strength had been weakened,—his blows could not tell at such a distance,—he was obliged to fling himself at his adversary, and could not strike from his feet; and almost as regularly as he flew at him with his right hand, Neate warded the blow, or drew back out of its reach, and felled him with the return of his left. There was little cautious sparring—no half-hits— no tapping and trifling, none of the *petit-maitreship*[2] of the art—they were almost all knock-down blows:—the fight was a good stand-up fight. The wonder was the half-minute time. If there had been a minute or more allowed between each round, it would have been intelligible how they should by degrees recover strength and resolution; but to see two men smashed to the ground, smeared with gore, stunned, senseless, the breath beaten out of their bodies, and then, before you recover from the shock, to see them rise up with new strength and courage, stand steady to inflict or receive mortal offence, and rush upon each other "like two clouds over the Caspian"[3]—this is the most astonishing thing of all.—This is the high and heroic state of man! From this time forward the event became more certain every round; and about the twelfth it seemed as if it must have been over. Hickman generally stood with his back to me; but in the scuffle, he had changed positions, and Neate just then made a tremendous lunge at him, and hit him full in the face. It was doubtful whether he would fall backwards or forwards; he hung suspended for a second or two, and then fell back, throwing his hands in the air, and with his face lifted up to the sky. I never saw anything more terrific than his aspect just before he fell. All traces of life, of natural expression, were gone from him. His face was like a human skull, a death's head, spouting blood. The eyes were filled with blood, the nose streamed with blood, the mouth gaped

[1] *Paradise Lost*, 2. 846.
[2] dandyism
[3] *Paradise Lost*, 2, 714.

blood. He was not like an actual man, but like a preternatural, spectral appearance, or like one of the figures in Dante's *Inferno*. Yet he fought on after this for several rounds, still striking the first desperate blow, and Neate standing on the defensive, and using the same cautious guard to the last, as if he had still all his work to do; and it was not till the Gas-man was so stunned in the seventeenth or eighteenth round, that his senses forsook him, and he could not come to time, that the battle was declared over.[1] Ye who despise the FANCY, do something to show as much *pluck*, or as much self-possession as this, before you assume a superiority which you have never given a single proof of by any one action in the whole course of your lives!—When the Gas-man came to himself, the first words he uttered were, "Where am I? What is the matter?"—"Nothing is the matter, Tom— you have lost the battle, but you are the bravest man alive." And Jackson whispered to him, "I am collecting a purse for you, Tom."—Vain sounds, and unheard at that moment! Neate instantly went up and shook him cordially by the hand, and seeing some old acquaintance, began to flourish with his fists, calling out, "Ah, you always said I couldn't fight—What do you think now?" But all in good humor, and without any appearance of arrogance; only it was evident Bill Neate was pleased that he had won the fight. When it was over I asked Cribb if he did not think it was a good one. He said, "*Pretty well!*" The carrier-pigeons now mounted into the air, and one of them flew with the news of her husband's victory to the bosom of Mrs. Neate. Alas, for Mrs. Hickman!

Mais au revoir,[2] as Sir Fopling Flutter says.[3] I went down with Toms; I returned with Jack Pigott, whom I met on the ground. Toms is a rattlebrain; Pigott is a sentimentalist. Now, under favor, I am a sentimentalist too—therefore I say nothing, but that the interest of the excursion did not flag as I came back. Pigott and I marched along the causeway leading from Hungerford to Newbury, now observing the effect of a brilliant sun on the tawny meads or moss-colored cottages, now exulting in the fight, now digressing to some topic of general and elegant literature. My friend was dressed in character for the occasion, or like one of the FANCY; that is, with a double portion of greatcoats, clogs,[1] and overalls: and just as we had agreed with a couple of country-lads to carry his superfluous wearing-apparel to the next town, we were overtaken by a return post-chaise, into which I got, Pigott preferring a seat on the bar.[2] There were two strangers already in the chaise, and on their observing they supposed I had been to the fight, I said I had, and concluded they had done the same. They appeared, however, a little shy and sore on the subject; and it was not till after several hints dropped, and questions put, that it turned out that they had missed it. One of these friends had undertaken to drive the other there in his gig: they had set out, to make sure work, the day before at three in the afternoon. The owner of the one-horse vehicle scorned to ask his way, and drove right on to Bagshot, instead of turning off at Hounslow: there they stopped all night, and set off the next day across the country to Reading, from whence they took coach, and got down within a mile or two of Hungerford, just half an hour after the fight was over. This might be safely set down as one of the miseries of human life. We parted with these two gentlemen who had been to see the fight, but had returned as they went, at Wolhampton, where we were promised beds (an irresistible temptation, for Pigott had passed the preceding night at Hungerford as we had done at Newbury), and we turned into an old bow-windowed parlor with carpet and a snug fire; and after devouring a quantity of tea, toast, eggs, sat down to consider, during an hour of philosophic leisure, what we should have for supper. In the midst of an Epicurean deliberation between a roasted fowl and mutton chops with mashed potatoes, we were interrupted by an inroad of Goths and Vandals—*O procul este profani*[3]—not real flash-men,[4] but interlopers, noisy pretenders, butchers from Tothill-fields, brokers from Whitechapel, who called immediately for pipes and tobacco, hoping it would not be disagreeable to the

---

[1] "Scroggins said of the Gas-man, that he thought he was a man of that courage that if his hands were cut off, he would still fight on with the stumps, like that of Widrington,—
    'In doleful dumps,
Who, when his legs were smitten off
Still fought upon his stumps.' "—Hazlitt.

These lines of verse are quoted from one of the versions of *Chevy Chase*, st. 50. For a variant reading, see p. 115, ll. 221-24.

[2] well, good-by
[3] In Etherege's *The Man of Mode*, III, 2 (ed. Verity, p. 299).

[1] shoes with thick wooden soles
[2] That is, on the seat with the driver.
[3] oh aloof, ye profane (*Æneid*, 6, 258)
[4] sporting men

gentlemen, and began to insist that it was *a cross.*[1] Pigott withdrew from the smoke and noise into another room, and left me to dispute the point with them for a couple of hours *sans intermission* by the dial. The next morning we rose refreshed; and on observing that Jack had a pocket volume in his hand, in which he read in the intervals of our discourse, I inquired what it was, and learned to my particular satisfaction that it was a volume of the *New Eloise.* Ladies, after this, will you contend that a love for the FANCY is incompatible with the cultivation of sentiment?—We jogged on as before, my friend setting me up in a genteel drab greatcoat and green silk handkerchief (which I must say became me exceedingly), and after stretching our legs for a few miles, and seeing Jack Randall, Ned Turner, and Scroggins pass on the top of one of the Bath coaches, we engaged with the driver of the second to take us to London for the usual fee. I got inside, and found three other passengers. One of them was an old gentleman with an aquiline nose, powdered hair,[2] and a pigtail, and who looked as if he had played many a rubber at the Bath rooms. I said to myself, he is very like Mr. Windham; I wish he would enter into conversation, that I might hear what fine observations would come from those finely-turned features. However, nothing passed, till, stopping to dine at Reading, some inquiry was made by the company about the fight, and I gave (as the reader may believe) an eloquent and animated description of it. When we got into the coach again, the old gentleman, after a graceful exordium, said he had, when a boy, been to a fight between the famous Broughton and George Stevenson, who was called the *Fighting Coachman,* in the year 1770, with the late Mr. Windham. This beginning flattered the spirit of prophecy within me and rivetted my attention. He went on— ''George Stevenson was coachman to a friend of my father's. He was an old man when I saw him some years afterwards. He took hold of his own arm and said, 'there was muscle here once, but now it is no more than this young gentleman's.' He added, 'Well, no matter; I have been here long, I am willing to go hence, and I hope I have done no more harm than another man.' Once,'' said my unknown companion, ''I asked him if he had ever beat

Broughton. He said Yes; that he had fought with him three times, and the last time he fairly beat him, though the world did not allow it. 'I'll tell you how it was, master. When the seconds lifted us up in the last round, we were so exhausted that neither of us could stand, and we fell upon one another, and as Master Broughton fell uppermost, the mob gave it in his favor, and he was said to have won the battle. But,' says he, 'the fact was, that as his second (John Cuthbert) lifted him up, he said to him, "I'll fight no more, I've had enough;" which,' says Stevenson, 'you know gave me the victory. And to prove to you that this was the case, when John Cuthbert was on his death-bed, and they asked him if there was anything on his mind which he wished to confess, he answered, "Yes, that there was one thing he wished to set right, for that certainly Master Stevenson won that last fight with Master Broughton; for he whispered him as he lifted him up in the last round of all, that he had had enough."'' This,'' said the Bath gentleman, ''was a bit of human nature;'' and I have written this account of the fight on purpose that it might not be lost to the world. He also stated as a proof of the candor of mind in this class of men, that Stevenson acknowledged that Broughton could have beat him in his best day; but that he (Broughton) was getting old in their last rencounter. When we stopped in Piccadilly, I wanted to ask the gentleman some questions about the late Mr. Windham, but had not courage. I got out, resigned my coat and green silk handkerchief to Pigott (loth to part with these ornaments of life), and walked home in high spirits.

P. S. Toms called upon me the next day, to ask me if I did not think the fight was a complete thing. I said I thought it was. I hope he will relish my account of it.

ON GOING A JOURNEY
1822

One of the pleasantest things in the world is going a journey; but I like to go by myself. I can enjoy society in a room; but out of doors, nature is company enough for me. I am then never less alone than when alone.

The fields his study, nature was his book.[1]

I cannot see the wit of walking and talking at the same time. When I am in the country, I wish to vegetate like the country.

---

[1] A match, the result of which was prearranged.
[2] The 18th century custom of powdering the hair still persisted.

[1] Bloomfield, *Spring,* 31.

I am not for criticizing hedge-rows and black cattle. I go out of town in order to forget the town and all that is in it. There are those who for this purpose go to watering-places, and carry the metropolis with them. I like more elbow-room, and fewer incumbrances. I like solitude, when I give myself up to it, for the sake of solitude; nor do I ask for

A friend in my retreat,
Whom I may whisper, solitude is sweet.[1]

The soul of a journey is liberty, perfect liberty, to think, feel, do, just as one pleases. We go a journey chiefly to be free of all impediments and of all inconveniences; to leave ourselves behind, much more to get rid of others. It is because I want a little breathing-space to muse on indifferent matters, where Contemplation

May plume her feathers and let grow her wings,
That in the various bustle of resort
Were all too ruffled, and sometimes impair'd,[2]

that I absent myself from the town for awhile, without feeling at a loss the moment I am left by myself. Instead of a friend in a post-chaise or in a Tilbury,[3] to exchange good things with, and vary the same stale topics over again, for once let me have a truce with impertinence. Give me the clear blue sky over my head, and the green turf beneath my feet, a winding road before me, and a three hours' march to dinner—and then to thinking! It is hard if I cannot start some game on these lone heaths. I laugh, I run, I leap, I sing for joy. From the point of yonder rolling cloud, I plunge into my past being, and revel there, as the sunburnt Indian plunges headlong into the wave that wafts him to his native shore. Then long-forgotten things, like "sunken wrack and sumless treasuries,"[4] burst upon my eager sight, and I begin to feel, think, and be myself again. Instead of an awkward silence, broken by attempts at wit or dull common-places, mine is that undisturbed silence of the heart which alone is perfect eloquence. No one likes puns, alliterations, antitheses, argument, and analysis better than I do; but I sometimes had rather be without them. "Leave, oh, leave me to my repose!"[5] I have just now other business in hand, which would seem idle to you, but is with me "very stuff of the con-

science."[1] Is not this wild rose sweet without a comment? Does not this daisy leap to my heart set in its coat of emerald? Yet if I were to explain to you the circumstance that has so endeared it to me, you would only smile. Had I not better then keep it to myself, and let it serve me to brood over, from here to yonder craggy point, and from thence onward to the far-distant horizon? I should be but bad company all that way, and therefore prefer being alone. I have heard it said that you may, when the moody fit comes on, walk or ride on by yourself, and indulge your reveries. But this looks like a breach of manners, a neglect of others, and you are thinking all the time that you ought to rejoin your party. "Out upon such half-faced fellowship,"[2] say I. I like to be either entirely to myself, or entirely at the disposal of others; to talk or be silent, to walk or sit still, to be sociable or solitary. I was pleased with an observation of Mr. Cobbett's, that "he thought it a bad French custom to drink our wine with our meals, and that an Englishman ought to do only one thing at a time." So I cannot talk and think, or indulge in melancholy musing and lively conversation by fits and starts. "Let me have a companion of my way," says Sterne, "were it but to remark how the shadows lengthen as the sun declines."[3] It is beautifully said: but in my opinion, this continual comparing of notes interferes with the involuntary impression of things upon the mind, and hurts the sentiment. If you only hint what you feel in a kind of dumb show, it is insipid: if you have to explain it, it is making a toil of a pleasure. You cannot read the book of nature, without being perpetually put to the trouble of translating it for the benefit of others. I am for the synthetical method on a journey, in preference to the analytical. I am content to lay in a stock of ideas then, and to examine and anatomize them afterwards. I want to see my vague notions float like the down of the thistle before the breeze, and not to have them entangled in the briars and thorns of controversy. For once, I like to have it all my own way; and this is impossible unless you are alone, or in such company as I do not covet. I have no objection to argue a point with anyone for twenty miles of measured road, but not for pleasure. If you remark the scent of a bean-field crossing the road, perhaps your fellow-traveller has no smell. If you point to a

---

[1] Cowper, *Retirement*, 741-42.   [2] *Comus*, 378-80.
[3] A kind of two-wheeled carriage without a top. It was named after the inventor, a coach-maker of the early 19th century.
[4] *Henry V*, I, 2, 165.
[5] Gray, *The Descent of Odin*, 50 (p. 67).

[1] *Othello*, I, 2, 2.
[2] *1 Henry IV*, I, 3, 208.   [3] Sterne, *Sermons*, 18.

distant object, perhaps he is short-sighted, and has to take out his glass to look at it. There is a feeling in the air, a tone in the color of a cloud which hits your fancy, but the effect of which you are unable to account for. There is then no sympathy, but an uneasy craving after it, and a dissatisfaction which pursues you on the way, and in the end probably produces ill humor. Now I never quarrel with myself, and take all my own conclusions for granted till I find it necessary to defend them against objections. It is not merely that you may not be of accord on the objects and circumstances that present themselves before you—these may recall a number of objects, and lead to associations too delicate and refined to be possibly communicated to others. Yet these I love to cherish, and sometimes still fondly clutch them, when I can escape from the throng to do so. To give way to our feelings before company, seems extravagance or affectation; and, on the other hand, to have to unravel this mystery of our being at every turn, and to make others take an equal interest in it (otherwise the end is not answered) is a task to which few are competent. We must "give it an understanding, but no tongue."[1] My old friend C——,[2] however, could do both. He could go on in the most delightful explanatory way over hill and dale, a summer's day, and convert a landscape into a didactic poem or a Pindaric ode. "He talked far above singing."[3] If I could so clothe my ideas in sounding and flowing words, I might perhaps wish to have some one with me to admire the swelling theme; or I could be more content, were it possible for me still to hear his echoing voice in the woods of All-Foxden. They had "that fine madness in them which our first poets had;"[4] and if they could have been caught by some rare instrument, would have breathed such strains as the following:

Here be woods as green
As any, air likewise as fresh and sweet
As when smooth Zephyrus plays on the fleet
Face of the curled streams, with flow'rs as
    many
As the young spring gives, and as choice as
    any;
Here be all new delights, cool streams and
    wells,
Arbors o'ergrown with woodbines, caves and
    dells;
Choose where thou wilt, whilst I sit by and sing,
Or gather rushes, to make many a ring

For thy long fingers; tell thee tales of love;
How the pale Phœbe, hunting in a grove,
First saw the boy Endymion, from whose eyes
She took eternal fire that never dies;
How she convey'd him softly in a sleep,
His temples bound with poppy, to the steep
Head of old Latmos, where she stoops each
    night,
Gilding the mountain with her brother's light,
To kiss her sweetest,[1]

Had I words and images at command like these, I would attempt to wake the thoughts that lie slumbering on golden ridges in the evening clouds: but at the sight of nature my fancy, poor as it is, droops and closes up its leaves, like flowers at sunset. I can make nothing out on the spot:—I must have time to collect myself.—

In general, a good thing spoils out-of-door prospects: it should be reserved for Table-talk. L——[2] is for this reason, I take it, the worst company in the world out of doors; because he is the best within. I grant, there is one subject on which it is pleasant to talk on a journey; and that is, what one shall have for supper when we get to our inn at night. The open air improves this sort of conversation or friendly altercation, by setting a keener edge on appetite. Every mile of the road heightens the flavor of the viands we expect at the end of it. How fine it is to enter some old town, walled and turreted just at approach of night-fall, or to come to some straggling village, with the lights streaming through the surrounding gloom; and then after inquiring for the best entertainment that the place affords, to "take one's ease at one's inn!"[3] These eventful moments in our lives' history are too precious, too full of solid, heart-felt happiness to be frittered and dribbled away in imperfect sympathy. I would have them all to myself, and drain them to the last drop: they will do to talk of or to write about afterwards. What a delicate speculation it is, after drinking whole goblets of tea,

The cups that cheer, but not inebriate,[4]

and letting the fumes ascend into the brain, to sit considering what we shall have for supper—eggs and a rasher, a rabbit smothered in onions, or an excellent veal-cutlet! Sancho in such a situation once fixed on cow-heel;[5] and his choice, though he could not help it, is not to be disparaged. Then, in the intervals of pictured scenery and Shandean[6] contemplation, to catch the

---

[1] *Hamlet*, I, 2, 250.   [2] Coleridge.
[3] Beaumont and Fletcher, *Philaster*, V, 5, 165.
[4] Drayton, *To My Dearly Loved Friend, Henry Reynolds, Esq.*, 109.

[1] Fletcher, *The Faithful Shepherdess*, I, 3, 27-43.
[2] Charles Lamb.   [3] *1 Henry IV*, III, 3, 93.
[4] Cowper, *The Task*, 4, 39.
[5] See Cervantes's *Don Quixote*, Part 2, ch. 59.
[6] discursive, like that of Tristram Shandy

preparation and the stir in the kitchen— *Procul, O procul este profani!*[1] These hours are sacred to silence and to musing, to be treasured up in the memory, and to feed the source of smiling thoughts hereafter. I would not waste them in idle talk; or if I must have the integrity of fancy broken in upon, I would rather it were by a stranger than a friend. A stranger takes his hue and character from the time and place; he is a part of the furniture and costume of an inn. If he is a Quaker, or from the West Riding of Yorkshire, so much the better. I do not even try to sympathize with him, and he breaks no squares. I associate nothing with my travelling companion but present objects and passing events. In his ignorance of me and my affairs, I in a manner forget myself. But a friend reminds one of other things, rips up old grievances, and destroys the abstraction of the scene. He comes in ungraciously between us and our imaginary character. Something is dropped in the course of conversation that gives a hint of your profession and pursuits; or from having someone with you that knows the less sublime portions of your history, it seems that other people do. You are no longer a citizen of the world: but your "unhoused free condition is put into circumspection and confine."[2] The *incognito* of an inn is one of its striking privileges—"lord of one's self, uncumber'd with a name."[3] Oh! it is great to shake off the trammels of the world and of public opinion—to lose our importunate, tormenting, everlasting personal identity in the elements of nature, and become the creature of the moment, clear of all ties—to hold to the universe only by a dish of sweet-breads, and to owe nothing but the score of the evening —and no longer seeking for applause and meeting with contempt, to be known by no other title than *the Gentleman in the parlor!* One may take one's choice of all characters in this romantic state of uncertainty as to one's real pretensions, and become indefinitely respectable and negatively right-worshipful. We baffle prejudice and disappoint conjecture; and from being so to others, begin to be objects of curiosity and wonder even to ourselves. We are no more those hackneyed common-places that we appear in the world: an inn restores us to the level of nature, and quits scores with society! I have certainly spent some enviable hours at inns—sometimes when I have been left entirely to myself, and have tried to solve some metaphysical problem, as once at Witham-common, where I found out the proof that likeness is not a case of the association of ideas—at other times, when there have been pictures in the room, as at St. Neot's (I think it was), where I first met with Gribelin's engravings of the Cartoons,[1] into which I entered at once, and at a little inn on the borders of Wales, where there happened to be hanging some of Westall's drawings, which I compared triumphantly (for a theory that I had, not for the admired artist) with the figure of a girl who had ferried me over the Severn, standing up in a boat between me and the twilight— at other times I might mention luxuriating in books, with a peculiar interest in this way, as I remember sitting up half the night to read *Paul and Virginia,* which I picked up at an inn at Bridgewater, after being drenched in the rain all day; and at the same place I got through two volumes of Madame D'Arblay's *Camilla.* It was on the 10th of April, 1798, that I sat down to a volume of *The New Eloise,* at the inn at Llangollen, over a bottle of sherry and a cold chicken. The letter I chose was that in which St. Preux describes his feelings as he first caught a glimpse from the heights of the Jura of the Pays de Vaud,[2] which I had brought with me as a *bon bouche*[3] to crown the evening with. It was my birth-day, and I had for the first time come from a place in the neighborhood to visit this delightful spot. The road to Llangollen turns off between Chirk and Wrexham; and on passing a certain point, you come all at once upon the valley, which opens like an amphitheatre, broad, barren hills rising in majestic state on either side, with "green upland swells that echo to the bleat of flocks"[4] below, and the river Dee babbling over its stony bed in the midst of them. The valley at this time "glittered green with sunny showers,"[5] and a budding ash-tree dipped its tender branches in the chiding stream. How proud, how glad I was to walk along the high road that overlooks the delicious prospect, repeating the lines which I have just quoted from Mr. Coleridge's poems! But besides the prospect which opened be-

[1] aloof, oh aloof, ye profane (*Æneid,* 6, 258)
[2] *Othello,* I, 2, 26.
[3] Dryden, *To my Honor'd Kinsman,* 18.

[1] Drawings of religious subjects by Raphael (1483-1520), the great Italian painter.
[2] See Rousseau's *La Nouvelle Héloïse,* 4, 17. The Jura is a chain of mountains on the border of Pays de Vaud, a canton of Switzerland.
[3] dainty morsel
[4] Coleridge, *Ode on the Departing Year,* 125-26 (p. 359).   [5] *Ibid.,* 124 (p. 359).

neath my feet, another also opened to my inward sight, a heavenly vision, on which were written, in letters large as Hope could make them, these four words, LIBERTY, GENIUS, LOVE, VIRTUE;[1] which have since faded into the light of common day,[2] or mock my idle gaze.

The beautiful is vanished and returns not.[3]

Still I would return some time or other to this enchanted spot; but I would return to it alone. What other self could I find to share that influx of thoughts, of regret, and delight, the fragments of which I could hardly conjure up to myself, so much have they been broken and defaced! I could stand on some tall rock, and overlook the precipice of years that separates me from what I then was. I was at that time going shortly to visit the poet whom I have above named. Where is he now?[4] Not only I myself have changed; the world, which was then new to me, has become old and incorrigible. Yet will I turn to thee in thought, O sylvan Dee, in joy, in youth and gladness as thou then wert; and thou shalt always be to me the river of Paradise, where I will drink of the waters of life freely![5]

There is hardly anything that shows the short-sightedness or capriciousness of the imagination more than travelling does. With change of place we change our ideas; nay, our opinions and feelings. We can by an effort indeed transport ourselves to old and long-forgotten scenes, and then the picture of the mind revives again; but we forget those that we have just left. It seems that we can think but of one place at a time. The canvas of the fancy is but of a certain extent, and if we paint one set of objects upon it, they immediately efface every other. We cannot enlarge our conceptions, we only shift our point of view. The landscape bares its bosom to the enraptured eye, we take our fill of it, and seem as if we could form no other image of beauty or grandeur. We pass on, and think no more of it: the horizon that shuts it from our sight, also blots it from our memory like a dream. In travelling through a wild barren

country, I can form no idea of a woody and cultivated one. It appears to me that all the world must be barren, like what I see of it. In the country we forget the town, and in town we despise the country. "Beyond Hyde Park," says Sir Fopling Flutter, "all is a desert."[1] All that part of the map that we do not see before us is a blank. The world in our conceit of it is not much bigger than a nutshell. It is not one prospect expanded into another, county joined to county, kingdom to kingdom, land to seas, making an image voluminous and vast;—the mind can form no larger idea of space than the eye can take in at a single glance. The rest is a name written in a map, a calculation of arithmetic. For instance, what is the true signification of that immense mass of territory and population, known by the name of China to us? An inch of pasteboard on a wooden globe, of no more account than a China orange! Things near us are seen of the size of life: things at a distance are diminished to the size of the understanding. We measure the universe by ourselves, and even comprehend the texture of our own being only piecemeal. In this way, however, we remember an infinity of things and places. The mind is like a mechanical instrument that plays a great variety of tunes, but it must play them in succession. One idea recalls another, but it at the same time excludes all others. In trying to renew old recollections, we cannot as it were unfold the whole web of our existence; we must pick out the single threads. So in coming to a place where we have formerly lived and with which we have intimate associations, everyone must have found that the feeling grows more vivid the nearer we approach the spot, from the mere anticipation of the actual impression: we remember circumstances, feelings, persons, faces, names that we had not thought of for years; but for the time all the rest of the world is forgotten!—To return to the question I have quitted above.

I have no objection to go to see ruins, aqueducts, pictures, in company with a friend or a party, but rather the contrary, for the former reason reversed. They are intelligible matters, and will bear talking about. The sentiment here is not tacit, but communicable and overt. Salisbury Plain is barren of criticism, but Stonehenge will bear a discussion antiquarian, picturesque,

---

[1] At the time referred to, 1798, Hazlitt shared with Coleridge and others a belief in the triumph of the principles of the French Revolution.

[2] See Wordsworth's *Ode: Intimations of Immortality*, 76 (p. 329).

[3] Coleridge, *The Death of Wallenstein*, V, 1, 68.

[4] When this essay was first published, in 1822, Coleridge's creative power had waned, and his vigor had been impaired by ill health and the use of laudanum.

[5] See *Revelation*, 22, 17.

[1] Etherege, *The Man of Mode*, V, 2 (ed. Verity, p. 361). The quotation is spoken by Harriet, not by Sir Fopling.

and philosophical. In setting out on a party of pleasure, the first consideration always is where we shall go to: in taking a solitary ramble, the question is what we shall meet with by the way. "The mind is its own place;"[1] nor are we anxious to arrive at the end of our journey. I can myself do the honors indifferently well to works of art and curiosity. I once took a party to Oxford with no mean *éclat*[2]—showed them that seat of the Muses at a distance,

With glistering spires and pinnacles adorn'd[3]—

descanted on the learned air that breathes from the grassy quadrangles and stone walls of halls and colleges—was at home in the Bodleian; and at Blenheim quite superseded the powdered Ciceroni[4] that attended us, and that pointed in vain with his wand to commonplace beauties in matchless pictures.— As another exception to the above reasoning, I should not feel confident in venturing on a journey in a foreign country without a companion. I should want at intervals to hear the sound of my own language. There is an involuntary antipathy in the mind of an Englishman to foreign manners and notions that requires the assistance of social sympathy to carry it off. As the distance from home increases, this relief, which was at first a luxury, becomes a passion and an appetite. A person would almost feel stifled to find himself in the deserts of Arabia without friends and countrymen: there must be allowed to be something in the view of Athens or old Rome that claims the utterance of speech; and I own that the Pyramids are too mighty for any single contemplation. In such situations, so opposite to all one's ordinary train of ideas, one seems a species by one's-self, a limb torn off from society, unless one can meet with instant fellowship and support.—Yet I did not feel this want or craving very pressing once, when I first set my foot on the laughing shores of France.[5] Calais was peopled with novelty and delight. The confused, busy murmur of the place was like oil and wine poured into my ears; nor did the mariners'

hymn, which was sung from the top of an old crazy vessel in the harbor, as the sun went down, send an alien sound into my soul. I only breathed the air of general humanity. I walked over "the vine-covered hills and gay regions of France,"[1] erect and satisfied; for the image of man was not cast down and chained to the foot of arbitrary thrones: I was at no loss for language, for that of all the great schools of painting was open to me. The whole is vanished like a shade. Pictures, heroes, glory, freedom, all are fled; nothing remains but the Bourbons and the French people![2]—There is undoubtedly a sensation in travelling into foreign parts that is to be had nowhere else: but it is more pleasing at the time than lasting. It is too remote from our habitual associations to be a common topic of discourse or reference, and, like a dream or another state of existence, does not piece into our daily modes of life. It is an animated but a momentary hallucination. It demands an effort to exchange our actual for our ideal identity; and to feel the pulse of our old transports revive very keenly, we must "jump"[3] all our present comforts and connections. Our romantic and itinerant character is not to be domesticated. Dr. Johnson remarked how little foreign travel added to the facilities of conversation in those who had been abroad.[4] In fact, the time we have spent there is both delightful and in one sense instructive; but it appears to be cut out of our substantial, downright existence, and never to join kindly on to it. We are not the same, but another, and perhaps more enviable individual, all the time we are out of our own country. We are lost to ourselves, as well as our friends. So the poet somewhat quaintly sings,

Out of my country and myself I go.

Those who wish to forget painful thoughts, do well to absent themselves for a while from the ties and objects that recall them: but we can be said only to fulfill our destiny in the place that gave us birth. I should on this account like well enough to spend the whole of my life in travelling abroad, if I could anywhere borrow another life to spend afterwards at home!

---

[1] *Paradise Lost*, 1, 254.
[2] display (Hazlitt accompanied Charles and Mary Lamb through Oxford and Blenheim on their way to London, in 1810. See Hazlitt's *On the Conversation of Authors* and *The Character of Country People;* also Lamb's letter to Hazlitt, Aug. 9, 1810.)
[3] *Paradise Lost*, 3, 550.
[4] guides (so named because of their talkativeness)
[5] In 1802, when he went to Paris to study the masterpieces of art collected there by Napoleon.

[1] William Roscoe, *Song* (written in 1791), 1.
[2] The Bourbons ruled France from 1589 to the French Revolution, and from the fall of Napoleon to 1830. They were noted for their policies of conservatism and repression.
[3] risk (*Macbeth*, I, 7, 7)
[4] See Boswell's *The Life of Samuel Johnson* (Oxford ed., 1904), 2, 267.

MY FIRST ACQUAINTANCE WITH POETS
1823

My father was a Dissenting Minister at
W——m[1] in Shropshire; and in the year
1798 (the figures that compose that date
are to me like the "dreaded name of Demogorgon"[2]) Mr. Coleridge came to Shrewsbury, to succeed Mr. Rowe in the spiritual
charge of a Unitarian congregation there.
He did not come till late on the Saturday
afternoon before he was to preach; and Mr.
Rowe, who himself went down to the coach
in a state of anxiety and expectation, to look
for the arrival of his successor, could find
no one at all answering the description but
a round-faced man in a short black coat
(like a shooting-jacket) which hardly seemed
to have been made for him, but who seemed
to be talking at a great rate to his fellow-
passengers. Mr. Rowe had scarce returned
to give an account of his disappointment,
when the round-faced man in black entered,
and dissipated all doubts on the subject by
beginning to talk. He did not cease while
he staid; nor has he since, that I know of.
He held the good town of Shrewsbury in
delightful suspense for three weeks that he
remained there, "fluttering the *proud Salo-
pians* like an eagle in a dove-cote;"[3] and
the Welsh mountains that skirt the horizon
with their tempestuous confusion, agree to
have heard no such mystic sounds since the
days of

High-born Hoel's harp or soft Llewellyn's
    lay![4]

As we passed along between W——m and
Shrewsbury, and I eyed their blue tops seen
through the wintry branches, or the red
rustling leaves of the sturdy oak-trees by
the roadside, a sound was in my ears as of
a Siren's song; I was stunned, startled with
it, as from deep sleep; but I had no notion
then that I should ever be able to express
my admiration to others in motley imagery
or quaint allusion, till the light of his genius
shone into my soul, like the sun's rays glittering in the puddles of the road. I was
at that time dumb, inarticulate, helpless, like
a worm by the way-side, crushed, bleeding,
lifeless; but now, bursting from the deadly
bands that "bound them,

With Styx nine times round them,[5]

---

1 Wem.
2 *Paradise Lost*, 2, 964.
3 *Coriolanus*, V, 6, 115. Shropshire is sometimes
   called Salop, from the Latin name *Salopia*.
4 Gray, *The Bard*, 28 (p. 63).
5 Pope, *Ode on St. Cecilia's Day*, 90.

my ideas float on winged words, and as they
expand their plumes, catch the golden light
of other years. My soul has indeed remained
in its original bondage, dark, obscure, with
longings infinite and unsatisfied; my heart,
shut up in the prison-house of this rude clay,
has never found, nor will it ever find, a
heart to speak to; but that my understanding also did not remain dumb and brutish,
or at length found a language to express
itself, I owe to Coleridge. But this is not
to my purpose.

My father lived ten miles from Shrewsbury, and was in the habit of exchanging
visits with Mr. Rowe, and with Mr. Jenkins
of Whitchurch (nine miles farther on) according to the custom of Dissenting Ministers in each other's neighborhood. A line
of communication is thus established, by
which the flame of civil and religious liberty
is kept alive, and nourishes its smouldering
fire unquenchable, like the fires in the
Agamemnon of Æschylus, placed at different stations, that waited for ten long years
to announce with their blazing pyramids
the destruction of Troy. Coleridge had
agreed to come over and see my father,
according to the courtesy of the country,
as Mr. Rowe's probable successor; but in
the meantime I had gone to hear him preach
the Sunday after his arrival. A poet and
a philosopher getting up into a Unitarian
pulpit to preach the Gospel, was a romance
in these degenerate days, a sort of revival
of the primitive spirit of Christianity,
which was not to be resisted.

It was in January, 1798, that I rose one
morning before daylight, to walk ten miles
in the mud, and went to hear this celebrated
person preach. Never, the longest day I
have to live, shall I have such another walk
as this cold, raw, comfortless one, in the
winter of the year 1798. *Il y a des impressions que ni le tems ni les circonstances
peuvent effacer. Dusse-je vivre des siècles
entiers, le doux tems de ma jeunesse ne peut
renaître pour moi, ni s'effacer jamais dans
ma mémoire.*[1] When I got there, the organ
was playing the 100th Psalm, and, when
it was done, Mr. Coleridge rose and gave
out his text, "And he went up into the
mountain to pray, HIMSELF, ALONE."[2] As
he gave out this text, his voice "rose like a

---

1 There are impressions which neither times nor
circumstances can efface. Were I enabled to
live entire ages, the sweet days of my youth
could not return for me, nor ever be obliterated from my memory.—Rousseau, *Confessions*. See Part II, Book VII.
2 *John*, 6 :15.

steam of rich distilled perfumes,''[1] and when he came to the two last words, which he pronounced loud, deep, and distinct, it seemed to me, who was then young, as if the sounds had echoed from the bottom of the human heart, and as if that prayer might have floated in solemn silence through the universe. The idea of St. John came into mind, ''of one crying in the wilderness, who had his loins girt about, and whose food was locusts and wild honey.''[2] The preacher then launched into his subject, like an eagle dallying with the wind. The sermon was upon peace and war; upon church and state —not their alliance, but their separation— on the spirit of the world and the spirit of Christianity, not as the same, but as opposed to one another. He talked of those who had ''inscribed the cross of Christ on banners dripping with human gore.'' He made a poetical and pastoral excursion, —and to show the fatal effects of war, drew a striking contrast between the simple shepherd boy, driving his team afield, or sitting under the hawthorn, piping to his flock, ''as though he should never be old,''[3] and the same poor country-lad, crimped, kidnapped, brought into town, made drunk at an ale-house, turned into a wretched drummer-boy, with his hair sticking on end with powder and pomatum, a long cue at his back, and tricked out in the loathsome finery of the profession of blood.

Such were the notes our once-lov'd poet sung.[4]

And for myself, I could not have been more delighted if I had heard the music of the spheres.[5] Poetry and Philosophy had met together, Truth and Genius had embraced,[6] under the eye and with the sanction of Religion. This was even beyond my hopes. I returned home well satisfied. The sun that was still laboring pale and wan through the sky, obscured by thick mists, seemed an emblem of the *good cause;* and the cold dank drops of dew that hung half melted on the beard of the thistle, had something genial and refreshing in them; for there was a spirit of hope and youth in all nature, that turned everything into good. The face of nature had not then the brand of Jus Divinum[7] on it:

Like to that sanguine flower inscrib'd with woe.[1]

On the Tuesday following, the half-inspired speaker came. I was called down into the room where he was, and went half-hoping, half-afraid. He received me very graciously, and I listened for a long time without uttering a word. I did not suffer in his opinion by my silence. ''For those two hours,'' he afterwards was pleased to say, ''he was conversing with W. H.'s forehead!'' His appearance was different from what I had anticipated from seeing him before. At a distance, and in the dim light of the chapel, there was to me a strange wildness in his aspect, a dusky obscurity, and I thought him pitted with the small-pox. His complexion was at that time clear, and even bright—

As are the children of yon azure sheen.[2]

His forehead was broad and high, light as if built of ivory, with large projecting eyebrows, and his eyes rolling beneath them like a sea with darkened lustre. ''A certain tender bloom his face o'erspread,''[3] a purple tinge as we see it in the pale thoughtful complexions of the Spanish portrait-painters, Murillo and Velasquez. His mouth was gross, voluptuous, open, eloquent; his chin good-humored and round; but his nose, the rudder of the face, the index of the will, was small, feeble, nothing—like what he has done. It might seem that the genius of his face as from a height surveyed and projected him (with sufficient capacity and huge aspiration) into the world unknown of thought and imagination, with nothing to support or guide his veering purpose, as if Columbus had launched his adventurous course for the New World in a scallop, without oars or compass. So at least I comment on it after the event. Coleridge in his person was rather above the common size, inclining to the corpulent, or like Lord Hamlet, ''somewhat fat and pursy.''[4] His hair (now, alas! gray) was then black and glossy as the raven's, and fell in smooth masses over his forehead. This long pendulous hair is peculiar to enthusiasts, to those whose minds tend heavenward; and is traditionally inseparable (though of a different color) from the pictures of Christ.

---

[1] *Comus,* 556.
[2] *Matthew,* 3:3-4.
[3] Sidney, *Arcadia,* 1, 2.
[4] Pope, *Epistle to Robert, Earl of Oxford,* 1.
[5] The ancients believed that the movement of the celestial spheres produced music.
[6] See *Psalms,* 85:10.
[7] divine law

[1] *Lycidas,* 106. The petals of the hyacinth were supposed to be marked with the exclamation *Ai* (woe) in lamentation for Hyacinthus, from whose blood the flower was said to have sprung.
[2] Thomson, *The Castle of Indolence,* 2, 295.
[3] *Ibid.,* 1, 507.
[4] *Hamlet,* V, 2, 298. *Pursy* means *scant of breath.*

It ought to belong, as a character, to all who preach *Christ crucified,* and Coleridge was at that time one of those!

It was curious to observe the contrast between him and my father, who was a veteran in the cause, and then declining into the vale of years. He had been a poor Irish lad, carefully brought up by his parents, and sent to the University of Glasgow (where he studied under Adam Smith) to prepare him for his future destination. It was his mother's proudest wish to see her son a Dissenting Minister. So if we look back to past generations (as far as eye can reach) we see the same hopes, fears, wishes, followed by the same disappointments, throbbing in the human heart; and so we may see them (if we look forward) rising up forever, and disappearing, like vaporish bubbles, in the human breast! After being tossed about from congregation to 'congregation in the heats of the Unitarian controversy, and squabbles about the American war, he had been relegated to an obscure village, where he was to spend the last thirty years of his life, far from the only converse that he loved, the talk about disputed texts of Scripture and the cause of civil and religious liberty. Here he passed his days, repining but resigned, in the study of the Bible, and the perusal of the Commentators, —huge folios, not easily got through, one of which would outlast a winter! Why did he pore on these from morn to night (with the exception of a walk in the fields or a turn in the garden to gather brocoli-plants[1] or kidney-beans of his own rearing, with no small degree of pride and pleasure)? Here was "no figures nor no fantasies,"[2] —neither poetry nor philosophy—nothing to dazzle, nothing to excite modern curiosity; but to his lacklustre eyes there appeared, within the pages of the ponderous, unwieldy, neglected tomes, the sacred name of JEHOVAH in Hebrew capitals: pressed down by the weight of the style, worn to the last fading thinness of the understanding, there were glimpses, glimmering notions of the patriarchal wanderings, with palm-trees hovering on the horizon, and processions of camels at the distance of three thousand years; there was Moses with the Burning Bush, the number of the Twelve Tribes, types, shadows, glosses on the law and the prophets; there were discussions (dull enough) on the age of Methuselah, a mighty speculation! there were outlines, rude guesses

at the shape of Noah's Ark and of the riches of Solomon's Temple; questions as to the date of the creation, predictions of the end of all things; the great lapses of time, the strange mutations of the globe were unfolded with the voluminous leaf, as it turned over; and though the soul might slumber with an hieroglyphic veil of inscrutable mysteries drawn over it, yet it was in a slumber ill-exchanged for all the sharpened realities of sense, wit, fancy, or reason. My father's life was comparatively a dream; but it was a dream of infinity and eternity, of death, the resurrection, and a judgment to come!

No two individuals were ever more unlike than were the host and his guest. A poet was to my father a sort of nondescript: yet whatever added grace to the Unitarian cause was to him welcome. He could hardly have been more surprised and pleased, if our visitor had worn wings. Indeed, his thoughts had wings; and as the silken sounds rustled round our little wainscoted parlor, my father threw back his spectacles over his forehead, his white hairs mixing with its sanguine hue; and a smile of delight beamed across his rugged cordial face, to think that Truth had found a new ally in Fancy![1] Besides, Coleridge seemed to take considerable notice of me, and that of itself was enough. He talked very familiarly, but agreeably, and glanced over a variety of subjects. At dinner-time he grew more animated, and dilated in a very edifying manner on Mary Wolstonecraft and Mackintosh. The last, he said, he considered (on my father's speaking of his *Vindiciæ Gallicæ* as a capital performance) as a clever scholastic man —a master of the topics,—or as the ready warehouseman of letters, who knew exactly where to lay his hand on what he wanted, though the goods were not his own. He thought him no match for Burke, either in style or matter. Burke was a metaphysician, Mackintosh a mere logician. Burke was an orator (almost a poet) who reasoned in figures, because he had an eye for nature: Mackintosh, on the other hand, was a rhetorician, who had only an eye to commonplaces. On this I ventured to say that I had always entertained a great opinion of Burke, and that (as far as I could find) the speaking of him with contempt might be made

---

[1] A variety of cauliflower.

[2] *Julius Cæsar,* II, 1, 231.

[1] "My father was one of those who mistook his talent after all. He used to be very much dissatisfied that I preferred his Letters to his Sermons. The last were forced and dry; the first came naturally from him. For ease, half-plays on words, and a supine, monkish, indolent pleasantry, I have never seen them equalled."—Hazlitt.

the test of a vulgar democratical mind. This was the first observation I ever made to Coleridge, and he said it was a very just and striking one. I remember the leg of Welsh mutton and the turnips on the table that day had the finest flavor imaginable. Coleridge added that Mackintosh and Tom Wedgwood (of whom, however, he spoke highly) had expressed a very indifferent opinion of his friend Mr. Wordsworth, on which he remarked to them—"He strides on so far before you, that he dwindles in the distance!" Godwin had once boasted to him of having carried on an argument with Mackintosh for three hours with dubious success; Coleridge told him—"If there had been a man of genius in the room, he would have settled the question in five minutes." He asked me if I had ever seen Mary Wolstonecraft, and I said, I had once for a few moments, and that she seemed to me to turn off Godwin's objections to something she advanced with quite a playful, easy air. He replied, that "this was only one instance of the ascendancy which people of imagination exercised over those of mere intellect." He did not rate Godwin very high[1] (this was caprice or prejudice, real or affected) but he had a great idea of Mrs. Wolstonecraft's powers of conversation, none at all of her talent for book-making. We talked a little about Holcroft. He had been asked if he was not much struck *with* him, and he said, he thought himself in more danger of being struck *by* him. I complained that he would not let me get on at all, for he required a definition of even the commonest word, exclaiming, "What do you mean by a *sensation*, Sir? What do you mean by an *idea?*" This, Coleridge said, was barricadoing the road to truth:—it was setting up a turnpike-gate at every step we took. I forget a great number of things, many more than I remember; but the day passed off pleasantly, and the next morning Mr. Coleridge was to return to Shrewsbury. When I came down to breakfast, I found that he had just received a letter from his friend, T. Wedgwood, making him an offer of £150 a year if he chose to waive his present pursuit, and devote himself entirely to the study of poetry and philosophy. Coleridge seemed to make up his mind to

close with this proposal in the act of tying on one of his shoes. It threw an additional damp on his departure. It took the wayward enthusiast quite from us to cast him into Deva's winding vales, or by the shores of old romance.[1] Instead of living at ten miles distance, and being the pastor of a Dissenting congregation at Shrewsbury, he was henceforth to inhabit the Hill of Parnassus, to be a Shepherd on the Delectable Mountains.[2] Alas! I knew not the way thither, and felt very little gratitude for Mr. Wedgwood's bounty. I was pleasantly relieved from this dilemma; for Mr. Coleridge asking for a pen and ink, and going to a table to write something on a bit of card, advanced towards me with undulating step, and giving me the precious document, said that that was his address, *Mr. Coleridge, Nether-Stowey, Somersetshire;* and that he should be glad to see me there in a few weeks' time, and, if I chose, would come half-way to meet me. I was not less surprised than the shepherd-boy (this simile is to be found in *Cassandra*) when he sees a thunder-bolt fall close at his feet. I stammered out my acknowledgments and acceptance of this offer (I thought Mr. Wedgwood's annuity a trifle to it) as well as I could; and this mighty business being settled, the poet-preacher took leave, and I accompanied him six miles on the road. It was a fine morning in the middle of winter, and he talked the whole way. The scholar in Chaucer is described as going

Sounding on his way.[3]

So Coleridge went on his. In digressing, in dilating, in passing from subject to subject, he appeared to me to float in air, to slide on ice. He told me in confidence (going along) that he should have preached two sermons before he accepted the situation at Shrewsbury, one on Infant Baptism, the other on the Lord's Supper, showing that he could not administer either, which would have effectually disqualified him for the object in view. I observed that he continually crossed me on the way by shifting from one side of the foot-path to the other. This struck me as an odd movement; but I did not at that time connect it with any instability of purpose or involuntary change of principle, as I have done since. He

---

[1] "He complained in particular of the presumption of his attempting to establish the future immortality of man, 'without' (as he said) 'knowing what Death was, or what Life was' —and the tone in which he pronounced these two words seemed to convey a complete image of both."—Hazlitt.

[1] See Wordsworth's *A Narrow Girdle of Rough Stones and Crags*, 38.
[2] In *Pilgrim's Progress*, Christian and Hopeful escape from Giant Despair and come to the Shepherds of the Delectable Mountain.
[3] Chaucer, *Prologue to the Canterbury Tales*, 307.

seemed unable to keep on in a straight line. He spoke slightingly of Hume (whose *Essay on Miracles* he said was stolen from an objection started in one of South's Sermons—*Credat Judæus Apella!*[1]) I was not very much pleased at this account of Hume, for I had just been reading, with infinite relish, that completest of all metaphysical *choke-pears,* his *Treatise on Human Nature,* to which the *Essays,* in point of scholastic subtlety and close reasoning, are mere elegant trifling, light summer-reading. Coleridge even denied the excellence of Hume's general style, which I think betrayed a want of taste or candor. He however made me amends by the manner in which he spoke of Berkeley. He dwelt particularly on his *Essay on Vision* as a masterpiece of analytical reasoning. So it undoubtedly is. He was exceedingly angry with Dr. Johnson for striking the stone with his foot, in allusion to this author's *Theory of Matter and Spirit,* and saying, "Thus I confute him, Sir."[2] Coleridge drew a parallel (I don't know how he brought about the connection) between Bishop Berkeley and Tom Paine. He said the one was an instance of a subtle, the other of an acute, mind, than which no two things could be more distinct. The one was a shop-boy's quality, the other the characteristic of a philosopher. He considered Bishop Butler as a true philosopher, a profound and conscientious thinker, a genuine reader of nature and his own mind. He did not speak of his *Analogy,* but of his *Sermons at the Rolls' Chapel,* of which I had never heard. Coleridge somehow always contrived to prefer the *unknown* to the *known.* In this instance he was right. The *Analogy* is a tissue of sophistry, of wiredrawn, theological special-pleading; the *Sermons* (with the Preface to them) are in a fine vein of deep, matured reflection, a candid appeal to our observation of human nature, without pedantry and without bias. I told Coleridge I had written a few remarks, and was sometimes foolish enough to believe that I had made a discovery on the same subject (the *Natural Disinterestedness of the Human Mind*)[3]—and I tried to explain my view of it to Coleridge, who listened with great willingness, but I did not succeed in making myself understood. I sat down to the task shortly afterwards

for the twentieth time, got new pens and paper, determined to make clear work of it, wrote a few meagre sentences in the skeleton-style of a mathematical demonstration, stopped half-way down the second page; and, after trying in vain to pump up any words, images, notions, apprehensions, facts, or observations, from that gulf of abstraction in which I had plunged myself for four or five years preceding, gave up the attempt as labor in vain, and shed tears of helpless despondency on the blank unfinished paper. I can write fast enough now. Am I better than I was then? Oh no! One truth discovered, one pang of regret at not being able to express it, is better than all the fluency and flippancy in the world. Would that I could go back to what I then was! Why can we not revive past times as we can revisit old places? If I had the quaint Muse of Sir Philip Sidney to assist me, I would write a *Sonnet to the Road between W——m and Shrewsbury,* and immortalize every step of it by some fond enigmatical conceit. I would swear that the very milestones had ears, and that Harmer-hill stooped with all its pines, to listen to a poet, as he passed! I remember but one other topic of discourse in this walk. He mentioned Paley, praised the naturalness and clearness of his style, but condemned his sentiments, thought him a mere time-serving casuist, and said that "the fact of his work on *Moral and Political Philosophy* being made a text-book in our Universities was a disgrace to the national character." We parted at the six-mile stone; and I returned homeward, pensive but much pleased. I had met with unexpected notice from a person, whom I believed to have been prejudiced against me. "Kind and affable to me had been his condescension, and should be honored ever with suitable regard."[1] He was the first poet I had known, and he certainly answered to that inspired name. I had heard a great deal of his powers of conversation, and was not disappointed. In fact, I never met with anything at all like them, either before or since. I could easily credit the accounts which were circulated of his holding forth to a large party of ladies and gentlemen, an evening or two before, on the Berkeleian Theory, when he made the whole material universe look like a transparency of fine words; and another story (which I believe he has somewhere told himself[2]—of his being asked to

[1] Let the Jew Apella,—*i. e.,* a credulous person, believe it; I shall not (Horace, *Satires,* I, 5, 101).

[2] See Boswell's *The Life of Samuel Johnson* (Oxford ed.), 1, 315.

[3] Not published by Hazlitt until 1805.

[1] *Paradise Lost,* 8, 648-50.

[2] See Coleridge's *Biographia Literaria,* 10.

a party at Birmingham, of his smoking tobacco and going to sleep after dinner on a sofa, where the company found him, to their no small surprise, which was increased to wonder when he started up of a sudden, and rubbing his eyes, looked about him, and launched into a three-hours' description of the third heaven, of which he had had a dream, very different from Mr. Southey's *Vision of Judgment*[1] and also from that other *Vision of Judgment*,[2] which Mr. Murray, the Secretary of the Bridge-street Junto, has taken into his especial keeping!

On my way back, I had a sound in my ears, it was the voice of Fancy: I had a light before me, it was the face of Poetry. The one still lingers there, the other has not quitted my side! Coleridge in truth met me half-way on the ground of philosophy, or I should not have been won over to his imaginative creed. I had an uneasy, pleasurable sensation all the time, till I was to visit him. During those months the chill breath of winter gave me a welcoming; the vernal air was balm and inspiration to me. The golden sunsets, the silver star of evening, lighted me on my way to new hopes and prospects. *I was to visit Coleridge in the spring.* This circumstance was never absent from my thoughts, and mingled with all my feelings. I wrote to him at the time proposed, and received an answer postponing my intended visit for a week or two, but very cordially urging me to complete my promise then. This delay did not damp, but rather increased, my ardor. In the meantime I went to Llangollen Vale, by way of initiating myself in the mysteries of natural scenery; and I must say I was enchanted with it. I had been reading Coleridge's description of England, in his fine *Ode on the Departing Year*,[3] and I applied it, *con amore*,[4] to the objects before me. That valley was to me (in a manner) the cradle of a new existence: in the river that winds through it, my spirit was baptized in the waters of Helicon!

I returned home, and soon after set out on my journey with unworn heart and untried feet. My way lay through Worcester and Gloucester, and by Upton, where I thought of Tom Jones and the adventure of the muff.[1] I remember getting completely wet through one day, and stopping at an inn (I think it was at Tewkesbury[2]) where I sat up all night to read *Paul and Virginia*. Sweet were the showers in early youth that drenched my body, and sweet the drops of pity that fell upon the books I read! I recollect a remark of Coleridge's upon this very book, that nothing could show the gross indelicacy of French manners and the entire corruption of their imagination more strongly than the behavior of the heroine in the last fatal scene, who turns away from a person on board the sinking vessel, that offers to save her life, because he has thrown off his clothes to assist him in swimming. Was this a time to think of such a circumstance? I once hinted to Wordsworth, as we were sailing in his boat on Grasmere lake, that I thought he had borrowed the idea of his *Poems on the Naming of Places*[3] from the local inscriptions of the same kind in *Paul and Virginia*. He did not own the obligation, and stated some distinction without a difference, in defence of his claim to originality. Any the slightest variation would be sufficient for this purpose in his mind; for whatever *he* added or omitted would inevitably be worth all that any one else had done, and contain the marrow of the sentiment. I was still two days before the time fixed for my arrival, for I had taken care to set out early enough. I stopped these two days at Bridgewater, and when I was tired of sauntering on the banks of its muddy river, returned to the inn, and read *Camilla*. So have I loitered my life away, reading books, looking at pictures, going to plays, hearing, thinking, writing on what pleased me best. I have wanted only one thing to make me happy; but wanting that, have wanted everything!

I arrived, and was well received. The country about Nether Stowey is beautiful, green and hilly, and near the sea-shore. I saw it but the other day, after an interval of twenty years, from a hill near Taunton. How was the map of my life spread out before me, as the map of the country lay at my feet! In the afternoon Coleridge took me over to All-Foxden, a romantic old family-mansion of the St. Aubins, where Wordsworth lived. It was then in the possession of a friend of the poet's, who gave

---

[1] See p. 435.
[2] By Lord Byron (p. 639). John Murray was publisher of *The Quarterly Review*, and of the works of Byron and other writers. The Bridge-Street Association (called "Gang" by its enemies) was organized in 1821 to prevent seditious publications and acts.
[3] See ll. 121-34 (p. 359).
[4] with love

---

[1] In Fielding's *The History of Tom Jones*, 10, 5. This was one of Hazlitt's favorite books.
[2] See Hazlitt's *On Going a Journey* (p. 1051b, 21).
[3] Wordsworth wrote seven poems of this character. See *It was an April Morning* (p. 299).

him the free use of it.[1] Somehow that period (the time just after the French Revolution) was not a time when *nothing was given for nothing.* The mind opened, and a softness might be perceived coming over the heart of individuals, beneath "the scales that fence" our self-interest. Wordsworth himself was from home, but his sister kept house, and set before us a frugal repast; and we had free access to her brother's poems, the *Lyrical Ballads,* which were still in manuscript, or in the form of *Sybilline Leaves.* I dipped into a few of these with great satisfaction, and with the faith of a novice. I slept that night in an old room with blue hangings, and covered with the round-faced family-portraits of the age of George I and II and from the wooded declivity of the adjoining park that overlooked my window, at the dawn of day, could

Hear the loud stag speak.

In the outset of life (and particularly at this time I felt it so) our imagination has a body to it. We are in a state between sleeping and waking, and have indistinct but glorious glimpses of strange shapes, and there is always something to come better than what we see. As in our dreams the fulness of the blood gives warmth and reality to the coinage of the brain, so in youth our ideas are clothed, and fed, and pampered with our good spirits; we breathe thick with thoughtless happiness, the weight of future years presses on the strong pulses of the heart, and we repose with undisturbed faith in truth and good. As we advance, we exhaust our fund of enjoyment and of hope. We are no longer wrapped in *lamb's-wool,* lulled in Elysium. As we taste the pleasures of life, their spirit evaporates, the sense palls; and nothing is left but the phantoms, the lifeless shadows of what *has been!*

That morning, as soon as breakfast was over, we strolled out into the park, and seating ourselves on the trunk of an old ash-tree that stretched along the ground, Coleridge read aloud with a sonorous and musical voice *The Ballad of Betty Foy.* I was not critically or skeptically inclined. I saw touches of truth and nature, and took the rest for granted. But in *The Thorn,*[2] *The Mad Mother,*[3] and *The Complaint of a Poor Indian Woman,* I felt that deeper power and

pathos which have been since acknowledged,

In spite of pride, in erring reason's spite,[1]

as the characteristics of this author; and the sense of a new style and a new spirit in poetry came over me. It had to me something of the effect that arises from the turning up of the fresh soil, or of the first welcome breath of spring:

While yet the trembling year is unconfirmed.[2]

Coleridge and myself walked back to Stowey that evening, and his voice sounded high

Of Providence, foreknowledge, will, and fate, Fix'd fate, free-will, foreknowledge absolute,[3]

as we passed through echoing grove, by fairy stream or waterfall, gleaming in the summer moonlight! He lamented that Wordsworth was not prone enough to believe in the traditional superstitions of the place, and that there was a something corporeal, a *matter-of-fact-ness,*[4] a clinging to the palpable, or often to the petty, in his poetry, in consequence. His genius was not a spirit that descended to him through the air; it sprung out of the ground like a flower, or unfolded itself from a green spray, on which the gold-finch sang. He said, however (if I remember right) that this objection must be confined to his descriptive pieces, that his philosophic poetry had a grand and comprehensive spirit in it, so that his soul seemed to inhabit the universe like a palace, and to discover truth by intuition, rather than by deduction.[5] The next day Wordsworth arrived from Bristol at Coleridge's cottage. I think I see him now. He answered in some degree to his friend's description of him, but was more gaunt and Don Quixote-like. He was quaintly dressed (according to the *costume* of that unconstrained period) in a brown fustian jacket and striped pantaloons. There was something of a roll, a lounge, in his gait, not unlike his own Peter Bell. There was a severe, worn pressure of thought about his temples, a fire in his eye (as if he saw something in objects more than the outward appearance), an intense high narrow forehead, a Roman nose, cheeks furrowed by strong purpose and feeling, and a convulsive inclination to laughter about the mouth, a good deal at variance with the solemn,

---

[1] Wordsworth paid £23 a year for Alfoxden.
[2] See p. 251.
[3] This poem was later entitled 'Her Eyes Are Wild. See p. 255.

[1] Pope, *Essay on Man,* 1, 293.
[2] Thomson, *The Seasons,* Spring, 293.
[3] *Paradise Lost,* 2, 559-60.
[4] See Coleridge's *Biographia Literaria,* 22 (p. 410a, 38 ff.).
[5] See *ibid.* (p. 418a, 26 ff.).

stately expression of the rest of his face. Chantry's bust wants the marking traits; but he was teased into making it regular and heavy: Haydon's head of him, introduced into *The Entrance of Christ into Jerusalem*, is the most like his drooping weight of thought and expression. He sat down and talked very naturally and freely, with a mixture of clear, gushing accents in his voice, a deep guttural intonation, and a strong tincture of the northern *burr*,[1] like the crust on wine. He instantly began to make havoc of the half of a Cheshire cheese on the table, and said triumphantly that "his marriage with experience had not been so productive as Mr. Southey's in teaching him a knowledge of the good things of life." He had been to see *The Castle Spectre*, by Monk Lewis, while at Bristol, and described it very well. He said "it fitted the taste of the audience like a glove." This *ad captandum*[2] merit was however by no means a recommendation of it, according to the severe principles of the new school,[3] which reject rather than court popular effect. Wordsworth, looking out of the low, latticed window, said, "How beautifully the sun sets on that yellow bank!" I thought within myself, "With what eyes these poets see nature!" and ever after, when I saw the sunset stream upon the objects facing it, conceived I had made a discovery, or thanked Mr. Wordsworth for having made one for me! We went over to All-Foxden again the day following, and Wordsworth read us the story of *Peter Bell* in the open air; and the comment made upon it by his face and voice was very different from that of some later critics! Whatever might be thought of the poem, "his face was as a book where men might read strange matters,"[4] and he announced the fate of his hero in prophetic tones. There is a *chaunt* in the recitation both of Coleridge and Wordsworth, which acts as a spell upon the hearer, and disarms the judgment. Perhaps they have deceived themselves by making habitual use of this ambiguous accompaniment. Coleridge's manner is more full, animated, and varied; Wordsworth's more equable, sustained, and internal. The one might be termed more *dramatic*, the other more *lyrical*. Coleridge has told me that he himself liked to compose in walking over uneven ground, or breaking

through the straggling branches of a copsewood; whereas Wordsworth always wrote (if he could) walking up and down a straight gravel-walk, or in some spot where the continuity of his verse met with no collateral interruption. Returning that same evening, I got into a metaphysical argument with Wordsworth, while Coleridge was explaining the different notes of the nightingale to his sister, in which we neither of us succeeded in making ourselves perfectly clear and intelligible. Thus I passed three weeks at Nether Stowey and in the neighborhood, generally devoting the afternoons to a delightful chat in an arbor made of bark by the poet's friend Tom Poole, sitting under two fine elm-trees, and listening to the bees humming round us, while we quaffed our *flip*.[1] It was agreed, among other things, that we should make a jaunt down the Bristol-Channel, as far as Linton. We set off together on foot, Coleridge, John Chester, and I. This Chester was a native of Nether Stowey, one of those who were attracted to Coleridge's discourse as flies are to honey, or bees in swarming-time to the sound of a brass pan. He "followed in the chase like a dog who hunts, not like one that made up the cry."[2] He had on a brown cloth coat, boots, and corduroy breeches, was low in stature, bow-legged, had a drag in his walk like a drover, which he assisted by a hazel switch, and kept on a sort of trot by the side of Coleridge, like a running footman by a state coach, that he might not lose a syllable or sound, that fell from Coleridge's lips. He told me his private opinion, that Coleridge was a wonderful man. He scarcely opened his lips, much less offered an opinion the whole way: yet of the three, had I to choose during that journey, I would be John Chester. He afterwards followed Coleridge into Germany,[3] where the Kantean philosophers were puzzled how to bring him under any of their categories.[4] When he sat down at table with his idol, John's felicity was complete; Sir Walter Scott's or Mr. Blackwood's, when they sat down at the same table with the King,[5] was not more so. We passed Dunster on our right, a small town between the brow of a hill and the sea. I remember eying it wistfully as it lay below

---

[1] A trilled pronunciation of the letter *r*, common in Northumberland.
[2] designed to catch popular applause
[3] The Lake School of poets,—Wordsworth, Coleridge, and Southey,—so called because of their residence in the lake district.
[4] *Macbeth*, I, 5, 63.

[1] A spiced drink.   [2] *Othello*, II, 3, 370.
[3] Coleridge, Wordsworth, and Dorothy Wordsworth went to Germany in September, 1798.
[4] With Kant, a category was one of the constitutional forms of the functioning of intellect in all kinds of judgment.
[5] Probably a reference to the banquet which the magistrates of Edinburgh gave to George IV on Aug. 24, 1822. Scott was present.

us: contrasted with the woody scene around, it looked as clear, as pure, as *embrowned* and ideal as any landscape I have seen since, of Gasper Poussin's or Domenichino's. We had a long day's march—(our feet kept time to the echoes of Coleridge's tongue)— through Minehead and by the Blue Anchor, and on to Linton, which we did not reach till near midnight, and where we had some difficulty in making a lodgment. We however knocked the people of the house up at last, and we were repaid for our apprehensions and fatigue by some excellent rashers of fried bacon and eggs. The view in coming along had been splendid. We walked for miles and miles on dark brown heaths overlooking the channel, with the Welsh hills beyond, and at times descended into little sheltered valleys close by the sea-side, with a smuggler's face scowling by us, and then had to ascend conical hills with a path winding up through a coppice to a barren top, like a monk's shaven crown, from one of which I pointed out to Coleridge's notice the bare masts of a vessel on the very edge of the horizon and within the red-orbed disk of the setting sun, like his own spectre-ship in *The Ancient Mariner.*[1] At Linton the character of the sea-coast becomes more marked and rugged. There is a place called *The Valley of Rocks* (I suspect this was only the poetical name for it) bedded among precipices overhanging the sea, with rocky caverns beneath, into which the waves dash, and where the sea-gull forever wheels its screaming flight. On the tops of these are huge stones thrown transverse, as if an earthquake had tossed them there, and behind these is a fretwork of perpendicular rocks, something like *The Giant's Causeway.* A thunder-storm came on while we were at the inn, and Coleridge was running out bareheaded to enjoy the commotion of the elements in *The Valley of Rocks,* but as if in spite, the clouds only muttered a few angry sounds, and let fall a few refreshing drops. Coleridge told me that he and Wordsworth were to have made this place the scene of a prose-tale, which was to have been in the manner of, but far superior to, *The Death of Abel,* but they had relinquished the design. In the morning of the second day, we breakfasted luxuriously in an old-fashioned parlor, on tea, toast, eggs, and honey, in the very sight of the bee-hives from which it had been taken, and a garden full of thyme and wild flowers that had produced it. On this occasion Coleridge spoke of Virgil's

[1] See ll. 143 ff. (p. 363).

Georgics, but not well. I do not think he had much feeling for the classical or elegant. It was in this room that we found a little worn-out copy of *The Seasons,* lying in a window-seat, on which Coleridge exclaimed, "*That* is true fame!" He said Thomson was a great poet, rather than a good one; his style was as meretricious as his thoughts were natural. He spoke of Cowper as the best modern poet. He said the *Lyrical Ballads* were an experiment about to be tried by him and Wordsworth, to see how far the public taste would endure poetry written in a more natural and simple style than had hitherto been attempted; totally discarding the artifices of poetical diction, and making use only of such words as had probably been common, in the most ordinary language since the days of Henry II.[1] Some comparison was introduced between Shakespear and Milton. He said "he hardly knew which to prefer. Shakespear appeared to him a mere stripling in the art; he was as tall and as strong, with infinitely more activity than Milton, but he never appeared to have come to man's estate; or if he had, he would not have been a man, but a monster." He spoke with contempt of Gray, and with intolerance of Pope.[2] He did not like the versification of the latter. He observed that "the ears of these couplet-writers might be charged with having short memories, that could not retain the harmony of whole passages." He thought little of Junius as a writer;[3] he had a dislike of Dr. Johnson; and a much higher opinion of Burke as an orator and politician, than of Fox or Pitt. He however thought him very inferior in richness of style and imagery to some of our elder prose-writers, particularly Jeremy Taylor. He liked Richardson, but not Fielding; nor could I get him to enter into the merits of *Caleb Williams.*[4] In short, he was profound and discriminating with respect to those authors whom he liked, and where he gave his judg-

[1] Henry II was King of England 1154-89.
[2] See Coleridge's *Biographia Literaria,* 1-2.
[3] For comments on Junius and the other writers here mentioned, see Coleridge's *Table Talk,* July 3, 1833; July 4, 1833; Apr. 8, 1833; and July 5, 1834. In the latter paper, Coleridge expresses a preference for Fielding over Richardson.
[4] "He had no idea of pictures, of Claude or Raphael, and at this time I had as little as he. He sometimes gives a striking account at present of the Cartoons at Pisa, by Buffamalco and others; of one in particular where Death is seen in the air brandishing his scythe, and the great and mighty of the earth shudder at his approach, while the beggars and the wretched kneel to him as their deliverer. He would of course understand so broad and fine a moral as this at any time."—Hazlitt.

ment fair play; capricious, perverse, and prejudiced in his antipathies and distastes. We loitered on the "ribbed sea-sands,"[1] in such talk as this, a whole morning, and I recollect met with a curious sea-weed, of which John Chester told us the country name! A fisherman gave Coleridge an account of a boy that had been drowned the day before, and that they had tried to save him at the risk of their own lives. He said "he did not know how it was that they ventured, but, sir, we have a *nature* towards one another." This expression, Coleridge remarked to me, was a fine illustration of that theory of disinterestedness which I (in common with Butler) had adopted. I broached to him an argument of mine to prove that *likeness* was not mere association of ideas. I said that the mark in the sand put one in mind of a man's foot, not because it was part of a former impression of a man's foot (for it was quite new) but because it was like the shape of a man's foot. He assented to the justness of this distinction (which I have explained at length elsewhere, for the benefit of the curious), and John Chester listened; not from any interest in the subject, but because he was astonished that I should be able to suggest anything to Coleridge that he did not already know. We returned on the third morning, and Coleridge remarked the silent cottage-smoke curling up the valleys where, a few evenings before, we had seen the lights gleaming through the dark.

In a day or two after we arrived at Stowey, we set out, I on my return home, and he for Germany. It was a Sunday morning, and he was to preach that day for Dr. Toulmin of Taunton. I asked him if he had prepared anything for the occasion? He said he had not even thought of the text, but should as soon as we parted. I did not go to hear him,—this was a fault,—but we met in the evening at Bridgewater. The next day we had a long day's walk to Bristol, and sat down, I recollect, by a well-side on the road, to cool ourselves and satisfy our thirst, when Coleridge repeated to me some descriptive lines of his tragedy of *Remorse*, which I must say became his mouth and that occasion better than they, some years after, did Mr. Elliston's and the Drury-lane boards,—

Oh memory! shield me from the world's poor
    strife,
And give those scenes thine everlasting life.

I saw no more of him for a year or two,

[1] *The Rime of the Ancient Mariner*, 227 (p. 364).

during which period he had been wandering in the Hartz Forest in Germany; and his return was cometary, meteorous, unlike his setting out. It was not till some time after that I knew his friends Lamb and Southey. The last always appears to me (as I first saw him) with a common-place-book under his arm, and the first with a *bon-mot*[1] in his mouth. It was at Godwin's that I met him with Holcroft and Coleridge,[2] where they were disputing fiercely which was the best— *Man as he was, or man as he is to be.* "Give me," says Lamb, "man as he is *not* to be."[?] This saying was the beginning of a friendship between us, which I believe still continues.—Enough of this for the present.

But there is matter for another rhyme,
And I to this may add a second tale.[3]

ON THE FEELING OF IMMORTALITY IN YOUTH
1827

Life is a pure flame, and we live by an invisible sun within us.—SIR THOMAS BROWNE.[4]

No young man believes he shall ever die. It was a saying of my brother's,[5] and a fine one. There is a feeling of Eternity in youth, which makes us amends for everything. To be young is to be as one of the Immortal Gods. One half of time indeed is flown— the other half remains in store for us with all its countless treasures; for there is no line drawn, and we see no limit to our hopes and wishes. We make the coming age our own.—

The vast, the unbounded prospect lies before
    us.[6]

Death, old age, are words without a meaning, that pass by us like the idle air which we regard not. Others may have undergone, or may still be liable to them—we "bear a charmed life,"[7] which laughs to scorn all such sickly fancies. As in setting out on a delightful journey, we strain our eager gaze forward—

Bidding the lovely scene at distance hail,[8]—

and see no end to the landscape, new objects presenting themselves as we advance; so, in the commencement of life, we set no bounds to our inclinations, nor to the unrestricted opportunities of gratifying them. We have as yet found no obstacle, no disposition to flag; and it seems that we can go on so for-

[1] clever or witty saying   [2] This was in 1804.
[3] Wordsworth, *Hart-Leap Well*, 95-96.
[4] *Urn Burial*, ch. 5.   [5] John Hazlitt (1767-1837).
[6] Addison, *Cato*, V, 1, 13.   [7] *Macbeth*, V, 8, 12.
[8] Collins, *The Passions*, 32 (p. 51).

ever. We look round in a new world, full of life, and motion, and ceaseless progress; and feel in ourselves all the vigor and spirit to keep pace with it, and do not foresee from any present symptoms how we shall be left behind in the natural course of things, decline into old age, and drop into the grave. It is the simplicity, and as it were *abstractedness* of our feelings in youth, that (so to speak) identifies us with nature, and (our experience being slight and our passions strong) deludes us into a belief of being immortal like it. Our short-lived connection with existence, we fondly flatter ourselves, is an indissoluble and lasting union—a honey-moon that knows neither coldness, jar, nor separation. As infants smile and sleep, we are rocked in the cradle of our wayward fancies, and lulled into security by the roar of the universe around us—we quaff the cup of life with eager haste without draining it, instead of which it only overflows the more —objects press around us, filling the mind with their magnitude and with the throng of desires that wait upon them, so that we have no room for the thoughts of death. From the plenitude of our being, we cannot change all at once to dust and ashes, we cannot imagine "this sensible, warm motion, to become a kneaded clod"[1]—we are too much dazzled by the brightness of the waking dream around us to look into the darkness of the tomb. We no more see our end than our beginning: the one is lost in oblivion and vacancy, as the other is hid from us by the crowd and hurry of approaching events. Or the grim shadow is seen lingering in the horizon, which we are doomed never to overtake, or whose last, faint, glimmering outline touches upon Heaven and translates us to the skies! Nor would the hold that life has taken of us permit us to detach our thoughts from the present objects and pursuits, even if we would. What is there more opposed to health, than sickness; to strength and beauty, than decay and dissolution; to the active search of knowledge than mere oblivion? Or is there none of the usual advantage to bar the approach of Death, and mock his idle threats; Hope supplies their place, and draws a veil over the abrupt termination of all our cherished schemes. While the spirit of youth remains unimpaired, ere the "wine of life is drank up,"[2] we are like people intoxicated or in a fever, who are hurried away by the violence of their own sensations: it is only as present objects begin

to pall upon the sense, as we have been disappointed in our favorite pursuits, cut off from our closest ties, that passion loosens its hold upon the breast, that we by degrees become weaned from the world, and allow ourselves to contemplate, "as in a glass, darkly,"[1] the possibility of parting with it for good. The example of others, the voice of experience, has no effect upon us whatever. Casualties we must avoid: the slow and deliberate advances of age we can play at *hide-and-seek* with. We think ourselves too lusty and too nimble for that blear-eyed decrepid old gentleman to catch us. Like the foolish fat scullion, in Sterne,[2] when she hears that Master Bobby is dead, our only reflection is—"So am not I!" The idea of death, instead of staggering our confidence, rather seems to strengthen and enhance our possession and our enjoyment of life. Others may fall around like leaves, or be mowed down like flowers by the scythe of Time: these are but tropes and figures to the unreflecting ears and overweening presumption of youth. It is not till we see the flowers of Love, Hope, and Joy, withering around us, and our own pleasures cut up by the roots, that we bring the moral home to ourselves, that we abate something of the wanton extravagance of our pretensions, or that the emptiness and dreariness of the prospect before us reconciles us to the stillness of the grave!

Life! thou strange thing, thou has a power to
feel
Thou art, and to perceive that others are.[3]

Well might the poet begin his indignant invective against an art, whose professed object is its destruction, with this animated apostrophe to life. Life is indeed a strange gift, and its privileges are most miraculous. Nor is it singular that when the splendid boon is first granted us, our gratitude, our admiration, and our delight should prevent us from reflecting on our own nothingness, or from thinking it will ever be recalled. Our first and strongest impressions are taken from the mighty scene that is opened to us, and we very innocently transfer its durability as well as magnificence to ourselves. So newly found, we cannot make up our minds to parting with it yet and at least put off that consideration to an indefinite term. Like a clown at a fair, we are full of amaze-

---

[1] *Measure for Measure*, III, 1, 120.
[2] *Macbeth*, II, 3, 100.

[1] *1 Corinthians*, 13:12.
[2] *The Life and Opinions of Tristram Shandy*, V, 7.
[3] "Fawcett's *Art of War*, a poem, 1794."—Hazlitt.

ment and rapture, and have no thoughts of
going home, or that it will soon be night.
We know our existence only from external
objects, and we measure it by them. We can
never be satisfied with gazing; and nature
will still want us to look on and applaud.
Otherwise, the sumptuous entertainment,
"the feast of reason and the flow of soul,"[1]
to which they were invited, seems little better
than mockery and a cruel insult. We do not
go from a play till the scene is ended, and
the lights are ready to be extinguished. But
the fair face of things still shines on; shall
we be called away, before the curtain falls,
or ere we have scarce had a glimpse of what
is going on? Like children, our step-mother
Nature holds us up to see the raree-show[2]
of the universe; and then, as if life were a
burthen to support, lets us instantly down
again. Yet in that short interval, what
"brave sublunary things"[3] does not the
spectacle unfold; like a bubble, at one minute reflecting the universe, and the next,
shook to air!—To see the golden sun and the
azure sky, the outstretched ocean, to walk
upon the green earth, and to be lord of a
thousand creatures, to look down the giddy
precipices or over the distant flowery vales,
to see the world spread out under one's
finger in a map, to bring the stars near,
to view the smallest insects in a microscope,
to read history, and witness the revolutions
of empires and the succession of generations, to hear of the glory of Sidon and
Tyre, of Babylon and Susa, as of a faded
pageant, and to say all these were, and are
now nothing, to think that we exist in such
a point of time, and in such a corner of
space, to be at once spectators and a part
of the moving scene, to watch the return of
the seasons of spring and autumn, to hear

The stockdove plain amid the forest deep,
That drowsy rustles to the sighing gale[4]—

to traverse desert wilderness, to listen to the
midnight choir, to visit lighted halls, or
plunge into the dungeon's gloom, or sit in
crowded theatres and see life itself mocked,
to feel heat and cold, pleasure and pain,
right and wrong, truth and falsehood, to
study the works of art and refine the sense
of beauty to agony, to worship fame and to
dream of immortality, to have read Shakspeare and belong to the same species as Sir

[1] Pope, *Imitations of Horace*, Satire 1, 128.
[2] cheap street show
[3] Drayton, *To My Dearly Loved Friend, Henry Reynolds, Esq.*, 106.
[4] Thomson, *The Castle of Indolence*, 1, 33-34 (p. 25).

Isaac Newton;[1] to be and to do all this, and
then in a moment to be nothing, to have it

[1] "Lady Wortley Montagu says, in one of her letters, that 'she would much rather be a rich *effendi*,[a] with all his ignorance, than Sir Isaac Newton, with all his knowledge.'[b] This was not perhaps an impolitic choice, as she had a better chance of becoming one than the other, there being many rich effendis to one Sir Isaac Newton. The wish was not a very intellectual one. The same petulance of rank and sex breaks out everywhere in these *Letters*. She is constantly reducing the poets or philosophers who have the misfortune of her acquaintance, to the figure they might make at her Ladyship's levee or toilette, not considering that the public mind does not sympathize with this process of a fastidious imagination. In the same spirit, she declares of Pope and Swift, that 'had it not been for the *good-nature* of mankind, these two superior beings were entitled, by their birth and hereditary fortune, to be only a couple of link-boys.[c] *Gulliver's Travels*, and *The Rape of the Lock*, go for nothing in this critical estimate, and the world raised the authors to the rank of superior beings, in spite of their disadvantages of birth and fortune, *out of pure good-nature!* So again, she says of Richardson, that he had never got beyond the servant's hall, and was utterly unfit to describe the manners of people of quality; till in the capricious workings of her vanity, she persuades herself that Clarissa is very like what she was at her age, and that Sir Thomas and Lady Grandison strongly resembled what she had heard of her mother and remembered of her father.[d] It is one of the beauties and advantages of literature, that it is the means of abstracting the mind from the narrowness of local and personal prejudices, and of enabling us to judge of truth and excellence by their inherent merits alone. Woe be to the pen that would undo this fine illusion (the only reality), and teach us to regulate our notions of genius and virtue by the circumstances in which they happen to be placed! You would not expect a person whom you saw in a servant's hall, or behind a counter, to write *Clarissa*; but after he had written the work, to *pre-judge* it from the situation of the writer, is an unpardonable piece of injustice and folly. His merit could only be the greater from the contrast. If literature is an elegant accomplishment, which none but persons of birth and fashion should be allowed to excel in, or to exercise with advantage to the public, let them by all means take upon them the task of enlightening and refining mankind; if they decline this responsibility as too heavy for their shoulders, let those who do the drudgery in their stead, however inadequately, for want of their polite example, receive the meed that is their due, and not be treated as low pretenders who have encroached upon the provinces of their betters. Suppose Richardson to have been acquainted with the great man's steward, or valet, instead of the great man himself, I will venture to say that there was more difference between him who lived in an *ideal world*, and had the genius and felicity to open that world to others, and his friend the steward, than between the lacquey and the mere lord, or between those who lived in different rooms of the same house, who dined on the same luxuries at different tables, who rode outside or inside of the same coach, and were proud of wearing or of be-

[a] A Turkish title of respect.
[b] Letter, May 17, 1717. For her comments on Fielding and Richardson, see letters dated Dec. 14, 1750, Dec. 8, 1751, Oct. 20, 1752, June 23, 1754, and Sept. 22, 1755.
[c] torch-bearers (See Works, 2, 254.)
[d] See Works, 2, 222 and 285.

all snatched from one like a juggler's ball or a phantasmagoria; there is something revolting and incredible to sense in the transition, and no wonder that, aided by youth and warm blood, and the flush of enthusiasm, the mind contrives for a long time to reject it with disdain and loathing as a monstrous and improbable fiction, like a monkey on a housetop, that is loath, amidst its fine discoveries and specious antics, to be tumbled headlong into the street, and crushed to atoms, the sport and laughter of the multitude!

The change, from the commencement to the close of life, appears like a fable, after it had taken place; how should we treat it

stowing the same tawdry livery. If the lord is distinguished from his valet by anything else, it is by education and talent, which he has in common with the author. But if the latter shows these in the highest degree, it is asked What are his pretensions? Not birth or fortune, for neither of these would enable him to write *Clarissa*. One man is born with a title and estate, another with genius. That is sufficient; and we have no right to question the genius for want of the *gentility*, unless the former ran in families, or could be bequeathed with a fortune, which is not the case. Were it so, the flowers of literature, like jewels and embroidery, would be confined to the fashionable circles; and there would be no pretenders to taste or elegance but those whose names were found in the court list. No one objects to Claude's Landscapes as the work of a pastry-cook, or withholds from Raphael the epithet of *divine*, because his parents were not rich. This impertinence is confined to men of letters; the evidence of the senses baffles the envy and foppery of mankind. No quarter ought to be given to this *aristocratic* tone of criticism whenever it appears. People of quality are not contented with carrying all the external advantages for their own share, but would persuade you that all the intellectual ones are packed up in the same bundle. Lord Byron was a later instance of this double and unwarrantable style of pretension—*monstrum ingens, biforme*.[a] He could not endure a lord who was not a wit, nor a poet who was not a lord. Nobody but himself answered to his own standard of perfection. Mr. Moore carries a proxy in his pocket from some noble persons to estimate literary merit by the same rule. Lady Mary calls Fielding names, but she afterwards makes atonement by doing justice to his frank, free, hearty nature, where she says 'his spirits gave him raptures with his cookmaid, and cheerfulness when he was starving in a garret, and his happy constitution made him forget everything when he was placed before a venison-pasty or over a flask of champagne.[b] She does not want shrewdness and spirit when her petulance and conceit do not get the better of her, and she has done ample and merited execution on Lord Bolingbroke. She is, however, very angry at the freedoms taken with the Great; *smells a rat* in this indiscriminate scribbling, and the familiarity of writers with the reading public; and inspired by her Turkish costume, foretells a French and English revolution as the consequence of transferring the patronage of letters from the *quality* to the mob, and of supposing that ordinary writers or readers can have any notions in common with their superiors."—Hazlitt.

[a] a monster, huge, misshaped (*Æneid*, 3, 658)
[b] See Works, 2, 283.

otherwise than as a chimera before it has come to pass. There are some things that happened so long ago, places or persons we have formerly seen, of which such dim traces remain, we hardly know whether it was sleeping or waking they occurred; they are like dreams within the dream of life, a mist, a film before the eye of memory, which, as we try to recall them more distinctly, elude our notice altogether. It is but natural that the lone interval that we thus look back upon, should have appeared long and endless in prospect. There are others so distinct and fresh, they seem but of yesterday—their very vividness might be deemed a pledge of their permanence. Then, however far back our impressions may go, we find others still older (for our years are multiplied in youth); descriptions of scenes that we had read, and people before our time, Priam and the Trojan war; and even then, Nestor was old and dwelt delighted on his youth, and spoke of the race, of heroes that were no more;—what wonder that, seeing this long line of beings pictured in our minds, and reviving as it were in us, we should give ourselves involuntary credit for an indeterminate existence? In the Cathedral at Peterborough there is a monument to Mary, Queen of Scots, at which I used to gaze when a boy, while the events of the period, all that had happened since, passed in review before me. If all this mass of feeling and imagination could be crowded into a moment's compass, what might not the whole of life be supposed to contain? We are heirs of the past; we count on the future as our natural reversion. Besides, there are some of our early impressions so exquisitely tempered, it appears that they must always last—nothing can add or take away from their sweetness and purity— the first breath of spring, the hyacinth dipped in the dew, the mild lustre of the evening-star, the rainbow after a storm— while we have the full enjoyment of these, we must be young; and what can ever alter us in this respect? Truth, friendship, love, books, are also proof against the canker of time; and while we live, but for them, we can never grow old. We take out a new lease of existence from the objects on which we set our affections, and become abstracted, impassive, immortal in them. We cannot conceive how certain sentiments should ever decay or grow cold in our breasts; and, consequently, to maintain them in their first youthful glow and vigor, the flame of life must continue to burn as bright as ever, or rather, they are the fuel that feed the sacred lamp, that kindle "the purple light of love,"[1] and spread a golden cloud around our heads! Again, we not only flourish and survive in our affections (in which we will not listen to the possibility of a change, any more than we foresee the wrinkles on the brow of a mistress), but we have a farther guarantee against the thoughts of death in our favorite studies and pursuits and in their continual advance. Art we know is long; life, we feel, should be so too. We see no end of the difficulties we have to encounter: perfection is slow of attainment, and we must have time to accomplish it in. Rubens complained that when he had just learned his art, he was snatched away from it: we trust we shall be more fortunate! A wrinkle in an old head takes whole days to finish it properly: but to catch "the Raphael grace, the Guido air,"[2] no limit should be put to our endeavors. What a prospect for the future! What a task we have entered upon! and shall we be arrested in the middle of it? We do not reckon our time thus employed lost, or our pains thrown away, or our progress slow—we do not droop or grow tired, but "gain a new vigor at our endless task;"[3] —and shall Time grudge us the opportunity to finish what we have auspiciously begun, and have formed a sort of compact with nature to achieve? The fame of the great names we look up to is also imperishable; and shall not we, who contemplate it with such intense yearnings, imbibe a portion of ethereal fire, the *divinæ particula auræ*,[4] which nothing can extinguish? I remember to have looked at a print of Rembrandt for hours together, without being conscious of the flight of time, trying to resolve it into its component parts, to connect its strong and sharp gradations, to learn the secret of its reflected lights, and found neither satiety nor pause in the prosecution of my studies. The print over which I was poring would last long enough; why should the idea of my mind, which was finer, more impalpable, perish before it? At this, I redoubled the ardor of my pursuit, and by the very subtlety and refinement of my inquiries, seemed to bespeak for them an exemption from corruption and the rude grasp of Death.[5]

Objects, on our first acquaintance with them, have that singleness and integrity of impression that it seems as if nothing could destroy or obliterate them, so firmly are they stamped and riveted on the brain. We repose on them with a sort of voluptuous indolence, in full faith and boundless confidence. We are absorbed in the present moment, or return to the same point—idling away a great deal of time in youth, thinking we have enough to spare. There is often a local feeling in the air, which is as fixed as if it were marble; we loiter in dim cloisters, losing ourselves in thought and in their glimmering arches; a winding road before us seems as long as the journey of life, and as full of events. Time and experience dissipate this illusion; and by reducing them to detail, circumscribe the limits of our expectations. It is only as the pageant of life passes by and the masques turn their backs upon us, that we see through the deception, or believe that the train will have an end. In many cases, the slow progress and monotonous texture of our lives, before we mingle with the world and are embroiled in its affairs, has a tendency to aid the same feeling. We have a difficulty, when left to ourselves, and without the resource of books or some more lively pursuit, to "beguile the slow and creeping hours of time,"[1] and argue that if it moves on always at this tedious snail's-pace, it can never come to an end. We are willing to skip over certain portions of it that separate us from favorite objects, that irritate ourselves at the unnecessary delay. The young are prodigal of life from a superabundance of it; the old are tenacious on the same score, because they have little left, and cannot enjoy even what remains of it.

For my part, I set out in life with the French Revolution, and that event had considerable influence on my early feelings, as on those of others. Youth was then doubly such. It was the dawn of a new era, a new impulse had been given to men's minds, and the sun of Liberty rose upon the sun of Life in the same day, and both were proud to run their race together. Little did I dream, while my first hopes and wishes went hand in hand with those of the human race, that long before my eyes should close, that dawn would be overcast, and set once more in the night of despotism[2]—"total eclipse!" Happy that I did not. I felt for years, and during the best part of my existence, *heart-whole* in that cause, and triumphed in the triumphs

[1] Gray, *The Progress of Poesy*, 41 (p. 62).
[2] Pope, *Moral Essays*, 8, 36. Raphael (1483-1520) and Guido Reni (1575-1642) were Italian painters.
[3] Cowper, *Charity*, 104.
[4] portions of the divine breath,—*i. e.*, inspiration
[5] "Is it not this that frequently keeps artists alive so long, *viz.*, the constant occupation of their minds with vivid images, with little of the *wear-and-tear* of the body?"—Hazlitt.

[1] *As You Like It*, II, 7, 112.
[2] A reference to the return of the Bourbons after the defeat of Napoleon.

over the enemies of man! At that time, while the fairest aspirations of the human mind seemed about to be realized, ere the image of man was defaced and his breast mangled in scorn, philosophy took a higher, poetry could afford a deeper range. At that time, to read *The Robbers,* was indeed delicious,[1] and to hear

From the dungeon of the tower time-rent,
That fearful voice, a famish'd father's cry[2]

could be borne only amidst the fulness of hope, the crash of the fall of the strong-holds of power, and the exulting sounds of the march of human freedom. What feel-ings the death-scene in *Don Carlos*[3] sent into the soul! In that headlong career of lofty enthusiasm, and the joyous opening of the prospects of the world and our own, the thought of death crossing it, smote doubly cold upon the mind; there was a stifling sense of oppression and confinement, an im-patience of our present knowledge, a desire to grasp the whole of our existence in one strong embrace, to sound the mystery of life and death, and in order to put an end to the agony of doubt and dread, to burst through our prison-house, and confront the King of Terrors in his grisly palace!—As I was writing out this passage, my miniature pic-ture when a child lay on the mantle-piece, and I took it out of the case to look at it. I could perceive few traces of myself in it; but there was the same placid brow, the dimpled mouth, the same timid, inquisitive glance as ever. But its careless smile did not seem to reproach me with having become recreant to the sentiments that were then sown in my mind, or with having written a sentence that could call up a blush in this image of ingenuous youth!

"That time is past with all its giddy rap-tures."[4] Since the future was barred to my progress, I have turned for consolation to the past, gathering up the fragments of my early recollections, and putting them into form that might live. It is thus, that when we find our personal and substantial identity vanishing from us, we strive to gain a re-flected and substituted one in our thoughts: we do not like to perish wholly, and wish to bequeath our names at least to posterity. As long as we can keep alive our cherished thoughts and nearest interests in the minds of others, we do not appear to have retired altogether from the stage, we still occupy a place in the estimation of mankind, exercise a powerful influence over them, and it is only our bodies that are trampled into dust or dis-persed to air. Our darling speculations still find favor and encouragement, and we make as good a figure in the eyes of our descend-ants, nay, perhaps, a better than we did in our life-time. This is one point gained; the demands of our self-love are so far satisfied. Besides, if by the proofs of intellectual supe-riority we survive ourselves in this world, by exemplary virtue or unblemished faith, we are taught to ensure an interest in another and a higher state of being, and to anticipate at the same time the applauses of men and angels.

Even from the tomb the voice of nature cries;
Even in our ashes live their wonted fires.[1]

As we advance in life, we acquire a keener sense of the value of time. Nothing else, indeed, seems of any consequence; and we become misers in this respect. We try to arrest its few last tottering steps, and to make it linger on the brink of the grave. We can never leave off wondering how that which has ever been should cease to be, and would still live on, that we may wonder at our own shadow, and when "all the life of life is flown,"[2] dwell on the retrospect of the past. This is accompanied by a mechanical tena-ciousness of whatever we possess, by a dis-trust and a sense of fallacious hollowness in all we see. Instead of the full, pulpy feeling of youth, everything is flat and insipid. The world is a painted witch, that puts us off with false shows and tempting appearances. The ease, the jocund gaiety, the unsuspecting security of youth are fled: nor can we, with-out flying in the face of common sense,

From the last dregs of life, hope to receive
What its first sprightly runnings could not give.[3]

If we can slip out of the world without notice or mischance, can tamper with bodily infirmity, and frame our minds to the becom-ing composure of *still-life*, before we sink into total insensibility, it is as much as we ought to expect. We do not in the regular course of nature die all at once: we have

[1] *The Robbers* is the most strongly revolutionary work of Schiller and of the Storm and Stress period in German literature. In *Don Carlos,* Schiller shows his impatience with the revo-lutionary struggle in so far as it concerns physical liberty only, and stresses the value of spiritual liberty.
[2] Coleridge, *To the Author of The Robbers,* 3-4.
[3] Act I, 1.
[4] Wordsworth. *Lines Composed a Few Miles Above Tintern Abbey,* 83-85 (p. 260).

[1] Gray, *Elegy, Written in a Country Churchyard,* 91-92 (p. 61).
[2] Burns, *Lament for James, Earl of Glencairn,* 46.
[3] Dryden, *Aurengzebe,* IV, 1, 41-42.

mouldered away gradually long before; faculty after faculty, attachment after attachment, we are torn from ourselves piece-meal while living; year after year takes something from us; and death only consigns the last remnant of what we were to the grave. The revulsion is not so great, and a quiet *euthanasia*[1] is a winding-up of the plot, that is not out of reason or nature.

That we should thus in a manner outlive ourselves, and dwindle imperceptibly into nothing, is not surprising, when even in our prime the strongest impressions leave so little traces of themselves behind, and the last object is driven out by the succeeding one. How little effect is produced on us at any time by the books we have read, the scenes we have witnessed, the sufferings we have gone through! Think only of the variety of feelings we experience in reading an interesting romance, or being present at a fine play—what beauty, what sublimity, what soothing, what heart-rending emotions! You would suppose these would last forever, or at least subdue the mind to a correspondent tone and harmony—while we turn over the page, while the scene is passing before us, it seems as if nothing could ever after shake our resolution, that "treason domestic, foreign levy, nothing could touch us farther!"[2] The first splash of mud we get, on entering the street, the first pettifogging shop-keeper that cheats us out of two-pence, and the whole vanishes clean out of our remembrance, and we become the idle prey of the most petty and annoying circumstances. The mind soars by an effort to the grand and lofty: it is at home, in the grovelling, the disagreeable, and the little. This happens in the height and hey-day of our existence, when novelty gives a stronger impulse to the blood and takes a faster hold of the brain, (I have known the impression on coming out of a gallery of pictures then last half a day) —as we grow old, we become more feeble and querulous, every object "reverbs its own hollowness,"[3] and both worlds are not enough to satisfy the peevish importunity and extravagant presumption of our desires! There are a few superior, happy beings, who are born with a temper exempt from every trifling annoyance. This spirit sits serene and smiling as in its native skies, and a divine harmony (whether heard or not) plays around them.[4] This is to be at peace. Without this, it is in vain to fly into

[1] easy death
[2] *Macbeth*, III, 2, 24.　　[3] *King Lear*, I, 1, 145.
[4] A reference to the ancient belief that the movement of the celestial spheres produced music.

deserts, or to build a hermitage on the top of rocks, if regret and ill-humor follow us there: and with this, it is needless to make the experiment. The only true retirement is that of the heart; the only true leisure is the repose of the passions. To such persons it makes little difference whether they are young or old; and they die as they have lived, with graceful resignation.

Thomas De Quincey 1785-1859

CONFESSIONS OF AN ENGLISH OPIUM-EATER

1820-22　　　*1821-22*

From PRELIMINARY CONFESSIONS

．　．　．　．　．

I have often been asked how I came to be a regular opium-eater; and have suffered, very unjustly, in the opinion of my acquaintance, from being reputed to have brought upon myself all the sufferings which I shall have to record, by a long course of indulgence in this practice purely for the sake of creating an artificial state of pleasurable excitement. This, however, is a misrepresentation of my case. True it is, that for nearly ten years I did occasionally take opium for the sake of the exquisite pleasure it gave me: but, so long as I took it with this view, I was effectually protected from all material bad consequences by the necessity of interposing long intervals between the several acts of indulgence, in order to renew the pleasurable sensations. It was not for the purpose of creating pleasure, but of mitigating pain in the severest degree, that I first began to use opium as an article of daily diet. In the twenty-eighth year of my age, a most painful affection of the stomach, which I had first experienced about ten years before, attacked me in great strength. This affection had originally been caused by extremities of hunger, suffered in my boyish days. During the season of hope and redundant happiness which succeeded (that is, from eighteen to twenty-four) it had slumbered: for the three following years it had revived at intervals: and now, under unfavorable circumstances, from depression of spirits, it attacked me with a violence that yielded to no remedies but opium. As the youthful sufferings which first produced this derangement of the stomach, were interesting in themselves, and in the circumstances that attended them, I shall here briefly retrace them.

My father died when I was about seven years old, and left me to the care of four guardians. I was sent to various schools,[1] great and small; and was very early distinguished for my classical attainments, especially for my knowledge of Greek. At thirteen I wrote Greek with ease; and at fifteen my command of that language was so great that I not only composed Greek verses in lyric metres, but could converse in Greek fluently, and without embarrassment—an accomplishment which I have not since met with in any scholar of my times, and which, in my case, was owing to the practice of daily reading off the newspapers into the best Greek I could furnish *extempore:* for the necessity of ransacking my memory and invention for all sorts and combinations of periphrastic expressions, as equivalents for modern ideas, images, relations of things, etc., gave me a compass of diction which would never have been called out by a dull translation of moral essays, etc. "That boy," said one of my masters,[2] pointing the attention of a stranger to me, "that boy could harangue an Athenian mob better than you or I could address an English one." He who honored me with this eulogy, was a scholar, "and a ripe and good one":[3] and, of all my tutors, was the only one whom I loved or reverenced. Unfortunately for me (and, as I afterwards learned, to this worthy man's great indignation), I was transferred to the care, first of a blockhead,[4] who was in a perpetual panic lest I should expose his ignorance; and finally, to that of a respectable scholar,[5] at the head of a great school on an ancient foundation. This man had been appointed to his situation by [Brasenose][6] College, Oxford; and was a sound, well-built scholar, but, like most men whom I have known from that college, coarse, clumsy, and inelegant. A miserable contrast he presented, in my eyes, to the Etonian brilliancy[7] of my favorite master: and, besides, he could not disguise from my hourly notice the poverty and meagreness of his understanding. It is a bad thing for a boy to be, and to know himself, far beyond his tutors, whether in knowledge or in power of mind. This was the case, so far as regarded knowledge at least, not with myself only: for the two boys, who

jointly with myself composed the first form, were better Grecians[1] than the head-master, though not more elegant scholars, nor at all more accustomed to sacrifice to the graces. When I first entered, I remember that we read Sophocles; and it was a constant matter of triumph to us, the learned triumvirate of the first form, to see our *Archididascalus,*[2] as he loved to be called, conning our lesson before we went up, and laying a regular train, with lexicon and grammar, for blowing up and blasting, as it were, any difficulties he found in the choruses; whilst *we* never condescended to open our books until the moment of going up, and were generally employed in writing epigrams upon his wig, or some such important matter. My two class-fellows were poor, and dependent for their future prospects at the university, on the recommendation of the head-master: but I, who had a small patrimonial property, the income of which was sufficient to support me at college, wished to be sent thither immediately. I made earnest representations on the subject to my guardians, but all to no purpose. One, who was more reasonable, and had more knowledge of the world than the rest, lived at a distance: two of the other three resigned all their authority into the hands of the fourth;[3] and this fourth, with whom I had to negotiate, was a worthy man in his way, but haughty, obstinate, and intolerant of all opposition to his will. After a certain number of letters and personal interviews, I found that I had nothing to hope for, not even a compromise of the matter, from my guardian: unconditional submission was what he demanded: and I prepared myself, therefore, for other measures. Summer was now coming on with hasty steps, and my seventeenth birthday was fast approaching, after which day I had sworn within myself that I would no longer be numbered amongst schoolboys. Money being what I chiefly wanted, I wrote to a woman of high rank,[4] who, though young herself, had known me from a child, and had latterly treated me with great distinction, requesting that she would "lend" me five guineas. For upwards of a week no answer came; and I was beginning to despond, when, at length,

---

[1] At Bath, at Winkfield, and at Manchester.
[2] Mr. Morgan, master of Bath School.
[3] *Henry VIII,* IV, 2, 51.
[4] Mr. Spencer, master of Winkfield School.
[5] Mr. Lawson, master of Manchester School. The School was founded by Hugh Oldham, Bishop of Exeter, in 1519.
[6] The bracketed words in the text are supplied from the 1856 edition of the *Confessions.*
[7] A reference to the emphasis placed upon the classical training at Eton.

[1] That is, had had more Greek.
[2] The word means *head master.*
[3] In his *Introduction to the World of Strife,* De Quincey mentions these guardians as B., E., G., and H. The fourth was the Reverend Samuel Hall, curate at Salford, a part of Manchester.
[4] Lady Carbery, a friend of De Quincey's mother.

a servant put into my hands a double letter, with a coronet on the seal. The letter was kind and obliging: the fair writer was on the sea-coast, and in that way the delay had arisen: she enclosed double of what I had asked, and good-naturedly hinted that if I should *never* repay her it would not absolutely ruin her. Now, then, I was prepared for my scheme: ten guineas, added to about two which I had remaining from my pocket money, seemed to me sufficient for an indefinite length of time: and at that happy age, if no *definite* boundary can be assigned to one's power, the spirit of hope and pleasure makes it virtually infinite.

It is a just remark of Dr. Johnson's, and, what cannot often be said of his remarks, it is a very feeling one, that we never do anything consciously for the last time—of things, that is, which we have long been in the habit of doing—without sadness of heart.[1] This truth I felt deeply, when I came to leave [Manchester], a place which I did not love, and where I had not been happy. On the evening before I left [Manchester] forever, I grieved when the ancient and lofty school-room resounded with the evening service, performed for the last time in my hearing; and at night, when the muster-roll of names was called over, and mine, as usual, was called first, I stepped forward, and, passing the head-master, who was standing by, I bowed to him, and looked earnestly in his face, thinking to myself, "He is old and infirm, and in this world I shall not see him again." I was right: I never *did* see him again, nor ever shall. He looked at me complacently, smiled good-naturedly, returned my salutation, or rather my valediction, and we parted, though he knew it not, forever. I could not reverence him intellectually: but he had been uniformly kind to me, and had allowed me many indulgences: and I grieved at the thought of the mortification I should inflict upon him.

The morning came which was to launch me into the world, and from which my whole succeeding life has, in many important points, taken its coloring. I lodged in the head-master's house, and had been allowed, from my first entrance, the indulgence of a private room, which I used both as a sleeping-room and as a study. At half after three I rose, and gazed with deep emotion at the ancient towers of [the Collegiate Church], "dressed in earliest light," and beginning

[1] See Johnson's *The Idler*, No. 103 (the last paper).

to crimson with the radiant lustre of a cloudless July morning. I was firm and immovable in my purpose: but yet agitated by anticipation of uncertain danger and troubles; and, if I could have foreseen the hurricane and perfect hail-storm of affliction which soon fell upon me, well might I have been agitated. To this agitation the deep peace of the morning presented an affecting contrast, and in some degree a medicine. The silence was more profound than that of midnight: and to me the silence of a summer morning is more touching than all other silence,[1] because, the light being broad and strong, as that of noon-day at other seasons of the year, it seems to differ from perfect day chiefly because man is not yet abroad; and thus the peace of nature, and of the innocent creatures of God, seems to be secure and deep, only so long as the presence of man, and his restless and unquiet spirit, are not there to trouble its sanctity. I dressed myself, took my hat and gloves, and lingered a little in the room. For the last year and a half this room had been my "pensive citadel":[2] here I had read and studied through all the hours of night: and, though true it was that for the latter part of this time I, who was framed for love and gentle affections, had lost my gaiety and happiness, during the strife and fever of contention with my guardian; yet, on the other hand, as a boy so passionately fond of books, and dedicated to intellectual pursuits, I could not fail to have enjoyed many happy hours in the midst of general dejection. I wept as I looked round on the chair, hearth, writing-table, and other familiar objects, knowing too certainly that I looked upon them for the last time. Whilst I write this, it is eighteen years ago: and yet, at this moment, I see distinctly as if it were yesterday the lineaments and expression of the object on which I fixed my parting gaze: it was a picture of the lovely ——,[3] which hung over the mantle-piece; the eyes and mouth of which were so beautiful, and the whole countenance so radiant with benignity and divine tranquillity, that I had a thousand times laid down my pen or my book, to gather consolation from it, as a devotee from his patron saint. Whilst I was yet gazing upon it, the deep tones of [Manchester] clock proclaimed that it was four o'clock. I went up to the picture, kissed it,

[1] See p. 1103b, 1-42; also *The English Mail-Coach*, 3, 1 (p. 1151b, 46 ff.).
[2] Wordsworth, *Nuns Fret not at their Convent's Narrow Room*, 3 (p. 326).
[3] The name of the subject of this picture is unknown.

and then gently walked out, and closed the door forever!

* * * * * *

So blended and intertwisted in this life are occasions of laughter and of tears, that I cannot yet recall, without smiling, an incident which occurred at that time, and which had nearly put a stop to the immediate execution of my plan. I had a trunk of immense weight; for, besides my clothes, it [10] contained nearly all my library. The difficulty was to get this removed to a carrier's: my room was at an aerial elevation in the house, and (what was worse) the staircase, which communicated with this angle of the [15] building, was accessible only by a gallery which passed the head-master's chamberdoor. I was a favorite with all the servants; and, knowing that any of them would screen me, and act confidentially, I communicated [20] my embarrassment to a groom of the headmaster's. The groom swore he would do anything I wished; and, when the time arrived, went up stairs to bring the trunk down. This I feared was beyond the strength [25] of any one man: however, the groom was a man—

Of Atlantean shoulders, fit to bear
The weight of mightiest monarchies[1]

[30] and had a back as spacious as Salisbury plain. Accordingly, he persisted in bringing down the trunk alone, whilst I stood waiting at the foot of the last flight, in anxiety for the event. For some time I heard him de-[35]scending with slow and firm steps: but, unfortunately, from his trepidation as he drew near the dangerous quarter, within a few steps of the gallery, his foot slipped; and the mighty burden, falling from his [40] shoulders, gained such increase of impetus at each step of the descent, that, on reaching the bottom, it tumbled, or rather leaped, right across, with the noise of twenty devils, against the very bedroom door of the Archi-[45]didascalus. My first thought was that all was lost, and that my only chance for executing a retreat was to sacrifice my baggage. However, on reflection, I determined to abide the issue. The groom was in the ut-[50]most alarm, both on his own account and on mine: but, in spite of this, so irresistibly had the sense of the ludicrous, in this unhappy contretemps,[2] taken possession of his fancy, that he sang out a long, loud, and [55] canorous[3] peal of laughter, that might have wakened the Seven Sleepers. At the sound

of this resonant merriment, within the very ears of insulted authority, I could not myself forbear joining in it: subdued to this, not so much by the unhappy étourderie[1] of [5] the trunk, as by the effect it had upon the groom. We both expected, as a matter of course, that Dr. [Lawson] would sally out of his room: for, in general, if but a mouse stirred, he sprang out like a mastiff from his [10] kennel. Strange to say, however, on this occasion, when the noise of laughter had ceased, no sound, or rustling even, was to be heard in the bedroom. Dr. [Lawson] had a painful complaint, which, sometimes [15] keeping him awake, made his sleep, perhaps, when it did come, the deeper. Gathering courage from the silence, the groom hoisted his burden again, and accomplished the remainder of his descent without accident. I [20] waited until I saw the trunk placed on a wheel-barrow, and on its road to the carrier's: then, "with Providence my guide,"[2] I set off on foot,—carrying a small parcel, with some articles of dress, under my arm; [25] a favorite English poet in one pocket; and a small 12mo volume, containing about nine plays of Euripides, in the other.

It had been my intention originally to proceed to Westmoreland, both from the [30] love I bore to that country, and on other personal accounts.[3] Accidents, however, gave a different direction to my wanderings, and I bent my steps towards North Wales.

After wandering about for some time in [35] Denbighshire, Merionethshire, and Carnarvonshire, I took lodgings in a small neat house in B[angor]. Here I might have stayed with great comfort for many weeks; for provisions were cheap at B[angor], [40] from the scarcity of other markets for the surplus produce of a wide agricultural district. An accident, however, in which, perhaps, no offence was designed, drove me out to wander again. I know not whether my [45] reader may have remarked, but I have often remarked, that the proudest class of people in England, or, at any rate, the class whose pride is most apparent, are the families of bishops. Noblemen and their children carry [50] about with them, in their very titles, a sufficient notification of their rank. Nay, their very names, and this applies also to the children of many untitled houses, are often to the English ear adequate exponents of [55] high birth or descent. Sackville, Manners, Fitzroy, Paulet, Cavendish, and scores of others, tell their own tale. Such persons,

---

[1] *Paradise Lost*, 2, 306-7.
[2] untoward accident   [3] resonant; ringing

[1] blunder   [2] *Paradise Lost*, 12, 647.
[3] For the purpose of visiting Wordsworth.

therefore, find everywhere a due sense of their claims already established, except among those who are ignorant of the world by virtue of their own obscurity: "Not to know *them*, argues one's self unknown."[1] Their manners take a suitable tone and coloring; and, for once that they find it necessary to impress a sense of their consequence upon others, they meet with a thousand occasions for moderating and tempering this sense by acts of courteous condescension. With the families of bishops it is otherwise: with them it is all uphill work to make known their pretensions: for the proportion of the episcopal bench taken from noble families is not at any time very large; and the succession to these dignities is so rapid that the public ear seldom has time to become familiar with them, unless where they are connected with some literary reputation. Hence it is, that the children of bishops carry about with them an austere and repulsive air, indicative of claims not generally acknowledged, a sort of *noli me tangere*[2] manner, nervously apprehensive of too familiar approach, and shrinking with the sensitiveness of a gouty man, from all contact with the οἱ πολλοί.[3] Doubtless, a powerful understanding, or unusual goodness of nature, will preserve a man from such weakness: but, in general, the truth of my representation will be acknowledged: pride, if not of deeper root in such families, appears, at least, more upon the surface of their manners. The spirit of manners naturally communicates itself to their domestics and other dependents. Now, my landlady had been a lady's maid, or a nurse, in the family of the Bishop of [Bangor]; and had but lately married away and "settled" (as such people express it) for life. In a little town like B[angor] merely to have lived in the bishop's family conferred some distinction: and my good landlady had rather more than her share of the pride I have noticed on that score. What "my lord" said, and what "my lord" did, how useful he was in Parliament, and how indispensable at Oxford, formed the daily burden of her talk. All this I bore very well: for I was too good-natured to laugh in anybody's face, and I could make an ample allowance for the garrulity of an old servant. Of necessity, however, I must have appeared in her eyes very inadequately impressed with the bishop's importance: and, perhaps, to punish me for

my indifference, or possibly by accident, she one day repeated to me a conversation in which I was indirectly a party concerned. She had been to the palace to pay her respects to the family; and, dinner being over, was summoned into the dining-room. In giving an account of her household economy, she happened to mention that she had let her apartments. Thereupon the good bishop (it seemed) had taken occasion to caution her as to her selection of inmates: "for," said he, "you must recollect, Betty, that this place is in the high road to the Head;[1] so that multitudes of Irish swindlers, running away from their debts into England—and of English swindlers, running away from their debts to the Isle of Man, are likely to take this place in their route." This advice was certainly not without reasonable grounds: but rather fitted to be stored up for Mrs. Betty's private meditations, than specially reported to me. What followed, however, was somewhat worse:— "Oh, my lord," answered my landlady (according to her own representation of the matter), "I really don't think this young gentleman is a swindler; because——" —"You don't *think* me a swindler?" said I, interrupting her, in a tumult of indignation: "for the future I shall spare you the trouble of thinking about it." And without delay I prepared for my departure. Some concessions the good woman seemed disposed to make: but a harsh and contemptuous expression which I fear that I applied to the learned dignitary himself, roused *her* indignation in turn: and reconciliation then became impossible. I was, indeed, greatly irritated at the bishop's having suggested any grounds of suspicion, however remotely, against a person whom he had never seen: and I thought of letting him know my mind in Greek: which, at the same time that it would furnish some presumption that I was no swindler, would also, I hoped, compel the bishop to reply in the same language; in which case, I doubted not to make it appear, that if I was not so rich as his lordship, I was a better Grecian. Calmer thoughts, however, drove this boyish design out of my mind: for I considered that the bishop was in the right to counsel an old servant; that he could not have designed that his advice should be reported to me; and that the same coarseness of mind which had led Mrs. Betty to repeat the advice at all might have colored it in a way more agreeable to her own style

---

[1] *Paradise Lost*, 4, 830.
[2] touch me not
[3] many ; multitude

[1] Probably Holyhead, from which travelers would embark for Ireland or the Isle of Man.

of thinking than to the actual expressions of the worthy bishop.

I left the lodgings the same hour; and this turned out a very unfortunate occurrence for me: because, living henceforward at inns, I was drained of my money very rapidly. In a fortnight I was reduced to short allowance; that is, I could allow myself only one meal a day. From the keen appetite produced by constant exercise and mountain air acting on a youthful stomach, I soon began to suffer greatly on this slender regimen; for the single meal which I could venture to order was coffee or tea. Even this, however, was at length withdrawn: and afterwards, so long as I remained in Wales, I subsisted either on blackberries, hips, haws, etc., or on the casual hospitalities which I now and then received, in return for such little service as I had an opportunity of rendering. Sometimes I wrote letters of business for cottagers, who happened to have relatives in Liverpool, or in London: more often I wrote love-letters to their sweethearts for young women who had lived as servants in Shrewsbury, or other towns on the English border. On all such occasions I gave great satisfaction to my humble friends, and was generally treated with hospitality: and once, in particular, near the village of Llan-y-styndw (or some such name), in a sequestered part of Merionethshire, I was entertained for upwards of three days by a family of young people, with an affectionate and fraternal kindness that left an impression upon my heart not yet impaired. The family consisted, at that time, of four sisters and three brothers, all grown up, and all remarkable for elegance and delicacy of manners. So much beauty, and so much native good-breeding and refinement, I do not remember to have seen before or since in any cottage, except once or twice in Westmoreland and Devonshire. They spoke English, an accomplishment not often met with in so many members of one family, especially in villages remote from the high road. Here I wrote, on my first introduction, a letter about prize-money, for one of the brothers, who had served on board an English man-of-war; and more privately, two love-letters for two of the sisters. They were both interesting looking girls, and one of uncommon loveliness. In the midst of their confusion and blushes, whilst dictating, or rather giving me general instructions, it did not require any great penetration to discover that what they wished was, that their letters should be as kind as was consistent with proper maidenly pride. I contrived so to temper my expressions as to reconcile the gratification of both feelings: and they were as much pleased with the way in which I had expressed their thoughts, as, in their simplicity, they were astonished at my having so readily discovered them. The reception one meets with from the women of a family generally determines the tenor of one's whole entertainment. In this case I had discharged my confidential duties as secretary so much to the general satisfaction, perhaps also amusing them with my conversation, that I was pressed to stay with a cordiality which I had little inclination to resist. I slept with the brothers, the only unoccupied bed standing in the apartment of the young women: but in all other points they treated me with a respect not usually paid to purses as light as mine; as if my scholarship were sufficient evidence that I was of "gentle blood." Thus I lived with them for three days, and a greater part of a fourth: and from the undiminished kindness which they continued to show me, I believe I might have stayed with them up to this time, if their power had corresponded with their wishes. On the last morning, however, I perceived upon their countenances, as they sat at breakfast, the expression of some unpleasant communication which was at hand; and soon after one of the brothers explained to me that their parents had gone, the day before my arrival, to an annual meeting of Methodists, held at Carnarvon, and were that day expected to return; "and if they should not be so civil as they ought to be," he begged, on the part of all the young people, that I would not take it amiss. The parents returned, with churlish faces, and *"Dym Sassenach"* (*no English*), in answer to all my addresses. I saw how matters stood; and so, taking an affectionate leave of my kind and interesting young hosts, I went my way. For, though they spoke warmly to their parents in my behalf, and often excused the manner of the old people, by saying that it was "only their way," yet I easily understood that my talent for writing love-letters would do as little to recommend me with two grave sexagenarian Welsh Methodists, as my Greek Sapphics or Alcaics:[1] and what had been hospitality, when offered to me with the gracious courtesy of my young friends,

[1] Greek love lyrics written after the manner of Sappho and Alcæus, famous Greek poets (600 B. C.).

would become charity, when connected with the harsh demeanor of these old people. Certainly, Mr. Shelley is right in his notions about old age:[1] unless powerfully counteracted by all sorts of opposite agencies, it is a miserable corrupter and blighter to the genial charities of the human heart.

Soon after this, I contrived, by means which I must omit for want of room,[2] to transfer myself to London. And now began the latter and fiercer stage of my long sufferings; without using a disproportionate expression, I might say, of my agony. For I now suffered, for upwards of sixteen weeks, the physical anguish of hunger in various degrees of intensity; but as bitter, perhaps, as ever any human being can have suffered who has survived it. I would not needlessly harass my reader's feelings by a detail of all that I endured: for extremities such as these, under any circumstances of heaviest misconduct or guilt, cannot be contemplated even in description without a rueful pity that is painful to the natural goodness of the human heart. Let it suffice, at least on this occasion, to say that a few fragments of bread from the breakfast-table of one individual,[3] who supposed me to be ill, but did not know of my being in utter want, and these at uncertain intervals, constituted my whole support. During the former part of my sufferings, that is, generally in Wales, and always for the first two months in London, I was houseless, and very seldom slept under a roof. To this constant exposure to the open air I ascribe it mainly that I did not sink under my torments. Latterly, however, when colder and more inclement weather came on, and when, from the length of my sufferings, I had begun to sink into a more languishing condition, it was, no doubt, fortunate for me that the same person to whose breakfast-table I had access allowed me to sleep in a large unoccupied house, of which he was tenant. Unoccupied, I call it, for there was no household or establishment in it; nor any furniture indeed, except for a table and a few chairs. But I found, on taking possession of my new quarters, that the house already contained one single inmate, a poor friendless child, apparently ten years old; but she seemed hunger-bitten; and sufferings of that

sort often make children look older than they are. From this forlorn child I learned that she had slept and lived there alone for some time before I came: and great joy the poor creature expressed, when she found that I was, in future, to be her companion through the hours of darkness. The house was large; and, from the want of furniture, the noise of the rats made a prodigious echoing on the spacious staircase and hall; and, amidst the real fleshly ills of cold, and, I fear, hunger, the forsaken child had found leisure to suffer still more, it appeared, from the self-created one of ghosts. I promised her protection against all ghosts whatsoever: but, alas! I could offer her no other assistance. We lay upon the floor, with a bundle of cursed law papers for a pillow: but with no other covering than a sort of large horseman's cloak: afterwards, however, we discovered, in a garret, an old sofa-cover, a small piece of rug, and some fragments of other articles, which added a little to our warmth. The poor child crept close to me for warmth, and for security against her ghostly enemies. When I was not more than usually ill, I took her into my arms, so that, in general, she was tolerably warm, and often slept when I could not: for, during the last two months of my sufferings, I slept much in the day-time, and was apt to fall into transient dozing at all hours. But my sleep distressed me more than my watching: for, besides the tumultuousness of my dreams, which were only not so awful as those which I shall have to describe hereafter as produced by opium, my sleep was never more than what is called *dogsleep;* so that I could hear myself moaning, and was often, as it seemed to me, wakened suddenly by my own voice; and, about this time, a hideous sensation began to haunt me as soon as I fell into a slumber, which has since returned upon me at different periods of my life, *viz.,* a sort of twitching, I know not where, but apparently about the region of the stomach, which compelled me violently to throw out my feet for the sake of relieving it. This sensation coming on as soon as I began to sleep, and the effort to relieve it constantly awaking me, at length I slept only from exhaustion; and from increasing weakness, as I said before, I was constantly falling asleep, and constantly awaking. Meantime, the master of the house sometimes came in upon us suddenly, and very early, sometimes not till ten o'clock, sometimes not at all. He was in constant fear of bailiffs: improving on

---

[1] Shelley says that old age is cold and cruel. See his *The Revolt of Islam,* 2, 33.
[2] He borrowed twelve guineas from two friends.
[3] A Mr. Brunell, an obscure lawyer, who had been recommended to De Quincey by a money-lender named Dell.

the plan of Cromwell,[1] every night he slept in a different quarter of London; and I observed that he never failed to examine through a private window the appearance of those who knocked at the door, before he would allow it to be opened. He breakfasted alone: indeed, his tea equipage would hardly have admitted of his hazarding an invitation to a second person—any more than the quantity of esculent *matériel*, which, for the most part, was little more than a roll, or a few biscuits, which he had bought on his road from the place where he had slept. Or, if he *had* asked a party, as I once learnedly and facetiously observed to him—the several members of it must have *stood* in the relation to each other (not *sat* in any relation whatever) of succession, as the metaphysicians have it, and not of coexistence; in the relation of the parts of time, and not of the parts of space. During his breakfast, I generally contrived a reason for lounging in; and, with an air of as much indifference as I could assume, took up such fragments as he had left—sometimes, indeed, there were none at all. In doing this, I committed no robbery except upon the man himself, who was thus obliged, I believe, now and then to send out at noon for an extra biscuit; for, as to the poor child, *she* was never admitted into his study, if I may give that name to his chief depository of parchments, law writings, etc.; that room was to her the Bluebeard room of the house, being regularly locked on his departure to dinner, about six o'clock, which usually was his final departure for the night. Whether this child were an illegitimate daughter of Mr. [Brunell], or only a servant, I could not ascertain; she did not herself know; but certainly she was treated altogether as a menial servant. No sooner did Mr. [Brunell] make his appearance, than she went below stairs, brushed his shoes, coat, etc.; and, except when she was summoned to run an errand, she never emerged from the dismal Tartarus of the kitchens, etc., to the upper air, until my welcome knock at night called up her little trembling footsteps to the front door. Of her life during the daytime, however, I knew little but what I gathered from her own account at night; for, as soon as the

hours of business commenced, I saw that my absence would be acceptable; and, in general, therefore, I went off, and sat in the parks, or elsewhere, until nightfall.

But who, and what, meantime, was the master of the house himself? Reader, he was one of those anomalous practitioners in lower departments of the law, who—what shall I say?—who, on prudential reasons, or from necessity, deny themselves all indulgence in the luxury of too delicate a conscience: (a periphrasis which might be abridged considerably, but *that* I leave to the reader's taste:) in many walks of life, a conscience is a more expensive encumbrance, than a wife or a carriage; and just as people talk of "laying down" their carriages, so I suppose my friend, Mr. [Brunell], had "laid down" his conscience for a time, meaning, doubtless, to resume it as soon as he could afford it. The inner economy of such a man's daily life would present a most strange picture, if I could allow myself to amuse the reader at his expense. Even with my limited opportunities for observing what went on, I saw many scenes of London intrigues, and complex chicanery "cycle and epicycle, orb in orb,"[1] at which I sometimes smile to this day—and at which I smiled then, in spite of my misery. My situation, however, at that time, gave me little experience, in my own person, of any qualities in Mr. [Brunell]'s character but such as did him honor; and of his whole strange composition I must forget everything but that towards me he was obliging and, to the extent of his power, generous.

That power was not, indeed, very extensive; however, in common with the rats, I sat rent free; and, as Dr. Johnson has recorded, that he never but once in his life had as much wall-fruit as he could eat,[2] so let me be grateful, that on that single occasion I had as large a choice of apartments in a London mansion as I could possibly desire. Except the Bluebeard room, which the poor child believed to be haunted, all others, from the attics to the cellars, were at our service; "the world was all before us";[3] and we pitched our tent for the night in any spot we chose. This house I have already described as a large one; it stands in a conspicuous situation, and in a well-known part of London. Many of my read-

---

[1] A reference to the precautions for safety which Cromwell is said to have taken after the dissolution of his last Parliament. According to Clarendon, Cromwell wore armor under his clothes and "rarely lodged two nights together in one chamber." See Clarendon's *The History of the Rebellion and Civil Wars in England* (Oxford ed.), 7, 345.

[1] *Paradise Lost*, 8, 84.
[2] The incident is recorded in Mrs. Piozzi's *Anecdotes of the late Samuel Johnson, LL.D., during the last Twenty Years of his Life* (1786), 102.
[3] *Paradise Lost*, 12, 646.

ers will have passed it, I doubt not, within a few hours of reading this. For myself, I never fail to visit it when business draws me to London; about ten o'clock, this very night, August 15, 1821, being my birthday, —I turned aside from my evening walk, down Oxford Street, purposely to take a glance at it: it is now occupied by a respectable family; and, by the lights in the front drawing-room, I observed a domestic party, assembled perhaps at tea, and apparently cheerful and gay. Marvellous contrast in my eyes to the darkness—cold—silence— and desolation of that same house eighteen years ago, when its nightly occupants were one famishing scholar, and a neglected child. —Her, by the bye, in after years, I vainly endeavored to trace. Apart from her situation, she was not what would be called an interesting child: she was neither pretty, nor quick in understanding, nor remarkably pleasing in manners. But, thank God! even in those years I needed not the embellishments of novel accessaries to conciliate my affections; plain human nature, in its humblest and most homely apparel, was enough for me: and I loved the child because she was my partner in wretchedness. If she is now living, she is probably a mother, with children of her own; but, as I have said, I could never trace her.

This I regret, but another person there was at that time, whom I have since sought to trace with far deeper earnestness, and with far deeper sorrow at my failure. This person was a young woman, and one of that unhappy class who subsist upon the wages of prostitution. I feel no shame, nor have any reason to feel it, in avowing that I was then on familiar and friendly terms with many women in that unfortunate condition. The reader needs neither smile at this avowal, nor frown. For, not to remind my classical readers of the old Latin proverb— *"Sine Cerere,"*[1] etc., it may well be supposed that in the existing state of my purse my connection with such women could not have been an impure one. But the truth is, that at no time of my life have I been a person to hold myself polluted by the touch or approach of any creature that wore a human shape: on the contrary, from my very earliest youth it has been my pride to converse familiarly, *more Socratico,*[2] with all human beings, man, woman, and child, that chance might fling in my way: a prac-

[1] without food and wine love grows cold (Terence, *Eunuchus,* IV, 5, 6)
[2] after the manner of Socrates,—*i. e.,* by questions and answers

tice which is friendly to the knowledge of human nature, to good feelings, and to that frankness of address which becomes a man who would be thought a philosopher. For a philosopher should not see with the eyes of the poor limitary creature calling himself a man of the world, and filled with narrow and self-regarding prejudices of birth and education, but should look upon himself as a catholic creature, and as standing in an equal relation to high and low—to educated and uneducated, to the guilty and the innocent. Being myself at that time of necessity a peripatetic, or a walker of the streets, I naturally fell in more frequently with those female peripatetics who are technically called street-walkers. Many of these women had occasionally taken my part against watchmen who wished to drive me off the steps of houses where I was sitting. But one amongst them, the one on whose account I have at all introduced this subject—yet no! let me not class thee, oh noble-minded Ann ——, with that order of women; let me find, if it be possible, some gentler name to designate the condition of her to whose bounty and compassion, ministering to my necessities when all the world had forsaken me, I owe it that I am at this time alive.— For many weeks I had walked at nights with this poor friendless girl up and down Oxford Street, or had rested with her on steps and under the shelter of porticoes. She could not be so old as myself: she told me, indeed, that she had not completed her sixteenth year. By such questions as my interest about her prompted, I had gradually drawn forth her simple history. Hers was a case of ordinary occurrence (as I have since had reason to think), and one in which, if London beneficence had better adapted its arrangements to meet it, the power of the law might oftener be interposed to protect, and to avenge. But the stream of London charity flows in a channel which, though deep and mighty, is yet noiseless and underground; not obvious or readily accessible to poor houseless wanderers: and it cannot be denied that the outside air and framework of London society is harsh, cruel, and repulsive. In any case, however, I saw that part of her injuries might easily have been redressed; and I urged her often and earnestly to lay her complaint before a magistrate: friendless as she was, I assured her that she would meet with immediate attention; and that English justice, which was no respecter of persons, would speedily and amply avenge her on the brutal ruffian who had plundered her little property. She promised me often that she would; but she delayed taking the steps I pointed out from time to time: for she was timid and dejected to a degree which showed how deeply sorrow had taken hold of her young heart: and perhaps she thought justly that the most upright judge, and the most righteous tribunals, could do nothing to repair her heaviest wrongs. Something, however, would perhaps have been done: for it had been settled between us at length, but unhappily on the very last time but one that I was ever to see her, that in a day or two we should go together before a magistrate, and that I should speak on her behalf. This little service it was destined, however, that I should never realize. Meantime, that which she rendered to me, and which was greater than I could ever have repaid her, was this:—One night, when we were pacing slowly along Oxford Street, and after a day when I had felt more than usually ill and faint, I requested her to turn off with me into Soho Square: thither we went; and we sat down on the steps of a house, which, to this hour, I never pass without a pang of grief, and an inner act of homage to the spirit of that unhappy girl, in memory of the noble action which she there performed. Suddenly, as we sat, I grew much worse: I had been leaning my head against her bosom; and all at once I sank from her arms and fell backwards on the step. From the sensations I then had, I felt an inner conviction of the liveliest kind that without some powerful and reviving stimulus, I should either have died on the spot—or should at least have sunk to a point of exhaustion from which all re-ascent under my friendless circumstances would soon have become hopeless. Then it was, at this crisis of my fate, that my poor orphan companion —who had herself met with little but injuries in this world—stretched out a saving hand to me. Uttering a cry of terror, but without a moment's delay, she ran off into Oxford Street, and in less time than could be imagined, returned to me with a glass of port wine and spices, that acted upon my empty stomach (which at that time would have rejected all solid food) with an instantaneous power of restoration: and for this glass the generous girl without a murmur paid out of her own humble purse at a time—be it remembered!—when she had scarcely wherewithal to purchase the bare necessaries of life, and when she could have no reason to expect that I should ever be able to reimburse her.——Oh! youthful benefactress! how often in succeeding years, standing in solitary places, and thinking of thee with grief of heart and perfect love, how often have I wished that, as in ancient times the curse of a father was believed to have a supernatural power, and to pursue its object with a fatal necessity of self-fulfillment,—even so the benediction of a heart oppressed with gratitude might have a like prerogative; might have power given it from above to chase—to haunt—to way-lay[1]—to overtake—to pursue thee into the central darkness of a London brothel, or, if it were possible, into the darkness of the grave—there to awaken thee with an authentic message of peace and forgiveness, and of final reconciliation!

I do not often weep: for not only do my thoughts on subjects connected with the chief interests of man daily, nay hourly, descend a thousand fathoms "too deep for tears";[2] not only does the sternness of my habits of thought present an antagonism to the feelings which prompt tears—wanting of necessity to those who, being protected usually by their levity from any tendency to meditative sorrow, would by that same levity be made incapable of resisting it on any casual access of such feelings:—but also, I believe that all minds which have contemplated such objects as deeply as I have done, must, for their own protection from utter despondency, have early encouraged and cherished some tranquillizing belief as to the future balances and the hieroglyphic meanings of human sufferings. On these accounts, I am cheerful to this hour; and, as I have said, I do not often weep. Yet some feelings, though not deeper or more passionate, are more tender than others; and often, when I walk at this time in Oxford Street by dreamy lamp-light, and hear those airs played on a barrel-organ which years ago solaced me and my dear companion, as I must always call her, I shed tears, and muse with myself at the mysterious dispensation which so suddenly and so critically separated us forever. How it happened, the reader will understand from what remains of this introductory narration.

Soon after the period of the last incident I have recorded, I met, in Albemarle Street, a gentleman of his late majesty's[3] household. This gentleman had received hospital-

---

[1] See Wordsworth's *She was a Phantom of Delight*, 10 (p. 321).

[2] Wordsworth, *Ode: Intimations of Immortality*, 203 (p. 331).

[3] George III, who had recently died (1820).

ities, on different occasions, from my family: and he challenged me upon the strength of my family likeness. I did not attempt any disguise: I answered his questions ingenuously,—and, on his pledging his word of honor that he would not betray me to my guardians, I gave him an address to my friend the attorney's. The next day I received from him a £10 Bank-note. The letter enclosing it was delivered with other letters of business to the attorney; but, though his look and manner informed me that he suspected its contents, he gave it up to me honorably and without demur.

This present, from the particular service to which it was applied, leads me naturally to speak of the purpose which had allured me up to London, and which I had been (to use a forensic word) *soliciting* from the first day of my arrival in London, to that of my final departure.

In so mighty a world as London, it will surprise my readers that I should not have found some means of staving off the last extremities of penury: and it will strike them that two resources at least must have been open to me,—*viz.*, either to seek assistance from the friends of my family, or to turn my youthful talents and attainments into some channel of pecuniary emolument. As to the first course, I may observe, generally, that what I dreaded beyond all other evils was the chance of being reclaimed by my guardians, not doubting that whatever power the law gave them would have been enforced against me to the utmost; that is, to the extremity of forcibly restoring me to the school which I had quitted: a restoration which as it would in my eyes have been a dishonor even if submitted to voluntarily, could not fail, when extorted from me in contempt and defiance of my known wishes and efforts, to have been a humiliation worse to me than death, and which would indeed have terminated in death. I was, therefore, shy enough of applying for assistance even in those quarters where I was sure of receiving it—at the risk of furnishing my guardians with any clue for recovering me. But, as to London in particular, though, doubtless, my father had in his lifetime had many friends there, yet, as ten years had passed since his death, I remembered few of them even by name: and never having seen London before, except once for a few hours, I knew not the address of even those few. To this mode of gaining help, therefore, in part the difficulty, but much more the paramount fear which I have men-

tioned, habitually indisposed me. In regard to the other mode, I now feel half inclined to join my reader in wondering that I should have overlooked it. As a corrector of Greek proofs, if in no other way, I might doubtless have gained enough for my slender wants. Such an office as this I could have discharged with an exemplary and punctual accuracy that would soon have gained me the confidence of my employers. But it must not be forgotten that, even for such an office as this, it was necessary that I should first of all have an introduction to some respectable publisher: and this I had no means of obtaining. To say the truth, however, it had never once occurred to me to think of literary labors as a source of profit. No mode sufficiently speedy of obtaining money had ever occurred to me but that of borrowing it on the strength of my future claims and expectations. This mode I sought by every avenue to compass, and amongst other persons I applied to a Jew named D[ell].[1]

To this Jew, and to other advertising money-lenders, some of whom were, I believe, also Jews, I had introduced myself with an account of my expectations; which account, on examining my father's will at Doctor's Commons, they had ascertained to be correct. The person there mentioned as

[1] "To this same Jew, by the way, some eighteen months afterwards, I applied again on the same business; and, dating at that time from a respectable college, I was fortunate enough to gain his serious attention to my proposals. My necessities had not arisen from any extravagance or youthful levities (these my habits and the nature of my pleasures raised me far above), but simply from the vindictive malice of my guardian, who, when he found himself no longer able to prevent me from going to the university, had, as a parting token of his good nature, refused to sign an order for granting me a shilling beyond the allowance made to me at school—*viz.*, £100 *per annum.* Upon this sum it was, in my time, barely possible to have lived in college, and not possible to a man who, though above the paltry affectation of ostentatious disregard for money, and without any expensive tastes, confided nevertheless rather too much in servants, and did not delight in the petty details of minute economy. I soon, therefore, became embarrassed; and at length, after a most voluminous negotiation with the Jew (some parts of which, if I had leisure to rehearse them, would greatly amuse my readers), I was put in possession of the sum I asked for, on the 'regular' terms of paying the Jew seventeen and a half per cent by way of annuity on all the money furnished, Israel, on his part, graciously resuming no more than about ninety guineas of the said money, on account of an attorney's bill (for what services, to whom rendered, and when, whether at the siege of Jerusalem—at the building of the Second Temple—or on some earlier occasion, I have not yet been able to discover). How many perches this bill measured I really forget: but I still keep it in a cabinet of natural curiosities, and sometime or other I believe I shall present it to the British Museum."—De Quincey.

the second son of ——, was found to have all the claims, or more than all, that I had stated: but one question still remained, which the faces of the Jews pretty significantly suggested,—was *I* that person? This doubt had never occurred to me as a possible one: I had rather feared, whenever my Jewish friends scrutinized me keenly, that I might be too well known to be that person—and that some scheme might be passing in their minds for entrapping me, and selling me to my guardians. It was strange to me to find my own self, *materialiter*[1] considered (so I expressed it, for I doted on logical accuracy of distinctions), accused, or at least suspected, of counterfeiting my own self, *formaliter*[2] considered. However, to satisfy their scruples, I took the only course in my power. Whilst I was in Wales, I had received various letters from young friends: these I produced: for I carried them constantly in my pocket—being, indeed, by this time, almost the only relics of my personal incumbrances (excepting the clothes I wore) which I had not in one way or other disposed of. Most of these letters were from the Earl of [Altamont], who was at this time my chief, or rather only, confidential friend. These letters were dated from Eton. I had also some from the Marquess of [Sligo], his father, who, though absorbed in agricultural pursuits, yet having been an Etonian himself, and as good a scholar as a nobleman needs to be—still retained an affection for classical studies, and for youthful scholars. He had, accordingly, from the time that I was fifteen, corresponded with me; sometimes upon the great improvements which he had made, or was meditating, in the counties of M[ayo] and Sl[igo] since I had been there; sometimes upon the merits of a Latin poet; at other times suggesting subjects to me on which he wished me to write verses.

On reading the letters, one of my Jewish friends agreed to furnish two or three hundred pounds on my personal security—provided I could persuade the young Earl, who was, by the way, not older than myself, to guarantee the payment on our coming of age: the Jew's final object being, as I now suppose, not the trifling profit he could expect to make by me, but the prospect of establishing a connection with my noble friend, whose immense expectations were well known to him. In pursuance of this proposal on the part of the Jew, about eight

or nine days after I had received the £10, I prepared to go down to Eton. Nearly £3 of the money I had given to my money-lending friend, on his alleging that the stamps must be bought, in order that the writings might be preparing whilst I was away from London. I thought in my heart that he was lying; but I did not wish to give him any excuse for charging his own delays upon me. A smaller sum I had given to my friend the attorney, who was connected with the money-lenders as their lawyer, to which, indeed, he was entitled for his unfurnished lodgings. About fifteen shillings I had employed in re-establishing, though in a very humble way, my dress. Of the remainder I gave one-quarter to Ann, meaning on my return to have divided with her whatever might remain. These arrangements made,—soon after six o'clock, on a dark winter evening, I set off, accompanied by Ann, towards Piccadilly, for it was my intention to go down as far as Salt Hill on the Bath or Bristol mail. Our course lay through a part of the town which has now all disappeared, so that I can no longer retrace its ancient boundaries: Swallow Street, I think it was called. Having time enough before us, however, we bore away to the left until we came into Golden Square: there, near the corner of Sherrard Street, we sat down; not wishing to part in the tumult and blaze of Piccadilly. I had told her of my plans some time before: and I now assured her again that she should share in my good fortune, if I met with any; and that I would never forsake her, as soon as I had power to protect her. This I fully intended, as much from inclination as from a sense of duty: for, setting aside gratitude, which in any case must have made me her debtor for life, I loved her as affectionately as if she had been my sister: and at this moment, with sevenfold tenderness, from pity at witnessing her extreme dejection. I had, apparently, most reason for dejection, because I was leaving the savior of my life: yet I, considering the shock my health had received, was cheerful and full of hope. She, on the contrary, who was parting with one who had little means of serving her, except by kindness and brotherly treatment, was overcome by sorrow; so that, when I kissed her at our final farewell, she put her arms about my neck, and wept without speaking a word. I hoped to return in a week at farthest, and I agreed with her that on the fifth night from that, and every night afterwards, she should wait for me at six o'clock

---

[1] with reference to material, or substance
[2] with reference to form, or appearance

near the bottom of Great Titchfield Street, which had been our customary haven, as it were, of rendezvous, to prevent our missing each other in the great Mediterranean of Oxford Street. This and other measures of precaution I took: one only I forgot. She had either never told me, or (as a matter of no great interest) I had forgotten, her surname. It is a general practice, indeed, with girls of humble rank in her unhappy condition, not (as novel-reading women of higher pretensions) to style themselves—*Miss Douglas, Miss Montague,* etc., but simply by their Christian names, *Mary, Jane, Frances,* etc. Her surname, as the surest means of tracing her hereafter, I ought now to have inquired: but the truth is, having no reason to think that our meeting could, in consequence of a short interruption, be more difficult or uncertain than it had been for so many weeks, I had scarcely for a moment adverted to it as necessary, or placed it amongst my memoranda against this parting interview: and, my final anxieties being spent in comforting her with hopes, and in pressing upon her the necessity of getting some medicines for a violent cough and hoarseness with which she was troubled, I wholly forgot it until it was too late to recall her.

It was past eight o'clock when I reached the Gloucester coffee-house: and, the Bristol mail being on the point of going off, I mounted on the outside. The fine fluent motion[1] of this mail soon laid me asleep: it is somewhat remarkable that the first easy or refreshing sleep which I had enjoyed for some months was on the outside of a mail-coach—a bed which, at this day, I find rather an uneasy one. Connected with this sleep was a little incident, which served, as hundreds of others did at that time, to convince me how easily a man who has never been in any great distress may pass through life without knowing, in his own person at least, anything of the possible goodness of the human heart—or, as I must add with a sigh, of its possible vileness. So thick a curtain of *manners* is drawn over the features and expression of men's *natures,* that to the ordinary observer the two extremities, and the infinite field of varieties which lie between them, are all confounded—the vast and multitudinous compass of their several harmonies reduced to the meagre outline of

[1] "The Bristol mail is the best appointed in the kingdom—owing to the double advantages of an unusually good road, and of an extra sum for expenses subscribed by the Bristol merchants."—De Quincey.

differences expressed in the gamut or alphabet of elementary sounds. The case was this: for the first four or five miles from London, I annoyed my fellow-passenger on the roof by occasionally falling against him when the coach gave a lurch to his side; and indeed, if the road had been less smooth and level than it is, I should have fallen off from weakness. Of this annoyance he complained heavily, as perhaps in the same circumstances most people would; he expressed his complaint, however, more morosely than the occasion seemed to warrant; and, if I had parted with him at that moment, I should have thought of him, if I had considered it worth while to think of him at all, as a surly and almost brutal fellow. However, I was conscious that I had given him some cause for complaint: and, therefore, I apologized to him, and assured him that I would do what I could to avoid falling asleep for the future; and, at the same time, in as few words as possible, I explained to him that I was ill and in a weak state from long suffering; and that I could not afford at that time to take an inside place. The man's manner changed, upon hearing this explanation, in an instant: and when I next woke for a minute from the noise and lights of Hounslow (for in spite of my wishes and efforts I had fallen asleep again within two minutes from the time I had spoken to him), I found that he had put his arm around me to protect me from falling off: and for the rest of my journey he behaved to me with the gentleness of a woman, so that, at length, I almost lay in his arms: and this was the more kind, as he could not have known that I was not going the whole way to Bath or Bristol. Unfortunately, indeed, I' *did* go rather farther than I intended: for so genial and refreshing was my sleep, that the next time after leaving Hounslow that I fully awoke, was upon the sudden pulling up of the mail, possibly at a post-office, and on inquiry, I found that we had reached Maidenhead—six or seven miles, I think, ahead of Salt Hill. Here I alighted: and for the half-minute that the mail stopped, I was entreated by my friendly companion, who, from the transient glimpse I had had of him in Piccadilly, seemed to me to be a gentleman's butler—or person of that rank, to go to bed without delay. This I promised, though with no intention of doing so: and in fact, I immediately set forward, or rather backward, on foot. It must then have been nearly midnight: but so slowly did I creep along, that I heard a clock in a cottage strike four before I turned down the lane from Slough to Eton. The air and the sleep had both refreshed me; but I was weary nevertheless. I remember a thought, obvious enough, and which has been prettily expressed by a Roman poet,[1] which gave me some consolation at that moment under my poverty. There had been some time before a murder committed on or near Hounslow Heath. I think I cannot be mistaken when I say that the name of the murdered person was Steele, and that he was the owner of a lavender[2] plantation in that neighborhood. Every step of my progress was bringing me nearer to the heath: and it naturally occurred to me that I and the accursed murderer, if he were that night abroad, might at every instant be unconsciously approaching each other through the darkness: in which case, said I,—supposing that I, instead of being, as indeed I am, little better than an outcast,—

Lord of my learning and no land beside,[3]

were, like my friend, Lord [Altamont], heir by general repute to £70,000 *per ann.*, what a panic should I be under at this moment about my throat!—indeed, it was not likely that Lord [Altamont] should ever be in my situation. But nevertheless, the spirit of the remark remains true—that vast power and possessions make a man shamefully afraid of dying: and I am convinced that many of the most intrepid adventurers who, by fortunately being poor, enjoy the full use of their natural courage, would, if at the very instant of going into action news were brought to them that they had unexpectedly succeeded to an estate in England of £50,000 a year, feel their dislike to bullets considerably sharpened[4]—and their efforts at perfect equanimity and self-possession proportionably difficult. So true it is, in the language of a wise man whose own experience had made him acquainted with both fortunes, that riches are better fitted—

To slacken virtue, and abate her edge,
Than tempt her to do aught may merit praise.
         —*Paradise Regained.*[5]

[1] "An empty-pocketed tramp will sing in the face of a robber."—Juvenal, *Satires*, 10, 22.
[2] A small shrub cultivated for its perfume.
[3] *King John*, I, 1, 137.
[4] "It will be objected that many men, of the highest rank and wealth, have in our own day, as well as throughout our history, been amongst the foremost in courting danger in battle. True; but this is not the case supposed; long familiarity with power has to them deadened its effect and attractions."—De Quincey.
[5] Book 2, 455-56.

I dally with my subject because, to myself, the remembrance of these times is profoundly interesting. But my reader shall not have any further cause to complain: for I now hasten to its close.—In the road between Slough and Eton, I fell asleep: and, just as the morning began to dawn, I was awakened by the voice of a man standing over me and surveying me. I know not what he was: he was an ill-looking fellow— but not therefore of necessity an ill-meaning fellow: or, if he were, I suppose he thought that no person sleeping out-of-doors in winter would be worth robbing. In which conclusion, however, as it regarded myself, I beg to assure him, if he should be among my readers, that he was mistaken. After a slight remark he passed on: and I was not sorry at his disturbance, as it enabled me to pass through Eton before people were generally up. The night had been heavy and lowering: but towards the morning it had changed to a slight frost: and the ground and the trees were now covered with rime. I slipped through Eton unobserved; washed myself, and, as far as possible, adjusted my dress at a little public-house in Windsor; and about eight o'clock went down towards Pote's. On my road I met some junior boys of whom I made inquiries: an Etonian is always a gentleman; and, in spite of my shabby habiliments, they answered me civilly. My friend, Lord [Altamont], was gone to the University of [Cambridge]. "*Ibi omnis effusus labor!*"[1] I had, however, other friends at Eton: but it is not to all who wear that name in prosperity that a man is willing to present himself in distress. On recollecting myself, however, I asked for the Earl of D[esart], to whom (though my acquaintance with him was not so intimate as with some others) I should not have shrunk from presenting myself under any circumstances. He was still at Eton, though I believe on the wing for Cambridge. I called, was received kindly, and asked to breakfast.

Here let me stop for a moment to check my reader from any erroneous conclusion: because I have had occasion incidentally to speak of various patrician friends, it must not be supposed that I have myself any pretensions to rank or high blood. I thank God that I have not:—I am the son of a plain English merchant, esteemed during his life for his great integrity, and strongly attached to literary pursuits; indeed, he

[1] There was all his labor lost.—Virgil, *Georgics*, 4, 490-91.

was himself, anonymously, an author: if he had lived, it was expected that he would have been very rich; but, dying prematurely, he left no more than about £30,000, amongst seven different claimants. My mother I may mention with honor, as still more highly gifted. For, though unpretending to the name and honors of a *literary* woman, I shall presume to call her (what many literary women are not) an *intellectual* woman: and I believe that if ever her letters should be collected and published,[1] they would be thought generally to exhibit as much strong and masculine sense, delivered in as pure "mother English," racy and fresh with idiomatic graces, as any in our language—hardly excepting those of Lady M. W. Montagu. —These are my honors of descent: I have no others: and I have thanked God sincerely that I have not, because, in my judgment, a station which raises a man too eminently above the level of his fellow-creatures is not the most favorable to moral, or to intellectual qualities.

Lord D[esart] placed before me a most magnificent breakfast. It was really so; but in my eyes it seemed trebly magnificent —from being the first regular meal, the first "good man's table," that I had sat down to for months. Strange to say, however, I could scarcely eat anything. On the day when I first received my £10 Bank-note, I had gone to a baker's shop and bought a couple of rolls: this very shop I had two months or six weeks before surveyed with an eagerness of desire which it was almost humiliating to me to recollect. I remembered the story about Otway,[2] and feared that there might be danger in eating too rapidly. But I had no need for alarm, my appetite was quite sunk, and I became sick before I had eaten half of what I had bought. This effect from eating what approached to a meal, I continued to feel for weeks: or, when I did not experience any nausea, part of what I ate was rejected, sometimes with acidity, sometimes immediately, and without any acidity. On the present occasion, at Lord D[esart]'s table, I found myself not at all better than usual: and, in the midst of luxuries, I had no appetite. I had, however, unfortunately, at all times a craving for wine: I explained my situation, therefore,

to Lord D[esart], and gave him a short account of my late sufferings, at which he expressed great compassion, and called for wine. This gave me a momentary relief and pleasure; and on all occasions when I had an opportunity, I never failed to drink wine —which I worshipped then as I have since worshipped opium. I am convinced, however, that this indulgence in wine contributed to strengthen my malady; for the tone of my stomach was apparently quite sunk; but by a better regimen it might sooner, and perhaps effectually, have been revived. I hope that it was not from this love of wine that I lingered in the neighborhood of my Eton friends: I persuaded myself *then* that it was from reluctance to ask of Lord D[esart], on whom I was conscious I had not sufficient claims, the particular service in quest of which I had come down to Eton. I was, however, unwilling to lose my journey, and—I asked it. Lord D[esart], whose good nature was unbounded, and which, in regard to myself had been measured rather by his compassion perhaps for my condition, and his knowledge of my intimacy with some of his relatives, than by an over-rigorous inquiry into the extent of my own direct claims, faltered, nevertheless, at this request. He acknowledged that he did not like to have any dealings with money-lenders, and feared lest such a transaction might come to the ears of his connections. Moreover, he doubted whether *his* signature, whose expectations were so much more bounded than those of [his cousin], would avail with my unchristian friends. However, he did not wish, as it seemed, to mortify me by an absolute refusal: for after a little consideration, he promised, under certain conditions which he pointed out, to give his security. Lord D[esart] was at this time not eighteen years of age: but I have often doubted, on recollecting since the good sense and prudence which on this occasion he mingled with so much urbanity of manner, an urbanity which in him wore the grace of youthful sincerity, whether any statesman —the oldest and the most accomplished in diplomacy—could have acquitted himself better under the same circumstances. Most people, indeed, cannot be addressed on such a business without surveying you with looks as austere and unpropitious as those of a Saracen's head.[1]

Recomforted by this promise, which was not quite equal to the best, but far above the

[1] A number of Mrs. De Quincey's letters are printed in Japp's *De Quincey Memorials* (1891).

[2] Thomas Otway (1652-85) is said to have choked to death from eating too rapidly after a period of enforced starvation. The tradition is related in Cibber's *Lives of the Poets* (1753), 2, 335.

[1] The head of a Saracen, Turk, or Arab, used as a tavern sign.

worst that I had pictured to myself as possible, I returned in a Windsor coach to
London three days after I had quitted it.
And now I come to the end of my story:—
the Jews did not approve of Lord D[esart]'s [5]
terms; whether they would in the end have
acceded to them, and were only seeking time
for making due inquiries, I know not; but
many delays were made—time passed on—
the small fragment of my Bank-note had [10]
just melted away; and before any conclusion could have been put to the business, I
must have relapsed into my former state of
wretchedness. Suddenly, however, at this
crisis, an opening was made, almost by acci- [15]
dent, for reconciliation with my friends.[1]
I quitted London, in haste, for a remote part
of England:[2] after some time, I proceeded
to the university;[3] and it was not until
many months had passed away that I had [20]
it in my power again to revisit the ground
which had become so interesting to me, and
to this day remains so, as the chief scene of
my youthful sufferings.

Meantime, what had become of poor Ann? [25]
For her I have reserved my concluding
words: according to our agreement, I sought
her daily, and waited for her every night,
so long as I stayed in London, at the corner
of Titchfield Street. I inquired for her of [30]
every one who was likely to know her; and
during the last hours of my stay in London
I put into activity every means of tracing
her that my knowledge of London suggested,
and the limited extent of my power made [35]
possible. The street where she had lodged
I knew, but not the house: and I remembered
at last some account which she had given
me of ill treatment from her landlord, which
made it probable that she had quitted those [40]
lodgings before we parted. She had few
acquaintance; most people, besides, thought
that the earnestness of my inquiries arose
from motives which moved their laughter,
or their slight regard; and others, thinking [45]
I was in chase of a girl who had robbed me
of some trifles, were naturally and excusably
indisposed to give me any clue to her, if,
indeed, they had any to give. Finally, as
my despairing resource, on the day I left [50]
London I put into the hands of the only
person who (I was sure) must know Ann by
sight, from having been in company with us
once or twice, an address to —— in
——shire,[4] at that time the residence of my [55]

family. But, to this hour, I have never
heard a syllable about her.[1] This, amongst
such troubles as most men meet with in this
life, has been my heaviest affliction.—If she
lived, doubtless we must have been some- [5]
times in search of each other, at the very
same moment, through the mighty labyrinths
of London; perhaps even within a few feet
of each other—a barrier no wider in a London street often amounting in the end to [10]
a separation for eternity! During some
years, I hoped that she *did* live; and I suppose that, in the literal and unrhetorical use
of the word *myriad,* I may say that on my
different visits to London, I have looked into [15]
many, many myriads of female faces, in the
hope of meeting her. I should know her
again amongst a thousand, if I saw her for
a moment; for, though not handsome, she
had a sweet expression of countenance, and [20]
a peculiar and graceful carriage of the head.
—I sought her, I have said, in hope. So it
was for years; but now I should fear to see
her; and her cough, which grieved me when
I parted with her, is now my consolation. [25]
I now wish to see her no longer; but think
of her, more gladly, as one long since laid
in the grave; in the grave, I would hope, of
a Magdalen; taken away, before injuries
and cruelty had blotted out and transfigured [30]
her ingenuous nature, or the brutalities of
ruffians had completed the ruin they had
begun.

So then, Oxford Street, stony-hearted
step-mother! thou that listenest to the sighs [35]
of orphans, and drinkest the tears of children, at length I was dismissed from thee:
the time was come at last that I no more
should pace in anguish thy never-ending
terraces; no more should dream, and wake [40]
in captivity to the pangs of hunger. Successors, too many, to myself and Ann, have,
doubtless, since trodden in our footsteps,—
inheritors of our calamities: other orphans
than Ann have sighed: tears have been shed [45]
by other children: and thou, Oxford Street,
hast since, doubtless, echoed to the groans
of innumerable hearts. For myself, however, the storm which I had outlived seemed
to have been the pledge of a long fair- [50]
weather; the premature sufferings which I
had paid down to have been accepted as a
ransom for many years to come, as a price

---

[1] He was accidentally discovered by his friends
   and taken home.
[2] Liverpool.
[3] He entered Worcester College Dec. 17, 1803.
[4] St. John's Priory, in Chester.

[1] Another meeting between the Opium-Eater and
   Anne is depicted by Alfred de Musset (1810-
   57) in his French continuation of the *Confes-
   sions.* See De Quincey's *Confessions of an
   English Opium-Eater* (ed. Garnett), 169-88.
   See also De Quincey's dream, p. 1104a, 20 ff.

of long immunity from sorrow: and if again I walked in London, a solitary and contemplative man (as oftentimes I did), I walked for the most part in serenity and peace of mind. And, although it is true that the calamities of my noviciate in London had struck root so deeply in my bodily constitution that afterwards they shot up and flourished afresh, and grew into a noxious umbrage that has overshadowed and darkened my latter years, yet these second assaults of suffering were met with a fortitude more confirmed, with the resources of a maturer intellect, and with alleviations from sympathizing affection—how deep and tender!

Thus, however, with whatsoever alleviations, years that were far asunder were bound together by subtle links of suffering derived from a common root. And herein I notice an instance of the short-sightedness of human desires, that oftentimes on moonlight nights, during my first mournful abode in London, my consolation was (if such it could be thought) to gaze from Oxford Street up every avenue in succession which pierces through the heart of Marylebone to the fields and the woods; and *that*, said I, travelling with my eyes up the long vistas which lay part in light and part in shade, *"that* is the road to the north, and therefore to [Grasmere], and if I had the wings of a dove, *that* way I would fly for comfort."[1] Thus I said, and thus I wished, in my blindness; yet, even in that very northern region it was, even in that very valley, nay, in that very house to which my erroneous wishes pointed, that this second birth of my sufferings began;[2] and that they again threatened to besiege the citadel of life and hope. There it was, that for years I was persecuted by visions as ugly, and as ghastly phantoms as ever haunted the couch of Orestes:[3] and in this unhappier than he, that sleep which comes to all as a respite and a restoration, and to him especially, as a blessed[4] balm for his wounded heart and his haunted brain, visited me as my bitterest scourge. Thus blind was I in my desires; yet, if a veil interposes between the dim-sightedness of man and his future calamities, the same veil hides from

him their alleviations; and a grief which had not been feared is met by consolations which had not been hoped. I, therefore, who participated, as it were, in the troubles of Orestes (excepting only in his agitated conscience), participated no less in all his supports: my Eumenides, like his, were at my bed-feet, and stared in upon me through the curtains: but, watching by my pillow, or defrauding herself of sleep to bear me company through the heavy watches of the night, sat my Electra: for thou, beloved [Margaret],[1] dear companion of my later years, thou wast my Electra! and neither in nobility of mind nor in long-suffering affection, wouldst permit that a Grecian sister should excel an English wife. For thou thoughtest not much to stoop to humble offices of kindness, and to servile[2] ministrations of tenderest affection;—to wipe away for years the unwholesome dews upon the forehead, or to refresh the lips when parched and baked with fever; nor, even when thy own peaceful slumbers had by long sympathy become infected with the spectacle of my dread contest with phantoms and shadowy enemies that oftentimes bade me "sleep no more!"[3]—not even then, didst thou utter a complaint or any murmur, nor withdraw thy angelic smiles, nor shrink from thy service of love more than Electra did of old. For she too, though she was a Grecian woman, and the daughter of the king[4] of men, yet wept sometimes, and hid her face[5] in her robe.

But these troubles are past; and thou wilt read these records of a period so dolorous to us both as the legend of some hideous dream that can return no more. Meantime, I am again in London: and again I pace the terraces of Oxford Street by night: and oftentimes, when I am oppressed by anxieties that demand all my philosophy and the

[1] See *Psalms*, 55. 6.
[2] The first period of De Quincey's sufferings was in 1813-14. See p. 1069b, 18 ff.
[3] After he had slain his mother and her lover in vengeance for their murder of his father, Orestes was pursued by the Furies (euphemistically called the Eumenides).
[4] "Φίλον ὕπνη θέλγητρον ἐπίκουρον νόσου."—De Quincey. (O sweet balm of sleep, cure of disease.—Euripides, *Orestes*, 211.)

[1] De Quincey's wife. She died in 1837.
[2] "ἡδὺ δούλευμα.—Eurip. *Orest.*"—De Quincey. (sweet service.—Euripides, *Orestes*, 221.)
[3] *Macbeth*, II, 2, 35.
[4] "ἄναξ ἀνδρῶν 'Αγαμέμνων."— De Quincey. (Agamemnon, king of men.—*Iliad*, 1, 172.)
[5] "ὄμμα θεῖσ' ἔἰσω πέπλων [covering your eye with your garments. — Euripides, *Orestes*, 280]. The scholar will know that throughout this passage I refer to the earlier scenes of the *Orestes*, one of the most beautiful exhibitions of the domestic affections which even the dramas of Euripides can furnish. To the English reader, it may be necessary to say that the situation at the opening of the drama is that of a brother attended only by his sister during the demoniacal possession of a suffering conscience (or, in the mythology of the play, haunted by the Furies) and in circumstances of immediate danger from enemies, and of desertion or cold regard from nominal friends."—De Quincey.

comfort of thy presence to support, and yet remember that I am separated from thee by three hundred miles, and the length of three dreary months,—I look up the streets that run northwards from Oxford Street, upon moonlight nights, and recollect my youthful ejaculation of anguish;—and remembering that thou art sitting alone in that same valley, and mistress of that very house to which my heart turned in its blindness nineteen years ago, I think that, though blind indeed, and scattered to the winds of late, the promptings of my heart may yet have had reference to a remoter time, and may be justified if read in another meaning:—and, if I could allow myself to descend again to the impotent wishes of childhood, I should again say to myself, as I look to the north, "Oh, that I had the wings of a dove—" and with how just a confidence in thy good and gracious nature might I add the other half of my early ejaculation—"And *that* way I would fly for comfort."

The Pleasures of Opium

It is so long since I first took opium that if it had been a trifling incident in my life I might have forgotten its date: but cardinal events are not to be forgotten; and from circumstances connected with it I remember that it must be referred to the autumn of 1804. During that season I was in London, having come thither for the first time since my entrance at college. And my introduction to opium arose in the following way. From an early age I had been accustomed to wash my head in cold water at least once a day: being suddenly seized with toothache, I attributed it to some relaxation caused by an accidental intermission of that practice; jumped out of bed; plunged my head into a basin of cold water; and with hair thus wetted went to sleep. The next morning, as I need hardly say, I awoke with excruciating rheumatic pains of the head and face, from which I had hardly any respite for about twenty days. On the twenty-first day, I think it was, and on a Sunday, that I went out into the streets, rather to run away, if possible, from my torments, than with any distinct purpose. By accident I met a college acquaintance who recommended opium. Opium! dread agent of unimaginable pleasure and pain! I had heard of it as I had of manna or of ambrosia, but no further: how unmeaning a sound was it at that time! what solemn chords does it now strike upon my heart!

what heart-quaking vibrations of sad and happy remembrances! Reverting for a moment to these, I feel a mystic importance attached to the minutest circumstances connected with the place and the time, and the man, if man he was, that first laid open to me the Paradise of Opium-eaters. It was a Sunday afternoon, wet and cheerless: and a duller spectacle this earth of ours has not to show than a rainy Sunday in London. My road homewards lay through Oxford Street; and near "the *stately* Pantheon,"[1] as Mr. Wordsworth has obligingly called it, I saw a druggist's shop. The druggist, unconscious minister of celestial pleasures!—as if in sympathy with the rainy Sunday, looked dull and stupid, just as any mortal druggist might be expected to look on a Sunday: and, when I asked for the tincture of opium, he gave it to me as any other man might do: and furthermore, out of my shilling, returned me what seemed to be real copper halfpence, taken out of a real wooden drawer. Nevertheless, in spite of such indications of humanity, he has ever since existed in my mind as the beatific vision of an immortal druggist, sent down to earth on a special mission to myself. And it confirms me in this way of considering him, that, when I next came up to London, I sought him near the stately Pantheon, and found him not: and thus to me, who knew not his name (if indeed he had one), he seemed rather to have vanished from Oxford Street than to have removed in any bodily fashion. The reader may choose to think of him as, possibly, no more than a sublunary druggist: it may be so: but my faith is better: I believe him to have evanesced,[2] or evaporated. So unwillingly would I connect any mortal remembrances with that hour, and place, and creature, that first brought me acquainted with the celestial drug.

[1] Wordsworth, *Power of Music*, 3 (p. 325). The Pantheon was a concert room or theatre.

[2] *"Evanesced:*—This way of going off the stage of life appears to have been well known in the seventeenth century, but at that time to have been considered a peculiar privilege of blood-royal, and by no means to be allowed to druggists. For about the year 1686, a poet of rather ominous name (and who, by the by, did ample justice to his name)—*viz.*, Mr. *Flatman*, in speaking of the death of Charles II, expresses his surprise that any prince should commit so absurd an act as dying: because, says he,

'Kings should disdain to die, and only disappear.'

They should *abscond*, that is, into the other world."—De Quincey. For the line quoted, see Thomas Flatman's *On the Much lamented Death of our late Sovereign Lord King Charles II of Blessed Memory*, 14, 25.

Arrived at my lodgings, it may be supposed that I lost not a moment in taking the quantity prescribed. I was necessarily ignorant of the whole art and mystery of opium-taking: and, what I took, I took under every disadvantage. But I took it:—and in an hour, oh! heavens! what a revulsion! what an upheaving, from its lowest depths, of the inner spirit! what an apocalypse of the world within me! That my pains had vanished, was now a trifle in my eyes:—this negative effect was swallowed up in the immensity of those positive effects which had opened before me—in the abyss of divine enjoyment thus suddenly revealed. Here was a panacea—a φάρμακον νηπενθές[1] for all human woes: here was the secret of happiness, about which philosophers had disputed for so many ages, at once discovered: happiness might now be bought for a penny, and carried in the waistcoat pocket: portable ecstasies might be had corked up in a pint bottle: and peace of mind could be sent down in gallons by the mail-coach. But, if I talk in this way, the reader will think I am laughing: and I can assure him, that nobody will laugh long who deals much with opium: its pleasures even are of a grave and solemn complexion; and in his happiest state, the opium-eater cannot present himself in the character of "L'Allegro":[2] even then, he speaks and thinks as becomes "Il Penseroso."[3] Nevertheless, I have a very reprehensible way of jesting at times in the midst of my own misery: and, unless when I am checked by some more powerful feelings, I am afraid I shall be guilty of this indecent practice even in these annals of suffering or enjoyment. The reader must allow a little to my infirm nature in this respect: and with a few indulgences of that sort, I shall endeavor to be as grave, if not drowsy, as fits a theme like opium, so anti-mercurial as it really is, and so drowsy as it is falsely reputed.

And, first, one word with respect to its bodily effects: for upon all that has been hitherto written on the subject of opium, whether by travellers in Turkey, who may plead their privilege of lying as an old immemorial right, or by professors of medicine, writing ex cathedra,[4]—I have but one emphatic criticism to pronounce—Lies! lies! lies! I remember once, in passing a book-

stall, to have caught these words from a page of some satiric author:—"By this time I became convinced that the London newspapers spoke truth at least twice a week, viz., on Tuesday and Saturday, and might safely be depended upon for —— the list of bankrupts." In like manner, I do by no means deny that some truths have been delivered to the world in regard to opium: thus it has been repeatedly affirmed by the learned that opium is a dusky brown in color; and this, take notice, I grant: secondly, that it is rather dear; which I also grant, for in my time, East-India opium has been three guineas a pound, and Turkey eight: and, thirdly, that if you eat a good deal of it, most probably you must do what is particularly disagreeable to any man of regular habits, viz., die.[1] These weighty propositions are, all and singular, true: I cannot gainsay them: and truth ever was, and will be, commendable. But in these three theorems, I believe we have exhausted the stock of knowledge as yet accumulated by man on the subject of opium. And therefore, worthy doctors, as there seems to be room for further discoveries, stand aside, and allow me to come forward and lecture on this matter.

First, then, it is not so much affirmed as taken for granted by all who ever mention opium, formally or incidentally, that it does, or can, produce intoxication. Now, reader, assure yourself, meo periculo,[2] that no quantity of opium ever did, or could intoxicate. As to the tincture of opium (commonly called laudanum) that might certainly intoxicate if a man could bear to take enough of it; but why? because it contains so much proof spirit, and not because it contains so much opium. But crude opium, I affirm peremptorily, is incapable of producing any state of body at all resembling that which is produced by alcohol: and not in degree only incapable, but even in kind: it is not in the quantity of its effects merely, but in the quality, that it differs altogether. The pleasure given by wine is always mounting, and tending to a crisis, after which it declines: that from opium, when once generated, is stationary for eight or ten hours: the first, to borrow a technical distinction from medi-

---

[1] sorrow-banishing drug (See the Odyssey, 4, 220-21.)
[2] In Milton's L'Allegro; the title means the cheerful man.
[3] In Milton's Il Penseroso; the title means the thoughtful man.
[4] with authority

[1] "Of this, however, the learned appear latterly to have doubted: for in a pirated edition of Buchan's Domestic Medicine, which I once saw in the hands of a farmer's wife who was studying it for the benefit of her health, the Doctor was made to say—'Be particularly careful never to take above five-and-twenty ounces of laudanum at once': the true reading being probably five-and-twenty drops, which are held equal to about one grain of crude opium."—De Quincey.
[2] at my own risk

cine, is a case of acute—the second, of chronic pleasure: the one is a flame, the other a steady and equable glow. But the main distinction lies in this, and whereas wine disorders the mental faculties, opium, on the contrary, if taken in a proper manner, introduces amongst them the most exquisite order, legislation, and harmony. Wine robs a man of his self-possession: opium greatly invigorates it. Wine unsettles and clouds the judgment, and gives a preternatural brightness and a vivid exaltation to the contempts and the admirations, the loves and the hatreds, of the drinker: opium on the contrary communicates serenity and equipoise to all the faculties, active or passive: and with respect to the temper and moral feelings in general, it gives simply that sort of vital warmth which is approved by the judgment, and which would probably always accompany a bodily constitution of primeval or antediluvian health. Thus, for instance, opium, like wine, gives an expansion to the heart and the benevolent affections: but then, with this remarkable difference, that in the sudden development of kind-heartedness which accompanies inebriation, there is always more or less of a maudlin character, which exposes it to the contempt of the bystander. Men shake hands, swear eternal friendship, and shed tears—no mortal knows why: and the sensual creature is clearly uppermost. But the expansion of the benigner feelings incident to opium, is no febrile access, but a healthy restoration to that state which the mind would naturally recover upon the removal of any deep-seated irritation of pain that had disturbed and quarrelled with the impulses of a heart originally just and good. True it is, that even wine, up to a certain point, and with certain men, rather tends to exalt and to steady the intellect: I myself, who have never been a great wine-drinker, used to find that half a dozen glasses of wine advantageously affected the faculties—brightened and intensified the consciousness—and gave to the mind a feeling of being "*ponderibus librata suis*":[1] and certainly it is most absurdly said in popular language of any man that he is *disguised* in liquor: for, on the contrary, most men are disguised by sobriety; and it is when they are drinking (as some old gentleman says in Athenæus), that men ἑαυτοὺς ἐμφανίζουσιν οἵτινές εἰσιν[2] — display

themselves in their true complexion of character,—which surely is not disguising themselves. But still, wine constantly leads a man to the brink of absurdity and extravagance; and, beyond a certain point, it is sure to volatilize and to disperse the intellectual energies: whereas opium always seems to compose what has been agitated, and to concentrate what had been distracted. In short, to sum up all in one word, a man who is inebriated, or tending to inebriation, is, and feels that he is, in a condition which calls up into supremacy the merely human, too often the brutal, part of his nature: but the opium-eater (I speak of him who is not suffering from any disease, or other remote effects of opium) feels that the diviner part of his nature is paramount; that is, the moral affections are in a state of cloudless serenity; and over all is the great light of the majestic intellect.

This is the doctrine of the true church on the subject of opium: of which church I acknowledge myself to be the only member —the alpha and the omega: but then it is to be recollected that I speak from the ground of a large and profound personal experience: whereas most of the unscientific[1] authors who have at all treated of opium, and even of those who have written expressly on the materia medica, make it evident, from the horror they express of it, that their experimental knowledge of its action is none at all. I will, however,

---

[1] balanced with its own weight; self-poised (See Ovid's *Metamorphoses*, 1, 13.)

[2] Quoted from the historian Philochorus (3rd cent. B. C.) by Athenæus (200) in his *Deipnosophistæ*, 37 E.

[1] "Amongst the great herd of travellers, etc., who show sufficiently by their stupidity that they never held any intercourse with opium, I must caution my readers especially against the brilliant author of *Anastasius*. This gentleman, whose wit would lead one to presume him an opium-eater, has made it impossible to consider him in that character from the grievous misrepresentation which he gives of its effects, at pp. 215-17 of vol. i. Upon consideration, it must appear such to the author himself; for, waiving the errors I have insisted on in the text, which (and others) are adopted in the fullest manner, he will himself admit, that an old gentleman, 'with a snow-white beard,' who eats 'ample doses of opium,' and is yet able to deliver what is meant and received as very weighty counsel on the bad effects of that practice, is but an indifferent evidence that opium either kills people prematurely, or sends them into a mad-house. But for my part, I see into this old gentleman and his motives; the fact is, he was enamored of 'the little golden receptacle of the pernicious drug' which Anastasius carried about him; and no way of obtaining it so safe and so feasible occurred as that of frightening its owner out of his wits (which, by the by, are none of the strongest). This commentary throws a new light upon the case, and greatly improves it as a story; for the old gentleman's speech, considered as a lecture on pharmacy, is highly absurd, but, considered as a hoax on Anastasius, it reads excellently."—De Quincey. The author of *Anastasius, or Memoirs of a Greek* (1819) is Thomas Hope (1770-1831).

candidly acknowledge that I have met with one person who bore evidence to its intoxicating power, such as staggered my own incredulity: for he was a surgeon, and had himself taken opium largely. I happened to say to him that his enemies, as I had heard, charged him with talking nonsense on politics, and that his friends apologized for him by suggesting that he was constantly in a state of intoxication from opium. Now the accusation, said I, is not *prima facie*,[1] and of necessity, an absurd one: but the defence *is*. To my surprise, however, he insisted that both his enemies and his friends were in the right: "I will maintain," said he, "that I *do* talk nonsense; and secondly, I will maintain that I do not talk nonsense upon principle, or with any view to profit, but solely and simply," said he, "solely and simply,—solely and simply" (repeating it three times over), "because I am drunk with opium; and *that* daily." I replied that, as to the allegation of his enemies, as it seemed to be established upon such respectable testimony, seeing that the three parties concerned all agreed in it, it did not become me to question it; but the defence set up I must demur to. He proceeded to discuss the matter, and to lay down his reasons; but it seemed to me so impolite to pursue an argument which must have presumed a man mistaken in a point belonging to his own profession, that I did not press him even when his course of argument seemed open to objection: not to mention that a man who talks nonsense, even though "with no view to profit," is not altogether the most agreeable partner in a dispute, whether as opponent or respondent. I confess, however, that the authority of a surgeon, and one who was reputed a good one, may seem a weighty one to my prejudice: but still I must plead my experience, which was greater than his greatest by 7000 drops a day; and, though it was not possible to suppose a medical man unacquainted with the characteristic symptoms of vinous intoxication, it yet struck me that he might proceed on a logical error of using the word intoxication with too great latitude, and extending it generally to all modes of nervous excitement, instead of restricting it as the expression for a specific sort of excitement, connected with certain diagnostics. Some people have maintained, in my hearing, that they have been drunk upon green tea: and a medical student in London, for whose knowledge in his profession I

[1] at first view

have reason to feel great respect, assured me, the other day, that a patient, in recovering from an illness, had got drunk on a beef-steak.

Having dwelt so much on this first and leading error in respect to opium, I shall notice very briefly a second and a third; which are, that the elevation of spirits produced by opium is necessarily followed by a proportionate depression, and that the natural and even immediate consequence of opium is torpor and stagnation, animal and mental. The first of these errors I shall content myself with simply denying, assuring my reader that for ten years, during which I took opium at intervals, the day succeeding to that on which I allowed myself this luxury was always a day of unusually good spirits.

With respect to the torpor supposed to follow, cr rather, if we were to credit the numerous pictures of Turkish opium-eaters, to accompany the practice of opium-eating, I deny that also. Certainly, opium is classed under the head of narcotics; and some such effect it may produce in the end: but the primary effects of opium are always, and in the highest degree, to excite and stimulate the system: this first stage of its action always lasted with me, during my noviciate, for upwards of eight hours; so that it must be the fault of the opium eater himself if he does not so time his exhibition of the dose, to speak medically, as that the whole weight of its narcotic influence may descend upon his sleep. Turkish opium-eaters, it seems, are absurd enough to sit, like so many equestrian statues, on logs of wood as stupid as themselves. But that the reader may judge of the degree in which opium is likely to stupify the faculties of an Englishman, I shall, by way of treating the question illustratively, rather than argumentatively, describe the way in which I myself often passed an opium evening in London, during the period between 1804 and 1812. It will be seen that at least opium did not move me to seek solitude, and much less to seek inactivity, or the torpid state of self-involution ascribed to the Turks. I give this account at the risk of being pronounced a crazy enthusiast or visionary: but I regard *that* little: I must desire my reader to bear in mind that I was a hard student, and at severe studies for all the rest of my time: and certainly I had a right occasionally to relaxations as well as other people: these, however, I allowed myself but seldom.

The late Duke of [Norfolk] used to say,

"Next Friday, by the blessing of Heaven, I purpose to be drunk": and in like manner I used to fix beforehand how often, within a given time, and when, I would commit a debauch of opium. This was seldom more than once in three weeks: for at that time I could not have ventured to call every day (as I did afterwards) for *"a glass of laudanum negus,*[1] *warm, and without sugar."* No: as I have said, I seldom drank laudanum, at that time, more than once in three weeks: this was usually on a Tuesday or a Saturday night; my reason for which was this. In those days Grassini sang at the Opera: and her voice was delightful to me beyond all that I had ever heard. I know not what may be the state of the Opera-house now, having never been within its walls for seven or eight years, but at that time it was by much the most pleasant place of public resort in London for passing an evening. Five shillings admitted one to the gallery, which was subject to far less annoyance than the pit of the theatres: the orchestra was distinguished by its sweet and melodious grandeur from all English orchestras, the composition of which, I confess, is not acceptable to my ear, from the predominance of the clangorous instruments, and the absolute tyranny of the violin. The choruses were divine to hear: and when Grassini appeared in some interlude,[2] as she often did, and poured forth her passionate soul as Andromache at the tomb of Hector,[3] etc., I question whether any Turk, of all that ever entered the paradise of opium-eaters, can have had half the pleasure I had. But, indeed, I honor the Barbarians too much by supposing them capable of any pleasures approaching to the intellectual ones of an Englishman. For music is an intellectual or a sensual pleasure, according to the temperament of him who hears it. And, by the by, with the exception of the fine extravaganza on that subject in *Twelfth Night,*[4] I do not recollect more than one thing said adequately on the subject of music in all literature: it is a passage in the *Religio Medici*[5] of Sir T. Brown; and,

[1] Negus is a beverage of wine, hot water, sugar, nutmeg, and lemon juice; it is said to be named after its first maker, Col. Francis Negus (d. 1732).
[2] Probably a vocal solo sung between the parts of some formal program.
[3] In Grétry's *Andromaque,* which was produced at Paris in 1780.
[4] Act I, 1.
[5] "I have not the book at this moment to consult; but I think the passage begins—'And even that tavern music, which makes one man merry, another mad, in me strikes a deep fit of devotion,' etc."—De Quincey. The passage occurs in Part 2, Sec. 9.

though chiefly remarkable for its sublimity, has also a philosophic value, inasmuch as it points to the true theory of musical effects. The mistake of most people is to suppose that it is by the ear they communicate with music, and, therefore, that they are purely passive to its effects. But this is not so: it is by the reaction of the mind upon the notices of the ear (the *matter* coming by the senses, the *form* from the mind) that the pleasure is constructed: and therefore it is that people of equally good ear differ so much in this point from one another. Now opium, by greatly increasing the activity of the mind generally, increases, of necessity, that particular mode of its activity by which we are able to construct out of the raw material of organic sound an elaborate intellectual pleasure. But, says a friend, a succession of musical sounds is to me like a collection of Arabic characters: I can attach no ideas to them. Ideas! my good sir? there is no occasion for them: all that class of ideas which can be available in such a case has a language of representative feelings. But this is a subject foreign to my present purposes: it is sufficient to say that a chorus, etc., of elaborate harmony, displayed before me, as in a piece of arras work, the whole of my past life— not as if recalled by an act of memory, but as if present and incarnated in the music: no longer painful to dwell upon: but the detail of its incidents removed, or blended in some hazy abstraction; and its passions exalted, spiritualized, and sublimed. All this was to be had for five shillings. And over and above the music of the stage and the orchestra, I had all around me, in the intervals of the performance, the music of the Italian language talked by Italian women: for the gallery was usually crowded with Italians: and I listened with a pleasure such as that with which Weld the traveller lay and listened, in Canada, to the sweet laughter of Indian women;[1] for the less you understand of a language the more sensible you are to the melody or harshness of its sounds: for such a purpose, therefore, it was an advantage to me that I was a poor Italian scholar, reading it but little, and not speaking it at all, nor understanding a tenth part of what I heard spoken.

These were my Opera pleasures: but another pleasure I had which, as it could be

[1] The incident is recorded by I. Weld, Jr., in his *Travels through the States of North Carolina and the Provinces of Upper and Lower Canada during the Years 1795, 1796, and 1797* (ed. 1800), 2, 288.

had only on a Saturday night, occasionally struggled with my love of the Opera; for, at that time, Tuesday and Saturday were the regular Opera nights. On this subject I am afraid I shall be rather obscure, but, I can assure the reader, not at all more so than Marinus in his *Life of Proclus,* or many other biographers and autobiographers of fair reputation. This pleasure, I have said, was to be had only on a Saturday night. What then was Saturday night to me more than any other night? I had no labors that I rested from; no wages to receive: what needed I to care for Saturday night, more than as it was a summons to hear Grassini? True, most logical reader: what you say is unanswerable. And yet so it was and is, that, whereas different men throw their feelings into different channels, and most are apt to show their interest in the concerns of the poor, chiefly by sympathy, expressed in some shape or other, with their distresses and sorrows, I, at that time, was disposed to express my interest by sympathizing with their pleasures. The pains of poverty I had lately seen too much of; more than I wished to remember: but the pleasures of the poor, their consolations of spirit, and their reposes from bodily toil, can never become oppressive to contemplate. Now Saturday night is the season for the chief, regular, and periodic return of rest to the poor: in this point the most hostile sects unite, and acknowledge a common link of brotherhood: almost all Christendom rests from its labors. It is a rest introductory to another rest: and divided by a whole day and two nights from the renewal of toil. On this account I feel always, on a Saturday night, as though I also were released from some yoke of labor, had some wages to receive, and some luxury of repose to enjoy. For the sake, therefore, of witnessing, upon as large a scale as possible, a spectacle with which my sympathy was so entire, I used often, on Saturday nights, after I had taken opium, to wander forth, without much regarding the direction or the distance, to all the markets and other parts of London to which the poor resort on a Saturday night for laying out their wages. Many a family party, consisting of a man, his wife, and sometimes one or two of his children, have I listened to, as they stood consulting on their ways and means, or the strength of their exchequer, or the price of household articles. Gradually I became familiar with their wishes, their difficulties, and their opinions. Sometimes there might be heard murmurs of discontent: but far oftener expressions on the countenance, or uttered in words, of patience, hope, and tranquillity. And taken generally, I must say that, in this point at least, the poor are far more philosophic than the rich—that they show a more ready and cheerful submission to what they consider as irremediable evils, or irreparable losses. Whenever I saw occasion, or could do it without appearing to be intrusive, I joined their parties; and gave my opinion upon the matter in discussion, which, if not always judicious, was always received indulgently. If wages were a little higher, or expected to be so, or the quartern loaf[1] a little lower, or it was reported that onions and butter were expected to fall, I was glad: yet, if the contrary were true, I drew from opium some means of consoling myself. For opium, like the bee, that extracts its materials indiscriminately from roses and from the soot of chimneys, can overrule all feelings into a compliance with the master key. Some of these rambles led me to great distances: for an opium-eater is too happy to observe the motion of time. And sometimes in my attempts to steer homewards upon nautical principles, by fixing my eye on the pole-star, and seeking ambitiously for a northwest passage, instead of circumnavigating all the capes and headlands I had doubled in my outward voyage, I came suddenly upon such knotty problems of alleys, such enigmatical entries, and such sphinx's riddles[2] of streets without thoroughfares, as must, I conceive, baffle the audacity of porters, and confound the intellects of hackney-coachmen. I could almost have believed, at times, that I must be the first discoverer of some of these *terræ incognitæ,*[3] and doubted whether they had yet been laid down in the modern charts of London. For all this, however, I paid a heavy price in distant years, when the human face tyrannized over my dreams, and the perplexities of my steps in London came back and haunted my sleep with the feeling of perplexities, moral or intellectual, that brought confusion to the reason, or anguish and remorse to the conscience.

Thus I have shown that opium does not, of necessity, produce inactivity or torpor; but that, on the contrary, it often led me into markets and theatres. Yet, in candor, I will admit that markets and theatres are

---

[1] A loaf of bread weighing about 4 lbs.
[2] The sphinx propounded a riddle to the Thebans and killed all passers-by who could not solve it. See De Quincey's *The Sphinx's Riddle.* [3] unknown lands

not the appropriate haunts of the opium-eater, when in the divinest state incident to his enjoyment. In that state, crowds become an oppression to him; music even, too sensual and gross. He naturally seeks solitude and silence, as indispensable conditions of those trances and profoundest reveries which are the crown or consummation of what opium can do for human nature. I, whose disease it was to meditate too much, and to observe too little, and who upon my first entrance at college was nearly falling into a deep melancholy from brooding too much on the sufferings which I had witnessed in London, was sufficiently aware of the tendencies of my own thoughts to do all I could to counteract them.—I was, indeed, like a person who, according to the old legend, had entered the cave of Trophonius:[1] and the remedies I sought were to force myself into society, and to keep my understanding in continual activity upon matters of science. But for these remedies, I should certainly have become hypochondriacally melancholy. In after years, however, when my cheerfulness was more fully re-established, I yielded to my natural inclination for a solitary life. And, at that time, I often fell into these reveries upon taking opium; and more than once it has happened to me, on a summer night, when I have been at an open window, in a room from which I could overlook the sea at a mile below me, and could command a view of the great town of L[iverpool], at about the same distance, that I have sat, from sunset to sun-rise, motionless, and without wishing to move.

I shall be charged with mysticism, Behmenism,[2] quietism,[3] etc., but that shall not alarm me. Sir H. Vane, the Younger,[4] was one of our wisest men: and let my readers see if he, in his philosophical works, be half as unmystical as I am.—I say, then, that it has often struck me that the scene itself was somewhat typical of what took place in such a reverie. The town of L[iverpool] represented the earth, with its sorrows and its graves left behind, yet not out of sight, nor wholly forgotten. The ocean, in everlasting but gentle agitation,

and brooded over by a dove-like calm,[1] might not unfitly typify the mind and the mood which then swayed it. For it seemed to me as if then first I stood at a distance, and aloof from the uproar of life, as if the tumult, the fever, and the strife, were suspended; a respite granted from the secret burthens of the heart; a sabbath of repose; a resting from human labors. Here were the hopes which blossom in the paths of life, reconciled with the peace which is in the grave; motions of the intellect as unwearied as the heavens, yet for all anxieties a halcyon calm:[2] a tranquillity that seemed no product of inertia, but as if resulting from mighty and equal antagonisms; infinite activities, infinite repose.

Oh! just, subtle, and mighty opium! that to the hearts of poor and rich alike, for the wounds that will never heal, and for "the pangs that tempt the spirit to rebel,"[3] bringest an assuaging balm; eloquent opium! that with thy potent rhetoric stealest away the purposes of wrath; and to the guilty man for one night givest back the hopes of his youth, and hands washed pure from blood; and to the proud man a brief oblivion for

Wrongs unredress'd and insults unavenged;[4]

that summonest to the chancery of dreams, for the triumphs of suffering innocence, false witnesses; and confoundest perjury; and dost reverse the sentences of unrighteous judges:—thou buildest upon the bosom of darkness, out of the fantastic imagery of the brain, cities and temples beyond the art of Phidias and Praxiteles—beyond the splendor of Babylon and Hekatompylos:[5] and "from the anarchy of dreaming sleep,"[6] callest into sunny light the faces of long-buried beauties, and the blessed household countenances, cleansed from the "dishonors of the grave."[7] Thou only givest these gifts to man; and thou hast the keys of Paradise, oh, just, subtle, and mighty opium![8]

---

[1] It was supposed that a visitor to this cave never smiled again.

[2] The teachings of the German Mystic, Jacob Behman (Böhme), who held that everything manifested its divine origin; that the material and moral powers were one; etc.

[3] A system of religious mysticism based on indifference to worldly interests, and on passive contemplation of spiritual interests.

[4] See Wordsworth's *Great Men Have Been Among Us* (p. 313).

[1] See *Paradise Lost*, 1, 21.

[2] The halcyon or kingfisher was fabled to nest on the sea and to calm the waves.

[3] Wordsworth, *The White Doe of Rylstone*, Dedication, 36.

[4] Wordsworth, *The Excursion*, 3, 374.

[5] The hundred-gated, an epithet applied by De Quincey to Thebes, the capital of Egypt. The Hanging Gardens at Babylon were regarded as one of the seven wonders of the world. See *Daniel* 4:29-30.

[6] Wordsworth, *The Excursion*, 4, 87.

[7] See *1 Corinthians*, 15:43. This verse is a portion of the lesson read at the burial service of the Church of England.

[8] Adapted from the address to Death with which Raleigh closes his *History of the World*.

From INTRODUCTION TO THE PAINS OF OPIUM

. . . . . .

If any man, poor or rich, were to say that he would tell us what had been the happiest day in his life, and the why, and the wherefore, I suppose that we should all cry out —Hear him! Hear him!—As to the happiest *day*, that must be very difficult for any wise man to name: because any event, that could occupy so distinguished a place in a man's retrospect of his life, or be entitled to have shed a special felicity on any one day, ought to be of such an enduring character, as that, accidents apart, it should have continued to shed the same felicity, or one not distinguishably less, on many years together. To the happiest *lustrum*,[1] however, or even to the happiest *year*, it may be allowed to any man to point without discountenance from wisdom. This year, in my case, reader, was the one which we have now reached;[2] though it stood, I confess, as a parenthesis between years of a gloomier character. It was a year of brilliant water, to speak after the manner of jewelers, set as it were, and insulated, in the gloom and cloudy melancholy of opium. Strange as it may sound, I had a little before this time descended suddenly, and without any considerable effort, from 320 grains of opium (*i. e.*, eight[3] thousand drops of laudanum) per day, to forty grains, or one-eighth part. Instantaneously, and as if by magic, the cloud of profoundest melancholy which rested upon my brain, like some black vapors that I have seen roll away from the summits of mountains, drew off in one day ($νυχθήμερον$[4]); passed off with its murky banners as simultaneously as a ship that has been stranded, and is floated off by a spring tide—

That moveth altogether, if it move at all.[5]

Now, then, I was again happy: I now took only 1000 drops of laudanum per day: and what was that? A latter spring had

[1] period of five years
[2] That is, 1816.
[3] "I here reckon twenty-five drops of laudanum as equivalent to one grain of opium, which, I believe, is the common estimate. However, as both may be considered variable quantities (the crude opium varying much in strength, and the tincture still more), I suppose that no infinitesimal accuracy can be had in such a calculation. Tea-spoons vary as much in size as opium in strength. Small ones hold about 100 drops; so that 8000 drops are about eighty times a tea-spoonful. The reader sees how much I kept within Dr. Buchan's indulgent allowance."—De Quincey. On Dr. Buchan's allowance, see p. 1087b, n. 1.
[4] a day and a night
[5] Wordsworth, *Resolution and Independence*, 77 (p. 310).

come to close up the season of youth: my brain performed its functions as healthily as ever before: I read Kant again; and again I understood him, or fancied that I did. Again my feelings of pleasure expanded themselves to all around me: and if any man from Oxford or Cambridge, or from neither, had been announced to me in my unpretending cottage, I should have welcomed him with as sumptuous a reception as so poor a man could offer. Whatever else was wanting to a wise man's happiness, —of laudanum I would have given him as much as he wished, and in a golden cup. And, by the way, now that I speak of giving laudanum away, I remember, about this time, a little incident, which I mention, because, trifling as it was, the reader will soon meet it again in my dreams, which it influenced more fearfully than could be imagined. One day a Malay knocked at my door. What business a Malay could have to transact amongst English mountains, I cannot conjecture: but possibly he was on his road to a seaport about forty miles distant.

The servant who opened the door to him was a young girl[1] born and bred amongst the mountains, who had never seen an Asiatic dress of any sort: his turban, therefore, confounded her not a little: and, as it turned out that his attainments in English were exactly of the same extent as hers in the Malay, there seemed to be an impassable gulf fixed between all communication of ideas, if either party had happened to possess any. In this dilemma, the girl, recollecting the reputed learning of her master, and doubtless giving me credit for a knowledge of all the languages of the earth, besides, perhaps, a few of the lunar ones, came and gave me to understand that there was a sort of demon below, whom she clearly imagined that my art could exorcise from the house. I did not immediately go down: but, when I did, the group which presented itself, arranged as it was by accident, though not very elaborate, took hold of my fancy and my eye in a way that none of the statuesque attitudes exhibited in the ballets at the Opera-house, though so ostentatiously complex, had ever done. In a cottage kitchen, but panelled on the wall with dark wood that from age and rubbing resembled oak, and looking more like a rustic hall of entrance than a kitchen, stood the Malay—his turban and loose trousers of dingy white relieved upon the dark panel-

[1] Barbara Lewthwaite. See Wordsworth's *The Pet Lamb*.

ling: he had placed himself nearer to the girl than she seemed to relish; though her native spirit of mountain intrepidity contended with the feeling of simple awe which her countenance expressed as she gazed upon the tiger-cat before her. And a more striking picture there could not be imagined, than the beautiful English face of the girl, and its exquisite fairness, together with her erect and independent attitude, contrasted with the sallow and bilious skin of the Malay, enamelled or veneered with mahogany, by marine air, his small, fierce, restless eyes, thin lips, slavish gestures and adorations. Half-hidden by the ferocious looking Malay was a little child from a neighboring cottage who had crept in after him, and was now in the act of reverting its head, and gazing upwards at the turban and the fiery eyes beneath it, whilst with one hand he caught at the dress of the young woman for protection. My knowledge of the Oriental tongues is not remarkably extensive, being indeed confined to two words—the Arabic word for barley, and the Turkish for opium (madjoon), which I have learnt from Anastasius. And, as I had neither a Malay dictionary, nor even Adelung's *Mithridates,* which might have helped me to a few words, I addressed him in some lines from the *Iliad,* considering that, of such languages as I possessed, Greek, in point of longitude, came geographically nearest to an Oriental one. He worshipped me in a most devout manner, and replied in what I suppose was Malay. In this way I saved my reputation with my neighbors for the Malay had no means of betraying the secret. He lay down upon the floor for about an hour, and then pursued his journey. On his departure, I presented him with a piece of opium. To him, as an Orientalist, I concluded that opium must be familiar: and the expression of his face convinced me that it was. Nevertheless, I was struck with some little consternation when I saw him suddenly raise his hand to his mouth, and, in the schoolboy phrase, bolt the whole, divided into three pieces, at one mouthful. The quantity was enough to kill three dragoons and their horses: and I felt some alarm for the poor creature: but what could be done? I had given him the opium in compassion for his solitary life, on recollecting that if he had travelled on foot from London it must be nearly three weeks since he could have exchanged a thought with any human being. I could not think of violating the laws of hospitality by having him seized

and drenched with an emetic, and thus frightening him into a notion that we were going to sacrifice him to some English idol. No: there was clearly no help for it:—he took his leave: and for some days I felt anxious: but as I never heard of any Malay being found dead, I became convinced that he was used[1] to opium: and that I must have done him the service I designed, by giving him one night of respite from the pains of wandering.

This incident I have digressed to mention, because this Malay, partly from the picturesque exhibition he assisted to frame, partly from the anxiety I connected with his image for some days, fastened afterwards upon my dreams, and brought other Malays with him worse than himself, that ran "a-muck"[2] at me, and led me into a world of troubles.—But to quit this episode, and to return to my intercalary[3] year of happiness. I have said already, that on a' subject so important to us all as happiness, we should listen with pleasure to any man's experience or experiments, even though he were but a plough-boy, who cannot be supposed to have ploughed very deep into such an intractable soil as that of human pains and pleasures, or to have conducted his researches upon any very enlightened principles. But I, who have taken happiness, both in a solid and a liquid shape, both boiled and unboiled, both East India and Turkey—who have conducted my experiments upon this interesting subject with a sort of galvanic battery—and have, for the general benefit of the world, inoculated myself, as it were, with the poison of 8000 drops of laudanum per day (just for the same reason as a French surgeon inoculated himself lately with cancer—an English one, twenty years ago, with plague—and a third,

---

[1] "This, however, is not a necessary conclusion; the varieties of effect produced by opium on different constitutions are infinite. A London Magistrate (Harriott's *Struggles through Life,* vol. iii, p. 391, Third Edition) has recorded that, on the first occasion of his trying laudanum for the gout, he took *forty* drops, the next night *sixty,* and on the fifth night *eighty,* without any effect whatever; and this at an advanced age. I have an anecdote from a country surgeon, however, which sinks Mr. Harriott's case into a trifle; and in my projected medical treatise on opium, which I will publish, provided the College of Surgeons will pay me for enlightening their benighted understandings upon this subject, I will relate it; but it is far too good a story to be published gratis."—De Quincey.

[2] "See the common accounts in any Eastern traveller or voyager of the frantic excesses committed by Malays who have taken opium, or are reduced to desperation by ill luck at gambling."—De Quincey.

[3] inserted among others in the calendar

I know not of what nation,[1] with hydrophobia),—*I*, it will be admitted, must surely know what happiness is, if anybody does. And, therefore, I will here lay down an analysis of happiness; and as the most interesting mode of communicating it, I will give it, not didactically, but wrapt up and involved in a picture of one evening, as I spent every evening during the intercalary year when laudanum, though taken daily, was to me no more than the elixir of pleasure. This done, I shall quit the subject of happiness altogether, and pass to a very different one—*the pains of opium.*

Let there be a cottage, standing in a valley, eighteen miles from any town—no spacious valley, but about two miles long, by three-quarters of a mile in average width, the benefit of which provision is that all the families resident within its circuit will compose, as it were, one larger household personally familiar to your eye, and more or less interesting to your affections. Let the mountains be real mountains, between three and four thousand feet high; and the cottage, a real cottage; not, as a witty author has it, "a cottage, with a double coach-house":[2] let it be, in fact—for I must abide by the actual scene—a white cottage, embowered with flowering shrubs, so chosen as to unfold a succession of flowers upon the walls, and clustering round the windows through all the months of spring, summer, and autumn—beginning, in fact, with May roses, and ending with jasmine. Let it, however, *not* be spring, nor summer, nor autumn—but winter, in his sternest shape. This is a most important point in the science of happiness. And I am surprised to see people overlook it, and think it matter of congratulation that winter is going; or, if coming, is not likely to be a severe one. On the contrary, I put up a petition annually for as much snow, hail, frost, or storm, of one kind or other, as the skies can possibly afford us. Surely everybody is aware of the divine pleasures which attend a winter fireside: candles at four o'clock, warm hearthrugs, tea, a fair tea-maker, shutters closed, curtains flowing in ample draperies on the floor, whilst the wind and rain are raging audibly without,

And at the doors and windows seemed to call,
As heav'n and earth they would together mell:[3]

[1] In the enlarged edition of the *Confessions*, De Quincey says that the third was an English surgeon at Brighton, in Sussex.
[2] Southey, *The Devil's Walk*, 37; Coleridge, *The Devil's Thoughts*, 21.　　[3] mingle

Yet the least entrance find they none at all:
Whence sweeter grows our rest secure in massy hall. 　—*Castle of Indolence.*[1]

All these are items in the description of a winter evening, which must surely be familiar to everybody born in a high latitude. And it is evident that most of these delicacies, like ice-cream, require a very low temperature of the atmosphere to produce them: they are fruits which cannot be ripened without weather stormy or inclement, in some way or other. I am not *"particular,"* as people say, whether it be snow, or black frost, or wind so strong that (as Mr. [Anti-Slavery Clarkson] says) "you may lean your back against it like a post." I can put up even with rain, provided it rains cats and dogs: but something of the sort I must have: and, if I have it not, I think myself in a manner ill-used: for why am I called on to pay so heavily for winter, in coals, and candles, and various privations that will occur even to gentlemen, if I am not to have the article good of its kind? No: a Canadian winter for my money: or a Russian one, where every man is but a co-proprietor with the north wind in the fee-simple[2] of his own ears. Indeed, so great an epicure am I in this matter, that I cannot relish a winter night fully if it be much past St. Thomas's day,[3] and have degenerated into disgusting tendencies to vernal appearances: no: it must be divided by a thick wall of dark nights from all return of light and sunshine.— From the latter weeks of October to Christmas-eve, therefore, is the period during which happiness is in season, which, in my judgment, enters the room with the tea-tray: for tea, though ridiculed by those who are naturally of coarse nerves, or are become so from wine-drinking, and are not susceptible of influence from so refined a stimulant, will always be the favorite beverage of the intellectual: and, for my part, I would have joined Dr. Johnson in a *bellum internecinum*[4] against Jonas Hanway, or any other impious person who should presume to disparage it.—But here, to save myself the trouble of too much verbal description, I will introduce a painter, and give him directions for the rest of the picture. Painters do not like white cottages, unless

[1] Thomson, *The Castle of Indolence*, 1, 383-87 (p. 31).
[2] unrestricted ownership (literally, an estate of inheritance in land, without restriction as to heirs)
[3] Dec. 21.
[4] civil war (See Boswell's *The Life of Samuel Johnson* [Oxford ed., 1904], 1, 209 and 281.)

a good deal weather-stained: but as the reader now understands that it is a winter night, his services will not be required, except for the inside of the house.

Paint me, then, a room seventeen feet by twelve, and not more than seven and a half feet high. This, reader, is somewhat ambitiously styled, in my family, the drawing-room: but, being contrived "a double debt to pay,"[1] it is also, and more justly, termed the library; for it happens that books are the only article of property in which I am richer than my neighbors. Of these, I have about five thousand, collected gradually since my eighteenth year. Therefore, painter, put as many as you can into this room. Make it populous with books: and, furthermore, paint me a good fire; and furniture, plain and modest, befitting the unpretending cottage of a scholar. And, near the fire, paint me a tea-table; and, as it is clear that no creature can come to see one such a stormy night, place only two cups and saucers on the tea-tray: and, if you know how to paint such a thing symbolically, or otherwise, paint me an eternal tea-pot—eternal *a parte ante,* and *a parte post;*[2] for I usually drink tea from eight o'clock at night to four o'clock in the morning. And, as it is very unpleasant to make tea, or to pour it out for oneself, paint me a lovely young woman, sitting at the table. Paint her arms like Aurora's, and her smiles like Hebe's.—But no, dear M[argaret],[3] not even in jest let me insinuate that thy power to illuminate my cottage rests upon a tenure so perishable as mere personal beauty; or that the witchcraft of angelic smiles lies within the empire of any earthly pencil. Pass, then, my good painter, to something more within its power: and the next article brought forward should naturally be myself—a picture of the Opium-eater with his "little golden receptacle of the pernicious drug,"[4] lying beside him on the table. As to the opium, I have no objection to see a picture of *that,* though I would rather see the original: you may paint it, if you choose; but I apprise you, that no "little" receptacle would, even in 1816, answer *my* purpose, who was at a distance from the "stately Pantheon,"[5] and all druggists (mortal or otherwise). No: you may as well paint the real receptacle, which was not of gold, but of glass, and as much like a wine-decanter as possible. Into

this you may put a quart of ruby-colored laudanum: that, and a book of German metaphysics[1] placed by its side, will sufficiently attest my being in the neighborhood; but, as to myself,—there I demur. I admit that, naturally, I ought to occupy the foreground of the picture; that being the hero of the piece, or (if you choose) the criminal at the bar, my body should be had into court. This seems reasonable: but why should I confess, on this point, to a painter? or why confess at all? If the public (into whose private ear I am confidentially whispering my confessions, and not into any painter's) should chance to have framed some agreeable picture for itself, of the Opium-eater's exterior,—should have ascribed to him, romantically, an elegant person, or a handsome face, why should I barbarously tear from it so pleasing a delusion—pleasing both to the public and to me? No: paint me, if at all, according to your own fancy; and, as a painter's fancy should teem with beautiful creations, I cannot fail, in that way, to be a gainer. And now, reader, we have run through all the ten categories of my condition, as it stood about 1816-17: up to the middle of which latter year I judge myself to have been a happy man: and the elements of that happiness I have endeavored to place before you, in the above sketch of the interior of a scholar's library, in a cottage among the mountains, on a stormy winter evening.

But now farewell—a long farewell to happiness—winter or summer! farewell to smiles and laughter! farewell to peace of mind! farewell to hope and to tranquil dreams, and to the blessed consolations of sleep! for more than three years and a half I am now summoned away from these: I am now arrived at an *Iliad* of woes:[2] for I have now to record

THE PAINS OF OPIUM

————as when some great painter dips
His pencil in the gloom of earthquake and eclipse.
—SHELLEY'S *Revolt of Islam.*[3]

Readers, who have thus far accompanied me, I must request your attention to a brief explanatory note on three points:

1. For several reasons, I have not been able to compose the notes for this part of my narrative into any regular and connected shape. I give the notes disjointed as I find

1 Goldsmith, *The Deserted Village,* 229.
2 from the part before and from the part after
3 De Quincey's wife.
4 See p. 1088b, n. 1.
5 See p. 1086b, 11-43, and n. 1.

1 He means by Kant, Fichte, or Schelling.
2 That is, unnumbered woes. See the opening lines of Homer's *Iliad.*
3 Canto 5, st. 23.

them, or have now drawn them up from memory. Some of them point to their own date; some I have dated; and some are undated. Whenever it could answer my purpose to transplant them from the natural or chronological order, I have not scrupled to do so. Sometimes I speak in the present, sometimes in the past tense. Few of the notes, perhaps, were written exactly at the period of time to which they relate; but this can little affect their accuracy, as the impressions were such that they can never fade from my mind. Much has been omitted. I could not, without effort, constrain myself to the task of either recalling, or constructing into a regular narrative, the whole burthen of horrors which lies upon my brain. This feeling partly I plead in excuse, and partly that I am now in London, and am a helpless sort of person, who cannot even arrange his own papers without assistance; and I am separated from the hands which are wont to perform for me the offices of an amanuensis.

2. You will think, perhaps, that I am too confidential and communicative of my own private history. It may be so. But my way of writing is rather to think aloud, and follow my own humors, than much to consider who is listening to me; and, if I stop to consider what is proper to be said to this or that person, I shall soon come to doubt whether any part at all is proper. The fact is, I place myself at a distance of fifteen or twenty years ahead of this time, and suppose myself writing to those who will be interested about me hereafter; and wishing to have some record of a time, the entire history of which no one can know but myself, I do it as fully as I am able with the efforts I am now capable of making, because I know not whether I can ever find time to do it again.

3. It will occur to you often to ask why did I not release myself from the horrors of opium, by leaving it off, or diminishing it. To this I must answer briefly: it might be supposed that I yielded to the fascinations of opium too easily; it cannot be supposed that any man can be charmed by its terrors. The reader may be sure, therefore, that I made attempts innumerable to reduce the quantity. I add that those who witnessed the agonies of those attempts, and not myself, were the first to beg me to desist. But could not I have reduced it a drop a day, or by adding water, have bisected or trisected a drop? A thousand drops bisected would thus have taken nearly six years to reduce; and that way would certainly not have answered. But this is a common mistake of those who know nothing of opium experimentally; I appeal to those who do, whether it is not always found that down to a certain point it can be reduced with ease and even pleasure, but that, after that point, further reduction causes intense suffering. Yes, say many thoughtless persons, who know not what they are talking of, you will suffer a little low spirits and dejection for a few days. I answer, no; there is nothing like low spirits; on the contrary, the mere animal spirits are uncommonly raised: the pulse is improved: the health is better. It is not there that the suffering lies. It has no resemblance to the sufferings caused by renouncing wine. It is a state of unutterable irritation of stomach (which surely is not much like dejection), accompanied by intense perspirations, and feelings such as I shall not attempt to describe without more space at my command.

I shall now enter in medias res,[1] and shall anticipate, from a time when my opium pains might be said to be at their acme, an account of their palsying effects on the intellectual faculties.

My studies have now been long interrupted. I cannot read to myself with any pleasure, hardly with a moment's endurance. Yet I read aloud sometimes for the pleasure of others; because reading is an accomplishment of mine; and, in the slang use of the word accomplishment as a superficial and ornamental attainment, almost the only one I possess: and formerly, if I had any vanity at all connected with any endowment or attainment of mine, it was with this; for I had observed that no accomplishment was so rare. Players are the worst readers of all: John Kemble reads vilely: and Mrs. Siddons, who is so celebrated, can read nothing well but dramatic compositions: Milton she cannot read sufferably. People in general either read poetry without any passion at all, or else overstep the modesty of nature,[2] and read not like scholars. Of late, if I have felt moved by anything in books, it has been by the grand lamentations of Samson Agonistes, or the great harmonies of the Satanic speeches in Paradise Regained, when read aloud by myself. A young lady[3] sometimes comes and drinks tea with us: at

[1] Into the midst of things (Horace, Ars Poetica, 148)
[2] See Hamlet, III, 2, 22.
[3] Probably Dorothy Wordsworth.

her request and M[argaret]'s I now and then read Wordsworth's poems to them. (Wordsworth, by the by, is the only poet I ever met who could read his own verses: often indeed he reads admirably.)

For nearly two years I believe that I read no book but one:[1] and I owe it to the author, in discharge of a great debt of gratitude, to mention what that was. The sublimer and more passionate poets I still read, as I have said, by snatches, and occasionally. But my proper vocation, as I well knew, was the exercise of the analytic understanding. Now, for the most part, analytic studies are continuous, and not to be pursued by fits and starts, or fragmentary efforts. Mathematics, for instance, intellectual philosophy, etc., were all become insupportable to me; and I shrunk from them with a sense of powerless and infantine feebleness that gave me an anguish the greater from remembering the time when I grappled with them to my own hourly delight; and for this further reason, because I had devoted the labor of my whole life, and had dedicated my intellect, blossoms and fruits, to the slow and elaborate toil of constructing one single work, to which I had presumed to give the title of an unfinished work of Spinoza's; viz., *De emendatione humani intellectus*.[2] This was now lying locked up, as by frost, like any Spanish bridge or aqueduct, begun upon too great a scale for the resources of the architect; and, instead of surviving me as a monument of wishes at least, and aspirations, and a life of labor dedicated to the exaltation of human nature in that way in which God had best fitted me to promote so great an object, it was likely to stand a memorial to my children of hopes defeated, of baffled efforts, of materials uselessly accumulated, of foundations laid that were never to support a superstructure,—of the grief and the ruin of the architect. In this state of imbecility, I had, for amusement, turned my attention to political economy; my understanding, which formerly had been as active and restless as a hyena, could not, I suppose (so long as I lived at all), sink into utter lethargy; and political economy offers this advantage to a person in my state, that though it is eminently an organic science (no part, that is to say, but what acts on the whole, as the whole again reacts on each part), yet the several parts may be detached and contemplated singly. Great as was the

1 *Political Economy*, by David Ricardo (1772-1823), a noted English Jewish political economist.
2 of the amendment of the human mind

prostration of my powers at this time, yet I could not forget my knowledge; and my understanding had been for too many years intimate with severe thinkers, with logic, and the great masters of knowledge, not to be aware of the utter feebleness of the main herd of modern economists. I had been led in 1811 to look into loads of books and pamphlets on many branches of economy; and, at my desire, M[argaret] sometimes read to me chapters from more recent works, or parts of parliamentary debates. I saw that these were generally the very dregs and rinsings of the human intellect: and that any man of sound head, and practiced in wielding logic with a scholastic adroitness, might take up the whole academy of modern economists, and throttle them between heaven and earth with his finger and thumb, or bray their fungus heads to powder with a lady's fan. At length, in 1819, a friend in Edinburgh sent me down Mr. Ricardo's book: and recurring to my own prophetic anticipation of the advent of some legislator for this science, I said, before I had finished the first chapter, "Thou art the man!" Wonder and curiosity were emotions that had long been dead in me. Yet I wondered once more: I wondered at myself that I could once again be stimulated to the effort of reading: and much more I wondered at the book. Had this profound work been really written in England during the nineteenth century? Was it possible? I supposed thinking had been extinct in England. Could it be that an Englishman, and he not in academic bowers, but oppressed by mercantile and senatorial cares, had accomplished what all the universities of Europe, and a century of thought, had failed even to advance by one hair's breadth? All other writers had been crushed and overlaid by the enormous weight of facts and documents; Mr. Ricardo had deduced, *a priori*, from the understanding itself, laws which first gave a ray of light into the unwieldy chaos of materials, and had constructed what had been but a collection of tentative discussions into a science of regular proportions, now first standing on an eternal basis.

Thus did one single work of a profound understanding avail to give me a pleasure and an activity which I had not known for years:—it roused me even to write, or, at least, to dictate what M[argaret] wrote for me. It seemed to me that some important truths had escaped even "the inevitable eye" of Mr. Ricardo: and, as these were, for the most part, of such a nature that I could express or illustrate them more briefly and elegantly by algebraic symbols than in the usual clumsy and loitering diction of economists, the whole would not have filled a pocket-book; and being so brief, with M[argaret] for my amanuensis, even at this time, incapable as I was of all general exertion, I drew up my *Prolegomena to all Future Systems of Political Economy*.[1] I hope it will not be found redolent of opium; though, indeed, to most people, the subject itself is a sufficient opiate.

This exertion, however, was but a temporary flash, as the sequel showed—for I designed to publish my work: arrangements were made at a provincial press, about eighteen miles distant, for printing it. An additional compositor was retained, for some days, on this account. The work was even twice advertised: and I was, in a manner, pledged to the fulfillment of my intention. But I had a preface to write; and a dedication, which I wished to make a splendid one, to Mr. Ricardo. I found myself quite unable to accomplish all this. The arrangements were countermanded: the compositor dismissed: and my *Prolegomena* rested peacefully by the side of its elder and more dignified brother.

I have thus described and illustrated my intellectual torpor, in terms that apply, more or less, to every part of the four years during which I was under the Circean[2] spells of opium. But for misery and suffering, I might, indeed, be said to have existed in a dormant state. I seldom could prevail on myself to write a letter; an answer of a few words, to any that I received, was the utmost that I could accomplish; and often *that* not until the letter had lain weeks, or even months, on my writing table. Without the aid of M[argaret] all records of bills paid, or *to be* paid, must have perished: and my whole domestic economy, whatever became of Political Economy, must have gone into irretrievable confusion. I shall not afterwards allude to this part of the case: it is one, however, which the opium-eater will find, in the end, as oppressive and tormenting as any other, from the sense of incapacity and feebleness, from the direct embarrassments incident to the neglect or procrastination of each day's appropriate duties, and from the remorse which must often exasperate the stings of these evils to a reflective and conscientious mind. The opium-eater loses none of his moral sensibilities, or aspirations: he wishes and longs, as earnestly as ever, to realize what he believes possible, and feels to be exacted by duty; but his intellectual apprehension of what is possible infinitely outruns his power, not of execution only, but even of power to attempt. He lies under the weight of incubus and night-mare: he lies in the sight of all that he would fain perform, just as a man forcibly confined to his bed by the mortal languor of a relaxing disease, who is compelled to witness injury or outrage offered to some object of his tenderest love:—he curses the spells which chain him down from motion:—he would lay down his life if he might but get up and walk; but he is powerless as an infant, and cannot even attempt to rise.

I now pass to what is the main subject of these latter confessions, to the history and journal of what took place in my dreams; for these were the immediate and proximate cause of my acutest suffering.

The first notice I had of any important change going on in this part of my physical economy, was from the reawakening of a state of eye generally incident to childhood, or exalted states of irritability. I know not whether my reader is aware that many children, perhaps most, have a power of painting, as it were, upon the darkness, all sorts of phantoms; in some, that power is simply a mechanic affection of the eye; others have a voluntary, or a semi-voluntary power to dismiss or to summon them; or, as a child once said to me when I questioned him on this matter, "I can tell them to go, and they go; but sometimes they come when I don't tell them to come." Whereupon I told him that he had almost as unlimited command over apparitions as a Roman centurion over his soldiers.—In the middle of 1817, I think it was, that this faculty became positively distressing to me: at night, when I lay awake in bed, vast processions passed along in mournful pomp; friezes of never-ending stories, that to my feelings were as sad and solemn as if they were stories drawn from times before Œdipus or Priam—before Tyre—before Memphis. And, at the same time, a corresponding change took place in my dreams; a theatre seemed suddenly opened and lighted up within my brain, which presented nightly spectacles of more than earthly splendor. And the four following facts may be mentioned, as noticeable at this time:

[1] A lost work.
[2] pleasing but harmful (Circe was the sorceress in the *Odyssey* who feasted mariners and then turned them into beasts.)

1. That, as the creative state of the eye increased, a sympathy seemed to arise between the waking and the dreaming states of the brain in one point—that whatsoever I happened to call up and to trace by a voluntary act upon the darkness was very apt to transfer itself to my dreams; so that I feared to exercise this faculty; for, as Midas turned all things to gold, that yet baffled his hopes and defrauded his human desires, so whatever things capable of being visually represented I did but think of in the darkness, immediately shaped themselves into phantoms of the eye; and, by a process apparently no less inevitable, when thus once traced in faint and visionary colors, like writings in sympathetic ink,[1] they were drawn out by the fierce chemistry of my dreams, into insufferable splendor that fretted my heart.

2. For this and all other changes in my dreams were accompanied by deep-seated anxiety and gloomy melancholy, such as are wholly incommunicable by words. I seemed every night to descend, not metaphorically, but literally to descend, into chasms and sunless abysses, depths below depths, from which it seemed hopeless that I could ever reascend. Nor did I, by waking, feel that I *had* reascended. This I do not dwell upon; because the state of gloom which attended these gorgeous spectacles, amounting at least to utter darkness, as of some suicidal despondency, cannot be approached by words.

3. The sense of space, and in the end, the sense of time, were both powerfully affected. Buildings, landscapes, etc., were exhibited in proportions so vast as the bodily eye is not fitted to receive. Space swelled, and was amplified to an extent of unutterable infinity. This, however, did not disturb me so much as the vast expansion of time; I sometimes seemed to have lived for 70 or 100 years in one night; nay, sometimes had feelings representative of a millennium passed in that time, or, however, of a duration far beyond the limits of any human experience.

4. The minutest incidents of childhood, or forgotten scenes of later years, were often revived: I could not be said to recollect them; for if I had been told of them when waking, I should not have been able to acknowledge them as parts of my past experience. But placed as they were before me, in dreams like intuitions, and clothed in all their evanescent circumstances and accompanying feelings, I *recognized* them instantaneously. I was once told by a near relative of mine, that having in her childhood fallen into a river, and being on the very verge of death but for the critical assistance which reached her, she saw in a moment her whole life, in its minutest incidents, arrayed before her simultaneously as in a mirror; and she had a faculty developed as suddenly for comprehending the whole and every part. This, from some opium experiences of mine, I can believe; I have, indeed, seen the same thing asserted twice in modern books, and accompanied by a remark which I am convinced is true; *viz.,* that the dread book of account[1] which the Scriptures speak of is, in fact, the mind itself of each individual. Of this, at least, I feel assured, that there is no such thing as *forgetting* possible to the mind; a thousand accidents may and will interpose a veil between our present consciousness and the secret inscriptions on the mind; accidents of the same sort will also rend away this veil; but alike, whether veiled or unveiled, the inscription remains forever; just as the stars seem to withdraw before the common light of day, whereas, in fact, we all know that it is the light which is drawn over them as a veil—and that they are waiting to be revealed, when the obscuring daylight shall have withdrawn.

Having noticed these four facts as memorably distinguishing my dreams from those of health, I shall now cite a case illustrative of the first fact; and shall then cite any others that I remember, either in their chronological order, or any other that may give them more effect as pictures to the reader.

I had been in youth, and even since, for occasional amusement, a great reader of Livy, whom I confess that I prefer, both for style and matter, to any other of the Roman historians; and I had often felt as most solemn and appalling sounds, and most emphatically representative of the majesty of the Roman people, the two words so often occurring in Livy—*Consul Romanus;* especially when the consul is introduced in his military character. I mean to say that the words *king—sultan—regent,* etc., or any other titles of those who embody in their own persons the collective majesty of a great people, had less power over my reverential feelings. I had also, though no great reader of history, made myself minutely and critically familiar with one period of English history; *viz.,* the period of the Parliamen-

---

[1] A fluid used for invisible writing, which becomes visible when heated.

[1] *Revelation,* 20 :12.

tary War,[1] having been attracted by the moral grandeur of some who figured in that day, and by the many interesting memoirs which survive these unquiet times. Both these parts of my lighter reading, having furnished me often with matter of reflection, now furnished me with matter for my dreams. Often I used to see, after painting upon the blank darkness a sort of rehearsal whilst waking, a crowd of ladies, and perhaps a festival, and dances. And I heard it said, or I said to myself, "These are English ladies from the unhappy times of Charles I. These are the wives and the daughters of those who met in peace, and sat at the same tables, and were allied by marriage or by blood; and yet, after a certain day in August, 1642,[1] never smiled upon each other again, nor met but in the field of battle; and at Marston Moor, at Newbury, or at Naseby, cut asunder all ties of love by the cruel sabre, and washed away in blood the memory of ancient friendship."—The ladies danced, and looked as lovely as the court of George IV. Yet I knew, even in my dream, that they had been in the grave for nearly two centuries.—This pageant would suddenly dissolve: and, at a clapping of hands, would be heard the heart-quaking sound of *Consul Romanus:* and immediately came "sweeping by,"[2] in gorgeous paludaments,[3] Paulus, or Marius, girt round by a company of centurions, with the crimson tunic hoisted on a spear,[4] and followed by the *alalagmos*[5] of the Roman legions.

Many years ago, when I was looking over Piranesi's Antiquities of Rome, Mr. Coleridge, who was standing by, described to me a set of plates by that artist, called his *Dreams,* and which record the scenery of his own visions during the delirium of a fever: some of them (I describe only from memory of Mr. Coleridge's account) representing vast Gothic halls, on the floor of which stood all sorts of engines and machinery, wheels, cables, pulleys, levers, catapults, etc., etc., expressive of enormous power put forth, and resistance overcome. Creeping along the sides of the walls, you perceived a staircase; and upon it, groping his way upwards, was Piranesi himself: follow the stairs a little further, and you perceive it come to a sudden abrupt termination, without any balustrade, and allowing no step onwards to him who had reached the extremity, except into the depths below. Whatever

is to become of poor Piranesi, you suppose, at least, that his labors must in some way terminate here. But raise your eyes, and behold a second flight of stairs still higher: on which again Piranesi is perceived, but this time standing on the very brink of the abyss. Again elevate your eye, and a still more aerial flight of stairs is beheld: and again is poor Piranesi busy on his aspiring labors: and so on, until the unfinished stairs and Piranesi both are lost in the upper gloom of the hall.—With the same power of endless growth and self-reproduction did my architecture proceed in dreams. In the early stage of my malady, the splendors of my dreams were indeed chiefly architectural: and I beheld such pomp of cities and palaces as was never yet beheld by the waking eye, unless in the clouds. From a great modern poet I cite part of a passage which describes, as an appearance actually beheld in the clouds, what in many of its circumstances I saw frequently in sleep:

The appearance, instantaneously disclosed,
Was of a mighty city—boldly say
A wilderness of building, sinking far
And self-withdrawn into a wondrous depth,
Far sinking into splendor—without end!
Fabric it seem'd of diamond, and of gold,
With alabaster domes, and silver spires,
And glazing terrace upon terrace, high
Uplifted; here, serene pavilions bright
In avenues disposed; there, towers begirt
With battlements that on their restless fronts
Bore stars—illumination of all gems!
By earthly nature had the effect been wrought
Upon the dark materials of the storm
Now pacified: on them, and on the coves,
And mountain-steeps and summits, whereunto
The vapors had receded,—taking there
Their station under a cerulean sky, etc., etc.[1]

The sublime circumstance—"battlements that on their *restless* fronts bore stars,"— might have been copied from my architectural dreams, for it often occurred.—We hear it reported of Dryden, and of Fuseli in modern times, that they though proper to eat raw meat for the sake of obtaining splendid dreams: how much better for such a purpose to have eaten opium, which yet I do not remember that any poet is recorded to have done, except the dramatist Shadwell: and in ancient days, Homer is, I think, rightly reputed to have known the virtues of opium.[2]

To my architecture succeeded dreams of lakes and silvery expanses of water:—these

---

[1] The war between Charles I and the Parliamentary party began Aug. 22, 1642.
[2] *Il Penseroso,* 98.
[3] military cloaks   [4] A signal for battle.
[5] battle cry (originally of the Greeks)

[1] Wordsworth, *The Excursion,* 2, 834 ff.
[2] In Homer's *Odyssey,* 4, 220-21, Helen gives to Telemachus a drug which banishes sorrow. This is thought by many persons to be opium. See p. 1087a, 16 and n. 1.

haunted me so much that I feared, though
possibly it will appear ludicrous to a medical man, that some dropsical state or tendency of the brain might thus be making
itself, to use a metaphysical word, *objective;*
and the sentient organ *project* itself as its
own object.—For two months I suffered
greatly in my head—a part of my bodily
structure which had hitherto been so clear
from all touch or taint of weakness, physi-
cally, I mean, that I used to say of it, as the
last Lord Orford said of his stomach, that it
seemed likely to survive the rest of my
person.—Till now I had never felt headache
even, or any the slightest pain, except rheumatic pains caused by my own folly. However, I got over this attack, though it must
have been verging on something very dangerous.

The waters now changed their character,—
from translucent lakes, shining like mirrors,
they now became seas and oceans. And now
came a tremendous change, which, unfolding
itself slowly like a scroll, through many
months, promised an abiding torment; and,
in fact, never left me until the winding up
of my case. Hitherto the human face had
mixed often in my dreams, but not despot-
ically, nor with any special power of tormenting. But now that which I have called
the tyranny of the human face began to
unfold itself. Perhaps some part of my
London life might be answerable for this.
Be that as it may, now it was that upon the
rocking waters of the ocean the human face
began to appear: the sea appeared paved
with innumerable faces, upturned to the
heavens: faces, imploring, wrathful, despairing, surged upwards by thousands, by
myriads, by generations, by centuries:—my
agitation was infinite,—my mind tossed—
and surged with the ocean.

May, 1818.

The Malay has been a fearful enemy for
months. I have been every night, through
his means, transported into Asiatic scenes.
I know not whether others share in my
feelings on this point; but I have often
thought that if I were compelled to forego
England, and to live in China, and among
Chinese manners and modes of life and scenery, I should go mad. The causes of my
horror lie deep and some of them must be
common to others. Southern Asia, in general, is the seat of awful images and associations. As the cradle of the human race, it
would alone have a dim and reverential feeling connected with it. But there are other
reasons. No man can pretend that the wild,

barbarous, and capricious superstitions of
Africa, or of savage tribes elsewhere, affect
him in the way that he is affected by the
ancient, monumental, cruel, and elaborate
religions of Indostan, etc. The mere antiquity of Asiatic things, of their institutions,
histories, modes of faith, etc., is so impressive, that to me the vast age of the race and
name overpowers the sense of youth in the
individual. A young Chinese seems to me
an antediluvian man renewed. Even Englishmen, though not bred in any knowledge of
such institutions, cannot but shudder at the
mystic sublimity of *castes* that have flowed
apart, and refused to mix, through such immemorial tracts of time; nor can any man
fail to be awed by the names of the Ganges
or the Euphrates. It contributes much to
these feelings that southern Asia is, and has
been for thousands of years, the part of the
earth most swarming with human life;
the great *officina gentium*.[1] Man is a weed
in those regions. The vast empires also, into
which the enormous population of Asia has
always been cast, give a further sublimity
to the feelings associated with all Oriental
names or images. In China, over and above
what it has in common with the rest of
southern Asia, I am terrified by the modes
of life, by the manners, and the barrier of
utter abhorrence, and want of sympathy,
placed between us by feelings deeper than I
can analyze. I could sooner live with luna-
tics, or brute animals. All this, and much
more than I can say, or have time to say, the
reader must enter into before he can comprehend the unimaginable horror which these
dreams of Oriental imagery, and mythological tortures, impressed upon me. Under
the connecting feeling of tropical heat and
vertical sunlights, I brought together all
creatures, birds, beasts, reptiles, all trees
and plants, usages and appearances, that are
found in all tropical regions, and assembled
them together in China or Indostan. From
kindred feelings, I soon brought Egypt and
all her gods under the same law. I was
stared at, hooted at, grinned at, chattered at,
by monkeys, by paroquets, by cockatoos. I
ran into pagodas: and was fixed for centuries at the summit, or in secret rooms; I
was the idol; I was the priest; I was worshipped; I was sacrificed. I fled from the
wrath of Brama[2] through all the forests of

[1] beehive of nations
[2] Brahma, the creator, Vishnu, the protector, and
Siva the destroyer, constitute the so-called
Triad of Hindu mythology. Osiris, the creator,
and Isis, his sister and wife, were Egyptian
deities. The ibis and the crocodile were
sacred animals among the Egyptians.

Asia: Vishnu hated me: Seeva laid wait for me. I came suddenly upon Isis and Osiris: I had done a deed, they said, which the ibis and the crocodile trembled at. I was buried for a thousand years in stone coffins, with mummies and sphinxes, in narrow chambers at the heart of eternal pyramids. I was kissed, with cancerous kisses, by crocodiles; and laid, confounded with all unutterable slimy things, amongst reeds and Nilotic[1] mud.

I thus give the reader some slight abstraction of my Oriental dreams, which always filled me with such amazement at the monstrous scenery, that horror seemed absorbed, for a while, in sheer astonishment. Sooner or later, came a reflux of feeling that swallowed up the astonishment, and left me, not so much in terror, as in hatred and abomination of what I saw. Over every form, and threat, and punishment, and dim sightless incarceration, brooded a sense of eternity and infinity that drove me into an oppression as of madness. Into these dreams only, it was, with one or two slight exceptions, that any circumstances of physical horror entered. All before had been moral and spiritual terrors. But here the main agents were ugly birds, or snakes, or crocodiles; especially the last. The cursed crocodile became to me the object of more horror than almost all the rest. I was compelled to live with him; and (as was always the case almost in my dreams) for centuries. I escaped sometimes, and found myself in Chinese houses, with cane tables, etc. All the feet of the tables, sofas, etc., soon became instinct with life: the abominable head of the crocodile, and his leering eyes, looked out at me, multiplied into a thousand repetitions: and I stood loathing and fascinated. And so often did this hideous reptile haunt my dreams, that many times the very same dream was broken up in the very same way: I heard gentle voices speaking to me (I hear everything when I am sleeping); and instantly I awoke: it was broad noon; and my children were standing, hand in hand, at my bedside; come to show me their colored shoes, or new frocks, or to let me see them dressed for going out. I protest that so awful was the transition from the damned crocodile, and the other unutterable monsters and abortions of my dreams, to the sight of innocent *human* natures and of infancy, that, in the mighty and sudden revulsion of mind, I wept, and could not forbear it, as I kissed their faces.

[1] belonging to the Nile

June, 1819.

I have had occasion to remark, at various periods of my life, that the deaths of those whom we love, and indeed the contemplation of death generally, is (*cæteris paribus*)[1] more affecting in summer than in any other season of the year.[2] And the reasons are these three, I think: first, that the visible heavens in summer appear far higher, more distant, and (if such a solecism may be excused) more infinite; the clouds, by which chiefly the eye expounds the distance of the blue pavilion stretched over our heads, are in summer more voluminous, massed, and accumulated in far grander and more towering piles: secondly, the light and the appearance of the declining and the setting sun are much more fitted to be types and characters of the Infinite: and, thirdly, which is the main reason, the exuberant and riotous prodigality of life naturally forces the mind more powerfully upon the antagonist thought of death, and the wintry sterility of the grave. For it may be observed, generally, that wherever two thoughts stand related to each other by a law of antagonism, and exist, as it were, by mutual repulsion, they are apt to suggest each other. On these accounts it is that I find it impossible to banish the thought of death when I am walking alone in the endless days of summer; and any particular death, if not more affecting, at least haunts my mind more obstinately and besiegingly in that season. Perhaps this cause, and a slight incident which I omit, might have been the immediate occasion of the following dream, to which, however, a predisposition must always have existed in my mind; but having been once roused, it never left me, and split into a thousand fantastic varieties, which often suddenly reunited, and composed again the original dream.

I thought that it was a Sunday morning in May, that it was Easter Sunday, and as yet very early in the morning. I was standing, as it seemed to me, at the door of my own cottage. Right before me lay the very scene which could really be commanded from that situation, but exalted, as was usual, and solemnized by the power of dreams. There were the same mountains, and the same lovely valley at their feet; but the mountains were raised to more than Alpine height, and there was interspace far larger between them of meadows and forest lawns; the hedges were rich with white roses; and no

[1] other conditions being the same
[2] See p. 1071b, 12-22; also, *Autobiographic Sketches* (p. 1118a, 26 ff.), and *The English Mail-Coach*, 3, 1 (p. 1151b, 45 ff.).

living creature was to be seen, excepting that in the green churchyard there were cattle tranquilly reposing upon the verdant graves, and particularly round about the grave of a child whom I had tenderly loved,[1] just as I had really beheld them, a little before sunrise in the same summer, when that child died. I gazed upon the well-known scene, and I said aloud (as I thought) to myself, "It yet wants much of sunrise; and it is Easter Sunday; and that is the day on which they celebrate the first-fruits of resurrection. I will walk abroad; old griefs shall be forgotten today; for the air is cool and still, and the hills are high, and stretch away to heaven; and the forest-glades are as quiet as the churchyard; and with the dew I can wash the fever from my forehead, and then I shall be unhappy no longer." And I turned, as if to open my garden gate; and immediately I saw upon the left a scene far different; but which yet the power of dreams had reconciled into harmony with the other. The scene was an Oriental one; and there also it was Easter Sunday, and very early in the morning. And at a vast distance were visible, as a stain upon the horizon, the domes and cupolas of a great city—an image or faint abstraction, caught perhaps in childhood from some picture of Jerusalem. And not a bowshot from me, upon a stone, and shaded by Judean palms, there sat a woman; and I looked; and it was—Ann![2] She fixed her eyes upon me earnestly; and I said to her at length: "So then I have found you at last." I waited: but she answered me not a word. Her face was the same as when I saw it last, and yet again how different! Seventeen years ago, when the lamplight fell upon her face, as for the last time I kissed her lips (lips, Ann, that to me were not polluted), her eyes were streaming with tears: the tears were now wiped away; she seemed more beautiful than she was at that time, but in all other points the same, and not older. Her looks were tranquil, but with unusual solemnity of expression; and I now gazed upon her with some awe, but suddenly her countenance grew dim, and, turning to the mountains, I perceived vapors rolling between us; in a moment, all had vanished; thick darkness came on; and, in the twinkling of an eye, I was far away from mountains, and by lamplight in Oxford Street, walking again with Ann—just as we walked seventeen years before, when we were both children.

[1] Catherine Wordsworth.
[2] See pp. 1077-86.

As a final specimen, I cite one of a different character, from 1820.

The dream commenced with a music which now I often heard in dreams—a music of preparation and of awakening suspense; a music like the opening of the Coronation Anthem, and which, like *that,* gave the feeling of a vast march—of infinite cavalcades filing off—and the tread of innumerable armies. The morning was come of a mighty day—a day of crisis and of final hope for human nature, then suffering some mysterious eclipse, and laboring in some dread extremity. Somewhere, I knew not where—somehow, I knew not how—by some beings, I knew not whom—a battle, a strife, an agony, was conducting,—was evolving like a great drama, or piece of music; with which my sympathy was the more insupportable from my confusion as to its place, its cause, its nature, and its possible issue. I, as is usual in dreams (where, of necessity, we make ourselves central to every movement), had the power, and yet had not the power, to decide it. I had the power, if I could raise myself, to will it, and yet again had not the power, for the weight of twenty Atlantics was upon me, or the oppression of inexpiable guilt. "Deeper than ever plummet sounded,"[1] I lay inactive. Then, like a chorus, the passion deepened. Some greater interest was at stake; some mightier cause than ever yet the sword had pleaded, or trumpet had proclaimed. Then came sudden alarms: hurryings to and fro: trepidations of innumerable fugitives, I knew not whether from the good cause or the bad: darkness and lights: tempest and human faces: and at last, with the sense that all was lost, female forms, and the features that were worth all the world to me, and but a moment allowed, —and clasped hands, and heart-breaking partings, and then—everlasting farewells! and with a sigh, such as the caves of hell sighed when the incestuous mother[2] uttered the abhorred name of death, the sound was reverberated—everlasting farewells! and again, and yet again reverberated—everlasting farewells!

And I awoke in struggles, and cried aloud—"I will sleep no more!"[3]

But I am now called upon to wind up a narrative which has already extended to an unreasonable length. Within more spacious limits, the materials which I have used might

[1] *The Tempest,* V, 1, 56.
[2] Sin. (See *Paradise Lost,* 2, 787 ff.)
[3] See *Macbeth,* II, 2, 35.

have been better unfolded; and much which I have not used might have been added with effect. Perhaps, however, enough has been given. It now remains that I should say something of the way in which this conflict of horrors was finally brought to its crisis. The reader is already aware (from a passage near the beginning of the introduction to the first part) that the opium-eater has, in some way or other, "unwound, almost to its final links, the accursed chain which bound him."[1] By what means? To have narrated this, according to the original intention, would have far exceeded the space which can now be allowed. It is fortunate, as such a cogent reason exists for abridging it, that I should, on a maturer view of the case, have been exceedingly unwilling to injure, by any such unaffecting details, the impression of the history itself, as an appeal to the prudence and the conscience of the yet unconfirmed opium-eater—or even, though a very inferior consideration, to injure its effect as a composition. The interest of the judicious reader will not attach itself chiefly to the subject of the fascinating spells, but to the fascinating power. Not the opium-eater, but the opium, is the true hero of the tale; and the legitimate center on which the interest revolves. The object was to display the marvellous agency of opium, whether for pleasure or for pain: if that is done, the action of the piece has closed.

However, as some people, in spite of all laws to the contrary, will persist in asking what became of the opium-eater, and in what state he now is, I answer for him thus: The reader is aware that opium had long ceased to found its empire on spells of pleasure; it was solely by the tortures connected with the attempt to abjure it, that it kept its hold. Yet, as other tortures, no less it may be thought, attended the non-abjuration of such a tyrant, a choice only of evils was left; and *that* might as well have been adopted, which, however terrific in itself, held out a prospect of final restoration to happiness. This appears true; but good logic gave the author no strength to act upon it. However, a crisis arrived for the author's life, and a crisis for other objects still dearer to him—and which will always be far dearer to him than his life, even now that it is again a happy one.— I saw that I must die if I continued the opium: I determined, therefore, if that should be required, to die in throwing it off. How much I was at that time taking I cannot

say; for the opium which I used had been purchased for me by a friend who afterwards refused to let me pay him; so that I could not ascertain even what quantity I had used within the year. I apprehend, however, that I took it very irregularly: and that I varied from about fifty or sixty grains, to 150 a day. My first task was to reduce it to forty, to thirty, and, as fast as I could, to twelve grains.

I triumphed: but think not, reader, that therefore my sufferings were ended; nor think of me as of one sitting in a *dejected* state. Think of me as of one, even when four months had passed, still agitated, writhing, throbbing, palpitating, shattered; and much, perhaps, in the situation of him who has been racked, as I collect the torments of that state from the affecting account of them left by the most innocent sufferer[1] of the times of James I. Meantime, I derived no benefit from any medicine, except one prescribed to me by an Edinburgh surgeon of great eminence, *viz.*, ammoniated tincture of valerian. Medical account, therefore, of my emancipation I have not much to give: and even that little, as managed by a man so ignorant of medicine as myself, would probably tend only to mislead. At all events, it would be misplaced in this situation. The moral of the narrative is addressed to the opium-eater; and, therefore, of necessity, limited in its application. If he is taught to fear and tremble, enough has been effected. But he may say, that the issue of my case is at least a proof that opium, after a seventeen years' use, and an eight years' abuse of its powers, may still be renounced: and that *he* may chance to bring to the task greater energy than I did, or that with a stronger constitution than mine he may obtain the same results with less. This may be true: I would not presume to measure the efforts of other men by my own: I heartily wish him more energy: I wish him the same success. Nevertheless, I had motives external to myself which he may unfortunately want: and these supplied me with conscientious supports which mere personal interests might fail to supply to a mind debilitated by opium.

Jeremy Taylor conjectures that it may be as painful to be born as to die:[2] I think

1 Quoted from the passage addressed to the reader, at the beginning of the *Confessions.*

1 "William Lithgow: his book (*Travels*, etc.) is ill and pedantically written: but the account of his own sufferings on the rack at Malaga is overpoweringly affecting."—De Quincey.
2 In the enlarged *Confessions*, De Quincey changes the name to Lord Bacon, and in a note refers to Bacon's *Essay on Death.*

it probable: and, during the whole period of diminishing the opium, I had the torments of a man passing out of one mode of existence into another. The issue was not death, but a sort of physical regeneration: and I may add, that ever since, at intervals, I have had a restoration of more than youthful spirits, though under the pressure of difficulties, which, in a less happy state of mind, I should have called misfortunes.

One memorial of my former condition still remains: my dreams are not yet perfectly calm: the dread swell and agitation of the storms have not wholly subsided: the legions that encamped in them are drawing off, but not all departed: my sleep is still tumultuous, and, like the gates of Paradise to our first parents when looking back from afar, it is still, in the tremendous line of Milton—

With dreadful faces throng'd and fiery arms.[1]

. . . .

ON THE KNOCKING AT THE GATE IN MACBETH[2]
1823

From my boyish days I had always felt a great perplexity on one point in *Macbeth*. It was this:—the knocking at the gate which succeeds to the murder of Duncan produced to my feelings an effect for which I never could account. The effect was that it reflected back upon the murderer a peculiar awfulness and a depth of solemnity; yet, however obstinately I endeavored with my understanding to comprehend this, for many years I never could see *why* it should produce such an effect.

Here I pause for one moment to exhort the reader never to pay any attention to his understanding when it stands in opposition to any other faculty of his mind. The mere understanding, however useful and indispensable, is the meanest faculty in the human mind and the most to be distrusted; and yet the great majority of people trust to nothing else,—which may do for ordinary life, but not for philosophical purposes. Of this, out of ten thousand instances that I might produce, I will cite one. Ask of any person whatsoever who is not previously prepared for the demand by a knowledge of perspective, to draw in the rudest way the commonest appearance which depends upon the laws of that science,—as, for instance, to represent the effect of two walls standing at right angles to each other, or the appearance of the houses on each side of a street, as seen by a person looking down the street from one extremity. Now, in all cases, unless the person has happened to observe in pictures how it is that artists produce these effects, he will be utterly unable to make the smallest approximation to it. Yet why? For he has actually seen the effect every day of his life. The reason is that he allows his understanding to overrule his eyes. His understanding, which includes no intuitive knowledge of the laws of vision, can furnish him with no reason why a line which is known and can be proved to be a horizontal line should not *appear* a horizontal line: a line that made any angle with the perpendicular less than a right angle would seem to him to indicate that his houses were all tumbling down together. Accordingly he makes the line of his houses a horizontal line, and fails of course to produce the effect demanded. Here then is one instance out of many in which not only the understanding is allowed to overrule the eyes, but where the understanding is positively allowed to obliterate the eyes, as it were; for not only does the man believe the evidence of his understanding in opposition to that of his eyes, but (which is monstrous) the idiot is not aware that his eyes ever gave such evidence. He does not know that he has seen (and therefore, *quoad*,[1] his consciousness has *not* seen) that which he *has* seen every day of his life. But to return from this digression,—my understanding could furnish no reason why the knocking at the gate in *Macbeth* should produce any effect, direct or reflected. In fact, my understanding said positively that it could *not* produce any effect. But I knew better; I felt that it did; and I waited and clung to the problem until further knowledge should enable me to solve it. At length, in 1812,[2] Mr. Williams made his *début* on the stage of Ratcliffe Highway, and executed those unparalleled murders which have procured for him such a brilliant and undying reputation. On which murders, by the way, I must observe, that in one respect they have had an ill effect, by making the connoisseur in murder very fastidious in his taste, and dissatisfied with anything that has been since done in that line. All other murders look pale by the deep crimson of his; and, as an amateur[3] once said to me in a querulous tone, "There has been absolutely nothing *doing* since his time, or noth-

[1] *Paradise Lost*, 12, 644.
[2] Act II, 2-3.

[1] therefore
[2] It was in December, 1811.
[3] A person fond of something.

ing that's worth speaking of." But this is wrong, for it is unreasonable to expect all men to be great artists, and born with the genius of Mr. Williams. Now it will be remembered that in the first of these murders (that of the Marrs) the same incident (of a knocking at the door soon after the work of extermination was complete) did actually occur which the genius of Shakspere has invented; and all good judges, and the most eminent dilettanti, acknowledged the felicity of Shakspere's suggestion as soon as it was actually realized. Here then was a fresh proof that I had been right in relying on my own feeling in opposition to my understanding; and again I set myself to study the problem. At length I solved it to my own satisfaction; and my solution is this:—Murder, in ordinary cases, where the sympathy is wholly directed to the case of the murdered person, is an incident of coarse and vulgar horror; and for this reason—that it flings the interest exclusively upon the natural but ignoble instinct by which we cleave to life: an instinct which, as being indispensable to the primal law of self-preservation, is the same in kind (though different in degree) amongst all living creatures. This instinct, therefore, because it annihilates all distinctions, and degrades the greatest of men to the level of "the poor beetle that we tread on,"[1] exhibits human nature in its most abject and humiliating attitude. Such an attitude would little suit the purposes of the poet. What then must he do? He must throw the interest on the murderer. Our sympathy must be with *him* (of course I mean a sympathy of comprehension, a sympathy by which we enter into his feelings, and are made to understand them—not a sympathy of pity or approbation).[2] In the murdered person all strife of thought, all flux and reflux of passion and of purpose, are crushed by one overwhelming panic; the fear of instant death smites him "with its petrific[3] mace." But in the murderer, such a murderer as a poet will condescend to, there must

<hr>

[1] *Measure for Measure*, III, 1, 78.

[2] "It seems almost ludicrous to guard and explain my use of a word in a situation where it would naturally explain itself. But it has become necessary to do so, in consequence of the unscholar-like use of the word *sympathy*, at present so general, by which, instead of taking it in its proper sense, as the act of reproducing in our minds the feelings of another, whether for hatred, indignation, love, pity, or approbation, it is made a mere synonym of the word *pity*; and hence, instead of saying, 'sympathy *with* another,' many writers adopt the monstrous barbarism of 'sympathy *for* another.'"—De Quincey.

[3] petrifying (*Paradise Lost*, 10, 293 ff.)

be raging some great storm of passion—jealousy, ambition, vengeance, hatred—which will create a hell within him; and into this hell we are to look.

In *Macbeth*, for the sake of gratifying his own enormous and teeming faculty of creation, Shakspere has introduced two murderers: and, as usual in his hands, they are remarkably discriminated: but—though in Macbeth the strife of mind is greater than in his wife, the tiger spirit not so awake, and his feelings caught chiefly by contagion from her—yet, as both were finally involved in the guilt of murder, the murderous mind of necessity is finally to be presumed in both. This was to be expressed; and on its own account, as well as to make it a more proportionable antagonist to the unoffending nature of their victim, "the gracious Duncan,"[1] and adequately to expound "the deep damnation of his taking off,"[2] this was to be expressed with peculiar energy. We were to be made to feel that the human nature,—*i. e.*, the divine nature of love and mercy, spread through the hearts of all creatures, and seldom utterly withdrawn from man—was gone, vanished, extinct, and that the fiendish nature had taken its place. And, as this effect is marvellously accomplished in the *dialogues* and *soliloquies* themselves, so it is finally consummated by the expedient under consideration; and it is to this that I now solicit the reader's attention. If the reader has ever witnessed a wife, daughter, or sister, in a fainting fit, he may chance to have observed that the most affecting moment in such a spectacle is *that* in which a sigh and a stirring announce the recommencement of suspended life. Or, if the reader has ever been present in a vast metropolis on the day when some great national idol was carried in funeral pomp to his grave, and, chancing to walk near the course through which it passed, has felt powerfully, in the silence and desertion of the streets and in the stagnation of ordinary business, the deep interest which at that moment was possessing the heart of man—if all at once he should hear the death-like stillness broken up by the sound of wheels rattling away from the scene, and making known that the transitory vision was dissolved, he will be aware that at no moment was his sense of the complete suspension and pause in ordinary human concerns so full and affecting as at that moment when the suspension ceases, and the goings-on of

<hr>

[1] *Macbeth*, III, 1, 65.

[2] *Ibid.*, I, 7, 20.

human life are suddenly resumed. All action in any direction is best expounded, measured, and made apprehensible, by reaction. Now apply this to the case in *Macbeth*. Here, as I have said, the retiring of the human heart and the entrance of the fiendish heart was to be expressed and made sensible. Another world has stepped in; and the murderers are taken out of the region of human things, human purposes, human desires. They are transfigured: Lady Macbeth is "unsexed";[1] Macbeth has forgot that he was born of woman; both are conformed to the image of devils; and the world of devils is suddenly revealed. But how shall this be conveyed and made palpable? In order that a new world may step in, this world must for a time disappear. The murderers, and the murder, must be insulated—cut off by an immeasurable gulf from the ordinary tide and succession of human affairs— locked up and sequestered in some deep recess; we must be made sensible that the world of ordinary life is suddenly arrested— laid asleep—tranced—racked into a dread armistice; time must be annihilated; relation to things without abolished; and all must pass self-withdrawn into a deep syncope and suspension of earthly passion. Hence it is that, when the deed is done, when the work of darkness is perfect, then the world of darkness passes away like a pageantry in the clouds: the knocking at the gate is heard, and it makes known audibly that the reaction has commenced; the human has made its reflux upon the fiendish: the pulses of life are beginning to beat again; and the re-establishment of the goings-on of the world in which we live first makes us profoundly sensible of the awful parenthesis that had suspended them.

O mighty poet! Thy works are not as those of other men, simply and merely great works of art, but are also like the phenomena of nature, like the sun and the sea, the stars and the flowers, like frost and snow, rain and dew, hail-storm and thunder, which are to be studied with entire submission of our own faculties, and in the perfect faith that in them there can be no too much or too little, nothing useless or inert, but that, the farther we press in our discoveries, the more we shall see proofs of design and self-supporting arrangement where the careless eye had seen nothing but accident!

[1] Macbeth, I, 5, 42.

From RECOLLECTIONS OF CHARLES LAMB
1838

Amongst the earliest literary acquaintances I made was that with the inimitable Charles Lamb: inimitable, I say, but the word is too limited in its meaning; for, as is said of Milton in that well-known life of him attached to all common editions of the *Paradise Lost* (Fenton's, I think), "in both senses he was above imitation." Yes; it was as impossible to the moral nature of Charles Lamb that he should imitate another as, in an intellectual sense, it was impossible that any other should successfully imitate him. To write with patience even, not to say genially, for Charles Lamb it was a very necessity of his constitution that he should write from his own wayward nature; and that nature was so peculiar that no other man, the ablest at mimicry, could counterfeit its voice. But let me not anticipate; for these were opinions about Lamb which I had not when I first knew him, nor could have had by any reasonable title. "Elia,"[1] be it observed, the exquisite "Elia," was then unborn; Lamb had as yet published nothing to the world which proclaimed him in his proper character of a most original man of genius:[2] at best, he could have been thought no more than a man of talent—and of talent moving in a narrow path, with a power rather of mimicking the quaint and the fantastic than any large grasp over catholic beauty. And, therefore, it need not offend the most doting admirer of Lamb as he is *now* known to us, a brilliant star forever

[1] The pseudonym of Charles Lamb.
[2] "'Man of genius' . . . 'man of talent':— I have, in another place, laid down what I conceive to be the true ground of distinction between *genius* and *talent:* which lies mainly in this—that genius is intellectual power impregnated with the *moral* nature, and expresses a synthesis of the active in man with his original organic capacity of pleasure and pain. Hence the very word *genius*, because the *genial* nature in its whole organization is expressed and involved in it. Hence, also, arises the reason that genius is always peculiar and individual; one man's genius never exactly repeats another man's. But talent is the same in all men; and that which is effected by talent can never serve to identify or indicate its author. Hence, too, that, although talent is the object of respect, it never conciliates love; you love a man of talent perhaps *in concreto*, but not talent; whereas genius, even for itself, is idolized. I am the more proud of this distinction since I have seen the utter failure of Mr. Coleridge, judging from his attempt in his *Table-Talk*." —De Quincey. For the other discussions referred to, see De Quincey's *Autobiographic Sketches*, The Nation of London (Works, ed. Masson, 1, 194 n.), and *John Keats* (Works, ed. Masson, 11, 382); also Coleridge's *Table Talk*, May 21, 1830, and Aug. 20, 1833.

fixed in the firmament of English Literature, that I acknowledge myself to have sought his acquaintance rather under the reflex honor he had enjoyed of being known as Coleridge's friend than for any which he yet held directly and separately in his own person. My earliest advances towards this acquaintance had an inauspicious aspect; and it may be worth while reporting the circumstances, for they were characteristic of Charles Lamb; and the immediate result was—that we parted, not perhaps (as Lamb says of his philosophic friend R. and the Parisians) "with mutual contempt," but at least with coolness; and, on my part, with something that might have even turned to disgust—founded, however, entirely on my utter misapprehension of Lamb's character and his manners—had it not been for the winning goodness of Miss Lamb,[1] before which all resentment must have melted in a moment.

It was either late in 1804 or early in 1805, according to my present computations, that I had obtained from a literary friend a letter of introduction to Mr. Lamb. All that I knew of his works was his play of *John Woodvil*, which I had bought in Oxford, and perhaps *I* only had bought throughout that great University, at the time of my matriculation there, about the Christmas of 1803. Another book fell into my hands on that same morning, I recollect—the *Gebir*[2] of Mr. Walter Savage Landor, which astonished me by the splendor of its descriptions (for I had opened accidentally upon the sea-nymph's marriage with Tamor, the youthful brother of Gebir—and I bought this also. Afterwards, when placing these two most unpopular of books on the same shelf with the other far holier idols of my heart, the joint poems of Wordsworth and Coleridge as then associated in the *Lyrical Ballads*—poems not equally unknown, perhaps a *little* better known, but only with the result of being more openly scorned, rejected—I could not but smile internally at the fair prospect I had of congregating a library which no man had read but myself. *John Woodvil* I had almost studied, and Miss Lamb's pretty *High-Born Helen*, and the ingenious imitations of Burton;[3] these I had read, and, to a certain degree, must have admired, for some parts of them had settled without effort in my memory. I

had read also the *Edinburgh*[1] notice of them; and with what contempt may be supposed from the fact that my veneration for Wordsworth transcended all that I felt for any created being, past or present; insomuch that, in the summer, or spring rather, of that same year, and full eight months before I first went to Oxford, I had ventured to address a letter to him, through his publishers, the Messrs. Longman (which letter, Miss Wordsworth in after years assured me they believed to be the production of some person much older than I represented myself), and that in due time I had been honored by a long answer from Wordsworth; an honor which, I well remember, kept me awake, from mere excess of pleasure, through a long night in June, 1803. It was not to be supposed that the very feeblest of admirations could be shaken by mere scorn and contumely, unsupported by any shadow of a reason. Wordsworth, therefore, could not have suffered in any man's opinion from the puny efforts of this new autocrat amongst reviewers; but what was said of Lamb, though not containing one iota of criticism, either good or bad, had certainly more point and cleverness. The supposition that *John Woodvil* might be a lost drama, recovered from the age of Thespis,[2] and entitled to the hircus,[3] etc., must, I should think, have won a smile from Lamb himself; or why say "Lamb himself," which means "*even* Lamb," when he would have been the *very* first to laugh (as he was afterwards among the first to hoot at his own farce),[4] provided only he could detach his mind from the ill-nature and hard contempt which accompanied the wit. This wit had certainly not dazzled my eyes in the slightest degree. So far as I was left at leisure by a more potent order of poetry to think of the *John Woodvil* at all, I had felt and acknowledged a delicacy and tenderness in the situations as well as the sentiments, but disfigured, as I thought, by quaint, grotesque, and *mimetic* phraseology. The main defect, however, of which I complained, was defect of power. I thought Lamb had no right to take his station amongst the inspired writers who had just then risen to throw new blood into

---

[1] Lamb's sister Mary.
[2] See p. 985. The marriage of Tamar and the sea-nymph is described in Book 6.
[3] Lamb's imitations were called *Curious Fragments*.

[1] *The Edinburgh Review*, April, 1803 (vol. 2, 90-98).
[2] That is, from the rudest age of the drama. Thespis (6th cent. B. C.) is the reputed founder of tragedy.
[3] goat (said to have been the prize of tragedy in the time of Thespis)
[4] Lamb's farce, *Mr. H.*, was hooted off the stage at its first appearance, in 1806.

our literature, and to breathe a breath of life through the worn-out, or, at least, torpid organization of the national mind. He belonged, I thought, to the old literature; and, as a poet, he certainly does. There were in his verses minute scintillations of genius—now and then, even a subtle sense of beauty; and there were shy graces, lurking half-unseen, like violets in the shade. But there was no power on a colossal scale; no breadth; no choice of great subjects; no wrestling with difficulty; no creative energy. So I thought then; and so I should think now, if Lamb were viewed chiefly as a poet. Since those days he has established his right to a seat in any company. But why? and in what character? As "Elia":—the essays of "Elia" are as exquisite a gem amongst the jewelry of literature as any nation can show. They do not, indeed, suggest to the typifying imagination a *Last Supper* of da Vinci or a *Group from the Sistine Chapel*, but they suggest some exquisite cabinet painting; such, for instance, as that Carlo Dolce known to all who have visited Lord Exeter's place of Burleigh (by the way, I bar the allusion to *Charles* Lamb which a shameless punster suggests in the name *Carlo Dolce*[1]); and in this also resembling that famous picture— that many critics (Hazlitt amongst others) can see little or nothing in it. *Quam nihil ad genium, Papiniane, tuum!*[2] Those, therefore, err, in my opinion, who present Lamb to our notice amongst the poets. Very pretty, very elegant, very tender, very beautiful verses he has written; nay, twice he has written verses of extraordinary force, almost demoniac force—*viz., The Three Graves,* and *The Gipsy's Malison.*[3] But speaking generally, he writes verses as one to whom that function was a secondary and occasional function, not his original and natural vocation—not an ἔργον, but a πάρεργον.[4]

For the reasons, therefore, I have given, never thinking of Charles Lamb as a poet, and, at that time, having no means for judging of him in any other character, I had requested the letter of introduction to him rather with a view to some further knowledge of Coleridge (who was then ab-

sent from England) than from any special interest about Lamb himself. However, I felt the extreme discourtesy of approaching a man and asking for his time and civility under such an avowal: and the letter, therefore, as I believe, or as I requested, represented me in the light of an admirer. I hope it did; for that character might have some excuse for what followed, and heal the unpleasant impression likely to be left by a sort of *fracas* which occurred at my first meeting with Lamb. This was so characteristic of Lamb that I have often laughed at it since I came to know what *was* characteristic of Lamb.

But first let me describe my brief introductory call upon him at the India House. I had been told that he was never to be found at home except in the evenings; and to have called then would have been, in a manner, forcing myself upon his hospitalities, and at a moment when he might have confidential friends about him; besides that, he was sometimes tempted away to the theatres. I went, therefore, to the India House; made inquiries amongst the servants; and, after some trouble (for *that* was early in his Leadenhall Street career, and possibly he was not much known), I was shown into a small room, or else a small section of a large one (thirty-four years affects one's remembrance of some circumstances), in which was a very lofty writing desk, separated by a still higher railing from that part of the floor on which the profane—the laity, like myself—were allowed to approach the *clerus,* or clerkly rulers of the room. Within the railing sat, to the best of my remembrance, six quill-driving gentlemen; not gentlemen whose duty or profession it was merely to drive the quill, but who were then driving it—*gens de plume,*[1] such *in esse,* as well as *in posse*—in act as well as habit; for, as if they supposed me a spy sent by some superior power to report upon the situation of affairs as surprised by me, they were all too profoundly immersed in their oriental studies to have any sense of my presence. Consequently, I was reduced to a necessity of announcing myself and my errand. I walked, therefore, into one of the two open doorways of the railing, and stood closely by the high stool of him who occupied the first place within the little aisle. I touched his arm, by way of recalling him from his lofty Leadenhall speculation to this sublunary world; and, presenting my letter,

---

[1] Italian for "sweet Charles."
[2] How not at all in accord with your taste, Papinianus. Papinianus (175-212) was a famous Roman lawyer and jurist. De Quincey means Hazlitt. The expression is found on the title page of the 2nd, 3rd, and 4th editions of Wordsworth and Coleridge's *Lyrical Ballads.*
[3] For these poems, see p. 943.
[4] Not a vocation, but an avocation.

[1] men of the pen

asked if that gentleman (pointing to the address) were really a citizen of the present room; for I had been repeatedly mislead, by the directions given me, into wrong rooms. The gentleman smiled; it was a smile not to be forgotten. This was Lamb. And here occurred a *very, very* little incident—one of those which pass so fugitively that they are gone and hurrying away into Lethe almost before your attention can have arrested them; but it was an incident which, to me, who happened to notice it, served to express the courtesy and delicate consideration of Lamb's manner. The seat upon which he sat was a very high one; so absurdly high, by the way, that I can imagine no possible use or sense in such an altitude, unless it were to restrain the occupant from playing truant at the fire by opposing Alpine difficulties to his descent.

Whatever might be the original purpose of this aspiring seat, one serious dilemma arose from it, and this it was which gave the occasion to Lamb's act of courtesy. Somewhere there is an anecdote, meant to illustrate the ultra-obsequiousness of the man,—either I have heard of it in connection with some actual man known to myself, or it is told in a book of some historical coxcomb,—that, being on horseback, and meeting some person or other whom it seemed advisable to flatter, he actually dismounted, in order to pay his court by a more ceremonious bow. In Russia, as we all know, this was, at one time, upon meeting any of the Imperial family, an act of legal necessity: and there, accordingly, but there only, it would have worn no ludicrous aspect. Now, in this situation of Lamb's, the act of descending from his throne, a very elaborate process, with steps and stages analogous to those on horseback—of slipping your right foot out of the stirrup, throwing your leg over the crupper, etc.—was, to all intents and purposes, the same thing as dismounting from a great elephant of a horse. Therefore it both was, and was felt to be by Lamb, supremely ludicrous. On the other hand, to have sate still and stately upon this aerial station, to have bowed condescendingly from this altitude, would have been—not ludicrous indeed; performed by a very superb person and supported by a superb bow, it might have been vastly fine, and even terrifying to many young gentlemen under sixteen; but it would have had an air of ungentlemanly assumption. Between these extremes, therefore, Lamb had to choose;—between appearing ridiculous himself for a moment, by going through a ridiculous evolution which no man could execute with grace; or, on the other hand, appearing lofty and assuming, in a degree which his truly humble nature (for he was the humblest of men in the pretensions which he put forward for himself) must have shrunk from with horror. Nobody who knew Lamb can doubt how the problem was solved: he began to dismount instantly; and, as it happened that the very first *round* of his descent obliged him to turn his back upon me as if for a sudden purpose of flight, he had an excuse for laughing; which he did heartily —saying, at the same time, something to this effect: that I must not judge from first appearances; that he should revolve upon me; that he was not going to fly; and other facetiæ, which challenged a general laugh from the clerical brotherhood.

When he had reached the basis of terra firma on which I was standing, naturally, as a mode of thanking him for his courtesy, I presented my hand; which, in a general case, I should certainly not have done; for I cherished, in an ultra-English degree, the English custom (a wise custom) of bowing in frigid silence on a first introduction to a stranger; but, to a man of literary talent, and one who had just practiced so much kindness in my favor at so probable a hazard to himself of being laughed at for his pains, I could not maintain that frosty reserve. Lamb took my hand; did not absolutely reject it: but rather repelled my advance by his manner. This, however, long afterwards I found, was only a habit derived from his too great sensitiveness to the variety of people's feelings, which run through a gamut so infinite of degrees and modes as to make it unsafe for any man who respects himself to be too hasty in his allowances of familiarity Lamb had, as he was entitled to have, a high self-respect; and me he probably suspected (as a young Oxonian) of some aristocratic tendencies. The letter of introduction, containing (I imagine) no matters of business, was speedily run through; and I instantly received an invitation to spend the evening with him. Lamb was not one of those who catch at the chance of escaping from a bore by fixing some distant day, when accidents (in duplicate proportion, perhaps, to the number of intervening days) may have carried you away from the place: he sought to benefit by no luck of that kind; for he was, with his limited income—and I say it deliberately—

positively the most hospitable man I have
known in this world. That night, the same
night, I was to come and spend the evening
with him. I had gone to the India House
with the express purpose of accepting whatever
invitation he should give me; and,
therefore, I accepted this, took my leave,
and left Lamb in the act of resuming his
aerial position.

I was to come so early as to drink tea with
Lamb; and the hour was seven. He lived
in the Temple; and I, who was not then,
as afterwards I became, a student and
member of "the Honorable Society of the
Middle Temple," did not know much of the
localities. However, I found out his abode,
not greatly beyond my time: nobody had
been asked to meet me,—which a little surprised
me, but I was glad of it; for, besides
Lamb, there was present his sister, Miss
Lamb, of whom, and whose talents and
sweetness of disposition, I had heard. I
turned the conversation, upon the first opening
which offered, to the subject of Coleridge;
and many of my questions were
answered satisfactorily, because seriously,
by Miss Lamb. But Lamb took a pleasure
in baffling me, or in throwing ridicule upon
the subject. Out of this grew the matter of
our affray. We were speaking of *The Ancient
Mariner*.[1] Now, to explain what followed,
and a little to excuse myself, I must
beg the reader to understand that I was
under twenty years of age, and that my
admiration for Coleridge (as, in perhaps
a still greater degree, for Wordsworth) was
literally in no respect short of a religious
feeling: it had, indeed, all the sanctity of
religion, and all the tenderness of a human
veneration. Then, also, to imagine the
strength which it would derive from circumstances
that do not exist now, but did then,
let the reader further suppose a case—not
such as he may have known since that era
about Sir Walter Scotts and Lord Byrons,
where every man you could possibly fall
foul of, early or late, night or day, summer
or winter, was in perfect readiness to feel
and express his sympathy with the admirer—
but when no man, beyond one or two in each
ten thousand, had so much as heard of either
Coleridge or Wordsworth, and that one, or
those two, knew them only to scorn them,
trample on them, spit upon them. Men so
abject in public estimation, I maintain, as
that Coleridge and that Wordsworth, had
not existed before, have not existed since,

will not exist again. We have heard in old
times of donkeys insulting effete or dying
lions by kicking them; but in the case of
Coleridge and Wordsworth it was effete
donkeys that kicked living lions. They,
Coleridge and Wordsworth, were the Pariahs[1]
of literature in those days: as much
scorned wherever they were known; but
escaping that scorn only because they were
as little known as Pariahs, and even more
obscure.

Well, after this bravura,[2] by way of conveying
my sense of the real position then
occupied by these two authors—a position
which thirty and odd years have altered, by
a revolution more astonishing and total than
ever before happened in literature or in
life—let the reader figure to himself the
sensitive horror with which a young person,
carrying his devotion about with him, of
necessity, as the profoundest of secrets, like
a primitive Christian amongst a nation of
Pagans, or a Roman Catholic convert
amongst the bloody idolators of Japan[3]—
in Oxford, above all places, hoping for no
sympathy, and feeling a daily grief, almost
a shame, in harboring this devotion to that
which, nevertheless, had done more for the
expansion and sustenance of his own inner
mind than all literature besides—let the
reader figure, I say, to himself, the shock
with which such a person must recoil from
hearing the very friend and associate of
these authors utter what seemed at that time
a burning ridicule of all which belonged to
them—their books, their thoughts, their
places, their persons. This had gone on for
some time before we came upon the ground
of *The Ancient Mariner;* I had been grieved,
perplexed, astonished; and how else could I
have felt reasonably, knowing nothing of
Lamb's propensity to mystify a stranger;
he, on the other hand, knowing nothing of
the depth of my feelings on these subjects,
and that they were not so much mere literary
preferences as something that went deeper
than life or household affections? At length,
when he had given utterance to some ferocious
canon of judgment, which seemed to
question the entire value of the poem, I said,
perspiring (I dare say) in this detestable
crisis—"But, Mr. Lamb, good heavens! how
is it possible you can allow yourself in such

---

[1] outcasts (A Pariah properly is a member of a
very extensive low caste in Southern India,
but the name was extended to members of
any low Hindu caste, and by Europeans applied
to persons of no caste.)

[2] Bravura is a brilliant style of music.

[3] Japan persecuted Christians until the middle of
the 19th century.

[1] See p. 361.

opinions? What instance could you bring from the poem that would bear you out in these insinuations?"—"Instances?" said Lamb: "oh, I'll instance you, if you come to that. Instance, indeed! Pray, what do you say to this—

> The many men so beautiful,
> And they all dead did lie?[1]

So beautiful, indeed! Beautiful! Just think of such a gang of Wapping vagabonds,[2] all covered with pitch, and chewing tobacco; and the old gentleman himself—what do you call him?—the bright-eyed fellow?"[3] What more might follow I never heard; for, at this point, in a perfect rapture of horror, I raised my hands—both hands—to both ears; and, without stopping to think or to apologize, I endeavored to restore equanimity to my disturbed sensibilities by shutting out all further knowledge of Lamb's impieties. At length he seemed to have finished; so I, on my part, thought I might venture to take off the embargo: and in fact he *had* ceased; but no sooner did he find me restored to my hearing than he said with a most sarcastic smile—which he could assume upon occasion—"If you please, sir, we'll say grace before we begin." I know not whether Lamb were really piqued or not at the mode by which I had expressed my disturbance: Miss Lamb certainly was not; her goodness led her to pardon me, and to treat me—in whatever light she might really view my almost involuntary rudeness—as the party who had suffered wrong; and, for the rest of the evening, she was so pointedly kind and conciliatory in her manner that I felt greatly ashamed of my boyish failure in self-command. Yet, after all, Lamb necessarily appeared so much worse, in my eyes, as a traitor is worse than an open enemy.

Lamb, after this one visit—not knowing at that time any particular reason for continuing to seek his acquaintance—I did not trouble with my calls for some years. At length, however, about the year 1808, and for the six or seven following years, in my evening visits to Coleridge, I used to meet him again; not often, but sufficiently to correct the altogether very false impression I had received of his character and manners. . . .

[1] *The Rime of the Ancient Mariner,* 236-7 (p. 364).
[2] The district of Wapping along the Thames in London, is the favorite haunt of sailors.
[3] *The Rime of the Ancient Mariner,* 20 (p. 361).

STYLE
1840-41

From PART I

.   .   .   .   .   .

It is a fault, amongst many faults, of such works as we have on this subject of style, that they collect the list of qualities, good or bad, to which composition is liable, not under any principle from which they might be deduced *à priori,* so as to be assured that all had been enumerated, but by a tentative groping, a mere conjectural estimate. The word *style* has with us a twofold meaning: one sense, the narrow one, expressing the mere *synthesis onomatōn,*[1] the syntaxis or combination of words into sentences; the other of far wider extent, and expressing all possible relations that can arise between thoughts and words—the total effect of a writer, as derived from manner. Style may be viewed as an *organic* thing and as a *mechanic* thing. By *organic,* we mean that which, being acted upon, reacts, and which propogates the communicated power without loss; by *mechanic,* that which, being impressed with motion, cannot throw it back without loss, and therefore soon comes to an end. The human body is an elaborate system of organs; it is sustained by organs. But the human body is exercised as a machine, and, as such, may be viewed in the arts of riding, dancing, leaping, etc., subject to the laws of motion and equilibrium. Now, the use of words is an organic thing, in so far as language is connected with thoughts and modified with thoughts. It is a mechanic thing, in so far as words in combination determine or modify each other. The science of style, as an organ of thought, of style in relation to the ideas and feelings, might be called the *organology* of style. The science of style, considered as a machine, in which words act upon words, and through a particular grammar, might be called the *mechanology* of style. It is of little importance by what name these two functions of composition are expressed. But it is of great importance not to confound the functions; that function by which style maintains a commerce with thought, and that by which it chiefly communicates with grammar and with words. A pedant only will insist upon the names; but the distinction in the ideas, under some name, can be neglected only by the man who is careless of logic.

We know not how far we may be ever

[1] putting together of nouns (See Aristotle's *Rhetoric,* III, 2, 2, 26.)

called upon to proceed with this discussion: if it should happen that we were, an interesting field of questions would lie before us for the first part, the organology. It would lead us over the ground trodden by the Greek and Roman rhetoricians; and over those particular questions which have arisen by the contrast between the circumstances of the ancients and our own since the origin of printing. Punctuation,[1] trivial as such an innovation may seem, was the product of typography; and it is interesting to trace the effects upon style even of that one slight addition to the resources of logic. Previously, a man was driven to depend for his security against misunderstanding upon the pure virtue of his syntax. Miscollocation or dislocation of related words disturbed the whole sense; its least effect was to give no sense; often it gave a dangerous sense. Now, punctuation was an artificial machinery for maintaining the integrity of the sense against all mistakes of the writer; and, as one consequence, it withdrew the energy of men's anxieties from the natural machinery, which lay in just and careful arrangement. Another and still greater machinery of art for the purpose of maintaining the sense, and with the effect of relaxing the care of the writer, lay in the exquisitely artificial structure of the Latin language, which, by means of its terminal forms, indicated the arrangement, and referred the proper predicate to the proper subject, spite of all that affectation or negligence could do to disturb the series of the logic or the succession of the syntax. Greek, of course, had the same advantage in kind, but not in degree; and thence rose some differences which have escaped all notice of rhetoricians. Here also would properly arise the question started by Charles Fox (but probably due originally

to the conversation of some far subtler friend, such as Edmund Burke), how far the practice of footnotes—a practice purely modern in its *form*—is reconcilable with the laws of just composition; and whether in virtue, though not in form, such footnotes did not exist for the ancients, by an evasion we could point out.[1] The question is clearly one which grows out of style in its relations to thought—how far, *viz.*, such an excrescence as a note argues that the sentence to which it is attached has not received the benefit of a full development for the conception involved; whether if thrown into the furnace again and remelted, it might not be so recast as to absorb the redundancy which had previously flowed over into a note. Under this head would fall not only all the differential questions of style and composition between us and the ancients, but also the questions of merit as fairly distributed amongst the moderns compared with each other. The French, as we recently insisted,[2] undoubtedly possess one vast advantage over all other nations in the good taste which governs the arrangement of their sentences; in the simplicity (a strange pretension to make for anything French) of the modulation under which their thoughts flow; in the absence of all cumbrous involution, and in the quick succession of their periods.[3] In reality this invaluable merit tends to an excess; and the *style coupé* as opposed to the *style soutenu*,[4] flippancy opposed to gravity, the subsultory[5] to the continuous, these are the two frequent extremities to which the French manner betrays men. Better, however, to be flippant than, by a revolting form of tumor and perplexity, to lead men into habits of intellect such as result from the modern vice of English style. Still, with all its practical value, it is evident that the intellectual merits of the French style are but small.[6] They are chiefly negative, in the first place; and, secondly, founded in the accident of their colloquial necessities. The law of conversation has prescribed the model of their sentences; and in that law there is quite as much of self-interest at work as of respect for equity. *Hanc veniam petimusque da-*

[1] "This is a most instructive fact, and it is an-other fact not less instructive, that lawyers in most parts of Christendom, I believe, certainly wherever they are wide awake professionally, tolerate no punctuation. But why? Are lawyers not sensible to the luminous effect from a point happily placed? Yes, they *are* sensible; but also they are sensible of the false prejudicating effect from a punctuation managed (as too generally it is) carelessly and illogically. Here is the brief abstract of the case. All punctuation narrows the path, which is else unlimited; and (*by* narrowing it) may chance to guide the reader into the right groove amongst several that are *not* right. But also punctuation has the effect very often (and almost always has the power) of biasing and predetermining the reader to an erroneous choice of meaning. Better, therefore, no guide at all than one which is likely enough to lead astray, and which must always be suspected and mistrusted, inasmuch as very nearly always it has the *power* to lead astray."—De Quincey.

[1] Probably a reference to the habit of the ancients of incorporating foot-note material in a parenthesis in the text.
[2] In an earlier part of the essay.
[3] sentences
[4] concise style as opposed to lofty style
[5] leaping; bounding
[6] For a corrective of this unsound view, see F. Brunetière's "The French Mastery of Style," *The Atlantic Monthly*, 80, 442.

musque vicissim.[1] Give and take is the rule, and he who expects to be heard must condescend to listen; which necessity, for both parties, binds over both to be brief. Brevity so won could at any rate have little merit; and it is certain that, for profound thinkers, it must sometimes be a hindrance. In order to be brief, a man must take a short sweep of view: his range of thought cannot be extensive; and such a rule, applied to a general method of thinking, is fitted rather to aphorisms and maxims as upon a known subject, than to any process of investigation as upon a subject yet to be fathomed. Advancing still further into the examination of style as the organ of thinking, we should find occasion to see the prodigious defects of the French in all the higher qualities of prose composition. One advantage, for a practical purpose of life, is sadly counterbalanced by numerous faults, many of which are faults of *stamina,* lying not in any corrigible defects, but in such as imply penury of thinking, from radical inaptitude in the thinking faculty to connect itself with the feeling, and with the creative faculty of the imagination. There are many other researches belonging to this subject of subjects, affecting both the logic and the ornaments of style, which would fall under the head of organology. But for instant practical use, though far less difficult for investigation, yet, for that reason, far more tangible and appreciable, would be all the suggestions proper to the other head of mechanology. Half a dozen rules for evading the most frequently recurring forms of awkwardness, of obscurity, of misproportion, and of double meaning, would do more to assist a writer in practice, laid under some necessity of hurry, than volumes of general disquisition. It makes us blush to add that even grammar is so little of a perfect attainment amongst us that, with two or three exceptions (one being Shakspeare, whom some affect to consider as belonging to a semi-barbarous age), we have never seen the writer, through a circuit of prodigious reading, who has not sometimes violated the accidence or the syntax of English grammar.[2]

Whatever becomes of our own possible speculations, we shall conclude with insisting on the growing necessity of style as a practical interest of daily life. Upon sub-

jects of public concern, and in proportion to that concern, there will always be a suitable (and as letters extend, a growing) competition. Other things being equal, or appearing to be equal, the determining principle for the public choice will lie in the style. Of a German book, otherwise entitled to respect, it was said—*er lässt sich nicht lesen,* it does not permit itself to be read: such and so repulsive was the style. Among ourselves, this has long been true of newspapers: they do not suffer themselves to be read *in extenso,* and they are read short—with what injury to the mind may be guessed. The same style of reading, once largely practiced, is applied universally. To this special evil an improvement of style would apply a special redress. The same improvement is otherwise clamorously called for by each man's interest of competition. Public luxury, which is gradually consulted by everything else, must at length be consulted in style.

From AUTOBIOGRAPHIC SKETCHES
1845-51
THE AFFLICTION OF CHILDHOOD

• • • • • •

The earliest incidents in my life, which left stings in my memory so as to be remembered at this day, were two, and both before I could have completed my second year; namely, 1st, a remarkable dream of terrific grandeur about a favorite nurse, which is interesting to myself for this reason—that it demonstrates my dreaming tendencies to have been constitutional, and not dependent upon laudanum;[1] and, 2dly, the fact of having connected a profound sense of pathos with the reappearance, very early in the spring, of some crocuses. This I mention as inexplicable; for such annual resurrections of plants and flowers affect us only as memorials, or suggestions of some higher change, and therefore in connection with the idea of death; yet of death I could, at that time, have had no experience whatever.

This, however, I was speedily to acquire. My two eldest sisters—eldest of three *then* living, and also elder than myself—were summoned to an early death. The first who

[1] We both seek and grant this indulgence in turn. —Horace, *Ars Poetica,* 11.
[2] De Quincey makes this statement evidently on the assumption that the laws of grammar are constant for all ages.

[1] "It is true that in those days *paregoric elixir* was occasionally given to children in colds; and in this medicine there is a small proportion of laudanum. But no medicine was ever administered to any member of our nursery except under medical sanction; and this, assuredly, would not have been obtained to the exhibition of laudanum in a case such as mine. For I was not more than twenty-one months old: at which age the action of opium is capricious, and therefore perilous."—De Quincey.

died was Jane, about two years older than myself.[1] She was three and a half, I one and a half, more or less by some trifle that I do not recollect. But death was then scarcely intelligible to me, and I could not so properly be said to suffer sorrow as a sad perplexity. There was another death in the house about the same time, namely, of a maternal grandmother; but, as she had come to us for the express purpose of dying in her daughter's society, and from illness had lived perfectly secluded, our nursery circle knew her but little, and were certainly more affected by the death (which I witnessed) of a beautiful bird—*viz.*, a kingfisher, which had been injured by an accident. With my sister Jane's death (though otherwise, as I have said, less sorrowful than perplexing) there was, however, connected an incident which made a most fearful impression upon myself, deepening my tendencies to thoughtfulness and abstraction beyond what would seem credible for my years. If there was one thing in this world from which, more than from any other, nature had forced me to revolt, it was brutality and violence. Now, a whisper arose in the family that a female servant, who by accident was drawn off from her proper duties to attend my sister Jane for a day or two, had on one occasion treated her harshly, if not brutally; and as this illtreatment happened within three or four days of her death, so that the occasion of it must have been some fretfulness in the poor child caused by her sufferings, naturally there was a sense of awe and indignation diffused through the family. I believe the story never reached my mother, and possibly it was exaggerated; but upon me the effect was terrific. I did not often see the person charged with this cruelty; but, when I did, my eyes sought the ground; nor could I have borne to look her in the face; not, however, in any spirit that could be called anger. The feeling which fell upon me was a shuddering horror, as upon a first glimpse of the truth that I was in a world of evil and strife. Though born in a large town (the town of Manchester, even then among the largest of the island), I had passed the whole of my childhood, except for the few earliest weeks, in a rural seclusion. With three innocent little sisters for playmates, sleeping always amongst them, and shut up for ever in a silent garden from all knowledge of poverty, or oppression, or outrage, I had

not suspected until this moment the true complexion of the world in which myself and my sisters were living. Henceforward the character of my thoughts changed greatly; for so *representative* are some acts, that one single case of the class is sufficient to throw open before you the whole theatre of possibilities in that direction. I never heard that the woman accused of this cruelty took it at all to heart, even after the event which so immediately succeeded had reflected upon it a more painful emphasis. But for myself, that incident had a lasting revolutionary power in coloring my estimate of life.

So passed away from earth one of those three sisters that made up my nursery playmates; and so did my acquaintance (if such it could be called) commence with mortality. Yet, in fact, I knew little more of mortality than that Jane had disappeared. She had gone away; but, perhaps, she would come back. Happy interval of heaven-born ignorance! Gracious immunity of infancy from sorrow disproportioned to its strength! I was sad for Jane's absence. But still in my heart I trusted that she would come again. Summer and winter came again—crocuses and roses; why not little Jane?

Thus easily was healed, then, the first wound in my infant heart. Not so the second. For thou, dear, noble Elizabeth, around whose ample brow, as often as thy sweet countenance rises upon the darkness, I fancy a *tiara*[1] of light or a gleaming *aureola*[2] in token of thy premature intellectual grandeur—thou whose head, for its superb developments, was the astonishment of science[3]—thou next, but after an inter-

---

[1] The record on the grave-stones makes Jane one year younger than De Quincey.

[1] A crownlike head ornament.

[2] "The *aureola* is the name given in the *Legends of the Christian Saints* to that golden diadem or circlet of supernatural light (that *glory*, as it is commonly called in English) which, amongst the great masters of painting in Italy, surrounded the heads of Christ and of distinguished saints."—De Quincey.

[3] "*The astonishment of science*':—Her medical attendants were Dr. Percival, a well-known literary physician, who had been a correspondent of Condorcet, D'Alembert, etc., and Mr. Charles White, the most distinguished surgeon at that time in the North of England. It was he who pronounced her head' to be the finest in its development of any that he had ever seen—an assertion which, to my own knowledge, he repeated in after years, and with enthusiasm. That he had some acquaintance with the subject may be presumed from this, that, at so early a stage of such inquiries, he had published a work on human craniology, supported by measurements of heads selected from all varieties of the human species. Meantime, as it would grieve me that any trait of what might seem vanity should creep into this record, I will admit that my sister died of hydrocephalus; and it has been often supposed that the pre-

val of happy years, thou also wert summoned away from our nursery; and the night which for me gathered upon that event ran after my steps far into life; and perhaps at this day I resemble little for good or for ill that which else I should have been. Pillar of fire that didst go before me[1] to guide and to quicken—pillar of darkness, when thy countenance was turned away to God, that didst too truly reveal to my dawning fears the secret shadow of death, by what mysterious gravitation was it that *my* heart had been drawn to thine? Could a child, six years old, place any special value upon intellectual forwardness? Serene and capacious as my sister's mind appeared to me upon after review, was *that* a charm for stealing away the heart of an infant? Oh no! I think of it *now* with interest, because it lends, in a stranger's ear, some justification to the excess of my fondness. But then it was lost upon me; or, if not lost, was perceived only through its effects. Hadst thou been an idiot, my sister, not the less I must have loved thee, having that capacious heart —overflowing, even as mine overflowed, with tenderness, strung, even as mine was strung, by the necessity of loving and being loved. This it was which crowned thee with beauty and power:—

Love, the holy sense,
Best gift of God, in thee was most intense[2]

That lamp of Paradise was, for myself, kindled by reflection from the living light which burned so steadfastly in thee; and never but to thee, never again since *thy* departure, had I power or temptation, courage or desire, to utter the feelings which possessed me. For I was the shyest of children; and, at all stages of life, a natural sense of personal dignity held me back from exposing the least ray of feelings which I was not encouraged *wholly* to reveal.

It is needless to pursue, circumstantially, the course of that sickness which carried off my leader and companion. She (according to my recollection at this moment) was just

as near to nine years as I to six. And perhaps this natural precedency in authority of years and judgment, united to the tender humility with which she declined to assert it, had been amongst the fascinations of her presence. It was upon a Sunday evening, if such conjectures can be trusted, that the spark of fatal fire fell upon that train of predispositions to a brain complaint which had hitherto slumbered within her. She had been permitted to drink tea at the house of a laboring man, the father of a favorite female servant. The sun had set when she returned, in the company of this servant, through meadows reeking with exhalations after a fervent day. From that day she sickened. In such circumstances, a child, as young as myself, feels no anxieties. Looking upon medical men as people privileged, and naturally commissioned, to make war upon pain and sickness, I never had a misgiving about the result. I grieved, indeed, that my sister should lie in bed; I grieved still more to hear her moan. But all this appeared to me no more than as a night of trouble, on which the dawn would soon arise. O! moment of darkness and delirium, when the elder nurse awakened me from that delusion, and launched God's thunderbolt at my heart in the assurance that my sister MUST die. Rightly is it said of utter, utter misery, that it "cannot be *remembered*."[1] Itself, as a remarkable thing, is swallowed up in its own chaos. Blank anarchy and confusion of mind fell upon me. Deaf and blind I was, as I reeled under the revelation. I wish not to recall the circumstances of that time, when *my* agony was at its height, and hers, in another sense, was approaching. Enough it is to say, that all was soon over; and the morning of that day had at last arrived which looked down upon her innocent face, sleeping the sleep from which there is no awaking, and upon me sorrowing the sorrow for which there is no consolation.

On the day after my sister's death, whilst the sweet temple of her brain was yet unviolated by human scrutiny, I formed my own scheme for seeing her once more. Not for the world would I have made this known, nor have suffered a witness to accompany me. I had never heard of feelings that take the name of "sentimental," nor dreamed of such a possibility. But grief, even in a child,

---

mature expansion of the intellect in cases of that class is altogether morbid—forced on, in fact, by the mere stimulation of the disease. I would however, suggest, as a possibility, the very opposite order of relation between the disease and the intellectual manifestations. Not the disease may always have caused the preternatural growth of the intellect; but, inversely, this growth of the intellect coming on spontaneously, and outrunning the capacities of the physical structure, may have caused the disease."—De Quincey.

[1] *Exodus,* 13 :21-22.
[2] Wordsworth, *Tribute to the Memory of the Same Dog,* 27.

[1] " 'I stood in unimaginable trance
And agony which cannot be remember'd.'
Speech of Alhadra in Coleridge's
Remorse, [IV, 3, 77-8]."—De Quincey.

hates the light, and shrinks from human eyes. The house was large enough to have two staircases; and by one of these I knew that about mid-day, when all would be quiet (for the servants dined at one o'clock), I could steal up into her chamber. I imagine that it was about an hour after high noon when I reached the chamber-door; it was locked, but the key was not taken away. Entering, I closed the door so softly, that, although it opened upon a hall which ascended through all the stories, no echo ran along the silent walls. Then, turning round, I sought my sister's face. But the bed had been moved, and the back was now turned towards myself. Nothing met my eyes but one large window, wide open, through which the sun of midsummer at mid-day was showering down torrents of splendor. The weather was dry, the sky was cloudless, the blue depths seemed to express types of infinity; and it was not possible for eye to behold, or for heart to conceive,[1] any symbols more pathetic of life and the glory of life.

Let me pause for one instant in approaching a remembrance so affecting for my own mind, to mention that, in the *Opium Confessions,* I endeavored to explain the reason why death, other conditions remaining the same, is more profoundly affecting in summer than in other parts of the year—so far, at least, as it is liable to any modification at all from accidents of scenery or season.[2] The reason, as I there suggested, lies in the antagonism between the tropical redundancy of life in summer, and the frozen sterilities of the grave. The summer we see, the grave we haunt with our thoughts; the glory is around us, the darkness is within us; and, the two coming into collision, each exalts the other into stronger relief. But, in my case, there was even a subtler reason why the summer had this intense power of vivifying the spectacle or the thoughts of death. And, recollecting it, I am struck with the truth, that far more of our deepest thoughts and feelings pass to us through perplexed combinations of *concrete* objects, pass to us as *involutes* (if I may coin that word) in compound experiences incapable of being disentangled, than ever reach us *directly,* and in their own abstract shapes. It had happened that amongst our vast nursery collection of books was the Bible illustrated with many pictures. And in long dark evenings, as my three sisters with myself sat by the firelight

round the *guard*[1] of our nursery, no book was so much in request amongst us. It ruled us and swayed us as mysteriously as music. Our younger nurse, whom we all loved, would sometimes, according to her simple powers, endeavor to explain what we found obscure. We, the children, were all constitutionally touched with pensiveness; the fitful gloom and sudden lambencies of the room by firelight suited our evening state of feelings; and they suited, also, the divine revelations of power and mysterious beauty which awed us. Above all, the story of a just man[2]—man and yet *not* man, real above all things, and yet shadowy above all things—who had suffered the passion of death in Palestine, slept upon our minds like early dawn upon the waters. The nurse knew and explained to us the chief differences in oriental climates; and all these differences (as it happens) express themselves, more or less, in varying relations to the great accidents and powers of summer. The cloudless sunlights of Syria —those seemed to argue everlasting summer; the disciples plucking the ears of corn[3]—that *must* be summer; but, above all, the very name of Palm Sunday (a festival in the English Church) troubled me like an anthem. "Sunday!" what was *that?* That was the day of peace which masked another peace deeper than the heart of man can comprehend. "Palms!" what were they? *That* was an equivocal word; palms, in the sense of trophies, expressed the pomps of life; palms, as a product of nature, expressed the pomps of summer. Yet still even this explanation does not suffice; it was not merely by the peace and by the summer, by the deep sound of rest below all rest and of ascending glory, that I had been haunted. It was also because Jerusalem stood near to those deep images both in time and in place. The great event of Jerusalem was at hand when Palm Sunday came; and the scene of that Sunday was near in place to Jerusalem. What then was Jerusalem? Did I fancy it to be the *omphalos* (navel) or physical centre of the earth? Why should *that* affect me? Such a pretension had once been made for Jerusalem,[4] and once for a Grecian city;[5]

[1] "*The guard*':—I know not whether the word is a local one in this sense. What I mean is a sort of fender, four or five feet high, which locks up the fire from too near an approach on the part of children."—De Quincey.
[2] A reference to Christ.
[3] See *Luke,* 6 :1.
[4] See *Ezekiel,* 5 :5. A round stone in the church of the Holy Sepulchre indicates what was said to be the center of the world.
[5] The stone on which Apollo sat in the temple at Delphi marked, supposedly, the center of the world.

[1] See *1 Corinthians,* 2 :9.
[2] See p. 1103b, 1-42.

and both pretensions had become ridiculous, as the figure of the planet became known. Yes; but if not of the earth, yet of mortality, for earth's tenant, Jerusalem, had now become the *omphalos* and absolute centre. Yet how? There, on the contrary, it was, as we infants understood, that mortality had been trampled under foot. True; but, for that very reason, there it was that mortality had opened its very gloomiest crater. There it was, indeed, that the human had risen on wings from the grave; but, for that reason, there also it was that the divine had been swallowed up by the abyss; the lesser star could not rise, before the greater should submit to eclipse. Summer, therefore, had connected itself with death, not merely as a mode of antagonism, but also as a phenomenon brought into intricate relations with death by scriptural scenery and events.

Out of this digression, for the purpose of showing how inextricable my feelings and images of death were entangled with those of summer, as connected with Palestine and Jerusalem, let me come back to the bed-chamber of my sister. From the gorgeous sunlight I turned round to the corpse. There lay the sweet childish figure; there the angel face; and, as people usually fancy, it was said in the house that no features had suffered any change. Had they not? The forehead, indeed—the serene and noble forehead—*that* might be the same; but the frozen eyelids, the darkness that seemed to steal from beneath them, the marble lips, the stiffening hands, laid palm to palm, as if repeating the supplications of closing anguish—could these be mistaken for life? Had it been so, wherefore did I not spring to those heavenly lips with tears and never-ending kisses? But so it was *not*. I stood checked for a moment; awe, not fear, fell upon me; and, whilst I stood, a solemn wind began to blow—the saddest that ear ever heard. It was a wind that might have swept the fields of mortality for a thousand centuries. Many times since, upon summer days, when the sun is about the hottest, I have remarked the same wind arising and uttering the same hollow, solemn, Memnonian,[1] but saintly swell: it is in this world

1 " 'Memnonian':—For the sake of many readers, whose hearts may go along earnestly with a record of infant sorrow, but whose course of life has not allowed them much leisure for study, I pause to explain—that the head of Memnon, in the British Museum, that sublime head which wears upon its lips a smile co-extensive with all time and all space, an Æonian smile of gracious love and Panlike mystery, the most diffusive and pathetically divine that the hand of man has created, is

the one great *audible* symbol of eternity. And three times in my life have I happened to hear the same sound in the same circumstances—namely, when standing between an open window and a dead body on a summer day.

Instantly, when my ear caught this vast Æolian intonation, when my eye filled with the golden fulness of life, the pomps of the heavens above, or the glory of the flowers below, and turning when it settled upon the frost which overspread my sister's face, instantly a trance fell upon me. A vault seemed to open in the zenith of the far blue sky, a shaft which ran up forever. I, in spirit, rose as if on billows that also ran up the shaft forever; and the billows seemed to pursue the throne of God; but *that* also ran before us and fled away continually. The flight and the pursuit seemed to go on forever and ever. Frost gathering frost, some Sarsar[1] wind of death, seemed to repel me; some mighty relation between God and death dimly struggled to evolve itself from the dreadful antagonism between them; shadowy meanings even yet continue to exer-

represented on the authority of ancient traditions to have uttered at sunrise, or soon after, as the sun's rays had accumulated heat enough to rarify the air within certain cavities in the bust, a solemn and dirge-like series of intonations; the simple explanation being, in its general outline, this—that sonorous currents of air were produced by causing chambers of cold and heavy air to press upon other collections of air, warmed, and therefore rarified, and therefore yielding readily to the pressure of heavier air. Currents being thus established, by artificial arrangements of tubes, a certain succession of notes could be concerted and sustained. Near the Red Sea lie a chain of sand hills, which, by a natural system of grooves inosculating with each other, become vocal under changing circumstances in the position of the sun, etc. I knew a boy who, upon observing steadily, and reflecting upon a phenomenon that met him in his daily experience—*viz.*, that tubes, through which a stream of water was passing, gave out a very different sound according to the varying slenderness or fulness of the current—devised an instrument that yielded a rude hydraulic gamut of sounds; and, indeed, upon this simple phenomenon is founded the use and power of the stethoscope. For exactly as a thin thread of water, trickling through a leaden tube, yields a stridulous and plaintive sound compared with the full volume of sound corresponding to the full volume of water—on parity of principles, nobody will doubt that the current of blood pouring through the tubes of the human frame will utter to the learned ear, when armed with the stethoscope, an elaborate gamut or compass of music, recording the ravages of disease, or the glorious plenitudes of health, as faithfully as the cavities within this ancient Memnonian bust reported this mighty event of sunrise to the rejoicing world of light and life—or, again, under the sad passion of the dying day, uttered the sweet requiem that belonged to its departure."—De Quincey.

1 An Arabic word meaning *cold wind*. See Southey's *Thalaba*, 1, st. 44.

cise and torment, in dreams, the deciphering oracle within me. I slept—for how long I cannot say; slowly I recovered my self-possession; and, when I woke, found myself standing, as before, close to my sister's bed.

I have reason to believe that a *very* long interval had elapsed during this wandering or suspension of my perfect mind. When I returned to myself, there was a foot (or I fancied so) on the stairs. I was alarmed; for, if anybody had detected me, means would have been taken to prevent my coming again. Hastily, therefore, I kissed the lips that I should kiss no more, and slunk, like a guilty thing, with stealthy steps from the room. Thus perished the vision, loveliest amongst all the shows which earth has revealed to me; thus mutilated was the parting which should have lasted forever; tainted thus with fear was that farewell sacred to love and grief, to perfect love and to grief that could not be healed.

O Ahasuerus, everlasting Jew![1] fable or not a fable, thou, when first starting on thy endless pilgrimage of woe—thou, when first flying through the gates of Jerusalem, and vainly yearning to leave the pursuing curse behind thee—couldst not more certainly in the words of Christ have read thy doom of endless sorrow, than I when passing forever from my sister's room. The worm was at my heart; and, I may say, the worm that could not die.[2] Man is doubtless *one* by some subtle *nexus*, some system of links, that we cannot perceive, extending from the new-born infant to the superannuated dotard: but, as regards many affections and passions incident to his nature at different stages, he is *not* one, but an intermitting creature, ending and beginning anew; the unity of man, in this respect, is co-extensive only with the particular stage to which the passion belongs. Some passions, as that of sexual love, are celestial by one half of their origin, animal and earthly by the other half. These will not survive their own appropriate stage. But love, which is *altogether* holy, like that between two children, is privileged to revisit by glimpses the silence and the darkness of declining years; and, possibly, this final experience in my sister's bedroom, or some other in which her innocence was concerned,

may rise again for me to illuminate the clouds of death.

On the day following this which I have recorded, came a body of medical men to examine the brain, and the particular nature of the complaint; for in some of its symptoms it had shown perplexing anomalies. An hour after the strangers had withdrawn, I crept again to the room; but the door was now locked, the key had been taken away— and I was shut out forever.

Then came the funeral. I, in the ceremonial character of *mourner,* was carried thither. I was put into a carriage with some gentlemen whom I did not know. They were kind and attentive to me; but naturally they talked of things disconnected with the occasion, and their conversation was a torment. At the church, I was told to hold a white handkerchief to my eyes. Empty hypocrisy! What need had *he* of masks or mockeries, whose heart died within him at every word that was uttered? During that part of the service which passed within the church, I made an effort to attend; but I sank back continually into my own solitary darkness, and I heard little consciously, except some fugitive strains from the sublime chapter of St. Paul, which in England is always read at burials.[1]

Lastly came that magnificent liturgical service which the English Church performs at the side of the grave; for this church does not forsake her dead so long as they continue in the upper air, but waits for her last "sweet and solemn farewell"[2] at the side of the grave. There is exposed once again, and for the last time, the coffin. All eyes survey the record of name, of sex, of age, and the day of departure from earth— records how shadowy! and dropped into darkness as messages addressed to worms. Almost at the very last comes the symbolic ritual, tearing and shattering the heart with volleying discharges, peal after peal, from the fine artillery of woe. The coffin is lowered into its home; it has disappeared from all eyes but those that look down into the abyss of the grave. The sacristan stands ready, with his shovel of earth and stones. The priest's voice is heard once more—*earth*

[1] "*Everlasting Jew*':—*der ewige Jude*—which is the common German expression for 'The Wandering Jew,' and sublimer even than our own." —De Quincey. For a full account of the widespread legend of The Wandering Jew, see *The Encyclopædia Britannica* (11th ed.).
[2] See *Isaiah,* 66:24; *Mark,* 9:44-48; also *Paradise Lost,* 6, 739.

[1] "*First Epistle to Corinthians,* chap. 15, beginning at verse 20."—De Quincey.
[2] "This beautiful expression, I am pretty certain, must belong to Mrs. Trollope; I read it, probably, in a tale of hers connected with the backwoods of America, where the absence of such a farewell must unspeakably aggravate the gloom at any rate belonging to a household separation of that eternal character occurring amongst the shadows of those mighty forests."—De Quincey.

to earth—and immediately the dread rattle ascends from the lid of the coffin; *ashes to ashes*—and again the killing sound is heard; *dust to dust*—and the farewell volley announces that the grave, the coffin, the face are sealed up forever and ever.

Grief! thou art classed amongst the depressing passions. And true it is that thou humblest to the dust, but also thou exaltest to the clouds. Thou shakest as with ague, but also thou steadiest like frost. Thou sickenest the heart, but also thou healest its infirmities. Among the very foremost of mine was morbid sensibility to shame. And, ten years afterwards, I used to throw my self-reproaches with regard to that infirmity into this shape—*viz.*, that if I were summoned to seek aid for a perishing fellow-creature, and that I could obtain that aid only by facing a vast company of critical or sneering faces, I might, perhaps, shrink basely from the duty. It is true that no such case had ever actually occurred; so that it was a mere romance of casuistry to tax myself with cowardice so shocking. But to feel a doubt was to feel condemnation; and the crime that *might* have been, was in my eyes the crime that *had* been. Now, however, all was changed; and, for anything which regarded my sister's memory, in one hour I received a new heart. Once in Westmoreland I saw a case resembling it. I saw a ewe suddenly put off and abjure her own nature, in a service of love—yes, slough it as completely as ever serpent sloughed his skin. Her lamb had fallen into a deep trench, from which all escape was hopeless without the aid of man. And to a man she advanced, bleating clamorously, until he followed her and rescued her beloved. Not less was the change in myself. Fifty thousand sneering faces would not have troubled me *now* in any office of tenderness to my sister's memory. Ten legions would not have repelled me from seeking her, if there had been a chance that she could be found. Mockery! it was lost upon me. Laughter! I valued it not. And when I was taunted insultingly with "my girlish tears," that word "*girlish*" had no sting for me, except as a verbal echo to the one eternal thought of my heart —that a girl was the sweetest thing which I, in my short life, had known—that a girl it was who had crowned the earth with beauty, and had opened to my thirst fountains of pure celestial love, from which, in this world, I was to drink no more.

Now began to unfold themselves the consolations of solitude, those consolations which only I was destined to taste; now, therefore, began to open upon me those fascinations of solitude, which, when acting as a co-agency with unresisted grief, end in the paradoxical result of making out of grief itself a luxury; such a luxury as finally becomes a snare, overhanging life itself, and the energies of life, with growing menaces. All deep feelings of a *chronic* class agree in this, that they seek for solitude, and are fed by solitude. Deep grief, deep love, how naturally do these ally themselves with religious feeling! and all three—love, grief, religion —are haunters of solitary places. Love, grief, and the mystery of devotion—what were these without solitude? All day long, when it was not impossible for me to do so, I sought the most silent and sequestered nooks in the grounds about the house, or in the neighboring fields. The awful stillness oftentimes of summer noons, when no winds were abroad, the appealing silence of gray or misty afternoons—these were fascinations as of witchcraft. Into the woods, into the desert air, I gazed, as if some comfort lay hid in *them*. I wearied the heavens with my inquest of beseeching looks. Obstinately I tormented the blue depths with my scrutiny, sweeping them forever with my eyes, and searching them for one angelic face that might, perhaps, have permission to reveal itself for a moment.

At this time, and under this impulse of rapacious grief, that grasped at what it could not obtain, the faculty of shaping images in the distance out of slight elements, and grouping them after the yearnings of the heart, grew upon me in morbid excess. And I recall at the present moment one instance of that sort, which may show how merely shadows, or a gleam of brightness, or nothing at all, could furnish a sufficient basis for this creative faculty.

On Sunday mornings I went with the rest of my family to church: it was a church, on the ancient model of England, having aisles, galleries,[1] organ, all things ancient and venerable, and the proportions majestic. Here, whilst the congregation knelt through the long litany, as often as we came to that passage, so beautiful amongst many that are so, where God is supplicated on behalf of "all sick persons and young children," and

[1] "*Galleries*:—These, though condemned on some grounds by the restorers of authentic church architecture, have, nevertheless, this one advantage—that, when the *height* of a church is that dimension which most of all expresses its sacred character, galleries expound and interpret that height."—De Quincey.

that he would "show his pity upon all prisoners and captives," I wept in secret; and raising my streaming eyes to the upper windows of the galleries, saw, on days when the sun was shining, a spectacle as affecting as ever prophet can have beheld. The *sides* of the windows were rich with storied glass; through the deep purples and crimsons streamed the golden light; emblazonries of heavenly illumination (from the sun) mingling with the earthly emblazonries (from art and its gorgeous coloring) of what is grandest in man. *There* were the apostles that had trampled upon earth, and the glories of earth, out of celestial love to man. *There* were the martyrs that had borne witness to the truth through flames, through torments, and through armies of fierce, insulting faces. *There* were the saints who, under intolerable pangs, had glorified God by meek submission to his will. And all the time whilst this tumult of sublime memorials held on as the deep chords from some accompaniment in the bass, I saw through the wide central field of the window, where the glass was *uncolored*, white, fleecy clouds sailing over the azure depths of the sky; were it but a fragment or a hint of such a cloud, immediately under the flash of my sorrow-haunted eye, it grew and shaped itself into visions of beds with white lawny curtains; and in the beds lay sick children, dying children, that were tossing in anguish, and weeping clamorously for death. God, for some mysterious reason, could not suddenly release them from their pain; but he suffered the beds, as it seemed, to rise slowly through the clouds; slowly the beds ascended into the chambers of the air; slowly also his arms descended from the heavens, that he and his young children, whom in Palestine, once and forever, he had blessed, though they *must* pass slowly through the dreadful chasm of separation, might yet meet the sooner. These visions were self-sustained. These visions needed not that any sound should speak to me, or music mould my feelings. The hint from the litany, the fragment from the clouds—those and the storied windows were sufficient. But not the less the blare of the tumultuous organ wrought its own separate creations. And oftentimes in anthems, when the mighty instrument threw its vast columns of sound, fierce yet melodious, over the voices of the choir—high in arches, when it seemed to rise, surmounting and overriding the strife of the vocal parts, and gathering by strong coercion the total storm into unity—sometimes I seemed to rise and walk triumphantly upon those clouds which, but a moment before, I had looked up to as mementos of prostrate sorrow; yes, sometimes under the transfigurations of music, felt of grief itself as of a fiery chariot for mounting victoriously above the causes of grief.

God speaks to children, also, in dreams, and by the oracles that lurk in darkness. But in solitude, above all things, when made vocal to the meditative heart by the truths and services of a national church, God holds with children "communion undisturbed."[1] Solitude, though it may be silent as light, is, like light, the mightiest of agencies; for solitude is essential to man. All men come into this world *alone;* all leave it *alone.* Even a little child has a dread, whispering consciousness, that, if he should be summoned to travel into God's presence, no gentle nurse will be allowed to lead him by the hand, nor mother to carry him in her arms, nor little sister to share his trepidations. King and priest, warrior and maiden, philosopher and child, all must walk those mighty galleries alone. The solitude, therefore, which in this world appals or fascinates a child's heart, is but the echo of a far deeper solitude, through which already he has passed, and of another solitude, deeper still, through which he *has* to pass: reflex of one solitude—prefiguration of another.

Oh, burden of solitude, that cleavest to man through every stage of his being! in his birth, which *has* been—in his life, which *is*—in his death, which *shall be*—mighty and essential solitude! that wast, and art, and art to be; thou broodest, like the Spirit of God moving upon the surface of the deeps,[2] over every heart that sleeps in the nurseries of Christendom. Like the vast laboratory of the air, which, seeming to be nothing, or less than the shadow of a shade, hides within itself the principles of all things, solitude for the meditating child is the Agrippa's mirror[3] of the unseen universe. Deep is the solitude of millions who, with hearts welling forth love, have none to love them. Deep is the solitude of those who, under secret griefs, have none to pity them. Deep is the solitude of those who, fighting with doubts or darkness, have none to counsel them. But deeper than the deepest of these solitudes is that

---

[1] Wordsworth, *The Excursion*, 4, 86.
[2] See *Genesis*, 1:2; also *Paradise Lost*, 1, 19-21.
[3] That is, the medium by which the unseen may be made visible. For an account of the alleged marvels performed by Cornelius Agrippa (1486-1535) by means of a wonderful glass, see Nash's *The Unfortunate Traveller, or The Life of Jack Wilton* (ed. Gosse), pp. 86 ff.

which broods over childhood under the passion of sorrow—bringing before it, at intervals, the final solitude which watches for it, and is waiting for it within the gates of death. Oh, mighty and essential solitude, that wast, and art, and art to be! thy kingdom is made perfect in the grave; but even over those that keep watch outside the grave, like myself, an infant of six years old, thou stretchest out a sceptre of fascination.

From SUSPIRIA DE PROFUNDIS[1]
1845-49
LEVANA AND OUR LADIES OF SORROW
1845

Oftentimes at Oxford I saw Levana in my dreams. I knew her by her Roman symbols. Who is Levana? Reader, that do not pretend to have leisure for very much scholarship, you will not be angry with me for telling you. Levana was the Roman goddess that performed for the new-born infant the earliest office of ennobling kindness,—typical, by its mode, of that grandeur which belongs to man everywhere, and of that benignity in powers invisible which even in Pagan worlds sometimes descends to sustain it. At the very moment of birth, just as the infant tasted for the first time the atmosphere of our troubled planet, it was laid on the ground. *That* might bear different interpretations. But immediately, lest so grand a creature should grovel there for more than one instant, either the paternal hand, as proxy for the goddess Levana, or some near kinsman, as proxy for the father, raised it upright, bade it look erect as the king of all this world, and presented its forehead to the stars, saying, perhaps, in his heart, "Behold what is greater than yourselves!" This symbolic act represented the function of Levana. And that mysterious lady, who never revealed her face (except to me in dreams), but always acted by delegation, had her name from the Latin verb (as still it is the Italian verb) *levare,* to raise aloft.

This is the explanation of Levana. And hence it has arisen that some people have understood by Levana the tutelary power that controls the education of the nursery. She, that would not suffer at his birth even a prefigurative or mimic degradation for her awful ward, far less could be supposed to suffer the real degradation attaching to the non-development of his powers. She therefore watches over human education. Now, the word *edŭco,* with the penultimate short, was derived (by a process often exemplified in the crystallization of languages) from the word *edūco,* with the penultimate long. Whatsoever *educes,* or develops, *educates.* By the education of Levana, therefore, is meant,—not the poor machinery that moves by spelling-books and grammars, but that mighty system of central forces hidden in the deep bosom of human life, which by passion, by strife, by temptation, by the energies of resistance, works forever upon children,—resting not day or night, any more than the mighty wheel of day and night themselves, whose moments, like restless spokes, are glimmering[1] forever as they revolve.

If, then, *these* are the ministries by which Levana works, how profoundly must she reverence the agencies of grief! But you, reader, think that children generally are not liable to grief such as mine. There are two senses in the world *generally,*—the sense of Euclid, where it means *universally* (or in the whole extent of the *genus*), and a foolish sense of this word, where it means *usually.* Now, I am far from saying that children universally are capable of grief like mine. But there are more than you ever heard of who die of grief in this island of ours. I will tell you a common case. The rules of Eton require that a boy on the *foundation*[2] should be there twelve years: he is superannuated at eighteen; consequently he must come at six. Children torn away from mothers and sisters at that age not unfrequently die. I speak of what I know. The complaint is not entered by the registrar as grief; but *that* it is. Grief of that sort, and at that age, has killed more than ever have been counted amongst its martyrs.

Therefore it is that Levana often communes with the powers that shake man's heart; therefore it is that she dotes upon grief. "These ladies," said I softly to myself, on seeing the ministers with whom Levana was conversing, "these are the Sorrows; and they are three in number: as the *Graces* are three, who dress man's life with beauty; the *Parcæ* are three, who weave the dark arras of man's life in their mysterious loom always with colors sad in part, sometimes angry with tragic crimson and black; the *Furies* are three, who visit with retributions called from the other side of the grave offences that walk upon this; and once even the *Muses* were but three, who fit the harp, the trumpet, or the lute, to the great burdens of man's impassioned creations. These are the Sorrows; all three of whom I know." The last words I say *now;* but in Oxford I said, "one of whom I know, and the others too surely I *shall* know." For already, in my fervent youth, I saw (dimly relieved upon the dark background of my dreams) the imperfect lineaments of the awful Sisters.

These Sisters—by what name shall we call them? If I say simply "The Sorrows," there will be a chance of mistaking the term; it might be understood of individual sorrow, —separate cases of sorrow,—whereas I want a term expressing the mighty abstractions that incarnate themselves in all individual sufferings of man's heart, and I wish to have these abstractions presented as impersonations,—that is, as clothed with human attributes of life, and with functions pointing to flesh. Let us call them, therefore, *Our Ladies of Sorrow.*

I know them thoroughly, and have walked in all their kingdoms. Three sisters they are, of one mysterious household; and their paths are wide apart; but of their dominion there is no end. Them I saw often conversing with Levana, and sometimes about myself. Do they talk, then? O no! Mighty phantoms like these disdain the infirmities of language. They may utter voices through the organs of man when they dwell in human hearts, but amongst themselves is no voice nor sound; eternal silence reigns in *their* kingdoms. They spoke not as they talked with Levana; they whispered not; they sang not; though oftentimes methought they *might* have sung: for I upon earth had heard their mysteries oftentimes deciphered by harp and timbrel, by dulcimer and organ. Like God, whose servants they are, they utter their pleasure not by sounds that perish, or by

words that go astray, but by signs in heaven, by changes on earth, by pulses in secret rivers, heraldries painted on darkness, and hieroglyphics written on the tablets of the brain. *They* wheeled in mazes; *I* spelled the steps. *They* telegraphed[1] from afar; *I* read the signals. *They* conspired together; and on the mirrors of darkness *my* eye traced the plots. *Theirs* were the symbols; *mine* are the words.

What is it the Sisters are? What is it that they do. Let me describe their form and their presence, if form it were that still fluctuated in its outline, or presence it were that forever advanced to the front or forever receded amongst shades.

The eldest of the three is named *Mater Lachrymarum,* Our Lady of Tears. She it is that night and day raves and moans, calling for vanished faces. She stood in Rama, where a voice was heard of lamentation,— Rachel weeping for her children,[2] and refusing to be comforted. She it was that stood in Bethlehem on the night when Herod's sword swept its nurseries of Innocents,[3] and the little feet were stiffened forever which, heard at times as they trotted along floors overhead, woke pulses of love in household hearts that were not unmarked in heaven. Her eyes are sweet and subtle, wild and sleepy, by turns; oftentimes rising to the clouds, oftentimes challenging the heavens. She wears a diadem round her head. And I knew by childish memories that she could go abroad upon the winds, when she heard the sobbing of litanies, or the thundering of organs, and when she beheld the mustering of summer clouds. This Sister, the elder, it is that carries keys more than papal at her girdle,[4] which open every cottage and every palace. She, to my knowledge, sat all last summer by the bedside of the blind beggar, him that so often and so gladly I talked with, whose pious daughter, eight years old, with the sunny countenance, resisted the temptations of play and village mirth, to travel all day long on dusty roads with her afflicted father. For this did God send her a great reward. In the springtime of the year, and whilst yet her own spring was budding, He recalled her to himself. But her blind father mourns forever over *her:* still he dreams at midnight that the little guiding hand is locked within his own; and still he wakens to a darkness that is now

[1] This word was formerly used of various methods of signalling.
[2] See *Jeremiah,* 31:15; also *Matthew,* 2:16-18.
[3] See *Matthew,* 2:16.
[4] See *Matthew,* 15:18-19.

within a second and a deeper darkness. This *Mater Lachrymarum* also has been sitting all this winter of 1844-5 within the bed-chamber of the Czar,[1] bringing before his eyes a daughter (not less pious) that vanished to God not less suddenly, and left behind her a darkness not less profound. By the power of the keys it is that Our Lady of Tears glides, a ghostly intruder, into the chambers of sleepless men, sleepless women, sleepless children, from Ganges to the Nile, from Nile to Mississippi. And her, because she is the first-born of her house, and has the widest empire, let us honor with the title of "Madonna."

The second Sister is called *Mater Suspiriorum*, Our Lady of Sighs. She never scales the clouds, nor walks abroad upon the winds. She wears no diadem. And her eyes, if they were ever seen, would be neither sweet nor subtle; no man could read their story; they would be found filled with perishing dreams, and with wrecks of forgotten delirium. But she raises not her eyes; her head, on which sits a dilapidated turban, droops forever, forever fastens on the dust. She weeps not. She groans not. But she sighs inaudibly at intervals. Her sister, Madonna, is oftentimes stormy and frantic, raging in the highest against heaven, and demanding back her darlings. But Our Lady of Sighs never clamors, never defies, dreams not of rebellious aspirations. She is humble to abjectness. Hers is the meekness that belongs to the hopeless. Murmur she may, but it is in her sleep. Whisper she may, but it is to herself in the twilight. Mutter she does at times, but it is in solitary places that are desolate as she is desolate, in ruined cities, and when the sun has gone down to his rest. This Sister is the visitor of the Pariah, of the Jew, of the bondsman to the oar in the Mediterranean galleys; of the English criminal in Norfolk Island, blotted out from the books of remembrance[2] in sweet far-off England; of the baffled penitent reverting his eyes forever upon a solitary grave, which to him seems the altar overthrown of some past and bloody sacrifice, on which altar no oblations can now be availing, whether towards pardon that he might implore, or towards reparation that he might attempt. Every slave that at noonday looks up to the tropical sun with timid reproach, as he points with one hand to the earth, our

general mother, but for *him* a stepmother, as he points with the other hand to the Bible, our general teacher, but against *him* sealed and sequestered;[1] every woman sitting in darkness, without love to shelter her head, or hope to illumine her solitude, because the heaven-born instincts kindling in her nature germs of holy affections, which God implanted in her womanly bosom, having been stifled by social necessities, now burn sullenly to waste, like sepulchral lamps amongst the ancients; every nun defrauded of her unreturning May-time by wicked kinsman, whom God will judge; every captive in every dungeon; all that are betrayed, and all that are rejected; outcasts by traditionary law, and children of *hereditary* disgrace: all these walk with Our Lady of Sighs. She also carries a key; but she needs it little. For her kingdom is chiefly amongst the tents of Shem,[2] and the houseless vagrant of every clime. Yet in the very highest ranks of man she finds chapels of her own; and even in glorious England there are some that, to the world, carry their heads as proudly as the reindeer, who yet secretly have received her mark upon their foreheads.

But the third Sister, who is also the youngest——! Hush! whisper whilst we talk of *her!* Her kingdom is not large, or else no flesh should live; but within that kingdom all power is hers. Her head, turreted like that of Cybele, rises almost beyond the reach of sight. She droops not; and her eyes, rising so high, *might* be hidden by distance. But, being what they are, they cannot be hidden: through the treble veil of crape which she wears the fierce light of a blazing misery, that rests not for matins or for vespers, for noon of day or noon of night, for ebbing or for flowing tide, may be read from the very ground. She is the defier of God. She also is the mother of lunacies, and the suggestress of suicides. Deep lie the roots of her power; but narrow is the nation that she rules. For she can approach only those in whom a profound nature has been upheaved by central convulsions; in whom the heart trembles and the brain rocks under conspiracies of tempest from without and

---

[1] Nicholas I, whose daughter Alexandra died in August, 1844.
[2] See *Revelation*, 3:5.

[1] "This, the reader will be aware, applies chiefly to the cotton and tobacco States of North America; but not to them only: on which account I have not scrupled to figure the sun which looks down upon slavery as *tropical*,— no matter if strictly within the tropics, or simply so near to them as to produce a similar climate."—De Quincey.
[2] That is, among outcasts; literally, among the Hebrews, Arabs, and other Semitic races, said to be descended from Shem, the son of Noah. See *Genesis*, 9:27.

tempest from within. Madonna moves with uncertain steps, fast or slow, but still with tragic grace. Our Lady of Sighs creeps timidly and stealthily. But this youngest Sister moves with incalculable motions, bounding, and with tiger's leaps. She carries no key; for, though coming rarely amongst men, she storms all doors at which she is permitted to enter at all. And *her* name is *Mater Tenebrarum,*—Our Lady of Darkness.

These were the *Semnai Theai* or Sublime Goddesses,[1] these were the *Eumenides* or Gracious Ladies (so called by antiquity in shuddering propitiation), of my Oxford dreams. Madonna spoke. She spoke by her mysterious hand. Touching my head, she beckoned to Our Lady of Sighs; and *what* she spoke, translated out of the signs which (except in dreams) no man reads, was this:—

"Lo! here is he whom in childhood I dedicated to my altars. This is he that once I made my darling. Him I led astray, him I beguiled; and from heaven I stole away his young heart to mine. Through me did he become idolatrous; and through me it was, by languishing desires, that he worshipped the worm, and prayed to the wormy grave. Holy was the grave to him; lovely was its darkness; saintly its corruption. Him, this young idolater, I have seasoned for thee, dear gentle Sister of Sighs! Do thou take him now to *thy* heart, and season him for our dreadful sister. And thou,"—turning to the *Mater Tenebrarum,* she said,—"wicked sister, that temptest and hatest, do thou take him from *her.* See that thy sceptre lie heavy on his head. Suffer not woman and her tenderness to sit near him in his darkness. Banish the frailties of hope; wither the relenting of love; scorch the fountains of tears;[2] curse him as only *thou* canst curse. So shall he be accomplished in the furnace; so shall he see the things that ought *not* to be seen, sights that are abominable, and secrets that are unutterable. So shall he read elder truths, sad truths, grand truths, fearful truths. So shall he rise again *before* he dies. And so shall our commission be accomplished which from God we had,—to plague his heart until we had unfolded the capacities of his spirit."

SAVANNAH-LA-MAR[1]

God smote Savannah-la-mar, and in one night, by earthquake, removed her, with all her towers standing and population sleeping, from the steadfast foundations of the shore to the coral floors of ocean. And God said,—"Pompeii did I bury and conceal from men through seventeen centuries; this city I will bury, but not conceal. She shall be a monument to men of my mysterious anger, set in azure light through generations to come; for I will enshrine her in a crystal dome of my tropic seas." This city, therefore, like a mighty galleon with all her apparel mounted, streamers flying, and tackling perfect, seems floating along the noiseless depths of ocean; and oftentimes in glassy calms, through the translucid atmosphere of water that now stretches like an air-woven awning above the silent encampment, mariners from every clime look down into her courts and terraces, count her gates, and number the spires of her churches. She is one ample cemetery, and *has* been for many a year; but, in the mighty calms that brood for weeks over tropic latitudes, she fascinates the eye with a *Fata-Morgana*[2] revelation, as of human life still subsisting in submarine asylums sacred from the storms that torment our upper air.

Thither, lured by the loveliness of cerulean depths, by the peace of human dwellings privileged from molestation, by the gleam of marble altars sleeping in everlasting sanctity, oftentimes in dreams did I and the Dark Interpreter[3] cleave the watery veil that divided us from her streets. We looked into the belfries, where the pendulous bells were waiting in vain for the summons which should awaken their marriage peals; together we touched the mighty organ-keys, that sang no *jubilates*[4] for the ear of heaven, that sang no requiems for the ear of human sorrow; together we searched the silent nurseries, where the children were all asleep, and *had* been asleep through five generations. "They are waiting for the heavenly dawn," whispered the Interpreter to himself: "and, when *that* comes, the bells and organs will utter a *jubilate* repeated by the echoes of Paradise." Then, turning to me, he said,—"This is sad, this is piteous; but

1 Plain of the Sea.
2 That is, mirage-like; *Fata Morgana* is the name of a mirage off the coast of Sicily, formerly regarded as the work of Morgana the Fairy, a famous necromancer in medieval legend.
3 One of the *Suspiria* papers is entitled "The Dark Interpreter."
4 Hymns of rejoicing (like the 100th Psalm).

less would not have sufficed for the purpose of God. Look here. Put into a Roman clepsydra[1] one hundred drops of water; let these run out as the sands in an hour-glass, every drop measuring the hundredth part of a second, so that each shall represent but the three-hundred-and-sixty-thousandth part of an hour. Now, count the drops as they race along; and, when the fiftieth of the hundred is passing, behold! forty-nine are not, because already they have perished, and fifty are not, because they are yet to come. You see, therefore, how narrow, how incalculably narrow, is the true and actual present. Of that time which we call the present, hardly a hundredth part but belongs either to a past which has fled, or to a future which is still on the wing. It has perished, or it is not born. It was, or it is not. Yet even this approximation to the truth is *infinitely* false. For again subdivide that solitary drop, which only was found to represent the present, into a lower series of similar fractions, and the actual present which you arrest measures now but the thirty-six-millionth of an hour; and so by infinite declensions the true and very present, in which only we live and enjoy, will vanish into a mote of a mote, distinguishable only by a heavenly vision. Therefore the present, which only man possesses, offers less capacity for his footing than the slenderest film that ever spider twisted from her womb. Therefore, also, even this incalculable shadow from the narrowest pencil of moonlight is more transitory than geometry can measure, or thought of angel can overtake. The time which *is* contracts into a mathematic point; and even that point perishes a thousand times before we can utter its birth. All is finite in the present; and even that finite is infinite in its velocity of flight towards death. But in God there is nothing finite; but in God there is nothing transitory; but in God there *can* be nothing that tends to death. Therefore it follows that for God there can be no present. The future is the present of God, and to the future it is that he sacrifices the human present. Therefore it is that he works by earthquake. Therefore it is that he works by grief. Therefore it is that he works by earthquake! O, deep is the ploughing of earthquake! O, deep''—(and his voice swelled like a *sanctus*[2] rising from a choir of a cathedral)—''O, deep is the ploughing of grief! But oftentimes less would not suffice for the agriculture of God. Upon a night of

earthquake he builds a thousand years of pleasant habitations for man. Upon the sorrow of an infant he raises oftentimes from human intellects glorious vintages that could not else have been. Less than these fierce ploughshares would not have stirred the stubborn soil. The one is needed for Earth, our planet,—for Earth itself as the dwelling-place of man; but the other is needed yet oftener for God's mightiest instrument,—yes,'' (and he looked solemnly at myself), ''is needed for the mysterious children of the Earth!''

From THE POETRY OF POPE
1848
LITERATURE OF KNOWLEDGE AND LITERATURE OF POWER

• • • • • •

What is it that we mean by *literature?* Popularly, and amongst the thoughtless, it is held to include everything that is printed in a book. Little logic is required to disturb *that* definition. The most thoughtless person is easily made aware that in the idea of *literature* one essential element is,—some relation to a general and common interest of man, so that what applies only to a local or professional or merely personal interest, even though presenting itself in the shape of a book, will not belong to literature. So far the definition is easily narrowed; and it is as easily expanded. For not only is much that takes a station in books not literature, but, inversely, much that really *is* literature never reaches a station in books. The weekly sermons of Christendom, that vast pulpit literature which acts so extensively upon the popular mind—to warn, to uphold, to renew, to comfort, to alarm—does not attain the sanctuary of libraries in the ten-thousandth part of its extent. The drama, again, as for instance the finest of Shakspeare's plays in England and all leading Athenian plays in the noontide of the Attic stage,[1] operated as a literature on the public mind, and were (according to the strictest letter of that term) *published* through the audiences that witnessed[2] their representation, some time before they were published as things to be read; and they were published in this scenical mode of publication with much more effect than they could have had as books

---

[1] water clock
[2] A part of the mass, beginning with the Latin words *sanctus, sanctus, sanctus* (holy, holy, holy).

[1] The time of Æschylus, Sophocles, and Euripides, 5th century B. C.
[2] "Charles I, for example, when Prince of Wales, and many others in his father's court, gained their known familiarity with Shakspeare—not through the original quartos, so slenderly diffused, nor through the first folio of 1623, but through the court representations of his chief dramas at Whitehall."—De Quincey.

during ages of costly copying or of costly printing.

Books, therefore, do not suggest an idea co-extensive and interchangeable with the idea of literature, since much literature, scenic, forensic, or didactic (as from lectures and public orators), may never come into books, and much that *does* come into books may connect itself with no literary interest. But a far more important correction, applicable to the common vague idea of literature, is to be sought, not so much in a better definition of literature, as in a sharper distinction of the two functions which it fulfils. In that great social organ which, collectively, we call literature, there may be distinguished two separate offices, that may blend and often *do* so, but capable, severally, of a severe insulation, and naturally fitted for reciprocal repulsion. There is, first, the literature of *knowledge,* and, secondly, the literature of *power.* The function of the first is to *teach;* the function of the second is to *move:* the first is a rudder; the second an oar or a sail. The first speaks to the *mere* discursive understanding; the second speaks ultimately, it may happen, to the higher understanding, or reason, but always *through* affections of pleasure and sympathy. Remotely it may travel towards an object seated in what Lord Bacon calls *dry* light;[1] but proximately it does and must operate—else it ceases to be a literature of *power*—on and through that *humid* light which clothes itself in the mists and glittering *iris*[2] of human passions, desires, and genial emotions. Men have so little reflected on the higher functions of literature as to find it a paradox if one should describe it as a mean or subordinate purpose of books to give information. But this is a paradox only in the sense which makes it honorable to be paradoxical. Whenever we talk in ordinary language of seeking information or gaining knowledge, we understand the words as connected with something of absolute novelty. But it is the grandeur of all truth which *can* occupy a very high place in human interests that it is never absolutely novel to the meanest of minds: it exists eternally, by way of germ or latent principle, in the lowest as in the highest, needing to be developed but never to be planted. To be capable of transplantation is the immediate criterion of a truth that ranges on a lower

scale. Besides which, there is a rarer thing than truth, namely, *power,* or deep sympathy with truth. What is the effect, for instance, upon society, of children? By the pity, by the tenderness, and by the peculiar modes of admiration, which connect themselves with the helplessness, with the innocence, and with the simplicity of children, not only are the primal affections strengthened and continually renewed, but the qualities which are dearest in the sight of heaven —the frailty, for instance, which appeals to forbearance, the innocence which symbolizes the heavenly, and the simplicity which is most alien from the worldly—are kept up in perpetual remembrance, and their ideals are continually refreshed. A purpose of the same nature is answered by the higher literature, *viz.,* the literature of power. What do you learn from *Paradise Lost?* Nothing at all. What do you learn from a cookery-book? Something new, something that you did not know before, in every paragraph. But would you therefore put the wretched cookery-book on a higher level of estimation than the divine poem? What you owe to Milton is not any knowledge, of which a million separate items are still but a million of advancing steps on the same earthly level; what you owe is *power,* that is, exercise and expansion to your own latent capacity of sympathy with the infinite, where every pulse and each separate influx is a step upwards, a step ascending as upon a Jacob's ladder[1] from earth to mysterious altitudes above the earth. *All* the steps of knowledge, from first to last, carry you further on the same plane, but could never raise you one foot above your ancient level of earth; whereas the very *first* step in power is a flight, is an ascending movement into another element where earth is forgotten.

Were it not that human sensibilities are ventilated and continually called out into exercise by the great phenomena of infancy, or of real life as it moves through chance and change, or of literature as it recombines these elements in the mimicries of poetry, romance, etc., it is certain that, like any animal power or muscular energy falling into disuse, all such sensibilities would gradually droop and dwindle. It is in relation to these great *moral* capacities of man that the literature of power, as contra-distinguished from that of knowledge, lives and has its field of action. It is concerned with what is highest in man; for the Scriptures themselves never condescended to deal by sug-

---

[1] "Heraclitus the Obscure said: *The dry light was the best soul.* Meaning, when the faculties intellectual are in vigor, not wet, nor, as it were, blooded by the affections."—Bacon, *Apophthegms New and Old,* 268 (188).

[2] rainbow (Iris was the personification of the rainbow.)

[1] See *Genesis,* 28 :12.

Pat Williams
610 W 113th
~~AC~~ UN 4-6862
after 6:00 —
      between 1.50 & 2.00 / hour
IBM electric

Not W.'s function obeying it may be a
tragic prisoner on the action it
supernature ranges. Whiremba
function on, so as in the
sense of little a lawerless colony; also
at minimum has type. —

gestion or co-operation with the mere discursive understanding: when speaking of man in his intellectual capacity, the Scriptures speak, not of the understanding, but of *"the understanding heart,"*[1] making the heart,—that is, the great *intuitive* (or non-discursive) organ, to be the interchangeable formula for man in his highest state of capacity for the infinite. Tragedy, romance, fairy tale, or epopee,[2] all alike restore to man's mind the ideals of justice, of hope, of truth, of mercy, of retribution, which else (left to the support of daily life in its realities) would languish for want of sufficient illustration. What is meant, for instance, by *poetic justice?* It does not mean a justice that differs by its object from the ordinary justice of human jurisprudence, for then it must be confessedly a very bad kind of justice; but it means a justice that differs from common forensic justice by the degree in which it *attains* its object, a justice that is more omnipotent over its own ends, as dealing, not with the refractory elements of earthly life, but with the elements of its own creation and with materials flexible to its own purest preconceptions. It is certain that, were it not for the literature of power, these ideals would often remain amongst us as mere arid notional forms; whereas, by the creative forces of man put forth in literature, they gain a vernal life of restoration and germinate into vital activities. The commonest novel, by moving in alliance with human fears and hopes, with human instincts of wrong and right, sustains and quickens those affections. Calling them into action, it rescues them from torpor. And hence the pre-eminency, over all authors that merely *teach,* of the meanest that moves, or that teaches, if at all, indirectly *by* moving. The very highest work that has ever existed in the literature of knowledge is but a provisional work, a book upon trial and sufferance, and *quamdiu bene se gesserit.*[3] Let its teaching be even partially revised, let it be but expanded, nay, even let its teaching be but placed in a better order, and instantly it is superseded. Whereas the feeblest works in the literature of power, surviving at all, survive as finished and unalterable among men. For instance, the *Principia* of Sir Isaac Newton was a book *militant* on earth from the first.[4] In all stages of its progress it would have to fight for its existence: first, as regards absolute truth; secondly, when that combat was over, as regards its form, or mode of presenting the truth. And as soon as a La Place, or anybody else, builds higher upon the foundations laid by this book, effectually he throws it out of the sunshine into decay and darkness; by weapons won from this book he superannuates and destroys this book, so that soon the name of Newton remains as a mere *nominis umbra,*[1] but his book, as a living power, has transmigrated into other forms. Now, on the contrary, the *Iliad,* the *Prometheus* of Æschylus, the *Othello* or *King Lear,* the *Hamlet* or *Macbeth,* and the *Paradise Lost* are not militant but triumphant forever, as long as the languages exist in which they speak or can be taught to speak. They never *can* transmigrate into new incarnations. To reproduce these in new forms or variations, even if in some things they should be improved, would be to plagiarize. A good steam-engine is properly superseded by a better. But one lovely pastoral valley is not superseded by another, nor a statue of Praxiteles by a statue of Michael Angelo.[2] These things are separated, not by imparity, but by disparity. They are not thought of as unequal under the same standard, but as different in *kind,* and, if otherwise equal, as equal under a different standard. Human works of immortal beauty and works of nature in one respect stand on the same footing: they never absolutely repeat each other, never approach so near as not to differ; and they differ not as better and worse, or simply by more and less; they differ by undecipherable and incommunicable differences, that cannot be caught by mimicries, that cannot be reflected in the mirror of copies, that cannot become ponderable in the scales of vulgar comparison.

. . . . . .

THE ENGLISH MAIL-COACH
1849

Section I—The Glory of Motion

Some twenty or more years before I matriculated at Oxford, Mr. Palmer, at that time M. P. for Bath, had accomplished two things, very hard to do on our little planet, the Earth, however cheap they may be held by eccentric people in comets: he

---

[1] *1 Kings*, 3 :9, 12.   [2] epic
[3] as long as it bore itself well
[4] The full title is *Philosophiæ Naturalis Principia Mathematica (The Mathematical Principles of Natural Philosophy).* It was published in 1687.

[1] shadow of a name
[2] The work of Praxiteles is noted for grace and beauty ; that of Michelangelo for power.

had invented mail-coaches, and he had married the daughter of a duke. He was, therefore, just twice as great a man as Galileo, who did certainly invent (or, which is the same thing,[1] discover) the satellites of Jupiter, those very next things extant to mail-coaches in the two capital pretensions of speed and keeping time, but, on the other hand, who did *not* marry the daughter of a duke.

These mail-coaches, as organized by Mr. Palmer, are entitled to a circumstantial notice from myself, having had so large a share in developing the anarchies of my subsequent dreams: an agency which they accomplished, 1st, through velocity at that time unprecedented—for they first revealed the glory of motion; 2dly, through grand effects for the eye between lamplight and the darkness upon solitary roads; 3dly, through animal beauty and power so often displayed in the class of horses selected for this mail service; 4thly, through the conscious presence of a central intellect, that, in the midst of vast distances[2]—of storms, of darkness, of danger—overruled all obstacles into one steady co-operation to a national result. For my own feeling, this post-office service spoke as by some mighty orchestra, where a thousand instruments, all disregarding each other, and so far in danger of discord, yet all obedient as slaves to the supreme *baton* of some great leader, terminate in a perfection of harmony like that of heart, brain, and lungs in a healthy animal organization. But, finally, that particular element in this whole combination which most impressed myself, and through which it is that to this hour Mr. Palmer's mail-coach system tyrannizes over my dreams by terror and terrific beauty, lay in the awful *political* mission which at that time it fulfilled. The mail-coach it was that distributed over the face of the land, like the opening of apocalyptic vials,[3] the heart-shaking news of Trafalgar, of Salamanca, of Vittoria, of Waterloo. These were the harvests that, in the grandeur of their reaping, redeemed the

tears and blood in which they had been sown. Neither was the meanest peasant so much below the grandeur and the sorrow of the times as to confound battles such as these, which were gradually moulding the destinies of Christendom, with the vulgar conflicts of ordinary warfare, so often no more than gladiatorial trials of national prowess. The victories of England in this stupendous contest rose of themselves as natural *Te Deums*[1] to heaven; and it was felt by the thoughtful that such victories, at such a crisis of general prostration, were not more beneficial to ourselves than finally to France, our enemy, and to the nations of all western or central Europe, through whose pusillanimity it was that the French domination had prospered.

The mail-coach, as the national organ for publishing these mighty events, thus diffusively influential, became itself a spiritualized and glorified object to an impassioned heart; and naturally, in the Oxford of that day, *all* hearts were impassioned, as being all (or nearly all) in *early* manhood. In most universities there is one single college; in Oxford there were five-and-twenty, all of which were peopled by young men, the *élite* of their own generation; not boys, but men: none under eighteen. In some of these many colleges the custom permitted the student to keep what are called "short terms"; that is, the four terms of Michaelmas, Lent, Easter, and Act,[2] were kept by a residence, in the aggregate, of ninety-one days, or thirteen weeks. Under this interrupted residence, it was possible that a student might have a reason for going down to his home four times in the year. This made eight journeys to and fro. But, as these homes lay dispersed through all the shires of the island, and most of us disdained all coaches except his Majesty's mail, no city out of London could pretend to so extensive a connection with Mr. Palmer's establishment as Oxford. Three mails, at the least, I remember as passing every day through Oxford, and benefiting by my personal patronage—*viz.*, the Worcester, the Gloucester, and the Holyhead mail. Naturally, therefore, it became a point of some interest with us, whose journeys revolved every six weeks on an average, to look a little into the executive details of

---

[1] *"The same thing'*:—Thus, in the calendar of the Church Festivals, the discovery of the true cross (by Helen, the mother of Constantine) is recorded (and, one might think, with the express consciousness of sarcasm) as the *Invention* of the Cross."—De Quincey.

[2] *"'Vast distances'*:—One case was familiar to mail-coach travellers where two mails in opposite directions, north and south, starting at the same minute from points six hundred miles apart, met almost constantly at a particular bridge which bisected the total distance."—De Quincey.

[3] Bowls mentioned in the Apocalypse, containing the wrath of God, which the angels are to pour out. See *Revelation*, 16.

[1] Hymns of praise: so called from the first words of a celebrated Christian hymn, *Te Deum laudamus* (we praise thee, O God).

[2] Corresponding roughly to autumn, winter, spring, and summer terms. Michaelmas, the feast of St. Michael, is celebrated Sept. 29; Lent is the period before Easter, never as late as May; Act is the last term of the academic year, the occasion of the public presentation of a thesis by a candidate for a degree.

the system. With some of these Mr. Palmer had no concern; they rested upon bye-laws enacted by posting-houses[1] for their own benefit, and upon other bye-laws, equally stern, enacted by the inside passengers for the illustration of their own haughty exclusiveness. These last were of a nature to rouse our scorn; from which the transition was not very long to systematic mutiny. Up to this time, say 1804, or 1805 (the year of Trafalgar), it had been the fixed assumption of the four inside people (as an old tradition of all public carriages derived from the reign of Charles II) that they, the illustrious quaternion[2] constituted a porcelain variety of the human race, whose dignity would have been compromised by exchanging one word of civility with the three miserable delf-ware outsides.[3] Even to have kicked an outsider might have been held to attaint[4] the foot concerned in that operation, so that, perhaps, it would have required an act of Parliament to restore its purity of blood. What words, then, could express the horror, and the sense of treason, in that case, which *had* happened, where all three outsides (the trinity of Pariahs) made a vain attempt to sit down at the same breakfast-table or dinner-table with the consecrated four? I myself witnessed such an attempt; and on that occasion a benevolent old gentleman endeavored to soothe his three holy associates, by suggesting that, if the outsides were indicted for this criminal attempt at the next assizes, the court would regard it as a case of lunacy or *delirium tremens* rather than of treason. England owes much of her grandeur to the depth of the aristocratic element in her social composition, when pulling against her strong democracy. I am not the man to laugh at it. But sometimes, undoubtedly, it expressed itself in comic shapes. The course taken with the infatuated outsiders, in the particular attempt which I have noticed, was that the waiter, beckoning them away from the privileged *salle-à-manger*,[5] sang out, "This way, my good men," and then enticed these good men away to the kitchen. But that plan had not always answered. Sometimes, though rarely, cases occurred where the intruders, being stronger than usual, or more vicious than usual, resolutely refused to budge, and so far carried their point as to have a separate table arranged for themselves in a corner of the general room. Yet, if an Indian screen could be found ample enough to plant them out from the very eyes of the high table, or *dais*, it then became possible to assume as a fiction of law that the three delf fellows, after all, were not present. They could be ignored by the porcelain men, under the maxim that objects not appearing and objects not existing are governed by the same logical construction.[1]

Such being, at that time, the usage of mail-coaches, what was to be done by us of young Oxford? We, the most aristocratic of people, who were addicted to the practice of looking down superciliously even upon the insides themselves as often very questionable characters—were we, by voluntarily going outside, to court indignities? If our dress and bearing sheltered us generally from the suspicion of being "raff" (the name at that period for "snobs"[2]), we really *were* such constructively by the place we assumed. If we did not submit to the deep shadow of eclipse, we entered at least the skirts of its penumbra.[3] And the analogy of theatres was valid against us,—where no man can complain of the annoyances incident to the pit[4] or gallery, having his instant remedy in paying the higher price of the boxes. But the soundness of this analogy we disputed. In the case of the theatre, it cannot be pretended that the inferior situations have any separate attractions, unless the pit may be supposed to have an advantage for the purposes of the critic or the dramatic reporter. But the critic or reporter is a rarity. For most people, the sole benefit is in the price. Now, on the contrary,

---

[1] Inns where horses were changed.
[2] group of four
[3] Delf is earthenware originally made at Delft, Holland, in imitation of porcelain. In the time of Charles II (1660-85) no one sat outside; later, servants occupied the outside places.
[4] disgrace (This is a legal term applied to persons convicted of treason. The property of a person so convicted was forfeited and his right to receive or transmit by inheritance was cancelled. The "attaint" was extended to his descendants unless Parliament removed the attainder.)
[5] dining room

[1] "*De non apparentibus, etc.*"—De Quincey.
    This is a Roman legal phrase, the full form of which is *De non apparentibus et non existentibus eadem est lex.*
[2] "'Snobs,' and its antithesis, 'nobs,' arose among the internal factions of shoemakers perhaps ten years later. Possibly enough, the terms may have existed much earlier; but they were then first made known, picturesquely and effectively, by a trial at some assizes which happened to fix the public attention."—De Quincey.
    In university speech, *snob* meant *townsman* as opposed to *gownsman.* Later, the name was applied to a workman who accepted lower wages during a strike.
[3] Partial shadow, in an eclipse when the light is only partly cut off by the intervening body.
[4] The high-priced place—the orchestra—in the American theater, corresponds with what formerly was the cheap pit of the English theater.

the outside of the mail had its own incommunicable advantages. These we could not forego. The higher price we would willingly have paid, but not the price connected with the condition of riding inside; whch condition we pronounced insufferable. The air, the freedom of prospect, the proximity to the horses, the elevation of seat: these were what we required; but, above all, the certain anticipation of purchasing occasional opportunities of driving.

Such was the difficulty which pressed us; and under the coercion of this difficulty we instituted a searching inquiry into the true quality and valuation of the different apartments about the mail. We conducted this inquiry on metaphysical principles; and it was ascertained satisfactorily that the roof of the coach, which by some weak men had been called the attics, and by some the garrets, was in reality the drawing-room; in which drawing-room the box[1] was the chief ottoman or sofa; whilst it appeared that the *inside,* which had been traditionally regarded as the only room tenantable by gentlemen, was, in fact, the coal-cellar in disguise.

Great wits jump.[2] The very same idea had not long before struck the celestial intellect of China. Amongst the presents carried out by our first embassy to that country was a state-coach. It had been specially selected as a personal gift by George III; but the exact mode of using it was an intense mystery to Pekin. The ambassador, indeed (Lord Macartney), had made some imperfect explanations upon this point; but, as His Excellency communicated these in a diplomatic whisper at the very moment of his departure, the celestial intellect was very feebly illuminated, and it became necessary to call a cabinet council on the grand state question, "Where was the Emperor to sit?" The hammer-cloth[3] happened to be unusually gorgeous; and, partly on that consideration, but partly also because the box offered the most elevated seat, was nearest to the moon, and undeniably went foremost, it was resolved by acclamation that the box was the imperial throne, and, for the scoundrel who drove,—he might sit where he could find a perch. The horses, therefore, being harnessed, solemnly his imperial majesty ascended his new English throne under a flourish of trumpets, having the first lord of the treasury on his right hand, and the chief

jester on his left. Pekin gloried in the spectacle; and in the whole flowery people, constructively present by representation, there was but one discontented person, and *that* was the coachman. This mutinous individual audaciously shouted, "Where am *I* to sit?" But the privy council, incensed by his disloyalty, unanimously opened the door, and kicked him into the inside. He had all the inside places to himself; but such is the rapacity of ambition that he was still dissatisfied. "I say," he cried out in an extempore petition addressed to the Emperor through the window—"I say, how am I to catch hold of the reins?"—"Anyhow," was the imperial answer; "don't trouble *me,* man, in my glory. How catch the reins? Why, through the windows, through the keyholes—*anyhow.*" Finally this contumacious coachman lengthened the check-strings[1] into a sort of jury-reins[2] communicating with the horses; with these he drove as steadily as Pekin had any right to expect. The Emperor returned after the briefest of circuits; he descended in great pomp from his throne, with the severest resolution never to remount it. A public thanksgiving was ordered for his majesty's happy escape from the disease of a broken neck; and the state-coach was dedicated thenceforward as a votive offering to the god Fo Fo[3]—whom the learned more accurately called Fi Fi.

A revolution of this same Chinese character did young Oxford of that era effect in the constitution of mail-coach society. It was a perfect French Revolution; and we had good reason to say, *ça ira.*[4] In fact, it soon became *too* popular. The "public"— a well-known character, particularly disagreeable, though slightly respectable, and notorious for affecting the chief seats in synagogues[5]—had at first loudly opposed this revolution; but, when the opposition showed itself to be ineffectual, our disagreeable friend went into it with headlong zeal. At first it was a sort of race between us; and, as the public is usually from thirty to fifty years old, naturally we of young Oxford, that averaged about twenty, had the advantage. Then the public took to bribing, giving fees to horse-keepers, etc., who hired out their persons as warming-pans on the box seat. *That,* you know, was shocking to

---

[1] The driver's seat; so called from the box underneath.
[2] agree   [3] cloth that covers the box-seat

[1] strings by which the occupant signals to the driver
[2] makeshift reins
[3] This is De Quincey's creation.
[4] it will go on (This was a popular expression of the French Revolutionists, taken from one of their songs.)
[5] See *Matthew,* 23:6.

all moral sensibilities. Come to bribery, said we, and there is an end to all morality,— Aristotle's, Zeno's, Cicero's, or anybody's. And, besides, of what use was it? For *we* bribed also. And, as our bribes, to those of the public, were as five shillings to sixpence, here again young Oxford had the advantage. But the contest was ruinous to the principles of the stables connected with the mails. This whole corporation was constantly bribed, rebribed, and often sur-rebribed; a mail-coach yard was like the hustings[1] in a contested election; and a horse-keeper, ostler, or helper, was held by the philosophical at that time to be the most corrupt character in the nation.

There was an impression upon the public mind, natural enough from the continually augmenting velocity of the mail, but quite erroneous, that an outside seat on this class of carriages was a post of danger. On the contrary, I maintained that, if a man had become nervous from some gipsy prediction in his childhood, allocating to a particular moon[2] now approaching some unknown danger, and he should inquire earnestly, "Whither can I fly for shelter? Is a prison the safest retreat? or a lunatic hospital? or the British Museum?" I should have replied, "Oh no; I'll tell you what to do. Take lodgings for the next forty days on the box of his Majesty's mail. Nobody can touch you there. If it is by bills[3] at ninety days after date that you are made unhappy —if noters and protesters[4] are the sort of wretches whose astrological shadows darken the house of life[5]—then note you what I vehemently protest; *viz.*, that, no matter though the sheriff and under-sheriff in every county should be running after you with his *posse*, touch a hair of your head he cannot whilst you keep house and have your legal domicile on the box of the mail. It is felony to stop the mail; even the sheriff cannot do that. And an *extra* touch of the whip to the leaders (no great matter if it grazes the sheriff) at any time guarantees your safety." In fact, a bedroom in a quiet house seems a safe enough retreat; yet it is liable to its own notorious nuisances—to

robbers by night, to rats, to fire. But the mail laughs at these terrors. To robbers, the answer is packed up and ready for delivery in the barrel of the guard's blunderbuss. Rats again! there *are* none about mail-coaches any more than snakes in Von Troil's Iceland;[1] except, indeed, now and then a parliamentary rat,[2] who always hides his shame in what I have shown to be the "coal-cellar." And, as to fire, I never knew but one in a mail-coach; which was in the Exeter mail, and caused by an obstinate sailor bound to Devonport. Jack, making light of the law and the lawgiver that had set their faces against his offence, insisted on taking up a forbidden seat[3] in the rear of the roof, from which he could exchange his own yarns with those of the guard. No greater offence was then known to mail-coaches; it was treason, it was *læsa majestas,*[4] it was by tendency arson; and the ashes of Jack's pipe, falling amongst the straw of the hinder boot,[5] containing the mail-bags, raised a flame which (aided by

---

[1] The platform from which candidates for Parliament were nominated.
[2] assigning to a particular planet
[3] bills of exchange; promissory notes
[4] A noter is one who notes a protested bill of exchange; a protester is one who protests a bill of exchange.
[5] For astrological purposes the sky is divided into 12 sections called houses. Astrologers hold that a person's fortunes are determined by the positions of the planets at the time of his birth.

[1] "'*Von Troil's Iceland*':—The allusion is to a well-known chapter in Von Troil's work, entitled 'Concerning the Snakes of Iceland.' The entire chapter consists of these six words—'*There are no snakes in Iceland.*'"—De Quincey.
The work here referred to, Von Troil's *Letters on Iceland*, contains no chapter of this nature. Such a chapter is found, however, in Horrebow's *Natural History of Iceland* (1758). Allusion is made to this chapter in Boswell's *The Life of Samuel Johnson* (Oxford ed., 1904), 2, 212.
[2] A member of Parliament who deserts his party when it is losing, as a rat is said to leave a sinking ship or a falling house.
[3] "'*Forbidden seat*':—The very sternest code of rules was enforced upon the mails by the Post-office. Throughout England, only three outsides were allowed, of whom one was to sit on the box, and the other two immediately behind the box; none, under any pretext, to come near the guard; an indispensable caution: since else, under the guise of a passenger, a robber might by any one of a thousand advantages—which sometimes are created, but always are favored, by the animation of frank social intercourse—have disarmed the guard. Beyond the Scottish border, the regulation was so far relaxed as to allow of *four* outsides, but not relaxed at all as to the mode of placing them. One, as before, was seated on the box, and the other three on the front of the roof, with a determinate and ample separation from the little insulated chair of the guard. This relaxation was conceded by way of compensating to Scotland her disadvantages in point of population. England, by the superior density of her population, might always count upon a large fund of profits in the fractional trips of chance passengers riding for short distances of two or three stages. In Scotland this chance counted for much less. And therefore, to make good the deficiency, Scotland was allowed a compensatory profit upon one *extra* passenger."—De Quincey.
[4] A crime committed against the sovereign power; often any offense violating the dignity of the sovereign power or its representative.
[5] The place for baggage on the roof of a coach, under the guard's seat.

the wind of our motion) threatened a revolution in the republic of letters.[1] Yet even this left the sanctity of the box unviolated. In dignified repose, the coachman and myself sat on, resting with benign composure upon our knowledge that the fire would have to burn its way through four inside passengers before it could reach ourselves. I remarked to the coachman, with a quotation from Virgil's *Æneid* really too hackneyed—

> Jam proximus ardet
> Ucalegon.[2]

But, recollecting that the Virgilian part of the coachman's education might have been neglected, I interpreted so far as to say that perhaps at that moment the flames were catching hold of our worthy brother and inside passenger, Ucalegon. The coachman made no answer,—which is my own way when a stranger addresses me either in Syriac or in Coptic; but by his faint skeptical smile he seemed to insinuate that he knew better,—for that Ucalegon, as it happened, was not in the way-bill,[3] and therefore could not have been booked.

No dignity is perfect which does not at some point ally itself with the mysterious. The connection of the mail with the state and the executive government—a connection obvious, but yet not strictly defined—gave to the whole mail establishment an official grandeur which did us service on the roads, and invested us with seasonable terrors. Not the less impressive were those terrors because their legal limits were imperfectly ascertained. Look at those turnpike gates: with what deferential hurry, with what an obedient start, they fly open at our approach! Look at that long line of carts and carters ahead, audaciously usurping the very crest of the road. Ah! traitors, they do not hear us as yet; but, as soon as the dreadful blast of our horn reaches them with proclamation of our approach, see with what frenzy of trepidation they fly to their horses' heads, and deprecate our wrath by the precipitation of their crane-neck quarterings.[4] Treason they feel to be their crime; each individual carter feels himself under the ban of confiscation and attainder,[5] his blood

is attained through six generations; and nothing is wanting but the headsman and his axe, the block and the sawdust, to close up the vista of his horrors. What! shall it be within benefit of clergy[1] to delay the king's message on the high road?—to interrupt the great respirations, ebb and flood, *systole* and *diastole*,[2] of the national intercourse?—to endanger the safety of tidings running day and night between all nations and languages? Or can it be fancied, amongst the weakest of men, that the bodies of the criminals will be given up to their widows for Christian burial?[3] Now, the doubts which were raised as to our powers did more to wrap them in terror, by wrapping them in uncertainty, than could have been effected by the sharpest definitions of the law from the Quarter Sessions.[4] We, on our parts (we, the collective mail, I mean), did our utmost to exalt the idea of our privileges by the insolence with which we wielded them. Whether this insolence rested upon law that gave it a sanction, or upon conscious power that haughtily dispensed with that sanction, equally it spoke from a potential station; and the agent, in each particular insolence of the moment, was viewed reverentially, as one having authority.

Sometimes after breakfast his Majesty's mail would become frisky; and, in its difficult wheelings amongst the intricacies of early markets, it would upset an apple-cart, a cart loaded with eggs, etc. Huge was the smash. Huge was the affliction and dismay, awful was the smash. I, as far as possible, endeavored in such a case to represent the conscience and moral sensibilities of the mail; and, when wildernesses of eggs were lying poached under our horses' hoofs, then would I stretch forth my hands in sorrow, saying (in words too celebrated at that time, from the false echoes of Marengo),[5] "Ah! wherefore have

---

[1] newspapers, letters, etc., in the mail-bags
[2] now next (to the house of Deiphobus) Ucalegon (*i. e.*, his house) begins to blaze (*Æneid*, 2, 311)
[3] list of passengers
[4] De Quincey derives *quartering* from the French *cartayer*, to evade a rut or any obstacle. The crane-neck, here used for wagon, is a bent iron bar that connects the front and back parts of a vehicle. See p. 1148b, n. 2.
[5] See p. 1131a, 20 and n. 4.

[1] The clergy, and afterwards all persons who could read, were exempt from trial in the secular courts until 1827.
[2] alternate contraction and expansion (of the heart)
[3] The bodies of criminals were used by hospitals as subjects for dissection.
[4] court sessions held in the counties by the Justices of the Peace
[5] "*False echoes*':—Yes, false! for the words ascribed to Napoleon, as breathed to the memory of Desaix, never were uttered at all. They stand in the same category of theatrical fictions as the cry of the foundering line-of-battle ship *Vengeur*, as the vaunt of General Cambronne at Waterloo, 'La Garde meurt, mais ne se rend pas,' or as the repartees of Talleyrand."—De Quincey.
The words quoted in the text were said to have been spoken by Napoleon when he heard that Desaix had been killed in the Battle of

we not time to weep over you?"—which was evidently impossible, since, in fact, we had not time to laugh over them. Tied to post-office allowance in some cases of fifty minutes for eleven miles, could the royal mail pretend to undertake the offices of sympathy and condolence? Could it be expected to provide tears for the accidents of the road? If even it seemed to trample on humanity, it did so, I felt, in discharge of its own more peremptory duties.

Upholding the morality of the mail, *a fortiori*[1] I upheld its rights; as a matter of duty, I stretched to the uttermost its privilege of imperial precedency, and astonished weak minds by the feudal powers which I hinted to be lurking constructively in the charters of this proud establishment. Once I remember being on the box of the Holyhead mail, between Shrewsbury and Oswestry, when a tawdry thing from Birmingham, some "Tallyho" or "Highflyer," all flaunting with green and gold, came up alongside of us. What a contrast to our royal simplicity of form and color in this plebeian wretch! The single ornament on our dark ground of chocolate color was the mighty shield of the imperial arms, but emblazoned in proportions as modest as a signet-ring bears to a seal of office. Even this was displayed only on a single panel, whispering, rather than proclaiming, our relations to the mighty state; whilst the beast from Birmingham, our green-and-gold friend from false, fleeting, perjured[2] Brummagem,[3] had as much writing and painting on its sprawling flanks as would have puzzled a decipherer from the tombs of Luxor. For some time this Birmingham machine ran along by our side—a piece of familiarity that already of itself seemed to me sufficiently jacobinical.[1] But all at once a movement of the horses announced a desperate intention of leaving us behind. "Do you see *that?*" I said to the coachman.—"I see," was his short answer. He was wide awake,—yet he waited longer than seemed prudent; for the horses of our audacious opponent had a disagreeable air of freshness and power. But his motive was loyal; his wish was that the Birmingham conceit should be full-blown before he froze it. When *that* seemed right, he unloosed, or, to speak by a stronger word, he *sprang*, his known resources: he slipped our royal horses like cheetahs,[2] or hunting-leopards, after the affrighted game. How they could retain such a reserve of fiery power after the work they had accomplished seemed hard to explain. But on our side, besides the physical superiority, was a tower of moral strength, namely, the king's name, "which they upon the adverse faction wanted."[3] Passing them without an effort, as it seemed, we threw them into the rear with so lengthening an interval between us as proved in itself the bitterest mockery of their presumption; whilst our guard blew back a shattering blast of triumph that was really too painfully full of derision.

I mention this little incident for its connection with what followed. A Welsh rustic, sitting behind me, asked if I had not felt my heart burn within me[4] during the progress of the race? I said, with philosophic calmness, *No;* because we were not racing with a mail, so that no glory could be gained. In fact, it was sufficiently mortifying that such a Birmingham thing should dare to challenge us. The Welshman replied that he didn't see *that;* for that a cat might look at a king, and a Brummagem coach might lawfully race the Holyhead mail. "*Race* us, if you like," I replied, "though even *that* has an air of sedition; but not *beat* us. This would have been treason; and for its own sake I am glad that the 'Tallyho' was disappointed." So dissatisfied did the Welshman seem with this opinion that at last I was obliged to tell him a very fine story from one of our elder dramatists:[5] *viz.*, that once,

Marengo, in 1800. In spite of the fact that Desaix was instantly killed, Napoleon published three versions of a message from Desaix to himself, the original version being, "Go, tell the First Consul that I die with this regret,—that I have not done enough for posterity." See Ashton's *English Caricature and Satire on Napoleon I* (1884), 1, 130-32; also Lanfrey's *The History of Napoleon the First* (London, 1886), 2, 39.

In a naval battle in 1794, the British fleet captured six French ships and sunk a seventh, the *Vengeur*. It was falsely reported that the Vengeur went down with her crew shouting *Vive la République*, whereas they were imploring aid, which there was not time to give them. See Carlyle's *On the Sinking of the Vengeur* and *The French Revolution*, 5, 6.

The phrase "The guard dies, and does not surrender," incorrectly said to have been spoken by Cambronne at Waterloo when he was asked to surrender, is thought to have been invented by Rougemont, a prolific author of pithy sayings. See Bartlett's *Familiar Quotations*, 661.

[1] with greater force   [2] See *Richard III*, I, 4, 55.
[3] A vulgar form of *Birmingham*. The city was a noted manufactory of gilt toys, cheap jewelry, etc. See p. 1136a, 29-31.

[1] revolutionary (The Jacobins were an extremely radical club during the French Revolution, so called from its being established at a former convent of the Jacobin friars in Paris.)
[2] That is, he let them run free of their reins, as cheetahs are freed from the leash to hunt game.
[3] *Richard III*, V, 3, 12-13.   [4] See *Luke*, 24 :32.
[5] Thomas Heywood (d. 1650?) in *The Royal King and Loyal Subject*.

in some far Oriental kingdom, when the sultan of all the land, with his princes, ladies, and chief omrahs,[1] were flying their falcons, a hawk suddenly flew at a majestic eagle, and, in defiance of the eagle's natural advantage, in contempt also of the eagle's traditional royalty, and before the whole assembled field of astonished spectators from Agra and Lahore, killed the eagle on the spot. Amazement seized the sultan at the unequal contest, and burning admiration for its unparalleled result. He commanded that the hawk should be brought before him; he caressed the bird with enthusiasm; and he ordered that, for the commemoration of his matchless courage, a diadem of gold and rubies should be solemnly placed on the hawk's head, but then that, immediately after this solemn coronation, the bird should be led off to execution, as the most valiant indeed of traitors, but not the less a traitor, as having dared to rise rebelliously against his liege lord and anointed sovereign, the eagle. "Now," said I to the Welshman, "to you and me, as men of refined sensibilities, how painful it would have been that this poor Brummagem brute, the 'Tallyho,' in the impossible case of a victory over us, should have been crowned with Birmingham tinsel, with paste diamonds and Roman pearls, and then led off to instant execution." The Welshman doubted if that could be warranted by law. And, when I hinted at the 6th of Edward Longshanks,[2] chap. 18, for regulating the precedency of coaches, as being probably the statute relied on for the capital punishment of such offences, he replied drily that, if the attempt to pass a mail really were treasonable, it was a pity that the "Tallyho" appeared to have so imperfect an acquaintance with law.

The modern modes of travelling cannot compare with the old mail-coach system in grandeur and power. They boast of more velocity,—not, however, as a consciousness, but as a fact of our lifeless knowledge, resting upon *alien* evidence: as, for instance, because somebody *says* that we have gone fifty miles in the hour, though we are far from feeling it as a personal experience; or upon the evidence of a result, as that actually we find ourselves in York four hours after leaving London. Apart from such an assertion, or such a result, I myself am little aware

of the pace. But seated on the old mail-coach, we needed no evidence out of ourselves to indicate the velocity. On this system the word was not *magna loquimur,* as upon railways, but *vivimus.*[1] Yes, "magna *vivimus*"; we do not make verbal ostentation of our grandeurs, we realize our grandeurs in act, and in the very experience of life. The vital experience of the glad animal sensibilities made doubts impossible on the question of our speed; we heard our speed, we saw it, we felt it as a thrilling; and this speed was not the product of blind insensate agencies, that had no sympathy to give, but was incarnated in the fiery eyeballs of the noblest amongst brutes, in his dilated nostril, spasmodic muscles, and thunder-beating hoofs. The sensibility of the horse, uttering itself in the maniac light of his eye, might be the last vibration of such a movement; the glory of Salamanca might be the first. But the intervening links that connected them, that spread the earthquake of battle into the eyeballs of the horse, were the heart of man and its electric thrillings—kindling in the rapture of the fiery strife, and then propagating its own tumults by contagious shouts and gestures to the heart of his servant the horse. But now, on the new system of travelling,[2] iron tubes and boilers have disconnected man's heart from the ministers of his locomotion. Nile nor Trafalgar has power to raise an extra bubble in a steam-kettle. The galvanic cycle is broken up forever; man's imperial nature no longer sends itself forward through the electric sensibility of the horse; the inter-agencies are gone in the mode of communication between the horse and his master out of which grew so many aspects of sublimity under accidents of mists that hid, or sudden blazes that revealed, of mobs that agitated, or midnight solitudes that awed. Tidings fitted to convulse all nations must henceforwards travel by culinary process; and the trumpet that once announced from afar the laurelled mail, heart-shaking when heard screaming on the wind and proclaiming itself through the darkness to every village or solitary house on its route, has now given way forever to the pot-wallopings[3] of the boiler. Thus have perished multiform openings for public expressions of interest, scenical yet natural, in great national tidings,—for revelations of faces and groups that could not

---

[1] noblemen (See Wordsworth's *The Prelude,* 10, 18-20.)
[2] Edward I. Laws passed in each Parliament are divided into chapters. During the 6th year of Edward's reign (1278), only 12 laws were passed. De Quincey's jest seems lost on the Welshman.

[1] not, we speak great things, but, we live them
[2] The first railway in England was completed between Manchester and Liverpool in 1830.
[3] pot-boilings

offer themselves amongst the fluctuating mobs of a railway station. The gatherings of gazers about a laurelled mail had one centre, and acknowledged one sole interest. But the crowds attending at a railway station have as little unity as running water, and own as many centres as there are separate carriages in the train.

How else, for example, than as a constant watcher for the dawn, and for the London 10 mail that in summer months entered about daybreak amongst the lawny thickets of Marlborough forest, couldst thou, sweet Fanny of the Bath road, have become the glorified inmate of my dreams? Yet Fanny, 15 as the loveliest young woman for face and person that perhaps in my whole life I have beheld, merited the station which even now, from a distance of forty years, she holds in my dreams; yes, though by links of natural 20 association she brings along with her a troop of dreadful creatures, fabulous and not fabulous, that are more abominable to the heart than Fanny and the dawn are delightful.

Miss Fanny of the Bath road, strictly 25 speaking, lived at a mile's distance from that road, but came so continually to meet the mail that I on my frequent transits rarely missed her, and naturally connected her image with the great thoroughfare where 30 only I had ever seen her. Why she came so punctually I do not exactly know; but I believe with some burden of commissions, to be executed in Bath, which had gathered to her own residence as a central rendezvous 35 for converging them. The mail-coachman who drove the Bath mail and wore the royal livery[1] happened to be Fanny's grandfather. A good man he was, that loved his beautiful granddaughter, and, loving her 40 wisely, was vigilant over her deportment in any case where young Oxford might happen to be concerned. Did my vanity then suggest that I myself, individually, could fall within the line of his terrors? Certainly not, 45 as regarded any physical pretensions that I could plead; for Fanny (as a chance passenger from her own neighborhood once told me) counted in her train a hundred and 50

ninety-nine professed admirers, if not open aspirants to her favor; and probably not one of the whole brigade but excelled myself in personal advantages. Ulysses even, with the unfair advantage of his accursed bow,[1] could hardly have undertaken that amount of suitors. So the danger might have seemed slight—only that woman is universally aristocratic; it is amongst her nobilities of heart that she *is* so. Now, the aristocratic distinctions in my favor might easily with Miss Fanny have compensated my physical deficiencies. Did I then make love to Fanny? Why, yes; about as much love as one *could* make whilst the mail was changing horses—a process which, ten years later, did not occupy above eighty seconds; but *then,—viz.,* about Waterloo[2]—it occupied five times eighty. Now, four hundred seconds offer a field quite ample enough for whispering into a young woman's ear a great deal of truth, and (by way of parenthesis) some trifle of falsehood. Grandpapa did right, therefore, to watch me. And yet, as happens too often to the grandpapas of earth in a contest with the admirers of granddaughters, how vainly would he have watched me had I meditated any evil whispers to Fanny! She, it is my belief, would have protected herself against any man's evil suggestions. But he, as the result showed, could not have intercepted the opportunities for such suggestions. Yet, why not? Was he not active? Was he not blooming? Blooming he was as Fanny herself.

Say, all our praises why should lords——[3]

Stop, that's not the line.

Say, all our roses why should girls engross?

The coachman showed rosy blossoms on his face deeper even than his granddaughter's —*his* being drawn from the ale-cask, Fanny's from the fountains of the dawn. But, in spite of his blooming face, some infirmities he had; and one particularly in which he too much resembled a crocodile. This lay in a monstrous inaptitude for turning round. The crocodile, I presume, owes that inaptitude to the absurd *length* of his back; but in our grandpapa it arose rather from the absurd *breadth* of his back, combined, possibly, with some growing stiffness in his legs. Now, upon this crocodile infirmity of

[1] *"Wore the royal livery"*:—The general impression was that the royal livery belonged of right to the mail-coachmen as their professional dress. But that was an error. To the guard it *did* belong, I believe, and was obviously essential as an official warrant, and as a means of instant identification for his person, in the discharge of his important public duties. But the coachman, and especially if his place in the series did not connect him immediately with London and the General Post-Office, obtained the scarlet coat only as an honorary distinction after long (or, if not long, trying and special) service."—De Quincey.

[1] An allusion to the slaughter of the suitors of Penelope, the wife of Ulysses, upon the latter's return to Ithaca from his wanderings after the fall of Troy. Homer, *Odyssey*, 21-22.

[2] That is, about 1815.

[3] Pope, *Moral Essays*, 3, 249.

his I planted a human advantage for tendering my homage to Miss Fanny. In defiance of all his honorable vigilance, no sooner had he presented to us his mighty Jovian back (what a field for displaying to mankind his royal scarlet!), whilst inspecting professionally the buckles, the straps, and the silvery turrets[1] of his harness, that I raised Miss Fanny's hand to my lips, and, by the mixed tenderness and respectfulness of my manner, caused her easily to understand how happy it would make me to rank upon her list as No. 10 or 12: in which case a few casualties amongst her lovers (and, observe, they *hanged* liberally in those days) might have promoted me speedily to the top of the tree; as, on the other hand, with how much loyalty of submission I acquiesced by anticipation in her award, supposing that she should plant me in the very rearward of her favor, as No. 199+1. Most truly I loved this beautiful and ingenuous girl; and, had it not been for the Bath mail, timing all courtships by post-office allowance, heaven only knows what might have come of it. People talk of being over head and ears in love; now, the mail was the cause that I sank only over ears in love,—which, you know, still left a trifle of brain to overlook the whole conduct of the affair.

Ah, reader! when I look back upon those days, it seems to me that all things change— all things perish. "Perish the roses and the palms of kings"[2]: perish even the crowns and trophies of Waterloo: thunder and lightning are not the thunder and lightning which I remember. Roses are degenerating. The Fannies of our island—though this I say with reluctance—are not visibly improving; and the Bath road is notoriously superannuated. Crocodiles, you will say, are stationary. Mr. Waterton tells me that the crocodile does *not* change,—that a cayman,[3] in fact, or an alligator, is just as good for riding upon as he was in the time of the Pharaohs. *That* may be; but the reason is that the crocodile does not live

fast—he is a slow coach. I believe it is generally understood among naturalists that the crocodile is a blockhead. It is my own impression that the Pharaohs were also blockheads. Now, as the Pharaohs and the crocodile domineered over Egyptian society,[1] this accounts for a singular mistake that prevailed through innumerable generations on the Nile. The crocodile made the ridiculous blunder of supposing man to be meant chiefly for his own eating. Man, taking a different view of the subject, naturally met that mistake by another: he viewed the crocodile as a thing sometimes to worship, but always to run away from. And this continued till Mr. Waterton[2] changed the relations between the animals. The mode of escaping from the reptile he showed to be not by running away, but by leaping on its back booted and spurred. The two animals had misunderstood each other. The use of the crocodile has now been cleared up—*viz.*, to be ridden; and the final cause of man[3] is that he may improve the health of the crocodile by riding him a-fox-hunting before breakfast. And it is pretty certain that any crocodile who has been regularly hunted through the season, and is master of the weight he carries, will take a six-barred gate now as well as ever he would have done in the infancy of the pyramids.

If, therefore, the crocodile does *not* change, all things else undeniably *do*: even the shadow of the pyramids grows less.[4] And often the restoration in vision of Fanny and the Bath road makes me too pathetically sensible of that truth. Out of the darkness, if I happen to call back the image of Fanny, up rises suddenly from a gulf of forty years a rose in June; or, if I think for an instant of the rose in June, up rises the heavenly face of Fanny. One after the other, like the antiphonies[5] in the choral service, rise

---

[1] "*Turrets*':—As one who loves and venerates Chaucer for his unrivalled merits of tenderness, of picturesque characterization, and of narrative skill, I noticed with great pleasure that the word *torrettes* is used by him to designate the little devices through which the reins are made to pass. This same word, in the same exact sense, I heard uniformly used by many scores of illustrious mail-coachmen to whose confidential friendship I had the honor of being admitted in my younger days."—De Quincey.

Chaucer uses the word *torets* in *The Knightes Tale*, 1294, where it means the ring on a dog's collar.

[2] Wordsworth, *The Excursion*, 7, 989.

[3] The South American alligator.

[1] The crocodile was a sacred animal among ancient Egyptians.

[2] "'*Mr. Waterton*':—Had the reader lived through the last generation, he would not need to be told that, some thirty or thirty-five years back, Mr. Waterton, a distinguished country gentleman of ancient family in Northumberland, publicly mounted and rode in top-boots a savage old crocodile, that was restive and very impertinent, but all to no purpose. The crocodile jibbed and tried to kick, but vainly. He was no more able to throw the squire than Sinbad was to throw the old scoundrel who used his back without paying for it, until he discovered a mode (slightly immoral, perhaps, though some think not) of murdering the old fraudulent jockey, and so circuitously of unhorsing him."—De Quincey.

[3] the purpose for which man exists

[4] The walls and temples of Cairo were built of the exterior blocks of the Great Pyramid of Cheops.

[5] Alternate singings of a choir.

Fanny and the rose in June, then back again the rose in June and Fanny. Then come both together, as in a chorus—roses and Fannies, Fannies and roses, without end, thick as blossoms in paradise. Then comes a venerable crocodile, in a royal livery of scarlet and gold, with sixteen capes; and the crocodile is driving four-in-hand from the box of the Bath mail. And suddenly we upon the mail are pulled up by a mighty dial, sculptured with the hours, that mingle with the heavens and the heavenly host. Then all at once we are arrived at Marlborough forest, amongst the lovely households[1] of the roe-deer; the deer and their fawns retire into the dewy thickets; the thickets are rich with roses; once again the roses call up the sweet countenance of Fanny; and she, being the granddaughter of a crocodile, awakens a dreadful host of semi-legendary animals—griffins, dragons, basilisks, sphinxes[2]—till at length the whole vision of fighting images crowds into one towering armorial shield, a vast emblazonry of human charities and human loveliness that have perished, but quartered heraldically with unutterable and demoniac natures, whilst over all rises, as a surmounting crest, one fair female hand, with the forefinger pointing, in sweet, sorrowful admonition, upwards to heaven, where is sculptured the eternal writings[3] which proclaims the frailty of earth and her children.

GOING DOWN WITH VICTORY

But the grandest chapter of our experience within the whole mail-coach service was on those occasions when we went down from London with the news of victory. A period of about ten years stretched from Trafalgar to Waterloo; the second and third years of which period (1806 and 1807 were comparatively sterile; but the other nine (from 1805 to 1815 inclusively) furnished a long succession of victories, the least of which, in such a contest of Titans, had an inappreciable[1] value of position: partly for its absolute interference with the plans of our enemy, but still more from its keeping alive through central Europe the sense of a deep-seated vulnerability in France. Even to tease the coasts of our enemy, to mortify them by continual blockades, to insult them by capturing if it were but a baubling[2] schooner under the eyes of their arrogant armies, repeated from time to time a sullen proclamation of power lodged in one quarter to which the hopes of Christendom turned in secret. How much more loudly must this proclamation have spoken in the audacity[3] of having bearded the *élite* of their troops, and having beaten them in pitched battles! Five years of life it was worth paying down for the privilege of an outside place on a mail-coach, when carrying down the first tidings of any such event. And it is to be noted that, from our insular situation, and the multitude of our frigates disposable for the rapid transmission of intelligence, rarely did any unauthorized rumor steal away a prelibation[4] from the first aroma of the regular despatches. The government news was generally the earliest news.

From eight P.M. to fifteen or twenty minutes later imagine the mails assembled on parade in Lombard Street; where, at that time,[5] and not in St. Martin's-le-Grand, was seated the General Post-Office. In what exact strength we mustered I do not remember; but, from the length of each separate *attelage*,[6] we filled the street, though a long one, and though we were drawn up in double file. On *any* night the spectacle was beauti-

[1] *'Households'*:—Roe-deer do not congregate in herds like the fallow or the red deer, but by separate families, parents and children, which feature of approximation to the sanctity of human hearths, added to their comparatively miniature and graceful proportions, conciliates to them an interest of peculiar tenderness, supposing even that this beautiful creature is less characteristically impressed with the grandeurs of savage and forest life."—De Quincey.

[2] Mythical monsters. A griffin has the head and wings of an eagle, and the body of a lion. A dragon is a fire-breathing serpent with wings. A basilisk is a serpent said to be hatched from a cock's egg: it is called a cockatrice, and is fabled to kill with a look. The sphinx was a legendary animal of ancient Egypt, half lion and half man.

[3] See *Ecclesiastes*, 1 :2.

[1] too great to be estimated
[2] trifling
[3] *'Audacity'*:—Such the French accounted it; and it has struck me that Soult would not have been so popular in London, at the period of her present Majesty's coronation, or in Manchester, on occasion of his visit to that town, if they had been aware of the insolence with which he spoke of us in notes written at intervals from the field of Waterloo. As though it had been mere felony in our army to look a French one in the face, he said in more notes than one, dated from two to four P. M. on the field of Waterloo, 'Here are the English—we have them; they are caught *en flagrant délit.'* Yet no man should have known us better; no man had drunk deeper from the cup of humiliation than Soult had in 1809, when ejected by us with headlong violence from Oporto, and pursued through a long line of wrecks to the frontier of Spain; and subsequently at Albuera, in the bloodiest of recorded battles, to say nothing of Toulouse, he should have learned our pretensions."—De Quincey.

[4] foretaste
[5] *"At that time"*:—I speak of the era previous to Waterloo."—De Quincey.
[6] team and coach

ful. The absolute perfection of all the appointments about the carriages and the harness, their strength, their brilliant cleanliness, their beautiful simplicity—but, more than all, the royal magnificence of the horses —were what might first have fixed the attention. Every carriage on every morning in the year was taken down to an official inspector for examination: wheels, axles, linchpins, pole, glasses, lamps, were all critically probed and tested. Every part of every carriage had been cleaned, every horse had been groomed, with as much rigor as if they belonged to a private gentleman; and that part of the spectacle offered itself always. But the night before us is a night of victory; and, behold! to the ordinary display what a heart-shaking addition!— horses, men, carriages, all are dressed in laurels and flowers, oak-leaves[1] and ribbons. The guards, as being officially his Majesty's servants, and of the coachmen such as are within the privilege of the post-office, wear the royal liveries of course; and, as it is summer (for all the *land* victories were naturally won in summer), they wear, on this fine evening, these liveries exposed to view, without any covering of upper coats. Such a costume, and the elaborate arrangement of the laurels in their hats, dilate their hearts, by giving to them openly a personal connection with the great news in which already they have the general interest of patriotism. That great national sentiment surmounts and quells all sense of ordinary distinctions. Those passengers who happen to be gentlemen are now hardly to be distinguished as such except by dress; for the usual reserve of their manner in speaking to the attendants has on this night melted away. One heart, one pride, one glory, connects every man by the transcendent bond of his national blood. The spectators, who are numerous beyond precedent, express their sympathy with these fervent feelings by continual hurrahs. Every moment are shouted aloud by the post-office servants, and summoned to draw up, the great ancestral names of cities known to history through a thousand years—Lincoln, Winchester, Portsmouth, Gloucester, Oxford, Bristol, Manchester, York, Newcastle, Edinburgh, Glasgow, Perth, Stirling, Aberdeen—expressing the grandeur of the empire by the antiquity of its towns, and the grandeur of the mail establishment by the diffusive radiation of

[1] The British oak always has been venerated in England, and its leaves frequently are used for garlands. The laurel is an emblem of victory.

its separate missions. Every moment you hear the thunder of lids locked down upon the mail-bags. That sound to each individual mail is the signal for drawing off, which process is the finest part of the entire spectacle. Then come the horses into play. Horses! can these be horses that bound off with the action and gestures of leopards? What stir!—what sea-like ferment!—what a thundering of wheels!—what a tramping of hoofs!—what a sounding of trumpets!—what farewell cheers—what redoubling peals of brotherly congratulation, connecting the name of the particular mail — "Liverpool forever!"—with the name of the particular victory—"Badajoz forever!" or "Salamanca forever!" The half-slumbering consciousness that all night long, and all the next day—perhaps for even a longer period—many of these mails, like fire racing along a train of gunpowder, will be kindling at every instant new successions of burning joy, has an obscure effect of multiplying the victory itself, by multiplying to the imagination into infinity the stages of its progressive diffusion. A fiery arrow seems to be let loose, which from that moment is destined to travel, without intermission, westwards for three hundred miles[1]

[1] *'Three hundred'*:—Of necessity, this scale of measurement, to an American, if he happens to be a thoughtless man, must sound ludicrous. Accordingly, I remember a case in which an American writer indulges himself in the luxury of a little fibbing, by ascribing to an Englishman a pompous account of the Thames, constructed entirely upon American ideas of grandeur, and concluding in something like these terms:—'And sir, arriving at London, this mighty father of rivers attains a breadth of at least two furlongs, having, in its winding course, traversed the astonishing distance of one hundred and seventy miles.' And this the candid American thinks it fair to contrast with the scale of the Mississippi. Now, it is hardly worth while to answer a pure fiction gravely; else one might say that no Englishman out of Bedlam ever thought of looking in an island for the rivers of a continent, nor, consequently, could have thought of looking for the peculiar grandeur of the Thames in the length of its course, or in the extent of soil which it drains. Yet, if he *had* been so absurd, the American might have recollected that a river, not to be compared with the Thames even as to volume of water —*viz.*, the Tiber—has contrived to make itself heard of in this world for twenty-five centuries to an extent not reached as yet by any river, however corpulent, of his own land. The glory of the Thames is measured by the destiny of the population to which it ministers, by the commerce which it supports, by the grandeur of the empire in which, though far from the largest, it is the most influential stream. Upon some such scale, and not by a transfer of Columbian standards, is the course of our English mails to be valued. The American may fancy the effect of his own valuations to our English ears by supposing the case of a Siberian glorifying his country in these terms:—'These wretches, sir, in France and England, cannot march half a mile in any

—northwards for six hundred; and the sympathy of our Lombard Street friends at parting is exalted a hundredfold by a sort of visionary sympathy with the yet slumbering sympathies which in so vast a succession we are going to awake.

Liberated from the embarrassments of the city, and issuing into the broad uncrowded avenues of the northern suburbs, we soon begin to enter upon our natural pace of ten miles an hour. In the broad light of the summer evening, the sun, perhaps, only just at the point of setting, we are seen from every story of every house. Heads of every age crowd to the windows; young and old understand the language of our victorious symbols; and rolling volleys of sympathizing cheers run along us, behind us, and before us. The beggar, rearing himself against the wall, forgets his lameness—real or assumed—thinks not of his whining trade, but stands erect, with bold exulting smiles, as we pass him. The victory has healed him, and says, Be thou whole![1] Women and children, from garrets alike and cellars, through infinite London, look down or look up with loving eyes upon our gay ribbons and our martial laurels; sometimes kiss their hands; sometimes hang out, as signals of affection, pocket-handkerchiefs, aprons, dusters, anything that, by catching the summer breezes, will express an aerial jubilation. On the London side of Barnet, to which we draw near within a few minutes after nine, observe that private carriage which is approaching us. The weather being so warm, the glasses are all down; and one may read, as on the stage of a theatre, everything that goes on within. It contains three ladies—one likely to be "mamma," and two of seventeen or eighteen, who are probably her daughters. What lovely animation, what beautiful unpremeditated pantomime, explaining to us every syllable that passes, in these ingenuous girls! By the sudden start and raising of the hands on first discovering our laurelled equipage, by the sudden movement and appeal to the elder lady from both of them, and by the heightened color on their animated countenances, we can almost hear them saying, "See, see! Look at their laurels! Oh, mamma! there has been a great battle in Spain; and it has been a

great victory." In a moment we are on the point of passing them. We passengers—I on the box, and the two on the roof behind me—raise our hats to the ladies; the coachman makes his professional salute with the whip; the guard even, though punctilious on the matter of his dignity as an officer under the crown, touches his hat. The ladies move to us, in return, with a winning graciousness of gesture; all smile on each side in a way that nobody could misunderstand, and that nothing short of a grand national sympathy could so instantaneously prompt. Will these ladies say that we are nothing to *them?* Oh no; they will not say *that.* They cannot deny —they do not deny—that for this night they are our sisters; gentle or simple, scholar or illiterate servant, for twelve hours to come, we on the outside have the honor to be their brothers. Those poor women, again, who stop to gaze upon us with delight at the entrance of Barnet, and seem, by their air of weariness, to be returning from labor— do you mean to say that they are washerwomen and charwomen?[1] Oh, my poor friend, you are quite mistaken. I assure you they stand in a far higher rank; for this one night they feel themselves by birthright to be daughters of England, and answer to no humbler title.

Every joy, however, even rapturous joy— such is the sad law of earth—may carry with it grief, or fear of grief, to some. Three miles beyond Barnet, we see approaching us another private carriage, nearly repeating the circumstances of the former case. Here, also, the glasses are all down; here, also, is an elderly lady seated; but the two daughters are missing; for the single young person sitting by the lady's side seems to be an attendant—so I judge from her dress, and her air of respectful reserve. The lady is in mourning; and her countenance expresses sorrow. At first she does not look up; so that I believe she is not aware of our approach, until she hears the measured beating of our horses' hoofs. Then she raises her eyes to settle them painfully on our triumphal equipage. Our decorations explain the case to her at once; but she beholds them with apparent anxiety, or even with terror. Some time before this, I, finding it difficult to hit a flying mark when embarrassed by the coachman's person and reins intervening, had given to the guard a *Courier* evening paper, containing the gazette,[2] for

direction without finding a house where food can be had and lodging; whereas such is the noble desolation of our magnificent country that in many a direction for a thousand miles I will engage that a dog shall not find shelter from a snow-storm, nor a wren find an apology for breakfast.'"—De Quincey.
[1] See *Luke,* 8 :48.

[1] women who do odd jobs of household work
[2] official lists of appointments, promotions, names of bankrupts, and other public notices

the next carriage that might pass. Accordingly he tossed it in, so folded that the huge capitals expressing some such legend as GLORIOUS VICTORY might catch the eye at once. To see the paper, however, at all, interpreted as it was by our ensigns of triumph, explained everything; and, if the guard were right in thinking the lady to have received it with a gesture of horror, it could not be doubtful that she had suffered some deep personal affliction in connection with this Spanish war.

Here, now, was the case of one who, having formerly suffered, might, erroneously perhaps, be distressing herself with anticipations of another similar suffering. That same night, and hardly three hours later, occurred the reverse case. A poor woman, who too probably would find herself, in a day or two, to have suffered the heaviest of afflictions by the battle, blindly allowed herself to express an exultation so unmeasured in the news and its details as gave to her the appearance which amongst Celtic Highlanders is called *fey*.[1] This was at some little town where we changed horses an hour or two after midnight. Some fair or wake had kept the people up out of their beds, and had occasioned a partial illumination of the stalls and booths, presenting an unusual but very impressive effect. We saw many lights moving about as we drew near; and perhaps the most striking scene on the whole route was our reception at this place. The flashing of torches and the beautiful radiance of blue lights (technically, Bengal lights) upon the heads of our horses; the fine effect of such a showery and ghostly illumination falling upon our flowers and glittering laurels;[2] whilst all around ourselves, that formed a centre of light, the darkness gathered on the rear and flanks in massy blackness: these optical splendors, together with the prodigious enthusiasm of the people, composed a picture at once scenical and affecting, theatrical and holy. As we stayed for three or four minutes, I alighted; and immediately from a dismantled stall in the street, where no doubt she had been presiding through the earlier part of the night, advanced eagerly a middle-aged woman. The sight of my newspaper it was that had drawn her attention upon myself. The victory which we were carrying down to the provinces on *this* occasion was

the imperfect one of Talavera—imperfect for its results, such was the virtual treachery of the Spanish general, Cuesta, but not imperfect in its ever-memorable heroism. I told her the main outline of the battle. The agitation of her enthusiasm had been so conspicuous when listening, and when first applying for information, that I could not but ask her if she had not some relative in the Peninsular army. Oh yes; her only son was there. In what regiment. He was a trooper in the 23d Dragoons. My heart sank within me as she made that answer. This sublime regiment, which an Englishman should never mention without raising his hat to their memory, had made the most memorable and effective charge recorded in military annals. They leaped their horses— *over* a trench where they could; *into* it, and with the result of death or mutilation, when they could *not*. What proportion cleared the trench is nowhere stated. Those who *did* closed up and went down upon the enemy with such divinity of fervor (I use the word *divinity* by design: the inspiration of God must have prompted this movement for those even then He was calling to His presence) that two results followed. As regarded the enemy, this 23d Dragoons, not, I believe, originally three hundred and fifty strong, paralyzed a French column six thousand strong, then ascended the hill, and fixed the gaze of the whole French army. As regarded themselves, the 23d were supposed at first to have been barely not annihilated; but eventually, I believe, about one in four survived. And this, then, was the regiment—a regiment already for some hours glorified and hallowed to the ear of all London, as lying stretched, by a large majority, upon one bloody aceldama[1]—in which the young trooper served whose mother was now talking in a spirit of such joyous enthusiasm. Did I tell her the truth? Had I the heart to break up her dreams? No. Tomorrow, said I to myself—tomorrow, or the next day, will publish the worst. For one night more wherefore should she not sleep in peace? After tomorrow the chances are too many that peace will forsake her pillow. This brief respite, then, let her owe to *my* gift and *my* forbearance. But, if I told her not of the bloody price that had been paid, not therefore was I silent on the contributions from her son's regiment to that day's service and glory. I showed her

---

[1] fated to suffer death or some other calamity

[2] "'*Glittering laurels*':—I must observe that the color of *green* suffers almost a spiritual change and exaltation under the effect of Bengal lights."—De Quincey.

[1] field of blood (A name given to the field that was bought with the money received by Judas for betraying Christ. See *Acts*, 1:18-19.)

not the funeral banners under which the noble regiment was sleeping. I lifted not the overshadowing laurels from the bloody trench in which horse and rider lay mangled together. But I told her how these dear children of England, officers and privates, had leaped their horses over all obstacles as gaily as hunters to the morning's chase. I told her how they rode their horses into the midst of death,—saying to myself, but not saying to *her*, "and laid down their young lives for thee, O mother England! as willingly—poured out their noble blood as cheerfully —as ever, after a long day's sport, when infants, they had rested their weary heads upon their mother's knees, or had sunk to sleep in her arms." Strange it is, yet true, that she seemed to have no fears for her son's safety, even after this knowledge that the 23d Dragoons had been memorably engaged; but so much was she enraptured by the knowledge that *his* regiment, and therefore that *he,* had rendered conspicuous service in the dreadful conflict—a service which had actually made them, within the last twelve hours, the foremost topic of conversation in London—so absolutely was fear swallowed up in joy—that, in the mere simplicity of her fervent nature, the poor woman threw her arms around my neck, as she thought of her son, and gave to *me* the kiss which secretly was meant for *him.*

Section II—The Vision of Sudden Death

What is to be taken as the predominant opinion of man, reflective and philosophic, upon SUDDEN DEATH? It is remarkable that, in different conditions of society, sudden death has been variously regarded as the consummation of an earthly career most fervently to be desired, or, again, as that consummation which is with most horror to be deprecated. Cæsar the Dictator, at his last dinner-party (*cœna*), on the very evening before his assassination, when the minutes of his earthly career were numbered, being asked what death, in *his* judgment, might be pronounced the most eligible, replied "That which should be most sudden."[1] On the other hand, the divine Litany of our English Church, when breathing forth supplications, as if in some representative character, for the whole human race prostrate before God, places such a death in the very van of horrors: "From lightning and tem-

pest; from plague, pestilence, and famine; from battle and murder, and from SUDDEN DEATH—*Good Lord, deliver us.*" Sudden death is here made to crown the climax in a grand ascent of calamities; it is ranked among the last of curses; and yet by the noblest of Romans it was ranked as the first of blessings. In that difference most readers will see little more than the essential difference between Christianity and Paganism. But this, on consideration, I doubt. The Christian Church may be right in its estimate of sudden death; and it is a natural feeling, though after all it may also be an infirm one, to wish for a quiet dismissal from life, as that which *seems* most reconcilable with meditation, with penitential retrospects, and with the humilities of farewell prayer. There does not, however, occur to me any direct scriptural warrant for this earnest petition of the English Litany, unless under a special construction of the word *sudden*. It seems a petition indulged rather and conceded to human infirmity than exacted from human piety. It is not so much a doctrine built upon the eternities of the Christian system as a plausible opinion built upon special varieties of physical temperament. Let that, however, be as it may, two remarks suggest themselves as prudent restraints upon a doctrine which else may wander, and *has* wandered, into an uncharitable superstition. The first is this: that many people are likely to exaggerate the horror of a sudden death from the disposition to lay a false stress upon words or acts simply because by an accident they have become *final* words or acts. If a man dies, for instance, by some sudden death when he happens to be intoxicated, such a death is falsely regarded with peculiar horror, as though the intoxication were suddenly exalted into a blasphemy. But *that* is unphilosophic. The man was or he was not, *habitually* a drunkard. If not, if his intoxication were a solitary accident, there can be no reason for allowing special emphasis to this act simply because through misfortune it became his final act. Nor, on the other hand, if it were no accident, but one of his *habitual* transgressions, will it be the more habitual or the more a transgression because some sudden calamity, surprising him, has caused this habitual transgression to be also a final one. Could the man have had any reason even dimly to foresee his own sudden death, there would have been a new feature in his act of intemperance— a feature of presumption and irreverence,

---

[1] This incident is related by Suetonius in his *Life of Julius Cæsar,* ch. 87; also by Plutarch and Appian.

as in one that, having known himself drawing near to the presence of God, should have suited his demeanor to an expectation so awful. But this is no part of the case supposed. And the only new element in the man's act is not any element of special immorality, but simply of special misfortune.

The other remark has reference to the meaning of the word *sudden*. Very possibly Cæsar and the Christian Church do not differ in the way supposed,—that is, do not differ by any difference of doctrine as between Pagan and Christian views of the moral temper appropriate to death; but perhaps they are contemplating different cases. Both contemplate a violent death, a βιαθάνατος—death that is βίαιος, or, in other words, death that is brought about, not by internal and spontaneous change, but by active force having its origin from without. In this meaning the two authorities agree. Thus far they are in harmony. But the difference is that the Roman by the word *sudden* means *unlingering,* whereas the Christian Litany by *sudden death* means a *death without warning,* consequently without any available summons to religious preparation. The poor mutineer who kneels down to gather into his heart the bullets from twelve firelocks of his pitying comrades dies by a most sudden death in Cæsar's sense; one shock, one mighty spasm, one (possibly *not* one) groan, and all is over. But, in the sense of the Litany, the mutineer's death is far from sudden: his offence originally, his imprisonment, his trial, the interval between his sentence and its execution, having all furnished him with separate warnings of his fate—having all summoned him to meet it with solemn preparation.

Here at once, in this sharp verbal distinction, we comprehend the faithful earnestness with which a holy Christian Church pleads on behalf of her poor departing children that God would vouchsafe to them the last great privilege and distinction possible on a death-bed—*viz.,* the opportunity of untroubled preparation for facing this mighty trial. Sudden death, as a mere variety in the modes of dying where death in some shape is inevitable, proposes a question of choice which, equally in the Roman and the Christian sense, will be variously answered according to each man's variety of temperament. Meantime, one aspect of sudden death there is, one modification, upon which no doubt can arise, that of all martyrdoms it is the most agitating—*viz.,* where it surprises a man under circumstances which

offer (or which seem to offer some hurrying, flying, inappreciably minute chance of evading it. Sudden as the danger which it affronts must be any effort by which such an evasion can be accomplished. Even *that,* even the sickening necessity for hurrying in extremity where all hurry seems destined to be vain,—even that anguish is liable to a hideous exasperation in one particular case: *viz.,* where the appeal is made not exclusively to the instinct of self-preservation, but to the conscience, on behalf of some other life besides your own, accidentally thrown upon *your* protection. To fail, to collapse in a service merely your own, might seem comparatively venial; though, in fact, it is far from venial. But to fail in a case where Providence has suddenly thrown into your hands the final interests of another,—a fellow-creature shuddering between the gates of life and death: this, to a man of apprehensive conscience, would mingle the misery of an atrocious criminality with the misery of a bloody calamity. You are called upon, by the case supposed, possibly to die, but to die at the very moment when, by any even partial failure or effeminate collapse of your energies, you will be self-denounced as a murderer. You had but the twinkling of an eye for your effort, and that effort might have been unavailing; but to have risen to the level of such an effort would have rescued you, though not from dying, yet from dying as a traitor to your final and farewell duty.

The situation here contemplated exposes a dreadful ulcer, lurking far down in the depths of human nature. It is not that men generally are summoned to face such awful trials. But potentially, and in shadowy outline, such a trial is moving subterraneously in perhaps all men's natures. Upon the secret mirror of our dreams such a trial is darkly projected, perhaps, to every one of us. That dream, so familiar to childhood, of meeting a lion, and, through languishing prostration in hope and the energies of hope, that constant sequel of lying down before the lion publishes the secret frailty of human nature—reveals its deep-seated falsehood to itself — records its abysmal treachery. Perhaps not one of us escapes that dream; perhaps, as by some sorrowful doom of man, that dream repeats for every one of us, through every generation, the original temptation in Eden. Every one of us, in this dream, has a bait offered to the infirm places of his own individual will; once again a snare is presented for tempting him into captivity to a luxury of ruin; once again, as in aboriginal Paradise, the man falls by his own choice; again, by infinite iteration, the ancient earth groans to Heaven, through her secret caves, over the weakness of her child. "Nature, from her seat, sighing through all her works," again "gives signs of woe that all is lost";[1] and again the counter-sigh is repeated to the sorrowing heavens for the endless rebellion against God. It is not without probability that in the world of dreams every one of us ratifies for himself the original transgression. In dreams, perhaps under some secret conflict of the midnight sleeper, lighted up to the consciousness at the time, but darkened to the memory as soon as all is finished, each several child of our mysterious race completes for himself the treason of the aboriginal fall.

The incident, so memorable in itself by its features of horror, and so scenical by its grouping for the eye, which furnished the text for this reverie upon *Sudden Death* occurred to myself in the dead of night, as a solitary spectator, when seated on the box of the Manchester and Glasgow mail, in the second or third summer after Waterloo.[2] I find it necessary to relate the circumstances, because they are such as could not have occurred unless under a singular combination of accidents. In those days, the oblique and lateral communications with many rural post-offices were so arranged, either through necessity or through defect of system, as to make it requisite for the main north-western mail (*i. e.*, the *down* mail) on reaching Manchester to halt for a number of hours; how many, I do not remember; six or seven, I think; but the result was that, in the ordinary course, the mail recommenced its journey northwards about midnight. Wearied with the long detention at a gloomy hotel, I walked out about eleven o'clock at night for the sake of fresh air; meaning to fall in with the mail and resume my seat at the post-office. The night, however, being yet dark, as the moon had scarcely risen, and the streets being at that hour empty, so as to offer no opportunities for asking the road, I lost my way, and did not reach the post-office until it was considerably past midnight; but, to my great relief (as it was important for me to be in Westmoreland by the morning), I saw in the huge saucer eyes of the mail, blazing through the gloom, an evidence that my chance was not yet lost.

Past the time it was; but, by some rare accident, the mail was not even yet ready to start. I ascended to my seat on the box, where my cloak was still lying as it had lain at the Bridgewater Arms. I had left it there in imitation of a nautical discoverer, who leaves a bit of bunting on the shore of his discovery, by way of warning off the ground the whole human race, and notifying to the Christian and the heathen worlds, with his best compliments, that he has hoisted his pocket-handkerchief once and forever upon that virgin soil: thenceforward claiming the *jus dominii*[1] to the top of the atmosphere above it, and also the right of driving shafts to the centre of the earth below it; so that all people found after this warning either aloft in upper chambers of the atmosphere, or groping in subterraneous shafts, or squatting audaciously on the surface of the soil, will be treated as trespassers—kicked, that is to say, or decapitated, as circumstances may suggest, by their very faithful servant, the owner of the said pocket-handkerchief. In the present case, it is probable that my cloak might not have been respected, and the *jus gentium*[2] might have been cruelly violated in my person—for, in the dark, people commit deeds of darkness, gas being a great ally of morality; but it so happened that on this night there was no other outside passenger; and thus the crime, which else was but too probable, missed fire for want of a criminal.

Having mounted the box, I took a small quantity of laudanum, having already travelled two hundred and fifty miles—*viz.*, from a point seventy miles beyond London. In the taking of laudanum there is nothing extraordinary. But by accident it drew upon me the special attention of my assessor on the box, the coachman. And in *that* also there was nothing extraordinary. But by accident, and with great delight, it drew my own attention to the fact that this coachman was a monster in point of bulk, and that he had but one eye. In fact, he had been foretold by Virgil as

Monstrum horrendum, informe, ingens, cui lumen ademptum.[3]

He answered to the conditions in every one of the items:—1, a monster he was; 2, dreadful; 3, shapeless; 4, huge; 5, who had lost an eye. But why should *that* delight *me?*

---

[1] *Paradise Lost*, 9, 782-84.
[2] That is, in 1817 or 1818.

[1] law of ownership
[2] law of nations
[3] *Æneid*, 3, 658. The reference is to Polyphemus, one of the Cyclopes, whose eye was put out by Ulysses.

Had he been one of the Calendars[1] in *The Arabian Nights,* and had paid down his eye as the price of his criminal curiosity, what right had *I* to exult in his misfortune? I did *not* exult; I delighted in no man's punishment, though it were even merited. But these personal distinctions (Nos. 1, 2, 3, 4, 5) identified in an instant an old friend of mine whom I had known in the south for some years as the most masterly of mail-coachmen. He was the man in all Europe that could (if *any* could) have driven six-in-hand full gallop over *Al Sirat*[2]—that dreadful bridge of Mahomet, with no side battlements, and of *extra* room not enough for a razor's edge—leading right across the bottomless gulf. Under this eminent man, whom in Greek I cognominated Cyclops *Diphrélates* (Cyclops the Charioteer), I, and others known to me, studied the diphrelatic art. Excuse, reader, a word too elegant to be pedantic. As a pupil, though I paid extra fees, it is to be lamented that I did not stand high in his esteem. It showed his dogged honesty (though, observe, not his discernment) that he could not see my merits. Let us excuse his absurdity in this particular by remembering his want of an eye. Doubtless *that* made him blind to my merits. In the art of conversation, however, he admitted that I had the whip-hand of him. On the present occasion great joy was at our meeting. But what was Cyclops doing here? Had the medical men recommended northern air, or how? I collected, from such explanations as he volunteered, that he had an interest at stake in some suit-at-law now pending at Lancaster; so that probably he had got himself transferred to this station for the purpose of connecting with his professional pursuits an instant readiness for the calls of his law-suit.

Meantime, what are we stopping for? Surely we have now waited long enough. Oh, this procrastinating mail, and this procrastinating post-office! Can't they take a lesson upon that subject from *me*? Some people have called *me* procrastinating. Yet you are witness, reader, that I was here kept waiting for the post-office. Will the post-office lay its hand on its heart, in its moments of sobriety, and assert that ever it waited for me? What are they about? The guard tells me that there is a large extra accumulation of foreign mails this night, owing to irregularities caused by war, by wind, by weather, in the packet service, which as yet does not benefit at all by steam. For an *extra* hour, it seems, the post-office has been engaged in threshing out the pure wheaten correspondence of Glasgow, and winnowing it from the chaff of all baser intermediate towns. But at last all is finished. Sound your horn, guard! Manchester, good-bye! we've lost an hour by your criminal conduct at the post-office: which, however, though I do not mean to part with a serviceable ground of complaint, and one which really *is* such for the horses, to me secretly is an advantage, since it compels us to look sharply for this lost hour amongst the next eight or nine, and to recover it (if we can) at the rate of one mile extra per hour. Off we are at last, and at eleven miles an hour; and for the moment I detect no changes in the energy or in the skill of Cyclops.

From Manchester to Kendal, which virtually (though not in law) is the capital of Westmoreland, there were at this time seven stages of eleven miles each. The first five of these, counting from Manchester, terminate in Lancaster; which is therefore fifty-five miles north of Manchester, and the same distance exactly from Liverpool. The first three stages terminate in Preston (called, by way of distinction from other towns of that name, *Proud* Preston), at which place it is that the separate roads from Liverpool and from Manchester to the north become confluent.[1] Within these first three stages lay the foundation, the progress, and termination of our night's adventure. During the first stage, I found out that Cyclops was mortal: he was liable to the shocking affection of sleep—a thing which previously I had never suspected. If a man indulges in the vicious habit of sleeping, all the skill in aurigation[2] of Apollo himself, with the horses of Aurora to execute his notions, avails him nothing. "Oh, Cyclops!" I exclaimed, "thou art mortal. My friend, thou snorest." Through the first eleven miles, however, this infirmity—which

---

[1] A calendar is a member of a mendicant order of friars in Turkey and Persia.

[2] The bridge which leads over Hades to Paradise. It is a sword's edge in width.

[1] "*Confluent*":—Suppose a capital Y (the Pythagorean letter) : Lancaster is at the foot of this letter; Liverpool at the top of the *right* branch; Manchester at the top of the *left;* Proud Preston at the centre, where the two branches unite. It is thirty-three miles along either of the two branches; it is twenty-two miles along the stem,—*viz.,* from Preston in the middle to Lancaster at the root. There's a lesson in geography for the reader."—De Quincey.

[2] The act of driving a chariot or a carriage.

I grieve to say that he shared with the whole Pagan Pantheon[1]—betrayed itself only by brief snatches. On waking up, he made an apology for himself which, instead of mending matters, laid open a gloomy vista of coming disasters. The summer assizes, he reminded me, were now going on at Lancaster: in consequence of which for three nights and three days he had not lain down on a bed. During the day he was waiting for his own summons as a witness on the trial in which he was interested, or else, lest he should be missing at the critical moment, was drinking with the other witnesses under the pastoral surveillance[2] of the attorneys. During the night, or that part of it which at sea would form the middle watch, he was driving. This explanation certainly accounted for his drowsiness, but in a way which made it much more alarming; since now, after several days' resistance to this infirmity, at length he was steadily giving way. Throughout the second stage he grew more and more drowsy. In the second mile of the third stage he surrendered himself finally and without a struggle to his perilous temptation. All his past resistance had but deepened the weight of this final oppression. Seven atmospheres of sleep rested upon him; and, to consummate the case, our worthy guard, after singing *Love Amongst the Roses* for perhaps thirty times, without invitation and without applause, had in revenge moodily resigned himself to slumber—not so deep, doubtless, as the coachman's, but deep enough for mischief. And thus at last, about ten miles from Preston, it came about that I found myself left in charge of his Majesty's London and Glasgow mail, then running at the least twelve miles an hour.

What made this negligence less criminal than else it must have been thought was the condition of the roads at night during the assizes. At that time, all the law business of populous Liverpool, and also of populous Manchester, with its vast cincture of populous rural districts, was called up by ancient usage to the tribunal of Lilliputian Lancaster. To break up this old traditional usage required, 1, a conflict with powerful established interests; 2, a large system of new arrangements, and 3, a new parliamentary statute. But as yet this change was merely in contemplation. As things

were at present, twice in the year[1] so vast a body of business rolled northwards from the southern quarter of the county that for a fortnight at least it occupied the severe exertions of two judges in its despatch. The consequence of this was that every horse available for such a service, along the whole line of road, was exhausted in carrying down the multitudes of people who were parties to the different suits. By sunset, therefore, it usually happened that, through utter exhaustion amongst men and horses, the road sank into profound silence. Except the exhaustion in the vast adjacent county of York from a contested election, no such silence succeeding to no such fiery uproar was ever witnessed in England.

On this occasion the usual silence and solitude prevailed along the road. Not a hoof nor a wheel was to be heard. And, to strengthen this false luxurious confidence in the noiseless roads, it happened also that the night was one of peculiar solemnity and peace. For my own part, though slightly alive to the possibilities of peril, I had so far yielded to the influence of the mighty calm as to sink into a profound reverie. The month was August; in the middle of which lay my own birthday—a festival to every thoughtful man suggesting solemn and often sigh-born[2] thoughts. The county was my own native county[3]—upon which, in its southern section, more than upon any equal area known to man past or present, had descended the original curse of labor in its heaviest form, not mastering the bodies only of men, as of slaves, or criminals in mines, but working through the fiery will. Upon no equal space of earth was, or ever had been, the same energy of human power put forth daily. At this particular season also of the assizes, that dreadful hurricane of flight and pursuit, as it might have seemed to a stranger, which swept to and from Lancaster all day long, hunting the county up and down, and regularly subsiding back into silence about sunset, could not fail (when united with this permanent

---

[1] That is, all the gods put together. The Pantheon contained statues and images of the gods and was dedicated to them.

[2] That is, he was watched as carefully as a shepherd watches his sheep.

[1] "*Twice in the year*':—There were at that time only two assizes even in the most populous counties—*viz.*, the Lent Assizes and the Summer Assizes."—De Quincey.

[2] "*'Sigh-born*':—I owe the suggestion of this word to an obscure remembrance of a beautiful phrase in 'Giraldus Cambrensis'—*viz.*, *suspiriosæ cogitationes*."—De Quincey.

[3] Lancashire, celebrated for its coal mines, commerce, and manufactures. Poor soil and excessive taxes made living conditions in this county, especially in the vicinity of Manchester, in the southern district, almost unbearable. Manchester was the leading center of reform agitation concerning labor and trade conditions in the early nineteenth century.

distinction of Lancashire as the very metropolis and citadel of labor) to point the thoughts pathetically upon that counter-vision of rest, of saintly repose from strife and sorrow, towards which, as to their secret haven, the profounder aspirations of man's heart are in solitude continually travelling. Obliquely upon our left we were nearing the sea; which also must, under the present circumstances, be repeating the general state of halcyon[1] repose. The sea, the atmosphere, the light, bore each an orchestral part in this universal lull. Moonlight and the first timid tremblings of the dawn were by this time blending; and the blendings were brought into a still more exquisite state of unity by a slight silvery mist, motionless and dreamy, that covered the woods and fields, but with a veil of equable transparency. Except the feet of our own horses, —which, running on a sandy margin of the road, made but little disturbance,—there was no sound abroad. In the clouds and on the earth prevailed the same majestic peace; and, in spite of all that the villain of a schoolmaster has done for the ruin of our sublimer thoughts, which are the thoughts of our infancy, we still believe in no such nonsense as a limited atmosphere. Whatever we may swear with our false feigning lips, in our faithful hearts we still believe, and must forever believe, in fields of air traversing the total gulf between earth and the central heavens. Still, in the confidence of children that tread without fear *every* chamber in their father's house, and to whom no door is closed, we, in that Sabbatic vision[2] which sometimes is revealed for an hour upon nights like this, ascend with easy steps from the sorrow-stricken fields of earth upwards to the sandals of God.

Suddenly, from thoughts like these I was awakened to a sullen sound, as of some motion on the distant road. It stole upon the air for a moment; I listened in awe; but then it died away. Once roused, however, I could not but observe with alarm the quickened motion of our horses. Ten years' experience had made my eye learned in the valuing of motion; and I saw that we were now running thirteen miles an hour. I pretend to no presence of mind. On the contrary, my fear is that I am miserably and shamefully deficient in that quality as regards action. The palsy of doubt and distraction hangs like some guilty weight of dark unfathomed remembrances upon my energies when the signal is flying for *action.* But, on the other hand, this accursed gift I have, as regards *thought,* that in the first step towards the possibility of a misfortune I see its total evolution; in the radix of the series I see too certainly and too instantly its entire expansion; in the first syllable of the dreadful sentence I read already the last. It was not that I feared for ourselves. *Us* our bulk and impetus charmed against peril in any collision. And I had ridden through too many hundreds of perils that were frightful to approach, that were matter of laughter to look back upon, the first face of which was horror, the parting face a jest—for any anxiety to rest upon *our* interests. The mail was not built, I felt assured, nor bespoke, that could betray *me* who trusted to its protection. But any carriage that we could meet would be frail and light in comparison of ourselves. And I remarked this ominous accident of our situation,—we were on the wrong side of the road. But then, it may be said, the other party, if other there was, might also be on the wrong side; and two wrongs might make a right. *That* was not likely. The same motive which had drawn *us* to the right-hand side of the road—*viz.,* the luxury of the soft beaten sand as contrasted with the paved centre—would prove attractive to others. The two adverse carriages would therefore, to a certainty, be travelling on the same side; and from this side, as not being ours in law, the crossing over to the other would, of course, be looked for from *us.*[1] Our lamps, still lighted, would give the impression of vigilance on our part. And every creature that met us would rely upon *us* for quartering.[2] All this, and if the separate links of the anticipation had been a thousand times more, I saw, not discursively, or by effort, or by succession, but by one flash of horrid simultaneous intuition.

Under this steady though rapid anticipation of the evil which *might* be gathering

---

[1] calm; peaceful (The halcyon, or kingfisher, was fabled to nest at sea about the time of the winter solstice, and to calm the waves during the period of incubation.)

[2] That is, a vision which comes only at rare intervals; perhaps, holy.

[1] "It is true that, according to the law of the case as established by legal precedents, all carriages were required to give way before royal equipages, and therefore before the mail as one of them. But this only increased the danger, as being a regulation very imperfectly made known, very unequally enforced, and therefore often embarrassing the movements on both sides."—De Quincey.

[2] "'*Quartering*':—This is the technical word, and, I presume, derived from the French *cartayer,* to evade a rut or any obstacle."—De Quincey.

ahead, ah! what a sullen mystery of fear, what a sigh of woe, was that which stole upon the air, as again the far-off sound of a wheel was heard! A whisper it was—a whisper from, perhaps, four miles off—secretly announcing a ruin that, being foreseen, was not the less inevitable; that, being known, was not therefore healed. What could be done—who was it that could do it—to check the storm-flight of these maniacal horses? Could I not seize the reins from the grasp of the slumbering coachman? You, reader, think that it would have been in *your* power to do so. And I quarrel not with your estimate of yourself. But, from the way in which the coachman's hand was viced between his upper and lower thigh, this was impossible. Easy was it? See, then, that bronze equestrian statue. The cruel rider has kept the bit in his horse's mouth for two centuries. Unbridle him for a minute, if you please, and wash his mouth with water. Easy was it? Unhorse me, then, that imperial rider; knock me those marble feet from those marble stirrups of Charlemagne.

The sounds ahead strengthened, and were now too clearly the sounds of wheels. Who and what could it be? Was it industry in a taxed cart?[1] Was it youthful gaiety in a gig? Was it sorrow that loitered, or joy that raced? For as yet the snatches of sound were too intermitting, from distance, to decipher the character of the motion. Whoever were the travellers, something must be done to warn them. Upon the other party rests the active responsibility, but upon *us* —and, woe is me! that *us* was reduced to my frail opium-shattered self—rests the responsibility of warning. Yet, how should this be accomplished? Might I not sound the guard's horn? Already, on the first thought, I was making my way over the roof of the guard's seat. But this, from the accident which I have mentioned, of the foreign mails being piled upon the roof, was a difficult and even dangerous attempt to one cramped by nearly three hundred miles of outside travelling. And, fortunately, before I had lost much time in the attempt, our frantic horses swept round an angle of the road which opened upon us that final stage where the collision must be accomplished and the catastrophe sealed. All was apparently finished. The court was sitting; the case was heard; the judge had

finished; and only the verdict was yet in arrear.

Before us lay an avenue straight as an arrow, six hundred yards, perhaps, in length; and the umbrageous trees, which rose in a regular line from either side, meeting high overhead, gave to it the character of a cathedral aisle. These trees lent a deeper solemnity to the early light; but there was still light enough to perceive, at the further end of this Gothic aisle, a frail reedy gig, in which were seated a young man, and by his side a young lady. Ah, young sir! what are you about? If it is requisite that you should whisper your communications to this young lady—though really I see nobody, at an hour and on a road so solitary, likely to overhear you—is it therefore requisite that you should carry your lips forward to hers? The little carriage is creeping on at one mile an hour; and the parties within it, being thus tenderly engaged, are naturally bending down their heads. Between them and eternity, to all human calculation, there is but a minute and a half. Oh heavens! what is it that I shall do? Speaking or acting, what help can I offer? Strange it is, and to a mere auditor of the tale might seem laughable, that I should need a suggestion from the *Iliad* to prompt the sole resource that remained. Yet so it was. Suddenly I remembered the shout of Achilles, and its effect.[1] But could I pretend to shout like the son of Peleus, aided by Pallas? No: but then I needed not the shout that should alarm all Asia militant; such a shout would suffice as might carry terror into the hearts of two thoughtless young people and one gig-horse. I shouted—and the young man heard me not. A second time I shouted— and now he heard me, for now he raised his head.

Here, then, all had been done that, by me, *could* be done; more on *my* part was not possible. Mine had been the first step; the second was for the young man; the third was for God. If, said I, this stranger is a brave man, and if indeed he loves the young girl at his side—or, loving her not, if he feels the obligation, pressing upon every man worthy to be called a man, of doing his utmost for a woman confided to his protection—he will at least make some effort to save her. If *that* fails, he will not perish the more, or by a death more cruel, for

---

[1] A reference to the excessive taxes imposed upon the farmers by the government during the early part of the nineteenth century.

[1] The shout of Achilles, son of Peleus, together with the cry of Pallas Athene, spread terror among the Trojans during the siege of Troy, and gave the Greeks a chance to rest from battle. See the *Iliad*, 18, 217-31.

having made it; and he will die as a brave man should, with his face to the danger, and with his arm about the woman that he sought in vain to save. But, if he makes no effort,—shrinking without a struggle from his duty,—he himself will not the less certainly perish for this baseness of poltroonery.[1] He will die no less: and why not? Wherefore should we grieve that there is one craven less in the world? No; *let* him perish, without a pitying thought of ours wasted upon him; and, in that case, all our grief will be reserved for the fate of the helpless girl who now, upon the least shadow of failure in *him,* must by the fiercest of translations—must without time for a prayer —must within seventy seconds—stand before the judgment-seat of God.

But craven he was not: sudden had been the call upon him, and sudden was his answer to the call. He saw, he heard, he comprehended, the ruin that was coming down: already its gloomy shadow darkened above him; and already he was measuring his strength to deal with it. Ah! what a vulgar thing does courage seem when we see nations buying it and selling it for a shilling a-day:[2] ah! what a sublime thing does courage seem when some fearful summons on the great deeps of life carries a man, as if running before a hurricane, up to the giddy crest of some tumultuous crisis from which lie two courses, and a voice says to him audibly, "One way lies hope; take the other, and mourn forever!" How grand a triumph if, even then, amidst the raving of all around him, and the frenzy of the danger, the man is able to confront his situation—is able to retire for a moment into solitude with God, and to seek his counsel from *Him!*

For seven seconds, it might be, of his seventy, the stranger settled his countenance steadfastly upon us, as if to search and value every element in the conflict before him. For five seconds more of his seventy he sat immovably, like one that mused on some great purpose. For five more, perhaps, he sat with eyes upraised, like one that prayed in sorrow, under some extremity of doubt, for light that should guide him to the better choice. Then suddenly he rose; stood upright; and, by a powerful strain upon the reins, raising his horse's fore-feet from the ground, he slewed[3] him round on the

pivot of his hind-legs, so as to plant the little equipage in a position nearly at right angles to ours. Thus far his condition was not improved; except as a first step had been taken towards the possibility of a second. If no more were done, nothing was done; for the little carriage still occupied the very centre of our path, though in an altered direction. Yet even now it may not be too late: fifteen of the seventy seconds may still be unexhausted; and one almighty bound may avail to clear the ground. Hurry, then, hurry! for the flying moments —*they* hurry. Oh, hurry, hurry, my brave young man! for the cruel hoofs of our horses—*they* also hurry! Fast are the flying moments, faster are the hoofs of our horses. But fear not for *him,* if human energy can suffice; faithful was he that drove to his terrific duty; faithful was the horse to *his* command. One blow, one impulse given with voice and hand, by the stranger, one rush from the horse, one bound as if in the act of rising to a fence, landed the docile creature's fore-feet upon the crown or arching centre of the road. The larger half of the little equipage had then cleared our overtowering shadow: *that* was evident even to my own agitated sight. But it mattered little that one wreck should float off in safety if upon the wreck that perished were embarked the human freightage. The rear part of the carriage—was *that* certainly beyond the line of absolute ruin? What power could answer the question? Glance of eye, thought of man, wing of angel, which of these had speed enough to sweep between the question and the answer, and divide the one from the other? Light does not tread upon the steps of light more indivisibly than did our all-conquering arrival upon the escaping efforts of the gig. *That* must the young man have felt too plainly. His back was now turned to us; not by sight could he any longer communicate with the peril; but, by the dreadful rattle of our harness, too truly had his ear been instructed that all was finished as regarded any effort of *his.* Already in resignation he had rested from his struggle; and perhaps in his heart he was whispering, "Father, which art in heaven, do Thou finish above what I on earth have attempted." Faster than ever mill-race we ran past them in our inexorable flight. Oh, raving of hurricanes that must have sounded in their young ears at the moment of our transit! Even in that moment the thunder of collision spoke aloud. Either with the swingle-

---

[1] cowardice

[2] The English soldier received a shilling a day. Probably, De Quincey refers to the practice of employing mercenaries.

[3] turned

bar,[1] or with the haunch of our near leader, we had struck the off-wheel of the little gig, which stood rather obliquely, and not quite so far advanced as to be accurately parallel with the near-wheel. The blow, from the fury of our passage, resounded terrifically. I rose in horror, to gaze upon the ruins we might have caused. From my elevated station I looked down, and looked back upon the scene; which in a moment told its own tale, and wrote all its records on my heart forever.

Here was the map of the passion[2] that now had finished. The horse was planted immovably, with his fore-feet upon the paved crest of the central road. He of the whole party might be supposed untouched by the passion of death. The little cany[3] carriage —partly, perhaps, from the violent torsion of the wheels in its recent movement, partly from the thundering blow we had given to it—as if it sympathized with human horror, was all alive with tremblings and shiverings. The young man trembled not, nor shivered. He sat like a rock. But *his* was the steadiness of agitation frozen into rest by horror. As yet he dared not to look round; for he knew that, if anything remained to do, by him it could no longer be done. And as yet he knew not for certain if their safety were accomplished. But the lady——

But the lady——! Oh, heavens! will that spectacle ever depart from my dreams, as she rose and sank upon her seat, sank and rose, threw up her arms wildly to heaven, clutched at some visionary object in the air, fainting, praying, raving, despairing? Figure to yourself, reader, the elements of the case; suffer me to recall before your mind the circumstances of that unparalleled situation. From the silence and deep peace of this saintly summer night—from the pathetic blending of this sweet moonlight, dawnlight, dreamlight—from the manly tenderness of this flattering, whispering, murmuring love—suddenly as from the woods and fields—suddenly as from the chambers of the air opening in revelation—suddenly as from the ground yawning at her feet, leaped upon her, with the flashing of cataracts, Death the crowned phantom, with all the equipage of his terrors, and the tiger roar of his voice.

The moments were numbered; the strife was finished; the vision was closed. In the twinkling of an eye, our flying horses had carried us to the termination of the umbra-

geous aisle; at the right angles we wheeled into our former direction; the turn of the road carried the scene out of my eyes in an instant, and swept it into my dreams forever.

SECTION III — DREAM-FUGUE:

FOUNDED ON THE PRECEDING THEME OF SUDDEN
DEATH

Whence the sound
Of instruments, that made melodious chime,
Was heard, of harp and organ ; and who moved
Their stops and chords was seen ; his volant touch
Instinct through all proportions, low and high,
Fled and pursued transverse the resonant fugue.
—*Paradise Lost,* Bk. 11 [558-63].

Tumultuosissimamente

Passion of sudden death! that once in youth I read and interpreted by the shadows of thy averted signs![1]—rapture of panic taking the shape (which amongst tombs in churches I have seen) of woman bursting her sepulchral bonds—of woman's Ionic form[2] bending forward from the ruins of her grave with arching foot, with eyes upraised, with clasped adoring hands—waiting, watching, trembling, praying for the trumpet's call to rise from dust forever! Ah, vision too fearful of shuddering humanity on the brink of almighty abysses!—vision that didst start back, that didst reel away, like a shrivelling scroll from before the wrath of fire racing on the wings of the wind! Epilepsy so brief of horror, wherefore is it that thou canst not die? Passing so suddenly into darkness, wherefore is it that still thou sheddest thy sad funeral blights upon the gorgeous mosaics of dreams? Fragment of music too passionate, heard once, and heard no more, what aileth thee, that thy deep rolling chords come up at intervals through all the worlds of sleep, and after forty years have lost no element of horror?

I

Lo, it is summer—almighty summer! The everlasting gates of life and summer are thrown open wide;[3] and on the ocean, tranquil and verdant as a savannah, the unknown lady from the dreadful vision and I myself are floating—she upon a fairy pinnace, and I upon an English three-decker. Both of us

1 whippletree   3 canelike
2 horror ; suffering

1 " '*Averted signs':*— I read the course and changes of the lady's agony in the succession of her involuntary gestures ; but it must be remembered that I read all this from the rear, never once catching the lady's full face, and even her profile imperfectly."—De Quincey.
2 A form characterized by simplicity and delicacy, qualities of Ionic architecture.
3 See *Confessions of an English Opium-Eater* (p. 1071b, 12-22 and 1103b, 1-42), and *Autobiographic Sketches* (p. 1118a, 26 ff.).

are wooing gales of festal happiness within the domain of our common country, within that ancient watery park, within the pathless chase of ocean, where England takes her pleasure as a huntress through winter and summer, from the rising to the setting sun. Ah, what a wilderness of floral beauty was hidden, or was suddenly revealed, upon the tropic islands through which the pinnace moved! And upon her deck what a bevy of human flowers: young women how lovely, young men how noble, that were dancing together, and slowly drifting towards *us* amidst music and incense, amidst blossoms from forests and gorgeous corymbi[1] from vintages, amidst natural carolling, and the echoes of sweet girlish laughter. Slowly the pinnace nears us, gaily she hails us, and silently she disappears beneath the shadow of our mighty bows. But then, as at some signal from heaven, the music, and the carols, and the sweet echoing of girlish laughter—all are hushed. What evil has smitten the pinnace, meeting or overtaking her? Did ruin to our friends couch within our own dreadful shadow? Was our shadow the shadow of death? I looked over the bow for an answer, and behold! the pinnace was dismantled; the revel and the revellers were found no more; the glory of the vintage was dust; and the forests with their beauty were left without a witness upon the seas. "But where," and I turned to our crew— "where are the lovely women that danced beneath the awning of flowers and clustering corymbi? Whither have fled the noble young men that danced with *them?*" Answer there was none. But suddenly the man at the mast-head, whose countenance darkened with alarm, cried out, "Sail on the weather beam! Down she comes upon us: in seventy seconds she also will founder."

II

I looked to the weather side, and the summer had departed. The sea was rocking, and shaken with gathering wrath. Upon its surface sat mighty mists, which grouped themselves into arches and long cathedral aisles. Down one of these, with the fiery pace of a quarrel[2] from a cross-bow, ran a frigate right athwart our course. "Are they mad?" some voice exclaimed from our deck. "Do they woo their ruin?" But in a moment, as she was close upon us, some impulse of a heady current or local vortex gave a wheeling bias to her course, and off

[1] Clusters of fruit or flowers.
[2] An arrow with a four-edged head.

she forged without a shock. As she ran past us, high aloft amongst the shrouds stood the lady of the pinnace. The deeps opened ahead in malice to receive her, towering surges of foam ran after her, the billows were fierce to catch her. But far away she was borne into desert spaces of the sea: whilst still by sight I followed her, as she ran before the howling gale, chased by angry sea-birds and by maddening billows; still I saw her, as at the moment when she ran past us, standing amongst the shrouds, with her white draperies streaming before the wind. There she stood, with hair dishevelled, one hand clutched amongst the tackling—rising, sinking, fluttering, trembling, praying; there for leagues I saw her as she stood, raising at intervals one hand to heaven, amidst the fiery crests of the pursuing waves and the raving of the storm; until at last, upon a sound from afar of malicious laughter and mockery, all was hidden forever in driving showers; and afterwards, but when I knew not, nor how.

III

Sweet funeral bells from some incalculable distance, wailing over the dead that die before the dawn, awakened me as I slept in a boat moored to some familiar shore. The morning twilight even then was breaking; and, by the dusky revelations which it spread, I saw a girl, adorned with a garland of white roses about her head for some great festival, running along the solitary strand in extremity of haste. Her running was the running of panic; and often she looked back as to some dreadful enemy in the rear. But, when I leaped ashore, and followed on her steps to warn her of a peril in front, alas! from me she fled as from another peril, and vainly I shouted to her of quicksands that lay ahead. Faster and faster she ran; round a promontory of rocks she wheeled out of sight; in an instant I also wheeled round it, but only to see the treacherous sands gathering above her head. Already her person was buried; only the fair young head and the diadem of white roses around it were still visible to the pitying heavens; and, last of all, was visible one white marble arm. I saw by the early twilight this fair young head, as it was sinking down to darkness—saw this marble arm, as it rose above her head and her treacherous grave, tossing, faltering, rising, clutching, as at some false deceiving hand stretched out from the clouds —saw this marble arm uttering her dying hope, and then uttering her dying despair.

The head, the diadem, the arm—these all had sunk; at last over these also the cruel quicksand had closed; and no memorial of the fair young girl remained on earth, except my own solitary tears, and the funeral bells from the desert seas, that, rising again more softly, sang a requiem over the grave of the buried child, and over her blighted dawn.

I sat, and wept in secret the tears that men have ever given to the memory of those that died before the dawn, and by the treachery of earth, our mother. But suddenly the tears and funeral bells were hushed by a shout as of many nations, and by a roar as from some great king's artillery, advancing rapidly along the valleys, and heard afar by echoes from the mountains. "Hush!" I said, as I bent my ear earthwards to listen —"hush!—this either is the very anarchy of strife, or else"—and then I listened more profoundly, and whispered as I raised my head—"or else, oh heavens! it is *victory* that is final, victory that swallows up all strife."

IV

Immediately, in trance, I was carried over land and sea to some distant kingdom, and placed upon a triumphal car, amongst companions crowned with laurel. The darkness of gathering midnight, brooding over all the land, hid from us the mighty crowds that were weaving restlessly about ourselves as a centre: we heard them, but saw them not. Tidings had arrived, within an hour, of a grandeur that measured itself against centuries; too full of pathos they were, too full of joy, to utter themselves by other language than by tears, by restless anthems, and *Te Deums*[1] reverberated from the choirs and orchestras of earth. These tidings we that sat upon the laurelled car had it for our privilege to publish amongst all nations. And already, by signs audible through the darkness, by snortings and tramplings, our angry horses, that knew no fear or fleshly weariness, upbraided us with delay. Wherefore *was* it that we delayed? We waited for a secret word, that should bear witness to the hope of nations as now accomplished forever. At midnight the secret word arrived; which word was—*Waterloo and Recovered Christendom!* The dreadful word shone by its own light; before us it went; high above our leaders' heads it rode, and spread a golden light over the paths which we traversed. Every city, at the presence of the secret word, threw open its gates. The rivers were conscious as we crossed. All the forests, as we ran along their margins, shivered in homage to the secret word. And the darkness comprehended it.[1]

Two hours after midnight we approached a mighty Minster. Its gates, which rose to the clouds, were closed. But, when the dreadful word that rode before us reached them with its golden light, silently they moved back upon their hinges; and at a flying gallop our equipage entered the grand aisle of the cathedral. Headlong was our pace; and at every altar, in the little chapels and oratories to the right hand and left of our course, the lamps, dying or sickening, kindled anew in sympathy with the secret word that was flying past. Forty leagues we might have run in the cathedral, and as yet no strength of morning light had reached us, when before us we saw the aerial galleries of organ and choir. Every pinnacle of fretwork, every station of advantage amongst the traceries, was crested by white-robed choristers that sang deliverance; that wept no more tears, as once their fathers had wept; but at intervals that sang together to the generations, saying,

"Chant the deliverer's praise in every tongue,"

and receiving answers from afar,

"Such as once in heaven and earth were sung."

And of their chanting was no end; of our headlong pace was neither pause nor slackening.

Thus as we ran like torrents—thus as we swept with bridal rapture over the Campo Santo[2] of the cathedral graves—suddenly we became aware of a vast necropolis rising upon the far-off horizon—a city of sepulchres, built within the saintly cathedral for the warrior dead that rested from their feuds on earth. Of purple granite was the

---

[1] See *John*, 1:5.

[2] "*Campo Santo*':—It is probable that most of my readers will be acquainted with the history of the Campo Santo (or cemetery) at Pisa, composed of earth brought from Jerusalem from a bed of sanctity as the highest prize which the noble piety of crusaders could ask or imagine. To readers who are unacquainted with England, or who (being English) are yet unacquainted with the cathedral cities of England, it may be right to mention that the graves within-side the cathedrals often form a flat pavement over which carriages and horses *might* run; and perhaps a boyish remembrance of one particular cathedral, across which I had seen passengers walk and burdens carried, as about two centuries back they were through the middle of St. Paul's in London, may have assisted my dream."—De Quincey.

---

[1] Hymns of praise; so called from the first words of a celebrated Christian hymn, *Te Deum laudamus* (we praise thee, O God).

necropolis; yet, in the first minute, it lay like a purple stain upon the horizon, so mighty was the distance. In the second minute it trembled through many changes, growing into terraces and towers of wondrous altitude, so mighty was the pace. In the third minute already, with our dreadful gallop, we were entering its suburbs. Vast sarcophagi rose on every side, having towers and turrets that, upon the limits of the central aisle, strode forward with haughty intrusion, that ran back with mighty shadows into answering recesses. Every sarcophagus showed many bas-reliefs—bas-reliefs of battles and of battle-fields; battles from forgotten ages, battles from yesterday; battle-fields that, long since, nature had healed and reconciled to herself with the sweet oblivion of flowers; battle-fields that were yet angry and crimson with carnage. Where the terraces ran, there did *we* run; where the towers curved, there did *we* curve. With the flight of swallows our horses swept round every angle. Like rivers in flood wheeling round headlands, like hurricanes that ride into the secrets of forests, faster than ever light unwove the mazes of darkness, our flying equipage carried earthly passions, kindled warrior instincts, amongst the dust that lay around us—dust oftentimes of our noble fathers that had slept in God from Crécy to Trafalgar.[1] And now had we reached the last sarcophagus, now were we abreast of the last bas-relief, already had we recovered the arrow-like flight of the illimitable central aisle, when coming up this aisle to meet us we beheld afar off a female child, that rode in a carriage as frail as flowers. The mists which went before her hid the fawns that drew her, but could not hide the shells and tropic flowers with which she played— but could not hide the lovely smiles by which she uttered her trust in the mighty cathedral, and in the cherubim that looked down upon her from the mighty shafts of its pillars. Face to face she was meeting us; face to face she rode, as if danger there were none. "Oh, baby!" I exclaimed, "shalt thou be the ransom for Waterloo? Must we, that carry tidings of great joy to every people,[2] be messengers of ruin to thee!" In horror I rose at the thought; but then also, in horror at the thought, rose one that was sculptured on a bas-relief—a Dying Trumpeter. Solemnly from the field of battle he rose to his feet; and, unslinging his stony

trumpet, carried it, in his dying anguish, to his stony lips—sounding once, and yet once again; proclamation that, in *thy* ears, oh baby! spoke from the battlements of death. Immediately deep shadows fell between us, and aboriginal silence. The choir had ceased to sing. The hoofs of our horses, the dreadful rattle of our harness, the groaning of our wheels, alarmed the graves no more. By horror the bas-relief had been unlocked unto life. By horror we, that were so full of life, we men and our horses, with their fiery fore-legs rising in mid air to their everlasting gallop, were frozen to a bas-relief. Then a third time the trumpet sounded; the seals were taken off all pulses; life, and the frenzy of life, tore into their channels again; again the choir burst forth in sunny grandeur, as from the muffling of storms and darkness; again the thunderings of our horses carried temptation into the graves. One cry burst from our lips, as the clouds, drawing off from the aisle, showed it empty before us.—"Whither has the infant fled?—is the young child caught up to God?" Lo! afar off, in a vast recess, rose three mighty windows to the clouds; and on a level with their summits, at height insuperable to man, rose an altar of purest alabaster. On its eastern face was trembling a crimson glory. A glory was it from the reddening dawn that now streamed *through* the windows? Was it from the crimson robes of the martyrs painted *on* the windows? Was it from the bloody bas-reliefs of earth? There suddenly, within that crimson radiance, rose the apparition of a woman's head, and then of a woman's figure. The child it was—grown up to woman's height. Clinging to the horns of the altar, voiceless she stood—sinking, rising, raving, despairing; and behind the volume of incense that, night and day, streamed upwards from the altar, dimly was seen the fiery font, and the shadow of that dreadful being who should have baptized her with the baptism of death. But by her side was kneeling her better angel, that hid his face with wings; that wept and pleaded for *her;* that prayed when *she* could *not;* that fought with Heaven by tears for *her* deliverance; which also, as he raised his immortal countenance from his wings, I saw, by the glory in his eye, that from Heaven he had won at last.

V

Then was completed the passion of the mighty fugue. The golden tubes of the organ, which as yet had but muttered at

[1] The Battle of Crécy was fought in 1346; Trafalgar in 1805.
[2] See *Luke* 2 :10.

intervals—gleaming amongst clouds and surges of incense—threw up, as from fountains unfathomable, columns of heart-shattering music. Choir and anti-choir were
5 filling fast with unknown voices. Thou also, Dying Trumpeter, with thy love that was victorious, and thy anguish that was finishing, didst enter the tumult; trumpet and echo—farewell love, and farewell anguish—
10 rang through the dreadful *sanctus*.[1] Oh, darkness of the grave! that from the crimson altar and from the fiery font wert visited and searched by the effulgence in the angel's eye—were these indeed thy children?
15 Pomps of life, that, from the burials of centuries, rose again to the voice of perfect joy, did ye indeed mingle with the festivals of Death? Lo! as I looked back for seventy leagues through the mighty cathedral, I saw
20 the quick and the dead that sang together to God, together that sang to the generations of man. All the hosts of jubilation, like armies that ride in pursuit, moved with one step. Us, that, with laurelled heads, were
25 passing from the cathedral, they overtook, and, as with a garment, they wrapped us round with thunders greater than our own. As brothers we moved together; to the dawn that advanced, to the stars that fled, render-
30 ing thanks to God in the highest[2]—that, having hid His face through one generation behind thick clouds of War, once again was ascending, from the Campo Santo of Waterloo was ascending, in the visions of Peace;
35 rendering thanks for thee, young girl! whom having overshadowed with His ineffable passion of death, suddenly did God relent, suffered thy angel to turn aside His arm, and even in thee, sister unknown! shown to
40 me for a moment only to be hidden forever, found an occasion to glorify His goodness. A thousand times, amongst the phantoms of sleep, have I seen thee entering the gates of the golden dawn, with the secret word rid-
45 ing before thee, with the armies of the grave behind thee,—seen thee sinking, rising, raving, despairing; a thousand times in the worlds of sleep have I seen thee followed by God's angel through storms, through des-
50 ert seas, through the darkness of quicksands, through dreams and the dreadful revelations that are in dreams; only that at the last, with one sling of His victorious arm, He might snatch thee back from ruin,
55 and might emblazon in thy deliverance the endless resurrections of His love!

[1] A part of the Mass, beginning with the Latin words *sanctus, sanctus, sanctus* (holy, holy, holy).
[2] See *Luke*, 2 :14.

Thomas Lovell Beddoes 1803-1849

LINES
WRITTEN IN A BLANK LEAF OF THE ''PROMETHEUS UNBOUND''[1]
1822

Write it in gold—A spirit of the sun,
An intellect ablaze with heavenly thoughts,
A soul with all the dews of pathos shining,
Odorous with love, and sweet to silent woe
5 With the dark glories of concentrate song,
Was sphered in mortal earth. Angelic sounds
Alive with panting thoughts sunned the dim world.
The bright creations of an human heart
Wrought magic in the bosoms of mankind.
10 A flooding summer burst on poetry;
Of which the crowning sun, the night of beauty,
The dancing showers, the birds, whose anthems wild
Note after note unbind the enchanted leaves
Of breaking buds, eve, and the flow of dawn,
15 Were centred and condensed in his one name
As in a providence—and that was Shelley.

From THE BRIDE'S TRAGEDY
1822   1822

POOR OLD PILGRIM MISERY

Poor old pilgrim Misery,
  Beneath the silent moon he sate,
A-listening to the screech owl's cry,
  And the cold wind's goblin prate;
5 Beside him lay his staff of yew
  With withered willow[2] twined,
His scant gray hair all wet with dew,
  His cheeks with grief ybrined;
    And his cry it was ever, alack!
10   Alack, and woe is me!

Anon a wanton imp astray
  His piteous moaning hears,
And from his bosom steals away
  His rosary of tears:
15 With his plunder fled that urchin elf,
  And hid it in your eyes,
Then tell me back the stolen pelf,
  Give up the lawless prize;
    Or your cry shall be ever, alack!
    Alack, and woe is me!

[1] Written by Shelley. See p. 688.
[2] The yew and the willow are emblems of mourning.

A Ho! A Ho!

A ho! A ho!
Love's horn doth blow,
And he will out a-hawking go.
His shafts are light as beauty's sighs,
5 And bright as midnight's brightest eyes,
And round his starry way
The swan-winged horses of the skies,
With summer's music in their manes,
Curve their fair necks to zephyr's reins,
10   And urge their graceful play.

A ho! A ho!
Love's horn doth blow,
And he will out a-hawking go.
The sparrows[1] flutter round his wrist.
15 The feathery thieves that Venus kissed
And taught their morning song,
The linnets seek the airy list,
And swallows too, small pets of Spring,
Beat back the gale with swifter wing,
20   And dart and wheel along.

A ho! A ho!
Love's horn doth blow,
And he will out a-hawking go.
Now woe to every gnat that skips
25 To filch the fruit of ladies' lips,
His felon blood is shed;
And woe to flies, whose airy ships
On beauty cast their anchoring bite,
And bandit wasp, that naughty wight,[2]
30   Whose sting is slaughter-red.

From THE SECOND BROTHER
1825   1851

STREW NOT EARTH WITH EMPTY STARS

Strew not earth with empty stars,
    Strew it not with roses,
Nor feathers from the crest of Mars,
    Nor summer's idle posies.
5 'Tis not the primrose-sandalled moon,
    Nor cold and silent morn,
Nor he that climbs the dusty noon,
Nor mower war with scythe that drops,
Stuck with helmed and turbaned tops
10   Of enemies new shorn.

Ye cups, ye lyres, ye trumpets know,
Pour your music, let it flow,
'Tis Bacchus' son who walks below.

1 Sparrows were sacred to Venus.
2 creature

From TORRISMOND
1825   1851

HOW MANY TIMES DO I LOVE THEE, DEAR?

How many times do I love thee, dear?
    Tell me how many thoughts there be
        In the atmosphere
        Of a new-fall'n year,
5 Whose white and sable hours appear
    The latest flake of Eternity:
So many times do I love thee, dear.

How many times do I love again?
    Tell me how many beads there are
10   In a silver chain
        Of evening rain,
Unravelled from the tumbling main,
    And threading the eye of a yellow star:
So many times do I love again.

From DEATH'S JEST BOOK
1825-32   1850

TO SEA, TO SEA!

To sea, to sea! The calm is o'er;
    The wanton water leaps in sport,
And rattles down the pebbly shore;
    The dolphin wheels, the sea-cow snorts,
5 And unseen mermaids' pearly song
Comes bubbling up, the weeds among.
    Fling broad the sail, dip deep the oar:
To sea, to sea! the calm is o'er.

To sea, to sea! our wide-winged bark
10   Shall billowy cleave its sunny way,
And with its shadow, fleet and dark,
    Break the caved Tritons' azure day,
Like mighty eagle soaring light
O'er antelopes on Alpine height.
15   The anchor heaves, the ship swings free,
The sails swell full. To sea, to sea!

THE SWALLOW LEAVES HER NEST

The swallow leaves her nest,
The soul my weary breast;
But therefore let the rain
    On my grave
5 Fall pure; for why complain?
Since both will come again
    O'er the wave.

The wind dead leaves and snow
Doth hurry to and fro;
10 And, once, a day shall break
    O'er the wave,
When a storm of ghosts shall shake
The dead, until they wake
    In the grave.

IF THOU WILT EASE THINE HEART

If thou wilt ease thine heart
Of love and all its smart,
    Then sleep, dear, sleep;
And not a sorrow
5   Hang any tear on your eyelashes;
    Lie still and deep,
Sad soul, until the sea-wave washes
The rim o' the sun tomorrow,
    In eastern sky.

10 But wilt thou cure thine heart
Of love and all its smart,
    Then die, dear, die;
'Tis deeper, sweeter,
    Than on a rose bank[1] to lie dreaming
15   With folded eye;
And then alone, amid the beaming
Of love's stars, thou'lt meet her
    In eastern sky.

LADY, WAS IT FAIR OF THEE

Lady, was it fair of thee
To seem so passing fair to me?
Not every star to every eye
    Is fair; and why
5 Art thou another's share?
Did thine eyes shed brighter glances,
Thine unkissed bosom heave more fair,
    To his than to my fancies?
    But I'll forgive thee still;
10   Thou'rt fair without thy will.
So be: but never know,
That 'tis the hue of woe.

Lady, was it fair of thee
To be so gentle still to me?
15 Not every lip to every eye
    Should let smiles fly.
Why didst thou never frown,
    To frighten from my pillow
Love's head, round which Hope wove a
    crown,
20 And saw not 'twas of willow?[2]
    But I'll forgive thee still,
    Thou knew'st not smiles could kill.
Smile on: but never know,
I die, nor of what woe.

A CYPRESS-BOUGH,[3] AND A ROSE-WREATH[1] SWEET

A cypress-bough, and a rose-wreath sweet,
A wedding-robe, and a winding-sheet,
    A bridal bed and a bier.

[1] The rose is an emblem of love and marriage.
[2] The willow is an emblem of mourning.
[3] The cypress is an emblem of mourning; it has long been associated with funerals.

5 Thine be the kisses, maid,
    And smiling Love's alarms;
And thou, pale youth, be laid
    In the grave's cold arms.
Each in his own charms,
    Death and Hymen both are here;
10   So up with scythe and torch,
    And to the old church porch,
    While all the bells ring clear:
And rosy, rosy the bed shall bloom,
And earthy, earthy heap up the tomb.

15 Now tremble dimples on your cheek,
Sweet be your lips to taste and speak,
    For he who kisses is near:
By her the bride-god[1] fair,
    In youthful power and force;
20 By him the grizard[2] bare,
    Pale knight[3] on a pale horse,
    To woo him to a corse.
    Death and Hymen both are here,
    So up with scythe and torch,
25   And to the old church porch,
    While all the bells ring clear:
And rosy, rosy the bed shall bloom,
And earthy, earthy heap up the tomb.

OLD ADAM, THE CARRION CROW

Old Adam, the carrion crow,
    The old crow of Cairo;
He sat in the shower, and let it flow
Under his tail and over his crest;
5   And through every feather
    Leaked the wet weather;
And the bough swung under his nest;
For his beak it was heavy with marrow.
    Is that the wind dying? O no;
10   It's only two devils, that blow
    Through a murderer's bones, to and
    fro,
    In the ghosts' moonshine.

Ho! Eve, my gray carrion wife,
    When we have supped on kings' marrow,
15 Where shall we drink and make merry our
    life?
Our nest it is queen Cleopatra's skull,
    'Tis cloven and cracked,
    And battered and hacked,
But with tears of blue eyes it is full:
20 Let us drink then, my raven of Cairo.
    Is that the wind dying? O no;
    It's only two devils, that blow
    Through a murderer's bones, to and
    fro,
    In the ghosts' moonshine.

[1] Hymen.   [2] gray-headed person
[3] Death. See *Revelation*. 6 :8.

WE DO LIE BENEATH THE GRASS

We do lie beneath the grass
    In the moonlight, in the shade
Of the yew-tree.[1] They that pass
    Hear us not. We are afraid
5   They would envy our delight,
    In our graves by glow-worm night.
Come follow us, and smile as we;
We sail to the rock in the ancient waves,
Where the snow falls by thousands into the
    sea,
10 And the drowned and the shipwrecked
    have happy graves.

THE BODING DREAMS
1851

In lover's ear a wild voice cried:
  "Sleeper, awake and rise!"
A pale form stood at his bedside,
  With heavy tears in her sad eyes.
5 "A beckoning hand, a moaning sound,
A new-dug grave in weedy ground
For her who sleeps in dreams of thee.
Awake! Let not the murder be!"
Unheard the faithful dream did pray,
10 And sadly sighed itself away.
  "Sleep on," sung Sleep, "tomorrow
  'Tis time to know thy sorrow."
  "Sleep on," sung Death, "tomorrow
  From me thy sleep thou'lt borrow."
15 Sleep on, lover, sleep on,
    The tedious dream is gone;
    The bell tolls one.

Another hour, another dream:
  "Awake! awake!" it wailed,
20 "Arise, ere with the moon's last beam
  Her dearest life hath paled."
A hidden light, a muffled tread,
A daggered hand beside the bed
Of her who sleeps in dreams of thee.
25 Thou wak'st not: let the murder be.
In vain the faithful dream did pray,
And sadly sighed itself away.
  "Sleep on," sung Sleep, "tomorrow
  'Tis Time to know thy sorrow."
30 "Sleep on," sung Death, "tomorrow
  From me thy sleep thou'lt borrow."
  Sleep on, lover, sleep on,
    The tedious dream is gone;
    Soon comes the sun.

35 Another hour, another dream:
  A red wound on a snowy breast,
A rude hand stifling the last scream,
  On rosy lips a death-kiss pressed.

[1]The yew is an emblem of mourning; it is a
common tree in graveyards.

Blood on the sheets, blood on the floor,
40 The murderer stealing through the door.
"Now," said the voice, with comfort deep,
"She sleeps indeed, and thou may'st
    sleep."
The scornful dream then turned away
To the first, weeping cloud of day.
45 "Sleep on," sung Sleep, "tomorrow
  'Tis time to know thy sorrow."
  "Sleep on," sung Death, "tomorrow
  From me thy sleep thou'lt borrow."
  Sleep on, lover, sleep on,
50   The tedious dream is gone;
    The murder's done.

DREAM-PEDLARY
1851

If there were dreams to sell,
  What would you buy?
Some cost a passing bell;
  Some a light sigh,
5 That shakes from Life's fresh crown
Only a rose-leaf down.
If there were dreams to sell,
Merry and sad to tell,
And the crier rang the bell,
10 What would you buy?

A cottage lone and still,
  With bowers nigh,
Shadowy, my woes to still,
  Until I die.
15 Such pearls from Life's fresh crown
Fain would I shake me down.
Were dreams to have at will,
This would best heal my ill,
  This would I buy.

20 But there were dreams to sell
  Ill didst thou buy;
Life is a dream, they tell,
  Waking, to die.
Dreaming a dream to prize,
25 Is wishing ghosts to rise;
And if I had the spell
To call the buried well,
  Which one would I?

If there are ghosts to raise,
30 What shall I call,
Out of hell's murky haze,
  Heaven's blue pall?
Raise my loved long-lost boy,
To lead me to his joy.—
35 There are no ghosts to raise;
Out of death lead no ways;
  Vain is the call.

Know'st thou not ghosts to sue,
  No love thou hast.
40 Else lie, as I will do,
  And breathe thy last.
So out of Life's fresh crown
Fall like a rose-leaf down.
Thus are the ghosts to woo;
45 Thus are all dreams made true,
  Ever to last!

LET DEW THE FLOWERS FILL
1851

Let dew the flowers fill;
  No need of fell despair,
  Though to the grave you bear
One still of soul—but now too still,
5   One fair—but now too fair.
For, beneath your feet, the mound,
And the waves, that play around,
Have meaning in their grassy, and their
  watery, smiles;
And, with a thousand sunny wiles,
10   Each says, as he reproves,
  Death's arrow oft is Love's.

John Keble 1792-1866

From THE CHRISTIAN YEAR
1827

FIRST SUNDAY AFTER TRINITY

So Joshua smote all the country and all their
kings; he left none remaining.—*Joshua* 10:40.

Where is the land with milk and honey
  flowing,[1]
The promise of our God, our fancy's
  theme?
Here over shatter'd walls dank weeds are
  growing,
And blood and fire have run in mingled
  stream;
5   Like oaks and cedars all around
  The giant corses strew the ground,
And haughty Jericho's cloud-piercing wall
Lies where it sank at Joshua's trumpet call.[2]

These are not scenes for pastoral dance at
  even,
10 For moonlight rovings in the fragrant
  glades,
Soft slumbers in the open eye of heaven,
And all the listless joy of summer shades.
  We in the midst of ruins live,
  Which every hour dread warning give,
15 Nor may our household vine or fig-tree
  hide[3]
The broken arches of old Canaan's pride.

[1] The land of Canaan. See *Exodus*, 3:8.
[2] See *Joshua*, 6:20.
[3] See *Deuteronomy*, 8:8.

Where is the sweet repose of hearts re-
  penting,
The deep calm sky, the sunshine of the
  soul,
Now heaven and earth are to our bliss con-
  senting,
20   And all the Godhead joins to make us
  whole?
  The triple crown of mercy[1] now
  Is ready for the suppliant's brow,
By the Almighty Three forever plann'd,
And from behind the cloud held out by
  Jesus' hand.

25 "Now, Christians, hold your own—the
  land before ye
Is open—win your way, and take your
  rest."[2]
So sounds our war-note; but our path of
  glory
By many a cloud is darken'd and unblest:
  And daily as we downward glide,
30   Life's ebbing stream on either side
Shows at each turn some mould'ring hope
  or joy,
The Man seems following still the funeral
  of the Boy.

Open our eyes, Thou Sun of life and gladness,
That we may see that glorious world of
  Thine!
35 It shines for us in vain, while drooping
  sadness
Enfolds us here like mist: come, Power
  benign,
  Touch our chill'd hearts with vernal
  smile,
  Our wintry course do Thou beguile,
Nor by the wayside ruins let us mourn,
40 Who have th' eternal towers for our appointed bourn.

TWENTIETH SUNDAY AFTER TRINITY

Hear ye, O mountains, the Lord's controversy, and ye strong foundations of the earth.
—Micah 6:7.

Where is Thy favor'd haunt, eternal Voice,
  The region of Thy choice,
Where, undisturb'd by sin and earth, the
  soul
  Owns Thy entire control?—
5 'Tis on the mountain's summit dark and
  high,
  When storms are hurrying by:

[1] A reference to the Trinity.
[2] See *Deuteronomy*, 1:8; also *Joshua*, 1:11-15.

'Tis 'mid the strong foundations of the
    earth,
    Where torrents have their birth.'

No sounds of worldly toil, ascending there,
10   Mar the full burst of prayer;
Lone Nature feels that she may freely
    breathe,
    And round us and beneath
Are heard her sacred tones: the fitful sweep
    Of winds across the steep,
15 Through wither'd bents[1]—romantic note
    and clear,
    Meet for a hermit's ear—

The wheeling kite's wild solitary cry,
    And, scarcely heard so high,
The dashing waters when the air is still
20   From many a torrent rill
That winds unseen beneath the shaggy
    fell,[2]
    Track'd by the blue mist well:
Such sounds as make deep silence in the
    heart
    For Thought to do her part.

25 'Tis then we hear the voice of God within,
    Pleading with care and sin:
"Child of My love! how have I wearied
    thee?
    Why wilt thou err[3] from Me?
Have I not brought thee from the house of
    slaves,
30   Parted the drowning waves,
And set My saints before thee in the way,
    Lest thou shouldst faint or stray?

"What! was the promise made to thee
    alone?
    Art thou th' excepted one?—
35 An heir of glory without grief or pain?
    O vision false and vain!
There lies thy cross; beneath it meekly
    bow;
    It fits thy stature now:
Who scornful pass it with averted eye,
40   'Twill crush them by-and-by.

"Raise thy repining eyes, and take true
    measure
    Of thine eternal treasure;
The Father of thy Lord can grudge thee
    naught.
    The world for thee was bought,
45 And as this landscape broad—earth, sea,
    and sky—

[1] Reedlike grasses.
[2] hill; mountain
[3] wander

All centres in thine eye,
So all God does, if rightly understood,
    Shall work thy final good.''

UNITED STATES
1836

Because that Tyrus hath said against Jerusalem, Aha, she is broken that was the gates of
the people; she is turned unto me; I shall be
replenished, now she is laid waste: Therefore
thus saith the Lord God; Behold, I am against
thee, O Tyrus.—*Ezekiel*, 26 :2-3.

Tyre of the *farther*[1] West! be thou too
    warn'd,
    Whose eagle wings thine own green
        world o'erspread,
Touching two Oceans: wherefore hast thou
    scorn'd
    Thy fathers' God, O proud and full of
        bread?[2]
5 Why lies the Cross unhonor'd on thy
    ground
    While in mid air thy stars and arrows
        flaunt?
That sheaf of darts,[3] will it not fall un-
    bound,
    Except, disrob'd of thy vain earthly
        vaunt,
Thou bring it to be bless'd where Saints
    and Angels haunt?

10 The holy seed, by Heaven's peculiar grace,
    Is rooted here and there in thy dark
        woods;
But many a rank weed round it grows
    apace,
    And Mammon builds beside thy mighty
        floods,
O'ertopping Nature, braving Nature's
    God;
15   O while thou yet hast room, fair fruitful
    land,
Ere war and want have stain'd thy virgin
    sod,
    Mark thee a place on high, a glorious
    stand,
    Whence Truth her sign may make o'er
    forest, lake, and strand.

Eastward, this hour, perchance thou turn'st
    thine ear,
20   Listening if haply with the surging sea,

[1] This expression refers to John Henry Newman's poem to England, beginning "Tyre of
the West," which preceded Keble's poem in
Lyra Apostolica. Tyre was the great trading center of ancient Phœnicia, and was
noted for its worldliness and commercial
prosperity.
[2] See *Ezekiel*, 16 :49; also *Hamlet*, III, 3, 80.
[3] A reference to the sheaf of arrows held in
the claw of the eagle on the American coat-
of-arms.

Blend sounds of Ruin from a land once
    dear
  To thee and Heaven. O trying hour for
    thee!
Tyre mock'd when Salem[1] fell; where
    now is Tyre?
  Heaven was against her. Nations thick
    as waves,
25 Burst o'er her walls, to Ocean doom'd and
    fire:
  And now the tideless water idly laves
  Her towers, and lone sands heap her
    crownèd merchants' graves.

Thomas Hood 1799-1845

SONG
1824

O lady, leave thy silken thread
And flowery tapestrie,
There's living roses on the bush,
And blossoms on the tree;
5 Stoop where thou wilt, thy careless hand
Some random bud will meet;
Thou canst not tread but thou wilt find
The daisy at thy feet.

'Tis like the birthday of the world,
10 When earth was born in bloom;
The light is made of many dyes,
The air is all perfume;
There's crimson buds, and white and blue—
The very rainbow show'rs
15 Have turn'd to blossoms where they fell,
And sown the earth with flow'rs.

There's fairy tulips in the East,
The garden of the sun;
The very streams reflect the hues,
20 And blossom as they run:
While morn opes like a crimson rose,
Still wet with pearly showers;
Then, lady, leave the silken thread
Thou twinest into flow'rs!

FAITHLESS NELLY GRAY

A PATHETIC BALLAD
1826

Ben Battle was a soldier bold,
  And used to war's alarms:
But a cannon-ball took off his legs,
  So he laid down his arms!

5 Now as they bore him off the field,
  Said he, "Let others shoot,
For here I leave my second leg,
  And the Forty-second Foot!"

[1] Jerusalem.

The army-surgeons made him limbs:
10 Said he,—"They're only pegs:
But there's as wooden members[1] quite
  As represent my legs!"

Now Ben he loved a pretty maid,
  Her name was Nelly Gray;
15 So he went to pay her his devours[2]
  When he'd devoured his pay!

But when he called on Nelly Gray,
  She made him quite a scoff;
And when she saw his wooden legs,
20 Began to take them off!

"O Nelly Gray! O, Nelly Gray!
  Is this your love so warm?
The love that loves a scarlet coat
  Should be more uniform!"

25 Said she, "I loved a soldier once,
  For he was blythe and brave;
But I will never have a man
  With both legs in the grave!

"Before you had those timber toes,
30 Your love I did allow,
But then, you know, you stand upon
  Another footing now!"

"O, Nelly Gray! O, Nelly Gray!
  For all your jeering speeches,
35 At duty's call, I left my legs
  In Badajos's *breaches!*"

"Why, then," said she, "you've lost the
    feet
  Of legs in war's alarms,
And now you cannot wear your shoes
40 Upon your feats of arms!"

"O, false and fickle Nelly Gray;
  I know why you refuse:—
Though I've no feet—some other man
  Is standing in my shoes!

45 "I wish I ne'er had seen your face;
  But, now, a long farewell!
For you will be my death;—alas!
  You will not be my *Nell!*"

Now when he went from Nelly Gray,
50 His heart so heavy got—
And life was such a burthen grown,
  It made him take a knot!

[1] A thrust at the Members of Parliament.
[2] respects

So round his melancholy neck,
  A rope he did entwine,
55 And, for his second time in life,
  Enlisted in the Line!

One end he tied around a beam,
  And then removed his pegs,
And, as his legs were off,—of course,
60 He soon was off his legs!

And there he hung, till he was dead
  As any nail in town,—
For though distress had cut him up,
  It could not cut him down!

65 A dozen men sat on[1] his corpse,
  To find out why he died—
And they buried Ben in four cross-roads,
  With a *stake* in his inside![2]

FAIR INES
1827

O saw ye not fair Ines?
  She's gone into the West,
To dazzle when the sun is down,
  And rob the world of rest:
5 She took our daylight with her,
  The smiles that we love best,
With morning blushes on her cheek,
  And pearls upon her breast.

O turn again, fair Ines,
10 Before the fall of night,
For fear the moon should shine alone,
  And stars unrivall'd bright;
And blessed will the lover be
  That walks beneath their light,
15 And breathes the love against thy cheek
  I dare not even write!

Would I had been, fair Ines,
  That gallant cavalier,
Who rode so gaily by thy side,
20 And whisper'd thee so near!—
Were there no bonny dames at home
  Or no true lovers here,
That he should cross the seas to win
  The dearest of the dear?

25 I saw thee, lovely Ines,
  Descend along the shore,

[1] held a session on
[2] It was the custom to bury suicides in some
  public place, usually at the intersection of
  four roads, a stake being driven through the
  body. This custom, which was discontinued
  in 1823, grew out of the practice of erecting
  a cross at cross-roads. A person who was
  excluded from holy rites was buried at the
  foot of the cross as the place next in sanctity to consecrated ground. See Martineau's
  The History of England, 2, 383.

With bands of noble gentlemen,
  And banners wav'd before;
And gentle youth and maidens gay,
30 And snowy plumes they wore;—
It would have been a beauteous dream,
  —If it had been no more!

Alas, alas, fair Ines,
  She went away with song,
35 With Music waiting on her steps,
  And shoutings of the throng;
But some were sad, and felt no mirth,
  But only Music's wrong,
In sounds that sang Farewell, Farewell,
40 To her you've loved so long.

Farewell, farewell, fair Ines,
  That vessel never bore
So fair a lady on its deck,
  Nor danc'd so light before,—
45 Alas for pleasure on the sea,
  And sorrow on the shore!
The smile that blest one lover's heart
  Has broken many more!

RUTH
1827

She stood breast high amid the corn,[1]
Clasp'd by the golden light of morn,
Like the sweetheart of the sun,
Who many a glowing kiss had won.

5 On her cheek an autumn flush,
Deeply ripened;—such a blush
In the midst of brown was born,
Like red poppies grown with corn.

Round her eyes her tresses fell,
10 Which were blackest none could tell,
But long lashes veil'd a light,
That had else been all too bright.

And her hat, with shady brim,
Made her tressy forehead dim;—
15 Thus she stood amid the stooks,[2]
Praising God with sweetest looks:—

Sure, I said, heav'n did not mean
Where I reap thou shouldst but glean,
Lay thy sheaf adown and come,
20 Share my harvest and my home.

I REMEMBER, I REMEMBER
1827

I remember, I remember,
  The house where I was born,
The little window where the sun
  Came peeping in at morn;

[1] wheat
[2] shocks of grain

5 He never came a wink too soon,
   Nor brought too long a day,
But now, I often wish the night
   Had borne my breath away!

I remember, I remember,
10   The roses, red and white,
The vi'lets, and the lily-cups,
   Those flowers made of light!
The lilacs where the robin built,
   And where my brother set
15 The laburnum on his birthday,—
   The tree is living yet!

I remember, I remember,
   Where I was used to swing,
And thought the air must rush as fresh
20   To swallows on the wing;
My spirit flew in feathers then,
   That is so heavy now,
And summer pools could hardly cool
   The fever on my brow!

25 I remember, I remember,
   The fir trees dark and high;
I used to think their slender tops
   Were close against the sky:
It was a childish ignorance,
30   But now 'tis little joy
To know I'm farther off from heav'n
   Than when I was a boy.

THE STARS ARE WITH THE VOYAGER
1827

The stars are with the voyager
   Wherever he may sail;
The moon is constant to her time;
   The sun will never fail;
5 But follow, follow round the world,
   The green earth and the sea;
So love is with the lover's heart,
   Wherever he may be.

Wherever he may be, the stars
10   Must daily lose their light;
The moon will veil her in the shade;
   The sun will set at night.
The sun may set, but constant love
   Will shine when he's away;
15 So that dull night is never night,
   And day is brighter day.

SILENCE
1827

There is a silence where hath been no sound,
There is a silence where no sound may be,
In the cold grave—under the deep, deep
   sea,
Or in wide desert where no life is found,

5 Which hath been mute, and still must sleep
   profound;
No voice is hush'd—no life treads silently,
But clouds and cloudy shadows wander
   free,
That never spoke, over the idle ground:
But in green ruins, in the desolate walls
10 Of antique palaces, where man hath been,
Though the dun fox, or wild hyena, calls,
And owls, that flit continually between,
Shriek to the echo, and the low winds moan,
There the true Silence is, self-conscious
   and alone.

FALSE POETS AND TRUE
TO WORDSWORTH

Look how the lark soars upward and is
   gone,
Turning a spirit as he nears the sky!
His voice is heard, but body there is none
To fix the vague excursions of the eye.
5 So, poets' songs are with us, tho' they die
Obscur'd, and hid by death's oblivious
   shroud,
And Earth inherits the rich melody
Like raining music from the morning
   cloud.
Yet, few there be who pipe so sweet and
   loud
10 Their voices reach us through the lapse of
   space:
The noisy day is deafen'd by a crowd
Of undistinguish'd birds, a twittering
   race;
But only lark and nightingale forlorn.
Fill up the silences of night and morn.

SONG

There is dew for the flow'ret
   And honey for the bee,
And bowers for the wild bird,
   And love for you and me.

5 There are tears for the many
   And pleasures for the few;
But let the world pass on, dear,
   There's love for me and you.

AUTUMN
1827

The autumn is old,
The sere leaves are flying;
He hath gathered up gold,
And now he is dying;
5 Old age, begin sighing!

The vintage is ripe,
The harvest is heaping;

But some that have sowed
Have no riches for reaping;
10 Poor wretch, fall a-weeping!

The year's in the wane,
There is nothing adorning,
The night has no eve,
And the day has no morning;
15 Cold winter gives warning.

The rivers run chill,
The red sun is sinking,
And I am grown old,
And life is fast shrinking;
20 Here's enow for sad thinking!

BALLAD
1827

It was not in the winter
Our loving lot was cast!
It was the time of roses,
We plucked them as we passed!

5 That churlish season never frowned
On early lovers yet!—
Oh no—the world was newly crowned
With flowers, when first we met.

'Twas twilight, and I bade you go,
10 But still you held me fast;—
It was the time of roses,—
We plucked them as we passed!

What else could peer[1] my glowing cheek
That tears began to stud?—
15 And when I asked the like of Love,
You snatched a damask bud,—

And oped it to the dainty core
Still glowing to the last:—
It was the time of roses,
20 We plucked them as we passed!

THE DREAM OF EUGENE ARAM, THE MURDERER[2]
1829

'Twas in the prime of summer time,
An evening calm and cool,
And four-and-twenty happy boys
Came bounding out of school:
5 There were some that ran and some that leapt,
Like troutlets in a pool.

Away they sped with gamesome minds,
And souls untouched by sin;

[1] equal; match
[2] This is a story of fact. See J. Ashton's "The True Story of Eugene Aram," *Eighteenth Century Waifs* (1887); also, Bulwer-Lytton's *Eugene Aram*, a novel published in 1832.

To a level mead they came, and there
10 They drave the wickets in:
Pleasantly shone the setting sun
Over the town of Lynn.

Like sportive deer they cours'd about,
And shouted as they ran,—
15 Turning to mirth all things of earth,
As only boyhood can;
But the Usher[1] sat remote from all,
A melancholy man!

His hat was off, his vest apart,
20 To catch heaven's blessed breeze;
For a burning thought was in his brow,
And his bosom ill at ease:
So he lean'd his head on his hands, and read
The book between his knees!

25 Leaf after leaf, he turn'd it o'er,
Nor ever glanc'd aside,
For the peace of his soul he read that book
In the golden eventide:
Much study had made him very lean,
30 And pale, and leaden-ey'd.[2]

At last he shut the ponderous tome,
With a fast and fervent grasp
He strain'd the dusky covers close,
And fix'd the brazen hasp:
35 "Oh God! could I so close my mind,
And clasp it with a clasp!"

Then leaping on his feet upright,
Some moody turns he took,—
Now up the mead, then down the mead,
40 And past a shady nook,—
And, lo! he saw a little boy
That pored upon a book!

"My gentle lad, what is't you read—
Romance or fairy fable?
45 Or is it some historic page,
Of kings and crowns unstable?"
The young boy gave an upward glance,—
"It is *The Death of Abel.*"

The Usher took six hasty strides,
50 As smit with sudden pain,—
Six hasty strides beyond the place,
Then slowly back again;
And down he sat beside the lad,
And talk'd with him of Cain;

55 And, long since then, of bloody men,
Whose deeds tradition saves;

[1] An under-teacher or assistant in a school.
[2] See *Julius Cæsar*, I, 2, 192-95.

Of lonely folk cut off unseen,
  And hid in sudden graves;
Of horrid stabs, in groves forlorn,
60   And murders done in caves;

And how the sprites of injur'd men
  Shriek upward from the sod,—
Aye, how the ghostly hand will point
  To show the burial clod;
65 And unknown facts of guilty acts
  Are seen in dreams from God!

He told how murderers walk the earth
  Beneath the curse of Cain,—
With crimson clouds before their eyes,
70   And flames about their brain:
For blood has left upon their souls
  Its everlasting stain!

"And well," quoth he, "I know, for truth,
  Their pangs must be extreme,—
75 Woe, woe, unutterable woe,—
  Who spill life's sacred stream!
For why? Methought, last night, I wrought
  A murder, in a dream!

"One that had never done me wrong—
80   A feeble man, and old;
I led him to a lonely field,—
  The moon shone clear and cold:
Now here, said I, this man shall die,
  And I will have his gold!

85 "Two sudden blows with a ragged stick,
  And one with a heavy stone,
One hurried gash with a hasty knife,—
  And then the deed was done;
There was nothing lying at my foot
90   But lifeless flesh and bone!

"Nothing but lifeless flesh and bone,
  That could not do me ill;
And yet I fear'd him all the more,
  For lying there so still:
95 There was a manhood in his look,
  That murder could not kill!

"And, lo! the universal air
  Seem'd lit with ghastly flame;—
Ten thousand thousand dreadful eyes
100 Were looking down in blame:
I took the dead man by his hand,
  And call'd upon his name!

"Oh, God! it made me quake to see
  Such sense within the slain!
105 But when I touch'd the lifeless clay,
  The blood gushed out amain!

For every clot, a burning spot,
  Was scorching in my brain!

"My head was like an ardent coal,
110 My heart as solid ice;
My wretched, wretched soul, I knew,
  Was at the Devil's price:
A dozen times I groan'd; the dead
  Had never groan'd but twice.

115 "And now, from forth the frowning sky
  From the heaven's topmost height,
I heard a voice—the awful voice
  Of the blood-avenging sprite:—
'Thou guilty man! take up thy dead,
120 And hide it from my sight!'

"I took the dreary body up,
  And cast it in a stream,—
A sluggish water, black as ink,
  The depth was so extreme:—
125 My gentle boy, remember this
  Is nothing but a dream!

"Down went the corse with a hollow plunge
  And vanish'd in the pool;
Anon I cleans'd my bloody hands,
130 And wash'd my forehead cool,
And sat among the urchins young
  That evening in the school.

"Oh, Heaven, to think of their white souls,
  And mine so black and grim!
135 I could not share in childish prayer,
  Nor join in evening hymn:
Like a devil of the pit, I seem'd,
  'Mid holy cherubim![1]

"And Peace went with them, one and all,
140 And each calm pillow spread;
But Guilt was my grim chamberlain
  That lighted me to bed;
And drew my midnight curtains round
  With fingers bloody red!

145 "All night I lay in agony,
  In anguish dark and deep;
My fever'd eyes I dared not close,
  But stared aghast at Sleep:
For Sin had render'd unto her
150 The keys of hell to keep!

"All night I lay in agony,
  From weary chime to chime,
With one besetting horrid hint,
  That rack'd me all the time,—
155 A mighty yearning, like the first
  Fierce impulse unto crime!

[1] Members of the celestial hierarchy.

"One stern tyrannic thought, that made
   All other thoughts its slave;
Stronger and stronger every pulse
160   Did that temptation crave,—
Still urging me to go and see
   The dead man in his grave!

"Heavily I rose up, as soon
   As light was in the sky,
165 And sought the black accursed pool
   With a wild misgiving eye;
And I saw the dead in the river bed,
   For the faithless stream was dry!

"Merrily rose the lark, and shook
170   The dew-drop from its wing;
But I never mark'd its morning flight,
   I never heard it sing:
For I was stooping once again
   Under the horrid thing.

175 "With breathless speed, like a soul in
       chase,
   I took him up and ran;—
There was no time to dig a grave
   Before the day began:
In a lonesome wood, with heaps of leaves,
180   I hid the murder'd man!

"And all that day I read in school,
   But my thought was other where;
As soon as the mid-day task was done,
   In secret I was there:
185 And a mighty wind had swept the leaves,
   And still the corse was bare!

"Then down I cast me on my face,
   And first began to weep,
For I knew my secret then was one
190   That earth refused to keep:
Or land, or sea, though he should be
   Ten thousand fathoms deep.

"So wills the fierce avenging sprite,
   Till blood for blood atones!
195 Ay, though he's buried in a cave,
   And trodden down with stones,
And years have rotted off his flesh,—
   The world shall see his bones!

"Oh, God! that horrid, horrid dream
200   Besets me now awake!
Again—again, with a dizzy brain,
   The human life I take;
And my red right hand grows raging hot,
   Like Cranmer's at the stake.

205 "And still no peace for the restless clay,
   Will wave or mould allow;

The horrid thing pursues my soul,—
   It stands before me now!"
The fearful boy look'd up, and saw
210   Huge drops upon his brow.

That very night, while gentle sleep
   The urchin eyelids kiss'd,
Two stern-faced men set out from Lynn,
   Through the cold and heavy mist;
215 And Eugene Aram walked between,
   With gyves upon his wrist.

THE DEATH-BED[1]
1831

We watch'd her breathing thro' the night,
   Her breathing soft and low,
As in her breast the wave of life
   Kept heaving to and fro!

5 So silently we seemed to speak—
   So slowly moved about!
As we had lent her half our powers
   To eke her living out!

Our very hopes belied our fears,
10   Our fears our hopes belied—
We thought her dying when she slept,
   And sleeping when she died!

For when the morn came dim and sad—
   And chill with early showers,
15 Her quiet eyelids closed—she had
   Another morn than ours!

SALLY SIMPKIN'S LAMENT

OR, JOHN JONES'S KIT-CAT-ASTROPHE
1839

     He left his body to the sea,
    And made a shark his legatee.
           —*Bryan and Perenne.*

"Oh! what is that comes gliding in,
   And quite in middling haste?
It is the picture of my Jones,
   And painted to the waist.

5 "It is not painted to the life,
   For where's the trousers blue?
Oh Jones, my dear!—O dear! my Jones,
   What is become of you?"

"Oh! Sally dear, it is too true,
10   The half that you remark
Is come to say my other half
   Is bit off by a shark!

"Oh! Sally, sharks do things by halves,
   Yet most completely do!

[1] This poem is supposed to have been written on the death of Hood's sister.

15 A bite in one place seems enough,
    But I've been bit in two.

"You know I once was all your own,
    But now a shark must share!
But let that pass—for now to you
20   I'm neither here nor there.

"Alas! death has a strange divorce
    Effected in the sea,
It has divided me from you,
    And even me from me!

25 "Don't fear my ghost will walk o' nights
    To haunt as people say;
My ghost *can't* walk, for, oh! my legs
    Are many leagues away!

"Lord! think when I am swimming round,
30   And looking where the boat is,
A shark just snaps away a *half*,
    Without "a *quarter's* notice."[1]

"One half is here, the other half
    Is near Columbia placed;
35 Oh! Sally, I have got the whole
    Atlantic for my waist.

"But now, adieu—a long adieu!
    I've solved death's awful riddle,
And would say more, but I am doomed
40   To break off in the middle."

THE SONG OF THE SHIRT
1843   1843

With fingers weary and worn,
    With eyelids heavy and red,
A woman sat, in unwomanly rags,
    Plying her needle and thread—
5   Stitch! stitch! stitch!
In poverty, hunger, and dirt,
    And still with a voice of dolorous pitch
She sang the "Song of the Shirt!"

"Work! work! work!
10   While the cock is crowing aloof!
And work—work—work,
    Till the stars shine through the roof!
It's O! to be a slave
    Along with the barbarous Turk,
15 Where woman has never a soul to save,
    If this is Christian work!

"Work—work—work
    Till the brain begins to swim;
Work—work—work

---

[1] A notice to vacate given a quarter in advance.

20   Till the eyes are heavy and dim!
Seam, and gusset, and band,
    Band, and gusset, and seam,
Till over the buttons I fall asleep,
    And sew them on in a dream!

25 "O! men with sisters dear!
    O! men with mothers and wives,
It is not linen you're wearing out,
    But human creatures' lives!
Stitch—stitch—stitch,
30   In poverty, hunger, and dirt,
Sewing at once, with a double thread,
    A shroud as well as a shirt.

"But why do I talk of Death?
    That phantom of grisly bone,
35 I hardly fear his terrible shape,
    It seems so like my own—
    It seems so like my own,
Because of the fasts I keep,
Oh! God! that bread should be so dear,
40   And flesh and blood so cheap!

"Work—work—work!
    My labor never flags;
And what are its wages? A bed of straw,
    A crust of bread—and rags.
45 That shatter'd roof,—and this naked floor—
    A table—a broken chair—
And a wall so blank, my shadow I thank
    For sometimes falling there!

"Work—work—work!
50   From weary chime to chime,
Work—work—work—
    As prisoners work for crime!
Band, and gusset, and seam,
    Seam, and gusset, and band,
55 Till the heart is sick, and the brain benumb'd,
    As well as the weary hand.

"Work—work—work,
    In the dull December light,
And work—work—work,
60   When the weather is warm and bright—
While underneath the eaves
    The brooding swallows cling,
As if to show me their sunny backs
    And twit me with the spring.

65 "Oh! but to breathe the breath
    Of the cowslip and primrose sweet—
With the sky above my head,
    And the grass beneath my feet,
For only one short hour
70   To feel as I used to feel,

Before I knew the woes of want
And the walk that costs a meal!

"Oh but for one short hour!
  A respite however brief!
75 No blessed leisure for love or hope,
  But only time for grief!
A little weeping would ease my heart,
  But in their briny bed
My tears must stop, for every drop
80 Hinders needle and thread!

Seam, and gusset, and band,
  Band, and gusset, and seam,
Work, work, work,
  Like the engine that works by steam!
85 A mere machine of iron and wood
  That toils for Mammon's sake—
Without a brain to ponder and craze,
  Or a heart to feel—and break!

With fingers weary and worn,
90 With eyelids heavy and red,
A woman sate in unwomanly rags,
  Plying her needle and thread—
    Stitch! stitch! stitch!
In poverty, hunger, and dirt,
95 And still with a voice of dolorous pitch,
Would that its tone could reach the rich!—
  She sang this "Song of the Shirt!"

THE BRIDGE OF SIGHS
1844

Drown'd! drown'd!—*Hamlet*.[1]

One more unfortunate,
Weary of breath,
Rashly importunate,
Gone to her death!

5 Take her up tenderly,
Lift her with care;
Fashion'd so slenderly,
Young, and so fair!

Look at her garments
10 Clinging like cerements;[2]
Whilst the wave constantly
Drips from her clothing;
Take her up instantly,
Loving, not loathing.—

15 Touch her not scornfully;
Think of her mournfully,
Gently and humanly;
Not of the stains of her,
All that remains of her
20 Now is pure womanly.

[1] Act IV, 7, 185.
[2] waxed cloths used for wrapping dead bodies

Make no deep scrutiny
Into her mutiny
Rash and undutiful:
Past all dishonor
25 Death has left on her
Only the beautiful.

Still, for all slips of hers,
One of Eve's family—
Wipe those poor lips of hers
30 Oozing so clammily.

Loop up her tresses
Escaped from the comb,
Her fair auburn tresses;
Whilst wonderment guesses
35 Where was her home?

Who was her father?
Who was her mother?
Had she a sister?
Had she a brother?
40 Or was there a dearer one
Still, and a nearer one
Yet, than all other?

Alas! for the rarity
Of Christian charity
45 Under the sun!
Oh! it was pitiful!
Near a whole city full,
Home she had none!

Sisterly, brotherly,
50 Fatherly, motherly,
Feelings had changed:
Love, by harsh evidence,
Thrown from its eminence;
Even God's providence
55 Seeming estranged.

Where the lamps quiver
So far in the river,
With many a light
From window and casement,
60 From garret to basement,
She stood, with amazement,
Houseless by night.

The bleak wind of March
Made her tremble and shiver;
65 But not the dark arch,
Or the black flowing river:
Mad from life's history,
Glad to death's mystery,
Swift to be hurl'd—
70 Anywhere, anywhere,
Out of the world!

In she plunged boldly,
No matter how coldly
The rough river ran,—
75 Over the brink of it,
Picture it—think of it,
Dissolute man!
Lave in it, drink of it,
Then, if you can!

80 Take her up tenderly,
Lift her with care;
Fashion'd so slenderly,
Young, and so fair!

Ere her limbs frigidly
85 Stiffen too rigidly,
Decently,—kindly,—
Smoothe and compose them:
And her eyes, close them,
Staring so blindly!

90 Dreadfully staring
Thro' muddy impurity,
As when with the daring
Last look of despairing,
Fix'd on futurity.

95 Perishing gloomily,
Spurr'd by contumely,
Cold inhumanity,
Burning insanity,
Into her rest.—
100 Cross her hands humbly,
As if praying dumbly,
Over her breast!

Owning her weakness,
Her evil behaviour,
105 And leaving, with meekness,
Her sins to her Savior!

THE LAY OF THE LABORER
1844   1844

A spade! a rake! a hoe!
A pickaxe, or a bill![1]
A hook to reap, or a scythe to mow,
A flail, or what ye will—
5 And here's a ready hand
To ply the needful tool,
And skill'd enough, by lessons rough,
In Labor's rugged school.

To hedge, or dig the ditch,
10 To lop or fell the tree,
To lay the swarth on the sultry field,
Or plough the stubborn lea;

[1] A kind of pruning tool.

The harvest stack to bind,
The wheaten rick to thatch,
15 And never fear in my pouch to find
The tinder or the match.[1]

To a flaming barn or farm
My fancies never roam;
The fire I yearn to kindle and burn
20 Is on the hearth of home;
Where children huddle and crouch
Through dark long winter days,
Where starving children huddle and crouch,
To see the cheerful rays,
25 A-glowing on the haggard cheek,
And not in the haggard's[2] blaze!

To Him who sends a drought
To parch the fields forlorn,
The rain to flood the meadows with mud,
30 The lights to blast the corn,[3]
To Him I leave to guide
The bolt in its crooked path.
To strike the miser's rick, and show
The skies blood-red with wrath.

35 A spade! a rake! a hoe!
A pickaxe, or a bill!
A hook to reap, or a scythe to mow,
A flail, or what ye will—
The corn to thrash, or the hedge to plash,[4]
40 The market-team to drive,
Or mend the fence by the cover side,[5]
And leave the game alive.

Ay, only give me work,
And then you need not fear
45 That I shall snare his worship's hare,
Or kill his grace's deer;
Break into his lordship's house,
To steal the plate so rich;
Or leave the yeoman that had a purse
50 To welter in a ditch.

Wherever Nature needs,
Wherever Labor calls,
No job I'll shirk of the hardest work,
To shun the workhouse walls;
55 Where savage laws begrudge
The pauper babe its breath,
And doom a wife to a widow's life,
Before her partner's death.

[1] A reference to the rick-burning disorders in the agricultural counties of southern England in 1830 ff. See Martineau's *The History of England*, 3, 236-38.
[2] stack-yard's
[3] wheat
[4] trim and intertwine
[5] That is, along the woods, undergrowth, etc., that serve to shelter wild animals and game. Game is not so sacred in America as in England.

My only claim is this,
60   With labor stiff and stark,
By lawful turn, my living to earn,
   Between the light and dark;
My daily bread, and nightly bed,
   My bacon, and drop of beer—
65 But all from the hand that holds the land,
   And none from the overseer.[1]

No parish money, or loaf,
   No pauper badges for me,
A son of the soil, by right of toil
70   Entitled to my fee.[2]
No alms I ask, give me my task:
   Here are the arm, the leg,
The strength, the sinews of a man,
   To work, and not to beg.

75 Still one of Adam's heirs,
   Though doom'd by chance of birth
To dress so mean, and to eat the lean
   Instead of the fat of the earth;[3]
To make such humble meals
80   As honest labor can,
A bone and a crust, with a grace to God,
   And little thanks to man!

A spade! a rake! a hoe!
   A pickaxe, or a bill!
85 A hook to reap, or a scythe to mow,
   A flail, or what ye will—
Whatever the tool to ply,
   Here is a willing drudge,
With muscle and limb, and woe to him
90   Who does their pay begrudge!

Who every weekly score
   Docks labor's little mite,
Bestows on the poor at the temple door,
   But robb'd them over night.
95 The very shilling he hoped to save,
   As health and morals fail,
Shall visit me in the New Bastille,
   The Spital,[4] or the Gaol!

STANZAS
1845

Farewell, life! My senses swim;
And the world is growing dim;
Thronging shadows cloud the light,
Like the advent of the night,—
5 Colder, colder, colder still
Upward steals a vapor chill—
Strong the earthy odor grows—
I smell the mould above the rose!

[1] The overseer of the poor.
[2] wages
[3] See *Genesis*, 45:18.
[4] hospital

Welcome, life! the Spirit strives!
10 Strength returns, and hope revives;
Cloudy fears and shapes forlorn
Fly like shadows at the morn,—
Oer the earth there comes a bloom—
Sunny light for sullen gloom,
15 Warm perfume for vapor cold—
I smell the rose above the mould!

QUEEN MAB

A little fairy comes at night,
   Her eyes are blue, her hair is brown,
With silver spots upon her wings,
   And from the moon she flutters down.

5 She has a little silver wand,
   And when a good child goes to bed
She waves her wand from right to left,
   And makes a circle round its head.

And then it dreams of pleasant things,
10   Of fountains filled with fairy fish,
And trees that bear delicious fruit,
   And bow their branches at a wish:

Of arbors filled with dainty scents
   From lovely flowers that never fade;
15 Bright flies that glitter in the sun,
   And glow-worms shining in the shade.

And talking birds with gifted tongues,
   For singing songs and telling tales,
And pretty dwarfs to show the way
20   Through fairy hills and fairy dales.

But when a bad child goes to bed,
   From left to right she weaves her
      rings,
And then it dreams all through the night
   Of only ugly horrid things!

25 Then lions come with glaring eyes,
   And tigers growl, a dreadful noise,
And ogres draw their cruel knives,
   To shed the blood of girls and boys.

Then stormy waves rush on to drown,
30   Or raging flames come scorching round,
Fierce dragons hover in the air,
   And serpents crawl along the ground.

Then wicked children wake and weep,
   And wish the long black gloom away;
35 But good ones love the dark, and find
   The night as pleasant as the day.

Winthrop M. Praed 1802-1839

From THE TROUBADOUR
1823-24

SPIRITS, THAT WALK AND WAIL TONIGHT

Spirits, that walk and wail tonight,
  I feel, I feel that ye are near;
There is a mist upon my sight,
  There is a murmur in mine ear,
5   And a dark, dark dread
     Of the lonely dead
Creeps through the whispering atmosphere!

Ye hover o'er the hoary trees,
  And the old oaks stand bereft and bare;
10 Ye hover o'er the moonlight seas,
  And the tall masts rot in the poisoned air;
     Ye gaze on the gate
     Of earthly state,
And the bandog[1] shivers in silence there.

15 Come hither to me upon your cloud,
  And tell me of your bliss or pain,
And let me see your shadowy shroud,
  And colorless lip, and bloodless vein;
     Where do ye dwell,
20   In heaven or hell?
And why do ye wander on earth again?

Tell me where and how ye died,
  Fell ye in darkness, or fell ye in day,
On lorn hill-side, or roaring tide,
25 In gorgeous feast, or rushing fray?
     By bowl or blow,
     From friend or foe,
  Hurried your angry souls away?

Mute ye come, and mute ye pass,
30 Your tale untold, your shrift unshriven;
But ye have blighted the pale grass,
  And scared the ghastly stars from heaven;
     And guilt hath known
     Your voiceless moan,
35 And felt that the blood is unforgiven!

OH FLY WITH ME! 'TIS PASSION'S HOUR

Oh fly with me! 'tis Passion's hour;
  The world is gone to sleep;
And nothing wakes in brake[2] or bower,
  But those who love and weep:
5 This is the golden time and weather,
When songs and sighs go out together,

And minstrels pledge the rosy wine
To lutes like this, and lips like thine!

Oh fly with me! my courser's flight
10 Is like the rushing breeze,   [night!"
And the kind moon has said "Good
  And sunk behind the trees:
The lover's voice—the loved one's ear—
There's nothing else to speak or hear;
15 And we will say, as on we glide,
That nothing lives on earth beside!

Oh fly with me! and we will wing
  Our white skiff o'er the waves,
And hear the Tritons revelling
20 Among their coral caves;
The envious mermaid, when we pass,
Shall cease her song, and drop her glass;
For it will break her very heart,
To see how fair and dear thou art.

25 Oh fly with me! and we will dwell
  Far over the green seas,
Where sadness rings no parting knell
  For moments such as these!
Where Italy's unclouded skies
30 Look brightly down on brighter eyes,
Or where the wave-wed City[1] smiles;
Enthroned upon her hundred isles.

Oh fly with me! by these sweet strings
  Swept o'er by Passion's fingers,
35 By all the rocks, and vales, and springs
  Where Memory lives and lingers,
By all the tongue can never tell,
By all the heart has told so well,
By all that has been or may be,
40 And by Love's self—Oh fly with me!

TIME'S SONG
1826

O'er the level plains, where mountains greet
  me as I go,
O'er the desert waste, where fountains at
  my bidding flow,
On the boundless beam by day, on the cloud
  by night,
I am riding hence away: who will chain
  my flight?

5 War his weary watch was keeping,—I have
  crushed his spear;
Grief within her bower was weeping,—I
  have dried her tear;
Pleasure caught a minute's hold,—then I
  hurried by,

---

[1] A dog kept tied either as a watch dog or because he is ferocious
[2] thicket

[1] Venice, which according to an old story was wed to the Adriatic Sea. See Wordsworth's *On the Extinction of the Venetian Republic* (p. 312 and n. 2).

Leaving all her banquet cold, and her goblet dry.

Power had won a throne of glory: where
is now his fame?
10 Genius said, "I live in story:" who hath
heard his name?
Love beneath a myrtle[1] bough whispered
"Why so fast?"
And the roses on his brow withered as I
past.

I have heard the heifer lowing o'er the
wild wave's bed;
I have seen the billow flowing where the
cattle fed;
15 Where began my wandering? Memory
will not say!
Where will rest my weary wings? Science
turns away!

From LETTERS FROM TEIGNMOUTH
1829

I—OUR BALL

Comment! c'est lui? que je le regarde encore!
C'est que vraiment il est bien changé; n'est-ce
pas, mon papa?[2]—*Les Premier Amours.*

You'll come to our ball;—since we parted
I've thought of you more than I'll say;
Indeed, I was half broken-hearted
For a week, when they took you away.
5 Fond fancy brought back to my slumbers
Our walks on the Ness and the Den,
And echoed the musical numbers
Which you used to sing to me then.
I know the romance, since it's over,
10 'Twere idle, or worse, to recall;—
I know you're a terrible rover;
But, Clarence, you'll come to our Ball!

It's only a year since, at College,
You put on your cap and your gown;
15 But, Clarence, you're grown out of knowl-
edge,
And changed from the spur to the crown;
The voice that was best when it faltered,
Is fuller and firmer in tone:
And the smile that should never have
altered,—
20 Dear Clarence,—it is not your own;
Your cravat was badly selected,
Your coat don't become you at all;
And why is your hair so neglected?
You must have it curled for our Ball.

25 I've often been out upon Haldon
To look for a covey with Pup;
I've often been over to Shaldon,
To see how your boat is laid up.
In spite of the terrors of Aunty,
30 I've ridden the filly you broke;
And I've studied your sweet little Dante
In the shade of your favorite oak:
When I sat in July to Sir Lawrence,
I sat in your love of a shawl;
35 And I'll wear what you brought me from
Florence,
Perhaps, if you'll come to our Ball.

You'll find us all changed since you van-
ished;
We've set up a National School;[1]
And waltzing is utterly banished;
40 And Ellen has married a fool;
The Major is going to travel;
Miss Hyacinth threatens a rout;[2]
The walk is laid down with fresh gravel;
Papa is laid up with the gout;
45 And Jane has gone on with her easels,
And Anne has gone off with Sir Paul;
And Fanny is sick with the measles,
And I'll tell you the rest at the Ball.

You'll meet all your beauties;—the Lily,
50 And the Fairy of Willowbrook Farm,
And Lucy, who made me so silly
At Dawlish, by taking your arm;
Miss Manners, who always abused you,
For talking so much about Hock;[3]
55 And her sister, who often amused you,
By raving of rebels and Rock;[4]
And something which surely would answer,
An heiress quite fresh from Bengal:—
So, though you were seldom a dancer,
60 You'll dance, just for once, at our Ball.

But out on the world!—from the flowers
It shuts out the sunshine of truth;
It blights the green leaves in the bowers,
It makes an old age of our youth;
65 And the flow of our feeling, once in it,
Like a streamlet beginning to freeze,
Though it cannot turn ice in a minute,
Grows harder by sudden degrees.
Time treads o'er the graves of affection;
70 Sweet honey is turned into gall;
Perhaps you have no recollection
That ever you danced at our Ball.

[1] The myrtle and the rose are emblems of love.
[2] What! is it he? Let me look at him again!
He certainly has changed considerably;
hasn't he, papa?

[1] A school established by a national society for
educating the poor.
[2] A large evening party or other fashionable
gathering.
[3] Hochheimer, a kind of wine.
[4] A fictitious name signed to public notices by
one of the Irish rebels of 1822.

You once could be pleased with our bal-
lads—
Today you have critical ears;
75 You once could be charmed with our
salads—
Alas! you've been dining with Peers;
You trifled and flirted with many;
You've forgotten the when and the how;
There was one you liked better than any—
80 Perhaps you've forgotten her now.
But of those you remember most newly,
Of those who delight or enthrall,
None love you a quarter so truly
As some you will find at our Ball.

85 They tell me you've many who flatter,
Because of your wit and your song;
They tell me (and what does it matter?)
You like to be praised by the throng;
They tell me you're shadowed with laurel,
90 They tell me you're loved by a Blue;[1]
They tell me you're sadly immoral—
Dear Clarence, that cannot be true!
But to me you are still what I found you
Before you grew clever and tall;
95 And you'll think of the spell that once
bound you;
And you'll come, WON'T you come? to
our Ball?

From EVERY-DAY CHARACTERS
1829-30
THE BELLE OF THE BALL-ROOM

Il faut juger des femmes depuis la chaussure
jusqu' à la coiffure exclusivement, à peu près
comme on mesure le poisson entre queue et
tête.[2]—LA BRUYÈRE.

Years—years ago,—ere yet my dreams
Had been of being wise or witty,—
Ere I had done with writing themes,
Or yawned o'er this infernal Chitty;—
5 Years—years ago,—while all my joy
Was in my fowling-piece and filly,—
In short, while I was yet a boy,
I fell in love with Laura Lily.

I saw her at the County Ball:
10 There, when the sounds of flute and fiddle
Gave signal sweet in that old hall
Of hands across and down the middle,
Hers was the subtlest spell by far
Of all that set young hearts romancing;
15 She was our queen, our rose, our star;
And then she danced—O Heaven, her
dancing!

[1] A "blue stocking," a woman affecting an interest in literature and politics. See
Byron's *Don Juan*, I, 206, 3, and n. 1 (p.
611).
[2] One ought to judge women exclusive of their
foot-wear and their head-wear, approxi-
mately as one measures fish between tail and
head.

Dark was her hair, her hand was white;
Her voice was exquisitely tender;
Her eyes were full of liquid light;
20 I never saw a waist so slender!
Her every look, her every smile,
Shot right and left a score of arrows;
I thought 'twas Venus from her isle,
And wondered where she'd left her spar-
rows.[1]

25 She talked,—of politics or prayers,—
Of Southey's prose or Wordsworth's
sonnets,—
Of danglers—or of dancing bears,
Of battles—or the last new bonnets,
By candlelight, at twelve o'clock,
30 To me it mattered not a tittle;
If those bright lips had quoted Locke,
I might have thought they murmured
Little.

Through sunny May, through sultry June,
I loved her with a love eternal;
35 I spoke her praises to the moon,
I wrote them to *The Sunday Journal:*
My mother laughed; I soon found out
That ancient ladies have no feeling:
My father frowned; but how should gout
40 See any happiness in kneeling?

She was the daughter of a Dean,
Rich, fat, and rather apoplectic;
She had one brother, just thirteen,
Whose color was extremely hectic;
45 Her grandmother for many a year
Had fed the parish with her bounty;
Her second cousin was a peer,
And Lord Lieutenant of the County.

But titles, and the three per cents,[2]
50 And mortgages, and great relations,
And India bonds, and tithes[3] and rents,
Oh, what are they to love's sensations?
Black eyes, fair forehead, clustering locks—
Such wealth, such honors, Cupid chooses;
55 He cares as little for the Stocks,
As Baron Rothschild for the Muses.

She sketched; the vale, the wood, the beach,
Grew lovelier from her pencil's shading:
She botanized; I envied each
60 Young blossom in her boudoir fading:
She warbled Handel; it was grand;
She made the Catalani jealous:
She touched the organ; I could stand
For hours and hours to blow the bellows.

[1] Sparrows were sacred to Venus.
[2] Government bonds yielding three per cent interest.
[3] A tithe is a tenth part of the yearly income
paid for the support of the clergy and the
church.

65 She kept an album, too, at home,
    Well filled with all an album's glories;
Paintings of butterflies, and Rome,
    Patterns for trimmings, Persian stories;
Soft songs to Julia's cockatoo,
70 Fierce odes to Famine and to Slaughter;
And autographs of Prince Leboo,
    And recipes for elder-water.[1]

And she was flattered, worshipped, bored;
    Her steps were watched, her dress was
        noted,
75 Her poodle dog was quite adored,
    Her sayings were extremely quoted;
She laughed, and every heart was glad,
    As if the taxes were abolished;
She frowned, and every look was sad,
80 As if the Opera were demolished.

She smiled on many, just for fun,—
    I knew that there was nothing in it;
I was the first—the only one
    Her heart had thought of for a minute.—
85 I knew it, for she told me so,
    In phrase which was divinely moulded;
She wrote a charming hand,—and oh!
    How sweetly all her notes were folded!

Our love was like most other loves;—
90 A little glow, a little shiver,
A rose-bud, and a pair of gloves,
    And "Fly not yet"—upon the river;
Some jealousy of some one's heir,
    Some hopes of dying broken-hearted;
95 A miniature, a lock of hair,
    The usual vows,—and then we parted.

We parted; months and years rolled by;
    We met again four summers after:
Our parting was all sob and sigh;
100 Our meeting was all mirth and laughter:
For in my heart's most secret cell
    There had been many other lodgers;
And she was not the ball-room's belle,
    But only—Mrs. Something Rogers!

TELL HIM I LOVE HIM YET

Tell him I love him yet,
    As in that joyous time;
Tell him I ne'er forget,
    Though memory now be crime;
5 Tell him, when sad moonlight
    Is over earth and sea,
I dream of him by night,—
    He must not dream of me!

---

[1] Probably some sort of lotion made from elder leaves or berries.

Tell him to go where Fame
10 Looks proudly on the brave;
Tell him to win a name
    By deeds on land and wave;
Green—green upon his brow
    The laurel wreath shall be;
15 Although the laurel now
    May not be shared with me.

Tell him to smile again
    In Pleasure's dazzling throng,
To wear another's chain,
20 To praise another's song.
Before the loveliest there
    I'd have him bend his knee,
And breathe to her the prayer
    He used to breathe to me.

25 And tell him, day by day,
    Life looks to me more dim;
I falter when I pray,
    Although I pray for him.
And bid him when I die,
30 Come to our favorite tree;
I shall not hear him sigh,—
    Then let him sigh for me!

FAIRY SONG

He has conn'd the lesson now;
    He has read the book of pain:
There are furrows on his brow;
    I must make it smooth again.

5 Lo! I knock the spurs away;
    Lo! I loosen belt and brand;
Hark! I hear the courser neigh
    For his stall in Fairy-land.

Bring the cap, and bring the vest;
10 Buckle on his sandal shoon;
Fetch his memory from the chest
    In the treasury of the moon.

I have taught him to be wise
    For a little maiden's sake;—
15 Lo! he opens his glad eyes,
    Softly, slowly: Minstrel, wake!

STANZAS

O'er yon churchyard the storm may lower;
    But, heedless of the wintry air,
    One little bud shall linger there,
A still and trembling flower.

5 Unscathed by long revolving years,
    Its tender leaves shall flourish yet,
    And sparkle in the moonlight, wet
With the pale dew of tears.

And where thine humble ashes lie,
10   Instead of 'scutcheon or of stone,
  It rises o'er thee, lonely one,
Child of obscurity!

Mild was thy voice as Zephyr's breath,
  Thy cheek with flowing locks was
    shaded!
15   But the voice hath died, the cheek
    hath faded
In the cold breeze of death!

Brightly thine eye was smiling, sweet!
  But now decay hath stilled its glancing;
  Warmly thy little heart was dancing,
20 But it hath ceased to beat!

A few short months—and thou wert here!
  Hope sat upon thy youthful brow;
  And what is thy memorial now?
A flower—and a Tear.

THE TALENTED MAN

A LETTER FROM A LADY IN LONDON TO A
LADY AT LAUSANNE
1831

Dear Alice! you'll laugh when you know
  it,—
  Last week, at the Duchess's ball,
I danced with the clever new poet,—
  You've heard of him,—Tully St. Paul.
5 Miss Jonquil was perfectly frantic;
  I wish you had seen Lady Anne!
It really was very romantic,
  He *is* such a talented man!

He came up from Brazenose College,
10   Just caught, as they call it, this spring;
And his head, love, is stuffed full of knowl-
    edge
Of every conceivable thing.
Of science and logic he chatters,
  As fine and as fast as he can;
15 Though I am no judge of such matters,
  I'm sure he's a talented man.

His stories and jests are delightful;—
  Not stories, or jests, dear, for you;
The jests are exceedingly spiteful,
20   The stories not always *quite* true.
Perhaps to be kind and veracious
  May do pretty well at Lausanne;
But it never would answer,—good gracious!
  Chez nous[1]—in a talented man.

25 He sneers,—how my Alice would scold
  him!—
  At the bliss of a sigh or a tear;

[1] with us

He laughed—only think!—when I told him
  How we cried o'er Trevelyan last year;
I vow I was quite in a passion;
30   I broke all the sticks of my fan;
But sentiment's quite out of fashion,
  It seems, in a talented man.

Lady Bab, who is terribly moral,
  Has told me that Tully is vain,
35 And apt—which is silly—to quarrel,
  And fond—which is sad—of champagne.
I listened, and doubted, dear Alice,
  For I saw, when my Lady began,
It was only the Dowager's malice;—
40   She *does* hate a talented man!

He's hideous, I own it. But fame, love,
  Is all that these eyes can adore;
He's lame,—but Lord Byron was lame,
  love,
  And dumpy,—but so is Tom Moore.
45 Then his voice,—*such* a voice! my sweet
    creature,
  It's like your Aunt Lucy's toucan:[1]
But oh! what's a tone or a feature,
  When once one's a talented man?

My mother, you know, all the season,
50   Has talked of Sir Geoffrey's estate;
And truly, to do the fool reason,
  He *has* been less horrid of late.
But today, when we drive in the carriage,
  I'll tell her to lay down her plan;—
55 If ever I venture on marriage
  It must be a talented man!

P. S.—I have found on reflection,
  One fault in my friend,—*entre nous*,[2]
Without it, he'd just be perfection;—
60   Poor fellow, he has not a *sou!*
And so, when he comes in September
  To shoot with my uncle, Sir Dan,
I've promised mamma to remember
  He's *only* a talented man!

STANZAS

ON SEEING THE SPEAKER ASLEEP IN HIS CHAIR
DURING ONE OF THE DEBATES OF THE
FIRST REFORMED PARLIAMENT[3]
1833   1833

Sleep, Mr. Speaker; it's surely fair
If you don't in your bed, that you should
  in your chair,
Longer and longer still they grow,

[1] A brilliantly-colored tropical bird with a
harsh voice.
[2] between you and me
[3] The Parliament which met in 1833, the year
following the passage of the Reform Bill.
Manners Sutton, a Tory, was Speaker of the
House of Commons. Praed was a Tory
member of the House at that time. He had
been a Whig until 1830.

Tory and Radical, Aye and No;
5 Talking by night, and talking by day;—
Sleep, Mr. Speaker; sleep, sleep while you
    may!

Sleep, Mr. Speaker; slumber lies
Light and brief on a Speaker's eyes;
Fielden or Finn, in a minute or two,
10 Some disorderly thing will do;
Riot will chase repose away;—
Sleep, Mr. Speaker; sleep, sleep while you
    may!

Sleep, Mr. Speaker; Cobbett will soon
Move to abolish the sun and moon;
15 Hume, no doubt, will be taking the sense
Of the House on a saving of thirteen pence;
Grattan will growl, or Baldwin bray;—
Sleep, Mr. Speaker; sleep, sleep while you
    may!

Sleep, Mr. Speaker; dream of the time
20 When loyalty was not quite a crime;
When Grant was a pupil in Canning's
    school;
When Palmerston fancied Wood a fool;
Lord, how principles pass away!
Sleep, Mr. Speaker; sleep, sleep while you
    may!

25 Sleep, Mr. Speaker; sweet to men
Is the sleep that cometh but now and then;
Sweet to the sorrowful, sweet to the ill,
Sweet to the children that work in a mill;
You have more need of sleep than they;—
30 Sleep, Mr. Speaker; sleep, sleep while you
    may!

Robert Stephen Hawker 1803-1875

THE SONG OF THE WESTERN MEN
1825   1826

A good sword and a trusty hand!
  A merry heart and true!
King James's[1] men shall understand
  What Cornish lads can do.

5 And have they fix'd the where and when?
  And shall Trelawny die?
Here's twenty thousand Cornish men
  Will know the reason why!

Out spake their captain brave and bold,
10 A merry wight[2] was he:
"If London Tower were Michael's hold,
  We'll set Trelawny free!

[1] James II (1685-88).   [2] creature; being

"We'll cross the Tamar, land to land,
  The Severn is no stay,
15 With 'one and all,' and hand in hand,
  And who shall bid us nay?

"And when we come to London Wall,
  A pleasant sight to view,
Come forth! come forth, ye cowards all,
20 Here's men as good as you!

"Trelawny he's in keep and hold,
  Trelawny he may die;
But here's twenty thousand Cornish bold
  Will know the reason why!"

CLOVELLY
1825   ·1832

Oh! laborum dulce lenimen![1]

'Tis eve! 'tis glimmering eve! how fair the
    scene,
  Touched by the soft hues of the dreamy
    west!
Dim hills afar, and happy vales between,
  With the tall corn's[2] deep furrow calmly
    blest:
5 Beneath, the sea, by eve's fond gale carest,
  'Mid groves of living green that fringe
    its side;
Dark sails that gleam on Ocean's heaving
    breast
  From the glad fisher-barks that home-
    ward glide,
  To make Clovelly's shores at pleasant
    evening-tide.

10 Hearken! the mingling sounds of earth
    and sea,
  The pastoral music of the bleating flock,
Blent with the sea-birds' uncouth melody,
  The waves' deep murmur to the unheed-
    ing rock,
And ever and anon the impatient shock
15 Of some strong billow on the sounding
    shore:
And hark! the rowers' deep and well-
    known stroke.
  Glad hearts are there, and joyful hands
    once more
  Furrow the whitening wave with their
    returning oar.

But turn where Art with votive hand hath
    twined
20 A living wreath for Nature's grateful
    brow,

[1] Oh! sweet solace of labors.—Horace, *Odes*, **1**, 32, 14.
[2] wheat's

Where the lone wanderer's raptur'd footsteps wind
'Mid rock, and glancing stream, and
shadowy bough,
Where scarce the valley's leafy depths
allow
The intruding sunbeam in their shade to
dwell,
25 There doth the seamaid breathe her human
vow—
So village maidens in their envy tell—
Won from her dark blue home by that
alluring dell.

A softer beauty floats along the sky;
The moonbeam dwells upon the voiceless
wave;
30 Far off, the night-winds steal away and die,
Or sleep in music in their ocean-cave:
Tall oaks, whose strength the Giant Storm
might brave,
Bend in rude fondness o'er the silvery
sea;
Nor can yon mountain raun[1] forbear to
lave
35 Her blushing clusters where the waters
be,
Murmuring around her home such touching melody.

Thou quaint Clovelly! in thy shades of rest,
When timid Spring her pleasant task
hath sped,
Or Summer pours from her redundant
breast
40 All fruits and flowers along thy valley's
bed:
Yes! and when Autumn's golden glories
spread,
Till we forget near Winter's withering
rage,
What fairer path shall woo the wanderer's
tread,
Soothe wearied hope, and worn regret
assuage?
45 Lo! for firm youth a bower—a home for
lapsing age.

THE FIRST FATHERS[2]

They rear'd their lodges in the wilderness,
Or built them cells beside the shadowy sea,
And there they dwelt with angels, like a
dream!
So they unroll'd the Volume of the Book
5 And fill'd the fields of the Evangelist
With thoughts as sweet as flowers.

[1] The Scottish rowan, or mountain ash.
[2] That is, of the church.

MAWGAN OF MELHUACH[1]
1832

'Twas a fierce night when old Mawgan died,
Men shudder'd to hear the rolling tide:
The wreckers fled fast from the awful
shore,
They had heard strange voices amid the
roar.

5 "Out with the boat there," some one
cried,—
"Will he never come? we shall lose the
tide:
His berth is trim and his cabin stor'd,
He's a weary long time coming on board."

The old man struggled upon the bed:
10 He knew the words that the voices said;
Wildly he shriek'd as his eyes grew dim,
"He was dead! he was dead! when I
buried him."

Hark yet again to the devilish roar,
"He was nimbler once with a ship on
shore;
15 Come! come! old man, 'tis a vain delay,
We must make the offing by break of day."

Hard was the struggle, but at the last,
With a stormy pang, old Mawgan past,
And away, away, beneath their sight,
20 Gleam'd the red sail at pitch of night.

FEATHERSTONE'S DOOM[2]
1831 1832

Twist thou and twine,[3] in light and gloom
A spell is on thine hand;
The wind shall be thy changeful loom,
Thy web the shifting sand.

5 Twine from this hour, in ceaseless toil,
On Blackrock's sullen shore;
Till cordage of the sand shall coil
Where crested surges roar.

'Tis for that hour, when, from the wave,
10 Near voices wildly cried;
When thy stern hand no succor gave,
The cable at thy side.

[1] Gilbert Mawgan, a noted wrecker on the sea-
shore at Melhuach, Cornwall, is said to
have buried alive a sea captain whom he
found exhausted on the shore. It is reported that as Mawgan lay dying a vessel
came into Melhuach Bay, and remained
there until his death.
[2] Featherstone was a wrecker whose troubled
spirit was supposed to be imprisoned on
Blackrock, a prominent rock in Bude Bay,
off the coast of Cornwall, until he should
have accomplished his doom.
[3] See Scott's *Twist Ye, Twine Ye,* 1 (p. 491).

Twist thou and twine! in light and gloom
  The spell is on thine hand;
15 The wind shall be thy changeful loom,
  Thy web the shifting sand.

THE SILENT TOWER OF BOTTREAUX
1831   1832

Tintadgel bells ring o'er the tide,
The boy leans on his vessel side;
He hears that sound, and dreams of home
Soothe the wild orphan of the foam.
5   "Come to thy God in time!"
  Thus saith their pealing chime:
  Youth, manhood, old age past,
  "Come to thy God at last."

But why are Bottreaux' echoes still?
10 Her tower stands proudly on the hill;
Yet the strange chough[1] that home hath
    found,
The lamb lies sleeping on the ground.
  "Come to thy God in time!"
  Should be her answering chime:
15 "Come to thy God at last!"
  Should echo on the blast.

The ship rode down with courses free,[2]
The daughter of a distant sea:
Her sheet was loose, her anchor stor'd,
20 The merry Bottreaux bells on board.
  "Come to thy God in time!"
  Rung out Tintadgel chime;
  Youth, manhood, old age past,
  "Come to thy God at last!"

25 The pilot heard his native bells
Hang on the breeze in fitful swells;
"Thank God," with reverent brow he cried,
"We make the shore with evening's tide."
  "Come to thy God in time!"
30 It was his marriage chime:
  Youth, manhood, old age past,
  His bell must ring at last.

"Thank God, thou whining knave, on land,
But thank, at sea, the steersman's hand,"
35 The captain's voice above the gale:
"Thank the good ship and ready sail."
  "Come to thy God in time!"
  Sad grew the boding chime:
  "Come to thy God at last!"
40 Boom'd heavy on the blast.

Uprose that sea! as if it heard
The mighty Master's signal-word:
What thrills the captain's whitening lip?
The death-groans of his sinking ship.

[1] A bird of the crow family.
[2] That is, with the sails attached to the lower
yards of the ship hanging loose.

45 "Come to thy God in time!"
  Swung deep the funeral chime:
  Grace, mercy, kindness past,
  "Come to thy God at last!"

Long did the rescued pilot tell—
50 When gray hairs o'er his forehead fell,
While those around would hear and weep—
That fearful judgment of the deep.
  "Come to thy God in time!"
  He read his native chime:
55 Youth, manhood, old age past,
  His bell rung out at last.

Still when the storm of Bottreaux' waves
Is wakening in his weedy caves,
Those bells, that sullen surges hide,
60 Peal their deep notes beneath the tide:
  "Come to thy God in time!"
  Thus saith the ocean chime:
  Storm, billow, whirlwind past,
  "Come to thy God at last!"

"PATER VESTER PASCIT ILLA"[1]
1835   1840

Our bark is on the waters: wide around
The wandering wave; above, the lonely sky.
Hush! a young sea-bird floats, and that
    quick cry
Shrieks to the levell'd weapon's echoing
    sound,
5 Grasps its lank wing, and on, with reckless
    bound!
Yet, creature of the surf, a sheltering breast
Tonight shall haunt in vain thy far-off nest,
A call unanswer'd search the rocky ground.
Lord of Leviathan! when Ocean heard
10 Thy gathering voice, and sought his native
    breeze;
When whales first plunged with life, and
    the proud deep
Felt unborn tempests heave in troubled
    sleep;
Thou didst provide, e'en for this nameless
    bird,
Home, and a natural love, amid the surging
    seas.

DEATH SONG
1835

There lies a cold corpse upon the sands
  Down by the rolling sea;
Close up the eyes and straighten the hands,
  As a Christian man's should be.

5 Bury it deep, for the good of my soul,
  Six feet below the ground,
Let the sexton come and the death-bell toll,
  And good men stand around.

[1] "Your Father feeds them."—*Matthew*, 6:26.

Lay it among the churchyard stones,
10 Where the priest hath blessed the clay;
I cannot leave the unburied bones,
And I fain would go my way.

ARE THEY NOT ALL MINISTERING SPIRITS?
1840

We see them not—we cannot hear
The music of their wing—
Yet know we that they sojourn near,
The Angels of the spring!

5 They glide along this lovely ground,
When the first violet grows;
Their graceful hands have just unbound
The zone of yonder rose!

I gather it for thy dear breast,
10 From stain and shadow free,
That which an Angel's touch hath blest
Is meet, my love, for thee!

QUEEN GUENNIVAR'S ROUND[1]
1841

Naiad for Grecian waters!
Nymph for the fountain-side!
But old Cornwall's bounding daughters
For gray Dundagel's tide.

5 The wild wind proudly gathers
Round the ladies of the land;
And the blue wave of their fathers
If joyful where they stand.

Naiad for Grecian waters!
10 Nymph for the fountain-side!
But old Cornwall's bounding daughters
For gray Dundagel's tide.

Yes! when memory rejoices
In her long belovèd theme,
15 Fair forms and thrilling voices
Will mingle with my dream.

Naiad for Grecian waters!
Nymph for the fountain-side!
But old Cornwall's bounding daughters
20 For gray Dundagel's tide.

TO ALFRED TENNYSON
1859

They told me in their shadowy phrase,
Caught from a tale gone by,
That Arthur, King of Cornish praise,
Died not, and would not die.

[1] A kind of song sung by two or more persons, each taking up a strain in turn.

5 Dreams had they, that in fairy bowers
Their living warrior lies,
Or wears a garland of the flowers
That grow in Paradise.

I read the rune[1] with deeper ken,
10 And thus the myth I trace:—
A bard should rise, mid future men,
The mightiest of his race.

He would great Arthur's deeds rehearse
On gray Dundagel's shore;
15 And so the King in laurell'd verse
Shall live, and die no more!

John Wilson 1785-1854
"Christopher North"

From NOCTES AMBROSIANÆ[2]
1822-35

No. XLII—APRIL, 1829

SCENE I.—*The snuggery.*[3]*—Time, Eight o'clock.—The Union-Table,*[4] *with tea and Coffee-pots, and the O'Doherty China-set—Cold Round—Pies—Oysters—Rizzars*[5]
5 *—Pickled Salmon, a How-Towdie*[6] *whirling before the fire over a large basin of mashed Potatoes.—The Boiler on.—A Bachelor's Kitchen*[7] *on the small Oval.*[8]*— A Dumb Waiter at each end of the Union.*

NORTH—SHEPHERD[9]

10 *Shepherd.* This I ca' comfort, sir. Everything within oursell—nae need to ring the bell the leevelang night—nae openin' o' cheepin',[10] nae shuttin' o' clashin' doors— nae trampin' o' waiters across the carpet
15 wi' creakin' shoon[11]—or stumblin', clumsy coofs[12]—to the great spillin' o' gravy—but a' things, eatable and uneatable, either hushed into a cosy calm, or——
North. Now light, James, the lamp of the
20 Bachelor's Kitchen with Tickler's card, and in a quarter of an hour, minus five minutes, you shall scent and see such steaks!
Shepherd. Only look at the towdy, sir, how she swings sae granly roun' by my
25 garters, after the fashion o' a planet. It's a beautiful example o' centrifugal attraction. See till the fat dreep-dreepin' intil the

[1] A story or poem written in runes, symbols used in writing by early Germanic peoples.
[2] Ambrosian Nights.   [3] A small room or den.
[4] joined table   [5] dried herring
[6] whole young hen
[7] A vessel in which food is prepared; a Dutch oven.
[8] An elevated stand having an oval shape.
[9] "Christopher North" is a pseudonym of John Wilson; the Shepherd is James Hogg, known as "The Ettrick Shepherd."
[10] of squeaking   [11] shoes   [12] blockheads

ashet[1] o' mashed potawtoes, oilifying the crusted brown intil a mair delicious richness o' mixed vegetable and animal maitter! As she swings slowly twirling roun', I really canna say, sir, for I dinna ken, whether bany[2] back or fleshy briest[3] be the maist temptin'! Sappy baith![4]

North. Right, James—baste her—baste her—don't spare the flour. Nothing tells like the dredge-box.[5]

Shepherd. You're a capital man-cook, sir.

North. For plain roast and boil, I yield to no mortal man. Nor am I inconsiderable shakes at stews. What a beautiful blue magical light glimmers from the wonder-working lamp, beneath whose necromancy you already hear the sweet low bubble and squeak of the maturing steak! Off with the lid, James.   [*The* Shepherd *doffs the lid of the Bachelor's Kitchen.*]

Shepherd. What a pabblin'![6] A hotch-in'[7] like a sea in a squall, or a patfu'[8] o' boilin' parritch![9] What a sweet savor! Is't na like honeysuckle, sir, or sweet-brier, or broom, or whuns,[10] or thyme, or roses, or carnations? Or rather like the scent o' these a' conglomerated thegither in the dewy mornin' air, when, as sune as you open the window, the haill house is overflowing wi' fragrance, and a body's a maist sick with the sweet, warm, thick air, that slowly wins its way, like palpable balm, arm in arm wi' the licht that waukens the yellow-billed blackbird in her nest amang the cottage creepers, or reopens the watchful een[11] o' her neighbor, the bonny spotted mavis![12] Let's pree't.[13]   [Shepherd *tastes.*]

North. Ay—I could have told you so. Rash man, to swallow liquid and solid fire! But no more spluttering. Cool your tongue with a caulker.[14]

Shepherd. That lamp's no canny.[15] It intensifies hetness intil an atrocity abune[16] natur. Is the skin flyped[17] aff my tongue, sir?   [Shepherd *shows his tongue.*]

North. Let me put on my spectacles. A slight incipient inflammation not worth mentioning.

Shepherd. I houp[18] an incipient inflammation's no a dangerous sort?

North. Is that indeed the tongue, my dear James, that trills so sweetly and so simply those wild Doric[19] strains? How deeply,

darkly, beautifully red! Just like a rag of scarlet. No scurf—say rather no haze around the lambent light. A rod of fire[1]— an arrow of flame.[2] A tongue of ten thousand, prophesying an eagle or raven life.

Shepherd. I aye like, sir, to keep a gude tongue in my head, ever since I wrote *The Chaldee Mannyscripp.*[3]

North. Humph!—no more infallible mark of a man of genius, James, than the shape of his tongue. It is uniformly long, so that he can shoot it out, with an easy grace, to the tip of his nose.

Shepherd. This way.

North. Precisely so. Fine all round the edge, from root to tip—underneath very veinous—surface in color near as may be to that of a crimson curtain shining in setting sunlight. But the tip—James—the tip——

Shepherd. Like that o' the serpent's that deceived Eve, sir—curlin' up and down like the musical leaf o' some magical tree——

North. It is a singular fact with regard to the tongue, that if you cut off the half of it, the proprietor of the contingent remainder can only mumble—but cut it off wholly, and he speaks fully better than before.

Shepherd. That's a hang'd lee.

North. As true a word as ever I spoke, James.

Shepherd. Perhaps it may, sir, but it's a hang'd lee, nevertheless.

North. Dish the steaks, my dear James, and I shall cut down the howtowdie.   [North *and the* Shepherd *furnish up the Ambrosial tables, and sit down to serious devouring.*]

North. Now, James, acknowledge it— don't you admire a miscellaneous meal?

Shepherd. I do. Breakfast, noony,[4] denner, four-hours,[5] and sooper a' in ane. A material emblem o' that spiritual substance, *Blackwood's Magazine!* Can it possibly be, sir, that we are twa gluttons?

North. Gluttons we most assuredly are not; but each of us is a man of good appetite. What is gluttony?

Shepherd. Some mair steaks, sir?

North. Very few, my dear James, very few.

Shepherd. What's gluttony?

North. Some eggs!

[1] dish ; platter
[2] bony
[3] breast
[4] juicy both
[5] flour-sifter
[6] bubbling
[7] shaking
[8] potful
[9] porridge
[10] furze ; gorse
[11] eyes
[12] thrush
[13] taste it
[14] drink of liquor
[15] not trustworthy
[16] above
[17] peeled
[18] hope
[19] simple ; natural

[1] See *James,* 3 :6.   [2] See *Jeremiah,* 9 :8.
[3] *The Chaldee MS.,* the joint work of Hogg, Wilson, and Lockhart, appeared in *Blackwood's Magazine,* October, 1817 (vol. 2, pp. 89 ff.). It was a bitter satire, written in Biblical language, against the notables of Edinburgh ; it gave such offense that it immediately was withdrawn.
[4] ten-o'clock lunch.   [5] four-o'clock lunch.

Shepherd. Ae[1] spoonfu'. What a layer she wad hae been. O but she's a prolific creature, Mr. North, your howtowdie! It's necessary to kill heaps o' yearocks,[2] or the hail kintra[3] wud be a-cackle frae John o' Groat's House to St. Michael's Mount.[4]

North. Sometimes I eat merely as an amusement or pastime—sometimes for recreation of my animal spirits—sometimes on the philosophical principle of sustenance— sometimes for the mere sensual, but scarcely sinful, pleasure of eating, or, in common language, gormandizing—and occasionally, once a month or so, for all these several purposes united, as at this present blessed moment; so a few flakes, dear Shepherd, of that Westmoreland ham—lay the knife on it, and its own weight will sink it down through the soft sweet sappiness of fat and lean, undistinguishably blended as the colors of the rainbow, and out of all sight incomparably more beautiful.

Shepherd. As for me, I care nae mair about what I eat, than I do what kind o' bed I sleep upon, sir. I hate onything stinkin' or mooldy at board—or onything damp or musty in bed. But let the vivres[5] be but fresh and wholesome—and if it's but scones[6] and milk, I shut my een, say a grace, fa' to, and am thankfu';—let the bed be dry, and whether saft or hard, feathers, hair, caff,[7] straw, or heather, I'm fast in ten minutes, and my soul waverin' awa like a butterfly intil the land o' dreams.

North. Not a more abstemious man than old Kit North in his Majesty's dominions, on which the sun never sets. I have the most accommodating of palates.

Shepherd. Yes—it's a universal genius. I ken naething like it, sir, but your stomach. "Sure such a pair were never seen!" Had ye never the colic?

North. Never, James, never. I confess that I have been guilty of many crimes, but never of a capital crime,—never of colic.

Shepherd. There's muckle[8] confusion o' ideas in the brains of the blockheads who accuse us o' gluttony, Mr. North. Gluttony may be defined "an immoral and unintellectual abandonment o' the sowl o' man to his gustative natur." I defy a brute animal to be a glutton. A swine's no a glutton. Nae

cretur but man can be a glutton. A' the rest are prevented by the definition.

North. Is there any test of gluttony, James?

Shepherd. Watch twa men eatin'. As lang's there's a power or capacity o' smilin' on their cheeks, and in and about their een,— as lang's they keep lookin' at you, and round about the table, attendin' to or joinin' in the tauk, or the speakin' cawm,[1]—as lang's they every noo an' than lay doon their knife and fork, to ca' for yill,[2] or ask a young leddy to tak wine, or tell an anecdote, —as lang's they keep frequently ca'in' on the servant lad or lass for a clean plate—as lang's they glower on the framed pictures or prents on the wa', and askin' if the tane's[3] originals and the tither[4] proofs,—as lang's they offer to carve the tongue or turkey— depend on 't they're no in a state o' gluttony, but are devourin' their soup, fish, flesh, and fowl, like men and Christians. But as sune's their chin gets creeshy[5]—their cheeks lank, sallow, and clunk-clunky[6]—their nostrils wide—their een fixed—their faces close to their trencher—and themsel's dumbies[7]— then you may see a specimen "o' the immoral and unintellectual abandonment o' the sowl o' man to his gustative natur;" then is the fast, foul, fat feeder a glutton, the maist disgustfuest cretur that sits—and far aneath the level o' them that feed on a' fowers, out o' trochs[8] on garbage.

North. Sensuality is the most shocking of all sins, and its name is Legion.

Shepherd. Ay, there may be as muckle gluttony on sowens[9] as on turtle soup. A ploughman may be as greedy and as gutsy[10] as an alderman. The sin lies not in the sense but in the sowl. Sir—a red-herring?

North. Thank ye, James.

Shepherd. Are you drinkin' coffee? Let me toast you a shave o' bread, and butter it for you on baith sides, sir?

[*The* SHEPHERD *kneels on the Tiger,*[11] *and stretches out the Trident*[12] *to Vulcan.*[13]]

North. Heaven will reward ye, James, for your piety to the old man.

Shepherd. Dinna think, sir, that I care about your last wull and testament. I'm

---

1 one　　2 hens one year old　　3 whole country
4 That is, from one end of the country to the other. John o' Groat's House is a locality in the extreme northeastern part of Scotland. Saint Michael's Mount is a rock off the coast of Cornwall.
5 victuals　　　　　　　　7 chaff
6 griddle cakes　　　　　 8 much ; great

1 calm　　　　　　　　6 flabby
2 ale　　　　　　　　　7 dummies
3 one's　　　　　　　　8 troughs
4 other　　　　　　　　9 porridge
5 greasy　　　　　　　10 gluttonous
11 hearthrug into which is woven the image of a tiger
12 fork (The Trident was a three-pronged spear carried by Neptune, god of the sea.)
13 the fire (Vulcan was the blacksmith of the gods.)

nae legacy-hunter—nae Post-obit.[1] But hae ye added the codicil?

North. The man who has not made his will at forty is worse than a fool—almost a knave.

Shepherd. I ken nae better test o' wisdom—wisdom in its highest sense—than a just last wull and testament. It blesseth generations yet unborn. It guardeth and strengthneth domestic peace—and maketh brethren to dwell together in unity.[2] Being dead, the wise testator yet liveth[3]—his spirit abideth invisible, but felt ower the roof-tree, and delighteth, morning and evening, in the thanksgiving Psalm.

North. One would think it were easy to act well in that matter.

Shepherd. One would think it were easy to act weel, sir, in a' matters. Yet hoo difficult! The sowl seems, somehow or ither, to lose her simplicity, to keep restlessly glourin' round and round about wi' a thousan' artificial ogles up a' the cross and by-paths leadin' nae single body kens whither, unless it be into brakes, and thickets, and quagmires, and wildernesses o' moss—where ane may wander wearily and drearily up and doon for years, and never recover the richt road again, till death touches him on the shouther, and doon he fa's amang them that were, leavin' a' that lucked up to him for his effecks in doubt and dismay and desolation, wi' sore and bitter hearts, uncertain whether to gie vent to their feelings in blessings or in curses, in execration or prayer.

North. Of all the vices of old age, may gracious Heaven, my dearest James, forever shield me from avarice!

Shepherd. Nae fear o' that. There's either just ae enjoyment o' siller,[4] or five hunder thousan' million. The rich maun either spend it thick and fast, as a nightingale scatters her notes on the happy air—or sit upon his guineas, like a clockin' hen on a heap o' yellow addled eggs amang the nettles.

North. Picturesquely true.

Shepherd. Oh, sir! what delicht to a wise rich man in being lavish—in being prodigal! For these two words only carry blame alang wi' them according to the character o' the giver or the receiver. Wha mair lavish—wha mair prodigal than the Sun? Yet let him shower his beams forever and ever all

ower the Planetary System, frae Venus wi' her cestus[1] to Saturn wi' his ring, and nane the poorer, either in licht or in heat, is he—and nane the poorer will he ever be, till the hand that hung him on high shall cut the golden cord[2] by which he liveth in the sky, and he falls, his duty done, into the bosom of Chaos and Old Night![3]

North. My dear Shepherd!

Shepherd. But the Sun he shineth wi' unborrowed licht. There's the bonnie moon, God bless her mildest face, that loveth still to cheer the pensive nicht wi' a lustre lent her by the joyful day—to give to earth a' she receives frae heaven. Puir, senseless, ungratefu' creturs we! Eyeing her frae our ain narrow vales, we ca' her changefu' and inconstant! But is na she, sweet satellite, forever journeying on her gracious round, and why will we grudge her smiles to them far frae us, seein' we are a' children to ae Maker, and according to his perfect laws, a' partakers in the same impartial bounty? Here's a nice brown shave for you, sir.

[*The* Shepherd *rises from his knees on the rug, takes the bread from the prongs of the Trident, and fresh butters it on both sides for* Mr. North, *who receives it with a benign bow.*]

North. Uncommonly yellow this butter, James, for the season. The grass must be growing——

Shepherd. Ay, you may hear 't growin'. What years for vegetation the last beautifu' and glorious Three! The ongoings o' natur are in the lang run regular and steady;—but noo and then the mighty mother seems to obey some uncontrollable impulse far within her fair large bosom, and "wantons as in her prime,"[4] outdoing her very self in beneficence to earth, and that mysterious concave we ca' heaven.

North. In spite of gout, rheumatism, lumbago, corns, and chilblains, into the Forest shall I wend my way, James, before midsummer.

Shepherd. And young and auld will be but ower happy to see you, sir, frae the lanely Douglas Tower to those o' Newark. Would ye believe 't, an old ash stullion[5] in the garden hedge of Mount Benger shot out six scions last year, the langest o' them nine, and the shortest seven feet lang? That was growin' for you, sir.

---

[1] A post-obit is a bond given to secure a loan, and payable after death.
[2] See *Psalms*, 133 :1.
[3] See *Hebrews*, 11 :4.
[4] one enjoyment of small change

[1] girdle
[2] See *Ecclesiastes*, 12 :6.
[3] See *Paradise Lost*, 1, 543 ; 2. 1036.
[4] *Paradise Lost*, 5, 295.
[5] tree

North. There has been much planting of trees lately, in the Forest, James?

Shepherd. To my taste, to tell the truth, rather ower muckle[1]—especially o' nurses.[2]

North. Nurses! wet or dry nurses, James?

Shepherd. Baith. Larches and Scotch firs; or you may ca' them schoolmasters, that teach the young idea how to shoot.[3] But thinnins[4] in the Forest never can pay, I suspeck; and except on bleaky knows,[5] the hard wood wad grow better, in my opinion, left to themsells, without either nurses or schoolmasters. The nurses are apt to overlay the weans,[6] and the schoolmasters to forget, or what's waur,[7] to flog their pupils; and thus the rising is a stunted generation.

North. Forty-five years ago, my dear James, when you were too young to remember much, I loved the Forest for its solitary single trees, ancient yew or sycamore, black in the distance, but when near, how gloriously green. Tall, delicately-feathered ash, whose limbs were still visible in latest summer's leafiness — birch, in early spring, weeping and whispering in its pensive happiness by the perpetual din of its own waterfall—oak, yellow in the suns of June——

Shepherd.—

> The grace of forest wood decayed,
> And pastoral melancholy![8]

North. What lovely lines! Who writes like Wordsworth!

Shepherd. Tuts! Me ower young to remember muckle forty-five years ago! You're speakin' havers.[9] I was then twal—and I remember everything I ever heard or saw since I was three year auld. I recolleck the mornin' I was pitten intil breeks[10] as distinckly as if it was this verra day. They hurt me sair atween the fork and the inside o' the knees—but oh! I was a prood man—and the lamb that I chased all the way frae my father's hut to Ettrick Manse, round about the kirk, till I caught it on a gowany[11] grave, and lay doon wi't in my arms on the sunny heap, had nae need to be ashamed o' itsel', for I hunted it like a colley—although when I grupped it at last, I held it to my beatin' bosom as tenderly as ever I hae since done wee Jamie, when pitten the dear cretur

intil the crib that stauns at the side o' his mither's bed, after e'enin' prayers.

North. I feel not undelightfully, my dear James, that I must be waxing old—very old —for of the last ten years of my life I remember almost nothing except by an effort— whereas the first ten—commencing with that bright, clear, undying light that borders the edge of the oblivion of infancy—have been lately becoming more intensely distinct—so that often the past is with me as it were the present—and the sad gray-haired ancient is again a blest golden-headed boy, singing a chorus with the breeze, and the birds and the streams. Alas! and alack a day!

Shepherd. 'Tis only sae that we ever renew our youth. Oh, sir! I hinna[1] forgotten the color o' the plumage o' ae single dove that ever sat cooin' of old on the growin' turf-riggin'[2] o' my father's hut! Ae great muckle, big, beautifu' ane in particular, blue as if it had dropt doon frae the sky— I see the noo,[3] a' neck and bosom, cooin' and cooin' deep as distant thunder, round and round his mate, wha was whiter than the white sae-faem, makin' love to the snawy creture—wha cowered doon in fear afore her imperious and impassioned lord—yet in love stronger than fear—showing hoo in a' leevin'[4] natur passions seemingly the maist remote frae ane anither, coalesce into mysterious union by means o' ae pervading and interfusing speerit, that quickens the pulses o' that inscrutable secret—life!

North. All linnets have died, James— that race of loveliest lilters[5] is extinct.

Shepherd. No thae.[6] Broom and bracken are tenanted by the glad, meek creturs still— but the chords o' music in our hearts are sair unstrung—the harp o' our heart has lost its melody. But come out to the Forest, my dear, my honored sir, and fear not then when we twa are walking thegither without speakin' among the hills, you

> Will feel the airs that from them blow
> A momentary bliss bestow.[7]

and the wild, uncertain, waverin' music o' the Eolian harp that natur plays upon in the solitude, will again echo far, far awa' amang the recesses o' your heart, and the linty[8] will sing as sweetly as ever amang the blossoms o' the milk-white thorn. Or, if you canna be brocht to feel sae, you'll

---

[1] over much
[2] trees planted to protect other trees while young
[3] Thomson, *The Seasons*, Spring, 1153.
[4] transplanted trees   [5] knolls
[6] the young ones   [7] worse
[8] Wordsworth, *Yarrow Visited*, 47-48 (p. 335).
[9] nonsense
[10] put into breeches   [11] daisy-covered

[1] have not   [4] all living
[2] earthen roof   [5] singers
[3] now   [6] those
[7] Gray, *Ode on a Distant Prospect of Eton College*, 15-16 (p. 57).
[8] linnet

hae but to look in my wee Jamie's face, and his glistening een will convince you that Scotia's nightingale[1] still singeth as sweetly as of yore! But let us sit into the fire, sir.

North. Thank you, Shepherd — thank you, James.

Shepherd (wheeling his father's chair to the ingle-corner, and singing the while)

"There's Christopher North, that wons[2] in yon glen,
He's the king o' gude fallows and wale[3] o' auld men!"

North. I cannot bear, James, to receive such attention paid to my bodily weakness —I had almost said, my decrepitude—by any living soul but yourself. How is that, my dear Shepherd?

Shepherd. Because I treat you wi' tenderness, but no wi' pity—wi' sympathy, but no wi' compassion—

North. My dear James, ye must give us a book on synonyms. What delicacy of distinction!

Shepherd. I suspeck, sir, that mother wut[4] and mother feelin' hae mair to do wi' the truth o' metaphysical etymology and grammar, than either lair[5] or labor. Ken the meanin', by self-experience, o' a' the nicest shades o' thoughts and feelings, and devil the fears but you'll ken the meanin's o' the nicest shades o' syllables and words.

North. Good, James. Language flows from two great sources—the head and the heart. Each feeds ten thousand rills[6]—

Shepherd. Reflectin' different imagery—but no sae very different either—for—you see—

North. I see nothing, James, little or nothing, till you blow away the intervening mist by the breath of genius, and then the whole world outshines, like a panorama with a central sun.

Shepherd. Ah! sir, you had seen the hale world afore ever I kent you—a perfect wandering Ulysses.

North. Yes, James, I have circumnavigated the globe, and intersected it through all its zones, and, by Jupiter, there is not a climate comparable to that of Scotland.

Shepherd. I believ't. Blest be Providence for having saved my life frae the curse o' stagnant sky—a monotonous heaven. On flat land, and aneath an ever blue lift,[7] I should soon hae been a perfeck idiwit.[8]

North. What a comical chap, James, you would have been, had you been born a negro!

Shepherd. Aye—I think I see you, sir, wi' great blubber lips, a mouthfu' o' muckle white horse's teeth, and a head o' hair like the woo[1] atween a ram's horns when he's grown ancient amang the mountains. What Desdemona could hae stood out against sic[2] an Othello?

North. Are negroes, gentlemen, to sit in both Houses of Parliament?[3]

Shepherd. Nae politics the nicht—nae politics. I'm sick o' politics. Let's speak about the weather. This has been a fine day, sirs.

North. A first-rate day, indeed, James. Commend me to a Day who does not stand shilly-shallying during the whole morning and forenoon, with hands in his breeches' pockets, or bitin' his nails, and scratching his head, unable to make up his mind in what fancy character he is to appear from meridian to sunset—but who—

Shepherd. Breaks out o' the arms o' the dark-haired bricht-eed night, with the power and pomp o' a Titan, and frightnin' that bit puir timid lassie the Dawn out o' her seven senses, in thunder and lightning a' at ance storms the sky, till creation is drenched in flood, bathed in fire, and rocked by earthquake. That's the day for a poet, sirs—that's a picture for the ee, and that's music for the lug[4] o' imagination, sirs, till ane's verra speerit cums to creawte the war it trummles[5] at, and to be composed o' the self-same yelements, gloomin' and boomin', blackenin' and brightenin', pourin' and roarin', and awsomely confusin' and confoundin' heaven and earth, and this life and the life that is to come, and a' the passions that loup up at sichts and souns, joy, hope, fear, terror, exultation, and that mysterious up-risin' and downfa'in'[6] o' our mortal hearts, connected some hoo or ither wi' the fleein' cluds, and the tossin' trees, and the red rivers in spate,[7] and the sullen looks o' black bits o' sky like faces, together wi' ane and a' o' thae[8] restless shows o' uneasy natur appertainin', God knows hoo, but maist certain sure it is so, to the region, the rueful region o' man's entailed inheritance —the grave!

North. James, you are very pale—very white about the gills—are you well enough?

---

[1] The linnet. [2] dwells [3] pick ; choice
[4] wit [5] learning
[6] See Gray's *The Progress of Poesy*, 3-4 (p. 61).
[7] sky [8] idiot

[1] wool [2] such
[3] A reference to the growing agitation for the abolition of negro slavery.
[4] ear [5] trembles [6] See *Psalms*, 139 :2.
[7] flood [8] those

Turn up your little finger. Pale! nay, now they are more of the color of my hat—as if

> In the scowl of heaven, his face
> Grew black as he was speaking.

The shadow of the thunder-cloud threatening the eyes of his imagination, has absolutely darkened his face of clay. He seems at a funeral, James!

Shepherd. Whare's the moral? What's the use of thunder, except in a free country? There's nae grandeur in the terror o' slaves flingin' themsells doon on their faces amang the sugar-canes, in a tornawdo. But the low quick beatin' at the heart o' a freeman, a bauld-faced son o' liberty, when simultawneous flash and crash rends Natur to her core, why that flutter, sir, that does homage to a Power aboon us, exalts the dreadful magnificence o' the instruments that Power employs to subjugate our sowls to his sway, and makes thunder and lichtnin', in sic a country as England and Scotland, sublime.

North. The short and long of the matter seems to be, James, that when it thunders you funk.[1]

Shepherd. Yes, sir, thunders frighten me *into* my senses.

North. Well said, James—well said.

Shepherd. Heaven forgive me, but ten out o' the eighteen wakin' hours, I am an atheist.

North. And I.

Shepherd. And a' men. Puir, pitifu', ungratefu', and meeserable wretches that we are—waur than worms. An atheist's a godless man. Sweep a' thoughts o' his Maker out o' ony man's heart—and what better is he, as lang's the floor o' his being continues bare, than an atheist?

North. Little better indeed.

Shepherd. I envy—I honor—I venerate —I love—I bless the man, who, like the patriarchs of old, ere sin drowned the world, ever walks with God.

North. James, here we must not get too solemn—

Shepherd. That's true; and let me hope that I'm no sae forgetfu' as I fear. In this season o' the year, especially when the flowers are a' seen again in lauchin'[2] flocks ower the braes,[3] like children returnin' to school after a lang snaw, I can wi' truth avoo,[4] that the sight of a primrose is to me like the soun' o' a prayer, and that I seldom

walk alone by myself for half a mile, without thochts sae calm and sae serene, and sae humble and sae grateful, that I houp I'm no deceivin' myself noo when I venture to ca' them—religious.

North. No, James, you are not self-deceived. Poetry melts into religion.

Shepherd. It is religion, sir, for what is religion but a clear—often a sudden—insicht, accompanied wi' emotion, into the dependence o' a' beauty and a' glory on the Divine Mind? A wee bit dew-wat gowany,[1] as it makes a scarcely perceptible sound and stir, which it often does, amang the grass that loves to shelter but not hide the bonnie earth-born star, glintin' up sae kindly wi' its face into mine, while by good fortune my feet touched it not, has hundreds o' times affected me as profoundly as ever did the Sun himsell setting in a' his glory—as profoundly—and, oh! far mair tenderly, for a thing that grows and grows, and becomes every hour mair and mair beautifu', and then hangs fixed for a season in the perfection o' its lovely delicht, and then—wae is me—begins to be a little dim— and then dimmer and dimmer, till we feel that it is indeed—in very truth, there's nae denyin't—fading—fading—faded—gone — dead—buried. Oh! sir, sic an existence as that has an overwhelmin' analogy to our ain life—and *that* I hae felt—nor doubt I that you, my dear sir, hae felt it too—when on some saft, sweet, silent incense-breathing morning[2] o' spring—far awa, perhaps, frae the smoke o' ony human dwellin', and walkin' ye cared na, kent na whither—sae early that the ground-bees were but beginnin' to hum out o' their bikes[3]—when, I say, some flower suddenly attracted the licht within your ee, wi' a power like that o' the loadstone, and though, perhaps, the commonest o' the flowers that beautify the braes o' Scotland—only, as I said, a bit ordinary gowan—yet, what a sudden rush o' thochts and feelings overflowed your soul at the simple sicht! while a' nature becam for a moment overspread wi' a tender haze belongin' not to hersell, for there was naething there to bedim her brightness, but existin' only in your ain two silly een, sheddin' in the solitude a few holy tears!

North. James, I will trouble you for the red-herrings.

. . . .

[1] become frightened
[2] laughing
[3] hills   [4] avow

[1] dew-wet daisy
[2] See Gray's *Elegy Written in a Country Churchyard*, 17 (p. 59).
[3] hives

Felicia Dorothea Hemans
1793-1835

A DIRGE
1822   1823

Calm on the bosom of thy God,
  Fair spirit, rest thee now!
E'en while with ours thy footsteps trod
  His seal was on thy brow.

5 Dust, to its narrow house beneath!
  Soul, to its place on high!
They that have seen thy look in death
  No more may fear to die.

ENGLAND'S DEAD
1822

Son of the Ocean Isle!
  Where sleep your mighty dead?
Show me what high and stately pile
  Is reared o'er Glory's bed.

5 Go, stranger! track the deep—
  Free, free the white sail spread!
Wave may not foam, nor wild wind sweep,
  Where rest not England's dead.

On Egypt's burning plains,
10   By the pyramid o'erswayed,
With fearful power the noonday reigns,
  And the palm trees yield no shade;—

But let the angry sun
  From heaven look fiercely red,
15 Unfelt by those whose task is done!—
  There slumber England's dead.[1]

The hurricane hath might
  Along the Indian shore,
And far by Ganges' banks at night
20   Is heard the tiger's roar:—

But let the sound roll on!
  It hath no tone of dread
For those that from their toils are gone,—
  There slumber England's dead.[2]

25 Loud rush the torrent-floods
  The Western wilds among,
And free, in green Columbia's woods,
  The hunter's bow is strung;—

But let the floods rush on!
30   Let the arrow's flight be sped!
Why should *They* reck whose task is
  done?—
  There slumber England's dead.[3]

[1] English and French armies fought before Alexandria, Egypt, in 1801.
[2] English and French armies fought a number of battles in India, 1748-1803.
[3] English armies fought against the French and Americans in America at various times, 1758-59, 1775-81, 1812-14.

The mountain-storms rise high
  In the snowy Pyrenees,
35 And tossed the pine-boughs through the
    sky
  Like rose-leaves on the breeze;—

But let the storm rage on!
  Let the fresh wreaths be shed!
For the Roncesvalles' field is won,—
40   *There* slumber England's dead.[1]

On the frozen deep's repose
  'Tis a dark and dreadful hour,
When round the ship the ice-fields close,
  And the northern night-clouds
    lower;—

45 But let the ice drift on!
  Let the cold blue desert spread!
Their course with mast and flag is done—
  Even there sleep England's dead.[2]

The warlike of the isles,
50   The men of field and wave!
Are not the rocks their funeral piles,
  The seas and shores their grave?

Go, stranger! track the deep—
  Free, free the white sails spread!
55 Wave may not foam, nor wild wind sweep,
  Where rest not England's dead.

THE GRAVES OF A HOUSEHOLD
1825

They grew in beauty side by side,
  They filled one home with glee;
Their graves are severed far and wide,
  By mount, and stream, and sea.

5 The same fond mother bent at night
  O'er each fair sleeping brow;
She had each folded flower in sight—
  Where are those dreamers now?

One, midst the forest of the West,
10   By a dark stream is laid—
The Indian knows his place of rest,
  Far in the cedar-shade.

The sea, the blue lone sea, hath one—
  He lies where pearls lie deep;

[1] Roncesvalles, the famous pass in the Pyrenees, in which the rear-guard of Charlemagne's army was overwhelmed by the Basques in 778, is here used figuratively for Spain. English armies engaged in numerous battles in Spain against the Spanish and the French, the most noted of which were fought 1706-08, 1808-13.
[2] The most famous English naval battles were fought against the Spanish and the French, 1588, 1782-1805.

15 *He* was the loved of all, yet none
    O'er his low bed may weep.

One sleeps where southern vines are drest
    Above the noble slain:
He wrapt his colors round his breast
20   On a blood-red field of Spain.

And one—o'er *her* the myrtle showers
    Its leaves, by soft winds fanned;
She faded midst Italian flowers—
    The last of that bright band.

25 And parted thus they rest, who played
    Beneath the same green tree;
Whose voices mingled as they prayed
    Around one parent knee!

They that with smiles lit up the hall,
30   And cheered with song the hearth!—
Alas, for love! if *thou* wert all,
    And naught beyond, O Earth!

THE LANDING OF THE PILGRIM FATHERS IN NEW ENGLAND
1826

The breaking waves dashed high
    On a stern and rock-bound coast,[1]
And the woods against a stormy sky
    Their giant branches tossed;

5 And the heavy night hung dark,
    The hills and waters o'er,
When a band of exiles moored their bark
    On the wild New England shore.

Not as the conqueror comes,
10   They, the true-hearted, came;
Not with the roll of the stirring drums,
    And the trumpet that sings of fame:

Not as the flying come,
    In silence and in fear;—
15 They shook the depths of the desert gloom
    With their hymns of lofty cheer.

Amidst the storm they sang,
    And the stars heard, and the sea;
And the sounding aisles of the dim woods
    rang
20   To the anthem of the free.

The ocean eagle soared
    From his nest by the white wave's foam,
And the rocking pines of the forest
    roared,—
    This was their welcome home.

[1] This is not exactly true to fact.

25 There were men with hoary hair
    Amidst that pilgrim-band:
Why had *they* come to wither there,
    Away from their childhood's land?

There was woman's fearless eye,
30   Lit by her deep love's truth;
There was manhood's brow serenely high,
    And the fiery heart of youth.

What sought they thus afar?
    Bright jewels of the mine?
35 The wealth of seas, the spoils of war?—
    They sought a faith's pure shrine!

Ay, call it holy ground,
    The soil where first they trod;
They have left unstained what there they
    found,—
40   Freedom to worship God.

THE HOMES OF ENGLAND
1827   1827

The stately Homes of England,
    How beautiful they stand!
Amidst their tall ancestral trees,
    O'er all the pleasant land;
5 The deer across their greensward bound
    Through shade and sunny gleam,
And the swan glides past them with the
    sound
    Of some rejoicing stream.

The merry Homes of England!
10   Around their hearths by night,
What gladsome looks of household love
    Meet in the ruddy light.
There woman's voice flows forth in song,
    Or childish tale is told;
15 Or lips move tunefully along
    Some glorious page of old.

The blessèd Homes of England!
    How softly on their bowers
Is laid the holy quietness
20 That breathes from Sabbath hours!
Solemn, yet sweet, the church-bell's chime
    Floats through their woods at morn;
All other sounds, in that still time,
    Of breeze and leaf are born.

25 The cottage Homes of England!
    By thousands on her plains,
They are smiling o'er the silvery brooks,
    And round the hamlet-fanes.
Through glowing orchards forth they peep,
30 Each from its nook of leaves;
And fearless there the lowly sleep,
    As the bird beneath their eaves.

The free, fair Homes of England!
Long, long in hut and hall,
35 May hearts of native proof be reared
To guard each hallowed wall!
And green forever be the groves,
And bright the flowery sod,
Where first the child's glad spirit loves
40 Its country and its God!

William Motherwell 1797-1835

THE SWORD CHANT OF THORSTEIN
RAUDI
1828

'Tis not the gray hawk's flight
O'er mountain and mere;
'Tis not the fleet hound's course
Tracking the deer;
5 'Tis not the light hoof print
Of black steed or gray,
Though sweltering it gallop
A long summer's day,
Which mete forth the lordships
10 I challenge as mine;
Ha! ha! 'tis the good brand
I clutch in my strong hand,
That can their broad marches
And numbers define.
15 Land Giver! I kiss thee.

Dull builders of houses,
Base tillers of earth,
Gaping, ask me what lordships
I owned at my birth;
20 But the pale fools wax mute
When I point with my sword
East, west, north, and south,
Shouting, "There am I lord!"
Wold and waste, town and tower,
25 Hill, valley, and stream,
Trembling, bow to my sway
In the fierce battle fray,
When the star that rules Fate, is
This falchion's[1] red gleam.
30 Mighty Giver. I kiss thee.

I've heard great harps sounding,
In brave bower and hall,[2]
I've drank the sweet music
That bright lips let fall,
35 I've hunted in greenwood,
And heard small birds sing;
But away with this idle
And cold jargoning;
The music I love, is

[1] A kind of sword.
[2] The hall was the public dwelling of the Teutonic chieftain; the bower was the private apartments, especially of the women.

40   The shout of the brave,
The yell of the dying,
The scream of the flying,
When this arm wields Death's sickle,
And garners the grave.
45 Joy Giver! I kiss thee.

Far isles of the ocean
Thy lightning have known,
And wide o'er the main land
Thy horrors have shone.
50 Great sword of my father,
Stern joy of his hand,
Thou hast carved his name deep on
The stranger's red strand,
And won him the glory
55 Of undying song.
Keen cleaver of gay crests,
Sharp piercer of broad breasts,
Grim slayer of heroes,
And scourge of the strong.
60 Fame Giver! I kiss thee.

In a love more abiding
Than that the heart knows,
For maiden more lovely
Than summer's first rose,
65 My heart's knit to thine,
And lives but for thee;
In dreamings of gladness,
Thou'rt dancing with me,
Brave measures of madness
70 In some battle-field,
Where armor is ringing,
And noble blood springing,
And cloven, yawn helmet,
Stout hauberk and shield.
75 Death Giver! I kiss thee.

The smile of a maiden's eye
Soon may depart;
And light is the faith of
Fair woman's heart;
80 Changeful as light clouds,
And wayward as wind,
Be the passions that govern
Weak woman's mind.
But thy metal's as true
85 As its polish is bright;
When ills wax in number,
Thy love will not slumber,
But starlike, burns fiercer,
The darker the night.
90 Heart Gladdener! I kiss thee.

My kindred have perished
By war or by wave—
Now, childless and sireless,
I long for the grave.

95 When the path of our glory
    Is shadowed in death,
With me thou wilt slumber
    Below the brown heath;
Thou wilt rest on my bosom,
100   And with it decay—
While harps shall be ringing,
    And scalds[1] shall be singing
The deeds we have done in
    Our old fearless day.
105 Song Giver! I kiss thee.

JEANIE MORRISON
1832

I've wandered east, I've wandered west,
    Through mony a weary way;
But never, never can forget
    The luve o' life's young day!
5 The fire that's blawn on Beltane[2] e'en,
    May weel be black gin[3] Yule;
But blacker fa' awaits the heart
    Where first fond luve grows cule.

Oh dear, dear Jeanie Morrison,
10   The thochts o' bygane years
Still fling their shadows ower my path,
    And blind my een wi' tears:
They blind my een wi' saut, saut tears,
    And sair and sick I pine,
15 As memory idly summons up
    The blithe blinks o' langsyne.

'Twas then we luvit ilk ither[4] weel,
    'Twas then we twa did part;
Sweet time—sad time! twa bairns at scule.
20   Twa bairns, and but ae[5] heart!
'Twas then we sat on ae laigh bink,[6]
    To leir ilk ither lear;[7]
And tones, and looks, and smiles were shed,
    Remembered evermair.

25 I wonder, Jeanie, aften yet
    When sitting on that bink,
Cheek touchin' cheek, loof[8] lock'd in loof,
    What our wee heads could think.
When baith bent doun ower ae braid page,
30   Wi' ae buik on our knee,
Thy lips were on thy lesson, but
    My lesson was in thee.

Oh, mind ye how we hung our heads,
    How cheeks brent red wi' shame,
35 Whene'er the school-weans laughin' said,
    We cleek'd[9] thegither hame?
And mind ye o' the Saturdays

(The scule then skail't[1] at noon)
When we ran aff to speel the braes[2]—
40   The broomy[3] braes o' June?

My head rins round and round about,
    My heart flows like a sea,
As ane by ane the thochts rush back
    O' scule-time and o' thee.
45 Oh, mornin' life! Oh, mornin' luve!
    Oh lichtsome days and lang,
When hinnied[4] hopes around our hearts,
    Like simmer blossoms sprang!

O mind ye, luve, how aft we left
50   The deavin', dinsome[5] toun,
To wander by the green burnside,[6]
    And hear its waters croon;
The simmer leaves hung ower our heads,
    The flowers burst round our feet,
55 And in the gloamin' o' the wood,
    The throssil whusslit[7] sweet.

The throssil whusslit in the wood,
    The burn sang to the trees,
And we with Nature's heart in tune,
60   Concerted harmonies;
And on the knowe abune the burn,[8]
    For hours thegither sat
In the silentness o' joy, till baith
    Wi' very gladness grat![9]

65 Aye, aye, dear Jeanie Morrison,
    Tears trinkled down your cheek,
Like dew-beads from a rose, yet nane
    Had ony power to speak!
That was a time, a blessed time,
70   When hearts were fresh and young,
When freely gushed all feelings forth,
    Unsyllabled—unsung!

I marvel, Jeanie Morrison,
    Gin[10] I hae been to thee
75 As closely twined wi' earliest thochts
    As ye hae been to me?
Oh! tell me gin their music fills
    Thine ear as it does mine;
Oh! say gin e'er your heart grows grit[11]
80   Wi' dreamings o' langsyne?

I've wandered east, I've wandered west,
    I've borne a weary lot;
But in my wanderings, far or near,
    Ye never were forgot.
85 The fount that first burst frae this heart,

---

1 scattered   2 climb the hills
3 covered with broom shrubs
4 honied   8 knoll above the brook
5 deafening, noisy   9 wept
6 brookside   10 whether; if
7 song thrush whistled   11 great

1 Norse singers of heroic poems
2 May-day   6 low bench
3 by the time of   7 teach each other learning
4 each other   8 hand
5 one   9 went arm in arm

Still travels on its way;
And channels deeper as it rins,
The luve o' life's young day.

O dear, dear Jeanie Morrison,
90 Since we were sindered young,
I've never seen your face, nor heard
The music o' your tongue;
But I could hug all wretchedness,
And happy could I die,
95 Did I but ken your heart still dreamed
O' bygane days and me!

MY HEID IS LIKE TO REND,[1] WILLIE
1832

My heid is like to rend, Willie,
My heart is like to break—
I'm wearin' aff my feet, Willie,
I'm dyin' for your sake!
5 Oh lay your cheek to mine, Willie,
Your hand on my briest-bane—
Oh say ye'll think on me, Willie,
When I am deid and gane!

It's vain to comfort me, Willie,
10 Sair grief maun hae[2] its will—
But let me rest upon your briest,
To sab and greet[3] my fill.
Let me sit on your knee, Willie,
Let me shed by[4] your hair,
15 And look into the face, Willie,
I never sall see mair!

I'm sittin' on your knee, Willie,
For the last time in my life—
A puir heart-broken thing, Willie,
20 A mither, yet nae wife.
Ay, press your hand upon my heart,
And press it mair and mair—
Or it will burst the silken twine
Sae strang[5] is its despair!

25 Oh wae's me for the hour, Willie,
When we thegither met—
Oh wae's me for the time, Willie,
That our first tryst was set!
Oh wae's me for the loanin'[6] green
30 Where we were wont to gae—
And wae's me for the destinie,
That gart[7] me love thee sae!

Oh! dinna[8] mind my words, Willie,
I downa[9] seek to blame—
35 But oh! it's hard to live, Willie,
And dree[10] a warld's shame!

Het tears are hailin'[1] ower your cheek,
And hailin' ower your chin;
Why weep ye sae for worthlessness,
40 For sorrow and for sin?

I'm weary o' this warld, Willie,
And sick wi' a' I see—
A canna live as I hae lived,
Or be as I should be.
45 But fauld unto your heart, Willie,
The heart that still is thine—
And kiss ance mair the white, white cheek,
Ye said was red langsyne.

A stoun'[2] gaes through my heid, Willie,
50 A sair stoun' through my heart—
Oh! haud me up and let me kiss
Thy brow ere we twa pairt.
Anither, and anither yet!—
How fast my life-strings break!
55 Fareweel! fareweel! through yon kirk-
yaird
Step lichtly for my sake!

The lav'rock[3] in the lift,[4] Willie,
That lilts[5] far ower our heid,
Will sing the morn as merrilie
60 Abune[6] the clay-cauld deid;
And this green turf we're sittin' on,
Wi' dew-draps' shimmerin' sheen,
Will hap[7] the heart that luvit thee
As warld has seldom seen.

65 But oh! remember me, Willie,
On land where'er ye be—
And oh! think on the leal,[8] leal heart,
That ne'er luvit ane but thee!
And oh! think on the cauld, cauld mools,[9]
70 That file[10] my yellow hair—
That kiss the cheek, and kiss the chin,
Ye never sall kiss mair!

THE FORESTER'S CAROL
1832

Lusty Hearts! to the wood, to the merry
green wood,
While the dew with strung pearls loads
each blade,
And the first blush of dawn brightly
streams o'er the lawn,
Like the smile of a rosy-cheeked maid.

5 Our horns with wild music ring glad
through each shaw,[11]
And our broad arrows rattle amain;

---

[1] burst	[6] lane
[2] sore grief must have	[7] made
[3] sob and weep	[8] do not
[4] part	[9] cannot
[5] so strong	[10] endure

[1] pouring	[7] cover
[2] pang	[8] loyal
[3] lark	[9] earth
[4] sky	[10] defile
[5] sings cheerfully	[11] grove
[6] above	

For the stout bows we draw, to the green
    woods give law,
  And the Might is the Right once again!

Mark yon herds, as they brattle[1] and brush
    down the glade;
10 Pick the fat, let the lean rascals go,
Under favor 'tis meet that we tall[2] men
    should eat,—
  Nock[3] a shaft and strike down that
    proud doe!

Well delivered, parfay![4] convulsive she
    leaps,—
  One bound more,—then she drops on
    her side;
15 Our steel hath bit smart the life-strings
    of her heart,
  And cold now lies the green forest's
    pride.

Heave her up, and away!—should any
    base churl
Dare to ask why we range in this wood,
There's a keen arrow yare,[5] in each broad
    belt to spare,
20 That will answer the knave in his blood!

Then forward my Hearts! like the bold
    reckless breeze
Our life shall whirl on in mad glee;
The long bows we bend, to the world's
    latter end,
  Shall be borne by the hands of the Free!

SONG
1853

If to thy heart I were as near
  As thou art near to mine,
I'd hardly care though a' the year
Nae sun on earth suld shine, my dear,
5 Nae sun on earth suld shine!

Twin starnies are thy glancin' een[6]—
  A warld they'd licht and mair—
And gin[7] that ye be my Christine,
Ae blink[8] to me ye'll spare, my dear,
10 Ae blink to me ye'll spare!

My leesome[9] May I've wooed too lang—
  Aneath the trystin' tree,
I've sung till a' the plantin'[10] rang,
Wi' lays o' love for thee, my dear,
15 Wi' lays o' love for thee.

The dew-draps glisten on the green,
  The laverocks lilt[1] on high,
We'll forth and doun the loan,[2] Christine,
And kiss when nane is nigh, my dear,
20 And kiss when nane is nigh!

Ebenezer Elliott 1781-1849
SONG
1831

Tune—Robin Adair

Child, is thy father dead?
  Father is gone!
Why did they tax his bread?
  God's will be done!
5 Mother has sold her bed;
Better to die than wed!
Where shall she lay her head?
  Home we have none!

Father clamm'd[3] thrice a week—
10 God's will be done!
Long for work did he seek,
  Work he found none.
Tears on his hollow cheek
Told what no tongue could speak:
15 Why did his master break?
  God's will be done!

Doctor said air was best—
  Food we had none;
Father, with panting breast,
20 Groan'd to be gone:
Now he is with the blest—
Mother says death is best!
We have no place of rest—
  Yes, we have one!

BATTLE SONG
1831

Day, like our souls, is fiercely dark;
  What then? 'Tis day!
We sleep no more; the cock crows—hark!
  To arms! away!
5 They come! they come! the knell is rung
  Of us or them;
Wide o'er their march the pomp is flung
  Of gold and gem.
What collar'd hound of lawless sway,
10 To famine dear—
What pension'd slave of Attila,
  Leads in the rear?
Come they from Scythian wilds afar,
  Our blood to spill?
15 Wear they the livery of the Czar?
  They do his will.
Nor tassell'd silk, nor epaulette,

1 scamper   6 flashing eyes
2 brave; bold   7 if
3 fit to the string   8 one glance
4 by my faith   9 pleasant
5 ready   10 grove

1 larks sing cheerfully
2 lane
3 went without food

Nor plume, nor torse[1]—
No splendor gilds, all sternly met,
20   Our foot and horse.
But, dark and still, we inly glow,
  Condensed in ire!
Strike, tawdry slaves, and ye shall know
  Our gloom is fire.
25 In vain your pomp, ye evil powers,
  Insults the land;
Wrongs, vengeance, and *the cause* are
  ours,
  And God's right hand!
Madmen! they trample into snakes
30   The wormy clod!
Like fire, beneath their feet awakes
  The sword of God!
Behind, before, above, below,
  They rouse the brave;
35 Where'er they go, they make a foe,
  Or find a grave.

THE PRESS

WRITTEN FOR THE PRINTERS OF SHEFFIELD,
ON THE PASSING OF THE REFORM BILL
1832

God said—"Let there be light!"[2]
Grim darkness felt his might,
  And fled away;
Then startled seas and mountains cold
5 Shone forth, all bright in blue and gold,
  And cried—"'Tis day! 'tis day!"
"Hail, holy light!" exclaim'd
  The thund'rous cloud, that flamed
  O'er daisies white;
10 And, lo! the rose, in crimson dress'd,
Lean'd sweetly on the lily's breast;
  And, blushing, murmur'd—"Light!"
Then was the skylark born;
  Then rose th' embattled corn;[3]
15   Then floods of praise
Flow'd o'er the sunny hills of noon;
And then, in stillest night, the moon
  Pour'd forth her pensive lays.
Lo, heaven's bright bow is glad!
20 Lo, trees and flowers all clad
  In glory, bloom!
And shall the mortal sons of God
Be senseless as the trodden clod,
  And darker than the tomb?
25 No, by the *mind* of man!
By the swart artisan!
  By God, our Sire!
Our souls have holy light within,
And every form of grief and sin
30   Shall see and feel its fire.
By earth, and hell, and heav'n,

---

[1] wreath used to support a crest
[2] See *Genesis*, 1 :3.   [3] wheat

The shroud of souls is riven!
  Mind, mind alone
Is light, and hope, and life, and power!
35 Earth's deepest night, from this bless'd
  hour,
  The night of minds is gone!
"The Press!" all lands shall sing;
The Press, the Press we bring,
  All lands to bless;
40 O pallid Want! O Labor stark!
Behold, we bring the second ark!
  The Press! the Press! the Press!

PRESTON MILLS

The day was fair, the cannon roar'd,
  Cold blew the bracing north,
And Preston's Mills, by thousands, pour'd
  Their little captives forth.

5 All in their best they paced the street,
  All glad that they were free;
And sung a song with voices sweet—
  They sung of Liberty!

But from their lips the rose had fled,
10   Like "death-in-life"[1] they smiled;
And still, as each pass'd by, I said,
  Alas! is that a child?

Flags waved, and men—a ghastly crew—
  March'd with them, side by side:
15 While, hand in hand, and two by two,
  They moved—a living tide.

Thousands and thousands—all so white!—
  With eyes so glazed and dull!
O God! it was indeed a sight
20   Too sadly beautiful!

And, oh, the pang their voices gave
  Refuses to depart!
This is a wailing for the grave!
  I whisper'd to my heart.

25 It was as if, where roses blush'd,
  A sudden blasting gale,
O'er fields of bloom had rudely rush'd,
  And turn'd the roses pale.

It was as if, in glen and grove,
30   The wild birds sadly sung;
And every linnet mourn'd its love,
  And every thrush its young.

It was as if, in dungeon gloom,
  Where chain'd despair reclined,
35 A sound came from the living tomb,
  And hymn'd the passing wind.

---

[1] See Coleridge's *The Rime of the Ancient
Mariner*, 193 (p. 364).

And while they sang, and though they
    smiled,
  My soul groan'd heavily—
  O who would be or have a child?
40   A mother who would be?

SPENSERIAN

I saw a horrid thing of many names,
  And many shapes. Some call'd it
    wealth, some power,
Some grandeur. From its heart it shot
    black flames,
  That scorch'd the souls of millions,
    hour by hour;
5 And its proud eyes rain'd everywhere a
    shower
  Of hopeless life, and helpless misery;
For, spoused to fraud, destruction was
    its dower!
  But its cold brightness could not hide
    from me
The parent base of crime, the nurse of
    poverty!

A POET'S EPITAPH

Stop, mortal! Here thy brother lies—
  The poet of the poor.
His books were rivers, woods, and skies,
  The meadow, and the moor;
5 His teachers were the torn heart's wail,
  The tyrant, and the slave,
The street, the factory, the jail,
  The palace--and the grave.
Sin met thy brother everywhere!
10   And is thy brother blam'd?
From passion, danger, doubt, and care,
  He no exemption claim'd.
The meanest thing, earth's feeblest worm,
  He fear'd to scorn or hate;
15 But, honoring in a peasant's form
  The equal of the great,
He bless'd the steward, whose wealth
    makes
  The poor man's little, more;
Yet loath'd the haughty wretch that takes
20   From plunder'd labor's store.
A hand to do, a head to plan,
  A heart to feel and dare--
Tell man's worst foes, here lies the man
  Who drew them as they are.

SABBATH MORNING

Rise, young mechanic! Idle darkness
    leaves
The dingy town, and cloudless morning
    glows:
O rise and worship Him who spins and
    weaves

Into the petals of the hedge-side rose
5 Day's golden beams and all-embracing
    air!
Rise! for the morn of Sabbath riseth
    fair!
The clouds expect thee—Rise! the stone-
    chat[1] hops
Among the mosses of thy granite chair:
Go tell the plover, on the mountain tops,
10 That *we* have cherish'd nests and hidden
    wings.
Wings? Ay, like those on which the
    seraph flings,
His sun-bright speed from star to star
    abroad;
And we have music, like the whisperings
Of streams in Heav'n—our *labor* is an
    ode
15 Of sweet sad praise to Him who loves the
    right.
And cannot He who spins the beauteous
    light,
And weaves the air into the wild flowers'
    hues,
Give to thy soul the mountain torrent's
    might,
Or fill thy veins with sunbeams, and dif-
    fuse
20 Over thy thoughts the greenwood's mel-
    ody?
Yea, this and more He can and will for
    thee,
If thou wilt read, engraven on the skies
And restless waves, that "sloth is misery;
And that our worth from our necessities
25 Flows, as the rivers from his clouds
    descend!"

THE WAY BROAD-LEAF[2]

When Winter howls along the hill,
We find the broad-leaf'd plantain still;
The way broad-leaf, of herbs the chief,
We never miss the way broad-leaf;
5 'Tis common as the poor.

To soothe the cruel scorner's woes,
Beneath the scorner's feet it grows;
Neglected, trampled, still it thrives,
A creature of unnumber'd lives;
10 How like the trampled poor!

When roses die, it still remains;
Hoof-crush'd, beneath unpitying rains,
Roll'd o'er by ringing carts and wains,[3]
It suffers still, but ne'er complains;
15 Just like the helpless poor!

[1] A common European singing bird.
[2] the broad-leaf along the roads
[3] wagons

Scorn'd by the bluebells—or bent o'er
Their graves beneath the sycamore—
Meek, modest, silent, useful still,
It loves to do the gentle will
20 Of Him who loves the poor!

RELIGION

What is religion? "Speak the truth in
  love."
Reject no good. Mend, if thou canst, thy
  lot.
Doubting, enquire,—nor dictate till thou
  prove.
Enjoy thy own—exceed not, tresspass not.
5 Pity the scorners of life's meanest thing.
If wrong'd, forgive—that Hate may lose
  his sting.
Think, speak, work, get—bestow, or wisely
  keep.
So live, that thou may'st smile, and no one
  weep.
Be bless'd—like birds, that sing because
  they love;
10 And bless—like rivers, singing to the sun,

Giving and taking blessings, as they run;
Or soft-voiced showers, that cool the answering grove,
When cloudy wings are wide in heav'n
  display'd,
And blessings brighten o'er the freshen'd
  sod,
15 Till earth is like the countenance of God.
This is religion! saith the bard of trade.[1]

PLAINT

Dark, deep, and cold the current flows
Unto the sea, where no wind blows,
Seeking the land which no one knows.

O'er its sad gloom still comes and goes
5 The mingled wail of friends and foes,
Borne to the land which no one knows.

Why shrieks for help yon wretch, who goes
With millions, from a world of woes,
Unto the land which no one knows?

10 Though myriads go with him who goes,
Alone he goes where no wind blows,
Unto the land which no one knows.

For all must go where no wind blows,
And none can go for him who goes;
15 None, none return whence no one knows.

[1] Elliott himself, who was known as "The Corn-
Law Rhymer" from his *Corn-Law Rhymes,*
written against the corn laws.

Yet why should he who shrieking goes
With millions, from a world of woes,
Reunion seek with it or those?

Alone with God, where no wind blows,
20 And Death, his shadow—doomed, he goes:
That God is there the shadow shows.

Oh, shoreless Deep, where no wind blows!
And, thou, oh, Land which no one knows!
That God is All, His shadow shows.

Bryan Waller Procter 1787-1874
"Barry Cornwall"

THE SEA
1832

The sea! the sea! the open sea!
The blue, the fresh, the ever free!
Without a mark, without a bound,
It runneth the earth's wide regions 'round;
5 It plays with the clouds; it mocks the
  skies;
Or like a cradled creature lies.

I'm on the sea! I'm on the sea!
I am where I would ever be;
With the blue above, and the blue below,
10 And silence wheresoe'er I go;
If a storm should come and awake the deep,
What matter? *I* shall ride and sleep.

I love (oh! *how* I love) to ride
On the fierce foaming bursting tide,
15 When every mad wave drowns the moon,
Or whistles aloft his tempest tune,
And tells how goeth the world below,
And why the southwest blasts do blow.

I never was on the dull tame shore,
20 But I lov'd the great sea more and more,
And backwards flew to her billowy breast,
Like a bird that seeketh its mother's nest;
And a mother she *was,* and *is* to me;
For I was born on the open sea!

25 The waves were white, and red the morn,
In the noisy hour when I was born;
And the whale it whistled, the porpoise
  rolled,
And the dolphins bared their backs of gold;
And never was heard such an outcry wild
30 As welcomed to life the ocean-child!

I've lived since then, in calm and strife,
Full fifty summers a sailor's life,
With wealth to spend and a power to range,
But never have sought, nor sighed for
  change;
35 And Death, whenever he come to me,
Shall come on the wide unbounded sea!

THE STORMY PETREL
1832

A thousand miles from land are we,
Tossing about on the roaring sea;
From billow to bounding billow cast,
Like fleecy snow on the stormy blast:
5 The sails are scatter'd abroad, like weeds,
The strong masts shake like quivering
    reeds,
The mighty cables, and iron chains,
The hull, which all earthly strength dis-
    dains,
They strain and they crack, and hearts like
    stone
10 Their natural hard, proud strength disown.

Up and down! up and down!
From the base of the wave to the billow's
    crown,
And midst the flashing and feathery foam
The stormy petrel finds a home,—
15 A home, if such a place may be,
For her who lives on the wide, wide sea,
On the craggy ice, in the frozen air,
And only seeketh her rocky lair
To warm her young, and to teach them
    spring
20 At once o'er the waves on their stormy
    wing.

O'er the deep! O'er the deep!
Where the whale, and the shark, and the
    sword-fish sleep,
Outflying the blast and the driving rain,
The petrel telleth her tale—in vain;
25 For the mariner curseth the warning bird
Who bringeth him news of the storms un-
    heard!
Ah! thus does the prophet, of good or ill,
Meet hate from the creatures he serveth
    still:
Yet he ne'er falters:—So, petrel! spring
30 Once more o'er the waves on thy stormy
    wing!

THE HUNTER'S SONG
1832

Rise! Sleep no more! 'Tis a noble morn:
The dews hang thick on the fringed thorn,
And the frost shrinks back, like a beaten
    hound,
Under the steaming, steaming ground.
5 Behold, where the billowy clouds flow by,
And leave us alone in the clear gray sky!
Our horses are ready and steady.—So, ho!
I'm gone, like a dart from the Tartar's
    bow.
    *Hark, hark!—Who calleth the maiden
    Morn*

10 *From her sleep in the woods and the
    stubble corn?*
    The horn,—the horn!
    *The merry, sweet ring of the hunter's
    horn.*

Now, thorough the copse, where the fox is
    found,
And over the stream, at a mighty bound,
15 And over the high lands, and over the low,
O'er furrows, o'er meadows, the hunters
    go!
Away!—as a hawk flies full at its prey,
So flieth the hunter, away,—away!
From the burst at the cover till set of sun,
20 When the red fox dies, and—the day is
    done!
    *Hark, hark!—What sound on the wind
    is borne?*
    *'Tis the conquering voice of the hunt-
    er's horn.*
    The horn,—the horn!
    *The merry, bold voice of the hunter's
    horn.*

25 Sound! Sound the horn! To the hunter
    good
What's the gulley deep or the roaring
    flood?
Right over he bounds, as the wild stag
    bounds,
At the heels of his swift, sure, silent
    hounds.
O, what delight can a mortal lack,
30 When he once is firm on his horse's back,
With his stirrups short, and his snaffle[1]
    strong,
And the blast of the horn for his morning
    song?
    *Hark, hark!—now, home! and dream
    till morn*
    *Of the bold, sweet sound of the hunt-
    er's horn!*
35   *The horn,—the horn!*
    *O, the sound of all sounds is the hunt-
    er's horn!*

LIFE
1832

We are born; we laugh; we weep;
    We love; we droop; we die!
Ah! wherefore do we laugh or weep?
    Why do we live, or die?
5 Who knows that secret deep?
    Alas, not I!

Why doth the violet spring
    Unseen by human eye?

[1] A kind of bridle

Who do the radiant seasons bring
10   Sweet thoughts that quickly fly?
Why do our fond hearts cling
    To things that die?

We toil,—through pain and wrong;
    We fight,—and fly;
15 We love; we lose; and then, ere long,
    Stone-dead we lie.
O life! is *all* thy song
    "Endure and—die"?

PEACE! WHAT DO TEARS AVAIL
1832

Peace! what do tears avail?
She lies all dumb and pale,
    And from her eye
The spirit of lovely life is fading,
5   And she must die!
Why looks the lover wroth? the friend up-
      braiding?
    Reply, reply!

Hath she not dwelt too long
'Midst pain, and grief, and wrong?
10   Then, why not die?
Why suffer again her doom of sorrow,
    And hopeless lie?
Why nurse the trembling dream until to-
      morrow?
    Reply, reply!

15 Death! Take her to thine arms,
In all her stainless charms,
    And with her fly
To heavenly haunts, where clad in bright-
      ness,
    The Angels lie.
20 Wilt bear her there, O Death! in all her
      whiteness?
    Reply, reply!

A POET'S THOUGHT
1832

Tell me, what is a poet's thought?
    Is it on the sudden born?
Is it from the starlight caught?
Is it by the tempest taught,
5   Or by whispering morn?

Was it cradled in the brain?
    Chain'd awhile, or nurs'd in night?
Was it wrought with toil and pain?
Did it bloom and fade again,
10   Ere it burst to light?

No more question of its birth:
    Rather love its better part!

'Tis a thing of sky and earth,
Gathering all its golden worth
15   From the poet's heart.

THE POET'S SONG TO HIS WIFE

How many summers, love,
    Have I been thine?
How many days, thou dove,
    Hast thou been mine?
5 Time, like the wingèd wind
    When 't bends the flowers,
Hath left no mark behind,
    To count the hours!

Some weight of thought, though loath
10   On thee he leaves;
Some lines of care round both
    Perhaps he weaves;
Some fears,—a soft regret
    For joys scarce known;
15 Some looks we half forget;—
    All else is flown.

Ah!—With what thankless heart
    I mourn and sing!
Look, where our children start,
20   Like sudden spring!
With tongues all sweet and low
    Like a pleasant rhyme,
They tell how much I owe
    To thee and time!

INSCRIPTION FOR A FOUNTAIN

Rest! This little fountain runs
    Thus for aye:—It never stays
For the look of summer suns,
    Nor the cold of winter days.
5 Whosoe'er shall wander near,
    When the Syrian heat is worst,
Let him hither come, nor fear
    Lest he may not slake his thirst:

He will find this little river
10 Running still, as bright as ever.
Let him drink, and onward hie,
Bearing but in thought, that I,
Erotas, bade the Naiad fall,
And thank the great god Pan for all!

A PETITION TO TIME
1850

Touch us gently, Time!
    Let us glide adown thy stream
Gently,—as we sometimes glide
    Through a quiet dream.
5 Humble voyagers are we,
Husband, wife, and children three—
(One is lost,—an angel, fled
To the azure overhead.)

Touch us gently, Time!
10   We've not proud nor soaring wings:
Our ambition, our content,
Lies in simple things.
Humble voyagers are we,
O'er life's dim, unsounded sea,
15 Seeking only some calm clime;—
Touch us gently, gentle Time!

Hartley Coleridge 1796-1849

SONG
1833

She is not fair to outward view
As many maidens be,
Her loveliness I never knew
Until she smil'd on me;
5 Oh! then I saw her eye was bright,
A well of love, a spring of light.

But now her looks are coy and cold,
To mine they ne'er reply,
And yet I cease not to behold
10   The love-light in her eye:
Her very frowns are fairer far
Than smiles of other maidens are.

AN OLD MAN'S WISH
1833

I have lived, and I have loved,
Have lived and loved in vain;
Some joys, and many woes have proved,
That may not be again;
5 My heart is cold, my eye is sere,
Joy wins no smile, and grief no tear.

Fain would I hope, if hope I could,
If sure to be deceived,
There's comfort in a thought of good,
10   Tho' 'tis not quite believed;
For sweet is hope's wild warbled air,
But, oh! its echo is despair.

WHITHER IS GONE THE WISDOM AND THE POWER
1833

Whither is gone the wisdom and the power
That ancient sages scatter'd with the notes
Of thought-suggesting lyres? The music floats
In the void air; e'en at this breathing hour,
5 In every cell and every blooming bower
The sweetness of old lays is hovering still:
But the strong soul, the self-constraining will,
The rugged root that bare the winsome flower
Is weak and wither'd. Were we like the Fays

10 That sweetly nestle in the foxglove bells,
Or lurk and murmur in the rose-lipp'd shells
Which Neptune to the earth for quit-rent[1] pays,
Then might our pretty modern Philomels
Sustain our spirits with their roundelays.

NOVEMBER
1833

The mellow year is hasting to its close;
The little birds have almost sung their last,
Their small notes twitter in the dreary blast—
That shrill-piped harbinger of early snows;
5 The patient beauty of the scentless rose,
Oft with the Morn's hoar crystal quaintly glass'd,
Hangs, a pale mourner for the summer past,
And makes a little summer where it grows:
In the chill sunbeam of the faint brief day
10 The dusky waters shudder as they shine,
The russet leaves obstruct the straggling way
Of oozy brooks, which no deep banks define,
And the gaunt woods, in ragged, scant array,
Wrap their old limbs with sombre ivy twine.

NIGHT
1833

The crackling embers on the hearth are dead;
The indoor note of industry is still;
The latch is fast; upon the window sill
The small birds wait not for their daily bread;
5 The voiceless flowers—how quietly they shed
Their nightly odors;—and the household rill
Murmurs continuous dulcet sounds that fill
The vacant expectation, and the dread
Of listening night. And haply now she sleeps;
10 For all the garrulous noises of the air
Are hush'd in peace; the soft dew silent weeps,
Like hopeless lovers for a maid so fair:—
Oh! that I were the happy dream that creeps
To her soft heart, to find my image there.

[1] rent paid in commutation of service

TO SHAKSPEARE
1833

The soul of man is larger than the sky,
Deeper than ocean, or the abysmal dark
Of the unfathom'd centre. Like that Ark,
Which in its sacred hold uplifted high,
5 O'er the drown'd hills, the human family,
And stock reserved of every living kind,[1]
So, in the compass of the single mind,
The seeds and pregnant forms in essence
   lie,
That make all worlds. Great poet, 'twas
   thy art
10 To know thyself, and in thyself to be
Whate'er love, hate, ambition, destiny,
Or the firm, fatal purpose of the heart,
Can make of man. Yet thou wert still the
   same,
Serene of thought, unhurt by thy own
   flame.

MAY, 1840
1840   1850

A lovely morn, so still, so very still,
It hardly seems a growing day of spring,
Though all the odorous buds are blossom-
   ing,
And the small matin[2] birds were glad and
   shrill
5 Some hours ago; but now the woodland rill
Murmurs along, the only vocal thing,
Save when the wee wren flits with stealthy
   wing,
And cons by fits and bits her evening trill.
Lovers might sit on such a morn as this
10 An hour together, looking at the sky,
Nor dare to break the silence with a kiss,
Long listening for the signal of a sigh;
And the sweet Nun, diffused in voiceless
   prayer,
Feel her own soul through all the brooding
   air.

"MULTUM DILEXIT"[3]
1848   1850

She sat and wept beside His feet; the
   weight
Of sin oppress'd her heart; for all the
   blame,
And the poor malice of the worldly shame,
To her was past, extinct, and out of date:
5 Only the sin remain'd,—the leprous state;
She would be melted by the heart of love,

[1] See *Genesis*, 7.
[2] morning
[3] "Much hath she loved." See *Luke*, 7:37-50.

By fires far fiercer than are blown to prove
And purge the silver ore adulterate.
She sat and wept, and with her untress'd
   hair
10 Still wip'd the feet she was so bless'd to
   touch;
And He wip'd off the soiling of despair
From her sweet soul, because she lov'd so
   much.
I am a sinner, full of doubts and fears:
Make me a humble thing of love and tears.

HOMER
1850

Far from the sight of earth, yet bright
   and plain
As the clear noon-day sun, an "orb of
   song"
Lovely and bright is seen, amid the throng
Of lesser stars, that rise and wax and wane,
5 The transient rulers of the fickle main,
One constant light gleams through the dark
   and long
And narrow aisle of memory. How strong,
How fortified with all the numerous train
Of truths wert thou, great poet of man-
   kind,
10 Who told'st in verse as mighty as the sea,
And various as the voices of the wind,
The strength of passion rising in the glee
Of battle. Fear was glorified by thee,
And Death is lovely in thy tale enshrined.

PRAYER
1850

There is an awful quiet in the air,
And the sad earth, with moist, imploring
   eye,
Looks wide and wakeful at the pondering
   sky,
Like Patience slow subsiding to Despair.
5 But see, the blue smoke as a voiceless
   prayer,
Sole witness of a secret sacrifice,
Unfolds its tardy wreaths, and multiplies
Its soft chameleon breathings in the rare
Capacious ether,—so it fades away,
10 And nought is seen beneath the pendent
   blue,
The undistinguishable waste of day.
So have I dream'd!—oh, may the dream be
   true!—
That praying souls are purged from mortal
   hue,
And grow as pure as He to whom they
   pray.

Appendix

1. PRINCIPAL WRITERS AND HISTORICAL BACKGROUNDS

2. THREE NEO-CLASSICISTS, A BASIS FOR COMPARISON

   POPE, JOHNSON, AND BURKE

3. CRITICAL NOTES

4. BIBLIOGRAPHIES

5. GLOSSARY OF PROPER NAMES

6. INDEX OF AUTHORS, TITLES AND FIRST LINES

The North Front of Strawberry Hill. From "A Description of the Villa of Mr. Horace Walpole at Strawberry Hill near Twickenham, Middlesex" . . .Strawberry Hill. Printed by Thomas Kirgate, MDCCLXXIV.

	ENGLISH AUTHORS AND EVENTS		GERMAN AUTHORS
1730	Pope, 1688-1744 Richardson, 1689-1761 Thomson, 1700-1748	George II ....1727-60 War of the Austrian Succession...1741-48 Jacobite Rebellion in Scotland, Headed by Charles Edward............1745-46 Battle of Culloden.................1746 French and Indian War.........1756-63	Gellert, 1715-1769
1760	Johnson, 1709-1784 Gray, 1716-1771 Collins, 1721-1759 Macpherson, 1738-1796	George III ....1760-1820 Lord North's Ministry..........1770-82 War with American Colonies......1775-83 War with France..............1778-83 War with Spain.................1779-83 Anti-Slavery Agitation........1780-1833	Klopstock, 1724-1803 Lessing, 1729-1781 Kant, 1724-1804

1790	Burke, 1729-1797
	Percy, 1729-1811
	Chatterton, 1752-1770
	Cowper, 1731-1800
	Gibbon, 1737-1794
	Crabbe, 1754-1832
	Godwin, 1756-1836
	Blake, 1757-1827
	Beckford, 1759-1844
	Burns, 1759-1796
		William Pitt's Ministry........1783-1806
		Birmingham Riots 1791
		Society of United Irishmen........1791
		War with France; First Coalition
		  (England, Germany, Austria, Prus-
		  sia, Holland, Spain, Naples)....1793-97
		War with Spain...................1796
		Bank of England Suspends Specie
		  Payments 1797
		Great Irish Rebellion..............1798
		Battle of the Nile................1798
			Wieland, 1733-1813
			Herder, 1744-1803

1800	Rogers, 1763-1855 Wordsworth, 1770-1850 Coleridge, 1772-1834	Second Coalition against France.1799-1801 Union of Great Britain and Ireland..1800 Battle of Copenhagen.............1801 Peace of Amiens...................1802 War with France.................1803 Irish Rebellion (Emmet)..........1803 Third Coalition against France......1805 Battle of Trafalgar...............1805 Fourth Coalition against France..1806-07 Abolition of Slave Trade...........1807 Convention of Cintra..............1808 Fifth Coalition against France.....1809	Goethe, 1749-1832 Klinger, 1752-1831 Schiller, 1759-1805 Richter, 1763-1825 Schleiermacher, 1768-1834

1810	Hogg, 1770-1835
	Scott, 1771-1832
	Southey, 1774-1843
	Campbell, 1777-1844
	Moore, 1779-1852
		The Regency 1810
		War with United States.........1812-14
		Sixth Coalition against France....1813-15
		Peace of Paris....................1814
		Battle of Waterloo................1815
		Agricultural and Weaving Riots; Agi-
		  tation for Parliamentary Reform.1816-19
		Manchester Massacre 1819
			Fichte, 1762-1814
			A. W. Schlegel, 1767-1845
			Hegel, 1770-1831
			Hardenburg (Novalis),
			  1772-1801
			F. Schlegel, 1772-1829
			Hoffmann, 1776-1822
			Kleist, 1777-1811

1820	Lamb, 1775-1834 Hazlitt, 1778-1830 Elliott, 1781-1849 Byron, 1788-1824 Shelley, 1792-1822 Keats, 1795-1821 Praed, 1802-1839	George IV ....1820-30 Cato Street Conspiracy............1820 Bank of England Resumes Specie Pay- ments ....1821 Catholic Emancipation ....1829 William IV ....1830-37 Manchester-Liverpool Railway.......1830 First Reform Bill...............1830-32 Abolition of Slavery..............1833	Schelling, 1775-1854 Arndt, 1769-1860 Tieck, 1773-1853 Görres, 1776-1848 Brentano, 1778-1842 Arnim, 1781-1831
1835	Jeffrey, 1773-1850 Austen, 1775-1817 Landor, 1775-1864 Hunt, 1784-1859 Wilson, 1785-1854 DeQuincey, 1785-1859 Peacock, 1785-1866 Hood, 1799-1845 Beddoes, 1803-1849	Victoria ....1837-1901 Birmingham Riots ....1838 Chartist Agitation ....1838 Anti-Corn-Law League ....1838 Repeal of Corn Laws..............1846 Irish Rebellion 1848	Ruckert, 1788-1866 Heine, 1797-1856 J. Grimm, 1785-1863 W. Grimm, 1786-1859 Uhland, 1787-1862 Eichendorff, 1788-1857

Historical Backgrounds

AND EVENTS	FRENCH AUTHORS AND EVENTS	
Frederick II (The Great), King of Prussia ....1740-86 War of the Austrian Succession 1741-48 Francis I, Emperor of Germany 1745-65 Seven Years' War...........1756-63	Voltaire, 1694-1778 Rousseau, 1712-1778	War of the Polish Succession..1733-35 War of the Austrian Succession 1741-48 Seven Years' War...........1756-63
Joseph II, Emperor of Germany 1765-90 First Partition of Poland.......1772 War of the Bavarian Succession 1778-79 Frederick William II, King of Prussia 1786-97	Diderot, 1713-1784 Saint-Pierre, 1737-1814 Chénier, 1762-1794	Louis XVI ....1774 French Revolution ....1789-95 Formation of National Assembly..1789 Destruction of the Bastille......1789
Leopold II, Emperor of Germany 1790-92 War with France...............1791 Francis II, Emperor of Germany 1792-1806 First Coalition against France.1793-97 Second Partition of Poland......1793 Third Partition of Poland.......1795	de Staël, 1766-1817	War with Austria...............1792 Activities of the Jacobins........1792 Execution of Louis XVI.........1793 War of the First Coalition.....1793-97 Reign of Terror.................1793 Fall of Robespierre.............1794 Napoleon's Invasion of Austria and Venice ....1797 Napoleon in Rome; Establishment of Helvetic Republic...........1798 Battle of the Nile...............1798 Napoleon Made First Consul......1799 War of the Second Coalition.1799-1801
Frederick William III, King of Prussia ....1797-1840 Second Coalition against France 1799-1801 Third Coalition against France...1805 Fourth Coalition against France 1806-07 Dissolution of the Holy Roman Empire 1806	Chateaubriand, 1768-1848	Battle of Marengo.............1800 Napoleon President of the Italian Republic ....1802 Peace of Amiens.................1802 Napoleon Crowned Emperor of the French ....1804-15 Napoleon Proclaimed King of Italy 1805 War of the Third Coalition......1805 War of the Fourth Coalition...1806-07 War of the Fifth Coalition.......1809
Napoleon Annexes North Germany 1810 Sixth Coalition against France.1813-15 Battle of Leipzig.................1813 Congress of Vienna..............1814 Russia, Prussia, and Austria Form the Holy Alliance ....1814 Diet of the German Confederation.1816	Béranger, 1780-1857	War with Russia; Burning of Moscow; Retreat of French.........1812 War of the Sixth Coalition....1813-15 Battle of Leipzig................1813 Louis XVIII, King of France; the First Restoration.............1814 Napoleon Abdicates ....1814 Battle of Waterloo..............1815 Second Restoration of Louis XVIII 1815 Napoleon Banished to St. Helena..1815
Congress at Vienna.............1820 Congress at Laybach............1821 Revolution in Brunswick.........1830 The Zollverein 1834	Stendhal, 1783-1842 Lamartine, 1790-1869 de Vigny, 1797-1863 Balzac, 1799-1850	Charles X, King of France.....1824-30 Bourbons Overthrown ....1830 Louis Philippe, King of the French 1830-48
Frederick William IV, King of Prussia ....1840-61 Revolutionary Movements ....1848 Constitution of German Empire Completed 1849	Dumas (père) 1802-1870 Hugo, 1802-1885 Sand, 1804-1876 de Musset, 1810-1857 Gautier, 1811-1872	Louis Philippe Abdicates.........1848 Louis Napoleon Bonaparte Elected President of the Republic..........1848 Louis Napoleon Made Emperor of the French as Napoleon III..1852-70

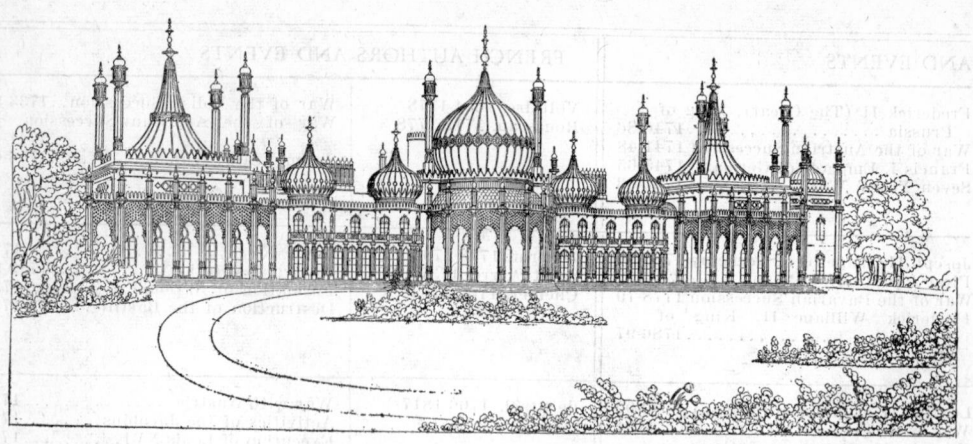

The Royal Pavilion at Brighton. From John Nash, "The Royal Pavilion at Brighton," London, R. Ackerman, 1825.

Three Neo-Classicists

A Basis for Comparison

IN ATTITUDE toward life, in subject matter, in manner of expression, the romantic writers differed greatly from their neoclassical forebears. Indeed, it was against the cold intellectuality, the appeal to reason and sense of fact, and the rigid formality of style which dominated the lives and the writings of the neo-classicists that the romanticists rebelled. Selections from three of the leading writers of the earlier period are here presented to show how they contrasted with the writings of the romantic period.

The high priest of neo-classical poetry was Alexander Pope (1688-1744). His verse conforms to the rules and standards of his age of convention and realism. It is characterized by extreme neatness, finish, orderliness, and perfection of form. It allows no play of the emotions or the imagination, qualities inherent in romantic writings.

The prose of Samuel Johnson (1709-1784), a late representative of the age, continues the neo-classical tradition. In method of expression Johnson's prose is elegant and pompous rather than free and natural. Judgments are expressed in the light of formal neo-classical standards.

Edmund Burke (1729-1797), the most significant political writer and speaker of his day, always expressed himself with considerable ardor and imagination. It was his faith that policies of government should be determined by expediency rather than by abstract right. Unlike the romanticists the conservative Burke could not approve the French Revolution, and he was horrified by its excesses.

Neo-classical formalities began to fade before the middle of the eighteenth century, and during the next sixty years there was an ever-increasing tendency toward the romantic way of life. Revolutionary ideas gradually affected political and social thinking as well as the subject matter and style of literature. As men became more liberal they thought and wrote more as individuals and thus hastened the advent of the romantic triumph.

Alexander Pope 1688-1744

From WINDSOR FOREST
1704   *1713*

Thy forests, Windsor! and thy green re-
  treats,
At once the Monarch's and the Muse's seats,
Invite my lays. Be present, sylvan maids!
Unlock your springs, and open all your
  shades.
Granville commands; your aid, O Muses,
  bring!   5
What Muse for Granville can refuse to
  sing?
  The groves of Eden, vanish'd now so long,
Live in description, and look green in song:[1]
These, were my breast inspir'd with equal
  flame,
Like them in beauty, should be like in
  fame.   10
Here hills and vales, the woodland and the
  plain,
Here earth and water, seem to strive again;
Not chaos-like together crush'd and bruis'd,
But, as the world, harmoniously confus'd,
Where order in variety we see,   15
And where, tho' all things differ, all agree.
Here waving groves a chequer'd scene dis-
  play,
And part admit, and part exclude the day,
As some coy nymph her lover's warm ad-
  dress
Nor quite indulges, nor can quite repress; 20
There, interspers'd in lawns and op'ning
  glades,
Thin trees arise, that shun each other's
  shades.
Here, in full light, the russet plains extend;
There wrapt in clouds, the bluish hills as-
  cend.
Ev'n the wild heath displays her purple
  dyes,   25
And 'midst the desert fruitful fields arise,
That, crown'd with tufted trees[2] and spring-
  ing corn,[3]
Like verdant isles the sable waste adorn.
Let India boast her plants, nor envy we
The weeping amber or the balmy tree,   30
While by our oaks the precious loads are
  borne,
And realms commanded which those trees
  adorn.
Not proud Olympus yields a nobler sight,
Tho' gods assembled grace his tow'ring
  height,

Than what more humble mountains offer
  here,   35
Where, in their blessings all those gods ap-
  pear:
See Pan with flocks, with fruits Pomona
  crown'd;
Here blushing Flora paints th' enamell'd
  ground;
Here Ceres' gifts in waving prospect stand,
And, nodding, tempt the joyful reaper's
  hand;   40
Rich Industry sits smiling on the plains,
And peace and plenty tell, a Stuart reigns.[1]
  Not thus the land appear'd in ages past,
A dreary desert, and a gloomy waste,
To savage beasts and savage laws a prey, 45
And kings more furious and severe than
  they;
Who claim'd the skies, dispeopled air and
  floods,
The lonely lords of empty wilds and woods:
Cities laid waste, they storm'd the dens and
  caves,
(For wiser brutes were backward to be
  slaves:)   50
What could be free, when lawless beasts
  obey'd,
And ev'n the elements a tyrant swayed?
In vain kind seasons swell'd the teeming
  grain,
Soft show'rs distill'd, and suns grew warm
  in vain;
The swain with tears his frustrate labor
  yields,   55
And famish'd dies amidst his ripen'd fields.
What wonder then, a beast or subject slain
Were equal crimes in a despotic reign?
Both doom'd alike, for sportive tyrants bled,
But while the subject starv'd, the beast was
  fed.   60
Proud Nimrod[2] first the bloody chase began,
A mighty hunter, and his prey was man:
Our haughty Norman boasts that barb'rous
  name,
And makes his trembling slaves, the royal
  game.
The fields are ravish'd from th' industrious
  swains,[3]
From men their cities, and from gods their
  fanes: 66
The levell'd towns with weeds lie cover'd
  o'er;
The hollow winds thro' naked temples roar;

[1] An allusion to *Paradise Lost.*
[2] See *L'Allegro,* 78.
[3] wheat

[1] Queen Anne (1702-14)
[2] William I, King of England (1066-87). See
  Genesis, 10:8-9.
[3] Among his other tyrannies, William I confiscated
  land in Hampshire, and made it into New Forest, a royal game preserve.

Round broken columns clasping ivy twin'd;
O'er heaps of ruin stalk'd the stately
    hind;[1]   70
The fox obscene to gaping tombs retires,
And savage howlings fill the sacred quires.[2]
Aw'd by the nobles, by his commons curst,
Th' oppressor rul'd tyrannic where he durst,
Stretch'd o'er the poor and church his iron
    rod,   75
And serv'd alike his vassals and his God.
Whom ev'n the Saxon spar'd and bloody
    Dane,
The wanton victims of his sport remain.
But see, the man who spacious regions gave
A waste for beasts, himself deny'd a
    grave![3]   80
Stretch'd on the lawn his second hope[4] sur-
    vey,
At once the chaser, and at once the prey:
Lo Rufus,[5] tugging at the deadly dart,
Bleeds in the Forest like a wounded hart.
Succeeding monarchs heard the subjects'
    cries,   85
Nor saw displeas'd the peaceful cottage rise.
Then gath'ring flocks on unknown moun-
    tains fed,
O'er sandy wilds were yellow harvests
    spread,
The forests wonder'd at th' unusual grain,
And secret transport touch'd the conscious
    swain.
Fair Liberty, Britannia's Goddess, rears   91
Her cheerful head, and leads the golden
    years.
    Ye vig'rous swains! while youth ferments
    your blood,
And purer spirits swell the sprightly flood,
Now range the hills, the gameful woods be-
    set,   95
Wind the shrill horn, or spread the waving
    net.
When milder autumn summer's heat suc-
    ceeds,
And in the new-shorn field the partridge
    feeds,
Before his lord the ready spaniel bounds, 99
Panting with hope, he tries the furrow'd
    grounds;
But when the tainted gales the game betray,
Couch'd close he lies, and meditates the
    prey;

Secure they trust th' unfaithful field beset,
'Till hov'ring o'er 'em sweeps the swelling
    net.
Thus (if small things we may with great
    compare)
When Albion sends her eager sons to
    war,   106
Some thoughtless town, with ease and
    plenty blest,
Near, and more near, the closing lines in-
    vest;
Sudden they seize th' amaz'd, defenceless
    prize,
And high in air Britannia's standard
    flies.[1]   110
    See! from the brake[2] the whirring pheas-
    ant springs,
And mounts exulting on triumphant wings!
Short is his joy; he feels the fiery wound,
Flutters in blood, and, panting, beats the
    ground.
Ah, what avail his glossy, varying dyes, 115
His purple crest and scarlet-circled eyes,
The vivid green his shining plumes unfold,
His painted wings, and breast that flames
    with gold?
    Nor yet, when moist Arcturus clouds the
    sky,
The woods and fields their pleasing toils
    deny.   120
To plains with well-breath'd beagles we re-
    pair,
And trace the mazes of the circling hare.
(Beasts, urg'd by us, their fellow-beasts
    pursue,
And learn of men each other to undo).   124
With slaught'ring guns th' unwearied fowler
    roves,
When frosts have whiten'd all the naked
    groves,
Where doves in flocks the leafless trees o'er-
    shade,
And lonely wood-cocks haunt the wat'ry
    glade.
He lifts the tube, and levels with his eye;
Straight a short thunder breaks the frozen
    sky: 130
Oft, as in airy rings they skim the heath,
The clam'rous lapwings feel the leaden
    death:
Oft, as the mounting larks their notes pre-
    pare,
They fall, and leave their little lives in air.
    In genial spring, beneath the quiv'ring
    shade,   135

---

[1] The female of the red deer.
[2] Parts of churches used by singers.
[3] The burial ground for William in Normandy had
    to be purchased.
[4] Richard, Duke of Bernay, said to have been killed
    by a stag.
[5] William II, King of England (1087-1100). He
    was killed (possibly by accident) by an arrow
    shot by one of his own men while hunting in
    New Forest.

[1] Probably an allusion to the easy capture of
    Gibraltar, in 1704.
[2] thicket

Where cooling vapors breathe along the
    mead,
The patient fisher takes his silent stand,
Intent, his angle trembling in his hand;
With looks unmov'd, he hopes the scaly
    breed,
And eyes the dancing cork and bending
    reed.   140
Our plenteous streams a various race sup-
    ply:
The bright-ey'd perch, with fins of Tyrian
    dye;[1]
The silver eel, in shining volumes[2] roll'd;
The yellow carp, in scales bedropp'd with
    gold;[3]
Swift trouts, diversified with crimson
    stains;   145
And pikes, the tyrants of the wat'ry plains.
    Now Cancer glows with Phœbus' fiery
    car,[4]
The youth rush eager to the sylvan war,
Swarm o'er the lawns, the forest walks
    surround,
Rouse the fleet hart, and cheer the opening
    hound.
Th' impatient courser pants in every
    vein,   151
And, pawing, seems to beat the distant
    plain:
Hills, vales, and floods appear already
    cross'd,
And ere he starts, a thousand steps are
    lost.   154
See the bold youth strain up the threat'ning
    steep,
Rush thro' the thickets, down the valleys
    sweep,
Hang o'er their coursers' heads with eager
    speed,
And earth rolls back beneath the flying
    steed.
Let old Arcadia boast her ample plain,
Th' immortal huntress,[5] and her virgin
    train;   160
Nor envy, Windsor! since thy shades have
    seen
As bright a Goddess and as chaste a Queen;[6]
Whose care, like hers, protects the sylvan
    reign,
The earth's fair light, and Empress of the
    main.

.   .   .   .

[1] A purple dye made by the natives of ancient
    Tyre, Asia Minor, from the juice of shellfish.
[2] coils
[3] See *Paradise Lost*, 7, 406.
[4] The sun was in the sign of Cancer,—*i. e.*, it was
    the time of the summer solstice.
[5] Diana, the goddess of the chase.
[6] Queen Anne.

From AN ESSAY ON CRITICISM
1709   1711

PART I

'Tis hard to say, if greater want of skill
Appear in writing or in judging ill;
But, of the two, less dangerous is th' offence
To tire our patience, than mislead our sense.
Some few in that, but numbers err in this, 5
Ten censure[1] wrong for one who writes
    amiss;
A fool might once himself alone expose,
Now one in verse makes many more in
    prose.
    'Tis with our judgments as our watches,
    none
Go just alike, yet each believes his own. 10
In poets as true genius is but rare,
True taste as seldom is the critic's share;
Both must alike from Heav'n derive their
    light,
These born to judge, as well as those to
    write.
Let such teach others who themselves
    excel,   15
And censure freely who have written well.
Authors are partial to their wit,[2] 'tis true,
But are not critics to their judgment too?
    Yet if we look more closely, we shall find
Most have the seeds of judgment in their
    mind: 20
Nature affords at least a glimm'ring light;
The lines, tho' touch'd but faintly, are drawn
    right.
But as the slightest sketch, if justly trac'd,
Is by ill-coloring but the more disgrac'd,
So by false learning is good sense de-
    fac'd;   25
Some are bewilder'd in the maze of schools,
And some made coxcombs Nature meant but
    fools.
In search of wit these lose their common
    sense,
And then turn critics in their own defence;
Each burns alike, who can, or cannot
    write,   30
Or with a rival's or an eunuch's spite.
All fools have still an itching to deride,
And fain would be upon the laughing side.
If Mævius scribbled in Apollo's spite,
There are who judge still worse than he can
    write.   35
    Some have at first for wits, then poets
    past,
Turned critics next, and prov'd plain fools
    at last.

[1] judge
[2] knowledge; intellect; genius; creative power

Some neither can for wits[1] nor critics pass,
As heavy mules are neither horse nor ass.
Those half-learn'd witlings, num'rous in our
    isle,   40
As half-form'd insects on the banks of Nile;
Unfinish'd things, one knows not what to
    call,
Their generation's[2] so equivocal:
To tell[3] 'em, would a hundred tongues re-
    quire,
Or one vain wit's, that might a hundred
    tire.   45
    But you who seek to give and merit fame,
And justly bear a critic's noble name,
Be sure yourself and your own reach to
    know,
How far your genius, taste, and learning
    go;
Launch not beyond your depth, but be dis-
    creet,   50
And mark that point where sense and dul-
    ness meet.
    Nature to all things fix'd the limits fit,
And wisely curb'd proud man's pretending
    wit.
As on the land while here the ocean gains,
In other parts it leaves wide sandy plains; 55
Thus in the soul while memory prevails,
The solid pow'r of understanding fails;
Where beams of warm imagination play,
The memory's soft figures melt away.
One science only will one genius fit;   60
So vast is art, so narrow human wit:
Not only bounded to peculiar arts,
But oft in those confined to single parts.
Like kings we lose the conquests gain'd be-
    fore,
By vain ambition still to make them
    more;   65
Each might his sev'ral province well com-
    mand,
Would all but stoop to what they under-
    stand.
    First follow Nature, and your judgment
    frame
By her just standard, which is still the
    same:
Unerring Nature, still divinely bright,   70
One clear, unchang'd, and universal light,
Life, force, and beauty, must to all impart,
At once the source, and end, and test of Art,
Art from that fund each just supply pro-
    vides,
Works without show, and without pomp
    presides: 75

In some fair body thus th' informing[1] soul
With spirits feeds, with vigor fills the whole,
Each motion guides, and ev'ry nerve sus-
    tains;
Itself unseen, but in th' effects, remains.
Some, to whom Heav'n in wit has been pro-
    fuse,   80
Want as much more, to turn it to its use;
For wit and judgment often are at strife,
Tho' meant each other's aid, like man and
    wife.
'Tis more to guide than spur the Muse's
    steed;
Restrain his fury, than provoke his speed; 85
The winged courser,[2] like a gen'rous[3] horse,
Shows most true mettle when you check his
    course.
    Those rules of old discovered, not devis'd,
Are Nature still, but Nature methodiz'd;
Nature, like liberty, is but restrain'd   90
By the same laws which first herself or-
    dain'd.
    Hear how learn'd Greece her useful rules
    indites,
When to repress and when indulge our
    flights;
High on Parnassus' top[4] her sons she
    show'd,
And pointed out those arduous paths they
    trod;   95
Held from afar, aloft, th' immortal prize,
And urged the rest by equal steps to rise.
Just precepts thus from great examples
    giv'n,
She drew from them what they deriv'd from
    Heav'n.
The gen'rous critic fann'd the poet's fire, 100
And taught the world with reason to admire.
Then Criticism the Muse's handmaid prov'd,
To dress her charms and make her more
    belov'd;
But following wits from that intention
    stray'd,
Who could not win the mistress, woo'd the
    maid;
Against the poets their own arms they
    turn'd,   106
Sure to hate most the men from whom they
    learn'd.
So modern 'pothecaries, taught the art
By doctor's bills[5] to play the doctor's part,
Bold in the practice of mistaken rules, 110
Prescribe, apply, and call their masters
    fools.
Some on the leaves of ancient authors prey,

---

[1] persons possessing learning or knowledge of hu-
    man nature
[2] begetting
[3] count

[1] animating
[2] Pegasus.
[3] of good stock; thoroughbred; mettlesome
[4] that is, on the heights of poetic fame.
[5] prescriptions

Nor time nor moths e'er spoil'd so much
    as they.
Some drily plain without invention's aid,
Write dull receipts how poems may be
    made; 115
These leave the sense, their learning to dis-
    play,
And those explain the meaning quite away.
    You then whose judgment the right course
      would steer,
Know well each ancient's proper character;
His fable,[1] subject, scope in ev'ry page; 120
Religion, country, genius of his age;
Without all these at once before your eyes,
Cavil you may, but never criticise.
Be Homer's works your study and delight,
Read them by day, and meditate by
    night; 125
Thence form your judgment, thence your
    maxims bring,
And trace the Muses upward to their spring.
Still with itself compar'd, his text peruse;
And let your comment be the Mantuan
    Muse.[2]
    When first young Maro[3] in his boundless
      mind 130
A work t' outlast immortal Rome design'd,
Perhaps he seemed above the critic's law,
And but from Nature's fountains scorned
    to draw;
But when t' examine every part he came,
Nature and Homer were, he found, the
    same. 135
Convinc'd, amaz'd, he checks the bold de-
    sign;
And rules as strict his labor'd work confine,
As if the Stagirite[4] o'erlooked each line.
Learn hence for ancient rules a just esteem;
To copy Nature is to copy them. 140
    Some beauties yet no precepts can de-
      clare,
For there's a happiness as well as care.
Music resembles poetry; in each
Are nameless graces which no methods teach,
And which a master-hand alone can
    reach. 145
If, where the rules not far enough extend,
(Since rules were made but to promote their
    end)
Some lucky licence answer to the full
Th' intent propos'd, that licence is a rule.

Thus Pegasus, a nearer way to take, 150
May boldly deviate from the common track;
From vulgar bounds with brave disorder
    part,
And snatch a grace beyond the reach of art,
Which, without passing thro' the judgment,
    gains
The heart, and all its end at once attains. 155
In prospects thus, some objects please our
    eyes,
Which out of Nature's common order rise,
The shapeless rock, or hanging precipice.
Great wits sometimes may gloriously offend,
And rise to faults true critics dare not
    mend; 160
But tho' the ancients thus their rules in-
    vade;
(As kings dispense with laws themselves
    have made)
Moderns beware! or if you must offend
Against the precept, ne'er transgress its
    end;
Let it be seldom, and compell'd by need; 165
And have, at least, their precedent to plead.
The critic else proceeds without remorse,
Seizes your fame and puts his laws in force.
    I know there are to whose presumptuous
      thoughts
Those freer beauties, ev'n in them, seem
    faults. 170
Some figures monstrous and mis-shap'd ap-
    pear,
Consider'd singly, or beheld too near,
Which, but proportion'd to their light or
    place,
Due distance reconciles to form and grace.
A prudent chief not always must display 175
His powers in equal ranks, and fair array,
But with th' occasion and the place comply,
Conceal his force, nay, seem sometimes to
    fly.
Those oft are stratagems which errors seem,
Nor is it Homer nods, but we that
    dream.[1] 180
    Still green with bays each ancient altar
      stands,
Above the reach of sacrilegious hands;
Secure from flames, from envy's fiercer
    rage,
Destructive war, and all-involving age. 184
See, from each clime the learn'd their in-
    cense bring!
Hear, in all tongues, consenting pæans ring!
In praise so just let ev'ry voice be joined,
And fill the general chorus of mankind.
Hail, bards triumphant! born in happier
    days;

---

[1] plot; story
[2] Virgil, who was born near Mantua, Italy.
[3] The family name of Virgil (Publius Virgilius
    Maro).
[4] Aristotle (384-322 B. C.), the famous Greek
    philosopher, who was born in Stagira, a city in
    Macedonia, now a part of Turkey. His *Poetics*
    laid the foundation of literary criticism, and
    for centuries, especially in Pope's time, enjoyed
    an almost superstitious reverence.

[1] See Horace's *Ars Poetica*, 359-60.

Immortal heirs of universal praise!   190
Whose honors with increase of ages grow,
As streams roll down, enlarging as they
      flow;
Nations unborn your mighty names shall
      sound,
And worlds applaud that must[1] not yet be
      found!
Oh, may some spark of your celestial fire, 195
The last, the meanest of your sons inspire,
(That on weak wings, from far, pursues
      your flights;
Glows while he reads, but trembles as he
      writes)
To teach vain wits a science little known,
T' admire superior sense, and doubt their
      own!   200

. . . .

From AN ESSAY ON MAN

EPISTLE I

Awake, my St. John! leave all meaner
      things
To low ambition, and the pride of kings.
Let us (since life can little more supply
Than just to look about us and to die)
Expatiate free[2] o'er all this scene of man; 5
A mighty maze! but not without a plan;
A wild, where weeds and flow'rs promiscu-
      ous shoot,
Or garden, tempting with forbidden fruit.
Together let us beat[3] this ample field,
Try what the open, what the covert yield; 10
The latent tracts, the giddy heights, explore
Of all who blindly creep, or sightless soar;
Eye Nature's walks, shoot folly as it flies,
And catch the manners living as they rise;
Laugh where we must, be candid[4] where we
      can;   15
But vindicate the ways of God to man.[5]

  I.   Say first, of God above, or man below,
What can we reason, but from what we
      know?
Of man, what see we but his station here
From which to reason or to which refer? 20
Thro' worlds unnumber'd tho' the God be
      known,
'Tis ours to trace him only in our own.
He, who through vast immensity can pierce,
See worlds on worlds compose one universe,
Observe how system into system runs,   25
What other planets circle other suns,
What varied being peoples every star,

May tell why Heav'n has made us as we are,
But of this frame[1] the bearings, and the ties,
The strong connections, nice dependencies, 30
Gradations just, has thy pervading soul
Look'd thro'? or can a part contain the
      whole?
Is the great chain, that draws all to agree,
And drawn supports, upheld by God, or
      thee?

  II.   Presumptuous man! the reason
      wouldst thou find,   35
Why form'd so weak, so little, and so blind?
First, if thou canst, the harder reason guess,
Why form'd no weaker, blinder, and no
      less?
Ask of thy mother earth, why oaks are made
Taller or stronger than the weeds they
      shade?   40
Or ask of yonder argent fields above,
Why Jove's satellites[2] are less than Jove.
Of systems possible, if 'tis confest
That Wisdom infinite must form the best,
Where all must full or not coherent be,   45
And all that rises, rise in due degree;
Then, in the scale of reas'ning life, 'tis
      plain,
There must be, somewhere, such a rank as
      man:
And all the question (wrangle e'er so long)
Is only this, if God has plac'd him wrong? 50
  Respecting man, whatever wrong we call,
May, must be right, as relative to all.
In human works, tho' labor'd on with pain,
A thousand movements scarce one purpose
      gain;
In God's, one single can its end produce; 55
Yet serves to second too some other use.
So man, who here seems principal alone,
Perhaps acts second to some sphere un-
      known,
Touches some wheel, or verges to some goal;
'Tis but a part we see, and not a whole.   60
  When the proud steed shall know why man
      restrains
His fiery course, or drives him o'er the
      plains;
When the dull ox, why now he breaks the
      clod,
Is now a victim, and now Egypt's god,[3]
Then shall man's pride and dullness com-
      prehend   65
His actions', passions', being's, use and end;
Why doing, suff'ring, check'd, impell'd; and
      why
This hour a slave, the next a deity.

---

[1] Used here in the original sense of *can*.
[2] wander at will
[3] scour; range over
[4] lenient; charitable
[5] See *Paradise Lost*, 1, 26.

[1] The structure of the universe.
[2] To be read as a four-syllable word.
[3] Apis, the sacred bull of Egypt.

Then say not man's imperfect, Heav'n in
    fault;
Say rather, man's as perfect as he ought: 70
His knowledge measur'd to his state and
    place,
His time a moment, and a point his space.
If to be perfect in a certain sphere,
What matter, soon or late, or here or there?
The blest today is as completely so,   75
As who began a thousand years ago.

   III.   Heav'n from all creatures hides the
    book of Fate,
All but the page prescrib'd, their present
    state:
From brutes what men, from men what
    spirits know:
Or who could suffer being here below?   80
The lamb thy riot dooms to bleed today,
Had he thy reason, would he skip and play?
Pleas'd to the last, he crops the flow'ry food,
And licks the hand just rais'd to shed his
    blood.
Oh, blindness to the future! kindly given, 85
That each may fill the circle mark'd by
    Heav'n:
Who sees with equal eye, as God of all,
A hero perish, or a sparrow fall,
Atoms or systems into ruin hurl'd,
And now a bubble burst, and now a world. 90
   Hope humbly then; with trembling pin-
    ions soar;
Wait the great teacher Death; and God
    adore.
What future bliss, he gives not thee to
    know,
But gives that hope to be thy blessing now.
Hope springs eternal in the human breast: 95
Man never is, but always to be blest.
The soul, uneasy and confin'd from home,
Rests and expatiates in a life to come.
   Lo, the poor Indian! whose untutor'd
    mind
Sees God in clouds, or hears him in the
    wind;   100
His soul, proud science never taught to
    stray
Far as the solar walk, or milky way;
Yet simple Nature to his hope has giv'n,
Behind the cloud-topt hill, an humbler
    Heav'n;
Some safer world in depths of woods em-
    brac'd   105
Some happier island in the watery waste,
Where slaves once more their native land
    behold,
No fiends torment, no Christians thirst for
    gold.
To be, contents his natural desire,

He asks no angel's wing, no seraph's fire; 110
But thinks, admitted to that equal sky
His faithful dog shall bear him company.

   IV.   Go, wiser thou! and, in thy scale of
    sense
Weigh thy opinion against Providence;
Call imperfection what thou fancy'st
    such,   115
Say, "Here he gives too little, there too
    much;"
Destroy all creatures for thy sport or gust,[1]
Yet cry, "If man's unhappy, God's unjust;"
If man alone engross not Heaven's high
    care,
Alone made perfect here, immortal there, 120
Snatch from his hand the balance and the
    rod,
Re-judge his justice, be the god of God.
In pride, in reas'ning pride, our error lies;
All quit their sphere, and rush into the
    skies.
Pride still is aiming at the blest abodes, 125
Men would be angels, angels would be gods.
Aspiring to be gods, if angels fell,
Aspiring to be angels, men rebel:
And who but wishes to invert the laws
Of order, sins against th' Eternal Cause. 130

   V.   Ask for what end the heav'nly bodies
    shine,
Earth for whose use? Pride answers, "'Tis
    for mine:
For me kind Nature wakes her genial pow'r,
Suckles each herb, and spreads out ev'ry
    flow'r;
Annual for me, the grape, the rose renew 135
The juice nectareous, and the balmy dew,
For me, the mine a thousand treasures
    brings;
For me, health gushes from a thousand
    springs;
Seas roll to waft me, suns to light me rise;
My footstool earth, my canopy the skies." 140
   But errs not Nature from this gracious
    end,
From burning suns when livid deaths de-
    scend,
When earthquakes swallow, or when tem-
    pests sweep
Towns to one grave, whole nations to the
    deep?
"No;" 'tis reply'd, "the first Almighty
    Cause   145
Acts not by partial, but by gen'ral laws;
Th' exceptions few; some change, since all
    began:

[1] pleasure of taste

And what created perfect?" — Why then
  man?
If the great end be human happiness,
Then Nature deviates; and can man do
  less?   150
As much that end a constant course requires
Of show'rs and sunshine, as of man's de-
  sires;
As much eternal springs and cloudless skies,
As men forever temp'rate, calm, and wise.
If plagues or earthquakes break not Heav-
  en's design,
Why then a Borgia, or a Catiline?   156
Who knows but He, whose hand the light-
  ning forms,
Who heaves old ocean, and who wings the
  storms;
Pours fierce ambition in a Cæsar's mind, 159
Or turns young Ammon loose to scourge
  mankind?
From pride, from pride, our very reas'ning
  springs.
Account for moral, as for nat'ral things:
Why charge we Heav'n in those, in these
  acquit?
In both, to reason right is to submit,
  Better for us, perhaps, it might ap-
    pear,   165
Were there all harmony, all virtue here;
That never air or ocean felt the wind;
That never passion discompos'd the mind.
But all subsists by elemental strife;
And passions are the elements of life.   170
The gen'ral order, since the whole began,
Is kept in Nature, and is kept in man.

  VI.   What would this man?   Now up-
    ward will he soar,
And little less than angel, would be more;
Now looking downwards, just as griev'd ap-
  pears   175
To want the strength of bulls, the fur of
  bears.
Made for his use all creatures if he call,
Say what their use, had he the pow'rs of
  all?
Nature to these, without profusion, kind,
The proper organs, proper pow'rs as-
  signed;   180
Each seeming want compensated of course,
Here with degrees of swiftness, there of
  force;
All in exact proportion to the state;
Nothing to add, and nothing to abate.
Each beast, each insect, happy in its
  own: 185
Is Heav'n unkind to man, and man alone?
Shall he alone, whom rational we call,

Be pleas'd with nothing, if not bless'd with
  all?
  The bliss of man (could pride that bless-
    ing find)
Is not to act or think beyond mankind; 190
No pow'rs of body or of soul to share,
But what his nature and his state can bear.
Why has not man a microscopic eye?
For this plain reason, man is not a fly.
Say what the use, were finer optics giv'n, 195
T' inspect a mite, not comprehend the
  heav'n?
Or touch, if tremblingly alive all o'er,
To smart and agonize at every pore?
Or, quick effluvia darting through the brain,
Die of a rose in aromatic pain?   200
If Nature thund'red in his op'ning ears,
And stunned him with the music of the
  spheres,[1]
How would he wish that Heav'n had left
  him still
The whisp'ring zephyr, and the purling rill?
Who finds not Providence all good and
  wise,   205
Alike in what it gives, and what denies?

  VII.   Far as Creation's ample range ex-
    tends,
The scale of sensual,[2] mental pow'rs ascends.
Mark how it mounts, to man's imperial race,
From the green myriads in the peopled
  grass: 210
What modes of sight betwixt each wide ex-
  treme,
The mole's dim curtain, and the lynx's
  beam:
Of smell, the headlong lioness between
And hound sagacious on the tainted green:
Of hearing, from the life that fills the
  flood,   215
To that which warbles thro' the vernal
  wood:
The spider's touch, how exquisitely fine!
Feels at each thread, and lives along the
  line:
In the nice bee, what sense so subtly true
From pois'nous herbs extracts the healing
  dew?   220
How instinct varies in the grov'lling swine,
Compar'd, half-reas'ning elephant, with
  thine!
'Twixt that and reason, what a nice barrier,
Forever sep'rate, yet forever near!

[1] According to the old Ptolemaic astronomy, the
earth was the center of the universe, with the
planets and stars revolving about it in concentric spheres. The revolution of these spheres
produced music too fine for mortal ears to hear.
[2] pertaining to the senses

Remembrance and reflection how ally'd; [225]
What thin partitions sense from thought
   divide:
And middle natures, how they long to join,
Yet never pass th' insuperable line!
Without this just gradation, could they be
Subjected, these to those, or all to thee? [230]
The pow'rs of all subdu'd by thee alone,
Is not thy reason all these pow'rs in one?

   VIII. See, through this air, this ocean,
   and this earth,
All matter quick,[1] and bursting into birth.
Above, how high, progressive life may
   go! [235]
Around, how wide! how deep extend below!
Vast chain of being! which from God began,
Natures ethereal, human, angel, man,
Beast, bird, fish, insect, what no eye can
   see,
No glass can reach; from infinite to thee, [240]
From thee to nothing.—On superior pow'rs
Were we to press, inferior might[2] on ours;
Or in the full creation leave a void,
Where, one step broken, the great scale's
   destroy'd:
From Nature's chain whatever link you
   strike, [245]
Tenth, or ten thousandth, breaks the chain
   alike.
   And, if each system in gradation roll
Alike essential to th' amazing whole,
The least confusion but in one, not all
That system only but the whole must
   fall. [250]
Let earth unbalanc'd from her orbit fly,
Planets and suns run lawless through the
   sky;
Let ruling angels from their spheres be
   hurl'd,
Being on being wreck'd, and world on
   world;
Heaven's whole foundations to their centre
   nod, [255]
And Nature tremble to the throne of God.
All this dread order break—for whom? for
   thee?
Vile worm!—Oh, madness! pride! impiety!

   IX. What if the foot, ordain'd the dust
   to tread,
Or, hand, to toil, aspir'd to be the head? [260]
What if the head, the eye, or ear repin'd
To serve mere engines to the ruling mind?
Just as absurd for any part to claim
To be another, in this gen'ral frame,[3]

[1] alive
[2] That is, inferior beings might press.
[3] universe

Just as absurd, to mourn the tasks or
   pains, [265]
The great directing Mind of all ordains.
   All are but parts of one stupendous
   whole,
Whose body Nature is, and God the soul;
That chang'd through all, and yet in all
   the same;
Great in the earth, as in th' ethereal
   frame; [270]
Warms in the sun, refreshes in the breeze,
Glows in the stars, and blossoms in the
   trees,
Lives thro' all life, extends thro' all extent,
Spreads undivided, operates unspent;
Breathes in our soul, informs our mortal
   part, [275]
As full, as perfect, in a hair as heart;
As full, as perfect, in vile man that mourns,
As the rapt seraph that adores and burns:[1]
To him no high, no low, no great, no small;
He fills, he bounds, connects, and equals
   all. [280]

   X. Cease then, nor order imperfection
   name:
Our proper bliss depends on what we blame.
Know thy own point: this kind, this due
   degree
Of blindness, weakness, Heav'n bestows on
   thee.
Submit.—In this, or any other sphere, [285]
Secure to be as blest as thou canst bear:
Safe in the hand of one disposing Pow'r,
Or in the natal, or the mortal hour.
All nature is but Art, unknown to thee;
All chance, direction, which thou canst not
   see; [290]
All discord, harmony not understood;
All partial evil, universal good:
And, spite of pride, in erring reason's spite,
One truth is clear,—Whatever is, is right.

. . . .

Samuel Johnson 1709-1784

From PREFACE TO SHAKSPEARE
1765

. . . .

   The poet, of whose works I have undertaken the revision, may now begin to assume
the dignity of an ancient, and claim the
privilege of established fame and prescrip-

[1] According to Jewish legend, the seraphs were
angels who lived only a day, being consumed by
fire in the ardor of their worship. See Longfellow's *Sandalphon*, which is based, in part, on
this legend.

tive veneration. He has long outlived his century, the term commonly fixed as the test of literary merit. Whatever advantages he might once derive from personal allusions, local customs, or temporary opinions, have for many years been lost; and every topic of merriment, or motive of sorrow, which the modes of artificial life afforded him, now only obscure the scenes which they once illuminated. The effects of favor and competition are at an end; the tradition of his friendships and his enmities has perished; his works support no opinion with arguments, nor supply any faction with invectives; they can neither indulge vanity, nor gratify malignity; but are read without any other reason than the desire of pleasure, and are therefore praised only as pleasure is obtained; yet, thus unassisted by interest or passion, they have passed through variations of taste and changes of manners, and, as they devolved from one generation to another, have received new honors at every transmission.

But because human judgment, though it be gradually gaining upon certainty, never becomes infallible, and approbation, though long continued, may yet be only the approbation of prejudice or fashion, it is proper to inquire by what peculiarities of excellence Shakspeare has gained and kept the favor of his countrymen.

Nothing can please many, and please long, but just representations of general nature. Particular manners can be known to few, and therefore few only can judge how nearly they are copied. The irregular combinations of fanciful invention may delight awhile, by that novelty of which the common satiety of life sends us all in quest; but the pleasures of sudden wonder are soon exhausted, and the mind can only repose on the stability of truth.

Shakspeare is, above all writers, at least above all modern writers, the poet of nature, the poet that holds up to his readers a faithful mirror of manners and of life. His characters are not modified by the customs of particular places, unpracticed by the rest of the world, by the peculiarities of studies or professions, which can operate but upon small numbers, or by the accidents of transient fashions or temporary opinions; they are the genuine progeny of common humanity, such as the world will always supply and observation will always find. His persons act and speak by the influence of those general passions and principles by which all minds are agitated and the whole system

of life is continued in motion. In the writings of other poets a character is too often an individual; in those of Shakspeare it is commonly a species.

It is from this wide extension of design that so much instruction is derived. It is this which fills the plays of Shakspeare with practical axioms and domestic wisdom. It was said of Euripides that every verse was a precept; and it may be said of Shakspeare that from his works may be collected a system of civil and economical prudence. Yet his real power is not shown in the splendor of particular passages, but by the progress of his fable[1] and the tenor of his dialogue; and he that tries to recommend him by select quotations will succeed like the pedant in Hierocles, who, when he offered his house to sale, carried a brick in his pocket as a specimen.

It will not easily be imagined how much Shakspeare excels in accommodating his sentiments to real life but by comparing him with other authors. It was observed of the ancient schools of declamation that the more diligently they were frequented the more was the student disqualified for the world, because he found nothing there which he should ever meet in any other place. The same remark may be applied to every stage[2] but that of Shakspeare. The theatre when it is under any other direction is peopled by such characters as were never seen, conversing in a language which was never heard, upon topics which will never arise in the commerce of mankind. But the dialogue of this author is often so evidently determined by the incident which produces it, and is pursued with so much ease and simplicity, that it seems scarcely to claim the merit of fiction but to have been gleaned by diligent selection out of common conversation and common occurrences.

Upon every other stage the universal agent is love, by whose power all good and evil is distributed and every action quickened or retarded. To bring a lover, a lady, and a rival into the fable; to entangle them in contradictory obligations, perplex them with oppositions of interest, and harass them with violence of desires inconsistent with each other; to make them meet in rapture and part in agony; to fill their mouths with hyperbolical joy and outrageous sorrow; to distress them as nothing human ever was distressed; to deliver them as nothing

---

[1] plot; story
[2] Johnson means the modern stage only.

human ever was delivered; is the business of a modern dramatist. For this, probability is violated, life is misrepresented, and language is depraved. But love is only one of many passions; and as it has no great influence upon the sum of life, it has little operation in the dramas of a poet who caught his ideas from the living world and exhibited only what he saw before him. He knew that any other passion, as[1] it was regular or exorbitant,[2] was a cause of happiness or calamity.

Characters thus ample and general were not easily discriminated and preserved, yet perhaps no poet ever kept his personages more distinct from each other. I will not say, with Pope, that every speech may be assigned to the proper speaker, because many speeches there are which have nothing characteristical; but, perhaps, though some may be equally adapted to every person, it will be difficult to find that any can be properly transferred from the present possessor to another claimant. The choice is right when there is reason for choice.

Other dramatists can only gain attention by hyperbolical or aggravated characters, by fabulous and unexampled excellence or depravity, as the writers of barbarous romances invigorated the reader by a giant and a dwarf; and he that should form his expectations of human affairs from the play or from the tale would be equally deceived. Shakspeare has no heroes; his scenes are occupied only by men, who act and speak as the reader thinks that he should himself have spoken or acted on the same occasion; even where the agency is supernatural, the dialogue is level with life. Other writers disguise the most natural passions and most frequent incidents, so that he who contemplates them in the book will not know them in the world. Shakspeare approximates the remote and familiarizes the wonderful; the event which he represents will not happen, but if it were possible its effects would probably be such as he has assigned; and it may be said that he has not only shown human nature as it acts in real exigencies but as it would be found in trials to which it cannot be exposed.

This, therefore, is the praise of Shakspeare, that his drama is the mirror of life; that he who has mazed his imagination in following the phantoms which other writers raise up before him may here be cured of his delirious ecstasies by reading human sentiments in human language, by scenes from which a hermit may estimate the transactions of the world and a confessor predict the progress of the passions.

His adherence to general nature has exposed him to the censure of critics who form their judgments upon narrower principles. Dennis and Rymer think his *Romans* not sufficiently *Roman*,[1] and Voltaire censures his kings as not completely royal.[2] Dennis is offended that Menenius, a senator of Rome, should play the buffoon; and Voltaire perhaps thinks decency violated when the Danish usurper[3] is represented as a drunkard. But Shakspeare always makes nature predominate over accident; and if he preserves the essential character, is not very careful of distinctions superinduced and adventitious. His story requires Romans or kings, but he thinks only on men. He knew that Rome, like every other city, had men of all dispositions; and, wanting a buffoon, he went into the senate-house for that which the senate-house would certainly have afforded him. He was inclined to show an usurper and a murderer not only odious but despicable; he therefore added drunkenness to his other qualities, knowing that kings love wine, like other men, and that wine exerts its natural powers upon kings. These are the petty cavils of petty minds. A poet overlooks the casual distinction of country and condition, as a painter, satisfied with the figure, neglects the drapery.

. . . .

Shakspeare, with his excellences, has likewise faults, and faults sufficient to obscure and overwhelm any other merit. I shall show them in the proportion in which they appear to me, without envious malignity or superstitious veneration. No question can be more innocently discussed than a dead poet's pretensions to renown, and little regard is due to that bigotry which sets candor higher than truth.

His first defect is that to which may be imputed most of the evil in books or in men. He sacrifices virtue to convenience, and is so much more careful to please than

---

[1] according as
[2] out of its orbit; irregular

[1] See Dennis's *On the Genius and Writings of Shakespeare* (1711), and Rymer's *A Short View of Tragedy* (1693).
[2] See Voltaire's "On Tragedy," in his *Letters on the English* (1733), and the Preface to *Semiramis*, Part 3 (1748); also "Dramatic Art," in his *Philosophical Dictionary* (1764-66), and the *Letter to the French Academy* (1776).
[3] Claudius in *Hamlet*.

to instruct that he seems to write without any moral purpose. From his writings, indeed, a system of social duty may be selected, for he that thinks reasonably must think morally; but his precepts and axioms drop casually from him; he makes no just distribution of good or evil, nor is always careful to show in the virtuous a disapprobation of the wicked; he carries his persons indifferently through right and wrong, and at the close dismisses them without further care and leaves their examples to operate by chance. This fault the barbarity of his age cannot extenuate, for it is always a writer's duty to make the world better, and justice is a virtue independent of time or place.

The plots are often so loosely formed that a very slight consideration may improve them, and so carelessly pursued that he seems not always fully to comprehend his own design. He omits opportunities of instructing or delighting, which the train of his story seems to force upon him, and apparently rejects those exhibitions which would be more affecting, for the sake of those which are more easy.

It may be observed that in many of his plays the latter part is evidently neglected. When he found himself near the end of his work and in view of his reward, he shortened the labor to snatch the profit. He therefore remits his efforts where he should most vigorously exert them, and his catastrophe is improbably produced or imperfectly represented.

He has no regard to distinction of time or place, but gives to one age or nation, without scruple, the customs, institutions, and opinions of another, at the expense not only of likelihood but of possibility. These faults Pope has endeavored, with more zeal than judgment, to transfer to his imagined interpolators.[1] We need not wonder to find Hector quoting Aristotle,[2] when we see the loves of Theseus and Hippolyta combined with the gothic mythology of fairies.[3] Shakspeare, indeed, was not the only violator of chronology, for in the same age Sidney, who wanted not the advantages of learning, has, in his *Arcadia,* confounded the pastoral with the feudal times,[1] the days of innocence, quiet, and security with those of turbulence, violence, and adventure.

In his comic scenes he is seldom very successful when he engages his characters in reciprocations of smartness and contests of sarcasm: their jests are commonly gross, and their pleasantry licentious; neither his gentlemen nor his ladies have much delicacy, nor are sufficiently distinguished from his clowns by any appearance of refined manners. Whether he represented the real conversation of his time is not easy to determine: the reign of Elizabeth is commonly supposed to have been a time of stateliness, formality, and reserve; yet perhaps the relaxations of that severity were not very elegant. There must, however, have been always some modes of gayety preferable to others, and a writer ought to choose the best.

In tragedy his performance seems constantly to be worse as his labor is more. The effusions of passion which exigence forces out are for the most part striking and energetic; but whenever he solicits his invention or strains his faculties, the offspring of his throes is tumor, meanness, tediousness, and obscurity.

In narration he effects a disproportionate pomp of diction and a wearisome train of circumlocution, and tells the incident imperfectly in many words which might have been more plainly delivered in few. Narration in dramatic poetry is naturally tedious, as it is unanimated and inactive and obstructs the progress of the action; it should therefore always be rapid, and enlivened by frequent interruption. Shakspeare found it an incumbrance, and, instead of lightening it by brevity, endeavored to recommend it by dignity and splendor.

His declamations, or set speeches, are commonly cold and weak, for his power was the power of nature; when he endeavored, like other tragic writers, to catch opportunities of amplification, and, instead of inquiring what the occasion demanded, to show how much his stores of knowledge could supply, he seldom escapes without the pity or resentment of his reader.

It is incident to him to be now and then entangled with an unwieldy sentiment, which he cannot well express and will not reject; he struggles with it a while, and, if it continues stubborn, comprises it in words such as occur, and leaves it to be dis-

---

[1] See Pope's Preface to the *Works of Shakespeare* (1725).

[2] In *Troilus and Cressida,* II, 2, 163-167. Hector was the bravest of the Trojan warriors in the Trojan War, which took place at least eight centuries before the time of Aristotle (384-322 B. C.), the great Greek philosopher.

[3] In *A Midsummer Night's Dream,* Theseus, an ancient Greek hero, and Hippolyta, Queen of the Amazons, are made contemporary with Oberon, Robin Goodfellow, and other characters of English folklore.

[1] The days of ancient Greece with those of the Middle Ages.

entangled and evolved by those who have more leisure to bestow upon it.

Not that always where the language is intricate the thought is subtle, or the image always great where the line is bulky; the equality of words to things is very often neglected, and trivial sentiments and vulgar ideas disappoint the attention, to which they are recommended by sonorous epithets and swelling figures.

But the admirers of this great poet have most reason to complain when he approaches nearest to his highest excellence, and seems fully resolved to sink them in dejection and mollify them with tender emotions by the fall of greatness, the danger of innocence, or the crosses of love. What he does best he soon ceases to do. He is not soft and pathetic without some idle conceit or contemptible equivocation. He no sooner begins to move than he counteracts himself; and terror and pity, as they are rising in the mind, are checked and blasted by sudden frigidity.

A quibble is to Shakspeare what luminous vapors are to the traveller; he follows it at all adventures; it is sure to lead him out of his way, and sure to engulf him in the mire. It has some malignant power over his mind, and its fascinations are irresistible. Whatever be the dignity or profundity of his disquisition, whether he be enlarging knowledge or exalting affection, whether he be amusing attention with incidents or enchaining it in suspense, let but a quibble spring up before him and he leaves his work unfinished. A quibble is the golden apple for which he will always turn aside from his career or stoop from his elevation. A quibble, poor and barren as it is, gave him such delight that he was content to purchase it by the sacrifice of reason, propriety, and truth. A quibble was to him the fatal Cleopatra[1] for which he lost the world and was content to lose it.

It will be thought strange that in enumerating the defects of this writer I have not yet mentioned his neglect of the unities,[2] his violation of those laws which have been instituted and established by the joint authority of poets and critics.

For his other deviations from the art of writing, I resign him to critical justice without making any other demand in his favor than that which must be indulged to all human excellence—that his virtues be rated with his failings; but from the censure which this irregularity may bring upon him I shall, with due reverence to that learning which I must oppose, adventure to try how I can defend him.

His histories, being neither tragedies nor comedies, are not subject to any of their laws: nothing more is necessary to all the praise which they expect than that the changes of action be so prepared as to be understood, that the incidents be various and affecting, and the characters consistent, natural, and distinct. No other unity is intended, and therefore none is to be sought.

In his other works he has well enough preserved the unity of action. He has not, indeed, an intrigue regularly perplexed and regularly unravelled; he does not endeavor to hide his design only to discover it, for this is seldom the order of real events and Shakspeare is the poet of nature: but his plan has commonly, what Aristotle requires, a beginning, a middle, and an end; one event is concatenated[1] with another, and the conclusion follows by easy consequence. There are perhaps some incidents that might be spared, as in other poets there is much talk that only fills up time upon the stage; but the general system makes gradual advances, and the end of the play is the end of expectation.

To the unities of time and place he has shown no regard; and perhaps a nearer view of the principles on which they stand will diminish their value and withdraw from them the veneration which, from the time of Corneille,[2] they have very generally received, by discovering that they have given more trouble to the poet than pleasure to the auditor.

The necessity of observing the unities of time and place arises from the supposed necessity of making the drama credible. The critics hold it impossible that an action of months or years can be possibly believed to pass in three hours, or that the spectator can suppose himself to sit in the theatre

---

[1] The beautiful queen of Egypt for whom Antony gave up his share in the Roman government. The subtitle of Dryden's *All for Love,* which deals with the love of Antony and Cleopatra, is *The World Well Lost.*

[2] The law of dramatic unities—that in a drama the action must spring from a single controlling purpose and be represented as occurring in one place, that the supposed time within which the action develops must not exceed the actual time of performance, and that the scene must not shift from place to place.

[1] connected; linked

[2] Pierre Corneille (1606-84), a noted French dramatist, whose late plays conformed rather closely to the classical rule regarding unities of place, time, and action.

while ambassadors go and return between distant kings, while armies are levied and towns besieged, while an exile wanders and returns, or till he whom they saw courting his mistress shall lament the untimely fall of his son. The mind revolts from evident falsehood, and fiction loses its force when it departs from the resemblance of reality. From the narrow limitation of time necessarily arises the contraction of place. The spectator, who knows that he saw the first act at Alexandria, cannot suppose that he sees the next at Rome,[1] at a distance to which not the dragons of Medea[2] could in so short a time have transported him; he knows with certainty that he has not changed his place, and he knows that place cannot change itself—that what was a house cannot become a plain, that what was Thebes can never be Persepolis.[3]

Such is the triumphant language with which a critic exults over the misery of an irregular poet, and exults commonly without resistance or reply. It is time, therefore, to tell him, by the authority of Shakspeare, that he assumes, as an unquestionable principle, a position, which, while his breath is forming it into words, his understanding pronounces to be false. It is false that any representation is mistaken for reality, that any dramatic fable in its materiality was ever credible or for a single moment was ever credited.

The objection arising from the impossibility of passing the first hour at Alexandria and the next at Rome, supposes that, when the play opens, the spectator really imagines himself at Alexandria, and believes that his walk to the theatre has been a voyage to Egypt and that he lives in the days of Antony and Cleopatra. Surely he that imagines this may imagine more. He that can take the stage at one time for the palace of the Ptolemies[4] may take it in half an hour for the promontory of Actium. Delusion, if delusion be admitted, has no certain limitation; if the spectator can be once persuaded that his old acquaintances are Alexander and Cæsar, that a room illuminated with candles is the plain of Pharsalia or the bank of Granicus, he is in a state of elevation above the reach of reason or of truth, and from the heights of empyrean poetry may despise the circumscriptions of terrestrial nature. There is no reason why a mind thus wandering in ecstasy should count the clock, or why an hour should not be a century in that calenture[1] of the brain that can make the stage a field.

The truth is that the spectators are always in their senses, and know, from the first act to the last, that the stage is only a stage and that the players are only players. They come to hear a certain number of lines recited with just gesture and elegant modulation. The lines relate to some action, and an action must be in some place; but the different actions that complete a story may be in places very remote from each other; and where is the absurdity of allowing that space to represent first Athens and then Sicily, which was always known to be neither Sicily nor Athens but a modern theatre?

By supposition, as place is introduced, time may be extended; the time required by the fable elapses for the most part between the acts, for of so much of the action as is represented the real and poetical duration is the same. If in the first act preparations for war against Mithridates are represented to be made in Rome, the event of the war may without absurdity be represented, in the catastrophe, as happening in Pontus:[2] we know that there is neither war nor preparation for war; we know that we are neither in Rome nor Pontus, that neither Mithridates nor Lucullus are before us. The drama exhibits succesive imitations of successive actions; and why may not the second imitation represent an action that happened years after the first, if it be so connected with it that nothing but time can be supposed to intervene? Time is, of all modes of existence, most obsequious to the imagination; a lapse of years is as easily conceived as a passage of hours. In contemplation we easily contract the time of real actions, and therefore willingly permit it to be contracted when we only see their imitation.

It will be asked how the drama moves[3] if

---

[1] In the first act of *Antony and Cleopatra,* the scene shifts from Alexandria to Rome and then back to Alexandria.
[2] Medea was an enchantress, the daughter of the King of Colchis, an ancient province in Asia. In *Medea,* a play by Euripides (480-406 B. C.), the famous Greek tragic poet, she is borne through the air in a chariot drawn by winged dragons.
[3] Thebes was the capital of Bœotia, in Greece: Persepolis was an ancient capital of Persia. The two places were far apart.
[4] The residence of Cleopatra, the last of the royal family of the Ptolemies, in Alexandria, Egypt.

---

[1] passion ; ardor
[2] See Racine's *Mithridates* (1673) and Nathaniel Lee's *Mithridates, King of Pontus* (1678).
[3] affects the audience

it is not credited. It is credited with all the credit due to a drama. It is credited, whenever it moves, as a just picture of a real original, as representing to the auditor what he would himself feel if he were to do or suffer what is there feigned to be suffered or to be done. The reflection that strikes the heart is not that the evils before us are real evils, but that they are evils to which we ourselves may be exposed. If there be any fallacy, it is not that we fancy the players, but that we fancy ourselves, unhappy for a moment; but we rather lament the possibility than suppose the presence of misery, as a mother weeps over her babe when she remembers that death may take it from her. The delight of tragedy proceeds from our consciousness of fiction; if we thought murders and treasons real, they would please no more.

. . . .

Voltaire expresses his wonder that our author's extravagances are endured by a nation which has seen the tragedy of *Cato*. Let him be answered that Addison speaks the language of poets, and Shakspeare of men. We find in *Cato* innumerable beauties which enamor us of its author, but we see nothing that acquaints us with human sentiments or human actions; we place it with the fairest and the noblest progeny which judgment propagates by conjunction with learning, but *Othello* is the vigorous and vivacious offspring of observation impregnated by genius. *Cato* affords a splendid exhibition of artificial and fictitious manners, and delivers just and noble sentiments, in diction easy, elevated, and harmonious, but its hopes and fears communicate no vibration to the heart; the composition refers us only to the writer; we pronounce the name of *Cato*, but we think on Addison.

The work of a correct and regular writer is a garden accurately formed and diligently planted, varied with shades, and scented with flowers; the composition of Shakspeare is a forest, in which oaks extend their branches, and pines tower in the air, interspersed sometimes with weeds and brambles, and sometimes giving shelter to myrtles and to roses; filling the eye with awful pomp, and gratifying the mind with endless diversity. Other poets display cabinets of precious rarities, minutely finished, wrought into shape, and polished into brightness. Shakspeare opens a mine which contains gold and diamonds in unexhaustible plenty, though clouded by incrustations,

debased by impurities, and mingled with a mass of meaner materials.

. . . .

THE LIVES OF THE ENGLISH POETS
1777-80   1779-81
From POPE

Of composition there are different methods. Some employ at once memory and invention, and, with little intermediate use of the pen, form and polish large masses by continued meditation, and write their productions only when, in their own opinion, they have completed them. It is related of Virgil that his custom was to pour out a great number of verses in the morning, and pass the day in retrenching exuberances, and correcting inaccuracies. The method of Pope, as may be collected from his translation,[1] was to write his first thoughts in his first words, and gradually to amplify, decorate, rectify, and refine them.

With such faculties, and such dispositions,[2] he excelled every other writer in poetical prudence: he wrote in such a manner as might expose him to few hazards. He used almost always the same fabric of verse;[3] and, indeed, by those few essays which he made of any other, he did not enlarge his reputation. Of this uniformity the certain consequence was readiness and dexterity. By perpetual practice, language had, in his mind, a systematical arrangement; having always the same use for words, he had words so selected and combined as to be ready at his call. This increase of facility he confessed himself to have perceived in the progress of his translation.

But what was yet of more importance, his effusions were always voluntary, and his subjects chosen by himself. His independence secured him from drudging at a task, and laboring upon a barren topic. He never exchanged praise for money,[4] nor opened a shop of condolence or congratulation. His poems, therefore, were scarcely ever temporary. He suffered coronations and royal

---

[1] Pope translated the *Iliad* and the *Odyssey*, and wrote imitations or translations of Horace and of several English poets, notably Chaucer.
[2] Eighteenth century writers frequently used the plural where we use the singular.
[3] That is, the heroic couplet.
[4] According to Warburton, Pope is said to have been offered a large sum of money by the Duchess of Marlborough to write a good character of her husband, but absolutely refused it. See J. Spence's *Anecdotes, Observations, and Characters, of Books and Men, Collected from the Conversation of Mr. Pope and Other Eminent Persons of His Time* (1820).

marriages to pass without a song; and derived no opportunities from recent events, nor any popularity from the accidental disposition of his readers. He never was reduced to the necessity of soliciting the sun to shine upon a birthday, of calling the graces and virtues to attend a wedding, or of saying what multitudes have said before him. When he could produce nothing new, he was at liberty to be silent.

His publications were for the same reason never hasty. He is said to have sent nothing to the press till it had lain two years under his inspection; it is at least certain that he ventured nothing without nice examination. He suffered the tumult of imagination to subside, and the novelties of invention to grow familiar. He knew that the mind is always enamored of its own productions, and did not trust his first fondness. He consulted his friends, and listened with great willingness to criticism; and what was of more importance, he consulted himself, and let nothing pass against his own judgment.

He professed to have learned his poetry from Dryden, whom, whenever an opportunity was presented, he praised through his whole life with unvaried liberality; and perhaps his character may receive some illustration if he be compared with his master.

Integrity of understanding and nicety of discernment were allotted in a less proportion to Dryden than to Pope. The rectitude of Dryden's mind was sufficiently shown by the dismission of his poetical prejudices,[1] and the rejection of unnatural thoughts and rugged numbers. But Dryden never desired to apply all the judgment that he had. He wrote, and professed to write, merely for the people; and when he pleased others, he contented himself. He spent no time in struggles to rouse latent powers; he never attempted to make that better which was already good, nor often to mend what he must have known to be faulty. He wrote, as he tells us, with very little consideration; when occasion or necessity called upon him, he poured out what the present moment happened to supply, and, when once it had passed the press, ejected it from his mind; for when he had no pecuniary interest, he had no further solicitude.

Pope was not content to satisfy, he desired to excel; and therefore always endeavored to do his best; he did not court the candor,[1] but dared the judgment, of his reader, and expecting no indulgence from others, he showed none to himself. He examined lines and words with minute and punctilious observations, and retouched every part with indefatigable diligence till he had left nothing to be forgiven.

For this reason he kept his pieces very long in his hands, while he considered and reconsidered them. The only poems which can be supposed to have been written with such regard to the times as might hasten their publication, were the two satires of *Thirty-eight*,[2] of which Dodsley told me that they were brought to him by the author that they might be fairly copied. "Almost every line," he said, "was then written twice over; I gave him a clean transcript, which he sent some time afterwards to me for the press, with almost every line written twice over a second time."

His declaration that his care for his works ceased at their publication was not strictly true. His parental attention never abandoned them; what he found amiss in the first edition, he silently corrected in those that followed. He appears to have revised the *Iliad*, and freed it from some of its imperfections; and the *Essay on Criticism* received many improvements after its first appearance. It will seldom be found that he altered without adding clearness, elegance, or vigor. Pope had perhaps the judgment of Dryden; but Dryden certainly wanted the diligence of Pope.

In acquired knowledge, the superiority must be allowed to Dryden, whose education was more scholastic, and who, before he became an author, had been allowed more time for study, with better means of information. His mind has a larger range, and he collects his images and illustrations from a more extensive circumference of science. Dryden knew more of man in his general nature, and Pope in his local manners. The notions of Dryden were formed by comprehensive speculation; and those of Pope by minute attention. There is more dignity in the knowledge of Dryden, and more certainty in that of Pope.

Poetry was not the sole praise of either, for both excelled likewise in prose; but Pope did not borrow his prose from his predecessor. The style of Dryden is capricious and varied; that of Pope is cautious and uniform. Dryden observes the motions

---

[1] indulgence; kindness

[2] Now known as *Epilogue to the Satires*, but first entitled *One Thousand Seven Hundred and Thirty-Eight*, from the year of publication.

---

[1] Dryden finally abandoned the heroic couplet for blank verse.

of his own mind; Pope constrains his mind to his own rules of composition. Dryden is sometimes vehement and rapid; Pope is always smooth, uniform, and gentle. Dryden's page is a natural field, rising into inequalities, and diversified by the varied exuberance of abundant vegetation; Pope's is a velvet lawn, shaven by the scythe, and levelled by the roller.

Of genius, that power which constitutes a poet; that quality without which judgment is cold, and knowledge is inert; that energy which collects, combines, amplifies, and animates; the superiority must, with some hesitation, be allowed to Dryden. It is not to be inferred that of this poetical vigor Pope had only a little because Dryden had more, for every other writer since Milton must give place to Pope; and even of Dryden it must be said that, if he has brighter paragraphs, he has not better poems. Dryden's performances were always hasty, either excited by some external occasion, or extorted by domestic necessity; he composed without consideration, and published without correction. What his mind could supply at call, or gather in one excursion, was all that he sought, and all that he gave. The dilatory caution of Pope enabled him to condense his sentiments, to multiply his images, and to accumulate all that study might produce, or chance might supply. If the flights of Dryden therefore are higher, Pope continues longer on the wing. If of Dryden's fire the blaze is brighter, of Pope's the heat is more regular and constant. Dryden often surpasses expectation, and Pope never falls below it. Dryden is read with frequent astonishment, and Pope with perpetual delight.

This parallel will, I hope, when it is well considered, be found just; and if the reader should suspect me, as I suspect myself, of some partial fondness for the memory of Dryden, let him not too hastily condemn me; for meditation and inquiry may, perhaps, show him the reasonableness of my determination.

. . . .

Edmund Burke 1729-1797

From REFLECTIONS ON THE REVOLUTION IN FRANCE
1790   1790

. . . .

On the forenoon of the fourth of November last, Doctor Richard Price, a Non-Conforming minister of eminence, preached at the Dissenting meeting-house of the Old Jewry,[1] to his club or society,[2] a very extraordinary miscellaneous sermon, in which there are some good moral and religious sentiments, and not ill expressed, mixed up in a sort of porridge of various political opinions and reflections; but the Revolution in France is the grand ingredient in the caldron.[3] I consider the address[4] transmitted by the Revolution Society to the National Assembly, through Earl Stanhope,[5] as originating in the principles of the sermon and as a corollary from them. It was moved by the preacher of that discourse. It was passed by those who came reeking from the effect of the sermon, without any censure or qualification, expressed or implied. If, however, any of the gentlemen concerned shall wish to separate the sermon from the revolution, they know how to acknowledge the one and to disavow the other. They may do it: I cannot.

For my part, I looked on that sermon as the public declaration of a man much connected with literary caballers and intriguing philosophers, with political theologians and theological politicians, both at home and abroad. I know they set him up as a sort of oracle; because, with the best intentions in the world, he naturally *philippizes*,[6] and chants his prophetic song in exact unison with their designs.

That sermon is in a strain which I believe has not been heard in this kingdom, in any of the pulpits which are tolerated or encouraged in it, since the year 1648, when a predecessor of Dr. Price, the Reverend Hugh Peters, made the vault of the king's own chapel at St. James's ring with the honor and privilege of the saints,[7] who, with the "high praises of God in their mouths and a *two*-edged sword in their hands, were to execute judgment on the heathen, and punishments upon the *people*, to bind their *kings* with chains and their *nobles* with fetters of iron."[8] Few harangues from the pulpit, except in the days

[1] A street in the center of London, so named from a synagogue which formerly stood there.
[2] The Revolution Society formed in commemoration of the English Revolution of 1688. It sympathized with the French Revolution.
[3] See *Macbeth*, IV, 1, 34.
[4] An address of sympathy to the National Assembly of France.
[5] Charles Stanhope, third Earl Stanhope (1753-1816), was chairman of the Revolution Society.
[6] That is, speaks as the mouthpiece of the politicians. Because the priestess at Delphi gave oracles favorable to Philip of Macedon (382-336 B. C.), who was invading Greece, Demosthenes accused her of "philippizing."
[7] The Puritans. They executed Charles I in 1649.
[8] *Psalms*, 149:6-8.

of your League[1] in France or in the days
of our Solemn League and Covenant[2] in
England, have ever breathed less of the
spirit of moderation than this lecture in the
Old Jewry. Supposing, however, that something like moderation were visible in this
political sermon, yet politics and the pulpit
are terms that have little agreement. No
sound ought to be heard in the Church but
the healing voice of Christian charity. The
cause of civil liberty and civil government
gains as little as that of religion by this
confusion of duties. Those who quit their
proper character, to assume what does not
belong to them, are, for the greater part,
ignorant both of the character they leave
and of the character they assume. Wholly
unacquainted with the world in which they
are so fond of meddling, and inexperienced
in all its affairs on which they pronounce
with so much confidence, they have nothing
of politics but the passions they excite.
Surely the Church is a place where one
day's truce ought to be allowed to the dis-
sensions and animosities of mankind.

.   .   .   .

Before I read that sermon, I really
thought I had lived in a free country; and it
was an error I cherished, because it gave me
a greater liking to the country I lived in. I
was, indeed, aware that a jealous, ever-wak-
ing vigilance, to guard the treasure of our
liberty, not only from invasion, but from
decay and corruption, was our best wisdom
and our first duty. However, I considered
that treasure rather as a possession to be
secured than as a prize to be contended for.
I did not discern how the present time came
to be so very favorable to all *exertions*[3] in
the cause of freedom. The present time
differs from any other only by the circumstance of what is doing in France. If the
example of that nation is to have an influence on this, I can easily conceive why
some of their proceedings which have an
unpleasant aspect, and are not quite reconcilable to humanity, generosity, good faith,
and justice, are palliated with so much milky

good-nature towards the actors, and borne
with so much heroic fortitude towards the
sufferers. It is certainly not prudent to dis-
credit the authority of an example we mean
to follow. But allowing this, we are led to a
very natural question:—What is that cause
of liberty, and what are those exertions in
its favor, to which the example of France
is so singularly auspicious? Is our monarchy to be annihilated, with all the laws,
all the tribunals, and all the ancient corporations of the kingdom? Is every landmark of the country to be done away in
favor of a geometrical and arithmetical constitution?[1] Is the House of Lords to be
voted useless? Is Episcopacy to be abolished? Are the Church lands to be sold
to Jews and jobbers,[2] or given to bribe new-
invented municipal republics[3] into a participation in sacrilege? Are all the taxes to be
voted grievances, and the revenue reduced
to a patriotic contribution or patriotic
presents? Are silver shoe-buckles to be
substituted in the place of the land-tax and
the malt-tax, for the support of the naval
strength of this kingdom? Are all orders,
ranks, and distinctions to be confounded,
that out of universal anarchy, joined to
national bankruptcy, three or four thousand democracies[4] should be formed into
eighty-three, and that they may all, by some
sort of unknown attractive power, be organized into one? For this end is the army to
be seduced from its discipline and its
fidelity, first by every kind of debauchery,
and then by the terrible precedent of a
donative[5] in the increase of pay? Are the
curates to be seduced from their bishops by
holding out to them the delusive hope of a
dole out of the spoils of their own order?
Are the citizens of London to be drawn
from their allegiance by feeding them at
the expense of their fellow-subjects? Is a
compulsory paper currency to be substituted
in the place of the legal coin of this kingdom? Is what remains of the plundered
stock of public revenue to be employed in
the wild project of maintaining two armies
to watch over and to fight with each other?
If these are the ends and means of the

---

[1] The Holy League (1576-93), formed by the
Roman Catholics of France to prevent the succession of Henry of Navarre, to suppress the
Huguenot party, and to enthrone the Catholic
house of Guise. The *Reflections* were published
in the form of a letter to Mr. Dupont, a young
gentleman of Paris.
[2] An agreement (1643) between the reform parties
of England and Scotland in support of Pres-
byterianism and the rights of Parliament.
[3] Dr. Price had asked his hearers to consider "the
favorableness of the present times to all exertions in the cause of liberty."

[1] The National Assembly abolished the old provinces of France, and divided the country into
eighty-three departments.
[2] brokers; speculators (The National Assembly of
France decreed that church property could be
confiscated for the uses of the state.)
[3] That is, city states, or republics.
[4] That is, English municipalities. Burke shared
with others the opinion that France would
break up into a number of independent republics.
[5] gift; present

Revolution Society, I admit that they are well assorted; and France may furnish them for both with precedents in point.

I see that your example is held out to shame us. I know that we are supposed a dull, sluggish race, rendered passive by finding our situation tolerable, and prevented by a mediocrity of freedom from ever attaining to its full perfection. Your leaders in France began by affecting to admire, almost to adore, the British Constitution; but as they advanced, they came to look upon it with a sovereign contempt. The friends of your National Assembly amongst us have full as mean an opinion of what was formerly thought the glory of their country. The Revolution Society has discovered that the English nation is not free. They are convinced that the inequality in our representation[1] is a "defect in our Constitution *so gross and palpable* as to make it excellent chiefly in *form and theory*,"[2]—that a representation in the legislature of a kingdom is not only the basis of all constitutional liberty in it, but of *"all legitimate government;* that without it a *government* is nothing but an *usurpation"; —that, "when the representation is partial, the kingdom possesses liberty only partially;* and if extremely partial, it gives only a *semblance;* and if not only extremely partial, but corruptly chosen, it becomes a *nuisance."* Dr. Price considers this inadequacy of representation as our *fundamental grievance;* and though, as to the corruption of this semblance of representation, he hopes it is not yet arrived to its full perfection of depravity, he fears that "nothing will be done towards gaining for us this *essential blessing,* until some *great abuse of power* again provokes our resentment, or some *great calamity* again alarms our fears, or perhaps till the acquisition of a *pure and equal representation by other countries,* whilst we are *mocked* with *the shadow,* kindles our shame." To this he subjoins a note in these words:—"A representation chosen chiefly by the Treasury,[3] and a *few* thousands of the *dregs* of the people, who are generally paid for their votes."

You will smile here at the consistency of those democratists who, when they are not on their guard, treat the humbler part of the community with the greatest contempt, whilst, at the same time, they pretend to make them the depositories of all power. It would require a long discourse to point out to you the many fallacies that lurk in the generality and equivocal nature of the terms "inadequate representation." I shall only say here, in justice to that old-fashioned Constitution under which we have long prospered, that our representation has been found perfectly adequate to all the purposes for which a representation of the people can be desired or devised. I defy the enemies of our Constitution to show the contrary. To detail the particulars in which it is found so well to promote its ends would demand a treatise on our practical Constitution. I state here the doctrine of the revolutionists, only that you and others may see what an opinion these gentlemen entertain of the Constitution of their country, and why they seem to think that some great abuse of power, or some great calamity, as giving a chance for the blessing of a Constitution according to their ideas, would be much palliated to their feelings; you see *why they* are so much enamored of your fair and equal representation, which being once obtained, the same effects might follow. You see they consider our House of Commons, as only "a semblance," "a form," "a theory," "a shadow," "a mockery," perhaps "a nuisance."

These gentlemen value themselves on being systematic, and not without reason. They must therefore look on this gross and palpable defect of representation, this fundamental grievance, (so they call it) as a thing not only vicious in itself, but as rendering our whole government absolutely *illegitimate,* and not at all better than a downright *usurpation.* Another revolution, to get rid of this illegitimate and usurped government, would of course be perfectly justifiable, if not absolutely necessary. Indeed, their principle, if you observe it with any attention, goes much further than to an alteration in the election of the House of Commons; for, if popular representation, or choice, is necessary to the *legitimacy* of all government, the House of Lords is, at one stroke, bastardized and corrupted in blood. That House is no representative of the people at all, even in "semblance" or in "form." The case of the crown is altogether as bad. In vain the crown may endeavor to screen itself against these gen-

[1] Some boroughs were not represented in Parliament.
[2] Price, *Discourse on the Love of our Country,* Nov. 4, 1789, 3rd edition, p. 39. The following quotations are from the same source.
[3] The Treasury Board, consisting of five or more Lords of the Treasury, including the Prime Minister and the Chancellor of the Exchequer.

tlemen by the authority of the establishment made on the Revolution.[1] The Revolution, which is resorted to for a title, on their system, wants a title itself. The Revolution is built, according to their theory, upon a basis not more solid than our present formalities, as it was made by a House of Lords not representing anyone but themselves, and by a House of Commons exactly such as the present, that is, as they term it, by a mere "shadow and mockery" of representation.

Something they must destroy, or they seem to themselves to exist for no purpose. One set is for destroying the civil power through the ecclesiastical; another for demolishing the ecclesiastic through the civil. They are aware that the worst consequences might happen to the public in accomplishing this double ruin of Church and State; but they are so heated with their theories that they give more than hints that this ruin, with all the mischiefs that must lead to it and attend it, and which to themselves appear quite certain, would not be unacceptable to them, or very remote from their wishes. A man amongst them of great authority, and certainly of great talents, speaking of a supposed alliance between Church and State, says, "Perhaps *we must wait for the fall of the civil powers*, before this most unnatural alliance be broken. Calamitous, no doubt, will that time be. But what convulsion in the political world ought to be a subject of lamentation, if it be attended with so desirable an effect?" You see with what a steady eye these gentlemen are prepared to view the greatest calamities which can befall their country!

It is no wonder, therefore, that, with these ideas of everything in their Constitution and government at home, either in Church or State, as illegitimate and usurped, or at best as a vain mockery, they look abroad with an eager and passionate enthusiasm. Whilst they are possessed by these notions, it is vain to talk to them of the practice of their ancestors, the fundamental laws of their country, the fixed form of a Constitution whose merits are confirmed by the solid test of long experience and an increasing public strength and national prosperity. They despise experience as the wisdom of unlettered men; and as for the rest, they have wrought under ground a mine

that will blow up, at one grand explosion, all examples of antiquity, all precedents, charters, and acts of Parliament. They have "the rights of men." Against these there can be no prescription; against these no argument is binding; these admit no temperament and no compromise; anything withheld from their full demand is so much of fraud and injustice. Against these their rights of men let no government look for security in the length of its continuance, or in the justice and lenity of its administration. The objections of these speculatists, if its forms do not quadrate[1] with their theories, are as valid against such an old and beneficent government as against the most violent tyranny or the greenest usurpation. They are always at issue with governments, not on a question of abuse, but a question of competency and a question of title. I have nothing to say to the clumsy subtilty of their political metaphysics. Let them be their amusement in the schools.

> *Illa se jactet in aula*
> Æolus, et clauso, ventorum carcere
> regnet.[2]

But let them not break prison to burst like a Levanter,[3] to sweep the earth with their hurricane, and to break up the fountains of the great deep to overwhelm us!

Far am I from denying in theory, full as far is my heart from withholding in practice (if I were of power to give or to withhold), the *real* rights of men. In denying their false claims of right, I do not mean to injure those which are real, and are such as their pretended rights would totally destroy. If civil society be made for the advantage of man, all the advantages for which it is made become his right. It is an institution of beneficence; and law itself is only beneficence acting by a rule. Men have a right to live by that rule; they have a right to do justice, as between their fellows, whether their fellows are in public function or in ordinary occupation. They have a right to the fruits of their industry; and to the means of making their industry fruitful. They have a right to the acquisitions of their parents; to the nourishment and improvement of their offspring; to instruction in life, and to consolation in

---

[1] At the time of the Revolution of 1688, William and Mary were appointed joint sovereigns by Parliament.

[1] square; agree; correspond
[2] Let Æolus pride himself in that court, and let him reign in the closed prison of winds (*Æneid*, 1, 140-41).
[3] A strong easterly wind peculiar to the Mediterranean.

death. Whatever each man can separately do, without trespassing upon others, he has a right to do for himself; and he has a right to a fair portion of all which society, with all its combinations of skill and force, can do in his favor. In this partnership all men have equal rights; but not to equal things. He that has but five shillings in the partnership has as good a right to it as he that has five hundred pounds has to his larger proportion; but he has not a right to an equal dividend in the product of the joint stock. And as to the share of power, authority, and direction which each individual ought to have in the management of the state, that I must deny to be amongst the direct original rights of man in civil society; for I have in my contemplation the civil social man,[1] and no other. It is a thing to be settled by convention.

If civil society be the offspring of convention, that convention must be its law. That convention must limit and modify all the descriptions of constitution which are formed under it. Every sort of legislative, judicial, or executory power are its creatures. They can have no being in any other state of things; and how can any man claim, under the conventions of civil society, rights which do not so much as suppose its existence,—rights which are absolutely repugnant to it? One of the first motives to civil society, and which becomes one of its fundamental rules, is, *that no man should be judge of his own cause.* By this each person has at once divested himself of the first fundamental right of uncovenanted man, that is, to judge for himself, and to assert his own cause. He abdicates all right to be his own governor. He inclusively, in a great measure, abandons the right of self-defence, the first law of nature. Men cannot enjoy the rights of an uncivil and of a civil state together. That he may obtain justice, he gives up his right of determining what it is in points the most essential to him. That he may secure some liberty, he makes a surrender in trust of the whole of it.

Government is not made in virtue of natural rights, which may and do exist in total independence of it,—and exist in much greater clearness, and in a much greater degree of abstract perfection; but their abstract perfection is their practical defect. By having a right to everything they want

everything. Government is a contrivance of human wisdom to provide for human *wants.* Men have a right that these wants should be provided for by this wisdom. Among these wants is to be reckoned the want, out of civil society, of a sufficient restraint upon their passions. Society requires not only that the passions of individuals should be subjected, but that even in the mass and body, as well as in the individuals, the inclinations of men should frequently be thwarted, their will controlled, and their passions brought into subjection. This can only be done *by a power out of themselves,* and not, in the exercise of its function, subject to that will and to those passions which it is its office to bridle and subdue. In this sense the restraints on men, as well as their liberties, are to be reckoned among their rights. But as the liberties and the restrictions vary with times and circumstances, and admit of infinite modifications, they cannot be settled upon any abstract rule; and nothing is so foolish as to discuss them upon that principle.

The moment you abate anything from the full rights of men, each to govern himself, and suffer any artificial, positive limitation upon those rights, from that moment the whole organization of government becomes a consideration of convenience. This it is which makes the constitution of a state, and the due distribution of its powers, a matter of the most delicate and complicated skill. It requires a deep knowledge of human nature and human necessities, and of the things which facilitate or obstruct the various ends, which are to be pursued by the mechanism of civil institutions. The state is to have recruits to its strength, and remedies to its distempers. What is the use of discussing a man's abstract right to food or medicine? The question is upon the method of procuring and administering them. In that deliberation I shall always advise to call in the aid of the farmer and the physician, rather than the professor of metaphysics.

The science of constructing a commonwealth, or renovating it, or reforming it, is, like every other experimental science, not to be taught *a priori.* Nor is it a short experience that can instruct us in that practical science; because the real effects of moral causes are not always immediate; but that which in the first instance is prejudicial may be excellent in its remoter operation, and its excellence may arise even from

---

[1] As distinguished from man in his aboriginal state, before the existence of society.

the ill effects it produces in the beginning. The reverse also happens; and very plausible schemes, with very pleasing commencements, have often shameful and lamentable conclusions. In states there are often some obscure and almost latent causes, things which appear at first view of little moment, on which a very great part of its prosperity or adversity may most essentially depend. The science of government being therefore so practical in itself, and intended for such practical purposes, a matter which requires experience, and even more experience than any person can gain in his whole life, however sagacious and observing he may be, it is with infinite caution that any man ought to venture upon pulling down an edifice, which has answered in any tolerable degree for ages the common purposes of society, or on building it up again, without having models and patterns of approved utility before his eyes.

These metaphysic rights entering into common life, like rays of light which pierce into a dense medium, are, by the laws of nature, refracted from their straight line. Indeed, in the gross and complicated mass of human passions and concerns, the primitive rights of men undergo such a variety of refractions and reflections that it becomes absurd to talk of them as if they continued in the simplicity of their original direction. The nature of man is intricate; the objects of society are of the greatest possible complexity: and therefore no simple disposition or direction of power can be suitable either to man's nature, or to the quality of his affairs. When I hear the simplicity of contrivance aimed at and boasted of in any new political constitutions, I am at no loss to decide that the artificers are grossly ignorant of their trade, or totally negligent of their duty. The simple governments are fundamentally defective, to say no worse of them. If you were to contemplate society in but one point of view, all the simple modes of polity[1] are infinitely captivating. In effect each would answer its single end much more perfectly than the more complex is able to attain all its complex purposes. But it is better that the whole should be imperfectly and anomalously answered than that, while some parts are provided for with great exactness, others might be totally neglected, or perhaps materially injured, by the over-care of a favorite member.

The pretended rights of these theorists are all extremes; and in proportion as they are metaphysically true, they are morally and politically false. The rights of men are in a sort of *middle,* incapable of definition, but not impossible to be discerned. The rights of men in governments are their advantages; and these are often in balances between differences of good,—in compromises sometimes between good and evil, and sometimes between evil and evil. Political reason is a computing principle: adding, subtracting, multiplying, and dividing, morally and not metaphysically, or mathematically, true moral denominations.

By these theorists the right of the people is almost always sophistically confounded with their power. The body of the community, whenever it can come to act, can meet with no effectual resistance; but till power and right are the same, the whole body of them has no right inconsistent with virtue, and the first of all virtues, prudence. Men have no right to what is not reasonable, and to what is not for their benefit; for though a pleasant writer said, *"Liceat perire poetis,"*[1] when one of them, in cold blood, is said to have leaped into the flames of a volcanic revolution, *"ardentem frigidus Ætnam insiluit,"*[2] I consider such a frolic rather as an unjustifiable poetic license than as one of the franchises of Parnassus; and whether he were poet, or divine, or politician, that chose to exercise this kind of right, I think that more wise, because more charitable, thoughts would urge me rather to save the man than to preserve his brazen slippers as the monuments of his folly.

The kind of anniversary sermons to which a great part of what I write refers, if men are not shamed out of their present course, in commemorating the fact, will cheat many out of the principles and deprive them of the benefits of the Revolution they commemorate. I confess to you, Sir, I never liked this continual talk of resistance and revolution, or the practice of making the extreme medicine of the Constitution its daily bread. It renders the habit of society dangerously valetudinary,[3] it is taking periodical doses of mercury sublimate, and

---

[1] government

[1] Poets have the right to die.
[2] In cold blood he leaped into glowing Ætna. Empedocles, a Greek philosopher (fifth century B. C.), is said to have died thus. A slipper, cast out in an eruption, was proof of his act.
[3] sickly; infirm

swallowing down repeated provocatives of cantharides[1] to our love of liberty.

This distemper of remedy, grown habitual, relaxes and wears out, by a vulgar and prostituted use, the spring of that spirit which is to be exerted on great occasions. It was in the most patient period of Roman servitude[2] that themes of tyrannicide made the ordinary exercise of boys at school,— *cum perimit sævos classis numerosa tyrannos.*[3] In the ordinary state of things, it produces in a country like ours the worst effects, even on the cause of that liberty which it abuses with the dissoluteness of an extravagant speculation. Almost all the high-bred republicans of my time have, after a short space, become the most decided, thorough-paced courtiers; they soon left the business of a tedious, moderate, but practical resistance, to those of us whom, in the pride and intoxication of their theories, they have slighted as not much better than Tories. Hypocrisy, of course, delights in the most sublime speculations; for, never intending to go beyond speculation, it costs nothing to have it magnificent. But even in cases where rather levity than fraud was to be suspected in these ranting speculations, the issue has been much the same. These professors, finding their extreme principles not applicable to cases which call only for a qualified, or, as I may say, civil and legal resistance, in such cases employ no resistance at all. It is with them a war or a revolution, or it is nothing. Finding their schemes of politics not adapted to the state of the world in which they live, they often come to think lightly of all public principle, and are ready, on their part, to abandon for a very trivial interest what they find of very trivial value. Some, indeed, are of more steady and persevering natures; but these are eager politicians out of Parliament, who have little to tempt them to abandon their favorite projects. They have some change in the Church or State, or both, constantly in their view. When that is the case, they are always bad citizens, and perfectly unsure connections. For, considering their speculative designs as of infinite value, and the actual arrangement of the state as of no estimation, they are, at best, indifferent about it. They see no merit in the good, and no fault in the vicious management of public affairs; they rather rejoice in the latter, as more propitious to revolution. They see no merit or demerit in any man, or any action, or any political principle, any further than as they may forward or retard their design of change; they therefore take up, one day, the most violent and stretched prerogative, and another time the wildest democratic ideas of freedom, and pass from the one to the other without any sort of regard to cause, to person, or to party.

In France you are now in the crisis of a revolution, and in the transit from one form of government to another: you cannot see that character of men exactly in the same situation in which we see it in this country. With us it is militant, with you it is triumphant; and you know how it can act, when its power is commensurate to its will. I would not be supposed to confine these observations to any description of men, or to comprehend all men of any description within them,—no, far from it! I am as incapable of that injustice as I am of keeping terms with those who profess principles of extremes, and who, under the name of religion, teach little else than wild and dangerous politics. The worst of these politics of revolution is this: they temper and harden the breast in order to prepare it for the desperate strokes which are sometimes used in extreme occasions. But as these occasions may never arrive, the mind receives a gratuitous taint; and the moral sentiments suffer not a little, when no political purpose is served by the depravation. This sort of people are so taken up with their theories about the rights of man that they have totally forgot his nature. Without opening one new avenue to the understanding, they have succeeded in stopping up those that lead to the heart. They have perverted in themselves, and in those that attend to them, all the well-placed sympathies of the human breast.

This famous sermon of the Old Jewry breathes nothing but this spirit through all the political part. Plots, massacres, assassinations, seem to some people a trivial price for obtaining a revolution. A cheap, bloodless reformation, a guiltless liberty, appear flat and vapid to their taste. There must be a great change of scene; there must be a magnificent stage effect; there must be a grand spectacle to rouse the imagination, grown torpid with the lazy enjoyment of

---

[1] A preparation of dried blister beetles.
[2] During the time of Quintilian (c. 35—95 A. D.) and Juvenal (c. 60—140 A. D.). See Friedländer's *Roman Life and Manners Under the Early Empire* (trans. by Freese), 3, pp. 14-15.
[3] When the class in large numbers slays the cruel tyrants (Juvenal, *Satires*, 7, 151).

sixty years' security, and the still unani-
mating repose of public prosperity. The
preacher found them all in the French
Revolution. This inspires a juvenile warmth
through his whole frame. His enthusiasm
kindles as he advances; and when he arrives at his peroration, it is in a full blaze.
Then viewing, from the Pisgah[1] of his pulpit, the free, moral, happy, flourishing, and
glorious state of France, as in a bird-eye
landscape of a promised land, he breaks
out into the following rapture:—

"What an eventful period is this! I am
thankful that I have lived to it; I could
almost say, *Lord, now lettest thou thy servant depart in peace, for mine eyes have
seen thy salvation.*[2]—I have lived to see a
diffusion of knowledge which has undermined superstition and error. — I have
lived to see *the rights of men* better understood than ever, and nations panting for
liberty which seemed to have lost the idea
of it.—I have lived to see *thirty millions
of people,* indignant and resolute, spurning
at slavery, and demanding liberty with an
irresistible voice; *their king led in triumph,
and an arbitrary monarch surrendering himself to his subjects.*"[3]

Before I proceed further, I have to remark that Dr. Price seems rather to over-
value the great acquisitions of light which
he has obtained and diffused in this age.
The last century appears to me to have
been quite as much enlightened. It had,
though in a different place, a triumph as
memorable as that of Dr. Price; and some
of the great preachers of that period partook of it as eagerly as he has done in the
triumph of France. On the trial of the
Reverend Hugh Peters for high treason,[4]
it was deposed that, when King Charles
was brought to London for his trial, the
Apostle of Liberty in that day conducted
the *triumph.* "I saw," says the witness, "his
Majesty in the coach with six horses, and
Peters riding before the king *triumphing.*"
Dr. Price, when he talks as if he had made
a discovery, only follows a precedent; for,
after the commencement of the king's trial,
this precursor, the same Dr. Peters, concluding a long prayer at the royal chapel
at Whitehall (he had very triumphantly
chosen his place), said, "I have prayed and

preached these twenty years; and now I
may say with old Simeon, *"Lord, now lettest thou thy servant depart in peace, for
mine eyes have seen thy salvation."* Peters
had not the fruits of his prayer; for he
neither departed so soon as he wished, nor
in peace. He became (what I heartily hope
none of his followers may be in this country) himself a sacrifice to the triumph
which he led as pontiff. They dealt at the
Restoration, perhaps, too hardly with this
poor good man. But we owe it to his memory and his sufferings, that he had as much
illumination and as much zeal, and had as
effectually undermined all *the superstition
and error* which might impede the great
business he was engaged in, as any who
follow and repeat after him in this age,
which would assume to itself an exclusive
title to the knowledge of the rights of men,
and all the glorious consequences of that
knowledge.

After this sally of the preacher of the
Old Jewry, which differs only in place and
time, but agrees perfectly with the spirit
and letter of the rapture of 1648, the Revolution Society, the fabricators of governments, the heroic band of *cashierers of
monarchs,*[1] electors of sovereigns, and leaders of kings in triumph, strutting with a
proud consciousness of the diffusion of
knowledge, of which every member had obtained so large a share in the donative,
were in haste to make a generous diffusion
of the knowledge they had thus gratuitously
received. To make this bountiful communication, they adjourned from the church
in the Old Jewry to the London Tavern,
where the same Dr. Price, in whom the
fumes of his oracular tripod were not entirely evaporated, moved and carried the
resolution, or address of congratulation,
transmitted by Lord Stanhope to the National Assembly of France.

I find a preacher of the Gospel profan-
ing the beautiful and prophetic ejaculation,
commonly called "Nunc dimittis,"[2] made on
the first presentation of our Savior in the
temple, and applying it, with an inhuman
and unnatural rapture, to the most horrid,
atrocious, and afflicting spectacle that perhaps ever was exhibited to the pity and

---

[1] The mountain, east of the Dead Sea, from which
Moses viewed the Promised Land just before
his death. See *Deuteronomy,* 34:1-4.
[2] See *Luke,* 2:25-30.
[3] See p. 1229a, 1 ff.
[4] Peters was found guilty of treason on Oct. 13,
1660, on the ground that he was an accomplice
in the death of Charles I (1625-49).

[1] Dr. Price asserted that by the principles of the
Revolution the people of England had acquired
three fundamental rights: to choose their own
governors; to cashier them for misconduct;
and to frame a government for themselves.
[2] Now lettest thou depart; the first words of the
Vulgate version of the song of Simeon (*Luke,*
2:29-32), which is used as a hymn or canticle
in many churches. See ll. 2-4 above.

indignation of mankind. This *"leading in triumph,"* a thing in its best form unmanly and irreligious, which fills our preacher with such unhallowed transports, must shock, I believe, the moral taste of every well-born mind. Several English were the stupefied and indignant spectators of that triumph. It was (unless we have been strangely deceived) a spectacle more resembling a procession of American savages entering into Onondaga after some of their murders called victories, and leading into hovels hung round with scalps their captives overpowered with the scoffs and buffets of women as ferocious as themselves, much more than it resembled the triumphal pomp of a civilized martial nation;—if a civilized nation, or any men who had a sense of generosity, were capable of a personal triumph over the fallen and afflicted.

This, my dear Sir, was not the triumph of France. I must believe that, as a nation, it overwhelmed you with shame and horror. I must believe that the National Assembly find themselves in a state of the greatest humiliation in not being able to punish the authors of this triumph or the actors in it, and that they are in a situation in which any inquiry they may make upon the subject must be destitute even of the appearance of liberty or impartiality. The apology of that assembly is found in their situation; but when we approve what they *must* bear, it is in us the degenerate choice of a vitiated mind.

With a compelled appearance of deliberation, they vote under the dominion of a stern necessity. They sit in the heart, as it were, of a foreign republic: they have their residence in a city whose constitution has emanated neither from the charter of their king nor from their legislative power. There they are surrounded by an army not raised either by the authority of their crown or by their command, and which, if they should order to dissolve itself, would instantly dissolve them. There they sit, after a gang of assassins had driven away some hundreds of the members; whilst those who held the same moderate principles, with more patience or better hope, continued every day exposed to outrageous insults and murderous threats. There a majority, sometimes real, sometimes pretended, captive itself, compels a captive king to issue as royal edicts, at third hand, the polluted nonsense of their most licentious and giddy coffee-houses. It is notorious that all their measures are decided before they are debated. It is beyond doubt that, under the terror of the bayonet, and the lamp-post, and the torch to their houses, they are obliged to adopt all the crude and desperate measures suggested by clubs composed of a monstrous medley of all conditions, tongues, and nations. Among these are found persons in comparison of whom Catiline would be thought scrupulous, and Cethegus a man of sobriety and moderation. Nor is it in these clubs alone that the public measures are deformed into monsters. They undergo a previous distortion in academies,[1] intended as so many seminaries for these clubs, which are set up in all the places of public resort. In these meetings of all sorts, every counsel, in proportion as it is daring and violent and perfidious, is taken for the mark of superior genius. Humanity and compassion are ridiculed as the fruits of superstition and ignorance. Tenderness to individuals is considered as treason to the public. Liberty is always to be estimated perfect as property is rendered insecure. Amidst assassination, massacre, and confiscation, perpetrated or meditated, they are forming plans for the good order of future society. Embracing in their arms the carcasses of base criminals, and promoting their relations on the title of their offences, they drive hundreds of virtuous persons to the same end, by forcing them to subsist by beggary or by crime.

The Assembly, their organ, acts before them the farce of deliberation with as little decency as liberty. They act like the comedians of a fair, before a riotous audience; they act amidst the tumultuous cries of a mixed mob of ferocious men, and of women lost to shame, who, according to their insolent fancies, direct, control, applaud, explode[2] them, and sometimes mix and take their seats amongst them, — domineering over them with a strange mixture of servile petulance and proud, presumptuous authority. As they have inverted order in all things, the gallery[3] is in the place of the house. This Assembly, which overthrows kings and kingdoms, has not even the physiognomy and aspect of a grave legislative body,—*nec color imperii, nec frons erat ulla senatus.*[4] They have a power given to them, like that of the Evil Principle, to

---

[1] learned societies
[2] In the obsolete sense: to drive out by noisy disapprobation.
[3] During legislative sessions the galleries are sometimes occupied by spectators.
[4] There was neither aspect of empire nor semblance of senate.

subvert and destroy,—but none to construct, except such machines as may be fitted for further subversion and further destruction.

Who is it that admires, and from the heart is attached to national representative assemblies, but must turn with horror and disgust from such a profane burlesque and abominable perversion of that sacred institute? Lovers of monarchy, lovers of republics, must alike abhor it. The members of your Assembly must themselves groan under the tyranny of which they have all the shame, none of the direction, and little of the profit. I am sure many of the members who compose even the majority of that body must feel as I do, notwithstanding the applause of the Revolution Society. Miserable king! miserable Assembly! How must that Assembly be silently scandalized with those of their members who could call a day which seemed to blot the sun out of heaven *"un beau jour!"*[1] How must they be inwardly indignant at hearing others who thought fit to declare to them, "that the vessel of the state would fly forward in her course towards regeneration with more speed than ever," from the stiff gale of treason and murder which preceded our preacher's triumph! What must they have felt, whilst, with outward patience and inward indignation, they heard of the slaughter of innocent gentlemen in their houses, that "the blood spilled was not the most pure!" What must they have felt, when they were besieged by complaints of disorders which shook their country to its foundations, at being compelled coolly to tell the complainants that they were under the protection of the law, and that they would address the king (the captive king) to cause the laws to be enforced for their protection, when the enslaved ministers of that captive king had formally notified to them that there were neither law nor authority nor power left to protect! What must they have felt at being obliged, as a felicitation on the present new year, to request their captive king to forget the stormy period of the last, on account of the great good which *he* was likely to produce to his people,—to the complete attainment of which good they adjourned the practical demonstrations of their loyalty, assuring him of their obedience when he should no longer possess any authority to command!

This address was made with much good-nature and affection, to be sure. But among the revolutions in France must be reckoned a considerable revolution in their ideas of politeness. In England we are said to learn manners at second-hand from your side of the water, and that we dress our behavior in the frippery of France. If so, we are still in the old cut, and have not so far conformed to the new Parisian mode of good breeding as to think it quite in the most refined strain of delicate compliment (whether in condolence or congratulation) to say, to the most humiliated creature that crawls upon the earth, that great public benefits are derived from the murder of his servants, the attempted assassination of himself and of his wife, and the mortification, disgrace, and degradation that he has personally suffered. It is a topic of consolation which our ordinary of Newgate[1] would be too humane to use to a criminal at the foot of the gallows. I should have thought that the hangman of Paris, now that he is liberalized by the vote of the National Assembly, and is allowed his rank and arms in the Heralds' College of the rights of men, would be too generous, too gallant a man, too full of the sense of his new dignity, to employ that cutting consolation to any of the persons whom the *lèze-nation*[2] might bring under the administration of his *executive powers*.

A man is fallen indeed, when he is thus flattered. The anodyne[3] draught of oblivion, thus drugged, is well calculated to preserve a galling wakefulness, and to feed the living ulcer of a corroding memory. Thus to administer the opiate potion of amnesty, powdered with all the ingredients of scorn and contempt, is to hold to his lips, instead of "the balm of hurt minds,"[4] the cup of human misery full to the brim, and to force him to drink it to the dregs.

Yielding to reasons at least as forcible as those which were so delicately urged in the compliment on the new year, the king of France will probably endeavor to forget these events and that compliment. But History, who keeps a durable record of all our acts, and exercises her awful censure[5] over the proceedings of all sorts of sovereigns, will not forget either those events, or the era of this liberal refinement in the

---

[1] Beautiful day. (Oct. 6, 1789, the day on which the King and Queen of France were forcibly taken from Versailles and marched to Paris. See p. 1229a, 1 ff.)

[1] The Chaplain of Newgate prison
[2] high treason against the nation
[3] soothing
[4] *Macbeth*, II, 2, 39. See also I, 7, 11
[5] judgment

intercourse of mankind. History will record that, on the morning of the sixth of October, 1789, the king and queen of France,[1] after a day of confusion, alarm, dismay, and slaughter, lay down, under the pledged security of public faith, to indulge nature in a few hours of respite, and troubled, melancholy repose. From this sleep the queen was first startled by the voice of the sentinel at her door, who cried out to her to save herself by flight,—that this was the last proof of fidelity he could give,— that they were upon him, and he was dead. Instantly he was cut down. A band of cruel ruffians and assassins, reeking with his blood, rushed into the chamber of the queen, and pierced with a hundred strokes of bayonets and poniards the bed, from whence this persecuted woman had but just time to fly almost naked, and, through ways unknown to the murderers, had escaped to seek refuge at the feet of a king and husband not secure of his own life for a moment.

This king, to say no more of him, and this queen, and their infant children (who once would have been the pride and hope of a great and generous people), were then forced to abandon the sanctuary of the most splendid palace in the world, which they left swimming in blood, polluted by massacre, and strewed with scattered limbs and mutilated carcasses. Thence they were conducted into the capital of their kingdom. Two had been selected from the unprovoked, unresisted, promiscuous slaughter which was made of the gentlemen of birth and family who composed the king's bodyguard. These two gentlemen, with all the parade of an execution of justice, were cruelly and publicly dragged to the block, and beheaded in the great court of the palace. Their heads were stuck upon spears, and led the procession; whilst the royal captives who followed in the train were slowly moved along, amidst the horrid yells, and shrilling screams, and frantic dances, and infamous contumelies, and all the unutterable abominations of the furies of hell, in the abused shape of the vilest of women. After they had been made to taste, drop by drop, more than the bitterness of death, in the slow torture of a journey of twelve miles, protracted to six hours, they were, under a guard composed of those very soldiers who had thus conducted them through this famous triumph, lodged in one of the old palaces of Paris, now converted into a Bastile for kings.

Is this a triumph to be consecrated at altars, to be commemorated with grateful thanksgiving, to be offered to the Divine Humanity with fervent prayer and enthusiastic ejaculation?—These Theban and Thracian orgies,[1] acted in France, and applauded only in the Old Jewry, I assure you, kindle prophetic enthusiasm in the minds but of very few people in this kingdom: although a saint and apostle, who may have revelations of his own, and who has so completely vanquished all the mean superstitions of the heart, may incline to think it pious and decorous to compare it with the entrance into the world of the Prince of Peace, proclaimed in an holy temple by a venerable sage, and not long before not worse announced by the voice of angels to the quiet innocence of shepherds.

At first I was at a loss to account for this fit of unguarded transport. I knew, indeed, that the sufferings of monarchs make a delicious repast to some sort of palates. There were reflections which might serve to keep this appetite within some bounds of temperance. But when I took one circumstance into my consideration, I was obliged to confess that much allowance ought to be made for the society, and that the temptation was too strong for common discretion: I mean, the circumstance of the Io Pæan[2] of the triumph, the animating cry which called for "all the BISHOPS to be hanged on the lamp posts,"[3] might well have brought forth a burst of enthusiasm on the foreseen consequences of this happy day. I allow to so much enthusiasm some little deviation from prudence. I allow this prophet to break forth into hymns of joy and thanksgiving on an event which appears like the precursor of the Millennium, and the projected Fifth Monarchy,[4] in the destruction of all Church establishments. There was, however, (as in all human affairs there is), in the midst of this joy, something to ex-

---

[1] A reference to the secret rites and ceremonies practiced in the worship of ancient Greek and Roman deities, especially those ceremonies connected with the festival of Bacchus, which was celebrated with much extravagance and license.

[2] A song of joy or exultation. Io is a Greek and Latin exclamation of joy or triumph.

[3] This was an actual cry of the Revolutionists.

[4] The kingdom which a sect of religious fanatics during the time of Cromwell attempted to establish in England. They maintained that Christ was coming to assume authority. This kingdom was to be the fifth and last in the series of which the kingdoms of Assyria, Persia, Greece, and Rome were the preceding four.

---

[1] Louis XVI and Marie Antoinette

ercise the patience of these worthy gentlemen, and to try the long-suffering of their faith. The actual murder of the king and queen, and their child, was wanting to the other auspicious circumstances of this *"beautiful day."* The actual murder of the bishops, though called for by so many holy ejaculations, was also wanting. A group of regicide and sacrilegious slaughter was, indeed, boldly sketched, but it was only sketched. It unhappily was left unfinished, in this great history-piece of the massacre of innocents. What hardy pencil of a great master, from the school of the rights of men, will finish it, is to be seen hereafter. The age has not yet the complete benefit of that diffusion of knowledge that has undermined superstition and error; and the king of France wants another object or two to consign to oblivion, in consideration of all the good which is to arise from his own sufferings, and the patriotic crimes of an enlightened age.

Although this work of our new light and knowledge did not go to the length that in all probability it was intended it should be carried, yet I must think that such treatment of any human creatures must be shocking to any but those who are made for accomplishing revolutions. But I cannot stop here. Influenced by the inborn feelings of my nature, and not being illuminated by a single ray of this new-sprung modern light, I confess to you, Sir, that the exalted rank of the persons suffering, and particularly the sex, the beauty, and the amiable qualities of the descendant of so many kings and emperors, with the tender age of royal infants, insensible only through infancy and innocence of the cruel outrages to which their parents were exposed, instead of being a subject of exultation, adds not a little to my sensibility on that most melancholy occasion.

I hear that the august person who was the principal object of our preacher's triumph, though he supported himself, felt much on that shameful occasion. As a man, it became him to feel for his wife and his children, and the faithful guards of his person that were massacred in cold blood about him; as a prince, it became him to feel for the strange and frightful transformation of his civilized subjects, and to be more grieved for them than solicitous for himself. It derogates little from his fortitude, while it adds infinitely to the honor of his humanity. I am very sorry to say it, very sorry indeed, that such person-

ages are in a situation in which it is not unbecoming in us to praise the virtues of the great.

I hear, and I rejoice to hear, that the great lady, the other object of the triumph, has borne that day (one is interested that beings made for suffering should suffer well), and that she bears all the succeeding days, that she bears the imprisonment of her husband, and her own captivity, and the exile of her friends, and the insulting adulation of addresses, and the whole weight of her accumulated wrongs, with a serene patience, in a manner suited to her rank and race, and becoming the offspring of a sovereign distinguished for her piety and her courage;[1] that, like her, she has lofty sentiments; that she feels with the dignity of a Roman matron; that in the last extremity she will save herself from the last disgrace; and that, if she must fall, she will fall by no ignoble hand.

It is now sixteen or seventeen years since I saw the queen of France, then the Dauphiness,[2] at Versailles; and surely never lighted on this orb, which she hardly seemed to touch, a more delightful vision. I saw her just above the horizon, decorating and cheering the elevated sphere she just began to move in,—glittering like the morning-star, full of life and splendor and joy. Oh! what a revolution! and what an heart must I have, to contemplate without emotion that elevation and that fall! Little did I dream, when she added titles of veneration to those of enthusiastic, distant, respectful love, that she should ever be obliged to carry the sharp antidote against disgrace concealed in that bosom! Little did I dream that I should have lived to see such disasters fallen upon her in a nation of gallant men, in a nation of men of honor, and of cavaliers! I thought ten thousand swords must have leaped from their scabbards to avenge even a look that threatened her with insult. But the age of chivalry is gone.[3] That of sophisters, economists, and calculators has succeeded; and the glory of Europe is extinguished forever. Never, never more, shall we behold that generous loyalty to rank and sex, that proud submission, that dignified obedience, that subordination of the heart, which kept alive, even in servitude itself,

---

[1] Maria Theresa, Empress of Austria and Queen of Hungary and Bohemia (1740-80).
[2] wife of the crown prince
[3] The phrasing of the following passage is admirable, but Burke's fervent imagination carries him somewhat beyond the bounds of strict truth.

the spirit of an exalted freedom! The unbought grace of life, the cheap defence of nations, the nurse of manly sentiment and heroic enterprise, is gone! It is gone, that sensibility of principle, that chastity of honor, which felt a stain like a wound, which inspired courage whilst it mitigated ferocity, which ennobled whatever it touched, and under which vice itself lost half its evil by losing all its grossness!

This mixed system of opinion and sentiment had its origin in the ancient chivalry; and the principle, though varied in its appearance by the varying state of human affairs, subsisted and influenced through a long succession of generations, even to the time we live in. If it should ever be totally extinguished, the loss, I fear, will be great. It is this which has given its character to modern Europe. It is this which has distinguished it under all its forms of government, and distinguished it to its advantage, from the states of Asia, and possibly from those states which flourished in the most brilliant periods of the antique world. It was this, which, without confounding ranks, had produced a noble equality, and handed it down through all the gradations of social life. It was this opinion which mitigated kings into companions, and raised private men to be fellows with kings. Without force or opposition, it subdued the fierceness of pride and power; it obliged sovereigns to submit to the soft collar of social esteem, compelled stern authority to submit to elegance, and gave a domination, vanquisher of laws, to be subdued by manners.

But now all is to be changed. All the pleasing illusions which made power gentle and obedience liberal, which harmonized the different shades of life, and which by a bland assimilation incorporated into politics the sentiments which beautify and soften private society, are to be dissolved by this new conquering empire of light and reason. All the decent drapery of life is to be rudely torn off. All the superadded ideas, furnished from the wardrobe of a moral imagination, which the heart owns and the understanding ratifies, as necessary to cover the defects of our naked, shivering nature, and to raise it to dignity in our own estimation, are to be exploded as a ridiculous, absurd, and antiquated fashion.

On this scheme of things, a king is but a man, a queen is but a woman, a woman is but an animal,—and an animal not of the highest order. All homage paid to the sex in general as such, and without distinct views, is to be regarded as romance and folly. Regicide, and parricide, and sacrilege, are but fictions of superstition, corrupting jurisprudence by destroying its simplicity. The murder of a king, or a queen, or a bishop, or a father, are only common homicide,—and if the people are by any chance or in any way gainers by it, a sort of homicide much the most pardonable and into which we ought not to make too severe a scrutiny.

On the scheme of this barbarous philosophy, which is the offspring of cold hearts and muddy understandings, and which is as void of solid wisdom as it is destitute of all taste and elegance, laws are to be supported only by their own terrors, and by the concern which each individual may find in them from his own private speculations, or can spare to them from his own private interests. In the groves of *their* academy,[1] at the end of every vista, you see nothing but the gallows. Nothing is left which engages the affections on the part of the commonwealth. On the principles of this mechanic philosophy, our institutions can never be embodied, if I may use the expression, in persons,—so as to create in us love, veneration, admiration, or attachment. But that sort of reason which banishes the affections is incapable of filling their place. These public affections, combined with manners, are required sometimes as supplements, sometimes as correctives, always as aids to law. The precept given by a wise man, as well as a great critic, for the construction of poems, is equally true as to states:— *"Non satis est pulchra esse poemata, dulcia sunto."*[2] There ought to be a system of manners in every nation which a well-formed mind would be disposed to relish. To make us love our country, our country ought to be lovely.

But power, of some kind or other, will survive the shock in which manners and opinions perish; and it will find other and worse means for its support. The usurpation, which, in order to subvert ancient institutions, has destroyed ancient principles, will hold power by arts similar to those by which it has acquired it. When the old feudal and chivalrous spirit of *fealty*, which, by freeing kings from fear, freed both kings and subjects from the pre-

---

[1] A reference to the Academy, or garden, in which Plato taught.
[2] It is not enough for poems to be beautiful; they must appeal to the heart. (Horace, *Ars Poetica*, 99)

cautions of tyranny,[1] shall be extinct in the minds of men, plots and assassinations will be anticipated by preventive murder and preventive confiscation, and that long roll of grim and bloody maxims which form the political code of all power not standing on its own honor and the honor of those who are to obey it. Kings will be tyrants from policy, when subjects are rebels from principle.

When ancient opinions and rules of life are taken away, the loss cannot possibly be estimated. From that moment we have no compass to govern us, nor can we know distinctly to what port we steer. Europe, undoubtedly, taken in a mass, was in a flourishing condition the day on which your Revolution was completed. How much of that prosperous state was owing to the spirit of our old manners and opinions is not easy to say; but as such causes cannot be indifferent in their operation, we must presume that, on the whole, their operation was beneficial.

We are but too apt to consider things in the state in which we find them, without sufficiently adverting to the causes by which they have been produced, and possibly may be upheld. Nothing is more certain than that our manners, our civilization, and all the good things which are connected with manners and with civilization, have, in this European world of ours, depended for ages upon two principles, and were, indeed, the result of both combined: I mean the spirit of a gentleman, and the spirit of religion. The nobility and the clergy, the one by profession, the other by patronage, kept learning in existence, even in the midst of arms and confusions, and whilst governments were rather in their causes than formed. Learning paid back what it received to nobility and to priesthood, and paid it with usury, by enlarging their ideas, and by furnishing their minds. Happy, if they had all continued to know their indissoluble union, and their proper place! Happy, if learning, not debauched by ambition, had been satisfied to continue the instructor, and not aspired to be master! Along with its natural protectors and guardians, learning will be cast into the mire and trodden down under the hoofs of a swinish multitude.

If, as I suspect, modern letters owe more than they are always willing to own to ancient manners, so do other interests which we value full as much as they are worth. Even commerce, and trade, and manufac-

ture, the gods of our economical politicians, are themselves perhaps but creatures, are themselves but effects, which, as first causes, we choose to worship. They certainly grew under the same shade in which learning flourished. They, too, may decay with their natural protecting principles. With you, for the present at least, they all threaten to disappear together. Where trade and manufactures are wanting to a people, and the spirit of nobility and religion remains, sentiment supplies, and not always ill supplies, their place; but if commerce and the arts should be lost in an experiment to try how well a state may stand without these old fundamental principles, what sort of a thing must be a nation of gross, stupid, ferocious, and at the same time poor and sordid barbarians, destitute of religion, honor, or manly pride, possessing nothing at present, and hoping for nothing hereafter?

I wish you may not be going fast, and by the shortest cut, to that horrible and disgustful situation. Already there appears a poverty of conception, a coarseness and vulgarity, in all the proceedings of the Assembly and of all their instructors. Their liberty is not liberal. Their science is presumptuous ignorance. Their humanity is savage and brutal.

It is not clear whether in England we learned those grand and decorous principles and manners, of which considerable traces yet remain, from you, or whether you took them from us. But to you, I think we trace them best. You seem to me to be *gentis incunabula nostræ.*[1] France has always more or less influenced manners in England; and when your fountain is choked up and polluted, the stream will not run long or not run clear with us, or perhaps with any nation. This gives all Europe, in my opinion, but too close and connected a concern in what is done in France. Excuse me, therefore, if I have dwelt too long on the atrocious spectacle of the sixth of October, 1789, or have given too much scope to the reflections which have arisen in my mind on occasion of the most important of all revolutions, which may be dated from that day: I mean a revolution in sentiments, manners, and moral opinions. As things now stand, with everything respectable destroyed without us, and an attempt to destroy within us every principle of respect, one is almost forced to apologize for harboring the common feelings of men.

---

[1] As a matter of fact, the opposite of this is nearer the truth.

[1] the cradle of our race

The following material is arranged in the order in which authors and titles appear in the text. It is intended to supply information helpful to a full understanding of each author and his writings, especially in relation to the times and to the literary trends. Quotations from eminent critics interpret both the writers and their individual works. Explanatory notes supply necessary backgrounds and meaning in harmony with the best scholarship.

Anne Finch, Countess of Winchilsea

Poems, p. 1 — Bibliography, p. 1452

"In general feeling an Augustan, with an undercurrent of real love for nature. It is in her fondness for country life, her love of outdoor beauty, and her accurate descriptions of nature, that she differs from her contemporaries. In these important points, she may certainly be classed as reactionary in tendency. Her octosyllabic ode *To the Nightingale* has true lyric quality, and her short poems *The Tree* and *A Nocturnal Reverie* are notable expressions of nature-worship."—Phelps, in *The Beginnings of the English Romantic Movement* (1893).

1. THE TREE

This poem was first published by T. H. Ward in *The English Poets*, Vol. 3 (1880).

2. THE PETITION FOR AN ABSOLUTE RETREAT

The meter of this poem is that of *L'Allegro.*

59. "Josephus says that every Monday Solomon went to the House of Lebanon in an open chariot, cloath'd in a robe most dazzling white, which makes that allusion not improper, and may give us grounds to believe that the lily mention'd by our Savior (compar'd to Solomon in his glory) might really be the common white lily, altho' the commentators seem in doubt what flowers are truly meant by the lilies, as thinking the plain lily not gay enough for the comparison; whereas this garment is noted by Josephus to be wonderfully beautiful tho' only white; nor can any flower, I believe, have a greater lustre than the common white lily."—Lady Winchilsea's note.

89. "These circumstances are related by Plutarch in his *Life of Sylla.*"—Lady Winchilsea's note. The passage referred to is as follows:

"At Fidentia, also, Marcus Lucullus, one of Sylla's commanders, reposed such confidence in the forwardness of the soldiers as to dare to face fifty cohorts of the enemy with only sixteen of his own; but because many of them were unarmed, delayed the onset. As he stood thus waiting and considering with himself, a gentle gale of wind, bearing along with it from the neighboring meadows a quantity of flowers, scattered them down upon the army, on whose shields and helmets they settled and arranged themselves spontaneously so as to give the soldiers, in the eyes of the enemy, the appearance of being crowned with chaplets. Upon this, being yet further animated, they joined battle, and victoriously slaying eight thousand men, took the camp."—Sec. 27, 16-29, Dryden's translation.

For other marvels attending the campaign of Lucullus, see Plutarch's *Life of Lucullus.*

TO THE NIGHTINGALE

12-13. Cf. Shelley's *To a Skylark*, 90 (p. 730): "Our sweetest songs are those that tell of saddest thought." See also Lamb's letter to Wordsworth, quoted in notes, p. 1375a l. 49.

Thomas Parnell

Poems, p. 3 — Bibliography, p. 1439

"We do not know how it is with others, but we never think of Parnell's *Hermit* without tranquilizing and grateful feelings. Parnell was a true poet of a minor order; he saw nature for himself, though he wrote a book style; and this, and one or two other poems of his, such as the eclogue on *Health* and the *Fairy Tale*, have inclined us to believe that there is something in the very name of 'Parnell' peculiarly gentle and agreeable."—Leigh Hunt, in *A Book for a Corner* (1849).

3.   A FAIRY TALE

This poem is meant to be written "in the ancient English style," but the vocabulary is characterized only by a timid and occasional pseudo-archaism, and the spirit of the whole piece is largely false; yet the poem does contain faint echoes of medievalism. For a crisp version of the incident of the hump, see *The Legend of Knockgrafton*, printed in Yeats's *Fairy and Folk Tales of the Irish Peasantry* (1888).

5. 183-92. These lines illustrate the moralizing tag habit of the eighteenth century.

A NIGHT-PIECE ON DEATH

This poem is an important forerunner of the so-called graveyard literature, which culminates in Gray's *Elegy*. In phrasing, Parnell is a slave to his time, but he gives an individual turn to the choice of subject. Goldsmith says in his *Life of Parnell* (1770) that "the *Night-Piece on Death*, with very little amendment, might be made to surpass all those night-pieces and churchyard scenes that have since appeared."—See note on Blair's *The Grave*, p. 1237a.

Allan Ramsay

Selections, p. 7 — Bibliography, **p. 1442**

7.   MY PEGGY

This poem was first published as part of *Patie and Roger*, later made the first scene of Act I of *The Gentle Shepherd*.

8.   SWEET WILLIAM'S GHOST

This is a genuine old ballad; it was used by the German poet Bürger in his *Lenore* (1774), which was translated into English by William Taylor and thus became the basis of Sir Walter Scott's *William and Helen* (see pp. 459 and 1315b).

9.   THE GENTLE SHEPHERD

"I spoke of Allan Ramsay's *Gentle Shepherd*, in the Scottish dialect, as the best pastoral that had ever been written; not only abounding with beautiful rural imagery, and just and pleasing sentiments, but being a real picture of the manners; and I offered to teach Dr. Johnson to understand it. 'No, sir,' said he; 'I won't learn it. You shall retain your superiority by my not knowing it.' "—Boswell, in *The Life of Samuel Johnson* (1773).

Patie and Peggy are conventional names in Scottish pastoral poetry.

11.   THE EVERGREEN

This was "a collection of Scots poems, wrote by the ingenious before 1600." It was compiled to arouse interest in old English poetry. It contained popular songs and ballads, new as well as old.

William Hamilton of Bangour

Poems, p. 13 — Bibliography, p. 1426

"Amid the generally vague verbiage of his [Hamilton's] descriptions, one effort of his genius stands out in vividness of human coloring, in depth and simplicity of feeling, and even to some extent in powerful and characteristic touches of scenery. This is a poem which owes its inspiration to the Yarrow. In fact it was suggested by the older poem of *The Dowie Dens*. It breathes the soul of the place, and it is so permeated by the spirit of its history and traditions, that when all the other writings of the author have fallen into oblivion, there will still be a nook in memory and a place in men's hearts for *The Braes of Yarrow*."—Veitch, in *The History and Poetry of the Scottish Border* (1878).

13.   THE BRAES OF YARROW

Yarrow is a beautiful river in Selkirkshire, Scotland; it is celebrated in many ballads and songs. See Wordsworth's *Yarrow Unvisited* (p. 319), *Yarrow Visited* (p. 334), and *Yarrow Revisited* (p. 338). Hamilton's poem is a dialogue spoken by three persons, designated A, B, and C. A has killed the lover of the maiden C; B is a bystander. The ghastly specter of l. 103 is that of the murdered lover.

David Mallet

Poems, p. 15 — Bibliography, p. 1438

15.   WILLIAM AND MARGARET

This was one of the most popular ballads of the eighteenth century. Mallet was not the author of it, but he was thought to be until 1878. See Phelps, *The Beginnings of the English Romantic Movement* (1893), Appendix II.

"*William and Margaret* is simply *Fair Margaret and Sweet William* rewritten in what used to be called an elegant style."—Child, in *English and Scottish Popular Ballads* (1882-98), II, 1, 200.

John Dyer

Poems, p. 16 — Bibliography, p. 1424

To the Poet John Dyer

Bard of the Fleece, whose skilful genius made
That work a living landscape fair and bright;
Nor hallowed less with musical delight
Than those soft scenes through which thy
    childhood strayed,
Those southern tracts of Cambria, "deep em-
    bayed,
With green hills fenced, with Ocean's murmur
    lulled";
Though hasty fame hath many a chaplet culled
For worthless brows, while in the pensive shade
Of cold neglect she leaves thy head ungraced,
Yet pure and powerful minds, hearts meek and
    still,
A grateful few, shall love thy modest lay,
Long as the shepherd's bleating flock shall
    stray
O'er naked Snowdon's wide aërial waste;
Long as the thrush shall pipe on Grongar Hill!
             —Wordsworth.

16.   GRONGAR HILL

"*Grongar Hill* is the happiest of his productions: it is not indeed very accurately
written; but the scenes which it displays are
so pleasing, the images which they raise so
welcome to the mind, and the reflections of the
writer so consonant to the general sense or
experience of mankind, that when it is once
read, it will be read again."—Johnson, in
"Dyer," *The Lives of the English Poets*
(1779-81).

Grongar Hill is a hill in southwestern
Wales. With respect to title and subject mat-
ter the poem is similar to Sir John Denham's
Cooper's Hill (1642).

James Thomson

Poems, p. 18 — Bibliography, p. 1450

"Thomson was blessed with a strong and
copious fancy; he hath enriched poetry with a
variety of new and original images, which he
painted from nature itself and from his own
actual observations: his descriptions have
therefore a distinctness and truth, which are
utterly wanting to those of poets who have
only copied from each other and have never
looked abroad on the objects themselves. Thomson was accustomed to wander away into the
country for days and for weeks, attentive to
'each rural sight, each rural sound,' while
many a poet who has dwelt for years in the
Strand has attempted to describe fields and
rivers and generally succeeded accordingly.

Hence that nauseous repetition of the same
circumstances; hence that disgusting impropriety of introducing what may be called a set
of hereditary images, without proper regard to
the age or climate or occasion in which they
were formerly used. Though the diction of
The Seasons is sometimes harsh and inharmonious, and sometimes turgid and obscure,
and though in many instances the numbers
are not sufficiently diversified by different
pauses, yet is this poem on the whole, from
the numberless strokes of nature in which it
abounds, one of the most captivating and
amusing in our language, and which, as its
beauties are not of a transitory kind, as depending on particular customs and manners,
will ever be perused with delight."—Joseph
Warton, in *An Essay on the Genius and Writings of Pope* (1756).

18.   THE SEASONS

"*The Seasons* shows that as far as intrinsic
worth is concerned the poems are marked with
a strange mingling of merits and defects, but
that considered in their historical place in the
development of the poetry of nature their importance and striking originality can hardly
be overstated. Though Thomson talked the
language of his day, his thought was a new
one. He taught clearly, though without emphasis, the power of nature to quiet the passions and elevate the mind of man, and he
intimated a deeper thought of divine immanence in the phenomena of nature. But his
great service to the men of his day was that he
shut up their books, led them out of their
parks, and taught them to look on nature with
enthusiasm."—Myra Reynolds, in *The Treatment of Nature in English Poetry between
Pope and Wordsworth* (1896).

The parts of this poem were first published
separately in the order—Winter, Summer,
Spring, Autumn. They were afterwards arranged in logical order. The poem is reminiscent of Milton and Spenser. That Thomson was consciously at variance with the prevailing school of early 18th century poetry
may be seen from the following extract from
his Preface to the second edition of *Winter*
(1726): "Nothing can have a better influence
towards the revival of poetry than the choosing
of great and serious subjects, such as at once
amuse the fancy, enlighten the head, and warm
the heart. These give a weight and dignity to
the poem; nor is the pleasure—I should say
rapture—both the writer and the reader feel
unwarranted by reason or followed by repentant disgust. To be able to write on a dry,
barren theme is looked upon by some as the
sign of a happy, fruitful genius:—fruitful

indeed! like one of the pendant gardens in Cheapside, watered every morning by the hand of the Alderman himself. And what are we commonly entertained with on these occasions save forced unaffecting fancies, little glittering prettinesses, mixed turns of wit and expression, which are as widely different from native poetry as buffoonery is from the perfection of human thinking? A genius fired with the charms of truth and nature is tuned to a sublimer pitch, and scorns to associate with such subjects. . . .

"I know no subject more elevating, more amusing; more ready to awake the poetical enthusiasm, the philosophical reflection, and the moral sentiment, than the works of nature. Where can we meet with such variety, such beauty, such magnificence? All that enlarges and transports the soul! What more inspiring than a calm, wide survey of them? In every dress nature is greatly charming—whether she puts on the crimson robes of the morning, the strong effulgence of noon, the sober suit of the evening, or the deep sables of blackness and tempest! How gay looks the spring! how glorious the summer! how pleasing the autumn! and how venerable the winter!—But there is no thinking of these things without breaking out into poetry; which is, by-the-by, a plain and undeniable argument of their superior excellence.

"For this reason the best, both ancient, and modern, poets have been passionately fond of retirement, and solitude. The wild romantic country was their delight. And they seem never to have been more happy, than when, lost in unfrequented fields, far from the little busy world, they were at leisure, to meditate, and sing the works of nature."

19a. Note. For an account of the conditions in jails and prisons in the early 18th century, see Lecky's *A History of England in the Eighteenth Century* (New York, Appleton, 1887), 6, 255ff.

22. 1004-29. With these lines cf. the following lyric from Tennyson's *The Princess,* 4, 21-40:

Tears, idle tears, I know not what they
    mean,
Tears from the depth of some divine despair
Rise in the heart, and gather to the eyes,
In looking on the happy autumn-fields,
And thinking of the days that are no more.

Fresh as the first beam glittering on a sail,
That brings our friends up from the under-
    world,
Sad as the last which reddens over one
That sinks with all we love below the verge;
So sad, so fresh, the days that are no more.

Ah, sad and strange as in dark summer
    dawns
The earliest pipe of half-awaken'd birds
To dying ears, when unto dying eyes
The casement slowly grows a glimmering
    square;
So sad, so strange, the days that are no more.

Dear as remember'd kisses after death,
And sweet as those by hopeless fancy feign'd
On lips that are for others; deep as love,
Deep as first love, and wild with all regret;
O Death in Life, the days that are no more.

24.   THE CASTLE OF INDOLENCE

"This poem being writ in the manner of Spenser, the obsolete words, and a simplicity of diction in some of the lines which borders on the ludicrous, were necessary to make the imitation more perfect. And the style of that admirable poet, as well as the measure in which he wrote, are as it were appropriated by custom to all allegorical poems writ in our language—just as in French the style of Marot, who lived under Francis I, has been used in tales and familiar epistles by the politest writers of the age of Louis XIV."—Thomson's prefatory Advertisement.

"It is an exquisite masterpiece, with not a grain of perishable matter in it. Completely free from all of Thomson's usual faults and less pleasing peculiarities, it is fresh, terse, and natural, perfectly melodious, and has a charming humor rarely displayed by the author in his other pieces."—F. J. Child, in Advertisement to *Poetical Works of James Thomson* (1863).

See note on Shenstone's *The Schoolmistress,* p. 1237b.

25. 10-19. Cf. this stanza with the following from *The Færie Queene,* I, 1, 34:

A litle lowly hermitage it was,
Downe in a dale, hard by a forests side,
Far from resort of people that did pas
In traveill to and froe: a litle wyde
There was an holy chappell edifyde,
Wherein the hermite dewly wont to say
His holy thinges each morne and eventyde;
Thereby a christall streame did gently play,
Which from a sacred fountaine welled forth
    alway.

29. 261. This line is a typical example of the eighteenth-century habit of inversion.

262-70. "I cannot at present recollect any solitude so romantic, or peopled with beings so proper to the place and the spectator. The mind naturally loves to lose itself in one of these wildernesses, and to forget the hurry,

the noise, and splendor of more polished life."
—Joseph Warton, in *An Essay on the Genius and Writings of Pope* (1756).

32. TO AMANDA

Amanda was Miss Elizabeth Young, daughter of Captain Gilbert Young of Dumfriesshire, Scotland. Thomson was devoted to her for several years, but she finally married a Mr. Campbell.

Edward Young

Selections, p. 33 — Bibliography, p. 1457

As a rule, Young's verse is hollow and formal, and his thought commonplace; yet his theme—an escape from manners and dress, etc.—and his use of blank verse make his work important among the forerunners of Romanticism.

33. NIGHT THOUGHTS

As originally published this poem was entitled *The Complaint; or, Night Thoughts.* Young prefixed to it the following Preface:

"As the occasion of this poem was *real*, not *fictitious*, so the method pursued in it was rather *imposed* by what spontaneously arose in the author's mind on that occasion, than *meditated* or *designed*, which will appear very probable from the nature of it. For it differs from the common mode of poetry, which is, from long narrations to draw short morals. Here, on the contrary, the narrative is short, and the morality arising from it makes the bulk of the poem. The reason of it is that the facts mentioned did naturally pour these moral reflections on the thought of the writer."
34a. *Narcissa.* With this passage compare Shelley's *Adonais*, st. 39-40 (p. 761).
36b. 51. Speaking of Dryden, Young says: "The strongest demonstration of his no-taste for the buskin are his tragedies fringed with rhyme, which in epic poetry is a sure disease, in the tragic, absolute death. To Dryden's enormity, Pope's was a slight offence. As lacemen are foes to mourning, these two authors, rich in rhyme, were no great friends to those solemn ornaments which the noble nature of their works required."—From *Conjectures on Original Composition* (1759).

Robert Blair

Poems, p. 37 — Bibliography, p. 1408

37. THE GRAVE

"*The Grave* was the first and best of a whole series of mortuary poems. In spite of the epigrams of conflicting partisans, *Night Thoughts* must be considered as contemporaneous with it, and neither preceding nor following it. There can be no doubt, however, that the success of Blair encouraged Young to persevere in his far longer and more laborious undertaking. Blair's verse is less rhetorical, more exquisite, than Young's, and, indeed, his relation to that writer, though too striking to be overlooked, is superficial. He forms a connecting link between Otway and Crabbe, who are his nearest poetical kinsmen. His one poem, *The Grave*, contains seven hundred and sixty-seven lines of blank verse. It is very unequal in merit, but supports the examination of modern criticism far better than most productions of the second quarter of the eighteenth century. As philosophical literature it is quite without value; and it adds nothing to theology; it rests solely upon its merit as romantic poetry."—Gosse, in *Dictionary of National Biography* (1886).

Bryant wrote *Thanatopsis* soon after reading this poem. Cf. Bryant's poem with lines 28-67 of *The Grave*.

William Shenstone

Poems, p. 40 — Bibliography, p. 1448

40. THE SCHOOLMISTRESS

One of the unmistakable signs of Romanticism was the reawakened interest in English literature of the past, especially in ballads, Spenser, and Milton. Although Spenser and Milton had never been completely forgotten, it was not until late in the eighteenth century that their influence became a real quickening force in English poetry; by the time of Keats, English poets had caught the spirit of these masters, and had reproduced it successfully.

The early eighteenth century poets did not take Spenser very seriously. They copied his language, his meter, and his stanza, all of which they used in comic verses, parodies, and mild satires. Of the numerous Spenserian imitations which appeared between 1735 and 1775, Shenstone's *The Schoolmistress* and Thomson's *The Castle of Indolence* are the best. Neither poem was written in any serious vein, although both were admired for their own sake.

"The inimitable *Schoolmistress* of Shenstone is one of the felicities of genius; but the purpose of this poem has been entirely misconceived. . . . *The Schoolmistress* of Shenstone has been admired for its simplicity and tenderness, not for its exquisitely ludicrous turn! This discovery I owe to the good fortune of possessing the original edition of *The Schoolmistress*, which the author printed under his own directions, and to his own fancy. To this piece of LUDICROUS POETRY, as he calls it, 'lest it should be mistaken,' he added a LUDICROUS INDEX, 'purely to show fools that I am in jest.' But 'the fool,' his subsequent editor, who I regret to say, was Robert Dodsley, thought proper to suppress this amusing 'ludicrous index,' and the consequence is, as the poet foresaw, that his aim has been 'mistaken.' "—Disraeli, in *Curiosities of Literature* (1791-1823).

Mark Akenside

Poems, p. 44 — Bibliography, p. 1406

44. THE PLEASURES OF THE IMAGINATION

The title and much of the thought of this poem were suggested by Addison's essays on the same subject (*Spectator*, 411-421). The selections here printed are taken from the enlarged version of the poem published in three Books (and a fragment of a fourth) in 1757. The poem originally was published anonymously in three Books in 1744. It was the parent of a number of similarly named poems, among which are Warton's *The Pleasures of Melancholy* (p. 75), Campbell's *The Pleasures of Hope* (p. 443), and Rogers's *The Pleasures of Memory* (p. 233).

45a. 227ff.—This passage should be compared with Addison's *Spectator*, 412.

47. ODE TO THE EVENING STAR

This poem is sometimes entitled *The Nightingale* and *Ode to Hesperus*.

William Collins

Poems, p. 48 — Bibliography, p. 1420

"Have you seen the works of two young authors, a Mr. Warton and Mr. Collins, both writers of odes? It is odd enough, but each is the half of a considerable man, and one the counterpart of the other. The first has but little invention, very poetical choice of expression, and a good ear; the second, a fine fancy, modelled upon the antique, a bad ear, great variety of words and images, with no choice at all. They both deserve to last some years, but will not."—Gray, in letter to Wharton, Dec. 27, 1746.

"He loved fairies, genii, giants, and monsters; he delighted to rove through the meanders of enchantment, to gaze on the magnificence of golden palaces, to repose by the water-falls of Elysian gardens. This was, however, the character rather of his inclination than his genius; the grandeur of wildness and the novelty of extravagance were always desired by him, but not always attained. Yet, as diligence is never wholly lost, if his efforts sometimes caused harshness and obscurity, they likewise produced in happier moments sublimity and splendor. This idea which he had formed of excellence led him to oriental fictions and allegorical imagery, and perhaps, while he was intent upon description, he did not sufficiently cultivate sentiment. . . . His diction was often harsh, unskilfully labored, and injudiciously selected. He affected the obsolete when it was not worthy of revival; and he puts his words out of the common order, seeming to think, with some later candidates for fame, that not to write prose is certainly to write poetry. His lines commonly are of slow motion, clogged and impeded with clusters of consonants. As men are often esteemed who cannot be loved, so the poetry of Collins may sometimes extort praise when it gives little pleasure."—Samuel Johnson, in "Collins," *The Lives of the English Poets* (1779-81).

"There are very few poets from whose wheat so little chaff has been winnowed as from that of Collins. His entire existing work does not extend to much more than fifteen hundred lines, at least two-thirds of which must live with the best poetry of the century. Collins has the touch of a sculptor; his verse is clearly-cut and direct; it is marble-pure, but also marble-cold. Each phrase is a wonder of felicitous workmanship, without emphasis, without sense of strain. His best strophes possess an extraordinary quiet melody, a soft harmonious smoothness as of some divine and aerial creature singing in artless, perfect numbers for its own delight."—Gosse, in *A History of Eighteenth Century Literature* (1888).

49. ODE ON THE POETICAL CHARACTER

This is supposed to be modeled on the Greek odes of Pindar, which were divided into a strophe and antistrophe of identical form, and an epode, or after-song, of different form. The strophe originally was the movement of the chorus in the Greek choral dance from the right to the left of the orchestra; the antistrophe was the return movement, and the epode a "stand" or pause.

23. *Band.* The band, or girdle, was the emblem of poetic genius.

23ff. In a letter to Thelwall, Dec., 1796, Coleridge states that this part of the poem "has inspired and whirled me along with greater agitations of enthusiasm than any of the most impassioned scenes in Schiller or Shakespeare."

55ff. The cliff is symbolical of Milton's poetry.

50. ODE WRITTEN IN THE BEGINNING OF
THE YEAR 1746

This ode probably commemorates the English who had fallen in recent battles: at Fontenoy, Belgium (May 11, 1745), in a battle with the French in the War of the Austrian Succession; at Prestonpans, Scotland (Sept. 21, 1745), and at Falkirk, Scotland (Jan. 17, 1746), in battles with the forces of Charles Edward Stuart, the Young Pretender. In all of these battles, the English were defeated with enormous losses.

ODE TO EVENING

"The most perfect and original poem of Collins, as well as the most finely appreciative of nature, is his *Ode to Evening*. No doubt evening is personified in his address as 'maid composed,' and 'calm votaress,' but the personification is so delicately handled, and in so subdued a tone, that it does not jar on the feelings as such personifications too often do. . . . There is about the whole ode a subdued twilight tone, a remoteness from men and human things, and a pensive evening musing, all the more expressive, because it does not shape itself into definite thoughts, but reposes in appropriate images."—Shairp, in *On Poetic Interpretation of Nature* (1877).

9-12. Cf. *Macbeth*, III, 2, 40-43:

. . . ere the bat hath flown
His cloistered flight, ere to black Hecate's
summons
The shard-borne beetle with his drowsy hums
Hath rung night's yawning peal, . . .

51.   THE PASSIONS

The thought of this poem should be compared with that of Blake's *To the Muses* (p. 168).

65-68. J. L. Lowes states (*The Road to Xanadu*, p. 400) that Coleridge had these lines in mind when he wrote *Kubla Khan* (p. 384).

52. 95. *Sphere-descended.* — Heaven-descended.

108. *Recording sister.*—Clio, the Muse of history.

ON THE DEATH OF MR. THOMSON

This poem is an elegy on James Thomson, the poet. See p. 18.

53. AN ODE ON THE POPULAR SUPERSTITIONS
OF THE HIGHLANDS OF SCOTLAND

This poem, which was left unfinished by Collins, was not published until after his death. Soon after it appeared in its incomplete form, what purported to be a perfect copy of the ode as revised by Collins was published in London. The bracketed passages in the text are supplied from this version, which is the one usually adopted.

"The whole Romantic School, in its germ, no doubt, but yet unmistakably foreshadowed, lies already in the *Ode on the Superstitions of the Highlands.* He [Collins] was the first to bring back into poetry something of the antique fervor, and found again the long-lost secret of being classically elegant without being pedantically cold."—Lowell, in "Pope," *My Study Windows* (1871).

56. 192-205. *Jerusalem Delivered*, by the Italian poet Torquato Tasso (1544-95), was translated into English by Fairfax in 1600. The following stanzas (13:41-43, 46) explain the allusions in Collins's lines:

He drew his sword at last and gaue the tree
A mightie blow, that made a gaping wound,
Out of the rift red streames he trickling see
That all bebled the verdant plaine around,
His haire start vp, yet once againe stroake he,
He nould giue ouer till the end he found
Of this aduenture, when with plaint and mone,
(As from some hollow graue) he heard one
grone.

Enough enough the voice lamenting said,
Tancred thou hast me hurt, thou didst me driue
Out of the bodie of a noble maid,
Who with me liu'd, whom late I kept on liue,
And now within this woeful Cipresse laid,
My tender rinde thy weapon sharpe doth riue,
Cruell, ist not enough thy foes to kill,
But in their graues wilt thou torment them
still?

I was *Clorinda*, now imprison'd heere,
(Yet not alone) within this plant I dwell,
For euerie Pagan Lord and Christian peere,
Before the cities walles last day that fell,
(In bodies new or graues I wote not cleere)
But here they are confin'd by magikes spell,
So that each tree hath life, and sense each bou,
A murderer if thou cut one twist art thou.

. . . .

Thus his fierce hart which death had scorned
oft,
Whom no strange shape, or monster could
dismay,
With faigned showes of tender loue made soft,
A spirit false did with vaine plaints betray,
A whirling winde his sword heau'd vp aloft,
And through the forrest bare it quite away.

Thomas Gray

Selections, p. 57 — Bibliography, p. 1425

Gray's poetry shows a distinct gain over his contemporaries in the number of poetic forms which he uses. The introduction of new poetic forms and new meters constituted one of the noticeable changes taking place in English poetry.

"In literature he was regarded as an innovator, for like Collins he revived the poetic diction of the past, and the adverse judgments of Johnson and others upon his work are in fact a defence of the current literary traditions. Few men have published so little to so much effect; few have attained to fame with so little ambition."—D. C. Tovey, in *Encyclopaedia Britannica*, 14th ed. (1929).

"Although Gray's biographers and critics have very seldom spoken of it, the most interesting thing in a study of his poetry . . . is his steady progress in the direction of Romanticism. Beginning as a classicist and disciple of Dryden, he ended in thorough-going Romanticism. His early poems contain nothing Romantic; his *Elegy* has something of the Romantic mood, but shows many conventional touches; in the Pindaric Odes the Romantic feeling asserts itself boldly; and he ends in enthusiastic study of Norse and Celtic poetry and mythology. Such a steady growth in the mind of the greatest poet of the time shows not only what he learned from the age, but what he taught it. Gray is a much more important factor in the Romantic Movement than seems to be commonly supposed."—Phelps, in *The Beginnings of the English Romantic Movement* (1893).

57.   ODE ON THE SPRING

The original title of this poem was *Noontide;* it is based upon Horace's *Spring's Lesson (Odes,* I, 4).

"His ode *On Spring* has something poetical, both in the language and the thought; but the language is too luxuriant, and the thoughts have nothing new. There has of late arisen a practice of giving to adjectives derived from substantives the termination of participles, such as the *cultured* plain, the *daisied* bank; but I was sorry to see in the lines of a scholar like Gray, the *honied* spring. The morality is natural, but too stale; the conclusion is pretty."—Samuel Johnson, in "Gray," *The Lives of the English Poets* (1779-81).

1.   In classic mythology the Hours are represented as accompanying Venus and as bringing the changes of the season. The epithet *rosy-bosom'd* is borrowed from Milton (*Comus,* 986).

21.   The pseudo-classic habit of personification is distinctly noticeable in this poem and others of Gray.

ODE ON A DISTANT PROSPECT OF ETON COLLEGE

This poem was written shortly after the death of Richard West, Gray's intimate friend.

Two other friends of college days, Ashton and Walpole, were estranged from Gray at the time.

"The *Prospect of Eton College* suggests nothing to Gray which every beholder does not equally think and feel. His supplication to father Thames, to tell him who drives the hoop or tosses the ball, is useless and puerile. Father Thames has no better means of knowing than himself."—Samuel Johnson, in "Gray," *The Lives of the English Poets* (1779-81).

6.   Windsor Castle is on the opposite side of the Thames from Eton College.

58a. 29.   In such phrases as this Gray shows the eighteenth-century pseudo-classic manner.

79.   In a note Gray refers to Dryden's *Palamon and Arcite,* 2, 582:

And Madness laughing in his ireful mood.

HYMN TO ADVERSITY

This poem was the model of Wordsworth's *Ode to Duty* (p. 322). It was itself modeled on Horace's *Ode to Fortune.*

7.   The phrase *purple tyrants* Gray borrowed from Horace (*Odes,* I, 35, 12). *Purple* refers to the robes worn by kings.

8.   See Milton's *Paradise Lost,* 2, 703:
Strange horror seize thee and pangs unfelt
    before.

59. 45-46.   See note above on *Ode on a Distant Prospect of Eton College.*

ELEGY WRITTEN IN A COUNTRY CHURCHYARD

"As you have brought me into a little sort of distress, you must assist me, I believe, to get out of it as well as I can. Yesterday I had the misfortune of receiving a letter from certain gentlemen (as their bookseller expresses it), who have taken the *Magazine of Magazines* into their hands. They tell me that an *ingenious* poem, called *Reflections in a Country Churchyard,* has been communicated to them, which they are printing forthwith; that they are informed that the *excellent* author of it is I by name, and that they beg not only his *indulgence,* but the *honor* of his correspondence, etc. As I am not at all disposed to be either so indulgent, or so correspondent, as they desire, I have but one bad way left to escape the honor they would inflict upon me; and therefore am obliged to desire you would make Dodsley print it immediately (which may be done in less than a week's time) from your copy, but without my name, in what form is most convenient for him, but on his best paper and character; he must correct the press himself, and print it without any interval between the stanzas, because the sense is in some places continued beyond them; and the title must be,—'Elegy, Written in a Country Churchyard.' If he would add a line or two to say it came into his hands by accident, I should like it better. If you behold the *Magazine of Magazines* in the light that I do, you will not refuse to give yourself this trouble on my account, which you have taken of your own accord before now. If Dodsley do not do this immediately, he may as well let it alone." —Gray's letter to Walpole, Feb. 11, 1751.

"The *Church-Yard* abounds with images which find a mirror in every mind, and with sentiments to which every bosom returns an echo. The four stanzas beginning 'Yet even these bones' are to me original: I have never seen the notions in any other place; yet he that reads them here persuades himself that he has always felt them. Had Gray written often thus, it had been vain to blame, and useless to praise him."—Samuel Johnson, in "Gray," *The Lives of the English Poets* (1779-81).

"Of all short poems—or indeed of all poems whatsoever—in the English language, which has been, for a century and a quarter past, the one most universally, persistently, and incessantly reproduced and quoted from? I suppose, beyond rivalry and almost beyond comparison, *The Elegy in a Country Churchyard* of Thomas Gray. Such is the glory which has waited upon scant productiveness and relative mediocrity—though undoubtedly nobly balanced and admirably grown and finished mediocrity—in the poetic art. The flute has overpowered the organ, the riding-horse has outstripped Pegasus, and the crescent moon has eclipsed the sun."—W. M. Rossetti, in *Lives of Famous Poets* (1878).

9-16. This is probably the scene of the church and graveyard at Stoke Poges.

60. 55-56. Cf. with the following lines from Ambrose Philips's *The Fable of Thule* (1748), 38-40:

In forests did the lonely beauty shine,
Like woodland flowers, which paint the desert glades,
And waste their sweets in unfrequented shades.

57-60. In an early manuscript version of the poem, the names used in this stanza are *Cato, Tully,* and *Cæsar.* The changes are significant of Gray's growing romanticism.

71-72. A reference to the custom, still common in Gray's time, of writing complimentary verses to noted persons to secure their patronage. After these lines, in an early manuscript version, the following stanzas are found:

The thoughtless world to majesty may bow,
Exalt the brave, and idolize success
But more to innocence their safety owe

Than pow'r and genius e'er conspired to bless.
And thou, who, mindful of th' unhonored dead,
Dost in these notes their artless tale relate,
By night and lonely contemplation led
To linger in the gloomy walks of Fate,
Hark! how the sacred calm, that broods around,
Bids ev'ry fierce tumultuous passion cease,
In still small accents whisp'ring from the ground
A grateful earnest of eternal peace.
No more, with reason and thyself at strife,
Give anxious cares and endless wishes room;
But through the cool sequestered vale of life
Pursue the silent tenor of thy doom.

81. A number of gravestones at Stoke Poges contain misspellings.
61. 105-12. These lines are inscribed on the monument to Gray at Stoke Poges.

THE PROGRESS OF POESY

This and the following poem are known as Gray's Pindaric Odes, perhaps the best ever written in the English language. They conform closely to the structure and manner of Pindar. See note on Collins's *Ode on the Poetical Character* (p. 1238b). *The Progress of Poesy* was announced by Gray in a letter to Walpole (undated; No. 97 in Tovey's ed.) in which he said that he might send very soon to Dodsley, his publisher, "an ode to his own tooth, a high Pindaric upon stilts, which one must be a better scholar than he is to understand a line of, and the very best scholars will understand but a little matter here and there." Gray's expectation was fulfilled. When this poem and *The Bard* were published, few persons read them with appreciation. In a letter to Mason (undated; No. 148 in Tovey's ed.), Gray says: "I would not have put another note to save the souls of all the owls in London. It is extremely well as it is—nobody understands me, and I am perfectly satisfied. Even *The Critical Review* (Mr. Franklin, I am told), that is rapt and surprised and shudders at me, yet mistakes the Æolian lyre for the harp of Æolus, which, indeed, as he observes, is a very bad instrument to dance to. If you hear anything (though it is not very likely, for I know my day is over), you will tell me. Lord Lyttleton[1] and Mr. Shenstone[2] admire me, but wish I had been a little clearer."

---

[1] George Lyttleton (1709-73), an English author and politician.
[2] William Shenstone (1714-63), an English poet. See p. 40.

In reply to Richard Hurd's letter of thanks for a present of these two odes, Gray wrote as follows (Aug. 25, 1757):

"I do not know why you should thank me for what you had a right and title to; but attribute it to the excess of your politeness; and the more so, because almost no one else has made me the same compliment. As your acquaintances in the University (you say) do me the honor to *admire*, it would be ungenerous in me not to give them notice, that they are doing a very unfashionable thing; for all people of condition are agreed not to admire, nor even to understand. One very great man, writing to an acquaintance of his and mine, says that he had read them seven or eight times; and that now, when he next sees him, he shall not have above *thirty questions* to ask. Another (a peer) believes that the last stanza of the second ode relates to King Charles the First and Oliver Cromwell. Even my friends tell me they do not *succeed*, and write me moving topics of consolation on that head. In short, I have heard of nobody but an actor[1] and a doctor of divinity[2] that profess their esteem for them. Oh yes, a lady of quality (a friend of Mason's), who is a great reader. She knew there was a compliment to Dryden, but never suspected there was anything said about Shakespeare or Milton, till it was explained to her; and wishes that there had been titles prefixed to tell what they were about."

"[The] *Progress of Poesy*, in reach, variety, and loftiness of poise, overflies all other English lyrics like an eagle. In spite of the dulness of contemporary ears, preoccupied with the continuous hum of the popular hurdy-gurdy, it was the prevailing blast of Gray's trumpet that more than anything else called man back to the legitimate standard."— Lowell, in "Pope," *My Study Windows* (1871).

61. I. 1. "The various sources of poetry, which gives life and lustre to all it touches, are here described; its quiet majestic progress enriching every subject (otherwise dry and barren) with a pomp of diction and luxuriant harmony of numbers; and its more rapid and irresistible course, when swoln and hurried away by the conflict of tumultuous passions."—Gray's note.

I. 2. "Power of harmony to calm the turbulent sallies of the soul."—Gray's note.

62. I. 3. "Power of harmony to produce all the graces of motion in the body."—Gray's note.

II. 1. "To compensate the real and imaginary ills of life, the Muse was given to

mankind by the same Providence that sends day by its cheerful presence to dispel the gloom and terrors of the night."—Gray's note.

II. 2. "Extensive influence of poetic genius over the remotest and most uncivilized nations: its connection with liberty, and the virtues that naturally attend on it. (See the Erse, Norwegian, and Welsh Fragments, the Lapland and American songs.)"—Gray's note.

62. II. 3. "Progress of poetry from Greece to Italy, and from Italy to England. Chaucer was not unacquainted with the writings of Dante or of Petrarch. The Earl of Surrey and Sir Tho. Wyatt had travelled in Italy, and formed their taste there; Spenser imitated the Italian writers; Milton improved on them; but this School expired soon after the Restoration, and a new one arose on the French model, which has subsisted ever since."— Gray's note.

63.   THE BARD

"The following ode is founded on a tradition current in Wales, that Edward the First, when he completed the conquest of the country, ordered all the bards that fell into his hands to be put to death."—Gray's prefatory Advertisement.

Gray's summary of the poem is as follows: "The army of Edward I as they march through a deep valley are suddenly stopped by the appearance of a venerable figure seated on the summit of an inaccessible rock, who, with a voice more than human, reproaches the King with all the misery and desolation which he had brought on his country; foretells the misfortunes of the Norman race, and with prophetic spirit declares that all his cruelty shall never extinguish the noble ardor of poetic genius in this island; and that men shall never be wanting to celebrate true virtue and valor in immortal strains, to expose vice and infamous pleasure, and boldly censure tyranny and oppression. His song ended, he precipitates himself from the mountain, and is swallowed up by the river that rolls at its foot."

"To select a singular event, and swell it to a giant's bulk by fabulous appendages of spectres and predictions, has little difficulty: for he that forsakes the probable may always find the marvellous. And it has little use; we are affected only as we believe; we are improved only as we find something to be imitated or declined. I do not see that *The Bard* promotes any truth, moral or political. His stanzas are too long, especially his epodes; the ode is finished before the ear has learned its measures, and consequently before it can receive pleasures from their consonance and recurrence. . . . In the second stanza the

[1] David Garrick (1717-79).
[2] William Warburton (1698-1779).

bard is well described; but in the third we have the puerilities of obsolete mythology. When we are told that 'Cadwallo hush'd the stormy main,' and that 'Modred made huge Plinlimmon bow his cloud-topp'd head,' attention recoils from the repetition of a tale that, even when it was first heard, was heard with scorn. . . . These odes are marked by glittering accumulation of ungraceful ornaments; they strike, rather than please; the images are magnified by affectation; the language is labored into harshness. The mind of the writer seems to work with unnatural violence. 'Double, double, toil and trouble.'[1] He has a kind of strutting dignity, and is tall by walking on tiptoe. His art and his struggle are too visible, and there is too little appearance of ease and nature."—Samuel Johnson, in "Gray," *The Lives of the English Poets* (1779-81).

"Mr. Fox, supposing the bard sung his song but once over, does not wonder if Edward the First did not understand him. This last criticism is rather unhappy, for though it had been sung a hundred times under his window, it was absolutely impossible King Edward should understand him; but that is no reason for Mr. Fox, who lives almost 500 years after him. It is very well; the next thing I print shall be in Welch,—that's all."—Gray, in letter to Mason (undated; No. 148 in Tovey's ed.).

19-20. "The image was taken from a well-known picture of Raphael, representing the Supreme Being in the vision of Ezekiel. There are two of these pictures (both believed original), one at Florence, the other at Paris."—Gray's note.

28. Hoel was a prince and poet of North-Wales. See note on *The Death of Hoel*, p. 1244a. *Soft Llewellyn's lay.*—A lay about the gentle Llewellyn, a Welsh prince.

65. ODE ON THE PLEASURE ARISING FROM VICISSITUDE

This poem, in its present unfinished form, was found after Gray's death in his notebook of the year 1754.

66. THE FATAL SISTERS

"Dodsley told me in the spring that the plates from Mr. Bentley's designs were worn out, and he wanted to have them copied and reduced to a smaller scale for a new edition. I dissuaded him from so silly an expense, and desired he would put in no ornaments at all. The *Long Story* was to be totally omitted, as its only use (that of explaining the prints)

[1] *Macbeth*, IV, 1, 20.

was gone: but to supply the place of it in bulk, lest *my works* should be mistaken for the works of a flea, or a pismire, I promised to send him an equal weight of poetry or prose: so, since my return hither, I put up about two ounces of stuff, viz. *The Fatal Sisters, The Descent of Odin* (of both which you have copies), a bit of something from the Welch, and certain little notes, partly from justice (to acknowledge the debt, where I had borrowed anything), partly from ill temper, just to tell the gentle reader that Edward I was not Oliver Cromwell, nor Queen Elizabeth the Witch of Endor. This is literally all; and with all this, I shall be but a shrimp of an author."—Gray, in letter to Walpole, Feb. 25, 1768.

The *Long Story* is a poem by Gray, written in a playful mood.

In a prefatory notice to *The Fatal Sisters*, Gray states that the poem is "an ode from the Norse tongue, in the *Orcades* of Thormodus Torfæus, Hafniæ, 1697, folio; and also in Bartholinus." Professor Kittredge has pointed out that the poem is really a free rendering of a Latin translation which accompanied the Norse text in the editions Gray refers to, and that Gray's knowledge of Old Norse was very slight. See Professor Kittredge's "Gray's Knowledge of Old Norse," printed as an appendix to the Introduction in the Athenæum Press ed. of Gray's Works. The Latin version is printed in the same text. The Norse poem, with a prose translation, may be found also in *Corpus Poeticum Boreale*, I, 281-83.

"In the eleventh century, *Sigurd*, earl of the Orkney Islands, went with a fleet of ships and a considerable body of troops into Ireland, to the assistance of *Sictryg with the Silken Beard*, who was then making war on his father-in-law, *Brian*, king of Dublin. The earl and all his forces were cut to pieces, and *Sictryg* was in danger of a total defeat; but the enemy had a greater loss by the death of *Brian* their king, who fell in the action. On Christmas day (the day of the battle), a native of Caithness in Scotland, of the name of Darrud, saw at a distance a number of persons on horseback riding full speed towards a hill, and seeming to enter into it. Curiosity led him to follow them, till looking through an opening in the rocks, he saw twelve gigantic figures resembling women. They were all employed about a loom, and as they wove, they sung the following dreadful song, which when they had finished, they tore the web into twelve pieces, and (each taking her portion) galloped six to the north, and as many to the south. These were the *Valkyriur*, female divinities, Parcæ

Militares, servants of *Odin* (or *Woden*) in the Gothic mythology. Their name signifies *Chusers of the Slain*. They were mounted on swift horses, with drawn swords in their hands; and in the throng of battle selected such as were destined to slaughter, and conducted them to *Valhalla*, the hall of *Odin*, or paradise of the brave; where they attended the banquet, and served the departed heroes with horns of mead and ale. Their numbers are not agreed upon, some authors representing them as *six*, some as *four*."—Gray's Preface.

67. THE DESCENT OF ODIN

"An ode from the Norse tongue, in Bartholinus, *De causis contemnendæ mortis*, Hafniæ, 1689, quarto."—Gray. The Norse poem is in the *Poetic Edda*, a collection of Old Norse poetry made probably in the thirteenth century. Gray's poem is a free rendering of the Latin translation which Bartholin prints with the Norse text.

In this poem, Odin, the supreme deity in Scandinavian mythology, descends to the lower world to learn from an ancient prophetess what danger threatened Balder, his favorite son. Balder had dreamed that his life was in danger, and Frigga, his mother, had made all things swear not to hurt Balder; but she had omitted the mistletoe, thinking it too insignificant to be dangerous.

55-56. Hoder was Balder's blind brother. Through the influence of the evil being Loki, Hoder unconsciously slew Balder with the mistletoe.

63-70. Vale, the son of Odin and Rinda, when only one night old slew Hoder.

75. The virgins were probably the Scandinavian Norns, or Sisters of Destiny. See *The Fatal Sisters* (p. 66) and Gray's Preface, above.

68. THE TRIUMPHS OF OWEN

This and the three following poems are fragments taken from Evans's *Specimens of the Antient Welsh Bards*, a collection of Welsh poems with English prose translations, followed by a *Dissertatio de Bardis*, published in 1764. *The Triumphs of Owen*, which is based on a prose version, commemorates a battle in which Owen, King of North-Wales, resisted the combined attack of Irish, Danish, and Norman fleets, about 1160.

THE DEATH OF HOEL

This and the two following poems are extracts from the *Gododin*, a relic of sixth century Welsh poetry, included in Evans's *Specimens*. (See note on *The Triumphs of Owen*.)

Gray used the Latin versions given by Evans in the *Dissertatio de Bardis*. These are printed in the Athenæum Press edition of Gray's Works. *The Death of Hoel* is supposed to celebrate a battle between the Strathclyde Britons and the Northumbrian Saxons. Hoel was a prince and poet of North-Wales.

69. GRAY'S LETTERS

"Everyone knows the letters of Gray, and remembers the lucid simplicity and directness, mingled with the fastidious sentiment of a scholar, of his description of such scenes as the Chartreuse. That is a well-known description, but those in his journal of a 'Tour in the North' have been neglected, and they are especially interesting since they go over much of the country in which Wordsworth dwelt, and of which he wrote. They are also the first conscious effort—and in this he is a worthy forerunner of Wordsworth—to describe natural scenery with the writer's eye upon the scene described, and to describe it in simple and direct phrase, in distinction to the fine writing that was then practiced. And Gray did this intentionally in the light prose journal he kept, and threw by for a time the refined carefulness and the insistence on human emotion which he thought necessary in poetic description of Nature. In his prose then, though not in his poetry, we have Nature loved for her own sake."—Stopford Brooke, in "From Pope to Cowper," *Theology in the English Poets* (1874).

The persons addressed in the letters printed in the text were Gray's mother and Gray's school and college friends. William Mason was his biographer.

73. JOURNAL IN THE LAKES

21. *Employment to the mirror*—Gray usually carried with him on his tours a plano-convex mirror, about four inches in diameter, which served the purpose of a camera-obscura.

27. *The Doctor.*—Dr. Thomas Wharton, Gray's friend, for whose amusement the Journal was composed.

55-56. *The jaws of Borrodale.* — See Wordsworth's *Yew-Trees* (p. 316).

74a. 30-31. *Lodoor waterfall.*—See Southey's *The Cataract of Lodore* (p. 436).

b. 27-28. Cf. Milton's *Samson Agonistes*, 86-89:

The sun to me is dark
And silent as the moon,
When she deserts the night,
Hid in her vacant interlunar cave.

35. *Helm-crag.*—This is "that ancient woman seated on Helm-crag" of Wordsworth in *To Joanna*, 56.

Thomas Warton

Selections, p. 75 — Bibliography, p. 1451

Thomas Warton thus describes his medieval studies:

"Long have I loved to catch the simple chime
Of minstrel-harps, and spell his fabling rime;
To view the festive rites, the knightly play,
That deck'd heroic Albion's elder day;
To mark the mouldering halls of barons bold,
And the rough castle, cast in giant mould;
With Gothic manners Gothic arts explore
And muse on the magnificence of yore."
—*Verses in Sir Joshua Reynolds's Painted
Window at New College, Oxford: 1782.*

"Warton's work is of interest because of the many attractive details scattered through his poems, but there is little unity of effect. The general impression is that he saw Nature first through Milton's eyes, and that when he afterward made many charming discoveries for himself he tried to express them in the *Il Penseroso* manner."—*Myra Reynolds*, in *The Treatment of Nature in English Poetry between Pope and Wordsworth* (1896).

75.   THE PLEASURES OF MELANCHOLY

With regard to title and subject, cf. this poem with Akenside's *The Pleasures of the Imagination* (p. 44), Rogers's *The Pleasures of Memory* (p. 233), and Campbell's *The Pleasures of Hope* (p. 443). With regard to subject it should be compared with *Il Penseroso.*

76. 153ff.   The attack on Pope contained in these lines was earlier than that of Joseph Warton's *Essay on Pope* (p. 85).

ODE ON THE APPROACH OF SUMMER

In form and language, this poem is a close imitation of *L'Allegro.*

77.   THE CRUSADE

"King Richard the First, celebrated for his achievements in the Crusades, was no less distinguished for his patronage of the Provençal minstrels, and his own compositions in their species of poetry. Returning from one of his expeditions in the Holy Land, in disguise, he was imprisoned in a castle of Leopold, Duke of Austria. His favorite minstrel, Blondel de Nesle, having traversed all Germany in search of his master, at length came to a castle, in which he found there was only one prisoner, and whose name was unknown. Suspecting that he had made the desired discovery, he seated himself under a window of the prisoner's apartment, and began a song, or ode, which the King and himself had formerly composed together. When the prisoner, who was King Richard, heard the song, he knew that Blondel must be the singer; and when Blondel paused about the middle, the King began the remainder and completed it. The following ode is supposed to be this joint composition of the minstrel and King Richard."—Warton's prefatory Advertisement.

WRITTEN IN A BLANK LEAF OF DUGDALE'S
MONASTICON

The *Monasticon Anglicanum* of Sir William Dugdale (1605-86) is a treatise on English Monasteries. It was published in three volumes (1655-73).

78.   WRITTEN AT STONEHENGE

In this sonnet, Warton summarizes several legends concerning the origin and meaning of Stonehenge, the celebrated prehistoric stone monument on Salisbury Plain, Wiltshire, England.

79. OBSERVATIONS ON THE FAIRY QUEEN OF
SPENSER

The selections here printed are taken from the second edition, 1762.

Joseph Warton

Selections, p. 80 — Bibliography, p. 1451

"Warton deserves remembrance as a learned and sagacious critic. He was a literary, not a philological scholar. His verse, although it indicates a true appreciation of natural scenery, is artificial and constrained in expression. He was well equipped for the role of literary historian, but his great designs in that field never passed far beyond the stage of preliminary meditation. It was as a leader of the revolution which overtook literary criticism in England in the eighteenth century that his chief work was done. In the preface to his volume of odes of 1746 he made a firm stand against the prevailing tendency of English poetry. He was convinced, he wrote, 'that the fashion of moralising in verse has been carried too far.' The true 'faculties of the poet' were invention and imagination."—*Dictionary of National Biography* (1885-1901).

See Gray's letter to Wharton, Dec. 27, 1746, in note on Collins, p. 1238a.

84. ODE TO FANCY

"The public has been so much accustomed of late to didactic poetry alone, and essays on moral subjects, that any work where the imagination is much indulged, will perhaps not be relished or regarded. The author therefore of these pieces is in some pain lest certain austere critics should think them too fanciful or descriptive. But as he is convinced that the fashion of moralizing in verse has been carried too far, and as he looks upon invention and imagination to be the chief faculties of a poet, so he will be happy if the following odes may be looked upon as an attempt to bring back poetry into its right channel."—From Warton's prefatory Advertisement to *Odes*, published in 1746.

The *Ode to Fancy* is imitative of *Il Penseroso*.

James Macpherson

Selections, p. 86 — Bibliography, p. 1438

"Apart from the doubtful morality of Macpherson's transactions he was a great writer. He did not transcribe actual Celtic poems, but he appreciated natural beauty and his art, with its tenderness, did more than any single work to bring about the romantic movement in European, and especially in German, literature."—*Encyclopaedia Britannica*, 14th ed. (1929).

". . . as a literary man, Macpherson was right—amazingly clever in his selections and rejections and in the whole frame of his policy, so far as it was intended to catch the greatest number of readers. Romance is to be found there in its two chief modes—superficial variety of scenes, and the opposite mode of intense feeling. There is also enough to conciliate a severer taste, in the motives of national heroism, and in the poet's conformity with the standards of epic. Thus, all sorts of readers were attracted—lovers of antiquity, lovers of romance, hearts of sensibility and those respectable critics who were not ashamed to follow Milton, Dryden and Pope in their devotion to the epic ideal." W. P. Ker, in *The Cambridge History of English Literature*, Vol. 10 (1933).

Macpherson's *Ossian* was greatly admired by Goethe and Schiller and was the favorite reading of Napoleon. The poems were translated into several European languages, and conscious imitators included Coleridge and Byron.

The passages reprinted are from the so-called Ossianic Poems, which Macpherson said were translations from an ancient Gaelic bard, Ossian, son of Fingal. A considerable controversy was waged as to the truth of Macpherson's statement; it is now generally agreed that the publications, though probably based upon genuine Gaelic remains, were largely the work of Macpherson himself. For Gray's interest in these productions, see his letters to Walpole, Stonehewer, Wharton, and Mason (pp. 71-72). In reply to a saucy letter from Macpherson in regard to the controversy, Samuel Johnson wrote Macpherson as follows (1775):

"I received your foolish and impudent letter. Any violence offered me I shall do my best to repel; and what I cannot do for myself the law shall do for me. I hope I shall never be deterred from detecting what I think a cheat, by the menaces of a ruffian.

"What would you have me retract? I thought your book an imposture; I think it an imposture still. For this opinion I have given my reasons to the public, which I here dare you to refute. Your rage I defy. Your abilities, since your *Homer*,[1] are not so formidable; and what I hear of your morals, inclines me to pay regard not to what you shall say, but to what you shall prove. You may print this if you will."

For a clear account of the whole matter, see J. S. Smart's *James Macpherson; An Episode in Literature* (1905).

"Homer has been superseded in my heart by the divine Ossian. Through what world does this angelic bard carry me! With him I wander over barren wastes and frightful wilds; surrounded by whirlwinds and hurricanes, trace by the feeble light of the moon the shades of our noble ancestors; hear from the mountainous heights, intermingled with the roaring of waves and cataracts, their plaintive tones stealing from cavernous recesses; while the pensive monody of some love-stricken maiden, who heaves her departing sighs over the moss-clad grave of the warrior by whom she was adored, makes up the inarticulate concert."—Goethe, in *The Sorrows of Werther*, Letter 68 (1774).

86. CARTHON

Macpherson's Argument to this poem is as follows: "This poem is complete, and the subject of it, as of most of Ossian's compositions, tragical. In the time of Comhal the son of Trathal, and father of the celebrated Fingal, Clessámmor the son of Thaddu and brother of Morna, Fingal's mother, was driven by a storm into the River Clyde, on the banks

---

[1] Macpherson published a prose translation of Homer's *Iliad* in 1773.

of which stood Balclutha, a town belonging to the Britons between the walls. He was hospitably received by Reuthámir, the principal man in the place, who gave him Moina his only daughter in marriage. Reuda, the son of Cormo, a Briton who was in love with Moina, came to Reuthámir's house, and behaved haughtily towards Clessámmor. A quarrel ensued, in which Reuda was killed; the Britons, who attended him, pressed so hard on Clessámmor, that he was obliged to throw himself into the Clyde, and swim to his ship. He hoisted sail, and the wind being favorable, bore him out to sea. He often endeavored to return, and carry off his beloved Moina by night; but the wind continuing contrary, he was forced to desist.

"Moina, who had been left with child by her husband, brought forth a son, and died soon after.—Reuthámir named the child Carthon, *i. e., the murmur of waves*, from the storm which carried off Clessámmor his father, who was supposed to have been cast away. When Carthon was three years old, Comhal the father of Fingal, in one of his expeditions against the Britons, took and burnt Balclutha. Reuthámir was killed in the attack; and Carthon was carried safe away by his nurse, who fled further into the country of the Britons. Carthon, coming to man's estate, was resolved to revenge the fall of Balclutha on Comhal's posterity. He set sail, from the Clyde, and falling on the coast of Morven, defeated two of Fingal's heroes, who came to oppose his progress. He was, at last, unwittingly killed by his father Clessámmor, in a single combat. This story is the foundation of the present poem, which opens on the night preceding the death of Carthon, so that what passed before is introduced by way of episode. The poem is addressed to Malvina the daughter of Toscar."

90b. 18-19. The incident of the father-and-son combat is also the basis of Arnold's *Sohrab and Rustum.* Arnold's direct source was a version of the Persian story, and his treatment of it was influenced both by Homer and by Greek tragedy. For a discussion of this theme in literature, see Potter's *Sohrab and Rustum* (Grimm Library Series, 1902).

91. OINA-MORUL

Macpherson's Argument to this poem is as follows: "After an address to Malvina, the daughter of Toscar, Ossian proceeds to relate his own expedition to Fuärfed, an island of Scandinavia. Mal-orchol, king of Fuärfed, being hard pressed in war, by Ton-thormod, chief of Sar-dronlo (who had demanded, in vain, the daughter of Mal-orchol in marriage),

Fingal sent Ossian to his aid. Ossian, on the day after his arrival, came to battle with Ton-thormod, and took him prisoner. Mal-orchol offers his daughter Oina-morul to Ossian; but he, discovering her passion for Ton-thormod, generously surrenders her to her lover, and brings about a reconciliation between the two kings."

91b. 5. *"Con-cathlin, 'mild beam of the wave.'*—What star was so called of old is not easily ascertained. Some now distinguish the pole-star by that name."—Macpherson.

92. FINGAL

Macpherson's Argument to Book 1 of *Fingal* is as follows: "Cuthullin (general of the Irish tribes, in the minority of Cormac, King of Ireland) sitting alone beneath a tree, at the gate of Tura, a castle of Ulster (the other chiefs having gone on a hunting party to Cromla, a neighboring hill), is informed of the landing of Swaran, King of Lochlin, by Moran, the son of Fithil, one of his scouts. He convenes the chiefs; a council is held, and disputes run high about giving battle to the enemy. Connal, the petty king of Togorma, and an intimate friend of Cuthullin, was for retreating, till Fingal, King of those Caledonians who inhabited the north-west coast of Scotland, whose aid had been previously solicited, should arrive; but Calmar, the son of Matha, lord of Lara, a country in Connaught, was for engaging the enemy immediately. Cuthullin, of himself willing to fight, went into the opinion of Calmar. Marching towards the enemy, he missed three of his bravest heroes, Fergus, Duchomar, and Cathba. Fergus arriving, tells Cuthullin of the death of the two other chiefs; which introduces the affecting episode of Morna, the daughter of Cormac. The army of Cuthullin is descried at a distance by Swaran, who sent the son of Arno to observe the motions of the enemy, while he himself ranged his forces in order of battle. The son of Arno returning to Swaran, describes to him Cuthullin's chariot, and the terrible appearance of that hero. The armies engage, but night coming on, leaves the victory undecided. Cuthullin, according to the hospitality of the times, sends to Swaran a formal invitation to a feast, by his bard Carril, the son of Knifena. Swaran refuses to come. Carril relates to Cuthullin the story of Grudar and Brassolis. A party, by Connal's advice, is sent to observe the enemy: which closes the action of the first day."

93b. 13. *Lochlin.*—"The Gaelic name of Scandinavia in general."—Macpherson.

16. *Inistore.*—"The Orkney Islands."—Macpherson.

56. *Four Stones.*—"This passage alludes to the manner of burial among the ancient Scots. They opened a grave six or eight feet deep; the bottom was lined with fine clay; and on this they laid the body of the deceased, and, if a warrier, his sword and the heads of twelve arrows by his side. Above they laid another stratum of clay, in which they placed the horn of a deer, the symbol of hunting. The whole was covered with a fine mould, and four stones were placed on end to mark the extent of the grave. These are the four stones alluded to here."—Macpherson.

95b. 53. "The Isle of Sky: not improperly called the 'isle of mist,' as its high hills, which catch the clouds from the Western Ocean, occasion almost continual rains."—Macpherson.

96b. 42. "The Coma here mentioned is that small river that runs through Glenco in Argyleshire. One of the hills which environ that romantic valley is still called Scornafena, or the hill of Fingal's people."—Macpherson.

97a. 3. "Lubar, a river in Ulster. *Labhar*, loud, noisy."—Macpherson.

Richard Hurd

Selections, p. 97 — Bibliography, p. 1430

"The *Lyrical Ballads* of 1798 were by no means the first indication of the change which was taking place in prevalent habits of thought and modes of expression. In criticism, men of letters early began, almost in spite of themselves, to reject the gods to whom they still professed allegiance. The citadel of classicism was first assaulted by the friends who claimed to defend it, and the attack was so insidious as to be irresistible. The very men who do most to bring about the Romantic Revival are strangely averse to its spirit of freedom and of individuality. Richard Hurd, the neoclassic upholder of Pope, the defender of *Poetical Imitation*, is one of the earliest to deviate from the beaten track, and is consequently of more importance than the ordinary neglect of his writings would lead one to suppose."—Edith J. Morley, in Introduction to Hurd's *Letters on Chivalry and Romance* (1911).

Horace Walpole

Selections, p. 100 — Bibliography, p. 1450

100. THE CASTLE OF OTRANTO

On the title page of the first edition, Walpole stated that *The Castle of Otranto* was "a Story, translated by William Marshal, Gent., from the original Italian of Onuphrio Muralto, Canon of the Church of St. Nicholas at Otranto."

The following account of the story is from Walpole's Preface to the first edition (1765):

"The following work was found in the library of an ancient Catholic family in the north of England. It was printed at Naples, in the black letter, in the year 1529. How much sooner it was written does not appear. The principal incidents are such as were believed in the darkest ages of Christianity; but the language and conduct have nothing that savors of barbarism. The style is the purest Italian. . . .

"If the story was written near the time when it is supposed to have happened, it must have been between 1095, the era of the first Crusade, and 1243, the date of the last, or not long afterwards. There is no other circumstance in the work that can lead us to guess at the period in which the scene is laid: the names of the actors are evidently fictitious, and probably disguised on purpose. . . .

"Miracles, visions, necromancy, dreams, and other preternatural events, are exploded now even from romances. That was not the case when our author wrote; much less when the story itself is supposed to have happened. Belief in every kind of prodigy was so established in those dark ages, that an author would not be faithful to the manners of the times, who would omit all mention of them. He is not bound to believe them himself, but he must represent his actors as believing them.

"If this air of the miraculous is excused, the reader will find nothing else unworthy of his perusal. Allow the possibility of the facts, and all the actors comport themselves as persons would do in their situation. There is no bombast, no similes, flowers, digressions, or unnecessary descriptions. Everything tends directly to the catastrophe. Never is the reader's attention relaxed. The rules of the drama are almost always observed throughout the conduct of the piece. The characters are well drawn, and still better maintained. Terror, the author's principal engine, prevents the story from ever languishing; and it is so often contrasted by pity, that the mind is kept up in a constant vicissitude of interesting passions. . . .

"Though the machinery is invention, and the names of the actors imaginary, I cannot but believe that the groundwork of the story is founded on truth. The scene is undoubtedly laid in some real castle. The author seems frequently, without design, to describe particular parts. 'The chamber,' says he, 'on the right hand;' 'the door on the left hand;' 'the distance from the chapel to Conrad's apartment;' these and other passages are strong presumptions that the author had some certain building in his eye. Curious persons, who have leisure to employ in such researches, may possibly discover in the Italian writers the foundation on which our author has built. If a catastrophe, at all resembling that which he describes, is believed to have given rise to this work, it will contribute to interest the reader, and will make *The Castle of Otranto* a still more moving story."

Walpole acknowledged the authorship of the story in the Preface to the second edition (1765) and gave further comment on the work, as follows: "It was an attempt to blend the two kinds of romance, the ancient and the modern. In the former, all was imagination and improbability; in the latter, nature is always intended to be, and sometimes has been, copied with success. Invention has not been wanting, but the great resources of fancy have been dammed up by a strict adherence to common life."

The origin of the romance is given by Walpole in a letter to the Rev. William Cole, dated March 9, 1765: "I had time to write but a short note with *The Castle of Otranto*, as your messenger called on me at four o'clock, as I was going to dine abroad. Your partiality to me and Strawberry have, I hope, inclined you to excuse the wildness of the story. You will even have found some traits to put you in mind of this place. When you read of the picture quitting its panel, did not you recollect the portrait of Lord Falkland, all in white, in my gallery? Shall I even confess to you, what was the origin of this romance! I waked one morning, in the beginning of last June, from a dream, of which, all I could recover was that I had thought myself in an ancient castle (a very natural dream for a head filled like mine with Gothic story), and that on the uppermost bannister of a great staircase I saw a gigantic hand in armor. In the evening I sat down, and began to write, without knowing in the least what I intended to say or relate. The work grew on my hands, and I grew fond of it—add that I was very glad to think of anything, rather than politics. In short, I was so engrossed with my tale, which I completed in less than two months, that one evening I wrote from the time I had drunk my tea, about six o'clock, till half an hour after one in the morning, when my hand and fingers were so weary that I could not hold the pen to finish the sentence, but

left Matilda and Isabella talking, in the middle of a paragraph. You will laugh at my earnestness; but if I have amused you by retracing with any fidelity the manners of ancient days, I am content, and give you leave to think me as idle as you please."

Thomas Percy

Poems, p. 110 — Bibliography, p. 1440

110.   RELIQUES OF ANCIENT
ENGLISH POETRY

The interest in old popular ballads is recognized as one of the important aspects of Romanticism, and selections from *Percy's Reliques* are included in this volume as representative of that phase of the movement. The *Reliques* is the most noted collection of ballads, songs, and other pieces of earlier poets, that was published in the eighteenth century. The materials were drawn from various sources, edited and discussed, expanded and compressed, as Percy pleased. The collection won an immediate popularity, and its influence upon subsequent writers of the Romantic period, notably Scott and Wordsworth, can hardly be overestimated. The text followed is that given by Percy.

"I remember well the spot where I read these volumes for the first time. It was beneath a huge platanus tree, in the ruins of what had been intended for an old-fashioned arbor in the *garden* I have mentioned. The summer-day sped onward so fast that notwithstanding the sharp appetite of thirteen, I forgot the hour of dinner, was sought for with anxiety, and was still found entranced in my intellectual banquet. To read and to remember was in this instance the same thing, and henceforth I overwhelmed my school-fellows, and all who would hearken to me, with tragical recitations from the ballads of Bishop Percy. The first time, too, I could scrape a few shillings together, which were not common occurrences with me, I bought unto myself a copy of these beloved volumes; nor do I believe I ever read a book half so frequently, or with half the enthusiasm."—Scott, in *Autobiography*, printed as Chapter 1 of Lockhart's *Memoirs of the Life of Sir Walter Scott, Bart.* (1837-39).

"I have already stated how Germany is indebted to this latter work; and for our own country, its poetry has been absolutely redeemed by it. I do not think there is a writer in verse of the present day who would not be proud to acknowledge his obligations to the *Reliques*. I know that it is so with my friends;

and for myself, I am happy in this occasion to make a public avowal of my own."—Wordsworth, in *Essay, Supplementary to the Preface* (1815).

ROBIN HOOD AND GUY OF GISBORNE

Robin Hood, the famous legendary English outlaw, is the subject of numerous songs and ballads. His chief resort was in Sherwood Forest, in Nottinghamshire. Of his followers, the most noted are Little John, Friar Tuck, and Maid Marian.

The scene of this ballad is in the vicinity of Gisborne, a town near the western border of Yorkshire. The two yeomen (l. 11) about whom Robin Hood dreams are Sir Guy and the Sheriff of Nottingham; Little John (l. 17) had been captured by the Sheriff.

112.   THE ANCIENT BALLAD OF
                      CHEVY-CHASE

This ballad is known also as *The Hunting of the Cheviot*. The scene of the action is the chase, or hunting ground, of Cheviot, a range of hills in Northumberlandshire, England, and Roxburghshire, Scotland.

The persons mentioned in the ballad belong to English and Scottish history of the fourteenth and fifteenth centuries.

"I never heard the old song of Percy and Douglas that I found not my heart moved more than with a trumpet; and yet it is sung but by some blind crowder with no rougher voice than rude style; which being so apparelled in the dust and cobwebs of that uncivil age, what would it work, trimmed in the gorgeous eloquence of Pindar?"—Sidney, in *The Defense of Poesy* (1595). See also Addison's praise of the ballad in *The Spectator*, Nos. 70 and 74.

James Beattie

Poems, p. 119 — Bibliography, p. 1406

"I thanked you in my last for Johnson; I now thank you, with more emphasis, for Beattie, the most agreeable and amiable writer I ever met with; the only author I have seen whose critical and philosophical researches are diversified and embellished by a poetical imagination, that makes even the driest subject, and the leanest, a feast for an epicure in books. He is so much at his ease too, that his own character appears in every page, and which is very rare, we see not only the writer but the man: and that man so gentle, so well-tempered, so happy in his religion, and so humane in his philosophy, that it is necessary to love him, if one has the least sense of what is lovely. If

you have not his poem called *The Minstrel*, and cannot borrow it, I must beg you to buy it for me; for though I cannot afford to deal largely in so expensive a commodity as books, I must afford to purchase at least the poetical works of Beattie."—Cowper, in letter to the Rev. William Unwin, April 5, 1784.

120.   THE MINSTREL

"The design was to trace the progress of a poetical genius, born in a rude age, from the first dawning of fancy and reason, till that period at which he may be supposed capable of appearing in the world as a minstrel, that is, as an itinerant poet and musician; a character which, according to the notions of our forefathers, was not only respectable, but sacred.

"I have endeavored to imitate Spenser in the measure of his verse, and in the harmony, simplicity, and variety of his composition. Antique expressions I have avoided, admitting, however, some old words, where they seemed to suit the subject; but I hope none will be found that are now obsolete, or in any degree not intelligible to a reader of English poetry.

"To those who may be disposed to ask what could induce me to write in so difficult a measure, I can only answer that it pleases my ear, and seems, from its Gothic structure and original, to bear some relation to the subject and spirit of the poem. It admits both simplicity and magnificence of sound and of language, beyond any other stanza I am acquainted with. It allows the sententiousness of the couplet, as well as the more complex modulation of blank verse. What some critics have remarked of its uniformity growing at last tiresome to the ear, will be found to hold true only when the poetry is faulty in other respects."—Beattie's Preface.

121. 50. Eighteenth-century writers idealized America as a land of gold and precious stones.

Thomas Chatterton

Poems, p. 125 — Bibliography, p. 1415

"I thought of Chatterton, the marvellous Boy,
The sleepless Soul that perished in his pride."
        —Wordsworth, *Resolution and Independence*, 43-44 (p. 310).

"The purest English, I think—or what ought to be purest—is Chatterton's. The language had existed long enough to be entirely uncorrupted of Chaucer's Gallicisms, and still the old words are used. Chatterton's language is entirely northern. I prefer the native music of it to Milton's, cut by feet."—Keats, in letter to George and Georgiana Keats, Sept. 22, 1819. See also Keats's *To Chatterton* (p. 778).

The following poems of Chatterton belong to what are known as the Rowley Poems. Chatterton invented a vocabulary, based upon the usage of the fourteenth and fifteenth centuries, and employed it in the composition of a number of poems, which he palmed off as the work of Thomas Rowley, a fictitious priest of fifteenth century Bristol. For an account of the controversy which was waged over these poems, see "History of the Rowley Controversy," in *Poetical Works* (British Poets ed., 1857). Chatterton's acknowledged poems are all written in the conventional eighteenth-century manner.

125. BRISTOWE TRAGEDIE

This poem is probably based upon the execution of Sir Baldwin Fulford for treason at Bristol (Bristowe) in 1461. During the Wars of the Roses, Fulford opposed the claim of Edward IV to the English throne.

130. THE ACCOUNTE OF W. CANYNGES FEAST

This poem is ascribed to William Canynge, whom Chatterton makes a friend and patron of Rowley. William Canynge (c. 1400-74) was a rich and influential citizen of Bristol. He was mayor of the city, and rebuilt at his own expense the famous Bristol Church of St. Mary. He appears as a defender of Fulford in *Bristowe Tragedie*.

9. Some editors print a comma after *keepe* and a semicolon after *stylle*, and interpret *heie stylle* as *high style*. Chatterton's Glossary defines *heie* only as *they*.

ÆLLA

"Ælla, a Tragycal Enterlude, or Discoorseynge Tragedie, wrotenn bie Thomas Rowleie; plaiedd before Mastre Canynge, atte hys Howse Nempte the Bodde Lodge; alsoe before the Duke of Norfolck, Johan Howard."—Chatterton's Title-Page.

132. AN EXCELENTE BALADE OF CHARITIE

"Thomas Rowley, the author, was born at Norton Malreward, in Somersetshire, educated at the Convent of St. Kenna, at Keynesham, and died at Westbury in Gloucestershire."—Chatterton.

134. EPITAPH ON ROBERT CANYNGE

Chatterton submitted this poem on vellum as a fragment of the original manuscript of Rowley.

William Beckford

Selections, p. 134 — Bibliography, p. 1407

134. VATHEK

This story originally was written in French. A surreptitious English translation, *The History of the Caliph Vathek*, by S. Henley, one of Beckford's friends, was published in 1786; in the Preface, Henley stated that the story was translated from the Arabic. Beckford published the original French text, in both Paris and Lausanne, in 1787.

"I do not know from what source the author of that singular volume may have drawn his materials; some of the incidents are to be found in the *Bibliotheque Orientale;* but for correctness of costume, beauty of description, and power of imagination, it far surpasses all European imitations, and bears such marks of originality that those who have visited the East will find some difficulty in believing it to be more than a translation. As an Eastern tale, even *Rasselas* must bow before it; his 'Happy Valley' will not bear a comparison with the 'Hall of Eblis.'"—Byron, in note on *The Giaour*, l. 1328 (1813).

"European literature has no Oriental fiction which impresses the imagination so powerfully and permanently as *Vathek*. Portions of the story may be tedious or repulsive, but the whole combines two things most difficult of alliance—the fantastic and the sublime."—Garnett, in *Dictionary of National Biography* (1885).

135a. 56. "In this heaven the paradise of Mahomet is supposed to be placed contiguous to the throne of Alla. Hagi Khalfah relates that Ben Iatmaiah, a celebrated Doctor of Damascus, had the temerity to assert that, when the Most High erected his throne, he reserved a vacant place for Mahomet upon it." —Henley's note in first edition.

138a. 37. "This is an apparent anachronism, but such frequently occur in reading the Arabian writers. . . . Though the origin of spectacles can be traced back with certainty no higher than the thirteenth century, yet the . . . . art of staining glass is sufficiently ancient to have suggested in the days of Vathek the use of green as a protection to the eye from a glare of light."—Henley.

139b. 14. "A phial of a similar potion is ordered to be instantaneously drank off in one of the Tales of Inatulla. 'These brewed enchantments' have been used in the East from the days of Homer. Milton in his *Comus* describes one of them, which greatly resembles the Indian's:

And first behold this cordial julep here,
That flames and dances in his crystal bounds,
With spirits of balm, and fragrant syrups
    mix'd.
Not that Nepenthes, which the wife of Thone
In Egypt gave to Jove-born Helena,
Is of such pow'r to stir up joy as this;
To life so friendly, or so cool to thirst."
                [ll. 672-78].—Henley.

56. In the portion omitted, the Indian, kicked from the palace because of his insolence, forms himself into a ball, rolls through the streets of the city and across the valley and plunges over the precipice into the gulf beneath. After many days and nights he reappears to Vathek, who has been waiting on the precipice, and promises to lead him to the palace of subterranean fire if he will abjure Mahomet. The promise is given, but before the journey can be begun, the Indian's thirst must be satisfied with the blood of fifty of the most beautiful sons of prominent men. Vathek treacherously makes the sacrifice, but the Indian immediately disappears. Endangered by the hostile attitude of the distracted parents of the sacrificed children, Vathek is advised by his mother to set out with a magnificent train in search of the region of wonders and delight. After numerous adventures, in which many of his company are lost, he comes to the happy valley of the Emir Fakreddin and is royally entertained in his beautiful palace. Vathek at once becomes enamored of Nouronihar, the Emir's daughter, and, contrary to the wishes of her father, induces her to accompany him to the subterranean kingdom. Various beneficent Genii warn Vathek, on the way, to abandon his purpose, with the result that nearly all of his attendants desert him. (At this point the concluding selection begins.)

143b. 41. In the third French edition of *Vathek*, Beckford inserted here the titles of three of these stories. They have been published as *The Episodes of Vathek* (1912).

48. "The expedition of the Afrit in fetching Carathis is characteristic of this order of dives. We read in the Koran that another of the fraternity offered to bring the Queen of Saba's throne to Solomon before he could rise from his place." Ch. 27.—Henley.

William Cowper

Poems, p. 145 — Bibliography, p. 1421

"What a world are you daily conversant with, which I have not seen these twenty years, and shall never see again! The arts of dissi-

pation (I suppose) are nowhere practiced with more refinement or success than at the place of your present residence. By your account of it, it seems to be just what it was when I visited it, a scene of idleness and luxury, music, dancing, cards, walking, riding, bathing, eating, drinking, coffee, tea, scandal, dressing, yawning, sleeping; the rooms perhaps more magnificent, because the proprietors are grown richer, but the manners and occupations of the company just the same. Though my life has long been like that of a recluse, I have not the temper of one, nor am I in the least an enemy to cheerfulness and good humor; but I cannot envy you your situation; I even feel myself constrained to prefer the silence of this nook, and the snug fireside in our own diminutive parlor, to all the splendor and gaiety of Brighton.

"You ask me, how I feel on the occasion of my approaching publication. Perfectly at my ease. If I had not been pretty well assured beforehand that my tranquillity would be but little endangered by such a measure, I would never have engaged in it; for I cannot bear disturbance. I have had in view two principal objects; first, to amuse myself,—and secondly, to compass that point in such a manner, that others might possibly be the better for my amusement. If I have succeeded, it will give me pleasure; but if I have failed, I shall not be mortified to the degree that might perhaps be expected. I remember an old adage (though not where it is to be found), '*bene vixit, qui bene latuit*,' [he has lived well who has kept hidden (Ovid, *Tristia*, III, 4, 25)], and if I had recollected it at the right time, it should have been the motto to my book. By the way, it will make an excellent one for *Retirement*, if you can but tell me whom to quote for it. The critics cannot deprive me of the pleasure I have in reflecting, that so far as my leisure has been employed in writing for the public, it has been conscientiously employed, and with a view to their advantage. There is nothing agreeable, to be sure, in being chronicled for a dunce; but I believe there lives not a man upon earth who would be less affected by it than myself. With all this indifference to fame, which you know me too well to suppose me capable of affecting, I have taken the utmost pains to deserve it. This may appear a mystery or a paradox in practice, but it is true. I considered that the taste of the day is refined, and delicate to excess, and that to disgust the delicacy of taste, by a slovenly inattention to it, would be to forfeit at once all hope of being useful; and for this reason, though I have written more verse this last year than perhaps any man in England, I have finished, and polished, and touched, and re-touched, with the utmost care. If after all I should be converted into waste paper, it may be my misfortune, but it will not be my fault. I shall bear it with the most perfect serenity."—Cowper, in letter to the Rev. William Unwin, Oct. 6, 1781.

"Your fear lest I should think you unworthy of my correspondence, on account of your delay to answer, may change sides now, and more properly belongs to me. It is long since I received your last, and yet I believe I can say truly, that not a post has gone by me since the receipt of it that has not reminded me of the debt I owe you, for your obliging and unreserved communications both in prose and verse, especially for the latter, because I consider them as marks of your peculiar confidence. The truth is, I have been such a verse-maker, myself, and so busy in preparing a volume for the press, which I imagine will make its appearance in the course of the winter, that I hardly had leisure to listen to the calls of any other engagement. It is however finished, and gone to the printer's, and I have nothing now to do with it, but to correct the sheets as they are sent to me, and consign it over to the judgment of the public. It is a bold undertaking at this time of day, when so many writers of the greatest abilities have gone before, who seem to have anticipated every valuable subject, as well as all the graces of poetical embellishment, to step forth into the world in the character of a bard, especially when it is considered that luxury, idleness, and vice, have debauched the public taste, and that nothing hardly is welcome but childish fiction, or what has at least a tendency to excite a laugh. I thought, however, that I had stumbled upon some subjects, that had never before been poetically treated, and upon some others, to which I imagined it would not be difficult to give an air of novelty by the manner of treating them. My sole drift is to be useful; a point which however I knew I should in vain aim at, unless I could be likewise entertaining. I have therefore fixed these two strings upon my bow, and by the help of both have done my best to send my arrow to the mark. My readers will hardly have begun to laugh, before they will be called upon to correct that levity, and peruse me with a more serious air. As to the effect, I leave it alone in His hands, who can alone produce it: neither prose nor verse can reform the manners of a dissolute age, much less can they inspire a sense of religious obligation, unless assisted and made efficacious by the

power who superintends the truth He has vouchsafed to impart."—Cowper, in letter to Mrs. Cowper, his cousin, Oct. 19, 1781.

"I did not write the line that has been tampered with, hastily, or without due attention to the construction of it; and what appeared to me its only merit is, in its present state, entirely annihilated.

"I know that the ears of modern verse-writers are delicate to an excess, and their readers are troubled with the same squeamishness as themselves. So that if a line do not run as smooth as quicksilver they are offended. A critic of the present day serves a poem as a cook serves a dead turkey, when she fastens the legs of it to a post, and draws out all the sinews. For this we may thank Pope; but unless we could imitate him in the closeness and compactness of his expression, as well as in the smoothness of his numbers, we had better drop the imitation, which serves no other purpose than to emasculate and weaken all we write. Give me a manly, rough line, with a deal of meaning in it, rather than a whole poem full of musical periods, that have nothing but their oily smoothness to recommend them!

"I have said thus much, as I hinted in the beginning, because I have just finished a much longer poem than the last, which our common friend will receive by the same messenger that has the charge of this letter. In that poem there are many lines, which an ear, so nice as the gentleman's who made the above-mentioned alteration, would undoubtedly condemn; and yet (if I may be permitted to say it) they cannot be made smoother without being the worse for it. There is a roughness on a plum, which nobody that understands fruit would rub off, though the plum would be much more polished without it. But lest I tire you, I will only add, that I wish you to guard me from all such meddling; assuring you that I always write as smoothly as I can; but that I never did, never will, sacrifice the spirit or sense of a passage to the sound of it."—Cowper, in letter to Mr. Johnson, his publisher, undated (No. 330 in Lucas's ed.).

145. OLNEY HYMNS

This was a collection of hymns written by Cowper and John Newton at Olney, Cowper's residence in Buckinghamshire from 1767 to 1786.

"The profound personal religion, gloomy even to insanity as it often became, which fills the whole of Cowper's poetry, introduced a theological element into English poetry which continually increased till it died out with Browning and Tennyson."—Stopford Brooke, in *English Literature* (1880).

LIGHT SHINING OUT OF DARKNESS

This hymn is often entitled *God Moves in a Mysterious Way*. According to legend, Cowper one day proposed to commit suicide at a certain place as a sacrifice required by God, but as the driver of the vehicle could not find the place, Cowper returned home and composed this poem.

THE TASK

"The history of the following production is briefly this:—A lady, fond of blank verse, demanded a poem of that kind from the author, and gave him the Sofa for a subject. He obeyed; and, having much leisure, connected another subject with it; and, pursuing the train of thought to which his situation and turn of mind led him, brought forth at length, instead of the trifle which he at first intended, a serious affair—a Volume!"—From Cowper's prefatory Advertisement. The lady referred to was Mrs. Austin, a friend of Cowper.

"I send you four quires of verse [*The Task*], which having sent, I shall dismiss from my thoughts, and think no more of, till I see them in print. I have not after all found time or industry enough to give the last hand to the points. I believe, however, they are not very erroneous, though in so long a work, and in a work that requires nicety in this particular, some inaccuracies will escape. Where you find any, you will oblige me by correcting them.

"In some passages, especially in the Second Book, you will observe me very satirical. Writing on such subjects I could not be otherwise. I can write nothing without aiming at usefulness: it were beneath my years to do it, and still more dishonorable to my religion. I know that a reformation of such abuses as I have censured is not to be expected from the efforts of a poet; but to contemplate the world, its follies, its vices, its indifference to duty, and its strenuous attachment to what is evil, and not to reprehend were to approve it. From this charge at least I shall be clear, for I have neither tacitly nor expressly flattered either its characters or its customs. I have paid one, and only one compliment, which was so justly due, that I did not know how to withhold it, especially having so fair an occasion;—I forget myself, there is another in the First Book to Mr. Throckmorton,—but the compliment I mean is to Mr. Smith. It

is, however, so managed, that nobody but himself can make the application, and you, to whom I disclose the secret: a delicacy on my part, which so much delicacy on his obliged me to the observance of.

"What there is of a religious cast in the volume I have thrown towards the end of it, for two reasons; first, that I might not revolt the reader at his entrance—and secondly, that my best impressions might be made last. Were I to write as many volumes as Lope de Vega, or Voltaire, not one of them would be without this tincture. If the world like it not, so much the worse for them. I make all the concessions I can, that I may please them, but I will not please them at the expense of conscience.

"My descriptions are all from nature: not one of them second-handed. My delineations of the heart are from my own experience: not one of them borrowed from books, or in the least degree conjectural. In my numbers, which I have varied as much as I could (for blank verse without variety of numbers is no better than bladder and string), I have imitated nobody, though sometimes perhaps there may be an apparent resemblance; because at the same time that I would not imitate, I have not affectedly differed.

"If the work cannot boast a regular plan (in which respect, however, I do not think it altogether indefensible), it may yet boast, that the reflections are naturally suggested always by the preceding passage, and that except in the Fifth Book, which is rather of a political aspect, the whole has one tendency: to discountenance the modern enthusiasm after a London life, and to recommend rural ease and leisure, as friendly to the cause of piety and virtue."—Cowper, in letter to the Rev. William Unwin, Oct. 10, 1784. Throckmorton and Smith were friends of Cowper. Lope de Vega, a Spanish dramatist and poet of the seventeenth century, is said to have written 1800 plays, besides 400 poems. Voltaire was a prolific French writer of the eighteenth century.

"How do you like Cowper? Is not *The Task* a glorious poem? The religion of *The Task*, bating a few scraps of Calvinist divinity, is the religion of God and nature, the religion that exalts, that ennobles man."—Robert Burns, in letter to Mrs. Dunlop, Dec. 25, 1795.

"I have been reading *The Task* with fresh delight. I am glad you love Cowper. I could forgive a man for not enjoying Milton, but I would not call that man my friend, who should be offended with the 'divine chit-chat of Cowper.'"—Lamb, in letter to Coleridge, Dec. 5, 1796. The phrase quoted by Lamb was Coleridge's.

"Is the kitchen-garden indeed poetical? To-day, perhaps; but tomorrow, if my imagination is barren, I shall see there nothing but carrots and other kitchen stuff. It is my sensation which is poetic, which I must respect, as the most precious flower of beauty. Hence a new style. It is no longer a question, after the old oratorical fashion, of boxing up a subject in a regular plan, dividing it into symmetrical portions, arranging ideas into files, like the pieces on a draught-board. Cowper takes the first subject that comes to hand—one which Lady Austin gave him at haphazard—*The Sofa*, and speaks about it for a couple of pages; then he goes whither the bent of his mind leads him, describing a winter evening, a number of interiors and landscapes, mingling here and there all kinds of moral reflections, stories, dissertations, opinions, confidences, like a man who thinks aloud before the most intimate and beloved of his friends. 'The best didactic poems,' says Southey [*Life of Cowper*, p. 341], 'when compared with *The Task*, are like formal gardens in comparison with woodland scenery.' This is his great poem, *The Task*. If we enter into details, the contrast is greater still. He does not seem to dream that he is being listened to; he only speaks to himself. He does not dwell on his ideas, to set them in relief, and make them stand out by repetitions and antitheses; he marks his sensation and that is all. We follow it in him as it is born, and we see it rising from a former one, swelling, falling, remounting, as we see vapor issuing from a spring, and insensibly rising, unrolling, and developing its shifting forms. Thought, which in others was curdled and rigid, becomes here mobile and fluent; the rectilinear verse grows flexible; the noble vocabulary widens its scope to let in vulgar words of conversation and life. At length poetry has again become lifelike; we no longer listen to words, but we feel emotions; it is no longer an author but a man who speaks. His life is there perfect, beneath its black lines, without falsehood or concoction; his whole effort is bent on removing falsehood and concoction. When he describes his little river, his dear Ouse, 'slow winding through a level plain of spacious meads, with cattle sprinkled o'er' [*The Task*, 1, 163-64 (p. 146)], he sees it with his inner eye, and each word, cæsura, sound, answers to a change of that inner vision. It is so in all his verses, they are full of personal emotions, genuinely felt, never al-

tered or disguised; on the contrary, fully expressed, with their transient shades and fluctuations; in a word, as they are, that is, in the process of production and destruction, not all complete, motionless, and fixed, as the old style represented them. Herein consists the great revolution of the modern style. The mind, outstripping the known rules of rhetoric and eloquence, penetrates into profound psychology, and no longer employs words except to mark emotions."—Taine, in *History of English Literature*, Book 4, 1 (1863).

148. 560ff. Cf. Blake's *The Book of Thel*, 93ff. (p. 174).

THE POPLAR-FIELD

"People nowadays, I believe, hold this style and metre light; I wish there were any one who could put words together with such exquisite flow and evenness."—Palgrave, in *Personal Recollections*, printed in *Alfred Lord Tennyson: A Memoir by his Son* (1897).

149. ON THE RECEIPT OF MY MOTHER'S PICTURE OUT OF NORFOLK

"I have lately received from a female cousin of mine in Norfolk, whom I have not seen these thirty years, a picture of my own mother. She died when I wanted two days of being six years old; yet I remember her perfectly, find the picture a strong likeness of her, because her memory has been ever precious to me, have written a poem on the receipt of it: a poem which, one excepted, I had more pleasure in writing, than any that I ever wrote. That one was addressed to a lady whom I expect in a few minutes to come down to breakfast, and who has supplied to me the place of my own mother—my own invaluable mother, these six-and-twenty-years. Some sons may be said to have had many fathers, but a plurality of mothers is not common."—Cowper, in letter to Mrs. King, March 12, 1790.

Cowper refers to Mrs. Unwin; the poem addressed to her is *To Mary* (p. 153).

150. 46ff. Cf. this passage with the following stanza from Tennyson's *In Memoriam* (102, 1-4):

We leave the well-beloved place
  Where first we gazed upon the sky;
  The roofs, that heard our earliest cry,
Will shelter one of stranger race.

151. YARDLEY OAK

Elton regards this fragment as the best work of Cowper's imagination. (*A Survey of English Literature, 1780-1830*, 1, 84). The tree described in this poem stood in Yardley hunting ground, near Cowper's house in Buck-inghamshire, England. It was nearly 23 feet in girth; it is said to have been planted by the daughter of William the Conqueror.

153. 143. The following lines, crossed through in the manuscript, are sometimes printed in the poem between lines 143 and 144.

Thou, like myself, hast stage by stage attain'd
Life's wintry bourn; thou, after many years,
I after few; but few or many prove
A span in retrospect; for I can touch
With my least finger's end my own decease
And with extended thumb my natal hour,
And hadst thou also skill in measurement
As I, the past would seem as short to thee. ·
Evil and few—said Jacob—at an age
Thrice mine, and few and evil, I may think
The Prediluvian race, whose buxom youth
Endured two centuries, accounted theirs.
"Shortliv'd as foliage is the race of man.
The wind shakes down the leaves, the budding
    grove
Soon teems with others, and in spring they
    grow.
So pass mankind. One generation meets
Its destin'd period, and a new succeeds."
Such was the tender but undue complaint
Of the Mæonian in old time; for who
Would drawl out centuries in tedious strife
Severe with mental and corporeal ill
And would not rather chuse a shorter race
To glory, a few decads here below?

The quoted lines are from Cowper's translation of the *Iliad*, 6, 175-79. The Mæonian is Homer, reputed to have been a native of ancient Mæonia, in Lydia, Asia Minor.

TO MARY

This poem is addressed to Mrs. Mary Unwin, Cowper's friend and companion for thirty-four years. See above note on *On the Receipt of my Mother's Picture.*

George Crabbe

Poems, p. 154 — Bibliography, p. 1421
"Yet Truth sometimes will lend her noblest
    fires,
And decorate the verse herself inspires:
This fact in Virtue's name let Crabbe attest;
Though nature's sternest painter, yet the
    best."
—Byron, in *English Bards and Scotch Reviewers*, 855-58 (p. 520).

"There was in each of the four British poets, who illuminated this darkest period just before the dawn, the determination to be natural and sincere. It was this that gave Cowper his directness and his delicacy; it was this which stamps with the harsh mark of truth the sombre vignettes of Crabbe, just as truly as it gave the voluptuous ecstasy to the songs of Blake, and to the strong, homely verse of Burns its potent charm and mastery. It was reality that was rising to drive back into oblivion the demons of conventionality, of 'regular diction,' of the proprieties and machinery of composition, of all the worn-out bogies with which poetical old women frightened the baby talents of the end of the eighteenth century. Not all was done, even by these admirable men: in Burns himself we constantly hear the old verbiage grating and grinding on; in his slow movements Crabbe is not to be distinguished from his predecessors of a hundred years; Cowper is forever showing qualities of grace and elegant amenity which tempt us to call him, not a forerunner of the nineteenth, but the finest example of the eighteenth-century type. Yet the revolt against rhetorical convention is uppermost, and that it is which is really the characteristic common feature of this singularly dissimilar quartette; and when the least inspired, the least revolutionary of the four takes us along the dismal coast that his childhood knew so well, and bids us mark how

'Here on its wiry stem, in rigid bloom,
Grows the salt lavender that lacks perfume;
Here the dwarf sallows creep, the septfoil
    harsh,
And the soft, shiny mallow of the marsh,'
    [Crabbe, *The Lover's Journey*, 120-23.]

we observe that the reign of empty verbiage is over, and that the poets who shall for the future wish to bring concrete ideas before us will do so in sincere and exact language. That position once regained, the revival of imaginative writing is but a question of time and of opportunity."—Gosse, in *A Short History of Modern English Literature* (1898).

For Jeffrey's criticism of Crabbe's poems, see p. 910. See also Wordsworth's note on *Lucy Gray* (p. 1280); and Byron's letter to Murray, Sept. 15, 1817 (p. 1326).

154.   THE VILLAGE

"*The Village* was intended as an antithesis to Goldsmith's idyllic sentimentalism. Crabbe's realism, preceding even Cowper and anticipating Wordsworth, was the first important indication of one characteristic movement in the contemporary school of poetry. His clumsy style and want of sympathy with the new world isolated him as a writer, as he was a recluse in his life. But the force and fidelity of his descriptions of the scenery of his native place and of the characteristics of the rural population give abiding interest to his work. His pathos is genuine and deep, and to some judgments his later works atone for the diminution in tragic interest by their gentleness and simple humor."—Stephen, in *Dictionary of National Biography* (1887).

160.   THE BOROUGH

"When the reader enters into the poem, he will find the author retired from view, and an imaginary personage brought forward to describe his Borough for him: to him it seemed convenient to speak in the first person: but the inhabitant of a village, in the center of the kingdom, could not appear in the character of a residing burgess in a large sea-port; and when, with this point, was considered what relations were to be given, what manners delineated, and what situations described, no method appeared to be so convenient as that of borrowing the assistance of an ideal friend: by this means the reader is in some degree kept from view of any particular place, nor will he perhaps be so likely to determine where those persons reside, and what their connections, who are so intimately known to this man of straw.

"From the title of this poem, some persons will, I fear, expect a political satire,—an attack upon corrupt principles in a general view, or upon the customs and manners of some particular place; of these they will find nothing satirized, nothing related. It may be that graver readers would have preferred a more historical account of so considerable a borough—its charter, privileges, trade, public structures, and subjects of this kind; but I have an apology for the omission of these things, in the difficulty of describing them, and in the utter repugnancy which subsists between the studies and objects of topography and poetry. What I thought I could best describe, that I attempted—the sea, and the country in the immediate vicinity; the dwellings, and the inhabitants; some incidents and characters, with an exhibition of morals and manners, offensive perhaps to those of extremely delicate feelings, but sometimes, I hope, neither unamiable nor unaffecting: an election indeed forms a part of one Letter, but the evil there described is one not greatly nor generally deplored, and there are probably many places of this kind where it is not felt.

"From the variety of relations, characters, and descriptions which a borough affords, several were rejected which a reader might reasonably expect to have met with: in this case he is entreated to believe that these, if they occurred to the author, were considered by him as beyond his ability, as subjects which he could not treat in a manner satisfactory to himself. Possibly the admission of some will be thought to require more apology than the rejection of others: in such variety, it is to be apprehended, that almost every reader will find something not according with his ideas of propriety, or something repulsive to the tone of his feelings; nor could this be avoided but by the sacrifice of every event, opinion, and even expression, which could be thought liable to produce such effect; and this casting away so largely of our cargo, through fears of danger, though it might help us to clear it, would render our vessel of little worth when she came into port. I may likewise entertain a hope, that this very variety, which gives scope to objection and censure, will also afford a better chance for approval and satisfaction. . . .

"In the first Letter is nothing which particularly calls for remark, except possibly the last line—giving a promise to the reader that he should both smile and sigh in the perusal of the following Letters. This may appear vain, and more than an author ought to promise; but let it be considered that the character assumed is that of a friend, who gives an account of objects, persons, and events to his correspondent, and who was therefore at liberty, without any imputation of this kind, to suppose in what manner he would be affected by such descriptions."—From Crabbe's Preface.

William Lisle Bowles

Poems, p. 164 — Bibliography, p. 1410

"I had just entered on my seventeenth year, when the sonnets of Mr. Bowles, twenty in number, and just then published in a quarto pamphlet, were first made known and presented to me, by a school-fellow who had quitted us for the University, and who, during the whole time that he was in our first form . . . had been my patron and protector. . . . It was a double pleasure to me, and still remains a tender recollection, that I should have received from a friend so revered the first knowledge of a poet by whose works, year after year, I was so enthusiastically delighted and inspired. My earliest acquaintances will not have forgotten the undisciplined eagerness and impetuous zeal, with which I labored to make proselytes, not only of my companions, but of all with whom I conversed, of whatever rank, and in whatever place. As my school finances did not permit me to purchase copies, I made, within less than a year and a half, more than forty transcriptions, as the best presents I could offer to those who had in any way won my regard. And with almost equal delight did I receive the three or four following publications of the same author. . . . My obligations to Mr. Bowles were indeed important, and for radical good. At a very premature age, even before my fifteenth year, I had bewildered myself in metaphysics, and in theological controversy. . . . This preposterous pursuit was, beyond doubt, injurious both to my natural powers, and to the progress of my education. It would perhaps have been destructive, had it been continued; but from this I was auspiciously withdrawn, partly indeed by an accidental introduction to an amiable family, chiefly, however, by the genial influence of a style of poetry, so tender and yet so manly, so natural, and real, and yet so dignified and harmonious, as the sonnets, etc., of Mr. Bowles!"—Coleridge, in *Biographia Literaria*, 1 (1817).

See Coleridge's *To the Reverend W. L. Bowles* (p. 355).

"As the English romantic poets went forth to combat the classic school with its supersense and pride of strict rules, and to endow the poetry of the fairy tale with new life, their first halt was under the shadow of Bowles. Compared with such a poet of the intellect as Pope, who had maintained that, with a clear head and dexterous style, nothing was too prosaic to be converted into poetry, such an elegist as Bowles, who aimed at all effect through the heart, was a most refreshing contrast."—A. Brandl, in *Samuel Taylor Coleridge and the English Romantic School*, English translation by Lady Eastlake (1887).

See Byron's *English Bards and Scotch Reviewers*, 327-84 (pp. 516-17).

164.   AT TYNEMOUTH PRIORY

Tynemouth Priory is a noted ruin of an ancient church in Tynemouth, a city at the mouth of the River Tyne, in Northumberland-shire, England. The city is noted as a watering-place and also for its picturesque cliffs.

THE BELLS, OSTEND

Ostend is a famous seaside resort in Belgium.

BAMBOROUGH CASTLE

Bamborough Castle is an ancient castle in Bamborough, a village on the coast of Northumberlandshire, England.

William Blake

Selections, p. 166 — Bibliography, p. 1408

"To define the poetry of Blake one must find new definitions for poetry; but, these definitions once found, he will seem to be the only poet who is a poet in essence; the only poet who could, in his own words, 'enter into Noah's rainbow, and make a friend and companion of one of these images of wonder, which always entreat him to leave mortal things.' In this verse there is, if it is to be found in any verse, the 'lyrical cry'; and yet, what voice is it that cries in this disembodied ecstasy? The voice of desire is not in it, nor the voice of passion, nor the cry of the heart, nor the cry of the sinner to God, nor of the lover of nature to nature. It neither seeks nor aspires nor laments nor questions. It is like the voice of wisdom in a child, who has not yet forgotten the world out of which the soul came. It is as spontaneous as the note of a bird, it is an affirmation of life; in its song, which seems mere music, it is the mind which sings; it is lyric thought. What is it that transfixes one in any couplet such as this:

'If the sun and moon should doubt
    They'd immediately go out.'

It is no more than a nursery statement, there is not even an image in it, and yet it sings to the brain, it cuts into the very flesh of the mind, as if there were a great weight behind it. Is it that it is an arrow, and that it comes from so far, and with an impetus gathered from its speed out of the sky? . . .

"The poetry of Blake is a poetry of the mind, abstract in substance, concrete in form; its passion is the passion of the imagination, its emotion is the emotion of thought, its beauty is the beauty of idea. When it is simplest, its simplicity is that of some 'infant joy' too young to have a name, or of some 'infant sorrow brought aged out of eternity into the dangerous world,' and there,

'Helpless, naked, piping loud,
    Like a fiend hid in a cloud.'

There are no men and women in the world of Blake's poetry, only primal instincts and the energies of the imagination."—Symons, in *The Romantic Movement in English Poetry* (1909).

168.   TO THE MUSES

For the names and offices of the Muses, see Glossary under *Muse*. The thought of this poem should be compared with that of Collins's *Ode on the Poetical Character* (p. 49).

SONGS OF INNOCENCE

For an interpretation of the poems published under this title see Berger's *William Blake*, pp. 284-304.

172. THE LITTLE BLACK BOY

Coleridge greatly admired this poem, as he did also *The Divine Image*.

173. THE BOOK OF THEL

This is one of Blake's so-called Prophetic or Symbolic Books, a series of writings in which he presents his ideas on ethics, morality, religion, etc. The names in the poem are of Blake's coinage.

"The regularity of its unrimed fourteeners, the idyllic gentleness of its imagery, and the not unpleasant blending of simplicity and formalism in the diction, proclaim the mood of *Songs of Innocence*. It treats of the same all-pervading spirit of mutual love and self-sacrifice. In response to the 'gentle lamentations' of the virgin Thel, to whom life seems vain, and death utter annihilation, the lily of the valley, the cloud, the worm, and the clod rise up to testify to the interdependence of all forms of being under the Divine Image, and to show that death is not final extinction, but the supreme manifestation of this impulse to 'willing sacrifice of self.' Blake's original conclusion to this argument is lost, for the last section has not any perceptible connection in its context. In it, the whole conception of life is changed. This world is a dark prison, and the physical senses are narrow windows darkening the infinite soul of man by excluding 'the wisdom and joy of eternity,' the condition of which is freedom. The source of this degradation is the tyranny of abstract moral law, the 'mind-forged manacles' upon natural and, therefore, innocent desires; its symbols are the silver rod of authority and the golden bowl of a restrictive ethic that would mete out the immeasurable spirit of love. Here, Blake is clearly enough in the grip of the formal antinomianism that produced the later 'prophecies.' "—J. P. R. Wallis, in *The Cambridge History of English Literature*, Vol. 11, ch. 9.

The *Motto* suggests that learning comes only from personal experience. Cf. *The Four Zoas*, 605ff. (p. 188).

1. *Mne Seraphim.*—In Blake's system, "Mnetha" was the name given to the Mother of All.

Keynes says (*Writings*, None such ed., I, 355): ". . . the apparently meaningless syllable was certainly intentional, probably being a corruption of the mystical name, Bne Seraphim, which is found in Agrippa's *Occult Philosophy* and elsewhere."

174. 51. Luvah is here represented as a sun god. Elsewhere in Blake the name symbolizes the Prince of Love, or passion.

175. THE MARRIAGE OF HEAVEN AND HELL

In this poem Blake opposes conventional moral and religious codes on the ground that they encourage fraud and deceit, and destroy spiritual integrity.

A MEMORABLE FANCY

18-19. Cf. Chatterton's *Bristowe Tragedie*, 133-136 (p. 126).

PROVERBS OF HELL

These cryptic sayings "deny the religious sanction of morality by denying the value of the restraint that is practised in obedience to external authority, including the authority of a transcendent deity; and condemn as futile prayer and all religious observances. On the positive side they affirm the value of enthusiasm, and of desire and passion carried to the degree conventionally condemned as excess."—Sloss and Wallis, I, 9.

8. Cf. Letter to Dr. Trusler (p. 195).

50. *apple tree . . . grow.* Cf. *Annotations to Sir Joshua Reynolds's Discourses* (p. 197).

177a. A MEMORABLE FANCY

35ff. In *All Religions Are One*, 5, Blake says: "The Religions of all Nations are derived from each Nation's different reception of the Poetic Genius, which is everywhere call'd the Spirit of Prophecy."

177b. A MEMORABLE FANCY

11-25. "It may possibly be that the stable, the church, and the vault represent the incarnation, the mortal life, and the death and resurrection of Jesus, while the mill and cave, which later become common symbols of religious error, image the repressive influence and the devious ways of the Christian Church, which offers, as rewards to its followers, an 'Eternal life' 'in an allegorical abode where existence hath never come' (*Europe*, 39), that is, the void immensity of the present parable." —Sloss and Wallis, I, 21.

178a. 18-20. Cf. *Proverbs of Hell*, 45 (p. 176).

178b. A SONG OF LIBERTY

This stirring song prophesies the destruction of all repressive codes and conventions—civil, social, religious—by the purifying power of native passion. The unrest in various nations is accepted as a sign of the emancipation of mankind.

179.   VISIONS OF THE DAUGHTERS
OF ALBION

This short poem of 218 lines opposes conventional moral standards. The daughters symbolize the souls of men under restrictions of the law. The theme developed is expressed in The Argument as follows:

I lovèd Theotormon,
And I was not ashamèd;
I trembled in my virgin fears,
And I hid in Leutha's vale!
I pluckèd Leutha's flower,
And I rose up from the vale;
But the terrible thunders tore
My virgin mantle in twain.

The Argument is spoken by Oothoon, one of the Daughters of Albion.
179. 63-81. These lines are spoken by Oothoon as she reflects on her feelings for Theotormon, the strict moralist. Lines 63-74 suggest Blake's belief in supersensuous knowledge.
83-97. Theotormon's reply shows how one may be deluded in both thought and morals.
181. 215. Cf. the last line of *A Song of Liberty* (p. 179a).

AMERICA

America continues the theme of *A Song of Liberty* (p. 178). In the poem Blake defines the forces inherent in the American Revolution, a symbol of the final overthrow of all forces of restraint. In his symbolic interpretation of the War of Independence Blake includes such actual persons as Washington, Franklin, and Hancock side by side with his usual imaginative creations. The lines printed here express the doctrine that man is free to put his impulses into action.
51. The lion and the wolf symbolize the tyranny of empire.

SONGS OF EXPERIENCE

When Blake published *Songs of Experience* and *Songs of Innocence* in one volume, he described the work as "Showing the Two Contrary States of the Human Soul." Poems from *Songs of Experience* should therefore be compared with any corresponding poems from *Songs of Innocence* (p. 168ff.). In the Rossetti MS. of Blake's poems the following poem appears under the title

MOTTO TO THE SONGS OF INNOCENCE
AND EXPERIENCE

The Good are attracted by Men's perceptions,
And think not for themselves;
Till Experience teaches them to catch

And to cage the Fairies & Elves.
And then the Knave begins to snarl
And the Hypocrite to howl!
And all his good Friends shew their private
ends,
And the Eagle is known from the Owl.

184.   THE TYGER

After reading this poem, Lamb declared the author to be "one of the most extraordinary persons of the age."

185.   A POISON TREE

This poem is sometimes entitled *Christian Forbearance*.

186.   A CRADLE SONG

This is from a notebook of Blake's; it was not included in *Songs of Experience* but was obviously intended for it. Cf. poem of same title in *Songs of Innocence*, p. 170.

A DIVINE IMAGE

Also obviously intended to be a part of *Songs of Experience*, though not included. See note on "A Cradle Song" above. For a contrast to this poem see "The Divine Image" from *Songs of Innocence* (p. 169).

TO TIRZAH

This poem was added to late editions of *Songs of Experience*.

LOVE'S SECRET

This poem is found without title in the Rossetti manuscript of Blake's poems. In the manuscript the last line is shown as a deleted line and "O, was no deny" is substituted.

THE FOUR ZOAS

The first title of this poem of 4000 lines was *Vala, or the Death and Judgment of the Eternal Man, and a Dream of Nine Nights*. In its final form the full title is *The Four Zoas; the Torments of Love and Jealousy in the Death and Judgment of Albion, the Ancient Man*. The chief interest of Blake is expressed in the Motto for the poem, quoted in Greek from *Ephesians*, 6:12—"For we wrestle not against flesh and blood, but against principalities, against powers, against the rulers of the darkness of this world, against spiritual wickedness in high places."
The four Zoas, symbolizing "the chief states through which the human spirit passes, the regulating principles of life," are thus interpreted by Berger:
"They are: (1st) *Urizen*, the firstborn of Eternity, the state of self-knowledge, arising

from experience, intelligence, and the reasoning faculty; (2nd) *Luvah*, the principle of human love, the state of the soul governed by the emotions; (3rd) *Tharmas*, the 'vegetative power,' that state of the spirit which feels only the blind forces of life and growth; (4th) *Urthona*, the instinct that binds the spirit of each individual to that of the whole universe; our last remaining recollection of the primeval unity. Urthona is also the spirit of art and of Prophecy."—*William Blake*, p. 130.

Los and Enitharmon are the offspring of Tharmas and his Emanation Enion, after she became a separate being. Enion is the "generative power in physical life." Los is the god of time; Enitharmon, his wife, represents space. Thus Blake suggests that time and space are necessary to vegetative life throughout its existence.

Before humanity became confined within the limits of the senses, all could walk forth as do Los and Enitharmon in the selection printed.

187. 532. *Ahania*. Ahania is an Emanation from Urizen. The two lived happily in Eden until Urizen transcended his own functions and assumed those that belonged to Luvah and regarded himself as the Supreme God. Then discord was born and laws were broken. Ahania left Urizen and became a "faint shadow, wandering in the void outside existence."

557-61. "These lines illustrate the repressive character of Natural Religion as symbolized by the Female."—Sloss and Wallis, *William Blake's Prophetic Writings*, I, 187.

574. *every thing . . . holy.* Cf. *Visions of the Daughters of Albion*, 215 (p. 181); and the last line of *A Song of Liberty* (p. 179).

188. 605. Cf. *Job*, 28:12-28—"But where shall wisdom be found? and where is the place of understanding?"

629. Urizen symbolizes in part the "principle of restrictive morality."

630. Other names for Non Entity are Chaos, Abyss, Void.

189.   AUGURIES OF INNOCENCE

1-4. With these lines compare Tennyson's *Flower in the Crannied Wall*, as follows:

Flower in the crannied wall,
I pluck you out of the crannies;
I hold you here, root and all, in my hand,
Little flower—but *if* I could understand
What you are, root and all, and all in all,
I should know what God and man is.

190.   THE MENTAL TRAVELLER

"*The Mental Traveller* indicates an explorer of mental phenomena. The mental phenomenon here symbolized seems to be the career of any great idea or intellectual movement—as, for instance, Christianity, chivalry, art, etc.—represented as going through the stages of—1, birth; 2, adversity and persecution; 3, triumph and maturity; 4, decadence through over-ripeness; 5, gradual transformation, under new conditions, into another renovated Idea, which again has to pass through all the same stages. In other words, the poem represents the action and re-action of Ideas upon society, and of society upon Ideas."—Rossetti's note in *Poetical Works* (1874). "The babe . . . I take to signify human genius or intellect, which none can touch and not be consumed except the 'woman old,' faith or fear: all weaker things, pain and pleasure, hatred and love, fly with shrieking, averted faces from before it. The gray and cruel nurse, custom or religion, crucifies and torments the child, feeding herself upon his agony to false fresh youth. Grown older, . . . he weds her; . . . custom, the daily life of men, once married to the fresh intellect, bears fruit to him of profit and pleasure; . . . but through such union he grows old the sooner, soon can but wander round and look over his finished work and gathered treasure, the tragic passions and splendid achievements of his spirit, kept fresh in verse or color . . . The 'female babe' sprung from the fire that burns always on his hearth is the issue or result of genius, which, being too strong for the father, flows into new channels and follows after fresh ways . . . The outcast intellect can then be vivified only by a new love. . . . Then follow the stages of love, and the phases of action and passion bred from either stage."—Swinburne, in *William Blake, a Critical Essay* (1868).

191.   MILTON

Milton is one of Blake's late Prophetic Books. See note on *The Book of Thel*, above. In *Milton*, Blake gives a mythical account of the progress of poetry. The poet Milton transmigrates into the body of Blake and through him gives assurance of the reign of the imagination and of the renewal of the human spirit in poetry.

Book the Second

61-96. Much of Blake's symbolic poetry was written during his three-year sojourn in Felpham, a seacoast town in Sussex. While there (1800-1803) he frequently wrote friends speaking of his delight in the wonders and beauties of nature. In these lines he rejoices in natural beauty, which communicates essential truth.

192. 78. Blake calls Beulah "a pleasant lovely Shadow Where no dispute can come, Because of those who Sleep." The weak and weary ones resting there are unable to face stern realities. Next to the highest of the four regions of humanity, Beulah is free from all kinds of doubt and error.

Ololon is an obscure symbol; it is found only in *Milton*. It is the name of a river in Eden, highest of the regions of humanity, and represents the Eternals who dwell on its banks. Eden is associated with perfect vision and vigorous spiritual activity. The other regions are Generation, associated with life on earth with its devastating errors in art and religion; and Ulro, which is chaos, a realm of complete error. Near the end of the poem Blake tells of meeting Ololon, a virgin of twelve years, as he walked in his cottage garden at Felpham; he addressed her as "a Daughter of Beulah."

82. Og and Anak symbolize the natural fears which prevent the free interplay of human hearts and minds.

497ff. Ololon is here the virgin who appeared in a vision before Blake at Felpham. She questions him about the poet Milton, who suddenly appears and holds converse with her. "Here, in this challenge, as vigorous as any Blake ever flung to the thought, art, and morality of his time, the identity of Blake and Milton is again clearly evident. This passage is also notable for the light it sheds upon the nature of the mystical Self-annihilation."—Sloss and Wallis, I, 423.

511. Francis Bacon (1561-1626), John Locke (1632-1704), and Sir Isaac Newton (1642-1727) represent the views of rationalistic philosophers. Albion, the symbol of mankind on earth, "is depicted as a victim of the cruelties of restrictive morality."—Sloss and Wallis, II, 131.

193.   JERUSALEM

Various meanings have been given to this poem. One meaning is that Jerusalem represents moral freedom, which can come to humanity, symbolized by Albion, only after the fetters of false religions are broken. Thus, true religion, which demands universal love and the achievement of man's desires, stands opposed to orthodox religions and moral codes that restrain desire, and also to those based solely on reason and science. Judaism represents the first type, Deism the other.

The poem consists of four chapters, each introduced by a short prologue. The first is addressed to the public; the second to the Jews; the third to the Deists; the fourth to the Christians.

193.   TO THE DEISTS

Blake's strangely arranged title for this selection is as follows:

Rahab is an Eternal State. } TO THE DEISTS { The Spiritual States of the Soul are all Eternal. Distinguish between the Man & his present State.

The Deists, who flourished in the seventeenth and eighteenth centuries, held that natural religion was the fruit of reason alone and had nothing to do with divine revelation and the supernatural doctrines of Christianity. Some of the leading Deists were Lord Edward Herbert (the Father of Deism), Charles Blount, John Toland, Matthew Tindal, Anthony Collins, Thomas Chubb, and Anthony Ashley Cooper, third Earl of Shaftesbury.

52. Rahab symbolizes religion of the strict law.

193b. 33. Voltaire, Rousseau, Gibbon, and Hume were supporters of the idea of natural religion.

44. Samuel Foote (1720-70) was the author of several satirical dramas. In *The Minor*, a farce directed against the Methodists, he represents Methodism as a covering for sin, and he mimics George Whitefield (1714-70), an evangelical preacher, as an overweening hypocrite, under the name of Mr. Squintum of the Tabernacle.

194a. 6. *Lewis.* The reference is to Matthew Gregory Lewis (1775-1818), author of *The Monk*, a novel in which the hero is a monk who falls into sin, becomes utterly depraved, commits murder, is sentenced to death, and compounds with the devil, who hurls him to destruction in another form.

Frederick. Frederic the Great, of Prussia (1712-86), who waged prolonged warfare against Austria. He was an intimate friend of Voltaire.

18. *The Monk of Charlemaine.* In this poem the monk is a symbol of condescending Christianity. Charlemagne, the great Emperor of the West (800), represents government by force.

23. Gibbon, Voltaire (l. 24), and Rousseau (l. 45) stand for skepticism.

44. Titus Livius (59 B.C.—17 A.D.) was a famous Roman historian. Constantine the Great (272-337) was the first Christian Emperor of Rome.

194. TO THE CHRISTIANS

58. *"Saul . . . me?"* The words heard by Saul as he journeyed toward Damascus. He had been persecuting the disciples of Jesus. See *Acts*, 9:1-9.

194b. 31. An allusion to Jesus's parable of the talents (*Matthew*, 25:1-30). The servant who had been entrusted with one talent only was condemned for hiding it in the earth instead of putting it to use. Cf. Milton's sonnet *On His Blindness*, 3: "And that one talent which is death to hide."

32. *treasures of Heaven.* From Christ's Sermon on the Mount (*Matthew*, 6:19-20): "Lay not up for yourselves treasures upon earth . . . But lay up for yourselves treasures in heaven."

45. *body . . . raiment.* From the Sermon on the Mount (*Matthew*, 6:25): "Is not the life more than meat, and the body than raiment?"

195. DEDICATION OF THE ILLUSTRATIONS TO BLAIR'S "THE GRAVE"

For a selection from Blair's *The Grave*, see pp. 37-40. Blake's poem, which he entitled *To the Queen*, is addressed to Queen Charlotte, wife of George III, King of England (1760-1820).

LETTER TO TRUSLER

This letter was written after Trusler had voiced dissatisfaction with some illustrations that he had engaged Blake to do for him. Lambeth is a section of London.

57. *Every body . . . alike.* Cf. *Proverbs of Hell*, 8 (p. 176).

196. LETTER TO FLAXMAN

John Flaxman (1755-1826) was a sculptor who had befriended Blake; he was one of the most important sculptors and designers of his period. His work is preserved in many of the churches of England. He is most widely known today for the clear-cut, classical drawings he made as illustrations for Pope's translations of the *Iliad* and the *Odyssey*. Blake lived at Felpham, a seashore town, near Chichester, in Sussex, from September 1800 to September 1803.

28. William Hayley (1745-1820) was an obscure poet, a country squire who lived near Blake at Felpham and who employed him to furnish illustrations and decorations for various purposes. Hayley was responsible for Blake's moving to Felpham and also, by his persistent interference, for Blake's returning to London.

197. ANNOTATIONS TO REYNOLDS'S DISCOURSES

Although Reynolds is frequently vague and inconsistent in his *Discourses*, many of his ideas are more valuable than Blake's attacks, based upon anti-romantic utterances, seem to indicate.

17. *Fuseli.* Henry Fuseli (1741-1825), a Swiss painter and art critic, who became a friend and near neighbor of Blake in London. In 1799-1800 he painted a series of forty-seven pictures from the poems of Milton. When these paintings were exhibited, they were not very well received by the public.

198. 5. *Apple tree . . . Fruit.* Cf. *Proverbs of Hell*, 50 (p. 176).

Robert Burns

Poems, p. 199 — Bibliography, p. 1411

"One song of Burns's is of more worth to you than all I could think for a whole year in his native country. His misery is a dead weight upon the nimbleness of one's quill—I tried to forget it—to drink toddy without any care—to write a merry sonnet—it won't do—he talked with bitches—he drank with blackguards, he was miserable—We can see horribly clear, in the works of such a man his whole life, as if we were God's spies."—Keats, in letter to Reynolds, July 13, 1818. "As if we were God's spies" is a phrase in *King Lear*, V, 3, 17.

"All that remains of Burns, the writings he has left, seem to us, as we hinted above, no more than a poor mutilated fraction of what was in him; brief, broken glimpses of a genius that could never show itself complete; that wanted all things for completeness: culture, leisure, true effort, nay, even length of life. His poems are, with scarcely any exception, mere occasional effusions; poured forth with little premeditation; expressing, by such means as offered, the passion, opinion, or humor of the hour. Never in one instance was it permitted him to grapple with any subject with the full collection of his strength, to fuse and mould it in the concentrated fire of his genius. To try by the strict rules of art such imperfect fragments, would be at once unprofitable and unfair. Nevertheless, there is something in these poems, marred and defective as they are, which forbids the most fastidious student of poetry to pass them by. Some sort of enduring quality they must have: for after fifty years of the wildest vicissitudes in poetic taste, they still continue to be read;

nay are read more and more eagerly, more and more extensively; and this not only by literary virtuosos, and that class upon whom transitory causes operate most strongly, but by all classes, down to the most hard, unlettered and truly natural class, who read little, and especially no poetry, except because they find pleasure in it. The grounds of so singular and wide a popularity, which extends, in a literal sense, from the palace to the hut, and over all regions where the English tongue is spoken, are well worth inquiring into. After every just deduction, it seems to imply some rare excellence in these works. What is that excellence?

"To answer this question will not lead us far. The excellence of Burns is, indeed, among the rarest, whether in poetry or prose; but, at the same time, it is plain and easily recognized: his *sincerity*, his indisputable air of truth. Here are no fabulous woes or joys; no hollow fantastic sentimentalities; no wire-drawn refinings, either in thought or feeling: the passion that is traced before us has glowed in a living heart; the opinion he utters has risen in his own understanding, and been a light to his own steps. He does not write from hearsay, but from sight and experience; it is the scenes that he has lived and labored amidst, that he describes: those scenes, rude and humble as they are, have kindled beautiful emotions in his soul, noble thoughts, and definite resolves; and he speaks forth what is in him, not from any outward call of vanity or interest, but because his heart is too full to be silent. He speaks it with such melody and modulation as he can; 'in homely rustic jingle'; but it is his own, and genuine."— Carlyle, in "Essay on Burns" (1828).

See Wordsworth's *At the Grave of Burns* (p. 317).

199.   O, ONCE I LOV'D A BONIE LASS

"For my own part, I never had the least thought or inclination of turning poet till I got once heartily in love, and then rhyme and song were in a manner the spontaneous language of my heart. The following composition was the first of my performances, and done at an early period of life, when my heart glowed with honest, warm simplicity; unacquainted and uncorrupted with the ways of a wicked world. The performance is, indeed, very puerile and silly; but I am always pleased with it, as it recalls to my mind those happy days when my heart was yet honest and my tongue was sincere. The subject of it was a young girl who really deserved all the praises I have bestowed on her. . . . The seventh stanza has several minute faults; but I re-

member I composed it in a wild enthusiasm of passion, and to this hour I never recollect it but my heart melts and my blood sallies at the remembrance."—Burns, *Commonplace Book*, 1783-85.

MARY MORISON

According to Gilbert Burns, Mary Morison was the subject of Burns's *And I'll Kiss Thee Yet, Yet*, the heroine of which has been thought to be either Mary Campbell or Elison Begbie. Henley and Henderson state (*The Poetry of Robert Burns*) that a Mary Morison lived at Mauchline from 1784, "said to have been as beautiful as amiable." She died in 1791.

MY NANIE, O

"As I have been all along a miserable dupe to love, and have been led into a thousand weaknesses and follies by it, for that reason I put the more confidence in my critical skill in distinguishing foppery and conceit from real passion and nature. Whether the following song will stand the test, I will not pretend to say, because it is my own; only I can say it was, at the time, real."—Burns, *Commonplace Book*, 1784.

200.   POOR MAILIE'S ELEGY

The stanza-form of this poem had been used for elegies by Sempill, Ramsay, and Fergusson, Scottish poets before Burns.

201.   TO DAVIE

This poem was addressed to David Sillar (1760-1830), son of a farmer near Tarbolton. He was a teacher in the parish school at Tarbolton, and a grocer in Irvine, before he published, in 1789, a volume of poems in imitation of Burns. Failing to get literary work in Edinburgh, he returned to Irvine, where he took up teaching again. He had considerable skill as a fiddler and as a poet.

EPISTLE TO J. LAPRAIK

John Lapraik (1727-1807) was an Ayrshire poet. Burns addressed two subsequent Epistles to him, both written in 1785.

202a. 13-17. The song referred to is Lapraik's *When I Upon Thy Bosom Lean*.

203. EPISTLE TO THE REV. JOHN M'MATH

John M'Math (1781-1825) was a convivial preacher, and a friend of Burns.

Holy Willie's[1] Prayer
And send the godly in a pet[2] to pray—Pope.[3]

Argument

Holy Willie was a rather oldish bachelor elder, in the parish of Mauchline, and much and justly famed for that polemical chattering which ends in tippling orthodoxy, and for that spiritualized bawdry which refines to liquorish devotion. In a sessional process with a gentleman in Mauchline—a Mr. Gavin Hamilton—Holy Willie and his priest, Father Auld, after full hearing in the Presbytery of Ayr, came off but second best, owing partly to the oratorical powers of Mr. Robert Aiken, Mr. Hamilton's counsel, but chiefly to Mr. Hamilton's being one of the most irreproachable and truly respectable characters in the country. On losing his process, the muse overheard him at his devotions as follows—

O Thou that in the heavens does dwell,
Wha, as it pleases best Thysel,
Sends ane to Heaven an' ten to Hell
    A' for Thy glory,
And no for onie guid or ill   5
    They've done before Thee!

I bless and praise Thy matchless might,
When thousands Thou hast left in night,
That I am here before Thy sight,
    For gifts an' grace   10
A burning and a shining light
    To a' this place.

What was I, or my generation,
That I should get sic exaltation?
I, wha deserv'd most just damnation   15
    For broken laws
Sax thousand years ere my creation,
    Thro' Adam's cause!

When from my mither's womb I fell,
Thou might hae plung'd me deep in Hell,   20
To gnash my gooms, and weep, and wail
    In burning lakes,
Whare damnèd devils roar and yell,
    Chain'd to their stakes.

Yet I am here, a chosen sample,   25
To show Thy grace is great and ample:
I'm here a pillar o' Thy temple,
    Strong as a rock,
A guide, a buckler, and example
    To a' Thy flock.   30

But yet, O Lord! confess I must:
At times I'm fash'd[4] wi' fleshly lust;

An' sometimes, too, in warldly trust,
    Vile self gets in;
But Thou remembers we are dust,   35
    Defiled wi' sin.

O Lord! yestreen, Thou kens, wi' Meg—
Thy pardon I sincerely beg—
O, may 't ne'er be a living plague
    To my dishonor!   40
An' I'll ne'er lift a lawless leg
    Again upon her.

Besides, I farther maun[1] avow—
Wi' Leezie's lass, three times, I trow—
But, Lord, that Friday I was fou,[2]   45
    When I cam near her,
Or else, Thou kens, Thy servant true
    Wad never steer[3] her.

Maybe Thou lets this fleshly thorn
Buffet Thy servant e'en and morn,   50
Lest he owre proud and high should turn
    That he's sae gifted:
If sae, Thy han' maun e'en be borne
    Until Thou lift it.

Lord, bless Thy chosen in this place,   55
For here Thou has a chosen race!
But God confound their stubborn face
    An' blast their name,
Wha bring Thy elders to disgrace
    An' open shame!   60

Lord, mind Gau'n Hamilton's deserts:
He drinks, an' swears, an' plays at cartes,[4]
Yet has sae monie takin arts
    Wi' great and sma',
Frae God's ain Priest the people's hearts   65
    He steals awa.

And when we chasten'd him therefore,
Thou kens how he bred sic a splore,[5]
And set the warld in a roar
    O' laughin at us: 70
Curse Thou his basket and his store,
    Kail an' potatoes!

Lord, hear my earnest cry and pray'r,
Against that Presbyt'ry of Ayr!
Thy strong right hand, Lord, mak it bare   75
    Upo' their heads!
Lord, visit them, and dinna spare,
    For their misdeeds!

O Lord, my God! that glib-tongu'd Aiken,
My vera heart and flesh are quakin,   80
To think how we stood sweatin, shakin,
    An' pish'd wi' dread,

---

[1] Holy Willie was William Fisher (1737-1809), a strict elder in the parish church at Mauchline.
[2] fit of peevishness
[3] *The Rape of the Lock*, 4, 64.
[4] troubled

[1] must
[2] full; drunk
[3] molest; meddle with
[4] cards
[5] such a fuss

While he, wi' hingin lip an' snakin,[1]
   Held up his head.

Lord, in Thy day o' vengeance try him!   85
Lord, visit him wha did employ him!
And pass not in Thy mercy by them,
   Nor hear their pray'r,
But for Thy people's sake destroy them,
   An' dinna spare!   90

But, Lord, remember me and mine
Wi' mercies temporal and divine,
That I for grace an' gear[2] may shine
   Excell'd by nane;
And a' the glory shall be Thine—   95
   Amen, Amen!

8. The gown and band were worn by clergymen; the black bonnet was worn by elders.

204.   THE JOLLY BEGGARS

"The Burns of this 'puissant and splendid production,' as Matthew Arnold calls it—this irresistible presentation of humanity caught in the act and summarized forever in the terms of art—comes into line with divers poets of repute, from our own Dekker and John Fletcher to the singer of *les Gueux* (1813) and *le Vieux Vagabond* (1830) [*The Beggars* and *The Old Vagabond*, written by the French poet, Jean de Béranger (1780-1857)] and approves himself their master in the matter of such qualities as humor, vision, lyrical potency, descriptive style, and the faculty of swift, dramatic presentation, to a purpose that may not be gainsaid. It was suggested by a chance visit (in company with Richmond and Smith) to the 'doss-house' of Poosie Nansie, as Agnes Gibson was nicknamed, in The Cowgate, Mauchline."—Henley and Henderson, in *The Poetry of Robert Burns* (1896-97). For Arnold's comment, see "The Study of Poetry," *Essays in Criticism*, Second Series (1888).

"Perhaps we may venture to say, that the most strictly poetical of all his poems is one which does not appear in Currie's Edition; but has been often printed before and since, under the humble title of *The Jolly Beggars*. The subject truly is among the lowest in Nature; but it only the more shows our poet's gift in raising it into the domain of art. To our minds, this piece seems thoroughly compacted; melted together, refined; and poured forth in one flood of true *liquid* harmony. It is light, airy, soft of movement; yet sharp and precise in its details; every face is a portrait: that *raucle carlin*, that *wee*

Apollo, that *Son of Mars*, are Scottish, yet ideal; the scene is at once a dream, and the very Ragcastle of 'Poosie-Nansie.' Farther, it seems in a considerable degree complete, a real self-supporting whole, which is the highest merit in a poem. The blanket of the night is drawn asunder for a moment; in full, ruddy, flaming light, these rough tatterdemalions are seen in their boisterous revel; for the strong pulse of life vindicates its right to gladness even here; and when the curtain closes, we prolong the action, without effort; the next day as the last, our *Caird* and our *Balladmonger* are singing and soldiering; their 'brats and callets' are hawking, begging, cheating; and some other night, in new combinations, they will wring from Fate another hour of wassail and good cheer. Apart from the universal sympathy with man which this again bespeaks in Burns, a genuine inspiration and no inconsiderable technical talent are manifested here. There is the fidelity, humor, warm life and accurate painting and grouping of some Teniers,[1] for whom hostlers and carousing peasants are not without significance. It would be strange, doubtless, to call this the best of Burns's writings: we mean to say only that it seems to us the most perfect of its kind, as a piece of poetical composition, strictly so called. In *The Beggar's Opera*,[2] in *The Beggar's Bush*,[3] as other critics[4] have already remarked, there is nothing which, in real poetic vigor, equals this *Cantata;* nothing, as we think, which comes within many degrees of it."—Carlyle, in "Essay on Burns" (1828).

9. The epithet *Poosie* is of doubtful meaning. A similar word, *pousie*, is a nickname for *cat;* and *cat* and *pousie* are both slang for *low woman*. *Pose* is Scotch for *purse* or *money*. *Pousse* means *pushing*, as in the word *poussecafe*, a glass of various liquors taken immediately after coffee. In eighteenth-century slang, a *pushing-school* is a brothel.

209.   THE HOLY FAIR

"The satire is chiefly concerned with the 'tent-preaching' outside the church while the communion services went on within. In Mauchline the preaching tent was pitched in the churchyard, whence a back entrance gave access to Nanse Tinnock's tavern; and the sacrament was observed once a year, on the second Sunday in August."—Henley and Henderson, in *The Poetry of Robert Burns* (1896-97). The stanza is an old one in Scotch poetry.

---

[1] sneering
[2] wealth

[1] David Teniers (1610-90), a Flemish painter of common scenes and characters.
[2] By John Gay (1685-1732).
[3] By John Fletcher (1579-1625).
[4] Particularly Lockhart, in his *Life of Burns*.

211a. 188. See *Hamlet*, I, 5, 15-16:
I could a tale unfold whose lightest word
Would harrow up thy soul.

212. THE COTTER'S SATURDAY NIGHT

Robert Aiken (1739-1807), to whom the poem is inscribed, was an old friend of the Burns family. He frequently read Burns's poems in public. As Burns had not read Spenser when he wrote this poem, he must have borrowed the stanza-form from the Spenserian imitators — Shenstone, Thomson, and Beattie—with whom he was familiar. According to Burns's brother Gilbert the plan and title of the poem were suggested by Fergusson's *The Farmer's Ingle*, the first two stanzas of which follow:

Whan gloamin' gray out owre the welkin keeks,[1]
  Whan Bawtie[2] ca's his owsen to the byre;[3]
  Whan Thrasher John sair dung,[4] his barn-door steeks,[5]
  And histy[6] lasses at the dightin'[7] tire;
What bangs fu' leal[8] the e'ening's comin' cauld,
  And gars[9] snaw-tappit winter freeze in vain;
Gars dowie[10] mortals look baith blithe and bauld,
  Nor fley'd[11] wi' a' the poortith[12] o' the plain;
Begin, my Muse, and chant in hamely strain.

Frae the big stack, weel winnow't on the hill,
  Wi' divots theekit[13] frae the weet and drift,
Sods, peats, and heathery turfs the chimely fill,
  And gar their thick'ning smeek salute the lift,[14]
The gudeman, new come hame, is blithe to find,
  Whan he out owre the hallan[15] flings his een,
That ilka[16] turn is handled to his mind,
  That a' his housie looks sae cash[17] and clean;
For cleanly house lo'es he, though e'er sae mean.

214. TO A MOUSE

Burns's brother Gilbert says that the poem was composed while Burns was plowing, after

[1] peeps; looks
[2] A pet name for a dog
[3] oxen to the cowhouse
[4] much wearied
[5] shuts; fastens
[6] dry; dusty
[7] winnowing
[8] overcomes full loyally
[9] makes; compels
[10] woeful
[11] scared
[12] poverty
[13] with turf thatched
[14] sky
[15] partition between the door and the fireplace
[16] every; each
[17] snug

he had turned up a mouse's nest and had saved the little creature from the "murdering pattle" of the boy who was leading the horses.

215. ADDRESS TO THE DEIL

"The Address is, in part, a good-natured burlesque of the Miltonic ideal of Satan; and this is effected 'by the introduction,' to use the words of Gilbert Burns, 'of ludicrous accounts and representations,' from 'various quarters,' of that 'august personage.' Burns in his despairing moods was accustomed to feign the strongest admiration for Milton's Arch-Fiend and his dauntless superiority of his desperate circumstances; and his farewell apostrophe, although it takes the form of an exclamation of pity—and was accepted merely as such by the too-too sentimental yet austere Carlyle—is in reality a satiric thrust at the old Satanic dogma."—Henley and Henderson, in *The Poetry of Robert Burns* (1896-97).

218. TO A MOUNTAIN DAISY

"I have here likewise enclosed a small piece, the very latest of my productions. I am a good deal pleased with some sentiments myself, as they are just the native querulous feelings of a heart which, as the elegantly melting Gray says, 'melancholy has marked for her own.'"—Burns, in a letter to John Kenedy, April 20, 1786. The poem was first entitled *The Gowan* [*The Daisy*].

Cf. Wordsworth's poems on the same subject (pp. 314-16).

1. The red tips on the white petals of the daisy are said to be the gift of Mars. Cf. Chaucer's *Prologue to The Legende of Good Women* (A, 519-22):

In remembrance of hir and in honour,
Cibella made the dayesy and the flour
Y-coroned al with whyt, as men may see;
And Mars yaf to hir coroun reed, pardee,
In stede of rubies, set among the whyte.

219. OF A' THE AIRTS

This song was written as a compliment to Mrs. Burns shortly after the poet's arrival in Ellisland, while his wife was still in Ayrshire. Additional stanzas, appearing in some versions of the poem, were the work of John Hamilton, an Edinburgh music-seller.

220. MY HEART'S IN THE HIGHLANDS

"The first half stanza of this song is old; the rest is mine."—Burns, in Interleaved Copy.

JOHN ANDERSON MY JO

This song is derived from a broad ditty current in the eighteenth century. The line

"John Anderson, My Jo, John," is found in a song composed as early as 1560.

SWEET AFTON

In a letter sent with the poem to Mrs. Dunlop Feb. 5, 1789, Burns states that the poem was written as a compliment to the "small river Afton that flows into Nith, near New Cummock, which has some charming, wild, romantic scenery on its banks." Probably no special heroine was in the poet's mind.

221. WILLIE BREW'D A PECK OF MAUT

"The air is Masterton's; the song mine. The occasion of it was this:—Mr. Wm. Nicol of the High School, Edinburgh, during the autumn vacation being at Moffat, honest Allan (who was at that time on a visit to Dalswinton) and I went to pay Nicol a visit. We had such a joyous meeting that Mr. Masterton and I agreed, each in our own way, that we should celebrate the business."—Burns, in Interleaved Copy. Allan Masterton was a teacher in the Edinburgh High School from 1789 to his death, in 1799.

TAM GLEN

21. It was a custom for young men and maidens to pair off by drawing slips of paper with names written on them.

222. THOU LING'RING STAR

This poem is sometimes entitled *To Mary in Heaven*. The subject of the song was Mary Campbell, daughter of a sailor at Clyde. She is commemorated in several other poems by Burns. "My 'Highland Lassie' was a warmhearted, charming young creature as ever blessed a man with generous love. After a pretty long tract of the most ardent reciprocal attachment, we met by appointment on the second Sunday of May, in a sequestered spot by the banks of Ayr, where we spent the day in taking farewell, before she should embark for the West Highlands to arrange matters for our projected change of life. At the close of the autumn following she crossed the sea to meet me at Greenock, where she had scarce landed when she was seized with a malignant fever, which hurried my dear girl to the grave in a few days, before I could even hear of her illness."—Burns's note to *My Highland Lassie, O*, in Interleaved Copy.

TAM O' SHANTER

This poem is based upon legends current in the neighborhood of Burns's birthplace, which is within a mile of Alloway Kirk and the old bridge over the River Doon. The following legend, sent by Burns to Francis Grose, is one of the many witch stories relating to Alloway Kirk:

"On a market-day in the town of Ayr, a farmer from Carrick, and consequently whose way lay by the very gate of Alloway Kirkyard, in order to cross the River Doon at the old bridge, which is about two or three hundred yards further on than the said gate, had been detained by his business till by the time he reached Alloway it was the wizard hour between night and morning. Though he was terrified with a blaze streaming from the Kirk, yet, as it is a well-known fact, that to turn back on these occasions is running by far the greatest risk of mischief, he prudently advanced on his road. When he had reached the gate of the Kirkyard, he was surprised and entertained, through the ribs and arches of an old Gothic window, which still faces the highway, to see a dance of witches merrily footing it around their old sooty blackguard master, who was keeping them all alive with the power of his bagpipe. The farmer, stopping his horse to observe them a little, could plainly descry the faces of many old women of his acquaintance and neighborhood. How the gentleman was dressed, tradition does not say, but that the ladies were all in their smocks; and one of them happening unluckily to have a smock which was considerably too short to answer all the purpose of that piece of dress, our farmer was so tickled that he involuntarily burst out with a loud laugh, 'Weel luppen, Maggy wi' the short sark!' and recollecting himself, instantly spurred his horse to the top of his speed. I need not mention the universally known fact, that no diabolical power can pursue you beyond the middle of a running stream. Lucky it was for the poor farmer that the River Doon was so near, for notwithstanding the speed of the horse, which was a good one, when he reached the middle of the arch of the bridge, and consequently the middle of the stream, the pursuing vengeful hags were so close at his heels that one of them actually sprang to seize him: but it was too late; nothing was on her side of the stream but the horse's tail, which immediately gave way at her infernal grip, as if blasted by a stroke of lightning; but the farmer was beyond her reach. However, the unsightly tailless condition of the vigorous steed was, to the last hour of the noble creature's life, an awful warning to the Carrick farmers not to stay too late in Ayr markets."

The poem was a favorite with Burns. "I look on *Tam o' Shanter* to be my standard performance in the poetical line. 'Tis true both the one [his new-born son] and the other discover a spice of roguish waggery that might perhaps be as well spared; but then they also show, in my opinion, a force of genius and a finishing polish that I despair of ever excelling."—Burns, in letter to Mrs. Dunlop, April 11, 1791.

"Probably Burns drew the suggestion of his hero, Tam o' Shanter, from the character and adventures of Douglas Graham (1739-1811), son of Robert Graham, farmer of Douglastown, tenant of the farm of Shanter on the Carrick Shore, and owner of a boat which he had named *Tam o' Shanter.* Graham was noted for his convivial habits, which his wife's rating tended rather to confirm than to eradicate. Tradition relates that once, when his long-tailed gray mare had waited even longer than usual for her master at the tavern door, certain humorists plucked her tail to such an extent as to leave it little better than a stump, and that Graham, on his attention being called to its state next morning, swore that it had been depilated by the witches at Alloway Kirk."—*MS. Notes* by D. Auld of Ayr in Edinburgh University Library, quoted by Henley and Henderson.

223. 56-66. Cf. Shelley's *Lines*, 6-10 (p. 769).

225. YE FLOWERY BANKS

Burns wrote three versions of this song; the others are entitled *Sweet are the Banks* and *The Banks o' Doon.*

"I do not know whether anybody, including the editor himself, has ever noticed a peculiar coincidence which may be found in the arrangement of the lyrics in Sir Francis Palgrave's *Golden Treasury.* However that may be, two poems, each of them extremely well known, are placed side by side, and their juxtaposition represents one vast revolution in the poetical manner of looking at things. The first is Goldsmith's almost too well known

When lovely woman stoops to folly
    And finds too late that men betray,
What charm can soothe her melancholy?
    What art can wash her guilt away?

"Immediately afterwards comes, with a sudden and thrilling change of note, the voice of Burns:

Ye banks and braes o' bonie Doon
    How can ye blume sae fair?
How can ye chant, ye little birds,
    And I sae fu' o' care?

Thou'll break my heart, thou bonie bird
    That sings upon the bough;

Thou minds me of the happy days,
    When my fause Love was true.

"A man might read those two poems a great many times without happening to realize that they are two poems on exactly the same subject—the subject of a trusting woman deserted by a man. And the whole difference—the difference struck by the very first note of the voice of anyone who reads them—is this fundamental difference that Goldsmith's words are spoken about a certain situation, and Burns's words are spoken in that situation. In the transition from one of these lyrics to the other, we have a vital change in the conception of the functions of the poet; a change of which Burns was in many ways the beginning."—Chesterton, in *Robert Browning* (1903).

AE FOND KISS

This poem was sent to a Mrs. Maclehose, of Edinburgh, with whom Burns had a love affair just before his marriage with Jean Armour. Scott once remarked that the first four lines of the poem were worth a thousand romances.

Cf. Burns's poem with the following opening stanza from *The Parting Kiss* by Robert Dodsley (1703-64):

One fond kiss before we part,
    Drop a tear and bid adieu;
Tho' we sever, my fond heart
    Till we meet shall pant for you.

226. SAW YE BONIE LESLEY

"Bonie Lesley" was Miss Leslie Baillie, of Mayfield, Ayrshire. "Mr. B., with his two daughters, . . . passing through Dumfries a few days ago on their way to England, did me the honor of calling on me; on which I took my horse—though God knows I could ill spare the time—and accompanied them fourteen or fifteen miles, and dined and spent the day with them. 'Twas about nine, I think, that I left them, and riding home I composed the following ballad."—Burns, in letter to Mrs. Dunlop, Aug. 22, 1792.

HIGHLAND MARY

The subject of this song was Mary Campbell. See note to *Thou Ling'ring Star*, p. 1268. "The foregoing song pleases me; I think it is in my happiest manner. . . . The subject of the song is one of the most interesting passages of my youthful days; and I own that I would be much flattered to see the verses set to an air which would ensure celebrity. Perhaps, after all, 'tis the still glowing prejudice of my heart that throws a borrowed lustre over the merits of the composition."—Burns, in letter to Thomson, Nov. 14, 1792.

227. SCOTS, WHA HAE

In a letter to Thomson, Sept., 1793, after remarking on the tradition that the old air *Hey Tutti Taitti* was Robert Bruce's march at the Battle of Bannockburn, Burns says: "This thought, in my solitary wanderings, roused me to a pitch of enthusiasm on the theme of liberty and independence, which I threw into a kind of Scottish ode, fitted to the air, that one might suppose to be the gallant royal Scot's address to his heroic followers on that eventful morning." That the French Revolution was partly responsible for the poem is clear from the Postscript, in which Burns says: "The accidental recollection of that glorious struggle for freedom, associated with the glowing ideas of some other struggles of the same nature, not quite so ancient, roused my rhyming mania."

Robert Bruce and the Scots won a decisive victory over the English at Bannockburn, June 24, 1314, and made Scotland independent until the kingdoms were united in 1603.

A RED, RED ROSE

The way in which Burns built up some of his poems from old songs and ballads is admirably shown by comparing this famous song with the following stanzas, taken from the songs indicated:

Her cheeks are like the roses
    That blossom fresh in June;
O, she's like a new-strung instrument
    That's newly put in tune.
        —*The Wanton Wife of Castle Gate.*

Now fare thee well, my dearest dear,
    And fare thee well awhile;
Altho' I go, I'll come again
    If I go ten thousand mile,
        Dear love,
    If I go ten thousand mile.
        —*The Unkind Parents.*

The day shall turn to night, dear love,
    And the rocks melt with the sun,
Before that I prove false to thee,
    Before my life be gone, dear love,
        Before my life be gone.
        —*The Loyal Lover's Faithful Promise.*

The seas they shall run dry,
    And rocks melt into sands;

Then I'll love you still, my dear,
    When all those things are done.
        —*The Young Man's Farewell to His Love.*

Fare you well, my own true love,
    And fare you well for a while,
And I will be sure to return back again,
    If I go ten thousand mile.
        —*The True Lover's Farewell.*

228. CONTENTED WI' LITTLE

"I have some thoughts of suggesting to you to prepare a vignette . . . to my song *Contented wi' Little and Cantie wi' Mair*, in order the portrait of my face and the picture of my mind may go down the stream of Time together."—Burns, in letter to Thomson, May 1795.

LASSIE WI' THE LINT-WHITE LOCKS

"The piece has at least the merit of being a regular pastoral; the vernal morn, the summer noon, the autumnal evening, the winter night, are regularly rounded."—Burns, in letter to Thomson, Nov., 1794. The subject of the poem was the daughter of William Lorimer, a farmer near Dumfries; she is commemorated in a number of Burns's songs. "I assure you that to my lovely friend you are indebted for many of your best songs of mine. Do you think that the sober gin-horse routine of existence could inspire a man with life, and love, and joy—could fire him with enthusiasm or melt him with pathos equal to the genius of your Book? No, No! Whenever I want to be more than ordinary in song—to be in some degree equal to your diviner airs—do you imagine I fast and pray for the celestial emanation? *Tout au contraire!* [all to the contrary] I have a glorious recipe; the very one that for his own use was invented to the Divinity of Healing and Poesy, when erst he piped to the flocks of Admetus. I put myself in the regimen of admiring a fine woman; and in proportion to the adorability of her charms, in proportion you are delighted with my verses."—Letter to Thomson.

The "Divinity of Healing and Poesy" is Apollo. For slaying the Cyclopes, Apollo was forced to serve as a shepherd to Admetus, King of Thessaly. See Lowell's *The Shepherd of King Admetus.*

IS THERE FOR HONEST POVERTY

The meter and the phrase "for a' that" Burns borrowed from older songs. A Jacobite song, published in 1750, has the following chorus:

For a' that and a' that,
　And twice as muckle's a' that,
He's far beyond the seas the night,
　Yet he'll be here for a' that.

See Burns's *The Jolly Beggars*, 255-82 (p. 208).

229. O, WERT THOU IN THE CAULD BLAST

This poem was written during Burns's last illness, in honor of Jessie Lewars, who was of great service to the Burns household at that time. Burns composed the verses to a favorite melody of Miss Lewars, after she had played it on the piano. She is commemorated also in other songs by Burns.

PREFACE TO THE FIRST, OR KILMARNOCK
EDITION OF BURNS'S POEMS

9-10. See *Song of Solomon*, 4:12.—"A garden inclosed is my sister, my spouse; a spring shut up, a fountain sealed;" also *Isaiah*, 29:11—"And the vision of all is become unto you as the words of a book that is sealed."

Samuel Rogers

Poems, p. 233 — Bibliography, p. 1442

"Rogers's title to a place among the representatives of the most brilliant age—the drama apart—of English poetry cannot now be challenged, but his rank is lower than that of any of his contemporaries, and his position is due in great measure to two fortunate accidents: the establishment of his reputation before the advent, or at least the recognition, of more potent spirits, and the intimate association of his name with that of greater men. He has, however, one peculiar distinction, that of exemplifying beyond almost any other poet what a moderate poetical endowment can effect when prompted by ardent ambition and guided by refined taste. Among the countless examples of splendid gifts marred or wasted, it is pleasing to find one of mediocrity elevated to something like distinction by fastidious care and severe toil. It must also be allowed that his inspiration was genuine as far as it went, and that it emanated from a store of sweetness and tenderness actually existing in the poet's nature."—R. Garnett, in the *Dictionary of National Biography* (1897).

233. THE PLEASURES OF MEMORY

"*The Pleasures of Memory* is an excellent specimen of what Wordsworth calls 'the *accomplishment* of verse': and it was well worthy to attract attention and admiration at the time when it appeared; for at that time poetry, with few exceptions, was to be distinguished from prose by versification and little else. *The Pleasures of Memory* is an essay in verse, not wanting in tender sentiment and just reflection, expressed, gracefully no doubt, but with a formal and elaborate grace, and in studiously pointed and carefully poised diction such as the heroic couplet had been trained to assume since the days of Pope."— Sir Henry Taylor, in Ward's *The English Poets*, Vol. 4 (1880).

Byron had a high opinion of Rogers. See *English Bards*, 803-808 (p. 519) and *Don Juan, Dedication*, st. 7 (p. 603).

With regard to title and subject, cf. this poem with Akenside's *The Pleasures of the Imagination* (p. 44), Warton's *The Pleasures of Melancholy* (p. 75), and Campbell's *The Pleasures of Hope* (p. 443).

235. WRITTEN IN THE HIGHLANDS
OF SCOTLAND

24. *Another flood.*—Loch Long, a narrow bay west of the county of Dumbarton, Scotland.

AN INSCRIPTION IN THE CRIMEA

236. 9. *To see his face no more.*—"There is a beautiful story, delivered down to us from antiquity, which will here perhaps occur to the reader.

"Icarius, when he gave Penelope in marriage to Ulysses, endeavored to persuade him to dwell in Lacedæmon; and, when all he urged was to no purpose, he entreated his daughter to remain with him. When Ulysses set out with his bride for Ithaca, the old man followed the chariot, till, overcome by his importunity, Ulysses consented that it should be left to Penelope to decide whether she would proceed with him or return with her father. It is related, says Pausanias, that she made no reply, but that she covered herself with her veil; and that Icarius, perceiving at once by it that she inclined to Ulysses, suffered her to depart with him.

"A statue was afterwards placed by her father as a memorial in that part of the road where she had covered herself with her veil. It was still standing there in the days of Pausanias, and was called the statue of Modesty."—Rogers's note.

THE BOY OF EGREMOND

"In the twelfth century William Fitz-Duncan laid waste the valleys of Craven with fire and sword; and was afterwards established there by his uncle, David, King of Scotland. He was the last of the race; his son, commonly called the Boy of Egremond, dying before him in the manner here related; then a Priory was removed from Embsay to Bolton, that it might be as near as possible to the place where the accident happened. That place is still known by the name of the *Strid;* and the mother's answer, as given in the first stanza, is to this day, often repeated in Wharfedale."—Rogers's note.

The places mentioned above are in the western part of Yorkshire, England.

237.   THE GONDOLA

238. 30. *Lay of love.*—"La Biondina in Gondoletta."—Rogers's note.

41. *Grass-grown.*—"When a despot lays his hand on a free city, how soon must he make the discovery of the rustic who bought Punch of the puppet-show man, and complained that he would not speak!"—Rogers's note.

50-52. "For this thought I am indebted to some unpublished travels by the author of *Vathek.*"—Rogers's note.

67. *Tancred and Erminia.*—"Goldoni, describing his excursion with the Passalacqua, has left us a lively picture of this class of men: 'We were no sooner in the middle of that great lagoon which encircles the city than our discreet gondolier drew the curtain behind us, and let us float at the will of the waves. At length night came on, and we could not tell where we were. "What is the hour?" said I to the gondolier.—"I cannot guess, sir; but, if I am not mistaken, it is the lover's hour."— "Let us go home," I replied; and he turned the prow homeward, singing, as he rowed, the twenty-ninth strophe of the sixteenth canto of the *Jerusalem Delivered.*'"—Rogers's note. Carlo Goldoni (1707-93) was a noted Italian dramatist.

90. *Bianca.*—"Bianca Capello. It had been shut, if we may believe the novelist Malespini, by a baker's boy, as he passed by at daybreak; and in her despair she fled with her lover to Florence, where he fell by assassination. Her beauty, and her love-adventure as here related, her marriage afterwards with the grand duke, and that fatal banquet at which they were both poisoned by the cardinal, his brother, have rendered her history a romance."—Rogers's note. Bianca Capello was a noted Italian adventuress of the sixteenth century. She eloped with Buonaventuri in 1563, and married Francesco, grand duke of Tuscany, in 1578.

William Godwin

Selections, p. 239 — Bibliography, p. 1424

"More than any English thinker, he [Godwin] resembles in intellectual temperament those French theorists who represented the early revolutionary impulse. His doctrines are developed with a logical precision which shrinks from no consequences, and which placidly ignores all inconvenient facts. The Utopia in which his imagination delights is laid out with geometrical symmetry and simplicity. Godwin believes as firmly as any early Christian in the speedy revelation of a new Jerusalem, four-square and perfect in its plan. . . . Godwin's intellectual genealogy may be traced to three sources. From Swift,[1] Mandeville,[2] and the Latin historian,[3] he had learnt to regard the whole body of ancient institutions as corrupt; from Hume[4] and Hartley,[5] of whom he speaks with enthusiasm, he derives the means of assault upon the old theories; from the French writers, such as Rousseau, Helvetius, and Holbach,[6] he caught, as he tells us, the contagion of revolutionary zeal. The *Political Justice* is an attempt to frame into a systematic whole the principles gathered from these various sources, and may be regarded as an exposition of the extremest form of revolutionary dogma. Though Godwin's idiosyncrasy is perceptible in some of the conclusions, the book is instructive, as showing, with a clearness paralleled in no other English writing, the true nature of those principles which excited the horror of Burke and the Conservatives."—Leslie Stephen, in *History of English Thought in the Eighteenth Century* (1876).

In his own day, both by his writings and by his conversation, Godwin exerted very great influence, especially upon young men, many of whom regarded his words as those of a prophet. His revolutionary zeal fired the enthusiasm of Wordsworth, Coleridge, and especially Shelley. Numerous instances of that influence may be observed in their writings. As a contrast to Godwin's ideas on the French Revolution, see Burke's *Reflections on the Revolution in France* (p. 1219).

[1] Jonathan Swift (1667-1745), a noted English satirist.
[2] Bernard Mandeville (c1670-1733), a Dutch-English writer.
[3] Tacitus (c55-118), who describes the century preceding his own as degenerate.
[4] David Hume (1711-76), a noted Scottish philosopher and historian.
[5] David Hartley (d. 1757), an English materialistic philosopher.
[6] Rousseau, Helvetius, and Holbach were noted French philosophers of the eighteenth century.

The text here followed is that of the 1796 American edition, a reprint of the second London edition. In editions subsequent to the first edition of the *Enquiry* (1793), Godwin's radicalism was slightly tempered.

William Wordsworth

Selections, p. 249 — Bibliography, p. 1452

From *Memorial Verses*
April, 1850

Goethe in Weimar sleeps, and Greece,
Long since, saw Byron's struggle cease.
But one such death remain'd to come;
The last poetic voice is dumb—
We stand today by Wordsworth's tomb.　5

. . . .

And Wordsworth!—Ah, pale ghosts, rejoice!
For never has such soothing voice　35
Been to your shadowy world convey'd,
Since erst, at morn, some wandering shade
Heard the clear song of Orpheus come
Through Hades, and the mournful gloom.
Wordsworth has gone from us—and ye,　40
Ah, may ye feel his voice as we!
He too upon a wintry clime
Had fallen—on this iron time
Of doubts, disputes, distractions, fears.
He found us when the age had bound　45
Our souls in its benumbing round;
He spoke, and loosed our heart in tears.
He laid us as we lay at birth
On the cool flowery lap of earth,
Smiles broke from us and we had ease;　50
The hills were round us, and the breeze
Went o'er the sun-lit fields again;
Our foreheads felt the wind and rain.
Our youth returned; for there was shed
On spirits that had long been dead,　55
Spirits dried up and closely furl'd,
The freshness of the early world.
Ah! since dark days still bring to light
Man's prudence and man's fiery might,
Time may restore us in his course　60
Goethe's sage mind and Byron's force;
But where will Europe's latter hour
Again find Wordsworth's healing power?
Others will teach us how to dare,
And against fear our breast to steel;　65
Others will strengthen us to bear—
But who, ah! who, will make us feel?
The cloud of mortal destiny,
Others will front it fearlessly—
But who, like him, will put it by?　70
Keep fresh the grass upon his grave
O Rotha, with thy living wave!
Sing him thy best! for few or none
Hears thy voice right, now he is gone.
　　　　　　—Matthew Arnold.

Rotha is a river near the Grasmere churchyard, in which Wordsworth is buried.

From *Wordsworth's Grave*[1]

Poet who sleepest by this wandering wave!　25
　When thou wast born, what birth-gift hadst thou then?
To thee what wealth was that the Immortals gave,
　The wealth thou gavest in thy turn to men?

Not Milton's keen, translunar music thine;
　Not Shakespeare's cloudless, boundless human view;　30
Not Shelley's flush of rose on peaks divine;
　Nor yet the wizard twilight Coleridge knew.

What hadst thou that could make such large amends
　For all thou hadst not and thy peers possessed,
Motion and fire, swift means to radiant ends?—　35
　Thou hadst, for weary feet, the gift of rest.

From Shelley's dazzling glow or thunderous haze,
　From Byron's tempest-anger, tempest-mirth,
Men turned to thee and found—not blast and blaze,
　Tumult of tottering heavens, but peace on earth.　40

Nor peace that grows by Lethe, scentless flower,
　There in white languors to decline and cease;
But peace whose names are also rapture, power,
　Clear sight, and love: for these are parts of peace.

. . . .

A hundred years ere he to manhood came,　65
　Song from celestial heights had wandered down,
Put off her robe of sunlight, dew and flame,
　And donned a modish dress to charm the town.

Thenceforth she but festooned the porch of things;
　Apt at life's lore, incurious what life meant.　70
Dextrous of hand, she struck her lute's few strings;
　Ignobly perfect, barrenly content.

Unflushed with ardor and unblanched with awe,
　Her lips in profitless derision curled,
She saw with dull emotion—if she saw—　75
　The vision of the glory of the world.

[1] From *Selected Poems of William Watson*, copyright 1902 by The John Lane Company.

The human masque she watched, with dream-
    less eyes
    In whose clear shallows lurked no trembling
        shade:
The stars, unkenned by her, might set and rise,
    Unmarked by her, the daisies bloom and
        fade.   80

The age grew sated with her sterile wit.
    Herself waxed weary on her loveless throne.
Men felt life's tide, the sweep and surge of it,
    And craved a living voice, a natural tone.

For none the less, though song was but half
        true,   85
    The world lay common, one abounding
        theme.
Man joyed and wept, and fate was ever new,
    And love was sweet, life real, death no
        dream.

In sad stern verse the rugged scholar-sage
    Bemoaned his toil unvalued, youth un-
        cheered,   90
His numbers wore the vesture of the age,
    But, 'neath it beating, the great heart was
        heard.

From dewy pastures, uplands sweet with thyme,
    A virgin breeze freshened the jaded day.
It wafted Collins' lonely vesper-chime,   95
    It breathed abroad the frugal note of Gray.

It fluttered here and there, nor swept in vain
    The dusty haunts where futile echoes
        dwell,—
Then, in a cadence soft as summer rain,
    And sad from Auburn voiceless, dropped
        and fell.   100

It dropped and fell, and one 'neath northern
        skies,
    With southern heart, who tilled his father's
        field,
Found Poesy a-dying, bade her rise
    And touch quick Nature's hem and go forth
        healed.

On life's broad plain the ploughman's con-
        quering share   105
    Upturned the fallow lands of truth anew,
And o'er the formal garden's trim parterre
    The peasant's team a ruthless furrow drew.

Bright was his going forth, but clouds ere long
    Whelmed him; in gloom his radiance set,
        and those   110
Twin morning stars of the new century's song,
    Those morning stars that sang together,
        rose.

In elvish speech the *Dreamer* told his tale
    Of marvellous oceans swept by fateful
        wings.—

The *Seër* strayed not from earth's human
        pale,   115
    But the mysterious face of common things

He mirrored as the moon in Rydal Mere
    Is mirrored, when the breathless night
        hangs blue:
Strangely remote she seems and wondrous near,
    And by some nameless difference born
        anew.   120

. . . .

The "scholar-sage" of l. 89 is Thomas Gray.
The reference in ll. 99-100 is to Goldsmith,
whose *The Deserted Village* begins: "Sweet
Auburn! loveliest village of the plain." The
reference in ll. 100-110 is to Burns. The
"morning stars" of l. 111 are Coleridge, the
Dreamer, and Wordsworth, the *Seër*. Cf. the
aim of the *Lyrical Ballads* as expressed in
Coleridge's *Biographia Literaria*, 14 (p. 398b).
On l. 104 see *Matthew*, 9:20-22.

For further comments and criticisms on
Wordsworth in this text see the following:

Coleridge's *To A Gentleman* (p. 391) and *Bio-
    graphia Literaria* (pp. 398-421).
Byron's *English Bards and Scotch Reviewers*,
    235-54 (p. 515) and *Don Juan, Dedica-
    tion*, stanzas 4-7 (p. 603); also *Canto
    III*, stanzas 93-100 (p. 621).
Shelley's *To Wordsworth* (p. 660).
Jeffrey's reviews of Crabbe's poems (p. 910)
    and Wordsworth's *The Excursion* (p.
    918); also *The White Doe of Rylstone*
    (p. 928).
Lamb's *Letter to Wordsworth* (p. 944).
Landor's *To Wordsworth* (p. 994).
Hood's *False Poets and True* (p. 1163).

249.   EXTRACT

These lines are sometimes entitled *Dear
Native Regions*. They were later recast and
incorporated in *The Prelude*, 8, 468-75 (p.
282).

AN EVENING WALK

This poem was addressed to Wordsworth's
sister Dorothy. "There is not an image in
it which I have not observed. . . . The
plan of it has not been confined to a particular walk or an individual place,—a proof (of
which I was unconscious at the time) of my
unwillingness to submit the poetic spirit to
the chains of fact and real circumstance. The
country is idealized rather than described in
any one of its local aspects."—Wordsworth's
note.

LINES LEFT UPON THE SEAT IN A YEW-TREE

"Composed in part at school at Hawkshead.
The tree has disappeared, and the slip of

Common on which it stood, that ran parallel to the lake and lay open to it, has long been enclosed; so that the road has lost much of its attraction. This spot was my favorite walk in the evenings during the latter part of my school-time."—Wordsworth's note.

The poem was published in Wordsworth and Coleridge's *Lyrical Ballads*, issued anonymously in 1798. The volume contained nineteen poems by Wordsworth and four by Coleridge. For a list of these poems see note, p. 1294. For statements of the occasion and object of the poems, see Wordsworth's Preface to the second edition (p. 343), Wordsworth's note on *We Are Seven*, below, and Coleridge's *Biographia Literaria*, 14 (p. 398).

250. THE REVERIE OF POOR SUSAN

"This arose out of my observation of the affecting music of these birds hanging in this way in the London streets during the freshness and stillness of the spring morning."— Wordsworth's note.

251. WE ARE SEVEN

"Written at Alfoxden in the spring of 1798, under circumstances somewhat remarkable. The little girl who is the heroine I met within the area of Goodrich Castle in the year 1793. Having left the Isle of Wight and crossed Salisbury Plain, as mentioned in the Preface to *Guilt and Sorrow*, I proceeded by Bristol up the Wye, and so on to North Wales, to the Vale of Clwydd, where I spent my summer under the roof of the father of my friend, Robert Jones. In reference to this poem I will here mention one of the most remarkable facts in my own poetic history and that of Mr. Coleridge. In the spring of the year 1798, he, my sister, and myself, started from Alfoxden, pretty late in the afternoon, with a view to visit Lenton and the valley of Stones near it; and as our united funds were very small, we agreed to defray the expense of the tour by writing a poem, to be sent to *The New Monthly Magazine* set up by Phillips the bookseller, and edited by Dr. Aikin. Accordingly we set off and proceeded along the Quantock Hills towards Watchet, and in the course of this walk was planned the poem of *The Ancient Mariner*, founded on a dream, as Mr. Coleridge said, of his friend, Mr. Cruikshank. Much the greatest part of the story was Mr. Coleridge's invention; but certain parts I myself suggested:—for example, some crime was to be committed which should bring upon the old navigator, as Coleridge afterwards delighted to call him, the spectral persecution, as a consequence of that crime, and his own wanderings. I had been reading in Shelvock's

Voyages a day or two before that while doubling Cape Horn they frequently saw albatrosses in that latitude, the largest sort of sea-fowl, some extending their wings twelve or fifteen feet. 'Suppose,' said I, 'you represent him as having killed one of these birds on entering the South Sea, and that the tutelary Spirits of those regions take upon them to avenge the crime.' The incident was thought fit for the purpose and adopted accordingly. I also suggested the navigation of the ship by the dead men, but do not recollect that I had anything more to do with the scheme of the poem. The Gloss with which it was subsequently accompanied was not thought of by either of us at the time; at least, not a hint of it was given to me, and I have no doubt it was a gratuitous afterthought. We began the composition together on that, to me, memorable evening. I furnished two or three lines at the beginning of the poem, in particular:—

'And listened like a three years' child;
The Mariner had his will.'

These trifling contributions, all but one (which Mr. C. has with unnecessary scrupulosity recorded) slipt out of his mind as they well might. As we endeavored to proceed conjointly (I speak of the same evening) our respective manners proved so widely different that it would have been quite presumptuous in me to do anything but separate from an undertaking upon which I could only have been a clog. We returned after a few days from a delightful tour, of which I have many pleasant, and some of them droll-enough, recollections. We returned by Dulverton to Alfoxden. *The Ancient Mariner* grew and grew till it became too important for our first object, which was limited to our expectation of five pounds, and we began to talk of a volume, which was to consist, as Mr. Coleridge has told the world, of poems chiefly on supernatural subjects taken from common life, but looked at, as much as might be, through an imaginative medium. Accordingly I wrote *The Idiot Boy, Her Eyes Are Wild,* etc., *We Are Seven, The Thorn,* and some others. To return to *We Are Seven,* the piece that called forth this note, I composed it while walking in the grove at Alfoxden. My friends will not deem it too trifling to relate that while walking to and fro I composed the last stanza first, having begun with the last line. When it was all but finished, I came in and recited it to Mr. Coleridge and my sister, and said, 'A prefatory stanza must be added, and I should sit down to our little tea-meal with greater pleasure if my task were finished.' I mentioned in substance what I wished to be expressed, and Coleridge immediately threw off the stanza thus:—

'A little child, dear brother Jem,'—

I objected to the rhyme, 'dear brother Jem,' as being ludicrous, but we all enjoyed the joke of hitching-in our friend, James T[obin]'s name, who was familiarly called Jem. He was the brother of the dramatist,[1] and this reminds me of an anecdote which it may be worth while here to notice. The said Jem got a sight of the *Lyrical Ballads* as it was going through the press at Bristol, during which time I was residing in that city. One evening he came to me with a grave face, and said, 'Wordsworth, I have seen the volume that Coleridge and you are about to publish. There is one poem in it which I earnestly entreat you to cancel, for, if published, it will make you everlastingly ridiculous.' I answered that I felt much obliged by the interest he took in my good name as a writer, and begged to know what was the unfortunate piece he alluded to. He said, 'It is called *We Are Seven.*'—'Nay,' said I, 'that shall take its chance, however,' and he left me in despair."—Wordsworth's note.

See Coleridge's comment on this poem, p. 415a, 30ff.

The utter simplicity of some of Wordsworth's early poems lent itself easily to imitation and ridicule. The following poem serves as an illustration. It was written by James Smith (1775-1839) and published in his *Rejected Addresses* (1812), a collection of imitative poems and other pieces purported to have been rejected as unsuitable for speaking at the opening of Drury Lane Theater, Oct. 10, 1812.

The Baby's Début

My brother Jack was nine in May,
And I was eight on New Year's Day;
  So in Kate Wilson's shop
Papa (he's my papa and Jack's)
Bought me, last week, a doll of wax,   5
  And brother Jack a top.

Jack's in the pouts, and thus it is,
He thinks mine came to more than his;
  So to my drawer he goes,
Takes out the doll, and, O my stars!   10
He pokes her head between the bars
  And melts off half her nose!

Quite cross, a bit of string I beg,
And tie it to his peg-top's peg,
  And bang, with might and main,   15

[1] John Tobin (1770-1804), author of *The Honey-Moon, The Curfew,* and other plays.

Its head against the parlor-door:
Off flies the head, and hits the floor,
  And breaks a window-pane.

This made him cry with rage and spite;
Well, let him cry, it serves him right.   20
  A pretty thing, forsooth!
If he's to melt, all scalding hot,
Half my doll's nose, and I am not
  To draw his peg-top's tooth!

Aunt Hannah heard the window break,   25
And cried, "O naughty Nancy Lake,
  Thus to distress your aunt;
No Drury Lane for you today!"
And while papa said, "Pooh, she may!"
  Mamma said, "No, she shan't!"   30

Well, after many a sad reproach,
They got into a hackney coach,
  And trotted down the street.
I saw them go: one horse was blind;
The tails of both hung down behind;   35
  Their shoes were on their feet.

The chaise in which poor brother Bill
Used to be drawn to Pentonville,
  Stood in the lumber-room:
I wiped the dust from off the top,   40
While Molly mopped it with a mop,
  And brushed it with a broom.

My uncle's porter, Samuel Hughes,
Came in at six to black the shoes
  (I always talk to Sam):   45
So what does he, but takes and drags
Me in the chaise along the flags,
  And leaves me where I am.

My father's walls are made of brick,
But not so tall, and not so thick   50
  As these; and, goodness me!
My father's beams are made of wood,
But never, never half so good
  As those that now I see.

What a large floor! 'tis like a town!   55
The carpet, when they lay it down,
  Won't hide it, I'll be bound:
And there's a row of lamps; my eye!
How they do blaze! I wonder why
  They keep them on the ground.   60

At first I caught hold of the wing,
And kept away; but Mr. Thing-
  umbob, the prompter man,
Gave with his hand my chaise a shove,
And said, "Go on, my pretty love;   65
  Speak to 'em, little Nan.

"You've only got to courtsey, whisper, hold your chin up, laugh, and lisp,
  And then you're sure to take:

I've known the day when brats not quite   70
Thirteen got fifty pounds a night,
    Then why not Nancy Lake?"

But while I'm speaking, where's papa?
And where's my aunt? and where's mamma?
    Where's Jack? O, there they sit!   75
They smile, they nod; I'll go my ways,
And order round poor Billy's chaise,
    To join them in the pit.

And now, good gentlefolks, I go
To join mamma, and see the show;   80
    So, bidding you adieu,
I courtsey, like a pretty miss,
And if you'll blow to me a kiss,
    I'll blow a kiss to you.

THE THORN

"Written at Alfoxden. Arose out of my observing, on the ridge of Quantock Hill, on a stormy day, a thorn which I had often past, in calm and bright weather, without noticing it. I said to myself, 'Cannot I by some invention do as much to make this thorn permanently an impressive object as the storm has made it to my eyes at this moment?' I began the poem accordingly, and composed it with great rapidity."—Wordsworth's note.

The poem was printed in *Lyrical Ballads*.

"This poem ought to have been preceded by an introductory poem, which I have been prevented from writing by never having felt myself in a mood when it was probable that I should write it well. The character which I have here introduced speaking is sufficiently common. The reader will perhaps have a general notion of it, if he has ever known a man, a captain of a small trading vessel, for example, who being past the middle age of life, had retired upon an annuity or small independent income to some village or country town of which he was not a native, or in which he had not been accustomed to live. Such men, having little to do, become credulous and talkative from indolence; and from the same cause, and other predisposing causes by which it is probable that such men may have been affected, they are prone to superstition. On which account it appeared to me proper to select a character like this to exhibit some of the general laws by which superstition acts upon the mind. Superstitious men are almost always men of slow faculties and deep feelings; their minds are not loose, but adhesive; they have a reasonable share of imagination, by which word I mean the faculty which produces impressive effects out of simple elements; but they are utterly destitute of fancy, the power by which pleasure and surprise are excited by sudden varieties of situation and by accumulated imagery.

"It was my wish in this poem to show the manner in which such men cleave to the same ideas; and to follow the turns of passion, always different, yet not palpably different, by which their conversation is swayed. I had two objects to attain; first, to represent a picture which should not be unimpressive, yet consistent with the character that should describe it; secondly, while I adhered to the style in which such persons describe, to take care that words, which in their minds are impregnated with passion, should likewise convey passion to readers who are not accustomed to sympathize with men feeling in that manner or using such language. It seemed to me that this might be done by calling in the assistance of lyrical and rapid metre. It was necessary that the poem, to be natural, should in reality move slowly; yet I hoped that, by the aid of the metre, to those who should at all enter into the spirit of the poem, it would appear to move quickly. The reader will have the kindness to excuse this note, as I am sensible that an introductory poem is necessary to give the poem its full effect.

"Upon this occasion I will request permission to add a few words closely connected with *The Thorn* and many other poems in these volumes. There is a numerous class of readers who imagine that the same words cannot be repeated without tautology: this is a great error: virtual tautology is much oftener produced by using different words when the meaning is exactly the same. Words, a poet's words more particularly, ought to be weighed in the balance of feeling, and not measured by the space which they occupy upon paper. For the reader cannot be too often reminded that poetry is passion: it is the history or science of feelings. Now every man must know that an attempt is rarely made to communicate impassioned feelings without something of an accompanying consciousness of the inadequateness of our own powers, or the deficiencies of language. During such efforts there will be a craving in the mind, and as long as it is unsatisfied the speaker will cling to the same words, or words of the same character. There are also various other reasons why repetition and apparent tautology are frequently beauties of the highest kind. Among the chief of these reasons is the interest which the mind attaches to words, not only as symbols of the passion, but as *things*, active and efficient, which are of themselves part of the passion. And further, from a spirit of fondness, exultation, and gratitude, the mind luxuriates in the repetition of words which appear successfully to communicate its feelings. The truth of these remarks might be shown by innumerable passages from the Bible, and from the impassioned poetry of every nation. 'Awake, awake, Deborah!' &c. *Judges*, chap. v., verses 12th, 27th, and part of 28th. See also the whole of that tumultuous and wonderful poem."—Wordsworth's Preface in *Lyrical Ballads* (1800).

See Coleridge's comment on this poem, p. 404b, 29ff.; also Jeffrey's comment, p. 913a, 13ff.

254. GOODY BLAKE AND HARRY GILL

The source of this poem was the following passage in Erasmus Darwin's *Zoönomia* (1794-96), Part 4: "I received good information of the truth of the following case, which was published a few years ago in the newspapers. A young farmer in Warwickshire, finding his hedges broke, and the sticks carried away during a frosty season, determined to watch for the thief. He lay many cold hours under a haystack, and at length an old woman, like a witch in a play, approached, and began to pull up the hedge; he waited till she had tied up her bottle of sticks, and was carrying them off, that he might convict her of the theft, and then springing from his concealment, he seized his prey with violent threats. After some altercation, in which her load was left upon the ground, she kneeled upon her bottle of sticks, and, raising her arms to Heaven beneath the bright moon then at the full, spoke to the farmer already shivering with cold, 'Heaven grant, that thou mayest never know again the blessing to be warm.' He complained of cold all the next day, and wore an upper coat, and in a few days another, and in a fortnight took to his bed, always saying nothing made him warm, he covered himself with many blankets, and had a sieve over his face, as he lay; and from this one insane idea he kept his bed above twenty years for fear of the cold air, till at length he died."

This poem was printed in *Lyrical Ballads*. See Coleridge's comment on it, p. 404a, 50ff.

255.   HER EYES ARE WILD

"The subject was reported to me by a lady of Bristol, who had seen the creature."— Wordsworth's note.

The poem was first entitled *The Mad Mother*. It was printed in *Lyrical Ballads*. See Coleridge's comment on the poem, p. 419a, 8ff.

256.   SIMON LEE

"This old man had been huntsman to the squires of Alfoxden, which, at the time we occupied it, belonged to a minor. The old man's cottage stood upon the common, a little way from the entrance to Alfoxden Park. But it had disappeared. Many other changes had taken place in the adjoining village, which I could not but notice with a regret more natural than well-considered. Improvements but rarely appear such to those who, after long intervals of time, revisit places they have had much pleasure in. It is unnecessary to add, the fact was as mentioned in the poem; and I have, after an interval of forty-five years, the image of the old man as fresh before my eyes as if I had seen him yesterday. The expression when the hounds were out, 'I dearly love their voice,' was word for word from his own lips."—Wordsworth's note.

The poem was printed in *Lyrical Ballads*.

257. LINES WRITTEN IN EARLY SPRING

"Actually composed while I was sitting by the side of the brook that runs down from the Comb, in which stands the village of Alford, through the grounds of Alfoxden. It was a chosen resort of mine. The brook fell down a sloping rock so as to make a waterfall considerable for that country, and across the pool below had fallen a tree, an ash, if I rightly remember, from which rose perpendicularly, boughs in search of the light intercepted by the deep shade above. The boughs bore leaves of green that for want of sunshine had faded into almost lily-white; and from the underside of this natural sylvan bridge depended long and beautiful tresses of ivy which waved gently in the breeze that might poetically speaking be called the breath of the waterfall. This motion varied of course in proportion to the power of water in the brook. When, with dear friends, I revisited this spot, after an interval of more than forty years, this interesting feature of the scene was gone. To the owner of the place I could not but regret that the beauty of this retired part of the grounds had not tempted him to make it more accessible by a path, not broad or obtrusive, but sufficient for persons who love such scenes to creep along without difficulty."—Wordsworth's note.

The poem was printed in *Lyrical Ballads*. The dell described is now known as Wordsworth's Glen.

See Coleridge's *This Lime-Tree Bower My Prison* (p. 360) and note, p. 1296.

TO MY SISTER

"Composed in front of Alfoxden House. My little boy-messenger on this occasion was the son of Basil Montagu. The larch mentioned in the first stanza was standing when I revisited the place in May, 1841, more than forty years after."—Wordsworth's note.

The poem was printed in *Lyrical Ballads* under the title *Lines Written at a Small Distance from My House and Sent by My Little Boy to the Person to Whom They are Addressed*.

Dorothy Wordsworth was her brother's most intimate companion during the years 1795-1802. She was not only the inspiration of many of his verses, but a most hallowing influence in his life. That she possessed a fine poetic instinct may be observed in her *Journals*, in which she wrote entertainingly of what she saw about her. See also the following selections from Wordsworth:

Lines Composed a Few Miles above Tintern Abbey, 111-59 (p. 260)
It Was an April Morning, 38-47 (p. 299)
The Prelude, 11, 333-56 (p. 287)
The Sparrow's Nest (p. 307)
It is a Beauteous Evening, Calm and Free (p. 312)

258. A WHIRL-BLAST FROM BEHIND THE HILL

"Observed in the holly-grove at Alfoxden. . . . I had the pleasure of again seeing, with dear friends, this grove in unimpaired beauty forty-one years after."—Wordsworth's note.

EXPOSTULATION AND REPLY

"This poem is a favorite among the Quakers, as I have learnt on many occasions."—Wordsworth's note.

This poem and the next, *The Tables Turned*, were published in *Lyrical Ballads*.

259. LINES COMPOSED A FEW MILES ABOVE TINTERN ABBEY

"No poem of mine was composed under circumstances more pleasant for me to remember than this. I began it upon leaving Tintern, after crossing the Wye, and concluded it just as I was entering Bristol, in the evening, after a ramble of four or five days,

with my sister. Not a line of it was altered, and not any part of it written down till I reached Bristol."—Wordsworth's note.

The poem was printed in *Lyrical Ballads*.

Tintern Abbey is a celebrated and beautiful ruin in Monmouthshire, England. See the engraving of it on the title page of this book. Samuel Ireland published this in his *Picturesque Views of the River Wye* in 1797, just a year before Wordsworth wrote his poem.

260. 97. Tennyson greatly praised this line; he spoke of it as giving the sense of "the permanent in the transitory."—See *Alfred Lord Tennyson: A Memoir by His Son* (New York, Macmillan, 1905), 2, 70.

104-07. Wordsworth noted the resemblance of these lines to Young's *Night Thoughts*, 6, 426-27:

Our senses, as our reason, are divine
And half create the wondrous world they see.

115. *My dearest friend.*—See note on *To My Sister*, above.

THE OLD CUMBERLAND BEGGAR

"Observed, and with great benefit to my own heart, when I was a child: written at Racedown and Alfoxden in my twenty-third year. The political economists were about that time beginning their war upon mendicity in all its forms, and by implication, if not directly, on alms-giving also. This heartless process has been carried as far as it can go by the AMENDED poor-law bill, though the inhumanity that prevails in this measure is somewhat disguised by the profession that one of its objects is to throw the poor upon the voluntary donations of their neighbors; that is, if rightly interpreted, to force them into a condition between relief in the Union poor-house, and alms robbed of their Christian grace and spirit, as being *forced* rather than given by them; while the avaricious and selfish, and all in fact but the humane and charitable, are at liberty to keep all they possess from their distressed brethren.

"The class of beggars, to which the old man here described belongs, will probably soon be extinct. It consisted of poor, and, mostly, old and infirm persons, who confined themselves to a stated round in their neighborhood, and had certain fixed days, on which, at different houses, they regularly received alms, sometimes in money, but mostly in provisions."—Wordsworth's note.

See Lamb's comment on this poem, p. 944b, 16ff.

For Wordsworth's views on pauperism, see his *Postscript*, 1835.

263. NUTTING

"Written in Germany; intended as part of a poem on my own life, but struck out as not being wanted there. Like most of my schoolfellows I was an impassioned nutter. For this pleasure, the vale of Esthwaite, abounding in coppice-wood, furnished a very wide range. These verses arose out of the remembrance of feelings I had often had when a boy, and particularly in the extensive woods that still [1843] stretch from the side of Esthwaite Lake towards Graythwaite, the seat of the ancient family of Sandys."—Wordsworth's note.

264. STRANGE FITS OF PASSION HAVE I KNOWN

This and the four following poems belong to what are known as the "Lucy poems," written in Germany in 1799. Nothing is known of the beautiful maiden immortalized in these verses. Wordsworth says nothing about them in his autobiographical notes.

265. A POET'S EPITAPH

See Lamb's comment on this poem, p. 945a, 3-8.

MATTHEW

"In the School of [Hawkshead] is a tablet, on which are inscribed, in gilt letters, the names of the several persons who have been schoolmasters there since the foundation of the school, with the time at which they entered upon and quitted their office. Opposite to one of those names the author wrote the following lines.

"Such a tablet as is here spoken of continued to be preserved in Hawkshead School, though the inscriptions were not brought down to our time. This and other poems connected with Matthew would not gain by a literal detail of facts. Like the Wanderer in *The Excursion*, this schoolmaster was made up of several both of his class and men of other occupations. I do not ask pardon for what there is of untruth in such verses, considered strictly as matters of fact. It is enough if, being true and consistent in spirit, they move and teach in a manner not unworthy of a poet's calling."—Wordsworth's note.

Some details of the character of Matthew are drawn from the Rev. William Taylor, Wordsworth's teacher at Hawkshead, 1782-86. This and the next two poems are known as the "Matthew poems."

267. LUCY GRAY

"Written at Goslar in Germany. It was founded on a circumstance told me by my sister, of a little girl who, not far from Halifax in Yorkshire, was bewildered in a snowstorm. Her footsteps were traced by her parents to the middle of the lock of a canal, and no other vestige of her, backward or forward, could be traced. The body however was found in the canal. The way in which the incident was treated and the spiritualizing of the character might furnish hints for contrasting the imaginative influences which I have endeavored to throw over common life with Crabbe's matter of fact style of treating subjects of the same kind. This is not spoken to his disparagement, far from it, but to direct the attention of thoughtful readers, into whose hands these notes may fall, to a comparison that may both enlarge the circle of their sensibilities, and tend to produce in them a catholic judgment."—Wordsworth's note.

268. THE PRELUDE

The design and occasion of *The Prelude* are thus described by Wordsworth in the Preface to *The Excursion*, written in 1814:

"Several years ago, when the author retired to his native mountains with the hope of being enabled to construct a literary work that might live, it was a reasonable thing that he should take a review of his own mind, and examine how far nature and education had qualified him for such an employment. As subsidiary to this preparation, he undertook to record, in verse, the origin and progress of his own powers, as far as he was acquainted with them. That work, addressed to a dear friend, most distinguished for his knowledge and genius, and to whom the author's intellect is deeply indebted, has been long finished; and the result of the investigation which gave rise to it, was a determination to compose a philosophical poem, containing views of man, nature, and society, and to be entitled *The Recluse*; as having for its principal subject the sensations and opinions of a poet living in retirement.

"The preparatory poem is biographical, and conducts the history of the author's mind to the point when he was emboldened to hope that his faculties were sufficiently matured for entering upon the arduous labor which he had proposed to himself; and the two works have the same kind of relation to each other, if he may so express himself, as the ante-chapel has to the body of a

Gothic church. Continuing this allusion, he may be permitted to add, that his minor pieces, which have been long before the public, when they shall be properly arranged, will be found by the attentive reader to have such connection with the main work as may give them claim to be likened to the little cells, oratories, and sepulchral recesses, ordinarily included in those edifices."

The Excursion was to be the second part of *The Recluse.*

The project was not completed. The "dear friend" to whom *The Prelude* is addressed was Coleridge.

274. 364-88. These lines are sometimes entitled *The Boy of Winander.* They were written in Germany in 1799, and published in 1800. Wordsworth sent them to Coleridge, who wrote in reply: "That

'uncertain heaven received
Into the bosom of the steady lake'

I should have recognized anywhere; and had I met these lines running wild in the deserts of Arabia, I should have instantly screamed out, 'Wordsworth!'"

The name of the Boy is unknown. He has been wrongly identified with Wordsworth's school-fellow, William Raincock of Rayrigg, who Wordsworth said took the lead of all the boys in the art of making a whistle of his fingers.

275. 52-65. See Wordsworth's *Personal Talk,* 51-56 (p. 327), and cf. with Milton's ambition to leave behind him "something the world would not willingly let die."

277. 76ff. Wordsworth had read Lord Macartney's description quoted by John Barrow in *Travels in China* (1804, pp. 127-133). The Chinese called the garden "a Paradise of ten thousand trees."

284. 660-64. These lines are quoted, with slight variation, from *Paradise Lost,* 11, 203-07.

287. 335. *Beloved sister.*—See note on *To My Sister,* p. 1279a.

290. 142-51. Cf. the following passage from Carlyle's *Sartor Resartus,* II, 2, 10: "In a like sense worked the *Postwagen* (Stage-coach), which, slow-rolling under its mountains of men and luggage, wended through our Village: northwards, truly, in the dead of night; yet southwards visibly at eventide. Not till my eighth year did I reflect that this Postwagen could be other than some terrestrial Moon, rising and setting by mere Law of Nature, like the heavenly one; that it came on made highways, from far cities toward far cities; weaving them like a monstrous shuttle into closer

and closer union. It was then that, independently of Schiller's *Wilhelm Tell,* I made this not quite insignificant reflection (so true also in spiritual things) : *Any road, this simple Entepfuhl road, will lead you to the end of the World!*"

180-85. For a reverse view, see Crabbe's *The Village* (p. 154).

221-78. "This passage is the finest in thought, and the most perfect in expression, of any of *The Prelude.* It illustrates the courage of the man who dared thus, in an age of superficiality and pride, to fly in the face of all the poetical creeds, and make the joys and sorrows that we encounter on the common highroad of life the subjects of his song."—George, in *The Complete Poetical Works of William Wordsworth* (Cambridge ed., 1904).

292. MICHAEL

"Written at Town-end, Grasmere, about the same time as *The Brothers.* The sheepfold, on which so much of the poem turns, remains, or rather the ruins of it. The character and circumstances of Luke were taken from a family to whom had belonged, many years before, the house we lived in at Town-end, along with some fields and woodlands on the eastern shore of Grasmere. The name of the Evening Star was not in fact given to this house, but to another on the same side of the valley, more to the north."—Wordsworth's note.

In a letter to his friend Thomas Poole, Wordsworth wrote of the poem (1801): "I have attempted to give a picture of a man, of strong mind and lively sensibility, agitated by two of the most powerful affections of the human heart: the parental affection, and the love of property (*landed* property), including the feelings of inheritance, home, and personal and family independence. . . . In writing it I had your character often before my eyes; and sometimes thought that I was delineating such a man as you yourself would have been under the same circumstances." In a letter to Charles James Fox, dated Jan. 14, 1801, he said: "In the two poems, *The Brothers* and *Michael,* I have attempted to draw a picture of the domestic affections, as I know they exist amongst a class of men who are now almost confined to the north of England. They are small independent *proprietors* of land, here called statesmen, men of respectable education, who daily labor on their own little properties. The domestic affections will always be strong amongst men who live in a country not crowded with population, if these men are

placed above poverty. But if they are proprietors of small estates which have descended
to them from their ancestors, the power which
these affections acquire amongst such men is
inconceivable by those who have only had
an opportunity of observing hired laborers,
farmers, and the manufacturing poor. Their
little tract of land serves as a kind of permanent rallying point for their domestic feelings, as a tablet on which they are written,
which makes them objects of memory in a
thousand instances, when they would otherwise be forgotten. It is a fountain fitted to
the nature of social man, from which supplies of affection, as pure as his heart was
intended for, are daily drawn. This class of
men is rapidly disappearing. . . . The two
poems which I have mentioned were written
with a view to show that men who do not
wear fine clothes can feel deeply. . . . The
poems are faithful copies from Nature."

296. 258. *Richard Bateman.*—"The story
alluded to is well known in the country."—
Wordsworth's note.

299. IT WAS AN APRIL MORNING

"Written at Grasmere. This poem was suggested on the banks of the brook that runs
through Easedale, which is, in some parts of
its course, as wild and beautiful as brook
can be. I have composed thousands of verses
by the side of it."—Wordsworth's note.

The poem is the first of a group of five
poems on the Naming of Places, to which
Wordsworth prefaced this Advertisement:
"By persons resident in the country and attached to rural objects, many places will be
found unnamed or of unknown names, where
little Incidents must have occurred, or feelings been experienced, which will have given
to such places a private and peculiar interest.
From a wish to give some sort of record to
such Incidents, and renew the gratification of
such feelings, names have been given to
places by the author and some of his friends,
and the following poems written in consequence."

39. *My Emma.*—See note on *To My
Sister*, p. 1279a.

'TIS SAID THAT SOME HAVE DIED FOR LOVE

300. 51. *Emma's voice.*—See note above.

THE EXCURSION

"The Title-page announces that this is only
a portion of a poem; and the reader must be
here apprised that it belongs to the second
part of a long and laborious work, which is
to consist of three parts.—The author will

candidly acknowledge that, if the first of
these had been completed, and in such a
manner as to satisfy his own mind, he should
have preferred the natural order of publication, and have given that to the world first;
but, as the second division of the work was
designed to refer more to passing events, and
to an existing state of things, than the others
were meant to do, more continuous exertion
was naturally bestowed upon it, and greater
progress made here than in the rest of the
poem; and as this part does not depend upon
the preceding to a degree which will materially injure its own peculiar interest, the
author, complying with the earnest entreaties
of some valued friends, presents the following
pages to the public."—From Wordsworth's
Preface to the ed. of 1814.

See note on *The Prelude*, the first part of
the "long and laborious work" referred to, p.
1280b.

The selection from *The Excursion* printed
here is usually referred to as *The Ruined
Cottage*. The portion omitted after line 37
gives an account of the peddler's boyhood,
education, and manner of life.

See Jeffrey's review of this poem, p. 918.

307. PELION AND OSSA

This is Wordsworth's first sonnet. It is
interesting for study in comparison with his
more mature work in the same form. Pelion,
Ossa, and Olympus were mountains in Thessaly, Greece, famous in Greek mythology.

THE SPARROW'S NEST

"Written in the orchard, Town-end, Grasmere. At the end of the garden of my father's
house at Cockermouth was a high terrace
that commanded a fine view of the River
Derwent and Cockermouth Castle. This was
our favorite play-ground. The terrace-wall,
a low one, was covered with closely-clipt privet
and roses, which gave an almost impervious
shelter to birds that built their nests there.
The latter of these stanzas alludes to one of
those nests."—Wordsworth's note.

9. *My Sister Emmeline.*—See note on *To
My Sister*, p. 1279a.

TO A BUTTERFLY

"Written in the orchard, Town-end, Grasmere. My sister and I were parted immediately after the death of our mother, who
died in 1778, both being very young."—Wordsworth's note. See note on l. 9 above.

Dorothy Wordsworth writes thus of the
poem in her *Journal* (March, 1802): "While
we were at breakfast . . . he wrote the

poem *To a Butterfly*. . . . The thought first came upon him as we were talking about the pleasure we both always felt at the sight of a butterfly. I told him that I used to chase them a little, but that I was afraid of brushing the dust off their wings, and did not catch them. He told me how he used to kill all the white ones when he went to school, because they were Frenchmen."

308. MY HEART LEAPS UP

The last three lines of this poem were adopted as the motto to the *Ode: Intimations of Immortality* (p. 329).

Piety (l. 9) is used here in the sense of *reverence, affection.*

WRITTEN IN MARCH

This poem is sometimes entitled *Brother's Water*. Wordsworth states that it was composed extempore. Dorothy Wordsworth writes thus about the poem in her *Journal* (April 16, 1802): "When we came to the foot of Brother's Water, I left William sitting on the bridge. . . . When I returned I found William writing a poem descriptive of the sights and sounds we saw and heard. There was the gentle flowing of the stream, the glittering, lively lake, green fields without a living creature to be seen on them; behind us, a flat pasture with forty-two cattle feeding; to our left, the road leading to the hamlet. No smoke there, the sun shone on the bare roofs. The people were at work ploughing, harrowing, and sowing: lasses working, a dog barking now and then; cocks crowing, birds twittering; the snow in patches at the top of the highest hills, yellow palms, purple and green twigs on the birches, ashes with their glittering spikes, stems quite bare. The hawthorn a bright green, with black stems under the oak. The moss of the oak glossy. . . . William finished the poem before we got to the foot of Kirkstone."

TO THE SMALL CELANDINE

"Written at Town-end, Grasmere. It is remarkable that this flower, coming out so early in the spring as it does, and so bright and beautiful, and in such profusion, should not have been noticed earlier in English verse. What adds much to the interest that attends it is its habit of shutting itself up and opening out according to the degree of light and temperature of the air."—Wordsworth's note.

309. RESOLUTION AND INDEPENDENCE

"Written at Town-end, Grasmere. This old man I met a few hundred yards from my cottage; and the account of him is taken from his own mouth. I was in the state of feeling described in the beginning of the poem, while crossing over Barton Fell from Mr. Clarkson's, at the foot of Ullswater, towards Askham. The image of the hare I then observed on the ridge of the Fell."—Wordsworth's note.

Dorothy Wordsworth gives in her *Journal* (Oct. 3, 1800) the following account of the origin of the poem: "When William and I returned, we met an old man almost double. He had on a coat, thrown over his shoulders, above his waistcoat and coat. Under this he carried a bundle, and had an apron on and a night-cap. His face was interesting. He had dark eyes and a long nose. John [Wordsworth's brother], who afterwards met him at Wytheburn, took him for a Jew. He was of Scotch parents, but had been born in the army. He had had a wife, and 'she was a good woman, and it pleased God to bless us with ten children.' All these were dead but one, of whom he had not heard for many years, a sailor. His trade was to gather leeches, but now leeches were scarce, and he had not strength for it. He lived by begging, and was making his way to Carlisle, where he should buy a few godly books to sell. He said leeches were very scarce, partly owing to this dry season, but many years they have been scarce. He supposed it owing to their being much sought after, that they did not breed fast, and were of slow growth. Leeches were formerly 2s 6d per 100; they are now 30s. He had been hurt in driving a cart, his leg broken, his body driven over, his skull fractured. He felt no pain till he recovered from his first insensibility. . . . It was then late in the evening when the light was just going away."

In a letter to friends, probably Mary and Sara Hutchinson, dated June 14, 1802, Wordsworth writes: "I will explain to you in prose my feelings in writing *that* poem. . . . I describe myself as having been exalted to the highest pitch of delight by the joyousness and beauty of nature; and then as depressed, even in the midst of those beautiful objects, to the lowest dejection and despair. A young poet in the midst of the happiness of nature is described as overwhelmed by the thoughts of the miserable reverses which have befallen the happiest of all men, *viz.*, poets. I think of this till I am so deeply impressed with it, that I consider the manner in which I was rescued from my dejection and despair almost as an interposition of Providence. A person reading the poem with feelings like mine will have been awed and controlled, expecting something spiritual or supernatural. What is brought forward? A lonely place, 'a pond by which an old man *was,* far from all house or home:' not *stood,* nor *sat,* but *was*—the figure presented in the most naked simplicity possible. This feeling of spirituality or supernaturalness is again referred to as being strong in my mind in this passage. How came he here? thought I, or what can he be doing? I then describe him, whether ill or well is not for me to judge with perfect confidence; but this I *can* confidently affirm, that though I believe God has given me a strong imagination, I cannot conceive a figure more impressive than that of an old man like this, the survivor of a wife and ten children, travelling alone among the mountains and all lonely places, carrying with him his own fortitude, and the necessities which an unjust state of society has laid upon him."—Quoted from C. Wordsworth's *Memoirs of William Wordsworth* (1851), I, 172-73.

See Coleridge's comment on this poem, p. 409b, 47ff.

311. I GRIEVED FOR BUONAPARTÉ

"In the cottage, Town-end, Grasmere, one afternoon in 1801, my sister read to me the sonnets of Milton. I had long been well acquainted with them, but I was particularly struck on that occasion with the dignified simplicity and majestic harmony that runs through most of them,—in character so totally different from the Italian, and still more so from Shakespeare's fine sonnets. I took fire, if I may be allowed to say so, and produced three sonnets the same afternoon, the first I ever wrote except an irregular one at school. Of these three, the only one I distinctly remember is—*I grieved for Buonaparté.* One was never written down: the third, which was, I believe, preserved, I cannot particularize."—Wordsworth's note.

COMPOSED UPON WESTMINSTER BRIDGE, SEPTEMBER 3, 1803

The date given in the title is wrong, and this poem was actually written in 1802. Wordsworth's recollection of the dates of writing some of his poems is not always correct. In 1843, he stated that this poem was "composed on the roof of a coach on my way to France Sept. 1802." Wordsworth and his sister Dorothy went to France in the fall of 1802 to see Annette Vallon, mother of Wordsworth's daughter Caroline, to make sure that nothing stood in the way of his projected marriage to Mary Hutchinson. The sonnet was composed sometime after the Wordsworths left London.

"We left London on Saturday morning at half-past five or six, the 30th of July. We mounted the Dover coach at Charing Cross. It was a beautiful morning. The city, St. Paul's, with the river, and a multitude of little boats, made a most beautiful sight as we crossed Westminster Bridge. The houses were not overhung by their cloud of smoke, and they were spread out endlessly; yet the sun shone so brightly, with such a fierce light, that there was even something like the purity of one of nature's own grand spectacles."—Dorothy Wordsworth, in *Journal,* July, 1802.

Westminster Bridge is next to the oldest bridge over the Thames at London. It was built in 1750 and replaced by the present structure in 1862.

312. COMPOSED BY THE SEA-SIDE, NEAR CALAIS

"We had delightful walks after the heat of the day was passed—seeing far off in the west the coast of England like a cloud crested with Dover Castle, which was but like the summit of the cloud—the evening star and the glory of the sky, the reflections in the water were more beautiful than the sky itself, purple waves brighter than precious stones, forever melting away upon the sands. . . . Nothing in romance was ever half so beautiful. Now came in view, as the evening star sunk down, and the colors of the west faded away, the two lights of England."—Dorothy Wordsworth, in *Journal,* August, 1802.

IT IS A BEAUTEOUS EVENING, CALM AND FREE

"This was composed on the beach near Calais, in the autumn of 1802."—Wordsworth's note.

Wordsworth was in France to see Annette Vallon, the mother of his daughter Caroline, to clear the way for his marriage with Mary Hutchinson.

TO TOUSSAINT L'OUVERTURE

Toussaint (surnamed L'Ouverture, the Opener, because he broke through the enemy's lines) was the noted negro liberator of San Domingo. In 1801 he attempted to free the Island from the control of Napoleon, but was captured and imprisoned for life. He was lying in the dungeon at Fort de Joux, France, when Wordsworth wrote this sonnet. He died in 1803.

313. WRITTEN IN LONDON, SEPTEMBER, 1802

"This was written immediately after my return from France to London, when I could not but be struck, as here described, with the vanity and parade of our own country, especially in great towns and cities, as contrasted with the quiet, and I may say the desolation, that the revolution had produced in France. This must be borne in mind, or else the reader may think that in this and the succeeding sonnets I have exaggerated the mischief engendered and fostered among us by undisturbed wealth. It would not be easy to conceive with what a depth of feeling I entered into the struggle carried on by the Spaniards for their deliverance from the usurped power of the French. Many times have I gone from Allan Bank in Grasmere Vale, where we were then residing, to the top of the Raise-gap as it is called, so late as two o'clock in the morning, to meet the carrier bringing the newspaper from Keswick. Imperfect traces of the state of mind in which I then was may be found in my Tract on the Convention of Cintra, as well as in these sonnets."—Wordsworth's note.

The Convention of Cintra, concluded between the French and the English in 1808, provided that the French should evacuate Portugal. They were taken to France in English vessels.

314. TO THE DAISY

"This poem and two others to the same flower, were written in the year 1802; which is mentioned, because in some of the ideas, though not in the manner in which those ideas are connected, and likewise even in some of the expressions, there is a resemblance to passages in a poem (lately published) of Mr. Montgomery's, entitled *A Field Flower*. This being said, Mr. Montgomery will not think any apology due to him; I cannot, however, help addressing him in the words of the father of English poets:

'Though it happe me to rehersin
That ye han in your freshe songis saied,
Forberith me, and beth not ill apaied,
Sith that ye se I doe it in the honour
Of Love, and eke in service of the Flour.'"
—Wordsworth's note (1807).

The lines quoted are from Chaucer's Prologue to *The Legende of Good Women*, B. 13, 78-82.

James Montgomery's *A Field Flower* was written before the publication of Wordsworth's poems. It is as follows:

A Field Flower

On Finding One in Full Bloom on Christmas Day, 1803

There is a flower, a little flower,
With silver crest and golden eye,

That welcomes every changing hour,
And weathers every sky.

The prouder beauties of the field   5
In gay but quick succession shine,
Race after race their honors yield,
They flourish and decline.

But this small flower, to Nature dear,
While moon and stars their courses run   10
Wreathes the whole circle of the year,
Companion of the Sun.

It smiles upon the lap of May,
To sultry August spreads its charms,
Lights pale October on his way,   15
And twines December's arms.

The purple heath and golden broom
On moory mountains catch the gale,
O'er lawns the lily sheds perfume,
The violet in the vale.   20

But this bold floweret climbs the hill,
Hides in the forest, haunts the glen,
Plays on the margin of the rill,
Peeps round the fox's den.

Within the garden's cultured round   25
It shares the sweet carnation's bed;
And blooms on consecrated ground
In honor of the dead.

The lambkin crops its crimson gem,
The wild-bee murmurs on its breast,   30
The blue-fly bends its pensile stem,
Light o'er the sky-lark's nest.

'Tis Flora's page;—in every place,
In every season fresh and fair,
It opens with perennial grace,   35
And blossoms everywhere.

On waste and woodland, rock and plain,
Its humble buds unheeded rise;
The Rose has but a summer reign,
The Daisy never dies.   40

Flora (l. 33) was the Roman goddess of flowers.

316. TO THE DAISY (*Bright Flower*)

"This and the other poems addressed to the same flower were composed at Town-end, Grasmere, during the earlier part of my residence there. I have been censured for the last line but one—'thy function apostolical'—as being little less than profane. How could it be thought so? The word is adopted with reference to its derivation, implying something sent on a mission; and assuredly this little flower, especially when the subject of verse, may be regarded, in its humble degree, as administering both to moral and to spiritual purposes."—Wordsworth's note.

YEW-TREES

"Written at Grasmere. These yew-trees are still standing, but the spread of that at Lorton is much diminished by mutilation. I will here mention that a little way up the hill, on the road leading from Rosthwaite to Stonethwaite (in Borrowdale), lay the trunk of a yew-tree, which appeared as you approached, so vast was its diameter, like the entrance of a cave, and not a small one. Calculating upon what I have observed of the slow growth of this tree in rocky situations, and of its durability, I have often thought that the one I am describing must have been as old as the Christian era. The tree lay in the line of a fence. Great masses of its ruins were strewn about, and some had been rolled down the hillside and lay near the road at the bottom. As you approached the tree, you were struck with the number of shrubs and young plants, ashes, etc., which had found a bed upon the decayed trunk and grew to no inconsiderable height, forming, as it were, a part of the hedgerow. In no part of England, or of Europe, have I ever seen a yew-tree at all approaching this in magnitude, as it must have stood. By the bye, Hutton, the old guide, of Keswick, had been so impressed with the remains of this tree, that he used gravely to tell strangers that there could be no doubt of its having been in existence before the flood."—Wordsworth's note.

Ruskin (*Modern Painters*, Part III, sec. 2, ch. 4) considers this poem as "the most vigorous and solemn bit of forest landscape ever painted." He calls attention especially to "the pure touch of color" in l. 22. Coleridge quotes from it (p. 419b) to illustrate Wordsworth's high imaginative faculty.

317.　AT THE GRAVE OF BURNS

This and the next four poems belong to a group of fifteen poems entitled *Memorials of a Tour in Scotland*. Wordsworth, his sister Dorothy, and Coleridge started the tour together on August 15, 1803. Coleridge, at that time in ill health, left them at Loch Lomond. See Dorothy Wordsworth's *Recollections of a Tour Made in Scotland*.

318.　TO A HIGHLAND GIRL

"This delightful creature and her demeanor are particularly described in my sister's *Journal*. The sort of prophecy with which the verses conclude has, through God's goodness, been realized; and now, approaching the close of my 73d year, I have a most vivid remembrance of her and the beautiful objects with which she was surrounded. She is alluded to in the poem of *The Three Cottage Girls* among my Continental Memorials. In illustration of this class of poems I have scarcely anything to say beyond what is anticipated in my sister's faithful and admirable *Journal*." —Wordsworth's note.

Dorothy Wordsworth writes thus in her *Recollections of a Tour Made in Scotland* (Aug. 28, 1803): "When beginning to descend the hill toward Loch Lomond, we overtook two girls, who told us we could not cross the ferry till evening, for the boat was gone with a number of people to church. One of the girls was exceedingly beautiful; and the figures of both of them, in gray plaids falling to their feet, their faces only being uncovered, excited our attention before we spoke to them; but they answered us so sweetly that we were quite delighted, at the same time that they stared at us with an innocent look of wonder. I think I never heard the English language sound more sweetly than from the mouth of the elder of these girls, while she stood at the gate answering our inquiries, her face flushed with the rain; her pronunciation was clear and distinct: without difficulty, yet slow, like that of a foreign speech. They told us we might sit in the ferry-house till the return of the boat, went in with us, and made a good fire as fast as possible to dry our wet clothes. We learnt that the taller one was the sister of the ferryman, and had been left in charge with the house for the day, that the other was his wife's sister, and was come with her mother on a visit,—an old woman, who sate in a corner beside the cradle, nursing her little grand-child. We were glad to be housed, with our feet upon a warm hearth-stone; and our attendants were so active and good-humored that it was pleasant to have to desire them to do anything. The younger was a delicate and unhealthy-looking girl; but there was an uncommon meekness in her countenance, with an air of premature intelligence, which is often seen in sickly young persons. The other made me think of Peter Bell's Highland Girl:

'As light and beauteous as a squirrel,
　As beauteous and as wild.'
　　　[Wordsworth's *Peter Bell*, 889-90].

She moved with unusual activity, which was chastened very delicately by a certain hesitation in her looks when she spoke, being able to understand us but imperfectly. . . .

"The hospitality we had met with . . . gave us very favorable impressions on this our first entrance into the Highlands, and at this day the innocent merriment of the girls, with their kindness to us, and the beautiful figure and face of the elder, come to my mind whenever I think of the ferry-house and waterfall of Loch Lomond, and I never think of the two girls but the whole image of that romantic spot is before me, a living image, as it will be to my dying day."

STEPPING WESTWARD

"While my fellow-traveller and I were walking by the side of Loch Ketterine, one fine evening after sunset, in our road to a hut where, in the course of our tour, we had been hospitably entertained some weeks before, we met, in one of the loneliest parts of that solitary region, two well-dressed women, one of whom said to us, by way of greeting, 'What, you are stepping westward?' "—Wordsworth's note.

Dorothy Wordsworth writes thus in her *Recollections of a Tour Made in Scotland* (Sept. 11, 1803): "We have never had a more delightful walk than this evening. Ben Lomond and the three pointed-topped mountains of Loch Lomond, which we had seen from the garrison, were very majestic under the clear sky, the lake perfectly calm, the air sweet and mild. I felt that it was much more interesting to visit a place where we have been before than it can possibly be the first time, except under peculiar circumstances. The sun had been set for some time, when, being within a quarter of a mile of the ferryman's hut, our path having led us close to the shore of the calm lake, we met two neatly dressed women, without hats, who had probably been taking their Sunday evening's walk. One of them said to us in a friendly, soft tone of voice, 'What! you are stepping westward?' I cannot describe how affecting this simple expression was in that remote place, with the western sky in front, yet glowing with the departed sun. William wrote the following poem long after, in remembrance of his feelings and mine."

In connection with this poem, see Wordsworth's *The Trosachs* (p. 340), composed on the same spot 27 years later.

319. THE SOLITARY REAPER

"As we descended, the scene became more fertile, our way being pleasantly varied—through coppices or open fields, and passing farm-houses, though always with an intermixture of uncultivated ground. It was harvest-time, and the fields were quietly—might I be allowed to say pensively?—enlivened by small companies of reapers. It is not uncommon in the more lonely parts of the Highlands to see a single person so employed.

The following poem was suggested to William by a beautiful sentence in Thomas Wilkinson's *Tour in Scotland*."—Dorothy Wordsworth in *Recollections of a Tour Made in Scotland*, Sept. 13, 1803.

The sentence from Wilkinson is as follows: "Passed a female who was reaping alone; she sung in Erse, as she bended over her sickle; the sweetest human voice I ever heard: her strains were tenderly melancholy, and felt delicious, long after they were heard no more."

YARROW UNVISITED

The River Yarrow, in southern Scotland, was a favorite scene of ballads and songs by the poets. See Child's *English and Scottish Popular Ballads*, Vol. 4, 160-84.

Of *Yarrow Unvisited*, Dorothy Wordsworth wrote thus in her *Recollections of a Tour Made in Scotland*, Sept. 8, 1803: "At Clovenford, being so near to the Yarrow, we could not but think of the possibility of going thither, but came to the conclusion of reserving the pleasure for some future time, in consequence of which, after our return, William wrote the poem." Upon receiving a copy of the poem from Wordsworth, Scott wrote: "I by no means admit your apology, however ingeniously and artfully stated, for not visiting the bonny holms of Yarrow, and certainly will not rest until I have prevailed upon you to compare the ideal with the real stream."—Wordsworth visited the Yarrow in 1814 and again in 1831. See his *Yarrow Visited* (p. 334) and *Yarrow Revisited* (p. 338).

320. OCTOBER, 1803

This sonnet and the two following were inspired by fears of an expected invasion of England by the French in 1803.

321. SHE WAS A PHANTOM OF DELIGHT

"Written at Town-end, Grasmere. The germ of this poem was four lines composed as a part of the verses on the Highland Girl. Though beginning in this way, it was written from my heart, as is sufficiently obvious."—Wordsworth's note.

The poem refers to Wordsworth's wife.

I WANDERED LONELY AS A CLOUD

"Written at Town-end, Grasmere. The daffodils grew and still grow on the margin of Ullswater, and probably may be seen to this day as beautiful in the month of March, nodding their golden heads beside the dancing and foaming waves."—Wordsworth's note.

Dorothy Wordsworth writes thus in her *Journal*, April 15, 1802: "When we were in the woods beyond Gowbarrow Park we saw a

few daffodils close to the water-side. . . .
As we went along there were more, and yet
more; and, at last, under the boughs of the
trees, we saw there was a long belt of them
along the shore. . . . I never saw daffodils so beautiful. They grew among the mossy
stones, about and above them; some rested
their heads on these stones as on a pillow for
weariness; and the rest tossed, and reeled, and
danced, and seemed as if they verily laughed
with the wind that blew upon them over the
lake. They looked so gay, ever glancing, ever
changing. . . . There was here and there
a little knot, and a few stragglers higher up;
but they were so few as not to disturb the
simplicity, unity, and life of that one busy
highway."

See Coleridge's comment on the poem, p.
413b, 27ff.

21-22. These two lines were written by
Wordsworth's wife.

THE AFFLICTION OF MARGARET

"Written at Town-end, Grasmere. This was
taken from the case of a poor widow who
lived in the town of Penrith. Her sorrow was
well known to Mrs. Wordsworth, to my sister,
and, I believe, to the whole town. She kept
a shop, and when she saw a stranger passing
by, she was in the habit of going out into
the street to enquire of him after her son."—
Wordsworth's note.

See Coleridge's comment on this poem, p.
419a, 2ff.

322. ODE TO DUTY

"This ode is on the model of Gray's *Ode to
Adversity* [p. 58], which is copied from Horace's *Ode to Fortune*. Many and many a
time have I been twitted by my wife and
sister for having forgotten this dedication of
myself to the stern lawgiver. Transgressor
indeed I have been, from hour to hour, from
day to day: I would fain hope, however, not
more flagrantly or in a worse way than most
of my tuneful brethren. But these last words
are in a wrong strain. We should be rigorous
to ourselves and forbearing, if not indulgent,
to others, and, if we make comparisons at
all, it ought to be with those who have morally excelled us."—Wordsworth's note.

323. TO A SKYLARK

Cf. this poem with Wordsworth's *To a Skylark* (p. 338), with Shelley's *To a Skylark* (p.
730), and with Hogg's *The Skylark* (p. 503).

ELEGIAC STANZAS

"Sir George Beaumont painted two pictures
of this subject, one of which he gave to Mrs.

Wordsworth, saying she ought to have it;
but Lady Beaumont interfered, and after Sir
George's death she gave it to Sir Uvedale
Price, in whose house at Foxley I have seen
it."—Wordsworth's note.

The Peele Castle here described is in Lancashire, England. Wordsworth visited his
cousin in the vicinity of Peele Castle during
one of his summer vacations. This poem
should be read in connection with *Character
of the Happy Warrior* (p. 324), and *Elegiac
Verses in Memory of My Brother*.

324. CHARACTER OF THE HAPPY WARRIOR

"The course of the great war with the
French naturally fixed one's attention upon the
military character, and, to the honor of our
country, there were many illustrious instances
of the qualities that constitute its highest
excellence. Lord Nelson carried most of the
virtues that the trials he was exposed to in his
department of the service necessarily call forth
and sustain, if they do not produce the contrary vices. But his public life was stained
with one great crime, so that, though many
passages of these lines were suggested by what
was generally known as excellent in his conduct, I have not been able to connect his name
with the poem as I could wish, or even to
think of him with satisfaction in reference to
the idea of what a warrior ought to be. For
the sake of such of my friends as may happen
to read this note I will add, that many elements of the character here portrayed were
found in my brother John, who perished by
shipwreck as mentioned elsewhere. His mess-
mates used to call him the Philosopher, from
which it must be inferred that the qualities
and dispositions I allude to had not escaped
their notice. He often expressed his regret,
after the war had continued some time, that
he had not chosen the naval, instead of the
East India Company's service, to which his
family connection had led him. He greatly
valued moral and religious instruction for
youth, as tending to make good sailors. The
best, he used to say, came from Scotland; the
next to them, from the North of England,
especially from Westmoreland and Cumberland, where, thanks to the piety and local
attachments of our ancestors, endowed, or, as
they are commonly called, free, schools
abound."—Wordsworth's note.

The "crime" of Nelson was his relations
with Lady Hamilton, a noted adventuress.
See Southey's *The Life of Nelson* (p. 442a,
10ff.).

325. POWER OF MUSIC

Wordsworth spent two months in London

in the spring of 1806. The poem, he says, was "taken from life."

326. YES, IT WAS THE MOUNTAIN ECHO

"Written at Town-end, Grasmere. The echo came from Nab-scar, when I was walking on the opposite side of Rydal Mere. I will here mention, for my dear sister's sake, that, while she was sitting alone one day high up on this part of Loughrigg Fell, she was so affected by the voice of the cuckoo heard from the crags at some distance that she could not suppress a wish to have a stone inscribed with her name among the rocks from which the sound proceeded. On my return from my walk I recited these verses to Mrs. Wordsworth."—Wordsworth's note.

PERSONAL TALK

"Written at Town-end, Grasmere. The last line but two stood, at first, better and more characteristically, thus:

'By my half-kitchen and half-parlor fire.'

My sister and I were in the habit of having the tea-kettle in our little sitting-room; and we toasted the bread ourselves, which reminds me of a little circumstance not unworthy of being set down among these minutiæ. Happening both of us to be engaged a few minutes one morning when we had a young prig of a Scotch lawyer to breakfast with us, my dear sister, with her usual simplicity, put the toasting-fork with a slice of bread into the hands of this Edinburgh genius. Our little book-case stood on one side of the fire. To prevent loss of time, he took down a book, and fell to reading, to the neglect of the toast, which was burnt to a cinder. Many a time have we laughed at this circumstance, and other cottage simplicities of that day. By the bye, I have a spite at one of this series of sonnets (I will leave the reader to discover which) as having been the means of nearly putting off forever our acquaintance with dear Miss Fenwick, who has always stigmatized one line of it as vulgar, and worthy only of having been composed by a country squire."—Wordsworth's note.

327. 25-26. Cf. these lines with Keats's *Ode on a Grecian Urn*, 11-12 (p. 853).

51-54. These lines are carved upon the pedestal of Wordsworth's statue in Westminster Abbey.

51-56. Cf. with Wordsworth's *The Prelude*, 6, 52-65 (p. 275) and with the *Immortality Ode* (p. 329) and Wordsworth's note on it (column b, this page).

ADMONITION

"Intended more particularly for the perusal of those who may have happened to be enamored of some beautiful place of retreat, in the country of the 'Lakes."—Wordsworth's note.

328. COMPOSED BY THE SIDE OF
GRASMERE LAKE

Grasmere Lake is in the county of Westmoreland, England.

329. ODE: INTIMATIONS OF IMMORTALITY

"This was composed during my residence at Town-end, Grasmere. Two years at least passed between the writing of the four first stanzas and the remaining part. To the attentive and competent reader the whole sufficiently explains itself; but there may be no harm in adverting here to particular feelings or *experiences* of my own mind on which the structure of the poem partly rests. Nothing was more difficult for me in childhood than to admit the notion of death as a state applicable to my own being. I have said elsewhere:—

'A simple child,
That lightly draws its breath,
And feels its life in every limb,
What should it know of death?'
[*We Are Seven*, 1-4 (p. 251)].

But it was not so much from feelings of animal vivacity that *my* difficulty came as from a sense of the indomitableness of the spirit within me. I used to brood over the stories of Enoch and Elijah, and almost to persuade myself that, whatever might become of others, I should be translated, in something of the same way, to heaven. With a feeling congenial to this, I was often unable to think of external things as having external existence, and I communed with all that I saw as something not apart from, but inherent in, my own immaterial nature. Many times while going to school have I grasped at a wall or tree to recall myself from this abyss of idealism to the reality. At that time I was afraid of such processes. In later periods of life I have deplored, as we have all reason to do, a subjugation of an opposite character, and have rejoiced over the remembrances, as is expressed in the lines—

'Obstinate questionings
Of sense and outward things,
Fallings from us, vanishings;' etc.
[ll. 141-43.]

To that dream-like vividness and splendor which invest objects of sight in childhood, every one, I believe, if he would look back, could bear testimony, and I need not dwell upon it here: but having in the poem regarded it as presumptive evidence of a prior state of existence, I think it right to protest against a conclusion, which has given pain to some good and pious persons, that I meant to inculcate such a belief. It is far too shadowy a notion to be recommended to faith, as more than an element in our instincts of immortality. But let us bear in mind that, though the idea is not advanced in revelation, there is nothing there to contradict it, and the fall of man presents an analogy in its favor. Accordingly, a pre-existent state has entered into the popular creeds of many nations; and, among all persons acquainted with classic literature, is known as an ingredient in Platonic philosophy. Archimedes said that he could move the world if he had a point whereon to rest his machine. Who has not felt the same aspirations as regards the world of his own mind? Having to wield some of its elements when I was impelled to write this poem on the Immortality of the Soul, I took hold of the notion of pre-existence as having sufficient foundation in humanity for authorizing me to make for my purpose the best use of it I could as a poet."—Wordsworth's note.

Cf. with Wordsworth's idea the following extract from Plato's *Phædo*, 72-76 (Jowett's trans.): "Your favorite doctrine, Socrates, that knowledge is simply recollection, if true, also necessarily implies a previous time in which we learned that which we now recollect. But this would be impossible unless our soul was in some place before existing in the human form; here then is another argument of the soul's immortality. . . . And if we acquired this knowledge before we were born and were born having it, then we also knew before we were born and at the instant of birth not only the equal or the greater or the less, but all other ideas; for we are not speaking only of equality absolute, but of beauty, good, justice, holiness, and all which we stamp with the name of essence in the dialectal process, when we ask and answer questions. . . . But if, after having acquired, we have not forgotten that which we acquired, then we must always have been born with knowledge, and shall always continue to know as long as life lasts—for knowing is the acquiring and retaining knowledge and not forgetting. . . . But if the knowledge which we acquired before birth was lost by us at birth, and if afterwards by the use of the senses we recovered that which we previously knew, will not that which we call learning be a process of recovering our knowl-

edge, and may not this be rightly termed recollection by us? . . . Then may we not say, Simmias, that if, as we are always repeating, there is an absolute beauty, and goodness, and essence in general, and to this, which is now discovered to be a previous condition of our being, we refer all our sensations, and with this compare them—assuming this to have a prior existence, then our souls must have had a prior existence, but if not, there would be no force in the argument. There can be no doubt that if these absolute ideas existed before we were born, then our souls must have existed before we were born, and if not the ideas, then not the souls."

Speaking of Wordsworth and this ode in *English Traits*, ch. 17, Emerson says: "Let us say of him that, alone in his time, he treated the human mind well, and with an absolute trust. His adherence to his poetic creed rested on real inspirations. The *Ode on Immortality* is the high water mark which the intellect has reached in this age. New means were employed, and new realms added to the empire of the muse, by his courage."

See Coleridge's comment on the poem, p. 414a, 35ff., and 417b, 44ff.

66-76. Ruskin cites these lines (*Modern Painters*, Part III, sec. 1, ch. 5) as revealing the words of "one whose authority is almost without appeal in all questions relating to the influence of external things upon the pure human soul."

330. 143. *Fallings from us, vanishings.*— "There was a time in my life when I had to push against something that resisted, to be sure that there was anything outside of me. I was sure of my own mind; everything else fell away, and vanished into thought."—Wordsworth, quoted by Knight in his edition of *Selections from Wordsworth*.

331. 202-03. "These lines have been often quoted as an illustration of Wordsworth's sensibility to external nature; in reality, they testify to his enriching the sentiment of nature with feeling derived from the heart of man and from the experience of human life."— Dowden, in his edition of Wordsworth's *Poems* (Athenæum Press ed., 1897).

332.   LAODAMÍA

"Written at Rydal Mount. The incident of the trees growing and withering put the subject into my thoughts, and I wrote with the hope of giving it a loftier tone than, so far as I know, has been given to it by any of the ancients who have treated of it. It cost me more trouble than almost anything of equal length I have ever written."—Wordsworth's note.

See Landor's comment on this poem in his *Imaginary Conversations*, "Southey and Porson," I.

Laodamia was the wife of Protesilaus, the first Greek killed at the siege of Troy. After his death she implored the gods to allow her to talk with him, and Mercury (Hermes) led him from the lower world. After the interview Protesilaus departed, and Laodamia died with grief. According to another tradition, she voluntarily accompanied him to the lower world.

334. YARROW VISITED

"As mentioned in my verses on the death of the Ettrick Shepherd [see p. 341], my first visit to Yarrow was in his company. We had lodged the night before at Traquhair, where Hogg had joined us and also Dr. Anderson, the editor of the *British Poets*, who was on a visit at the Manse. Dr. A. walked with us till we came in view of the Vale of Yarrow, and, being advanced in life, he then turned back. The old man was passionately fond of poetry, though with not much of a discriminating judgment, as the volumes he edited sufficiently show. But I was much pleased to meet with him, and to acknowledge my obligation to his collection, which had been my brother John's companion in more than one voyage to India, and which he gave me before his departure from Grasmere, never to return. Through these volumes I became first familiar with Chaucer, and so little money had I then to spare for books, that, in all probability, but for this same work, I should have known little of Drayton, Daniel, and other distinguished poets of the Elizabethan age, and their immediate successors, till a much later period of my life. I am glad to record this, not from any importance of its own, but as a tribute of gratitude to this simple-hearted old man, whom I never again had the pleasure of meeting. I seldom read or think of this poem without regretting that my dear sister was not of the party, as she would have had so much delight in recalling the time when, travelling together in Scotland, we declined going in search of this celebrated stream, not altogether, I will frankly confess, for the reason assigned in the poem on the occasion."—Wordsworth's note.

"We have there the true Yarrow, the truest Yarrow that ever was pictured; real yet not literal—Yarrow as it is for the spiritual sense made keen, quick, sensitive, and deep through the brooding over the stories of the years and living communion with the heart of things."—

J. Veitch, in *The History and Poetry of the Scottish Border* (1878).

This poem should be read in connection with Wordsworth's *Yarrow Unvisited* (p. 319) and *Yarrow Revisited* (p. 338). See notes, pp. 1287b and 1292b.

335. HAST THOU SEEN, WITH FLASH INCESSANT

This is the third of a group of poems entitled *Inscriptions Supposed to be Found in and near a Hermit's Cell.*

"Where the second quarry now is, as you pass from Rydal to Grasmere, there was formerly a length of smooth rock that sloped towards the road, on the right hand. I used to call it Tadpole Slope, from having frequently observed there the water-bubbles gliding under the ice, exactly in the shape of that creature."—Wordsworth's note.

COMPOSED UPON AN EVENING OF EXTRAORDINARY SPLENDOR AND BEAUTY

"Felt and in a great measure composed upon the little mount in front of our abode at Rydal. In concluding my notices of this class of poems it may be as well to observe that among the Miscellaneous Sonnets are a few alluding to morning impressions which might be read with mutual benefit in connection with these Evening Voluntaries. See, for example, that one on Westminster Bridge [p. 311], that composed on a May morning, the one on the song of the thrush [p. 342], and that beginning—'While beams of orient light shoot wide and high.' "—Wordsworth's note.

336. 41ff. "The multiplication of mountain-ridges, described at the commencement of the third stanza of this ode, as a kind of Jacob's Ladder, leading to Heaven, is produced either by watery vapors, or sunny haze;—in the present instance by the latter cause. Allusions to the ode, entitled *Intimations of Immortality*, pervade the last stanza."—Wordsworth's note.

THERE IS A LITTLE UNPRETENDING RILL

"This rill trickles down the hill-side into Windermere, near Lowwood. My sister and I, on our first visit together to this part of the country, walked from Kendal, and we rested to refresh ourselves by the side of the lake where the streamlet falls into it. This sonnet was written some years after in recollection of that happy ramble, that most happy day and hour."—Wordsworth's note.

BETWEEN NAMUR AND LIEGE

This and the following poem are from a group of 37 poems entitled *Memorials of a*

Tour on the Continent, 1820. Wordsworth's wife and sister Dorothy and other friends accompanied him on this tour. Namur and Liège are cities in Belgium.

Of the scenery described in this sonnet, Wordsworth says in a note: "The scenery on the Meuse pleases me more, upon the whole, than that of the Rhine, though the river itself is much inferior in grandeur. The rocks both in form and color, especially between Namur and Liège, surpass any upon the Rhine, though they are in several places disfigured by quarries, whence stones were taken for the new fortifications. This is much to be regretted, for they are useless, and the scars will remain perhaps for thousands of years."

337.   COMPOSED IN ONE OF THE
CATHOLIC CANTONS

See note on preceding poem. This poem refers to the Cantons or States of the Swiss federation.

THE RIVER DUDDON

The two following sonnets are the fifth and the last of a series of sonnets on the River Duddon. The following quotation is from Wordsworth's prefatory note on the series:

"It is with the little River Duddon as it is with most other rivers, Ganges and Nile not excepted,—many springs might claim the honor of being its head. In my own fancy I have fixed its rise near the noted Shire-stones placed at the meeting-point of the counties, Westmoreland, Cumberland, and Lancashire. They stand by the wayside on the top of the Wrynose Pass, and it used to be reckoned a proud thing to say that, by touching them at the same time with feet and hands, one had been in the three counties at once. At what point of its course the stream takes the name of Duddon I do not know. I first became acquainted with the Duddon, as I have good reason to remember, in early boyhood. Upon the banks of the Derwent I had learnt to be very fond of angling. Fish abound in that large river; not so in the small streams in the neighborhood of Hawkshead; and I fell into the common delusion that the farther from home the better sport would be had. Accordingly, one day I attached myself to a person living in the neighborhood of Hawkshead, who was going to try his fortune as an angler near the source of the Duddon. We fished a great part of the day with very sorry success, the rain pouring torrents, and long before we got home I was worn out with fatigue; and, if the good man had not carried me on his back, I must have lain down under

the best shelter I could find. Little did I think then it would be my lot to celebrate, in a strain of love and admiration, the stream which for many years I never thought of without recollections of disappointment and distress.

"During my college vacation, and two or three years afterwards, before taking my Bachelor's degree, I was several times resident in the house of a near relative who lived in the small town of Broughton. I passed many delightful hours upon the banks of this river, which becomes an estuary about a mile from that place."

ECCLESIASTICAL SONNETS

"During the month of December, 1820, I accompanied a much-beloved and honored friend in a walk through different parts of his estate, with a view to fix upon the site of a new church which he intended to erect. It was one of the most beautiful mornings of a mild season,—our feelings were in harmony with the cherishing influences of the scene; and such being our purpose, we were naturally led to look back upon past events with wonder and gratitude, and on the future with hope. Not long afterwards, some of the sonnets which will be found towards the close of this series were produced as a private memorial of that morning's occupation.

"The Catholic question, which was agitated in Parliament about that time, kept my thoughts in the same course; and it struck me that certain points in the ecclesiastical history of our country might advantageously be presented to view in verse. Accordingly, I took up the subject, and what I now offer to the reader was the result."—Wordsworth's note.

338.   TO A SKYLARK

Cf. this poem with Wordsworth's earlier poem on the same subject (p. 323), with Shelley's poem (p. 730) and Hogg's (p. 503).

SCORN NOT THE SONNET

2-3. This is poetic exaggeration; many of Shakespeare's sonnets are conventional in both subject matter and style.

YARROW REVISITED

This and the two following poems are the 1st, 2nd, and 6th of a number of poems written as the result of a tour in Scotland in 1831, and published under the title *Yarrow Revisited and Other Poems.* In the Preface to these poems, Wordsworth says: "In the autumn of 1831, my daughter and I set off from Rydal to visit Sir Walter Scott before his departure for Italy. . . . How sadly changed did I find him from the man I had seen so healthy, gay, and hopeful, a few years before, when he said at the inn at Paterdale, in my presence: 'I mean to live till I am *eighty*, and shall write as long as I live.' . . . On Tuesday morning Sir Walter Scott accompanied us and most of the party to Newark Castle on the Yarrow. When we alighted from the carriages he walked pretty stoutly, and had great pleasure in revisiting those his favorite haunts. Of that excursion the verses *Yarrow Revisited* are a memorial. Notwithstanding the romance that pervades Sir Walter's works and attaches to many of his habits, there is too much pressure of fact for these verses to harmonize as much as I could wish with other poems. On our return in the afternoon we had to cross the Tweed directly opposite Abbotsford. The wheels of our carriage grated upon the pebbles in the bed of the stream, that there flows somewhat rapidly; a rich but sad light of rather a purple than a golden hue was spread over the Eildon hills at that moment; and, thinking it probable that it might be the last time Sir Walter would cross the stream, I was not a little moved, and expressed some of my feelings in the sonnet beginning—'A trouble, not of clouds, or weeping rain.' At noon on Thursday we left Abbotsford, and in the morning of that day Sir Walter and I had a serious conversation *tête-á-tête*, when he spoke with gratitude of the happy life which upon the whole he had led. He had written in my daughter's Album, before he came into the breakfast-room that morning, a few stanzas addressed to her, and, while putting the book into her hand, in his own study, standing by his desk, he said to her in my presence—'I should not have done anything of this kind but for your father's sake: they are probably the last verses I shall ever write.' They show how much his mind was impaired, not by the strain of thought but by the execution, some of the lines being imperfect, and one stanza wanting corresponding rhymes: one letter, the initial *S*, had been omitted in the spelling of his own name."

Cf. this poem with Wordsworth's *Yarrow Unvisited* (p. 319) and *Yarrow Visited* (p. 334). See notes, pp. 1287b and 1291a.

340. ON THE DEPARTURE OF SIR WALTER SCOTT

See note on preceding poem.

THE TROSACHS

The Trosachs is the name given to a ro-mantic valley in the Highlands of western Perthshire, Scotland.

"As recorded in my sister's *Journal*, I had first seen the Trosachs in her and Coleridge's company. The sentiment that runs through this sonnet was natural to the season in which I again saw this beautiful spot; but this and some other sonnets that follow were colored by the remembrance of my recent visit to Sir Walter Scott, and the melancholy errand on which he was going."—Wordsworth's note.

See note on *Yarrow Revisited*, above.

Cf. this poem with *Stepping Westward* (p. 318), composed in the same region, 27 years earlier.

IF THOU INDEED DERIVE THY LIGHT FROM HEAVEN

"These verses were written some time after we had become residents at Rydal Mount, and I will take occasion from them to observe upon the beauty of that situation, as being backed and flanked by lofty fells, which bring the heavenly bodies to touch, as it were, the earth upon the mountain-tops, while the prospect in front lies open to a length of level valley, the extended lake, and a terminating ridge of low hills; so that it gives an opportunity to the inhabitants of the place of noticing the stars in both the positions here alluded to, namely, on the tops of the mountains, and as winter-lamps at a distance among the leafless trees."—Wordsworth's note.

"THERE!" SAID A STRIPLING, POINTING WITH MEET PRIDE

This and the following sonnet belong to a group of 48 poems "composed or suggested during a tour in the summer of 1833." Wordsworth's companions were his son John and his friend H. Crabb Robinson.

Wordsworth's note on the first of the sonnets here printed is as follows: "Mosgiel was thus pointed out to me by a young man on the top of the coach on my way from Glasgow to Kilmarnock. It is remarkable that, though Burns lived some time here, and during much the most productive period of his poetical life, he nowhere adverts to the splendid prospects stretching towards the sea and bounded by the peaks of Arran on one part, which in clear weather he must have had daily before his eyes. In one of his poetical effusions he speaks of describing 'fair Nature's face'[1] as a privilege on which he sets a high value; nevertheless, natural appearances rarely take a lead in his poetry. It is as a human being, eminently sensitive and intelligent, and not

---

[1] *To William Simpson*, st. 16, l. 3.

as a poet, clad in his priestly robes and carrying the ensigns of sacerdotal office, that he interests and affects us. Whether he speaks of rivers, hills, and woods, it is not so much on account of the properties with which they are absolutely endowed, as relatively to local patriotic remembrances and associations, or as they ministered to personal feelings, especially those of love, whether happy or otherwise;—yet it is not always so. Soon after we had passed Mosgiel Farm we crossed the Ayr, murmuring and winding through a narrow woody hollow. His line—'Auld hermit Ayr strays through his woods'[1]—came at once to my mind with Irwin, Lugar, Ayr, and Doon,[2]—Ayrshire streams over which he breathes a sigh as being unnamed in song; and surely his own attempts to make them known were as successful as his heart would desire."

341.   TO A CHILD

"This quatrain was extempore on observing this image, as I had often done, on the lawn of Rydal Mount."—Wordsworth's note.

EXTEMPORE EFFUSION UPON THE DEATH OF
JAMES HOGG

"These verses were written extempore, immediately after reading a notice of the Ettrick Shepherd's death in the Newcastle paper, to the editor of which I sent a copy for publication. The persons lamented in these verses were all either of my friends or acquaintance."—Wordsworth's note.

342. A POET!—HE HATH PUT HIS HEART
TO SCHOOL

"I was impelled to write this sonnet by the disgusting frequency with which the word *artistical*, imported with other impertinences from the Germans, is employed by writers of the present day: for *artistical* let them substitute *artificial*, and the poetry written on this system, both at home and abroad, will be for the most part much better characterized."—Wordsworth's note.

343.   PREFACE

This Preface first appeared in the second edition of *Lyrical Ballads*, published in 1800. In subsequent editions of Wordsworth's poems it was enlarged and modified, as here given, and transferred to the end of the volume. The phrase "several of the foregoing poems" in the title refers to the original *Lyrical Ballads*, which included the following poems by Wordsworth:

[1] *The Vision.* Duan 1, st. 14, l. 3.
[2] See *To William Simpson*, st. 8, l. 5.

For the other poems which appeared in the second edition of *Lyrical Ballads*, see the Glossary under *Lyrical Ballads*.

343b. 25ff. That is, one expects a poem written in a given period to exemplify the characteristics peculiar to the poetry of that period. The poetry of the age of Catullus, Terence, and Lucretius was less artificial than that of the age of Statius and Claudian. The poetry of the age of Shakespeare and Beaumont and Fletcher was characterized by spontaneity and naturalness; that of Donne and Cowley, by extravagant refinements; that of Dryden and Pope, by precision and conformity to set rules.

344b. 3. *Creation.*—"It is worth while here to observe that the affecting parts of Chaucer are almost always expressed in language pure and universally intelligible even to this day."—Wordsworth's note.

346b. 33. *Poetry.*—"I here used the word *poetry* (though against my own judgment) as opposed to the word *prose*, and synonymous with *metrical composition*. But much confusion has been introduced into criticism by this contradistinction of poetry and prose, instead of the more philosophical one of poetry and matter of fact, or science. The only strict antithesis to prose is metre: nor is this, in truth, a *strict* antithesis, because lines and passages of metre so naturally occur in writing prose, that it would be scarcely possible to avoid them, even were it desirable."—Wordsworth's note.

348a. 28ff. Cf. Shelley's *A Defense of Poetry* (p. 772b, 31ff.).

Samuel Taylor Coleridge

Selections, p. 354 — Bibliography, p. 1417

"His best work is but little, but of its kind it is perfect and unique. For exquisite music of metrical movement and for an imaginative phantasy, such as might belong to a world where men always dreamt, there is nothing in our language to be compared with *Christabel,* 1805, and *Kubla Khan,* and to *The Ancient Mariner* published as one of the *Lyrical Ballads,* in 1798. The little poem called *Love* is not so good, but it touches with great grace that with which all sympathize. All that he did excellently might be bound up in twenty pages, but it should be bound in pure gold."—S. A. Brooke, in *English Literature* (1876).

"You will see Coleridge—he who sits obscure
In the exceeding lustre and the pure
Intense irradiation of a mind,
Which, with its own internal lightning blind,
Flags wearily through darkness and despair—
A cloud-encircled meteor of the air,
A hooded eagle among blinking owls."
—Shelley, in *Letter to Maria Gisborne,*
ll. 202-08 (1820).

See Lamb's *Christ's Hospital Five and Thirty Years Ago* (p. 957) and note, p. 1373; Byron's *Don Juan, Dedication,* 2 (p. 603); and Hazlitt's *My First Acquaintance with Poets* (p. 1054).
Coleridge is caricatured in Mr. Flosky in Thomas Love Peacock's *Nightmare Abbey.*

354.   TO A YOUNG ASS

See Byron's satiric reference to this poem in *English Bards and Scotch Reviewers,* 261-64 (p. 515).
27-31. A reference to Pantisocracy. See Coleridge's *Pantisocracy* and note 1 (p. 354).

355.   LA FAYETTE

Marquis de Lafayette (1757-1834) was a celebrated French general and statesman. He left France in 1792 to avoid the consequences of his opposition to the Jacobins, and was imprisoned as a political suspect by the Prussians and Austrians, 1792-97. He returned to France in 1799.

KOSKIUSKO

Thaddeus Kosciusko (1746-1817) was a famous Polish patriot and general. He was commander of the Polish insurrection of 1794, and was defeated and taken prisoner on Oct. 10 of that year. He was released in 1796. See Campbell's *The Pleasures of Hope,* 349-418 (pp. 444-445).

TO THE REVEREND W. L. BOWLES

Coleridge probably intended to dedicate the 1797 edition of his poems to Bowles. On Nov. 14, 1796, Lamb wrote as follows: "Coleridge, I love you for dedicating your poetry to Bowles. Genius of the sacred fountain of tears, it was he who led you gently by the hand through all this valley of weeping; showed you the dark-green yew trees, and the willow shades."
See Coleridge's comment on Bowles, p. 1257b.

THE EOLIAN HARP

This poem was written Aug. 24, 1795, nearly two months before Coleridge's marriage (Oct. 4, 1795). The Æolian harp is a musical instrument consisting of a box with strings stretched across it. It is usually placed at a window, where the wind striking it produces music. It is named from Æolus, god of the winds.

357.   ODE ON THE DEPARTING YEAR

This poem, in a shorter form, was first entitled *Ode for the Last Day of the Year 1796.* In the early version, the first stanza was called Strophe I; the second, Strophe II; the third, Epode; the fourth, Antistrophe I; the fifth Antistrophe II; the remaining stanzas, Epode II. In the 1797 edition Coleridge prefixed the following Argument, which in the 1803 edition was distributed in notes:
"The Ode commences with an address to the Divine Providence that regulates into one vast harmony all the events of time, however calamitous some of them may appear to mortals. The second strophe calls on men to suspend their private joys and sorrows, and devote them for a while to the cause of human nature in general. The first epode speaks of the Empress of Russia, who died of an apoplexy on the 17th of November, 1796, having just concluded a subsidiary treaty with the kings combined against France. The first and second antistrophe describe the Image of the Departing Year, etc., as in a vision. The second epode prophesies, in anguish of spirit, the downfall of this country."

358. 40. "A subsidiary Treaty had been just concluded; and Russia was to have furnished more effectual aid than that of pious manifestoes to the Powers combined against France. I rejoice—not over the deceased Woman (I never dared figure the Russian Sovereign to my imagination under the dear and venerable Character of WOMAN—WOMAN, that complex term for Mother, Sister, Wife!) I rejoice, as at the disenshrining of a Daemon! I rejoice, as at the extinction of the evil Principle impersonated! This very day, six years ago, the massacre of Ismail was perpetrated. THIRTY THOUSAND HUMAN BEINGS, MEN, WOMEN, AND CHILDREN, murdered in cold blood, for no other crime than that their garrison had defended the place with perseverance and bravery. Why should I recall the poisoning of her husband, her iniquities in Poland, or her late unmotived attack on Persia, the desolating ambition of her public life, or the libidinous excesses of her private hours! I have no wish to qualify myself for the office of Historiographer to the King of Hell!"—Coleridge.

359. 135. *Abandon'd of Heaven.*—"The poet from having considered the peculiar advantages, which this country has enjoyed, passes in rapid transition to the uses, which we have made of these advantages. We have been preserved by our insular situation, from suffering the actual horrors of war ourselves, and we have shown our gratitude to Providence for this immunity by our eagerness to spread those horrors over nations less happily situated. In the midst of plenty and safety we have raised or joined the yell for famine and blood. Of the one hundred and seven last years, fifty have been years of war. Such wickedness cannot pass unpunished. We have been proud and confident in our alliances and our fleets—but God has prepared the cankerworm, and will smite the *gourds* of our pride. 'Art thou better than populous No, that was situate among the rivers, that had the waters round about it, whose rampart was the Sea? Ethiopia and Egypt were her strength and it was infinite: Put and Lubim were her helpers. Yet she was carried away, she went into captivity: and they cast lots for her honorable men, and all her great men were bound in chains. Thou also shalt be drunken: all thy strongholds shall be like fig trees with the first ripe figs; if they be shaken, they shall even fall into the mouth of the eater. Thou hast multiplied thy merchants above the stars of heaven. Thy crowned are as the locusts; and thy captains as the great grasshoppers which camp in the hedges in the cool

day; but when the sun ariseth they flee away, and their place is not known where they are. There is no healing of thy bruise; thy wound is grievous: all, that hear the report of thee, shall clap hands over thee: for upon whom hath not thy wickedness passed continually?' *Nahum*, chap. iii."—Coleridge.

360. THIS LIME-TREE BOWER MY PRISON

"In the June of 1797 some long-expected friends paid a visit to the author's cottage; and on the morning of their arrival, he met with an accident, which disabled him from walking during the whole time of their stay. One evening, when they had left him for a few hours, he composed the following lines in the garden-bower."—Coleridge's prefatory note.

The friends referred to were Wordsworth and his sister Dorothy, and Lamb. Coleridge wrote Southey in July about the visit, as follows: "Charles Lamb has been with me for a week. He left me Friday morning. The second day after Wordsworth came to me dear Sara accidentally emptied a skillet of boiling milk on my foot, which confined me during the whole of C. Lamb's stay and still prevents me from all walks longer than a furlong."

8-20. The spot here described was a favorite meeting place of Wordsworth, Coleridge, and their Alfoxden friends. See Wordsworth's *Lines Written in Early Spring* (p. 257), and note, p. 1278b.

361. THE RIME OF THE ANCIENT MARINER

This poem was first printed anonymously in the first edition of *Lyrical Ballads* (1798). Many archaisms intended to make it resemble the old popular ballads were removed in the second edition (1800). It was first published under the author's name in *Sibylline Leaves* (1817), where it appeared with a marginal gloss (printed in this text in footnotes) and a Latin motto from T. Burnet's *Archæologiæ Philosophicæ* (1692), of which the following is a translation:

"I readily believe that there are more invisible beings in the universe than visible. But who shall explain to us the nature, the rank and kinship, the distinguishing marks and graces of each? What do they do? Where do they dwell? The human mind has circled round this knowledge, but never attained to it. Yet there is profit, I do not doubt, in sometimes contemplating in the mind, as in a picture, the image of a greater and better world: lest the intellect, habituated to the petty details of daily life, should be

contracted within too narrow limits and settle down wholly on trifles. But, meanwhile,
a watchful eye must be kept on truth, and
proportion observed, that we may distinguish
the certain from the uncertain, day from
night."

For the origin of the poem, see Coleridge's
Biographia Literaria, 14 (pp. 398-399), and
Wordsworth's note on *We Are Seven* (p. 1275).
The following additional statement by Wordsworth was reported to H. N. Coleridge by the
Rev. Alexander Dyce: "*The Ancient Mariner*
was founded on a strange dream, which a
friend of Coleridge had, who fancied he saw
a skeleton ship, with figures in it. We had
both determined to write some poetry for a
monthly magazine, the profits of which were
to defray the expenses of a little excursion
we were to make together. *The Ancient
Mariner* was intended for this periodical, but
was too long. I had very little share in the
composition of it, for I soon found that the
style of Coleridge and myself would not assimilate. Besides the lines (in the fourth
part):

'And thou art long, and lank, and brown,
As is the ribbed sea-sand'—

I wrote the stanza (in the first part):

'He holds him with his glittering eye—
The Wedding-Guest stood still,
And listens like a three-years' child:
The Mariner hath his will'—

and four or five lines more in different parts
of the poem, which I could not now point
out. The idea of *'shooting an albatross' was
mine; for I had been reading Shelvocke's
Voyages, which probably Coleridge never saw*.
I also suggested the reanimation of the dead
bodies, to work the ship." (Note printed in
Campbell's ed. of *Poetical Works of Coleridge*
[1893], S. T. C. ed. 1852.) See Lamb's comment on Wordsworth's note on the poem,
published in the second edition of *Lyrical Ballads* (p. 945a, 49ff.).

In his masterful *Road to Xanadu*, J. L.
Lowes shows that many incidents and descriptive details of the poem were drawn from
actual human experience as related by various
writers in travel books that Coleridge had
read. This fact, however, does not lessen the
glory of Coleridge's imaginative achievement.

Regarding the probability of the poem, and
its moral, Coleridge remarked as follows
(*Table Talk*, May 31, 1800): "Mrs. Barbauld
once told me that she admired *The Ancient
Mariner* very much, but that there were two
faults in it,—it was improbable, and had no
moral. As for the probability, I owned that
that might admit some question; but as to
the want of a moral, I told her that in my
own judgment the poem had too much; and
that the only, or chief fault, if I might say
so, was the obtrusion of the moral sentiment
so openly on the reader as a principle or
cause of action in a work of pure imagination. It ought to have had no more moral
than the *Arabian Nights'* tale of the merchant's sitting down to eat dates by the side
of a well and throwing the shells aside, and
lo! a genie starts up and says he *must* kill
the aforesaid merchant *because* one of the
date shells had, it seems, put out the eye of
the genie's son." Mrs. Barbauld (1743-1825)
was an English poet and essayist.

"It is enough for us here that he has
written some of the most poetical poetry in
the language, and one poem, *The Ancient
Mariner*, not only unparalleled, but unap-
proached in its kind, and that kind of the
rarest. It is marvellous in its mastery over
that delightfully fortuitous inconsequence that
is the adamantine logic of dreamland. Coleridge has taken the old ballad measure and
given to it by an indefinable charm, wholly
his own, all the sweetness, all the melody and
compass of a symphony. And how picturesque
it is in the proper sense of the word. I know
nothing like it. There is not a description
in it. It is all picture."—J. R. Lowell, in
"Address on Unveiling the Bust of Coleridge
in Westminster Abbey, 7 May, 1885," *Democracy and Other Addresses* (1887).

The poem is here printed from the revised
text of 1829.

363. 125-30. Lowes (p. 81) quotes the following passage from Capt. James Cook's
Voyage to the Pacific Ocean: "During a calm
. . . some parts of the sea seemed covered
with a kind of slime; and some small sea animals were swimming about . . . that had
a white, or shining appearance. . . . When
they began to swim about, which they did,
with equal ease, upon their back, sides, or
belly, they emitted the brightest colors of the
most precious gems. . . . Sometimes they
. . . assumed various tints of blue. . . .
But . . . the color was, chiefly, a beautiful, pale green, tinged with a burnished gloss;
and, in the dark, it had a faint appearance of
glowing fire. They proved to be . . .
probably, an animal which has a share in producing . . . that lucid appearance, often
observed near ships at sea, in the night."

164. "I took the thought of *'grinning for
joy'* from poor Burnett's remark to me, when

we had climbed to the top of Plinlimmon, and were nearly dead with thirst. We could not speak for the constriction, till we found a little puddle under a stone. He said to me, 'You grinned like an idiot!' He had done the same."—Coleridge, in *Table Talk*, May 31, 1830. George Burnett (c1766-1811) was a miscellaneous writer, interested with Coleridge and Southey in the scheme of Pantisocracy. Plinlimmon is a mountain in Wales.

167-98. Tales of specter-ships, moving freely without wind or tide, were traditional, as was also the story of two spectral figures casting dice for the soul of an eternal wanderer, like Falkenberg in the Dutch folk tale. Living in a seaport town, Coleridge must have heard many of the current strange tales about phantom ships. See Lowes, pp. 261-94.

364. 210-11. "It is a common superstition among sailors that something evil is about to happen whenever a star dogs the moon."—Coleridge, in a manuscript note.

Coleridge had read Cotton Mather's report that "in November, 1668, a Star appear'd below the Body of the Moon within the Horns of it." The phenomenon belongs to a waning moon rising in the early morning. See Lowes, pp. 179-93.

365. 314-17. Coleridge had read accounts of travelers describing stars seen through the Northern Lights, or Aurora Borealis.

369.   CHRISTABEL

"The first part of the following poem was written in the year 1797, at Stowey, in the county of Somerset. The second part, after my return from Germany, in the year 1800, at Keswick, Cumberland. Since the latter date, my poetic powers have been, till very lately, in a state of suspended animation. But as, in my very first conception of the tale, I had the whole present to my mind, with the wholeness, no less than the liveliness of a vision, I trust that I shall be able to embody in verse the three parts yet to come, in the course of the present year. It is probable that if the poem had been finished at either of the former periods, or if even the first and second part had been published in the year 1800, the impression of its originality would have been much greater than I dare at present expect. But for this I have only my own indolence to blame. The dates are mentioned for the exclusive purpose of precluding charges of plagiarism or servile imitation from myself. For there is amongst us a set of critics, who seem to hold, that every possible thought and image is traditional; who have no notion that there are such things as fountains in the world, small

as well as great; and who would therefore charitably derive every rill they behold flowing, from a perforation made in some other man's tank. I am confident, however, that as far as the present poem is concerned, the celebrated poets whose writings I might be suspected of having imitated, either in particular passages, or in the tone and the spirit of the whole, would be among the first to vindicate me from the charge, and who, on any striking coincidence, would permit me to address them in this doggerel version of two monkish Latin hexameters:

'Tis mine and it is likewise yours;
But an if this will not do;
Let it be mine, good friend! for I
Am the poorer of the two.

"I have only to add that the metre of the *Christabel* is not, properly speaking, irregular, though it may seem so from its being founded on a new principle: namely, that of counting in each line the accents, not the syllables. Though the latter may vary from seven to twelve, yet in each line the accents will be found to be only four. Nevertheless, this occasional variation in number of syllables is not introduced wantonly, or for the mere ends of convenience, but in correspondence with some transition in the nature of the imagery or passion."—Coleridge's original Preface.

The poets referred to above are Scott, who heard the poem read in 1801, and Byron, who heard it in 1811.

The poem was intended for publication in the second edition of *Lyrical Ballads* (1800); but Coleridge never completed it. In *Table Talk*, July 6, 1833, Coleridge said: "I could write as good verses now as ever I did, if I were perfectly free from vexations, and were I in the *ad libitum* hearing of fine music, which has a sensible effect in harmonizing my thoughts, and in animating and, as it were, lubricating my inventive faculty. The reason of my not finishing *Christabel* is not that I don't know how to do it—for I have, as I always had, the whole plan entire from beginning to end in my mind; but I fear I could not carry on with equal success the execution of the idea, an extremely subtle and difficult one." The poem was finally published by Murray on the recommendation of Byron.

Coleridge's plan for the completion of the story is thus related by Mr. Gillman, who cared for Coleridge during the last years of his life: "The following relation was to have occupied a third and fourth canto, and to have closed the tale. Over the mountains, the Bard, as directed by Sir Leoline, hastes with his disciple; but in consequence of one of those inundations supposed to be common to this country, the spot only where the castle once stood is discovered—the edifice itself being washed away. He determines to return. Geraldine, being acquainted with all that is passing, like the weird sisters in *Macbeth*, vanishes. Reappearing, however, she awaits the return of the Bard, exciting in the meantime, by her wily arts, all the anger she could rouse in the Baron's breast, as well as that jealousy of which he is described to have been susceptible. The old Bard and the youth at length arrive, and therefore she can no longer personate the character of Geraldine, the daughter of Lord Roland de Vaux, but changes her appearance to that of the accepted though absent lover of Christabel. Now ensues a courtship most distressing to Christabel, who feels, she knows not why, great disgust for her once favored knight. This coldness is very painful to the Baron, who has no more conception than herself of the supernatural transformation. She at last yields to her father's entreaties, and consents to approach the altar with this hated suitor. The real lover, returning, enters at this moment, and produces the ring which she had once given him in sign of her betrothment. Thus defeated, the supernatural being Geraldine disappears. As predicted, the castle bell tolls, the mother's voice is heard, and, to the exceeding great joy of the parties, the rightful marriage takes place, after which follows a reconciliation and explanation between the father and daughter."—Quoted from Gillman's *The Life of Samuel Taylor Coleridge* (1838).

"For my part, I cannot compare *Kubla Khan* with *Christabel*. The magical beauty of the latter has been so long canonized in the world's estimate, that to praise it now would be unseemly. It brought into English poetry an atmosphere of wonder and mystery, of weird beauty and pity combined, which was quite new at the time it appeared, and has never since been approached. The movement of its subtle cadences has a union of grace with power, which only the finest lines of Shakespeare can parallel. As we read *Christabel* and a few other of Coleridge's pieces, we recall his own words:

'In a half-sleep we dream,
And dreaming hear thee still, O singing lark!
That singest like an angel in the clouds.' "

—J. C. Shairp, in "Poetic Style in Modern English Poetry," *Aspects of Poetry* (1881).

The meter of *Christabel* was used by Scott in *The Lay of the Last Minstrel*, and by other poets in imitation or ridicule of Coleridge's poem. The following poem was written by James Hogg, and published with other pieces imitative of his contemporaries in a volume entitled *The Poet's Mirror* (1816):

Isabelle

Can there be a moon in heaven tonight,
That the hill and the gray cloud seem so light?
The air is whitened by some spell,
For there is no moon, I know it well;
On this third day the sages say   5
('Tis wonderful how well they know)
The moon is journeying far away,
Bright somewhere in a heaven below,
It is a strange and lovely night,
A grayish pale, but not white!   10
Is it rain, or is it dew,
That falls so thick I see its hue?
In rays it follows, one, two, three,
Down the air so merrily,
Said Isabelle; so let it be!   15
Why does the Lady Isabelle
Sit in the damp and dewy dell,
Counting the racks of drizzly rain,
And how often the rail cries over again?
For she's harping, harping in the brake,   20
Craik, craik——Craik, craik,—
Ten times nine, and thrice eleven;—
The last call was an hundred and seven.
Craik, craik—the hour is near—
Let it come, I have no fear!   25
Yet it is a dreadful work, I wis,
Such doings in a night like this!
Sounds the river harsh and loud?
The stream sounds harsh, but not loud.
There is a cloud that seems to hover   30
By western hill the churchyard over;
What is it like?—'Tis like a whale;
'Tis like a shark with half the tail,
Not half, but third and more;
Now 'tis a wolf, and now a boar;   35
Its face is raised—it cometh here;
Let it come—there is no fear.
There's two for heaven, and ten for hell,
Let it come—'tis well—'tis well!
Said the Lady Isabelle.   40
What ails that little cut-tailed whelp,
That it continues to yelp, yelp?
Yelp, yelp, and it turns its eye
Up to the tree and half to the sky;
Half to the sky and full to the cloud,   45
And still it whines and barks aloud.
Why I should dread I cannot tell.
There is a spirit; I know it well!
I see it in yon falling beam—
Is it a vision or a dream?   50
It is no dream, full well I know
I have a woeful deed to do!

Hush, hush, thou little murmurer;
I tell thee, hush—the dead are near!

    If thou knewest all, poor tail-less whelp, 55
Well mightest thou tremble, growl, and yelp,
But thou knowest nothing, hast no part
(Simple and stupid as thou art)
Save gratitude and truth of heart.
But they are coming by this way   60
That have been dead for a year and a day;
Without challenge, without change,
They shall have their full revenge!
They have been sent to wander in woe
In the lands of flame and the lands of snow; 65
But those that are dead
Shall the greensward tread,
And those that are living
Shall soon be dead!
None to pity them, none to help;   70
Thou mayest quake, my cut-tailed whelp!
    There are two from the grave
That I fain would save;
Full hard is the weird
For the young and the brave!   75
Perchance they are wrapt in vision sweet,
While the passing breezes kiss their feet;
And they are dreaming of joy and love!—
Well, let them go—there's room above.
*   *   *   *   *   *   *   *   *   *
Yet they are coming! and they are three! 80
Jesu Maria! can it be?

The Conclusion

    Sleep on! fair maiden of Borrowdale!
Sleep, O sleep, and do not wake;
Dream of the dance, till the foot so pale,
And the beauteous ankle shiver and shake; 85
Till thou shalt press, with feeling bland,
Thine own fair breast for lover's hand.
Thy heart is light as summer breeze.
Thy heart is joyous as the day;
Man never form of angel sees,   90
But thou art fair as they.
So lovers ween, and so they say,
So thine shall ween for many a day.
The hour's at hand, O woe is me!
For they are coming, and they are three. 95

369. 49-52. Cf. these lines with the following entry in Dorothy Wordsworth's *Journal:* "March 7, 1798. William and I drank tea at Coleridge's. A cloudy sky. Observed nothing particularly interesting—the distant prospect obscured. One only leaf upon the top of a tree—the sole remaining leaf—danced round and round like a rag blown by the wind."

    Of these lines, Ruskin says ("Of the Pathetic Fallacy," *Modern Painters*, Part IV, ch. 12, sec. 6): "When Coleridge speaks of

    'The one red leaf, the last of its clan,
    That dances as often as dance it can,'

he has a morbid, that is to say, a so far false, idea about the leaf: he fancies a life in it, and will, which there are not; confuses its powerlessness with choice, its fading death with merriment, and the wind that shakes it with music. Here, however, there is some beauty, even in the morbid passage."

372. Part II.—The inspiration for Part II of the poem was the *Hymn to Teresa* by Richard Crashaw, an English poet of the 16th century. The scenery in Part II is that of the Lake district, England.

373. 408-26. Coleridge regarded these lines as "the best and sweetest passage" he ever wrote. Southey may be referred to in the passage. See Byron's *Childe Harold's Pilgrimage*, III, 94 (p. 563).

375. The Conclusion to Part II.—These lines have little obvious relation to the rest of the poem and probably were not meant originally to be a part of it. They were sent to Southey in a letter of May 6, 1801, and probably were written about that time. J. D. Campbell, in his edition of *Poetical Works of Coleridge*, says that these lines do not occur in any of the three extant manuscripts of the poem.

376.   FROST AT MIDNIGHT

    7. *My cradled infant.*—His son Hartley.

    24. *At school.*—Coleridge entered Christ's Hospital in 1782, and remained there until he went to Cambridge University in 1791. See Lamb's *Christ's Hospital Five and Thirty Years Ago* (p. 957).

    37. *Stern preceptor.*—Bowyer, the famous master of Christ's Hospital, noted for his flogging proclivities. In *Table Talk*, May 27, 1830, Coleridge says: "I had *one* just flogging. When I was about thirteen, I went to a shoemaker, and begged him to take me as his apprentice. He, being an honest man, immediately took me to Bowyer, who got into a great rage, knocked me down, and even pushed Crispin rudely out of the room. Bowyer asked me why I had made myself such a fool? to which I answered, that I had a great desire to be a shoemaker, and that I hated the thought of being a clergyman. 'Why so?' said he—'Because, to tell you the truth, sir,' said I, 'I am an infidel!' For this, without more ado, Bowyer flogged me,—wisely, as I think, —soundly, as I know. Any whining or sermonizing would have gratified my vanity, and confirmed me in my absurdity; as it was, I was laughed at, and got heartily ashamed of my folly."

    42. *Sister.*—Coleridge was very fond of his sister Ann, who was five years his senior. She died in 1791.

53. While at school, Coleridge used to lie upon the roof and gaze at the clouds and stars.

54ff. The prophecy expressed in these lines was fulfilled in 1800, when Coleridge moved to Greta Hall, Keswick, in the Lake district.

377.   FRANCE: AN ODE

Inspired by the French invasion of Switzerland (Helvetia) in 1798, this poem was printed in *The Morning Post*, April 16, 1798, with this introduction, entitled *Original Poetry:*

"The following excellent ode will be in unison with the feelings of every friend to liberty and foe to oppression; of all who, admiring the French Revolution, detest and deplore the conduct of France towards Switzerland. It is very satisfactory to find so zealous and steady an advocate for freedom as Mr. Coleridge concur with us in condemning the conduct of France towards the Swiss Cantons. Indeed his concurrence is not singular; we know of no friend to liberty who is not of his opinion. What we most admire is the *avowal* of his sentiments, and public censure of the unprincipled and atrocious conduct of France. The poem itself is written with great energy. The second, third, and fourth stanzas contain some of the most vigorous lines we have ever read. The lines in the fourth stanza:—

'To scatter rage and trait'rous guilt
Where Peace her jealous home had built,'

to the end of the stanza are particularly expressive and beautiful."

Argument prefixed to an 1802 edition: "*First Stanza.* An invocation to those objects in nature the contemplation of which had inspired the poet with a devotional love of liberty. *Second Stanza.* The exultation of the poet at the commencement of the French Revolution, and his unqualified abhorrence of the Alliance against the Republic. *Third Stanza.* The blasphemies and horrors during the domination of the Terrorists regarded by the poet as a transient storm, and as the natural consequence of the former despotism and of the foul superstition of Popery. Reason, indeed, began to suggest many apprehensions; yet still the poet struggled to retain the hope that France would make conquests by no other means than by presenting to the observation of Europe a people more happy and better instructed than under other forms of government. *Fourth Stanza.* Switzerland, and the poet's recantation. *Fifth Stanza.* An address to liberty, in which the poet expresses his conviction that those feelings and that grand *ideal* of freedom which the mind attains by its con-

templation of its individual nature, and of the sublime surrounding objects (see stanza the first) do not belong to men, as a society, nor can possibly be either gratified or realized, under any form of human government; but belong to the individual man, so far as he is pure, and inflamed with the love and adoration of God in nature."

378.   LEWTI

This poem, claimed by Coleridge as his own and certainly much revised by him, is now believed to have been written by Wordsworth in his youth, under the title *Beauty and Moonlight*; see Jane W. Smyser's "Coleridge's Use of Wordsworth's Juvenilia," *Pub. Mod. Lang. Assn.*, 65: 419-26 (1950). See also Lowes, *The Road to Xanadu*, pp. 514-16.

382.   THE NIGHTINGALE

The scenery of this poem is that of the Quantock hills about Nether Stowey and Alfoxden, in Somersetshire, England. The poem was first published in *Lyrical Ballads*, in 1798.

384.   THE BALLAD OF THE DARK LADIE

A manuscript note by Coleridge states that this poem was intended originally to contain 190 lines. See note on *Love*, p. 1302.

KUBLA KHAN

When first published this poem was prefaced with the following note:

Of The Fragment of Kubla Khan

"The following fragment is here published at the request of a poet of great and deserved celebrity [Lord Byron], and, as far as the author's own opinions are concerned, rather as a psychological curiosity, than on the ground of any supposed *poetic* merits.

"In the summer of the year 1797, the author, then in ill health, had retired to a lonely farmhouse between Porlock and Linton, on the Exmoor confines of Somerset and Devonshire. In consequence of a slight indisposition, an anodyne had been prescribed, from the effects of which he fell asleep in his chair at the moment that he was reading the following sentence, or words of the same substance, in *Purchas's Pilgrimage:* 'Here the Khan Kubla commanded a palace to be built, and a stately garden thereunto. And thus ten miles of fertile ground were inclosed with a wall.'[1] The author

[1] "In Xamdu did Cublai Can build a stately Pallace, encompassing sixteene miles of plaine ground with a wall, wherein are fertile Meddowes, pleasant Springs, delightful Streames, and all sorts of beasts of chase and game, and in the middest thereof a sumptuous house of pleasure."—*Purchas his Pilgrimage* (1626 ed.), 4, 13, 418.

continued for about three hours in a profound sleep, at least of the external senses, during which time he had the most vivid confidence, that he could not have composed less than from two to three hundred lines; if that indeed can be called composition in which all the images rose up before him as *things*, with a parallel production of the correspondent expressions, without any sensation or consciousness of effort. On awaking he appeared to himself to have a distinct recollection of the whole, and taking his pen, ink, and paper, instantly and eagerly wrote down the lines that are here preserved. At this moment he was unfortunately called out by a person on business from Porlock, and detained by him above an hour, and on his return to his room, found, to his no small surprise and mortification, that though he still retained some vague and dim recollection of the general purport of the vision, yet, with the exception of some eight or ten scattered lines and images, all the rest had passed away like the images on the surface of a stream into which a stone has been cast, but, alas! without the after restoration of the latter!

> Then all the charm
> Is broken—all that phantom-world so fair
> Vanishes, and a thousand circlets spread,
> And each mis-shape[s] the other. Stay awhile,
> Poor youth! who scarcely dar'st lift up thine
>   eyes—
> The stream will soon renew its smoothness,
>   soon
> The visions will return! And lo, he stays,
> And soon the fragments dim of lovely forms
> Come trembling back, unite, and now once more
> The pool becomes a mirror.

[From Coleridge's *The Picture; or, the Lover's Resolution*, 91-100.]

"Yet from the still surviving recollections in his mind, the author has frequently purposed to finish for himself what had been originally, as it were, given to him. Αὔριον ἄδιον ἄσω;[1] but the tomorrow is yet to come."

"Were we compelled to the choice, I for one would rather preserve *Kubla Khan* and *Christabel* than any other of Coleridge's poems. It is more conceivable that another man should be born capable of writing *The Ancient Mariner* than one capable of writing these. The former is perhaps the most wonderful of all poems. In reading it we seem rapt into that paradise revealed to Swedenborg, where music and color and perfume were one, where you could hear the hues and see the har-

monies of heaven. For absolute melody and splendor it were hardly rash to call it the first poem in the language."—A. C. Swinburne, in *Essays and Studies* (1875).

"In Coleridge's *Kubla Khan* we have no wrestling with spiritual questions, no lofty solution of the problem of conduct found through brooding on the beauties of nature. Instead, a thousand impressions received from the senses, from records of Oriental travel, from numberless romantic tales, have been taken in by the author, dissolved as in a crucible by the fierce heat of his imagination, and are poured forth in a molten stream of sensuous imagery, incalculable in its variety of suggestion, yet homogeneous, unified, and, despite its fragmentary character, the ultimate expression of a whole romantic world." —Neilson, in *Essentials of Poetry* (1912).

384. 14-16. These are three of the lines referred to by Kipling in his *Wireless:* "Remember that in all the millions permitted there are no more than five—five little lines—of which one can say, 'These are the magic. These are the vision. The rest is only poetry.'" The other two lines are in Keats's *Ode to a Nightingale*, 69-70 (p. 858).

385.   LINES

Coleridge sent this poem in a letter to his wife with the following comment: "At the inn they brought us an Album, or Stamm-Buch, requesting that we would write our names and something or other as a remembrance that we had been there. I wrote the following lines which I send to you, not that they possess a grain of merit as poetry, but because they contain a true account of my journey from the Brocken to Elbinrode."

LOVE

This poem was first published in *The Morning Post*, Dec. 21, 1799, under the title *Introduction to the Tale of the Dark Ladie*, and with the following introductory letter, addressed to the editor of *The Morning Post:*

"Sir,

"The following poem is the Introduction to a somewhat longer one, for which I shall solicit insertion on your next open day. The use of the old ballad word *Ladie* for *Lady* is the only piece of obsoleteness in it; and as it is professedly a tale of ancient times, I trust, that 'the affectionate lovers of venerable antiquity' (as Camden[1] says) will grant me their pardon, and perhaps may be induced to admit a force and propriety in it. A heavier objection may be adduced against the author, that

---

[1] Tomorrow, I shall sing a sweeter song.—Theocritus, *Idyls*, 1, 132.

[1] William Camden (1551-1623), an English antiquary and historian.

in these times of fear and expectation, when novelties *explode* around us in all directions, he should presume to offer to the public a silly tale of old-fashioned love; and, five years ago, I own, I should have allowed and felt the force of this objection. But, alas! explosion has succeeded explosion so rapidly that novelty itself ceases to appear new; and it is possible that now, even a simple story, wholly unspiced with politics or personality, may find some attention amid the hubbub of revolutions, as to those who have resided a long time by the falls of Niagara, the lowest whispering becomes distinctly audible. S. T. COLERIDGE."

O leave the lily on its stem;
O leave the rose upon the spray;
O leave the elder-bloom, fair maids!
 And listen to my lay.

A cypress and a myrtle bough,
This morn around my harp you twin'd,
Because it fashion'd mournfully
 Its murmurs in the wind.

And now a tale of love and woe,
A woeful tale of love I sing:
Hark, gentle maidens, hark! it sighs
 And trembles on the string.

But most, my own dear Genevieve!
It sighs and trembles most for thee!
O come and hear the cruel wrongs
 Befel the Dark Ladie!

Few sorrows hath she of her own,
My hope, my joy, my Genevieve!
She loves me best when'er I sing
 The songs that make her grieve.

Then came *Love* as we know it, with slight changes, and the following concluding stanzas:

And now once more a tale of woe,
A woeful tale of love, I sing:
For thee, my Genevieve! it sighs,
 And trembles on the string.

When last I sang the cruel scorn
That craz'd this bold and lonely Knight,
And how he roam'd the mountain woods,
 Nor rested day or night;

I promis'd thee a sister tale
Of man's perfidious cruelty:
Come, then, and hear what cruel wrong
 Befel the Dark Ladie.

386. DEJECTION: AN ODE

This poem was first addressed to Wordsworth and was printed in *The Morning Post* on his wedding day, Oct. 4, 1802. In this version Wordsworth was referred to as "Edmund," and that name occurred where "Lady" is found in the present text, and where "Otway" appears in l. 120. An earlier version contained the name "William" throughout. An estrangement between the two poets was the cause of the later substitutions.

Compare Wordsworth's *Immortality Ode* (p. 329).

388. HYMN BEFORE SUNRISE IN THE VALE OF CHAMOUNI

This poem was first printed in *The Morning Post*, Sept. 11, 1802, with the following introductory note by the author:

"Chamouni is one of the highest mountain valleys of the Barony of Faucigny in the Savoy Alps; and exhibits a kind of fairy world, in which the wildest appearances (I had almost said horrors) of nature alternate with the softest and most beautiful. The chain of Mont Blanc is its boundary; and besides the Arve it is filled with sounds from the Arveiron, which rushes from the melted glaciers, like a giant, mad with joy, from a dungeon, and forms other torrents of snow-water, having their rise in the glaciers which slope down into the valley. The beautiful *Gentiana Major*, or great gentian, with blossoms of the brightest blue, grows in large companies a few steps from the never-melted ice of the glaciers. I thought it an affecting emblem of the boldness of human hope, venturing near, and, as it were, leaning over the brink of the grave. Indeed, the whole vale, its every light, its every sound, must needs impress every mind not utterly callous with the thought—Who *would* be, who *could* be an atheist in this valley of wonders! If any of the readers of *The Morning Post* have visited this vale in their journeys among the Alps, I am confident that they will not find the sentiments and feelings expressed, or attempted to be expressed, in the following poem, extravagant."

In later editions the poem was preceded by the following note:

"Besides the rivers, Arve and Arveiron, which have their sources in the foot of Mont Blanc, five conspicuous torrents rush down its sides; and within a few paces of the glaciers, the *Gentiana Major* grows in immense numbers, with its 'flowers of loveliest blue.'"

As a matter of fact, Coleridge never was at Chamouni; his poem is based upon a translation of *Ode to Chamouny*, a German poem by Friederike Brûn (1765-1835) addressed to Klopstock (1724-1803). See Shelley's *Mont Blanc* (p. 672).

390. INSCRIPTION FOR A FOUNTAIN ON
A HEATH

Cf. this poem with the following concise lines from Tennyson's *Balin and Balan* (21-25):

So coming to the fountain-side beheld
Balin and Balan sitting statuelike,
Brethren to right and left the spring, that down,
From underneath a plume of lady-fern,
Sang, and the sand danced at the bottom of it.

THE PAINS OF SLEEP

"God forbid that my worst enemy should ever have the nights and the sleeps that I have had night after night—surprised by sleep, while I struggled to remain awake, starting up to bless my own loud scream that had awakened me—yea, dear friend! till my repeated night-yells had made me a nuisance in my own house. As I live and am a man, this is an unexaggerated tale. My dreams became the substance of my life."—Coleridge, in letter to Thomas Poole, Oct. 3, 1803.

391.　　　TO A GENTLEMAN

61-62. In place of these lines, the manuscript copy of January 1807 contained the following:

Dear shall it be to every human heart,
To me how more than dearest! me, on whom
Comfort from thee, and utterance of thy love,
Came with such heights and depths of harmony.
Such sense of wings uplifting, that its might
Scatter'd and quell'd me, till my thoughts became
A bodily tumult; and thy faithful hopes,
Thy hopes of me, dear friend, by me unfelt!
Were troublous to me, almost as a voice,
Familiar once, and more than musical;
As a dear woman's voice to one cast forth,
A wanderer with a worn-out heart forlorn,
Mid strangers pining with untended wounds.
O friend, too well thou know'st, of what sad years
The long suppression had benumb'd my soul.

392.　　TIME REAL AND IMAGINARY

"There is a fine prophecy here of the two main activities of the coming century—Science and Poetry. Tennyson's *Parnassus* should be read as expressing a similar truth a century later. In this notion of the sister we have an idea which was fundamental with Wordsworth, as in *We are Seven* and *Intimations of Immortality*."—George, in his edition of Coleridge's *Select Poems* (1902).

HEAR, SWEET SPIRIT, HEAR THE SPELL

This song is found in Act III, sc. 1, 69-82, of *Remorse*. It is sung from behind the scenes in proof of the power of Alvar, disguised as a sorcerer, to call up spirits of the departed.

A SUNNY SHAFT DID I BEHOLD

This song is found in Act II, sc. 1, 65-80, of *Zapolya*. It is sung by Glycine, the orphan daughter of a military chief, as she carries food to a friend who has gone to seek an enemy in a savage wood.

393.　　　THE KNIGHT'S TOMB

Coleridge states that these lines were composed as a metrical experiment.

YOUTH AND AGE

As first printed in 1828, this poem closed with 1. 38. The first draft, entitled *Aria Spontanea*, was written in 1823. The remaining lines, added in 1834, were first written and published, in a slightly different form, in 1832, under the title of *The Old Man's Sigh; a Sonnet*.

394.　　　WORK WITHOUT HOPE

"Though I am at present sadly below even *my* par of health, or rather unhealth, and am the more depressed thereby from the consciousness that in this yearly resurrection of Nature from her winter sleep, amid young leaves and blooms and twittering nest-building birds, the sun so gladsome, the breezes with such healing on their wings, all good and lovely things are beneath me, above me, and everywhere around me, and all from God, while my incapability of enjoying, or, at best, languor in receiving them, is directly or indirectly from myself, from past procrastination, and cowardly impatience of pain."—Coleridge, in letter to Lady Beaumont, March 18, 1826.

THE GARDEN OF BOCCACCIO

This poem was first published in *The Keepsake* for 1829, to accompany *The Garden of Boccaccio*, an engraving by Thomas Stothard (1755-1834), an English painter and illustrator. Boccaccio was a noted Italian writer of the fourteenth century.

395. 100. "I know few more striking or more interesting proofs of the overwhelming influence which the study of the Greek and Roman classics exercised on the judgments, feelings, and imaginations of the literati of Europe at the commencement of the restoration of literature, than the passage in the *Filocopo* of Boccaccio, where the sage instructor, Racheo, as soon as the young prince and the beautiful girl Biancofiore had learned their letters, sets them to study the Holy Book, Ovid's *Art of Love*."—Coleridge's note.

Filocopo, Coleridge's spelling, is meant to refer to Boccaccio's well known title *Filocolo*.

PHANTOM OR FACT

"This picture of the poet's spiritual youth returning from heaven, and at the same time not recognizing its former dwelling-place, is full of the most piteous pathos yet imagined; it is a bit of darkness from the depths of his soul. It is full of the mystery of Hamlet's riddling speeches."—George, in *Select Poems* (1902).

396.   THE WANDERINGS OF CAIN

"A prose composition, one not in metre at least, seems *prima facie* to require explanation or apology. It was written in the year 1798, near Nether Stowey, in Somersetshire, at which place (*sanctum et amabile nomen!* rich by so many associations and recollections) the author had taken up his residence in order to enjoy the society and close neighborhood of a dear and honored friend, T. Poole, Esq. The work was to have been written in concert with another [Wordsworth], whose name is too venerable within the precincts of genius to be unnecessarily brought into connection with such a trifle, and who was then residing at a small distance from Nether Stowey. The title and subject were suggested by myself, who likewise drew out the scheme and the contents for each of the three books or cantos, of which the work was to consist, and which, the reader is to be informed, was to have been finished in one night! My partner undertook the first canto: I the second: and which ever had *done first*, was to set about the third. Almost thirty years have passed by; yet at this moment I cannot without something more than a smile moot the question which of the two things was the more impracticable, for a mind so eminently original to compose another man's thoughts and fancies, or for a taste so austerely pure and simple to imitate *The Death of Abel?* Methinks I see his grand and noble countenance as at the moment when having despatched my own portion of the task at full finger-speed, I hastened to him with my manuscript—that look of humorous despondency fixed on his almost blank sheet of paper, and then its silent mock-piteous admission of failure struggling with the sense of the exceeding ridiculousness of the whole scheme—which broke up in a laugh: and *The Ancient Mariner* was written instead.

"Years afterward, however, the draft of the plan and proposed incidents, and the portion executed, obtained favor in the eyes of more than one person, whose judgment on a poetic work could not but have weighed with me, even though no parental partiality had been thrown into the same scale, as a make-weight: and I determined on commencing anew, and composing the whole in stanzas, and made some progress in realizing this intention, when adverse gales drove my bark off the 'Fortunate Isles' of the Muses: and then other and more momentous interests prompted a different voyage, to firmer anchorage and a securer port. I have in vain tried to recover the lines from the palimpsest tablet of my memory: and I can only offer the introductory stanza, which had been committed to writing for the purpose of procuring a friend's judgment on the metre, as a specimen:—

Encinctured with a twine of leaves,
That leafy twine his only dress!
A lovely boy was plucking fruits,
By moonlight, in a wilderness.
The moon was bright, the air was free,
And fruits and flowers together grew
On many a shrub and many a tree:
And all put on a gentle hue,
Hanging in the shadowy air
Like a picture rich and rare.
It was a climate where, they say,
The night is more belov'd than day.
But who that beauteous boy beguil'd,
That beauteous boy to linger here?
Alone, by night, a little child,
In place so silent and so wild—
Has he no friend, no loving mother near?

"I have here given the birth, parentage, and premature decease of *The Wanderings of Cain, a Poem*,—intreating, however, my readers, not to think so meanly of my judgment as to suppose that I either regard or offer it as any excuse for the publication of the following fragment (and I may add, of one or two others in its neighborhood) in its primitive crudity. But I should find still greater difficulty in forgiving myself were I to record *pro tædio publico* a set of petty mishaps and annoyances which I myself wish to forget. I must be content therefore with assuring the friendly reader, that the less he attributes its appearance to the author's will, choice, or judgment, the nearer to the truth he will be."—Coleridge (1828).

The Death of Abel is a drama by Salomon Gessner (1730-88), a Swiss poet and painter.

398.   BIOGRAPHIA LITERARIA

"It has been my lot to have had my name introduced both in conversation, and in print, more frequently than I find it easy to explain, whether I consider the fewness, unimportance, and limited circulation of my writings, or the retirement and distance, in which I have lived, both from the literary and political world. Most often it has been connected with some charge which I could not acknowledge, or some principle which I had never entertained. Nevertheless, had I had no other motive or incitement, the reader would not have been troubled with this exculpation. What my additional purposes were, will be seen in the following pages. It will be found, that the least of what I have written concerns myself personally. I have used the narration chiefly for the purpose of giving a continuity to the work, in part for the sake of the miscellaneous reflections suggested to me by particular events, but still more as introductory to a statement of my principles in politics, religion, and philosophy, and an application of the rules, deduced from philosophical principles, to poetry and criticism. But of the objects, which I proposed to myself, it was not the least important to effect, as far as possible, a settlement of the long continued controversy concerning the true nature of poetic diction; and at the same time to define with the utmost impartiality the real poetic character of the poet, by whose writings this controversy was first kindled, and has been since fuelled and fanned."—Opening paragraph of *Biographia Literaria*, ch. 1.

401. In Chapter 15 Coleridge discusses the symptoms of poetic power as elucidated in an analysis of Shakespeare's *Venus and Adonis* and *Lucrece;* Chapter 16 considers the points of difference between the poets of the early nineteenth century and those of the fifteenth and sixteenth centuries.

404a. 49-51. See *Her Eyes Are Wild* (p. 255). The following stanzas are from *The Idiot Boy:*

'Tis eight o'clock,—a clear March night,
The moon is up,—the sky is blue,
The owlet, in the moonlight air,
Shouts from nobody knows where;
He lengthens out his lonely shout,   5
Halloo! halloo! a long halloo!

—Why bustle thus about your door,
What means this bustle, Betty Foy?
Why are you in this mighty fret?
And why on horseback have you set   10
Him whom you love, your Idiot Boy?

Scarcely a soul is out of bed;
Good Betty, put him down again;

His lips with joy they burr at you;
But, Betty! what has he to do   15
With stirrup, saddle, or with rein?

But Betty's bent on her intent;
For her good neighbor Susan Gale,
Old Susan, she who dwells alone,
Is sick, and makes a piteous moan,   20
As if her very life would fail.

There's not a house within a mile,
No hand to help them in distress;
Old Susan lies a-bed in pain,
And sorely puzzled are the twain,   25
For what she ails they cannot guess.

And Betty's husband's at the wood,
Where by the week he doth abide,
A woodman in the distant vale;
There's none to help poor Susan Gale;   30
What must be done? what will betide?

And Betty from the lane has fetched
Her pony, that is mild and good;
Whether he be in joy or pain,
Feeding at will along the lane,   35
Or bringing fagots from the wood.

And he is all in travelling trim,—
And, by the moonlight, Betty Foy
Has on the well-girt saddle set
(The like was never heard of yet)   40
Him whom she loves, her Idiot Boy.

And he must post without delay
Across the bridge and through the dale,
And by the church, and o'er the down,
To bring a doctor from the town,   45
Or she will die, old Susan Gale.

There is no need of boot or spur,
There is no need of whip or wand;
For Johnny has his holly-bough,
And with a *hurly-burly* now   50
He shakes the green bough in his hand.

And Betty o'er and o'er has told
The Boy, who is her best delight,
Both what to follow, what to shun,
What do, and what to leave undone,   55
How turn to left, and how to right.

And Betty's most especial charge,
Was, "Johnny! Johnny! mind that you
Come home again, nor stop at all,—
Come home again, whate'er befall,   60
My Johnny, do, I pray you, do."

To this did Johnny answer make,
Both with his head and with his hand,
And proudly shook the bridle too;

And then! his words were not a few, 65
Which Betty well could understand.

And now that Johnny is just going,
Though Betty's in a mighty flurry,
She gently pats the pony's side,
On which her Idiot Boy must ride, 70
And seems no longer in a hurry.

But when the pony moved his legs,
Oh! then for the poor Idiot Boy!
For joy he cannot hold the bridle,
For joy his head and heels are idle, 75
He's idle all for very joy.

And, while the pony moves his legs,
In Johnny's left hand you may see
The green bough motionless and dead:
The moon that shines above his head 80
Is not more still and mute than he.

His heart it was so full of glee
That, till full fifty yards were gone,
He quite forgot his holly whip,
And all his skill in horsemanship: 85
Oh! happy, happy, happy John.

And while the mother, at the door,
Stands fixed, her face with joy o'erflows,
Proud of herself, and proud of him,
She sees him in his travelling trim, 90
How quietly her Johnny goes.

The silence of her Idiot Boy,
What hopes it sends to Betty's heart!
He's at the guide-post—he turns right;
She watches till he's out of sight, 95
And Betty will not then depart.

Burr, burr—now Johnny's lips they burr,
As loud as any mill, or near it;
Meek as a lamb the pony moves,
And Johnny makes the noise he loves, 100
And Betty listens, glad to hear it.

Away she hies to Susan Gale:
Her Messenger's in merry tune;
The owlets hoot, the owlets curr,
And Johnny's lips they burr, burr, burr, 105
As on he goes beneath the moon.

. . . .

407. Chapter 18. — Coleridge's prefatory
summary of Chapter 18 is all that is omitted
here.

408. The rest of Chapter 18 contains a discussion of the origin and elements of meter.

Chapters 19-21 are concerned with an examination and application of Wordsworth's object as expressed in the Preface to the *Lyrical
Ballads*.

410b. 5. *Prefatory letter to Hobbes.*—William Davenant (1605-68), an English poet and
dramatist, addressed the Preface to *Gondibert*
(1650) to his friend Thomas Hobbes (1588-
1679), a celebrated English philosopher.
421a. 48. Cf. Chapman's *An Humorous
Day's Mirth*, 8, 225: "Black is a pearl in a
woman's eye."

Robert Southey

Selections, p. 426 — Bibliography, p. 1449

"The poetry of sober feeling is rare in
lyrical verse. This may be found admirably
rendered in some of Southey's shorter pieces.
Although his temper was ardent and hopeful,
his poems of pensive remembrance, of meditative calm, are perhaps the most characteristic. . . . On the whole, judged by the
highest standard, Southey's poetry takes a
midmost rank; it neither renders into art a
great body of thought and passion, nor does
it give faultless expression to lyrical moments.
But it is the output of a large and vigorous
mind, amply stored with knowledge; its breath
of life is the moral ardor of a nature strong
and generous, and therefore it can never cease
to be of worth. . . . Southey is at his best
in prose. . . . History as written by
Southey is narrative rendered spiritual by
moral ardor. . . . In biography, at least,
one may be well pleased with clear and charming narrative. Here Southey has not been
surpassed. . . . Because his style is natural, it is inimitable."—Dowden, in *Southey*.

"Poetical criticism, whether of his own
writings or of those of others, was one of
Southey's weakest points. But while egregious-
ly deceived as to the absolute worth of his
epics, he obeyed a happy instinct in selecting
epic as his principal field in poetry. The gifts
which he possessed—ornate description, stately
diction, invention on a large scale—required
an ample canvas for their display. Although
the concise humor and simplicity of his lines
on *The Battle of Blenheim* ensure it a place
among the best known short poems in the
language, there are not half a dozen of his
lyrical pieces, some of his racy ballads excepted, that have any claim to poetic distinction."—Garnett, in *Dictionary of National Biography* (1898).

See Byron's *English Bards and Scotch Reviewers*, 189-234 (p. 514); *Don Juan*, Dedication (p. 603); *The Vision of Judgment* (p.
639), and note, p. 1333-34.

Southey is caricatured in Mr. Sackbut in
Thomas Love Peacock's *Nightmare Abbey*.

426. THE BATTLE OF BLENHEIM

In the Battle of Blenheim, Bavaria, Aug. 13, 1704, an allied army of English, Dutch, and Austrians under the command of the English Duke of Marlborough and the Austrian Prince Eugene delivered a crushing defeat to the French forces. Other allied victories followed; but subsequent political discord in England and the accession of the ambitious Charles VI to the crown of Austria led the English and the Dutch to make a separate peace with Louis XIV of France (1713). The result was the partition of the Spanish dominions and the French achievement of the recognition of Philip V as King of Spain.

427. THE OLD MAN'S COMFORTS

This poem is chiefly notable as the original of Lewis Carroll's brilliant parody in *Alice's Adventures in Wonderland*. Carroll's poem is as follows:

" 'You are old, Father William,' the young man said,
'And your hair has become very white;
And yet you incessantly stand on your head—
Do you think, at your age, it is right?'

" 'In my youth,' Father William replied to his son,   5
'I feared it would injure the brain;
But now that I'm perfectly sure I have none,
Why, I do it again and again.'

" 'You are old,' said the youth, 'as I mentioned before,
And have grown most uncommonly fat;   10
Yet you turned a back-somersault in at the door—
Pray, what is the reason of that?'

" 'In my youth,' said the sage, as he shook his gray locks,
'I kept all my limbs very supple
By the use of this ointment—one shilling the box—   15
Allow me to sell you a couple.'

" 'You are old,' said the youth, 'and your jaws are too weak
For anything tougher than suet;
Yet you finished the goose, with the bones and the beak:
Pray, how did you manage to do it?'   20

" 'In my youth,' said his father, 'I took to the law,
And argued each case with my wife;
And the muscular strength, which it gave to my jaw,
Has lasted the rest of my life.'

" 'You are old,' said the youth; 'one would hardly suppose   25
That your eye was as steady as ever;
Yet you balanced an eel on the end of your nose—
What made you so awfully clever?'

" 'I have answered three questions, and that is enough,'
Said his father; 'don't give yourself airs!   30
Do you think I can listen all day to such stuff?
Be off, or I'll kick you downstairs!' "

GOD'S JUDGMENT ON A WICKED BISHOP

" 'Here followeth the History of Hatto, Archbishop of Mentz.

" 'It hapned in the year 914, that there was an exceeding great famine in Germany, at what time Otho, surnamed the Great, was Emperor, and one Hatto, once Abbot of Fulda, was Archbishop of Mentz, of the Bishops after Crescens and Crescentius the two and thirtieth, of the Archbishops after St. Bonifacius the thirteenth. This Hatto, in the time of this great famine afore-mentioned, when he saw the poor people of the country exceedingly oppressed with famine, assembled a great company of them together into a barne, and, like a most accursed and mercilesse caitiffe, burnt up those poor innocent souls, that were so far from doubting any such matter, that they rather hoped to receive some comfort and relief at his hands. The reason that moved the prelat to commit that execrable impiety was, because he thought the famine would the sooner cease, if those unprofitable beggars that consumed more bread than they were worthy to eat, were dispatched out of the world. For he said that those poor folks were like to mice, that were good for nothing but to devour corne. But God Almighty, the just avenger of the poor folks' quarrel, did not long suffer this heinous tyranny, this most detestable fact, unpunished. For he mustered up an army of mice against the Archbishop, and sent them to persecute him as his furious Alastors,[1] so that they afflicted him both day and night, and would not suffer him to take his rest in any place. Whereupon the Prelate, thinking that he should be secure from the injury of mice if he were in a certain tower, that standeth in the Rhine near to the towne, betook himself unto the said tower as to a safe refuge and sanctuary from his enemies, and locked himself in. But the innumerable troupes of mice chased him continually very

---

[1] avenging spirits

eagerly, and swumme unto him upon the top of the water to execute the just judgment of God, and so at last he was most miserably devoured by those sillie creatures; who pursued him with such bitter hostility, that it is recorded they scraped and knawed out his very name from the walls and tapistry wherein it was written, after they had so cruelly devoured his body. Wherefore the tower wherein he was eaten up by the mice is shewn to this day, for a perpetual monument to all succeeding ages of the barbarous and inhuman tyranny of this impious Prelate, being situate in a little green island in the midst of the Rhine near to the towne of Bingen, and is commonly called in the German tongue the MOWSE-TURN.' "—*Coryat's Crudities*, pp. 571-572.

"Other authors who record this tale say that the Bishop was eaten by rats."—Southey's introductory note.

429. THE CURSE OF KEHAMA

"In the religion of the Hindoos, which of all false religions is the most monstrous in its fables, and the most fatal in its effects, there is one remarkable peculiarity. Prayers, penances, and sacrifices are supposed to possess an inherent and actual value, in no degree depending upon the disposition or motive of the person who performs them. They are drafts upon Heaven, for which the Gods cannot refuse payment. The worst men, bent upon the worst designs, have in this manner obtained power which has made them formidable to the Supreme Deities themselves, and rendered an *Avatar*, or Incarnation of Veshnoo the Preserver, necessary. This belief is the foundation of the following poem. The story is original; but, in all its parts, consistent with the superstition upon which it is built: and however startling the fictions may appear, they might almost be called credible when compared with the genuine tales of Hindoo mythology."—From Southey's Preface.

The poem takes its name from the following curse which Kehama, an Indian rajah, or king, pronounces upon the murderer of his son Arvalan:

"I charm thy life
From the weapons of strife,
From stone and from wood,
From fire and from flood,
From the serpent's tooth,
And the beasts of blood:
From Sickness I charm thee,
And Time shall not harm thee;
But Earth which is mine,

Its fruits shall deny thee;
And Water shall hear me,
And know thee and fly thee;
And the Winds shall not touch thee
When they pass by thee,
And the Dews shall not wet thee,
When they fall nigh thee:
And thou shalt seek Death
To release thee, in vain;
Thou shalt live in thy pain
While Kehama shall reign,
With a fire in thy heart,
And a fire in thy brain;
And Sleep shall obey me,
And visit thee never,
And the Curse shall be on thee
For ever and ever."
—Section 2, ll. 144-69.

The funeral of Arvalan is celebrated in Section 1.

431. THE MARCH TO MOSCOW

In this poem Southey treats satirically Napoleon's famous march to Moscow in 1812, and his unfortunate retreat after the burning of the city. The names used in the poem are said to indicate real persons. For a similar use of Russian names, cf. the following stanzas from Byron's *Don Juan* (7, 14-17):

The Russians now were ready to attack;
  But oh, ye goddesses of War and Glory!
How shall I spell the name of each Cossacque
  Who were immortal, could one tell their story?
Alas! what to their memory can lack?
  Achilles' self was not more grim and gory
Than thousands of this new and polished nation,
Whose names want nothing but—pronunciation.

Still I'll record a few, if but to increase
  Our euphony: there was Strongenoff, and Strokonoff,
Meknopp, Serge Lwow, Arséniew of modern Greece,
  And Tschitsshakoff, and Roguenoff, and Chokenoff,
And others of twelve consonants apiece;
  And more might be found if I could poke enough
Into gazettes; but Fame (capricious strumpet),
It seems, has got an ear as well as trumpet,

And cannot tune those discords of narration,
  Which may be names at Moscow, into rhyme;

Yet there were several worth commemora-
tion,
As e'er was virgin of a nuptial chime;
Soft words, too, fitted for the peroration
Of Londonderry[1] drawling against time.
Ending in "ischskin," "ousckin," "iffskchy,"
"ouski,"
Of whom we can insert but Rousamouski.

Scherematoff and Chrematoff, Koklophti,
Koclobski, Kourakin, and Mouskin Pouskin,
All proper men of weapons, as e'er scoffed high
Against a foe, or ran a sabre through skin...

The poem, which Southey wrote to amuse
his children, should be read as complementary
to the *Ode Written During the Negotiations
with Buonaparte* (p. 432). At an early date,
Southey was an ardent supporter of the
French Revolution, but its excesses and failures led him finally to become a Tory.

432. ODE WRITTEN DURING THE NEGOTIA-
TIONS WITH BUONAPARTE

Dowden characterizes this ode as "perhaps
the loftiest chant of political invective, inspired by moral indignation, which our literature possesses. . . . Southey stood erect
in the presence of power which he believed to
be immoral, defied it and execrated it. That
he did not perceive how, in driving the ploughshare of Revolution across Europe of the old
régime Napoleon was terribly accomplishing
an inevitable and a beneficent work, may have
been an error; but it was an error to which
no blame attaches, and in his fierce indict-
ment he states, with ample support of facts,
one entire side of the case. The ode is indeed more than a poem; it is a historical
document expressing the passion which filled
many of the highest minds in England, and
which at a later date was the justification of
Saint Helena."—In introduction to *Poems by
Robert Southey* (Golden Treasury ed., 1895).

434. MY DAYS AMONG THE DEAD ARE PAST

This poem is sometimes entitled *The
Scholar* and *In a Library*. According to Cuthbert Southey (*Life and Correspondence of
Robert Southey*, 1849), Wordsworth once remarked that these lines possessed a peculiar
interest as a most true and touching representation of Southey's character. Southey's
library contained nearly 14,000 volumes. His
son Cuthbert says (work cited): "On some
authors, such as the old divines, he 'fed,' as he

[1] Robert Stewart (1769-1822), Viscount Castlereagh and Earl of Londonberry, a British
statesman. See note on *Lines Written during
the Castlereagh Administration*, p. 1341.

expressed it, slowly and carefully, dwelling on
the page, and taking in its contents deeply
and deliberately, like an epicure with his
wine, 'searching the subtle flavor.' . . .
For a considerable time after he had ceased
to compose, he took pleasure in reading, and
the habit continued after the power of comprehension was gone. His dearly prized books,
indeed, were a pleasure to him almost to the
end, and he would walk slowly round his
library, looking at them and taking them down
mechanically."

435. A VISION OF JUDGMENT

This is the poem which inspired Byron's
more famous *The Vision of Judgment.* (See
p. 639 and note p. 1333) Southey's poem was
written as a tribute to the memory of George
III, who died in 1820. In two respects
Southey stirred the wrath of the critics: he
gave unstinted praise to George III as sovereign and man, and he wrote the poem in
dactylic hexameter measure. The incidents of
the poem appear to the author in a trance.
In the portion of the poem omitted before
the selection given here, George III is summoned before the judgment throne where testimony is heard from his accusers and his
absolvers. The Spirit of Washington has
just stated that George III

"didst act with upright heart, as befitted a
sovereign
True to his sacred trust, to his crown, his
kingdom, and people."

436. THE CATARACT OF LODORE

Lodore is a famous cascade in the Derwent
River, Cumberlandshire, England. See Gray's
description of it in his *Journal in the Lakes,*
Oct. 3, 1769 (p. 74a, 16-46).
The origin of this poem is thus given in a
letter by Southey to his brother Thomas, dated
Oct. 18, 1809: "I hope . . . you will
approve of a description of the water at
Lodore, made originally for Edith, and greatly
admired by Herbert. In my mind it surpasses
any that the tourists have yet printed. Thus
it runs—'Tell the people how the water comes
down at *Lodore?* Why it comes thundering,
and floundering, and thumping, and flumping,
and bumping, and jumping, and hissing, and
whizzing, and dripping, and skipping, and
grumbling, and rumbling, and tumbling, and
falling, and brawling, and dashing, and clashing, and splashing, and pouring, and roaring,
and whirling, and curling, and leaping, and
creeping, and sounding, and bounding, and
clattering, and chattering, with a dreadful up-

roar,—and that way the water comes down at *Lodore.*'"

437. THE LIFE OF NELSON

Southey's *The Life of Nelson* was written to furnish young seamen with a simple narrative of the exploits of England's greatest naval hero. It is usually regarded not only as the best of Southey's works, but as the best biography of its day, and as a model of directness and simplicity.

Thomas Campbell

Poems, p. 443 — Bibliography, p. 1415

443. THE PLEASURES OF HOPE

This poem should be compared as to subject and title with Akenside's *The Pleasures of the Imagination* (p. 44). Warton's *The Pleasures of Melancholy* (p. 75), and Rogers's *The Pleasures of Memory* (p. 233).

"Much of the success of the poem was no doubt due to the circumstance that it touched with such sympathy on the burning questions of the hour. If, as Stevenson remarks, the poet is to speak efficaciously, he must say what is already in his hearer's mind. This Campbell did, as perhaps no English poet had done before. The French Revolution, the partition of Poland, the abolition of negro-slavery —these had set the passion for freedom burning in many breasts, and *The Pleasures of Hope* gave at once vigorous and feeling expression to the doctrine of the universal brotherhood of man. . . . It is not easy at this time of day to approach *The Pleasures Of Hope* without a want of sympathy, if not an absolute prejudice, resulting from a whole century of poetical development."—J. C. Hadden, in *Thomas Campbell* (1899).

"The very name of this work discovered its adhesion to eighteenth-century tradition. It was a tame, 'correct' essay, in a mode already entirely outworn."—Gosse, in *A Short History of Modern English Literature* (1897).

445. YE MARINERS OF ENGLAND

"The *Battle of the Baltic* and *Ye Mariners of England* are without rivals in their own class, and Campbell deserves recognition as a true romanticist and revolutionary force in poetry, although fighting for his own hand, and never under the flag of Wordsworth and Coleridge. For the time being, however, Campbell did more than they . . . to break down in popular esteem the didactic convention of the classic school."—Gosse, in *A Short History of Modern English Literature* (1897).

15. This poem is said to have been written in 1799-1800, on the prospect of a war with Russia (ll. 5-6); but it must have been revised later, for Nelson fell at Trafalgar in 1805. He was severely wounded at the Battle of Copenhagen, April 2, 1801.

31. *Meteor flag.*—A reference to the color of the British flag and to the old belief that meteors portend calamity.

446. HOHENLINDEN

At the village of Hohenlinden, Bavaria, the Austrian army, the "Hun" in this poem, was defeated by the French (the "Frank") in December 1800. Campbell did not witness the battle, as was erroneously believed, but he was on the continent at the time and witnessed at least one skirmish. Scott was fond of this ballad; but Campbell himself spoke rather contemptuously of its "drum and trumpet lines."

"In the genuine success of *Hohenlinden* every line is a separate emphasis, but all the emphasis is required by the subject, is in its place. The thud and brief repeated monotony of the metre give the very sound of cannonading; each line is like a crackle of musketry. What is obvious in it, even, comes well into a poem which depends on elements so simple for its success; indeed, its very existence."— Symons, in *The Romantic Movement in English Poetry* (1909).

LOCHIEL'S WARNING

Donald Cameron, a Scottish Highland chieftain known as "Gentle Lochiel," joined the Young Pretender, Charles Edward, in the Jacobite uprising of 1745. He was wounded at Culloden in a battle against the English forces under the Duke of Cumberland, and fled to France, where he died in 1748. The Wizard in this poem forecasts the defeat of Cameron at Culloden.

448. THE BATTLE OF THE BALTIC

"It is an attempt to write an English ballad on the Battle of Copenhagen, as much as possible in that plain, strong style peculiar to our old ballads which tell us the when, where, and how the event happened—without gaud or ornament but what the subject essentially and easily affords."—Campbell, in letter to Dr. Currie, April 24, 1805, quoted in Beattie's *The Life and Letters of Thomas Campbell* (1849).

The Battle of Copenhagen was fought on April 2, 1801. Russia, Prussia, Sweden, and Denmark formed a neutrality league against England in December, 1800. England declared war, and a fleet under Parker and Nelson was dispatched against the Danish fleet at Copenhagen. Parker held eight ships in reserve while Nelson led twelve to the attack. The engagement was so fierce that Parker signaled to "Discontinue the action." In reading the signal Nelson applied his blind eye to the telescope; all the time he kept his own signal flying—"Move in closer." He finally won a decisive victory.

In its first form the poem contained 162 lines. Following are the first four stanzas as originally written:

Of Nelson and the North
  Sing the day,
When, their haughty powers to vex,
He engaged the Danish decks,
And with twenty floating wrecks   5
  Crowned the fray.

All bright, in April's sun,
  Shone the day,
When a British fleet came down,
Through the islands of the crown   10
And by Copenhagen town
  Took their stay.

In arms the Danish shore
  Proudly shone;
By each gun the lighted brand   15
In a bold determined hand;
And the Prince of all the land
  Led them on.

For Denmark here had drawn
  All her might;   20
From her battle-ships so vast
She had hewn away the mast,
And at anchor to the last
  Bade them fight.

23. *"Hearts of oak."*—The phrase is quoted from the old ballad *Ye Gentlemen of England.*

449.   THE LAST MAN

"Did you see *The Last Man* in my last number? Did it immediately remind you of Lord Byron's poem of *Darkness?* [See p. 547.] I was a little troubled about this appearance of my having been obliged to him for the idea. The fact is, many years ago I had the idea of this Last Man in my head, and distinctly remember speaking of the subject to Lord B. I recognized when I read his poem *Darkness,* some traits of the picture which I meant to draw, namely, the ships floating without living hands to guide them— the earth being blank—and one or two more circumstances. On soberly considering the

matter, I am entirely disposed to acquit Lord Byron of having intentionally taken the thoughts. It is consistent with my own experience to suppose that an idea, which is actually one of memory, may start up, appearing to be one of the imagination, in a mind that has forgot the source from which it borrowed that idea. I believe this. Nevertheless, to have given the poem to the world with a note, stating this fact, would have had the appearance of picking a quarrel with the noble bard, and this appearance I much dislike, from the kindly feeling I have towards him, in consequence of his always having dealt kindly by me."—Campbell, in a letter to Mr. Gray, Sept. 5, 1823, quoted in Beattie's *The Life and Letters of Thomas Campbell.* An article in *The London Magazine and Review,* 1825, suggests as the source of this poem, a former popular novel entitled *The Last Man, or Omegarus and Syderia, a Romance in Futurity* (2 vols., 1806).

450.   THE DEATH-BOAT OF HELIGOLAND

This poem probably refers to the Jacobites, who, under the leadership of Charles Edward Stuart, the Young Pretender, instituted a rebellion in Scotland in 1745. The badge of the Stuarts was the white rose; the standard of Charles Edward was white, blue, and red. The reference in line 36 is probably made to clarify the fact that the faction did not belong to the Irish revolutionists, whose badge was green. Heligoland is an island in the North Sea; it was ceded by Great Britain to Germany in 1890.

Thomas Moore

Poems, p. 450 — Bibliography, p. 1438

From *For the Moore Centennial Celebration, May 28, 1879*

Enchanter of Erin, whose magic has bound us,
  Thy wand for one moment we fondly would claim,
Entranced while it summons the phantoms around us
  That blush into life at the sound of thy name.

The tell-tales of memory wake from their slumbers!
  I hear the old song with its tender refrain,—
What passion lies hid in those honey-voiced numbers!
  What perfume of youth in each exquisite strain!

  •   •   •   •   •   •   •   •   •

The land where the staff of Saint Patrick was
   planted,
  Where the shamrocks grow green from the
     cliffs to the shore,
The land of fair maidens and heroes un-
   daunted,
  Shall wreathe her bright harp with the
     garlands of Moore!
          —Oliver Wendell Holmes (1879).

"It has been the fashion of late days to
deny Moore imagination, while granting him
fancy—a distinction originating with Coleridge—than whom no man more fully comprehended the great powers of Moore. The fact
is, that the fancy of this poet so far predominates over all his other faculties, and over
the fancy of all other men, as to have induced,
very naturally, the idea that he is fanciful
only. But never was there a greater mistake.
Never was a grosser wrong done the fame of
a true poet."—Poe, in *The Poetic Principle*
(1850).

See Byron's *English Bards and Scotch
Reviewers*, 283-94 (p. 515).

450. THE LAKE OF THE DISMAL SWAMP

This and the following poem, *A Canadian
Boat Song*, are part of a collection of poems
relating to America, first published in 1806
in the volume entitled *Odes and Epistles*.

"The Great Dismal Swamp is ten or twelve
miles distant from Norfolk, and the Lake in
the middle of it (about seven miles long) is
called Drummond's Pond."—Moore's note.

Moore prefixed to the poem the following
account:

" 'They tell of a young man, who lost his
mind upon the death of a girl he loved, and
who, suddenly disappearing from his friends,
was never afterwards heard of. As he had
frequently said, in his ravings, that the girl
was not dead, but gone to the Dismal Swamp,
it is supposed he had wandered into that
dreary wilderness, and had died of hunger,
or been lost in some of its dreadful morasses.'
—*Anon*."

451. A CANADIAN BOAT SONG

"I wrote these words to an air which our
boatmen sung to us frequently. The wind
was so unfavorable that they were obliged to
row all the way, and we were five days in
descending the river from Kingston to Mon-
treal, exposed to an intense sun during the
day, and at night forced to take shelter from
the dews in any miserable hut upon the banks
that would receive us. But the magnificent

scenery of the St. Lawrence repays all such
difficulties.

"Our *voyageurs* had good voices, and sung
perfectly in tune together. The original words
of the air, to which I adapted these stanzas,
appeared to be a long, incoherent story, of
which I could understand but little, from
the barbarous pronunciation of the Canadi-
ans. . . .

"I ventured to harmonize this air, and have
published it. Without that charm which association gives to every little memorial of
scenes or feelings that are past, the melody
may, perhaps, be thought common and trifling;
but I remember when we have entered, at sunset, upon one of those beautiful lakes, into
which the St. Lawrence so grandly and unexpectedly opens, I have heard this simple air
with a pleasure which the finest compositions
of the first masters have never given me;
and now there is not a note of it which does
not recall to my memory the dip of our oars
in the St. Lawrence, the flight of our boat
down the Rapids, and all those new and fanciful impressions to which my heart was alive
during the whole of this very interesting voyage."—Moore's note.

IRISH MELODIES

"In one only of his writings Moore attained
a positive perfection of style. Those homely
and sentimental lyrics which have endeared
themselves to thousands of hearts under the
name of the *Irish Melodies* form a part and
parcel of our literature the extinction of
which would leave a sad blank behind it.
When they were first produced, in slender
instalments spread over a period of more than
twenty-five years, they seemed universally
brilliant and fascinating to the ears on whom
their fresh tunes and dulcet numbers fell in
a most amiable union. Here for once, it
seemed, music and sweet poetry agreed in
complete harmony, the one not brighter or
more dainty than the other. Exposed to the
wear and tear of sixty years, all the jewels
in the casket do not now, any longer, look
equally brilliant. Some have wholly faded,
others have become weak or crude in coloring, while a few, perhaps one eighth of the
whole, are as glowing and exquisite as ever,
and shine like real stones in a heap of false
jewelry. It is upon these fifteen or sixteen
songs, amatory, patriotic, and jocose, that
Moore's fame mainly rests, but though the
support has become slender, it is lifted beyond
all further fear of disintegration."—E. W.
Gosse, in Ward's *The English Poets*, Vol. 4
(1880).

OH, BREATHE NOT HIS NAME!

This poem refers to Robert Emmet, the famous Irish revolutionist executed in 1803 because of his part in stirring up a rebellion in Dublin. He was a leader of *The United Irishmen*, a prominent revolutionary society. Emmet was affianced to Sarah Curran, commemorated in the following poem by Moore:

She Is Far From the Land

She is far from the land where her young
 hero sleeps,
And lovers are round her, sighing:
But coldly she turns from their gaze, and
 weeps,
 For her heart in his grave is lying.

She sings the wild song of her dear native
 plains,   5
 Every note which he lov'd awaking;—
Ah! little they think who delight in her strains,
 How the heart of the Minstrel is breaking.

He had liv'd for his love, for his country he
 died,
 They were all that to life had entwin'd
 him;   10
Nor soon shall the tears of his country be dried,
 Nor long will his love stay behind him.

Oh! make her a grave where the sunbeams rest,
 When they promise a glorious morrow;
They'll shine o'er her sleep, like a smile from
 the West,   15
 From her own lov'd island of sorrow.

WHEN HE WHO ADORES THEE

This poem is an appeal to Ireland to remember Robert Emmet. See note on *Oh, Breathe not his Name*, above.

452. THE HARP THAT ONCE THROUGH
TARA'S HALLS

Tara, near Dublin, was famous in early history as a residence of Irish kings.

454.   NATIONAL AIRS

"It is Cicero, I believe, who says, '*natura ad modos ducimur*' [by nature we are led to melody]; and the abundance of wild, indigenous airs, which almost every country, except England, possesses, sufficiently proves the truth of his assertion. The lovers of this simple, but interesting kind of music, are here presented with the first number of a collection, which, I trust, their contributions will enable us to continue. A pretty air without words resembles one of those *half* creatures of Plato, which are described as wandering in search of the remainder of them-

selves through the world. To supply this other half, by uniting with congenial words the many fugitive melodies which have hitherto had none,—or only such as are unintelligible to the generality of their hearers,—is the object and ambition of the present work. Neither is it our intention to confine ourselves to what are strictly called National Melodies, but, wherever we meet with any wandering and beautiful air, to which poetry has not yet assigned a worthy home, we shall venture to claim it as an *estray* swan, and enrich our humble Hippocrene with its song."—Moore's prefatory Advertisement. Hippocrene was a fountain in Greece supposed to give poetic inspiration.

455.   LALLA ROOKH

This is a series of four Oriental tales connected with a slight prose narrative showing how the poems were recited for the entertainment of Lalla Rookh, a beautiful Indian princess, on her journey from Delhi, India, to her betrothed, the Prince of Bucharia, in the Vale of Cashmere, a district north of India. The name *Lalla Rookh* means tulip cheek. The "Light of the Haram" is the Sultana Nourmahal.

"It is still possible to read *Lalla Rookh* with pleasure, and even with a sort of indulgent enthusiasm. . . . Underneath the smooth and faded surface lie much tenderness and pathos in the story of the Peri, much genuine patriotism in the fate of the Fire-Worshippers, much tropical sweetness in the adventures of the Light of the Haram."— E. W. Gosse, in Ward's *The English Poets*, Vol. 4 (1880).

456. FABLES FOR THE HOLY ALLIANCE

This is a collection of eight satires on the league formed by the rulers of Russia, Austria, England, and Prussia, after the downfall of Napoleon in 1815. This Quadruple Alliance was formed for the purpose of opposing all changes in existing dynasties, and was popularly confused with the Holy Alliance, an idealistic peace organization formed by the same powers.

20. A congress of European powers held at Laybach, Austria, in 1821, decided to use arms in repressing revolutions in Piedmont and Verona, in northern Italy. A congress of the monarchs of Russia, Austria, and Prussia was held at Troppau, Austria, in 1820, to consider the revolution at Naples, and to make plans for preserving the Quadruple Alliance. The congress of European powers held at Verona in 1822 was occasioned by recent disturbances in Spain and southeastern Europe.

Charles Wolfe

Poems, p. 458 — Bibliography, p. 1452

458. THE BURIAL OF SIR JOHN MOORE

Sir John Moore (1761-1809) was a British general who was killed in the Battle of Corunna (Spain) against the French. He had the reputation of being the best trainer of men that the British army ever had. Wolfe's poem is said to be based on the following paragraph, which appeared in *The Edinburgh Annual Register*, 1808:

"Sir John Moore had often said that if he was killed in battle he wished to be buried where he fell. The body was removed at midnight to the citadel of Corunna. A grave was dug for him on the rampart there, by a party of the 9th Regiment, the Aides-de-Camp attending by turns. No coffin could be procured, and the officers of his staff wrapped his body, dressed as it was, in a military cloak and blankets. The interment was hastened: for, about eight in the morning, some firing was heard, and the officers feared that if a serious attack was made, they should be ordered away, and not suffered to pay him their last duty. The officers of his regiment bore him to the grave; the funeral service was read by the chaplain; and the corpse was covered with earth."

Sir Walter Scott

Poems, p. 459 — Bibliography, p. 1442

"It is a platitude, taking all his work into account, to say that Scott was a far greater poet than his poetry reveals. . . . He essayed a new type of poetic narrative, a kind of miniature epic. He discovered a measure which was apt for both rapid movement and detailed description. . . . Scott's octosyllables embrace . . . surprising varieties of manner, and they are far more artful than they appear. . . . They can gallop and they can jig; they can move placidly in some piece of argument, and now and then they can sing themselves into a lyrical exaltation. . . . A rarer magic reveals itself . . . in the interspersed lyrics; and it is in such pieces . . . that Scott attains his real poetic stature. . . . He is in the first place a master of the pure lyric, the song for music. . . . But there is a second type of lyric or lyrical ballad . . . which mounts still higher, which at its best, indeed, is beyond analysis, producing that sense of something inexplicable and overwhelming which is the token of genius. Its subjects are the mysteries of life, not its gallant bustle, and the supreme mystery of death. . . . Sometimes the atmosphere of them is translunary, not of this earth. Sometimes they are sober reflections upon the transience of mortal things, and the minstrel becomes the prophet. They are Scott's final credentials as a poet, even as a great poet, for they have the *desiderium* of great poetry."—John Buchan, in *Sir Walter Scott* (1932).

"The perennial charm of the Waverley Novels resides very largely in their healthfulness. They take us entirely out of ourselves, and absorb us in the world of incident and action. If they are not always great as works of art, they are always great in that health of mind and soul which is elemental in all true living. Men cannot be too grateful for a mass of writing so genuine in tone, so free from morbid tendencies, so true to the fundamental ethics of living."—H. W. Mabie, in *My Study Fire*, Second Series (1896).

"Scott's is almost the only poetry in the English language that not only runs in the head of average men, but heats the head in which it runs by the mere force of its hurried frankness of style. . . . No poet ever equalled Scott in the description of wild and simple feelings."—R. H. Hutton, in *Sir Walter Scott* (English Men of Letters Series, 1878).

See Wordsworth's *Yarrow Revisited* (p. 338), and *On the Departure of Sir Walter Scott from Abbotsford, for Naples* (p. 340); also Byron's *English Bards and Scotch Reviewers*, 153-84 (pp. 513-14).

459. WILLIAM AND HELEN

Scott's first publication was a translation or imitation of two German ballads written by G. A. Bürger (1748-94), a noted German poet. One of these was *Lenore* (1774), the basis of Scott's *William and Helen*. Scott gives in a note the following account of how he became acquainted with *Lenore:* "A lady of high rank in the literary world read this romantic tale, as translated by Mr. Taylor, in the house of the celebrated Professor Dugald Stewart, of Edinburgh. The author was not present, nor indeed in Edinburgh at the time; but a gentleman who had the pleasure of hearing the ballad, afterwards told him the story, and repeated the remarkable chorus—

'Tramp, tramp, across the land they speede,
  Splash, splash, across the sea;
Hurrah, the dead can ride apace!
  Dost fear to ride with me?'

"In attempting a translation, then intended only to circulate among friends, the present author did not hesitate to make use of this impressive stanza; for which freedom he has since obtained the forgiveness of the ingenious gentleman to whom it properly belongs."

The lady referred to was Mrs. Anna Letitia Barbauld (1743-1825). Mr. Taylor was William Taylor of Norwich (1765-1836).

462. THE VIOLET

This is usually regarded as one of the most beautiful and delicate of Scott's poems. It refers to his love, never directly expressed, for Williamina Stuart. The poem was written immediately after it became evident that his hopes were in vain. Miss Stuart, who married Sir William Forbes, died in 1810. Seventeen years later Scott wrote in his Journal (Nov. 7 and 10, 1827), after a visit to Miss Stuart's aged mother: "I went to make another visit, and fairly softened myself like an old fool, with recalling old stories till I was fit for nothing but shedding tears and repeating verses for the whole night. This is sad work. The very grave gives up its dead, and time rolls back thirty years to add to my perplexities. I don't care. I begin to grow over-hardened, and, like a stag turning at bay, my naturally good temper grows fierce and dangerous. Yet what a romance to tell, and told I fear it will one day be. And then my three years of dreaming and my two years of wakening will be chronicled doubtless. But the dead will feel no pain. . . . At twelve o'clock I went to poor lady J. S. to talk over old stories. I am not clear that it is right or healthful indulgence to be ripping up old sorrows, but it seems to give her deep-seated sorrow words, and that is a mental blood-letting. To me these things are now matter of calm and solemn recollection, never to be forgotten, yet scarce to be remembered with pain."

For a full account of the story, see Lockhart's *Memoirs of the Life of Sir Walter Scott*, ch. 8, and Miss F. M. F. Skene's "Sir Walter Scott's First Love," *The Century Magazine*, July, 1899 (58:368).

GLENFINLAS

This ballad was first published in Monk Lewis's *Tales of Wonder*. The following account of the ballad was there given by Scott in a preface: "The simple tradition upon which this ballad is founded runs thus: While two Highland hunters were passing the night in a solitary *bothy* (a hut built for the

purpose of hunting) and making merry over their venison and whisky, one of them expressed a wish that they had pretty lasses to complete their party. The words were scarcely uttered, when two beautiful young women, habited in green, entered the hut, dancing and singing. One of the hunters was seduced by the siren who attached herself particularly to him, to leave the hut: the other remained, and, suspicious of the fair seducers, continued to play upon a trump, or Jew's harp, some strain, consecrated to the Virgin Mary. Day at length came, and the temptress vanished. Searching in the forest, he found the bones of his unfortunate friend, who had been torn to pieces and devoured by the fiend into whose toils he had fallen. The place was from thence called the Glen of the Green Women.

"Glenfinlas is a tract of forest-ground, lying in the Highlands of Perthshire, not far from Callender in Menteith. It was formerly a royal forest, and now belongs to the Earl of Moray. This country, as well as the adjacent district of Balquidder, was, in times of yore, chiefly inhabited by the Macgregors. To the west of the Forest of Glenfinlas lies Loch Katrine, and its romantic avenue, called the Trosachs. Benledi, Benmore, and Benvoirlich, are mountains in the same district, and at no great distance from Glenfinlas. The River Teith passes Callender and the Castle of Doune, and joins the Forth near Stirling. The Pass of Lenny is immediately above Callender, and is the principal access to the Highlands from that town. Glenartney is a forest, near Benvoirlich. The whole forms a sublime tract of Alpine scenery."

465. CADYOW CASTLE

This ballad was included in the third volume of Scott's *The Minstrelsy of the Scottish Border*. Scott gives the following historical basis for the ballad:

"The ruins of Cadyow, or Cadzow Castle, the ancient baronial residence of the family of Hamilton, are situated upon the precipitous banks of the River Evan, about two miles above its junction with the Clyde. It was dismantled, in the conclusion of the Civil Wars, during the reign of the unfortunate Mary, to whose cause the house of Hamilton devoted themselves with a generous zeal, which occasioned their temporary obscurity, and, very nearly, their total ruin. The situation of the ruins, embosomed in wood, darkened by ivy and creeping shrubs, and overhanging the brawling torrent, is romantic in the highest degree. In the immediate vicinity of Cadyow is a grove of immense oaks, the remains of the Caledonian Forest, which anciently extended through the south of Scotland, from the eastern to the Atlantic Ocean. Some of these trees measure twenty-five feet and upwards in circumference, and the state of decay in which they now appear shows that they have witnessed the rites of the Druids. The whole scenery is included in the magnificent and extensive park of the Duke of Hamilton. . . .

"In detailing the death of the Regent Murray, which is made the subject of the ballad, it would be injustice to my reader to use other words than those of Dr. Robertson, whose account of that memorable event forms a beautiful piece of historical painting:

" 'Hamilton of Bothwellhaugh was the person who committed this barbarous action. He had been condemned to death soon after the battle of Langside, as we have already related, and owed his life to the Regent's clemency. But part of his estate had been bestowed upon one of the Regent's favorites, who seized his house, and turned out his wife, naked, in a cold night, into the open fields, where, before next morning, she became furiously mad. This injury made a deeper impression on him than the benefit he had received, and from that moment he vowed to be revenged of the Regent. Party rage strengthened and inflamed his private resentment. His kinsmen, the Hamiltons, applauded the enterprise. The maxims of that age justified the most desperate course he could take to obtain vengeance. He followed the Regent for some time, and watched for an opportunity to strike the blow. He resolved at last to wait till his enemy should arrive at Linlithgow, through which he was to pass in his way from Stirling to Edinburgh. He took his stand in a wooden gallery, which had a window towards the street; spread a featherbed on the floor to hinder the noise of his feet from being heard; hung up a black cloth behind him, that his shadow might not be observed from without; and, after all this preparation, calmly expected the Regent's approach, who had lodged, during the night, in a house not far distant. Some indistinct information of the danger which threatened him had been conveyed to the Regent, and he paid so much regard to it, that he resolved to return by the same gate through which he had entered, and to fetch a compass round the town. But, as the crowd about the gate was great, and he himself unacquainted with fear, he proceeded directly along the street;

and the throng of people obliging him to move very slowly, gave the assassin time to take so true an aim, that he shot him, with a single bullet, through the lower part of his belly, and killed the horse of a gentleman who rode on his other side. His followers instantly endeavored to break into the house whence the blow had come; but they found the door strongly barricaded, and, before it could be forced open, Hamilton had mounted a fleet horse, which stood ready for him at a back passage, and was got far beyond their reach. The Regent died the same night [Jan. 23, 1569] of his wound.' [*History of Scotland*, Book v.]"

466. 45. *The Chief.*—"The head of the family of Hamilton, at this period, was James, Earl of Arran, Duke of Chatelherault in France, and first peer of the Scottish realm. In 1569 he was appointed by Queen Mary her lieutenant-general in Scotland."—Scott's note.

467. 141. *Dark Morton.*—"He was concerned in the murder of David Rizzio, and at least privy to that of Darnley."—Scott's note. Rizzio (d. 1566) was secretary to Mary Queen of Scots; Lord Darnley (d. 1567) was Mary's second husband.

THE MINSTRELSY OF THE SCOTTISH BORDER

This was a collection of ballads and songs which Scott gathered together with the help of friends and published in three volumes, 1802-03. It contained, besides genuine ballads, a number of pieces which were the work, in part or entirely, of Scott.

KINMONT WILLIE

"This ballad is preserved by tradition in the West Borders, but much mangled by reciters, so that some conjectural emendations have been absolutely necessary to render it intelligible."—Scott's note. It is believed that most of this ballad is the work of Scott. If that is so, the ballad is perhaps the one example of a completely successful imitation of the genuine ballads. The ballad which may have furnished the basis for *Kinmont Willie* is *Jock o' the Side*. See Child's *English and Scottish Popular Ballads*, 3, 475.

The ballad is based upon a Border incident of 1596. Kinmont Willie, or William Armstrong, of Kinmouth, near the southern border of Scotland, was captured for freebooting by the English and shut up in Carlisle Castle, under the wardenship of Lord Scroop and his deputy Sakeld. Failing to secure the release of Armstrong, Sir Walter Scott of Branxholm, Lord of Buccleugh, led a troop of horsemen to the Castle, surprised the watchmen, set the prisoner free, and escaped across the River Eden.

470.   LORD RANDAL

This is a genuine ballad, versions of which are widely distributed throughout Europe and in the Appalachians. See the account of it in Child's *The English and Scottish Popular Ballads*, 1, 151ff.

THE LAY OF THE LAST MINSTREL

In the Preface to the first edition, Scott states that the poem was intended "to illustrate the customs and manners which anciently prevailed on the Borders of Scotland and England. The inhabitants living in a state partly pastoral and partly warlike, and combining habits of constant depredation with the influence of a rude spirit of chivalry, were often engaged in scenes highly susceptible of poetical ornament. As the description of scenery and manners was more the object of the author than a combined and regular narrative, the plan of the ancient metrical romance was adopted, which allows greater latitude, in this respect than would be consistent with the dignity of a regular poem. . . . For these reasons, the poem was put into the mouth of an ancient minstrel, the last of the race, who, as he is supposed to have survived the Revolution, might have caught somewhat of the refinement of modern poetry, without losing the simplicity of his original model. The date of the tale itself is about the middle of the sixteenth century, when most of the persons actually flourished."

The poem is written in honor of Lady Dalkeith (afterwards Duchess of Buccleuch), of Branksholm Hall on the River Teviot in Roxburghshire. She suggested to Scott that he write a ballad on the legend of the goblin page, Gilpin Horner, and this poem was the result. It is sung by the minstrel in the presence of the Duchess and her ladies.

The meter of the poem was taken from Coleridge's *Christabel*, which Scott had heard recited in 1801. Scott's meter, however, does not possess the infinite variety and beauty of Coleridge's. The indebtedness was acknowledged in 1831.

See Byron's *English Bards and Scotch Reviewers*, 150-64 (p. 513).

471.   HAROLD

This song is sometimes entitled *The Lay of Rosabelle*. The poem is supposed to be sung, after the espousal of Margaret of Buccleuch to Lord Cranstoun, by Harold, the minstrel of the house of St. Clair. It tells of the death of Rosabelle as she was returning from Ravensheuch Castle to Roslin, the family seat of the St. Clairs, in Edinburghshire, Scotland.

472.   THE MAID OF NEIDPATH

The following explanatory note is prefixed to this poem in the Cambridge edition of Scott's *Complete Poetical Works*, ed. by H. E. Scudder (1900): " 'There is a tradition in Tweeddale,' says Scott, 'that, when Neidpath Castle, near Peebles, was inhabited by the Earls of March, a mutual passion subsisted between a daughter of that noble family and a son of the Laird of Tushielaw, in Ettrick Forest. As the alliance was thought unsuitable by her parents, the young man went abroad. During his absence the lady fell into a consumption; and at length, as the only means of saving her life, her father consented that her lover should be recalled. On the day when he was expected to pass through Peebles, on the road to Tushielaw, the young lady, though much exhausted, caused herself to be carried to the balcony of a house in Peebles belonging to the family, that she might see him as he rode past. Her anxiety and eagerness gave such force to her organs that she is said to have distinguished the horse's footsteps at an incredible distance. But Tushielaw, unprepared for the change in her appearance, and not expecting to see her in that place, rode on without recognizing her, or even slackening his pace. The lady was unable to support the shock; and, after a short struggle, died in the arms of her attendants.' Published in 1806, in Haydn's *Collection of Scottish Airs*."

HUNTING SONG

This song is found in Scott's continuation of Strutt's *Queenhoo-Hall* printed in the Appendix to the General Preface to *Waverley*. The song is sung by three minstrels preparatory to a hunting expedition.

WHERE SHALL THE LOVER REST

This song is found in Canto 3 of *Marmion*, lines 148-83. It is sung by the youth Fitz-Eustace, in response to a request from Marmion, "To speed the lingering night away." It is thus introduced:

A mellow voice Fitz-Eustace had,
The air he chose was wild and sad;
Such have I heard in Scottish land
Rise from the busy harvest band,
When falls before the mountaineer

On Lowland plains the ripened ear.
Now one shrill voice the notes prolong,
Now a wild chorus swells the song:
Oft have I listened and stood still
As it came softened up the hill,
And deemed it the lament of men
Who languished for their native glen,
And thought how sad would be such sound
On Susquehanna's swampy ground,
Kentucky's wood-encumbered brake,
Or wild Ontario's boundless lake,
Where heart-sick exiles in the strain
Recalled fair Scotland's hills again!

473.   LOCHINVAR

This familiar ballad is found in Canto 5
of *Marmion*, lines 313-60. It is sung by Lady
Heron, who has come to the court of King
James of Scotland to make peace between
him and her husband, who was held prisoner
because of alleged connection with the death
of Sir Robert Kerr, Warden of the Middle
Marches. James's defeat at Flodden is by
some historians imputed to his infatuation
for Lady Heron.

The ballad is based on the ballad *Katharine
Jaffray*, first published by Scott, under the
title of *The Laird of Laminton*, in *The Minstrelsy of the Scottish Border*, 1802. The
names in the ballad are traditional.

20.   The Firth of Solway is noted for its
strong tides.

474.   THE LADY OF THE LAKE

"The scene of the following poem is laid
chiefly in the vicinity of Loch Katrine, in the
Western Highlands of Perthshire. The time
of action includes six days, and the transactions of each day occupy a canto."—Scott's
prefatory Argument.

Scott gives the following account of the
poem in the Introduction prefixed to the
edition of 1830: "After the success of *Marmion*, I felt inclined to exclaim with Ulysses
in the *Odyssey* [22:5]—

'One venturous game my hand has won today—
Another, gallants, yet remains to play.'

"The ancient manners, the habits, and customs of the aboriginal race by whom the
Highlands of Scotland were inhabited, had
always appeared to me peculiarly adapted to
poetry. The change in their manners, too,
had taken place almost within my own time,
or at least I had learned many particulars
concerning the ancient state of the Highlands
from the old men of the last generation. I

had always thought the old Scottish Gael
highly adapted for poetical composition. . . .

"I had also read a great deal, seen much,
and heard more, of that romantic country,
where I was in the habit of spending some
time every autumn; and the scenery of Loch
Katrine was connected with the recollection
of many a dear friend and merry expedition
of former days. This poem, the action of
which lay among scenes so beautiful, and so
deeply imprinted on my recollection, was a
labor of love; and it was no less so to recall
the manners and incidents introduced. The
frequent custom of James IV, and particularly of James V, to walk through their kingdom in disguise, afforded me the hint of an
incident, which never fails to be interesting,
if managed with the slightest address or
dexterity."

479. 585.   *Though all unask'd his birth and
name.*—"The Highlanders, who carried hospitality to a punctilious excess, are said to
have considered it as churlish, to ask a stranger his name or lineage, before he had taken
refreshment. Feuds were so frequent among
them, that a contrary rule would in many
cases have produced the discovery of some
circumstance which might have excluded the
guest from the benefit of the assistance he
stood in need of."—Scott's note.

481.   BOAT SONG

This song (lines 399-438 of Canto 2) is
sung by a group of boatmen as they bring
their chieftain to shore. Scott states that the
song is intended to imitate the boat songs of
the Highlanders, "which were usually composed in honor of a favorite chief. They are
so adapted as to keep time with the sweep of
the oars, and it is easy to distinguish between
those intended to be sung to the oars of a
galley, where the stroke is lengthened and
doubled, as it were, and those which were
timed to the rowers of an ordinary boat."

482.   CORONACH

This song (lines 370-93 of Canto 3) is sung
by a group of village maids and matrons as a
lament over Duncan, their dead leader.

CANTO VI. THE GUARD-ROOM

Summary of Cantos II-V: Shortly after
the departure of James Fitz-James the next
morning, Roderick Dhu, one of the proudest
of Highland chieftains, returns with his
clansmen from a foray on the Lowlands. At
the same time, Douglas, who has been sheltered by his nephew, Roderick, from the

King's hatred, returns from hunting, bringing
with him young Malcolm Graeme, Ellen's
lover. That night Roderick suggests that
Douglas give him Ellen to wed, and that they
join forces against the King. Douglas, knowing Ellen's love for Malcolm, refuses to join
Roderick against the King. Malcolm leaves,
hoping to secure protection for Douglas.

All the next day, Roderick's messenger
rides through the Highlands, rousing the men
to arms. The day following, James Fitz-James
again discovers Ellen, this time in hiding
with old Allan, and he proposes to carry her
to the court as his wife. Upon her refusal,
he gives her a ring, which he says will secure
for her any boon that she may ask from the
King. On the fifth day, James meets with
Roderick in single combat and overcomes him.
A little later, Douglas, who has been performing feats of strength at the court, arouses
the anger of the King and is thrown into
prison.

486.   BATTLE OF BEAL' AN DUINE

"A skirmish actually took place at a pass
thus called in the Trosachs, and closed with
the remarkable incident mentioned in the text.
It was greatly posterior in date to the reign
of James V."—Scott's note. "Beal' an Duine"
means "The pass of the man."

384-91.   Cf. the following lines from the
Anglo-Saxon poem *The Fight at Finnsburg,*
describing the approach of an armed troop:
"This is not day that dawns from the east, nor
here flies the dragon, nor here burn the gables
of this hall; but hither come bearing a hostile
band its bright battle-gear, fowls sing, the
gray-coated one [the wolf] howls, the war-
wood resounds, shield answers shaft."

490.   BRIGNALL BANKS

This song is found in Canto 3 of *Rokeby,*
lines 394-453. It is sung in a scene of revel
by a youth, Edmund of Winston
        "as the aptest mate
    For jovial song and merry feat."

The song is sung after Edmund dreams of
early scenes and incidents in his own life.
Brignall was the name of an estate along the
Greta River, in Yorkshire. Edmund sings
also the next song, *Allen-a-Dale,* lines 718-47
of the same Canto.

491.   ALLEN-A-DALE

The subject of this song was a legendary
outlaw minstrel, a companion of Robin Hood
in Sherwood Forest.

HIE AWAY, HIE AWAY

This song is found in Chapter 12 of *Waverley.* It is sung by Davie, a simple-minded
youth, to his two large deer greyhounds.

TWIST YE, TWINE YE

This song is found in Chapter 4 of *Guy
Mannering.* It is sung by Meg Merrilies, a
gypsy, as she spins the charm of the new-born
son and heir of her master. The next song,
Wasted, Weary, Wherefore Stay, found in
Chapter 27, is sung also by Meg Merrilies as
a sort of spell or prayer to speed the passage
of a dying smuggler.

492. LINES ON THE LIFTING OF THE
         BANNER OF THE HOUSE OF BUCCLEUCH

The football match described in this poem
took place on Dec. 4, 1815, on the plain of
Carterhaugh, near the junction of the Ettrick
and Yarrow rivers in Selkirkshire, Scotland.
The game was arranged by Scott's friend, the
Duke of Buccleuch, between the men of the
Vale of Yarrow and the Burghers of Selkirk.
The names mentioned in the poem are those of
the players and partisans of the two teams.
For a full account of the event see Lockhart's
Memoirs of the Life of Sir Walter Scott, 4,
271 (ch. 36).

14. *A stripling's weak hand.*—This was
Scott's eldest son Walter.

493.   JOCK OF HAZELDEAN

The first stanza of this poem is old. See
Child's *English and Scottish Popular Ballads,*
5, 159ff.

PIBROCH OF DONUIL DHU

"This is a very ancient pibroch belonging
to Clan MacDonald, and supposed to refer
to the expedition of Donald Balloch, who, in
1431, launched from the Isles with a considerable force, invaded Lochaber, and at Inverlochy defeated and put to flight the Earls of
Mar and Caithness, though at the head of an
army superior to his own."—Scott's note.

WHY SITT'ST THOU BY THAT RUIN'D HALL?

This song is sometimes entitled *Time.* It
is found in Chapter 10 of *The Antiquary.*
Lovel, one of the chief characters in the story,
hears it early in the morning as it is sung by
a woman in a turret opposite his window.

494. AND WHAT THOUGH WINTER WILL
              PINCH SEVERE

This song is sometimes entitled *Cavalier
Song.* It is found in Chapter 19 of *Old Mor-*

tality, where it is sung by a Major Bellenden to his sister, after he had been refused a request by Colonel Grahame.

494. CLARION

This poem, the motto to Chapter 34, is ascribed to an anonymous poet. It is found, with slight change, in *Verses Written during the War 1756-1763*, a poem by T. O. Mordaunt (1730-1809).

"It may be worth noting that it was in correcting the proof-sheets of *The Antiquary* that Scott first took to equipping his characters with mottoes of his own fabrication. On one occasion he happened to ask John Ballantyne, who was sitting by him, to hunt for a particular passage in Beaumont and Fletcher. John did as he was bid, but did not succeed in discovering the lines. 'Hang it Johnnie!' cried Scott. 'I believe I can make a motto sooner than you will find one.' He did so accordingly; and from that hour, whenever memory failed to suggest an appropriate epigraph, he had recourse to the inexhaustible mines of '*old play*' or '*old ballad*' to which we owe some of the most exquisite verse that ever flowed from his pen."—Lockhart, in *Memoirs of the Life of Sir Walter Scott*, ch. 27.

THE DREARY CHANGE

"It was while struggling with such languor, on one lovely evening of this autumn [1817], that he composed the following beautiful verses. They mark the very spot of their birth,—namely, the then naked height overhanging the northern side of the Cauldshields Loch, from which Melrose Abbey to the eastward, and the hills of Ettrick and Yarrow to the west, are now visible over a wide range of rich woodland,—all the work of the poet's hand."—Lockhart, in *Memoirs of the Life of Sir Walter Scott*, ch. 39.

FAREWELL TO THE LAND

This poem stands as the motto of Chapter 36 of *Rob Roy*. See note on *Clarion*, above.

PROUD MAISIE

This song is found in Chapter 40 of *The Heart of Midlothian*. It is sung by the insane Madge Wildfire on her deathbed.

THE BAREFOOTED FRIAR

This song is found in Chapter 17 of *Ivanhoe*. It is sung by the friar of Copmanhurst to entertain his guest, the Black Knight.

495. REBECCA'S HYMN

This hymn is found in Chapter 39 of *Ivanhoe*. It follows this statement: "It was in the twilight of the day when her trial, if it could be called such, had taken place, that a low knock was heard at the door of Rebecca's prison-chamber. It disturbed not the inmate, who was then engaged in the evening prayer recommended by her religion, and which concluded with a hymn we have ventured thus to translate into English."

The original of Rebecca was an American Jewess named Rebecca Gratz. The story of her fruitless love for a Christian was told to Scott by Washington Irving at Abbotsford in 1817. See Van Rensselaer's "The Original of Rebecca in *Ivanhoe*," *The Century Magazine*, Sept. 1882 (24:679).

BORDER MARCH

This song is found in Chapter 25 of *The Monastery*. It is sung by a follower of Baron Avenel as he sits over his meal with a small company of Border-riders.

The following interesting parody is by Thomas Love Peacock. It is one of his so-called Paper Money Lyrics.

Chorus of Northumbrians

On the Prohibition of Scotch One-Pound Notes in England

1825 1837

March, march, Make-rags of Borrowdale,[1]
    Whether ye promise to bearer or order;
March, march, Take-rag and Bawbee tail,[2]
    All the Scotch flimsies must over the
        Border:
    Vainly you snarl anent
    New Act of Parliament,
Bidding you vanish from dairy and "lauder";[3]
    Dogs, you have had your day,
    Down tail and slink away;
You'll pick no more bones on this side of the
        Border.

[1] "Not the Cumberland Borrodaile, but the genuine ancient name of that district of Scotland, whatever it be called now, from which was issued the first promise to pay, that was made with the express purpose of being broken."—Peacock's note.

[2] "Scoticé for Tag-rag and Bob-tail; 'a highly respectable old firm.' A paper kite with a bawbee at its tail is perhaps a better emblem of the safe currency of Scotland than Mr. Canning's mountain of paper irrigated by a rivulet of gold."—Peacock's note. George Canning (1770-1827) was a noted English statesman, Secretary of Foreign Affairs, 1822-27, and Premier, 1827.

[3] larder

Hence to the hills where your fathers stole
 cattle;
Hence to the glens where they skulked from
 the law;
Hence to the moors where they vanished from
 battle,
 Crying "De'll tak the hindmost," and
 "Charlie's awa'."
  Metal is clanking here;
  Off with your banking gear;
Off, ere you're paid "to Old Harry or order";
 England shall many a day
 Wish you'd been far away,
Long ere your kite-wings flew over the Border.

March, march, Ettrick and Teviotdale,
 Pay-day's the word, lads, and gold is the
 law,
March, march, Eskdale and Liddesdale;
 Tagdale, and Ragdale, and Bobdale, and a';
  Persons or purse, they say;
  Purse you have none to pay;
Your persons who'll deal with, except the
 Recorder
 Yet, to retrieve your freaks,
 You can just leave your breeks;[1]
You'll want them no more when you're over
 the Border.

High on a pole in the vernal sun's baskings,
 When April has summoned you ragships
 away,
We'll hoist up a pair of your best galligaskins,
 Entwined with young thistles to usher in
 May.
  Types of Scotch "copital,"
  They shall o'er-top-it-all,
Stripped off from bearer and brushed into
 order;
  Then if you tarry, rogues,
  Nettles you'll get for brogues,[1]
And to the Rogue's March be drummed o'er
 the Border.

496. THE SONG OF THE REIM-KENNAR

This song is found in Chapter 6 of *The Pirate*. It is sung by the witch Norna, and is thus introduced: "Having looked on the sky for some time in a fixed attitude, and with the most profound silence, Norna at once, yet with a slow and elevated gesture, extended her staff of black oak toward that part of the heavens from which the blast came hardest, and in the midst of its fury chanted a Norwegian invocation, still preserved in the Island of Uist, under the name of *The Song of the Reim-kennar*, though some

---

[1] breeches; trousers

call it *The Song of the Tempest*. The following is a free translation, it being impossible to render literally many of the elliptical and metaphorical terms of expression peculiar to the ancient Northern poetry."

497. COUNTY GUY

This poem is found in Chapter 4 of *Quentin Durward*. It is thus introduced: "The maid of the little turret, of the veil, and of the lute, sung exactly such an air as we are accustomed to suppose flowed from the lips of the high-born dames of chivalry, when knights and troubadours listened and languished. The words had neither so much sense, wit, or fancy, as to withdraw the attention from the music, nor the music so much of art, as to drown all feeling of the words. The one seemed fitted to the other; and if the song had been recited without the notes, or the air played without the words, neither would have been worth noting. It is, therefore, scarcely fair to put upon record lines intended not to be said or read, but only to be sung. But such scraps of old poetry had always had a sort of fascination for us; and as the tune is lost forever—unless Bishop happens to find the notes, or some lark teaches Stephens to warble the air—we will risk our credit, and the taste of the Lady of the Lute, by preserving the verses, simple and even rude as they are."

Bishop and Stephens were contemporary English musicians and composers.

WHAT BRAVE CHIEF

This song is found in Chapter 11 of *The Talisman*. It is sung by a minstrel as a compliment to Leopold, Archduke of Austria, to glorify him as equal to Richard the Lion-Hearted of England. Both were leaders in the Crusades.

ROBIN HOOD

This song is found in Act II, sc. 1, of Scott's drama *The Doom of Devorgoil*. It is sung by Blackthorn, a forest ranger, in love with Kathleen, who has just skipped away from him.

BONNY DUNDEE

This and the following song, *When Friends are Met*, are found in Act II, sc. 2, of *The Doom of Devorgoil*. *Bonny Dundee* is sung by Leonard, a forest ranger, in recounting an incident in which Oswald of Devorgoil, a Scottish baron, had a part thirty years before.

Bonny Dundee was John Graham of Claverhouse (1649-89), Viscount Dundee, a staunch Scottish supporter of Charles II and James

II of England. His strict enforcement of the laws against the Scottish Covenanters won him the title "Bloody Claver'se." After the flight of James into France, Claverhouse supported his cause against William III, going so far as to defy the Convention, or Scotch Parliament, which had accepted William. Failing in his attempt to persuade the Duke of Gordon to hold Edinburgh Castle, on Castle Rock, for King James, he raised an army which met and defeated the government forces at the Battle of Killiecrankie, in 1689. He died of a wound the night of the victory.

499.   WHEN FRIENDS ARE MET

This was sung as a duet by Leonard and Flora, Oswald's daughter, after *Bonny Dundee* was finished.

GLEE FOR KING CHARLES

This song is found in Chapter 20 of *Woodstock*. It is sung by a merry group, just before they separate for the night, in honor of Charles I, King of England (1625-49).

Joanna Baillie

Poems, p. 500 — Bibliography, p. 1406

"In reading Joanna Baillie's poetry we find her to possess a quickness of observation that nearly supplies the place of insight; a strongly moralized temperament delighting in natural things; a vigorous, simple style. These are not especially dramatic qualities, and although she won her reputation through her plays, the poetry by which she is remembered is chiefly of a pastoral kind. . . . Her country songs, written in the language of her early home, have the best qualities of Scottish national poetry; their simplicity, their cautious humor, endeared them at once to the national heart; they have the shrewdness and the freshness of the morning airs, the homeliness of unsophisticated feeling. Such songs as *Woo'd and Married and A'*, *The Weary Pund o' Tow*, *My Nanny O*, and the lovely trysting song beginning 'The gowan glitters on the sward,' are among the treasures of Scottish minstrelsy."—A. Mary F. Robinson, in Ward's *The English Poets*, 4.

"Or, if to touch such chord be thine,
Restore the ancient tragic line.
And emulate the notes that rung
From the wild harp, which silent hung
By silver Avon's holy shore,
Till twice an hundred years roll'd o'er;

When she, the bold Enchantress, came
With fearless hand and heart on flame!
From the pale willow snatch'd the treasure,
And swept it with a kindred measure,
Till Avon's swans, while rung the grove
With Montfort's hate and Basil's love,
Awakening at the inspired strain,
Deem'd their own Shakespeare liv'd again."
    —Scott, in Introduction to Canto 3
of *Marmion*.

These lines are quoted as if they were spoken to Scott by his chief literary counselor, William Erskine, Esq., to whom the Introduction is addressed. Montfort and Basil are characters in Joanna Baillie's dramas *Basil* and *De Montfort*, respectively. In contemporary criticism Miss Baillie was frequently declared equal to Shakespeare.

500.   THE BEACON

In the subtitle, this play is characterized as "a serious musical drama"; it contains a number of songs. The one printed here, found in Act II, sc. 1, is sung at night by a fisherman to his mate as they keep a beacon burning on the cliff to guide an expected boat to shore.

Allan Cunningham

Poems, p. 501 — Bibliography, p. 1422

501. THE LOVELY LASS OF PRESTON MILL

Preston Mill is a rustic village on Solway Firth, Dumfriesshire, Scotland.

502.   A WET SHEET AND A FLOWING SEA

Scott classed this poem "as among the best songs going," and regarded Cunningham as "a man of genius, besides, who only requires the tact of knowing when and where to stop, to attain the universal praise which ought to follow it."—Scott's *Journal, 1825-32*, Nov. 14, 1826.

James Hogg

Poems, p. 502 — Bibliography, p. 1428

"No Scottish poet has dealt with the power and realm of Fairy more vividly and impressively than the Bard of Ettrick. He caught up several of the floating traditions which actually localized the fairy doings, and this, as he haunted the hills and moors where they were said to have taken place, brought the old legend home to his everyday life and feeling. He was thus led to an accurate observation and description of the reputed scenes of the story, and of the haunts of the Fairies. These had only received rare mention in the tradition itself, and little more than this even when they had been put into verse in the older time. But all these spots he knew well; many of them were the daily round of the shepherd and his collie. The legends he had learned thus acquired something of the reality which he felt. Hence Hogg's poems of Fairy are remarkable for the fullness, the richness, and the accuracy of the description of the country—of hill, glen, and moor."—John Veitch, in *The History and Poetry of the Scottish Border* (1878).

See Wordsworth's *Extempore Effusion upon the Death of James Hogg* (p. 341); also Wilson's *Noctes Ambrosianæ* (p. 1179).

503. THE SKYLARK

See Wordsworth's and Shelley's poems on the same subject (pp. 323, 338, and 730).

THE QUEEN'S WAKE

The Queen's Wake consists of a group of fifteen poems supposed to have been sung by Scottish minstrels before Mary, Queen of Scots, at Christmastide, 1561, after her return to her native land. According to the story, she was so struck with the song of an aged minstrel who played to her as she rode from the pier of Leith to Holyrood, and by the reports she heard of the great body of tradition belonging to Scotland, that she straightway announced a poetical competition —the prize to be a beautiful harp. The fifteen songs were the result.

"*The Queen's Wake* is a garland of fair forest-flowers, bound with a band of rushes from the moor. It is not a poem,—not it; nor was it intended to be so; you might as well call a bright bouquet of flowers a flower, which, by-the-by, we do in Scotland. Some of the ballads are very beautiful; one or two even splendid; most of them spirited; and the worst far better than the best that ever was written by any bard in danger of being a blockhead. *Kilmeny* alone places our (*ay, our*) Shepherd among the Undying Ones."— John Wilson, in *Christopher North's Recreations: An Hour's Talk about Poetry* (1831).

Kilmeny is the story, common in Celtic folklore and still believed in by the Irish peasantry, of a maiden stolen by the fairies and brought back to earth after seven years, devoid of all human desires.

508. M'KIMMAN

This and the next poem are stirring national songs reminiscent of border conflicts between Scotland and England (the Saxons) during the 18th century. The persons named in the poems were probably actual participants in the conflicts.

509. LOCK THE DOOR, LARISTON

See note on *M'Kimman*, above. Cf. Scott's *Border March* (p. 495), and Peacock's parody *Chorus of Northumbrians* (p. 1321).

THE MAID OF THE SEA

"This is one of the many songs which Moore caused me to cancel, for nothing that I know of, but because they ran counter to his. It is quite natural and reasonable that an author should claim a copyright of a sentiment; but it never struck me that it could be so exclusively his, as that another had not a right to contradict it. This, however, seems to be the case in the London law; for true it is that my songs were cancelled, and the public may now judge on what grounds, by comparing them with Mr. Moore's. I have neither forgot nor forgiven it; and I have a great mind to make him cancel *Lalla Rookh* for stealing it wholly from *The Queen's Wake*, which is so apparent in the plan, that every London judge will give it in my favor, although he ventured only on the character of one accomplished bard, and I on seventeen. He had better have let my few trivial songs alone."—Hogg's Introduction.

George Gordon Byron

Poems, p. 510 — Bibliography, p. 1413

"The great thing in Byron is *genius*, that quality so perilous to define, so evanescent in its aroma, so impossible to mistake. If ever a man breathed whom we recognize (athwart much poor and useless work, when strictly tested) as emphatically the genius, that man was Byron; and, if ever genius made poetry its mouthpiece, covering with its transcendent utterances a multitude of sins whether against art or against the full stature of perfect manhood, Byron's is that poetry."—W. M. Rossetti, in *Lives of Famous Poets* (1878).

"Few poets excel him in the instantaneous sympathy he creates, even among minds having no mental affinity with his own. He is eminently the poet of passion. In almost all the changes of his mood, the same energy of feeling glows in his verse. The thought or emotion uppermost in his mind at any one time, whether it be bad or good, seems to sway, for the moment, all the faculties of his nature.

He has a passionate love for evil, a passionate love for nature, for goodness, for beauty, and, we may add, a passionate love for himself. When he sits in the place of the scoffer, his words betray the same inspiration from impulse,—the same passion, though condensed into bitterness and mockery."—E. P. Whipple, in *Essays and Reviews* (1845).

"It is . . . useless to seek in Byron any such singleness of vision as resolves all the manifold speculations of a Milton or a Wordsworth. Central vision, indeed, is the quality of greatness in which chiefly his poetry is deficient; but he does everything that genius can in compensation by recording one impression after another with a point and spirit that have hardly been excelled in verse. These are the terms upon which we have to take Byron's poetry, or leave it. He excites, but he does not notably enlarge, our experience; and yet, what a splendid excitement it is. While we are with him we know admiration, delight, exultation even in a faculty so rich and ardent, everything indeed but the glory of the tabernacle. That too we see sometimes far off, but it is for rare moments only. Spiritual revelation, then, it was not Byron's destiny to make. Also we must endure . . . infelicities of style and taste. But we have our reward, almost on every page, in the supple, light-limbered verse that Byron stamped with his eager, if variable, mastery for fifteen years or more without tiring."—John Drinkwater, in *The Pilgrim of Eternity* (1925).

See Keats's *To Byron* (p. 778); also Jeffrey's criticism on Byron (pp. 930 ff.).

Byron is caricatured as Mr. Cypress in Thomas Love Peacock's *Nightmare Abbey*.

510.   LACHIN Y GAIR

This is one of the poems in *Hours of Idleness*. Byron wrote in his Preface:

"Lachin y Gair, or, as it is pronounced in the Erse, Loch na Garr, towers proudly preeminent in the Northern Highlands. One of our modern tourists mentions it as the highest mountain, perhaps, in Great Britain. Be that as it may, it is certainly one of the most sublime and picturesque amongst our 'Caledonian Alps.' Its appearance is of a dusky hue, but the summit is the seat of eternal snows. Near Lachin y Gair I spent some of the early part of my life, the recollection of which has given birth to the following stanzas."

17-18; 25-26. The two quotations in this poem have not been identified. In phrasing they bear striking similarity to expressions in Macpherson's *Ossian*, of which Byron was a great admirer. Note the following, which occur frequently in *Ossian:* "ghosts of the dead," "night came rolling down," "sweet as breathing gale." Numerous rhythmic sentences like the following also are found: "Her voice was like the harp, when the distant sound comes, in the evening, on the soft rustling breeze of the vale!"—(*The War of Inis-Thona*).

511.   ENGLISH BARDS AND SCOTCH
REVIEWERS

A hostile criticism of Byron's *Hours of Idleness* in *The Edinburgh Review*, Jan. 1808, inspired Byron to write this satire, which was first published anonymously. The following selection from the review of *Hours of Idleness* shows the tenor of that criticism:

"The poesy of this young lord belongs to the class which neither gods nor men are said to permit. Indeed we do not recollect to have seen a quantity of verse with so few deviations in either direction from that exact standard. His effusions are spread over a dead flat, and can no more get above or below the level than if they were so much stagnant water. . . . We must beg leave seriously to assure him that the mere rhyming of the final syllable, even when accompanied by the presence of a certain number of feet,—nay, although (which does not always happen) those feet should scan regularly, and have been all counted accurately upon the fingers,—is not the whole art of poetry. We could entreat him to believe that a certain portion of liveliness, somewhat of fancy, is necessary to constitute a poem; and that a poem in the present day, to be read, must contain at least one thought either in a little degree different from the ideas of former writers or differently expressed. . . . But whatever judgment may be passed on the poems of this noble minor, it seems we must take them as we find them, and be content; for they are the last we shall ever have from him. He is at best, he says, but an intruder into the groves of Parnassus; he never lived in a garret, like thoroughbred poets; and 'though he once roved a careless mountaineer in the Highlands of Scotland,' he has not of late enjoyed this advantage. Moreover, he expects no profit from his publication; and whether it succeeds or not, 'it is highly improbable, from his situation and pursuits hereafter,' that he should again condescend to be an author. Therefore let us take what we get and be thankful. What right have we poor devils to be nice? We are well off to have got so much from a man of this lord's station, who does not live in a garret, but 'has the sway' of Newstead Abbey. Again we say, let us be thankful; and, with honest Sancho, bid God bless the giver, nor look the gift-horse in the mouth."—*The Edinburgh Review*, January, 1808. (The article, formerly attributed to Francis Jeffrey, was written by Henry Brougham, one of the founders of *The Edinburgh Review*, and Lord Chancellor of England, 1830-34.)

Byron's original purpose was to satirize only contemporary poetry, of which he held a very low opinion. After reading *Lalla Rookh*, by Thomas Moore, Byron wrote Murray, Sept. 15, 1817, as follows: "With regard to poetry in general, I am convinced, the more I think of it, that he and *all* of us—Scott, Southey, Wordsworth, Moore, Campbell, I—are all in the wrong, one as much as another; that we are upon a wrong revolutionary poetical system, or systems, not worth a damn in itself, and from which none but Rogers and Crabbe are free. . . . I am the more confirmed in this by having lately gone over some of our classics, particularly Pope, whom I tried in this way—I took Moore's poems and my own and some others, and went over them side by side with Pope's, and I was really astonished (I ought not to have been so) and mortified at the ineffable distance in point of sense, harmony, effect, and even imagination, passion, and *invention*, between the little Queen Anne's man and us of the Lower Empire." Byron shortly came to disapprove of his *English Bards and Scotch Reviewers*. In 1816, he wrote in the margin, "The greater part of this satire I most sincerely wish had never been written—not only on account of the injustice of much of the critical and some of the personal part of it, but the tone and temper are such as I cannot approve."

512. 82. "This was not just. Neither the heart nor the head of these gentlemen are at all what they are here represented. At the time this was written, I was personally unacquainted with either."—Byron, in ed. of 1816.

514. 221-22. Southey's *Madoc* is in two parts; the first is "Madoc in Wales"; the second is "Madoc in Aztlan" (Mexico, from a tribe of Indians living there).

515. 235ff. In the annotated copy of the fourth edition Byron has written "Unjust" opposite the criticism on Wordsworth and Coleridge, lines 235-48 and 255-58.

516. 331. In 1807, Bowles issued an edition of Pope's works in which he declared that Pope was only a second-class poet. A heated controversy followed, in which Byron and

Bowles were the chief opponents. For a summary of the dispute see Byron's *Letters and Journals* (ed. by R. E. Prothero), Vol. 5, p. 522; also Saintsbury's *A History of Criticism*, 3, 279-82.

517. 391. Byron first wrote *Helicon* instead of *Hippocrene*. He made the correction in the edition of 1816.

406. "Mr. Cottle, Amos, Joseph, I don't know which, but one or both, once sellers of books they did not write, and now writers of books they do not sell, have published a pair of epics—*Alfred* (poor Alfred! Pye has been at him too!)—*Alfred* and *The Fall of Cambria*." —Byron, in ed. of 1816.

418ff. In these lines Byron refers to the religious poet James Montgomery, who is called Alcaeus after the Greek poet of that name. Many of Montgomery's early poems were published in the *Sheffield Register*.

518. 432-53. "Too ferocious—this is mere insanity."—Byron, in ed. of 1816. Byron thought that Jeffrey wrote the review of *Hours of Idleness*. When Jeffrey praised Byron's later poems, Byron wrote to Moore (April 9, 1814): "As for Jeffrey, it is a very handsome thing of him to speak well of an old antagonist, and what a mean mind dared not do."

464. "All this is bad, because personal."— Byron, in ed. of 1816.

519. 539. In the portions omitted, Byron pays his respects to a number of minor writers including the dramatists of the period.

520. 857. "I consider Crabbe and Coleridge as the first of these times, in point of power and genius."—Byron, in ed. of 1816.

522.   THE BRIDE OF ABYDOS

This was first entitled *Zuleika*. Byron says that he wrote it in four nights. "Whether it succeeds or not is no fault of the public, against whom I have no complaint. But I am much more indebted to the tale than I can ever be to the most partial reader, as it wrung my thoughts from reality to imagination— from selfish regrets to vivid recollections—and recalled me to a country replete with the *brightest* and *darkest*, but always most *lively* colors of my memory."—Byron, in *Journal*, Dec. 5, 1813.

Byron had fallen in love with Lady Frances, wife of his friend James Wedderburn Webster, whom he had been visiting at Ashton Hall, Rotherham. From Byron's letters it is to be inferred that he sought safety in flight. The poem was written to allay the distress of the love affair. Abydos is a town in Asia Minor on the Hellespont, the scene of the romance of Hero and Leander.

"The undoubted fact that *The Bride of Abydos*, as well as *The Giaour*, embodies recollections of actual scenes and incidents which had burnt themselves into the memory of an eye-witness, accounts not only for the fervent heat at which these Turkish tales were written, but for the extraordinary glamor which they threw over contemporary readers, to whom the local coloring was new and attractive, and who were not out of conceit with 'good Monsieur Melancholy.' "—E. H. Coleridge, in Introduction to *The Bride of Abydos*.

1. This line was probably suggested by Goethe's "Kennst du das Land wo die Citronen blühn?"

528. 70. The Koorsee text, or verse of the throne (Sura II, "Chapter of the Heifer," 257), is as follows: "God, there is no God but He, the living, the self-subsistent. Slumber takes Him not, nor sleep. His is what is in the heavens and what is in the earth. Who is it that intercedes with Him, save by His permission? He knows what is before them and what behind them, and they comprehend not aught of His knowledge but of what He pleases. His throne extends over the heavens and the earth, and it tires Him not to guard them both, for He is high and grand."—The *Qur'ân*, translated by E. H. Palmer, *Sacred Books of the East* (1880), 6, 40.

532. 388. *Ocean-Patriarch.*—Noah.

536. ODE TO NAPOLEON BUONAPARTE

"I don't know—but I think *I*, even *I* (an insect compared with this creature), have set my life on casts not a millionth part of this man's. But, after all, a crown may not be worth dying for. Yet, to outlive *Lodi*[1] for this ! ! ! Oh that Juvenal or Johnson could rise from the dead! 'Expende—quot libras in duce summo invenies?'[2] I knew they were light in the balance of mortality; but I thought their living dust weighed more *carats*. Alas! this imperial diamond hath a flaw in it, and is now hardly fit to stick in a glazier's pencil;—the pen of the historian won't rate it worth a ducat. Psha! 'something too much of this.'[3] But I won't give him up even now; though all his admirers have, 'like the thanes, fallen from him.' "[4]—Byron, in *Journal*, April 9, 1814.

---

[1] Napoleon won a victory over the Austrians at Lodi, Italy, on May 10, 1796. The victory gained him the epithet, "Little Corporal."
[2] Weigh [the ashes of Hannibal]—how many pounds do you find in that great leader?— Juvenal, *Satires*, 10, 47.
[3] *Hamlet*, III, 2, 79.
[4] *Macbeth*, V, 3, 49.

537. SHE WALKS IN BEAUTY

The following six poems were included in Byron's *Hebrew Melodies*. The first two are not Hebrew melodies, but genuine love-songs. This one was written the day after Byron first met his beautiful cousin, Mrs. Wilmot.

538. MY SOUL IS DARK

See Macpherson's *Oina-Morul* (p. 92a, 32-33).

HEROD'S LAMENT FOR MARIAMNE

Herod, surnamed "The Great," was King of Judea (40-4 B. C.). In a fit of jealousy he executed his beautiful wife Mariamne. The story is the theme of Stephen Phillips's *Herod, A Tragedy* (1900).

539. THE DESTRUCTION OF SENNACHERIB

Sennacherib was a king of Assyria who invaded Palestine in the 7th century B. C. See *2 Kings*, 18-19.

STANZAS FOR MUSIC

In a letter to Moore (March 8, 1816) Byron says of this poem: "I pique myself on these lines as being the *truest*, though the most melancholy I ever wrote." The poem was inspired by the death of a friend and the recollection of what Byron "once felt, and ought to have felt now, but could not."

541. THE PRISONER OF CHILLON

This poem was written in two days at a small inn, where Byron and Shelley were detained by bad weather during a tour of Lake Geneva. François Bonivard (1493-c1570) was prior of a small monastery outside Geneva. Being a lover of independence, he joined the patriots who were trying to make Geneva a republic, free from the control of Charles III, Duke of Savoy. Charles, therefore, removed Bonivard from office and imprisoned him in the Castle of Chillon, from 1530 to 1536. When Chillon was captured by the Bernese in 1536, he was released, made a member of the Council of Geneva, and awarded a house and a pension of 200 crowns a year.

542. 107-111. In respect of accuracy and inaccuracy of detail, Ruskin states that these lines fulfill the conditions of poetry in contradistinction to history. "Instead of finding, as we expected, the poetry distinguished from the history by the omission of details, we find it consisting entirely in the *addition* of details; and instead of its being characterized by regard only of the invariable, we find its whole power to consist in the clear expression of what is singular and particular!"—Ruskin, *Modern Painters*, Part IV, ch. 1, sec. 9.

545.   EPISTLE TO AUGUSTA

The Quarterly Review for January 1831 (44:202) says that there is nothing in the whole body of Byron's poetry "more mournfully and desolately beautiful" than these stanzas.

547.   DARKNESS

This poem should be compared with Campbell's *The Last Man* (p. 449) and note (p. 1312).

548.   PROMETHEUS

Byron was always a lover and a worshiper of Prometheus and frequently alludes to him in his poems. "The conception of an immortal sufferer at once beneficent and defiant, appealed alike to his passions and his convictions and awoke a peculiar enthusiasm."—E. H. Coleridge, Note to *Prometheus* in his edition of Byron's *Poetical Works*.

SONNET TO LAKE LEMAN

Lake Leman is Lake Geneva, situated between Switzerland and France.

549.   CHILDE HAROLD'S PILGRIMAGE

"The following poem was written, for the most part, amidst the scenes which it attempts to describe. It was begun in Albania; and the parts relative to Spain and Portugal were composed from the author's observations in those countries. Thus much it may be necessary to state for the correctness of the descriptions. The scenes attempted to be sketched are in Spain, Portugal, Epirus, Acarnania, and Greece. There, for the present, the poem stops; its reception will determine whether the author may venture to conduct his readers to the capital of the East, through Ionia and Phrygia: these two cantos are merely experimental.

"A fictitious character is introduced for the sake of giving some connection to the piece, which, however, makes no pretension to regularity. It has been suggested to me by friends, on whose opinions I set a high value, that in this fictitious character, Childe Harold, I may incur the suspicion of having intended some real personage: this I beg leave, once for all, to disclaim—Harold is the child of imagination, for the purpose I have stated. In some very trivial particulars, and those merely local, there might be grounds for such a notion; but in the main points, I should hope, none whatever. . . ."—From Preface to the First and Second Cantos.

"What helps it now, that Byron bore,
With haughty scorn which mock'd the smart,
Through Europe to the Ætolian shore
The pageant of his bleeding heart?
That thousands counted every groan,
And Europe made his woe her own?"
          —Arnold, in *Stanzas from the Grande*
                    Chartreuse.

Childe is used by Byron as in the old ballads and romances, signifying a youth of noble birth, usually one awaiting knighthood.
554. 32, 9. "Have you never seen a stick broken in the middle, and yet cohering by the rind? The fibres, half of them actually broken and the rest sprained, and, though tough, unsustaining? Oh, many, many are the brokenhearted for those who know what the moral and practical heart of the man is."—Coleridge, *Anima Poetæ* (ed. E. H. Coleridge, 1895), 303.
563. 90. See Shelley's *Adonais*, 54 (p. 763). Shelley's idealistic pantheism evidently influenced Byron here; the two were frequently together during the week when this Canto was written.

91. "It is to be recollected that the most beautiful and impressive doctrines of the divine Founder of Christianity were delivered, not in the *Temple*, but on the *Mount*. . . . Were the early and rapid progress of what is called Methodism to be attributed to any cause beyond the enthusiasm excited by its vehement faith and doctrines (the truth or error of which I presume neither to canvass nor to question), I should venture to ascribe it to the practice of preaching in the *fields*, and the unstudied and extemporaneous effusions of its teachers. The Mussulmans, whose erroneous devotion (at least in the lower orders) is most sincere, and therefore impressive, are accustomed to repeat their prescribed orisons and prayers, wherever they may be, at the stated hours—of course, frequently in the open air, kneeling upon a light mat (which they carry for the purpose of a bed or cushion as required); the ceremony lasts some minutes, during which they are totally absorbed, and only living in their supplication: nothing can disturb them. On me the simple and entire sincerity of these men, and the spirit which appeared to be within and upon them, made a far greater impression than any general rite which was ever performed in places of worship."—Byron.
92. "The thunder-storm to which these lines refer occurred on the 13th of June, 1816, at midnight. I have seen, among the Acroceraunian mountains of Chimari, several more terrible, but none more beautiful."—Byron.

94. 1-9. The similarity between these lines and Coleridge's probably is due to the fact that Byron had seen *Christabel* in manuscript.

566. 111. Cf. this stanza with Burns's *Epistle to the Rev. John M'Math*, 43-48 (p. 204).

567. 117, 1. "His allusions to me in *Childe Harold* are cruel and cold, but with such a semblance as to make *me* appear so, and to attract sympathy to himself. It is said in this poem that hatred of him will be taught as a lesson to his child. I might appeal to all who have ever heard me speak of him, and still more to my own heart, to witness that there has been no moment when I have remembered injury otherwise than affectionately and sorrowfully. It is not my duty to give way to hopeless and wholly unrequited affection, but so long as I live my chief struggle will be probably not to remember him too kindly."—Lady Byron, in letter to Lady Anne Lindsay, quoted by E. H. Coleridge in his edition of Byron's *Poetical Works*.

567b. 1, 1-2. "The Bridge of Sighs (*i. e.*, *Ponte dei Susperi)* is that which divides, or rather joins the palace of the Doge to the prison of the state. It has two passages: the criminal went by the one to judgment, and returned by the other to death, being strangled in a chamber adjoining, where there was a mechanical process for the purpose."—Byron, in letter to Murray (July 1, 1817), in which was enclosed the first stanza of Canto III.

568. 13. In the stanzas omitted Byron reflects upon the possibility of his name's being barred by Oblivion

". . . from out the temple where the dead
Are honor'd by the nations."

569. 25. In the stanzas omitted Byron reflects upon the influence of suffering upon the human heart and mind.

570. 79. In the stanzas omitted Byron writes of various Italian cities, temples, castles, etc., and of the famous men associated with each—Petrarch, Tasso, Galileo, Michelangelo, Dante, Boccaccio, and others.

80. The Goths sacked Rome in 410 and later. The Christians destroyed temples to satisfy religious frenzy and to secure building material.

95. In the stanzas omitted Byron writes of the great conquerors of Rome—Sylla, Pompey, and Cæsar— and of the nothingness of man.

97, 7. Some editors take the "base pageant" to be the empire and court of Napoleon.

571. 98. This stanza furnishes an example of Byron's vigorous optimism and keen political foresight. His passion for freedom led him to believe and to proclaim that democracy was the most powerful force of the time and that it finally would prevail.

128. In the stanzas omitted Byron writes of several tombs, columns, and other objects and places of note, of the persons concerned with each, and of the influence of love on human life.

130. 2. When visited by Byron, and for long afterwards, the ruins of the Coliseum were covered with shrubs and flowers.

132. The appeal to Nemesis in this stanza should be compared with Byron's *Fare Thee Well* (p. 539), *Stanzas to Augusta* (p. 544), *Epistle to Augusta* (p. 545), *Childe Harold's Pilgrimage*, 3, 69-75 and 111-18 (pp. 560-67), and *Manfred*, I, 1, 192-261 (p. 578).

573. 175. In the stanzas omitted Byron writes of the Pantheon, the dungeon of the Church of St. Nicholas, the Mole of Hadrian, the Church of St. Peter's, the art treasures in the Vatican, the death of Princess Charlotte, and the village of Nemi.

574. 180, 9. Byron made the same error in *The Adieu*, 94: "Where now my head must lay." This error was more common in Byron's day than it is now.

575.   MANFRED

John Wilson suggested in an article in *Blackwood's Edinburgh Magazine*, July, 1817, that *Manfred* was borrowed from Marlowe's *Dr. Faustus*. From this opinion Jeffrey dissented in his review of *Manfred* published in *The Edinburgh Review*, Aug. 1817 (Vol. 28, 430-31). He says: "It is suggested in an ingenious paper in a late number of *The Edinburgh Magazine* that the general conception of this piece and much of what is excellent in the manner of its execution have been borrowed from *The Tragical History of Dr. Faustus* of Marlow, and a variety of passages are quoted which the author considers as similar and, in many respects, superior to others in the poem before us. We cannot agree in the general terms of this conclusion, but there is, no doubt, a certain resemblance, both in some of the topics that are suggested and in the cast of the diction in which they are expressed. . . . But these and many other smooth and fanciful verses in this curious old drama prove nothing, we think, against the originality of *Manfred;* for there is nothing to be found there of the pride, the abstraction, and the heart-rooted misery in which that originality consists. Faustus is a vulgar sorcerer, tempted to sell his soul to the devil for the ordinary price of sensual pleasure and earthly power and glory—and who shrinks and shudders in agony when the forfeit comes to be exacted. The style, too, of Marlow, though elegant and scholar-like, is weak and childish compared with the depth and force of much of what we have quoted from Lord Byron; and the disgusting buffoonery and low farce of which his piece is principally made up place it much more in contrast, than in any terms of comparison, with that of his noble successor. In the tone and pitch of the composition, as well as in the character of the diction in the more solemn parts, the piece before us reminds us much more of the *Prometheus* of Æschylus than of any more modern performance. The tremendous solitude of the principal person—the supernatural beings with whom alone he holds communion—the guilt—the firmness—the misery—are all points of resemblance to which the grandeur of the poetic imagery only gives a more striking effect. The chief differences are that the subject of the Greek poet was sanctified and exalted by the established belief of his country, and that his terrors are nowhere tempered with the sweetness which breathes from so many passages of his English rival." Murray sent this review to Byron, who replied (Oct. 12, 1817) as follows:

"Many thanks for *The Edinburgh Review*, which is very kind about *Manfred*, and defends its originality, which I did not know that anybody had attacked. I *never read*, and do not know that I ever saw, the *Faustus* of Marlow, and had, and have, no dramatic works by me in English, except the recent things you sent me; but I heard Mr. Lewis translate verbally some scenes of Goethe's *Faust* (which were some good, and some bad) last summer;—which is all I know of the history of that magical personage; and as to the germs of *Manfred*, they may be found in the Journal which I sent to Mrs. Leigh . . . shortly before I left Switzerland. I have the whole scene of *Manfred* before me, as if it was but yesterday, and could point it out, spot by spot, torrent and all. Of the *Prometheus* of Æschylus I was passionately fond as a boy (it was one of the Greek plays we read thrice a year at Harrow). . . . As to the *Faustus* of Marlow, I never read, never saw, nor heard of it—at least, thought of it, except that I think Mr. Gifford mentioned in a note of his which you sent me, something about the catastrophe, but not as having anything to do with mine, which may or may not resemble it, for anything I know.

The *Prometheus*, if not exactly in my plan, has always been so much in my head that I can easily conceive its influence over all or anything that I have written;—but I deny Marlow and his progeny, and beg that you will do the same."

In June, 1820, Goethe published his review of *Manfred*. "Byron's tragedy, *Manfred*, was to me a wonderful phenomenon, and one that closely touched me. This singular intellectual poet has taken my *Faustus* to himself, and extracted from it the strangest nourishment for his hypochondriac humor. He has made use of the impelling principles in his own way, for his own purposes, so that no one of them remains the same; and it is particularly on this account that I cannot enough admire his genius. The whole is in this way so completely formed anew that it would be an interesting task for the critic to point out, not only the alterations he has made, but their degree of resemblance with, or dissimilarity to, the original; in the course of which I cannot deny that the gloomy heat of an unbounded and exuberant despair becomes at last oppressive to us. Yet is the dissatisfaction we feel always connected with esteem and admiration."—From Hoppner's Translation (Moore's *Life of Byron*, 448). Goethe's review was first published in *Kunst und Alterthum*, 2, 2, 191. See Goethe's *Sämmtliche Werke* (Stuttgart, 1874), 13, 640-42.

On June 7, 1820, Byron sent Goethe's comment to Murray, with the following letter: "Enclosed is something which will interest you, to-wit, the opinion of *the* Greatest man of Germany—perhaps of Europe—upon one of the great men of your advertisements, (all 'famous hands,' as Jacob Tonson used to say of his ragamuffins,)—in short, a critique of *Goethe's* upon Manfred. There is the original, Mr. Hoppner's translation, and an Italian one; keep them all in your archives,—for the opinions of such a man as Goethe, whether favorable or not, are always interesting, and this is, moreover, favorable. His *Faust* I never read, for I don't know German; but Matthew Monk Lewis, in 1816, at Coligny, translated most of it to me *viva voce*, and I was naturally much struck with it; but it was the *Staubach* and the *Jungfrau*, and something else, much more than *Faustus*, that made me write *Manfred*. The first scene, however, and that of *Faustus* are very similar."

582. Scene II. The following passages are quoted from Byron's Swiss Journal: "Arrived at the foot of the mountain (the Jungfrau, that is, the Maiden); glaciers; torrents: one of these torrents *nine hundred feet* in height of visible descent. Lodged at the curate's. Set out to see the valley; heard an avalanche fall, like thunder; glaciers enormous; storm came on—thunder, lightning, hail; all in perfection, and beautiful. . . . The torrent is in shape curving over the rock, like the tail of a white horse streaming in the wind, such as it might be conceived would be that of the 'pale horse' on which Death is mounted in the *Apocalypse*. It is neither mist nor water, but a something between both; its immense height (900 feet) gives it a wave or curve, a spreading here or condensation there, wonderful and indescribable."—Sept. 22, 1816.

"Before ascending the mountain, went to the torrent (seven in the morning) again; the sun upon it, forming a *rainbow* of the lower part of all colors, but principally purple and gold; the bow moving as you move; I never saw anything like this; it is only in the sunshine."—Sept. 23, 1816.

585. Scene III. "Came to a morass; Hobhouse dismounted to get over well; I tried to pass my horse over; the horse sunk up to the chin, and of course he and I were in the mud together; bemired, but not hurt; laughed and rode on. Arrived at the Grindlewald; dined; mounted again, and rode to the higher glacier —like *a frozen hurricane*."—Sept. 23, 1816.

594. SO, WE'LL GO NO MORE A-ROVING

This poem was sent in a letter to Thomas Moore, dated Feb. 28, 1817, following this statement: "At present, I am on the invalid regimen myself. The Carnival—that is, the latter part of it, and sitting up late o' nights, had knocked me up a little. But it is over,—and it is now Lent, with all its abstinence and sacred music. The mumming closed with a masked ball at the Fenice, where I went, as also to most of the ridottos, etc., etc.; and, though I did not dissipate much upon the whole, yet I find 'the sword wearing out the scabbard,' though I have but just turned the corner of twenty-nine."

The Fenice is a theatre in Venice. A ridotto is a public entertainment consisting of music and dancing, often in masquerade. "The sword wearing out the scabbard" is a French saying.

MY BOAT IS ON THE SHORE

This poem is sometimes entitled *To Thomas Moore*. It was incorporated in a letter to Moore, dated July 10, 1817. The first stanza was written in April, 1816.

STRAHAN, TONSON, LINTOT OF THE TIMES

This poem is sometimes entitled *To Mr. Murray*. William Strahan (1715-85). Jacob

Tonson (c1656-1736), and Barnaby Lintot (1675-1736) were prominent publishers of their times.

11. Murray bought an interest in *Blackwood's Edinburgh Monthly Magazine* in August 1818, and held it until Blackwood purchased the magazine in December 1819.

595. MAZEPPA

This poem is based on a passage in Voltaire's *Histoire de Charles XII*, which Byron printed as the "Advertisement" to his poem.

Ivan Stepánovitch Mazeppa (1644-1710) was a Cossack chief, a native of Poland. He made love to the wife (Theresa, line 202) of Lord Falbowski (the Palatine, line 155), and being discovered in the intrigue was bound to a horse which was furiously terrorized and turned loose. Mazeppa later became a chief and fought against Russia on the side of Charles XII of Sweden.

600. 549. Cf. *Christabel*, 216-17 (p. 371).

603. DON JUAN

This poem is usually regarded as Byron's masterpiece. Goethe described it as "a work of boundless genius" (*Kunst und Alterthum*, 1821). After receiving Cantos III, IV, and V, Shelley wrote Byron (Oct. 21, 1821): "This poem carries with it at once the stamp of originality and defiance of imitation. Nothing has ever been written like it in English, nor, if I may venture to prophesy, will there be, unless carrying upon it the mark of a secondary and borrowed light. . . . You are building up a drama such as England has not yet seen, and the task is sufficiently noble and worthy of you." In the introductory note to the poem in the Cambridge edition of Byron, Paul Elmer More says, "In one sense *Don Juan* is a satire, to many critics the greatest satire ever written; but it is something still more than that. It is the epic of modern life."

The first five cantos of *Don Juan* were published by Murray (1819-21) without name of author or publisher, but Byron's authorship was readily recognized. The name of the hero was taken from a Spanish traditional story regarding the profligacy of one Don Juan de Tenorio. With the exception of his libertinism, Byron's hero bears no likeness to the legendary character. For the history of the legend, see Ticknor's *History of Spanish Literature* (Boston, Houghton, 1888) 2, 380-81. Don Juan figures also in comedies by the Spaniard Tóllez, Molière, T. Corneille, and Goldini, in an opera by Mozart, and in a ballet by Glück. The stanza form of *Don Juan* is *ottava rima*, the same as Byron had used in *Beppo* in 1817. In a letter to Murray dated March 25, 1818, he says of *Beppo*: "Whistlecraft was my immediate model. . . . But . . . Berni is the father of that kind of writing, which, I think, suits our language, too, very well—we shall see by the experiment. If it does, I shall send you a volume in a year or two." Francesco Berni was an Italian poet of the early 16th century. "Whistlecraft" was the pseudonym of J. H. Frere in *The Monks and the Giants* (1817); the first two stanzas of his poem are as follows:

I've often wished that I could write a book
  Such as all English people might peruse;
I never should regret the pains it took,
  That's just the sort of fame that I should choose.
To sail about the world like Captain Cook,
  I'd sling a cot up for my favorite Muse,
And we'd take verses out to Demarara,
To New South Wales, and up to Niagara.

Poets consume exciseable commodities,
  They raise the nation's spirit when victorious,
They drive an export trade in whims and oddities,
  Making our commerce and revenue glorious;
As an industrious and pains-taking body 'tis
  That poets should be reckoned meritorious:
And therefore I submissively propose
To erect one Board for Verse and one for Prose.

Captain James Cook (1728-79) was a noted English navigator. Demarara is a city and county in British Guiana, South America. The pronunciation of Niagara required by Frere's rhyme was common in England.

Writing to Moore, Sept. 19, 1818, Byron says: "I have finished the first Canto (a long one, of about 180 octaves) of a poem in the style and manner of *Beppo*, encouraged by the good success of the same. It is called *Don Juan*, and is meant to be a little quietly facetious upon everything. But I doubt whether it is not—at least, as far as it has yet gone—too free for these very modest days. However, I shall try the experiment, anonymously; and if it don't take, it will be discontinued. It is dedicated to Southey in good, simple, savage verse, upon the Laureate's politics, and the way he got them." After Cantos I and II were published on July 15, 1819, Murray asked Byron for the plan of the poem. Byron wrote him in part as follows (Aug. 12, 1819): "You ask me for the plan of

Donny Johnny: I *have* no plan—I *had* no plan; but I had or have materials. . . . You are too earnest and eager about a work never intended to be serious. Do you suppose that I have any intention but to giggle and make giggle?—a playful satire, with as little poetry as could be helped, was what I meant." After the completion of Canto V, Byron again wrote Murray (Feb. 16, 1821): "The 5th is so far from being the last of *D. J.* that it is hardly the beginning. I meant to take him the tour of Europe, with a proper mixture of siege, battle, and adventure, and to make him finish as Anacharsis Cloots in the French Revolution. To how many cantos this may extend, I know not, nor whether (even if I live) I shall complete it; but this was my notion: I meant to have him a Cavalier Servente in Italy, and a cause for a divorce in England, and a Sentimental 'Werther-faced man' in Germany, so as to show the different ridicules of the society in each of those countries, and to have displayed him gradually *gâté* and *blasé* [spoiled and satiated with pleasure] as he grew older, as is natural. But I had not quite fixed whether to make him end in Hell, or in an unhappy marriage, not knowing which would be the severest. The Spanish tradition says Hell: but it is probably only an Allegory of the other state. You are now in possession of my notions on the subject." Cloots was condemned to death by Robespierre and executed in 1794. "Werther-faced man" is a phrase from Moore's *The Fudge Family in Paris*, 5, 98. Werther is the sentimental hero of Goethe's *The Sorrows of Werther*.

605. 5. In the stanzas omitted, Byron enumerates a number of possible epic heroes, all of whom are rejected as unsuited to his purpose.

609. 36, 6. "I could have forgiven the dagger or the bowl,—anything, but the deliberate desolation piled upon me, when I stood alone upon my hearth, with my household gods shivered around me. * * * Do you suppose I have forgotten it? It has comparatively swallowed up in me every other feeling, and I am only a spectator upon earth, till a tenfold opportunity offers."—Byron, in letter to Moore, Sept. 19, 1818. See *Marino Faliero*, III, 2, 361-64.

610. 44, 7-8. "Fact! There is, or was, such an edition, with all the obnoxious epigrams of Martial placed by themselves at the end."—Byron.

611. 200. In the stanzas omitted, Byron tells the story of Don Juan's infatuation for a married woman named Donna Julia, which resulted in his being sent abroad to "mend his former morals."

613. Canto II, 44.—In the stanzas omitted, Juan embarks for Leghorn, Italy, the home of relatives. On the way the vessel is wrecked in a prolonged storm, described in the poem in detail. Byron's indebtedness for the shipwreck to G. Dalzell's *Shipwrecks and Disasters at Sea* (1812) was pointed out in an article in *The Monthly Magazine*, Aug., 1821. In a letter to Murray, dated Aug. 23, 1821, Byron wrote: "With regard to the charges about the shipwreck, I think that I told you and Mr. Hobhouse, years ago, that there was not a *single circumstance* of it *not* taken from *fact;* not, indeed, from any *single* shipwreck, but all from *actual* facts of different wrecks. Almost all *Don Juan* is *real* life, either my own, or from people I know." J. C. Hobhouse, Lord Broughton (1786-1869), was an English statesman and writer, and a friend of Byron.

615. 103. Of the survivors of the wreck only four are alive as the longboat approaches one of the Cyclades, in the Ægean Sea.

619. 174. The stanzas omitted record Haidée's daily ministrations to Juan, which result in a love-affair.

625. 98, 4. One of Wordsworth's poems is entitled *The Waggoner;* it was published in 1815.

635. Canto XI.—In the cantos omitted, Juan recovers and is sent as a captive slave to a Turkish market, where he is purchased by the Sultana. He finally escapes, and after numerous adventures at the Court of Russia and elsewhere, he finally arrives in London, where he is well received by persons of high society.

636. 60, 1. Regarding the hostile attack upon Keats, published in *The Edinburgh Review,* April, 1818, Keats wrote George and Georgiana Keats (Oct. 14 or 15, 1818) as follows: "Reynolds has returned from a six weeks' enjoyment in Devonshire—he is well, and persuades me to publish my *Pot of Basil* as an answer to the attacks made on me in *Blackwood's Magazine* and *The Quarterly Review.* There have been two Letters in my defence in *The Chronicle* and one in *The Examiner,* copied from the Alfred Exeter Paper, and written by Reynolds. I do not know who wrote those in *The Chronicle.* This is a mere matter of the moment—I think I shall be among the English Poets after my death. Even as a matter of present interest the attempt to crush me in *The Quarterly* has only brought me more into notice, and it is a common expression among book men 'I wonder *The Quarterly* should cut its own throat.'

"It does me not the least harm in society to make me appear little and ridiculous: I know when a man is superior to me and give him all due respect—he will be the last to laugh at me, and as for the rest I feel that I make an impression upon them which insures me personal respect while I am in sight whatever they may say when my back is turned."

J. H. Reynolds was an intimate friend of Keats. For the letters published in *The Chronicle,* see Keats's letter to Hessey (p. 890), and note (p. 1363).

For a full account of the matter of Keats's suffering under these attacks, see Colvin's *Keats,* ch. 6, and Rossetti's *Life of John Keats,* ch. 5.

638. 86. The stanzas omitted contain reflections on the transitoriness of worldly fame.

639. 90. Byron conducts his hero through five more cantos without bringing him back to Spain, and leaves the story unfinished.

WHEN A MAN HATH NO FREEDOM TO FIGHT FOR AT HOME

This poem was sent in a letter to Moore, dated Nov. 5, 1820, as a memorial chant for one who might be killed fighting for the cause of the Italian Revolution.

FOR ORFORD AND FOR WALDEGRAVE

This poem is sometimes entitled *To Mr. Murray.* It was sent in a letter to Murray, dated Aug. 23, 1821, refusing an offer of £2000 for *Sardanapalus, The Two Foscari,* and three cantos of *Don Juan.* Murray had previously published works of Horace Walpole, Earl of Orford (1717-97), and of James Earl Waldegrave (1685-1741).

THE VISION OF JUDGMENT

This poem was written as a satire upon Robert Southey, the author of *A Vision of Judgment* (see p. 435), in which George III, who had just died (1820), was completely vindicated. In the Preface to his poem, Southey went out of his way to attack the moral character of Byron. Following is the Preface to Byron's poem:

"It hath been wisely said, that 'One fool makes many;'[1] and it hath been poetically observed—

'That fools rush in where angels fear to tread.' —Pope.[2]

---

[1] An old proverb found in many languages.
[2] *An Essay on Criticism,* 3, 66.

"If Mr. Southey had not rushed in where he had no business, and where he never was before, and never will be again, the following poem would not have been written. It is not impossible that it may be as good as his own, seeing that it cannot, by any species of stupidity, natural or acquired, be *worse*. The gross flattery, the dull impudence, the renegado intolerance, and impious cant, of the poem by the author of *Wat Tyler*,[1] are something so stupendous as to form the sublime of himself—containing the quintessence of his own attributes.

"So much for his poem—a word on his Preface. In this Preface it has pleased the magnanimous Laureate to draw the picture of a supposed 'Satanic School,' the which he doth recommend to the notice of the legislature; thereby adding to his other laurels the ambition of those of an informer. If there exists anywhere, except in his imagination, such a School, is he not sufficiently armed against it by his own intense vanity? The truth is that there are certain writers whom Mr. S. imagines, like Scrub, to have 'talked of *him;* for they laughed consumedly.'[2]

"I think I know enough of most of the writers to whom he is supposed to allude, to assert, that they, in their individual capacities, have done more good, in the charities of life, to their fellow-creatures, in any one year, than Mr. Southey has done harm to himself by his absurdities in his whole life; and this is saying a great deal. But I have a few questions to ask.

"1stly, Is Mr. Southey the author of *Wat Tyler?*

"2ndly, Was he not refused a remedy at law by the highest judge of his beloved England, because it was a blasphemous and seditious publication?

"3rdly, Was he not entitled by William Smith, in full parliament, 'a rancorous renegado'?[3]

"4thly, Is he not poet laureate, with his own lines on Martin the regicide staring him in the face?[4]

"And, 5thly, Putting the four preceding items together, with what conscience dare *he* call the attention of the laws to the publications of others, be they what they may?

"I say nothing of the cowardice of such a proceeding, its meanness speaks for itself; but I wish to touch upon the *motive*, which is neither more nor less than that Mr. S. has been laughed at a little in some recent publications, as he was of yore in the *Anti-Jacobin*,[1] by his present patrons. Hence all this 'skimble-scamble stuff' about 'Satanic,' and so forth. However, it is worthy of him—'*qualis ab incepto.*'[2]

"If there is anything obnoxious to the political opinions of a portion of the public in the following poem, they may thank Mr. Southey. He might have written hexameters, as he has written everything else, for aught that the writer cared—had they been upon another subject. But to attempt to canonize a monarch, who, whatever were his household virtues, was neither a successful nor a patriot king,—inasmuch as several years of his reign passed in war with America and Ireland, to say nothing of the aggression upon France,—like all other exaggeration, necessarily begets opposition. In whatever manner he may be spoken of in this new *Vision*, his *public* career will not be more favorably transmitted by history. Of his private virtues (although a little expensive to the nation) there can be no doubt.

"With regard to the supernatural personages treated of, I can only say that I know as much about them, and (as an honest man) have a better right to talk of them than Robert Southey. I have also treated them more tolerantly. The way in which that poor insane creature, the Laureate, deals about his judgments in the next world, is like his own judgment in this. If it was not completely ludicrous, it would be something worse. I don't think that there is much more to say at present.

Quevedo Redivivus."[3]

643. 34, 1-3. In 1812, John Mason Good had published an edition of *The Book of Job* translated from the original Hebrew. He included in the notes numerous quotations from the Hebrew and the Arabic versions and in an introduction supported the historical character of the Book.

650. 94, 1. "Yesterday, at Holland House, I was introduced to Southey—the best-looking bard I have seen for some time. To have that poet's head and shoulders, I would almost have written his *Sapphics*. He is certainly a

---

[1] A violent revolutionary epic written by Southey in 1794.
[2] Farquhar, *The Beaux' Stratagem*, III, 1, 81-84.
[3] William Smith (1756-1835), an English politician, and member of Parliament, attacked Southey in the House of Commons on March 14, 1817. See Southey's reply *To William Smith, Esq., M. P.*
[4] See p. 651a, n. 1.

[1] A paper originated in 1797 with the purpose of ridiculing the French Revolution and its supporters in England.
[2] Such he has been from the first.—Horace, *Ars Poetica*, 127.
[3] Quevedo revived. Francis Gómez de Quevedo (1580-1645) was a vigorous Spanish writer of satire and polemical verse. He was called "The Captain of Combat." He was also noted as a duelist.

prepossessing person to look on, and a man of talent, and all that, and—there is his eulogy."—Byron, in letter to Moore, Sept. 27, 1813.

652. ON THIS DAY I COMPLETE MY
THIRTY-SIXTH YEAR

"This morning Lord Byron came from his bedroom into the apartment where Colonel Stanhope and some friends were assembled, and said with a smile—'You were complaining, the other day, that I never write any poetry now:—this is my birthday, and I have just finished something, which I think, is better than what I usually write.' He then produced these noble and affecting verses, which were afterwards found written in his journals, with only the following introduction: 'Jan. 22; on this day I complete my 36th year.' "—Gamba, in *A Narrative of Lord Byron's Last Journey to Greece* (1825).

Percy Bysshe Shelley

Selections, p. 653 — Bibliography, p. 1445

"The grounds . . . on which Shelley's eminence is based are mainly three. He is unexcelled in his ideality, unexcelled in his music and unexcelled in his importance. By importance we here mean the direct import of the work performed, its controlling power over the reader's thought and feeling, the contagious fire of its white-hot intellectual passion, and the long reverberation of its appeal. Shelley is emphatically the poet of the future. . . . Shelley appeared at the time when the sublime frenzies of the French revolutionary movement had exhausted the elasticity of men's thought—at least in England—and had left them flaccid and stolid; but that movement prepared another in which revolution was to assume the milder guise of reform, conquering and to conquer. Shelley was its prophet. . . . To outrage his contemporaries was the condition of leading his successors to triumph and of personally triumphing in their victories. Shelley had the temper of an innovator and a martyr; he united speculative keenness and humanitarian zeal in a degree for which we might vainly seek his precursor. We have already named ideality as one of his leading excellences. This Shelleian quality combines, as its constituents, sublimity, beauty and the abstract passion for good. Perhaps no outstanding English poet, and he was essentially an English poet, has used a greater variety of forms and measures than Shelley. In the pure lyrics the rap-

ture, the music and the emotion are in exquisite balance, and the work has often as much of delicate simplicity as of fragile and flower-like perfection."—W. M. Rossetti and R. Ingpen, in *Encyclopaedia Britannica*, 14th ed. (1929).

Shelley's Centenary[1]
4th August, 1892

Within a narrow span of time,
Three princes of the realm of rhyme,
At height of youth or manhood's prime
 From earth took wing,
To join the fellowship sublime 5
 Who, dead, yet sing.

He, first, his earliest wreath who wove
Of laurel grown in Latmian grove,
Conquered by pain and hapless love
 Found calmer home, 10
Roofed by the heaven that glows above
 Eternal Rome.

A fiercer soul, its own fierce prey,
And cumbered with more mortal clay,
At Missolonghi flamed away, 15
 And left the air
Reverberating to this day
 Its loud despair.

Alike remote from Byron's scorn
And Keats's magic as of morn 20
Bursting forever newly-born
 On forest old,
To wake a hoary world forlorn
 With touch of gold,

Shelley, the cloud-begot, who grew 25
Nourished on air and sun and dew,
Into that Essence whence he drew
 His life and lyre
Was fittingly resolved anew
 Through wave and fire. 30

'Twas like his rapid soul! 'Twas meet
That he, who brooked not Time's slow feet,
With passage thus abrupt and fleet
 Should hurry hence,
Eager the Great Perhaps to greet 35
 With Why? and Whence?

Impatient of the world's fixed way,
He ne'er could suffer God's delay,
But all the future in a day
 Would build divine, 40
And the whole past in ruins lay,
 An emptied shrine.

[1] From *Selected Poems of William Watson*, copyright 1902 by the John Lane Company.

Vain vision! but the glow, the fire,
The passion of benign desire,
The glorious yearning, lift him higher   45
  Than many a soul
That mounts a million paces nigher
  Its meaner goal.

And power is his, if naught besides,
In that thin ether where he rides,   50
Above the roar of human tides
  To ascend afar,
Lost in a storm of light that hides
  His dizzy car.

Below, the unhasting world toils on,   55
And here and there are victories won,
Some dragon slain, some justice done,
  While, through the skies,
A meteor rushing on the sun,
  He flares and dies.   60

But, as he cleaves yon ether clear,
Notes from the unattempted Sphere
He scatters to the enchanted ear
  Of earth's dim throng,
Whose dissonance doth more endear   65
  The showering song.

In other shapes than he forecast
The world is moulded: his fierce blast,—
His wild assault upon the Past,—
  These things are vain;   70
Revolt is transient: what *must* last
  Is that pure strain

Which seems the wandering voices blent
Of every virgin element,—
A sound from ocean caverns sent,—   75
  An airy call
From the pavilioned firmament
  O'erdoming all.

And in this world of worldlings, where
Souls rust in apathy, and ne'er   80
A great emotion shakes the air,
  And life flags tame,
And rare is noble impulse, rare
  The impassioned aim,

'Tis no mean fortune to have heard   85
A singer who, if errors blurred
His sight, had yet a spirit stirred
  By vast desire,
And ardor fledging the swift word
  With plumes of fire.   90

A creature of impetuous breath,
Our torpor deadlier than death

He knew not; whatsoe'er he saith
  Flashes with life:
He spurreth men, he quickeneth   95
  To splendid strife.

And in his gusts of song he brings
Wild odors shaken from strange wings,
And unfamiliar whisperings
  From far lips blown,   100
While all the rapturous heart of things
  Throbs through his own,—

His own that from the burning pyre
One who had loved his wind-swept lyre
Out of the sharp teeth of the fire   105
  Unmolten drew,
Beside the sea that in her ire
  Smote him and slew.
               —William Watson.

The second stanza refers to Keats and his poem on Endymion, the shepherd on Mount Latmus. Keats died and was buried in Rome, in 1821. The third stanza refers to Byron, who died at Missolonghi, Greece, in 1824, while fighting for the independence of the Greeks. Line 30 and the the last stanza of the poem refer to the death of Shelley by drowning, in 1822, and to the cremation of his body. While the body was burning, Shelley's unconsumed heart was snatched from the flames by Shelley's faithful friend and admirer, E. J. Trelawny.

From *Pauline*

Sun-treader—life and light be thine for-
  ever!   151
Thou art gone from us—years go by, and
  spring
Gladdens, and the young earth is beautiful,
Yet thy songs come not—other bards arise,
But none like thee;—they stand—thy majes-
  ties,   155
Like mighty works which tell some Spirit there
Hath sat regardless of neglect and scorn,
Till, its long task completed, it hath risen
And left us, never to return: and all
Rush in to peer and praise when all in vain. 160
The air seems bright with thy past presence
  yet,
But thou art still for me, as thou hast been
When I have stood with thee, as on a throne
With all thy dim creations gathered round
Like mountains—and I felt of mould like
  them,   165
And with them creatures of my own were
  mixed,
Like things half-lived, catching and giving
  life.

But thou art still for me, who have adored,
Tho' single, panting but to hear thy name,
Which I believed a spell to me alone,   170
Scarce deeming thou wast as a star to men.
      —Robert Browning (1832).

Browning's more familiar tribute to Shelley is his short poem *Memorabilia*.

"The poetic ecstasy took him constantly upwards; and, the higher he got, the more thoroughly did his thoughts and words become one exquisite and intense unit. With elevation of meaning, and splendor and beauty of perception, he combined the most searching, the most inimitable loveliness of verse-music; and he stands at this day, and perhaps will always remain, the poet who, by instinct of verbal selection and charm of sound, comes nearest to expressing the half-inexpressible—the secret thing of beauty, the intolerable light of the arcane."—W. M. Rossetti, in *Lives of Famous Poets* (1878).

Shelley has been immortalized in the character of Scythrop, in Thomas Love Peacock's *Nightmare Abbey*.

653.   QUEEN MAB

This is a philosophical poem in which Shelley expresses his radical opinion about the society and orthodox Christianity of his day. In a note on the poem Mrs. Shelley says of Shelley: "He was animated to greater zeal by compassion for his fellow-creatures. His sympathy was excited by the misery with which the world is burning. He witnessed the sufferings of the poor, and was aware of the evils of ignorance. He desired to induce every rich man to despoil himself of superfluity, and to create a brotherhood of property and service, and was ready to be the first to lay down the advantages of his birth. He was of too uncompromising a disposition to join any party. He did not in his youth look forward to gradual improvement; nay, in those days of intolerance, now almost forgotten, it seemed as easy to look forward to the sort of millennium of freedom and brotherhood which he thought the proper state of mankind as to the present reign of moderation and improvement. Ill-health made him believe that his race would soon be run; that a year or two was all he had of life. He desired that these years should be useful and illustrious. He saw, in a fervent call on his fellow-creatures to share alike the blessings of the creation, to love and serve each other, the noblest work that life and time permitted him. In this spirit he composed *Queen Mab*."

Shelley himself was not blind to the crudeness of the poem. In a letter to the Editor of *The Examiner*, dated June 22, 1821, he said: "A poem entitled *Queen Mab* was written by me at the age of eighteen, I daresay in a sufficiently intemperate spirit—but even then was not intended for publication, and a few copies only were struck off, to be distributed among my personal friends. I have not seen this production for several years. I doubt not but that it is perfectly worthless in point of literary composition; and that, in all that concerns moral and political speculation, as well as in the subtler discriminations of metaphysical and religious doctrine, it is still more crude and immature."

In the poem, Ianthe, the central figure, falls asleep and dreams that she is transported to the court of Queen Mab, conceived by Shelley as the ruler over men's thoughts. After showing Ianthe visions of the past, present, and future, Queen Mab instructs her regarding the true doctrine of God and man. In connection with this poem, cf. the selections from Godwin's *An Enquiry Concerning Political Justice* (pp. 239 ff.).

655. 93-94.   *And statesmen boast of wealth!*
—"There is no real wealth but the labor of man. Were the mountains of gold and the valleys of silver, the world would not be one grain of corn the richer; no one comfort would be added to the human race. In consequence of our consideration for the precious metals, one man is enabled to heap to himself luxuries at the expense of the necessaries of his neighbor; a system admirably fitted to produce all the varieties of disease and crime, which never fail to characterize the two extremes of opulence and penury. A speculator takes pride to himself as the promoter of his country's prosperity, who employs a number of hands in the manufacture of articles avowedly destitute of use, or subservient only to the unhallowed cravings of luxury and ostentation. . . . The poor are set to labor,—for what? Not the food for which they famish: not the blankets for want of which their babes are frozen by the cold of their miserable hovels: not those comforts of civilization without which civilized man is far more miserable than the meanest savage; oppressed as he is by all its insidious evils, within the daily and taunting prospect of its innumerable benefits assiduously exhibited before him:—no; for the pride of power, for the miserable isolation of pride, for the false pleasures of the hundredth part of society. No greater evidence is afforded of the wide extended and radical

mistakes of civilized man than this fact:
those arts which are essential to his very
being are held in the greatest contempt;
employments are lucrative in an inverse ratio
to their usefulness: the jeweler, the toy-
man, the actor gains fame and wealth by the
exercise of his useless and ridiculous art;
whilst the cultivator of the earth, he without whom society must cease to subsist,
struggles through contempt and penury, and
perishes by that famine which but for his
unceasing exertions would annihilate the rest
of mankind."—Shelley's note.

659. 166-86. Cf. with this passage, Cowper's
The Task, II, 1-47 (p. 147), and *The Negro's
Complaint* (p. 148); also Southey's *Sonnet
Concerning the Slave Trade* (p. 426).

211-12. "I hold that the depravity of the
physical and moral nature of man originated
in his unnatural habits of life. The origin of
man, like that of the universe of which he
is a part, is enveloped in impenetrable mystery. His generations either had a beginning, or they had not. The weight of evidence
in favor of each of these suppositions seems
tolerably equal; and it is perfectly unimportant to the present argument which is
assumed. The language spoken, however, by
the mythology of nearly all religions seems
to prove that at some distant period man
forsook the path of nature, and sacrificed the
purity and happiness of his being to unnatural
appetites. The date of this event seems to
have also been that of some great change
in the climates of the earth, with which it
has an obvious correspondence. The allegory
of Adam and Eve eating of the tree of evil,
and entailing upon their posterity the wrath
of God and the loss of everlasting life, admits
of no other explanation than the disease and
crime that have flowed from unnatural
diet."—Shelley's note.

Shelley then gives a long discussion of the
necessity and the value of a vegetable diet.
See Shelley's *Alastor,* 98-106 (p. 662).

660.   TO WORDSWORTH

Wordsworth was at one time an enthusiastic supporter of the French Revolution, but
its excesses and failures led him finally to
become a conservative. This poem indicates
the contemporary feeling of the ardent rad-
icals toward his change of politics. See
Browning's *The Lost Leader,* which also was
suggested by Wordsworth's action.

661.   ALASTOR

"The poem entitled *Alastor* may be considered as allegorical of one of the most
interesting situations of the human mind. It
represents a youth of uncorrupted feelings
and adventurous genius led forth by an imagination inflamed and purified through
familiarity with all that is excellent and
majestic, to the contemplation of the universe.
He drinks deep of the fountains of knowledge,
and is still insatiate. The magnificence and
beauty of the external world sinks profoundly
into the frame of his conceptions, and affords
to their modifications a variety not to be exhausted. So long as it is possible for his
desires to point towards objects thus infinite
and unmeasured, he is joyous, and tranquil,
and self-possessed. But the period arrives
when these objects cease to suffice. His mind
is at length suddenly awakened and thirsts for
intercourse with an intelligence similar to
itself. He images to himself the being whom
he loves. Conversant with speculations of the
sublimest and most perfect natures, the vision
in which he embodies his own imaginations
unites all of wonderful, or wise, or beautiful,
which the poet, the philosopher, or the lover
could depicture. The intellectual faculties,
the imagination, the functions of sense, have
their respective requisitions on the sympathy
of corresponding powers in other human
beings. The poet is represented as uniting
these requisitions, and attaching them to a
single image. He seeks in vain for a prototype
of his conception. Blasted by his disappointment, he descends to an untimely grave.

"The picture is not barren of instruction
to actual men. The poet's self-centered
seclusion was avenged by the furies of an
irresistible passion pursuing him to speedy
ruin. But that power which strikes the luminaries of the world with sudden darkness and
extinction, by awakening them to too exquisite
a perception of its influences, dooms to a slow
and poisonous decay those meaner spirits
that dare to abjure its dominion. Their destiny is more abject and inglorious as their
delinquency is more contemptible and pernicious. They who, deluded by no generous
error, instigated by no sacred thirst of doubtful knowledge, duped by no illustrious superstition, loving nothing on this earth, and
cherishing no hopes beyond, yet keep aloof
from sympathies with their kind, rejoicing
neither in human joy nor mourning with
human grief; these, and such as they, have
their apportioned curse. They languish, because none feel with them their common
nature. They are morally dead. They are
neither friends, nor lovers, nor fathers, nor
citizens of the world, nor benefactors of their
country. Among those who attempt to exist

without human sympathy, the pure and tender-hearted perish through the intensity and passion of their search after its communities, when the vacancy of their spirit suddenly makes itself felt. All else, selfish, blind, and torpid, are those unforeseeing multitudes who constitute, together with their own, the lasting misery and loneliness of the world. Those who love not their fellow-beings live unfruitful lives, and prepare for their old age a miserable grave.

'The good die first,
And those whose hearts are dry as summer dust,
Burn to the socket!' "
—Shelley's Preface.

The lines of verse quoted by Shelley are from Wordsworth's *The Excursion*, 1, 500-02 (p. 301). With respect to style and love of nature, *Alastor* should be compared with Wordsworth's *Lines Composed a Few Miles above Tintern Abbey* (p. 259).

Alastor was written on Shelley's return from a trip up the Thames. Mrs. Shelley says in her note on the poem: "He spent his days under the oak-shades of Windsor Great Park; and the magnificent woodland was a fitting study to inspire the various descriptions of forest-scenery we find in the poem. "None of Shelley's poems is more characteristic than this. The solemn spirit that reigns throughout, the worship of the majesty of nature, the broodings of a poet's heart in solitude—the mingling of the exulting joy which the various aspects of the visible universe inspires with the sad and struggling pangs which human passion imparts—give a touching interest to the whole. The death which he had often contemplated during the last months as certain and near he here represented in such colors as had, in his lonely musings, soothed his soul to peace. The versification sustains the solemn spirit which breathes throughout: it is peculiarly melodious. The poem ought rather to be considered didactic than narrative: it was the outpouring of his own emotions, embodied in the purest form he could conceive, painted in the ideal hues which his brilliant imagination inspired, and softened by the recent anticipation of death."

662. 101. *Bloodless food.*—Shelley himself favored a vegetable diet. See *Queen Mab*, 211-12 (p. 659) and note (p. 1338).

670. HYMN TO INTELLECTUAL BEAUTY

Mrs. Shelley states in a note that this poem was conceived during Shelley's voyage around Lake Geneva, in Switzerland, with Lord Byron. Shelley's idea of the Eternal Beauty is borrowed from Plato's *The Symposium*, 211-12. Cf. the following passage as translated by Shelley (*Prose Works*, ed. Forman, Vol. 3, 219-222): "He who has been disciplined to this point in love, by contemplating beautiful objects gradually, and in their order, now arriving at the end of all that concerns love, on a sudden beholds a beauty wonderful in its nature. . . . It is eternal, unproduced, indestructible; neither subject to increase nor decay; not, like other things, partly beautiful and partly deformed; not at one time beautiful and at another time not; not beautiful in relation to one thing and deformed in relation to another; not here beautiful and there deformed; not beautiful in the estimation of one person and deformed in that of another; nor can this supreme beauty be figured to the imagination, like a beautiful face or beautiful hands or any portion of the body, nor like any discourse nor any science. Nor does it subsist in any other that lives or is, either in earth, or in heaven, or in any other place; but it is eternally uniform and consistent, and monoeidic with itself. All other things are beautiful through a participation of it, with this one condition, that, although they are subject to production and decay, it never becomes more or less, or endures any change. When any one, ascending from the correct system of love, begins to contemplate this supreme beauty, he already touches the consummation of his labor. For such as discipline themselves upon this system, or are conducted by another beginning to ascend through these transitory objects which are beautiful, toward that which is beauty itself, proceeding as on steps from the love of one form to that of two, and from that of two, to that of all forms which are beautiful; and from beautiful forms to beautiful habits and institutions, and from institutions to beautiful doctrines; until, from the meditation of many doctrines, they arrive at that which is nothing else than the doctrine of supreme beauty itself, in the knowledge and contemplation of which at length they repose. Such a life as this . . . spent in the contemplation of the beautiful, is the life for men to live; which if you chance ever to experience you will esteem far beyond gold and rich garments and even those lovely persons whom you and many others now gaze on with astonishment, and are prepared neither to eat nor drink so that you may behold and live forever with these objects of your love! What then shall we imagine to be the aspect of the supreme beauty itself, simple, pure, uncontaminated with the intermixture of human flesh and colors, and all other idle and unreal shapes attendant on mortality; the divine, the original, the supreme, the monoeidic beautiful itself? What must be the life of him who dwells with and gazes on that which it becomes us all to seek? Think you not that to him alone is accorded the prerogative of bringing forth, not images and shadows of virtue, for he is in contact not with a shadow but with reality, with virtue itself, in the production and nourishment of which he becomes dear to the gods, and, if such a privilege is conceded to any human being, himself immortal."

672.   MONT BLANC

Mrs. Shelley states that this poem was inspired by a view of Mont Blanc (the highest peak of the Alps) and its surrounding peaks and valleys as Shelley lingered on the Bridge of Arve on his way through the Valley of Chamouni. Shelley says, "It was composed under the immediate impression of the deep and powerful feelings excited by the objects which it attempts to describe; and, as an undisciplined overflowing of the soul, rests its claim to approbation on an attempt to imitate the untamable wildness and inaccessible solemnity from which those feelings sprang."—Quoted in Mrs. Shelley's note.

Cf. Coleridge's *Hymn before Sunrise in the Vale of Chamouni* (p. 388).

674. DEDICATION TO THE REVOLT OF ISLAM

The Revolt of Islam, entitled in an earlier version *Laon and Cythna*, is a social-political poem embodying opinions similar to those expressed by Shelley in *Queen Mab*. See note on *Queen Mab* (p. 1337).

676.   OZYMANDIAS

The statue of the Egyptian king Ozymandias was reputed, according to the Greek historian Diodorus of Sicily (1st century B. C.), to be the largest in Egypt. It bore the following inscription: "I am Ozymandias, king of kings; if any one wishes to know what I am and where I lie, let him surpass me in some of my exploits." See Diodorus's *Bibliotheca Historica* (Lipsiæ, 1853), I, 47.

677.   ON A FADED VIOLET

This poem was sent in a letter to Miss Sophia Stacey, dated March 7, 1820, with the following comment: "I promised you what I cannot perform: a song on singing:—

there are only two subjects remaining. I have a few old stanzas on one which, though simple and rude, look as if they were dictated by the heart.—And so—if you tell no one *whose* they are, you are welcome to them. Pardon these dull verses from one who is dull—but who is not the less, ever yours, P. B. S."

LINES WRITTEN AMONG THE EUGANEAN HILLS

Shelley states in the Preface that this poem "was written after a day's excursion among those lovely mountains which surround what was once the retreat, and where is now the sepulchre, of Petrarch. If any one is inclined to condemn the insertion of the introductory lines, which image forth the sudden relief of a state of deep despondency by the radiant visions disclosed by the sudden burst of an Italian sunrise in autumn, on the highest peak of those delightful mountains, I can only offer as my excuse that they were not erased at the request of a dear friend, with whom added years of intercourse only add to my apprehension of its value, and who would have had more right than any one to complain, that she has not been able to extinguish in me the very power of delineating sadness."

The experience described here occurred during a visit to Byron, who is praised in lines 167-205. The "dear friend" was Mary Shelley. The Shelleys had recently lost a child.

The Euganean Hills are a chain of volcanic hills in northeastern Italy, not far from Padua, where Petrarch (1304-74), the great Italian poet, once lived.

680.   STANZAS WRITTEN IN DEJECTION, NEAR NAPLES

"At this time, Shelley suffered greatly in health. He put himself under the care of a medical man, who promised great things, and made him endure severe bodily pain, without any good results. Constant and poignant physical suffering exhausted him; and though he preserved the appearance of cheerfulness, and often greatly enjoyed our wanderings in the environs of Naples, and our excursions on its sunny sea, yet many hours were passed when his thoughts, shadowed by illness, became gloomy,—and then he escaped to solitude, and in verses, which he hid from fear of wounding me, poured forth morbid but too natural bursts of discontent and sadness. One looks back with unspeakable regret and gnawing remorse to such periods; fancying that, had one been more alive to the nature of his feelings, and more attentive to soothe them, such would not have existed. And yet, enjoying as he appeared to do every sight or influence of earth or sky, it was difficult to imagine that any melancholy he showed was aught but the effect of the constant pain to which he was a martyr.

"We lived in utter solitude. And such is often not the nurse of cheerfulness; for then, at least with those who have been exposed to adversity, the mind broods over its sorrows too intently; while the society of the enlightened, the witty, and the wise, enables us to forget ourselves by making us the sharers of the thoughts of others, which is a portion of the philosophy of happiness. Shelley never liked society in numbers,—it harassed and wearied him; but neither did he like loneliness, and usually, when alone, sheltered himself against memory and reflection in a book. But, with one or two whom he loved, he gave way to wild and joyous spirits, or in more serious conversation expounded his opinions with vivacity and eloquence."—Mrs. Shelley's note.

681. LINES WRITTEN DURING THE
CASTLEREAGH ADMINISTRATION

Robert Stewart (1769-1822), Viscount Castlereagh, and Earl of Londonderry (1796), had been Secretary for Ireland and Secretary of War before he was appointed Foreign Secretary in 1812. At the time of the Irish rebellion in 1798, he was charged with encouraging inhuman punishments of the rebels; and during his whole administration he was noted for his contempt for all persons who did not belong to the aristocracy. In 1822 he committed suicide in a fit of insanity.

THE MASK OF ANARCHY

"Though Shelley's first eager desire to excite his countrymen to resist openly the oppression existent during 'the good old times' had faded with early youth, still his warmest sympathies were for the people. He was a republican, and loved a democracy. He looked on all human beings as inheriting an equal right to possess the dearest privileges of our nature; the necessaries of life when fairly earned by labor, and intellectual instruction. His hatred of any despotism that looked upon the people as not to be consulted, or protected from want and ignorance, was intense. He was residing near Leghorn, at Villa Valsovano, writing *The Cenci,* when the news of the Manchester Massacre reached us; it aroused in him violent emotions of indignation and compassion. The great truth that the many, if accordant and resolute, could

control the few, as was shown some years after, made him long to teach his injured countrymen how to resist. Inspired by these feelings, he wrote *The Mask of Anarchy,* which he sent to his friend Leigh Hunt, to be inserted in *The Examiner,* of which he was then the Editor.

" 'I did not insert it,' Leigh Hunt writes in his valuable and interesting preface to this poem, when he printed it in 1832, 'because I thought that the public at large had not become sufficiently discerning to do justice to the sincerity and kind-heartedness of the spirit that walked in this flaming robe of verse.' Days of outrage have passed away, and with them the exasperation that would cause such an appeal to the many to be injurious. Without being aware of them, they at one time acted on his suggestions, and gained the day. But they rose when human life was respected by the Minister in power; such was not the case during the Administration which excited Shelley's abhorrence.

"The poem was written for the people, and is therefore in a more popular tone than usual: portions strike as abrupt and unpolished, but many stanzas are all his own. I heard him repeat, and admired, those beginning

'My Father Time is old and gray,'

before I knew to what poem they were to belong. But the most touching passage is that which describes the blessed effects of liberty; it might make a patriot of any man whose heart was not wholly closed against his humbler fellow-creatures."—Mrs. Shelley's note.

The mask described in the poem is simply a procession with masks and disguises.

685. SONG TO THE MEN OF ENGLAND

This and the following poem, *England in 1819,* were inspired by Shelley's interest in the Manchester Massacre. See *The Mask of Anarchy* and note, above.

ENGLAND IN 1819

See note on preceding poem.

686. ODE TO THE WEST WIND

"This poem was conceived and chiefly written in a wood that skirts the Arno, near Florence, and on a day when that tempestuous wind, whose temperature is at once mild and animating, was collecting the vapors which pour down the autumnal rains. They began, as I foresaw, at sunset with a violent tempest of hail and rain, attended by that magnificent thunder and lightning peculiar to the Cisalpine regions."—Shelley's note.

9. *Sister of the Spring.*—The south wind.

38-42. "The phenomenon alluded to at the conclusion of the third stanza is well known to naturalists. The vegetation at the bottom of the sea, of rivers, and of lakes, sympathizes with that of the land in the change of seasons, and is consequently influenced by the winds which announce it."—Shelley's note.

Note the careful structure of this poem.

688.   PROMETHEUS UNBOUND

"*Prometheus Unbound* best combines the various elements of Shelley's genius in their most complete expression, and unites harmoniously his lyrically creative power of imagination and his 'passion for reforming the world.' It is the fruit of an outburst of poetic energy under the double stimulus of his enthusiastic Greek studies, begun under Peacock's influence, and of his delight in the beauty of Italy, whither he had removed for health and rest. It marks his full mastery of his powers. It is, not less than *Queen Mab* and *The Revolt of Islam,* a poem of the moral perfection of man; and, not less than *Alastor* and *Epipsychidion,* a poem of spiritual ideality. He was himself in love with it: 'a poem of a higher character than anything I have yet attempted and perhaps less an imitation of anything that has gone before it,' he writes to Ollier; and again, 'a poem in my best style, whatever that may amount to, . . . the most perfect of my productions,' and 'the best thing I ever wrote.' "—Woodberry, in prefatory note to the poem, in his edition of Shelley's *Complete Poetical Works* (Cambridge ed., 1901).

Shelley's Preface

"The Greek tragic writers, in selecting as their subject any portion of their national history or mythology, employed in their treatment of it a certain arbitrary discretion. They by no means conceived themselves bound to adhere to the common interpretation or to imitate in story as in title their rivals and predecessors. Such a system would have amounted to a resignation of those claims to a preference over their competitors which incited the composition. The Agamemnonian story was exhibited on the Athenian theatre with as many variations as dramas.

"I have presumed to employ a similar license. The *Prometheus Unbound* of Æschylus supposed the reconciliation of Jupiter with his victim as the price of the disclosure of the danger threatened to his empire by the consummation of his marriage with Thetis. Thetis, according to this view of the subject, was given in marriage to Peleus, and Prometheus, by the permission of Jupiter, delivered from his captivity by Hercules. Had I framed my story on this model, I should have done no more than have attempted to restore the lost drama of Æschylus; an ambition which, if my preference to this mode of treating the subject had incited me to cherish, the recollection of the high comparison such an attempt would challenge might well abate. But, in truth, I was averse from a catastrophe so feeble as that of reconciling the champion with the oppressor of mankind. The moral interest of the fable, which is so powerfully sustained by the sufferings and endurance of Prometheus, would be annihilated if we could conceive of him as unsaying his high language and quailing before his successful and perfidious adversary. The only imaginary being resembling in any degree Prometheus, is Satan; and Prometheus is, in my judgment, a more poetical character than Satan, because, in addition to courage, and majesty, and firm and patient opposition to omnipotent force, he is susceptible of being described as exempt from the taints of ambition, envy, revenge, and a desire for personal aggrandizement, which, in the hero of *Paradise Lost,* interfere with the interest. The character of Satan engenders in the mind a pernicious casuistry which leads us to weigh his faults with his wrongs, and to excuse the former because the latter exceed all measure. In the minds of those who consider that magnificent fiction with a religious feeling it engenders something worse. But Prometheus is, as it were, the type of the highest perfection of moral and intellectual nature, impelled by the purest and the truest motives to the best and noblest ends.

"This poem was chiefly written upon the mountainous ruins of the Baths of Caracalla, among the flowery glades, and thickets of odoriferous blossoming trees, which are extended in ever winding labyrinths upon its immense platforms and dizzy arches suspended in the air. The bright blue sky of Rome, and the effect of the vigorous awakening spring in that divinest climate, and the new life with which it drenches the spirits even to intoxication, were the inspiration of this drama.

"The imagery which I have employed will be found, in many instances, to have been drawn from the operations of the human mind, or from those external actions by which they are expressed. This is unusual in modern poetry, although Dante and Shakespeare are full of instances of the same kind: Dante indeed more than any other poet, and with greater success. But the Greek poets, as writers to whom no resource of awakening the sympathy of their contemporaries was unknown, were in the habitual use of this power; and it is the study of their works (since a higher merit would probably be denied me) to which I am willing that my readers should impute this singularity.

"One word is due in candor to the degree in which the study of contemporary writings may have tinged my composition, for such has been a topic of censure with regard to poems far more popular, and indeed more deservedly popular, than mine. It is impossible that any one who inhabits the same age with such writers as those who stand in the foremost ranks of our own, can conscientiously assure himself that his language and tone of thought may not have been modified by the study of the productions of those extraordinary intellects. It is true that, not the spirit of their genius, but the forms in which it has manifested itself, are due less to the peculiarities of their own minds than to the peculiarity of the moral and intellectual condition of the minds among which they have been produced. Thus a number of writers possess the form, whilst they want the spirit of those whom, it is alleged, they imitate; because the former is the endowment of the age in which they live, and the latter must be the uncommunicated lightning of their own mind.

"The peculiar style of intense and comprehensive imagery which distinguishes the modern literature of England, has not been, as a general power, the product of the imitation of any particular writer. The mass of capabilities remains at every period materially the same; the circumstances which awaken it to action perpetually change. If England were divided into forty republics, each equal in population and extent to Athens, there is no reason to suppose but that, under institutions not more perfect than those of Athens, each would produce philosophers and poets equal to those who (if we except Shakespeare) have never been surpassed. We owe the great writers of the golden age of our literature to that fervid awakening of the public mind which shook to dust the oldest and most oppressive form of the Christian religion. We owe Milton to the progress and development of the same spirit: the sacred Milton was, let it ever be remembered, a republican, and a bold inquirer into morals and religion. The great writers of our own age are, we have reason to suppose, the companions and forerunners of some unimagined change in our social condition or the opinions which cement it. The cloud of mind is discharging its collected lightning, and the equilibrium between institutions and opinions is now restoring, or is about to be restored.

"As to imitation, poetry is a mimetic art. It creates, but it creates by combination and representation. Poetical abstractions are beautiful and new, not because the portions of which they are composed had no previous existence in the mind of man or in nature, but because the whole produced by their combination has some intelligible and beautiful analogy with those sources of emotion and thought, and with the contemporary condition of them: one great poet is a masterpiece of nature which another not only ought to study but must study. He might as wisely and as easily determine that his mind should no longer be the mirror of all that is lovely in the visible universe, as exclude from his contemplation the beautiful which exists in the writings of a great contemporary. The pretence of doing it would be a presumption in any but the greatest; the effect, even in him, would be strained, unnatural, and ineffectual. A poet is the combined product of such internal powers as modify the nature of others; and of such external influences as excite and sustain these powers; he is not one, but both. Every man's mind is, in this respect, modified by all the objects of nature and art; by every word and every suggestion which he ever admitted to act upon his consciousness; it is the mirror upon which all forms are reflected, and in which they compose one form. Poets, not otherwise than philosophers, painters, sculptors, and musicians, are, in one sense, the creators, and, in another, the creations, of their age. From this subjection the loftiest do not escape. There is a similarity between Homer and Hesiod, between Æschylus and Euripides, between Virgil and Horace, between Dante and Petrarch, between Shakespeare and Fletcher, between Dryden and Pope; each has a generic resemblance under which their specific distinctions are arranged. If this similarity be the result of imitation, I am willing to confess that I have imitated.

"Let this opportunity be conceded to me of acknowledging that I have, what a Scotch philosopher characteristically terms, 'a passion for reforming the world': what passion incited him to write and publish his book, he omits to explain. For my part I had rather be damned with Plato and Lord Bacon, than go to Heaven with Paley and Malthus.[1] But it is a mistake to suppose that I dedicate my poetical compositions solely to the direct enforcement of reform, or that I consider them in any degree as containing a reasoned system on the theory of human life. Didactic poetry is my abhorrence; nothing can be equally well expressed in prose that is not tedious and supererogatory in verse. My purpose has hitherto been simply to familiarize the highly refined imagination of the more select classes of poetical readers with beautiful idealisms of moral excellence; aware that until the mind can love, and admire, and trust, and hope, and endure, reasoned principles of moral conduct are seeds cast upon the highway of life which the unconscious passenger tramples into dust, although they would bear the harvest of his happiness. Should I live to accomplish what I purpose, that is, produce a systematical history of what appear to me to be the genuine elements of human society, let not the advocates of injustice and superstition flatter themselves that I should take Æschylus rather than Plato as my model.

"The having spoken of myself with unaffected freedom will need little apology with the candid, and let the uncandid consider that they injure me less than their own hearts and minds by misrepresentation. Whatever talents a person may possess to amuse and instruct others, be they ever so inconsiderable, he is yet bound to exert them: if his attempt be ineffectual, let the punishment of an unaccomplished purpose have been sufficient; let none trouble themselves to heap the dust of oblivion upon his efforts; the pile they raise will betray his grave which might otherwise have been unknown."

From *Mrs. Shelley's Note*

"The first aspect of Italy enchanted Shelley; it seemed a garden of delight placed beneath a clearer and brighter heaven than any he had lived under before. He wrote long

---

[1] William Paley (1743-1805) was an English orthodox theologian and philosopher, who preached the necessity of religion on the basis of logic. T. R. Malthus (1766-1834) was an English political economist, who advanced the idea that vice and crime are necessary checks upon population. Essentially, Shelley says that he would rather be damned with the heretical reformers than go to heaven with the orthodox.

descriptive letters during the first year of his residence in Italy, which, as compositions, are the most beautiful in the world, and show how truly he appreciated and studied the wonders of nature and art in that divine land.

"The poetical spirit within him speedily revived with all the power and with more than all the beauty of his first attempts. He meditated three subjects as the groundwork for lyrical dramas. One was the story of Tasso; of this a slight fragment of a song of Tasso remains. The other was one founded on the *Book of Job*, which he never abandoned in idea, but of which no trace remains among his papers. The third was the *Prometheus Unbound*. The Greek tragedians were now his most familiar companions in his wanderings, and the sublime majesty of Æschylus filled him with wonder and delight. The father of Greek tragedy does not possess the pathos of Sophocles, nor the variety and tenderness of Euripides; the interest on which he founds his dramas is often elevated above human vicissitudes into the mighty passions and throes of gods and demi-gods; such fascinated the abstract imagination of Shelley.

. . . .

"At first he completed the drama in three acts. It was not till several months after, when at Florence, that he conceived that a fourth act, a sort of hymn of rejoicing in the fulfillment of the prophecies with regard to Prometheus, ought to be added to complete the composition.

"The prominent feature of Shelley's theory of the destiny of the human species was that evil is not inherent in the system of the creation, but an accident that might be expelled. This also forms a portion of Christianity: God made earth and man perfect, till he, by his fall,

'Brought death into the world and all
    our woe.'   [*Paradise Lost*, 1, 3].

Shelley believed that mankind had only to will that there should be no evil, and there would be none. It is not my part in these notes to notice the arguments that have been urged against this opinion, but to mention the fact that he entertained it, and was indeed attached to it with fervent enthusiasm. That man could be so perfectionized as to be able to expel evil from his own nature, and from the greater part of the creation, was the cardinal point of his system. And the subject he loved best to dwell on was the image of One warring with the Evil Principle, oppressed not only by it, but by all—even the good, who were deluded into considering evil a necessary portion of humanity; a victim full of fortitude and hope and the spirit of triumph emanating from a reliance in the ultimate omnipotence of Good. Such he had depicted in his last poem [*The Revolt of Islam*] when he made Laon the enemy and the victim of tyrants. He now took a more idealized image of the same subject. He followed certain classical authorities in figuring Saturn as the good principle, Jupiter the usurping evil one, and Prometheus as the regenerator, who, unable to bring mankind back to primitive innocence, used knowledge as a weapon to defeat evil, by leading mankind, beyond the state wherein they are sinless through ignorance, to that in which they are virtuous through wisdom. Jupiter punished the temerity of the Titan by chaining him to a rock of Caucasus, and causing a vulture to devour his still-renewed heart. There was a prophecy afloat in heaven portending the fall of Jove, the secret of averting which was known only to Prometheus; and the god offered freedom from torture on condition of its being communicated to him. According to the mythological story, this referred to the offspring of Thetis, who was destined to be greater than his father. Prometheus at last bought pardon for his crime of enriching mankind with his gifts, by revealing the prophecy. Hercules killed the vulture, and set him free; and Thetis was married to Peleus, the father of Achilles.

"Shelley adapted the catastrophe of this story to his peculiar views. The son greater than his father, born of the nuptials of Jupiter and Thetis, was to dethrone Evil, and bring back a happier reign than that of Saturn. Prometheus defies the power of his enemy, and endures centuries of torture; till the hour arrives when Jove, blind to the real event, but darkly guessing that some great good to himself will flow, espouses Thetis. At the moment, the Primal Power of the world drives him from his usurped throne, and Strength, in the person of Hercules, liberates Humanity, typified in Prometheus, from the tortures generated by evil done or suffered. Asia, one of the Oceanides, is the wife of Prometheus—she was, according to other mythological interpretations, the same as Venus and Nature. When the benefactor of mankind is liberated, Nature resumes the beauty of her prime, and is united to her husband, the emblem of the human race, in perfect and happy union. In the Fourth Act, the poet gives further scope to his imagination, and idealizes the forms of creation—such as we know them, instead of such as they appeared to the Greeks. Maternal Earth, the mighty parent, is superseded by the Spirit of the Earth, the guide of our planet through the realms of sky; while his fair and weaker companion and attendant, the Spirit of the Moon, receives bliss from the annihilation of Evil in the superior sphere.

"Shelley develops, more particularly in the lyrics of this drama, his abstruse and imaginative theories with regard to the Creation. It requires a mind as subtle and penetrating as his own to understand the mystic meanings scattered throughout the poem. They elude the ordinary reader by their abstraction and delicacy of distinction, but they are far from vague. It was his design to write prose metaphysical essays on the nature of man, which would have served to explain much of what is obscure in his poetry; a few scattered fragments of observations and remarks alone remain. He considered these philosophical views of mind and nature to be instinct with the intensest spirit of poetry.

"More popular poets clothe the ideal with familiar and sensible imagery. Shelley loved to idealize the real—to gift the mechanism of the material universe with a soul and a voice, and to bestow such also on the most delicate and abstract emotions and thoughts of the mind. . . .

"Through the whole poem there reigns a sort of calm and holy spirit of love; it soothes the tortured, and is hope to the expectant, till the prophecy is fulfilled, and love, untainted by any evil, becomes the law of the world. . . .

"The charm of the Roman climate helped to clothe his thoughts in greater beauty than they had ever worn before. And, as he wandered among the ruins made one with nature in their decay, or gazed on the Praxitelean shapes that throng the Vatican, the Capitol, and the palaces of Rome, his soul imbibed forms of loveliness which became a portion of itself. There are many passages in the *Prometheus* which show the intense delight he received from such studies, and give back the impression with a beauty of poetical description peculiarly his own."

For the general form of the drama, including the choruses, for the situation and scenery of Act I, and for a few scattered phrases and passages, Shelley is indebted to Æschylus. There are echoes also from Milton, Shakespeare, and Goethe.

The characters in *Prometheus Unbound* are impersonations of abstract qualities—those which were the occasion of suffering and evil in society and those which through the power of the spirit of democracy were to usher in the Golden Age. Prometheus represents humanity in general. Jupiter represents evil and unrighteous power; he stands for civil and religious institutions, all of which interfere with progress. Thetis, the wife of Jupiter, is arrogance, display, and false ideal. Demogorgon, the child of Jupiter and Thetis, is necessity, fate, wisdom; the force that presides over the destinies of the universe. Asia is the spirit of ideal beauty and divine love; Panthea, the spirit of faith; Ione, the spirit of hope. Hercules is strength. The Furies are the various causes of pain and suffering among men. The Spirits sent by the Earth to comfort Prometheus are embodiments of the happiness which comes from good impulses and good actions. The scenery also is allegorical. In the intricacies of the symbolism of the drama, however, one should not lose sight of its lyric greatness. Shelley called it a lyrical drama, and as such it deals with thought and emotion rather than with action.

Shelley's approach to the world-problem as expressed in this drama should be compared with Byron's as expressed in *Manfred* (pp. 575ff).

696. 546-66; 586-631. These lines contain a vision of the crucifixion of Christ and of the development of Christianity. Lines 567-77, 648-54 contain a vision of the French Revolution. These events, good in themselves, are thought of as resulting in evil.

697. 672-751. These spirits of consolation suggest that evil is merely the occasion for greater good.

698. 737-51. This lyric has been regarded as the most complete expression of poetic idealism.

702. Scene II.—The forest scenery represents the ordinary experiences of human life, as concerns physical senses, emotions, and intellectual impulses.

704. Scene III.—The mountain scenery represents elevated heights of thought.

708. 72-81. Cf. Shelley's fragment entitled *To One Singing*, written in 1817:

My spirit like a charmèd bark doth swim
  Upon the liquid waves of thy sweet singing,
Far, far away into the regions dim

Of rapture—as a boat, with swift sails winging
  Its way adown some many-winding river,

Speeds through dark forests o'er the waters
  swinging.

710. Scene II.—Ocean and Apollo have no allegorical significance; they are simply classical figures.

716. Act IV.—This is simply a concluding chorus of rejoicing over the fulfillment of the prophecies in the other acts. It was an afterthought; see Mrs. Shelley's note, p. 1344.

719. 202. *Two visions* . . . The strange images in the next 116 lines are among the passages which may reflect Shelley's knowledge of science, especially electricity and meteorology. See Carl Grabo, *A Newton Among Poets;* also his study entitled *Prometheus Unbound*.

725. THE SENSITIVE PLANT

"This is primarily a descriptive poem. The poet, with evident delight and exquisite power, produces his picture of the garden and its mistress, and enters into and sympathizes with the imagined life of the flowers. Secondarily, this concrete picture is symbolic of other things. The Sensitive Plant, with its isolation, its intensity, its yearnings, is Shelley himself. The lady of the garden is the mystical Spirit of Beauty 'whose smile kindles the universe.' The change which comes over the garden and the Sensitive Plant at the approach of winter typifies the evil and ugly side of things—death and the other ills which quench the joy of life. The Conclusion (as the close of *Adonais*) suggests that this change is transitory or unreal, that the Spirit of Beauty abides, and that the soul of man does not altogether pass away at death, but is united to the *one* spirit which is eternal."— W. J. Alexander, in *Select Poems of Shelley* (Athenæum Press ed., 1898).

729. Conclusion.—Cf. these stanzas with *Adonais*, 39 (p. 761) and with the quotation from Plato's *Phædo*, p. 1290.

THE CLOUD

"There are others, such as the *Ode to the Skylark* and *The Cloud*, which in the opinion of many critics bear a purer poetical stamp than any other of his productions. They were written as his mind prompted, listening to the caroling of the bird, aloft in the azure sky of Italy, or marking the cloud as it sped across the heavens, while he floated in his boat on the Thames."—Mrs. Shelley, in Preface to Shelley's *Poetical Works* (1839).

730. TO A SKYLARK

"It was on a beautiful summer evening, while wandering among the lanes, whose myrtle hedges were the bowers of the butterflies, that we heard the caroling of the skylark, which inspired one of the most beautiful of his poems."—Mrs. Shelley's note.

See note on preceding poem.

Cf. this poem with Wordsworth's poems on the same subject, pp. 323 and 338, and with Hogg's poem, p. 503.

732. ARETHUSA

This poem was written to be inserted in *Proserpine*, a drama by Shelley's friend, Edward Williams. Arethusa was a fountain in the island of Ortygia, near Syracuse, in Sicily. Alpheus is a river in the Peloponnesus which in part of its course flows underground. According to the legend, the wood nymph Arethusa, pursued by her lover Alpheus, the river god, was changed by Diana into a stream which ran under the sea and rose again as the fountain of Arethusa.

733. HYMN OF APOLLO

This and the next poem, *Hymn of Pan*, were written to be inserted in *Midas*, a projected drama by Shelley's friend, Edward Williams. Apollo and Pan were represented as contending before Tmolus, the mountain god, for a prize in music. Apollo was the sun god.

HYMN OF PAN

See note on preceding poem. Pan was the god of flocks and shepherds. He invented the shepherd's flute, which he made out of a reed. See Mrs. Browning's poem *A Musical Instrument*.

736. THE WITCH OF ATLAS

In her notes, Mrs. Shelley says of this poem and its author: "This poem is peculiarly characteristic of his tastes—wildly fanciful, full of brilliant imagery, and discarding human interest and passion, to revel in the fantastic ideas that his imagination suggested.

"The surpassing excellence of *The Cenci* had made me greatly desire that Shelley should increase his popularity, by adopting subjects that would more suit the popular taste than a poem conceived in the abstract and dreamy spirit of *The Witch of Atlas*. It was not only that I wished him to acquire popularity as redounding to his fame; but I believed that he would obtain a greater mastery over his own powers, and greater happiness in his mind, if public applause crowned his endeavors. The few stanzas that precede the poem were addressed to me on my representing these ideas to him. Even now I believe that I was in the right. Shel-

ley did not expect sympathy and approbation from the public; but the want of it took away a portion of the ardor that ought to have sustained him while writing. He was thrown on his own resources and on the inspiration of his own soul, and wrote because his mind overflowed, without the hope of being appreciated. I had not the most distant wish that he should truckle in opinion, or submit his lofty aspirations for the human race to the low ambition and pride of the many, but I felt sure that if his poems were more addressed to the common feelings of men, his proper rank among the writers of the day would be acknowledged; and that popularity as a poet would enable his countrymen to do justice to his character and virtues; which, in those days, it was the mode to attack with the most flagitious calumnies and insulting abuse. That he felt these things deeply cannot be doubted, though he armed himself with the consciousness of acting from a lofty and heroic sense of right. The truth burst from his heart sometimes in solitude, and he would write a few unfinished verses that showed that he felt the sting. . . .

"I believed that all this morbid feeling would vanish, if the chord of sympathy between him and his countrymen were touched. But my persuasions were vain; the mind could not be bent from its natural inclination. Shelley shrunk instinctively from portraying human passion, with its mixture of good and evil, of disappointment and disquiet. Such opened again the wounds of his own heart, and he loved to shelter himself rather in the airiest flights of fancy, forgetting love and hate and regret and lost hope, in such imaginations as borrowed their hues from sunrise or sunset, from the yellow moonshine or paly twilight, from the aspect of the far ocean or the shadows of the woods; which celebrated the singing of the winds among the pines, the flow of a murmuring stream, and the thousand harmonious sounds which nature creates in her solitudes. These are the materials which form *The Witch of Atlas*; it is a brilliant congregation of ideas, such as his senses gathered, and his fancy colored, during his rambles in the sunny land he so much loved."

Atlas is the name of a mountain system in northwestern Africa.

746. EPIPSYCHIDION

The meaning of the title of this poem, according to Stopford Brooke (*Publications of the Shelley Society*, 1887), is "this soul out of my soul" (l. 238). Forman (*Complete*

Poetical Works) sees no meaning in it beyond "a little poem about the soul." The "noble and unfortunate lady" who inspired the poem was Teresa Emilia Viviani, the beautiful and sentimental daughter of an Italian nobleman of Pisa. She had been placed by her family in the neighboring Convent of St. Anna, where Shelley met her in 1820, became interested in her, and idealized her as the embodiment of perfect love and beauty of which he was ever in search. Dowden says of her (*Life of Shelley*, 2, 378): "Emilia, beautiful, spiritual, sorrowing, became for him a type and symbol of all that is most radiant and divine in nature, all that is most remote and unattainable, yet ever to be pursued—the ideal of beauty, truth, and love. She was at once a breathing and living woman, young, lovely, ardent, afflicted, and the avatar of the Ideal." Shelley's interest in her, however, soon declined into that of mere sympathy.

In a letter to his friend Gisborne, dated Oct. 22, 1821, Shelley says of the poem: "The *Epipsychidion* is a mystery; as to real flesh and blood, you know that I do not deal in those articles; you might as well go to a gin-shop for a leg of mutton, as expect anything human or earthly from me." On June 18, 1822, he again wrote Gisborne: "The *Epipsychidion* I cannot look at; the person whom it celebrates was a cloud instead of a Juno, and poor Ixion[1] starts from the centaur that was the offspring of his own embrace. If you are curious, however, to hear what I am and have been, it will tell you something thereof. It is an idealized history of my life and feelings. I think one is always in love with something or other; the error, and I confess it is not easy for spirits cased in flesh and blood to avoid it, consists in seeking in a mortal image the likeness of what is, perhaps, eternal."

The poem represents the pursuit of an ideal, the nature of which may be gained from Shelley's prose fragment *On Love*, as follows:

"*Thou* demandest what is love? It is that powerful attraction towards all that we conceive, or fear or hope beyond ourselves, when we find within our own thoughts the chasm of an insufficient void, and seek to awaken in all things that are, a community with what we experience within ourselves. If we reason, we would be understood; if we imagine, we would that the airy children of our brain were born anew within another's; if we feel, we would that another's nerves should vibrate to our own, that the beams of their eyes

should kindle at once and mix and melt into our own, that lips of motionless ice should not reply to lips quivering and burning with the heart's best blood. This is love. This is the bond and the sanction which connects not only man with man, but with everything which exists. We are born into the world, and there is something within us which, from the instant that we live, more and more thirsts after its likeness. It is probably in correspondence with this law that the infant drains milk from the bosom of its mother; this propensity develops itself with the development of our nature. We dimly see within our intellectual nature a miniature as it were of our entire self, yet deprived of all that we condemn or despise; the ideal prototype of everything excellent or lovely that we are capable of conceiving as belonging to the nature of man. Not only the portrait of our external being, but an assemblage of the minutest particles of which our nature is composed; a mirror whose surface reflects only the forms of purity and brightness; a soul within our soul that describes a circle around its proper paradise, which pain, and sorrow, and evil dare not overleap. To this we eagerly refer all sensations, thirsting that they should resemble or correspond with it. The discovery of its anti-type; the meeting with an understanding capable of clearly estimating our own; an imagination which should enter into and seize upon the subtle and delicate peculiarities which we have delighted to cherish and unfold in secret; with a frame whose nerves, like the chords of two exquisite lyres, strung to the accompaniment of one delightful voice, vibrate with the vibrations of our own; and of a combination of all these in such proportion as the type within demands; this is the invisible and unattainable point to which love tends; and to attain which, it urges forth the powers of man to arrest the faintest shadow of that without the possession of which there is no rest nor respite to the heart over which it rules. Hence in solitude, or in that deserted state when we are surrounded by human beings, and yet they sympathize not with us, we love the flowers, the grass, and the waters and the sky. In the motion of the very leaves of spring in the blue air, there is then found a secret correspondence with our heart. There is eloquence in the tongueless wind, and a melody in the flowing brooks and the rustling of the reeds beside them, which by their inconceivable relation to something within the soul, awaken the spirits to a dance of breathless rapture, and bring tears of mysterious tenderness to the eyes, like the en-

[1] See Glossary.

thusiasm of patriotic success, or the voice of one beloved singing to you alone. Sterne says that if he were in a desert he would love some cypress. So soon as this want or power is dead, man becomes the living sepulchre of himself, and what yet survives is the mere husk of what once he was."

The poem was first published anonymously with Shelley's Advertisement describing the imaginary author.

749. 236. Cf. the prose fragment *On Love,* quoted above.

256-66. No satisfactory identification of the person here described has been made; nor is any needed. The passage describes sensual love.

267-383. Of the many attempts to identify details of this passage with incidents in Shelley's life, the most convincing explanation is found in K. N. Cameron's article in *Pub. Mod. Lang. Assn.,* 63:950-72 (1948).

267. *Mortal forms.* These include several women known by Shelley before he met Mary.

271. *One was true.* Harriet, Shelley's first wife. Lines 272-75 mark the beginning of the breaking up of the marriage of Shelley and Harriet in the spring of 1814.

277. *One stood on my path.* Mary, Shelley's second wife. Shelley first met her in the summer of 1814. She delivered him from his emotional crisis of the preceding months. The Moon (l. 279) is Mary.

750. 308-320. *What storms* . . . These lines refer to several crises in Shelley's life from 1816 to 1820. The first crisis was caused by the suicide of Harriet by drowning in December 1816. She was "The Planet of that hour" (l. 313). A second crisis was the "earthquakes" (l. 317), the result of legal action taken in 1817 which deprived Shelley of his two children, a boy and a girl (l. 303).

311-312. Cameron suggests that the Tempest that harassed the sea of Shelley's life was Eliza Westbrook, Harriet's sister. She would thus be blamed by Shelley for the suicide of Harriet and for the litigation over the two children.

321-322. These lines refer to Shelley's meeting with Emilia Viviani (see l. 344) in December 1820.

751. 368. The Comet, who is to be made the Evening Star, is Claire Clairmont, whom Shelley had previously loved, probably in 1815.

372. *Thine went astray.* A reference to Claire's affair with Byron in 1816.

755. TO EMILIA VIVIANI

Shelley sent this poem to Emilia Viviani in return for a bouquet which he received from her. See note on *Epipsychidion,* above.

756. ADONAIS

The title of this poem is evidently derived from *Adonis,* the name of the beautiful youth who was loved by Venus and who was killed by a wild boar. Shelley's belief that Keats was killed by "savage criticism on his *Endymion*" makes the analogy clear.

Shelley and Keats first met at the house of their friend Leigh Hunt, in 1817, and in 1820 Shelley invited Keats to be his guest at Pisa, Italy; but Keats did not accept the invitation, and they never became intimate. See Keats's letter to Shelley (pp. 891-92). Keats died in Rome on February 23, 1821, and soon afterwards Shelley wrote the poem, to which he later added the following Preface.

"It is my intention to subjoin to the London edition of this poem a criticism upon the claims of its lamented object to be classed among the writers of the highest genius who have adorned our age. My known repugnance to the narrow principles of taste on which several of his earlier compositions were modeled prove at least that I am an impartial judge. I consider the fragment of *Hyperion* as second to nothing that was ever produced by a writer of the same years.

"John Keats died at Rome of a consumption, in his twenty-fourth year, on the [23rd] of [Feb.], 1821; and was buried in the romantic and lonely cemetery of the Protestants in that city, under the pyramid which is the tomb of Cestius, and the massy walls and towers, now mouldering and desolate, which formed the circuit of ancient Rome. The cemetery is an open space among the ruins, covered in winter with violets and daisies. It might make one in love with death, to think that one should be buried in so sweet a place.

"The genius of the lamented person to whose memory I have dedicated these unworthy verses was not less delicate and fragile than it was beautiful; and where cankerworms abound, what wonder if its young flower was blighted in the bud? The savage criticism on his *Endymion,* which appeared in *The Quarterly Review,*[1] produced the most violent effect on his susceptible mind; the agitation thus originated ended in the rupture of a blood-vessel in the lungs; a rapid consumption ensued, and the succeeding acknowledgements from more candid critics of the

---

[1] The criticism of *Endymion* referred to was written by J. W. Croker and published in *The Quarterly Review,* April 1818 (see p. 939). Shelley thought it was written by H. H. Milman (1791-1868), an English clergyman. It was not responsible for the death of Keats. See Colvin's *Life of Keats,* ch. 6, and Rossetti's *Life of Keats,* ch. 5.

true greatness of his powers were ineffectual to heal the wound thus wantonly inflicted.

"It may be well said that these wretched men know not what they do. They scatter their insults and their slanders without heed as to whether the poisoned shaft lights on a heart made callous by many blows or one like Keats's composed of more penetrable stuff.[1] One of their associates is, to my knowledge, a most base and unprincipled calumniator. As to *Endymion*, was it a poem, whatever might be its defects, to be treated contemptuously by those who had celebrated, with various degrees of complacency and panegyric, *Paris*, and *Woman*, and a *Syrian Tale*, and Mrs. Lefanu, and Mr. Barrett, and Mr. Howard Payne, and a long list of the illustrious obscure? Are these the men who in their venal good nature presumed to draw a parallel between the Rev. Mr. Milman and Lord Byron? What gnat did they strain at here, after having swallowed all those camels?[2] Against what woman taken in adultery dares the foremost of these literary prostitutes to cast his opprobrious stone?[3] Miserable man! you, one of the meanest, have wantonly defaced one of the noblest specimens of the workmanship of God. Nor shall it be your excuse, that, murderer as you are, you have spoken daggers, but used none.[4]

"The circumstances of the closing scene of poor Keats's life were not made known to me until the *Elegy* was ready for the press. I am given to understand that the wound which his sensitive spirit had received from the criticism of *Endymion* was exasperated by the bitter sense of unrequited benefits; the poor fellow seems to have been hooted from the stage of life, no less by those on whom he had wasted the promise of his genius, than those on whom he had lavished his fortune and his care. He was accompanied to Rome, and attended in his last illness by Mr. Severn, a young artist of the highest promise, who, I have been informed, 'almost risked his own life, and sacrificed every prospect to unwearied attendance upon his dying friend.' Had I known these circumstances before the completion of my poem, I should have been tempted to add my feeble tribute of applause to the more solid recompense which the virtuous man finds in the recollection of his own

motives. Mr. Severn can dispense with a reward from 'such stuff as dreams are made of.'[1] His conduct is a golden augury of the success of his future career—may the unextinguished Spirit of his illustrious friend animate the creations of his pencil, and plead against Oblivion for his name!"

Adonais is based upon two Greek pastoral elegies of the third cent. B. C.—Bion's *Lament for Adonis* and Moschus's *Epitaph on Bion*. Milton's *Lycidas* also was probably in Shelley's mind, and a number of ideas expressed in the poem go back to Plato. Cf. *Adonais* with the following fragments of Shelley's translation of the two Greek poems referred to:

Fragment of the Elegy on the Death of Adonis

I mourn Adonis dead—loveliest Adonis—
Dead, dead Adonis—and the Loves lament.
Sleep no more, Venus, wrapped in purple woof—
Wake, violet-stolèd queen, and weave the crown
Of Death,—'tis Misery calls,—for he is dead. 5

The lovely one lies wounded in the mountains,
His white thigh struck with the white tooth; he scarce
Yet breathes; and Venus hangs in agony there.
The dark blood wanders o'er his snowy limbs,
His eyes beneath their lids are lustreless. 10
The rose has fled from his wan lips, and there
That kiss is dead, which Venus gathers yet.

A deep, deep wound Adonis * * *
A deeper Venus bears upon her heart.
See, his belovèd dogs are gathering round— 15
The Oread nymphs are weeping—Aphrodite
With hair unbound is wandering through the woods,
'Wildered, ungirt, unsandalled — the thorns pierce
Her hastening feet and drink her sacred blood.
Bitterly screaming out, she is driven on 20
Through the long vales; and her Assyrian boy,
Her love, her husband, calls—the purple blood
From his struck thigh stains her white navel now,
Her bosom, and her neck before like snow.

Alas for Cytherea—the Loves mourn— 25
The lovely, the beloved is gone!—and now
Her sacred beauty vanishes away.
For Venus whilst Adonis lived was fair—
Alas! her loveliness is dead with him.
The oaks and mountains cry, Ai! ai! Adonis! 30

[1] See *Hamlet*, III, 4, 35-36 :—
"And let me wring your heart; for so I shall,
If it be made of penetrable stuff."
[2] See *Matthew*, 23 :24.
[3] See *John*, 8 :3-7.
[4] *Hamlet*, III, 2, 414. Before going to meet his mother Hamlet says, "I will speak daggers to her but use none."

[1] *The Tempest*, IV, 1, 155-56.

The springs their waters change to tears and
    weep—
The flowers are withered up with grief. * * *

Ai! ai!   Adonis is dead
Echo resounds   Adonis dead.
Who will weep not thy dreadful woe, O
    Venus?   35
Soon as she saw and knew the mortal wound
Of her Adonis—saw the life-blood flow
From his fair thigh, now wasting,—wailing
    loud
She clasped him, and cried "Stay, Adonis!
Stay, dearest one. * * *   40

        and mix my lips with thine—
Wake yet a while, Adonis—oh, but once,
That I may kiss thee now for the last time—
But for as long as one short kiss may live—
Oh, let thy breath flow from thy dying soul 45
Even to my mouth and heart, that I may suck
That * * *"

Fragment of the Elegy on the Death of Bion

Ye Dorian woods and waves, lament aloud,—
Augment your tide, O streams, with fruitless
    tears,
For the belovèd Bion is no more.
Let every tender herb and plant and flower,
From each dejected bud and drooping bloom, 5
Shed dews of liquid sorrow, and with breath
Of melancholy sweetness on the wind
Diffuse its languid love; let roses blush,
Anemones grow paler for the loss
Their dells have known; and thou, O
    hyacinth,   10
Utter thy legend now—yet more, dumb flower,
Than "Ah! alas!"—thine is no common grief—
Bion the sweetest singer is no more.

757. 10-11. Cf. Bion's *Lament for Adonis*
(Lang's trans.): "He reclines, the delicate
Adonis, in his raiment of purple, and around
him the Loves are weeping, and groaning
aloud, clipping their locks for Adonis. And
one upon his shafts, another on his bow is
treading, and one hath loosed the sandal of
Adonis, and another hath broken his own
feathered quiver, and one in a golden vessel
bears water, and another laves the wound,
and another from behind him with his wings
is fanning Adonis."

14-17. Cf. Moschus's *Elegy on Bion*
(Lang's trans.): "Ye flowers, now in sad clusters breathe yourselves away. Now redden, ye
roses, in your sorrow, and now wax red, ye
wind-flowers; now, thou hyacinth, whisper
the letters on thee graven, and add a deeper
ai ai to thy petals; he is dead, the beautiful
singer. . . . Ye nightingales that lament

among the thick leaves of the trees, tell ye
to the Sicilian waters of Arethusa the tidings that Bion the herdsman is dead. . . .
And Echo in the rocks laments that thou art
silent, and no more she mimics thy voice.
And in sorrow for thy fall the trees cast
down their fruit, and all the flowers have
faded."

761. 39. Cf. the closing stanzas of *The
Sensitive Plant* (p. 729). See also Plato's
Phædo, 67-68; and *Narcissa*, in Young's *Night
Thoughts* (p. 34).

762. 46, 9. Cf. Plato's epigram on *Aster*,
thus translated by Shelley under the title of
To Stella and applied to Keats:

Thou wert the morning star among the living,
    Ere thy fair light had fled;—
Now, having died, thou art as Hesperus, giving
    New splendor to the dead.

763.   HELLAS

Hellas is a lyrical drama inspired by the
Greek war for independence from the Turks,
fought in 1821. Shelley looked upon this
manifestation of a free spirit as a prophecy
of the dawning Golden Age of love and
freedom. *Life May Change, But It May Fly
Not* occupies lines 34-45 of the drama; *Worlds
on Worlds are Rolling Ever*, lines 197-238;
Darkness has Dawned in the East, lines 1023-
59; *The World's Great Age Begins Anew* is
the closing chorus, lines 1060-1101.

764b. 8. *The Evening land.*—A reference to
America.

765.   THE WORLD'S GREAT AGE
            BEGINS ANEW

At the end of the "great age" of the
ancients, the sun, moon, and planets were
to return to their original positions, and the
history of the world would repeat itself; the
Golden Age would return and be followed by
ages of degradation and evil. Cf. this chorus
with Byron's *The Isles of Greece* (p. 622).

THE EVENING

The Ponte al Mare is the seaward bridge
of Pisa.

766.   REMEMBRANCE

This song was sent by Shelley with the following letter to his friend, Mrs. Williams:
"Dear Jane,—If this melancholy old song suits
any of your tunes, or any that humor of the
moment may dictate, you are welcome to it.
Do not say it is mine to any one, even if you
think so; indeed, it is from the torn leaf of a
book out of date. How are you today, and how

is Williams? Tell him that I dreamed of nothing but sailing and fishing up coral. Your ever affectionate P. B. S."

TO EDWARD WILLIAMS

This poem was inspired by Mary Shelley's jealousy of Jane Williams, the wife of Edward Williams, both intimate friends of the Shelleys. The following letter from Shelley to Williams (Jan. 26, 1822) refers to the poem: "My dear Williams: Looking over the portfolio in which my friend used to keep his verses, and in which those I sent you the other day were found, I have lit upon these; which, as they are too dismal for *me* to keep, I send you. If any of the stanzas should please you, you may read them to Jane, but to no one else. And yet, on second thoughts, I had rather you would not. Yours ever affectionately,   P. B. S."

768.   WITH A GUITAR: TO JANE

Woodberry gives the following note on the poem (Cambridge ed. of Shelley's *Poetical Works*): "The suggestion for the poem is found by Dr. Garnett in the fact that 'the front portion of the guitar is made of Swiss pine.' He continues: 'It is now clear how the poem took shape in Shelley's mind. The actual thought of the imprisonment of the Spirit of Music in the material of the instrument suggested Ariel's penance in the cloven pine; the identification of himself with Ariel and of Jane Williams with Miranda was the easiest of feats to his brilliant imagination; and hence an allegory of unequalled grace and charm, which could never have existed if the instrument had not been partly made of pine wood. The back, it should be added, is of mahogany, the finger board of ebony, and minor portions, chiefly ornamental, of some wood not identified. It was made by Ferdinando Bottari of Pisa in 1816. Having been religiously preserved since Shelley's death, it is in as perfect condition as when made. The strings, it is said, are better than those that are produced now.

" 'This guitar is also in a measure the subject of another of Shelley's most beautiful lyrics, *The Keen Stars Were Twinkling*. In a letter dated June 18, 1822, speaking of his cruises "in the evening wind under the summer moon," he adds, "Jane brings her guitar." There is probably no other relic of a great poet so intimately associated with the arts of poetry and music, or ever will be, unless Milton's organ should turn up at a broker's or some excavating explorer should bring to light the lyre of Sappho.' "

TO JANE

This poem was sent in a letter to Mrs. Jane Williams. See note on preceding poem.

769.   CHARLES THE FIRST

This is an unfinished tragedy on the subject of Charles I, King of England, who was beheaded in 1649. The song given here is found in scene 5, ll. 6-17. It is sung by the court fool.

A DEFENSE OF POETRY

In a letter to Peacock, dated March 21, 1821, Shelley states that this essay was written "as an antidote" to Peacock's *Four Ages of Poetry*. "You will see," he says, "that I have taken a more general view of poetry than you have."

771b. 22-27. Cf. this sentence with Plato's *The Symposium*, 205 (Shelley's trans.): "Poetry, which is a general name signifying every cause whereby anything proceeds from that which is not into that which is; so that the exercise of every inventive art is poetry, and all such artists poets. Yet they are not called poets, but distinguished by other names; and one portion or species of poetry, that which has relation to music and rhythm, is divided from all others, and known by the name belonging to all."

772b. 31ff. Cf. this passage with Wordsworth's *Preface* (p. 348a, 28ff.) and with Aristotle's *Poetics* (Butcher's translation), 9, 1-3: "It is, moreover, evident from what has been said that it is not the function of the poet to relate what has happened, but what may happen,—what is possible according to the law of probability or necessity. The poet and the historian differ not by writing in verse or in prose. The work of Herodotus might be put into verse, and it would be still a species of history, with metre no less than without it. The true difference is that one relates what has happened, the other what may happen. Poetry, therefore, is a more philosophical and a higher thing than history; for poetry tends to express the universal, history the particular."

774a. 46. The passage omitted contains a historical review of European poetry and a discussion of the superiority of poetry to science and political philosophy.

775a. 32-33. Cf. with Plato's *Ion*, 533-34 (Shelley's trans.): "For the authors of those great poems which we admire do not attain to excellence through the rules of any art, but they utter their beautiful melodies of verse in a state of inspiration, and, as it were, *possessed* by a spirit not their own. Thus the composers of lyrical poetry create those admired songs of theirs in a state of divine insanity, like the Corybantes, who lose all control over their reason in the enthusiasm of the sacred dance, and during this supernatural possession are excited to the rhythm and harmony which they communicate to men. . . . For a poet is indeed a thing ethereally light, winged, and sacred, nor can he compose anything worth calling poetry until he becomes inspired and, as it were, mad, or whilst any reason remains in him. For whilst a man retains any portion of the thing called reason, he is utterly incompetent to produce poetry, or to vaticinate. Thus, those who declaim various and beautiful poetry upon any subject, as for instance upon Homer, are not enabled to do so by art or study; but every rhapsodist or poet, whether dithyrambic, encomiastic, choral, epic, or iambic, is excellent in proportion to the extent of his participation in the divine influence and the degree in which the Muse itself has descended on him. In other respects, poets may be sufficiently ignorant and incapable. For they do not compose according to any art which they have acquired, but from the impulse of the divinity within them; for did they know any rules of criticism, according to which they could compose beautiful verses upon one subject, they would be able to exert the same faculty with respect to all or any other."

John Keats

Selections, p. 777 — Bibliography, p. 1432

"Every one of Keats's poems was a sacrifice of vitality; a virtue went away from him into every one of them; even yet, as we turn the leaves, they seem to warm and thrill our fingers with the flush of his fine senses, and the flutter of his electrical nerves, and we do not wonder he felt that what he did was to be done swiftly. . . . Keats certainly had more of the penetrative and sympathetic imagination which belongs to the poet, of that imagination which identifies itself with the momentary object of its contemplation, than any man of these later days. It is not merely that he has studied the Elizabethans and caught their turn of thought, but that he really sees things with their sovereign eye, and feels them with their electrified senses. . . . We are apt to talk of the classic *renaissance* as of a phenomenon long past, nor ever to be renewed, and to think the Greeks and Romans alone had the mighty

magic to work such a miracle. To me one of the most interesting aspects of Keats is that in him we have an example of the *renaissance* going on almost under our own eyes, and that the intellectual ferment was in him kindled by a purely English leaven. He had properly no scholarship, any more than Shakespeare had, but like him he assimilated at a touch whatever could serve his purpose. His delicate senses absorbed culture at every pore. Of the self-denial to which he trained himself (unexampled in one so young) the second draft of *Hyperion* as compared with the first is a conclusive proof. And far indeed is his *Lamia* from the lavish indiscrimination of *Endymion*. In his odes he showed a sense of form and proportion which we seek vainly in almost any other English poet, and some of his sonnets (taking all qualities into consideration) are the most perfect in our language. No doubt there is something tropical and of strange overgrowth in his sudden maturity, but it *was* maturity nevertheless. Happy the young poet who has the saving fault of exuberance, if he have also the shaping faculty that sooner or later will amend it!"—J. R. Lowell, in *Among My Books* (1876).

"Not since Spenser had there been a purer gift of poetry among English-speaking peoples; not since Milton a line of nobler balance of sound, thought, and cadence. There is no magic of color in written speech that is not mixed in the diction of *The Eve of St. Agnes*, —a vision of beauty, deep, rich, and glowing as one of those dyed windows in which the heart of the Middle Ages still burns. While of the odes, so perfect in form, so ripe with thought, so informed and irradiated by the vision and the insight of the imagination, what remains to be said save that they furnish us with the tests and standards of poetry itself? They mark the complete identification of thought with form, of vision with faculty, of life with art."—H. W. Mabie, in *Essays in Literary Interpretation* (1892-93).

See Shelley's *Adonais* (p. 756), and Hunt's *Proem to Selection from Keats's Poetry* (p. 908).

777. IMITATION OF SPENSER

"Probably no English poet who has used the Spenserian stanza, first assimilated so fully the spirit of Spenser, before using the stanza, as did Keats; and to this fact may be partly attributed his effective use of it as an organ for his imagination in its 'lingering, loving, particularizing mood.' "—Hiram Corson, in *A Primer of English Verse* (1892).

778.   TO CHATTERTON

Keats was an early and constant admirer of Chatterton. *Endymion* was dedicated to him.

779. HOW MANY BARDS GILD THE
                  LAPSES OF TIME

This sonnet gained Keats an introduction to the literary circle of which Leigh Hunt was the center.

ON FIRST LOOKING INTO CHAPMAN'S HOMER

After Charles Cowden Clarke and Keats had read over Chapman's translation of Homer together, Keats composed this sonnet, which he presented to Clarke the next morning. George Chapman was an Elizabethan poet and dramatist; his translation of Homer was published in 1598-1616.

As a contrast to Keats's interest in Chapman's translation, cf. Cowper's remarks in a letter to Thomas Park, dated July 15, 1793:

"Within these few days I have received . . . . your acceptable present of Chapman's translation of the *Iliad*. I know not whether the book be a rarity, but a curiosity it certainly is. I have as yet seen but little of it, enough, however, to make me wonder that any man, with so little taste for Homer, or apprehension of his manner, should think it worth while to undertake the laborious task of translating him; the hope of pecuniary advantage may perhaps account for it. His information, I fear, was not much better than his verse, for I have consulted him in one passage of some difficulty, and find him giving a sense of his own, not at all warranted by the words of Homer. Pope sometimes does this, and sometimes omits the difficult part entirely. I can boast of having done neither, though it has cost me infinite pains to exempt myself from the necessity."

Pope's translation of Homer's *Iliad* and *Odyssey* appeared in 1715-26; Cowper's, in 1791.

780.   SONNET TO SOLITUDE

This was the first poem of Keats's to be published. It was printed by Leigh Hunt in *The Examiner*, May 3, 1816.

I STOOD TIPTOE UPON A LITTLE HILL

"When Keats wrote the lines which here follow he was living in the Vale of Health in Hampstead, happy in the association of Hunt and kindred spirits, and trembling with the consciousness of his own poetic power. He had not yet essayed a long flight, as in *Endym-*

ion; but these lines indeed were written as a prelude to a poem which he was devising, which should narrate the loves of Diana, and it will be seen how, with circling flight, he draws nearer and nearer to his theme; but after all his songs end with a half agitated and passionate speculation over his own poetic birth."—Scudder's note in his edition of Keats's *Complete Poetical Works* (1899).

782. 141. The story of Cupid and Psyche was first told in Latin, by Apuleius in his *Metamorphoses, or the Golden Ass,* in the second century.

784.   SLEEP AND POETRY

This poem was written in Leigh Hunt's library, which had been temporarily fitted up as a sleeping room. "It originated in sleeping in a room adorned with busts and pictures, and is a striking specimen of the restlessness of the young poetical appetite, obtaining its food by the very desire of it, and glancing for fit subjects of creation 'from earth to heaven.' Nor do we like it the less for an impatient, and as it may be thought by some, irreverent assault upon the late French school of criticism and monotony, which has held poetry chained long enough to render it somewhat indignant when it has got free."—Hunt, in a review of Keats's first volume of poems; the review was published in *The Examiner*, July, 1817.

785. 96-98. Cf. these lines with *When I Have Fears That I May Cease to Be* (p. 791).

786. 162-229. "Both the strength and the weakness of this are typically characteristic of the time and of the man. The passage is likely to remain for posterity the central expression of the spirit of literary emancipation then militant and about to triumph in England. The two great elder captains of revolution, Coleridge and Wordsworth, have both expounded their cause, in prose, with much more maturity of thought and language. . . . But neither has left any enunciation of theory having power to thrill the ear and haunt the memory like the rhymes of this young untrained recruit in the cause of poetic liberty and the return to nature. It is easy, indeed, to pick these verses of Keats to shreds, if we choose to fix a prosaic and rational attention on their faults. . . . But controversy apart, if we have in us a touch of instinct for the poetry of imagination and beauty, as distinct from that of taste and reason, however clearly we may see the weak points of a passage like this, however much we may wish that taste and reason had had more to do with it, yet we cannot but feel that Keats touches truly the root of the matter; we cannot but admire the elastic life and variety of his verse, his fine spontaneous and effective turns of rhetoric, the ring and power of his appeal to the elements, and the glow of his delight in the achievements and promise of the new age."—Sidney Colvin, in *Keats* (English Men of Letters Series, 1901).

787. 230-247. An attack upon Byron, whose tempestuous poetic power Keats thought was misdirected.

789. ADDRESSED TO BENJAMIN ROBERT HAYDON

Haydon (1786-1840) was an historical painter, a member of the literary circle composed of Hunt, Keats, Shelley, and others. As originally written the thirteenth line of this sonnet was filled out with the words "in the human mart." Haydon suggested omitting them and sending the sonnet to Wordsworth. Keats replied in a note as follows (Nov. 20, 1816):

"Your letter has filled me with a proud pleasure, and shall be kept by me as a stimulus to exertion—I begin to fix my eye upon one horizon. My feelings entirely fall in with yours in regard to the ellipsis, and I glory in it. The idea of your sending it to Wordsworth put me out of breath—you know with what reverence I would send my wellwishes to him."

STANZAS

This poem is sometimes entitled *Happy Insensibility*. It is thought to be a set of album verses.

790. ON THE GRASSHOPPER AND CRICKET

This sonnet was written at Hunt's cottage in friendly competition with Hunt. See his *On the Grasshopper and the Cricket* (p. 894).

ON A PICTURE OF LEANDER

In Greek legend Leander of Abydos, Asia Minor, swam the Hellespont nightly to visit Hero, a priestess of Aphrodite, at Sestos in ancient Thrace. One night he was drowned, and Hero, in grief, cast herself into the sea.

TO LEIGH HUNT, ESQ.

This sonnet was the Dedication to the 1817 volume of Keats's poems.

791. ON THE SEA

This sonnet was inserted in a letter to Reynolds, dated April 17, 1817, following this

statement: "From want of regular rest I have been rather narvus—and the passage in Lear—'Do you not hear the sea?' has haunted me intensely." The words quoted by Keats are found in Act IV, 6, 4.

LINES

This is possibly the "Song" to which Keats refers in his letter to Bailey, Nov. 22, 1817. See p. 888a, 7ff.

WHEN I HAVE FEARS THAT I MAY CEASE TO BE

This sonnet was sent in a letter to Reynolds, dated Jan. 31, 1818. Cf. with *Sleep and Poetry*, 96-98 (p. 785).

792. ON SITTING DOWN TO READ "KING LEAR" ONCE AGAIN

This sonnet was inserted in a letter to Keats's brothers, dated Jan. 23, 1818, after the following statement: "I think a little change has taken place in my intellect lately —I cannot bear to be uninterested or unemployed, I, who for so long a time have been addicted to passiveness. Nothing is finer for the purposes of great productions than a very gradual ripening of the intellectual powers. As an instance of this—observe—I sat down yesterday to read *King Lear* once again: the thing appeared to demand the prologue of a sonnet. I wrote it, and began to read—(I know you would like to see it)."

LINES ON THE MERMAID TAVERN

This and the following poem were sent in a letter to Reynolds, dated Feb. 3, 1818, in return for two sonnets on Robin Hood which Reynolds had sent Keats. For the letter to Reynolds, see p. 888. Both Reynolds and Keats were in full sympathy with the spirit of the Elizabethans. The Mermaid Tavern in London was famous as the resort of Ben Jonson, Beaumont, Fletcher, and other Elizabethan dramatists.

ROBIN HOOD

See note to previous poem. Keats was fond of the legendary medieval hero Robin Hood.

793. TO THE NILE

Keats, Hunt, and Shelley all wrote sonnets on the Nile on the same day, Feb. 4, 1818. For Hunt's sonnet, see p. 894; for Shelley's, see note on *The Nile*, p. 1366.

THE HUMAN SEASONS

This sonnet was sent by Keats in a letter to Bailey, dated Mar. 13, 1818, after the following statement: "You know my ideas about religion. I do not think myself more in the right than other people, and that nothing in this world is provable. I wish I could enter into all your feelings on the subject, merely for one short 10 minutes, and give you a page or two to your liking. I am sometimes so very skeptical as to think poetry itself a mere Jack o' Lantern to amuse whoever may chance to be struck with its brilliance. As tradesmen say everything is worth what it will fetch, so probably every mental pursuit takes its reality and worth from the ardor of the pursuer—being in itself a nothing. Ethereal things may at least be thus real, divided under three heads—things real— things semireal—and nothings. Things real, such as existences of sun, moon, and stars— and passages of Shakespeare.—Things semi-real, such as love, the clouds, etc., which require a greeting of the spirit to make them wholly exist—and nothings, which are made great and dignified by an ardent pursuit— which, by the by, stamp the Burgundy mark on the bottles of our minds, insomuch as they are able to *'consecrate whate'er they look upon.'* I have written a sonnet here of a some-what collateral nature—so don't imagine it an 'apropos des bottes'—."

"Apropos des bottes" means literally "apropos of boots,"—*i.e.*, without any reason or motive.

The Human Seasons and *To Ailsa Rock* (p. 851) were first published, with the signature *I*, in Hunt's *Literary Pocket-Book*, 1819. The Blackwood reviewer described the poems as "two feats of Johnny Keats."

793. ENDYMION

The story of Endymion, the beautiful youth beloved by Diana, the moon goddess, had been in Keats's mind for about a year before he actually began to write it. The spirit of romance and of the classics abode with him constantly and stimulated him to poetic production. In a letter to Reynolds, dated April 17, 1817, he says: "I find I cannot exist without poetry—without eternal poetry—half the day will not do—the whole of it—I began with a little, but habit has made me a leviathan. I had become all in a tremble from not having written anything of late—the sonnet overleaf did me good. I slept the better last night for it—this morning, however, I am nearly as bad again. Just now I opened Spenser, and the first lines I saw were these— 'The noble heart that harbors virtuous thought, And is with child of glorious great intent, Can never rest until it forth have brought Th' eternal brood of glory excellent—'

"I shall forthwith begin my *Endymion*, which I hope I shall have got some way with by the time you come, when we will read our verses in a delightful place I have set my heart upon."

The "sonnet overleaf" was *On the Sea* (p. 791). The lines quoted by Keats are found in Spenser's *The Faerie Queene*, I, 5, 1, 1-4.

In a letter to Bailey, dated Oct. 8, 1817, Keats quotes as follows from a letter written to his brother George "in the spring": " 'As to what you say about my being a poet, I can return no answer but by saying that the high idea I have of poetical fame makes me think I see it towering too high above me. At any rate, I have no right to talk until *Endymion* is finished—it will be a test, a trial of my powers of imagination, and chiefly of my invention, which is a rare thing indeed—by which I must make 4000 lines of one bare circumstance, and fill them with poetry: and when I consider that this is a great task, and that when done it will take me but a dozen paces towards the temple of fame—it makes me say—God forbid that I should be without such a task! I have heard Hunt say, and I may be asked—*why endeavor after a long Poem?* To which I should answer, Do not the lovers of poetry like to have a little region to wander in, where they may pick and choose, and in which the images are so numerous that many are forgotten and found new in a second reading: which may be food for a week's stroll in the summer? Do not they like this better than what they can read through before Mrs. Williams comes down stairs? a morning work at most.

" 'Besides, a long poem is a test of invention, which I take to be the Polar star of poetry, as fancy is the sails—and imagination the rudder. Did our great poets ever write short pieces? I mean in the shape of tales— this same invention seems indeed of late years to have been forgotten as a poetical excellence —But enough of this, I put on no laurels till I shall have finished *Endymion*.' "

The poem was finished Nov. 28, 1817, and "inscribed, with every feeling of pride and regret and with 'a bowed mind' to the memory of the most English of poets except Shakespeare, Thomas Chatterton."

The poem was published in April, 1818, with the following Preface: "Knowing within myself the manner in which this poem has been produced, it is not without a feeling of regret that I make it public.

"What manner I mean, will be quite clear to the reader, who must soon perceive great inexperience, immaturity, and every error denoting a feverish attempt, rather than a deed accomplished. The two first books, and indeed the two last, I feel sensible are not of such completion as to warrant their passing the press; nor should they if I thought a year's castigation would do them any good:— it will not: the foundations are too sandy. It is just that this youngster should die away: a sad thought for me, if I had not some hope that while it is dwindling I may be plotting, and fitting myself for verses fit to live.

"This may be speaking too presumptuously, and may deserve a punishment: but no feeling man will be forward to inflict it: he will leave me alone, with the conviction that there is not a fiercer hell than the failure in a great object. This is not written with the least atom of purpose to forestall criticisms of course, but from the desire I have to conciliate men who are competent to look, and who do look with a zealous eye, to the honor of English literature.

"The imagination of a boy is healthy, and the mature imagination of a man is healthy; but there is a space of life between, in which the soul is in a ferment, the character undecided, the way of life uncertain, the ambition thick-sighted: thence proceeds mawkishness and all the thousand bitters which those men I speak of must necessarily taste in going over the following pages.

"I hope I have not in too late a day touched the beautiful mythology of Greece, and dulled its brightness: for I wish to try once more, before I bid it farewell."

In the last line Keats has in mind a poem on the fall of Hyperion, the sun god.

An earlier preface had been discarded because of objections by Reynolds. Keats's defense of it is contained in the following interesting letter to Reynolds, dated April 9, 1818: "Since you all agree that the thing is bad, it must be so—though I am not aware there is anything like Hunt in it (and if there is, it is my natural way, and I have something in common with Hunt). Look it over again, and examine into the motives, the seeds, from which any one sentence sprung— I have not the slightest feeling of humility towards the public—or to anything in existence,—but the eternal Being, the principle of

beauty, and the memory of great men. When I am writing for myself for the mere sake of the moment's enjoyment, perhaps nature has its course with me—but a preface is written to the public; a thing I cannot help looking upon as an enemy, and which I cannot address without feelings of hostility. If I write a preface in a supple or subdued style, it will not be in character with me as a public speaker—I would be subdued before my friends, and thank them for subduing me— but among multitudes of men—I have no feel of stooping, I hate the idea of humility to them.

"I never wrote one single line of poetry with the least shadow of public thought.

"Forgive me for vexing you and making a Trojan horse of such a trifle, both with respect to the matter in question, and myself—but it eases me to tell you—I could not live without the love of my friends—I would jump down Ætna for any great public good—but I hate a mawkish popularity. I cannot be subdued before them—My glory would be to daunt and dazzle the thousand jabberers about pictures and books—I see swarms of porcupines with their quills erect 'like lime-twigs set to catch my winged book,' [*2 Henry VI*, III. 3, 16] and I would fright them away with a torch. You will say my preface is not much of a torch. It would have been too insulting 'to begin from Jove,' and I could not set a golden head upon a thing of clay. If there is any fault in the preface it is not affectation, but an undersong of disrespect to the public— if I write another preface it must be done without a thought of those people—I will think about it. If it should not reach you in four or five days, tell Taylor to publish it without a preface, and let the dedication simply stand—'inscribed to the memory of Thomas Chatterton.'"

The new preface was sent to Reynolds in a letter dated April 10, 1818, with the following comment: "I am anxious you should find this preface tolerable. If there is an affectation in it 'tis natural to me. Do let the printer's devil cook it, and let me be as 'the casing air' [*Macbeth*, III, 4, 23].

"You are too good in this matter—were I in your state, I am certain I should have no thought but of discontent and illness—I might though be taught patience: I had an idea of giving no preface; however, don't you think this had better go? O, let it—one should not be too timid—of committing faults."

794. 34-62. Cf. Keats's letter to Hessey, Oct. 9, 1818, in which he says: "In *Endymion*

I leaped headlong into the sea, and thereby have become better acquainted with the soundings, the quicksands, and the rocks than if I had stayed upon the green shore, and piped a silly pipe, and took tea and comfortable advice. I was never afraid of failure; for I would sooner fail than not be among the greatest."

796. 208. The review of *Endymion* in *The Quarterly Review* (see p. 939) accused Keats of introducing new words into the language. *Needments*, which Keats borrowed from Spenser's *The Faerie Queene* (I, 6, 35, 56), is one of the words objected to.

232-306. This Hymn to Pan, recited by Keats to Wordsworth when they met at Haydon's house, Dec. 28, 1817, was dismissed by Wordsworth as "a pretty piece of paganism."

798. 411. This is one of nine unrhyming lines in *Endymion*. These are probably the result of changes made in revising the poem. The other lines are as follows: I, 796; II, 143, 362; III, 767, 1016; IV, 510, 758, 799.

800. 534. *Steed from Araby.*—This is an anachronism.

810. 376 ff. Cf. this passage with the account of the garden of Adonis in Spenser's *The Faerie Queene*, III, 6, 29-50.

819. Book   .—Keats is said to have remarked to a friend: "It will be easily seen what I think of the present ministers, by the beginning of the third Book." Bates suggests (Athenæum Press ed.) that "the pseudopolitical effusion with which the third Book opens is rather a reflection of the opinion of the Leigh Hunt circle than the spontaneous expression of Keats, who at heart was too fully absorbed in literature to feel deeply upon such subjects as these."

835. 244. *Arabians prance.*—This is an anachronism. See Book I, 534 (p. 800).

844.   ISABELLA: OR THE POT OF BASIL

This poem was originally intended to be printed in a projected volume of metrical tales translated by Reynolds and Keats from Boccaccio; but Keats published his poem in 1820 without waiting for Reynolds, who published his in 1821. In the Preface to his volume, Reynolds said: "The stories from Boccaccio (*The Garden of Florence*, and *The Ladye of Provence*) were to have been associated with tales from the same source, intended to have been written by a friend:— but illness on his part, and distracting engagements on mine, prevented us from accomplishing our plan at the time; and Death now, to my deep sorrow, has frustrated it forever!

He, who is gone, was one of the very kindest friends I possessed, and yet he was not kinder perhaps to me, than to others. His intense mind and powerful feeling would, I truly believe, have done the world some service, had his life been spared—but he was of too sensitive a nature—and thus he was destroyed! One story he completed, and that is to me now the most pathetic poem in existence!"

851.   FRAGMENT OF AN ODE TO MAIA

This fragment was written in a letter to Reynolds, dated May 3, 1818, after the following statement: "With respect to the affections and poetry you must know by a sympathy my thoughts that way, and I daresay these few lines will be but a ratification: I wrote them on May-day—and intend to finish the ode all in good time—"

Arnold quotes this ode in the closing paragraph of his essay on Keats prefixed to the selections in Ward's *The English Poets*, following this statement regarding Keats's poetic work: "Shakespearian work it is; not imitative, indeed, of Shakespeare, but Shakespearian, because its expression has that rounded perfection and felicity of loveliness of which Shakespeare is the great master. To show such work is to praise it. Let us now end by delighting ourselves with a fragment of it, too broken to find a place among the pieces which follow, but far too beautiful to be lost. It is a fragment of an ode for May-day."

TO AILSA ROCK

While journeying through Scotland, Keats wrote his brother as follows (July 10, 1818): "Yesterday we came 27 miles from Stranraer—entered Ayrshire a little beyond Cairn, and had our path through a delightful country. I shall endeavor that you may follow our steps in this walk—it would be uninteresting in a book of travels—it can not be interesting but by my having gone through it. When we left Cairn our road lay half way up the sides of a green mountainous shore, full of clefts of verdure and eternally varying—sometimes up sometimes down, and over little bridges going across green chasms of moss, rock, and trees—winding about everywhere. After two or three miles of this we turned suddenly into a magnificent glen finely wooded in parts—seven miles long—with a mountain stream winding down the midst—full of cottages in the most happy situations—the sides of the hills covered with sheep—the effect of cattle lowing I never had so finely. At the end we had a gradual ascent and got among the tops of the mountains whence in a little time I descried in the sea Ailsa Rock 940 feet high—it was 15 miles distant and seemed close upon us. The effect of Ailsa with the peculiar perspective of the sea in connection with the ground we stood on, and the misty rain then falling gave me a complete idea of a deluge. Ailsa struck me very suddenly— really I was a little alarmed."

See note on *The Human Seasons* (p. 1356).

852.   FANCY

"I know of no other poem which so closely rivals the richness and melody,—and that in this very difficult and rarely attempted meter, —of Milton's *Allegro* and *Penseroso*."—Palgrave's note in his edition of *The Poetical Works of John Keats.*

ODE

This poem was written on a blank page before Beaumont and Fletcher's tragi-comedy *The Fair Maid of the Inn.* In his poem Keats refers especially to these Elizabethan dramatists.

853.   ODE ON MELANCHOLY

Early in January, 1819, Keats wrote Haydon as follows: "I have been writing a little now and then lately: but nothing to speak of—being discontented and as it were moulting. Yet I do not think I shall ever come to the rope or the pistol, for after a day or two's melancholy, although I smoke more and more my own insufficiency—I see by little and little more of what is to be done, and how it is to be done, should I ever be able to do it. On my soul, there should be some reward for that continual *agonie ennuyeuse*."

ODE ON A GRECIAN URN

There is a tradition that the urn which inspired this poem was one still preserved in the garden of Holland House, a noted mansion in Kensington, London. But many such treasures in the British Museum were easily accessible to Keats.

This ode is one of Keats's most famous and best loved poems. A few critics insist that the last two lines spoil an otherwise good poem. Others find in those lines a summation of an eternal principle in human experience. See Keats's letter to Benjamin Bailey, Nov. 22, 1817 (p. 887b, 1. 50 ff.).

11-12. Cf. Wordsworth's *Personal Talk*, 25-26 (p. 327).

854.   ODE ON INDOLENCE

In a letter to George and Georgiana Keats, dated March 19, 1819, Keats wrote as follows: "This morning I am in a sort of temper, indolent and supremely careless—I long after a stanza or two of Thomson's *Castle of Indolence*—my passions are all asleep, from my having slumbered till nearly eleven, and weakened the animal fibre all over me, to a delightful sensation, about three degrees on this side of faintness. If I had teeth of pearl and the breath of lilies I should call it languor, but as I am I must call it laziness. In this state of effeminacy the fibres of the brain are relaxed in common with the rest of the body, and to such a happy degree that pleasure has no show of enticement and pain no unbearable power. Neither poetry, nor ambition, nor love have any alertness of countenance as they pass by me; they seem rather like figures on a Greek vase—a man and two women whom no one but myself could distinguish in their disguisement. This is the only happiness, and is a rare instance of the advantage of the body overpowering the mind."

855.   LA BELLE DAME SANS MERCI

When Hunt printed this poem in *The Indicator*, May 10, 1820, he stated that Keats was inspired to write it by a poem of the same title written by Alain Chartier which was found in a translation in a volume of Chaucer's works and formerly ascribed to Chaucer.

856.   ANOTHER ON FAME

10. Fame personified is conventionally characterized as jealous, like Potiphar, and as faithless, like Potiphar's wife. The word *sister-in-law* would seem to identify the characteristics of fame and Potiphar's wife.

ODE TO PSYCHE

This poem was written in a letter to George and Georgiana Keats following this statement: "The following poem—the last I have written—is the first and the only one with which I have taken even moderate pains. I have for the most part dash'd off my lines in a hurry. This I have done leisurely—I think it reads the more richly for it, and will I hope encourage me to write other things in even a more peaceable and healthy spirit. You must recollect that Psyche was not embodied as a goddess before the time of Apuleius the Platonist who lived after the Augustan age, and consequently the Goddess was never worshipped or sacrificed to with any of the ancient fervor—and perhaps never thought of in the old religion—I am more orthodox than to let a heathen Goddess be so neglected—"

857. 50-67. Ruskin quotes these lines to illustrate Keats's power in describing the pine (*Modern Painters*, Pt. VI, ch. 9, sec. 9, note). He says: "Keats (as is his way) puts nearly all that may be said of the pine into one verse [line 55], though they are only figurative pines of which he is speaking. I have come to that pass of admiration for him now, that I dare not read him, so discontented he makes me with my own work; but others must not leave unread, in considering the influence of trees upon the human soul, that marvellous *Ode to Psyche.*"

ODE TO A NIGHTINGALE

In the Aldine edition of 1876, Lord Houghton prefixes this note to the poem: "In the spring of 1819 a nightingale built her nest next Mr. Bevan's house. Keats took great pleasure in her song, and one morning took his chair from the breakfast table to the grass plot under a plum tree, where he remained between two and three hours. He then reached the house with some scraps of paper in his hand, which he soon put together in the form of this ode."

858. 26. This line may refer to Keats's brother Tom, who died in December, 1818. Shortly after this date, Haydon wrote Miss Mitford: "The death of his brother wounded him deeply, and it appeared to me from the hour he began to droop. He wrote his exquisite *Ode to the Nightingale* at this time, and as we were one evening walking in the Kilburn meadows he repeated it to me, before he put it to paper, in a low, tremulous undertone which affected me extremely."

52. *In love with easeful Death.*—Cf. Keats's statement in a letter to Bailey, dated June 10, 1818: "I was in hopes some little time back to be able to relieve your dulness by my spirits—to point out things in the world worth your enjoyment—and now I am never alone without rejoicing that there is such a thing as death—without placing my ultimate in the glory of dying for a great human purpose. Perhaps if my affairs were in a different state, I should not have written the above—you shall judge: I have two brothers; one is driven by the 'burden of society,' to America; the other with an exquisite love of life, is in a lingering state—My love for my brothers, from the early loss of our parents, and even from earlier mis-

fortunes,[1] has grown into an affection 'passing the love of women.'[2] I have been ill-tempered with them—I have vexed them—but the thought of them has always stifled the impression that any woman might otherwise have made upon me. I have a sister too, and may not follow them either to America or to the grave. Life must be undergone, and I certainly derive some consolation from the thought of writing one or two more poems before it ceases."

In a letter to Charles Brown, dated Nov. 30, 1820, Keats said, "It runs in my head, we shall all die young."

65-70. See Hood's *Ruth* (p. 1162).

69-70. These are two of the lines referred to by Kipling in his *Wireless*. See also note on Coleridge's *Kubla Khan*, 14-16 (p. 1302).

LAMIA

Keats is said to have written this poem after studying Dryden's versification. It is based upon the old legend of Lamia, a beautiful woman loved by Zeus and turned into a man-eating monster by Herè; later Lamia was regarded as an evil spirit who enticed youths by her beauty and fed upon their flesh and blood. Keats found the germ of the story in the following passage from Burton's *The Anatomy of Melancholy* (1621): "Philostratus, in his fourth book *de Vita Apollonii*, hath a memorable instance in this kind, which I may not omit, of one Menippus Lycius, a young man twenty-five years of age, that going betwixt Cenchreas and Corinth, met such a phantasm in the habit of a fair gentlewoman, which, taking him by the hand, carried him home to her house, in the suburbs of Corinth, and told him she was a Phœnician by birth, and if he would tarry with her, he should hear her sing and play, and drink such wine as never any drank, and no man should molest him; but she, being fair and lovely, would live and die with him, that was fair and lovely to behold. The young man, a philosopher, otherwise staid and discreet, able to moderate his passions, though not this of love, tarried with her a while to his great content, and at last married her, to whose wedding, amongst other guests, came Apollonius; who, by some probable conjectures, found her out to be a serpent, a lamia; and that all her furniture was, like Tantalus' gold, described by Homer, no substance but mere illusions. When she saw herself descried, she

---

[1] Probably a reference to the unfortunate second marriage of their mother.
[2] *2 Samuel*, 2:26.

wept, and desired Apollonius to be silent, but he would not be moved, and thereupon she, plate, house, and all that was in it, vanished in an instant: many thousands took notice of this fact, for it was done in the midst of Greece." (III, 2, 1, 1)

This passage appeared as a note to the last line in the first edition of *Lamia*.

868. THE EVE OF ST. AGNES

St. Agnes was a Roman virgin who suffered martyrdom about the year 300. Formerly, in the Catholic church, upon St. Agnes Day, January 21, while the *Agnus Dei* (Lamb of God) was chanted, two lambs were sacrificed and their wool was afterwards woven by nuns. The poem is based on the superstition that it was possible for a girl, on the eve of St. Agnes, to obtain knowledge of her future husband; as she lay on her back, with her hands under her head, he was supposed to appear before her in a dream, to salute her with a kiss, and to feast with her.

H. N. MacCracken suggests (*Modern Philology*, 5:145, Oct. 1907) that "for most of the numerous and essential details of the charming episode of Porphyro and Madeline, Keats is indebted to the *Filocolo* of Boccaccio."

871. 23-25. Keats devoted especial care to the composition of these three stanzas, as is shown by the manuscript changes. Hunt says of stanza 24, in his comment on the poem published in *Imagination and Fancy* (1844): "Could all the pomp and graces of aristocracy, with Titian's and Raphael's aid to boot, go beyond the rich religion of this picture, with its 'twilight saints,' and its 'scutcheons 'blushing with the blood of queens'?" The haunting quality of several of these lines is aptly portrayed by Kipling in his *Wireless*, printed in *Traffics and Discoveries*.

872. 27, 7. *Clasp'd like a missal where swart Paynims pray.*—Several interpretations have been given for this line. Hunt interprets it as follows: "Where Christian prayer-books must not be seen, and are, therefore, doubly cherished for the danger." Other interpretations suggested are: "Her soul was clasped as tightly in sleep as a prayer-book would be by a Christian in a land of Pagans!"—"A prayer-book bearing upon its margin pictures of converted heathen in the act of prayer." Keats originally wrote "shut like a missal"; so *clasp'd* must mean *fastened by clasps*. The meaning given on p. 872a, n. 1, seems to fit best.

28, 7. The suggestiveness of this line has frequently been called worthy of Shakespeare.

30. "It is, apparently, as a poetical contrast to the fasting which was generally accepted as the method by which a maiden was to prepare herself for the vision, that the gorgeous supper-picture of st. xxx was introduced. Keats, who was Leigh Hunt's guest at the time this volume appeared, read aloud the passage to Hunt, with manifest pleasure in his work: the sole instance I can recall where the poet—modest in proportion to his greatness—yielded even to so innocent an impulse of vanity."—Palgrave, in his edition of *The Poetical Works of John Keats* (1884).

874. 40, 9. *Carpets.*—The use of carpets in the poem is an anachronism.

THE EVE OF ST. MARK

This poem was written in a letter to George and Georgiana Keats, dated Sept. 20, 1819, following this statement: "The great beauty of poetry is that it makes everything in every place interesting. The palatine Venice and the abbotine Winchester are equally interesting. Some time since I began a poem called *The Eve of St. Mark*, quite in the spirit of town quietude. I think it will give you the sensation of walking about an old country town in a coolish evening. I know not whether I shall ever finish it; I will give it as far as I have gone."

Regarding the superstition on which the poem is based, Dante Gabriel Rossetti wrote Forman as follows: "Keats's unfinished poem on that subject is perhaps, with *La Belle Dame sans Merci*, the chastest and choicest example of his maturing manner, and shows astonishingly real mediævalism for one not bred as an artist. I copy an extract [from *The Unseen World* (Masters, 1853), p. 72] which I have no doubt embodies the superstition in accordance with which Keats meant to develop his poem. It is much akin to the belief connected with the Eve of St. Agnes. 'It was believed that if a person, on St. Mark's Eve, placed himself near the church-porch when twilight was thickening, he would behold the apparition of those persons in the parish who were to be seized with any severe disease that year, go into the church. If they remained there it signified their death; if they came out again it portended their recovery; and the longer or shorter the time they remained in the building, the severer or less dangerous their illness. Infants, under age to walk, rolled in.' "
—Quoted from Forman's edition of Keats's *Poetical Works*.

875. HYPERION

In a letter to George and Georgiana Keats, dated Dec. 25, 1818, Keats announced that his next poem would be on the fall of Hyperion, the sun god. On Sept. 22, 1819, he wrote Reynolds: "I have given up *Hyperion*—there were too many Miltonic inversions in it—Miltonic verse cannot be written but in an artful, or, rather, artist's humor. I wish to give myself up to other sensations. English ought to be kept up. It may be interesting to you to pick out some lines from *Hyperion*, and put a mark × to the false beauty proceeding from art, and one ‖ to the true voice of feeling. Upon my soul 'twas imagination—I cannot make the distinction—Every now and then there is a Miltonic intonation—But I cannot make the division properly."

Keats's friend, Woodhouse, in his annotated copy of *Endymion*, says of *Hyperion*: "The structure of the verse, as well as the subject, are colossal. It has an air of calm grandeur about it which is indicative of true power.—I know of no poem with which in this respect it can be compared.—It is that in poetry, which the Elgin and Egyptian marbles are in sculpture."—Quoted from Forman's edition of Keats's *Poetical Works*.

At the close of his extracts from the manuscript of the poem, Woodhouse says: "The above lines, separated from the rest, give but a faint idea of the sustained grandeur and quiet power which characterize the poem; but they are sufficient to lead us to regret that such an attempt should have been abandoned. The poem if completed, would have treated of the dethronement of Hyperion, the former God of the Sun, by Apollo,—and incidentally of those of Oceanus by Neptune, of Saturn by Jupiter etc., and of the war of the Giants for Saturn's reëstablishment—with other events, of which we have but very dark hints in the mythological poets of Greece and Rome. In fact the incidents would have been pure creations of the poet's brain. How he is qualified for such a task, may be seen in a trifling degree by the few mythological glimpses afforded in *Endymion*."—Quoted from Forman's edition of Keats's *Poetical Works*.

886. TO AUTUMN

Autumn always had a peculiar attraction for Keats. On Sept. 22, 1819, he wrote Reynolds: "How beautiful the season is now—How fine the air. A temperate sharpness about it. Really, without joking, chaste weather—Dian skies—I never liked stubble-fields so much as now—Aye better than the chilly green of the spring. Somehow, a stubble-field looks warm—in the same way that some pictures look warm. This struck me so much in my Sunday's walk that I composed upon it." He refers to the ode *To Autumn*.

887. BRIGHT STAR, WOULD I WERE STEADFAST AS THOU ART

The original version of this sonnet, composed in April, 1819, is as follows:

Bright star! would I were steadfast as thou
  art!
  Not in lone splendour hung amid the
    night;
Not watching, with eternal lids apart,
  Like Nature's devout sleepless Eremite,
The morning waters at their priestlike task
  Of pure ablution round earth's human
    shores;
Or, gazing on the new soft fallen mask
  Of snow upon the mountains and the
    moors:—
No;—yet still steadfast, still unchangeable,
  Cheek-pillow'd on my Love's white ripening
    breast,
To touch, for ever, its warm sink and swell,
  Awake, for ever, in a sweet unrest;
To hear, to feel her tender-taken breath,
  Half passionless, and so swoon on to death.

On July 25, 1819, Keats wrote Fanny Brawne: "I have two luxuries to brood over in my walks, your Loveliness and the hour of my death. O that I could have possession of them both in the same minute. I hate the world: it batters too much the wings of my self-will, and would I could take a sweet poison from your lips to send me out of it. . . . I am distracted with a thousand thoughts. I will imagine you Venus tonight and pray, pray, pray to your star like a He[a]then.

Your's ever, fair Star,
  John Keats"

In September, 1820, while waiting on a ship that would take him to Italy, Keats transcribed the final version in a copy of Shakespeare's poems given to him by his friend Reynolds. The volume was given to his companion, Severn, in memory of the voyage.

KEATS'S LETTERS

In the Preface to his edition of Keats's letters, Colvin says that Keats "is one of those poets whose genius makes itself felt in prose-writing almost as decisively as in verse, and at their best these letters are among the most beautiful in our language." The letters here printed were addressed to the following: (1) Benjamin Bailey (1794-1852), undergraduate of Magdalen Hall, Oxford, afterwards Archdeacon of Colombo; (2) John Hamilton Reynolds (1796-1852), poet, critic, and lawyer; (3) John Taylor (1781-1864), publisher, of the firm of Taylor and Hessey, and proprietor and editor of *The London Magazine;* (4) James Augustus Hessey, publisher, of the firm of Taylor and Hessey; (5) George and Georgiana Keats, Keats's brother and his brother's wife; (6) Percy Bysshe Shelley (1792-1822), the poet.

TO BENJAMIN BAILEY

b. 2. *Unsaid.*—Colvin, in his edition of Keats's letters, suggests that this is probably an error for *unpaid.* As the first part of the word is italicized, it may, however, be simply a play on the phrase "the said letter."

890. TO JAMES AUGUSTUS HESSEY

a. 2. The first letter, which appeared in *The Morning Chronicle,* Oct. 3, 1818, was written by John Scott. It is as follows: "Sir, Although I am aware that literary squabbles are of too uninteresting and interminable a nature for your Journal, yet there are occasions when acts of malice and gross injustice towards an author may be properly brought before the public through such a medium.— Allow me, then, without further preface, to refer you to an article in the last number of *The Quarterly Review,* professing to be a critique on *The Poems of John Keats.* Of John Keats I know nothing; from his Preface I collect that he is very young—no doubt a heinous sin; and I have been informed that he has incurred the additional guilt of an acquaintance with Mr. Leigh Hunt. That this latter gentleman and the editor of *The Quarterly Review* have long been at war, must be known to every one in the least acquainted with the literary gossip of the day. Mr. L. Hunt, it appears, has thought highly of the poetical talents of Mr. Keats; hence Mr. K. is doomed to feel the merciless tomahawk of the Reviewers, termed *Quarterly,* I presume from the *modus operandi.* From a perusal of the criticism, I was led to the work itself. I would, Sir, that your limits would permit a few extracts from this poem. I dare appeal to the taste and judgment of your readers, that beauties of the highest order may be found in almost every page—that there are

also many, very many passages indicating haste and carelessness, I will not deny; I will go further, and assert that a real friend of the author would have dissuaded him from an immediate publication.

"Had the genius of Lord Byron sunk under the discouraging sneers of an *Edinburgh Review* the nineteenth century would scarcely yet have been termed the Augustan era of poetry. Let Mr. Keats too persevere—he has talents of [no] common stamp; this is the hastily written tribute of a stranger, who ventures to predict that Mr. K. is capable of producing a poem that shall challenge the admiration of every reader of true taste and feeling; nay if he will give up his acquaintance with Mr. Leigh Hunt, and apostatize in his friendships, his principles, and his politics (if he have any), he may even command the approbation of *The Quarterly Review.*

"I have not heard to whom public opinion has assigned this exquisite morceau of critical acumen. If the Translator of Juvenal be its author, I would refer him to the manly and pathetic narrative prefixed to that translation, to the touching history of genius oppressed by and struggling with innumerable difficulties, yet finally triumphing under patronage and encouragement. If the Biographer of Kirke White have done Mr. Keats this cruel wrong, let him remember his own just and feeling expostulation with *The Monthly Reviewer,* who 'sat down to blast the hopes of a boy, who had confessed to him all his hopes and all his difficulties.' If the 'Admiralty Scribe' (for he too is a Reviewer) be the critic, let him compare *The Battle of Talavera* with *Endymion.*

I am, Sir, Your obedient servant,
J. S."

The "Translator of Juvenal" was William Gifford, editor of *The Quarterly Review;* the "Biographer of Kirke White" was Southey; the author of *The Battle of Talavera* was John Wilson Croker, Secretary of the Admiralty, the actual author of the article in question (see p. 939).

The second letter, which appeared October 8, is as follows. The author has not been identified: "Sir,—The spirited and feeling remonstrance of your correspondent J. S. against the cruelty and injustice of *The Quarterly Review,* has most ably anticipated the few remarks which I had intended to address to you on the subject. But your well known liberality in giving admission to everything calculated to do justice to oppressed and injured merit, induces me to trespass further on your valuable columns, by a few extracts from Mr. Keat's [sic] poem. As the Reviewer professes to have read only the first book, I have confined my quotations to that part of the poem; and I leave your readers to judge whether the critic who could pass over such beauties as these lines contain, and condemn the whole poem as 'consisting of the most incongruous ideas in the most uncouth language,' is very implicitly to be relied on.

I am, Sir, Your obedient servant,
Temple, Oct. 3rd, 1818.   R. B."

James Henry Leigh Hunt

Selections, p. 892 — Bibliography, p. 1429

"An essayist, poet, and translator, full (at his best) of grace and charm in a kind quite of his own, he lacked both the stamina and the piercing imaginative vision which make Hazlitt so great. In temperament he was more akin to Lamb, but he equally lacked Lamb's rarer qualities both as a man and as a writer; and his chief function in literature was to further the ease, vivacity, and grace of which, though in a far choicer kind, Lamb was a master in prose, and Chaucer and Ariosto in verse."— C. H. Herford, in *The Age of Wordsworth* (1897).

From *Letter to Maria Gisborne*

You will see Hunt—one of those happy souls
Which are the salt of the earth, and without
        whom
This world would smell like what it is—a
        tomb;
Who is, what others seem; his room no doubt
Is still adorned with many a cast from Shout,
With graceful flowers tastefully placed about;
And coronals of bay from ribbons hung,
And brighter wreaths in neat disorder flung;
The gifts of the most learned among some
        dozens
Of female friends, sisters-in-law, and cousins.
And there is he with his eternal puns,
Which beat the dullest brain for smiles, like
        duns
Thundering for money at a poet's door;
Alas! it is no use to say, "I'm poor!"
Or oft in graver mood, when he will look
Things wiser than were ever read in book,
Except in Shakespeare's wisest tenderness.—
        —Shelley (1820).

Shelley dedicated *The Cenci* to Hunt in the following words: "MY DEAR FRIEND—I in-

scribe with your name, from a distant country, and after an absence whose months have seemed years, this the latest of my literary efforts.

"Those writings which I have hitherto published, have been little else than visions which impersonate my own apprehensions of the beautiful and the just. I can also perceive in them the literary defects incidental to youth and impatience; they are dreams of what ought to be, or may be. The drama which I now present to you is a sad reality. I lay aside the presumptuous attitude of an instructor, and am content to paint, with such colors as my own heart furnishes, that which has been.

"Had I known a person more highly endowed than yourself with all that it becomes a man to possess, I had solicited for this work the ornament of his name. One more gentle, honorable, innocent and brave; one of more exalted toleration for all who do and think evil, and yet himself more free from evil; one who knows better how to receive, and how to confer a benefit, though he must ever confer far more than he can receive; one of simpler, and, in the highest sense of the word, of purer life and manners I never knew: and I had already been fortunate in friendships when your name was added to the list.

"In that patient and irreconcilable enmity with domestic and political tyranny and imposture which the tenor of your life has illustrated, and which, had I health and talents, should illustrate mine, let us, comforting each other in our task, live and die.

"All happiness attend you! Your affectionate friend,   Percy B. Shelley.
"Rome, May 29, 1819."

See Keats's sonnets *Written on the Day that Mr. Leigh Hunt Left Prison* (p. 779) and *To Leigh Hunt, Esq.* (p. 790); also Dickens's genial caricature of Hunt as Harold Skimpole in *Bleak House*.

892.   THE STORY OF RIMINI

"The following story is founded on a passage in Dante, the substance of which is contained in the concluding paragraph of the second [fifth] Canto. For the rest of the incidents, generally speaking, the praise or blame remains with myself. The passage in question—the episode of Paulo and Francesca—has long been admired by the readers of Italian poetry, and is indeed the most cordial and refreshing one in the whole of that singular poem the *Inferno*, which some call a satire, and some an epic, and which, I confess, has always appeared to me a kind of sublime night-mare. We even lose sight of the place, in which the saturnine poet, according to his summary way of disposing both of friends and enemies, has thought proper to put the sufferers; and see the whole melancholy absurdity of his theology, in spite of itself, falling to nothing before one genuine impulse of the affections.

"The interest of the passage is greatly increased by its being founded on acknowledged matter of fact. Even the particular circumstance which Dante describes as having hastened the fall of the lovers,—the perusal of *Launcelot of the Lake*,[1]—is most likely a true anecdote; for he himself, not long after the event, was living at the court of Guido Novella da Polenta, the heroine's father; and indeed the very circumstance of his having related it at all, considering its nature, is a warrant of its authenticity. . . .

"There are no notes to the present poem. I have done my best, as every writer should, to be true to costume and manners, to time and place; and if the reader understands me as he goes, and feels touched where I am most ambitious he should be, I can be content that he shall miss an occasional nicety or so in other matters, and not be quite sensible of the mighty extent of my information. If the poem reach posterity, curiosity may find commentators enough for it, and the sanction of time give interest to whatever they may trace after me. If the case be otherwise, to write notes is only to show to how little purpose has been one's reading. . . .

". . . I suppress a good deal which I had intended to say on the versification of the poem,—or of that part of it, at least, where, in coming upon household matters calculated to touch us nearest, it takes leave, as it were, of a more visible march and accompaniment. I do not hesitate to say, however, that Pope and the French school of versification have known the least on the subject, of any poets perhaps that ever wrote.[2] They have mistaken mere smoothness for harmony; and, in fact, wrote as they did, because their ears were only sensible of a marked and uniform regularity. One of the most successful of Pope's imitators, Dr. Johnson, was confessedly insensible to music. In speaking of such men, I allude, of course, only to their style in poetry, and not to their undisputed excellence in other matters. The great masters of modern versifi-

cation are, Dryden for common narrative, though he wanted sentiment, and his style in some respects was apt to be artificial,—Spenser, who was musical from pure taste,—Milton, who was learnedly so,—Ariosto, whose fine ear and animal spirits gave so frank and exquisite a tone to all he said,—Shakspeare, whose versification escapes us, only because he over-informed it with knowledge and sentiment;—and, though the name may appear singular to those who have not read him with due attention to the nature of the language then existing,—Chaucer,—to whom it sometimes appears to me, that I can trace Dryden himself, though the latter spoke on the subject without much relish, or, in fact, knowledge of it. All these are about as different from Pope, as the church organ is from the bell in the steeple, or, to give him a more decorous comparison, the song of the nightingale, from that of the cuckoo.

"With the endeavor to recur to a freer spirit of versification, I have joined one of still greater importance,—that of having a free and idiomatic cast of language. There is a cant of art as well as of nature, though the former is not so unpleasant as the latter, which affects non-affectation. But the proper language of poetry is in fact nothing different from that of real life, and depends for its dignity upon the strength and sentiment of what it speaks. It is only adding musical modulation to what a fine understanding might actually utter in the midst of its griefs or enjoyments. The poet therefore should do as Chaucer or Shakspeare did,—not copy what is obsolete or peculiar in either, any more than they copied from their predecessors,—but use as much as possible an actual, existing language,—omitting of course mere vulgarisms and fugitive phrases, which are the cant of ordinary discourse, just as tragedy phrases, dead idioms, and exaggerations of simplicity, are of the natural. The artificial style, it is true, has its beauties, as some great poets have proved; but I am here speaking of the style that is most beautiful; and these poets, it is to be observed, were not the greatest. Of the style, to which I allude, exquisite specimens, making allowances for what is obsolete, are to be found in *The Canterbury Tales* of Chaucer, and his *Troilus and Cressida;* and you have only to open the first books of Pulci[1] and Ariosto[2] to meet with two charming ones,

---

[1] *Launcelot of the Lake* was a popular medieval romance.
[2] Cf. Coleridge's remarks in *Biographia Literaria,* ch. 1 (p. 1384), and Keats's denunciation in *Sleep and Poetry* (p. 786, ll. 181-206).

[1] Luigi Pulci (1432-87) was an Italian romantic poet, author of the burlesque epic *Il Morgante Maggiore.*
[2] Ludovico Ariosto (1474-1533) was a celebrated Italian romantic poet, author of *Orlando Furioso.*

the interview of Orlando with the Abbott, in the *Morgante Maggiore* (Canto 1 towards the conclusion), and the flight of Angelica, her meeting with Rinaldo's horse, etc., in the *Orlando Furioso.* Homer abounds with them, though, by the way, not in the translation; and I need not, of course, warn any reader of taste against trusting Mr. Hoole[1] for a proper representation of the delightful Italian. Such versions, more or less, resemble bad engravings, in which all the substances, whether flesh, wood, or cloth, are made of one texture, and that a bad one. With the Greek dramatists I am ashamed to say I am unacquainted; and of the Latin writers, though Horace, for his delightful companionship, is my favorite, Catullus appears to me to have the truest taste for nature. But an Englishman need go no farther than Shakspeare. Take a single speech of Lear's, such for instance as that heart-rending one,

'I am a very foolish fond old man,
Fourscore and upward,' etc.[2]

and you have all that criticism can say, or poetry can do.

"In making these observations, I do not demand the reader to conclude that I have succeeded in my object, whatever may be my own opinion of the matter. All the merit I claim is that of having made an attempt to describe natural things in a language becoming to them, and to do something towards a revival of what appears to me a proper English versification. There are narrative poets now living who have fine eyes for the truth of things, and it remains with them perhaps to perfect what I may suggest. If I have succeeded at all, the lovers of nature have still to judge in what proportion the success may be; but let me take them with me a while, whether in doors or out of doors, whether in the room or the green fields,—let my verses, in short, come under the perusal of ingenuous eyes, and be felt a little by the hearts that look out of them, and I am satisfied."—Hunt, in Preface to *The Story of Rimini* (1816). The poem was dedicated to Lord Byron.

See Keats's *On Leigh Hunt's Poem "The Story of Rimini"* (p. 791).

In the portion of the poem omitted Paulo, the brother of Giovanni, Lord of Rimini, goes to Ravenna to bring back Giovanni's bride, Francesca, the daughter of Duke Guido. A proxy wedding is held, and Paulo and Fran-

cesca return to Rimini. From their first meeting Paulo and Francesca had grown to love each other, and as Giovanni was ill-tempered and uncongenial the relationship between him and his beautiful bride was not cordial. He often gave vent to his wrath and ill-treated Francesca. At such times, Francesca sought solace in the garden described in the text, the place where she and Paulo first confessed their love for each other.

893.   TO HAMPSTEAD

Hampstead is a borough and parish in northwestern London; it was the home of Hunt and the center of a literary circle including Hunt, Keats, Shelley, Hazlitt, Lamb, and others.

894.   TO THE GRASSHOPPER AND
THE CRICKET

This sonnet was written in friendly competition with Keats. See his *On the Grasshopper and Cricket* (p. 790).

THE NILE

Hunt, Keats, and Shelley all wrote sonnets on the Nile on the same day, Feb. 4, 1818. For Keats's sonnet, see p. 793. Shelley's is as follows:

Month after month the gathered rains descend
Drenching yon secret Ethiopian dells,
And from the desert's ice-girt pinnacles
Where Frost and Heat in strange embraces blend
On Atlas, fields of moist snow half depend.
Girt there with blasts and meteors Tempest dwells
By Nile's aëreal urn, with rapid spells
Urging those waters to their mighty end.
O'er Egypt's land of Memory floods are level
And they are thine, O Nile—and well thou knowest
That soul-sustaining airs and blasts of evil
And fruits and poisons spring where'er thou flowest.
Beware, O Man—for knowledge must to thee,
Like the great flood to Egypt ever be.

MAHMOUD

The subject of this poem is Mahmoud the Gaznevide, a famous Turkish prince, who reigned in one of the eastern provinces of Persia during the first part of the eleventh century. The incident on which this poem is based is related in Gibbon's *The History of the Decline and Fall of the Roman Empire,* ch. 57. Gibbon found the story in D'Herbelot's *Bibliothèque Orientale* (1697).

---

[1] John Hoole (1727-1803) was an English poet, now known only as the translator of Tasso's *Jerusalem Delivered* (1763), Ariosto's *Orlando Furioso* (1773-83), and other Italian poems.
[2] *King Lear,* IV, 7, 60-61.

895. SONG OF FAIRIES ROBBING ORCHARD

This poem is sometimes entitled *Fairies Song*. It is taken from some Latin verses in Thomas Randolph's drama of *Amyntas, or the Impossible Dowry* (1638), Act III, sc. 4.

ABOU BEN ADHEM AND THE ANGEL

This poem is based on an incident recorded in D'Herbelot's *Bibliothèque Orientale* (1697).

896. THE GLOVE AND THE LIONS

This poem is based on an incident quoted from Brantome (d. 1614) in St. Felix's *History of Paris*. Browning's *The Glove* treats the same story in a quite different way.

RONDEAU

The Jenny of this poem was Jane Welsh, wife of Thomas Carlyle. When Hunt visited her and announced that the publishers had accepted one of Carlyle's writings, she impetuously jumped up and kissed him.

899. GETTING UP ON COLD MORNINGS

For the point of view opposite to that expressed in this essay, see Hunt's *A Word on Early Rising*.

874. ON THE REALITIES OF IMAGINATION

902b. 21. The passage omitted consists of quotations from Milton's *L'Allegro* and *Arcades*, illustrating his love of nature.

903a. 55. The passage omitted consists of a quotation from Ben Jonson's *To Penshurst*, illustrating his method of enlivening description by the use of classical mythology and of manners of the time.

A "NOW"

"The paper that was most liked by Keats, if I remember, was the one on a hot summer's day, entitled *A Now*. He was with me when I was writing and reading it to him, and contributed one or two of the passages." —Hunt, in *Autobiography*, ch. 16 (1850).

908. PROEM TO SELECTION FROM KEATS'S POETRY

In his volume entitled *Imagination and Fancy* (1844), Hunt printed as a selection from Keats's poetry *The Eve of St. Agnes*, three pages of extracts from *Endymion* and *Hyperion*, the *Ode to a Nightingale*, and *On First Looking into Chapman's Homer*. The essay here printed served as an introduction to the selections.

909a. 10ff. Hunt's enthusiasm for Keats accounts for this extravagant and unsound statement.

910a. 14. *Denied it to no one.*—"Allusion, of course, is not here made to *all* the critics of the time, but only to such reigning reviewers as took earliest and most frequent notice of Keats. *The Edinburgh Review*, though not quick to speak of him, did so before he died, with a fervor of eulogy at least equal to its objections; and I think I may add that its then distinguished editor [Jeffrey], now a revered ornament of the Scottish bench, has since felt his admiration of the young poet increase, instead of diminish."—Hunt's note.

Francis Jeffrey

Selections, p. 910 — Bibliography, p. 1430

"Jeffrey was before all things a literary critic, and, within the limits of his discernment, one of the acutest and liveliest of his time. His point of view was that of refined but positive common-sense, qualified by a rooted distrust of innovation. To the simple and obvious poetry of Rogers, Campbell, Crabbe, he brought a keen if somewhat excessive appreciation; mawkish sentiment and pseudo-mediævalism he exposed with signal effect. We cannot now wholly disapprove of the stricture upon *Marmion* which angered Scott, nor share his effusive penitence for those upon Byron's *Hours of Idleness*. But he was, unfortunately, as proof against the true Romantics as against the false, and comprehended the mysticism of imaginative poetry in the same anathema with the crude supernaturalism of the school of horrors. The manifesto against the 'Lake school' with which he opened the review is one of the most striking examples in literature of the fatuous efforts of a clever man to interpret a larger world than his own. The naked simplicity of Wordsworth, the tumultuous energy of Coleridge, the irregular metres of Southey were equally offensive to him, and he classed them together, as if innovators formed one brotherhood."—C. H. Herford, in *The Age of Wordsworth* (1897).

"He is a Whig in taste as in politics, and desires in both spheres the supremacy of a chosen aristocracy. In his essay on Scott's *Lady of the Lake* he declares the standard of literary excellence to reside in 'the taste of a few . . . persons, eminently qualified, by natural sensibility, and long experience and reflection, to perceive all beauties that really exist, as well as to settle the relative value and importance of all the different sorts of beauty.' Jeffrey regards himself as one of the choicest spirits of this chosen aristocracy, and it is as the exponent of the best current opinion that he speaks on all questions of taste. His business, then, is to dogmatize, to pronounce this right and that wrong, to praise this author and blame that one; but his dogmatism is not the dogmatism of reason, but the dogmatism of taste; he justifies his decisions, not by referring to a code of written laws from which there is no appeal, but by a more or less direct suggestion that he has all the best instructed opinion behind him."— Gates, in *Selections from the Essays of Francis Jeffrey* (Athenæum Press ed., 1894).

See Byron's *English Bards and Scotch Reviewers*, 438-539 (pp. 518-519).

Speaking in the Preface to *Contributions to The Edinburgh Review*, Jeffrey says of his connection with *The Edinburgh Review:* "It will not, I think, be expected or required of me, that I should look back—from *any* station —upon the part I took in originating and conducting such a work, without some mixture of agreeable feelings. And, while I seek not to decline my full share of the faults and follies to which I have alluded, I trust I may be allowed to take credit, at the same time, for some participation in the merits by which these were, to a certain extent at least, redeemed or atoned for. If I might be permitted farther to state, in what particular department, and generally, on account of what, I should most wish to claim a share of those merits, I should certainly say, that it was by having constantly endeavored to combine ethical precepts with literary criticism, and earnestly sought to impress my readers with a sense, both of the close connection between sound intellectual attainments and the higher elements of duty and enjoyment; and of the just and ultimate subordination of the former to the latter. The praise in short to which I aspire, and to merit which I am conscious that my efforts were most constantly directed, is, that I have, more uniformly and earnestly than any preceding critic, made the moral tendencies of the works under consideration a leading subject of discussion, and neglected no opportunity, in reviews of poems and novels as well as of graver productions, of elucidating the true constituents of human happiness and virtue: and combating those besetting prejudices and errors of opinion which appear so often to withhold men from the path of their duty—or to array them in foolish and fatal hostility to each other. I cannot, of course, do more, in this place, than intimate this proud claim. But for the proof—or at least the explanation of it,—I think I may venture to refer to the greater part of the papers that follow."

910.   CRABBE'S POEMS

"I have given a larger space to Crabbe in this republication than to any of his contemporary poets; not merely because I think more highly of him than of most of them, but also because I fancy that he has had less justice done him. The nature of his subjects was not such as to attract either imitators or admirers, from among the ambitious or fanciful lovers of poetry; or, consequently, to set him at the head of a school, or let him surround himself with the zealots of a sect. And it must also be admitted, that his claims to distinction depend fully as much on his great powers of observation, his skill in touching the deeper sympathies of our nature, and his power of inculcating, by their means, the most impressive lessons of humanity, as on any fine play of fancy, or grace and beauty in his delineations. I have great faith, however, in the intrinsic worth and ultimate success of those more substantial attributes; and have, accordingly, the strongest impression that the citations I have here given from Crabbe will strike more, and sink deeper into the minds of readers to whom they are new (or by whom they may have been partially forgotten), than any I have been able to present from other writers. It probably is idle enough (as well as a little presumptuous) to suppose that a publication like this will afford many opportunities of testing the truth of this prediction. But as the experiment is to be made, there can be no harm in mentioning this as one of its objects.

"It is but candid, however, after all, to add, that my concern for Mr. Crabbe's reputation would scarcely have led me to devote near one hundred pages to the estimate of his poetical merits, had I not set some value on the speculations as to the elements of poetical excellence in general, and its moral bearings and affinities—for the introduction of which this estimate seemed to present an occasion, or apology."—Jeffrey's note in *Contributions to the Edinburgh Review.*

Besides the essay given here, Jeffrey reprinted in his *Contributions to The Edinburgh Review* essays on Crabbe's *The Borough, Tales*, and *Tales of the Hall*, which had originally appeared in *The Edinburgh Review*, April, 1808, April, 1810, Nov., 1812, and July, 1819.

Jeffrey never escaped from the narrow and prejudiced view that poetry was something artificial, to be composed with strict adherence to rules and conventions. See Wordsworth's Preface to *Lyrical Ballads* (p. 348a, 20-27).

911b. 31-38. See Coleridge's *Biographia Literaria*, 14 (p. 398b, 22-41).

912b. 28-32. This is an inaccurate and unfair characterization of Wordsworth's poem.

913. ALISON'S ESSAYS ON THE NATURE AND PRINCIPLES OF TASTE

This review was afterwards expanded and included in *The Encyclopædia Britannica* as the discussion on Beauty. It was omitted in the ninth and subsequent editions. Alison's *Essay*, the work of the Reverend Archibald Alison (1757-1839), a clergyman of the English Church, appeared in 1790; the second edition, printed in 1811, gave occasion for Jeffrey's review.

Jeffrey's theory of the nature of beauty should be compared with his principles of literary criticism, especially with his ethical interpretation of literature. See note on *Crabbe's Poems*, above.

913b. 28-35. Upon receiving a copy of the *Essay*, Burns wrote Alison as follows (Feb. 14, 1791): "You must by this time have set me down as one of the most ungrateful of men. You did me the honor to present me with a book which does honor to science and the intellectual powers of man, and I have not even so much as acknowledged the receipt of it. The fact is, you yourself are to blame for it. Flattered as I was by your telling me that you wished to have my opinion of the work, the old spiritual enemy of mankind, who knows well that vanity is one of the sins that most easily beset me, put it into my head to ponder over the performance with the look-out of a critic, and to draw up, forsooth! a deep learned digest of strictures on a composition of which, in fact, until I read the book, I did not even know the first principles. I own, sir, that at first glance several of your propositions startled me as paradoxical. That the martial clangor of a trumpet had something in it vastly more grand, heroic, and sublime, than the twingle-twangle of a jews-harp; that the delicate flexure of a rose-twig, when the half-blown flower is heavy with the tears of the dawn, was infinitely more beautiful and elegant than the upright stub of a burdock, and that from something innate and independent of all associations of ideas;—these I had set down as irrefragable, orthodox truths, until perusing your book shook my faith. In short, sir, except Euclid's *Elements of Geometry*, which I made a shift to unravel by my father's fireside, in the winter evenings of the first season I held the plough, I never read a book which gave me such a quantum of information, and added so much to my stock of ideas, as your *Essays on the Principles of Taste*."

918. WORDSWORTH'S THE EXCURSION

"I have spoken in many places rather too bitterly and confidently of the faults of Mr. Wordsworth's poetry; and forgetting that, even on my own view of them, they were but faults of taste, or venial self-partiality, have sometimes visited them, I fear, with an asperity which should be reserved for objects of moral reprobation. If I were now to deal with the whole question of his poetical merits, though my judgment might not be substantially different, I hope I should repress the greater part of these *vivacités* of expression: and indeed so strong has been my feeling in this way, that, considering how much I have always loved many of the attributes of his genius, and how entirely I respect his character, it did at first occur to me whether it was quite fitting that, in my old age and his, I should include in this publication any of those critiques which may have formerly given pain or offence, to him or his admirers. But, when I reflected that the mischief, if there really ever was any, was long ago done, and that I still retain, in substance, the opinions which I should now like to have seen more gently expressed, I felt that to omit all notice of them on the present occasion, might be held to import a retraction which I am as far as possible from intending; or even be represented as a very shabby way of backing out of sentiments which should either be manfully persisted in, or openly renounced, and abandoned as untenable.

"I finally resolved, therefore, to reprint my review of *The Excursion*, which contains a pretty full view of my griefs and charges against Mr. Wordsworth; set forth too, I believe, in a more temperate strain than most of my other inculpations,—and of which I think I may now venture to say farther that if the faults are unsparingly noted, the beauties are not penuriously or grudgingly allowed, but commended to the admiration of the reader with at least as much heartiness and good-will.

"But I have also reprinted a short paper on the same author's *White Doe of Rylstone*,—in which there certainly is no praise, or notice of beauties, to set against the very unqualified censures of which it is wholly made up. I have done this, however, not merely because I adhere to these censures, but chiefly because it seemed necessary to bring me fairly to issue with those who may not concur in them. I can easily understand that many whose admiration of *The Excursion*, or the *Lyrical Ballads*, rests substantially on the passages which I too should join in admiring, may view with greater indulgence than I can do, the tedious and flat passages with which they are interspersed, and may consequently think my censure of these works a great deal too harsh and uncharitable. Between such persons and me, therefore, there may be no radical difference of opinion, or contrariety as to principles of judgment. But if there be any who actually admire this *White Doe of Rylstone*, or *Peter Bell the Waggoner*, or the *Lamentations of Martha Rae*, or the *Sonnets on the Punishment of Death*, there can be no such ambiguity, or means of reconcilement. Now I have been assured not only that there are such persons, but that almost all those who seek to exalt Mr. Wordsworth as the founder of a new school of poetry, consider these as by far his best and most characteristic productions, and would at once reject from their communion anyone who did not acknowledge in them the traces of a high inspiration. Now I wish it to be understood, that when I speak with general intolerance or impatience of the school of Mr. Wordsworth, it is to the school holding these tenets, and applying these tests, that I refer: and I really do not see how I could better explain the grounds of my dissent from their doctrines, than by republishing my remarks on this *White Doe*."

919b. 3-8. Through his failure to appreciate the influence of solitude upon poets, Jeffrey is led into this unsound statement. See p. 680b, n. 1; also Thomson's Preface to *Winter*, p. 1235.

920a. 7ff. Jeffrey never understood Wordsworth's theory of poetry or his doctrine of the immanence of God in nature. What is perfectly sincere and distinctive in Wordsworth's mystical interpretation of nature, Jeffrey regards as merely affectation or madness.

928. WORDSWORTH'S THE WHITE DOE OF RYLSTONE

In connection with this review, cf. the following passage from Wordsworth's prefatory note on the poem:

"Let me here say a few words of this poem in the way of criticism. The subject being taken from the feudal times has led to its being compared to some of Walter Scott's poems that belong to the same age and state of society. The comparison is inconsiderate. Sir Walter pursued the customary and very natural course of conducting an action, presenting various turns of fortune, to some outstanding point on which the mind might rest as a termination or catastrophe. The course I attempted to pursue is entirely different. Everything that is attempted by the principal personages in *The White Doe* fails, so far as its object is external and substantial. So far as it is moral and spiritual it succeeds. The heroine of the poem knows that her duty is not to interfere with the current of events, either to forward or delay them, but

> 'To abide
> The shock, and finally secure
> O'er pain and grief a triumph pure.'

This she does in obedience to her brother's injunction, as most suitable to a mind and character that, under previous trials, had been proved to accord with his. She achieves this not without aid from the communication with the inferior creature, which often leads her thoughts to revolve upon the past with a tender and humanizing influence that exalts rather than depresses her. The anticipated beatification, if I may so say, of her mind, and the apotheosis of the companion of her solitude, are the points at which the poem aims, and constitute its legitimate catastrophe, far too spiritual a one for instant or widely-spread sympathy, but not therefore the less fitted to make a deep and permanent impression upon that class of minds who think and feel more independently, than the many do, of the surfaces of things and interests transitory because belonging more to the outward and social forms of life than to its internal spirit. How insignificant a thing, for example, does personal prowess appear compared with the fortitude of patience and heroic martyrdom; in other words, with struggles for the sake of principle, in preference to victory glorified in for its own sake."

930.   CHILDE HAROLD'S PILGRIMAGE

"I have already said so much of Lord Byron with reference to his dramatic productions, that I cannot now afford to republish more than one other paper on the subject of his poetry in general and I select this, rather because it refers to a greater variety of these compositions, than because it deals with such as are either absolutely the best, or the most characteristic of his genius. The truth is, however, that all his writings are characteristic, and lead, pretty much alike, to those views of the dark and the bright parts of his nature, which have led me, I fear (though almost irresistibly) into observations more personal to the character of the author, than should generally be permitted to a mere literary censor."—Jeffrey's note in *Contributions to The Edinburgh Review.*

933b. 13-18. At an earlier date *The Edinburgh Review* had severely criticized Byron's first work, *Hours in Idleness.* The article, however, was written by Lord Brougham. See note on *English Bards and Scotch Reviewers,* p. 1325.

John Wilson Croker

Croker had the reputation of being a great talker. Hazlitt, in his *Pulpit Oratory (Collected Works,* ed. Waller and Glover, 12, 276) records an incident which gave Croker the nickname of "Talking Potato":—"Some years ago, a periodical paper was published in London, under the title of the *Pic-Nic.* It was got up under the auspices of a Mr. Fulke Greville, and several writers of that day contributed to it, among whom were Mr. Horace Smith, Mr. Dubois, Mr. Prince Hoare, Mr. Cumberland, and others. On some dispute arising between the proprietor and the gentlemen-contributors on the subject of an advance in the remuneration for articles, Mr. Fulke Greville grew heroic, and said, 'I have got a young fellow just come from Ireland, who will undertake to do the whole, verse and prose, politics and scandal, for two guineas a week, and if you will come and sup with me tomorrow night, you shall see him, and judge whether I am not right in closing with him.' Accordingly, they met the next evening, and the WRITER OF ALL WORK was introduced. He began to make a display of his native ignorance and impudence on all subjects immediately, and no one else had occasion to say anything. When he was gone, Mr. Cumberland exclaimed, 'A talking potato, by God!' The talking potato was Mr. Croker, of the Admiralty. Our adventurer shortly, however, returned to his own country, and passing accidentally through a town where they were in want of a ministerial candidate at an Election, the gentleman of modest assurance offered himself, and succeeded. 'They wanted a Jack-pudding,' said the father of the hopeful youth, 'and so they chose my son.'"

The following note by Hazlitt is found in his *The New School for Reform (Collected Works,* 7, 183): "A certain *Talking Potatoe* (who is now one of the props of Church and State), when he first came to this country, used to frighten some respectable old gentlewomen, who invited him to supper, by asking them for a slice of the 'leg of the Savior,' meaning a leg of lamb; or a bit of 'the Holy Ghost pie,' meaning a pigeon-pie on the table. Ill-nature and impertinence are the same in all schools."

939. ENDYMION: A POETIC ROMANCE

This is the review which Shelley, Byron, and others erroneously thought hastened the death of Keats. See Shelley's Preface to *Adonais* (p. 1349) and stanzas 36-37 (p. 761); also Byron's *Don Juan,* XI, 60, and note 5 (p. 636), and note (p. 1333).

Charles Lamb

Written after the Death of Charles Lamb

To a good man of most dear memory
This stone is sacred. Here he lies apart
From the great city where he first drew breath,
Was reared and taught; and humbly earned
    his bread,
To the strict labors of the merchant's desk   5
By duty chained. Not seldom did those tasks
Tease, and the thought of time so spent depress
His spirit, but the recompense was high;
Firm Independence, Bounty's rightful sire;
Affections, warm as sunshine, free as air;   10
And when the precious hours of leisure came,
Knowledge and wisdom, gained from converse
    sweet
With books, or while he ranged the crowded
    streets
With a keen eye, and overflowing heart:
So genius triumphed over seeming wrong,   15
And poured out truth in works by thoughtful
    love
Inspired—works potent over smiles and tears.
And as round mountain-tops the lightning
    plays,
Thus innocently sported, breaking forth
As from a cloud of some grave sympathy,   20
Humor and wild instinctive wit, and all
The vivid flashes of his spoken words.
From the most gentle creature nursed in fields
Had been derived the name he bore—a name,
Wherever Christian altars have been raised,   25
Hallowed to meekness and to innocence;
And if in him meekness at times gave way,
Provoked out of herself by troubles strange,
Many and strange, that hung about his life;
Still, at the centre of his being, lodged   30
A soul by resignation sanctified:
And if too often, self-reproached, he felt
That innocence belongs not to our kind,
A power that never ceased to abide in him,

Charity, 'mid the multitude of sins				35
That she can cover, left not his exposed
To an unforgiving judgment from just Heaven.
O, he was good, if e'er a good man lived!

. . . .

—Wordsworth (1835).

Lines on the Death of Charles Lamb
Once, and once only, have I seen thy face,
Elia! once only has thy tripping tongue
Run o'er my breast, yet never has been left
Impression on it stronger or more sweet.
Cordial old man! what youth was in thy years,
What wisdom in thy levity, what truth
In every utterance of that purest soul!
Few are the spirits of the glorified
I'd spring to earlier at the gate of heaven.
—Landor (1846).

"There was L—— himself, the most delightful, the most provoking, the most witty and sensible of men. He always made the best pun, and the best remark in the course of the evening. His serious conversation, like his serious writing, is his best. No one ever stammered out such fine, piquant, deep, eloquent things in half a dozen half-sentences as he does. His jests scald like tears: and he probes a question with a play upon words. . . . There was no fuss or cant about him: nor were his sweets or his sours ever diluted with one particle of affectation."—William Hazlitt, in "On the Conversation of Authors," *The Plain Speaker* (1826).

"Charles Lamb's nosegay of verse may be held by the small hand of a maiden, and there is not in it one flaunting, gallant flower; it is, however, fragrant with the charities of home, like blossoms gathered in some old cottage croft."—Edward Dowden, in Ward's *The English Poets,* Vol. 4 (1880).

See Landor's *To the Sister of Elia* (p. 996) and Hazlitt's *On Familiar Style* (p. 1038b, 31ff.).

942. IF FROM MY LIPS SOME ANGRY
ACCENTS FELL

This sonnet was addressed to Lamb's sister Mary.

THE OLD FAMILIAR FACES

This is the best known of Lamb's poems. It was probably inspired by his sister Mary's being taken to an asylum as the result of a second attack of insanity in January, 1798. Other incidents referred to in the poem account equally well for its composition. The text here given is that of the first edition.

Subsequent editions omitted the first four lines, perhaps the most strikingly effective in the poem.

943.			THE THREE GRAVES

This poem was written during the time of the spy system, a protective movement inaugurated by Lord Sidmouth (1757-1844), the Home Secretary, in 1817, as the result of several riots and conspiracies and general dissatisfaction in the country. George Edwards, named in the last line of the poem, was a government spy who revealed the Cato Street Conspiracy, a plot to murder the ministers in 1820. Castles and Oliver were other contemporary spies. William Bedloe (1650-80), and Titus Oates (1649-1705), mentioned in the second line, were lying informers on whose testimony and forged documents a number of persons were executed as conspirators in an alleged plot of the Roman Catholics in 1678 to murder Charles II and gain control of the government.

The title of the poem was borrowed from Coleridge's *The Three Graves.* This poem of Lamb's and the next were highly praised by De Quincey for what he called their "almost demoniac force." See p. 1110a, 35-40.

THE GIPSY'S MALISON

This poem was first printed in *Blackwood's Magazine,* Jan., 1829, after it had been declined by *The Gem,* of which Hood was then editor. Upon its publication Lamb wrote B. W. Procter as follows (Jan. 22, 1829): "Did you see a sonnet of mine in Blackwood's last? Curious construction! *Elaborata facilitas!* And now I'll tell. 'Twas written for *The Gem*; but the editors declined it, on the plea that it would *shock all mothers;* so they published *The Widow* instead. I am born out of time. I have no conjecture about what the present world calls delicacy. I thought *Rosamund Gray* was a pretty modest thing. Hessey assures me that the world would not bear it. I have lived to grow into an indecent character. When my sonnet was rejected, I exclaimed, 'Damn the age; I will write for Antiquity!' "

The Widow is a parody of Lamb written by Hood. *Rosamund Gray* is a brief story by Lamb written in 1798. Hessey was one of the publishers of *The London Magazine.*

ON AN INFANT DYING AS SOON AS BORN

Lucas *(Works of Charles and Mary Lamb)* regards this as "in some ways, Lamb's most remarkable poem."

944.   SHE IS GOING

The subject of this poem has not been identified.

LETTER TO WORDSWORTH

945b. 42-43. *I have passed all my days in London.*—Lamb's fondness for the city is admirably expressed in the following poem by William Watson (1893):

At the Grave of Charles Lamb in Edmonton[1]

Not here, O teeming City, was it meet
Thy lover, thy most faithful, should repose,
But where the multitudinous life-tide flows
Whose ocean-murmur was to him more sweet
Than melody of birds at morn, or bleat
Of flocks in spring-time, *there* should Earth
   enclose
His earth, amid thy thronging joys and woes,
There, 'neath the music of thy million feet.
In love of thee this lover knew no peer.
Thine eastern or thy western fane had made
Fit habitation for his noble shade.
Mother of mightier, nurse of none more dear,
Not here, in rustic exile, O not here,
Thy Elia like an alien should be laid.

947.   THOMAS HEYWOOD

a. 23. *The English Traveller.*—Heywood's Preface to this play, published in 1633, is as follows: "If, reader, thou hast of this play been an auditor, there is less apology to be used by intreating thy patience. This tragicomedy (being one reserved amongst 220 in which I had either an entire hand or at the least a main finger) coming accidentally to the press, and I having intelligence thereof, thought it not fit that it should pass as *filius populi* a bastard without a father to acknowledge it: true it is that my plays are not exposed to the world in volumes, to bear the titles of works (as others): one reason is, that many of them by shifting and change of companies have been negligently lost. Others of them are still retained in the hands of some actors, who think it against their peculiar profit to have them come in print, and a third that it never was any great ambition in me to be in this kind voluminously read. All that I have further to say at this time is only this: censure I entreat as favorably as it is exposed to thy view freely.

        Ever
Studious of thy Pleasure and Profit,
        Th. Heywood."

[1] From *Selected Poems of William Watson*, copyright 1902 by the John Lane Company.

By "others," Heywood probably means Ben Jonson, who had recently published his *Works*. Jonson's use of this title for a collection of plays was regarded as presumptuous.

949.   THE TRAGEDIES OF SHAKSPEARE

b. 46. *Ore rotundo.*—The phrase is quoted from Horace's *Ars Poetica*, 323.
952a. 55. *Contemptible machinery.* — One method of producing rain was to tear up rejected manuscripts and drop the pieces upon the stage from above.

953.   THE SOUTH-SEA HOUSE

Most of Lamb's essays were contributed to *The London Magazine* under the pseudonym of "Elia," the name of an obscure Italian clerk whom he had known at the South-Sea House, the headquarters of the South-Sea Company, incorporated in 1710 to monopolize the trade with Spanish South America. Lamb held a subordinate position with this company, probably from Sept., 1791 to Feb., 1792. His brother John was with the company when Lamb entered its employ.

b. 48-49. *Living accounts . . . puzzle me.*—"Here Elia begins his 'matter-of-lie' career. Lamb was at this time in the Accountants' Office of the India House, living among figures all day."—Lucas in his edition of *The Works of Charles and Mary Lamb* (1903).
954b. 9. *Picture still hangs.*—This picture, if it ever existed, has been lost.
956b. 45-47. These names are borrowed from Shakespeare's *The Taming of the Shrew*, Induction, sc. 2, 93-98, in which one of the servants says to Christopher Sly:

Why, sir, you know no house nor no such maid,
Nor no such men as you have reckon'd up,
As Stephen Sly, and old John Naps of Greece,
And Peter Turph, and Henry Pimpernell,
And twenty more such names and men as these
Which never were, nor no man ever saw.

957. CHRIST'S HOSPITAL FIVE AND THIRTY
        YEARS AGO

This essay combines Lamb's experiences at school with those of Coleridge. Both boys entered Christ's Hospital, the famous charity school, on July 17, 1782; Coleridge was nearly ten years old, Lamb was seven and a half. From the opening of the essay to the paragraph beginning "I was a hypochondriac lad" (p. 959b, 41), Lamb writes under the character of Coleridge: with that paragraph he assumes his own character.

963. THE TWO RACES OF MEN

Lucas suggests, in his edition of *The Works of Charles and Mary Lamb*, that the germ of this essay is probably found in the following passage from a letter to Wordsworth, dated April 9, 1816: "Thanks for the books you have given me and for all the books you mean to give me. I will bind up the *Political Sonnets* and *Ode* according to your suggestion. I have not bound the poems yet. I wait till people have done borrowing them. I think I shall get a chain and chain them to my shelves *More Bodleiano,* and people may come and read them at chain's length. For of these who borrow, some read slow, some mean to read but don't read, and some neither read nor meant to read, but borrow to leave you an opinion of their sagacity. I must do my money-borrowing friends the justice to say that there is nothing of this caprice or wantonness of alienation in them. When they borrow my money, they never fail to make use of it."

More Bodleiano.—Until the middle of the eighteenth century it was the custom in the Bodleian Library to have some books fastened with chains.

965b. 10ff. Lamb's letters contain several references to Coleridge's habit of borrowing books. See especially the letters to Coleridge dated June 7, 1809, and Autumn, 1820 (Lucas's ed., pp. 400 and 544).

13. *Bloomsbury.*—A noted district in London; Lamb never lived there.

15-16. *Reformed posture.*—These figures, which once guarded the entrance, had been removed to the rear of the hall.

966a. 1. *Widower-volume.* — *John Buncle* was originally published in two volumes, only one of which remained on Lamb's shelf.

38-40. The authorship of these lines is credited to Lamb.

MRS. BATTLE'S OPINIONS ON WHIST

Hunt reprinted this essay in *The London Journal* after the following statement: "Here followeth, gentle reader, the immortal record of Mrs. Battle and her whist; a game which the author, as thou wilt see, wished that he could play forever; and, accordingly, in the deathless pages of his wit, forever will he play it."

Critics have identified Mrs. Battle with Mary Field, Lamb's grandmother, and with Sarah Burney, the wife of Lamb's friend James Burney, and the center of a prominent whist club. If any identification is necessary, the latter suits well.

968a. 32-33. Lamb is here echoing Burke. See page 1230b, 45ff.

970. MACKERY END, IN HERTFORDSHIRE

Mackery End was the name of a farm in Hertfordshire. Lamb had visited there once before, about 1780.

b. 11-12. *Freethinkers.* — The following among Lamb's friends might be included in this description: Godwin, Hazlitt, Hunt, Thomas Holcroft, and John Thelwall.

971a. 1. *In this fashion.*—Cf. the following statement by Ruskin in his "Of Queen's Gardens," *Sesame and Lilies, II:* "Without, however, venturing here on any attempt at decision how much novel-reading should be allowed, let us at least clearly assert this, that whether novels, or poetry, or history be read, they should be chosen, not for their freedom from evil, but for their possession of good. The chance and scattered evil that may here and there haunt, or hide itself in, a powerful book, never does any harm to a noble girl; but the emptiness of an author oppresses her, and his amiable folly degrades her. And if she can have access to a good library of old and classical books, there need be no choosing at all. Keep the modern magazine and novel out of your girl's way; turn her loose into the old library every wet day, and let her alone. She will find what is good for her; you cannot; for there is just this difference between the making of a girl's character and a boy's—you may chisel a boy into shape, as you would a rock, or hammer him into it, if he be of a better kind, as you would a piece of bronze. But you cannot hammer a girl into anything. She grows as a flower does,—she will wither without sun; she will decay in her sheath, as a narcissus will, if you do not give her air enough; she may fall, and defile her head in dust, if you leave her without help at some moments of her life; but you cannot fetter her; she must take her own fair form and way, if she take any, and in mind as in body, must have always

'Her household motions light and free, And steps of virgin liberty.'

Let her loose in the library, I say, as you do a fawn in the field. It knows the bad weeds twenty times better than you; and the good ones too, and will eat some bitter and prickly ones, good for it, which you had not the slightest thought would have been so."

The lines quoted by Ruskin are from Wordsworth's *She Was a Phantom of Delight,* 13-14 (p. 321).

972.   DREAM-CHILDREN

This reverie is as exquisite a piece of prose as anything Lamb ever wrote; it is one of the choicest bits of prose writing in English literature. The essay was inspired by the death of Lamb's brother John, which occurred on Oct. 26, 1821. Writing to Wordsworth March 20, 1822, Lamb said: "We are pretty well save colds and rheumatics, and a certain deadness to everything, which I think may date from poor John's loss, and another accident or two at the same time, that has made me almost bury myself at Dalston, where yet I see more faces than I could wish. Deaths over-set one and put one out long after the recent grief. Two or three have died within this last two twelve^{ths}, and so many parts of me have been numbed. One sees a picture, reads an anecdote, starts a casual fancy, and thinks to tell of it to this person in preference to every other—the person is gone whom it would have peculiarly suited. It won't do for *another*. Every departure destroys a class of sympathies. There's Capt. Burney gone!—what fun has whist now? what matters it what you lead, if you can no longer fancy him looking over you? One never hears anything, but the image of the particular person occurs with whom alone almost you would care to share the intelligence. Thus one distributes oneself about—and now for so many parts of me I have lost the market. Common natures do not suffice me. Good people, as they are called, won't serve. I want individuals. I am made up of queer points and I want so many answering needles. The going away of friends does not make the remainder more precious. It takes so much from them, as there was a common link. . . . I grow ominously tired of official confinement. Thirty years have I served the Philistines, and my neck is not subdued to the yoke. You don't know how wearisome it is to breathe the air of four pent walls without relief day after day, all the golden hours of the day between 10 and 4 without ease or interposition. . . . O for a few years between the grave and the desk! they are the same, save that at the latter you are outside the machine. . . . I sit like Philomel all day (but not singing) with my breast against this thorn of a desk, with the only hope that some pulmonary affliction may relieve me."

Alfred Ainger, in *Charles Lamb* (English Men of Letters Series), writes of the death of Lamb's brother as follows:

"The death of this brother, wholly unsympathetic as he was with Charles, served to bring home to him his loneliness. He was left in the world with but one near relation [his sister Mary], and that one too often removed from him for months at a time by the saddest of afflictions. No wonder if he became keenly aware of his solitude. No wonder if his thoughts turned to what *might* have been, and he looked back to those boyish days when he wandered in the glades of Blakesware with Alice by his side. . . . For no reason that is apparent, while he retains his grandmother's real name, he places the house in Norfolk, but all the details that follow are drawn from Blakesware. . . . Inexpressibly touching, when we have once learned to penetrate the thin disguise in which he clothes them, are the hoarded memoirs, the tender regrets, which Lamb, writing by his 'lonely hearth,' thus ventures to commit to the uncertain sympathies of the great public. More touching still is the almost superhuman sweetness with which he deals with the character of his lately lost brother. . . . And there is something of the magic of genius, unless, indeed, it was a burst of uncontrollable anguish, in the revelation with which his dream ends."

974.   A DISSERTATION UPON ROAST PIG

In a letter written to his friend Bernard Barton, March 11, 1823, Lamb says that the idea of the discovery of roasting pigs was borrowed from his friend Manning. The fact that Manning had spent some years in China may account for the fantastic scenery of the story. The central idea of the essay, however, has been found in *The Turkish Spy*, an Italian work by Giovanni Paulo Marana (1684), and elsewhere. Lamb writes of the subject of the essay in a letter to Coleridge dated March 9, 1822. Influenced by this essay, several persons sent pigs to Lamb.

977.   OLD CHINA

This essay was one of Wordsworth's favorites. It completes the sympathetic portrait of Mary Lamb begun in *Mackery End, in Hertfordshire.*

980.   POOR RELATIONS

This essay is noted for Lamb's marvelous command of words.

983.   SANITY OF TRUE GENIUS

This essay was originally published as one of the Popular Fallacies under the title *That Great Wit is Allied to Madness.* The subject is a common one among essayists and scientists. See Dryden's *Absalom and Achitophel,* 1, 163-164:

Great wits are sure to madness near allied,
And thin partitions do their bounds divide.

Cf. the essay with Lamb's *On the Tragedies of Shakspeare* (p. 949).

985.   THE DEATH OF COLERIDGE

These reflections were written by Lamb in an album of Mr. Keymer, a London bookseller, at the suggestion of Lamb's friend John Forster. Lamb never fully recovered from the death of Coleridge.

Walter Savage Landor

Selections, p. 985 — Bibliography, p. 1437

In Memory of Walter Savage Landor

Back to the flower-town, side by side,
    The bright months bring,
New-born, the bridegroom and the bride,
    Freedom and spring.

The sweet land laughs from sea to sea,   5
    Filled full of sun;
All things come back to her, being free,—
    All things but one.

In many a tender wheaten plot
    Flowers that were dead   10
Live, and old suns revive; but not
    That holier head.

By this white wandering waste of sea,
    Far north, I hear
One face shall never turn to me   15
    As once this year:

Shall never smile and turn and rest
    On mine as there,
Nor one most sacred hand be pressed
    Upon my hair   20

I came as one whose thoughts half linger,
    Half run before;
The youngest to the oldest singer
    That England bore.

I found him whom I shall not find   25
    Till all grief end,
In holiest age our mightiest mind,
    Father and friend.

But thou, if anything endure,
    If hope there be,   30
O spirit that man's life left pure,
    Man's death set free,

Not with disdain of days that were
    Look earthward now:

Let dreams revive the reverend hair,   35
    The imperial brow;

Come back in sleep, for in the life
    Where thou art not
We find none like thee. Time and strife
    And the world's lot   40

Move thee no more; but love at least
    And reverent heart
May move thee, royal and released,
    Soul, as thou art.

And thou, his Florence, to thy trust   45
    Receive and keep,
Keep safe his dedicated dust,
    His sacred sleep.

So shall thy lovers, come from far,
    Mix with thy name   50
As morning-star with evening-star
    His faultless fame.
                    —A. C. Swinburne (1866).

"Few men have ever impressed their peers so much, or the general public so little, as Walter Savage Landor. Of all celebrated authors, he has hitherto been one of the least popular. Nevertheless he is among the most striking figures in the history of English literature; striking alike by his character and his powers. . . . The place occupied by Landor among English men of letters is a place apart. He wrote on many subjects and in many forms, and was strong both in imagination and criticism. He was equally master of Latin and English, and equally at home in prose and verse. He cannot properly be associated with any given school, or, indeed, with any given epoch of our literature, as epochs are usually counted, but stands alone, alike by the character of his mind and by the tenor and circumstances of his life. . . . Everything he says must be his own. On the other hand, it is no part of Landor's originality to provoke attention, as many even of illustrious writers have done, by emphasis or singularity of style. Arbitrary and vehement beyond other men in many of his thoughts, in their utterance he is always sober and decorous. He delivers himself of whatever is in his mind with an air, to borrow an expression of his own, 'majestically sedate.' "—Sidney Colvin, in *Landor* (English Men of Letters Series, 1881).

"I claim no place in the world of letters; I am alone, and will be alone, as long as I live, and after."—Landor, in a letter to Lord Brougham on the neglect of Southey, printed in *The Last Fruit off an Old Tree* (1853).

985. GEBIR

This poem was suggested to Landor by an Arabian tale, *The History of Charoba, Queen of Egypt,* which he found in Clara Reeve's *The Progress of Romance* (1785), lent him by his friend Rose Aylmer. Gebir is a prince of Spain who makes war upon Charoba in fulfillment of a vow to avenge hereditary wrongs. Charoba is aided by her nurse, the sorceress Dalicia. Although the first meeting of Gebir and Charoba changes their enmity to love, the story ends tragically as a result of Dalicia's misunderstanding of the true situation. Landor first attempted the poem in Latin and in English, but finally decided to write it in English. Later he translated it into Latin. It was republished in 1859 as one of the Hellenics. (See p. 1001a, n. 2.)

"*Gebir* was published in 1798, the year of the *Lyrical Ballads*, and, in its individual way, it marks an epoch almost as distinctly. No blank verse of comparable caliber had appeared since the death of Milton, and, though the form was at times actually reminiscent both of Milton and of the Latin structure of some of the portions as they were originally composed, it has a quality which still remains entirely its own. Cold, sensitive, splendid, so precise, so restrained, keeping step with such a stately music, scarcely any verse in English has a more individual harmony, more equable, more refreshingly calm to the ear."—Symons, in *The Romantic Movement in English Poetry* (1909).

In the selections printed here, Landor's spelling has been somewhat modernized, such forms as *toucht, fixt,* and *lookt* being changed to *touch'd, fix'd, look'd*. On Landor's spelling see his *Imaginary Conversations*, "Archdeacon Hare and Walter Landor," and De Quincey's *Orthographic Mutineers* (*Collected Writings,* ed. Masson, 11, 437).

986. 90ff. The passage upon which the incident of the wrestling match is based is as follows: "Now the chief shepherd was a beautiful person, and of a goodly stature and aspect. One day when he had committed his flocks to the other shepherds, and wandered far away from them, he saw a fair young lady rising out of the sea, who walked towards him and saluted him graciously.—He returned her salutation, and she began to converse with him.—'Young man,' said she, 'will you wrestle with me for a wager that I shall lay against you?'—'What will you lay, fair lady,' said the shepherd, 'and what can I stake against you?' —'If you give me a fall,' said the lady, 'I will be yours, and at your disposal,—and if I

give you a fall you shall give me a beast out of your flock.'—'I am content,' said the shepherd,—so he went towards her, and she met him, and wrestled with him, and presently gave him a fall. She then took a beast out of the flock, and carried it away with her into the sea.

"She came every evening afterwards, and did the same, until the shepherd was desperately in love with her:—So the flock was diminished, and the shepherd was pining away with love and grief.

"One day King *Gebirus,* passing by the shepherd, found him sitting very pensive by his flocks; so he came near and spoke to him.—'What misfortune hath befallen thee, shepherd? why art thou so altered and dejected? thy flock also diminishes, and gives less milk every day?'—Upon this the shepherd took courage, and told the king all that had befallen him by the lady of the sea."

987. 159. "W. Wordsworth borrowed this shell, and filled it to overflowing for the refreshment of the wayfarers in his *Excursion.* The Lord of a Manor may wink at small encroachments on the common, but the steward must note them in his book."—Landor's note, ed. of 1859.

989. ROSE AYLMER

The subject of this little elegy, the daughter of Henry, Baron Aylmer, was Landor's friend and companion during his early years in Wales (1795-98). He was indebted to her for the book which gave him his hint for *Gebir*. The poem was written after hearing the news of her death in India in 1800. Colvin says of this poem (*Landor:* English Men of Letters Series): "Just, natural, simple, severely and at the same time hauntingly melodious, however baldly or stoically they may strike the ear attuned to more high-pitched lamentations, these are the lines which made afterwards so deep an impression upon Charles Lamb. Tipsy or sober, it is reported of that impressionable spirit a few years before his death, he would always be repeating *Rose Aylmer*."

LYRICS, TO IANTHE

A number of lyrics referring to Ianthe, written and published at various times, are here grouped together in the order suggested by Colvin in the Golden Treasury edition of *Selections from Landor*. It is probable that a number of Landor's other lyrics also were addressed to Ianthe. Colvin says of these poems (*Landor:* English Men of Letters Series): "From these years, about 1802-1806, dates the chief part of Landor's verses written to or about Ianthe. Whether in the form of praise, of complaint, or of appeal, these verses are for the most part general in their terms, and do not enable us definitely to retrace the course of an attachment on which Landor never ceased to look back as the strongest of his life, and for the object of which he continued until her death to entertain the most chivalrous and tender friendship. Landor's verses in this class, although not in the first rank of love-poetry, nevertheless express much contained passion in their grave, concise way, and seldom fail to include, within the polished shell of verse, a solid and appropriate kernel, however minute, of thought."

990. PAST RUIN'D ILION HELEN LIVES

Helen was the wife of Menelaus, King of Sparta. Paris carried her off to Troy (Ilion), and by so doing caused the Trojan War. After the fall of Troy, Helen returned to Menelaus.

991. A FIESOLAN IDYL

This poem admirably phrases Landor's passion for flowers. In a letter to H. Crabb Robinson, Landor writes: "I like white flowers better than any others; they resemble fair women. Lily, tuberose, orange, and the truly English syringa are my heart's delight. I do not mean to say that they supplant the rose and violet in my affections, for these are our first loves, before we grew too fond of considering and too fond of displaying our acquaintance with others of sounding titles." —H. C. Robinson's *Diary, Reminiscences, and Correspondence,* 2:518 (1869).

This poem should be compared with Tennyson's *The Gardener's Daughter,* printed some ten years later.

992. THE CITATION AND EXAMINATION OF WILLIAM SHAKSPEARE

This is one of Landor's longer prose works, which aims to reproduce Shakespeare's trial for deer-stealing. The humorous account is supposed to be written by the magistrate's clerk. The work contains several lyrics, the best of which are those printed here. *The Maid's Lament* is found in Shakespeare's pocket by the examiners and read in court. *Upon a Sweet Briar* is recited by Shakespeare after he has heard some lines on dogroses.

993. PERICLES AND ASPASIA

This is a long prose work by Landor composed in the form of imaginary letters written by Pericles, the famous Athenian statesman and orator (fifth century B. C.), and his mistress Aspasia, and some of their friends. Some of the letters are in verse; others contain verses. For the letters written in prose, see p. 1019. Edmund Clarence Stedman says of this work *(Victorian Poets):* "As an exhibition of intellectual beauty [it] may be termed the masterpiece of Landor's whole career. Critics are not wanting who maintain *Pericles and Aspasia* to be the purest creation of sustained art in English prose. . . . [It] is clear as noonday, a book for thinkers,—but a book for lovers also, and should be as immortal as the currents which flow between young hearts."

CORINNA TO TANAGRA

This poem is found in Letter 44, Aspasia to Cleone, following this statement: "To compensate the disappointment you complained of, I will now transcribe for you an ode of Corinna to her native town, being quite sure it is not in your collection. Let me first inform you that the exterior of the best houses in Tanagra is painted with historical scenes, adventures of gods, allegories, and other things; and under the walls of the city flows the Thermodon. This it is requisite to tell you of so small and so distant a place."

I WILL NOT LOVE

This poem is found in Letter 52, Aspasia to Cleone; it purports to be an autograph from the library of Pericles. It follows this statement: "Men may be negligent in their hand-writing, for men may be in a hurry about the business of life; but I never knew either a sensible woman or an estimable one whose writing was disorderly. Well, the verses are prettier than my reflection, and equally true."

THE DEATH OF ARTEMIDORA

This poem is found in Letter 85, Cleone to Aspasia, following this statement: "We are losing, day by day, one friend or other. Artemidora of Ephesus was betrothed to Elpenor, and their nuptials, it was believed, were at hand. How gladly would Artemidora have survived Elpenor. I pitied her almost as much as if she had. I must ever love true lovers on the eve of separation. These indeed were little known to me until a short time before.

We became friends when our fates had made us relatives. On these occasions there are always many verses, but not always so true in feeling and in fact as those which I shall now transcribe for you."

The text here given is that of the first edition. The poem was later included in *The Hellenics* with the last three lines dropped and a few other slight changes.

994. LIFE PASSES NOT AS SOME MEN SAY

This poem is found in Letter 91, Aspasia to Cleone, following this statement: "Nothing is pleasanter to me than exploring in a library. What a delight in being a discoverer! Among a loose accumulation of poetry, the greater part excessively bad, the verses I am about to transcribe are perhaps the least so." Ardalia, of line 7, is the person whom the poet addresses.

LITTLE AGLAE

This poem is found in Letter 113, Cleone to Aspasia, following this statement: "In case of necessity, everything is ready for my departure to the sources of the Meander. I will prove to you that I am not hurried nor frightened; I have leisure to write out what perhaps may be the last verses written in Miletus, unless we are relieved."

WE MIND NOT HOW THE SUN IN THE MID-SKY

This poem is found in Letter 119, Cleone to Aspasia, following this statement: "Worse verses, it may be, than any of those which you lately sent to me affect me more. There is no giddiness in looking down the precipices of youth: it is the rapidity and heat of its course that brings the giddiness. When we are near its termination a chilly thrill comes over us, whether we look before or behind. Yet there is something like enchantment in the very sound of the word *youth*, and the calmest heart, at every season of life, beats in double time to it. Never expect a compensation for what you send me, whether prose or poetry: but expect a pleasure, because it has given me one. Now here are the worse verses for the better, the Milesian for the Attic."

SAPPHO TO HESPERUS

This poem is found in Letter 150, Cleone to Aspasia, where it is quoted as the authentic work of Sappho, the famous Greek lyric poetess of the seventh century B. C. Hesperus is the evening star.

DIRCE

This poem is found in Letter 230, Aspasia to Cleone. Aspasia states that it was sent to her by Pericles to prove that his Athenians could sport with Charon. Dirce, the wife of Lycus, King of Thebes, was murdered by Amphion and Zethus because of her ill treatment of their mother Antiope. Charon was the ferryman who transported the souls of the dead over the River Styx in the lower world.

ON SEEING A HAIR OF LUCRETIA BORGIA

Lucretia Borgia (1480-1519) was an Italian woman, noted for her rare beauty and ability, her patronage of learning and the arts, and notorious for her wickedness.

995. TO JOSEPH ABLETT

The subject of this poem was a Welsh gentleman of considerable means who admired and befriended Landor. Among other things he advanced the money for the purchase of Landor's home near Fiesole, Italy. The poem was written after the two friends had made a tour from Ablett's home to the lakes, and after Landor had returned to Italy.

996. TO THE SISTER OF ELIA

This poem was sent in a letter to H. Crabb Robinson, following this statement: "The death of Charles Lamb has grieved me very bitterly. Never did I see a human being with whom I was more inclined to sympathize. There is something in the recollection that you took me with you to see him which affects me greatly more than writing or speaking of him could do with any other. When I first heard of the loss that all his friends, and many that never were his friends, sustained in him, no thought took possession of my mind except the anguish of his sister. That very night before I closed my eyes I composed this."

997. ON HIS OWN AGAMEMNON AND
IPHIGENEIA

This poem was written as a criticism of Landor's earlier poem *The Shades of Agamemnon and Iphigeneia*, included in Letter 225 of *Pericles and Aspasia*. Agamemnon was the leader of the Greek expedition against Troy. Iphigeneia was his daughter. When the Greek fleet was becalmed at Aulis, a seaport on the east coast of Greece, through the anger of Artemis, the seer of Colchas declared that the death of Iphigeneia was the only means of appeasing the goddess. At the time of the sacrifice Artemis carried Iphigeneia away in a cloud to Tauris, and made her a priestess. See Landor's *Iphigeneia and Agamemnon* (p. 1002).

1. *From eve to morn.*—Cf. Milton's *Paradise Lost*, 1, 742-43: "From morn to noon he fell, from noon to dewy eve."

1001.   ON THE HELLENICS

This poem was prefixed to the second edition of Landor's *The Hellenics* (1847).

THRASYMEDES AND EUNÖE

Thrasymedes eloped with Eunöe, the daughter of Pisistratos, tyrant of Athens, sixth century B. C. In this poem Eunöe's brother Hippias overhauls the fleeing pair and brings them back to Athens.

1002. IPHIGENEIA AND AGAMEMNON

See note above on *On His Own Agamemnon and Iphigeneia.*

1003.   THE HAMADRYAD

A hamadryad was a nymph who was born and who died at the same time as the tree (usually an oak) of which she was the spirit (ἅμα, with + δρυς, tree). The legend traces back to the fifth century B. C.

1008. ON HIS SEVENTY-FIFTH BIRTHDAY

"How definite is the picture of the old man bending with outstretched hands over the dying embers; with what dignity is the emotion repressed. We feel the modern spirit if we contrast this with Browning's *Prospice*, with its cry of exulting struggle, or with Tennyson's *Crossing the Bar*, with its music, its twilight tones, its mystery of the sea."— Reed, in *English Lyrical Poetry* (1912).

1010.   THESEUS AND HIPPOLYTA

Hippolyta, daughter of Ares and Otrera, was Queen of the Amazons, a tribe of warlike women reputed to live in Asia Minor. Theseus, the son of Ægeus, King of Athens, was the national hero of Attica, Greece. In his exploit against the Amazons, he carried off their queen.

1011. IMAGINARY CONVERSATIONS

This work consists of a number of prose dialogues or conversations between illustrious personages chiefly of the past. In "Archdeacon Hare and Walter Landor," Landor says: "Poetry was always my amusement, prose my study and business. I have pub-

lished five volumes of *Imaginary Conversations:* cut the worst of them through the middle, and there will remain in this decimal fraction quite enough to satisfy my appetite for fame. I shall dine late; but the dining-room will be well lighted, the guests few and select."

TIBERIUS AND VIPSANIA

Vipsania was the daughter of Agrippa, a Roman general and consul of the first century B. C. Tiberius, her husband, was the son of Tiberius Nero and Livia (later the wife of Augustus Cæsar) and heir to the throne. Upon the birth of a son (Drusus) to Vipsania, Tiberius was compelled to divorce his wife and marry Julia, the daughter of Augustus, in order that the crown might be held by inheritance. Landor here represents an unexpected meeting between Tiberius and Vipsania.

1013. MARCELLUS AND HANNIBAL

Hannibal, the famous general of Carthage, overcame Marcellus, the Roman general, in southern Italy, in 208 B. C. In this scene, Marcellus lies before his conqueror mortally wounded.

1015. METELLUS AND MARIUS

In this conversation, the Roman centurion Caius Marius, at the request of the tribune Cæcilius Metellus, enters Numantia, a city in Spain besieged by the Romans in 132 B. C., and reports what he has seen.

1017. LEOFRIC AND GODIVA

This conversation is based on the legend that Leofric, Earl of Mercia (eleventh century), consented to the plea of his wife Godiva to relieve the people of a burdensome tax on condition that she should ride through the streets of Coventry naked at noon-day. She fulfilled the condition, covered only by her luxuriant hair. The festival of Godiva is still celebrated in Coventry. See Tennyson's *Godiva.*

1019. PERICLES AND ASPASIA

See note on *Pericles and Aspasia,* p. 1378.

1022.   THE PENTAMERON

The Pentameron (πέντα, five + μέρος, part) is a series of five interviews held on successive days between Giovanni Boccaccio and Francesco Petrarca, famous Italian writers of the fourteenth century. In the selection given here, Boccaccio relates how his former love Fiametta, daughter of the King of Naples, appeared to him in a dream.

"In *The Pentameron* Landor is again at his very best. All his study of the great Italian writers of the 14th century, and all his recent observations of Tuscan scenery and Tuscan character are turned to skilful and harmonious account. Landor loved and understood Boccaccio through and through; and if he over-estimated that prolific and amiable genius in comparison with other and greater men, it was an error which for the present purpose was almost an advantage. Nothing can be pleasanter than the intercourse of the two friendly poets as Landor had imagined it; nothing more classically idyllic than the incidental episodes."—Colvin, in *Landor: English Men of Letters* Series (1878).

Thomas Love Peacock

Poems, p. 1024 — Bibliography, p. 1439

From *Letter to Maria Gisborne*

And there
Is English Peacock, with his mountain Fair
Turned into a Flamingo;—that shy bird
That gleams i' the Indian air—have you not
 heard   235
When a man marries, dies, or turns Hindoo,
His best friends hear no more of him?—but
 you
Will see him, and will like him too, I hope,
With the milk-white Snowdonian Antelope
Matched with this cameleopard—his fine wit 240
Makes such a wound, the knife is lost in it;
A strain too learnèd for a shallow age,
Too wise for selfish bigots; let his page,
Which charms the chosen spirits of the time,
Fold itself up for the serener clime 245
Of years to come, and find its recompense
In that just expectation.
      —Shelley (1820).

The "Snowdonian Antelope" is Peacock's wife, a Welsh girl, who lived near Mt. Snowdon in Wales. The marriage took place on March 20, 1820.

"His learned wit, his satire upon the vulgarity of progress, are more continuously present in his prose than in his verse; but the novels are filled with cheerful scraps of rhyming, wine-songs, love-songs, songs of mockery, and nonsense jingles, some of which are no more than the scholar's idle diversions, but others of a singular excellence. They are like no other verse; they are startling, grotesque, full of hearty extravagances, at times thrilling with unexpected beauty."—Symons, in *The Romantic Movement in English Poetry* (1909).

1024.   HAIL TO THE HEADLONG

This song is found in Chapter 13 of *Headlong Hall*. It is sung as a toast "To the immortal memory of Headlong Ap-Rhaider, and to the health of his noble descendant and worthy representative," Squire Headlong, master of Headlong Hall.

SEAMEN THREE! WHAT MEN BE YE?

This song is sometimes entitled *The Men of Gotham*. It is found in a drinking scene in Chapter 11 of *Nightmare Abbey*.

FOR THE SLENDER BEECH AND THE SAPLING OAK

This poem is recited in Chapter 2 of *Maid Marian* to illustrate the impossibility of a certain young lady's being other than a lover of the birds and the forests.

1025.   THOUGH I BE NOW A GRAY, GRAY FRIAR

This song is sung by a bibulous Friar in Chapter 4 of *Maid Marian*.

OH! BOLD ROBIN HOOD IS A FORESTER GOOD

This song is found in Chapter 11 of *Maid Marian*. It is sung at the end of the day's festivities in Sherwood Forest, the haunt of Robin Hood and his followers.

YE WOODS, THAT OFT AT SULTRY NOON

This song is found in Chapter 18 of *Maid Marian*. It is sung by the Friar as he bids farewell to the forest.

1026. THE CIRCLING OF THE MEAD HORNS

This song is found in Chapter 2 of *The Misfortunes of Elphin*. It is the chorus which greets Elphin, the hero of the story, as he approaches the castle of Seithenyn, one of the "immortal drunkards of the Isle of Britain."

THE WAR SONG OF DINAS VAWR

This song is found in Chapter 11 of *The Misfortunes of Elphin*. The castle of Dinas Vawr, a petty Welsh king of the days of King Arthur, had been seized by King Melvas from east of the Severn. The song is preceded by the following comment: "The hall of Melvas was full of magnanimous heroes, who were celebrating their own exploits in sundry choruses, especially that which follows, which is here put upon record as being the quintessence of all the war-songs that ever were written, and the sum and substance of all the appetencies, tendencies, and consequences of military glory."

1027.   IN THE DAYS OF OLD

This song is found in Chapter 18 of *Crotchet Castle*. It is sung by a Lady Clarinda during an interval at a dancing-party.

LOVE AND AGE

This song is found in Chapter 15 of *Gryll Grange*. It is sung by one of a company of young people. It was probably inspired by Peacock's memory of a young woman to whom he was engaged in 1807, but who married another. She died in 1808. Peacock's *Newark Abbey* was written in her memory.

William Cobbett

Selections, p. 1028 — Bibliography, p. 1416

From *Elegy on William Cobbett*

O bear him where the rain can fall,
  And where the winds can blow;
And let the sun weep o'er his pall
  As to the grave ye go!
And in some little lone churchyard,
  Beside the growing corn,
Lay gentle Nature's stern prose bard,
  Her mightiest peasant-born.
Yes, let the wild-flower wed his grave,
  That bees may murmur near,
When o'er his last home bend the brave
  And say—"A man lies here!"
For Britons honor Cobbett's name,
  Though rashly oft he spoke;
And none can scorn, and few will blame,
  The low-laid heart of oak.
See, o'er his prostrate branches, see!
  E'en factious hate consents
To reverence, in the fallen tree,
  His British lineaments.
        —Ebenezer Elliott (1835).

". . . Peasant-bred, with a passion for farming, and a most genuine, if quite unpoetic, love of the open country and all that it could offer eye or ear, he depicted, with Dutch honesty, the rural England that he knew how to see, its fertility and beauty, the misery that had descended on many of its inhabitants, the decent prosperity remaining to others. And he was master of a style in which to express his knowledge. It is not one of those great styles which embalm their authors' memory; but it was serviceable. He is vigorous, plain, and absolutely unaffected. The aptest words come to him with most per-fect ease. His eloquence springs from vivid insight into the heart of his theme, and from a native fervor and energy that do not need art to blow them into flame. Apart from his plebeian virulence, he shows a natural good taste in writing. The flaccid elegance and pompous rotund verbiage then in vogue are, by him, left on one side. If he cannot frame a period, every sentence has its work to do, and every sentence tells. What mars his farmer's Odyssey, *Rural Rides*, is, perhaps, the excess of this very disregard for fine writing. They are notes of what he saw, and notes must often be brief, formless, and disconnected. Imagination and the charm it gives are, indeed, absent throughout; but his sympathetic realism has an attraction of its own. He scans the look and manners of the laborers; he calculates whether they have bacon to eat; he descants on the capabilities of the soil; and he is able to impress upon his readers the strength of his interest in these things and of his enjoyment of field and woods and streams and the palatable salmon that inhabit the latter. He seems to give an unconscious demonstration how excellent a tongue English could be for a man, who saw and felt keenly, to express the facts as he saw them, and the emotions which possessed him."—C. W. Previté-Orton, in *The Cambridge History of English Literature*, 11, ch. 2.

1033b. 20-30. "To refute lies is not, at present, my business; but it is my business to give you, in as small a compass as possible, one striking proof that they are lies; and thereby to put you well upon your guard for the whole of the rest of your life. The opinion sedulously inculcated by these '*historians*' is this; that, before the *Protestant* times came, England was, comparatively, an insignificant country, *having few people in it, and those few wretchedly poor and miserable.* Now, take the following *undeniable facts.* All the parishes in England are now (except where they have been *united*, and two, three, or four, have been made into one) in point of *size*, what they were *a thousand years ago.* The county of Norfolk is the best cultivated of any one in England. This county has *now* 731 parishes; and the number was formerly greater. Of these parishes 22 *have now no churches at all*; 74 contain less than 100 souls each: and 268 have *no parsonage-houses.* Now, observe, every parish had, in old times, a church and a parsonage-house. The county contains 2092 square miles; that is to say, something less than 3 square miles to each parish, and that is 1920 statute acres of land; and the *size* of each parish is, on an average, that of a piece of ground about one mile and a half each way; so that the churches are, even now, on an average, only about *a mile and a half from each other*. Now, the questions for you to put to yourself are these: Were churches formerly built and kept up *without being wanted*, and especially by a poor and miserable people? Did these miserable people build 74 churches out of 731, each of which 74 had not a hundred souls belonging to it? Is it a sign of an augmented population, that 22 churches out of 731 have tumbled down and been effaced? Was it a country *thinly* inhabited by miserable people that could build and keep a church in every piece of ground a mile and a half each way, besides having, in this same county, 77 monastic establishments and 142 free chapels? Is it a sign of augmented population, ease, and plenty, that, out of 731 parishes, 268 have suffered the parsonage-houses to fall into ruins, and their sites to become patches of nettles and of brambles? Put these questions calmly to yourself: common sense will dictate the answers; and truth will call for an expression of your indignation against the lying historians and the still more lying population-mongers."—Cobbett, in *Advice to Young Men*, Letter I, 52.

See Praed's *Stanzas on Seeing the Speaker Asleep* (pp. 1175-6) and note (p. 1395a).

William Hazlitt

Selections, p. 1033 — Bibliography, p. 1427

"The various critical writings of William Hazlitt are laden with original and striking thoughts, and indicate an intellect strong and intense, but narrowed by prejudice and personal feeling. He was an acute but somewhat bitter observer of life and manners, and satirized rather than described them. Though bold and arrogant in the expression of his opinions, and continually provoking opposition by the hardihood of his paradoxes, he does not appear to have been influenced so much by self-esteem as sensibility. He was naturally shy and despairing of his own powers, and his dogmatism was of that turbulent kind which comes from passion and self-distrust. He had little repose of mind or manner, and in his works almost always appears as if his faculties had been stung and spurred into action."—E. P. Whipple, in *Essays and Reviews* (1849).

"If not the first, he was the most influential of those who bent the essay to this purely literary purpose, and he may be regarded as standing midway between the old essayists and the new. It was a fashion in his own time, and one that has often since been followed, to insist too strongly on Hazlitt's limitations as a critic. Yet, after all has been said, his method was essentially the same as Sainte-Beuve's, and his essays cannot even now be safely neglected by students of the literary developments with which they deal. It is impossible to read them without catching something of the ardor of his own enthusiasm, and it says much for the soundness of his taste and judgment that the great majority of his criticisms emerged undistorted from the glowing crucible of his thoughts."—J. H. Lobban, in Introduction to *English Essayists* (1896).

"Read a dozen of his essays, with their constant play of allusion, their apt—if overabundant—quotation; their fleeting glimpses of imagination, now august, now beautiful, now pathetic, but always vivid; their brilliant, half-earnest paradox; their mild tone of melancholy reflection; their flashes of cynical satire; all flowing in a rhythm, unstudied yet varied and musical—and then you understand why many of the best masters of modern prose—Macaulay, Walter Bagehot, Robert Louis Stevenson, Augustine Birrell—have given to the style of Hazlitt their praise and the better tribute of imitation. 'We are fine fellows,' said Stevenson once, in despairing admiration, 'but we can't write like William Hazlitt.' "—C. T. Winchester, in *A Group of English Essayists of the Early Nineteenth Century* (1910).

The numerous quotations in Hazlitt's writings were written largely from memory and are very often inaccurate. Yet many of them were purposely changed by him in order to be more serviceable and applicable. Frequently he uses earlier phrases of his own as if they were taken from some other author. A number of the quotations found in his writings have not yet been identified.

1033. CHARACTERS OF SHAKESPEAR'S
PLAYS

Hazlitt shares with Hunt the distinction of having introduced a type of theatrical criticism which is frank and honest at the same time that it is keenly appreciative. His criticisms of Shakespeare's plays usually appeared in the papers immediately after the performance of the plays. His criticism of *Hamlet*, a review of Kean's playing, appeared in *The Morning Chronicle*, March 14, 1814. The text here given is that of the first edition of the *Characters of Shakespear's Plays* (1817), which was a reprint, with slight changes, of the earlier reviews.

1034b. 14. *There is no attempt to force an interest.*—Saintsbury regards the criticism expressed in this sentence as one of "the *apices* of Shakespearian criticism" (*History of Criticism and Literary Taste in Europe*, 3:258).

1037. ON FAMILIAR STYLE

"In reading this essay and rereading it, one has the feeling that here are some of the best words ever written on the subject and written by a man who had thought of style and what it means."—Howe, in *Selections from William Hazlitt* (1913). Cf. Lamb's *The Genteel Style of Writing.*

b. 9. *"Tall, opaque words."*—"I hate set dissertations—and above all things in the world, 'tis one of the silliest things in one of them, to darken your hypothesis by placing a number of tall, opake words, one before another, in a right line, betwixt your own and your reader's conception."—Sterne, in *The Life and Opinions of Tristram Shandy*, 3, 20, the Author's Preface. In his review of Miss O'Neill's *Elwina*, in *A View of the English Stage* (*Collected Works*, 8:257), Hazlitt uses the phrase as follows: "We should not have made these remarks, but that the writers in the above paper have a greater knack than any others, by putting a parcel of tall opaque words before them, to blind the eyes of their readers, and hoodwink their own understandings."

1040. THE FIGHT

Henley remarks that the summary of the fight is "alone in literature, as also in the annals of the Ring." (Introduction to *Collected Works*, 1 :xxiii). For an account of the fight and the journey home, see P. G. Patmore's *My Friends and Acquaintance.* Hazlitt's *The Indian Jugglers* is another good essay on sport, especially the latter part, which contains the famous characterization of John Cavanaugh the fives-player (*Collected Works*, 6:77).

1042b. 38. Hazlitt is here echoing *Othello*, I, 3, and he is thinking of his own marital troubles.

1048. ON GOING A JOURNEY

With this essay compare Stevenson's *Walking Tours* (*Works*, Scribner ed., 9:138).

1053b. 43. *Out of my country and myself I go.*—This quotation has not yet been identified.

1054. MY FIRST ACQUAINTANCE WITH POETS

"Any sketch of William Hazlitt may fitly begin with an extract from his most familiar essay—the most delightful essay of personal reminiscence in the English language. It is the story of his spiritual birth."—C. T. Winchester, in *A Group of English Essayists of the Early Nineteenth Century* (1910).

1058a. 38. *Prefer the unknown to the known.*—Cf. Hazlitt's remarks in *On the Conversation of Authors* (*Collected Works*, 7, 29): "Coleridge withholds his tribute of applause from every person, in whom any mortal but himself can descry the least glimpse of understanding. He would be thought to look farther into a millstone than anybody else. He would have others see with his eyes, and take their opinions from him on trust, in spite of their senses. The more obscure and defective the indications of merit, the greater his sagacity and candor in being the first to point them out. He looks upon what he nicknames *a man of genius*, but as the breath of his nostrils, and the clay in the potter's hands. If any such inert, unconscious mass, under the fostering care of the modern Prometheus, is kindled into life,—begins to see, speak, and move, so as to attract the notice of other people,—our jealous patronizer of latent worth in that case throws aside, scorns, and hates his own handy-work; and deserts his intellectual offspring from the moment they can go alone and shift for themselves."

1060a. 21. *Hear the loud stag speak.*—This quotation has not yet been identified.

1062b. 28. *Contempt of Gray.*—See *Biographia Literaria*, ch. 2, note: "I felt almost as if I had been newly couched, when, by Mr. Wordsworth's conversation, I had been induced to re-examine with impartial strictness Gray's celebrated *Elegy*. I had long before detected the defects in *The Bard;* but the *Elegy* I had considered as proof against all fair attacks; and to this day I can not read either without delight, and a portion of enthusiasm."

28-29. *Intolerance of Pope*—See *Biographia Literaria*, ch. 1: "Among those with whom I conversed, there were, of course, very many who had formed their taste, and learned their notions of poetry, from the writings of Mr. Pope and his followers: or to speak more generally, in that school of French poetry, condensed and invigorated by English understanding, which had predominated from the last century. I was not blind to the merits of this school, yet, as from inexperience of the world, and consequent want of sympathy with the general subjects of these poems, they gave me little pleasure, I doubtless undervalued the *kind*, and with the presumption of youth withheld from its masters the legitimate name of poets. I saw that the excellence of this kind consisted in just and acute observations on men and manners in an artificial state of society, as its matter and substance, and in the logic of wit, conveyed in smooth and strong epigrammatic couplets, as its *form;* that even when the subject was addressed to fancy, or the intellect, as in *The Rape of the Lock,* or the *Essay on Man;* nay, when it was a consecutive narration, as in that astonishing product of matchless talent and ingenuity, Pope's Translation of the *Iliad;* still a *point* was looked for at the end of each second line, and the whole was, as it were, a *sorites,*[1] or, if I may exchange a logical for a grammatical metaphor, a *conjunction disjunctive,* of epigrams. Meantime, the matter and diction seemed to me characterized not so much by poetic thoughts, as by thoughts *translated* into the language of poetry."

1063a. 54. *Oh memory!* etc.—This quotation has not yet been identified.

Thomas De Quincey

Selections, p. 1069 — Bibliography, p. 1423

"De Quincey himself, in descanting on the Dream-faculty, says, 'Habitually to dream magnificently, a man must have a constitutional determination to reverie.' In that sentence he announces the true law of all literature that comes under the order of pure phantasy. But in his case, in spite of the strength of the dream-element, we cannot proceed far till we discover that his determination to reverie was but the extreme projection of one phase of a phenomenal nature balancing its opposite. . . . He was skilled in the exercises of the analytic understanding—a logician exacting and precise—else his dreaming had never gained for him the eminence it has gained. Surely it is calculated to strike the most casual reader on a perusal of that first edition of the *Confessions,* that his power of following up sensational effects and tracing with absolute exactness the most delicately varying shades of experience, and recording them with conscientious precision, were as noticeable as were the dreams to which they served to give effect. No proper ground has been laid for a liberal and sympathetic appreciation of De Quincey till these points have been clearly apprehended; and assuredly this is one of the cases where, as he himself has well said, 'not to sympathize is not to

[1] A *sorites* in an abridged form of stating a series of syllogisms, arranged in such a way that the predicate of one member becomes the subject of the following member.

understand.'"—A. H. Japp, in *Thomas De Quincey; His Life and Writings* (1877).

"He represents the reaction from the polish, reserve, and coldness of the eighteenth century to the warmth and glow of the seventeenth century,—the golden period of English prose. His masters are Milton, Jeremy Taylor, Fuller, and Browne, whose eloquence, rich coloring, and elaborate ornamentation he inherits. To these qualities he has added the finish and elegance of the eighteenth century writers, and the freedom, deep feeling, and lofty spiritual tone of our own age. In fineness of texture and in beauty of coloring he is unequalled save by Ruskin, whom he surpasses in form and general pictorial and sound effects. He is sometimes guilty of bad taste or bathos, but when at his best is a supreme master of the 'grand style.' With an imagination as great as Carlyle's, his style is more chastened, rhythmical, and exquisite, though not showing so much industry or moral earnestness. He has a finer rhetorical and critical faculty than Macaulay, and is more stately and vivacious than Landor. De Quincey's unique power lies in his imagination, which is extraordinary. In his best passages there is a poetic loftiness, a phantasmagoric charm, and a spectacular gorgeousness which seizes and holds the mind of the reader with its subtle power. Even when we cannot accept the soundness of his conclusions on philosophical questions, or the accuracy of his statements in the historical and biographical essays, we delight in surrendering ourselves to his wonderful fancy. When he has on his magic robes, few can mount so high."—Wauchope, in his edition of *Confessions of an English Opium-Eater* (1898).

1069. CONFESSIONS OF AN ENGLISH
OPIUM-EATER

"I here present you, courteous reader, with the record of a remarkable period in my life: according to my application of it, I trust that it will prove, not merely an interesting record, but, in a considerable degree, useful and instructive. In *that* hope it is, that I have drawn it up: and *that* must be my apology for breaking through that delicate and honorable reserve, which, for the most part, restrains us from the public exposure of our own errors and infirmities. Nothing, indeed, is more revolting to English feelings, than the spectacle of a human being obtruding on our notice his moral ulcers and scars, and tearing away that 'decent drapery,' which time, or indulgence to human frailty, may have drawn over them: accordingly, the greater part of *our* confessions (that is, spontaneous and extra-judicial confessions) proceed from demireps, adventurers, or swindlers: and for any such acts of gratuitous self-humiliation from those who can be supposed in sympathy with the decent and self-respecting part of society, we must look to French literature, or to that part of the German which is tainted with the spurious and defective sensibility of the French. All this I feel so forcibly, and so nervously am I alive to reproach of this tendency, that I have for many months hesitated about the propriety of allowing this, or any part of my narrative, to come before the public eye, until after my death, when, for many reasons, the whole will be published: and it is not without an anxious review of the reasons for and against this step that I have, at last, concluded on taking it."—De Quincey, in introductory remarks to the reader.

The text here followed is that of the first edition of 1821-22.

In the portion omitted from the *Preliminary Confessions* De Quincey states that he wrote this part as an introduction to the *Confessions* proper for three reasons:

1. As forestalling and answering the question as to how a reasonable being could become a slave to opium.

2. As furnishing a key to some parts of that tremendous scenery which afterwards peopled his dreams.

3. As creating a previous personal interest in his subject apart from the matter of the confessions.

1071b. 45. *A picture of the lovely ——.* "The housekeeper was in the habit of telling me that the lady had *lived* (meaning, perhaps, had been *born*) two centuries ago; that date would better agree with the tradition that the portrait was a copy from Vandyke. All that she knew further about the lady was that either to the grammar school, or to that particular college at Oxford with which the school was connected, or else to that particular college at Oxford with which Mr. Lawson personally was connected, or else, fourthly, to Mr. Lawson himself as a private individual, the unknown lady had been a special benefactress. She was also a special benefactress to me, through eighteen months, by means of her sweet Madonna countenance. And in some degree it serves to spiritualize and to hallow this service that of her who unconsciously rendered it I know neither the name, nor the exact rank or age, nor the place where she lived and died. She was parted from me by perhaps two centuries; I

from her by the gulf of eternity."—De Quincey's note in enlarged *Confessions* (*Collected Writings*, ed. Masson, 3:297). Sir Anthony Vandyke (1599-1641) was a Flemish portrait painter; he lived for some years in England. **1073b. 34-35.** *A harsh and contemptuous expression.*—"I was wrong if I said anything in my anger that was disparaging or skeptical as to the bishop's intellectual pretensions; which were not only very sound, but very appropriate to the particular stations which he filled. For the Bishop of Bangor (at that time Dr. Cleaver) was also the head of Brasenose, Oxford—which college was indebted to him for its leadership at that era in scholarship and discipline. In this academic character I learned afterwards that he might be called almost a reformer,—a wise, temperate, and successful reformer; and, as a scholar, I saw many years later that he had received the laudatory notice of Porson."—De Quincey, in enlarged *Confessions* (*Collected Writings*, ed. Masson, 3:323-24). Richard Porson (1759-1808) was a famous Greek scholar and critic. **1075a. 11.** In the enlarged *Confessions*, De Quincey inserted an admirable passage, describing the journey to London. See *Collected Writings*, ed. Masson, 3:339-348.

b. 7ff. One cannot be sure of the accuracy of De Quincey's account of the house and of his residence there.

1076a. 38. *Whether this child.*—Garnett suggests, in his edition of the *Confessions*, that Dickens must have had this whole situation in mind when he drew the Marchioness and Sally Brass in *Old Curiosity Shop*.

1082a. 10. *Murder committed.*—"Two men, Holloway and Haggerty, were long afterwards convicted, upon very questionable evidence, as the perpetrators of this murder. The main testimony against them was that of a Newgate turnkey, who had imperfectly overheard a conversation between the two men. The current impression was that of great dissatisfaction with the evidence; and this impression was strengthened by the pamphlet of an acute lawyer, exposing the unsoundness and incoherency of the statements relied upon by the court. They were executed, however, in the teeth of all opposition. And, as it happened that an enormous wreck of life occurred at the execution (not fewer, I believe, than sixty persons having been trampled under foot by the unusual pressure of some brewers' draymen forcing their way with linked arms to the space below the drop), this tragedy was regarded for many years by a section of the London mob as a providential judgment upon the passive metropolis."—De

Quincey's note in enlarged *Confessions* (*Collected Writings*, ed. Masson, 3:370).

1090a. 20-21. *The most pleasant place.*—"I trust that my reader has not been so inattentive to the windings of my narrative as to fancy me speaking here of the Brown-Brunell and Pyment [Brunell's clerk] period. Naturally I had no money disposable at that period for the opera. I am speaking here of years stretching far beyond those boyish scenes—interludes in my Oxford life, or long after Oxford."—De Quincey's note in enlarged *Confessions* (*Collected Writings*, ed. Masson, 3:389).

1092b. 20ff. Cf. with the following closing lines of Raleigh's *History of the World*:—"O, eloquent, just, and mighty Death! whom none could advise, thou hast persuaded; what none have dared, thou hast done; and whom all the world flattered, thou only hast cast out of the world and despised: thou hast drawn together all the far stretched greatness, all the pride, cruelty, and ambition of man, and covered it all over with these two narrow words, *Hic jacet.*"

1093. INTRODUCTION TO THE PAINS OF OPIUM

The portion omitted recounts the changes that took place between 1804 and 1813 at the school De Quincey attended and in his own life. Mention is made of De Quincey's sufferings of 1813, in which his old dreams were revived, and as a result of which he became a "regular and confirmed opium-eater." The selection printed continues the record from 1816.

1095a. 16ff. "The cottage and the valley concerned in this description were not imaginary: the valley was the lovely one, *in those days*, of Grasmere; and the cottage was occupied for more than twenty years by myself, as immediate successor, in the year 1809, to Wordsworth. Looking to the limitation here laid down—*viz.*, *in those days*—the reader will inquire in what way *Time* can have affected the beauty of Grasmere. Do the Westmoreland valleys turn gray-headed? O reader! this is a painful memento for some of us! Thirty years ago, a gang of Vandals (nameless, I thank heaven, to me), for the sake of building a mail-coach road that never would be wanted, carried, at a cost of £3000 to the defrauded parish, a horrid causeway of sheer granite masonry, for three-quarters of a mile, right through the loveliest succession of secret forest dells and sly recesses of the lake, margined by unrivalled ferns, amongst which was the *Osmunda regalis*. This sequestered angle

of Grasmere is described by Wordsworth, as it unveiled itself on a September morning, in the exquisite poems on the 'Naming of Places.' From this also—*viz.*, this spot of ground, and this magnificent crest (the Osmunda)—was suggested that unique line, the finest independent line through all the records of verse,

'Or lady of the lake,
Sole-sitting by the shores of old romance.'

Rightly therefore did I introduce this limitation. The Grasmere before and after this outrage were two different vales."—De Quincey's note in enlarged *Confessions* (*Collected Writings*, ed. Masson, 3:406). The poem referred to begins "A narrow girdle of rough stones and crags."

1097b. 35-36. *Reading is an accomplishment of mine.*—Some persons admired the soft, clear tone of De Quincey's voice in conversation, but others found much fault with his reading. "It seems to me, from the manner in which the Opium-Eater recited a few lines occasionally which he had occasion to quote, that the reading upon which in his *Confessions* he piques himself would scarcely appear good to most people. He reads with too inward a voice; he dwells much upon the long vowels (this he does in his conversation, which makes it resemble more a speech delivered in a debating society than the varitonous discourse usually held among friends); he ekes out particular syllables, has generally much appearance of intensity, and, in short, removes his tone and manner too much from the mode of common language. Hence I could not always catch the words in his quotations, and though one acquainted with the quotation beforehand would relish it the more from having an opportunity afforded of dwelling upon it, and from hearing the most made of those particular parts for the sake of which it is brought forward, yet general hearers would be left far behind, and in a state of wonder at the quoter."—From Woodhouse's *Conversations*, quoted by Garnett in his edition of the *Confessions* (1885).

1098a. 5. An early manuscript of the *Confessions* contains at this point the following entertaining paragraph: "This, then, has been the extent of my reading for upwards of sixteen months. It frets me to enter those rooms of my cottage in which the books stand. In one of them, to which my little boy has access, he has found out a use for some of them. Somebody has given him a bow and arrows—God knows who, certainly not I, for I have not energy or ingenuity to invent a walking-stick—thus equipped for action, he rears up the largest of the folios that he can lift, places them on a tottering base, and then shoots until he brings down the enemy. He often presses me to join him; and sometimes I consent, and we are both engaged together in these intellectual labors. We build up a pile, having for its base some slender modern metaphysician, ill able (poor man!) to sustain such a weight of philosophy. Upon this we place the Dutch quartos of Descartes[1] and Spinoza;[2] then a third story of Schoolmen[3] in folio—the Master of Sentences,[4] Suarez,[5] Picus Mirandula[6] and the Telemonian bulk of Thomas Aquinas;[7] and when the whole architecture seems firm and compact, we finish our system of metaphysics by roofing the whole with Duval's enormous Aristotle.[8] So far there is some pleasure—building up is something, but what is that to destroying? Thus thinks, at least, my little companion, who now, with the wrath of the Pythian Apollo,[9] assumes his bow and arrows; plants himself in the remotest corner of the room, and prepares his fatal shafts. The bowstring twangs, flights of arrows are in the air, but the Dutch impregnability of the Bergen-op-Zooms[10] at the base receives the few which reach the mark, and they recoil without mischief done. Again the baffled archer collects his arrows, and again he takes his station. An arrow issues forth and takes effect on a weak side of Thomas. Symptoms of disillusion appear—the cohesion of the system is loosened—the Schoolmen begin to totter; the Stagyrite[11] trembles; Philosophy rocks to its centre; and, before it can be seen

[1] Descartes (1596-1650) was a noted French philosopher; he lived in Holland from 1629 to 1649.
[2] Spinoza (1632-77) was a noted Dutch philosopher.
[3] The Schoolmen were medieval Christian philosophers, who tried to reconcile Christian faith with reason.
[4] The Master of Sentences was Peter Lombard, an Italian theologian of the twelfth century; he was so called from his Latin work Four Books of Sentences.
[5] Suarez (1548-1617) was a noted Spanish Jesuit philosopher and theologian.
[6] Picus Mirandula was Pico, Count of Mirandola (1463-94), an Italian humanist and philosopher.
[7] Thomas Aquinas was an Italian theologian and scholastic philosopher of the thirteenth century; he was a prolific writer; his works are called "Telemonian" from Telamon, a famous legendary Greek hero.
[8] Duval was probably an editor of the works of Aristotle (fourth century B. C.), the famous Greek philosopher.
[9] Apollo, the god of the sun, was given the epithet Pythian, because he slew the Python, the serpent at Delphi.
[10] Bergen-op-Zoom was formerly a strongly fortified town in the Netherlands.
[11] Aristotle, so called from Stagira, his birthplace, a city on the coast of Macedonia.

whether time will do anything to heal their wounds, another arrow is planted in the schism of their ontology; the mighty structure heaves—reels—seems in suspense for one moment, and then, with one choral crash—to the frantic joy of the young Sagittary—lies subverted on the floor! Kant[1] and Aristotle, Nominalists and Realists,[2] Doctors Seraphic[3] or Irrefragable,[4] what cares he? All are at his feet—the Irrefragable has been confuted by his arrows, the Seraphic has been found mortal, and the greatest philosopher and the least differ but according to the brief noise they have made."—Posthumous Works, ed. Japp, 1:318-19.

45ff. "For this, as for some other passages, I was justly attacked by an able and liberal critic in The New Edinburgh Review, as for so many absurd irrelevancies: in that situation no doubt they were so; and of this, in spite of the haste in which I had written the greater part of the book, I was fully aware. However, as they said no more than what was true, I was glad to take that, or any occasion which I could invent, for offering my public testimony of gratitude to Mr. Ricardo. The truth is, I thought that something might occur to intercept any more appropriate mode of conveying my homage to Mr. Ricardo's ear, which should else more naturally have been expressed in a direct work on political economy. This fear was at length realized—not in the way I had apprehended, viz., by my own death, but by Mr. Ricardo's. And now, therefore, I felt happy that, at whatever price of good taste, I had in some imperfect way made known my sense of his high pretensions—although, unfortunately, I had given him no means of judging whether my applause were of any value. For during the interval between September, 1821, and Mr. Ricardo's death in September, 1823, I had found no leisure for completing my work on political economy."—De Quincey, in Dialogues of Three Templars on Political Economy (Collected Writings, ed. Masson, 9:39-40). This article first appeared in The London Magazine, March, 1824.

1099b. 43-44. Roman centurion over his soldiers.—A reference to the reply of the cen-

[1] Kant (1724-1804) was a noted German philosopher.
[2] The Nominalists were a school of philosophers who held that universal and collective terms have no real existences corresponding to them; the Realists held an opposite view.
[3] The Seraphic Doctor was St. Bonaventura (1221-74), an Italian scholastic philosopher noted for the religious fervor of his style.
[4] The Irrefragable Doctor was Alexander of Hales, an English scholastic philosopher of the thirteenth century.

turion to Christ, *Matthew*, 8:9: "For I am a man under authority, having soldiers under me; and I say to this man, Go, and he goeth; and to another, Come, and he cometh; and to my servant, Do this, and he doeth it."

1100b. 2-3. *Relative of mine.*—"The heroine of this remarkable case was a girl about nine years old; and there can be little doubt that she looked down as far within the *crater* of death—that awful volcano—as any human being ever *can* have done that has lived to draw back and report her experience. Not less than ninety years did she survive this memorable escape; and I may describe her as in all respects a woman of remarkable and interesting qualities. She enjoyed throughout her long life, as the reader will readily infer, serene and cloudless health; had a masculine understanding; reverenced truth not less than did the Evangelists; and led a life of saintly devotion, such as might have glorified '*Hilarion or Paul.*'—(The words in italics are Ariosto's.)—I mention these traits as characterizing her in a memorable extent, that the reader may not suppose himself relying upon a dealer in exaggerations, upon a credulous enthusiast, or upon a careless wielder of language. Forty-five years had intervened between the first time and the last time of her telling me this anecdote, and not one iota had shifted its ground amongst the incidents, nor had any the most trivial of the circumstantiations suffered change. The scene of the accident was the least of valleys,—what the Greeks of old would have called an ἄγκος, and we English should properly call a dell. Human tenant it had none: even at noonday it was a solitude, and would oftentimes have been a silent solitude, but for the brawling of a brook—not broad, but occasionally deep—which ran along the base of the little hills. Into this brook, probably into one of its dangerous pools, the child fell: and, according to the ordinary chances, she could have had but a slender prospect indeed of any deliverance; for, although a dwelling-house was close by, it was shut out from view by the undulations of the ground. How long the child lay in the water was probably never inquired earnestly until the answer had become irrecoverable: for a servant, to whose care the child was then confided, had a natural interest in suppressing the whole case. From the child's own account, it should seem that *asphyxia* must have announced its commencement. A process of struggle and deadly suffocation was passed through half consciously. This process terminated by a sudden blow apparently *on* or *in* the brain, after which there was no pain or conflict; but in

an instant succeeded a dazzling rush of light; immediately after which came the solemn apocalypse of the entire past life. Meantime, the child's disappearance in the water had happily been witnessed by a farmer who rented some fields in this little solitude, and by a rare accident was riding through them at the moment. Not being very well mounted, he was retarded by the hedges and other fences in making his way down to the water; some time was thus lost; but, once at the spot, he leaped in, booted and spurred, and succeeded in delivering one that must have been as nearly counted amongst the populations of the grave as perhaps the laws of the shadowy world can suffer to return!"—De Quincey's note in enlarged *Confessions* (*Collected Writings*, ed. Masson, 3:435). The relative mentioned is said to be De Quincey's mother. The quotation from Ariosto is found in *Orlando Furioso*, VIII, 45, 8.

1101a. 39-40. *Set of plates . . . called his "Dreams."*—No plates of this title were ever published by Piranesi.

b. 19-20. *Great modern poet.*—"What poet? It was Wordsworth; and why did I not formally name him? This throws a light backwards upon the strange history of Wordsworth's reputation. The year in which I wrote and published these Confessions was 1821; and at that time the name of Wordsworth, though beginning to emerge from the dark cloud of scorn and contumely which had hitherto overshadowed it, was yet most imperfectly established. Not until ten years later was his greatness cheerfully and generally acknowledged. I, therefore, as the very earliest (without one exception) of all who came forward, in the beginning of his career, to honor and welcome him, shrank with disgust from making any sentence of mine the occasion for an explosion of vulgar malice against him. But the grandeur of the passage here cited inevitably spoke for itself; and he that would have been most scornful on hearing the name of the poet coupled with this epithet of 'great' could not but find his malice intercepted, and himself cheated into cordial admiration, by the splendor of the verses."—De Quincey's note in enlarged *Confessions* (*Collected Writings*, ed. Masson, 3:439).

1102a. 5. *Objective.*—"This word, so nearly unintelligible in 1821, so intensely scholastic, and, consequently, when surrounded by familiar and vernacular words, so apparently pedantic, yet, on the other hand, so indispensable to accurate thinking, and to *wide* thinking, has since 1821 become too common to need any apology."—De Quincey's note in enlarged *Confessions* (*Collected Writings*, ed. Masson, 3:440).

Cf. the following passage from Ruskin's *Modern Painters*, Part IV, ch. 12, "Of the Pathetic Fallacy," sec. 1: "German dulness and English affectation have of late much multiplied among us the use of two of the most objectionable words that were ever coined by the troublesomeness of metaphysicians,—namely, *Objective* and *Subjective*. No words can be more exquisitely, and in all points, useless; and I merely speak of them that I may, at once and forever, get them out of my way, and out of my reader's."

1104a. 57. The original manuscript contained at this point the following passage: "This dream at first brought tears to one who had been long familiar only with groans: but afterwards it fluctuated and grew unsteady: the passions and the scenery changed countenance, and the whole was transposed into another key. Its variations, though interesting, I must omit.

"At length I grew afraid to sleep, and I shrunk from it as from the most savage torture. Often I fought with my drowsiness, and kept it aloof by sitting up the whole night and following day. Sometimes I lay down only in the daytime: and sought to charm away the phantoms by requesting my family to sit around me and to talk: hoping thus to derive an influence from what affected me externally into my internal world of shadows: but, far from this, I infected and stained as it were the whole of my waking experience with feelings derived from sleep. I seemed indeed to live and to converse even when awake with my visionary companions much more than with the realities of life. 'Oh, X, what do you see? dear X, what is it that you see?' was the constant exclamation of M[argaret], by which I was awakened as soon as I had fallen asleep, though to me it seemed as if I had slept for years. My groans had, it seems, wakened her, and, from her account, they had commenced immediately on my falling asleep.

"The following dream, as an impressive one to me, I shall close with: it grew up under the influence of that misery which I have described above as resulting from the almost paralytic incapacity to do anything towards completing my intellectual labors, combined with a belief which at the time I reasonably entertained that I should soon be called on to quit forever this world and those for whom I still clung to it."—Quoted by Garnett in his edition of the *Confessions*, 263. Margaret was De Quincey's wife.

1105b. 11. *I triumphed.*—This was true when the *Confessions* was first written in 1821; but De Quincey later suffered prostrations under the influence of opium, notably in 1823-24 and in 1841-44.

1106a. 20. The *Confessions* closes with an Appendix, in which De Quincey rather apologizes for conveying the impression that he had wholly renounced the use of opium.

ON THE KNOCKING AT THE GATE IN MACBETH

"The little paper *On the Knocking at the Gate in Macbeth* is interesting in several ways. It is a classical instance of the peculiar faculty of discovering hidden analogies of which De Quincey boasts; like Lamb's essay on the tragedies of Shakspere considered as to their fitness for stage representation, it is an early note of the great burden of rational Shakspere appreciation that took its rise, in England, in the lectures of Coleridge; and it is a contribution from one who does not rank among the great commentators upon the Elizabethan drama, which no such commentator can afford to neglect. There is, in fact, no part of De Quincey's additions to literature in which he has more clearly redeemed for all time a bit of the unknown."— Turk, in Introduction to *Selections from De Quincey* (Athenæum Press ed.), 1.

For another example of the same kind of writing see the Postscript to *On Murder Considered as One of the Fine Arts* (*Collected Writings*, ed. Masson, 13:70).

1115. AUTOBIOGRAPHIC SKETCHES

The Affliction of Childhood is mainly a reproduction, with alterations, of portions of De Quincey's *Suspiria de Profundis* articles printed in *Blackwood's Magazine* in 1845, and of the first Autobiographic Sketch printed in *Hogg's Instructor* in 1851. In the portion omitted De Quincey tells of the status of the family.

1126. SAVANNAH-LA-MAR

Savannah-la-Mar is the name of a small coast town in Jamaica, where De Quincey's brother Richard lost his life during a hunting trip.

1127. THE POETRY OF POPE

The following selection is part of an article printed in *The North British Review*, Aug., 1848, in the form of a review of W. Roscoe's edition of *The Works of Alexander Pope* (1847). When reprinted by De Quincey the article was entitled *Alexander Pope;* but Masson's title (*Collected Writings*, 11:51) is used here to distinguish this article from another one by De Quincey entitled *Alexander Pope*, printed in *The Encyclopædia Britannica*.

1129. THE ENGLISH MAIL-COACH

"This little paper, according to my original intention, formed part of the *Suspiria de Profundis*, from which, for a momentary purpose, I did not scruple to detach it, and to publish it apart, as sufficiently intelligible even when dislocated from its place in a larger whole. To my surprise, however, one or two critics, not carelessly in conversation, but deliberately in print, professed their inability to apprehend the meaning of the whole, or to follow the links of the connection between its several parts. I am myself as little able to understand where the difficulty lies, or to detect any lurking obscurity, as these critics found themselves to unravel my logic. Possibly I may not be an indifferent and neutral judge in such a case. I will therefore sketch a brief abstract of the little paper according to my original design, and then leave the reader to judge how far this design is kept in sight through the actual execution.

"Thirty-seven years ago, or rather more, accident made me, in the dead of night, and of a night memorably solemn, the solitary witness of an appalling scene, which threatened instant death in a shape the most terrific to two young people whom I had no means of assisting, except in so far as I was able to give them a most hurried warning of their danger; but even *that* not until they stood within the very shadow of the catastrophe, being divided from the most frightful of deaths by scarcely more, if more at all, than seventy seconds.

"Such was the scene, such in its outline, from which the whole of this paper radiates as a natural expansion. This scene is circumstantially narrated in Section the Second, entitled 'The Vision of Sudden Death.'

"But a movement of horror, and of spontaneous recoil from this dreadful scene, naturally carried the whole of that scene, raised and idealized, into my dreams, and very soon into a rolling succession of dreams. The actual scene, as looked down from the box of the mail, was transformed into a dream, as tumultuous and changing as a musical fugue. This troubled dream is circumstantially reported in Section the Third, entitled 'Dream-Fugue on the theme of Sudden Death.' What I had beheld from my seat upon the mail,—the scenical strife of action and passion, of anguish and fear, as I had there witnessed them moving in ghostly silence,—this

duel between life and death narrowing itself to a point of such exquisite evanescence as the collision neared: all these elements of the scene blended, under the law of association, with the previous and permanent features of distinction investing the mail itself; which features at that time lay—1st, in velocity unprecedented; 2dly, in the power and beauty of the horses; 3dly, in the official connection with the government of a great nation; and, 4thly, in the function, almost a consecrated function, of publishing and diffusing through the land the great political events, and especially the great battles, during a conflict of unparalleled grandeur. These honorary distinctions are all described circumstantially in the First or introductory Section ('The Glory of Motion'). The three first were distinctions maintained at all times; but the fourth and grandest belonged exclusively to the war with Napoleon; and this it was which most naturally introduced Waterloo into the dream. Waterloo, I understand, was the particular feature of the 'Dream-Fugue' which my censors were least able to account for. Yet surely Waterloo, which, in common with every other great battle, it had been our special privilege to publish over all the land, most naturally entered the dream under the license of our privilege. If not—if there be anything amiss —let the Dream be responsible. The Dream is a law to itself; and as well quarrel with a rainbow for showing or for *not* showing, a secondary arch. So far as I know, every element in the shifting movements of the Dream derived itself either primarily from the incidents of the actual scene, or from secondary features associated with the mail. For example, the cathedral aisle derived itself from the mimic combination of features which grouped themselves together at the point of approaching collision—*viz.*, an arrow-like section of the road, six hundred yards long, under the solemn lights described, with lofty trees meeting overhead in arches. The guard's horn, again—a humble instrument in itself— was yet glorified as the organ of publication for so many great national events. And the incident of the Dying Trumpeter, who rises from a marble bas-relief, and carries a marble trumpet to his marble lips for the purpose of warning the female infant, was doubtless secretly suggested by my own imperfect effort to seize the guard's horn, and to blow the warning blast. But the Dream knows best; and the Dream, I say again, is the responsible party."—De Quincey, in Preface to the volume of his *Collected Writings* (1854) containing *The English Mail-Coach*. It is printed by

Masson as the Author's Postscript (*Collected Writings*, 13:328-30).

1132a. 28ff. "This paragraph is a caricature of a story told in Staunton's *Account of the Earl of Macartney's Embassy to China in 1792.*"—Masson's note in *Collected Writings*, 13:277. The account was published in 1797.

1135a. 22. *"Tallyho"* or *"Highflyer."*—A tallyho was a kind of four-in-hand pleasure coach, so called from a popular coach named "The Tallyho." A highflyer was a fast stage coach.

1147a. 49-50. *Lilliputian Lancaster.*—Lancaster, the county seat of Lancashire, was much smaller than Liverpool or Manchester, both situated in the same county.

Thomas Lovell Beddoes

Poems, p. 1155 — Bibliography, p. 1407

"Beddoes has sometimes been treated as a mainly bookish poet deriving from the Elizabethans and Shelley. I cannot agree with this. His very earliest work, written when he could not know much either of Shelley or Keats, shows, as they do, technique caught from Leigh Hunt. But this is quite dropped later; and his Elizabethanism is not imitation but inspiration. In this inspiration he does not follow but shares with his greater contemporaries. He is a younger and tragic counterpart to Charles Lamb in the intensity with which he has imbibed the Elizabethan spirit, rather from the night-shade of Webster and Tourneur than from the vine of Shakespeare. As wholes, his works are naught, or naught but night-shade. . . . But they contain passages, especially lyrics, of the most exquisite fancy and music, such as since the seventeenth century none but Blake and Coleridge had given."—Saintsbury, in *A History of Nineteenth Century Literature* (1896).

"In his lyric form, Beddoes has a preference for brief lines skilfully combined into intricate stanzas. He was too modest when he said that he could not 'manage rhyme well or easily,' or 'order complicated verse harmoniously'; for this is just what he can do. His best songs are frail-seeming but unbreakable fabrics, like the fairy chain that was woven out of the sound of cats' footsteps and the roots of the hills. They did not come easily, but the result shows no effort; and not many wise, not many learned amongst the English poets have risen so lightly into so pure a lyric atmosphere as this specialist, with his somewhat unblessed life and his death-engrossed imagination."—O. Elton, in *A Survey of English Literature, 1780-1880* (1928).

1155. POOR OLD PILGRIM MISERY

This song is found in Act I, sc. 1, of *The Bride's Tragedy*. Hesperus sings it to his bride Floribel, after she has related a dream in which she was told to beware "of love, of fickleness, and woe, and mad despair."

1156. A HO! A HO!

This song is found in Act II, sc. 1, of *The Bride's Tragedy*. It is sung by a boy in response to his master's request for a song. It is sometimes entitled *Love Goes A-Hawking*.

STREW NOT EARTH WITH EMPTY STARS

This song is found in Act I, sc. 1, of *The Second Brother*. It is sung by female attendants to Orazio, a self-proclaimed son of Bacchus, god of wine.

HOW MANY TIMES DO I LOVE THEE, DEAR?

This song is found in Act I, sc. 3, of *Torrismond*. It is sung by female attendants, at night in a garden, to their mistress, Veronica, to induce her to sleep.

TO SEA! TO SEA!

This song is found in Act I, sc. 1, of *Death's Jest Book*. It is sung on a ship by sailors about to depart on a voyage to rescue their duke from captivity in a foreign country.

THE SWALLOW LEAVES HER NEST

This song is found in Act I, sc. 4, of *Death's Jest Book*. It is heard from the waters after Sibylla has thrown herself upon the dead body of her lover, Wolfram, who has just been killed by the duke, his rival. Wolfram had learned that the duke had tried to poison him, and was killed because of this knowledge.

1157. IF THOU WILT EASE THINE HEART

This song is found in Act II, sc. 1, of *Death's Jest Book*. It is a dirge sung at the funeral of Wolfram in the presence of the duke, Sibylla, and others.

LADY, WAS IT FAIR OF THEE

This and the next song are found in Act IV, sc. 3, of *Death's Jest Book*. The first is sung by Siegfried, a dejected courtier, beneath the window of his lady love, Amala. The second is sung to Amala by Athulf, another lover, who has taken poison because his brother has married her.

OLD ADAM, THE CARRION CROW

This and the next song are found in Act V, sc. 3, of *Death's Jest Book*. The first is sung by the ghost of Wolfram, disguised as a fool, after he has listened to a drinking song by Siegfried. The second is a dirge sung by a funeral procession bearing Sibylla to her grave.

John Keble

Poems, p. 1159 — Bibliography, p. 1435

"There can be no doubt that Keble had, in even an eminent degree, some of the higher qualities which make the true poet. His fancy was lively and fertile in images full of beauty. His observation of outward nature, such as it may be seen in the rich lowlands of England, was accurate; and his feeling for the quiet and tender beauty of grove and stream, and field and English wild flowers was exquisitely quick and true. His sympathy with all that is pure and sweet in home affections, with the joys and sorrows of family life, with the ways and the feelings of children, was almost unequalled. . . . He had learnt, too, from Cowper and Wordsworth in England, and from the early poets of ancient Greece, whom he loved so well, to express his thought by preference directly and truthfully, avoiding artificial 'poetic diction.'"—E. T. Vaughan, in "The Life of Keble," *The Contemporary Review* (1869).

1159.   THE CHRISTIAN YEAR

This was a collection of poems characterized by Keble as "thoughts in verse for the Sundays and Holydays throughout the year."

Thomas Hood

Poems, p. 1161 — Bibliography, p. 1428

". . . apart even from the very best of the comic work . . . apart from the 'sensational pieces' *The Song* and *The Bridge*, which make their appeal at once to all those who are likely to appreciate them, Hood has to his credit a body of purely serious poetical work neither aiming at mere popularity, nor deliberately eschewing it, work to be taken at a purely poetic valuation and judged on that, which (even though fifteen editions of it sold in as many years after his death) is still far too often neglected, and, even when not quite neglected, is far too seldom accorded its proper rank."—G. Saintsbury, in *The Cambridge History of English Literature*, XII.

To the Memory of Hood

Another star 'neath Time's horizon dropped,
  To gleam o'er unknown lands and seas;
Another heart that beat for freedom stopped,—
  What mournful words are these!

O Love Divine, that claspest our tired earth,
  And lullest it upon thy heart,
Thou knowest how much a gentle soul is worth
  To teach men what thou art!

His was a spirit that to all thy poor
  Was kind as slumber after pain:
Why ope so soon thy heaven-deep Quiet's door
  And call him home again?

Freedom needs all her poets: it is they
  Who give her aspirations wings,
And to the wiser law of music sway
  Her wild imaginings.

Yet thou hast called him, nor art thou unkind,
  O Love Divine, for 'tis thy will
That gracious natures leave their love behind
  To work for Freedom still.

Let laurelled marbles weigh on other tombs,
  Let anthems peal for other dead,
Rustling the bannered depth of minster-glooms
  With their exulting spread.

His epitaph shall mock the short-lived stone,
  No lichen shall its lines efface,
He needs these few and simple lines alone
  To mark his resting place:—

"Here lies a Poet. Stranger, if to thee
  His claim to memory be obscure,
If thou wouldst learn how truly great was he,
  Go ask it of the poor."
                        —J. R. Lowell (1845).

Jealous, I own it, I was once—
That wickedness I here renounce.
I tried at wit—it would not do;
At tenderness—that failed me too.
Before me on each path there stood
The witty and the tender Hood!
                    —Walter Savage Landor.

1162.   FAIR INES

"One of the noblest—and, speaking of Fancy, one of the most singularly fanciful of modern poets, was Thomas Hood. His *Fair Ines* had always, for me, an inexpressible charm."—Edgar Allan Poe, in *The Poetic Principle* (1850).

RUTH

This poem is based on the Book of *Ruth.*— Cf. Keats's *Ode to a Nightingale*, 65-70 (p. 858).

I REMEMBER, I REMEMBER

The house described in this poem has not been accurately identified. It may be the house at Islington Green where Hood lived during the early days of his childhood.

1164. THE DREAM OF EUGENE ARAM, THE MURDERER

"The remarkable name of Eugene Aram [1704-59], belonging to a man of unusual talents and acquirements, is unhappily associated with a deed of blood as extraordinary in its details as any recorded in our calendar of crime. In the year 1745, being then an Usher and deeply engaged in the study of Chaldee, Hebrew, Arabic, and the Celtic dialects, for the formation of a Lexicon, he abruptly turned over a still darker page in human knowledge, and the brow that learning might have made illustrious was stamped ignominiously forever with the brand of Cain. To obtain a trifling property he concerted with an accomplice, and with his own hand effected the violent death of one Daniel Clarke, a shoemaker of Knaresborough, in Yorkshire. For fourteen years nearly the secret slept with the victim in the earth of St. Robert's Cave, and the manner of its discovery would appear a striking example of the Divine Justice, even amongst those marvels narrated in that curious old volume alluded to in *The Fortunes of Nigel*, under its quaint title of *God's Revenge against Murther*.

"The accidental digging up of a skeleton, and the unwary and emphatic declaration of Aram's accomplice that it could not be that of Clarke, betraying a guilty knowledge of the true bones, he was wrought to a confession of their deposit. The learned homicide was seized and arraigned; and a trial of uncommon interest was wound up by a defense as memorable as the tragedy itself for eloquence and ingenuity—too ingenious for innocence, and eloquent enough to do credit even to that long premeditation which the interval between the deed and its discovery had afforded. That this dreary period had not passed without paroxysms of remorse, may be inferred from a fact of affecting interest. The late Admiral Burney was a scholar, at the school at Lynn in Norfolk, where Aram was an Usher, subsequent to his crime. The Admiral stated that Aram was beloved by the boys, and that he used to discourse to them of murder, not occasionally, as I have written elsewhere, but constantly, and in somewhat of the spirit ascribed to him in the poem.

"For the more imaginative part of the version I must refer back to one of those unaccountable visions, which come upon us like frightful monsters thrown up by storms from the great black deeps of slumber. A lifeless body, in love and relationship the nearest

and dearest, was imposed upon my back, with an overwhelming sense of obligation—not of filial piety merely, but some awful responsibility equally vague and intense, and involving, as it seemed, inexpiable sin, horrors unutterable, torments intolerable,—to bury my dead, like Abraham, out of my sight.[1] In vain I attempted, again and again, to obey the mysterious mandate—by some dreadful process the burthen was replaced with a more stupendous weight of injunction, and an appalling conviction of the impossibility of its fulfilment. My mental anguish was indescribable;—the mighty agonies of souls tortured on the supernatural racks of sleep are not to be penned—and if in sketching those that belong to blood-guiltiness I have been at all successful, I owe it mainly to the uninvoked inspiration of that terrible dream."—Hood's Preface.

1167. THE SONG OF THE SHIRT

This poem was inspired by an incident which recently had drawn attention to the conditions of workers in London. A woman whose husband had been killed in an accident and who was left with two infant children to support, was charged with having pawned articles belonging to her employer. It was brought out at the trial that she had been trying to support herself and family by making trousers at seven shillings a week, what her master called a "good living."

The poem won instant popularity in France and Germany as well as in England. It was printed on cotton handkerchiefs and sung about the streets. It is said to have trebled the circulation of *Punch*, in which it was first printed. Hood's monument bears the inscription "He sang the Song of the Shirt."

1168. THE BRIDGE OF SIGHS

"The vigor of this poem is no less remarkable than its pathos. The versification, although carrying the fanciful to the very verge of the fantastic, is nevertheless admirably adapted to the wild insanity which is the thesis of the poem."—E. A. Poe, in *The Poetic Principle* (1850).

Among Hood's papers after his death was found a fragment entitled *Bridge of Sighs.—Part II.* This aimed to tell the story of a mother who threw her illegitimate child into the river and who was sentenced to death for her act.

---

[1] When Sarah, Abraham's wife, died in a foreign land, Abraham said to the people: "Give me a possession of a buryingplace with you, that I may bury my dead out of my sight."—*Genesis*, 23:4.

1169. THE LAY OF THE LABORER

This poem in behalf of the starving unemployed was inspired by an incident that happened in the spring of 1844. A young Huntingdon laborer threatened to burn the property of the local farmers if they would not give him work. He was convicted and sentenced to transportation for life. Haunted by the subject, Hood wrote this poem and set it in a vigorous prose appeal, which he sent to the Home Secretary, Sir James Graham. It had no effect on the minister, but it won a pension for Hood's wife, and popular esteem for himself.

1170. STANZAS

This poem was written on Hood's deathbed, 1845. Jerrold (*Thomas Hood: his Life and Times*, p. 395) calls it "the swan-song of a suffering man possessed of unconquerable optimism."

Winthrop Mackworth Praed

Poems, p. 1171 — Bibliography, p. 1441

Praed is best known as a writer of social satire and *vers de société*; and among writers of such verse he has never been equalled. Austin Dobson says of him (Miles's *The Poets and the Poetry of the Century*, 1889): "In ease of wit and humor, in spontaneity and unflagging vivacity of rhythm, in sparkle of banter and felicity of rhyme, no imitator, whom we can recall, has ever come within measurable distance of Winthrop Mackworth Praed."

1171. SPIRITS, THAT WALK AND WAIL TONIGHT

This song is found in Canto 1 of *The Troubadour*. It is sung by the troubadour in response to a request for a song of witchery.

OH FLY WITH ME! 'TIS PASSION'S HOUR

This song is found in Canto 2 of *The Troubadour*. It is sung by the troubadour beneath his sweetheart's window in a convent.

1172. OUR BALL

This is one of two "letters" written from Teignmouth, a fashionable watering-place in Devonshire, England. The places mentioned in the poem belong to the vicinity.

1175. STANZAS

1176. 14. *Move to abolish the sun and moon.*—Cobbett was a member of the House of Commons who was known for his virulent attacks upon all sorts of institutions and measures. James Sayers (1748-1823), the caricaturist, thus characterizes him:

Mr. Cobbett ask'd leave to bring in very soon
A Bill to abolish the Sun and the Moon.
The Honorable Member proceeded to state
Some arguments, used in a former debate,
On the subject of sinecures, taxes, vexations,
The Army and Navy, and old Corporations:—
The Heavenly Bodies, like those upon Earth,
Had, he said, been corrupt from the day of
    their birth,
With reckless profusion expending their light,
One after another, by day and by night.
And what class enjoy'd it?—The upper alone—
Upon such they had always exclusively shone.
. . . .
These abuses must cease—they had lasted too
    long—
Was there anything right? was not everything
    wrong?
The Crown was too costly,—the Church was a
    curse,—
Old Parliament's bad, Reform'd Parliament's
    worse,—
All revenues ill-manag'd,—all wants ill-provided,—
Equality,—Liberty,—Justice, divided.
—Quoted from Melville's *The Life and Letters of William Cobbett* (1913).

Robert Stephen Hawker

Poems, p. 1176 — Bibliography, p. 1426

"The simple legends connected with the wild and singular scenery of my own country appear to me not undeserving of record. These which I have published were related to me, and that chiefly by the common people, in the course of my solitary rambles in the West. They were 'done into verse,' also, during these my walks and rides."—From Hawker's Preface to *Records of the Western Shore* (1832).

1176. THE SONG OF THE WESTERN MEN

In 1688, Sir Jonathan Trelawney, a native of Cornwall, was imprisoned in the Tower of London with six other bishops for resisting James II's Declaration of Indulgence. The refrain in Hawker's poem dates from that time, but the rest is original. It was first published anonymously, and Scott, Macaulay, and Dickens all thought it a genuine ballad.

CLOVELLY

Clovelly is a picturesque village on the north coast of Devonshire, England.

1178. THE SILENT TOWER OF BOTTREAUX

"The rugged heights that line the sea-shore in the neighborhood of Tintadgel Castle and Church [on the coast of Cornwall] are crested with towers. Among these, that of Bottreaux, or, as it is now written, Boscastle, is without bells. The silence of this wild and lonely churchyard on festive or solemn occasions is not a little striking. On enquiry I was told that the bells were once shipped for this church, but that when the vessel was within sight of the tower the blasphemy of her captain was punished in the manner related in the poem. The bells, they told me, still lie in the bay, and announce by strange sounds the approach of a storm."—Hawker's note.

11. *Chough.*—"This wild bird chiefly haunts the coasts of Devon and Cornwall. The common people believe that the soul of King Arthur inhabits one of these birds, and no entreaty or bribe would induce an old Tintadgel quarryman to kill me one."—Hawker's note.

"PATER VESTER PASCIT ILLA"

This poem is sometimes entitled *A Sonnet of the Sea*.

1179. QUEEN GUENNIVAR'S ROUND

Guennivar is Guinevere, the wife of King Arthur.

TO ALFRED TENNYSON

This poem was written to Tennyson on the publication of his *Idylls of the King*.

John Wilson ("Christopher North")

Selections, p. 1179 — Bibliography, p. 1451

"Poetry, sport, and revelry were three fountains of inexhaustible inspiration; and it was from an intimate blending of the most vivid joys of all three that his most original and lasting work proceeded. Tavern meetings with good cheer and good society, long tramps among the heathery glens—'glorious guffawing,' as the Wilsonian Hogg put it, 'all night, and immeasurable murder all day,'—were the elements which, flung across the rich refracting medium of his imagination, evolved those unique compounds of poetry, wit, humor, drama, high spirits, and balderdash—the *Noctes Ambrosianæ.*"—Herford, in *The Age of Wordsworth* (1897).

Felicia Dorothea Hemans

Poems, p. 1186 — Bibliography, p. 1428

"Accomplishment without genius, and amiability without passion, reappear, translated into an atmosphere of lyric exaltation, in the once famous poetry of Mrs. Hemans. . . . Of all the English Romantic poets, Mrs. Hemans expresses with the richest intensity the more superficial and transient elements of Romanticism. She is at the beck and call of whatever is touched with the pathos of the far away, of the bygone—scenes of reminiscence or farewell, laments of exile and dirges for the dead. Her imagination floats romantically aloof from actuality, but it quite lacks the creative energy of the great Romantics, and her fabrics are neither real substance nor right dreams. Her expression is spontaneously picturesque and spontaneously melodious; and both qualities captivated her public; but she never learned to modulate or to subdue her effects. She paints with few colors, all bright. Her pages are a tissue of blue sky, golden corn, flashing swords and waving banners, the murmur of pines, and the voices of children." —C. H. Herford, in *The Age of Wordsworth* (1897).

See Wordsworth's *Extempore Effusion upon the Death of James Hogg*, 37-40 (p. 341).

William Motherwell

Poems, p. 1188 — Bibliography, p. 1439

Motherwell was an antiquarian who was interested in the ballads and folklore of Scotland and Scandinavia, and nearly all of his poems are of a ballad character. His martial pieces are noted for their stirring life and action, and his love poems for their tenderness and simplicity.

1189. JEANIE MORRISON

"Motherwell's reputation in his own country as a poet was made by the plaintive song of *Jeanie Morrison*, a sweet and touching reminiscence of pleasant days spent with a school playfellow and child sweetheart. This and another song in the Scotch dialect, *My Heid is Like to Break*, in which a betrayed damsel harrows up the feelings of her seducer with pitiless pathos, may be said to be the only two lyrics of his that have taken any hold of fame. They prove him to have been a man of keen sensibility; he was also a man of vigorous intellect and large culture, more of a student and a scholar than any contemporary Scotch lyricist."—Minto, in Ward's *The English Poets*, Vol. 4 (1880).

1190. MY HEID IS LIKE TO REND, WILLIE

See note on preceding poem.

Ebenezer Elliott

Poems, p. 1191 — Bibliography, p. 1424

From *On the Statue of Ebenezer Elliott*

Three Elliotts there have been, three glorious men
Each in his generation. One was doom'd

By Despotism and Prelaty to pine
In the damp dungeon, and to die for Law, 20
Rackt by slow tortures ere he reacht the grave.[1]
A second[2] hurl'd his thunderbolt and flame
When Gaul and Spaniard moor'd their pin-
    naces,
Screaming defiance at Gibraltar's frown,
Until one moment more, and other screams 25
And other writhings rose above the wave,
From sails afire and hissing where they fell,
And men half burnt along the buoyant mast.
A third[3] came calmly on, and askt the rich
To give laborious hunger daily bread, 30
As they in childhood had been taught to pray
By God's own Son, and sometimes have prayed
    since.
God heard; but they heard not: God sent down
    bread;
They took it, kept it all, and cried for more,
Hollowing both hands to catch and clutch the
    crumbs. 35
I may not live to hear another voice,
Elliott, of power to penetrate, as thine,
Dense multitudes; another none may see
Leading the Muses from unthrifty shades
To fields where corn gladdens the heart of
    man, 40
And where the trumpet with defiant blast
Blows in the face of War, and yields to Peace.
. . . .
                —Walter Savage Landor (1853).

"No man could be more happy than Elliott
in a green lane; though an indefatigable and
successful man of business, he devoutly and de-
votedly loved Nature. If absolutely rabid when
he wrote of the 'tax-fed aristocracy'—senten-
tious, bitter, sarcastic, loud with his pen in
hand and class sympathies and antipathies for
his inspiration—all evil thoughts evaporated
when communing in the woods and fields with
the God by whom the woods and fields were
made; among them his spirit was as fresh and
gentle as the dew by which they were
nourished."—S. C. Hall, in *Retrospect of a
Long Life* (1883).

"Nothing of worth that Elliott wrote was
caught out of the air; each poem had its
roots in fact; but the coloring in his earlier
pieces is sometimes extravagant; as he matured, his imagination gravitated from the
romantic to the real. . . . The sorrows of
oppressed toil were sung by Elliott with a sincerity which makes amends for some imagina-

[1] Sir John Eliot (1592-1632), an English patriot
who was imprisoned because of his opposition
to the government of Charles I. He died in
the Tower of London.
[2] George Augustus Eliot (1717-90), an English
general and Governor of Gibraltar, which he
defended against the French and Spanish,
1779-83.
[3] Ebenezer Elliott.

tive crudeness. His pathos is not hard and
dry like that of Crabbe; it is not that of a
student of human misery, but that of a loving
fellow-sufferer. And his ideal of happiness for
the working man is simple and refined—some
leisure, flowers, a good book, a neat home,
a happy wife, and glad, innocent children."—
E. Dowden, in Ward's *The English Poets*.

From his bold and vigorous attack upon
the Corn Laws, which placed restrictions upon
the grain trade, Elliott won the name of "The
Corn-Law Rhymer." A volume of his verse,
published in 1831, was entitled *Corn-Law
Rhymes*. It was inscribed to "all who revere
the memory of Jeremy Bentham, wise to promote the greatest happiness to the greatest
number for the greatest length of time."
Bentham was an English utilitarian philosopher (1748-1832).

1191.   BATTLE SONG

This is a workman's song which grew out
of the labor troubles of the early nineteenth
century. It applies, possibly, to the Peterloo
Massacre of Aug. 16, 1819. On that date, a
large assembly, chiefly of the laboring classes,
which met at St. Peter's Field, Manchester,
in behalf of reform legislation, was charged
by the militia and many were killed and
wounded.

1192.   THE PRESS

The Reform Bill of 1832, which greatly
extended the franchise, had been strongly supported by the press. Elliott was engaged in
the iron trade in Sheffield from 1821 to 1842.

PRESTON MILLS

Preston is a manufacturing town in Lancashire, England, noted for its cotton, linen,
and iron industries.

Bryan Waller Procter ("Barry Cornwall")

Poems, p. 1194 — Bibliography, p. 1441

"There never was a poet more honest in the
expression of his nature. His songs are the
reflections of all moods of his mind, and he
cares not if the sentiment of one contradicts
that of another. In grief, or love, or fear, or
despair, at the festive board, or the bed of sickness, wherever and whenever the spirit of song
comes to him, it takes the color of the emotion
which animates or saddens the moment. He is
a large-hearted and most lovable man; and
his poetry is admired because it is the expression of his character."—E. P. Whipple, in
Essays and Reviews (1845).

1194.   THE SEA

24. *I was born on the open sea.*—Procter was born at Leeds, a large inland city in the western part of Yorkshire.

25-30. Cf. with Glendower's account of his birth in *1 Henry IV*, III, 1, 13-16:

> At my nativity
> The front of heaven was full of fiery shapes,
> Of burning cressets; and at my birth
> The frame and huge foundation of the earth
> Shak'd like a coward.

Hartley Coleridge

Poems, p. 1197 — Bibliography, p. 1416

"His poems are full of graceful beauty, but almost all fall below the level of high poetry. They are not sufficiently powerful for vivid remembrance, and are much too good for oblivion. . . . The one species of composition in which he is a master is the sonnet, which precisely suited both his strength and his limitations. His sonnets are among the most perfect in the language."—Richard Garnett, in *Dictionary of National Biography* (1887).

See Wordsworth's *To H. C.* (p. 314).

1198.   HOMER

An earlier but inferior version of this sonnet was printed in 1833.

Alexander Pope

Poems, p. 1203 — Bibliography, p. 1441

See selection from Warton's *Essay on the Genius and Writings of Pope*, p. 85; Johnson's *Pope*, p. 1217; Coleridge's comment on Pope, p. 1384b; and Hunt's Preface to *Rimini*, p. 1364ff.

1203.   WINDSOR FOREST

Windsor Forest is near the town of Windsor, in Berkshire, the seat of the famous royal residence Windsor Castle, founded by William the Conqueror.

1205.   AN ESSAY ON CRITICISM

In this *Essay*, Pope presents in concise form the accepted rules of poetic composition as they had been formulated in the works of the ancients and of Italian, French, and English critics of the seventeenth and eighteenth centuries. Cf. especially Horace's *Ars Poetica*, Vida's *De Arte Poetica*, and Boileau's *L'Art Poétique*, all of which are founded on Aristotle's *Poetics*.

The importance of Pope's poem lies in the skill with which these rules are presented.

1208.   AN ESSAY ON MAN

This is a treatise in four Epistles on the moral order of the universe. For much of the thought Pope was indebted to Henry St. John, Lord Bolingbroke, a contemporary politician and philosopher, to whom the poem is addressed. The poem should be compared with Bolingbroke's *Fragments*, 43-63. Bolingbroke belonged to the school of Deistic philosophers, who discredited revelation and endeavored to construct a religion solely by the light of reason.

Pope's reasons for treating his subject in verse rather than in prose are thus set forth in his Preface: "If I could flatter myself that this essay has any merit, it is in steering betwixt the extremes of doctrines seemingly opposite, in passing over terms utterly unintelligible, and in forming a temperate yet not inconsistent, and a short yet not imperfect, system of ethics. This I might have done in prose; but I chose verse, and even rhyme, for two reasons. The one will appear obvious; that principles, maxims, or precepts so written both strike the reader more strongly at first, and are more easily retained by him afterwards. The other may seem odd, but is true: I found I could express them more shortly this way than in prose itself; and nothing is more certain than that much of the force as well as grace of arguments or instructions depends on their conciseness."

1211. 237-46. The biological idea expressed in these lines is false; evolution, however, predicates just such a chain, but with a difference.

Samuel Johnson

Selections, p. 1211 — Bibliography, p. 1430

1211.   PREFACE TO SHAKSPEARE

Johnson published an edition of Shakespeare's Works in 1765. The selection here printed is from the Preface to that work.

1217. 25. *Cato.*—Voltaire says of this play (*Letters on the English*, 18, "On Tragedy"): "The first English writer who composed a regular tragedy, and infused a spirit of elegance through every part of it, was the illustrious Mr. Addison. His *Cato* is a masterpiece, both with regard to the diction and to the beauty and harmony of the numbers. . . . Mr. Addison's Cato appears to me the greatest character that was ever brought upon any stage."

In contrast to Voltaire's extravagant praise of *Cato*, cf. the following criticism from Ward's *A History of English Dramatic Literature*, 3, 441-42: "When we view this famous tragedy as it now lies dead and cold before us, and examine it, as we needs must, on its own merits, there remains surprisingly little to account for its unprecedented success. *Cato* is full of effective commonplaces, many of which are to this day current as familiar quotations; but otherwise it would be difficult to find in it any distinguishing feature. . . . Such as *Cato* was, it helped to make English tragedy pursue more resolutely than before the path into which it had unfortunately entered. . . . The play which Addison had written and which Voltaire eulogized marks no doubt with incontestable definiteness an epoch in the history of English tragedy; but this epoch was one of decay, holding out no prospect of recovery by any signs easily admitting of interpretation."

Edmund Burke

Selection, p. 1219 — Bibliography, p. 1410

1219. REFLECTIONS ON THE REVOLUTION IN FRANCE

"This extraordinary book was published near the outbreak of the French Revolution and justly takes rank as one of the masterpieces of English literature. It is at once a condemnation of the Revolution, and a prophecy of the evils the Revolution would produce. As a specimen of denunciatory writing, it is probably one of the most remarkable ever produced in any language. It pours out torrent after torrent, Niagara after Niagara. But though it is repetitious, and therefore somewhat monotonous, it abounds in shrewd judgments, in brilliant pictures, and in prophecies that seem inspired. At times it is so unfair and so unjust that some have attempted to explain its excesses by the presumption that Burke had lost his reason. There is no need, however, of resorting to this violent hypothesis. Burke's mind was always essentially denunciatory in its nature; and he was never able to be quite just either to men or to political methods he disliked. Moreover, though he was a passionate friend of liberty, he never believed liberty was to be secured or preserved by submitting political affairs to the control of masses of ignorant men. These characteristics of his mind and of his political doctrines are quite sufficient to account for the peculiarities of what, with all its drawbacks, must probably be considered the greatest work of the greatest writer of English prose."—C. K. Adams, in *A Manual of Historical Literature* (1882).

During the period 1789-92, the French Revolution found many supporters in England among poets, political philosophers, and clergymen. Most prominent among these groups were Wordsworth, Coleridge, and Southey; Godwin, Fox, and Wilkes; and Priestley and Price. All of these openly and fervently glorified everything that was being done in the name of Liberty. With these enthusiasts, Burke was entirely at variance. To him the Revolution meant only the overthrow of an established civilization, and he vigorously protested. For the contrasting view, see the selections from Godwin's *An Enquiry concerning Political Justice* (pp. 239 ff.).

The style of Burke's prose, so far as form goes, is neither Classic nor Romantic.

The *Reflections* opens with a statement of Burke's attitude toward the Constitution Society and the Revolution Society, English clubs which approved of the proceedings in France. **1220a. 28.** In the portion omitted, Burke discusses the style of Price's sermon and his assertions that the people of England have the right to choose their own governors, to cashier them for misconduct, and to frame a government for themselves.

1222a. 27. *A man amongst them.*—A reference probably to Fox, Godwin, or Wilkes, all of whom vigorously supported the French Revolution.

1222b. 25-32. Burke here compares the results of the Revolution to the Flood in *Genesis.* He echoes the language of *Genesis,* 7:11.

1225a. 18. *Thorough-paced courtiers.* — Wordsworth, Coleridge, and Southey were at first ardent Republicans, but the excesses and the failures of the French Revolution led them finally to become Tories.

1227b. 46. *Inverted Order.* — Cf. with the story of the Englishman who once satirically remarked that French infantry could not be good—it wore blue, a color meant by God for cavalry.

Bibliographies

The following bibliographies are meant to serve as convenient reference lists for a study of the literature of the English romantic movement. Books containing critical discussions of the movement or period in general or of special phases of romanticism are listed in the General Bibliography.

Memoirs of nearly all the writers are found in various editions of their works, together with critical introductions, and brief biographical accounts of each appear in *The Encyclopædia Britannica* and in the *Dictionary of National Biography*. Critical material, supplementary to the special critical references, is found in virtually all of the biographies listed.

The editions of each writer's works are arranged usually in three groups—complete works, selections, important single works. Complete works and selections are arranged chronologically; single works, alphabetically. Unless otherwise specified, editions are in one volume. The biographies and the criticisms are arranged alphabetically by authors. Critical essays bearing simply names of writers as titles are listed only by the title of the volume in which they are found; other essays are listed by title as well as by volume.

More extended bibliographies than those given here may be found, some with critical comments on individual entries, in the following publications:

The Cambridge Bibliography of English Literature, 4 vols., ed. by F. W. Bateson (London, Cambridge Univ. Press, 1941; New York, Macmillan).

"The Romantic Movement: A Selective and Critical Bibliography," in *Journal of English Literary History*, annually in March, 1937 ff.

Annual Bibliography of English Language and Literature, Modern Humanities Research Association, 1920 ff. (Retarded by war. Vol. 20 for 1939 published in 1948.)

"American Bibliography," in Supplement to *Publications of the Modern Language Association* annually 1933 ff.

The Year's Work in English Studies, ed. by F. S. Boas (The Eng. Assoc., London), annually 1919 ff.

"English Literature, 1660-1800," in *Philological Quarterly*, April, annually.

General Bibliography

POLITICAL AND SOCIAL HISTORY, 1720-1850

Bryant, A.: *The Years of Endurance: 1793-1802* (New York, Harper, 1942).

Bryant, A.: *The Years of Victory: 1802-1812* (New York, Harper, 1944).

The Cambridge Modern History, 14 vols., ed. by Ward, Prothero, and Leathes, Vols. 6 and 8 (London, Macmillan, 1902).

Lecky, W. E. H.: *A History of England in the Eighteenth Century*, 8 vols. (London, Longmans, 1878-90; New York, Appleton, 1883-90).

Macaulay, T. B.: *The History of England from the Accession of James II*, 5 vols. (London and New York, Longmans, 1849-61).

Martineau, Harriet: *The History of England from the Commencement of the XIXth Century to the Crimean War*, 4 vols. (London, Bell, 1849-51; Philadelphia, Potter, 1864).

McCarthy, J., and McCarthy, J. H.: *A History of the Four Georges and of William IV*, 4 vols. (London, Chatto, 1884-1901; New York, Harper, 1890-1901).

Mowat, R. B.: *The Romantic Age: Europe in the Nineteenth Century* (London, Harrap, 1937).

The Political History of England, 12 vols., ed. by W. Hunt and R. L. Poole, Vols. 9-11 (London and New York, Longmans, 1905-06).

Social England, 6 vols., ed. by H. D. Traill and J. S. Mann, Vols. 5 and 6 (London, Cassell, 1896-97; New York, Putnam, 1905).

Thompson, J. M.: *The French Revolution* (Toronto, Oxford Univ. Press, 1945).

Trevelyan, G. M.: *English Social History* (London, Longmans, 1942).

Walpole, S.: *A History of England from the Conclusion of the Great War in 1815*, 6 vols. (new and rev. ed., London and New York, Longmans, 1890).

HISTORY OF LITERATURE

Abercrombie, L.: *Romanticism* (London, Secker, 1926).

Addison, A. E.: *Romanticism and the Gothic Revival* (New York, Richard R. Smith, 1938).

Allen, B. S.: *Tides in English Taste: 1619-1800*, 2 vols. (Cambridge, Mass., Harvard Univ. Press, 1937).

Archbold, W. A. J.: *The Romantic Movement in English Literature* (London, Longmans, 1921).

Ash, D.: "Creative Romanticism," *Coll. Eng.*, 4:100 (1942).

Babbitt, I.: *On Being Creative, and Other Essays* (Boston, Houghton, 1932).

Babbitt, I.: *Rousseau and Romanticism* (Boston, Houghton, 1919).

Bailey, J. C.: *Dr. Johnson and His Circle* (Home Univ. Lib.: London, Williams, 1913; New York, Holt).

Baker, E. A.: *The History of the English Novel*, vols. 6-8 (London, Witherby, 1935-37).

Baldensperger, F.: "1793-1794: Climacteric Times for 'Romantic' Tendencies in English Ideology," *Jour. Hist. Ideas*, 5:3 (1944).

Barzun, J. M.: "To the Rescue of Romanticism," *Amer. Scholar*, 9:147 (1940).

Barzun, J. M.: *Romanticism and the Modern Ego* (Boston, Little, 1943).

Bate, W. J.: *From Classic to Romantic: Premises of Taste in Eighteenth-Century England* (Cambridge, Mass., Harvard Univ. Press, 1946).

Beach, J. W.: *The Concept of Nature in Nineteenth Century English Poetry* (New York, Macmillan, 1936).

Beach, J. W.: *A Romantic View of Poetry* (New York, Oxford Univ. Press, 1941, 1945).

Beers, H. A.: *A History of English Romanticism in the Eighteenth Century* (New York, Holt, 1898, 1910).

Beers, H. A.: *A History of English Romanticism in the Nineteenth Century* (New York, Holt, 1901, 1910).

Bentley, E. R.: "Romanticism: A Re-Evaluation," *Antioch Rev.*, 4:6 (1944).

Bernbaum, E.: *Guide Through the Romantic Movement*, 2nd ed. (New York, Ronald, 1949).

Birkhead, E.: *The Tale of Terror; A Study of the Gothic Romance* (New York, Dutton, 1921).

Bradbury, R.: *The Romantic Theories of Architecture of the Nineteenth Century in Germany, England, and France* (New York, Dorothy Press, 1934).

Bradley, A. C.: *English Poetry and German Philosophy in the Age of Wordsworth* (Manchester, Sherrat, 1909); rptd. in *A Miscellany* (London, Macmillan, 1929).

Bradley, A. C.: *Oxford Lectures on Poetry* (London, Macmillan, 1909, 1911).

Brandes, G.: *Main Currents in Nineteenth Century Literature*, 6 vols. (London, Heinemann, 1901-05; New York, Macmillan, 1906).

Brawley, B.: "English Hymnody and Romanticism," *Sewanee Rev.*, 24:476 (1916).

Brinton, C. C.: *The Political Ideas of the English Romanticists* (London, Oxford Univ. Press, 1926).

Bronowski, J.: *The Poet's Defence* (London, Cambridge Univ. Press, 1939).

Brooks, C.: *Modern Poetry and the Tradition* (Chapel Hill, Univ. of N. C. Press, 1939).

Brooks, C.: *The Well Wrought Urn; Studies in the Structure of Poetry* (New York, Reynal, 1947).

Bush, D.: *Mythology and the Romantic Tradition in English Poetry* (Cambridge, Mass., Harvard Univ. Press, 1937).

The Cambridge History of English Literature, 14 vols., ed. by Ward and Waller, Vols. 9-11 (London, Cambridge Univ. Press, 1908; New York, Putnam).

Campbell, O. W.: "Some Suggestions on the Romantic Revival and Its Effects," *Shelley and the Unromantics* (New York, Scribner, 1924).

Clark, K.: *The Gothic Revival* (London, Constable, 1928).

Clement, N. H.: *Romanticism in France* (New York, Mod. Lang. Assn. Amer., 1939).

Colum, M. G.: *From These Roots: The Ideas That Have Made Modern Literature* (New York, Scribner, 1937).

Conant, M. P.: *The Oriental Tale in England in the Eighteenth Century* (New York, Columbia Univ. Press, 1908).

Courthope, W. J.: *A History of English Poetry*, 6 vols., Vol. 3-5 (London and New York, Macmillan, 1903-05).

Courthope, W. J.: *The Liberal Movement in English Literature* (London, Murray, 1885, 1895).

Crane, R. S.: "Cleanth Brooks; or, The Bankruptcy of Critical Monism," *Mod. Phil.*, 45:226 (1948).

Cyclopædia of English Literature, 3 vols., ed. by R. Chambers (new ed., Philadelphia, Lippincott, 1902-04).

Dawson, C.: "The Origins of the Romantic Tradition," *Medieval Religion and Other Essays* (London, Sheed, 1934).

Dawson, W. J.: *The Makers of English Poetry* (New York and London, Revell, 1906).

Dawson, W. J.: *The Makers of English Prose* (New York and London, Revell, 1906).

Deane, C. V.: *Aspects of Eighteenth Century Nature Poetry* (Oxford, Blackwell, 1935).

Dennis, J.: *The Age of Pope* (London, Bell, 1894, 1909; New York, Macmillan).

Dictionary of National Biography, 22 vols., ed. by L. Stephen and S. Lee (London, Smith, 1885-1901; Macmillan).

Dodds, Mrs. A. E. Powell: *The Romantic Theory of Poetry* (New York, Longmans, 1926).

Doughty, O.: *English Lyric in the Age of Reason* (London, O'Connor, 1922).

Dowden, E.: *The French Revolution and English Literature* (New York and London, Scribner, 1897).

Dowden, E.: *Studies in Literature, 1789-1877* (London, Paul, 1878).

Dowden, E.: *Transcripts and Studies* (London, Paul, 1888).

Draper, J. W.: *The Funeral Elegy and the Rise of English Romanticism* (New York, New York Univ. Press, 1929).

Dutt, S.: *The Supernatural in English Romantic Poetry: 1780-1830* (London, Longmans, 1938).

Dykes, E. B.: *The Negro in English Romantic Thought; or, A Study of Sympathy for the Oppressed* (Washington, D. C., Assoc. Pubs., 1942).

Early Reviews of English Poets, 1757-1885, ed. by J. L. Haney (Philadelphia, Egerton Press, 1904).

Early Reviews of Great Writers, 1786-1832, ed. by E. Stevenson (London, Scott, 1906).

Eastlake, C. L.: *A History of the Gothic Revival* (London, Longmans, 1872).

Einstein, A.: *Music in the Romantic Era* (New York, Norton, 1947).

Eliot, T. S.: *The Sacred Wood: Essays on Poetry and Criticism* (London, Methuen, 1920, 1934).

Eliot, T. S.: *The Use of Poetry and Criticism* (Cambridge, Mass., Harvard Univ. Press, 1933).

Elliott, W. Y.: "The Political Application of Romanticism," *Pol. Sci. Quart.*, 39:234 (1924).

Elton, O.: *A Survey of English Literature, 1730-80*, 2 vols. (London, Arnold, 1928; New York, Macmillan).

Elton, O.: *A Survey of English Literature, 1780-1880*, 4 vols. (New York, Macmillan, 1920).

Elwin, M.: *The First Romantics* (London, Macdonald, 1947; New York, Longmans, 1948).

The Encyclopædia Britannica, fourteenth ed., 24 vols. (London and New York, The Encyclopædia Britannica Co., 1929).

Evans, B. I.: *Tradition and Romanticism* (London, Methuen, 1940).

Eyre-Todd, G.: *Scottish Poetry of the Eighteenth Century* (Glasgow, Hodge, 1896).

Fairchild, H. N.: *The Noble Savage: A Study in Romantic Naturalism* (New York, Columbia Univ. Press, 1928).

Fairchild, H. N.: *Religious Trends in English Poetry*, 2 vols. (New York, Columbia Univ. Press, 1939, 1942).

Fairchild, H. N.: *The Romantic Quest* (New York, Columbia Univ. Press, 1931).

Fairchild, H. N., Nitchie, and others: "Romanticism: A Symposium," *Pub. Mod. Lang. Assn.*, 55:1 (1940).

Farley, F. E.: *Scandinavian Influence on the English Romantic Movement* (Studies and Notes in Phil. and Lit., Vol. 9, Cambridge, Mass., Harvard Univ. Press, 1903).

Fausset, H. I'A.: *The Proving of Psyche* (New York, Harcourt, 1929).

Fogle, R. H.: "Romantic Bards and Metaphysical Reviewers," *Jour. Eng. Lit. Hist.*, 12:221 (1945).

Frye, P. H.: "The Terms Classic and Romantic," *Romance and Tragedy* (Boston, Marshall, Jones, 1922).

Garnett, R. and Gosse, E.: *English Literature, an illustrated Record*, 4 vols., Vols. 3 and 4 (London, Macmillan, 1903-04).

Gates, L. E.: *Studies and Appreciations* (New York, Macmillan, 1900).

Gilfillan, G.: *Galleries of Literary Portraits*, 3 vols. (London, Groombridge, 1845-54; New York, Appleton, 1850-55; Everyman's Lib., Dutton).

Gill, F. C.: *The Romantic Movement and Methodism* (London, Epworth Press, 1937).

Gosse, E.: *From Shakespeare to Pope* (London, Cambridge Univ. Press, 1885; New York, Dodd).

Gosse, E.: *History of Eighteenth Century Literature* (London, Macmillan, 1889).

Graham, W.: "The Politics of the Greater Romantic Poets," *Pub. Mod. Lang. Assn.*, 36:60 (1921).

Gregory, A.: *The French Revolution and the English Novel* (New York, Putnam, 1915).

Grierson, H. J. C.: "Classical and Romantic," (1923), rptd. in *The Background of English Literature* (New York, Holt, 1925).

Guérard, A., Jr.: "Prometheus and the Aeolian Lyre," *Yale Rev.*, n.s. 33:482 (1944).

Hamilton, G. R.: *Poetry and Contemplation* (New York, Macmillan; London, Cambridge Univ. Press, 1937).

Hancock, A. E.: *The French Revolution and the English Poets* (New York, Holt, 1899).

Havens, R. D.: *The Influence of Milton on English Poetry* (Cambridge, Mass., Harvard Univ. Press, 1922).

Havens, R. D.: "Romantic Aspects of the Age of Pope," *Pub. Mod. Lang. Assn.*, 20:297 (1912).

Hedge, F. H.: "Classic and Romantic," *The Atlantic Monthly*, 57:309 (1886).

Heine, H.: *Die romantische Schule* (Hamburg, 1836); English translation by Fleishman (New York, Holt, 1882).

Herford, C. H.: *The Age of Wordsworth* (London, Bell, 1897, 1899; New York, Macmillan).

Herford, C. H.: "Romanticism in the Modern World," *Eng. Assn. Essays and Studies*, 8:109 (1922).

Hinchman, W. S. and Gummere, F. B.: *Lives of Great English Writers* (Boston, Houghton, 1908).

Hungerford, E. B.: *Shores of Darkness* (New York, Columbia Univ. Press, 1941).

Inge, W. R.: *The Platonic Tradition in English Religious Thought* (New York, Longmans, 1926).

Inge, W. R.: "Romanticism," *Lay Thoughts of a Dean* (New York, Putnam, 1926).

Jack, A. A.: *Poetry and Prose* (London, Constable, 1911).

James, D. G.: *Scepticism and Poetry: An Essay on the Poetic Imagination* (London, Allen, 1937).

Johnson, Samuel: *The Lives of the English Poets* (1779-81); 3 vols., ed. by G. B. Hill (London, Clarendon Press, 1905).

Jones, R. E.: "Romanticism Reconsidered: Humanism and Romantic Poetry," *Sewanee Rev.*, 41:396 (1933).

Ker, W. P.: "On the Value of the Terms 'Classical' and 'Romantic' as Applied to Literature," *Collected Essays*, 2 vols. (London, Macmillan, 1925).

King, R. W.: "Italian Influence on English Scholarship and Literature during the Romantic Revival," *Mod. Lang. Rev.*, 20:48, 295; 21:24 (1925; 1926).

Knight, G. W.: *The Burning Oracle: Studies in the Poetry of Action* (London, Oxford Univ. Press, 1939).

Knight, G. W.: *The Starlit Dome: Studies in the Poetry of Vision* (London, Oxford Univ. Press, 1941).

Lamont, C.: "Naturalism and the Appreciation of Nature," *Jour. of Philos.*, 44:597 (1947).

Larrabee, S. A.: *English Bards and Grecian Marbles: The Relationship Between Sculpture and Poetry, Especially in the Romantic Period* (New York, Columbia Univ. Press, 1943).

Law, M. H.: *The English Familiar Essay in the Early Nineteenth Century* (Philadelphia, Univ. of Pennsylvania Press, 1934).

Leavis, F. R.: *Revaluation: Tradition and Development in English Poetry* (London, Chatto, 1936).

Legouis, E. and Cazamian, L.: *A History of English Literature*, 2 vols., trans. from the French by H. D. Irvine, W. D. MacInnes, and L. Cazamian (New York, Macmillan, 1926; 2 vols. in 1, 1935, 1937).

Lehman, B. H.: "The Doctrine of Leadership in the Greater Romantic Poets," *Pub. Mod. Lang. Assn.*, 37:639 (1922).

Levin, H.: *The Broken Column: A Study in Romantic Hellenism* (Cambridge, Mass., Harvard Univ. Press, 1931).

Lovejoy, A. O.: "On the Discrimination of Romanticisms," *Pub. Mod. Lang. Assn.*, 39:229 (1924).

Lovejoy, A. O.: *The Great Chain of Being: A Study of the History of an Idea* (Cambridge, Mass., Harvard Univ. Press, 1933).

Lovejoy, A. O.: "The Meaning of Romanticism for the Historian of Ideas," *Jour. Hist. Ideas*, 2 (1941).

Lovejoy, A. O.: "Optimism and Romanticism," *Pub. Mod. Lang. Assn.*, 42:921 (1927).

Lovejoy, A. O.: "Schiller and the Genesis of Romanticism," *Mod. Lang. Notes*, 35:1, 136 (1920).

Lucas, F. L.: *The Decline and Fall of the Romantic Ideal* (New York, Macmillan, 1936).

Maar, H. G. de: *A History of Modern English Romanticism* (London and New York, Oxford Univ. Press, 1924).

MacClintock, W. D.: "The Romantic and Classical in English Literature," *The Chautauquan*, 14:187 (1891).

Mackail, J. W.: *Lectures on Poetry* (London and New York, Longmans, 1911).

McKeehan, I. P.: "The Vocabulary of Landscape Description among the Early Romanticists," *Univ. of Colorado Studies in the Humanities* (1945).

McKillop, A. D.: *English Literature from Dryden to Burns* (New York, Appleton, 1948).

Miles, J.: *The Vocabulary of Poetry* (Berkeley, Univ. of Calif. Press, 1946).

Millar, J. H.: *A Literary History of Scotland* (London, Unwin, 1903; New York, Scribner).

Millar, J. H.: *The Mid-Eighteenth Century* (Edinburgh, Blackwood, 1902; New York, Scribner).

Monk, S. H.: *The Sublime: A Study of Critical Theories in Eighteenth-Century England* (New York, Mod. Lang. Assn., 1935).

Moore, C. A.: "The Return to Nature in English Poetry of the Eighteenth Century," *Stud. in Phil.*, 14:243 (1917).

More, P. E.: "The Drift of Romanticism," *Shelburne Essays*, Eighth Ser. (Boston, Houghton, 1913).

Murry, J. M.: *Heroes of Thought* (New York, Messner, 1938).

Neilson, W. A.: *Essentials of Poetry* (Boston, Houghton, 1913).

Nicoll, A.: *A History of Early Nineteenth Century Drama*, 2 vols. (New York, Macmillan, 1930).

Nicolson, M. H.: *Newton Demands the Muse* (Princeton, Princeton Univ. Press, 1945).

Omond, T. S.: *The Romantic Triumph* (Edinburgh, Blackwood, 1900; New York, Scribner, 1909).

Palgrave, F. T.: *Landscape in Poetry* (London and New York, Macmillan, 1897).

Parrington, V. L.: *The Romantic Revolution in America, 1800-1860* (New York, Harcourt, 1927).

Partridge, E. H.: *Eighteenth Century English Romantic Poetry (up till the Publication of the "Lyrical Ballads," 1798)* (Paris, Champion, 1924).

Pater, W.: "Romanticism," *Macmillan's Mag.*, 35:64 (1876).

Pater, W.: *Appreciations* (London and New York, Macmillan, 1889, 1895).

Pellissier, G.: *The Literary Movement in France during the Nineteenth Century;* English translation by Britton (New York, Putnam, 1897).

Perry, T.: *English Literature in the Eighteenth Century*, 2 vols. (New York, Harper, 1883).

Peyre, H. M.: *Writers and Their Critics: A Study of Misunderstanding* (Ithaca, Cornell Univ. Press, 1944).

Phelps, W. L.: *The Beginnings of the English Romantic Movement* (Boston, Ginn, 1893).

Pierce, F. E.: *Currents and Eddies in the English Romantic Generation* (New Haven, Yale Univ. Press, 1918).

Pierce, F. E.: "Romanticism and Other Isms," *Jour. of Eng. and Ger. Phil.*, 26:451 (1926).

Porterfield, A. W.: *An Outline of German Romanticism* (Boston, Ginn, 1914).

Praz, M.: *The Romantic Agony*, trans. from the Italian by A. Davidson (New York, Oxford Univ. Press, 1933).

Prescott, F. C.: *The Poetic Mind* (New York, Macmillan, 1922).

Quiller-Couch, Sir A.: "On the Terms 'Classical' and 'Romantic,'" *Studies in Literature*, 2 vols. (New York, Putnam, 1922; London, Cambridge Univ. Press).

Railo, Eino: *The Haunted Castle, a Study of the Elements of English Romanticism* (New York, Dutton, 1927).

Ransom, J. C.: *The World's Body* (New York, Scribner, 1938).

Rawnsley, H. D.: *Literary Associations of the English Lakes*, 2 vols. (Glasgow, Maclehose, 1894, 1906).

Read, H.: *Reason and Romanticism* (London, Faber and Gwyer, 1926).

Reed, A. L.: *The Background of Gray's Elegy: Melancholy Poetry, 1700-51* (New York, Columbia Univ. Press, 1924).

Reed, E. B.: *English Lyrical Poetry* (New Haven, Yale Univ. Press, 1912).

Reynolds, Myra: *The Treatment of Nature in Poetry between Pope and Wordsworth* (Chicago, Univ. of Chicago Press, 1896, 1909).

Rhys, E.: *Lyric Poetry* (London, Dent, 1913; New York, Dutton).

Richards, I. A.: *Principles of Literary Criticism* (New York, Harcourt, 1924).

Richardson, G. F.: *A Neglected Aspect of the English Romantic Revolt* (Berkeley, Univ. of Calif. Press, 1915).

Robertson, J. G.: *The Reconciliation of Classic and Romantic* (Cambridge, Bowes, 1925).

Robertson, J. G.: *Studies in the Genesis of Romantic Theory in the Eighteenth Century* (London, Cambridge Univ. Press, 1923; New York, Macmillan).

Robinson, H. Crabb: *Diary, Reminiscences, and Correspondence*, 2 vols., ed. by T. Sadler (London, Macmillan, 1872; Cambridge, Mass., Riverside Press, 1877).

Saintsbury, G.: *A History of Criticism and Literary Taste in Europe*, 3 vols. (Edinburgh, Blackwood, 1900-04, 1908; New York, Dodd).

Saintsbury, G.: *A History of English Prose Rhythm* (London and New York, Macmillan, 1912).

Saintsbury, G.: *A History of English Prosody*, 3 vols. (London and New York, Macmillan, 1906-10).

Saintsbury, G.: *A History of Nineteenth Century Literature* (London and New York, Macmillan, 1896).

Saintsbury, G.: *Essays in English Literature, 1780-1860,* First Ser. (London, Percival, 1890); Second Ser. (London, Dent, 1895; New York, Scribner).

Saurat, D.: *Literature and Occult Tradition: Studies in Philosophical Poetry,* trans. from the French by D. Bolton (New York, Dial Press, 1930).

Seccombe, T.: *The Age of Johnson* (London, Bell, 1899, 1909; New York, Macmillan; New Haven, Yale Univ. Press, 1949).

Shairp, J. C.: *Aspects of Poetry* (Oxford, Clarendon Press, 1881; Boston, Houghton, 1882).

Shairp, J. C.: *On Poetic Interpretation of Nature* (Edinburgh, Douglas, 1877; New York, Hurd, 1878; Boston, Houghton, 1885).

Shepherd, T. B.: *Methodism and the Literature of the Eighteenth Century* (London, Epworth Press, 1940).

Sherwood, M. P.: *Undercurrents of Influence in English Romantic Poetry* (Cambridge, Mass., Harvard Univ. Press, 1934; London, Oxford Univ. Press, 1935).

Sickells, E. M.: *The Gloomy Egoist. Moods and Themes of Melancholy from Gray to Keats* (New York, Columbia Univ. Press, 1932).

Sitwell, S.: *British Architects and Craftsmen: A Survey of Taste, Design, and Style: 1600-1830* (London, Batsford, 1945, 1947).

Smith, D. N.: *Shakespeare in the Eighteenth Century* (Oxford, Clarendon Press, 1928).

Smith, L. P.: "Four Words: Romantic, Originality, Creative, Genius" (Oxford, Clarendon Press, 1924); rptd. as "Four Romantic Words" in *Words and Idioms* (London, Constable, 1933).

Snyder, E. D.: *The Celtic Revival in English Literature, 1760-1800* (Cambridge, Mass., Harvard Univ. Press, 1923).

Stephen, L.: *English Literature and Society in the Eighteenth Century* (London, Duckworth, 1904; New York, Putnam).

Stephen, L.: *History of English Thought in the Eighteenth Century,* 2 vols. (London, Smith, 1876, 1880; New York, Putnam, 1876, 1902).

Stephen, L.: *Hours in a Library,* 3 vols. (London, Smith, 1874-79; New York and London, Putnam, 1899); 4 vols. (1907).

Stephen, L.: *Studies of a Biographer,* 4 vols. (London, Duckworth, 1898-1902; New York, Putnam).

Stewart, H. L.: "Theology and Romanticism," *Harvard Theol. Rev.,* 13:362 (1920).

Stockley, V.: *German Literature as Known in England: 1750-1830* (London, Routledge, 1929).

Stokoe, F. W.: *German Influence in the English Romantic Period, 1788-1818* (London, Cambridge Univ. Press, 1926; New York, Macmillan).

Summers, M.: *The Gothic Quest: A History of the Gothic Novel* (New York, Columbia Univ. Press, 1941).

Symons, A.: *The Romantic Movement in English Poetry* (London, Constable, 1909; New York, Dutton).

Taine, H. A.: *Histoire de la Littérature Anglaise,* 2 vols. (Paris, 1863); trans. by H. Van Laun (Edinburgh, The Academy, 1871; New York, Holt, 1872, 1896).

Tate, A.: *Reason in Madness* (New York, Putnam, 1941).

Texte, J.: *J. J. Rousseau et les origines du cosmopolitisme littéraire* (Paris, 1895); trans. by J. W. Matthews (London, Duckworth, 1899; New York, Macmillan).

Tinker, C. B.: *Nature's Simple Plan: Radical Thought in the Mid-Eighteenth Century* (Princeton, Princeton Univ. Press, 1922).

Tinker, C. B.: *Painter and Poet: Studies in the Literary Relations of English Painting* (Cambridge, Mass., Harvard Univ. Press, 1938).

Van Tieghem, P.: *L'Ère Romantique; Le Romantisme dans la Littérature Européenne* (Paris, A. Michel, 1948).

Van Tieghem, P.: *Le Mouvement Romantique* (Paris, Vuibert, 1923).

Van Tieghem, P.: *La Poésie de la Nuit et des Tombeaux en Europe au XVIIIᵉ Siècle* (Paris, Rieder, 1921).

Van Tieghem, P.: *Le Préromantisme* (Paris, Rieder, 1924; second ser., 1930); trans. by A. L. McKenzie, with a Preface by R. S. Crane (New York, Century, 1930).

Vaughan, C. E.: *The Romantic Revolt* (Edinburgh, Blackwood, 1900; New York, Scribner, 1907).

Veitch, J.: *The History and Poetry of the Scottish Border* (Glasgow, MacLehose, 1878).

Vines, S.: *The Course of English Classicism* (London, Hogarth Press, 1930).

Walker, H.: *The English Essay and Essayists* (London, Dent, 1915; New York, Dutton).

Walker, H.: *The Literature of the Victorian Era* (London, Cambridge Univ. Press, 1910; New York, Putnam).

Walker, H.: *Three Centuries of Scottish Literature,* 2 vols. (Glasgow, MacLehose, 1893; New York, Macmillan).

Warner, W. J.: *The Wesleyan Movement and the Industrial Revolution* (London, Longmans, 1930).

Wasserman, E. R.: *Elizabethan Poetry in the Eighteenth Century* (Urbana, Univ. of Ill. Press, 1947).

Watts-Dunton, T.: "The Renascence of Wonder in Poetry," *Chambers's Cyclopaedia of English Literature*, 3 (1903).

Weisinger, H.: "English Treatment of the Classical-Romantic Problem," *Mod. Lang. Quart.*, 7:477 (1946).

Wernaer, R. M.: *Romanticism and the Romantic School in Germany* (New York, Appleton, 1909).

Whipple, E. P.: *Essays and Reviews*, 2 vols. (Boston, Osgood, 1849; Ticknor, 1861).

White, N. I.: "The English Romantic Writers as Dramatists," *Sewanee Rev.*, 30:206 (1922).

Whitford, R. C.: "Satire's View of Sentimentalism in the Days of George the Third," *Jour. of Eng. and Ger. Phil.*, 18:155 (1919).

Whitney, L.: *Primitivism and the Idea of Progress in English Popular Literature of the Eighteenth Century* (Baltimore, Johns Hopkins Press, 1934).

Willey, B.: *The Eighteenth Century Background: Studies on the Idea of Nature in the Thought of the Period* (London, Chatto, 1940; New York, Columbia Univ. Press, 1941).

Williams, C.: *The English Poetic Mind* (London, Oxford Univ. Press, 1932).

Williams, G. C.: "The Beginnings of Nature Poetry in the Eighteenth Century," *Stud. in Phil.*, 27:583 (1930).

Willoughby, L. A.: *The Romantic Movement in Germany* (London, Oxford Univ. Press, 1930).

Wilson, J. G.: *The Poets and Poetry of Scotland*, 2 vols. (Glasgow, Blackie, 1876, 1877; New York, Harper).

Woodberry, G. E.: *Makers of Literature* (London and New York, Macmillan, 1901); first published as *Studies in Letters and Life* (Boston, Houghton, 1890).

Wright, C. H. C.: *A History of French Literature* (London and New York, Oxford Univ. Press, 1912).

Mark Akenside 1721-1770

Poems, p. 44 — Critical Notes, p. 1238

EDITIONS

Poetical Works, ed., with a Life, by A. Dyce (Aldine ed.: Edinburgh, Bell, 1835; New York, Macmillan).

Poetical Works, with Beattie, Text and Life by Dyce (British Poets ed.: Boston, Houghton, 1854, 1880).

Poetical Works, with Dyer, ed. by R. A. Willmott (London and New York, Routledge, 1855).

Poetical Works, ed., with a Life, by G. Gilfillan (Edinburgh, Nichol, 1857).

BIOGRAPHY AND CRITICISM

Aldridge, A. O.: "Akenside and Imagination," *Stud. in Phil.*, 42:769 (1945).

Bucke, C.: *On the Life, Writings, and Genius of Akenside; with some Account of his Friends* (London, Cochrane, 1832).

Dowden, E.: in Ward's *The English Poets*, Vol. 3 (London and New York, Macmillan, 1880, 1909).

Gosse, E.: "Mark Akenside, Poet and Physician," *Living Age*, 311:787 (1916).

Gosse, E.: *More Books on the Table* (London, Heinemann, 1923).

Houpt, C. T.: *Mark Akenside: A Biographical and Critical Study* (Philadelphia, Univ. of Pa. Press, 1944).

Johnson, Samuel: *The Lives of the English Poets* (London, 1779-81); 3 vols., ed. by G. B. Hill (London, Clarendon Press, 1905).

Potter, G. R.: "Mark Akenside, Prophet of Evolution," *Mod. Phil.*, 24:55 (1926).

BIBLIOGRAPHY

Williams, Iolo A.: *Seven Eighteenth Century Bibliographies* (London, Dulau, 1924).

Joanna Baillie 1762-1851

Poems, p. 500 — Critical Notes, p. 1323

EDITIONS

Dramatic and Poetical Works (London, Longmans, 1851).

BIOGRAPHY AND CRITICISM

Carhart, Margaret S.: *The Life and Work of Joanna Baillie* (New Haven, Yale Univ. Press, 1923; London, Milford).

Hamilton, Catharine J.: *Women Writers*, 2 vols. (London, Ward and Lock, 1892).

Jeffrey, F.: "Miss Baillie's Plays on the Passions," *The Edinburgh Rev.*, 2:269 (1803).

Mitford, Mary R.: *Recollections of a Literary Life*, 3 vols. (London, Bentley, 1852, 1888).

Plarr, G.: "Walter Scott and Joanna Baillie," *The Edinburgh Rev.*, 216:355; 217:170 (1912; 1913).

Wilson, J. G.: *The Poets and Poetry of Scotland*, 2 vols. (Glasgow, Blackie, 1876; New York, Harper).

James Beattie 1735-1803

Poems, p. 119 — Critical Notes, p. 1250

EDITIONS

Poetical Works, ed., with a Life, by A. Dyce (Aldine ed.: Edinburgh, Bell, 1831; New York, Macmillan, 1891).

Poetical Works, with Collins, ed., with a Memoir, by T. Miller (1846).

Poetical Works, with Akenside (British Poets ed.: Boston, Houghton, 1854, 1880).

Poetical Works, with Blair and Falconer, ed., with Lives, by G. Gilfillan (Edinburgh, Nimmo, 1868; London, Cassell, 1879).

Letters, ed. by A. Mackie (Aberdeen, 1908).

BIOGRAPHY AND CRITICISM

Forbes, Margaret: *Beattie and His Friends* (London, Constable, 1904).

Forbes, W.: *An Account of the Life and Writings of James Beattie, Including Many of His Original Letters*, 2 vols. (London, Roper, 1824).

Graham, H. G.: *Scottish Men of Letters in the Eighteenth Century* (London, Black, 1901; New York, Macmillan).

Jeffrey, F.: "Sir William Forbes's Life of Dr. Beattie," *The Edinburgh Rev.*, 10:171 (1807).

McCosh, J.: *The Scottish Philosophy* (London, Macmillan, 1874; New York, Carter, 1875).

Perry, T. S.: "Gray, Collins, and Beattie," *The Atlantic Monthly*, 46:810 (1880).

Walker, H.: *Three Centuries of Scottish Literature*, 2 vols. (Glasgow, MacLehose, 1893; New York, Macmillan).

William Beckford 1759-1844

EDITIONS

The History of the Caliph Vathek; and European Travels, ed., with a Biographical Introduction, by G. T. Bettany (London and New York, Ward and Lock, 1891).

Vathek; an Arabian Tale, ed., with an Introduction, by R. Garnett (London, Lawrence, 1893, 1900; Philadelphia, Lippincott, 1901).

The History of the Caliph Vathek, ed., with an Introduction, by E. D. Ross (London, Methuen, 1901).

Vathek, ed., with an Introduction, by R. Brimley Johnson (London, Chapman and Dodd, 1922).

Vathek, trans. by H. B. Grimsditch (New York, Random House, 1929).

Vathek, with *The Episodes of Vathek*, 2 vols., ed., with an Introduction and Notes, by G. Chapman (London, Constable, 1929).

The Episodes of Vathek, French texts with English translation by F. T. Marzials, and with an Introduction by L. Melville (London, Swift, 1912; Philadelphia, Lippincott).

The Episodes of Vathek, trans. by F. T. Marzials (London, Chapman and Dodd, 1922).

BIOGRAPHY AND CRITICISM

Benjamin, L. S. (L. Melville): *The Life and Letters of William Beckford of Fonthill* (New York, Duffield, 1910).

Benjamin, L. S. (L. Melville): "William Beckford of Fonthill Abbey," *The Fortnightly Rev.*, 86:1011 (1909).

Chapman, G.: *Beckford* (New York, Scribner, 1937).

Conant, M. P.: *The Oriental Tale in England in the 18th Century* (New York, Columbia Univ. Press, 1908).

Garnett, R.: *Essays of an Ex-Librarian* (London, Heinemann, 1901; New York, Dodd).

More, P. E.: "The Drift of Romanticism," *Shelburne Essays*, Eighth Ser. (Boston, Houghton, 1913).

Oliver, J. W.: *The Life of William Beckford* (London, Oxford Univ. Press, 1932).

Sitwell, S.: *Beckford and Beckfordism* (London, Duckworth, 1930).

BIBLIOGRAPHY

Benjamin, L. S. (L. Melville): In his *The Life and Letters of William Beckford of Fonthill* (1910).

Chapman, G. and Hodgkin, J.: *A Bibliography of William Beckford of Fonthill* (London, Constable, 1930).

Thomas Lovell Beddoes 1803-1849

EDITIONS

Poetical Works, 2 vols., ed., with a Memoir, by E. Gosse (London, Dent, 1890; New York, Macmillan); reprinted in Temple Lib. ed.

Poems, ed. by R. Colles (Muses' Lib.: London, Dent, 1906; New York, Dutton, 1907).

The Complete Works, 2 vols., ed., with a Memoir, by E. Gosse (London, Fanfrolico Press, 1928).

The Works, ed. by H. W. Donner (London, Oxford Univ. Press, 1935).

Letters, ed. by E. Gosse (London, Mathews, 1894).

BIOGRAPHY AND CRITICISM

Donner, H. W.: *Thomas Lovell Beddoes: the Making of a Poet* (Oxford, Blackwell, 1935).

Gosse, E.: *Critical Kit-Kats* (New York, Dodd, 1903): a reprint, with slight additions, of the Memoir in *Poetical Works* (1890).

Moldauer, Grete: *Thomas Lovell Beddoes* (Wien and Leipzig, Braumüller, 1924; *Wiener Beiträge*, 52).

Pierce, F. E.: "Beddoes and Continental Romanticists," *Phil. Quart.*, 6:123 (1927).

Potter, G. R.: "Did Thomas Lovell Beddoes Believe in the Evolution of Species?" *Mod. Phil.*, 21:89 (1923).

Rickword, E.: "Thomas Lovell Beddoes," *London Mercury*, 9:162 (1923-24).

Snow, R. H.: *Thomas Lovell Beddoes: Eccentric and Poet* (New York, Covici, 1928).

Stoddard, R. H.: *Under the Evening Lamp* (New York, Scribner, 1892).

Symons, A.: *Figures of Several Centuries* (London, Constable, 1916).

Wood, H.: "T. L. Beddoes, a Survival in Style," *Amer. Jour. of Phil.*, 4:445 (1883).

Robert Blair 1699-1746

Poems, p. 37 — Critical Notes, p. 1237

EDITIONS

Poetical Works, with Beattie and Falconer, ed., with Lives, by G. Gilfillan (Edinburgh, Nimmo, 1868; London, Cassell, 1879).

The Grave, illustrated by Schiavonetti, from the original inventions of William Blake, 1808, 1813 (London, Methuen, 1903; New York, Appleton).

The Grave, ed., with a Preface, by F. W. Farrar (Philadelphia, Lippincott, 1860).

BIOGRAPHY AND CRITICISM

Graham, H. G.: *Scottish Men of Letters in the Eighteenth Century* (London, Black, 1901; New York, Macmillan).

Wilson, J. G.: *The Poets and Poetry of Scotland*, 2 vols. (Glasgow, Blackie, 1876; New York, Harper).

William Blake 1757-1827

Selections, p. 166 — Critical Notes, p. 1258

EDITIONS

Poetical Works, ed., with a Memoir, by W. M. Rossetti (Aldine ed.: London, Bell, 1874, 1890; New York, Macmillan).

Works, Poetic, Symbolic, and Critical, 3 vols., ed., with a Memoir and Interpretation, by E. J. Ellis and W. B. Yeats (London, Quaritch, 1893).

Poetical Works, ed. by J. Sampson (London and New York, Oxford Univ. Press, 1905).

Poetical Works, 2 vols., ed. by E. J. Ellis (London, Chatto, 1906).

Poetical Works, including Minor Prophetic Books, ed. by J. Sampson (London, Oxford Univ. Press, 1913).

Writings, 3 vols., ed. by G. Keynes (London, Nonesuch Press, 1925).

Complete Poetry, ed., with an Introduction, by R. S. Hillyer (New York, Random House, 1941).

Complete Poetry and Selected Prose (Modern Lib. ed.: New York, Random House, 1946).

Poetry and Prose, 3 vols., ed. by G. Keynes (London, Nonesuch Press, 1927, 1939).

The Prophetic Writings, 2 vols., ed., with an Introduction and a Commentary, by D. J. Sloss and J. P. R. Wallis (Oxford, Clarendon Press, 1926).

Poems, ed. by W. B. Yeats (Muses' Lib. ed.: London, Lawrence, 1893; New York, Scribner; London, Routledge, 1905; New York, Dutton).

Lyrical Poems, ed., with an Introduction by W. Raleigh, by J. Sampson (Oxford, Clarendon Press, 1906).

Selections from the Symbolical Poems, ed. by F. E. Pierce (New Haven, Yale Univ. Press, 1915).

Songs of Innocence and Experience (Chicago, Doubleday, 1916).

Selected Poems, ed., with an Introduction, by B. De Sélincourt (World's Classics: New York, Oxford Univ. Press, 1927).

Poems, ed., with an Introduction, by L. Binyon (London, Macmillan, 1931).

Selected Poems, ed., with an Introduction, by D. Saurat (London, Westhouse, 1947).

The Portable Blake, ed. by A. Kazin (New York, Viking Press, 1946).

Etchings, arranged by W. B. Scott (London, Chatto, 1906).

Paintings, ed. by D. Figgis (London, Benn, 1925, New York, Scribner).

The Engraved Designs of William Blake, ed. by L. Binyon (New York, Scribner, 1926).

Letters, ed., with a Life by F. Tatham, by A. G. B. Russell (London, Methuen, 1906; New York, Scribner).

BIOGRAPHY

Burdett, O.: *William Blake* (English Men of Letters Ser.: New York, Macmillan, 1926).

Clutton-Brock, A.: *Blake* (London, Macmillan, 1933).

De Sélincourt, B.: *William Blake* (London, Duckworth, 1909; New York, Scribner).

Ellis, E. J.: *The Real Blake, a Portrait Biography* (London, Chatto, 1907; New York, Doubleday).

Gilchrist, A.: *Life of William Blake*, 2 vols. (London, Macmillan, 1863); ed. by W. G. Robertson (London and New York, Lane,

1906; New York, Dodd, 1922; New York, Dutton, 1942).

Jenkins, H. G.: *William Blake; Studies of His Life and Personality*, ed., with an Introduction, by C. E. Lawrence (London, Jenkins, 1925).

Robinson, H. C.: *Blake, Coleridge, Wordsworth, Lamb, Etc.*, being Selections from the *Remains* of Henry Crabb Robinson, ed. by Edith J. Morley (Manchester, The Univ. Press, 1922; London and New York, Longmans).

Short, E. H.: *Blake* (British Artists Ser.: London, Allen, 1925; New York, Stokes).

Story, A. T.: *William Blake: His Life, Character, and Genius* (London, Sonnenschein, 1893).

Wilson, M.: *The Life of William Blake* (New York, Random House, 1927, 1928; London, Hart-Davis, 1932, 1948).

Wright, T.: *The Life of William Blake*, 2 vols. (Olney, Wright, 1929).

CRITICISM

Beeching, H. C.: *Essays and Studies by Members of the English Association*, Vol. 3 (1912).

Benson, A. C.: *Essays* (London, Heinemann, 1895; New York, Dutton).

Berger, P.: *Mysticisme et Poésie* (Paris, 1907); English translation by D. H. Conner, *William Blake, Poet and Mystic* (New York, Dutton, 1915).

Berger, P.: *Mercure de France*, 198:5 (1927).

Blackstone, B.: *English Blake* (London, Cambridge Univ. Press, 1949; New York, Macmillan).

Bronowski, J.: *William Blake, 1757-1827: A Man Without a Mask* (London, Secker and Warburg, 1943; New York, Transatlantic, 1945).

Brooke, S. A.: *Studies in Poetry* (London, Duckworth, 1907; New York, Putnam).

Bruce, H. L.: "William Blake and His Companions from 1818 to 1827," *Pub. Mod. Lang. Assn.*, 39:358 (1924).

Bruce, H. L.: *William Blake in This World* (New York, Harcourt, 1925).

Butterworth, Adeline M.: *William Blake, Mystic* (Liverpool, Liverpool Booksellers, 1911).

Cary, E. L.: *The Art of William Blake* (New York, Moffat, 1907).

Cheney, S.: *Men Who Have Walked with God* (New York, Knopf, 1945).

Chesterton, G. K.: *Blake* (New York, Dutton, 1910).

Damon, S. F.: *William Blake: His Philosophy and Symbols* (Boston, Houghton, 1924; New York, P. Smith, 1947).

Davies, J. G.: *The Theology of William Blake* (New York, Oxford Univ. Press, 1948).

De Casseres, B.: *Forty Immortals* (New York, Joseph Lawren, 1926).

De Sélincourt, B.: *William Blake* (London, Duckworth, 1909; New York, Scribner).

De Sélincourt, E.: *Oxford Lectures on Poetry* (New York, Oxford Univ. Press, 1934).

Dodds, Mrs. A. E. Powell: *The Romantic Theory of Poetry* (New York, Longmans, 1926).

Doughty, O.: *English Lyric in the Age of Reason* (London, O'Connor, 1922).

Fausset, H. I'A.: *Studies in Idealism* (London, Dent, 1923; New York, Dutton).

Fletcher, J. G.: "William Blake," *North Amer. Rev.*, 218:518 (1923).

Frye, N.: *Fearful Symmetry: A Study of William Blake* (Princeton, Princeton Univ. Press, 1947).

Gardner, C.: *Vision and Vesture; a Study of William Blake in Modern Thought* (London, Dent, 1916, 1929).

Gardner, C.: *William Blake, the Man* (London, Dent, 1919; New York, Dutton).

Gosse, E.: *More Books on the Table* (London, Heinemann, 1923).

Grierson, H. J. C.: *The Background of English Literature and Other Collected Essays and Addresses* (London, Chatto and Windus, 1925).

Herford, C. H.: *William Blake* (London, Longmans, 1928).

Keeble, S. E.: "Imagination and William Blake," *London Quart. Rev.* 127:215 (1917).

Keynes, G. L.: *Blake Studies* (London, Hart-Davis, 1949).

Langridge, I.: *William Blake* (New York, Macmillan, 1904).

Lowery, M. R.: *Windows of the Morning: A Critical Study of the "Poetical Sketches"* (New Haven, Yale Univ. Press, 1940).

Moore, T. S.: "William Blake and His Aesthetic," *Art and Life* (London, Methuen, 1910).

Moore, T. S.: "William Blake, Poet and Painter," *Quart. Rev.*, 208:24 (1908).

More, P. E.: *Shelburne Essays*, Fourth Ser. (New York, Putnam, 1906).

Morris, H. N.: *Flaxman, Blake, Coleridge, and Other Men of Genius Influenced by Swedenborg* (London, New Church Press, 1915).

Morris, L. R.: "William Blake: the First of the Moderns," *The Forum*, 51:932 (1914).

Murry, J. M.: *William Blake* (London, Cape, 1933).

Nicoll, A.: *William Blake and His Poetry* (London, Harrap, 1922).

Nicolson, M. H.: "Epilogue on Blake," *Newton*

Demands the Muse (Princeton, Princeton Univ. Press, 1946).

Percival, M. O.: *William Blake's Circle of Destiny* (New York, Columbia Univ. Press, 1938).

Plowman, M.: *An Introduction to the Study of Blake* (New York, Dutton, 1927).

Powys, J. C.: *Suspended Judgments* (New York, G. Arnold Shaw, 1916).

Preston, K.: *Blake and Rossetti* (London, Moring, 1944).

Saurat, D.: *Blake and Milton* (New York, L. MacVeagh, Dial Press, 1924).

Saurat, D.: *Blake and Modern Thought* (London, Constable, 1929).

Schorer, M.: *William Blake; the Politics of Vision* (New York, Holt, 1946).

Sitwell, S.: *The Hunters and the Hunted* (London, Macmillan, 1948).

Swinburne, A. C.: *William Blake, a Critical Essay* (London, Chatto, 1868; New York, Dutton, 1906; London, Heinemann, 1925).

Symons, A.: *The Romantic Movement in English Poetry* (London, Constable, 1909; New York, Dutton).

Symons, A.: *William Blake* (New York, Dutton, 1907).

Todd, R.: "William Blake and the Eighteenth-Century Mythologists," *Tracks in the Snow* (London, Grey Walls Press, 1946).

White, H. C.: *The Mysticism of William Blake* (Madison, Univ. of Wis. Stud. in Lang. and Lit., No. 23, 1927).

Wicksteed, J. H.: *Blake's Innocence and Experience* (London, Dent, 1928).

Witcutt, W. P.: *Blake: A Psychological Study* (London, Hollis and Carter, 1946).

Yeats, W. B.: "William Blake and the Imagination," (1897) in *Essays* (London, Macmillan, 1924).

BIBLIOGRAPHY

Jagaku, B.: *Bibliography of William Blake* (Kobe, Japan, Grolier Society, 1929).

Keynes, G. L.: *A Bibliography of William Blake* (New York, Grolier Club, 1921).

William Lisle Bowles 1762-1850

Poems, p. 164 — Critical Notes, p. 1257

EDITIONS

Poetical Works, 2 vols., ed., with a Memoir and critical Dissertation, by G. Gilfillan (Edinburgh, 1855).

Poetical Works (London, Cassell, 1879).

Poetical Works, with Lamb and H. Coleridge, ed. by W. Tirebuck (Canterbury Poets ed.: London, Scott, 1887).

BIOGRAPHY AND CRITICISM

Beers, H. A.: "Coleridge, Bowles, and the Pope Controversy," *A History of English Romanticism in the Nineteenth Century* (New York, Holt, 1901; 1910).

Casson, T. E.: *Eighteenth Century Literature; an Oxford Miscellany* (London, Frowde, 1909).

Coleridge, S. T.: *Biographia Literaria*, ch. 1 (London, 1817; Oxford, Clarendon Press, 1907).

Greever, G.: *A Wiltshire Parson and His Friends* (London, Constable, 1924; Boston, Houghton, 1926).

Hazlitt, W.: "Pope, Lord Byron, and Mr. Bowles," *The London Mag.*, 1821; *Collected Works*, ed. by Waller and Glover (London, Dent, 1902-06; New York, McClure), 11, 486.

Moore, J. R.: "The Mood of Pessimism in Nature Poetry: Bowles, Coleridge, and Arnold," *Sewanee Rev.*, 30:454 (1922).

Quarterly Review, The, 2:281 (1809).

Saintsbury, G.: *A History of Criticism* (Edinburgh and London, Blackwood, 1900-04; 1908; New York, Dodd).

Symons, A.: *The Romantic Movement in English Poetry* (London, Constable, 1909; New York, Dutton).

Edmund Burke 1729-1797

Selections, p. 1219 — Critical Notes, p. 1399

EDITIONS

Complete Works, 6 vols., ed., with an Introduction and Prefaces, by F. H. Willis and F. W. Raffety (World's Classics: London, Oxford Univ. Press, 1906-08).

Selections, 3 vols., ed. by E. J. Payne (Oxford, Clarendon Press, 1874, 1892-98).

Selections, ed. by L. N. Broughton (New York, Scribner, 1925).

American Speeches and Letters, ed. by H. Law (Everyman's Lib. ed.: New York, Dutton, 1908).

Reflections on the Revolution in France, ed. by E. Rhys (Everyman's Lib. ed.: New York, Dutton, 1935).

Correspondence, 4 vols., ed. by E. Fitzwilliam and R. Bourke (London, Rivington, 1844).

Letters, Selections, ed. by H. J. Laski (London, Oxford Univ. Press, 1922).

Speeches on America, ed. by F. G. Selby (London, Macmillan, 1895).

Speeches on Irish Affairs, ed. by M. Arnold (London, Macmillan, 1881).

BIOGRAPHY AND CRITICISM

Baumann, A. A.: *Burke, the Founder of Conservatism* (London, Eyre, 1929).

Birrell, A.: *Collected Essays and Addresses*, 3 vols. (London and Toronto, Dent, 1922).

Cobban, A.: *Edmund Burke and the Revolt against the Eighteenth Century* (London, Allen, 1929).

Dawson, W. J.: *The Makers of English Prose* (New York and London, Revell, 1906).

Dowden, E.: "Anti-Revolution: Edmund Burke," *The French Revolution and English Literature* (New York and London, Scribner, 1897).

Einaudi, M.: "The British Background of Burke's Political Philosophy," *Pol. Sci. Quart.*, 49:576 (1934).

Hazlitt, W.: "Character of Mr. Burke," *Political Essays* (London, 1819); *Collected Works*, ed. Waller and Glover (London, Dent, 1902-06; New York, McClure), 3:250, 325.

Hearnshaw, F. J. C.: *Social and Political Ideas of Some Representative Thinkers of the Revolutionary Era* (London, Harrap, 1930).

MacCunn, J.: *The Political Philosophy of Burke* (London, Arnold, 1913; New York, Longmans).

Magnus, P. M.: *Edmund Burke* (London, Murray, 1939).

Morley, J.: *Edmund Burke* (English Men of Letters Ser.: London, Macmillan, 1879; New York, Harper).

Morley, J.: *Edmund Burke, a Historical Study* (New York, Knopf, 1924).

Newman, B.: *Edmund Burke* (London, Bell, 1927).

O'Brien, W.: *Edmund Burke as an Irishman* (Dublin, Gill, 1924).

Oliver, R. T.: *Four Who Spoke Out* (Syracuse, N. Y.; Syracuse Univ. Press, 1946).

Osborn, A. M.: *Rousseau and Burke* (London and New York, Oxford Univ. Press, 1940).

Pillans, T. D.: *Edmund Burke, Apostle of Justice and Liberty* (London, Watts, 1905).

Rogers, A. K.: "Burke's Social Philosophy," *The Amer. Jour. of Soc.*, 18:51 (1912).

Stephen, L.: *History of English Thought in the Eighteenth Century*, 2 vols. (London, Smith, 1876, 1902; New York, Putnam).

Robert Burns 1759-1796

Selections, p. 199 — Critical Notes, p. 1263

EDITIONS

Life and Works, 4 vols., ed. by R. Chambers (1851-52); rev. by W. Wallace (Edinburgh, Chambers, 1896-97; New York, Longmans).

Poems, Songs, and Letters, ed. by E. Smith (Globe ed.: London and New York, Macmillan, 1868).

Works, 6 vols., ed. by W. S. Douglas (Edinburgh, W. Paterson, 1877-79).

Poetical Works, 3 vols., ed., with a Memoir, by G. A. Aitken (Aldine ed.: London, Bell, 1892-93; New York, Macmillan).

Poetical Works, 3 vols., ed. by J. L. Robertson (London, Oxford Univ. Press, 1896).

Poetry, 4 vols., ed., with an Essay on Burns's Life, Genius, and Achievement, by W. E. Henley and T. F. Henderson (Centenary ed.: Edinburgh, Jack, 1896-97; Boston, Houghton).

Complete Poetical Works, ed., with Henley's essay from the Centenary ed., by W. E. Henley (Cambridge ed.: Boston, Houghton, 1897).

Complete Writings, 10 vols., containing an Essay on Burns's life, genius, and achievement by W. E. Henley, and an Introduction by John Buchan (Boston and New York, Houghton, 1926).

Poetical Works, ed., with a Life, by W. Wallace (London and Edinburgh, Chambers, 1902; 1947).

Complete Poetical Works, ed., with an Appreciation, by Lord Rosebery (London, Nelson, 1902).

Complete Poems, ed. by J. L. Robertson (London, Oxford Univ. Press, 1906).

Selections from the Poems, ed. by J. G. Dow (Athenæum Press ed.: Boston, Ginn, 1898).

Songs now First Printed with the Melodies for Which They Were Written, ed. by J. C. Dick (London, Oxford Univ. Press, 1907).

Scottish Poems in his Native Dialect, ed. by Sir James Wilson (London, Oxford Univ. Press, 1925).

Selected Poems, ed., with an Introduction, by J. De L. Ferguson (New York, Macmillan, 1926).

The Poems, Epistles, Songs, Epigrams, and Epitaphs, ed. by C. S. Dougall (New York, Macmillan, 1927).

Correspondence, 2 vols., ed. by W. Wallace (New York, Dodd, 1898).

Letters, selections, ed., with an Introduction, by J. L. Robertson (Camelot ed.: London, Scott, 1887).

Sylvander and Clarinda; the Love Letters of Robert Burns and Agnes M'Lehose, ed. by A. J. Burr (New York, Doran, 1917).

Letters, ed., with an Introduction, by R. B. Johnson (New York, Dodd, 1928).

Letters, 2 vols., ed. from the original manuscripts by J. De L. Ferguson (New York and London, Oxford Univ. Press, 1931).

BIOGRAPHY

Blackie, J. S.: *Life of Robert Burns* (Great Writers Ser.: London, Scott, 1888).

Carswell, C.: *The Life of Robert Burns* (London, Chatto, 1930; New York, Harcourt, 1931).

Dakers, A.: *Robert Burns, His Life and Genius* (London, Chapman and Hall, 1923).

Dougall, C. S.: *The Burns Country* (London and New York, Macmillan, 1911).

Henderson, T. F.: *Robert Burns* (London, Methuen, 1904).

Lockhart, J. G.: *Life of Robert Burns* (1828); enlarged ed. by W. S. Douglas (London, Bohn, 1882).

Mackenzie, J.: *A New Life and Vindication of Robert Burns* (Edinburgh, Henderson, 1924).

Setoun, G. (T. N. Hepburn): *Robert Burns* (Famous Scots Ser.: Edinburgh and London, Anderson, 1896).

Shairp, J. C.: *Robert Burns* (English Men of Letters Ser.: London, Macmillan, 1879; New York, Harper).

Snyder, F. B.: *The Life of Robert Burns* (New York, Macmillan, 1932).

CRITICISM

Arnold, M.: "The Study of Poetry," *Essays in Criticism*, Second Ser. (London, Macmillan, 1888).

Brooke, S. A.: *Theology in the English Poets* (London, King, 1874, 1880; New York, Dutton, 1910).

Brooke, S. A.: *Naturalism in English Poetry* (New York, Dutton, 1920).

Carlyle, T.: "Essay on Burns," *The Edinburgh Rev.*, 48:27 (1828); *Critical and Miscellaneous Essays*, 4 vols. (Boston, Houghton, 1880).

Dawson, W. J.: *The Makers of English Poetry* (New York and London, Revell, 1906).

Dowden, E.: "Early Revolutionary Group and Antagonists," *The French Revolution and English Literature* (New York and London, Scribner, 1897).

Ferguson, J. De L.: *Pride and Passion, Robert Burns 1759-1796* (London, Oxford Univ. Press, 1939).

Fitzhugh, R. T. (ed.): *Robert Burns, His Associates and Contemporaries* (Chapel Hill, Univ. of N. C. Press, 1943).

Graham, H. G.: *Scottish Men of Letters in the Eighteenth Century* (London, Black, 1901; New York, Macmillan).

Hazlitt, W.: "On Burns and the Old English Ballads," *Lectures on the English Poets* (London, 1818); *Collected Works*, 13 vols., ed. by A. R. Waller and A. Glover (London,

Dent, 1902-06; New York, McClure), 5:123.

Hughes, J. L.: *The Real Robert Burns* (London, Chambers, 1922; New York, Stokes, 1923).

Jack, A. A.: "Burns (Natural or Spontaneous Poetry)," *Poetry and Prose* (London, Constable, 1911).

Jeffrey, F.: "Reliques of Burns," *The Edinburgh Rev.*, 13:249 (1809); *Contributions to the Edinburgh Review* (Modern British Essayists: Philadelphia, Carey, 1849).

Kellow, H. A.: *Burns and His Poetry* (New York, Dodge, 1912).

Lang, A.: *Letters to Dead Authors* (London and New York, Longmans, 1886, 1892; New York, Scribner, 1893).

Lowe, C.: "Robert Burns, Poet; Can English People Understand Him?" *Nine. Cent.*, 93:850 (1923).

MacGowan, R.: *Robert Burns: His Contribution to Democracy* (New York, Arts and Letters Pub., 1939).

Muriel, J. St. C.: *Robert Burns* (New York, Liveright, 1947).

Neilson, W. A.: *Robert Burns, How to Know Him* (Indianapolis, Bobbs-Merrill, 1917).

Noyes, R.: "Wordsworth and Burns," *Pub. Mod. Lang. Assn.*, 59:813 (1944).

Quiller-Couch, A. T.: *Adventures in Criticism* (New York, Scribner, 1896).

Raleigh, W.: *Some Authors* (Oxford, Clarendon Press, 1923).

Shairp, J. C.: "Nature in Collins, Gray, Goldsmith, Cowper, and Burns," *On the Poetic Interpretation of Nature* (Edinburgh, Douglas, 1877; New York, Hurd, 1878; Boston, Houghton, 1885).

Shairp, J. C.: "Scottish Song and Burns," *Aspects of Poetry* (Oxford, Clarendon Press, 1881; Boston, Houghton, 1882).

Snyder, F. B.: *Robert Burns; His Personality, His Reputation, and His Art* (Toronto, Univ. of Toronto Press, 1936).

Stevenson, R. L.: "Some Aspects of Robert Burns," *Familiar Studies of Men and Books* (1882); *Works*, 10 vols. (New York, Scribner, 1914).

Walker, H.: *Three Centuries of Scottish Literature*, 2 vols. (Glasgow, MacLehose, 1893; New York, Macmillan).

Watson, John (Ian Maclaren): "Robert Burns: the Voice of the Scots People," *Concerning Books and Bookmen* (London, Nisbet, 1912; New York, Doran).

CONCORDANCE

Reid, J. B.: *Complete Concordance to the Poetry and Songs of Burns* (Glasgow, Kerr, 1889).

BIBLIOGRAPHY

Angus, W. C.: *The Printed Works of Robert Burns* (Glasgow, Hodge, 1899).

Ewing, J. C.: *Bibliography of Robert Burns to 1796* (Privately printed, 1909).

Gibson, James: *Bibliography of Robert Burns* (Kilmarnock, McKie, 1881).

McKie, J. J.: *Bibliography of Burns* (Kilmarnock, 1881).

George Noel Gordon, Lord Byron 1788-1824

Poems, p. 510 — Critical Notes, p. 1324

EDITIONS

Poetical Works (London, Oxford Univ. Press, 1896).

Poetical Works, ed., with a Memoir, by E. H. Coleridge (London, Murray, 1905; New York, Scribner).

Works: Poetry, 7 vols., ed. by E. H. Coleridge; Letters and Journals, 6 vols., ed. by R. E. Prothero (London, Murray, 1898-1904; New York, Scribner, 1922).

Complete Poetical Works, ed., with a Biographical Sketch, by P. E. More (Cambridge ed., Boston, Houghton, 1906, 1947).

Byron: A Self-Portrait. Letters & Diaries, 1798 to 1824, 2 vols., ed. by P. Quennell (New York, Scribners, 1950).

Letters, 1804-1813, ed. by W. E. Henley (Vol. 1 of "Works"; no more published. London, Macmillan, 1897).

Letters and Journals, selections, ed. with an Introduction, by Mathilde Blind (Camelot ed.; London, Scott, 1886).

Letters, ed. by R. G. Howarth (Everyman's Lib. ed.: New York, Dutton, 1933, 1936).

The Best of Byron, ed., with an Introduction and Notes by R. A. Rice (New York, Nelson, 1933; New York, Ronald, 1942).

Don Juan: ed. by H. Ristine (New York, Macmillan, 1927).

Don Juan, ed. by L. I. Bredvold (New York, Doubleday, 1935).

Lord Byron's Correspondence Chiefly with Lady Melbourne, Mr. Hobhouse, the Hon. Douglas Kinnaird, and P. B. Shelley, 2 vols., ed. by John Murray (London, Murray, 1922; New York, Scribner).

BIOGRAPHY

Beck, Mrs L. (E. Barrington): *Glorious Apollo* (New York, Dodd, 1925).

Bellamy, R. L.: *Byron the Man* (London, Paul, 1924).

Borst, W. A.: *Lord Byron's First Pilgrimage, 1809-1811* (New Haven, Yale Univ. Press, 1948).

Chew, S. C.: *Byron in England, His Fame and After-Fame* (London, Murray, 1924; New York, Scribner).

Clarke, I. C.: *Shelley and Byron* (London, Hutchinson, 1934).

Drinkwater, J.: *The Pilgrim of Eternity: Byron—A Conflict* (London, Hodder and Stoughton, 1925; New York, Doran).

Erdman, D. V.: "Byron and Revolt in England," *Science and Society*, 11:234 (1947).

Fox, Sir J. C.: *The Byron Mystery* (London, Richards, 1924).

Gordon, A. C.: *Allegra: The Story of Byron and Miss Clairmont* (New York, Minton, Balch, 1926).

Graham, W.: *Last Links with Byron, Shelley, and Keats* (London, Smithers, 1899).

Gray, A. K.: *Teresa, or Her Demon Lover* (New York, Scribner, 1945).

Gribble, F. H.: *The Love Affairs of Lord Byron* (New York, Scribner, 1910).

Hobhouse, J. C. (Lord Broughton): *Recollections of a Long Life*, 6 vols. (London, Murray, 1909-11).

Lovelace, R. G. N. K.: *Astarte: a Fragment of Truth concerning George Gordon Byron* (London, Christophers, 1921).

Lovell, E. J.: *Byron: The Record of a Quest* (Austin, Univ. of Texas Press, 1950).

Maurois, André (E. S. W. Herzog): *Byron*, 2 vols. (Paris, Grasset, 1930); trans. by H. Miles (London, Cape, 1930; Lane, 1933).

Mayne, Ethel C.: *Byron*, 2 vols. (New York, Scribner, 1913); rev., 1 vol. (1924).

Mayne, E. C.: *The Life and Letters of Anne Isabella, Lady Noel Byron* (London, Constable, 1929, 1932).

Monvel, R. B. de: *La Vie de Lord Byron* (Paris, Plon-Nourrit, 1924; New York, Brentano).

Moore, T.: *The Life of Lord Byron with his Letters and Journals and Illustrative Notes* (London, Murray, 1830).

Murray, J.: *Lord Byron and His Detractors* (London, Ballantyne, 1906).

Nichol, J.: *Byron* (English Men of Letters Ser.: London, Macmillan, 1880; New York, Harper, 1887).

Nicolson, H. G.: *Byron: the Last Journey, April, 1823—April, 1824* (London, Constable, 1924, 1948).

Noel, R.: *Life of Lord Byron* (Great Writers Ser.: London, Scott, 1890; New York, Scribner).

Origo, I.: *Allegra* (London, Hogarth, 1935).

Origo, I., *The Last Attachment* (New York, Scribner, 1949).

Quennell, P. C.: *Byron: the Years of Fame* (New York, Viking Press, 1935).

Quennell, P. C.: *Byron in Italy* (New York, Viking Press, 1941).

Raymond, D. N.: *The Political Career of Lord Byron* (New York, Holt, 1924).

Spender, H.: *Byron and Greece* (London, Murray, 1924; New York, Scribner).

Trelawny, E. J.: *Recollections of the Last Days of Shelley and Byron* (London, Moxon, 1858); *Records of Shelley, Byron, and the Author,* 2 vols. (London, Pickering, 1878; Frowde, 1906; New York, Dutton, 1905; London, Oxford Univ. Press, 1906).

Vulliamy, C. E.: *Byron: With a View of the Kingdom of Cant and a Dissection of the Byronic Ego* (London, M. Joseph, 1948).

CRITICISM

Arnold, M.: *Essays in Criticism,* Second Ser. (London, Macmillan, 1888).

Boyd, E. F.: *Byron's Don Juan: A Critical Study* (New Brunswick, N. J., Rutgers Univ. Press, 1945).

Brandes, G.: "Byron, The Passionate Personality," *Main Currents in Nineteenth Century Literature,* 4 vols. (London, Heinemann, 1901-05; New York, Macmillan, 1906).

Brinton, C.: *The Political Ideas of the English Romanticists* (London, Oxford Univ. Press, 1926).

Briscoe, W. A. (ed.): *Byron the Poet.* A Collection of addresses and essays. A centenary volume (London, Routledge, 1924).

Brown, W. C.: "Byron and the English Interest in the Near East," *Stud. in Phil.,* 34:55 (1937).

Calvert, W. J.: *Byron: Romantic Paradox* (Chapel Hill, Univ. of N. C. Press, 1935).

Chambers, R. W. (ed.): *Ruskin and Others on Byron* (London, Oxford Univ. Press, 1925); reprinted in *Man's Unconquerable Mind* (New York, Transatlantic, 1939).

Chesterton, G. K.: "The Optimism of Byron," *Twelve Types* (London, Humphreys, 1902, 1910); *Varied Types* (New York, Dodd, 1903, 1909).

Chew, S. C.: *The Dramas of Lord Byron* (Baltimore, Johns Hopkins Press, 1915).

Collins, J. C.: "The Collected Works of Byron," *Studies in Poetry and Criticism* (London, Bell, 1905; New York, Macmillan, 1906); printed in *The Quart. Rev.,* 202:429 (1905).

Dawson, W. J.: *The Makers of English Poetry* (New York and London, Revell, 1906).

Dick, W.: *Byron and His Poetry* (London, Harrap, 1918).

Elliott, G. R.: "Byron and the Comic Spirit," *Pub. Mod. Lang. Assn.,* 39:897 (1924).

Fuess, C. M.: *Lord Byron as a Satirist in Verse* (New York, Columbia Univ. Press, 1912).

Garrod, H. W.: "Byron 1824-1924." Lecture, University of Oxford, May 14, 1924 (Oxford, Clarendon Press, 1924).

Goode, C. T.: *Byron as a Critic* (Weimar, Wagner, 1923).

Hancock, A. E.: *The French Revolution and the English Poets* (New York, Holt, 1899).

Jack, A. A.: "Byron (Oratorical Poetry)," *Poetry and Prose* (London, Constable, 1911).

Ker, W. P.: *Collected Essays,* 2 vols. (London, Macmillan, 1925).

Knight, G. W.: *The Burning Oracle: Studies in the Poetry of Action* (London, Oxford Univ. Press, 1939).

Leonard, W.: *Byron and Byronism in America* (New York, Lemcke, 1907).

Mackerness, E. D.: "Byron, the Satirist," *Contemp. Rev.,* 172:112 (1947).

Marjarum, E. W.: *Byron as a Skeptic and Believer* (Princeton, Princeton Univ. Press, 1938).

Mirsky, Prince D. S.: *London Mercury,* 9:603 (1923-24).

More, P. E.: "The Wholesome Revival of Byron," *The Atlantic Monthly,* 82:801 (1898).

More, P. E.: "A Note on Byron's Don Juan," *Shelburne Essays,* Third Ser. (New York and London, Putnam, 1906).

Morley, J.: *Critical Miscellanies,* First Ser. (London, Macmillan, 1871).

Payne, W. M.: *The Greater English Poets of the Nineteenth Century* (New York, Holt, 1907, 1909).

Pierce, F. E.: *Currents and Eddies in the English Romantic Generation* (New Haven, Yale Univ. Press, 1918).

Pyre, J. F. A.: "Byron in Our Day," *The Atlantic Monthly,* 99:542 (1907).

Quiller-Couch, Sir A.: *Studies in Literature,* 2 vols. (New York, Putnam, 1922; London, Cambridge Univ. Press).

Rice, R. A.: "Lord Byron's British Reputation," *Smith College Studies in Mod. Lang.,* Vol. 5, No. 2 (1924).

Stokoe, F. W.: *German Influence in the English Romantic Period, 1788-1818* (London, Cambridge Univ. Press, 1926; New York, Macmillan).

Swinburne, A. C.: *Essays and Studies* (London, Chatto, 1875).

Swinburne, A. C.: "Wordsworth and Byron," *Miscellanies* (London, Chatto, 1886, 1911; New York, Scribner).

Symons, A.: *The Romantic Movement in English Poetry* (London, Constable, 1909; New York, Dutton).

Taine, H. A.: *History of English Literature;* trans. from the French by H. Van Laun (New York, Holt, 1872, 1896).

Trueblood, P. G.: *The Flowering of Byron's Genius* (Palo Alto, Calif., Stanford Univ. Press, 1945).

Van Rennes, J. J.: *Bowles, Byron and the Pope Controversy* (New York, Stechert, 1927).

Vincent, E. R. P.: *Byron, Hobhouse, and Foscolo* (London, Cambridge Univ. Press, 1949).

Wiener, H. S. L.: *Byron and the East: Sources of the "Turkish Tales"* (Ithaca, Cornell Univ. Press, 1940).

Woodberry, G. E.: "Byron's Centenary," *Studies in Letters and Life* (Boston, Houghton, 1890); *Makers of Literature* (London and New York, Macmillan, 1900).

Woodberry, G. E.: *Literary Essays* (New York, Harcourt, 1920).

BIBLIOGRAPHY

Anderson, J. P.: In Noel's *Life of Lord Byron* (Great Writers Ser.: London, Scott, 1890; New York, Scribner).

Chew, S. C.: In *Byron in England: His Fame and After-Fame* (New York, Scribner, 1924).

Coleridge, E. H.: In *Works of Lord Byron, Poetry,* Vol. 7 (London, Murray, 1898-1904; New York, Scribner, 1922).

Wise, T. J.: *A Bibliography of the Writings in Verse and Prose of Lord Byron,* 2 vols. (London, Maggs Bros., 1932-33).

Thomas Campbell 1777-1844

Poems, p. 443 — Critical Notes, p. 1311

EDITIONS

Poetical Works, ed., with a Sketch of Campbell's Life, by W. Allingham (Aldine ed.: London, Bell, 1875).

Complete Poetical Works, ed., with Notes, by J. L. Robertson (London, Oxford Univ. Press, 1907).

Selected Poems, ed., with a Prefatory Notice, by J. Hogben (Canterbury Poets ed.: London, Scott, 1885).

Poems, selected by L. Campbell (Golden Treasury Ser.: London, Macmillan, 1904).

BIOGRAPHY AND CRITICISM

Beattie, W.: *The Life and Letters of Thomas Campbell,* 3 vols. (London, Moxon, 1850).

Dixon, W. M.: *An Apology for the Arts* (London, Arnold, 1944; New York, Longmans, 1945).

Elton, O.: *A Survey of English Literature, 1780-1830,* 2 vols. (London, Arnold, 1928, 1933; New York, Macmillan).

Hadden, J. C.: *Thomas Campbell* (Famous Scots Ser.: Edinburgh, Anderson, 1899).

Hazlitt, W.: *The Spirit of the Age* (London, 1825); *Collected Works,* ed. Waller and Glover (London, Dent, 1902-1906; New York, McClure), 4, 343.

Redding, C.: *Literary Reminiscences and Memoirs of Thomas Campbell,* 2 vols. (London, Skeet, 1860).

Saintsbury, G.: *Essays in English Literature, Second Ser.* (London, Dent, 1895; New York, Scribner).

Symons, A.: *The Romantic Movement in English Poetry* (London, Constable, 1909; New York, Dutton).

Tuckerman, H. T.: "Thomas Campbell, the Popular Poet," *Essays Biographical and Critical* (Boston, Phillips, 1857).

Turner, A. M.: "Wordsworth's Influence on Thomas Campbell," *Pub. Mod. Lang. Assn.,* 38:253 (1923).

Wilson, J. G.: *The Poets and Poetry of Scotland,* Vol. 2 (Glasgow, Blackie, 1876; New York, Harper).

Thomas Chatterton 1752-1770

Poems, p. 125 — Critical Notes, p. 1250

EDITIONS

Poetical Works, 2 vols. (British Poets ed.: Boston, Houghton, 1857).

Poetical Works, 2 vols., ed., with an Essay on the Rowley Poems, by W. W. Skeat, and a Memoir by E. Bell (Aldine ed.: London, Bell, 1871, 1875; New York, Macmillan).

Complete Poetical Works, 2 vols., ed., with a Biographical Introduction, by H. D. Roberts (Muses' Lib.: London, Routledge, 1906; New York, Dutton).

The Rowley Poems, ed., with an Introduction, by M. E. Hare (Oxford, Clarendon Press, 1911).

Poems, ed. by J. Richmond (Canterbury Poets ed.: London, Scott, 1885).

BIOGRAPHY AND CRITICISM

Beers, H.: *A History of English Romanticism in the Eighteenth Century* (New York, Holt, 1898, 1910).

Browning, R.: *Essay on Chatterton* (Cambridge, Mass., Harvard Univ. Press, 1948).

Doughty, O.: *English Lyric in the Age of Reason* (London, O'Connor, 1922).

Ellinger, E. P.: *Thomas Chatterton the Marvelous Boy* (Philadelphia, Univ. of Pa. Press, 1930; London, Oxford Univ. Press).

Ingram, J. H.: *Chatterton and His Poetry* (London, Harrap, 1916).

Ingram, J. H.: *The True Chatterton* (New York, Scribner, 1910).

Masson, D.: *Chatterton* (Edinburgh, Constable, 1899; New York, Dodd, 1901).

Meyerstein, E. H. W.: *A Life of Thomas Chatterton* (London, Ingpen, 1930).

Nevill, J. C.: *Thomas Chatterton* (London, Muller, 1948).

Russell, C. E.: *Thomas Chatterton, the Marvellous Boy* (New York, Moffat, 1908; London, Richards, 1909).

Scott, W.: "The Works of Thomas Chatterton," *The Edinburgh Rev.*, 4:214 (1804).

Watts-Dunton, T.: In Ward's *The English Poets*, Vol. 3 (London and New York, Macmillan, 1880, 1909).

BIBLIOGRAPHY

Hare, M. E.: In his edition of Chatterton's *The Rowley Poems* (1911).

Hyett, F. A. and Bazeley, W.: *Chattertoniana* (Gloucester, Bellows, 1914).

Roberts, H. D.: In his edition of Chatterton's *Complete Poetical Works* (1906).

William Cobbett 1763-1835

Selections, p. 1028 — Critical Notes, p. 1382

EDITIONS

Works of Peter Porcupine, 12 vols. (London, at the Crown and Mitre, 1801).

Selections from Political Works, 6 vols., ed., with a Biographical Preface, by J. M. and J. P. Cobbett (London, Cobbett, 1835).

Selections, ed., with an Introduction and Notes, by A. M. D. Hughes (Oxford, Clarendon Press, 1923).

A Year's Residence in America, ed., with an Introduction, by John Freeman (London, Chapman and Dodd, 1922).

Advice to Young Men (London, Oxford Univ. Press, 1906); ed. by P. Snowden (1926); ed. by E. E. Fisk (London, Knopf, 1930).

English Grammar (London, 1817); ed., with a Memoir, by R. Waters (1883); ed. by H. L. Stephen (London, Oxford Univ. Press, 1906).

Opinions of William Cobbett, ed. by G. D. H. and M. Cole (London, Cobbett, 1945).

Political Register (1802-35).

The Progress of a Ploughboy, reprinted as *Autobiography of William Cobbett*, ed. by W. Reitzel (London, Faber, 1947).

Rural Rides, 2 vols. (London, Cuilley, 1910); 2 vols., ed., with an Introduction, by E. Thomas (Everyman's Lib. ed.: New York, Dutton, 1912); selected and ed. by J. H.

Lobban (Cambridge Univ. Press, 1908); 3 vols., ed. by G. D. H. and M. Cole (London, P. Davies, 1930), contains *Tour in Scotland* and *Letters from Ireland*.

Letters, ed. by G. D. H. Cole (New York and London, Oxford Univ. Press, 1937).

BIOGRAPHY AND CRITICISM

Benjamin, L. S. (L. Melville): *Life and Letters of William Cobbett in England and America*, 2 vols. (London and New York, Lane, 1913).

Bowen, M. (Mrs. G. M. V. Long): *Peter Porcupine: A Study of William Cobbett* (London, Longmans, 1935).

Carlyle, E. I.: *William Cobbett. A Study of his Life as Shown in his Writings* (London, Constable, 1904).

Chesterton, G. K.: *William Cobbett* (London, Hodder and Stoughton, 1925; New York, Dodd, 1926).

Cole, G. D. H.: *The Life of William Cobbett* (London, W. Collins, 1924; New York, Harcourt, 1925; London, Horne and Van Thal, 1947).

Freeman, J.: *English Portraits and Essays* (London, Hodder and Stoughton, 1924). Same article in *The London Mercury*, 3:407 (1920).

Hazlitt, W.: "The Character of Cobbett," *Table Talk* (London, 1821); *The Spirit of the Age* (London, 1817); *Collected Works*, ed. Waller and Glover (London, Dent, 1902-06; New York, McClure), 6, 50; 4, 334.

Massingham, H. J.: *Wisdom of the Fields* (London, Collins, 1945).

Saintsbury, G.: *Essays in English Literature*, Second Ser. (London, Dent, 1895; New York, Scribner).

Hartley Coleridge 1796-1849

Poems, p. 1197 — Critical Notes, p. 1398

EDITIONS

Complete Poetical Works, ed. by R. Colles (New York, Dutton, 1908).

Poetical Works, with Bowles and Lamb, ed., with a Biographical Introduction, by W. Tirebuck (Canterbury Poets ed.: London, Scott, 1887).

New Poems, ed. by E. L. Griggs (London, Oxford Univ. Press, 1942).

Essays and Marginalia, 2 vols., ed. by D. Coleridge (London, Moxon, 1851).

Essays, ed., with an Introduction, by J. Drinkwater (New York, Duffield, 1925).

Letters, ed. by G. E. and E. L. Griggs (New York and London, Oxford Univ. Press, 1937, 1941).

BIOGRAPHY AND CRITICISM

Bagehot, W.: *Literary Studies*, 3 vols., ed. by R. H. Hutton (London and New York, Longmans, 1878-79, 1895).

Blunden, E. C.: "Coleridge the Less," *Votive Tablets* (London, Cobden-Sanderson, 1931).

Caine, T. Hall: *Cobwebs of Criticism* (London, Stock, 1882, 1885).

Dawson, J., Jr.: "Hartley Coleridge and Wordsworth," *Macmillan's Mag.*, 13:232 (1866).

Dowden, E.: In Ward's *The English Poets*, Vol. 4 (London and New York, Macmillan, 1880, 1910).

Graham, H.: *Splendid Failures* (London and New York, Longmans, 1913).

Griggs, E. L.: *Hartley Coleridge, His Life and Work* (London, Univ. of London Press, 1929).

Hartman, H.: *Hartley Coleridge, Poet's Son and Poet* (London, Oxford Univ. Press, 1931).

Pomeroy, Sister Mary Joseph: *The Poetry of Hartley Coleridge* (Washington, D. C., Catholic Univ. Press, 1927).

Towle, Eleanor A.: *A Poet's Children, Hartley and Sara Coleridge* (London, Methuen, 1912).

Turner, A. M.: "Wordsworth and Hartley Coleridge," *Jour. of Eng. and Ger. Phil.*, 22:538 (1923).

Williams, S. T.: "Hartley Coleridge as a Critic of Literature," *South Atl. Quart.*, 23:73 (1924).

Samuel Taylor Coleridge
1772-1834

Selections, p. 354 — Critical Notes, p. 1295

EDITIONS

Works, 8 vols., ed. by T. Ashe; *Poetical Works*, 2 vols. (Aldine ed.: London, Bell, 1885; New York, Macmillan); *Prose Works*, 6 vols. (Bohn Lib.: London, Bell, 1885; New York, Macmillan).

Poetical Works, ed., with a Biographical Introduction, by J. D. Campbell (Globe ed.: London, Macmillan, 1893, 1909).

Poems and Dramatic Works, ed. by W. Knight (New York, Scribner, 1906).

Poems, ed., with an Introduction, by E. H. Coleridge (London and New York, Lane, 1907).

Complete Poetical Works, 2 vols., ed. by E. H. Coleridge (London, Oxford Univ. Press, 1912).

Poems, ed. by E. H. Coleridge (London, Oxford Univ. Press, 1912).

Poetry, ed. by R. Garnett (Muses' Lib.: London, Lawrence, 1898; New York, Scribner).

Poetry and Prose, ed., with Essays by Hazlitt, Jeffrey, De Quincey, Carlyle, and Others by H. W. Garrod (London, Oxford Univ. Press, 1925).

Select Poetry and Prose, ed. by S. Potter (New York, Random House, 1933).

The Best of Coleridge, ed. by E. L. Griggs (New York, Nelson, 1934).

Select Poems, ed., with a Critical Introduction, by A. J. George (Boston, Heath, 1902).

Lyrical Ballads, ed. by E. Dowden (London, Nutt, 1890, 1898); ed. by T. Hutchinson (London, Duckworth, 1898, 1907); ed., with an Introduction, by H. Littledale (London and New York, Oxford Univ. Press, 1911).

Anima Poetæ, ed. by E. H. Coleridge (Boston, Houghton, 1895).

Biographia Epistolaris, 2 vols., ed. by A. Turnbull (Bohn Lib.: London, Bell, 1911; New York, Macmillan).

Biographia Literaria, 2 vols., ed. by J. Shawcross (Oxford, Clarendon Press, 1907).

Biographia Literaria, ed. by J. C. Metcalf (New York, Macmillan, 1926).

Letters, 1785-1834, 2 vols., ed. by E. H. Coleridge (London, Heinemann, 1895; Boston, Houghton).

Unpublished Letters, 2 vols., ed. by E. L. Griggs (London, Constable, 1932; New Haven, Yale Univ. Press, 1933).

Literary Criticism, ed., with an Introduction, by J. Mackail (London, Frowde, 1908).

Shakespearean Criticism, 2 vols., ed., with Introduction and Notes, by T. M. Raysor (Cambridge, Mass., Harvard Univ. Press, 1930).

Miscellaneous Criticism, ed. by T. M. Raysor (Cambridge, Mass., Harvard Univ. Press, 1936).

Table Talk, ed. by H. Morley (Morley's Universal Lib.: London, Routledge, 1883).

The Political Thought of Samuel Taylor Coleridge, ed. by R. J. White (London, Cape, 1938).

BIOGRAPHY

Armour, R. W. and Howes, R. F.: *Coleridge the Talker* (Ithaca, Cornell Univ. Press, 1940).

Brandl, A.: *Samuel Taylor Coleridge und die englische Romantik* (Berlin, 1886); English translation by Lady Eastlake (London, Murray, 1887).

Caine, T. H.: *Life of Samuel Taylor Coleridge* (Great Writers Ser.: London, Scott, 1887).

Campbell, J. D.: *Samuel Taylor Coleridge* (London, Macmillan, 1894).

Chambers, E. K.: *S. T. Coleridge: A Biographical Study* (Oxford, Clarendon Press, 1938).

Coleridge, Mrs. S. T.: *Minnow Among Tritons: Letters to Thomas Poole, 1799-1834*, ed. by S. Potter (London, Nonesuch Press, 1934).

Fausset, H. I'A.: *Samuel Taylor Coleridge* (London, Cape, 1926; New York, Harcourt).

Hanson, L.: *The Life of S. T. Coleridge: The Early Years* (New York, Oxford Univ. Press, 1938).

Knight, W. A.: *Coleridge and Wordsworth in the West Country* (New York, Scribner, 1914).

Robinson, H. C.: *Blake, Coleridge, Wordsworth, Lamb, Etc.*, being Selections from the *Remains* of Henry Crabb Robinson, ed. by Edith J. Morley (New York, Longmans, 1922).

Sandford, Mrs. H.: *Thomas Poole and his Friends*, 2 vols. (London, Macmillan, 1888).

Traill, H. D.: *Coleridge* (English Men of Letters Ser.: London, Macmillan, 1884; New York, Harper).

Watson, Lucy E.: *Coleridge at Highgate* (London and New York, Longmans, 1925).

Wright, H.: "The Tour of Coleridge and His Friend Hucks in Wales in 1794," *Nine. Cent.* 99:732 (1926).

CRITICISM

Abrams, M. H.: *The Milk of Paradise: The Effect of Opium Visions on the Works of De Quincey, Crabbe, Francis Thompson, and Coleridge* (Cambridge, Mass., Harvard Univ. Press, 1934).

Babbitt, I.: "Coleridge and Imagination," *Nineteenth Century and After*, 106:383 (1929); reprinted in *On Being Creative, and Other Essays* (Boston, Houghton, 1932).

Beers, H. A.: "Coleridge, Bowles and the Pope Controversy," *A History of English Romanticism in the Nineteenth Century* (New York, Holt, 1901, 1910).

Birrell, A.: *More Obiter Dicta* (London, Heinemann, 1924; New York, Scribner).

Blunden, E. C. and Griggs, E. L.: *Coleridge: Studies by Several Hands on the Hundredth Anniversary of His Death* (London, Constable, 1934).

Boas, G.: *Wordsworth and Coleridge Contrasted* (London and Edinburgh, T. Nelson, 1925).

Bradley, A. C.: "Coleridge's Use of Light and Color," *A Miscellany* (London, Macmillan, 1929).

Brandes, G.: "Naturalistic Romanticism," *Main Currents of Nineteenth Century Literature*, vol. 4 (London, Heinemann, 1905; New York, Macmillan, 1906).

Brewster, P. G.: "The Influence of Popular Ballads on Wordsworth and Coleridge," *Stud. in Phil.*, 35:588 (1938).

Brinton, C.: *The Political Ideas of the English Romanticists* (London, Oxford Univ. Press, 1926).

Brooke, S. A.: *Theology in the English Poets* (London, King, 1874, New York, Dutton, 1910).

Charpentier, J.: "Coleridge, Père du Romantisme Anglais; les Années d'Or du Poète," *Mercure de France*, 198:556 (1927).

Charpentier, J.: *Coleridge, the Sublime Somnambulist*, trans. from the French by M. V. Nugent (New York, Dodd, 1929).

Cobban, A.: *Edmund Burke and the Revolt against the Eighteenth Century. A Study of the Political and Social Thinking of Burke, Wordsworth, Coleridge, and Southey* (London, Allen, 1929).

Creed, H. H.: "Coleridge on Taste," *Jour. Eng. Lit. Hist.*, 13:143 (1946).

Dawson, W. J.: *The Makers of English Poetry* (New York and London, Revell, 1906).

Dodds, Mrs. A. E. Powell: *The Romantic Theory of Poetry* (New York, Longmans, 1926).

Dowden, E.: "Early Revolutionary Group and Antagonists," *The French Revolution and English Literature* (New York and London, Scribner, 1897).

Dowden, E.: "Coleridge as a Poet," *New Studies in Literature* (London, Paul, 1895, 1902).

Drinkwater, J.: *A Book for Bookmen* (London, Dulau, 1926).

Dunstan, A. C.: "The German Influence on Coleridge," *Mod. Lang. Rev.*, 17:272 (1922); 18:183 (1923).

Edinburgh Review, The: "Christabel, Kubla Khan, The Pains of Sleep," 27:58 (1816).

Elwin, M.: *The First Romantics* (London, Macdonald, 1947; New York, Longmans, 1948).

Fairchild, H. N.: *The Romantic Quest* (New York, Columbia Univ. Press, 1931).

Forster, J.: *Great Teachers* (London, Redway, 1898).

Garnett, R.: "The Poetry of Coleridge," *Essays of an Ex-Librarian* (London, Heinemann, 1901).

Garrod, H. W.: *The Profession of Poetry and Other Lectures* (London, Oxford Univ. Press, 1929).

Gingerich, S. F.: *Essays in the Romantic Poets* (New York, Macmillan, 1924).

Gingerich, S. F.: "From Necessity to Transcendentalism in Coleridge," *Pub. Mod. Lang. Assn.*, 35:1 (1920).

Graham, W.: "Contemporary Critics of Coleridge, the Poet," *Pub. Mod. Lang. Assn.*, 38:278 (1923).

Greever, G.: *A Wiltshire Parson and His Friends* (London, Constable, 1926; Boston, Houghton).

Hancock, A. E.: *The French Revolution and the English Poets* (New York, Holt, 1899).

Haney, J. L.: *The German Influence on S. T. Coleridge* (Philadelphia, Univ. of Pa. Press, 1902).

Harper, G. M.: "The Wordsworth-Coleridge Combination," *Sewanee Rev.*, 31:258 (1923).

Hazlitt, W.: "Mr. Coleridge," *The Spirit of the Age* (London, 1825); "On the Living Poets," *Lectures on the English Poets* (London, 1818); "My First Acquaintance with Poets," *The Liberal*, 1823:—*Collected Works*, ed. Waller and Glover (London, Dent, 1902-06; New York, McClure), 4, 212; 5, 143; 12, 259.

Helmholz, A. A.: *The Indebtedness of S. T. Coleridge to A. W. Schlegel* (Madison, Univ. of Wis. Press, 1907).

Howard, C.: *Coleridge's Idealism: a Study of Its Relationship to Kant and to the Cambridge Platonists* (Boston, Badger, 1924).

Kaufman, P.: "The Reading of Southey and Coleridge," *Mod. Phil.* 21:317 (1924).

Knight, G. W.: *The Burning Oracle: Studies in the Poetry of Action* (London, Oxford Univ. Press, 1939).

Knight, G. W.: *The Starlit Dome: Studies in the Poetry of Vision* (London, Oxford Univ. Press, 1941).

Lowell, J. R.: *Democracy and Other Addresses* (Boston, Houghton, 1887).

Lowes, J. L.: *The Road to Xanadu* (Boston and New York, Houghton, 1927, 1930).

Marshall, E. G.: *Poetical Theories and Criticisms of the Chief Romantic Poets* (Ann Arbor, Edwards Brothers, 1926).

Moore, J. R.: "The Mood of Pessimism in Nature Poetry: Bowles, Coleridge, and Arnold," *Sewanee Rev.*, 30:454 (1922).

Muirhead, J. H.: *Coleridge as Philosopher* (London, Allen, 1930; New York, Macmillan).

Murry, J. M.: *Aspects of Literature* (London, Collins, 1920).

Pater, W.: *Appreciations* (London and New York, Macmillan, 1889, 1895).

Payne, W. M.: *The Greater English Poets of the Nineteenth Century* (New York, Holt, 1907, 1909).

Potter, G. R.: "Coleridge and the Idea of Evolution," *Pub. Mod. Lang. Assn.*, 40:379 (1925).

Potter, S.: *Coleridge and S. T. C.* (New York, P. Smith, 1935).

Quiller-Couch, Sir A.: *Studies in Literature*, 2 vols. (New York, Putnam, 1922; London, Cambridge Univ. Press).

Rawnsley, H. D.: *Literary Associations of the English Lakes*, 2 vols. (Glasgow, Mac-Lehose, 1894, 1906).

Raysor, T. M.: "Coleridge's Criticism of Wordsworth," *Pub. Mod. Lang. Assn.*, 54:496 (1934).

Richards, I. A.: *Coleridge on Imagination* (London, K. Paul, Trench, 1934; New York, Harcourt, 1935).

Robertson, J. M.: *New Essays towards a Critical Method* (London and New York, Lane, 1897).

Royds, Kathleen: *Coleridge and His Poetry* (New York, Dodge, 1912).

Saintsbury, G.: "Coleridge and Southey," *Essays in English Literature*, Second Ser. (London, Dent, 1895; New York, Scribner).

Sanders, C. R.: *Coleridge and the Broad Church Movement* (Durham, Duke Univ. Press, 1942).

Shafer, R.: *Christianity and Naturalism* (New Haven, Yale Univ. Press, 1926).

Shairp, J. C.: *Studies in Poetry and Philosophy* (Edinburgh, Douglas, 1872, 1886; Boston, Houghton, 1880, 1887).

Smyser, Jane: "Coleridge's Use of Wordsworth's Juvenilia," *Pub. Mod. Lang. Assn.*, 6:419-26 (1950).

Snyder, A. D.: *The Critical Principle of the Reconciliation of Opposites as Employed by Coleridge* (Ann Arbor, Ann Arbor Press, 1918).

Stephen, L.: *Hours in a Library*, 3 vols. (London, Smith, 1874-79; New York and London, Putnam, 1899); 4 vols. (1907).

Stewart, H. L.: "The Place of Coleridge in English Theology," *Harvard Theol. Rev.*, 11:1 (1918).

Stokoe, F. W.: *German Influence in the English Romantic Period, 1788-1818* (London, Cambridge Univ. Press, 1926; New York, Macmillan).

Stoll, E. E.: "Symbolism in Coleridge," *Pub. Mod. Lang. Assn.*, 63:214 (1948).

Stork, C. W.: "The Influence of the Popular Ballad on Wordsworth and Coleridge," *Pub. Mod. Lang. Assn.*, 22:299 (1914).

Swinburne, A. C.: *Essays and Studies* (London, Chatto, 1875).

Symons, A.: *The Romantic Movement in English Poetry* (London, Constable, 1909; New York, Dutton).

Thorpe, C. D.: "The Imagination: Coleridge vs. Wordsworth," *Phil. Quart.*, 18:1(1939).

Watson, W.: "Coleridge's Supernaturalism," *Excursions in Criticism* (London, Mathews, 1893; New York, Macmillan).

Watts-Dunton, W. T.: "The Renascence of Wonder," *Chambers's Cyclopaedia of English Literature*, 3:1 (1903).

Whipple, E. P.: "Coleridge as a Philosophic Critic," *Essays and Reviews* (Boston, Osgood, 1849; Ticknor, 1861).

Wilde, N.: "The Development of Coleridge's Thought," *Phil. Rev.*, 28:147 (1919).

Willey, B.: *Coleridge on Imagination and Fancy* (London, Oxford Univ. Press, 1946).

Woodberry, G. E.: *Literary Essays* (New York, Harcourt, 1920).

Woodberry, G. E.: *Makers of Literature* (New York and London, Macmillan, 1900).

CONCORDANCE

Logan, Sister Eugenia: *A Concordance to the Poetry of Samuel Taylor Coleridge* (Saint Mary-of-the-Woods, Ind., The Editor, 1940).

BIBLIOGRAPHY

Anderson, J. P.: In Caine's *Life of Samuel Taylor Coleridge* (1887).

Haney, J. L.: *A Bibliography of S. T. Coleridge* (Philadelphia, Egerton Press, 1903; London, Gay, 1904).

Jack, A. A. and Bradley, A. C.: *A Short Bibliography of Coleridge* (1912).

Kennedy, V. W. and Barton, M. N.: *Samuel Taylor Coleridge; a Selected Bibliography* (Baltimore, Enoch Pratt Free Lib., 1935).

Shepherd, R. H.: *The Bibliography of Coleridge*, rev. by W. F. Prideaux (London, Hollings, 1901).

Wise, T. J.: *A Bibliography of the Writings in Prose and Verse of S. T. Coleridge* (London, Bibliographical Soc., 1913).

William Collins 1721-1759

Poems, p. 48 — Critical Notes, p. 1238

EDITIONS

Poetical Works, ed. by W. M. Thomas (Aldine ed.: London, Bell, 1858, 1894; New York, Macmillan).

Poetical Works (with Gray), ed. by E. C. Stone and A. L. Poole (London, Oxford Univ. Press, 1917); rev. by F. Page (1937).

Poems, ed., with a Life and Critical Study, by W. C. Bronson (Athenæum Press ed.: Boston, Ginn, 1898).

Poems, with Johnson, Goldsmith, and Gray, ed. by T. M. Ward (Muses' Lib.: London, Routledge, 1905; New York, Dutton).

Poems, ed. by C. Stone (London, Oxford Univ. Press, 1907).

Poems, ed. by E. C. Blunden (London, Etchells, 1929).

Minor Poets of the Eighteenth Century, ed. by H. I'A. Fausset (Everyman's Lib. ed.: New York, Dutton, 1930).

BIOGRAPHY AND CRITICISM

Ainsworth, E. G.: *Poor Collins; His Life, His Art, and His Influence* (Ithaca, Cornell Univ. Press, 1937).

Brooke, S. A.: *Naturalism in English Poetry* (New York, Dutton, 1920).

Doughty, O.: *English Lyric in the Age of Reason* (London, O'Connor, 1922).

Falls, C.: "The Poetry of William Collins," *Nine. Cent.* 88:824 (1915).

Garrod, H. W.: *Collins* (London, Oxford Univ. Press, 1928).

Hazlitt, W.: "On Swift, Young, Gray, Collins, Etc.," *Lectures on the English Poets* (London, 1818); *Collected Works*, ed. Waller and Glover (London, Dent, 1902-1906; New York, McClure), 5, 104.

Johnson, S.: *The Lives of the English Poets* (1779-81), 3 vols., ed. by G. B. Hill (London, Clarendon Press, 1905).

Mackail, J. W.: *Studies of English Poets* (London and New York, Longmans, 1926).

McKillop, A. D.: "The Romanticism of William Collins," *Stud. in Phil.*, 20:1 (1923).

Murry, J. M.: *Countries of the Mind* (London, Collins, 1922).

Shairp, J. C.: "Nature in Collins, Gray, Goldsmith, Cowper and Burns," *On Poetic Interpretation of Nature* (Edinburgh, Douglas, 1877; New York, Hurd, 1878; Boston, Houghton, 1885).

Swinburne, A. C.: *Miscellanies* (London, Chatto, 1886, 1911; New York, Scribner).

CONCORDANCE

Booth, B. A. and Jones, C. E.: *Concordance of the Poetical Works of William Collins* (Berkeley, Univ. of Calif. Press, 1939).

BIBLIOGRAPHY

Bronson, W. C.: In *Poems* (Athenaeum Press ed.: Boston, Ginn, 1898).

"Barry Cornwall" (See *Procter*)

William Cowper 1731-1800

Poems, p. 145 — Critical Notes, p. 1252

EDITIONS

Works, 15 vols., ed., with a Life, by R. Southey (London, Baldwin, 1836-37, 8 vols., 1853-55).

Poetical Works, 3 vols., ed., with a Memoir by T. Mitford, by J. Bruce (Aldine ed.: London, Bell, 1830-31, 1865; New York, Macmillan).

Poetical Works, ed., with a Biographical Introduction, by W. Benham (Globe ed.: London, Macmillan, 1870).

Complete Poetical Works, ed. by H. S. Milford (London, Oxford Univ. Press, 1906; rev. ed., 1926, 1934).

Selections from the Poetical Works, ed., with an Introduction, by J. O. Murray (Athenæum Press ed.: Boston, Ginn, 1898).

Poetry and Prose, ed., with Essays by Hazlitt and Bagehot, by H. S. Milford (London, Oxford Univ. Press, 1921).

Poems, ed. by H. I'A. Fausset (Everyman's Lib. ed.: New York, Dutton, 1931).

Correspondence, 4 vols., ed. by T. Wright (London, Hodder, 1904; New York, Dodd).

Letters, ed. by W. Benham (Golden Treasury ed.: London, Macmillan, 1884).

Letters, selected and edited by E. V. Lucas (World's Classics: London, Oxford Univ. Press, 1908, 1911).

Selected Letters, 2 vols. ed., with a Memoir, by J. G. Frazer (New York, Macmillan, 1912).

Selected Letters, ed. by W. Hadley (Everyman's Lib. ed.: New York, Dutton, 1926).

BIOGRAPHY AND CRITICISM

Brooke, S. A.: *Naturalism in English Poetry* (New York, Dutton, 1920).

Brooke, S. A.: *Theology in the English Poets* (London, King, 1874; New York, Dutton, 1910).

Cecil, E. C. D.: *The Stricken Deer; or, The Life of Cowper* (London, Constable, 1929, 1933, 1943; New York, Oxford Univ. Press).

Fausset, H. I'A.: *William Cowper* (London, Cape, 1928; New York, Harcourt; reprint, New York, P. Smith, 1934).

Hartley, L. C.: *William Cowper, Humanitarian* (Chapel Hill, Univ. of N. Carolina Press, 1938).

Hazlitt, W.: "On Thomson and Cowper," *Lectures on the English Poets* (London, 1818); *Collected Works*, ed. Waller and Glover (London, Dent, 1902-06; New York, McClure), 5, 85.

More, P. E.: "The Correspondence of William Cowper," *Shelburne Essays*, Third Ser. (New York and London, Putnam, 1906).

Price, W. J.: "Cowper's *Task*: a Literary Milestone," *Sewanee Rev.*, 24:155 (1916).

Roy, J. A.: *Cowper and His Poetry* (London, Harrap, 1914).

Shairp, J. C.: "Nature in Collins, Gray, Goldsmith, Cowper, and Burns," *On Poetic Interpretation of Nature* (Edinburgh, Douglas, 1877; New York, Hurd, 1878; Boston, Houghton, 1885).

Smith, G.: *Cowper* (English Men of Letters Ser.: London, Macmillan, 1880; New York, Harper).

Stephen, L.: "Cowper and Rousseau," *Hours in a Library*, 3 vols. (London, Smith, 1874-79; New York and London, Putnam, 1899); 4 vols. (1907).

Thomas, G. O.: *William Cowper and the Eighteenth Century* (London, Nicholson, 1935; rev. ed., G. Allen, 1949).

Woodberry, G. E.: "Three Men of Piety," *Makers of Literature* (New York, Macmillan, 1901).

Wright, T.: *The Life of Cowper* (London, Unwin, 1902; rev., 1921).

CONCORDANCE

Neve, J.: *A Concordance to the Poetical Works of William Cowper* (London, Low, 1887).

BIBLIOGRAPHY

Murray, J. O.: In *Selections from the Poetical Works* (Athenæum Press ed.: Boston, Ginn, 1898).

George Crabbe 1754-1832

Poems, p. 154 — Critical Notes, p. 1256

EDITIONS

Poetical Works, 8 vols., ed., with his Letters and Journals and a Life, by his son (London, Murray, 1834); in 1 vol. (1901).

Poems, 3 vols., ed. by A. W. Ward (Cambridge English Classics: London, Cambridge Univ. Press, 1905-07; New York, Putnam).

Poetical Works, ed., with a Critical Introduction, by A. J. and R. M. Carlyle (London, Oxford Univ. Press, 1914).

Selections from the Poems, ed., with an Introduction, by A. Deane (London, Methuen, 1903, 1932).

Poems. Selections, with an Introduction by A. Quiller-Couch (London, Oxford Univ. Press, 1912).

Poems, selected by P. Henderson (London, Lawson, 1946).

George Crabbe, ed. by F. L. Lucas (London, Cambridge Univ. Press, 1933).

BIOGRAPHY AND CRITICISM

Abrams, M. H.: *The Milk of Paradise: The Effect of Opium Visions on the Works of De Quincey, Crabbe, Francis Thompson, and Coleridge* (Cambridge, Mass., Harvard Univ. Press, 1934).

Ainger, A.: *Crabbe* (English Men of Letters Ser.: New York and London, Macmillan, 1903).

Bailey, J.: *Poets and Poetry* (Oxford, Clarendon Press, 1911).

Broadley, A. M. and Jerrold, W.: *The Romance of an Elderly Poet* (London, Paul, 1913).

Brooke, S. A.: *Naturalism in English Poetry* (New York, Dutton, 1920).

Collins, J. C.: "The Poetry of Crabbe," *The Fort. Rev.*, 82:575 (1907).

Crabbe, G.: *Life of George Crabbe*, by his son, with an Introduction by E. Blunden (London, Cresset, 1947).

Elton, O.: "The Poetry of Crabbe," *Blackwood's Mag.*, 185:78 (1909).

Evans, J. H.: *The Poems of George Crabbe: a Literary and Historical Study* (London, Sheldon Press, 1933; New York, Macmillan).

Huchon, R. L.: *George Crabbe and His Time*, trans. from the French by F. Clarke (London, Murray, 1907).

Kebbel, T. E.: *Life of George Crabbe* (Great Writers Ser.: London, Scott, 1888; New York, Scribner).

More, P. E.: *Shelburne Essays*, First Ser. (New York and London, Putnam, 1906).

Saintsbury, G.: *Essays in English Literature, 1780-1860*, First Ser. (London, Percival, 1890; New York, Scribner).

Shorter, C. K.: *Immortal Memories* (New York, Harper, 1907).

Stephen, L.: *Hours in a Library*, 3 vols. (London, Smith, 1874-79; New York and London, Putnam, 1899); 4 vols. (1907).

Symons, A.: *The Romantic Movement in English Poetry* (London, Constable, 1909; New York, Dutton).

Wylie, Laura Johnson: *Social Studies in English Literature* (Boston, Houghton, 1916).

BIBLIOGRAPHY

Anderson, J. P.: In Kebbel's *Life of George Crabbe* (Great Writers Ser.: London, Scott, 1888; New York, Scribner).

Bartholomew, A. T.: In *Poems*, ed. by A. W. Ward (Cambridge English Classics: London, Cambridge Univ. Press, 1905-07; New York, Putnam).

Huchon, R.: In *George Crabbe and His Time*, trans. by F. Clarke (New York, Dutton, 1907).

John Wilson Croker 1780-1857

Selections, p. 939 — Critical Notes, p. 1371

EDITIONS

The Croker Papers: Correspondence and Diaries of J. W. Croker, 3 vols., ed. by L. J. Jennings (London, Murray, 1884; New York, Scribner).

Essays on the Early Period of the French Revolution (London, Murray, 1857).

History of the Guillotine (London, Murray, 1853).

BIOGRAPHY AND CRITICISM

Brightfield, M. F.: *John Wilson Croker* (Berkeley, Univ. of Calif. Press, 1940).

Dicey, A. V.: *The Nation*, 40:121 (1885).

Fortesque, G. K.: "The French Revolution in Contemporary Literature," *The Quart. Rev.*, 218:353 (1913).

Grant, J.: *Random Recollections of the House of Commons*, 2 vols. (London, Smith, 1837).

Kebbel, T. E.: *The Fort. Rev.*, 42:688 (1884).

Littell's Living Age, "A Quartet of Quarterly Reviewers," 51:240 (1856).

Martineau, Harriet: *Biographical Sketches* (New York, Hurst, 1869).

The Quarterly Review, 210:748 (1909).

Sillard, P. A.: *The Gentleman's Mag.*, 285:145 (1898).

Walpole, S.: "The Croker Papers," *Essays, Political and Biographical* (New York, Dutton, 1908).

Allan Cunningham 1784-1842

Poems, p. 501 — Critical Notes, p. 1323

EDITIONS

Songs and Poems, ed., with an Introduction, by P. Cunningham (London, Murray, 1847, 1875).

Traditional Tales of the English and Scottish Peasantry, 2 vols., ed. by H. Morley (London and New York, Routledge, 1887).

BIOGRAPHY AND CRITICISM

Elton, O.: *A Survey of English Literature, 1780-1830*, 2 vols. (London, Arnold, 1912, 1924).

Gilfillan, G.: *A First Gallery of Literary Portraits* (Edinburgh, Hogg, 1851).

Hogg, D.: *The Life of Allan Cunningham, with Selections from His Works and Correspondence* (Dumfries, Anderson, 1875).

Wilson, J. G.: *The Poets and Poetry of Scotland*, 2 vols. (Glasgow, Blackie, 1876; New York, Harper).

Thomas De Quincey 1785-1859

EDITIONS

Works, 12 vols. (Riverside ed.: Boston, Houghton, 1877).

Collected Writings, 14 vols., ed. by D. Masson (Edinburgh, Black, 1889-90; cheaper ed., 1896-97; New York, Macmillan).

Uncollected Writings, 2 vols., ed., with a Preface, by J. Hogg (London, Swan, 1890).

Posthumous Works, 2 vols., ed. by A. H. Japp (London, Heinemann, 1891-93).

Selections, ed., with an Introduction, by M. H. Turk (Athenæum Press ed.: Boston, Ginn, 1902).

Selections, ed. by S. Low (New York, Macmillan, 1911).

Selections, ed. by Bliss Perry (Garden City, Doubleday, 1924).

Selections, ed., with an Introduction and Notes, by M. R. Ridley, with Essays by L. Stephen and F. Thompson (London, Oxford Univ. Press, 1927).

Selected Writings, ed. by P. Van D. Stern (New York, Random House, 1937).

Literary Criticism, ed., with an Introduction, by H. Darbishire (London, Frowde, 1909).

The Confessions of An English Opium-Eater, ed., with de Musset's French Continuation, and with other matter, by R. Garnett (London, Paul, 1885); ed. by E. Rhys (New York, Dutton, 1927).

Recollections of the Lake Poets, ed., with an Introduction, by E. Sackville-West (London, Lehmann, 1948).

The Revolt of the Tartars, ed. by C. W. French (Chicago, Scott, 1898).

The English Mail-Coach and Other Essays (Everyman's Lib. ed.: New York, Dutton, 1914).

A Diary of Thomas De Quincey: 1803, ed. by H. A. Eaton (London, Douglas, 1927).

De Quincey at Work: As Seen in One Hundred and Thirty New Letters, ed. by W. H. Bonner (Buffalo, N. Y., Airport Pubs., 1936).

BIOGRAPHY

Eaton, H. A.: *Thomas De Quincey* (New York and London, Oxford Univ. Press, 1936).

Elwin, M.: *De Quincey* (London, Duckworth, 1935).

Findlay, J. R.: *Personal Recollections of De Quincey* (Edinburgh, Black, 1886).

Hogg, J.: *De Quincey and His Friends* (London, Low, 1895).

Japp, A. H. (H. A. Page): *Thomas De Quincey: His Life and Writings, with Unpublished Correspondence*, 2 vols. (London, Heinemann, 1877; New York, Scribner, 1890).

Japp, A. H.: *De Quincey Memorials: Being Letters and other Records, here first Published*, 2 vols. (London, Heinemann, 1891).

Martineau, Harriet: *Biographical Sketches* (London, Macmillan, 1869).

Masson, D.: *Thomas De Quincey* (English Men of Letters Ser.: London, Macmillan, 1881; New York, Harper).

Sackville-West, E.: *Thomas De Quincey: His Life and Works* (New Haven, Yale Univ. Press, 1936).

Salt, H. S.: *De Quincey* (London, Bell, 1904; New York, Macmillan).

CRITICISM

Abrams, M. H.: *The Milk of Paradise; the Effect of Opium Visions on the Works of De Quincey, Crabbe, Francis Thompson, and Coleridge* (Cambridge, Mass., Harvard Univ. Press, 1934).

Bayne, P.: "Thomas De Quincey and His Works," *Essays in Biography and Criticism* (Boston, Gould, 1857; New York, Sheldon).

Birrell, A.: *Essays about Men, Women, and Books* (London, Stock, 1894; New York, Scribner, 1901).

Cooper, L.: *Prose-Poetry of Thomas De Quincey* (Leipzig, Seele, 1902).

Dawson, W. J.: *The Makers of English Prose* (New York and London, Revell, 1906).

Dodds, Mrs. A. E. Powell: *The Romantic Theory of Poetry* (New York, Longmans, 1926).

Dowden, E.: "How De Quincey Worked," *The Saturday Rev.*, 79:246 (1895).

Dunn, W. A.: *Thomas De Quincey's Relation to German Literature and Philosophy* (Strasbourg, Heitz, 1900).

Fowler, J. H.: *De Quincey as Literary Critic* (London, Oxford Univ. Press, 1922).

Hudson, H. H.: "De Quincey on Rhetoric and Public Speaking," *Stud. in Rhet. and Pub. Speak.* (New York, Century, 1925).

Leonard, L. P.: "De Quincey's Dream-Fugue," *Poet Lore*, 28:680 (1922).

Masson, D.: *Wordsworth, Shelley, Keats, and Other Essays* (London, Macmillan, 1874).

Metcalf, J. C.: *De Quincey: A Portrait* (Cambridge, Mass., Harvard Univ. Press, 1940).

Procter, S. K.: *Thomas De Quincey's Theory of Literature* (Ann Arbor, Univ. of Mich. Press, 1943).

Rawnsley, H. D.: *Literary Associations of the English Lakes*, 2 vols. (Glasgow, Mac-Lehose, 1894, 1906).

Rickett, A.: "The Vagabond," *Personal Forces in Modern Literature* (London, Dent, 1906; New York, Dutton).

Saintsbury, G.: *Essays in English Literature, 1780-1860* (London, Percival, 1890; New York, Scribner).

Stephen, L.: *Hours in a Library*, 3 vols. (London, Smith, 1874-79; New York and London, Putnam, 1899); 4 vols. (1907).

Symons, A.: "A Word on De Quincey," *Studies in Prose and Verse* (London, Dent, 1904).

Walker, H.: "The Early Magazines of the Nineteenth Century," *The English Essay and Essayists* (London, Dent, 1915; New York, Dutton).

Wellek, R.: "De Quincey's Status in the History of Ideas," *Phil. Quart.*, 23:248 (1944).

Winchester, C. T.: *A Group of English Essayists* (New York, Macmillan, 1910).

BIBLIOGRAPHY

Green, J. A.: *Thomas De Quincey: A Bibliography based upon the De Quincey Collection in the Moss Side Library, Manchester* (Manchester, Moss Side Public Library, 1908).

Masson, D.: In *Collected Writings of Thomas De Quincey*, Vol. 14 (Edinburgh, Black, 1889-90; 1896-97; New York, Macmillan).

John Dyer c. 1700-1758

Poems, p. 16 — Critical Notes, p. 1235

EDITIONS

Poems, ed., with a Biographical Introduction, by E. Thomas (Welsh Lib.: London, Unwin, 1903).

Minor Poets of the Eighteenth Century, ed. by H. I'A. Fausset (Everyman's Lib. ed.: New York, Dutton, 1930; contains all of Dyer's poems).

Grongar Hill, ed., with an Introduction and Notes, by R. C. Boys (Baltimore, Johns Hopkins Press, 1941).

BIOGRAPHY AND CRITICISM

Dowden, E.: In Ward's *The English Poets*, Vol. 3 (London, Macmillan, 1880, 1909).

Johnson, S.: *The Lives of the English Poets* (1779-81); 3 vols., ed. by G. B. Hill (London, Clarendon Press, 1905).

Ebenezer Elliott 1781-1849

Poems, p. 1191 — Critical Notes, p. 1396

EDITIONS

Works, 2 vols., ed. by his son E. Elliott (London, King, 1876).

BIOGRAPHY AND CRITICISM

Carlyle, T.: "Corn-Law Rhymes," *The Edinburgh Rev.*, 55:338 (1832); *Critical and Miscellaneous Essays*, 3 vols. (Boston, Houghton, 1880).

Howitt, W.: *Homes and Haunts of the Most Eminent British Poets*, 2 vols. (London, 1847, 1856; Routledge, 1894; New York, Dutton).

Odom, W.: *Two Sheffield Poets: James Montgomery and Ebenezer Elliott* (Sheffield, Leng, 1929).

Phillips, G. S. (J. Searle): *Memoirs of Ebenezer Elliott* (London, Gilpin, 1850, 1852).

Smiles, S.: *Brief Biographies* (Boston, Ticknor, 1860).

Stoddard, R. H.: *Under the Evening Lamp* (New York, Scribner, 1892; London, Gay).

Watkins, J.: *The Life, Poetry, and Letters of Ebenezer Elliott, the Corn-Law Rhymer* (London, Mortimer, 1850).

Wilson, John: "Poetry of Ebenezer Elliott," *Blackwood's Mag.*, 35:815 (1834).

William Godwin 1756-1836

Selections, p. 239 — Critical Notes, p. 1272

EDITIONS

An Enquiry Concerning Political Justice, 2 vols. (1793, 1796; London, Sonnenschein, 1890; New York, Scribner).

An Enquiry Concerning Political Justice, 2 vols., ed. and abridged by R. A. Preston (London and New York, Knopf, 1926).

Enquiry Concerning Political Justice and Its Influence on Morals and Happiness, 3 vols., ed., with a Critical Introduction and Notes, by F. E. Priestley (Toronto, Univ. of Toronto Press, 1946).

Caleb Williams, or Things as They Are, 3 vols. (1794); 1 vol. (London, Newnes, n. d.; New York, Scribner, 1904).

The Adventures of Caleb Williams (New York, Greenberg, 1926).

BIOGRAPHY AND CRITICISM

Allen, B. S.: "William Godwin as a Sentimentalist," *Pub. Mod. Lang. Assn.*, 33:1 (1918).

Brailsford, H. N.: *Shelley, Godwin, and their Circle* (Home Univ. Lib.: New York, Holt, 1913; London, Williams).

Brown, F. K.: *The Life of William Godwin* (London, Dent, 1926; New York, Dutton).

Dowden, E.: "Theorists of Revolution," *The French Revolution and English Literature* (New York, Scribner, 1897, 1908).

Harper, G. M.: "Rousseau, Godwin, and Wordsworth," *The Atlantic Monthly*, 109: 639 (1912).

Hazlitt, W.: *Contributions to The Edinburgh Review*, April, 1830; *The Spirit of the Age* (London, 1825); *Collected Works*, ed. by Waller and Glover (London, Dent, 1902-06; New York, McClure), 10, 385; 4, 200.

Paul, C. K.: *William Godwin, His Friends and Contemporaries*, 2 vols. (London, Paul, 1876; Boston, Roberts).

Roussin, H.: *William Godwin* (Paris, Plon-Nourrit, 1913).

Simon, Helene: *William Godwin und Mary Wollstonecraft* (München, Beck, 1909).

Stephen, L.: "Godwin and Shelley," *Hours in a Library*, 3 vols. (London, Smith, 1874-79; New York and London, Putnam, 1899); 4 vols. (1907).

Stephen, L.: *History of English Thought in the Eighteenth Century*, 2 vols. (London, Smith, 1876, 1902; New York, Putnam, 1902).

Stephen, L.: "William Godwin's Novels," *Studies of a Biographer*, 4 vols. (London, Duckworth, 1898-1902; New York, Putnam).

Woodcock, G.: *William Godwin* (London, Porcupine, 1946).

BIBLIOGRAPHY

Brown, F. K.: In his *The Life of William Godwin* (London, Dent, 1926; New York, Dutton).

Thomas Gray 1716-1771

Selections, p. 57 — Critical Notes, p. 1239

EDITIONS

Works, 4 vols., ed. by E. Gosse (London, Macmillan, 1884).

Poetical Works, ed. by J. Bradshaw (Aldine ed.: London, Bell, 1891; New York, Macmillan).

English Poems, ed. by D. C. Tovey (London, Cambridge Univ. Press, 1898).

Poetical Works (with Collins), ed. by A. L. Poole (London, Oxford Univ. Press, 1917; rev. by P. Toynbee and L. Whibley, 1937).

Selections from the Poetry and Prose, ed. by W. L. Phelps (Athenæum Press ed.: Boston, Ginn, 1894).

The Correspondence of Gray, Walpole, West, and Ashton, 2 vols., ed. by P. Toynbee (Oxford, Clarendon Press, 1915).

Letters, 3 vols., ed. by D. C. Tovey (London, Bell, 1900-12).

Letters, selected by J. Beresford (London and New York, Oxford Univ. Press, 1925).

Essays and Criticisms, ed., with an Introduction, by C. S. Northrup (Belles Lettres Ser.: Boston, Heath, 1911).

BIOGRAPHY AND CRITICISM

Arnold, M.: In Ward's *The English Poets*, Vol. 3 (London and New York, Macmillan, 1880, 1909); *Essays in Criticism*, Second Ser. (London and New York, Macmillan, 1888).

Beers, H. A.: "The Miltonic Group," *A History of English Romanticism in the Eighteenth Century* (New York, Holt, 1898, 1910).

Benson, A. C.: *Essays* (London, Heinemann, 1895; New York, Dutton).

Bradford, G.: *Bare Souls* (New York and London, Harper, 1924). Same article in *Harper's Magazine*, 148:734 (1923).

Brooke, S. A.: *Naturalism in English Poetry* (New York, Dutton, 1920).

Carlton, W. N. C.: *Thomas Gray's "Elegy Written in a Country Church Yard"* (New York, George D. Smith, 1925).

Cecil, E. C. D.: "The Poetry of Thomas Gray," *Yale Rev.*, n.s. 36, No. 4: 611 (1947).

Cecil, Lord David: *Two Quiet Lives: Dorothy Osborne, Thomas Gray* (London, Constable, 1948).

Gosse, E.: *Gray* (English Men of Letters Ser.: London, Macmillan, 1882; New York, Harper).

Hudson, W. H.: *Gray and His Poetry* (New York, Dodge, 1912).

Jack, A. A.: "Gray (Social or Prose Poetry)," *Poetry and Prose* (London, Constable, 1911).

Johnson, S.: *The Lives of the English Poets* (1779-81); ed. by G. B. Hill, 3 vols. (London, Clarendon Press, 1905).

Jones, W. P.: *Thomas Gray, Scholar* (Cambridge, Mass., Harvard Univ. Press, 1937).

Ketton-Cremer, R. W.: *Thomas Gray* (London, Duckworth, 1935).

Kittredge, G. L.: "Gray's Knowledge of Old Norse," in Appendix to Introduction to W. L. Phelps's *Selections from the Poetry and Prose of Thomas Gray* (Boston, Ginn, 1894).

Lowell, J. R.: *Latest Literary Essays* (*Collected Writings*, Boston, Houghton, 1890-92), Vol. 9.

More, P. E.: "With the Wits," *Shelburne Essays*, Tenth Ser. (Boston and New York, Houghton, 1919).

Norton, C. E.: *The Poet Gray as a Naturalist* (Boston, Goodspeed, 1903).

Reed, Amy Louise: *The Background of Gray's "Elegy"; a Study in the Taste for Melancholy Poetry, 1700-1751* (New York, Columbia Univ. Press, 1924).

Shairp, J. C.: "Nature in Collins, Gray, Goldsmith, Cowper, and Burns," *On Poetic Interpretation of Nature* (Edinburgh, Douglas, 1877; New York, Hurd, 1878; Boston, Houghton, 1885).

Snyder, E. D.: *The Celtic Revival in English Literature, 1760-1800* (Cambridge, Mass., Harvard Univ. Press, 1923).

Starr, H. W.: *Gray as a Literary Critic* (Philadelphia, Univ. of Pa. Press, 1941).

Stephen, L.: "Gray and his School," *Hours in a Library*, 3 vols. (London, Smith, 1874-79; New York and London, Putnam, 1899); 4 vols. (1907).

Tovey, D. C.: *Gray and His Friends* (London, Cambridge Univ. Press, 1890).

Warren, T. H.: "Letters of Thomas Gray," *The Quart. Rev.*, 220:390 (1914).

Woodberry, G. E.: *The Inspiration of Poetry* (New York, Macmillan, 1910).

CONCORDANCE

Cook, A. S.: *A Concordance to the English Poems of Thomas Gray* (Boston and New York, Houghton, 1908).

BIBLIOGRAPHY

Northrup, C. S.: *A Bibliography of Thomas Gray* (New Haven, Yale Univ. Press, 1917).

William Hamilton of Bangour
1704-1754

Poems, p. 13 — Critical Notes, p. 1234

EDITIONS

Poems and Songs, ed., with a Life, by James Paterson (London, Stephenson, 1852).

BIOGRAPHY AND CRITICISM

Bushnell, N. S.: *Stud. in Phil.*, 35:131 (1938).

Chalmers, A.: *Works of the English Poets*, Vol. 15 (London, Johnson, 1810).

Eyre-Todd, G.: *Scottish Poetry of the Eighteenth Century* (Glasgow, Hodge, 1896).

Veitch, J.: *The History and Poetry of the Scottish Border* (London, Macmillan, 1877, 1878).

Walker, H.: *Three Centuries of Scottish Literature*, 2 vols. (Glasgow, MacLehose, 1893).

Wilson, J. G.: *The Poets and Poetry of Scotland*, 2 vols. (Glasgow, Blackie, 1876; New York, Harper).

Robert Stephen Hawker 1803-1875

Poems, p. 1176 — Critical Notes, p. 1395

EDITIONS

Poetical Works, ed. by J. G. Godwin (London, Paul, 1879).

Poetical Works, ed., with a Preface and Bibliography, by A. Wallis (London, Lane, 1899).

Cornish Ballads, and Other Poems, ed. by C. E. Byles (London and New York, Lane, 1904).

Twenty Poems, ed., with an Introduction, by John Drinkwater (Oxford, Blackwell, 1925).

Hawker of Morwenstow (Augustan Books of Poetry: London, Benn, 1932).

BIOGRAPHY AND CRITICISM

"A Famous Cornish Character," *The Dial*, 38:308 (1905).

Baring-Gould, S.: *Robert Stephen Hawker, Vicar of Morwenstow* (London, Paul, 1876, 1886; Methuen, 1939).

Burrows, M. F.: *Robert Stephen Hawker: a Study of His Thought and Poetry* (Oxford, Blackwell, 1926).

Byles, C. E.: *Life and Letters of R. S. Hawker* (London and New York, Lane, 1905).

Drinkwater, J.: *A Book for Bookmen* (London, Dulau, 1926).

Kelly, R. M.: "Hawker of Morwenstow," *Catholic World*, 103:487 (1916).

Macartney, C. E.: "The Vicar of Morwenstow," *Sewanee Rev.*, 24:193 (1916).

More, P. E.: "The Vicar of Morwenstow," *Shelburne Essays*, Fourth Ser. (New York and London, Putnam, 1906).

Noble, J. A.: "Hawker of Morwenstow," *The Sonnet in England and Other Essays* (London, Mathews, 1893).

BIBLIOGRAPHY

Byles, C. E.: In *Life and Letters of R. S. Hawker* (London and New York, Lane, 1905).

Wallis, A.: In his edition of Hawker's *Poetical Works* (London, Lane, 1899).

William Hazlitt 1778-1830

EDITIONS

Collected Works, 12 vols., and Index, with an Introduction by W. E. Henley, ed. by A. R. Waller and A. Glover (London, Dent, 1902-06; New York, McClure).

The Complete Works, 20 vols. and Index, ed. by P. P. Howe (a re-issue of the Waller-Glover edition: London, Dent, 1930-34).

Works, 4 vols. (Everyman's Lib. ed.: New York, Dutton, 1906-10).

Selections, ed., with a Biographical and Critical Introduction, by W. D. Howe (Boston, Ginn, 1913).

Hazlitt on English Literature, Selections of Critical Essays, ed., with a Critical Introduction, by J. Zeitlin (London, Oxford Univ. Press, 1913).

Dramatic Essays, ed., with an Introduction, by W. Archer and R. W. Lowe (London, Scott, 1894).

Lectures on the English Poets (London and New York, Oxford Univ. Press, 1924).

Lectures on English Comic Writers, ed., with an Introduction, by R. B. Johnson (London and New York, Oxford Univ. Press, 1920).

Liber Amoris and Dramatic Criticisms, ed., with an Introduction, by C. Morgan (London, Peter Nevill, 1948).

Essays, selected and ed., with an Introduction, by Percy Van Dyke Shelley (New York and Chicago, Scribner, 1924).

Selected Essays, ed. by George Sampson (London, Cambridge Univ. Press, 1917).

Selected Essays, ed. by G. Keynes (London, Nonesuch Press, 1930).

Essays, selected and ed. by C. H. Gray (New York, Macmillan, 1926).

The Best of Hazlitt, compiled by P. P. Howe (London, Methuen, 1923; New York, Doran).

BIOGRAPHY

Birrell, A.: *William Hazlitt* (English Men of Letters Ser.: New York and London, Macmillan, 1902).

Hazlitt, W. C.: *Four Generations of a Literary Family*: the Hazlitts in England, Ireland, and America; their Friends and Fortunes, 1725-1896, 2 vols. (London, Redway, 1897).

Hazlitt, W. C.: *Lamb and Hazlitt: Letters and Records* (London, Mathews, 1899).

Hazlitt, W. C.: *Memoirs of William Hazlitt*, 2 vols. (London, Bentley, 1867).

Hazlitt, W. C.: *The Hazlitts: an Account of Their Origin and Descent* (Edinburgh, Ballantyne, 1911).

Howe, P. P.: *The Life of William Hazlitt* (London, Secker, 1922; Dent, 1928; H. Hamilton, 1947; New York, Doran).

Maclean, C. M.: *Born under Saturn, a Biography of William Hazlitt* (London, Collins, 1943; New York, Macmillan, 1944).

CRITICISM

Bullitt, J. M.: "Hazlitt and the Romantic Conception of the Imagination," *Phil. Quart.*, 24:343 (1945).

Chase, S. P.: "Hazlitt as a Critic of Art," *Pub. Mod. Lang. Assn.*, 39:179 (1924).

Elton, O.: *A Survey of English Literature, 1780-1830*, 2 vols. (London, Arnold, 1912, 1924).

Garrod, H. W.: "The Place of Hazlitt in English Criticism," *The Profession of Poetry and Other Lectures* (Oxford, Clarendon Press, 1929).

Ker, W. P.: *Collected Essays*, 2 vols. (London, Macmillan, 1925).

Law, M. H.: *The English Familiar Essay in the Early Nineteenth Century* (Philadelphia, Univ. of Pa. Press, 1934).

Lucas, E. V.: *The Life of Charles Lamb*, 2 vols. (London, Methuen, 1905); 1 vol. (1910).

More, P. E.: "The First Complete Edition of Hazlitt," *Shelburne Essays*, Second Ser. (New York and London, Putnam, 1905).

Patmore, P. G.: *My Friends and Acquaintance*, 3 vols. (New York, Saunders, 1854).

Saintsbury, G.: *A History of Criticism*, 3 vols. (Edinburgh and London, Blackwood, 1901-04, 1908; New York, Dodd), Book 8.

Saintsbury, G.: *Essays in English Literature, 1780-1860*, First Ser. (London, Percival, 1890; New York, Scribner).

Schneider, E.: *The Aesthetics of William Hazlitt* (Philadelphia, Univ. of Pa. Press, 1933).

Sichel, W.: "William Hazlitt—Romantic and Amorist," *The Fort. Rev.*, 101:94 (1914).

Stephen, L.: *Hours in a Library*, 3 vols. (London, Smith, 1874-79; New York and London, Putnam, 1899); 4 vols. (1907).

Stoddard, R. H.: *Personal Recollections of Lamb, Hazlitt, and Others* (New York, Scribner, 1875, 1903).

Thorpe, C. D.: "Keats and Hazlitt," *Pub. Mod. Lang. Assn.*, 62:487 (1947).

Walker, H.: *The English Essay and Essayists* (London, Dent, 1915; New York, Dutton), ch. 7.

Winchester, C. T.: *A Group of English Essayists* (New York, Macmillan, 1910).

BIBLIOGRAPHY

Keynes, G. L.: *Bibliography of William
Hazlitt* (New York, Random House, 1931).
Zeitlin, J.: In *Hazlitt on English Literature*
(London, Oxford Univ. Press, 1913).

Felicia Dorothea Hemans
1793-1835

Poems, p. 1186 — Critical Notes, p. 1396

EDITIONS

Collected Works, 7 vols. ed., with a Memoir,
by her Sister (London, Blackwood, 1839).
Complete Works, 2 vols., ed. by her Sister
(New York, Appleton, 1869).
Poetical Works, ed., with a Prefatory Notice,
by W. M. Rossetti (London and Edinburgh, Moxon, 1873; New York, Burt).
Poetical Works (London, Oxford Univ. Press,
1914).

BIOGRAPHY AND CRITICISM

Bancroft, G.: "Mrs. Hemans's Poems," *North
Amer. Rev.,* 24:443 (1827).
Bethune, G. W.: *The British Female Poets*
(Philadelphia, Lindsay, 1848).
Courtney, Mrs. W. L.: "Lesser Literary
Lights: Nineteenth Century Poetesses,"
North Amer. Rev., 211:793 (1920).
Hamilton, Catherine J.: *Women Writers: their
Works and Ways,* 2 Ser. (London and New
York, Ward, 1892).
Robinson, E. S.: *English Poetesses* (London
and New York, Cassell, 1883).
Walford, L. B.: *Twelve English Authoresses*
(London, Longmans, 1892).

James Hogg 1770-1835

Poems, p. 502 — Critical Notes, p. 1323

EDITIONS

Works in Poetry and Prose, 2 vols., ed., with a
Memoir, by J. Thomson (London, Blackie,
1865, 1874); 6 vols. (Edinburgh, Nimmo,
1878).
Works (Centenary Illustrated ed., 1876).
Poems, selected and edited with an Introduc-
tion, by Mrs. Garden (Canterbury Poets
ed.: London, Scott, 1886; New York,
Simmons).
*Private Memoirs and Confessions of a Justi-
fied Sinner,* ed., with an Introduction, by
A. Gide (London, Cresset, 1947).

Selected Poems, ed. by J. W. Oliver (Edinburgh, Oliver, 1940).

BIOGRAPHY AND CRITICISM

Batho, Edith C.: *The Ettrick Shepherd* (Lon-
don, Cambridge Univ. Press, 1927).
Douglas, G. B. S.: *James Hogg* (Famous Scots
Ser.: London, Oliphant, 1899).
Memorials of James Hogg, ed. by his daugh-
ter, Mrs. M. G. Garden, with a Preface
by J. Veitch (Paisley, Gardner, 1885,
1903).
Minto, W.: In Ward's *The English Poets,*
Vol. 4 (London and New York, Macmillan,
1880, 1911).
Saintsbury, G.: *Essays in English Literature,
1780-1860,* First Ser. (London, Percival,
1890; New York, Scribner).
Shairp, J. C.: "The Ettrick Shepherd,"
Sketches in History and Poetry, ed. by
J. Veitch (Edinburgh, Douglas, 1887).
Stephenson, H. T.: *The Ettrick Shepherd: a
Biography* (Bloomington, Indiana Univ.
Stud., 9, 1922).
Stoddard, R. H.: *Under the Evening Lamp*
(New York, Scribner, 1892; London,
Gay).
Strout, A. L.: *Life and Letters of James Hogg*
(Lubbock, Texas Tech. Press, 1946).
"The Real Ettrick Shepherd," *The Dial,*
28:205 (1900).
Thomson, J.: *Biographical and Critical Studies*
(London, Reeves, 1896).
Veitch, J.: *The History and Poetry of the
Scottish Border* (London, Macmillan, 1877,
1878).

Thomas Hood 1799-1845

Poems, p. 1161 — Critical Notes, p. 1393

EDITIONS

Complete Works, 11 vols. (London, Ward and
Lock, 1870-73, 1889).
Poetical Works, ed. by W. M. Rossetti (Lon-
don, Ward, 1880).
Poems, 2 vols. (Miniature Poets ed.: London,
Cassell, 1882-84).
Poems, 2 vols. ed. by A. Ainger (New York,
Macmillan, 1897).
Complete Poetical Works, ed. by W. Jerrold
(London, Oxford Univ. Press, 1906, 1911).
Poems, with Hunt (selections), ed. by J. H.
Panting (Canterbury Poets ed.: London,
Scott, 1889).
Prose Works, 3 vols., ed. by E. Sargent (New
York, Putnam, 1865).

BIOGRAPHY AND CRITICISM

Dawson, W. J.: "The Humanitarian Movement in Poetry—Thomas Hood and Mrs. Browning," *The Makers of English Poetry* (New York and London, Revell, 1906).

Dobson, A.: In Ward's *The English Poets*, Vol. 4 (London and New York, Macmillan, 1880, 1911).

Henley, W. E.: *Views and Reviews* (New York, Scribners, 1890).

Hudson, W. H.: *A Quiet Corner in a Library* (Chicago, Rand-McNally, 1915).

Jerrold, W. C.: *Thomas Hood, His Life and Times* (New York, Lane, 1909).

Jerrold, W. C.: *Thomas Hood and Charles Lamb* (London, Benn, 1930).

More, P. E.: *Shelburne Essays*, Seventh Ser. (New York and London, Putnam, 1910).

Saintsbury, G.: *Essays in English Literature, 1780-1860*, Second Ser. (London, Dent, 1895; New York, Scribner).

Shelley, H. C.: *Literary By-Paths in Old England* (Boston, Little, 1906).

Shillito, E.: "Tom Hood," *Christian Century*, 61:968 (1944).

Stedman, E. C.: *Victorian Poets* (Boston, Houghton, 1875, 1888).

James Henry Leigh Hunt 1784-1859

Selections, p. 892 — Critical Notes, p. 1364

EDITIONS

The Poetical Works, ed. by H. S. Milford (London and New York, Oxford Univ. Press, 1923).

Poems, with Hood, selected and ed. by J. H. Panting (Canterbury Poets ed.: London, Scott, 1889; New York, Simmons).

Essays and Poems, 2 vols., selected and ed. by R. B. Johnson (Temple Lib.: London, Dent, 1891).

Essays, selected and edited by A. Seymour (New York, Dutton, 1904).

Essays (Everyman's Lib. ed.: New York, Dutton, 1948).

Essays and Sketches, ed., with an Introduction, by R. B. Johnson (London and New York, Oxford Univ. Press, 1912).

Prefaces, ed. by R. B. Johnson (Chicago, Hill, 1927).

Dramatic Essays, ed. by W. Archer and R. W. Lowe (London, Scott, 1894).

Autobiography, 2 vols., ed. by R. Ingpen (London, Constable, 1903; New York, Dutton); ed. by E. C. Blunden (World's Classics: London, Oxford Univ. Press, 1928).

Autobiography, ed., with an Introduction, by J. E. Morpurgo (London, Cresset, 1949).

BIOGRAPHY AND CRITICISM

Blunden, E. C.: *Leigh Hunt and His Circle* (New York, Harper, 1930); published as *Leigh Hunt: A Biography* (London, Cobden-Sanderson).

Dowden, E.: In Ward's *The English Poets*, Vol. 4 (London and New York, Macmillan, 1880, 1911).

Gosse, E.: *More Books on the Table* (London, Heinemann, 1923).

Graham, W.: "Shelley's Debt to Leigh Hunt and the *Examiner*," *Pub. Mod. Lang. Assn.*, 40:185 (1925).

Houchens, L. H. and Houchens, C. W. (ed.): *Leigh Hunt's Dramatic Criticism, 1808-1831* (New York, Columbia Univ. Press, 1949).

Johnson, R. B.: *Leigh Hunt* (London, Sonnenschein, 1896).

Johnson, R. B. (ed.): *Shelley-Leigh Hunt* (London, Ingpen, 1928).

Landré, L.: *Leigh Hunt (1784-1859): Contribution à l'Histoire du Romantisme anglais*, 2 vols. (Paris, 1935-36).

Law, M. H.: *The English Familiar Essay in the Early Nineteenth Century* (Philadelphia, Univ. of Pa. Press, 1934).

Miller, B.: *Leigh Hunt's Relations with Byron, Shelley, and Keats* (New York, Columbia Univ. Press, 1910).

Monkhouse, C.: *Life of Leigh Hunt* (Great Writers Ser.: London, Scott, 1893).

Pickering, L. P.: *Lord Byron, Leigh Hunt, and the "Liberal"* (London, Drane's Limited, 1925).

Pierce, F. E.: *Currents and Eddies in the English Romantic Generation* (New Haven, Yale Univ. Press, 1918).

Punchard, C. D.: *Helps to the Study of Leigh Hunt's Essays* (London, Macmillan, 1899).

Saintsbury, G.: *Essays in English Literature, 1780-1860*, First Ser. (London, Percival, 1890; New York, Scribner).

Walker, H.: *The English Essay and Essayists*, ch. 7 (London, Dent, 1915; New York, Dutton).

Whipple, E. P.: "British Critics" and "Leigh Hunt's Poems," *Essays and Reviews*, 2 vols. (Boston, Osgood, 1849, 1878).

Winchester, C. T.: *A Group of English Essayists of the Early Nineteenth Century* (New York, Macmillan, 1910).

BIBLIOGRAPHY

Johnson, R. B.: In his edition of Hunt's *Essays and Poems* (1891).

Landré, L.: In his *Leigh Hunt* (Paris, 1935-36).

Milford, H. S.: In his edition of *The Poetical Works* (London and New York, Oxford Univ. Press, 1923).

Richard Hurd 1720-1808

EDITIONS

Complete Works, 8 vols. (1811).

Moral and Political Dialogues, with Letters on Chivalry and Romance, 3 vols. (London, Cadell, 1788).

Letters on Chivalry and Romance (1762) ; ed., with an Introduction, by Edith J. Morley (London, Frowde, 1911).

Correspondence, ed. by E. H. Pearce and L. Whibley (London, Cambridge Univ. Press, 1932).

BIOGRAPHY AND CRITICISM

Evans, A. W.: *Warburton and the Warburtonians* (London, Oxford Univ. Press, 1932).

Kilvert, F.: *Memoirs of the Life and Writings of the Right Rev. Richard Hurd* (London, Bentley, 1860).

Pearce, E. H.: *Hartlebury Castle* (London, Soc. Prom. Christian Knowledge, 1926).

Saintsbury, G.: *A History of Criticism*, 3 vols. (Edinburgh and London, Blackwood, 1901-04, 1908; New York, Dodd).

Stephen, L.: *History of English Thought in the Eighteenth Century*, 2 vols. (London, Smith, 1876, 1902; New York, Putnam).

Francis Jeffrey 1773-1850

EDITIONS

Essays on English Poets and Poetry from The Edinburgh Review (New Universal Lib.: New York, Dutton, 1913).

Literary Criticism, ed., with an Introduction, by D. N. Smith (London, Frowde, 1910).

Selections, ed., with an Introduction, by L. E. Gates (Athenæum Press ed.: Boston, Ginn, 1894).

BIOGRAPHY AND CRITICISM

Bagehot, W.: "The First Edinburgh Reviewers," *The National Rev.*, 1855; *Literary Stud.*, 3 vols. (London, Longmans, 1878-79, 1895).

Bald, R. C.: "Francis Jeffrey as a Literary Critic," *Nine. Cent.*, 97:201 (1925).

Beatty, J. M.: "Lord Jeffrey and Wordsworth," *Pub. Mod. Lang. Assn.*, 38:221 (1923).

Cockburn, H.: *Life of Lord Jeffrey, with a Selection from his Correspondence*, 2 vols. (London, Black, 1852, 1874).

Gates, L. E.: *Three Studies in Literature* (New York, Macmillan, 1899).

Greig, J. A.: *Francis Jeffrey of the Edinburgh Review* (Edinburgh, Oliver, 1948).

Hughes, M. Y.: "The Humanism of Francis Jeffrey," *Mod. Lang. Rev.*, 16:243 (1921).

Saintsbury, G.: "Jeffrey and Sydney Smith," *Essays in English Literature, 1780-1860*, First Ser. (London, Percival, 1890; New York, Scribner).

Walker, H.: *The English Essay and Essayists*, ch. 8 (London, Dent, 1915; New York, Dutton).

Whipple, E. P.: "British Critics," *Essays and Reviews*, 2 vols. (Boston, Osgood, 1849, 1878).

Winchester, C. T.: "The New Essay—Jeffrey as a Critic," *A Group of English Essayists of the Early Nineteenth Century* (New York, Macmillan, 1910).

BIBLIOGRAPHY

Smith, D. N.: "List of Jeffrey's Articles in *The Edinburgh Review*," Appendix to *Literary Criticism* (London, Frowde, 1910).

Samuel Johnson 1709-1784

EDITIONS

Works, 16 vols. (Literary Club ed.: New York, Lamb, 1903).

Complete Works, 8 vols. (New York, Bigelow, 1912).

Lives of the English Poets, ed. by W. E. Henley (London, Methuen, 1896).

The Lives of the Most Eminent English Poets, with Critical Observations on their Works, 3 vols., ed. by G. B. Hill and H. S. Scott (Oxford, Clarendon Press, 1905).

Select Essays, 2 vols., ed. by G. B. Hill (Temple Library ed.: London, Dent, 1889).

Miscellanies, ed. by G. B. Hill (London, Oxford Univ. Press, 1897).

Johnson on Shakespeare, selected and ed. by W. A. Raleigh (London, Oxford Univ. Press, 1908).

The Critical Opinions of Samuel Johnson, compiled, with an Introduction, by J. E. Brown (Princeton, Princeton Univ. Press, 1926).

Samuel Johnson: Writer, a Selection, ed., with an Introduction, by S. C. Roberts (London, Jenkins, 1927).

The Reader's Johnson, selections, ed. by C. H. Conley (New York, Amer. Book Co., 1940).

Journey to the Western Islands of Scotland; and Boswell's *Journal of a Tour to the Hebrides with Samuel Johnson*, ed. by R. W. Chapman (London, Milford, 1924).

The History of Rasselas, ed., with an Introduction, by G. B. Hill (Oxford, Clarendon Press, 1889).

Letters, 2 vols., ed. by G. B. Hill (Oxford, Clarendon Press, 1892; New York, Harper).

Poems, with Goldsmith, Collins, and Gray, ed. by T. M. Ward (Muses' Lib.: London, Routledge, 1905; New York, Dutton).

Prose and Poetry, ed., with an Introduction and Notes, by R. W. Chapman (Oxford, Clarendon Press, 1922).

The Poems, ed. by D. N. Smith and E. L. McAdam (London and New York, Oxford Univ. Press, 1941, 1942).

BIOGRAPHY

Bailey, J.: *Dr. Johnson and His Circle* (Home Univ. Lib.: London, Williams, 1913; New York, Holt; rev. ed., London, Oxford Univ. Press, 1944).

Boswell, J.: *The Life of Samuel Johnson;* with the Journal of a Tour to the Hebrides, ed. by G. B. Hill, 6 vols. (London, Macmillan, 1887).

Boswell, J.: *The Life of Samuel Johnson* (Globe ed.: London, Macmillan, 1893); 6 vols. (Temple Lib.: London, Dent, 1898); 2 vols. in 1 (Oxford ed.: London, Frowde, 1904).

Boswell, J.: *Life of Johnson*, abridged and ed., with an Introduction, by C. G. Osgood (New York and Chicago, Scribner, 1917).

Boswell, J.: *Life of Samuel Johnson* (New York, Doubleday, 1946).

Broadley, A. M.: *Dr. Johnson and Mrs. Thrale* (London and New York, Lane, 1910).

Grant, F.: *Life of Samuel Johnson* (Great Writers Ser.: London, Scott, 1887).

Stephen, L.: *Samuel Johnson* (English Men of Letters Ser.: London, Macmillan, 1878; New York, Harper).

Tinker, C. B.: *Dr. Johnson and Fanny Burney* (New York, Moffat, 1911).

CRITICISM

Arnold, M.: "Johnson's Lives," *Essays in Criticism*, Third Ser. (Boston, Ball, 1910).

Birrell, A.: *Collected Essays and Addresses*, 3 vols. (London and Toronto, Dent, 1922).

Boynton, P. H.: "Johnson's London," *London in English Literature* (Chicago, Univ. of Chicago Press, 1913).

Bracey, R.: *Eighteenth Century Studies* (Oxford, Blackwell, 1925).

Bronson, B. H.: *Johnson Agonistes and Other Essays* (New York, Macmillan, 1946).

Bronson, B. H.: *Johnson and Boswell* (Berkeley, Univ. of Calif. Press, 1944).

Carlyle, T.: "Boswell's Life of Johnson," *Fraser's Mag.*, 5:379 (1832); *Critical and*

Miscellaneous Essays, 4 vols. (Boston, Houghton, 1880).

Christie, O. F.: *Johnson the Essayist* (London, Richards, 1924; New York, Doran, 1925).

Collins, J. C.: "Johnson's Lives of the Poets," *The Quart. Rev.*, 208:72 (1908).

Dawson, W. J.: *The Makers of English Prose* (New York and London, Revell, 1906).

Hill, G. B.: *Dr. Johnson: His Friends and His Critics* (London, Smith, 1878).

Hollis, C.: *Dr. Johnson* (London, Gollancz, 1928).

Houston, P. H.: *Doctor Johnson; a Study in Eighteenth Century Humanism* (Cambridge, Harvard Univ. Press, 1923).

Hudson, W. H.: *Johnson and Goldsmith and Their Poetry* (London, Harrap, 1918).

Krutch, J. W.: *Samuel Johnson* (New York, Holt, 1944).

Krutch, J. W.: "Samuel Johnson as Critic," *The Nation*, 158:218 (1944).

Lunn, H. K.: *Samuel Johnson* (New York, Viking Press, 1933).

Macaulay, T. B.: "Boswell's Life of Johnson," *The Edinburgh Rev.*, 54:1 (1831); *Critical and Historical Essays*, 2 vols. (London and New York, Longmans, 1898).

McNair, A. D.: *Dr. Johnson and the Law* (London, Cambridge Univ. Press, 1948).

Raleigh, Sir W.: *Johnson on Shakespeare* (London, Frowde, 1908).

Raleigh, Sir W.: *Six Essays on Johnson* (London, Frowde, 1910).

Roberts, S. C.: *The Story of Doctor Johnson* (London, Cambridge Univ. Press, 1919).

Secombe, T.: *The Age of Johnson* (London, Bell, 1900; New Haven, Yale Univ. Press, 1949).

Spittal, J. K. (ed.): *Contemporary Criticisms of Dr. Samuel Johnson, His Works, and His Biographers* (London, Murray, 1923; New York, Dutton).

Stephen, L.: "Dr. Johnson's Writings," *Hours in a Library*, 3 vols. (London, Smith, 1874-79; New York and London, Putnam, 1899); 4 vols. (1907).

Struble, M. C.: *A Johnson Handbook* (New York, Crofts, 1933).

Taggart, S.: "Dr. Johnson as a Literary Critic," *The Westminster Rev.*, 180:291 (1913).

Trent, W. P.: "Bicentenary of Dr. Johnson," *Longfellow and Other Essays* (New York, Crowell, 1910).

Vulliamy, C. E.: *Ursa Major* (London, M. Joseph, 1946).

Walker, H.: *The English Essay and Essayists*, ch. 6 (London, Dent, 1915; New York, Dutton).

Wimsatt, W. K.: *The Prose Style of Samuel Johnson* (New Haven, Yale Univ. Press, 1941).

BIBLIOGRAPHY

Anderson, J. P.: In Grant's *Life of Samuel Johnson* (Great Writers Ser.: London, Scott, 1887).

Courtney, W. P. and Smith, D. N.: *A Bibliography of Samuel Johnson* (Oxford, Clarendon Press, 1925).

John Keats 1795-1821

Selections, p. 777 — Critical Notes, p. 1353

EDITIONS

Complete Works, 5 vols., ed., with a Memoir, by H. B. Forman (Glasgow, Gowans, 1900-01; New York, Crowell).

Complete Poetical Works and Letters, ed., with a Biographical Sketch, by H. E. Scudder (Cambridge ed.: Boston, Houghton, 1899, 1948).

Complete Poems and Selected Letters, ed. by C. DeW. Thorpe (New York, Doubleday, 1935).

Complete Poetry, ed., with an Introduction, by G. R. Elliott (New York, Macmillan, 1927).

Complete Poetical Works, ed. by M. B. Forman and L. Bacon (New York, Oxford Univ. Press, 1935).

Poetical Works and Other Writings, 8 vols., ed. by H. B. Forman (Hampstead ed.: New York, Scribner, 1938-39).

The Poetical Works, ed. by H. W. Garrod (London, Oxford Univ. Press, 1939).

Poetical Works (Globe ed.: London and New York, Macmillan, 1902).

Poetical Works, ed., with an Introduction, by H. B. Forman (Oxford ed.: London, Oxford Univ. Press, 1906, 1908, 1926).

Poems, ed. by Arlo Bates (Athenæum Press ed.: Boston, Ginn, 1896).

Poems, ed., with an Introduction and Notes, by E. De Sélincourt (New York, Dodd, 1905, 1912).

Poems, 2 vols., ed., with a Preface, by S. Colvin (London, Chatto, 1915; New York, Brentano).

Poems, ed., with an Introduction, by J. M. Murry (London, P. Nevill, 1948).

Poems and Verses, ed. by J. M. Murry (London, Eyre, 1949).

Letters, Papers, and Other Relics, ed., with Forewords by T. Watts-Dunton, and an Introduction by H. B. Forman, by G. C. Williamson (London and New York, Lane, 1914).

The Letters, 2 vols., ed. by M. B. Forman (London, Oxford Univ. Press, 1931, 1935, 1947).

Letters to His Family and Friends, ed. by S. Colvin (London, Macmillan, 1937).

Letters, ed., with an Introduction, by H. I'A. Fausset (New York, Nelson, 1938).

BIOGRAPHY

Askwith, B.: *Keats* (London, Collins, 1941).

Brown, C. A.: *Life of John Keats*, ed. by D. H. Bodwitha and W. B. Pope (London, Oxford Univ. Press, 1937).

Colvin, S.: *John Keats; His Life and Poetry, His Friends, Critics, and After-Fame* (New York, Scribner, 1925).

Colvin, S.: *Life of John Keats*, New Ed. (London and New York, Macmillan, 1921).

Evans, B. I.: *Keats* (Great Lives: London, Duckworth, 1934).

Garrod, H. W.: *Keats* (Oxford, Clarendon Press, 1926, 1939).

Hale-White, W.: *Keats as Doctor and Patient* (London, Oxford Univ. Press, 1938).

Hale-White, W.: *Keats as a Medical Student* (London, Wakley, 1925).

Hancock, A. E.: *John Keats, A Literary Biography* (London, Constable, 1908; Boston, Houghton).

Hewlett, D.: *Adonais: a Life of John Keats* (London, Hurst, 1937, 1939).

Houghton, Lord (R. M. Milnes) (ed.): *Life, Letters, and Literary Remains of John Keats*, 2 vols. (London, Moxon, 1848, 1867; New Universal Lib.: London, Routledge, 1906; Everyman's Lib. ed.: New York, Dutton, 1927).

Lindon, Mrs. Frances (Brawne): *Letters of Fanny Brawne to Fanny Keats, 1820-1824*, ed. by F. Edgcumbe (London, Oxford Univ. Press, 1936, 1939).

Lowell, Amy: *John Keats*, 2 vols. (Boston and New York, Houghton, 1925).

Rollins, H. E.: *Keats' Reputation in America to 1848* (Harvard Memorial Keats Stud., No. 1: Cambridge, Mass., Harvard Univ. Press, 1948).

Rollins, H. E. (ed.): *The Keats Circle; Letters and Papers, 1816-1878*, 2 vols. (Cambridge, Mass., Harvard Univ. Press, 1948).

Rossetti, W. M.: *Life of John Keats* (Great Writers Ser.: London, Scott, 1887).

Weller, E. V.: *Keats and Mary Tighe* (New York, Century, 1928).

Williams, B. C.: *Forever Young: A Life of John Keats* (New York, Putnam, 1943).

Wolff, L.: *John Keats, sa Vie et son Œuvre* (Paris, Hachette, 1910).

CRITICISM

Arnold, M.: *Essays in Criticism*, Second Ser. (London and New York, Macmillan, 1888).

Bate, W. J.: *Negative Capability; the Intuitive Approach in Keats* (Cambridge, Mass., Harvard Univ. Press, 1939).

Bate, W. J.: *The Stylistic Development of Keats* (London, Oxford Univ. Press, 1945).

Beyer, W. W.: *Keats and the Daemon King* (London, Oxford Univ. Press, 1947).

Blackwood's Magazine: "On the Cockney School of Poetry" (*Endymion*), 3:519 (1818).

Blunden, E. C. (ed.): *Shelley and Keats as They Struck Their Contemporaries* (London, Beaumont, 1925).

Bradford, G.: *Bare Souls* (New York and London, Harper, 1924). Same article in *Harper's Mag.*, 149:259 (1937).

Bradley, A. C.: "Keats and Philosophy," *The John Keats Memorial Volume*, ed. by G. C. Williamson (London and New York, Lane, 1921); also in *A Miscellany* (London, Macmillan, 1929).

Bradley, A. C.: "The Letters of Keats," *Oxford Lectures on Poetry* (London, Macmillan, 1909, 1911).

Bridges, R.: *John Keats, a Critical Essay* 1895); *Collected Essays, Papers, Etc.*, 4 vols. (London, Oxford Univ. Press, 1929).

Brooke, S. A.: *Studies in Poetry* (New York, Putnam, 1907; London, Duckworth).

Brooks, C.: *The Well Wrought Urn* (New York, Reynal and Hitchcock, 1947).

Brown, L.: "The Genesis, Growth, and Meaning of *Endymion*," *Stud. in Phil.*, 30:618 (1933).

Bush, D.: *Mythology and the Romantic Tradition in English Poetry* (Cambridge, Mass., Harvard Univ. Press, 1937).

Caldwell, J. R.: *John Keats' Fancy; the Effect on Keats of the Psychology of His Day* (Ithaca, N. Y., Cornell Univ. Press, 1945).

Clutton-Brock, A.: *Essays on Books* (London, Methuen, 1920).

Crawford, A. W.: *The Genius of Keats: An Interpretation* (London, Stockwell, 1932).

Croker, J. W.: "Endymion," *The Quart. Rev.*, 19:204 (1818).

Dawson, W. J.: *The Makers of English Poetry* (New York and London, Revell, 1906).

De Sélincourt, E.: *Keats* (London, Oxford Univ. Press, 1921).

Dodds, Mrs. A. E. Powell: *The Romantic Theory of Poetry* (New York, Putnam, 1926).

Du Bos, C.: *What Is Literature?* (London, Sheed, 1940).

Elliott, G. R.: "The Real Tragedy of Keats; a Post-Centenary View," *Pub. Mod. Lang. Assn.*, 36:315 (1921); in *The Cycle of Modern Poetry* (Princeton, Princeton Univ. Press, 1929).

Elton, O.: *A Survey of English Literature, 1780-1830*, 2 vols. (London, Arnold, 1912, 1924).

Evans, B. I.: *Tradition and Romanticism* (New York, Longmans, 1940; London, Methuen).

Fairchild, H. N.: *The Romantic Quest* (New York, Columbia Univ. Press, 1931).

Fausset, H. I'A.: *Keats: a Study in Development* (London, Secker, 1922).

Finney, C. L.: *The Evolution of Keats's Poetry*, 2 vols. (Cambridge, Mass., Harvard Univ. Press, 1936).

Fogle, R. H.: "Empathic Imagery in Keats and Shelley," *Pub. Mod. Lang. Assn.*, 61:163 (1946).

Ford, G. H.: *Keats and the Victorians, 1821-95* (New Haven, Yale Univ. Press, 1944).

Gorell, R. G. B.: *John Keats: The Principle of Beauty* (London, Sylvan Press, 1948).

Graham, W.: "Sensuousness in the Poetry of Milton and Keats," *South Atl. Quart.*, 16:346 (1917).

Haber, T. B.: "The Unifying Principle of Love in Keats's Poetry," *Phil. Quart.*, 16:192 (1937).

Harvard Memorial Keats Studies (Cambridge, Mass., Harvard Univ. Press, 1946).

Havens, R. D.: "Concerning the *Ode on a Grecian Urn*," *Mod. Phil.*, 24:209 (1926).

Havens, R. D.: *The Influence of Milton on English Poetry* (Cambridge, Mass., Harvard Univ. Press, 1922).

Havens, R. D.: "Unreconciled Opposites in Keats," *Phil. Quart.*, 14:289 (1935).

Hudson, W. H.: *Keats and His Poetry* (New York, Dodge, 1912).

James, D. G.: *Scepticism and Poetry* (London, G. Allen, 1937).

Jeffrey, F.: "Endymion, Lamia, Isabella, The Eve of St. Agnes, and Other Poems," *The Edinburgh Rev.*, 34:203 (1820).

Ker, W. P.: *Collected Essays*, 2 vols. (London, Macmillan, 1925).

Knight, G. W.: *The Burning Oracle: Studies in the Poetry of Action* (London, Oxford Univ. Press, 1939).

Knight, G. W.: *The Starlit Dome: Studies in the Poetry of Vision* (London, Oxford Univ. Press, 1941).

Landrum, Grace W.: "More concerning Chapman's Homer and Keats," *Pub. Mod. Lang. Assn.*, 42:986 (1927).

Lowell, J. R.: *Among My Books*, Second Ser.

(Boston, Houghton, 1884); *Collected Writings* (Boston, Houghton, 1890-92).

Lynd, R.: *Books and Authors* (New York and London, Putnam, 1923).

Lynd, R.: *Old and New Masters* (London, Unwin, 1919).

Mabie, H. W.: *Essays in Literary Interpretation* (New York, Dodd, 1892).

MacCracken, H.: "The Source of Keats's *Eve of St. Agnes*," *Mod. Phil.*, 5:145 (1907).

Mackail, J. W.: *Lectures on Poetry* (London, Longmans, 1911).

Mackail, J. W.: *Studies of English Poets* (London and New York, Longmans, 1926).

Marshall, E. G.: *Poetical Theories and Criticism of the Chief Romantic Poets* (Ann Arbor, Mich., Edwards Brothers, 1926).

Masson, D.: *Wordsworth, Shelley, Keats, and other Essays* (London, Macmillan, 1874, 1881).

Miles, J.: *Major Adjectives in English Poetry* (Berkeley, Univ. of Calif. Publ., 1946).

Miller, B.: *Leigh Hunt's Relations with Byron, Shelley, and Keats* (New York, Columbia Univ. Press, 1910).

More, P. E.: *Shelburne Essays*, Fourth Ser. (New York and London, Putnam, 1906).

Murry, J. M.: *Aspects of Literature* (London, Collins, 1920).

Murry, J. M.: *Heroes of Thought: A Study of Keats' Poetic Life from 1816 to 1820* (New York, Messner, 1938).

Murry, J. M.: *Keats and Shakespeare* (London, Oxford Univ. Press, 1925).

Murry, J. M.: *Studies in Keats: New and Old* (London, Oxford Univ. Press, 1930, 1939).

Murry, J. M.: *The Mystery of Keats* (London, Nevill, 1949).

Payne, W. M.: *The Greater English Poets of the Nineteenth Century* (New York, Holt, 1907, 1909).

Rickett, A.: "The Poets: Keats and Rossetti," *Personal Forces in Modern Literature* (London, Dent, 1906; New York, Dutton).

Ridley, M. R.: *Keats's Craftsmanship: A Study in Poetic Development* (London, Oxford Univ. Press, 1934).

Roberts, J. H.: "Poetry of Sensation or of Thought," *Pub. Mod. Lang. Assn.*, 45:1129 (1930).

Robertson, J. M.: "The Art of Keats," *New Essays Toward a Critical Method* (New York, Lane, 1897).

Saito, T.: *Keats's View of Poetry* (London, Cobden-Sanderson, 1929).

Shackford, M. H.: "*The Eve of St. Agnes* and *The Mysteries of Udolpho*," *Pub. Mod. Lang. Assn.*, 36:104 (1921).

Shackford, M. H.: "*Hyperion*," *Stud. in Phil.*, 22:48 (1925).

Shackford, M. H.: "John Keats and Adversity," *Sewanee Rev.*, 32:474 (1924).

Shanks, E.: *First Essays on Literature* (London, W. Collins, 1923).

Shipman, M. E.: "Orthodoxy concerning Keats," *Pub. Mod. Lang. Assn.*, 44:929 (1929).

Stedman, E. C.: *Genius and Other Essays* (New York, Moffat, 1911).

Suddard, S. J. M.: *Keats, Shelley, and Shakespeare Studies* (London, Cambridge Univ. Press, 1912; New York, Broadway).

Swinburne, A. C.: *Miscellanies* (London, Chatto, 1886, 1911; New York, Scribner).

Symons, A.: *The Romantic Movement in English Poetry* (London, Constable, 1909; New York, Dutton).

Thomas, E.: *A Literary Pilgrim in England* (London, Methuen, 1917; New York, Dodd).

Thorpe, C. De W.: *The Mind of John Keats* (New York and London, Oxford Univ. Press, 1926).

Thorpe, C. De W.: "Wordsworth and Keats," *Pub. Mod. Lang. Assn.*, 42:1010 (1927).

Thorpe, C. De W.: "Keats and Hazlitt," *Pub. Mod. Lang. Assn.*, 62:487 (1947).

Thorpe, C. De W.: "Keats's Interest in Politics," *Pub. Mod. Lang. Assn.*, 46:1228 (1931).

Torrey, B.: *Friends on the Shelf* (Boston, Houghton, 1906).

Van Dyke, H.,: "The Influence of Keats," *The Century Mag.*, 50:910 (1895).

Wagenblass, J. H.: "Keats's Roaming Fancy," *Harvard Stud. and Notes*, 20:123 (1938).

Watson, W.: "Keats's Letters," *Excursions in Criticism* (New York, Macmillan, 1893).

White, I. H.: "John Keats as a Critic," *Sewanee Rev.*, 34:451 (1926).

Williams, C.: *Reason and Beauty in the Poetic Mind* (London, Oxford Univ. Press, 1933).

Williamson, C. C. H.: *Writers of Three Centuries, 1789-1914* (London, Richards, 1920).

Williamson, G. C. (ed.): *The John Keats Memorial Volume* (London, Lane, 1921).

Wolff, L.: *An Essay on Keats's Treatment of the Heroic Rhythm and Blank Verse* (Paris, 1909).

Woodberry, G. E.: *Literary Essays* (New York, Harcourt, 1920).

Zillman, L. J.: *John Keats and the Sonnet Tradition* (Los Angeles, Lymanhouse, 1939).

CONCORDANCE

Baldwin, D. L., and others: *A Concordance to*

the Poems of John Keats (Washington, D. C., Carnegie Institution, 1917).

BIBLIOGRAPHY

Finney, C. L.: In *The Evolution of Keats's Poetry*, Vol. 2 (Cambridge, Mass., Harvard Univ. Press, 1936).

Forman, H. B.: In his edition of Keats's *Complete Works* (Glasgow, Gowans, 1900-01; New York, Crowell).

Forman, H. B.: "List of Principal Works concerning Keats," in the Hampstead edition of *Poetical Works and Other Writings*, Vol. 1 (New York, Scribner, 1938-39).

MacGillivray, J. R.: *John Keats: A Bibliography & Reference Guide, with an Essay on Keats' Reputation* (Toronto, Univ. of Toronto Press, 1949).

Wise, T. J.: In *The John Keats Memorial Volume*, ed. by G. C. Williamson (London, Lane, 1921).

John Keble 1792-1866

Poems, p. 1159 — Critical Notes, p. 1393

EDITIONS

The Christian Year, Lyra Innocentium and Other Poems (London, Oxford Univ. Press, 1914).

The Christian Year (World's Classics: London, Oxford Univ. Press, 1914).

Lectures on Poetry, 1832-1841, 2 vols., trans. from the Latin by E. K. Francis (London, Oxford Univ. Press, 1912).

BIOGRAPHY AND CRITICISM

Coleridge, J. T.: *A Memoir of John Keble*, 2 vols. (Oxford, Parker, 1869, 1874).

Ingram, K.: *John Keble* (London, Allan, 1933).

Lock, W.: *John Keble* (London, Methuen, 1893, 1895).

Shairp, J. C.: *Studies in Poetry and Philosophy* (Edinburgh, Douglas, 1872, 1886; Boston, Houghton, 1880).

Smith, E. F.: "The Centenary of *The Christian Year*," *Church Quart. Rev.*, 105:99 (1929).

Wood, E. F. L. (Baron Irwin): *John Keble* (London, Mowbray, 1909; Milwaukee, Morehouse, 1932).

Charles Lamb 1775-1834

Selections, p. 941 — Critical Notes, p. 1371

EDITIONS

Complete Works in Prose and Verse, ed. by R. H. Shepherd (London, Chatto, 1874, 1901).

Works, 12 vols., ed., with a Biographical and Critical Essay, by W. Macdonald (London, Dent, 1903; New York, Dutton).

Works of Charles and Mary Lamb, 7 vols., ed. by E. V. Lucas (New York, Putnam, 1903-05; London, Methuen); 6 vols. (New York, 1913).

The Works of Charles and Mary Lamb, 2 vols., ed. by T. Hutchinson (London, Oxford Univ. Press, 1924).

The Life, Letters, and Writings of Charles Lamb, 6 vols., ed. by P. Fitzgerald (London, Navarre Society, 1924).

Prose and Poetry, ed., with an Introduction, by G. Gordon (Oxford, Clarendon Press, 1921).

The Complete Elia, illus. by G. Ross (New York, Heritage, 1943).

Essays of Elia, ed. by H. E. Woodbridge (New York, Macmillan, 1927).

The Letters of Charles Lamb, 3 vols., ed. by E. V. Lucas (New Haven, Yale Univ. Press, 1935).

Selected Letters, ed. by G. T. Clapton (London, Methuen, 1925).

Letters, 2 vols., ed. by G. Pocock (Everyman's Lib. ed.: New York, Dutton, 1946).

Lamb's Criticism, ed., with an Introduction, by E. M. W. Tillyard (London, Cambridge Univ. Press, 1923; New York, Macmillan).

The Best of Lamb, ed. by E. V. Lucas (London, Methuen, 1914).

Essays and Letters, ed. by J. M. French (New York, Doubleday, 1937).

Everybody's Lamb, ed. by A. C. Ward (New York, Harcourt, 1933).

The Portable Lamb, ed., with an Introduction, by J. M. Brown (New York, Viking Press, 1949).

BIOGRAPHY

Ainger, A.: *Charles Lamb* (English Men of Letters Ser.: London, Macmillan, 1882; New York, Harper).

Anthony, K. S.: *The Lambs* (New York, Knopf, 1945).

Blunden, E. C.: *Charles Lamb and His Contemporaries* (London, Cambridge Univ. Press, 1933, 1937).

Blunden, E. C. (ed): *Charles Lamb: His Life Recorded by His Contemporaries* (London, Woolf, 1934).

Fitzgerald, P.: *Charles Lamb, His Friends, His Haunts, and His Books* (London, Bentley, 1866).

Gilchrist, Mrs. Anne: *Life of Mary Lamb* (Eminent Women Ser.: London, Allen, 1883, 1890).

Hazlitt, W. C.: *The Lambs: their Lives, their*

Friends, and their Correspondence, etc.
(London, E. Mathews, 1896).

Howe, W. D.: Charles Lamb and His Friends
(Indianapolis, Bobbs, 1944).

Lucas, E. V.: The Life of Charles Lamb, fifth
ed., 2 vols. (London, Methuen, 1921).

McKechnie, S.: "Charles Lamb of the India
House," Notes and Queries, 191 and 192
(1946-47).

Ridley, H. M.: "Great Friendships: Samuel
Taylor Coleridge and Charles Lamb,"
Canadian Mag., 61:21 (1923).

Robinson, H. C.: Blake, Coleridge, Wordsworth, Lamb, Etc., being Selections from
the Remains of Henry Crabb Robinson, ed.
by E. J. Morley (New York, Longmans,
1922).

Wherry, G.: Cambridge and Charles Lamb
(London, Cambridge Univ. Press, 1925).

CRITICISM

Ainger, A.: "The Letters of Charles Lamb"—
"How I Traced Charles Lamb in Hertfordshire," Lectures and Essays, 2 vols. (London and New York, Macmillan, 1905).

Baker, H. T.: "Lamb and the Periodical
Essay," North Amer. Rev., 215:519 (1922).

Bald, R. C.: "Lamb and the Elizabethans," in
Studies in Honor of A. H. R. Fairchild, ed.
by C. J. Prouty (Columbia, Univ. of Mis-
souri, 1946).

Bensusan, S. L.: Charles Lamb (New York,
Dodge, 1912).

Birrell, A.: Obiter Dicta, Second Ser. (London,
Stock, 1885, 1888; New York, Scribner).

Bradford, G.: Bare Souls (New York, Harper,
1924). Same article in Century Mag.,
109:73 (1924).

Dawson, W. J.: The Makers of English Prose
(New York and London, Revell, 1906).

De Quincey, T.: "Recollections of Charles
Lamb," Tait's Mag., April and June, 1838;
Collected Writings, ed. by Masson (Lon-
don, Black, 1889-90, 1896-97), 3, 85.

Dobell, B.: Sidelights on Charles Lamb (London, Dobell, 1903; New York, Scribner).

Elton, O.: A Survey of English Literature,
1780-1830, 2 vols. (London, Arnold, 1912,
1924).

Evans, B. I.: "Charles Lamb," Nine. Cent.,
116:674 (1934).

Foster, W.: The East India House (London,
Lane, 1924).

Harrison, F.: "Lamb and Keats," Tennyson,
Ruskin, Mill, and Other Literary Estimates
(New York and London, Macmillan, 1900,
1902).

Hazlitt, W.: "Of Persons One Would Wish to

Have Seen," The New Monthly Mag., Jan.,
1826; Collected Works, ed. Waller and
Glover (London, Dent, 1902-06; New York,
McClure), 12, 26.

Hine, R. L.: Charles Lamb and His Hertfordshire (New York, Macmillan, 1949).

Hunt, Leigh: Autobiography (London, Smith,
1850, 1906); 2 vols., ed. by R. Ingpen
(London, Constable, 1903; New York,
Dutton).

Hutton, L.: Literary Landmarks of London
(London, Unwin, 1885, 1888).

Iseman, J. S.: Charles Lamb and Sir Thomas
Browne (Cambridge, Mass., Harvard Univ.
Press, 1937).

Jerrold, W. C.: Charles Lamb (London, Bell,
1905).

Jerrold, W. C.: Thomas Hood and Charles
Lamb (London, Benn, 1930).

Johnson, E. C.: Lamb Always Elia (Boston,
Jones Marshall, 1935).

Johnson, E. C.: "Lamb and Coleridge," The
Amer. Scholar, 6:152 (1937).

Lake, B.: A General Introduction to Charles
Lamb (Leipzig, Seele, 1903).

Law, M. H.: The English Familiar Essay in
the Early Nineteenth Century (Philadelphia, Univ. of Pa. Press, 1934).

Macdonald, W. L.: "Charles Lamb, the Greatest of the Essayists," Pub. Mod. Lang.
Assn., 32:547 (1917).

May, J. L.: Charles Lamb (London, Bles,
1934).

More, P. E.: Shelburne Essays, First and
Fourth Ser. (New York and London, Putnam, 1906).

Morley, F. V.: Lamb before Elia (London,
Cape, 1932).

Pater, W.: Appreciations (London and New
York, Macmillan, 1889, 1895).

Patmore, P. G.: My Friends and Acquaintance,
3 vols. (New York, Saunders, 1854).

Paul, H.: Stray Leaves (London, Lane, 1906).

Robinson, H. C.: On Books and Their Writers,
3 vols., ed. by E. J. Morley (London, Dent,
1938).

Swinburne, A. C.: "Charles Lamb and George
Wither," Miscellanies (London, Chatto,
1886, 1911).

Symons, A.: Figures of Several Centuries
(London, Constable, 1916).

Tillyard, E. M. W.: Introduction to Lamb's
Criticism (New York, Macmillan, 1923).

Walker, H.: The English Essay and Essayists,
Chaps. 7, 9 (London, Dent, 1915; New
York, Dutton).

Williamson, C. C. H.: Writers of Three Centuries, 1789-1914 (London, Richards, 1920).

Winchester, C. T.: A Group of English Essay-

ists of the Early Nineteenth Century (New York, Macmillan, 1910).

Woodberry, G. E.: *Makers of Literature* (New York, Macmillan, 1901).

BIBLIOGRAPHY

Hutchinson, T.: In his edition of *The Works of Charles and Mary Lamb*, 2 vols. (London, Oxford Univ. Press, 1924).

Thomson, J. C.: *Bibliography of the Writings of Charles and Mary Lamb* (Hull, Tutin, 1908).

Walter Savage Landor 1775-1864

Selections, p. 985 — Critical Notes, p. 1376

EDITIONS

Works, 10 vols., ed. by C. G. Crump (London, Dent, 1891-93).

Complete Works, 16 vols., ed. by T. E. Welby and S. Wheeler (London, Chapman, 1927, 1936).

Poetical Works, 3 vols., ed. by S. Wheeler (Oxford, Clarendon Press, 1937).

Selections, ed., with a Preface, by S. Colvin (Golden Treasury ed.: London and New York, Macmillan, 1882, 1895).

Selections, ed. by W. B. S. Clymer (Athenæum Press ed.: Boston, Ginn, 1898).

Poetry and Prose, ed., with an Introduction and Notes, by E. K. Chambers (London, Oxford, 1946).

The Shorter Poems, ed. by J. B. Sidgwick (London, Cambridge Univ. Press, 1946; New York, Macmillan, 1947).

The Sculptured Garland (lyrical poems), ed. by R. Buxton (London, Dropmore, 1948).

Imaginary Conversations and Poems, a Selection, ed. by H. Ellis (Everyman's Lib. ed.: New York, Dutton, 1933).

Imaginary Conversations, selections, ed. by F. A. Cavenagh (London, Oxford Univ. Press, 1914).

Imaginary Conversations, ed., with an Introduction, by E. De Sélincourt (London, Oxford, 1914, 1931).

Imaginary Conversations, selected by T. E. Welby; ed. by F. A. Cavenagh and A. C. Ward (Bombay, Oxford Univ. Press, 1934).

The Pentameron and Other Imaginary Conversations, ed., with a Preface, by H. Ellis (Camelot ed.: London, Scott, 1889).

Last Days, Letters, and *Conversations*, ed. by H. C. Minchin (London, Methuen, 1934).

Letters and Other Unpublished Writings, ed. by S. Wheeler (London, Bentley, 1897).

Letters, Private and Public, ed. by S. Wheeler, (London, Duckworth, 1899).

BIOGRAPHY

Colvin, S.: *Landor* (English Men of Letters Ser.: London, Macmillan, 1878; New York, Harper).

Elwin, M.: *Savage Landor* (London and New York, Macmillan, 1941).

Forster, J.: *Walter Savage Landor*, 2 vols. (London, Chapman, 1869).

Whiting, L.: *The Florence of Landor* (Boston, Little, 1905, 1912).

CRITICISM

Aldington, R.: *Literary Studies and Reviews* (New York, Dial Press, 1924).

Bailey, J.: *Essays by Divers Hands*, 5, 63 (1925).

Boynton, H. W.: "The Poetry of Landor," *The Atlantic Monthly*, 90:126 (1902).

Bradley, W.: *The Early Poems of Walter Savage Landor. A Study of his Development and Debt to Milton.* (London, Bradbury, 1914).

Dawson, W. J.: *The Makers of English Prose* (New York and London, Revell, 1906).

De Sélincourt, E.: *Classicism and Romanticism in the Poetry of Walter Savage Landor* (Berlin, 1932).

De Sélincourt, E.: "Landor's Prose," *Wordsworthian and Other Studies* (Oxford, Clarendon Press, 1947).

De Vere, A.: "Landor's Poetry," *Essays, Chiefly on Poetry*, 2 vols. (New York, Macmillan, 1887).

Dowden, E.: *Studies in Literature* (London, Paul, 1878).

Elkin, F.: *Walter Savage Landor's Studies of Italian Life and Literature* (Philadelphia, Univ. of Pa. Press, 1934).

Elton, O.: *A Survey of English Literature, 1830-1880* (London, Arnold, 1920, 1932).

Evans, E. W.: *Walter Savage Landor: A Critical Study* (New York, Putnam, 1892).

Fyvie, J.: *Some Literary Eccentrics* (New York, Pott, 1906).

Goldmark, Mrs. Ruth I.: "The Influence of Greek Literature on Walter Savage Landor," *Studies in the Influence of the Classics on English Literature* (New York, Columbia Univ. Press, 1918).

Henderson, W. B. D.: *Swinburne and Landor* (London, Macmillan, 1918).

Henley, W. E.: *Views and Reviews* (Chicago, Scribner, 1890).

Mason, A. H.: *Walter Savage Landor, Poète Lyrique* (Paris, Les Presses Universitaires de France, 1924).

Morgan, C.: *Reflections in a Mirror*, Second Ser. (New York, Macmillan, 1947).

Payne, W. M.: *The Greater English Poets of*

the Nineteenth Century (New York, Holt, 1907, 1909).

Robinson, H. C.: *On Books and Their Writers*, 3 vols., ed. by E. J. Morley (London, Dent, 1938).

Saintsbury, G.: *Essays in English Literature, 1780-1860*, Second Ser. (London, Dent, 1895; New York, Scribner).

Scudder, H. E.: "Landor as a Classic," *Men and Letters* (Boston, Houghton, 1887).

Stedman, E. C.: "Introduction to Cameos," *Genius and Other Essays* (New York, Moffat, 1911).

Stephen, L.: "Landor's Imaginary Conversations," *Hours in a Library*, 3 vols. (London, Smith, 1874-79; New York and London, Putnam, 1897) ; 4 vols. (1907).

Swinburne, A. C.: *Miscellanies* (London, Chatto, 1886, 1911; New York, Scribner).

Symons, A.: "The Poetry of Landor," *The Atlantic Monthly*, 97:808 (1906) ; *The Romantic Movement in English Poetry* (London, Constable, 1909; New York, Dutton).

Wheeler, S.: "Landor: The Man and the Poet," *Nine. Cent.*, 91:236 (1922).

Williams, S. T.: "Walter Savage Landor as a Critic of Literature," *Pub. Mod. Lang. Assn.*, 38:906 (1923).

Woodberry, G. E.: *Literary Essays* (New York, Harcourt, 1920).

Woodberry, G. E.: *Makers of Literature* (New York, Macmillan, 1900).

BIBLIOGRAPHY

Welby, T. E. and Wheeler, S.: In *The Complete Works of Walter Savage Landor* (London, Chapman, 1936).

Wise, T. J. and Wheeler, S.: *A Bibliography of the Writings in Prose and Verse of Walter Savage Landor* (London, Blades, 1919).

James Macpherson 1738-1796

Selections, p. 86 — Critical Notes, p. 1246

EDITIONS

Poems of Ossian, trans. by James Macpherson (Boston, Phillips, 1852).

Works of Ossian, trans. by James Macpherson, ed. by W. Sharp (Edinburgh, Geddes, 1896).

Poems of Ossian, trans. by James Macpherson, ed., with an Introduction, Historical and Critical, by G. Eyre-Todd (Canterbury Poets ed.: London, Scott, 1888).

BIOGRAPHY AND CRITICISM

Fraser, G. M.: "The Truth about Macpherson's *Ossian*," *Quart. Rev.*, 245:331 (1925).

Moore, J. R.: "Wordsworth's Unacknowledged Debt to Macpherson's *Ossian*," *Pub. Mod. Lang. Assn.*, 40:362 (1925).

Nutt, A.: *Ossian and the Ossianic Literature* (Popular Studies in Mythology, Romance, and Folk-Lore, Ser. 3: London, Nutt, 1899).

Saunders, (T.) B.: *The Life and Letters of James Macpherson* (London, Sonnenschein, 1894; New York, Macmillan).

Shairp, J. C.: "The Poetry of the Scottish Highlands—Ossian," *Aspects of Poetry* (Oxford, Clarendon Press, 1881; Boston, Houghton, 1882).

Smart, J. S.: *James Macpherson: An Episode in Literature* (London, Nutt, 1905).

Snyder, E. D.: *The Celtic Revival in English Literature 1760-1800* (Cambridge, Mass., Harvard Univ. Press, 1923).

Van Tieghem, P.: *Ossian et l'Ossianisme dans le Littérature Européenne au XVIIIe Siècle* (Groningen, den Haag, Wolters, 1920). Same article in Van Tieghem's *Le Préromantisme* (Paris, Rieder, 1924).

BIBLIOGRAPHY

Black, G. F.: "Macpherson's *Ossian* and the Ossianic Controversy: a Contribution towards a Bibliography," *Bulletin of The New York Public Library*, 30:424, 508 (1926).

Nutt, A.: In his *Ossian and the Ossianic Literature* (1899).

David Mallet 1705-1765

Poems, p. 15 — Critical Notes, p. 1234

EDITIONS

Works, 3 vols. (London, Millar, 1759).

BIOGRAPHY AND CRITICISM

Johnson, S.: *The Lives of the English Poets* (London, 1779-81) ; 3 vols., ed. by G. B. Hill (London, Clarendon Press, 1905).

Thomas Moore 1779-1852

Poems, p. 450 — Critical Notes, p. 1312

EDITIONS

Poetical Works, ed. by W. M. Rossetti (Popular Poets ed.: London, Moxon, 1872, 1880).

Complete Poetical Works, ed., with a Biographical Sketch, by N. H. Dole (New York, Crowell, 1895).

Poetical Works (Home Lib.: New York, Burt, 1900).

Poetical Works, ed., with an Introduction, by A. D. Godley (London, Oxford Univ. Press, 1910; Boston, 1930).

Poems, selected by C. L. Falkiner (Golden Treasury ed.: London and New York, Macmillan, 1903).

Irish Melodies and Songs, ed., with an Introduction, by S. Gwynn (Muses' Lib.: London, Routledge, 1908; New York, Dutton).

Lalla Rookh (Home Lib.: New York, Burt, 1900).

Lalla Rookh (Handy Volume Classics: New York, Crowell, 1912).

Lyrics and Satires, ed. by S. O'Faoláin (Dublin, Cuala Press, 1929).

Tom Moore's Diary, a Selection, ed., with an Introduction, by J. B. Priestley (London, Cambridge Univ. Press, 1925).

BIOGRAPHY AND CRITICISM

Brandes, G.: *Main Currents in Nineteenth Century Literature*, 6 vols. (London, Heinemann, 1901-05; New York, Macmillan, 1906).

Brown, W. C.: "Thomas Moore and English Interest in the East," *Stud. in Phil.*, 34:576 (1937).

Garnett, R.: *Essays of an Ex-Librarian* (London, Heinemann, 1901).

Gosse, E.: *Leaves and Fruit* (New York, Scribner, 1927).

Gunning, J. P.: *Moore: Poet and Patriot* (Dublin, Gill, 1900).

Gwynn, S.: *Thomas Moore* (English Men of Letters Ser.: New York and London, Macmillan, 1924).

Jones, H. M.: *The Harp That Once—a Chronicle of the Life of Thomas Moore* (New York, Holt, 1937).

MacCall, S.: *Thomas Moore* (London, Duckworth, 1935; New York, Nelson).

Previté-Orton, C. W.: *Political Satire in English Poetry* (London, Cambridge Univ. Press, 1910).

Russell, Lord J.: *Memoirs, Journal, and Correspondence of Thomas Moore*, 8 vols. (1853-56; abridged ed., 1860).

Saintsbury, G.: *Essays in English Literature, 1780-1860*, First Ser. (London, Percival, 1890; New York, Scribner).

Stockley, W. F. P.: *Essays in Irish Biography* (Cork, University Press, 1933).

Strong, L. A. G.: *The Minstrel Boy: A Portrait of Tom Moore* (New York, Knopf, 1937).

Travis, J.: "Moore's *Irish Melodies*," *Cath. World*, 158:539 (1944).

William Motherwell 1797-1835

Poems, p. 1188 — Critical Notes, p. 1396

EDITIONS

Minstrelsy, Ancient and Modern, ed. by W.

Motherwell (Glasgow, 1827; Paisley, Gardner, 1873).

Poetical Works, ed., with a Memoir, by J. M'Conechy (Paisley, Gardner, 1881).

BIOGRAPHY AND CRITICISM

Minto, W.: In Ward's *The English Poets*, Vol. 4 (London and New York, Macmillan, 1880, 1911).

Stoddard, R. H.: *Under the Evening Lamp* (New York, Scribner, 1892; London, Gay).

Wilson, J.: "Motherwell's Poems," *Blackwood's Mag.*, 33:668 (1833).

"Christopher North" (See *Wilson*)

Thomas Parnell 1679-1718

Poems, p. 3 — Critical Notes, p. 1233

EDITIONS

Poetical Works, ed., with a Memoir, by G. A. Aitken (Aldine ed.: London, Bell, 1846, 1894; New York, Macmillan).

Poetical Works, with Churchill and Tickell (British Poets ed.: Boston, Houghton, 1854).

Minor Poets of the Eighteenth Century, ed. by H. I'A. Fausset (Everyman's Lib. ed.: New York, Dutton, 1930); contains all of Parnell's poems.

BIOGRAPHY AND CRITICISM

Cruickshank, A. H.: "Thomas Parnell; or, What Was Wrong with the Eighteenth Century," *Essays and Studies*, 11:57 (1925).

Doughty, O.: *English Lyric in the Age of Reason* (London, O'Connor, 1922).

Goldsmith, O.: *Life of Dr. Parnell* (1770), ed. by J. W. M. Gibbs in Goldsmith's *Works*, 5 vols. (Bohn Lib.: London, Bohn, 1884-86).

Johnson, S.: *The Lives of the English Poets* (1779-81), 3 vols., ed. by G. B. Hill (London, Clarendon Press, 1905).

Thomas Love Peacock 1785-1866

Poems, p. 1024 — Critical Notes, p. 1381

EDITIONS

Works, 3 vols., ed. by H. Cole, with a Preface by Lord Houghton (London, Bentley, 1875, 1888).

Collected Prose Works, 10 vols., ed. by R. Garnett (London, Dent, 1891).

Works, Halliford Edition in 10 vols., ed. by H. F. B. Brett-Smith and C. E. Jones (London, Constable, 1924-34; New York, Wells).

Poems, ed., with a Biographical Preface, by R. B. Johnson (Muses' Lib.: London, Routledge, 1906; New York, Dutton).

Novels, 2 vols. (New Universal Lib.: London, Routledge, 1905; New York, Dutton).

Novels, ed., with Introduction and Notes, by D. Garnett (London, Hart-Davis, 1948).

Pleasures of Peacock, comprising in whole or in part the seven novels, ed., with an Introduction, by B. R. Redman (New York, Farrar, Straus, 1947).

Letters to Edward Hookham and Percy B. Shelley, ed. by R. Garnett (London, 1910).

Plays, ed. by A. B. Young (London, Nutt, 1910).

Four Ages of Poetry, ed. by H. F. B. Brett-Smith (Oxford, Blackwell, 1921).

BIOGRAPHY AND CRITICISM

Able, A.: *George Meredith and Thomas Love Peacock* (Philadelphia, Univ. of Pa. Press, 1933).

Burdett, O.: *Critical Essays* (London, Faber and Gwyer, 1925; New York, Holt).

Draper, J. W.: "The Social Satires of Thomas Love Peacock," *Mod. Lang. Notes*, 33:456, 34:23 (1918; 1919).

Fedden, H. R.: "Peacock," in *English Novelists*, ed. by D. Verschoyle (New York, Harcourt, 1936).

Freeman, A. M.: *Thomas Love Peacock, A Critical Survey* (London, Secker, 1911; New York, Kennerley, 1913).

Garnett, R.: *Essays of an Ex-Librarian* (London, Heinemann, 1901).

Helm, W. H.: *Thomas Love Peacock* (Chicago, Browne, 1913).

Paul, H.: "The Novels of Peacock," *Stray Leaves* (London and New York, Lane, 1906).

Priestley, J. B.: *Thomas Love Peacock* (English Men of Letters Ser.: New York, Macmillan, 1927).

Saintsbury, G.: *Essays in English Literature, 1780-1860*, First Ser. (London, Percival, 1890; New York, Scribner).

Van Doren, C.: *Life of Thomas Love Peacock* (London, Dent, 1911; New York, Dutton).

Thomas Percy 1729-1811

Poems, p. 110 — Critical Notes, p. 1249

EDITIONS

Reliques of Ancient English Poetry (1765), 2 vols., ed. by C. C. Clarke (London, Cassell, 1877); 3 vols., ed. by H. B. Wheatley (London, Sonnenschein, 1876-77, 1891; New York, Macmillan, 1910).

Folio MS., 4 vols., ed. by J. W. Hales, F. J.

Furnivall, and F. J. Child, with a Life by J. Pickford (London, Trübner, 1867-68); ed. by I. Gollancz (London, De La More Press, 1905-10).

Northern Antiquities, 2 vols., translated from the French of P. H. Mallet (1770; Edinburgh, 1809; London, Bohn, 1844).

Percy Letters, 2 vols., ed. by D. N. Smith and C. Brooks (New Orleans, Louisiana State Univ. Press, 1944-46).

BIOGRAPHY AND CRITICISM

Dennis, L. A.: "Thomas Percy: Antiquarian vs. Man of Taste," *Pub. Mod. Lang. Assn.*, 57:140 (1942).

Doughty, O.: *English Lyric in the Age of Reason* (London, O'Connor, 1922).

Gaussen, A. C. C.: *Percy, Prelate and Poet*, with a Preface by Sir G. Douglas (London, Smith, 1908).

Watkin-Jones, A.: "Bishop Percy and the Scottish Ballads," English Association, London, *Essays and Studies*, 18:110 (1933).

OTHER BALLAD COLLECTIONS

Child, F. J.: *The English and Scottish Popular Ballads*, 5 vols. (Boston and New York, Houghton, 1882-98).

Gummere, F. B.: *Old English Ballads* (Athenæum Press ed.: Boston, Ginn, 1894, 1904).

Hazlitt, W. C.: *Remains of the Early Popular Poetry of England*, 4 vols. (London, Smith, 1864-66).

Laing, D.: *Select Remains of the Ancient Popular Poetry of Scotland* (Edinburgh, 1822); 2 vols. (London, Reeves, 1895).

Motherwell, W.: *Minstrelsy, Ancient and Modern* (Glasgow, 1827; Paisley, Gardner, 1873).

Ramsay, A.: *The Tea-Table Miscellany*, 4 vols. (Edinburgh, Donaldson, 1760; 4 vols. in 1, Dublin, Smith, 1794; 2 vols., Glasgow, Forrester, 1876).

Ritson, Joseph: *Ancient English Metrical Romances*, 3 vols. (London, Bulmer, 1802; Edinburgh, Goldsmid, 1884-86). *Ancient Songs and Ballads*, ed. by W. C. Hazlitt (London, Reeves, 1877). *Robin Hood*, 2 vols. (London, Nimmo, 1887).

Sargent, Helen Child, and Kittredge, G. L.: *English and Scottish Popular Ballads*, with an Introduction by G. L. Kittredge (Cambridge ed.: Boston, Houghton, 1904).

Scott, Sir Walter: *The Minstrelsy of the Scottish Border*, 3 vols. (Edinburgh, 1802-03); 4 vols., ed. by T. F. Henderson (Edinburgh, Blackwood, 1902); 1 vol., with an Introduction by A. Noyes (Edinburgh, Melrose, 1908; New York, Stokes, 1913).

Alexander Pope 1688-1744

Poems, p. 1203 — Critical Notes, p. 1398

EDITIONS

Works, 10 vols., ed., with an Introduction, by W. Elwin and W. J. Courthope (London, Murray, 1871-89).
Poetical Works, ed., with an Introductory Memoir, by A. W. Ward (Globe ed.: London and New York, Macmillan, 1869, 1896, 1907).
Complete Poems, ed. by H. W. Boynton; includes translation of Homer (Cambridge ed.: Boston, Houghton, 1903).
Prose Works, 2 vols., ed. by N. Ault (Oxford, Blackwell, 1936).
Selected Poems, ed. by L. I. Bredvold (New York, Crofts, 1926).
The Best of Pope, ed., with an Introduction, by G. Sherburn (New York, Nelson, 1929).
Poetry and Prose, ed. by H. V. Dyson (Oxford, Clarendon Press, 1933).
Selected Works, ed., with an Introduction, by L. Kronenberger (Modern Lib.: New York, Random House, 1948).

BIOGRAPHY AND CRITICISM

Chesterton, G. K.: "Pope and the Art of Satire," *Twelve Types* (London, Humphreys, 1902, 1910); *Varied Types* (New York, Dodd, 1903, 1909).
Edmunds, E. W.: *Pope and His Poetry* (London, Harrap, 1913).
Johnson, S.: *The Lives of the English Poets* (1779-81), 3 vols., ed. by G. B. Hill (Oxford, Clarendon Press, 1905).
Lowell, J. R.: *My Study Windows* (Boston, Osgood, 1871; Houghton, 1899).
Mackail, J. W.: *Studies of English Poets* (London and New York, Longmans, 1926).
More, P. E.: "With the Wits," *Shelburne Essays*, Tenth Ser. (Boston, Houghton, 1919).
Paston, G. (E. M. Symonds): *Mr. Pope, His Life and Times*, 2 vols. (New York, Putnam, 1909).
Root, R. K.: *The Poetical Career of Alexander Pope* (Princeton, Princeton Univ. Press, 1938).
Sherburn, G.: *The Early Career of Alexander Pope* (London, Oxford Univ. Press, 1934).
Sitwell, E.: *Alexander Pope* (London, Faber, 1930; New York, P. Smith, 1936).
Stephen, L.: *Alexander Pope* (English Men of Letters Ser.: London, Macmillan, 1880; New York, Harper).
Stephen, L.: "Pope as a Moralist," *Hours in a Library*, 3 vols. (London, Smith, 1874-79; New York, Putnam, 1899); 4 vols. (1907).
Stevenson, S. W.: *Romantic Tendencies in the*

Works of Dryden, Addison, and Pope (Baltimore, Johns Hopkins Press, 1934).
Sutherland, J. R.: *Wordsworth and Pope* (London, Oxford Univ. Press, 1944).
Tillotson, G.: *On the Poetry of Pope* (London and New York, Oxford Univ. Press, 1938).
Warren, A. A.: *Alexander Pope as Critic and Humanist* (Princeton, Princeton Univ. Press, 1929).

CONCORDANCE AND BIBLIOGRAPHY

Abbott, E.: *A Concordance to the Works of Alexander Pope* (London, Chapman, 1875; New York, Appleton).
Griffith, R. H.: *Alexander Pope; a Bibliography* (Austin, Univ. of Texas Press, 1922-27).

Winthrop Mackworth Praed
1802-1839

Poems, p. 1171 — Critical Notes, p. 1395

EDITIONS

Poems, 2 vols., ed., with a Memoir, by D. Coleridge (London, Moxon, 1864; New York, Widdleton, 1865; London, Ward and Lock, 1889).
Political and Occasional Poems, ed., with an Introduction, by G. Young (London, Ward and Lock, 1889).
Poems, ed., with an Introductory Note, by F. Cooper (Canterbury Poets ed.: London, Scott, 1888).
Poems, selections, ed., with an Introduction, by F. Greenslet (Boston, Houghton, 1909).
Select Poems, ed., with an Introduction, by A. D. Godley (London, Frowde, 1909).
Essays, ed. by G. Young, with an Introduction by H. Morley (London, Routledge, 1887).

BIOGRAPHY AND CRITICISM

Hudson, D.: *A Poet in Parliament* (London, Murray, 1939).
Previté-Orton, C. W.: *Political Satire in English Poetry* (London, Cambridge Univ. Press, 1910; New York, Macmillan).
Saintsbury, G.: *Essays in English Literature, 1780-1860*, First Ser. (London, Percival, 1890; New York, Scribner).
Smith, G. B.: "English Fugitive Poets," *Poets and Novelists* (London, Smith, 1876).
Whitmore, W. H.: "Praed and His Poems," *The North Amer. Rev.*, 89:536 (1859).

Bryan Waller Procter 1787-1874

Poems, p. 1194 — Critical Notes, p. 1397

EDITIONS

English Songs and Lyrics (1844; London, Bell, 1870).

*An Autobiographical Fragment and Biographi-
cal Notes*, ed. by C. Patmore (London,
Bell, 1877) ; ed. as *The Literary Recollections of Barry Cornwall* by R. W. Armour
(Boston, Meador, 1936).

BIOGRAPHY AND CRITICISM

Armour, R. W.: *Barry Cornwall: a Biography
of Bryan Waller Procter* (Boston, Meador,
1935).
Patmore, P. G.: *My Friends and Acquaintance*,
3 vols. (New York, Saunders, 1854).
Stedman, E. C.: *Victorian Poets* (Boston,
Houghton, 1875, 1884).
Symons, A.: *The Romantic Movement in English Poetry* (London, Constable, 1909 ; New
York, Dutton).
Whipple, E. P.: "English Poets of the Nineteenth Century," *Essays and Reviews*, 2
vols. (Boston, Osgood, 1849, 1878).

Allan Ramsay 1686-1758

Selections, p. 7 — Critical Notes, p. 1234

EDITIONS

Poetical Works, 2 vols., ed., with a Memoir,
by C. Mackay (London, Virtue, 1870).
Works, 2 vols., with a Life (Paisley, Gardner,
1877).
Poems (selections) ed., with a Biographical
Introduction, by J. L. Robertson (Canter-
bury Poets ed.: London, Scott, 1887).
Poems, ed. by H. H. Wood (Edinburgh, Oliver,
1940).
The Evergreen, 2 vols., ed. by A. Ramsay
(Edinburgh, Donaldson, 1761; Glasgow,
Forrester, 1876).
The Gentle Shepherd (London, Simpkin,
1891).
The Tea-Table Miscellany, ed. by A. Ramsay,
3 vols. (Edinburgh, 1724-27) ; 4 vols. in 1
(London, 1750) ; 2 vols. (Glasgow, 1876).

BIOGRAPHY AND CRITICISM

Eyre-Todd, G.: *Scottish Poetry of the Eight-
eenth Century*, 2 vols. (Glasgow, Hodge,
1896).
Gibson, A.: *New Light on Allan Ramsay*
(Edinburgh, Brown, 1927).
Holmes, D. T.: *Lectures on Scottish Literature*
(Paisley, Gardner, 1903).
Mackail, J. W.: "Allan Ramsay and the Ro-
mantic Revival," *Essays and Studies*,
10:137 (1924).
Martin, B.: *Allan Ramsay* (Cambridge, Mass.,
Harvard Univ. Press, 1931).
Shairp, J. C.: "Return to Nature Begun by
Allan Ramsay and Thomson," *On Poetic
Interpretation of Nature* (Edinburgh,

Douglas, 1877; New York, Hurd, 1878;
Boston, Houghton, 1885).
Smeaton, O.: *Allan Ramsay* (Famous Scots
Ser.: Edinburgh, Oliphant, 1896).
Walker, H.: *Three Centuries of Scottish Lit-
erature*, 2 vols. (Glasgow, MacLehose,
1893; New York, Macmillan).
Wilson, J. G.: *The Poets and Poetry of Scot-
land*, 2 vols. (Glasgow, Blackie, 1876; New
York, Harper).

Samuel Rogers 1763-1855

Poems, p. 233 — Critical Notes, p. 1271

EDITIONS

Poetical Works, ed., with a Memoir, by E.
Bell (Aldine ed.: London, Bell, 1856, 1892;
New York, Macmillan).
Poems (London, Routledge, 1890).
Reminiscences and Table-Talk, collected by
G. H. Powell (London, Johnson, 1903).

BIOGRAPHY AND CRITICISM

Boyle, E.: "Samuel Rogers, the Banker Poet,"
National Rev., 85:883 (1925).
Clayden, P. W.: *Rogers and his Contem-
poraries*, 2 vols. (London, Smith, 1889).
Patmore, P. G.: *My Friends and Acquaint-
ance*, 3 vols. (New York, Saunders, 1854).
Roberts, R. E.: *Samuel Rogers and his Circle*
(London, Methuen, 1910; New York, Dut-
ton).
Symons, A.: *The Romantic Movement in Eng-
lish Poetry* (London, Constable, 1909;
New York, Dutton).

Sir Walter Scott 1771-1832

Poems, p. 459 — Critical Notes, p. 1315

EDITIONS

Poetical Works, with a Biographical and Critical Memoir, by F. T. Palgrave (Globe ed.:
London and New York, Macmillan, 1866,
1907).
Poems, 5 vols., ed. by J. Dennis (Aldine ed.:
London, Bell, 1892; New York, Macmillan).
Poetical Works, 4 vols., with the Author's Introductions and Notes, and the Annotations
of J. G. Lockhart (Edinburgh, Oliphant,
1898; Philadelphia, Lippincott, 1900).
Complete Poetical Works, ed., with a Biographical Sketch, by H. E. Scudder (Cambridge ed.: Boston, Houghton, 1900).
Complete Poetical Works, 6 vols., ed., with
Introductions, by A. Lang (Boston, Estes,
1902) ; 1 vol. (London, Nimmo, 1905).

Poetical Works, ed. by J. L. Robertson (London, Oxford Univ. Press, 1904, 1913).

Poems (selections), ed. by J. C. Jordan (New York, Macmillan, 1928).

The Heart of Scott's Poetry, ed. by J. H. Holmes (London, Oxford Univ. Press, 1932).

Waverley Novels, 25 vols., ed. by Andrew Lang (Border ed.: London, Macmillan, 1902-04).

Waverley Novels, 25 vols. (Everyman's Lib. ed.: New York, Dutton, 1906).

Waverley Novels, 25 vols. (London, Oxford Univ. Press, 1912).

Miscellaneous Prose Works, 30 vols. (Edinburgh, Cadell, 1834-71; Black, 1870-82).

Journal, 1825-32, 2 vols., ed. by D. Douglas (Edinburgh, Douglas, 1890; New York, Harper, 1890, 1900).

The Journal of Sir Walter Scott, 3 vols., ed. by J. G. Tait and W. M. Parker (Edinburgh, Oliver, 1939-47).

Familiar Letters, 2 vols., ed. by D. Douglas (Edinburgh, Simpkin, 1893; Boston, Houghton, 1894).

Letters, 12 vols., ed. by H. J. C. Grierson, D. Cook, and Others (London, Constable, 1932-37).

Minstrelsy of the Scottish Border, 4 vols., ed. by T. F. Henderson (Edinburgh, Blackwood, 1902, 1932); 1 vol., with an Introduction by A. Noyes (Edinburgh, Melrose, 1908; New York, Stokes, 1913); ed. by T. F. Henderson (New York, Crowell, 1931).

BIOGRAPHY

Baikie, J.: *The Charm of the Scott Country* (New York, Macmillan, 1927).

Bayne, M.: *Sir Walter Scott: the Wizard of the North* (Edinburgh, Chambers, 1931).

Boas, L. C.: *A Great Rich Man: the Romance of Sir Walter Scott* (New York, Longmans, 1929).

Buchan, J.: *Sir Walter Scott* (London, Cassell, 1932).

Carswell, D.: *Sir Walter Scott: a Four-Part Study in Biography* (London, Murray, 1930, 1932); *Scott and His Circle* (New York, Doubleday, 1930).

Cruse, A.: *Sir Walter Scott* (London, Harrap, 1915).

Emerson, O. F.: "The Early Literary Life of Sir Walter Scott," *Jour. Eng. and Ger. Phil.*, 23:28, 241, 389 (1924).

Findlay, J. P.: *Sir Walter Scott, the Great Unknown* (Edinburgh, Nimmo, 1911).

Grierson, H. J. C.: *Sir Walter Scott, Bart.* (New York, Columbia Univ. Press, 1938).

Gwynn, S. L.: *The Life of Sir Walter Scott*

(Boston, Little, 1930; London, T. Butterworth, 1936).

Hudson, W. H.: *Sir Walter Scott* (London, Sands, 1901).

Hutton, R. H.: *Sir Walter Scott* (English Men of Letters Ser.: London, Macmillan, 1878, 1896; New York, Harper).

Ker, J. I.: *The Land of Scott* (London, Burrow, 1931).

Lang, A.: *Sir Walter Scott* (Literary Lives Ser.: London, Hodder, 1906; New York, Scribner).

Lockhart, J. G.: *Memoirs of the Life of Sir Walter Scott, Baronet*, 10 vols. (Edinburgh, 1839); 3 vols. (Boston, Houghton, 1881); abridged ed., 1 vol. (New York, Crowell, 1871; London, Black, 1880; Boston, Houghton, 1901).

MacCunn, F. A.: *Sir Walter Scott's Friends* (Edinburgh, Blackwood, 1909; New York, Lane, 1910).

Napier, G. G.: *Homes and Haunts of Scott* (London, Macmillan, 1907).

Norgate, G. Le G.: *Life of Sir Walter Scott* (London, Methuen, 1906).

Olcott, C. S.: *The Country of Sir Walter Scott* (London, Cassell, 1913; Boston, Houghton).

Olcott, C. S.: "The Courtship of Sir Walter Scott," *The Bookman*, 34:488 (1912).

Pagan, A. M.: *Scott and His Times* (Glasgow, Blackie, 1935).

Patten, J. A.: *Sir Walter Scott: a Character Study* (London, James Clarke, 1932).

Saintsbury, G.: *Sir Walter Scott* (Famous Scots Ser.: Edinburgh and London, Oliphant, 1897; New York, Scribner).

Stalker, A.: *The Intimate Life of Sir Walter Scott* (London, Black, 1921).

Stephen, L.: "The Story of Scott's Ruin," *Studies of a Biographer*, 3 vols. (London, Duckworth, 1898-1902; New York, Putnam).

Yonge, C. D.: *Life of Sir Walter Scott* (Great Writers Ser.: London, Scott, 1888).

CRITICISM

Ainger, A.: *Lectures and Essays*, 2 vols. (New York and London, Macmillan, 1905).

Bagehot, W.: "The Waverley Novels," *The National Rev.*, April, 1858; *Literary Studies*, 3 vols., ed. by R. H. Hutton (London and New York, Longmans, 1878-79, 1895).

Baker, E. A.: *The History of the English Novel*, 10 vols. (London, Witherby, 1924-1939).

Baldensperger, F.: "La Grande Communion Romantique de 1827: sous le Signe de

Walter Scott," *Revue de Littérature Comparée*, 7:47 (1927).

Ball, Margaret: *Sir Walter Scott as a Critic of Literature* (New York, Columbia Univ. Press, 1907).

Beers, H. A.: *A History of English Romanticism in the Nineteenth Century* (New York, Holt, 1901).

Brandes, G.: "Historical Naturalism," *Main Currents in Nineteenth Century Literature*, Vol. 4 (London, Heinemann, 1905; New York, Macmillan, 1906).

Brinton, C.: *The Political Ideas of the English Romanticists* (London, Oxford Univ. Press, 1926).

Brooke, S. A.: *Studies in Poetry* (New York, Putnam, 1907; London, Duckworth).

Canning, A. S. G.: *Sir Walter Scott Studied in Eight Novels* (London, Unwin, 1910; New York, Wessels).

Canning, A. S. G.: *History in Scott's Novels* (London, Unwin, 1905, 1907).

Carlyle, T.: *The London and Westminster Review* (1838); *Critical and Miscellaneous Essays*, 4 vols. (Boston, Houghton, 1880).

Cecil, E. C. D.: *Sir Walter Scott* (London, Constable, 1933).

Chesterton, G. K.: "The Position of Sir Walter Scott," *Twelve Types* (London, Humphreys, 1902, 1910); *Varied Types* (New York, Dodd, 1903, 1909).

Crockett, W. S.: *Footsteps of Scott* (New York, Jacobs, 1908; Boston, Phillips, 1914).

Crockett, W. S.: *The Scott Country* (Edinburgh, Black, 1902, 1911; New York, Macmillan).

Crockett, W. S.: *The Scott Originals* (Edinburgh, Foulis, 1911; New York, Scribner).

Dawson, W. J.: *The Makers of English Poetry* (New York and London, Revell, 1906).

Dawson, W. J.: "The Waverley Novels" and "Scott's Greatness," *The Makers of English Fiction* (New York and London, Revell, 1905).

Dixon, W. M.: *An Apology for the Arts* (London, E. Arnold, 1944; New York, Longmans, 1945).

Elliot, Col. F.: *Trustworthiness of the Border Ballads* (London, Blackwood, 1906).

Elliot, Col. F.: *Further Essays on the Border Ballads* (Edinburgh, A. Eliot, 1910).

Elton, O.: *A Survey of English Literature, 1780-1830*, 2 vols. (London, Arnold, 1912, 1924).

Fyfe, W. G.: *Edinburgh under Sir Walter Scott* (Edinburgh, Constable, 1906; New York, Dutton).

Gates, L. E.: *Studies and Appreciations* (New York, Macmillan, 1900).

Gray, W. F.: *The Scott Centenary Handbook* (Edinburgh, Grant and Murray, 1932).

Hay, J.: "Address at the Unveiling of the Bust of Scott in Westminster Abbey, 1897," *Addresses* (New York, Century, 1906).

Hazlitt, W.: *The Spirit of the Age* (London, Oxford, 1825); *Collected Works*, ed. by Waller and Glover (London, Dent, 1902-06; New York, McClure), 4, 241.

Herford, C. H.: *The Age of Wordsworth* (London, Bell, 1897, 1899; New York, Macmillan).

Hillhouse, J. T.: *The Waverley Novels and Their Critics* (Minneapolis, Univ. of Minn. Press, 1936).

Ker, W. P.: *Collected Essays*, 2 vols. (London, Macmillan, 1925).

Lang, A.: *Sir Walter Scott and the Border Minstrelsy* (London and New York, Longmans, 1910).

Lieder, P. R.: *Scott and Scandinavian Literature* (Northampton, Mass., Smith College Studies in Mod. Lang., 1920).

Macintosh, W.: *Scott and Goethe: German Influence on the Writings of Sir Walter Scott* (Glasgow, Fraser, 1925).

Marshall, E. G.: *Poetical Theories and Criticisms of the Chief Romantic Poets* (Ann Arbor, Mich., Edwards Brothers, 1926).

Morgan, A. E.: *Scott and His Poetry* (London, Harrap, 1913).

Muir, E.: *Scott and Scotland: the Predicament of the Scottish Writer* (London, Routledge, 1936).

Omond, T. S.: *The Romantic Triumph* (Edinburgh, Blackwood, 1900; New York, Scribner, 1900, 1909).

Pierce, F. E.: *Currents and Eddies in the English Romantic Generations* (New Haven, Yale Univ. Press, 1918).

Plarr, G.: "Walter Scott and Joanna Baillie," *The Edinburgh Rev.*, 216:355; 217:170 (1912, 1913).

Saintsbury, G.: "The Historical Novel," *Essays in English Literature, 1780-1860*, Second Ser. (London, Dent, 1895; New York, Scribner).

Shairp, J. C.: "The Homeric Spirit in Walter Scott," *Aspects of Poetry* (Oxford, Clarendon Press, 1881; Boston, Houghton).

Smith, J. C.: "Scott and Shakespeare," English Association, London, *Essays and Studies*, 24:114 (1939).

Stephen, L.: *Hours in a Library*, 3 vols. (London, Smith, 1874-79; New York and London, Putnam, 1899); 4 vols. (1907).

Stevenson, R. L.: "A Gossip on Romance," *Memories and Portraits* (London, Chatto, 1887).

Stokoe, F. W.: *German Influence in the English Romantic Period, 1788-1818* (Cambridge, Eng., The Univ. Press, 1926; New York, Macmillan).

Swinburne, A. C.: "The Journal of Sir Walter Scott," *Studies in Prose and Poetry* (London, Chatto, 1897).

Symons, A.: "Was Sir Walter Scott a Poet?" *The Atlantic Monthly*, 94:664 (1904); *The Romantic Movement in English Poetry* (London, Constable, 1909; New York, Dutton).

Vaughan, C. E.: *The Romantic Revolt* (Edinburgh, Blackwood, 1900; New York, Scribner, 1907).

Veitch, J.: *The History and Poetry of the Scottish Border*, 2 vols. (Glasgow, MacLehose, 1878).

Verrall, A. W.: "The Prose of Sir Walter Scott," *Collected Literary Essays* (London, Cambridge Univ. Press, 1913).

Watt, L. M.: *Scottish Life and Poetry* (London, Nisbet, 1912).

White, H. A.: *Sir Walter Scott's Novels on the Stage* (New Haven, Yale Univ. Press, 1927).

Williams, A. M.: "Scott as a Man of Letters," *Eng. Stud.*, 37:100 (1907).

Woodberry, G. E.: "The Prince of Prose Romancers," *Great Writers* (New York, McClure, 1907; Macmillan, 1912).

Woolf, V. S.: *The Moment and Other Essays* (New York, Harcourt, 1948).

Wyndham, G.: *Sir Walter Scott* (London, Macmillan, 1908).

Young, C. A.: *The Waverley Novels* (Glasgow, MacLehose, 1907).

KEY, DICTIONARY, AND SYNOPSES

Burr, A.: *Sir Walter Scott: an Index* (Cambridge, Mass., Harvard Univ. Press, 1936).

Grey, H.: *Key to the Waverley Novels* (London, Griffith, 1884; Long, 1898; Sonnenschein, 1899; New York, Bowman, 1910).

Husband, M. F. A.: *Dictionary of Characters in the Waverley Novels* (London, Routledge, 1910; New York, Dutton).

McSpadden, J. W.: *Waverley Synopses* (New York, Crowell, 1909, 1914).

BIBLIOGRAPHY

Anderson, J. P.: In Yonge's *Life of Sir Walter Scott* (Great Writers Ser.: London, Scott, 1888).

Ball, Margaret: In *Sir Walter Scott as a Critic of Literature* (New York, Columbia Univ. Press, 1907).

Corson, J. C.: *A Bibliography of Sir Walter Scott, 1797-1940* (Edinburgh, Oliver, 1943).

Ruff, W.: *A Bibliography of the Poetical Works of Sir Walter Scott* (Transactions of the Edinburgh Bibliog. Soc., 1937-38).

Worthington, G.: *A Bibliography of the Waverley Novels* (London, Constable, 1931).

Percy Bysshe Shelley 1792-1822

Selections, p. 653 — Critical Notes, p. 1335

EDITIONS

The Complete Works, 10 vols., newly ed. by R. Ingpen and W. E. Peck (London, Benn, 1926-30; New York, Scribner).

Poetical Works, 3 vols., ed. by R. H. Shepherd (London, Chatto, 1888); 2 vols. (1912).

Poetical Works, ed. by E. Dowden (Globe ed.: London and New York, Macmillan, 1890, 1907).

Complete Poetical Works, 4 vols., ed., with a Memoir, by G. E. Woodberry (Centenary ed.: Boston, Houghton, 1892; London, Paul, 1893).

Complete Poetical Works, ed., with a Memoir, by G. E. Woodberry (Cambridge ed.: Boston, Houghton, 1901, 1947).

Complete Poetical Works, ed. by T. Hutchinson (London and New York, Oxford Univ. Press, 1904, 1907, 1919); rev., with an introduction by B. P. Kurtz (1934).

Poems, 2 vols., ed., with an Introduction by A. Clutton-Brock, by C. D. Locock (London, Methuen, 1911).

Prose Works, 2 vols., ed. by R. H. Shepherd (London, Chatto, 1888, 1912).

Select Poems, ed., with an Introduction, by W. J. Alexander (Athenæum Press ed.: Boston, Ginn, 1898).

Select Poems, ed., with an Introduction, by G. E. Woodberry (Belles Lettres ed.: Boston, Heath, 1908).

Selected Poems, Essays, and Letters, ed. by E. Barnard (New York, Odyssey Press, 1944).

Poems, a selection with an Introduction by M. Bishop (London, Macdonald, 1949).

The Lyrical Poems and Translations, ed. by C. H. Herford (London, Chatto and Windus, 1918).

The Dramatic Poems, ed. by C. H. Herford (London, Chatto and Windus, 1922).

Correspondence of Shelley, 3 vols., ed. by W. Scott (London, Golden Cockerel Press, 1944-45).

Letters, 2 vols., ed. by R. Ingpen (London, Pitman, 1909, 1912; New York, Scribner, 1909; Macmillan, 1915).

Letters, ed. by R. B. Johnson (New York, Dodd, 1929).

New Shelley Letters, ed. by W. S. Scott (London, Lane, 1948).

The Best of Shelley, ed., with an Introduction, by N. I. White (New York, Nelson, 1932).

The Reader's Shelley, selections with Introduction, Bibliography, and Notes, by C. H. Grabo and M. J. Freeman (New York, Amer. Book Co., 1942).

Literary and Philosophical Criticism, ed. by J. Shawcross (London, Frowde, 1909).

Note Books, 3 vols., ed. by H. B. Forman (St. Louis, privately printed for W. K. Bixby, 1911).

The Cenci, ed. by G. E. Woodberry (Belles Lettres ed.: Boston, Heath, 1909).

A Defense of Poetry, ed., with an Introduction, by A. S. Cook (Athenæum Press ed.: Boston, Ginn, 1890).

An Apology for Poetry, with Browning's Essay on Shelley, ed. by L. Winstanley (Belles Lettres ed.: Boston, Heath, 1911).

Peacock's *Four Ages of Poetry*, Shelley's *Defense of Poetry*, Browning's *Essay on Shelley*, ed. by H. F. B. Brett-Smith (Oxford, Blackwell, 1921).

BIOGRAPHY

Angeli, H. R.: *Shelley and His Friends in Italy* (London, Methuen, 1911; New York, Brentano).

Blunden, E. C.: *Shelley: a Life Story* (London, Collins, 1946; New York, Viking Press, 1947).

Clutton-Brock, A.: *Shelley, the Man and the Poet* (New York, Putnam, 1909; London, Methuen).

Dowden, E.: *The Life of P. B. Shelley*, 2 vols. (London, Paul, 1886, 1896; New York, Scribner).

Godwin, W.: *The Elopement of Shelley and Mary Wollstonecraft Godwin*, ed. by H. B. Forman (St. Louis, privately printed for W. K. Bixby, 1912).

Gribble, F.: *The Romantic Life of Shelley, and the Sequel* (New York, Putnam, 1911).

Grylls, R. G.: *Mary Shelley: a Biography* (London, Oxford, 1938).

Hogg, T. J.: *The Life of Percy Bysshe Shelley*, 2 vols. (London, Moxon, 1858); 1 vol., with an Introduction, by E. Dowden (London, Routledge, 1906; New York, Dutton).

Hogg, T. J.: *Shelley at Oxford*, with an Introduction by R. A. Streatfeild (London, Methuen, 1904).

Ingpen, R.: *Shelley in England* (Boston, Houghton, 1916; London, Paul, 1917).

Liptzin, S.: *Shelley in Germany* (New York, Columbia Univ. Press, 1924).

Marshall, Mrs. J.: *Life and Letters of Mary Wollstonecraft Shelley*, 2 vols. (London, Bentley, 1889).

Maurois, A.: *Ariel, a Shelley Romance*, trans. from the French by Ella D'Arcy (London, Lane, 1924, 1930; New York, Appleton).

Medwin, T.: *Life of Shelley*, 2 vols. (1847); ed. by H. B. Forman (Oxford, Clarendon Press, 1913).

Peacock, T. L.: *Memoirs of Shelley, with Shelley's Letters to Peacock* (London, Bentley, 1875; Frowde, 1909; New York, Oxford Univ. Press).

Peck, W. E.: *Shelley, His Life and Work*, 2 vols. (Boston, Houghton, 1927).

Reed, M.: *Love Affairs of Literary Men* (New York, Putnam, 1907).

Salt, H. S.: *P. B. Shelley, Poet and Pioneer*, a Biographical Study (London, Reeves, 1896).

Sharp, William: *Life of Shelley* (Great Writers Ser.: London, Scott, 1887; New York, Scribner).

Shelley, Mary W. G.: *Journal*, ed. by F. L. Jones (Norman, Univ. of Okla. Press, 1947).

Shelley, Mary W. G.: *Letters*, 2 vols., ed. by F. L. Jones (Norman, Univ. of Okla. Press, 1944).

Symonds, J. A.: *Shelley* (English Men of Letters Ser.: London, Macmillan, 1878, 1887; New York, Harper).

Trelawny, E. J.: *Recollections of the Last Days of Shelley and Byron* (London, Moxon, 1858); *Records of Shelley, Byron, and the Author* (London, Pickering, 1878; Frowde, 1906; New York, Dutton, 1905; Oxford Univ. Press, 1906).

White, N. I.: *Shelley*, 2 vols. (New York, Knopf, 1940; London, Secker and Warburg, 1947; rev. as *Portrait of Shelley*, 1 vol., New York, Knopf, 1945).

CRITICISM

Arnold, M.: *Essays in Criticism*, Second Ser. (London and New York, Macmillan, 1888).

Bailey, R.: *Shelley* (London, Duckworth, 1934).

Baker, C.: *Shelley's Major Poetry: the Fabric of a Vision* (Princeton, Princeton Univ. Press, 1948).

Bald, M. A.: "Shelley's Mental Progress," *Essays and Studies*, 10:112 (Oxford, Clarendon Press, 1928).

Barnard, E.: *Shelley's Religion* (Minneapolis, Univ. of Minn. Press, 1937).

Barrell, J.: *Shelley and the Thought of His Time* (New Haven, Yale Univ. Press, 1947).

Bates, E. S.: "Mad Shelley: a Study in the Origins of English Romanticism," *Fred Newton Scott Anniversary Papers* (Chicago, Univ. of Chicago Press, 1929).

Blunden, E. C. (ed.): *Shelley and Keats as They Struck Their Contemporaries* (London, Beaumont, 1925).

Bradley, A. C.: "Shelley's View of Poetry," *Oxford Lectures on Poetry* (London, Macmillan, 1909, 1911).

Brailsford, H. N.: *Shelley, Godwin, and Their Circle* (Home Univ. Lib.: New York, Holt, 1913; London, Williams).

Brandes, G.: *Main Currents in Nineteenth Century Literature*, Vol. 4 (London, Heinemann, 1905; New York, Macmillan, 1906).

Brinton, C.: *The Political Ideas of the English Romanticists* (London, Oxford Univ. Press, 1926).

Brooke, S. A.: *Naturalism in English Poetry* (New York, Dutton, 1920).

Buck, P. M.: "The Empire of Beauty: Shelley," *Social Forces in Modern Literature* (Boston, Ginn, 1913).

Bush, D.: *Mythology and the Romantic Tradition in English Poetry* (Cambridge, Mass., Harvard Univ. Press, 1937).

Cameron, K. N.: "The Political Symbolism of Prometheus Unbound," *Pub. Mod. Lang. Assn.*, 58:728 (1943).

Cameron, K. N.: "The Social Philosophy of Shelley," *Sewanee Rev.*, 50:457 (1942).

Campbell, Mrs. O. W.: *Shelley and the Unromantics* (London, Methuen, 1924; New York, Scribner).

Carpenter, E. and Barnefield, G.: *The Psychology of the Poet Shelley* (London, Allen and Unwin, 1925; New York, Dutton).

Clark, D. L.: "Shelley and Shakespeare," *Pub. Mod. Lang. Assn.*, 54:216 (1939).

Clark, D. L.: "What Was Shelley's Indebtedness to Keats?" *Pub. Mod. Lang. Assn.*, 56:479 (1941).

Clarke, I. C.: *Shelley and Byron* (London, Hutchinson, 1934).

Dawson, W. J.: *The Makers of English Poetry* (New York and London, Revell, 1906).

Dodds, Mrs. A. E. Powell: *The Romantic Theory of Poetry* (New York, Longmans, 1926).

Dowden, E.: "Last Words on Shelley," "Shelley's Philosophical View of Reform," *Transcripts and Studies* (London, Paul, 1888, 1910).

Dowden, E., Garnett, R., and Rossetti, W. M.: *Letters about Shelley* (London and New York, Hodder and Stoughton, 1917).

Edmunds, E. W.: *Shelley and His Poetry* (New York, Dodge, 1912).

Elton, O.: *A Survey of English Literature, 1780-1830*, 2 vols. (London, Arnold, 1912, 1924).

Fairchild, H. N.: "Shelley and Transcendentalism," *The Romantic Quest* (New York, Columbia Univ. Press, 1931).

Firkins, O. W.: *Power and Elusiveness in Shelley* (Minneapolis, Univ. of Minn. Press, 1937).

Fogle, R. H.: "Romantic Bards and Metaphysical Reviewers," *Jour. of Eng. Lit. Hist.*, 12:221 (1945).

Fogle, R. N.: "Empathic Imagery in Keats and Shelley," *Pub. Mod. Lang. Assn.*, 61:163 (1946).

Gingerich, S. F.: *Essays in the Romantic Poets* (New York, Macmillan, 1924).

Gordon, G.: *Shelley and the Oppressors of Mankind* (London, Oxford Univ. Press, 1923).

Grabo, C. H.: *The Magic Plant: the Growth of Shelley's Thought* (Chapel Hill, Univ. of N. C. Press, 1936).

Grabo, C. H.: *A Newton among Poets: Shelley's Use of Science in "Prometheus Unbound"* (Chapel Hill, Univ. of N. C. Press, 1930).

Grabo, C. H.: *The Meaning of "The Witch of Atlas"* (Chapel Hill, Univ. of N. C. Press, 1935).

Grabo, C. H.: *"Prometheus Unbound," An Interpretation* (Chapel Hill, Univ. of N. C. Press, 1935).

Hughes, A. M. D.: *The Nascent Mind of Shelley* (London, Oxford Univ. Press, 1947).

Jack, A. A.: *Shelley: an Essay* (Edinburgh, Constable, 1904).

Jeaffreson, J. C.: *The Real Shelley*, 2 vols. (London, Hurst, 1885).

Jones, F. L.: "The Shelley Legend: a Refutation of the Book by R. M. Smith and Others," *Pub. Mod. Lang. Assn.*, 61:848 (1946).

Knight, G. W.: "The Naked Seraph," *The Starlit Dome: Studies in the Poetry of Vision* (London, Oxford Univ. Press, 1941).

Kurtz, B. P.: *The Pursuit of Death. A Study of Shelley's Poetry* (New York, Oxford Univ. Press, 1933).

Lea, F. A.: *Shelley and the Romantic Revolution* (London, Routledge, 1945).

MacDonald, D. J.: *The Radicalism of Shelley and Its Sources* (Washington, D.C., Catholic Univ., 1912).

Madariaga, S. De: *Shelley and Calderon* (London, Constable, 1920).

Marsh, G. L.: "The Early Reviews of Shelley," *Mod. Phil.*, 27:73 (1929).

Marshall, E. G.: *Poetical Theories and Criticisms of the Chief Romantic Poets* (Ann Arbor, Mich., Edwards Bros., 1926).

Meldrum, E.: "The Classical Background of Shelley," *Contemp. Rev.*, 173:160 (1948).

More, P. E.: *Shelburne Essays*, Seventh Ser. (New York and London, Putnam, 1910).

Norman, S.: "Shelley and the Greeks," *Nine. Cent.*, 137:245 (1945).

Payne, W. M.: *The Greater English Poets of the Nineteenth Century* (New York, Holt, 1907, 1909).

Power, J.: *Shelley in America in the Nineteenth Century* (Lincoln, Univ. of Neb. Press, 1940).

Propst, L.: *An Analytical Study of Shelley's Versification* (Iowa City, *Univ. of Iowa Humanistic Studies*, 1932).

Quiller-Couch, Sir A.: *Studies in Literature*, 2 vols. (New York, Putnam, 1922; London, Cambridge Univ. Press).

Raleigh, W.: *Some Authors* (Oxford, Clarendon Press, 1923).

Read, H. E.: *In Defense of Shelley, and Other Essays* (London, Heinemann, 1936).

Robertson, J. M.: *New Essays Towards a Critical Method* (London, Lane, 1897).

Rolleston, T. W.: *Introduction to Shelley's Philosophical View of Reform* (London, Milford, 1920).

Santayana, G.: *Winds of Doctrine* (London, Dent, 1913).

Shairp, J. C.: "Shelley as a Lyric Poet," *Aspects of Poetry* (Oxford, Clarendon Press, 1881; Boston, Houghton).

Shanks, E.: *First Essays on Literature* (London, Collins, 1923).

Shelley Society Papers (London, 1886-91).

Sickels, E. M.: *The Gloomy Egoist: Moods and Themes of Melancholy from Gray to Keats* (New York, Columbia Univ. Press, 1932).

Slicer, T. R.: *P. B. Shelley: An Appreciation* (New York, Everett, 1903).

Smith, R. M. and Others: *The Shelley Legend* (New York, Scribner, 1945).

Solve, M. T.: *Shelley: His Theory of Poetry* (Chicago, Univ. of Chicago Press, 1927).

Stephen, L.: "Godwin and Shelley," *Hours in a Library*, 3 vols. (London, Smith, 1874-79; New York and London, Putnam, 1899); 4 vols. (1907).

Stokoe, F. W.: *German Influence in the English Romantic Period, 1788-1818* (London, Cambridge Univ. Press, 1926; New York, Macmillan).

Stovall, F.: *Desire and Restraint in Shelley* (Durham, N. C., Duke Univ. Press, 1932).

Strong, A. T.: *Three Studies in Shelley* (London, Oxford Univ. Press, 1921).

Symons, A.: *The Romantic Movement in English Poetry* (London, Constable, 1909; New York, Dutton).

Thompson, F.: *Works*, 3 vols. (New York, Scribner, 1909, 1913).

Thompson, F.: *Shelley* (London, Burns, 1909).

Tinker, C. B.: "Shelley Once More," *Yale Rev.*, n.s. 31, 1:87 (1941).

Ullman, J. R.: *Mad Shelley* (Princeton, Princeton Univ. Press, 1930).

Walker, A. S.: "Peterloo, Shelley, and Reform, The Mask of Anarchy," *Pub. Mod. Lang. Assn.*, 40:128 (1925).

Weaver, B.: *Toward the Understanding of Shelley* (Ann Arbor, Univ. of Mich. Press, 1932).

White, N. I.: "Shelley's *Prometheus Unbound*: or, Every Man His Own Allegorist," *Pub. Mod. Lang. Assn.*, 40:172 (1925).

White, N. I.: *The Unextinguished Hearth: Shelley and His Contemporary Critics* (Durham, N. C., Duke Univ. Press, 1938).

Winwar, F.: *Romantic Rebels* (Boston, Little, 1935).

Woodberry, G. E.: *Literary Essays* (New York, Harcourt, 1920).

Woodberry, G. E.: *Literary Memoirs of the Nineteenth Century* (New York, Harcourt, 1921).

Woodberry, G. E.: *Makers of Literature* (New York, Macmillan, 1901).

Wylie, L. J.: *Social Studies in English Literature* (Boston, Houghton, 1916).

Yeats, W. B.: "The Philosophy of Shelley's Poetry," *Ideas of Good and Evil* (London, Bullen, 1903; New York, Macmillan).

CONCORDANCE

Ellis, F. S.: *A Lexical Concordance to the Poetical Works of Shelley* (London, Quaritch, 1892).

BIBLIOGRAPHY

De Ricci, S.: *A Bibliography of Shelley's Letters, Published and Unpublished* (London, Maggs Bros., 1927).

Forman, H. B.: *The Shelley Library*, an Essay in Bibliography (London, Reeves, 1886).

Wise, T. J.: *A Shelley Library* (Privately printed, 1925).

William Shenstone 1714-1763

EDITIONS

Poetical Works, ed., with a Critical Dissertation, by G. Gilfillan (London, Nisbet, 1854).

Poetical Works, ed. by C. C. Clarke (London, Cassell, 1880).

The Letters, ed. by M. Williams (Oxford, Blackwell, 1939).

Letters, ed., with an Introduction, by D. Mallam (Minneapolis, Univ. of Minn. Press, 1939).

The School-Mistress, a Poem, 1742 (London, Milford, 1924).

BIOGRAPHY AND CRITICISM

Ellis, H.: "William Shenstone," *The Dial*, 82:381 (1927).

Hazeltine, A. I.: *A Study of William Shenstone and of His Critics* (Menasha, Wis., Banta, 1918).

Humphreys, A. R.: *William Shenstone* (New York, Macmillan, 1937).

Johnson, S.: *The Lives of the English Poets* (1779-81); 3 vols., ed. by G. B. Hill (London, Clarendon Press, 1905).

Purkis, E. M.: *William Shenstone: Poet and Landscape Gardener* (Wolverhampton, Whitehead, 1931).

BIBLIOGRAPHY

Williams, I. A.: *Seven Eighteenth Century Bibliographies* (London, Dulau, 1924).

Robert Southey 1774-1843

Selections, p. 426 — Critical Notes, p. 1307

EDITIONS

Poetical Works, 10 vols. with a Memoir, by H. T. Tuckerman (Boston, Little, 1860); 10 vols. in 5 (British Poets ed.: Boston, Houghton, 1880).

Poems, ed. by M. H. Fitzgerald (London and New York, Oxford Univ. Press, 1909).

Poems, selections, ed. by E. Dowden (Golden Treasury ed.: London, Macmillan, 1895, 1930).

Ballads and Other Poems, ed. by C. J. Battersby (London, Blackie, 1899).

Correspondence with Caroline Bowles, ed. by E. Dowden (London and New York, Longmans, 1881).

Letters, ed., with a Preface, by J. Dennis (New York, Macmillan, 1881).

Letters, selected and ed., with an Introduction, by M. H. Fitzgerald (World's Classics: London, Oxford Univ. Press, 1912).

Select Prose, ed., with an Introduction, by J. Zeitlin (New York, Macmillan, 1916).

The Doctor (abridged), ed. by M. H. Fitzgerald (London, Bell, 1930).

The Life of Nelson, ed., with an Introduction, by H. B. Butler (London, Frowde, 1911); ed. by H. Newbolt (New York, Macmillan, 1925).

The Life of Wesley, 2 vols., ed. by M. H. Fitzgerald (New York, Oxford Univ. Press, 1925).

Journal of a Tour in Scotland in 1819, ed. by C. H. Herford (London, Murray, 1929).

BIOGRAPHY AND CRITICISM

Brinton, C.: *The Political Ideas of the English Romanticists* (London, Oxford Univ. Press, 1926).

Cameron, K. N.: "Shelley vs. Southey," *Pub. Mod. Lang. Assn.*, 57:489 (1942).

Cobban, A.: *Edmund Burke and the Revolt against the Eighteenth Century. A Study of the Political and Social Thinking of Burke, Wordsworth, Coleridge, and Southey* (London, Allen, 1929).

Dawson, W. J.: *The Makers of English Poetry* (New York and London, Revell, 1906).

Dennis, J.: *Studies in English Literature* (London, Stanford, 1876).

De Quincey, T.: "The Lake Poets," *Tait's Mag.*, July and August, 1839; *Collected Writings*, ed. by Masson (London, Black, 1889-90, 1896-97), 2, 303, 335.

Dowden, E.: *Southey* (English Men of Letters Ser.: London, Macmillan, 1876; New York, Harper).

Dowden, E.: "Early Revolutionary Group and Antagonists," *The French Revolution and English Literature* (New York, Scribner, 1897, 1908).

Elwin, M.: *The First Romantics* (London, Macdonald, 1947; New York, Longmans, 1948).

Haller, W.: *The Early Life of Robert Southey, 1774-1803* (New York, Columbia Univ. Press, 1917).

Haller, W.: "Southey's Later Radicalism," *Pub. Mod. Lang. Assn.*, 37:281 (1922).

Marshall, E. G.: *Poetical Theories and Criticism of the Chief Romantic Poets* (Ann Arbor, Mich., Edwards Bros., 1926).

Rawnsley, H. D.: *Literary Associations of the English Lakes*, 2 vols. (Glasgow, MacLehose, 1894, 1906).

Saintsbury, G.: *Essays in English Literature, 1780-1860*, Second Ser. (London, Dent, 1895; New York, Scribner).

Simmons, J.: *Southey* (London, Collins, 1945; New Haven, Yale Univ. Press, 1948).

Southey, C. C.: *Life and Correspondence of Robert Southey*, ed. in 6 vols. (London, Longmans, 1849-50).

Stephen, L.: "Southey's Letters," *Studies of a Biographer*, 4 vols. (London, Duckworth, 1898-1902; New York, Putnam).

Symons, A.: *The Romantic Movement in English Poetry* (London, Constable, 1909; New York, Dutton).

James Thomson 1700-1748

Poems, p. 18 — Critical Notes, p. 1235

EDITIONS

Poetical Works, 2 vols., ed. by B. Dobell (London, Reeves, 1895).

Poetical Works, 2 vols., ed. by D. C. Tovey (Aldine ed.: London, Bell, 1897; New York, Macmillan).

Complete Poetical Works, ed. by J. L. Robertson (London, Oxford Univ. Press, 1908).

The Seasons, The Castle of Indolence, and Other Poems, 2 vols., ed., with a Critical Study by E. Gosse, by H. D. Roberts (Muses' Lib.: London, Routledge, 1906; New York, Dutton).

BIOGRAPHY AND CRITICISM

Bayne, W.: *James Thomson* (Famous Scots Ser.: Edinburgh, Oliphant, 1898).

Brooke, S. A.: *Naturalism in English Poetry* (New York, Dutton, 1920).

Cory, H. E.: "Spenser, Thomson, and Romanticism," *Pub. Mod. Lang. Assn.*, 19:51 (1911).

Douglas, G. B. S.: *Scottish Poetry* (New York, Macmillan, 1911).

Hazlitt, W.: *Lectures on the English Poets* (London, 1818); *Collected Works*, ed. by Waller and Glover (London, Dent, 1902-06; New York, McClure), 5, 85.

Johnson, S.: *The Lives of the English Poets* (1779-81); 3 vols., ed. by G. B. Hill (London, Clarendon Press, 1905).

Macaulay, G. C.: *James Thomson* (English Men of Letters Ser.: London and New York, Macmillan, 1908).

Mackail, J. W.: *Studies of English Poets* (London and New York, Longmans, 1926).

McKillop, A. D.: *The Background of Thomson's "Seasons"* (Minneapolis, Univ. of Minn. Press, 1942).

Shairp, J. C.: "Return to Nature Begun by Allan Ramsay and Thomson," *On Poetic Interpretation of Nature* (Edinburgh, Douglas, 1877; New York, Hurd, 1878; Boston, Houghton, 1885).

Horace Walpole 1717-1797

Selections, p. 100 — Critical Notes, p. 1248

EDITIONS

Works, 5 vols. (London, Robinson, 1798); 9 vols., ed. by Mary Berry (1798-1825).

The Castle of Otranto, ed., with Sir Walter Scott's Introduction and Preface, by Caroline Spurgeon (London, Chatto and Windus, 1923).

The Castle of Otranto and the Mysterious Mother, ed., with an Introduction, by M. Summers (London, Constable, 1924).

The Castle of Otranto (Everyman's Lib. ed.: New York, Dutton, 1930).

Last Journals: Memoirs of the Reign of George IV from 1771 to 1783, 2 vols., ed. by A. F. Steuart (London and New York, Lane, 1909).

Letters, 16 vols., ed. by Mrs. Paget Toynbee (Oxford, Clarendon Press, 1903).

Correspondence, 14 vols., ed. by W. S. Lewis, W. H. Smith, and Others (Yale ed.: New Haven, Yale Univ. Press, 1937-48).

Letters, selections, ed. by C. B. Lucas (London, Newnes, 1904; New York, Scribner).

Letters, 2 vols., selected and ed. by W. S. Lewis (New York and London, Harper, 1926).

Correspondence with Thomas Gray, Richard West, and Thomas Ashton, ed. by W. S. Lewis and Others (New Haven, Yale Univ. Press, 1948).

BIOGRAPHY AND CRITICISM

Benjamin, L. S. (L. Melville): *Horace Walpole* (London, Hutchinson, 1930).

Birkhead, Edith: *The Tale of Terror. A Study of the Gothic Romance* (New York, Dutton, 1921; London, Hodder).

Bradford, G.: *Bare Souls* (New York and London, Harper, 1924). Same article in *Harper's Mag.*, 149:114 (1924).

Dobson, A.: *Horace Walpole, A Memoir* (New York, Harper, 1890, 1910); ed. by P. Toynbee (1927); rev. (New York, Oxford Univ. Press, 1932).

Edge, J. H.: *Horace Walpole, the Great Letter-Writer* (Dublin, 1913).

Greenwood, Alice D.: *Horace Walpole's World* (London, Bell, 1913; New York, Macmillan).

Gwynn, S. L.: *The Life of Horace Walpole* (Boston, Houghton, 1932).

Ker, W. P.: *Collected Essays*, 2 vols. (London, Macmillan, 1925).

Ketton-Cremer, R. W.: *Horace Walpole* (New York, Longmans, 1940; London, Faber, 1946).

Mehrotra, K. K.: *Horace Walpole and the English Novel* (Oxford, Blackwell, 1934).

More, P. E.: "The Letters of Horace Walpole," *Shelburne Essays*, Fourth Ser. (New York and London, Putnam, 1906).

Morley, J.: *Walpole* (Twelve English Statesmen Ser.: London, Macmillan, 1889).

Railo, E.: *The Haunted Castle, a Study of the Elements of English Romanticism* (New York, Dutton, 1927).

Ridley, H. M.: "Great Friendships: Thomas Gray and Horace Walpole," *Canadian Mag.*, 60:328 (1922).

Robertson, W. G.: *Neglected English Classics* (Aberdeen, Wylie, 1920).

Stuart, Dorothy M.: *Horace Walpole* (English Men of Letters Ser.: New York, Macmillan, 1927).

Whibley, L.: "The Foreign Tour of Gray and Walpole," *Blackwood's Mag.*, 227:813 (1930).

BIBLIOGRAPHY

Hazen, A. T.: *Bibliography of Horace Walpole* (New Haven, Yale Univ. Press, 1948).

Hazen, A. T.: *Bibliography of the Strawberry Hill Press* (New Haven, Yale Univ. Press, 1942).

Joseph Warton 1722-1800

Selections, p. 80 — Critical Notes, p. 1245

EDITIONS

Essay on the Genius and Writings of Pope, 2 vols. (1765-82; London, Cadell, 1806).

The Three Wartons: a Choice of Their Verse, ed. by E. Partridge (London, Scholartis Press, 1927).

BIOGRAPHY AND CRITICISM

Chalmers, A.: *Works of the English Poets*, 21 vols. (London, Johnson, 1810).

Dennis, J.: "The Wartons," *Studies in English Literature* (London, Stanford, 1876).

Doughty, O.: *English Lyric in the Age of Reason* (London, O'Connor, 1922).

Gosse, E.: *Two Pioneers of Romanticism, Joseph and Thomas Warton* (London, Oxford Univ. Press, 1915).

MacClintock, W. D.: *Joseph Warton's "Essay on Pope,"* (Chapel Hill, Univ. of N. C. Press, 1933).

Morley, Edith J.: "Joseph Warton: a Comparison of His *Essay on the Genius and Writings of Pope* with His Edition of Pope's Works," *Essays and Studies*, 9:98 (1924).

Morley, Edith J.: "Joseph Warton's Criticism of Pope," *Mod. Lang. Notes*, 36:276 (1921).

Pattison, M.: "Pope and His Editors," *Essays, 1854-82*, 2 vols., ed. by H. Nettleship (Oxford, Oxford Warehouse, 1889).

Trowbridge, H.: "Joseph Warton on the Imagination," *Mod. Phil.*, 35:73 (1937).

Thomas Warton 1728-1790

Selections, p. 75 — Critical Notes, p. 1245

EDITIONS

Poetical Works, 2 vols., ed., with a Memoir, by R. Mant (Oxford, Rivington, 1802).

Observations on the Fairy Queen of Spenser, 2 vols. (London, Dodsley, 1762; London, Stower, 1807).

The History of English Poetry, 3 vols. (1774-81; London, Ward and Lock, 1870); 4 vols., ed. by W. C. Hazlitt (London, Tegg, 1871, 1875).

The Three Wartons: a Choice of Their Verse, ed. by E. Partridge (London, Scholartis Press, 1927).

BIOGRAPHY AND CRITICISM

Chalmers, A.: *The Life of Thomas Warton, B.D.*, in Chalmers's *British Poets* (London, 1810).

Dennis, J.: "The Wartons," *Studies in English Literature* (London, Stanford, 1876).

Doughty, O.: *English Lyric in the Age of Reason* (London, O'Connor, 1922).

Gosse, E.: "The Oxford Sausage," *Selected Essays* (London, Heinemann, 1928).

Havens, R. D.: *The Influence of Milton on English Poetry* (Cambridge, Mass., Harvard Univ. Press, 1922).

Havens, R. D.: "Thomas Warton and the Eighteenth Century Dilemma," *Stud. in Phil.*, 25:36 (1928).

Ker, W. P.: *Thomas Warton* (London, Oxford Univ. Press, 1911).

Ker, W. P.: *Collected Essays*, 2 vols. (London, Macmillan, 1925).

Rinaker, Clarissa: *Thomas Warton: a Biographical and Critical Study* (Urbana, Ill., Univ. of Ill. Stud. in Lang. and Lit., Vol. 2, No. 1, Feb. 1916).

John Wilson 1785-1854
"Christopher North"

Selections, p. 1179 — Critical Notes, p. 1396

EDITIONS

Works, 12 vols., ed. by J. F. Ferrier (Edinburgh, Blackwood, 1865-68).

Essays, Critical and Imaginative, 4 vols., ed. by J. F. Ferrier (Edinburgh, Blackwood, 1866).

Noctes Ambrosianæ, 4 vols., ed. by J. F. Ferrier (Edinburgh, Blackwood, 1864); 5 vols., ed. by R. S. Mackenzie (New York, Widdleton, 1872).

The Recreations of Christopher North, 2 vols. (Edinburgh, Blackwood, 1864).

Selections, ed. by J. S. Moncrieff and J. H. Millar (London, Isbister, 1904).

BIOGRAPHY AND CRITICISM

Douglas, G. P. S.: *The Blackwood Group* (Famous Scots Ser.: Edinburgh, Oliphant, 1897).

Elwin, M.: *Victorian Wallflowers* (New York, P. Smith, 1934).

Gordon, Mary: *Christopher North: A Memoir*, 2 vols. (Edinburgh, Edmonston, 1862).

Lowell, C. T.: *Christopher North and the "Noctes Ambrosianæ"* (Boston, Luce, 1928).

Saintsbury, G.: *Essays in English Literature, 1780-1860*, First Ser. (London, Percival, 1890; New York, Scribner).

Swann, E.: *Christopher North* (Edinburgh, Oliver, 1934).

Thomson, James: *Biographical and Critical Studies* (London, Reeves, 1896).

Walker, H.: *The English Essay and Essayists*, ch. 9 (London, Dent, 1915; New York, Dutton).

Winchester, C. T.: *A Group of English Essayists of the Early Nineteenth Century* (New York, Macmillan, 1910).

Anne Finch, Countess of Winchilsea 1661-1720

Poems, p. 1 — Critical Notes, p. 1233

EDITIONS

Poems, ed., with an Introduction, by Myra Reynolds (Chicago, Univ. of Chicago Press, 1903).

Poems (selections) ed. by J. M. Murry (London, Cape, 1928).

Minor Poets of the Eighteenth Century, ed. by H. I'A. Fausset (Everyman's Lib. ed.: New York, Dutton, 1930).

BIOGRAPHY AND CRITICISM

Doughty, O.: *English Lyric in the Age of Reason* (London, O'Connor, 1922).

Dowden, E.: "Noble Authoress," *Essays, Modern and Elizabethan* (New York, Dutton, 1910).

Gosse, E.: "Lady Winchilsea's Poems," *Gossip in a Library* (London, Heinemann, 1891).

Reynolds, Myra: *The Treatment of Nature in English Poetry between Pope and Wordsworth* (Chicago, Univ. of Chicago Press, 1896, 1909).

Robinson, Mabel: "Lady Winchilsea: a Modernist," *Sewanee Rev.*, 25:412 (1917).

Charles Wolfe 1791-1823

Poems, p. 458 — Critical Notes, p. 1315

EDITIONS

Remains of the Rev. Charles Wolfe, 2 vols., ed. by J. A. Russell (Dublin, Watson, 1825, 1846).

The Burial of Sir John Moore, and Other Poems, ed., with an Introductory Memoir, by C. L. Falkiner (London, Sidgwick, 1909).

William Wordsworth 1770-1850

Selections, p. 249 — Critical Notes, p. 1273

EDITIONS

Poetical Works, 11 vols., ed., with a Life by W. Knight (London, Simpkin, 1882-89); 8 vols. (London, Paterson, 1896; New York, Macmillan).

Complete Poetical Works, with an Introduction by J. Morley (Globe ed.: London and New York, Macmillan, 1888, 1905).

Poetical Works, 7 vols., ed., with a Memoir, by E. Dowden (Aldine ed.: London, Bell, 1892-93; New York, Macmillan).

Poetical Works, 5 vols., ed., with an Introduction, by T. Hutchinson (Oxford, Clarendon Press, 1895).

Poetical Works, ed. by T. Hutchinson (London, Oxford Univ. Press, 1896, 1911).

Complete Poetical Works, ed., with a Biographical Sketch, by A. J. George (Cambridge ed.: Boston, Houghton, 1904, 1947).

Poetical Works, 5 vols., ed., with Textual and Critical Notes, by E. De Sélincourt and H. Darbishire (London, Oxford Univ. Press, 1940-48).

Poems, 3 vols., ed., with an Introduction, by N. C. Smith (London, Methuen, 1908).

Poems (selections) ed. by E. Dowden (Athenæum Press ed.: Boston, Ginn, 1897).

Poems, selected and ed., with an Introduction, by G. M. Harper (New York, Scribner, 1923).

Selected Poems, ed. by A. Beatty (New York, Doubleday, 1937).

Lyrical Ballads, Reprints, ed. by E. Dowden (London, Nutt, 1891, 1898); ed. by T. Hutchinson (London, Duckworth, 1898, 1920); ed. by H. Littledale (London, Oxford Univ. Press, 1911).

Prose Works, 2 vols., ed. by W. Knight (Eversley ed.: London and New York, Macmillan, 1896).

Prefaces and Essays on Poetry, ed., with an Introduction, by A. J. George (Boston, Heath, 1892).

Prefaces, with Coleridge's Chapters on Wordsworth in *Biographia Literaria*, ed. by A. J. George (Belles Lettres ed.: Boston, Heath, 1906).

Literary Criticism, ed., with an Introduction, by N. C. Smith (London, Frowde, 1906).

Guide to the Lakes, ed., with an Introduction,

by E. De Sélincourt (London, Oxford Univ. Press, 1906, 1926).

Letters of the Wordsworth Family from 1787 to 1855, 3 vols., ed. by W. A. Knight (Boston and London, Ginn, 1907).

Letters of William and Dorothy Wordsworth, 7 vols., ed. by E. De Sélincourt (London, Oxford Univ. Press, 1935-38).

The Ecclesiastical Sonnets, a Critical Edition by A. F. Potts (New Haven, Yale Univ. Press, 1922).

The Prelude, ed., with an Introduction and Notes, by E. De Sélincourt (Oxford, Clarendon Press, 1926, 1934).

The Prelude, ed. by E. E. Reynolds (London and New York, Macmillan, 1932).

BIOGRAPHY

Bensusan, S. L.: *William Wordsworth: His Homes and Haunts* (New York, Dodge, 1912).

De Quincey, T.: "The Lake Poets," *Tait's Magazine*, Jan.-Aug., 1839; *Collected Writings*, ed. by Masson (London, Black, 1889-90; 1896-97), 2, 229, 303, 335.

De Sélincourt, E.: *Dorothy Wordsworth* (New York and London, Oxford Univ. Press, 1933).

Harper, G. M.: *William Wordsworth: His Life, Works, and Influence*, 2 vols. (New York, Scribner, 1916, 1929).

Harper, G. M.: *Wordsworth's French Daughter* (Princeton, Princeton Univ. Press, 1921).

Hazlitt, W.: "My First Acquaintance with Poets," *The Liberal*, 1823; *Collected Works*, ed. Waller and Glover (London, Dent, 1902-06; New York, McClure), 12, 259.

Herford, C. H.: *Wordsworth* (London, Routledge, 1930).

Knight, W. A.: *Coleridge and Wordsworth in the West Country* (New York, Scribner, 1914).

Legouis, E.: *La Jeunesse de William Wordsworth, 1770-98* (Paris, 1896); English translation by J. W. Mathews, as *The Early Life of William Wordsworth* (London, Dent, 1897, 1921).

Legouis, E.: *William Wordsworth and Annette Vallon* (London, Dent, 1922; New York, Dutton).

Legouis, E.: *Wordsworth in a New Light* (London, Milford, 1923; Cambridge, Mass., Harvard Univ. Press).

MacLean, C. M.: *Dorothy and William Wordsworth* (New York, Macmillan, 1927).

MacLean, C. M.: *Dorothy Wordsworth: The Early Years* (New York, Viking Press, 1932).

Meyer, G. W.: *Wordsworth's Formative Years* (Ann Arbor, Univ. of Mich. Press, 1943).

Moorhouse, E. H.: *Wordsworth* (Chicago, Browne, 1913).

Myers, F. W. H.: *Wordsworth* (English Men of Letters Ser.: London, Macmillan, 1881; New York, Harper).

Punch, C.: *Wordsworth: An Introduction to his Life and Works* (London, Allman, 1907).

Rannie, D. W.: *Wordsworth and His Circle* (New York, Putnam, 1907).

Rawnsley, H. D.: *Literary Associations of the English Lakes*, 2 vols. (Glasgow, MacLehose, 1894, 1906).

Robinson, H. C.: *Correspondence with the Wordsworth Circle (1808-66)*, 2 vols., ed. by E. J. Morley (London, Oxford Univ. Press, 1927).

Stephen, L.: "Wordsworth's Youth," *Studies of a Biographer*, 4 vols. (London, Duckworth, 1898-1902; New York, Putnam).

Woods, Margaret L.: *A Poet's Youth: Dealing with the Early Life of William Wordsworth* (New York, Liveright, 1924; London, Chapman and Dodd).

Wordsworth, Dorothy: *Journals*, 2 vols., ed. by W. A. Knight (London and New York, Macmillan, 1924).

Wordsworth, D.: *Journals*, 2 vols., ed. by E. De Sélincourt (London, Macmillan, 1942).

Wordsworth, D.: *Recollections of a Tour Made in Scotland*, ed. by J. C. Shairp (Edinburgh, Douglas, 1875, 1894).

Wordsworth, G. G.: "The Boyhood of Wordsworth," *Living Age*, 305:471 (1920).

Wordsworth, W.: *Letters, Prefaces, The Prelude*.

CRITICISM

Arnold, M.: *Essays in Criticism*, Second Ser. (London and New York, Macmillan, 1888).

Babbitt, I.: "The Primitivism of Wordsworth," *On Being Creative* (Boston, Houghton, 1932).

Babenroth, A. C.: *English Childhood; Wordsworth's Treatment of Childhood in the Light of English Poetry from Prior to Crabbe* (New York, Columbia Univ. Press, 1922).

Bagehot, W.: "Wordsworth, Tennyson, and Browning," *The National Rev.*, Nov. 1864; *Literary Studies*, 3 vols., ed. by R. H. Hutton (London, Longmans, 1878-79, 1895).

Barstow, M. L.: *Wordsworth's Theory of Poetic Diction: a Study of the Historical and Personal Background of the "Lyrical Ballads"* (New Haven, Yale Univ. Press, 1917).

Batho, E. C.: *The Later Wordsworth* (New York, Macmillan, 1933).

Beach, J. W.: *The Concept of Nature in Nineteenth Century English Poetry* (New York, Macmillan, 1936).

Beach, J. W.: "Expostulation and Reply," *Pub. Mod. Lang. Assn.*, 40:346 (1925).

Beach, J. W.: "Reason and Nature in Wordsworth," *Jour. Hist. Ideas*, 1:335 (1940).

Beatty, A.: *William Wordsworth: His Doctrine and Art in Their Historical Relations*, (Madison, Univ. of Wis. Studies in Lang. and Lit., No. 17, 1922, 1927).

Blunden, E. C.: *Nature in English Literature* (London, Hogarth Press, 1929).

Boas, F. S.: *Wordsworth's Patriotic Poems and Their Significance Today* (Eng. Assn. Pamph. No. 30, 1914).

Bradley, A. C.: *Oxford Lectures on Poetry* (London, Macmillan, 1909, 1911).

Brandes, G.: *Main Currents in Nineteenth Century Literature*, Vol. 4 (London, Heinemann, 1905; New York, Macmillan, 1906).

Brewster, P. G.: "The Influence of Popular Ballads on Wordsworth and Coleridge," *Stud. in Phil.*, 35:588 (1938).

Brinton, C.: *The Political Ideas of the English Romanticists* (London, Oxford Univ. Press, 1926).

Brooke, S. A.: *Naturalism in English Poetry* (New York, Dutton, 1920).

Brooke, S. A.: *Theology in the English Poets* (London, King, 1874; N. Y., Dutton, 1910).

Brooks, B. G.: "Wordsworth Reconsidered," *Nine. Cent.*, 126:577 (1939).

Brooks, C.: *The Well Wrought Urn* (New York, Harcourt, 1947).

Broughton, L. N.: *The Theocritean Element in the Works of William Wordsworth* (Halle, Niemeyer, 1920).

Buck, P. M.: "The Beginnings of Romanticism in England—Wordsworth," *Social Forces in Modern Literature* (Boston, Ginn, 1913).

Burton, M. E.: *The One Wordsworth* (Chapel Hill, Univ. of N. C. Press, 1942).

Bush, D.: *Mythology and the Romantic Tradition in English Poetry* (Cambridge, Mass., Harvard Univ. Press, 1937).

Caird, E.: *Essays on Literature and Philosophy* (New York, Macmillan, 1892, 1909).

Campbell, O. J.: "Sentimental Morality in Wordsworth's Narrative Poetry," (Madison, *Univ. of Wis. Stud. in Lang. and Lit.*, No. 11:21, 1920).

Campbell, O. J.: "Wordsworth Bandies Jests with Matthew," *Mod. Lang. Notes*, 36:408 (1922).

Campbell, O. J.: "Wordsworth's Aesthetic Development, 1795-1802," (Ann Arbor, *Univ. of Mich. Essays and Studies*, 1933).

Cerf, B.: "Wordsworth's Gospel of Nature," *Pub. Mod. Lang. Assn.*, 37:615 (1922).

Cobban, A.: *Edmund Burke and the Revolt against the Eighteenth Century: a Study of the Political and Social Thinking of Burke, Wordsworth, Coleridge, and Southey* (London, Allen, 1929).

Coleridge, S. T.: *Biographia Literaria* (1817), 2 vols., ed. by J. Shawcross (Oxford, Clarendon Press, 1907), chaps. 5, 14, 17-22.

Cooper, L.: "A Glance at Wordsworth's Reading," *Mod. Lang. Notes*, 22:83, 110 (1907); in *Methods and Aims in the Study of Literature* (New York, Harcourt, 1915, 1921).

Crofts, E. V.: *Wordsworth and the Seventeenth Century* (London, Oxford Univ. Press, 1940).

Dawson, W. J.: *The Makers of English Poetry* (New York and London, Revell, 1906).

De Quincey, T.: "On Wordsworth's Poetry," *Tait's Mag.*, 1845; *Collected Writings*, ed. Masson (London, Black, 1889-90; 1896-97), 11, 294.

De Sélincourt, E.: *Wordsworthian and Other Studies* (London, Oxford Univ. Press, 1947).

Dicey, A. V.: *The Statesmanship of Wordsworth* (Oxford, Clarendon Press, 1917).

Dodds, Mrs. A. E. Powell: *The Romantic Theory of Poetry* (New York, Longmans, 1926).

Duffin, H. C.: *The Way of Happiness: a Reading of Wordsworth* (Bristol, Sidgwick, 1947; New York, Macmillan, 1948).

Dunne, M. A.: "Wordsworthian Theory of Solitude," *Amer. Cath. Quart.*, 36:610 (1911).

Elwin, M.: *The First Romantics* (London, Macdonald, 1947; New York, Longmans, 1948).

Fink, Z. S.: "Wordsworth and the English Republican Tradition," *Jour. Eng. and Ger. Phil.*, 47:107 (1948).

Garrod, H. W.: *Wordsworth* (London, Oxford Univ. Press, 1923, 1927).

Garrod, H. W.: *The Profession of Poetry* (London, Clarendon Press, 1929).

Geen, E.: "The Concept of Grace in Wordsworth's Poetry," *Pub. Mod. Lang. Assn.*, 58:689 (1943).

Gingerich, S. F.: *Essays in the Romantic Poets* (New York, Macmillan, 1924).

Graham, W.: "The Politics of the Greater Romantic Poets," *Pub. Mod. Lang. Assn.*, 36:60 (1921).

Greenbie, Mrs. M. L.: *Wordsworth's Theory of Poetic Diction* (New Haven, Yale Univ. Press, 1917).

Grey, Edward (Viscount): *Wordsworth's Pre-*

lude. (London, Oxford Univ. Press, 1924) ;
in *Fallodon Papers* (London, Constable,
1926, 1927; Boston, Houghton, 1926).

Grierson, H. J. C.: *Milton and Wordsworth*
(London, Cambridge Univ. Press, 1937).

Griggs, E. L. (ed.): *Wordsworth and Coleridge: Studies in Honor of G. M. Harper*
(Princeton, Princeton Univ. Press, 1939).

Havens, R. D.: *The Mind of a Poet* (Baltimore, Johns Hopkins Press, 1941).

Hazlitt, W.: "On the Living Poets," *Lectures
on the English Poets* (London, 1818);
"Mr. Wordsworth," *The Spirit of the Age*
(London, 1825); *Collected Works*, ed.
Waller and Glover (London, Dent, 1902-
06; New York, McClure), 5, 156; 4, 270.

Herford, C. H.: *The Age of Wordsworth*
(London, Bell, 1897, 1899; New York,
Macmillan).

Housman, L.: "What Happened to Wordsworth," *The Atlantic Monthly*, 174:66
(1944).

Hudson, W. H.: *Wordsworth and His Poetry*
(London, Harrap, 1918).

Hutton, R. H.: "Dorothy Wordsworth's Scotch
Journal," "Mr. Morley on Wordsworth,"
"Wordsworth the Man," *Brief Literary
Criticisms* (London, Macmillan, 1906).

Hutton, R. H.: "The Genius of Wordsworth,"
Literary Essays (London, Strahan, 1871;
Macmillan, 1888, 1908).

Huxley, A.: "Wordsworth in the Tropics,"
Holy Face and Other Essays (London,
Fleuron, 1929).

Jack, A. A.: "Wordsworth (Basic or Elemental Poetry)," *Poetry and Prose* (London, Constable, 1911).

James, D. G.: *Scepticism and Poetry* (London,
G. Allen, 1937).

Knight, G. W.: *The Starlit Dome: Studies in
the Poetry of Vision* (London, Oxford
Univ. Press, 1941).

Knowlton, E. C.: "The Novelty of Wordsworth's *Michael* as a Pastoral," *Pub. Mod.
Lang. Assn.*, 35:432 (1920).

Lacey, N.: *Wordsworth's View of Nature, and
Its Ethical Consequences* (New York, Macmillan, 1948).

Leavis, F. R.: *Revaluation* (London, Chatto,
1936).

Lowell, J. R.: *Among My Books*, Second Ser.
(Boston, Houghton, 1876, 1884).

Lowell, J. R.: *Democracy and Other Addresses*
(Boston, Houghton, 1886).

Mabie, H. W.: "The Lake Country and Wordsworth," *Backgrounds of Literature* (New
York, Outlook, 1903).

Mackail, J. W.: *Studies of English Poets*
(London and New York, Longmans, 1926).

Madariaga, S. de: "The Case of Wordsworth,"

Shelley and Calderon (London, Constable,
1920).

Marshall, E. G.: *Poetical Theories and Criticisms of the Chief Romantic Poets* (Ann
Arbor, Mich., Edwards Bros., 1926).

Martin, A. D.: *The Religion of Wordsworth*
(London, G. Allen, 1936).

McKinsey, J. O.: *Wordsworth in a New Light*
(Cambridge, Mass., Harvard Univ. Press,
1923).

McNulty, J. B.: "Milton's Influence on Wordsworth's Early Sonnets," *Pub. Mod. Lang.
Assn.*, 62:745 (1947).

Mead, M.: *Four Studies in Wordsworth* (Menasha, Wis., Banta, 1928).

Miles, J.: *Wordsworth and the Vocabulary
of Emotion* (Berkeley, Univ. of Calif.
Press, 1942).

Moore, J. R.: "Wordsworth's Unacknowledged
Debt to Macpherson's *Ossian*," *Pub. Mod.
Lang. Assn.*, 40:362 (1925).

More, P. E.: *Shelburne Essays*, Seventh Ser.
(New York, Putnam, 1910).

Murry, J. M.: *Heroes of Thought* (New York,
Messner, 1938).

Myers, F. W. H.: *Wordsworth* (English Men
of Letters Ser.: London, Macmillan, 1881;
New York, Harper).

Noyes, R.: *Wordsworth and Jeffrey in Controversy* (Bloomington, Ind. Univ. Press,
1941).

Noyes, R.: "Wordsworth and Burns," *Pub.
Mod. Lang. Assn.*, 69:813 (1944).

Pater, W.: *Appreciations* (London and New
York, Macmillan, 1889, 1895).

Patton, C. H.: *The Rediscovery of Wordsworth*
(Boston, Stratford, 1935).

Payne, W. M.: *The Greater English Poets of
the Nineteenth Century* (New York, Holt,
1907, 1909).

Peek, K. M.: *Wordsworth in England* (Rosemont, Pa., Rosemont College, Peek,
1943).

Rader, M. M.: *Presiding Ideas in Wordsworth's Poetry* (Seattle, Univ. of Wash.
Press, 1931).

Rader, M. M.: "The Transcendentalism of
William Wordsworth," *Mod. Phil.*, 26:169
(1928).

Raleigh, W. A.: *Wordsworth* (London, Arnold,
1903; New York, Longmans, 1913).

Ralli, A.: "Wordsworth and His Critics,"
Queen's Quart., 49, No. 2, 101 (1942).

Read, H. E.: *Wordsworth* (London, Faber,
1949).

Rice, R. A.: *Wordsworth's Mind* (Bloomington, Indiana Univ. Studies, 1913).

Rice, R. A.: "Wordsworth Since 1916"
(Northampton, Mass., Smith College Stud.
in Mod. Lang., Jan., 1924).

Rickett, A.: "The Poet—William Wordsworth," *Personal Forces in Modern Literature* (London, Dent, 1906; New York, Dutton).

Roberts, E. C.: "The Ascendancy of Wordsworth," *The Contemporary Rev.*, 103:703 (1913).

Robertson, F. W.: *Lectures on the Influence of Poetry, and Wordsworth* (London, Paul, 1906).

Scudder, V. D.: "Wordsworth and the New Democracy," *The Life of the Spirit in Modern English Poets* (Boston, Houghton, 1895).

Shackford, M. H.: *Wordsworth's Interest in Painters and Pictures* (Wellesley, Mass., Wellesley Press, 1945).

Shackford, M. H.: "Wordsworth's *Michael*," *Sewanee Rev.*, 31:275 (1923).

Shairp, J. C.: "The Three Yarrows," "The White Doe of Rylstone," *Aspects of Poetry* (Oxford, Clarendon Press, 1881; Boston, Houghton).

Shairp, J. C.: "Wordsworth as an Interpreter of Nature," *On Poetic Interpretation of Nature* (Edinburgh, Douglas, 1877; New York, Hurd, 1878; Boston, Houghton, 1885).

Shairp, J. C.: "Wordsworth, the Man and the Poet," *Stud. in Poetry and Philosophy* (Edinburgh, Douglas, 1868, 1886; Boston, Houghton, 1880, 1887).

Sherwood, M.: *Undercurrents of Influence in English Romantic Poetry* (Cambridge, Mass., Harvard Univ. Press, 1934).

Smith, E.: *An Estimate of William Wordsworth by His Contemporaries, 1793-1822* (Oxford, Blackwell, 1932).

Smith, J. C.: *A Study of Wordsworth* (London, Oliver, 1944, 1946).

Smyser, Jane W., "Coleridge's Use of Wordsworth's Juvenilia," *Pub. Mod. Lang. Assn.*, 6: 419-26 (1950).

Sneath, E. H.: *Wordsworth: Poet of Nature and Poet of Man* (Boston and London, Ginn, 1912).

Sperry, W. L.: *Wordsworth's Anti-Climax* (Cambridge, Mass., Harvard Univ. Press, 1935).

Stallknecht, N. P.: *Strange Seas of Thought: Studies in Wordsworth's Philosophy of Man and Nature* (Durham, N. C., Duke Univ. Press, 1945).

Stephen, L.: "Wordsworth's Ethics," *Hours in a Library*, 3 vols. (London, Smith, 1874-79; New York and London, Putnam, 1899); 4 vols. (1907).

Stephen, L.: "Wordsworth's Youth," *Studies of a Biographer*, 4 vols. (London, Duckworth, 1898-1902; New York, Putnam).

Stork, C. W.: "The Influence of the Popular Ballad on Wordsworth and Coleridge," *Pub. Mod. Lang. Assn.*, 22:299 (1914).

Sutherland, J. R.: *Wordsworth and Pope* (London, Oxford Univ. Press, 1944).

Swinburne, A. C.: "Wordsworth and Byron," *Miscellanies* (London, Chatto, 1886, 1911; New York, Scribner).

Symons, A.: *The Romantic Movement in English Poetry* (London, Constable, 1909; New York, Dutton).

Thorpe, C. D.: "The Imagination: Coleridge vs. Wordsworth," *Phil. Quart.*, 18:1 (1939).

Thorpe, C. D.: "Wordsworth and Keats," *Pub. Mod. Lang. Assn.*, 42:1010 (1927).

Trilling, L.: "Wordsworth's *Ode: Intimations of Immortality*," *Eng. Inst. Annual for 1941* (New York, Columbia University Press, 1942).

Van Doren, M.: *The Noble Voice: a Study of Ten Great Poems* (New York, Holt, 1946).

Whitehead, A. N.: *Science and the Modern World* (New York, Macmillan, 1925).

Willey, B.: *The Eighteenth Century Background: Studies on the Idea of Nature in the Thought of the Period* (London, Chatto, 1940; New York, Columbia Univ. Press, 1941).

Wilson, J. D.: *Leslie Stephen and Matthew Arnold as Critics of Wordsworth* (New York, Macmillan, 1939).

Winchester, C. T.: *William Wordsworth* (Indianapolis, Bobbs, 1916).

Woodberry, G. E.: "Sir George Beaumont, Coleridge, and Wordsworth," *Stud. in Letters and Life* (Boston, Houghton, 1890); *Makers of Literature* (New York, Macmillan, 1901).

Woodberry, G. E.: *The Torch* (New York, Macmillan, 1905, 1912).

Worthington, J.: *Wordsworth's Reading of Roman Prose* (New Haven, Yale Univ. Press, 1946).

Wylie, L. J.: *Social Studies in English Literature* (Boston, Houghton, 1916).

CONCORDANCE

Cooper, L.: *A Concordance to the Poems of William Wordsworth* (New York, Dutton, 1911).

BIBLIOGRAPHY

Dowden, E.: In his edition of Wordsworth's *Poetical Works*, Vol. 7 (Aldine ed.: London, Bell, 1892-93; New York, Macmillan).

Knight, W.: In his edition of Wordsworth's *Poetical Works*, Vol. 8 (London, Paterson, 1896; New York, Macmillan).

Logan, J. V.: *Wordsworthian Criticism: a*

Guide and Bibliography (Columbus, Ohio State Univ. Press, 1947).

Tutin, J. R.: In the Globe ed. of Wordsworth's *Complete Poetical Works* (1888, 1905).

Wise, T. J.: *A Bibliography of the Writings in Prose and Verse of William Wordsworth* (London, R. Clay, 1916).

Edward Young 1683-1765

Selections, p. 33 — Critical Notes, p. 1237

EDITIONS

Poetical Works, 2 vols., ed., with a Life, by J. Mitford (Aldine ed.: London, Bell, 1834, 1871; New York, Macmillan).

Poems, ed., with a Memoir, by W. M. Rossetti (London, Ward and Lock, 1871).

Prose Works (London, 1765).

Conjectures on Original Composition, ed. by E. J. Morley (Manchester, Univ. Press; London and New York, Longmans, 1918).

BIOGRAPHY AND CRITICISM

Brooke, S. A.: *Naturalism in English Poetry* (New York, Dutton, 1920).

Clark, H. H.: "A Study of Melancholy in Edward Young," *Mod. Lang. Notes,* 39:129, 193 (1924).

Clark, H. H.: "The Romanticism of Edward Young," *Trans. of the Wis. Acad.,* 24:1 (1929).

Hazlitt, W.: "On Swift, Young, Gray, Collins, etc.," *Lectures on the English Poets* (London, 1818); *Collected Works*, ed. Waller and Glover (London, Dent, 1902-06; New York, McClure), 5, 104.

Johnson, S.: *The Lives of the English Poets* (1779-81); 3 vols., ed. by G. B. Hill (Oxford, Clarendon Press, 1905).

Kaufman, P.: "Heralds of Original Genius," *Essays in Memory of Barrett Wendell* (Cambridge, Harvard Univ. Press, 1926).

Lynd, R.: *The Art of Letters* (London, Unwin, 1920).

Mackail, J. W.: *Studies of English Poets* (London and New York, Longmans, 1926).

McKillop, A. D.: "Richardson, Young, and the *Conjectures,*" *Mod. Phil.,* 22:391 (1924).

Shelley, H. C.: *The Life and Letters of Edward Young* (Boston, Little, 1914).

Steinke, M. W.: *Edward Young's "Conjectures on Original Composition" in England and Germany* (New York, Stechert, 1917).

Thomas, W.: *Le Poète Edward Young* (Paris, Hachette, 1901).

Glossary
of Proper Names

The following glossary is meant to include all the proper names occurring in the text, with the following exceptions: names explained in the text itself; names explained in the footnotes or in the critical notes, especially names found in titles; names of imaginary persons and places, and of other persons and places not identified; names of very familiar persons and places reference to which is immediately clear.

The glossary aims to supply merely the specific information that is needed in connection with the names as they occur in the text.

Aaron. A high priest of the Israelites, and the brother of Moses. When the twelve rods of the tribes of Israel were placed in the tabernacle, Aaron's alone budded in confirmation of his appointment to the priesthood.

Abassides. A famous dynasty of caliphs at Bagdad, Asiatic Turkey, 749-1258.

Abbotsford. The residence of Sir Walter Scott on the River Tweed, Roxburghshire, Scotland.

Abel. The second son of Adam. He offered a more acceptable sacrifice than his brother Cain, and was slain by him out of jealousy.

Abelard. Peter Abelard (1079-1142), a noted French philosopher and theologian. He was the instructor and paramour of Héloïse. After their marriage, Abelard became a monk, and Héloïse retired to a convent. The story of their love is preserved in their letters, which have been frequently published. See Pope's *Eloisa to Abelard*.

Aberdeen. 1—(519, 521)—George Gordon, (1784-1860), 4th Earl of Aberdeen, a member of the Athenian Society, and the author of *An Inquiry into the Principles of Beauty in Grecian Architecture.* 2—(1140)—An important seaport in the county of Aberdeen, Scotland.

Aberdour. A small place on the Firth of Forth, near Edinburgh, Scotland.

Aberfoyle. A small village in Perthshire, central Scotland, near Loch Katrine.

Abora, Mount. See **Mount Abora.**

Aboukir. A seacoast village near Alexandria, Egypt, on the west side of Aboukir Bay. Here Admiral Nelson gained a decisive victory over the French fleet, Aug. 1, 1798.

Abram. First of the patriarchs and founder of the Hebrew race.

Abram, Heights of. The scene of Wolfe's victory over Montcalm, before Quebec, Sept. 13, 1759.

Abydos. A town in Asia Minor on the Hellespont, the scene of the romance of Hero and Leander.

Abyssinia. An empire in northeastern Africa.

Academy of Compliments. A popular treatise with the sub-title, *The Whole Art of Courtship, Being the Rarest and Most Exact Way of Wooing a Maid or Widow, by Way of Dialogue or Complimental Expressions.* Books of similar titles were published in 1655 and 1669.

Achilles. A Greek legendary warrior, son of Peleus and Thetis. He is the principal character in the *Iliad*, which is largely occupied with a quarrel with Agamemnon, leader of the Greek army, and his martial exploits. Achilles was noted for his heroism and his fierce passions. After defeating Hector, Achilles dragged his body around the walls of Troy.

Achitophel. A character in Dryden's *Absalom and Achitophel,* representing Anthony Ashley Cooper (1621-83), Earl of Shaftesbury, a noted English statesman.

Achray. A lake in western Perthshire, Scotland, near Stirling.

Acon. Acre (Akka), a seaport of Syria, which was taken by Richard Cœur de Lion in 1191.

Acroceraunian. The ancient name of a promontory in Epirus, Greece, formed by the end of a chain of hills called the Ceraunii Montes.

Acron. A Sicilian physician said to have conquered the plague in Athens in 430 B. C.

Actæa. A river goddess.

Actæon. A hunter, who saw Diana bathing, and who was changed by her into a stag, and killed by his own hounds.

Actium. A promontory on the coast of Acarnania, ancient Greece.

Addison. Joseph Addison (1672-1719), a noted English essayist; principal contributor to *The Spectator*.

Adelung. Johann Christoph Adelung (1732-1806), a noted German philologist and lexicographer; author of *Mithridates*, a general treatise on language, and of a Grammatico-critical Dictionary, regarded as superior to Johnson's.

Admetus. A mythological king of Thessaly, the husband of Alcestis.

Adon'. See **Adonis.**

Adonais. The name given by Shelley to Keats, and used by him as the title of a poem. See note on *Adonais*, p. 1349b.

Adonis. A beautiful youth, beloved by Venus. He was slain by a wild boar, and at Venus's request it was decreed that he should spend half the year in the upper world and the other half in the lower.

Adria; Adrian. The Adriatic Sea, lying east of Italy.

Adriatic. A sea lying east of Italy.

Adventures of the Hon. Capt. Robert Boyle. A book by W. R. Cheterode (1726).

Æææ. An island lying between Italy and Sicily, and fabled as the abode of Circe.

Ægean. A sea east of Greece.

Ægeria. In Roman mythology, one of the Camenæ (identified with the Muses), by whom Numa was instructed with regard to the forms of worship he was to introduce into Roman temples.

Ægeus. A mythological king of Athens. The Ægean Sea was, by tradition, named after him because he drowned himself in it.

Ægisthus. Son of Thyestes, in Greek mythology, slayer of Atreus, and paramour of Clytemnestra, whom he aided in the slaying of her husband, Agamemnon. He was slain by Orestes.

Æneas. The hero of Virgil's *Æneid*, and a prominent defender of Troy in Homer's *Iliad*. He was the son of Anchises and Aphrodite.

Æneid. An epic poem by Virgil, relating the wanderings of Æneas from Troy to various countries around the Mediterranean.

Æol. Æolus, god of winds.

Æolia. In ancient geography, the western coast of Asia Minor.

Æolian. Of or pertaining to Æolus, god of winds; of or pertaining to Æolia, in Asia Minor. The **Æolian harp** was a stringed instrument, usually placed where the wind would strike it and produce music. The **Æolian lyre** was the lyre of Pindar, a famous lyric poet, who belonged to the Æolian division of the Greek race.

Æolus. God of the winds.

Æonian. Eternal; lasting for eons.

Æschylus (5th century B. C.). One of the great tragic poets of Greece. He left Athens for the court of Syracuse in 468, in humiliation, according to Plutarch, at being defeated for the tragic prize by Sophocles.

Æson. In classic mythology, the father of Jason (noted for his quest of the Golden Fleece). Medea, the sorceress, at Jason's request, restored aged Æson to the vigor of youth.

Æsop. According to tradition, a Greek fabulist of the 6th century B. C.

Æthiopia. In ancient times, a country south of Egypt.

Æthon. One of the horses of the sun, named in Ovid's *Metamorphoses*.

Ætnean. Of or resembling Mt. Etna, a volcano in Sicily.

Affrico. A small stream near Landor's home in Fiesole, Italy. It was celebrated by Boccaccio in his *Ninfale*, and near it the stories of his *Decameron* were related.

Afton. A small river in Ayrshire, Scotland.

Agamemnon. An ancient king of Mycenæ and leader of the Greeks in the Trojan War. He is the subject of a tragedy by Æschylus, a Greek dramatist of the 5th century B. C.

Agave. Mother of Pentheus, King of Thebes. Pentheus was discovered watching the orgies of the Bacchæ in a wood near Thebes, and was torn to pieces by his mother and two sisters, in their frenzy.

Agra. A military and commercial city in a northwestern province of India, taken by the British in 1803.

Agrippa. Cornelius Heinrich Agrippa (1486-1533), a German philosopher and student of alchemy and magic. Numerous marvels are ascribed to him. See Thomas Nash's *The Unfortunate Traveller; or, The Life of Jack Wilton* (1594).

Ahasuerus. The name of a Jewish cobbler, according to a late legend, who refused Christ permission to rest when passing his house on the way to Calvary. The sentence pronounced by Christ was, "Thou shalt wander on the earth till I return." The story has frequently been used in literature and art.

Ailsa Rock. Ailsa Crag, a rocky island on the coast of Ayrshire, Scotland.

Aix. A city of France, near Marseilles, famous for its hot saline spring used by the Romans.

Ajax. A leading Greek hero in the Trojan War, noted for his size and strength.

Alban Mount. A mountain near Rome, Italy.

Alban's. See **Saint Alban's.**

Albin. A poetic name for Scotland.

Albion. A poetic name for England.

Albuera. A town in Spain; the scene of a victory of the British and their allies over the French in 1811.

Albyn. Same as Albin.

Alcæus (fl. 600 B. C.). A famous Greek poet.

Alcestis. A daughter of Pelias, and wife of Admetus, a king in Thessaly. She voluntarily died to save the life of Admetus, and was brought back from Hades by Hercules, or, according to another version of the story, by Proserpina. The legend is the subject of a tragedy by Euripides, a Greek dramatist of the 5th century B. C.

Alcibiades (5th century B. C.). An Athenian statesman and general.

Alcina. A fairy in *Orlando Innamorato*, an Italian romance by Boiardo (1434 ?-94).

Alexander the Great. King of Macedonia (336-323 B. C.). Immediately upon his accession he made himself master of all Greece. After conquering Persia and Egypt, he crossed the Indus River (327 B. C.), and invaded India.

Alexandria. A seaport of Egypt, near the westernmost branch of the Nile delta, on the Mediterranean.

Alexis. In Virgil's second *Eclogue* a beautiful youth beloved by the shepherd Corydon.

Alfonso. 1—(102)—Alfonso IX, King of Castile (1158-1214), surnamed "The Noble" and "The Good." 2—(651)—Alfonso X, King of Leon and Castile (1252-82), surnamed "The Wise" and "The Astronomer."

Alford. Halford, a village in Somersetshire, England.

Alfoxden. The large mansion and park, the home of Wordsworth in Somersetshire. See *My First Acquaintance with Poets* (p. 1059b, 51ff.).

Alfred. Alfred the Great, the famous King of the West Saxons (871-901), noted for his generous service to his people.

Allan-Bane. A gray-haired bard in *The Lady of the Lake.*

Allen. Bob Allen, a student at Christ's Hospital, contemporary with Lamb.

All-Foxden. See **Alfoxden.**

Alloway. A church not far from Burns's birthplace near Ayr, Ayrshire, Scotland.

Alp. Any one of the Alps Mountains.

Alpheus. In Greek mythology, a river god, represented originally as a hunter who fell in love with the nymph Arethusa. She fled from him and was transformed into a fountain; Alpheus then became a river.

Alphonso. See **Alfonso X.**

Amalek. A grandson of Esau, and prince of an Arab tribe, the Amalekites. When they attacked the Israelites in the desert, the Amalekites were driven off by Joshua and doomed to extermination.

Amalfi. A seaport of Italy, south of Naples.

Amalthea. A nymph who nursed the infant Jupiter.

Amarillis. The name of a rustic maiden or shepherdess, in various pastorals.

Amasis. An Egyptian king of the 6th century B. C.

Amazon. One of a race of female warriors, said to have dwelt in Scythia, famous in literature for their contests with the Greeks.

Amber. A name given by the Greeks to the Islands in the North Sea.

Amiens. A character in *As You Like It.*

Amiens, Peace of. A peace concluded at Amiens, France, between Great Britain, on the one hand, and France, Spain, and the Batavian Republic on the other.

Ammon. 1—The ancestor of a people called Ammonites, frequently mentioned in the Old Testament. 2—(1210)—Alexander the Great, King of Macedonia (336-323 B. C.), who boasted that he was a son of the Egyptian god Ammon.

Amoret. In Spenser's *The Faerie Queene*, the wife of Sir Scudamore. She is a type of feminine loveliness.

Amphion. A son of Jupiter and Antiope. By the music of his lyre, he caused stones to move and form themselves into a wall around Thebes.

Amphitrite. The wife of Neptune, god of the sea.

Anacreon (6th century B. C.). A Greek lyric poet.

Analogy. A theological treatise by Joseph Butler (1692-1752), an English theologian. The full title is *Analogy of Religion, Natural and Revealed, to the Constitution and Course of Nature.*

Anapos. A river in Sicily.

Anastasius. The title of a work by the English writer, Thomas Hope (1770-1831).

Anatomy of Melancholy, The. A book by Robert Burton (1576-1640), an English divine.

Anaxagoras (5th century B. C.). A famous Greek philosopher.

Ancient Pistol. See p. 1039b, n. 5.

Anderton's. A coffee house in Fleet St., London.

Andes. A mountain range along the west side of South America.

Andromache. The wife of Hector, leader of the Trojans in the Trojan War. The French Opera *Andromaque* was written by André Grétry (1741-1813).

Andromeda. A northern constellation, supposed to represent the figure of a woman chained. According to Greek legend, Andromeda was exposed to a sea monster, rescued by Perseus, and changed, after her death, into a constellation.

Angelo. See **Michelangelo**.

Angerbode. A famous giantess in Norse mythology.

Anio. A river in central Italy. It is noted for its beautiful valley and waterfall, 330 ft. high.

Ann, St. See **St. Ann**.

Annabella. A character in John Ford's *'Tis Pity She's a Whore* (1633).

Annan. A river in Dumfriesshire, Scotland.

Anne. Queen of England (1702-14).

Annecy. A town in eastern France.

Anson, Lord George. (1697-1762). An English Admiral.

Antiparos, Grotto of. Antiparos is an island of the Greek Archipelago, celebrated for a stalactite cavern.

Antoinette, Marie. See **Marie Antoinette**.

Antonine. Marcus Aurelius Antoninus (121-180), a celebrated Roman emperor and Stoic philosopher.

Antony and Cleopatra. A tragedy by Shakespeare.

Aonian Muses. The Muses of Aonia, an ancient district in Bœotia, Greece.

Aornos. In ancient geography, a rocky stronghold, situated near the Indus, taken by Alexander the Great from native defenders in 327 B. C.

Apennine. The central mountain system of Italy.

Aphrodite. At the marriage of Peleus and Thetis in Thessaly, Greece, Paris, son of Priam, King of Troy, awarded the golden apple to Aphrodite (Venus, goddess of love and beauty) as the most beautiful woman. This pleased Ares (Mars), the lover of Aphrodite, but aroused the wrath of Athena and Hera (Pallas, goddess of wisdom and war, and Juno, queen of heaven), and led to the fall of Troy. Aphrodite (Venus) fell in love with Adonis. See **Adonis**.

Apicius. A famous Roman epicure of the 1st century A. D.

Apis. The sacred bull worshiped by the ancient Egyptians.

Apocalypse. The revelation made to the Apostle John and recorded in *Revelation*.

Apollonian. Resembling Apollo, noted for his youthful beauty.

Apollo. One of the great Olympian gods; son of Jupiter and Latona. He was the god of music, poetry, and healing. As god of the sun, he was represented as driving the chariot of the sun through the sky and as sinking into the western ocean at evening. He slew the Python, a monstrous serpent dwelling in the caves of Mount Parnassus. He loved a beautiful youth named Hyacinthus, but accidentally slew him with a quoit. He was inspired by Cupid with love for a maiden, Daphne, who fled his advances, and escaped him by being changed into a laurel tree. Apollo's constant attributes were the bow, the lyre, and the laurel wreath.

Apollo Belvedere. A celebrated antique statue of Apollo in the Belvedere, a portion of the Vatican Palace in Rome.

Apollyon. The angel of the bottomless pit, in *Revelation*.

Appian. A Roman historian of the 2nd century A. D.

Appleby. A town in the county of Westmoreland, England.

Aquarius. A constellation supposed to represent a man standing with his left hand extended upward, and with his right pouring a stream of water out of a vase.

Arabia. A country of southwestern Asia, between the Red Sea and the Persian Gulf.

Arabian Nights, The. A famous and ancient collection of Eastern stories.

Arabic. The language spoken originally by the Arabians.

Arabie; Araby. Poetic names for Arabia.

Aragon. An ancient kingdom, now a part of northeastern Spain.

Arcadia; Arcadian. A picturesque district of the Peloponnesus, praised for the simplicity and contentment of its people, and represented as the home of pastoral poetry.

Arcadian Evocators. Beings of Phigalia, Greece who summoned up spirits of the dead.

Arcady. A poetic name for Arcadia.

Arcturi; Arcturus. A brilliant star in the northern hemisphere, the fourth in order of brightness in the entire heavens.

Ardalia. See note on *Life Passes not as Some Men Say*, p. 1379a.

Arden. A forest in *As You Like It;* the retreat of the banished Duke and of Rosalind.

Ardennes. In ancient times a large forest in Gaul (modern France).

Ares. Mars, god of war. See **Aphrodite.**

Arethusa. A nymph who, while bathing, was pursued by her lover, Alpheus, the river god. She fled under the sea to the island of Ortygia, where she was transformed into a fountain. Alpheus was changed into a river.

Argenis. A political allegory by John Barclay (1582-1621), said by Cowper to be the most amusing romance ever written.

Argo. The ship of the Argonauts.

Argonauts. The sailors who accompanied Jason in the Argo, in quest of the Golden Fleece.

Argos. The most ancient city in Greece.

Argus. In Greek legend, the guardian of Io. He was famous for his one hundred eyes. He was slain by Hermes.

Argyleshire. A county in western Scotland.

Ariadne. Daughter of Minos, King of Crete. She fell in love with Theseus, and gave him a clew of thread to guide him out of the labyrinth in case he should slay the Minotaur. Having fled with Theseus, she was abandoned by him on the Isle of Naxos. There Bacchus found her and married her.

Ariel. A tricky spirit in Shakespeare's *The Tempest.* See note on *With a Guitar: to Jane,* p. 1352a.

Arion. A Greek poet and musician in Lesbos. Returning from Sicily, after a successful musical competition, he was compelled to leap into the sea by sailors who are said to have robbed him; he was carried to shore by dolphins which had gathered to listen to his music.

Ariosto (1474-1533). A famous Italian poet.

Aristides. A celebrated Athenian statesman and general who was exiled through the influence of Themistocles, his rival, in 483 B. C. He was recalled in 480 because of his service at the Battle of Salamis, against the Persians.

Aristotle (384-322 B. C.). The most famous and influential of Greek philosophers. He was the author of a treatise on moral philosophy entitled *Nicomachean Ethics,* of a treatise on poetry entitled *Poetics,* and of other works.

Ark. See *Genesis* 6:14ff.

Armada. The fleet sent against England by Philip II of Spain in 1588.

Armida. A beautiful sorceress who ensnared Rinaldo, in Tasso's epic poem *Jerusalem Delivered* (1581).

Arno. 1—(95)—See note on *Fingal,* p. 1247b. 2—(395, 847)—A river of Tuscany, which flows into the Mediterranean.

Arpinum. An ancient town in Caserta province, Italy, the birthplace of Marius.

Arran. An island on the west coast of Scotland, noted for its lofty mountain peaks. It is the ancient seat of the Hamiltons, a noted Scotch family.

Art of Cookery. A cookbook by Mrs. Rundell, first entitled *Family Receipt-Book* (1810); in later editions, *Domestic Cookery.* It was one of Murray's most successful books. He paid £2,000 for the copyright.

Artemis. Diana, goddess of the moon and the chase. See **Diana.**

Arthur. A British chieftain of the 6th century, celebrated in Welsh, Breton, and old French romance.

Arve. A river in France and Switzerland, which waters the valley of Chamouni.

Arveiron. A small stream in eastern France, a branch of the River Arve.

Arviragus. Cymbeline's son, in Shakespeare's *Cymbeline,* who assumes the name of Cadwal.

Arvon. Carnarvonshire, a county in Wales, opposite the Isle of Anglesey.

Ascabart; Ascapart. A giant in the medieval romance *Bevis of Hampton,* said to have been 30 feet high. He was overthrown by Sir Bevis.

Ashe. A small village in the county of Surrey, England.

Ashtaroth. A general name of the Syrian deities. See *Paradise Lost,* 1, 422.

Ashur. Asshur, the highest god of the Assyrians.

Asmodeus. King of the Demons.

Aspatia. A character in Beaumont and Fletcher's *The Maid's Tragedy* (c1610).

Asphaltes. Asphaltites, an ancient name of the Dead Sea.

Assyria. An ancient empire in southwestern Asia.

Astræa. The goddess of justice.

Atalantis. A scandalous romance entitled *Memoirs of the New Atalantis,* written by Mrs. Mary Manley, a popular English writer of the early 18th century. The story is an account of the crimes of thinly disguised persons of high rank.

Athena. Goddess of wisdom and war. See **Aphrodite.**

Athenæus. A Greek rhetorician and philosopher of the 2nd century A. D. His *Deipnosophistæ* is a storehouse of quotations.

Athenè. See **Athena.**

Athol. A district in northern Perthshire, Scotland.

Atlantean. Resembling Atlas. See **Atlas.**

Atlantides. The Pleiades, daughters of Atlas.

Athenian Aberdeen. See **Aberdeen** (1).

Atlas. In classic mythology, a Titan, who was

supposed to support the pillars of heaven on his shoulders as a punishment for making war against Zeus.

Attic; Attica. Of or belonging to Attica, an ancient kingdom of Greece.

Attila. A famous King of the Huns (406?-453), surnamed "The Scourge of God" on account of the terrible destruction wrought by his armies.

Aubert, Peter. Probably Peter Auber, assistant secretary of the East India Company in 1820.

Auerstadt. A town in Saxony where the French defeated the Prussians in 1806.

Augereau. Pierre François Charles Augereau (1757-1816), a noted French marshal.

Augustine, St. Aurelius Augustinus (354-430), the most celebrated father of the Latin Church; author of *Confessions.*

Augustus. Augustus Cæsar, the first Roman emperor (31 B. C.-14 A. D.). During his reign, Roman literature reached its highest point. See note on *Tiberius and Vipsania,* p. 1380b.

Aulis. A town on the eastern coast of Bœotia, Greece. It was the rendezvous of the Greek fleet in the expedition against Troy.

Aurora. Goddess of the dawn, represented as rising from the ocean in a chariot, with her fingers dripping dew. She was attended by the Hours. She fell in love with Tithonus, the son of Laomedon, King of Troy. She prevailed on the gods to grant Tithonus immortality, but forgot to ask immortal youth for him. He grew old, and was changed by Aurora into a grasshopper.

Aurora Borealis. A phenomenon of the atmosphere, often seen during the night in high northern latitudes, called commonly "Northern Lights."

Ausonia. A poetical name for Italy.

Auster. The south wind.

Austral. Pertaining to the south.

Aventicum. The ancient name of Avenches, a town in Switzerland. It was an important Roman city, destroyed by the Huns in 447. It contains walls and other ancient remains.

Avon. A river in the midland counties of England, on which Stratford, where Shakespeare lived, is located.

Axumé. An ancient city in Abyssinia, noted for its antiquities.

Aylmer, Rose. A daughter of Lord Aylmer, a friend of Landor's.

Ayr. The name of a city and a river in Ayrshire, Scotland.

Azincour. Agincourt, a village in France, southeast of Boulogne; the scene of an English victory over the French in 1415.

Azrael. The angel of death.

B. One of De Quincey's guardians. He was a merchant.

Baal. The supreme divinity of the ancient Syro-Phœnician nations. He was also worshiped as the sun god.

Babel. 1—(495)—The city of Babylon. 2—(603)—The tower described in *Genesis,* 11, during the building of which occurred the confusion of tongues. 3—(638, 772)—Tumult; confusion.

Babes in the Wood, The. In Percy's *Reliques,* a ballad of two children who perished in Wayland Wood, Norfolkshire, England.

Bab'lon; Babylon. The capital of ancient Babylonia, in Asia, situated on the Euphrates River. For the destruction of the city, see *Revelation,* 14:8 and 18:10-21. It is noted for its Hanging Gardens, one of the seven wonders of the world.

Bacchanal; Bacchanalian. Pertaining to Bacchanalia, the worship of Bacchus, or a festival in his honor, usually a drunken revel.

Bacchic Nysa. See **Nysa.**

Bacchus. (Dionysus). The son of Jupiter, and the god of wine. His forehead was crowned with vine leaves or ivy. He rode upon the tiger, the panther, or the lynx, and was drawn by them in a car. His worshipers were Bacchanals, or Bacchantes. He was attended by Satyrs and Sileni, and women called Mænads, who, as they danced and sang, waved in the air the thyrsus, a staff entwined with ivy and surmounted by a pine cone. He gained the love of Ariadne, daughter of King Minos of Crete.

Bacleuch; Buccleuch. Sir Walter Scott of Branxholm (Branksome), in Roxburghshire, Scotland.

Bacon. Francis Bacon (1561-1626), a celebrated English philosopher, jurist, statesman, and essayist.

Badajoz. A town and fortress in Spain; stormed by Wellington in 1812.

Bagdat. Bagdad, an ancient city in Asiatic Turkey.

Bagshot. A village in the county of Surrey, England.

Baia; Baiæ. A small seaport of Italy, west of Naples.

Bailey. Benjamin Bailey (1749-1852), an intimate friend of Keats.

Bajazet. A Turkish sultan (1389-1402) who appears as a character in Marlowe's *Tamburlaine the Great* (c1588), Racine's *Bajazet* (1672), and other plays.

Balaam. The prophet to whom Balak, King of Moab, sent presents to induce him to curse Israel, and who was rebuked by the ass he rode. His utterance, by God's power, was a blessing instead of a curse.

Balbec. An ancient city of Syria, Asia Minor, famous for its ruins; it was sacred to the worship of Baal, the sun god.

Balboa. A Spanish navigator who discovered the Pacific Ocean in 1513.

Balclutha. See note on *Carthon*, p. 1246b.

Balder. See note on *The Descent of Odin*, p. 1244a.

Baldwin. C. B. Baldwin or Herbert Baldwin, both of whom were members of the House of Commons, 1830-33.

Balk. Balkh, a region of Turkestan, in Asia.

Ballad of Betty Foy. A poem by Wordsworth.

Banborowe. A district in Northumberland-shire, England. It contains Bamborough Castle, which is built on a high rock projecting into the North Sea.

Bangor. A city on the coast of Carnarvon-shire, North Wales.

Bank; Bank of England. The custodian of the public money of Great Britain, and manager of the public debt; now the largest bank in the world.

Banks. John Banks (fl. 1696), author of *The Unhappy Favorite* and other melodramatic plays.

Bannister. Jack Bannister (1760-1836), an English comedian.

Bannochar. A valley on the borders of Loch Lomond, in the county of Dumbarton, Scotland.

Banquo. A Scottish thane and general, the legendary ancestor of the Stuarts; he appears in Shakespeare's *Macbeth.*

Baramoule. A locality in the western part of Cashmere, which is bounded by Eastern Turkestan, Tibet, and India.

Barbara. A child mentioned in Wordsworth's *'Tis Said That Some Have Died for Love.* Not to be confused with Barbara Lewth-waite, mentioned in Wordsworth's *The Pet Lamb.*

Barbary. The Mohammedan countries on the north coast of Africa, not including Egypt.

Barbican. A street in London, so called from a former watch tower, which stood on it.

Barclay. John Barclay (1582-1621), a Scottish poet.

Barden. A moor in Cumberlandshire, England.

Bardie clan. Bards, or poets.

Barker's. A former bookshop in what is now Russell Street, London.

Barleycorn, John. The personification of malt liquor, as being made from barley.

Barnesdale. A woodland region in the western part of Yorkshire, England.

Barnet. A village in Hertfordshire, north of London.

Barnwell, George. A character in George Lillo's tragedy *The London Merchant; or the History of George Barnwell* (1731).

Barrett, Elizabeth. An English poet (1806-61).

Barrow. John Barrow (1764-1848), an English writer and traveler.

Bartholinus. Thomas Bartholin (1616-80), a Danish physician and scholar.

Bartholomew, St. One of the twelve apostles.

Bartram. William Bartram (1739-1823), an American botanist and ornithologist, who wrote *Travels Through North and South Carolina, Georgia, East and West Florida, etc.*

Basques. A race of unknown origin inhabiting the Basque provinces and other parts of Spain in the neighborhood of the Pyrenees.

Bateable Land. Debatable Land, a region on the border of England and Scotland, formerly claimed by both kingdoms; it comprised about 30 square miles north and east of the mouth of the River Esk.

Bath. A town in Somersetshire, England. It is one of the leading watering places of England, and is noted for its hot springs.

Bathyllus. A poem by Anacreon, a Greek lyric poet of the fifth century B. C.

Battle. A town in the county of Sussex, which received its name from the Battle of Hastings, fought there in 1066.

Battle Abbey. A large Benedictine monastery, built by William the Conqueror in 1067 on the spot where Harold's banner had been planted in the Battle of Hastings.

Battle of Hexham. A comedy by George Colman the Younger (1762-1836).

Bavius. An inferior Roman poet of the first century B. C.; an enemy of Virgil and Horace.

Beacon-hill. A prominent hill near Penrith, Cumberlandshire, England.

Bear, The Great. Ursa Major, a large northern constellation, containing the seven conspicuous stars called the Great Dipper.

Beattie. James Beattie (1735-1803), a Scotch poet, essayist, and philosophical writer. See p. 119.

Beatty, Mr. Sir William Beatty (d. 1842), an English surgeon, for many years in the service of the navy.

Beaumont. Francis Beaumont (1584-1616), an Elizabethan dramatist, collaborator with John Fletcher.

Beaumont, Sir George (1753-1827). An English landscape painter and patron of art.

Bede (673-735). A celebrated English monk and ecclesiastical writer.

Bedford. John Plantagenet (1389-1435), Duke of Bedford, an English general and statesman. He abetted the execution of Joan of Arc in 1431.

Bedlam. The hospital of St. Mary of Bethlehem in London, founded about 1247. On the suppression of religious houses by Henry VIII, it was incorporated as a hospital for the insane in 1547.

Bedlamites. —(290)—Discharged inmates of Bedlam Hospital, licensed to beg.

Bedouin Arab. One of the nomadic Arabs of Syria, Arabia, and northern Africa.

Beelzebub. Prince of the demons; the devil.

Behman. Jacob Behman (1575-1624), a noted German mystic.

Bela. A town in the district of Lus, in southeastern Baluchistan, west of India.

Belcher. Tom Belcher (1783-1854), younger brother of James Belcher, a well-known prize fighter, who kept a tavern in Holborn, a district in the central part of London.

Belial. The ancient Hebrew personification of recklessness or lawlessness; hence, the devil.

Bellarmine. Cardinal Roberto Bellarmino (1542-1621), an Italian divine.

Bellini. Vincenzo Bellini (1802-35), a famous Italian operatic composer.

Bembo, Cardinal (1470-1547). An Italian cardinal and writer.

Ben-an. A mountain north of the Trosachs, a valley of western Perthshire, Scotland.

Benbecula, Island of. An island of the Hebrides, between North Uist and South Uist, west of Scotland.

Bengal. A province in northeastern British India.

Benledi. A mountain in Perthshire, Scotland. The name signifies *Mountain of God*.

Ben-Lomond. A mountain in Stirlingshire, Scotland.

Benmore. A mountain near Loch Katrine in Perthshire, Scotland.

Benvenue. A mountain in Perthshire, Scotland.

Benvoirlich. A mountain in Perthshire, Scotland.

Berkeley. George Berkeley (1685-1753), an Irish bishop and philosopher.

Berkeley Castle. A Norman stronghold, Gloucestershire, England. Here Edward II was murdered in 1327.

Bermoothes. An old form of *Bermudas*.

Bermudas. A British island group in the North Atlantic Ocean.

Bernard, Abbot of Clairvaux (1091-1153). A celebrated French ecclesiastic.

Berwick-Law. North Berwick Law, a prominent height in Hoddingtonshire, Scotland, overlooking the Firth of Forth.

Bess, Queen. Elizabeth, Queen of England (1558-1603).

Bethlehem. An ancient city in Palestine; the birthplace of Christ.

Betterton. Thomas Betterton (1635?-1710), a noted English actor.

Bey. A title given to sons of Pashas, and to the nobility. It is conferred by the Sultan.

Bey Oglou. The title of a Turkish nobleman.

Bigod, Ralph. John Fenwick, an early nineteenth-century editor. His life was full of misfortunes. Lamb borrowed the name *Bigod* from the old family name of the Earls of Norfolk.

Billet, Mr. Lamb's "poor relation."

Birkbeck. George Birkbeck (1766-1841), a London physician, founder of Mechanics' Institute, Birkbeck College, and University College, London.

Birmingham. A large manufacturing city in Warwickshire, England.

Bishopsgate. The principal entrance through the northern wall of Old London.

Black. John Black (1783-1855), a distinguished journalist, editor of *The Morning Chronicle*, a prominent London paper, from 1819 to 1843.

Black Prince, The. Edward, Prince of Wales (1330-76), a son of Edward III of England; so named by "terror of his arms."

Blackwood. 1—(438)—Sir Henry Blackwood (1770-1832), an English naval captain. 2—(890, 1061)—William Blackwood (1776-1834), a Scotch publisher and bookseller, founder of *The Edinburgh Magazine*. He was a rank Tory.

Blackwood's Magazine. A magazine of Edinburgh, Scotland, founded and edited by William Blackwood (1776-1834).

Blake. Robert Blake (1598-1657), a famous British admiral who won notable victories over the Dutch and Spanish. He died at sea, and was buried in Westminster Abbey.

Blanc, Mont. See **Mont Blanc**.

Bland, Mrs. Maria Theresa Bland (Dorothea Jordan) (1769-1838), a well-known Irish actress.

Blenheim. 1—(426)—See note on *The Battle of Blenheim*, p. 1308a. 2—(1053)—A village in Oxfordshire, England. It is the seat of Blenheim Palace, noted for its fine apartments.

Bloomfield. Robert Bloomfield (1766-1823), an English pastoral poet.

Bloomsbury. A noted district in London. Lamb never lived there.

Blue Anchor. Probably the name of a hill near Minehead, in Somersetshire, England.

Blue Bonnets. Scotchmen, so called from the broad, flat cap of blue wool which they wore.

Bluebeard. The hero of a popular story, who gave his wives, in turn, a key to a certain room, and forbade their opening it on penalty of death.

Bobby, Master. A character in *The Life and Opinions of Tristram Shandy* (v, 7), a novel by Laurence Sterne (1713-68).

Boccace; Boccaccio. Giovanni Boccaccio (1313-75), a noted Italian writer.

Bochastle. A moor in Perthshire, Scotland.

Bodleian. The library of Oxford University; named after Sir Thomas Bodley, who re-established it, 1597-1602.

Bœotian. Belonging to or having the traits of the inhabitants of Bœotia, Greece, proverbial for their dullness.

Boetius. Boethius (475-524), a Roman philosopher. His most famous work is the *De Consolatione Philosophiæ*.

Boileau. Nicholas Boileau-Despréaux (1636-1711), a famous French critic and poet.

Bolingbroke. Henry St. John (1678-1751), Lord Bolingbroke, an English statesman, political writer, and Deistic philosopher.

Bolton Priory. An abbey in the western part of Yorkshire, England.

Bond-street. In the West End of London; the fashionable shopping district.

Bonnivard. François de Bonnivard (1496-1570), a French reformer who aided the Genevese against Charles of Savoy. He was imprisoned at Chillon.

Boreas. The god of the north wind.

Borgia. Cesare Borgia (1478-1507), an Italian cardinal, soldier, and adventurer, noted for the murder of his brother and as an adept in perfidious politics.

Borgia, Lucretia. See note on *On Seeing a Hair of Lucretia Borgia*, p. 1379b.

Borrodale. Borrowdale, a romantic vale in the lake country, Cumberlandshire, England.

Borrowgate. A small place in Cumberlandshire, England.

Borysthenes. The ancient name of the River Dnieper, in Russia.

Bosniac. A poetic name for Bosnian. Bosnia was a province of Austria-Hungary.

Boswell. James Boswell (1740-1795), a Scotch lawyer; biographer of Samuel Johnson.

Botany Bay. An inlet on the east coast of New South Wales, Australia. The British formerly used it as a convict station.

Bothwellhaugh. See note on *Cadyow Castle*, p. 1316b.

Bowles. William Lisle Bowles (1762-1850), an English clergyman and minor poet. He published an edition of Pope in 1806. See p. 164.

Bracklinn. A beautiful cascade in the River Keltie, near Callander, Perthshire, Scotland.

Braemar. The highland portion of the district of Mar, Aberdeenshire, Scotland. It is famed for its deer and its forests.

Brahma. The creator in Hindu mythology.

Bramins. Members of the first of the four castes of India.

Branksome Ha; Branxholm. A castle and an estate three miles southwest of the village of Hawick, in Roxburghshire, Scotland. It was the residence of the Buccleuch family.

Bratha Head. The source of the River Bratha, which flows through the county of Westmoreland into Lake Windermere, England.

Brazenose College. A college of Oxford University, so named from the sign of the former Brazenose Hall, a brazen nose.

Breadalbane. A district in Perthshire, Scotland, north of Loch Lomond.

Brenta. A river of northern Italy, flowing into the Gulf of Venice.

Brentford. A town in the county of Middlesex, England, on the Thames, nine miles west of London.

Brian. King of Dublin in the eleventh century.

Briareus. A son of Uranus and Gæa; a monster with a hundred arms.

Bridge of Sighs. The covered bridge in Venice leading from the Doge's Palace to the state prison; so called because condemned prisoners formerly passed over it from the judgment hall to the place of execution.

Bridge Street Junto. See p. 1059a, n. 2.

Bridgewater. A seaport in Somersetshire, England.

Brigg of Turk. An old stone bridge over the Turk, a small stream in Glenfinlas Valley, in Perthshire, Scotland.

Brinsley. Richard Brinsley Sheridan (1751-1816), an Irish dramatist and politician.

Bristol; Bristowa. A town in Gloucestershire, England.

Britannia. A poetical name for Great Britain.

British Fairfax. See Fairfax.

British Museum. A national institution in London. It contains collections of antiquities and a library of more than 2,000,000 books.

Britomart. A lady knight in Spenser's *The Faerie Queene*, representing chastity.

Britonferry. A seaport in Glamorganshire, Wales.

Brocken. One of the Hartz Mountains in Saxony, famous for its "specter" caused by the shadow cast upon the clouds.

Bronte. A title of Lord Nelson.

Brooke, Lord. Fulke Greville (1554-1628), an English poet and philosopher.

Brougham. Henry Peter, Baron Brougham and Vaux (1778-1868), a celebrated British statesman, jurist, and scientist. He became Chancellor in 1830. He was one of the founders of *The Edinburgh Review*, in 1802.

Broughton. Jack Broughton (1704-89), a prize fighter; he fought with George Stevenson in 1771.

Brown. Tom Brown (1663-1704), an English satirical poet and prose writer.

Browne. Sir Thomas Browne (1605-82), an English physician, author of *Religio Medici, Urn Burial*, etc.

Bruce. Robert de Bruce (1274-1329), King of Scotland; he defeated Edward II of England at Bannockburn in 1314.

Brunetière. Ferdinand Brunetière (1849-1906), a French literary critic.

Bruno, St. An eleventh-century monk, founder of the order of Carthusian monks, at Chartreuse, France.

Brunswick. A duchy in Germany.

Brusa. A city in Turkey, Asia Minor.

Brussels. Capital of the kingdom of Belgium. In 1830 it was the scene of the outbreak of the Belgian Revolution.

Brutus. The legendary king and founder of Britain.

Bryan and Perenne. A West Indian ballad, founded on an actual occurrence, which happened in the Island of St. Christopher, about 1760.

Buccleuch. See **Bacleuch.**

Bucephalus. The war horse of Alexander the Great; hence, any saddle horse.

Buchan. William Buchan (1729-1805), a Scottish physician.

Bucks. Buckingham, an inland county of England.

Buffamalco. Buonamico Buffalmacco (c. 1262-1340), a Florentine painter, celebrated in Boccaccio's *Decameron*.

Bull.—(956)—William Bull (1738-1814), Lord Mayor of London in 1773.

Bull, John. A name that stands for England or an Englishman.

Bulwer-Lytton. Edward Robert, Earl of Lytton (1831-91), an English poet and diplomat.

Bunbury, H. Henry William Bunbury (1750-1811), an English artist and caricaturist.

Buncle, John. See **John Buncle.**

Burford Bridge. A small village near Dorking, in the county of Surrey, England.

Bürger. Gottfried August Bürger (1748-94), a noted German poet.

Burgoyne. John Burgoyne (1723-92), an English general in the American Revolution.

Burgundy. A former province in east-central France, famous for its wines.

Burke. Edmund Burke (1729-97), an Irish orator, statesman, and writer. See p. 1219.

Burleigh. See **Exeter, Lord.**

Burnet. Thomas Burnet (1635-1715), an English writer, noted chiefly as the author of *Telluris Theoria Sacra*, remarkable for its vivid imagery and purity of style.

Burn-mill. A meadow in the Yarrow Valley, Selkirkshire, Scotland.

Burton. Robert Burton (1577-1640), a noted English writer, author of *The Anatomy of Melancholy*.

Busyrane. An enchanter in Spenser's *The Faerie Queene.*

Bute. John Stuart (1713-92), Earl of Bute, an English statesman and leader of the party of George III.

Butler, Bishop. Joseph Butler (1672-1752), an English theologian.

Byzantine. Of ancient Byzantium.

Byzantium. An ancient Greek city on the site of modern Constantinople.

Cadiz. A seaport of southwestern Spain.

Cadmæn forest. A forest near Cadmeia, the citadel or acropolis of Thebes, in Bœotia, Greece.

Cadmus. The reputed founder of Thebes in Bœotia, Greece. He brought the old Phœnician, or Cadmean, alphabet of sixteen letters to Greece.

Cadwallader (d. 703). The last king of Wales; the hero of Welsh poems.

Cadwallo. An ancient Welsh poet.

Cæcilia. See **Cecilia, Saint.**

Cæsar, Augustus. See **Augustus.**

Cæsar. Julius Cæsar (100-44 B. C.), a famous Roman general, statesman, and writer. He was assassinated by Brutus, Cassius, and others.

Cæsarean. Belonging to Julius Cæsar.

Caf. In Mohammedan mythology, a mountain, consisting of a single emerald, said to surround the whole earth.

Cain. The eldest son of Adam and Eve, and the murderer of his brother Abel. He was condemned to be a fugitive for his sin.

Cairo. The capital of Egypt, on the east bank of the Nile.

Calais. A fortified seaport on the north coast of France.

Calantha. A character in John Ford's tragedy, *The Broken Heart* (1633). She drops dead of a broken heart after an extraordinary ballroom scene during which, with apparent calm and while continuing her dance, she listens to the announcement of the deaths, one after another, of her father, lover, and brother.

Calchas. In Greek legend, the wisest soothsayer who accompanied the expedition against Troy.

Calcutta. The capital of Bengal, India.

Calder, Sir Robert (1745-1818). A British admiral who fought an indecisive naval battle with the Franco-Spanish fleet in 1805, and was severely blamed for not continuing the action to the finish.

Calderon. Pedro Calderon (1600-81), a Spanish dramatist.

Caleb Williams. A famous political novel by William Godwin (1756-1836), published in 1794.

Caledon; Caledonia; Caledonie. Ancient and poetical names for Scotland.

Caliban. A deformed savage slave of Prospero, in Shakespeare's *The Tempest*.

Calidore. A courteous knight in Spenser's *The Faerie Queene*.

Caligula. A Roman emperor (37-41 A. D.).

Calne in Wiltshire. A mystification for Ottery St. Mary in Devonshire, England, the early home of Coleridge.

Calpe. The ancient name of Gibraltar.

Calvary. The place where Christ was crucified.

Calypso. A nymph of Ogygia, the island on which Ulysses was shipwrecked. She detained him seven years, and promised him immortal youth if he would remain there, but he refused.

Cambria. The ancient name of Wales.

Cambridge. Capital of Cambridgeshire, England, and the seat of Cambridge University.

Cambro-Briton. A Welshman.

Cambronne. Baron Pierre Jacques de Cambronne (1770-1843), a celebrated French marshal, who commanded a division at Waterloo.

Cambusmore. The estate of a family named Buchanan, near Callander, Perthshire, Scotland.

Cambyses. A king of ancient Persia. As a character in several dramas, he became proverbial for his ranting speeches.

Camilla. An English novel by Madame D'Arblay (Frances Burney, 1752-1840), published in 1796.

Camoens. Luis de Camoens (1524-80), a noted Portuguese poet.

Campania. A province in Italy.

Campbell. Thomas Campbell (1777-1844), a British poet, critic, and miscellaneous writer. See p. 443.

Campbells. A powerful Highland Scotch

family, the descendants of Colin Campbell, first Earl of Argyle (d. 1493).

Canaan. The part of Palestine between the Mediterranean and the Dead Sea.

Canary. Islands in the North Atlantic Ocean, northwest of Africa, famous for their wines.

Cancer. A constellation represented by the form of a crab, and showing the limits of the sun's course northward in summer.

Candlemas. The feast of the Purification of the Virgin Mary, or presentation of Christ in the Temple, celebrated Feb. 2, with the burning of many candles. In England this was one of the customary dates for settling debts.

Canidia. A sorceress reviled by Horace in *Epode 5*.

Cannæ. A village in Italy where Hannibal defeated the Romans, 216 B. C.; called "The Field of Blood," from the heavy losses suffered by the Romans.

Canning. George Canning (1770-1827), a British Tory statesman, famous for his foreign policy of nonintervention. His wit made many believe he was insincere.

Canobie. A village near the Esk River in Dumfriesshire, Scotland.

Canongate. The principal thoroughfare in the Old Town of Edinburgh.

Canopus. The second brightest star in the heavens.

Canova. Antonio Canova (1757-1822), an Italian sculptor.

Canzoni. Italian song.

Cape St. Vincent. See **St. Vincent.**

Capitol, The. 1—(81, 236, 1017)—A temple of Jupiter, in Rome, called the Capitolium. It stood on the Capitoline Hill. 2—(570)—The part of the Capitoline Hill occupied by the temple of Jupiter.

Caracci, Annibal (1560-1609). An Italian painter, celebrated for his ceiling decorations in the Farnese Palace, Rome.

Caràdoc. Caractacus (1st century A. D.), a king of a British tribe in South Wales.

Carasman. Carasman Oglou, the principal land holder in Turkey. The line of Carasman dates back to the fourteenth century.

Cardigan. A county in South Wales.

Caria. An ancient division of Asia Minor.

Carlisle. A city in Cumberlandshire, England.

Carlo Dolce. See **Dolce.**

Carmanian waste. A frightful salt desert in Carmania, an ancient province of Asia, on the Persian Gulf.

Carmel. A famous mountain in central Palestine, near the Mediterranean.

Carnarvonshire. A county in Wales.

Carr. Sir John Carr (1772-1832), author of

several books of travel, one of which, *The Stranger in Ireland*, was ridiculed by Edward Du Bois by the publication of his *My Pocket Book* (1807). An unsuccessful suit for damages resulted.

Carrick. The southern district of Ayrshire, Scotland. It is south of the River Doon.

Carterhaugh. An extensive plain near the junction of the Ettrick and Yarrow rivers in Selkirkshire, Scotland.

Carthage. An ancient city and state in northern Africa, famous for its wars with Rome, called the Punic Wars.

Cartoons. Seven drawings done by Raphael, an Italian painter, in 1515-16 for Leo X, to be reproduced in Flemish tapestry.

Cary, Sir Lucius (1610-43). An English politician and writer.

Cashmere, Vale of. A beautiful and fertile valley in the state of Kashmir, a native state bounded by eastern Turkestan, Tibet, and India. It is now a part of India.

Casimir. King of Poland (1040-58). He is called "The Restorer of Poland."

Caspian. An inland salt sea between Europe and Asia.

Cassandra. 1—(521, 633)—In Greek legend a prophetess, the daughter of Priam and Hecuba. By command of Apollo (whose advances she had repelled), her predictions, though true, were always discredited. She was made a slave by Agamemnon after the fall of Troy. 2—(1057)—A French historical romance by La Calprenède (1610-63).

Castalia. A fountain on Mt. Parnassus near Delphi, Greece, supposed to give inspiration to those who drank of it. It was sacred to the Muses.

Castaly. A poetical name for Castalia.

Castile. A former kingdom in the north central part of Spain.

Castilian. A native of Castile, Spain.

Castle of Otranto. The romance by Horace Walpole, published in 1765. See p. 100.

Castle Spectre, The. A drama presented at Drury Lane theatre in 1797.

Castle hill. A hill in Cumberlandshire, England.

Castlereagh. See note on *Lines Written During the Castlereagh Administration*, p. 1341a.

Castor. In Greek mythology, twin brother of Pollux. The brothers were placed in the heavens as a constellation, Gemini.

Catalani. Angelica Catalani (1779-1849), a noted Italian singer.

Cathay. A Chinese province; it is a poetical name for China.

Catiline (1st century B. C.). A Roman politi-

cian and conspirator. He is the subject of plays by S. Gosson (1579), H. Chettle (1598), Ben Jonson (1611), and G. Croly (1811).

Cato. Marcus Porcius Cato (234-149 B. C.), a Roman statesman, general, and writer.

Cattræth's vale. A valley in Yorkshire, England. Cattræth may be Catterick, a town in Yorkshire.

Catullus. Caius Valerius Catullus (87-45? B. C.), a famous Latin lyric poet.

Caucasus. A mountain range between the Caspian and Black seas.

Cave. Edward Cave (1691-1754), a noted English printer and bookseller.

Cavendish. The name of a family of the English nobility.

Cecil, Earl of Salisbury. Robert Cecil (1563-1612), an English statesman, minister to Queen Elizabeth, 1598-1603, and to James I, 1603-12.

Cecelia, Saint (third century A. D.). A Christian martyr; she is generally regarded as the patron saint of music, particularly church music.

Cecropian port. Athens. Cecrops was the traditional first king of Athens.

Celt. A member of the western European branch of the Aryan family that includes the Irish, Welsh, Cornish, and Low Bretons.

Cenchreas. A small seaport in Greece, southeast of Corinth.

Cenci, The. A tragedy by Shelley dealing with the story of Beatrice Cenci (1577-1599), an Italian woman, beheaded for taking part in the murder of her father.

Cenis, Mont. See **Mont Cenis.**

Centaur. A fabled monster having the head, arms, and body of a man from waist up, united to the body and legs of a horse.

Cephisus. A river in Attica, Greece.

Cerberus. In classic mythology, the sleepless watchdog at the entrance of the infernal regions, usually represented with three heads.

Cereate. The rustic home of Marius's childhood, near Arpinum.

Ceres. 1—(61, 852, 866, 1203)—In classic mythology, the goddess of corn and harvests. 2—(819)—An asteroid discovered in 1801.

Cervantes. Miguel de Cervantes (1547-1616), a noted Spanish writer.

Cethegus. Gaius Cornelius Cethegus (1st century B. C.), a Roman of the most corrupt and profligate character; one of the accomplices of Catiline.

Ceylon. An island south of India, noted for its pearl fisheries.

Chaldean. An inhabitant of Chaldea, an ancient kingdom at the head of the Persian Gulf.

Chaldee land. Chaldea.

Chamberry. A city in southeastern France.

Chamouni. A beautiful valley at the foot of Mont Blanc on the eastern border of France.

Chancery-lane. A street in London leading from Fleet Street to Holborn, and passing by the Inns of Court.

Channel. The English Channel, a strait between England and France.

Chantry. Sir Francis Chantry (1781-1842), a noted English sculptor and portrait painter. He executed the bust of Wordsworth about 1820.

Chaos. The first state of the universe. In Greek mythology, the most ancient of the gods.

Chapman. George Chapman (c1559-1634), an English poet, dramatist, and translator.

Charlemagne. Charles the Great (742-814), the great King of France, and Emperor of the West.

Charles. 1—(499)—Charles I, King of England (1625-49). 2—(510)—Charles Edward, "The Young Pretender" (1720-88), who headed an insurrection to recover the British crown for his father, called James III. At first he was successful, but finally was routed at Culloden, in the county of Inverness, Scotland, in 1746. 3—(1131)— Charles II, King of England (1649-85).

Charlotte, Princess. Charlotte Augusta (1796-1817), daughter of George IV of England. In 1816, she married Leopold, Duke of Saxe-Coburg, later King of Belgium (1831-65).

Charon. In classic mythology, the ferryman who transported the souls of the dead over the Styx, a river in Hades.

Chartier, Alain. A French writer of the fifteenth century.

Chartreuse, La Grande. A former monastery in Isère department, France, altitude 4000 feet; it was founded by St. Bruno in 1084.

Chatham. William Pitt (1708-78), first Earl of Chatham, a famous English Whig statesman and orator.

Chatterton. Thomas Chatterton (1752-70), an English poet who committed suicide in a fit of despondency. See p. 125.

Cheap; Cheapside. The central, east-and-west thoroughfare of London.

Chenars, Isle of. Probably an island in the ancient lake of Cashmere, India.

Cheops. A king of Egypt (fourth century B. C.), said to have built the first pyramid, at Gizeh, near Cairo.

Chepstow Castle. A famous castle in Chepstow, a town in Monmouthshire, England.

Chersonese. An ancient name of several peninsulas: the Malay Peninsula, Jutland (Denmark), Crimea (Russia), and Gallipoli (southern Turkey).

Cherubim. A high order of angels, excelling in knowledge.

Cherwell's flood. A small river in England, which joins the Thames at Oxford.

Cheshire. A county in western England, noted for its dairy products.

Chester. The capital of Cheshire, England.

Cheviot Hills. A mountain range between Scotland and England.

Childe Harold. See page 549.

Children in the Wood, The. A comedy by Thomas Morton (1769-1838). It was also the title of an old ballad included in Percy's *Reliques of Ancient English Poetry*.

Chimæra. In Greek mythology, a fire-breathing monster, variously described as a combination of lion, goat, and serpent.

Chirk. A small town in Denbigshire, Wales.

Chitty. Joseph Chitty (1776-1841), a noted English writer of legal treatises.

Chorasmian shore. Chorasmia, or Khiva, a portion of central Asia in Russian Turkestan. The country is almost wholly a sandy desert.

Christ's Hospital. A famous charity school for boys, founded in 1552 by Edward VI in the buildings formerly belonging to the dissolved order of Grey Friars.

Chrysostom. Saint John Chrysostomus (fourth century), a celebrated father of the Greek church; the author of *Commentaries*.

Chyviat. Same as Cheviot.

Cibber. Theophilus Cibber (1703-58), an English actor and dramatist.

Cicero. Marcus Tullius Cicero (106-43 B. C.), a celebrated Roman orator, philosopher, and statesman; the author of a treatise on moral philosophy entitled *De Officiis (Of Duties)*.

Cicilie, Sainte. See **Cecelia, Saint.**

Cimmerian. Pertaining to the Cimmerii, a mythical people mentioned by Homer as living in perpetual darkness.

Cincinnatus. Lucius Quinctius Cincinnatus (fifth century B. C.), a Roman legendary hero. He distinguished himself in 462-454 as an opponent of the plebians in their struggle against the patricians. He was appointed dictator in 458.

Circassian. Pertaining to Circassia, a former country northwest of the Caucasus Mountains, now part of Russia.

Circe. The sorceress in the *Odyssey* who feasted the mariners and then turned them into beasts.

Circean. Bewitching like Circe.

Circus. A large enclosure used frequently for gladiatorial combats in Roman times.

Clair, St. See **St. Clair.**

Clarendon. Edward Hyde (1608-74), Earl of Clarendon, an English royalist statesman and historian.

Clarens. A village in Switzerland, situated near the east end of Lake Geneva. It is celebrated as the scene of Rousseau's *La Nouvelle Héloïse.*

Clarissa; Clarissa Harlowe. A novel by Samuel Richardson (1689-1761); it takes its name from the leading character.

Clarke. Samuel Clarke (1675-1729), a celebrated English philosopher and theologian.

Clarkson. Thomas Clarkson (1760-1846), an English philanthropist, devoted to the abolition of slave-trade.

Claud.—(466)—Lord Claud Hamilton, son of the Duke of Chatelherault; he was a loyal supporter of Queen Mary and her cause.

Claude. Claude Lorrain (1600-82), a celebrated French landscape painter.

Claudian. Claudius Claudianus, a noted Latin poet of the fourth century.

Claver'se. See note on *Bonny Dundee*, p. 1322b.

Cleone. 1—(861)—A town in Greece, southwest of Corinth. 2—(1020)—A friend and correspondent of Aspasia, in Landor's *Pericles and Aspasia.*

Cleopatra. Queen of Egypt (69-30 B. C.).

Clevedon. A town in Somersetshire, England.

Clinkumbell. A humorous name for a bellman.

Clinton. Sir Henry Clinton (1738-95), an English general in the American Revolution.

Clitumnus. A river of Umbria, Italy. It is celebrated for its sanctity and beauty.

Clotho. In Greek mythology, one of the three Fates; she spins the thread of life.

Clyde. A river in southwestern Scotland.

Clydesdale. The valley of the River Clyde, in southwestern Scotland, noted for its horses.

Clymene. In Greek mythology, a daughter of Oceanus and Tethys; mother of Atlas and Prometheus.

Cobbett. William Cobbett (1762-1835), an English politician and writer who was continually getting into trouble because of the views he expressed in his political publications. He was the author also of an English grammar. See p. 1028.

Coblentz. An important city in Prussia. It suffered in the Thirty Years' War and in the wars of Louis XIV.

Clovenford. A fishing station on the road from Edinburgh to Selkirk, Scotland, within a few miles of the Yarrow and Ettrick rivers.

Clwyd. A river in North Wales.

Cochrane, Thomas Lord. A Scottish noble and British naval commander (1775-1860), noted for his brilliant service against Spanish and French vessels. In 1814, he was accused of starting, for personal gain, a report of Napoleon's death, was imprisoned, fined, and expelled from the navy and from the House of Commons. He was exonerated from the charges in 1832.

Cockshut. A hill in Cumberlandshire, England.

Codri. Codrus was an alleged author of a tragedy on the subject of Theseus. See Juvenal's *Satires*, 1, 1-2.

Cœlebs' Wife. A novel by Hannah More (1809).

Cœlus. The sky, father of Saturn (Cronos).

Cœus. One of the Titans, a family of giants.

Coliseum. An amphitheater in Rome, the greatest architectural monument left by the Romans.

Collingwood. Lord Cuthbert Collingwood (1750-1810), an English admiral, second in command at Trafalgar.

Collins. Anthony Collins (1676-1729), a noted English Deist; a friend of John Locke.

Colloquies. A Latin work by Desiderius Erasmus (1466-1536), a Dutch scholar and theologian.

Colnaghi. A London printseller of the eighteenth century.

Colonsay. An island of the Inner Hebrides, in Argyllshire, Scotland. It is noted for its ecclesiastical antiquities.

Columbia. A poetical name for America.

Columbian. Pertaining to the United States.

Columbus. Christopher Columbus (1446-1506), an Italian navigator; discoverer of America.

Comberbatch. Silas Titus Comberbatch, the name assumed by S. T. Coleridge when he enlisted in the 15th Light Dragoons, in 1793.

Commons. A college boarding-hall.

Complaint of a Poor Indian Woman, The. A poem by Wordsworth.

Compleat Angler, The. A celebrated work by Izaak Walton (1593-1683), an English writer.

Comus. The evil spirit in Milton's *Comus*, who, like his mother, Circe, the enchantress, could transform human beings into swine.

Condé. Prince de Condé (1530-69), a French general, leader of the Huguenot army, who was captured in 1569 and treacherously shot after he surrendered his sword.

Condorcet. Marquis de Condorcet (1743-94), a celebrated French philosopher and mathematician.

Conduit in Cheap. A leaden cistern built in the middle of Cheapside Street, London, in 1285, for holding water brought underground from Paddington, a western division of London. In times of public festivity the conduit ran wine instead of water.

Confucius (551-478 B.C.). A celebrated Chinese philosopher; founder of the Confucian religion.

Congress. A meeting for deliberation and negotiation.

Congress of Vienna. An assembly, held at Vienna, Austria in 1814-1815, at which the rulers of Austria, Bavaria, Denmark, Prussia, Russia, and other states settled the affairs of Europe after the Napoleonic wars.

Congreve. William Congreve (1670-1729), an English dramatist.

Constantine. Constantine I, surnamed "The Great" (272-337), the first Christian Emperor of Rome.

Conway. 1—(63)—A picturesque river in North Wales. 2—(251)—An ancient walled seaport in Carnarvonshire, Wales.

Cook, Captain. James Cook (1728-79), a celebrated English navigator. He discovered the Sandwich Islands in 1778.

Coomb. In England or Scotland, the name for any short, steep valley or hollow.

Copenhagen. The capital of Denmark; it was bombarded by the British fleet under Parker and Nelson in 1807.

Coptic. Language of the Copts, the name given to the Christians who lived in Egypt at the time of the Mohammedan conquest, 639.

Cordara, Guilio (1704-85). An Italian poet and historiographer of the Jesuits.

Cordelia. In Shakespeare's *King Lear*, Lear's youngest and best loved daughter.

Corin. A conventional name for a shepherd in pastoral poetry.

Corinth. An ancient fortified city in Greece.

Corinthians. Inhabitants of Corinth, Greece.

Coriolanus. A tragedy by Shakespeare.

Cornish. Of or belonging to Cornwall, a southwestern county in England.

Cornwall. A county in southwestern England.

Corsican. Napoleon, who was born in Corsica, an island in the Mediterranean Sea.

Cortez. Hernando Cortez (1485-1547), a famous Spanish soldier, who conquered Mexico and discovered California.

Corunna. A seaport on the northwestern coast of Spain.

Coryate. Thomas Coryate (1577-1617), an English traveler, author of *Coryate's Crudities*.

Corybantes. The attendants of the goddess Cybele in ancient Phrygia, whose rites were conducted with wild revelry.

Corydons. Corydon is a conventional name for a shepherd in pastoral poetry.

Cossack. A member of the race inhabiting eastern Russia on the lower Don and Dnieper rivers.

Cottle, Amos (1768-1800). An English writer, elder brother of Joseph Cottle.

Cottle, Joseph (1770-1853). An English bookseller and poet; a friend of Coleridge, Southey, and Wordsworth, and the publisher of several of their works.

Cotton, Charles (1630-87). A minor English poet, author of *The New Year*.

Cottus. In Greek mythology, a giant having a hundred hands. He was the son of Uranus and Gæa.

Covenanters. Scottish Presbyterians, who in 1638-43 engaged in a struggle against the Pope and prelacy.

Covent Garden. A square in the center of London, famous for its fruit and flower markets.

Coventry. A town of Warwickshire, England.

Cowgate. A street in the village of Mauchline, Ayrshire, Scotland.

Cowley. Abraham Cowley (1618-67), an English poet, one of the founders of the Royal Society.

Cowper. William Cowper (1731-1800), a noted English poet. See p. 145.

Coxe, Archdeacon. William Coxe (1747-1828), Archdeacon of Wiltshire, an English historian and writer of travels. His *Memoirs of the Duke of Marlborough* appeared in 1817-19.

Crabbe. George Crabbe (1754-1832), an English poet. See p. 154.

Cranmer. Thomas Cranmer (1489-1556), an English Protestant divine and reformer, burned at the stake by Mary I.

Crashaw. Richard Crashaw, a seventeenth-century English poet.

Craven. A district in western Yorkshire, England.

Crécy. A small town in northern France, where Edward III of England defeated the French in 1346.

Creolian negro. A negro born in Africa.

Cressid. Cressida, the heroine of several medieval stories and later dramas, depicting the love between her and Troilus, a noted Trojan hero. The story is an offshoot of Benoit de Ste.-Maure's *Le Roman de Troie* (12th century). See also Boccaccio's *Il Filostrato*, Chaucer's *Troilus and Creseyde*, and Shakespeare's *Troilus and Cressida*.

Cretan. A native of Crete.

Crete. An island in the Mediterranean Sea.

Creüs. A Titan, probably a divinity of the sea.

Cribbs. Tom Cribbs (1781-1848), an English champion pugilist.

Criffel. A mountain in the county of Kircudbright, Scotland.

Crimea. A peninsula in southern Russia extending into the Black Sea.

Cripps. A young painter in whom Keats and his friend Haydon were interested.

Crœsus. King of Lydia, Asia Minor, noted for his fabulous wealth.

Croly. George Croly (1780-1860), an Irish poet, divine, novelist, and miscellaneous writer.

Cromwell. Oliver Cromwell, Lord Protector of England (1653-58).

Cronus. See **Saturn.**

Crosthwait Church. A church in Langdale, Westmoreland; the burial place of Southey.

Crow-park. A hill in Cumberlandshire, England.

Crusade, Third. A warlike enterprise undertaken by Christians against the Saracens late in the 12th century.

Cuesta. Don Gregorio dello Cuesta. A Spanish general in the Napoleonic wars. He refused to follow Wellington's advice with regard to the part that he should play preparatory to the Battle of Talavera, Spain, 1809.

Culloden. A village in Inverness-shire, Scotland, the scene of the bloody defeat of the Pretender Charles Edward by the Duke of Cumberland, 1746.

Cumæan shore. Cumæ, an ancient city in Campania, Italy. Near by was Liturnum, the native country seat of Scipio Africanus, who retired there in 185 B. C., after a life of warfare.

Cumberland. 1—A county in northwestern England. 2—(412)—Richard Cumberland (1732-1811), an English dramatist and essayist.

Cumbria. An ancient British kingdom, which comprised what is now the greater part of Cumberlandshire.

Cunningham. The northern division of Ayrshire, Scotland.

Cupid. The god of love.

Curll. Edmund Curll (1675-1747), a notorious London bookseller and piratical publisher.

Currie. Doctor James Currie (1756-1805), a Scottish physician.

Curteis, Mr. One of the members of Parliament for Sussex, whose political policies were held in contempt by Cobbett.

Curtis. Sir Roger Curtis (1746-1816), an English admiral who defeated the French before Gibraltar, Sept. 13, 1782.

Cybele. Mother of the Olympian gods. She was represented in art with a turreted crown.

Cyclades. A group of islands in the Ægean Sea, east of Greece.

Cyclops. One of a race of giants having but one eye, and said to assist Vulcan, the blacksmith of the gods.

Cynthia. One of the names of Artemis, or Diana, the moon goddess. Her birthplace was Mt. Cynthus, in Delos, an island in the Ægean Sea, east of Greece.

Cyprus. An island in the Mediterranean, south of Asia Minor.

Cyrus (6th century B.C.). Surnamed "The Great"; the founder of the Persian Empire.

Cytherea. In Greek mythology, the surname of Aphrodite, one of whose shrines was on the Island of Cythera, south of Greece.

Dacre, Lord. Thomas Fiennes (1517-41), Baron Dacre, an English nobleman. He engaged in a poaching expedition which resulted in the death of one of the keepers and was condemned to death for murder.

Dædalian wings. Dædalus was a legendary sculptor noted for the wings, made of wax, with which he and his son Icarus escaped imprisonment from the labyrinth. See **Icarus.**

D'Alembert. Jean le Rond d'Alembert (1717-83), a noted French philosopher and mathematician.

Dalgarnock. The name of a romantic spot near the Nith, a river in Ayrshire, Scotland.

Dalston. Formerly a suburb of London, now an outlying district of the city itself.

Damascus. A city of Syria, famous for its silks and steel.

Damocles. A courtier of the 4th century B. C., who, having praised the pleasures of kingly estate, was placed, by order of Dionysius, at a banquet with a sword suspended over his head by a single hair, that he might learn the insecurity of such happiness.

Damon (5th century B.C.). An Athenian musician and sophist; a teacher and close friend of Pericles.

Danaë. In Greek mythology, the daughter of Acrisius and Eurydice; beloved of Zeus and by him mother of Perseus.

Daniel. Samuel Daniel (1562-1619), an English poet and historian.

Dante. Alighieri Dante (1265-1321), the most famous of Italian poets.

Danube. A river of Europe flowing through

Germany, Austria, Hungary, and Roumania to the Black Sea.

Daphne. In Greek mythology, the daughter of the river god, Peneus. She was changed to a laurel while fleeing from Apollo.

D'Arblay. Madame d'Arblay (Frances Burney, 1752-1840), an English novelist.

Dardan. Trojan.

Dardanelles. The strait between Europe and Asia, connecting the Sea of Marmora with the Ægean Sea; in ancient times known as the Hellespont.

Darien. Another name for the Isthmus of Panama.

Davenant. Sir William Davenant (1605-68), an English poet and dramatist.

David. Second king of Israel (1055-1015 B.C.), noted in his youth for his playing on the harp.

Davies, Sir John (1569-1626). An English statesman and poet.

Dawlish. A seaside resort in Devonshire, England.

Dead Sea. A salt lake in Palestine.

Death of Abel, The. A prose idyl, *Der Tod Abels* (1758), by Salomon Gessner (1730-88), a Swiss poet and painter.

Deborah. A Hebrew prophetess who helped to free the Israelites from the Canaanites, and who celebrated the victory in a famous song of triumph. See *Judges*, 4-5.

Decalogue. The Ten Commandments.

Dee. A river on the boundary of Denbighshire, Wales.

De Foe. Daniel Defoe (1661-1731), an English political writer and adventurer, author of *Robinson Crusoe*.

Deira. An Anglian kingdom extending from the Humber to the Lees; it included about what is now Yorkshire.

Delis. Turkish soldiers who form the forlorn hope of the cavalry, always beginning the action.

Delphi. In ancient geography, a town in Greece situated at the foot of Mount Parnassus; the seat of a world-renowned oracle of Apollo.

Delphic. Relating to the oracle of Apollo at Delphi.

Delphos. See **Delphi**.

Delos. An island off the coast of Greece.

Demetrius. An Ephesian silversmith who assailed Paul.

Democritus. A famous Greek philosopher (5th century B. C.).

Demogorgon. An evil spirit or magician. See note on *Prometheus Unbound*, p. 1342a.

Den. A promenade between Teignmouth and the sea, in Devonshire, England.

Denbighshire. A county in Wales.

Dennis. John Dennis (1657-1734), an English critic. He incurred the enmity of Pope and was ridiculed by him in *The Dunciad*.

Derwent. A river of Cumberlandshire, England.

Derwentwater, House of. The earls of Derwentwater, zealous supporters of the Stuarts. James Radcliffe (1689-1716), 3rd Earl of Derwentwater, was a leader in the Jacobite rebellion of 1715. He was captured and executed in 1716.

Desaix. Louis Charles Desaix (1768-1800), a noted French general killed in the Battle of Marengo, Italy.

Desdemona. The beautiful white wife of Othello the Moor, in Shakespeare's *Othello*.

De Staël. Madame de Staël (1766-1817), a celebrated French writer.

Deucalion. In Greek mythology, a king of Thessaly. He and his wife, Pyrrha, survived a nine days' deluge, their ark grounding on Mount Parnassus. To replenish the earth, an oracle commanded them to cast stones behind them, those of Deucalion becoming men and those of Pyrrha, women.

Deva. The old Latin name for the River Dee, in North Wales.

Devon. Devonshire, a county in southwestern England.

Devonport. A fortified seaport in Devonshire, England.

Devonshire. A county in southwestern England.

Dian; Diana. Goddess of the moon and the chase. She fell in love with the shepherd boy Endymion, found sleeping in a cave on Mt. Latmos, Asia Minor.

Dickie of Dryhope. A member of the Armstrong family who assisted in the rescue of Kinmont Willie. He lived in Liddesdale, Dumfriesshire, Scotland. He was outlawed in 1603.

Dido. The Queen of Carthage, who killed herself for love of Æneas. See Virgil's *Æneid*, Books 1 and 2.

Diogenes. A Greek cynic philosopher (4th century B. C.), who is said to have lived in a tub. He searched Corinth with a lantern to find an honest man.

Diomed. Diomedes, one of the bravest of the Greeks in the Trojan War.

Dionysius, the Younger. A tyrant of Syracuse (367-356 B. C.).

Dirce. 1—(993)—A fountain on Mt. Cithæron, near Thebes, Greece. It took its name from (2) Dirce—(994)—wife of Lycus, King of Thebes. She was put to death by the two sons of Antiope, divorced wife of Lycus;

her body was thrown into the fountain which bears her name. According to another legend, her body was changed by Dionysus into the fountain.

Dis. Pluto, god of the lower world, who bore away Proserpina, daughter of Demeter (Ceres).

Dives. 1—(143, 144)—Evil spirits of Persian mythology. 2—(964)—The rich man who, when he died, looked up from hell and saw Lazarus the beggar in Abraham's bosom (*Luke* 16:19-31).

Dnieper. A river in southwestern Russia, flowing to the Black Sea.

Dodsley. Robert Dodsley (1703-64), an English bookseller and playwright. He was the publisher of *A Select Collection of Old Plays*, 12 vols. (1744).

Dog of Darkness. Cerberus, the watchdog at the entrance to Hades.

Doge. The elective chief magistrate, holding princely rank in the republics of Venice and Genoa, Italy.

Dolce. Carlo Dolce (1616-86), a Florentine painter, best known through his Madonnas. The painting referred to on p. 1110a, 24, is *Christ Breaking the Bread.*

Dolor. One of the Titans, who warred against the Olympian gods.

Domdaniel. In *The Arabian Tales* a seminary for evil magicians and a resort of evil spirits; it was an immense cavern "under the roots of the ocean" off the coast of Tunis, in North Africa.

Domenichino. Zampieri Domenichino (1581-1641), a noted Italian painter.

Domingo's Shore. San Domingo, an island republic of the West Indies. Under the negro leader Toussaint L'Ouverture, the island rebelled against the French in 1801, but was subdued by Napoleon.

Don. A river of Aberdeenshire, Scotland, which flows into the North Sea.

Donald. —(553)—Donald Cameron (1695?-1748), a Scottish Highland chieftain known as "Gentle Lochiel." He was a descendant of Sir Evan Cameron of Lochiel.

Donne. John Donne (1573-1631), an English divine, founder of the so-called metaphysical school of poetry.

Don Quixote. The gaunt hero of *Don Quixote*, a Spanish romance by Cervantes (1547-1616).

Doon. A small river in Ayrshire, Scotland, flowing into the Clyde.

Dorian; Doric. Relating to the Doric race, which originated in Doris, an ancient province in Northern Greece.

Doris. —(832)—In Greek mythology, a sea goddess, the daughter of Oceanus, and mother of the Nereids.

Douglas. 1—(481)—James Douglas (d. 1488), a Scottish nobleman, who headed the rebellion against James II of Scotland, 1452-55, as a result of which he was banished. 2—(492)—See note on *Lines on the Lifting of the Banner of the House of Buccleuch*, p. 1320b.

Douglas Tower. A ruined castle in Douglas, a village in Lanarkshire, Scotland.

Dove. A river of England forming part of the boundary between the counties of Derby and Stafford.

Dover. A fortified seaport in the county of Kent, England.

Drachenfels. A mountain in the Siebengebirge, a mountain range on the Rhine in Germany.

Drayton. Michael Drayton (1563-1631), an English poet.

Drontheim. Trondhiem, a province and seaport on the west coast of Norway.

Druid. A priest of religion among the ancient Celts of Gaul, Britain, and Ireland. The Druids were supposed to have some knowledge of geometry, natural philosophy, etc.

Drummond, William (1585-1649). A Scottish poet of Hawthornden, near Edinburgh.

Drury-lane. A street in London near the Strand.

Dryad. In Greek mythology, one of the nymphs of trees. The life of each Dryad was bound up with the tree, usually an oak, in which she lived.

Dryades. The Dryads.

Dryborough. A beautiful monastic ruin on the River Tweed, in Berwickshire, Scotland.

Dryden. John Dryden (1631-1700), a noted English poet and dramatist.

Dryope. A shepherdess in Greek mythology, the playmate of the Hamadryads, changed by them into a poplar.

Duck. Stephen Duck (1705-56), an English farm laborer who won some distinction as a poet.

Duddon. A river in the counties of Cumberland and Lancashire, England.

Dudley, Earl of Leicester. An English statesman and soldier (1533-88), the favorite of Elizabeth.

Dumferling. Dunfermline, a town in Fifeshire, Scotland. It has a noted abbey and was formerly a royal residence.

Duncan. In Shakespeare's *Macbeth*, King of Scotland, murdered by Macbeth.

Dunciad. A satirical poem by Alexander Pope (1688-1744).

Dundagel. A castle near the shore of Cornwall, England.

Dunedin. A poetical name for Edinburgh, Scotland.

Dungeon-gyll. A steep narrow valley at the head of Langdale Vale in the county of Westmoreland, England. See Wordsworth's *The Idle Shepherd-Boys.*

Dunmailraise. Dunmail Raise, a pass in the Lake district of England, on the borders of the counties of Westmoreland and Cumberland.

Dunning. John Dunning (1731-83), an English lawyer and politician.

Dunster. A town in Somersetshire, England.

Dyfed. An old British name for a region in southwestern Wales.

E. One of De Quincey's guardians. He was a rural magistrate in a populous district close to Manchester.

Easedale. A valley in the county of Westmoreland, England.

East Everly. A small town in Wiltshire, England.

Echelles. Les Echelles, a village in eastern France, near the Italian border. It is named from the stairs which formerly existed there and have now been replaced by a road.

Echo. A nymph who by her prattling kept Hera from surprising her husband Zeus in the company of the nymphs. For this, she was punished by being compelled never to speak first and never to be silent when anyone else spoke. She pined away to an echo for love of Narcissus.

Eden. 1—(216, etc.)—In Biblical history, the Garden of Eden. 2—(469)—A river in the counties of Westmoreland and Cumberland, England. It is 8 miles northwest of Carlisle.

Edgeworth, Miss. Maria Edgeworth (1764-1849), and English novelist.

Edina. A poetic name of Edinburgh.

Edinburgh Review, The. A literary and political journal, founded at Edinburgh in 1802. It was the organ of the Whig Party.

Edward the Confessor. King of the West Saxons (1042-66).

Edward I. King of England (1272-1307).

Edward II. King of England (1307-27).

Edward III. King of England (1327-77).

Edward IV. King of England (1461-83).

Egina. Ægina, an island of Greece in the Gulf of Ægina, on the east side of Greece.

Egremond. Egremont, a town in Cumberlandshire, England.

Egremont, Lord. Sir George O'Brien Wyndham (1751-1837), an English patron of art, much interested in agriculture.

Egripo. A former name for Chalcis, a seaport of Eubœ Island, Greece.

Ehrenbreitstein. A town and fortress in Prussia, Germany. It was taken by the French in 1790.

Eildon-hills. Three conical peaks in northwestern Roxburghshire, Scotland.

Eirin. Ireland.

Elamites. People of an ancient kingdom, now part of Persia.

Elba. An island on the Tuscan coast of Italy.

Elbe. A river of Germany flowing from the Bohemian Alps to the North Sea.

Elbingerode. A town in the province of Hanover, Prussia, situated in the Hartz Mountains.

Eldon. John Scott (1751-1838), 1st Earl Eldon, a jurist, twice Lord Chancellor.

Elector of Hanover. One of the seven great princes, who, from the 12th century to the dissolution of the Holy Roman Empire in 1806, had the right of electing the emperor.

Electra. The heroine of *Electra*, a Greek tragedy by Sophocles (5th century B. C.).

Elfins. Elves, tiny spirits in human form, without a soul.

Elgin. Thomas Bruce (1777-1841), Earl of Elgin, a British diplomat. He collected the "Elgin Marbles," ancient Greek sculptures brought from the Parthenon in Athens, Greece, in 1811, and now in the British Museum.

Elia. The pseudonym of Charles Lamb (1775-1834) in his essays contributed to *The London Magazine*, beginning in 1820. The name was borrowed from an Italian, Lamb's fellow-clerk at the South-Sea House.

Elia, Bridget. Charles Lamb's sister Mary.

Elia, James. Charles Lamb's elder brother.

Elijah. A Hebrew prophet of the 9th century B. C.

Eliott. George Eliott (1717-90), an English general. He defended Gibraltar against the Spaniards and French in 1779-83.

Elisha. A Hebrew prophet of the 9th century B. C. He was the attendant and successor of Elijah.

Elizabeth. Queen of England (1558-1603).

Elliot, Sir Gilbert. —(468)—One of the rescuers of Kinmont Willie.

Elliston, Mr. Robert William Elliston (1774-1831), a noted English actor and theatrical manager.

Elpenor. One of the companions of Odysseus in Homer's *Odyssey*.

Elsinore. A seaport near Copenhagen. It was at the entrance of the sound where the Battle of Copenhagen was fought April 2, 1801.

Elwina. A character in *Percy*, a tragedy by Miss Hannah More (1745-1833); it was first acted in 1777.

Elysian. Of or pertaining to Elysium.

Elysium. The abode of the blessed after death.

Emily. See note on *Epipsychidion*, p. 1347b.

Emma. A name given to Wordsworth's sister Dorothy.

Emmet, Robert (1778-1803). An Irish patriot, leader of the United Irishmen. He attempted an uprising in 1803 and was hanged.

Empedocles. (490-430 B. C.). A Greek philosopher, poet, and statesman.

Enceladus. In Greek mythology, a giant with one hundred arms. He was killed by Zeus and buried under Mt. Ætna.

Endor. A village in Palestine, where Saul consulted the female soothsayer (witch of Endor) on the eve of his last battle with the Philistines. At Saul's request she called up Samuel to advise Saul regarding the battle.

Endymion. A beautiful youth, a shepherd of Mt. Latmus, in Caria, Asia Minor, who was beloved by Selene (Diana), the moon goddess.

Enfield. A suburb of London.

Engaddi. Engedi, in scriptural geography, a place abounding in caverns, situated on the shore of the Dead Sea, southeast of Jerusalem. In the desert of Engedi, David hid from Saul.

Enna. An ancient city in Sicily. It was from a flowery meadow near this place that Pluto, ruler of Hades, carried off Proserpina, daughter of Ceres.

Entrance of Christ into Jerusalem, The. A famous painting by Benjamin Robert Haydon (1786-1846), a noted English painter.

Eolian. See Æolian.

Ephesian. Of Ephesus, a city in Asia Minor.

Epictetus (1st century A. D.). A noted Greek Stoic philosopher; he was born a slave in Phrygia, Asia Minor.

Epicurean. Pertaining to the Greek philosopher Epicurus, or to his doctrine.

Epicurus (342-270 B. C.). A Greek philosopher who taught that pleasure is the only good and the end of all morality.

Epirus. An ancient country in northwestern Greece.

Epithalamium. A lyric poem in celebration of a marriage.

Epsom. A town in the county of Surrey, England, famous for its mineral spring and its race course.

Erasmus. Desiderius Erasmus (1466-1536), a famous Dutch classical scholar.

Erebus. A place of utter darkness between the earth and Hades.

Erin. A poetic name for Ireland; *ear, iar,* meaning west, and *in,* an island.

Erminia. In Tasso's *Jerusalem Delivered*, the heroine, who goes in armor with her lover Tancred to Jerusalem.

Erse. The language of the Celts in the Highlands of Scotland.

Erymanthus. A mountain of Arcadia in Greece.

Esau. The oldest son of Isaac, who sold his birthright to Jacob (*Genesis* 25:25).

Eskdale. The valley of the Esk River, in Dumfriesshire, Scotland.

Eske. A river in Dumfriesshire, Scotland, near the English border.

Essex. Robert Devereaux (1567-1601), 2nd Earl of Essex, a favorite of Queen Elizabeth.

Etherege. Sir George Etherege, a seventeenth-century English dramatist.

Ethiop. Archaic for *Ethiopian;* a native of Ethiopia, an ancient country south of Egypt.

Esthwaite. A lake and valley south of Hawkshead, in Lancashire, England.

Eton. A town on the Thames, opposite Windsor, in Buckinghamshire, England; the seat of Eton College.

Etrurians. The ancient inhabitants of Etruria, the modern Tuscany, in Italy.

Ettrick. A river in Selkirkshire, Scotland, which joins the Tweed near Selkirk. The wood adjoining it was formerly known as Ettrick Forest.

Euclid (c. 300 B. C.). A famous Greek geometrician.

Euganean Hills. A chain of volcanic hills in northeastern Italy.

Eugene, Prince. François of Savoy (1663-1736), an Austrian general.

Eumenides. Originally, a euphemistic title of the Furies.

Euphrates. A river of Turkey, Syria, and Iraq.

Euphues. In John Lyly's *Euphues* (1578-79), an Athenian youth who embodies qualities of elegance, beauty, and amorousness.

Euripides (5th century B.C.). One of the greatest tragic poets of Greece; a friend of Socrates.

Eurus. The god of the east wind.

Eurydice. In Greek mythology, a nymph, the wife of Orpheus. After her death, her husband was allowed to follow her to the lower regions, and lead her thence on condition that he should not look around at her during the passage. He violated the condition and she was returned to Hades.

Euxine. The Black Sea, an inland sea bounded by Russia, Asia Minor, European Turkey, and Bulgaria.

Evan. 1—A river in Scotland; it merges with the Clyde near Greenock, in the country of Renfrew. 2—(553)—Sir Evan Cameron (1629-1719), a noted Scottish Highland chieftain of Lochiel; the head of the Cameron clan.

Evandale. A wooded region in the valley of the River Evan, Scotland.

Evander. A son of Hermes, and the leader of an Arcadian colony into Italy, some years before the Trojan War.

Evans. William Evans, a clerk in the South-Sea House, who became deputy cashier in 1792.

Examiner, The. A weekly liberal and literary journal, established in January 1808. Leigh Hunt was at one time editor.

Exciseman. A tax officer who collects duties on domestic goods and guards against violation of the tax laws.

Exeter. The capital city of Devonshire, England.

Exeter, Lord. A member of the titled Cecil family, residing at Burleigh House, Stamford, Lincolnshire, England.

Ezzelin. Ezzelino da Romano (1194-1259), an Italian tyrant who conquered Verona, Padua, and other Italian cities. His name became proverbial for cruelty.

Fairfax, British. Edward Fairfax (1580-1635), an English writer and poet, translator of Tasso.

Faliero. Marino Faliero, the hero of Byron's tragedy, *Marino Faliero*. He was a doge of Venice, beheaded for treason in 1355.

Falkirk. A town in Sterlingshire, Scotland, where Charles Edward, The Young Pretender, defeated the English in 1746.

Falstaff. A fat, witty, and bibulous old knight in Shakespeare's *The Merry Wives of Windsor* and *Henry IV*.

Fanny, Lord. Lord John Hervey (1696-1743), an English writer and politician, called "Lord Fanny" on account of the effeminacy of his habits.

Farnham. A town in the county of Surrey, England.

Fates. In Greek mythology, the goddesses Clotho, Lachesis, and Atropos, who were supposed to control destinies.

Fatima. A common name of Turkish women.

Fauns. In Roman mythology, deities of the woods, represented as half human, with pointed ears, a tail, and goat's feet.

Faunus. A mythical king of Latium, worshiped as a god of agriculture; sometimes identified with the Arcadian Pan.

Fawcett. Henry Fawcett (1833-84), a noted English statesman and political economist.

Fays. Fairies.

Feinagle. Gregor von Feinagle (1765?-1819), an inventor of a system of rules to assist the memory.

Fenelon (1651-1715). A French ecclesiastic and writer.

Fenton. Elijah Fenton (1683-1730), an English versifier, who was associated with Pope in translating the *Odyssey*; he edited the works of Milton and Waller.

Ferdinand. A character in Shakespeare's *The Tempest*, in love with Miranda.

Fergusson. Robert Fergusson (1750-74), a Scottish poet.

Ferney. A village in France, near the Swiss border, the residence of Voltaire.

Ferragus. A giant celebrated in medieval romance. He appears as Ferrau in Ariosto's *Orlando Furioso*, an Italian romance of the 16th century.

Fez. An ancient province and city in Morocco, North Africa.

Fiametta. Maria, daughter of the King of Naples, beloved by Boccaccio.

Fichte. Johann Fichte (1762-1814), a German philosopher, one of the founders of transcendental philosophy.

Fidentia. A town in northern Italy, the scene of the victory of Lucullus, a noted Roman general, over Carbo, the leader of the civil war against Sulla the dictator, in 82 B. C.

Field. Barron Field (1786-1846), an English lawyer and friend of Charles Lamb.

Fielden. John Fielden (1784-1849), a radical reformer who because of his pertinacious advocacy of factory legislation was called, "The Self-acting Mule."

Fielding. Henry Fielding (1707-54), an English novelist and dramatist.

Fiesole. A small village on a hill near Florence, Italy. Landor lived there for some years.

Fife. A county on the east coast of Scotland.

Fillan, Saint. A Scottish abbot of the 7th century. His name was given to several towns and to many chapels and holy fountains in Scotland.

Fingal. See note on *Fingal*, p. 1247b.

Finn. An Irish politician who took an active part in attacking and breaking up the Orangemen, an anti-Catholic organization.

Fitzgerald. William Thomas Fitzgerald (1759-1829), a minor British poet.

Fitzjames, James. James V, King of Scotland (1513-42).

Fitzroy. The name of a titled family in England. See **Grafton.**

Fives Court. A place for playing fives, a game similar to tennis.

Flaccus. Caius Valerius Flaccus (1st century A.D.), a Roman poet.

Flatman. Thomas Flatman (1637-88), a well-known lawyer, painter, and poet.

Flavius. A steward of Timon, in Shakespeare's *Timon of Athens*.

Fleet Street. A prominent street in London.

Fleming. A native of Flanders, an ancient district now divided among France, Belgium, and Holland.

Fletcher. John Fletcher (1579-1625), an English dramatist and poet, collaborator with Francis Beaumont.

Flora. In Roman mythology, the goddess of flowers and spring.

Florence. A large city in north-central Italy, noted for its art treasures and former prominence in literature.

Florentines. Inhabitants of Florence, Italy.

Florizel. A prince in Shakespeare's *The Winter's Tale*, in love with Perdita.

Flower Pot, The. An inn in Bishopsgate Street, the starting place of coaches for the north of London.

Flutter, Sir Fopling. An affected and fashionable fop in George Etherege's comedy, *The Man of Mode* (1676).

Ford. John Ford (1586?-1639), an English dramatist.

Forth. The Firth of Forth, a bay on the east coast of Scotland.

Fortinbras. The warlike Prince of Norway in Shakespeare's *Hamlet*.

Fortunate Blue-Coat Boy, The. A romance (1770) which shows how a Blue-coat boy marries a rich woman of rank.

Fox. Charles James Fox (1749-1806), a celebrated English statesman and orator.

Franche-Comté (*i.e.,* free country). The old County of Burgundy, in eastern France.

Francis I. —(938)—King of France (1515-47), conqueror of Milan (1515) and Burgundy (1544).

Francis, Sir Philip (1740-1818), an English political writer.

Frank. A member of one of the Germanic tribes which conquered Gaul in the 6th century, and from whom the country was named France. In the Orient, any European.

Franklin. Benjamin Franklin (1706-90), a noted American printer and diplomat.

Frederick Barbarossa. Frederick I, the most noted emperor (1155-1190) of the Holy Roman Empire.

Freers. Friars.

Friar Bacon. The Friar Roger Bacon, an English philosopher and scientist of the 13th century, the hero of popular legend.

Friuli. An ancient duchy in northern Italy, now partly included in Austria.

Fuller. Thomas Fuller (1608-61), an English preacher, author of *History of the Worthies of England*.

Furies. The goddesses of vengeance; sometimes synonymous with Fates.

Furness-fells. Upland tracts in northern Lancashire, England.

Fuseli. John Henry Fuseli (1741-1825), a Swiss painter and art critic.

G. One of De Quincey's guardians. He was a banker in Lincolnshire.

Gaelic. Belonging to the Celtic Gaels or Highland Scotch, or their language.

Galaxy. Popularly known as the Milky Way.

Galesus. An Italian river valley famous for fine-fleeced sheep.

Galilee. A sea in Palestine frequented by Christ and his disciples. It is nearly 700 feet below sea level.

Galileo (1564-1642). A famous Italian physicist and astronomer.

Galla Water. A small stream in Roxburghshire, Scotland; it flows into the Tweed near Abbotsford, Scott's home.

Gallic. Pertaining to ancient Gaul, modern France.

Gallican land. France.

Galston Muirs. The moorlands near Galston, a small town in Ayrshire, Scotland.

Gamelyn. The hero of a medieval tale, once attributed to Chaucer.

Gamester, The. A tragedy by Edward Moore (1753) depicting the horrors of gambling.

Ganges. A river in northern India, venerated by Hindus.

Ganymede. The beautiful youth who succeeded Hebe as cupbearer to the gods.

Gaol. Same as *jail*.

Garamant. Fezzan, a province in northern Africa.

Garrick. David Garrick (1717-79), a noted English actor and dramatist.

Garth. Samuel Garth (1661-1719), an English physician and poet.

Gascoigne. Bamber Gascoigne (1725-91), a British Member of Parliament from the county of Essex.

Gate Slack. A passage among the Lowther hills on the border of Dumfriesshire, Scotland.

Gath. A Philistine city in Judah.

Gaul. Ancient Gallia, which in the time of the Romans included what is now France, northern Italy, Belgium, and parts of Switzerland, Germany, and Holland.

Gay. John Gay (1685-1732), an English poet.

Geira. One of the Fatal Sisters.

Gell. Sir William Gell (1777-1836), a writer of travels and topography, especially of Greece and Troy.

Geneva. The name of a canton, a city, and a lake in Switzerland.

Genii. (Tutelary spirits.)

Genoa. A seaport and province in Liguria, Italy.

Genoese. A native of Genoa, Italy.

Gentile. A non-Jewish people.

George. —(512a, 57)—See **Lambe, George.**

George Barnwell. A tragedy by George Lillo (1693-1739), an English dramatist.

George I. King of England (1714-27).

George II. King of England (1727-60).

George III. King of England (1760-1820).

George IV. King of England (1820-30).

George Rex. George III.

George, St. (d. 303?). The patron saint of England.

Georgics. A Latin poem treating of agriculture, trees, animals, etc., written by Virgil about 35 B. C.

Geryon. A fabulous monster with three heads; it was killed by Hercules.

Ghent. A prominent commercial and manufacturing city of East Flanders, Belgium.

Giant Despair. The owner of Doubting Castle in John Bunyan's *Pilgrim's Progress* (1678-84).

Giants. A mythological race of monstrous beings, who assaulted the gods and were imprisoned by them.

Giant's Causeway, The. A famous rock formation on the north coast of Ireland.

Gibbon. Edward Gibbon (1737-94), an English historian; author of *The History of the Decline and Fall of the Roman Empire.*

Gibraltar. A fortified rock and town on the southern coast of Spain; a British possession since 1704.

Gideon. A judge of Israel. As a sign that Israel should be saved through his hand, Gideon asked that God should let dew fall upon a fleece of wool and not upon the earth around it.

Gierusalemme Liberata. *Jerusalem Delivered,* an Italian epic poem by Torquato Tasso (1544-95) on the deliverance of Jerusalem by Godfrey of Bouillon, leader of the First Crusade (1096-1100).

Gieta. A loyal subject of Charles XII, King of Sweden (1697-1718).

Gifford. William Gifford (1756-1826), editor of *The Quarterly Review;* he was hostile to Keats. His satires, *The Baviad* and *The Mæviad,* were published in 1797.

Gilbert. Sir William Schwenck Gilbert (1836-1911), an English poet and dramatist.

Gilpin. The hero of William Cowper's poem *The Diverting History of John Gilpin* (1782).

Gilpin Horner. See **Horner.**

Giovanni. 1—(948)—A character in John Ford's *'Tis Pity She's a Whore* (1633). 2—(1022)—The Christian name of Boccaccio (1313-75), a great Italian poet.

Giraldus Cambrensis. A Welsh ecclesiastic and historian of the early 13th century.

Gisborne. A town on the western border of Yorkshire.

Glaramara. A rugged mountain in Borrowdale Valley, in the western part of Cumberlandshire, England.

Glasgow. The industrial and commercial metropolis of Scotland. It is the seat of the University of Glasgow, founded in 1451.

Glasse, Mrs. Hannah Glasse, author of *The Art of Cookery* (1747), and similar works.

Glaucus. A sea god, originally a fisherman, who became immortal by tasting magic grass.

Gleim. Johann W. Gleim (1719-1803), a German poet.

Glen Fruin. A valley southwest of Loch Lomond, in Dumbartonshire, Scotland.

Glen Luss. A valley southwest of Loch Lomond, in Dumbartonshire, Scotland.

Glenalvon. A character in John Home's tragedy, *Douglas* (1756).

Glenartney. A forest in Perthshire, Scotland.

Glencairn, Earl of. A staunch supporter of Regent Murray of Scotland.

Glenfinlas. A tract of forest ground in the Highlands of Perthshire, Scotland.

Glo'ster. —(63)—"Gilbert de Clare, surnamed the Red, Earl of Gloucester and Hertford, son-in-law to King Edward."—Gray.

Gloucester. A city in Gloucestershire, England.

Gloucester, Duke of. Later Richard III, King of England (1483-85). On the death of Edward IV, his older brother, Richard seized the young Edward V and in 1483 assumed the crown. The deaths of Edward V and his brother in prison were announced shortly after.

Gnidos. Cnidus, an ancient city of Caria, Asia Minor, a seat of the worship of Aphrodite.

Godwin. William Godwin (1756-1836), an English novelist and political writer. See p. 239.

Godwin, Earl. An English statesman (990?-1053), chief minister of Edward the Confessor.

Godwin, Mary Wollstonecraft. An English author (1797-1851), daughter of William and Mary Godwin; second wife of Shelley.

Goethe. Johann W. Goethe (1749-1832), a famous German poet and dramatist.

Gog and Magog. Fabulous giants; names of

two wooden statues in the London Guildhall supposed to represent the survivors of a race of giants which formerly inhabited Britain.

Golconda. A town in India, once famous as a diamond market.

Golden Age. A mythical period of perfect innocence, peace, and happiness. In Roman literature, the period (31 B. C.-14 A. D.) of the greatest classical writers, Virgil, Horace, Livy, Ovid, and others.

Golden Square. A prominent square in London.

Goldsmith. Oliver Goldsmith (1728-74), an Irish poet, novelist, and dramatist.

Gondula. One of the Fatal Sisters.

Gorges, Tyb. Theobald Gorges, a knight of an ancient family near Bristol. He appeared as an actor in Chatterton's *Ælla* and *Goddwyn*.

Gorgon. A fabulous female monster said to inhabit the Western Ocean. The name is usually applied to Medusa, whose hair was transformed into serpents so terrible that all who looked upon them were turned to stone. She was slain by Perseus and her head set on the shield of Athena.

Goshen. The district in Egypt allotted to the Children of Israel for their residence.

Goslar. An ancient city in the province of Hanover, Prussia.

Goth; Goths. A low German tribe that overran the Roman Empire in the 3rd and 4th centuries. They founded kingdoms in Italy, Spain, and southern France. The name is used of any barbaric or uncivilized person or people.

Gotham. A village in Northamptonshire, England, famous for the proverbial follies of its inhabitants. Irving applied the name to New York.

Gothic. Pertaining (1) to the ancient Goths or their language; (2) to the so-called pointed types of medieval architecture; (3) —(97)—to the Middle Ages in general; or (4) characterized by display.

Gowder crag. A rocky eminence in Cumberlandshire, England.

Græmes. The old and powerful family of Graham, which held extensive possessions in the counties of Dumbarton and Stirling, in Scotland.

Grace. One of three goddesses embodying and conferring grace, beauty, and joy, and represented as attending on Venus. The names usually given them are Euphrosyne, Aglaia, and Thalia.

Grafton. A. H. Fitzroy (1735-1811), Duke of Grafton, an English political leader during the reign of George III (1760-1820).

Grahame. James Grahame (1765-1811), a Scottish poet, whose chief work is *The Sabbath* (1804).

Grammaticus, Saxo. A Danish historian of the 12th and 13th centuries.

Granby, Marquis of. John Manners (1721-70), a British general.

Grande Chartreuse. See **Chartreuse**.

Grandison, Lady. A character in Samuel Richardson's *The History of Sir Charles Grandison* (1754).

Granicus. A river in Mysia, Asia Minor, the scene of Alexander the Great's victory over the Persians in 334 B. C.

Grant. Charles Grant (1778-1866), a very unpopular statesman. In 1827 he entered Canning's last ministry as President of the Board of Trade and Treasurer of the Navy.

Granville. George Granville (1667-1735), an English poet, dramatist, and politician.

Grasmere. A village in the county of Westmoreland, at the head of Grasmere Lake.

Grass Market. The place of executions in Edinburgh in the 17th century.

Grassini. Josephina Grassini (1773-1850), a famous Italian opera singer.

Grattan. Henry Grattan, Jr. (1789-1859), an Irish Member of Parliament who was noted for his quarrels in regard to legislation.

Gray. Thomas Gray (1716-71), an English poet. See p. 57.

Great Bear, The. See **Bear**.

Grecian. —(963, 985)—A name given to students of the first class who were preparing for a university.

Greenhead Ghyll. A small valley near Grasmere, in the county of Westmoreland, England.

Grenada. Granada, a province in southern Spain.

Grenville. W. W. Grenville (1759-1834), an English statesman, Secretary of Foreign Affairs in Pitt's ministry (1791-1801).

Greta Woods. A wood along the River Greta in northern Yorkshire, England.

Grétry. André Grétry (1741-1813), a French opera composer.

Greville. Fulke Greville (1554-1628), Lord Brook, author of poems and tragedies, and a biography of Sir Philip Sidney.

Grey Friars. A school established on the site of the old Grey Friars' Monastery, London. Christ's Hospital, founded on this site by Edward VI, was moved to Horsham, Sussex, in 1902.

Gribelin. Simon Gribelin (1661-1733), an engraver who in 1707 drew plates of the *Cartoons* of Raphael (1483-1520), the Italian painter.

Griffin. A fanciful creature, half lion and half eagle.

Groat's House, John o'. See **John o' Groat.**

Grosvenor Place. A fashionable square in London; it has been the residence of many famous men.

Grotto of Antiparos. See **Antiparos.**

Group from the Sistine Chapel. The Sistine, or Sixtine, chapel is the private chapel of the Pope. Its walls and ceilings are decorated with paintings, most noted of which are pictures of the Creation, the Deluge, and the Judgment, by Michelangelo.

Grub Street. A London street (now Milton Street) formerly noted as the residence of poor and needy authors.

Guadalquivir. A river in southern Spain.

Guardian, The. An 18th century periodical published by Addison, Steele, and others.

Guelphs. (Guelfs, Welfs). A powerful family in Germany and Italy from the 9th to the 15th century.

Guildenstern. A courtier in Shakespeare's *Hamlet.*

Guildford. A town in the county of Surrey, England.

Guildhall. The corporation hall of the city of London, England.

Guinea. The coast land of western Africa.

Gulliver's Travels. A social and political satire in the form of a book of travels, written by Jonathan Swift (1726).

Gully. John Gully (1783-1863), a prize fighter and sportsman.

Gwyneth. North Wales.

Gyges. A son of Uranus and Gæa; one of the giants; he was killed by Hercules.

Hadrian. Publius Ælius Hadrianus, a Roman emperor (117-138). He constructed a wall against the Picts and Scots in northern England, between Solway Firth and the mouth of the River Tyne.

Hag of Endor. See **Endor.**

Hagar. Concubine of Abraham.

Hairibee. A place of execution near Carlisle, Cumberlandshire, England.

Haldon. A range of hills in Devonshire, England.

Hallam. Henry Hallam (1777-1859), a noted English historian.

Hallowell, Captain. Benjamin Hallowell, a British naval captain with Nelson at the Battle of Trafalgar (1805).

Hamadryades. See note on *The Hamadryad,* p. 1380.

Hamelin. A town in Hanover province, Prussia.

Hamet. Cid Hamet Benengeli, the imaginary chronicler from whom Cervantes said he got the account of Don Quixote. Byron states that Hamet promises repose to his pen, in the last chapter of *Don Quixote.*

Hamilton. —(465, 467)—See note on *Cadyow Castle,* p. 1316.

Hamilton, Gavin. A Scottish painter and antiquarian (1730-97).

Hamilton, Lady. —(437, 442)—Emma Lyon Hamilton (c1761-1815), the wife of Sir William Hamilton, a British Ambassador at Naples. She was the mistress of Lord Nelson, whom she met in Naples in 1793, and the cause of his separation from his wife.

Hamlet. The leading character in Shakespeare's *Hamlet.*

Hampden. John Hampden (1594-1643), an English patriot and statesman who refused to pay ship-money exacted by Charles I.

Hampshire. A county in South England.

Hampstead. See note on *To Hampstead,* p. 1366.

Handel. George Frederick Handel (1685-1759), a famous German musical composer; he lived in London for some years.

Hanging Gardens of Babylon. A four-acre terraced garden, 300 feet high, built on a raised base supported by pillars. It was constructed by Nebuchadnezzar (6th cent. B. C.), and is known as one of the seven wonders of the world.

Hannibal. The famous general of Carthage. He overcame Marcellus, the Roman general, in southern Italy, in 208 B. C.

Hanover. A province in Prussia.

Hanway, Jonas (1712-86). An author and tourist. He was a vehement opponent of tea, over which he got into conflict with Samuel Johnson, an inveterate tea drinker.

Haram. Harem.

Hardy. Sir Thomas Hardy (1769-1839), an English rear admiral.

Harfleur. A seaport in northern France, taken by the English, Sept. 1415; retaken by the French, 1449.

Harmer-hill. A prominent hill on the road between Wem and Shrewsbury in Shropshire, England.

Harmodius. See p. 720a, n. 3.

Haroun Al Raschid. (Haroun the Just). Caliph or Prince of Bagdad (786-809). He is an important character in *The Arabian Nights' Entertainment.*

Harrington. Charles Stanhope (1753-1829), Third Earl of Harrington, an English general; aide-de-camp of Burgoyne in the American Revolution.

Harriott. John Harriott, author of *Struggles*

Through Life (1807), a work which contains an interesting account of the author's adventures in New England.

Harrison. John Harrison (1693-1776), a noted English mechanician and watchmaker.

Henry the V. Henry V, King of England (1413-22).

Hartz Mountains. A mountain range in Brunswick and Anhalt, Germany, and in the provinces of Hanover and Saxony in Prussia.

Harvey, Captain. Sir Eliab Harvey (1759-1830), an English Admiral.

Hascombe. A hill in the county of Surrey, England.

Hassan. An Arabian prince of the 7th century. He was the grandson of Mohammed.

Hathaway. Mr. Mathias Hathaway, steward at Christ's Hospital from 1790 to 1813.

Hawkshead. A village in northern Lancashire, England.

Hawthornden. A town in the county of Edinburgh, Scotland; it is famous for its caves.

Haydon. Benjamin Robert Haydon (1786-1846), a noted English historical painter.

Hayley. William Hayley (1745-1820), an English writer, author of *The Triumphs of Temper* (1781), *The Triumph of Music* (1804), and various biographies.

Hazlitt. William Hazlitt (1778-1830), an English author and critic. See p. 1033.

Hebe. The cup bearer of the gods.

Hebrid Isles; Hebrides. A group of islands on the west coast of Scotland.

Hecate. An ancient goddess combining traits of moon goddess, earth goddess, and underworld goddess.

Hecla. A volcano in Iceland.

Hector. In Greek legend, the son of Priam and Hecuba, and the leader of the Trojans in the Trojan War. He was slain by Achilles. He is a prominent character in Homer's *Iliad*.

Hela. The goddess of death, who presided over Niflheimr, the hell of the Gothic nations.

Helen. 1—(990, 1101)—Helen of Troy, wife of Menelaus, King of Sparta, carried off on account of her beauty by Paris, son of Priam, King of Troy. She was the Trojan war heroine of Homer's *Iliad*. 2—(1130) Julia Flavia Saint Helen (247-328) mother of Constantine.

Helicon. A part of the Parnassus, a mountain range in Bœotia, in Greece. It had two springs, Aganippe and Hippocrene, sacred to the Muses.

Heligoland. An island and fortress in the North Sea.

Helios. The sun god, called Hyperion by Homer; later he was identified with Apollo.

Hellas. Greece.

Helle. The Hellespont. See **Hellespont.**

Hellenics. A group of poems on Greek topics.

Hellespont. The ancient name of the Strait of Dardanelles, between Europe and Asia. It took its name from Helle (daughter of Athamas and Nephele), who was drowned in it.

Héloïse. —(70)—A French abbess of the 12th century. See **Abelard.**

Helots. The slave class of Laconia, or Sparta, Greece.

Helvellyn. A mountain in Cumberlandshire, England.

Helvetia. The ancient Latin (now poetical) name for Switzerland.

Hengest. A fifth century chief of the Jutes; founder of the Kingdom of Kent, in Britain.

Henry. The name of a number of English Kings: I, 1100-35; II, 1154-89; III, 1216-72; IV, 1399-1413; V, 1413-22; VI, 1422-61; VII, 1485-1509; VIII, 1509-47.

Henry VIII. A chronicle-history play, partly written by Shakespeare.

Heraclea. An ancient Greek city on the coast of Asia Minor.

Heracles. See **Hercules.**

Heraclitus (fl. 500 B.C.). A Greek philosopher of Ephesus, surnamed "The Obscure" because of his style; he was known also as "The Weeping Philosopher" because of the solemnity of his bearing and the hopelessness of his view of life.

Heralds' College. A body of officials, instituted in 1484 to determine rights and titles in heraldry and to regulate the use of heraldic devices.

Herbert. William Herbert (1778-1847), a translator of Icelandic and other poetry. One of his principal pieces is entitled *Song on the Recovery of Thor's Hammer.*

Herculaneum. An Italian city buried with Pompeii in 79 A. D. by the eruption of Mount Vesuvius.

Herculean. Resembling Hercules in strength; requiring great strength or labor.

Hercules. The son of Zeus; he was noted for his gigantic strength; hero of numerous mighty labors, one of which was the securing of the girdle of the Amazon queen Hippolyta.

Hercynian forest. A forest near the Rhine in southern and central Germany.

Herè. Queen of heaven. See **Aphrodite.**

Hermaphroditus. The fabled son of Hermes and Aphrodite, combining both sexes in one body, having been joined to Salmacis, a nymph presiding over a fountain near Halicarnassus. He is regarded as an emblem of indissoluble marriage.

Hermes. Greek god who was the messenger of Zeus and the other gods, identified by the Romans with Mercury.

Hero. —(528, 790, 806, 820)—A priestess of Aphrodite; beloved by Leander, who swam nightly across the Hellespont from Abydos, Asia Minor, to meet her. Leander was drowned during a storm, and Hero, in despair, threw herself into the sea.

Herod. Surnamed "The Great," King of Judea (40-4 B. C.). He is alleged to have ordered the massacre of the infants in Bethlehem, in order to kill the child Jesus. See *Herod's Lament for Mariamne* (p. 538) and note, p. 1327; also Stephen Phillips's *Herod, a Tragedy* (1900).

Herodotus (5th century B. C.). A noted Greek historian.

Herry the fourth. Henry IV, King of England (1399-1413).

Hertford. A branch of Christ's Hospital School for girls, located in Hertford, Hertfordshire, England.

Hertfordshire. A county in the south-central part of England.

Hertha. (Nerthus). A German goddess of fertility and growth.

Hervey, William. An English soldier and nobleman of the early 17th century.

Hesiod (8th century B.C.). A celebrated Greek poet.

Hesper; Hesperus. The evening star in Greek mythology.

Hesperean. Of or pertaining to Hesperus, the evening star.

Hesperides. The maidens who guarded the golden apples in the garden of the gods; also, the garden itself, on the borders of eternal darkness.

Hessey. James Augustus Hessey. A member of the publishing firm of Taylor & Hessey, Keats's publishers.

Heywood. Thomas Heywood. A noted English dramatist of the early 17th century.

Hibernian Strangford. See **Strangford.**

Hierarch. A leader of celestial hosts.

High-Born Helen. This poem appears as *Helen* in most editions of Lamb's works.

Highflyer. A fast stage coach.

Highgate. A suburb of London.

Highland Mary. A name given by Burns to Mary Campbell and to Mary Morison.

Hilda. One of the Fatal Sisters.

Himera. An ancient town in Sicily.

Hincklean. Of Hinckley, a town in Leicestershire, England.

Hindu. A member of one of the native races of Hindustan, the central peninsula of Asia.

Hindhead. A ridge in the southwest part of the county of Surrey, England.

Hinnom; Hinnom's Vale. The ancient valley of Hinnom, south of Jerusalem. It was called also Gehenna and Tophet, and in later times it became the prototype of the place of punishment, and was regarded as the mouth of Hell.

Hippias. Son of Pisistratus; he became ruler and tyrant of Athens in 527 B. C. and was expelled in 510.

Hippocrates. A celebrated physician who served Athens at the time of the great plague, 420 B. C. He was a native of Cos, an island in the Ægean Sea.

Hippocrene. A fountain sacred to the Muses, on Helicon, a part of the Parnassus, a mountain range in Bœotia, in Greece. The fable was that the fountain gushed out where the hoof of Pegasus struck the ground.

Hippolyta. See note on *Theseus and Hippolyta*, p. 1380.

Hobbs. Thomas Hobbes (1588-1679), a celebrated English philosopher.

Hoder. See note on Gray's *The Descent of Odin*, 67b, 55-56, p. 1244a.

Hodges. A student at Christ's Hospital with Lamb.

Hoel. The son of Prince Owain Gwynedd of North Wales; he was a poet and a warrior.

Hofer. Andreas Hofer (1767-1810), a Tyrolese patriot and insurgent leader, executed by the French under Napoleon.

Hogarth. William Hogarth (1697-1764), a noted English painter and engraver.

Hogg, James. A Scottish poet (1770-1835). See p. 502.

Hog-lane. A disreputable street in London; now Middlesex Street.

Hog's Back. A mountain ridge in the county of Surrey, England.

Holcroft. Thomas Holcroft (1745-1809), an English dramatist, actor, and miscellaneous writer.

Holland. Henry Richard Vassall (1773-1840), 3rd Lord Holland, who Byron thought wrote the hostile attack upon his *Hours of Idleness.* Byron says that Holland was "applauded for dinners and translations."

Holy Alliance. An alliance made in 1815 by the Emperors of Austria and Russia and the King of Prussia; subsequently joined by all the European sovereigns except the Pope and the King of England.

Holyhead. A seaport in Anglesea, Wales.

Holy Paul. —(960)—St. Paul's Cathedral,

London; it contains a statue of John Howard (1726-90), the prison reformer.

Holy Roman Empire. Certain portions of the old Roman Empire, together with the Frankish possessions of Charlemagne, who was crowned Emperor at Rome, 800, by Pope Leo III. In 962 the real Holy Roman German Empire began. It became extinct in 1806 when Francis II resigned for the hereditary crown of Austria.

Holy Thursday. Thursday of Holy Week— i. e., the week before Easter.

Homer. An ancient Greek poet, variously assigned to the 8th to 12th century B. C.; the reputed author of the *Iliad* and the *Odyssey* and of the so-called Homeric hymns. According to tradition he lived in Smyrna and on the Islands of Chios and Ios, in the Ægean Sea, and in his old age was blind.

Honorable Society of the Middle Temple. See **Temple.**

Hooker. Richard Hooker (1553-1600), a noted English divine.

Horace. Quintus Horatius Flaccus (65-8 B.C.), a Roman lyric and satirical poet.

Horatio. A character in Shakespeare's *Hamlet.*

Horner, Gilpin. The goblin page in Scott's *The Lay of the Last Minstrel.*

Hornie. The devil.

Horton, Lady Wilmot. Anne Beatrix Horton, wife of Byron's second cousin, Robert John Wilmot (1784-1841). She died in 1871.

Hounslow. A town in the county of Middlesex, England.

Houris. The beautiful damsels who, according to the Moslem faith, are to be companions of the faithful in Paradise.

Hours. Mythological beings represented as accompanying Venus, and as bringing the changes of the seasons.

House of Commons. The lower legislative body of England.

House of Tudor. An English dynasty, descended on the male side from Owen Tudor, on the female side from John of Gaunt through the Beauforts. It comprised the sovereigns Henry VII, Henry VIII, Edward VI, Mary, and Elizabeth.

Houses of Parliament. The legislative body of England consisting of the House of Commons, and the House of Lords.

Howard. 1—(357, 960)—John Howard (1726-90), an English philanthropist, noted for his efforts in behalf of prison reform. 2—(508)—See note on *M'Kimman,* p. 1324. 3—See p. 553b, n. 2.

Howard, Earl of Nottingham. —(246)— Charles Howard (1536-1624), an English admiral.

Howe. William Howe (1729-1814), a British general in the American Revolution.

Hoyle. Edmund Hoyle (1672-1769), an English writer on whist and other card games.

Hubert, Saint (656?-727). A bishop of Liége, Belgium; the patron saint of hunters.

Huguenot. French Protestants who suffered great persecution during the religious wars of the 16th and 17th centuries.

Hull. A seaport on the east coast of Yorkshire, England.

Humboldt. F. H. A. Humboldt (1769-1859), a German naturalist and statesman.

Hume, David (1711-76). A famous Scottish philosopher and historian.

Hume, Joseph (1777-1855). An English politician who devoted himself to financial questions, and was indefatigable in exposing extravagance and abuse. *Retrenchment* was his watchword.

Hun. One of an obscure Asiatic nomadic and warlike race living between the Ural and Volga about the dawn of the Christian era. —(446)—Austrians.

Hungerford. A city in western Berkshire, England.

Hunt. James Henry Leigh Hunt (1784-1859), an English poet and essayist. See p. 892.

Hyacinth; Hyacinthus. A beautiful youth beloved of Apollo and accidentally killed by him while playing at discus throwing. From the blood of Hyacinthus sprang the flower called hyacinth.

Hybla. An ancient town of Sicily, famous for its honey.

Hydaspes. The ancient name of the River Jhelum in India.

Hyde Park Corner. Hyde Park is a park in Westminster, London, one of the largest of the London parks.

Hymen. The god of marriage.

Hyperion. A Titan, father of Helios, the sun god; also the sun god himself, the incarnation of light and beauty.

Iago. The villain in Shakespeare's *Othello.*

Ianthe. Sophia Jane Swift, Landor's early sweetheart. Her first husband died in 1812 and she soon afterwards married M. de Molandé. They went to live in Paris, where her second husband died. She spent two years (1829-31) in Florence, and passed the remainder of her life in England and France. She died in Paris in 1851.

Iäpetus. A Titan, father of Prometheus and Atlas, and fabled ancestor of the human race.

Iberian. Of Iberia, the ancient name of the Spanish peninsula.

Icarus. A youth who, flying with his father, Dædalus, on wings fastened with wax, soared so high that the sun melted the wax and he fell into the Icarian Sea and was drowned.

Icolmkill. Iona, an island of the inner Hebrides on the west coast of Scotland.

Ida. An ancient mountain in the Island of Crete, southeast of Greece, connected with the worship of Zeus.

Idalia. A town in the Island of Cyprus, in the Mediterranean, containing a temple for the worship of Venus, goddess of love.

Iliad. A Greek epic poem dealing with the story of the siege of Ilium (Troy). It is ascribed to Homer.

Ilion. See **Troy.**

Ilissus. A small river in Attica, Greece.

Ilium. See **Troy.**

Imogen. A character in Shakespeare's *Cymbeline.*

Inde. 1—(642)—Indus, a river in India. 2—(835)—India.

India House. The London headquarters of the East India Company, a trading company formed in 1600 to carry on commerce with the East Indies. It became also a great political power, until in 1858 it practically governed India.

Indostan. India.

Indus. A river in India.

Inferno. The first part of Dante's *The Divine Comedy,* describing the poet's journey through hell under the guidance of Virgil.

Inner Temple. See **Temple.**

Inquisition. The Roman Catholic court for examination and punishment of heretics. It came into being in 1231, and took its most severe form in Spain where torture, as a means of eliciting evidence, was generally employed.

Inverlochy. A place in Argyllshire, Scotland, where James Graham (1612-50), Earl of Montrose, defeated the Scottish Covenanters in 1645.

Inverness. A county in north-central Scotland.

Inversneyde. A village in Stirlingshire, Scotland, near the head of Loch Lomond.

Io. A beautiful nymph beloved of Jupiter; she aroused the jealousy of Juno.

Iona, Island of. One of the Inner Hebrides, off the west coast of Scotland.

Ionian; Ionic. Pertaining to Ionia, the ancient name of the coast district and islands of western Asia Minor, peopled by Greek colonists.

Iphigeneia. See note on *On His Own Agamemnon and Iphigeneia,* p. 1379.

Iran. Persia.

Iris. The personification of the rainbow, regarded as the swift messenger of the gods. She was supposed to loosen the hair of dying persons so that their spirits might depart.

Irish Rebellion. A rebellion fostered in 1798 by the Society of United Irishmen for the avowed purpose of separating Ireland from the British Empire.

Iron Age. In Greek mythology, the last and most degraded period of the ages preceding the human era. Opposed to Golden Age.

"Iron Mask." An allusion to the "Man in the Iron Mask," a mysterious figure of the late 17th century in Italy. He has been identified as Count Mattioli, Secretary of State at the Court of Gonzaga, Duke of Mantua.

Irthing. A river in the northeastern part of Cumberlandshire, England.

Isaiah. A Hebrew prophet (740-701 B. C.).

Iscamm. A boon companion of Canyng. He appears as an actor in Chatterton's *Ælla* and *Goddwyn.*

Iser. A river in Bavaria, Germany.

Isle of Man. An island in the Irish sea.

Islington. A parish in northern London.

Ismail. A town of Russia, formerly a Turkish fortress. The massacre which followed the storming of the city by the Russians in 1790 was one of the bloodiest events in the annals of European warfare.

Israel. The kingdom of the northern tribes of the Israelites, who seceded from the southern tribes in the reign of Rehoboam, 953 B. C.

Israel's sons. Children of Israel; descendants of Jacob.

Istambol. Istanbul, a Turkish name for Constantinople.

Italia. The ancient name of Italy.

Ithaca. An island of the Ionian group, Greece; in classical legend, the home of Odysseus.

Ixion. In Greek legend, a king of a wild people of Thessaly, Greece, in the heroic age. He made love to Hera, by whom (in the form of a cloud sent by Zeus) he became father of the Centaurs. For boasting of the favors of Hera, Ixion was bound to an endlessly revolving wheel in Tartarus.

Jack. The conventional name of a sailor.

Jack Cade. Jack Cade was the leader of "Cade's Rebellion," a political uprising in Kent, in 1450.

Jack Horner. An old nursery rhyme, the hero of which "sat in a corner eating his Christmas pie."

Jackson. John Jackson (1769-1845), a well-known prize fighter.

Jacob. The son of Isaac, and ancestor of the Israelites.

Jacobi. Friedrich Heinrich Jacobi (1743-1819), a noted German philosopher.

Jaffa. A seaport of Palestine. It was stormed by the French under Napoleon in 1799.

Jamblichus. One of the Neo-Platonic philosophers of the 4th century.

Janus. An ancient Roman deity, god of gates and doors. He was represented with two faces looking in opposite directions, thus seeing the past and the future at the same time.

James. 1—(469)—James VI, King of Scotland (1567-1625) and—(653)—King of England as James I (1603-25); 2—(481)—James V, King of Scotland (1513-42); 3—(1105)—James I, King of Scotland (1406-37); 4—(1176)—King of England (1685-88).

Jamy, the Skottishe Kyng. —(116)—James I, King of Scotland (1406-37).

Jason. See **Medea.**

Jean. Burns's wife.

Jeffrey. Francis Jeffrey (1773-1850), a Scottish critic, essayist, and jurist. He was editor of *The Edinburgh Review.* See p. 910.

Jenkins. A dissenting minister in Whitchurch, Shropshire, England.

Jephthah. A judge of Israel who sacrificed his daughter in fulfillment of a vow that if he subdued the Ammonites he would kill whatever came out of his house to meet him on his return.

Jericho. An ancient walled city of Palestine. When attacked by the invading Israelites under the command of Joshua, its walls were miraculously destroyed.

Jerome. St. Jerome (c340-420), one of the fathers of the Latin Church. He published a Latin version of the Bible known as the Vulgate.

Jesuit. One of a Catholic religious order founded by Ignatius Loyola in 1534, under the title of The Society of Jesus, whence its name—Jesuits.

Jewel. John Jewel (1522-71), Bishop of Salisbury, an English divine.

Joan of Arc. "The Maid of Orleans" (1412-31), the French national heroine. She won a great battle against the English in 1429.

Jock of Hazeldean. A traditional ballad hero.

Job. The chief personage in the book of *Job,* in the Old Testament.

John Buncle. A novel by Thomas Amory (1691?-1788), an English humorist and moralist. The hero, John Buncle, is noted for his amorousness; he was married seven times.

John o' Groat's House. A building near Duncansby Head, the northernmost point of Scotland, said to have been erected by John o' Groat, a Dutchman who probably settled there about 1489.

John, Saint. One of the twelve apostles; author of the book of *John.*

Johnson. Samuel Johnson (1709-84), a celebrated English essayist and lexicographer. He wrote in the conventional classical manner.

Jonathan. —(646)—See **Bull, John.**

Jonson. Ben Jonson (c1573-1637), a celebrated English poet and dramatist.

Josephus. Flavius Josephus (37-96?), a celebrated Jewish historian.

Joshua. A leader of the Israelites who conquered Canaan. He is the subject of the book of *Joshua.*

Jove. Same as Jupiter or Zeus.

Jovian. Resembling Jove.

Judah. The tribe descended from Judah, or the territory in Palestine assigned to it.

Judaism. The Jewish civil and religious law.

Judas. Judas Iscariot, the betrayer of Christ.

Judean. Of Judea, a southern division of Palestine in the Roman period.

Julian, Count. The hero of Landor's dramatic poem *Count Julian.*

Julian, Emperor. Emperor of Rome (361-363).

Juliet. The heroine in Shakespeare's *Romeo and Juliet.*

Jungfrau. A high mountain of the Alps, in Switzerland.

Junius. The signature of an unknown writer of letters attacking the British government, published 1769-72.

Juno. The wife of Jupiter and queen of heaven. She was identified with the Greek goddess Hera. See **Ixion.**

Junot. Andoche Junot (1771-1813), a French general.

Jupiter. The supreme deity in Roman mythology. He was worshiped on the Capitoline Hill at Rome. His weapon was the thunderbolt; the eagle was sacred to him.

Jura. A chain of mountains in eastern France and western and northern Switzerland.

Juvenal (c55-125). A Roman satiric poet.

Kaf. In oriental legend a mountain range consisting of a single emerald, said to surround the world.

Kaff. Caucasus, a mountain system in Russia, between Europe and Asia.

Kaliburn. Excalibur, the sword of King Arthur. Monkish historians say it came into the possession of Richard I and was given by him during the Crusades to Tancred, King of Sicily, as a royal present, about 1190.

Kant. Immanuel Kant (1724-1804), founder of the so-called Critical System of Philosophy.

Kathay (Cathay). A poetical name for China.

Katrine. A lake in the western highlands of Perthshire, Scotland.

Kean, Mr. Edmund Kean (1787-1833), a celebrated English actor.

Keats, George and Georgiana. George Keats was the brother of John Keats the poet. Georgiana was George Keats's wife.

Kemble, Mr. John Philip Kemble (1757-1823), a noted English actor.

Kendal. A town in the county of Westmoreland, England.

Kensington. A western section of London.

Kent. 1—(81)—William Kent (1684-1748), an English painter, sculptor, architect, and landscape gardener. 2—(313, 320)—A county in southeastern England. 3—(984) —The servant of Lear in *King Lear*.

Kentish Town. A district in the northwestern part of London.

Keppel. Augustus Keppel (1725-86), an English admiral.

Keswick. A town in Cumberlandshire, England, the burial place of Southey.

Keymer. Mr. Keymer, a London bookseller.

Kilda (St. Kilda). A small island outside of the Hebrides, west of Scotland.

Kilmarnock. An ancient mining and manufacturing town in Ayrshire, Scotland.

King of Day. Hyperion, god of the sun.

King of Terrors. Death. See *Job* 18.

King's College. A college of Cambridge University, Cambridge, England.

Kirk-Alloway. See **Alloway.**

Klopstock. Friedrich Gottlieb Klopstock (1724-1803), a German lyric and epic poet, author of *The Messiah.*

Knox. John Knox (1505-72), a celebrated Scottish reformer, statesman, and writer.

Koran. The Mohammedan sacred scripture.

Koskiusko. See note on *Koskiusko,* p. 1295.

Kotzebue. See p. 424b, n. 2.

Krudener, Madame. Barbara von Vietinghoff-Scheel (1764-1824), Baroness of Krüdener, a Russian mystic, friend of the Czar, Alexander I (1775-1825).

Kyrkesly; Kirkless. A priory in western Yorkshire.

Labrador. A peninsula between Hudson Bay and the Atlantic Ocean in Canada.

Lady Blanch. A picture known as *Modesty and Vanity.*

Laertes. A character in Shakespeare's *Hamlet.*

Lahore. An important trade and educational city in India, annexed by the British in 1849.

Laian. Laius, legendary King of Thebes, upon learning from the oracle that he would be killed by his son, who would wed his own mother, left his infant son Œdipus in an exposed place. The boy was rescued, and later slew his father unwittingly.

Lake District; Lakes. The region in northern England including the counties of Lancaster, Cumberland, and Westmoreland, so called because of its beautiful lakes.

Lake Leman. See **Leman.**

Lakers. A name given to Wordsworth, Coleridge, Southey, and others because of their residence in the Lake district of England.

Lamb. Charles Lamb (1775-1834), a noted English essayist. See p. 941.

Lamb, Miss. Charles Lamb's sister Mary (1764-1847).

Lambe. 1—(512a, 55)—William Lamb (1779-1848); 2—(512a, 57; 512b, 82; 519; 522) —George Lamb (1784-1834). Both were cousins of Byron's wife. George Lamb was a contributor to *The Edinburgh Review,* and the author of an unsuccessful farce, *Whistle for It.* At the time of Byron's separation from his wife, George Lamb supported Byron; the wives of George and William Lamb supported Lady Byron. William Lamb supported neither.

Lambro. 1—(532)—Lambros Katzones, a noted Greek revolutionist and pirate, of the late 18th century. 2—(631)—Haidée's father, in Byron's *Don Juan,* probably identified with 1.

Lancashire. A county in northwestern England.

Lancaster. 1—(64, 132, 247)—The name of a line of English kings descended from John of Gaunt, Duke of Lancaster, third son of Edward III. In the 15th century, the House of Lancaster contested for the throne with the House of York, descendants of Edmund, Duke of York, fourth son of Edward III, in the War of the Roses, so called from the red rose and the white rose, badges of the adherents of the respective houses. 2—(1146)—A city in Lancashire, England.

Lane's novels. The novels published by William Lane at the Minerva Press, in London.

Langdale Pike. A hill in the county of Westmoreland, England, at the head of Langdale Vale, near Ambleside.

Laocoön. An antique group in marble representing the death of the Trojan priest Laocoön and his two sons, who are represented as crushed by huge serpents.

Laodamia. See note on *Laodamia*, p. 1290.

La Place. Pierre Laplace (1749-1827), a French astronomer and mathematician.

Lapland. A region in the northern parts of Norway, Sweden, and Russia.

Lapponian. Belonging to Lapland.

Lara. 1—(93)—See note on *Fingal*, p. 1247. 2—(932)—A poem by Byron.

Last Supper. A famous painting by Leonardo da Vinci (1452-1519), in Milan, Italy. It was finished in 1498.

Latian. Of or pertaining to ancient Latium in Italy.

Latimer. Hugh Latimer (1488-1555), an English Protestant martyr, Bishop of Worcester.

Latium. An ancient country in Italy, between Etruria and Campania; the home of the Latin or Roman people.

Latmian. Endymion, a shepherd on Mt. Latmus, Asia Minor, who was loved by Diana.

Latmos. Latmus, a mountain in Caria, Asia Minor, where Diana found the shepherd boy Endymion, sleeping.

Latona. Same as Leto, mother of Apollo and Artemis. She personifies night.

Laura. The sweetheart of Petrarch, immortalized in his sonnets.

Lausanne. A city in Switzerland.

Lawrence, Sir. Sir Thomas Lawrence (1769-1830), a noted portrait painter.

Lawson, Dr. The Master of Manchester School when De Quincey was a student there, in 1800.

Laybach (Laibach). A city in Austria.

Lazarus. The beggar "full of sores" who desired to be fed with the crumbs from the table of the rich man Dives (*Luke* 16: 19-31). See **Dives.**

Lea. A river in Bedfordshire, England, famous for its fish.

Leadenhall Street. A street in London on which was located the East India House, where Lamb served as a clerk from 1792 to 1825.

Leader Haughs. Lowlands along the River Leader, which joins the Tweed, near Melrose, in Roxburghshire, Scotland.

Leander. See **Hero** (1).

Lear. King Lear in Shakespeare's *King Lear*.

Lebanon. A mountain range in Syria, once famous for its forests of cedar.

Leboo, Prince. Jean Louis Joseph Lebeau (1779-1863), a Belgian diplomat, who carried on important negotiations with England, 1830-31.

Leda. Zeus, in the form of a swan, made love to Leda, and from this amour, according to one legend, were born Castor and Pollux, Helena and Clytemnestra.

Leicestershire. An inland county of England.

Leigh, Mrs. Byron's half sister Augusta.

Leipsic. Leipzig, a city in Saxony, Germany.

Leith. A seaport of Scotland, near Edinburgh.

Leman, Lake. Lake of Geneva, Switzerland.

Lemnos (Limno). An island in the Ægean Sea, belonging to Turkey.

Lennox. A district at the lower extremity of Loch Lomond, in the county of Dumbarton, Scotland. It was the residence of the Lennox family, and was frequently raided by the mountaineers.

Lenny. A pass from the village of Callander, Perthshire, Scotland, to the Highlands.

Lent. A fasting period of forty days immediately preceding Easter.

Leo X. Pope from 1513 to 1521. His pontificate was marked by great political changes and a revival of literature and the fine arts.

Leopold, Prince. Duke of Saxe-Coburg (1790-1865), afterwards, Leopold I, King of Belgium (1831-65). He married Princess Charlotte, daughter of George IV of England, in 1816.

Lepanto. A naval battle fought in the Bay of Lepanto, on the west coast of Greece, between the fleet of Turkey and the allied fleets of Spain and Italy, Oct. 7, 1571. The Turks were defeated with great loss.

Lessing. Gotthold E. Lessing (1729-81), a celebrated German critic and dramatist.

L'Estrange. Sir Roger L'Estrange (1616-1704), an English journalist and pamphleteer.

Lethe, Lethean. Lethe was the river of forgetfulness in Hades.

Leuctra. A village in ancient Bœotia, Greece, the scene of a victory by the Thebans over the Spartans, in 371 B. C.

Leven-glen. The valley of the River Leven, which connects Loch Lomond with the River Clyde in Dumbartonshire, Scotland.

Leviathan. A large unidentified animal mentioned in the Bible; hence, anything huge or colossal.

Lewis; Monk Lewis. Matthew Gregory Lewis (1775-1818), an English novelist and dramatist, author of the romance *Ambrosio, or the Monk* (1795).

Libs. The west-southwest wind.

Libyan. Of ancient Libya, a part of northern Africa west of Egypt.

Liddesdale. A valley in Dumfriesshire, Scotland, on the English border.

Life and Opinions of Tristram Shandy, The. A discursive novel by Laurence Sterne (1713-68), an English novelist and humorist.

Lilliputian. Very small, like the people of Lilliput, an imaginary island in Swift's *Gulliver's Travels* (1726).

Lillo. George Lillo (1693-1739), an English dramatist, author of *George Barnwell* and other plays.

Lima. A city and province in Peru, South America.

Limbo-lake. The "pit" of Hell.

Lincoln. A city in Lincolnshire, England.

Lincoln green. A cloth made in the city of Lincoln, and worn by huntsmen.

Linden. Hohenlinden, a village in Bavaria.

Lindsay. Lord Lindsay, a staunch supporter of Regent Murray of Scotland. He was noted for his fierceness and brutality.

Linlithgow. A town in the county of Linlithgow (West Lothian), Scotland.

Linton. A parish near Cambridge, in Cambridgeshire, England.

Lion. —(839)—The constellation Leo.

Lion of St. Mark. A winged lion holding an open book with the inscription "Pax tibi, Marce, Evangelista meus"; the national emblem of Venice. It was cast in the 12th century.

Lisbon. The capital of Portugal.

Lithgow. William Lithgow (1582-1645?), a noted English traveler. He is said to have walked over 36,000 miles through Europe, Asia, and Africa. He is the author of a book of travel and of other works.

Little. A pseudonym of Thomas Moore (1779-1852), an Irish poet. See p. 450.

Little John. A lieutenant of Robin Hood, noted for his skill with the bow.

Liverpool. A large seaport in Lancashire, England.

Livia. The wife of Augustus Cæsar, Emperor of Rome (31 B.C.-14 A.D.).

Livy. Titus Livius (59 B.C.-17 A.D.), a famous Roman historian.

Llangollen. A town in Denbighshire, Wales.

Llewellyn. A Welsh prince noted for his mild temperament.

Lloyd. Charles Lloyd (1775-1839), a minor English poet. Charles Lamb and Lloyd were classed with Coleridge and Southey, in *The Anti-Jacobin*, as advocates of French socialism.

Loch-Achray. A small lake in Perthshire, Scotland.

Lochard. A small lake near the village of Aberfoyle, in Perthshire, Scotland.

Lochgyle. A partially landlocked arm of the sea on the west coast of Scotland.

Lochiel. The chief of the Camerons. See note on *Lochiel's Warning*, p. 1311.

Loch Lomond. The largest lake of Scotland, situated in the counties of Stirling and Dumbarton. It is noted for scenes of grandeur and beauty.

Lochlin. The Gaelic name of Scandinavia.

Locke, John (1632-1704). A noted English philosopher.

Lockhart. J. G. Lockhart (1794-1854), a Scottish critic and biographer; son-in-law of Sir Walter Scott.

Lo-door banks. Craglike heights in Cumberlandshire, England.

Lodore. A famous cataract of a branch of the River Derwent, in Cumberlandshire, England.

Logan. John Logan (1748-88), a Scottish lyric poet.

Lok (Loki). In Norse mythology, the god of discord and evil, sometimes classed with the Aesir, sometimes with the Jotunns.

Lombard Street. An important street in London occupied by many banks.

Lomond, Loch. See **Loch Lomond.**

Lomonds. Ben-Lomond is a mountain in Stirlingshire, Scotland. West of it is the beautiful lake Loch Lomond.

London Gazette, The. The official government newspaper of London.

London Magazine, The. A monthly magazine founded in London in 1820 under the editorship of John Scott. In 1821, it passed into the ownership of the publishing firm of Taylor and Hessey. Among its contributors were Lamb, Hazlitt, De Quincey, Hood, Keats, and Carlyle.

London Tower. Originally a royal residence and citadel, situated on the River Thames, in London. It was long famous as a state prison for political offenders.

Longinus. Dionysius Cassius Longinus (213?-273), a Greek Platonic philosopher and critic.

Longman, Messrs. A long-established English publishing house.

Lopé. Lopé de Vega (1562-1635), a celebrated Spanish poet and dramatist.

Lord Lieutenant of the County. A deputy of the sovereign who had wide military powers.

Lords and Commons. Members of the upper and lower houses of Parliament.

Lords of Convention, The. Scottish Parliament.

Lorenzo. —(35)—Probably Philip, Duke of Wharton (1698-1731), an English political intriguer noted for his profligacy.

Lorrain. Claude Gelée (1600-82), a celebrated French landscape painter.

Lorton Vale. A small valley in Cumberland-shire, England.

Lothbury. A street in London, near the Bank of England; it is frequented by business-men and clerks.

Lothian. The county in which Edinburgh is situated.

Louis XIV. King of France (1643-1715).

Lowe. Sir Hudson Lowe (1769-1844), a British general, governor of St. Helena dur-ing Napoleon's captivity.

Lowth, Dr. Robert Lowth (1710-87), an Eng-lish scholar and theologian.

Lowther Park. A small place on the River Lowther, in Cumberlandshire, England.

Lucan. Marcus Annæus Lucanus (39-65), a Roman poet and prose writer, author of *Pharsalia.*

Lucifer. Satan, the prince of darkness; so called from the impression the church fathers had that he had fallen from heaven. Also, the morning star.

Lucretilis. A hill near the farm of Horace, among the Sabine Hills, east of Rome.

Lucretius. Titus Lucretius Carus (c95-55 B.C.), a Roman poet and philosopher.

Lucullus. Lucius Licinius Lucullus (c110-57 B.C.), a Roman general and consul. He defeated Carbo, the leader of the civil war against Sulla the dictator, in 82 B. C., and other noted generals. He was famous for his wealth and luxury.

Lugar. —(199)—A small stream near the village of Lugar, in Ayrshire, Scotland.

Lunardi. Vincenzo Lunardi (1759-1806), a famous Italian aeronaut, who made several successful ascents in England and Scotland in 1784-86. He was secretary to the Neapoli-tan ambassador in England at the time.

Luss. A small village on the west shore of Loch Lomond, in Dumbarton, Scotland.

Luxor. A winter resort on the Nile River in upper Egypt; the site of ancient Thebes. It is famous for its antiquities.

Lycean, Mount. Lycæum, a mountain in Ar-cadia, Greece, the chief seat of the worship of Pan, god of flocks and shepherds.

Lycid; Lycidas. In Milton's *Lycidas,* a name given to Milton's friend Edward King, lamented in the poem.

Lyncolne. See **Lincoln Green.**

Lynn. A seaport in Norfolkshire, England.

Lyons (Lyon). An important city in the De-partment of Rhone, France.

Lyrical Ballads. A collection of poems by Wordsworth and Coleridge published in 1798. For contents of the first edition see p. 1294. The second edition, published in two volumes in 1800, contained all of the poems of the first edition, Wordsworth's *Preface,* and a number of additional poems, including *The Two April Mornings* (p. 266), *The Fountain* (p. 266), *The Brothers, Ruth, The Two Thieves, Michael* (p. 292), and *The Old Cumberland Beggar* (p. 260),—by Wordsworth; and *Love,* by Coleridge.

Lysicrates. See **Monument of Lysicrates.**

Lyttleton, Lord. George Lyttleton (1709-73), an English author and politician.

Mab. A fairy queen who delivers men of their dreams. See *Romeo and Juliet,* I, 4.

Macartney, Lord. George Macartney (1737-1806), an Irish diplomat, Governor of Madras, a province in India.

Macassar. A former kingdom in one of the East India Islands.

Macbeth. A character in Shakespeare's *Mac-beth.*

Maccaronies. Fops or dandies. The word came into use in England between 1750 and 1775. Horace Walpole tells about the Mac-caroni Club, composed of "all the traveled young men who wear long curls and spying-glasses."

Macculloch. John Ramsay Macculloch (1789-1864), Professor of Political Economy, Lon-don University (1828-32).

Macedonia. An ancient country in northern Greece; the most powerful seat of empire of its time, under Alexander the Great (4th century B. C.).

Macfarlane. A clan of Scottish Highlanders attached to the Regent Murray. They re-sided in Lennox, the ancient name of a district comprising parts of the counties of Stirling, Perth, Renfrew, and Dumbarton.

Machiavel. Niccolo Machiavelli (1469-1527), a celebrated Italian statesman and political writer.

Mackenzie. Dr. James Mackenzie (d. 1837), a practicing physician at Mauchline, Irvine, and Edinburgh, Scotland. He was one of Burns's warmest friends.

Mackintosh. Sir James Mackintosh (1765-1832), a Scottish philosopher and historian; he published *Vindiciæ Gallicæ* in 1791 in answer to Burke's *Reflections on the Revolu-tion in France.*

Macneil. Hector Macneil (1746-1818), a popular Scottish poet.

Macon. An obsolete form of *Mahound,* often used as a name for the devil.

Macpherson. James Macpherson (1738-96), a Scottish writer and politician; translator or author of *Ossian.* See p. 86.

Madeira. A Portuguese island northwest of Africa; it is noted for its wines.

Madison, James. President of the United States (1809-17).

Madoc. A legendary Welsh prince, said to have discovered America about 1170.

Madonna. An old Italian form of address equivalent to *Madam*. Also, an Italian designation of the Virgin Mary.

Mænad. A priestess or female votary of Bacchus; hence, a woman given to revelry and debauchery.

Mænalus. A mountain in Arcadia, Greece, the favorite haunt of Pan, god of flocks and shepherds.

Mæander. In ancient geography, a winding river which rose in Asia Minor and flowed into the Ægean Sea near Samos. Its modern name is Menderez.

Mæonides. A poetical epithet of Homer, from his reputed native place, Mæonia, the ancient name of Lydia, a district in Asia Minor.

Mævius. An inferior Roman poet of the first century B.C., an enemy of Virgil and Horace.

Magdalen. Mary Magdalen, traditionally regarded as the repentant sinner forgiven by Christ. See *Luke* 7:36.

Magi; Magian. The learned and priestly caste of the ancient Medes and Persians; the keepers of sacred articles, tutors of the kings, philosophers, augurs, and astrologers.

Magog. See **Gog.**

Magus Zoroaster. See **Zoroaster.**

Mahomet. See **Mohammed.**

Maia. The eldest of the Pleiades, and mother of Hermes. She was identified by the Romans with an old Italian goddess of spring.

Maiano. Benedetto Maiano (1424?-98), an eminent Italian sculptor and architect.

Maid Marian. A companion of Robin Hood, a legendary medieval outlaw hero.

Maidenhead. A borough in Berkshire, England, situated on the Thames.

Malaga. The name of a city and a province on the southern coast of Spain.

Malaprop, Mrs. A character in Richard Sheridan's *The Rivals* (1775).

Malay. The most southern portion of continental Asia. The name is also applied to inhabitants of the country.

Mallet. David Mallet (1705-65), a Scottish poet and author. See p. 15.

Mammon. The god of riches and the personification of wealth. He is one of the fallen angels in Milton's *Paradise Lost.*

Man, Isle of. An island in the Irish Sea.

Manasseh. One of the ten tribes of the He-

brews dwelling along the Jordan River, named from Manasseh, the son of Joseph.

Manchester. A large manufacturing city in Lancashire, England.

Mandarin. A Chinese public official.

Mandeville. Sir John Mandeville, the reputed author of a 14th-century book of travels.

Manners. The name of a titled English family, prominent in the 18th century.

Manning. Thomas Manning (1774-1840), an English linguist, who spent a number of years in Tibet and China.

Mantuan. A surname of Virgil, a native of Mantua, in Lombardy, Italy.

Marathon. A plain in Attica, Greece, the scene of the Battle of Marathon, in which the Athenian general Miltiades defeated the Persian army and saved Greece, 490 B.C.

Marceau. François Marceau (1769-96), a general of the French Republic, killed in a battle at Altenkirchen, Prussia.

Marcellus. A famous Roman general. See **Hannibal.**

Marengo. A village in northwestern Italy, the scene of Napoleon's victory over the Austrians on June 14, 1800.

Mareotid. Mareotis is a lake in the northwestern part of Lower Egypt.

Margaret. 1—(301-305, 925)—The Weaver's wife in Book 1 of Wordsworth's *The Excursion.* 2—(466)—The wife of Hamilton of Bothwellhaugh in Scott's *Cadyow Castle.* 3—(480)—A character in Scott's *The Lady of the Lake.* 4—(944)—Unidentified. 5—(1085)—De Quincey's wife.

Margaret of Anjou. Queen of Henry VI, King of England (1422-61).

Marian, Maid. See **Maid Marian.**

Marie Antoinette. Daughter of Emperor Francis I and Maria Theresa, of Austria; Queen of France, and wife of Louis XVI, King of France (1774-92); she was executed by the Jacobins in 1793.

Marinus. Marinus of Flavia Neopolis, in Palestine, a philosopher and rhetorician of the 5th century A.D. He was a disciple of Proclus.

Marius, Caius. A Roman general of the 2nd century B.C. He served in the siege of Numantia, a famous city in Spain, 132 B.C., under Scipio Africanus the Younger.

Mark, St. See **St. Mark.**

Marlborough; Marlbro. 1—(426, 624)—John Churchill (1650-1722), Duke of Marlborough, a famous English general and statesman. He defeated the French in the Battle of Blenheim in Bavaria, in 1704. 2—(1033)—A town in Wiltshire, England. 3—(1137)—A forest near Marlborough, Wiltshire.

Marlowe. Christopher Marlowe (1564-93), an English dramatist, who developed blank verse.

Marmaduke Thompson. See **Thompson.**

Marmion. The hero of Scott's tale *Marmion.*

Maro. The family name of Virgil (Publius Virgilius Maro, 70-19 B.C.), a Latin poet.

Marrs. Marr was the name of a family murdered by the notorious John Williams in the early 19th century. See De Quincey's Postscript to *On Murder Considered as One of the Fine Arts.*

Mars. 1—God of War. 2—(737)—One of the planets.

Marshal Ney. See **Ney.**

Marston Moor. A plain in Yorkshire, England, the scene of a victory of the Parliamentary forces and Scots over the Royalists, July 2, 1644.

Martial. Marcus Valerius Martialis (1st century A. D.), a Latin poet, author of 14 books of epigrams.

Martin. —(1042)—Jack Martin, a prize fighter.

Martin, M. An author of books of travels, born in the Island of Skye, west of Scotland. He died in 1719.

Martinmas. A festival in honor of St. Martin of Tours, France (4th century A. D.), that took the place of an old pagan festival. It was celebrated Nov. 11.

Marvel. Andrew Marvel (1621-78), a minor English poet.

Mary. 1—(153)—See note on *To Mary,* p. 1256a. 2—(222, 226)—Mary Campbell, see note on *Thou Ling'ring Star,* p. 1268a. 3—(472)—See note on *The Maid of Neidpath,* p. 1318b. 4—(675, 1030)—Mary II, wife of William III, and Queen of England (1689-94).

Mary Mother; Mary Queen. —(365, 598)—The Virgin Mary, mother of Christ.

Mary Queen of Scots. Mary Stuart (1542-87). She laid claim to the English throne in 1558, as the great-granddaughter of Henry VII, on the ground of Elizabeth's illegitimacy. She was beheaded by Queen Elizabeth in 1587.

Masons. Members of an old and extensive secret order or fraternity dating from the Middle Ages.

Massinger. Philip Massinger (1583-1640), an English dramatist and poet.

Matilda. —(520)—Probably Rosa Matilda, author of *The Libertine,* 4 vols. (1807), and *The Passions,* 4 vols. (1811).

Matthew. See note on *Matthew,* p. 1280a.

Mauchline. A small town in Ayrshire, Scotland. Burns lived there eleven years.

Maurice. The Rev. Thomas Maurice (1754-1824), an English clergyman, scholar, and poet. He wrote various works on India. His *History of Ancient and Modern Hindostan* was severely attacked in *The Edinburgh Review.*

Meander. See **Mæander.**

Mecca. A city in Arabia. As the birthplace of Mohammed, it is a sacred city of Mohammedans and the object of pilgrimages to Kaaba, the shrine of Mecca.

Medea. An enchantress, the daughter of the King of Colchis. She aided her lover, Jason, to get the golden fleece, and fled with him to Thessaly, preventing her father, who pursued them, from overtaking them by strewing the sea with the limbs of her young brother. She restored Jason's father, Æson, by replacing his blood with magic liquid. Jason deserted her for Creüsa, Princess of Corinth, and Medea took vengeance upon her rival by sending her a poisoned robe. She also killed her own children, set fire to the palace, and then fled to Athens.

Medes. The people of an ancient kingdom, now part of Persia.

Medorus. Probably Medoro, a beautiful Moorish youth in Ariosto's romance *Orlando Furioso.* His elopement with Angelica causes the madness of Orlando.

Medusa. See **Gorgon.**

Mejnoun. The ideal lover of Persian legend. For the story of "Leila and Mujnoon," see Francis Gladwin's translation of Saadi's *The Gulistan, or Rose Garden,* Tale 19 (Boston 1865).

Melbourne House. The house of Peniston Lamb (1748-1819), Viscount Melbourne, the father of William and George Lamb, cousins of Lady Byron.

Melpomene. A muse of tragedy, usually represented as bearing a tragic mask.

Melrose Abbey. The ruins of a famous monastery in Melrose, a village in Roxburghshire, Scotland. The abbey was founded in 1136.

Melville's Sound. Melville Bay is an inlet of northwestern Greenland.

Memnon. Memnonian. A name given to a colossal statue of Amenhotep III, an Egyptian king, who reigned about 1500 B. C. See p. 884b, n. 1.

Memphian. Of or pertaining to Memphis.

Memphis. An ancient capital of Egypt, on the Lower Nile. It is now in ruins.

Menai. A narrow strait separating the Island of Anglesey from Wales.

Menander. A Greek dramatic poet who flourished in the 2nd and 3rd centuries B. C.

Menenius. Menenius Agrippa, a Roman senator and a friend of Coriolanus in Shakespeare's *Coriolanus*.

Menteith. A district north of Loch Lomond, in Perthshire, Scotland.

Merches. Same as Marches, or borders.

Mercury. Herald and messenger of the gods.

Merionethshire. A county in western Wales.

Merlin. A famous magician in medieval romance, especially in the cycle of stories dealing with King Arthur.

Mermaid in the Zodiac. The sign of the Virgin in the Zodiac.

Merton. A village in the county of Surrey, England.

Mestastasio. Assumed name of Pietro Bonaventura Trapassi (1698-1782), a noted Italian poet and dramatist.

Methuselah. The oldest man mentioned in the Bible, said to have lived 969 years. See *Genesis* 5:27.

Meton (5th century B. C.). A famous Greek astronomer.

Meuse. A river in France, Belgium, and the Netherlands.

Michael. 1—(134, 643, 964, 1017, 1130)—An archangel mentioned in the Bible; regarded as the leader of the host of angels. By the Roman Catholic Church, he is considered as representative of the church triumphant. His feast occurs on Sept. 29. A noted Church of St. Michael is in Coventry, a city in Warwickshire, England. 2—(216)—An archangel in *Paradise Lost* (Book 6) sent to wage battle against Satan and his angels. 3—(404)—The hero of Wordsworth's *Michael*.

Michael's hold. —(1176)—St. Michael's Mount, a lofty pyramidal rock in Mount Bay, off the coast of Cornwall, England. It was once a fortified post of importance.

Michelangelo. A famous Italian painter and sculptor (1475-1564).

Midas, Lord. A mythological King of Phrygia, who, upon being promised anything he might ask, asked that everything he touched might turn to gold. For his decision in a musical contest between Pan and Apollo in favor of Pan, Apollo changed Midas's ears into ass's ears. His barber discovered them and, to relieve himself of the secret, dug a hole into which he whispered, "King Midas has ass's ears," and then filled it up. A reed, however, grew there and betrayed the secret by its whispers.

Middle Temple. See **Temple**.

Middleton, Thomas Fanshaw (1769-1822). An English divine. He was made Bishop of Calcutta in 1814.

Midgard Serpent, The. The world-serpent, hidden in the ocean, whose coils gird the whole earth.

Milan. A city in northern Italy, noted for its manufactures of steel and other products.

Miletus. A coast city in Caria, Asia Minor.

Milky-Way. An irregular luminous band encircling the heavens, consisting of numberless stars too small to be seen separately by the naked eye.

Miller. 1—(210)—Alexander Miller (d. 1804), a parish preacher in Ayrshire, Scotland. 2—(512)—"Joe" Miller (1684-1758), an uneducated man, noted for his many jokes. These were compiled after his death, by John Mottley. 3—(514)—William Miller (1769-1844), a London publisher and bookseller.

Millwood. An adventurer in George Lillo's *The London Merchant or the History of George Barnwell* (1751).

Milman. Henry Hart Milman (1791-1868), an English clergyman and author; he was Professor of Poetry at Oxford University.

Miltiades (5th century B. C.). A celebrated Athenian general, tyrant of Chersonesus. Unable to pay a fine of 50 talents, imposed because he failed in an expedition against Paros, an island in the Ægean Sea, he was imprisoned, and died without being freed.

Mincio. A river in northern Italy.

Minehead. A small seaport of Somersetshire, England.

Minerva. The daughter of Jupiter; the goddess of invention, thought, and intelligence. She was ultimately identified with the Greek goddess of wisdom, Pallas or Athena.

Minos. A king and lawgiver of Crete, an island in the Mediterranean; after death he was made a judge in Hades.

Minster-square. The portion of a city adjacent to a monastery church.

Miranda. A character in Shakespeare's *The Tempest*.

Mirandula. Giovanni Pico della Mirandola (1463-94), a young Italian nobleman of refined character and extraordinary intellect and accomplishments.

Miserere. A musical setting of the 51st Psalm, beginning "Miserere mei, Domine" (Have mercy upon me, O God!).

Mista. One of the Fatal Sisters.

Mithridates. 1—(1094)—See **Adelung**. 2—(1216)—King of Pontus, Asia Minor (120-63 B. C.). He subjugated the nations around the Black Sea, and made himself master of nearly all the Roman possessions in Asia Minor. He was defeated by Lucullus in 69 B. C., and by Pompey in 66 B. C.

Mnemosyne. The goddess of memory, daughter of Heaven and Earth, and the mother of the Muses by Zeus.

Mœris. A large lake of ancient Egypt.

Mohammed (570-632). The founder of the Mohammedan religion.

Mona. Anglesea, an island and county of North Wales, northwest of the mainland.

Monan's rill. St. Monan was a Scotch martyr of the 4th century. No stream of this name has been identified.

Moneira. A name given to a brook in Glenartney forest, in the Highlands of Perthshire, Scotland.

Mont Blanc. The highest mountain of the Alps, situated on the boundary of France, Italy, and Switzerland.

Mont Cenis. A summit of the Alps between France and Italy.

Mont Saint Jean. A village near Waterloo, Belgium, which sometimes gives its name to the Battle of Waterloo, in which Napoleon was defeated by Wellington, in 1815.

Montagu. —(125)—John Montagu (1718-92), an English politician. He was Secretary of State in 1770, and first Lord of the Admiralty, 1771-82.

Montague, Lady Mary Wortley (1689-1762). An English author and letter writer.

Montague, Wortley. Edward Wortley Montague (1713-76), an English author, son of Lady Mary Wortley Montague.

Montgomery. James Montgomery (1771-1854), an English poet and hymn writer, bitterly reviled by *The Edinburgh Review*.

Montmorenci. A river in the Province of Quebec, Canada, noted for its torrent and its waterfalls, 265 feet high, near the city of Quebec.

Montrose. James Graham (1612-50), Earl and Marquis of Montrose, a noted Scottish statesman and soldier. As a royalist supporter, he led an attack on Scotland in 1650, was captured, and executed.

Monument of Lysicrates. A celebrated monument in Athens, Greece, erected by the chorus trainer Lysicrates as the result of a victory by his musicians in a Dionysiac festival at Athens, 335 B. C. The monument was in honor of Dionysus (Bacchus), god of wine.

Moodie. Alexander Moodie (1722-99), a Scottish clergyman at Riccarton, a small town in Ayrshire, Scotland. He was noted for his strict enforcement of law.

Moor. 1—(531, 605)—A member of the mixed Mauritanian-Arab race inhabiting Morocco or other North African states. 2—(568)—Othello, in Shakespeare's *Othello*.

Moore. Thomas Moore (1779-1852), an Irish poet. See p. 450.

Moorish. Of or pertaining to the Moors, inhabiting North African states.

Morat. A small town in Switzerland, celebrated for the victory of the forces of the republic over the invading tyrant Charles the Bold, Duke of Burgundy (1433-77), on June 22, 1476. Fifteen thousand men were killed in the engagement.

Moray (Murray). —(447, 480, 508)—A Scotch name common in Border warfare and poetry.

Mordecai. A Jew who accepted a position at court in order to be near his adopted daughter Esther, who had been raised to the rank of queen. Haman, the court favorite, was distressed when he came to the queen's banquet at seeing Mordecai sitting at the gate. See *Esther*, 3-5.

More, Dr. Henry (1614-87). An English theologian.

More, Sir Thomas (1478-1535). An English statesman and author, beheaded on a charge of treason.

Morgana. A fairy in *Orlando Innamorato*, an Italian romance by Boiardo (1434?-94).

Morning Post. A London newspaper started in 1772. Sir J. Mackintosh and Coleridge were among its contributors.

Moro. El Moro, the castle at Santiago harbor, Cuba. It was stormed by the English in 1762.

Morphean. Of or pertaining to Morpheus.

Morpheus. The son of Sleep, and god of dreams.

Morris. William Morris (1834-96), an English poet, decorative artist, and socialist.

Mortimer. Roger Mortimer (1287?-1330), Earl of March, a favorite of Isabella, Queen of Edward II of England.

Moscovy; Muscovy. A name given to Russia, derived from Moscow, the ancient capital.

Moses. The great Hebrew prophet and lawgiver who led the Israelites out of Egypt and through the wilderness to Canaan.

Moslem. Mohammedan.

Mossgiel Farm. The home of Burns in Ayrshire, Scotland.

Mount Abora. Apparently a mountain of Coleridge's imagination. Professor Lane Cooper (*Mod. Phil.*, Jan., 1906) suggests that it is a variant of *Amara*, the name of a hill in Abyssinia and the seat of a terrestrial paradise like that described in Coleridge's *Kubla Khan* (p. 385).

Muezzin. A public crier, in Mohammedan countries, who calls the faithful to prayer at the appointed hours.

Mulberry-Gardens. A noted London pleasure resort of the 17th century, containing a number of mulberry trees planted by James I, King of England (1603-25). The Garden occupied the present site of Buckingham Palace and Garden.

Mulciber. A surname of Vulcan, the blacksmith of the gods.

Munich. A city, capital of Bavaria, in Germany.

Muirkirk. A manufacturing town in East Ayrshire, Scotland.

Murillo. Bartolomé Esteban Murillo (1617-82), a Spanish painter, chiefly of religious subjects.

Murray. 1—(466)—James Stuart (1533-70), Earl of Murray, Regent of Scotland. He was half-brother of Mary Queen of Scots. See note on *Cadyow Castle*, p. 1316b. 2—(514, 594, 639, 1059)—John Murray (1778-1843), a famous English publisher; founder of *The Edinburgh Review*. He was the publisher of Byron's works.

Muse. 1—One of the nine goddesses who preside over poetry, art, and science: Calliope, muse of epic poetry; Clio, muse of history; Erato, muse of love poetry; Euterpe, muse of lyric poetry; Melpomene, muse of tragedy; Polymnia, muse of sacred poetry; Terpsichore, muse of dancing; Thalia, muse of comedy; Urania, muse of astronomy. 2—The inspiring power of poetry.

Museum of the Capitol. A famous museum at Rome.

Musset, Alfred de (1810-57). A noted French poet, novelist, and dramatist.

Mussulman. A Mohammedan.

Mycenæ. An ancient city in Argolis, Greece.

Mychael. See Michael (1).

Mysteries of Udolpho, The. A Gothic romance by Anne Radcliffe (1764-1823), an English novelist.

Naiad. One of the nymphs believed to live in lakes, rivers, springs, and fountains, and to give life to them.

Nais. A naiad; a river nymph.

Namur. A strongly fortified city of Belgium.

Narcissus. A beautiful youth, who, having rejected the love of Echo, is fabled to have fallen in love with his own reflection in the water, to have pined away, and to have been changed into the flower which bears his name.

Naseby. A parish in Northamptonshire, England, the scene of the Battle of Naseby, in which the forces of Charles I were defeated by the Parliamentary army in 1645.

Nash. Thomas Nash (1567-1601), an English author and satirist. He wrote *The Unfortunate Traveler, or Jack Wilton*.

Naxos (Naxia). An island belonging to the Cyclades group, in the Ægean Sea, southeast of Greece.

Nazareth. A city of Galilee in northeastern Palestine.

Neapolitans. Citizens of Naples, Italy.

Nelson. Horatio Nelson (1758-1805), the greatest of English naval commanders. He was killed on board his ship, in the Battle of Trafalgar, 1805. He was buried in St. Paul's Cathedral. (See p. 437.)

Nemesis. An ancient goddess of retributive justice.

Neo-Platonic. Relating to Neo-Platonism, a system of philosophy in the third century which endeavored to reconcile the teachings of Plato and Aristotle with Oriental mysticism.

Neptune; Neptunus. God of the sea, represented as bearing a trident for a scepter.

Nereids. Sea nymphs attendant upon Neptune, god of the sea.

Nero. Lucius Domitius Nero (37-68), a Roman Emperor (54-68) notorious for his profligacy and cruelties.

Ness. A promontory near Teignmouth, a seaport in Devonshire, England.

Nessus. A mythical character shot with a poisoned arrow by Hercules for making love to Hercules's wife Deianira. In compliance with the last request of Nessus, Deianira steeped her husband's shirt in the blood of Nessus, as a love charm; but the shirt poisoned Hercules, causing such agony that he killed himself.

Nestor. Counselor of the Greeks in the Trojan War.

Netherby. A village near the northern boundary of Cumberlandshire, England.

Nether-Stowey. A town in Somersetshire, England.

Neva. A river near Petrograd, Russia.

Nevis. An island of the Leeward group, British West Indies.

New Bastille. —(1170)—Probably a name given to the state prison.

New Eloise. A French novel by J. J. Rousseau (1712-78).

New-River. —(957)—An artificial stream that brings water for the supply of the City of London.

Newark. A manufacturing city in Nottinghamshire, England, situated on the River Trent. It contains the ruins of a 12th century castle in which King John of England died, in 1216.

Newbury. A city in Berkshire, England, the scene of two battles between the forces of Charles I and of the Parliamentary Party, Sept. 1643 and Oct. 1644.

Newcastle. A large manufacturing city in Northumberlandshire, England, on the River Tyne.

Newcastle, Margaret. Margaret Cavendish (1624-73), Duchess of Newcastle, an eccentric Restoration noblewoman. She entitled her life of her husband *The Life of the Thrice Noble, High, and Puissant Prince William Cavendish, and Earl of Newcastle, by the Thrice Noble, Illustrious, and Excellent Princess, Margaret Duchess of Newcastle, his Wife.*

Newland valley. A small valley in Cumberlandshire, England.

Newman, John Henry (1801-90). An English divine and philosopher. He is the author of *Lead, Kindly Light.*

Newstead Abbey. The home of Lord Byron, the poet; an estate in Nottinghamshire, England, bestowed by Henry VIII on Sir John Byron in 1538.

Newton. 1—(154)—John Newton (1725-1807), an English clergyman; a friend of Cowper, and associated with him in writing the *Olney Hymns.* 2—(210)—A village in Ayrshire, Scotland, at the mouth of the River Ayr. 3—(353, 656, 938, 956, 1065, 1129)—Sir Isaac Newton (1647-1721), a celebrated English mathematician, scientist, and natural philosopher.

Ney, Marshal. Michel Ney (1769-1815), a famous French marshal. He commanded the rear guard in the retreat from Moscow in 1812. He was defeated by Wellington at Quatre-Bras, Belgium, June 16, 1815, and at Waterloo two days later. When summoned to capitulate, he is alleged to have said, "A marshal of France never surrenders." (See p. 1134b, n. 5.)

Nicholas, St. A noted bishop of Myra, Asia Minor, of the 4th century. He is a prominent saint of the Greek church.

Nick. A name of the devil.

Niger. One of the chief rivers of Africa.

Nilus. The god of the River Nile.

Nimrod. A grandson of Ham; a mighty hunter. See *Genesis* 10:8.

Nineveh. An ancient city, the capital of Assyria, noted for its vast royal palaces.

Niobe. A mythological character noted for her pride in her twelve children, which led her to compare herself with Leto, the wife of Zeus, who had only two. In punishment, Apollo and Artemis, Leto's children, slew Niobe's children, and Niobe was changed by Zeus into a rock, and in that form she continued to weep her loss.

Nithsdale. A dale along the River Nith in Dumfriesshire, Scotland.

Noah. A patriarch who built an ark to save his family and representatives of all living creatures at the time of the Flood. See *Genesis,* 5-10.

Nominis Umbra. See p. 649a, n. 3.

Norfolk. A county on the east coast of England.

Norfolk, Duke of. Thomas Howard (1473-1554), an English general, diplomat, and statesman.

Norfolk Island. An island in the South Pacific used by England as a penal colony.

Norman. Pertaining to Normandy, in northern France. The Norman Conquest was the subjugation of England by William of Normandy, in the 11th century.

Norris, Randal (1751-1827). A friend of Lamb. For many years he was Sub-Treasurer and Librarian of the Inner Temple, London. See **Temple.**

Northombarlande; Northumberland. A northern county of England.

Norton, Richard. The head of a 16th-century English family loyal to Mary Queen of Scots.

Nottingham. An east-central county in England. In the western part is Sherwood Forest, the haunt of Robin Hood and his followers.

Notus. The south wind.

Nox. The goddess of night.

Nubian. A native of Nubia, a region in eastern Africa.

Nuceus. Joseph Nutt, an 18th-century apothecary at Hinckley, a town in Leicestershire, England.

Numa. Numa Pompilius, the legendary second King of Rome (715-672 B. C.), and reputed founder of many Roman institutions.

Numantia. A famous ancient city in Spain, taken and destroyed by the Romans in 133 B. C.

Numidian. Of Numidia, an ancient country of North Africa, corresponding to modern Algeria.

Nymphs. Inferior divinities of nature represented as beautiful maidens dwelling in the mountains, forests, meadows, waters, etc.

Nysa. In ancient geography, the birthplace of Bacchus. Of several cities so named, the chief city was in Caria, Asia Minor.

Oban's bay. A beautiful bay on the west coast of Argyllshire, Scotland.

Oberon. The king of the fairies.

Ocean Isle. England.

Oceanus. The god of the stream Oceanus, believed to encircle the earth.

Octavius. Augustus Cæsar, the first Roman emperor (31 B. C.-14 A. D.).

Odin. The supreme deity of Scandinavian mythology, same as Woden.

Odysseus. Ulysses, King of Ithaca, one of the Greek heroes in the Trojan War. He is a leading character in Homer's *Iliad*, and the hero of Homer's *Odyssey*. He was famed for his wisdom and craftiness.

Odyssey. An epic poem by Homer, recounting the adventures of Odysseus (Ulysses), one of the Greek heroes of the Trojan War.

Œdipus. A legendary king of Thebes, an ancient city of Bœotia, Greece. See **Laian.**

Olympian. Inhabiting Olympus.

Olympians. The gods who were said to inhabit Mt. Olympus.

Olympus. A famous mountain in Thessaly, Greece, the home of the gods. It is often celebrated in poetry.

Omphale. A queen of Lydia, Asia Minor, whom Hercules was compelled to serve for three years, wearing female apparel and spinning with the maids, while she wore his lion skin.

O'Neill, Miss. Eliza O'Neill (1791-1872), a noted Irish tragic actress.

Onondaga. A tribe of North American Indians whose chief seat was in the vicinity of Lake Onondaga, New York.

Ophelia. A character in Shakespeare's *Hamlet*.

Oporto. A district in Portugal.

Ops. The goddess of agriculture, the harvest, and plenty.

Oran, St. (6th century A. D.). A friend and follower of St. Columba (521-97), a Celtic missionary in Scotland. According to legend, Oran consented to be buried alive in order to propitiate certain demons of the soil who hindered Columba in building a chapel. A chapel and a cemetery in Icolmkill, an island west of Scotland, were named after him.

Oreads. Mountain nymphs.

Orestes. A son of the Greek king Agamemnon and Clytemnestra, who slew his mother and her lover Ægisthus in revenge for their murder of Agamemnon.

Orford, Lord. Horace Walpole (1717-97), 4th Earl of Orford, an English author. See p. 100.

Orion. A famous hunter of giant stature, beloved by the goddess Artemis, but accidentally slain by her, and after his death transformed into a constellation.

Orkney. An island group north of Scotland.

Orlando Furioso. A romance by Ariosto (1474-1533), a famous Italian poet.

Orphean. Resembling Orpheus, or possessing the quality of his lyre.

Orpheus. A mythological poet and musician whose lyre could charm beasts and move trees and stones. When his wife Eurydice died, Orpheus descended to the lower world and gained permission from Pluto to lead her back to the upper world on condition that he should not look back at her until they had reached the upper air. Orpheus broke the condition, and Eurydice vanished.

Ortygian. Of Ortygia, an ancient island near Sicily.

Oscar. —(72)—The name of a warrior in Macpherson's *Ossian*.

Osirian. Belonging or relating to Osiris, the most popular of Egyptian gods.

Osman. The name of a line of Turkish sultans tracing to Osman I, who founded the Ottoman Empire about 1300.

Osman Bey. The nobleman Osman.

Ossian. 1—A semi-fabulous Scottish bard of the 3rd century, said to be the son of Fingal, King of Morven. 2—A pretended translation of the poems of Ossian, published by James Macpherson in 1765. See p. 86.

Ostend. A noted seaport of Belgium.

Oswestry. A town in Shropshire, England.

Otaheite. Tahiti, the principal island of the Society Archipelago in the South Pacific Ocean.

Othello. The chief character in Shakespeare's *Othello*.

Otter. A river in Devonshire, England.

Ottomite. A native of Turkey.

Otway. Thomas Otway (1651-85), an English tragic dramatist.

Ouse. A small river in Sussex county, England.

Ovid. Publius Ovidius Nasco (43 B. C.-17 A.D.), a famous Roman poet. He was banished by Augustus and died in exile.

Oxford. The county town of Oxfordshire, England; the seat of Oxford University.

Oxonian. Of or pertaining to Oxford, England, or its university.

Oxus. Amu-Daria, a river in central Asia.

Pacha. Same as Pasha.

Padua. The capital of Padua province, Italy; seat of the University of Padua.

Paine, Tom. Thomas Paine (1737-1809), an English political writer; author of *Common Sense* and *The Rights of Man*.

Paisley. A manufacturing town in the county of Renfrew, Scotland.

Palestine. A country in southwestern Syria. Its capital is Jerusalem.

Paley. William Paley (1743-1805), an English orthodox theologian and philosopher.

Palladian. Introduced by or in the pompous Renaissance style of Andrea Palladio (1518-80), an Italian architect and author, who had much influence in shaping the modern Italian school of architecture.

Pallas. Pallas Athena, goddess of wisdom and war.

Palm. Johann Philipp Palm (1766-1800), a German publisher, shot because of the publication of a pamphlet against Napoleon.

Palm Sunday. The Sunday before Easter.

Palmer. John Palmer (1742-1818), noted for his reform in the mail service of England.

Palmerston. John Temple Palmerston (1784-1865), an English statesman, the enemy of slavery, injustice, and oppression. In private life his personality made his opponents forget their differences.

Pan. An Arcadian woodland spirit and god of hills and woods, flocks and herds. He is represented as horned, goat-footed, playing on his pipes, and as exciting sudden fear. It was because they believed him to have caused the panic among the Persians at Marathon that the Athenians instituted his worship on the Acropolis.

Panama, Bay of. The Gulf of Panama on the west coast of Panama.

Pandion. An early king of Athens.

Pandora. A beautiful but deceitful woman sent to earth by the gods to bring misery upon the human race in revenge for Prometheus's theft of fire from heaven. Some say that she brought with her a box from which escaped all human ills, hope alone remaining. Others say that she brought blessings, all of which, when she opened the box, escaped and departed, excepting hope.

Pantheists. Believers in pantheism, a doctrine which identifies the universe with God.

Pantheon. 1—(325, 1086)—A building in Oxford Street, London, formerly a concert hall. 2—(423, 1147)—A circular temple at Rome with a fine Corinthian portico and a great domed roof, originally built by Agrippa, 27 B. C. In its present form it represents the building by Hadrian.

Paphian. Of or belonging to Paphos.

Paphos. Paphos was an ancient city on the Island of Cyprus, containing a temple of Aphrodite, goddess of love and beauty.

Parcæ. The three Fates of the Greeks. See **Fates.**

Parga. A seaport of Turkey, in Epirus on a rocky height, opposite the Island of Paxos.

Pariahs. See p. 1112b, n. 1.

Parian. Of or pertaining to Paros, an island in the Ægean sea, noted for its white marble.

Parkhead. George Douglas of Parkhead, a staunch supporter of Regent Murray of Scotland.

Parnassus. A mountain range in Bœotia, Greece, celebrated as the haunt of the Muses of poetry and music.

Paroles. A son of Pericles.

Parry, Captain. Sir Edward Parry (1790-1855). He made unsuccessful attempts to find the Northwest Passage in 1819, 1821, and later. He passed the winter of 1819 on Melville Island, in the Arctic Ocean.

Parthenon. The official temple of Pallas in Athens.

Parthenope. One of the sirens who, unable to charm Ulysses by her singing, cast herself into the sea.

Parthians. People of an ancient kingdom, now part of Persia.

Pasha. The title of a high official or prince in Turkey and Egypt.

Pastorella. A character in Spenser's *The Faerie Queene*, VI, 2.

Paswan. Passwan Oglou (1758-1807), a famous rebel of Widdin, a department in northwestern Bulgaria.

Patmos. An island of the Sporades, off the west coast of Asia Minor.

Paul and Virginia. A French story by Bernardin de Saint Pierre (1737-1814).

Paul Potters. See **Potters.**

Paul, St. 1—(618, 642, 960, 1120)—An apostle of the Gentiles, who was called, before his conversion, Saul of Tarsus. 2—Sir Paul (1172) and Tully St. Paul (1175) are unidentified.

Paulet. William Pawlett, Marquis of Winchester, an English courtier of the 16th century.

Paulus (d. 160 B. C.). A noted Roman general and consul.

Paynim. Mohammedan.

Peacock. Thomas Love Peacock (1785-1866), an English novelist and poet. See p. 1024.

Peebles. The Rev. William Peebles, minister at Newton-on-Ayr, Ayrshire, Scotland.

Peele Castle. A castle on the Isle of Man, west of England.

Pegasus. A winged horse fabled to have sprung from the body of Medusa at her death. With a blow of his foot he caused Hippocrene, the inspiring fountain of the Muses, to spring from Mount Helicon. Hence, he is associated with poetic inspiration.

Peggy. A conventional name for a Scottish shepherdess.

Pelasgian. The Pelasgians were prehistoric inhabitants of Greece.

Peleus. A king of Thessaly, father of Achilles.

Pelion. A mountain of Thessaly, Greece, famous in mythology.

Pembroke Hall. A college of Cambridge University, Cambridge, England.

Pendragon. An ancient British chief, the father of King Arthur.

Peneus. A river in Arcadia, Greece.

Pennant. Thomas Pennant (1726-98), an English naturalist and antiquary.

Pentameron, The. See note on *The Pentameron*, p. 1380b.

Pentland. A range of hills in the counties of Peebles, Lanark, and Edinburgh, Scotland.

Pentonville. A district in the north central part of London.

Peona. The sister of Endymion in Keats's *Endymion*.

Peræan. Of Pera, a city in Greece, northeast of Corinth.

Percy. Henry Percy, Earl of Northumberland, a distinguished English military leader of the early 15th century.

Perdita. A character in Shakespeare's *The Winter's Tale*.

Peri. An imaginary being, like a fairy, originally regarded as evil, but later regarded as benevolent and beautiful.

Pericles. A celebrated Athenian statesman of the 5th century B. C. See **Aspasia**.

Peris. See **Peri**.

Perry. John Perry, steward at Christ's Hospital from 1761 to 1785.

Persè. See **Percy**.

Perseus. A hero of classical mythology.

Perth. The capital of Perthshire, Scotland.

Peter Bell. A poetical tale by Wordsworth (1819). It was burlesqued by Shelley in *Peter Bell the Third*.

Peter, St. One of the twelve apostles.

Peter Wilkins. *The Life and Adventures of Peter Wilkins* (1750), a grotesque romance by Robert Paltock.

Peterborough. A city in the counties of Northampton and Huntingdon, England. It is noted for the famous Cathedral of Peterborough.

Petra. An ancient city in the rocky region of northwestern Arabia.

Petrarca; Petrarch. A famous Italian poet of the 14th century.

Petronius Arbiter. A Roman satirist of the 1st century A. D. He arranged the entertainments of Nero, and hence was known as *arbiter elegans*.

Phædrus. A Latin writer of fables in the 1st century A. D. He was originally a slave.

Phaeton. A mythical son of Helios, the sun god. He was allowed to guide for one day the chariot of the sun; he lost control of the steeds, was killed by Jupiter with a thunderbolt, and fell into the River Po.

Pharaoh(s). A line of kings of ancient Egypt, under whom the Exodus took place.

Pharsalia. A district of Thessaly, ancient Greece.

Phidian. Of or resembling Phidias.

Phidias. A celebrated Greek sculptor of the 5th century B. C.

Phigalia. An ancient city of Greece, modern Pavlitza in Messenia.

Philip. Philip II (382-336 B. C.), King of Macedon, and father of Alexander the Great.

Philippi. An ancient city of Macedonia, the scene of the victory of Octavius and Antony over Brutus and Cassius, 42 B. C.

Phillis. See **Phyllis**.

Philomel; Philomela. The nightingale. Philomela, daughter of Pandion, King of Athens, was violated and deprived of her tongue by Tereus, the husband of her sister Procne. In revenge, the sisters served up Tereus's own son to Tereus as a meal and fled. As Tereus pursued them, all three were turned into birds: Philomela into a swallow, Procne into a nightingale, Tereus into a hawk. According to Ovid, Philomela was turned into a nightingale.

Phoebe. 1—(81)—A poetic name for a shepherdess or rustic maiden. 2—(278)—A character in Shakespeare's *As You Like It*. 3—(833, 1050)—A surname of Diana, goddess of the moon. See **Diana**.

Phoebus. An epithet of Apollo. See **Apollo**.

Phœnicia. An ancient country in Asia Minor.

Phorcus. The old man of the sea in classic mythology; the father of the Gorgons and the Hesperides.

Phyllis. A poetic name for a shepherdess or rustic maiden.

Phyxian Jove. Jupiter Phyxius, the protector of exiles.

Piccadilly. The great thoroughfare in London between Hyde Park Corner and the Haymarket.

Pichegru. Charles Pichegru (1761-1804), a French general, said to have been assassinated in prison because he engaged in a conspiracy against Napoleon in 1803-04.

Pictish. Scottish. The Picts were an early race inhabiting the Highlands of Scotland. They carried on border wars with the Romans.

Piedmont. A province in northern Italy.

Pierre. The hero of Thomas Otway's tragedy *Venice Preserved* (1682). He was a favorite character of great actors. Byron was an admirer of Otway.

Pigmies. An African race of dwarfs.

Pigott, Jack. Peter George Patmore (1786-1855), an active journalist and writer in London, and an intimate friend of Hazlitt and Lamb.

Pilate. A Roman governor of Judea of the 1st century A. D. When Christ was tried before him, Pilate allowed him to be condemned, and washed his own hands as symbolical of innocence of guilt. See *Matthew*, 27:24.

Pilgrim's Progress. A religious allegory by John Bunyan (1628-88).

Pillans. James Pillans (1778-1864), a Scottish educational reformer, at one time a private tutor at Eton; later, Professor of Humanity at Edinburgh University. He was the supposed author of an unfriendly review of a translation of Juvenal, by his friend Francis Hodgson (1781-1852). The review was published in *The Edinburgh Review*, April 1808. Pillans was an intimate friend of Byron.

Pindar (5th century B. C.). A celebrated Greek lyric poet.

Pindus. A range of mountains in Greece between Thessaly and Epirus.

Piozzi. Mrs. Piozzi (Esther Lynch Salusbury, 1739-1821), an English author.

Piræeus. The seaport of Athens.

Piranesi. Giovanni Battista Piranesi (1720-78), an Italian engraver, who was especially interested in restoring in engravings the ruined architecture of Rome.

Pisa. Capital of the province of Pisa, Italy.

Piscator. A character in Walton's *The Complete Angler* (1653).

Pisistratos (6th century B. C.). A tyrant of Athens.

Pistol, Ancient. See p. 1039b, n. 4.

Pitt. William Pitt (1708-1778), a celebrated English statesman and orator. He was premier, 1766-68.

Plancus. Lucius Plancus, a profligate Roman politician, who was a partisan of Cæsar in the Civil War. He was consul in 42 B. C.

Plato (427-347 B. C.). A celebrated Greek philosopher.

Pleiad. One of a group of small stars in the constellation Taurus.

Plinlimmon. A mountain in Montgomeryshire and Cardiganshire, Wales.

Pliny. Caius Plinius Secundus (23-79), a celebrated Roman naturalist.

Plotinus (3rd century A. D.). A Greek philosopher who founded the Neo-Platonic school of philosophy, a system of refined Platonic doctrines combined with Oriental mysticism.

Plumer. Richard Plumer, deputy-secretary in the South-Sea House in 1800.

Plutarch (1st century A. D.). A famous Greek historian, celebrated as the author of a number of Lives of Greeks and Romans.

Pluto. In Roman mythology, the god of the infernal regions.

Po. The largest river of Italy. It empties into the Adriatic Sea.

Poictiers. Poitiers, the capital of the department of Vienne, France; the scene of an English victory over the French in 1356.

Pollux. See **Castor**.

Polonius. The father of Ophelia, and the king's chamberlain, in Shakespeare's *Hamlet*.

Poltava. Capital of the government of Pultowa, Russia, where the Russians defeated the Swedes in 1709.

Polybius (204-125 B. C.). A celebrated Greek historian.

Polycrates. Tyrant of Samos (536-522 B. C.). He was a patron of literature and art.

Polyphemes. In Homer's *Odyssey*, the one-eyed giant who imprisoned Ulysses.

Pomona. In Roman mythology, the goddess of fruit trees.

Pompeii. An ancient city of Italy, buried by an eruption from Mt. Vesuvius in 79 A. D.

Pompey. Cneius Pompeius Magnus (106-48 B. C.), a famous Roman general.

Pontus. An ancient country in Asia Minor, south of the Black Sea.

Poole, Tom (1765-1837). A wealthy tanner; Coleridge's friend, correspondent, and patron, who lived at Stowey. He was noted for his kindness to authors.

Pope. Alexander Pope (1688-1744), a famous English poet.

Porphyrion. In Greek mythology, the fire king of the giants.

Portland. William Henry Cavendish Bentinck (1738-1809), Duke of Portland, an English Whig statesman, prime minister, 1783 and 1807-09.

Portsmouth. A seaport in Hampshire, England, situated on the English Channel.

Poseidon. In Greek mythology, god of the sea and brother of Zeus.

Posilippo. A hill west of Naples, Italy.

Potiphar. One of Pharaoh's officers, who bought Joseph.

Potter's Bar. A village in Hertfordshire, England.

Potters, Paul. Paintings by Paul Potter

(1625-54), a noted Dutch painter of land-scapes and cattle.

Poule. St. Paul.

Poussin. Gaspard Poussin (1613-75), a noted Italian painter.

Powle, Seyncte. See **Seyncte Powle.**

Powley. The Reverend George Croly, D.D. (1780-1860), at one time a dramatic critic of *The London Times.*

Prague. Formerly the capital of Bohemia, Austria; seat of a university founded by Charles IV in 1345.

Pratt. Charles Pratt (1713-94), Chief Justice and Lord Chancellor of England.

Praxitelean. Of or relating to Praxiteles.

Praxiteles (4th century B. C.). A Greek sculptor, noted for the grace and natural-ness of his feminine figures.

Pre-adamite kings. Seventy-two kings or sul-tans, each said to govern a distinct species of rational beings before the existence of Adam.

Preston. 1—(54)—Prestonpans, a small town in Haddingtonshire, Scotland, the scene of a Jacobite victory over the English in 1745. 2—(1146)—A city in Lancashire, England, noted as an industrial center.

Preston Mill. —(501)—A rustic village in Dumfriesshire, Scotland.

Priam. Legendary King of Troy, a city of Asia Minor.

Priapus. The god of fruitfulness and pro-creative power, of horticulture and vine-growing.

Prince Eugene. See **Eugene.**

Prior. Matthew Prior (1664-1721), an English diplomat and lyric and humorous poet.

Priuli. A character in *Venice Preserved*, a tragedy by Thomas Otway (1651-85).

Proclus (412-485). A Greek philosopher and religious commentator.

Promethean. Of or pertaining to Prometheus.

Prometheus. In Greek mythology, regarded as the founder of civilization and the bene-factor of mankind. For an act of deception by Prometheus, Zeus denied mankind the use of fire; but Prometheus stole fire from heaven and carried it to earth in a hollow tube. For this act he was chained, by order of Zeus, on Mt. Caucasus, where a vulture fed daily upon his liver, which grew again at night. The vulture was finally slain by Hercules and Prometheus released.

Propontic. The present Sea of Marmara, be-tween European and Asiatic Turkey. It is not subject to tides.

Proserpina; Proserpine. The wife of Pluto, and queen of the lower regions. While gathering flowers in the Valley of Enna,

Sicily, she was carried off by Pluto. Zeus allowed her to spend half of her time on earth with her mother, Ceres.

Prospero. In Shakespeare's *The Tempest*, the banished Duke of Milan. He is shipwrecked on an island, where he works enchantments, and after sixteen years of exile raises a storm to shipwreck the usurper of his right-ful title.

Protagoras (5th century B. C.). A famous Greek philosopher.

Protean. Pertaining to Proteus.

Proteus. A sea god in the service of Neptune, god of the sea. Proteus had the power of assuming different shapes.

Prowse, Captain. William Prowse (1752 ?-1826). A famous English naval commander and rear admiral.

Pryocles. A character in Sir Philip Sidney's pastoral romance *Arcadia* (1590).

Psellus, Michael. Michael Constantinus Psel-lus (11th century). A celebrated Greek writer and scholar. He was born in Con-stantinople.

Psyche. In classical mythology, the name given to a personified soul. She was beloved by Eros, god of love. She is represented in art as a maiden with the wings of a butter-fly.

Ptolemean. Of Ptolemy (2nd century A. D.), a celebrated Egyptian astronomer and mathematician.

Pulci. Luigi Pulci (1432-87), an Italian ro-mantic poet.

Pultowa. See **Poltava.**

Punic War, Second (218-201 B. C.). A war waged between Carthage and Rome. By the peace Carthage was forced to cede her pos-sessions in Spain and the Mediterranean, and to pay a heavy tribute.

Pye. Henry James Pye (1745-1813). A minor English poet.

Pygmalion. In Greek legend, a sculptor, King of Cyprus, who fell in love with a statue he had carved and which came to life.

Pyrenees. A mountain range between Spain and France.

Pyrrhic. Pertaining to Pyrrhus (318?-272 B. C.), King of Epirus, Greece.

Pyrrho (360-270 B. C.). A Greek skeptic and philosopher.

Pythagorean. Referring to Pythagoras (6th century B. C.), a Greek philosopher of Samos, an island west of Asia Minor.

Pythian. Referring to Python.

Python. In classical mythology, a soothsaying spirit or demon. The serpent Python de-livered oracles at Delphi before the coming of Apollo, who slew it.

Quarles. John Quarles (1624-65), a minor English poet.

Quarterly; Quarterly Review, The. A periodical started in 1809 in opposition to *The Edinburgh Review,* the organ of the Whig party. William Gifford was the first editor.

Quatre-Bras. A place in Belgium, near Brussels. It was the scene of a battle between the French under Ney and the Allies under Wellington, in 1815; Ney was forced to retreat.

Queen Bess. See **Bess.**

Queen of Numbers. The goddess of poetry.

Queen of Scots. Mary Stuart (1542-87), who was beheaded by Queen Elizabeth.

Quixotic. Resembling Don Quixote, an adventurous knight, the hero of *Don Quixote,* a Spanish romance by Cervantes (1547-1616).

Racer Jess. Janet Gibson, the half-witted daughter of Mrs. Gibson or "Poosie Nansie"; being fleet of foot, she often ran errands.

Rachel. In the Old Testament, the wife of Jacob.

Radcleves. Same as Radcliffe.

Radcliffe. Mrs. Anne Radcliffe (1764-1823), a popular English romantic novelist.

Radical. A member of a political party holding the most progressive views; opposed to *Conservative.*

Ragusan. Of Ragusa, a seaport of Dalmatia, situated on the Adriatic.

Rajah. A Hindu prince in a tribal state in India.

Ralph. James Ralph, a minor English poet of the eighteenth century.

Rama. A place near ancient Bethlehem, Judea.

Ramsay. Allan Ramsay (1685-1758), a Scottish poet. See p. 7.

Randall's, Jack. A tavern, known as "The Hole in the Wall," in Chancery Lane, London, kept by Jack Randall, a noted pugilist.

Raphael (1483-1520). A noted Italian painter.

Rapp, General. Count Jean Rapp (1772-1821), a noted French general who accompanied Napoleon on the march to Moscow.

Ratcliffe Highway. A public thoroughfare in a disreputable quarter of eastern or nautical London.

Ravenna. A city and province of Italy.

Ravensheuch, Castle. A large castle on the Firth of Forth, Fifeshire, Scotland. It was given to William St. Clair by James III in 1471.

Reading. A city in Berkshire, England.

Rebecca; Rebekah. The wife of the patriarch Isaac, and mother of Jacob and Esau.

Red Cross Knight. A character in Spenser's *The Faerie Queene* (Bk. I), who personifies St. George, patron saint of England, and typifies Christian holiness.

Red Rowan. "Red Rowy Forster," one of the rescuers of Kinmont Willie. He lived about 1550.

Red Sea. An inland sea between Egypt and Arabia, joined to the Mediterranean by the Suez Canal.

Redi. Francesco Redi (1626-95), an Italian poet. Landor uses the name (996) for himself.

Reform Bill. An electoral reform bill passed by the British Parliament in 1832 for the correction and extension of the suffrage.

Reign of Terror, The. In French history that period of the first revolution (1793-94) when the faction in power recklessly executed persons opposed to their measures.

Religio Medici. A religious treatise by Sir Thomas Browne (1605-82), an English physician and author.

Rembrandt (1606-69). A celebrated Dutch painter.

Reni, Guido (1575-1642). An Italian painter.

Rere-cross. A fragment of an old cross on the summit of Stanmore, a ridge which divides the mountains of Cumberland and Westmoreland, England. The cross was originally intended as a landmark.

Reynolds, J. H. See note on *Keats's Letters,* p. 1362b.

Reynolds. Sir Joshua Reynolds (1723-92). An English portrait painter.

Rhadamanthus. A son of Zeus, and a judge in Hades.

Rhætian. Of or pertaining to ancient Rhætia, a province of the Roman Empire.

Rhea. See **Ops.**

Rhine. The chief river of Germany.

Rhodes. An island in the Ægean Sea, southwest of Asia Minor.

Rhone. A river in Switzerland and France.

Rhymes on Blenheim. *The Battle of Blenheim.* See p. 426.

Rialto. A bridge over the Grand Canal, in Venice, Italy. Byron uses the word (568) figuratively for Venetian commerce.

Rice. James Rice, a London solicitor of the early 19th century; a friend of Keats and J. H. Reynolds.

Richard, English. Richard I, surnamed "The Lion-Hearted," King of England (1189-99).

Richard I. King of England (1189-99).

Richard II. King of England (1377-99).

Richard III. 1—King of England (1483-85). 2—(951)—King of England in Shakespeare's *Richard III.*

Richards. George Richards (1767-1837), author of a poem, *Aboriginal Britons,* and a governor of Christ's Hospital.

Richardson. Samuel Richardson (1689-1761), an English novelist.

Richmond. 1—(491, 517)—A town in the county of Surrey, England. It is built on a hill. 2—(956)—Charles Lennox (1735-1806), 3rd Duke of Richmond, an English politician. 3—(1042)—Bill Richmond, a veteran Negro boxing teacher of the early 19th century.

Rimini. See note on *The Story of Rimini,* p. 1364b.

Riou. Captain Edward Riou, commander of the frigates and smaller craft in the Battle of Copenhagen, April 2, 1801. He was killed in that battle.

Rob Roy (Red Rob). Robert McGregor (1671-1734), a Scotch freebooter and outlaw. He took the name of Campbell after he was outlawed, in 1712.

Robbers, The. A German drama by Schiller (1759-1805).

Robert. The husband of Margaret in Wordsworth's *The Excursion.*

Robert Boyle. A story by W. R. Chetwood, an 18th-century English dramatist.

Robin Good-fellow. A merry and mischievous sprite of folklore.

Robin Hood. A legendary medieval hero in England, celebrated as a bold, chivalrous, and generous outlaw.

Robinson Crusoe. A novel of adventure by Daniel Defoe (1661-1731).

Rockingham. Charles Wentworth (1730-82), Marquis of Rockingham, Prime Minister of England (1765-66).

Roderic. Said to have been Prince of all Wales in the 10th century.

Roderick Random. A novel by Tobias Smollett (1721-71), a British novelist.

Rogers. Samuel Rogers (1763-1855), an English poet. See p. 233.

Roland de Vaux. See **Tryermaine.**

Romeo. The lover of Juliet in Shakespeare's *Romeo and Juliet.*

Romilly. Sir Samuel Romilly (1757-1818). An English lawyer and philanthropist.

Rosa. Salvator Rosa (1615-73), a famous Italian painter of history, landscapes, and battles. He was partial to desolate, wild, and romantic scenery.

Rosalind. A character in Shakespeare's *As You Like It.*

Rosamond's Pond. A pond in the southwest corner of St. James's Park, London, which was the scene of many suicides of unhappy lovers. It was filled in in 1770.

Roscoe, Mr. William Roscoe (1753-1831), historian, banker, and Whig Member of Parliament (1806-07); a strong advocate of peace with France.

Rosenberg, Mount. Rossberg, a mountain in Switzerland. A landslide from it buried the village of Goldau in 1806, killing over 450 persons.

Rosencrans. A courtier in Shakespeare's *Hamlet.*

Roses, Wars of the. In English history, the prolonged armed struggle between the rival houses of Lancaster and York, beginning about 1455 and ending in 1485; so called from the. red rose and the white rose, badges, respectively, of the followers of the two families.

Roslin. The family seat of the St. Clairs near Hawthornden, in the county of Edinburgh, Scotland. Roslin Castle stands on a woody bank of the North Esk River. Wordsworth and his sister Dorothy visited it in 1803. For the account of the visit and a description of the scenery, see Dorothy Wordsworth's *Recollections of a Tour Made in Scotland,* Sept. 17, 1803.

Ross-dhu. A valley on the western border of Loch Lomond, Dumbartonshire, Scotland.

Rotherham. Edward Rotherham (1753 ?-1830), an English naval captain.

Rothschild, Baron. Nathan Meyer Rothschild (1777-1836), a rich financier in London, founder of the English branch of the banking house of Rothschild.

Roumelie. Rumelia, a name applied to the eastern portion of the Turkish dominions in Europe.

Rousseau. Jean Jacques Rousseau (1712-78), a celebrated Swiss-French philosopher and writer on educational subjects.

Rowe, Mr. A Unitarian minister at Shrewsbury, later at Bristol, Somersetshire, England, in the early nineteenth century.

Rowe, Mrs. Elizabeth Rowe (1674-1737), daughter of a Dissenting minister in Somersetshire, England; author of a number of poems and treatises.

Rowleie, Thomas. A fictitious priest of Bristol, invented by Chatterton.

Rowley, William. An English dramatist of the early 17th century.

Rowley Powley. See **Powley.**

Rubens. Peter Paul Rubens (1577-1640), a Flemish painter.

Rudesheimer. A famous Rhenish wine named after Rudesheim, a town in Prussia, in which it was made.

Russel, Lord John (1792-1878). A famous English statesman and author.

Russell, Black. John Russel (1740?-1817), a minister in Kilmarnock, Ayrshire, Scotland. He was a Calvinist of the sternest type.

Ruth. A Moabite woman who was married to Boaz. Her story is the subject of the book of *Ruth.*

Rylstone. The property and residence of the Nortons, a 16th-century English family loyal to Mary Queen of Scots.

Rymer. Thomas Rymer (c1641-1713), a noted English antiquary and critic.

S. T. C. Samuel Taylor Coleridge.

Sackville. The family name of the English noble family of Dorset.

Sadi (c1190-1291). A celebrated Persian poet and moralist.

Saint Alban's. A cathedral city in Hertfordshire, England.

St. Ann. A river of Quebec, which empties into the St. Lawrence.

St. Augustine. See **Augustine.**

St. Bartholomew. One of the twelve apostles.

St. Bruno. See **Bruno, St.**

St. Clair. A noted Norman family which settled in Scotland in the 11th century.

Saint Fillan. See **Fillan, Saint.**

St. George. See **George, St.**

Saint Hubert. See **Hubert.**

St. Helena. An island in the South Atlantic belonging to Great Britain.

St. John. 1—See **John, St.** 2—See **Bolingbroke.**

St. John, Henry. See **Bolingbroke.**

St. Kits. An abbreviation for St. Christopher's, an island in the British West Indies.

St. Leons. *St. Leon,* a novel by William Godwin (1756-1836), written in 1799.

St. Mark. 1—(238)—St. Mark's Square, the principal square in Venice. It contains St. Mark's Church; near it are the Ducal Palace, the Bridge of Sighs, etc. 2—(568)—St. Mark's Church, a famous Venetian basilica, the most superb piece of architectural coloring in the world. 3—(874)—See note on *The Eve of St. Mark,* p. 1361b.

St. Martin's-le-Grand. A monastery and church formerly in London, dating from very early times.

St. Mary's Lake. A lake at the source of the River Yarrow in Selkirkshire, Scotland.

St. Maurice. An abbey in the town of St. Maurice, Switzerland; it was founded in the 6th century.

St. Michael. See **Michael** (1).

St. Neots. A town in Huntingdonshire, England.

St. Nicholas. See **Nicholas.**

St. Oran. See **Oran.**

St. Paul. See **Paul, St.**

St. Peter. See **Peter, St.**

St. Peter's Field. The scene of the Manchester massacre, Manchester, England, August 16, 1819.

St. Preux. A character in Rousseau's *La Nouvelle Héloïse.*

St. Sebastian. A seaport on the north coast of Spain.

St. Vincent, Cape. The southwest extremity of Portugal.

Sakelde. Deputy to Lord Scroop, the warden of the West-Marches of England, in the late 16th century.

Saladin (1137-93). Sultan of Egypt and Syria; he defended Acre for two years against the Crusaders.

Salamanca. A famous British victory over the French and Spanish, fought in the province of Salamanca, western Spain, in 1812.

Salamis. An island of Greece in the Gulf of Ægina, west of Athens.

Salem. An ancient name of Jerusalem.

Salisbury. A town in Wiltshire, England.

Salisbury Plain. A region in Wiltshire, England. It contains Stonehenge, a famous prehistoric ruin.

Salt, Samuel (d. 1792). A friend of the Lambs. He was instrumental in getting Charles Lamb into Christ's Hospital and into the East India House. He gave Charles and Mary Lamb the freedom of his library.

Samarah. In his notes on *Vathek,* Henley says that Samarah is a city of Babylonia, supposed to have stood on the site where Nimrod erected his tower.

Samarcand. A city of Turkestan. It is noted for its silver and gold wares, leather goods, silks, wine, and pottery.

Samian. Of or relating to the Island of Samos.

Samos. An island in the Ægean Sea.

Samson Agonistes. A drama by Milton.

Samuel. A Hebrew judge and prophet.

San Benito. The yellow garment worn by persons condemned by the Spanish Inquisition. The name is derived from the robes worn by members of the order of St. Benedict, founded about 529.

Sancho. The ignorant but clever squire in the Spanish romance *Don Quixote* by Cervantes (1547-1616).

Sandham. 1—A town on the Isle of Wight, south of England. 2—(968)—An imaginary residence.

Sangrida. One of the Fatal Sisters.

Sappho (7th century B. C.). A Greek lyric poetess of Lesbos; she was known as the Tenth Muse.

Saracen. In general, a Mohammedan or other enemy of medieval Christians.

Sarmatia. The ancient name of Poland.

Saturn. A Roman deity, supposed to have ruled in the golden age. He was identified with the Greek Cronus, father of Zeus.

Saturnalia. In Roman antiquity, the annual festival of Saturn held at Rome in mid-December, a form of harvest-home, an occasion of riotous indulgence.

Saturnian. Pertaining to the god Saturn; hence, characterized by simplicity, virtue, and happiness.

Saturnus. Same as Saturn.

Satyrs. In Greek mythology, woodland deities in the train of Dionysus, god of wine; depicted as shy creatures with goatlike ears, tail, and horns, who delight in music and revelry.

Saul. First king of the Hebrews (1055-1033 B. C.).

Savoy. A former duchy, now divided into the departments of Savoie and Haute-Savoie in France.

Sawbridge. John Sawbridge (1732-1795), Lord Mayor of London in 1775.

Saxon. The people that formerly dwelt in the northern part of Germany, and invaded England in the 5th and 6th centuries; hence, the English-speaking peoples.

Scamander. The ancient name of a river in Mysia, Asia Minor; the Mæander, now known as the Mendere. The river is mentioned by Homer in the *Iliad* (Bk. 21).

Scaramouch. A cowardly, foolish boaster; a stock character in 17 c. Italian farce.

Scarlet. Will Scarlet, one of the companions of Robin Hood.

Schelling. F. W. Schelling (1775-1854), an eminent German philosopher.

Schiller. Johann C. F. Schiller (1759-1805), a famous German poet and dramatist.

Scio (Chios). An island in the Ægean Sea, west of Asia Minor, formerly celebrated for its wines and figs.

Scipio. 1—(27)—Publius Scipio Africanus Major (c 234-183 B. C.), a famous Roman general, who, after a life of warfare, retired in 185 B. C. to his native seat near Cumæa, a city in Campania, Italy. 2—(1016)—Publius Scipio Africanus Minor (c 185-129 B.C.), a famous Roman general who captured Carthage in 146 B. C. and Numantia, Spain, in 133 B. C.

Scipios' Tomb. A group of ancient Roman tombs on the Appian Way, near Rome.

Scone. A village in Perthshire, Scotland; the coronation place of Scottish kings from 1153 to 1488.

Scotia. Scotland.

Scott. 1—(339, etc.)—Sir Walter Scott (1771-1832), a famous Scottish poet and novelist. See p. 459. 2—(890)—John Scott (1751-1838), an English jurist, Lord Chancellor of England, 1801-1806, and 1807-1827.

Scroggins. Jack Scroggins, a prize fighter.

Scroope, Lord. Warder of the West-Marches of England late in the 16th century.

Scylla. The monster inhabiting Scylla, a rock on the coast of Italy opposite Sicily. She was beloved by Glaucus, and from jealousy was changed by Circe into a monster surrounded with barking dogs.

Scythia. In ancient times, the whole north and northeast of Europe and Asia, called such by the Greeks.

Scythian. The Scythians were a nomadic people of Europe and Asia, expert in horsemanship and archery. They often made raids upon neighboring peoples.

Seasons, The. A poem by James Thomson, an English poet of the 18th century. See p. 18.

Seeva (Siva). The usual name of one of the gods of the Hindu triad. He represented the destructive power of nature.

Seine. A river of France which empties into the English channel.

Selkirk. The capital of Selkirkshire, Scotland.

Semele. In Greek mythology, beloved of Zeus and mother of Dionysus, god of wine.

Sennacherib. King of Assyria (705-681 B. C.), well-known in Biblical history. He was engaged in numerous wars.

Seraphim. One of the highest orders of angels, excelling in wisdom and in zeal in the service of God.

Sesostris. A legendary king of Egypt, said to have conquered the world.

Sestos. A ruined town in European Turkey on the Dardanelles.

Seven Dials. A locality in London, notorious for its poverty and crime. It took its name from a column which stood at the junction of seven streets and which bore a sundial facing each street.

Seven Sleepers. Seven Christian youths, said to have hidden in a cave near Ephesus, Asia Minor, during the persecution under Decius (249-51 A. D.), and to have fallen asleep, awaking two or three hundred years later when Christianity had become established.

Severn. A river in southwestern England.

Seville. A city in southwestern Spain.

Seyncte Powle.—(129)—St. Paul's Cathedral, London.

Sforza, Ludovico (1451-1510). Duke of Milan, Italy.

Shacklewell. Formerly a suburb of London, now an outlying district of the city itself.

Shadwell. Thomas Shadwell (1640-92), a Restoration dramatist, satirized by Dryden in *Mac Flecknoe* and in *Absalom and Achitophel.*

Shaldon. A village on the River Teign, across from Teignmouth, Devonshire, England.

Shanklin. A seaside resort on the coast of the Isle of Wight, south of England.

Sheeraz (Shiraz). A city in Persia.

Sheffield. 1—(517)—John Sheffield (1648-1721), Duke of Buckingham, an English statesman and author. 2—(1192)—A manufacturing town in Yorkshire, England, famous for its works in steel and cutlery.

Shelburne. William Petty (1737-1805), Earl of Shelburne, an English statesman.

Shem. The son of Noah and reputed ancestor of the Hebrew, Arabic, and other Semitic races. See *Genesis* 9:27.

Shenstone. William Shenstone (1714-63), an English poet. See p. 40.

Sheridan. Richard Brinsley Sheridan (1751-1816), a noted Irish dramatist, orator, and politician.

Sherwood. A forest in Nottinghamshire, England, the principal scene of the legendary exploits of Robin Hood.

Shrewsbury. A town in Shropshire, England.

Shropshire. An inland county of England, bordering on Wales; sometimes called Salop, from the Latin name *Salopia.*

Shylock. The Jew in Shakespeare's *The Merchant of Venice.*

Siam. A kingdom in southeastern Asia.

Siberia. A country of Asiatic Russia; it is noted for its mines.

Sibir. Siberia.

Sibyl. In ancient mythology, one of several women reputed to possess powers of prophecy or divination. They spoke their utterances in a frenzied state.

Sicily. An island in the Mediterranean, belonging to Italy; situated southwest of the mainland.

Siddons, Mrs. Sarah Kemble Siddons (1755-1831), a noted English actress.

Sidmouth. Henry Addington (1757-1844), Viscount Sidmouth, an English politician noted for his repressive measures.

Sidney. 1—(313, 406)—Algernon Sidney (c1622-83), an English politician and patriot. 2—(443, 948, 1055, 1058)—Sir Philip Sidney (1554-86), an English author and general. His chief works are *Arcadia* and *The Defense of Poesy.*

Sidney, Smug. See **Smug Sidney.**

Sidon. An ancient city in Asia Minor.

Sidonius Apollinarius (c430-482). A Christian author.

Siege of Corinth, The. A narrative poem by Lord Byron, published in 1816.

Sienna (Siena). A city and province in central Italy, noted for its works of art.

Sigæum. In ancient geography, a promontory and town in Asia Minor, at the entrance to the Hellespont. It was the legendary station of the Greek fleet in the Trojan War.

Sigtrygg (Sictryg). See Gray's preface to *The Fatal Sisters,* p. 1243b.

Sileni. Woodland nymphs, companions of Bacchus, god of wine. See **Silenus.**

Silenus. The eldest of the Satyrs, sometimes regarded as the son of Hermes, or of Pan. He was the fosterer and later the companion of Bacchus. He was represented as a jovial old man, corpulent, bald, and commonly tipsy. He carried a wine bag in his hand and rode on an ass. He was fond of sleep, music, and dancing. He is sometimes said to be the inventor of Pan's pipes. See **Pan.**

Silius Italicus (d. 100 A. D.). A Roman poet, imitator of Virgil; the author of *Punica,* a dull poem giving an account of the Second Punic War.

Simois. A small river in Asia Minor.

Simoom. A hot dry wind of the desert.

Sinbad. Sindbad, a character in the *Arabian Nights' Entertainments.* He was once shipwrecked on an island where the Old Man of the Sea, a monster, got on his back and would not dismount until finally Sindbad succeeded in killing him.

Sion (Zion). A hill on which was situated the old city of Jerusalem.

Sir Charles Grandison. A novel written by Samuel Richardson (1689-1761).

Siren. One of the sea nymphs said to inhabit an island near Italy, and by their singing to lure mariners to destruction.

Sistine Chapel. The Sistine, or Sixtine, Chapel is the papal private chapel built by Pope Sixtus IV in 1473. Its walls and ceilings are covered with magnificent paintings, of which the most famous are those of the Creation, the Deluge, and the Judgment, all by Michelangelo.

Sisyphus. A legendary character condemned in the lower world to roll up a hill, without ceasing, a huge stone which when he reached the top always rolled back to the valley.

Skiddaw. A mountain in Cumberlandshire, England.

Sky(e). A rocky, mountainous island off the western coast of Scotland; the largest of the Inner Hebrides.

Slough. A town in the county of Buckingham, England.

Smith, Adam (1723-90). A celebrated Scottish political economist.

Smithfield. A locality in London near St. Paul's; it was formerly used as a recreation yard.

Smug Sidney. The Rev. Sidney Smith (1771-1845), a Canon of St. Paul's, one of the founders and editors of *The Edinburgh Review.*

Snowdon. The highest mountain in Wales.

Snowdoun, Knight of. James V of Scotland, who chose this name to disguise his identity. Snowdoun refers to Stirling Castle, one of the Scottish royal palaces.

Soare. A river in Leicestershire, England.

Society of the Middle Temple. See **Temple.**

Socrates (5th century B. C.). A famous Greek philosopher.

Soho Square. A square in London, south of Oxford Street.

Sol. The sun.

Solomon. A king of Israel famous for his great wisdom.

Solway. The Solway Firth, a large inlet of the Irish Sea, partly separating England and Scotland.

Somersetshire. A county in southwestern England.

Sophia. The capital of Bulgaria, formerly a portion of the Turkish Kingdom.

Sophocles (5th century B. C.). One of the greatest tragic poets of Greece.

Sorento; Sorrento. A town on the west coast of Italy, across the bay from Naples.

Sotheby. William Sotheby (1757-1833), an English scholar and poet.

Soult. Nicolas Jean de Dieu Soult (1769-1851), a French marshal. He was engaged in many important battles, and was ambassador at the coronation of Queen Victoria in 1838.

South. Robert South (1634-1716), a celebrated English divine.

South-Sea House. See note on *The South-Sea House,* p. 1373b.

Spartan. Pertaining to Sparta, capital of Laconia in ancient Greece; hence, resembling the Spartans in discipline or courage.

Spectator. An 18th-century periodical published by Addison, Steele, and others.

Spey. A river in northern Scotland.

Sphinx. In Greek mythology, a winged monster represented with a woman's head and a lion's body; she sat on a high rock by the roadside in Thebes, Bœotia, and killed all passers-by who could not guess a riddle which she proposed. When Œdipus finally guessed the riddle she cast herself down from the rock and was killed.

Spinoza. Baruch de Spinoza (1632-77), a Dutch pantheistic philosopher.

Sporus. The name under which Lord John Hervey (1696-1743), an English writer and politician, was satirized by Pope in his *Epistle to Dr. Arbuthnot,* 305 ff.

Stamboul. Constantinople.

Staneshaw-bank. A place on the River Eden, in Cumberlandshire, England, near the Scottish border.

Stanhope, Lord. See p. 1219b, n. 5.

Stanmore. A ridge which divides the mountains of the counties of Westmoreland and Cumberland, England.

Statius. Publius Papinius Statius (60-100), a Roman poet.

Staubach. A famous waterfall in the canton of Berne, Switzerland.

Steele. Sir Richard Steele (1672-1729), an English essayist, contributor to *The Spectator.*

Sterne. Laurence Sterne (1713-68), an English novelist and humorist, author of *Tristram Shandy.*

Sternhold. Thomas Sternhold (d. 1549), an English writer.

Stevenson, George. An 18th-century English pugilist. He fought with Jack Broughton in 1771.

Stewart, Mr. Dugald Stewart (1753-1828), an eminent Scottish philosopher.

Stirling. A city and county in Scotland, noted for its picturesque buildings.

Stobs, Laird of. Sir Gilbert Elliot, a Scottish Border Warrior of the 16th century. He lived near Hawick, Roxburghshire, Scotland.

Stonehenge. A famous prehistoric stone ruin in Salisbury Plain, Wiltshire, England.

Stothard. Thomas Stothard (1755-1834), an English painter and illustrator.

Stott. Robert Stott, a minor English poet of the early 19th century. He contributed articles to *The Morning Post,* under the name of "Hafiz."

Stow. Stowe, a village in Buckinghamshire, England, noted for its castle and park.

Stowey. Nether Stowey, a village in Somersetshire, England.

Strabo (c63 B. C.-24 A. D.). A Greek geographer and historian.

Strand. A long prominent London street running parallel with the Thames.

Strangford, Hibernian. P. C. Smythe (1780-1855), Viscount Strangford, an Irish diplomat, and translator of poems of Camœns, a noted 16th-century Portuguese poet. In a note on one of the love songs, Strangford said that "eyes of blue have been ever dear to the sons of song."

Stygian. Pertaining or belonging to the River Styx, or to the infernal regions in general.

Styx. A fabulous river in Hades, over which all newcomers were ferried by Charon. Before it the most solemn oaths were sworn. Violation of such oaths was punished by deprivation of nectar and ambrosia, and by loss of all heavenly privileges for ten years.

Suckling, Captain. Sir John Suckling (1609-42), an English poet and soldier.

Suetonius. Caius Tranquillus Suetonius (c70-140), a Roman historian.

Suli. A mountainous district in Albania, European Turkey.

Sultan. A Mohammedan sovereign ruler.

Sunium. In ancient geography, the promontory at the southeastern extremity of Attica, Greece, now known as Cape Colonna.

Surrender of Calais. A comedy by George Colman, the Younger (1762-1836).

Surrey; Surry. A county in southeastern England.

Susa. An ancient city in Asia Minor.

Sussex. A county in southeastern England.

Swift. Jonathan Swift (1667-1745), a celebrated English satirist and man of letters.

Sybilline Leaves. A collection of poems by Coleridge, published in 1817.

Sydney. Algernon Sydney (1622-83), an eminent English Republican patriot.

Sylvans. Fabled spirits or deities of the wood.

Symplegades. Two island rocks on the Strait of Constantinople (or Bosphorus), a narrow passage which separates Europe from Asia.

Syracuse. A province in the southeastern part of Sicily. It was conquered by Marcellus in 212 B. C.

Syriac. The language of Syria, a country in Asia.

Syrian. Pertaining to Syria.

Syrinx. In Greek mythology, a nymph who was pursued by Pan and who was changed into a reed, out of which Pan then constructed his musical pipe. See **Pan.**

Tacitus. Cornelius Tacitus (55-117?), a celebrated Roman historian and legal orator.

Talavera. A town in the province of Toledo, Spain. Near it, in 1809, the allied English and Spanish army under Wellington and Cuesta defeated the French under King Joseph.

Taliessin. Taliesin, a Cymric or Welsh bard said to have lived in the 6th century.

Talleyrand. Charles Maurice de Talleyrand-Périgord (1754-1838), a famous French statesman and diplomatist.

Talymalpa. A small bay on the northeast coast of Anglesea, an island of Wales in the Irish Sea.

Tamar. 1—(986, 1109)—The brother of Gebir. 2—(1176)—A river on the border of Cornwall and Devonshire, England.

Tame, Thomas. A deputy-cashier in the South-Sea House in 1793.

Tamerlane (1336-1405). A Tartar conqueror of India and Asia.

Tanagra. In ancient geography, a town in Bœotia, Greece.

Tancred. One of the chief heroes of the First Crusade, 1096-99. His virtues are celebrated in Tasso's *Jerusalem Delivered.*

Tantalus. A mythological king, punished for betraying the secrets of the gods by being placed in the midst of a lake. The waters reached to his chin but receded whenever he attempted to drink.

Tara. A place in the county of Meath, Ireland. It was famous in the early history of Ireland as a royal residence.

Tarbat (Tarbet). The name of a village and a narrow neck of land between Loch Lomond and Loch Long, forming the northern end of the county of Dumbarton, Scotland. *Tarbat* is Gaelic for *isthmus.*

Tartar. The Tartars were mixed tribes, Mongolian or Turkish, inhabiting Russia and Central and Eastern Asia. They were warlike tribes, noted for their skill in archery.

Tartarian. Of or pertaining to the Tartars or Tartary, a name formerly applied to the middle portion of the Eurasiatic continent.

Tartarly. In the manner of a Tartar, *i.e.,* savagely.

Tartarus. The lowest portion of hell, the place of punishment for the spirits of the wicked.

Tartary. A name formerly applied to the middle portion of the Eurasiatic continent. Its people were warlike tribes.

Tasso. Torquato Tasso (1544-95), a celebrated Italian epic poet.

Tate. Nahum Tate (1652-1715), an English poet and dramatist.

Taunton. A town in Somersetshire, England.

Tay. The longest river of Scotland; it empties into the North Sea.

Taylor, Bishop. Jeremy Taylor (1613-67), an English bishop and theological writer, author of *Holy Living* (1650), *Holy Dying* (1651), and other works.

Teesdale. The valley of the River Tees in northern England; it flows into the North Sea.

Teignmouth. A bathing resort in Devonshire, England.

Teith. A small river chiefly in Perthshire, Scotland.

Telemachus. In Greek legend, the son of Odysseus and Penelope. He slew the suitors of Penelope while his father was away from home.

Tell, William. One of the legendary heroes of Switzerland in the struggle for independence. The story is that Tell, having refused to salute the cap which the Austrian governor had placed in the market place for that purpose, was ordered to shoot an apple from his little son's head. He did so successfully.

Tellus. A Roman goddess, the personification of the earth.

Tempe. A valley in eastern Thessaly, Greece. It has been celebrated from ancient times for its beauty.

Temple. Originally, a lodge of the medieval religious Order of Knights Templars. After this Order was abolished in 1312, the property passed to the crown and thence to the religious military Order of Knights Hospitalers, who in 1346 leased part of it to the students of law. On its site now stand two Inns of Court, known as the Inner and the Middle Temple. These are occupied by barristers, and are owned by the Societies of the Inner and Middle Temple, which have the right to admit students to the bar. The Inner Temple is so called because it is within the old City of London; the Middle Temple was between the Inner and the Outer Temples. The Outer Temple became a part of the Exeter Buildings, used for religious, charitable, and other assemblies.

Teneriff. The largest of the Canary Islands, in the Atlantic Ocean, northwest of Africa.

Tenos. An island of the Cyclades in the Ægean Sea, southeast of Greece.

Terence. Publius Terentius Afer (c185-159 B. C.), a noted Roman writer of comedies.

Termagaunt. A name given in medieval romances to the god of the Saracens.

Tethys. A sea goddess, the wife of Oceanus.

Teviot. A river in Roxburghshire, Scotland.

Teviotdale. Roxburghshire, Scotland, so called from the River Teviot, which flows through it.

Tewkesbury. A town in Gloucestershire, England.

Thalaba. The hero of *Thalaba*, an Oriental epic by Robert Southey (1744-1843).

Thalia. One of the Muses; she inspired gaiety, and favored rural pursuits and pleasures.

Thamondocana. A town of Africa near the border of the Sahara Desert.

Thebes. 1—(423, 693, 765)—The chief city of Bœotia, Greece. 2—(662)—The ancient capital of Upper Egypt.

Themis. The personification of divine justice; represented as the wife or companion of Zeus. In art Themis is represented as carrying scales in one hand and a horn of plenty in the other.

Theocritus (3rd century B. C.). A famous Greek idyllic poet.

Thermodon. A river, now Thermeh, in Pontus, Asia Minor, the reputed home of Hippolyta.

Thermopylæ. A pass in northern Greece, famous for the valiant stand made there in 480 B. C. by Leonidas and his band of Spartans against the Persian host of Xerxes.

Theseids. The *Theseid* is a tragedy on the subject of Theseus, of which Codrus is the alleged author.

Theseus. A legendary hero of Attica, Greece. In his exploit against the Amazons, he carried off their queen.

Thespis (6th century B. C.). An Attic poet, the reputed founder of tragedy.

Thessalian. Of or pertaining to Thessaly.

Thessaly. A province in northern Greece.

Thetis. The chief of the Nereids; the mother of Achilles, whom she dipped in the River Styx, thus making him invulnerable except in the heel, by which she held him. The story of the marriage of Thetis and Peleus, King of Thessaly, Greece, was a favorite subject in early painting, especially on vases.

Thomas, Holy. St. Thomas Aquinas (1225-74), a noted Italian divine.

Thomson. James Thomson (1700-48), a British poet. See p. 18.

Thone, Wife of. Polydamna, daughter of Zeus. See the *Odyssey*, 4, 220 ff.

Thor. In Scandinavian mythology, the god of thunder; always represented as carrying a hammer.

Thorn, The. A poem by Wordsworth. See p. 251.

Thrace. In ancient times a name applied by the Greeks to the regions northeast of Macedonia, and later to the greater part of the eastern half of the Balkan Peninsula.

Thracia. Thrace.

Thucydides (5th century B. C.). A celebrated Greek historian.

Thursley. A town in the county of Surrey, England.

Thurston-mere. Coniston Lake, west of Hawkshed, Lancashire, England.

Thyrsis. A common name in literature for a rustic or shepherd.

Tiber. A river of central Italy which enters the Mediterranean below Rome.

Tiberius. See note on *Tiberius and Vipsania*, p. 1380b.

Tickler. "Timothy Tickler," an Edinburgh lawyer named Sym; an uncle of John Wilson's wife.

Timon. A typical hater of mankind, in Shakespeare's *Timon of Athens*.

Timour. See **Tamerlane.**

Tintadgel. Tintagel, a village in Cornwall, England. Near it is the ruined Tintagel Castle, celebrated in Arthurian legend as the birthplace of King Arthur.

Tipp, John. An accountant in the South-Sea House about 1794.

Titan. One of a mythological race of giants, said to have piled mountain upon mountain to scale heaven.

Titanic. Resembling the Titans, a race of giants.

Titchfield Street. A prominent street in London.

Tithon; Tithonus. A legendary character loved by Aurora, who prevailed on the gods to grant him immortal life but forgot to ask for him immortal youth. He grew old and shriveled and was changed by Aurora into a grasshopper.

Titian. Tiziano Vecelli (1477-1576), a famous Venetian painter.

Tityrus. —(155)—A freedman in Virgil's *Eclogues,* supposed to represent Virgil himself.

Tividale. See **Teviotdale.**

Tiviot. See **Teviot.**

Tmolus. A mountain range in Asia Minor.

Tobin. James Webbe Tobin (d. 1814), an English lawyer. See note on Wordsworth's *We Are Seven,* p. 1275b.

Tolbooth. The principal prison in Edinburgh. Many criminals were executed in front of it.

Tom Thumb. A legendary diminutive personage celebrated in English literature.

Toms, Jo. Joseph Parkes (1796-1865), a Radical politician.

Tonson, Jacob (c1656-1736). A prominent London publisher.

Tooke. John Horne Tooke (1726-1812), an English politician, philosopher, and philologist; he opposed the war with America in 1776.

Torfæus. Thormodr Torfason (1636-1719), an Icelandic antiquary and historian.

Tory. The Tories, in English history, were members of one of the two great political parties which arose at the end of the 17th century. They favored conservative principles in church and state.

Toulmin, Dr. Joshua Toulmin (1740-1815), a dissenting historian and theologian. He preached at Taunton, Somersetshire, England, for nearly 40 years.

Toulouse. A city in southern France; the scene of massacres of Huguenots in 1562 and 1572.

Tourneur. Cyril Tourneur, an English tragic poet of the early 17th century.

Toussaint L'Ouverture (1743-1803). A Haitian revolutionist and liberator. He was captured by the French and imprisoned for life.

Tower; Tower of London. An ancient palace-citadel near the eastern wall of London. It was long a prison for political offenders.

Towy. A river in Carmarthenshire, South Wales.

Trafalgar. The name of a famous British naval victory over the French and Spanish, off Cape Trafalgar, on the southern coast of Spain, 1805. See p. 437.

Trajan. Marcus Ulpius Trajanus, a famous Roman emperor (98-117).

Trent. A river flowing through the counties of Stafford, Derby, Nottingham, and Lincoln, England.

Trevelyan. Raleigh Trevelyan (1781-1865), a miscellaneous English writer.

Trimmer, Mrs. Sarah Trimmer (1741-1810), whose original name was Kirby, the author of various juvenile and educational works of great merit.

Tristram Shandy. The hero of *Tristram Shandy,* a novel by Laurence Sterne (1713-68), an English novelist.

Triton. One of the sea gods; son of Poseidon.

Troilus. 1—(806)—In medieval romance, a son of Priam, King of Troy; lover of Cressida. 2—(890)—The hero of Shakespeare's *Troilus and Cressida.*

Troilus and Cressida. A tragedy by Shakespeare.

Trojan. 1—(332, 995, 1149)—Pertaining to ancient Troy. 2—(965, 1066)—The Trojan War, the ten years' war between Greeks and Trojans, described in the *Iliad.*

Trollope, Mrs. Frances Trollope (1790-1863), a popular English novelist.

Troppau. A city in Austria.

Trosachs; Trossachs. A romantic and beautiful valley between lakes Achray and Katrine in Perthshire, Scotland.

Trout Hall. In *The Complete Angler,* a treatise by Izaak Walton (1593-1683), an English writer.

Troy. An ancient city in Troas, Asia Minor, the scene of Homer's *Iliad.*

Tryermaine. A fief of the Barony of Gilsland, in Cumberlandshire, England. Roland Vaux was the name of successive owners of Tryermaine during the 14th and 15th centuries.

Tullibardine. The name of an old seat of the

Murrays, a powerful family of Scotland, near Stirling in Stirlingshire. See **Murray.**

Tura. A castle of Ulster, North Ireland.

Turin. A city of Italy, capital of the province of Turin.

Turkish Spy, The. An Italian romance by Giovanni Paolo Marana (1684). Defoe wrote a continuation of it.

Turner, Ned. A well-known English pugilist of the early 19th century.

Turtle, Tom. John Thurtell (1794-1824), an English fighter, gambler, and murderer.

Tuscan; Tuscany. A territorial division of west central Italy.

Tweed. A river on the border of England and Scotland.

Tygris. Tigris, a river in Asiatic Turkey.

Typhon. Typhœus, a giant monster with a hundred snake heads. He contended for the throne of the lower world with Zeus, who cast him into Tartarus or, according to another account, buried him under Mt. Ætna.

Tyre. One of the most important cities of Phœnicia, noted at one time for its magnificence and luxury. Alexander the Great reduced the city after a nine-months' siege.

Tyrian. Of or pertaining to Tyre.

Tyrolese. The inhabitants of Tyrol, an Austrian Alpine province.

Tyrtæus. A Greek poet of about 650 B. C., who inspired the Spartans by his patriotic elegies and war songs.

Uam-Var. A mountain in Menteith, a district in Perthshire, Scotland.

Ucalegon. A close companion and counselor of Priam, King of Troy.

Uist. Either of two Scottish islands of the Outer Hebrides, North Uist or South Uist.

Ukraine. The name of a region of European Russia, lying in the valley of the River Dnieper.

Ulysses. See **Odysseus.**

Ulva's Isle. A small island off the west coast of Scotland.

Ulz-water. Ullswater, a large lake between the counties of Cumberland and Westmoreland, England.

Umfraville. Probably Sir Robert de Umfraville (d. 1436), Earl of Angus, a member of an influential Norman family in Northumberlandshire, England. He fought on the side of Henry IV and Henry Percy (Hotspur) against the Scots. The Umfravilles and the Percys were closely related.

Una. In Spenser's *The Faerie Queene,* a beautiful maiden, the personification of truth.

Upton. A town in Worcestershire, England, midway between Worcester and Gloucester.

Urania. The Muse of astronomy. The name was applied also to Aphrodite as the goddess of spiritual love.

Uranus. With the exception of Neptune and Pluto, the outermost of the planets.

Urien. An ancient Welsh poet; nothing is extant of his works.

Urthona. Instinct that binds the spirit of each individual to that of the universe; also, the spirit of art and of prophecy.

Utopia. An imaginary island having a perfect political system, described by Sir Thomas More in a romance entitled *Utopia* (1516).

Valdarno. A beautiful valley near Florence, Italy.

Valerius Maximus (1st century A. D.). A Roman historian.

Vallombrosa. A famous monastery east of Florence, Italy.

Vandals. A Teutonic race formerly inhabiting the southern shores of the Baltic.

Vandykes. Paintings by Sir Anthony Vandyke (1599-1641), a Flemish portrait painter.

Vane. Sir Henry Vane (1612-62), an English Puritan statesman, one time governor of Massachusetts Bay.

Vaux, Roland de. See **Tryermaine.**

Velasquez. Diego Velasquez (1599-1660), a noted Spanish painter.

Vennachar. The "Lake of the Fair Valley," in Perthshire, Scotland.

Venta. Venta Belgarum, the ancient name of Winchester, a city in Hampshire, England.

Venus. The goddess of love and beauty. See **Aphrodite.**

Venus de' Medici. A marble statue of Venus in the Uffizi Gallery, Florence, by the Greek sculptor Cleomenes (3rd century B.C.).

Verona. The capital of a province in northeast Italy.

Verrio. Antonio Verrio (c1639-1707), an Italian painter. He was employed by Charles II of England to paint frescoes in the royal residence, Windsor Castle.

Versailles. A city in France, near Paris.

Vertumnus. A god of the changing seasons who presided over orchards and gardens.

Vesper. Venus when an evening star; also, the evening.

Vesta. The goddess of the hearth.

Vesuvio. Vesuvius, a mountain of southern Italy; the only active volcano in Europe.

Vevey. A town on Lake Geneva, Switzerland.

Vicar of Wakefield, The. A novel by Oliver Goldsmith (1728-74).

Villeneuve. Pierre Charles Jean de Villeneuve (1763-1806), a French admiral who commanded the French fleet at Trafalgar.

Vinci, da. Leonardo da Vinci (1452-1519), a noted Italian painter, sculptor, architect, and engineer.

Viola. The heroine of Shakespeare's *Twelfth Night*; she was shipwrecked on the coast of Illyria, a region in the Balkan peninsula.

Virgil. Publius Virgilius Maro (70-19 B. C.), a famous Roman epic, didactic, and idyllic poet.

Virgin's picture. The picture of the Virgin Mary.

Victoria. A famous British victory over the French and Spanish at Vittoria, a city in northern Spain, in 1813.

Vittoria Corombona. A tragedy written by John Webster (1580?-1625?), an English dramatist.

Voltaire. François Voltaire (1694-1778), a famous French writer and skeptic.

Vulcan. The blacksmith of the gods.

Wakefield. A small town in the south-central part of Yorkshire, England.

Wallace. William Wallace (c1270-1305), a celebrated Scottish hero and patriot. His achievements have been a favorite theme with Scottish poets and writers of romance.

Walla-crag. A rocky eminence in Cumberland-shire, England.

Waller. Edmund Waller (1606-87), an English poet.

Walpole. Horace Walpole (1717-97), an English author and wit. See p. 100.

Waltham. A suburb of London.

Walter, Sir. Sir Walter Scott (1771-1832).

Walton. Izaak Walton (1593-1683), an English writer.

Wandering Jew. The shoemaker Ahasuerus, fabled to be condemned to wander on the earth till the end of the world for driving Christ from his door when he rested there while bearing the cross.

Wapping. A quarter of London along the Thames, frequented by sailors.

War of the Second Coalition. The war conducted by the allied European powers against Napoleon, 1799-1801.

Warden. The title of a chief executive officer.

Ware. A town in Hertfordshire, England.

Warsaw. The capital of the Kingdom of Poland from 1609 to 1813.

Wat Tyler. A revolutionary epic by Robert Southey, dealing with the English rebel Wat Tyler and the insurrection started by him in 1381, because of the levying of a capitation tax.

Waterloo. A decisive victory gained by the allies over Napoleon at Waterloo, a village near Brussels, Belgium, on June 18, 1815.

Water-Monarch. Neptune, god of the sea.

Waterton, Mr. Charles Waterton (1782-1865), an English naturalist.

Webster. John Webster, an English tragic dramatist of the early 17th century.

Wedgewood, Tom. An Englishman who, with his brother Josiah (1730-95), paid Coleridge an annuity of £150 as the result of his preaching in Shrewsbury, Shropshire, England.

Weirdlaw Hill. A hill in the Ettrick Valley, Selkirkshire, Scotland.

Welborn. A character in Philip Massinger's *A New Way to Pay Old Debts* (1632).

Wellington, Duke of. Arthur Wellesley (1769-1852), a celebrated British general.

Wem. A town in Shropshire, England.

Went. A small river in the southern part of Yorkshire, England.

Wesley. John Wesley (1703-91), a distinguished religious reformer, founder of Methodism.

Westall. Richard Westall (1765-1836), a prominent historical painter.

Westbrook, Harriet. The first wife of the poet Shelley.

Westminster Abbey. A famous church in Westminster, London.

Westminster Bridge. The oldest bridge but one built over the Thames at London.

Westmoreland. A northern county of England.

West Riding. The western division of a county.

Wharfe. A river flowing through the central part of Yorkshire, England.

Wheathampstead. A small station near Mackery End in Hertfordshire, England.

Whigs. In English history, members of one of the two great political parties which arose at the end of the 17th century. They professed more liberal principles than did the Tories.

Whinfield. A place in Cumberlandshire, England.

Whitchurch. A small town north of Wem in Shropshire, England.

White. Henry Kirke White (1785-1806), a minor poet, who died at Cambridge as a result of too much exertion in the pursuit of studies, which increased his tendency to epilepsy.

White Horse Cellar. Probably the name of a London tavern.

Whitechapel. A district in London inhabited by the poorer classes and criminals.

Whitehall. In modern London, the main thoroughfare between Trafalgar Square and the Houses of Parliament. On it is Whitehall Chapel, formerly a royal palace.

Whole Duty of Man. A once popular ethical

treatise of unknown authorship, published in 1659.

Widdin. A town in Bulgaria, situated on the Danube. It was formerly a fortress.

Wilkes, Jack. John Wilkes (1727-97), an English politician, publicist, and political agitator.

Will o' the Wisp. Ignis fatuus—a misleading or illusive thing.

William. 1—(54, 1030)—William of Orange, King of England (1689-1702). 2—(258)—William Wordsworth.

Williams, Mr. John Williams, an English seaman and a noted murderer of the early 19th century. See De Quincey's postscript to *On Murder Considered as One of the Fine Arts.*

Wilmot. John Wilmot (1750-1815), an English politician and author.

Wilson. Thomas Wilson (1663-1755), a noted English theologian.

Wiltshire. An inland county of England.

Winander. Windermere, a large lake on the borders of the counties of Westmoreland and Lancaster, England.

Winchester. A city in Hampshire, England.

Windham. William Windham (1750-1810), an eminent English orator and statesman.

Windsor. A town in Berkshire, England, situated on the Thames, 23 miles from London. It contains Windsor Castle, a famous royal residence founded by William the Conqueror. Nearly opposite the castle is Eton College.

Winkfield. A village in Wiltshire, England; the seat of a private school attended by De Quincey.

Wirtemberg. Same as Würtemberg, a kingdom of southern Germany.

Witham-common. Witham is a town in the county of Essex, England.

Withers. George Withers (1588-1667), a minor English poet.

Wittenberg. A town in the province of Saxony, Prussia.

Wollstonecraft, Mary (1759-97). An English author, wife of William Godwin and mother of the second wife of Shelley. Her chief work is *Vindication of the Rights of Women* (1792).

Woman Killed with Kindness. A tragedy by Thomas Heywood, an English dramatist of the early 17th century.

Wood. Sir Matthew Wood (1768-1843), an English political reformer, a consistent and strenuous supporter of the Whig ministries.

Wood Street. A street in London; it is off Cheapside, the leading east and west thoroughfare.

Woodhouse. Robert Woodhouse (1773-1827),

an English astronomer and mathematician.

Woodhouslee. A barony belonging to Bothwellhaugh, along the banks of the Esk River, in Dumfriesshire, on the Scottish Border.

Woollett. William Woollett (1735-85), a noted English landscape engraver.

Woolston. Thomas Woolston (1669-1733), an English theological writer.

Worcester. A city in Worcestershire, England.

Wrexham. A town in Denbigshire, Wales.

Wright. John W. Wright (1769-1805), an Irish naval officer. He was captured by the French in 1804, and confined in the Temple at Paris. In 1805 he was found dead in prison, and it was suspected that he had been murdered.

Wye. A river in Wales and England, noted for its picturesque scenery.

Wyndermere. Lake Windermere, on the borders of the counties of Westmoreland and Lancaster; one of the finest and largest lakes of England.

Xanthippos. A son of Pericles.

Xenophon (430-357 B. C.). A celebrated Greek historian and essayist; author of the *Anabasis* and the *Memorabilia.*

Xerxes (c519-465 B. C.). King of Persia.

Yardley. A parish in Worcestershire, England.

Yarrow. A river in Selkirkshire, Scotland.

York. 1—(73, 929, 1140)—A city in Yorkshire, England. 2—(247)—A branch of the English royal dynasty, descended from Edmund, Duke of York, fourth son of Edward III, King of England (1327-77).

York, Duke of. —(899)—Frederick Augustus (1763-1827), second son of George III, King of England (1760-1820).

Yule. Christmas time (from Anglo-Saxon *geol*, December).

Zeno (3rd century B. C.). A Greek philosopher, founder of the Stoic school of philosophy, known for the sternness of its doctrines.

Zephyrus. The West Wind, regarded as the mildest of all the sylvan deities.

Zeus. In Greek mythology, the chief of the gods.

Zimmerman. Johann Georg von Zimmerman (1728-95), a Swiss philosopher and physician, who wrote a book entitled *On Solitude.*

Zion. A hill on which was situated the heavenly Jerusalem.

Zoe. Haidée's maid in Byron's *Don Juan.*

Zoroaster (fl. 600 B. C.). The traditional founder of the ancient Irano-Persian religion.

Index of Authors, Titles, and First Lines

In the following index, the names of authors represented in this text are printed in heavy type, and page references to selections, bibliography, and critical notes are given for each. The titles of selections are printed in italics, and first lines of poems are printed in ordinary Roman type. Poems having titles and first lines identical are entered only under titles.

Poems from the critical notes are included in this listing. Since the poems in "Romanticism in Illustration" (p. ix) serve as explanatory material and are easily found, they are not listed here.